2018
STANDARD POSTAGE STAMP CATALOGUE

ONE HUNDRED AND SEVENTY-FOURTH EDITION IN SIX VOLUMES

VOLUME 4B

M

EDITOR	Donna Houseman
MANAGING EDITOR	Charles Snee
EDITOR EMERITUS	James E. Kloetzel
SENIOR EDITOR /NEW ISSUES & VALUING	Martin J. Frankevicz
SENIOR VALUING ANALYST	Steven R. Myers
ADMINISTRATIVE ASSISTANT/CATALOGUE LAYOUT	Eric Wiessinger
PRINTING AND IMAGE COORDINATOR	Stacey Mahan
SENIOR GRAPHIC DESIGNER	Cinda McAlexander
ADVERTISING/SALES – EAST	David Pistello
ADVERTISING/SALES – WEST & FL	Eric Roth

Released July 2017
Includes New Stamp Listings through the May 2017 *Linn's Stamp News Monthly* Catalogue Update

AMOS MEDIA

911 Vandemark Road, Sidney, OH 45365-0828
Publishers of *Linn's Stamp News, Linn's Stamp News Monthly, Coin World* and *Coin World Monthly.*

Table of Contents

See the following volumes for other country listings:
Volume 1A: United States, United Nations, Abu Dhabi-Australia; Volume 1B: Austria-B
Volume 2A: C-Cur; Volume 2B: Cyp-F
Volume 3A: G; Volume 3B: H-I
Volume 4A: J-L
Volume 5A: N-Phil; Volume 5B: Pit-Sam
Volume 6A: San-Tete; Volume 6B: Thai-Z

Scott Catalogue Mission Statement

The Scott Catalogue Team exists to serve the recreational, educational and commercial hobby needs of stamp collectors and dealers.

We strive to set the industry standard for philatelic information and products by developing and providing goods that help collectors identify, value, organize and present their collections.

Quality customer service is, and will continue to be, our highest priority. We aspire toward achieving total customer satisfaction.

Copyright Notice

Trademark Notice

ISBN 978-0-89487-524-3

Library of Congress Card No. 2-3301

SCOTT

What's new for 2018 Scott Standard Volume 4B?

Greetings, Fellow Scott Catalog User:

The 2018 edition of the Scott *Standard Postage Stamp Catalogue* celebrates the 150th anniversary of the Scott catalogs. The title page of this volume and other volumes in the 2018 Scott Standard catalog states that this is the 174th edition of the catalogs (and it is). In September 1868, John Walter Scott published his first stamp catalog. The catalog, titled *A Descriptive Catalogue of America and Foreign Postage Stamps, Issued from 1840 to Date*, is considered to be the first Scott stamp catalog.

The Scott catalog has come a long way since its humble beginnings as a 24-page bound pamphlet. The Scott Standard catalog lists more than 700,000 stamps from more than 600 stamp-issuing entities. Because the catalog volumes had grown so large that they were literally bursting at the seams, each 2018 Scott Standard catalog has been split into two volumes, A and B.

• Scattered value changes occur among the listings for stamps of Mexico. Among the provisional stamps issued for the city of Guadalajara, the 1867 un real black on gray blue paper with serrate perforations (Scott 10) skyrockets from $400 used to $900. The value is in italics to indicate that this stamp trades infrequently and is difficult to value. Numerous counterfeits exist of the stamps of Guadalajara.

Madeira Scott 16, the 1871 5r black overprinted in red, jumps from $14 unused to $15.

• Value changes for classic and modern issues of Macau reflect mostly increases. The surcharged 1902 6-avos-on-10-rupee red violet (Scott 120) jumps from $40 unused to $60. The 1989 souvenir sheet of six honoring World Stamp Expo 89 (610) reflects an increase of 20 percent, from $50 mint to $60. The value is in italics to indicate that this item is difficult to value because it trades infrequently.

• Scattered decreases in values are seen throughout the Balkan country of Macedonia.

• The 1884 6-penny violet stamp of Madagascar with the handstamped "British Vice-Consulate" seal in black (Scott 5) jumps from $475 unused to $500.

• The Portugal 1870 240-reis blue King Luiz stamp overprinted "Madeira" in black or red for use on the island (Madeira Scott 15) soars from $600 unused to $700. The 1871 5r black overprinted in red (16) rises from $14 unused to $15.

• A review of Maldive Islands results in almost 1,700 value changes. Most values show decreases as a result of a weakening of the market.

• A few value changes were made to the stamp listings of Moheli, one of the Comoro Islands located in the Mozambique Channel in Africa. The 1906 5-franc lilac on lavender paper (Scott 16) jumps from $130 unused and used to $140 both ways.

• Among the changes for Mozambique, the 1985 16-metical stamp celebrating the 40th anniversary of the United Nations (Scott 955) climbs from $1.40 mint to $2.50.

Mozambique issued a 16-metical stamp in 1985 honoring the 40th anniversary of the United Nations. The value for the stamp in mint condition increases from $1.40 to $2.50.

Editorial enhancements for Vol. 4B

Various notes and footnotes have been clarified or expanded throughout the catalog to further explain complicated listings, and other notes have been screened carefully to ensure accuracy.

• Among the Maldive Islands listings, several imperforate varieties were added to footnotes from 1972 onward.

• The Montenegro 1894-98 set of overprinted Prince Nicholas I stamps (Scott 32-44) has been expanded to include new listings for stamps perforated gauge 11½ with small holes and perforated gauge 11½ with large holes. Similar reorganizations are made for Scott 45-56. The perforation varieties for Montenegro's first postage due stamps (Scott J1-J8) also have been broken out into new minor listings.

The 1942 overprints of the Federated Malay State of Perak issued under Japanese occupation are now organized by the color of the handstamp.

Among the listings of the Federated Malay State of Pahang issued under Japanese occupation, the 1942 overprints (Scott N1-N12) are now organized by the color of the handstamp (black, red, brown, or violet). The same is true for the stamps of Perak issued under Japanese occupation (N1-N16).

As with the stock market, a softening in the stamp market for some countries can be looked upon as an opportunity to buy stamps to fill spaces in your stamp albums.

As always, we encourage you to pay special attention to the Number Additions, Deletions & Changes found on page 748 in this volume.

While you settle in with your stamp album and Scott catalog, relax and enjoy the world's greatest hobby.

Donna Houseman

Donna Houseman/Catalogue Editor

Acknowledgments

Our appreciation and gratitude go to the following individuals who have assisted us in preparing information included in this year's Scott Catalogues. Some helpers prefer anonymity. These individuals have generously shared their stamp knowledge with others through the medium of the Scott Catalogue.

Those who follow provided information that is in addition to the hundreds of dealer price lists and advertisements and scores of auction catalogues and realizations that were used in producing the catalogue values. It is from those noted here that we have been able to obtain information on items not normally seen in published lists and advertisements. Support from these people goes beyond data leading to catalogue values, for they also are key to editorial changes.

A special acknowledgment to Liane and Sergio Sismondo of The Classic Collector for their assistance and knowledge sharing that have aided in the preparation of this year's Standard and Classic Specialized Catalogues.

Roland Austin
Robert Ausubel (Great Britain Collectors Club)
John Birkinbine II
Thurston Bland (Bubba Bland Philatelics)
Roger S. Brody
Peter Bylen
Tina & John Carlson (JET Stamps)
Richard A Champagne (Richard A. Champagne, Ltd.)
Henry Chlanda
David & Julia Crawford
Steven D. Crippe (Gradedstamps.com)
Tony L. Crumbley (Carolina Coin & Stamp, Inc.)
Christopher Dahle
Ubaldo Del Toro
Leon Djerahian
Bob & Rita Dumaine (Sam Houston Duck Co.)
Sister Theresa Durand
Mark Eastzer (Markest Stamp Co.)
Paul G. Eckman
George Epstein (Allkor Stamp Co.)
Henry Fisher
Robert A. Fisher
Jeffrey M. Forster
Robert S. Freeman
Michael Fuchs
Bob Genisol (Sultan Stamp Center)
Stan Goldfarb
Allen Grant (Rushstamps (Retail) Ltd.)
Daniel E. Grau
Jan E. Gronwall
Bruce Hecht (Bruce L. Hecht Co.)
Peter Hoffman
Armen Hovsepian (Armenstamp)
Philip J. Hughes
Doug Iams
Chris Jackson (Society for Czechoslovak Philately)
John Jamieson (Saskatoon Stamp and Coin)
N. M. Janoowalla
Peter Jeannopoulos
Stephen Joe (International Stamp Service)
William A. Jones
Allan Katz (Ventura Stamp Co.)
Stanford M. Katz
Lewis Kaufman (The Philatelic Foundation)
Jon Kawaguchi (Ryukyu Philatelic Specialist Society)
Roland Kretschmer
William V. Kriebel (Brazil Philatelic Association)
George Krieger
Victor Krievans
Frederick P. Lawrence
Ken Lawrence
John R. Lewis (The William Henry Stamp Co.)
Ulf Lindahl
Ignacio Llach (Filatelia Llach S.L.)
Marilyn R. Mattke
Gary Morris (Pacific Midwest Co.)
Peter Mosiondz, Jr.
Bruce M. Moyer (Moyer Stamps & Collectibles)
Richard H. Muller
Leonard Nadybal
Dr. Tiong Tak Ngo
Nik & Lisa Oquist
Dr. Everett Parker
Don Peterson (International Philippine Philatelic Society)
Stanley M. Piller (Stanley M. Piller & Associates)
Virgil Pirvulescu
Todor Drumev Popov
Peter W. W. Powell
Siddique Mahmudur Rahman
Ghassan D. Riachi
Omar Rodriguez
Mehrdad Sadri (Persiphila)
Theodosios Sampson PhD
Alexander Schauss (Schauss Philatelics)
Jacques C. Schiff, Jr. (Jacques C. Schiff, Jr., Inc.)
Chuck & Joyce Schmidt
Michael Schreiber
Jeff Siddiqui
Sergio & Liane Sismondo (The Classic Collector)
Jay Smith
Frank J. Stanley, III
Alfred E. Staubus
Peter Thy
Scott R. Trepel (Siegel Auction Galleries)
Dan Undersander (United Postal Stationery Society)
Herbert R. Volin
Philip T. Wall
Giana Wayman
Gary B. Weiss
Ralph Yorio
Val Zabijaka (Zabijaka Auctions)
Michal Zika
Steven Zirinsky (Zirinsky Stamps)
Alfonso G. Zulueta, Jr.

Addresses, Telephone Numbers, Web Sites, E-Mail Addresses of General & Specialized Philatelic Societies

Collectors can contact the following groups for information about the philately of the areas within the scope of these societies, or inquire about membership in these groups. Aside from the general societies, we limit this list to groups that specialize in particular fields of philately, particular areas covered by the Scott Standard Postage Stamp Catalogue, and topical groups. Many more specialized philatelic society exist than those listed below. These addresses are updated yearly, and they are, to the best of our knowledge, correct and current. Groups should inform the editors of address changes whenever they occur. The editors also want to hear from other such specialized groups not listed. Unless otherwise noted all website addresses begin with http://

American Philatelic Society
100 Match Factory Place
Bellefonte PA 16823-1367
Ph: (814) 933-3803
www.stamps.org
E-mail: apsinfo@stamps.org

American Stamp Dealers Association, Inc.
P.O. Box 692
Leesport PA 19553
Ph: (800) 369-8207
www.americanstampdealer.com
E-mail: asda@americanstampdealer.com

National Stamp Dealers Association
Richard Kostka, President
3643 Private Road 18
Pinckneyville IL 62274-3426
Ph: (800) 875-6633
www.nsdainc.org
E-mail: nsda@nsdainc.org

International Society of Worldwide Stamp Collectors
Joanne Berkowitz, MD
P.O. Box 19006
Sacramento CA 95819
www.iswsc.org
E-mail: executivedirector@iswsc.org

Royal Philatelic Society
41 Devonshire Place
London, W1G 6JY
UNITED KINGDOM
www.rpsl.org.uk
E-mail: secretary@rpsl.org.uk

Royal Philatelic Society of Canada
P.O. Box 929, Station Q
Toronto, ON, M4T 2P1
CANADA
Ph: (888) 285-4143
www.rpsc.org
E-mail: info@rpsc.org

Young Stamp Collectors of America
Janet Houser
100 Match Factory Place
Bellefonte PA 16823-1367
Ph: (814) 933-3820
www.stamps.org/ysca/intro.htm
E-mail: ysca@stamps.org

Philatelic Research Resources

(The Scott editors encourage any additional research organizations to submit data for inclusion in this listing category)

American Philatelic Research Library
Tara Murray
100 Match Factory Place
Bellefonte PA 16823
Ph: (814) 933-3803
www.stamplibrary.org
E-mail: libraryestamps.org

Institute for Analytical Philately, Inc.
P.O. Box 8035
Holland MI 49422-8035
Ph: (616) 399-9299
www.analyticalphilately.org
E-mail: info@analyticalphilately.org

The Western Philatelic Library
P.O. Box 2219
1500 Partridge Ave.
Sunnyvale CA 94087
Ph: (408) 733-0336
www.fwpf.org

Groups focusing on fields or aspects found in worldwide philately (some might cover U.S. area only)

American Air Mail Society
Stephen Reinhard
P.O. Box 110
Mineola NY 11501
www.americanairmailsociety.org
E-mail: sreinhard1@optonline.net

American First Day Cover Society
Douglas Kelsey
P.O. Box 16277
Tucson AZ 85732-6277
Ph: (520) 321-0880
www.afdcs.org
E-mail: afdcs@afdcs.org

American Revenue Association
Eric Jackson
P.O. Box 728
Leesport PA 19533-0728
Ph: (610) 926-6200
www.revenuer.org
E-mail: eric@revenuer.com

American Topical Association
Vera Felts
P.O. Box 8
Carterville IL 62918-0008
Ph: (618) 985-5100
www.americantopicalassn.org
E-mail: americantopical@msn.com

Christmas Seal & Charity Stamp Society
John Denune
234 E. Broadway
Granville OH 43023
Ph: (740) 587-0276
www.seal-society.org
E-mail: john@christmasseals.net

Errors, Freaks and Oddities Collectors Club
Scott Shaulis
P.O. Box 549
Murrysville PA 15668-0549
Ph: (724) 733-4134
www.efocc.org

First Issues Collectors Club
Kurt Streepy, Secretary
3128 E. Mattatha Drive
Bloomington IN 47401
www.firstissues.org
E-mail: secretary@firstissues.org

International Society of Reply Coupon Collectors
Peter Robin
P.O. Box 353
Bala Cynwyd PA 19004
E-mail: peterrobin@verizon.net

The Joint Stamp Issues Society
Richard Zimmermann
29A Rue Des Eviats
Lalaye F-67220
FRANCE
www.philarz.net
E-mail: richard.zimmermann@club-internet.fr

National Duck Stamp Collectors Society
Anthony J. Monico
P.O. Box 43
Harleysville PA 19438-0043
www.ndscs.org
E-mail: ndscs@ndscs.org

No Value Identified Club
Albert Sauvanet
Le Clos Royal B, Boulevard des Pas Enchantes
St. Sebastien-sur Loire, 44230
FRANCE
E-mail: alain.vailly@irin.univ nantes.fr

The Perfins Club
Ken Masters
111 NW 94th Street Apt. 102
Kansas City MO 64155-2993
Ph: (816) 835-5907
www.perfins.org
E-mail: kmasters@aol.com

Postage Due Mail Study Group
John Rawlins
13, Longacre
Chelmsford, CM1 3BJ
UNITED KINGDOM
E-mail: john.rawlins2@ukonline.co.uk.

Post Mark Collectors Club
Bob Milligan
7014 Woodland Oaks
Magnolia TX 77354
Ph: (281) 259-2735
www.postmarks.org
E-mail: bob.milligan@gmail.net

Postal History Society
George McGowan
P.O. Box 482
East Schodack NY 12063-0482
www.postalhistorysociety.org
E-mail: geolotus2003@nycap.rr.com

Precancel Stamp Society
Charles Adrion
P.O. Box 10295
Rochester NY 14610
Ph: (585) 319-0600
www.precancels.com
E-mail: pss.promotion@rochester.rr.com

United Postal Stationery Society
Stuart Leven
1659 Branham Lane Suite F-307
San Jose CA 95118-2291
www.upss.org
E-mail: poststat@gmail.com

United States Possessions Philatelic Society
Daniel F. Ring
P.O. Box 113
Woodstock IL 60098
www.uspps.net
E-mail: danielfring@hotmail.com

Groups focusing on U.S. area philately as covered in the Standard Catalogue

Canal Zone Study Group
Tom Brougham
737 Neilson St.
Berkeley CA 94707
www.CanalZoneStudyGroup.com
E-mail: czsgsecretary@gmail.com

Carriers and Locals Society
Martin Richardson
P.O. Box 74
Grosse Ile MI 48138
www.pennypost.org
E-mail: martinr362@aol.com

Confederate Stamp Alliance
Patricia A. Kaufmann
10194 N. Old State Road
Lincoln DE 19960
Ph. (302) 422-2656
www.csalliance.org
E-mail: trishkauf@comcast.net

Hawaiian Philatelic Society
Kay H. Hoke
P.O. Box 10115
Honolulu HI 96816-0115
Ph: (808) 521-5721

Plate Number Coil Collectors Club
Gene Trinks
16415 W. Desert Wren Court
Surprise AZ 85374
Ph: (623) 322-4619
www.pnc3.org
E-mail: gctrinks@cox.net

Ryukyu Philatelic Specialist Society
Laura Edmonds, Secy.
P.O. Box 240177
Charlotte NC 28224-0177
Ph: (336) 509-3739
www.ryukyustamps.org
E-mail: secretary@ryukyustamps.org

United Nations Philatelists
Blanton Clement, Jr.
P.O. Box 146
Morrisville PA 19067-0146
www.unpi.com
E-mail: bclemjr@yahoo.com

United States Stamp Society
Executive Secretary
P.O. Box 6634
Katy TX 77491-6634
www.usstamps.org

U.S. Cancellation Club
Joe Crosby
E-mail: joecrosby@cox.nat

U.S. Philatelic Classics Society
Rob Lund
2913 Fulton St.
Everett WA 98201-3733
www.uspcs.org
E-mail: membershipchairman@uspcs.org

Groups focusing on philately of foreign countries or regions

Aden & Somaliland Study Group
Gary Brown
P.O. Box 106
Briar Hill, Victoria, 3088
AUSTRALIA
E-mail: garyjohn951@optushome.com.au

American Society of Polar Philatelists (Antarctic areas)
Alan Warren
P.O. Box 39
Exton PA 19341-0039
www.polarphilatelists.org

Andorran Philatelic Study Circle
D. Hope
17 Hawthorn Drive
Stalybridge, Cheshire, SK15 1UE
UNITED KINGDOM
E-mail: andorranpsc@btinternet.com

Australian States Study Circle of The Royal Sydney Philatelic Club
Ben Palmer
GPO 1751
Sydney, N.S.W., 2001
AUSTRALIA
www.philas.org.au/states

Austria Philatelic Society
Ralph Schneider
P.O. Box 23049
Belleville IL 62223
Ph: (618) 277-6152
www.austriaphilatelicsociety.com
E-mail: rschneiderstamps@att.net

American Belgian Philatelic Society
Edward de Bary
11 Wakefield Drive Apt. 2105
Asheville NC 28803
E-mail: emdeb@charter.net

Bechuanalands and Botswana Society
Neville Midwood
69 Porlock Lane
Furzton, Milton Keynes, MK4 1JY
UNITED KINGDOM
www.nevsoft.com
E-mail: bbsoc@nevsoft.com

Bermuda Collectors Society
John Pare
405 Perimeter Road
Mount Horeb WI 53572
www.bermudacollectorssociety.com
E-mail: pare16@mhtc.net

Brazil Philatelic Association
William V. Kriebel
1923 Manning St.
Philadelphia PA 19103-5728
www.brazilphilatelic.org
E-mail: info@brazilphilatelic.org

British Caribbean Philatelic Study Group
Duane Larson
2 Forest Blvd.
Park Forest IL 60466
www.bcpsg.com
E-mail: dlarson283@aol.com

The King George VI Collectors Society (British Commonwealth)
Brian Livingstone
21 York Mansions, Prince of Wales Drive
London, SW11 4DL
UNITED KINGDOM
www.kg6.info
E-mail: livingstone484@btinternet.com

British North America Philatelic Society (Canada & Provinces)
Andy Ellwood
10 Doris Avenue
Gloucester, ON, KIT 3W8
CANADA
www.bnaps.org
E-mail: secretary@bnaps.org

British West Indies Study Circle
John Seidl
4324 Granby Way
Marietta GA 30062
Ph: (770) 642-6424
www.bwisc.org
E-mail: john.seidl@gmail.com

Burma Philatelic Study Circle
Michael Whittaker
1, Ecton Leys, Hillside
Rugby, Warwickshire, CV22 5SL
UNITED KINGDOM
www.burmastamps.homecall.co.uk
E-mail: manningham8@mypostoffice.co.uk

Cape and Natal Study Circle
Dr. Guy Dillaway
P.O. Box 181
Weston MA 02493
www.nzsc.demon.co.uk

Ceylon Study Circle
R. W. P. Frost
42 Lonsdale Road, Cannington
Bridgewater, Somerset, TA5 2JS
UNITED KINGDOM
www.ceylonsc.org
E-mail: rodney.frost@tiscali.co.uk

Channel Islands Specialists Society
Richard Flemming
64, Falconers Green, Burbage
Hinckley, Leicestershire, LE10 2SX
UNITED KINGDOM
www.ciss1950.org.uk
E-mail: secretary@ciss1950.org.uk

China Stamp Society
H. James Maxwell
1050 West Blue Ridge Boulevard
Kansas City MO 64145-1216
www.chinastampsociety.org
E-mail: president@chinastampsociety.org

Colombia/Panama Philatelic Study Group (COPAPHIL)
Thomas P. Myers
P.O. Box 522
Gordonsville VA 22942
www.copaphil.org
E-mail: tpmphil@hotmail.com

Association Filatelic de Costa Rica
Giana Wayman
c/o Interlink 102, P.O. Box 52-6770
Miami FL 33152
E-mail: scotland@racsa.co.cr

Society for Costa Rica Collectors
Dr. Hector R. Mena
P.O. Box 14831
Baton Rouge LA 70808
www.socorico.org
E-mail: hrmena@aol.com

International Cuban Philatelic Society
Ernesto Cuesta
P.O. Box 34434
Bethesda MD 20827
www.cubafil.org
E-mail: ecuesta@philat.com

Cuban Philatelic Society of America ®
P.O. Box 141656
Coral Gables FL 33114-1656
www.cubapsa.com
E-mail: cpsa.usa@gmail.com

Cyprus Study Circle
Colin Dear
10 Marne Close, Wem
Shropshire, SY4 5YE
UNITED KINGDOM
www.cyprusstudycircle.org/index.htm
E-mail: colindear@talktalk.net

Society for Czechoslovak Philately
Tom Cossaboom
P.O. Box 4124
Prescott AZ 86302
Ph: (928) 771-9097
www.csphilately.org
E-mail: klfck1@aol.com

Danish West Indies Study Unit of the Scandinavian Collectors Club
Arnold Sorensen
7666 Edgedale Drive
Newburgh IN 47630
Ph: (812) 480-6532
www.scc-online.org
E-mail: valbydwi@hotmail.com

East Africa Study Circle
Michael Vesey-Fitzgerald
Gambles Cottage, 18 Clarence Road
Lyndhurst, SO43 7AL
UNITED KINGDOM
www.easc.org.uk
E-mail: secretary@easc.org.uk

Egypt Study Circle
Mike Murphy
109 Chadwick Road
London, SE15 4PY
UNITED KINGDOM
Trent Ruebush: North American Agent
E-mail: tkruebrush@gmail.com
www.egyptstudycircle.org.uk
E-mail: egyptstudycircle@hotmail.com

Estonian Philatelic Society
Juri Kirsimagi
29 Clifford Ave.
Pelham NY 10803
Ph: (914) 738-3713

Ethiopian Philatelic Society
Ulf Lindahl
21 Westview Place
Riverside CT 06878
Ph: (203) 722-0769
http://ethiopianphilatelicsociety.weebly.com
E-mail: ulindahl@optonline.net

Falkland Islands Philatelic Study Group
Carl J. Faulkner
615 Taconic Trail
Williamstown MA 01267-2745
Ph: (413) 458-4421
www.fipsg.org.uk
E-mail: cfaulkner@taconicwilliamstown.com

Faroe Islands Study Circle
Norman Hudson
40 Queen's Road, Vicar's Cross
Chester, CH3 5HB
UNITED KINGDOM
www.faroeislandssc.org
E-mail: jntropics@hotmail.com

Former French Colonies Specialist Society
COLFRA
BP 628
75367 Paris, Cedex 08
FRANCE
www.colfra.org
E-mail: secretaire@colfra.org

France & Colonies Philatelic Society
Edward Grabowski
111 Prospect St., 4C
Westfield NJ 07090
www.franceandcolps.org
E-mail: edjjg@alum.mit.edu

Gibraltar Study Circle
Susan Dare
22, Byways Park, Strode Road
Clevedon, North Somerset, BS21 6UR
UNITED KINGDOM
E-mail: smldare@yahoo.co.uk

Germany Philatelic Society
P.O. Box 6547
Chesterfield MO 63006
www.germanyphilatelicusa.org

Plebiscite-Memel-Saar Study Group of the German Philatelic Society
Clayton Wallace
100 Lark Court
Alamo CA 94507
E-mail: claytonwallace@comcast.net

Great Britain Collectors Club
Steve McGill
10309 Brookhollow Circle
Highlands Ranch CO 80129
www.gbstamps.com/gbcc
E-mail: steve.mcgill@comcast.net

International Society of Guatemala Collectors
Jaime Marckwordt
449 St. Francis Blvd.
Daly City CA 94015-2136
www.guatemalastamps.com
E-mail:
membership@guatamalastamps.com

Haiti Philatelic Society
Ubaldo Del Toro
5709 Marble Archway
Alexandria VA 22315
www.haitiphilately.org
E-mail: u007ubi@aol.com

Federacion Filatelica de la Republica de Honduras (Honduran Philatelic Federation, FFRH)
Mauricio Mejia
Apartado postal 1465
Tegucigalpa
HONDURAS

Hong Kong Stamp Society
Ming W. Tsang
P.O. Box 206
Glenside PA 19038
www.hkss.org
E-mail: hkstamps@yahoo.com

Society for Hungarian Philately
Robert Morgan
2201 Roscomare Road
Los Angeles CA 90077-2222
Ph: (978) 682-0242
www.hungarianphilately.org
E-mail: alan@hungarianstamps.com

India Study Circle
John Warren
P.O. Box 7326
Washington DC 20044
Ph: (202) 564-6876
www.indiastudycircle.org
E-mail: warren.john@epa.gov

Indian Ocean Study Circle
E. S. Hutton
29 Patermoster Close
Waltham Abby, Essex, EN9 3JU
UNITED KINGDOM
www.indianoceanstudycircle.com
E-mail: secretary@indianoceanstudy-circle.com

Society of Indo-China Philatelists
Ron Bentley
2600 N. 24th St.
Arlington VA 22207
www.sicp-online.org
E-mail: ron.bentley@verizon.net

Iran Philatelic Study Circle
Mehdi Esmaili
P.O. Box 750096
Forest Hills NY 11375
www.iranphilatelic.org
E-mail: m.esmaili@earthlink.net

Eire Philatelic Association (Ireland)
David J. Brennan
P.O. Box 704
Bernardsville NJ 07924
www.eirephilatelicassoc.org
E-mail: brennan704@aol.com

Society of Israel Philatelists
Becky Dean
100 Match Factory Place
Bellefonte PA 16823-1367
Ph: (814) 933-3802 ext. 212
www.israelstamps.com
E-mail: israelstamps@gmail.com

Italy and Colonies Study Circle
Richard Harlow
7 Duncombe House, 8 Manor Road
Teddington, TW11 8BE
UNITED KINGDOM
www.icsc.pwp.blueyonder.co.uk
E-mail: harlowr@gmail.com

International Society for Japanese Philately
William Eisenhauer
P.O. Box 230462
Tigard OR 97281
www.isjp.org
E-mail: secretary@isjp.org

Latin American Philatelic Society
Jules K. Beck
30½ St. #209
St. Louis Park MN 55426-3551

Liberian Philatelic Society
William Thomas Lockard
P.O. Box 106
Wellston OH 45692
Ph: (740) 384-2020
E-mail: tlockard@zoomnet.net

Liechtenstudy USA (Liechtenstein)
Paul Tremaine
410 SW Ninth St.
Dundee OR 97115
Ph: (503) 538-4500
www.liechtenstudy.org
E-mail: editor@liechtenstudy.org

Lithuania Philatelic Society
John Variakojis
8472 Carlisle Court
Burr Ridge IL 60527
Ph: (630) 974-6525
www.lithuanianphilately.com/lps
E-mail: variakojis@sbcglobal.net

Luxembourg Collectors Club
Gary B. Little
7319 Beau Road
Sechelt, BC, VON 3A8
CANADA
lcc.luxcentral.com
E-mail: gary@luxcentral.com

Malaya Study Group
David Tett
16 Broadway, Gustard Wood
Wheathampstead, Herts, AL4 8LN
UNITED KINGDOM
www.m-s-g.org.uk
E-mail: davidtett@aol.com

Malta Study Circle
Rodger Evans
Ravensbourne, Hook Heath Road
Woking, Surrey, GU22 OLB
UNITED KINGDOM
www.maltastudycircle.org.uk
E-mail: carge@hotmail.co.uk

Mexico-Elmhurst Philatelic Society International
Thurston Bland
50 Regato
Rancho Santa Margarita CA 92688-3003
www.mepsi.org

Asociacion Mexicana de Filatelia
AMEXFIL
Jose Maria Rico, 129, Col. Del Valle
Mexico City DF, 03100
MEXICO
www.amexfil.mx
E-mail: amexfil@gmail.com

Society for Moroccan and Tunisian Philately
S.P.L.M.
206, bld. Pereire
Paris 75017
FRANCE
splm-philatelie.org
E-mail: splm206@aol.com

Nepal & Tibet Philatelic Study Group
Ken Goss
2643 Wagner Place
EL Dorado Hills CA 95762
Ph: (510) 207-5369
www.fuchs-online.com/ntpsc/
E-mail: kfgoss@comcast.net

American Society for Netherlands Philately
Hans Kremer
50 Rockport Court
Danville CA 94526
Ph: (925) 820-5841
www.asnp1975.com
E-mail: hkremer@usa.net

New Zealand Society of Great Britain
Michael Wilkinson
121 London Road
Sevenoaks, Kent, TN13 1BH
UNITED KINGDOM
www.nzsgb.org.uk
E-mail: mwilkin799@aol.com

Nicaragua Study Group
Erick Rodriguez
11817 SW 11th St.
Miami FL 33184-2501
clubs.yahoo.com/clubs/
nicaraguastudygroup
E-mail: nsgsec@yahoo.com

Society of Australasian Specialists/Oceania
David McNamee
P.O. Box 37
Alamo CA 94507
www.sasoceania.org
E-mail: treasurer@sasoceania.com

Orange Free State Study Circle
J. R. Stroud
24 Hooper Close
Burnham-on-sea, Somerset, TA8 1JQ
UNITED KINGDOM
orangefreestatephilately.org.uk
E-mail: richardstroudph@gofast.co.uk

Pacific Islands Study Circle
John Ray
24 Woodvale Ave.
London, SE25 4AE
UNITED KINGDOM
www.pisc.org.uk
E-mail: info@pisc.org.uk

Pakistan Philatelic Study Circle
Jeff Siddiqui
P.O. Box 7002
Lynnwood WA 98046
E-mail: jeffsiddiqui@msn.com

Centro de Filatelistas Independientes de Panama
Vladimir Berrio-Lemm
Apartado 0823-02748
Plaza Concordia Panama
PANAMA
E-mail: panahistoria@gmail.com

Papuan Philatelic Society
Steven Zirinsky
P.O. Box 49, Ansonia Station
New York NY 10023
Ph: (718) 706-0616
www.communigate.co.uk/york/pps
E-mail: szirinsky@cs.com

International Philippine Philatelic Society
Donald J. Peterson
P.O. Box 122
Brunswick MD 21716
Ph: (301) 834-6419
www.theipps.info
E-mail: dpeterson4526@gmail.com

Pitcairn Islands Study Group
Dr. Everett L. Parker
117 Cedar Breeze South
Glenburn ME 04401-1734
Ph: (386) 688-1358
www.pisg.net
E-mail: eparker@hughes.net

Polonus Philatelic Society (Poland)
Daniel Lubelski
P.O. Box 60438
Rossford OH 43460
Ph: (419) 410-9115
www.polonus.org
E-mail: info@polonus.org

International Society for Portuguese Philately
Clyde Homen
1491 Bonnie View Road
Hollister CA 95023-5117
www.portugalstamps.com
E-mail: ispp1962@sbcglobal.net

Rhodesian Study Circle
William R. Wallace
P.O. Box 16381
San Francisco CA 94116
www.rhodesianstudycircle.org.uk
E-mail: bwall8rscr@earthlink.net

Rossica Society of Russian Philately
Alexander Kolchinsky
1506 Country Lake Drive
Champaign IL 6821-6428
www.rossica.org
E-mail: alexander.kolchinsky@rossica.org

St. Helena, Ascension & Tristan Da Cunha Philatelic Society
Dr. Everett L. Parker
117 Cedar Breeze South
Glenburn ME 04401-1734
Ph: (386) 688-1358
www.shatps.org
E-mail: eparker@hughes.net

St. Pierre & Miquelon Philatelic Society
James R. (Jim) Taylor
2335 Paliswood Road SW
Calgary, AB, T2V 3P6
CANADA
www.stamps.org/spm

Associated Collectors of El Salvador
Joseph D. Hahn
1015 Old Boalsburg Road Apt G-5
State College PA 16801-6149
www.elsalvadorphilately.org
E-mail: jdhahn2@gmail.com

Fellowship of Samoa Specialists
Donald Mee
23 Leo St.
Christchurch, 8051
NEW ZEALAND
www.samoaexpress.org
E-mail: donanm@xtra.co.nz

Sarawak Specialists' Society
Stephen Schumann
2417 Cabrillo Drive-
Hayward CA 94545
Ph: (510) 785-4794
www.britborneostamps.org.uk
E-mail: sdsch@earthlink.net

Scandinavian Collectors Club
Steve Lund
P.O. Box 16213
St. Paul MN 55116
www.scc-online.org
E-mail: steve88h@aol.com

Slovakia Stamp Society
Jack Benchik
P.O. Box 555
Notre Dame IN 46556

Philatelic Society for Greater Southern Africa
Alan Hanks
34 Seaton Drive
Aurora, ON, L4G 2K1
CANADA
www.psgsa.thestampweb.com

South Sudan Philatelic Society
William Barclay
1370 Spring Hill Road
South Londonderry VT 05155
E-mail: barclayphilatelics@gmail.com

Spanish Philatelic Society
Robert H. Penn
1108 Walnut Drive
Danielsville PA 18038
Ph: (610) 844-8963
E-mail: roberthpenn43@gmail.com

Sudan Study Group
Paul Grigg
19 Howmead
Berkeley, GLOS, GL13 9AR
England
UNITED KINGDOM
www.sudanstamps.org

American Helvetia Philatelic Society (Switzerland, Liechtenstein)
Richard T. Hall
P.O. Box 15053
Asheville NC 28813-0053
www.swiss-stamps.org
E-mail: secretary2@swiss-stamps.org

Tannu Tuva Collectors Society
Ken R. Simon
P.O. Box 385
Lake Worth FL 33460-0385
Ph: (561) 588-5954
www.tuva.tk
E-mail: yurttuva@yahoo.com

Society for Thai Philately
H. R. Blakeney
P.O. Box 25644
Oklahoma City OK 73125
E-mail: HRBlakeney@aol.com

Transvaal Study Circle
Chris Board
36 Wakefield Gardens
London, SE19 2NR
UNITED KINGDOM
www.transvaalstamps.org.uk
E-mail: c.board@macace.net

Ottoman and Near East Philatelic Society (Turkey and related areas)
Bob Stuchell
193 Valley Stream Lane
Wayne PA 19087
www.oneps.org
E-mail: rstuchell@msn.com

Ukrainian Philatelic & Numismatic Society
Martin B. Tatuch
5117 8th Road N.
Arlington VA 22205-1201
www.upns.org
E-mail: treasurer@upns.org

Vatican Philatelic Society
Sal Quinonez
1 Aldersgate, Apt. 1002
Riverhead NY 11901-1830
Ph: (516) 727-6426
www.vaticanphilately.org

British Virgin Islands Philatelic Society
Giorgio Migliavacca
P.O. Box 7007
St. Thomas VI 00801-0007
www.islandsun.com/category/collectables/
E-mail: issun@candwbvi.net

West Africa Study Circle
Martin Bratzel
1233 Virginia Ave.
Windsor, ON, N8S 2Z1
CANADA
www.wasc.org.uk
E-mail: marty_bratzel@yahoo.ca

Western Australia Study Group
Brian Pope
P.O. Box 423
Claremont, Western Australia, 6910
AUSTRALIA
www.wastudygroup.com
E-mail: black5swan@yahoo.com.au

Yugoslavia Study Group of the Croatian Philatelic Society
Michael Lenard
1514 N. Third Ave.
Wausau WI 54401
Ph: (715) 675-2833
E-mail: mjlenard@aol.com

Topical Groups

Americana Unit
Dennis Dengel
17 Peckham Road
Poughkeepsie NY 12603-2018
www.americanaunit.org
E-mail: ddengel@americanaunit.org

Astronomy Study Unit
John Budd
728 Sugar Camp Way
Brooksville FL 34604
Ph: (352) 345-4799
E-mail: jwgbudd@gmail.com

Bicycle Stamp Club
Steve Andreasen
2000 Alaskan Way, Unit 157
Seattle WA 98121
E-mail: steven.w.andreasen@gmail.com

Biology Unit
Alan Hanks
34 Seaton Drive
Aurora, ON, L4G 2K1
CANADA
Ph: (905) 727-6993

Bird Stamp Society
S. A. H. (Tony) Statham
Ashlyns Lodge, Chesham Road,
Berkhamsted, Hertfordshire HP4 2ST
UNITED KINGDOM
www.bird-stamps.org/bss
E-mail: tony.statham@sky.com

Captain Cook Society
Jerry Yucht
8427 Leale Ave.
Stockton CA 95212
www.captaincooksociety.com
E-mail: US@captaincooksociety.com

The CartoPhilatelic Society
Marybeth Sulkowski
2885 Sanford Ave, SW, #32361
Grandville MI 49418-1342
www.mapsonstamps.org
E-mail: secretary@mapsonstamps.org

Casey Jones Railroad Unit
Roy W. Menninger MD
P.O. Box 5511
Topeka KS 66605
Ph: (785) 231-8366
www.uqp.de/cjr/index.htm
E-mail: roymenn85@gmail.com

Cats on Stamps Study Unit
Robert D. Jarvis
2731 Teton Lane
Fairfield CA 94533
www.catstamps.info
E-mail: bobmarci@aol.com

Chemistry & Physics on Stamps Study Unit
Dr. Roland Hirsch
20458 Water Point Lane
Germantown MD 20874
www.cpossu.org
E-mail: rfhirsch@cpossu.org

Chess on Stamps Study Unit
Ray C. Alexis
608 Emery St.
Longmont CO 80501
E-mail: chessstuff911459@aol.com

Christmas Philatelic Club
Jim Balog
P.O. Box 774
Geneva OH 44041
www.christmasphilatelicclub.org
E-mail: jpb4stamps@windstream.net

Cricket Philatelic Society
A.Melville-Brown, President
11 Weppons, Ravens Road
Shoreham-by-Sea
West Sussex, BN43 5AW
UNITED KINGDOM
www.cricketstamp.net
E-mail: mel.cricket.100@googlemail.com

Dogs on Stamps Study Unit
Morris Raskin
202A Newport Road
Monroe Township NJ 08831
Ph: (609) 655-7411
www.dossu.org
E-mail: mraskin@cellurian.com

Earth's Physical Features Study Group
Fred Klein
515 Magdalena Ave.
Los Altos CA 94024
epfsu.jeffhayward.com

Ebony Society of Philatelic Events and Reflections, Inc. (African-American topicals)
Manuel Gilyard
800 Riverside Drive, Suite 4H
New York NY 10032-7412
www.esperstamps.org
E-mail: gilyardmani@aol.com

Europa Study Unit
Tonny E. Van Loij
3002 S. Xanthia St.
Denver CO 80231-4237
Ph: (303) 752-0189
www.europastudyunit.org
E-mail: tvanloij@gmail.com

Fine & Performing Arts
Deborah L. Washington
6922 S. Jeffery Blvd., #7 - North
Chicago IL 60649
E-mail: brasslady@comcast.net

Fire Service in Philately
John Zaranek
81 Hillpine Road
Cheektowaga NY 14227-2259
Ph: (716) 668-3352
E-mail: jczaranek@roadrunner.com

Gay & Lesbian History on Stamps Club
Joe Petronie
P.O. Box 190842
Dallas TX 75219-0842
www.facebook.com/glhsc
E-mail: glhsc@aol.com

Gems, Minerals & Jewelry Study Unit
Mrs. Gilberte Proteau
138 Lafontaine
Beloeil QC J3G 2G7
CANADA
Ph: (978) 851-8283
E-mail: gilberte.ferland@sympatico.ca

Graphics Philately Association
Mark H. Winnegrad
P.O. Box 380
Bronx NY 10462-0380
www.graphics-stamps.org
E-mail: indybruce1@yahoo.com

Journalists, Authors & Poets on Stamps
Ms. Lee Straayer
P.O. Box 6808
Champaign IL 61826
E-mail: lstraayer@dcbnet.com

Lighthouse Stamp Society
Dalene Thomas
1805 S Balsam St., #106
Lakewood CO 80232
Ph: (303) 986-6620
www.lighthousestampsociety.org
E-mail: dalene@lighthousestampsociety.org

Lions International Stamp Club
John Bargus
108-2777 Barry Road RR 2
Mill Bay, BC, V0R 2P2
CANADA
Ph: (250) 743-5782

Mahatma Gandhi On Stamps Study Circle
Pramod Shivagunde
Pratik Clinic, Akluj
Solapur, Maharashtra, 413101
INDIA
E-mail: drnanda@bom6.vsnl.net.in

Masonic Study Unit
Stanley R. Longenecker
930 Wood St.
Mount Joy PA 17552-1926
Ph: (717) 669-9094
E-mail: natsco@usa.net

Mathematical Study Unit
Monty Strauss
4209 88th St.
Lubbock TX 79423-2941
www.mathstamps.org

Medical Subjects Unit
Dr. Frederick C. Skvara
P.O. Box 6228
Bridgewater NJ 08807
E-mail: fcskvara@optonline.net

Military Postal History Society
Ed Dubin
1 S. Wacker Drive, Suite 3500
Chicago IL 60606
www.militaryPHS.org
E-mail: dubine@comcast.net

Mourning Stamps and Covers Club
James Camak, Jr.
3801 Acapulco Ct.
Irving TX 75062
www.mscc.ms
E-mail: jamescamak7@gmail.com

Napoleonic Age Philatelists
Ken Berry
4117 NW 146th St.
Oklahoma City OK 73134-1746
Ph: (405) 748-8646
www.nap-stamps.org
E-mail: krb4117@att.net

Old World Archeological Study Unit
Caroline Scannell
11 Dawn Drive
Smithtown NY 11787-1761
www.owasu.org
E-mail: editor@owasu.org

Petroleum Philatelic Society International
Feitze Papa
922 Meander Dr.
Walnut Creek CA 94598-4239
E-mail: oildad@astound.net

Rotary on Stamps Unit
Gerald L. Fitzsimmons
105 Calla Ricardo
Victoria TX 77904
rotaryonstamps.org
E-mail: glfitz@suddenlink.net

Scouts on Stamps Society International
Lawrence Clay
P.O. Box 6228
Kennewick WA 99336
Ph: (509) 735-3731
www.sossi.org
E-mail: rfrank@sossi.org

Ships on Stamps Unit
Les Smith
302 Conklin Ave.
Penticton, BC, V2A 2T4
CANADA
Ph: (250) 493-7486
www.shipsonstamps.org
E-mail: lessmith440@shaw.ca

Space Unit
David Blog
P.O. Box 174
Bergenfield NJ 07621
www.space-unit.com
E-mail: davidblognj@gmail.com

Sports Philatelists International
Mark Maestrone
2824 Curie Place
San Diego CA 92122-4110
www.sportstamps.org
Email: president@sportstamps.org

Stamps on Stamps Collectors Club
Alf Jordan
156 W. Elm St.
Yarmouth ME 04096
www.stampsonstamps.org
E-mail: ajordan1@maine.rr.com

Windmill Study Unit
Orville Tysseling
9740 Washington Church Rd.
Miamisburg OH 45342-4510
www.wsu.world

Wine On Stamps Study Unit
David Wolfersberger
768 Chain Ridge Road
St. Louis MO 63122-3259
Ph: (314) 961-5032
www.wine-on-stamps.org
E-mail: dewolf2@swbell.net

Women on Stamps Study Unit
Hugh Gottfried
2232 26th St.
Santa Monica CA 90405-1902
E-mail: hgottfried@adelphia.net

Expertizing Services

The following organizations will, for a fee, provide expert opinions about stamps submitted to them. Collectors should contact these organizations to find out about their fees and requirements before submiting philatelic material to them. The listing of these groups here is not intended as an endorsement by Amos Media Co.

General Expertizing Services

American Philatelic Expertizing Service (a service of the American Philatelic Society)
100 Match Factory Place
Bellefonte PA 16823-1367
Ph: (814) 237-3803
Fax: (814) 237-6128
www.stamps.org
E-mail: ambristo@stamps.org
Areas of Expertise: Worldwide

B. P. A. Expertising, Ltd.
P.O. Box 1141
Guildford, Surrey, GU5 0WR
UNITED KINGDOM
E-mail: sec@bpaexpertising.org
Areas of Expertise: British Commonwealth, Great Britain, Classics of Europe, South America and the Far East

Philatelic Foundation
341 W. 38th St., 5th Floor
New York NY 10018
Ph: (212) 221-6555
Fax: (212) 221-6208
www.philatelicfoundation.org
E-mail: philatelicfoundation@verizon.net
Areas of Expertise: U.S. & Worldwide

Philatelic Stamp Authentication and Grading, Inc.
P.O. Box 41-0880
Melbourne FL 32941-0880
Customer Service: (305) 345-9864
www.psaginc.com
E-mail: info@psaginc.com
Areas of Expertise: U.S., Canal Zone, Hawaii, Philippines, Canada & Provinces

Professional Stamp Experts
P.O. Box 6170
Newport Beach CA 92658
Ph: (877) STAMP-88
Fax: (949) 833-7955
www.collectors.com/pse
E-mail: pseinfo@collectors.com
Areas of Expertise: Stamps and covers of U.S., U.S. Possessions, British Commonwealth

Royal Philatelic Society Expert Committee
41 Devonshire Place
London, W1N 1PE
UNITED KINGDOM
www.rpsl.org.uk/experts.html
E-mail: experts@rpsl.org.uk
Areas of Expertise: Worldwide

Expertizing Services Covering Specific Fields Or Countries

China Stamp Society Expertizing Service
1050 W. Blue Ridge Blvd.
Kansas City MO 64145
Ph: (816) 942-6300
E-mail: hjmesq@aol.com
Areas of Expertise: China

Confederate Stamp Alliance Authentication Service
Gen. Frank Crown, Jr.
P.O. Box 278
Capshaw AL 35742-0396
Ph: (302) 422-2656
Fax: (302) 424-1990
www.csalliance.org
E-mail: csaas@knology.net
Areas of Expertise: Confederate stamps and postal history

Errors, Freaks and Oddities Collectors Club Expertizing Service
138 East Lakemont Drive
Kingsland GA 31548
Ph: (912) 729-1573
Areas of Expertise: U.S. errors, freaks and oddities

Estonian Philatelic Society Expertizing Service
39 Clafford Lane
Melville NY 11747
Ph: (516) 421-2078
E-mail: esto4@aol.com
Areas of Expertise: Estonia

Hawaiian Philatelic Society Expertizing Service
P.O. Box 10115
Honolulu HI 96816-0115
Areas of Expertise: Hawaii

Hong Kong Stamp Society Expertizing Service
P.O. Box 206
Glenside PA 19038
Fax: (215) 576-6850
Areas of Expertise: Hong Kong

International Association of Philatelic Experts United States Associate members:

Paul Buchsbayew
119 W. 57th St.
New York NY 10019
Ph: (212) 977-7734
Fax: (212) 977-8653
Areas of Expertise: Russia, Soviet Union

William T. Crowe
P.O. Box 2090
Danbury CT 06813-2090
E-mail: wtcrowe@aol.com
Areas of Expertise: United States

John Lievsay
(see American Philatelic Expertizing Service and Philatelic Foundation)
Areas of Expertise: France

Robert W. Lyman
P.O. Box 348
Irvington on Hudson NY 10533
Ph and Fax: (914) 591-6937
Areas of Expertise: British North America, New Zealand

Robert Odenweller
P.O. Box 401
Bernardsville NJ 07924-0401
Ph and Fax: (908) 766-5460
Areas of Expertise: New Zealand, Samoa to 1900

Sergio Sismondo
The Regency Tower, Suite 1109
770 James Street
Syracuse NY 13203
Ph: (315) 422-2331
Fax: (315) 422-2956
Areas of Expertise: British East Africa, Camerouns, Cape of Good Hope, Canada, British North America

International Society for Japanese Philately Expertizing Committee
132 North Pine Terrace
Staten Island NY 10312-4052
Ph: (718) 227-5229
Areas of Expertise: Japan and related areas, except WWII Japanese Occupation issues

International Society for Portuguese Philately Expertizing Service
P.O. Box 43146
Philadelphia PA 19129-3146
Ph and Fax: (215) 843-2106
E-mail: s.s.washburne@worldnet.att.net
Areas of Expertise: Portugal and Colonies

Mexico-Elmhurst Philatelic Society International Expert Committee
P.O. Box 1133
West Covina CA 91793
Areas of Expertise: Mexico

Ukrainian Philatelic & Numismatic Society Expertizing Service
30552 Dell Lane
Warren MI 48092-1862
Areas of Expertise: Ukraine, Western Ukraine

V. G. Greene Philatelic Research Foundation
P.O. Box 204, Station Q
Toronto, ON, M4T 2M1
CANADA
Ph: (416) 921-2073
Fax: (416) 921-1282
www.greenefoundation.ca
E-mail: vggfoundation@on.aibn.com
Areas of Expertise: British North America

Information on Catalogue Values, Grade and Condition

Catalogue Value

The Scott Catalogue value is a retail value; that is, an amount you could expect to pay for a stamp in the grade of Very Fine with no faults. Any exceptions to the grade valued will be noted in the text. The general introduction on the following pages and the individual section introductions further explain the type of material that is valued. The value listed for any given stamp is a reference that reflects recent actual dealer selling prices for that item.

Dealer retail price lists, public auction results, published prices in advertising and individual solicitation of retail prices from dealers, collectors and specialty organizations have been used in establishing the values found in this catalogue. Amos Media Co. values stamps, but Amos Media is not a company engaged in the business of buying and selling stamps as a dealer.

Use this catalogue as a guide for buying and selling. The actual price you pay for a stamp may be higher or lower than the catalogue value because of many different factors, including the amount of personal service a dealer offers, or increased or decreased interest in the country or topic represented by a stamp or set. An item may occasionally be offered at a lower price as a "loss leader," or as part of a special sale. You also may obtain an item inexpensively at public auction because of little interest at that time or as part of a large lot.

Stamps that are of a lesser grade than Very Fine, or those with condition problems, generally trade at lower prices than those given in this catalogue. Stamps of exceptional quality in both grade and condition often command higher prices than those listed.

Values for pre-1900 unused issues are for stamps with approximately half or more of their original gum. Stamps with most or all of their original gum may be expected to sell for more, and stamps with less than half of their original gum may be expected to sell for somewhat less than the values listed. On rarer stamps, it may be expected that the original gum will be somewhat more disturbed than it will be on more common issues. Post-1900 unused issues are assumed to have full original gum. From breakpoints in most countries' listings, stamps are valued as never hinged, due to the wide availability of stamps in that condition. These notations are prominently placed in the listings and in the country information preceding the listings. Some countries also feature listings with dual values for hinged and never-hinged stamps.

Grade

A stamp's grade and condition are crucial to its value. The accompanying illustrations show examples of Very Fine stamps from different time periods, along with examples of stamps in Fine to Very Fine and Extremely Fine grades as points of reference. When a stamp seller offers a stamp in any grade from fine to superb without further qualifying statements, that stamp should not only have the centering grade as defined, but it also should be free of faults or other condition problems.

FINE stamps (illustrations not shown) have designs that are quite off center, with the perforations on one or two sides very close to the design but not quite touching it. There is white space between the perforations and the design that is minimal but evident to the unaided eye. Imperforate stamps may have small margins, and earlier issues may show the design just touching one edge of the stamp design. Very early perforated issues normally will have the perforations slightly cutting into the design. Used stamps may have heavier than usual cancellations.

FINE-VERY FINE stamps will be somewhat off center on one side, or slightly off center on two sides. Imperforate stamps will have two margins of at least normal size, and the design will not touch any edge. For perforated stamps, the perfs are well clear of the design, but are still noticeably off center. *However, early issues of a country may be printed in such a way that the design naturally is very close to the edges. In these cases, the perforations may cut into the design very slightly.* Used stamps will not have a cancellation that detracts from the design.

VERY FINE stamps will be just slightly off center on one or two sides, but the design will be well clear of the edge. The stamp will present a nice, balanced appearance. Imperforate stamps will be well centered within normal-sized margins. *However, early issues of many countries may be printed in such a way that the perforations may touch the design on one or more sides. Where this is the case, a boxed note will be found defining the centering and margins of the stamps being valued.* Used stamps will have light or otherwise neat cancellations. This is the grade used to establish Scott Catalogue values.

EXTREMELY FINE stamps are close to being perfectly centered. Imperforate stamps will have even margins that are slightly larger than normal. Even the earliest perforated issues will have perforations clear of the design on all sides.

Amos Media Co. recognizes that there is no formally enforced grading scheme for postage stamps, and that the final price you pay or obtain for a stamp will be determined by individual agreement at the time of transaction.

Condition

Grade addresses only centering and (for used stamps) cancellation. *Condition* refers to factors other than grade that affect a stamp's desirability.

Factors that can increase the value of a stamp include exceptionally wide margins, particularly fresh color, the presence of selvage, and plate or die varieties. Unusual cancels on used stamps (particularly those of the 19th century) can greatly enhance their value as well.

Factors other than faults that decrease the value of a stamp include loss of original gum, regumming, a hinge remnant or foreign object adhering to the gum, natural inclusions, straight edges, and markings or notations applied by collectors or dealers.

Faults include missing pieces, tears, pin or other holes, surface scuffs, thin spots, creases, toning, short or pulled perforations, clipped perforations, oxidation or other forms of color changelings, soiling, stains, and such man-made changes as reperforations or the chemical removal or lightening of a cancellation.

Grading Illustrations

On the following two pages are illustrations of various stamps from countries appearing in this volume. These stamps are arranged by country, and they represent early or important issues that are often found in widely different grades in the marketplace. The editors believe the illustrations will prove useful in showing the margin size and centering that will be seen on the various issues.

In addition to the matters of margin size and centering, collectors are reminded that the very fine stamps valued in the Scott catalogues also will possess fresh color and intact perforations, and they will be free from defects.

Examples shown are computer-manipulated images made from single digitized master illustrations.

Stamp Illustrations Used in the Catalogue

It is important to note that the stamp images used for identification purposes in this catlaogue may not be indicative of the grade of stamp being valued. Refer to the written discussion of grades on this page and to the grading illustrations on the following two pages for grading information.

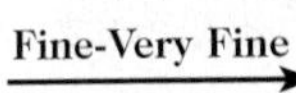
Fine-Very Fine

SCOTT CATALOGUES VALUE STAMPS IN THIS GRADE

Very Fine

Extremely Fine

Fine-Very Fine

SCOTT CATALOGUES VALUE STAMPS IN THIS GRADE

Very Fine

Extremely Fine

Fine-Very Fine →

SCOTT CATALOGUES VALUE STAMPS IN THIS GRADE

Very Fine →

Extremely Fine →

Fine-Very Fine →

SCOTT CATALOGUES VALUE STAMPS IN THIS GRADE

Very Fine →

Extremely Fine →

For purposes of helping to determine the gum condition and value of an unused stamp, Scott presents the following chart which details different gum conditions and indicates how the conditions correlate with the Scott values for unused stamps. Used together, the Illustrated Grading Chart on the previous pages and this Illustrated Gum Chart should allow catalogue users to better understand the grade and gum condition of stamps valued in the Scott catalogues.

Gum Categories:	MINT N.H.	ORIGINAL GUM (O.G.)				NO GUM
	 **Mint Never Hinged** *Free from any disturbance*	 **Lightly Hinged** *Faint impression of a removed hinge over a small area*	 **Hinge Mark or Remnant** *Prominent hinged spot with part or all of the hinge remaining*	 **Large part o.g.** *Approximately half or more of the gum intact*	 **Small part o.g.** *Approximately less than half of the gum intact*	**No gum** *Only if issued with gum*
Commonly Used Symbol:	★★	★	★	★	★	(★)
Pre-1900 Issues (Pre-1881 for U.S.)	*Very fine pre-1900 stamps in these categories trade at a premium over Scott value*			Scott Value for "Unused"		Scott "No Gum" listings for selected unused classic stamps
From 1900 to breakpoints for listings of never-hinged stamps	Scott "Never Hinged" listings for selected unused stamps	Scott Value for "Unused" (Actual value will be affected by the degree of hinging of the full o.g.)				
From breakpoints noted for many countries	Scott Value for "Unused"					

Never Hinged (NH; ★★): A never-hinged stamp will have full original gum that will have no hinge mark or disturbance. The presence of an expertizer's mark does not disqualify a stamp from this designation.

Original Gum (OG; ★): Pre-1900 stamps should have approximately half or more of their original gum. On rarer stamps, it may be expected that the original gum will be somewhat more disturbed than it will be on more common issues. Post-1900 stamps should have full original gum. Original gum will show some disturbance caused by a previous hinge(s) which may be present or entirely removed. The actual value of a post-1900 stamp will be affected by the degree of hinging of the full original gum.

Disturbed Original Gum: Gum showing noticeable effects of humidity, climate or hinging over more than half of the gum. The significance of gum disturbance in valuing a stamp in any of the Original Gum categories depends on the degree of disturbance, the rarity and normal gum condition of the issue and other variables affecting quality.

Regummed (RG; (★)): A regummed stamp is a stamp without gum that has had some type of gum privately applied at a time after it was issued. This normally is done to deceive collectors and/or dealers into thinking that the stamp has original gum and therefore has a higher value. A regummed stamp is considered the same as a stamp with none of its original gum for purposes of grading.

Understanding the Listings

On the opposite page is an enlarged "typical" listing from this catalogue. Below are detailed explanations of each of the highlighted parts of the listing.

❶ **Scott number** — Scott catalogue numbers are used to identify specific items when buying, selling or trading stamps. Each listed postage stamp from every country has a unique Scott catalogue number. Therefore, Germany Scott 99, for example, can only refer to a single stamp. Although the Scott catalogue usually lists stamps in chronological order by date of issue, there are exceptions. When a country has issued a set of stamps over a period of time, those stamps within the set are kept together without regard to date of issue. This follows the normal collecting approach of keeping stamps in their natural sets.

When a country issues a set of stamps over a period of time, a group of consecutive catalogue numbers is reserved for the stamps in that set, as issued. If that group of numbers proves to be too few, capital-letter suffixes, such as "A" or "B," may be added to existing numbers to create enough catalogue numbers to cover all items in the set. A capital-letter suffix indicates a major Scott catalogue number listing. Scott generally uses a suffix letter only once. Therefore, a catalogue number listing with a capital-letter suffix will seldom be found with the same letter (lower case) used as a minor-letter listing. If there is a Scott 16A in a set, for example, there will seldom be a Scott 16a. However, a minor-letter "a" listing may be added to a major number containing an "A" suffix (Scott 16Aa, for example).

Suffix letters are cumulative. A minor "b" variety of Scott 16A would be Scott 16Ab, not Scott 16b.

There are times when a reserved block of Scott catalogue numbers is too large for a set, leaving some numbers unused. Such gaps in the numbering sequence also occur when the catalogue editors move an item's listing elsewhere or have removed it entirely from the catalogue. Scott does not attempt to account for every possible number, but rather attempts to assure that each stamp is assigned its own number.

Scott numbers designating regular postage normally are only numerals. Scott numbers for other types of stamps, such as air post, semi-postal, postal tax, postage due, occupation and others have a prefix consisting of one or more capital letters or a combination of numerals and capital letters.

❷ **Illustration number** — Illustration or design-type numbers are used to identify each catalogue illustration. For most sets, the lowest face-value stamp is shown. It then serves as an example of the basic design approach for other stamps not illustrated. Where more than one stamp use the same illustration number, but have differences in design, the design paragraph or the description line clearly indicates the design on each stamp not illustrated. Where there are both vertical and horizontal designs in a set, a single illustration may be used, with the exceptions noted in the design paragraph or description line.

When an illustration is followed by a lower-case letter in parentheses, such as "A2(b)," the trailing letter indicates which overprint or surcharge illustration applies.

Illustrations normally are 70 percent of the original size of the stamp. Oversized stamps, blocks and souvenir sheets are reduced even more. Overprints and surcharges are shown at 100 percent of their original size if shown alone, but are 70 percent of original size if shown on stamps. In some cases, the illustration will be placed above the set, between listings or omitted completely. Overprint and surcharge illustrations are not placed in this catalogue for purposes of expertizing stamps.

❸ **Paper color** — The color of a stamp's paper is noted in italic type when the paper used is not white.

❹ **Listing styles** — There are two principal types of catalogue listings: major and minor.

Major listings are in a larger type style than minor listings. The catalogue number is a numeral that can be found with or without a capital-letter suffix, and with or without a prefix.

Minor listings are in a smaller type style and have a small-letter suffix or (if the listing immediately follows that of the major number) may show only the letter. These listings identify a variety of the major item. Examples include perforation and shade differences, multiples (some souvenir sheets, booklet panes and se-tenant combinations), and singles of multiples.

Examples of major number listings include 16, 28A, B97, C13A, 10N5, and 10N6A. Examples of minor numbers are 16a and C13Ab.

❺ **Basic information about a stamp or set** — Introducing each stamp issue is a small section (usually a line listing) of basic information about a stamp or set. This section normally includes the date of issue, method of printing, perforation, watermark and, sometimes, some additional information of note. *Printing method, perforation and watermark apply to the following sets until a change is noted.* Stamps created by overprinting or surcharging previous issues are assumed to have the same perforation, watermark, printing method and other production characteristics as the original. Dates of issue are as precise as Scott is able to confirm and often reflect the dates on first-day covers, rather than the actual date of release.

❻ **Denomination** — This normally refers to the face value of the stamp; that is, the cost of the unused stamp at the post office at the time of issue. When a denomination is shown in parentheses, it does not appear on the stamp. This includes the non-denominated stamps of the United States, Brazil and Great Britain, for example.

❼ **Color or other description** — This area provides information to solidify identification of a stamp. In many recent cases, a description of the stamp design appears in this space, rather than a listing of colors.

❽ **Year of issue** — In stamp sets that have been released in a period that spans more than a year, the number shown in parentheses is the year that stamp first appeared. Stamps without a date appeared during the first year of the issue. Dates are not always given for minor varieties.

❾ **Value unused and Value used** — The Scott catalogue values are based on stamps that are in a grade of Very Fine unless stated otherwise. Unused values refer to items that have not seen postal, revenue or any other duty for which they were intended. Pre-1900 unused stamps that were issued with gum must have at least most of their original gum. Later issues are assumed to have full original gum. From breakpoints specified in most countries' listings, stamps are valued as never hinged. Stamps issued without gum are noted. Modern issues with PVA or other synthetic adhesives may appear ungummed. Unused self-adhesive stamps are valued as appearing undisturbed on their original backing paper. Values for used self-adhesive stamps are for examples either on piece or off piece. For a more detailed explanation of these values, please see the "Catalogue Value," "Condition" and "Understanding Valuing Notations" sections elsewhere in this introduction.

In some cases, where used stamps are more valuable than unused stamps, the value is for an example with a contemporaneous cancel, rather than a modern cancel or a smudge or other unclear marking. For those stamps that were released for postal and fiscal purposes, the used value represents a postally used stamp. Stamps with revenue cancels generally sell for less.

Stamps separated from a complete se-tenant multiple usually will be worth less than a pro-rated portion of the se-tenant multiple, and stamps lacking the attached labels that are noted in the listings will be worth less than the values shown.

❿ **Changes in basic set information** — Bold type is used to show any changes in the basic data given for a set of stamps. These basic data categories include perforation gauge measurement, paper type, printing method and watermark.

⓫ **Total value of a set** — The total value of sets of three or more stamps issued after 1900 are shown. The set line also notes the range of Scott numbers and total number of stamps included in the grouping. The actual value of a set consisting predominantly of stamps having the minimum value of 25 cents may be less than the total value shown. Similarly, the actual value or catalogue value of se-tenant pairs or of blocks consisting of stamps having the minimum value of 25 cents may be less than the catalogue values of the component parts.

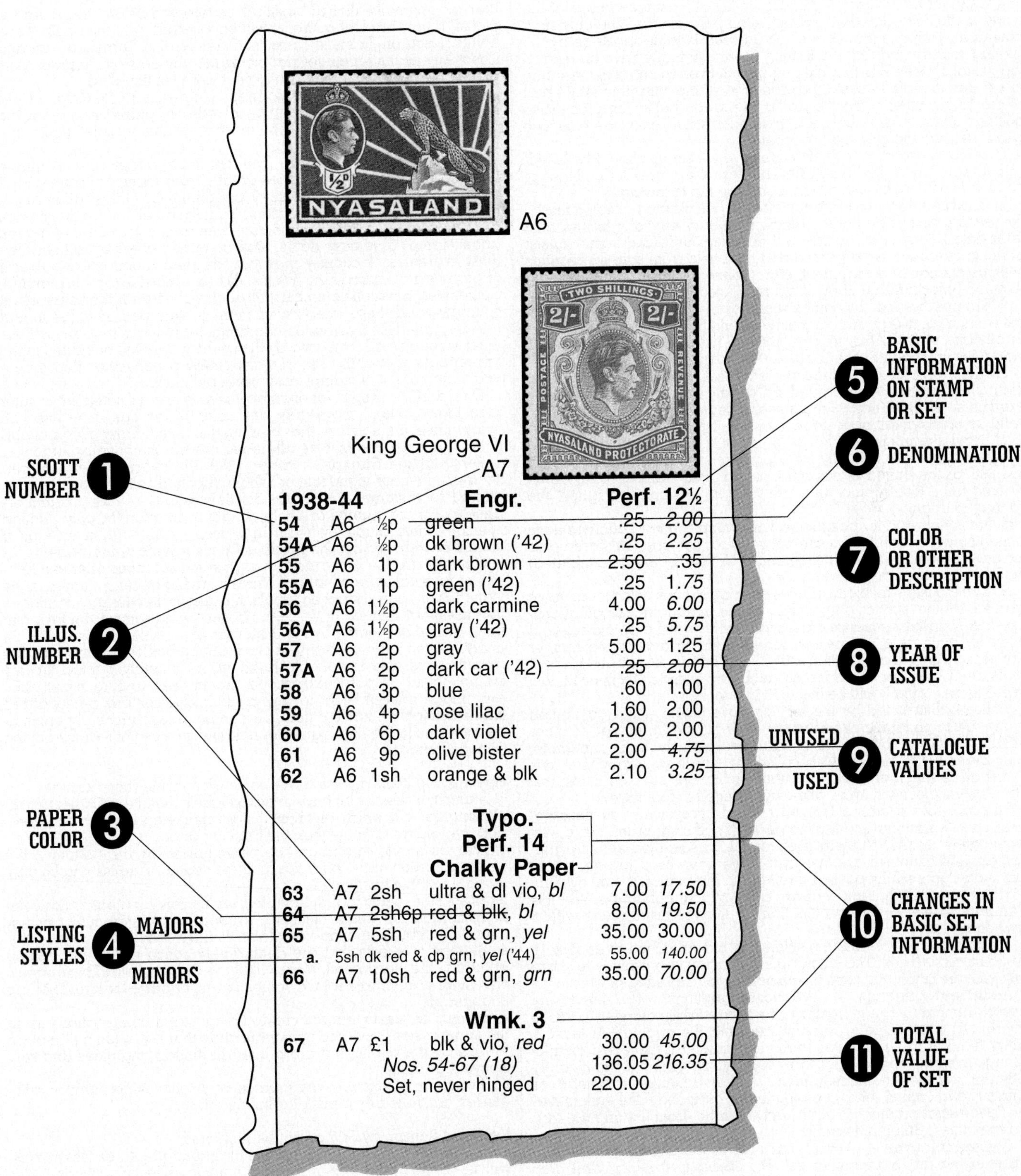

NYASALAND
1/2D
A6
TWO SHILLINGS
2/-
POSTAGE
REVENUE
NYASALAND PROTECTORATE
King George VI
A7
1938-44 Engr. Perf. 12½
54 A6 ½p green .25 2.00
54A A6 ½p dk brown ('42) .25 2.25
55 A6 1p dark brown 2.50 .35
55A A6 1p green ('42) .25 1.75
56 A6 1½p dark carmine 4.00 6.00
56A A6 1½p gray ('42) .25 5.75
57 A6 2p gray 5.00 1.25
57A A6 2p dark car ('42) .25 2.00
58 A6 3p blue .60 1.00
59 A6 4p rose lilac 1.60 2.00
60 A6 6p dark violet 2.00 2.00
61 A6 9p olive bister 2.00 4.75
62 A6 1sh orange & blk 2.10 3.25
Typo.
Perf. 14
Chalky Paper
63 A7 2sh ultra & dl vio, bl 7.00 17.50
64 A7 2sh6p red & blk, bl 8.00 19.50
65 A7 5sh red & grn, yel 35.00 30.00
a. 5sh dk red & dp grn, yel ('44) 55.00 140.00
66 A7 10sh red & grn, grn 35.00 70.00
Wmk. 3
67 A7 £1 blk & vio, red 30.00 45.00
Nos. 54-67 (18) 136.05 216.35
Set, never hinged 220.00
1 SCOTT NUMBER
2 ILLUS. NUMBER
3 PAPER COLOR
4 LISTING STYLES
MAJORS
MINORS
5 BASIC INFORMATION ON STAMP OR SET
6 DENOMINATION
7 COLOR OR OTHER DESCRIPTION
8 YEAR OF ISSUE
UNUSED
USED
9 CATALOGUE VALUES
10 CHANGES IN BASIC SET INFORMATION
11 TOTAL VALUE OF SET

Catalogue Listing Policy

It is the intent of Amos Media Co. to list all postage stamps of the world in the *Scott Standard Postage Stamp Catalogue*. The only strict criteria for listing is that stamps be decreed legal for postage by the issuing country and that the issuing country actually have an operating postal system. Whether the primary intent of issuing a given stamp or set was for sale to postal patrons or to stamp collectors is not part of our listing criteria. Scott's role is to provide basic comprehensive postage stamp information. It is up to each stamp collector to choose which items to include in a collection.

It is Scott's objective to seek reasons why a stamp should be listed, rather than why it should not. Nevertheless, there are certain types of items that will not be listed. These include the following:

1. Unissued items that are not officially distributed or released by the issuing postal authority. If such items are officially issued at a later date by the country, they will be listed. Unissued items consist of those that have been printed and then held from sale for reasons such as change in government, errors found on stamps or something deemed objectionable about a stamp subject or design.

2. Stamps "issued" by non-existent postal entities or fantasy countries, such as Nagaland, Occusi-Ambeno, Staffa, Sedang, Torres Straits and others. Also, stamps "issued" in the names of legitimate, stamp-issuing countries that are not authorized by those countries.

3. Semi-official or unofficial items not required for postage. Examples include items issued by private agencies for their own express services. When such items are required for delivery, or are valid as prepayment of postage, they are listed.

4. Local stamps issued for local use only. Postage stamps issued by governments specifically for "domestic" use, such as Haiti Scott 219-228, or the United States non-denominated stamps, are not considered to be locals, since they are valid for postage throughout the country of origin.

5. Items not valid for postal use. For example, a few countries have issued souvenir sheets that are not valid for postage. This area also includes a number of worldwide charity labels (some denominated) that do not pay postage.

6. Egregiously exploitative issues such as stamps sold for far more than face value, stamps purposefully issued in artificially small quantities or only against advance orders, stamps awarded only to a selected audience such as a philatelic bureau's standing order customers, or stamps sold only in conjunction with other products. All of these kinds of items are usually controlled issues and/or are intended for speculation. These items normally will be included in a footnote.

7. Items distributed by the issuing government only to a limited group, club, philatelic exhibition or a single stamp dealer or other private company. These items normally will be included in a footnote.

8. Stamps not available to collectors. These generally are rare items, all of which are held by public institutions such as museums. The existence of such items often will be cited in footnotes.

The fact that a stamp has been used successfully as postage, even on international mail, is not in itself sufficient proof that it was legitimately issued. Numerous examples of so-called stamps from non-existent countries are known to have been used to post letters that have successfully passed through the international mail system.

There are certain items that are subject to interpretation. When a stamp falls outside our specifications, it may be listed along with a cautionary footnote.

A number of factors are considered in our approach to analyzing how a stamp is listed. The following list of factors is presented to share with you, the catalogue user, the complexity of the listing process.

Additional printings — "Additional printings" of a previously issued stamp may range from an item that is totally different to cases where it is impossible to differentiate from the original. At least a minor number (a small-letter suffix) is assigned if there is a distinct change in stamp shade, noticeably redrawn design, or a significantly different perforation measurement. A major number (numeral or numeral and capital-letter combination) is assigned if the editors feel the "additional printing" is sufficiently different from the original that it constitutes a different issue.

Commemoratives — Where practical, commemoratives with the same theme are placed in a set. For example, the U.S. Civil War Centennial set of 1961-65 and the Constitution Bicentennial series of 1989-90 appear as sets. Countries such as Japan and Korea issue such material on a regular basis, with an announced, or at least predictable, number of stamps known in advance. Occasionally, however, stamp sets that were released over a period of years have been separated. Appropriately placed footnotes will guide you to each set's continuation.

Definitive sets — Blocks of numbers generally have been reserved for definitive sets, based on previous experience with any given country. If a few more stamps were issued in a set than originally expected, they often have been inserted into the original set with a capital-letter suffix, such as U.S. Scott 1059A. If it appears that many more stamps than the originally allotted block will be released before the set is completed, a new block of numbers will be reserved, with the original one being closed off. In some cases, such as the U.S. Transportation and Great Americans series, several blocks of numbers exist. Appropriately placed footnotes will guide you to each set's continuation.

New country — Membership in the Universal Postal Union is not a consideration for listing status or order of placement within the catalogue. The index will tell you in what volume or page number the listings begin.

"No release date" items — The amount of information available for any given stamp issue varies greatly from country to country and even from time to time. Extremely comprehensive information about new stamps is available from some countries well before the stamps are released. By contrast some countries do not provide information about stamps or release dates. Most countries, however, fall between these extremes. A country may provide denominations or subjects of stamps from upcoming issues that are not issued as planned. Sometimes, philatelic agencies, those private firms hired to represent countries, add these later-issued items to sets well after the formal release date. This time period can range from weeks to years. If these items were officially released by the country, they will be added to the appropriate spot in the set. In many cases, the specific release date of a stamp or set of stamps may never be known.

Overprints — The color of an overprint is always noted if it is other than black. Where more than one color of ink has been used on overprints of a single set, the color used is noted. Early overprint and surcharge illustrations were altered to prevent their use by forgers.

Personalized Stamps — Since 1999, the special service of personalizing stamp vignettes, or labels attached to stamps, has been offered to customers by postal administrations of many countries. Sheets of these stamps are sold, singly or in quantity, only through special orders made by mail, in person, or through a sale on a computer website with the postal administrations or their agents for which an extra fee is charged, though some countries offer to collectors at face value personalized stamps having generic images in the vignettes or on the attached labels. It is impossible for any catalogue to know what images have been chosen by customers. Images can be 1) owned or created by the customer, 2) a generic image, or 3) an image pulled from a library of stock images on the stamp creation website. It is also impossible to know the quantity printed for any stamp having a particular image. So from a valuing standpoint, any image is equivalent to any other image for any personalized stamp having the same catalogue number. Illustrations of personalized stamps in the catalogue are not always those of stamps having generic images.

Personalized items are listed with some exceptions. These include:

1. Stamps or sheets that have attached labels that the customer cannot personalize, but which are nonetheless marketed as "personalized," and are sold for far more than the franking value.
2. Stamps or sheets that can be personalized by the customer, but where a portion of the print run must be ceded to the issuing country for sale to other customers.
3. Stamps or sheets that are created exclusively for a particular commercial client, or clients, including stamps that differ from any similar stamp that has been made available to the public.
4. Stamps or sheets that are deliberately conceived by the issuing authority that have been, or are likely to be, created with an excessive number of different face values, sizes, or other features that are changeable.
5. Stamps or sheets that are created by postal administrations using the same system of stamp personalization that has been put in place for use by the public that are printed in limited quantities and sold above face value.
6. Stamps or sheets that are created by licensees not directly affiliated or controlled by a postal administration.

Excluded items may or may not be footnoted.

Se-tenants — Connected stamps of differing features (se-tenants) will be listed in the format most commonly collected. This includes pairs, blocks or larger multiples. Se-tenant units are not always symmetrical. An example is Australia Scott 508, which is a block of seven stamps. If the stamps are primarily collected as a unit, the major number may be assigned to the multiple, with minors going to each component stamp. In cases where continuous-design or other unit se-tenants will receive significant postal use, each stamp is given a major Scott number listing. This includes issues from the United States, Canada, Germany and Great Britain, for example.

Special Notices

Classification of stamps

The *Scott Standard Postage Stamp Catalogue* lists stamps by country of issue. The next level of organization is a listing by section on the basis of the function of the stamps. The principal sections cover regular postage, semi-postal, air post, special delivery, registration, postage due and other categories. Except for regular postage, catalogue numbers for all sections include a prefix letter (or number-letter combination) denoting the class to which a given stamp belongs. When some countries issue sets containing stamps from more than one category, the catalogue will at times list all of the stamps in one category (such as air post stamps listed as part of a postage set).

The following is a listing of the most commonly used catalogue prefixes.

Prefix ....Category
C.........Air Post
M........Military
P.........Newspaper
N.........Occupation - Regular Issues
O........Official
Q........Parcel Post
J..........Postage Due
RA......Postal Tax
B.........Semi-Postal
E.........Special Delivery
MR......War Tax

Other prefixes used by more than one country include the following:
H.........Acknowledgment of Receipt
I..........Late Fee
CO......Air Post Official
CQ......Air Post Parcel Post
RAC....Air Post Postal Tax
CF......Air Post Registration
CB......Air Post Semi-Postal
CBO...Air Post Semi-Postal Official
CE......Air Post Special Delivery
EY.......Authorized Delivery
S.........Franchise
G........Insured Letter
GY......Marine Insurance
MC.....Military Air Post
MQ.....Military Parcel Post
NC......Occupation - Air Post
NO......Occupation - Official
NJ........Occupation - Postage Due
NRA....Occupation - Postal Tax
NB......Occupation - Semi-Postal
NE......Occupation - Special Delivery
QY......Parcel Post Authorized Delivery
AR......Postal-fiscal
RAJ.....Postal Tax Due
RAB....Postal Tax Semi-Postal
F.........Registration
EB.......Semi-Postal Special Delivery
EO......Special Delivery Official
QE......Special Handling

New issue listings

Updates to this catalogue appear each month in the *Linn's Stamp News* monthly magazine. Included in this update are additions to the listings of countries found in the *Scott Standard Postage Stamp Catalogue* and the *Specialized Catalogue of United States Stamps and Covers*, as well as corrections and updates to current editions of this catalogue.

From time to time there will be changes in the final listings of stamps from the *Linn's Stamp News* magazine to the next edition of the catalogue. This occurs as more information about certain stamps or sets becomes available.

The catalogue update section of the *Linn's Stamp News* magazine is the most timely presentation of this material available. Annual subscriptions to *Linn's Stamp News* are available from Linn's Stamp News, Box 926, Sidney, OH 45365-0926.

Number additions, deletions & changes

A listing of catalogue number additions, deletions and changes from the previous edition of the catalogue appears in each volume. See Catalogue Number Additions, Deletions & Changes in the table of contents for the location of this list.

Understanding valuing notations

The *minimum catalogue value* of an individual stamp or set is 25 cents. This represents a portion of the cost incurred by a dealer when he prepares an individual stamp for resale. As a point of philatelic-economic fact, the lower the value shown for an item in this catalogue, the greater the percentage of that value is attributed to dealer mark up and profit margin. In many cases, such as the 25-cent minimum value, that price does not cover the labor or other costs involved with stocking it as an individual stamp. The sum of minimum values in a set does not properly represent the value of a complete set primarily composed of a number of minimum-value stamps, nor does the sum represent the actual value of a packet made up of minimum-value stamps. Thus a packet of 1,000 different common stamps — each of which has a catalogue value of 25 cents — normally sells for considerably less than 250 dollars!

The *absence of a retail value* for a stamp does not necessarily suggest that a stamp is scarce or rare. A dash in the value column means that the stamp is known in a stated form or variety, but information is either lacking or insufficient for purposes of establishing a usable catalogue value.

Stamp values in *italics* generally refer to items that are difficult to value accurately. For expensive items, such as those priced at $1,000 or higher, a value in italics indicates that the affected item trades very seldom. For inexpensive items, a value in italics represents a warning. One example is a "blocked" issue where the issuing postal administration may have controlled one stamp in a set in an attempt to make the whole set more valuable. Another example is an item that sold at an extreme multiple of face value in the marketplace at the time of its issue.

One type of warning to collectors that appears in the catalogue is illustrated by a stamp that is valued considerably higher in used condition than it is as unused. In this case, collectors are cautioned to be certain the used version has a genuine and contemporaneous cancellation. The type of cancellation on a stamp can be an important factor in determining its sale price. Catalogue values do not apply to fiscal, telegraph or non-contemporaneous postal cancels, unless otherwise noted.

Some countries have released back issues of stamps in canceled-to-order form, sometimes covering as much as a 10-year period. The Scott Catalogue values for used stamps reflect canceled-to-order material when such stamps are found to predominate in the marketplace for the issue involved. Notes frequently appear in the stamp listings to specify which items are valued as canceled-to-order, or if there is a premium for postally used examples.

Many countries sell canceled-to-order stamps at a marked reduction of face value. Countries that sell or have sold canceled-to-order stamps at *full* face value include United Nations, Australia, Netherlands, France and Switzerland. It may be almost impossible to identify such stamps if the gum has been removed, because official government canceling devices are used. Postally used examples of these items on cover, however, are usually worth more than the canceled-to-order stamps with original gum.

Abbreviations

Scott uses a consistent set of abbreviations throughout this catalogue to conserve space, while still providing necessary information.

COLOR ABBREVIATIONS

amb. amber
anil.. aniline
ap.... apple
aqua aquamarine
az .... azure
bis ... bister
bl..... blue
bld... blood
blk ... black
bril... brilliant
brn... brown
brnsh brownish
brnz. bronze
brt.... bright
brnt . burnt
car... carmine
cer ... cerise
chlky chalky
chamchamois
chnt . chestnut
choc chocolate
chr... chrome
cit .... citron
cl...... claret
cob .. cobalt
cop .. copper
crim. crimson
cr..... cream
dk .... dark
dl ..... dull
dp.... deep
db.... drab
emer emerald
gldn. golden
gryshgrayish
grn... green
grnsh greenish
hel ... heliotrope
hn .... henna
ind ... indigo
int .... intense
lav ... lavender
lem .. lemon
lil ..... lilac
lt ...... light
mag. magenta
man. manila
mar.. maroon
mv ... mauve
multi multicolored
mlky milky
myr .. myrtle
ol ..... olive
olvn . olivine
org... orange
pck .. peacock
pnksh pinkish
Prus. Prussian
pur... purple
redsh reddish
res ... reseda
ros ... rosine
ryl .... royal
sal ... salmon
saph sapphire
scar. scarlet
sep .. sepia
sien . sienna
sil..... silver
sl...... slate
stl ...... steel
turq.. turquoise
ultra ultramarine
Ven .. Venetian
ver ... vermilion
vio ... violet
yel ... yellow
yelsh yellowish

When no color is given for an overprint or surcharge, black is the color used. Abbreviations for colors used for overprints and surcharges include: "(B)" or "(Blk)," black; "(Bl)," blue; "(R)," red; and "(G)," green.

Additional abbreviations in this catalogue are shown below:

Adm. ....Administration
AFL...............American Federation of Labor
Anniv. ....Anniversary
APS ....American Philatelic Society
Assoc. ....Association
ASSR. ....Autonomous Soviet Socialist Republic
b. ....Born
BEP...............Bureau of Engraving and Printing
Bicent. ....Bicentennial
Bklt. ....Booklet
Brit................British
btwn. ....Between
Bur. ....Bureau
c. or ca. ....Circa
Cat. ....Catalogue
Cent. ....Centennial, century, centenary
CIO ....Congress of Industrial Organizations
Conf. ....Conference
Cong. ....Congress
Cpl. ....Corporal
CTO ....Canceled to order
d. ....Died
Dbl. ....Double
EDU..............Earliest documented use
Engr. ....Engraved
Exhib. ....Exhibition
Expo. ....Exposition
Fed. ....Federation
GB ....Great Britain
Gen. ....General
GPO ....General post office
Horiz. ....Horizontal
Imperf. ....Imperforate
Impt. ....Imprint
Intl. ....International
Invtd. ....Inverted
L ....Left
Lieut., lt. ....Lieutenant
Litho. ....Lithographed
LL ....Lower left
LR.................Lower right
mm ....Millimeter
Ms. ....Manuscript
Natl. ....National
No.................Number
NY ....New York
NYC ....New York City
Ovpt. ....Overprint
Ovptd. ....Overprinted
P ....Plate number
Perf. ....Perforated, perforation
Phil. ....Philatelic
Photo. ....Photogravure
PO ....Post office
Pr. ....Pair
P.R. ....Puerto Rico
Prec. ....Precancel, precanceled
Pres. ....President
PTT ....Post, Telephone and Telegraph
R ....Right
Rio ....Rio de Janeiro
Sgt. ....Sergeant
Soc. ....Society
Souv. ....Souvenir
SSR ....Soviet Socialist Republic, see ASSR
St. ....Saint, street
Surch. ....Surcharge
Typo. ....Typographed
UL.................Upper left
Unwmkd. ......Unwatermarked
UPU..............Universal Postal Union
UR ....Upper Right
US ....United States
USPOD ....United States Post Office Department
USSR ....Union of Soviet Socialist Republics
Vert. ....Vertical
VP.................Vice president
Wmk. ....Watermark
Wmkd. ....Watermarked
WWI ....World War I
WWII ....World War II

Examination

Amos Media Co. will not comment upon the genuineness, grade or condition of stamps, because of the time and responsibility involved. Rather, there are several expertizing groups that undertake this work for both collectors and dealers. Neither will Amos Media Co. appraise or identify philatelic material. The company cannot take responsibility for unsolicited stamps or covers sent by individuals.

All letters, E-mails, etc. are read attentively, but they are not always answered due to time considerations.

How to order from your dealer

When ordering stamps from a dealer, it is not necessary to write the full description of a stamp as listed in this catalogue. All you need is the name of the country, the Scott catalogue number and whether the desired item is unused or used. For example, "Japan Scott 422 unused" is sufficient to identify the unused stamp of Japan listed as "422 A206 5y brown."

Basic Stamp Information

A stamp collector's knowledge of the combined elements that make a given stamp issue unique determines his or her ability to identify stamps. These elements include paper, watermark, method of separation, printing, design and gum. On the following pages each of these important areas is briefly described.

Paper

Paper is an organic material composed of a compacted weave of cellulose fibers and generally formed into sheets. Paper used to print stamps may be manufactured in sheets, or it may have been part of a large roll (called a web) before being cut to size. The fibers most often used to create paper on which stamps are printed include bark, wood, straw and certain grasses. In many cases, linen or cotton rags have been added for greater strength and durability. Grinding, bleaching, cooking and rinsing these raw fibers reduces them to a slushy pulp, referred to by paper makers as "stuff." Sizing and, sometimes, coloring matter is added to the pulp to make different types of finished paper.

After the stuff is prepared, it is poured onto sieve-like frames that allow the water to run off, while retaining the matted pulp. As fibers fall onto the screen and are held by gravity, they form a natural weave that will later hold the paper together. If the screen has metal bits that are formed into letters or images attached, it leaves slightly thinned areas on the paper. These are called watermarks.

When the stuff is almost dry, it is passed under pressure through smooth or engraved rollers - dandy rolls - or placed between cloth in a press to be flattened and dried.

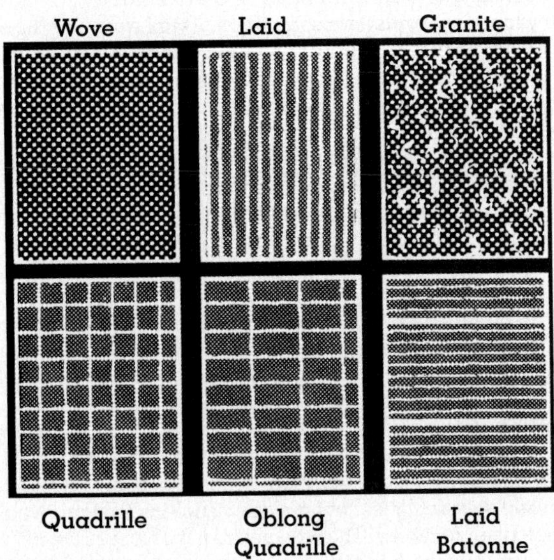

Stamp paper falls broadly into two types: wove and laid. The nature of the surface of the frame onto which the pulp is first deposited causes the differences in appearance between the two. If the surface is smooth and even, the paper will be of fairly uniform texture throughout. This is known as *wove paper*. Early papermaking machines poured the pulp onto a continuously circulating web of felt, but modern machines feed the pulp onto a cloth-like screen made of closely interwoven fine wires. This paper, when held to a light, will show little dots or points very close together. The proper name for this is "wire wove," but the type is still considered wove. Any U.S. or British stamp printed after 1880 will serve as an example of wire wove paper.

Closely spaced parallel wires, with cross wires at wider intervals, make up the frames used for what is known as *laid paper*. A greater thickness of the pulp will settle between the wires. The paper, when held to a light, will show alternate light and dark lines. The spacing and the thickness of the lines may vary, but on any one sheet of paper they are all alike. See Russia Scott 31-38 for examples of laid paper.

Batonne, from the French word meaning "a staff," is a term used if the lines in the paper are spaced quite far apart, like the printed ruling on a writing tablet. Batonne paper may be either wove or laid. If laid, fine laid lines can be seen between the batons.

Quadrille is the term used when the lines in the paper form little squares. *Oblong quadrille* is the term used when rectangles, rather than squares, are formed. Grid patterns vary from distinct to extremely faint. See Mexico-Guadalajara Scott 35-37 for examples of oblong quadrille paper.

Paper also is classified as thick or thin, hard or soft, and by color. Such colors may include yellowish, greenish, bluish and reddish.

Brief explanations of other types of paper used for printing stamps, as well as examples, follow.

Colored — Colored paper is created by the addition of dye in the paper-making process. Such colors may include shades of yellow, green, blue and red. *Surface-colored papers*, most commonly used for British colonial issues in 1913-14, are created when coloring is added only to the surface during the finishing process. Stamps printed on surface-colored paper have white or uncolored backs, while true colored papers are colored through. See Jamaica Scott 71-73.

Pelure — Pelure paper is a very thin, hard and often brittle paper that is sometimes bluish or grayish in appearance. See Serbia Scott 169-170.

Native — This is a term applied to handmade papers used to produce some of the early stamps of the Indian states. Stamps printed on native paper may be expected to display various natural inclusions that are normal and do not negatively affect value. Japanese paper, originally made of mulberry fibers and rice flour, is part of this group. See Japan Scott 1-18.

Manila — This type of paper is often used to make stamped envelopes and wrappers. It is a coarse-textured stock, usually smooth on one side and rough on the other. A variety of colors of manila paper exist, but the most common range is yellowish-brown.

Silk — Introduced by the British in 1847 as a safeguard against counterfeiting, silk paper contains bits of colored silk thread scattered throughout. The density of these fibers varies greatly and can include as few as one fiber per stamp or hundreds. U.S. revenue Scott R152 is a good example of an easy-to-identify silk paper stamp.

Silk-thread paper has uninterrupted threads of colored silk arranged so that one or more threads run through the stamp or postal stationery. See Great Britain Scott 5-6 and Switzerland Scott 14-19.

Granite — Filled with minute cloth or colored paper fibers of various colors and lengths, granite paper should not be confused with either type of silk paper. Austria Scott 172-175 and a number of Swiss stamps are examples of granite paper.

Chalky — A chalk-like substance coats the surface of chalky paper to discourage the cleaning and reuse of canceled stamps, as well as to provide a smoother, more acceptable printing surface. Because the designs of stamps printed on chalky paper are imprinted on what is often a water-soluble coating, any attempt to remove a cancellation will destroy the stamp. *Do not soak these stamps in any fluid.* To remove a stamp printed on chalky paper from an envelope, wet the paper from underneath the stamp until the gum dissolves enough to release the stamp from the paper. See St. Kitts-Nevis Scott 89-90 for examples of stamps printed on this type of chalky paper.

India — Another name for this paper, originally introduced from China about 1750, is "China Paper." It is a thin, opaque paper often used for plate and die proofs by many countries.

Double — In philately, the term double paper has two distinct meanings. The first is a two-ply paper, usually a combination of a thick and a thin sheet, joined during manufacture. This type was used experimentally as a means to discourage the reuse of stamps.

The design is printed on the thin paper. Any attempt to remove a cancellation would destroy the design. U.S. Scott 158 and other Banknote-era stamps exist on this form of double paper.

The second type of double paper occurs on a rotary press, when the end of one paper roll, or web, is affixed to the next roll to save time feeding the paper through the press. Stamp designs are printed over the joined paper and, if overlooked by inspectors, may get into post office stocks.

Goldbeater's Skin — This type of paper was used for the 1866 issue of Prussia, and was a tough, translucent paper. The design was printed in reverse on the back of the stamp, and the gum applied over the printing. It is impossible to remove stamps printed on this type of paper from the paper to which they are affixed without destroying the design.

Ribbed — Ribbed paper has an uneven, corrugated surface made by passing the paper through ridged rollers. This type exists on some copies of U.S. Scott 156-165.

Various other substances, or substrates, have been used for stamp manufacture, including wood, aluminum, copper, silver and gold foil, plastic, and silk and cotton fabrics.

Watermarks

Watermarks are an integral part of some papers. They are formed in the process of paper manufacture. Watermarks consist of small designs, formed of wire or cut from metal and soldered to the surface of the mold or, sometimes, on the dandy roll. The designs may be in the form of crowns, stars, anchors, letters or other characters or symbols. These pieces of metal - known in the paper-making industry as "bits" - impress a design into the paper. The design sometimes may be seen by holding the stamp to the light. Some are more easily seen with a watermark detector. This important tool is a small black tray into which a stamp is placed face down and dampened with a fast-evaporating watermark detection fluid that brings up the watermark image in the form of dark lines against a lighter background. These dark lines are the thinner areas of the paper known as the watermark. Some watermarks are extremely difficult to locate, due to either a faint impression, watermark location or the color of the stamp. There also are electric watermark detectors that come with plastic filter disks of various colors. The disks neutralize the color of the stamp, permitting the watermark to be seen more easily.

Multiple watermarks of Crown Agents and Burma

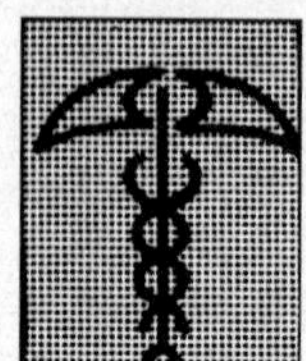

Watermarks of Uruguay, Vatican City and Jamaica

WARNING: Some inks used in the photogravure process dissolve in watermark fluids (Please see the section on Soluble Printing Inks). Also, see "chalky paper."

Watermarks may be found normal, reversed, inverted, reversed and inverted, sideways or diagonal, as seen from the back of the stamp. The relationship of watermark to stamp design depends on the position of the printing plates or how paper is fed through the press. On machine-made paper, watermarks normally are read from right to left. The design is repeated closely throughout the sheet in a "multiple-watermark design." In a "sheet watermark," the design appears only once on the sheet, but extends over many stamps. Individual stamps may carry only a small fraction or none of the watermark.

"Marginal watermarks" occur in the margins of sheets or panes of stamps. They occur on the outside border of paper (ostensibly outside the area where stamps are to be printed). A large row of letters may spell the name of the country or the manufacturer of the paper, or a border of lines may appear. Careless press feeding may cause parts of these letters and/or lines to show on stamps of the outer row of a pane.

Soluble Printing Inks

WARNING: Most stamp colors are permanent; that is, they are not seriously affected by short-term exposure to light or water. Many colors, especially of modern inks, fade from excessive exposure to light. There are stamps printed with inks that dissolve easily in water or in fluids used to detect watermarks. Use of these inks was intentional to prevent the removal of cancellations. Water affects all aniline inks, those on so-called safety paper and some photogravure printings - all such inks are known as fugitive colors. *Removal from paper of such stamps requires care and alternatives to traditional soaking.*

Separation

"Separation" is the general term used to describe methods used to separate stamps. The three standard forms currently in use are perforating, rouletting and die-cutting. These methods are done during the stamp production process, after printing. Sometimes these methods are done on-press or sometimes as a separate step. The earliest issues, such as the 1840 Penny Black of Great Britain (Scott 1), did not have any means provided for separation. It was expected the stamps would be cut apart with scissors or folded and torn. These are examples of imperforate stamps. Many stamps were first issued in imperforate formats and were later issued with perforations. Therefore, care must be observed in buying single imperforate stamps to be certain they were issued imperforate and are not perforated copies that have been altered by having the perforations trimmed away. Stamps issued imperforate usually are valued as singles. However, imperforate varieties of normally perforated stamps should be collected in pairs or larger pieces as indisputable evidence of their imperforate character.

PERFORATION

The chief style of separation of stamps, and the one that is in almost universal use today, is perforating. By this process, paper between the stamps is cut away in a line of holes, usually round, leaving little bridges of paper between the stamps to hold them together. Some types of perforation, such as hyphen-hole perfs, can be confused with roulettes, but a close visual inspection reveals that paper has been removed. The little perforation bridges, which project from the stamp when it is torn from the pane, are called the teeth of the perforation.

As the size of the perforation is sometimes the only way to differentiate between two otherwise identical stamps, it is necessary to be able to accurately measure and describe them. This is done with a perforation gauge, usually a ruler-like device that has dots or graduated lines to show how many perforations may be counted in the space of two centimeters. Two centimeters is the space universally adopted in which to measure perforations.

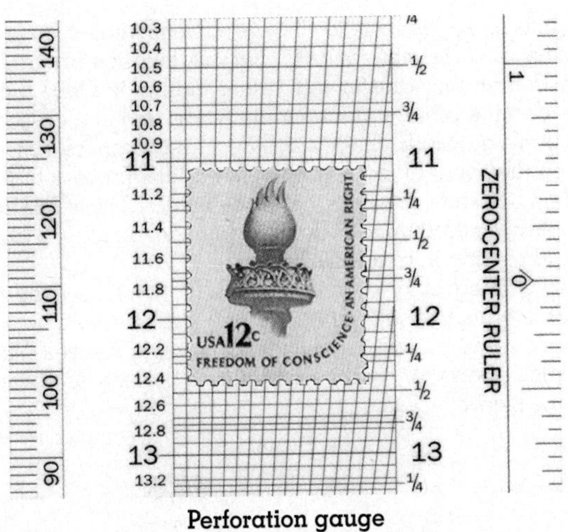

Perforation gauge

To measure a stamp, run it along the gauge until the dots on it fit exactly into the perforations of the stamp. If you are using a graduated-line perforation gauge, simply slide the stamp along the surface until the lines on the gauge perfectly project from the center of the bridges or holes. The number to the side of the line of dots or lines that fit the stamp's perforation is the measurement. For example, an "11" means that 11 perforations fit between two centimeters. The description of the stamp therefore is "perf. 11." If the gauge of the perforations on the top and bottom of a stamp differs from that on the sides, the result is what is known as *compound perforations*. In measuring compound perforations, the gauge at top and bottom is always given first, then the sides. Thus, a stamp that measures 11 at top and bottom and 10½ at the sides is "perf. 11 x 10½." See U.S. Scott 632-642 for examples of compound perforations.

Stamps also are known with perforations different on three or all four sides. Descriptions of such items are clockwise, beginning with the top of the stamp.

A perforation with small holes and teeth close together is a "fine perforation." One with large holes and teeth far apart is a "coarse perforation." Holes that are jagged, rather than clean-cut, are "rough perforations." *Blind perforations* are the slight impressions left by the perforating pins if they fail to puncture the paper. Multiples of stamps showing blind perforations may command a slight premium over normally perforated stamps.

The term *syncopated perfs* describes intentional irregularities in the perforations. The earliest form was used by the Netherlands from 1925-33, where holes were omitted to create distinctive patterns. Beginning in 1992, Great Britain has used an oval perforation to help prevent counterfeiting. Several other countries have started using the oval perfs or other syncopated perf patterns.

A new type of perforation, still primarily used for postal stationery, is known as microperfs. Microperfs are tiny perforations (in some cases hundreds of holes per two centimeters) that allows items to be intentionally separated very easily, while not accidentally breaking apart as easily as standard perforations. These are not currently measured or differentiated by size, as are standard perforations.

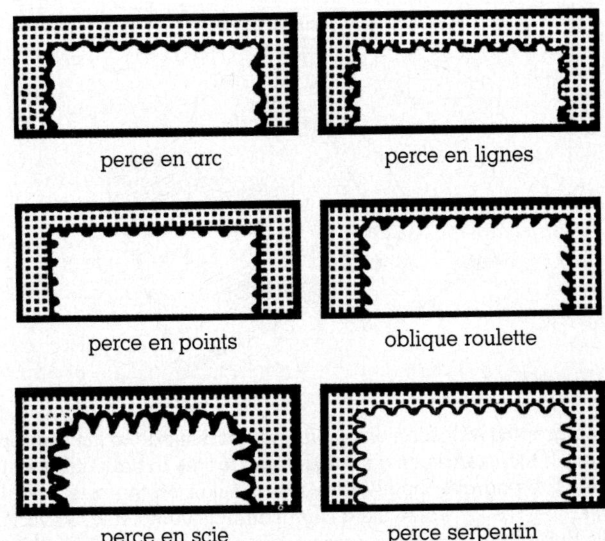

ROULETTING

In rouletting, the stamp paper is cut partly or wholly through, with no paper removed. In perforating, some paper is removed. Rouletting derives its name from the French roulette, a spur-like wheel. As the wheel is rolled over the paper, each point makes a small cut. The number of cuts made in a two-centimeter space determines the gauge of the roulette, just as the number of perforations in two centimeters determines the gauge of the perforation.

The shape and arrangement of the teeth on the wheels varies. Various roulette types generally carry French names:

Perce en lignes - rouletted in lines. The paper receives short, straight cuts in lines. This is the most common type of rouletting. See Mexico Scott 500.

Perce en points - pin-rouletted or pin-perfed. This differs from a small perforation because no paper is removed, although round, equidistant holes are pricked through the paper. See Mexico Scott 242-256.

Perce en arc and *perce en scie* - pierced in an arc or saw-toothed designs, forming half circles or small triangles. See Hanover (German States) Scott 25-29.

Perce en serpentin - serpentine roulettes. The cuts form a serpentine or wavy line. See Brunswick (German States) Scott 13-18.

Once again, no paper is removed by these processes, leaving the stamps easily separated, but closely attached.

DIE-CUTTING

The third major form of stamp separation is die-cutting. This is a method where a die in the pattern of separation is created that later cuts the stamp paper in a stroke motion. Although some standard stamps bear die-cut perforations, this process is primarily used for self-adhesive postage stamps. Die-cutting can appear in straight lines, such as U.S. Scott 2522, shapes, such as U.S. Scott 1551, or imitating the appearance of perforations, such as New Zealand Scott 935A and 935B.

Printing Processes

ENGRAVING (Intaglio, Line-engraving, Etching)

Master die — The initial operation in the process of line engraving is making the master die. The die is a small, flat block of softened steel upon which the stamp design is recess engraved in reverse.

Master die

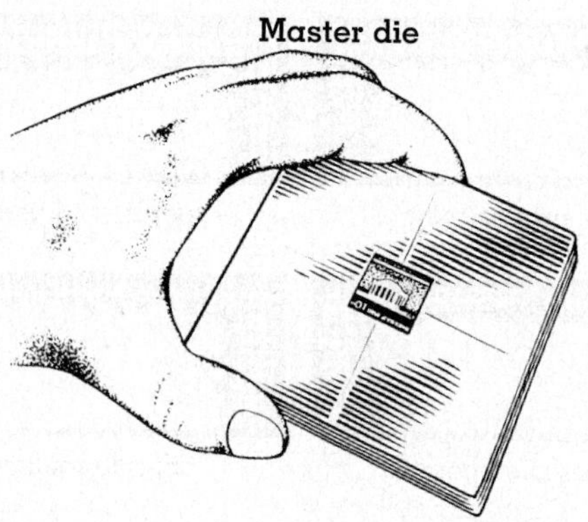

Photographic reduction of the original art is made to the appropriate size. It then serves as a tracing guide for the initial outline of the design. The engraver lightly traces the design on the steel with his graver, then slowly works the design until it is completed. At various points during the engraving process, the engraver hand-inks the die and makes an impression to check his progress. These are known as progressive die proofs. After completion of the engraving, the die is hardened to withstand the stress and pressures of later transfer operations.

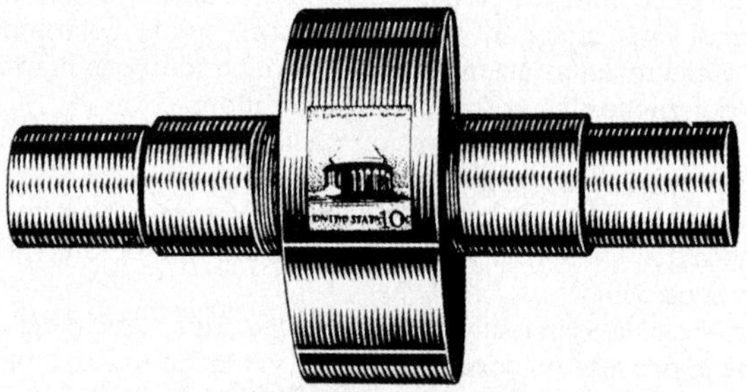

Transfer roll

Transfer roll — Next is production of the transfer roll that, as the name implies, is the medium used to transfer the subject from the master die to the printing plate. A blank roll of soft steel, mounted on a mandrel, is placed under the bearers of the transfer press to allow it to roll freely on its axis. The hardened die is placed on the bed of the press and the face of the transfer roll is applied to the die, under pressure. The bed or the roll is then rocked back and forth under increasing pressure, until the soft steel of the roll is forced into every engraved line of the die. The resulting impression on the roll is known as a "relief" or a "relief transfer." The engraved image is now positive in appearance and stands out from the steel. After the required number of reliefs are "rocked in," the soft steel transfer roll is hardened.

Different flaws may occur during the relief process. A defective relief may occur during the rocking in process because of a minute piece of foreign material lodging on the die, or some other cause. Imperfections in the steel of the transfer roll may result in a breaking away of parts of the design. This is known as a relief break, which will show up on finished stamps as small, unprinted areas. If a damaged relief remains in use, it will transfer a repeating defect to the plate. Deliberate alterations of reliefs sometimes occur. "Altered reliefs" designate these changed conditions.

Plate — The final step in pre-printing production is the making of the printing plate. A flat piece of soft steel replaces the die on the bed of the transfer press. One of the reliefs on the transfer roll is positioned over this soft steel. Position, or layout, dots determine the correct position on the plate. The dots have been lightly marked on the plate in advance. After the correct position of the relief is determined, the design is rocked in by following the same method used in making the transfer roll. The difference is that this time the image is being transferred from the transfer roll, rather than to it. Once the design is entered on the plate, it appears in reverse and is recessed. There are as many transfers entered on the plate as there are subjects printed on the sheet of stamps. It is during this process that double and shifted transfers occur, as well as re-entries. These are the result of improperly entered images that have not been properly burnished out prior to rocking in a new image.

Modern siderography processes, such as those used by the U.S. Bureau of Engraving and Printing, involve an automated form of rocking designs in on preformed cylindrical printing sleeves. The same process also allows for easier removal and re-entry of worn images right on the sleeve.

Transferring the design to the plate

Following the entering of the required transfers on the plate, the position dots, layout dots and lines, scratches and other markings generally are burnished out. Added at this time by the siderographer are any required *guide lines, plate numbers* or other *marginal markings*. The plate is then hand-inked and a proof impression is taken. This is known as a plate proof. If the impression is approved, the plate is machined for fitting onto the press, is hardened and sent to the plate vault ready for use.

On press, the plate is inked and the surface is automatically wiped clean, leaving ink only in the recessed lines. Paper is then forced under pressure into the engraved recessed lines, thereby receiving the ink. Thus, the ink lines on engraved stamps are slightly raised, and slight depressions (debossing) occur on the back of the stamp. Prior to the advent of modern high-speed presses and more advanced ink formulations, paper had to be dampened before receiving the ink. This sometimes led to uneven shrinkage by the time the stamps were perforated, resulting in improperly perforated stamps, or misperfs. Newer presses use drier paper, thus both *wet* and *dry printings* exist on some stamps.

Rotary Press — Until 1914, only flat plates were used to print engraved stamps. Rotary press printing was introduced in 1914, and slowly spread. Some countries still use flat-plate printing.

After approval of the plate proof, older *rotary press plates* require additional machining. They are curved to fit the press cylinder. "Gripper slots" are cut into the back of each plate to receive the "grippers," which hold the plate securely on the press. The plate is then hardened. Stamps printed from these bent rotary press plates are longer or wider than the same stamps printed from flat-plate presses. The stretching of the plate during the curving process is what causes this distortion.

Re-entry — To execute a re-entry on a flat plate, the transfer roll is re-applied to the plate, often at some time after its first use on the press. Worn-out designs can be resharpened by carefully burnishing out the original image and re-entering it from the transfer roll. If the original impression has not been sufficiently removed and the transfer roll is not precisely in line with the remaining impression, the resulting double transfer will make the re-entry obvious. If the registration is true, a re-entry may be difficult or impossible to distinguish. Sometimes a stamp printed from a successful re-entry is identified by having a much sharper and clearer impression than its neighbors. With the advent of rotary presses, post-press re-entries were not possible. After a plate was curved for the rotary press, it was impossible to make a re-entry. This is because the plate had already been bent once (with the design distorted).

However, with the introduction of the previously mentioned modern-style siderography machines, entries are made to the preformed cylindrical printing sleeve. Such sleeves are dechromed and softened. This allows individual images to be burnished out and re-entered on the curved sleeve. The sleeve is then rechromed, resulting in longer press life.

Double Transfer — This is a description of the condition of a transfer on a plate that shows evidence of a duplication of all, or a portion of the design. It usually is the result of the changing of the registration between the transfer roll and the plate during the rocking in of the original entry. Double transfers also occur when only a portion of the design has been rocked in and improper positioning is noted. If the worker elected not to burnish out the partial or completed design, a strong double transfer will occur for part or all of the design.

It sometimes is necessary to remove the original transfer from a plate and repeat the process a second time. If the finished re-worked image shows traces of the original impression, attributable to incomplete burnishing, the result is a partial double transfer.

With the modern automatic machines mentioned previously, double transfers are all but impossible to create. Those partially doubled images on stamps printed from such sleeves are more than likely re-entries, rather than true double transfers.

Re-engraved — Alterations to a stamp design are sometimes necessary after some stamps have been printed. In some cases, either the original die or the actual printing plate may have its "temper" drawn (softened), and the design will be re-cut. The resulting impressions from such a re-engraved die or plate may differ slightly from the original issue, and are known as "re-engraved." If the alteration was made to the master die, all future printings will be consistently different from the original. If alterations were made to the printing plate, each altered stamp on the plate will be slightly different from each other, allowing specialists to reconstruct a complete printing plate.

Dropped Transfers — If an impression from the transfer roll has not been properly placed, a dropped transfer may occur. The final stamp image will appear obviously out of line with its neighbors.

Short Transfer — Sometimes a transfer roll is not rocked its entire length when entering a transfer onto a plate. As a result, the finished transfer on the plate fails to show the complete design, and the finished stamp will have an incomplete design printed. This is known as a "short transfer." U.S. Scott No. 8 is a good example of a short transfer.

TYPOGRAPHY (Letterpress, Surface Printing, Flexography, Dry Offset, High Etch)

Although the word "Typography" is obsolete as a term describing a printing method, it was the accepted term throughout the first century of postage stamps. Therefore, appropriate Scott listings in this catalogue refer to typographed stamps. The current term for this form of printing, however, is "letterpress."

As it relates to the production of postage stamps, letterpress printing is the reverse of engraving. Rather than having recessed areas trap the ink and deposit it on paper, only the raised areas of the design are inked. This is comparable to the type of printing seen by inking and using an ordinary rubber stamp. Letterpress includes all printing where the design is above the surface area, whether it is wood, metal or, in some instances, hardened rubber or polymer plastic.

For most letterpress-printed stamps, the engraved master is made in much the same manner as for engraved stamps. In this instance, however, an additional step is needed. The design is transferred to another surface before being transferred to the transfer roll. In this way, the transfer roll has a recessed stamp design, rather than one done in relief. This makes the printing areas on the final plate raised, or relief areas.

For less-detailed stamps of the 19th century, the area on the die not used as a printing surface was cut away, leaving the surface area raised. The original die was then reproduced by stereotyping or electrotyping. The resulting electrotypes were assembled in the required number and format of the desired sheet of stamps. The plate used in printing the stamps was an electroplate of these assembled electrotypes.

Once the final letterpress plates are created, ink is applied to the raised surface and the pressure of the press transfers the ink impression to the paper. In contrast to engraving, the fine lines of letterpress are impressed on the surface of the stamp, leaving a debossed surface. When viewed from the back (as on a typewritten page), the corresponding line work on the stamp will be raised slightly (embossed) above the surface.

PHOTOGRAVURE (Gravure, Rotogravure, Heliogravure)

In this process, the basic principles of photography are applied to a chemically sensitized metal plate, rather than photographic paper. The design is transferred photographically to the plate through a halftone, or dot-matrix screen, breaking the reproduction into tiny dots. The plate is treated chemically and the dots form depressions, called cells, of varying depths and diameters, depending on the degrees of shade in the design. Then, like engraving, ink is applied to the plate and the surface is wiped clean. This leaves ink in the tiny cells that is lifted out and deposited on the paper when it is pressed against the plate.

Gravure is most often used for multicolored stamps, generally using the three primary colors (red, yellow and blue) and black. By varying the dot matrix pattern and density of these colors, virtually any color can be reproduced. A typical full-color gravure stamp will be created from four printing cylinders (one for each color). The original multicolored image will have been photographically separated into its component colors.

Modern gravure printing may use computer-generated dot-matrix screens, and modern plates may be of various types including metal-coated plastic. The catalogue designation of Photogravure (or "Photo") covers any of these older and more modern gravure methods of printing.

For examples of the first photogravure stamps printed (1914), see Bavaria Scott 94-114.

LITHOGRAPHY (Offset Lithography, Stone Lithography, Dilitho, Planography, Collotype)

The principle that oil and water do not mix is the basis for lithography. The stamp design is drawn by hand or transferred from engraving to the surface of a lithographic stone or metal plate in a greasy (oily) substance. This oily substance holds the ink, which will later be transferred to the paper. The stone (or plate) is wet with an acid fluid, causing it to repel the printing ink in all areas not covered by the greasy substance.

Transfer paper is used to transfer the design from the original stone or plate. A series of duplicate transfers are grouped and, in turn, transferred to the final printing plate.

Photolithography — The application of photographic processes to lithography. This process allows greater flexibility of design, related to use of halftone screens combined with line work. Unlike photogravure or engraving, this process can allow large, solid areas to be printed.

Offset — A refinement of the lithographic process. A rubber-covered blanket cylinder takes the impression from the inked lithographic plate. From the "blanket" the impression is *offset* or transferred to the paper. Greater flexibility and speed are the principal reasons offset printing has largely displaced lithography. The term "lithography" covers both processes, and results are almost identical.

EMBOSSED (Relief) Printing

Embossing, not considered one of the four main printing types, is a method in which the design first is sunk into the metal of the die. Printing is done against a yielding platen, such as leather or linoleum. The platen is forced into the depression of the die, thus forming the design on the paper in relief. This process is often used for metallic inks.

Embossing may be done without color (see Sardinia Scott 4-6); with color printed around the embossed area (see Great Britain Scott 5 and most U.S. envelopes); and with color in exact registration with the embossed subject (see Canada Scott 656-657).

HOLOGRAMS

For objects to appear as holograms on stamps, a model exactly the same size as it is to appear on the hologram must be created. Rather than using photographic film to capture the image, holography records an image on a photoresist material. In processing, chemicals eat away at certain exposed areas, leaving a pattern of constructive and destructive interference. When the photoresist is developed, the result is a pattern of uneven ridges that acts as a mold. This mold is then coated with metal, and the resulting form is used to press copies in much the same way phonograph records are produced.

A typical reflective hologram used for stamps consists of a reproduction of the uneven patterns on a plastic film that is applied to a reflective background, usually a silver or gold foil. Light is reflected off the background through the film, making the pattern present on the film visible. Because of the uneven pattern of the film, the viewer will perceive the objects in their proper three-dimensional relationships with appropriate brightness.

The first hologram on a stamp was produced by Austria in 1988 (Scott 1441).

FOIL APPLICATION

A modern technique of applying color to stamps involves the application of metallic foil to the stamp paper. A pattern of foil is applied to the stamp paper by use of a stamping die. The foil usually is flat, but it may be textured. Canada Scott 1735 has three different foil applications in pearl, bronze and gold. The gold foil was textured using a chemical-etch copper embossing die. The printing of this stamp also involved two-color offset lithography plus embossing.

THERMOGRAPHY

In the 1990s stamps began to be enhanced with thermographic printing. In this process, a powdered polymer is applied over a sheet that has just been printed. The powder adheres to ink that lacks drying or hardening agents and does not adhere to areas where the ink has these agents. The excess powder is removed and the sheet is briefly heated to melt the powder. The melted powder solidifies after cooling, producing a raised, shiny effect on the stamps. See Scott New Caledonia C239-C240.

COMBINATION PRINTINGS

Sometimes two or even three printing methods are combined in producing stamps. In these cases, such as Austria Scott 933 or Canada 1735 (described in the preceding paragraph), the multiple-printing technique can be determined by studying the individual characteristics of each printing type. A few stamps, such as Singapore Scott 684-684A, combine as many as three of the four major printing types (lithography, engraving and typography). When this is done it often indicates the incorporation of security devices against counterfeiting.

INK COLORS

Inks or colored papers used in stamp printing often are of mineral origin, although there are numerous examples of organic-based pigments. As a general rule, organic-based pigments are far more subject to varieties and change than those of mineral-based origin.

The appearance of any given color on a stamp may be affected by many aspects, including printing variations, light, color of paper, aging and chemical alterations.

Numerous printing variations may be observed. Heavier pressure or inking will cause a more intense color, while slight interruptions in the ink feed or lighter impressions will cause a lighter appearance. Stamps printed in the same color by water-based and solvent-based inks can differ significantly in appearance. This affects several stamps in the U.S. Prominent Americans series. Hand-mixed ink formulas (primarily from the 19th century) produced under different conditions (humidity and temperature) account for notable color variations in early printings of the same stamp (see U.S. Scott 248-250, 279B, for example). Different sources of pigment can also result in significant differences in color.

Light exposure and aging are closely related in the way they affect stamp color. Both eventually break down the ink and fade colors, so that a carefully kept stamp may differ significantly in color from an identical copy that has been exposed to light. If stamps are exposed to light either intentionally or accidentally, their colors can be faded or completely changed in some cases.

Papers of different quality and consistency used for the same stamp printing may affect color appearance. Most pelure papers, for example, show a richer color when compared with wove or laid papers. See Russia Scott 181a, for an example of this effect.

The very nature of the printing processes can cause a variety of differences in shades or hues of the same stamp. Some of these shades are scarcer than others, and are of particular interest to the advanced collector.

Luminescence

All forms of tagged stamps fall under the general category of luminescence. Within this broad category is fluorescence, dealing with forms of tagging visible under longwave ultraviolet light, and phosphorescence, which deals with tagging visible only under shortwave light. Phosphorescence leaves an afterglow and fluorescence does not. These treated stamps show up in a range of different colors when exposed to UV light. The differing wavelengths of the light activates the tagging material, making it glow in various colors that usually serve different mail processing purposes.

Intentional tagging is a post-World War II phenomenon, brought about by the increased literacy rate and rapidly growing mail volume. It was one of several answers to the problem of the need for more automated mail processes. Early tagged stamps served the purpose of triggering machines to separate different types of mail. A natural outgrowth was to also use the signal to trigger machines that faced all envelopes the same way and canceled them.

Tagged stamps come in many different forms. Some tagged stamps have luminescent shapes or images imprinted on them as a form of security device. Others have blocks (United States), stripes, frames (South Africa and Canada), overall coatings (United States), bars (Great Britain and Canada) and many other types. Some types of tagging are even mixed in with the pigmented printing ink (Australia Scott 366, Netherlands Scott 478 and U.S. Scott 1359 and 2443).

The means of applying taggant to stamps differs as much as the intended purposes for the stamps. The most common form of tagging is a coating applied to the surface of the printed stamp. Since the taggant ink is frequently invisible except under UV light, it does not interfere with the appearance of the stamp. Another common application is the use of phosphored papers. In this case the paper itself either has a coating of taggant applied before the stamp is printed, has taggant applied during the papermaking process (incorporating it into the fibers), or has the taggant mixed into the coating of the paper. The latter method, among others, is currently in use in the United States.

Many countries now use tagging in various forms to either expedite mail handling or to serve as a printing security device against counterfeiting. Following the introduction of tagged stamps for public use in 1959 by Great Britain, other countries have steadily joined the parade. Among those are Germany (1961); Canada and Denmark (1962); United States, Australia, France and Switzerland (1963); Belgium and Japan (1966); Sweden and Norway (1967); Italy (1968); and Russia (1969). Since then, many other countries have begun using forms of tagging, including Brazil, China, Czechoslovakia, Hong Kong, Guatemala, Indonesia, Israel, Lithuania, Luxembourg, Netherlands, Penrhyn Islands, Portugal, St. Vincent, Singapore, South Africa, Spain and Sweden to name a few.

In some cases, including United States, Canada, Great Britain and Switzerland, stamps were released both with and without tagging. Many of these were released during each country's experimental period. Tagged and untagged versions are listed for the aforementioned countries and are noted in some other countries' listings. For at least a few stamps, the experimentally tagged version is worth far more than its untagged counterpart, such as the 1963 experimental tagged version of France Scott 1024.

In some cases, luminescent varieties of stamps were inadvertently created. Several Russian stamps, for example, sport highly fluorescent ink that was not intended as a form of tagging. Older stamps, such as early U.S. postage dues, can be positively identified by the use of UV light, since the organic ink used has become slightly fluorescent over time. Other stamps, such as Austria Scott 70a-82a (varnish bars) and Obock Scott 46-64 (printed quadrille lines), have become fluorescent over time.

Various fluorescent substances have been added to paper to make it appear brighter. These optical brightners, as they are known, greatly affect the appearance of the stamp under UV light. The brightest of these is known as Hi-Brite paper. These paper varieties are beyond the scope of the Scott Catalogue.

Shortwave UV light also is used extensively in expertizing, since each form of paper has its own fluorescent characteristics that are impossible to perfectly match. It is therefore a simple matter to detect filled thins, added perforation teeth and other alterations that involve the addition of paper. UV light also is used to examine stamps that have had cancels chemically removed and for other purposes as well.

Gum

The Illustrated Gum Chart in the first part of this introduction shows and defines various types of gum condition. Because gum condition has an important impact on the value of unused stamps, we recommend studying this chart and the accompanying text carefully.

The gum on the back of a stamp may be shiny, dull, smooth, rough, dark, white, colored or tinted. Most stamp gumming adhesives use gum arabic or dextrine as a base. Certain polymers such as polyvinyl alcohol (PVA) have been used extensively since World War II.

The *Scott Standard Postage Stamp Catalogue* does not list items by types of gum. The *Scott Specialized Catalogue of United States Stamps and Covers* does differentiate among some types of gum for certain issues.

Reprints of stamps may have gum differing from the original issues. In addition, some countries have used different gum formulas for different seasons. These adhesives have different properties that may become more apparent over time.

Many stamps have been issued without gum, and the catalogue will note this fact. See, for example, United States Scott 40-47. Sometimes, gum may have been removed to preserve the stamp. Germany Scott B68, for example, has a highly acidic gum that eventually destroys the stamps. This item is valued in the catalogue with gum removed.

Reprints and Reissues

These are impressions of stamps (usually obsolete) made from the original plates or stones. If they are valid for postage and reproduce obsolete issues (such as U.S. Scott 102-111), the stamps are *reissues.* If they are from current issues, they are designated as *second, third, etc., printing.* If designated for a particular purpose, they are called *special printings.*

When special printings are not valid for postage, but are made from original dies and plates by authorized persons, they are *official reprints. Private reprints* are made from the original plates and dies by private hands. An example of a private reprint is that of the 1871-1932 reprints made from the original die of the 1845 New Haven, Conn., postmaster's provisional. *Official reproductions* or imitations are made from new dies and plates by government authorization. Scott will list those reissues that are valid for postage if they differ significantly from the original printing.

The U.S. government made special printings of its first postage stamps in 1875. Produced were official imitations of the first two stamps (listed as Scott 3-4), reprints of the demonetized pre-1861 issues (Scott 40-47) and reissues of the 1861 stamps, the 1869 stamps and the then-current 1875 denominations. Even though the official imitations and the reprints were not valid for postage, Scott lists all of these U.S. special printings.

Most reprints or reissues differ slightly from the original stamp in some characteristic, such as gum, paper, perforation, color or watermark. Sometimes the details are followed so meticulously that only a student of that specific stamp is able to distinguish the reprint or reissue from the original.

Remainders and Canceled to Order

Some countries sell their stock of old stamps when a new issue replaces them. To avoid postal use, the *remainders* usually are canceled with a punch hole, a heavy line or bar, or a more-or-less regular-looking cancellation. The most famous merchant of remainders was Nicholas F. Seebeck. In the 1880s and 1890s, he arranged printing contracts between the Hamilton Bank Note Co., of which he was a director, and several Central and South American countries. The contracts provided that the plates and all remainders of the yearly issues became the property of Hamilton. Seebeck saw to it that ample stock remained. The "Seebecks," both remainders and reprints, were standard packet fillers for decades.

Some countries also issue stamps *canceled-to-order (CTO),* either in sheets with original gum or stuck onto pieces of paper or envelopes and canceled. Such CTO items generally are worth less than postally used stamps. In cases where the CTO material is far more prevalent in the marketplace than postally used examples, the catalogue value relates to the CTO examples, with postally used examples noted as premium items. Most CTOs can be detected by the presence of gum. However, as the CTO practice goes back at least to 1885, the gum inevitably has been soaked off some stamps so they could pass as postally used. The normally applied postmarks usually differ slightly from standard postmarks, and specialists are able to tell the difference. When applied individually to envelopes by philatelically minded persons, CTO material is known as *favor canceled* and generally sells at large discounts.

Cinderellas and Facsimiles

Cinderella is a catch-all term used by stamp collectors to describe phantoms, fantasies, bogus items, municipal issues, exhibition seals, local revenues, transportation stamps, labels, poster stamps and many other types of items. Some cinderella collectors include in their collections local postage issues, telegraph stamps, essays and proofs, forgeries and counterfeits.

A *fantasy* is an adhesive created for a nonexistent stamp-issuing authority. Fantasy items range from imaginary countries (Occusi-Ambeno, Kingdom of Sedang, Principality of Trinidad or Torres Straits), to non-existent locals (Winans City Post), or nonexistent transportation lines (McRobish & Co.'s Acapulco-San Francisco Line).

On the other hand, if the entity exists and could have issued stamps (but did not) or was known to have issued other stamps, the items are considered *bogus* stamps. These would include the Mormon postage stamps of Utah, S. Allan Taylor's Guatemala and Paraguay inventions, the propaganda issues for the South Moluccas and the adhesives of the Page & Keyes local post of Boston.

Phantoms is another term for both fantasy and bogus issues.

Facsimiles are copies or imitations made to represent original stamps, but which do not pretend to be originals. A catalogue illustration is such a facsimile. Illustrations from the Moens catalogue of the last century were occasionally colored and passed off as stamps. Since the beginning of stamp collecting, facsimiles have been made for collectors as space fillers or for reference. They often carry the word "facsimile," "falsch" (German), "sanko" or "mozo" (Japanese), or "faux" (French) overprinted on the face or stamped on the back. Unfortunately, over the years a number of these items have had fake cancels applied over the facsimile notation and have been passed off as genuine.

Forgeries and Counterfeits

Forgeries and counterfeits have been with philately virtually from the beginning of stamp production. Over time, the terminology for the two has been used interchangeably. Although both forgeries and counterfeits are reproductions of stamps, the purposes behind their creation differ considerably.

Among specialists there is an increasing movement to more specifically define such items. Although there is no universally accepted terminology, we feel the following definitions most closely mirror the items and their purposes as they are currently defined.

Forgeries (also often referred to as *Counterfeits*) are reproductions of genuine stamps that have been created to defraud collectors. Such spurious items first appeared on the market around 1860, and most old-time collections contain one or more. Many are crude and easily spotted, but some can deceive experts.

An important supplier of these early philatelic forgeries was the Hamburg printer Gebruder Spiro. Many others with reputations in this craft included S. Allan Taylor, George Hussey, James Chute, George Forune, Benjamin & Sarpy, Julius Goldner, E. Oneglia and L.H. Mercier. Among the noted 20th-century forgers were Francois Fournier, Jean Sperati and the prolific Raoul DeThuin.

Forgeries may be complete replications, or they may be genuine stamps altered to resemble a scarcer (and more valuable) type. Most forgeries, particularly those of rare stamps, are worth only a small fraction of the value of a genuine example, but a few types, created by some of the most notable forgers, such as Sperati, can be worth as much or more than the genuine. Fraudulently produced copies are known of most classic rarities and many medium-priced stamps.

In addition to rare stamps, large numbers of common 19th- and early 20th-century stamps were forged to supply stamps to the early packet trade. Many can still be easily found. Few new philatelic forgeries have appeared in recent decades. Successful imitation of well-engraved work is virtually impossible. It has proven far easier to produce a fake by altering a genuine stamp than to duplicate a stamp completely.

Counterfeit (also often referred to as *Postal Counterfeit* or *Postal Forgery*) is the term generally applied to reproductions of stamps that have been created to defraud the government of revenue. Such items usually are created at the time a stamp is current and, in some cases, are hard to detect. Because most counterfeits are seized when the perpetrator is captured, postal counterfeits, particularly used on cover, are usually worth much more than a genuine example to specialists. The first postal counterfeit was of Spain's 4-cuarto carmine of 1854 (the real one is Scott 25). Apparently, the counterfeiters were not satisfied with their first version, which is now very scarce, and they soon created an engraved counterfeit, which is common. Postal counterfeits quickly followed in Austria, Naples, Sardinia and the Roman States. They have since been created in many other countries as well, including the United States.

An infamous counterfeit to defraud the government is the 1-shilling Great Britain "Stock Exchange" forgery of 1872, used on telegraph forms at the exchange that year. The stamp escaped detection until a stamp dealer noticed it in 1898.

Fakes

Fakes are genuine stamps altered in some way to make them more desirable. One student of this part of stamp collecting has estimated that by the 1950s more than 30,000 varieties of fakes were known. That number has grown greatly since then. The widespread existence of fakes makes it important for stamp collectors to study their philatelic holdings and use relevant literature. Likewise, collectors should buy from reputable dealers who guarantee their stamps and make full and prompt refunds should a purchased item be declared faked or altered by some mutually agreed-upon authority. Because fakes always have some genuine characteristics, it is not always possible to obtain unanimous agreement among experts regarding specific items. These students may change their opinions as philatelic knowledge increases. More than 80 percent of all fakes on the philatelic market today are regummed, reperforated (or perforated for the first time), or bear forged overprints, surcharges or cancellations.

Stamps can be chemically treated to alter or eliminate colors. For example, a pale rose stamp can be re-colored to resemble a blue shade of high market value. In other cases, treated stamps can be made to resemble missing color varieties. Designs may be changed by painting, or a stroke or a dot added or bleached out to turn an ordinary variety into a seemingly scarcer stamp. Part of a stamp can be bleached and reprinted in a different version, achieving an inverted center or frame. Margins can be added or repairs done so deceptively that the stamps move from the "repaired" into the "fake" category.

Fakers have not left the backs of the stamps untouched either. They may create false watermarks, add fake grills or press out genuine grills. A thin India paper proof may be glued onto a thicker backing to create the appearance an issued stamp, or a proof printed on cardboard may be shaved down and perforated to resemble a stamp. Silk threads are impressed into paper and stamps have been split so that a rare paper variety is added to an otherwise inexpensive stamp. The most common treatment to the back of a stamp, however, is regumming.

Some in the business of faking stamps have openly advertised fool-proof application of "original gum" to stamps that lack it, although most publications now ban such ads from their pages. It is believed that very few early stamps have survived without being hinged. The large number of never-hinged examples of such earlier material offered for sale thus suggests the widespread extent of regumming activity. Regumming also may be used to hide repairs or thin spots. Dipping the stamp into watermark fluid, or examining it under longwave ultraviolet light often will reveal these flaws.

Fakers also tamper with separations. Ingenious ways to add margins are known. Perforated wide-margin stamps may be falsely represented as imperforate when trimmed. Reperforating is commonly done to create scarce coil or perforation varieties, and to eliminate the naturally occurring straight-edge stamps found in sheet margin positions of many earlier issues. Custom has made straight-edged stamps less desirable. Fakers have obliged by perforating straight-edged stamps so that many are now uncommon, if not rare.

Another fertile field for the faker is that of overprints, surcharges and cancellations. The forging of rare surcharges or overprints began in the 1880s or 1890s. These forgeries are sometimes difficult to detect, but experts have identified almost all. Occasionally, overprints or cancellations are removed to create non-overprinted stamps or seemingly unused items. This is most commonly done by removing a manuscript cancel to make a stamp resemble an unused example. "SPECIMEN" overprints may be removed by scraping and repainting to create non-overprinted varieties. Fakers use inexpensive revenues or pen-canceled stamps to generate unused stamps for further faking by adding other markings. The quartz lamp or UV lamp and a high-powered magnifying glass help to easily detect removed cancellations.

The bigger problem, however, is the addition of overprints, surcharges or cancellations - many with such precision that they are very difficult to ascertain. Plating of the stamps or the overprint can be an important method of detection.

Fake postmarks may range from many spurious fancy cancellations to a host of markings applied to transatlantic covers, to adding normally appearing postmarks to definitives of some countries with stamps that are valued far higher used than unused. With the increased popularity of cover collecting, and the widespread interest in postal history, a fertile new field for fakers has come about. Some have tried to create entire covers. Others specialize in adding stamps, tied by fake cancellations, to genuine stampless covers, or replacing less expensive or damaged stamps with more valuable ones. Detailed study of postal rates in effect at the time a cover in question was mailed, including the analysis of each handstamp used during the period, ink analysis and similar techniques, usually will unmask the fraud.

Restoration and Repairs

Scott bases its catalogue values on stamps that are free of defects and otherwise meet the standards set forth earlier in this introduction. Most stamp collectors desire to have the finest copy of an item possible. Even within given grading categories there are variances. This leads to a controversial practice that is not defined in any universal manner: stamp *restoration*.

There are broad differences of opinion about what is permissible when it comes to restoration. Carefully applying a soft eraser to a stamp or cover to remove light soiling is one form of restoration, as is washing a stamp in mild soap and water to clean it. These are fairly accepted forms of restoration. More severe forms of restoration include pressing out creases or removing stains caused by tape. To what degree each of these is acceptable is dependent upon the individual situation. Further along the spectrum is the freshening of a stamp's color by removing oxide build-up or the effects of wax paper left next to stamps shipped to the tropics.

At some point in this spectrum the concept of *repair* replaces that of restoration. Repairs include filling thin spots, mending tears by reweaving or adding a missing perforation tooth. Regumming stamps may have been acceptable as a restoration or repair technique many decades ago, but today it is considered a form of fakery.

Restored stamps may or may not sell at a discount, and it is possible that the value of individual restored items may be enhanced over that of their pre-restoration state. Specific situations dictate the resultant value of such an item. Repaired stamps sell at substantial discounts from the value of sound stamps.

Terminology

Booklets — Many countries have issued stamps in small booklets for the convenience of users. This idea continues to become increasingly popular in many countries. Booklets have been issued in many sizes and forms, often with advertising on the covers, the panes of stamps or on the interleaving.

The panes used in booklets may be printed from special plates or made from regular sheets. All panes from booklets issued by the United States and many from those of other countries contain stamps that are straight edged on the sides, but perforated between. Others are distinguished by orientation of watermark or other identifying features. Any stamp-like unit in the pane, either printed or blank, that is not a postage stamp, is considered to be a *label* in the catalogue listings.

Scott lists and values booklet panes. Modern complete booklets also are listed and valued. Individual booklet panes are listed only when they are not fashioned from existing sheet stamps and, therefore, are identifiable from their sheet stamp counterparts.

Panes usually do not have a used value assigned to them because there is little market activity for used booklet panes, even though many exist used and there is some demand for them.

Cancellations — The marks or obliterations put on stamps by postal authorities to show that they have performed service and to prevent their reuse are known as cancellations. If the marking is made with a pen, it is considered a "pen cancel." When the location of the post office appears in the marking, it is a "town cancellation." A "postmark" is technically any postal marking, but in practice the term generally is applied to a town cancellation with a date. When calling attention to a cause or celebration, the marking is known as a "slogan cancellation." Many other types and styles of cancellations exist, such as duplex, numerals, targets, fancy and others. See also "precancels," below.

Coil Stamps — These are stamps that are issued in rolls for use in dispensers, affixing and vending machines. Those coils of the United States, Canada, Sweden and some other countries are perforated horizontally or vertically only, with the outer edges imperforate. Coil stamps of some countries, such as Great Britain and Germany, are perforated on all four sides and may in some cases be distinguished from their sheet stamp counterparts by watermarks, counting numbers on the reverse or other means.

Covers — Entire envelopes, with or without adhesive postage stamps, that have passed through the mail and bear postal or other markings of philatelic interest are known as covers. Before the introduction of envelopes in about 1840, people folded letters and wrote the address on the outside. Some people covered their letters with an extra sheet of paper on the outside for the address, producing the term "cover." Used airletter sheets, stamped envelopes and other items of postal stationery also are considered covers.

Errors — Stamps that have some major, consistent, unintentional deviation from the normal are considered errors. Errors include, but are not limited to, missing or wrong colors, wrong paper, wrong watermarks, inverted centers or frames on multicolor printing, inverted or missing surcharges or overprints, double impressions, missing perforations, unintentionally omitted tagging and others. Factually wrong or misspelled information, if it appears on all examples of a stamp, are not considered errors in the true sense of the word. They are errors of design. Inconsistent or randomly appearing items, such as misperfs or color shifts, are classified as freaks.

Color-Omitted Errors — This term refers to stamps where a missing color is caused by the complete failure of the printing plate to deliver ink to the stamp paper or any other paper. Generally, this is caused by the printing plate not being engaged on the press or the ink station running dry of ink during printing.

Color-Missing Errors — This term refers to stamps where a color or colors were printed somewhere but do not appear on the finished stamp. There are four different classes of color-missing errors, and the catalog indicates with a two-letter code appended to each such listing what caused the color to be missing. These codes are used only for the United States' color-missing error listings.

FO = A *foldover* of the stamp sheet during printing may block ink from appearing on a stamp. Instead, the color will appear on the back of the foldover (where it might fall on the back of the selvage or perhaps on the back of the stamp or another stamp). FO also will be used in the case of foldunders, where the paper may fold underneath the other stamp paper and the color will print on the platen.

EP = A piece of *extraneous paper* falling across the plate or stamp paper will receive the printed ink. When the extraneous paper is removed, an unprinted portion of stamp paper remains and shows partially or totally missing colors.

CM = A misregistration of the printing plates during printing will result in a *color misregistration*, and such a misregistraion may result in a color not appearing on the finished stamp.

PS = *A perforation shift* after printing may remove a color from the finished stamp. Normally, this will occur on a row of stamps at the edge of the stamp pane.

Measurements - When measurements are given in the Scott catalogues for stamp size, grill size or any other reason, the first measurement given is always for the top and bottom dimension, while the second measurement will be for the sides (just as perforation gauges are measured). Thus, a stamp size of 15mm x 21mm will indicate a vertically oriented stamp 15mm wide at top and bottom, and 21mm tall at the sides. The same principle holds for measuring or counting items such as U.S. grills. A grill count of 22x18 points (B grill) indicates that there are 22 grill points across by 18 grill points down.

Overprints and Surcharges — Overprinting involves applying wording or design elements over an already existing stamp. Overprints can be used to alter the place of use (such as "Canal Zone" on U.S. stamps), to adapt them for a special purpose ("Porto" on Denmark's 1913-20 regular issues for use as postage due stamps, Scott J1-J7) or to commemorate a special occasion (United States Scott 647-648).

A *surcharge* is a form of overprint that changes or restates the face value of a stamp or piece of postal stationery.

Surcharges and overprints may be handstamped, typeset or, occasionally, lithographed or engraved. A few hand-written overprints and surcharges are known.

Personalized Stamps — In 1999, Australia issued stamps with se-tenant labels that could be personalized with pictures of the customer's choice. Other countries quickly followed suit, with some offering to print the selected picture on the stamp itself within a frame that was used exclusively for personalized issues. As the picture used on these stamps or labels vary, listings for such stamps are for any picture within the common frame (or any picture on a se-tenant label), be it a "generic" image or one produced especially for a customer, almost invariably at a premium price.

Precancels — Stamps that are canceled before they are placed in the mail are known as precancels. Precanceling usually is done to expedite the handling of large mailings and generally allow the affected mail pieces to skip certain phases of mail handling.

In the United States, precancellations generally identified the point of origin; that is, the city and state. This information appeared across the face of the stamp, usually centered between parallel lines. More recently, bureau precancels retained the parallel lines, but the city and state designations were dropped. Recent coils have a service inscription that is present on the original printing plate. These show the mail service paid for by the stamp. Since these stamps are not intended to receive further cancellations when used as intended, they are considered precancels. Such items often do not have parallel lines as part of the precancellation.

In France, the abbreviation *Affranchts* in a semicircle together with the word *Postes* is the general form of precancel in use. Belgian precancellations usually appear in a box in which the name of the city appears. Netherlands precancels have the name of the city enclosed between concentric circles, sometimes called a "lifesaver." Precancellations of other countries usually follow these patterns, but may be any arrangement of bars, boxes and city names.

Precancels are listed in the Scott catalogues only if the precancel changes the denomination (Belgium Scott 477-478); if the precanceled stamp is different from the non-precanceled version (such as untagged U.S. precancels); or if the stamp exists only precanceled (France Scott 1096-1099, U.S. Scott 2265).

Proofs and Essays — Proofs are impressions taken from an approved die, plate or stone in which the design and color are the same as the stamp issued to the public. Trial color proofs are impressions taken from approved dies, plates or stones in colors that vary from the final version. An essay is the impression of a design that differs in some way from the issued stamp. "Progressive die proofs" generally are considered to be essays.

Provisionals — These are stamps that are issued on short notice and intended for temporary use pending the arrival of regular issues. They usually are issued to meet such contingencies as changes in government or currency, shortage of necessary postage values or military occupation.

During the 1840s, postmasters in certain American cities issued stamps that were valid only at specific post offices. In 1861, postmasters of the Confederate States also issued stamps with limited validity. Both of these examples are known as "postmaster's provisionals."

Se-tenant — This term refers to an unsevered pair, strip or block of stamps that differ in design, denomination or overprint.

Unless the se-tenant item has a continuous design (see U.S. Scott 1451a, 1694a) the stamps do not have to be in the same order as shown in the catalogue (see U.S. Scott 2158a).

Specimens — The Universal Postal Union required member nations to send samples of all stamps they released into service to the International Bureau in Switzerland. Member nations of the UPU received these specimens as samples of what stamps were valid for postage. Many are overprinted, handstamped or initial-perforated "Specimen," "Canceled" or "Muestra." Some are marked with bars across the denominations (China-Taiwan), punched holes (Czechoslovakia) or back inscriptions (Mongolia).

Stamps distributed to government officials or for publicity purposes, and stamps submitted by private security printers for official approval, also may receive such defacements.

The previously described defacement markings prevent postal use, and all such items generally are known as "specimens."

Tete Beche — This term describes a pair of stamps in which one is upside down in relation to the other. Some of these are the result of intentional sheet arrangements, such as Morocco Scott B10-B11. Others occurred when one or more electrotypes accidentally were placed upside down on the plate, such as Colombia Scott 57a. Separation of the tete-beche stamps, of course, destroys the tete beche variety.

Pronunciation Symbols

ə .... banana, collide, abut

ˈə, ˌə .... humdrum, abut

ə .... immediately preceding \l\, \n\, \m\, \ŋ\, as in battle, mitten, eaten, and sometimes open \ˈō-pᵊm\, lock and key \-ᵊŋ-\; immediately following \l\, \m\, \r\, as often in French table, prisme, titre

ər .... further, merger, bird

ˈər-, ˈə-r .... as in two different pronunciations of hurry \ˈhər-ē, ˈhə-rē\

a .... mat, map, mad, gag, snap, patch

ā .... day, fade, date, aorta, drape, cape

ä .... bother, cot, and, with most American speakers, father, cart

ȧ .... father as pronounced by speakers who do not rhyme it with *bother*; French patte

au̇ .... now, loud, out

b .... baby, rib

ch .... chin, nature \ˈnā-chər\

d .... did, adder

e .... bet, bed, peck

ˈē, ˌē .... beat, nosebleed, evenly, easy

ē .... easy, mealy

f .... fifty, cuff

g .... go, big, gift

h .... hat, ahead

hw .... whale as pronounced by those who do not have the same pronunciation for both *whale* and *wail*

i .... tip, banish, active

ī .... site, side, buy, tripe

j .... job, gem, edge, join, judge

k .... kin, cook, ache

k̲ .... German ich, Buch; one pronunciation of loch

l .... lily, pool

m .... murmur, dim, nymph

n .... no, own

ⁿ .... indicates that a preceding vowel or diphthong is pronounced with the nasal passages open, as in French *un bon vin blanc* \œⁿ-bōⁿ-vaⁿ-bläⁿ\

ŋ .... sing \ˈsiŋ\, singer \ˈsiŋ-ər\, finger \ˈfiŋ-gər\, ink \ˈiŋk\

ō .... bone, know, beau

ȯ .... saw, all, gnaw, caught

œ .... French boeuf, German Hölle

œ̄ .... French feu, German Höhle

ȯi .... coin, destroy

p .... pepper, lip

r .... red, car, rarity

s .... source, less

sh .... as in shy, mission, machine, special (actually, this is a single sound, not two); with a hyphen between, two sounds as in *grasshopper* \ˈgras-ˌhä-pər\

t .... tie, attack, late, later, latter

th .... as in thin, ether (actually, this is a single sound, not two); with a hyphen between, two sounds as in *knighthood* \ˈnīt-ˌhu̇d\

t̲h̲ .... then, either, this (actually, this is a single sound, not two)

ü .... rule, youth, union \ˈyün-yən\, few \ˈfyü\

u̇ .... pull, wood, book, curable \ˈkyu̇r-ə-bəl\, fury \ˈfyu̇r-ē\

ue .... German füllen, hübsch

ue̅ .... French rue, German fühlen

v .... vivid, give

w .... we, away

y .... yard, young, cue \ˈkyü\, mute \ˈmyüt\, union \ˈyün-yən\

ʸ .... indicates that during the articulation of the sound represented by the preceding character the front of the tongue has substantially the position it has for the articulation of the first sound of *yard*, as in French *digne* \dēnʸ\

z .... zone, raise

zh .... as in vision, azure \ˈa-zhər\ (actually, this is a single sound, not two); with a hyphen between, two sounds as in *hogshead* \ˈhȯgz-ˌhed, ˈhägz-\

\ .... slant line used in pairs to mark the beginning and end of a transcription: \ˈpen\

ˈ .... mark preceding a syllable with primary (strongest) stress: \ˈpen-mən-ˌship\

ˌ .... mark preceding a syllable with secondary (medium) stress: \ˈpen-mən-ˌship\

\- .... mark of syllable division

( ) .... indicate that what is symbolized between is present in some utterances but not in others: *factory* \ˈfak-t(ə-)rē\

÷ .... indicates that many regard as unacceptable the pronunciation variant immediately following: *cupola* \ˈkyü-pə-lə, ÷-ˌlō\

Currency Conversion

Country	Dollar	Pound	S Franc	Yen	HK $	Euro	Cdn $	Aus $
Australia	1.3053	1.6070	1.2914	0.0115	0.1681	1.3749	0.9792	—
Canada	1.3330	1.6411	1.3188	0.0117	0.1717	1.4040	—	1.0212
European Union	0.9494	1.1688	0.9393	0.0083	0.1223	—	0.7122	0.7273
Hong Kong	7.7630	9.5570	7.6801	0.0682	—	8.1767	5.8237	5.9473
Japan	113.91	140.23	112.69	—	14.674	119.98	85.454	87.267
Switzerland	1.0108	1.2444	—	0.0089	0.1302	1.0647	0.7583	0.7744
United Kingdom	0.8123	—	0.8036	0.0071	0.1046	0.8556	0.6094	0.6223
United States	—	1.2311	0.9893	0.0088	0.1288	1.0533	0.7502	0.7661

Country	Currency	U.S. $ Equiv.
Jamaica	dollar	.0078
Japan	yen	.0088
Jordan	dinar	1.4114
Kazakhstan	tenge	.0032
Kenya	shilling	.0097
Kiribati	Australian dollar	.7661
Korea (South)	won	.0009
Korea (North)	won	.0077
Kosovo	euro	1.0533
Kuwait	dinar	3.2712
Kyrgyzstan	som	.0145
Laos	kip	.0001
Latvia	euro	1.0533
Lebanon	pound	.0007
Lesotho	maloti	.0763
Liberia	dollar	.0106
Libya	dinar	.7003
Liechtenstein	Swiss franc	.9893
Lithuania	euro	1.0533
Luxembourg	euro	1.0533

Source: **xe.com** *Mar. 1, 2017. Figures reflect values as of Mar. 1, 2017.*

COMMON DESIGN TYPES

Pictured in this section are issues where one illustration has been used for a number of countries in the Catalogue. Not included in this section are overprinted stamps or those issues which are illustrated in each country. Because the location of Never Hinged breakpoints varies from country to country, some of the values in the listings below will be for unused stamps that were previously hinged.

EUROPA

Europa, 1956

The design symbolizing the cooperation among the six countries comprising the Coal and Steel Community is illustrated in each country.

Belgium	*496-497*
France	*805-806*
Germany	*748-749*
Italy	*715-716*
Luxembourg	*318-320*
Netherlands	*368-369*

Nos. 496-497 (2)	9.00	.70
Nos. 805-806 (2)	5.25	1.00
Nos. 748-749 (2)	7.30	1.20
Nos. 715-716 (2)	11.50	1.25
Nos. 318-320 (3)	65.50	42.00
Nos. 368-369 (2)	72.50	1.75
Set total (13) Stamps	171.05	47.90

Europa, 1958

"E" and Dove — CD1

European Postal Union at the service of European integration.

1958, Sept. 13

Belgium	527-528
France	889-890
Germany	790-791
Italy	750-751
Luxembourg	341-343
Netherlands	375-376
Saar	317-318

Nos. 527-528 (2)	4.25	.60
Nos. 889-890 (2)	1.65	.55
Nos. 790-791 (2)	3.65	.65
Nos. 750-751 (2)	1.85	.60
Nos. 341-343 (3)	2.35	1.15
Nos. 375-376 (2)	2.50	.75
Nos. 317-318 (2)	1.05	2.30
Set total (15) Stamps	17.30	6.60

Europa, 1959

6-Link Enless Chain — CD2

1959, Sept. 19

Belgium	536-537
France	929-930
Germany	805-806
Italy	791-792
Luxembourg	354-355
Netherlands	379-380

Nos. 536-537 (2)	1.55	.60
Nos. 929-930 (2)	1.40	.80
Nos. 805-806 (2)	1.55	.65
Nos. 791-792 (2)	.80	.50
Nos. 354-355 (2)	3.50	1.40
Nos. 379-380 (2)	9.90	1.25
Set total (12) Stamps	18.70	5.20

Europa, 1960

19-Spoke Wheel CD3

First anniversary of the establishment of C.E.P.T. (Conference Europeenne des Administrations des Postes et des Telecommunications.) The spokes symbolize the 19 founding members of the Conference.

1960, Sept.

Belgium	553-554
Denmark	379
Finland	376-377
France	970-971
Germany	818-820
Great Britain	377-378
Greece	688
Iceland	327-328
Ireland	175-176
Italy	809-810
Luxembourg	374-375
Netherlands	385-386
Norway	387
Portugal	866-867
Spain	941-942
Sweden	562-563
Switzerland	400-401
Turkey	1493-1494

Nos. 553-554 (2)	1.25	.55
No. 379 (1)	.55	.50
Nos. 376-377 (2)	1.70	1.80
Nos. 970-971 (2)	.50	.50
Nos. 818-820 (3)	2.25	1.50
Nos. 377-378 (2)	9.00	5.00
No. 688 (1)	5.00	2.00
Nos. 327-328 (2)	1.30	1.85
Nos. 175-176 (2)	75.00	14.00
Nos. 809-810 (2)	.70	.50
Nos. 374-375 (2)	1.00	.80
Nos. 385-386 (2)	3.65	1.50
No. 387 (1)	1.25	1.25
Nos. 866-867 (2)	2.25	1.25
Nos. 941-942 (2)	1.50	.75
Nos. 562-563 (2)	1.05	.55
Nos. 400-401 (2)	1.25	.65
Nos. 1493-1494 (2)	2.10	1.35
Set total (34) Stamps	111.30	36.30

Europa, 1961

19 Doves Flying as One — CD4

The 19 doves represent the 19 members of the Conference of European Postal and Telecommunications Administrations C.E.P.T.

1961-62

Belgium	572-573
Cyprus	201-203
France	1005-1006
Germany	844-845
Great Britain	382-384
Greece	718-719
Iceland	340-341
Italy	845-846
Luxembourg	382-383
Netherlands	387-388
Spain	1010-1011
Switzerland	410-411
Turkey	1518-1520

Nos. 572-573 (2)	.75	.50
Nos. 201-203 (3)	*2.10*	*1.20*
Nos. 1005-1006 (2)	.50	.50
Nos. 844-845 (2)	.60	.75
Nos. 382-384 (3)	.75	.90
Nos. 718-719 (2)	.80	.50
Nos. 340-341 (2)	1.10	1.60
Nos. 845-846 (2)	.55	.50
Nos. 382-383 (2)	.70	.70
Nos. 387-388 (2)	.55	.50
Nos. 1010-1011 (2)	.70	.55
Nos. 410-411 (2)	1.25	.60
Nos. 1518-1520 (3)	2.45	1.30
Set total (29) Stamps	12.80	10.10

Europa, 1962

Young Tree with 19 Leaves CD5

The 19 leaves represent the 19 original members of C.E.P.T.

1962-63

Belgium	582-583
Cyprus	219-221
France	1045-1046
Germany	852-853
Greece	739-740
Iceland	348-349
Ireland	184-185
Italy	860-861
Luxembourg	386-387
Netherlands	394-395
Norway	414-415
Switzerland	416-417
Turkey	1553-1555

Nos. 582-583 (2)	.65	.65
Nos. 219-221 (3)	*76.25*	*4.40*
Nos. 1045-1046 (2)	.60	.50
Nos. 852-853 (2)	.70	.80
Nos. 739-740 (2)	2.25	1.15
Nos. 348-349 (2)	.85	.85
Nos. 184-185 (2)	2.00	1.50
Nos. 860-861 (2)	1.35	.55
Nos. 386-387 (2)	.85	.70
Nos. 394-395 (2)	1.40	.75
Nos. 414-415 (2)	2.25	2.25
Nos. 416-417 (2)	1.65	1.00
Nos. 1553-1555 (3)	*3.00*	1.55
Set total (28) Stamps	93.80	16.65

Europa, 1963

Stylized Links, Symbolizing Unity — CD6

1963, Sept.

Belgium	598-599
Cyprus	229-231
Finland	419
France	1074-1075
Germany	867-868
Greece	768-769
Iceland	357-358
Ireland	188-189
Italy	880-881
Luxembourg	403-404
Netherlands	416-417
Norway	441-442
Switzerland	429
Turkey	1602-1603

Nos. 598-599 (2)	1.60	.55
Nos. 229-231 (3)	*54.75*	*5.15*
No. 419 (1)	1.25	.55
Nos. 1074-1075 (2)	.60	.50
Nos. 867-868 (2)	.50	.55
Nos. 768-769 (2)	5.25	1.90
Nos. 357-358 (2)	1.20	1.20
Nos. 188-189 (2)	4.75	3.25
Nos. 880-881 (2)	.65	.50
Nos. 403-404 (2)	1.00	.80
Nos. 416-417 (2)	2.25	1.00
Nos. 441-442 (2)	4.75	3.00
No. 429 (1)	.90	.60
Nos. 1602-1603 (2)	1.40	.60
Set total (27) Stamps	80.85	20.15

Europa, 1964

Symbolic Daisy — CD7

5th anniversary of the establishment of C.E.P.T. The 22 petals of the flower symbolize the 22 members of the Conference.

1964, Sept.

Austria	738
Belgium	614-615
Cyprus	244-246
France	1109-1110
Germany	897-898
Greece	801-802
Iceland	367-368
Ireland	196-197
Italy	894-895
Luxembourg	411-412
Monaco	590-591
Netherlands	428-429
Norway	458
Portugal	931-933
Spain	1262-1263
Switzerland	438-439
Turkey	1628-1629

No. 738 (1)	1.20	.80
Nos. 614-615 (2)	1.40	.60
Nos. 244-246 (3)	*35.75*	*3.45*
Nos. 1109-1110 (2)	.50	.50
Nos. 897-898 (2)	.50	.50
Nos. 801-802 (2)	5.00	1.90
Nos. 367-368 (2)	1.40	1.15
Nos. 196-197 (2)	20.00	4.25
Nos. 894-895 (2)	.55	.50
Nos. 411-412 (2)	.90	.55
Nos. 590-591 (2)	2.50	.70
Nos. 428-429 (2)	1.80	.60
No. 458 (1)	4.50	4.50
Nos. 931-933 (3)	*10.00*	*2.00*
Nos. 1262-1263 (2)	1.30	.80
Nos. 438-439 (2)	1.60	.50
Nos. 1628-1629 (2)	2.65	1.35
Set total (34) Stamps	91.55	24.65

Europa, 1965

Leaves and "Fruit" CD8

1965

Belgium	636-637
Cyprus	262-264
Finland	437
France	1131-1132
Germany	934-935
Greece	833-834
Iceland	375-376
Ireland	204-205
Italy	915-916
Luxembourg	432-433
Monaco	616-617
Netherlands	438-439
Norway	475-476
Portugal	958-960
Switzerland	469
Turkey	1665-1666

Nos. 636-637 (2)	.50	.50
Nos. 262-264 (3)	*25.35*	*3.80*
No. 437 (1)	1.25	.55
Nos. 1131-1132 (2)	.70	.55
Nos. 934-935 (2)	.50	.50
Nos. 833-834 (2)	2.25	1.15
Nos. 375-376 (2)	2.50	1.75
Nos. 204-205 (2)	20.00	3.35
Nos. 915-916 (2)	.50	.50
Nos. 432-433 (2)	.80	.60
Nos. 616-617 (2)	3.25	1.65
Nos. 438-439 (2)	.75	.55
Nos. 475-476 (2)	4.00	3.10
Nos. 958-960 (3)	*10.00*	*2.75*
No. 469 (1)	1.15	.25
Nos. 1665-1666 (2)	3.50	2.10
Set total (32) Stamps	77.00	23.65

Europa, 1966

Symbolic Sailboat — CD9

1966, Sept.

Andorra, French	172
Belgium	675-676
Cyprus	275-277
France	1163-1164
Germany	963-964

Greece	862-863
Iceland	384-385
Ireland	216-217
Italy	942-943
Liechtenstein	415
Luxembourg	440-441
Monaco	639-640
Netherlands	441-442
Norway	496-497
Portugal	980-982
Switzerland	477-478
Turkey	1718-1719

No. 172 (1)	3.00	3.00
Nos. 675-676 (2)	.80	.50
Nos. 275-277 (3)	*4.75*	*1.90*
Nos. 1163-1164 (2)	.55	.50
Nos. 963-964 (2)	.50	.55
Nos. 862-863 (2)	2.25	1.05
Nos. 384-385 (2)	4.50	3.50
Nos. 216-217 (2)	7.00	2.00
Nos. 942-943 (2)	.50	.50
No. 415 (1)	.40	.35
Nos. 440-441 (2)	.80	.60
Nos. 639-640 (2)	2.00	.65
Nos. 441-442 (2)	1.50	.65
Nos. 496-497 (2)	5.00	3.00
Nos. 980-982 (3)	*9.75*	2.25
Nos. 477-478 (2)	1.60	.60
Nos. 1718-1719 (2)	3.35	1.75
Set total (34) Stamps	48.25	23.35

Europa, 1967

Cogwheels
CD10

1967

Andorra, French	174-175
Belgium	688-689
Cyprus	297-299
France	1178-1179
Germany	969-970
Greece	891-892
Iceland	389-390
Ireland	232-233
Italy	951-952
Liechtenstein	420
Luxembourg	449-450
Monaco	669-670
Netherlands	444-447
Norway	504-505
Portugal	994-996
Spain	1465-1466
Switzerland	482
Turkey	B120-B121

Nos. 174-175 (2)	10.75	6.25
Nos. 688-689 (2)	1.05	.55
Nos. 297-299 (3)	*4.25*	*1.75*
Nos. 1178-1179 (2)	.55	.50
Nos. 969-970 (2)	.55	.55
Nos. 891-892 (2)	3.75	1.00
Nos. 389-390 (2)	3.00	2.00
Nos. 232-233 (2)	6.15	2.30
Nos. 951-952 (2)	.60	.50
No. 420 (1)	.45	.40
Nos. 449-450 (2)	1.00	.70
Nos. 669-670 (2)	2.75	.70
Nos. 444-447 (4)	5.00	1.85
Nos. 504-505 (2)	3.25	2.75
Nos. 994-996 (3)	*9.50*	1.85
Nos. 1465-1466 (2)	.50	.50
No. 482 (1)	.70	.25
Nos. B120-B121 (2)	3.50	2.75
Set total (38) Stamps	57.30	27.15

Europa, 1968

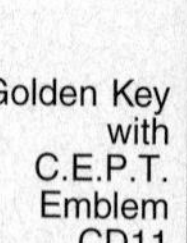

Golden Key
with
C.E.P.T.
Emblem
CD11

1968

Andorra, French	182-183
Belgium	705-706
Cyprus	314-316
France	1209-1210
Germany	983-984
Greece	916-917
Iceland	395-396
Ireland	242-243
Italy	979-980
Liechtenstein	442
Luxembourg	466-467
Monaco	689-691
Netherlands	452-453
Portugal	1019-1021
San Marino	687
Spain	1526
Switzerland	488
Turkey	1775-1776

Nos. 182-183 (2)	16.50	10.00
Nos. 705-706 (2)	1.25	.50
Nos. 314-316 (3)	*2.90*	*1.75*
Nos. 1209-1210 (2)	.85	.55
Nos. 983-984 (2)	.50	.55
Nos. 916-917 (2)	3.75	1.65
Nos. 395-396 (2)	3.00	2.20
Nos. 242-243 (2)	3.75	3.00
Nos. 979-980 (2)	.50	.50
No. 442 (1)	.45	.40
Nos. 466-467 (2)	.80	.70
Nos. 689-691 (3)	*5.40*	.95
Nos. 452-453 (2)	2.10	.70
Nos. 1019-1021 (3)	*9.75*	2.10
No. 687 (1)	.55	.35
No. 1526 (1)	.25	.25
No. 488 (1)	.45	.25
Nos. 1775-1776 (2)	5.00	2.00
Set total (35) Stamps	57.75	28.40

Europa, 1969

"EUROPA"
and "CEPT"
CD12

Tenth anniversary of C.E.P.T.

1969

Andorra, French	188-189
Austria	837
Belgium	718-719
Cyprus	326-328
Denmark	458
Finland	483
France	1245-1246
Germany	996-997
Great Britain	585
Greece	947-948
Iceland	406-407
Ireland	270-271
Italy	1000-1001
Liechtenstein	453
Luxembourg	475-476
Monaco	722-724
Netherlands	475-476
Norway	533-534
Portugal	1038-1040
San Marino	701-702
Spain	1567
Sweden	814-816
Switzerland	500-501
Turkey	1799-1800
Vatican	470-472
Yugoslavia	1003-1004

Nos. 188-189 (2)	18.50	12.00
No. 837 (1)	.65	.30
Nos. 718-719 (2)	.75	.50
Nos. 326-328 (3)	*3.00*	*1.35*
No. 458 (1)	.75	.75
No. 483 (1)	3.50	.75
Nos. 1245-1246 (2)	.55	.50
Nos. 996-997 (2)	.80	.50
No. 585 (1)	.25	.25
Nos. 947-948 (2)	5.00	1.50
Nos. 406-407 (2)	4.20	2.40
Nos. 270-271 (2)	4.00	2.00
Nos. 1000-1001 (2)	.70	.50
No. 453 (1)	.45	.45
Nos. 475-476 (2)	1.00	.70
Nos. 722-724 (3)	*10.50*	2.00
Nos. 475-476 (2)	2.60	1.15
Nos. 533-534 (2)	3.75	2.35
Nos. 1038-1040 (3)	17.85	2.40
Nos. 701-702 (2)	.90	.90
No. 1567 (1)	.25	.25
Nos. 814-816 (3)	4.00	2.85
Nos. 500-501 (2)	1.85	.60
Nos. 1799-1800 (2)	3.85	2.25
Nos. 470-472 (3)	.75	.75
Nos. 1003-1004 (2)	4.00	4.00
Set total (51) Stamps	94.40	43.95

Europa, 1970

Interwoven
Threads
CD13

1970

Andorra, French	196-197
Belgium	741-742
Cyprus	340-342
France	1271-1272
Germany	1018-1019
Greece	985, 987
Iceland	420-421
Ireland	279-281
Italy	1013-1014
Liechtenstein	470
Luxembourg	489-490
Monaco	768-770
Netherlands	483-484
Portugal	1060-1062
San Marino	729-730
Spain	1607
Switzerland	515-516
Turkey	1848-1849
Yugoslavia	1024-1025

Nos. 196-197 (2)	20.00	8.50
Nos. 741-742 (2)	1.10	.55
Nos. 340-342 (3)	*2.70*	*1.90*
Nos. 1271-1272 (2)	.65	.50
Nos. 1018-1019 (2)	.60	.50
Nos. 985,987 (2)	7.75	2.00
Nos. 420-421 (2)	6.00	4.00
Nos. 279-281 (3)	9.50	3.30
Nos. 1013-1014 (2)	.65	.50
No. 470 (1)	.45	.45
Nos. 489-490 (2)	.80	.80
Nos. 768-770 (3)	*6.35*	2.10
Nos. 483-484 (2)	2.50	1.15
Nos. 1060-1062 (3)	*9.85*	2.35
Nos. 729-730 (2)	.90	.55
No. 1607 (1)	.25	.25
Nos. 515-516 (2)	1.85	.60
Nos. 1848-1849 (2)	5.00	2.25
Nos. 1024-1025 (2)	.80	.80
Set total (40) Stamps	77.70	33.05

Europa, 1971

"Fraternity,
Cooperation,
Common
Effort"
CD14

1971

Andorra, French	205-206
Belgium	803-804
Cyprus	365-367
Finland	504
France	1304
Germany	1064-1065
Greece	1029-1030
Iceland	429-430
Ireland	305-306
Italy	1038-1039
Liechtenstein	485
Luxembourg	500-501
Malta	425-427
Monaco	797-799
Netherlands	488-489
Portugal	1094-1096
San Marino	749-750
Spain	1675-1676
Switzerland	531-532
Turkey	1876-1877
Yugoslavia	1052-1053

Nos. 205-206 (2)	20.00	7.75
Nos. 803-804 (2)	1.30	.55
Nos. 365-367 (3)	*2.60*	*1.75*
No. 504 (1)	5.00	.75
No. 1304 (1)	.45	.40
Nos. 1064-1065 (2)	.60	.50
Nos. 1029-1030 (2)	4.00	1.80
Nos. 429-430 (2)	5.00	3.75
Nos. 305-306 (2)	5.00	1.50
Nos. 1038-1039 (2)	.65	.50
No. 485 (1)	.45	.45
Nos. 500-501 (2)	1.00	.80
Nos. 425-427 (3)	*.80*	*.80*
Nos. 797-799 (3)	*15.00*	2.80
Nos. 488-489 (2)	2.50	1.15
Nos. 1094-1096 (3)	*9.75*	1.75
Nos. 749-750 (2)	.65	.55
Nos. 1675-1676 (2)	.75	.55
Nos. 531-532 (2)	1.85	.65
Nos. 1876-1877 (2)	5.60	2.50
Nos. 1052-1053 (2)	.50	.50
Set total (43) Stamps	83.45	31.75

Europa, 1972

Sparkles, Symbolic
of Communications
CD15

1972

Andorra, French	210-211
Andorra, Spanish	62
Belgium	825-826
Cyprus	380-382
Finland	512-513
France	1341
Germany	1089-1090
Greece	1049-1050
Iceland	439-440
Ireland	316-317
Italy	1065-1066
Liechtenstein	504
Luxembourg	512-513
Malta	450-453
Monaco	831-832
Netherlands	494-495
Portugal	1141-1143
San Marino	771-772
Spain	1718
Switzerland	544-545
Turkey	1907-1908
Yugoslavia	1100-1101

Nos. 210-211 (2)	21.00	7.00
No. 62 (1)	45.00	45.00
Nos. 825-826 (2)	.95	.55
Nos. 380-382 (3)	*5.95*	*2.45*
Nos. 512-513 (2)	7.00	1.40
No. 1341 (1)	.50	.35
Nos. 1089-1090 (2)	1.30	.50
Nos. 1049-1050 (2)	2.00	1.55
Nos. 439-440 (2)	2.90	2.65
Nos. 316-317 (2)	13.00	4.50
Nos. 1065-1066 (2)	.65	.50
No. 504 (1)	.45	.45
Nos. 512-513 (2)	1.00	.80
Nos. 450-453 (4)	1.05	1.40
Nos. 831-832 (2)	5.00	1.40
Nos. 494-495 (2)	3.25	1.15
Nos. 1141-1143 (3)	*9.85*	1.50
Nos. 771-772 (2)	.70	.50
No. 1718 (1)	.50	.40
Nos. 544-545 (2)	1.65	.60
Nos. 1907-1908 (2)	7.50	3.00
Nos. 1100-1101 (2)	1.20	1.20
Set total (44) Stamps	132.40	78.85

Europa, 1973

Post Horn
and Arrows
CD16

1973

Andorra, French	219-220
Andorra, Spanish	76
Belgium	839-840
Cyprus	396-398
Finland	526
France	1367
Germany	1114-1115
Greece	1090-1092
Iceland	447-448
Ireland	329-330
Italy	1108-1109
Liechtenstein	528-529
Luxembourg	523-524
Malta	469-471
Monaco	866-867
Netherlands	504-505
Norway	604-605
Portugal	1170-1172
San Marino	802-803
Spain	1753
Switzerland	580-581
Turkey	1935-1936
Yugoslavia	1138-1139

Nos. 219-220 (2)	20.00	11.00
No. 76 (1)	.65	.55
Nos. 839-840 (2)	1.00	.65
Nos. 396-398 (3)	*4.25*	*2.10*
No. 526 (1)	1.25	.55
No. 1367 (1)	1.25	.75
Nos. 1114-1115 (2)	.90	.50
Nos. 1090-1092 (3)	2.10	1.40
Nos. 447-448 (2)	6.65	3.35

Nos. 329-330 (2)	5.25	2.00
Nos. 1108-1109 (2)	.65	.50
Nos. 528-529 (2)	.60	.60
Nos. 523-524 (2)	.90	1.00
Nos. 469-471 (3)	.90	1.20
Nos. 866-867 (2)	15.00	2.40
Nos. 504-505 (2)	2.85	1.10
Nos. 604-605 (2)	6.25	2.40
Nos. 1170-1172 (3)	*13.00*	2.15
Nos. 802-803 (2)	*1.00*	.60
No. 1753 (1)	.35	.25
Nos. 580-581 (2)	1.55	.60
Nos. 1935-1936 (2)	10.00	4.50
Nos. 1138-1139 (2)	1.15	1.10
Set total (46) Stamps	97.50	41.25

Europa, 2000

CD17

2000

Albania....2621-2622
Andorra, French....522
Andorra, Spanish....262
Armenia....610-611
Austria....1814
Azerbaijan....698-699
Belarus....350
Belgium....1818
Bosnia & Herzegovina (Moslem)....358
Bosnia & Herzegovina (Serb)....111-112
Croatia....428-429
Cyprus....959
Czech Republic....3120
Denmark....1189
Estonia....394
Faroe Islands....376
Finland....1129
Aland Islands....166
France....2771
Georgia....228-229
Germany....2086-2087
Gibraltar....837-840
Great Britain (Jersey)....935-936
Great Britain (Isle of Man)....883
Greece....1959
Greenland....363
Hungary....3699-3700
Iceland....910
Ireland....1230-1231
Italy....2349
Latvia....504
Liechtenstein....1178
Lithuania....668
Luxembourg....1035
Macedonia....187
Malta....1011-1012
Moldova....355
Monaco....2161-2162
Poland....3519
Portugal....2358
Portugal (Azores)....455
Portugal (Madeira)....208
Romania....4370
Russia....6589
San Marino....1480
Slovakia....355
Slovenia....424
Spain....3036
Sweden....2394
Switzerland....1074
Turkey....2762
Turkish Rep. of Northern Cyprus....500
Ukraine....379
Vatican City....1152

Nos. 2621-2622 (2)	11.00	11.00
No. 522 (1)	2.00	1.00
No. 262 (1)	1.60	.70
Nos. 610-611 (2)	4.75	4.75
No. 1814 (1)	1.40	1.40
Nos. 698-699 (2)	6.00	6.00
No. 350 (1)	1.75	1.75
No. 1818 (1)	1.40	.60
No. 358 (1)	4.75	4.75
Nos. 111-112 (2)	110.00	110.00
Nos. 428-429 (2)	6.25	6.25
No. 959 (1)	2.10	1.40
No. 3120 (1)	1.00	.40
No. 1189 (1)	3.50	2.25
No. 394 (1)	1.25	1.25
No. 376 (1)	2.40	2.40
No. 1129 (1)	2.00	.60
No. 166 (1)	2.00	1.10
No. 2771 (1)	1.25	.40
No. 228-229 (1)	9.00	9.00
Nos. 2086-2087 (2)	4.15	1.90
Nos. 837-840 (4)	5.50	5.30
Nos. 935-936 (2)	2.40	2.40
No. 883 (1)	1.50	1.50
No. 1959 (1)	3.00	3.00
No. 363 (1)	1.90	1.90
Nos. 3699-3700 (2)	6.50	2.50
No. 910 (1)	1.60	1.60
Nos. 1230-1231 (2)	4.75	4.75
No. 2349 (1)	1.50	.40
No. 504 (1)	5.00	2.40
No. 1178 (1)	2.25	1.75
No. 668 (1)	1.50	1.50
No. 1035 (1)	1.40	1.00
No. 187 (1)	3.25	3.25
Nos. 1011-1012 (2)	4.35	4.35
No. 355 (1)	3.50	3.50
Nos. 2161-2162 (2)	2.80	1.40
No. 3519 (1)	1.10	.50
No. 2358 (1)	1.25	.65
No. 455 (1)	1.25	.50
No. 208 (1)	1.25	.50
No. 4370 (1)	2.50	1.25
No. 6589 (1)	2.00	.85
No. 1480 (1)	1.00	1.00
No. 355 (1)	1.25	.55
No. 424 (1)	3.25	1.60
No. 3036 (1)	.75	.40
No. 2394 (1)	3.00	2.25
No. 1074 (1)	2.10	.75
No. 2762 (1)	2.00	2.00
No. 500 (1)	2.50	2.50
No. 379 (1)	4.50	3.00
No. 1152 (1)	1.25	1.25
Set total (68) Stamps	263.20	230.95

The Gibraltar stamps are similar to the stamp illustrated, but none have the design shown above. All other sets listed above include at least one stamp with the design shown, but some include stamps with entirely different designs. Bulgaria Nos. 4131-4132, Guernsey Nos. 802-803 and Yugoslavia Nos. 2485-2486 are Europa stamps with completely different designs.

PORTUGAL & COLONIES
Vasco da Gama

Fleet Departing CD20

Fleet Arriving at Calicut — CD21

Embarking at Rastello CD22

Muse of History CD23

San Gabriel, da Gama and Camoens CD24

Archangel Gabriel, the Patron Saint CD25

Flagship San Gabriel — CD26

Vasco da Gama — CD27

Fourth centenary of Vasco da Gama's discovery of the route to India.

1898

Azores....93-100
Macao....67-74
Madeira....37-44
Portugal....147-154
Port. Africa....1-8
Port. Congo....75-98
Port. India....189-196
St. Thomas & Prince Islands....170-193
Timor....45-52

Nos. 93-100 (8)	122.00	76.25
Nos. 67-74 (8)	136.00	96.75
Nos. 37-44 (8)	44.55	34.00
Nos. 147-154 (8)	169.30	43.45
Nos. 1-8 (8)	23.95	21.70
Nos. 75-98 (24)	41.15	34.45
Nos. 189-196 (8)	20.25	12.95
Nos. 170-193 (24)	38.75	34.30
Nos. 45-52 (8)	21.50	10.45
Set total (104) Stamps	617.45	364.30

Pombal
POSTAL TAX
POSTAL TAX DUES

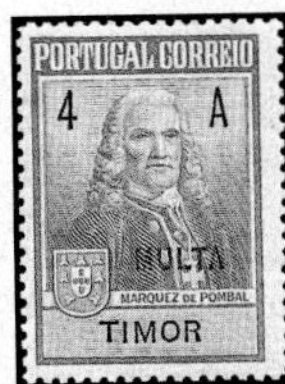

Marquis de Pombal — CD28

Planning Reconstruction of Lisbon, 1755 — CD29

Pombal Monument, Lisbon — CD30

Sebastiao Jose de Carvalho e Mello, Marquis de Pombal (1699-1782), statesman, rebuilt Lisbon after earthquake of 1755. Tax was for the erection of Pombal monument. Obligatory on all mail on certain days throughout the year. Postal Tax Dues are inscribed "Multa."

1925

Angola.... RA1-RA3, RAJ1-RAJ3
Azores.... RA9-RA11, RAJ2-RAJ4
Cape Verde.... RA1-RA3, RAJ1-RAJ3
Macao.... RA1-RA3, RAJ1-RAJ3
Madeira.... RA1-RA3, RAJ1-RAJ3
Mozambique.... RA1-RA3, RAJ1-RAJ3
Nyassa.... RA1-RA3, RAJ1-RAJ3
Portugal.... RA11-RA13, RAJ2-RAJ4
Port. Guinea.... RA1-RA3, RAJ1-RAJ3
Port. India.... RA1-RA3, RAJ1-RAJ3
St. Thomas & Prince Islands.... RA1-RA3, RAJ1-RAJ3
Timor.... RA1-RA3, RAJ1-RAJ3

Nos. RA1-RA3,RAJ1-RAJ3 (6)	6.60	6.60
Nos. RA9-RA11,RAJ2-RAJ4 (6)	6.60	9.30
Nos. RA1-RA3,RAJ1-RAJ3 (6)	6.00	5.40
Nos. RA1-RA3,RAJ1-RAJ3 (6)	18.50	10.50
Nos. RA1-RA3,RAJ1-RAJ3 (6)	4.35	12.45
Nos. RA1-RA3,RAJ1-RAJ3 (6)	2.55	2.70
Nos. RA1-RA3,RAJ1-RAJ3 (6)	52.50	38.25
Nos. RA11-RA13,RAJ2-RAJ4 (6)	5.80	5.20
Nos. RA1-RA3,RAJ1-RAJ3 (6)	3.30	2.70
Nos. RA1-RA3,RAJ1-RAJ3 (6)	3.45	3.45
Nos. RA1-RA3,RAJ1-RAJ3 (6)	3.60	3.60
Nos. RA1-RA3,RAJ1-RAJ3 (6)	2.10	3.90
Set total (72) Stamps	115.35	104.05

Vasco da Gama CD34

Mousinho de Albuquerque CD35

Dam CD36

Prince Henry the Navigator CD37

Affonso de Albuquerque CD38

Plane over Globe CD39

1938-39

Angola....274-291, C1-C9
Cape Verde....234-251, C1-C9
Macao....289-305, C7-C15
Mozambique....270-287, C1-C9
Port. Guinea....233-250. C1-C9
Port. India....439-453, C1-C8
St. Thomas & Prince Islands... 302-319, 323-340, C1-C18
Timor....223-239, C1-C9

Nos. 274-291,C1-C9 (27)	132.90	22.85
Nos. 234-251,C1-C9 (27)	100.00	31.20
Nos. 289-305,C7-C15 (26)	701.70	135.60
Nos. 270-287,C1-C9 (27)	63.45	11.20
Nos. 233-250,C1-C9 (27)	88.05	30.70
Nos. 439-453,C1-C8 (23)	74.75	25.50
Nos. 302-319,323-340,C1-C18 (54)	319.25	190.35
Nos. 223-239,C1-C9 (26)	149.25	73.15
Set total (237) Stamps	1,629.	520.55

Lady of Fatima

Our Lady of the Rosary, Fatima, Portugal — CD40

1948-49

Angola....315-318
Cape Verde....266
Macao....336
Mozambique....325-328
Port. Guinea....271
Port. India....480
St. Thomas & Prince Islands....351
Timor....254

Nos. 315-318 (4)	68.00	17.25
No. 266 (1)	8.50	4.50
No. 336 (1)	40.00	12.00
Nos. 325-328 (4)	20.00	4.50
No. 271 (1)	3.25	3.00
No. 480 (1)	2.50	2.25
No. 351 (1)	7.25	6.50
No. 254 (1)	3.00	3.00
Set total (14) Stamps	152.50	53.00

A souvenir sheet of 9 stamps was issued in 1951 to mark the extension of the 1950 Holy Year. The sheet contains: Angola No. 316, Cape Verde No. 266, Macao No. 336, Mozambique No. 325, Portuguese Guinea No. 271, Portuguese India Nos. 480, 485, St. Thomas & Prince Islands No. 351, Timor No. 254. The sheet also contains a portrait of Pope Pius XII and is inscribed "Encerramento do

"Ano Santo, Fatima 1951." It was sold for 11 escudos.

Holy Year

Church Bells and Dove
CD41

Angel Holding Candelabra
CD42

Holy Year, 1950.

1950-51

Angola	331-332
Cape Verde	268-269
Macao	339-340
Mozambique	330-331
Port. Guinea	273-274
Port. India	490-491, 496-503
St. Thomas & Prince Islands	353-354
Timor	258-259

Nos. 331-332 (2)	7.60	1.35
Nos. 268-269 (2)	4.75	2.20
Nos. 339-340 (2)	55.00	12.50
Nos. 330-331 (2)	1.75	.85
Nos. 273-274 (2)	3.50	2.60
Nos. 490-491,496-503 (10)	12.80	5.40
Nos. 353-354 (2)	7.50	4.40
Nos. 258-259 (2)	3.75	3.25
Set total (24) Stamps	96.65	32.55

A souvenir sheet of 8 stamps was issued in 1951 to mark the extension of the Holy Year. The sheet contains: Angola No. 331, Cape Verde No. 269, Macao No. 340, Mozambique No. 331, Portuguese Guinea No. 275, Portuguese India No. 490, St. Thomas & Prince Islands No. 354, Timor No. 258, some with colors changed. The sheet contains doves and is inscribed 'Encerramento do Ano Santo, Fatima 1951.' It was sold for 17 escudos.

Holy Year Conclusion

Our Lady of Fatima — CD43

Conclusion of Holy Year. Sheets contain alternate vertical rows of stamps and labels bearing quotation from Pope Pius XII, different for each colony.

1951

Angola	357
Cape Verde	270
Macao	352
Mozambique	356
Port. Guinea	275
Port. India	506
St. Thomas & Prince Islands	355
Timor	270

No. 357 (1)	5.25	1.50
No. 270 (1)	1.50	1.25
No. 352 (1)	37.50	10.00
No. 356 (1)	2.25	1.00
No. 275 (1)	1.00	.65
No. 506 (1)	1.60	1.00
No. 355 (1)	2.50	2.00
No. 270 (1)	2.00	1.75
Set total (8) Stamps	53.60	19.15

Medical Congress

CD44

First National Congress of Tropical Medicine, Lisbon, 1952. Each stamp has a different design.

1952

Angola	358
Cape Verde	287
Macao	364
Mozambique	359
Port. Guinea	276
Port. India	516
St. Thomas & Prince Islands	356
Timor	271

No. 358 (1)	1.50	.50
No. 287 (1)	.70	.50
No. 364 (1)	9.75	4.25
No. 359 (1)	1.10	.55
No. 276 (1)	.45	.35
No. 516 (1)	4.75	2.00
No. 356 (1)	.30	.30
No. 271 (1)	1.00	1.00
Set total (8) Stamps	19.55	9.45

Postage Due Stamps

CD45

1952

Angola	J37-J42
Cape Verde	J31-J36
Macao	J53-J58
Mozambique	J51-J56
Port. Guinea	J40-J45
Port. India	J47-J52
St. Thomas & Prince Islands	J52-J57
Timor	J31-J36

Nos. J37-J42 (6)	4.05	3.15
Nos. J31-J36 (6)	2.80	2.30
Nos. J53-J58 (6)	17.45	6.85
Nos. J51-J56 (6)	1.80	1.55
Nos. J40-J45 (6)	2.55	2.55
Nos. J47-J52 (6)	6.10	6.10
Nos. J52-J57 (6)	4.15	4.15
Nos. J31-J36 (6)	3.50	3.50
Set total (48) Stamps	42.40	30.15

Sao Paulo

Father Manuel da Nobrega and View of Sao Paulo — CD46

Founding of Sao Paulo, Brazil, 400th anniv.

1954

Angola	385
Cape Verde	297
Macao	382
Mozambique	395
Port. Guinea	291
Port. India	530
St. Thomas & Prince Islands	369
Timor	279

No. 385 (1)	.80	.50
No. 297 (1)	.70	.60
No. 382 (1)	14.00	3.00
No. 395 (1)	.40	.30
No. 291 (1)	.35	.25
No. 530 (1)	.80	.40
No. 369 (1)	.80	.60
No. 279 (1)	.85	.70
Set total (8) Stamps	18.70	6.35

Tropical Medicine Congress

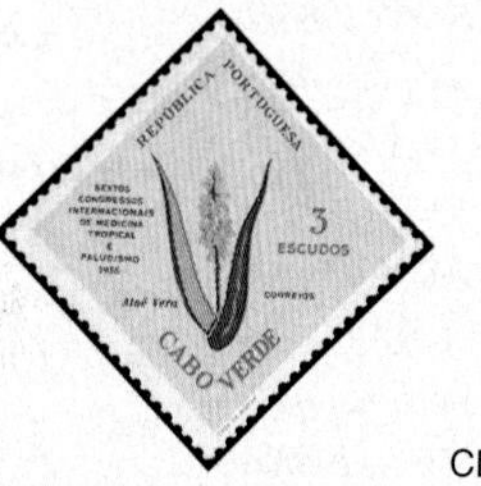

CD47

Sixth International Congress for Tropical Medicine and Malaria, Lisbon, Sept. 1958. Each stamp shows a different plant.

1958

Angola	409
Cape Verde	303
Macao	392
Mozambique	404
Port. Guinea	295
Port. India	569
St. Thomas & Prince Islands	371
Timor	289

No. 409 (1)	3.50	1.10
No. 303 (1)	5.50	2.10
No. 392 (1)	8.00	3.00
No. 404 (1)	4.00	.85
No. 295 (1)	2.75	1.10
No. 569 (1)	1.75	.75
No. 371 (1)	2.75	2.25
No. 289 (1)	3.00	2.75
Set total (8) Stamps	31.25	13.90

Sports

CD48

Each stamp shows a different sport.

1962

Angola	433-438
Cape Verde	320-325
Macao	394-399
Mozambique	424-429
Port. Guinea	299-304
St. Thomas & Prince Islands	374-379
Timor	313-318

Nos. 433-438 (6)	5.50	3.20
Nos. 320-325 (6)	15.25	5.20
Nos. 394-399 (6)	74.00	14.60
Nos. 424-429 (6)	5.70	2.45
Nos. 299-304 (6)	4.95	2.15
Nos. 374-379 (6)	6.75	3.20
Nos. 313-318 (6)	6.40	3.70
Set total (42) Stamps	118.55	34.50

Anti-Malaria

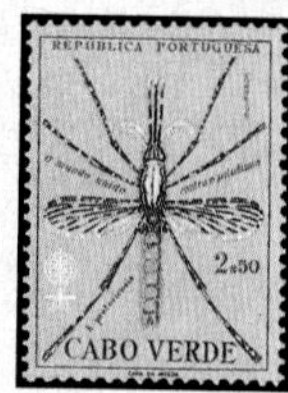

Anopheles Funestus and Malaria Eradication Symbol — CD49

World Health Organization drive to eradicate malaria.

1962

Angola	439
Cape Verde	326
Macao	400
Mozambique	430
Port. Guinea	305
St. Thomas & Prince Islands	380
Timor	319

No. 439 (1)	1.75	.90
No. 326 (1)	1.40	.90
No. 400 (1)	6.50	2.00
No. 430 (1)	1.40	.40
No. 305 (1)	1.25	.45
No. 380 (1)	2.00	1.50
No. 319 (1)	.75	.60
Set total (7) Stamps	15.05	6.75

Airline Anniversary

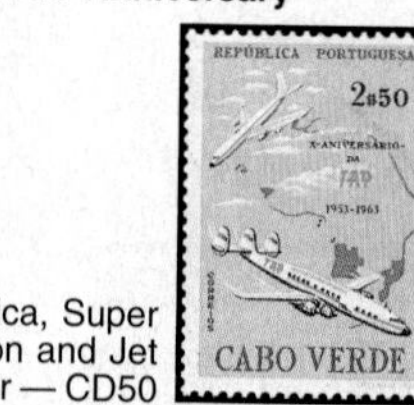

Map of Africa, Super Constellation and Jet Liner — CD50

Tenth anniversary of Transportes Aereos Portugueses (TAP).

1963

Angola	490
Cape Verde	327
Mozambique	434
Port. Guinea	318
St. Thomas & Prince Islands	381

No. 490 (1)	1.00	.35
No. 327 (1)	1.10	.70
No. 434 (1)	.40	.25
No. 318 (1)	.65	.35
No. 381 (1)	.70	.60
Set total (5) Stamps	3.85	2.25

National Overseas Bank

Antonio Teixeira de Sousa — CD51

Centenary of the National Overseas Bank of Portugal.

1964, May 16

Angola	509
Cape Verde	328
Port. Guinea	319
St. Thomas & Prince Islands	382
Timor	320

No. 509 (1)	.90	.30
No. 328 (1)	1.10	.75
No. 319 (1)	.65	.40
No. 382 (1)	.70	.50
No. 320 (1)	.75	.60
Set total (5) Stamps	4.10	2.55

ITU

ITU Emblem and the Archangel Gabriel — CD52

International Communications Union, Cent.

1965, May 17

Angola	511
Cape Verde	329
Macao	402
Mozambique	464
Port. Guinea	320
St. Thomas & Prince Islands	383
Timor	321

No. 511 (1)	1.25	.65
No. 329 (1)	2.10	1.40
No. 402 (1)	5.00	2.00
No. 464 (1)	.40	.25
No. 320 (1)	1.90	.75
No. 383 (1)	1.50	1.00
No. 321 (1)	1.50	.90
Set total (7) Stamps	13.65	6.95

National Revolution

CD53

40th anniv. of the National Revolution. Different buildings on each stamp.

1966, May 28

Angola	525
Cape Verde	338
Macao	403
Mozambique	465
Port. Guinea	329
St. Thomas & Prince Islands	392
Timor	322

No. 525 (1)	.50	.25
No. 338 (1)	.60	.45
No. 403 (1)	5.00	2.00
No. 465 (1)	.50	.30
No. 329 (1)	.55	.35
No. 392 (1)	.75	.50
No. 322 (1)	1.50	.90
Set total (7) Stamps	9.40	4.75

Navy Club

CD54

Centenary of Portugal's Navy Club. Each stamp has a different design.

1967, Jan. 31

Angola 527-528
Cape Verde 339-340
Macao....................412-413
Mozambique....................478-479
Port. Guinea....................330-331
St. Thomas & Prince Islands...393-394
Timor 323-324

Nos. 527-528 (2)	1.75	.75
Nos. 339-340 (2)	2.00	1.40
Nos. 412-413 (2)	9.50	3.75
Nos. 478-479 (2)	1.20	.65
Nos. 330-331 (2)	1.20	.90
Nos. 393-394 (2)	3.20	1.25
Nos. 323-324 (2)	4.00	2.00
Set total (14) Stamps	22.85	10.70

Admiral Coutinho

CD55

Centenary of the birth of Admiral Carlos Viegas Gago Coutinho (1869-1959), explorer and aviation pioneer. Each stamp has a different design.

1969, Feb. 17

Angola 547
Cape Verde 355
Macao....................417
Mozambique....................484
Port. Guinea....................335
St. Thomas & Prince Islands..........397
Timor 335

No. 547 (1)	.85	.35
No. 355 (1)	.35	.25
No. 417 (1)	3.75	1.50
No. 484 (1)	.25	.25
No. 335 (1)	.35	.25
No. 397 (1)	.50	.35
No. 335 (1)	1.10	.85
Set total (7) Stamps	7.15	3.80

Administration Reform

Luiz Augusto Rebello da Silva — CD56

Centenary of the administration reforms of the overseas territories.

1969, Sept. 25

Angola 549
Cape Verde 357
Macao....................419
Mozambique....................491
Port. Guinea....................337
St. Thomas & Prince Islands..........399
Timor 338

No. 549 (1)	.35	.25
No. 357 (1)	.35	.25
No. 419 (1)	5.00	1.00
No. 491 (1)	.25	.25
No. 337 (1)	.25	.25
No. 399 (1)	.45	.45
No. 338 (1)	.40	.25
Set total (7) Stamps	7.05	2.70

Marshal Carmona

CD57

Birth centenary of Marshal Antonio Oscar Carmona de Fragoso (1869-1951), President of Portugal. Each stamp has a different design.

1970, Nov. 15

Angola 563
Cape Verde 359
Macao....................422
Mozambique....................493
Port. Guinea....................340
St. Thomas & Prince Islands..........403
Timor 341

No. 563 (1)	.45	.25
No. 359 (1)	.55	.35
No. 422 (1)	2.25	1.25
No. 493 (1)	.40	.25
No. 340 (1)	.35	.25
No. 403 (1)	.75	.45
No. 341 (1)	.25	.25
Set total (7) Stamps	5.00	3.05

Olympic Games

CD59

20th Olympic Games, Munich, Aug. 26-Sept. 11. Each stamp shows a different sport.

1972, June 20

Angola 569
Cape Verde 361
Macao....................426
Mozambique....................504
Port. Guinea....................342
St. Thomas & Prince Islands..........408
Timor 343

No. 569 (1)	.65	.25
No. 361 (1)	.65	.30
No. 426 (1)	3.25	1.00
No. 504 (1)	.30	.25
No. 342 (1)	.45	.25
No. 408 (1)	.35	.25
No. 343 (1)	.50	.50
Set total (7) Stamps	6.15	2.80

Lisbon-Rio de Janeiro Flight

CD60

50th anniversary of the Lisbon to Rio de Janeiro flight by Arturo de Sacadura and Coutinho, March 30-June 5, 1922. Each stamp shows a different stage of the flight.

1972, Sept. 20

Angola 570
Cape Verde 362
Macao....................427
Mozambique....................505
Port. Guinea....................343
St. Thomas & Prince Islands..........409
Timor 344

No. 570 (1)	.35	.25
No. 362 (1)	1.50	.30
No. 427 (1)	22.50	7.50
No. 505 (1)	.25	.25
No. 343 (1)	.25	.25
No. 409 (1)	.35	.25
No. 344 (1)	.25	.40
Set total (7) Stamps	25.45	9.20

WMO Centenary

WMO Emblem — CD61

Centenary of international meterological cooperation.

1973, Dec. 15

Angola 571
Cape Verde 363
Macao....................429
Mozambique....................509
Port. Guinea....................344
St. Thomas & Prince Islands..........410
Timor 345

No. 571 (1)	.45	.25
No. 363 (1)	.65	.30
No. 429 (1)	6.25	1.75
No. 509 (1)	.30	.25
No. 344 (1)	.45	.35
No. 410 (1)	.60	.50
No. 345 (1)	1.75	2.00
Set total (7) Stamps	10.45	5.40

FRENCH COMMUNITY

Upper Volta can be found under Burkina Faso in Vol. 1
Madagascar can be found under Malagasy in Vol. 3

Colonial Exposition

People of French Empire CD70

Women's Heads CD71

France Showing Way to Civilization CD72

"Colonial Commerce" CD73

International Colonial Exposition, Paris.

1931

Cameroun....................213-216
Chad....................60-63
Dahomey 97-100
Fr. Guiana 152-155
Fr. Guinea 116-119
Fr. India 100-103
Fr. Polynesia....................76-79
Fr. Sudan....................102-105
Gabon....................120-123
Guadeloupe....................138-141
Indo-China....................140-142
Ivory Coast....................92-95
Madagascar....................169-172
Martinique....................129-132
Mauritania....................65-68
Middle Congo....................61-64
New Caledonia....................176-179
Niger....................73-76
Reunion....................122-125
St. Pierre & Miquelon..............132-135
Senegal 138-141
Somali Coast....................135-138
Togo....................254-257
Ubangi-Shari 82-85
Upper Volta....................66-69
Wallis & Futuna Isls. 85-88

Nos. 213-216 (4)	23.00	18.25
Nos. 60-63 (4)	22.00	22.00
Nos. 97-100 (4)	26.00	26.00
Nos. 152-155 (4)	22.00	22.00
Nos. 116-119 (4)	19.75	19.75
Nos. 100-103 (4)	18.00	*18.00*
Nos. 76-79 (4)	30.00	30.00
Nos. 102-105 (4)	19.00	19.00
Nos. 120-123 (4)	17.50	17.50
Nos. 138-141 (4)	19.00	19.00
Nos. 140-142 (3)	11.50	11.50
Nos. 92-95 (4)	22.50	22.50
Nos. 169-172 (4)	7.90	5.00
Nos. 129-132 (4)	21.00	21.00
Nos. 65-68 (4)	22.00	22.00
Nos. 61-64 (4)	20.50	20.50
Nos. 176-179 (4)	24.00	24.00
Nos. 73-76 (4)	21.50	21.50
Nos. 122-125 (4)	22.00	22.00
Nos. 132-135 (4)	24.00	24.00
Nos. 138-141 (4)	20.00	20.00
Nos. 135-138 (4)	22.00	22.00
Nos. 254-257 (4)	22.00	22.00
Nos. 82-85 (4)	21.00	21.00
Nos. 66-69 (4)	19.00	19.00
Nos. 85-88 (4)	35.00	35.00
Set total (103) Stamps	552.15	544.50

Paris International Exposition
Colonial Arts Exposition

"Colonial Resources"
CD74 CD77

Overseas Commerce CD75

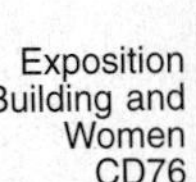

Exposition Building and Women CD76

"France and the Empire" CD78

Cultural Treasures of the Colonies CD79

Souvenir sheets contain one imperf. stamp.

1937

Cameroun....................217-222A
Dahomey 101-107
Fr. Equatorial Africa 27-32, 73
Fr. Guiana 162-168
Fr. Guinea 120-126
Fr. India 104-110
Fr. Polynesia....................117-123
Fr. Sudan....................106-112
Guadeloupe....................148-154
Indo-China....................193-199
Inini....................41
Ivory Coast....................152-158
Kwangchowan 132
Madagascar....................191-197
Martinique....................179-185
Mauritania....................69-75
New Caledonia....................208-214
Niger....................73-83
Reunion....................167-173
St. Pierre & Miquelon..............165-171
Senegal 172-178
Somali Coast....................139-145
Togo....................258-264
Wallis & Futuna Isls. 89

Nos. 217-222A (7)	18.80	20.30
Nos. 101-107 (7)	23.60	27.60
Nos. 27-32, 73 (7)	28.10	32.10
Nos. 162-168 (7)	22.50	24.50
Nos. 120-126 (7)	24.00	28.00
Nos. 104-110 (7)	21.15	36.50
Nos. 117-123 (7)	58.50	75.00
Nos. 106-112 (7)	23.60	27.60
Nos. 148-154 (7)	19.55	21.05
Nos. 193-199 (7)	17.70	19.70
No. 41 (1)	19.00	22.50
Nos. 152-158 (7)	22.20	26.20
No. 132 (1)	9.25	11.00
Nos. 191-197 (7)	19.25	21.75
Nos. 179-185 (7)	19.95	21.70
Nos. 69-75 (7)	20.50	24.50
Nos. 208-214 (7)	39.00	50.50
Nos. 73-83 (11)	42.70	46.70
Nos. 167-173 (7)	21.70	23.20
Nos. 165-171 (7)	49.60	64.00
Nos. 172-178 (7)	21.00	23.80
Nos. 139-145 (7)	25.60	32.60
Nos. 258-264 (7)	20.40	20.40
No. 89 (1)	28.50	37.50
Set total (154) Stamps	616.15	738.70

Curie

Pierre and Marie Curie CD80

40th anniversary of the discovery of radium. The surtax was for the benefit of the Intl. Union for the Control of Cancer.

1938

Cameroun.. B1
Cuba..B1-B2
Dahomey.. B2
France.. B76
Fr. Equatorial Africa........................ B1
Fr. Guiana.. B3
Fr. Guinea.. B2
Fr. India.. B6
Fr. Polynesia.. B5
Fr. Sudan.. B1
Guadeloupe.. B3
Indo-China.. B14
Ivory Coast.. B2
Madagascar.. B2
Martinique.. B2
Mauritania.. B3
New Caledonia.. B4
Niger.. B1
Reunion.. B4
St. Pierre & Miquelon........................ B3
Senegal.. B3
Somali Coast.. B2
Togo.. B1

No. B1 (1)	10.00	10.00
Nos. B1-B2 (2)	8.50	2.40
No. B2 (1)	9.50	9.50
No. B76 (1)	21.00	12.50
No. B1 (1)	24.00	24.00
No. B3 (1)	13.50	13.50
No. B2 (1)	8.75	8.75
No. B6 (1)	10.00	10.00
No. B5 (1)	20.00	20.00
No. B1 (1)	12.50	12.50
No. B3 (1)	11.00	10.50
No. B14 (1)	12.00	12.00
No. B2 (1)	11.00	7.50
No. B2 (1)	11.00	11.00
No. B2 (1)	13.00	13.00
No. B3 (1)	7.75	7.75
No. B4 (1)	16.50	17.50
No. B1 (1)	15.00	15.00
No. B4 (1)	14.00	14.00
No. B3 (1)	21.00	22.50
No. B3 (1)	10.50	10.50
No. B2 (1)	7.75	7.75
No. B1 (1)	20.00	20.00
Set total (24) Stamps	308.25	292.15

Caillie

Rene Caillie and Map of Northwestern Africa — CD81

Death centenary of Rene Caillie (1799-1838), French explorer. All three denominations exist with colony name omitted.

1939

Dahomey..108-110
Fr. Guinea..161-163
Fr. Sudan..113-115
Ivory Coast..160-162
Mauritania..109-111
Niger..84-86
Senegal..188-190
Togo..265-267

Nos. 108-110 (3)	1.20	3.60
Nos. 161-163 (3)	1.20	3.20
Nos. 113-115 (3)	1.20	3.20
Nos. 160-162 (3)	1.05	2.55
Nos. 109-111 (3)	1.05	3.80
Nos. 84-86 (3)	1.05	2.35
Nos. 188-190 (3)	1.05	2.90
Nos. 265-267 (3)	1.05	3.30
Set total (24) Stamps	8.85	24.90

New York World's Fair

Natives and New York Skyline CD82

1939

Cameroun..223-224
Dahomey..111-112
Fr. Equatorial Africa........................78-79
Fr. Guiana..169-170
Fr. Guinea..164-165
Fr. India..111-112
Fr. Polynesia..124-125
Fr. Sudan..116-117
Guadeloupe..155-156
Indo-China..203-204
Inini..42-43
Ivory Coast..163-164
Kwangchowan..133-134
Madagascar..209-210
Martinique..186-187
Mauritania..112-113
New Caledonia..215-216
Niger..87-88
Reunion..174-175
St. Pierre & Miquelon........................205-206
Senegal..191-192
Somali Coast..179-180
Togo..268-269
Wallis & Futuna Isls.........................90-91

Nos. 223-224 (2)	2.80	2.40
Nos. 111-112 (2)	1.60	3.20
Nos. 78-79 (2)	1.60	3.20
Nos. 169-170 (2)	2.60	2.60
Nos. 164-165 (2)	1.60	3.20
Nos. 111-112 (2)	3.00	*8.00*
Nos. 124-125 (2)	4.80	4.80
Nos. 116-117 (2)	1.60	3.20
Nos. 155-156 (2)	2.50	2.50
Nos. 203-204 (2)	2.05	2.05
Nos. 42-43 (2)	7.50	9.00
Nos. 163-164 (2)	1.50	3.00
Nos. 133-134 (2)	2.50	2.50
Nos. 209-210 (2)	1.50	2.50
Nos. 186-187 (2)	2.35	2.35
Nos. 112-113 (2)	1.40	2.80
Nos. 215-216 (2)	3.35	3.35
Nos. 87-88 (2)	1.40	2.80
Nos. 174-175 (2)	2.80	2.80
Nos. 205-206 (2)	4.80	6.00
Nos. 191-192 (2)	1.40	2.80
Nos. 179-180 (2)	1.40	2.80
Nos. 268-269 (2)	1.40	2.80
Nos. 90-91 (2)	6.00	6.00
Set total (48) Stamps	63.45	86.65

French Revolution

Storming of the Bastille CD83

French Revolution, 150th anniv. The surtax was for the defense of the colonies.

1939

Cameroun..B2-B6
Dahomey..B3-B7
Fr. Equatorial Africa.......... B4-B8, CB1
Fr. Guiana........................ B4-B8, CB1
Fr. Guinea..B3-B7
Fr. India..B7-B11
Fr. Polynesia.................. B6-B10, CB1
Fr. Sudan..B2-B6
Guadeloupe..B4-B8
Indo-China.................... B15-B19, CB1
Inini..B1-B5
Ivory Coast..B3-B7
Kwangchowan..B1-B5
Madagascar...................... B3-B7, CB1
Martinique..B3-B7
Mauritania..B4-B8
New Caledonia.................. B5-B9, CB1
Niger..B2-B6
Reunion........................ B5-B9, CB1
St. Pierre & Miquelon........................B4-B8
Senegal........................ B4-B8, CB1
Somali Coast..B3-B7
Togo..B2-B6
Wallis & Futuna Isls.........................B1-B5

Nos. B2-B6 (5)	60.00	60.00
Nos. B3-B7 (5)	47.50	47.50
Nos. B4-B8,CB1 (6)	120.00	120.00
Nos. B4-B8,CB1 (6)	79.50	79.50
Nos. B3-B7 (5)	47.50	47.50
Nos. B7-B11 (5)	28.75	*32.50*
Nos. B6-B10,CB1 (6)	122.50	122.50
Nos. B2-B6 (5)	50.00	50.00
Nos. B4-B8 (5)	50.00	50.00
Nos. B15-B19,CB1 (6)	85.00	85.00
Nos. B1-B5 (5)	75.00	87.50
Nos. B3-B7 (5)	43.75	43.75
Nos. B1-B5 (5)	46.25	46.25
Nos. B3-B7,CB1 (6)	65.50	65.50
Nos. B3-B7 (5)	52.50	52.50
Nos. B4-B8 (5)	42.50	42.50
Nos. B5-B9,CB1 (6)	101.50	101.50
Nos. B2-B6 (5)	60.00	60.00
Nos. B5-B9,CB1 (6)	87.50	87.50
Nos. B4-B8 (5)	67.50	72.50
Nos. B4-B8,CB1 (6)	56.50	56.50
Nos. B3-B7 (5)	45.00	45.00
Nos. B2-B6 (5)	42.50	42.50
Nos. B1-B5 (5)	95.00	95.00
Set total (128) Stamps	1,572.	1,593.

Plane over Coastal Area CD85

All five denominations exist with colony name omitted.

1940

Dahomey..C1-C5
Fr. Guinea..C1-C5
Fr. Sudan..C1-C5
Ivory Coast..C1-C5
Mauritania..C1-C5
Niger..C1-C5
Senegal..C12-C16
Togo..C1-C5

Nos. C1-C5 (5)	4.00	4.00
Nos. C1-C5 (5)	4.00	4.00
Nos. C1-C5 (5)	4.00	4.00
Nos. C1-C5 (5)	3.80	3.80
Nos. C1-C5 (5)	3.50	3.50
Nos. C1-C5 (5)	3.50	3.50
Nos. C12-C16 (5)	3.50	3.50
Nos. C1-C5 (5)	3.15	3.15
Set total (40) Stamps	29.45	29.45

Defense of the Empire

Colonial Infantryman — CD86

1941

Cameroun..B13B
Dahomey..B13
Fr. Equatorial Africa........................B8B
Fr. Guiana..B10
Fr. Guinea..B13
Fr. India..B13
Fr. Polynesia..B12
Fr. Sudan..B12
Guadeloupe..B10
Indo-China..B19B
Inini..B7
Ivory Coast..B13
Kwangchowan..B7
Madagascar..B9
Martinique..B9
Mauritania..B14
New Caledonia..B11
Niger..B12
Reunion..B11
St. Pierre & Miquelon........................B8B
Senegal..B14
Somali Coast..B9
Togo..B10B
Wallis & Futuna Isls.........................B7

No. B13B (1)	1.60
No. B13 (1)	1.20
No. B8B (1)	3.50
No. B10 (1)	1.40
No. B13 (1)	1.40
No. B13 (1)	1.25
No. B12 (1)	3.50
No. B12 (1)	1.40
No. B10 (1)	1.00
No. B19B (1)	1.60
No. B7 (1)	1.75
No. B13 (1)	1.25
No. B7 (1)	.85
No. B9 (1)	1.50
No. B9 (1)	1.40
No. B14 (1)	.95
No. B12 (1)	1.40
No. B11 (1)	1.60
No. B8B (1)	3.75
No. B14 (1)	1.25
No. B9 (1)	1.60
No. B10B (1)	1.10
No. B7 (1)	2.40
Set total (23) Stamps	38.65

Each of the CD86 stamps listed above is part of a set of three stamps. The designs of the other two stamps in the set vary from country to country. Only the values of the Common Design stamps are listed here.

Colonial Education Fund

CD86a

1942

Cameroun..CB3
Dahomey..CB4
Fr. Equatorial Africa........................CB5
Fr. Guiana..CB4
Fr. Guinea..CB4
Fr. India..CB3
Fr. Polynesia..CB4
Fr. Sudan..CB4
Guadeloupe..CB3
Indo-China..CB5
Inini..CB3
Ivory Coast..CB4
Kwangchowan..CB4
Malagasy..CB5
Martinique..CB3
Mauritania..CB4
New Caledonia..CB4
Niger..CB4
Reunion..CB4
St. Pierre & Miquelon........................CB3
Senegal..CB5
Somali Coast..CB3
Togo..CB3
Wallis & Futuna..CB3

No. CB3 (1)	1.10	
No. CB4 (1)	.80	5.50
No. CB5 (1)	.80	
No. CB4 (1)	1.10	
No. CB4 (1)	.40	5.50
No. CB3 (1)	.90	
No. CB4 (1)	2.00	
No. CB4 (1)	.40	5.50
No. CB3 (1)	1.10	
No. CB5 (1)	1.10	
No. CB3 (1)	1.25	
No. CB4 (1)	1.00	5.50
No. CB4 (1)	1.00	
No. CB5 (1)	.65	
No. CB3 (1)	1.00	
No. CB4 (1)	.80	
No. CB4 (1)	2.25	
No. CB4 (1)	.35	
No. CB4 (1)	.90	
No. CB3 (1)	5.25	
No. CB5 (1)	.80	6.50
No. CB3 (1)	.70	
No. CB3 (1)	.35	
No. CB3 (1)	2.25	
Set total (24) Stamps	28.25	28.50

Cross of Lorraine & Four-motor Plane CD87

1941-5

Cameroun..C1-C7
Fr. Equatorial Africa........................C17-C23
Fr. Guiana..C9-C10
Fr. India..C1-C6
Fr. Polynesia..C3-C9
Fr. West Africa..C1-C3
Guadeloupe..C1-C2
Madagascar..C37-C43

Martinique C1-C2
New Caledonia C7-C13
Reunion C18-C24
St. Pierre & Miquelon C1-C7
Somali Coast C1-C7

Nos. C1-C7 (7)	6.30	6.30
Nos. C17-C23 (7)	10.40	6.35
Nos. C9-C10 (2)	3.80	3.10
Nos. C1-C6 (6)	9.30	*15.00*
Nos. C3-C9 (7)	13.75	10.00
Nos. C1-C3 (3)	9.50	3.90
Nos. C1-C2 (2)	3.75	2.50
Nos. C37-C43 (7)	5.60	3.80
Nos. C1-C2 (2)	3.00	1.60
Nos. C7-C13 (7)	8.85	7.30
Nos. C18-C24 (7)	7.05	5.00
Nos. C1-C7 (7)	11.60	9.40
Nos. C1-C7 (7)	13.95	11.10
Set total (71) Stamps	106.85	85.35

Transport Plane CD88

Caravan and Plane CD89

1942

Dahomey C6-C13
Fr. Guinea C6-C13
Fr. Sudan C6-C13
Ivory Coast C6-C13
Mauritania C6-C13
Niger C6-C13
Senegal C17-C25
Togo C6-C13

Nos. C6-C13 (8)	7.15
Nos. C6-C13 (8)	5.75
Nos. C6-C13 (8)	8.00
Nos. C6-C13 (8)	11.15
Nos. C6-C13 (8)	9.75
Nos. C6-C13 (8)	6.90
Nos. C17-C25 (9)	9.45
Nos. C6-C13 (8)	6.75
Set total (65) Stamps	64.90

Red Cross

Marianne CD90

The surtax was for the French Red Cross and national relief.

1944

Cameroun B28
Fr. Equatorial Africa B38
Fr. Guiana B12
Fr. India B14
Fr. Polynesia B13
Fr. West Africa B1
Guadeloupe B12
Madagascar B15
Martinique B11
New Caledonia B13
Reunion B15
St. Pierre & Miquelon B13
Somali Coast B13
Wallis & Futuna Isls. B9

No. B28 (1)	2.00	1.60
No. B38 (1)	1.60	1.20
No. B12 (1)	1.75	1.25
No. B14 (1)	1.50	1.25
No. B13 (1)	2.00	1.60
No. B1 (1)	6.50	4.75
No. B12 (1)	1.40	1.00
No. B15 (1)	.90	.90
No. B11 (1)	1.20	1.20
No. B13 (1)	1.50	1.50
No. B15 (1)	1.60	1.10
No. B13 (1)	2.75	2.40
No. B13 (1)	1.75	2.00
No. B9 (1)	4.50	3.25
Set total (14) Stamps	30.95	25.00

Eboue

CD91

Felix Eboue, first French colonial administrator to proclaim resistance to Germany after French surrender in World War II.

1945

Cameroun 296-297
Fr. Equatorial Africa 156-157
Fr. Guiana 171-172
Fr. India 210-211
Fr. Polynesia 150-151
Fr. West Africa 15-16
Guadeloupe 187-188
Madagascar 259-260
Martinique 196-197
New Caledonia 274-275
Reunion 238-239
St. Pierre & Miquelon 322-323
Somali Coast 238-239

Nos. 296-297 (2)	2.40	1.95
Nos. 156-157 (2)	2.55	2.00
Nos. 171-172 (2)	2.45	2.00
Nos. 210-211 (2)	2.20	1.95
Nos. 150-151 (2)	3.60	2.85
Nos. 15-16 (2)	2.40	2.40
Nos. 187-188 (2)	2.05	1.60
Nos. 259-260 (2)	2.00	1.45
Nos. 196-197 (2)	2.05	1.55
Nos. 274-275 (2)	3.40	3.00
Nos. 238-239 (2)	2.40	2.00
Nos. 322-323 (2)	4.40	3.45
Nos. 238-239 (2)	2.45	2.10
Set total (26) Stamps	34.35	28.30

Victory

Victory — CD92

European victory of the Allied Nations in World War II.

1946, May 8

Cameroun C8
Fr. Equatorial Africa C24
Fr. Guiana C11
Fr. India C7
Fr. Polynesia C10
Fr. West Africa C4
Guadeloupe C3
Indo-China C19
Madagascar C44
Martinique C3
New Caledonia C14
Reunion C25
St. Pierre & Miquelon C8
Somali Coast C8
Wallis & Futuna Isls. C1

No. C8 (1)	1.60	1.20
No. C24 (1)	1.60	1.25
No. C11 (1)	1.75	1.25
No. C7 (1)	1.00	4.00
No. C10 (1)	2.75	2.00
No. C4 (1)	1.60	1.20
No. C3 (1)	1.25	1.00
No. C19 (1)	1.00	.55
No. C44 (1)	1.00	.35
No. C3 (1)	1.30	1.00
No. C14 (1)	1.50	1.25
No. C25 (1)	1.10	.90
No. C8 (1)	2.10	1.75
No. C8 (1)	1.75	1.40
No. C1 (1)	2.50	1.90
Set total (15) Stamps	23.80	21.00

Chad to Rhine

Leclerc's Departure from Chad — CD93

Battle at Cufra Oasis — CD94

Tanks in Action, Mareth — CD95

Normandy Invasion — CD96

Entering Paris — CD97

Liberation of Strasbourg — CD98

"Chad to the Rhine" march, 1942-44, by Gen. Jacques Leclerc's column, later French 2nd Armored Division.

1946, June 6

Cameroun C9-C14
Fr. Equatorial Africa C25-C30
Fr. Guiana C12-C17
Fr. India C8-C13
Fr. Polynesia C11-C16
Fr. West Africa C5-C10
Guadeloupe C4-C9
Indo-China C20-C25
Madagascar C45-C50
Martinique C4-C9
New Caledonia C15-C20
Reunion C26-C31
St. Pierre & Miquelon C9-C14
Somali Coast C9-C14
Wallis & Futuna Isls. C2-C7

Nos. C9-C14 (6)	12.05	9.70
Nos. C25-C30 (6)	14.70	10.80
Nos. C12-C17 (6)	12.65	10.35
Nos. C8-C13 (6)	12.80	*15.00*
Nos. C11-C16 (6)	17.55	13.40
Nos. C5-C10 (6)	16.05	11.95
Nos. C4-C9 (6)	12.00	9.60
Nos. C20-C25 (6)	6.40	6.40
Nos. C45-C50 (6)	10.30	8.40
Nos. C4-C9 (6)	8.85	7.30
Nos. C15-C20 (6)	13.40	11.90
Nos. C26-C31 (6)	10.25	6.55
Nos. C9-C14 (6)	17.30	14.35
Nos. C9-C14 (6)	18.10	12.65
Nos. C2-C7 (6)	13.75	10.45
Set total (90) Stamps	196.15	158.80

UPU

French Colonials, Globe and Plane — CD99

Universal Postal Union, 75th anniv.

1949, July 4

Cameroun C29
Fr. Equatorial Africa C34
Fr. India C17
Fr. Polynesia C20
Fr. West Africa C15
Indo-China C26
Madagascar C55
New Caledonia C24
St. Pierre & Miquelon C18
Somali Coast C18
Togo C18
Wallis & Futuna Isls. C10

No. C29 (1)	8.00	4.75
No. C34 (1)	16.00	12.00
No. C17 (1)	11.50	8.75
No. C20 (1)	20.00	15.00
No. C15 (1)	12.00	8.75
No. C26 (1)	4.75	4.00
No. C55 (1)	4.00	2.75
No. C24 (1)	7.50	5.00
No. C18 (1)	20.00	12.00
No. C18 (1)	14.00	10.50
No. C18 (1)	8.50	7.00
No. C10 (1)	12.50	8.25
Set total (12) Stamps	138.75	98.75

Tropical Medicine

Doctor Treating Infant CD100

The surtax was for charitable work.

1950

Cameroun B29
Fr. Equatorial Africa B39
Fr. India B15
Fr. Polynesia B14
Fr. West Africa B3
Madagascar B17
New Caledonia B14
St. Pierre & Miquelon B14
Somali Coast B14
Togo B11

No. B29 (1)	7.25	5.50
No. B39 (1)	7.25	5.50
No. B15 (1)	6.00	4.00
No. B14 (1)	10.50	8.00
No. B3 (1)	9.50	7.25
No. B17 (1)	5.50	5.50
No. B14 (1)	6.75	5.25
No. B14 (1)	17.00	13.00
No. B14 (1)	7.75	6.25
No. B11 (1)	5.00	3.50
Set total (10) Stamps	82.50	63.75

Military Medal

Medal, Early Marine and Colonial Soldier — CD101

Centenary of the creation of the French Military Medal.

1952

Cameroun 322
Comoro Isls. 39
Fr. Equatorial Africa 186

Fr. India 233
Fr. Polynesia 179
Fr. West Africa 57
Madagascar 286
New Caledonia 295
St. Pierre & Miquelon 345
Somali Coast 267
Togo 327
Wallis & Futuna Isls. 149

No. 322 (1) 7.25 3.25
No. 39 (1) 50.00 40.00
No. 186 (1) 8.00 5.50
No. 233 (1) 5.50 7.00
No. 179 (1) 13.50 10.00
No. 57 (1) 8.75 6.50
No. 286 (1) 3.75 2.50
No. 295 (1) 6.50 6.00
No. 345 (1) 17.00 13.00
No. 267 (1) 9.00 8.00
No. 327 (1) 5.50 4.75
No. 149 (1) 9.50 7.00
Set total (12) Stamps 144.25 113.50

Liberation

Allied Landing, Victory Sign and Cross of Lorraine — CD102

Liberation of France, 10th anniv.

1954, June 6

Cameroun C32
Comoro Isls. C4
Fr. Equatorial Africa C38
Fr. India C18
Fr. Polynesia C22
Fr. West Africa C17
Madagascar C57
New Caledonia C25
St. Pierre & Miquelon C19
Somali Coast C19
Togo C19
Wallis & Futuna Isls. C11

No. C32 (1) 7.25 4.75
No. C4 (1) 35.00 20.00
No. C38 (1) 12.00 8.00
No. C18 (1) 11.00 8.00
No. C22 (1) 10.00 8.00
No. C17 (1) 12.00 5.50
No. C57 (1) 3.25 2.00
No. C25 (1) 7.50 5.00
No. C19 (1) 18.00 12.00
No. C19 (1) 10.50 8.50
No. C19 (1) 7.00 5.50
No. C11 (1) 12.50 8.25
Set total (12) Stamps 146.00 95.50

FIDES

Plowmen CD103

Efforts of FIDES, the Economic and Social Development Fund for Overseas Possessions (Fonds d' Investissement pour le Developpement Economique et Social). Each stamp has a different design.

1956

Cameroun 326-329
Comoro Isls. 43
Fr. Equatorial Africa 189-192
Fr. Polynesia 181
Fr. West Africa 65-72
Madagascar 292-295
New Caledonia 303
St. Pierre & Miquelon 350
Somali Coast 268-269
Togo 331

Nos. 326-329 (4) 6.90 3.20
No. 43 (1) 2.25 1.60
Nos. 189-192 (4) 3.20 1.65
No. 181 (1) 4.00 2.00
Nos. 65-72 (8) 16.00 6.35
Nos. 292-295 (4) 2.25 1.20
No. 303 (1) 1.90 1.10
No. 350 (1) 6.50 3.50
Nos. 268-269 (2) 5.35 3.15
No. 331 (1) 4.25 2.10
Set total (27) Stamps 52.60 25.85

Flower

CD104

Each stamp shows a different flower.

1958-9

Cameroun 333
Comoro Isls. 45
Fr. Equatorial Africa 200-201
Fr. Polynesia 192
Fr. So. & Antarctic Terr. 11
Fr. West Africa 79-83
Madagascar 301-302
New Caledonia 304-305
St. Pierre & Miquelon 357
Somali Coast 270
Togo 348-349
Wallis & Futuna Isls. 152

No. 333 (1) 1.60 .80
No. 45 (1) 5.50 4.50
Nos. 200-201 (2) 3.60 1.60
No. 192 (1) 6.50 4.00
No. 11 (1) 10.00 8.00
Nos. 79-83 (5) 10.45 5.60
Nos. 301-302 (2) 1.60 .60
Nos. 304-305 (2) 8.00 3.00
No. 357 (1) 4.50 2.40
No. 270 (1) 4.25 1.40
Nos. 348-349 (2) 1.10 .50
No. 152 (1) 4.50 2.50
Set total (20) Stamps 61.60 34.90

Human Rights

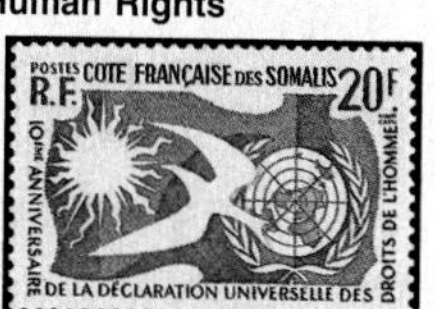

Sun, Dove and U.N. Emblem CD105

10th anniversary of the signing of the Universal Declaration of Human Rights.

1958

Comoro Isls. 44
Fr. Equatorial Africa 202
Fr. Polynesia 191
Fr. West Africa 85
Madagascar 300
New Caledonia 306
St. Pierre & Miquelon 356
Somali Coast 274
Wallis & Futuna Isls. 153

No. 44 (1) 11.00 11.00
No. 202 (1) 2.40 1.25
No. 191 (1) 13.00 8.75
No. 85 (1) 2.40 2.00
No. 300 (1) .80 .40
No. 306 (1) 2.00 1.50
No. 356 (1) 3.50 2.50
No. 274 (1) 3.50 2.10
No. 153 (1) 5.75 4.00
Set total (9) Stamps 44.35 33.50

C.C.T.A.

CD106

Commission for Technical Cooperation in Africa south of the Sahara, 10th anniv.

1960

Cameroun 339
Cent. Africa 3
Chad 66
Congo, P.R. 90
Dahomey 138
Gabon 150
Ivory Coast 180
Madagascar 317
Mali 9
Mauritania 117
Niger 104
Upper Volta 89

No. 339 (1) 1.60 .75
No. 3 (1) 1.90 .65
No. 66 (1) 1.90 .50
No. 90 (1) 1.00 1.00
No. 138 (1) .50 .25
No. 150 (1) 1.40 1.10
No. 180 (1) 1.10 .50
No. 317 (1) .60 .30
No. 9 (1) 1.20 .50
No. 117 (1) .75 .40
No. 104 (1) .85 .45
No. 89 (1) .45 .40
Set total (12) Stamps 13.25 6.80

Air Afrique, 1961

Modern and Ancient Africa, Map and Planes — CD107

Founding of Air Afrique (African Airlines).

1961-62

Cameroun C37
Cent. Africa C5
Chad C7
Congo, P.R. C5
Dahomey C17
Gabon C5
Ivory Coast C18
Mauritania C17
Niger C22
Senegal C31
Upper Volta C4

No. C37 (1) 1.00 .50
No. C5 (1) 1.00 .55
No. C7 (1) 1.00 .25
No. C5 (1) 1.75 .90
No. C17 (1) .80 .40
No. C5 (1) 11.00 6.00
No. C18 (1) 2.00 1.25
No. C17 (1) 2.50 1.25
No. C22 (1) 1.75 .90
No. C31 (1) .80 .30
No. C4 (1) .65 .45
Set total (11) Stamps 24.25 12.75

Anti-Malaria

CD108

World Health Organization drive to eradicate malaria.

1962, Apr. 7

Cameroun B36
Cent. Africa B1
Chad B1
Comoro Isls. B1
Congo, P.R. B3
Dahomey B15
Gabon B4
Ivory Coast B15
Madagascar B19
Mali B1
Mauritania B16
Niger B14
Senegal B16
Somali Coast B15
Upper Volta B1

No. B36 (1) 1.00 .45
No. B1 (1) 1.40 1.40
No. B1 (1) 1.25 .50
No. B1 (1) 4.00 4.00
No. B3 (1) 1.40 1.00
No. B15 (1) .75 .75
No. B4 (1) 1.00 1.00
No. B15 (1) 1.25 1.25
No. B19 (1) .75 .50
No. B1 (1) 1.25 .60
No. B16 (1) .80 .80
No. B14 (1) .60 .60
No. B16 (1) 1.10 .65
No. B15 (1) 7.00 7.00
No. B1 (1) .95 .95
Set total (15) Stamps 24.50 21.45

Abidjan Games

CD109

Abidjan Games, Ivory Coast, Dec. 24-31, 1961. Each stamp shows a different sport.

1962

Cent. Africa 19-20, C6
Chad 83-84, C8
Congo, P.R. 103-104, C7
Gabon 163-164, C6
Niger 109-111
Upper Volta 103-105

Nos. 19-20,C6 (3) 3.90 2.60
Nos. 83-84,C8 (3) 6.30 1.55
Nos. 103-104,C7 (3) 3.85 1.80
Nos. 163-164,C6 (3) 5.00 3.00
Nos. 109-111 (3) 2.60 1.10
Nos. 103-105 (3) 3.15 1.80
Set total (18) Stamps 24.80 11.85

African and Malagasy Union

Flag of Union CD110

First anniversary of the Union.

1962, Sept. 8

Cameroun 373
Cent. Africa 21
Chad 85
Congo, P.R. 105
Dahomey 155
Gabon 165
Ivory Coast 198
Madagascar 332
Mauritania 170
Niger 112
Senegal 211
Upper Volta 106

No. 373 (1) 2.00 .75
No. 21 (1) 1.25 .60
No. 85 (1) 1.25 .25
No. 105 (1) 1.50 .50
No. 155 (1) 1.25 .90
No. 165 (1) 1.60 1.25
No. 198 (1) 2.10 .75
No. 332 (1) .80 .80
No. 170 (1) .75 .50
No. 112 (1) .80 .40
No. 211 (1) .80 .50
No. 106 (1) 1.50 .90
Set total (12) Stamps 15.60 8.10

Telstar

Telstar and Globe Showing Andover and Pleumeur-Bodou — CD111

First television connection of the United States and Europe through the Telstar satellite, July 11-12, 1962.

1962-63

Andorra, French 154
Comoro Isls. C7
Fr. Polynesia C29
Fr. So. & Antarctic Terr. C5
New Caledonia C33
St. Pierre & Miquelon C26
Somali Coast C31
Wallis & Futuna Isls. C17

No. 154 (1) 2.00 1.60
No. C7 (1) 5.00 3.00
No. C29 (1) 11.50 8.00

No. C5 (1)	29.00	21.00
No. C33 (1)	25.00	18.50
No. C26 (1)	7.25	5.50
No. C31 (1)	1.00	1.00
No. C17 (1)	3.50	3.50
Set total (8) Stamps	84.25	62.10

Freedom From Hunger

World Map and Wheat Emblem CD112

U.N. Food and Agriculture Organization's "Freedom from Hunger" campaign.

1963, Mar. 21

Cameroun B37-B38
Cent. Africa B2
Chad B2
Congo, P.R. B4
Dahomey B16
Gabon B5
Ivory Coast B16
Madagascar B21
Mauritania B17
Niger B15
Senegal B17
Upper Volta B2

Nos. B37-B38 (2)	2.25	.75
No. B2 (1)	1.25	1.25
No. B2 (1)	2.00	.50
No. B4 (1)	1.40	1.00
No. B16 (1)	.80	.80
No. B5 (1)	1.00	1.00
No. B16 (1)	1.50	1.50
No. B21 (1)	.60	.45
No. B17 (1)	.80	.80
No. B15 (1)	.60	.60
No. B17 (1)	.80	.50
No. B2 (1)	.95	.95
Set total (13) Stamps	13.95	10.10

Red Cross Centenary

CD113

Centenary of the International Red Cross.

1963, Sept. 2

Comoro Isls. 55
Fr. Polynesia 205
New Caledonia 328
St. Pierre & Miquelon 367
Somali Coast 297
Wallis & Futuna Isls. 165

No. 55 (1)	9.50	7.00
No. 205 (1)	15.00	12.00
No. 328 (1)	8.00	6.75
No. 367 (1)	12.00	6.75
No. 297 (1)	6.25	6.25
No. 165 (1)	4.00	3.50
Set total (6) Stamps	54.75	42.25

African Postal Union, 1963

UAMPT Emblem, Radio Masts, Plane and Mail CD114

Establishment of the African and Malagasy Posts and Telecommunications Union.

1963, Sept. 8

Cameroun C47
Cent. Africa C10
Chad C9
Congo, P.R. C13
Dahomey C19
Gabon C13
Ivory Coast C25
Madagascar C75
Mauritania C22
Niger C27
Rwanda 36
Senegal C32
Upper Volta C9

No. C47 (1)	2.25	1.00
No. C10 (1)	1.90	.85
No. C9 (1)	2.40	.60
No. C13 (1)	1.40	.75
No. C19 (1)	.75	.25
No. C13 (1)	1.90	.80
No. C25 (1)	2.50	1.50
No. C75 (1)	1.25	.80
No. C22 (1)	1.50	.60
No. C27 (1)	1.25	.60
No. 36 (1)	.90	.55
No. C32 (1)	1.75	.50
No. C9 (1)	1.50	.75
Set total (13) Stamps	21.25	9.55

Air Afrique, 1963

Symbols of Flight — CD115

First anniversary of Air Afrique and inauguration of DC-8 service.

1963, Nov. 19

Cameroun C48
Chad C10
Congo, P.R. C14
Gabon C18
Ivory Coast C26
Mauritania C26
Niger C35
Senegal C33

No. C48 (1)	1.25	.40
No. C10 (1)	2.40	.60
No. C14 (1)	1.60	.60
No. C18 (1)	1.40	.65
No. C26 (1)	1.00	.50
No. C26 (1)	.70	.25
No. C35 (1)	.90	.50
No. C33 (1)	2.00	.65
Set total (8) Stamps	11.25	4.15

Europafrica

Europe and Africa Linked — CD116

Signing of an economic agreement between the European Economic Community and the African and Malagasy Union, Yaounde, Cameroun, July 20, 1963.

1963-64

Cameroun 402
Cent. Africa C12
Chad C11
Congo, P.R. C16
Gabon C19
Ivory Coast 217
Niger C43
Upper Volta C11

No. 402 (1)	2.25	.60
No. C12 (1)	2.50	1.75
No. C11 (1)	2.00	.50
No. C16 (1)	1.60	1.00
No. C19 (1)	1.40	.75
No. 217 (1)	1.10	.35
No. C43 (1)	.85	.50
No. C11 (1)	1.50	.80
Set total (8) Stamps	13.20	6.25

Human Rights

Scales of Justice and Globe CD117

15th anniversary of the Universal Declaration of Human Rights.

1963, Dec. 10

Comoro Isls. 56
Fr. Polynesia 206
New Caledonia 329
St. Pierre & Miquelon 368
Somali Coast 300
Wallis & Futuna Isls. 166

No. 56 (1)	9.50	7.50
No. 205 (1)	15.00	12.00
No. 329 (1)	7.00	6.00
No. 368 (1)	6.50	3.50
No. 300 (1)	8.50	8.50
No. 166 (1)	8.00	7.50
Set total (6) Stamps	54.50	45.00

PHILATEC

Stamp Album, Champs Elysees Palace and Horses of Marly CD118

Intl. Philatelic and Postal Techniques Exhibition, Paris, June 5-21, 1964.

1963-64

Comoro Isls. 60
France 1078
Fr. Polynesia 207
New Caledonia 341
St. Pierre & Miquelon 369
Somali Coast 301
Wallis & Futuna Isls. 167

No. 60 (1)	4.50	4.00
No. 1078 (1)	.25	.25
No. 206 (1)	15.00	10.00
No. 341 (1)	6.50	6.50
No. 369 (1)	11.00	8.00
No. 301 (1)	7.75	7.75
No. 167 (1)	3.50	3.50
Set total (7) Stamps	48.50	40.00

Cooperation

CD119

Cooperation between France and the French-speaking countries of Africa and Madagascar.

1964

Cameroun 409-410
Cent. Africa 39
Chad 103
Congo, P.R. 121
Dahomey 193
France 1111
Gabon 175
Ivory Coast 221
Madagascar 360
Mauritania 181
Niger 143
Senegal 236
Togo 495

Nos. 409-410 (2)	2.50	.50
No. 39 (1)	1.00	.55
No. 103 (1)	1.00	.25
No. 121 (1)	.80	.35
No. 193 (1)	.80	.35
No. 1111 (1)	.25	.25
No. 175 (1)	.90	.60
No. 221 (1)	1.10	.35

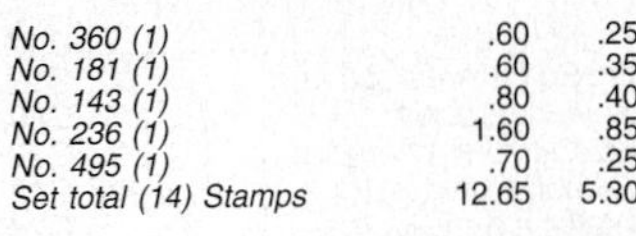

No. 360 (1)	.60	.25
No. 181 (1)	.60	.35
No. 143 (1)	.80	.40
No. 236 (1)	1.60	.85
No. 495 (1)	.70	.25
Set total (14) Stamps	12.65	5.30

ITU

Telegraph, Syncom Satellite and ITU Emblem CD120

Intl. Telecommunication Union, Cent.

1965, May 17

Comoro Isls. C14
Fr. Polynesia C33
Fr. So. & Antarctic Terr. C8
New Caledonia C40
New Hebrides 124-125
St. Pierre & Miquelon C29
Somali Coast C36
Wallis & Futuna Isls. C20

No. C14 (1)	20.00	10.00
No. C33 (1)	80.00	52.50
No. C8 (1)	200.00	160.00
No. C40 (1)	10.00	8.00
Nos. 124-125 (2)	40.50	34.00
No. C29 (1)	24.00	11.00
No. C36 (1)	15.00	9.00
No. C20 (1)	21.00	15.00
Set total (9) Stamps	410.50	299.50

French Satellite A-1

Diamant Rocket and Launching Installation — CD121

Launching of France's first satellite, Nov. 26, 1965.

1965-66

Comoro Isls. C16a
France 1138a
Reunion 359a
Fr. Polynesia C41a
Fr. So. & Antarctic Terr. C10a
New Caledonia C45a
St. Pierre & Miquelon C31a
Somali Coast C40a
Wallis & Futuna Isls. C23a

No. C16a (1)	11.00	11.00
No. 1138a (1)	.65	.65
No. 359a (1)	3.50	3.00
No. C41a (1)	14.00	14.00
No. C10a (1)	29.00	24.00
No. C45a (1)	7.00	7.00
No. C31a (1)	15.00	15.00
No. C40a (1)	7.00	7.00
No. C23a (1)	9.25	9.25
Set total (9) Stamps	96.40	90.90

French Satellite D-1

D-1 Satellite in Orbit — CD122

Launching of the D-1 satellite at Hammaguir, Algeria, Feb. 17, 1966.

1966

Comoro Isls. C17
France 1148

Fr. Polynesia....................................C42
Fr. So. & Antarctic Terr. C11
New Caledonia..............................C46
St. Pierre & Miquelon....................C32
Somali Coast..................................C49
Wallis & Futuna Isls. C24

No. C17 (1)	4.00	4.00
No. 1148 (1)	.25	.25
No. C42 (1)	7.00	4.75
No. C11 (1)	57.50	40.00
No. C46 (1)	2.25	2.00
No. C32 (1)	10.50	6.50
No. C49 (1)	4.25	2.75
No. C24 (1)	3.50	3.50
Set total (8) Stamps	89.25	63.75

Air Afrique, 1966

Planes and Air Afrique Emblem — CD123

Introduction of DC-8F planes by Air Afrique.

1966

Cameroun..C79
Cent. Africa C35
Chad...C26
Congo, P.R......................................C42
Dahomey C42
Gabon..C47
Ivory Coast......................................C32
Mauritania.......................................C57
Niger...C63
Senegal C47
Togo..C54
Upper Volta.....................................C31

No. C79 (1)	.80	.25
No. C35 (1)	1.00	.40
No. C26 (1)	1.00	.25
No. C42 (1)	1.00	.25
No. C42 (1)	.75	.25
No. C47 (1)	.90	.35
No. C32 (1)	1.00	.60
No. C57 (1)	.80	.30
No. C63 (1)	.65	.35
No. C47 (1)	.80	.30
No. C54 (1)	.80	.25
No. C31 (1)	.75	.50
Set total (12) Stamps	10.25	4.05

African Postal Union, 1967

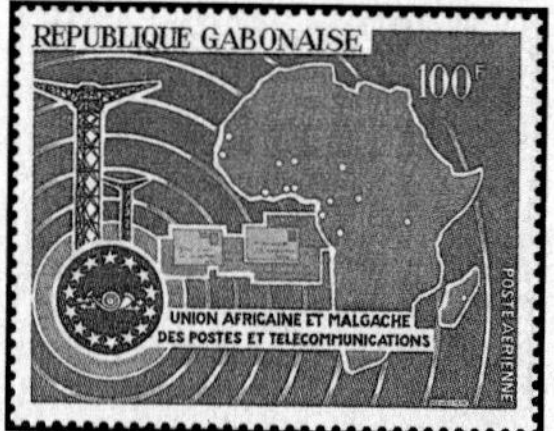

Telecommunications Symbols and Map of Africa — CD124

Fifth anniversary of the establishment of the African and Malagasy Union of Posts and Telecommunications, UAMPT.

1967

Cameroun..C90
Cent. Africa C46
Chad...C37
Congo, P.R......................................C57
Dahomey C61
Gabon..C58
Ivory Coast......................................C34
Madagascar.....................................C85
Mauritania.......................................C65
Niger...C75
Rwanda C1-C3
Senegal C60
Togo..C81
Upper Volta.....................................C50

No. C90 (1)	2.40	.65
No. C46 (1)	2.25	.85
No. C37 (1)	2.00	.60
No. C57 (1)	1.60	.60
No. C61 (1)	1.75	.95
No. C58 (1)	2.25	.95
No. C34 (1)	3.50	1.50
No. C85 (1)	1.25	.60
No. C65 (1)	1.25	.60
No. C75 (1)	1.40	.60
Nos. C1-C3 (3)	2.30	1.25
No. C60 (1)	1.75	.50
No. C81 (1)	1.90	.30
No. C50 (1)	1.80	.70
Set total (16) Stamps	27.40	10.65

Monetary Union

Gold Token of the Ashantis, 17-18th Centuries — CD125

West African Monetary Union, 5th anniv.

1967, Nov. 4

Dahomey 244
Ivory Coast......................................259
Mauritania.......................................238
Niger...204
Senegal 294
Togo..623
Upper Volta.....................................181

No. 244 (1)	.65	.65
No. 259 (1)	.85	.40
No. 238 (1)	.45	.25
No. 204 (1)	.45	.25
No. 294 (1)	.60	.25
No. 623 (1)	.60	.25
No. 181 (1)	.70	.35
Set total (7) Stamps	4.30	2.40

WHO Anniversary

Sun, Flowers and WHO Emblem CD126

World Health Organization, 20th anniv.

1968, May 4

Afars & Issas...................................317
Comoro Isls. 73
Fr. Polynesia............................241-242
Fr. So. & Antarctic Terr. 31
New Caledonia...............................367
St. Pierre & Miquelon.....................377
Wallis & Futuna Isls. 169

No. 317 (1)	3.00	3.00
No. 73 (1)	2.75	2.00
Nos. 241-242 (2)	22.00	12.75
No. 31 (1)	65.00	45.00
No. 367 (1)	4.00	2.25
No. 377 (1)	12.00	8.00
No. 169 (1)	6.50	4.50
Set total (8) Stamps	115.25	77.50

Human Rights Year

Human Rights Flame — CD127

1968, Aug. 10

Afars & Issas...........................322-323
Comoro Isls. 76
Fr. Polynesia............................243-244
Fr. So. & Antarctic Terr. 32
New Caledonia...............................369
St. Pierre & Miquelon.....................382
Wallis & Futuna Isls. 170

Nos. 322-323 (2)	6.50	3.70
No. 76 (1)	3.50	3.50
Nos. 243-244 (2)	24.00	14.00
No. 32 (1)	60.00	45.00
No. 369 (1)	2.75	1.50
No. 382 (1)	10.00	5.50
No. 170 (1)	3.75	3.75
Set total (9) Stamps	110.50	76.95

2nd PHILEXAFRIQUE

CD128

Opening of PHILEXAFRIQUE, Abidjan, Feb. 14. Each stamp shows a local scene and stamp.

1969, Feb. 14

Cameroun......................................C118
Cent. Africa C65
Chad...C48
Congo, P.R.......................................C77
Dahomey C94
Gabon...C82
Ivory Coast C38-C40
Madagascar......................................C92
Mali...C65
Mauritania..C80
Niger...C104
Senegal C68
Togo..C104
Upper Volta......................................C62

No. C118 (1)	3.25	1.25
No. C65 (1)	1.90	1.90
No. C48 (1)	2.40	1.00
No. C77 (1)	2.00	1.75
No. C94 (1)	2.25	2.25
No. C82 (1)	2.25	2.25
Nos. C38-C40 (3)	14.50	14.50
No. C92 (1)	1.75	.85
No. C65 (1)	1.75	1.00
No. C80 (1)	1.90	.75
No. C104 (1)	2.75	1.90
No. C68 (1)	2.00	1.40
No. C104 (1)	2.25	.45
No. C62 (1)	4.00	3.75
Set total (16) Stamps	44.95	35.00

Concorde

Concorde in Flight CD129

First flight of the prototype Concorde supersonic plane at Toulouse, Mar. 1, 1969.

1969

Afars & Issas...................................C56
Comoro Isls. C29
France..C42
Fr. Polynesia...................................C50
Fr. So. & Antarctic Terr. C18
New Caledonia................................C63
St. Pierre & Miquelon......................C40
Wallis & Futuna Isls. C30

No. C56 (1)	25.00	16.00
No. C29 (1)	24.00	16.00
No. C42 (1)	.75	.35
No. C50 (1)	55.00	35.00
No. C18 (1)	55.00	37.50
No. C63 (1)	27.50	20.00
No. C40 (1)	32.50	12.00
No. C30 (1)	15.00	10.00
Set total (8) Stamps	234.75	146.85

Development Bank

Bank Emblem — CD130

African Development Bank, fifth anniv.

1969

Cameroun..499
Chad...217
Congo, P.R..................................181-182
Ivory Coast.......................................281
Mali..127-128
Mauritania.......................................267
Niger...220
Senegal 317-318
Upper Volta.....................................201

No. 499 (1)	.80	.25
No. 217 (1)	.70	.25
Nos. 181-182 (2)	.80	.50
No. 281 (1)	.70	.40
Nos. 127-128 (2)	1.00	.50
No. 267 (1)	.60	.25
No. 220 (1)	.60	.30
Nos. 317-318 (2)	1.55	.50
No. 201 (1)	.70	.30
Set total (12) Stamps	7.45	3.25

ILO

ILO Headquarters, Geneva, and Emblem — CD131

Intl. Labor Organization, 50th anniv.

1969-70

Afars & Issas...................................337
Comoro Isls. 83
Fr. Polynesia.............................251-252
Fr. So. & Antarctic Terr. 35
New Caledonia.................................379
St. Pierre & Miquelon......................396
Wallis & Futuna Isls. 172

No. 337 (1)	2.75	2.00
No. 83 (1)	1.25	.75
Nos. 251-252 (2)	24.00	12.50
No. 35 (1)	18.50	11.00
No. 379 (1)	2.25	1.10
No. 396 (1)	10.00	5.50
No. 172 (1)	3.00	2.90
Set total (8) Stamps	61.75	35.75

ASECNA

Map of Africa, Plane and Airport CD132

10th anniversary of the Agency for the Security of Aerial Navigation in Africa and Madagascar (ASECNA, Agence pour la Securite de la Navigation Aerienne en Afrique et a Madagascar).

1969-70

Cameroun..500
Cent. Africa 119
Chad..222
Congo, P.R......................................197
Dahomey 269
Gabon..260
Ivory Coast......................................287
Mali..130
Niger..221
Senegal 321
Upper Volta......................................204

No. 500 (1)	2.00	.60
No. 119 (1)	2.25	.80
No. 222 (1)	1.00	.25
No. 197 (1)	2.00	.40
No. 269 (1)	.90	.55
No. 260 (1)	1.75	.75
No. 287 (1)	.90	.40
No. 130 (1)	.90	.40
No. 221 (1)	1.25	.70
No. 321 (1)	1.60	.50
No. 204 (1)	1.75	1.00
Set total (11) Stamps	16.30	6.35

U.P.U. Headquarters

CD133

New Universal Postal Union headquarters, Bern, Switzerland.

1970

Afars & Issas....342
Algeria....443
Cameroun....503-504
Cent. Africa....125
Chad....225
Comoro Isls.....84
Congo, P.R.....216
Fr. Polynesia....261-262
Fr. So. & Antarctic Terr.....36
Gabon....258
Ivory Coast....295
Madagascar....444
Mali....134-135
Mauritania....283
New Caledonia....382
Niger....231-232
St. Pierre & Miquelon....397-398
Senegal....328-329
Tunisia....535
Wallis & Futuna Isls.....173

No. 342 (1) 2.50 1.40
No. 443 (1) 1.10 .40
Nos. 503-504 (2) 2.60 .55
No. 125 (1) 1.90 .70
No. 225 (1) 1.00 .25
No. 84 (1) 5.50 2.00
No. 216 (1) .80 .25
Nos. 261-262 (2) 20.00 10.00
No. 36 (1) 45.00 29.00
No. 258 (1) .90 .55
No. 295 (1) 1.10 .50
No. 444 (1) .55 .25
Nos. 134-135 (2) 1.05 .50
No. 283 (1) .60 .30
No. 382 (1) 3.00 1.50
Nos. 231-232 (2) 1.20 .60
Nos. 397-398 (2) 34.00 17.50
Nos. 328-329 (2) 1.55 .55
No. 535 (1) .60 .25
No. 173 (1) 4.00 4.00
Set total (26) Stamps 128.95 71.05

De Gaulle

CD134

First anniversay of the death of Charles de Gaulle, (1890-1970), President of France.

1971-72

Afars & Issas....356-357
Comoro Isls.....104-105
France....1325a
Fr. Polynesia....270-271
Fr. So. & Antarctic Terr.....52-53
New Caledonia....393-394
Reunion....380a
St. Pierre & Miquelon....417-418
Wallis & Futuna Isls.....177-178

Nos. 356-357 (2) 14.50 9.50
Nos. 104-105 (2) 9.00 5.75
No. 1325a (1) 3.00 2.50
Nos. 270-271 (2) 51.50 29.50
Nos. 52-53 (2) 47.00 33.50
Nos. 393-394 (2) 23.00 11.75
No. 380a (1) 9.25 8.00
Nos. 417-418 (2) 57.50 30.00
Nos. 177-178 (2) 24.00 16.25
Set total (16) Stamps 238.75 146.75

African Postal Union, 1971

UAMPT Building, Brazzaville, Congo — CD135

10th anniversary of the establishment of the African and Malagasy Posts and Telecommunications Union, UAMPT. Each stamp has a different native design.

1971, Nov. 13

Cameroun....C177
Cent. Africa....C89
Chad....C94
Congo, P.R.....C136
Dahomey....C146
Gabon....C120
Ivory Coast....C47
Mauritania....C113
Niger....C164
Rwanda....C8
Senegal....C105
Togo....C166
Upper Volta....C97

No. C177 (1) 2.00 .50
No. C89 (1) 2.25 .85
No. C94 (1) 1.50 .50
No. C136 (1) 1.60 .75
No. C146 (1) 1.75 .80
No. C120 (1) 1.75 .70
No. C47 (1) 2.00 1.00
No. C113 (1) 1.20 .65
No. C164 (1) 1.25 .60
No. C8 (1) 2.75 2.25
No. C105 (1) 1.60 .50
No. C166 (1) 1.25 .40
No. C97 (1) 1.50 .70
Set total (13) Stamps 22.40 10.20

West African Monetary Union

African Couple, City, Village and Commemorative Coin — CD136

West African Monetary Union, 10th anniv.

1972, Nov. 2

Dahomey....300
Ivory Coast....331
Mauritania....299
Niger....258
Senegal....374
Togo....825
Upper Volta....280

No. 300 (1) .65 .25
No. 331 (1) 1.00 .50
No. 299 (1) .75 .25
No. 258 (1) .55 .30
No. 374 (1) .50 .30
No. 825 (1) .60 .25
No. 280 (1) .60 .25
Set total (7) Stamps 4.65 2.10

African Postal Union, 1973

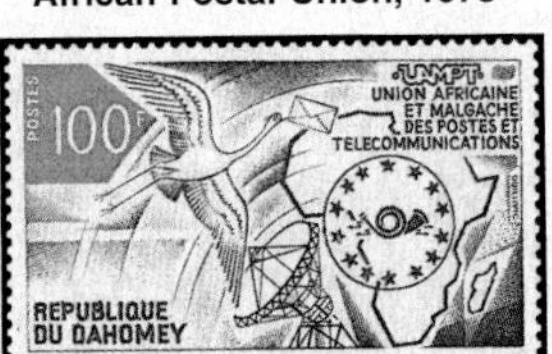

Telecommunications Symbols and Map of Africa — CD137

11th anniversary of the African and Malagasy Posts and Telecommunications Union (UAMPT).

1973, Sept. 12

Cameroun....574
Cent. Africa....194
Chad....294
Congo, P.R.....289
Dahomey....311
Gabon....320
Ivory Coast....361
Madagascar....500
Mauritania....304
Niger....287
Rwanda....540
Senegal....393
Togo....849
Upper Volta....297

No. 574 (1) 1.75 .40
No. 194 (1) 1.25 .75
No. 294 (1) 1.75 .40
No. 289 (1) 1.60 .50
No. 311 (1) 1.25 .55
No. 320 (1) 1.40 .75
No. 361 (1) 2.50 1.00
No. 500 (1) 1.10 .35
No. 304 (1) 1.10 .40
No. 287 (1) .90 .60
No. 540 (1) 3.75 2.00
No. 393 (1) 1.60 .50
No. 849 (1) 1.00 .35
No. 297 (1) 1.25 .70
Set total (14) Stamps 22.20 9.25

Philexafrique II — Essen

CD138

CD139

Designs: Indigenous fauna, local and German stamps. Types CD138-CD139 printed horizontally and vertically se-tenant in sheets of 10 (2x5). Label between horizontal pairs alternately commemoratives Philexafrique II, Libreville, Gabon, June 1978, and 2nd International Stamp Fair, Essen, Germany, Nov. 1-5.

1978-1979

Benin....C286a
Central Africa....C201a
Chad....C239a
Congo Republic....C246a
Djibouti....C122a
Gabon....C216a
Ivory Coast....C65a
Mali....C357a
Mauritania....C186a
Niger....C292a
Rwanda....C13a
Senegal....C147a
Togo....C364a

No. C286a (1) 9.00 8.50
No. C201a (1) 7.50 7.50
No. C239a (1) 8.00 4.00
No. C246a (1) 7.00 7.00
No. C122a (1) 8.50 8.50
No. C216a (1) 6.50 4.00
No. C65a (1) 9.00 9.00
No. C357a (1) 5.00 3.00
No. C186a (1) 4.50 4.00
No. C292a (1) 6.00 5.00
No. C13a (1) 4.00 4.00
No. C147a (1) 10.00 4.00
No. C364a (1) 3.00 1.50
Set total (13) Stamps 88.00 70.00

BRITISH COMMONWEALTH OF NATIONS

The listings follow established trade practices when these issues are offered as units by dealers. The Peace issue, for example, includes only one stamp from the Indian state of Hyderabad. The U.P.U. issue includes the Egypt set. Pairs are included for those varieties issued with bilingual designs se-tenant.

Silver Jubilee

Windsor Castle and King George V
CD301

Reign of King George V, 25th anniv.

1935

Antigua....77-80
Ascension....33-36
Bahamas....92-95
Barbados....186-189
Basutoland....11-14
Bechuanaland Protectorate....117-120
Bermuda....100-103
British Guiana....223-226
British Honduras....108-111
Cayman Islands....81-84
Ceylon....260-263
Cyprus....136-139
Dominica....90-93
Falkland Islands....77-80
Fiji....110-113
Gambia....125-128
Gibraltar....100-103
Gilbert & Ellice Islands....33-36
Gold Coast....108-111
Grenada....124-127
Hong Kong....147-150
Jamaica....109-112
Kenya, Uganda, Tanzania....42-45
Leeward Islands....96-99
Malta....184-187
Mauritius....204-207
Montserrat....85-88
Newfoundland....226-229
Nigeria....34-37
Northern Rhodesia....18-21
Nyasaland Protectorate....47-50
St. Helena....111-114
St. Kitts-Nevis....72-75
St. Lucia....91-94
St. Vincent....134-137
Seychelles....118-121
Sierra Leone....166-169
Solomon Islands....60-63
Somaliland Protectorate....77-80
Straits Settlements....213-216
Swaziland....20-23
Trinidad & Tobago....43-46
Turks & Caicos Islands....71-74
Virgin Islands....69-72

The following have different designs but are included in the omnibus set:

Great Britain....226-229
Offices in Morocco (Sp. Curr.)....67-70
Offices in Morocco (Br. Curr.)....226-229
Offices in Morocco (Fr. Curr.)....422-425
Offices in Morocco (Tangier)....508-510
Australia....152-154
Canada....211-216
Cook Islands....98-100
India....142-148
Nauru....31-34
New Guinea....46-47
New Zealand....199-201
Niue....67-69
Papua....114-117
Samoa....163-165
South Africa....68-71
Southern Rhodesia....33-36
South-West Africa....121-124

Nos. 77-80 (4) 20.25 *20.50*
Nos. 33-36 (4) 58.50 *120.00*
Nos. 92-95 (4) 25.00 *43.00*
Nos. 186-189 (4) 30.15 49.30
Nos. 11-14 (4) 12.10 *23.00*
Nos. 117-120 (4) 17.00 *31.25*
Nos. 100-103 (4) 18.00 *58.25*
Nos. 223-226 (4) 18.35 35.50
Nos. 108-111 (4) 15.25 *15.35*
Nos. 81-84 (4) 19.95 19.50
Nos. 260-263 (4) 10.15 19.10
Nos. 136-139 (4) 39.75 *34.40*
Nos. 90-93 (4) 18.85 19.85
Nos. 77-80 (4) 51.00 13.75
Nos. 110-113 (4) 15.25 29.00
Nos. 125-128 (4) 12.20 *25.25*
Nos. 100-103 (4) 28.75 42.75
Nos. 33-36 (4) 31.50 *50.00*
Nos. 108-111 (4) 26.25 *62.85*
Nos. 124-127 (4) 16.70 *40.60*
Nos. 147-150 (4) 59.00 18.75
Nos. 109-112 (4) 17.00 39.00
Nos. 42-45 (4) 8.75 *11.00*
Nos. 96-99 (4) 35.75 49.60
Nos. 184-187 (4) 22.00 33.70
Nos. 204-207 (4) 47.60 58.25
Nos. 85-88 (4) 10.25 *30.25*
Nos. 226-229 (4) 17.50 12.05
Nos. 34-37 (4) 13.25 *59.75*
Nos. 18-21 (4) 16.75 16.25
Nos. 47-50 (4) 39.75 *80.25*
Nos. 111-114 (4) 31.15 *33.25*
Nos. 72-75 (4) 11.55 *18.50*
Nos. 91-94 (4) 16.00 *20.80*
Nos. 134-137 (4) 9.45 *21.25*
Nos. 118-121 (4) 17.50 *32.50*
Nos. 166-169 (4) 24.25 *56.00*
Nos. 60-63 (4) 27.25 38.00
Nos. 77-80 (4) 18.75 *50.75*
Nos. 213-216 (4) 15.00 *25.10*
Nos. 20-23 (4) 6.80 18.25
Nos. 43-46 (4) 14.05 27.75
Nos. 71-74 (4) 9.25 16.25
Nos. 69-72 (4) 24.20 55.25

Nos. 226-229 (4) 7.25 *7.45*

Nos. 67-70 (4)	14.35	*26.10*
Nos. 226-229 (4)	8.20	*28.90*
Nos. 422-425 (4)	3.90	2.00
Nos. 508-510 (3)	18.80	*23.85*
Nos. 152-154 (3)	45.75	60.35
Nos. 211-216 (6)	26.30	13.35
Nos. 98-100 (3)	9.65	*12.00*
Nos. 142-148 (7)	23.25	11.80
Nos. 31-34 (4)	9.90	*9.90*
Nos. 46-47 (2)	4.35	1.70
Nos. 199-201 (3)	21.75	*31.75*
Nos. 67-69 (3)	10.55	*26.50*
Nos. 114-117 (4)	9.20	*17.00*
Nos. 163-165 (3)	4.40	5.50
Nos. 68-71 (4)	57.00	*155.00*
Nos. 33-36 (4)	27.75	*45.25*
Nos. 121-124 (4)	14.50	*36.10*
Set total (245) Stamps	1,315.	2,090.

Coronation

Queen Elizabeth and King George VI
CD302

1937

Aden....13-15
Antigua....81-83
Ascension....37-39
Bahamas....97-99
Barbados....190-192
Basutoland....15-17
Bechuanaland Protectorate....121-123
Bermuda....115-117
British Guiana....227-229
British Honduras....112-114
Cayman Islands....97-99
Ceylon....275-277
Cyprus....140-142
Dominica....94-96
Falkland Islands....81-83
Fiji....114-116
Gambia....129-131
Gibraltar....104-106
Gilbert & Ellice Islands....37-39
Gold Coast....112-114
Grenada....128-130
Hong Kong....151-153
Jamaica....113-115
Kenya, Uganda, Tanzania....60-62
Leeward Islands....100-102
Malta....188-190
Mauritius....208-210
Montserrat....89-91
Newfoundland....230-232
Nigeria....50-52
Northern Rhodesia....22-24
Nyasaland Protectorate....51-53
St. Helena....115-117
St. Kitts-Nevis....76-78
St. Lucia....107-109
St. Vincent....138-140
Seychelles....122-124
Sierra Leone....170-172
Solomon Islands....64-66
Somaliland Protectorate....81-83
Straits Settlements....235-237
Swaziland....24-26
Trinidad & Tobago....47-49
Turks & Caicos Islands....75-77
Virgin Islands....73-75

The following have different designs but are included in the omnibus set:

Great Britain....234
Offices in Morocco (Sp. Curr.)....82
Offices in Morocco (Fr. Curr.)....439
Offices in Morocco (Tangier)....514
Canada....237
Cook Islands....109-111
Nauru....35-38
Newfoundland....233-243
New Guinea....48-51
New Zealand....223-225
Niue....70-72
Papua....118-121
South Africa....74-78
Southern Rhodesia....38-41
South-West Africa....125-132

Nos. 13-15 (3)	3.00	*5.75*
Nos. 81-83 (3)	1.85	*3.75*
Nos. 37-39 (3)	2.75	*2.75*
Nos. 97-99 (3)	1.15	3.05
Nos. 190-192 (3)	1.10	1.95
Nos. 15-17 (3)	1.15	*3.00*
Nos. 121-123 (3)	.95	3.35
Nos. 115-117 (3)	1.25	5.00
Nos. 227-229 (3)	1.45	3.05
Nos. 112-114 (3)	1.20	2.35
Nos. 97-99 (3)	1.10	2.30
Nos. 275-277 (3)	8.25	10.35
Nos. 140-142 (3)	3.75	6.50
Nos. 94-96 (3)	.85	2.40
Nos. 81-83 (3)	2.90	*2.30*
Nos. 114-116 (3)	1.35	5.75
Nos. 129-131 (3)	.95	3.95
Nos. 104-106 (3)	2.25	6.45
Nos. 37-39 (3)	.85	2.00
Nos. 112-114 (3)	3.10	*10.00*
Nos. 128-130 (3)	1.00	.85
Nos. 151-153 (3)	23.00	12.50
Nos. 113-115 (3)	1.25	1.25
Nos. 60-62 (3)	1.00	2.35
Nos. 100-102 (3)	1.55	4.00
Nos. 188-190 (3)	1.25	1.60
Nos. 208-210 (3)	2.05	3.75
Nos. 89-91 (3)	1.00	3.35
Nos. 230-232 (3)	7.00	2.80
Nos. 50-52 (3)	3.25	8.50
Nos. 22-24 (3)	.95	2.25
Nos. 51-53 (3)	1.05	1.30
Nos. 115-117 (3)	1.45	2.05
Nos. 76-78 (3)	.95	2.05
Nos. 107-109 (3)	1.05	2.05
Nos. 138-140 (3)	.80	*4.75*
Nos. 122-124 (3)	1.20	*1.90*
Nos. 170-172 (3)	1.95	5.65
Nos. 64-66 (3)	.90	2.00
Nos. 81-83 (3)	1.10	*3.40*
Nos. 235-237 (3)	3.25	1.60
Nos. 24-26 (3)	1.05	1.75
Nos. 47-49 (3)	1.00	1.00
Nos. 75-77 (3)	1.30	1.55
Nos. 73-75 (3)	2.20	6.90

No. 234 (1)	.25	.25
No. 82 (1)	.80	.80
No. 439 (1)	.35	.25
No. 514 (1)	.55	.55
No. 237 (1)	.35	.25
Nos. 109-111 (3)	.85	.80
Nos. 35-38 (4)	1.10	*5.50*
Nos. 233-243 (11)	42.20	30.40
Nos. 48-51 (4)	1.40	*7.90*
Nos. 223-225 (3)	1.40	*2.75*
Nos. 70-72 (3)	.80	*2.05*
Nos. 118-121 (4)	1.60	*5.25*
Nos. 74-78 (5)	9.25	10.80
Nos. 38-41 (4)	3.55	15.50
Nos. 125-132 (8)	5.50	8.45
Set total (189) Stamps	173.70	258.65

Peace

King George VI and Parliament Buildings, London
CD303

Return to peace at the close of World War II.

1945-46

Aden....28-29
Antigua....96-97
Ascension....50-51
Bahamas....130-131
Barbados....207-208
Bermuda....131-132
British Guiana....242-243
British Honduras....127-128
Cayman Islands....112-113
Ceylon....293-294
Cyprus....156-157
Dominica....112-113
Falkland Islands....97-98
Falkland Islands Dep....1L9-1L10
Fiji....137-138
Gambia....144-145
Gibraltar....119-120
Gilbert & Ellice Islands....52-53
Gold Coast....128-129
Grenada....143-144
Jamaica....136-137
Kenya, Uganda, Tanzania....90-91
Leeward Islands....116-117
Malta....206-207
Mauritius....223-224
Montserrat....104-105
Nigeria....71-72
Northern Rhodesia....46-47
Nyasaland Protectorate....82-83
Pitcairn Islands....9-10
St. Helena....128-129
St. Kitts-Nevis....91-92
St. Lucia....127-128
St. Vincent....152-153
Seychelles....149-150
Sierra Leone....186-187
Solomon Islands....80-81
Somaliland Protectorate....108-109
Trinidad & Tobago....62-63
Turks & Caicos Islands....90-91
Virgin Islands....88-89

The following have different designs but are included in the omnibus set:

Great Britain....264-265
Offices in Morocco (Tangier)....523-524
Aden
Kathiri State of Seiyun....12-13
Qu'aiti State of Shihr and Mukalla....12-13
Australia....200-202
Basutoland....29-31
Bechuanaland Protectorate....137-139
Burma....66-69
Cook Islands....127-130
Hong Kong....174-175
India....195-198
Hyderabad....51-53
New Zealand....247-257
Niue....90-93
Pakistan-Bahawalpur....O16
Samoa....191-194
South Africa....100-102
Southern Rhodesia....67-70
South-West Africa....153-155
Swaziland....38-40
Zanzibar....222-223

Nos. 28-29 (2)	.95	2.50
Nos. 96-97 (2)	.50	*.80*
Nos. 50-51 (2)	.90	1.80
Nos. 130-131 (2)	.50	1.40
Nos. 207-208 (2)	.50	1.10
Nos. 131-132 (2)	.55	.55
Nos. 242-243 (2)	1.05	*1.40*
Nos. 127-128 (2)	.50	.50
Nos. 112-113 (2)	.60	.80
Nos. 293-294 (2)	.60	*2.10*
Nos. 156-157 (2)	1.00	.70
Nos. 112-113 (2)	.50	.50
Nos. 97-98 (2)	.90	1.35
Nos. 1L9-1L10 (2)	1.40	1.00
Nos. 137-138 (2)	.50	*1.75*
Nos. 144-145 (2)	.50	.95
Nos. 119-120 (2)	.75	*1.00*
Nos. 52-53 (2)	.50	.50
Nos. 128-129 (2)	1.85	*3.75*
Nos. 143-144 (2)	.50	*.95*
Nos. 136-137 (2)	.80	*12.50*
Nos. 90-91 (2)	.65	.65
Nos. 116-117 (2)	.50	1.50
Nos. 206-207 (2)	.65	2.00
Nos. 223-224 (2)	.50	1.05
Nos. 104-105 (2)	.50	.50
Nos. 71-72 (2)	.70	*2.75*
Nos. 46-47 (2)	1.25	*2.00*
Nos. 82-83 (2)	.50	.50
Nos. 9-10 (2)	1.40	1.40
Nos. 128-129 (2)	.65	.70
Nos. 91-92 (2)	.50	.50
Nos. 127-128 (2)	.50	.60
Nos. 152-153 (2)	.50	.50
Nos. 149-150 (2)	.55	.50
Nos. 186-187 (2)	.50	.50
Nos. 80-81 (2)	.50	1.30
Nos. 108-109 (2)	.70	.50
Nos. 62-63 (2)	.50	.50
Nos. 90-91 (2)	.50	.50
Nos. 88-89 (2)	.50	.50

Nos. 264-265 (2)	.50	.70
Nos. 523-524 (2)	1.50	3.00
Nos. 12-13 (2)	.50	.90
Nos. 12-13 (2)	.50	*1.25*
Nos. 200-202 (3)	1.60	*3.00*
Nos. 29-31 (3)	2.10	2.60
Nos. 137-139 (3)	2.05	*4.75*
Nos. 66-69 (4)	1.60	1.30
Nos. 127-130 (4)	2.00	1.85
Nos. 174-175 (2)	6.75	3.15
Nos. 195-198 (4)	4.75	3.60
Nos. 51-53 (3)	1.50	1.70
Nos. 247-257 (11)	3.95	3.90
Nos. 90-93 (4)	1.70	*2.20*
No. O16 (1)	5.50	*7.00*
Nos. 191-194 (4)	2.05	1.00
Nos. 100-102 (3)	1.20	4.00
Nos. 67-70 (4)	1.40	1.75
Nos. 153-155 (3)	2.55	3.50
Nos. 38-40 (3)	2.40	*5.50*
Nos. 222-223 (2)	.65	1.00
Set total (151) Stamps	75.15	114.50

Silver Wedding

King George VI and Queen Elizabeth
CD304 CD305

1948-49

Aden....30-31
Kathiri State of Seiyun....14-15
Qu'aiti State of Shihr and Mukalla....14-15
Antigua....98-99
Ascension....52-53
Bahamas....148-149
Barbados....210-211
Basutoland....39-40
Bechuanaland Protectorate....147-148
Bermuda....133-134
British Guiana....244-245
British Honduras....129-130
Cayman Islands....116-117
Cyprus....158-159
Dominica....114-115
Falkland Islands....99-100
Falkland Islands Dep....1L11-1L12
Fiji....139-140
Gambia....146-147
Gibraltar....121-122
Gilbert & Ellice Islands....54-55
Gold Coast....142-143
Grenada....145-146
Hong Kong....178-179
Jamaica....138-139
Kenya, Uganda, Tanzania....92-93
Leeward Islands....118-119
Malaya
Johore....128-129
Kedah....55-56
Kelantan....44-45
Malacca....1-2
Negri Sembilan....36-37
Pahang....44-45
Penang....1-2
Perak....99-100
Perlis....1-2
Selangor....74-75
Trengganu....47-48
Malta....223-224
Mauritius....229-230
Montserrat....106-107
Nigeria....73-74
North Borneo....238-239
Northern Rhodesia....48-49
Nyasaland Protectorate....85-86
Pitcairn Islands....11-12
St. Helena....130-131
St. Kitts-Nevis....93-94
St. Lucia....129-130
St. Vincent....154-155
Sarawak....174-175
Seychelles....151-152
Sierra Leone....188-189
Singapore....21-22
Solomon Islands....82-83
Somaliland Protectorate....110-111
Swaziland....48-49
Trinidad & Tobago....64-65
Turks & Caicos Islands....92-93
Virgin Islands....90-91
Zanzibar....224-225

The following have different designs but are included in the omnibus set:

Great Britain....267-268
Offices in Morocco (Sp. Curr.)....93-94
Offices in Morocco (Tangier)....525-526
Bahrain....62-63
Kuwait....82-83
Oman....25-26
South Africa....106
South-West Africa....159

Nos. 30-31 (2)	37.90	45.00
Nos. 14-15 (2)	18.85	*17.50*
Nos. 14-15 (2)	18.55	*14.75*
Nos. 98-99 (2)	12.55	*12.75*
Nos. 52-53 (2)	60.55	*57.95*
Nos. 148-149 (2)	45.25	40.30
Nos. 210-211 (2)	18.35	13.05
Nos. 39-40 (2)	52.80	*55.25*
Nos. 147-148 (2)	45.35	*50.25*
Nos. 133-134 (2)	47.75	*55.25*
Nos. 244-245 (2)	24.25	*28.45*
Nos. 129-130 (2)	22.75	*53.20*
Nos. 116-117 (2)	22.75	28.50
Nos. 158-159 (2)	58.50	*78.05*
Nos. 114-115 (2)	25.25	*32.75*
Nos. 99-100 (2)	112.10	83.60
Nos. 1L11-1L12 (2)	4.25	6.00
Nos. 139-140 (2)	18.20	10.75
Nos. 146-147 (2)	21.25	21.25
Nos. 121-122 (2)	61.00	*78.00*
Nos. 54-55 (2)	14.25	*22.75*
Nos. 142-143 (2)	35.25	37.75
Nos. 145-146 (2)	21.75	21.75
Nos. 178-179 (2)	303.50	96.50
Nos. 138-139 (2)	27.85	*60.25*
Nos. 92-93 (2)	50.25	*67.75*
Nos. 118-119 (2)	7.00	8.25
Nos. 128-129 (2)	29.25	*53.25*
Nos. 55-56 (2)	35.25	*50.25*
Nos. 44-45 (2)	35.75	*62.75*
Nos. 1-2 (2)	35.40	*49.75*
Nos. 36-37 (2)	28.10	*38.20*
Nos. 44-45 (2)	28.00	*38.05*
Nos. 1-2 (2)	40.50	37.80

Nos. 99-100 (2)	27.80	*37.75*
Nos. 1-2 (2)	33.50	*58.00*
Nos. 74-75 (2)	30.25	25.30
Nos. 47-48 (2)	35.25	*62.75*
Nos. 223-224 (2)	40.55	45.25
Nos. 229-230 (2)	17.75	*45.25*
Nos. 106-107 (2)	9.25	*18.25*
Nos. 73-74 (2)	17.85	*22.80*
Nos. 238-239 (2)	35.30	*45.75*
Nos. 48-49 (2)	92.80	90.25
Nos. 85-86 (2)	19.25	*32.75*
Nos. 11-12 (2)	49.25	51.00
Nos. 130-131 (2)	32.80	*42.80*
Nos. 93-94 (2)	11.25	7.25
Nos. 129-130 (2)	22.25	*45.25*
Nos. 154-155 (2)	27.75	*30.25*
Nos. 174-175 (2)	55.40	*60.40*
Nos. 151-152 (2)	16.25	*45.75*
Nos. 188-189 (2)	24.75	*26.25*
Nos. 21-22 (2)	116.25	45.40
Nos. 82-83 (2)	13.40	13.40
Nos. 110-111 (2)	8.40	*8.75*
Nos. 48-49 (2)	40.30	*47.75*
Nos. 64-65 (2)	32.75	*38.25*
Nos. 92-93 (2)	15.25	*20.30*
Nos. 90-91 (2)	15.35	21.35
Nos. 224-225 (2)	29.60	38.00
Nos. 267-268 (2)	40.40	40.25
Nos. 93-94 (2)	20.10	25.35
Nos. 525-526 (2)	23.10	29.25
Nos. 62-63 (2)	38.45	*72.50*
Nos. 82-83 (2)	45.50	45.50
Nos. 25-26 (2)	46.00	*47.50*
No. 106 (1)	.90	1.25
No. 159 (1)	1.25	.35
Set total (136) Stamps	2,507.	2,716.

U.P.U.

Mercury and Symbols of Communications — CD306

Plane, Ship and Hemispheres — CD307

Mercury Scattering Letters over Globe CD308

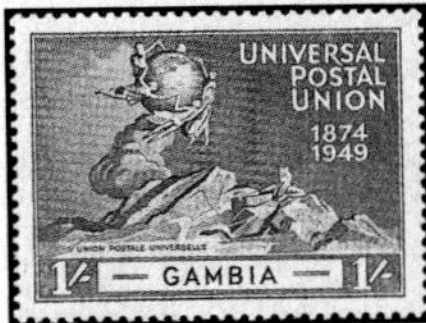

U.P.U. Monument, Bern CD309

Universal Postal Union, 75th anniversary.

1949

Aden....................................32-35
Kathiri State of Seiyun..............16-19
Qu'aiti State of Shihr and Mukalla 16-19
Antigua....................................100-103
Ascension....................................57-60
Bahamas....................................150-153
Barbados....................................212-215
Basutoland....................................41-44
Bechuanaland Protectorate......149-152
Bermuda....................................138-141
British Guiana....................................246-249
British Honduras....................................137-140
Brunei....................................79-82
Cayman Islands....................................118-121
Cyprus....................................160-163
Dominica....................................116-119
Falkland Islands....................................103-106
Falkland Islands Dep...........1L14-1L17
Fiji....................................141-144
Gambia....................................148-151
Gibraltar....................................123-126
Gilbert & Ellice Islands................56-59
Gold Coast....................................144-147
Grenada....................................147-150
Hong Kong....................................180-183
Jamaica....................................142-145
Kenya, Uganda, Tanzania...........94-97
Leeward Islands....................................126-129
Malaya
Johore....................................151-154
Kedah....................................57-60
Kelantan....................................46-49
Malacca....................................18-21
Negri Sembilan....................................59-62
Pahang....................................46-49
Penang....................................23-26
Perak....................................101-104
Perlis....................................3-6
Selangor....................................76-79
Trengganu....................................49-52
Malta....................................225-228
Mauritius....................................231-234
Montserrat....................................108-111
New Hebrides, British....................................62-65
New Hebrides, French....................................79-82
Nigeria....................................75-78
North Borneo....................................240-243
Northern Rhodesia....................................50-53
Nyasaland Protectorate....................................87-90
Pitcairn Islands....................................13-16
St. Helena....................................132-135
St. Kitts-Nevis....................................95-98
St. Lucia....................................131-134
St. Vincent....................................170-173
Sarawak....................................176-179
Seychelles....................................153-156
Sierra Leone....................................190-193
Singapore....................................23-26
Solomon Islands....................................84-87
Somaliland Protectorate...........112-115
Southern Rhodesia....................................71-72
Swaziland....................................50-53
Tonga....................................87-90
Trinidad & Tobago....................................66-69
Turks & Caicos Islands...........101-104
Virgin Islands....................................92-95
Zanzibar....................................226-229

The following have different designs but are included in the omnibus set:

Great Britain....................................276-279
Offices in Morocco (Tangier).......546-549
Australia....................................223
Bahrain....................................68-71
Burma....................................116-121
Ceylon....................................304-306
Egypt....................................281-283
India....................................223-226
Kuwait....................................89-92
Oman....................................31-34
Pakistan-Bahawalpur 26-29, O25-O28
South Africa....................................109-111
South-West Africa....................................160-162

Nos. 32-35 (4)	5.50	*7.80*
Nos. 16-19 (4)	3.10	*3.60*
Nos. 16-19 (4)	2.95	3.95
Nos. 100-103 (4)	4.15	*6.85*
Nos. 57-60 (4)	12.40	10.00
Nos. 150-153 (4)	5.60	9.55
Nos. 212-215 (4)	4.40	14.15
Nos. 41-44 (4)	4.75	*10.00*
Nos. 149-152 (4)	3.35	*7.25*
Nos. 138-141 (4)	4.75	5.55
Nos. 246-249 (4)	2.75	4.20
Nos. 137-140 (4)	3.35	4.75
Nos. 79-82 (4)	7.75	6.75
Nos. 118-121 (4)	4.00	6.40
Nos. 160-163 (4)	4.60	8.30
Nos. 116-119 (4)	2.30	5.65
Nos. 103-106 (4)	14.90	17.10
Nos. 1L14-1L17 (4)	15.50	14.00
Nos. 141-144 (4)	3.35	14.00
Nos. 148-151 (4)	3.10	7.10
Nos. 123-126 (4)	5.90	*8.75*
Nos. 56-59 (4)	4.70	*7.85*
Nos. 144-147 (4)	3.05	*6.95*
Nos. 147-150 (4)	2.15	3.55
Nos. 180-183 (4)	57.25	18.25
Nos. 142-145 (4)	2.25	2.45
Nos. 94-97 (4)	2.90	3.40
Nos. 126-129 (4)	3.05	*9.60*
Nos. 151-154 (4)	4.70	8.90
Nos. 57-60 (4)	4.80	12.00
Nos. 46-49 (4)	4.25	12.65
Nos. 18-21 (4)	4.25	*17.30*
Nos. 59-62 (4)	3.50	10.75
Nos. 46-49 (4)	3.00	7.25
Nos. 23-26 (4)	5.10	11.75
Nos. 101-104 (4)	3.65	10.75
Nos. 3-6 (4)	3.95	14.25
Nos. 76-79 (4)	4.90	12.30
Nos. 49-52 (4)	4.95	9.75
Nos. 225-228 (4)	4.50	4.85
Nos. 231-234 (4)	4.35	6.70
Nos. 108-111 (4)	3.40	3.85
Nos. 62-65 (4)	1.60	*4.25*
Nos. 79-82 (4)	24.25	24.25
Nos. 75-78 (4)	2.80	*9.25*
Nos. 240-243 (4)	7.15	6.50
Nos. 50-53 (4)	5.00	*6.50*
Nos. 87-90 (4)	4.05	4.05
Nos. 13-16 (4)	18.50	16.50
Nos. 132-135 (4)	4.85	7.10
Nos. 95-98 (4)	3.35	4.70
Nos. 131-134 (4)	2.55	*3.85*
Nos. 170-173 (4)	2.20	*5.05*
Nos. 176-179 (4)	9.00	11.10
Nos. 153-156 (4)	3.25	4.10
Nos. 190-193 (4)	3.00	5.10
Nos. 23-26 (4)	20.75	14.20
Nos. 84-87 (4)	4.35	4.90
Nos. 112-115 (4)	3.95	8.70
Nos. 71-72 (2)	1.95	*2.25*
Nos. 50-53 (4)	2.80	4.65
Nos. 87-90 (4)	3.25	*5.25*
Nos. 66-69 (4)	3.15	3.15
Nos. 101-104 (4)	3.65	4.00
Nos. 92-95 (4)	2.60	5.90
Nos. 226-229 (4)	5.45	13.50
Nos. 276-279 (4)	1.35	*2.10*
Nos. 546-549 (4)	3.20	*10.15*
No. 223 (1)	.60	.55
Nos. 68-71 (4)	5.00	*16.75*
Nos. 116-121 (6)	7.15	5.30
Nos. 304-306 (3)	3.35	4.25
Nos. 281-283 (3)	5.75	2.70
Nos. 223-226 (4)	35.50	10.50
Nos. 89-92 (4)	6.10	10.25
Nos. 31-34 (4)	5.55	15.75
Nos. 26-29,O25-O28 (8)	2.00	*42.00*
Nos. 109-111 (3)	2.20	3.00
Nos. 160-162 (3)	3.95	6.00
Set total (313) Stamps	478.25	678.90

University

Arms of University College CD310

Alice, Princess of Athlone CD311

1948 opening of University College of the West Indies at Jamaica.

1951

Antigua....................................104-105
Barbados....................................228-229
British Guiana....................................250-251
British Honduras....................................141-142
Dominica....................................120-121
Grenada....................................164-165
Jamaica....................................146-147
Leeward Islands....................................130-131
Montserrat....................................112-113
St. Kitts-Nevis....................................105-106
St. Lucia....................................149-150
St. Vincent....................................174-175
Trinidad & Tobago....................................70-71
Virgin Islands....................................96-97

Nos. 104-105 (2)	1.35	*3.25*
Nos. 228-229 (2)	1.85	1.55
Nos. 250-251 (2)	1.10	*1.25*
Nos. 141-142 (2)	1.40	2.15
Nos. 120-121 (2)	1.40	*1.75*
Nos. 164-165 (2)	1.20	*1.60*
Nos. 146-147 (2)	.90	.70
Nos. 130-131 (2)	1.35	4.00
Nos. 112-113 (2)	.85	*1.50*
Nos. 105-106 (2)	.90	1.50
Nos. 149-150 (2)	1.40	1.50
Nos. 174-175 (2)	1.00	*2.15*
Nos. 70-71 (2)	.75	.75
Nos. 96-97 (2)	1.50	*3.40*
Set total (28) Stamps	16.95	27.05

Coronation

Queen Elizabeth II — CD312

1953

Aden....................................47
Kathiri State of Seiyun....................................28
Qu'aiti State of Shihr and Mukalla 28
Antigua....................................106
Ascension....................................61
Bahamas....................................157
Barbados....................................234
Basutoland....................................45
Bechuanaland Protectorate....................................153
Bermuda....................................142
British Guiana....................................252
British Honduras....................................143
Cayman Islands....................................150
Cyprus....................................167
Dominica....................................141
Falkland Islands....................................121
Falkland Islands Dependencies....1L18
Fiji....................................145
Gambia....................................152
Gibraltar....................................131
Gilbert & Ellice Islands....................................60
Gold Coast....................................160
Grenada....................................170
Hong Kong....................................184
Jamaica....................................153
Kenya, Uganda, Tanzania....................................101
Leeward Islands....................................132
Malaya
Johore....................................155
Kedah....................................82
Kelantan....................................71
Malacca....................................27
Negri Sembilan....................................63
Pahang....................................71
Penang....................................27
Perak....................................126
Perlis....................................28
Selangor....................................101
Trengganu....................................74
Malta....................................241
Mauritius....................................250
Montserrat....................................127
New Hebrides, British....................................77
Nigeria....................................79
North Borneo....................................260
Northern Rhodesia....................................60
Nyasaland Protectorate....................................96
Pitcairn Islands....................................19
St. Helena....................................139
St. Kitts-Nevis....................................119
St. Lucia....................................156
St. Vincent....................................185
Sarawak....................................196
Seychelles....................................172
Sierra Leone....................................194
Singapore....................................27
Solomon Islands....................................88
Somaliland Protectorate....................................127
Swaziland....................................54
Trinidad & Tobago....................................84
Tristan da Cunha....................................13
Turks & Caicos Islands....................................118
Virgin Islands....................................114

The following have different designs but are included in the omnibus set:

Great Britain....................................313-316
Offices in Morocco (Tangier).......579-582
Australia....................................259-261
Bahrain....................................92-95
Canada....................................330
Ceylon....................................317
Cook Islands....................................145-146
Kuwait....................................113-116
New Zealand....................................280-284
Niue....................................104-105
Oman....................................52-55
Samoa....................................214-215
South Africa....................................192
Southern Rhodesia....................................80
South-West Africa....................................244-248
Tokelau Islands....................................4

No. 47 (1)	1.25	1.25
No. 28 (1)	.40	*1.50*
No. 28 (1)	1.10	.60
No. 106 (1)	.50	*.75*
No. 61 (1)	1.25	2.50
No. 157 (1)	1.25	.75
No. 234 (1)	1.00	.25
No. 45 (1)	.50	*.60*
No. 153 (1)	.75	.35
No. 142 (1)	.85	.40
No. 252 (1)	.45	.25
No. 143 (1)	.55	.40
No. 150 (1)	.40	*1.00*
No. 167 (1)	1.50	1.00
No. 141 (1)	.40	.40
No. 121 (1)	.90	1.50
No. 1L18 (1)	1.50	1.50
No. 145 (1)	1.75	.60
No. 152 (1)	.50	.50
No. 131 (1)	.50	.50
No. 60 (1)	.65	2.25
No. 160 (1)	.95	.25

No. 170 (1)	.30	.25
No. 184 (1)	6.00	.35
No. 153 (1)	.70	.25
No. 101 (1)	.40	.25
No. 132 (1)	1.00	2.25
No. 155 (1)	1.40	.30
No. 82 (1)	2.25	.60
No. 71 (1)	1.60	1.60
No. 27 (1)	1.10	1.50
No. 63 (1)	1.40	.65
No. 71 (1)	2.25	.25
No. 27 (1)	1.75	.30
No. 126 (1)	1.60	.25
No. 28 (1)	1.75	4.00
No. 101 (1)	1.75	.25
No. 74 (1)	1.50	1.00
No. 241 (1)	.50	.25
No. 250 (1)	1.00	.25
No. 127 (1)	.65	.50
No. 77 (1)	.75	.60
No. 79 (1)	.45	.25
No. 260 (1)	2.00	1.00
No. 60 (1)	.70	.25
No. 96 (1)	.75	.75
No. 19 (1)	2.25	2.25
No. 139 (1)	1.25	1.25
No. 119 (1)	.35	.25
No. 156 (1)	.70	.35
No. 185 (1)	.50	.30
No. 196 (1)	2.25	2.25
No. 172 (1)	.80	.80
No. 194 (1)	.40	.40
No. 27 (1)	2.50	.40
No. 88 (1)	1.10	1.10
No. 127 (1)	.40	.25
No. 54 (1)	.30	.25
No. 84 (1)	.25	.25
No. 13 (1)	1.00	1.75
No. 118 (1)	.40	1.10
No. 114 (1)	.40	1.00
Nos. 313-316 (4)	16.35	8.75
Nos. 579-582 (4)	7.40	5.20
Nos. 259-261 (3)	4.60	3.25
Nos. 92-95 (4)	15.25	12.75
No. 330 (1)	.25	.25
No. 317 (1)	1.50	.25
Nos. 145-146 (2)	2.65	2.65
Nos. 113-116 (4)	16.00	8.50
Nos. 280-284 (5)	5.65	6.85
Nos. 104-105 (2)	1.75	1.75
Nos. 52-55 (4)	15.25	6.50
Nos. 214-215 (2)	2.10	1.00
No. 192 (1)	.30	.25
No. 80 (1)	7.25	7.25
Nos. 244-248 (5)	4.90	3.50
No. 4 (1)	2.75	2.75
Set total (106) Stamps	171.25	122.40

Separate designs for each country for the visit of Queen Elizabeth II and the Duke of Edinburgh.

Royal Visit 1953

1953

Aden 62
Australia 267-269
Bermuda 163
Ceylon 318
Fiji 146
Gibraltar 146
Jamaica 154
Kenya, Uganda, Tanzania 102
Malta 242
New Zealand 286-287

No. 62 (1)	.65	2.00
Nos. 267-269 (3)	2.35	1.90
No. 163 (1)	.50	.25
No. 318 (1)	1.25	.25
No. 146 (1)	.65	.35
No. 146 (1)	.50	.30
No. 154 (1)	.50	.25
No. 102 (1)	.50	.25
No. 242 (1)	.35	.25
Nos. 286-287 (2)	.50	.50
Set total (13) Stamps	7.75	6.30

West Indies Federation

Map of the Caribbean CD313

Federation of the West Indies, April 22, 1958.

1958

Antigua 122-124
Barbados 248-250
Dominica 161-163
Grenada 184-186
Jamaica 175-177
Montserrat 143-145
St. Kitts-Nevis 136-138
St. Lucia 170-172
St. Vincent 198-200
Trinidad & Tobago 86-88

Nos. 122-124 (3)	5.80	3.80
Nos. 248-250 (3)	1.60	2.90
Nos. 161-163 (3)	1.95	1.85
Nos. 184-186 (3)	1.50	1.20
Nos. 175-177 (3)	2.65	3.45
Nos. 143-145 (3)	2.35	1.35
Nos. 136-138 (3)	3.00	1.85
Nos. 170-172 (3)	2.05	2.80
Nos. 198-200 (3)	1.50	1.75
Nos. 86-88 (3)	.75	.90
Set total (30) Stamps	23.15	21.85

Freedom from Hunger

Protein Food CD314

U.N. Food and Agricultural Organization's "Freedom from Hunger" campaign.

1963

Aden 65
Antigua 133
Ascension 89
Bahamas 180
Basutoland 83
Bechuanaland Protectorate 194
Bermuda 192
British Guiana 271
British Honduras 179
Brunei 100
Cayman Islands 168
Dominica 181
Falkland Islands 146
Fiji 198
Gambia 172
Gibraltar 161
Gilbert & Ellice Islands 76
Grenada 190
Hong Kong 218
Malta 291
Mauritius 270
Montserrat 150
New Hebrides, British 93
North Borneo 296
Pitcairn Islands 35
St. Helena 173
St. Lucia 179
St. Vincent 201
Sarawak 212
Seychelles 213
Solomon Islands 109
Swaziland 108
Tonga 127
Tristan da Cunha 68
Turks & Caicos Islands 138
Virgin Islands 140
Zanzibar 280

No. 65 (1)	1.75	1.75
No. 133 (1)	.35	.35
No. 89 (1)	1.00	1.00
No. 180 (1)	.65	.65
No. 83 (1)	.50	.25
No. 194 (1)	.50	.50
No. 192 (1)	1.00	.50
No. 271 (1)	.45	.25
No. 179 (1)	.65	.25
No. 100 (1)	3.25	2.25
No. 168 (1)	.50	.30
No. 181 (1)	.30	.30
No. 146 (1)	11.50	3.50
No. 198 (1)	5.25	2.75
No. 172 (1)	.50	.25
No. 161 (1)	4.00	2.25
No. 76 (1)	1.40	.40
No. 190 (1)	.30	.25
No. 218 (1)	47.50	7.50
No. 291 (1)	2.00	2.00
No. 270 (1)	.50	.50
No. 150 (1)	.55	.45
No. 93 (1)	.60	.25
No. 296 (1)	1.90	.75
No. 35 (1)	10.00	4.50
No. 173 (1)	2.25	1.10
No. 179 (1)	.40	.40
No. 201 (1)	.90	.50
No. 212 (1)	1.60	1.75
No. 213 (1)	.85	.35
No. 109 (1)	2.00	.85
No. 108 (1)	.50	.50
No. 127 (1)	.70	.35
No. 68 (1)	.90	.40
No. 138 (1)	.50	.50
No. 140 (1)	.50	.50
No. 280 (1)	1.50	.80
Set total (37) Stamps	109.50	41.70

Red Cross Centenary

Red Cross and Elizabeth II CD315

1963

Antigua 134-135
Ascension 90-91
Bahamas 183-184
Basutoland 84-85
Bechuanaland Protectorate 195-196
Bermuda 193-194
British Guiana 272-273
British Honduras 180-181
Cayman Islands 169-170
Dominica 182-183
Falkland Islands 147-148
Fiji 203-204
Gambia 173-174
Gibraltar 162-163
Gilbert & Ellice Islands 77-78
Grenada 191-192
Hong Kong 219-220
Jamaica 203-204
Malta 292-293
Mauritius 271-272
Montserrat 151-152
New Hebrides, British 94-95
Pitcairn Islands 36-37
St. Helena 174-175
St. Kitts-Nevis 143-144
St. Lucia 180-181
St. Vincent 202-203
Seychelles 214-215
Solomon Islands 110-111
South Arabia 1-2
Swaziland 109-110
Tonga 134-135
Tristan da Cunha 69-70
Turks & Caicos Islands 139-140
Virgin Islands 141-142

Nos. 134-135 (2)	1.10	1.50
Nos. 90-91 (2)	8.25	2.70
Nos. 183-184 (2)	2.30	2.55
Nos. 84-85 (2)	1.20	.90
Nos. 195-196 (2)	.95	.85
Nos. 193-194 (2)	2.75	2.55
Nos. 272-273 (2)	1.05	.80
Nos. 180-181 (2)	1.00	2.25
Nos. 169-170 (2)	.95	2.00
Nos. 182-183 (2)	.70	1.05
Nos. 147-148 (2)	19.75	6.00
Nos. 203-204 (2)	4.00	3.55
Nos. 173-174 (2)	.75	1.00
Nos. 162-163 (2)	6.25	5.40
Nos. 77-78 (2)	2.25	3.25
Nos. 191-192 (2)	.80	.50
Nos. 219-220 (2)	35.00	7.35
Nos. 203-204 (2)	.75	1.65
Nos. 292-293 (2)	2.50	4.75
Nos. 271-272 (2)	.90	.90
Nos. 151-152 (2)	1.00	.80
Nos. 94-95 (2)	1.00	.50
Nos. 36-37 (2)	6.50	5.50
Nos. 174-175 (2)	1.70	2.30
Nos. 143-144 (2)	.90	.90
Nos. 180-181 (2)	1.25	1.25
Nos. 202-203 (2)	.90	.90
Nos. 214-215 (2)	1.10	.90
Nos. 110-111 (2)	1.25	1.15
Nos. 1-2 (2)	1.25	1.25
Nos. 109-110 (2)	1.10	1.10
Nos. 134-135 (2)	1.00	1.25
Nos. 69-70 (2)	1.50	1.00
Nos. 139-140 (2)	.95	1.10
Nos. 141-142 (2)	.80	.80
Set total (70) Stamps	115.40	72.20

Shakespeare

Shakespeare Memorial Theatre, Stratford-on-Avon — CD316

400th anniversary of the birth of William Shakespeare.

1964

Antigua 151
Bahamas 201
Bechuanaland Protectorate 197
Cayman Islands 171
Dominica 184
Falkland Islands 149
Gambia 192
Gibraltar 164
Montserrat 153
St. Lucia 196
Turks & Caicos Islands 141
Virgin Islands 143

No. 151 (1)	.40	.25
No. 201 (1)	.60	.35
No. 197 (1)	.35	.35
No. 171 (1)	.35	.30
No. 184 (1)	.35	.35
No. 149 (1)	1.75	.50
No. 192 (1)	.35	.25
No. 164 (1)	.65	.55
No. 153 (1)	.35	.25
No. 196 (1)	.45	.25
No. 141 (1)	.40	.40
No. 143 (1)	.45	.45
Set total (12) Stamps	6.45	4.25

ITU

ITU Emblem CD317

Intl. Telecommunication Union, cent.

1965

Antigua 153-154
Ascension 92-93
Bahamas 219-220
Barbados 265-266
Basutoland 101-102
Bechuanaland Protectorate 202-203
Bermuda 196-197
British Guiana 293-294
British Honduras 187-188
Brunei 116-117
Cayman Islands 172-173
Dominica 185-186
Falkland Islands 154-155
Fiji 211-212
Gibraltar 167-168
Gilbert & Ellice Islands 87-88
Grenada 205-206
Hong Kong 221-222
Mauritius 291-292
Montserrat 157-158
New Hebrides, British 108-109
Pitcairn Islands 52-53
St. Helena 180-181
St. Kitts-Nevis 163-164
St. Lucia 197-198
St. Vincent 224-225
Seychelles 218-219
Solomon Islands 126-127
Swaziland 115-116
Tristan da Cunha 85-86
Turks & Caicos Islands 142-143
Virgin Islands 159-160

Nos. 153-154 (2)	1.65	1.35
Nos. 92-93 (2)	1.90	1.50
Nos. 219-220 (2)	1.35	1.35
Nos. 265-266 (2)	1.50	1.25
Nos. 101-102 (2)	.85	.65
Nos. 202-203 (2)	1.10	.75
Nos. 196-197 (2)	2.15	2.25
Nos. 293-294 (2)	.60	.55
Nos. 187-188 (2)	.85	.85
Nos. 116-117 (2)	1.75	1.75
Nos. 172-173 (2)	1.00	1.00
Nos. 185-186 (2)	.55	.55
Nos. 154-155 (2)	7.75	3.65
Nos. 211-212 (2)	2.70	2.70
Nos. 167-168 (2)	9.00	5.95
Nos. 87-88 (2)	.95	.75
Nos. 205-206 (2)	.50	.50
Nos. 221-222 (2)	24.50	3.80
Nos. 291-292 (2)	1.20	.65
Nos. 157-158 (2)	1.25	1.15
Nos. 108-109 (2)	.65	.50
Nos. 52-53 (2)	6.25	4.30
Nos. 180-181 (2)	.80	.60
Nos. 163-164 (2)	.60	.60
Nos. 197-198 (2)	1.25	1.25
Nos. 224-225 (2)	.80	.90
Nos. 218-219 (2)	.90	.60
Nos. 126-127 (2)	.70	.55
Nos. 115-116 (2)	.75	.75
Nos. 85-86 (2)	1.15	.65
Nos. 142-143 (2)	.90	.90
Nos. 159-160 (2)	.95	.95
Set total (64) Stamps	78.80	45.50

Intl. Cooperation Year

ICY Emblem
CD318

1965

Antigua 155-156
Ascension 94-95
Bahamas 222-223
Basutoland 103-104
Bechuanaland Protectorate 204-205
Bermuda 199-200
British Guiana 295-296
British Honduras 189-190
Brunei 118-119
Cayman Islands 174-175
Dominica 187-188
Falkland Islands 156-157
Fiji 213-214
Gibraltar 169-170
Gilbert & Ellice Islands 104-105
Grenada 207-208
Hong Kong 223-224
Mauritius 293-294
Montserrat 176-177
New Hebrides, British 110-111
New Hebrides, French 126-127
Pitcairn Islands 54-55
St. Helena 182-183
St. Kitts-Nevis 165-166
St. Lucia 199-200
Seychelles 220-221
Solomon Islands 143-144
South Arabia 17-18
Swaziland 117-118
Tristan da Cunha 87-88
Turks & Caicos Islands 144-145
Virgin Islands 161-162

Nos. 155-156 (2)	.60	.50
Nos. 94-95 (2)	1.30	1.50
Nos. 222-223 (2)	.65	1.40
Nos. 103-104 (2)	.75	.85
Nos. 204-205 (2)	.85	1.00
Nos. 199-200 (2)	2.25	1.25
Nos. 295-296 (2)	.65	.60
Nos. 189-190 (2)	.60	.55
Nos. 118-119 (2)	.85	.85
Nos. 174-175 (2)	1.00	.95
Nos. 187-188 (2)	.55	.55
Nos. 156-157 (2)	7.00	1.90
Nos. 213-214 (2)	2.60	2.35
Nos. 169-170 (2)	1.25	*2.75*
Nos. 104-105 (2)	.95	.60
Nos. 207-208 (2)	.50	.50
Nos. 223-224 (2)	22.00	3.10
Nos. 293-294 (2)	.70	.70
Nos. 176-177 (2)	.80	.65
Nos. 110-111 (2)	.50	.50
Nos. 126-127 (2)	12.00	12.00
Nos. 54-55 (2)	6.35	4.50
Nos. 182-183 (2)	.95	.50
Nos. 165-166 (2)	.70	.60
Nos. 199-200 (2)	.55	.55
Nos. 220-221 (2)	.90	.65
Nos. 143-144 (2)	.70	.60
Nos. 17-18 (2)	1.20	.50
Nos. 117-118 (2)	.75	.75
Nos. 87-88 (2)	1.35	.75
Nos. 144-145 (2)	.85	.85
Nos. 161-162 (2)	.80	.80
Set total (64) Stamps	73.45	46.10

Churchill Memorial

Winston Churchill and St. Paul's, London, During Air Attack
CD319

1966

Antigua 157-160
Ascension 96-99
Bahamas 224-227
Barbados 281-284
Basutoland 105-108
Bechuanaland Protectorate 206-209
Bermuda 201-204
British Antarctic Territory 16-19
British Honduras 191-194
Brunei 120-123
Cayman Islands 176-179
Dominica 189-192
Falkland Islands 158-161
Fiji 215-218
Gibraltar 171-174
Gilbert & Ellice Islands 106-109
Grenada 209-212
Hong Kong 225-228
Mauritius 295-298
Montserrat 178-181
New Hebrides, British 112-115
New Hebrides, French 128-131
Pitcairn Islands 56-59
St. Helena 184-187
St. Kitts-Nevis 167-170
St. Lucia 201-204
St. Vincent 241-244
Seychelles 222-225
Solomon Islands 145-148
South Arabia 19-22
Swaziland 119-122
Tristan da Cunha 89-92
Turks & Caicos Islands 146-149
Virgin Islands 163-166

Nos. 157-160 (4)	3.05	2.55
Nos. 96-99 (4)	10.00	7.15
Nos. 224-227 (4)	2.30	*3.20*
Nos. 281-284 (4)	3.00	4.45
Nos. 105-108 (4)	2.80	3.25
Nos. 206-209 (4)	2.50	2.50
Nos. 201-204 (4)	4.00	4.00
Nos. 16-19 (4)	41.35	20.00
Nos. 191-194 (4)	2.55	1.80
Nos. 120-123 (4)	8.00	7.25
Nos. 176-179 (4)	3.40	3.55
Nos. 189-192 (4)	1.15	1.15
Nos. 158-161 (4)	12.75	7.80
Nos. 215-218 (4)	5.15	3.45
Nos. 171-174 (4)	3.05	5.30
Nos. 106-109 (4)	1.75	1.30
Nos. 209-212 (4)	1.10	1.10
Nos. 225-228 (4)	52.50	11.40
Nos. 295-298 (4)	4.05	4.05
Nos. 178-181 (4)	1.60	1.55
Nos. 112-115 (4)	2.30	1.00
Nos. 128-131 (4)	10.25	10.25
Nos. 56-59 (4)	11.00	6.75
Nos. 184-187 (4)	1.85	1.95
Nos. 167-170 (4)	1.70	1.70
Nos. 201-204 (4)	1.50	1.50
Nos. 241-244 (4)	1.50	1.75
Nos. 222-225 (4)	3.20	3.60
Nos. 145-148 (4)	1.75	1.75
Nos. 19-22 (4)	2.95	2.20
Nos. 119-122 (4)	1.70	2.55
Nos. 89-92 (4)	5.95	2.70
Nos. 146-149 (4)	1.60	1.75
Nos. 163-166 (4)	1.90	1.90
Set total (136) Stamps	215.20	138.15

Royal Visit, 1966

Queen Elizabeth II and Prince Philip
CD320

Caribbean visit, Feb. 4 - Mar. 6, 1966.

1966

Antigua 161-162
Bahamas 228-229
Barbados 285-286
British Guiana 299-300
Cayman Islands 180-181
Dominica 193-194
Grenada 213-214
Montserrat 182-183
St. Kitts-Nevis 171-172
St. Lucia 205-206
St. Vincent 245-246
Turks & Caicos Islands 150-151
Virgin Islands 167-168

Nos. 161-162 (2)	3.80	2.60
Nos. 228-229 (2)	3.05	3.05
Nos. 285-286 (2)	3.00	2.00
Nos. 299-300 (2)	3.35	1.60
Nos. 180-181 (2)	3.45	1.80
Nos. 193-194 (2)	3.00	.60
Nos. 213-214 (2)	.80	.50
Nos. 182-183 (2)	1.70	1.00
Nos. 171-172 (2)	.80	.75
Nos. 205-206 (2)	1.50	1.35
Nos. 245-246 (2)	2.75	1.35
Nos. 150-151 (2)	1.20	.70
Nos. 167-168 (2)	2.25	2.25
Set total (26) Stamps	30.65	19.55

World Cup Soccer

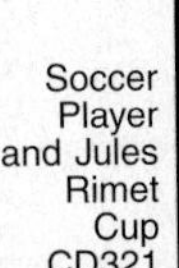

Soccer Player and Jules Rimet Cup
CD321

World Cup Soccer Championship, Wembley, England, July 11-30.

1966

Antigua 163-164
Ascension 100-101
Bahamas 245-246
Bermuda 205-206
Brunei 124-125
Cayman Islands 182-183
Dominica 195-196
Fiji 219-220
Gibraltar 175-176
Gilbert & Ellice Islands 125-126
Grenada 230-231
New Hebrides, British 116-117
New Hebrides, French 132-133
Pitcairn Islands 60-61
St. Helena 188-189
St. Kitts-Nevis 173-174
St. Lucia 207-208
Seychelles 226-227
Solomon Islands 167-168
South Arabia 23-24
Tristan da Cunha 93-94

Nos. 163-164 (2)	.85	.50
Nos. 100-101 (2)	2.50	1.80
Nos. 245-246 (2)	.65	.65
Nos. 205-206 (2)	1.75	1.75
Nos. 124-125 (2)	1.40	1.00
Nos. 182-183 (2)	.75	.75
Nos. 195-196 (2)	1.20	.75
Nos. 219-220 (2)	2.00	1.20
Nos. 175-176 (2)	1.85	1.75
Nos. 125-126 (2)	.80	.60
Nos. 230-231 (2)	.65	*.95*
Nos. 116-117 (2)	1.00	1.00
Nos. 132-133 (2)	7.00	7.00
Nos. 60-61 (2)	5.50	5.00
Nos. 188-189 (2)	1.25	.60
Nos. 173-174 (2)	.85	.80
Nos. 207-208 (2)	1.15	.90
Nos. 226-227 (2)	.85	.85
Nos. 167-168 (2)	.70	.70
Nos. 23-24 (2)	1.90	.55
Nos. 93-94 (2)	1.25	.80
Set total (42) Stamps	35.85	29.90

WHO Headquarters

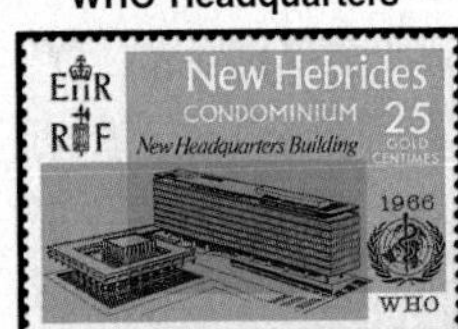

World Health Organization Headquarters, Geneva — CD322

1966

Antigua 165-166
Ascension 102-103
Bahamas 247-248
Brunei 126-127
Cayman Islands 184-185
Dominica 197-198
Fiji 224-225
Gibraltar 180-181
Gilbert & Ellice Islands 127-128
Grenada 232-233
Hong Kong 229-230
Montserrat 184-185
New Hebrides, British 118-119
New Hebrides, French 134-135
Pitcairn Islands 62-63
St. Helena 190-191
St. Kitts-Nevis 177-178
St. Lucia 209-210
St. Vincent 247-248
Seychelles 228-229
Solomon Islands 169-170
South Arabia 25-26
Tristan da Cunha 99-100

Nos. 165-166 (2)	1.05	.55
Nos. 102-103 (2)	6.60	3.50
Nos. 247-248 (2)	.80	.80
Nos. 126-127 (2)	1.35	1.00
Nos. 184-185 (2)	2.25	1.40
Nos. 197-198 (2)	.75	.75
Nos. 224-225 (2)	5.10	3.90
Nos. 180-181 (2)	6.50	4.50
Nos. 127-128 (2)	.80	.70
Nos. 232-233 (2)	.80	.50
Nos. 229-230 (2)	11.25	2.30
Nos. 184-185 (2)	1.00	1.00
Nos. 118-119 (2)	.75	.50
Nos. 134-135 (2)	8.75	8.75
Nos. 62-63 (2)	7.25	6.50
Nos. 190-191 (2)	3.50	1.50
Nos. 177-178 (2)	.65	.65
Nos. 209-210 (2)	.80	.80
Nos. 247-248 (2)	1.15	1.05
Nos. 228-229 (2)	1.25	.75
Nos. 169-170 (2)	.80	.80
Nos. 25-26 (2)	2.10	.70
Nos. 99-100 (2)	1.90	1.25
Set total (46) Stamps	67.15	44.15

UNESCO Anniversary

"Education" — CD323

"Science" (Wheat ears & flask enclosing globe). "Culture" (lyre & columns). 20th anniversary of the UNESCO.

1966-67

Antigua 183-185
Ascension 108-110
Bahamas 249-251
Barbados 287-289
Bermuda 207-209
Brunei 128-130
Cayman Islands 186-188
Dominica 199-201
Gibraltar 183-185
Gilbert & Ellice Islands 129-131
Grenada 234-236
Hong Kong 231-233
Mauritius 299-301
Montserrat 186-188
New Hebrides, British 120-122
New Hebrides, French 136-138
Pitcairn Islands 64-66
St. Helena 192-194
St. Kitts-Nevis 179-181
St. Lucia 211-213
St. Vincent 249-251
Seychelles 230-232
Solomon Islands 171-173
South Arabia 27-29
Swaziland 123-125
Tristan da Cunha 101-103
Turks & Caicos Islands 155-157
Virgin Islands 176-178

Nos. 183-185 (3)	1.90	*2.50*
Nos. 108-110 (3)	11.00	6.15
Nos. 249-251 (3)	2.35	2.35
Nos. 287-289 (3)	2.50	2.15
Nos. 207-209 (3)	4.30	3.90
Nos. 128-130 (3)	5.00	*7.40*
Nos. 186-188 (3)	2.50	1.70
Nos. 199-201 (3)	1.60	.75
Nos. 183-185 (3)	6.50	3.25
Nos. 129-131 (3)	2.50	1.65
Nos. 234-236 (3)	1.10	1.20
Nos. 231-233 (3)	69.50	17.50
Nos. 299-301 (3)	2.10	1.50
Nos. 186-188 (3)	2.40	2.40
Nos. 120-122 (3)	1.90	1.90
Nos. 136-138 (3)	7.75	7.75
Nos. 64-66 (3)	7.10	4.75
Nos. 192-194 (3)	5.25	3.65
Nos. 179-181 (3)	.90	.90
Nos. 211-213 (3)	1.15	1.15
Nos. 249-251 (3)	2.30	1.35
Nos. 230-232 (3)	2.40	2.40
Nos. 171-173 (3)	2.00	1.50
Nos. 27-29 (3)	5.50	5.50
Nos. 123-125 (3)	1.45	1.45
Nos. 101-103 (3)	2.00	1.40
Nos. 155-157 (3)	1.05	1.05
Nos. 176-178 (3)	1.30	1.30
Set total (84) Stamps	157.30	90.45

Silver Wedding, 1972

Queen Elizabeth II and Prince Philip — CD324

Designs: borders differ for each country.

1972

Anguilla 161-162
Antigua 295-296
Ascension 164-165
Bahamas 344-345
Bermuda 296-297
British Antarctic Territory 43-44
British Honduras 306-307
British Indian Ocean Territory 48-49

Brunei 186-187
Cayman Islands 304-305
Dominica 352-353
Falkland Islands 223-224
Fiji 328-329
Gibraltar 292-293
Gilbert & Ellice Islands 206-207
Grenada 466-467
Hong Kong 271-272
Montserrat 286-287
New Hebrides, British 169-170
Pitcairn Islands 127-128
St. Helena 271-272
St. Kitts-Nevis 257-258
St. Lucia 328-329
St.Vincent 344-345
Seychelles 309-310
Solomon Islands 248-249
South Georgia 35-36
Tristan da Cunha 178-179
Turks & Caicos Islands 257-258
Virgin Islands 241-242

Nos. 161-162 (2)	1.30	*1.50*
Nos. 295-296 (2)	.50	.50
Nos. 164-165 (2)	.80	.80
Nos. 344-345 (2)	.60	.60
Nos. 296-297 (2)	.50	.50
Nos. 43-44 (2)	7.75	6.10
Nos. 306-307 (2)	.90	.90
Nos. 48-49 (2)	2.30	1.00
Nos. 186-187 (2)	.65	.85
Nos. 304-305 (2)	.75	.75
Nos. 352-353 (2)	.65	.65
Nos. 223-224 (2)	1.10	1.10
Nos. 328-329 (2)	1.00	1.00
Nos. 292-293 (2)	.50	.50
Nos. 206-207 (2)	.50	.50
Nos. 466-467 (2)	.70	.70
Nos. 271-272 (2)	1.70	1.50
Nos. 286-287 (2)	.55	.55
Nos. 169-170 (2)	.50	.50
Nos. 127-128 (2)	.90	.85
Nos. 271-272 (2)	.70	1.20
Nos. 257-258 (2)	.65	.50
Nos. 328-329 (2)	.75	.75
Nos. 344-345 (2)	.55	.55
Nos. 309-310 (2)	.95	.95
Nos. 248-249 (2)	.60	.60
Nos. 35-36 (2)	1.40	1.40
Nos. 178-179 (2)	.70	.70
Nos. 257-258 (2)	.50	.50
Nos. 241-242 (2)	.50	.50
Set total (60) Stamps	31.45	29.00

Princess Anne's Wedding

Princess Anne and Mark Phillips — CD325

Wedding of Princess Anne and Mark Phillips, Nov. 14, 1973.

1973

Anguilla 179-180
Ascension 177-178
Belize 325-326
Bermuda 302-303
British Antarctic Territory 60-61
Cayman Islands 320-321
Falkland Islands 225-226
Gibraltar 305-306
Gilbert & Ellice Islands 216-217
Hong Kong 289-290
Montserrat 300-301
Pitcairn Islands 135-136
St. Helena 277-278
St. Kitts-Nevis 274-275
St. Lucia 349-350
St. Vincent 358-359
St. Vincent Grenadines 1-2
Seychelles 311-312
Solomon Islands 259-260
South Georgia 37-38
Tristan da Cunha 189-190
Turks & Caicos Islands 286-287
Virgin Islands 260-261

Nos. 179-180 (2)	.55	.55
Nos. 177-178 (2)	.65	.65
Nos. 325-326 (2)	.50	.50
Nos. 302-303 (2)	.50	.50
Nos. 60-61 (2)	1.10	1.10
Nos. 320-321 (2)	.55	.55
Nos. 225-226 (2)	.75	.75
Nos. 305-306 (2)	.55	.55
Nos. 216-217 (2)	.50	.50
Nos. 289-290 (2)	2.65	2.00
Nos. 300-301 (2)	.65	.65
Nos. 135-136 (2)	.70	.60
Nos. 277-278 (2)	.50	.50
Nos. 274-275 (2)	.50	.50
Nos. 349-350 (2)	.50	.50
Nos. 358-359 (2)	.50	.50
Nos. 1-2 (2)	.50	.50
Nos. 311-312 (2)	.70	.70
Nos. 259-260 (2)	.70	.70
Nos. 37-38 (2)	.75	.75
Nos. 189-190 (2)	.50	.50
Nos. 286-287 (2)	.50	.50
Nos. 260-261 (2)	.50	.50
Set total (46) Stamps	15.80	15.05

Elizabeth II Coronation Anniv.

CD326

CD327

CD328

Designs: Royal and local beasts in heraldic form and simulated stonework. Portrait of Elizabeth II by Peter Grugeon. 25th anniversary of coronation of Queen Elizabeth II.

1978

Ascension 229
Barbados 474
Belize 397
British Antarctic Territory 71
Cayman Islands 404
Christmas Island 87
Falkland Islands 275
Fiji 384
Gambia 380
Gilbert Islands 312
Mauritius 464
New Hebrides, British 258
St. Helena 317
St. Kitts-Nevis 354
Samoa 472
Solomon Islands 368
South Georgia 51
Swaziland 302
Tristan da Cunha 238
Virgin Islands 337

No. 229 (1)	2.25	2.25
No. 474 (1)	1.35	1.35
No. 397 (1)	1.75	1.75
No. 71 (1)	6.00	6.00
No. 404 (1)	2.00	2.50
No. 87 (1)	3.50	*4.00*
No. 275 (1)	4.00	4.00
No. 384 (1)	2.75	2.75
No. 380 (1)	1.50	1.50
No. 312 (1)	1.25	1.25
No. 464 (1)	2.75	2.75
No. 258 (1)	1.75	1.75
No. 317 (1)	1.75	1.75
No. 354 (1)	1.00	1.00
No. 472 (1)	2.00	2.00
No. 368 (1)	3.00	3.00
No. 51 (1)	3.00	3.00
No. 302 (1)	1.75	1.75
No. 238 (1)	1.50	1.50
No. 337 (1)	2.25	2.25
Set total (20) Stamps	47.10	48.10

Queen Mother Elizabeth's 80th Birthday

CD330

Designs: Photographs of Queen Mother Elizabeth. Falkland Islands issued in sheets of 50; others in sheets of 9.

1980

Ascension 261
Bermuda 401
Cayman Islands 443
Falkland Islands 305
Gambia 412
Gibraltar 393
Hong Kong 364
Pitcairn Islands 193
St. Helena 341
Samoa 532
Solomon Islands 426
Tristan da Cunha 277

No. 261 (1)	.50	.50
No. 401 (1)	.45	.45
No. 443 (1)	.45	.45
No. 305 (1)	.40	.40
No. 412 (1)	.40	.50
No. 393 (1)	.35	.35
No. 364 (1)	1.10	1.00
No. 193 (1)	.60	.60
No. 341 (1)	.50	.50
No. 532 (1)	.55	.55
No. 426 (1)	.50	.50
No. 277 (1)	.45	.45
Set total (12) Stamps	6.25	6.25

Royal Wedding, 1981

Prince Charles and Lady Diana — CD331

CD331a

Wedding of Charles, Prince of Wales, and Lady Diana Spencer, St. Paul's Cathedral, London, July 29, 1981.

1981

Antigua 623-627
Ascension 294-296
Barbados 547-549
Barbuda 497-501
Bermuda 412-414
Brunei 268-270
Cayman Islands 471-473
Dominica 701-705
Falkland Islands 324-326
Falkland Islands Dep. 1L59-1L61
Fiji 442-444
Gambia 426-428
Ghana 759-764
Grenada 1051-1055
Grenada Grenadines 440-443
Hong Kong 373-375
Jamaica 500-503
Lesotho 335-337
Maldive Islands 906-909
Mauritius 520-522
Norfolk Island 280-282
Pitcairn Islands 206-208
St. Helena 353-355
St. Lucia 543-549
Samoa 558-560
Sierra Leone 509-518
Solomon Islands 450-452
Swaziland 382-384
Tristan da Cunha 294-296
Turks & Caicos Islands 486-489
Caicos Island 8-11
Uganda 314-317
Vanuatu 308-310
Virgin Islands 406-408

Nos. 623-627 (5)	7.55	2.55
Nos. 294-296 (3)	1.10	1.10
Nos. 547-549 (3)	.90	.90
Nos. 497-501 (5)	10.95	10.95
Nos. 412-414 (3)	2.00	2.00
Nos. 268-270 (3)	2.15	*4.50*
Nos. 471-473 (3)	1.35	1.35
Nos. 701-705 (5)	8.35	2.35
Nos. 324-326 (3)	1.65	1.70
Nos. 1L59-1L61 (3)	1.45	1.45
Nos. 442-444 (3)	1.70	1.70
Nos. 426-428 (3)	.80	.80
Nos. 759-764 (9)	6.20	6.20
Nos. 1051-1055 (5)	9.85	1.85
Nos. 440-443 (4)	2.35	2.35
Nos. 373-375 (3)	3.30	3.10
Nos. 500-503 (4)	1.45	1.35
Nos. 335-337 (3)	.90	.90
Nos. 906-909 (4)	1.55	1.55
Nos. 520-522 (3)	2.75	2.75
Nos. 280-282 (3)	1.35	1.35
Nos. 206-208 (3)	1.10	1.10
Nos. 353-355 (3)	.85	.85
Nos. 543-549 (5)	8.50	8.50
Nos. 558-560 (3)	.85	.85
Nos. 509-518 (10)	15.50	15.50
Nos. 450-452 (3)	1.05	1.05
Nos. 382-384 (3)	1.30	1.25
Nos. 294-296 (3)	.90	.90
Nos. 486-489 (4)	2.20	2.20
Nos. 8-11 (4)	6.25	6.25
Nos. 314-317 (4)	3.30	3.00
Nos. 308-310 (3)	1.15	1.15
Nos. 406-408 (3)	1.30	1.30
Set total (131) Stamps	113.90	96.65

Princess Diana

CD332

CD333

Designs: Photographs and portrait of Princess Diana, wedding or honeymoon photographs, royal residences, arms of issuing country. Portrait photograph by Clive Friend. Souvenir sheet margins show family tree, various people related to the princess. 21st birthday of Princess Diana of Wales, July 1.

1982

Antigua 663-666
Ascension 313-316
Bahamas 510-513
Barbados 585-588
Barbuda 544-547
British Antarctic Territory 92-95
Cayman Islands 486-489
Dominica 773-776
Falkland Islands 348-351
Falkland Islands Dep. 1L72-1L75
Fiji 470-473
Gambia 447-450
Grenada 1101A-1105
Grenada Grenadines 485-491
Lesotho 372-375
Maldive Islands 952-955
Mauritius 548-551
Pitcairn Islands 213-216
St. Helena 372-375
St. Lucia 591-594
Sierra Leone 531-534
Solomon Islands 471-474
Swaziland 406-409
Tristan da Cunha 310-313
Turks and Caicos Islands 531-534
Virgin Islands 430-433

Nos. 663-666 (4)	9.70	9.70
Nos. 313-316 (4)	3.95	3.95
Nos. 510-513 (4)	6.00	3.85
Nos. 585-588 (4)	3.40	3.25
Nos. 544-547 (4)	9.75	7.70
Nos. 92-95 (4)	5.30	3.45
Nos. 486-489 (4)	*5.40*	*2.70*
Nos. 773-776 (4)	7.05	7.05
Nos. 348-351 (4)	3.10	3.10
Nos. 1L72-1L75 (4)	2.50	2.60
Nos. 470-473 (4)	4.50	4.50
Nos. 447-450 (4)	2.85	2.85
Nos. 1101A-1105 (7)	16.05	15.55
Nos. 485-491 (7)	17.65	17.65
Nos. 372-375 (4)	4.00	4.00
Nos. 952-955 (4)	5.50	3.90
Nos. 548-551 (4)	5.50	5.50
Nos. 213-216 (4)	2.15	2.15
Nos. 372-375 (4)	2.95	2.95
Nos. 591-594 (4)	9.90	9.90
Nos. 531-534 (4)	7.20	7.20
Nos. 471-474 (4)	2.90	2.90
Nos. 406-409 (4)	3.85	2.25
Nos. 310-313 (4)	3.65	1.45
Nos. 486-489 (4)	2.20	2.20
Nos. 430-433 (4)	3.55	3.55
Set total (110) Stamps	150.55	135.85

250th anniv. of first edition of Lloyd's List (shipping news publication) & of Lloyd's marine insurance.

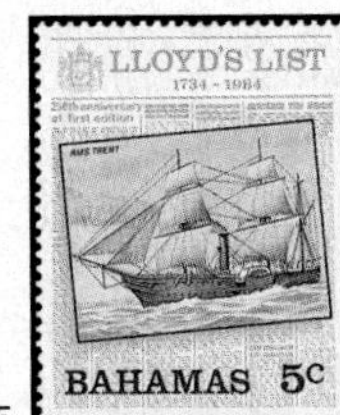

CD335

Designs: First page of early edition of the list; historical ships, modern transportation or harbor scenes.

1984

Ascension	351-354
Bahamas	555-558
Barbados	627-630
Cayes of Belize	10-13
Cayman Islands	522-526
Falkland Islands	404-407
Fiji	509-512
Gambia	519-522
Mauritius	587-590
Nauru	280-283
St. Helena	412-415
Samoa	624-627
Seychelles	538-541
Solomon Islands	521-524
Vanuatu	368-371
Virgin Islands	466-469

Nos. 351-354 (4)	3.30	2.55
Nos. 555-558 (4)	4.55	2.95
Nos. 627-630 (4)	6.10	5.15
Nos. 10-13 (4)	3.05	3.05
Nos. 522-526 (5)	9.30	8.45
Nos. 404-407 (4)	3.65	4.00
Nos. 509-512 (4)	6.15	6.15
Nos. 519-522 (4)	4.20	4.30
Nos. 587-590 (4)	8.95	8.95
Nos. 280-283 (4)	2.40	2.35
Nos. 412-415 (4)	2.40	2.40
Nos. 624-627 (4)	2.75	2.55
Nos. 538-541 (4)	5.25	5.25
Nos. 521-524 (4)	4.65	3.95
Nos. 368-371 (4)	2.40	2.40
Nos. 466-469 (4)	5.00	5.00
Set total (65) Stamps	74.10	69.45

Queen Mother 85th Birthday

CD336

Designs: Photographs tracing the life of the Queen Mother, Elizabeth. The high value in each set pictures the same photograph taken of the Queen Mother holding the infant Prince Henry.

1985

Ascension	372-376
Bahamas	580-584
Barbados	660-664
Bermuda	469-473
Falkland Islands	420-424
Falkland Islands Dep.	1L92-1L96
Fiji	531-535
Hong Kong	447-450
Jamaica	599-603
Mauritius	604-608
Norfolk Island	364-368
Pitcairn Islands	253-257
St. Helena	428-432
Samoa	649-653
Seychelles	567-571
Zil Elwannyen Sesel	101-105
Solomon Islands	543-547
Swaziland	476-480
Tristan da Cunha	372-376
Vanuatu	392-396

Nos. 372-376 (5)	5.35	5.35
Nos. 580-584 (5)	7.95	6.45
Nos. 660-664 (5)	8.00	6.70
Nos. 469-473 (5)	9.90	9.90
Nos. 420-424 (5)	8.25	7.60
Nos. 1L92-1L96 (5)	8.25	8.25
Nos. 531-535 (5)	7.05	7.05
Nos. 447-450 (4)	10.25	8.50
Nos. 599-603 (5)	6.15	7.00
Nos. 604-608 (5)	11.80	11.80
Nos. 364-368 (5)	5.05	5.05
Nos. 253-257 (5)	5.25	5.95
Nos. 428-432 (5)	5.25	5.25
Nos. 649-653 (5)	8.65	7.80
Nos. 567-571 (5)	8.70	8.70
Nos. 101-105 (5)	7.15	7.15
Nos. 543-547 (5)	4.20	4.20
Nos. 476-480 (5)	8.00	7.50
Nos. 372-376 (5)	5.40	5.40
Nos. 392-396 (5)	5.25	5.25
Set total (99) Stamps	145.85	140.85

Queen Elizabeth II, 60th Birthday

CD337

1986, April 21

Ascension	389-393
Bahamas	592-596
Barbados	675-679
Bermuda	499-503
Cayman Islands	555-559
Falkland Islands	441-445
Fiji	544-548
Hong Kong	465-469
Jamaica	620-624
Kiribati	470-474
Mauritius	629-633
Papua New Guinea	640-644
Pitcairn Islands	270-274
St. Helena	451-455
Samoa	670-674
Seychelles	592-596
Zil Elwannyen Sesel	114-118
Solomon Islands	562-566
South Georgia	101-105
Swaziland	490-494
Tristan da Cunha	388-392
Vanuatu	414-418
Zambia	343-347

Nos. 389-393 (5)	2.80	2.80
Nos. 592-596 (5)	2.75	*3.70*
Nos. 675-679 (5)	3.35	3.20
Nos. 499-503 (5)	4.90	4.90
Nos. 555-559 (5)	4.55	4.45
Nos. 441-445 (5)	3.95	*4.95*
Nos. 544-548 (5)	4.05	4.05
Nos. 465-469 (5)	9.60	6.85
Nos. 620-624 (5)	2.75	2.70
Nos. 470-474 (5)	2.10	2.10
Nos. 629-633 (5)	3.70	3.70
Nos. 640-644 (5)	4.50	4.50
Nos. 270-274 (5)	2.70	2.70
Nos. 451-455 (5)	3.05	3.05
Nos. 670-674 (5)	2.90	2.90
Nos. 592-596 (5)	2.70	2.70
Nos. 114-118 (5)	2.25	2.25
Nos. 562-566 (5)	2.50	2.50
Nos. 101-105 (5)	3.55	3.55
Nos. 490-494 (5)	2.30	2.30
Nos. 388-392 (5)	3.00	3.00
Nos. 414-418 (5)	3.10	3.10
Nos. 343-347 (5)	1.75	1.75
Set total (115) Stamps	78.80	77.70

Royal Wedding

Marriage of Prince Andrew and Sarah Ferguson CD338

1986, July 23

Ascension	399-400
Bahamas	602-603
Barbados	687-688
Cayman Islands	560-561
Jamaica	629-630
Pitcairn Islands	275-276
St. Helena	460-461
St. Kitts	181-182
Seychelles	602-603
Zil Elwannyen Sesel	119-120
Solomon Islands	567-568
Tristan da Cunha	397-398
Zambia	348-349

Nos. 399-400 (2)	1.60	1.60
Nos. 602-603 (2)	2.75	2.75
Nos. 687-688 (2)	2.25	1.25
Nos. 560-561 (2)	1.50	*2.15*
Nos. 629-630 (2)	1.35	1.35
Nos. 275-276 (2)	2.40	2.40
Nos. 460-461 (2)	1.05	1.05
Nos. 181-182 (2)	1.50	1.50
Nos. 602-603 (2)	2.50	2.50
Nos. 119-120 (2)	2.30	2.30
Nos. 567-568 (2)	1.00	1.00
Nos. 397-398 (2)	1.40	1.40
Nos. 348-349 (2)	1.10	1.30
Set total (26) Stamps	22.70	22.55

Queen Elizabeth II, 60th Birthday

Queen Elizabeth II & Prince Philip, 1947 Wedding Portrait — CD339

Designs: Photographs tracing the life of Queen Elizabeth II.

1986

Anguilla	674-677
Antigua	925-928
Barbuda	783-786
Dominica	950-953
Gambia	611-614
Grenada	1371-1374
Grenada Grenadines	749-752
Lesotho	531-534
Maldive Islands	1172-1175
Sierra Leone	760-763
Uganda	495-498

Nos. 674-677 (4)	8.00	8.00
Nos. 925-928 (4)	6.75	6.75
Nos. 783-786 (4)	23.15	23.15
Nos. 950-953 (4)	7.25	7.25
Nos. 611-614 (4)	8.25	7.90
Nos. 1371-1374 (4)	6.80	6.80
Nos. 749-752 (4)	6.75	6.75
Nos. 531-534 (4)	5.25	5.25
Nos. 1172-1175 (4)	6.25	6.25
Nos. 760-763 (4)	6.30	6.30
Nos. 495-498 (4)	8.50	8.50
Set total (44) Stamps	93.25	92.90

Royal Wedding, 1986

CD340

Designs: Photographs of Prince Andrew and Sarah Ferguson during courtship, engagement and marriage.

1986

Antigua	939-942
Barbuda	809-812
Dominica	970-973
Gambia	635-638
Grenada	1385-1388
Grenada Grenadines	758-761
Lesotho	545-548
Maldive Islands	1181-1184
Sierra Leone	769-772
Uganda	510-513

Nos. 939-942 (4)	8.25	8.25
Nos. 809-812 (4)	14.55	14.55
Nos. 970-973 (4)	7.25	7.25
Nos. 635-638 (4)	8.55	8.55
Nos. 1385-1388 (4)	8.30	8.30
Nos. 758-761 (4)	9.00	9.00
Nos. 545-548 (4)	7.45	7.45
Nos. 1181-1184 (4)	8.45	8.45
Nos. 769-772 (4)	5.35	5.35
Nos. 510-513 (4)	9.25	10.00
Set total (40) Stamps	86.40	87.15

Lloyds of London, 300th Anniv.

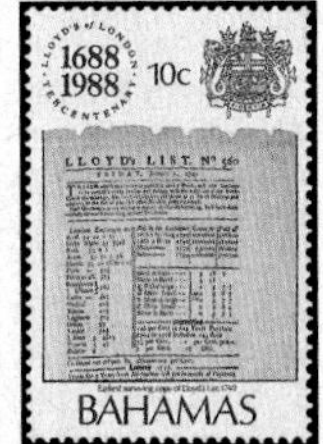

CD341

Designs: 17th century aspects of Lloyds, representations of each country's individual connections with Lloyds and publicized disasters insured by the organization.

1986

Ascension	454-457
Bahamas	655-658
Barbados	731-734
Bermuda	541-544
Falkland Islands	481-484
Liberia	1101-1104
Malawi	534-537
Nevis	571-574
St. Helena	501-504
St. Lucia	923-926
Seychelles	649-652
Zil Elwannyen Sesel	146-149
Solomon Islands	627-630
South Georgia	131-134
Trinidad & Tobago	484-487
Tristan da Cunha	439-442
Vanuatu	485-488

Nos. 454-457 (4)	5.00	5.00
Nos. 655-658 (4)	8.90	4.95
Nos. 731-734 (4)	12.50	8.35
Nos. 541-544 (4)	8.25	5.60
Nos. 481-484 (4)	6.30	4.55
Nos. 1101-1104 (4)	4.25	4.25
Nos. 534-537 (4)	11.00	7.85
Nos. 571-574 (4)	8.35	8.35
Nos. 501-504 (4)	8.70	7.15
Nos. 923-926 (4)	9.40	9.40
Nos. 649-652 (4)	13.10	13.10
Nos. 146-149 (4)	11.25	11.25
Nos. 627-630 (4)	7.90	4.45
Nos. 131-134 (4)	6.30	3.70
Nos. 484-487 (4)	10.25	6.35
Nos. 439-442 (4)	7.60	7.60
Nos. 485-488 (4)	5.90	5.90
Set total (68) Stamps	144.95	117.80

Moon Landing, 20th Anniv.

CD342

Designs: Equipment, crew photographs, spacecraft, official emblems and report profiles created for the Apollo Missions. Two stamps in each set are square in format rather than like the stamp shown; see individual country listings for more information.

1989

Ascension	468-472
Bahamas	674-678
Belize	916-920
Kiribati	517-521
Liberia	1125-1129
Nevis	586-590
St. Kitts	248-252
Samoa	760-764
Seychelles	676-680
Zil Elwannyen Sesel	154-158
Solomon Islands	643-647
Vanuatu	507-511

Nos. 468-472 (5)	9.40	8.60
Nos. 674-678 (5)	23.00	19.70
Nos. 916-920 (5)	27.40	23.50
Nos. 517-521 (5)	12.50	12.50
Nos. 1125-1129 (5)	8.50	8.50
Nos. 586-590 (5)	7.50	7.50
Nos. 248-252 (5)	8.00	8.00
Nos. 760-764 (5)	9.60	9.05
Nos. 676-680 (5)	16.05	16.05
Nos. 154-158 (5)	26.85	26.85

Nos. 643-647 (5)	12.75	11.60
Nos. 507-511 (5)	9.90	9.90
Set total (60) Stamps	171.45	161.75

Queen Mother, 90th Birthday

CD343

CD344

Designs: Portraits of Queen Elizabeth, the Queen Mother. See individual country listings for more information.

1990

Ascension 491-492
Bahamas 698-699
Barbados 782-783
British Antarctic Territory 170-171
British Indian Ocean Territory 106-107
Cayman Islands 622-623
Falkland Islands 524-525
Kenya 527-528
Kiribati 555-556
Liberia 1145-1146
Pitcairn Islands 336-337
St. Helena 532-533
St. Lucia 969-970
Seychelles 710-711
Zil Elwannyen Sesel 171-172
Solomon Islands 671-672
South Georgia 143-144
Swaziland 565-566
Tristan da Cunha 480-481

Nos. 491-492 (2)	4.75	5.65
Nos. 698-699 (2)	5.65	5.65
Nos. 782-783 (2)	4.00	3.70
Nos. 170-171 (2)	6.75	6.75
Nos. 106-107 (2)	20.75	21.25
Nos. 622-623 (2)	5.10	*6.75*
Nos. 524-525 (2)	5.25	5.25
Nos. 527-528 (2)	7.00	7.00
Nos. 555-556 (2)	4.75	4.75
Nos. 1145-1146 (2)	3.25	3.25
Nos. 336-337 (2)	4.25	4.25
Nos. 532-533 (2)	5.25	5.25
Nos. 969-970 (2)	5.25	5.25
Nos. 710-711 (2)	6.60	6.60
Nos. 171-172 (2)	8.25	8.25
Nos. 671-672 (2)	6.50	*6.40*
Nos. 143-144 (2)	5.75	5.75
Nos. 565-566 (2)	4.35	4.35
Nos. 480-481 (2)	5.60	5.60
Set total (38) Stamps	119.05	121.70

Queen Elizabeth II, 65th Birthday, and Prince Philip, 70th Birthday

CD345

CD346

Designs: Portraits of Queen Elizabeth II and Prince Philip differ for each country. Printed in sheets of 10 + 5 labels (3 different) between. Stamps alternate, producing 5 different triptychs.

1991

Ascension 506a
Bahamas 731a
Belize 970a
Bermuda 618a
Kiribati 572a
Mauritius 734a
Pitcairn Islands 349a
St. Helena 555a
St. Kitts 319a
Samoa 791a
Seychelles 724a
Zil Elwannyen Sesel 178a
Solomon Islands 689a
South Georgia 150a
Swaziland 587a
Vanuatu 541a

No. 506a (1)	3.50	3.75
No. 731a (1)	4.00	4.00
No. 970a (1)	3.75	3.75
No. 618a (1)	4.00	4.00
No. 572a (1)	4.00	4.00
No. 734a (1)	3.75	3.75
No. 349a (1)	3.25	3.25
No. 555a (1)	2.75	2.75
No. 319a (1)	3.00	3.00
No. 791a (1)	4.25	4.25
No. 724a (1)	5.00	5.00
No. 178a (1)	6.50	6.50
No. 689a (1)	4.50	4.50
No. 150a (1)	7.00	7.00
No. 587a (1)	4.25	4.25
No. 541a (1)	2.50	2.50
Set total (16) Stamps	66.00	66.25

Royal Family Birthday, Anniversary

CD347

Queen Elizabeth II, 65th birthday, Charles and Diana, 10th wedding anniversary: Various photographs of Queen Elizabeth II, Prince Philip, Prince Charles, Princess Diana and their sons William and Henry.

1991

Antigua 1446-1455
Barbuda 1229-1238
Dominica 1328-1337
Gambia 1080-1089
Grenada 2006-2015
Grenada Grenadines 1331-1340
Guyana 2440-2451
Lesotho 871-875
Maldive Islands 1533-1542
Nevis 666-675
St. Vincent 1485-1494
St. Vincent Grenadines 769-778
Sierra Leone 1387-1396
Turks & Caicos Islands 913-922
Uganda 918-927

Nos. 1446-1455 (10)	21.95	20.30
Nos. 1229-1238 (10)	125.00	119.50
Nos. 1328-1337 (10)	30.20	30.20
Nos. 1080-1089 (10)	24.65	24.40
Nos. 2006-2015 (10)	25.45	22.10
Nos. 1331-1340 (10)	23.85	23.35
Nos. 2440-2451 (12)	21.40	21.15
Nos. 871-875 (5)	13.55	13.55
Nos. 1533-1542 (10)	28.10	28.10
Nos. 666-675 (10)	25.65	25.65
Nos. 1485-1494 (10)	26.75	25.90
Nos. 769-778 (10)	25.40	25.40
Nos. 1387-1396 (10)	26.55	26.55
Nos. 913-922 (10)	31.65	30.00
Nos. 918-927 (10)	26.60	26.60
Set total (147) Stamps	476.75	462.75

Queen Elizabeth II's Accession to the Throne, 40th Anniv.

CD348

Various photographs of Queen Elizabeth II with local Scenes.

1992

Antigua 1513-1518
Barbuda 1306-1311
Dominica 1414-1419
Gambia 1172-1177
Grenada 2047-2052
Grenada Grenadines 1368-1373
Lesotho 881-885
Maldive Islands 1637-1642
Nevis 702-707
St. Vincent 1582-1587
St. Vincent Grenadines 829-834
Sierra Leone 1482-1487
Turks and Caicos Islands 978-987
Uganda 990-995
Virgin Islands 742-746

Nos. 1513-1518 (6)	16.00	14.10
Nos. 1306-1311 (6)	125.25	83.65
Nos. 1414-1419 (6)	12.50	12.50
Nos. 1172-1177 (6)	16.60	16.35
Nos. 2047-2052 (6)	15.95	15.95
Nos. 1368-1373 (6)	17.00	15.35
Nos. 881-885 (5)	11.90	11.90
Nos. 1637-1642 (6)	17.55	17.55
Nos. 702-707 (6)	13.80	13.80
Nos. 1582-1587 (6)	14.40	14.40
Nos. 829-834 (6)	19.65	19.65
Nos. 1482-1487 (6)	22.50	22.50
Nos. 913-922 (10)	31.65	30.00
Nos. 990-995 (6)	19.50	19.50
Nos. 742-746 (5)	15.50	15.50
Set total (92) Stamps	369.75	322.70

CD349

1992

Ascension 531-535
Bahamas 744-748
Bermuda 623-627
British Indian Ocean Territory 119-123
Cayman Islands 648-652
Falkland Islands 549-553
Gibraltar 605-609
Hong Kong 619-623
Kenya 563-567
Kiribati 582-586
Pitcairn Islands 362-366
St. Helena 570-574
St. Kitts 332-336
Samoa 805-809
Seychelles 734-738
Zil Elwannyen Sesel 183-187
Solomon Islands 708-712
South Georgia 157-161
Tristan da Cunha 508-512
Vanuatu 555-559
Zambia 561-565

Nos. 531-535 (5)	6.35	6.35
Nos. 744-748 (5)	6.90	4.70
Nos. 623-627 (5)	8.20	7.30
Nos. 119-123 (5)	24.75	*21.00*
Nos. 648-652 (5)	7.60	7.10
Nos. 549-553 (5)	6.80	8.20
Nos. 605-609 (5)	5.15	*5.50*
Nos. 619-623 (5)	5.65	2.65
Nos. 563-567 (5)	9.10	9.10
Nos. 582-586 (5)	3.85	3.85
Nos. 362-366 (5)	5.35	5.35
Nos. 570-574 (5)	5.70	5.70
Nos. 332-336 (5)	6.60	5.50
Nos. 805-809 (5)	8.10	6.15
Nos. 734-738 (5)	10.80	10.80
Nos. 183-187 (5)	9.40	9.40
Nos. 708-712 (5)	7.95	7.30
Nos. 157-161 (5)	5.85	5.75
Nos. 508-512 (5)	8.75	8.30
Nos. 555-559 (5)	3.65	3.65
Nos. 561-565 (5)	5.60	5.60
Set total (105) Stamps	162.10	149.25

Royal Air Force, 75th Anniversary

CD350

1993

Ascension 557-561
Bahamas 771-775
Barbados 842-846
Belize 1003-1008
Bermuda 648-651
British Indian Ocean Territory 136-140
Falkland Is. 573-577
Fiji 687-691
Montserrat 830-834
St. Kitts 351-355

Nos. 557-561 (5)	16.70	14.85
Nos. 771-775 (5)	26.00	22.20
Nos. 842-846 (5)	13.65	12.35
Nos. 1003-1008 (6)	19.40	18.70
Nos. 648-651 (4)	10.50	9.95
Nos. 136-140 (5)	17.50	17.50
Nos. 573-577 (5)	11.25	11.25
Nos. 687-691 (5)	18.95	18.95
Nos. 830-834 (5)	14.35	14.35
Nos. 351-355 (5)	24.45	23.95
Set total (50) Stamps	172.75	164.05

Royal Air Force, 80th Anniv.

Design CD350 Re-inscribed

1998

Ascension 697-701
Bahamas 907-911
British Indian Ocean Terr 198-202
Cayman Islands 754-758
Fiji 814-818
Gibraltar 755-759
Samoa 957-961
Turks & Caicos Islands 1258-1265
Tuvalu 763-767
Virgin Islands 879-883

Nos. 697-701 (5)	17.35	17.35
Nos. 907-911 (5)	14.25	13.55
Nos. 136-140 (5)	17.50	17.50
Nos. 754-758 (5)	15.75	15.75
Nos. 814-818 (5)	15.50	15.50
Nos. 755-759 (5)	9.70	9.70
Nos. 957-961 (5)	16.70	15.90
Nos. 1258-1265 (2)	32.00	32.00
Nos. 763-767 (5)	9.75	9.75
Nos. 879-883 (5)	17.00	17.00
Set total (47) Stamps	165.50	164.00

End of World War II, 50th Anniv.

CD351

CD352

1995

Ascension 613-617
Bahamas 824-828
Barbados 891-895
Belize 1047-1050
British Indian Ocean Territory 163-167
Cayman Islands 704-708
Falkland Islands 634-638
Fiji 720-724
Kiribati 662-668
Liberia 1175-1179
Mauritius 803-805
St. Helena 646-654
St. Kitts 389-393
St. Lucia 1018-1022
Samoa 890-894
Solomon Islands 799-803
South Georgia 198-200
Tristan da Cunha 562-566

Nos. 613-617 (5)	21.50	21.50
Nos. 824-828 (5)	22.00	18.70
Nos. 891-895 (5)	14.20	11.90
Nos. 1047-1050 (4)	7.45	6.75
Nos. 163-167 (5)	16.25	16.25

Nos. 704-708 (5)	18.15	14.45
Nos. 634-638 (5)	17.90	17.40
Nos. 720-724 (5)	21.35	21.35
Nos. 662-668 (7)	16.30	16.30
Nos. 1175-1179 (5)	15.25	11.15
Nos. 803-805 (3)	7.50	7.50
Nos. 646-654 (9)	26.10	26.10
Nos. 389-393 (5)	13.60	13.60
Nos. 1018-1022 (5)	14.25	11.15
Nos. 890-894 (5)	14.25	13.50
Nos. 799-803 (5)	17.50	17.50
Nos. 198-200 (3)	14.00	14.00
Nos. 562-566 (5)	20.10	20.10
Set total (91) Stamps	297.65	279.20

UN, 50th Anniv.

CD353

1995

Bahamas 839-842
Barbados 901-904
Belize 1055-1058
Jamaica 847-851
Liberia 1187-1190
Mauritius 813-816
Pitcairn Islands 436-439
St. Kitts 398-401
St. Lucia 1023-1026
Samoa 900-903
Tristan da Cunha 568-571
Virgin Islands 807-810

Nos. 839-842 (4)	8.00	7.05
Nos. 901-904 (4)	7.00	5.75
Nos. 1055-1058 (4)	5.70	5.60
Nos. 847-851 (5)	5.40	5.45
Nos. 1187-1190 (4)	9.65	9.65
Nos. 813-816 (4)	3.90	3.90
Nos. 436-439 (4)	8.15	8.15
Nos. 398-401 (4)	6.15	6.15
Nos. 1023-1026 (4)	7.50	7.25
Nos. 900-903 (4)	9.35	8.20
Nos. 568-571 (4)	13.50	13.50
Nos. 807-810 (4)	9.45	9.45
Set total (49) Stamps	93.75	90.10

Queen Elizabeth, 70th Birthday

CD354

1996

Ascension 632-635
British Antarctic Territory 240-243
British Indian Ocean Territory 176-180
Falkland Islands 653-657
Pitcairn Islands 446-449
St. Helena 672-676
Samoa 912-916
Tokelau 223-227
Tristan da Cunha 576-579
Virgin Islands 824-828

Nos. 632-635 (4)	5.90	5.90
Nos. 240-243 (4)	10.50	8.90
Nos. 176-180 (5)	11.50	11.50
Nos. 653-657 (5)	14.35	11.90
Nos. 446-449 (4)	8.60	8.60
Nos. 672-676 (5)	12.70	12.70
Nos. 912-916 (5)	11.50	11.50
Nos. 223-227 (5)	11.35	11.35
Nos. 576-579 (4)	8.35	8.35
Nos. 824-828 (5)	12.30	12.30
Set total (46) Stamps	107.05	103.00

Diana, Princess of Wales (1961-97)

CD355

1998

Ascension 696
Bahamas 901A-902
Barbados 950
Belize 1091
Bermuda 753
Botswana 659-663
British Antarctic Territory 258
British Indian Ocean Terr. 197
Cayman Islands 752A-753
Falkland Islands 694
Fiji 819-820
Gibraltar 754
Kiribati 719A-720
Namibia 909
Niue 706
Norfolk Island 644-645
Papua New Guinea 937
Pitcairn Islands 487
St. Helena 711
St. Kitts 437A-438
Samoa 955A-956
Seycelles 802
Solomon Islands 866-867
South Georgia 220
Tokelau 252B-253
Tonga 980
Niuafo'ou 201
Tristan da Cunha 618
Tuvalu 762
Vanuatu 718A-719
Virgin Islands 878

No. 696 (1)	5.50	5.50
Nos. 901A-902 (2)	5.30	5.30
No. 950 (1)	5.00	5.00
No. 1091 (1)	5.50	5.50
No. 753 (1)	5.50	5.50
Nos. 659-663 (5)	10.25	10.10
No. 258 (1)	6.25	6.25
No. 197 (1)	6.50	6.50
Nos. 752A-753 (3)	7.75	7.75
No. 694 (1)	4.75	4.75
Nos. 819-820 (2)	6.00	6.00
No. 754 (1)	4.75	4.75
Nos. 719A-720 (2)	4.85	4.85
No. 909 (1)	1.90	1.90
No. 706 (1)	5.50	5.50
Nos. 644-645 (2)	5.25	5.25
No. 937 (1)	6.50	6.50
No. 487 (1)	4.75	4.75
No. 711 (1)	4.25	4.25
Nos. 437A-438 (2)	5.15	5.15
Nos. 955A-956 (2)	7.00	7.00
No. 802 (1)	6.25	6.25
Nos. 866-867 (2)	6.90	6.90
No. 220 (1)	5.25	5.25
Nos. 252B-253 (2)	6.75	6.75
No. 980 (1)	5.75	5.75
No. 201 (1)	7.75	7.75
No. 618 (1)	5.00	5.00
No. 762 (1)	4.00	4.00
Nos. 718A-719 (2)	8.00	8.00
No. 878 (1)	5.50	5.50
Set total (46) Stamps	179.35	179.20

Wedding of Prince Edward and Sophie Rhys-Jones

CD356

1999

Ascension 729-730
Cayman Islands 775-776
Falkland Islands 729-730
Pitcairn Islands 505-506
St. Helena 733-734
Samoa 971-972
Tristan da Cunha 636-637
Virgin Islands 908-909

Nos. 729-730 (2)	5.90	5.90
Nos. 775-776 (2)	5.50	5.50
Nos. 729-730 (2)	15.00	15.00
Nos. 505-506 (2)	7.00	7.00
Nos. 733-734 (2)	5.00	5.00
Nos. 971-972 (2)	5.00	5.00
Nos. 636-637 (2)	7.50	7.50
Nos. 908-909 (2)	8.30	8.30
Set total (16) Stamps	59.20	59.20

1st Manned Moon Landing, 30th Anniv.

CD357

1999

Ascension 731-735
Bahamas 942-946
Barbados 967-971
Bermuda 778
Cayman Islands 777-781
Fiji 853-857
Jamaica 889-893
Kirbati 746-750
Nauru 465-469
St. Kitts 460-464
Samoa 973-977
Solomon Islands 875-879
Tuvalu 800-804
Virgin Islands 910-914

Nos. 731-735 (5)	13.90	13.90
Nos. 942-946 (5)	14.10	14.10
Nos. 967-971 (5)	8.65	7.75
No. 778 (1)	8.00	8.00
Nos. 777-781 (5)	10.30	10.30
Nos. 853-857 (5)	10.40	10.40
Nos. 889-893 (5)	8.30	7.18
Nos. 746-750 (5)	8.85	8.85
Nos. 465-469 (5)	8.90	10.15
Nos. 460-464 (5)	12.00	12.00
Nos. 973-977 (5)	13.45	13.30
Nos. 875-879 (5)	10.00	9.85
Nos. 800-804 (5)	7.45	7.45
Nos. 910-914 (5)	15.00	15.00
Set total (66) Stamps	149.30	148.23

Queen Mother's Century

CD358

1999

Ascension 736-740
Bahamas 951-955
Cayman Islands 782-786
Falkland Islands 734-738
Fiji 858-862
Norfolk Island 688-692
St. Helena 740-744
Samoa 978-982
Solomon Islands 880-884
South Georgia 231-235
Tristan da Cunha 638-642
Tuvalu 805-809

Nos. 736-740 (5)	17.00	17.00
Nos. 951-955 (5)	14.00	12.90
Nos. 782-786 (5)	9.15	9.15
Nos. 734-738 (5)	30.75	27.75
Nos. 858-862 (5)	15.00	15.00
Nos. 688-692 (5)	10.30	10.30
Nos. 740-744 (5)	16.15	16.15
Nos. 978-982 (5)	12.50	12.10
Nos. 880-884 (5)	10.00	9.45
Nos. 231-235 (5)	30.25	29.75
Nos. 638-642 (5)	18.00	18.00
Nos. 805-809 (5)	8.65	8.65
Set total (60) Stamps	191.75	186.20

Prince William, 18th Birthday

CD359

2000

Ascension 755-759
Cayman Islands 797-801
Falkland Islands 762-766
Fiji 889-893
South Georgia 257-261
Tristan da Cunha 664-668
Virgin Islands 925-929

Nos. 755-759 (5)	17.75	17.75
Nos. 797-801 (5)	13.05	12.75
Nos. 762-766 (5)	27.15	23.75
Nos. 889-893 (5)	14.00	14.00
Nos. 257-261 (5)	29.00	29.00
Nos. 664-668 (5)	21.50	21.50
Nos. 925-929 (5)	14.75	14.75
Set total (35) Stamps	137.20	133.50

Reign of Queen Elizabeth II, 50th Anniv.

CD360

2002

Ascension 790-794
Bahamas 1033-1037
Barbados 1019-1023
Belize 1152-1156
Bermuda 822-826
British Antarctic Territory 307-311
British Indian Ocean Territory 239-243
Cayman Islands 844-848
Falkland Islands 804-808
Gibraltar 896-900
Jamaica 952-956
Nauru 491-495
Norfolk Island 758-762
Papua New Guinea 1019-1023
Pitcairn Islands 552
St. Helena 788-792
St. Lucia 1146-1150
Solomon Islands 931-935
South Georgia 274-278
Swaziland 706-710
Tokelau 302-306
Tonga 1059
Niuafo'ou 239
Tristan da Cunha 706-710
Virgin Islands 967-971

Nos. 790-794 (5)	16.25	16.25
Nos. 1033-1037 (5)	15.75	15.75
Nos. 1019-1023 (5)	13.15	13.15
Nos. 1152-1156 (5)	15.50	15.15
Nos. 822-826 (5)	18.50	18.50
Nos. 307-311 (5)	25.00	25.00
Nos. 239-243 (5)	22.00	22.00
Nos. 844-848 (5)	14.25	14.25
Nos. 804-808 (5)	23.50	22.50
Nos. 896-900 (5)	6.65	6.65
Nos. 952-956 (5)	16.65	16.65
Nos. 491-495 (5)	18.75	18.75
Nos. 758-762 (5)	19.50	19.50
Nos. 1019-1023 (5)	14.50	14.50
No. 552 (1)	9.25	9.25
Nos. 788-792 (5)	19.75	19.75
Nos. 1146-1150 (5)	12.25	12.25
Nos. 931-935 (5)	16.00	16.00
Nos. 274-278 (5)	28.50	28.50
Nos. 706-710 (5)	12.75	12.75
Nos. 302-306 (5)	17.00	17.00
No. 1059 (1)	8.00	8.00
No. 239 (1)	7.00	7.00
Nos. 706-710 (5)	18.50	18.50
Nos. 967-971 (5)	19.00	19.00
Set total (113) Stamps	407.95	406.60

Queen Mother Elizabeth (1900-2002)

CD361

2002

Ascension 799-801
Bahamas 1044-1046
Bermuda 834-836
British Antarctic Territory 312-314
British Indian Ocean Territory 245-247
Cayman Islands 857-861
Falkland Islands 812-816
Nauru 499-501
Pitcairn Islands 561-565
St. Helena 808-812
St. Lucia 1155-1159
Seychelles 830
Solomon Islands 945-947
South Georgia 281-285
Tokelau 312-314
Tristan da Cunha 715-717
Virgin Islands 979-983

Nos. 799-801 (3)	9.75	9.75
Nos. 1044-1046 (3)	9.35	9.35
Nos. 834-836 (3)	12.50	12.50
Nos. 312-314 (3)	19.25	19.25
Nos. 245-247 (3)	19.50	19.50
Nos. 857-861 (5)	15.00	15.00
Nos. 812-816 (5)	31.50	31.50
Nos. 499-501 (3)	16.00	16.00
Nos. 561-565 (5)	15.25	15.25
Nos. 808-812 (5)	12.00	12.00
Nos. 1155-1159 (5)	13.00	13.00
No. 830 (1)	6.50	6.50
Nos. 945-947 (3)	11.00	11.00
Nos. 281-285 (5)	20.00	20.00
Nos. 312-314 (3)	14.25	13.75
Nos. 715-717 (3)	16.25	16.25
Nos. 979-983 (5)	26.50	26.50
Set total (63) Stamps	267.60	267.10

Head of Queen Elizabeth II

CD362

2003

Ascension 822
Bermuda 865
British Antarctic Territory 322
British Indian Ocean Territory 261
Cayman Islands 878
Falkland Islands 828
St. Helena 820
South Georgia 294
Tristan da Cunha 731
Virgin Islands 1003

No. 822 (1)	13.50	13.50
No. 865 (1)	55.00	55.00
No. 322 (1)	10.00	10.00
No. 261 (1)	12.50	12.50
No. 878 (1)	17.00	17.00
No. 828 (1)	10.00	10.00
No. 820 (1)	9.00	9.00
No. 294 (1)	9.00	9.00
No. 731 (1)	10.00	10.00
No. 1003 (1)	10.00	10.00
Set total (10) Stamps	156.00	156.00

Coronation of Queen Elizabeth II, 50th Anniv.

CD363

2003

Ascension 823-825
Bahamas 1073-1075
Bermuda 866-868
British Antarctic Territory 323-325
British Indian Ocean Territory 262-264
Cayman Islands 879-881
Jamaica 970-972
Kiribati 825-827
Pitcairn Islands 577-581
St. Helena 821-823
St. Lucia 1171-1173
Tokelau 320-322
Tristan da Cunha 732-734
Virgin Islands 1004-1006

Nos. 823-825 (3)	13.50	13.50
Nos. 1073-1075 (3)	13.00	13.00
Nos. 866-868 (3)	14.25	14.25
Nos. 323-325 (3)	26.00	26.00
Nos. 262-264 (3)	31.00	31.00
Nos. 879-881 (3)	20.25	20.25
Nos. 970-972 (3)	10.00	10.00
Nos. 825-827 (3)	13.50	13.50
Nos. 577-581 (5)	14.40	14.40
Nos. 821-823 (3)	7.25	7.25
Nos. 1171-1173 (3)	8.75	8.75
Nos. 320-322 (3)	20.00	20.00
Nos. 732-734 (3)	16.75	16.75
Nos. 1004-1006 (3)	25.00	25.00
Set total (44) Stamps	233.65	233.65

Prince William, 21st Birthday

CD364

2003

Ascension 826
British Indian Ocean Territory 265
Cayman Islands 882-884
Falkland Islands 829
South Georgia 295
Tokelau 323
Tristan da Cunha 735
Virgin Islands 1007-1009

No. 826 (1)	7.50	7.50
No. 265 (1)	9.00	9.00
Nos. 882-884 (3)	7.65	7.65
No. 829 (1)	14.50	14.50
No. 295 (1)	9.00	9.00
No. 323 (1)	7.25	7.25
No. 735 (1)	6.00	6.00
Nos. 1007-1009 (3)	10.00	10.00
Set total (12) Stamps	70.90	70.90

2016 Minkus Supplements

Whether you're updating your album or decided to start collecting a new country, Minkus supplements are the way to go. Heavy acid-free paper and the use of Scott numbers for easy identification makes collecting easy.

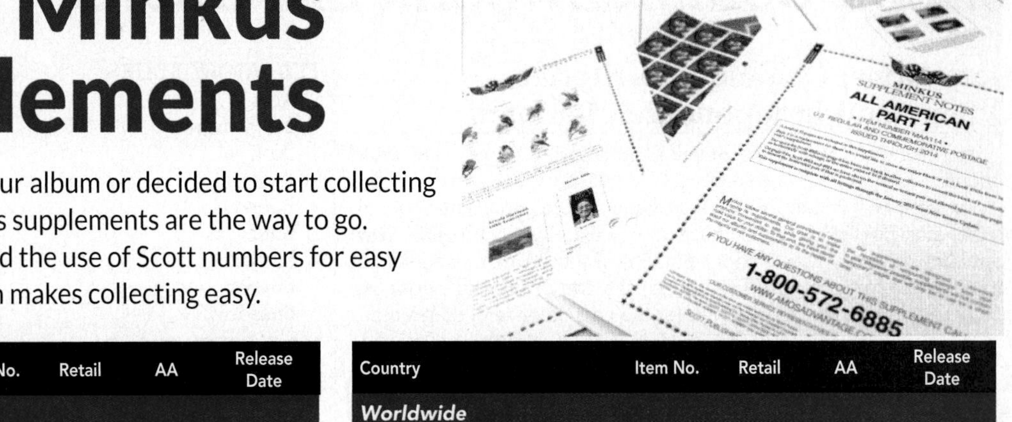

Country	Item No.	Retail	AA	Release Date
All-American				
All-American Part 1: US Reg Issues & Commems	MAA116	22.99	19.99	February
All-American Part 3: United Nations	MAA316	25.99	21.99	March
All-American Part 4: US Booklet Panes	MAA416	16.99	13.99	April
All-American Part 5: US Sheetlets	MAA516	22.99	19.99	April
All-American Part 6: US Plate Number Coils	MAA616	11.99	9.99	January
U.S. & U.N 3-Ring				
U.S. Booklet Panes	MUBK16	19.99	16.99	April
U.S. Commemoratives	MUSC16	16.99	13.99	February
U.S. Plate Blocks	MSPB16	22.99	19.99	April
U.S. Plate Number Coils	MPNC16	11.99	9.99	January
U.S. Regular Issues	MUSR16	16.99	13.99	February
U.S. Sheetlets	MSH16	22.99	19.99	April
U.N. Imprint Blocks	MUIB16	22.99	19.99	March
U.N. Postal Stationery	MNPS16	11.99	9.99	March
U.N. Singles	MUN16	25.99	21.99	March
Worldwide				
Andorra - French & Spanish	MAND16	11.99	9.99	July
Australia	MBO116	22.99	19.99	September
Austria	MAU16	19.99	16.99	May
Belgium	MBL16	22.99	19.99	August
Dependencies of Australia	MBO216	22.99	19.99	September
Brazil	MBR16	19.99	16.99	September
Canada	MCA16	34.99	29.99	May
Cyprus	MBE516	16.99	13.99	May
Czech Republic & Slovakia	MCZ16	22.99	19.99	August
Denmark/Faroe Islands/ Greenland/Iceland	MSC116	28.99	24.99	June
Finland	MSC216	22.99	19.99	June
France	MFR16	34.99	29.99	May
Germany	MGM16	16.99	13.99	May
Gibraltar	MBE416	16.99	13.99	May

Country	Item No.	Retail	AA	Release Date
Worldwide				
Great Britian, Ireland	MBE116	28.99	24.99	May
Greece	MGR16	22.99	19.99	June
Guernsey, Jersey, Isle of Man	MBE216	37.99	32.99	May
Hong Kong	MBA216	22.99	19.99	May
Hungary	MHU16	22.99	19.99	August
India	MIN116	22.99	19.99	July
Ireland	MIR16	16.99	13.99	May
Israel Singles	MIS16	16.99	13.99	August
Israel Tab Singles	MIST16	19.99	16.99	August
Italy	MIT16	22.99	19.99	July
Japan	MJA16	45.99	39.99	July
Latvia, Lithuania, Estonia	MSC516	19.99	16.99	August
Liechtenstein	MLT16	16.99	13.99	June
Luxembourg	MLX16	11.99	9.99	August
Malta	MBE316	16.99	13.99	May
Mexico	MMX16	19.99	16.99	September
Monaco	MMO16	16.99	13.99	May
Netherlands	MNE16	37.99	32.99	August
New Zealand	MBO316	22.99	19.99	September
Norway	MSC316	11.99	9.99	June
People's Republic of China	MPRC16	22.99	19.99	July
Poland	MPO16	19.99	16.99	August
Portugal	MPT16	22.99	19.99	July
Republic of China-Taiwan	MCT16	22.99	19.99	July
Russia	MRU16	34.99	29.99	September
San Marino	MSM16	11.99	9.99	July
Spain	MSP16	22.99	19.99	July
Sweden	MSC416	16.99	13.99	September
Switzerland	MSWZ16	16.99	13.99	June
Vatican City	MVA16	11.99	9.99	July
Global				
Global Part 1 (Countries U.S. & A-K)	MGL117	160.99	140.00	December
Global Part 2 (Countries L-Z)	MGL217	160.99	140.00	December

Visit AmosAdvantage.com

or Call 1-800-572-6885

Outside U.S. & Canada 937-498-0800
Mail to: P.O. Box 4129, Sidney OH 45365

SHIPPING & HANDLING: United States: order total $0-$10.00 charged $3.99 shipping. United States - order total $10.01-$79.99 charged $7.99 shipping. United States - order total $80.00 or more charged 10% of order total for shipping. Maximum Freight Charge $45.00. Canada: 20% of order total. Minimum charge $19.99 Maximum charge $200.00. Foreign orders are shipped via FedExl Intl. or USPS and billed actual freight.
ORDERING INFORMATION: *AA prices apply to paid subscribers of Amos Media titles, or orders placed online. Prices, terms and product availability subject to change. Shipping and handling rates will apply.

British Commonwealth of Nations

Dominions, Colonies, Territories, Offices and Independent Members

Comprising stamps of the British Commonwealth and associated nations.

A strict observance of technicalities would bar some or all of the stamps listed under Burma, Ireland, Kuwait, Nepal, New Republic, Orange Free State, Samoa, South Africa, South-West Africa, Stellaland, Sudan, Swaziland, the two Transvaal Republics and others but these are included for the convenience of collectors.

1. Great Britain

Great Britain: Including England, Scotland, Wales and Northern Ireland.

2. The Dominions, Present and Past

AUSTRALIA

The Commonwealth of Australia was proclaimed on January 1, 1901. It consists of six former colonies as follows:

New South Wales
Queensland
South Australia
Victoria
Tasmania
Western Australia

The following islands and territories are, or have been, administered by Australia: Australian Antarctic Territory, Christmas Island, Cocos (Keeling) Islands, Nauru, New Guinea, Norfolk Island, Papua.

CANADA

The Dominion of Canada was created by the British North America Act in 1867. The following provinces were former sepa- rate colonies and issued postage stamps:

British Columbia and Vancouver Island
New Brunswick
Newfoundland
Nova Scotia
Prince Edward Island

FIJI

The colony of Fiji became an independent nation with dominion status on Oct. 10, 1970.

GHANA

This state came into existence Mar. 6, 1957, with dominion status. It consists of the former colony of the Gold Coast and the Trusteeship Territory of Togoland. Ghana became a republic July 1, 1960.

INDIA

The Republic of India was inaugurated on January 26, 1950. It succeeded the Dominion of India which was proclaimed August 15, 1947, when the former Empire of India was divided into Pakistan and the Union of India. The Republic is composed of about 40 predominantly Hindu states of three classes: governor's provinces, chief commissioner's provinces and princely states. India also has various territories, such as the Andaman and Nicobar Islands.

The old Empire of India was a federation of British India and the native states. The more important princely states were autonomous. Of the more than 700 Indian states, these 43 are familiar names to philatelists because of their postage stamps.

CONVENTION STATES

Chamba
Faridkot
Gwalior
Jhind
Nabha
Patiala

FEUDATORY STATES

Alwar
Bahawalpur
Bamra
Barwani
Bhopal
Bhor
Bijawar
Bundi
Bussahir
Charkhari
Cochin
Dhar
Dungarpur
Duttia
Faridkot (1879-85)
Hyderabad
Idar
Indore
Jaipur
Jammu
Jammu and Kashmir
Jasdan
Jhalawar
Jhind (1875-76)
Kashmir
Kishangarh
Kotah
Las Bela
Morvi
Nandgaon
Nowanuggur
Orchha
Poonch
Rajasthan
Rajpeepla
Sirmur
Soruth
Tonk
Travancore
Wadhwan

NEW ZEALAND

Became a dominion on September 26, 1907. The following islands and territories are, or have been, administered by New Zealand:

Aitutaki
Cook Islands (Rarotonga)
Niue
Penrhyn
Ross Dependency
Samoa (Western Samoa)
Tokelau Islands

PAKISTAN

The Republic of Pakistan was proclaimed March 23, 1956. It succeeded the Dominion which was proclaimed August 15, 1947. It is made up of all or part of several Moslem provinces and various districts of the former Empire of India, including Bahawalpur and Las Bela. Pakistan withdrew from the Commonwealth in 1972.

SOUTH AFRICA

Under the terms of the South African Act (1909) the self-governing colonies of Cape of Good Hope, Natal, Orange River Colony and Transvaal united on May 31, 1910, to form the Union of South Africa. It became an independent republic May 3, 1961.

Under the terms of the Treaty of Versailles, South-West Africa, formerly German South-West Africa, was mandated to the Union of South Africa.

SRI LANKA (CEYLON)

The Dominion of Ceylon was proclaimed February 4, 1948. The island had been a Crown Colony from 1802 until then. On May 22, 1972, Ceylon became the Republic of Sri Lanka.

3. Colonies, Past and Present; Controlled Territory and Independent Members of the Commonwealth

Aden
Aitutaki
Anguilla
Antigua
Ascension
Bahamas
Bahrain
Bangladesh
Barbados
Barbuda
Basutoland
Batum
Bechuanaland
Bechuanaland Prot.
Belize
Bermuda
Botswana
British Antarctic Territory
British Central Africa
British Columbia and Vancouver Island
British East Africa
British Guiana

British Honduras
British Indian Ocean Territory
British New Guinea
British Solomon Islands
British Somaliland
Brunei
Burma
Bushire
Cameroons
Cape of Good Hope
Cayman Islands
Christmas Island
Cocos (Keeling) Islands
Cook Islands
Crete,
 British Administration
Cyprus
Dominica
East Africa & Uganda
 Protectorates
Egypt
Falkland Islands
Fiji
Gambia
German East Africa
Gibraltar
Gilbert Islands
Gilbert & Ellice Islands
Gold Coast
Grenada
Griqualand West
Guernsey
Guyana
Heligoland
Hong Kong
Indian Native States
 (see India)
Ionian Islands
Jamaica
Jersey
Kenya
Kenya, Uganda & Tanzania
Kuwait
Labuan
Lagos
Leeward Islands
Lesotho
Madagascar
Malawi
Malaya
 Federated Malay States
 Johore
 Kedah
 Kelantan
 Malacca
 Negri Sembilan
 Pahang
 Penang
 Perak
 Perlis
 Selangor
 Singapore
 Sungei Ujong
 Trengganu
Malaysia
Maldive Islands
Malta
Man, Isle of
Mauritius
Mesopotamia
Montserrat
Muscat
Namibia
Natal
Nauru
Nevis
New Britain
New Brunswick
Newfoundland
New Guinea
New Hebrides
New Republic
New South Wales
Niger Coast Protectorate
Nigeria
Niue
Norfolk Island
North Borneo
Northern Nigeria
Northern Rhodesia
North West Pacific Islands
Nova Scotia
Nyasaland Protectorate
Oman
Orange River Colony
Palestine
Papua New Guinea
Penrhyn Island
Pitcairn Islands
Prince Edward Island
Queensland
Rhodesia
Rhodesia & Nyasaland
Ross Dependency
Sabah
St. Christopher
St. Helena
St. Kitts
St. Kitts-Nevis-Anguilla
St. Lucia
St. Vincent
Samoa
Sarawak
Seychelles
Sierra Leone
Solomon Islands
Somaliland Protectorate
South Arabia
South Australia
South Georgia
Southern Nigeria
Southern Rhodesia
South-West Africa
Stellaland
Straits Settlements
Sudan
Swaziland
Tanganyika
Tanzania
Tasmania
Tobago
Togo
Tokelau Islands
Tonga
Transvaal
Trinidad
Trinidad and Tobago
Tristan da Cunha
Trucial States
Turks and Caicos
Turks Islands
Tuvalu
Uganda
United Arab Emirates
Victoria
Virgin Islands
Western Australia
Zambia
Zanzibar
Zululand

POST OFFICES IN FOREIGN COUNTRIES

Africa
 East Africa Forces
 Middle East Forces
Bangkok
China
Morocco
Turkish Empire

Colonies, Former Colonies, Offices, Territories Controlled by Parent States

Belgium

Belgian Congo
Ruanda-Urundi

Denmark

Danish West Indies
Faroe Islands
Greenland
Iceland

Finland

Aland Islands

France

COLONIES PAST AND PRESENT, CONTROLLED TERRITORIES

Afars & Issas, Territory of
Alaouites
Alexandretta
Algeria
Alsace & Lorraine
Anjouan
Annam & Tonkin
Benin
Cambodia (Khmer)
Cameroun
Castellorizo
Chad
Cilicia
Cochin China
Comoro Islands
Dahomey
Diego Suarez
Djibouti (Somali Coast)
Fezzan
French Congo
French Equatorial Africa
French Guiana
French Guinea
French India
French Morocco
French Polynesia (Oceania)
French Southern & Antarctic Territories
French Sudan
French West Africa
Gabon
Germany
Ghadames
Grand Comoro
Guadeloupe
Indo-China
Inini
Ivory Coast
Laos
Latakia
Lebanon
Madagascar
Martinique
Mauritania
Mayotte
Memel
Middle Congo
Moheli
New Caledonia
New Hebrides
Niger Territory
Nossi-Be
Obock
Reunion
Rouad, Ile
Ste.-Marie de Madagascar
St. Pierre & Miquelon
Senegal
Senegambia & Niger
Somali Coast
Syria
Tahiti
Togo
Tunisia
Ubangi-Shari
Upper Senegal & Niger
Upper Volta
Viet Nam
Wallis & Futuna Islands

POST OFFICES IN FOREIGN COUNTRIES

China
Crete
Egypt
Turkish Empire
Zanzibar

Germany

EARLY STATES

Baden
Bavaria
Bergedorf
Bremen
Brunswick
Hamburg
Hanover
Lubeck
Mecklenburg-Schwerin
Mecklenburg-Strelitz
Oldenburg
Prussia
Saxony
Schleswig-Holstein
Wurttemberg

FORMER COLONIES

Cameroun (Kamerun)
Caroline Islands
German East Africa
German New Guinea
German South-West Africa
Kiauchau
Mariana Islands
Marshall Islands
Samoa
Togo

Italy

EARLY STATES

Modena
Parma
Romagna
Roman States
Sardinia
Tuscany
Two Sicilies
  Naples
  Neapolitan Provinces
  Sicily

FORMER COLONIES, CONTROLLED TERRITORIES, OCCUPATION AREAS

Aegean Islands
  Calimno (Calino)
  Caso
  Cos (Coo)
  Karki (Carchi)
  Leros (Lero)
  Lipso
  Nisiros (Nisiro)
  Patmos (Patmo)
  Piscopi
  Rodi (Rhodes)
  Scarpanto
  Simi
  Stampalia
Castellorizo
Corfu
Cyrenaica
Eritrea
Ethiopia (Abyssinia)
Fiume
Ionian Islands
  Cephalonia
  Ithaca
  Paxos
Italian East Africa
Libya
Oltre Giuba
Saseno
Somalia (Italian Somaliland)
Tripolitania

POST OFFICES IN FOREIGN COUNTRIES

"ESTERO"*
Austria
China
  Peking
  Tientsin
Crete
Tripoli
Turkish Empire
  Constantinople
  Durazzo
  Janina
Jerusalem
Salonika
Scutari
Smyrna
Valona

*Stamps overprinted "ESTERO" were used in various parts of the world.

Netherlands

Aruba
Caribbean Netherlands
Curacao
Netherlands Antilles (Curacao)
Netherlands Indies
Netherlands New Guinea
St. Martin
Surinam (Dutch Guiana)

Portugal

COLONIES PAST AND PRESENT, CONTROLLED TERRITORIES

Angola
Angra
Azores
Cape Verde
Funchal
Horta
Inhambane
Kionga
Lourenco Marques
Macao
Madeira
Mozambique
Mozambique Co.
Nyassa
Ponta Delgada
Portuguese Africa
Portuguese Congo
Portuguese Guinea
Portuguese India
Quelimane
St. Thomas & Prince Islands
Tete
Timor
Zambezia

Russia

ALLIED TERRITORIES AND REPUBLICS, OCCUPATION AREAS

Armenia
Aunus (Olonets)
Azerbaijan
Batum
Estonia
Far Eastern Republic
Georgia
Karelia
Latvia
Lithuania
North Ingermanland
Ostland
Russian Turkestan
Siberia
South Russia
Tannu Tuva
Transcaucasian Fed. Republics
Ukraine
Wenden (Livonia)
Western Ukraine

Spain

COLONIES PAST AND PRESENT, CONTROLLED TERRITORIES

Aguera, La
Cape Juby
Cuba
Elobey, Annobon & Corisco
Fernando Po
Ifni
Mariana Islands
Philippines
Puerto Rico
Rio de Oro
Rio Muni
Spanish Guinea
Spanish Morocco
Spanish Sahara
Spanish West Africa

POST OFFICES IN FOREIGN COUNTRIES

Morocco
Tangier
Tetuan

Dies of British Colonial Stamps

DIE A:

1. The lines in the groundwork vary in thickness and are not uniformly straight.

2. The seventh and eighth lines from the top, in the groundwork, converge where they meet the head.

3. There is a small dash in the upper part of the second jewel in the band of the crown.

4. The vertical color line in front of the throat stops at the sixth line of shading on the neck.

DIE B:

1. The lines in the groundwork are all thin and straight.

2. All the lines of the background are parallel.

3. There is no dash in the upper part of the second jewel in the band of the crown.

4. The vertical color line in front of the throat stops at the eighth line of shading on the neck.

DIE I:

1. The base of the crown is well below the level of the inner white line around the vignette.

2. The labels inscribed "POSTAGE" and "REVENUE" are cut square at the top.

3. There is a white "bud" on the outer side of the main stem of the curved ornaments in each lower corner.

4. The second (thick) line below the country name has the ends next to the crown cut diagonally.

DIE Ia.	DIE Ib.
1 as die II.	1 and 3 as die II.
2 and 3 as die I.	2 as die I.

DIE II:

1. The base of the crown is aligned with the underside of the white line around the vignette.

2. The labels curve inward at the top inner corners.

3. The "bud" has been removed from the outer curve of the ornaments in each corner.

4. The second line below the country name has the ends next to the crown cut vertically.

British Colonial and Crown Agents Watermarks

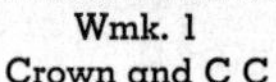

Wmk. 1
Crown and C C

Wmk. 2
Crown and C A

Wmk. 3
Multiple Crown and C A

Wmk. 4
Multiple Crown and Script C A

Wmk. 4a

Wmk. 314
St. Edward's Crown and C A Multiple

Wmk. 373

Wmk. 384

Wmk. 406

Watermarks 1 to 4, 314, 373, 384 and 406, common to many British territories, are illustrated here to avoid duplication.

The letters "CC" of Wmk. 1 identify the paper as having been made for the use of the Crown Colonies, while the letters "CA" of the others stand for "Crown Agents." Both Wmks. 1 and 2 were used on stamps printed by De La Rue & Co.

Wmk. 3 was adopted in 1904; Wmk. 4 in 1921; Wmk. 314 in 1957; Wmk. 373 in 1974; Wmk. 384 in 1985; Wmk 406 in 2008.

In Wmk. 4a, a non-matching crown of the general St. Edwards type (bulging on both sides at top) was substituted for one of the Wmk. 4 crowns which fell off the dandy roll. The non-matching crown occurs in 1950-52 printings in a horizontal row of crowns on certain regular stamps of Johore and Seychelles, and on various postage due stamps of Barbados, Basutoland, British Guiana, Gold Coast, Grenada, Northern Rhodesia, St. Lucia, Swaziland and Trinidad and Tobago. A variation of Wmk. 4a, with the non-matching crown in a horizontal row of crown-CA-crown, occurs on regular stamps of Bahamas, St. Kitts-Nevis and Singapore.

Wmk. 314 was intentionally used sideways, starting in 1966. When a stamp was issued with Wmk. 314 both upright and sideways, the sideways varieties usually are listed also – with minor numbers. In many of the later issues, Wmk. 314 is slightly visible.

Wmk. 373 is usually only faintly visible.

MACAO

mə-ˈkau

LOCATION — Off the Chinese coast at the mouth of the Canton River
GOVT. — Special Administrative Area of China (PRC) (as of 12/20/99)
AREA — 8 sq. mi.
POP. — 415,850 (1998)
CAPITAL — Macao

Formerly a Portuguese overseas territory. The territory includes the two small adjacent islands of Coloane and Taipa.

1000 Reis = 1 Milreis
78 Avos = 1 Rupee (1894)
100 Avos = 1 Pataca (1913)

Catalogue values for unused stamps in this country are for Never Hinged items, beginning with Scott 339 in the regular postage section, Scott C16 in the air post section, Scott J50 in the semi-postal section, and Scott RA11 in the postal tax section.

Watermarks

Wmk. 232 — Maltese Cross

Portuguese Crown — A1

Perf. 12½, 13½

1884-85 Typo. Unwmk.

1	A1	5r black	15.00	9.00
2	A1	10r orange	25.00	12.00
3	A1	10r green ('85)	30.00	9.00
4	A1	20r bister	32.50	22.50
5	A1	20r rose ('85)	45.00	18.00
6	A1	25r rose	22.50	5.25
7	A1	25r violet ('85)	30.00	13.50
8	A1	40r blue	115.00	40.00
9	A1	40r yellow ('85)	42.50	20.00
10	A1	50r green	250.00	75.00
11	A1	50r blue ('85)	57.50	25.00
12	A1	50r gray ('85)	57.50	30.00
13	A1	100r red lilac	75.00	24.00
a.		100r lilac	75.00	24.00
14	A1	200r orange	70.00	20.00
15	A1	300r chocolate	100.00	25.00
		Nos. 1-15 (15)	967.50	348.25

All values exist both perf 12½ and 13½. The cheaper variety is listed above. For detailed listings, see the Scott Classic Specialized Catalogue of stamps and Covers.

The reprints of the 1885 issue are printed on smooth, white chalky paper, ungummed and on thin white paper with shiny white gum and clean-cut perforation 13½.

For surcharges see Nos. 16-28, 108-109.

No. 13a Surcharged in Black

1884 Without Gum *Perf. 12½*

16	A1	80r on 100r lilac	90.00	45.00
a.		Inverted surcharge	*200.00*	*75.00*
b.		Without accent on "e" of "reis"	80.00	47.50
c.		Perf. 13½	125.00	55.00
d.		As "b," perf. 13½	140.00	62.50

Nos. 6 and 10 Surcharged in Black, Blue or Red

b

1885 Without Gum

17	A1(b)	5r on 25r rose, perf. 12½ (Bk)	21.00	6.50
a.		With accent on "e" of "Reis"	35.00	12.00
b.		Double surcharge	225.00	160.00
c.		Inverted surcharge	200.00	125.00
d.		Perf. 13½	125.00	100.00
e.		As "d," inverted surcharge	*200.00*	*140.00*
18	A1(b)	10r on 25r rose (Bl)	47.50	18.00
a.		Accent on "e" of "Reis"		
b.		Pair, one without surcharge	—	
19	A1(b)	10r on 50r grn, perf. 13½ (Bl)	625.00	225.00
a.		Perf. 12½	625.00	260.00
20	A1(b)	20r on 50r green, perf. 12½ (Bk)	47.50	10.00
a.		Double surcharge		160.00
b.		Accent on "e" of "Reis"	—	—
21	A1(b)	40r on 50r grn, perf. 12½ (R)	175.00	50.00
a.		Perf. 13½	240.00	50.00
		Nos. 17-21 (5)	916.00	309.50

c

1885 Without Gum

22	A1(c)	5r on 25r rose (Bk)	32.50	18.00
a.		Original value not obliterated		
23	A1(c)	10r on 50r green (Bk)	32.50	18.00
a.		Inverted surcharge		
b.		Perf. 12½	32.50	18.00

Nos. 12, 13a and 14 Surcharged in Black

1887

24	A1	5r on 80r gray	35.00	9.00
a.		"R" of "Reis" 4mm high	125.00	50.00
b.		Perf. 12½	150.00	45.00
25	A1	5r on 100r lilac	150.00	90.00
a.		Perf. 12½	95.00	60.00
26	A1	10r on 80r gray	65.00	20.00
a.		"R" 4mm high	140.00	47.50
27	A1	10r on 200r orange	160.00	62.50
a.		"R" 4mm high, "e" without accent	200.00	80.00
b.		Perf. 13½	140.00	62.50
28	A1	20r on 80r gray	125.00	35.00
a.		"R" 4mm high	175.00	47.50
b.		Perf. 12½	100.00	50.00
c.		"R" 4mm high, "e" without accent	160.00	47.50
		Nos. 24-28 (5)	535.00	216.50

The surcharges with larger "R" (4mm) have accent on "e." Smaller "R" is 3mm high.

Occasionally Nos. 24, 26 and 28 may be found with original gum. Values the same.

Coat of Arms — A6

Red Surcharge Without Gum

1887, Oct. 20 *Perf. 12½*

32	A6	5r green & buff	15.00	7.00
a.		With labels, 5r on 10r	77.50	65.00
b.		With labels, 5r on 20r	90.00	65.00
c.		With labels, 5r on 60r	77.50	65.00
33	A6	10r green & buff	22.50	9.00
a.		With labels, 10r on 10r	95.00	75.00
b.		With labels, 10r on 60r	110.00	75.00
34	A6	40r green & buff	37.50	*14.00*
a.		With labels, 40r on 20r	150.00	*110.00*
		Nos. 32-34 (3)	75.00	30.00

Nos. 32-34 were local provisionals, created by perforating contemporary revenue stamps to remove the old value inscriptions and then surcharging the central design portion. The unused portion of the design was normally removed prior to use. For simplicity's sake, we refer to these extraneous portions of the original revenue stamps as "labels."

The 10r also exists with 20r labels, and 40r with 10r labels. Value, $250 each.

King Luiz — A7

Typographed and Embossed

1888, Jan. *Perf. 12½, 13½*

Chalk-surfaced Paper

35	A7	5r black	21.00	4.00
36	A7	10r green	21.00	6.00
a.		Perf. 13½	75.00	37.50
37	A7	20r rose	35.00	13.00
38	A7	25r violet	35.00	13.00
39	A7	40r chocolate	35.00	18.00
a.		Perf. 13½	60.00	26.00
40	A7	50r blue	60.00	13.50
41	A7	80r gray	95.00	22.50
a.		Imperf., pair	—	
42	A7	100r brown	45.00	22.50
43	A7	200r gray lilac	90.00	45.00
44	A7	300r orange	72.50	45.00
		Nos. 35-44 (10)	509.50	202.50

Nos. 37-44 were issued without gum.

For surcharges and overprints see Nos. 45, 58-66B, 110-118, 164-170, 239, Timor Nos. P1-P3.

No. 43 Surcharged in Red

1892 Without Gum *Perf. 13½*

45	A7	30r on 200r gray lil	80.00	24.00
a.		Inverted surcharge	275.00	165.00

King Carlos — A9

1894, Nov. 15 Typo. *Perf. 11½*

46	A9	5r yellow	9.00	3.75
47	A9	10r redsh violet	9.00	3.75
48	A9	15r chocolate	12.50	5.25
49	A9	20r lavender	14.00	6.00
50	A9	25r green	35.00	11.25
51	A9	50r lt blue	37.50	22.50
a.		Perf. 13½	*550.00*	*400.00*
52	A9	75r carmine	70.00	30.00
53	A9	80r yellow green	37.50	22.50
54	A9	100r brown, *buff*	40.00	22.50
55	A9	150r carmine, *rose*	45.00	22.50
56	A9	200r dk blue, *blue*	62.50	34.00
57	A9	300r dk blue, *sal*	82.50	45.00
		Nos. 46-57 (12)	454.50	229.00

Nos. 49-57 were issued without gum, No. 49 with or without gum.

For surcharges and overprints see Nos. 119-130, 171-181, 183-186, 240-251, 257-258.

Stamps of 1888 Surcharged in Red, Green or Black

1894 Without Gum *Perf. 12½*

58	A7	1a on 5r black (R)	11.00	4.50
a.		Short "1"	11.00	4.50
b.		Inverted surcharge	100.00	100.00
c.		Double surcharge	*400.00*	
d.		Surch. on back instead of face	*200.00*	*200.00*
59	A7	3a on 20r car (G)	19.00	4.50
a.		Inverted surcharge	—	—
60	A7	4a on 25r violet (Bk)	21.00	9.00
a.		Inverted surcharge	60.00	50.00
61	A7	6a on 40r choc (Bk)	25.00	6.75
a.		Perf. 13½	19.00	12.00
62	A7	8a on 50r blue (R)	55.00	18.00
a.		Double surch., one inverted	*225.00*	*200.00*
b.		Inverted surcharge	125.00	60.00
c.		Perf. 13½	62.50	40.00
d.		As #62, double surch.	150.00	120.00
63	A7	13a on 80r gray (Bk)	30.00	7.00
a.		Double surcharge	*150.00*	*110.00*
64	A7	16a on 100r brn (Bk)	60.00	18.00
a.		Inverted surcharge	*200.00*	*125.00*
b.		Perf. 13½	115.00	110.00
65	A7	31a on 200r gray lil (Bk)	90.00	25.00
a.		Inverted surcharge	150.00	125.00
b.		Perf. 13½	75.00	25.00
66	A7	47a on 300r org (G)	72.50	11.00
a.		Double surcharge	*160.00*	*120.00*
		Nos. 58-66 (9)	383.50	103.75

The style of type used for the word "PROVISÓRIO" on Nos. 58 to 66 differs for each value.

A 2a on 10r green was unofficially surcharged and denounced by the authorities. Value, $500.

On No. 45

66B	A7	5a on 30r on 200r	160.00	50.00

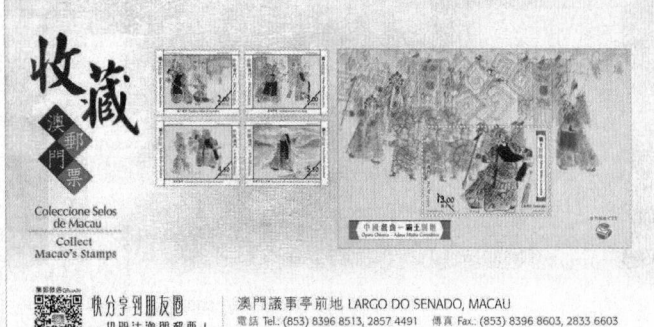

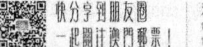

Common Design Types pictured following the introduction.

Vasco da Gama Issue
Common Design Types

1898, Apr. 1 Engr. *Perf. 12½ to 16*

67 CD20 ½a blue green 7.00 2.25
68 CD21 1a red 7.00 3.75
69 CD22 2a red violet 7.00 5.25
70 CD23 4a yellow green 10.00 7.50
71 CD24 8a dark blue 19.00 12.00
72 CD25 12a violet brown 30.00 22.00
73 CD26 16a bister brown 26.00 22.00
74 CD27 24a bister 30.00 22.00
Nos. 67-74 (8) 136.00 96.75

For overprints and surcharges see Nos. 187-194.

King Carlos — A11

1898-1903 Typo. *Perf. 11½*
Name and Value in Black except #103

75 A11 ½a gray 4.50 1.00
a. Perf. 12½ 15.00 7.50
b. As #75, black ("MACAU" and denom.) inverted 100.00 90.00
76 A11 1a orange 4.50 1.00
a. Perf. 12½ 15.00 7.50
b. As #76, black ("MACAU" and denom.) inverted 175.00 150.00
77 A11 2a yellow green 5.75 1.50
a. Black ("MACAU" and denom.) inverted 140.00 110.00
78 A11 2a gray grn ('03) 6.25 1.50
79 A11 2½a red brown 7.50 2.25
80 A11 3a gray violet 7.50 2.25
81 A11 3a slate ('03) 6.25 1.65
82 A11 4a sea green 9.00 5.00
83 A11 4a carmine ('03) 6.25 1.50
84 A11 5a gray brn ('00) 15.00 3.75
85 A11 5a pale yel brn ('03) 9.00 2.25
86 A11 6a red brn ('03) 10.00 2.00
87 A11 8a blue 12.50 3.75
88 A11 8a gray brn ('03) 16.00 4.00
89 A11 10a sl bl ('00) 15.00 3.75
90 A11 12a rose 15.00 6.50
91 A11 12a red lil ('03) 62.50 15.00
92 A11 13a violet 18.00 6.50
93 A11 13a gray lilac ('03) 22.50 6.00
94 A11 15a pale ol grn ('00) 90.00 23.00
95 A11 16a dk blue, *bl* 17.00 7.50
96 A11 18a org brn, *pink* ('03) 32.50 11.50
97 A11 20a brn, *yelsh* ('00) 45.00 11.50
98 A11 24a brown, *buff* 27.50 7.50
99 A11 31a red lilac 27.50 9.00
100 A11 31a red lil, *pink* ('03) 32.50 11.50
101 A11 47a dk blue, *rose* 50.00 11.50
102 A11 47a dull bl, *straw* ('03) 60.00 13.00
103 A11 78a blk & red, *bl* ('00) 85.00 17.50
Nos. 75-103 (29) 720.00 194.65

Issued without gum: Nos. 76a, 77, 79-80, 82, 84, 89, 94, 97 and 103.

For surcharges and overprints see Nos. 104-107, 132-136, 141, 147-157D, 159-161, 182, 195-209, 253-255, 258A.

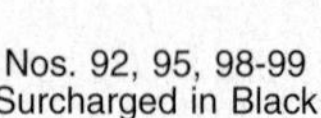

Nos. 92, 95, 98-99 Surcharged in Black

1900 Without Gum

104 A11 5a on 13a violet 20.00 3.50
105 A11 10a on 16a dk bl, *bl* 22.50 5.00
106 A11 15a on 24a brn, *buff* 22.50 8.25
107 A11 20a on 31a red lilac 25.00 13.50
Nos. 104-107 (4) 90.00 30.25

Nos. 106-107 were issued with and without gum.

Regular Issues Surcharged

On Stamps of 1884-85

1902 Black Surcharge *Perf. 11½*

108 A1 6a on 10r orange 30.00 9.75
a. Double surcharge *300.00 175.00*
109 A1 6a on 10r green 21.00 6.00

On Stamps of 1888
Red Surcharge
Perf. 12½, 13½

110 A7 6a on 5r black 10.00 3.50
a. Inverted surcharge 110.00 60.00

Black Surcharge

111 A7 6a on 10r green 8.25 3.50
112 A7 6a on 40r choc 8.25 3.50
a. Double surcharge 125.00 50.00
b. Perf. 13½ 30.00 10.00
113 A7 18a on 20r rose 17.00 4.50
a. Double surcharge 160.00 70.00
b. Inverted surcharge 175.00 —
114 A7 18a on 25r violet 250.00 60.00
115 A7 18a on 80r gray 250.00 67.50
a. Double surcharge 275.00 175.00
116 A7 18a on 100r brown 42.50 26.00
a. Perf. 13½ 90.00 35.00
117 A7 18a on 200r gray lil 250.00 67.50
a. Perf. 12½ 190.00 60.00
118 A7 18a on 300r orange 30.00 10.00
a. Perf. 13½ 57.50 25.00

Issued without gum: Nos. 110-118.

Nos. 109 to 118 inclusive, except No. 111, have been reprinted. The reprints have white gum and clean-cut perforation 13½ and the colors are usually paler than those of the originals.

On Stamps of 1894

1902-10 *Perf. 11½, 13½*

119 A9 6a on 5r yellow 7.75 2.75
a. Inverted surcharge 82.50 65.00
120 A9 6a on 10r red vio 60.00 5.25
121 A9 6a on 15r choc 26.00 5.25
122 A9 6a on 25r green 7.75 2.75
123 A9 6a on 80r yel grn 7.75 2.75
124 A9 6a on 100r brn, *buff* 15.00 6.00
a. Perf. 11½ 26.00 10.00
125 A9 6a on 200r bl, *bl* 10.00 2.75
a. Vert. half used as 3a on cover ('10) *40.00*
126 A9 18a on 20r lavender 21.00 6.75
127 A9 18a on 50r lt blue 26.00 6.75
a. Perf. 13½ 77.50 17.00
128 A9 18a on 75r carmine 21.00 6.75
129 A9 18a on 150r car, *rose* 21.00 7.50
130 A9 18a on 300r bl, *salmon* 26.00 6.75

On Newspaper Stamp of 1893
Perf. 12½

131 N3 18a on 2½r brown 10.00 3.25
a. Perf. 13½ 27.50 9.00
b. Perf. 11½ 45.00 14.00
Nos. 108-131 (24) 1,176. 327.00

Issued without gum: Nos. 122-130, 131b.

Stamps of 1898-1900 Overprinted in Black

1902 *Perf. 11½*

132 A11 2a yellow green 21.00 4.00
133 A11 4a sea green 32.50 10.00
134 A11 8a blue 21.00 7.00
135 A11 10a slate blue 26.00 8.00
136 A11 12a rose 70.00 26.00
Nos. 132-136 (5) 170.50 55.00

Issued without gum: Nos. 133, 135.

Reprints of No. 133 have shiny white gum and clean-cut perforation 13½. Value $1.

No. 91 Surcharged

1905 Without Gum

141 A11 10a on 12a red lilac 30.00 12.50

For overprint see No. 182.

Nos. J1-J3 Overprinted

1910, Oct. *Perf. 11½x12*

144 D1 ½a gray green 10.00 6.75
a. Inverted overprint 35.00 30.00
b. Double overprint 40.00 40.00
c. Pair, one without ovpt.
145 D1 1a yellow green 12.00 6.75
a. Inverted overprint 35.00 30.00
146 D1 2a slate 20.00 7.50
a. Inverted overprint *65.00* 45.00
Nos. 144-146 (3) 42.00 21.00

No. 144 issued without gum, Nos. 145-146 with and without gum.

Stamps of 1898-1903 Overprinted in Carmine or Green

Overprint 24½mm long. "A" has flattened top.

Lisbon Overprint

1911, Apr. 2 *Perf. 11½*

147 A11 ½a gray 2.10 .75
a. Inverted overprint 20.00 20.00
147B A11 1a orange 2.00 .75
c. Inverted overprint 20.00 20.00
148 A11 2a gray green 2.00 .75
a. Inverted overprint 12.50 12.50
149 A11 3a slate 6.25 .75
a. Inverted overprint 12.50 12.50
150 A11 4a carmine (G) 6.25 2.00
a. 4a pale yel brn (error) *75.00 50.00*
b. As No. 150, inverted overprint 50.00 50.00
151 A11 5a pale yel brn 6.25 4.00
152 A11 6a red brown 6.25 4.00
153 A11 8a gray brown 6.25 4.00
154 A11 10a slate blue 6.25 4.00
155 A11 13a gray lilac 10.00 5.00
a. Inverted overprint 60.00 60.00
156 A11 16a dk blue, *bl* 10.00 5.00
a. Inverted overprint 60.00 60.00
157 A11 18a org brn, *pink* 16.00 6.00
157A A11 20a brown, *straw* 16.00 6.00
157B A11 31a red lil, *pink* 30.00 8.00
157C A11 47a dull bl, *straw* 50.00 10.00
157D A11 78a blk & red, *bl* 82.50 12.00
Nos. 147-157D (16) 258.10 73.00

Issued without gum: Nos. 151, 153-157D.

Coat of Arms — A14

Red Surcharge

1911 *Perf. 11½x12*

158 A14 1a on 5r brn & buff 32.50 12.50
a. "1" omitted 80.00 60.00
b. Inverted surcharge 100.00 55.00

Stamps of 1900-03 Surcharged

Diagonal Halves
Black Surcharge

1911 Without Gum *Perf. 11½*

159 A11 2a on half of 4a car 50.00 32.50
a. "2" omitted 100.00 80.00
b. Inverted surcharge *150.00* 82.50
d. Entire stamp 180.00
159C A11 5a on half of 10a sl bl (#89) *900.00 400.00*
e. Entire stamp *8,500. 4,000.*

Red Surcharge

160 A11 5a on half of 10a sl bl (#89) *700.00 400.00*
a. Inverted surcharge *750.00 500.00*
b. Entire stamp *11,000. 5,000.*
161 A11 5a on half of 10a sl bl (#135) 150.00 120.00
a. Inverted surcharge 350.00 200.00
b. Entire stamp 500.00

Nos. 159-161 normally were bisected by the government before being placed on sale.

A15

Laid or Wove Paper

1911 *Perf. 12x11½*

162 A15 1a black 525.00 —
a. "Correio" 2,000. —
163 A15 2a black 600.00 —
a. "Correio" 2,000. —

The vast majority of used stamps were not canceled.

Surcharged Stamps of 1902 Overprinted in Red or Green

Overprint 23mm long. "A" has pointed top.

Local Overprint

1913 Without Gum *Perf. 11½*

164 A1 6a on 10r grn (R) 37.50 12.00
a. "REPUBLICA" double 70.00 70.00

Perf. 12½, 13½

165 A7 6a on 5r black (G) 15.00 3.50
166 A7 6a on 10r grn (R) 31.00 8.00
167 A7 6a on 40r choc (R) 10.50 3.00
a. Perf. 13½ 50.00 20.00
168 A7 18a on 20r car (G) 21.00 6.00
169 A7 18a on 100r brn (R) 82.50 40.00
a. Perf. 13½ 100.00 50.00
170 A7 18a on 300r org (R) 32.50 9.00
a. Perf. 13½ 50.00 10.00
Nos. 164-170 (7) 230.00 81.50

"Republica" overprint exists inverted on Nos. 164-170.

1913 Without Gum *Perf. 11½, 13½*

171 A9 6a on 10r red vio (G) 14.50 4.50
172 A9 6a on 10r red vio (R) 300.00 26.00
173 A9 6a on 15r choc (R) 14.50 5.00
174 A9 6a on 25r grn (R) 16.00 5.00
175 A9 6a on 80r yel grn (R) 14.50 5.00
176 A9 6a on 100r brn, *buff* (R) 30.00 7.00
a. Perf. 11½ 32.50 8.00
177 A9 18a on 20r lav (R) 19.00 5.00
178 A9 18a on 50r lt bl (R) 19.00 5.00
a. Perf. 13½ 21.00 6.00
179 A9 18a on 75r car (G) 19.00 5.50
180 A9 18a on 150r car, *rose* (G) 21.00 6.00
181 A9 18a on 300r dk bl, *sal* (R) 32.50 10.00

On No. 141

182 A11 10a on 12a red lil (R) 13.00 4.50
Nos. 171-182 (12) 513.00 88.50

"Republica" overprint exists inverted on Nos. 171-181.

Stamps of Preceding Issue Surcharged

1913 Without Gum *Perf. 11½*

183 A9 2a on 18a on 20r (R) 15.00 4.00
184 A9 2a on 18a on 50r (R) 15.00 4.00
a. Perf. 13½ 16.00 4.25
185 A9 2a on 18a on 75r (G) 15.00 4.00
186 A9 2a on 18a on 150r (G) 15.00 4.00
Nos. 183-186 (4) 60.00 16.00

"Republica" overprint exists inverted on Nos. 183-186. Value, each $20.

The 2a surcharge exists inverted or double on Nos. 183-186. For values, see Classic Specialized Catalogue.

Vasco da Gama Issue Overprinted or Surcharged

j 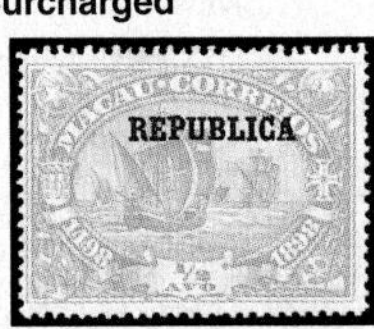

k 

187 CD20 (j) ½a blue green 7.75 2.00
188 CD21 (j) 1a red 8.50 2.00
189 CD22 (j) 2a red violet 8.50 2.00
a. Double ovpt., one inverted 100.00
190 CD23 (j) 4a yellow grn 7.75 2.00
191 CD24 (j) 8a dk blue 13.00 2.00
192 CD25 (k) 10a on 12a vio brn 24.00 5.00
193 CD26 (j) 16a bister brn 17.00 4.00
194 CD27 (j) 24a bister 27.50 5.00
Nos. 187-194 (8) 114.00 24.00

Stamps of 1898-1903 Overprinted in Red or Green

1913 Without Gum *Perf. 11½*

195 A11 4a carmine (G) 250.00 100.00
a. Double overprint 400.00 175.00
b. Inverted overprint 400.00
196 A11 5a yellow brn 30.00 20.00
a. Inverted overprint *50.00 40.00*
197 A11 6a red brown 77.50 40.00
a. Inverted overprint 95.00
198 A11 8a gray brown 625.00 300.00
b. Inverted overprint 1,000. *1,500.*
198A A11 10a dull blue 1,000.
199 A11 13a violet 77.50 32.50
a. Inverted overprint 95.00
200 A11 13a gray lilac 40.00 20.00
a. Inverted overprint 95.00
201 A11 16a blue, *bl* 50.00 20.00
202 A11 18a org brn, *pink* 50.00 20.00
a. Inverted overprint 95.00
203 A11 20a brown, *yelsh* 50.00 20.00
204 A11 31a red lil, *pink* 67.50 30.00
a. Inverted overprint 95.00
205 A11 47a dull bl, *straw* 100.00 40.00

Only 20 examples of No. 198A were sold by the Post Office.

Stamps of 1911-13 Surcharged

On Stamps of 1911 With Lisbon "Republica"

1913

206 A11 ½a on 5a yel brn (R) 15.00 3.00
a. "½ Avo" inverted 125.00 70.00
207 A11 4a on 8a gray brn (R) 30.00 4.00
a. "4 Avos" inverted 150.00 70.00

On Stamps of 1913 With Local "Republica"

208 A11 1a on 13a violet (R) 250.00 30.00
209 A11 1a on 13a gray lil (R) 15.00 3.00
a. Surch. on #155 (error) — —
Nos. 206-209 (4) 310.00 40.00

Issued without gum: Nos. 207-209.

"Ceres" — A16

Name and Value in Black

1913 Chalky Paper *Perf. 15x14*

210 A16 ½a olive brown 1.75 .25
211 A16 1a black 1.75 .25
212 A16 2a blue green 1.75 .25
213 A16 4a carmine 6.75 1.00
214 A16 5a lilac brown 7.75 3.00
215 A16 6a lt violet 7.75 3.00
216 A16 8a lilac brown 7.75 3.00
217 A16 10a deep blue 7.75 3.00
218 A16 12a yellow brn 11.00 3.00
219 A16 16a slate 20.00 5.00
220 A16 20a orange brn 20.00 5.00
221 A16 40a plum 21.00 5.00
222 A16 58a brown, *grn* 35.00 12.00
223 A16 76a brown, *pink* 75.00 14.00
224 A16 1p orange, *sal* 100.00 20.00
225 A16 3p green, *bl* 200.00 55.00
Nos. 210-225 (16) 525.00 132.75

Nos. 210, 211 and 212 exist on glazed paper.

1919 Ordinary Paper *Perf. 15x14*

226 A16 ½a olive brown 5.50 2.25
a. Inscriptions inverted 50.00
227 A16 1a black 5.50 2.25
a. Inscriptions inverted 50.00
b. Inscriptions double 50.00
228 A16 2a blue green 14.50 7.00
a. Inscriptions inverted 40.00
229 A16 4a carmine 42.50 21.00
Nos. 226-229 (4) 68.00 32.50

1922-24 *Perf. 12x11½*

230 A16 ½a olive brown 2.75 1.10
231 A16 1a black 2.75 1.10
232 A16 1½a yel grn ('24) 1.75 .25
233 A16 2a blue green 6.00 3.00
234 A16 3a org brn 10.00 3.00
235 A16 4a carmine 20.00 5.00
236 A16 4a lemon ('24) 14.00 5.00
237 A16 6a gray ('23) 47.50 7.50
238 A16 8a lilac brown 17.50 5.50
238A A16 10a pale bl ('23) 27.50 6.00
238B A16 12a yellow brown 30.00 6.50
238C A16 14a lilac ('24) 42.50 12.00
238D A16 16a slate 67.50 20.00
238E A16 24a sl grn ('23) 25.00 7.00
238F A16 32a org brn ('24) 25.00 8.00
238G A16 56a dl rose ('24) 50.00 15.00
238H A16 72a brown ('23) 67.50 20.00
238I A16 1p org ('24) 200.00 30.00

Glazed Paper

238J A16 3p pale turq ('24) 425.00 95.00
238K A16 5p car rose ('24) 350.00 82.50
Nos. 230-238K (20) 1,432. 333.45

For surcharges see Nos. 256, 259-267.

Preceding Issues and No. P4 Overprinted in Carmine

On Stamps of 1902

Perf. 11½, 12, 12½, 13½, 11½x12

1915

239 A7 6a on 10r green 14.50 4.00
240 A9 6a on 5r yellow 14.50 4.00
241 A9 6a on 10r red vio 14.50 4.00
242 A9 6a on 15r choc 12.50 3.25
243 A9 6a on 25r green 12.00 4.00
244 A9 6a on 80r yel grn 12.00 4.00
245 A9 6a on 100r brn, *buff* 21.00 4.00
246 A9 6a on 200r bl, *bl* 11.00 6.00
247 A9 18a on 20r lav 21.00 6.00
248 A9 18a on 50r lt bl 45.00 6.75
249 A9 18a on 75r car 40.00 6.75
250 A9 18a on 150r car, *rose* 45.00 8.00
251 A9 18a on 300r bl, *sal* 40.00 10.00
252 N3 18a on 2½r brn 32.50 6.00

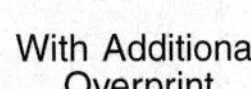

With Additional Overprint

253 A11 8a blue 14.50 8.25
254 A11 10a slate blue 14.50 6.00
a. "Provisorio" double 110.00

On Stamp of 1905

255 A11 10a on 12a red lil 19.00 9.75
Nos. 239-255 (17) 383.50 100.75

Issued without gum: Nos. 243-251 and 255.

No. 217 Surcharged

Without Gum

1919-20 *Perf. 15x14*

256 A16 ½a on 5a lilac brn 100.00 32.50
Never hinged 125.00

Nos. 243 and 244 Surcharged

257 A9 2a on 6a on 25r green 500.00 125.00
258 A9 2a on 6a on 80r yel grn 100.00 70.00

No. 152 Surcharged

258A A11 2a on 6a red brown 175.00 70.00
Nos. 256-258A (4) 875.00 297.50

Issued without gum: Nos. 256-258A.

Stamps of 1913-24 Surcharged

1931-33 *Perf. 12x11½*

259 A16 1a on 24a slate grn ('33) 14.50 4.00
260 A16 2a on 32a org brn ('33) 14.50 4.00
261 A16 4a on 12a bis brn ('33) 14.50 4.00
262 A16 5a on 6a lt gray ('33) 57.50 35.00
264 A16 7a on 8a lil brn 24.00 5.00
265 A16 12a on 14a lilac 24.00 5.00
266 A16 15a on 16a dk gray ('33) 24.00 5.00
267 A16 20a on 56a dull rose ('33) 50.00 11.00

Chalky Paper

Perf. 15x14

263 A16 5a on 6a lt vio ('33) 30.00 11.00
Nos. 259-267 (9) 253.00 84.00

"Portugal" and Vasco da Gama's Flagship "San Gabriel" — A17

Wmk. 232

1934, Feb. 1 Typo. *Perf. 11½*

268 A17 ½a bister .45 .40
269 A17 1a olive brown .45 .25
270 A17 2a blue green 1.10 .50
271 A17 3a violet 1.40 .50
272 A17 4a black 1.75 .50
273 A17 5a gray 1.75 .80
274 A17 6a brown 1.75 .80
275 A17 7a brt rose 3.25 1.00
276 A17 8a brt blue 3.25 1.00
277 A17 10a red orange 7.25 2.00
278 A17 12a dark blue 7.25 2.00
279 A17 14a olive green 7.25 2.00
280 A17 15a maroon 7.25 2.00
281 A17 20a orange 7.25 2.00
282 A17 30a apple green 14.00 3.50
283 A17 40a violet 14.00 3.50
284 A17 50a olive bister 21.00 5.00
285 A17 1p lt blue 75.00 20.00
286 A17 2p brown org 90.00 27.50
287 A17 3p emerald 150.00 45.00
288 A17 5p dark violet 225.00 67.50
Nos. 268-288 (21) 640.40 187.75

See Nos. 316-323. For overprints and surcharges see Nos. 306-315, C1-C6, J43-J49.

Common Design Types

Perf. 13½x13

1938, Aug. 1 Engr. Unwmk.

Name and Value in Black

289 CD34 1a gray green 1.00 .35
290 CD34 2a orange brown 1.25 .55
291 CD34 3a dk vio brn 1.25 .55
292 CD34 4a brt green 1.25 .55
293 CD35 5a dk carmine 1.25 .55
294 CD35 6a slate 1.25 .55
295 CD35 8a rose violet 2.10 2.25
296 CD36 10a brt red vio 2.50 2.25
297 CD36 12a red 3.25 2.60
298 CD36 15a orange 3.25 2.60
299 CD37 20a blue 16.50 2.90
300 CD37 40a gray black 16.50 3.50
301 CD37 50a brown 16.50 3.75
302 CD38 1p brown car 50.00 7.25
303 CD38 2p olive green 85.00 17.50
304 CD38 3p blue violet 115.00 25.00
305 CD38 5p red brown 200.00 37.50
Nos. 289-305 (17) 517.85 110.20

For surcharge see No. 315A.

Stamps of 1934 Surcharged in Black

a

b

1941 Wmk. 232 *Perf. 11½x12*

306 A17(a) 1a on 6a brown 7.50 3.50
307 A17(b) 2a on 6a brown 3.00 2.00
308 A17(b) 3a on 6a brown 3.00 2.00
309 A17(a) 5a on 7a brt rose 120.00 60.00
310 A17(b) 5a on 7a brt rose 17.50 8.50
311 A17(a) 5a on 8a brt blue 19.50 10.00
312 A17(b) 5a on 8a brt blue 12.00 8.50
313 A17(b) 8a on 30a apple grn 9.50 5.00
314 A17(b) 8a on 40a violet 9.50 5.00
315 A17(b) 8a on 50a olive bis 9.50 5.50
Nos. 306-315 (10) 211.00 110.00

No. 294 Surcharged in Black

1941 Unwmk. *Perf. 13½x13*

315A CD35 3a on 6a slate 75.00 35.00

Counterfeits exist.

"Portugal" Type of 1934

1934 Issue

1942 Issue

The lines in the background are more widely spaced than on the original 1934 issue; also the 1942 issue has no imprint at Lower Right.

1942 Litho. *Rough Perf. 12*
Thin Paper Without Gum

316 A17 1a olive brown 2.00 1.25
317 A17 2a blue green 2.00 1.25
318 A17 3a vio, perf. 11 20.00 4.00
a. Perf. 12 25.00 4.75
319 A17 6a brown 20.00 5.50
a. Perf. 10 45.00 25.00
b. Perf. 11 37.50 15.00
320 A17 10a red orange 12.50 4.50
321 A17 20a orange 12.50 4.00
a. Perf. 11 45.00 17.50
322 A17 30a apple green 15.00 6.50
323 A17 40a violet 30.00 9.50
Nos. 316-323 (8) 114.00 36.50

Nos. 316-323 doesn't have imprint on lower right and lines in background are more widely spaced than on the original 1934 issue.

Macao Dwelling A18

Pagoda of Barra — A19

Designs: 2a, Mountain fort. 3a, View of Macao. 8a, Praia Grande Bay. 10a, Leal Senado Square. 20a, Sao Jeronimo Hill. 30a, Marginal Ave. 50a, Relief of Goddess Ma. 1p, Gate of Cerco. 3p, Post Office. 5p, Solidao Walk.

1948, Dec. 20 Litho. *Perf. 10½*

324 A18 1a dk brn & org 2.25 .50
325 A19 2a rose brn & rose 1.60 .50
326 A18 3a brn vio & lil 3.75 1.00
327 A18 8a rose car & rose 2.25 1.40
328 A18 10a lilac rose & rose 3.75 1.60
329 A18 20a dk blue & gray 4.75 2.00
330 A18 30a black & gray 15.00 4.00
331 A18 50a brn & pale bis 27.50 9.00
332 A19 1p emer & pale grn 125.00 16.00
333 A19 2p scarlet & rose 100.00 18.00
334 A19 3p dl grn & gray grn 125.00 20.00
335 A18 5p vio bl & gray 200.00 22.50
Nos. 324-335 (12) 610.85 96.50

See Nos. 341-347A.

Catalogue values for unused stamps in this section, from this point to the end of the section, are for Never Hinged items.

Lady of Fatima Issue
Common Design Type

1949, Feb. 1 Unwmk. *Perf. 14½*
336 CD40 8a scarlet 40.00 12.00

Symbols of the UPU — A20

1949, Dec. 24 Litho. Unwmk.
337 A20 32a claret & rose 75.00 27.50

75th anniv. of the formation of the UPU.

Holy Year Issue
Common Design Types

1950, July 26 *Perf. 13x13½*
339 CD41 32a dk slate gray 27.50 6.00
340 CD42 50a carmine 27.50 6.50

Scenic Types of 1948

Designs as before.

1950-51 *Perf. 14*

341 A18 1a violet & rose 2.75 1.00
342 A19 2a ol bis & yel 2.75 1.00
343 A18 3a org red & buff 8.50 1.25
344 A18 8a slate & gray 11.00 1.75
345 A18 10a red brn & org 15.00 3.75
346 A18 30a vio bl & bl 19.00 4.50
347 A18 50a ol grn & yel grn 42.50 5.00
347A A19 1p dk org brn & org brn 115.00 25.00
Nos. 341-347A (8) 216.50 43.25

A 1p ultra & vio, perf. 11, was not sold in Macao. Value $150.

Nos. 341-347 issued in 1951, the 1p in 1950.

Dragon — A21

1951 *Perf. 11½x12*
348 A21 1a org yel, *lemon* 2.50 1.25
349 A21 2a dk grn, *blue* 2.50 1.25

Shaded Background

350 A21 10a vio brn, *blue* 8.00 2.75
351 A21 10a brt pink, *blue* 7.00 2.75
Nos. 348-351 (4) 20.00 8.00

Nos. 348-351 were isuued without gum. For overprints see Nos. J50-J52.

Holy Year Extension Issue
Common Design Type

1951, Dec. 3 Litho. *Perf. 14*
352 CD43 60a magenta & pink + label *37.50* 10.00

Stamp without label sells for much less.

Fernao Mendes Pinto — A22

Portraits: 2a and 10a, St. Francis Xavier. 3a and 50a, Jorge Alvares. 6a and 30a, Luis de Camoens.

1951, Aug. 27 *Perf. 11½*

353 A22 1a steel bl & gray bl 1.00 .50
354 A22 2a dk brown & ol grn 2.00 .50
355 A22 3a deep grn & grn 2.75 .75
356 A22 6a purple 4.00 1.00
357 A22 10a red brn & org 8.00 1.75
358 A22 20a brown car 15.00 3.75
359 A22 30a dk brn & ol grn 30.00 6.00
360 A22 50a red & orange 60.00 14.00
Nos. 353-360 (8) 122.75 28.25

Sampan — A23

Junk — A24

Design: 5p, Junk.

1951, Nov. 1 Unwmk.
361 A23 1p vio bl & bl 37.50 3.25
362 A24 3p black & vio 130.00 15.00
363 A23 5p henna brown 160.00 32.50
Nos. 361-363 (3) 327.50 50.75

Medical Congress Issue
Common Design Type

Design: Sao Rafael Hospital.

1952, June 16 Unwmk. *Perf. 13½*
364 CD44 6a black & purple 9.75 4.25

St. Francis Xavier Issue

Statue of St. Francis Xavier — A25

16a, Arm of St. Francis. 40a, Tomb of St. Francis.

1952, Nov. 28 Litho. *Perf. 14*
365 A25 3a blk, *grnsh gray* 4.00 .90
366 A25 16a choc, *buff* 17.00 3.00
367 A25 40a blk, *blue* 21.00 5.25
Nos. 365-367 (3) 42.00 9.15

400th anniv. of the death of St. Francis Xavier.

Statue of Virgin Mary — A26

1953, Apr. 28 Unwmk. *Perf. 13½*
368 A26 8a choc & dull ol 3.50 1.00
369 A26 10a blue blk & buff 13.50 3.75
370 A26 50a slate grn & ol grn 23.00 5.50
Nos. 368-370 (3) 40.00 10.25

Exhibition of Sacred Missionary Art, held at Lisbon in 1951.

Stamp of Portugal and Arms of Colonies — A27

1954, Mar. 9 Photo. *Perf. 13*
371 A27 10a multicolored 10.00 2.00

Cent. of Portugal's first postage stamps.

Firecracker Flower — A28

Flowers: 3a, Forget-me-not. 5a, Dragon claw. 10a, Nunflower. 16a, Narcissus. 30a, Peach flower. 39a, Lotus flower. 1p, Chrysanthemum. 3p, Cherry blossoms. 5p, Tangerine blossoms.

1953, Sept. 22 *Perf. 11½*
Flowers in Natural Colors

372 A28 1a dark red .60 .35
373 A28 3a dark green .60 .35
374 A28 5a dark brown .75 .40
375 A28 10a dp grnsh blue .75 .40
376 A28 16a yellow brown 1.25 .45
377 A28 30a dk olive grn 3.00 1.00
378 A28 39a violet blue 3.25 1.00
379 A28 1p deep plum 7.25 1.25
380 A28 3p dark gray 14.00 2.50
381 A28 5p deep carmine 27.50 4.25
Nos. 372-381 (10) 58.95 11.95

For surcharges see Nos. 443-444.

Sao Paulo Issue
Common Design Type

1954, Aug. 4 Litho. *Perf. 13½*
382 CD46 39a org, cream & blk 14.00 3.00

Sao Paulo founding, 400th anniversary.
For surcharge see No. 445.

Map of Colony — A29

Inscriptions and design in brown, red, green, ultra & yellow (buff on 10a, 40a, 90a)

Perf. 12½x13½

1956, May 10 Photo.

383 A29 1a pale green .50 .40
384 A29 3a pale gray 1.10 .50
385 A29 5a pale pink 1.50 .75
386 A29 10a buff 3.00 .90
387 A29 30a lt blue 6.00 1.25
388 A29 40a pale green 9.00 1.75
389 A29 90a pale gray 14.00 3.25
390 A29 1.50p pink 22.50 4.00
Nos. 383-390 (8) 57.60 12.80

Exhibition Emblems and View — A30

1958, Nov. 8 Litho. *Perf. 14½*
391 A30 70a multicolored 6.00 1.75

World's Fair, Brussels, Apr. 17-Oct. 19.

Tropical Medicine Congress Issue
Common Design Type

Design: Cinnamomum camphora.

1958, Nov. 15 *Perf. 13½*
392 CD47 20a multicolored 8.00 3.00

Armillary Sphere — A31

1960, June 25 Litho. *Perf. 13½*
393 A31 2p multicolored 11.50 4.00

500th anniversary of the death of Prince Henry the Navigator.

Sports Issue

Common Design Type

Sports: 10a, Field hockey. 16a, Wrestling. 20a, Table tennis. 50a, Motorcycling. 1.20p, Relay race. 2.50p, Badminton.

1962, Feb. 9 ***Perf. 13½***

Multicolored Design

394 CD48 10a blue & yel grn 2.00 .45
395 CD48 16a brt pink 2.50 .90
396 CD48 20a orange 3.50 1.00
397 CD48 50a rose 6.00 1.25
398 CD48 1.20p blue & beige 25.00 3.00
399 CD48 2.50p gray & brown 35.00 8.00
Nos. 394-399 (6) 74.00 14.60

Anti-Malaria Issue

Common Design Type

Design: Anopheles hyrcanus sinensis.

1962, Apr. 7 **Litho.** ***Perf. 13½***
400 CD49 40a multicolored 6.50 2.00

Bank Building — A32

1964, May 16 **Unwmk.** ***Perf. 13½***
401 A32 20a multicolored 9.50 2.50

Centenary of the National Overseas Bank of Portugal.

ITU Issue

Common Design Type

1965, May 17 **Litho.** ***Perf. 14½***
402 CD52 10a pale grn & multi 5.00 2.00

National Revolution Issue

Common Design Type

Design: 10a, Infante D. Henrique School and Count de S. Januario Hospital.

1966, May 28 **Litho.** ***Perf. 11½***
403 CD53 10a multicolored 5.00 2.00

Drummer, 1548 — A32a

Designs: 15a, Soldier with sword, 1548. 20a, Harquebusier, 1649. 40a, Infantry officer, 1783. 50a, Infantry soldier, 1783. 60a, Colonial infantry soldier (Indian), 1902. 1p, Colonial infantry soldier (Chinese), 1903. 3p, Colonial infantry soldier (Chinese) 1904.

1966, Aug. 8 **Litho.** ***Perf. 13***

404 A32a 10a multicolored 1.25 .40
405 A32a 15a multicolored 2.25 .75
406 A32a 20a multicolored 2.50 .75
407 A32a 40a multicolored 4.50 .85
408 A32a 50a multicolored 5.00 1.50
409 A32a 60a multicolored 12.00 1.75
410 A32a 1p multicolored 15.00 3.00
411 A32a 3p multicolored 27.50 7.50
Nos. 404-411 (8) 70.00 16.50

Navy Club Issue, 1967

Common Design Type

Designs: 10a, Capt. Oliveira E. Carmo and armed launch Vega. 20a, Capt. Silva Junior and frigate Dom Fernando.

1967, Jan. 31 **Litho.** ***Perf. 13***
412 CD54 10a multicolored 3.25 1.00
413 CD54 20a multicolored 6.25 2.75

Arms of Pope Paul VI and Golden Rose — A33

1967, May 13 ***Perf. 12½x13***
414 A33 50a multicolored 5.25 2.00

50th anniversary of the apparition of the Virgin Mary to three shepherd children at Fatima.

Cabral Issue

Cabral Monument, Lisbon — A34

Design: 70a, Cabral monument, Belmonte.

1968, Apr. 22 **Litho.** ***Perf. 14***
415 A34 20a multicolored 4.25 1.00
416 A34 70a multicolored 6.00 2.75

500th anniversary of the birth of Pedro Alvares Cabral, navigator who took possession of Brazil for Portugal.

Admiral Coutinho Issue

Common Design Type

Design: 20a, Adm. Coutinho with sextant, vert.

1969, Feb. 17 **Litho.** ***Perf. 14***
417 CD55 20a multicolored 3.75 1.50

Church of Our Lady of the Relics, Vidigueira — A35

Vasco da Gama Issue

1969, Aug. 29 **Litho.** ***Perf. 14***
418 A35 1p multicolored 11.00 1.75

Vasco da Gama (1469-1524), navigator.

Administration Reform Issue

Common Design Type

1969, Sept. 25 **Litho.** ***Perf. 14***
419 CD56 90a multicolored 5.00 1.00

Bishop D. Belchior Carneiro — A36

1969, Oct. 16 **Litho.** ***Perf. 13***
420 A36 50a multicolored 3.25 .75

4th centenary of the founding of the Santa Casa da Misericordia in Macao.

King Manuel I Issue

Portal of Mother Church, Golega — A37

1969, Dec. 1 **Litho.** ***Perf. 14***
421 A37 30a multicolored 5.75 1.00

500th anniversary of the birth of King Manuel I.

Marshal Carmona Issue

Common Design Type

5a, Antonio Oscar Carmona in general's uniform.

1970, Nov. 15 **Litho.** ***Perf. 14***
422 CD57 5a multicolored 2.25 1.25

Dragon Mask — A38

1971, Sept. 30 ***Perf. 13½***
423 A38 5a lt blue & multi 1.10 .50
424 A38 10a Lion mask 2.25 .75

Lusiads Issue

Portuguese Delegation at Chinese Court — A39

1972, May 25 **Litho.** ***Perf. 13***
425 A39 20a citron & multi 13.00 3.75

4th centenary of publication of The Lusiads by Luiz Camoens.

Olympic Games Issue

Common Design Type

Design: Hockey and Olympic emblem.

1972, June 20 ***Perf. 14x13½***
426 CD59 50a multicolored 3.25 1.00

Lisbon-Rio de Janeiro Flight Issue

Common Design Type

Design: "Santa Cruz" landing in Rio de Janeiro.

1972, Sept. 20 **Litho.** ***Perf. 13½***
427 CD60 5p multicolored 22.50 7.50

Pedro V Theater and Lyre — A42

1972, Dec. 25 **Litho.** ***Perf. 13½***
428 A42 2p multicolored 8.00 2.50

Centenary of Pedro V Theater, Macao.

WMO Centenary Issue

Common Design Type

1973, Dec. 15 **Litho.** ***Perf. 13***
429 CD61 20a blue grn & multi 6.25 1.75

Viscount St. Januario — A44

Design: 60a, Hospital, 1874 and 1974.

1974, Jan. 25 **Litho.** ***Perf. 13½***
430 A44 15a multicolored 1.00 .75
431 A44 60a multicolored 3.75 1.00

Viscount St. Januario Hospital, Macao, cent. For surcharge see No. 457.

George Chinnery, Self-portrait A45

1974, Sept. 23 **Litho.** ***Perf. 14***
432 A45 30a multicolored 3.50 1.50

George Chinnery (1774-1852), English painter who lived in Macao.

Macao-Taipa Bridge — A46

Design: 2.20p, Different view of bridge.

1974, Oct. 7 **Litho.** ***Perf. 14x13½***
433 A46 20a multicolored 1.50 .75
434 A46 2.20p multicolored 12.50 1.50

Inauguration of the Macao-Taipa Bridge. For surcharge see No. 446.

Man Raising Banner A47

1975, Apr. 25 ***Perf. 12***
435 A47 10a ocher & multi 3.00 1.75
436 A47 1p multicolored 13.50 4.00

Revolution of Apr. 25, 1974, 1st anniv.

Pou Chai Pagoda — A48

Design: 20p, Tin Hau Pagoda.

1976, Jan. 30 **Litho.** ***Perf. 13½x13***
437 A48 10p multicolored *15.00* 3.00
438 A48 20p multicolored *32.50* 5.00

A 1p stamp for the 400th anniv. of the Macao Diocese was prepared but not issued. Some stamps were sold in Lisbon. Value $150.

"The Law" — A50

1978 **Litho.** ***Perf. 13½***
440 A50 5a blk, dk & lt blue *3.00* 2.75
441 A50 2p blk, org brn & buff *125.00* 10.00
442 A50 5p blk, ol & yel grn *25.00* 12.50
Nos. 440-442 (3) *153.00* 25.25

Legislative Assembly, Aug. 9, 1976.

Nos. 376, 378, 382, 434 Surcharged

1979, Nov.

443 A28 10a on 16a *9.00* 3.00
444 A28 30a on 39a (#378) *11.00* 3.00
445 CD46 30a on 39a (#382) *50.00* *15.00*
446 A46 2p on 2.20p *10.00* 6.00
Nos. 443-446 (4) *80.00* 27.00

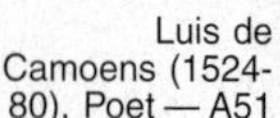

Luis de Camoens (1524-80), Poet — A51

1981, June Litho. *Perf. 13½*

447 A51 10a multicolored *.95* .45
448 A51 30a multicolored *1.90* .50
449 A51 1p multicolored *4.25* 1.50
450 A51 3p multicolored *6.25* 2.25
Nos. 447-450 (4) *13.35* 4.70

Buddha, Macao Cathedral — A52

1981, Sept.

451 A52 15a multicolored .50 .40
452 A52 40a multicolored .75 .40
453 A52 50a multicolored 1.25 .50
454 A52 60a multicolored 1.90 .75
455 A52 1p multicolored 2.40 1.00
456 A52 2.20p multicolored 6.00 1.40
Nos. 451-456 (6) 12.80 4.45

Transcultural Psychiatry Symposium.

No. 431 Surcharged

1981 Litho. *Perf. 13½*

457 A44 30a on 60a multi 7.50 1.00

Health Services Building A53

Designs: Public Buildings and Monuments: 40a, Guia Lighthouse. 1p, Portas do Cerco. 2p, Luis de Camoes Museum. 10p, School Welfare Service Building.

1982, June 10 Litho. *Perf. 12x12½*

458 A53 30a shown .50 .25
459 A53 40a multicolored .65 .25
460 A53 1p multicolored 1.25 .30
461 A53 2p multicolored 2.50 .50
462 A53 10p multicolored 11.00 3.50
Nos. 458-462 (5) 15.90 4.80

See Nos. 472-476, 489-493.

Autumn Festivals A54

Designs: Painted paper lanterns.

1982, Oct. 1 *Perf. 12x11½*

463 A54 40a multicolored 3.25 1.00
464 A54 1p multicolored 8.75 2.25
465 A54 2p multicolored 10.50 4.25
466 A54 5p multicolored 25.00 7.00
Nos. 463-466 (4) 47.50 14.50

Geographical Position — A55

1982, Dec. 1 Litho. *Perf. 13*

467 A55 50a Aerial view *10.00* 1.75
468 A55 3p Map *37.50* 6.50

World Communications Year — A56

No. 469, Telephone operators. No. 470, Mailman, mailbox. No. 471, Globe, satellites.

1983, Feb. 16 *Perf. 13½*

469 A56 60a multicolored 1.50 .35
470 A56 3p multicolored 3.25 2.00
471 A56 6p multicolored 6.25 3.50
Nos. 469-471 (3) 11.00 5.85

Architecture Type of 1982

No. 472, Social Welfare Institute. No. 473, St. Joseph's Seminary. No. 474, St. Dominic's Church. No. 475, St. Paul's Church ruins. No. 476, Senate House.

1983, May 12 Litho. *Perf. 13*

472 A53 10a multi .50 .25
473 A53 80a multi 1.00 .40
474 A53 1.50p multi 1.75 .75
475 A53 2.50p multi 2.50 1.40
476 A53 7.50p multi 8.00 3.25
Nos. 472-476 (5) 13.75 6.05

Medicinal Plants A57

No. 477, Asclepias curassavica. No. 478, Acanthus ilicifolius. No. 479, Melastoma sanguineum. No. 480, Nelumbo nucifera. No. 481, Bombax malabaricum. No. 482, Hibiscus mutabilis.

1983, July 14 Litho. *Perf. 13½x14*

477 A57 20a multi 1.00 .70
478 A57 40a multi 1.50 .70
479 A57 60a multi 2.00 1.00
480 A57 70a multi 2.75 1.50
481 A57 1.50p multi 4.25 2.25
482 A57 2.50p multi 8.00 4.25
a. Souvenir sheet of 6, #477-482 *175.00*
Nos. 477-482 (6) 19.50 10.40

No. 482a sold for 6.50p.

16th Century Discoveries — A58

1983, Nov. 15 Litho. *Perf. 13½x14*

483 4p multicolored *7.00* 2.00
484 4p multicolored *7.00* 2.00
a. A58 Pair, #483-484 *19.50* 9.00

A60

1984, Jan. 25 Litho. *Perf. 13½*

485 A60 60a multicolored *9.00* 2.50
a. Booklet pane of 5 *45.00*

New Year 1984 (Year of the Rat).
No. 485a has straight edges.
See Nos. 504, 522, 540, 560, 583, 611, 639, 662, 684, 718, 757, 804.

A61

Design of First Stamp Issue, 1884.

1984, Mar. 1 Litho. *Perf. 12½*

486 A61 40a orange & blk 1.25 .40
487 A61 3p gray & blk 3.00 1.50
488 A61 5p sepia & blk 6.50 2.50
a. Souvenir sheet of 3, #486-488 *40.00*
Nos. 486-488 (3) 10.75 4.40

Centenary of Macao postage stamps.

Architecture Type of 1982

No. 489, Holy House of Mercy. No. 490, St. Lawrence Church. No. 491, King Peter V Theater. No. 492, Palace of St. Sancha. No. 493, Moorish barracks.

1984, May 18 Litho. *Perf. 13½*

489 A53 20a multicolored .35 .25
490 A53 60a multicolored .60 .30
491 A53 90a multicolored .90 .45
492 A53 3p multicolored 2.10 .60
493 A53 15p multicolored 6.75 2.00
Nos. 489-493 (5) 10.70 3.60

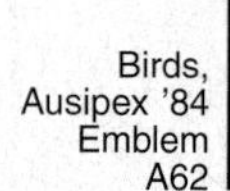

Birds, Ausipex '84 Emblem A62

1984, Sept. 21 Litho. *Perf. 13*

494 A62 30a Kingfishers .85 .35
495 A62 40a European jay .90 .40
496 A62 50a White eyes 1.50 .40
497 A62 70a Hoopoe 2.50 .70
498 A62 2.50p Peking nightingale 5.00 2.00
499 A62 6p Wild duck 9.00 3.00
Nos. 494-499 (6) 19.75 6.85

Philakorea '84 Emblem, Fishing Boats A63

1984, Oct. 22 Litho.

500 A63 20a Hok lou t'eng .75 .25
501 A63 60a Tai t'ong 1.40 .65
502 A63 2p Tai mei chai 3.50 1.25
503 A63 5p Ch'at pong t'o 7.50 3.00
Nos. 500-503 (4) 13.15 5.15

New Year Type of 1984

1985, Feb. 13 Litho. *Perf. 13½*

504 A60 1p Buffalo 7.00 2.75
a. Booklet pane of 5 *35.00*

Intl. Youth Year — A65

1985, Apr. 19 Litho. *Perf. 13½*

505 A65 2.50p shown *3.75* .75
506 A65 3p Clasped hands *4.75* 2.25

Visit of President Eanes of Portugal A66

1985, May 27 Litho.

507 A66 1.50p multicolored 2.75 .90

Luis de Camoens Museum, 25th Anniv. — A67

Silk paintings by Chen Chi Yun. No. 508, Two travelers, hermit. No. 509, Traveling merchant. No. 510, Conversation in a garden. No. 511, Veranda of a house.

1985, June 27 Litho.

508 A67 2.50p multi 5.00 1.60
509 A67 2.50p multi 5.00 1.60
510 A67 2.50p multi 5.00 1.60
511 A67 2.50p multi 5.00 1.60
a. Block or strip of 4, #508-511 30.00 *15.00*
Nos. 508-511 (4) 20.00 6.40

Butterflies, World Tourism Assoc. Emblem — A68

No. 512, Euploea midamus. No. 513, Hebomoia glaucippe. No. 514, Lethe confusa. No. 515, Heliophorus epicles. No. 516, Euthalia phemius seitzi. No. 517, Troides helena.

1985, Sept. 27 Litho.

512 A68 30a multi 1.00 .25
513 A68 50a multi 1.25 .35
514 A68 70a multi 2.00 .40
515 A68 2p multi 2.75 1.00
516 A68 4p multi 5.75 1.75
517 A68 7.50p multi 8.00 3.50
a. Sheet of 6, #512-517 *160.00*
Nos. 512-517 (6) 20.75 7.25

World Tourism Day.

Cargo Boats A69

Designs: 50a, Tou. 70a, Veng Seng Lei motor junk. 1p, Tong Heng Long No. 2 motor junk. 6p, Fong Vong San cargo ship.

1985, Oct. 25 *Perf. 14*

518 A69 50a multicolored .75 .25
519 A69 70a multicolored 2.00 .50
520 A69 1p multicolored 3.50 1.10
521 A69 6p multicolored 6.00 3.00
Nos. 518-521 (4) 12.25 4.85

New Year Type of 1984

1986, Feb. 3 *Perf. 13½*

522 A60 1.50p Tiger 6.00 1.25
a. Booklet pane of 5 30.00

No. 522a has straight edges.

City of Macau, 400th Anniv. A71

1986, Apr. 10 Litho. *Perf. 13½*

523 A71 2.20p multicolored *4.00* 1.60

Musical Instruments A72

1986, May 22

524 A72 20a Suo-na *3.50* .90
525 A72 50a Sheng *4.00* 1.25
526 A72 60a Er-hu *5.00* 1.50
527 A72 70a Ruan *8.00* 2.00
528 A72 5p Cheng *19.00* 2.75
529 A72 8p Pi-pa *22.50* 5.00
a. Souvenir sheet of 6, #524-529 *225.00*
Nos. 524-529 (6) *62.00* 13.40

AMERIPEX '86.

Ferries A73

1986, Aug. 28 Litho. *Perf. 13*

530 A73 10a Hydrofoil .50 .35
531 A73 40a Hovermarine 2.25 .65
532 A73 3p Jetfoil 3.50 1.40
533 A73 7.5p High-speed ferry 8.00 3.00
Nos. 530-533 (4) 14.25 5.40

Fortresses — A74

No. 534, Taipa. No. 535, Sao Paulo do Monte. No. 536, Our Lady of Guia. No. 537, Sao Francisco.

1986, Oct. 3 Litho. *Perf. 12½*

534 A74 2p multi *10.00* 2.40
535 A74 2p multi *10.00* 2.40
536 A74 2p multi *10.00* 2.40
537 A74 2p multi *10.00* 2.40
a. Block or strip of 4, #534-537 *80.00* *20.00*
Nos. 534-537 (4) *40.00* 9.60

Macao Security Forces, 10th anniv. No. 537a has continuous design.

A75

Dr. Sun Yat-sen — A76

1986, Nov. 12 Litho. *Perf. 12½*

538 A75 70a multicolored *3.25* *2.25*

Souvenir Sheet

539 A76 1.30p shown *50.00* *30.00*

New Year Type of 1984

1987, Jan. 21 *Perf. 13½*

540 A60 1.50p Hare *6.00* 1.25
a. Booklet pane of 5 *30.00*

No. 540a has straight edges.

Shek Wan Ceramic Figures in the Luis de Camoens Museum — A78

No. 541, Medicine man (4/1). No. 542, Choi San, god of good fortune (4/2). No. 543, Yi, sun god (4/3). No. 544, Chung Kuei, conqueror of demons (4/4).

1987, Apr. 10 Litho. *Perf. 13½*

541 A78 2.20p multi 6.75 2.50
542 A78 2.20p multi 6.75 2.50
543 A78 2.20p multi 6.75 2.50
544 A78 2.20p multi 6.75 2.50
a. Block or strip of 4, #541-544 40.00 26.50
Nos. 541-544 (4) 27.00 10.00

Dragon Boat Festival A79

1987, May 29 Litho. *Perf. 13½*

545 A79 50a Dragon boat race 3.50 .90
546 A79 5p Figurehead 9.50 3.00

Decorated Fans — A80

1987, July 29 Litho. *Perf. 12½*

547 A80 30a multicolored 3.50 1.00
548 A80 70a multi, diff. 7.50 1.75
549 A80 1p multi, diff. 17.50 3.00
550 A80 6p multi, diff. 24.50 6.50
a. Souvenir sheet of 4, #547-550 *250.00* *125.00*
Nos. 547-550 (4) 53.00 12.25

Casino Gambling — A81

1987, Sept. 30 *Perf. 13½*

551 A81 20a Fan-tan 9.50 3.00
552 A81 40a Cussec 9.50 3.00
553 A81 4p Baccarat 9.50 3.00
554 A81 7p Roulette 9.50 3.00
Nos. 551-554 (4) 38.00 12.00

Traditional Transportation — A82

1987, Nov. 18 Litho. *Perf. 13½*

555 A82 10a Market wagon .75 .50
556 A82 70a Sedan chair 2.25 .75
557 A82 90a Rickshaw 3.25 .90
558 A82 10p Tricycle rickshaw 10.00 4.00
Nos. 555-558 (4) 16.25 6.15

Souvenir Sheet

559 A82 7.50p Sedan chair, diff. *47.50* —

New Year Type of 1984

1988, Feb. 10 Litho. *Perf. 13½*

560 A60 2.50p Dragon 5.00 2.50
a. Booklet pane of 5 25.00

No. 560a has straight edges.

Wildlife Protection A84

1988, Apr. 14 Litho. *Perf. 12½x12*

561 A84 3p Erinaceus europaeus 4.75 1.75
562 A84 3p Meles meles 4.75 1.75
563 A84 3p Lutra lutra 4.75 1.75
564 A84 3p Manis pentadactyla 4.75 1.75
a. Block or strip of 4, #561-564 27.50 *15.00*
Nos. 561-564 (4) 19.00 7.00

World Health Organization, 40th Anniv. — A85

1988, June 1 Litho. *Perf. 13½*

565 A85 60a Breast-feeding 2.00 .55
566 A85 80a Immunization 3.50 .65
567 A85 2.40p Blood donation 5.50 2.00
Nos. 565-567 (3) 11.00 3.20

Modes of Transportation — A86

20a, Bicycles. 50a, Vespa, Lambretta. 3.30p, 1907 Rover 20hp. 5p, 1912 Renault delivery truck.
7.50p, 1930s Sedan.

1988, July 15 Litho.

568 A86 20a multi .75 .40
569 A86 50a multi 1.50 .80
570 A86 3.30p multi 4.00 1.50
571 A86 5p multi 6.75 3.25
Nos. 568-571 (4) 13.00 5.95

Souvenir Sheet

572 A86 7.50p multi *52.50*

1988 Summer Olympics, Seoul A87

1988, Sept. 19 Litho.

573 A87 40a Hurdles 1.25 .50
574 A87 60a Basketball 2.00 .60
575 A87 1p Soccer 3.50 1.25
576 A87 8p Table tennis 6.50 3.00
Nos. 573-576 (4) 13.25 5.35

Souvenir Sheet

577 Sheet of 5, #573-576, 577a *55.00*
a. A87 5p Tae kwon do *30.00*

World Post Day — A88

1988, Oct. 10 Litho. *Perf. 14*

578 A88 13.40p Electronic mail 6.00 1.75
579 A88 40p Express mail 10.50 5.00

35th Macao Grand Prix — A89

1988, Nov. 24 Litho. *Perf. 12½*

580 A89 80a Sedan 1.25 .50
581 A89 2.80p Motorcycle 3.75 1.25
582 A89 7p Formula 3 10.00 2.75
a. Souvenir sheet of 3, #580-582 *80.00*
Nos. 580-582 (3) 15.00 4.50

New Year Type of 1984

1989, Jan. 20 Litho. *Perf. 13½*

583 A60 3p Snake 9.00 2.00
a. Booklet pane of 5 45.00

No. 583a has straight edges. Value for No. 583 is for stamp perfed on 4 sides.

Occupations A91

1989, Mar. 1 Litho. *Perf. 12x12½*

584 A91 50a Water carrier .75 .25
585 A91 1p Tan-kya woman 1.50 .50
586 A91 4p Tin-tin (junk) man 3.00 1.75
587 A91 5p Tofu peddler 4.00 2.00
Nos. 584-587 (4) 9.25 4.50

See Nos. 612-615, 640-643.

Watercolors by George Smirnoff in the Luis de Camoens Museum — A92

1989, Apr. 10 Litho. *Perf. 12½x12*

588 A92 2p multi (4-1) 2.10 .90
589 A92 2p multi (4-2) 2.10 .90
590 A92 2p multi (4-3) 2.10 .90
591 A92 2p multi (4-4) 2.10 .90
a. Block or strip of 4, #588-591 12.50 5.75
Nos. 588-591 (4) 8.40 3.60

Snakes A93

No. 592, Naja naja. No. 593, Bungarus fasciatus. No. 594, Trimeresurus albolabris. No. 595, Elaphe radiata.

1989, July 7 **Litho.**

592 A93 2.50p multicolored 3.50 1.25
593 A93 2.50p multicolored 3.50 1.25
594 A93 2.50p multicolored 3.50 1.25
595 A93 2.50p multicolored 3.50 1.25
a. Block or strip of 4, #592-595 16.00 7.00
Nos. 592-595 (4) 14.00 5.00

Traditional Games — A94

1989, July 31 **Litho.** ***Perf. 13½***

596 A94 10a Talu .75 .40
597 A94 60a Triol 2.25 .50
598 A94 3.30p Chiquia 3.00 1.40
599 A94 5p Xadrez Chines 4.00 2.50
Nos. 596-599 (4) 10.00 4.80

Airplanes A95

1989, Oct. 9 **Litho.**

600 A95 50a Over church .50 .30
601 A95 70a American over lighthouse 1.00 .40
602 A95 2.80p Over wharf 1.50 .90
603 A95 4p Over junk 2.75 1.50
Nos. 600-603 (4) 5.75 3.10

Souvenir Sheet

604 A95 7.50p Over harbor *30.00* 15.00

No. 604 contains one 40x30mm stamp.

World Stamp Expo '89, Washington, DC — A96

1989, Nov. 17 **Litho.** ***Perf. 12½***

605 A96 40a Malacca .45 .25
606 A96 70a Thailand .90 .30
607 A96 90a India 1.40 .50
608 A96 2.50p Japan 2.25 1.00
609 A96 7.50p China 4.50 2.00
Nos. 605-609 (5) 9.50 4.05

Souvenir Sheet

610 Sheet of 6, #605-609, 610a *60.00* 37.50
a. A96 3p Macao *18.00* 18.00

Influence of the Portuguese in the Far East.

New Year Type of 1984

1990, Jan. 19 **Litho.** ***Perf. 13½***

611 A60 4p Horse 5.00 1.75
a. Booklet pane of 5 25.00

No. 611a has straight edges. Value for No. 611 is for stamp perfed on 4 sides.

Occupations Type of 1989

1990, Mar. 1 **Litho.** ***Perf. 12x12½***

612 A91 30a Long chau singer .90 .45
613 A91 70a Cobbler 1.75 .85
614 A91 1.50p Scribe 2.75 1.00
615 A91 7.50p Net fisherman 8.00 2.50
Nos. 612-615 (4) 13.40 4.80

Souvenir Sheet

Penny Black, 150th Anniv. — A99

1990, May 3 **Litho.** ***Perf. 12***

616 A99 10p multicolored *30.00 19.00*

Stamp World London 90.

Lutianus Malabaricus — A100

No. 618, Epinephelus megachir. No. 619, Macropodus opercularis. No. 620, Ophiocephalus maculatus.

1990, June 8 ***Perf. 12x12½***

617 A100 2.40p shown 2.00 1.10
618 A100 2.40p multicolored 2.00 1.10
619 A100 2.40p multicolored 2.00 1.10
620 A100 2.40p multicolored 2.00 1.10
a. Block or strip of 4, #617-620 14.00 7.00
Nos. 617-620 (4) 8.00 4.40

Decorative Porcelain A101

1990, Aug. 24 **Litho.** ***Perf. 12½***

621 A101 3p shown 2.25 1.25
622 A101 3p Furniture 2.25 1.25
623 A101 3p Toys 2.25 1.25
624 A101 3p Artificial flowers 2.25 1.25
a. Souvenir sheet of 4, #621-624 *35.00 15.00*
b. Block or strip of 4, #621-624 16.00 8.00
Nos. 621-624 (4) 9.00 5.00

Asian Games, Beijing — A102

1990, Sept. 22 **Litho.** ***Perf. 13½***

625 A102 80a Cycling .70 .40
626 A102 1p Swimming 1.00 .50
627 A102 3p Judo 3.50 1.10
628 A102 4.20p Shooting 5.25 1.75
Nos. 625-628 (4) 10.45 3.75

Souvenir Sheet

629 Sheet of 5, #625-628, 629a *40.00 20.00*
a. A102 6p Martial arts *13.00 13.00*

Compass Roses from Portuguese Charts — A103

Charts by 16th century cartographers: Lazaro Luis, Diogo Homem, Fernao Vaz Dourado, and Luiz Teixeira.

1990, Oct. 9 **Litho.** ***Perf. 13½***

630 A103 50a shown .90 .45
631 A103 1p multi, diff. 1.50 .50
632 A103 3.50p multi, diff. 3.50 1.25
633 A103 6.50p multi, diff. 7.00 2.00
Nos. 630-633 (4) 12.90 4.20

Souvenir Sheet

634 A103 5p multi, diff. *55.00 27.50*

Games with Animals A104

1990, Nov. 15 **Litho.** ***Perf. 14***

635 A104 20a Cricket fight .75 .30
636 A104 80a Bird fight 2.00 .55
637 A104 1p Greyhound race 2.75 .75
638 A104 10p Horse race 8.00 2.25
Nos. 635-638 (4) 13.50 3.85

New Year Type of 1984

1991, Feb. 8 **Litho.** ***Perf. 13½***

639 A60 4.50p Sheep 5.00 1.10
b. Booklet pane of 5 *28.00*

No. 639b has straight edges.

Occupations Type of 1987

1991, Mar. 1 ***Perf. 14***

640 A91 80a Knife grinder .75 .45
641 A91 1.70p Flour puppet vender 1.50 .50
642 A91 3.50p Street barber 3.50 1.00
643 A91 4.20p Fortune teller 6.00 2.00
Nos. 640-643 (4) 11.75 3.95

Shells A106

1991, Apr. 18 **Litho.** ***Perf. 14***

644 A106 3p Murex pecten 2.00 1.40
645 A106 3p Harpa harpa 2.00 1.40
646 A106 3p Chicoreus rosarius 2.00 1.40
647 A106 3p Tonna zonata 2.00 1.40
a. Strip of 4, #644-647 13.00 9.50
Nos. 644-647 (4) 8.00 5.60

Chinese Opera — A107

Various performers in costume.

1991, June 5 **Litho.** ***Perf. 13½***

648 A107 60a multicolored 1.25 .35
649 A107 80a multicolored 2.25 .40
650 A107 1p multicolored 3.25 .85
651 A107 10p multicolored 10.00 2.75
Nos. 648-651 (4) 16.75 4.35

Flowers A108

Designs: 1.70p, Delonix regia. 3p, Ipomoea cairica. 3.50p, Jasminum mesnyi. 4.20p, Bauhinia variegata.

1991, Oct. 9 **Litho.** ***Perf. 13½***

652 A108 1.70p multicolored 1.50 .45
653 A108 3p multicolored 2.25 .90
654 A108 3.50p multicolored 3.75 1.25
655 A108 4.20p multicolored 4.50 2.25
a. Souvenir sheet of 4, #652-655 *52.50 27.50*
Nos. 652-655 (4) 12.00 4.85

Cultural Exchange A109

Namban screen: No. 656, Unloading boat.

1991, Nov. 16 **Litho.** ***Perf. 12***

656 A109 4.20p multicolored 3.00 .95
657 A109 4.20p shown 3.00 .95
a. Souvenir sheet of 2, #656-657 *35.00 20.00*

Holiday Greetings A110

1.70p, Lunar New Year. 3p, Santa Claus, Christmas. 3.50p, Old man. 4.20p, Girl at New Year party.

1991, Nov. 29 **Litho.** ***Perf. 14½***

658 A110 1.70p multicolored 1.00 .45
659 A110 3p multicolored 1.75 .65
660 A110 3.50p multicolored 2.75 .90
661 A110 4.20p multicolored 5.75 1.60
Nos. 658-661 (4) 11.25 3.60

New Year Type of 1984

1992, Jan. 28 **Litho.** ***Perf. 13½***

662 A60 4.50p Monkey 3.75 2.00
a. Booklet pane of 5 22.50

No. 662a has straight edges.

Paintings of Doors and Windows A111

1992, Mar. 1 ***Perf. 14***

663 A111 1.70p multicolored 1.00 .50
664 A111 3p multi, diff. 2.00 1.00
665 A111 3.50p multi, diff. 3.00 1.50
666 A111 4.20p multi, diff. 4.00 2.00
Nos. 663-666 (4) 10.00 5.00

Mythological Chinese Gods — A112

No. 667, T'it Kuai Lei (4-1). No. 668, Chong Lei Kun (4-2). No. 669, Cheong Kuo Lou (4-3). No. 670, Loi Tong Pan (4-4).

1992, Apr. 3 Litho. *Perf. 14*

667 A112 3.50p multi 6.00 3.00
668 A112 3.50p multi 6.00 3.00
669 A112 3.50p multi 6.00 3.00
670 A112 3.50p multi 6.00 3.00
a. Block or strip of 4, #667-670 *42.50 24.00*
Nos. 667-670 (4) 24.00 12.00

See Nos. 689-692.

Lion Dance Costume A113

Designs: 2.70p, Lion, diff. 6p, Dragon.

1992, May 18

671 A113 1p multicolored .90 .40
672 A113 2.70p multicolored 1.50 .60
673 A113 6p multicolored 3.50 1.25
Nos. 671-673 (3) 5.90 2.25

World Columbian Stamp Expo '92, Chicago.

1992 Summer Olympics, Barcelona — A114

1992, July 1 Litho. *Perf. 13*

674 A114 80a High jump .75 .30
675 A114 4.20p Badminton 1.60 .75
676 A114 4.70p Roller hockey 2.25 1.10
677 A114 5p Yachting 3.50 1.40
a. Souvenir sheet of 4, #674-677 *18.00 12.00*
Nos. 674-677 (4) 8.10 3.55

Temples A115

1992, Oct. 9 *Perf. 14*

678 A115 1p Na Cha .85 .40
679 A115 1.50p Kun Iam 1.10 .55
680 A115 1.70p Hong Kon 1.75 .90
681 A115 6.50p A Ma 3.50 2.00
Nos. 678-681 (4) 7.20 3.85

See Nos. 685-688.

Portuguese-Chinese Friendship — A116

1992, Nov. 1 Litho. *Perf. 14*

682 A116 10p multicolored 3.50 2.00
a. Souv. sheet, perf. 13½ *15.00 10.00*

Tung Sin Tong Charity Organization, Cent. — A117

1992, Nov. 27 *Perf. 12x11½*

683 A117 1p multicolored 1.50 .40

New Year Type of 1984

1993, Jan. 18 Litho. *Perf. 13½*

684 A60 5p Rooster 3.25 1.40
a. Booklet pane of 5 16.00

No. 684a has straight edges.

Temple Type of 1992

1993, Mar. 1 Litho. *Perf. 14*

685 A115 50a T'am Kong .30 .25
686 A115 2p T'in Hau 1.00 .35
687 A115 3.50p Lin Fong 1.50 .70
688 A115 8p Pau Kong 2.00 1.50
Nos. 685-688 (4) 4.80 2.80

Mythological Chinese Gods Type of 1992

Designs: No. 689, Lam Ch'oi Wo seated on crane in flight. No. 690, Ho Sin Ku, seated on peach flower.No. 691, Hon Seong Chi throwing peonies from basket. No. 692, Ch'ou Kuok K'ao seated on gold plate.

1993, Apr. 1 Litho. *Perf. 14*

689 A112 3.50p multi (4-1) *2.25 1.75*
690 A112 3.50p multi (4-2) *2.25 1.75*
691 A112 3.50p multi (4-3) *2.25 1.75*
692 A112 3.50p multi (4-4) *2.25 1.75*
a. Strip of 4, #689-692 *11.00 9.00*

Chinese Wedding — A118

No. 693, Three children celebrating. No. 694, Bride. No. 695, Groom. No. 696, Woman with parasol, person being carried. 8p, Bride & groom.

1993, May 19 *Perf. 14*

693 A118 3p multicolored *1.50 1.25*
694 A118 3p multicolored *1.50 1.25*
695 A118 3p multicolored *1.50 1.25*
696 A118 3p multicolored *1.50 1.25*
a. Strip of 4, #693-696 *8.00 8.00*

Souvenir Sheet

Perf. 14½x14

697 A118 8p multicolored *15.00 11.50*

No. 697 contains one 50x40mm stamp.

World Environment Day — A119

1993, June 5 Litho. *Perf. 14*

698 A119 1p multicolored 1.75 .55

Birds — A120

No. 699, Falco peregrinus. No. 700, Aquila obrysaetos. No. 701, Asio otus. No. 702, Tyto alba.

1993, June 27

699 A120 3p multicolored 1.50 1.00
700 A120 3p multicolored 1.50 1.00
701 A120 3p multicolored 1.50 1.00
702 A120 3p multicolored 1.50 1.00
a. Block or strip of 4, #699-702 7.50 6.00
b. Souvenir sheet of 4, #699-702 *14.00 10.00*

Union of Portuguese Speaking Capitals — A121

1993, July 30 Litho. *Perf. 13½*

703 A121 1.50p multicolored 1.10 .50

Portuguese Arrival in Japan, 450th Anniv. A122

50a, Japanese using musket. 3p, Catholic priests. 3.50p, Exchanging items of trade.

1993, Sept. 22 Litho. *Perf. 12x11½*

704 A122 50a multicolored .60 .25
705 A122 3p multicolored 1.50 .70
706 A122 3.50p multicolored 1.90 .80
Nos. 704-706 (3) 4.00 1.75

See Portugal Nos. 1964-1966.

Flowers A123

Designs: 1p, Spathodea campanulata. 2p, Tithonia diversifolia. 3p, Rhodomyrtus tomentosa. 8p, Passiflora foetida.

1993, Oct. 9 *Perf. 14½*

707 A123 1p multicolored .65 .25
708 A123 2p multicolored 1.25 .45
709 A123 3p multicolored 1.50 .65
710 A123 8p multicolored 2.50 1.75
a. Souvenir sheet of 4, #707-710 *13.00 12.50*
Nos. 707-710 (4) 5.90 3.10

Portuguese Ships A124

1993, Nov. 5 Litho. *Perf. 14*

711 A124 1p Caravel .60 .30
712 A124 2p Round caravel 1.00 .25
713 A124 3.50p Nau 1.40 .40
714 A124 4.50p Galleon 2.00 1.00
a. Souvenir sheet of 4, #711-714 *8.00 7.00*
Nos. 711-714 (4) 5.00 1.95

Macao Grand Prix, 40th Anniv. A125

1993, Nov. 16 Litho. *Perf. 13½*

715 A125 1.50p Stock car .75 .40
716 A125 2p Motorcycle 1.25 .55
717 A125 4.50p Formula 1 race car 2.00 1.40
Nos. 715-717 (3) 4.00 2.35

New Year Type of 1984

1994, Feb. 3 Litho. *Perf. 13½*

718 A60 5p Dog 3.00 1.25
a. Booklet pane of 5 20.00

New Year 1994 (Year of the Dog). No. 718a has straight edges.

Prince Henry the Navigator (1394-1460) — A126

1994, Mar. 4 Litho. *Perf. 12*

719 A126 3p multicolored 2.25 1.00

See Portugal No. 1987.

Scenes of Macao, by George Chinnery (1774-1852) — A127

Designs: No. 720, Hut, natives. No. 721, S. Tiago Fortress. No. 722, Overview of Praia Grande. No. 723, S. Francisco Church.

1994, Mar. 21 *Perf. 14*

720 A127 3.50p multi (4-1) 1.40 .90
721 A127 3.50p multi (4-2) 1.40 .90
722 A127 3.50p multi (4-3) 1.40 .90
723 A127 3.50p multi (4-4) 1.40 .90
a. Block or strip of 4, #720-723 7.00 4.00
b. Souvenir sheet of 4, #720-723 *15.00 10.00*

Spring Festival of New Lunar Year A128

Designs: 1p, Girl, woman shopping. 2p, Celebration. 3.50p, Couple preparing food at table. 4.50p, Old man making decorations.

1994, Apr. 6

724 A128 1p multicolored .50 .25
725 A128 2p multicolored 1.00 .40
726 A128 3.50p multicolored 1.25 .75
727 A128 4.50p multicolored 1.75 1.10
Nos. 724-727 (4) 4.50 2.50

Mythological Chinese Gods — A129

Statuettes: No. 728, Happiness. No. 729. Prosperity. No. 730, Longevity.

1994, May 9 Litho. *Perf. 12*

728 A129 3p multi (3-1) *2.50 1.50*
729 A129 3p multi (3-2) *2.50 1.50*
730 A129 3p multi (3-3) *2.50 1.50*
a. Strip of 3, #728-730 *9.50 7.00*
b. Souvenir sheet of 3, #728-730 *14.00 12.00*

A130

1994 World Cup Soccer Championships, US: Various soccer players.

1994, June 1

731	A130	2p multicolored	.65	.40
732	A130	3p multicolored	1.00	.60
733	A130	3.50p multicolored	1.25	.75
734	A130	4.50p multicolored	1.50	1.25
a.		Souvenir sheet of 4, #731-734	12.00	10.00
		Nos. 731-734 (4)	4.40	3.00

A131

Traditional Chinese shops: 1p, Rice shop. 1.50p, Medicinal drink shop. 2p, Salt fish shop. 3.50p, Pharmacy.

1994, June 27 Litho. *Perf. 12*

735	A131	1p multi	.50	.35
736	A131	1.50p multi	.55	.45
737	A131	2p multi	1.25	.65
738	A131	3.50p multi	1.75	.90
		Nos. 735-738 (4)	4.05	2.35

Navigation Instruments A132

1994, Sept. 13 Litho. *Perf. 12*

739	A132	3p Astrolabe	1.00	.80
740	A132	3.50p Quadrant	1.40	1.10
741	A132	4.50p Sextant	1.60	1.25
		Nos. 739-741 (3)	4.00	3.15

12th Asian Games, Hiroshima 1994 A133

1994, Sept. 30 Litho. *Perf. 12*

742	A133	1p Fencing	.40	.30
743	A133	2p Gymnastics	.85	.40
744	A133	3p Water polo	1.25	.60
745	A133	3.50p Pole vault	1.50	1.00
		Nos. 742-745 (4)	4.00	2.30

Bridges A134

1994, Oct. 8

746	A134	1p Nobre de Carvalho	.40	.45
747	A134	8p Friendship	2.60	1.50

Fortune Symbols — A135

Designs: 3p, Child, carp, water lily. 3.50p, Basket of peaches, child, bats. 4.50p, Flower, child playing mouth organ.

1994, Nov. 7 Litho. *Perf. 12*

748	A135	3p multicolored	1.40	.60
749	A135	3.50p multicolored	1.60	.80
750	A135	4.50p multicolored	2.00	1.25
		Nos. 748-750 (3)	5.00	2.65

Religious Art — A136

Designs: 50a, Stained glass, angel's head. 1p, Stained glass, Holy Ghost. 1.50p, Silver sacrarium. 2p, Silver salver. 3p, Ivory sculpture, Escape to Egypt. 3.50p, Gold & silver chalice.

1994, Nov. 30

751	A136	50a multicolored	.25	.25
752	A136	1p multicolored	.40	.25
753	A136	1.50p multicolored	.60	.30
754	A136	2p multicolored	.85	.45
755	A136	3p multicolored	1.10	.65
756	A136	3.50p multicolored	1.25	.85
		Nos. 751-756 (6)	4.45	2.75

New Year Type of 1984

1995, Jan. 23 Litho. *Perf. 13½*

757	A60	5.50p Boar	2.75	1.10
a.		Booklet pane of 5	18.00	

Tourism A138

Scenes of Macao, by Lio Man Cheong: 50a, Walkway beside pond. 1p, Lighthouse. 1.50p, Temple. 2p, Buildings along coast. 2.50p, Columns, temple. 3p, Ruins on hill overlooking city. 3.50p, Bridge. 4p, Trees in park.

1995, Mar. 1 Litho. *Perf. 12*

758	A138	50a multicolored	.25	.25
759	A138	1p multicolored	.45	.30
760	A138	1.50p multicolored	.60	.35
761	A138	2p multicolored	.85	.50
762	A138	2.50p multicolored	.95	.60
763	A138	3p multicolored	1.10	.75
764	A138	3.50p multicolored	1.40	.85
765	A138	4p multicolored	1.75	1.10
		Nos. 758-765 (8)	7.35	4.70

World Day of the Consumer A139

1995, Mar. 15

766	A139	1p multicolored	.85	.40

Asian Pangolin — A140

No. 767, Facing left (4-1). No. 768, Hanging by tail (4-2). No. 769, On tree limb (4-3). No. 770, On tree stump (4-4).

1995, Apr. 10

767	A140	1.50p multi	*1.40*	.50
768	A140	1.50p multi	*1.40*	.50
769	A140	1.50p multi	*1.40*	.50
770	A140	1.50p multi	*1.40*	.50
a.		Block or strip of 4, #767-770	*7.50*	6.50

World wildlife Fund.
Issued in sheets of 16 stamps.

Legend of Buddhist Goddess Kun Iam — A141

No. 772, Seated atop dragon, holding flower. No. 773, Meditating. No. 774, Holding infant.
8p, Goddess with many faces, hands.

1995, May 5 Litho. *Perf. 12*

771	A141	3p multicolored	1.75	.80
772	A141	3p multicolored	1.75	.80
773	A141	3p multicolored	1.75	.80
774	A141	3p multicolored	1.75	.80
a.		Block or strip of 4, #771-774	*10.00*	*9.00*

Souvenir Sheet

775	A141	8p multicolored	*20.00*	*14.00*

Senado Square — A142

Designs: No. 776, Street, bell tower. No. 777, Street, plaza, shops. No. 778, Fountain, plaza. No. 779, Plaza, buildings.
8p, Bell tower, building, horiz.

1995, June 24 Litho. *Perf. 12*

776	A142	2p multicolored	.90	.55
777	A142	2p multicolored	.90	.55
778	A142	2p multicolored	.90	.55
779	A142	2p multicolored	.90	.55
a.		Strip of 4, #776-779	5.00	3.50

Souvenir Sheet

780	A142	8p multicolored	*11.00*	*8.00*

Temple Type of 1992

1995, July 17 Litho. *Perf. 12*

781	A115	50a Kuan Tai	.25	.25
782	A115	1p Pak Tai	.40	.25
783	A115	1.50p Lin K'ai	.65	.35
784	A115	3p Sek Kam Tong	1.25	.75
785	A115	3.50p Fok Tak	1.40	.90
		Nos. 781-785 (5)	3.95	2.50

Singapore '95 — A143

Birds: No. 786, Gurrulax canorus. No. 787, Serinus canarius. No. 788, Zosterops japonica. No. 789, Leiothrix lutea. 10p, Copsychus saularis.

1995, Sept. 1 Litho. *Perf. 12*

786	A143	2.50p multicolored	1.40	.65
787	A143	2.50p multicolored	1.40	.65
788	A143	2.50p multicolored	1.40	.65
789	A143	2.50p multicolored	1.40	.65
a.		Strip of 4, #786-789	*8.50*	*4.00*

Souvenir Sheet

790	A143	10p multicolored	*17.50*	*11.00*

Intl. Music Festival — A144

1995, Oct. 9 Litho. *Perf. 12*

791	A144	1p Pipa (6-1)	.90	.35
792	A144	1p Erhu (6-2)	.90	.35
793	A144	1p Gongo (6-3)	.90	.35
794	A144	1p Sheng (6-4)	.90	.35
795	A144	1p Xiao (6-5)	.90	.35
796	A144	1p Tambor (6-6)	.90	.35
a.		Block of 6, #791-796	*8.50*	*5.00*

Souvenir Sheet

797	A144	8p Musicians, horiz.	*10.00*	*6.00*

UN, 50th Anniv. A145

1995, Oct. 24 Litho. *Perf. 12*

798	A145	4.50p multicolored	1.75	1.10

Macao Intl. Airport A146

Designs: 1p, Airplane above terminal. 1.50p, Boeing 747 on ground, terminal. 2p, Hangars, 747 with boarding ramp at door. 3p, Airplane, control tower. 8p, Boeing 747 over runway.

1995, Dec. 8 Litho. *Perf. 12*

799	A146	1p multicolored	.50	.25
800	A146	1.50p multicolored	.75	.35
801	A146	2p multicolored	1.00	.45
802	A146	3p multicolored	1.25	.70
		Nos. 799-802 (4)	3.50	1.75

Souvenir Sheet

Perf. 12½

803	A146	8p multicolored	*15.00*	*8.50*

No. 803 contains one 51x38mm stamp.

New Year Type of 1984

Miniature Sheet of 12

Designs: a, like #485. b, like #504. c, like #522. d, like #540. e, like #560. f, like #583. g, like #611. h, like #639. i, like #662. j, like #684. k, like #718. l, like #757.

1995, Dec. 15 Litho. *Perf. 13½*

804	A60	1.50p #a.-l. + label	*20.00*	*10.00*

New Year 1996 (Year of the Rat) A147

1996, Feb. 12 Litho. *Perf. 12*

805	A147	5p multicolored	3.75	1.75

Souvenir Sheet

806	A147	10p like No. 805	*10.00*	*7.50*

Traditional Chinese Bird Cages — A148

Various styles.

1996, Mar. 1 Litho. *Perf. 12*

807	A148	1p multi (4-1)	.35	.25
808	A148	1.50p multi (4-2)	.55	.35
809	A148	3p multi (4-3)	1.00	.60
810	A148	4.50p multi (4-4)	1.60	.90
		Nos. 807-810 (4)	3.50	2.10

Souvenir Sheet

811 A148 10p purple & multi *12.50 8.50*

Paintings, by Herculano Estorninho A149

Scenes of Macao: 50a, Boats. 1.50p, Street, buildings at night, vert. 3p, Fronts of buildings during day, vert. 5p, Townhouse complex.
10p, Entrance to building, vert.

1996, Apr. 1

812	A149	50a multi (4-1)	.25	.25
813	A149	1.50p multi (4-2)	.65	.45
814	A149	3p multi (4-3)	1.10	.85
815	A149	5p multi (4-4)	2.00	1.40
		Nos. 812-815 (4)	4.00	2.95

Souvenir Sheet

816 A149 10p multi *9.00* 5.00

Myths and Legends — A150

Designs: No. 817, Man holding staff, Tou Tei (3-1). No. 818, Man riding tiger, Choi San (3-2). No. 819, Man on top of fireplace, Chou Kuan (3-3).

1996, Apr. 30 Litho. *Perf. 12*

817	A150	3.50p multi	1.20	.90
818	A150	3.50p multi	1.20	.90
819	A150	3.50p multi	1.20	.90
a.		Strip of 3, #817-819	4.50	4.50
b.		Souvenir sheet of 3, #817-819	*11.00*	*8.00*

Traditional Chinese Tea Houses A151

Designs: No. 820, Two men seated at table. No. 821, Cook holding steaming tray of food, woman, baby. No. 822, Woman holding up papers. No. 823, Waiter pouring tea, man seated.
8p, Food, serving bowl.

1996, May 17 *Perf. 12*

820	A151	2p multi (4-1)	1.10	.55
821	A151	2p multi (4-2)	1.10	.55
822	A151	2p multi (4-3)	1.10	.55
823	A151	2p multi (4-4)	1.10	.55
a.		Block of 4, #820-823	6.00	4.00

Souvenir Sheet

824 A151 8p multi *11.00 8.00*

No. 823a is a continuous design. China '96 (No. 824).

Greetings Stamps A152

Designs: 50a, Get well. 1.50p, Congratulations on new baby. 3p, Happy birthday. 4p, Marriage congratulations.

1996, June 14 Litho. *Perf. 12*

825	A152	50a multi (4-1)	.25	.25
826	A152	1.50p multi (4-2)	.50	.35
827	A152	3p multi (4-3)	1.25	.60
828	A152	4p multi (4-4)	1.50	.90
		Nos. 825-828 (4)	3.50	2.10

1996 Summer Olympic Games, Atlanta A153

2p, Swimming (4-1). 3p, Soccer (4-2). 3.50p, Gymnastics (4-3). 4.50p, Sailboarding (4-4).
10p, Boxing.

1996, July 19

829	A153	2p multi	.50	.35
830	A153	3p multi	.80	.55
831	A153	3.50p multi	.90	.60
832	A153	4.50p multi	1.10	.80
		Nos. 829-832 (4)	3.30	2.30

Souvenir Sheet

833 A153 10p multi *7.50 5.00*

Civil and Military Emblems A154

No. 834, Bird looking left. No. 835, Dragon. No. 836, Bird looking right. No. 837, Leopard.

1996, Sept. 18

834	A154	2.50p bl & multi (4-1)	1.20	.60
835	A154	2.50p grn & multi (4-2)	1.20	.60
836	A154	2.50p grn & multi (4-3)	1.20	.60
837	A154	2.50p pur & multi (4-4)	1.20	.60
a.		Block of 4, #834-837	6.50	4.00

See Nos. 947-951.

Fishing with Nets — A155

Boats, fish in sea: No. 838, Six small nets extended from mast of boat. No. 839, Modern trawler. No. 840, Junk trawling. No. 841, Sailboat with nets extended from both sides.

1996, Oct. 9 Litho. *Perf. 12*

838	A155	3p multi (4-1)	1.20	.60
839	A155	3p multi (4-2)	1.20	.60
840	A155	3p multi (4-3)	1.20	.60
841	A155	3p multi (4-4)	1.20	.60
a.		Strip of 4, #838-841	6.50	5.25

Legislative Assembly, 20th Anniv. — A156

1996, Oct. 15 Litho. *Perf. 12x12½*

842 A156 2.80p multicolored .95 .60

Souvenir Sheet

843 A156 8p like No. 842 *9.00 6.00*

Paper Kites A157

No. 844, Dragonfly (4-1). No. 845, Butterfly (4-2). No. 846, Owl in flight (4-3). No. 847, Standing owl (4-4).
No. 848, Dragon.

1996, Oct. 21 Litho. *Perf. 12*

844	A157	3.50p multi	1.50	1.00
845	A157	3.50p multi	1.50	1.00
846	A157	3.50p multi	1.50	1.00
847	A157	3.50p multi	1.50	1.00
a.		Strip or block of 4, #844-847	*8.00*	*8.00*

Souvenir Sheet

Perf. 12½

848 A157 8p multi *12.00 9.00*

No. 848 contains one 51x38mm stamp.

Traditional Chinese Toys — A158

1996, Nov. 13 Litho. *Perf. 12*

849	A158	50a shown	.40	.25
850	A158	1p Fish	1.00	.65
851	A158	3p Doll	3.00	1.25
852	A158	4.50p Dragon	5.00	1.75
		Nos. 849-852 (4)	9.40	3.90

New Year 1997 (Year of the Ox) A159

1997, Jan. 23 Litho. *Perf. 12*

853 A159 5.50p multicolored *3.00 2.00*

Souvenir Sheet

854 A159 10p multicolored *8.00 6.25*

No. 854 is a continuous design.

Lucky Numbers A160

1997, Feb. 12 Litho. *Perf. 12*

855	A160	2p "2," Simplicity	.70	.50
856	A160	2.80p "8," Prosperity	.90	.60
857	A160	3p "3," Progress	1.00	.65
858	A160	3.90p "9," Longevity	1.40	1.00
		Nos. 855-858 (4)	4.00	2.75

Souvenir Sheet

859 A160 9p Man outside house *6.00 4.00*

Hong Kong '97 (No. 859).

Paintings of Macao, by Kwok Se — A161

2p, Junks. 3p, Fortress on side of mountain. 3.50p, Retreat house. 4.50p, Cerco Gate.
8p, Rooftop of building, horiz.

1997, Mar. 1 Litho. *Perf. 12*

860	A161	2p multicolored	.65	.35
861	A161	3p multicolored	1.10	.55
862	A161	3.50p multicolored	1.25	.75
863	A161	4.50p multicolored	1.80	1.00
		Nos. 860-863 (4)	4.80	2.65

Souvenir Sheet

864 A161 8p multicolored *7.50 6.25*

A162

Boat People: 1p, Old woman seated. 1.50p, Woman wearing hat. 2.50p, Woman carrying baby. 5.50p, Man, boy.

1997, Mar. 26 Litho. *Perf. 12*

865	A162	1p multicolored	.60	.40
866	A162	1.50p multicolored	.70	.50
867	A162	2.50p multicolored	1.10	.80
868	A162	5.50p multicolored	2.60	1.75
a.		Block of 4, #865-868	5.00	4.00

Temple A-Ma — A163

No. 869, Steps leading to entrance. No. 870, People strolling past temple, one with umbrella. No. 871, People outside pagoda, pedicab. No. 872, Towers from temple, one emiting smoke.

1997, Apr. 29 Litho. *Perf. 12*

869	A163	3.50p multicolored	.60	.40
870	A163	3.50p multicolored	.60	.40
871	A163	3.50p multicolored	.60	.40
872	A163	3.50p multicolored	.60	.40
a.		Strip of 4, #869-872	3.25	3.25

Souvenir Sheet

873 A163 8p Boat *4.50 4.50*

Drunken Dragon Festival — A164

Stylized designs: 2p, Two men, one holding dragon. 3p, Man holding up dragon. 5p, Two men, one holding horn.
9p, Dragon, man, horiz.

1997, May 14

874	A164	2p multicolored	.60	.35
875	A164	3p multicolored	1.00	.55
876	A164	5p multicolored	1.60	1.10
a.		Strip of 3, #874-876	3.50	3.50

Souvenir Sheet

877 A164 9p multicolored *4.25 4.25*

Father Luís Fróis, 400th Death Anniv. A165

No. 879, Father Fróis, cathedral, vert.

1997, June 9 Litho. *Perf. 12*

878	A165	2.50p multi (2-1)	.75	.75
879	A165	2.50p multi (2-2)	.75	.75

See Portugal Nos. 2165-2167.

Legends and Myths — A166

Gods of Protection: No. 880, Wat Lot. No. 881, San Su. No. 882, Chon Keng. No. 883, Wat Chi Kong.
10p, Chon Keng and Wat Chi Kong.

1997, June 18 Litho. *Perf. 12*

880 A166 2.50p multicolored .65 .65
881 A166 2.50p multicolored .65 .65
882 A166 2.50p multicolored .65 .65
883 A166 2.50p multicolored .65 .65
a. Strip or block of 4, #880-883 3.50 3.50
Nos. 880-883 (4) 2.60 2.60

Souvenir Sheet

884 A166 10p multicolored 4.00 4.00

No. 884 contains one 40x40mm stamp.

Macao Red Cross, 77th Anniv. — A167

1997, July 12 *Perf. 12½*

885 A167 1.50p multicolored .40 .40

No. 885 is printed se-tenant with label.

Verandas A168

Various architectural styles.
8p, Close up of veranda, vert.

1997, July 30 Litho. *Perf. 12*

886 A168 50a multi (6-1) .25 .25
887 A168 1p multi (6-2) .25 .25
888 A168 1.50p multi (6-3) .40 .40
889 A168 2p multi (6-4) .50 .50
890 A168 2.50p multi (6-5) .65 .65
891 A168 3p multi (6-6) .75 .75
a. Block of 6, #886-891 2.75 2.75

Souvenir Sheet

892 A168 8p multicolored 2.75 2.75

Traditional Chinese Fans — A169

1997, Sept. 24 Litho. *Perf. 12*

893 A169 50a Planta (4-1) .25 .25
894 A169 1p Papel (4-2) .30 .30
895 A169 3.50p Seda (4-3) .85 .85
896 A169 4p Pluma (4-4) 1.10 1.10
a. Strip or block of 4, #893-896 3.00 3.00

Souvenir Sheet

897 A169 9p Sandalo 4.00 3.75

Fong Soi (Chinese Geomancy) A170

Chinese principles of Yin and Yang related to the five elements of the ancient Zodiac.

1997, Oct. 9 Litho. *Perf. 12*

898 A170 50a green & multi .25 .25
899 A170 1p orange & multi .30 .30
900 A170 1.50p brown & multi .45 .45
901 A170 2p yellow & multi .60 .60
902 A170 2.50p blue & multi .70 .70
a. Strip of 5, #898-902 2.50 2.50

Souvenir Sheet

903 A170 10p green & multi 3.75 3.75

Martial Arts — A171

1997, Nov. 19

904 A171 1.50p Kung Fu .40 .40
905 A171 3.50p Judo .90 .60
906 A171 4p Karate 1.00 .80
a. Strip of 3, #904-906 2.50 2.50

New Year 1998 (Year of the Tiger) A172

1998, Jan. 18 Litho. *Perf. 12*

907 A172 5.50p multicolored 1.75 1.75

Souvenir Sheets

908 A172 10p multicolored 2.75 2.75
a. Ovptd. in sheet margin 2.75 2.75

No. 908 is a continuous design.
No. 908a overprinted in Gold in Sheet Margin with "Amizade Luso-Chinesa / Festival de Macao" & Chinese Text.

Street Vendors A173

Vendors at stands, carts: No. 909, 1p, Frying foods. 1.50p, Food products, eggs. 2p, Clothing items. 2.50p, Balloons. 3p, Flowers. 3.50p, Fruits and vegetables.
6p, Vendor at fruit and vegetable stand, diff.

1998, Feb. 13 Litho. *Perf. 12*

909 A173 1p multi (6-1) .25 .25
910 A173 1.50p multi (6-2) .35 .30
911 A173 2p multi (6-3) .50 .45
912 A173 2.50p multi (6-4) .60 .50
913 A173 3p multi (6-5) .75 .65
914 A173 3.50p multi (6-6) .90 .70
a. Block of 6, #909-914 3.60 3.60

Souvenir Sheets

915 A173 6p multicolored 1.75 1.75
a. Ovptd. in sheet margin 2.00 2.00

No. 915a overprinted in Gold in Sheet Margin with "Amizade Luso-Chinesa / Festival de Macao" & Chinese Text.

Traditional Gates A174

Inscriptions: 50a, "Beco da Sé." 1p, "Pátio da Ilusao." 3.50p, "Travessa da galinhas." 4p, "Beco das Felicidades."
9p, "Seminário d S. José," vert.

1998, Mar. 1

916 A174 50a multi (4-1) .25 .25
917 A174 1p multi (4-2) .25 .25
918 A174 3.50p multi (4-3) .95 .95
919 A174 4p multi (4-4) 1.10 1.10
Nos. 916-919 (4) 2.55 2.55

Souvenir Sheets

920 A174 9p multicolored 2.40 2.40
a. Ovptd. in sheet margin 2.50 2.50

No. 920a overprinted in Gold in Sheet Margin with "Amizade Luso-Chinesa / Festival de Macao" & Chinese Text.

Myths and Legends — A175

Gods of Ma Chou: No. 921, Holding baby. No. 922, Watching image appear in smoke. No. 923, With cherubs. No. 924, Hovering over junks.
10p, Face.

1998, Apr. 23 Litho. *Perf. 12*

921 A175 4p multi (4-1) .95 .85
922 A175 4p multi (4-2) .95 .85
923 A175 4p multi (4-3) .95 .85
924 A175 4p multi (4-4) .95 .85
a. Strip of 4, #921-924 4.25 4.25

Souvenir Sheets

925 A175 10p multicolored 2.50 2.50
a. Ovptd. in sheet margin 2.60 2.60

No. 925a overprinted in Gold in Sheet Margin with "Amizade Luso-Chinesa / Festival de Macao" & Chinese Text.

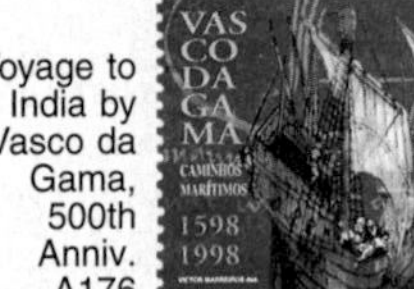

Voyage to India by Vasco da Gama, 500th Anniv. A176

Designs: 1p, Sailing ship. 1.50p, Vasco da Gama. 2p, Map, sailing ship.
8p, Compass rose.

1998, May 20 Litho. *Perf. 12*

926 A176 1p multi (3-1) *.35 .35*
927 A176 1.50p multi (3-2) *.55 .55*
928 A176 2p multi (3-3) *.75 .75*
a. Strip of 3, #926-928 *2.00 2.00*

Souvenir Sheet

929 A176 8p multicolored *3.75 3.75*

Nos. 926-929 are inscribed "1598" instead of "1498," and were withdrawn after two days. For corrected version, see Nos. 943-946.

Oceans A177

Stylized designs: 2.50p, Mermaid, shells, sailing ship, compass rose. 3p, Compass rose, fish, oil derrick.
9p, Sailing ship, seagull, fish, cloud, sun.

1998, May 22

930 A177 2.50p multi (2-1) .65 .65
931 A177 3p multi (2-2) .75 .75
a. Pair, #930-931 2.00 2.00

Souvenir Sheets

932 A177 9p multicolored 2.75 2.75
a. Ovptd. in sheet margin *3.00 3.00*

No. 932a overprinted in Gold in Sheet Margin with "Amizade Luso-Chinesa / Festival de Macao" & Chinese Text.

1998 World Cup Soccer Championships, France — A178

Various soccer plays.

1998, June 10 Litho. *Perf. 12*

933 A178 3p multicolored .75 .45
934 A178 3.50p multicolored .90 .65
935 A178 4p multicolored .95 .75
936 A178 4.50p multicolored 1.10 .95
Nos. 933-936 (4) 3.70 2.80

Souvenir Sheets

937 A178 9p multicolored 2.75 2.75
a. Ovptd. in sheet margin *3.75 3.75*

No. 937a overprinted in Gold in Sheet Margin with "Amizade Luso-Chinesa / Festival de Macao" & Chinese Text.

Chinese Opera Masks A179

1.50p, Lio, Seak Chong (4-1). 2p, Wat, Chi Kong (4-2). 3p, Kam, Chin Pao (4-3). 5p, Lei, Kwai (4-4).
8p, Masked player.

1998, July 28 Litho. *Perf. 12*

938 A179 1.50p multi .35 .25
939 A179 2p multi .50 .45
940 A179 3p multi .75 .60
941 A179 5p multi 1.10 .95
a. Strip of 4, #938-941 3.25 3.25

Souvenir Sheets

942 A179 8p multi 2.25 2.25
a. Ovptd. in sheet margin *3.75 3.75*

No. 942a overprinted in Gold in Sheet Margin with "Amizade Luso-Chinesa / Festival de Macao" & Chinese Text.

Vasco da Gama Type of 1998 Inscribed "1498"

1998, Sept. 4 Litho. *Perf. 12*

943 A176 1p like #926 .30 .30
944 A176 1.50p like #927 .60 .60
945 A176 2p like #928 .75 .75
a. Strip of 3, #943-945 1.90 1.90

Souvenir Sheets

946 A176 8p like #929 2.00 2.00
a. Ovptd. in sheet margin *3.75 3.75*

Issued to correct the error on Nos. 926-929.
No. 946a overprinted in Gold in Sheet Margin with "Amizade Luso-Chinesa / Festival de Macao" & Chinese Text.

Civil and Military Emblems Type of 1996

Designs: 50a, Lion. 1p, Dragon. 1.50p, Bird looking right. 2p, Bird looking left.
9p, Bird flying.

1998, Sept. 9

947 A154 50a multi (4-1) .25 .25
948 A154 1p multi (4-2) .30 .25
949 A154 1.50p multi (4-3) .40 .30
950 A154 2p multi (4-4) .60 .40
a. Strip of 4, #947-950 1.50 1.50

Souvenir Sheets

951 A154 9p multicolored 2.50 2.50
a. Ovptd. in sheet margin *3.75 3.75*

No. 951a overprinted in Gold in Sheet Margin with "Amizade Luso-Chinesa / Festival de Macao" & Chinese Text.

Kun Iam Temple A180

Scenes inside temple compound: No. 952, Buddha figure standing. No. 953, Entrance gate, man running, benches. No. 954, Entrance to building, people. No. 955, People, stream, pagoda, flowers.
10p, Table, chairs, top of incense burner.

1998 Litho. *Perf. 12*

952 A180 3.50p multicolored .85 .75
953 A180 3.50p multicolored .85 .75
954 A180 3.50p multicolored .85 .75

955 A180 3.50p multicolored .85 .75
a. Block of 4, #952-955 3.60 3.60

Souvenir Sheets

956 A180 10p multicolored 2.50 2.50
a. Ovptd. in sheet margin *3.75 3.75*

No. 956a overprinted in Gold in Sheet Margin with "Amizade Luso-Chinesa / Festival de Macao" & Chinese Text.

Paintings of Macao, by Didier Rafael Bayle
A181

Designs: 2p, Street scene, buggy, vert. 3p, People standing outside of buildings. 3.50p, Building atop wall. 4.50p, Buildings, house along street, vert.
8p, Top of building.

1998, Nov. 11 Litho. *Perf. 12*
957 A181 2p multi (4-1) .50 .40
958 A181 3p multi (4-2) .75 .60
959 A181 3.50p multi (4-3) .90 .70
960 A181 4.50p multi (4-4) 1.10 .90
Nos. 957-960 (4) 3.25 2.60

Souvenir Sheets

961 A181 8p multicolored 2.25 2.25
a. Ovptd. in sheet margin *3.75 3.75*

No. 961a overprinted in Gold in Sheet Margin with "Amizade Luso-Chinesa / Festival de Macao" & Chinese Text.

Tiles
A182

Designs: 1p, Dragon. 1.50p, Sailing ship. 2.50p, Chinese junk. 5.50p, Peacock.
10p, Building, lighthouse.

1998, Dec. 8
962 A182 1p multi (4-1) .25 .25
963 A182 1.50p multi (4-2) .35 .30
964 A182 2.50p multi (4-3) .60 .45
965 A182 5.50p multi (4-4) 1.20 .90
a. Block of 4, #962-965 2.75 2.75

Souvenir Sheets

966 A182 10p multicolored 3.25 3.25
a. Ovptd. in sheet margin *4.50 4.50*

No. 966a overprinted in Gold in Sheet Margin with "Amizade Luso-Chinesa / Festival de Macao" & Chinese Text.

New Year 1999 (Year of the Rabbit)
A183

1999, Feb. 8 Litho. *Perf. 12*
967 A183 5.50p multicolored 1.40 1.40

Souvenir Sheet

968 A183 10p multicolored 2.75 2.75
a. Ovptd. in sheet margin 2.75 2.75

No. 968 is a continuous design.
No. 968a overprinted in gold in sheet margin with "Amizade Luso-Chinesa / Transferencia da Soberania de / MACAU 1999 / Sichuan Chengdu," dates and Chinese text.

Characters from Novel, "Dream of the Red Mansion," by Cao Xuequin — A184

1999, Mar. 1 Litho. *Perf. 12*
969 A184 2p Bao Yu (6-1) .60 .45
970 A184 2p Dayiu (6-2) .60 .45
971 A184 2p Bao Chai (6-3) .60 .45
972 A184 2p Xi Feng (6-4) .60 .45
973 A184 2p San Jie (6-5) .60 .45
974 A184 2p Qing Wen (6-6) .60 .45
a. Block of 6, #969-974 3.60 3.60

Souvenir Sheet

975 A184 8p Bao Yu & Dayiu 2.25 2.25
a. Ovptd. in sheet margin 2.25 2.25

No. 975a overprinted in gold in sheet margin with "Amizade Luso-Chinesa / Transferencia da Soberania de / MACAU 1999 / Sichuan Chengdu," dates and Chinese text.

Maritime Heritage
A185

1999, Mar. 19 Litho. *Perf. 12*
976 A185 1.50p Sailing ships .45 .30
977 A185 2.50p Marine life .70 .60
a. Pair, #976-977 1.25 1.25

Souvenir Sheet

978 A185 6p Whale, vert. 2.00 2.00
a. Ovptd. in sheet margin 2.50 2.50

Australia '99, World Stamp Expo.
No. 978a overprinted in gold in sheet margin with "Amizade Luso-Chinesa / Transferencia da Soberania de / MACAU 1999 / Sichuan Chengdu," dates and Chinese text.

First Portugal-Macao Flight, 75th Anniv. — A186

Airplanes: No. 979, Breguet 16 Bn2, "Patria." No. 980, DH9.

1999, Apr. 19 Litho. *Perf. 12*
979 A186 3p multicolored 1.10 1.10
980 A186 3p multicolored 1.10 1.10
a. Souvenir sheet, #979-980 2.50 2.50
b. As "a," ovptd. in sheet margin *3.00 3.00*

See Portugal Nos. 2289-2290.
No. 980a is a continuous design.
No. 980b overprinted in gold in sheet margin with "Amizade Luso-Chinesa / Transferencia da Soberania de / MACAU 1999 / Sichuan Chengdu," dates and Chinese text.

A187

Traditional Water Carrier: a, 1p, Woman carrying container (4-1). b, 1.50p, Filling container from pump (4-2). c, 2p, Drawing water from well (4-3). d, 2.50p, Filling containers from faucet (4-4).
7p, Woman carrying containers up stairs.

1999, Apr. 28 *Perf. 12*
Horiz. Strip or Block of 4
981 A187 #a.-d. 2.00 2.00

Souvenir Sheet

982 A187 7p multicolored 2.00 2.00
a. Ovptd. in sheet margin 2.25 2.25

No. 981 was issued in sheets of 4 strips or blocks, each in a different order.
No. 982a overprinted in gold in sheet margin with "Amizade Luso-Chinesa / Transferencia de Soberania de / MACAU 1999 / China Shanghai," date and Chinese text.

A188

Telecommunications — No. 983: a, 50a, Sea-Me-We cable. b, 1p, Satellite dishes. c, 3.50p, Cellular phones. d, 4p, Television. e, 4.50p, Internet.
8p, Computer mouse.

1999, May 5 Litho. *Perf. 12*
983 A188 Strip of 5, #a.-e. 3.50 3.50

Souvenir Sheet

984 A188 8p multi 2.50 2.50
a. Ovptd. in sheet margin *3.50 3.50*

No. 984 has a holographic image. Soaking in water may affect hologram.
No. 984a is overprinted in gold in sheet margin with "Amizade Luso-Chinesa / Transferencia de Soberania de / MACAU 1999 / China Shanghai," date and Chinese text.

Modern Buildings, Construction — A189

1p, Cultural Center. 1.50p, Museum of Macao. 2p, Maritime Museum. 2.50p, Maritime Terminal. 3p, University of Macao. 3.50p, Public Administration Building. 4.50p, World Trade Center. 5p, Coloane Go-kart Track. 8p, Bank of China. 12p, Ultramarine National Bank.

1999, June 2 Litho. *Perf. 12*
989 A189 1p multi .25 .25
990 A189 1.50p multi .40 .30
991 A189 2p multi .55 .45
992 A189 2.50p multi .65 .50
993 A189 3p multi .75 .55
994 A189 3.50p multi, vert. .85 .70
995 A189 4.50p multi, vert. 1.10 .90
996 A189 5p multi, vert. 1.25 1.00
997 A189 8p multi, vert. 2.00 1.50
998 A189 12p multi, vert. 2.50 2.00
Nos. 989-998 (10) 10.30 8.15

TAP SEAC Buildings — A190

No. 999 — Various buildings with enominations in: a, Greenish blue. b, Orange. c, Dull yellow. d, Blue green (blue door).
10p, Orange.

1999, June 24
999 A190 1.50p Strip of 4, #a.-d. 1.60 1.60

Souvenir Sheet

1000 A190 10p multicolored 2.50 2.50
a. Ovptd. in sheet margin 2.50 2.50

No. 1000a overprinted in gold in sheet margin with "Amizade Luso-Chinesa / Transferencia de Soberania de / MACAU 1999 / Guangdong Cantao," date and Chinese text.

Dim Sum — A191

No. 1001 — Table settings with: a, Brown teapot. b, Two food platters. c, Two bamboo steamers. d, Flowered teapot.
9p, Various platters.

1999, Aug. 21
1001 A191 2.50p Strip of 4, #a.-d. 2.50 2.50

Souvenir Sheet

1002 A191 9p multicolored 2.50 2.50
a. Ovptd. in sheet margin 2.25 2.25

China 1999 World Philatelic Exhibition (No. 1002).
No. 1002a overprinted in gold in sheet margin with "Amizade Luso-Chinesa / Transferencia de Soberania de / MACAU 1999 / Guangdong Cantao," date and Chinese text.

Modern Sculpture
A192

Various unidentified sculptures.

1999, Oct. 9 Litho. *Perf. 12*
Background Color
1003 A192 1p red violet .30 .25
1004 A192 1.50p brown, vert. .45 .25
1005 A192 2.50p gray brn, vert. .75 .45
1006 A192 3.50p blue grn 1.00 .65
Nos. 1003-1006 (4) 2.50 1.60

Souvenir Sheet

1007 A192 10p blue gray 2.75 2.75
a. Ovptd. in sheet margin 2.75 2.75

No. 1007a overprinted in gold in sheet margin with "Amizade Luso-Chinesa / Transferencia da Soberania de / MACAU 1999 / Zhejiang Hangzhou," date and Chinese text.

Meeting of Portuguese and Chinese Cultures — A193

No. 1008: a, 1p, Ships. b, 1.50p, Building. c, 2p, Bridge. d, 3p, Fort.
10p, Fort, diff.

1999, Nov. 19 Litho. *Perf. 12¼*
1008 A193 Strip of 4, #a.-d. 2.25 2.25

Souvenir Sheet

1009 A193 10p multi 2.75 2.75
a. Ovptd. in sheet margin 2.50 2.50

Perforations in corners of stamps on Nos. 1008-1009 are star-shaped.
No. 1009a overprinted in gold in sheet margin with "Amizade Luso-Chinesa / Transferencia da Soberania de / MACAU 1999 / Zhejiang Hangzhou," date and Chinese text.
See Portugal No. 2339.

Retrospective of Macao's Portuguese History — A194

No. 1010: a, 1p, Globe. b, 1.50p, Fort. c, 2p, Chinese, Portuguese people. d, 3.50p, Skyline, Nobre de Carvalho bridge.
9p, Arms.

1999, Dec. 19
1010 A194 Block or strip of 4, #a.-d. 2.75 2.75

Souvenir Sheet

1011 A194 9p multi 2.75 2.75
a. Ovptd. in sheet margin 2.50 2.50

No. 1011a overprinted in gold in sheet margin with "Amizade Luso-Chinesa / Transferencia da Soberania de / MACAU 1999 / Macau," date and Chinese text.
Perforations in corners of stamps on Nos. 1010-1011 are star-shaped.
See Portugal No. 2340.

Special Administrative Region of People's Republic of China

Establishment of Special Administrative Region — A195

No. 1012: a, 1p, Temple, dragon. b, 1.50p, Friendship Bridge, dragon boats. c, 2p, Cathedral, Santa Claus, Christmas tree. d, 2.50p, Lighthouse, race cars. e, 3p, Building, dragons. f, 3.50p, Building, crowd.
8p, Flower.

1999, Dec. 20 Litho. *Perf. 12*
1012 A195 Block of 6, #a.-f. 3.50 3.50

Souvenir Sheet

1013 A195 8p multi 2.75 2.75
a. Ovptd. in sheet margin 2.75 2.75

No. 1013a overprinted in gold in sheet margin with "Amizade Luso-Chinesa / Transferencia da Soberania de / MACAU 1999 / China — Macau," dte, "O futuro de Macau será melhor" and Chinese text.

Souvenir Sheet

Millennium — A196

2000, Jan. 1 Litho. *Perf. 12¼*
1014 A196 8p multi 2.75 2.75

Perforations in corners of stamp are star-shaped.

New Year 2000 (Year of the Dragon) A197

2000, Jan. 28 *Perf. 12¼*
1015 A197 5.50p multi 1.60 1.60

Souvenir Sheet

1016 A197 10p multi 2.75 2.75

Perforations in corners of stamps on Nos. 1015-1016 are star-shaped.

Historic Buildings — A198

2000, Mar. 1 Litho. *Perf. 12¼*
1017 Strip of 4 2.25 2.25
a. A198 1p green circles .25 .25
b. A198 1.50p pink circles .40 .40
c. A198 2p brown circles .50 .50
d. A198 3p blue circles .75 .75

Souvenir Sheet

1018 A198 9p Brown circles 2.50 2.50

Perforations in corners of stamps are star-shaped.

Chinese Calligraphy A199

No. 1019 — Characters: a, Rectangle with bisecting line. b, Rectangle with lines inside. c, 8 horizontal lines, 3 vertical lines. d, 3 spots to left of 6 touching lines.
8p, Characters shown on Nos. 1019a-1019d.

2000, Mar. 23
1019 Block of 4 3.50 3.50
a.-d. A199 3p any single .75 .75

Souvenir Sheet

1020 A199 8p multi 2.50 2.50

Bangkok 2000 Stamp Exhibition (No. 1020).
Perforations in corners of stamps are star-shaped.

Scenes From "A Journey to the West" — A200

No. 1021: a, 1p, Monkey and tiger. b, 1.50p, Monkey on tree. c, 2p, Monkey and spear carrier. d, 2.50p, Spear carrier and dog. e, 3p, Man in robe. f, 3.50p, Monkey in palm of hand.
9p, Monkey with stick, horiz.

2000, May 5 Litho. *Perf. 12¼*
1021 A200 Block of 6, #a-f 3.50 3.50

Souvenir Sheet

1022 A200 9p multi 3.00 3.00

Perforations in corners of stamps are star-shaped.

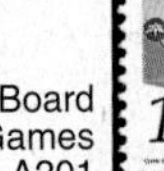

Board Games A201

Designs: 1p, Chinese chess. 1.50p, Chess. 2p, Go. 2.50p, Parcheesi.

2000, June 8
1023-1026 A201 Set of 4 2.25 2.25

Souvenir Sheet

1027 A201 9p Chinese checkers 2.50 2.50

Perforations in corners of stamps are star-shaped.

Tea Rituals A202

2000, July 7
1028 Horiz. strip of 4 4.00 4.00
a. A202 2p Square table, 4 people .50 .40
b. A202 3p Round table, 5 people .75 .60
c. A202 3.50p Round table, 3 people 1.00 .90
d. A202 4.50p Square table, 3 people 1.25 1.10

Souvenir Sheet

1029 A202 8p Woman pouring tea 2.50 2.50

Perforations in corners are star-shaped.
World Stamp Expo 2000, Anaheim (No. 1029).

Tricycle Drivers — A203

No. 1030: a, Driver pointing. b, Driver wearing yellow cap. c, Driver sitting on saddle. d, Driver with feet on saddle. e, Driver with crossed legs. f, Driver repairing tricycle.
8p, Driver standing next to tricycle, vert.

2000, Sept. 1 Granite Paper
1030 A203 2p Block of 6, #a-f 4.00 4.00

Souvenir Sheet

1031 A203 8p multi 2.75 2.75

Perforations in corners of stamps are star-shaped.

Sculpture Type of 1999 Inscribed "Macau, China"

Various unidentified sculptures with background colors of: 1p, Brown. 2p, Green, vert. 3p, Purple, vert. 4p, Purple.
10p, Gray blue.

2000, Oct. 9 Granite Paper
1032-1035 A192 Set of 4 3.00 3.00

Souvenir Sheet

1036 A192 10p multi 3.25 3.25

Perforations in corners of stamps are star-shaped.

Ceramics and Chinaware — A204

No. 1037; a, Style. b, Color. c, Form. d, Function. e, Design. f, Export.

2000, Oct. 31 Granite Paper
1037 A204 2.50p Sheet of 6, #a-f 4.75 4.75

Souvenir Sheet

1038 A204 8p Plate design 2.25 2.25

No. 1038 contains one 38mm diameter stamp. Perforations in corners of No. 1037 are star-shaped.

Jade Ornaments A205

Various ornaments. Colors of country name: 1.50p, Purple. 2p, Green, vert. 2.50p, Red, vert. 3p, Blue.
9p, Red, vert.

2000, Nov. 22 Granite Paper
1039-1042 A205 Set of 4 2.75 2.75

Souvenir Sheet

1043 A205 9p multi 2.75 2.75

Perforations in corners of stamps are star-shaped.

Special Administrative Region, 1st Anniv. — A206

No. 1044: a, 2p, Dancers, flags. b, 3p, Monument, dragon.

2000, Dec. 20 Litho. *Perf. 12¼*
Granite Paper (#1044)
1044 A206 Horiz. pair, #a-b 1.75 1.75

Souvenir Sheet
Litho. & Embossed
Perf. 13½x13

1045 A206 18p Flags, monument 5.25 5.25

No. 1045 contains one 60x40mm stamp. Perforations in corners of No. 1044 are star-shaped.

New Year 2001 (Year of the Snake) A207

2001, Jan. 18 Litho. *Perf. 13x13¼*
1046 A207 5.50p multi 1.75 1.75

Souvenir Sheet
Granite Paper

1047 A207 10p multi 3.25 3.25

Seng-Yu Proverbs — A208

Designs: No. 1048, Sleeping on a woodpile and tasting gall (4-1). No. 1049, Watching over a stump waiting for a rabbit (4-2). No. 1050, The fox making use of the tiger's fierceness (4-3). No. 1051, Meng Mu moving house three times (4-4).
8p, Man and bell.

2001, Feb. 1 Photo. *Perf. 11¾*
Granite Paper
1048 A208 2p multi .60 .60
a. Booklet pane of 1, plain paper 3.50

1049 A208 2p multi .60 .60
a. Booklet pane of 1, plain paper 3.50
1050 A208 2p multi .60 .60
a. Booklet pane of 1, plain paper 3.50
1051 A208 2p multi .60 .60
a. Booklet pane of 1, plain paper 3.50
Booklet, #1048a-1051a 18.00
Nos. 1048-1051 (4) 2.40 2.40

Souvenir Sheet

1052 A208 8p multi 2.75 2.75

Hong Kong 2001 Stamp Exhibition (No. 1052). Booklet containing Nos. 1048a-1051a sold for 35p.

Traditional Implements A209

Designs: 1p, Abacus. 2p, Plane. 3p, Iron. 4p, Balance scale.
8p, Abacus, plane, iron, balance scale.

2001, Mar. 1 Litho. *Perf. 14½x14*
1053-1056 A209 Set of 4 3.00 3.00

Souvenir Sheet

1057 A209 8p multi 2.75 2.75

Religious Beliefs A210

No. 1058: a, Buddha. b, People in prayer. c, Re-enactment of Christ carrying cross. d, People in procession.
8p, Symbols.

2001, Apr. 12 Litho. *Perf. 14½x14*
1058 Horiz. strip of 4 2.75 2.75
a. A210 1p multi .30 .30
b. A210 1.50p multi .50 .45
c. A210 2p multi .70 .65
d. A210 2.50p multi .90 .85

Souvenir Sheet
Photo.
Perf.

1059 A210 8p multi 3.00 3.00

No. 1059 contains one 60mm diameter stamp.

Rescue Workers A211

No. 1060: a, Fireman. b, Hazardous materials worker. c, Fireman, diff. d, Ambulance crew.
8p, Firemen, diff

2001, May 2 Litho. *Perf. 14½x14*
1060 Horiz. strip of 4 4.00 4.00
a. A211 1.50p multi .55 .45
b. A211 2.50p multi .85 .80
c. A211 3p multi .95 .90
d. A211 4p multi 1.30 1.25

Souvenir Sheet
Perf. 14x14½

1061 A211 8p multi 5.00 5.00

No. 1061 contains one 60x40mm stamp.

Internet and E-Commerce — A212

Designs: 1.50p, Keys. 2p, Envelope with "@" symbol. 2.50p, Hand-held computer. 3p, Computer.
6p, Linked computers.

2001, June 30 Litho. *Perf. 14½x14*
1062-1065 A212 Set of 4 3.00 3.00

Souvenir Sheet

1066 A212 6p multi 2.50 2.50

Emblem of 2008 Summer Olympics, Beijing — A213

2001, July 14 Photo. *Perf. 13x13¼*
1067 A213 1p multi + label 1.00 .60

No. 1067 printed in sheets of 12 stamp + label pairs with one large central label. See People's Republic of China No. 3119, Hong Kong No. 940. No. 1067 with different label is from People's Republic of China No. 3119a.

The Romance of Three Kingdoms — A214

Designs: a, Men praying (4-1). b, Man with spear (4-2). c, Men at outdoors table (4-3). d, Man on horseback (4-4).
7p, Man with sword, horiz.

2001, Aug. 1 Litho. *Perf. 14x14½*
1068 A214 3p Block of 4, #a-d 4.00 4.00

Souvenir Sheet
Perf. 14½x14

1069 A214 7p multi 3.00 3.00

2001 Census — A215

Designs: 1p, Buildings, students, child health care. 1.50p, Buildings, street scene. 2.50p, Bridge, people.
6p, Buildings, students, child health care, street scene, bridge, people.

2001, Aug. 23 Litho. *Perf. 14x14½*
1070-1072 A215 Set of 3 2.00 2.00

Souvenir Sheet

1073 A215 6p multi 2.00 2.00

No. 1073 contains one 89x39mm stamp.

Stores — A216

No. 1074: a, 1.50p, Municipal market. b, 2.50p, Store with red window frames. c, 3.50p, Store, parked bicycles. d, 4.50p, Store, parked cars.
7p, Store tower and windows.

2001, Sept. 13 *Perf. 14½x14*
1074 A216 Block of 4, #a-d 3.50 3.50

Souvenir Sheet
Perf. 14x14½

1075 A216 7p multi 2.75 2.75

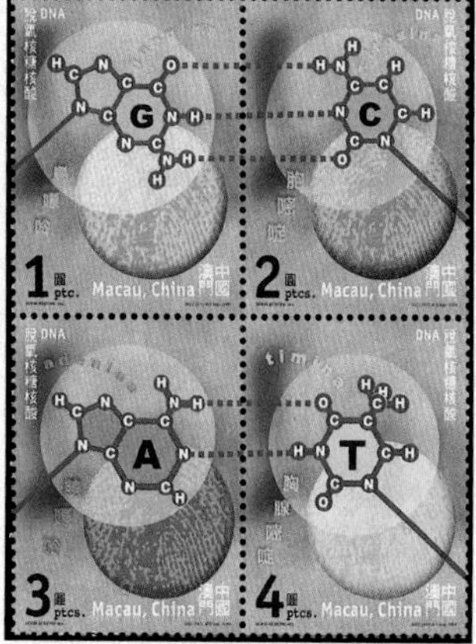
DNA — A217

Fingerprint and: a, 1p, Guanine. b, 2p, Cytosine. c, 3p, Adenine. d, 4p, Thymine.
8p, Adenine, horiz.

2001, Oct. 9 Photo. *Perf. 14x13½*
Granite Paper
1076 A217 Block of 4, #a-d 4.00 4.00

Souvenir Sheet
Perf. 13½x14

1077 A217 8p multi 3.25 3.25

No. 1077 contains one 44x29mm stamp.

Parks and Gardens — A218

No. 1078: a, 1.50p, Comendador Ho Yin Garden. b, 2.50p, Mong Há Hill Municipal Park. c, 3p, City of Flowers Garden. 4.50p, Taipa Grande Nature Park.
8p, Art Garden.

2001, Nov. 30 Litho. *Perf. 13½x14*
Granite Paper
1078 A218 Block of 4, #a-d 3.75 3.75

Souvenir Sheet

1079 A218 8p multi 3.00 3.00

I Ching A219

A219a

No. 1080 — Position of broken bars in trigrams (pa kua): a, No broken bars. b, First and second. c, Second and third. d, Second. e, First and third. f, First. g, Third. h, First, second and third.

2001, Dec. 10 Photo. *Perf. 13*
Granite Paper
1080 A219 2p Sheet of 8, #a-h 5.75 5.75

Souvenir Sheet
Perf. 13½x13¼

1081 A219a 8p shown 3.00 3.00

No. 1080 contains eight 39x34mm hexagonal stamps. See Nos. 1111, 1126, 1135, 1203, 1241, 1306, 1360.

New Year 2002 (Year of the Horse) A220

Horse's head: 5.50p, With frame. 10p, With continuous design.

2002, Jan. 28 Litho. *Perf. 14½x14*
1082 A220 5.50p multi 2.00 2.00

Souvenir Sheet

1083 A220 10p multi 3.50 3.50

Characters From Novel "Dream of the Red Mansion II," by Cao Xuequin — A221

No. 1084: a, Lao Lao (6/1). b, Jin Chuan (6/2). c, Zi Juan (6/3). d, Xiang Yun (6/4). e, Liu Lang (6/5). f, Miao Yu (6/6).
8d, Woman reading book.

2002, Mar. 1 *Perf. 14x14½*
1084 A221 2p Block of 6, #a-f 5.00 5.00

Souvenir Sheet

1085 A221 8p multi 5.00 5.00

Tou-tei Festival — A222

No. 1086: a, 1.50p, Opera. b, 2.50p, Dinner in appreciation of the elderly. c, 3.50p, Burning of religious objects. d, 4.50p, Preparing roasted pork.
8p, People watching performance, vert.

2002, Mar. 15 *Perf. 14½x14*
1086 A222 Block of 4, #a-d 4.25 4.25

Souvenir Sheet
Perf. 14x14½

1087 A222 8p multi 3.00 3.00

Church of St. Paul, 400th Anniv. — A223

Various church statues: 1p, 3.50p.
8p, Statue in niche.

2002, Apr. 12 *Perf. 14½x14*
1088-1089 A223 Set of 2 1.75 1.75

Souvenir Sheet
Perf. 14x14½

1090 A223 8p multi 3.00 3.00

No. 1090 contains one 30x40mm stamp.

Participation of Chinese Team in 2002 World Cup Soccer Championships — A224

No. 1091: a, 1p, Goalie. b, 1.50p, Two players.

Perf. 12 Syncopated
2002, May 16 **Photo.**
1091 A224 Horiz. pair, #a-b 1.25 1.25

A souvenir sheet containing Nos. 1091a-1091b, People's Republic of China No. 3198 and Hong Kong Nos. 978a-978b exists.

Environmental Protection — A225

Designs: 1p, Conservation of maritime resources. 1.50p, Reforestation. 2p, Recycling. 2.50p, Protection of swamps. 3p, Reuse of resources. 3.50p, Municipal cleaning. 4p, Air purification. 4.50p, Health and hygiene. 8p, Quiet and comfort.

2002, June 5 **Litho.** *Perf. 13x13¼*
1092-1100 A225 Set of 9 9.00 7.00

Zheng Guanying (1842-1921), Reformer and Author — A226

Zheng and: a, 1p, Another man. b, 2p, Harbor scene. c, 3p, Men at table. d, 3.50p, Chinese text.
6p, Zheng seated at table.

2002, July 24 *Perf. 14*
1101 A226 Strip or block of 4, #a-d 3.75 3.75

Souvenir Sheet

1102 A226 6p multi 2.50 2.50

No. 1102 contains one 40x60mm stamp.

Honesty and Equality A227

Various buildings: 1p, 3.50p.

2002, Sept. 13 **Litho.** *Perf. 14½x14*
1103-1104 A227 Set of 2 1.50 1.50

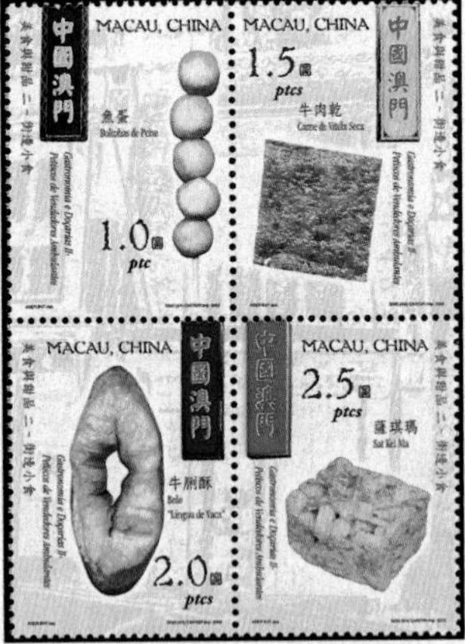
Macao Snack Food — A228

No. 1105: a, 1p, Bolinhas de peixe (fish balls). b, 1.50p, Carne de vitela seca (dried veal). c, 2p, Bolo (cake). d, 2.50p, Sat Kei Ma.
7p, Pastry.

2002, Sept. 26 **Litho.** *Perf. 13¼x13*
1105 A228 Block of 4, #a-d 3.00 2.00

Souvenir Sheet

1106 A228 7p multi 3.00 2.00

Portions of Nos. 1105-1106 were applied by a thermographic process, producing a raised, shiny effect. No. 1106 contains one 50x50mm diamond-shaped stamp.

Filial Love — A229

No. 1107: a, 1p, Farmer and elephant (O amor filial comove a Deus). b, 1.50p, Man and woman (Abanar a almofada e aquecer a manta). c, 2p, Man and bamboo plants (Chorar sobre o bambu fez crescer rebentos). d, 2.50p, Man and fish (Pescar para a mae deitado no gelo).
No. 1107E: f, Man with arms extended (Mal agasalhado mas tolerante com a madrasta). g, Man and woman (Saltaram carpas da nascente). h, Man with hat (Quem tem amor filial é também fiel). i, Man (Lealdade de pai, amor filial do filho).
7p, Man wearing deer's head (Dar leite de veado aos pais).

2002, Oct. 9 **Litho.** *Perf. 14*
1107 A229 Block of 4, #a-d 2.75 2.75
1107E Souvenir booklet 8.00
f.-i. A229 4.50p Any booklet pane of 1 1.60 1.60

Souvenir Sheet
Perf. 13½x13

1108 A229 7p multi 2.50 2.50

Particle Physics — A230

No. 1109: a, Unified electroweak interaction theory developed by Steven Weinberg, Sheldon Lee Glashow and Abdus Salam. b, Discovery of W and Z subatomic particles by Carlo Rubbia, 1983. c, Higgs diagram, developed by Richard Feynman and Peter Higgs. d, CERN large electron positron collider, 1989. e, Classification of particles and prediction of quarks by Murray Gell-Mann and George Zweig. f, Unification theory of Albert Einstein.
8p, Detection of positive and negative W particles, CERN LEP, 1996.

2002, Nov. 22 *Perf. 14x14½*
1109 A230 1.50p Block of 6, #a-f 5.00 5.00

Souvenir Sheet

1110 A230 8p multi 3.00 3.00

I Ching Type of 2001 and

Peace Dance — A231

No. 1111 — Position of broken bars in trigrams (pa kua): a, Fourth. b, First, second and fourth. c, Second, third and fourth. d, Second and fourth. e, First, third and fourth. f, First and fourth. g, Third and fourth. h, First, second, third and fourth.

2002, Dec. 13 *Perf. 14*
Granite Paper

1111 A219 2p Sheet of 8, #a-h 4.75 4.75

Souvenir Sheet
Perf. 11¼x13½

1112 A231 8p multi 2.75 2.75

No. 1111 contains eight 39x34 hexagonal stamps. Stamps from No. 1111 have Roman numeral II below "I Ching" and "Pa Kua."

New Year 2003 (Year of the Ram) A232

2003, Jan. 2 *Perf. 14½x14*
1113 A232 5.50p multi 1.75 1.75

Souvenir Sheet

1113A A232 10p multi 3.00 3.00

Legend of Liang Shanbo and Zhu Yingtai A233

No. 1114: a, People seated and reading. b, People on bridge. c, People, tea pot and cups. d, Man holding red paper.
9p, People with butterfly wings.

2003, Feb. 15 **Litho.** *Perf. 13x13½*
1114 Horiz. strip of 4 4.25 4.25
a.-d. A233 3.50p Any single .90 .90

Souvenir Sheet

1115 A233 9p multi 3.25 3.25

No. 1115 contains one 40x60mm stamp.

The Outlaws of the Marsh — A234

No. 1116: a, Song Jiang. b, Lin Chong. c, Wu Song. d, Lu Zhishen. e, Wu Yong. f, Hua Rong.
8p, Heróis do Monte Liang Shan.

2003, Mar. 1 *Perf. 13½x14*
Granite Paper (#1116)

1116 A234 2p Block of 6, #a-f 5.00 5.00

Souvenir Sheet
Perf. 14x14½

1117 A234 8p multi 3.00 3.00

Basic Law of Macao, 10th Anniv. A235

Designs: 1p, Building, doves, cover of book of laws. 4.50p, Children, dove, flags of Macao and People's Republic of China, law book

2003, Mar. 31 *Perf. 14*
1118-1119 A235 Set of 2 1.75 1.75

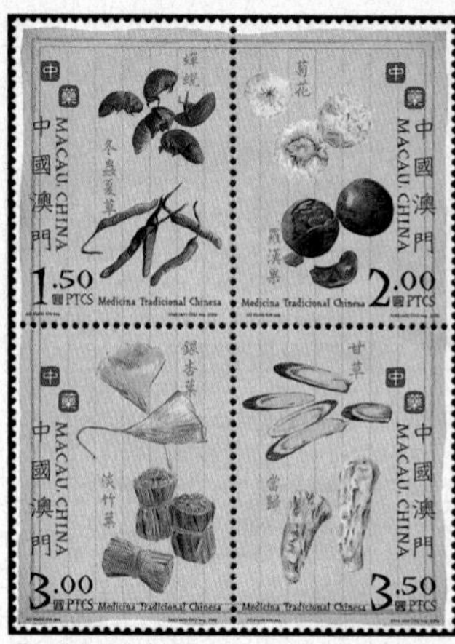

Traditional Chinese Medicine — A236

No. 1120 — Various medicines: a, 1.50p. b, 2p. c, 3p. d, 3.50p.
8p, Man holding bowl of medicine, horiz.

2003, May 28

1120 A236 Block of 4, #a-d 4.00 4.00

Souvenir Sheet

1121 A236 8p multi 3.00 3.00

Historic Buildings on Taipa and Coloane Islands — A237

Various buildings.

2003, June 18

1122 Horiz. strip of 4 2.50 2.50
a. A237 1p multi .25 .25
b. A237 1.50p multi .40 .40
c. A237 2p multi .50 .50
d. A237 3.50p multi .85 .85

Souvenir Sheet

1123 A237 9p multi 2.50 2.50

Everyday Life in the Past — A238

No. 1124: a, Calligrapher at table. b, Puppet maker. c, Man with food cart. d, Washerwoman. e, Woman with decorative lanterns. f, Man carrying food tray above head, man with baskets. g, Photographer. h, Man in chicken costume playing horn.
8p, Barber.

2003, July 30 ***Perf. 13½x13***

1124 Block of 8 3.75 3.75
a.-h. A238 1.50p Any single .40 .40

Souvenir Sheet

Perf. 14x14½

1125 A238 8p multi 2.50 2.50

I Ching Type of 2001 and

Woman and Child — A239

No. 1126 — Position of broken bars in trigrams (pa kua): a, Second. b, Second, fifth and sixth. c, Second, fourth and fifth. d, Second and fifth. e, Second, fourth and sixth. f, Second and sixth. g, Second and fourth. h, Second, fourth, fifth and sixth.

2003, Sept. 10 ***Perf. 14***

Granite Paper

1126 A219 2p Sheet of 8, #a-h 5.00 5.00

Souvenir Sheet

Perf. 14x13½

1127 A239 8p multi 3.00 3.00

No. 1126 contains eight 39x34mm hexagonal stamps. Stamps from No. 1126 have Roman numeral III below text "Pa Kua" and "I Ching."

Launch of First Manned Chinese Spacecraft A240

No. 1128: a, 1p, Astronaut. b, 1.50p, Ship, Shenzhou spacecraft.

2003, Oct. 16 ***Perf. 13x13½***

1128 A240 Pair, #a-b 1.25 1.25

A booklet containing No. 1128, People's Republic of China No. 3314 and Hong Kong No. 1062 exists. The booklet sold for a premium over face value. Value $30.

50th Grand Prix of Macao — A241

No. 1129: a, 1p, Race car #5. b, 1.50p, Yellow race car #11. c, 2p, Red race car #11. d, 3p, Motorcycle #5. e, 3.50p, Race car #15. f, 4.50p, Race car #3.
12p, Race car and motorcycle.

Litho. & Embossed

2003, Oct. 29 ***Perf. 14***

1129 A241 Sheet of 6, #a-f 5.00 5.00

Souvenir Sheet

Litho. With Hologram Applied

Perf.

1130 A241 12p multi 5.00 5.00

No. 1129 contains six 36x27mm stamps that have varnish applied to raised portions.

Macao Museum of Art — A242

No. 1131 — Artwork depicting: a, 1p, Man in hooded cloak. b, 1.50p, Hill overlooking harbor. c, 2p, Ruins of St. Paul's Church. d, 2.50p, Two men.
7p, Waterfront buildings, boats in harbor.

2003, Dec. 1 Litho. ***Perf. 14½x14***

1131 A242 Block of 4 #a-d 2.25 2.25

Souvenir Sheet

1132 A242 7p multi 2.25 2.25

No. 1132 contains one 57x55mm stamp.

New Year 2004 (Year of the Monkey) A243

2004, Jan. 8 ***Perf. 14½x14***

1133 A243 5.50p shown 1.75 1.75

Souvenir Sheet

1134 A243 10p Monkey, diff. 3.00 3.00

I Ching Type of 2001 and

Man Chiseling Stone — A244

No. 1135 — Position of broken bars in trigrams (pa kua): a, Second and third. b, Second, third, fifth and sixth. c, Second, third, fourth and fifth. d, Second, third and fifth. e, Second, third, fourth and sixth. f, Second, third and sixth. g, Second, third and fourth. h, Second, third, fourth, fifth and sixth.

2004, Mar. 1 ***Perf. 14***

Granite Paper

1135 A219 2p Sheet of 8, #a-h 5.00 5.00

Souvenir Sheet

Perf. 14x13½

1136 A244 8p multi 4.00 4.00

No. 1135 contains eight 39x34mm hexagonal stamps. Stamps from No. 1135 have Roman numeral IV below text "Pa Kua" and "I Ching."

Li Sao — A245

No. 1137: a, Orientaçao. b, Cultivo. c, Aconselhamento pela Irma. d, Transmissao de esperança pela fénix. e, Viagens e reflexoes. f, Local da vida eterna.
8p, Li Sao, horiz.

2004, May 28 ***Perf. 13½x14***

Granite Paper

1137 A245 1.50p Block of 6, #a-f 4.00 4.00

Souvenir Sheet

Perf. 14x13½

1138 A245 8p multi 4.00 4.00

God of Guan Di — A246

2004, June 30 ***Perf. 13½x14***

Granite Paper

1139 Horiz. strip of 4 3.25 3.25
a. A246 1.50p shown .35 .30
b. A246 2.50p God, diff. .65 .60
c. A246 3.50p God, diff. .90 .80
d. A246 4.50p God, diff. 1.10 1.00

Souvenir Sheet

Perf. 14x13½

1140 A246 9p God, diff. *4.00* 4.00

No. 1140 contains one 40x40mm stamp.

2004 Summer Olympics, Athens — A247

Designs: 1p, Woman runner. 1.50p, Long jump. 2p, Discus. 3.50p, Javelin.

2004, July 30 ***Perf. 13¼***

Granite Paper

1141-1144 A247 Set of 4 2.25 2.25

Deng Xiaoping (1904-97), Chinese Leader A248

Designs: 1p, Saluting. 1.50p, Wearing white shirt.
8p, As young man.

2004, Aug. 22 Litho. ***Perf. 13x13¼***

1145-1146 A248 Set of 2 .65 .65

Souvenir Sheet

Litho. & Embossed

Perf.

1147 A248 8p multi 2.25 2.25

No. 1147 contains one 40mm diameter stamp.

Intl. Fireworks Display Contest — A249

No. 1148 — Various landmarks and fireworks displays: a, 1p. b, 1.50p. c, 2p. d, 4.50p.
9p, Statue and fireworks, vert.

Litho. & Silk Screened

2004, Sept. 2 ***Perf. 13¼***

Granite Paper

1148 A249 Block of 4, #a-d 2.50 2.50

Souvenir Sheet

Perf. 13x13¼

1149 A249 9p multi 2.50 2.50

No. 1149 contains one 40x60mm stamp.

People's Republic of China, 55th Anniv. — A250

No. 1150 — Buildings and: a, 1p, Flag of People's Republic of China. b, 1.50p, Flag of Macao. c, 2p, Arms of People's Republic of China. d, 3p, Arms of Macao.
7p, Buildings.

2004, Oct. 1 Litho. *Perf. 13x13¼*
Granite Paper
1150 A250 Block of 4, #a-d 2.00 2.00
Souvenir Sheet
Perf. 13¼x13
1151 A250 7p multi 2.50 2.50

No. 1151 contains one 60x40mm stamp.

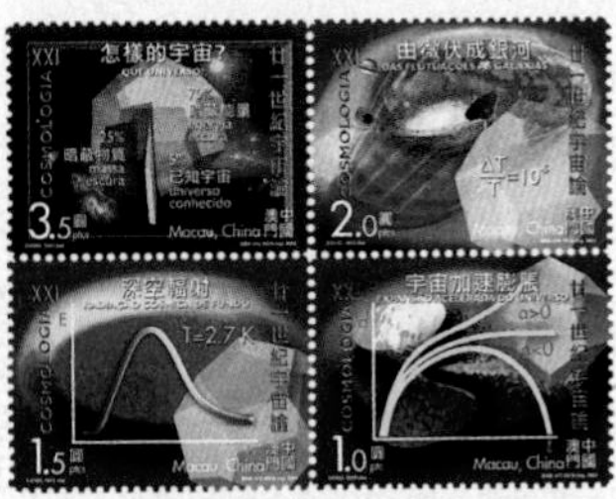
Cosmology — A251

No. 1152: a, 1p, Expansion and acceleration of the Universe. b, 1.50p, Cosmic radiation. c, 2p, Fluctuations of galaxies. d, 3.50p, What is the Universe?
8p, Big Bang Theory.

2004, Oct. 9 *Perf. 12¼*
1152 A251 Block of 4, #a-d 2.50 2.50
Souvenir Sheet
1153 A251 8p multi 2.50 2.50

Macao Garrison of the People's Liberation Army — A252

No. 1154 — Flag and, in foreground: a, 1p, Soldier holding sword. b, 1p, Soldier in tank. c, 1.50p, Soldiers in car. d, 1.50p, Soldiers giving blood. e, 3.50p, Soldier at attention holding gun. f, 3.50p, Soldier with helmet and rifle with bayonet.
8p, Soldiers in car, vert.

2004, Dec. 1 *Perf. 13x13¼*
1154 A252 Block of 6, #a-f 3.00 3.00
Souvenir Sheet
1155 A252 8p multi 2.25 2.25

No. 1155 contains one 40x60mm stamp.

Establishment of Special Administrative District, 5th Anniv. — A253

Lotus flowers and various buildings.

2004, Dec. 20 Litho. *Perf. 14½x14*
1156 Horiz. strip of 4 2.50 2.50
a. A253 1.50p multi .45 .30
b. A253 2p multi .55 .40
c. A253 2.50p multi .65 .50
d. A253 3p multi .80 .65
Souvenir Sheet
Litho. & Embossed
1157 A253 10p multi 3.25 3.25

Souvenir Sheet

Air Macau, 10th Anniv. — A254

2004, Dec. 28 Litho. *Perf. 14*
1158 A254 8p multi 2.25 2.25

New Year 2005 (Year of the Rooster) A255

2005, Jan. 13 Litho. *Perf. 14½x14*
1159 A255 5.50p shown 1.60 1.60
Souvenir Sheet
1160 A255 10p Rooster, diff. 2.75 2.75

Everyday Life in the Past — A256

No. 1161: a, Cook (8/1). b, Man holding pole with hanging bottles (8/2). c, Man at work at small table (8/3). d, Textile worker (8/4). e, Man cutting coconuts (8/5). f, Cook at cart (8/6). g, Cook under lantern (8/7). h, Seamstress (8/8).
8p, Mailman on bicycle.

2005, Mar. 1 *Perf. 12¼*
1161 Block of 8 3.00 3.00
a.-h. A256 1.50p Any single .35 .35
Souvenir Sheet
1162 A256 8p multi 2.40 2.40

Sai Van Bridge A257

Designs: 1p, Bridge. 3.50p, Bridge and approaches.
8p, Bridge tower, vert.

2005, Mar. 23 *Perf. 14*
1163-1164 A257 Set of 2 1.10 1.10
Souvenir Sheet
1165 A257 8p multi 2.25 2.25

Libraries A258

2005, Apr. 15
1166 Horiz. strip of 4 2.25 2.25
a. A258 1p Central Library .25 .25
b. A258 1.50p Sir Robert Ho Tung Library .35 .30
c. A258 2p Coloane Library .50 .45
d. A258 3.50p Mong Há Library .90 .75
Souvenir Sheet
1167 A258 8p Public Commercial Assoc. Library 2.00 2.00

No. 1167 contains one 60x40mm stamp.

Mothers and Offspring — A259

2005, May 8 *Perf. 14½x14*
1168 Horiz. strip of 4 + 4 alternating labels 2.00 2.00
a. A259 1p Humans + label .25 .25
b. A259 1.50p Kangaroos + label .35 .30
c. A259 2p Birds and nest + label .50 .40
d. A259 3.50p Ducks + label .90 .80

Labels could be personalized, with sheets containing 5 strips and 20 labels selling for 60p.

The Romance of the Western Chamber — A260

No. 1169 — Inscriptions: a, Espreitando a Beldade à Luz da Lua (6/1). b, Ying Ying Ouvindo Música (6/2). c, O Amor e Ansiedade de Zhang Sheng (6/3). d, A Interrogaçao da Dama (6/4). e, Sonhando com Ying Ying na Pensao (6/5). f, A Uniao dos Amados (6/6).
8p, A Espera da Lua.

2005, June 10 *Perf. 13¼x14*
Granite Paper
1169 A260 2p Block of 6, #a-f 4.00 4.00
Souvenir Sheet
Perf. 14x13¼
1170 A260 8p multi *3.00 3.00*

Voyages of Admiral Zheng He, 600th Anniv. A261

No. 1171: a, Admiral Zheng He. b, Giraffe. c, Ship and map.
8p, Ships.

2005, June 28 Litho. *Perf. 13x13½*
1171 Horiz. strip of 3 3.25 3.25
a. A261 1p multi .70 .50
b.-c. A261 1.50p Either single .95 .75
Souvenir Sheet
Perf. 13¼
1172 A261 8p multi 3.25 3.25

No. 1172 contains one 50x30mm stamp.

UNESCO World Heritage Sites — A262

Various buildings in Historical Center of Macao World Heritage Site with background colors of: a, 1p, White. b, 1.50p, Red. c, 2p, Orange. d, 3.50p, Dark green.
8p, Green.

2005, July 16 *Perf. 14*
1173 A262 Block of 4, #a-d 2.25 2.25
Souvenir Sheet
1174 A262 8p multi 2.25 2.25

4th East Asian Games, Macao — A263

No. 1175 — Stylized athletes and: a, 1p, Olympic Swimming Pool of Macao. b, 1.50p, Nautical Center, Praia Grande. c, 2p, Tennis Academy. d, 2.50p, IPM Sports Pavilion. e, 3.50p, Macao Stadium. f, 4.50p, Tap Seac Sports Pavilion.
8p, Sports Arena.

2005, Aug. 30 *Perf. 14x13¼*
Granite Paper
1175 A263 Block of 6, #a-f 3.75 3.75
Souvenir Sheet
Perf.
1176 A263 8p multi 2.25 2.25

No. 1176 contains one 55x38mm oval stamp.

Macao Bank Notes, Cent. — A264

Designs: 1p, 1 pataca note. 1.50p, 5 pataca note. 3p, 10 pataca note. 4.50p, 50 pataca note.
8p, 100 pataca note.

2005, Sept. 2 *Perf. 13½x14*
Granite Paper
1177-1180 A264 Set of 4 2.75 2.75
Souvenir Sheet
1181 A264 8p multi *4.00 4.00*

Great Chinese Inventions — A265

No. 1182: a, 1p, Textile loom. b, 1.50p, Paper. c, 2p, Metal smelting. d, 4.50p, Calendar.
8p, Seismograph.

2005, Oct. 9 ***Perf. 14x13½***

Granite Paper

1182 A265 Block of 4, #a-d 2.50 2.50

Souvenir Sheet

1183 A265 8p multi 2.25 2.25

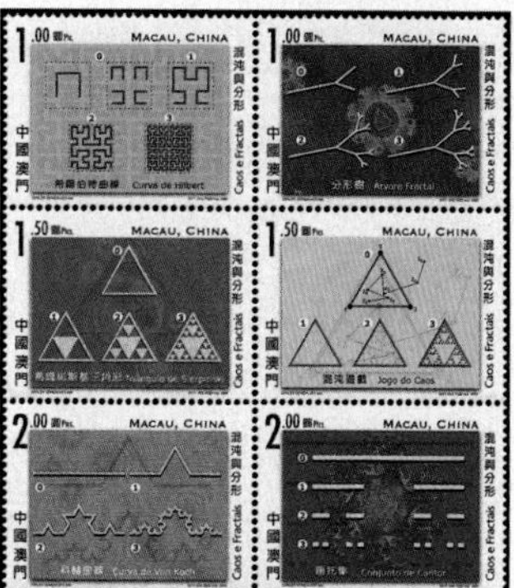

Chaos and Fractal Mathematics — A266

No. 1184: a, 1p, Hilbert's Curve. b, 1p, Tree Fractal. c, 1.50p, Sierpinski Triangle. d, 1.50p, Chaos Game. e, 2p, Von Koch Curve. f, 2p, Cantor Set.

8p, Julia Set.

2005, Nov. 16 ***Perf. 14***

1184 A266 Block of 6, #a-f 2.50 2.50

Souvenir Sheet

1185 A266 8p multi 2.25 2.25

New Year 2006 (Year of the Dog) A267

2006, Jan. 9 **Litho.** ***Perf. 13x13¼***

1186 A267 5.50p multi 1.60 1.60

Souvenir Sheet

1187 A267 10p multi 2.75 2.75

Lanterns — A268

No. 1188 — Various lanterns: a, (4/1). b, (4/2). c, (4/3). d, (4/4).

2006, Feb. 12 ***Perf. 13¼x13***

1188 Horiz. strip of 4 1.60 1.60
a.-b. A268 1p Either single .30 .25
c.-d. A268 1.50p Either single .40 .30

Souvenir Sheet

Perf. 13x13¼

1189 A268 8p multi 2.25 2.25

Everyday Life in the Past — A269

No. 1190: a, Cook (8/1). b, Food vendor (8/2). c, Man holding scissors (8/3). d, Man with small round table (8/4). e, Cobbler (8/5). f, Man with pots (8/6). g, Man hammering pails (8/7). h, Man carrying goods suspended from stick (8/8).

8p, Man looking at kettle.

2006, Mar. 1 ***Perf. 14***

1190 Block of 8 3.25 3.25
a.-h. A269 1.50p Any single .35 .35

Souvenir Sheet

1191 A269 8p multi 2.25 2.25

Items from Communications Museum — A270

No. 1192: a, Rubber stamp (8/1). b, Scale (8/2). c, Mail box (8/3). d, Mail sorting boxes (8/4). e, Telephone (8/5). f, Telephone switching equipment (8/6). g, Radio (8/7). h, Submarine cable (8/8).

10p, Macao #1, horiz.

2006, May 18 ***Perf. 13¼x14***

Granite Paper

1192 Block of 8 3.25 3.25
a.-h. A270 1.50p Any single .35 .35

Souvenir Sheet

1193 A270 10p multi 2.50 2.50

2006 World Cup Soccer Championships, Germany — A271

Various soccer players.

Litho. & Embossed

2006, June 9 ***Perf. 13¼***

1194 A271 Block of 4 3.00 3.00
a. 1.50p multi .35 .35
b. 2.50p multi .65 .65
c. 3.50p multi .90 .90
d. 4p multi 1.00 1.00

Fans — A272

No. 1195 — Various pictures on fans: a, (5/1). b, (5/2). c, (5/3). d, (5/4). e, (5/5).

10p, Three children.

2006, June 28 **Litho.** ***Perf. 14x13¼***

Granite Paper

1195 Vert. strip of 5 3.00 3.00
a.-b. A272 1.50p Either single .35 .35
c.-d. A272 2.50p Either single .65 .65
e. A272 3.50p multi .90 .90

Souvenir Sheet

1196 A272 10p multi 2.50 2.50

No. 1196 contains one 40x30mm stamp.

21st China Adolescents Invention Contest — A273

No. 1197: a, 1.50p, Models of molecules, laboratory equipment (4/1). b, 2p, Dish antenna, Earth, windmills (4/2). c, 2.50p, Gear, compass, pyramid and diagrams (4/3). d, 3.50p, Invention, computer keyboard and mouse (4/4).

10p, Atomic model, contest venue, vert.

2006, July 28 ***Perf. 14***

1197 A273 Block of 4, #a-d 2.40 2.40

Souvenir Sheet

1198 A273 10p multi 2.50 2.50

No. 1198 contains one 40x60mm stamp.

Street Scenes — A274

No. 1199: a, Rua de S. Domingos (4/1). b, Rua de Camilo Pessanha (4/2). c, Calcada de S. Francisco Xavier (4/3). d, Travessa da Paixao (4/4).

10p, Largo de Santo Agostinho.

2006, Sept. 13 ***Perf. 13½x14***

Granite Paper

1199 Block of 4 2.25 2.25
a.-b. A274 1.50p Either single .35 .35
c. A274 2.50p multi .65 .65
d. A274 3.50p multi .90 .90

Souvenir Sheet

Perf. 14x13½

1200 A274 10p multi 2.50 2.50

University of Macao, 25th Anniv. A275

No. 1201 — Inscriptions for Faculty of: a, Social Sciences and Humanities (5/1). b, Law (5/2). c, Science and Education (5/3). d, Science and Technology (5/4). e, Business Management (5/5).

10p, University emblem.

2006, Sept. 28 ***Perf. 13x13½***

1201 Horiz. strip of 5 2.50 2.50
a.-e. A275 1.50p Any single .40 .35

Souvenir Sheet

1202 A275 10p multi 2.50 2.50

I Ching Type of 2001 and

Two Women — A276

No. 1203 — Position of broken bars in trigrams (pa kua): a, Sixth. b, First, second and sixth. c, Second, third and sixth. d, Second and sixth. e, First, third and sixth. f, First and sixth. g, Third and sixth. h, First, second, third and sixth.

2006, Oct. 9 ***Perf. 13***

1203 A219 2p Sheet of 8, #a-h 5.00 5.00

Souvenir Sheet

1204 A276 10p shown 4.00 4.00

No. 1204 contains eight 39x34mm hexagonal stamps. Stamps from No. 1135 have Roman numeral "V" below text "Pa Kua" and "I Ching."

Jesuits — A277

Designs: No. 1205, 1.50p, Matteo Ricci (1552-1610), missionary, and red Chinese chop. No. 1206, 1.50p, St. Francis Xavier (1506-52), missionary, and cross. No. 1207, 3.50p, Allesandro Valignano (1539-1606), missionary, and capital. No. 1208, 3.50p, Melchior Carneiro (c. 1516-83), in red bishop's stole.

10p, St. Ignatius Loyola (1491-1556), founder of Society of Jesus.

2006, Nov. 30 **Litho.** ***Perf. 13½x14***

1205-1208 A277 Set of 4 2.75 2.75

Souvenir Sheet

Perf. 14x13½

1209 A277 10p multi 2.50 2.50

New Year 2007 (Year of the Pig) A278

2007, Jan. 8 **Litho.** ***Perf. 13x13¼***

1210 A278 5.50p multi 1.50 1.50

Souvenir Sheet

1211 A278 10p multi *5.00 5.00*

Shek Wan Ceramics — A279

No. 1212: a, 1.50p, Lao Zi (4/1). b, 1.50p, Lu Yu (4/2). c, 1.50p, Philosopher (4/3). d, 2.50p, Luo Han Seated (4/4).

8p, Concubine After Bath.

2007, Feb. 3

1212 A279 Block of 4, #a-d 2.00 2.00

Souvenir Sheet

1213 A279 8p multi 2.25 2.25

Everyday Life in the Past — A280

No. 1214: a, Man carrying tray on head (8/1). b, Man pouring tea into bowls (8/2). c, Rickshaw (8/3). d, People around table looking into bowl (8/4). e, Seamstress (8/5). f, Shoemaker (8/6). g, Ceramics artists (8/7). h, Embroiderer at booth (8/8).

10p, Festival dragon.

2007, Mar. 1 ***Perf. 14***

1214 Block of 8 3.00 3.00
a.-h. A280 1.50p Any single .35 .35

Souvenir Sheet

1215 A280 10p multi 2.50 2.50

Traditional Chinese Shops — A281

No. 1216: a, 1.50p, Seamstress's shop (4/1). b, 1.50p, Acupuncturist and herbalist (4/2). c, 2.50p, Print shop (4/3). d, 3.50p, Restaurant (4/4).

10p, Street scene with man carting sign from shop.

2007, May 8 ***Perf. 14½x14***

1216 A281 Block of 4, #a-d 2.40 2.40

Souvenir Sheet

1217 A281 10p multi 2.50 2.50

Seng Yu Proverbs — A282

Designs: Nos. 1218, 1223a, 1.50p, The Foolish Old Man Moved a Mountain (pink frame, 4/1). Nos. 1219, 1223b, 1.50p, The Friendship Between Guan and Bao (blue green frame, 4/2). Nos. 1220, 1223c, 3.50p, Calling Black White (lilac frame, 4/3). Nos. 1221, 1223d, 3.50p, The Quarrel Between Snipe and Clam (orange frame, 4/4).

10p, Horses and riders before riderless horse pulling cart, horiz.

2007, June 1 ***Perf. 14***

1218-1221 A282 Set of 4 *13.00 13.00*

Souvenir Sheet

1222 A282 10p multi *13.00 13.00*

Self-Adhesive

Booklet Stamps

Serpentine Die Cut 14

1223 Booklet pane, #1223a-1223d *16.00 16.00*
Complete booklet, 2 #1223 *32.00*

No. 1222 contains one 60x40mm stamp.

A Journey to the West — A283

No. 1224: a, 1.50p, King and entourage, sprite with stick on cloud (6/1). b, 1.50p, Sprite on cloud, woman dreaming of horned spirit (6/2). c, 2p, Man with foot pierced by spear tip, woman, sprite without stick on cloud (6/3). d, 2p, Sprite on cloud battling other sprites (6/4). e, 2.50p, Sprite with stick, sprite with rake, sprite with swords (6/5). f, 2.50p, Sprite with rake on cloud, spirit with eight hands, spider (6/6).

10p, Sprite and sun.

2007, June 18 ***Perf. 14***

1224 A283 Block of 6, #a-f 3.25 3.25

Souvenir Sheet

1225 A283 10p multi 2.50 2.50

Scouting, Cent. A284

Lord Robert Baden-Powell, Macao Scouting emblem, flag ceremony and: 1.50p, Scout with semaphore flags. 2p, Scouts saluting. 2.50p, Scouts setting up campfire. No. 1229, 3.50p, Scouts lashing sticks together. No. 1230, 3.50p, Scout giving directions to other Scout.

10p, Flag, cannon and buildings, vert.

2007, July 9 ***Perf. 13x13¼***

1226-1230 A284 Set of 5 3.25 3.25

Souvenir Sheet

Perf. 13¼x13

1231 A284 10p multi 2.50 2.50

Arrival of Robert Morrison (1782-1834), First Protestant Missionary in China, Bicent. — A285

Morrison and: 1.50p, Lilac panel. 3.50p, Yellow panel.

2007, Sept. 28 **Litho.** ***Perf. 13x13¼***

1232-1233 A285 Set of 2 1.40 1.40

Souvenir Sheet

Mount Kangrinboqe, Tibet — A286

2007, Oct. 9 ***Perf. 14***

1234 A286 10p multi 2.50 2.50

Applications of the Golden Ratio — A287

No. 1235: a, 1.50p, Fibonacci sequence. b, 2p, Sunflower spirals. c, 2.50p, Penrose tiling. d, 3.50p, Nautilus shell.

10p, Phi and equation.

2007, Oct. 26 ***Perf. 13¼x13***

1235 A287 Block of 4, #a-d 2.50 2.50

Souvenir Sheet

1236 A287 10p multi 2.50 2.50

Chinese Philosophers — A288

No. 1237 Chinese character and: a, 1.50p, Lao Tzu (Lao Zi). b, 2.50p, Chuang Tzu (Zhuang Zi). c, 3.50p, Confucius (Confúcio). d, 4p, Meng Tzu (Méncio).

10p, Lao Tzu, Chuang Tzu, Confucius, Meng Tzu.

Litho. & Embossed

2007, Nov. 30 ***Perf. 13x13¼***

1237 A288 Block of 4, #a-d 3.00 3.00

Souvenir Sheet

Perf.

1238 A288 10p multi 2.50 2.50

No. 1238 contains one 42mm diameter stamp.

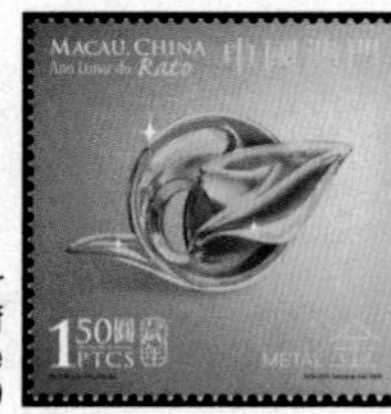

New Year 2008 (Year of the Rat) — A289

No. 1239: a, Metal sculpture of rat. b, Wood carving of rat. c, Watercolor painting of rat. d, Fireworks and laser light image of rat. e, Clay teapot depicting rat.

10p, Clay teapot depicting rat and 2008 Beijing Summer Olympics emblem.

Litho., Litho. & Embossed with Foil and Hologram Application (#1239e, 1240)

2008, Jan. 23 ***Perf. 14¼***

1239 Horiz. strip of 5 2.75 2.75
a.-d. A289 1.50p Any single .35 .35
e. A289 5p multi 1.25 1.25

Souvenir Sheet

1240 A289 10p multi 2.50 2.50

No. 1240 contains one 50x50mm diamond-shaped stamp.

I Ching Type of 2001 and

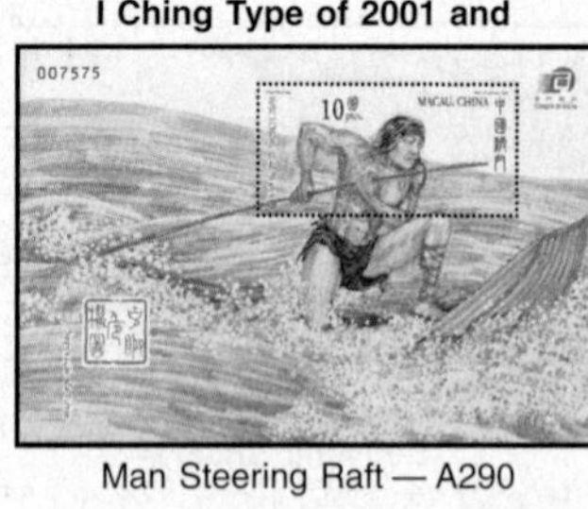

Man Steering Raft — A290

No. 1241 — Position of broken bars in trigrams (pa kua): a, Fourth and sixth. b, First, second, fourth and sixth. c, Second, third, fourth and sixth. d, Second, fourth and sixth. e, First, third, fourth and sixth. f, First, fourth and sixth. g, Third, fourth and sixth. h, First, second, third, fourth and sixth.

2008, Mar. 1 **Litho.** ***Perf. 14***

Granite Paper

1241 A219 2p Sheet of 8, #a-h 4.00 4.00

Souvenir Sheet

1242 A290 10p multi 2.50 2.50

No. 1241 contains eight 39x34mm hexagonal stamps. Stamps from No. 1241 have Roman numeral "VI" below text "Pa Kua" and "I Ching."

Olympic Torch Relay A291

Designs: 1.50p, Man holding Olympic torch, Parthenon. 3.50p, Mascot holding Olympic torch, lotus flower.

10p, Olympic torch, doves, vert.

2008, May 3 ***Perf. 13x13¼***

1243-1244 A291 Set of 2 1.25 1.25

Souvenir Sheet

Perf. 13

1245 A291 10p multi 2.50 2.50

No. 1245 contains one 40x70mm stamp.

Western Legends — A292

No. 1246: a, The Golden Apple. b, The Gordian Knot. c, The Trojan Horse. d, The Riddle of the Sphinx.

10p, Cupid and Psyche, horiz.

2008, June 2 ***Perf. 13¼x14***

Granite Paper

1246 Horiz. strip of 4 3.00 3.00
a. A292 1.50p multi .35 .35
b. A292 2.50p multi .65 .65
c. A292 3.50p multi .90 .90
d. A292 4.00p multi 1.00 1.00

Souvenir Sheet

Perf. 14x13¼

1247 A292 10p multi 2.50 2.50

Native Cuisine of Macao and Singapore A293

No. 1248: a, Panqueca Indiana. b, Arroz de Frango à Hainan. c, Carne de Porco à Alentejana. d, Lombo de Bacalhau Braseado em Lascas. e, Laksa. f, Saté. g, Arroz Frito à Yangzhou. h, Frango Frito.

No. 1249, vert.: a, Arroz no Tacho de Porcelana. b, Caranguejo con Piri-piri.

2008, July 4 ***Perf. 13¼x14***

Granite Paper

1248 Block of 8 5.00 5.00
a.-d. A293 1.50p Any single .35 .35
e.-h. A293 3.50p Any single .90 .90

Souvenir Sheet

1249 Sheet of 2 2.50 2.50
a.-b. A293 5p Either single 1.25 1.25

See Singapore Nos. 1318-1320.

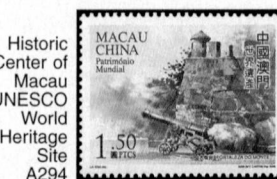

Historic Center of Macau UNESCO World Heritage Site A294

Designs: 1.50p, Fortaleza do Monte. 2p, Largo do Lilau. 2.50p, Lou Kau House. 3p, Largo do Senado. 3.50p, Sam Kai Vui Kun. 4p, Igreja da Sé. 4.50p, Quartel dos Mouros. 5p, St. Anthony's Church.

2008, July 31 **Litho.** ***Perf. 13x13½***

1250 A294 1.50p multi .35 .35
1251 A294 2p multi .50 .50
1252 A294 2.50p multi .65 .65
1253 A294 3p multi .75 .75
1254 A294 3.50p multi .90 .90
1255 A294 4p multi 1.10 1.10

1256 A294 4.50p multi 1.25 1.25
1257 A294 5p multi 1.40 1.40
Nos. 1250-1257 (8) 6.90 6.90

2008 Summer Olympics, Beijing A295

Designs: 5p, National Aquatics Center. 10p, National Stadium.

2008, Aug. 8 ***Perf. 13x13½***
1258 A295 5p multi 1.40 1.40

Souvenir Sheet
Perf. 13
1259 A295 10p multi 2.75 2.75

No. 1259 contains one 54x74mm irregular, six-sided stamp.

20th Macao Intl. Fireworks Display Contest — A296

No. 1260 — Fireworks displays over various sections of Macao: a, 1.50p. b, 2.50p. c, 3.50p. d, 5p.

2008, Oct. 1 **Litho.** ***Perf. 14x13½***
Granite Paper
1260 A296 Sheet of 4, #a-d 3.50 3.50

Souvenir Sheet
1261 A296 10p shown 2.75 2.75

Celebration — A297

No. 1262: a, 1.50p, "Celebration" in many languages. b, 3.50p, UPU emblem.

2008, Oct. 9 ***Perf. 14***
1262 A297 Horiz. pair, #a-b 1.25 1.25

The images in the frames of Nos. 1262a-1262b could be personalized for an additional fee. The generic images are shown.

Souvenir Sheet

Lijiang, People's Republic of China — A298

2008, Nov. 7
1263 A298 10p multi 3.00 3.00

Traditional Handicrafts A299

Designs: 1.50p, Ivory carving. 2p, Ceramic painting. 2.50p, Basket weaving. 3.50p, Wood carving. 10p, Beaded embroidery.

2008, Dec. 1 ***Perf. 13x13¼***
1264-1267 A299 Set of 4 2.50 2.50

Souvenir Sheet
Perf. 13¼x13
1268 A299 10p multi 2.75 2.75

No. 1268 contains one 60x40mm stamp.

Louis Braille (1809-52), Educator of the Blind — A300

2009, Jan. 4 **Litho.** ***Perf. 13¼***
1269 A300 5p black 1.40 1.40

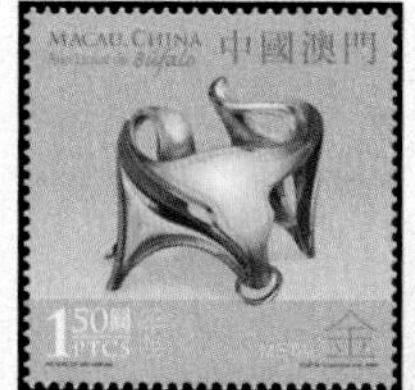

New Year 2009 (Year of the Buffalo) A301

No. 1270: a, Metal sculpture of buffalo head. b, Wood carving of buffalo head. c, Watercolor drawing of buffalo head. d, Fireworks display of buffalo head. e, Clay teapot with buffalo design.
10p, Clay teapot with buffalo design, diff.

Litho. (1.50p), Litho. & Embossed With Foil Application (5p, 10p)

2009, Jan. 8 ***Perf. 14¼***
1270 Horiz. strip of 5 3.00 3.00
a.-d. A301 1.50p Any single .35 .35
e. A301 5p multi 1.25 1.25

Souvenir Sheet
1271 A301 10p multi 2.75 2.75

No. 1271 contains one 50x50mm diamond-shaped stamp.

Opening of Kun Iam Treasury — A302

No. 1272 — Crowd of worshipers and holders of incense sticks with red chop at: a, Top. b, Lower left. c, Lower right. d, Left.
10p, Woman praying, horiz.

2009, Feb. 20 **Litho.** ***Perf. 13¼x13***
1272 Horiz. strip of 4 3.25 3.25
a. A302 1.50p multi .40 .40
b. A302 2.50p multi .65 .65
c. A302 3.50p multi .90 .90
d. A302 4p multi 1.00 1.00

Souvenir Sheet
Perf. 13x13¼
1273 A302 10p multi 2.75 2.75

Traditional Tools A303

Designs: 1.50p, Sand basin for compacting firecrackers. 2.50p, Whetstone. 3.50p, Stone grain mill. 4p, Cake mold.
10p, All four tools.

2009, Mar. 1 ***Perf. 14½x14***
1274-1277 A303 Set of 4 3.00 3.00

Souvenir Sheet
Perf. 14x14½
1278 A303 10p multi 2.75 2.75

No. 1278 contains one 60x40mm stamp.

Souvenir Sheet

Buddha, Longmen Cave — A304

2009, Apr. 8 ***Perf. 14***
1279 A304 10p multi 2.75 2.75

China 2009 World Stamp Exhibition, Luoyang.

Labor Day A305

"5," "1" and: 1.50p, Construction workers, Macao Tower. 5p, Haulers, ruins of St. Paul's Church.
10p, Men lifting diamond-shaped "5.1." box.

2009, May 1 ***Perf. 13x13¼***
1280-1281 A305 Set of 2 1.75 1.75

Souvenir Sheet
1282 A305 10p multi 2.75 2.75

The Mantis Stalking the Cicada — A306

A Fond Dream on Nanke — A307

Songs of Chu on All Sides — A308

Give the Last Measure of Devotion — A309

Design: 10p, Marking the boat to find the sword, horiz.

2009, June 1 **Litho.** ***Perf. 14***
1283 A306 1.50p multi .40 .40
1284 A307 1.50p multi .40 .40
1285 A308 3.50p multi .90 .90
1286 A309 3.50p multi .90 .90
Nos. 1283-1286 (4) 2.60 2.60

Souvenir Sheet
1287 A309 10p multi 2.75 2.75

Booklet Stamps
Self-Adhesive
Serpentine Die Cut 14
1288 A306 1.50p multi .75 .75
1289 A307 1.50p multi .75 .75
1290 A308 3.50p multi 1.50 1.50
1291 A309 3.50p multi 1.50 1.50
a. Booklet pane of 8, 2 each #1288-1291 9.50
Nos. 1288-1291 (4) 2.60 2.60

Seng Yu proverbs. No. 1287 contains one 60x40mm stamp.

People's Republic of China, 60th Anniv. — A310

No. 1292 — Lanterns and: a, 1.50p, Archway. b, 2.50p, Soldier in tank. c, 3.50p, Children exercising. d, 4p, Soldiers and flag of People's Republic of China.
10p, Archway, soldiers and flag of People's Republic of China, horiz.

2009, Oct. 1 **Litho.** ***Perf. 13¼x13***
1292 A310 Block of 4, #a-d 3.00 3.00

Souvenir Sheet
Photo.
Perf. 13
1293 A310 10p multi 2.75 2.75

No. 1293 contains one 60x40mm stamp.

Porcelain Plate Paintings by Sou Farong A311

Designs: 1.50p, Bodhisattva Ksitigarbha. 5p, Bodhisattva Avalokitsavara.

2009, Oct. 9 **Litho.** ***Perf. 13x13¼***
1294-1295 A311 Set of 2 1.75 1.75

Pui Ching Middle School, 120th Anniv. — A312

No. 1296: a, 1.50p, Building and basketball court. b, 2p, Building, diff. c, 2.50d, Buildings. d, 3.50p, Bust and fireplace.
10p, Building and fountain.

2009, Nov. 29 Litho. *Perf. 13½x14*

Granite Paper

1296 A312 Block or strip of 4, #a-d 2.50 2.50

Souvenir Sheet

1297 A312 10p multi 2.75 2.75

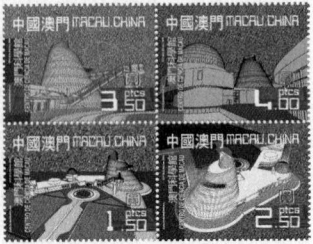

Macao Science Center — A313

No. 1298: a, 1.50p, Aerial view of entire complex. b, 2.50p, Exhibition Center and Planetarium. c, 3.50p, Ground-level view of entire complex. d, 4p, Ground-level view of Exhibition Center and Convention Center.
10p, Top of Exhibition Center.

2009, Dec. 19 *Perf. 13½x14*

Granite Paper

1298 A313 Block or strip of 4, #a-d 3.00 3.00

Souvenir Sheet

1299 A313 10p multi 2.75 2.75

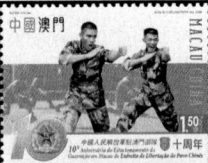

People's Liberation Army Garrison in Macao, 10th Anniv. A314

No. 1300: a, Soldiers with martial arts stances. b, Two women officers. c, Soldiers with gun. d, Soldiers and children with cannon. e, Soldiers and children planting tree. f, Soldiers repairing tank.
10p, Soldiers on parade, vert.

2009, Dec. 20 *Perf. 13x13¼*

1300 Block of 6 2.40 2.40
a.-f. A314 1.50p Any single .35 .35

Souvenir Sheet

Perf. 13x13½

1301 A314 10p multi 2.75 2.75

No. 1301 contains one 40x60mm stamp.

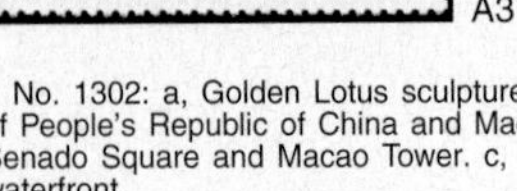

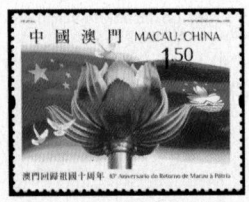

Return of Macao to China, 10th Anniv. A315

No. 1302: a, Golden Lotus sculpture, flags of People's Republic of China and Macao. b, Senado Square and Macao Tower. c, Macao waterfront.
10p, Golden Lotus, gate, vert.

Perf. 13¼x13 Syncopated

2009, Dec. 20 Photo.

1302 Horiz. strip of 3 1.25 1.25
a.-c. A315 1.50p Any single .35 .35

Souvenir Sheet

Perf. 13x13½

1303 A315 10p multi 2.75 2.75

No. 1303 contains one 40x60mm stamp. See People's Republic of China Nos. 3791-3793.

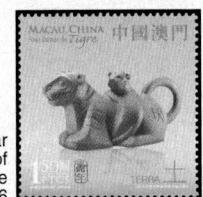

New Year 2010 (Year of the Tiger) — A316

No. 1304: a, Clay sculpture of tiger and cub. b, Fireworks display of tiger's head. c, Watercolor drawing of tiger. d, Wood carving of tiger. e, Metal sculpture of tiger.
10p, Metal sculpture of tiger, diff.

Litho. (1.50p), Litho. & Embossed with Hologram and Foil Application (5p, 10p)

2010, Jan. 2 *Perf. 14¼*

1304 Horiz. strip of 5 3.00 3.00
a.-d. A316 1.50p Any single .35 .35
e. A316 5p multi 1.25 1.25

Souvenir Sheet

1305 A316 10p multi 2.75 2.75

No. 1305 contains one 50x50mm diamond-shaped stamp.

I Ching Type of 2001 and

Child With Toy — A317

No. 1306 — Position of broken bars in trigrams (pa kua): a, First and second. b, First, second, fifth and sixth. c, First, second, fourth and fifth. d, First, second and fifth. e, First, second, fourth and sixth. f, First, second and sixth. g, First, second and fourth. h, First, second, fourth, fifth and sixth.

2010, Mar. 1 Litho. *Perf. 13*

Granite Paper

1306 A219 2p Sheet of 8, #a-h 5.00 5.00

Souvenir Sheet

Perf. 13½

1307 A317 10p multi 3.00 3.00

No. 1306 contains eight 39x34 hexagonal stamps. Stamps from No. 1306 have Roman numeral "VII" below text "Pa Kua" and "I Ching."

Intl. Women's Day, Cent. — A318

No. 1308 — Women in various costumes: a, 1.50p. b, 2.50p. c, 3.50p. d, 4p.
10p, Three women, vert.

2010, Mar. 8 *Perf. 13¼x14*

Granite Paper

1308 A318 Block of 4, #a-d 4.00 4.00

Souvenir Sheet

1309 A318 10p multi 3.00 3.00

No. 1309 contains one 40x60mm stamp.

Expo 2010, Shanghai — A319

Designs: 3.50p, Rabbits. 4p, Chinese lanterns.
10p, Rabbit and Chinese lanterns.

2010, May 1 *Perf. 13¼x14*

Granite Paper

1310-1311 A319 Set of 2 2.00 2.00

Souvenir Sheet

1312 A319 10p multi 2.75 2.75

Macau Branch of Bank of China, 60th Anniv. — A320

No. 1313 — Yellow ribbons forming "60," Bank of China emblem and: a, 1.50p, Street lamp, ruins of St. Paul's Church. b, 2.50p, Buildings. c, 3.50p, "10" from banknote, 1000-pataca banknote. d, 4p, Child, stylized people, people shaking hands.
10p, Buildings, lotus flower, Bank of China emblem.

2010, June 21 *Perf. 13¼x14*

Granite Paper

1313 A320 Block of 4, #a-d 3.00 3.00

Souvenir Sheet

1314 A320 10p multi 3.00 3.00

No. 1314 contains one 60x40mm stamp.

Historic Center of Macao UNESCO World Heritage Site — A321

No. 1315 — Buildings near St. Augustine's Square: a, 1.50p, Dom Pedro V Theater. b, 2.50p, Sir Robert Ho Tung Library. c, 3.50p, St. Augustine's Church. d, 4p, Seminary and Church of St. Joseph.
10p, Building on Square.

2010, July 15 *Perf. 14x13¼*

Granite Paper

1315 A321 Block of 4, #a-d 3.50 3.50

Souvenir Sheet

1316 A321 10p multi 3.00 3.00

Stained-Glass Windows — A322

Stained-glass window from St. Lawrence's Church, Macao: 5.50p, Detail. 10p, Entire window, horiz.

2010, Aug. 30 *Perf. 13¼x13*

Granite Paper

1317 A322 5.50p multi 1.50 1.50

Souvenir Sheet

Perf. 13x13¼

1318 A322 10p multi 3.00 3.00

See Aland Islands Nos. 306-307.

Carvings of Religious Figures — A323

No. 1319: a, 1.50p, Buddha. b, 2.50p, Na Tcha. c, 3.50p, Kun Iam. d, 4p, Tin Hau.
10p, The Eight Immortals, horiz.

2010, Sept. 7 *Perf. 14*

1319 A323 Block or strip of 4, #a-d 3.00 3.00

Souvenir Sheet

1320 A323 10p multi 3.00 3.00

No. 1320 contains one 60x30mm stamp.

Old Telephones — A324

No. 1321 — Various old telephones with background color of: a, 1.50p, Green. b, 2.50p, Pink. c, 3.50p, Yellow. d, 4p, Blue.
10p, Old telephone, horiz.

2010, Sept. 1 Litho. *Perf. 14*

1321 A324 Block or strip of 4, #a-d 3.00 3.00

Souvenir Sheet

1322 A324 10d multi 2.75 2.75

No. 1322 contains one 60x40mm stamp.

Macao Food Festival, 10th Anniv. — A325

Designs: 1.50p, Wonton soup. 2.50p, Xiao Long Bao (steamed buns). 3.50p, Sushi. 4p, Pastel de nata (egg tart).
10p, Portuguese chicken.

2010, Nov. 5 *Perf. 13¼x13*
1323-1326 A325 Set of 4 3.00 3.00

Souvenir Sheet

1327 A325 10p multi 2.75 2.75

Traditional Clothing — A326

No. 1328: a, 1.50p, Man in Tang suit. b, 2.50p, Woman in qipao. c, 3.50p, Woman in blouse and long skirt. d, 4p, Man in tunic suit.
10p, Two women, horiz.

2010, Nov. 30
1328 A326 Block of 4, #a-d 3.00 3.00

Souvenir Sheet

1329 A326 10p multi 2.75 2.75

No. 1329 contains one 60x40mm stamp.

Giant Pandas — A327

Panda, domed building and: 1.50p, Chapel of Our Lady of Penha. 5p, Ruins of St. Paul's Church.
10p, Two pandas, domed building, Ruins of St. Paul's Church.

2010, Dec. 18 *Perf. 13¼x13*
1330-1331 A327 Set of 2 3.00 3.00

Souvenir Sheet
Perf. 13x13¼

1332 A327 10p multi 3.00 3.00

No. 1332 contains one 40x60mm stamp.

New Year 2011 (Year of the Rabbit) A328

No. 1333: a, Clay sculpture of rabbit. b, Fireworks and laser light image of rabbit. c, Watercolor painting of rabbit. d, Wood carving rabbit. e, Metal sculpture of rabbit.
10p, Metal sculpture of rabbit, diff.

Litho., Litho. & Embossed with Foil and Hologram Application (5p, 10p)

2011, Jan. 5 *Perf. 13¼x13*
1333 Horiz. strip of 5 2.75 2.75
a.-d. A328 1.50p Any single .35 .35
e. A328 5p multi 1.25 1.25

Souvenir Sheet
Perf. 14¼

1334 A328 10p multi 2.50 2.50

No. 1334 contains one 50x50mm diamond-shaped stamp.

Souvenir Sheet

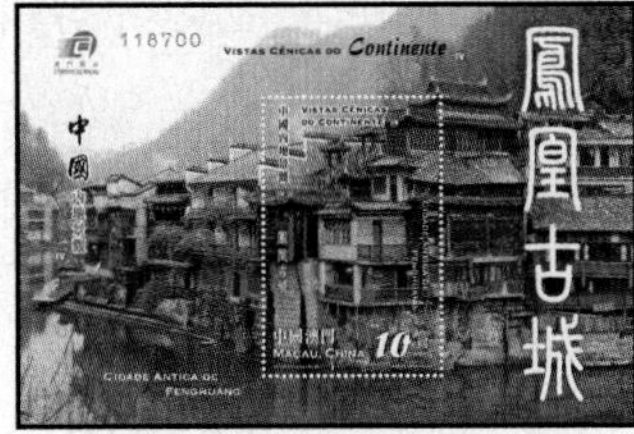

Ancient City of Fenghuang — A329

2011, Mar. 1 Litho. *Perf. 13x13¼*
1335 A329 10p multi 3.00 3.00

Public Buildings A330

Designs: 1.50p, Government Headquarters. 2.50p, Monetary Authority. 3.50p, Holy House of Mercy Hospice. 4p, Macao Foundation.

2011, Apr. 19 *Perf. 14*
1336-1339 A330 Set of 4 3.50 3.50

Cantonese Naamyam — A331

No. 1340 — Musician near: a, 1.50p, Building archway. b, 2,50p, Junk with sails up. c, 3.50p, Wall and awning. d, 4p, Harbor.
10p, Musician near wall.

2011, May 30 *Perf. 13¼x13*
1340 A331 Block of 4, #a-d 3.00 3.00

Souvenir Sheet

1341 A331 10p multi 2.75 2.75

Legend of the White Snake — A332

No. 1342: a, 1.50p, Lady Bai Suzhen and Xu Xian meeting when traveling the lake (6/1). b, 1.50p, Revelation to Xu Xian that Lady Bai is a snake during Dragon Boat Festival (6/2). c, 2p, Lady Bai steals herb to save husband (6/3). d, 2p, Fight between dragon and white snake (6/4). e, 2.50p, Lady Bai captive in pagoda (6/5). f, 2.50p, Flooding of the Jinshan Temple (6/6).
10p, Lacy Bai with sword, horiz.

2011, July 28 *Perf. 13¼x13*
1342 A332 Block of 6, #a-f 3.00 3.00

Souvenir Sheet
Perf. 13¼

1343 A332 10p multi 2.75 2.75

No. 1343 contains one 60x30mm stamp.

Worldwide Fund for Nature, 50th Anniv. — A333

No. 1344 — Birds: a, 1.50p, Pycnonotus sinensis. b, 2.50p, Streptopelia chinensis. c, 3.50p, Ixobrychus sinensis. d, 4.50p, Centropus sinensis.

2011, Sept. 11 Litho. *Perf. 14x13¼*

Granite Paper

1344 A333 Block of 4, #a-d 3.50 3.50
e. Souvenir sheet, #1344a-1344d 3.50 3.50

Famous Men — A334

No. 1345: a, 1.50p, Lin Zexu (1785-1850), scholar. b, 2.50p, Ye Ting (1896-1946), military leader. c, 3.50p, Xian Xinghai (1905-45), composer. d, 4p, Ho Yin, industrialist and philanthropist.
10p, Lin Zexu, Ye Ting, Xian Xinghai and Ho Yin, vert.

2011, Oct. 9 Litho. *Perf. 14*
1345 A334 Block or strip of 4, #a-d 3.00 3.00

Souvenir Sheet
Litho. With Foil Application

1346 A334 10p multi 2.75 2.75

No. 1346 contains one 40x60mm stamp.

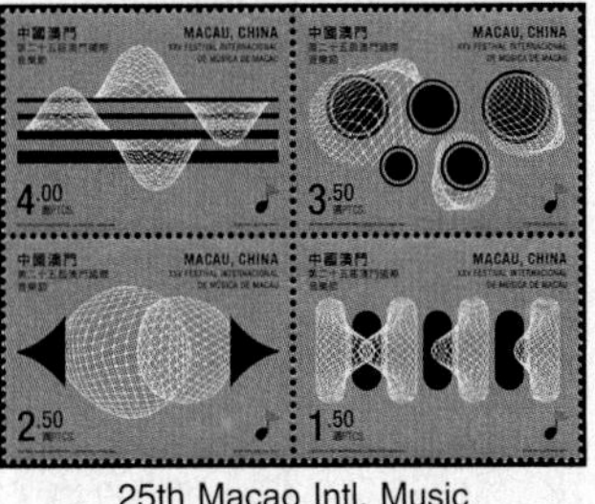

25th Macao Intl. Music Festival — A335

No. 1347 — Musical note, web and: a, 1.50p, Vertical ovals. b, 2.50p, Parabolas. c, 3.50p, Circles. d, 4p, Lines.
10p, Horizontal oval.

2011, Oct. 9 *Perf. 14x13½*

Granite Paper

1347 A335 Block or strip of 4, #a-d 3.00 3.00

Souvenir Sheet

1348 A335 10p multi 2.75 2.75

Chinese Revolution, Cent. — A336

No. 1349 — Flags and: a, 1.50p, Gao Jianfu (1879-1951), painter, Macao office of Chinese Revolutionary League. b, 2.50p, Huang Xing (1874-1916), revolutionary leader, Huanghuagang Mausoleum of 72 Martyrs. c, 3.50p, Xiong Bingkun (1885-1969, revolutionary leader, Uprising Gate. d, 4p, Dr. Sun Yat-sen (1866-1925), President of Republic of China, office of Provisional President.
10p, Flags, China #185.

2011, Oct. 10 Litho. *Perf. 13x13¼*
1349 A336 Block or strip of 4, #a-d 3.00 3.00

Souvenir Sheet
Photo.
Perf. 13¼x13

1350 A336 10p multi 2.75 2.75

No. 1350 contains one 60x40mm stamp.

Kiang Wu Hospital Charitable Association, 140th Anniv. — A337

Building and: 1.50p, Plaque. 2.50p, Statue of Dr. Sun Yat-sen. 3.50p, Crushing wheel. 4p, Magnetic resonance imaging machine.
10p, Statue of Dr. Sun Yat-sen, scenes from modern hospital.

2011, Oct. 28 Litho. *Perf. 14x13½*

Granite Paper

1351-1354 A337 Set of 4 3.00 3.00

Souvenir Sheet

1355 A337 10p multi 2.75 2.75

No. 1355 contains one 40x40mm stamp.

New Year 2012 (Year of the Dragon) A338

No. 1356: a, Metal sculpture of dragon. b, Wood carving of dragon. c, Fireworks display of dragon. d, Clay sculpture of dragon. e, Watercolor painting of dragon.
12p, Watercolor painting of dragon, diff.

Litho., Litho. & Embossed with Foil and Hologram Application (5p)

2012, Jan. 5 *Perf. 14¼*
1356 Horiz. strip of 5 3.00 3.00
a.-d. A338 1.50p Any single .40 .40
e. A338 5p multi 1.25 1.25

Souvenir Sheet
Litho. & Embossed With Foil Application
Perf. 13¼

1357 A338 12p multi 3.00 3.00

No. 1357 contains one 50x50mm diamond-shaped stamp.

Smoke-Free Macao — A339

Macao skyline and: 1.50p, "2012" with "no smoking" symbol replacing zero. 5p, "No smoking" symbol.

2012, Jan. 31 Litho. *Perf. 14*
1358-1359 A339 Set of 2 1.75 1.75

I Ching Type of 2001 and

Woman and Child — A340

No. 1360 — Position of broken bars in trigrams (pa kua): a, First, second and third. b, First, second, third, fifth and sixth. c, First, second, third, fourth and fifth. d, First, second, third and fifth. e, First, second, third, fourth and sixth. f, First, second, third and sixth. g, First, second, third and fourth. h, First, second, third, fourth, fifth and sixth.

2012, Mar. 1 *Perf. 14*
Granite Paper
1360 A219 2p Sheet of 8, #a-h 4.00 4.00
Souvenir Sheet
Perf. 14x13¼
1361 A340 10p multi 2.50 2.50

No. 1360 contains eight 39x34mm hexagonal stamps. Stamps from No. 1360 have Roman numeral "VIII" below text "Pa Kuand "I Ching."

Tai Fung Bank, 70th Anniv. A341

Designs: 1.50p, Man, rectangular emblem with Portuguese and Chinese text. 2.50p, Building, emblem with Chinese characters. 3.50p, Building, round emblem with Portuguese and Chinese text. 4p, Emblem with serpents.
10p, 70th anniversary emblem.

2012, Mar. 28 *Perf. 13x13¼*
Granite Paper
1362-1365 A341 Set of 4 3.00 3.00
Souvenir Sheet
Perf. 13¼x13
1366 A341 10p multi 2.75 2.75

No. 1366 contains one 60x40mm stamp.

Historic Views of Fishing Harbor A342

Various views of harbor, boats and structures.

2012, May 18 *Perf. 13x13¼*
Granite Paper
1367 Horiz. strip of 4 3.00 3.00
a. A342 1.50p multi .40 .40
b. A342 2.50p multi .65 .65
c. A342 3.50p multi .90 .90
d. A342 4p multi 1.00 1.00

Souvenir Sheet
Perf. 13½x13
1368 A342 10p multi 2.75 2.75

No. 1368 contains one 60x40mm stamp.

Hou Kong Middle School, 80th Anniv. — A343

No. 1369: a, 1.50p, Students working on models of Chinese junks, students painting and writing Chinese characters. b, 2.50p, Students participating in sporting events. c, 3.50p, Students participating in performing arts. d, 4p, Teacher and student in classroom, student taking piano lesson, child holding artwork, children at play.
10p, Students parading on track with school emblem and banner, school band, vert.

2012, June 10 *Perf. 13x13¼*
Granite Paper
1369 A343 Block of 4, #a-d 3.00 3.00
Souvenir Sheet
Perf. 13½
1370 A343 10p multi 2.50 2.50

No. 1370 contains one 40x40mm stamp.

Tung Sin Tong Charitable Society, 120th Anniv. — A344

No. 1371: a, 1.50p, Woman playing piano, line of children. b, 2.50p, Students in classroom. c, 3.50p, Health care. d, 4p, People of various ages.
10p, Roof of building, fireworks.

2012, Aug. 8 *Perf. 14x13¼*
Granite Paper
1371 A344 Block of 4, #a-d 3.00 3.00
Souvenir Sheet
1372 A344 10p multi 2.50 2.50

Legend of the Cowherd and the Weaving Maid — A345

No. 1373: a, 1.50p, Cowherd and cow, denomination at LR. b, 1.50p, Cowherd taking clothes of bathing maid, denomination at LL. c, 2p, Children playing with cow, cowherd watching maid weaving, denomination at LR. d, 2p, Maid being abducted, denomination at LL. e, 2.50p, Children and cowherd on knees at edge of sea, denomination at LR. f, 2.50p, Cowherd tossing water, old man and woman, denomination at LL.
10p, Cowherd, maid, children, birds, vert.

2012, Aug. 23 *Perf. 14x13¼*
Granite Paper
1373 A345 Block of 6, #a-f 3.00 3.00
Souvenir Sheet
1374 A345 10p multi 2.50 2.50

No. 1374 contains one 40x60mm stamp.

Safeguarding of Honesty and Transparency, 20th Anniv. — A346

20th anniversary emblem and: 2p, Buildings and bridge. 5p, Buildings.

2012, Sept. 20 *Perf. 14x13¼*
Granite Paper
1375-1376 A346 Set of 2 1.75 1.75

Paintings of Macao Scenes by Lok Cheong — A347

No. 1377: a, 1.50p, Temple, painting of boat on rock. b, 2.50p, Trees. c, 3.50p, People in park. d, 4p, People walking near large trees.
10p, Macao skyline, vert.

2012, Sept. 21 *Perf. 13x13¼*
Granite Paper
1377 A347 Block of 4, #a-d 3.00 3.00
Souvenir Sheet
Perf. 13½
1378 A347 10p multi 2.50 2.50

No. 1378 contains one 40x40mm stamp.

Henrique de Senna Fernandes (1923-2010), Writer — A348

2012, Oct. 9 Litho. *Perf. 14*
1379 A348 5p multi 1.25 1.25

Scenes From *The Peony Pavilion* — A349

No. 1380: a, 1.50p, Du Liniang falls asleep under tree (6/1). b, 1.50p, Du Liniang drawing (6/2). c, 2p, Lord of the Underworld and Du Liniang (6/3). d, 2p, Du Liniang and Liu Mengmei (6/4). e, 2.50p, Du Liniang and Liu Mengmei under tree (6/5). f, 2.50p, Wedding (6/6).
12p, Du Liniang and Liu Mengmei, diff.

2012, Nov. 30 *Perf. 13¼x13*
Granite Paper
1380 A349 Block of 6, #a-f 3.00 3.00
Souvenir Sheet
Perf. 13¼
1381 A349 12p multi 3.00 3.00

No. 1381 contains one 30x60mm stamp.

New Year 2013 (Year of the Snake) A350

No. 1382: a, Metal sculpture of snake. b, Wood carving of snake. c, Fireworks display of snake. d, Clay sculpture of snake. e, Watercolor painting of snake.
12p, Watercolor painting of snake, diff.

Litho., Litho. & Embossed with Foil and Hologram Application (5p)

2013, Jan. 3 *Perf. 14¼*
1382 Horiz. strip of 5 3.00 3.00
a.-d. A350 1.50p Any single .40 .40
e. A350 5p multi 1.25 1.25

Souvenir Sheet
Litho. & Embossed With Foil Application
1383 A350 12p multi 3.00 3.00

No. 1383 contains one 50x50mm diamond-shaped stamp.

Macao Chamber of Commerce, Cent. — A351

No. 1384 — Chamber of Commerce emblem and: a, 1.50p, Chamber of Commerce leader, building, abacus. b, 2.50p, Chamber of Commerce leader, documents, Chamber of Commerce members clapping. c, 3.50p, Chamber of Commerce leader, leaders shaking hands, Chamber of Commerce seal and embosser. d, 4p, Chamber of Commerce members casting ballots, building.
12p, Building.

2013, Jan. 23 Litho. *Perf. 14x13½*
Granite Paper
1384 A351 Block of 4, #a-d 3.00 3.00
Souvenir Sheet
1385 A351 12p multi 3.00 3.00

No. 1385 contains one 40x40mm stamp.

Souvenir Sheet

Diaolou (Watchtower), Kaiping, People's Republic of China — A352

2013, Mar. 1 *Perf. 14x13¼*
Granite Paper
1386 A352 12p multi 3.00 3.00

Basic Law of Macao, 20th Anniv. A353

Various people with denomination in: 1.50p, Green square. 5p, Red square.

2013, Mar. 31 ***Perf. 14***

1387-1388 A353 Set of 2 1.75 1.75

First Macao Fire Brigade, 130th Anniv. — A354

No. 1389: a, 1.50p, Manual pump wagon, c. 1877, Central Fire Station (4/1). b, 2.50p, 1955 Ladder truck, Taipa Fire Station (4/2). c, 3.50p, 2008 Aerial ladder truck, Areia Preta Fire Station (4/3). d, 4p, 2007 High Reach Extendable Turret Stinger, Fire Brigade Headquarters and Sai Van Lake Fire Station (4/4).

12p, 19th cent. horse-drawn steam pump, Fire Brigade Command Building, vert.

2013, Apr. 25 ***Perf. 14x13¼***

Granite Paper

1389 A354 Block of 4, #a-d 3.00 3.00

Souvenir Sheet

1390 A354 12p multi 3.00 3.00

No. 1390 contains one 40x60mm stamp.

Items in Macao Museum — A355

No. 1391: a, 1.50p, Nativity scene carved in mother-of-pearl (4/1). b, 2.50p, Painted stone sculpture of Madonna and Child (4/2). c, 3.50p, Elephant-shaped Kraak porcelain vessel (4/3). d, 4p, Bronze bell of St. Paul's Church (4/4).

12p, 16th cent. copperplate engraving of Macao, by Theodore de Bry, horiz.

2013, May 10 ***Perf. 13¼x13***

1391 A355 Block of 4, #a-d 3.00 3.00

Souvenir Sheet

1392 A355 12p multi 3.00 3.00

No. 1392 contains one 60x40mm stamp.

Na Tcha, Child God of War — A356

No. 1393 — Various depictions of Na Tcha with background color of: a, 2p, Pale orange (4/1). b, 2.50p, Blue black (4/2). c, 3.50p, Red (4/3). d, 4p, Dull blue (4/4).

12p, Na Tcha, orange background.

2013, June 25 ***Perf. 13¼x13***

1393 A356 Block of 4, #a-d 3.00 3.00

Souvenir Sheet

1394 A356 12p multi 3.00 3.00

Scenes From *The Romance of the Three Kingdoms* — A357

No. 1395: a, 2p, Rescue of the young prince (4/1). b, 2.50p, Control of Yi Province (4/2). c, 3.50p, Drowning of the Seven Armies (4/3). d, 4p, Zhuge Liang prays to the stars (4/4).

12p, Unification of the Three Kingdoms under the Jin Dynasty, horiz.

2013, Sept. 13 Litho. ***Perf. 13¼x13***

Granite Paper

1395 A357 Block of 4, #a-d 3.00 3.00

Souvenir Sheet

Perf. 13x13¼

1396 A357 12p multi 3.00 3.00

Streets of Macao — A358

No. 1397: a, 2p, Avenida de Almeida Ribiero (4/1). b, 2.50p, Calçada dos Quartéis (4/2). c, 3.50p, Calçada do Teatro (4/3). d, 4p, Beco do Lilau (4/4).

12p, Calçada da Igreja de Sao Lázaro, vert.

2013, Oct. 9 Litho. ***Perf. 14x13¼***

Granite Paper

1397 A358 Block of 4, #a-d 3.00 3.00

Souvenir Sheet

Perf. 13¼x14

1398 A358 12p multi 3.00 3.00

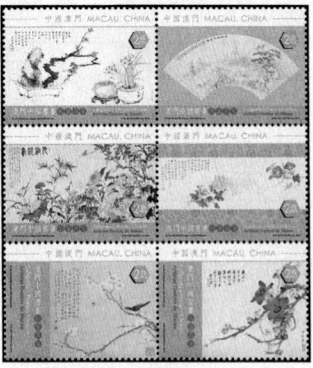

Christmas A359

Designs: 3.50p, Church, statue of angel (2/1). 5p, Church, statue of angel, diff. (2/2).

12p, Statue of Madonna and Child.

2013, Oct. 21 Litho. ***Perf. 14x13¼***

Granite Paper

1399-1400 A359 Set of 2 2.25 2.25

Souvenir Sheet

1401 A359 12p multi 3.00 3.00

Chinese Calligraphy and Painting — A360

No. 1402: a, Yu Un, by Leong Chong Hin, Guan Wanli, Situ Qi, Chui Tak Kei and Lin Jin (potted plants, 6/1). b, Literary Meeting in Goi Meng House, by Gu Danming (fan, 6/2). c, Blessings of Autumn, by Huang Yunyu, Guan Wanli, U Kuan Wai, Zhou Paiyun, Zhao Wenfeng, Tam Van Iao, Kam Hang, Chan Chi Vai, Chui Tak Kei and Lin Jin (flowers, 6/3). d, Autumn, by Situ Qi, Chui Tak Kei and Huang Haoming (yellow and blue flowers, 6/4). e, Announcement of Spring, by Chui Tak Kei (bird in blossoming tree, 6/5). f, Heroic Kapok, by Chui Tak Kei (tree with red blossoms, 6/6).

12p, Sparrows and Red Leaves, by Deng Fen, Situ Qi and Lin Jin.

2013, Nov. 1 Litho. ***Perf. 13x13¼***

Granite Paper

1402 A360 2p Block of 6, #a-f 3.00 3.00

Souvenir Sheet

1403 A360 12p multi 3.00 3.00

60th Macao Grand Prix — A361

No. 1404 — Race cars or motorcyles (#1404c) from: a, 1954 (6/1). b, 1963 (6/2). c, 1973 (6/3). d, 1983 (6/4). e, 1993 (6/5). f, 2003 (6/6).

12p, 2013 race car, older car.

2013, Nov. 8 Litho. ***Perf. 14x13¼***

Granite Paper

1404 A361 2p Block of 6, #a-f 3.00 3.00

Souvenir Sheet

Litho. With Foil Application

Perf.

1405 A361 12p multi 3.00 3.00

No. 1405 contains one 55x38mm oval stamp.

Trade and Cooperation Agreement Between Macao and the European Union, 20th Anniv. — A362

Flags of Macao and the European Union, "20" and various symbols with denomination color of: 1.50p, Green (2/1). 5p, Dark blue (2/2).

2013, Nov. 23 Litho. ***Perf. 14***

1406-1407 A362 Set of 2 1.75 1.75

New Year 2014 (Year of the Horse) — A363

No. 1408: a, Metal sculpture of horse (5/1). b, Watercolor painting of horse (5/2). c, Horse in fireworks (5/3). d, Clay figurine of horse (5/4). e, Wood carving of horse (5/5).

12p, Wood carving of horse, diff.

Litho., Litho. & Embossed With Foil Application (5p, 12p)

2014, Jan. 3 ***Perf. 13¾***

Granite Paper

1408 Horiz. strip of 5 3.25 3.25

a.-d. A363 2p Any single .50 .50

e. A363 5p multi 1.25 1.25

Souvenir Sheet

Perf. 14¼

1409 A363 12p multi 3.00 3.00

No. 1409 contains one 50x50mm diamond-shaped stamp.

Conde de Sao Januário General Hospital, 140th Anniv. A364

Designs: 2p, Old hospital building (4/1). 2.50p, Modern hospital building (4/2). 3.50p, Accreditation emblem, surgeons (4/3). 4p, 140th anniversary emblem, doctors examining patient (4/4).

12p, Old and new hospital buildings, 140th anniversary emblem.

2014, Jan. 6 Litho. ***Perf. 13x13¼***

Granite Paper

1410-1413 A364 Set of 4 3.00 3.00

Souvenir Sheet

Perf. 13¼x13

1414 A364 12p multi 3.00 3.00

No. 1414 contains one 60x40mm stamp.

Macao Post, 130th Anniv. — A365

No. 1415: a, 2p, Macao Post Headquarters (4/1). b, 2.50p, Arch of post office (4/2). c, 3.50p, Museum of Communications (4/3). d, 4p, Emblems for postal services (4/4).

12p, Macao Post Headquarters (2/1). 50p, Tower and arches of Macao Post Headquarters (2/2), vert.

2014, Mar. 1 Litho. *Perf. 14x13¼*

Granite Paper

1415 A365 Block or strip of 4, #a-d 3.00 3.00

Souvenir Sheets

Litho. With Foil Application

Perf. 13½x14

1416 A365 12p multi 3.00 3.00

Litho.

Perf. 13½

Silk-Faced Granite Paper

1417 A365 50p multi 12.50 12.50

No. 1416 contains one 40x40mm stamp. No. 1417 contains one 30x60mm stamp.

Animal Protection — A366

No. 1418: a, 2p, Dog (4/1). b, 2.50p, Cat (4/2). c, 3.50p, Cat, diff. (4/3). d, 4p, Dog, diff. (4/4).

12p, Dog and chain-link fence.

2014, Apr. 28 Litho. *Perf. 14x13¼*

Granite Paper

1418 A366 Block or strip of 4, #a-d 3.00 3.00

Souvenir Sheet

Perf. 13½x14

1419 A366 12p multi 3.00 3.00

No. 1419 contains one 60x40mm stamp.

Characters From *The Outlaws of the Marsh* — A367

No. 1420: a, Shi Jin, with tattooed back (6/1). b, Chai Jin, wearing purple robe (6/2). c, Yang Zhi, unsheathing sword (6/3). d, Chao Gai, holding spear (6/4). e, Ruan Xiaoqi, holding oar (6/5). f, Gongsun Sheng, holding leaf (6/6).

12p, Chao Gai and Chai Jin, horiz.

2014, June 26 Litho. *Perf. 13¼x13*

Granite Paper

1420 A367 2p Block of 6, #a-f 3.00 3.00

Souvenir Sheet

Perf. 13x13¼

1421 A367 12p multi 3.00 3.00

New Campus of the University of Macao — A368

No. 1422 — Various buildings with stamps numbered: a, (4/1). b, (4/2). c, (4/3). d, (4/4).

12p, Building, diff.

2014, Sept. 5 Litho. *Perf. 13x13¼*

Granite Paper

1422 A368 2p Block or strip of 4, #a-d 2.00 2.00

Souvenir Sheet

1423 A368 12p multi 3.00 3.00

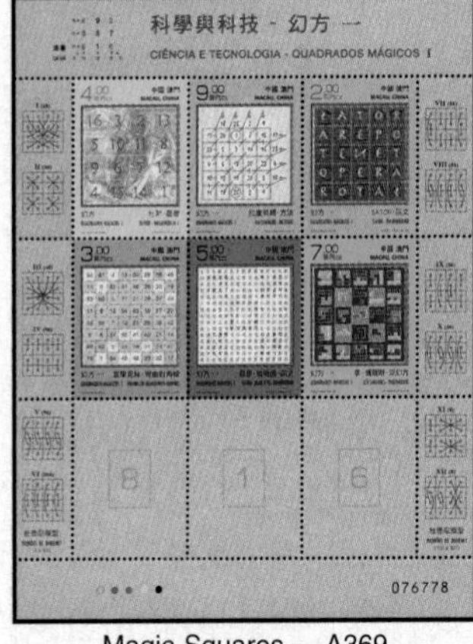

Magic Squares — A369

No. 1424: a, 2p, Magic word square (6/1). b, 3p, Bent diagonal square by Benjamin Franklin (6/2). c, 4p, Melancolia I magic square by Albrecht Dürer (6/3). d, 5p, Xuan Ji Tu Chinese palindromic square by Su Hui (6/4). e, 7p, Panmagic square by Lee Sallows (6/5). f, 9p, Magic square construction method by Simon de la Loubère (6/6).

12p, Magic square of dots on turtle shell, by Luo Shu, horiz.

2014, Oct. 9 Litho. *Perf. 13¼x13*

Granite Paper

1424 A369 Sheet of 6, #a-f, + 3 labels 7.50 7.50

Souvenir Sheet

1425 A369 12p multi 3.00 3.00

No. 1425 contains one 60x40mm stamp. See Nos. 1465-1466.

General Post Offices — A370

No. 1426 — General Post Office in: a, Macao. b, Bangkok, Thailand.

2014, Nov. 1 Litho. *Perf. 13x13¼*

Granite Paper

1426 A370 5.50p Horiz. pair, #a-b 2.75 2.75

See Thailand No. 2825.

Lin Zexu Memorial Museum — A371

No. 1427 — Lin Zexu (1785-1850), Qing Dynasty official: a, Wearing robe depicting crane (4/1). b, With Opium War battle in background (4/2). c, Seated with Portuguese naval officer (4/3). d, Meeting Portuguese naval officer at harbor (4/4).

12p, Lin Zexu, diff.

2014, Nov. 5 Litho. *Perf. 13x13¼*

Granite Paper

1427 A371 2p Block of 4, #a-d 2.00 2.00

Souvenir Sheet

Perf. 13¼x13

1428 A371 12p multi 3.00 3.00

No. 1428 contains one 60x40mm stamp.

Paintings of Macao by Kam Cheong Ling (1911-91) — A372

No. 1429 — Paintings depicting: a, 2p, Ships (4/1). b, 2p, Fountain and street scene (4/2). c, 3p, Market stalls near building (4/3). d, 5p, Gate near church (4/4).

12p, People on verandah.

2014, Nov. 12 Litho. *Perf. 13x13¼*

Granite Paper

1429 A372 Block of 4, #a-d 3.00 3.00

Souvenir Sheet

Perf. 13½

1430 A372 12p multi 3.00 3.00

No. 1430 contains one 40x40mm stamp.

Macao Special Administrative Region, 15th Anniv. — A373

No. 1431: a, Clothing on mannequins in store, building, gears (4/1). b, Buildings, blue sky (4/2). c, Buildings, orange sky (4/3). d, Building and world map (4/4).

12p, Building with flags.

2014, Dec. 20 Litho. *Perf. 13x13¼*

Granite Paper

1431 A373 2p Block of 4, #a-d 2.00 2.00

Souvenir Sheet

Perf. 13¼x13

1432 A373 12p multi 3.00 3.00

No. 1432 contains one 60x40mm stamp.

People's Liberation Army Garrison in Macao, 15th Anniv. — A374

No. 1433: a, Soldiers at flag ceremony (6/1). b, Soldier in camouflage uniform (6/2). c, Soldiers looking at sign (6/3). d, Soldier putting military helmet on child (6/4). e, Musicians (6/5). f, Soldier guiding shooter (6/6).

12p, Soldiers at attention in front of building.

2014, Dec. 20 Litho. *Perf. 13x13¼*

1433 A374 2p Block of 6, #a-f 3.00 3.00

Souvenir Sheet

Perf. 13¼x13

1434 A374 12p multi 3.00 3.00

No. 1434 contains one 60x40mm stamp.

New Year 2015 (Year of the Goat) — A375

No. 1435: a, Metal sculpture of goat (5/1). b, Watercolor of goat (5/2). c, Goat in fireworks (5/3). d, Clay figurine of goat (5/4). e, Wood carving of goat (5/5).

12p, Wood carving of goat, diff.

Litho., Litho & Embossed With Foil Application (5p, 12p)

2015, Jan. 5 *Perf. 13¾*

Granite Paper (#1435)

1435 Horiz. strip of 5 3.25 3.25
a.-d. A375 2p Any single .50 .50
e. A375 5p multi 1.25 1.25

Souvenir Sheet

Perf. 14¼

1436 A375 12p multi 3.00 3.00

No. 1436 contains one 50x50mm diamond-shaped stamp.

Rotary International, 110th Anniv. — A376

Rotary International emblem and: 5.50p, Rotary International founder Paul Harris (1868-1947). 12p, People tending to child in wheelchair, vert.

2015, Feb. 16 Litho. *Perf. 13x13¼*

Granite Paper

1437 A376 5.50p multi 1.40 1.40

Souvenir Sheet

1438 A376 12p multi 3.00 3.00

No. 1438 contains one 40x60mm stamp.

Souvenir Sheet

Crescent Lake, Dunhuang, People's Republic of China — A377

2015, Mar. 1 Litho. *Perf. 13x13¼*

Granite Paper

1439 A377 12p multi 3.00 3.00

Intl. Association of Portuguese-Speaking Countries, 25th Anniv. — A378

2015, Apr. 27 Litho. *Perf. 13¼x13*

Granite Paper

1440 A378 5.50p multi 1.40 1.40

See Angola No. , Brazil No. 3300, Cape Verde No. 1004, Guinea-Bissau No. , Mozambique No. , Portugal No. , St. Thomas & Prince Islands No. 2954, Timor No.

Wetlands Wildlife — A379

No. 1441: a, 2p, Uca arcuata (4/1). b, 3p, Boleophthalmus pectinirostris (4/2). c, 4.50p, Microhyla ornata (4/3). d, 5.50p, Trithemis aurora (4/4).
12p, Platalea minor.

2015, May 5 Litho. *Perf. 14x13½*
Granite Paper

1441 A379 Block or strip of 4, #a-d 3.75 3.75

Souvenir Sheet

1442 A379 12p multi 3.00 3.00

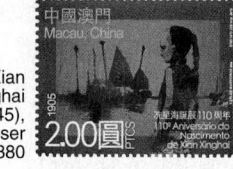

Xian Xinghai (1905-45), Composer A380

Stamps dated: a, 2p, 1905 (4/1). b, 3p, 1934 (4/2). c, 4.50p, 1939 (4/3). d, 5.50p, 1945 (4/4).
12p, Xian Xinghai conducting.

2015, June 13 Litho. *Perf. 14x13½*
Granite Paper

1443 Horiz. strip of 4 3.75 3.75
a. A380 2p multi .50 .50
b. A380 3p multi .75 .75
c. A380 4.50p multi 1.10 1.10
d. A380 5.50p multi 1.40 1.40

Souvenir Sheet

1444 A380 12p multi 3.00 3.00

Guia Lighthouse, 150th Anniv. A381

Designs: 2p, Top of lighthouse (2/1). 5.50p, Doorway (2/2).
12p, Lighthouse and flag, vert.

2015, July 8 Litho. *Perf. 13x13¼*
Granite Paper

1445-1446 A381 Set of 2 1.90 1.90

Souvenir Sheet
Perf. 13¼x13

1447 A381 12p multi 3.00 3.00

Historic Center of Macao's Designation as UNESCO World Heritage Site, 10th Anniv. — A382

No. 1448 — Various buildings, Macao residents and tourists: a, 2p (4/1). b, 3p (4/2). c, 4.50p (4/3). d, 5.50p (4/4).
12p, Tourists at food cart.

2015, July 15 Litho. *Perf. 14x13½*
Granite Paper

1448 A382 Block or strip of 4, #a-d 3.75 3.75

Souvenir Sheet

1449 A382 12p multi 3.00 3.00

Water and Life — A383

No. 1450: a, 2p, Woman getting water from hydrant, leaf, technician monitoring computers (4/1). b, 3p, Fish, technician examining test tube of water (4/2). c, 4.50p, Fountain, water purification plant (4/3). d, 5.50p, Bowl of soup, glass of water, building near waterfront (4/4).
12p, Fountain near waterfront.

2015, July 31 Litho. *Perf. 14x13½*
Granite Paper

1450 A383 Block of 4, #a-d 3.75 3.75

Souvenir Sheet
Perf. 13½x14

1451 A383 12p multi 3.00 3.00

No. 1451 contains one 60x40mm stamp.

End of World War II, 70th Anniv. A384

Designs: 2p, Soldier with rifle, Marco Polo Bridge, Beijing (2/1). 5.50p, Chinese soldiers, Great Wall of China (2/2).

2015, Sept. 3 Litho. *Perf. 14x13½*
Granite Paper

1452-1453 A384 Set of 2 1.90 1.90

Old Streets and Alleys — A385

Designs: 2p, Rua da Sé (8/1). 2.50p, Rua dos Ervanários (8/2). 3p, Rua da Felicidade (8/3). 3.50p, Rua da Figueira (8/4). 4p, Rua de Eduardo Marques (8/5). 4.50p, Calçada do Embaixador (8/6). 5p, Rua da Erva (8/7). 5.50p, Calçada das Verdades (8/8).

2015, Sept. 22 Litho. *Perf. 13½x14*
Granite Paper

1454-1461 A385 Set of 8 7.50 7.50

Festivities — A386

No. 1462: a, 2p, Lion dancers (2/1). b, 4.50p, Balloons (2/2).

2015, Oct. 9 Litho. *Perf. 13x13¼*
Granite Paper

1462 A386 Horiz. pair, #a-b 1.60 1.60

The images in the frames of Nos. 1462a-1462b could be personalized for an additional fee. The generic images are shown.

Scenes from *Jiu Ge,* Poem by Qu Yuan — A387

No. 1463: a, The God and Goddess of River Xiang (6/1). b, The Lords of Fate - the Greater and Lesser (6/2). c, The Lord of the East (6/3). d, The Mountain Spirit (6/4). e, Hymn to the Fallen (6/5). f, Honoring the Spirits (6/6).
12p, Jiu Ge.

2015, Oct. 30 Litho. *Perf. 13½x14*
Granite Paper

1463 A387 2p Block of 6, #a-f 3.00 3.00

Souvenir Sheet

1464 A387 12p multi 3.00 3.00

No. 1464 contains one 30x60mm stamp.

Magic Squares Type of 2014

No. 1465: a, 1p, Most Perfect magic square, by Emory McClintock and Kathleen Timpson Ollerenshaw (3/1). b, 6p, Patchwork magic square, by David M. Collison (3/2). c, 8p, Ixohoxi 88 magic square, by Inder Taneja (3/3).
12p, Method of Knight's Tour magic square, by Joseph S. Madachy, horiz.

2015, Nov. 12 Litho. *Perf. 13½x14*
Granite Paper

1465 A369 Sheet of 3, #a-c, + 6 labels 3.75 3.75

Souvenir Sheet

1466 A369 12p multi 3.00 3.00

No. 1466 contains one 60x40mm stamp.

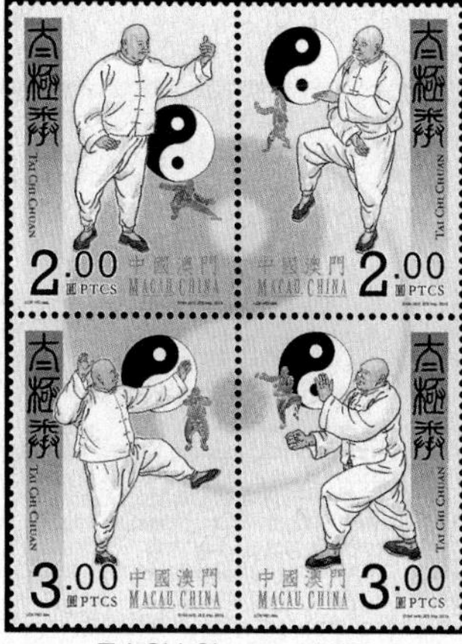
Tai Chi Chuan — A388

No. 1467 — Various body positions with denomination at: a, 2p, LL (4/1). b, 2p, LR (4/2). c, 3p, LL (4/3). d, 3p, LR (4/4).

2015, Nov. 30 Litho. *Perf. 13½x14*
Granite Paper

1467 A388 Block of 4, #a-d 2.50 2.50

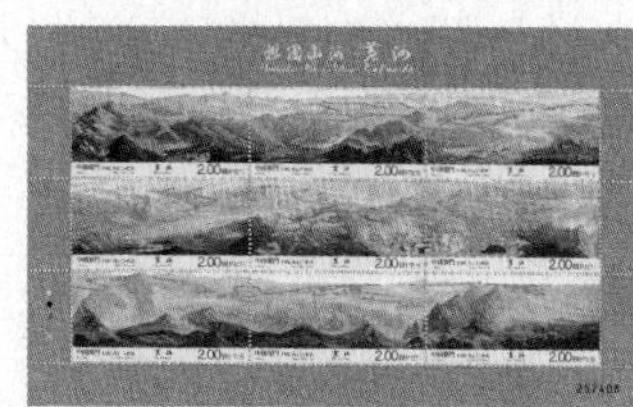
Yellow River — A389

Nos. 1468 and 1469: a, Headwaters (9/1). b, Winding River, Lanzhou (9/2). c, Ningxia Alluvial Plains (9/3). d, Vast Terrirory of Hetao (9/4). e, Hukou Golden Waterfall (9/5). f, Hukou Golden Waterfall and river running through Shanxi (9/6). g, Mountainous region of Luoyang (9/7). h, River running through Henan (9/8). i, Clear River reaching East China Sea (9/9).

Litho. With Foil Application
2015, Dec. 10 *Perf. 13¼*
Granite Paper

1468 A389 Sheet of 9 4.50 4.50
a.-i. 2p Any single .50 .50

Litho.
Perf. 14x13½

1469 A389 Booklet pane of 9 6.25 —
a.-i. 2p Any single .65 .65
Complete booklet, #1469 6.25

Complete booklet sold for 25p

New Year 2016 (Year of the Monkey) A390

No. 1470: a, Metal sculpture of monkey (5/1). b, Wood carving of monkey (5/2). c, Watercolor painting of monkey (5/3). d, Clay figurine of monkey (5/4). e, Monkey in fireworks (5/5).
12p, Monkey in fireworks, diff.

Litho., Litho. & Embossed With Foil Application (5.50p, 12p)
2016, Jan. 22 *Perf. 13¾*
Granite Paper

1470 Horiz. strip of 5 4.00 4.00
a.-b. A390 2p Either single .50 .50
c.-d. A390 3p Either single .75 .75
e. A390 5.50p multi 1.40 1.40

Souvenir Sheet
Perf. 14¼

1471 A390 12p multi 3.00 3.00

No. 1471 contains one 50x50mm diamond-shaped stamp.

Structures at the Imperial Palace, Beijing — A391

No. 1472: a, 2p, Palace of Peace and Longevity (4/1). b, 3p, Gate of Divine Prowess (4/2). c, 4.50p, Hall of Radiating Justice (4/3). d, 5.50p Hall of Spring and Happiness (4/4).
12p, Hall of Supreme Harmony.

2016, Mar. 1 Litho. *Perf. 13x13¼*
Granite Paper

1472 A391 Block or strip of 4, #a-d 3.75 3.75

Souvenir Sheet
Perf. 13¼x13

1473 A391 12p multi 3.00 3.00

No. 1473 contains one 60x40mm stamp.

Macao Police Force, 325th Anniv. — A392

No. 1474: a, 2p, Policeman and policewoman (4/1). b, 3p, Police officers with drawn weapons, police at flag ceremony (4/2). c, 4.50p, Policewoman checking identity card

(4/3). d, 5.50p, Policeman on motorcycle, police officer on traffic duty (4/4).
12p, Police officers in various uniforms.

2016, Mar. 14 Litho. *Perf. 13x13¼*

1474 A392 Block or strip of 4, #a-d 3.75 3.75

Souvenir Sheet

Perf. 13¼x13

1475 A392 12p multi 3.00 3.00

No. 1475 contains one 60x40mm stamp.

Ballad of Mulan — A393

No. 1476: a, Mulan decides to replace her father in the army (4/1). b, Mulan becomes a heroine in war (4/2). c, Mulan refusing honors and returning home (4/3). d, Mulan reveals her identity as a woman (4/4).
12p, Mulan on horseback.

2016, Apr. 8 Litho. *Perf. 13¼x13*

Granite Paper

1476	Horiz. strip of 4	3.75	3.75
a.	A393 2p multi	.50	.50
b.	A393 3p multi	.75	.75
c.	A393 4.50p multi	1.10	1.10
d.	A393 5.50p multi	1.40	1.40

Souvenir Sheet

Perf. 13¼

1477 A393 12p multi 3.00 3.00

No. 1477 contains one 30x60mm stamp.

Paintings of Macao, by Chan Chi Vai — A394

No. 1478 — Various paintings depicting: a, 2p, Octagon Pavilion (4/1). b, 3p, Skyline (4/2). c, 4.50p, Street view and Our Lady of Penha Church on hill (4/3). d, 5.50p, St. Lawrence's Church (4/4).
12p, Fishermen, boats and nets.

2016, Apr. 28 Litho. *Perf. 14x13½*

Granite Paper

1478 A394 Block or strip of 4, #a-d 3.75 3.75

Souvenir Sheet

Perf. 13½x14

1479 A394 12p multi 3.00 3.00

No. 1479 contains one 60x40mm stamp.

Items in Maritime Museum — A395

No. 1480: a, 2p, Chu Tai Sin, protector god of fishermen (4/1). b, 3p, Octant (4/2). c, 4.50p, Tai To Junk (4/3). d, 5.50p, Black ship (4/4).
12p, Compass.

2016, May 18 Litho. *Perf. 13x13¼*

Granite Paper

1480 A395 Block of 4, #a-d 3.75 3.75

Souvenir Sheet

Perf.

1481 A395 12p multi 3.00 3.00

No. 1481 contains one 38mm diameter stamp.

2016 Volleyball World Grand Prix Preliminary Matches, Macao — A396

No. 1482: a, 2p, Three women volleyball players. b, 5.50p, Two women volleyball players.
12p, Woman player and volleyball.

2016, June 17 Litho. *Perf. 14x13½*

Granite Paper

1482 A396 Horiz. pair, #a-b 1.90 1.90

Souvenir Sheet

Perf. 13½x14

1483 A396 12p multi 3.00 3.00

No. 1483 contains one 60x40mm stamp.

2016 Summer Olympics, Rio de Janeiro — A397

No. 1484: a, 2p, Runner. b, 3p, Gymnast. c, 4.50p, High jumper. d, 5.50p, Diver.

2016, July 29 Litho. *Perf. 14x13½*

Granite Paper

1484 A397 Block of 4, #a-d 3.50 3.50

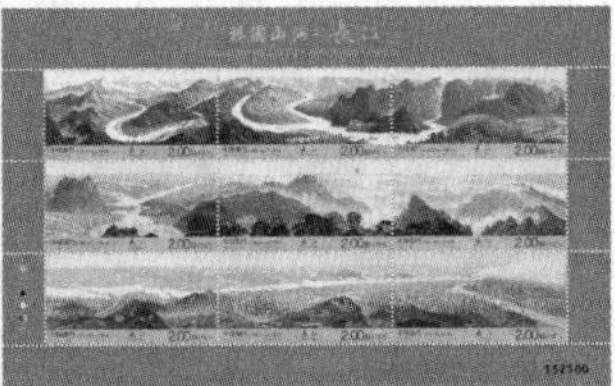

Yangtze River — A398

No. 1485: a, Geladaindong Snow Mountain, Tiger Leaping Gorge (9/1). b, Yuzhong Peninsula, Chaotian Gate and Dongsui Gate Yangtze River Bridge, Chongqing (9/2). c, Baidicheng Temple, Qutang Gorge, Wu Gorge, Xiling Gorge (9/3). d, Gezhouba Dam, Wuhan Yangtze River Bridge, Dongting Lake, Yueyang Tower (9/4). e, Lushan Mountain, Lushan Conference Site, Fairy Cave of Lushan, Lushan Hydroelectric Power Station (9/5). f, Huangshan Mountain, Lotus Peak (9/6). g, Nanjing Yangtze River Bridges, Purple Mountain Observatory (9/7). h, Plum Garden, Wuxi, Tiger Hill Pagoda, Langshan Mountain, Jiangyin Bridge (9/8). i, Bund, Pudong, Pudong International Airport, China Expo 2010 Pavilion, Nanpu Bridge, Sutong Bridge, Chongming Island, Shanghai (9/9).

2016, July 11 Litho. *Perf. 14x13¼*

Granite Paper

1485	A398 2p Sheet of 9, #a-i	4.50	4.50
j.	Booklet pane of 9, #1485a-1485i	6.25	—
	Complete booklet, #1485j	6.25	

Complete booklet sold for 25p.

Paintings by Macao Artists — A399

No. 1486: a, 2p, Nest-bound Birds, by Lok Cheong (6/1). b, 2p, Post Office, by Kwok Se (6/2). c, 2p, Meeting at the Later Year, by Ng Meng (6/3). d, 3p, Fishing Alone in the Willow Shade, by Kuan Man Le (6/4). e, 3p, The Lifestyle of Fishing Harbor, by Kam Cheong Ling (6/5). f, 3p, A Ma temple, by Tam Chi Sang (6/6).
12p, Sai Van Waterfront, by Lok Cheong, The Convent of the Precious Blood, by Kam Cheong Ling. Sailing Boats, by Kwok Se.

2016, Aug. 25 Litho. *Perf. 13x13¼*

1486 A399 Block of 6, #a-f 3.75 3.75

Souvenir Sheet

Perf. 13¼x13

1487 A399 12p multi 3.00 3.00

No. 1487 contains one 60x40mm stamp.

Ye Ting (1896-1946), General — A400

Ye Ting wearing: 2p, Suit and tie. 5.50p, Military uniform.
12p, Ye Ting seated on chair.

2016, Sept. 10 Litho. *Perf. 13½x14*

Granite Paper

1488-1489 A400 Set of 2 1.90 1.90

Souvenir Sheet

Perf. 14x13½

1490 A400 12p multi 3.00 3.00

No. 1490 contains one 40x40mm stamp.

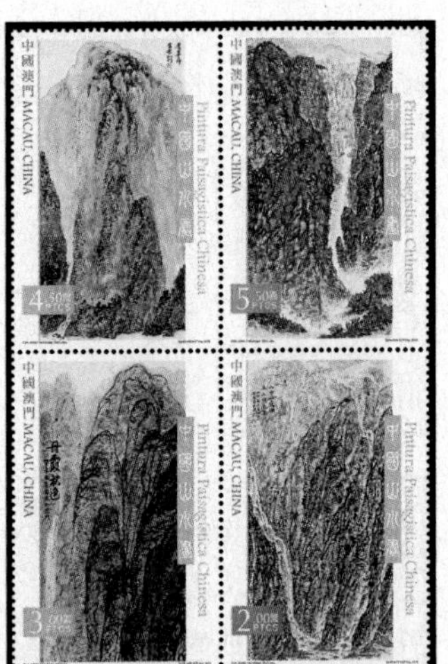

Chinese Landscape Paintings — A401

No. 1491 — Various paintings by unattributed artists: a, 2p, (4/1). b, 3p, (4/2). c, 4.50p, (4/3). d, 5.50p, (4/4).
12p, Waterfall.

2016, Oct. 9 Litho. *Perf. 13½*

Granite Paper

1491 A401 Block or horiz. strip of 4, #a-d 3.75 3.75

Souvenir Sheet

Perf. 13¼x13

1492 A401 12p multi 3.00 3.00

Sun Yat-sen (1866-1925), President of the Republic of China — A402

No. 1493 — Sun Yat-sen: a, 2p, Wearing traditional Chinese clothing (4/1). b, 3p, Wearing suit and tie (4/2). c, 3.50p, With wife (4/3). d, 4.50p, Wearing military uniform (4/4).
12p, Sun Yat-sen and soldiers.

Perf. 13 Syncopated

2016, Nov. 12 Photo.

Granite Paper

1493 A402 Block or strip of 4, #a-d 3.25 3.25

Souvenir Sheet

Perf. 14 Syncopated

1494 A402 12p multi 3.00 3.00

No. 1494 contains one 60x40mm stamp.

50th Macao Motorcycle Grand Prix — A403

No. 1495 — Rider on: a, 2p, Motorcycle No. 28 (4/1). b, 3p, Motorcycle No. 4 (4/2). c, 4.50p, Motorcycle No. 5 (4/3). d, 5.50p, Motorcycle with Pepsi emblems (4/4).
12p, Rider on motorcycle No. 1.

Perf. 13x13¼ Syncopated

2016, Nov. 18 Litho.

Granite Paper

1495 A403 Block or strip of 4, #a-d 3.75 3.75

Souvenir Sheet

1496 A403 12p multi 3.00 3.00

Strange Tales of Liao Zhai, by Pu Songling (1640-1715) — A404

No. 1497 — Story scenes: a, Mural (8/1). b, Qing Feng (8/2). c, Judge Lu (8/3). d, Nie Xiaoqian (8/4). e, The Magnanimous Girl (8/5). f, Lian Xiang (8/6). g, Zhang Cheng (8/7). h, Exchange of Brides (8/8).
12p, Painted Skin, horiz.

2016, Dec. 1 Litho. *Perf. 14¼*

Granite Paper

1497 A404 Block of 8, #a-h 4.00 4.00

Souvenir Sheet

Perf. 14 Syncopated

1498 A404 12p multi 3.00 3.00

No. 1498 contains one 60x40mm stamp.

New Year 2017 (Year of the Rooster) A405

No. 1499: a, Metal sculpture of rooster (5/1). b, Wood carving of rooster (5/2). c, Watercolor painting of rooster (5/3). d, Clay figurine of rooster (5/4). e, Rooster in fireworks (5/5).
12p, Rooster in fireworks, diff.

Litho., Litho. & Embossed With Foil Application (5.50p, 12p)

2017, Jan. 5 *Perf. 14¼x14*

Granite Paper

1499	Horiz. strip of 5	4.00	4.00
a.-b.	A405 2p Either single	.50	.50
c.-d.	A405 3p Either single	.75	.75

e.	A405 5.50p multi	1.40	1.40

Souvenir Sheet

Perf. 14¼

1500	A405	12p multi	3.00	3.00

No. 1500 contains one 50x50mm diamond-shaped stamp.

Common Roots — A406

No. 1501: a, 2p, Artisans at work (4/1). b, 3p, Parade (4/2). c, 4.50p, Angels, ruins of St. Paul's Church (4/3). d, 5.50p, Dancers (4/4).
12p, Ship.

Perf. 13x13¼ Syncopated

2017, Feb. 10 Litho.

Granite Paper

1501	A406	Block or strip of 4, #a-d	3.75	3.75

Souvenir Sheet

Perf. 14x13½

1502	A406	12p multi	3.00	3.00

No. 1502 contains one 40x40mm stamp.

SEMI-POSTAL STAMPS

Orbis International, 30th Anniv. — SP1

No. B1: a, 1.50p+1p, Orbis airplane, surgeons. b, 5p+1p, Doctor administering eye examination, eye chart.

2012, Oct. 9 Litho. *Perf. 13x13¼*

Granite Paper

B1	SP1	Horiz. pair, #a-b	2.25	2.25

AIR POST STAMPS

Stamps of 1934 Overprinted or Surcharged in Black

a

b

1936 Wmk. 232 *Perf. 11½*

C1	A17 (a)	2a blue green	3.00	1.00
C2	A17 (a)	3a violet	4.50	1.50
C3	A17 (b)	5a on 6a brown	4.50	1.90
C4	A17 (a)	7a brt rose	4.50	1.90
C5	A17 (a)	8a brt blue	12.00	5.00
C6	A17 (a)	15a maroon	29.00	11.50
		Nos. C1-C6 (6)	57.50	22.80

Common Design Type

Name and Value in Black

Perf. 13½x13

1938, Aug. 1 Engr. Unwmk.

C7	CD39	1a scarlet	.90	.50
C8	CD39	2a purple	1.10	.65
C9	CD39	3a orange	1.60	.90
C10	CD39	5a ultra	3.25	1.25
C11	CD39	10a lilac brn	5.50	1.75
C12	CD39	20a dk green	11.00	3.00
C13	CD39	50a red brown	18.00	4.00
C14	CD39	70a rose car	22.50	5.00
C15	CD39	1p magenta	45.00	18.00
		Nos. C7-C15 (9)	108.85	35.05

No. C13 exists with overprint "Exposicao Internacional de Nova York, 1939-1940" and Trylon and Perisphere. Value $325.

Catalogue values for unused stamps in this section, from this point to the end of the section, are for never hinged items.

Plane over Bay of Grand Beach — AP1

1960, Dec. 11 Litho. *Perf. 14*

C16	AP1	50a shown	2.50	.40
C17	AP1	76a Penha Chapel	5.00	1.25
C18	AP1	3p Macao	14.00	2.00
C19	AP1	5p Bairro de Mong Ha	17.50	2.00
C20	AP1	10p Penha and Bay	28.00	2.25
		Nos. C16-C20 (5)	67.00	7.90
		Set, hinged	37.50	

No. C17 Surcharged

1979, Aug. 3 Litho. *Perf. 14*

C21	AP1	70a on 76a multi	*30.00*	4.50

POSTAGE DUE STAMPS

Numeral of Value — D1

Name and Value in Black

Perf. 11½x12

1904, July Typo. Unwmk.

J1	D1	½a gray green	1.50	1.25
a.		Name & value inverted	125.00	60.00
J2	D1	1a yellow grn	2.00	1.25
J3	D1	2a slate	2.00	1.25
J4	D1	4a pale brown	2.75	1.25
J5	D1	5a red orange	3.50	2.00
J6	D1	8a gray brown	4.00	2.00
J7	D1	12a red brown	6.00	2.00
J8	D1	20a dull blue	10.00	4.50
J9	D1	40a carmine	20.00	6.00
J10	D1	50a orange	26.50	12.00
J11	D1	1p gray violet	52.50	25.00
		Nos. J1-J11 (11)	130.75	58.50

Issued without gum: Nos. J7-J11. Issued with or without gum: No. J4. Others issued with gum.

For overprints see Nos. 144-146, J12-J32.

Issue of 1904 Overprinted in Carmine or Green

Overprint 24½mm long. "A" has flattened top.

1911 Lisbon Overprint

J12	D1	½a gray green	.50	.50
J13	D1	1a yellow green	1.00	1.00
J14	D1	2a slate	1.25	1.40
J15	D1	4a pale brown	1.50	1.50
J16	D1	5a orange	2.00	1.60
J17	D1	8a gray brown	4.00	1.75
J18	D1	12a red brown	7.00	2.00
J19	D1	20a dull blue	9.50	3.00
J20	D1	40a carmine (G)	12.50	6.00
J21	D1	50a orange	16.00	8.50
J22	D1	1p gray violet	30.00	14.00
		Nos. J12-J22 (11)	85.25	41.25

Issued without gum: Nos. J19-J22.

Issue of 1904 Overprinted in Red or Green

Overprint 23mm long. "A" has pointed top.

1914 Local Overprint

J22A	D1	½a gray green	*1,600.*	*600.00*
J23	D1	1a yellow green	3.00	1.00
J24	D1	2a slate	3.00	1.00
J25	D1	4a pale brown	3.00	1.25
J26	D1	5a orange	4.50	1.25
J27	D1	8a gray brown	5.00	1.50
J28	D1	12a red brown	7.00	2.00
J29	D1	20a dull blue	13.50	5.50
J30	D1	40a car (G)	20.00	7.50
a.		Double ovpt., red and green	100.00	27.50
J31	D1	50a orange	27.50	10.00
J32	D1	1p gray violet	45.00	15.00
		Nos. J23-J32 (10)	131.50	46.00

Issued without gum: Nos. J28, J30-J32.

D2

Name and Value in Black

1947 Typo. *Perf. 11½x12*

J33	D2	1a red violet	1.50	1.25
J34	D2	2a purple	2.00	1.50
J35	D2	4a dark blue	2.50	2.00
J36	D2	5a chocolate	3.50	2.25
J37	D2	8a red violet	5.00	2.50
J38	D2	12a orange brown	10.00	2.50
J39	D2	20a yellow green	12.00	5.00
J40	D2	40a brt carmine	15.00	7.00
J41	D2	50a orange yellow	20.00	9.00
J42	D2	1p blue	25.00	11.00
		Nos. J33-J42 (10)	96.50	44.00

Stamps of 1934 Surcharged "PORTEADO" and New Values in Carmine

1949, May 1 Wmk. 232

J43	A17	1a on 4a black	2.75	1.25
J44	A17	2a on 6a brown	2.75	1.25
J45	A17	4a on 8a brt blue	3.00	1.50
J46	A17	5a on 10a red org	3.00	1.75
J47	A17	8a on 12a dk blue	4.25	2.75
J48	A17	12a on 30a apple grn	7.00	3.75
J49	A17	20a on 40a violet	7.50	5.00
		Nos. J43-J49 (7)	30.25	17.25

Catalogue values for unused stamps in this section, from this point to the end of the section, are for Never Hinged items.

Nos. 348, 349 and 351 Overprinted or Surcharged in Black or Carmine

1951, June 6 Unwmk.

J50	A21	1a org yel, *lem*	1.40	.90
J51	A21	2a dk grn, *bl* (C)	1.75	.90
J52	A21	7a on 10a brt pink, *bl*	2.25	1.10
		Nos. J50-J52 (3)	5.40	2.90

Common Design Type

1952 Photo. & Typo. *Perf. 14*

Numeral in Red; Frame Multicolored

J53	CD45	1a violet blue	1.00	.40
J54	CD45	3a chocolate	1.10	.40
J55	CD45	5a indigo	1.10	.50
J56	CD45	10a dark red	2.00	.90
J57	CD45	30a indigo	3.75	1.40
J58	CD45	1p chocolate	8.50	3.25
		Nos. J53-J58 (6)	17.45	6.85

WAR TAX STAMPS

Victory WT1

Overprinted in Black or Carmine

1919, Aug. 11 Unwmk. *Perf. 15x14*

MR1	WT1	2a green	5.50	4.50
MR2	WT1	11a green (C)	10.00	*14.00*

Nos. MR1-MR2 were also for use in Timor.

A 9a value was issued for revenue use. Value $30.

NEWSPAPER STAMPS

Nos. P1-P2

No. P3

Typographed and Embossed

1892-93 Unwmk. *Perf. 12½*

Black Surcharge

Without Gum

P1	A7	2½r on 40r choc	7.00	4.00
a.		Inverted surcharge	70.00	65.00
b.		Perf. 13½	8.00	6.00
P2	A7	2½r on 80r gray	9.00	4.00
a.		Inverted surcharge	70.00	65.00
b.		Double surcharge	70.00	65.00
c.		Perf. 13½	90.00	70.00
P3	A7	2½r on 10r grn ('93)	8.00	4.00
a.		Double surcharge	—	70.00
b.		Perf. 13½	9.00	9.00
		Nos. P1-P3 (3)	24.00	12.00

N3

N4

1893-94 Typo. *Perf. 11½*

P4	N3	2½r brown	7.00	4.25
a.		Perf. 12½	6.00	4.00
b.		Perf. 13½	7.00	4.00
P5	N4	½a on 2½r brn (Bk) ('94)	6.00	4.00
a.		Double surcharge		

For surcharges see Nos. 131, 252.

POSTAL TAX STAMPS

Pombal Commemorative Issue

Common Design Types

Perf. 12½

1925, Nov. 3 Engr. Unwmk.

RA1	CD28	2a red org & blk	2.50	1.25
RA2	CD29	2a red org & blk	3.00	1.50
RA3	CD30	2a red org & blk	3.25	1.75
		Nos. RA1-RA3 (3)	8.75	4.50

Symbolical of Charity — PT1

1930, Dec. 25 Litho. *Perf. 11*

RA4	PT1	5a dk brown, *yel*	*37.50*	*17.50*

PT2

1945-47 ***Perf. 11½, 12, 10***

RA5 PT2 5a blk brn, *yel* 11.00 8.50
RA6 PT2 5a bl, *bluish* ('47) 35.00 20.00
RA7 PT2 10a grn, *citron* 20.00 17.50
RA8 PT2 15a org, *buff* 20.00 15.00
RA9 PT2 20a rose red, *sal* 50.00 17.50
RA10 PT2 50a red vio, *pnksh* 40.00 22.50
Nos. RA5-RA10 (6) 176.00 101.00

Catalogue values for unused stamps in this section, from this point to the end of the section, are for Never Hinged items.

1953-56 ***Perf. 10½x11½***

RA11 PT2 10a bl, *pale grn* ('56) 2.50 1.75
RA12 PT2 20a chocolate, *yel* 9.00 6.00
RA13 PT2 50a car, *pale rose* 15.00 9.00
Nos. RA11-RA13 (3) 26.50 16.75

1958 ***Perf. 12x11½***

RA14 PT2 1a gray grn, *grnsh* 1.00 .50
RA15 PT2 2a rose lilac, *grysh* 1.50 .85

Type of 1945-47 Redrawn
Imprint: "Lito. Imp. Nac.-Macau"

1961-66 ***Perf. 11***

RA16 PT2 1a gray grn, *grnsh* 1.50 1.00
RA17 PT2 2a rose lil, *grysh* 1.50 1.00
RA18 PT2 10a bl, *pale grn* ('62) 1.50 1.00
RA19 PT2 20a brn, *yel* ('66) 1.75 1.10
Nos. RA16-RA19 (4) 6.25 4.10

Nos. RA16-RA19 have accent added to "E" in "Assistencia."
Nos. RA4-RA19 were issued without gum.

Type of 1945-47 Redrawn and Surcharged

1979 **Litho.** ***Perf. 11x11½***

RA20 PT2 20a on 1p yel grn, *cream* 5.00 2.00

No. RA20 has no accent above "E," no imprint and was not issued without surcharge.

No. RA8 Surcharged

Methods and Perfs As Before

1981

RA20A PT2 10a on 15a #RA8 7.00 3.00

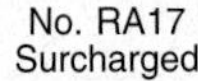
No. RA17 Surcharged

Methods and Perfs As Before

1981 **Without Gum**

RA21 PT2 20a on 2a #RA17 8.00 2.00

POSTAL TAX DUE STAMPS

Pombal Commemorative Issue
Common Design Types

1925 **Unwmk.** ***Perf. 12½***

RAJ1 CD28 4a red orange & blk 3.25 2.00
RAJ2 CD29 4a red orange & blk 3.25 2.00
RAJ3 CD30 4a red orange & blk 3.25 2.00
Nos. RAJ1-RAJ3 (3) 9.75 6.00

MACEDONIA

ˌma-sə-ˈdō-nē-ə

LOCATION — Central Balkans, bordered on the north by Serbia, to the east by Bulgaria, on the south by Greece and by Albania on the west.
GOVT. — Republic
AREA — 9,928 sq. mi.
POP. — 2,022,604 (1999 est.)
CAPITAL — Skopje

Formerly a constituent republic in the Socialist Federal Republic of Yugoslavia. Declared independence on Nov. 21, 1991.

100 Deni (de) = 1 Denar (d)

Catalogue values for all unused stamps in this country are for Never Hinged items.

Watermark

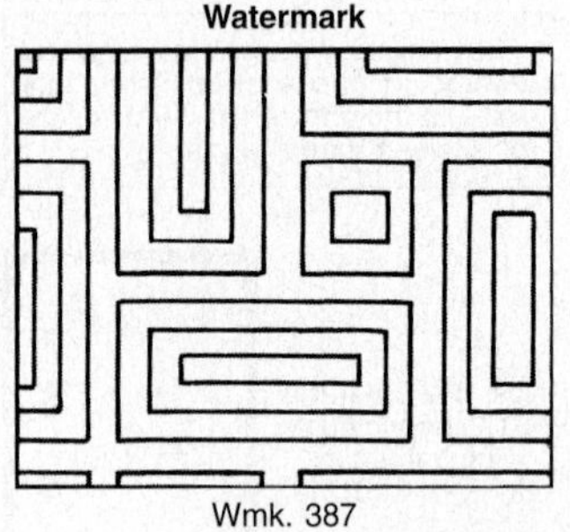
Wmk. 387

Bas Relief — A1

1992-93 **Litho.** ***Perf. 13½x13***

1 A1 30d multicolored .65 .40

Perf. 10

2 A1 40d multicolored .60 .30

Issued: 30d, 9/8/92; 40d, 3/15/93.
For surcharges see Nos. 21, 42.

Christmas — A2

Frescoes: 100d, Nativity Scene, 16th cent. 500d, Virgin and Child, 1422.

1992, Dec. 10 **Litho.** ***Perf. 13x13½***

3 A2 100d multicolored 1.10 1.10
4 A2 500d multicolored 2.50 2.50

Natl. Flag — A3

1993, Mar. 15 ***Perf. 13½x13***

5 A3 10d multicolored .75 .35
6 A3 40d multicolored 2.00 .95
7 A3 50d multicolored 2.25 1.25
Nos. 5-7 (3) 5.00 2.55

For surcharges see Nos. 23, 40-41.

Fish — A4

Designs: 50d, 1000d, Rutilus macedonicus. 100d, 2000d, Salmothymus achridanus.

1993, Mar. 15 ***Perf. 10***

8 A4 50d multicolored .35 .25
9 A4 100d multicolored .45 .25
10 A4 1000d multicolored 3.00 2.00
11 A4 2000d multicolored 4.00 3.00
Nos. 8-11 (4) 7.80 5.50

Easter — A5

1993, Apr. 16

12 A5 300d multicolored 3.50 2.50

Trans-Balkan Telecommunications Network — A6

1993, May 6

13 A6 500d multicolored 1.30 .80

Admission to the UN, Apr. 8, 1993 — A7

1993, July 28

14 A7 10d multicolored 1.60 .95

Ilinden Uprising, 90th Anniv. — A8

1993, Aug. 2

15 A8 10d multicolored 1.60 .95

Souvenir Sheet

Imperf

16 A8 30d multicolored 4.50 4.50

A9

1993, Nov. 4

17 A9 4d multicolored .65 .60

Size: 85x67mm

Imperf

18 A9 40d multicolored 5.50 5.50

Macedonian Revolutionary Organization, cent.

Christmas A10

1993, Dec. 31 ***Perf. 10***

19 A10 2d Nativity Scene .75 .50
20 A10 20d Adoration of the Magi 3.25 2.50

Nos. 1, 5, RA1 Surcharged

1994, Apr. 2 ***Perfs., Etc. as Before***

21 A1 2d on 30d multi .40 .40
22 PT1 8d on 2.50d multi 1.50 1.50
23 A3 15d on 10d multi 3.25 3.25
Nos. 21-23 (3) 5.15 5.15

Size and location of surcharge varies.

Easter — A11

1994, Apr. 29 **Litho.** ***Perf. 10***

24 A11 2d multicolored .60 .30

Revolutionaries — A12

Designs: 8d, Kosta Racin (1908-43), writer. 15d, Grigor Prlicev (1830-93), writer. 20d, Nikola Vapzarov (1909-42), poet. 50d, Goce Delchev (1872-1903), politician.

1994, May 23

25 A12 8d multicolored *.75 .50*
26 A12 15d multicolored *1.25 1.00*
27 A12 20d multicolored *2.50 1.50*
28 A12 50d multicolored *3.50 2.50*
Nos. 25-28 (4) 8.00 5.50

Intl. Year of the Family — A13

1994, June 21

29 A13 2d multicolored *.70 .25*

Liberation Day, 50th Anniv. — A14

Designs: 5d, St. Prohor Pcinski Monastery, up close. 50d, View of entire grounds.

1994, Aug. 2 Litho. *Perf. 10*

30 A14 5d multicolored *.70 .45*

Size: 108x73mm

Imperf

31 A14 50d multicolored *4.50 3.50*

Swimming Marathon, Ohrid Lake — A15

1994, Aug. 22

32 A15 8d multicolored *.90 .55*

Stamp Day — A16

1994, Sept. 12

33 A16 2d multicolored *1.25 .75*

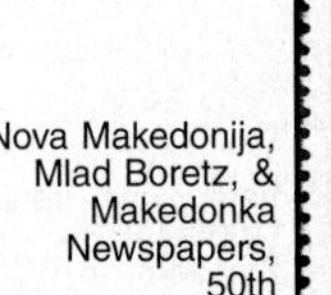

Nova Makedonija, Mlad Boretz, & Makedonka Newspapers, 50th Anniv. — A17

1994, Sept. 13 Litho. *Perf. 10*

34 A17 2d multicolored *1.30 .65*

St. Kliment of Ohrid Library, 50th Anniv. A18

Manuscripts: 2d, 15th cent. 10d, 13th cent.

1994, Sept. 29 Litho. *Perf. 10*

35 A18 2d multi *.30 .25*
36 A18 10d multi, vert. *1.60 1.30*

Macedonian Radio, 50th Anniv. — A19

1994, Dec. 26 Litho. *Perf. 10*

37 A19 2d multicolored *.65 .30*

Wildlife Conservation — A20

1994, Dec. 26 Litho. *Perf. 10*

38 A20 5d Pinus peluse *.55 .45*
39 A20 10d Lynx lynx martinoi *1.40 1.10*

Nos. 2, 6 Surcharged in Black or Gold

a

b

Perfs., Etc. as Before

1995, Mar. 13 Litho.

40 A3(a) 2d on 40d #6 *1.75 1.75*
41 A3(b) 2d on 40d #6 *1.00 1.00*
42 A1(a) 5d on 40d #2 (G) *.75 .75*
Nos. 40-42 (3) 3.50 3.50

Easter — A21

1995, Apr. 23 Litho. *Perf. 10*

43 A21 4d multicolored *.60 .35*

End of World War II, 50th Anniv. A22

1995, May 9 Litho. *Perf. 10*

44 A22 2d multicolored *1.25 .75*

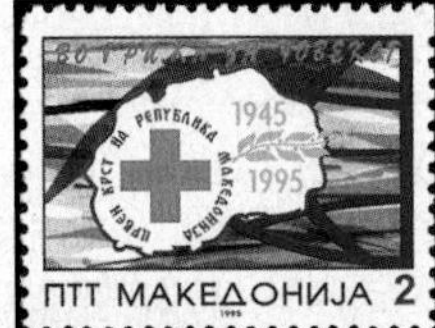

Macedonian Red Cross, 50th Anniv. — A23

1995, May 20 Litho. *Perf. 10*

45 A23 2d multicolored *1.30 .75*

Wilhelm Röntgen (1845-1923), Discovery of the X-Ray, Cent. — A24

1995, May 20

46 A24 2d multicolored *1.40 .75*

Vojdan Cernodrinski (1875-1951), Theater Festival, 50th Anniv. — A25

1995, June 8

47 A25 10d multicolored *1.30 .65*

Death of Prince Marko Kraljevic, 600th Anniv. A26

1995, June 22

48 A26 20d multicolored *2.40 1.50*

Gorgi Puleski (1818-95), Writer A27

1995, July 8

49 A27 2d multicolored *1.25 .65*

Writer's Festival, Struga A28

1995, Aug. 23 Litho. *Perf. 10*

50 A28 2d multicolored *1.75 1.25*

Mosque of Tetovo — A29

1995, Oct. 4

51 A29 15d multicolored *1.75 1.25*

Architecture A30

1995, Oct. 4 Litho. *Perf. 10*

52 A30 2d Malesevija *.35 .25*
53 A30 20d Krakornica *2.25 1.25*

See Nos. 81-83 and design A63a.

Motion Pictures, Cent. — A31

Film strip of early movie and: No. 54, Auguste and Louis Lumiére. No. 55, Milton and Janaki Manaki, Macedonian cinematographers.

1995, Oct. 6 *Perf. 10 on 3 Sides*

54 10d multicolored *1.50 1.50*
55 10d multicolored *1.50 1.50*
a. A31 Pair, #54-55 *4.75 4.75*

UN, 50th Anniv. A32

1995, Oct. 24

56 A32 20d Blocks, globe in nest *2.25 1.50*
57 A32 50d Blocks, sun *4.50 3.00*

Christmas
A33

1995, Dec. 13
58 A33 15d multicolored *1.75 1.25*

Birds
A34

15d, Pelecanus crispus. 40d, Gypaetus barbatus.

1995, Dec. 14
59 A34 15d multicolored *2.00 1.50*
60 A34 40d multicolored *4.00 3.00*

Reform of Macedonian Language, 50th Anniv. — A35

1995, Dec. 18
61 A35 5d multicolored *.65 .50*

St. Bogorodica Church, Ohrid, 700th Anniv. — A36

Designs: 8d, Detail of fresco, exterior view, St. Kliment of Ohrid (840-916). 50d, Portion of fresco inside church, #62.

1995, Dec. 19
62 A36 8d multicolored *1.00 1.00*

Size: 80x61mm

Imperf

62A A36 50d multicolored *50.00 50.00*

Macedonia's Admission to UPU, 1st Anniv. — A37

1995, Dec. 27
62B A37 10d Post office, Skopje *1.25 1.25*

Admission to Council of Europe (CE) and Organization for Security and Cooperation in Europe (OSCE) — A37a

1995, Dec. 27
62C A37a 20d multicolored *2.75 2.75*

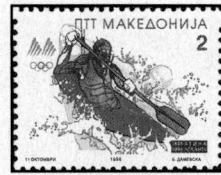

Modern Olympic Games, Cent., 1996 Summer Olympic Games, Atlanta
A38

1996, May 20 Litho. *Perf. 10*
63 A38 2d Kayak race *.65 .65*
64 A38 8d Basketball, vert. *.85 .85*
65 A38 15d Swimming *1.75 1.75*
66 A38 20d Wrestling *2.75 2.75*
67 A38 40d Boxing, vert. *4.25 4.25*
68 A38 50d Running, vert *6.00 6.00*
Nos. 63-68 (6) *16.25 16.25*

Intl. Decade to Fight Illegal Drugs — A39

1996, July 11 Litho. *Perf. 10*
69 A39 20d multicolored *2.00 2.00*

Children's Paintings — A40

1996, July 15
70 A40 2d Boy *.30 .30*
71 A40 8d Girl *.85 .85*

Peak of Czar Samuel of Bulgaria's Power, 1000th Anniv. A41

1996, July 19
72 A41 40d multicolored *5.00 5.00*

G. Petrov (1865-1921), Revolutionary A42

1996, Aug. 2
73 A42 20d multicolored *2.00 2.00*

Independence, 5th Anniv. — A43

1996, Sept. 8
74 A43 10d multicolored *1.00 1.00*

Vera Ciriviri-Trena (1920-44), Freedom Fighter — A44

Mother Teresa (1910-97) — A45

1996, Nov. 22 Litho. *Perf. 13x13½*
75 A44 20d multicolored *4.00 4.00*
76 A45 40d multicolored *8.00 7.50*

Europa.

Christmas — A46

Designs: No. 77, Tree, children caroling in snow. No. 78, Candle, nuts, apples.

1996, Dec. 14 Litho. *Perf. 10*
77 A46 10d multicolored *.75 .60*
78 A46 10d multicolored *.75 .60*
a. Pair, #77-78 *2.40 2.40*

Terra Cotta Tiles — A47

Nos. 79a, 80a, 4d, Daniel in lions den. Nos. 79b, 80b, 8d, Sts. Christopher & George. Nos. 79c, 80c, 20d, Joshua, Caleb. Nos. 79d, 80d, 50d, Unicorn.

1996, Dec. 19 Blocks of 4, #a.-d.
79 A47 bl grn & multi *7.50 7.50*
80 A47 yel grn & multi *7.50 7.50*

Traditional Architecture Type of 1995

1996
81 A30 2d House, Nistrovo *.25 .25*
82 A30 8d House, Brodets *.80 .80*
83 A30 10d House, Niviste *.90 .90*
Nos. 81-83 (3) *1.95 1.95*

Issued: 8d, 12/20; 2d, 10d, 12/25.
See Nos. 112-116.

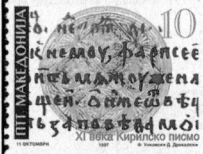

Butterflies
A49

4d, Pseudochazara cingovskii. 40d, Colias balcanica.

1996, Dec. 21
84 A49 4d multicolored *.35 .35*
85 A49 40d multicolored *4.75 4.75*

UNICEF, 50th Anniv. A50

40d, UNESCO, 50th anniv.

1996, Dec. 31 *Perf. 14½*
86 A50 20d shown *2.00 2.00*
87 A50 40d multicolored *4.00 4.00*

Alpine Skiing Championships, 50th Anniv. — A51

1997, Feb. 7 *Perf. 10*
88 A51 20d multicolored *2.00 2.00*

Alexander Graham Bell (1847-1922) — A52

1997, Mar. 12
89 A52 40d multicolored *3.00 3.00*

Ancient Roman Mosaics, Heraklia and Stobi A53

1997, Mar. 26 *Perf. 10*
90 A53 2d Wild dog *.35 .35*
91 A53 8d Bull *.60 .60*
92 A53 20d Lion *1.50 1.50*
93 A53 40d Leopard with prey *3.25 3.25*
Nos. 90-93 (4) *5.70 5.70*

Size: 79x56mm

Imperf

94 A53 50d Deer, peacocks *6.00 6.00*

No. 94 has simulated perforations within the design.

Cyrilic Alphabet, 1100th Anniv. A54

Cyrillic inscriptions and: No. 95, Gold embossed plate. No. 96, St. Cyril (827-69), St. Methodius (825-84), promulgators of Cyrillic alphabet.

1997, May 2 *Perf. 10*
95 A54 10d multicolored *.75 .60*
96 A54 10d multicolored *.75 .60*
a. Pair, #95-96 *2.10 2.10*

A55

Europa (Stories and Legends): 20d, Man kneeling down, another seated in background. 40d, Man, tree, bird dressed as man.

1997, June 6 ***Perf. 15x14***

97 A55 20d multicolored *2.25 2.00*
98 A55 40d multicolored *5.00 3.50*

5th Natl. Ecology Day — A56

1997, June 5 ***Perf. 10***

99 A56 15d multicolored *1.50 1.50*

St. Naum A57

1997, July 3 ***Perf. 10***

100 A57 15d multicolored *1.60 1.60*

Mushrooms — A58

2d, Cantharellus cibarius. 15d, Boletus aereus. 27d, Amanita caesarea. 50d, Morchella conica.

1997, Nov. 7 Litho. ***Perf. 10***

101 A58 2d multicolored *.60 .60*
102 A58 15d multicolored *1.25 1.25*
103 A58 27d multicolored *2.00 2.00*
104 A58 50d multicolored *3.50 3.50*
Nos. 101-104 (4) *7.35 7.35*

Week of the Child — A59

1997, Oct. 11

105 A59 27d multicolored *2.25 2.25*

Minerals — A60

1997, Oct. 10

106 A60 27d Stibnite *2.25 2.25*
107 A60 40d Lorandite *3.75 3.75*

Mahatma Gandhi (1869-1948) A61

1998, Feb. 4 Litho. ***Perf. 13½***

108 A61 30d multicolored *1.75 1.75*

Pythagoras (c. 570-c. 500 BC), Greek Philosopher, Mathematician — A62

1998, Feb. 6

109 A62 16d multicolored *1.40 1.40*

1998 Winter Olympic Games, Nagano — A63

1998, Feb. 7

110 A63 4d Slalom skier + label *.55 .55*
111 A63 30d Cross country skiers + label *3.75 3.75*

Nos. 110-111 were each printed with a se-tenant label.

Traditional Architecture A63a

Location of home: 2d, Novo Selo. 4d, Jablanica. 16d, Kiselica. 20d, Konopnica. 30d, Ambar. 50d, Galicnik.

1998

112 A63a 2d multicolored *.25 .25*
113 A63a 4d multicolored *.30 .30*
113A A63a 16d multicolored *.80 .80*
114 A63a 20d multicolored *.95 .95*
115 A63a 30d multicolored *1.50 1.50*
116 A63a 50d multicolored *2.50 2.50*
Nos. 112-116 (6) *6.30 6.30*

Issued: 2d, 4d, 30d, 2/9; 20d, 50d, 2/12; 16d, 6/10.
See Nos. 146-148.

Painting, "Exodus," by Kole Manev A64

1998, Feb. 11

117 A64 30d multicolored *3.00 3.00*

Exodus from Aegean Macedonia, 50th anniv.

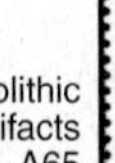

Neolithic Artifacts A65

Designs: 4d, Water flasks. 18d, Animal-shaped bowl. 30d, Woman figure. 60d, Bowl.

1998, Apr. 29 Litho. ***Perf. 13½***

118 A65 4d multicolored *.25 .25*
119 A65 18d multicolored *.85 .85*
120 A65 30d multicolored *1.25 1.25*
121 A65 60d multicolored *3.50 3.50*
Nos. 118-121 (4) *5.85 5.85*

1998 World Cup Soccer Championships, France — A66

4d, Looking down at soccer field, ball. 30d, Soccer field with world map in center.

1998, Apr. 30

122 A66 4d multicolored *.30 .30*
123 A66 30d multicolored *2.25 2.25*

Natl. Festivals A67

Europa: 30d, Dancers, Strumica. 40d, People wearing masks, Vevcani.

1998, May 5 Litho. ***Perf. 13½***

124 A67 30d multicolored *3.25 1.75*
125 A67 40d multicolored *3.75 2.25*

Carnival Cities Congress, Strumica — A68

1998, May 10 Litho. ***Perf. 13½***

126 A68 30d multicolored *2.50 2.50*

World Ecology Day — A69

4d, Stylized flower. 30d, Smokestack uprooting tree.

1998, June 5 Litho. ***Perf. 13½***

127 A69 4d multicolored .35 .35
128 A69 30d multicolored 2.00 2.00

Dimitri Cupovski, 120th Birth Anniv. — A70

1998, June 30

129 A70 16d multicolored 1.10 1.10

Railroads in Macedonia, 125th Anniv. — A72

30d, Document, building, early steam locomotive, vert. 60d, Locomotive, 1873.

1998, Aug. 9 Litho. ***Perf. 13½***

130 A72 30d multicolored 2.00 2.00
131 A72 60d multicolored 4.00 4.00

Fossil Skulls Found in Macedonia A73

Designs: 4d, Ursus spelaeus. 8d, Mesopithecus pentelici. 18d, Tragoceros. 30d, Aceratherium incisivum.

1998, Sept. 17

132 A73 4d multicolored .30 .30
133 A73 8d multicolored .50 .50
134 A73 18d multicolored 1.10 1.10
135 A73 30d multicolored 2.00 2.00
Nos. 132-135 (4) 3.90 3.90

The Liturgy of St. John Chrysostom, Cent. — A74

Design: Atanas Badev, composer.

1998, Sept. 21

136 A74 25d multicolored 1.60 1.60

Children's Day — A75

1998, Oct. 5

137 A75 30d multicolored 2.10 2.10

Beetles A76

4d, Cerambyx cerdo. 8d, Rosalia alpina. 20d, Oryctes nasicornis. 40d, Lucanus cervus.

1998, Oct. 20

138	A76	4d multicolored	.25	.25
139	A76	8d multicolored	.45	.45
140	A76	20d multicolored	1.10	1.10
141	A76	40d multicolored	2.25	2.25
		Nos. 138-141 (4)	4.05	4.05

A77

Christmas and New Year A77a

1998, Nov. 20

142	A77	4d multicolored	.25	.25
143	A77a	30d multicolored	2.00	2.00

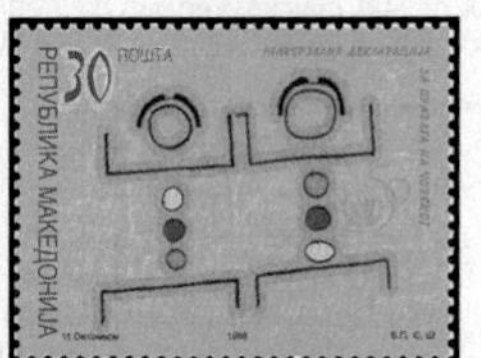

Universal Declaration of Human Rights, 50th Anniv. — A78

1998, Dec. 10

144	A78	30d multicolored	2.00	2.00

Sharplaninec Dog — A79

1999, Jan. 20 Litho. *Perf. 13¼*

145	A79	15d multi	1.25	1.25

Architecture Type of 1998
"Republica Macedonia" in Cyrillic

Location of home: 1d, Bogomila. 4d, Svekani. 5d, Teovo.

1999 Litho. *Perf. 13¼*

146	A63a	1d multi	.25	.25
147	A63a	4d multi	.25	.25
148	A63a	5d multi	.30	.30
		Nos. 146-148 (3)	.80	.80

Issued: 4d, 2/1; 5d, 2/25; 1d, 11/5.

Icons — A80

Designs: 4d, 1535 Slepche Monastery Annunciation icon, Demir Hisar, by Dimitar Zograf. 8d, 1862 St. Nicholas Church icon, Ohrid. 18d, 1535 Slepche Monastery Madonna and Child icon, Demir Hisar. 30d, 1393-94 Zrze Monastery Jesus icon, Prilep.

50d, 1626 Lesnovo Monastery Jesus icon, Probishtip.

1999, Mar. 3 *Perf. 11¾*

149	A80	4d multi	.30	.30
150	A80	8d multi	.50	.50
151	A80	18d multi	1.10	1.10
152	A80	30d multi	1.75	1.75
		Nos. 149-152 (4)	3.65	3.65

Souvenir Sheet

153	A80	50d multi	3.25	3.25

Dimitar A. Pandilov (1899-1963), Painter — A81

1999, Mar. 14 *Perf. 13¼*

154	A81	4d multi	.40	.40

Telegraphy in Macedonia, Cent. A82

1999, Apr. 22

155	A82	4d multi	.40	.40

Saints Cyril and Methodius University, Skopje, 50th Anniv. A83

1999, Apr. 24

156	A83	8d multi	.55	.55

Issued in sheets of 8 + label.

Council of Europe, 50th Anniv. A84

1999, May 5

157	A84	30d multi	2.00	2.00

Europa A85

Natl. Parks: 30d, Pelister. 40d, Mavrovo.

1999, May 5

158	A85	30d multi	*2.50*	*1.25*
159	A85	40d multi	*3.50*	*1.75*

Ecology — A86

1999, June 5

160	A86	30d multi	1.75	1.75

Macedonian Leaders from the Middle Ages — A87

Designs: a, 30d, Strez (1204-14). b, 8d, Gorgi Voytech (1072-1073). c, 18d, Dobromir Hrs (1195-1203). d, 4d, Petar Deljan (1040-41).

1999, June 25

161	A87	Block of 4, #a.-d.	4.00	4.00

Kuzman Sapkarev (1834-1909), Folklorist — A88

1999, Sept. 1 Litho. *Perf. 13¼*

162	A88	4d multi	.50	.50

Flowers — A89

Designs: 4d, Crocus scardicus. 8d, Astragalus mayeri. 18d, Campanula formanekiana. 30d, Viola kosaninii.

1999, Sept. 16

163	A89	4d multi	.25	.25
164	A89	8d multi	.50	.50
165	A89	18d multi	1.10	1.10
166	A89	30d multi	1.75	1.75
		Nos. 163-166 (4)	3.60	3.60

Children's Day — A90

1999, Oct. 4

167	A90	30d multi	1.75	1.75

UPU, 125th Anniv. A91

1999, Oct. 9

168	A91	5d Post horn, emblem	.30	.30
169	A91	30d Emblem, post horn	1.75	1.75

Krste Petkov Misirkov (1875-1926), Writer — A92

1999, Nov. 18

170	A92	5d multi	.50	.50

Christmas — A93

1999, Nov. 24

171	A93	30d multi	1.60	1.60

New Year's Day — A94

1999, Nov. 24 *Perf. 13¼*

172	A94	5d multi	.35	.35

Slavic Presence in Macedonia, 1400th Anniv. — A95

1999, Oct. 27 Litho. *Perf. 13¼*

173	A95	5d multi	.45	.45

Christianity, 2000th Anniv. — A96

Icons and frescoes: 5d, Altar cross, St. Nikita Monastery, vert. 10d, Fresco of Holy Mother of God, St. Mark's Monastery. 15d, St. Clement of Ohrid, vert. 30d, Fresco of Apostle Paul St. Andrew's Monastery, vert.

50d, St. Sophia's Cathedral, Ohrid, vert.

2000, Jan. 19

174-177	A96	Set of 4	2.75	2.75

Souvenir Sheet

178	A96	50d multi	2.00	2.00

No. 178 contains one 30x31mm stamp.

Millennium A97

No. 179: a, 5d, "2000." b, 30d, Religious symbols.

2000, Feb. 16
179 A97 Vert. pair, #a-b 2.25 2.25

Silver Jewelry — A98

Designs: 5d, Pin with icon, Ohrid, 19th cent. 10d, Bracelet, Bitola, 20th cent. 20d, Earrings, Ohrid, 18th cent. 30d, Brooch, Bitola, 19th-20th cent.

2000, Mar. 1 Litho. *Perf. 13¼*
180-183 A98 Set of 4 3.75 3.75

Macedonian Philatelic Society, 50th Anniv. — A99

2000, Mar. 19
184 A99 5d multi .45 .45

World Meteorological Organization, 50th Anniv. — A100

2000, Mar. 23 Litho. *Perf. 13¼*
185 A100 30d multi 1.75 1.75

Easter — A101

2000, Apr. 21 Litho. *Perf. 13¼*
186 A101 5d multi .35 .35

Europa, 2000
Common Design Type

2000, May 9 *Perf. 14*
187 CD17 30d multi *3.25 3.25*

2000 Summer Olympics, Sydney A102

Designs: 5d: Runners. 30d, Wrestlers.

2000, May 17 *Perf. 13¼*
188-189 A102 Set of 2 2.50 2.50

Ecology — A103

2000, June 5 Litho. *Perf. 13¼*
190 A103 5d multi .45 .45

Architecture Type of 1998

2000, July 28
191 A63a 6d House, Zdunje .45 .45

Printing Pioneers — A104

Designs: 6d, Theodosius Sinaitski. 30d, Johannes Gutenberg.

2000, July 28
192-193 A104 Set of 2 2.00 2.00

Mother Teresa (1910-97) A105

2000, Aug. 26
194 A105 6d multi .45 .45

Birds — A106

Designs: 6d, Egretta garzeta. 10d, Ardea cinerea. 20d, Ardea purpurea. 30d, Plegadis falcinellus.

2000, Sept. 14
195-198 A106 Set of 4 3.00 3.00

Children's Week A107

2000, Oct. 2 Litho. *Perf. 13¼*
199 A107 6d multi .45 .45

Duke Dimo Hadi Dimov (1875-1924) A108

2000, Oct. 20
200 A108 6d multi .45 .45

Economics Faculty of Sts. Cyril & Methodius Univ., 50th Anniv. — A109

2000, Nov. 1
201 A109 6d multi .45 .45

Joachim Krchovski, 250th Anniv. of Birth A110

2000, Nov. 8
202 A110 6d multi .50 .50

Christmas A111

2000, Nov. 22
203 A111 30d multi 1.90 1.90

UN High Commissioner For Refugees, 50th Anniv. — A112

Designs: 6d, Handprints. 30d, Globe, hands.

2001, Jan. 10 Litho. *Perf. 13¼*
204-205 A112 Set of 2 2.00 2.00

Worldwide Fund for Nature (WWF) — A113

Imperial eagle: a, 6d, Facing right. b, 8d, With chick. c, 10d, In flight, and close-up of head. d, 30d, Close-up of head.

2001, Feb. 1 Litho. *Perf. 14*
206 A113 Block of 4, #a-d 3.50 3.50

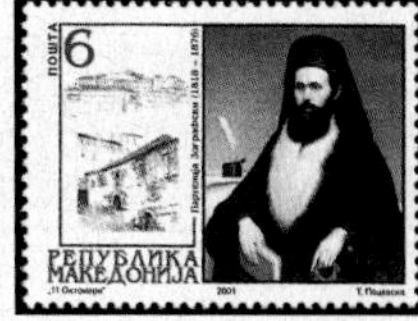
Partenija Zografski (1818-1876) A114

2001, Feb. 6 Litho. *Perf. 13¼*
207 A114 6d multi .35 .35

A115

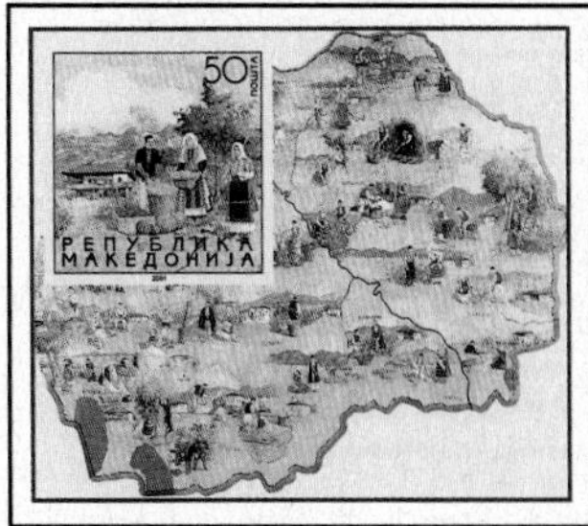
Native Costumes — A116

Designs: 6d, Dolmi Polog. 12d, Albanian. 18d, Reka. 30d, Skopska Crna Gora.
50d, Women, men in costumes, house, vegetables.

2001, Mar. 1 *Perf. 13¼*
208-211 A115 Set of 4 3.50 3.50

Souvenir Sheet
Imperf
Granite Paper

212 A116 50d multi 3.00 3.00

Lazar Licenoski (1901-64), Painter — A117

2001, Mar. 23 *Perf. 13¼*
213 A117 6d multi .50 .50

National Archives, 50th Anniv. — A118

2001, Apr. 1
214 A118 6d multi .35 .35

Easter A119

2001, Apr. 15
215 A119 6d multi .50 .50

Europa — A120

No. 216, Boat on lake: a, 18d. b, 36d.

2001, May 16 **Granite Paper**
216 A120 Horiz. pair, #a-b *3.00 3.00*

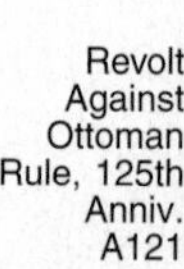

Revolt Against Ottoman Rule, 125th Anniv. A121

2001, May 20 **Litho.** ***Perf. 13¼***
217 A121 6d multi .45 .45

2nd Individual European Chess Championships A122

2001, June 1 **Litho.** ***Perf. 13¼***
218 A122 36d multi 1.75 1.75
a. Booklet pane of 4 10.00 —
Booklet, #218a 10.00

Booklet sold for 145d.

Boats in Lake Dojran A123

2001, June 5 **Litho.** ***Perf. 13¼***
219 A123 6d multi .50 .50

Architecture Type of 1998
Perf. 13¼
2001, June 25 **Litho.** **Unwmk.**
220 A63a 6d House, Mitrasinci .50 .50

Independence, 10th Anniv. — A124

2001, Sept. 8 **Wmk. 387**
221 A124 6d multi .55 .55

Trees A125

Designs: 6d, Juniperus excelsa. 12d, Quercus macedonica. 24d, Arbutus andrachne. 36d, Quercus coccifera.

Perf. 13¼
2001, Sept. 12 **Litho.** **Unwmk.**
222-225 A125 Set of 4 4.75 4.75

Children's Day — A126

Perf. 13¼
2001, Oct. 1 **Litho.** **Unwmk.**
226 A126 6d multi .45 .45

Year of Dialogue Among Civilizations A127

2001, Oct. 9 **Granite Paper**
227 A127 36d multi 2.50 2.50

Nature Museum, 75th Anniv. A128

2001, Oct. 26
228 A128 6d multi .50 .50

Christmas — A129

2001, Nov. 22
229 A129 6d multi .45 .45

Nobel Prizes, Cent. A130

2001, Dec. 10 **Litho.** ***Perf. 13¼***
230 A130 36d multi 2.50 2.50

2002 Winter Olympics, Salt Lake City — A131

Designs: 6d, Skier. 36d, Skier, diff.

2002, Jan. 16 **Litho.** ***Perf. 14***
231-232 A131 Set of 2 2.50 2.50

Ancient Coins A132

Designs: 6d, King Lykkeios of Paeonia obol, 359-340 B.C. 12d, Alexander III tetradrachm. 24d, Kings of Macedon tetrobol, 185-165 B.C. 36d, Philip II of Macedon gold stater.
50d, Kings of Macedon coin.

2002, Mar. 1
233-236 A132 Set of 4 5.50 5.50

Souvenir Sheet
237 A132 50d multi 3.50 3.50

Petar Mazev (1927-93), Painter A133

2002, Apr. 15
238 A133 6d multi .50 .50

Dimitar Kondovski (1927-93), Painter A134

2002, Apr. 15
239 A134 6d multi .50 .50

Leonardo da Vinci (1452-1519) and Mona Lisa A135

2002, Apr. 15
240 A135 36d multi 1.75 1.75

Easter — A136

2002, Apr. 24
241 A136 6d multi .50 .50

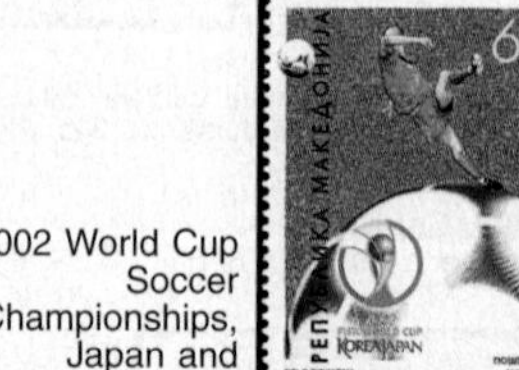
Europa A137

Designs: 6d, Acrobat, bicycle on wire, seal. 36d, Ball on wire, bicycle.

2002, May 9
242-243 A137 Set of 2 *3.00 3.00*

2002 World Cup Soccer Championships, Japan and Korea — A138

2002, May 15
244 A138 6d multi 2.00 2.00

Environmental Protection — A139

2002, June 5
245 A139 6d multi .45 .45

National Arms — A140

Background colors: 10d, Blue. 36d, Greenish blue.

2002, June 18
246-247 A140 Set of 2 3.00 3.00

Architecture A141

Buildings in: 36d, Krushevo. 50d, Bitola.

2002, June 26 ***Perf. 13¼***
248-249 A141 Set of 2 5.00 5.00

Metodija Andonov Cento (1902-57), 1st President of Antifascist Council for the Natl. Liberation of Macedonia A142

2002, Aug. 18 **Litho.** ***Perf. 13¼***
250 A142 6d multi .55 .55

Nikola Karev (1877-1905), President of Krushevo Republic, Aug. 1903 — A143

2002, Aug. 18
251 A143 18d multi 1.10 1.10

Fauna — A144

No. 252: a, 6d, Perdix perdix. b, 12d, Sus scrofa. c, 24d, Rupicapra rupicapra. d, 36d, Alectoris graeca.

2002, Sept. 11 ***Perf. 14***
252 A144 Block of 4, #a-d 5.00 5.00

Children's Day — A145

2002, Oct. 1
253 A145 6d multi .50 .50

Architecture Type of 1998

2002, Nov. 5 *Perf. 13¼*
254 A63a 3d House, Jachince .25 .25
255 A63a 9d House, Ratevo .40 .40

Christmas — A146

2002, Nov. 20
256 A146 9d multi .50 .50

Andreja Damjanov (1813-78), Builder of Churches A147

2003, Jan. 21
257 A147 36d multi 2.25 2.25

Musical Instruments A148

Designs: 9d, Gajda. 10d, Tambura. 20d, Kemene. 50d, Tapan.

2003, Feb. 19 Litho. *Perf. 13¼*
258-261 A148 Set of 4 6.00 6.00

Scouting In Macedonia, 50th Anniv. A149

2003, Feb. 22
262 A149 9d multi .65 .65

Krste Petkov Misirkov Macedonian Language Institute, 50th Anniv. A150

2003, Mar. 5
263 A150 9d multi .60 .60

Europa — A151

Poster art: No. 264, 36d, 1966 poster. No. 265, 36d, 1994 Intl. Triennial of Graphic Art poster.

2003, May 9 *Perf. 13¼x13½*
Granite Paper
264-265 A151 Set of 2 *4.00 3.00*

Ursus Arctos A152

2003, June 5 *Perf. 13½x13¼*
266 A152 9d multi .85 .85

Building, Skopje A153

Building, Resen A154

2003, June 16
267 A153 10d multi .60 .60
268 A154 20d multi 1.10 1.10

Macedonian Arms — A155

Designs: 9d, Latin lettering. 36d, Cyrillic lettering.

2003, June 23 *Perf. 13¼x13½*
269-270 A155 Set of 2 3.00 3.00

World Youth Handball Championships A156

2003, July 30
271 A156 36d multi 2.25 2.25

Printed in sheets of 8 + label.

Ilinden Uprising, Cent. A157

Uprising participants and: 9d, Seal. 36d, Memorial.
50d, Seal, diff.

2003, Aug. 2 *Perf. 13½x13¼*
272-273 A157 Set of 2 2.50 2.50
Souvenir Sheet
274 A157 50d multi + label 2.50 2.50

Paintings — A158

Paintings by: 9d, Nikola Martinovski (1903-73), vert. 36d, Vincent van Gogh (1853-90)

Perf. 13½x13¼, 13¼x13½
2003, Aug. 18
275-276 A158 Set of 2 2.10 2.10

Flowers — A159

Designs: 9d, Colchicum macedonicum. 20d, Viola allchariensis. 36d, Tulipa mariannae. 50d, Thymus oehmianus.

Perf. 13¼x13½
2003, Sept. 25 Litho.
277-280 A159 Set of 4 6.50 6.50

Writers A160

Designs: No. 281, 9d, Jeronim de Rada (1814-1903). No. 282, 9d, Said Najdeni (1864-1903).

2003, Sept. 30 *Perf. 13½x13¼*
281-282 A160 Set of 2 1.10 1.10

Children's Day — A161

2003, Oct. 6 *Perf. 13¼x13½*
283 A161 9d multi .60 .60

Kresnensko Uprising, 125th Anniv. A162

2003, Oct. 17 *Perf. 13½x13¼*
284 A162 9d multi .60 .60

Dimitar Vlahov (1878-1953), Politician — A163

2003, Nov. 8 Litho. *Perf. 13½x13¼*
285 A163 9d multi .60 .60

Christmas A164

2003, Nov. 19
286 A164 9d multi .65 .65

Handicrafts A165

DesignsL 5d, Tassels. 9d, Pitcher. 10d, Kettle. 20d, Ornament.

2003-04 Litho. *Perf. 13¼x13½*
287 A165 3d multi .30 .30
288 A165 5d multi .35 .35
289 A165 9d multi .55 .55
290 A165 10d multi .65 .65
291 A165 12d multi .75 .75
292 A165 20d multi 1.25 1.25
Nos. 287-292 (6) 3.85 3.85

Issued: 9d, 12/16; 10d, 1/21/04; 5d, 20d, 6/4/04; 3d, 12d, 6/4/04.

Powered Flight, Cent. A166

Perf. 13½x13¼
2003, Dec. 17 Litho.
293 A166 50d multi 3.25 3.25

Paintings Type of 2003

Designs: No. 294, 9d, Street and Buildings, by Tomo Vladimirski (1904-71), vert. No. 295, 9d, Street Scene, by Vangel Kodzoman (1904-94).

Perf. 13½x13¼, 13¼x13½
2004, Feb. 14
294-295 A158 Set of 2 1.10 1.10

Decorated Weapons — A167

Designs: 10d, Sword, 1806. 20d, Saber, 19th cent. 36d, Gun, 18th cent. 50d, Rifle, 18th cent.

2004, Mar. 10 *Perf. 13¼x13½*
Stamps + Labels
296-299 A167 Set of 4 5.00 5.00

Rugs — A168

Various rugs: 36d, 50d.

2004, Mar. 24
300-301 A168 Set of 2 5.50 5.50

Konstandin Kristoforidhi, Publisher of First Albanian Dictionary in Macedonia
A169

2004, Apr. 19
302 A169 36d multi 2.00 2.00

House, Kratovo
A170

2004, Apr. 23 ***Perf. 13½x13¼***
303 A170 20d multi 1.25 1.25

Macedonian Intention to Enter European Union — A171

2004, May 4
304 A171 36d multi 2.00 2.00

Europa — A172

No. 305 — People at beach: a, Denomination at left. b, Denomination at right.

Perf. 13¼x13½
2004, May 7 **Wmk. 387**
305 A172 50d Horiz. pair, #a-b *4.00 4.00*

Prespa Ecopark — A173

Perf. 13¼x13½
2004, June 5 **Litho.** **Unwmk.**
306 A173 36d multi 2.00 2.00

2004 Summer Olympics, Athens — A174

No. 307 — Map of Europe, Olympic rings with flags and 2004 Summer Olympics emblem at: a, Left. b, Right.

Perf. 13½x13¼
2004, June 16 **Wmk. 387**
307 A174 50d Horiz. pair, #a-b 4.00 4.00

Sami Frasheri (1850-1904), Writer — A175

Perf. 13½x13¼
2004, June 18 **Litho.** **Unwmk.**
308 A175 12d multi .80 .80

FIFA (Fédération Internationale de Football Association), Cent. — A176

2004, July 3
309 A176 100d multi 5.00 5.00

Marko Cepenkov (1829-1920), Writer — A177

2004, Sept. 1
310 A177 12d multi .80 .80

Vasil Glavinov (1869-1929), Politician — A178

2004, Sept. 1 ***Perf. 13¼x13½***
311 A178 12d multi .80 .80

Birds — A179

Designs: 12d, Bombycilla garrulus. 24d, Lanius senator. 36d, Monticola saxatilis. 48d, Pyrrhula pyrrhula.
60d, Tichodroma muraria.

Perf. 13¼x13½
2004, Sept. 25 **Litho.**
312-315 A179 Set of 4 7.50 7.50

Souvenir Sheet

Imperf
316 A179 60d multi 4.00 4.00

No. 316 contains one 27x36mm stamp.

Children's Day
A180

2004, Oct. 4 **Litho.** ***Perf. 13½x13¼***
317 A180 12d multi .85 .85

Information Technology Society Summit
A181

2004, Oct. 16
318 A181 36d multi 2.25 2.25

Aseman Gospel, 1000th Anniv.
A182

2004, Oct. 27 **Litho.** ***Perf. 13½x13¼***
319 A182 12d multi .85 .85

Marco Polo (1254-1324), Explorer — A183

2004, Nov. 10
320 A183 36d multi 2.25 2.25

Christmas
A184

2004, Nov. 24 ***Perf. 13¼x13½***
321 A184 12d multi .85 .85

Konstantin Miladinov (1830-62), Poet
A185

2005, Feb. 4 ***Perf. 13½x13¼***
322 A185 36d multi 1.90 1.90

Illuminated Manuscripts
A186

Designs: 12d, Manuscript from 16th-17th cent. 24d, Manuscript from 16th cent.

2005, Mar. 9 ***Perf. 13¼x13½***
323-324 A186 Set of 2 2.25 2.25

A187

Embroidery — A188

2005, Mar. 23 ***Perf. 13½x13¼***
325 A187 36d multi 2.25 2.25
326 A188 50d multi 3.00 3.00

Art — A189

Designs: 36d, Sculpture by Ivan Mestrovic. 50d, Painting by Paja Jovanovic, horiz.

Perf. 13½x13¼, 13¼x13½
2005, Apr. 6
327-328 A189 Set of 2 5.25 5.25

First Book in Albanian Language, 450th Anniv. — A190

2005, Apr. 27 ***Perf. 13¼x13½***
329 A190 12d multi .80 .80

Skanderbeg (1405-68), Albanian National Hero — A191

2005, Apr. 27
330 A191 36d multi 2.25 2.25

Europa — A192

Designs: a, 36d, Wheat, bread. b, 60d, Peppers, plate of food.

2005, May 9 ***Perf. 13½x13¼***
331 A192 Horiz. pair, #a-b *6.00 6.00*

Vlachs' Day, Cent. A193

2005, Apr. 27 Litho. ***Perf. 13½x13¼***
332 A193 12d multi .80 .80

Environmental Protection — A194

2005, June 4 ***Perf. 13¼x13½***
333 A194 36d multi 2.25 2.25

Friezes — A195

Frieze from: 3d, 16th cent. 4d, 15th cent. 6d, 16th cent., diff. 8d, 1883-84. 12d, 16th cent., diff.

2005, June 8 Litho. ***Perf. 13¼x13½***
334-338 A195 Set of 5 2.25 2.25

First Automobile in Macedonia, Cent. — A196

First Glider in Macedonia, 50th Anniv. — A197

Perf. 13½x13¼
2005, June 15 **Litho.**
339 A196 12d multi .75 .75
340 A197 36d multi 2.25 2.25

Intl. Year of Physics A198

2005, June 30
341 A198 60d multi 3.25 3.25

Fruit A199

Designs: 12d, Malus Miller (apples). 24d, Prunus persica (peaches). 36d, Prunus avium (cherries). 48d, Prunus sp. (plums). 100d, Pyrus sp. (pears), vert.

Perf. 13½x13¼
2005, Sept. 14 Litho. Wmk. 387
342-345 A199 Set of 4 7.00 7.00

Souvenir Sheet
Perf. 13¼x13½
346 A199 100d multi 6.50 6.50

Smolar Waterfall — A200

Perf. 13¼x13½
2005, Sept. 28 **Unwmk.**
347 A200 24d multi 1.60 1.60

Hans Christian Andersen (1805-75), Author A201

2005, Oct. 3 Litho. ***Perf. 13½x13¼***
348 A201 12d multi .85 .85

Kozjak Dam A202

2005, Oct. 25
349 A202 12d multi .80 .80

Brsjac Rebellion, 125th Anniv. A203

2005, Oct. 28
350 A203 12d multi .80 .80

Rila Congress, Cent. — A204

2005, Oct. 28 ***Perf. 13¼x13½***
351 A204 12d multi .80 .80

Europa Stamps, 50th Anniv. (in 2006) — A205

Emblems and Europa stamps: Nos. 352a, 353a, 60d, #243. Nos. 352b, 353b, 170d, #158. Nos. 352c, 353c, 250d, #97. Nos. 352d, 353d, 350d, #76.

2005, Nov. 14 ***Perf. 13½x13¼***
352 A205 Block of 4, #a-d *50.00 50.00*

Souvenir Sheet
353 A205 Sheet of 4, #a-d *50.00 50.00*

Stamp sizes: Nos. 352a-352d, 40x30mm; Nos. 353a-353d, 40x29mm.

Whitewater Kayaker A206

2005, Nov. 23
354 A206 36d multi 2.25 2.25

Christmas — A207

2005, Nov. 23 ***Perf. 13¼x13½***
355 A207 12d multi .85 .85

Macedonia Post Emblem — A208

Perf. 13¼x13½
2005, Dec. 14 **Litho.**
356 A208 12d multi .80 .80

2006 Winter Olympics, Turin — A209

Designs: 36d, Skiing. 60d, Ice hockey.

2006, Jan. 26
357-358 A209 Set of 2 6.25 6.25

Fresco and Matejce Monastery A210

Isaac Celebi Mosque — A211

2006, Mar. 8
359 A210 12d multi .65 .65
360 A211 24d multi 1.60 1.60

Léopold Sédar Senghor (1906-2001), First President of Senegal — A212

2006, Mar. 20 ***Perf. 13½x13¼***
361 A212 36d multi 2.25 2.25

Handicrafts With Inlaid Mother-of-Pearl A213

Designs: 12d, Wooden shoes. 24d, Decorative objects.

2006, Mar. 22 ***Perf. 13¼x13½***
362-363 A213 Set of 2 2.25 2.25

Wood Carving by Makarie Negriev Frckovski A214

Cupola of St. Peter's Basilica, Vatican City, 450th Anniv. A215

2006, Apr. 5 ***Perf. 13½x13¼***

364 A214 12d multi .65 .65
365 A215 36d multi 2.00 2.00

Zivko Firfov (1906-84), Composer A216

2006, Apr. 26 ***Perf. 13¼x13½***

366 A216 24d multi 1.50 1.50

Wolfgang Amadeus Mozart (1756-91), Composer A217

2006, Apr. 26

367 A217 60d multi 4.00 4.00

Europa A218

Designs: 36d, Lettered balls. 60d, Lettered blocks.

2006, May 9 ***Perf. 13½x13¼***

368-369 A218 Set of 2 *5.00 5.00*

Souvenir Sheet

Macedonian Europa Stamps, 10th Anniv. — A219

No. 370: a, Pope John Paul II (1920-2005). b, Mother Teresa (1910-97).

2006, May 9 ***Perf. 13¼x13½***

370 A219 60d Sheet of 2, #a-b 5.00 5.00

Fight Against Desertification — A220

2006, June 5 Litho. ***Perf. 13½x13¼***

371 A220 12d multi .80 .80

Grand Prix Racing, Cent. A221

Perf. 13½x13¼

2006, June 14 Litho.

372 A221 36d multi 2.25 2.25

Nikola Tesla (1856-1943), Electrical Engineer — A222

Perf. 13½x13¼

2006, June 28 Litho.

373 A222 24d multi 1.50 1.50

Christopher Columbus (1451-1506), Explorer — A223

2006, June 28

374 A223 36d multi 2.00 2.00

Containers — A224

2006, Aug. 30 Litho. ***Perf. 12¾x13***

375 A224 3d Carafe .25 .25
376 A224 6d Pitcher, bowl .40 .40

Shells — A225

Designs: 12d, Ancylus scalariformis. 24d, Macedopyrgula pavlovici. 36d, Gyraulus trapezoides. 48d, Valvata hirsutecostata. 72d, Ochridopyrgula macedonica.

2006, Sept. 6 Litho. ***Perf. 13¼x13½***

377-380 A225 Set of 4 7.00 7.00

Souvenir Sheet

381 A225 72d multi 4.25 4.25

UNICEF, 60th Anniv. A226

2006, Oct. 2 ***Perf. 13½x13¼***

382 A226 12d multi .80 .80

Lynx and Galicica Natl. Park A227

2006, Oct. 2

383 A227 24d multi 1.50 1.50

World Senior Men's and Women's Bowling Championships — A228

2006, Oct. 20

384 A228 36d multi 2.10 2.10

Bishop Frang Bardhi (1606-43) A229

Pres. Boris Trajkovski (1956-2004) A230

Kemal Ataturk (1881-1938), Turkish Statesman A231

Archbishop Dositheus, 100th Anniv. of Birth — A232

2006, Oct. 25 ***Perf. 13¼x13½***

385 A229 12d multi .60 .60
386 A230 12d multi .60 .60
387 A231 24d multi 1.40 1.40
388 A232 24d multi 1.40 1.40
Nos. 385-388 (4) 4.00 4.00

Christmas A233

2006, Nov. 22 ***Perf. 13½x13¼***

389 A233 12d multi .75 .75

Metal Objects — A234

Designs: 4d, Handled container, Bitola, 19th cent. 5d, Wine flask, Skopje, 20th cent., vert. 10d, Bell, Skopje, 18th cent., vert. 12d, Lidded container, Prilep, 18th-19th cent., vert.

Perf. 13x12¾, 12¾x13

2006, Nov. 30

390 A234 4d multi .25 .25
391 A234 5d multi .25 .25
392 A234 10d multi .55 .55
393 A234 12d multi .70 .70
Nos. 390-393 (4) 1.75 1.75

Kokino Megalithic Observatory A235

Designs: 12d, Mold for amulet. 36d, Sunrise over observatory.

2007, Jan. 31 ***Perf. 13¼x13½***

394-395 A235 Set of 2 2.75 2.75

Nos. 394-395 each were printed in sheets of 8 + label.

Monastery Anniversaries — A236

Designs: 12d, Slivnica Monastery, 400th anniv. 36d, St. Nikita Monastery, 700th anniv., vert.

Perf. 13½x13¼, 13¼x13½

2007, Jan. 31

396-397 A236 Set of 2 3.00 3.00

Handicrafts A237

Designs: 12d, Tepelak, Kicevo, 18th-19th cent. 36d, Casket, Ohrid, 19th cent.

2007, Feb. 14 ***Perf. 13½x13¼***

398-399 A237 Set of 2 2.75 2.75

Fish A238

Designs: 12d, Cobitis vardarensis. 36d, Zingel balcanicus. 60d, Chondrostoma vardarense. No. 403, 100d, Barbus macedonicus.
No. 404, 100d, Leuciscus cephalus.

2007, Feb. 28

400-403	A238	Set of 4	11.00 11.00

Souvenir Sheet

404	A238	100d multi	5.25 5.25

Epos of Freedom, Mosaic by Borko Lazeski
A239

Head of a Woman, by Pablo Picasso — A240

2007, Mar. 14 ***Perf. 13½x13¼***

405	A239	36d multi	2.00 2.00

Perf. 13¼x13½

406	A240	100d multi	6.00 6.00

Cubism, cent.

Intl. Francophone Day — A241

2007, Mar. 20 ***Perf. 13½x13¼***

407	A241	12d multi	.70 .70

Cat — A242

2007, Apr. 9 ***Perf. 13¼x13½***

408	A242	12d multi	.75 .75

Europa
A243

Macedonian Scouting emblem and: 60d, Scout camp. 100d, Scout, tent, vert.

Perf. 13½x13¼, 13¼x13½

2007, May 9 **Litho.**

409-410	A243	Set of 2	*9.00 9.00*

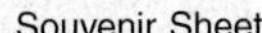
Souvenir Sheet

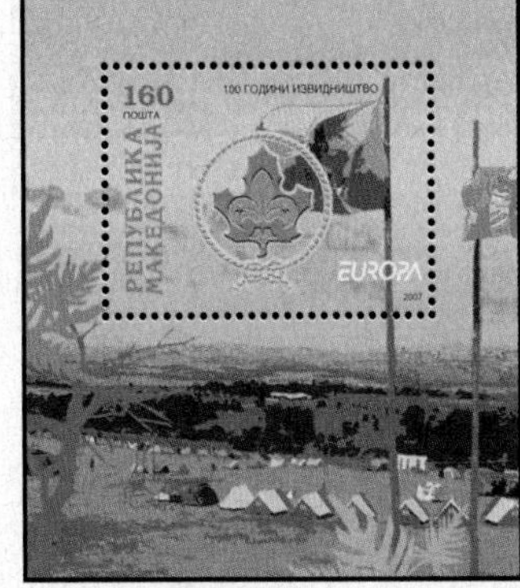
Europa — A243a

2007, May 9 Litho. ***Perf. 13½x13¼***

411	A243a	160d multi	*40.00 40.00*

Scouting, cent.

Discovery of St. Cyril's Grave, 150th Anniv. — A244

2007, May 23 ***Perf. 13¼x13½***

412	A244	50d multi	2.75 2.75

Smokestacks and Clock — A245

2007, June 5 Litho. ***Perf. 13¼x13½***

413	A245	12d multi	.75 .75

Carl von Linné (1707-78), Botanist — A246

Notes of Dmitri Mendeleev (1834-1907), Chemist — A247

2007, June 20 ***Perf. 13¼x13½***

414	A246	36d multi	2.10 2.10

Perf. 13½x13¼

415	A247	36d multi	2.10 2.10

Euro-Atlantic Partnership Council Security Forum, Ohrid — A248

2007, June 28 ***Perf. 13½x13¼***

416	A248	60d multi	3.25 3.25

Intl. Sailing Federation, Cent.
A249

2007, July 31 Litho. ***Perf. 13½x13¼***

417	A249	35d multi	2.10 2.10

Maminska River Waterfall — A250

Perf. 13¼x13½

2007, Sept. 19 **Litho.**

418	A250	12d multi	.75 .75

Mitrush Kuteli (1907-67), Writer — A251

Fan S. Noli (1882-1965), Albanian Prime Minister — A252

2007, Sept. 25

419	A251	12d multi	.75 .75
420	A252	12d multi	.75 .75

Children's Day
A253

2007, Oct. 1 Litho. ***Perf. 13½x13¼***

421	A253	12d multi	.75 .75

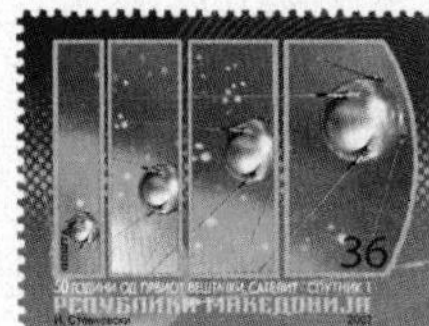
Launch of Sputnik 1, 50th Anniv.
A254

2007, Oct. 4 Litho. ***Perf. 13½x13¼***

422	A254	36d multi	2.10 2.10

Petre Prlicko (1905-95), Actor
A255

2007, Oct. 31 Litho. ***Perf. 13½x13¼***

423	A255	12d multi	.75 .75

Jordan Hadzi Konstantinov-Dzinot (1821-82), Educator — A256

2007, Oct. 31

424	A256	12d multi	.75 .75

Handbag — A257

2007, Nov. 9 Litho. ***Perf. 12¾x13***

425	A257	12d multi	.75 .75

Christmas
A258

Perf. 13½x13¼

2007, Nov. 21 **Litho.**

426	A258	12d multi	.75 .75

Tose Proeski (1981-2007), Singer — A259

2007, Dec. 15 ***Perf. 13¼x13½***

427	A259	12d multi	.75 .75

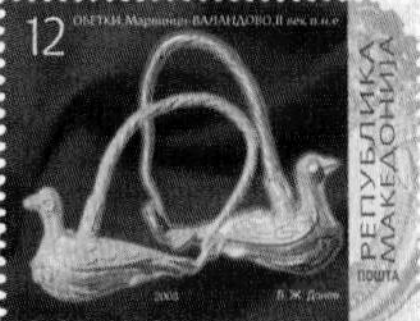
Earrings
A260

Designs: 12d, Earrings with pigeon design, 2nd cent. B.C. 24d, Earring with lion design, 4th cent. B.C., vert.

Perf. 13½x13¼, 13¼x13½

2008, Jan. 23 Litho.

428-429 A260 Set of 2 1.75 1.75

Launch of Explorer 1 Satellite, 50th Anniv. — A261

2008, Jan. 31 Litho. *Perf. 13¼x13½*

430 A261 24d multi 1.60 1.60

High-speed Train — A262

2008, Feb. 27 *Perf. 13½x13¼*

431 A262 100d multi 6.50 6.50

Worldwide Fund for Nature (WWF) — A263

No. 432 — Upupa epops: a, 12d, In flight. b, 24d, Head. c, 48d, On branch, facing left with insect in beak. d, 60d, On branch, facing right.

Perf. 13½x13¼

2008, Mar. 28 Litho.

432 A263 Block of 4, #a-d 6.50 6.50

Bulldog — A264

2008, Apr. 16 Litho. *Perf. 13¼x13½*

433 A264 30d multi 2.00 2.00

Europa — A265

No. 434 — Envelopes over: a, 50d, Western Hemisphere, dark blue panel at top, country name in yellow. b, 100d, Asia, Eastern Europe and Africa, dark blue panel at top, country name in pink.

No. 435, 50d: a, As No. 434a, green panel at top. b, As No. 434b, green panel at top. c, As No. 434a, blue panel at top, country name in orange. d, As No. 434b, blue panel at top, country name in orange.

2008, May 7 Litho. *Perf. 13½x13¼*

434 A265 Horiz. pair, #a-b *7.00 7.00*

Miniature Sheet

435 A265 50d Sheet of 4, #a-d *11.00 11.00*

No. 435 was sold with, but not attached to, a booklet cover.

Robert Schuman, Macedonian and European Union Flags — A266

Macedonian and European Union Flags, Eiffel Tower, Paris — A267

Macedonian and European Union Flags, Ljubljana, Slovenia — A268

Perf. 13¼x13½, 13½x13¼

2008, May 22

436	A266 36d multi		2.10	2.10
437	A267 50d multi		3.00	3.00
438	A268 50d multi		3.00	3.00
	Nos. 436-438 (3)		8.10	8.10

Environmental Protection — A269

2008, June 5 Litho. *Perf. 13½x13¼*

439 A269 12d multi .75 .75

Rudolf Diesel (1858-1918), Inventor — A270

2008, June 18 *Perf. 13¼x13½*

440 A270 30d multi 2.00 2.00

2008 Summer Olympics, Beijing A271

Designs: 12d, Sailing. 18d, Rhythmic gymnastics. 20d, Tennis. 36d, Equestrian.

Perf. 13½x13¼

2008, June 25 Litho.

441-444 A271 Set of 4 5.50 5.50

Eqrem Cabej (1908-80), Linguist A272

2008, Aug. 6 Litho. *Perf. 13½x13¼*

445 A272 12d multi .75 .75

14th Intl. Congress of Slavists, Ohrid A273

2008, Sept. 10

446 A273 12d multi .75 .75

Flowers — A274

Designs: 1d, Helichrysum zivojinii. 12d, Pulsatilla halleri, horiz. 50d, Stachys iva, horiz. No. 450, 72d, Fritillaria macedonica.

No. 451, 72d, Centaurea grbavacensis.

Perf. 13¼x13½, 13½x13¼

2008, Sept. 10

447-450 A274 Set of 4 8.00 8.00

Souvenir Sheet

451 A274 72d multi 4.25 4.25

Matka Cave A275

2008, Sept. 24 *Perf. 13½x13¼*

452 A275 12d multi .75 .75

Children's Day A276

2008, Oct. 6

453 A276 12d multi .75 .75

European Women's Handball Championships — A277

2008, Oct. 15

454 A277 30d multi 1.40 1.40

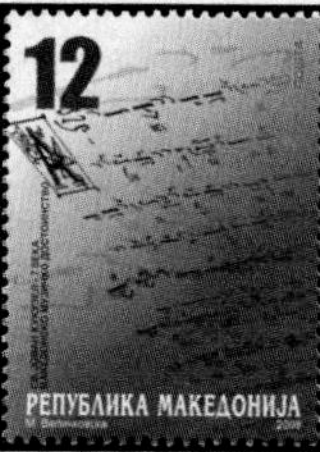

Religious Song Lyrics by St. John Kukuzel (c. 1280-1360) A278

2008, Oct. 22 Litho. *Perf. 13¼x13½*

455 A278 12d multi .75 .75

Giacomo Puccini (1858-1924), Opera Composer — A279

2008, Oct. 22 *Perf. 13½x13¼*

456 A279 100d multi 5.25 5.25

Kosta Racin (1908-43), Poet — A280

2008, Nov. 5 *Perf. 13¼x13½*

457 A280 12d multi .75 .75

Albanian Language, Cent. — A281

Perf. 13¼x13½

2008, Nov. 14 Litho.

458 A281 12d multi .75 .75

Christmas A282

Perf. 13½x13¼

2008, Nov. 19 Litho.

459 A282 12d multi .65 .65

Cities

A283 A284

Designs: No. 460, Bitola. No. 461, Ohrid. No. 462, Tetovo. No. 463, Skopje. No. 464, Stip.

2008, Dec. 4 Litho. *Perf. 12¾x13*

Denomination Color

460	A283	12d blue	.70	.70
461	A283	12d black	.70	.70
462	A283	12d red	.70	.70

463 A284 12d gray blue .70 .70
464 A284 12d gray green .70 .70
Nos. 460-464 (5) 3.50 3.50

See Nos. 484-485, 499, 500.

Lech Walesa and Solidarity Emblem — A285

2008, Dec. 8 ***Perf. 13¼x13½***
465 A285 50d multi 3.00 3.00

Friendship between Macedonia and Poland. Printed in sheets of 8 + label.

Blacksmithing A286

Designs: 10d, Blacksmiths and anvil. 20d, Horseshoe.

2009, Jan. 21
466-467 A286 Set of 2 1.90 1.90

Yuri Gagarin (1934-68), First Man in Space A287

2009, Feb. 4 ***Perf. 13½x13¼***
468 A287 50d multi 3.00 3.00

Printed in sheets of 8 + label.

Campaign Against Breast Cancer — A288

2009, Mar. 2 ***Perf. 13¼x13½***
469 A288 15d multi 1.00 1.00

Composers — A289

Designs: 12d, Trajko Prokopiev (1909-79) and Todor Skalovski (1909-2004). 60d, George Friedrich Handel (1685-1759) and Joseph Haydn (1732-1809).

2009, Mar. 18 ***Perf. 13½x13¼***
470-471 A289 Set of 2 3.50 3.50

No. 471 was printed in sheets of 8 + label.

A290

Horses — A291

2009, Apr. 15 Litho. ***Perf. 13¼x13½***
Granite Paper
472 A290 20d multi .95 .95
473 A291 50d multi 2.40 2.40

Europa A292

Design: 50d, Hen, chicks, wolf, sheep, Pleiades and Venus. 100d, Cowherd, cows and Orion. 150d, Rooster and Moon, vert.

2009, May 6 Litho. ***Perf. 13½x13¼***
474 A292 50d multi *3.75 3.75*
475 A292 100d multi *7.00 7.00*

Souvenir Sheet
Perf. 13x13½
476 A292 150d multi *20.00 20.00*

Intl. Year of Astronomy.

Prague, Flags of Czech Republic and Macedonia A293

Pippi Longstocking, Flag of Macedonia A294

2009, May 9 Litho. ***Perf. 13½x13¼***
477 A293 10d multi .65 .65

Perf. 13¼x13½
478 A294 60d multi 3.75 3.75

Macedonia in the European Union. No. 478 was printed in sheets of 8 + label.

Vrelo Cave A295

2009, June 5 ***Perf. 13½x13¼***
479 A295 12d multi .80 .80

Louis Braille (1809-52), Educator of the Blind A296

Perf. 13½x13¼
2009, June 17 **Litho.**
480 A296 18d multi 1.00 1.00

Charles Darwin (1809-82), Naturalist A297

2009, June 17
481 A297 18d multi 1.25 1.25

Boat and Compass Rose A298

Boat's Bow — A299

2009, June 24 ***Perf. 13½x13¼***
482 A298 18d multi 1.10 1.10

Perf. 13¼x13½
483 A299 18d multi 1.10 1.10

Cities Type of 2008

Designs: 16d, Strumica. 18d, Prilep.

2009 ***Perf. 12¾x13***
Denomination Color
484 A283 16d brown .90 .90
485 A283 18d blue 1.10 1.10

Issued: 16d, 8/7; 18d, 7/27.

Organized Soccer in Macedonia, Cent. — A300

2009, Aug. 12 ***Perf. 13¼x13½***
486 A300 18d multi 1.10 1.10

Cyclist — A301

Bicycle Pedal A302

2009, Sept. 2 Litho. ***Perf. 13¼x13½***
487 A301 18d multi 1.00 1.00

Perf. 13½x13¼
488 A302 18d multi 1.00 1.00

Giro d'Italia bicycle race, cent.

Fauna A303

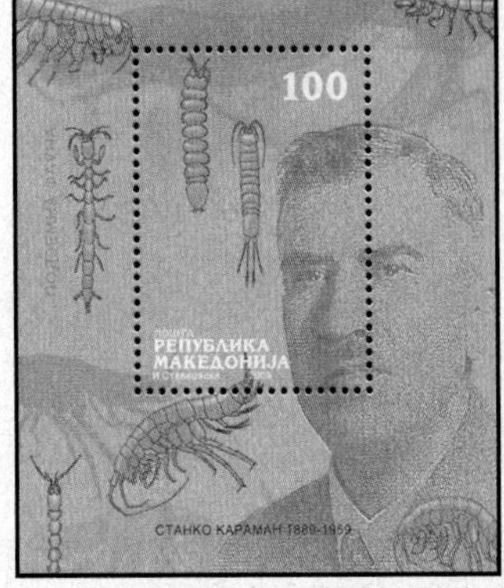

Dr. Stankos Karaman (1889-1959), Zoologist, and Crustaceans — A304

Designs: 2d, Pelobates syriacus balcanicus. 3d, Salmo letnica. 6d, Austropotamobius torrentium macedonicus. 8d, Triturus macedonicus.

2009, Sept. 9 Litho. ***Perf. 13½x13¼***
489-492 A303 Set of 4 1.40 1.40

Souvenir Sheet
Perf. 13¼x13½
493 A304 100d multi 5.00 5.00

Dimitar Andronov Papardishki (1859-1954), Painter — A305

2009, Sept. 30 ***Perf. 13½x13¼***
494 A305 16d multi .95 .95

Elbasan Normal School and Pedagogical High School, 150th Anniv. — A306

2009, Oct. 14 ***Perf. 13¼x13½***
495 A306 16d multi .95 .95

Filip Shiroka (1859-1935), Poet — A307

Krume Kepeski (1909-88), Linguist — A308

Petre M. Amdreevski (1934-2006), Writer — A309

2009, Nov. 4 Litho. *Perf. 13¼x13½*

496 A307 16d multi .95 .95
497 A308 16d multi .95 .95

Perf. 13½x13¼

498 A309 16d multi .95 .95
Nos. 496-498 (3) 2.85 2.85

Cities Type of 2008 and

Struga — A309a

Delchevo — A309b

Kumanovo — A309c

Resen — A309d

Designs: No. 499, Gostivar. No. 500, Kichevo.

2009, Nov. 11 Litho. *Perf. 12¾x13*

Denomination Color

499	A283	16d gray blue	.70	.70
500	A283	16d Prus blue	.70	.70
501	A309a	16d brown	.70	.70
502	A309b	16d brown	.70	.70
503	A309c	18d brown	.75	.75
504	A309d	18d black	.75	.75
		Nos. 499-504 (6)	5.00	5.00

Christmas A310

Perf. 13¼x13½

2009, Nov. 18 Litho.

505 A310 16d multi .95 .95

Helicopter A311

2010, Feb. 10 *Perf. 13½x13¼*

506 A311 50d multi 2.75 2.75

2010 Winter Olympics, Vancouver A312

Olympic rings, Vancouver Olympics emblem, inukshuk and: 50d, Ski jumper. 100d, Ice hockey goalie.

2010, Feb. 12 *Perf. 13¼x13½*

507-508 A312 Set of 2 7.25 7.25

Nos. 507-508 each were printed in sheets ot 8 + label.

Souvenir Sheet

International Women's Day — A313

No. 509 — Flower with denomination in: a, UL. b, UR.

2010, Mar. 8

509 A313 18d Sheet of 2, #a-b 2.00 2.00

St. Peter's Church, Golem Grad Island, 650th Anniv. A314

Perf. 13½x13¼

2010, Mar. 25 Litho.

510 A314 18d multi 1.00 1.00

A315

Parrots A316

2010, Apr. 14 *Perf. 13¼x13½*

511 A315 20d multi 1.25 1.25

Perf. 13½x13¼

512 A316 40d multi 2.25 2.25

Europa A317

2010, May 5

513 A317 100d multi *8.00 8.00*

Macedonian Chairmanship of the Council of Europe — A318

2010, May 8

514 A318 18d multi 1.00 1.00

Macedonia in the European Union A319

Buildings: 20d, European Parliament, Brussels. 50d, Main Post Office, Madrid.

2010, May 8

515-516 A319 Set of 2 3.75 3.75

Debar — A319a

Gevgelija — A319b

Kratovo — A319c

Veles — A319d

Krusevo — A319e

2010 Litho. *Perf. 12¾x13*

Denomination Color

517	A319a	16d brown	.65	.65
518	A319b	16d white	.65	.65
519	A319c	16d orange brown	.65	.65
520	A319d	18d olive brown	.70	.70
521	A319e	18d blue	.70	.70
		Nos. 517-521 (5)	3.35	3.35

Issued: No. 520, 5/8; others, 6/2.

Castanea Sativa A320

2010, June 5 Litho. *Perf. 13½x13¼*

522 A320 20d multi .95 .95

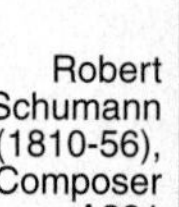

Robert Schumann (1810-56), Composer A321

Frédéric Chopin (1810-49), Composer A322

2010, June 8 *Perf. 13½x13¼*

523 A321 50d multi 2.75 2.75

Perf. 13¼x13½

524 A322 60d multi 3.25 3.25

2010 World Cup Soccer Championships, South Africa — A323

Emblem and: 50d, Soccer ball in goal net. 100d, Soccer ball at midfield, vert.
150d, Soccer ball, map of South Africa.

Perf. 13½x13¼, 13¼x13½

2010, June 11

525-526 A323 Set of 2 8.50 8.50

Souvenir Sheet

527 A323 150d multi 8.50 8.50

50th Ohrid Summer Festival — A324

2010, June 30 *Perf. 13¼x13½*

528 A324 18d multi 1.00 1.00

Mother Teresa (1910-97), Humanitarian A325

2010, Aug. 26 Litho. *Perf. 13*

529 A325 60d multi 2.25 2.25

See Albania No. 2889, Kosovo No. 154.

Bayram Festival — A326

2010, Sept. 9 Litho. *Perf. 13¼x13½*

530 A326 50d multi 2.40 2.40

Awarding of First Prize in Poetry Contest to "The Serdar," by Gligor Prlicev, 150th Anniv. A327

2010, Sept. 10 *Perf. 13¼*
531 A327 100d multi 3.75 3.75

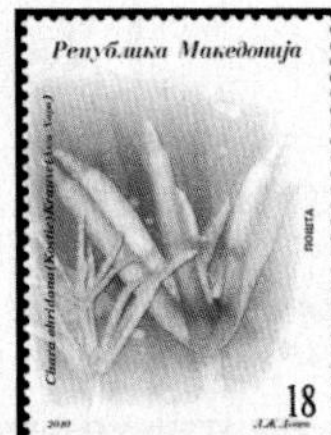

A328

Flora and Fauna — A329

Designs: 18d, Chara ohridana. 20d, Gocea ohridana. 44d, Surirella spiralis. 100d, Ochridaspongia rotunda.

Perf. 13¼x13½

2010, Sept. 10 **Litho.**
532 A328 18d multi .85 .85
533 A329 20d multi 1.10 1.10
534 A328 44d multi 2.25 2.25
535 A329 100d multi 4.75 4.75
Nos. 532-535 (4) 8.95 8.95

Henri Dunant (1828-1910), Founder of Red Cross — A330

Robert Koch (1843-1910), Bacteriologist — A331

Jacques Cousteau (1910-97), Marine Conservationist — A332

2010, Oct. 20 *Perf. 13¼x13½*
536 A330 10d multi .50 .50

Perf. 13½x13¼

537 A331 20d multi .95 .95
538 A332 20d multi .95 .95
Nos. 536-538 (3) 2.40 2.40

St. Naum (c. 830-910) A333

Dimitar Miladinov (1810-62), Folklorist A334

2010, Nov. 5 *Perf. 13½x13¼*
539 A333 18d multi .85 .85

Perf. 13¼x13½

540 A334 18d multi .85 .85

First Multiparty Elections in Macedonia A335

2010, Nov. 11 *Perf. 13½x13¼*
541 A335 16d multi .75 .75

Marin Barleti (c. 1450-c. 1512), Historian — A336

2010, Nov. 15 *Perf. 13¼x13½*
542 A336 20d multi .85 .85

Jama, Sculpture by Dimo Todorovski (1910-83) A337

Painting by Dimce Koco (1910-93) A338

2010, Nov. 15 *Perf. 13½x13¼*
543 A337 50d multi 2.50 2.50
544 A338 50d multi 2.50 2.50

Christmas A339

2010, Nov. 22 **Litho.**
545 A339 16d multi .75 .75

Kavadarci A340

Kriva Palanka A341

Negotin A342

Probistip A343

Kocani — A344

Sveti Nikole — A345

Radovici — A346

2010, Dec. 11 *Perf. 12¾x13*

Denomination Color

546 A340 16d aquamarine .75 .75
547 A341 16d aquamarine .75 .75
548 A342 16d purple .75 .75
549 A343 16d black .75 .75
550 A344 18d red .85 .85
551 A345 18d black .85 .85

Perf. 13x12¾

552 A346 18d red .85 .85
Nos. 546-552 (7) 5.55 5.55

Coin From Reign of Constantine Dragas, c. 1371-95 — A347

2011, Feb. 28 *Perf. 13½x13¼*
553 A347 50d multi 2.50 2.50

First Man in Space, 50th Anniv. — A348

2011, Mar. 4 **Litho.** *Perf. 13¼x13½*
554 A348 40d multi *11.00 11.00*

Opening of Holocaust Memorial Center of the Jews From Macedonia, Skopje — A349

2011, Mar. 8 *Perf. 13½x13¼*
555 A349 100d multi 5.00 5.00

Macedonian Shepherd A350

2011, Apr. 11 *Perf. 13¼x13½*
556 A350 50d multi 2.50 2.50

Princess Diana (1961-97) A351

2011, Apr. 12
557 A351 100d multi 5.00 5.00

Intl. Year of Chemistry A352

2011, Apr. 13 *Perf. 13½x13¼*
558 A352 60d multi 3.00 3.00

First Automobile, 125th Anniv. — A353

First Automobile in Skopje, Cent. — A354

2011, Apr. 15 *Perf. 13½x13¼*
559 A353 20d multi 1.10 1.10

Perf. 13¼x13½

560 A354 70d multi 3.50 3.50

Statue of James Watt (1736-1819), Engineer, and Diagram of His Steam Engine — A355

2011, Apr. 20 ***Perf. 13½x13¼***
561 A355 60d multi 3.00 3.00

European Capitals A356

Designs: No. 562, 40d, Warsaw, Poland. No. 563, 40d, Budapest, Hungary.

2011, May 4
562-563 A356 Set of 2 4.25 4.25

Europa A357

Designs: 50d, Forest in autumn. No. 565, 100d, Forest in winter.
No. 566, 100d, Forest in spring.

2011, May 5 ***Perf. 13½x13¼***
564-565 A357 Set of 2 7.25 7.25

Souvenir Sheet

566 A357 100d multi 4.75 4.75

Intl. Year of Forests.

Albanian Language Newspaper, Shkupi, Cent. — A358

2011, June 10
567 A358 60d multi 3.00 3.00

Struga Poetry Evenings, 50th Anniv. A359

2011, June 15
568 A359 40d multi 2.00 2.00

Souvenir Sheet

Iustinianus Primus Law Faculty, Saints Cyril and Methodius University, Skopje, 60th Anniv. — A360

2011, July 1
569 A360 100d multi 5.00 5.00

Vinica — A361

2011, July 27 ***Perf. 13x12¾***
570 A361 10d multi .55 .55

Bayram Festival A362

Perf. 13½x13¼

2011, Aug. 30 **Litho.**
571 A362 50d multi 2.25 2.25

2011 European Basketball Championships, Lithuania — A363

2011, Aug. 31 ***Perf. 13¼***
572 A363 70d multi 3.25 3.25

Values are for stamps with surrounding selvage.

Independence, 20th Anniv. — A364

2011, Sept. 5 ***Perf. 13½x13¼***
573 A364 20d multi 1.25 1.25

Ljubomir Belogaski (1912-94), Painter A365

2011, Sept. 14
574 A365 20d multi 1.00 1.00

Franz Liszt (1811-86), Composer A366

2011, Sept. 21 ***Perf. 13¼x13½***
575 A366 50d black & silver 2.40 2.40

Ernest Hemingway (1899-1961), Writer — A367

2011, Oct. 11 ***Perf. 13½x13¼***
576 A367 50d multi 2.40 2.40

Migjeni (Millos Gjergj Nikolla, 1911-38), Writer A368

2011, Oct. 19
577 A368 20d multi 1.00 1.00

Angelarios (1911-86), Archbishop of Ohrid — A369

2011, Oct. 26 ***Perf. 13¼x13½***
578 A369 40d multi 2.00 2.00

Buildings
A370 A371

Buildings in: 16d, Demir Hisar. 18d, Dojran.

2011, Nov. ***Perf. 12¾x13***
579 A370 16d multi .80 .80
580 A371 18d multi .90 .90

Worldwide Fund for Nature (WWF) — A372

No. 581 — Spermophilus citellus: a, 12d, Two adults and butterfly. b, 24d, Adult and three juveniles. c, 48d, Adult and juvenile. d, 60d, Six adults and den.

2011, Dec. 13 ***Perf. 13¼x13½***
581 A372 Block of 4, #a-d 5.75 5.75

Butterflies A373

Designs: 12d, Parnassius apollo. 24d, Zerynthia polyxena. 48d, Parnassius mnemosyne. 60d, Elphinstonia penia.

2011, Dec. 19 ***Perf. 13½x13¼***
582-585 A373 Set of 4 6.25 6.25

Christmas A374

2011, Dec. 20 **Litho.**
586 A374 18d multi 1.00 1.00

Gjerasim Qiriazi (1858-94), Founder of Protestant Church of Albania A375

2011, Dec. 28
587 A375 20d multi 1.10 1.10

Tapestry — A376

2012, Feb. 20 ***Perf. 13¼x13½***
588 A376 20d multi 1.00 1.00

Turtle A377

2012, Apr. 3 ***Perf. 13½x13¼***
589 A377 100d multi 4.25 4.25

A378

Jets A379

2012, Apr. 4
590 A378 40d multi *14.00 14.00*
a. With corrected spelling of country name (added Cyrillic "E") 2.50 2.50
591 A379 60d multi 2.60 2.60

Country name is misspelled on No. 590.

Invention of the Telegraph, 175th Anniv. A380

2012, Apr. 5 **Litho.**
592 A380 100d multi 4.00 4.00

European Capitals — A381

Designs: 20d, Nicosia, Cyprus. 40d, Copenhagen, Denmark.

2012, Apr. 9 ***Perf. 13¼x13½***
593-594 A381 Set of 2 22.50 22.50
593a With corrected spelling of country name (added Cyrillic "E" 1.25 1.25
594a With corrected spelling of country name (added Cyrillic "E" 2.40 2.40

Country name is misspelled on Nos. 593-594.

Europa — A382

Designs: 20d, Building and aerial view of city. No. 596, 100d, Equestrian statue.
No. 597, 100d, Bridge, horiz.

2012, Apr. 13 ***Perf. 13¼x13½***
595-596 A382 Set of 2 5.25 5.25

Souvenir Sheet

Perf. 13½x13¼

597 A382 100d multi 4.25 4.25

Sinking of the Titanic, Cent. A383

2012, Apr. 17
598 A383 100d multi 4.00 4.00

Introduction of Denar as Currency, 20th Anniv. — A384

2012, Apr. 26
599 A384 50d multi 2.40 2.40

Berovo A385

Valandovo A386

Makedonska Kamenica — A387

2012 ***Perf. 12¾x13***

Denomination Color

600 A385 2d gray .25 .25
601 A386 16d blue .65 .65
602 A387 18d rose .75 .75
Nos. 600-602 (3) 1.65 1.65

Issued: 2d, 6/4; 16d, 18d, 6/6.

Zani i Maleve Orchestra, Cent. A388

2012, June 12 ***Perf. 13½x13¼***
603 A388 40d multi 2.00 2.00

2012 Summer Olympics, London A389

Designs: 50d, Hurdles. 100d, Wrestling.

2012, June 24
604-605 A389 Set of 2 6.50 6.50

Bayram Festival — A390

2012, Aug. 19 ***Perf. 13¼x13½***
606 A390 50d multi 2.40 2.40

Premiere of Opera "Otello," by Giuseppe Verdi, 125th Anniv. A391

2012, Sept. 11 ***Perf. 13½x13¼***
607 A391 40d multi 2.00 2.00

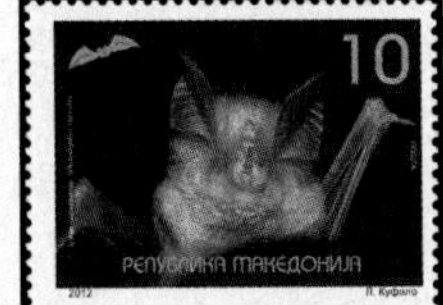
Bats A392

Designs: 10d, Rhinolophus euryale. 20d, Rhinolophus ferrumequinum. 50d, Rhinolophus hipposideros. 100d, Miniopterus schreibersii.

2012, Sept. 18
608-611 A392 Set of 4 6.50 6.50

Kole Nedelkovski (1912-41), Poet A393

2012, Oct. 16
612 A393 50d multi 2.10 2.10

Gabriel II (1912-92), Archbishop of Ohrid — A394

2012, Oct. 16 ***Perf. 13¼x13½***
613 A394 60d multi 2.25 2.25

Grimm's Fairy Tales, 200th Anniv. A395

2012, Dec. 3 **Litho.** ***Perf. 13½x13¼***
614 A395 20d multi .95 .95

Christmas A396

Perf. 13¼x13½

2012, Dec. 11 **Litho.**
615 A396 50d multi 2.10 2.10

Kitchenware A397

Designs: 40d, Lidded bowl and decorative pattern. 50d, Plate and decorative pattern.

2013, Feb. 27 ***Perf. 13½x13¼***
616-617 A397 Set of 2 4.00 4.00

Rabbit — A398

Perf. 13¼x13½

2013, Mar. 14 **Litho.**
618 A398 60d multi 3.00 3.00

Motorcycle A399

Perf. 13¼x13½

2013, Mar. 21 **Litho.**
619 A399 50d multi 2.50 2.50

Invention of Pneumatic Tires by John Boyd Dunlop (1840-1921), 125th Anniv. — A400

2013, Apr. 3 ***Perf. 13½x13¼***
620 A400 40d multi 1.75 1.75

Vladimir Zworykin (1888-1982), Inventor, Diagram, and Television — A401

2013, Apr. 3 **Litho.** ***Perf. 13½x13¼***
621 A401 50d multi 2.10 2.10

European Capitals A402

Designs: 40d, Dublin, Ireland. 60d, Vilnius, Lithuania.

2013, Apr. 17 **Litho.** ***Perf. 13½x13¼***
622-623 A402 Set of 2 4.50 4.50

Europa A403

Designs: 40d, Postal van facing left. 60d, Postal van facing right.
100d, Postal truck and van.

2013, Apr. 22 **Litho.** ***Perf. 13½x13¼***
624-625 A403 Set of 2 4.75 4.75

Souvenir Sheet

Perf. 13¾x13

626 A403 100d multi 4.75 4.75

Ali Riza Ulqinaku (1855-1913), Writer — A404

Perf. 13¼x13½

2013, June 10 **Litho.**
627 A404 16d multi .85 .85

Rexhep Mitrovica (1887-1967), Prime Minister of Albania — A405

Perf. 13½x13¼

2013, June 10 **Litho.**
628 A405 18d multi .80 .80

Mission of Saints Cyril and Methodius to Slavic Lands, 1150th Anniv. A406

Perf. 13½x13¼

2013, June 24 **Litho.**
629 A406 40d multi 1.75 1.75

Building, Demir Kapija — A407

Building, Makedonski Brod — A408

2013 **Litho.** ***Perf. 12¾x13***
630 A407 16d multi .70 .70
631 A408 16d multi .70 .70

Issued: No. 630, 7/5; No. 631, 7/18.

Skopje Earthquake, 50th Anniv. — A409

2013, July 26 **Litho.** ***Perf. 13½x13¼***
632 A409 100d multi 3.75 3.75

Bayram Festival A410

2013, July 30 **Litho.** ***Perf. 13½x13¼***
633 A410 40d multi 1.75 1.75

Vasil Chekalarov (1874-1913), Bulgarian Revolution Leader — A411

Perf. 13¼x13½

2013, Sept. 10 **Litho.**
634 A411 16d multi .70 .70

Gjurchin Kokaleski (1775-1863), Local Chieftain, Writer of First Macedonian Autobiography — A412

Perf. 13½x13¼

2013, Sept. 10 **Litho.**
635 A412 18d multi .80 .80

Ohrid-Debar Rebellion, Cent. — A413

Perf. 13¼x13½

2013, Sept. 19 **Litho.**
636 A413 60d multi 2.75 2.75

2013 Men's European Basketball Championships, Slovenia — A414

2013, Sept. 20 **Litho.** ***Perf. 13¼***
637 A414 90d multi 3.50 3.50

Values are for stamps with surrounding selvage.

Diplomatic Relations Between Macedonia and People's Republic of China, 20th Anniv. A415

2013, Oct. 15 **Litho.** ***Perf. 13½x13¼***
638 A415 100d multi 4.50 4.50

Mushrooms A416

No. 639: a, Boletus satanas, butterfly, ladybug. b, Myriostoma coliforme, butterfly, lizard. c, Caloscypha fulgens, insect. d, Terana caerulea, insect.

2013, Oct. 16 **Litho.** ***Perf. 13¼x13½***
639 Horiz. strip of 4 8.25 8.25
a. A416 10d multi .45 .45
b. A416 20d multi .90 .90
c. A416 50d multi 2.25 2.25
d. A416 100d multi 4.50 4.50

Petre Bogdanov-Kocko (1913-88), Composer — A417

Perf. 13½x13¼

2013, Nov. 13 **Litho.**
640 A417 20d multi .90 .90

Richard Wagner (1883-83), Composer A418

Perf. 13½x13¼

2013, Nov. 13 **Litho.**
641 A418 40d multi 1.90 1.90

Christmas A419

Perf. 13½x13¼

2013, Dec. 11 **Litho.**
642 A419 40d multi 1.90 1.90

Vegetables — A420

2013, Dec. 28 **Litho.** ***Perf. 12¾x13***
643 A420 8d Tomatoes .35 .35
644 A420 10d Eggplants .45 .45

Calculator A421

Shopping Cart A422

2014, Jan. 14 **Litho.** ***Perf. 12¾x13***
645 A421 8d multi .35 .35
646 A422 8d multi .35 .35

Decorative Jewelry A423

Various pieces from 19th-20th cent. from Bitola: 24d, 40d, vert.

Perf. 13½x13¼, 13¼x13½

2014, May 22 **Litho.**
647-648 A423 Set of 2 3.00 3.00

2014 Winter Olympics, Sochi, Russia — A424

Designs: 50d, Ice hockey. 100d, Ski jumping.

2014, May 23 **Litho.** ***Perf. 13¼***
649-650 A424 Set of 2 6.75 6.75

Values are for stamps with surrounding selvage.

Michelangelo (1475-1564), Sculptor and Painter — A425

2014, May 27 **Litho.** ***Perf. 13½x13¼***
651 A425 144d multi 6.50 6.50

Goldfish A426

Designs: 21d, Goldfish in water. 60d, Goldfish and air bubbles.

2014, May 28 **Litho.** ***Perf. 13½x13¼***
652-653 A426 Set of 2 3.75 3.75

Truck A427

2014, May 29 **Litho.** ***Perf. 13½x13¼***
654 A427 50d multi 2.25 2.25

No. 654 was printed in sheets of 8 + central label.

Galileo Galilei (1564-1642), Astronomer — A428

2014, May 30 **Litho.** ***Perf. 13½x13¼***
655 A428 20d multi .90 .90

No. 655 was printed in sheets of 8 + central label.

George Stepehenson (1781-1848), Railway Builder, and Rocket Locomotive — A429

2014, May 30 Litho. *Perf. 13½x13¼*
656 A429 40d multi 1.75 1.75

No. 656 was printed in sheets of 8 + central label.

European Capitals A430

Designs: 40d, Acropolis, Athens, Greece. 60d, Colosseum, Rome, Italy.

2014, June 3 Litho. *Perf. 13½x13¼*
657-658 A430 Set of 2 4.50 4.50

Nos. 657-658 were each printed in sheets of 8 + central label.

Europa A431

Designs: 40d, Zurna. No. 660, 50d, Three-holed ocarina (light green background).
No. 661, 50d: a, Tambura (gray green background). b, Two tamburas (pale pink background). c, Kemene and bow (pale orange background). d, Gajda (pale blue background).
60d, Drum.

2014, June 4 Litho. *Perf. 13½x13¼*
659-660 A431 Set of 2 4.00 4.00

Miniature Sheet

661 Sheet of 4 9.00 9.00
a.-d. A431 50d Any single 2.25 2.25

Souvenir Sheet

662 A431 60d multi 2.75 2.75

No. 661 was sold with but unattached to a booklet cover.

Peoni Spelunking Club, 50th Anniv. — A432

2014, June 4 Litho. *Perf. 13¼x13½*
663 A432 80d multi 3.75 3.75

2014 World Cup Soccer Championships, Brazil — A433

Designs: 50d, Soccer ball and emblem. 100d, Soccer ball, emblem and Christ the Redeemer statue.

Perf. 13¼x13½
2014, June 12 Litho.
664-665 A433 Set of 2 14.50 14.50

Nos. 664-665 were each printed in sheets of 8 + central label.

Vegetables — A434

2014 Litho. *Perf. 12¾*
666 A434 6d Cabbage .30 .30
667 A434 16d Beans .70 .70
668 A434 18d Cauliflower .80 .80
Nos. 666-668 (3) 1.80 1.80

Issued: 6d, 7/2; 16d, 6/13; 18d, 6/20.
See Nos. 715-717.

Bayram Festival A435

Perf. 13½x13¼
2014, June 15 Litho.
669 A435 40d multi 1.75 1.75

Battle of Belasitsa (Kleidion), 1000th Anniv. A436

Perf. 13½x13¼
2014, June 29 Litho.
670 A436 50d multi 2.25 2.25

Charlie Chaplin (1889-1977), Actor — A437

2015, Apr. 21 Litho. *Perf. 13½x13¼*
671 A437 50d multi 1.90 1.90

Dated 2014.

Vladimir Komarov (1927-67), Cosmonaut A438

2015, Apr. 21 Litho. *Perf. 13½x13¼*
672 A438 50d multi 1.90 1.90

Dated 2014.

Famous Men — A439

Designs: 16d, Tashko Karadza (1914-42), resistance leader. 18d, Ivan Tocko (1914-73), writer. 20d, Nexhat Agolli (1914-49), politician. 24d, Sterjo Spasse (1914-89), writer.

2015, Apr. 21 Litho. *Perf. 13¼x13½*
673-676 A439 Set of 4 3.00 3.00

Dated 2014.

Pigeons A440

No. 677: a. Columba palumbus. b, Columba oenas. c, Columba livia. d, Columba livia forma domestica.

2015, Apr. 21 Litho. *Perf. 13½x13¼*
677 Vert. strip of 4 6.75 6.75
a. A440 11d multi .40 .40
b. A440 20d multi .75 .75
c. A440 50d multi 1.90 1.90
d. A440 100d multi 3.75 3.75

Dated 2014.

Christmas — A441

2015, Apr. 21 Litho. *Perf. 13¼x13½*
678 A441 40d multi 1.50 1.50

Dated 2014.

2015 Men's World Handball Championships, Qatar — A442

2015, Apr. 22 Litho. *Perf. 13¼x13½*
679 A442 100d multi 3.75 3.75

Serinus Canaria Domestica A443

Designs: 31d, One bird. 50d, Two birds.

2015, Apr. 23 Litho. *Perf. 13¼x13½*
680-681 A443 Set of 2 3.00 3.00

No. 680 has incorrect Latin name for bird depicted (Carduelis carduelis).

20th Century Ceramic Pitcher — A444

2015, Apr. 24 Litho. *Perf. 13¼x13½*
682 A444 50d multi 1.90 1.90

Battle of Gallipoli, Cent. A445

2015, Apr. 27 Litho. *Perf. 13½x13¼*
683 A445 70d multi 2.60 2.60

Benjamin Franklin (1706-90) A446

2015, Apr. 29 Litho. *Perf. 13½x13¼*
684 A446 60d multi 2.25 2.25

Cat and Bicycle A447

2015, Apr. 29 Litho. *Perf. 13½x13¼*
685 A447 100d multi 3.75 3.75

European Capitals A448

Designs: 40d, Riga, Latvia. 60d, Luxembourg, Luxembourg.

2015, Apr. 29 Litho. *Perf. 13½x13¼*
686-687 A448 Set of 2 3.75 3.75

Nos. 686-687 were each printed in sheets of 8 + central label.

Europa A449

Old toys: 50d, Yo-yo. 100d, Rocking horse. 150d, Spinning top.

2015, May 6 Litho. *Perf. 13½x13¼*
688-689 A449 Set of 2 5.50 5.50

Souvenir Sheet

690 A449 150d multi 5.50 5.50

Souvenir Sheet

2015 Eurovision Song Contest — A450

2015, May 7 Litho. *Perf. 13½x13¼*
691 A450 100d multi 3.75 3.75

Invention of the Saxophone, 175th Anniv. — A451

2015, May 8 Litho. *Perf. 13¼x13½*
692 A451 44d multi 1.60 1.60

No. 692 was printed in sheets of 8 + central label.

Pyotr I. Tchaikovsky (1840-93), Composer — A452

2015, May 8 Litho. *Perf. 13½x13¼*
693 A452 100d multi 3.75 3.75

No. 693 was printed in sheets of 8 + central label.

Carrots — A453

2015, July 2 Litho. *Perf. 12¾*
694 A453 2d multi .25 .25

Bayram Festival — A454

2015, July 15 Litho. *Perf. 13¼x13½*
695 A454 40d multi 1.50 1.50

2015 European Basketball Championships A455

2015, Sept. 4 Litho. *Perf. 13¼x13½*
696 A455 50d multi 1.90 1.90

No. 696 was printed in sheets of 8 + central label.

Mirce Acev (1915-43), Resistance Leader — A456

Ibrahim Temo (1865-1939), Politician — A457

Jane Sandanski (1872-1915), Revolution Leader — A458

Ali Pasha of Tepelena (1740-1822), Ruler of Albania — A459

Arthur Miller (1915-2005), Playwright — A460

Perf. 13¼x13½
2015, Sept. 17 Litho.
697 A456 16d multi .60 .60
698 A457 16d multi .60 .60
699 A458 18d multi .65 .65

Perf. 13½x13¼
700 A459 18d multi .65 .65
701 A460 20d multi .75 .75
Nos. 697-701 (5) 3.25 3.25

Flowers — A461

No. 702: a, 11d, Thymus serpyllum. b, 20d, Calendula officinalis. c, 50d, Hypericum perforatum. d, 100d, Urtica dioica.

2015, Oct. 14 Litho. *Perf. 13¼x13½*
702 A461 Block of 4, #a-d 6.50 6.50

Christmas A462

2015, Dec. 8 Litho. *Perf. 13½x13¼*
703 A462 40d multi 1.50 1.50

Souvenir Sheet

Mountain Tourism — A463

Perf. 13½x13¼
2016, Mar. 23 Litho.
704 A463 144d multi + label 5.50 5.50

See Kosovo No. 300.

St. Clement of Ohrid (c. 840-916) — A464

2016, Apr. 25 Litho. *Perf. 13¼x13½*
705 A464 18d multi .70 .70

Hamster A465

2016, Apr. 26 Litho. *Perf. 13½x13¼*
706 A465 81d multi 3.00 3.00

Donatello (c. 1386-1466), Sculptor — A466

2016, Apr. 27 Litho. *Perf. 13¼x13½*
707 A466 40d multi 1.50 1.50

European Capitals A467

Designs: 40d, Houses, Amsterdam, Netherlands. 60d, Bratislava Castle, Bratislava, Slovakia.

2016, Apr. 29 Litho. *Perf. 13½x13¼*
708-709 A467 Set of 2 3.75 3.75

A468

A469

A470

Europa — A471

No. 712: a, Fishing boat on lake, bird in flight. b, Foliage near shore. c, Dock. d, Pelican.

2016, May 10 Litho. *Perf. 13½x13¼*
710 A468 50d multi 1.90 1.90
711 A469 100d multi 3.75 3.75

Miniature Sheet
712 A470 50d Sheet of 4, #a-d 7.25 7.25

Souvenir Sheet
Perf. 13¼x13½
713 A471 144d multi 5.25 5.25

Train A472

2016, Apr. 28 Litho. *Perf. 13½x13¼*
714 A472 44d multi 1.60 1.60

Vegetables Type of 2014

2016, May 13 Litho. *Perf. 12¾*
715 A434 3d Garlic .25 .25
716 A434 6d Beets .25 .25
717 A434 13d Peppers .50 .50
Nos. 715-717 (3) 1.00 1.00

Bayram Festival — A473

2016, June 9 Litho. *Perf. 13¼x13½*
718 A473 44d multi 1.60 1.60

2016 European Soccer Championships, France — A474

Perf. 13½x13¼
2016, June 10 Litho.
719 A474 101d multi 3.75 3.75

René Laennec (1781-1826), Inventor of Stethoscope — A475

2016, July 12 Litho. *Perf. 13½x13¼*
720 A475 40d multi 1.50 1.50

Claude Elwood Shannon (1916-2001), Mathematician and Electrical Engineer — A476

2016, July 12 Litho. *Perf. 13½x13¼*
721 A476 50d multi 1.90 1.90

2016 Summer Olympics, Rio de Janeiro A477

Designs: 40d, Wrestling. 60d, Judo. 50d, Macedonian Olympic emblem, vert.

2016, Aug. 5 Litho. *Perf. 13½x13¼*
722-723 A477 Set of 2 3.75 3.75

Souvenir Sheet
Perf. 13¼x13½
724 A477 50d multi 1.90 1.90

First Albanian Language School in Macedonia, 75th Anniv. A478

2016, Sept. 7 Litho. *Perf. 13½x13¼*
725 A478 50d multi 1.90 1.90

Independence, 25th Anniv. — A479

2016, Sept. 8 Litho. *Perf. 13¼x13½*
726 A479 18d multi .65 .65

Lorenc Antoni (1909-91), Composer A480

Perf. 13¼x13½
2016, Sept. 12 Litho.
727 A480 20d multi .75 .75

Antonio Vivaldi (1678-1741), Composer — A481

Perf. 13½x13¼
2016, Sept. 12 Litho.
728 A481 40d multi 1.50 1.50

Orce Nikolov (1916-42), Syndicalist Movement Leader — A483

Perf. 13¼x13½
2016, Sept. 20 Litho.
730 A483 18d multi .65 .65

Tajar Zavalani (1903-66), Historian — A484

Perf. 13¼x13½
2016, Sept. 20 Litho.
731 A484 18d multi .65 .65

Churches — A487

No. 734: a, 44d, Trinity Cathedral, St. Petersburg, Russia. b, 100d, Church of St. John the Theologian, Ohrid, Macedonia.

Perf. 13½x13¼
2016, Dec. 23 Litho.
734 A487 Horiz. pair, #a-b 5.00 5.00

See Russia No. 7796.

POSTAL TAX STAMPS

Men Blowing Horns — PT1

1991, Dec. 30 Litho. *Perf. 13½*
RA1 PT1 2.50d multicolored *.90 .90*

No. RA1 was required on mail Dec. 31, 1991-Sept. 8, 1992. For surcharge see No. 22.

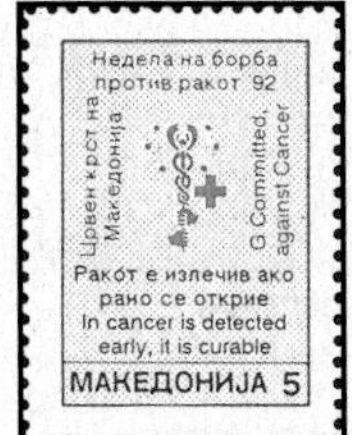

Anti-Cancer Week — PT2

Designs: Nos. RA2, RA6, Emblems, inscriptions. Nos. RA3, RA7, Magnetic resonance imaging scanner. Nos. RA4, RA8, Overhead scanner, examination table. No. RA5, RA9c, Mammography imager. No. RA9, Ultra sound computer.

1992, Mar. 1	**Litho.**	***Perf. 10***	
RA2	PT2 5d multicolored	*.65*	*.65*
RA3	PT2 5d multicolored	*.65*	*.65*
RA4	PT2 5d multicolored	*.65*	*.65*
RA5	PT2 5d multicolored	*.65*	*.65*
a.	Block of 4, #RA2-RA5	*3.75*	*3.75*
RA6	PT2 5d multicolored	*.25*	*.25*
RA7	PT2 5d multicolored	*.25*	*.25*
RA8	PT2 5d multicolored	*.25*	*.25*
RA9	PT2 5d multicolored	*.25*	*.25*
a.	Block of 4, #RA6-RA9	*1.25*	*1.25*
b.	Souv. sheet of 3, #RA7-RA9, RA9c	*22.50*	*22.50*
c.	PT2 5d multicolored	*.40*	*.40*
	Nos. RA2-RA9 (8)	*3.60*	*3.60*

Inscription at right reads up on No. RA2 and down on No. RA6. Designs on Nos. RA7-RA8, RA9c are without red cross symbol.

Souvenir folders with perf. and imperf. sheets of RA9b sold for 40d. Value for both sheets in folder, $50.

Obligatory on mail Mar. 1-8.

See Nos. RA28-RA31.

Red Cross Week — PT3

Designs: RA10, Slogans. No. RA11, Airplanes dropping supplies. No. RA12, Aiding traffic accident victim. No. RA13, Evacuating casualties from building.

1992, May 8		***Perf. 10***	
RA10	10d multicolored	*.25*	*.25*
RA11	10d multicolored	*.25*	*.25*
RA12	10d multicolored	*.25*	*.25*
RA13	10d multicolored	*.25*	*.25*
a.	PT3 Block of 4, #RA10-RA13	*.65*	*.65*

Nos. RA10-RA13 exist with silver-colored borders in perf. and imperf. miniature sheets that sold for 80d. Value for both sheets $7.50.

Obligatory on mail May 8-15.

PT4

Solidarity Week: No. RA14, Skopje earthquake. No. RA15, Woman holding girl. No. RA16, Mother carrying infant. No. RA17, Mother, children, airplane.

130d, Woman, child, airport control tower.

1992, June 1		***Perf. 10***	
RA14	PT4 20d multicolored	*.25*	*.25*
RA15	PT4 20d multicolored	*.25*	*.25*
RA16	PT4 20d multicolored	*.25*	*.25*
RA17	PT4 20d multicolored	*.25*	*.25*
a.	Block of 4	*.65*	*.65*

Size: 74x97mm

Imperf

RA18 PT4 130d multicolored *3.00 3.00*

No. RA18 also exists with perf. vignette. Same value.

Obligatory on mail June 1-7.

See No. RA55.

PT5

Anti-Tuberculosis Week: No. RA20, Nurse, infant. No. RA21, Nurse giving oxygen to patient. No. RA22, Infant in bed.

200d, Child being treated by nurse.

1992, Sept. 14		***Perf. 10***	
RA19	PT5 20d multicolored	*.25*	*.25*
RA20	PT5 20d multicolored	*.25*	*.25*
RA21	PT5 20d multicolored	*.25*	*.25*
RA22	PT5 20d multicolored	*.25*	*.25*
a.	Block of 4, #RA19-RA22	*.65*	*.65*

Size: 74x97mm

Imperf

RA23 PT5 200d vermilion & multi *2.50 2.50*

No. RA23 exists with magenta inscriptions, and also with perf. vignette and either magenta or vermilion inscriptions. Obligatory on mail Sept. 14-21.

Red Cross Fund PT6

1993, Feb. 1	**Litho.**	***Perf. 10***	
RA24	PT6 20d Shown	*.30*	*.30*
RA25	PT6 20d Marguerites	*.30*	*.30*
RA26	PT6 20d Carnations	*.30*	*.30*
RA27	PT6 20d Mixed bouquet	*.30*	*.30*
a.	Block of 4, #RA24-RA27	*1.25*	*1.25*

Nos. RA24-RA27 exist in perf. or imperf. miniature sheets with either gold or silver backgrounds and inscriptions, that sold for 500d each. Value for both sheets $12.

Obligatory on mail Feb. 1-28.

Cancer Therapy Type of 1992

Designs: No. RA28, Nuclear medicine caduceus, inscriptions. No. RA29, Radiographic equipment. No. RA30, Radiology machine. No. RA31, Scanner.

1993, Mar. 1	**Litho.**	***Perf. 10***	
RA28	PT2 20d multicolored	*.30*	*.30*
RA29	PT2 20d multicolored	*.30*	*.30*
RA30	PT2 20d multicolored	*.30*	*.30*
RA31	PT2 20d multicolored	*.30*	*.30*
a.	Block of 4, #RA28-RA31	*1.25*	*1.25*

Nos. RA28-RA31 exist in perf. & imperf. miniature sheets with gold background or inscription, that sold for 500d each. Value for both sheets $6.50.

Obligatory on mail Mar. 1-8.

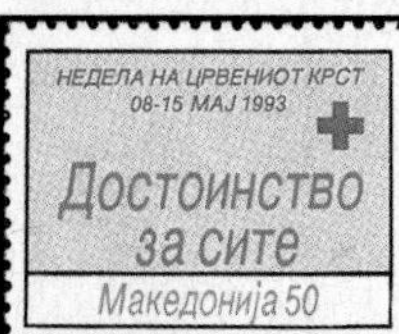

Red Cross Week PT7

No. RA32, Inscriptions. No. RA33, Man holding baby. No. RA34, Patient in wheelchair. No. RA35, Carrying stretcher.

1993, May 8 Litho. *Perf. 10*

RA32 PT7 50d multicolored .25 .25
RA33 PT7 50d multicolored .25 .25
RA34 PT7 50d multicolored .25 .25
RA35 PT7 50d multicolored .25 .25
a. Block of 4, #RA32-RA35 1.20 1.20

Perf. & imperf. miniature sheets of Nos. RA32-RA35 exist with yellow inscription tablets that sold for 700d each. Value for both sheets $7.

Obligatory on mail May 8-15.

1993, June 1 *Perf. 10*

No. RA36, Skopje earthquake. No. RA37, Unloading boxes. No. RA38, Labeling boxes. No. RA39, Boxes, fork lift.

RA36 PT7 50de multi .25 .25
RA37 PT7 50de multi .25 .25
RA38 PT7 50de multi .25 .25
RA39 PT7 50de multi .25 .25
a. Block of 4, #RA36-RA39 1.20 1.20

Perf. & imperf. miniature sheets of Nos. RA36-RA39 exist with gold inscription tablets that sold for 7d each. Value for both sheets $5.

Obligatory on mail June 1-7.

1993, Sept. 14 *Perf. 10*

Designs: Nos. RA40, Inscriptions. Nos. RA41, Children in meadow. Nos. RA42, Bee on flower. No. RA43, Goat behind rock.

RA40 PT7 50de black, gray & red .25 .25
RA41 PT7 50de green & multi .25 .25
RA42 PT7 50de green & multi .25 .25
RA43 PT7 50de green & multi .25 .25
a. Block of 4, #RA40-RA43 .65 .65

Nos. RA41-RA43 exist in perf. & imperf. miniature sheets that sold for 15d each. Values for both sheets $3.25. Nos. RA40-RA43 exist with yellow omitted, resulting in blue stamps. Value of the blue set $4.25.

Obligatory on mail Sept. 14-21.

See Nos. RA52-RA54.

Anti-Cancer Week — PT8

No. RA44, Inscription, emblem. No. RA45, Lily. No. RA46, Mushroom. No. RA47, Swans.

1994, Mar. 1 *Perf. 10*

RA44 PT8 1d multi .25 .25
RA45 PT8 1d multi .25 .25
RA46 PT8 1d multi .25 .25
RA47 PT8 1d multi .25 .25
a. Block of 4, #RA44-RA47 .90 .90

Nos. RA44-RA47 without silver color exist in perf. & imperf. miniature sheets and sold for 20d. Value for both sheets $7.

Obligatory on mail Mar. 1-8.

Red Cross Type of 1993 and

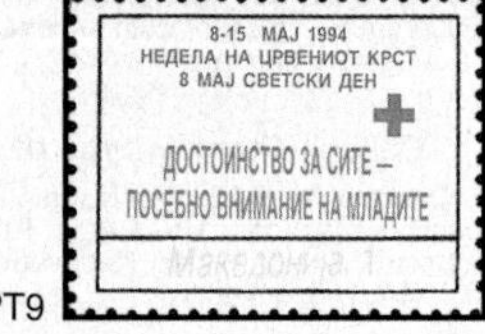

PT9

1994, May 8 Litho. *Perf. 10*

RA51 PT9 1d shown .25 .25
RA52 PT7 1d like #RA41 .25 .25
RA53 PT7 1d like #RA39 .25 .25
RA54 PT7 1d like #RA33 .25 .25
a. Block of 4, #RA51-RA54 .65 .65

Nos. RA51-RA54 exist without denomination in perf. & imperf. miniature sheets and sold for 30d each. Value for both sheets $9.

Obligatory on mail May 8-15, 1994.

Skopje Earthquake Type of 1993

1994, June 1

RA55 PT4 1d like #RA14 .65 .65

Obligatory on mail June 1-7, 1994.

Red Cross Fund PT10

1994, Dec. 1 Litho. *Perf. 10*

RA56 PT10 2d shown .25 .25
RA57 PT10 2d Globe .25 .25
RA58 PT10 2d AIDS awareness .25 .25
RA59 PT10 2d Condoms .25 .25
a. Block of 4, Nos. RA56-RA59 1.15 1.15

Size: 80x95mm

Imperf

RA60 PT10 40d like RA57 3.00 3.00

Country name and value omitted from vignette on No. RA60, which also exists with perf. vignette. Obligatory on mail Dec. 1-8.

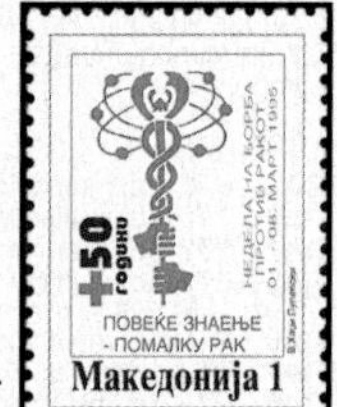

Anti-Cancer Week — PT11

1995, Mar. 1

RA61 PT11 1d shown .25 .25
RA62 PT11 1d White lilies .25 .25
RA63 PT11 1d Red lilies .25 .25
RA64 PT11 1d Red roses .25 .25
a. Block of 4, Nos. RA61-RA64 1.15 1.15

Size: 97x74mm

Imperf

RA65 PT11 30d like #RA61, RA64 2.25 2.25

Blue inscriptions, country name, and value omitted from vignette on No. RA65, which also exists with perf. vignette. Obligatory on mail Mar. 1-8.

Red Cross Fund — PT12

Designs: No. RA66, Red Cross emblem. No. RA67, Red Cross volunteers holding clipboards. No. RA68, Young volunteers wearing white shirts. No. RA69, RA70, Red Cross, Red Crescent symbols, globe.

1995, May 8

RA66 PT12 1d multicolored .25 .25
RA67 PT12 1d multicolored .25 .25
RA68 PT12 1d multicolored .25 .25
RA69 PT12 1d blue & multi .25 .25
a. Strip of 4, Nos. RA70-RA73 1.15 1.15

Size: 68x85mm

Imperf

RA70 PT12 30d multicolored 2.25 2.25

No. RA70 also exists with perf. vignette. Obligatory on mail May 8-15.

Solidarity Week PT13

1995, June 1

RA71 PT13 1d shown .45 .45

Size: 85x70

Imperf

RA72 PT13 30d like No. RA75 2.00 2.00

No. RA72 also exists with perf. vignette. Obligatory on mail June 1-7.

Robert Koch (1843-1910), Bacteriologist — PT14

1995, Sept. 14 Litho. *Perf. 10*

RA73 PT14 1d shown .60 .60

Size: 90x73mm

Imperf

RA74 PT14 30d like No. RA73 2.00 2.00

No. RA74 exists with perf. vignette. Obligatory on mail Sept. 14-21.

Children's Week — PT15

1995, Oct. 2 Litho. *Die Cut*

Self-Adhesive

RA75 PT15 2d blue violet & red .45 .45

Obligatory on mail 10/2-8.

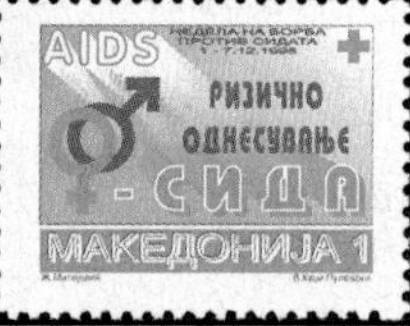

PT16

1995, Nov. 1 Litho. *Perf. 10*

RA76 PT16 1d multicolored .40 .40

Size: 90x72mm

Imperf

RA77 PT16 30d like #RA76 2.00 2.00

Red Cross, AIDS awareness. No. RA77 also exists with perf. vignette. Obligatory on mail Nov. 1-7.

Red Cross PT17

1996, Mar. 1 Litho. *Perf. 10*

RA78 PT17 1d multicolored .60 .60

Size: 98x76mm

Imperf

RA79 PT17 30d like #RA78 2.25 2.25

No. RA79 also exists with perf. vignette. Obligatory on mail Mar. 1-8.

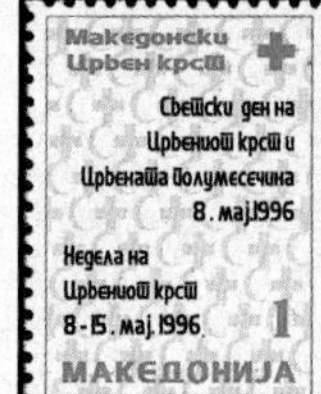

PT18

Red Cross Week — PT19

Fundamental principles of Red Cross, Red Crescent Societies, inscriptions in: No. RA81, Macedonian. No. RA82, English. No. RA83, French. RA84, Spanish.

1996, May 8 Litho. *Perf. 10*

RA80 PT18 1d multicolored .25 .25
RA81 PT19 1d multicolored .25 .25
RA82 PT19 1d multicolored .25 .25
RA83 PT19 1d multicolored .25 .25
RA84 PT19 1d multicolored .25 .25
a. Strip of 5, #RA80-RA84 1.30 1.30

Obligatory on mail May 8-15.

Red Cross, Solidarity Week — PT20

1996, June 1 Litho. *Perf. 10*

RA86 PT20 1d multicolored .50 .50

No. RA86 exists without country name or denomination in perf. & imperf. miniature sheets and sold for 30d each. Value for both sheets $5.50. Obligatory on mail June 1-7, 1996.

Red Cross, Fight Tuberculosis Week — PT21

1996, Sept. 14 Litho. *Perf. 10*

RA87 PT21 1d multicolored .55 .55

Size: 80x90mm

Imperf

RA88 PT21 30d like #RA87 2.00 2.00

No. RA88 also exists with perf. vignette. Obligatory on mail Sept. 14-21.

Red Cross, AIDS Awareness PT22

1996, Dec. 6

RA89 PT22 1d multicolored .55 .55

Size: 90x73mm

Imperf

RA90 PT22 30d like #RA89 2.00 2.00

No. RA90 also exists with perf. vignette. Obligatory on mail Dec. 1-7.

Red Cross, Cancer Week — PT23

1997, Apr. 1

RA91 PT23 1d Cross in pale org .50 .50
a. Cross in red .70 .70

No. RA91 obligatory on mail Apr. 1-8. No. RA91a issued 5/8.

Red Cross — PT24

1997, May 8

RA92 PT24 1d multicolored *1.75 1.75*

Obligatory on mail May 8-15.

Children's Day — PT25

1997, June 1

RA93 PT25 1d Cross in deep vermilion .50 .50
a. Cross in red .70 .70

Obligatory on mail June 1-8.

Red Cross, Anti-Tuberculosis PT26

1997, Sept. 14

RA94 PT26 1d multicolored .50 .50

Obligatory on mail, Sept. 14-21.

Red Cross — PT27

1997, Dec. 1 Litho. *Perf. 10*

RA95 PT27 1d multicolored .50 .50

Obligatory on mail Dec. 1-7.

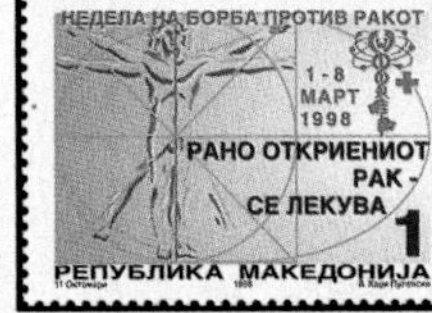

Red Cross Fight Against Cancer PT28

1998, Mar. 1 *Perf. 13½*

RA96 PT28 1d multicolored .50 .50

Obligatory on mail Mar. 1-8.

Red Cross, Humanity PT29

1998, May 8

RA97 PT29 2d multicolored .50 .50

Obligatory on mail May 8-15.

Red Cross — PT30

1998, June 1 Litho. *Perf. 13½*

RA98 PT30 2d multicolored .50 .50

Obligatory on mail June 1-7, 1998.

Fight Tuberculosis PT31

1998, Sept. 14 Litho. *Perf. 13½*

RA99 PT31 2d multicolored .50 .50

Obligatory on mail Sept. 14-21, 1998.

AIDS Awareness PT32

1998, Dec. 1

RA100 PT32 2d multicolored .50 .50

Obligatory on mail Dec. 1-7, 1998.

Red Cross Fight Against Cancer — PT33

1999, Mar. 1 Litho. *Perf. 13¼*

RA101 PT33 2d multi .50 .50

Obligatory on mail Mar. 1-7, 1999.

Red Cross PT34

1999, May 8

RA102 PT34 2d multi .50 .50

Obligatory on mail May 8-15, 1999.

Red Cross, Solidarity Week — PT35

1999, June 1

RA103 PT35 2d multi .50 .50

Obligatory on mail June 1-7, 1999.

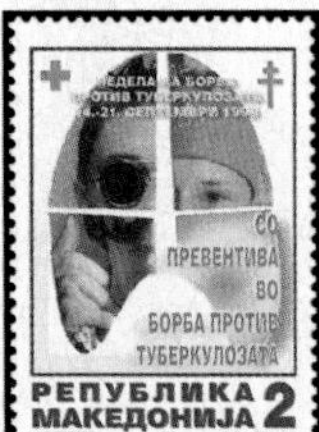

Fight Tuberculosis PT36

1999, Sept. 14 Litho. *Perf. 13¼*

RA104 PT36 2d multi .50 .50

Obligatory on mail Sept. 14-21.

AIDS Awareness PT37

1999, Dec. 1

RA105 PT37 2.50d multi .55 .55

Obligatory on mail Dec. 1-7.

Anti-Cancer Week — PT38

2000, Mar. 1 Litho. *Perf. 13¼*

RA106 PT38 2.50d multi .50 .50

Obligatory on mail Mar. 1-8.

Red Cross PT39

2000, May 8

RA107 PT39 2.50d multi .50 .50

Obligatory on mail May 8-15.

Red Cross — PT40

2000, June 1

RA108 PT40 2.50d multi .30 .30

Obligatory on mail June 1-7.

Red Cross — PT41

2000 Sept. 14 Litho. *Perf. 13¼*

RA109 PT41 3d multi .50 .50

Obligatory on mail Sept. 14-21.

Fight Against AIDS — PT42

2000 Dec. 1

RA110 PT42 3d multi .55 .55

Obligatory on mail Dec. 1-7.

Fight Against Cancer — PT43

2001, Mar. 1 Litho. *Perf. 13¼*

RA111 PT43 3d multi .50 .50

Obligatory on mail Mar. 1-8.

Red Cross PT44

2001, May 8

RA112 PT44 3d multi .50 .50

Obligatory on mail May 8-15.

Red Cross Solidarity Week — PT45

2001, June 1
RA113 PT45 3d multi .50 .50
Obligatory on mail June 1-7.

Fight Against Tuberculosis PT46

2001, Sept. 14
RA114 PT46 3d multi .50 .50
Obligatory on mail Sept. 14-21.

Campaign Against AIDS — PT47

2001, Dec. 1 Litho. ***Perf. 13¼***
RA115 PT47 3d multi .55 .55
Obligatory on mail Dec. 1-7.

Campaign Against Cancer PT48

2002, Mar. 1
RA116 PT48 3d multi .50 .50
Obligatory on mail Mar. 1-8.

Red Cross Week PT49

2002, May 8 Litho. ***Perf. 13¼***
RA117 PT49 3d multi .50 .50
Obligatory on mail May 8-15.

Red Cross Solidarity Week PT50

2002, June 1
RA118 PT50 3d multi .50 .50
Obligatory on mail June 1-7.

Tuberculosis Prevention PT51

2002, Sept. 14
RA119 PT51 3d multi .50 .50
Obligatory on mail Sept. 14-21.

Campaign Against AIDS PT52

2002, Dec. 1
RA120 PT52 3d multi .50 .50

Campaign Against Cancer — PT53

2003, Mar. 1 Litho. ***Perf. 13¼***
RA121 PT53 4d multi .50 .50
Obligatory on mail Mar. 1-8.

Campaign Against AIDS — PT54

2003, May 8
RA122 PT54 4d multi .55 .55
Obligatory on mail May 8-15.

Red Cross Solidarity — PT55

2003, June 1 ***Perf. 13¼x13½***
RA123 PT55 4d multi .50 .50
Obligatory on mail June 1-7.

Tuberculosis Prevention PT56

Perf. 13½x13¼
2003, Sept. 14 Litho.
RA124 PT56 4d multi .50 .50
Obligatory on mail Sept. 14-21.

Campaign Against AIDS — PT57

2003, Dec. 1 Litho. ***Perf. 13¼x13½***
RA125 PT57 4d multi .50 .50
Obligatory on mail Dec. 1-7.

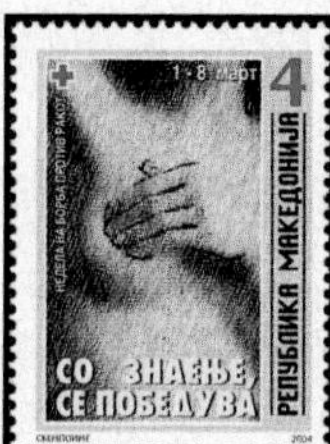
Campaign Against Cancer — PT58

2004, Mar. 1
RA126 PT58 4d multi .50 .50
Obligatory on mail Mar. 1-8.

Red Cross Week — PT59

2004, May 8
RA127 PT59 4d multi .50 .50
Obligatory on mail May 8-15.

Red Cross Solidarity Week — PT60

2004, June 1 Litho. ***Perf. 13¼x13½***
RA128 PT60 6d multi .50 .50
Obligatory on mail June 1-7.

Tuberculosis Week — PT61

2004, Sept. 14 ***Perf. 13½x13¼***
RA129 PT61 6d multi .50 .50
Obligatory on mail Sept. 14-21.

Campaign Against AIDS PT62

2004, Dec. 1 Litho. ***Perf. 13½x13¼***
RA130 PT62 6d multi .60 .60
Obligatory on mail Dec. 1-7.

Campaign Against Cancer — PT63

2005, Mar. 1 ***Perf. 13¼x13½***
RA131 PT63 6d multi .60 .60
Obligatory on mail Mar. 1-8.

Red Cross PT64

2005, May 8 Litho. ***Perf. 13½x13¼***
RA132 PT64 6d multi .60 .60
Obligatory on mail May 8-15.

Campaign Against Tuberculosis — PT65

Perf. 13½x13¼
2005, Sept. 14 Litho.
RA133 PT65 6d multi .60 .60
Obligatory on mail Sept. 14-21.

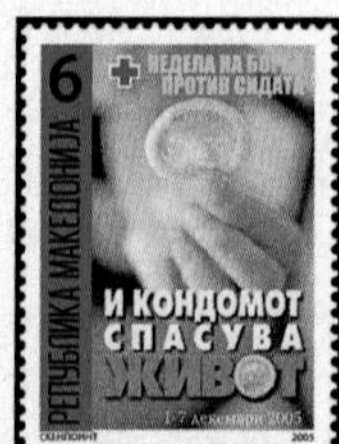
Campaign Against AIDS — PT66

2005, Dec. 1 ***Perf. 13¼x13½***
RA134 PT66 6d multi .60 .60
Obligatory on mail Dec. 1-7.

Campaign Against Breast Cancer — PT67

2006, Mar. 1 Litho. *Perf. 13¼x13½*
RA135 PT67 6d multi .60 .60
Obligatory on mail Mar. 1-7.

Red Cross Week — PT68

2006, May 18 Litho. *Perf. 13¼x13½*
RA136 PT68 6d multi .60 .60
Obligatory on mail May 8-15.

Campaign Against Tuberculosis — PT69

2006, Sept. 14 *Perf. 13½x13¼*
RA137 PT69 6d multi .60 .60
Obligatory on mail Sept. 14-21.

Campaign Against AIDS PT70

2006, Dec. 1
RA138 PT70 6d multi .60 .60
Obligatory on mail Dec. 1-7.

Campaign Against Cancer — PT71

2007, Mar. 1 Litho. *Perf. 13¼x13½*
RA139 PT71 6d multi .60 .60
Obligatory on mail Mar. 1-8.

Red Cross Week — PT72

2007, May 8
RA140 PT72 6d multi .60 .60
Obligatory on mail May 8-15.

Campaign Against Tuberculosis PT73

2007, Sept. 14
RA141 PT73 6d multi .60 .60
Obligatory on mail Sept. 14-21.

Campaign Against AIDS PT74

2007, Dec. 1 *Perf. 13½x13¼*
RA142 PT74 6d multi .60 .60
Obligatory on mail Dec. 1-8.

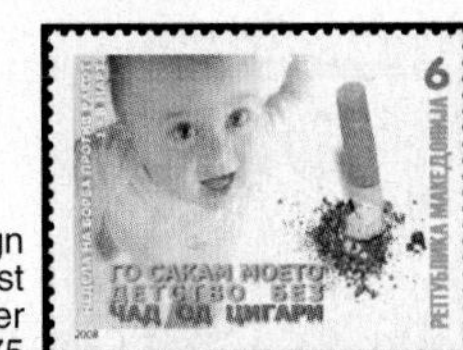

Campaign Against Cancer PT75

2008, Mar. 1 Litho. *Perf. 13½x13¼*
RA143 PT75 6d multi .50 .50
Obligatory on mail Mar. 1-8.

Red Cross Week PT76

2008, May 8
RA144 PT76 6d multi .50 .50
Obligatory on mail May 8-15.

Campaign Against Tuberculosis PT77

2008, Sept. 14 *Perf. 13¼x13½*
RA145 PT77 6d multi .50 .50
Obligatory on mail Sept. 14-21.

Campaign Against AIDS PT78

2008, Dec. 1 *Perf. 13½x13¼*
RA146 PT78 6d multi .60 .60
Obligatory on mail Dec. 1-8.

Campaign Against Cancer — PT79

2009, Mar. 1 *Perf. 13¼x13½*
RA147 PT79 6d multi .50 .50
Obligatory on mail Mar. 1-8.

Red Cross Week PT80

2009, May 8 *Perf. 13½x13¼*
RA148 PT80 6d multi .50 .50
Obligatory on mail May 8-15.

Campaign Against Tuberculosis — PT81

2009, Sept. 14
RA149 PT81 6d multi .60 .60
Obligatory on mail Sept. 14-21.

Campaign Against AIDS PT82

2009, Dec. 1
RA150 PT82 8d multi .60 .60
Obligatory on mail Dec. 1-7.

Campaign Against Cancer — PT83

2010, Mar. 1 *Perf. 13¼x13½*
Granite Paper
RA151 PT83 8d multi .60 .60
Obligatory on mail Mar. 1-7.

Red Cross Week — PT84

2010, May 8 Litho.
Granite Paper
RA152 PT84 8d multi .50 .50
Obligatory on mail May 8-15.

Campaign Against Tuberculosis — PT85

Perf. 13½x13¼
2010, Sept. 14 Litho.
Granite Paper
RA153 PT85 8d multi .50 .50
Obligatory on mail Sept. 14-21.

Campaign Against AIDS — PT86

2010, Dec. 1 *Perf. 13¼x13½*
Granite Paper
RA154 PT86 8d multi .50 .50
Obligatory on mail Dec. 1-7.

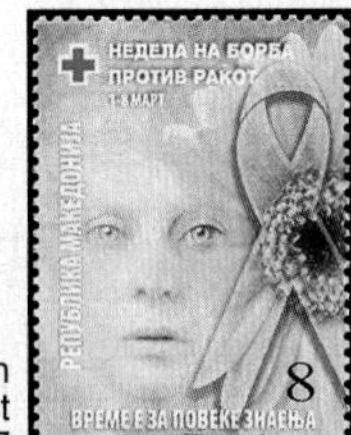

Campaign Against Cancer — PT87

2011, Mar. 1 Granite Paper
RA155 PT87 8d multi .50 .50
Obligatory on mail Mar. 1-8.

Red Cross Week — PT88

2011, May 8
RA156 PT88 8d multi .50 .50
Obligatory on mail May 8-15.

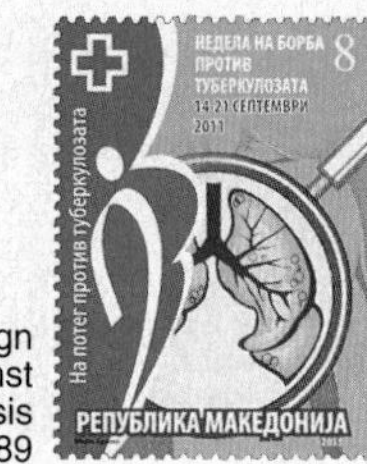

Campaign Against Tuberculosis PT89

2011, Sept. 14

RA157 PT89 8d multi .50 .50

Obligatory on mail Sept. 14-21.

Campaign Against AIDS — PT90

2011, Dec. 1

RA158 PT90 8d multi .50 .50

Obligatory on mail Dec. 1-7.

Campaign Against Cancer — PT91

2012, Mar. 1

RA159 PT91 8d multi .35 .35

Obligatory on mail Mar. 1-8.

Red Cross Week — PT92

2012, May 8

RA160 PT92 8d multi .35 .35

Obligatory on mail May 8-15.

Campaign Against Tuberculosis PT93

2012, Sept. 14

RA161 PT93 8d multi .35 .35

Obligatory on mail Sept. 14-21.

Campaign Against AIDS — PT94

2012, Dec. 1 Litho. ***Perf. 13¼x13½***

RA162 PT94 8d multi .35 .35

Obligatory on mail Dec. 1-7.

Campaign Against Cancer — PT95

2013, Mar. 1 Litho. ***Perf. 13¼x13½***

RA163 PT95 8d multi .35 .35

Obligatory on mail Mar. 1-8.

Red Cross Week — PT96

2013, May 8 Litho. ***Perf. 13¼x13½***

RA164 PT96 8d multi .35 .35

Intl. Red Cross, 150th anniv. Obligatory on mail May 8-15.

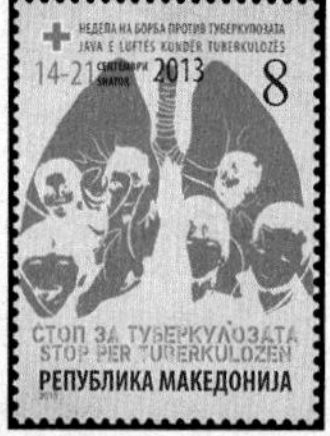

Campaign Against Tuberculosis PT97

Perf. 13¼x13½

2013, Sept. 14 Litho.

RA165 PT97 8d multi .35 .35

Obligatory on mail Sept. 14-21.

Campaign Against AIDS — PT98

2013, Dec. 1 Litho. ***Perf. 13¼x13½***

RA166 PT98 8d multi .35 .35

Obligatory on mail Dec. 1-7.

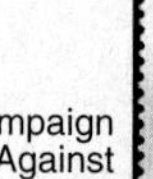

Campaign Against Cancer — PT99

2014, Mar. 1 Litho. ***Perf. 13¼x13½***

RA167 PT99 8d multi .35 .35

Obligatory on mail Mar. 1-8.

Red Cross Week — PT100

2014, May 8 Litho. ***Perf. 13¼x13½***

RA168 PT100 8d multi .35 .35

Obligatory on mail May 8-15.

Red Cross, 50th Anniv. — PT101

2015, May 8 Litho. ***Perf. 13¼x13½***

RA169 PT101 8d multi .30 .30

Obligatory on mail May 8-15.

Campaign Against Tuberculosis PT102

Perf. 13¼x13½

2015, Sept. 14 Litho.

RA170 PT102 9d multi .35 .35

Obligatory on mail Sept. 14-21.

Red Cross Week — PT103

2016, May 8 Litho. ***Perf. 13¼x13½***

RA171 PT103 8d multi .30 .30

Obligatory on mail May 8-15.

ISSUED UNDER GERMAN OCCUPATION

During World War II, Yugoslav Macedonia was annexed by Bulgaria. From April 1941 until Sept. 8, 1944, Bulgarian stamps were used in the region. On Sept. 8, 1944, Bulgaria signed an armistace with the Allies, and Macedonia was occupied by German forces. A puppet state was created, which collapsed upon the German withdrawal on Nov. 13.

Catalogue values for all unused stamps in this section are for Never Hinged examples. Hinged stamps are worth approximately 60% of the values shown.

Bulgaria Nos 364//413 Overprinted in Black or Red (R)

Ovpt. I Ovpt. II

Photo., Typo. (#N1, N2)

1944, Oct. 28 ***Perf. 13***

Overprinted I

N1	A177	1 l on 10st red org (#364)	6.50	*16.00*
N2	A178	3 l on 15st blue (#365) (R)	6.50	*16.00*

Overprinted II

N3	A201	6 l on 10st dk blue (#398) (R)	8.00	*26.00*
N4	A201	9 l on 15st Prus blue (#399) (R)	8.00	*26.00*
N5	A201	9 l on 15st dk ol brn (#400) (R)	12.00	*30.00*
N6	A209	15 l on 4 l ol gray (#411) (R)	40.00	*60.00*
N7	A210	20 l on 7 l dp blue (#412) (R)	60.00	*60.00*
N8	A211	30 l on 14 l fawn (#413)	65.00	*110.00*
		Nos. N1-N8 (8)	206.00	*344.00*

There are two types of both overprints, differing in the font of the "9" in the year date. Values for the more common types are given above.

MADAGASCAR

ˌmad-ə-ˈgas-kər

British Consular Mail

Postage stamps issued by the British Consulate in Madagascar were in use for a short period until the British relinquished all claims to this territory in favor of France in return for which France recognized Great Britain's claims in Zanzibar.

See Malagasy Republic for stamps inscribed "Madagascar."

12 Pence = 1 Shilling

British Consular Mail stamps of Madagascar were gummed only in one corner. Unused values are for stamps without gum. Examples having the original corner gum will command higher prices. Most used examples of these stamps have small faults and values are for stamps in this condition. Used stamps without faults are scarce and are worth more. Used stamps are valued with the commonly used crayon or pen cancellations.

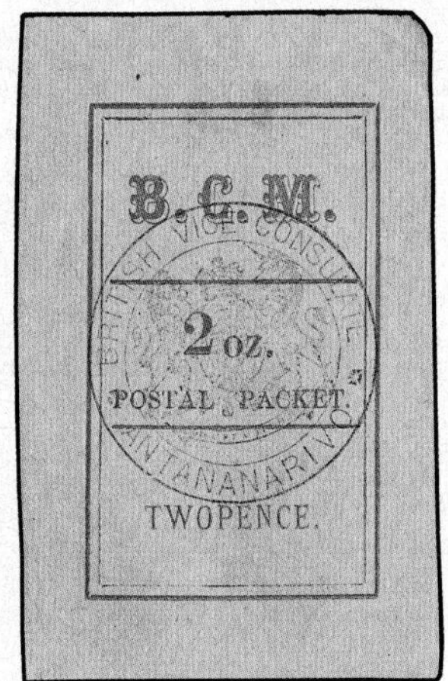

"B C M" and Arms — A1

Handstamped "British Vice-Consulate"

Black Seal Handstamped

1884 Unwmk. Typo. *Rouletted*

No.	Type	Description	Unused	Used
1	A1	1p violet	550.	450.
b.		Seal omitted	10,000.	10,000.
2	A1	2p violet	375.	325.
3	A1	3p violet	425.	350.
4	A1	4p violet 1 oz.	6,000.	5,250.
a.		"1 oz." corrected to "4 oz." in mss.	1,000.	725.
b.		Seal omitted	*9,000.*	9,000.
5	A1	6p violet	500.	*500.*
6	A1	1sh violet	525.	*475.*
7	A1	1sh6p violet	525.	*525.*
8	A1	2sh violet	850.	*900.*
9	A1	1p on 1sh vio		
10	A1	4½ on 1sh vio		
11	A1	6p red	1,325.	825.

1886 Violet Seal Handstamped

No.	Type	Description	Unused	Used
12	A1	4p violet	1,800.	—
13	A1	6p violet	2,750.	—

Handstamped "British Consular Mail" as on A3

Black Seal Handstamped

No.	Type	Description	Unused	Used
14	A1	4p violet	1,850.	—

Violet Seal Handstamped

No.	Type	Description	Unused	Used
15	A1	4p violet	7,500.	—

The 1, 2, 3 and 4 pence are inscribed "POSTAL PACKET," the other values of the series are inscribed "LETTER."

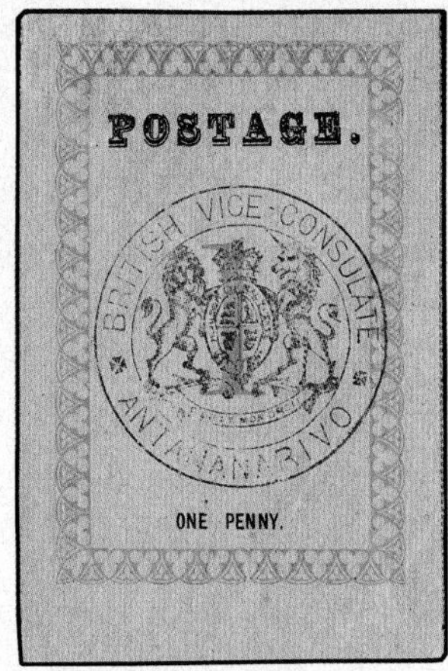

"British Vice-Consulate" — A2

Three types of A2 and A3:

I — "POSTAGE" 29½mm. Periods after "POSTAGE" and value.

II — "POSTAGE" 29½mm. No periods.

III — "POSTAGE" 24½mm. Period after value.

1886 Violet Seal Handstamped

No.	Type	Description	Unused	Used
16	A2	1p rose, I	400.	—
a.		Type II	1,350.	—
17	A2	1½p rose, I	1,500.	*875.*
a.		Type II	3,000.	—
18	A2	2p rose, I	400.	—
19	A2	3p rose, I	575.	*400.*
a.		Type II	1,350.	—
20	A2	4p rose, III	500.	—
21	A2	4½p rose, I	725.	*350.*
a.		Type II	2,250.	—
22	A2	6p rose, II	1,700.	—
23	A2	8p rose, I	2,750.	*1,900.*
a.		Type III	700.	—
24	A2	9p rose	1,350.	—
24A	A2	1sh rose, III	22,500.	
24B	A2	1sh6p rose, III	12,500.	—
25	A2	2sh rose, III	6,500.	—

Black Seal Handstamped

Type I

No.	Type	Description	Unused	Used
26	A2	1p rose	145.	*275.*
27	A2	1½p rose	3,000.	*1,300.*
28	A2	2p rose	200.	—
29	A2	3p rose	4,000.	*1,450.*
30	A2	4½p rose	3,850.	*575.*
31	A2	8p rose	5,000.	*3,150.*
32	A2	9p rose	4,750.	*2,900.*
32A	A2	2sh rose, III	—	—

"British Consular Mail" — A3

1886 Violet Seal Handstamped

No.	Type	Description	Unused	Used
33	A3	1p rose, II	175.	—
34	A3	1½p rose, II	275.	—
35	A3	2p rose, II	325.	—
36	A3	3p rose, II	210.	—
37	A3	4p rose, III	475.	—
38	A3	4½p rose, II	225.	—
39	A3	6p rose, II	500.	—
40	A3	8p rose, III	1,450.	—
a.		Type I	1,750.	—
41	A3	9p rose, I	475.	—
42	A3	1sh rose, III	1,750.	—
43	A3	1sh6p rose, III	1,750.	—
44	A3	2sh rose, III	1,750.	—

Black Seal Handstamped

No.	Type	Description	Unused	Used
45	A3	1p rose, I	135.	—
a.		Type II	135.	*210.*
46	A3	1½p rose, I	170.	*300.*
a.		Type II	145.	*200.*
47	A3	2p rose, I	190.	—
a.		Type II	150.	200.
48	A3	3p rose, I	170.	*260.*
a.		Type II	170.	*210.*
49	A3	4p rose, III	375.	—
50	A3	4½p rose, I	190.	*240.*
a.		Type II	160.	*200.*
51	A3	6p rose, II	170.	*260.*
52	A3	8p rose, I	200.	—
a.		Type III	2,250.	—
53	A3	9p rose, I	225.	*375.*
54	A3	1sh rose, III	625.	—
55	A3	1sh6p rose, III	775.	—
56	A3	2sh rose, III	775.	—

Seal Omitted

No.	Type	Description	Unused	Used
45b	A3	1p rose, II	5,000.	
46b	A3	1½p rose, II	5,250.	
48b	A3	3p rose, II	8,000.	
49a	A3	4p rose, III	6,250.	
50b	A3	4½p rose, II	8,750.	
51a	A3	6p rose, II	9,500.	
52b	A3	8p rose, III	6,250.	
53a	A3	9p rose, I	8,250.	
54a	A3	1sh rose, III	8,500.	
55a	A3	1sh6p rose, III	7,250.	
56a	A3	2sh rose, III	8,500.	

Some students of these issues doubt that the 1886 "seal omitted" varieties were regularly issued.

Red Seal Handstamped

No.	Type	Description	Unused	Used
57	A3	3p rose, I	*20,000.*	
58	A3	4½p rose, I	*12,750.*	

MADEIRA

mə-ˈdir-ə

LOCATION — A group of islands in the Atlantic Ocean northwest of Africa

GOVT. — Part of the Republic of Portugal

AREA — 314 sq. mi.

POP. — 150,574 (1900)

CAPITAL — Funchal

These islands are considered an integral part of Portugal and since 1898 postage stamps of Portugal have been in use. See Portugal for issues also inscribed Madeira, starting in 1980.

1000 Reis = 1 Milreis

100 Centavos = 1 Escudo (1925)

It is recommended that the rare overprinted 1868-81 stamps be purchased accompanied by certificates of authenticity from competent experts.

King Luiz — A1

Stamps of Portugal Overprinted

1868, Jan. 1 Unwmk. *Imperf.*

Black Overprint

No.	Type	Description	Unused	Used
2	A1	20r bister	210.00	120.00
a.		Inverted overprint	—	
b.		Rouletted		—
3	A1	50r green	210.00	120.00
4	A1	80r orange	225.00	125.00
a.		Double overprint	—	
5	A1	100r lilac	225.00	125.00
		Nos. 2-5 (4)	870.00	490.00

The 5r black does not exist as a genuinely imperforate original.

Reprints of 1885 are on stout white paper, ungummed. (Also, 5r, 10r and 25r values were overprinted.) Reprints of 1905 are on ordinary white paper with shiny gum and have a wide "D" and "R." Value, $12 each.

Lozenge Perf.

No.	Type	Description	Unused	Used
2c	A1	20r		—
3a	A1	50r		—
4b	A1	80r		—
5a	A1	100r		—

Overprinted in Red or Black

1868-70 *Perf. 12½*

No.	Type	Description	Unused	Used
6	A1	5r black (R)	50.00	37.50
8	A1	10r yellow	90.00	80.00
9	A1	20r bister	140.00	110.00
10	A1	25r rose	50.00	12.00
a.		Inverted overprint	—	
11	A1	50r green	200.00	140.00
a.		Inverted overprint	—	
12	A1	80r orange	180.00	140.00
13	A1	100r lilac	190.00	140.00
a.		Inverted overprint	—	
14	A1	120r blue	110.00	80.00
15	A1	240r violet ('70)	700.00	425.00
		Nos. 6-15 (9)	1,710.	1,165.

Two types of 5r differ in the position of the "5" at upper right.

The reprints are on stout white paper, ungummed, with rough perforation 13½, and on thin white paper with shiny white gum and clean-cut perforation 13½. The overprint has the wide "D" and "R" and the first reprints included the 5r with both black and red overprint. Value $10 each.

King Luiz — A2

Overprinted in Red or Black

1871-80 *Perf. 12½, 13½*

No.	Type	Description	Unused	Used
16	A2	5r black (R)	15.00	8.00
a.		Inverted overprint	—	
b.		Double overprint	55.00	55.00
c.		Perf. 14	90.00	55.00
18	A2	10r yellow	35.00	22.50
19	A2	10r bl grn ('79)	140.00	110.00
a.		Perf. 13½	160.00	140.00
20	A2	10r yel grn ('80)	65.00	52.50
21	A2	15r brn ('75)	19.00	11.50
22	A2	20r bister	30.00	22.50
23	A2	25r rose	13.50	4.50
a.		Inverted overprint	50.00	40.00
b.		Double overprint	50.00	40.00
24	A2	50r green ('72)	67.50	30.00
a.		Double overprint	—	
b.		Inverted overprint	200.00	200.00
25	A2	50r blue ('80)	125.00	55.00
26	A2	80r orange ('72)	77.50	67.50
27	A2	100r pale lil ('73)	90.00	60.00
a.		Perf. 14	200.00	85.00
b.		Perf. 13½	160.00	75.00
28	A2	120r blue	110.00	80.00
29	A2	150r blue ('76)	160.00	140.00
a.		Perf. 13½	175.00	150.00
30	A2	150r yel ('79)	350.00	240.00
31	A2	240r vio ('74)	750.00	500.00
32	A2	300r vio ('76)	75.00	67.50
		Nos. 16-32 (16)	2,123.	1,472.

There are two types of the overprint, the second one having a broad "D."

The reprints have the same characteristics as those of the 1868-70 issues.

A3

A4

King Luiz — A5

1880-81

No.	Type	Description	Unused	Used
33	A3	5r black	40.00	21.00
34	A4	25r pearl gray	50.00	21.00
a.		Inverted overprint	75.00	75.00
35	A5	25r lilac	50.00	11.00
a.		25r purple brown	32.50	11.00
b.		25r gray	35.00	10.00
		Nos. 33-35 (3)	140.00	53.00

Nos. 33, 34 and 35 have been reprinted on stout white paper, ungummed, and the last three on thin white paper with shiny white gum. The perforations are as previously described.

Common Design Types pictured following the introduction.

Vasco da Gama Issue

Common Design Types

1898, Apr. 1 Engr. *Perf. 14-15*

No.	Type	Description	Unused	Used
37	CD20	2½r blue grn	2.40	1.25
38	CD21	5r red	2.40	1.25
39	CD22	10r red violet	3.00	1.50
40	CD23	25r yel green	2.75	1.25
41	CD24	50r dk blue	6.00	3.25
42	CD25	75r vio brown	8.00	7.00

43 CD26 100r bister brn 8.00 7.00
44 CD27 150r bister 12.00 11.50
Nos. 37-44 (8) 44.55 34.00

Nos. 37-44 with "REPUBLICA" overprint and surcharges are listed as Portugal Nos. 199-206.

Ceres — A6

1928, May 1 Engr. *Perf. 13½*
Value Typographed in Black

45 A6 3c deep violet .40 *.60*
46 A6 4c orange .40 *.60*
47 A6 5c light blue .40 *.60*
48 A6 6c brown .40 *.60*
49 A6 10c red .40 *.60*
50 A6 15c yel green .40 *.60*
51 A6 16c red brown .40 *.60*
52 A6 25c violet rose 1.00 .60
53 A6 32c blue grn 1.00 .60
54 A6 40c yel brown 1.50 *1.75*
55 A6 50c slate 1.50 *1.75*
56 A6 64c Prus blue 1.50 *3.00*
57 A6 80c dk brown 1.50 *5.00*
58 A6 96c carmine rose 5.00 *3.00*
59 A6 1e black 2.00 3.00
a. Value omitted 42.50 *45.00*
60 A6 1.20e light rose 2.00 *3.00*
61 A6 1.60e ultra 2.00 *3.00*
62 A6 2.40e yellow 3.00 *3.50*
63 A6 3.36e dull green 4.00 *5.75*
64 A6 4.50e brown red 5.00 *9.00*
65 A6 7e dark blue 6.00 *17.50*
Nos. 45-65 (21) 39.80 *64.65*

It was obligatory to use these stamps in place of those in regular use on May 1, June 5, July 1 and Dec. 31, 1928, Jan. 1 and 31, May 1 and June 5, 1929. The amount obtained from this sale was donated to a fund for building a museum.

Less than very fine examples sell for much less.

NEWSPAPER STAMP

Numeral of Value — N1

Newspaper Stamp of Portugal Overprinted in Black

Perf. 12½, 13½

1876, July 1 Unwmk.
P1 N1 2½r olive 9.00 4.25
a. Inverted overprint 30.00

The reprints have the same papers, gum, perforations and overprint as the reprints of the regular issues.

POSTAL TAX STAMPS

Pombal Commemorative Issue
Common Design Types

1925 Unwmk. Engr. *Perf. 12½*
RA1 CD28 15c gray & black .60 .65
RA2 CD29 15c gray & black .60 .65
RA3 CD30 15c gray & black .60 .65
Nos. RA1-RA3 (3) 1.80 1.95

POSTAL TAX DUE STAMPS

Pombal Commemorative Issue
Common Design Types

1925 Unwmk. *Perf. 12½*
RAJ1 CD28 30c gray & black .85 3.50
RAJ2 CD29 30c gray & black .85 3.50
RAJ3 CD30 30c gray & black .85 3.50
Nos. RAJ1-RAJ3 (3) 2.55 10.50

MALAGASY REPUBLIC

ˌmal-ə-ˈgə-sē

Madagascar (French)

Malagasy Democratic Republic

Republic of Madagascar

LOCATION — Large island off the coast of southeastern Africa
GOVT. — Republic
AREA — 226,658 sq. mi.
POP. — 14,062,000 (1995 est.)
CAPITAL — Antananarivo

Madagascar became a French protectorate in 1885 and a French colony in 1896 following several years of dispute among France, Great Britain, and the native government. The colony administered the former protectorates of Anjouan, Grand Comoro, Mayotte, Diego-Suarez, Nossi-Be and Sainte-Marie de Madagascar. Previous issues of postage stamps are found under these individual headings. The Malagasy Republic succeeded the colony in 1958 and became the Democratic Republic of Malagasy in 1975. The official name was again changed in 1993 to Republic of Madagascar.

For British Consular Mail stamps of 1884-1886, see Madagascar.

100 Centimes = 1 Franc
100 Centimes = 1 Ariary (1976)

See France No. 2767 for stamp inscribed "Madagascar."

Catalogue values for unused stamps in this country are for Never Hinged items, beginning with Scott 241 in the regular postage section, Scott B15 in the semi-postal section, Scott C37 in the airpost section, and Scott J31 in the postage due section.

French Offices in Madagascar

The general issues of French Colonies were used in these offices in addition to the stamps listed here.

Stamps of French Colonies Surcharged in Black

a

b

c

Overprint Type "a"

1889 Unwmk. *Perf. 14x13½*
1 A9 05c on 10c blk, *lav* 725. 220.
a. Inverted surcharge 1,950. 1,300.
2 A9 05c on 25c blk, *rose* 725. 220.
a. Inverted surcharge 1,950. 1,300.
b. 25c on 10c lav (error) 11,500. 10,000.
3 A9 25c on 40c red, *straw* 650. 200.
a. Inverted surcharge 1,700. 1,300.

1891 Overprint Type "b"
4 A9 05c on 40c red, *straw* *235.00 100.00*
5 A9 15c on 25c blk, *rose* *235.00 110.00*
a. Surcharge vertical *275.00 145.00*

Overprint Type "c"
6 A9 5c on 10c blk, *lav* *275.00 125.00*
a. Double surcharge *1,000.* 900.00
7 A9 5c on 25c blk, *rose* *275.00 125.00*

See Senegal Nos. 4, 8 for similar surcharge on 20c, 30c.

Forgeries of Nos. 1-7 exist.

A4

Without Gum

1891 Type-set *Imperf.*
8 A4 5c blk, *green* 165.00 32.50
9 A4 10c blk, *lt bl* 125.00 40.00
10 A4 15c ultra, *pale bl* 125.00 47.50
11 A4 25c brn, *buff* 30.00 22.50
12 A4 1fr blk, *yellow* 1,300. 300.00
13 A4 5fr vio & blk, *lil* 2,400. 1,275.

Stamps of France 1876-90, Overprinted in Red or Black

1895 *Perf. 14x13½*
14 A15 5c grn, *grnsh* (R) 22.50 11.00
15 A15 10c blk, *lav* (R) 50.00 32.50
16 A15 15c bl (R) 72.50 22.00
17 A15 25c blk, *rose* (R) 100.00 25.00
18 A15 40c red, *straw* (Bk) 95.00 45.00
19 A15 50c rose, *rose* (Bk) 110.00 55.00
20 A15 75c dp vio, *org* (R) 125.00 62.50
21 A15 1fr brnz grn, *straw* (Bk) 135.00 72.50
22 A15 5fr vio, *lav* (Bk) 220.00 100.00
Nos. 14-22 (9) 930.00 425.50

Majunga Issue
Stamps of France, 1876-86, Surcharged with New Value

1895
Manuscript Surcharge in Red
22A A15 0,15c on 25c blk, *rose* *8,000.*
22B A15 0,15c on 1fr brnz grn, *straw* *6,000.*

Handstamped in Black
22C A15 15c on 25c blk, *rose* *12,750.*
22D A15 15c on 1fr brnz grn, *straw* *11,750.*

On most of No. 22C and all of No. 22D the manuscript surcharge of Nos. 22A-22B was washed off. Three types of "15" were used for No. 22C.

Stamps of France, 1876-84, Surcharged

1896
23 A15 5c on 1c blk, *bl* *6,400. 2,500.*
24 A15 15c on 2c brn, *buff* *2,600. 1,000.*
25 A15 25c on 3c gray, *grysh* *3,400. 1,100.*
26 A15 25c on 4c cl, *lav* *6,400. 1,950.*
27 A15 25c on 40c red, *straw* *1,650. 875.*

The oval of the 5c and 15c surcharges is smaller than that of the 25c, and it does not extend beyond the edges of the stamp as the 25c surcharge does.

Excellent counterfeits of the surcharges on Nos. 22A to 27 exist.

Issues of the Colony

Navigation and Commerce — A7

1896-1906 Typo. *Perf. 14x13½*
Colony Name in Blue or Carmine

28 A7 1c blk, *lil bl* 1.50 1.10
29 A7 2c brn, *buff* 2.25 1.50
a. Name in blue black 4.25 4.50
30 A7 4c claret, *lav* 2.50 1.80
31 A7 5c grn, *grnsh* 8.00 1.50
32 A7 5c yel grn ('01) 1.80 1.10
33 A7 10c blk, *lav* 8.00 2.25
34 A7 10c red ('00) 3.00 1.10
35 A7 15c blue, quadrille paper 14.00 1.50
36 A7 15c gray ('00) 2.50 1.50
37 A7 20c red, *grn* 7.25 2.25
38 A7 25c blk, *rose* 11.00 4.50
39 A7 25c blue ('00) 25.00 32.50
40 A7 30c brn, *bis* 8.75 3.75
41 A7 35c blk, *yel* ('06) 45.00 7.25
42 A7 40c red, *straw* 11.00 6.00
43 A7 50c car, *rose* 14.50 3.00
44 A7 50c brn, *az* ('00) 32.50 45.00
45 A7 75c dp vio, *org* 6.25 4.50
46 A7 1fr brnz grn, *straw* 14.50 3.75
a. Name in blue ('99) 30.00 22.00
47 A7 5fr red lil, *lav* ('99) 37.50 32.50
Nos. 28-47 (20) 256.80 158.35

Perf. 13½x14 stamps are counterfeits.

For surcharges see Nos. 48-55, 58-60, 115-118, 127-128.

Nos. 32, 43, 44 and 46, affixed to pressboard with animals printed on the back, were used as emergency currency in the Comoro Islands in 1920.

Surcharged in Black

1902
48 A7 05c on 50c car, *rose* 7.25 6.00
a. Inverted surcharge 120.00 120.00
49 A7 10c on 5fr red lil, *lav* 25.00 22.00
a. Inverted surcharge 125.00 125.00
50 A7 15c on 1fr ol grn, *straw* 9.50 8.75
a. Inverted surcharge 120.00 120.00
b. Double surcharge 400.00 400.00
Nos. 48-50 (3) 41.75 36.75

Surcharged in Black

51 A7 0,01 on 2c brn, *buff* 11.50 11.50
a. Inverted surcharge 72.50 72.50
b. "00,1" instead of "0,01" 150.00 155.00
c. As "b" inverted — —
d. Comma omitted 210.00 210.00
e. Name in blue black 11.50 11.50
52 A7 0,05 on 30c brn, *bis* 11.50 11.50
a. Inverted surcharge 72.50 72.50
b. "00,5" instead of "0,05" 100.00 100.00
c. As "b" inverted 2,550.
d. Comma omitted 210.00 210.00
53 A7 0,10 on 50c car, *rose* 9.50 9.50
a. Inverted surcharge 72.50 72.50
b. Comma omitted 210.00 210.00
54 A7 0,15 on 75c vio, *org* 7.25 7.25
a. Inverted surcharge 72.50 72.50
b. Comma omitted 210.00 210.00
55 A7 0,15 on 1fr ol grn, *straw* 14.50 14.50
a. Inverted surcharge 110.00 110.00
b. Comma omitted 275.00 275.00
Nos. 51-55 (5) 54.25 54.25

Surcharged On Stamps of Diego-Suarez

56 A11 0,05 on 30c brn, *bis* 165.00 145.00
a. "00,5" instead of "0,05" 1,350. 1,350.
b. Inverted surcharge 1,450. 1,450.
57 A11 0,10 on 50c car, *rose* *5,000. 5,000.*

Counterfeits of Nos. 56-57 exist with surcharge both normal and inverted.

Surcharged in Black

58 A7 0,01 on 2c brn, *buff* 11.50 11.50
a. Inverted surcharge 72.50 72.50
b. Comma omitted 210.00 210.00
59 A7 0,05 on 30c brn, *bis* 11.50 11.50
a. Inverted surcharge 72.50 72.50
b. Comma omitted 210.00 210.00
60 A7 0,10 on 50c car, *rose* 9.50 9.50
a. Inverted surcharge 72.50 72.50
b. Comma omitted 210.00 210.00
Nos. 58-60 (3) 32.50 32.50

Surcharged On Stamps of Diego-Suarez

61 A11 0,05 on 30c brn, *bis* 165.00 145.00
a. Inverted surcharge 1,450. 1,450.
62 A11 0,10 on 50c car, *rose* *5,000.* *5,000.*

BISECTS

During alleged stamp shortages at several Madagascar towns in 1904, it is claimed that bisects were used. After being affixed to letters, these bisects were handstamped "Affranchissement - exceptionnel - (faute de timbres)" and other inscriptions of similar import. The stamps bisected were 10c, 20c, 30c and 50c denominations of Madagascar type A7 and Diego-Suarez type A11. The editors believe these provisionals were unnecessary and speculative.

Zebu, Traveler's Tree and Lemur — A8

1903 Engr. *Perf. 11½*

63 A8 1c dk violet .90 .90
a. On bluish paper 5.00 5.00
64 A8 2c olive brn .90 .90
65 A8 4c brown 1.20 1.25
66 A8 5c yellow grn 6.00 1.90
67 A8 10c red 11.00 1.25
68 A8 15c carmine 14.00 1.25
a. On bluish paper *150.00* *150.00*
69 A8 20c orange 5.25 2.50
70 A8 25c dull blue 25.00 5.00
71 A8 30c pale red 37.50 13.00
72 A8 40c gray vio 25.00 5.25
73 A8 50c brown org 40.00 25.00
74 A8 75c orange yel 52.50 25.00
75 A8 1fr dp green 52.50 25.00
76 A8 2fr slate 72.50 26.00
77 A8 5fr gray black 82.50 *85.00*
Nos. 63-77 (15) 426.75 219.20

Nos. 63-77 exist imperf. Value of set, $600.
For surcharges see Nos. 119-124, 129.

Transportation by Sedan Chair — A9

1908-28 Typo. *Perf. 13½x14*

79 A9 1c violet & ol .25 .25
80 A9 2c red & ol .25 .25
81 A9 4c ol brn & brn .25 .25
82 A9 5c bl grn & ol 1.00 .30
83 A9 5c blk & rose ('22) .30 .30
84 A9 10c rose & brown 1.00 .30
85 A9 10c bl grn & ol grn ('22) .60 .40
86 A9 10c org brn & vio ('25) .35 .35
87 A9 15c dl vio & rose ('16) .35 .35
88 A9 15c dl grn & lt grn ('27) .70 .70
89 A9 15c dk bl & rose red ('28) 1.60 1.00
90 A9 20c org & brn .70 .45
91 A9 25c blue & blk 3.00 1.00
92 A9 25c vio & blk ('22) .40 .30
93 A9 30c brown & blk 3.00 1.35
94 A9 30c rose red & brn ('22) .55 .40
95 A9 30c grn & red vio ('25) .55 .45
96 A9 30c dp grn & yel grn ('27) 1.35 1.00
97 A9 35c red & black 2.00 1.00
98 A9 40c vio brn & blk 1.35 .70
99 A9 45c bl grn & blk 1.00 .70
100 A9 45c red & ver ('25) .45 .45
101 A9 45c gray lil & mag ('27) 1.25 1.00
102 A9 50c violet & blk 1.00 .70
103 A9 50c blue & blk ('22) .85 .60
104 A9 50c blk & org ('25) 1.00 .40
105 A9 60c vio, *pnksh* ('25) .70 .70
106 A9 65c black & bl ('25) 1.00 .75
107 A9 75c rose red & blk 1.00 .70
108 A9 85c grn & ver ('25) 1.35 .85
109 A9 1fr brown & ol 1.00 .70
110 A9 1fr dull blue ('25) 1.00 1.00
111 A9 1fr rose & grn ('28) 5.75 4.50
112 A9 1.10fr bis & bl grn ('28) 2.00 2.00
113 A9 2fr blue & olive 4.00 1.60
114 A9 5fr vio & vio brn 12.50 5.50
Nos. 79-114 (36) 55.40 33.25

75c violet on pinkish stamps of type A9 are No. 138 without surcharge.
For surcharges and overprints see Nos. 125-126, 130-146, 178-179, B1, 212-214.

Preceding Issues Surcharged in Black or Carmine

1912, Nov. *Perf. 14x13½*

115 A7 5c on 15c gray (C) 1.00 1.00
116 A7 5c on 20c red, *grn* 1.35 1.35
a. Inverted surcharge 175.00
117 A7 5c on 30c brn, *bis* (C) 1.00 1.00
118 A7 10c on 75c vio, *org* 12.50 11.50
a. Double surcharge 310.00
119 A8 5c on 2c ol brn (C) 1.00 1.00
120 A8 5c on 20c org 1.00 1.00
121 A8 5c on 30c pale red 1.75 1.75
122 A8 10c on 40c gray vio (C) 1.75 1.75
123 A8 10c on 50c brn org 3.50 4.50
124 A8 10c on 75c org yel 6.00 7.25
a. Inverted surcharge 230.00
Nos. 115-124 (10) 30.85 32.10

Two spacings between the surcharged numerals are found on Nos. 115 to 118. For detailed listings, see the *Scott Classic Specialized Catalogue of Stamps and Covers.*

Stamps of Anjouan, Grand Comoro Island, Mayotte and Mohéli with similar surcharges were also available for use in Madagascar and the entire Comoro archipelago.

Preceding Issues Surcharged in Red or Black

g

h

1921 On Nos. 98 & 107

125 A9 (g) 30c on 40c (R) 2.50 2.50
126 A9 (g) 60c on 75c 3.25 3.25

On Nos. 45 & 47

127 A7 (g) 60c on 75c (R) 12.50 12.50
a. Inverted surcharge 220.00 220.00
128 A7 (h) 1fr on 5fr 1.10 1.10

On No. 77

129 A8 (h) 1fr on 5fr (R) 100.00 100.00
Nos. 125-129 (5) 119.35 119.35

Stamps and Type of 1908-16 Surcharged in Black or Red

No. 130

No. 131

130 A9 1c on 15c dl vio & rose 1.10 1.10
131 A9 25c on 35c red & blk 6.50 6.50
132 A9 25c on 35c red & blk (R) 32.50 32.50
133 A9 25c on 40c brn & blk 5.00 5.00
134 A9 25c on 45c grn & blk 4.50 4.50
Nos. 130-134 (5) 49.60 49.60
Nos. 125-134 (10) 168.95 168.95

Stamps and Type of 1908-28 Surcharged with New Value and Bars

1922-27

135 A9 25c on 15c dl vio & rose .35 .35
a. Double surcharge 95.00
136 A9 25c on 2fr bl & ol .50 .50
137 A9 25c on 5fr vio & vio brn .35 .35
138 A9 60c on 75c vio, *pnksh* .60 .60
139 A9 65c on 75c rose red & blk 1.10 1.10
140 A9 85c on 45c bl grn & blk 1.90 1.45
141 A9 90c on 75c dl red & rose red 1.10 1.10
142 A9 1.25fr on 1fr lt bl (R) .75 .50
143 A9 1.50fr on 1fr dp bl & dl bl .75 .60
144 A9 3fr on 5fr grn & vio 2.25 1.45
145 A9 10fr on 5fr org & rose lil 9.50 6.00
146 A9 20fr on 5fr rose & sl bl 10.00 8.00
Nos. 135-146 (12) 29.15 22.00

Years of issue: No. 138, 1922; Nos. 136, 137, 1924; Nos. 135, 139-140, 1925; No. 142, 1926; Nos. 141, 143-146, 1927.
See Nos. 178-179.

Sakalava Chief — A10

Hova Woman — A12

Hova with Oxen A11

Bétsiléo Woman A13

Perf. 13½x14, 14x13½

1930-44 Typo.

147 A11 1c dk bl & bl grn ('33) .25 .25
148 A10 2c brn red & dk brn .25 .25
149 A10 4c dk brn & vio .25 .25
150 A11 5c lt grn & red .25 .25
151 A12 10c ver & dp grn .40 .25
152 A13 15c dp red .25 .25
153 A11 20c yel brn & dk bl .25 .25
154 A12 25c vio & dk brn .25 .25
155 A13 30c Prus blue .65 .45
156 A10 40c grn & red .75 .50
157 A13 45c dull violet .90 .55
158 A11 65c brn & vio 1.10 .80
159 A13 75c dk brown .85 .50
160 A11 90c brn red & dk red 1.40 .90
161 A12 1fr yel brn & dk bl 1.75 1.10
162 A12 1fr dk red & car rose ('38) .95 .90
163 A12 1.25fr dp bl & dk brn ('33) 1.60 .90
164 A10 1.50fr dk & dp bl 5.50 1.10
165 A10 1.50fr brn & dk red ('38) .75 .50
165A A10 1.50fr dk red & brn ('44) .50 .50
166 A10 1.75fr dk brn & dk red ('33) 4.25 1.60
167 A10 5fr vio & dk brn 1.25 .70
168 A10 20fr yel brn & dk bl 2.00 1.75
Nos. 147-168 (23) 26.35 14.75

Common Design Types pictured following the introduction.

Colonial Exposition Issue
Common Design Types

1931 Engr. *Perf. 12½*
Name of Country in Black

169 CD70 40c deep green 1.40 1.00
170 CD71 50c violet 2.00 1.25
171 CD72 90c red orange 2.00 1.25
172 CD73 1.50fr dull blue 2.50 1.50
Nos. 169-172 (4) 7.90 5.00

General Joseph Simon Galliéni — A14

Size: 21½x34½mm

1931 Engr. *Perf. 14*

173 A14 1c ultra .50 .45
174 A14 50c orange brn 1.40 .35
175 A14 2fr deep red 5.75 4.25
176 A14 3fr emerald 5.50 3.00
177 A14 10fr dp orange 4.00 3.00
Nos. 173-177 (5) 17.15 11.05

Nos. 113 and 109 Surcharged

1932 *Perf. 13½x14*

178 A9 25c on 2fr bl & ol .75 .50
179 A9 50c on 1fr brn & ol .75 .50

No. 178 has numerals in thick block letters. No. 136 has thin shaded numerals.

Galliéni Type of 1931

1936-40 Photo. *Perf. 13½, 13x13½*
Size: 21x34mm

180 A14 3c sapphire ('40) .25 .25
181 A14 45c brt green ('40) .50 .40
182 A14 50c yellow brown .25 .25
183 A14 60c brt red lil ('40) .40 .25
184 A14 70c brt rose ('40) .60 .40
185 A14 90c copper brn ('39) .50 .40
186 A14 1.40fr org yel ('40) .90 .50
187 A14 1.60fr purple ('40) .90 .60
188 A14 2fr dk carmine .50 .25
189 A14 3fr green 4.50 2.25
190 A14 3fr olive blk ('39) .90 .70
Nos. 180-190 (11) 10.20 6.25

Paris International Exposition Issue
Common Design Types

1937, Apr. 15 Engr. *Perf. 13*

191 CD74 20c dp violet 1.60 1.60
192 CD75 30c dk green 1.60 1.60
193 CD76 40c car rose 1.60 1.60
194 CD77 50c dk brn & blk 1.25 1.25
195 CD78 90c red 1.60 1.60
196 CD79 1.50fr ultra 1.60 1.60
Nos. 191-196 (6) 9.25 9.25

Colonial Arts Exhibition Issue
Common Design Type
Souvenir Sheet

1937 *Imperf.*
197 CD74 3fr orange red 10.00 *12.50*

Jean Laborde A15

1938-40 *Perf. 13*
198 A15 35c green .60 .35
199 A15 55c dp purple .60 .35
200 A15 65c orange red .80 .35
201 A15 80c violet brn .60 .35
202 A15 1fr rose car .80 .35
203 A15 1.25fr rose car ('39) .35 .25
204 A15 1.75fr dk ultra 1.60 .65
205 A15 2.15fr yel brn 2.25 1.60
206 A15 2.25fr dk ultra ('39) .55 .45
207 A15 2.50fr blk brn ('40) .60 .45
208 A15 10fr dk green ('40) 1.10 .80
Nos. 198-208 (11) 9.85 5.95

New York World's Fair Issue
Common Design Type

1939, May 10 Engr. *Perf. 12½x12*
209 CD82 1.25fr car lake .75 1.25
210 CD82 2.25fr ultra .75 1.25

Porters Carrying Man in Chair, and Marshal Petain — A15a

1941 Engr. *Perf. 12x12½*
210A A15a 1fr bister brn .35
210B A15a 2.50fr blue .35

Nos. 210A-210B were issued by the Vichy government in France but were not placed on sale in Madagascar.

For overprints see Nos. B13-B14.

Type of 1930-44 Surcharged in Black with New Value

1942 *Perf. 14x13½*
211 A11 50c on 65c dk brn & mag 2.50 .75

French Explorers de Hell, Passot & Jehenne — A15b

1942 Engr. *Perf. 13x13½*
211A A15b 1.50fr blue & red brn 1.10

Centenary of French colonies of Mayotte and Nossi Bé.

No. 211A was issued by the Vichy government in France, but was not placed on sale in Madagascar.

Nos. 143, 145-146 with Additional Overprint in Red or Black

1942 Unwmk. *Perf. 14x13½*
212 A9 1.50fr on 1fr (R) 1.75 1.75
213 A9 10fr on 5fr (Bk) 10.00 10.00
214 A9 20fr on 5fr (R) 12.50 12.50

Stamps of 1930-40 Overprinted Like Nos. 212-214 in Black or Red or

215 A10 2c brn red & dk brn 2.25 2.25
216 A14 3c sapphire (R) 115.00 115.00
217 A13 15c deep red 12.00 12.00
218 A11 65c dk brn & mag 5.00 5.00
219 A14 70c brt rose 2.50 2.50
220 A15 80c violet brn 5.00 5.00
221 A14 1.40fr orange yel 2.50 2.50
222 A10 1.50fr dk bl & dp bl (R) 2.50 2.25
223 A10 1.50fr brn & dk red 5.00 5.00
224 A14 1.60fr purple 2.50 2.50
225 A15 2.25fr dk ultra (R) 5.00 5.00
226 A15 2.50fr black brn (R) 6.00 6.00
227 A15 10fr dk green 9.00 9.00
228 A10 20fr yel brn & dk bl (R) *725.00 750.00*

Stamps of 1930-40 Surcharged in Black or Red

229 A11 5c on 1c dk bl & bl grn 1.25 1.25
230 A15 10c on 55c dp pur 1.75 1.75
231 A15 30c on 65c org red 1.75 1.75
232 A14 50c on 90c cop brn 1.25 1.25
233 A12 1fr on 1.25fr dp bl & dk brn 12.00 12.00
234 A15 1fr on 1.25fr rose car 12.50 12.50
235 A10 1.50fr on 1.75fr dk brn & dk red 1.25 1.25
236 A15 1.50fr on 1.75fr ultra (R) 1.25 1.25
237 A15 2fr on 2.15fr yel brn 1.75 1.75

No. 211 with additional Overprint Like Nos. 217-218 in Black
239 A11 50c on 65c dk brn & mag 2.25 2.25

New York World's Fair Stamp Overprinted Like Nos. 217-218 in Red
Perf. 12½x12
240 CD82 2.25fr ultra 5.00 5.00
Nos. 212-227,229-240 (27) 240.50 240.25

Catalogue values for unused stamps in this section, from this point to the end of the section, are for Never Hinged items.

Traveler's Tree — A16

1943 Unwmk. Photo. *Perf. 14x14½*
241 A16 5c ol gray .25 .25
242 A16 10c pale rose vio .25 .25
243 A16 25c emerald .25 .25
244 A16 30c dp orange .25 .25
245 A16 40c slate bl .25 .25
246 A16 80c dk red brn .25 .25
247 A16 1fr dull blue .30 .25
248 A16 1.50fr crim rose .55 .40
249 A16 2fr dull yel .55 .45
250 A16 2.50fr brt ultra .55 .45
251 A16 4fr aqua & red .70 .55
252 A16 5fr green & blk .70 .55
253 A16 10fr sal pink & dk bl 1.00 .85
254 A16 20fr dl vio & brn 1.40 1.20
Nos. 241-254 (14) 7.25 6.20

For surcharges see Nos. 255-256, 261-268.

Types of 1930-44 without "RF"

1943-44
254A A11 20c yel brn & dk bl .75
254B A14 60c lilac rose 1.10
254C A12 1fr dk red & car rose 1.90
254D A10 1.50fr brn & dk red 1.50
254E A10 5fr vio & dk brn 3.75
Nos. 254A-254E (5) 9.00

On type A10, the two panels at the top of the frame have been reversed, with the value at the left and a blank (RF removed) panel at right.

Nos. 254A-254E were issued by the Vichy government in France, but were not placed on sale in Madagascar.

Nos. 241 and 242 Surcharged with New Values and Bars in Red or Blue

1944
255 A16 1.50fr on 5c (R) 1.25 .55
256 A16 1.50fr on 10c (Bl) 1.75 .85

Nos. 229 and 224 Surcharged with New Values and Bars in Red or Black
Perf. 14x13½, 14
257 A11 50c on 5c on 1c (R) 3.00 .70
258 A14 1.50fr on 1.60fr (Bk) 3.00 .95
Nos. 255-258 (4) 9.00 3.05

Eboue Issue
Common Design Type

1945 Engr. *Perf. 13*
259 CD91 2fr black .75 .50
260 CD91 25fr Prus green 1.25 .95

Nos. 241, 243 and 250 Surcharged with New Values and Bars in Carmine or Black

1945 *Perf. 14x14½*
261 A16 50c on 5c ol gray (C) .55 .45
262 A16 60c on 5c ol gray (C) .70 .55
263 A16 70c on 5c ol gray (C) 1.00 .50
264 A16 1.20fr on 5c ol gray (C) .85 .70
265 A16 2.40fr on 25c emer .85 .70
266 A16 3fr on 25c emer .85 .70
267 A16 4.50fr on 25c emer 1.25 1.00
268 A16 15fr on 2.50fr brt ultra (C) 1.25 1.00
Nos. 261-268 (8) 7.30 5.60

Southern Dancer — A17

Gen. J. S. Galliéni — A20

Herd of Zebus A18

Sakalava Man and Woman A19

Betsimisaraka Mother and Child — A21

General Jacques C. R. A. Duchesne A22

Marshal Joseph J. C. Joffre A23

Perf. 13x13½, 13½x13
1946 Photo. Unwmk.
269 A17 10c green .25 .25
270 A17 30c orange .25 .25
271 A17 40c brown ol .25 .25
272 A17 50c violet brn .25 .25
273 A18 60c dp ultra .40 .25
274 A18 80c blue grn .50 .25
275 A19 1fr brown .40 .25
276 A19 1.20fr green .40 .25
276A A20 1.50fr dk red .40 .25
277 A20 2fr slate blk .40 .25
278 A20 3fr dp claret .60 .25
278A A21 3.60fr dk car rose 1.00 .65
279 A21 4fr dp ultra .60 .25
280 A21 5fr red orange .85 .25
281 A22 6fr dk grnsh bl .60 .25
282 A22 10fr red brn .85 .25
283 A23 15fr violet brn 1.20 .30
284 A23 20fr dk vio bl 1.60 .65
285 A23 25fr brown 2.40 1.00
Nos. 269-285 (19) 13.20 6.35

Military Medal Issue
Common Design Type
Engraved and Typographed

1952, Dec. 1 Unwmk. *Perf. 13*
286 CD101 15fr multicolored 3.75 2.50

Creation of the French Military Medal, cent.

Tropical Flowers — A24

Long-tailed Ground Roller A25

1954 **Engr.**
287 A24 7.50fr ind & gray grn 1.50 .25
288 A25 8fr brown carmine 1.25 .35
289 A25 15fr dk grn & dp ultra 2.50 .35
Nos. 287-289 (3) 5.25 .95

Colonel Lyautey and Royal Palace, Tananarive A26

1954-55
290 A26 10fr vio bl, ind & bl ('55) 1.20 .25
291 A26 40fr dk sl bl & red brn 1.75 .25

FIDES Issue
Common Design Type

Designs: 3fr, Tractor and modern settlement. 5fr, Gallieni school. 10fr, Pangalanes Canal. 15fr, Irrigation project.

1956, Oct. 22 Engr. *Perf. 13x12½*
292 CD103 3fr gray vio & vio brn .40 .25
293 CD103 5fr org brn & dk vio brn .40 .35
294 CD103 10fr indigo & lilac .60 .35
295 CD103 15fr grn & bl grn .85 .25
Nos. 292-295 (4) 2.25 1.20

Coffee
A26a

1956, Oct. 22 ***Perf. 13***
296 A26a 20r red brn & dk brn .90 .25

Manioc — A27 Vanilla — A28

Design: 4fr, Cloves.

1957, Mar. 12 **Unwmk.** ***Perf. 13***
297 A27 2fr bl, grn & sepia .35 .25
298 A28 4fr dp grn & red .75 .25
299 A28 12fr dk vio, dl grn & sepia .75 .35
Nos. 297-299 (3) 1.85 .85

Malagasy Republic Human Rights Issue

Common Design Type

1958, Dec. 10 **Engr.** ***Perf. 13***
300 CD105 10fr brn & dk bl .80 .40

Universal Declaration of Human Rights, 10th anniversary.
"CF" stands for "Communauté française."

> Imperforates
> Most Malagasy stamps from 1958 onward exist imperforate in issued and trial colors, and also in small presentation sheets in issued colors.

Flower Issue

Common Design Type

Perf. 12½x12, 12x12½

1959, Jan. 31 **Photo.**
301 CD104 6fr Datura, horiz. .40 .25
302 CD104 25fr Poinsettia 1.20 .35

Flag and Assembly Building
A29

Flag and Map — A30

1959, Feb. 28 **Engr.** ***Perf. 13***
303 A29 20fr brn vio, car & emer .35 .25
304 A30 25fr gray, red & emer .70 .25

Proclamation of the Malagasy Republic.

French and Malagasy Flags and Map — A31

1959, Feb. 28
305 A31 60fr multi 1.60 .50

Issued to honor the French Community.

Chionaema Pauliani
A32

Ylang-ylang — A33

Designs: 30c, 40c, 50c, 3fr, Various butterflies. 5fr, Sisal. 8fr, Pepper. 10fr, Rice. 15fr, Cotton.

1960 **Unwmk.** ***Perf. 13***
306 A32 30c multicolored .25 .25
307 A32 40c emer, sep & red brn .25 .25
308 A32 50c vio brn, blk & stl bl .25 .25
309 A32 1fr ind, red & dl pur .25 .25
310 A32 3fr ol, vio blk & org .25 .25
311 A32 5fr red, brn & emer .35 .25
312 A33 6fr dk grn & brt yel .40 .25
313 A32 8fr crim rose, emer & blk .40 .25
314 A33 10fr dk grn, yel grn & lt brn .80 .25
315 A32 15fr brown & grn .80 .25
Nos. 306-315 (10) 4.00 2.50

Family Planting Trees — A34

1960, Feb. 1 **Engr.** ***Perf. 13***
316 A34 20fr red brn, buff & grn .90 .30

Issued for the "Week of the Tree," Feb. 1-7.

C.C.T.A. Issue

Common Design Type

1960, Feb. 22
317 CD106 25fr lt bl grn & plum .60 .30

Pres. Philibert Tsiranana and Map — A36

1960, Mar. 25 **Unwmk.** ***Perf. 13***
318 A36 20fr green & brn .35 .25

Athletes of Two Races — A37

1960 **Engr.** ***Perf. 13***
319 A37 25fr choc, org brn & ultra .60 .30

First Games of the French Community, Apr. 13-18, at Tananarive.

Pres. Philibert Tsiranana — A38

1960, July 29 **Unwmk.** ***Perf. 13***
320 A38 20fr red, blk & brt grn .35 .25

Issued to honor Pres. Tsiranana, "Father of Independence." For surcharge see No. B18.

Gray Lemur — A39

Designs: 4fr, Ruffed lemur, horiz. 12fr, Mongoose lemur.

1961, Dec. 9 ***Perf. 13***
321 A39 2fr brn & grnsh bl .25 .25
322 A39 4fr brn, grn & blk .25 .25
323 A39 12fr grn & red brn .55 .25
Nos. 321-323,C67-C69 (6) 12.80 5.20

Pres. Tsiranana Bridge, Sofia River
A40

1962, Jan. 4 **Unwmk.** ***Perf. 13***
324 A40 25fr bright blue 1.00 .25

First Train Built at Tananarive
A41

1962, Feb. 1
325 A41 20fr dk grn 1.10 .30

UN and Malagasy Flags over Government Building, Tananarive
A42

1962, Mar. 14 ***Perf. 13***
326 A42 25fr multicolored .45 .25
327 A42 85fr multicolored 1.90 .55

Malagasy Republic's admission to the UN.
For surcharge see No. 409.

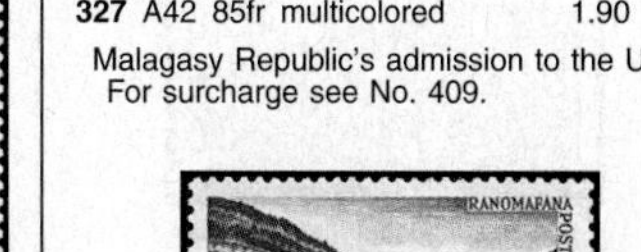

Ranomafana Village — A43

Designs: 30fr, Tritriva crater lake. 50fr, Foulpointe shore. 60fr, Fort Dauphin.

1962, May 7 **Engr.** ***Perf. 13***
328 A43 10fr sl grn, grnsh bl & cl .25 .25
329 A43 30fr sl grn, cl & grnsh bl .65 .25
330 A43 50fr ultra, cl & sl grn .90 .30
331 A43 60fr cl, ultra & sl grn 1.10 .40
Nos. 328-331,C70 (5) 4.65 1.80

African and Malgache Union Issue

Common Design Type

1962, Sept. 8 **Photo.** ***Perf. 12½x12***
332 CD110 30fr grn, bluish grn, red & gold .80 .80

First anniversary of the African and Malgache Union.

Arms of Republic and UNESCO Emblem
A44

1962, Sept. 3 **Unwmk.**
333 A44 20fr rose, emer & blk .60 .25

First Conference on Higher Education in Africa, Tananarive, Sept. 3-12.

Power Station — A45

Designs: 8fr, Atomic reactor and atom symbol, horiz. 10fr, Oil derrick. 15fr, Tanker, horiz.

Perf. 12x12½, 12½x12

1962, Oct. 18 **Litho.**
334 A45 5fr blue, yel & red .25 .25
335 A45 8fr blue, red & yel .30 .25
336 A45 10fr multicolored .40 .25
337 A45 15fr bl, red brn & blk .50 .25
Nos. 334-337 (4) 1.45 1.00

Industrialization of Madagascar.

Factory and Globe
A46

1963, Jan. 7 **Typo.** ***Perf. 14x13½***
338 A46 25fr dp org & blk .55 .25

International Fair at Tamatave.

Hertzian Cable, Tananarive-Fianarantsoa — A47

1963, Mar. 7 Photo. *Perf. 12½x12*

339 A47 20fr multi .55 .25

Madagascar Blue Pigeon — A48

Gastrorchis Humblotii — A49

Birds: 2fr, Blue coua. 3fr, Red fody. 6fr, Madagascar pigmy kingfisher.

Orchids: 10fr, Eulophiella roempleriana. 12fr, Angraecum sesquipedale.

1963 Unwmk. *Perf. 13*

340 A48 1fr multi .55 .30
341 A48 2fr multi .55 .30
342 A48 3fr multi .75 .30
343 A48 6fr multi .75 .30
344 A49 8fr multi .60 .30
345 A49 10fr multi .75 .45
346 A49 12fr multi .75 .50
Nos. 340-346,C72-C74 (10) 17.45 6.60

Arms — A50

Arms of: 1.50fr, Antsirabe. 5fr, Antalaha. 10fr, Tulear. 15fr, Majunga. 20fr, Fianarantsoa. 25fr, Tananarive. 50fr, Diégo-Suarez.

Imprint: "R. Louis del. So. Ge. Im."

1963-65 Litho. *Perf. 13*
Size: 23½x35½mm

347 A50 1.50fr multi ('64) .25 .25
348 A50 5fr multi ('65) .25 .25
349 A50 10fr multi ('64) .25 .25
350 A50 15fr multi ('64) .35 .25
351 A50 20fr multi .50 .25
352 A50 25fr multi .55 .25
353 A50 50fr multi ('65) 1.25 .50
Nos. 347-353 (7) 3.40 2.00

See Nos. 388-390, 434-439.
For surcharge see No. 503.

Map and Centenary Emblem — A51

1963, Sept. 2 *Perf. 12x12½*

354 A51 30fr multi 1.00 .50

Centenary of the International Red Cross.

Globe and Hands Holding Torch — A52

1963, Dec. 10 Engr. *Perf. 12½*

355 A52 60fr ol, ocher & car .85 .40

Universal Declaration of Human Rights, 15th anniv.

Scouts and Campfire A53

1964, June 6 Engr. *Perf. 13*

356 A53 20fr dk red, org & car .70 .30

40th anniv. of the Boy Scouts of Madagascar.

Europafrica Issue

Dove and Globe A54

1964, July 20 Engr.

357 A54 45fr ol grn, brn red & blk 1.00 .35

First anniversary of economic agreement between the European Economic Community and the African and Malgache Union.

Carved Statue of Woman — A55

Malagasy Art: 30fr, Statue of sitting man.

1964, Oct. 20 Unwmk. *Perf. 13*

358 A55 6fr dk bl, brt bl & sepia .45 .25
359 A55 30fr dp grn, ol bis & dk brn .80 .30
Nos. 358-359,C79 (3) 3.00 1.45

Cooperation Issue
Common Design Type

1964, Nov. 7 Engr. *Perf. 13*

360 CD119 25fr blk, dk brn & org brn .60 .25

University Emblem — A56

1964, Dec. 5 Litho. *Perf. 13x12½*

361 A56 65fr red, blk & grn .60 .35

Founding of the University of Madagascar, Tannanarive. The inscription reads: "Foolish is he who does not do better than his father."

Jejy — A57

Valiha Player A58

Musical instruments: 3fr, Kabosa (lute). 8fr, Hazolahy (sacred drum).

1965 Engr. *Perf. 13*
Size: 22x36mm

362 A57 3fr mag, vio bl & dk brn .50 .25
363 A57 6fr emer, rose lil & dk brn .60 .25
364 A57 8fr brn, grn & blk .90 .25

Photo. *Perf. 12½x13*

365 A58 25fr multi 1.75 .60
Nos. 362-365,C80 (5) 8.25 3.35

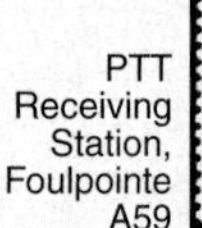

PTT Receiving Station, Foulpointe A59

1965, May 8 Engr. *Perf. 13*

366 A59 20fr red org, dk grn & ocher .50 .25

Issued for Stamp Day, 1965.

ITU Emblem, Old and New Telecommunication Equipment — A60

1965, May 17

367 A60 50fr ultra, red & grn 1.00 .40

ITU, centenary.

Jean Joseph Rabearivelo — A61

1965, June 22 Photo. *Perf. 13x12½*

368 A61 40fr dk brn & org .60 .30

Issued to honor the poet Jean Joseph Rabearivelo, pen name of Joseph Casimir, (1901-37).

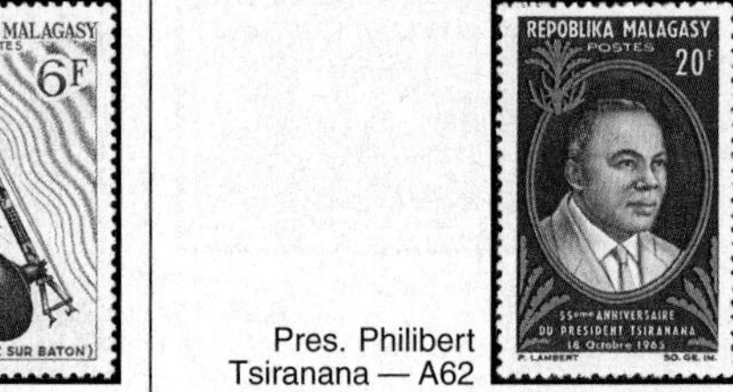

Pres. Philibert Tsiranana — A62

1965, Oct. 18 *Perf. 13x12½*

369 A62 20fr multi .25 .25
a. Souv. sheet of 4 1.00 1.00
370 A62 25fr multi .40 .25
a. Souv. sheet of 4 2.00 2.00

55th birthday of President Philibert Tsiranana.

Mail Coach A63

History of the Post: 3fr, Early automobile. 4fr, Litter. 10fr, Mail runner, vert. 12fr, Mail boat. 25fr, Oxcart. 30fr, Old railroad mail car. 65fr, Hydrofoil.

1965-66 Engr. *Perf. 13*

371 A63 3fr vio, dp bis & sky bl ('66) .40 .25
372 A63 4fr ultra, grn & dk brn ('66) .35 .25
373 A63 10fr multi .35 .25
374 A63 12fr multi .40 .25
375 A63 20fr bis, grn & red brn .90 .30
376 A63 25fr sl grn, dk brn & org .85 .30
377 A63 30fr pck bl, red & sep ('66) 2.50 .50
378 A63 65fr vio, brn & Prus bl ('66) 2.00 .50
Nos. 371-378 (8) 7.75 2.60

Leper's Crippled Hands A64

1966, Jan. 30

379 A64 20fr dk grn, dk brn & red .70 .30

Issued for the 13th World Leprosy Day.

Couple Planting Trees A65

1966, Feb. 21

380 A65 20fr dk brn, pur & bl grn .60 .25

Reforestation as a national duty.

Tiger Beetle A66

Insects: 6fr, Mantis. 12fr, Long-horned beetle. 45fr, Weevil.

1966 Photo. *Perf. 12½x12*
Insects in Natural Colors

381 A66 1fr brick red .95 .25
382 A66 6fr rose claret 1.25 .25
383 A66 12fr Prus blue 2.40 .40
384 A66 45fr lt yel grn 3.25 .75
Nos. 381-384 (4) 7.85 1.65

Stamp of 1903 — A67

1966, May 8 Engr. *Perf. 13*

385 A67 25fr red & sepia .80 .30

Issued for Stamp Day 1966.

Betsileo Dancers A68

1966, June 13 Photo. *Perf. 12½x13*

Size: 36x23mm

386 A68 5fr multi .55 .25

See No. C83.

Symbolic Tree and Emblems — A69

1966, June 26

387 A69 25fr multi .60 .25

Conference of the Organisation Commune Africaine et Malgache (OCAM), Tananarive.

No. 387 dated "JUIN 1966," original date "Janvier 1966" obliterated with bar. Exists without overprint "JUIN 1966" and bar. Value $100.

Arms Type of 1963-65

Imprint: "S. Gauthier So. Ge. Im."

20fr, Mananjary. 30fr, Nossi-Bé. 90fr, Antsohihy.

1966-68 Litho. *Perf. 13*

Size: 23½x35½mm

388 A50 20fr multi ('67) .40 .25
389 A50 30fr multi .45 .25
390 A50 90fr multi ('68) 1.50 .40
Nos. 388-390 (3) 2.35 .90

For surcharge see No. 503.

Singers and Map of Madagascar — A70

1966, Oct. 14 Engr. *Perf. 13*

392 A70 20fr red brn, grn & dk car rose .60 .25

Issued in honor of the National Anthem.

UNESCO Emblem A71

1966, Nov. 4

393 A71 30fr red, yel & slate .60 .25

UNESCO, 20th anniv.

Lions Emblem — A72

1967, Jan. 14 Photo. *Perf. 13x12½*

394 A72 30fr multi .60 .30

50th anniversary of Lions International.

Rice Harvest A73

1967, Jan. 27 *Perf. 12½x13*

395 A73 20fr multi .60 .25

FAO International Rice Year.

Adventist Temple, Tanambao-Tamatave — A74

Designs: 5fr, Catholic Cathedral, Tananarive, vert. 10fr, Mosque, Tamatave.

1967, Feb. 20 Engr. *Perf. 13*

396 A74 3fr lt ultra, grn & bis .25 .25
397 A74 5fr brt rose lil, grn & vio .25 .25
398 A74 10fr dp bl, brn & grn .30 .25
Nos. 396-398 (3) .80 .75

Norbert Raharisoa at Piano A75

1967, Mar. 23 Photo. *Perf. 12½x12*

399 A75 40fr citron & multi .70 .25

Norbert Raharisoa (1914-1963), composer.

Jean Raoult Flying Blériot Plane, 1911 A76

45fr, Georges Bougault and hydroplane, 1926.

1967, Apr. 28 Engr. *Perf. 13*

Size: 35½x22mm

400 A76 5fr gray bl, brn & grn .80 .30
401 A76 45fr brn, stl bl & blk 1.60 .60
Nos. 400-401,C84 (3) 11.40 4.90

History of aviation in Madagascar.

Ministry of Equipment and Communications — A77

1967, May 8 Engr. *Perf. 13*

402 A77 20fr ocher, ultra & grn .60 .25

Issued for Stamp Day, 1967.

Lutheran Church, Tananarive, Madagascar Map — A78

1967, Sept. 24 Photo. *Perf. 12x12½*

403 A78 20fr multi .70 .25

Lutheran Church in Madagascar, cent.

Map of Madagascar and Emblems — A79

1967, Oct. 16 Engr. *Perf. 13*

404 A79 90fr red brn, bl & dk red 1.10 .40

Hydrological Decade (UNESCO), 1965-74.

Dance of the Bilo Sakalavas — A80

Design: 30fr, Atandroy dancers.

1967, Nov. 25 Photo. *Perf. 13x12½*

Size: 22x36mm

405 A80 2fr lt grn & multi .30 .25
406 A80 30fr multi .60 .25
Nos. 405-406,C86-C87 (4) 6.90 2.50

Woman's Face, Scales and UN Emblem A81

1967, Dec. 16 *Perf. 12½x13*

407 A81 50fr emer, dk bl & brn .70 .30

UN Commission on the Status of Women.

Human Rights Flame — A82

1968, Mar. 16 Litho. *Perf. 13x12½*

408 A82 50fr blk, ver & grn .70 .30

International Human Rights Year.

No. 327 Surcharged with New Value and 3 Bars

1968, June 4 Engr. *Perf. 13*

409 A42 20fr on 85fr multi .70 .40

"Industry" A83

Designs: 20fr, "Agriculture" (mother and child carrying fruit and grain, and cattle), vert. 40fr, "Communications and Investments," (train, highway, factory and buildings).

1968, July 15

410 A83 10fr rose car, grn & dk pur .25 .25
411 A83 20fr dp car, grn & blk .30 .25
412 A83 40fr brn, vio & sl bl .60 .25
Nos. 410-412 (3) 1.15 .75

Completion of Five-year Plan, 1964-68.

Church, Translated Bible, Cross and Map of Madagascar — A84

1968, Aug. 18 Photo. *Perf. 12½x12*

413 A84 20fr multi .55 .25

Sesquicentennial of Christianity in Madagascar.

Isotry-Fitiavana Protestant Church — A85

12fr, Catholic Cathedral, Fianarantsoa. 50fr, Aga Khan Mosque, Tananarive.

1968, Sept. 10 Engr. *Perf. 13*

414 A85 4fr red brn, brt grn & dk brn .25 .25
415 A85 12fr plum, bl & hn brn .30 .25
416 A85 50fr brt grn, bl & indigo .60 .25
Nos. 414-416 (3) 1.15 .75

Madagascar Map and Cornucopia with Coins — A87

President and Mrs. Tsiranana A86

1968, Oct. 14 Photo. *Perf. 12½x12*

417 A86 20fr car, org & blk .30 .25
418 A86 30fr car, grnsh bl & blk .50 .25
a. Souv. sheet of 4, 2 each #417-418 1.50 1.00

10th anniv. of the Republic.

1968, Nov. 3 Photo. *Perf. 12x12½*

419 A87 20fr multi .60 .25

50th anniversary of the Malagasy Savings Bank.

Striving Mankind — A88

15fr, Mother, child and physician, horiz.

1968, Dec. 3 Photo. *Perf. 12½x12*

420 A88 15fr ultra, yel & crim .30 .25
421 A88 45fr vio bl & multi .55 .25

Completion of Five-Year Plan, 1964-68.

Queen Adelaide Receiving Malagasy Delegation, London, 1836 — A89

1969, Mar. 29 Photo. *Perf. 12x12½*

422 A89 250fr multi 4.75 2.50

Malagasy delegation London visit, 1836-37.

Cogwheels, Wrench and ILO Emblem A90

1969, Apr. 11 *Perf. 12½x12*

423 A90 20fr grn & multi .50 .25

ILO, 50th anniv.

Telecommunications and Postal Building, Tananarive — A91

1969, May 8 Engr. *Perf. 13*

424 A91 30fr bl, brt grn & car lake .60 .25

Issued for Stamp Day 1969.

Steering Wheel, Map, Automobiles — A92

1969, June 1 Photo. *Perf. 12*

425 A92 65fr multi 1.00 .30

Automobile Club of Madagascar, 20th anniv.

Pres. Philibert Tsiranana — A93

1969, June 26 Photo. *Perf. 12x12½*

426 A93 20fr multi .60 .25

10th anniversary of the inauguration of Pres. Philibert Tsiranana.

Banana Plants — A94

1969, July 7 Engr. *Perf. 13*

427 A94 5fr shown .65 .25
428 A94 15fr Lichi tree 1.25 .25

Runners A95

1969, Sept. 9 Engr. *Perf. 13*

429 A95 15fr yel grn, brn & red .55 .25

Issued to commemorate the 19th Olympic Games, Mexico City, Oct. 12-27, 1968.

Malagasy House, Highlands — A96

Malagasy Houses: No. 430, Betsileo house, Highlands. No. 431, Tsimihety house, West Coast, horiz. 60fr, Malagasy house, Highlands.

1969-70 Engr. *Perf. 13*

430 A96 20fr bl, ol & ver .25 .25
431 A96 20fr sl, brt grn & red .25 .25
432 A96 40fr blk, bl & dk red .45 .25
433 A96 60fr vio bl, dp grn & brn .75 .30
Nos. 430-433 (4) 1.70 1.05

Issued: 40fr, 60fr, 11/25/69; others, 11/25/70.

Arms Type of 1963-65

1fr, Maintirano. 10fr, Ambalavao. No. 436, Morondava. No. 437, Ambatondrazaka. No. 438, Fenerive-Est. 80fr, Tamatave.

1970-72 Photo. *Perf. 13*

434 A50 1fr multi ('72) .30 .25
435 A50 10fr multi ('72) .50 .25
436 A50 25fr multi ('71) .75 .25
437 A50 25fr multi ('71) .75 .25
438 A50 25fr multi ('72) 1.10 .25
439 A50 80fr pink & multi 1.75 .30
Nos. 434-439 (6) 5.15 1.55

The 10fr, 80fr are dated "1970." No. 437 is dated "1971." Nos. 434, 438 are dated "1972."

Sizes: Nos. 434, 438, 22x37mm; others, 25½x36mm.

Imprints: "S. Gauthier" on Nos. 434, 438; "S. Gauthier Delrieu" on others.

Carnelian — A97

Semi-precious Stones: 12fr, Yellow calcite. 15fr, Quartz. 20fr, Ammonite.

Perf. 12x12½ (5, 20fr), 13 (12, 15fr)

1970-71 Photo.

440 A97 5fr brn, dl rose & yel 4.25 1.00
441 A97 12fr multi ('71) 4.75 1.00
442 A97 15fr multi ('71) 6.25 1.50
443 A97 20fr grn & multi 17.50 2.00
Nos. 440-443 (4) 32.75 5.50

UPU Headquarters Issue
Common Design Type

1970, May 20 Engr. *Perf. 13*

444 CD133 20fr lil rose, brn & ultra .55 .25

UN Emblem and Symbols of Justice A98

1970, June 26 Engr. *Perf. 13*

445 A98 50fr blk, ultra & org .70 .30

25th anniversary of the United Nations.

Fruits of Madagascar — A99

1970, Aug. 18 Photo. *Perf. 13*

446 A99 20fr multi 1.00 .25

Volute Delessertiana — A100

Shells: 10fr, Murex tribulus. 20fr, Spondylus.

1970, Sept. 9 Photo. *Perf. 13*

447 A100 5fr Prus bl & multi .80 .25
448 A100 10fr vio & multi .95 .25
449 A100 20fr multi 2.40 .30
Nos. 447-449 (3) 4.15 .80

Aye-aye — A101

1970, Oct. 7 Photo. *Perf. 12½*

450 A101 20fr multi 2.00 .35

Intl. Conference for Nature Conservation, Tananarive, Oct. 7-10.

Pres. Tsiranana A102

1970, Dec. 30 Photo. *Perf. 12½*

451 A102 30fr grn & lt brn .60 .25

60th birthday of Pres. Philibert Tsiranana.

Tropical Soap Factory, Tananarive A103

Designs: 15fr, Comina chromium smelting plant, Andriamena. 50fr, Textile mill, Majunga.

1971, Apr. 14 Photo. *Perf. 12½x12*

452 A103 5fr multi .30 .25

Engr. *Perf. 13*

453 A103 15fr vio bl, blk & ocher .35 .25

Photo. *Perf. 13*

454 A103 50fr multi .65 .25
Nos. 452-454 (3) 1.30 .75

Economic development.

Globe, Agriculture, Industry, Science A104

1971, Apr. 22 Photo. *Perf. 12½x12*

455 A104 5fr multi .30 .25

Extraordinary meeting of the Council of the C.E.E.-E.A.M.A. (Communauté Economique Européen-Etats Africains et Malgache Associés).

Mobile Rural Post Office A105

1971, May 8 *Perf. 13*

456 A105 25fr multi .60 .25

Stamp Day.

Gen. Charles de Gaulle — A106

1971, June 26 Engr. *Perf. 13*

457 A106 30fr ultra, blk & rose 1.00 .35

In memory of Charles de Gaulle (1890-1970), President of France.

For surcharge see No. B24.

Madagascar Hilton, Tananarive A107

Design: 25fr, Hotel Palm Beach, Nossi-Bé.

1971, July 23 Photo.

458 A107 25fr multi .50 .25

Engr.

459 A107 65fr vio bl, brn & lt grn .85 .30

Trees and Post Horn A108

1971, Aug. 6 Photo. *Perf. 12½x12*
460 A108 3fr red, yel & grn .50 .25

Forest preservation campaign.

House, South West Madagascar — A109

10fr, House from Southern Madagascar.

1971, Nov. 25 *Perf. 13x12½*
461 A109 5fr lt bl & multi .25 .25
462 A109 10fr lt bl & multi .35 .25

Children Playing, and Cattle A110

1971, Dec. 11 Litho. *Perf. 13*
463 A110 50fr grn & multi 1.10 .30

UNICEF, 25th anniv.

Cable-laying Railroad Car, PTT Emblem — A111

1972, Apr. 8 Engr. *Perf. 13*
464 A111 45fr slate grn, red & choc 2.00 .40

Coaxial cable connection between Tananarive and Tamatave.

Philibert Tsiranana Radar Station — A112

1972, Apr. 8 Photo. *Perf. 13½*
465 A112 85fr bl & multi 1.00 .40

A113

Voters and Pres. Tsiranana.

1972, May 1 *Perf. 12½x13*
466 A113 25fr yel & multi .55 .35

Presidential election, Jan. 30, 1972.

Stamp Day — A114

1972, May 30 Photo. *Perf. 12x12½*
467 A114 10fr Mail delivery .60 .25

Emblem and Stamps of Madagascar A115

Stamps shown are #352, 410, 429, 449.

1972, June 26 *Perf. 13*
468 A115 25fr org & multi .50 .25
469 A115 40fr org & multi .60 .30
470 A115 100fr org & multi 1.50 .50
a. Souv. sheet of 3, #468-470 3.50 3.50
Nos. 468-470 (3) 2.60 1.05

2nd Malgache Philatelic Exhibition, Tananarive, June 26-July 9.

Andapa-Sambava Road and Monument — A116

1972, July 6 *Perf. 12½x12*
471 A116 50fr multi .60 .30

Opening of the Andapa-Sambava road.

Diesel Locomotive A117

1972, July 6 Engr. *Perf. 13*
472 A117 100fr multicolored 4.00 .50

Razafindrahety College — A118

1972, Aug. 6
473 A118 10fr choc, bl & red brn .45 .25

Razafindrahety College, Tananarive, sesqui.

Volleyball A119

1972, Aug. 6 Typo. *Perf. 12½x13*
474 A119 12fr orange, blk & brn .60 .25

African volleyball championship.

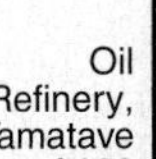

Oil Refinery, Tamatave A120

1972, Sept. 18 Engr. *Perf. 13*
475 A120 2fr bl, bister & slate grn .50 .25

Ravoahangy Andrianavalona Hospital — A121

1972, Oct. 14 Photo. *Perf. 13x12½*
476 A121 6fr multi .45 .25

Plowing A122

1972, Nov. 15 Photo. *Perf. 13½x14*
477 A122 25fr gold & multi .70 .30

Betsimisaraka Costume — A123

Design: 15fr, Merina costume.

1972, Dec. 30 Photo. *Perf. 13x12½*
478 A123 10fr blue & multi .35 .25
479 A123 15fr brown & multi .65 .25

Farmer and Produce — A124

1973, Feb. 6 Photo. *Perf. 13*
480 A124 25fr lt blue & multi .60 .25

10th anniversary of the Malagasy Committee of "Freedom from Hunger Campaign."

For surcharge see No. 499.

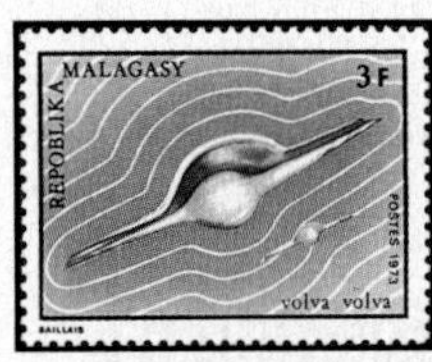

Volva Volva A125

Shells: 10fr, 50fr, Lambis chiragra. 15fr, 40fr, Harpa major. 25fr, Like 3fr.

1973, Apr. 5 Litho. *Perf. 13*
481 A125 3fr olive & multi .25 .25
482 A125 10fr blue grn & multi .45 .25
483 A125 15fr brt blue & multi .70 .25
484 A125 25fr lt blue & multi 1.10 .30
485 A125 40fr multicolored 1.40 .30
486 A125 50fr red lilac & multi 2.10 .40
Nos. 481-486 (6) 6.00 1.75

Tsimandoa Mail Carrier — A126

1973, May 13 Engr. *Perf. 13*
487 A126 50fr ind, ocher & sl grn .75 .30

Stamp Day 1973.

Builders and Map of Africa — A127

1973, May 25 Photo. *Perf. 13*
488 A127 25fr multicolored .60 .25

Organization for African Unity, 10th anniversary.

Campani Chameleon A128

Various Chameleons: 5fr, 40fr, Male nasutus. 10fr, 85fr, Female nasutus. 60fr, Like 1fr.

1973, June 15 Photo. *Perf. 13x12½*
489 A128 1fr dp car & multi .30 .25
490 A128 5fr brown & multi .30 .25
491 A128 10fr green & multi .45 .25
492 A128 40fr red lilac & multi 1.20 .25
493 A128 60fr dk blue & multi 1.75 .40
494 A128 85fr brown & multi 2.50 .60
Nos. 489-494 (6) 6.50 2.00

Lady's Slipper A129

Orchids: 25fr, 40fr, Pitcher plant.

1973, Aug. 6 Photo. *Perf. 12½*
495 A129 10fr multicolored .55 .25
496 A129 25fr rose & multi .75 .30
497 A129 40fr lt blue & multi 1.75 .35
498 A129 100fr multicolored 3.75 .70
Nos. 495-498 (4) 6.80 1.60

No. 480 Surcharged with New Value, 2 Bars, and Overprinted in Ultramarine

"SECHERESSE / SOLIDARITE AFRICAINE"

1973, Aug. 16 *Perf. 13*
499 A124 100fr on 25fr multi 1.40 .50

African solidarity in drought emergency.

African Postal Union Issue
Common Design Type

1973, Sept. 12 Engr. *Perf. 13*
500 CD137 100fr vio, red & slate grn 1.10 .35

Greater Dwarf Lemur
A131

Design: 25fr, Weasel lemur, vert.

1973, Oct. 9 Engr. *Perf. 13*
501 A131 5fr brt green & multi .75 .30
502 A131 25fr ocher & multi 1.75 .60
Nos. 501-502,C117-C118 (4) 9.50 3.20

Lemurs of Madagascar.

No. 389 Surcharged

1974, Feb. 9 Litho. *Perf. 13*
503 A50 25fr on 30fr multi .50 .25

Scouts Helping to Raise Cattle — A132

Design: 15fr, Scouts building house; African Scout emblem.

1974, Feb. 14 Engr. *Perf. 13*
504 A132 4fr blue, slate & emer .25 .25
505 A132 15fr chocolate & multi .30 .25
Nos. 504-505,C122-C123 (4) 4.55 1.85

Malagasy Boy Scouts.

Mother with Children and Clinic — A133

1974, May 24 Photo. *Perf. 13*
506 A133 25fr multicolored .45 .25

World Population Year.

Rainibetsimisaraka — A134

1974, July 26 Photo. *Perf. 13*
507 A134 25fr multicolored .65 .30

In memory of Rainibetsimisaraka, independence leader.

Marble Blocks A135

Design: 25fr, Marble quarry.

1974, Sept. 27 Photo. *Perf. 13*
508 A135 4fr multicolored .80 .25
509 A135 25fr multicolored 2.10 .45

Malagasy marble.

Europafrica Issue

Links, White and Black Faces, Map of Europe and Africa — A136

1974, Oct. 17 Engr. *Perf. 13*
510 A136 150fr dk brown & org 1.75 .60

Grain and Hand A137

1974, Oct. 29
511 A137 80fr light blue & ocher 1.00 .35

World Committee against Hunger.

Tuléar Dog A138

Design: 100fr, Hunting dog.

1974, Nov. 26 Photo. *Perf. 13x13½*
512 A138 50fr multicolored 2.50 .50
513 A138 100fr multicolored 3.50 .90

Malagasy Citizens — A139

1974, Dec. 9 *Perf. 13½x13*
514 A139 5fr blue grn & multi .25 .25
515 A139 10fr multicolored .25 .25
516 A139 20fr yellow grn & multi .35 .25
517 A139 60fr orange & multi .90 .25
Nos. 514-517 (4) 1.75 1.00

Introduction of "Fokonolona" community organization.

Symbols of Development — A140

1974, Dec. 16 Photo. *Perf. 13x13½*
518 A140 25fr ultra & multi .30 .25
519 A140 35fr blue grn & multi .50 .25

National Council for Development.

Woman, Rose, Dove and Emblem — A141

1975, Jan. 21 Engr. *Perf. 13*
520 A141 100fr brown, emer & org 1.10 .40

International Women's Year 1975.

Col. Richard Ratsimandrava — A142

1975, Apr. 25 Photo. *Perf. 13*
521 A142 15fr brown & salmon .25 .25
522 A142 25fr black, bl & brn .35 .25
523 A142 100fr black, lt grn & brn 1.25 .30
Nos. 521-523 (3) 1.85 .80

Ratsimandrava (1933-1975), head of state.

Sofia Bridge A143

1975, May 29 Litho. *Perf. 12½*
524 A143 45fr multicolored .80 .30

Count de Grasse and "Randolph" — A144

Design: 50fr, Marquis de Lafayette, "Lexington" and HMS "Edward."

1975, June 30 Litho. *Perf. 11*
525 A144 40fr multicolored .50 .25
526 A144 50fr multicolored .65 .30
Nos. 525-526,C137-C139 (5) 7.15 2.10

American Bicentennial.

For overprints see Nos. 564-565, C164-C167.

Euphorbia Viguieri A145

Tropical Plants: 25fr, Hibiscus. 30fr, Plumieria rubra acutitolia. 40fr, Pachypodium rosulatum.

1975, Aug. 4 Photo. *Perf. 12½*
527 A145 15fr lemon & multi .25 .25
528 A145 25fr black & multi .45 .25
529 A145 30fr orange & multi .60 .30
530 A145 40fr dk red & multi 1.00 .30
Nos. 527-530,C141 (5) 4.20 2.00

Brown, White, Yellow and Black Hands Holding Globe — A146

1975, Aug. 26 Litho. *Perf. 12*
531 A146 50fr multicolored .70 .25

Namibia Day (independence for South-West Africa.)

Woodpecker — A147

1975, Sept. 16 Litho. *Perf. 14x13½*
532 A147 25fr shown .55 .25
533 A147 40fr Rabbit .85 .25
534 A147 50fr Frog 1.10 .30
535 A147 75fr Tortoise 1.60 .45
Nos. 532-535,C145 (5) 6.00 1.70

International Exposition, Okinawa.

Lily Waterfall A148

Design: 40fr, Lily Waterfall, different view.

1975, Sept. 17 Litho. *Perf. 12½*
536 A148 25fr multicolored .50 .25
537 A148 40fr multicolored .65 .25

4-man Bob Sled — A149

100fr, Ski jump. 140fr, Speed skating.

1975, Nov. 19 Litho. *Perf. 14*
538 A149 75fr multicolored .60 .25
539 A149 100fr multicolored 1.00 .30
540 A149 140fr multicolored 1.50 .40
Nos. 538-540,C149-C150 (5) 7.75 2.15

12th Winter Olympic games, Innsbruck, 1976.

For overprints see Nos. 561-563, C161-C163.

Pirogue A150

Designs: 45fr, Boutre (Arabian coastal vessel).

1975, Nov. 20 Photo. *Perf. 12½*

541 A150 8fr multicolored .50 .25
542 A150 45fr ultra & multi 1.75 .40

Canadian Canoe and Kayak — A151

Design: 50fr, Sprint and Hurdles.

1976, Jan. 21 Litho. *Perf. 14x13½*

543 A151 40fr multicolored .45 .25
544 A151 50fr multicolored .55 .25
Nos. 543-544,C153-C155 (5) 6.65 2.30

21st Summer Olympic games, Montreal.

For overprints see Nos. 571-572, C168-C171.

Count Zeppelin and LZ-127 over Fujiyama, Japan — A152

Designs (Count Zeppelin and LZ-127 over): 50fr, Rio. 75fr, NYC. 100fr, Sphinx.

1976, Mar. 3 *Perf. 11*

545 A152 40fr multicolored .40 .25
546 A152 50fr multicolored .50 .25
547 A152 75fr multicolored 1.00 .30
548 A152 100fr multicolored 1.20 .35
Nos. 545-548,C158-C159 (6) 9.35 2.65

75th anniversary of the Zeppelin.

Worker, Globe, Eye Chart and Eye — A153

1976, Apr. 7 Photo. *Perf. 12½*

549 A153 100fr multicolored 1.40 .50

World Health Day: "Foresight prevents blindness."

Aragonite A154

50fr, Petrified wood. 150fr, Celestite.

1976, May 7 Photo. *Perf. 12½*

550 A154 25fr blue & multi 1.40 .50
551 A154 50fr blue grn & multi 3.50 1.00
552 A154 150fr orange & multi 10.50 2.00
Nos. 550-552 (3) 15.40 3.50

Alexander Graham Bell and First Telephone — A155

50fr, Telephone lines, 1911. 100fr, Central office, 1895. 200fr, Cable ship, 1925. 300fr, Radio telephone. 500fr, Telstar satellite and globe.

1976, May 13 Litho. *Perf. 14*

553 A155 25fr multicolored .25 .25
554 A155 50fr multicolored .45 .25
555 A155 100fr multicolored .75 .30
556 A155 200fr multicolored 1.50 .45
557 A155 300fr multicolored 2.40 .50
Nos. 553-557 (5) 5.35 1.75

Souvenir Sheet

558 A155 500fr multicolored 4.25 1.40

Cent. of 1st telephone call by Alexander Graham Bell, Mar. 10, 1876.

Children with Books A156

Design: 25fr, Children with books, vert.

1976, May 25 Litho.

559 A156 10fr multicolored .25 .25
560 A156 25fr multicolored .50 .25

Books for children.

Nos. 538-540 Overprinted

a. VAINQUEUR ALLEMAGNE FEDERALE
b. VAINQUEUR KARL SCHNABL AUTRICHE
c. VAINQUEUR SHEILA YOUNG ETATS-UNIS

1976, June 17

561 A149 (a) 75fr multi .60 .30
562 A149 (b) 100fr multi 1.00 .45
563 A149 (c) 140fr multi 1.50 .60
Nos. 561-563,C161-C162 (5) 6.80 2.75

12th Winter Olympic games winners.

Nos. 525-526 Overprinted "4 Juillet / 1776-1976"

1976, July 4

564 A144 40fr multicolored .45 .30
565 A144 50fr multicolored .60 .40
Nos. 564-565,C164-C166 (5) 6.80 2.50

American Bicentennial.

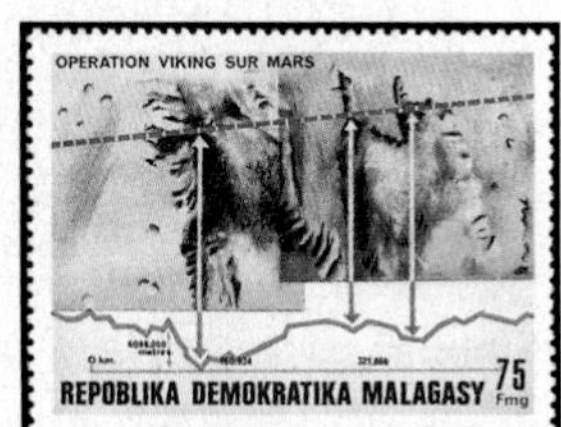

Graph of Projected Landing Spots on Mars — A157

Viking project to Mars: 100fr, Viking probe in flight. 200fr, Viking probe on Mars. 300fr, Viking probe over projected landing spot. 500fr, Viking probe approaching Mars.

1976, July 17 Litho. *Perf. 14*

566 A157 75fr multicolored .45 .25
567 A157 100fr multicolored .75 .30
568 A157 200fr multicolored 1.50 .40
569 A157 300fr multicolored 2.25 .60
Nos. 566-569 (4) 4.95 1.55

Souvenir Sheet

570 A157 500fr multicolored 4.50 1.00

Nos. 543-544 Overprinted

a. A. ROGOV / V. DIBA
b. H. CRAWFORD / J. SCHALLER

1977, Jan.

571 A151 (a) 40fr multi .45 .25
572 A151 (b) 50fr multi .60 .30
Nos. 571-572,C168-C170 (5) 6.80 2.40

21st Summer Olympic games winners.

Rainandriamampandry — A158

Portrait: No. 574, Rabezavana.

1976-77 Litho. *Perf. 12x12½*

573 A158 25fr multicolored .75 .25
574 A158 25fr multicolored .25 .25

Rainandriamampandry was Malagasy Foreign Minister who signed treaties in 1896. Issued: No. 573, 10/15; No. 574, 3/29/77.

"Indian Ocean - Zone of Peace." A159

Design: 60fr, Globe with Africa and Indian Ocean, doves, vert. 160fr, Doves, Indian Ocean on Globe.

Perf. 12½x12, 12x12½

1976, Nov. 18

575 A159 60fr multicolored .60 .25
576 A159 160fr shown 1.40 .50

Coat of Arms — A160

1976, Dec. 30 Litho. *Perf. 12*

577 A160 25fr multicolored .40 .25

Democratic Republic of Malagasy, 1st anniv.

Lt. Albert Randriamaromanana — A161

Portrait: No. 578, Avana Ramanantoanina.

1977, Mar. 29

578 A161 25fr multicolored .30 .25
579 A161 25fr multicolored .30 .25

National Mausoleum — A162

1977, Mar. 29 *Perf. 12½x12*

580 A162 100fr multicolored 1.25 .40

Family A163

1977, Apr. 7 *Perf. 12x12½*

581 A163 5fr yellow & multi .40 .25

World Health Day: Immunization protects the children.

Tananarive Medical School — A164

1977, June 30 Litho. *Perf. 12½x12*

582 A164 250fr multicolored 2.10 .80

80th anniversary of Tananarive Medical School.

Mail Bus — A165

1977, Aug. 18 Litho. *Perf. 12½x12*

583 A165 35fr multicolored .50 .25

Rural mail delivery.

Telegraph Operator — A166

1977, Sept. 13 Litho. ***Perf. 12½x12***
584 A166 15fr multicolored .50 .25

Telegraph service Tananarive-Tamatave, 90th anniv.

Malagasy Art — A167

1977, Sept. 29 ***Perf. 12x12½***
585 A167 10fr multicolored .50 .25

Malagasy Academy, 75th anniversary.

Lenin and Russian Flag — A168

1977, Nov. 7 Litho. ***Perf. 12½x12***
586 A168 25fr multicolored 2.60 .35

60th anniversary of Russian October Revolution.

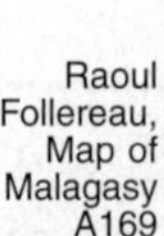

Raoul Follereau, Map of Malagasy A169

1978, Jan. 28 Litho. ***Perf. 12x12½***
587 A169 5fr multicolored 1.75 .30

25th anniversary of Leprosy Day.

Antenna, ITU Emblem A170

1978, May 17 Litho. ***Perf. 12x12½***
588 A170 20fr multicolored .50 .25

10th World Telecommunications Day.

Black and White Men Breaking Chains of Africa — A171

1978, June 22 Photo. ***Perf. 12½x12***
589 A171 60fr multicolored .75 .25

Anti-Apartheid Year.

Boy and Girl, Arch: Pen, Gun and Hoe — A172

1978, July 28 Litho. ***Perf. 12½x12***
590 A172 125fr multicolored 1.25 .40

Youth, the pillar of revolution.

Farm Workers, Factory, Tractor — A173

1978, Aug. 24
591 A173 25fr multicolored .50 .25

Socialist cooperation.

Women — A174

1979, Mar. 8 Litho. ***Perf. 12½x12***
592 A174 40fr multicolored .50 .25

Women, supporters of the revolution.

Children Bringing Gifts — A175

1979, June 1 Litho. ***Perf. 12x12½***
593 A175 10fr multicolored .50 .25

International Year of the Child.

Lemur Macaco A176

Fauna: 25fr, Lemur catta, vert. 1000fr, Foussa.

Perf. 12½x12, 12x12½
1979, July 6 Litho.
594 A176 25fr multi .60 .25
595 A176 125fr multi 2.25 .35
596 A176 1000fr multi 8.25 1.50
Nos. 594-596,C172-C173 (5) 12.75 2.60

Jean Verdi Salomon A177

1979, July 25 ***Perf. 12x12½***
597 A177 25fr multicolored .50 .25

Jean Verdi Salomon (1913-1978), poet.

Talapetraka (Medicinal Plant) — A178

1979, Sept. 27 Litho. ***Perf. 12½***
598 A178 25fr multicolored .75 .25

Map of Magagascar, Dish Antenna — A179

1979, Oct. 12
599 A179 25fr multicolored .50 .25

Stamp Day 1979 A180

1979, Nov. 9
600 A180 500fr multicolored 4.50 1.40

Jet, Map of Africa A181

1979, Dec. 12 ***Perf. 12½***
601 A181 50fr multicolored .75 .25

ASECNA (Air Safety Board), 20th anniversary.

Lenin Addressing Workers in the Winter Palace A182

1980, Apr. 22 Litho. ***Perf. 12x12½***
602 A182 25fr multicolored .70 .25

Lenin's 110th birth anniversary.

Bus and Road in Madagascar Colors A183

1980, June 15 Litho. ***Perf. 12x12½***
603 A183 30fr multicolored .50 .25

Socialist Revolution, 5th anniversary.

Flag and Map under Sun — A184

1980, June 26 ***Perf. 12½x12***
604 A184 75fr multicolored .75 .25

Independence, 20th anniversary.

Armed Forces Day — A185

1980, Aug. Litho. ***Perf. 12½x12***
605 A185 50fr multicolored .60 .25

Dr. Joseph Raseta (1886-1979) A186

1980, Oct. 15 Litho. ***Perf. 12x12½***
606 A186 30fr multicolored .50 .25

Anatirova Temple Centenary — A187

1980, Nov. 27 Litho. ***Perf. 12½x12***
607 A187 30fr multicolored .50 .25

Hurdles, Olympic Torch, Moscow '80 Emblem — A188

1980, Dec. 29
608 A188 30fr shown .45 .25
609 A188 75fr Boxing .85 .30
Nos. 608-609,C175-C176 (4) 6.95 2.75

22nd Summer Olympic Games, Moscow, July 19-Aug. 3.

Democratic Republic of Madagascar, 5th Anniversary A189

1980, Dec. 30 ***Perf. 12x12½***
610 A189 30fr multicolored .50 .25

Downhill Skiing — A190

1981, Jan. 26 Litho. ***Perf. 12½x12***
611 A190 175fr multicolored 1.60 .60

13th Winter Olympic Games, Lake Placid, Feb. 12-24, 1980.

Angraecum Leonis A191

80fr, Angraecum ramosum. 170fr, Angraecum sesquipedale.

1981, Mar. 23 Litho. ***Perf. 11½***
612 A191 5fr shown .40 .25
613 A191 80fr multicolored 1.40 .30
614 A191 170fr multicolored 2.25 .65
Nos. 612-614 (3) 4.05 1.20

For surcharge, see No. 1474B.

Intl. Year of the Disabled — A192

1981, June 12 Litho. ***Perf. 12***
615 A192 25fr Student at desk .35 .25
616 A192 80fr Carpenter .75 .30

A193

1981, July 10 Litho. ***Perf. 12½x12***
617 A193 15fr multicolored .25 .25
618 A193 45fr multicolored .55 .25

13th World Telecommunications Day.

Neil Armstrong on Moon (Apollo 11) — A194

Space Anniversaries: 30fr, Valentina Tereshkova. 90fr, Yuri Gagarin.

1981, July 23 ***Perf. 11½***
619 A194 30fr multicolored .30 .25
620 A194 80fr shown .80 .25
621 A194 90fr multicolored .90 .25
Nos. 619-621 (3) 2.00 .75

Brother Raphael Louis Rafiringa (1854-1919) A195

1981, Aug. 10 Litho. ***Perf. 12***
622 A195 30fr multi .50 .25

World Literacy Day — A196

1981, Sept. 8
623 A196 30fr multi .50 .25

World Food Day — A197

1981, Oct. 16 Litho. ***Perf. 12x12½***
624 A197 200fr multi 1.90 .60

See No. 635.

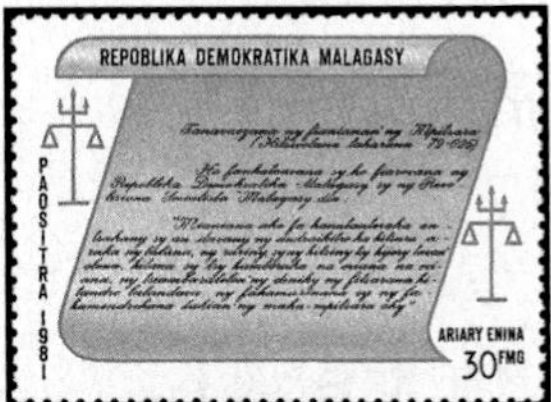
Oaths of Magistracy Renewal — A198

1981, Oct. 30 ***Perf. 12½x12***
625 A198 30fr blk & lil rose .50 .25

Dove, by Pablo Picasso (1881-1973) — A199

1981, Nov. 18 Photo. ***Perf. 11½x12***
626 A199 80fr multi 1.00 .30

20th Anniv. of UPU Membership — A200

Design: Nos. C76, C77, emblem.

1981, Nov. 19 Litho. ***Perf. 12***
627 A200 5fr multi .25 .25
628 A200 30fr multi .45 .25

TB Bacillus Centenary A201

1982, June 21 Litho. ***Perf. 12***
629 A201 30fr multi .60 .25

Jeannette Mpihira (1903-1981), Actress and Singer — A202

1982, June 24 ***Perf. 12½***
630 A202 30fr multi .50 .25

Haliaeetus Vociferoides A203

25fr, Vanga curvirostris, horiz. 30fr, Leptostomus discolor, horiz.

1982, July
631 A203 25fr multi 1.10 .25
632 A203 30fr multi 1.40 .25
633 A203 200fr shown 4.75 .70
Nos. 631-633 (3) 7.25 1.20

Pierre Louis Boiteau (1911-1980), Educator A204

1982, Sept. 13
634 A204 30fr multi .50 .25

World Food Day Type of 1981

1982, Oct. 16 ***Perf. 12x12½***
635 A197 80fr multi .75 .25

No. 635 is overprinted "EFA POLO ARIARY" on the text.

25th Anniv. of Launching of Sputnik I — A205

10fr, Sputnik I. 80fr, Yuri Gagarin, Vostok I. 100fr, Soyuz-Salyut.

1982, Oct. 4 Litho. ***Perf. 12***
636 A205 10fr mulitcolored .25 .25
637 A205 80fr multicolored .65 .25
638 A205 100fr multicolored .85 .30
Nos. 636-638 (3) 1.75 .80

1982 World Cup — A206

Designs: Various soccer players.

1982, Oct. 14 ***Perf. 12x12½***
639 A206 30fr multi .30 .25
640 A206 40fr multi .40 .25
641 A206 80fr multi .80 .25
Nos. 639-641 (3) 1.50 .75

Souvenir Sheet

Perf. 11½x12½
642 A206 450fr multi 3.75 1.60

Scene at a Bar, by Edouard Manet (1832-1883) — A207

30fr, Lady in a White Dress. 170fr, Portrait of Mallarme.
400fr, The Fifer, vert.

1982, Nov. 25 ***Perf. 12½x12***

643 A207 5fr shown .55 .25
644 A207 30fr multicolored .75 .30
645 A207 170fr multicolored 3.50 .70
Nos. 643-645 (3) 4.80 1.25

Souvenir Sheet

Perf. 11½x12½

646 A207 400fr multi 8.00 2.00

For surcharge, see No. 1475B.

Local Fish — A208

5fr, Lutianus sebae. 20fr, Istiophorus platypterus. 30fr, Pterois volitans. 50fr, Thunnus albacares. 200fr, Epinephelus fasciatus.
450fr, Latimeria chalumnae.

1982, Dec. 14 ***Perf. 11½***

647 A208 5fr multi .30 .25
648 A208 20fr multi .30 .25
649 A208 30fr multi .55 .25
650 A208 50fr multi 1.00 .25
651 A208 200fr multi 3.00 .60
Nos. 647-651 (5) 5.15 1.60

Souvenir Sheet

Perf. 12½x12

652 A208 450fr multi 5.00 2.00

No. 652 contains one stamp 38x26mm.

Fort Mahavelona Ruins — A209

30fr, Ramena Beach. 400fr, Flowering jacaranda trees.

1982, Dec. 22 ***Perf. 12½x12***

653 A209 10fr shown .25 .25
654 A209 30fr multicolored .25 .25
655 A209 400fr multicolored 3.00 1.00
Nos. 653-655 (3) 3.50 1.50

60th Anniv. of USSR — A210

1982, Dec. 29

656 A210 10fr Tractors .25 .25
657 A210 15fr Pylon .25 .25
658 A210 30fr Kremlin, Lenin .25 .25
659 A210 150fr Arms 1.25 .50
Nos. 656-659 (4) 2.00 1.25

World Communications Year — A211

80fr, Stylized figures holding wheel.

1983, May 17 **Litho.** ***Perf. 12***

660 A211 30fr multi .30 .25
661 A211 80fr multi .95 .30

Organization of African Unity, 20th Anniv. A212

1983, May 25 **Litho.** ***Perf. 12***

662 A212 30fr multi .50 .25

Henri Douzon, Lawyer and Patriot — A213

1983, June 27 **Litho.** ***Perf. 12***

663 A213 30fr multi .50 .25

Souvenir Sheet

Manned Flight Bicentenary — A214

500fr, Montgolfiere balloon.

1983, July 20 **Litho.** ***Perf. 12***

664 A214 500fr multicolored 5.00 2.00

Souvenir Sheet

Raphael, 500th Birth Anniv. — A215

500fr, The Madonna Connestable.

1983, Aug. 10 **Litho.** ***Perf. 12***

665 A215 500fr multi 5.00 2.00

Lemur — A216

Various lemurs: No. 666, Daubentonia madagascariensis. No. 667, Microcebus murinus. No. 668, Lemur variegatus, vert. No. 669, Propithecus verreauxi, vert. No. 670, Indri indri.
No. 671, Perodicticus potto, vert.

Perf. 12½x12, 12x12½

1983, Dec. 6 **Litho.**

666 A216 30fr multicolored .55 .25
667 A216 30fr multicolored .55 .25
668 A216 30fr multicolored .55 .25
669 A216 30fr multicolored .55 .25
670 A216 200fr multicolored 3.50 .80
Nos. 666-670 (5) 5.70 1.80

Souvenir Sheet

671 A216 500fr multicolored 6.50 2.00

1984 Winter Olympics A217

1984, Jan. 20 **Litho.** ***Perf. 11½***

672 A217 20fr Ski jumping .25 .25
673 A217 30fr Speed skating .25 .25
674 A217 30fr Downhill skiing .25 .25
675 A217 30fr Hockey .25 .25
676 A217 200fr Figure skating 2.00 .60
Nos. 672-676 (5) 3.00 1.60

Souvenir Sheet

677 A217 500fr Cross-country skiing 4.50 2.00

No. 677 contains one stamp 48x32mm.

Vintage Cars — A218

1984, Jan. 27 ***Perf. 12½x12***

678 A218 15fr Renault, 1907 .25 .25
679 A218 30fr Benz, 1896 .30 .25
680 A218 30fr Baker, 1901 .30 .25
681 A218 30fr Blake, 1901 .30 .25
682 A218 200fr FIAL, 1908 2.40 .60
Nos. 678-682 (5) 3.55 1.60

Souvenir Sheet

Perf. 12½x11½

683 A218 450fr Russo-Baltique, 1909 4.50 2.00

Pastor Ravelojaona (1879-1956), Encyclopedist A219

1984, Feb. 14 ***Perf. 12x12½***

684 A219 30fr multi .50 .25

See No. 704.

Madonna and Child, by Correggio (1489-1534) A220

Various Correggio paintings.

1984, May 5 **Litho.** ***Perf. 12x12½***

685 A220 5fr multi .25 .25
686 A220 20fr multi .25 .25
687 A220 30fr multi .35 .25
688 A220 80fr multi .75 .30
689 A220 200fr multi 2.10 .60
Nos. 685-689 (5) 3.70 1.65

Souvenir Sheet

690 A220 400fr multi 5.50 2.00

World Chess Federation, 60th Anniv. — A221

No. 691, Paris landmarks. No. 692, Wilhelm Steinitz. No. 693, Champion, cup. No. 694, Vera Menchik. No. 695, Champion, cup, diff.
No. 696, Children playing chess.

1984, July 27

691 A221 5fr multi .25 .25
692 A221 20fr multi .35 .25
693 A221 30fr multi .55 .25
694 A221 30fr multi .55 .25
695 A221 215fr multi 3.25 .80
Nos. 691-695 (5) 4.95 1.80

Souvenir Sheet

696 A221 400fr multi 6.00 2.00

1984 Summer Olympics — A222

1984, Aug. 10

697 A222 100fr Soccer 1.00 .35

Butterflies A223

No. 698, Eudaphaenura splendens. No. 699, Othreis boseae. No. 700, Pharmacophagus antenor. No. 701, Acraea hova. No. 702, Epicausis smithii.
400fr, Papilio delandii.

1984, Aug. 30 **Litho.** ***Perf. 11½***

698 A223 15fr multicolored .60 .25
699 A223 50fr multicolored 1.25 .25
700 A223 50fr multicolored 1.25 .25
701 A223 50fr multicolored 1.25 .25
702 A223 200fr multicolored 4.50 .65
Nos. 698-702 (5) 8.85 1.65

Miniature Sheet

Perf. 11½x12½

703 A223 400fr multicolored 5.50 2.00

No. 703 contains one stamp 37x52mm.

Famous People Type

Jean Ralaimongo (1884-1944).

1984, Oct. 4 *Perf. 12x12½*
704 A219 50fr Portrait .60 .25

Children's Rights A225

1984, Nov. 20 Litho. *Perf. 12½x12*
705 A225 50fr Youths in school bag .50 .25

Malagasy Orchids — A226

20fr, Disa incarnata. 235fr, Eulophiella roempleriana.
400fr, Gastrorchis tuberculosa.

1984, Nov. 20 Litho. *Perf. 12*
706 A226 20fr multi .30 .25
707 A226 235fr multi 3.25 .70
Nos. 706-707,C180-C182 (5) 6.55 1.70

Miniature Sheet

Perf. 12x12½

708 A226 400fr multi 7.50 2.00

No. 708 contains one stamp 30x42mm.

Cotton Seminar, UN Trade and Development Conference A227

1984, Dec. 15 Litho. *Perf. 13x12½*
709 A227 100fr UN emblem, cotton bolls 1.00 .30

Malagasy Language Bible, 150th Anniv. A228

1985, Feb. 11 Litho. *Perf. 12½x12*
710 A228 50fr multi .50 .25

1985 Agricultural Census — A229

1985, Feb. 21 Litho. *Perf. 12x12½*
711 A229 50fr Census taker, farmer .50 .25

Allied Defeat of Nazi Germany, 40th Anniv. — A230

20fr, Russian flag-raising, Berlin, 1945. 50fr, Normandy-Niemen squadron shooting down German fighter planes. No. 714, Soviet Victory Parade, Red Square, Moscow. No. 715, Victorious French troops marching through Arc de Triomphe, vert.

1985 *Perf. 12½x12, 12x12½*
712 A230 20fr multi .30 .25
713 A230 50fr multi .30 .35
714 A230 100fr multi .90 .35
715 A230 100fr multi 3.00 .70
Nos. 712-715 (4) 4.50 1.65

Issue dates: Nos. 712-714, 5/9; No. 715, Oct.

Cats and Dogs A231

1985, Apr. 25 *Perf. 12x12½, 12½x12*
716 A231 20fr Siamese .30 .25
717 A231 20fr Bichon .30 .25
718 A231 50fr Abyssinian, vert. .75 .25
719 A231 100fr Cocker spaniel, vert. 1.40 .35
720 A231 235fr Poodle 3.50 .80
Nos. 716-720 (5) 6.25 1.90

Souvenir Sheet

721 A231 400fr Kitten 6.00 2.00

No. 721 contains one stamp 42x30mm, perf. 12½x12.

Gymnastic Event, Natl. Stadium, Atananarivo — A232

1985, July 9 *Perf. 12½x12*
722 A232 50fr multi .45 .25

Natl. Socialist Revolution, 10th anniv.

Commemorative Medal, Memorial Stele — A233

1985, July 9
723 A233 50fr multi 1.25 .25

Independence, 25th anniv.

Intl. Youth Year — A234

1985, Sept. 18 *Perf. 12*
724 A234 100fr Emblem, map 1.00 .25

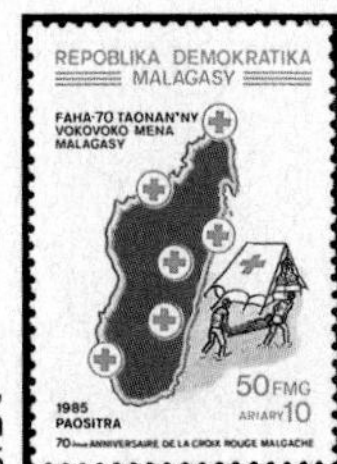

Natl. Red Cross, 70th Anniv. — A235

1985, Oct. 3 *Perf. 12x12½*
725 A235 50fr multi .90 .25

Indira Gandhi — A236

1985, Oct. 31 *Perf. 13½*
726 A236 100fr multi 1.25 .35

22nd World Youth and Student's Festival, Moscow — A237

1985, Nov. *Perf. 12*
727 A237 50fr multi .50 .25

Rouen Cathedral at Night, by Monet — A238

Impressionist paintings: No. 729, View of Sea at Sainte-Marie, by van Gogh, horiz. 45fr, Young Women in Black, by Renoir. 50fr, The Red Vineyard at Arles, by van Gogh, horiz. 100fr, Boulevard des Capucines in Paris, by Monet, horiz. 400fr, In the Garden, by Renoir.

1985, Oct. 25 Litho. *Perf. 12*
728 A238 20fr multi .50 .25
729 A238 20fr multi .50 .25
730 A238 45fr multi .90 .25
731 A238 50fr multi 1.10 .25
732 A238 100fr multi 2.40 .50
Nos. 728-732 (5) 5.40 1.50

Souvenir Sheet

Perf. 12x12½

733 A238 400fr multi 6.00 2.75

No. 733 contains one 30x42mm stamp.

UN, 40th Aniv. — A239

1985, Oct. 31 *Perf. 12*
734 A239 100fr multi 1.00 .30

Orchids A240

No. 735, Aeranthes grandiflora, vert. No. 736, Angraecum magdalanae. No. 737, Aerangis stylosa, vert. No. 738, Angraecum eburneum longicalcar, vert. No. 739, Angraecum sesquipedale, vert.
No. 740, Angraecum aburneum superbum, vert.

1985, Nov. 8
735 A240 20fr multi 1.00 .25
736 A240 45fr multi 1.50 .25
737 A240 50fr multi 1.75 .30
738 A240 100fr multi 3.25 .50
739 A240 100fr multi 3.25 .50
Nos. 735-739 (5) 10.75 1.80

Souvenir Sheet

Perf. 12x12½

740 A240 400fr multi 8.00 2.50

No. 740 contains one 30x42mm stamp.

INTERCOSMOS — A241

Cosmonauts, rockets, satellites, probes and natl. flags of: No. 741, USSR, Czechoslovakia. No. 742, Soyuz-Apollo emblem. No. 743, USSR, India. No. 744, USSR, Cuba. No. 745, USSR, France.
No. 746, Halley's Comet, probe.

1985, Nov. *Perf. 12x12½*
741 A241 20fr multicolored .25 .25
742 A241 20fr multicolored .25 .25
743 A241 50fr multicolored .55 .25
744 A241 100fr multicolored 1.00 .30
745 A241 200fr multicolored 1.90 .65
Nos. 741-745 (5) 3.95 1.70

Souvenir Sheet

746 A241 400fr multicolored 5.50 1.75

No. 746 contains one stamp 42x30mm.

Democratic Republic, 10th Anniv. — A242

1985, Dec. 30 Litho. *Perf. 12½x12*
747 A242 50fr Industrial symbols .45 .25

Natl. Insurance and Securities Co. (ARO), 10th Anniv. — A243

1986, Jan. 20 *Perf. 12x12½*
748 A243 50fr dk brn, yel org & gray brn .45 .25

Paintings in the Tretyakov Gallery, Moscow — A244

Designs: 20fr, Still-life with Flowers and Fruit, 1839, by I. Chroutzky. No. 750, Portrait of Alexander Pushkin, 1827, by O. Kiprenski, vert. No. 751, Portrait of an Unknown Woman, 1883, by I. Kramskoi. No. 752, The Crows Have Returned, 1872, by A. Sakrassov, vert. 100fr, March, 1895, by I. Levitan. 450fr, Portrait of Pavel Tretyakov, 1883, by I. Repin, vert.

Perf. 12½x12, 12x12½

1986, Apr. 26 **Litho.**

749 A244 20fr multi .25 .25
750 A244 50fr multi .80 .25
751 A244 50fr multi .80 .25
752 A244 50fr multi .80 .25
753 A244 100fr multi 2.25 .40
Nos. 749-753 (5) 4.90 1.40

Souvenir Sheet

754 A244 450fr multi 4.50 2.00

1986 World Cup Soccer Championships, Mexico — A245

1986, May 31 ***Perf. 13½***

755 A245 150fr multi 1.40 .45

Paintings in Russian Museums — A246

No. 756, David and Urie, by Rembrandt, vert. No. 757, Danae, by Rembrandt. No. 758, Portrait of the Nurse of the Infant Isabella, by Rubens, vert. No. 759, The Alliance of Earth and Water, by Rubens, vert. No. 760, Portrait of an Old Man in Red, by Rembrandt. No. 761, The Holy Family, by Raphael.

Perf. 12x12½, 12½x12

1986, Mar. 24 **Litho.**

756 A246 20fr multi .25 .25
757 A246 50fr multi .70 .25
758 A246 50fr multi .70 .25
759 A246 50fr multi .70 .25
760 A246 50fr multi .75 .25
Nos. 756-760 (5) 3.10 1.25

Souvenir Sheet

Perf. 11½x12½

761 A246 450fr multi 3.50 2.50

UN Child Survival Campaign A247

1986, June 1 **Litho.** ***Perf. 12x12½***

762 A247 60fr multi .80 .25

A248

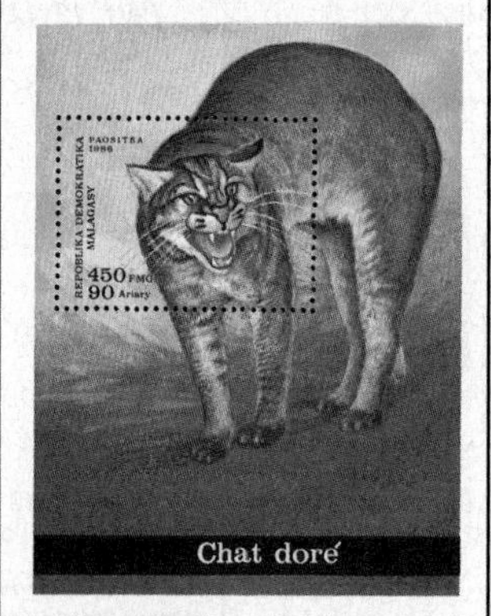

Wildcats — A249

1986, July 17

763 A248 10fr Sable .25 .25
764 A248 10fr Chaus .25 .25
765 A248 60fr Serval .70 .25
766 A248 60fr Caracal .70 .25
767 A248 60fr Bengal .70 .25
Nos. 763-767 (5) 2.60 1.25

Souvenir Sheet

Perf. 12½x12

768 A249 450fr Golden 4.75 2.00

Intl. Peace Year A249a

150fr, Hemispheres, emblem, vert.

1986, Sept. 12 ***Perf. 12***

769 A249a 60fr shown .55 .25
770 A249a 150fr multicolored 1.25 .40

World Post Day — A250

1986, Oct. 9 **Litho.** ***Perf. 13x12½***

771 A250 60fr multi .60 .25
772 A250 150fr multi 1.40 .40

No. 772 is airmail.

A251

Birds — A252

No. 773, Xenopirostris daimi, vert. No. 774, Falculea palliata. No. 775, Coua gigas. No. 776, Coua cristata. No. 777, Cianolanius madagascariensis, vert.
450fr, Bubulcus ibis ibis.

Perf. 12x12½, 12½x12

1986, Dec. 23 **Litho.**

773 A251 60fr multicolored .80 .25
774 A251 60fr multicolored .80 .25
775 A251 60fr multicolored .80 .25
776 A251 60fr multicolored .80 .25
777 A251 60fr multicolored .80 .25
Nos. 773-777 (5) 4.00 1.25

Souvenir Sheet

778 A252 450fr multi 6.00 2.00

A253

Endangered Species — A254

No. 779, Lophotibis cristata, vert. No. 780, Coracopsis nigra. No. 781, Crocodylus niloticus. No. 782, Geochelone yniphora.
450fr, Centropus toulou, vert.

Perf. 12x12½, 12½x12

1987, Mar. 13 **Litho.**

779 A253 60fr multicolored .90 .25
780 A253 60fr multicolored .90 .25
781 A254 60fr multicolored .90 .25
782 A254 60fr multicolored .90 .25
Nos. 779-782 (4) 3.60 1.00

Souvenir Sheet

783 A253 450fr multicolored 5.50 2.00

Anti-Colonial Revolt, 40th Anniv. — A255

A256

1987, Mar. 29 ***Perf. 12***

784 A255 60fr multicolored .50 .25
785 A256 60fr multicolored .50 .25

1st Games of Indian Ocean Towns A257

1987, Apr. 15 ***Perf. 13½***

786 A257 60fr multicolored .55 .25
787 A257 150fr multicolored 1.25 .40

Le Sarimanok — A258

1987, Apr. 15

788 A258 60fr Port side .60 .25
789 A258 150fr Starboard side 1.40 .40

African and Madagascar Coffee Organization, 25th Anniv. — A259

1987, Apr. 24 **Litho.** ***Perf. 12***

790 A259 60fr Coffee plant .60 .25
791 A259 150fr Map 1.50 .40

Halley's Comet — A260

Space probes: 60fr, Giotto, ESA. 150fr, Vega 1, Russia. 250fr, Vega 2, Russia. 350fr, Planet-A1, Japan. 400fr, Planet-A2, Japan. 450fr, ICE, US.
600fr, Halley, Giotto.

1987, May 13 ***Perf. 13½***

792 A260 60fr multi .40 .25
793 A260 150fr multi .90 .25
794 A260 250fr multi 1.75 .40
795 A260 350fr multi 2.50 .60
796 A260 400fr multi 2.75 .65
797 A260 450fr multi 3.25 .70
Nos. 792-797 (6) 11.55 2.85

Souvenir Sheet

798 A260 600fr multi 4.50 1.00

Litho. & Embossed 'Gold Foil' Stamps
These stamps generally are of a different design format than the rest of the issue. Since there is a commemorative inscription tying them to the issue a separate illustration is not being shown.

1988 Calgary Winter Olympics — A261

Men's Downhill — A262

No. 799, Biathlon. No. 801, Luge. No. 802, Speed skating. No 803, Hockey. No. 804, Pairs figure skating. No. 804A, Speed skating.
No. 805A, Slalom skiing.

1987, May 13

799	A261	60fr multi	.40	.25
800	A261	150fr shown	.90	.25
801	A261	250fr multi	1.75	.40
802	A261	350fr multi	2.50	.60
803	A261	400fr multi	2.75	.65
804	A261	450fr multi	3.25	.70
		Nos. 799-804 (6)	11.55	2.85

Litho. & Embossed

804A A261 1500fr multi 10.00

Souvenir Sheets

Litho.

805 A262 600fr shown 4.75 1.25

Litho. & Embossed

805A A262 1500fr multi 7.50

No. 804A exists in souvenir sheet of 1. Value, $40.

Jean-Joseph Rabearivelo (d. 1937), Poet — A263

1987, June 22 *Perf. 13½*

806 A263 60fr multi .50 .25

1992 Summer Olympics, Barcelona — A264

Athletes, emblem and art or architecture: 60fr, Equestrian, and the Harlequin, by Picasso. 150fr, Weight lifting, church. 250fr, Hurdles, Canaletas Fountain. 350fr, High jump, amusement park. 400fr, Men's gymnastics, abbey. 450fr, Rhythmic gymnastics, Arc de Triomphe. 600fr, Equestrian, Columbus monument.

1987, Oct. 7 **Litho.** *Perf. 13½*

807	A264	60fr multi	.25	.25
808	A264	150fr multi	.80	.25
809	A264	250fr multi	1.40	.40
810	A264	350fr multi	2.00	.60
811	A264	400fr multi	2.25	.65
812	A264	450fr multi	2.50	.70
		Nos. 807-812 (6)	9.20	2.85

Souvenir Sheet

813 A264 600fr multi 3.75 1.25

Nos. 811-813 are airmail.

A265

Discovery of America, 500th Anniv. (in 1992) — A266

Anniv. emblem and: 60fr, Bartolomeu Dias (c. 1450-1500), Portuguese navigator, departure from De Palos, 1492. 150fr, Henry the Navigator (1394-1460), prince of Portugal, Samana Cay. 250fr, A. De Marchena landing, 1492. 350fr, Paolo Toscanelli dal Pozzo (1397-1482), Italian physician and cosmographer, La Navidad Fort. 400fr, Queen Isabella I, Barcelona, 1493. 450fr, Christopher Columbus, the Nina. 600fr, Landing in New World, 1492.

1987, Sept. 24 **Litho.** *Perf. 13½*

814	A265	60fr multi	.30	.25
815	A265	150fr multi	.80	.30
816	A265	250fr multi	1.25	.55
817	A265	350fr multi	1.90	.85
818	A265	400fr multi	2.25	1.00
819	A265	450fr multi	2.50	1.10
		Nos. 814-819 (6)	9.00	4.05

Souvenir Sheet

820 A266 600fr multi 4.00 1.50

A267

1987, July 27 *Perf. 12½x12*

821 A267 60fr multicolored .50 .25

Natl. telecommunications research laboratory.

A268

1987, Aug. 14

822 A268 60fr lt blue, blk & brt ultra .50 .25

Rafaravavy Rasalama (d. 1837), Christian martyr.

Antananarivo-Tamatave Telegraph Link, Cent. — A269

1987, Sept. 15 *Perf. 12x12½*

823 A269 60fr multicolored .50 .25

Pasteur Institute, Paris, Cent. A270

1987, Oct. 26 *Perf. 13½*

824 A270 250fr multicolored 1.25 .50

City of Berlin, 750th Anniv. — A271

Design: Anniv. emblem, television tower and the Interhotel in East Berlin.

1987, Oct. 18 **Litho.** *Perf. 12½x12*

825 A271 150fr multicolored .50 .30

Schools Festival A272

1987, Oct. 23 *Perf. 12x12½*

826 A272 60fr multicolored .50 .25

Paintings in the Pushkin Museum, Moscow — A273

Designs: 10fr, After the Shipwreck (1847), by Eugene Delacroix (1798-1863). No. 828, Still-life with Swan (c. 1620), by Frans Snyders (1579-1647). No. 829, Jupiter and Callisto (1744), by Francois Boucher (1703-1770), vert. No. 830, Chalet in the Mountains (1874), by Jean Desire Gustav Courbet (1819-1877). 150fr, At the Market (1564), by Joachim Bueckelaer. 1000fr, Minerva (1560), by Paolo Veronese (1528-1588), vert.

Perf. 12½x12, 12x12½

1987, Nov. 10

827	A273	10fr multi	.55	.25
828	A273	60fr multi	.70	.25
829	A273	60fr multi	.70	.25
830	A273	60fr multi	.70	.25
831	A273	150fr multi	1.40	.25
		Nos. 827-831 (5)	4.05	1.25

Souvenir Sheet

832 A273 1000fr multi 7.00 2.75

Pan-African Telecommunications Union, 10th Anniv. — A274

1987, Dec. 28 *Perf. 13x12½*

833 A274 250fr multicolored .60 .45

Intl. Year of Shelter for the Homeless A275

250fr, Family in shelter, rain, vert.

1988, Feb. 15 **Litho.** *Perf. 12*

834 A275 80fr shown .25 .25
835 A275 250fr multicolored .60 .25

Fauna A276

Designs: 60fr, Hapalemur simus. 150fr, Propithecus diadema diadema. 250fr, Indri indri. 350fr, Varecia variegata variegata. 550fr, Madagascar young heron. No. 841, Nossi-Be chameleon. No. 842, Uratelornis (bird).

1988, Apr. 18 **Litho.** *Perf. 13½*

836	A276	60fr multicolored	1.75	.75
837	A276	150fr multicolored	2.25	.75
838	A276	250fr multicolored	3.25	1.00
839	A276	350fr multicolored	5.00	1.25
840	A276	550fr multicolored	1.50	.60
841	A276	1500fr multicolored	3.50	1.60
		Nos. 836-841 (6)	17.25	5.95

Souvenir Sheet

842 A276 1500fr multicolored 6.50 6.50

Conservation and service organization emblems: World Wildlife Fund (60fr, 150fr, 250fr and 350fr); Rotary Intl. (550fr and No. 842); and Scouting trefoil (No. 841).

Nos. 840-841 exist in souvenir sheet of 2.

For overprints see Nos. 1134, 1154.

October Revolution, Russia, 70th Anniv. A277

No. 843, Lenin. No. 844, Revolutionaries. No. 845, Lenin, revolutionaries.

1988, Mar. 7 **Litho.** *Perf. 12x12½*

843	A277	60fr multi	.60	.25
844	A277	60fr multi	.60	.25
845	A277	150fr multi	1.25	.25
		Nos. 843-845 (3)	2.45	.75

1988 Winter Olympics, Calgary A278

No. 846, Pairs figure skating. No. 847, Slalom. No. 848, Speed skating. No. 849, Cross-country skiing. No. 850, Ice hockey.
No. 851, Ski jumping.

1988, May 11 *Perf. 11½*

846	A278	20fr multicolored	.25	.25
847	A278	60fr multicolored	.25	.25
848	A278	60fr multicolored	.25	.25
849	A278	100fr multicolored	.30	.25
850	A278	250fr multicolored	.70	.30
		Nos. 846-850 (5)	1.75	1.30

Souvenir Sheet

851 A278 800fr multicolored 2.50 1.75

Discovery of Radium by Pierre and Marie Curie, 90th Anniv. A279

1988, July 14 **Litho.** ***Perf. 12***

852 A279 150fr blk & rose lil .50 .25

OAU, 25th Anniv. A280

1988, May 25 **Litho.** ***Perf. 13***

853 A280 80fr multi .50 .25

Natl. Telecommunications and Posts Institute, 20th Anniv. — A281

1988, June 22 ***Perf. 13½***

854 A281 80fr multi .50 .25

Saint-Michel College, Cent. — A282

1988, July 9

855 A282 250fr multi .55 .30

Alma-Ata Declaration, 10th Anniv. — A283

1988, Aug. 11 **Litho.** ***Perf. 12***

856 A283 60fr multi .50 .25

WHO, 40th Anniv. — A284

1988, Aug. 11

857 A284 150fr multi .50 .25

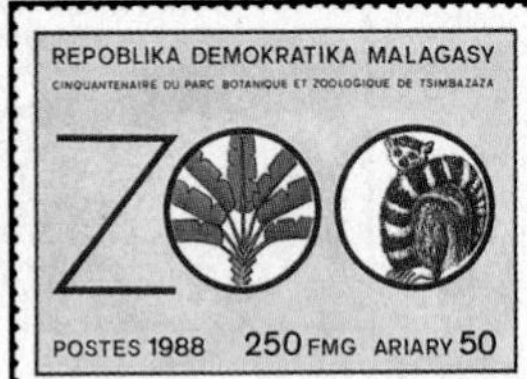

Tsimbazaza Botanical and Zoological Park, 150th Anniv. — A285

20fr, Lemur habitat. 80fr, Lemur and young. 1000fr, Lemur and mate.

Perf. 12x12½, 12½x12

1988, Aug. 22

858	A285	20fr multi	.25	.25
859	A285	80fr multi	.45	.25
860	A285	250fr shown	1.10	.40
		Nos. 858-860 (3)	1.80	.90

Souvenir Sheet

861 A285 1000fr multi 3.50 2.25

Size of No. 859: 25x37mm.

Boy Scouts Studying Birds and Butterflies A286

Designs: 80fr, Upupa epops maginata, Coua caerulea and scout photographing bird. 250fr, Chrysiridia croesus and comparing butterfly to a sketch. 270fr, Nelicurvius nelicourvi, Foudia omissa and constructing bird feeder. 350fr, Papilio dardanus and studying butterflies with magnifying glass. 550fr, Coua critata and tagging bird. No. 867, Argema mittrei and writing observations. No. 868, Merops superciliosus and recording bird calls. No. 868A, Euchloron megaera. No. 868B, Rhynchee.

1988, Sept. 29

862	A286	80fr multi	.25	.25
863	A286	250fr multi	.55	.30
864	A286	270fr multi	.60	.30
865	A286	350fr multi	.80	.40
866	A286	550fr multi	1.25	.60
867	A286	1500fr multi	3.75	1.60
		Nos. 862-867 (6)	7.20	3.45

Souvenir Sheet

868 A286 1500fr multi 3.50 2.25

Litho. & Embossed

Perf. 13½

868A A286 5000fr gold & multi 8.00

Souvenir Sheet

868B A286 5000fr gold & multi 8.00

No. 868 contains one stamp 36x51mm. Nos. 868A-868B dated 1989. Nos. 868A-868B exist imperf.

Composers and Entertainers A287

Designs: 80fr, German-made clavier and Carl Philipp Emanuel Bach (1714-1788), organist and composer. 250fr, Piano and Franz Peter Schubert (1797-1828), Austrian composer. 270fr, Scene from opera Carmen, 1875, and Georges Bizet (1838-1875), French composer. 350fr, Scene from opera Pelleas et Melisande, 1902, and Claude Debussy (1862-1918), French composer. 550fr, George Gershwin (1898-1937), American composer. No. 874, Elvis Presley (1935-1977), American entertainer. No. 875, Rimsky-Korsakov (1844-1908), Russian composer, and Le Coq d'Or from the opera of the same name.

1988, Oct. 28 ***Perf. 12x12½, 12½x12***

869	A287	80fr multi	.25	.25
870	A287	250fr multi	.55	.30
871	A287	270fr multi	.60	.30
872	A287	350fr multi	.80	.40
873	A287	550fr multi	1.25	.60
874	A287	1500fr multi	3.50	1.60
		Nos. 869-874 (6)	6.95	3.45

Souvenir Sheet

875 A287 1500fr multi 3.25 3.25

For overprints see Nos. 1135-1136.

Intl. Fund for Agricultural Development (IFAD), 10th Anniv. — A288

1988, Sept. 4 **Litho.** ***Perf. 12***

876 A288 250fr multi .50 .25

School Feast — A289

1988, Nov. 22

877 A289 80fr multi .50 .25

A290

Ships — A291

Paintings: 20fr, The Squadron of the Sea, Black Feodossia, by Ivan Aivazovski, vert. No. 879, Seascape with Sailing Ships, by Simon de Vlieger, vert. No. 880, The Ship Lesnoie, by N. Semenov, vert. 100fr, The Merchantman, Orel, by N. Golitsine. 250fr, Naval Exercises, by Adam Silo, vert. 550fr, On the River, by Abraham Beerstraten.

1988, Dec. 5 ***Perf. 12x12½, 12½x12***

878	A290	20fr multi	.25	.25
879	A290	80fr multi	.30	.25
880	A290	80fr multi	.30	.25
881	A290	100fr shown	.40	.25
882	A290	250fr multi	.90	.25
		Nos. 878-882 (5)	2.15	1.25

Souvenir Sheet

Perf. 11½x12½

883 A291 550fr shown 2.00 1.00

World Wildlife Fund — A292

Insect species in danger of extinction: 20fr, Tragocephala crassicornis. 80fr, Polybothris symptuosa-gema. 250fr, Euchroea auripigmenta. 350fr, Stellognata maculata.

1988, Dec. 13 ***Perf. 12***

884	A292	20fr multi	*1.00*	—
885	A292	80fr multi	*6.50*	—
886	A292	250fr multi	*22.50*	—
887	A292	350fr multi	*30.00*	—
		Nos. 884-887 (4)	*60.00*	

Intl. Red Cross and Red Crescent Organizations, 125th Annivs. — A293

80fr, Globe, stretcher-bearers, vert. 250fr, Emblems, Dunant.

1988, Dec. 27 **Litho.** ***Perf. 12***

888	A293	80fr multicolored	.25	.25
889	A293	250fr multicolored	.55	.30

UN Declaration of Human Rights, 40th Anniv. (in 1988) — A294

1989, Jan. 10

890	A294	80fr shown	.25	.25
891	A294	250fr Hands, "4" and "0"	.60	.30

Dated 1988.

Transportation — A295

Designs: 80fr, 1909 Mercedes-Benz Blitzen Benz. 250fr, Micheline ZM 517 Tsikirity, Tananarive-Moramanga line. 270fr, Bugatti Coupe Binder 41. 350fr, Electric locomotive 1020-DES OBB, Germany. 1500fr, Souleze Autorail 701 DU CFN, Madagascar. No. 897, 1913 Opel race car. No. 898, Bugatti Presidential Autorail locomotive and Bugatti Type 57 Atalante automobile.

1989, Jan. 24 ***Perf. 13½***

892	A295	80fr multi	.25	.25
893	A295	250fr multi	.40	.25
894	A295	270fr multi	.50	.25
895	A295	350fr multi	.60	.35
896	A295	1500fr multi	2.50	1.00
897	A295	2500fr multi	3.50	2.00
		Nos. 892-897 (6)	7.75	4.10

Souvenir Sheet

898 A295 2500fr multi 5.00 3.50

Nos. 893-897 exist imperf. Value, set $13.

Dinosaurs — A296

20fr, Tyrannosaurus. 80fr, Stegosaurus. 250fr, Arsinoitherium. 450fr, Triceratops. 600fr, Sauralophus, vert.

1989, Feb. 1 Litho. *Perf. 12½x12*

899 A296 20fr multicolored .25 .25
900 A296 80fr multicolored 1.10 .25
901 A296 250fr multicolored 3.25 .50
902 A296 450fr multicolored 4.50 1.00
Nos. 899-902 (4) 9.10 2.00

Souvenir Sheet

Perf. 11½x12½

903 A296 600fr multicolored 2.75 1.25

Women as the Subject of Paintings — A297

Designs: 20fr, *Tahitian Pastorales,* by Gauguin. No 905, *Portrait of a Young Woman,* by Titian, vert. No. 906, *Portrait of a Little Girl,* by Jean-Baptiste Greuze (1725-1805), vert. 100fr, *Woman in Black,* by Renoir, vert. 250fr, *Lacemaker,* by Vassili Tropinine, vert. 550fr, *The Annunciation,* by Cima Da Conegliano (c. 1459-1517), vert.

1989, Feb. 10 *Perf. 12½x12, 12x12½*

904 A297 20fr multi .25 .25
905 A297 80fr multi .25 .25
906 A297 80fr multi .25 .25
907 A297 100fr multi .35 .25
908 A297 250fr multi .75 .30
Nos. 904-908 (5) 1.85 1.30

Souvenir Sheet

Perf. 11½x12½

909 A297 550fr multi 1.60 1.00

Orchids A298

No. 910, Sobennikoffia robusta, vert. No. 911, Grammangis fallax. No. 912, Cymbidiella humblotii, vert. No. 913, Angraecum sororium, vert. No. 914, Oenia oncidiiflora, vert. 1000fr, Aerangis curnowiana.

1989, Feb. 28 Litho. *Perf. 12*

910 A298 5fr multicolored .30 .25
911 A298 10fr multicolored .30 .25
912 A298 80fr multicolored .60 .25
913 A298 80fr multicolored .60 .25
914 A298 250fr multicolored 1.60 .35
Nos. 910-914 (5) 3.40 1.35

Souvenir Sheet

915 A298 1000fr multi 3.00 2.00

Jawaharlal Nehru (1889-1964), 1st Prime Minister of Independent India — A299

1989, Mar. 7 Litho. *Perf. 13*

916 A299 250fr multi .50 .25

Ornamental Mineral Industry A300

1989, Apr. 12 Litho. *Perf. 13½*

917 A300 80fr Rose quartz .30 .25
918 A300 250fr Petrified wood .90 .30

Views of Antananarivo A301

Designs: 5fr, Mahamasina Sports Complex, Ampefiloha Quarter. 20fr, Andravoahangy and Anjanahary Quarters. No. 921, Zoma Market and Faravohitra Quarter. No. 922, Andohan'Analakely Quarter and March 29th monument. 250fr, Independence Avenue and Jean Ralaimongo monument. 550fr, Queen's Palace and Andohalo School on Lake Anosy.

1989, Mar. 31 Litho. *Perf. 13½*

919 A301 5fr multi .25 .25
920 A301 20fr multi .25 .25
921 A301 80fr multi .25 .25
922 A301 80fr multi .25 .25
923 A301 250fr multi .50 .25
924 A301 550fr multi .90 .35
Nos. 919-924 (6) 2.40 1.60

Visit of Pope John Paul II — A302

1989, Apr. 28 *Perf. 12x12½*

925 A302 80fr shown .30 .25
926 A302 250fr Pope, map 1.00 .25

French Revolution, Bicent. A303

250fr, Storming of the Bastille.

1989, July 7 Litho. *Perf. 12½*

927 A303 250fr multicolored .60 .25

Phobos Space Program for the Exploration of Mars — A304

1989, Aug. 29 Litho. *Perf. 12½x12*

928 A304 20fr Mars 1 .25 .25
929 A304 80fr Mars 3 .25 .25
930 A304 80fr Zond 2 .25 .25
931 A304 250fr Mariner 9 .55 .25
932 A304 270fr Viking 2 .65 .30
Nos. 928-932 (5) 1.95 1.30

Souvenir Sheet

933 A304 550fr Phobos 1.50 .60

PHILEXFRANCE '89 and French Revolution, Bicent. — A305

Exhibition emblems, key people and scenes from the revolution: 250fr, Honore-Gabriel Riqueti (1749-1791), Count of Mirabeau, at the meeting of Estates-General, June 23, 1789. 350fr, Camille Desmoulins (1760-1794), call to arms, July 12, 1789. 1000fr, Lafayette (1757-1834), women's march on Versailles, Oct. 5, 1789. 1500fr, King tried by the National Convention, Dec. 26, 1792. 2500fr, Charlotte Corday (1768-1793), assassination of Marat, July 13, 1793. 3000fr, Bertrand Barere de Vieuzac, Robespierre, Jean-Marie Collot D'Herbois, Lazare Nicolas Carnot, George Jacques Danton, Georges Auguste Couthon, Pierre-Louis Prieur, Antoine Saint-Just and Marc Guillaume Vadier, Committee of Public Safety, July, 1793. No. 939A, Family saying farewell to Louis XVI. No. 939B, Danton and the Club of the Cordeliers.

1989, July 14 Litho. *Perf. 13½*

934 A305 250fr multicolored .35 .25
935 A305 350fr multicolored .50 .25
936 A305 1000fr multicolored 1.20 .65
937 A305 1500fr multicolored 2.00 1.00
938 A305 2500fr multicolored 3.50 1.60
Nos. 934-938 (5) 7.55 3.75

Souvenir Sheet

939 A305 3000fr multicolored 4.00 4.00

Litho. & Embossed

939A A305 5000fr gold & multi 6.00

Souvenir Sheet

939B A305 5000fr gold & multi 6.00

Nos. 939A-939B exist imperf.

For overprints see Nos. 1161-1165, 1166A-1166B.

French Revolution, Bicent. — A306

Paintings and sculpture: 5fr, *Liberty Guiding the People,* by Eugene Delacroix. 80fr, "La Marseillaise" from *Departure of the Volunteers in 1792,* high relief on the Arc de Triomphe, 1833-35, by Francois Rude. 250fr, *The Tennis Court Oath,* by David.

1989, Oct. 25 *Perf. 12½x12*

940 A306 5fr multicolored .25 .25
941 A306 80fr multicolored .45 .25
942 A306 250fr multicolored .90 .25
Nos. 940-942 (3) 1.60 .75

No. 942 is airmail.

Rene Cassin (1887-1976), Nobel Peace Prize Winner and Institute Founder — A307

1989, Nov. 21 *Perf. 12*

943 A307 250fr multicolored .50 .25

Intl. Law Institute of the French-Speaking Nations, 25th anniv.

Hapalemur aureus A308

1989, Dec. 5 Litho. *Perf. 12*

944 A308 250fr multicolored 1.00 .35

A309

A309a

Various athletes, cup and: 350fr, Cavour Monument, Turin. 1000fr, Christopher Columbus Monument, Genoa, 1903. 1500fr, Michelangelo's *David.* 2500fr, *Abduction of Proserpina,* by Bernini, Rome. 3000fr, Statue of Leonardo da Vinci, 1903. 5000fr, Castel Nuovo, Naples.

1989, Dec. 12 Litho. *Perf. 13½*

945 A309 350fr multicolored .45 .25
946 A309 1000fr multicolored 1.20 .65
947 A309 1500fr multicolored 2.00 1.00
948 A309 2500fr multicolored 3.00 1.60
Nos. 945-948 (4) 6.65 3.50

Souvenir Sheet

949 A309 3000fr multicolored 3.50 2.00

Litho. & Embossed

949A A309a 5000fr gold & multi 8.00

1990 World Cup Soccer Championships, Italy.

For overprints see Nos. 1137-1140.

A310

1989, Oct. 7 Litho. *Perf. 13½*

950 A310 80fr Long jump .25 .25
951 A310 250fr Pole vault .35 .25
952 A310 550fr Hurdles .80 .40
953 A310 1500fr Cycling 2.25 1.10

954 A310 2000fr Baseball 3.00 1.45
955 A310 2500fr Tennis 3.75 1.75
Nos. 950-955 (6) 10.40 5.20

Souvenir Sheet

956 A310 3000fr Soccer 4.50 2.10

1992 Summer Olympics, Barcelona.

Scenic Views and Artifacts A311

No. 957, Queen Isalo Rock. No. 958, Sakalava pipe. No. 959, Sakalava combs. No. 960, Lowry Is., Diego Suarez Bay.

1990, May 29

Size: 47x33mm (#958, 960)

957 A311 70fr multi .25 .25
958 A311 70fr multi .25 .25
959 A311 150fr multi .30 .25
960 A311 150fr multi .30 .25
Nos. 957-960 (4) 1.10 1.00

Fish A312

5fr, Heniochus acuminatus. 20fr, Simenhelys dofleinl. 80fr, Rhinobatos percellens. 250fr, Epinephelus fasciatus. 320fr, Sphyrna zygaena.
550fr, Latimeria chalumnae.

1990, Apr. 26 Litho. *Perf. 12*

961 A312 5fr multicolored .25 .25
962 A312 20fr multicolored .25 .25
963 A312 80fr multicolored .25 .25
964 A312 250fr multicolored 1.00 .25
965 A312 320fr multicolored 1.40 .35
Nos. 961-965 (5) 3.15 1.35

Souvenir Sheet

966 A312 550fr multicolored 3.50 1.50

Nos. 962-963 vert. Nos. 961-966 inscribed 1989.

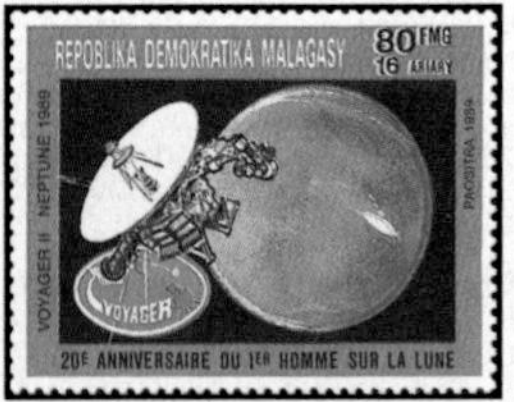

Moon Landing, 20th Anniv. — A314

Designs: 80fr, Voyager 2, Neptune. 250fr, Hydro 2000 flying boat. 550fr, NOAA satellite. 1500fr, Magellan probe, Venus. 2000fr, Concorde. 2500fr, Armstrong, Aldrin, Collins, lunar module. 3000fr, Apollo 11 astronauts, first step on moon.

1990, June 19 Litho. *Perf. 13½*

967 A314 80fr multicolored .25 .25
968 A314 250fr multicolored .25 .25
969 A314 550fr multicolored .65 .40
970 A314 1500fr multicolored 1.75 .85
971 A314 2000fr multicolored 2.40 1.00
972 A314 2500fr multicolored 2.90 1.25
Nos. 967-972 (6) 8.20 4.00

Souvenir Sheet

973 A314 3000fr multicolored 3.50 2.00

For overprint see No. 1304.
Nos. 967-972 exist in souvenir sheets of 1, and se-tenant in a sheet of 6.

1992 Winter Olympics, Albertville — A315

350fr, Bobsled. 1000fr, Speed skating. 1500fr, Nordic skiing. 2500fr, Super giant slalom.
No. 978, Giant slalom. No. 978A, Pairs figure skating. No. 978B, Ice hockey.

1990, July 17

974 A315 350fr multi .50 .25
975 A315 1000fr multi 1.50 .75
976 A315 1500fr multi 2.25 1.10
977 A315 2500fr multi 3.75 1.90
Nos. 974-977 (4) 8.00 4.00

Souvenir Sheet

978 A315 3000fr multi 4.50 2.25

Litho. & Embossed

978A A315 5000fr multi 8.00

Souvenir Sheet

978B A315 5000fr multi 8.00

Nos. 978A-978B exist imperf.
For overprints see Nos. 1141-1145.

A316

1990, June 19 Litho. *Perf. 12*

979 A316 250fr blk, ultra & bl .50 .25

Intl. Maritime Organization, 30th anniv.

African Development Bank, 25th Anniv. A317

1990, June 19

980 A317 80fr multicolored .50 .25

Campaign Against Polio — A318

1990, June 28

981 A318 150fr multicolored .50 .25

Independence, 30th Anniv. — A319

1990, Aug. 22

982 A319 100fr multicolored .50 .25

3rd Indian Ocean Games — A320

1990, Aug. 24 *Perf. 12½x12*

983 A320 100fr yellow & multi .35 .25
984 A320 350fr lil rose & multi .65 .30

A322

1990, Oct. 19 Litho. *Perf. 12*

986 A322 350fr multicolored .75 .30

Ho Chi Minh (1890-1969), Vietnamese leader.

Lemurs A323

No. 987, Avahi laniger. No. 988, Lemur fulvus sanfordi. No. 989, Lemur fulvus albifrons. No. 990, Lemur fulvus collaris. No. 991, Lepulemur ruficaudatus.
No. 992, Lemur fulvus fulvus.

1990, Nov. 23 Litho. *Perf. 11½*

987 A323 10fr multi .25 .25
988 A323 20fr multi .35 .25
989 A323 20fr multi .35 .25
990 A323 100fr multi .80 .25
991 A323 100fr multi .80 .25
Nos. 987-991 (5) 2.55 1.25

Souvenir Sheet

992 A323 350fr multi 3.00 .50

Shells A324

40fr, Tridacna squamosa. 50fr, Terebra demidiata, Terebra subulata.

1990, Dec. 21 *Perf. 12½*

993 A324 40fr multicolored .80 .25
994 A324 50fr multicolored .80 .25

Anniversaries and Events A325

100fr, Charles de Gaulle, liberation of Paris, 1944. 350fr, Galileo probe orbiting Jupiter. 800fr, Apollo 11 crew & Columbia command module, 1st Moon landing, 1969. 900fr, De Gaulle, 1942. 1250fr, Concorde jet, TGV high-speed train. 2500fr, De Gaulle as head of provisional government, 1944. 3000fr, Apollo 11 crew, Eagle lunar module. No. 1001A, De Gaulle with Roosevelt & Churchill. No. 1001B, Charles de Gaulle.

1990, Dec. 28 Litho. *Perf. 13½*

995 A325 100fr multi .25 .25
996 A325 350fr multi .60 .30
997 A325 800fr multi 1.40 .70
998 A325 900fr multi 1.60 .80
999 A325 1250fr multi 2.25 1.10
1000 A325 2500fr multi 4.50 2.25
Nos. 995-1000 (6) 10.60 5.40

Souvenir Sheet

1001 A325 3000fr multi 4.00 2.00

Litho. & Embossed

1001A A325 5000fr gold & multi 7.50

Souvenir Sheet

1001B A325 5000fr gold & multi 7.50

Nos. 995-1000, 1001A exist in souvenir sheets of 1. A souvenir sheet containing Nos. 996-997 exists.

Mushrooms — A325b

Designs: 25fr, Boletus edulis. 100fr, Suillus luteus. 350fr, Amanita muscaria. 450fr, Boletus calopus. 680fr, Boletus erythropus. 800fr, Leccinum scabrum. 900fr, Leccinum testaceoscabrum.
1500fr, Lycoperdon perlatum.

1990, Dec. 28 Litho. *Perf. 12*

1001C A325b 25fr multi .25 .25
1001D A325b 100fr multi .40 .25
1001E A325b 350fr multi .85 .25
1001F A325b 450fr multi 1.25 .30
1001G A325b 680fr multi 1.75 .45
1001H A325b 800fr multi 1.90 .50
1001I A325b 900fr multi 2.10 .60

Imperf

Size: 71x91mm

1001J A325b 1500fr multi 4.50 4.50
Nos. 1001C-1001J (8) 13.00 7.10

For surcharge, see No. 1478A.

Intl. Literacy Year A326

20fr, Book, guiding hands, vert. 100fr, Open Book, hand holding pencil.

1990, Dec. 30 *Perf. 12*

1002 A326 20fr multi .25 .25
1003 A326 100fr multi .25 .25

Dogs — A326a

Designs: 30fr,Greyhound. 50fr, Japanese spaniel. 140fr, Toy terrier. 350fr, Chow. 500fr, Miniature pinscher. 800fr, Afghan. 1140fr, Papillon. 1500fr, Shih tzu.

1991, Mar. 20 Litho. *Perf. 12*

1003A	A326a	30fr	multi	.25	.25
1003B	A326a	50fr	multi	.25	.25
1003C	A326a	140fr	multi	.60	.25
1003D	A326a	350fr	multi	.90	.25
1003E	A326a	500fr	multi	1.25	.30
1003F	A326a	800fr	multi	2.10	.50
1003G	A326a	1140fr	multi	3.00	.75

Imperf

Size: 70x90mm

1003H	A326a	1500fr	multi	4.00	1.40
	Nos. 1003A-1003H (8)			12.35	3.95

Nos. 1003D-1003H are airmail.

Democratic Republic of Madagascar, 15th Anniv. (in 1990) — A327

1991, Apr. 8 Litho. *Perf. 12*

1004	A327	100fr	multicolored	.25	.25

Dated 1990.

Trees — A328

140fr, Adansonia fony. 500fr, Didierea madagascariensis.

1991, June 20 Litho. *Perf. 13½*

1005	A328	140fr	multi	.55	.25
1006	A328	500fr	multi	1.25	.40

Scouts, Insects and Mushrooms A329

Insects: 140fr, Helictopleurus splendidicollis. 640fr, Cocles contemplator. 1140fr, Euchroea oberthurii.

Mushrooms: 500fr, Russula radicans. 1025fr, Russula singeri. 3500fr, Lactariopsis pandani.

4500fr, Euchroea spinnasuta fairmaire and Russula aureotacta.

1991, Aug. 2 Litho. *Perf. 13½*

1007	A329	140fr	multicolored	.35	.25
1008	A329	500fr	multicolored	.90	.30
1009	A329	640fr	multicolored	1.00	.40
1010	A329	1025fr	multicolored	1.75	.65
1011	A329	1140fr	multicolored	2.10	.70
1012	A329	3500fr	multicolored	5.25	2.25
	Nos. 1007-1012 (6)			11.35	4.55

Souvenir Sheet

1013	A329	4500fr	multicolored	7.00	5.75

Nos. 1007-1012 exist in souvenir sheets of 1. For overprints see Nos. 1149-1156.

Discovery of America, 500th Anniv. A330

Designs: 15fr, Ship, 9th cent.. 65fr, Clipper ship, 1878. 140fr, Golden Hind. 500fr, Galley, 18th cent. 640fr, Galleon Ostrust, 1721, vert. 800fr, Caravel Amsterdam, 1539, vert. 1025fr, Santa Maria, 1492. 1500fr, Map.

1991, Sept. 10 Litho. *Perf. 12*

1014	A330	15fr	multicolored	.25	.25
1015	A330	65fr	multicolored	.25	.25
1016	A330	140fr	multicolored	.55	.25
1017	A330	500fr	multicolored	1.25	.30
1018	A330	640fr	multicolored	1.50	.40
1019	A330	800fr	multicolored	1.60	.50
1020	A330	1025fr	multicolored	1.75	.65

Size: 90x70mm

1021	A330	1500fr	multicolored	3.50	1.50
	Nos. 1014-1021 (8)			10.65	4.10

No. 1021 contains one 40x27mm perf. 12 label in center of stamp picturing ships and Columbus.

Domesticated Animals A331

Designs: 140fr, Dog. 500fr, Arabian horse. 640fr, House cats. 1025fr, Himalayan cats. 1140fr, Draft horse. 5000fr, German shepherd. 10,000fr, Horse, cat & dog.

1991, Sept. 27 Litho. *Perf. 13½*

1022	A331	140fr	multicolored	.25	.25
1023	A331	500fr	multicolored	.90	.30
1024	A331	640fr	multicolored	1.00	.40
1025	A331	1025fr	multicolored	1.75	.65
1026	A331	1140fr	multicolored	2.25	.70
1027	A331	5000fr	multicolored	7.25	3.25
	Nos. 1022-1027 (6)			13.40	5.55

Souvenir Sheet

1028	A331	10,000fr	multicolored	13.00	6.50

Nos. 1022-1028 exist imperf. and in souvenir sheets of 1.

Birds — A332

Designs: 40fr, Hirundo rustica. 55fr, Circus melanoluecos, vert. 60fr, Cuculas canorus, vert. 140fr, Threskiornis aethiopicus. 210fr, Porphyrio poliocephalus. 500fr, Coracias garrulus. 2000fr, Oriolus oriolus. 1500fr, Upupa epops.

Perf. 12½x12, 12x12½

1991, Dec. 10 Litho.

1029	A332	40fr	multicolored	.25	.25
1030	A332	55fr	multicolored	.25	.25
1031	A332	60fr	multicolored	.25	.25
1032	A332	140fr	multicolored	.45	.25
1033	A332	210fr	multicolored	.70	.25
1034	A332	500fr	multicolored	1.00	.35
1035	A332	2000fr	multicolored	3.00	1.10

Size: 70x90mm

Imperf

1036	A332	1500fr	multicolored	3.00	1.40
	Nos. 1029-1036 (8)			8.90	4.10

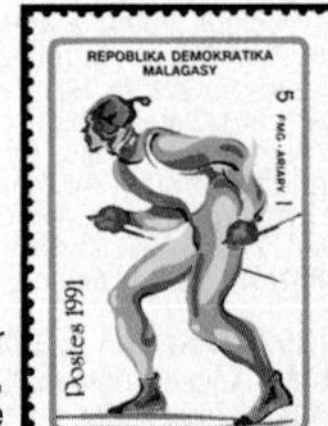

1992 Winter Olympics, Albertville A333

5fr, Cross-country skiing. 15fr, Biathlon. 60fr, Ice hockey. 140fr, Downhill skiing. 640fr, Figure skating. 1000fr, Ski jumping. 1140fr, Speed skating. 1500fr, Three hockey players.

1991, Dec. 30 Litho. *Perf. 12x12½*

1037	A333	5fr	multi	.25	.25
1038	A333	15fr	multi	.25	.25
1039	A333	60fr	multi	.25	.25
1040	A333	140fr	multi	.45	.25
1041	A333	640fr	multi	1.25	.40
1042	A333	1000fr	multi	1.60	.70
1043	A333	1140fr	multi	2.00	.75

Imperf

Size: 90x70mm

1044	A333	1500fr	multi	3.00	1.40
	Nos. 1037-1044 (8)			9.05	4.25

For surcharge see No. 1482.

Paul Minault College, 90th Anniv. A333a

1991 Litho. *Perf. 13½*

1044A	A333a	140fr	multicolored	.65	.30

Space Program A334

Designs: 140fr, Astronaunts repairing space telescope. 500fr, Soho solar observation probe. 640fr, Topex-Poseidon, observing oceans. 1025fr, Hipparcos probe, Galaxy 3C75. 1140fr, Voyager II surveying Neptune. 5000fr, Adeos, ETS VI, earth observation and communications satellites. 7500fr, Crew of Apollo 11.

1992, Apr. 22 *Perf. 13½*

1045	A334	140fr	multi	.25	.25
1046	A334	500fr	multi	.70	.30
1047	A334	640fr	multi	.90	.40
1048	A334	1025fr	multi	1.40	.65
1049	A334	1140fr	multi	1.60	.70
1050	A334	5000fr	multi	6.75	3.25
a.	Souvenir sheet of 6, #1045-1050			19.00	19.00
	Nos. 1045-1050 (6)			11.60	5.55

Souvenir Sheet

1051	A334	7500fr	multi	12.00	9.75

Nos. 1045-1050 exist in souvenir sheets of one.

Entertainers A335

100fr, Ryuichi Sakamoto. 350fr, John Lennon. 800fr, Bruce Lee. 900fr, Sammy Davis, Jr. 1250fr, John Wayne. 2500fr, James Dean. 3000fr, Clark Gable & Vivien Leigh.

1992, Apr. 29

1052	A335	100fr	multi	.25	.25
1053	A335	350fr	multi	.60	.25
1054	A335	800fr	multi	1.50	.50
1055	A335	900fr	multi	1.75	.60
1056	A335	1250fr	multi	1.90	.80
1057	A335	2500fr	multi	3.50	1.60
	Nos. 1052-1057 (6)			9.50	4.00

Souvenir Sheet

1058	A335	3000fr	multi	5.25	2.00

Nos. 1052-1057 exist in souvenir sheets of one.

Fight Against AIDS — A336

1992, July 29 Litho. *Perf. 12*

1059	A336	140fr	lil rose & black	.40	.25

Dated 1991.

Reforestation — A337

1992, July 29 Litho. *Perf. 12*

1060	A337	140fr	black & green	.30	.25

Dated 1991.

1990 Sports Festival — A338

1992, Aug. 20

1061	A338	140fr	multicolored	.35	.25

Dated 1991.

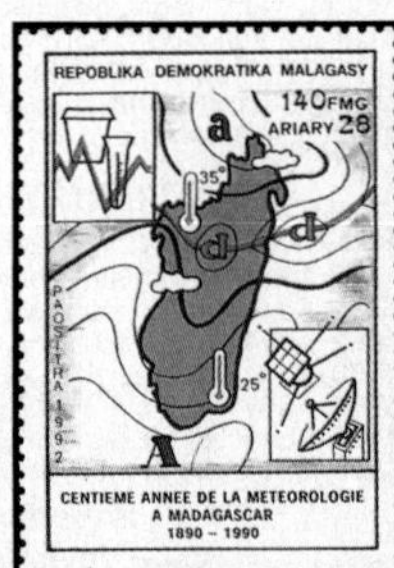

Meteorology in Madagascar, Cent. A339

1992, Nov. 10 Litho. *Perf. 12x12½*

1062	A339	140fr	multicolored	.40	.25

Fruit — A341

10fr, Litchis. 50fr, Oranges. 60fr, Apples. 140fr, Peaches. 555fr, Bananas, vert. 800fr, Avocados, vert. 1400fr, Mangoes, vert. 1600fr, Mixed fruit.

Perf. 12½x12, 12x12½

1992, May 27 **Litho.**

1064	A341	10fr multi	.30	.25
1065	A341	50fr multi	.30	.25
1066	A341	60fr multi	.35	.25
1067	A341	140fr multi	.50	.25
1068	A341	555fr multi	1.25	.45
1069	A341	800fr multi	1.75	.60
1070	A341	1400fr multi	3.00	1.25

Size: 89x70mm

Imperf

1071	A341	1600fr multi	3.25	1.40
		Nos. 1064-1071 (8)	10.70	4.70

For surcharges, see Nos. 1477, 1486.

1992 Summer Olympics, Barcelona A342

65fr, Women's gymnastics. 70fr, High jump. 120fr, Archery. 140fr, Cycling. 675fr, Weight lifting. 720fr, Boxing. 1200fr, Canoeing. 1600fr, Volleyball. 5000fr, Judo.

1992, June 30 *Perf. 11½*

1072	A342	65fr multi	.25	.25
1073	A342	70fr multi	.25	.25
1074	A342	120fr multi	.25	.25
1075	A342	140fr multi	.30	.25
1076	A342	675fr multi	1.10	.45
1077	A342	720fr multi	1.10	.50
1078	A342	1200fr multi	1.75	.75

Imperf

Size: 90x70mm

1078A	A342	1600fr multi	3.00	1.40
		Nos. 1072-1078A (8)	8.00	4.10

Litho. & Embossed

Perf. 13½

1079	A342	5000fr multi	8.00	

For surcharge, see No. 1473A.

Butterflies — A344

Designs: 15fr, Eusemia bisma. 35fr, Argema mittrei, vert. 65fr, Alcidis aurora. 140fr, Agarista agricola. 600fr, Trogonoptera croesus. 850fr, Trogonodtera priamus. 1300fr, Pereute leucodrosime. 1500fr, Chrysirridia madagaskariensis.

Perf. 12½x12, 12x12½

1992, June 24 **Litho.**

1080	A344	15fr multicolored	.25	.25
1081	A344	35fr multicolored	.25	.25
1082	A344	65fr multicolored	.45	.25
1083	A344	140fr multicolored	.70	.25
1084	A344	600fr multicolored	1.50	.45
1085	A344	850fr multicolored	2.00	.60
1086	A344	1300fr multicolored	2.50	.85

Imperf

Size: 70x90mm

1087	A344	1500fr multicolored	4.75	1.50
		Nos. 1080-1087 (8)	12.40	4.40

For surcharge, see No. 1485.

Anniversaries and Events — A345

Designs: 500fr, Jean-Henri Dunant, delivery of Red Cross supplies. 640fr, Charles de Gaulle, battle of Bir Hacheim. 1025fr, Brandenburg Gate, people on Berlin wall. 1500fr, Village health clinic, Rotary, Lions emblems. 3000fr, Konrad Adenauer. 3500fr, Dirigible LZ4, hanger on Lake Constance, Ferdinand von Zeppelin. 7500fr, Wolfgang Amadeus Mozart at piano, palace, cathedral in Salzburg.

1992, Dec. 8 **Litho.** *Perf. 13½*

1088	A345	500fr multicolored	.70	.30
1089	A345	640fr multicolored	.90	.45
1090	A345	1025fr multicolored	1.50	.75
1091	A345	1500fr multicolored	2.00	1.00
1092	A345	3000fr multicolored	4.25	2.00
1093	A345	3500fr multicolored	5.00	2.50
		Nos. 1088-1093 (6)	14.35	7.00

Souvenir Sheet

1094	A345	7500fr multicolored	10.00	5.00

Intl. Red Cross (No. 1088). Battle of Bir Hacheim, 50th anniv. (No. 1089). Brandenburg Gate, bicent. and destruction of Berlin Wall, 3rd anniv. (No. 1090). Konrad Adenauer, 25th death anniv. (No. 1092). Ferdinand von Zeppelin, 75th death anniv. (No. 1093). Mozart, death bicent. (in 1991), (No. 1094).

For overprint see No. 1146.

1994 World Cup Soccer Championships, U.S. — A346

Soccer players, Georgia landmarks: 140fr, Ficklin Home, Macon. 640fr, Herndon Home, Atlanta. 1025fr, Cultural Center, Augusta. 5000fr, Old Governor's Mansion, Milledgeville. 7500fr, Player, stars, stripes.

1992, Dec. 15 **Litho.** *Perf. 13½*

1095	A346	140fr multicolored	.25	.25
1096	A346	640fr multicolored	.90	.45
1097	A346	1025fr multicolored	1.40	.75
1098	A346	5000fr multicolored	7.00	3.50
		Nos. 1095-1098 (4)	9.55	4.95

Souvenir Sheet

1099	A346	7500fr multicolored	10.25	5.25

Miniature Sheet

Inventors and Inventions — A347

No. 1100: a, Gutenberg (1394?-1468), printing press. b, Newton (1642-1727), telescope. c, John Dalton (1766-1844), atomic theory. d, Louis-Jacques-Mande Daguerre (1789-1851), photographic equipment. e, Faraday (1791-1867), electric motor. f, Orville (1871-1948), Wilbur Wright (1867-1912), motor-powered airplane. g, Bell (1847-1922), telephone. h, Edison (1847-1931), phonograph. i, Benz (1844-1929), motor-driven vehicle. j, Charles Parsons (1854-1931), steam turbine. k, Diesel (1858-1913), Diesel engine. l, Marconi, radio. m, Auguste-Marie-Louis Lumiere (1862-1954), Louis-Jean Lumiere (1864-1948), motion pictures. n, Oberth (1894-1989), rocketry. o, John W. Mauchly (1907-1980), John P. Eckert, electronic computer. p, Arthur Schawlow, laser.

1993, Apr. 27

1100	A347	500fr Sheet of 16, #a.-p.	11.00	5.50

Dated 1990.

Transportation — A348

No. 1101 — Race cars: a, 20fr, 1956 Bugatti. b, 20fr, 1968 Ferrari. c, 140fr, 1962 Lotus MK25. d, 140fr, 1970 Matra. e, 1250fr, 1963 Porsche. f, 1250fr, 1980 Ligier JS11. g, 3000fr, 1967 Honda. h, 3000fr, 1992 B192 Benetton.

No. 1102 — Locomotives: a, 20fr, C62, Japan, 1948. b, 20fr, SZD, USSR, 1975. c, 140fr, MU A1A-A1A, Norway, 1954. d, 140fr, Series 26 2-D-2, Africa, 1982. e, 1250fr, Amtrak Metroliner, US, 1967. f, 1250fr, VIA, Canada, 1982. g, 3000fr, Diesel, Union Pacific RR, US, 1969. h, 3000fr, Atlantic, TGV, France, 1990.

1993, Mar. 23

1101	A348	Block of 8, #a.-h.	12.00	6.00
1102	A348	Block of 8, #a.-h.	12.00	6.00

Dated 1990.

Wildlife — A349

No. 1103 — Birds: a, 45fr, Coua verreauxi. b, 45fr, Asio helvola hova. c, 60fr, Coua cristata. d, 60fr, Euryceros prevostii. e, 140fr, Coua gigas. f, 140fr, Foudia madagascariensis. g, 3000fr, Falculea palliata. h, 3000fr, Eutriorchis astur.

No. 1104 — Butterflies: a, 45fr, Chrysiridia madagascariensis. b, 45fr, Hypolimnas misippus. c, 60fr, Charaxes antamboulou. d, 60fr, Papilio antenor. e, 140fr, Hypolimnas dexithea. f, 140fr, Charaxes andranodorus. g, 3000fr, Euxanthe madagascariensis. h, 3000fr, Papilio grosesmithi.

1993, May 27

1103	A349	Block of 8, #a.-h.	8.75	4.25
1104	A349	Block of 8, #a.-h.	8.75	4.25

Dated 1991.

Intl. Conference on Nutrition, Rome — A350

1992, Nov. 3

1105	A350	500fr multicolored	1.00	.40

Automobiles — A351

1993, Jan. 28 **Litho.** *Perf. 12*

1106	A351	20fr BMW	.25	.25
1107	A351	40fr Toyota	.25	.25
1108	A351	60fr Cadillac	.25	.25
1109	A351	65fr Volvo	.25	.25
1110	A351	140fr Mercedes Benz	.25	.25
1111	A351	640fr Ford	1.00	.50
1112	A351	3000fr Honda	5.00	2.50

Size: 90x70mm

Imperf

1113	A351	2000fr Renault	3.00	1.50
		Nos. 1106-1113 (8)	10.25	5.75

Birds — A352

Designs: 50fr, Anodorhynchus hyacinthinus. 60fr, Nymphicus hollandicus. 140fr, Melopsittacus undulatus. 500fr, Aratinga jandaya. 675fr, Melopsittacus undulatus, diff. 800fr, Cyanoramphus novaezelandiae. 1750fr, Nestor notabilis. 2000fr, Ara militaris.

1993, Feb. 24

1114	A352	50fr multicolored	.40	.25
1115	A352	60fr multicolored	.40	.25
1116	A352	140fr multicolored	.50	.25
1117	A352	500fr multicolored	1.75	.45
1118	A352	675fr multicolored	2.50	.65
1119	A352	800fr multicolored	2.75	.70
1120	A352	1750fr multicolored	6.00	1.50

Size: 71x91mm

Imperf

1121	A352	2000fr multicolored	5.00	2.00
		Nos. 1114-1121 (8)	19.30	6.05

For surcharges, see Nos. 1473B, 1488.

Mollusks A353

40fr, Turbo marmoratus. 60fr, Mitra mitra. 65fr, Argonauta argo. 140fr, Conus textile. 500fr, Aplysia depilans. 675fr, Harpa amouretta. 2500fr, Cypraea tigris.

2000fr, Architectonica maxima.

1993, Feb. 3

1122	A353	40fr multi	.25	.25
1123	A353	60fr multi	.25	.25
1124	A353	65fr multi	.25	.25
1125	A353	140fr multi	.30	.25
1126	A353	500fr multi	1.10	.45
1127	A353	675fr multi	1.50	.70
1128	A353	2500fr multi	4.50	2.25

Size: 70x90mm

Imperf

1129	A353	2000fr multi	5.00	1.75
		Nos. 1122-1129 (8)	13.15	6.15

For surcharge, see No. 1478.

Boat, Barges, Pangalanes Canal A354

1993, Jan. 29 **Litho.** *Perf. 12*

1130	A354	140fr multicolored	.40	.25

Miniature Sheet

Ships — A355

No. 1131: a, 5fr, Egyptian ship. b, 5fr, Mediterranean galley. c, 5fr, Great Western, England, 1837. d, 5fr, Mississippi River sidewheeler, US, 1850. e, 15fr, Bireme, Phoenicia. f, 15fr, Viking long ship. g, 15fr, Clermont, US, 1806. h, 15fr, Pourquoi-pas, France, 1936. i, 140fr, Santa Maria, Spain, 1492. j, 140fr, HMS Victory, England, 1765. k, 140fr, Fast motor yacht, Monaco. l, 140fr, Bremen, Germany, 1950. m, 10,000fr, Sovereign of the Seas, England, 1637. n, 10,000fr, Cutty Sark, England, 1869. o, 10,000fr, Savannah, US, 1959. p, 10,000fr, Condor, Australia.

1993, Apr. 6 Litho. *Perf. 13½*

1131 A355 Sheet of 16, #a.-p. 50.00 25.00

Miniature Sheet

Nobel Prize Winners in Physics, Chemistry and Medicine — A356

No. 1132: a, Albert Einstein, Niels Bohr. b, Wolfgang Pauli, Max Born. c, Joseph Thomson, Johannes Stark. d, Otto Hahn, Hideki Yukawa. e, Owen Richardson, William Shockley. f, Albert Michelson, Charles Townes. g, Wilhelm Wien, Lev Landau. h, Karl Braun, Sir Edward Appleton. i, Percy Bridgman, Nikolai Semenov. j, Sir William Ramsay, Glenn Seaborg. k, Otto Wallach, Hermann Staudinger. l, Richard Synge, Alex Theorell. m, Thomas Morgan, Hermann Muller. n, Allvar Gullstrand, Willem Einthoven. o, Sir Charles Sherrington, Otto Loewi. p, Jules Bordet, Sir Alexander Fleming.

1993, Mar. 11

1132 A356 500fr Sheet of 16, #a.-p. 11.00 5.50

Alex misspelled on No. 1132l.

Miniature Sheet

Lemurs — A357

No. 1133: a, 60fr, Hapalemur simus. b, 150fr, Propithecus diadema. c, 250fr Indri indri. d, 350fr, Varecia variegata.

1992, Oct. 9 Litho. *Perf. 13½*

1133 A357 Sheet of 4, #a.-d. 5.50 2.00

World Post Day.

No. 840 Ovptd. in Silver

1993, Sept. 28 Litho. *Perf. 13½*

1134 A276 550fr multicolored *3.75 1.90*

Exists in souvenir sheet of 1.

No. 874 Ovptd. in Silver Overprint includes Guitar and reads "THE ELVIS'S GUITAR / 15th ANNIVERSARY OF HIS DEATH / 1977-1992" in English or French

1993, Sept. 28

1135 A287 1500fr English ovpt. 2.50 1.10
1136 A287 1500fr French ovpt. 2.50 1.10
a. Pair, #1135-1136 5.00 2.25

No. 1135 exists in souvenir sheet of 1.

Nos. 945-948 Ovptd. in Gold

1993, Sept. 28

1137 A309 350fr multicolored .50 .30
1138 A309 1000fr multicolored 1.50 .75
1139 A309 1500fr multicolored 2.25 1.25
1140 A309 2500fr multicolored 3.75 1.90
Nos. 1137-1140 (4) 8.00 4.20

Nos. 974-978 Ovptd. in Gold

1993, Sept. 28

1141 A315 350fr multicolored .50 .25
1142 A315 1000fr multicolored 1.50 .75
1143 A315 1500fr multicolored 2.25 1.10
1144 A315 2500fr multicolored 3.75 1.90
Nos. 1141-1144 (4) 8.00 4.00

Souvenir Sheet

1145 A315 3000fr multicolored 4.75 2.50

No. 1088 Overprinted in Red

1993, Sept. 28

1146 A345 500fr multicolored 3.50 1.75

Exists in souvenir sheet of 1, overprinted in red or green.

Miniature Sheet

Commercial Airlines — A358

No. 1147: a, 10fr, Lufthansa, Germany. b, 10fr, Air France. c, 10fr, Air Canada. d. 10fr, ANA, Japan. e, 60fr, British Airways. f, 60fr, DO-X, Germany. g, 60fr, Shinmeiwa, Japan. h, 60fr, Royal Jordanian. i, 640fr, Alitalia, Italy. j, 640fr, Hydro 2000, France-Europe. k, 640fr, Boeing 314 Clipper, US. l, 640fr, Air Madagascar. m, 5000fr, Emirates Airlines, United Arab Emirates n, 5000fr, Scandinavian Airways. o, 5000fr, KLM, Netherlands. p, 5000fr, Air Caledonia.

1993, Nov. 22 Litho. *Perf. 13½*

1147 A358 Sheet of 16, #a.-p. 30.00 15.00

Dated 1990.

Miniature Sheet

Painters — A359

No. 1148: a, 50fr, Leonardo Da Vinci. b, 50fr, Titian. c, 50fr, Rembrandt. d, 50fr, J.M.W. Turner (1775-1851). e, 640fr, Michelangelo. f, 640fr, Rubens. g, 640fr, Goya. h, 640fr, Delacroix (1798-1863). i, 1000fr, Monet. j, 1000fr, Gauguin. k, 1000fr, Toulouse Lautrec (1864-1901). l, 1000fr, Dali (1904-89). m, 2500fr, Renoir. n, 2500fr, Van Gogh. o, 2500fr, Picasso. p, 2500fr, Andy Warhol.

1993, May 10

1148 A359 Sheet of 16, #a.-p. 22.50 11.50

The local currency on Nos. 1148m-1148p is obliterated by a black overprint.

Nos. 1007-1013 Ovptd. in Gold

No. 841 Ovptd. in Metallic Green

1993, Sept. 28 Litho. *Perf. 13½*

1149 A329 140fr multicolored .25 .25
1150 A329 500fr multicolored .65 .30
1151 A329 640fr multicolored .90 .40
1152 A329 1025fr multicolored 1.25 .60
1153 A329 1140fr multicolored 1.50 .75
1154 A276 1500fr multicolored 2.00 1.00
1155 A329 3500fr multicolored 4.50 2.25
Nos. 1149-1155 (7) 11.05 5.55

Souvenir Sheet

1156 A329 4500fr multicolored 6.00 3.00

Fauna A360

No. 1157 — Dogs: a, 40fr, Golden retriever. b, 140fr, Fox terrier. c, 40fr, Coton de tulear. d, 140fr, Langhaar.

No. 1158 — Cats: a, 40fr, Birman. b, 140fr, Egyptian. c, 40fr, European creme. d, 140fr, Rex du Devon.

No. 1159 — Reptiles: a, 1000fr, Phelsuma madagascariensis. b, 2000fr, Cameleon de parson. c, 1000fr, Laticauda laticaudate. d, 2000fr, Testudo radiata.

No. 1160 — Beetles: a, 1000fr, Euchroea spininasuta. b, 2000fr, Orthophagus minnulus klug. c, 1000fr, Helictopleurus radicollis. d, 2000fr, Euchroea coelestis.

1993, Dec. 7 Litho. *Perf. 13½*

1157 A360 Block of 4, #a.-d. .50 .25
1158 A360 Block of 4, #a.-d. .50 .25
1159 A360 Block of 4, #a.-d. 8.00 4.00
1160 A360 Block of 4, #a.-d. 8.00 4.00
e. Sheet of 16, #1157-1160 18.00 8.50

Dated 1991.

Nos. 934-938 Ovptd. in Metallic Blue Nos. 939-939B Ovptd. in Metallic Red Lilac

1993, Sept. 28

1161 A305 250fr multicolored .35 .25
1162 A305 350fr multicolored .50 .25
1163 A305 1000fr multicolored 1.50 .75
1164 A305 1500fr multicolored 2.25 1.10
1165 A305 2500fr multicolored 3.75 1.90
Nos. 1161-1165 (5) 8.35 4.25

Souvenir Sheet

1166 A305 3000fr multi 4.50

Litho. & Embossed

Perf. 13½

1166A A305 5000fr gold & multi 8.00

Souvenir Sheet

1166B A305 5000fr gold & multi 8.00

Nos. 1161-1165 exist in souvenir sheets of 1, and in a sheet containing Nos. 1161-1165 plus label.

A number has been reserved for an additional value in this set.

Marine Life — A361

No. 1167 — Shells: a, 15fr, Chicoreus torrefactus. b, 15fr, Fasciolaria filamentosa. c, 30fr, Stellaria solaris. d, 30fr, Harpa ventricosa lamarck.

No. 1168 — Crustaceans: a, 1250fr, Panulirus. b, 1250fr, Stenopus hispidus. c, 1500fr, Pagure. d, 1500fr, Bernard l'hermite.

No. 1169 — Fish: a, 15fr, Pigopytes diacanthus. b, 15fr, Coelacanth latimeria chalumnae. c, 30fr, Ostracion cyanurus. d, 30fr, Coris gaimardi. e, 1250fr, Balistapus undulatus. f, 1250fr, Forcipiger longirostris. g, 1500fr, Adioryx diadema. h, 1500fr, Pterois lunulata.

1993, Nov. 26 *Perf. 13½*

1167 A361 Block of 4, #a.-d. .25 .25
1168 A361 Block of 4, #a.-d. 7.25 3.50
1169 A361 Block of 8, #a.-h. 7.25 3.50
i. Sheet of 16, #1167-1169 16.50 7.50

Dated "1991."

Flora — A362

No. 1170 — Orchids: a, 45fr, Oceonia oncidiflora. b, 60fr, Cymbidella rhodochica. c,

140fr, Vanilla planifolia. d, 3000fr, Phaius humblotii.

No. 1171 — Fruits: a, 45fr, Artocarpus altilis. b, 60fr, Eugenia malaceensis. c, 140fr, Jambosa domestica. d, 3000fr, Papaya.

No. 1172 — Mushrooms: a, 45fr, Russula annulata. b, 60fr, Lactarius claricolor. c, 140fr, Russula tuberculosa. d, 3000fr, Russula fistulosa.

No. 1173 — Vegetables: a, 45fr, Sweet potatoes. b, 60fr, Yams. c, 140fr, Avocados. d, 3000fr, Mangoes.

1993, Dec. 15 Litho. *Perf. 13*

1170 A362 Strip of 4, #a.-d. 4.25 2.25
1171 A362 Strip of 4, #a.-d. 4.25 2.25
1172 A362 Strip of 4, #a.-d. 4.25 2.25
1173 A362 Strip of 4, #a.-d. 4.25 2.25
e. Sheet of 16, #1170-1173 18.00 9.00

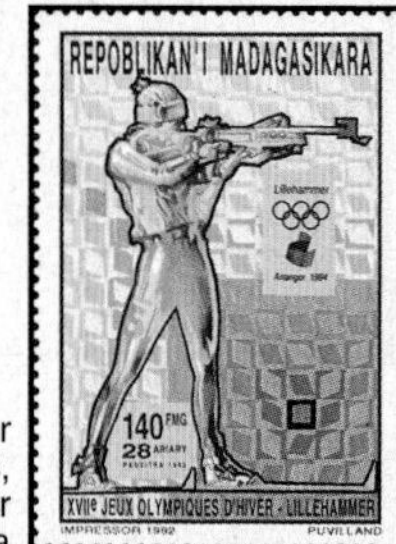
1994 Winter Olympics, Lillehammer A362a

Designs: 140fr, Biathlon. 1250fr, Ice hockey. 2000fr, Figure skating. 2500fr, Slalom skiing. 5000fr, Downhill skiing. No. 1173K, Ski jumping. No. 1173L, Speed skating.

1994, Jan. 19 Litho. *Perf. 13*

1173F-1173I A362a Set of 4 *18.50 9.25*

Souvenir Sheet

1173J A362a 5000fr multi *7.25 3.50*

Litho. & Embossed

1173K A362a 10,000fr gold & multi 13.00

Souvenir Sheet

1173L A362a 10,000fr gold & multi 13.00

No. 1173K exists in a souvenir sheet of 1.
For overprints see Nos. 1288A-1288E.

1996 Summer Olympics, Atlanta — A362b

Scene in Atlanta, event: 640fr, 1892 Windsor Hotel Americus, dressage. 1000fr, Covington Courthouse, women's shot put. 1500fr, Carolton Community Activities Center, table tennis. 3000fr, Newman Historic Commercial Court Square, soccer.

7500fr, Relay race runner. No. 1173R, Pole vault, vert. No. 1173S, Hurdles, vert.

1994, Jan. 19

1173M-1173P A362b Set of 4 *19.50 9.50*

Souvenir Sheet

1173Q A362b 7500fr multi *27.00 13.50*

Litho. & Embossed

1173R A362b 5000fr gold & multi 7.50

Souvenir Sheet

1173S A362b 5000fr gold & multi 8.00

Prehistoric Animals — A363

Designs: 35fr, Dinornis maximus, vert. 40fr, Ceratosaurus, vert. 140fr, Mosasavrus, vert. 525fr, Protoceratops. 640fr, Styvacosaurus. 755fr, Smilodon. 1800fr, Uintatherium.

2000fr, Tusks of mammuthus, trees, vert.

1995, Feb. 23 Litho. *Perf. 12*

1174-1180 A363 Set of 7 4.50 4.50

Souvenir Sheet

1181 A363 2000fr multicolored 3.50 1.50

For surcharge see No. 1474A.

Wild Animals A364

Designs: 10fr, Panthera pardus. 30fr, Martes. 60fr, Vulpes vulpes. 120fr, Canis lupus. 140fr (No. 1186), Fennecus zerda. 140fr (No. 1187), Panthera leo. 3500fr, Uncia uncia.

2000fr, Panthera onca.

1995, Mar. 21

1182-1188 A364 Set of 7 5.00 5.00

Souvenir Sheet

1189 A364 2000fr multicolored 3.50 3.50

D-Day Landings, Normandy, 50th Anniv. — A365

No. 1190: a, 3000fr, American troops, flamethrower. b, 1500fr, Coming ashore. c, 3000fr, Explosion, German commander pointing.

No. 1191 — Liberation of Paris, 50th anniv.: a, 3000fr, Notre Dame, resistance fighters, crowd. b, 1500fr, Arch de Triomphe, woman cheering. c, 3000fr, Eiffel Tower, parade, French troops.

1994 *Perf. 13½*

1190 A365 Strip of 3, #a.-c. 6.75 3.50
1191 A365 Strip of 3, #a.-c. 6.75 3.50

Nos. 1190b, 1191b are 30x47mm. Nos. 1190-1191 are continuous design.

Aquarium Fish A366

Designs: 10fr, Pomacanthus imperator. 30fr, Betta splendens. 45fr, Trichogaster leeri. 95fr, Labrus bimaculatus. No. 1196, 140fr, Synodontis nigreventris. No. 1197, 140fr, Cichlasoma biocellatum. 3500fr, Fudulus heteroclitus.

2000fr, Carassius auratus, vert.

1994, June 28 Litho. *Perf. 12½x12*

1192-1198 A366 Set of 7 5.75 5.75

Souvenir Sheet

Perf. 12x12½

1199 A366 2000fr multicolored 3.25 3.25

Modern Locomotives — A367

Designs: 5fr, Superviem Odoriko. 15fr, Morrison Knudsen Corporation. 140fr, ER-200. 265fr, General Motors. 300fr, New Jersey Transit. 575fr, Siemens Inter-City Express. 2500fr, Sweden's Fast Train.

2000fr, Alstham T60.

1993, Nov. 10 *Perf. 12*

1200-1206 A367 Set of 7 5.00 4.50

Souvenir Sheet

1207 A367 2000fr multicolored 3.25 1.50

For surcharge, see No. 1475A, 1477A.

Cathedrals A368

Cathedral, location: 10fr, Antwerp, Belgium. 100fr, Cologne, Germany. 120fr, Antsirabe, Masdagascar. 140fr, Kremlin, Moscow. 525fr, Notre Dame, Paris. 605fr, Toledo, Spain. 2500fr, St. Stephens, Vienna.

2000fr, Westminster Abbey, London.

1995, Feb. 14 *Perf. 12x12½*

1208-1214 A368 Set of 7 4.50 4.50

Souvenir Sheet

1215 A368 2000fr multicolored 2.75 2.75

Dated 1994.

No. 1215 is inscribed with country name only in the sheet margin.

For surcharge, see No. 1472B.

Insects — A369

Designs: 20fr, Necrophorus tomentosus. 60fr, Dynastes tityus. 140fr, Megaloxantha bicolor. 605fr, Calosoma sycophanta. 720fr, Chrysochroa mirabilis. 1000fr, Crioceris asparaqi. 1500fr, Cetonia aurata.

2000fr, Goliathus goliathus.

1994, Feb. 2 *Perf. 12*

1216-1222 A369 Set of 7 5.50 5.50

Size: 85x58mm

Imperf

1223 A369 2000fr multicolored 2.25 1.25

For surcharge, see No. 1478B.

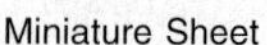
Miniature Sheet

PHILAKOREA '94 — A370

No. 1224: a, 100fr, John Lennon, Ella Fitzgerald. b, 140fr, Marilyn Monroe, Elvis Presley. c, 550fr, U.S. Pres. Bill Clinton, Louis Armstrong.

1995, Feb. 23 *Perf. 12*

1224 A370 Sheet of 2 each, #a.-c. + 3 labels 4.75 2.25

Ancient Art & Architecture — A371

Designs: No. 1225, 350fr, Statue of Augustus, vert. No. 1226, 350fr, Statue, Land Surveyor, vert. No. 1227, 350fr, Painting, "Child of Thera," vert. No. 1228, 350fr, Sarcophagous, Cerveteri and Wife, vert. No. 1229, 350fr, Statue, Athena of Fidia, vert. No. 1230, 405fr, Colosseum, Rome. No. 1231, 405fr, Mask of Agamemnon, vert. No. 1232, 405fr, Forum of Caesar. No. 1233, 405fr, She-Wolf suckling Romulus & Remus. No. 1234, 405fr, Parthenon, Athens. No. 1235, 525fr, Carthaginian mask, vert. No. 1236, 525fr, Bust of Emperor Tiberius, vert. No. 1237, 525fr, Statue of Alexandar the Great, vert. No. 1238, 525fr, Detail, Taormina Theater, vert. No. 1239, 525fr, Denarius of Caesar. No. 1240, 605fr, Forum, Pompeii, vert. No. 1241, 605fr, Bronze statue, Riace, vert. No. 1242, 605fr, Venus de Milo, vert. No. 1243, 605fr, Bronze statue, Archer, vert. No. 1244, 605fr, Pont Du Gard Aqueduct, Nimes.

1994 Litho. *Perf. 13½*

1225-1244 A371 Set of 20 6.50 3.25

Elvis Presley (1935-77) A371a

Design: No. 1244B, "The King," "Presley," Elvis wearing black.

Litho. & Embossed

1994, June 8 *Perf. 13½*

1244A A371a 10,000fr gold & multi 12.00

Souvenir Sheet

1244B A371a 10,000fr gold & multi 12.00

Exists in sheets of 4.

The Stuff of Heroes, by Philip Kaufman — A372

No. 1245: a, 140fr, Astronaut. b, 140fr, Astronaut up close, walking. c, 5000fr, Spacecraft, astronaut.

1994

1245 A372 Strip of 3, #a.-c. 3.75 1.90

Motion pictures, cent. No. 1245 is a continuous design and exists in souvenir sheet of 1 with scenes from the film "Blade Runner."

No. 1245c is 60x47mm.

Intl. Olympic Committee, Cent. — A373

No. 1246: a, 2500fr, Flag. b, 2500fr, Olympic flame. c, 3500fr, Pierre de Coubertin.

1994

1246 A373 Strip of 3, #a.-c. 5.75 2.75

No. 1246 is a continuous design and exists in souvenir sheet of 1. No. 1246c is 60x47mm.

ILO, 75th Anniv. — A374

1994 Litho. *Perf. 13½*
1247 A374 140fr multicolored .25 .25

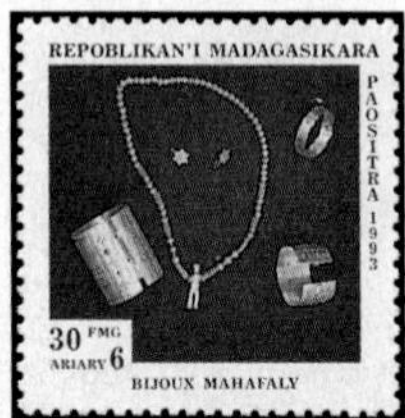
A374a

Designs: 30fr, Mahafaly jewelry. 60fr, Sakalava fork and spoon. 140fr, Antandroy jewelry. 430fr, Sakalava jewelry. 580fr, Antaimoro Ambalavao paper. 1250fr Sakalava jewelry, diff. 1500fr, Inlaid cabinet.
2000fr, Ampanihy tapestry.

1995, Feb. 2 Litho. *Perf. 11¼*
1247A A374a 30fr multi
1247B A374a 60fr multi
1247C A374a 140fr multi
1247D A374a 430fr multi
1247E A374a 580fr multi
1247F A374a 1250fr multi
1247G A374a 1500fr multi

Souvenir Sheet

Imperf

1247H A374a 2000fr multi

For surcharge, see No. 1472.

Modern Ships — A375

Ships: 45fr, Russian car ferry. 50fr, Australian cargo. 100fr, Japanese cruise. 140fr, US cruise. 300fr, English hovercraft. 350fr, Danish cargo. 3000fr, Korean container ship.
2000fr, Finnish car ferry, vert.

1994 Litho. *Perf. 12*
1248-1254 A375 Set of 7 4.50 4.50

Souvenir Sheet

1255 A375 2000fr multicolored 3.25 3.25

1994 World Cup Soccer Championships, U.S. — A375a

Player at: No. 1255A, Left. No. 1255B, Right.

Litho. & Embossed

1994, Aug. 24 *Perf. 13½*
1255A A375a 10,000fr gold & multi 12.00

Souvenir Sheet

1255B A375a 10,000fr gold & multi 12.00

Sports — A377

5fr, Hurdles. 140fr, Boxing. 525fr, Gymnastics. 550fr, Weight lifting. 640fr, Swimming. 720fr, Equestrian. 1500fr, Soccer.
2000fr, Running, horiz.

1995, Apr. 4 Litho. *Perf. 12*
1264-1270 A377 Set of 7 5.00 2.50

Souvenir Sheet

1271 A377 2000fr multicolored 3.25 1.25

A378

Orchids: 50fr, Paphiopedilum siamense. 65fr, Cypripedium calceolus. 70fr, Ophrys oestrifera. 140fr, Cephalanthera rubra. 300fr, Cypripedium macranthon. 640fr, Calanthe vestita. 2500fr, Cypripedium guttatum. 2000fr, Oncidium tigrinum.

1993, Nov. 10 Litho. *Perf. 12*
1272-1278 A378 Set of 7 6.00 2.50

Size: 90x70mm

Imperf

1279 A378 2000fr multicolored 3.25 1.25

Sharks A379

Designs: 10fr, Galeocerdo cuvieri. 45fr, Pristiophorus japonicus. 140fr, Rhincodon typus. 270fr, Sphyrna zygaena. 600fr, Carcharhinus longimanus. 1200fr, Stegostoma tigrinum. 1500fr, Scapanorhynchus owstoni. 2000fr, Galeorhinus zyopterus.

1993, Sept. 22 *Perf. 12*
1280-1286 A379 Set of 7 5.00 2.50

Size: 70x90mm

Imperf

1287 A379 2000fr multicolored 3.25 1.25

Archaea Workmani A380

1994 *Perf. 15*
1288 A380 500fr multicolored 1.00 .75

Nos. 1173F-1173J Ovptd. With Names of Winners in Silver or Gold

Overprinted in silver: 140fr, "M. BEDARD / CANADA." 1250fr, "MEDAILLE D'OR / SUEDE." 2000fr, "O. BAYUL / UKRAINE." 2500fr, "M. WASMEIER / ALLEMAGNE." 5000fr,
Overprinted in gold: 5000fr, "D. COMPAGNONI / ITALIE."

1994, Aug. 30 Litho. *Perf. 13*
1288A-1288D A362a Set of 4 *18.50 9.25*

Souvenir Sheet

1288E A362a 5000fr multi *7.25 3.50*

Marilyn Monroe (1926-62), Elvis Presley (1935-77) — A381

Scenes from films: No. 1289, 100fr, Gentlemen Prefer Blondes. No. 1290, 100fr, Clambake, Roustabout, Viva Las Vegas. 550fr, Some Like it Hot. 1250fr, Girls, Girls, Girls, King Creole. 5000fr, Niagara. 10,000fr, Double Trouble, Kid Gallahad, Speedway.

1995, Aug. 15 Litho. *Perf. 13½*
1289-1294 A381 Set of 6 12.50 12.50

Nos. 1289-1294 exist in souvenir sheets of 1.

Motion Pictures, Cent. A382

Actor, film: No. 1295, 140fr, James Dean, Rebel Without a Cause. No. 1296, 140fr, Burt Lancaster, Vera Cruz. 5000fr, Elvis Presley, Speedway. 10,000fr, Marilyn Monroe, How to Marry a Millionaire.

1995, Aug. 16 Litho. *Perf. 13½*
1295-1298 A382 Set of 4 11.00 11.00
a. Miniature sheet of 4, #1295-1298 *17.50 17.50*

Nos. 1295-1298 exist in souvenir sheets of 1.

Locusts A383

Designs: No. 1299, Assylidae, natural enemy of the locust. No. 1300, Locust eating corn, vert. No. 1301, Gathering locusts for consumption.

1995, Sept. 26 Litho. *Perf. 13½*
1299 A383 140fr multicolored .90 .25
1300 A383 140fr multicolored .90 .25
1301 A383 140fr multicolored .90 .25
Nos. 1299-1301 (3) 2.70 .75

Malagasyan Bible, 160th Anniv. — A384

1995, June 21 Litho. *Perf. 15*
1302 A384 140fr multicolored .25 .25

World Post Day — A385

1995, Oct. 9 *Perf. 13½*
1303 A385 500fr multicolored .80 .35

Nos. 967-972 Ovptd. in Silver

1996, Jan. 21 Litho. *Perf. 13½*
1304 A314 2000fr on No. 971 *3.50 1.75*
1304A A314 Sheet of 6, #b-g, 1304

No. 1304 exists in souvenir sheet of 1, overprinted in gold or silver. No. 1304A exists with gold overprint.

Death of Charles de Gaulle, 25th Anniv. — A386

No. 1305: a, 100fr, World War I battle. b, 100fr, As President of France. c, 100fr, Brazzaville, 1940. d, 500fr, Pierre Brossolette, Churchill, De Gaulle. e, 500fr, Young woman. f, 500fr, Yak 9T, Gen. Leclerc. g, 1500fr, Liberation of Paris. h, 1500fr, De Gaulle as younger man. i, 1500fr, Jean Moulin, Free French barricade in Paris. j, 7500fr, Writing Tourbillon de L'Histoire, Colombey Les Deux Eglises. k, 7500fr, Giving speech as older diplomat. l, 7500fr, Doves, French flag, older De Gaulle standing on hilltop.

1996, Apr. 28 Litho. *Perf. 13½*
1305 A386 Sheet of 12, #a.-l. 21.50 10.75

See design A390.

Famous People A387

Designs: 1500fr, Wilhelm Steinitz (1836-1900), American chess master. 1750fr,

Emmanuel Lasker (1868-1941), German chess master. 2000fr, Enzo Ferrari (1898-1988), automobile designer. 2500fr, Thomas Stafford, American astronaut, A.A. Leonov, Russian cosmonaut. 3000fr, Jerry Garcia (d. 1995), musician. 3500fr, Ayrton Senna (1960-94), race car driver. 5000fr, Paul-Emile Victor (1907-95), polar explorer. 7500fr, Paul Harris (1868-1947), founder of Rotary Intl.

1996, Feb. 20
1306-1313 A387 Set of 8 20.00 10.00

Nos. 1306-1313 exist in souvenir sheets of 1.

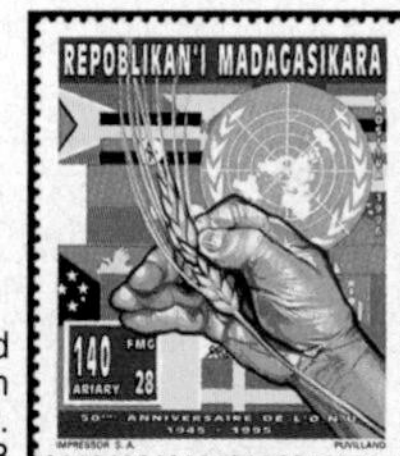

UN and UNICEF, 50th Anniv. A388

Designs: No. 1314, 140fr, Hand holding shaft of grain, UN emblem. No. 1315, 140fr, UN building, flags, map, woman feeding child. No. 1316, 140fr, Child holding plate of food, child holding UNICEF emblem. 7500fr, Two children, UNICEF emblem.

1996, Aug. 30
1314-1317 A388 Set of 4 5.25 2.50

Nos. 1314-1317 exist in souvenir sheets of 1.

Jade — A389

No. 1318, 175fr: a, People on mountain. b, Carving of insect, leaves. c, Chops on a chain. d, Insect in stone.

1996, Apr. 20 Litho. *Perf. 13½*
1318 A389 Sheet of 4, #a.-d. 2.50 1.25

A390

No. 1319: Bruce Lee (1940-73), various portraits.

No. 1320: John Lennon (1940-80), various portraits.

No. 1321: Locomotives: a, Train going left. b, Train going right. c, ICE Train, Germany. d, Eurostar.

No. 1322: Louis Pasteur (1822-95), various portraits.

No. 1323: Francois Mitterrand (1916-96), various portraits.

No. 1324: Intl. Space Station: a, Shuttle Atlantis, MIR Space Station. b, MIR. c, Intl. Space Station. d, Shuttle, Alpha section of station.

Sheets of 4, #a.-d.

1996 Litho. *Perf. 13½*
1319 A390 500fr multicolored 2.25 1.10
1320 A390 1500fr multicolored 3.75 1.90
1321 A390 1500fr multicolored 3.75 1.90
1322 A390 1750fr multicolored 4.25 2.10
1323 A390 2000fr multicolored 5.00 2.50
1324 A390 2500fr multicolored 6.25 3.00

Post Day — A396

Various local post offices: a, 500fr. b, 1000fr. c, 3500fr. d, 5000fr.

1996, Oct. 16 Litho. *Perf. 13½*
1325 A396 Sheet of 4, #a.-d. 6.25 3.00

United Nations Program for International Drug Control — A396a

Perf. 11¾x11½
1996, Oct. 23 Photo.
1325E A396a 140fr multi —

Sports Cars — A397

No. 1326: a, Mercedes W196 driven by Juan Manuel Fangio. b, Porsche 911 Carrera. c, Porsche 917-30. d, Mercedes 600 SEC.

1996
1326 A397 3000fr Sheet of 4, #a.-d. 7.50 3.75

1996 Olympic Games, Atlanta

Perf. 11¾x11½
1996, Dec. 27 Litho.
Granite Paper
1326E A397a 140fr Judo
1326F A397a 140fr Tennis

UN, 50th Anniv. — A398

140fr, Private sector promotion. 500fr, Lemur, tortoise. 1500fr, Grain stalks.

1995, Oct. 24 Litho. *Perf. 11½x11¾*
1327 A398 140fr multi
1328 A398 500fr multi
1330 A398 1500fr multi

An additional stamp exists in this set. The editors would like to examine it.

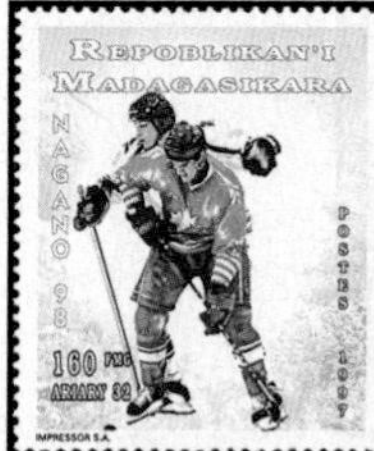

1998 Winter Olympics, Nagano A399

Designs: 160fr, Ice hockey. 350fr, Pairs figure skating. 5000fr, Biathlon. 7500fr, Freestyle skiing.
12,500fr, Speed skating.

1997 Litho. *Perf. 13½*
1331-1334 A399 Set of 4 6.75 3.50

Souvenir Sheet

1335 A399 12,500fr multicolored 6.50 3.25

No. 1335 contains one 42x60mm stamp.

1998 World Cup Soccer Championships, France — A400

Various soccer plays: 300fr, 1350fr, 3000fr, 10,000fr.

1997
1336-1339 A400 Set of 4 7.75 4.00

Souvenir Sheet

1340 A400 12,500fr Player, ball 6.50 3.25

No. 1340 contains one 42x60mm stamp.

Greenpeace, 25th Anniv. — A401

Views of Rainbow Warrior I: 1500fr, At anchor. 3000fr, Under sail. 3500fr, Going left, small raft. 5000fr, Going forward at full speed.
12,500fr, Under sail, vert.

1996, Apr. 16 Litho. *Perf. 13½*
1341-1344 A401 Set of 4 5.50 2.75

Souvenir Sheet

1345 A401 12,500fr multicolored 5.50 2.75

Dinosaurs — A402

No. 1346: a, Herrerasaurus, archaeopteryx. b, Segnosaurus, dimorphodon. c, Sauropelta, proavis.

No. 1347: a, Eudimorphodon, eustreptospondylus. b, Triceratops, rhamphorychus. c, Pteranodon, segnosaurus.

12,500fr, Tenontosaurus, deinonychus, vert.

1998, Feb. 25
1346 A402 1350fr Sheet of 3, #a.-c. 2.25 1.10
1347 A402 5000fr Sheet of 3, #a.-c. 8.00 4.00

Souvenir Sheet

1348 A402 12,500fr multicolored 6.50 3.25

Dated 1997.

Meteorites and Minerals — A403

No. 1349 — Meteorites: a, Iron, found in Chile. b, Iron, found in Alvord, Iowa. c, Silicate in lunar meteorite, found in Antarctica.

No. 1350 — Minerals: a, Agate, dioptase. b, Malachite, garnet. c, Chrysolile, wulfenite.

12,500fr, Mars meterorite, found in Antarctica.

1998, Feb. 25
1349 A403 3000fr Sheet of 3, #a.-c. 5.00 2.50
1350 A403 7500fr Sheet of 3, #a.-c. 12.00 6.00

Souvenir Sheet

1351 A403 12,500fr multicolored 6.50 3.25

Dated 1997.

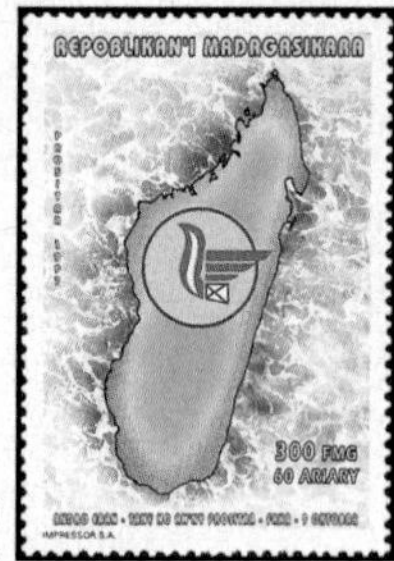

World Post Day — A404

1997, Oct. 21 Litho. *Perf. 13½*
1352 A404 300fr multicolored 5.50 2.75

Radio Nederland in Madagascar, 25th Anniv. — A404a

Perf. 11¾x11½
1997, Sept. 18 Litho.
Granite Paper
1352A A404a 500fr multi — —

Third Francophone Games — A404b

Background colors: 300fr, Light blue. 1850fr, Beige.

1997, Oct. 9 Litho. *Perf. 11½x11¾*
Granite Paper
1352B-1352C A404b Set of 2 1.75 1.75

For surcharge, see No. 1490.

Diana, Princess of Wales (1961-97) — A405

No. 1353 — Diana wearing: a, High-collared white dress. b, Halter-style dress. c, Choker necklace, purple dress. d, Wide-brimmed hat. e, Jeweled choker necklace. f, White dress, no necklace. g, Black dress. h, White dress, pearls. i, Red dress.

No. 1354 — Portraits of Diana: a, Wearing jeweled necklace. b, With Pope John Paul II. c, Wearing beaded jacket. d, With Nelson Mandela. e, With man from India. f, With Emperor Akihito. g, Holding infant. h, Receiving flowers from child. i, Visiting sick child.

No. 1355, 12,500fr, With Mother Teresa (in margin). No. 1356, 12,500fr, With Princess Grace (in margin). No. 1357, 12,500fr, With land mine victim. No. 1358, 12,500fr, Rose-colored dress, hat.

1998, Feb. 18 Litho. *Perf. 13½*

1353	A405	1350fr Sheet of 9, #a.-i.	6.50	3.25
1354	A405	1750fr Sheet of 9, #a.-i.	8.50	4.25

Souvenir Sheets

1355-1358	A405	Set of 4	27.00	14.00

Nos. 1355-1358 each contain one 42x60mm stamp.

Pasteur Institute of Madagascar, Cent. — A405a

1998 Litho. *Perf. 11¾x11½*

1358A	A405a	500fr multi	—	—
1358B	A405a	2500fr multi		—

An additional stamp was issued in this set. The editors would like to examine it.

1998 World Cup Soccer Championships, France — A406

No. 1359 — Group A: a, Brazil. b, Scotland. c, Morocco. d, Norway.

No. 1360 — Group B: a, Italy. b, Chile. c, Cameroun. d, Austria.

No. 1361 — Group C: a, France. b, South Africa. c, Saudi Arabia. d, Denmark.

No. 1362 — Group D: a, Spain. b, Nigeria. c, Paraguay. d, Bulgaria.

No. 1363 — Group E: a, Netherlands. b, Belgium. c, South Korea. d, Mexico.

No. 1364 — Group F: a, Germany. b, US. c, Yugoslavia. d, Iran.

No. 1365 — Group G: a, Romania. b, Colombia. c, England. d, Tunisia.

No. 1366 — Group H: a, Argentina. b, Japan. c, Jamaica. d, Croatia.

1998, July 10 Litho. *Perf. 13½*
Sheets of 4, #a.-d.

1359	A406	1350fr multi	2.75	1.40
1360	A406	1500fr multi	3.00	1.50
1361	A406	1700fr multi	3.50	1.75
1362	A406	2000fr multi	4.00	2.00
1363	A406	2500fr multi	5.00	2.50
1364	A406	3000fr multi	6.00	3.00
1365	A406	3500fr multi	7.00	3.50
1366	A406	5000fr multi	10.00	5.00

Sheets exist without Group A-Group H inscriptions. Stamps on these sheets have different denominations, and some design details differ. These sheets were allegedly on sale for a brief time before withdrawal.

Antsirabe Military Academy, 30th Anniv. — A406a

1998 Litho. *Perf. 11½x11¾*

1366E	A406a	500fr multi	—	—
1366F	A406a	2500fr multi		—

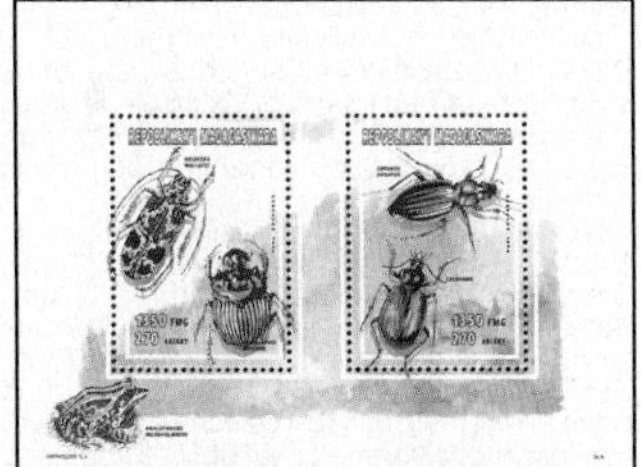

Insects, Butterflies, Mushrooms, Minerals — A407

No. 1367 — Insects: a, Batocera wallacei, heliocopris antenor. b, Carabus auratus, calosome.

No. 1368 — Butterflies: a, Catopsilia thauruma. b, Iphiclides podalirius.

No. 1369 — Mushrooms: a, Hygrocybe punicea. b, Lepista nuda.

No. 1370 — Insects: a, Euchroma gigantea, goliathus goliathus. b, Pyrrbocor apterus, Acroninus longimanus.

No. 1371 — Butterflies: a, Hypolimnas dexithea. b, Colotis zoe.

No. 1372 — Mushrooms: a, Boletus edulis bull. b, Hygrophorus hypotheium.

No. 1373 — Minerals: a, Vanadinite. b, Carnotite.

No. 1374, 12,500fr, Papilio dardanus. No. 1375, 12,500fr, Albatrellus ovinus.

1998 Litho. *Perf. 13½*
Sheets of 2, #a.-b.

1367	A407	1350fr multi	1.60	.70
1368	A407	2500fr multi	3.00	1.25
1369	A407	3000fr multi	3.50	1.50
1370	A407	3500fr multi	4.00	1.75
1371	A407	5000fr multi	5.75	2.50
1372	A407	7500fr multi	8.25	3.75
1373	A407	10,000fr multi	11.00	5.00

Souvenir Sheets

1374-1375	A407	Set of 2	14.00	6.50

Nos. 1374-1375 each contain one 36x42mm stamp.

Personalities A408

Designs: No. 1376, Andrianary Ratianarivo (1895-1949). No. 1377, Odeam Rakoto (1922-73). No. 1378, Fredy Rajaofera (1902-68).

1997, Aug. 21

1376-1378	A408	140fr Set of 3	.45	.25

The Titanic — A409

No. 1379 — Faces of the Titanic: a, 1300fr, J. Pierpont Morgan, owner, White Star Line. b, 1300fr, J. Bruce Ismay, director, White Star Line. c, 1300fr, Lord James Pirrie, builder, Harland & Wolff. d, 1300fr, Alexander Carlisle, designer, Harland & Wolff. e, 1300fr, Edward John Smith, Captain of Titanic. f, 1750fr, Arthur Rostron, Captain of Carpathia.

No. 1380 — Rescue: a, 1350fr, Women and children first. b, 1350fr, Lifeboats lowered. c, 1350fr, Lifeboats called back. d, 1350fr, Captain Smith hands child to safety. e, 1700fr, Few saved from water. f, 1700fr, Reaching Carpathia.

No. 1381, vert. — Various pictures of ship taken from period postcards: a, 300fr. b, 5000fr. c, 1200fr. d, 7500fr.

No. 1382 — Interior of ship: a, 800fr, Grand staircase. b, 800fr, Reception area. c, 850fr, Restaurant. d, 850fr, Stateroom. e, 1300fr, Turkish baths. f, 10.000fr, Swimming pool.

No. 1383 — Building the ship: a, 1450fr, Drafting room, 1907-08. b, 2050fr, Hull constructed, 1909-11. c, 5000fr, Launch, Belfast, May 31, 1911. d, 7500fr, Fitting out, 1911-12.

No. 1384 — The aftermath: a, 300fr, "The Sun" post lastest bulletins. b, 450fr, Paperboys on street. c, 1050fr, Hearses, coffins at dock. d, 5000fr, Wallace Hartley, "The Last Tune." e, 10,000fr, Engineers Monument, 1914.

1998, Sept. 10 Litho. *Perf. 13½*

1379	A409	Sheet of 6, #a.-f.	3.50	1.50
1380	A409	Sheet of 6, #a.-f.	3.75	1.60
1381	A409	Sheet of 4, #a.-d.	6.25	2.50
1382	A409	Sheet of 6, #a.-f.	6.50	2.75
1383	A409	Sheet of 4, #a.-d.	7.00	3.00
1384	A409	Sheet of 5, #a.-e.	7.25	3.25

No. 1381 contains four 37½x49mm stamps. No. 1382 contains six 49x38mm stamps. No. 1384, five 28x35mm stamps.

Famous Disasters at Sea — A410

No. 1385: a, 160fr, Sinking of the Titanic, 1912. b, 160fr, Torpedoing of the Lusitania, 1915. c, 1350fr, Burning of the Atlantique, 1933. d, 1350fr, Burning of the Normandie, 1942. e, 1350fr, Wilhelm Gustloff being torpedoed, 1945. f, 1350fr, Sinking of the Andrea Doria, 1956. g, 3500fr, Burning of the Queen Elizabeth, 1972. h, 3500fr, Sinking of the Amoco Cadiz, 1978. i, 3500fr, Sinking of the Estonia, 1994.

No. 1386, Various scenes of Titanic disaster.

1998, Nov. 6 Litho. *Perf. 13½*

1385	A410	Sheet of 9, #a.-i.	7.75	3.75

Souvenir Sheet

1386	A410	12,500fr multicolored	6.25	3.00

No. 1386 contains one 120x51mm stamp.

Trains, Sports Cars, Airplanes — A411

No. 1387 — Trains: a, Steam locomotive, 477.043, China. b, Kruckenberg Zeppelin Train, Germany. c, Mountain 498, China. d, Gottardo tram, Switzerland. e, TGV 001, France. f, ET-403, Germany. g, Le Shuttle, France. h, Shinkansen, Japan. i, TGV Alexander Dumas, France.

No. 1388 — Sports cars: a, Opel Kapitan, Germany. b, Volkswagen Beetle, Germany. c, Fiat Topolino, Italy. d, Facel Delahaye, France-England. e, Bristol Series 407, England. f, Alfa Romeo 2500, Italy. g, Chrysler Viper GTS, US. h, McLaren FI, England. i, Mercedes Brabus SLK, Germany.

No. 1389 — Airplanes: a, Aerospatiale STS 2000, France. b, Piggyback Space Shuttle, US. c, Hermes Rocket, France, Germany, Italy. d, Northrop B-35, US. e, Airbus A310, A321, A340, Europe. f, Armstrong Whitworth A.W52, Great Britain. g, Concorde, UK, France, going right. h, Tupolev, Russia. i, Concorde, France, UK, going left.

1998, Nov. 6

1387	A411	1700fr Sheet of 9, #a.-i.	7.50	3.75
1388	A411	2000fr Sheet of 9, #a.-i.	9.00	4.50
1389	A411	3000fr Sheet of 9, #a.-i.	13.50	6.75

Balloons A412

No. 1390: a, 300fr, "Pilatre de Rozier," Montgolfier, 1783. b, 300fr, Charles and Robert, 1783. c, 300fr, Blanchard and Jeffries, 1785. d, 350fr, "Pilatre de Rozier," 1785. e, 350fr, "Testu-Brissy," 1798. f, 350fr, "Atlantic," 1858. g, 5000fr, "Small World," 1959. h, 5000fr, "Strato-lab High 5", 1961. i, 5000fr, "Double Eagle II", 1978.

10,000fr, Auguste Piccard (1884-1962), balloon.

1998, Nov. 6

1390	A412	Sheet of 9, #a.-i.	8.50	4.25

Souvenir Sheet

1391	A412	10,000fr multicolored	5.00	2.50

No. 1391 contains one 42x51mm stamp.

Butterflies and Moths — A413

No. 1392: a, 1950fr, Citrus swallowtail. b, 1950fr, Mocker swallowtail. c, 1950fr, Striped policeman. d, 1950fr, Golden piper. e, 1950fr, Painted lady. f, 1950fr, Monarch. g, 250fr, Gold-banded forester. h, 250fr, Madagascan sunset moth. i, 250fr, Palla butterfly. j, 250fr, Blue pansy. k, 250fr, Common grass blue. l, 250fr, Crimson tip.

1800fr, Cabbage butterfly, vert. No. 1394, Broad-bordered grass yellow. 2250fr, Figtree blue. 3500fr, African migrant, vert.

1999, Mar. 24

1392	A413	Sheet of 12, #a.-l.	7.50	3.50

Souvenir Sheets

1393 A413 1800fr multicolored 1.25 .55
1394 A413 1950fr multicolored 1.40 .60
1395 A413 2250fr multicolored 1.50 .65
1396 A413 3500fr multicolored 2.50 1.00

Birds — A414

No. 1397: a, 250fr, Madagascar blue pigeon. b, 250fr, White-tailed tropicbird. c, 1350fr, Madagascan red fody. d, 1350fr, Crested drongo. e, 250fr, Namaqua dove. f, 250fr, Helmet bird. g, 1350fr, Blue-crowned roller. h, 1350fr, Red-eyed roller. i, 250fr, Coral-billed nuthatch. j, 250fr, Wattled false sunbird. k, 1350fr, Short-legged ground roller. l, 1350fr, Pied crow.

No. 1398, 4000fr, Barn owl. No. 1399, 4000fr, Goliath heron.

No. 1400, 7200fr, Marah harrier hawk, horiz. No. 1401, 7200fr, Vasa parrot, horiz.

1999, Feb. 17 Litho. *Perf. 13½*
1397 A414 Sheet of 12, #a.-l. 4.75 1.75

Souvenir Sheets

1398-1399 A414 Set of 2 4.25 1.50
1400-1401 A414 Set of 2 7.75 2.75

New Year 1999 (Year of the Rabbit) — A415

No. 1402 — Stylized rabbits: a, Facing right. b, Looking right over shoulder. c, Looking left over shoulder. d, Facing left.
10,000fr, Facing forward.

1999, Apr. 7 Litho. *Perf. 14*
1402 A415 1500fr Sheet of 4, #a.-d. 3.00 1.25

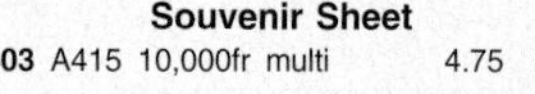

Souvenir Sheet

1403 A415 10,000fr multi 4.75 3.75

Grain and Map — A415a

1999 Litho. *Perf. 13½*
1403A A415a 450fr brn & multi — —
1403B A415a 900fr red & multi
1403C A415a 900fr green & multi — —
1403D A415a 1500fr (300a) blue & multi — —
1403E A415a 5600fr multi — —

Nos. 1403Dand 1403E are airmail. Denomination is at bottom on No. 1403A. Nos. 1403A and 1403C are dated "2000." On No. 1403D, the denomination is at the bottom with large capital and lower case letters.

Lizards — A416

World Wildlife Fund: a, 1700fr, Chamaeleo minor (on branch). b, 2400fr, Phelsuma standingi. c, 300fr, Chamaeleo balteatus. d, 2050fr, Chamaeleo minor (on rock). e, 2050fr, as "d," inscribed "Urplatus fimbriatus."

1999, Apr. 7
1404 A416 Block of 4, #a.-d. 8.75 8.75
f. Block of 4, #1404a-1404c, 1404e 5.25 5.25

Issued in sheets of 16 stamps.
Issued: No. 1404e, 7/23.

Fauna A417

Designs: No. 1405, 1950fr, Toucan. No. 1406, 1950fr, Hummingbird. No. 1407, 1950fr, Dendrobates pumilis. No. 1408, 1950fr, Jaguar, vert. No. 1409, 1950fr, Dendrobate (frog). No. 1410, 1950fr, Pangolin.

No. 1411: a, Three-toed sloth (d). b, Chameleon (e). c, Loris (f). d, Tree frog. e, Tarsier. f, Civet (i). g, Cicada. h, Callicore butterfly. i, Python (f).

No. 1412: a, Flying fox (bat). b, Galago (a, d, e). c, Squirrel monkey (f). d, Red kingfisher. e, Blue parrot (h). f, Heliconide butterfly. g, Oranutan (d). h, Tamarin. i, Ocelot (h).

No. 1413, 10,000fr, Tiger. No. 1414, 10,000fr, Leopard.

1999, Apr. 7
1405-1410 A417 Set of 6 4.50 4.50
1411 A417 2250fr Sheet of 9, #a.-i. 7.50 7.50
1412 A417 2450fr Sheet of 9, #a.-i. 7.75 7.75

Souvenir Sheets

1413-1414 A417 Set of 2 7.50 7.50

Film Stars — A418

No. 1414A: b, Antonio Banderas. c, Glenn Close. d, Harrison Ford. e, Pamela Anderson. f, Tom Hanks. g, Michelle Pfeiffer. h, Leonardo Di Caprio. i, Sharon Stone. j, Tom Cruise.

No. 1415: a. Catherine Deneuve. b, Gérard Depardieu. c, John-Paul Belmondo. d, John Reno. e, Johnny Hallyday. f, Christopher Lambert. g, Jean Gabin. h, Alain Delon. i, Brigitte Bardot.

1999 Litho. *Perf. 13½*
1414A A418 2500fr Sheet of 9, #b.-j. 12.00 12.00
1415 A418 3500fr Sheet of 9, #a.-i. 11.50 11.50

Fauna — A419

No. 1416: a, Rotary International emblem and Hapalemur gris, satellite. b, Rotary International emblem and Lemur vari, satellite. c, Rotary International emblem and Hanka. d, Scouting emblem, comet ,and Sifaka de verreaux. e, Scouting emblem, comet, and Euplere de goudot. f, Scouting emblem, comet, and Potamochere. g, Lions International emblem and Rousette geante, satellite. h, Lions International emblem, Lampira, comet. i, Lions International emblem, Maki catta, satellite.

No. 1416J — Butterfly and : k, Gibbon lar. l, Macaque rhesus. m, Maki macaco. n, Gélada. o, Maki brun. p, Nasique. q, Maki vari. r, Mandrill. s, Hapalémur gris.

1999 Sheets of 9 + 3 Labels
1416 A419 2500fr #a.-i., + 3 labels 10.00 10.00
1416J A419 3500fr #k.-s., + 3 labels 14.00 14.00

Intl. Year of the Ocean A420

Designs: No. 1417, Scarus gibbus. No, 1418, Gramma loreto. No. 1419, Arusetta asfur. No. 1420, Daseyllus trimaculatus.

No. 1421: a, Hyporhamphus unifasciatus. b, Delphinus delphis. c, Cetorhinus maximus. d, Manta birostris. e, Chactodon capistratus. f, Microspathodon chysurus.

No. 1422: a, Coryphaena hippurus. b, Diodon holacanthus. c, Aequorea aequorea. d, Sphyraena barracuda. e, Octopus vulgaris. f, Acanthurus bahianus. g, Gymnothorax moringa. h, Limulus polyphemus. i, Pristis pictinata.

No. 1423: a, 1350fr, Balistoides niger. b, 1350fr, Isiophorus platypterus. c, 2750fr, Carcharhinus limbatus. d, 2750fr, Carcharodon carcharias. e, 1350fr, Zanclus cornutus. f, 1350fr, Mermaid's face. g, 2750fr, Gramma loreto. h, 2750fr, Rhinecanthus aculeatus. i, 1350fr, Lactoria cornuta. j, 1350fr, Hippocampus kuda. k, 2750fr, Pygoplites diancanthus. l, 2750fr, Epinephelus lanceolatus. m, 1350fr, Echinaster sepositus. n, 1350fr, Ocypede quadrata. o, 2750fr, Amphiprion clarkii. p, 2750fr, Cyphoma gibbosum.

No. 1424, 7200fr, Odontaspis taurus, vert. No. 1425, 7200fr, Stenalla plagiodon.

1999, June 10 *Perf. 14*
1417-1420 A420 550fr Set of 4 1.75 1.75

Sheets of 6, 9 or 16

1421 A420 550fr Sheet of 6, #a.-f. 1.60 1.60
1422 A420 3500fr Sheet of 9, #a.-i. 15.00 15.00
1423 A420 Sheet of 16, #a.-p. 15.00 15.00

Souvenir Sheets

1424-1425 A420 Set of 2 7.25 7.25

No. 1423a-1423p are each 33x52mm. Dated 1998.

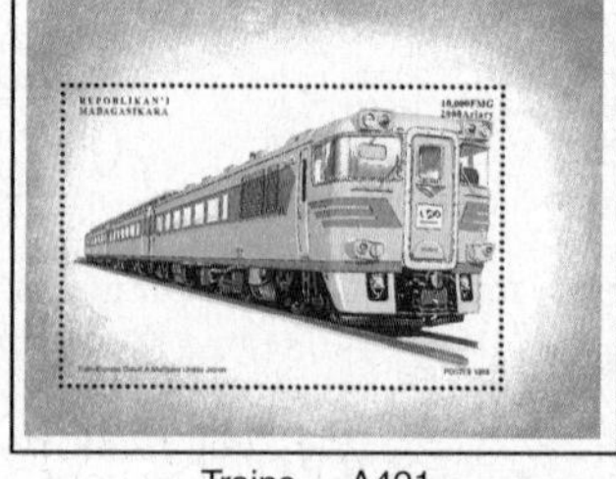

Trains — A421

No. 1426, 4000fr: a, Danish State Railways, 1950-59. b, France, 1963. c, East Germany, 1980. d, Finnish State Railways, 1950. e, Canada, 1949. f, West Germany, 1952.

No. 1427, 4000fr: a, Light Branch 4-4-0 locomotive, Ireland, 1948. b, 4-8-0 locomotive, Argentina, 1949. c, 2-8-0 locomotive, US, 1943. d, Gold rush steam engine, US, 1870. e, Royal Blue, US, 1870-80. f, Queensland Railways, Australia, 1952.

No. 1428, 4000fr: a, 0-4-0 Lightning, England, 1829. b, Grampton, Namur, Belgium, 1848. c, Lion, England, 1838. d, Borsig, Germany, 1841. e, Baldwin "Eight-coupled" locomotive, US, 1846. f, Crampton, England, 1848.

No. 1429, 10,000fr, Diesel multiple-unit express train, Japan. No. 1430, 10,000fr, 4-8-0 steam locomotive, US, 19th cent.

1999, June 22 Sheets of 6, #a-f
1426-1428 A421 Set of 3 27.00 27.00

Souvenir Sheets

1429-1430 A421 Set of 2 7.50 7.50

Nos. 1429-1430 each contain one 76x50mm stamp. No. 1426c is incorrectly inscribed with date, "1930."

A422

Dinosaurs A423

Designs: No. 1431, 500fr, Stenonychosaurus, vert. No. 1432, 500fr, Iguanodon, vert. No. 1433, 500fr, Staurikosaurus, vert. No. 1434, 500fr, Plateosaurus, vert.

No. 1435, 500fr, Antrodemus. No. 1436, 500fr, Corythosaurus, vert. No. 1437, 500fr, Stegosaurus, vert. No. 1438, 500fr, Lambeosaurus, vert. No. 1439, 500fr, Hypsilophodon, vert.

No. 1440: a, Psittacosaurus. b, Allosaurus. c, Stegosaurus. d, Hypsilophodon. e, Triceratops. f, Camptosaurus. g, Compsognathus. h, Carnotaurus.

No. 1441, vert: a, Brachiosaurus. b, Tyrannosaurus. c, Plateosaurus. d, Hadrosaurus. e, Triceratops. f, Iguanodon.

No. 1442, 12,500fr, Styracosaurus. No. 1443, 12,500fr, Brachiosaurus, vert. No. 1444, 12,500fr, Tyrannosaurus rex, vert.

1999, July 6 Litho. *Perf. 14*
1431-1434 A422 Set of 4 1.10 1.10
1435-1439 A423 Set of 5 1.40 1.40
1440 A422 1850fr Sheet of 8, #a.-h. 5.50 5.50
1441 A422 1950fr Sheet of 6, #a.-f. 4.50 4.50

Souvenir Sheets

1442-1444 A422 Set of 3 13.50 13.50

Nos. 1431-1439 dated 1998. Numbers have been reserved for additional values in this set.

Princess Diana — A424

1999, Aug. 10 Litho. *Perf. 13½*
1446 A424 1950fr multicolored 1.00 1.00

Issued in sheets of six stamps.
Compare with Type A434.

Picasso Paintings A425

Designs: 2750fr, Bacchanalia, 1955. 7200fr, Picador, 1971, vert. 7500fr Seated Nude, 1906-07, vert.
12,500fr, The Two Saltimbanques, 1901, vert.

1999, Aug. 10 Litho. *Perf. 13x13¼*
1447-1449 A425 Set of 3 6.75 6.75

Souvenir Sheet

1450 A425 12,500fr multi 4.75 4.75

Dated 1998.

Mahatma Gandhi — A426

Perf. 13½x13¼

1999, Aug. 10 **Litho.**

1451	A426	2250fr Profile	1.25	1.25

Souvenir Sheet

1452	A426	12,500fr Gandhi shirtless	4.75	4.75

No. 1451 issued in sheets of four stamps. Dated 1998.

Indian Ocean Commission, 15th Anniv. A427

1999 **Litho.** ***Perf. 13¼***

1453	A427	500fr multicolored	.60	.60

Fire Fighting Apparatus — A429

No. 1456, 2500fr: a, Pumper Boat "Dauphin," Africa. b, 60T Pumper, US. c, Fire train, Switzerland.

No. 1457, 2500fr: a, Gillois amphibian engine, Germany. b, Ford FMC pumper. c, Cherry picker pumper, Iraq.

1999 **Sheets of 3, #a-c**

1456-1457	A429	Set of 2	7.00	7.00

Trains — A430

No. 1458, 3500fr: a, Pen-y-Darren, England. b, Pennsylvania Railroad locomotive. c, Norfolk and Western locomotive.

No. 1459, 3500fr: a, TGV Postal, France. b, TGV, Sweden. c, Magnetic train "Europa."

1999 **Sheets of 3, #a-c**

1458-1459	A430	Set of 2	9.50	9.50

Airplanes — A431

No. 1460, 5000fr: a, Short-Mayo Composite. b, Boeing 747. c, Concorde, Air France poster.

No. 1461, 5000fr: a, Concorde, KLM poster. b, 1931 Curtiss F9C. c, Macchi-Castoldi MC72.

1999 **Sheets of 3, #a-c**

1460-1461	A431	Set of 2	13.00	13.00

Space Achievements — A432

No. 1462, 7500fr: a, Viking. b, Voyager. c, Apollo 11.

No. 1463, 7500fr: a, Dog Laika. b, Yuri Gagarin, Vostok spacecraft. c, Mir space station.

1999 **Sheets of 3, #a-c**

1462-1463	A432	Set of 2	20.00	20.00

Boy Scouts — A433

Scouts, No. 1464: a, Bandaging thigh. b, Splinting arm. c, Making sling. d, Pulling tape from roll.

No. 1464E: f, Oeniella polystachys. g, Cynorkis lowiana. h, Oeceoclades saundersiana. i, Cynorkis purpurascens.

No. 1465: a, Upupa epops. b, Nettapus auritus. c, Leptosomus discolor. d, Brachypteracias squamigera.

No. 1465E: f, Euchraca spinnasuta. g, Cricket. h, Scorpion. i, Euchroea nigrostellata.

No. 1466: a, Charaxes antamboulou. b, Hypolimnas misippus. c, Papilio demodocus. d, Papilio antenor.

No. 1467: a, Eucalyptoboletus. b, Cantharllus congolensis. c, Gomphus. d, Russula.

No. 1468: a, Jasper. b, Granite. c, Rhodonite. d, Morganite.

No. 1469: a, Soccer. b, Chess. c, Table tennis. d, Cycling.

1999 **Litho.** ***Perf. 13¼***

Sheets of 4, #a.-d.

1464	A433	1350fr multi	2.25	2.75
1464E	A433	1500fr multi	3.00	3.00
1465	A433	1950fr multi	4.00	4.00
1465E	A433	2000fr multi	4.00	4.00
1466	A433	2500fr multi	4.75	4.75
1467	A433	3000fr multi	5.50	5.50
1468	A433	5000fr multi	8.75	8.75
1469	A433	7500fr multi	13.50	13.50
		Nos. 1464-1469 (8)	45.75	46.25

No. B27 Handstamp Surcharged in Violet

Printing Methods and Perfs as before

1999 (?)

1471	SP7	60fr on 350fr+20fr on 250fr+20fr	

Various Stamps Surcharged

No. 1472

No. 1472B

No. 1473B

No. 1473A

No. 1474A

No. 1474B

No. 1475A

No. 1477

No. 1478

No. 1478B

No. 1485

No. 1487

No. 1488

No. 1489

Printing Methods and Perfs as Before

1998-99 (?)

1472	A374a	300fr on 430fr #1247D		—
1472A	A369	300fr on 605fr #1219		—
1472B	A368	300fr on 605fr #1213	—	—
1473A	A342	300fr on 675fr #1076		—
1473B	A352	300fr on 675fr #1118	—	—
1474	A342	300fr on 720fr #1077		—
1474A	A363	300fr on 755fr #1179	—	—
1474B	A191	400fr on 170fr #614	—	—
1475A	A367	400fr on 265fr #1203		—
1475B	A207	500fr on 170fr #645	—	—
1477	A341	500fr on 555fr #1068		—
1477A	A367	500fr on 575fr #1205	—	—
1478	A353	500fr on 675fr #1127		—
1478A	A325b	500fr on 680fr #1001G	—	—
1478B	A369	500fr on 720fr #1220		—
1482	A333	500fr on 1140fr #1043	—	—
1483	A379	500fr on 1200fr #1285		—
1485	A344	500fr on 1300fr #1086		—

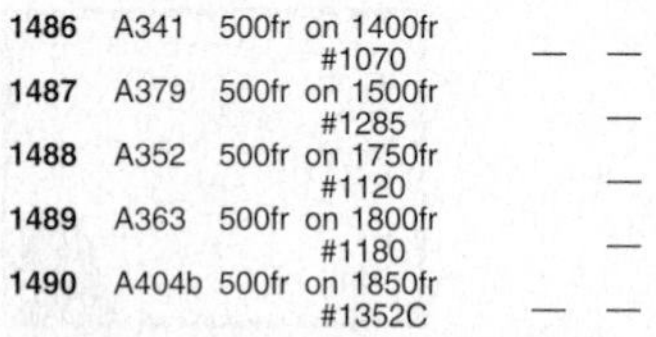

1486	A341	500fr on 1400fr #1070	—	—
1487	A379	500fr on 1500fr #1285		—
1488	A352	500fr on 1750fr #1120		—
1489	A363	500fr on 1800fr #1180		—
1490	A404b	500fr on 1850fr #1352C	—	—

At least 14 additional surcharges have been reported. The editors would like to examine them.

20th Century Celebrities — A434

No. 1491: a, Princess Diana. b, Kwame Nkrumah. c, Gen. Georgy Zhukov. d, Samora Machel. e, Gen. Moshe Dayan. f, Mahatma Gandhi. g, Jacqueline Kennedy. h, Gen. John Pershing.

1999 Litho. ***Perf. 13½***

1491 A434 1950fr Sheet of 8, #a.-h. 7.25 7.25

Famous People — A435

Designs: No. 1492, 900fr, Razafindrakotohasina Rahantavololona. No. 1493, 900fr, Gen. Gabriel Ramanantsoa. No. 1494, 900fr, Rasalama. No. 1495, 900fr, Dr. Ralivao Ramiaramanana. No. 1496, 900fr, Jérôme-Henri Cardinal Rakotomalala. No. 1497, 900fr, Rakotovao Razakaboana.

2000, Jan. 12 Litho. ***Perf. 14***

1492-1497 A435 Set of 6 3.00 3.00

UPU, 125th Anniv. — A436

UPU emblem, postmen of various eras and: 1000fr, Mailbox. 1200fr, Postmen, space shuttle, airplane, cargo. 1800fr, Cable-laying ships. 3200fr, 19th century diligence, modern mail truck. 3500fr, balloon, Apollo 15 astronaut. 5000fr, Stentor satellite, Claude Chappe's semaphore. 5600fr, Micheline ZM 517, Autorail Bouleze 701. 7500fr, Old and modern mail trains.

1999 Litho. ***Perf. 13¼***

1498-1505 A436 Set of 8 13.00 13.00

Nos. 1498-1505 exist in souvenir sheets of 1.

The Incredible Hulk — A437

No. 1506: a, Hulk with gray skin, wearing white shirt. b, Head of Hulk, red background. c, Hulk with fist raised, blue background. d, Hulk with red violet pants, lilac background. e, Hulk with ripped shirt, orange background. f, Hulk wearing sunglasses. g, Hulk shirtless, orange and red background. h, Hulk holding shirt, red violet and orange background. i, Hulk, multicolored striped background.

12,500fr, Hulk, yellow and orange background.

1999, Apr. 29 Litho. ***Perf. 13¼***

1506 A437 1800fr Sheet of 9, #a-i 7.00 7.00

Souvenir Sheet

1507 A437 12,500fr multi 6.00 6.00

No. 1507 contains one 36x42mm stamp.

Silver Surfer — A438

No. 1509: a, Silver Surfer at left, dark blue green background. b, Head of Silver Surfer, red brown background. c, Silver Surfer at right, black background with large star. d, Silver Surfer on surfboard, purple background. e, Head of Silver Surfer, green background. f, Silver Surfer carrying surfboard, purple background. g, Silver Surfer, Earth and outer space in background. h, Silver Surfer, multicolored striped background. i, Silver Surfer on surfboard, outer space background with red and blue spots.

12,500fr, Silver Surfer, diff.

1999, Apr. 29

1508 A438 1800fr Sheet of 9, #a-i 7.00 7.00

Souvenir Sheet

1509 A438 12,500fr multi 6.00 6.00

No. 1509 contains one 36x42mm stamp.

Spiderman — A439

No. 1510: a, Peter Parker turning into Spiderman. b, Spiderman with fist at upper right. c, Spiderman crouching. d, Spiderman holding silk at top. e, Head of Spiderman. f, Spiderman with rays around head. g, Spiderman with arms together, on silk. h, Spiderman with two strands of silk. i, Spiderman with large black spider on front of costume, and netting under arms.

12,500fr, Spiderman with arms raised.

1999, Apr. 29

1510 A439 3200fr Sheet of 9, #a-i 11.50 11.50

Souvenir Sheet

1511 A439 12,500fr multi 6.00 6.00

No. 1511 contains one 30x42mm stamp.

Garfield — A440

No. 1512: a, Garfield sitting. b, Garfield looking between legs. c, Garfield holding teddy bear. d, Garfield climbing wall. e, Garfield sticking out tongue. f, Garfield with legs crossed. g, Garfield asleep. h, Garfield standing. i, Odie.

1999, Apr. 29

1512 A440 3200fr Sheet of 9, #a-i 11.50 11.50

Miniature Sheets

Trains — A441

No. 1513, 800fr: a, Locomotive PK 102 on Brickaville to Fonavana line. b, Locomotive in Diego-Suarez region, 1904. c, 030T locomotive, 1922. d, BBB Alsthom Diesel-electric, 1937.

No. 1514, 1500fr: a, Locomotive 42104, 1906. b, Decauville 60 gauge locomotive. c, Mallet 020+020T locomotive, 1916. d, Garratt No. 101 locomotive, 1925.

No. 1515, 2000fr: a, Billard ZM 111 rail car, 1938. b, BB AD16 locomotive. c, Brissoneau Diesel-electric rail car, 1958. d, BBB 2nd Series 106-112, 1958.

No. 1516, 3500fr: a, Train at Fianarantsoa Station. b, AD 12 Alsthom locomotive. c, Mallet 131+131 St. Leonard. d, Micheline ZM 514.

No. 1517, 4000fr: a, Decauville 0.20 gauge 1m locomotive. b, BB235 Diesel. c, Baldwin 031 T locomotive. d, BBB Alsthom Diesel locomotive, 1935.

No. 1518, 4400fr: a, Decauville 60 gauge Montagne d'Ambre locomotive. b, Brissoneau & Lotz Diesel, 1938. c, Mallet 120+020 T locomotive, 1902. d, Corpet-Louvet locomotive.

No. 1519, 5200fr: a, Adiz BB229 locomotive. b, 030T Weidnecht locomotive, 1901. c, Jung locomotive, 1922. d, Billard rail car, 1934.

No. 1520, 10,000fr: a, Mallet 020+020 locomotive, 1925. b, Decauville 030 locomotive, 1907. c, Garratt 130+031 locomotive, 1925. d, Nosy Be 030N1, 1868.

2000, July 21 ***Perf. 13¼***

Sheets of 4, #a-d

1513-1520 A441 Set of 8 45.00 45.00

Miniature Sheets

2000 Summer Olympics, Sydney — A442

No. 1521, 500fr: a, Soccer. b, Handball. c, Judo. d, Kayaking.

No. 1522, 1350fr: a, Cycling. b, Swimming. c, Boxing. d, Fencing.

No. 1523, 2500fr: a, Basketball. b, Cycling, diff. c, Equestrian. d, Running.

No. 1524, 3200fr: a, Weight lifting. b, Javelin. c, Equestrian, diff. d, Yachting.

No. 1525, 5000fr: a, Shot put. b, Women's gymnastics. c, Men's tennis. d, High jump.

No. 1526, 7500fr: a, Diving. b, Wrestling. c, Table tennis. d, Pole vault.

12,500fr, Kayaking and equestrian, horiz.

2000, Aug. 2 Litho.

Sheets of 4, #a-d

1521-1526 A442 Set of 6 25.00 25.00

Souvenir Sheet

1527 A442 12,500fr multi 4.00 4.00

No. 1527 contains one 57x51mm stamp and exists imperf.

Space Achievements A443

Launches of: No. 1528, 1500fr, Gemini 1. No. 1529, 1500fr, Saturn 1. No. 1530, 1500fr, Apollo 6. No. 1531, 1500fr, Mariner 3. No. 1532, 1500fr, Mariner 4. No. 1533, 1500fr, Titan IIIC. No. 1534, 1500fr, Discovery. No. 1535, 1500fr, Soyuz 19.

No. 1536, 3500fr — Spacecraft: a, Cassini-Huygens. b, Exosat. c, ICE. d, Solar Mesosphere Explorer. e, Mir Space Station. f, Observer.

No. 1537, 3500fr — Spacecraft: a, Mars 1. b, Solar Max. c, Venera 4. d, Skylab. e, Space Shuttle Challenger. f, Mars 3.

No. 1538, 4400fr — Spacecraft: a, Ranger 1. b, Mariner 4. c, Gemini 9. d, Gemini 2. e, Apollo 15. f, Gemini 12.

No. 1539, 5000fr — Spacecraft: a, Agena. b, Syncom 1. c, Olympus 1. d, FLT Satcom. e, Skynet 4B. f, COBE.

No. 1540, 6800fr, horiz.: a, Skylab. b, Agena 1. c, Agena 2. d, X-36. e, Space Shuttle. f, Dale Gardner spacewalking.

No. 1541, 6800fr, horiz.: a, Hermes prototype. b, Pioneeer 10. c, Venture Star. d, Viking. e, Spacecraft landing on Mars. f, Mars Rover.

No. 1542, 10,000fr, Apollo 1 mission patch. No. 1543, 10,000fr, Apollo 9 mission patch. No. 1544, 10,000fr, Apollo 11 mission patch.

No. 1545, 10,000fr, Apollo-Soyuz mission patch. No. 1546, 10,000fr, Columbia Space Shuttle mission patch. No. 1547, 12,500fr, Gemini 4 mission patch. No. 1548, 12,500fr, Gemini 12 mission patch. No. 1549, 12,500fr, Gemini 9 mission patch, horiz. No. 1550, 12,700fr, Huygens Probe approaching Titan. No. 1551, 12,700fr, Space Shuttle at Space Station, horiz.

Perf. 14, 14¾ (#1540-1541, 1550-1551)

2000, Sept. 22
1528-1535 A443 Set of 8 3.75 3.75

Sheets of 6, #a-f

1536-1541 A443 Set of 6 55.00 55.00

Souvenir Sheets

1542-1551 A443 Set of 10 35.00 35.00

June 21, 2001 Solar Eclipse A444

2001, June 21 ***Perf. 13x13¼***
1552 A444 5600fr multi — —

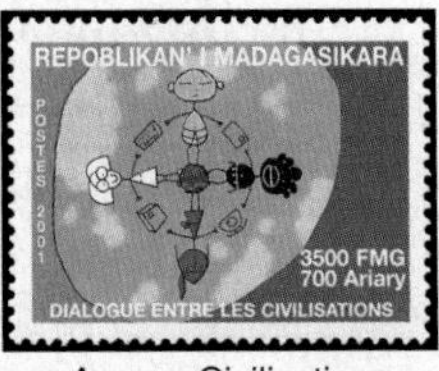

Dialogue Among Civilizations — A445

2001, Oct. 12 ***Perf. 13½x13¼***
1553 A445 3500fr multi 2.50 2.50

Miniature Sheets

Flora and Fauna — A446

No. 1554, 250fr — Turtles: a, Tortue geante des Seychelles. b, Tortue luth. c, Tortue panthere. d, Caouanne. e, Cistude d'Europe. f, Chelonee.

No. 1555, 400fr — Fish: a, Astronotus ocellatus. b, Cyphotilapia frontosa. c, Bothriolepis. d, Pseudanthias tuka. e, Cleidopus gloriamaris. f, Ablabys taenionotus.

No. 1556, 500fr — Owls: a, Grand duc de Virginie. b, Chouette cheveche Brahmans. c, Grand duc du cap. d, Grand duc d'Afrique. e, Hibou moyen duc. f, Petit duc Choliba.

No. 1557, 1500fr, vert. — Turtles: a, Tortue à cou cache d'Afrique. b, Tortue à dos diamante. c, Tortue d'Hermann. d, Tortue Grecque. e, Tortue caret. f, Geochelone denticulata.

No. 1558, 2500fr, vert. — Parrots: a, Ara militaire. b, Ara vert. c, Ara macao. d, Ara hyacinthe. e, Perroquet de Meyer. f, Ara ararauna.

No. 1559, 3400fr, vert. — Bears and pandas: a, Ours lippu. b, Ours noir. c, Ours polaire. d, Petit panda. e, Ours des cocotiers. f, Ours à collier.

No. 1560, 3500fr — Insects and spiders: a, Xylocopa violacea. b, Triatoma infestans. c, Myrmecia gulosa. d, Mantis religiosa. e, Atrax robustus. f, Euglosse.

No. 1561, 4000fr, vert. — Primates: a, Ouistiti mignon. b, Tamarin lion d'ore. c, Singe de nuit. d, Magot. e, Vervet. f, Ouakari.

No. 1562, 4200fr — Flowers: a, Stapelia wilmaniae. b, Centaurea montana. c, Pagonia suffruticosa. d, Acanthosicyos horrida. e, Erimophila colorhabdos. f, Amaryllis belladonna.

No. 1563, 4400fr — Orchids: a, Cattleya amethystoglossa. b, Vanda coerulea. c, Orchis robusta. d, Orchis papilionacea. e, Orchis fragrans. f, Orchis italica.

Perf. 13½x13¼, 13¼x13½

2001, Oct. 25

Sheets of 6, #a-f

1554-1563 A446 Set of 10 47.50 47.50

The following items inscribed "Repoblikan'i Madigaskara" have been declared "illegal" by Madagascar postal officials:

Sheets of nine 2000fr stamps: Motorbikes; Concorde; Elephants; Birds (2 different).

Sheets of nine stamps: Dinosaurs.

Sheet of six 5600fr stamps: Mars Exploration.

Sheets of four 5600fr stamps: Chess; Prehistoric horses; Mushrooms and eagles; Mushrooms and cats; Mushrooms and butterflies; Mushrooms and owls (2 different).

Sheet of three 5600fr stamps: Nude females (3 different).

Sheet of four 5000fr stamps: Monet paintings.

Souvenir sheets of one 1750fr stamp: Marilyn Monroe (8 different).

Souvenir sheets of two 7500fr stamps: Marilyn Monroe.

Souvenir sheet of one 12,500fr stamp: J. Baptiste Simeon Chardin.

Souvenir sheets of one: Actors Robert De Niro, Robert Redford and Leonardo DiCaprio; Actress Michelle Pfeiffer; Concorde (2 different); Fire fighting (4 different).

Famous Men — A447

Designs: No. 1564, 1500fr, Rakoto Frah (1925-2001), flutist. No. 1565, 1500fr, Albert Rakoto Ratsimamanga (1907-2001), ambassador.

2002, Oct. 9 **Litho.** ***Perf. 13x12¾***
1564-1565 A447 Set of 2 2.75 2.75

Primates — A448

Design: 1000fr, Verreaux's sifaka (prophiteque de Verreauxi). 2500fr, Lemur catta.

2002, Oct. 9 **Litho.** ***Perf. 13x12¾***
1566 A448 1000fr multi
1567 A448 2500fr multi 1.75 1.75

Furcifer Pardalis — A448a

2002, Oct. 9 **Litho.** ***Perf. 12¾x13***
1568 A448a 3000fr multi —

Flora A449

Designs: 100fr, Chorisia ventricosa. 350fr, Eichhornia crassipes, vert. 400fr, Didieraceae. 500fr, Palm tree, Nosy Iranja, vert. 900fr, Ravinala, vert. 4400fr, Takhtajania perrieri. 6800fr, Ravinala, diff., vert.

Perf. 12¾x13, 13x12¾

2002, Oct. 9 **Litho.**
1569-1575 A449 Set of 7 12.50 12.50

For surcharge, see No. 1621.

Diplomatic Relations Between Madagascar and People's Republic of China, 30th Anniv. — A450

2002, Nov. 6 ***Perf. 12***
1576 A450 2500fr multi 1.90 1.90

5 Iraimbilanja = 1 Ariary

Establishment of Japan International Cooperation Agency Bureau in Madagascar — A451

2003, Dec. 4 **Litho.** ***Perf. 13x13¼***
1577 A451 300a multi 2.25 2.25

The ariary officially replaced the franc on Aug. 1, 2003.

Indri Indri — A452

Denomination color: 500a, Bister. 3000a, White.

2003, Dec. 4 **Litho.** ***Perf. 13¼x13***
1578 A452 500a multi 1.75 1.75
1579 A452 3000a multi — —

First Catholic Church in Madagascar — A453

House, Falafa A454

House in High Plateaus A455

Pirate Cemetery, Ste. Marie A456

2003, Dec. 4 **Litho.** ***Perf. 13¼x13½***
1580 A453 800a multi 2.50 2.50
1581 A454 900a multi 3.00 3.00
1582 A455 1100a multi 3.50 3.50
1583 A456 2000a multi 6.25 6.25
Nos. 1580-1583 (4) 15.25 15.25

Indian Ocean Commission, 20th Anniv. — A457

2003, Dec. 4 **Litho.** ***Perf. 13¼x13***
1584 A457 1200a multi —

Flowers — A458

Designs: 20a, Xyloolaena perrieri. 100a, Megistostegium microphyllum. 120a, Tambourissa, horiz. 200a, Leptolaena diospyroidea. 300a, Ochna greveanum. 1500a, Schizolaena tampoketsana.

Perf. 13¼x13, 13x13¼

2003, Dec. 4 **Litho.**
1585 A458 20a multi — —
1586 A458 100a multi —
1587 A458 120a multi —
1588 A458 200a multi —
1589 A458 300a multi — —
1590 A458 1500a multi —

World Health Day — A459

2004, Oct. 9 **Litho.** ***Perf. 13½x13***
1591 A459 300a multi 1.75 1.75

Isalo Wolf Rock Formation A460

Nosy Mitsio — A461

Fort Dauphin A462

Tamatave A463

Dancers at Rova of Ambohimanga — A464

Red Tsingy, Irodo A465

Lemur and Ostriches A466

Perf. 13¼x13, 13x13¼

2004, Nov. 15 **Litho.**

1592 A460	400a multi		1.25	.50
1593 A461	600a multi			.60
1594 A462	1000a multi		2.75	1.00
1595 A463	1200a multi			1.25
1596 A464	2000a multi		5.25	1.50
1597 A465	5000a multi		13.00	3.25
1598 A466	10,000a multi		30.00	6.00

Royalty — A467

Designs: 20a, Ranavalona I, 1828-61. 80a, Ranavalona III, 1883-96. 100a, Radama I, 1810-28. 200a, Radama II, 1861-63. 500a, Rasoherina, 1863-68. 800a, Andrianampoinimerina, 1787-1810. 1500a, Ranavalona II, 1863-83.

2004, Nov. 15 **Litho.** ***Perf. 13¼x13***
1599-1605 A467 Set of 7 15.00 15.00

Rotary International, Cent. — A468

2005, Feb. 23 ***Perf. 13x13¼***
1606 A468 2100a multi 2.60 2.60

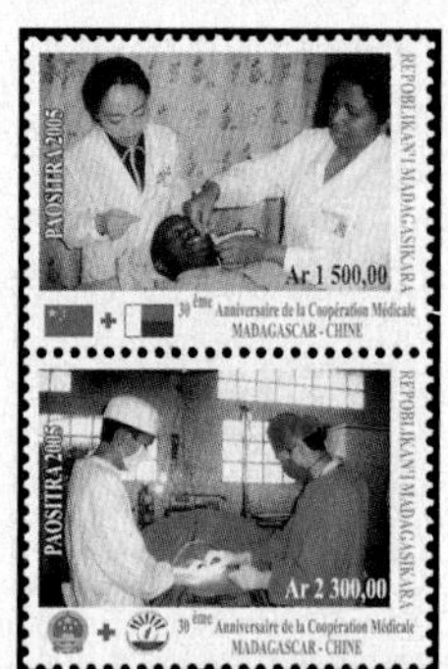

Medical Cooperation Between Madagascar and People's Republic of China, 30th Anniv. — A469

No. 1607 — Medical workers, patients and Chinese and Madagascar: a, 1500a, Flags. b, 2300a, Arms.

2005, Dec. 8 ***Perf. 12***
1607 A469 Pair, #a-b 3.50 3.50

Miniature Sheet

Orchids — A470

No. 1608, 1500a: a, Aerangis cryptodon. b, Aeranthes grandiflora. c, Aeranthes henrici. d, Aeranthes peyrotii. e, Oeccoclades spathulifera. f, Angraecum sesquipedale. g, Cynorchis elata. h, Angraecum viguieri. i, Gastrochis humblotii. j, Gastrorchis lutea. k, Gastrorchis pulcher. l, Jumellea sagittata. m, Microcoelia gilpinae. n, Angraecum praestans.

2005, Dec. 29 ***Perf. 13¼x13***
1608 A470 Sheet of 14, #a-n, + 2 labels 19.50 19.50

Campaign Against AIDS — A471

2006, Feb. 10
1609 A471 300a multi .40 .40

Mpitandrina Rainimamonjisoa (1805-82) A472

2006, Mar. 1
1610 A472 300a blk & lt blue .40 .40

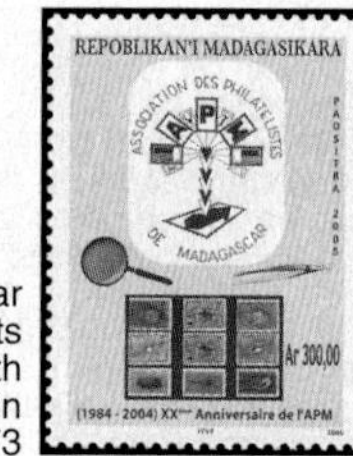

Madagascar Philatelists Association, 20th Anniv. (in 2004) — A473

2006, Mar. 1
1611 A473 300a multi .40 .40

Léopold Sédar Senghor (1906-2001), First President of Senegal — A474

2006, Mar. 20
1612 A474 2000a multi 2.00 2.00

Seventh Indian Ocean Islands Games — A475

2007, June 22 **Litho.** ***Perf. 13***
1613 A475 300a multi .40 .40

Ile Sainte Marie Whale Festival A476

Designs: 1100a, Two whales. 3000a, Whale and two fish, vert.

Perf. 13x13¼, 13¼x13
2007, Aug. 2 **Litho.**
1614-1615 A476 Set of 2 8.50 8.50

Régis Rajemisa-Raolison (1913-90), Linguist, Founder of Havatsa Upem — A477

2008, May 15 **Litho.** ***Perf. 13***
1616 A477 300a red & black .40 .40

No. 1403E Surcharged

No. 1600 Surcharged

Methods and Perfs As Before
2008, Sept. 29
1617 A415a 300a on 5600fr #1403E 1.10 1.10
1618 A467 300a on 80a #1600 1.10 1.10

No. 1617 is airmail.

Postman Delivering Mail — A478

2008, Oct. 21 **Litho.** ***Perf. 13¼x13***
1619 A478 100a multi .25 .25

"Post For All" — A479

2009, Oct. 9 **Litho.** ***Perf. 13x13¼***
1620 A479 300a multi —

No. 1573 Surcharged

Method and Perf. As Before
2010, May 14
1621 A449 300a on 900fr #1573 .55 .55

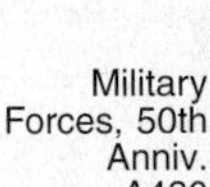

Military Forces, 50th Anniv. A480

Perf. 13¼x13½

2010, June 26 **Litho.**
1622 A480 300a multi .65 .65

Flowers A481

Designs: 100a, Physena sessiliflora. 200a, Pentachlaena latifolia. 300a, Rhopalocarpus similis. 500a, Asteropeia amblyocarpa, vert.

2011, Feb. 16 *Perf. 13½*
1623 A481 100a multi — —
1624 A481 200a multi — —
1625 A481 300a multi — —
1626 A481 500a multi — —

Dated 2010.

Antananarivo City Hall — A482

Jean Laborde Blast Furnace A483

Red Cirque of Mahajanga A484

2013, Jan. 30 **Litho.** *Perf. 13½*
1627 A482 300a multi 1.25 1.25
1628 A483 1600a multi 4.25 4.25
1629 A484 1900a multi 5.25 5.25
Nos. 1627-1629 (3) 10.75 10.75

Green Turtle A486

2014, Oct. 9 **Litho.** *Perf. 13x13¼*
1637 A486 1500a multi 1.10 1.10

See Comoro Islands No. , France No. 4695, French Southern & Antarctic Territories No. 511, Mauritius No. 1144, Seychelles No. 904.

SEMI-POSTAL STAMPS

No. 84 Surcharged in Red

1915, Feb. **Unwmk.** *Perf. 13½x14*
B1 A9 10c + 5c rose & brn 1.50 1.50

Curie Issue
Common Design Type

1938, Oct. 24 *Perf. 13*
B2 CD80 1.75fr + 50c brt ultra 11.00 11.00

French Revolution Issue
Common Design Type
Name and Value Typographed in Black

1939, July 5 **Photo.**
B3 CD83 45c + 25c grn 9.50 9.50
B4 CD83 70c + 30c brn 9.50 9.50
B5 CD83 90c + 35c red org 9.50 9.50
B6 CD83 1.25fr + 1fr rose pink 9.50 9.50
B7 CD83 2.25fr + 2fr blue 9.50 9.50
Nos. B3-B7 (5) 47.50 47.50

Common Design Type and

Malgache Sharpshooter — SP1

Tank Corpsman SP2

1941 **Photo.** *Perf. 13½*
B8 SP1 1fr + 1fr red 1.50
B9 CD86 1.50fr + 3fr maroon 1.50
B10 SP2 2.50fr + 1fr blue 1.75
Nos. B8-B10 (3) 4.75

Nos. B8-B10 were issued by the Vichy government in France, but were not placed on sale in Madagascar.

Nos. 162, 190 Surcharged "SECOURS +50c NATIONAL"

1942
B11 A12 1fr + 50c dk red & car rose .40
B12 A14 3fr + 50c olive black .40

Nos. B11-B12 were issued by the Vichy government in France, but were not placed on sale in Madagascar.

Petain Type of 1941Surcharged in Black or Blue (Bl)

1944 **Engr.** *Perf. 12½x12*
B13 50c + 1.50fr on 2.50fr deep blue (Bl) .80
B14 + 2.50fr on 1fr bister brown .80

Colonial Development Fund.

Nos. B13-B14 were issued by the Vichy government in France, but were not placed on sale in Madagascar.

Catalogue values for unused stamps in this section, from this point to the end of the section, are for Never Hinged items.

Red Cross Issue
Common Design Type

1944 **Unwmk.** *Perf. 14½x14*
B15 CD90 5fr + 20fr dk grn .90 .90

The surtax was for the French Red Cross and national relief.

Gen. J. S. Galliéni and Malagasy Plowing — SP3

1946, Nov. **Engr.** *Perf. 13*
B16 SP3 10fr + 5fr dk vio brn .40 .40

50th anniv. of Madagascar's as a French Colony.

Tropical Medicine Issue
Common Design Type

1950, May 15
B17 CD100 10fr + 2fr dk Prus grn & brn vio 5.50 5.50

The surtax was for charitable work.

Malagasy Republic
No. 320 Surcharged in Ultramarine with New Value and: "FETES DE L'INDEPENDANCE"

1960, July 29 **Engr.** *Perf. 13*
B18 A38 20fr + 10fr red, blk & brt grn .60 .35

Anti-Malaria Issue
Common Design Type

1962, Apr. 7 *Perf. 12½x12*
B19 CD108 25fr + 5fr yel grn .75 .50

Post Office, Tamatave SP4

1962, May 8 **Engr.** *Perf. 13*
B20 SP4 25fr + 5fr sl grn, bl & lt red brn .70 .35

Issued for Stamp Day, 1962.

Freedom from Hunger Issue
Common Design Type

1963, Mar. 21 *Perf. 13*
B21 CD112 25fr + 5fr red org, plum & brn .60 .45

FAO "Freedom from Hunger" campaign.

Type of 1962

20fr+5fr, Central Parcel P. O., Tananarive.

1963, May 8 **Engr.**
B22 SP4 20fr + 5fr bl grn & red brn .60 .35

Issued for Stamp Day, 1963.

Postal Savings and Checking Accounts Building, Tananarive — SP5

1964, May 8 **Unwmk.** *Perf. 13*
B23 SP5 25fr + 5fr bl, bis & dk grn .80 .50

Issued for Stamp Day, 1964.

No. 457 Surcharged in Violet Blue

1972, June 26 **Engr.** *Perf. 13*
B24 A106 30fr + 20fr multi .90 .50

Charles de Gaulle memorial.

SP6

1989, June 15 **Litho.**
B25 SP6 80fr +20fr Torch bearer .50 .25

Village games.

SP7

1990, Aug. 7 **Litho.** *Perf. 12*
B26 SP7 100fr+20fr on 80fr+20fr .45 .25
B27 SP7 350fr+20fr on 250fr+20fr .80 .35

3rd Indian Ocean Games. Nos. B26-B27 were not issued without surcharge.
For surcharge see No. 1471.

AIR POST STAMPS

Airplane and Map of Madagascar — AP1

Perf. 13x13½

1935-41 Photo. Unwmk.

Map in Red

C1 AP1 50c yellow green .65 .45
C2 AP1 90c yel grn ('41) .50
C3 AP1 1.25fr claret .50 .50
C4 AP1 1.50fr bright blue .50 .50
C5 AP1 1.60fr br blue ('41) .25 .25
C6 AP1 1.75fr orange 8.75 3.75
C7 AP1 2fr Prus blue .85 .45
C8 AP1 3fr dp org ('41) .25 .25
C9 AP1 3.65fr ol blk ('38) .85 .50
C10 AP1 3.90fr turq grn ('41) .25 .25
C11 AP1 4fr rose 45.00 3.25
C12 AP1 4.50fr black 27.50 2.50
C13 AP1 5.50fr ol blk ('41) .25 .25
C14 AP1 6fr rose lil ('41) .35 .25
C15 AP1 6.90fr dl vio ('41) .25 .25
C16 AP1 8fr rose lilac 1.50 .90
C17 AP1 8.50fr green 1.50 1.10
C18 AP1 9fr ol grn ('41) .35 .35
C19 AP1 12fr violet brown .80 .55
C20 AP1 12.50fr dull violet 1.90 .90
C21 AP1 15fr org yel ('41) .80 .55
C22 AP1 16fr olive green 1.75 1.10
C23 AP1 20fr dark brown 2.50 1.75
C24 AP1 50fr brt ultra ('38) 4.75 4.50
Nos. C1,C3-C24 (23) 102.05 25.10

According to some authorities the 90c was not placed on sale in Madagascar.

Airplane and Map of Madagascar — AP1a

Type of 1935-41 without "RF"

1942-44

Map in Red,
Tablet & Value in Blue (except #C25)

C25 AP1a 50c yel grn .25
C25A AP1a 90c yel grn .55
C25B AP1a 1.25fr claret .30
C25C AP1a 1.50fr brt blue .50
C25D AP1a 2fr Prus blue .50
C25E AP1a 3.65fr ol blk .65
C25F AP1a 4fr rose .65
C25G AP1a 4.50fr black .50
C25H AP1a 5fr red brown .90
C25I AP1a 8fr rose lilac .90
C25J AP1a 8.50fr green .90
C25K AP1a 10fr green .65
C25L AP1a 12.50fr dull violet .70
C25M AP1a 16fr ol grn .70
C25N AP1a 20fr dk brn 1.25
C25O AP1a 50fr brt ultra 1.75
Nos. C25-C25O (16) 11.65

Nos. C25-C25O were issued by the Vichy government in France, but were not placed on sale in Madagascar.

Airplane Over Farm — AP1b

1942-44 Engr. *Perf. 13*

C26 AP1b 100fr red brown .65

No. C26 was issued by the Vichy government in France, but was not placed on sale in Madagascar.

Air Post Stamps of 1935-38 Overprinted in Black

1942 *Perf. 13x13½*

C27 AP1 1.50fr brt bl & red 6.50 6.50
C28 AP1 1.75fr org & red 92.50 92.50
C29 AP1 8fr rose lil & red 2.10 2.10
C30 AP1 12fr vio brn & red 4.00 4.00
C31 AP1 12.50fr dl vio & red 2.50 2.50
C32 AP1 16fr ol grn & red 6.50 6.50
C33 AP1 50fr brt ultra & red 4.00 4.00

Nos. C3, C9, C17 Surcharged in Black

C34 AP1 1fr on 1.25fr 4.75 4.75
C35 AP1 3fr on 3.65fr 1.25 1.25
C36 AP1 8fr on 8.50fr 1.40 1.40
Nos. C27-C36 (10) 125.50 125.50

Catalogue values for unused stamps in this section, from this point to the end of the section, are for Never Hinged items.

Common Design Type

1943 Photo. *Perf. 14½x14*

C37 CD87 1fr dk orange .25 .25
C38 CD87 1.50fr brt red .25 .25
C39 CD87 5fr brown red .40 .35
C40 CD87 10fr black .40 .35
C41 CD87 25fr ultra .90 .55
C42 CD87 50fr dk green 1.40 .80
C43 CD87 100fr plum 2.00 1.25
Nos. C37-C43 (7) 5.60 3.80

Victory Issue

Common Design Type

Perf. 12½

1946, May 8 Unwmk. Engr.

C44 CD92 8fr brown red 1.00 .35

European victory of the Allied Nations in World War II.

Chad to Rhine Issue

Common Design Types

1946, June 6

C45 CD93 5fr brt blue 1.50 1.25
C46 CD94 10fr dk car rose 1.60 1.25
C47 CD95 15fr gray grn 1.60 1.25
C48 CD96 20fr brown olive 1.75 1.40
C49 CD97 25fr dk violet 1.75 1.50
C50 CD98 50fr brown org 2.10 1.75
Nos. C45-C50 (6) 10.30 8.40

Tamatave — AP2

Allegory of Air Mail — AP3

Plane over Map of Madagascar — AP4

Perf. 13½x12½, 12½x13½

1946 Photo. Unwmk.

C51 AP2 50fr bl vio & car 1.50 .50
C52 AP3 100fr brn & car 4.00 .90
C53 AP4 200fr bl grn & brn 7.50 2.00
Nos. C51-C53 (3) 13.00 3.40

No. C52 Overprinted in Carmine

1948, Oct. 26 *Perf. 12½x13½*

C54 AP3 100fr brn & car 45.00 *65.00*

Issued to publicize the French claim to Antarctic Adelie Land, discovered by Jules S. C. Dumont d'Urville in 1840.

UPU Issue

Common Design Type

1949, July 4 Engr. *Perf. 13*

C55 CD99 25fr multi 4.00 2.75

Scene Near Bemananga — AP5

1952, June 30 Unwmk. *Perf. 13*

C56 AP5 500fr brn, blk brn & dk grn 25.00 6.50

Liberation Issue

Common Design Type

1954, June 6

C57 CD102 15fr vio & vio brn 3.25 2.00

Pachypodes — AP6

Designs: 100fr, Antsirabé viaduct, grey-headed gull. 200fr, Ring-tailed lemurs.

1954, Sept. 20

C58 AP6 50fr dk bl grn & dk grn 3.50 .70
C59 AP6 100fr dp ultra, blk & choc 5.75 1.40
C60 AP6 200fr dk grn & sep 19.00 4.50
Nos. C58-C60 (3) 28.25 6.60

Malagasy Republic

Sugar Cane Harvest — AP7

Charaxes Antamboulou — AP8

Designs: 40fr, Tobacco field. 100fr, Chrysiridia Madagascariensis. 200fr, Argema mittrel, vert. 500fr, Mandrare bridge.

1960 Unwmk. Engr. *Perf. 13*

C61 AP7 30fr grn, vio brn & pale brn 2.00 .25
C62 AP7 40fr Prus grn & ol gray 2.00 .25
C63 AP8 50fr multi 3.50 .35
C64 AP8 100fr sl grn, emer & org 5.00 .50
C65 AP8 200fr pur & yel 7.50 1.40
C66 AP7 500fr Prus grn, bis & ultra 12.00 2.50
Nos. C61-C66 (6) 32.00 5.25

Diademed Sifakas — AP9

Lemurs: 85fr, Indri. 250fr, Verreaux's sifaka.

1961, Dec. 9 Unwmk. *Perf. 13*

C67 AP9 65fr slate grn & red brn 1.50 .70
C68 AP9 85fr olive, blk & brn 3.75 1.00
C69 AP9 250fr Prus grn, blk & mar 6.50 2.75
Nos. C67-C69 (3) 11.75 4.45

For surcharge see No. C90.

Plane over Nossi-Bé AP10

1962, May 7 Engr. *Perf. 13*

C70 AP10 100fr red brn, bl & dk grn 1.75 .60
a. Souv. sheet of 5, #328-331, C70 5.00 1.50

1st Malagasy Philatelic Exhibition, Tananarive, May 5-13.

Turbojet Airliner, Emblem — AP11

1963, Apr. 18 Unwmk. *Perf. 13*

C71 AP11 500fr dk bl, red & grn 8.00 3.25

Madagascar commercial aviation.

Helmet Bird — AP12

Birds: 100fr, Pitta-like ground roller. 200fr, Crested wood ibis.

1963, Aug. 12 Photo. *Perf. 13x12½*

C72 AP12 40fr multi 1.75 .65
C73 AP12 100fr multi 4.00 1.25
C74 AP12 200fr multi 7.00 2.25
Nos. C72-C74 (3) 12.75 4.15

African Postal Union Issue
Common Design Type

1963, Sept. 8 ***Perf. 12½***
C75 CD114 85fr grn, ocher & red 1.25 .80

Map of Madagascar, Jet Plane and UPU Emblem — AP13

1963, Nov. 2 **Engr.** ***Perf. 13***
C76 AP13 45fr dk car, grnsh bl & ultra .65 .25
C77 AP13 85fr dk car, vio & bl 1.10 .50

Malagasy Republic's admission to the UPU, Nov. 2, 1961.

Meteorological Center, Tananarive and Tiros Satellite — AP14

1964, Mar. 23 **Unwmk.**
C78 AP14 90fr org brn, ultra & grn 1.50 .90

UN 4th World Meteorological Day, Mar. 23.

Zebu, Wood Sculpture AP15

1964, Oct. 20 **Engr.** ***Perf. 13***
C79 AP15 100fr lil rose, dk vio & brn 1.75 .90

Musical Instrument Type of Regular Issue

200fr, Lokanga bara (stringed instrument).

1965, Feb. 16 **Unwmk.** ***Perf. 13***
Size: 26x47mm
C80 A57 200fr grn, org & choc 4.50 2.00

Nurse Weighing Infant, and ICY Emblem — AP16

Design: 100fr, Small boy and girl, child care scenes and ICY emblem.

1965, Sept. 20 **Engr.** ***Perf. 13***
C81 AP16 50fr multi .55 .25
C82 AP16 100fr multi 1.10 .55

International Cooperation Year.

Dance Type of Regular Issue

250fr, Dance of a young girl, Sakalava, vert.

1966, June 13 **Photo.** ***Perf. 13***
Size: 27x49mm
C83 A68 250fr multi 4.75 2.00

Aviation Type of Regular Issue

Design: 500fr, Dagnaux and his Bréguet biplane, 1927.

1967, Apr. 28 **Engr.** ***Perf. 13***
Size: 48x27mm
C84 A76 500fr Prus bl, blk & brn 9.00 4.00

No. C84 for the 40th anniv. of the 1st Majunga-Tananarive flight.

African Postal Union Issue, 1967
Common Design Type

1967, Sept. 9 **Engr.** ***Perf. 13***
C85 CD124 100fr ol bis, red brn & brt pink 1.25 .60

Dancer Type of Regular Issue

Designs: 100fr, Tourbillon dance, horiz. 200fr, Male dancer from the South.

1967-68 **Photo.** ***Perf. 11½***
Size: 38x23mm
C86 A80 100fr multi ('68) 2.00 .60
Perf. 13
Size: 27x48mm
C87 A80 200fr multi 4.00 1.40

Issue dates: 100fr, Nov. 25; 200fr, Nov. 25.

WHO Emblem, Bull's Head Totem and Palm Fan — AP17

1968, Apr. 7 **Photo.** ***Perf. 12½x13***
C88 AP17 200fr bl, yel brn & red 2.00 .90

WHO, 20th anniv.; Intl. Congress of Medical Science, Apr. 2-12.

Tananarive-Ivato International Airport — AP18

1968, May 8 **Engr.** ***Perf. 13***
C89 AP18 500fr lt red brn, dl bl & dl grn 6.75 3.00

Issued for Stamp Day.

No. C68 Surcharged in Vermilion with New Value and 2 Bars

1968, June 24 **Engr.** ***Perf. 13***
C90 AP9 20fr on 85fr multi .75 .25

PHILEXAFRIQUE Issue

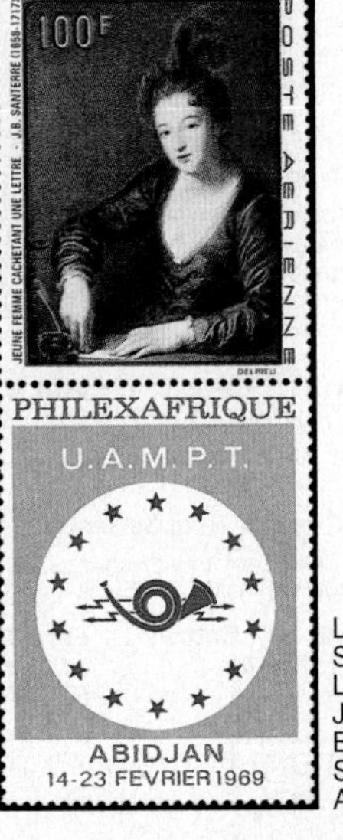

Lady Sealing Letter, by Jean Baptiste Santerre AP19

1968, Dec. 30 **Photo.** ***Perf. 12½x12***
C91 AP19 100fr lilac & multi, with label 3.25 .70

Issued to publicize PHILEXAFRIQUE Philatelic Exhibition in Abidjan, Feb. 14-23. Printed with alternating lilac label.

2nd PHILEXAFRIQUE Issue
Common Design Type

Design: 50fr, Madagascar No. 274, map of Madagascar and Malagasy emblem.

1969, Feb. 14 **Engr.** ***Perf. 13***
C92 CD128 50fr gray, brn red & sl grn 1.75 .85

Sunset over Madagascar Highlands, by Henri Ratovo — AP20

Painting: 100fr, On the Seashore of the East Coast of Madagascar, by Alfred Razafinjohany.

1969, Nov. 5 **Photo.** ***Perf. 12x12½***
C93 AP20 100fr brn & multi 1.50 .65
C94 AP20 150fr multi 3.00 1.25

Lunar Landing Module and Man on the Moon — AP21

1970, July 20 **Engr.** ***Perf. 13***
C95 AP21 75fr ultra, dk gray & sl grn 1.25 .40

1st anniv. of man's 1st landing on the moon.

Boeing 737 — AP22

1970, Dec. 18 **Engr.** ***Perf. 13***
C96 AP22 200fr bl, red brn & grn 3.00 .90

Jean Ralaimongo (1884-1944) AP23

Portraits: 40fr, René Rakotobe (1918-71). 65fr, Albert Sylla (1909-67). 100fr, Joseph Ravoahangy Andrianavalona (1893-1970).

1971-72 **Photo.** ***Perf. 12½; 13 (40fr)***
C97 AP23 25fr red brn, org & blk .40 .25
C98 AP23 40fr dp cl, ocher & blk .60 .25
C99 AP23 65fr grn, lt grn & blk .50 .25
C100 AP23 100fr vio bl, lt bl & blk 1.25 .35
Nos. C97-C100 (4) 2.75 1.10

Famous Malagasy men.
Issued: No. C98, 7/25/72; others, 10/14/71.

African Postal Union Issue

"Mpisikidy" by G. Rakotovao and UAMPT Building, Brazzaville, Congo — AP24

1971, Nov. 13 **Photo.** ***Perf. 13x13½***
C105 AP24 100fr bl & multi 1.25 .45

10th anniv. of African and Malagasy Posts and Telecommunications Union (UAMPT).

Running, Olympic Village AP25

Design: 200fr, Judo, Olympic Stadium.

1972, Sept. 11 **Photo.** ***Perf. 13½***
C106 AP25 100fr multi 1.40 .60
C107 AP25 200fr multi 2.50 .85

20th Olympic Games, Munich, 8/26-9/11.

Mohair Goat AP26

1972, Nov. 15
C108 AP26 250fr multi 5.00 1.60

Adoration of the Kings, by Andrea Mantegna — AP27

Christmas: 85fr, Virgin and Child, Florentine School, 15th century, vert.

1972, Dec. 15 Photo. *Perf. 13*
C109 AP27 85fr gold & multi 1.00 .45
C110 AP27 150fr gold & multi 2.25 .70

Landing Module, Astronauts and Lunar Rover AP28

1973, Jan. 25 Engr. *Perf. 13*
C111 AP28 300fr dp cl, gray & brn 4.00 1.40

Apollo 17 moon mission, Dec. 7-19, 1972.

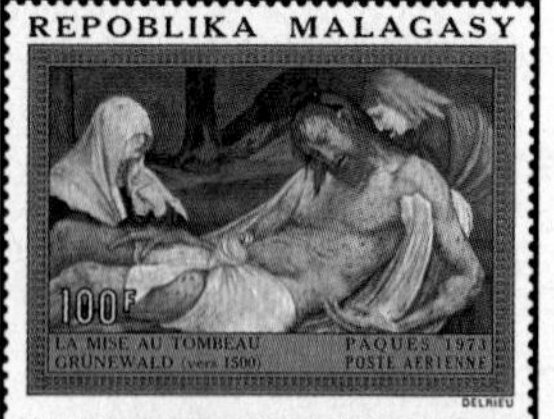

The Burial of Christ, by Grunewald — AP29

Easter: 200fr, Resurrection, by Mattias Grunewald, vert. Both paintings from panels of Issenheim altar.

1973, Mar. 22 Photo. *Perf. 13*
C112 AP29 100fr gold & multi 1.25 .45
C113 AP29 200fr gold & multi 2.75 .70

Early Excursion Car — AP30

Design: 150fr, Early steam locomotive.

1973, July 25 Photo. *Perf. 13x12½*
C114 AP30 100fr multi 1.50 .70
C115 AP30 150fr multi 2.25 1.00

WMO Emblem, Radar, Map of Madagascar, Hurricane AP31

1973, Sept. 3 Engr. *Perf. 13*
C116 AP31 100fr blk, ultra & org 1.50 .50

Cent. of intl. meteorological cooperation.

Lemur Type of Regular Issue

Designs: 150fr, Lepilemur mustelinus, vert. 200fr, Cheirogaleus major.

1973, Oct. 9 Engr. *Perf. 13*
C117 A131 150fr multi 2.75 .90
C118 A131 200fr multi 4.25 1.40

Pres. John F. Kennedy, US Flag — AP32

1973, Nov. 22 Photo. *Perf. 13*
C119 AP32 300fr multi 3.00 1.40

10th anniv. of the death of John F. Kennedy.

Soccer — AP33

1973, Dec. 20 Engr. *Perf. 13*
C120 AP33 500fr lil rose, dk brn & org brn 5.50 2.00

World Soccer Cup, Munich, 1974.
For overprint see No. C130.

Copernicus, Ranger and Heliocentric System — AP34

1974, Jan. 22
C121 AP34 250fr multi 4.00 1.10

500th anniversary of the birth of Nicolaus Copernicus (1473-1543), Polish astronomer.

Scout Type of Regular Issue

Designs (African Scout Emblem and): 100fr, Scouts bringing sick people to Red Cross tent, horiz. 300fr, Scouts fishing and fish, horiz.

1974, Feb. 14 Engr. *Perf. 13*
C122 A132 100fr multi 1.00 .35
C123 A132 300fr multi 3.00 1.00

Camellia, Hummingbird, Table Tennis Player — AP35

100fr, Girl player, flower and bird design.

1974, Mar. 19 Engr. *Perf. 13*
C124 AP35 50fr bl & multi 1.00 .30
C125 AP35 100fr multi 1.75 .60

Table Tennis Tournament, Peking.

Autorail Micheline — AP36

Malagasy Locomotives: 85fr, Track inspection trolley. 200fr, Garratt (steam).

1974, June 7 Engr. *Perf. 13*
C126 AP36 50fr multi .75 .35
C127 AP36 85fr multi 1.25 .45
C128 AP36 200fr multi 3.00 .95
Nos. C126-C128 (3) 5.00 1.75

Letters and UPU Emblem — AP37

1974, July 9 Engr. *Perf. 13*
C129 AP37 250fr multi 3.50 1.10

Centenary of Universal Postal Union.
For overprint see No. C133.

No. C120 Overprinted: "R.F.A. 2 / HOLLANDE 1"

1974, Aug. 20 Engr. *Perf. 13*
C130 AP33 500fr multi 5.00 2.00

World Cup Soccer Championship, 1974, victory of German Federal Republic.

Link-up in Space, Globe, Emblem — AP38

250fr, Link-up, globe and emblem, diff.

1974, Sept. 12
C131 AP38 150fr org, bl & slate grn 1.25 .65
C132 AP38 250fr bl, brn & slate grn 2.75 .90

Russo-American space cooperation.
For overprints see Nos. C142-C143.

No. C129 Overprinted

1974, Oct. 9 Engr. *Perf. 13*
C133 AP37 250fr multi 2.00 .70

100 years of international collaboration.

Adoration of the Kings, by J. L. David AP39

Christmas: 300fr, Virgin of the Cherries and Child, by Quentin Massys.

1974, Dec. 20 Photo. *Perf. 13*
C134 AP39 200fr gold & multi 2.25 .60
C135 AP39 300fr gold & multi 3.50 1.10

UN Emblem and Globe — AP40

1975, June 24 Litho. *Perf. 12½*
C136 AP40 300fr grn, bl & blk 3.00 .90

United Nations Charter, 30th anniversary.

American Bicentennial Type, 1975

Designs: 100fr, Count d'Estaing and "Languedoc." 200fr, John Paul Jones, "Bonhomme Richard" and "Serapis." 300fr, Benjamin Franklin, "Millern" and "Montgomery." 500fr, George Washington and "Hanna."

1975, June 30 Litho. *Perf. 11*
C137 A144 100fr multi 1.00 .30
C138 A144 200fr multi 2.00 .50
C139 A144 300fr multi 3.00 .75
Nos. C137-C139 (3) 6.00 1.55

Souvenir Sheet

C140 A144 500fr multi 7.00 1.50

For overprints see Nos. C164-C167.

Flower Type of 1975

Design: 85fr, Turraea sericea.

1975, Aug. 4 Photo. *Perf. 12½*
C141 A145 85fr dp grn, yel & org 1.90 .90

Nos. C131-C132 Overprinted

1975, Aug. 5 Engr. *Perf. 13*
C142 AP38 150fr multi 1.25 .45
C143 AP38 250fr multi 2.40 .75

Apollo Soyuz link-up in space, July 17, 1975.

Bas-relief and Stupas — AP41

1975, Aug. 10 Engr. *Perf. 13*
C144 AP41 50fr bl, car & bister 1.40 .35

UNESCO campaign to save Borobudur Temple, Java.

Exposition Type, 1975

1975, Sept. 16 Litho. *Perf. 14x13½*
C145 A147 125fr Deer 1.90 .45

Souvenir Sheet

C146 A147 300fr Jay 4.75 1.00

Hurdling and Olympic Rings — AP42

200fr, Weight lifting and Olympic rings, vert.

1975, Oct. 9 Litho. *Perf. 12½*
C147 AP42 75fr multi .90 .25
C148 AP42 200fr multi 2.10 .70

Pre-Olympic Year 1975.

12th Winter Olympics Type, 1975

Designs: 200fr, Cross-country skiing. 245fr, Down-hill skiing. 450fr, Figure skating, pairs.

1975, Nov. 19 *Perf. 14*
C149 A149 200fr multi 2.25 .55
C150 A149 245fr multi 2.40 .65

Souvenir Sheet

C151 A149 450fr multi 3.75 1.40

For overprints see Nos. C161-C163.

Landing Module, Apollo 14 Emblem — AP43

1976, Jan. 18 Engr. *Perf. 13*
C152 AP43 150fr red, grn & ind 1.50 .50

Apollo 14 moon landing, 5th anniversary. For overprint see No. C157.

21st Summer Olympics Type, 1976

Designs: 100fr, Shot-put and long jump. 200fr, Gymnastics, horse and balance bar. 300fr, Diving, 3-meter and platform. 500fr, Swimming, free-style and breast stroke.

1976, Jan. 21 Litho. *Perf. 13½*
C153 A151 100fr multi 1.00 .30
C154 A151 200fr multi 1.90 .60
C155 A151 300fr multi 2.75 .90
Nos. C153-C155 (3) 5.65 1.80

Souvenir Sheet

C156 A151 500fr multi 4.50 1.40

For overprints see Nos. C168-C171.

No. C152 Overprinted: "5e Anniversaire / de la mission / APOLLO XIV"

1976, Feb. 5 Engr. *Perf. 13*
C157 AP43 150fr red, grn & indigo 1.75 .70

Apollo 14 moon landing, 5th anniversary.

Zeppelin Type of 1976

Designs (Count Zeppelin and LZ-127 over): 200fr, Brandenburg Gate, Berlin 300fr, Parliament, London. 450fr, St. Peter's Cathedral, Rome.

1976, Mar. 3 Litho. *Perf. 11*
C158 A152 200fr multi 2.50 .60
C159 A152 300fr multi 3.75 .90

Souvenir Sheet

C160 A152 450fr multi 5.50 1.40

Nos. C149-C151 Overprinted

(a)

(b)

(c)

1976, June 17
C161 A149 (a) 200fr multi 1.60 .60
C162 A149 (b) 245fr multi 2.10 .80

Souvenir Sheet

C163 A149 (c) 450fr multi 4.50 2.75

12th Winter Olympic games winners.

Nos. C137-C140 Overprinted in Black

1976, July 4
C164 A144 100fr multi 1.00 .30
C165 A144 200fr multi 2.00 .60
C166 A144 300fr multi 2.75 .90
Nos. C164-C166 (3) 5.75 1.80

Souvenir Sheet

C167 A144 500fr multi 4.00 2.75

American Bicentennial.

Nos. C153-C156 Overprinted

(a)

(b)

(c)

(d)

1977, Jan.
C168 A151 (a) 100fr multi 1.00 .30
C169 A151 (b) 200fr multi 2.00 .65
C170 A151 (c) 300fr multi 2.75 .90
Nos. C168-C170 (3) 5.75 1.85

Souvenir Sheet

C171 A151 (d) 500fr multi 4.50 2.75

21st Summer Olympic Games winners.

Fauna Type of 1979

1979, July 6
C172 A176 20fr Tortoises .45 .25
C173 A176 95fr Macaco lemurs 1.20 .25

International Palestinian Solidarity Day — AP44

1979, Nov. 29 Litho. *Perf. 12x12½*
C174 AP44 60fr multi .60 .25

Olympic Type of 1980

1980, Dec. 29 Litho. *Perf. 12½x12*
C175 A188 250fr Judo 1.90 .70
C176 A188 500fr Swimming 3.75 1.50

Stamp Day — AP45

1981, Dec. 17 Litho. *Perf. 12x12½*
C177 AP45 90fr multi .75 .25

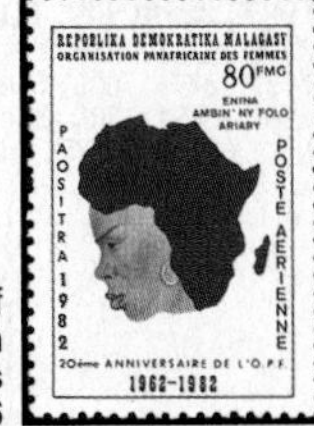
20th Anniv. of Pan-African Women's Org. — AP46

1982, Aug. 6 Litho. *Perf. 12*
C178 AP46 80fr dk brn & lt brn .70 .25

Hydroelectric Plant, Andekaleka — AP47

1982, Sept. 13 *Perf. 12½x12*
C179 AP47 80fr multi .70 .25

Orchid Type of 1984

No. C180, Eulophiella elisabethae, horiz. No. C181, Grammangis ellisii, horiz. No. C182, Grammangis spectabilis.

1984, Nov. 20 Litho. *Perf. 12*
C180 A226 50fr multi 1.00 .25
C181 A226 50fr multi 1.00 .25
C182 A226 50fr multi 1.00 .25
Nos. C180-C182 (3) 3.00 .75

Solar Princess, by Sadiou Diouf AP48

1984, Dec. 22 Litho. *Perf. 12*
C183 AP48 100fr multi .90 .25

Intl. Civil Aviation Org., 40th anniv.

Halley's Comet AP49

1986, Apr. 5 Litho. *Perf. 12½x13*
C184 AP49 150fr multi 1.25 .50

Admission of Madagascar into the UPU, 25th Anniv. AP50

1986, Dec. 23 Litho. *Perf. 11½*
C185 AP50 150fr multi 1.25 .40

Air Madagascar, 25th Anniv. — AP51

1987, June 17 Litho. *Perf. 12x12½*

C186 AP51 60fr Piper Aztec .55 .25
C187 AP51 60fr Twin Otter .55 .25
C188 AP51 150fr Boeing 747 1.10 .30
Nos. C186-C188 (3) 2.20 .80

Socialist Revolution, 15th Anniv. — AP52

1990, June 16 Litho. *Perf. 13½*

C189 AP52 100fr Map .25 .25
C190 AP52 350fr Architecture .60 .30

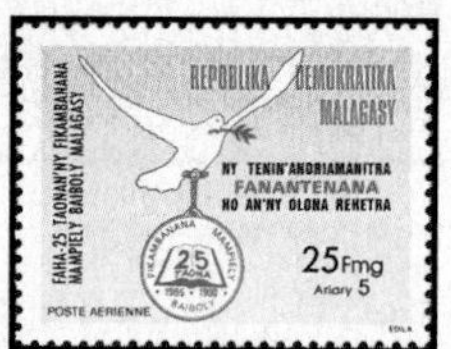

Madagascan Bible Society, 25th Anniv. — AP53

1990, Sept. 17 *Perf. 12½*

C191 AP53 25fr lt bl & multi .25 .25
C192 AP53 100fr bl, blk & grn, vert. .30 .25

Stamp Day — AP54

1990, Oct. 9 Litho. *Perf. 13x12½*

C193 AP54 350fr multicolored 1.25 .30

World Environment Day — AP55

1992, June 5 Litho. *Perf. 12½*

C194 AP55 140fr multicolored .50 .25

World Post Day — AP56

1992, Oct. 9 Litho. *Perf. 13½*

C195 AP56 500fr multicolored .80 .35

Girl Guides, 50th Anniv. AP57

1993, Aug. Litho. *Perf. 11½*

C196 AP57 140fr multicolored .50 .25

AP58

1993, Nov. 20 Litho. *Perf. 12*

C197 AP58 500fr multicolored .90 .40

African Industrialization Day.

Zone A Conference AP59

1994 Litho. *Perf. 11½x11, 11x11½*

C198 AP59 140fr shown .25 .25
C199 AP59 500fr Logo, vert. .70 .40

Madagascar Hilton, 25th Anniv.—AP60

1995, Oct. 8 Litho. *Perf. 13½*

C200 AP60 500fr black, blue & bister .80 .60

ACCT, 25th Anniv. — AP60a

1996, Aug. 9 Litho. *Perf. 14¾x15*

C200A AP60a 500fr multi .70 .45

FAO, 50th Anniv. — AP60b

Designs: 140fr, Map, FAO emblem, grains. 500fr, FAO emblem, map, grains, diff.

1995, Aug. 16 Litho. *Perf. 15*

C200B AP60b 140fr multi — —
C200C AP60b 500fr multi — —
Set of 2 130.00 130.00

UN Industrial Development Organization, 30th Anniv. — AP60c

Perf. 11¾x11½

1996, June 17 Litho.

Granite Paper

C200D AP60c 140fr multi .25 .25

Souvenir Sheet

Zheng He, Chinese Navigator — AP61

1998 Litho. *Perf. 13½*

C201 AP61 5700fr multicolored 3.00 1.50

AIR POST SEMI-POSTAL STAMPS

French Revolution Issue

Common Design Type

Unwmk.

1939, July 5 Photo. *Perf. 13*

Name and Value in Orange

CB1 CD83 4.50fr + 4fr brn blk 18.00 18.00

"Maternity" Statue at Tannarive City Hall — SPAP1

Manankavaly Free Milk Station — SPAP2

Mother & Children — SPAP3

1942, June 22 Engr. *Perf. 13*

CB2 SPAP1 1.50fr + 3.50fr lt grn .65
CB3 SPAP2 2fr + 6fr yel brn .65
CB4 SPAP3 3fr + 9fr car red .65
Nos. CB2-CB4 (3) 1.95

Native children's welfare fund.

Nos. CB2-CB4 were issued by the Vichy government in France, but were not placed on sale in Madagascar.

Colonial Education Fund

Common Design Type

1942, June 22

CB5 CD86a 1.20fr + 1.80fr blue & red .65

No. CB5 was issued by the Vichy government in France, but was not placed on sale in Madagascar.

POSTAGE DUE STAMPS

Postage Due Stamps of French Colonies Overprinted in Red or Blue — D1

1896 Unwmk. *Imperf.*

J1 D1 5c blue (R) 12.00 9.50
J2 D1 10c brown (R) 11.00 8.00
J3 D1 20c yellow (Bl) 10.00 8.00
J4 D1 30c rose red (Bl) 11.00 8.00
J5 D1 40c lilac (R) 80.00 50.00
J6 D1 50c gray vio (Bl) 14.50 10.00
J7 D1 1fr dk grn (R) 80.00 65.00
Nos. J1-J7 (7) 218.50 158.50

Governor's Palace — D2

1908-24 Typo. *Perf. 13½x14*

J8 D2 2c vio brn .25 .25
J9 D2 4c violet .25 .25
J10 D2 5c green .25 .25
J11 D2 10c deep rose .25 .25
J12 D2 20c olive green .40 .40
J13 D2 40c brn, *straw* .45 .45
J14 D2 50c brn, *bl* .60 .60
J15 D2 60c orange ('24) .60 .60
J16 D2 1fr dark blue 1.10 1.10
Nos. J8-J16 (9) 4.15 4.15

Type of 1908 Issue Surcharged

1924-27

J17 D2 60c on 1fr org 1.90 1.90

Surcharged

J18 D2 2fr on 1fr lil rose ('27) .90 .90
J19 D2 3fr on 1fr ultra ('27) .90 .90

Postage Due Stamps of 1908-27 Ovptd. or Srchd. in Black

1943 *Perf. 13½x14*

J20 D2 10c dp rose .95 .95
J21 D2 20c olive grn .95 .95
J22 D2 30c on 5c green .95 .95
J23 D2 40c brn, *straw* 1.00 1.00
J24 D2 50c brn, *blue* 1.40 1.40
J25 D2 60c orange .95 .95
J26 D2 1fr dark blue .95 .95
J27 D2 1fr on 2c vio brn 4.50 4.50
J28 D2 2fr on 1fr lil rose 1.10 1.10
J29 D2 2fr on 4c vio 2.10 2.10
J30 D2 3fr on 1fr ultra 1.25 1.25
Nos. J20-J30 (11) 16.10 16.10

Catalogue values for unused stamps in this section, from this point to the end of the section, are for Never Hinged items.

D3

1947 Photo. *Perf. 13*

No.	Type	Description	Unused	Used
J31	D3	10c dk violet	.25	.25
J32	D3	30c brown	.25	.25
J33	D3	50c dk bl grn	.25	.25
J34	D3	1fr dp orange	.25	.25
J35	D3	2fr red violet	.45	.45
J36	D3	3fr red brown	.45	.45
J37	D3	4fr blue	.50	.50
J38	D3	5fr henna brown	.55	.55
J39	D3	10fr slate green	.70	.70
J40	D3	20fr vio blue	1.75	1.75
		Nos. J31-J40 (10)	5.40	5.40

Malagasy Republic

Independence Monument — D4

Engraved; Denomination Typographed

1962, May 7 Unwmk. *Perf. 13*

No.	Type	Description	Unused	Used
J41	D4	1fr brt green	.25	.25
J42	D4	2fr copper brn	.25	.25
J43	D4	3fr brt violet	.25	.25
J44	D4	4fr slate	.25	.25
J45	D4	5fr red	.25	.25
J46	D4	10fr yellow grn	.25	.25
J47	D4	20fr dull claret	.25	.25
J48	D4	40fr blue	.55	.55
J49	D4	50fr rose red	.85	.85
J50	D4	100fr black	1.60	1.60
		Nos. J41-J50 (10)	4.75	4.75

MALAWI

mə-ˈlä-wē

LOCATION — Southeast Africa
GOVT. — Republic in British Commonwealth
AREA — 36,100 sq. mi.
POP. — 10,000,416 (1999 est.)
CAPITAL — Lilongwe

The British Protectorate of Nyasaland became the independent state of Malawi on July 6, 1964, and a republic on July 6, 1966.

12 Pence = 1 Shilling
20 Shillings = 1 Pound
100 Tambalas = 1 Kwacha (1970)

Catalogue values for all unused stamps in this country are for Never Hinged items.

Watermark

Wmk. 357 — Multiple Cockerel

Dr. H. Kamuzu Banda and Independence Monument — A1

Prime Minister Banda and: 6p, Sun rising from lake. 1sh3p, National flag. 2sh6p, Coat of Arms.

Perf. 14½

1964, July 6 Unwmk. Photo.

No.	Type	Description	Unused	Used
1	A1	3p dk gray & lt ol green	.25	.25
2	A1	6p car rose, red, gold & bl	.25	.25
3	A1	1sh3p dull vio, blk, red & grn	.30	.25
4	A1	2sh6p multicolored	.50	.75
a.		Blue omitted	2,750.	
		Nos. 1-4 (4)	1.30	1.50

Malawi's independence, July 6, 1964.

Mother and Child — A2

Designs: 1p, Chambo fish. 2p, Zebu bull. 3p, Peanuts. 4p, Fishermen in boat. 6p, Harvesting tea. 9p, Tung nut, flower and leaves. 1sh, Lumber and tropical pine branch. 1sh3p, Tobacco drying and Turkish tobacco plant. 2sh6p, Cotton industry. 5sh, Monkey Bay, Lake Nyasa. 10sh, Afzelia tree (pod mahogany). £1, Nyala antelope, vert.

1964, July 6 Size: 23x19mm

No.	Type	Description	Unused	Used
5	A2	½p lilac	.30	.30
6	A2	1p green & black	.30	.25
7	A2	2p red brown	.30	.25
8	A2	3p pale brn, brn red & grn	.30	.25
9	A2	4p org yel & indigo	1.10	.25
		Size: 41½x25, 25x41½mm		
10	A2	6p bl, vio bl & brt yel grn	1.00	.25
11	A2	9p grn, yel & brn	.50	.25
12	A2	1sh yel, brn & dk green	.35	.25
13	A2	1sh3p red brn & olive	.75	*.85*
14	A2	2sh6p blue & brown	1.75	1.10
15	A2	5sh multicolored	1.00	*3.25*
16	A2	10sh org brn, grn & gray	2.25	*2.25*
17	A2	£1 yel & dk brn	9.50	6.25
		Nos. 5-17 (13)	19.40	15.75

See Nos. 26, 41-51. For surcharges see Nos. 27-28.

Star of Bethlehem over World — A3

1964, Dec. 1 Photo. *Perf. 14½*

No.	Type	Description	Unused	Used
18	A3	3p brt green & gold	.25	.25
19	A3	6p lilac rose & gold	.25	.25
20	A3	1sh3p lilac & gold	.25	.25
21	A3	2sh6p ultra & gold	.25	.30
a.		Souvenir sheet of 4	1.25	*1.50*
		Nos. 18-21 (4)	1.00	1.05

Christmas. No. 21a contains Nos. 18-21 with simulated perforations.

Sixpence, Shilling, Florin and Half-Crown Coins — A4

1965, Mar. 1 Unwmk. *Perf. 13x13½*
Coins in Silver and Black

No.	Type	Description	Unused	Used
22	A4	3p green	.25	.25
23	A4	9p rose	.25	.25
a.		Silver omitted		
24	A4	1sh6p rose violet	.25	.25
25	A4	3sh dark blue	.35	*.75*
a.		Souvenir sheet of 4	1.75	1.50
		Nos. 22-25 (4)	1.10	1.50

First coinage of Malawi. No. 25a contains Nos. 22-25 with simulated perforations. Sold for 6sh.

Type of 1964 Redrawn

1965, June 1 Photo. *Perf. 14½*

No.	Type	Description	Unused	Used
26	A2	5sh "Monkey Bay-Lake Malawi"	8.50	1.25

Nos. 13-14 Surcharged with New Value and Two Bars

1965, June 14

No.	Type	Description	Unused	Used
27	A2	1sh6p on 1sh3p	.30	.25
28	A2	3sh on 2sh6p	.30	.25

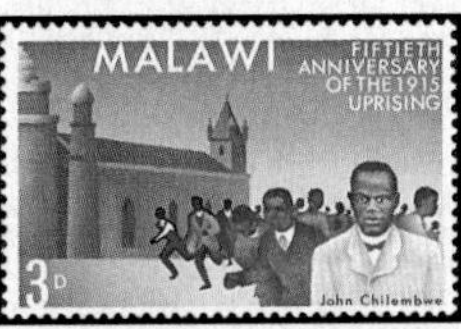

John Chilembwe, Rebels and Church at Mbwombwe — A5

1965, Aug. 20 Photo. *Perf. 14½*

No.	Type	Description	Unused	Used
29	A5	3p yel grn & purple	.25	.25
30	A5	9p red org & olive	.25	.25
31	A5	1sh6p dk blue & red brn	.25	.25
32	A5	3sh dull bl & green	.25	.25
a.		Souvenir sheet of 4, #29-32	6.00	6.00
		Nos. 29-32 (4)	1.00	1.00

50th anniversary of the revolution of Jan. 23, 1915, led by John Chilembwe (1871-1915), missionary.

Microscope and Open Book — A6

1965, Oct. 6 *Perf. 14*

No.	Type	Description	Unused	Used
33	A6	3p emer & slate	.25	.25
34	A6	9p brt rose & slate	.25	.25
35	A6	1sh6p purple & slate	.25	.25
36	A6	3sh ultra & slate	.25	.30
a.		Souvenir sheet of 4, #33-36	4.25	4.25
		Nos. 33-36 (4)	1.00	1.05

Opening of the University of Malawi in temporary quarters in Chichiri secondary school, Blantyre. The University will be located in Zomba.

African Danaine A7

Designs: Various butterflies.

Perf. 13x13½

1966, Feb. 15 Unwmk.

No.	Type	Description	Unused	Used
37	A7	4p multicolored	1.10	.25
38	A7	9p multicolored	1.75	.25
39	A7	1sh6p lil, blk & blue	2.00	.45
40	A7	3sh blue, dk brn & bis	2.75	*6.75*
a.		Souvenir sheet of 4, #37-40	18.00	18.00
		Nos. 37-40 (4)	7.60	7.70

See No. 51.

Type of 1964

Designs: 1sh6p, Curing tobacco and Burley tobacco plant. £2, Cyrestis camillus sublineatus (butterfly). Other designs as in 1964.

Wmk. 357

1966-67 Photo. *Perf. 14½*
Size: 23x19mm

No.	Type	Description	Unused	Used
41	A2	½p lilac	.25	.25
42	A2	1p green & black	.25	.25
43	A2	2p red brown ('67)	.25	.25
44	A2	3p multi ('67)	.25	.25
		Size: 41½x25mm		
45	A2	6p blue, vio bl & brt yel grn ('67)	2.00	.80
46	A2	9p grn, yel & brn ('67)	2.25	.25
47	A2	1sh yel, brn & dk green	.30	.25
48	A2	1sh6p choc & emer	.50	.25
49	A2	5sh multi ('67)	7.00	2.75
50	A2	10sh org brn, grn & gray ('67)	16.50	*17.50*
51	A2	£2 dl vio, yel & blk	25.00	26.00
		Nos. 41-51 (11)	54.55	48.80

British Central Africa Stamp 1891 — A8

1966, May 4 *Perf. 14½*

No.	Type	Description	Unused	Used
54	A8	4p yel grn & sl blue	.25	.25
55	A8	9p dull rose & sl blue	.25	.25
56	A8	1sh6p lil & slate blue	.25	.25
57	A8	3sh blue & slate blue	.25	.50
a.		Souvenir sheet of 4, #54-57	5.75	5.75
		Nos. 54-57 (4)	1.00	1.25

Postal service, 75th anniv.

President Kamuzu Banda — A9

Perf. 14x14½

1966, July 6 Wmk. 357

No.	Type	Description	Unused	Used
58	A9	4p green, sil & brn	.25	.25
59	A9	9p magenta, sil & brn	.25	.25
60	A9	1sh6p violet, sil & brn	.25	.25
61	A9	3sh blue, sil & brn	.25	.25
a.		Souvenir sheet of 4, #58-61	2.50	2.50
		Nos. 58-61 (4)	1.00	1.00

Republic Day, July 6, 1966; 2nd anniv. of Independence.

Star over Bethlehem — A10

1966, Oct. 12 Photo. *Perf. 14½x14*

No.	Type	Description	Unused	Used
63	A10	4p dp grn & gold	.25	.25
64	A10	9p plum & gold	.25	.25
65	A10	1sh6p orange & gold	.25	.25
66	A10	3sh deep blue & gold	.25	.50
		Nos. 63-66 (4)	1.00	1.25

Christmas.

Ilala I, 1875 A11

Steamers on Lake Malawi: 9p, Dove, 1892. 1sh6p, Chauncey Maples, 1901. 3sh, Guendolen, 1899.

1967, Jan. 4 *Perf. 14½x14*

No.	Type	Description	Unused	Used
67	A11	4p emer, black & yel	.45	.25
a.		Yellow omitted		*650.00*
68	A11	9p car rose, blk & yellow	.50	.35
69	A11	1sh6p lt vio, blk & red	.75	.60
70	A11	3sh ultra, black & red	1.50	1.75
		Nos. 67-70 (4)	3.20	2.95

Pseudotropheus Auratus — A12

Fish of Lake Malawi: 9p, Labeotropheus trewavasae. 1sh6p, Pseudotropheus zebra. 3sh, Pseudotropheus tropheops.

1967, May 3 Photo. *Perf. 12½x12*

71	A12	4p green & multi	.55	.25
72	A12	9p ocher & multi	.70	.25
73	A12	1sh6p multicolored	.90	.25
74	A12	3sh ultra & multi	1.40	*1.75*
		Nos. 71-74 (4)	3.55	2.50

Nos. 73 and 74 exist imperf. Value, pairs, each, $400.

Rising Sun and Cogwheel — A13

Perf. 13½x13

1967, July 5 Litho. Unwmk.

75	A13	4p black & brt grn	.25	.25
76	A13	9p black & car rose	.25	.25
77	A13	1sh6p black & brt pur	.25	.25
78	A13	3sh black & brt ultra	.25	.25
a.		Souvenir sheet of 4, #75-78	1.10	1.10
		Nos. 75-78 (4)	1.00	1.00

Malawi industrial development.

Nativity A14

Perf. 14x14½

1967, Oct. 12 Photo. Wmk. 357

79	A14	4p vio blue & green	.25	.25
80	A14	9p vio blue & red	.25	.25
81	A14	1sh6p vio blue & yel	.25	.25
82	A14	3sh bright blue	.25	.25
a.		Souvenir sheet of 4, #79-82, perf. 14x13½	1.25	1.25
		Nos. 79-82 (4)	1.00	1.00

Christmas.

Calotropis Procera — A15

Wild Flowers: 9p, Borreria dibrachiata. 1sh6p, Hibiscus rhodanthus. 3sh, Bidens pinnatipartita.

1968, Apr. 24 Litho. *Perf. 13½x13*

83	A15	4p green & multi	.25	.25
84	A15	9p pale grn & multi	.25	.25
85	A15	1sh6p lt green & multi	.25	.25
86	A15	3sh brt blue & multi	.25	.80
a.		Souvenir sheet of 4, #83-86	2.50	2.50
		Nos. 83-86 (4)	1.00	1.55

Thistle No. 1, 1902 A16

Locomotives: 9p, G-class steam engine, 1954. 1sh6p, "Zambesi" diesel locomotive No. 202, 1963. 3sh, Diesel rail car No. 1, 1955.

1968, July 24 Photo. *Perf. 14x14½*

87	A16	4p gray grn & multi	.25	.25
88	A16	9p red & multi	.55	.50
89	A16	1sh6p cream & multi	.90	.80
90	A16	3sh lt ultra & multi	1.25	2.50
a.		Souv. sheet of 4, #87-90, perf. 14	4.00	4.00
		Nos. 87-90 (4)	2.95	4.05

Nativity, by Piero della Francesca A17

Paintings: 9p, Adoration of the Shepherds, by Murillo. 1sh6p, Adoration of the Shepherds, by Guido Reni. 3sh, Nativity with God the Father and the Holy Ghost, by Giovanni Batista Pittoni.

1968, Nov. 6 Photo. Wmk. 357

91	A17	4p black & multi	.25	.25
92	A17	9p multicolored	.25	.25
93	A17	1sh6p multicolored	.25	.25
94	A17	3sh blue & multi	.25	.25
a.		Souvenir sheet of 4, #91-94, perf. 14x13½	.70	.70
		Nos. 91-94 (4)	1.00	1.00

Christmas.

Scarlet-chested Sunbird — A18

Nyasa Lovebird — A19

Birds: 2p, Violet-backed starling. 3p, White-browed robin-chat. 4p, Red-billed firefinch. 9p, Yellow bishop. 1sh, Southern carmine bee-eater. 1sh6p, Grayheaded bush shrike. 2sh, Paradise whydah. 3sh, African paradise fly-catcher. 5sh, Bateleur. 10sh, Saddlebill. £1, Purple heron. £2, Livingstone's lorie.

1968, Nov. 13 *Perf. 14½*

Size: 23x19, 19x23mm

95	A18	1p multicolored	.25	.25
96	A18	2p multicolored	.25	.25
97	A18	3p multicolored	.25	.25
98	A18	4p multicolored	.35	.35
99	A19	6p multicolored	1.00	.25
100	A19	9p multicolored	1.00	.60

Perf. 14

Size: 42x25, 25x42mm

101	A18	1sh multicolored	.85	.25
102	A18	1sh6p multicolored	3.25	*6.00*
103	A18	2sh multicolored	5.75	*6.00*
104	A19	3sh multicolored	4.75	4.00
105	A19	5sh multicolored	3.75	4.00
106	A19	10sh multicolored	7.00	7.00
107	A19	£1 multicolored	9.00	*15.00*
109	A18	£2 multicolored	27.50	*32.50*
		Nos. 95-109 (14)	64.95	*76.70*

No. 104 was surcharged "30t Special United Kingdom Delivery Service" in 5 lines and issued Feb. 8, 1971, during the British postal strike. The 30t was to pay a private postal service. Values: unused 50c, used $2.25.

See Nos. 136-137. For overprint see No. 131.

ILO Emblem A20

Photo., Gold Impressed (Emblem)

Perf. 14x14½

1969, Feb. 5 Wmk. 357

110	A20	4p deep green	.25	.25
111	A20	9p dk rose brown	.25	.25
112	A20	1sh6p dark gray	.25	.25
113	A20	3sh dark blue	.25	.25
a.		Souvenir sheet of 4, #110-113	1.60	1.60
		Nos. 110-113 (4)	1.00	1.00

ILO, 50th anniversary.

White Fringed Ground Orchid A21

Malawi Orchids: 9p, Red ground orchid. 1sh6p, Leopard tree orchid. 3sh, Blue ground orchid.

1969, July 9 Litho. *Perf. 13½*

114	A21	4p gray & multi	.30	.30
115	A21	9p gray & multi	.50	.50
116	A21	1sh6p gray & multi	.70	.70
117	A21	3sh gray & multi	1.50	1.50
a.		Souvenir sheet of 4, #114-117	2.75	2.75
		Nos. 114-117 (4)	3.00	3.00

African Development Bank Emblem — A22

1969, Sept. 10 *Perf. 14*

118	A22	4p multicolored	.25	.25
119	A22	9p multicolored	.25	.25
120	A22	1sh6p multicolored	.25	.25
121	A22	3sh multicolored	.25	.25
a.		Souvenir sheet of 4, #118-121	1.10	1.10
		Nos. 118-121 (4)	1.00	1.00

African Development Bank, 5th anniv.

"Peace on Earth" A23

1969, Nov. 5 Photo. *Perf. 14x14½*

122	A23	2p citron & blk	.25	.25
123	A23	4p Prus blue & blk	.25	.25
124	A23	9p scarlet & blk	.25	.25
125	A23	1sh6p purple & blk	.25	.25
126	A23	3sh ultra & blk	.25	.25
a.		Souvenir sheet of 5, #122-126	1.25	1.25
		Nos. 122-126 (5)	1.25	1.25

Christmas.

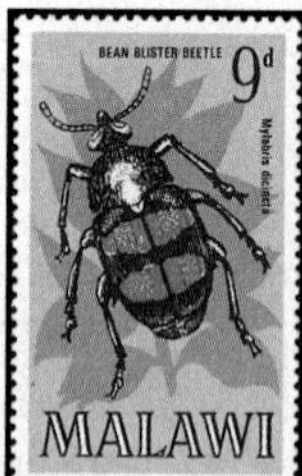

Bean Blister Beetle — A24

Insects: 4p, Elegant grasshopper. 1sh6p, Pumpkin ladybird. 3sh, Praying mantis.

1970, Feb. 4 Litho. *Perf. 14x14½*

127	A24	4p multicolored	.30	.25
128	A24	9p multicolored	.30	.25
129	A24	1sh6p multicolored	.55	.50
130	A24	3sh multicolored	1.00	1.00
a.		Souvenir sheet of 4, #127-130	2.25	2.25
		Nos. 127-130 (4)	2.15	2.00

No. 102 Overprinted in Black

1970, Mar. 18 Photo. *Perf. 14*

131	A18	1sh6p multicolored	1.00	*2.00*

75th Anniversary Rand Easter Show, Johannesburg, South Africa, Mar. 24-Apr. 6.

Runner — A25

1970, June 3 Litho. *Perf. 13*

132	A25	4p green & dk blue	.25	.25
133	A25	9p rose & dk bl	.25	.25
134	A25	1sh6p dull yel & dk bl	.25	.25
135	A25	3sh blue & dk blue	.25	.25
a.		Souvenir sheet of 4, #132-135	1.10	1.10
		Nos. 132-135 (4)	1.00	1.00

9th Commonwealth Games, Edinburgh, Scotland, July 16-25.

Dual Currency Issue

Bird Type of 1968 with Denominations in Tambalas

Designs: 10t/1sh, Southern carmine bee-eater. 20t/2sh, Paradise whydah.

1970, Sept. 2 Photo. *Perf. 14½*

Size: 42x25mm

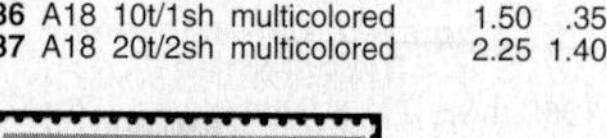

136	A18	10t/1sh multicolored	1.50	.35
137	A18	20t/2sh multicolored	2.25	1.40

Aegocera Trimenii A26

Moths of Malawi: 9p, Epiphora bauhiniae. 1sh6p, Parasa karschi. 3sh, Teracotona euprepia.

Perf. 11x11½

1970, Sept. 30 Wmk. 357

138	A26	4p multicolored	.35	.35
139	A26	9p multicolored	.50	.50
140	A26	1sh6p lt vio & multi	.85	.85
141	A26	3sh multicolored	1.90	1.90
a.		Souvenir sheet of 4, #138-141	7.50	7.50
		Nos. 138-141 (4)	3.60	3.60

Mother and Child A27

1970, Nov. 4 Litho. *Perf. 14½*

142	A27	2p black & yel	.25	.25
143	A27	4p black & emer	.25	.25
144	A27	9p black & dp org	.25	.25
145	A27	1sh6p black & red lil	.25	.25
146	A27	3sh black & ultra	.25	.25
a.		Souv. sheet of 5, #142-146 + label	1.40	1.40
		Nos. 142-146 (5)	1.25	1.25

Christmas.

Decimal Currency

Greater Kudu — A28

Eland — A29

Antelopes: 2t, Nyala. 3t, Reedbuck. 5t, Puku. 8t, Impala. 15t, Klipspringer. 20t, Livingstone's suni. 30t, Roan antelope. 50t, Waterbuck. 1k, Bushbuck. 2k, Red duiker. 4k, Gray bush duiker.

Perf. 13½x14 (A28), 14x14½ (A29)

1971, Feb. 15 Litho. Wmk. 357

148 A28 1t dull vio & multi .25 .25
a. Perf. 14½x14, coil .55 .40
b. Perf. 14 ('74) .45 1.50
149 A28 2t dp yel & multi .25 .25
150 A28 3t ap grn & multi .25 .25
a. Perf. 14 ('74) .65 1.25
151 A28 5t multicolored .35 *1.00*
a. Perf. 14 ('74) .65 1.75
152 A28 8t org red & multi .35 *.75*
153 A29 10t green & multi .50 .35
154 A29 15t brt pur & multi 1.00 .40
155 A29 20t bl gray & multi 1.25 .90
156 A29 30t dull blue & multi 7.50 1.50
157 A29 50t multicolored 1.10 .75
158 A29 1k multicolored 2.50 1.00
159 A29 2k gray & multi 3.50 2.25
160 A29 4k multicolored 17.50 *20.00*
Nos. 148-160 (13) 36.30 29.65

Decimal Coins A30

1971, Feb. 15 ***Perf. 14½***

161 A30 3t multicolored .25 .25
162 A30 8t dull red & multi .25 .25
163 A30 15t purple & multi .30 .30
164 A30 30t brt blue & multi .40 .40
a. Souvenir sheet of 4, #161-164 1.60 1.60
Nos. 161-164 (4) 1.20 1.20

Introduction of decimal currency and coinage.

Engravings by Albrecht Dürer — A31

Design: Nos. 165, 167, 169, 171, Christ on the Cross. Nos. 166, 168, 170, 172, The Resurrection.

1971, Apr. 7 Litho. ***Perf. 14x13½***

165 3t emerald & black .25 .25
166 3t emerald & black .25 .25
a. A31 Pair, #165-166 .25 .25
167 8t orange & black .25 .25
168 8t orange & black .25 .25
a. A31 Pair, #167-168 .25 .25
169 15t red lilac & black .25 .25
170 15t red lilac & black .25 .25
a. A31 Pair, #169-170 .40 .40
171 30t blue & black .25 .25
a. Souv. sheet of 4, #165, 167, 169, 171 1.75 1.75
172 30t blue & black .25 .25
a. Souv. sheet of 4, #166, 168, 170, 172 1.75 1.75
b. A31 Pair, #171-172 .50 .50
Nos. 165-172 (8) 2.00 2.00

Easter. Printed checkerwise in sheets of 25.

Holarrhena Febrifuga — A32

Flowering Shrubs and Trees: 8t, Brachystegia spiciformis. 15t, Securidaca longepedunculata. 30t, Pterocarpus rotundifolius.

1971, July 14 Litho. Wmk. 357

173 A32 3t gray & multi .25 .25
174 A32 8t gray & multi .25 .25
175 A32 15t gray & multi .35 .30
176 A32 30t gray & multi .50 .50
a. Souvenir sheet of 4, #173-176 2.00 2.00
Nos. 173-176 (4) 1.35 1.30

Drum Major — A33

1971, Oct. 5 ***Perf. 14x14½***

177 A33 30t lt blue & multi .90 .90

50th anniversary of Malawi Police Force.

Madonna and Child, by William Dyce — A34

Paintings of Holy Family by: 8t, Martin Schongauer. 15t, Raphael. 30t, Bronzino.

1971, Nov. 10 ***Perf. 14½***

178 A34 3t green & multi .25 .25
179 A34 8t carmine & multi .25 .25
180 A34 15t dp claret & multi .30 .30
181 A34 30t dull blue & multi .60 .60
a. Souvenir sheet of 4, #178-181 2.00 2.00
Nos. 178-181 (4) 1.40 1.40

Christmas.

Vickers Viscount — A35

Airplanes: 8t, Hawker Siddeley 748. 15t, Britten Norman Islander. 30t, B.A.C. One Eleven.

1972, Feb. 9 Litho. ***Perf. 13½x14***

182 A35 3t brt grn, blk & red .30 .25
183 A35 8t red org & black .50 .25
184 A35 15t dp rose lil, red & black .80 .75
185 A35 30t vio blue & multi 1.40 1.40
a. Souvenir sheet of 4, #182-185 9.00 9.00
Nos. 182-185 (4) 3.00 2.65

Publicity for Air Malawi.

Figures, Chencherere Hill — A36

Rock Paintings: 8t, Lizard and cat, Chencherere Hill. 15t, Symbols, Diwa Hill. 30t, Sun behind rain, Mikolongwe Hill.

1972, May 10 ***Perf. 13½***

186 A36 3t black & yel grn .30 .25
187 A36 8t black & dp car .35 .25
188 A36 15t black, vio & car .55 .45
189 A36 30t black, blue & yel 1.00 1.00
a. Souv. sheet of 4, #186-189, perf. 15 4.25 4.25
Nos. 186-189 (4) 2.20 1.95

Athlete and Olympic Rings — A37

1972, Aug. 9 ***Perf. 14x14½***

190 A37 3t gray, black & green .25 .25
191 A37 8t gray, black & scar .25 .25
192 A37 15t gray, black & lilac .25 .25
193 A37 30t gray, black & blue .40 .40
a. Souvenir sheet of 4, #190-193 2.10 2.10
Nos. 190-193 (4) 1.15 1.15

20th Olympic Games, Munich, 8/26-9/10.

Malawi Coat of Arms — A38

1972, Oct. 20 Litho. ***Perf. 13½x14***

194 A38 15t blue & multi .65 .65

18th Commonwealth Parliamentary Conference, Malawi, Oct. 1972.

Adoration of the Kings, by Orcagna — A39

Paintings of the Florentine School: 8t, Madonna and Child Enthroned, anonymous. 15t, Madonna and Child with Sts. Bonaventura and Louis of Toulouse, by Carlo Crivelli. 30t, Madonna and Child with St. Anne, by Jean de Bruges.

Perf. 14½x14

1972, Nov. 8 Wmk. 357

195 A39 3t lt olive & multi .25 .25
196 A39 8t carmine & multi .25 .25
197 A39 15t purple & multi .25 .25
198 A39 30t blue & multi .50 .50
a. Souvenir sheet of 4, #195-198 1.50 1.50
Nos. 195-198 (4) 1.25 1.25

Christmas.

Charaxes Bohemani — A40

8t, Uranothauma crawshayi. 15t, Charaxes acuminatus. No. 202, "Euphaedra zaddachi". No. 203, Amauris ansorgei.

1973 ***Perf. 13½x14***

199 A40 3t shown .55 .25
200 A40 8t multicolored .85 .25
201 A40 15t multicolored 1.00 .40
202 A40 30t multicolored 4.75 *7.00*
a. Souvenir sheet of 4, #199-202 13.50 13.50
203 A40 30t multicolored 5.00 *7.00*
Nos. 199-203 (5) 12.15 14.90

Issued: Nos. 199-202, 2/7; No. 203, 4/5.

Dr. Livingstone and Map of West Africa — A41

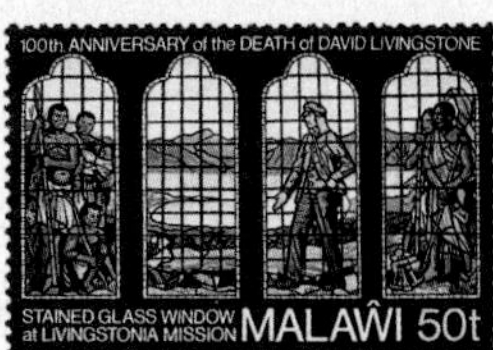

Livingstone Choosing Site for Mission — A42

1973 Litho. ***Perf. 13½x14***

204 A41 3t apple grn & multi .25 .25
205 A41 8t red orange & multi .25 .25
206 A41 15t multicolored .25 .25
207 A41 30t blue & multi .45 .45
a. Souvenir sheet of 4, #204-207 1.40 1.40
208 A42 50t black & multi .50 .50
a. Souvenir sheet of 1 1.25 1.25
Nos. 204-208 (5) 1.70 1.70

Dr. David Livingstone (1813-73), medical missionary and explorer.

Issued: Nos. 204-207, 207a, 5/1; Nos. 208, 208a, 12/12.

Thumb Dulcitone (Kalimba) A43

African Musical Instruments: 8t, Hand zither (bangwe; vert.). 15t, Hand drum (ng'oma; vert.). 30t, One-stringed fiddle (kaligo).

1973, Aug. 8 Wmk. 357 ***Perf. 14***

209 A43 3t brt green & multi .25 .25
210 A43 8t red & multi .25 .25
211 A43 15t violet & multi .25 .25
212 A43 30t blue & multi .25 .25
a. Souvenir sheet of 4, #209-212 3.25 3.25
Nos. 209-212 (4) 1.00 1.00

The Three Kings A44

1973, Nov. 8 ***Perf. 13½x14***

213 A44 3t blue & multi .25 .25
214 A44 8t ver & multi .25 .25
215 A44 15t multicolored .25 .25
216 A44 30t orange & multi .25 .25
a. Souvenir sheet of 4, #213-216 1.25 1.25
Nos. 213-216 (4) 1.00 1.00

Christmas.

Largemouth Black Bass — A45

Designs: Game fish.

1974, Feb. 20 Litho. ***Perf. 14x14½***

217 A45 3t shown .40 .25
218 A45 8t Rainbow trout .45 .30
219 A45 15t Lake salmon 1.00 .75
220 A45 30t Triggerfish 2.00 2.00
a. Souvenir sheet of 4, #217-220 5.25 5.25
Nos. 217-220 (4) 3.85 3.30

30th anniv. of Angling Society of Malawi.

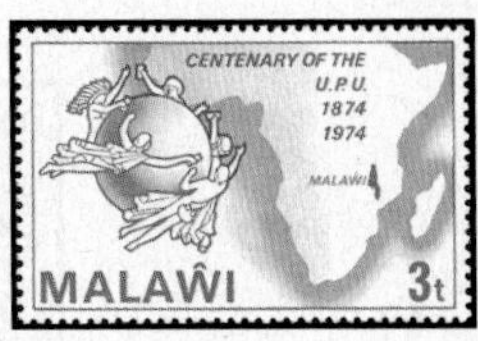

UPU Emblem, Map of Africa with Malawi A46

1974, Apr. 24 ***Perf. 13½***

221 A46 3t green & bister .25 .25
222 A46 8t ver & bister .25 .25
223 A46 15t lilac & bister .25 .25

224 A46 30t gray & bister .35 .35
a. Souvenir sheet of 4, #221-224 1.60 1.60
Nos. 221-224 (4) 1.10 1.10

Centenary of Universal Postal Union.

Capital Hill, Lilongwe and Pres. Kamuzu Banda A47

1974, July 3 Litho. *Perf. 14*

225 A47 3t emerald & multi .25 .25
226 A47 8t red & multi .25 .25
227 A47 15t lilac & multi .25 .25
228 A47 30t vio blue & multi .25 .25
a. Souvenir sheet of 4, #225-228 1.10 1.10
Nos. 225-228 (4) 1.00 1.00

10th anniversary of independence.

Madonna of the Meadow, by Giovanni Bellini — A48

Paintings: 8t, Holy Family, by Jacob Jordaens. 15t, Nativity, by Peter F. de Grebber. 30t, Adoration of the Shepherds, by Lorenzo di Credi.

1974, Dec. 4 Litho. *Perf. 13½x14*

229 A48 3t dk green & multi .25 .25
230 A48 8t multicolored .25 .25
231 A48 15t purple & multi .25 .25
232 A48 30t dk blue & multi .25 .25
a. Souvenir sheet of 4, #229-232 1.10 1.10
Nos. 229-232 (4) 1.00 1.00

Christmas.

African Snipe A49

Double-banded Sandgrouse A50

Birds: 3t, Blue quail. 5t, Red-necked francolin. 8t, Harlequin quail. 10t, Spurwing goose. 15t, Denham's bustard. 20t, Knob-billed duck. 30t, Helmeted guinea fowl. 50t, Pigmy goose. 1k, Garganey. 2k, White-faced tree duck. 4k, Green pigeon.

Wmk. 357

1975, Feb. 19 Litho. *Perf. 14*

Size: 17x21, 21x17mm

233 A49 1t multicolored .25 .40
234 A50 2t multicolored .35 .40
235 A50 3t multicolored 1.40 1.60
236 A49 5t multicolored 3.25 2.00
237 A50 8t multicolored 4.50 1.60

Perf. 14½

Size: 25x41, 41x25mm

238 A49 10t multicolored 4.00 .80
239 A49 15t multicolored 3.25 4.00
240 A49 20t multicolored 1.10 1.60
241 A49 30t multicolored 1.40 1.25
242 A50 50t multicolored 2.25 2.00
243 A50 1k multicolored 3.75 5.00
244 A49 2k multicolored 9.00 8.00
245 A50 4k multicolored 18.00 16.00
Nos. 233-245 (13) 52.50 44.65

See Nos. 270-279. For overprints see Nos. 263, 294.

Malawi Coat of Arms — A51

Coil Stamps

1975-84 *Perf. 14½x14*

246 A51 1t dark violet blue .50 .30
247 A51 5t red ('84) 1.40 1.40

"Mpasa" A52

Designs: Lake Malawi ships.

1975, Mar. 12 Wmk. 357 *Perf. 13½*

251 A52 3t shown .35 .30
252 A52 8t "Ilala II" .55 .45
253 A52 15t "Chauncy Maples" 1.00 1.00
254 A52 30t "Nkwazi" 1.75 *2.75*
a. Souvenir sheet of 4, #251-254, perf. 14½ 4.50 4.50
Nos. 251-254 (4) 3.65 4.50

Habenaria Splendens — A53

Orchids of Malawi: 10t, Eulophia cucullata. 20t, Disa welwitschii. 40t, Angraecum conchiferum.

1975, June 6 Litho. *Perf. 14½*

255 A53 3t lt green & multi .55 .25
256 A53 10t red org & multi .65 .25
257 A53 20t dull vio & multi 1.00 .40
258 A53 40t multicolored 1.50 *2.25*
a. Souvenir sheet of 4, #255-258 9.00 9.00
Nos. 255-258 (4) 3.70 3.15

Bush Baby — A54

1975, Sept. 3 Litho. *Perf. 14*

259 A54 3t shown .25 .25
260 A54 10t Leopard .40 .30
261 A54 20t Roan antelope .80 .80
262 A54 40t Burchell's zebra 1.60 *2.00*
a. Souvenir sheet of 4, #259-262 5.00 5.00
Nos. 259-262 (4) 3.05 3.35

Animals of Malawi.

No. 242 Overprinted in Black

1975, Dec. 9 Litho. *Perf. 14½*

263 A50 50t multicolored 1.75 *2.25*

10th African, Caribbean and Pacific Ministerial Conference.

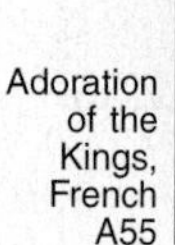

Adoration of the Kings, French A55

Christmas: 10t, Nativity, 16th century, Spanish. 20t, Nativity, by Pierre Raymond, 16th century. 40t, Angel Appearing to the Shepherds, 14th century, English.

1975, Dec. 12 *Perf. 13x13½*

264 A55 3t multicolored .25 .25
265 A55 10t multicolored .25 .25
266 A55 20t purple & multi .25 .25
267 A55 40t blue & multi .25 .25
a. Souv. sheet of 4, #264-267, perf. 14 2.60 2.60
Nos. 264-267 (4) 1.00 1.00

Bird Types of 1975

1975 Litho. Unwmk. *Perf. 14*

Size: 21x17mm

270 A50 3t multicolored 5.00 3.50

Perf. 14½

Size: 25x41mm

273 A49 10t multicolored 3.00 3.75
274 A49 15t multicolored 3.00 4.25
279 A49 2k multicolored 8.00 *15.00*
Nos. 270-279 (4) 19.00 26.50

For overprint see No. 293.

Alexander Graham Bell — A56

Perf. 14x14½

1976, Mar. 24 Litho. Wmk. 357

281 A56 3t green & black .25 .25
282 A56 10t dp lilac rose & blk .25 .25
283 A56 20t brt purple & blk .25 .25
284 A56 40t brt blue & blk .50 .50
a. Souvenir sheet of 4, #281-284 2.00 2.00
Nos. 281-284 (4) 1.25 1.25

Centenary of first telephone call by Alexander Graham Bell, Mar. 10, 1876.

President Kamuzu Banda — A57

1976, July 1 Photo. *Perf. 13*

285 A57 3t brt green & multi .25 .25
286 A57 10t multicolored .25 .25
287 A57 20t violet & multi .25 .25
288 A57 40t dull blue & multi .55 .55
a. Souvenir sheet of 4, #285-288 1.75 1.75
Nos. 285-288 (4) 1.30 1.30

10th anniversary of the Republic.

Bagnall Diesel No. 100 A58

Diesel Locomotives: 10t, Shire class No. 503. 20t, Nippon Sharyo No. 301. 40t, Hunslet No. 110.

1976, Oct. 1 Litho. *Perf. 14½*

289 A58 3t emerald & multi .50 .30
290 A58 10t red & multi 1.00 .40
291 A58 20t lilac & multi 1.75 1.75
292 A58 40t blue & multi 3.00 3.00
a. Souvenir sheet of 4, #289-292 7.00 7.00
Nos. 289-292 (4) 6.25 5.45

Malawi Railways.

Nos. 274 and 241 Overprinted

1976, Oct. 22 Litho. Unwmk.

293 A49 15t multicolored 2.75 1.40

Wmk. 357

294 A49 30t multicolored 3.25 3.25

Blantyre Mission centenary.

Christ Child on Straw Bed — A59

1976, Dec. 6 Wmk. 357 *Perf. 14*

295 A59 3t green & multi .25 .25
296 A59 10t magenta & multi .25 .25
297 A59 20t purple & multi .25 .25
298 A59 40t dk blue & multi .25 .25
a. Souvenir sheet of 4, #295-298 2.25 2.25
Nos. 295-298 (4) 1.00 1.00

Christmas.

Ebony Ancestor Figures — A60

Handicrafts: 10t, Ebony elephant, horiz. 20t, Ebony rhinoceros, horiz. 40t, Wooden antelope.

1977, Apr. 1 Litho. Wmk. 357

299 A60 4t yellow & multi .25 .25
300 A60 10t black & multi .25 .25
301 A60 20t ocher & multi .25 .25
302 A60 40t ver & multi .25 .25
a. Souvenir sheet of 4, #299-302 2.00 2.00
Nos. 299-302 (4) 1.00 1.00

Chileka Airport, Blantyre, and VC10 A61

Transportation in Malawi: 10t, Leyland bus on Blantyre-Lilongwe Road. 20t, Ilala II on Lake Malawi. 40t, Freight train of Blantyre-Nacala line on overpass.

1977, July 12 Litho. *Perf. 14½*

303 A61 4t multicolored .45 .25
304 A61 10t multicolored .45 .40
305 A61 20t multicolored 1.10 .95
306 A61 40t multicolored 1.75 *3.25*
a. Souvenir sheet of 4, #303-306 4.25 4.25
Nos. 303-306 (4) 3.75 4.85

Pseudotropheus Johanni — A62

Lake Malawi Fish: 10t, Pseudotropheus livingstoni. 20t, Pseudotropheus zebra. 40t, Genyochromis mento.

Wmk. 357, Unwmkd.

1977, Oct. 4 Litho. *Perf. 13½x14*

No.	Type	Description	Unused	Used
307	A62	4t multicolored	.40	.25
308	A62	10t multicolored	.60	.30
309	A62	20t multicolored	1.40	.60
310	A62	40t multicolored	1.60	1.50
a.		Souvenir sheet of 4, #307-310	5.00	5.00
		Nos. 307-310 (4)	4.00	2.65

Virgin and Child, by Bergognone A63

Virgin and Child: 10t, with God the Father and Angels, by Ambrogio Bergognone. 20t, detail from Bottigella altarpiece, by Vincenzo Foppa. 40t, with the fountain, by Jan Van Eyck.

Perf. 14x13½

1977, Nov. 21 Unwmk.

No.	Type	Description	Unused	Used
311	A63	4t multicolored	.25	.25
312	A63	10t red & multi	.25	.25
313	A63	20t lilac & multi	.25	.25
314	A63	40t vio blue & multi	.40	.40
a.		Souvenir sheet of 4, #311-314	3.25	3.25
		Nos. 311-314 (4)	1.15	1.15

Christmas.

Entry into Jerusalem, by Giotto — A64

Giotto Paintings: 10t, Crucifixion. 20t, Descent from the Cross. 40t, Jesus Appearing to Mary.

1978, Mar. 1 Litho. *Perf. 12x12½*

No.	Type	Description	Unused	Used
315	A64	4t multicolored	.25	.25
316	A64	10t multicolored	.25	.25
317	A64	20t multicolored	.30	.25
318	A64	40t multicolored	.60	.60
a.		Souvenir sheet of 4, #315-318	2.50	2.50
		Nos. 315-318 (4)	1.40	1.35

Easter.

Lions, Wildlife Fund Emblem A65

Animals and Wildlife Fund Emblem: 4t, Nyala, vert. 20t, Burchell's zebras. 40t, Reedbuck, vert.

1978, June 1 Unwmk. *Perf. 13x13½*

No.	Type	Description	Unused	Used
319	A65	4t multicolored	*4.00*	*1.00*
320	A65	10t multicolored	*10.00*	*2.00*
321	A65	20t multicolored	*17.50*	*3.00*
322	A65	40t multicolored	*25.00*	*10.00*
a.		Souvenir sheet of 4, #319-322, perf. 13½	*65.00*	*50.00*
		Nos. 319-322 (4)	*56.50*	*16.00*

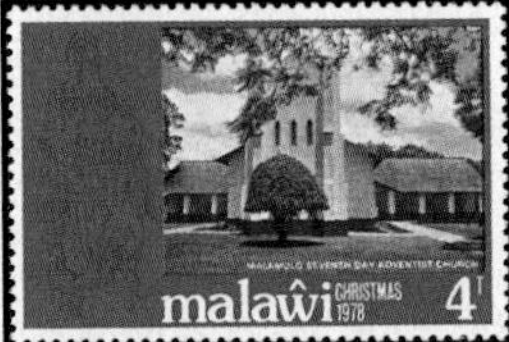

Malamulo Seventh Day Adventist Church — A66

Virgin and Child and: 10t, Likoma Cathedral. 20t, St. Michael's and All Angel's, Blantyre. 40t, Zomba Catholic Cathedral.

1978, Nov. 15 Wmk. 357 *Perf. 14*

No.	Type	Description	Unused	Used
323	A66	4t multicolored	.25	.25
324	A66	10t multicolored	.25	.25
325	A66	20t multicolored	.25	.25
326	A66	40t multicolored	.40	.40
a.		Souvenir sheet of 4, #323-326	1.25	1.25
		Nos. 323-326 (4)	1.15	1.15

Christmas.

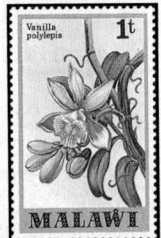

Vanilla Polylepis — A67

Orchids of Malawi: 2t, Cirrhopetalum umbellatum. 5t, Calanthe natalensis. 7t, Ansellia gigantea. 8t, Tridactyle bicaudata. 10t, Acampe pachyglossa. 15t, Eulophia quartiniana. 20t, Cyrtorchis arcuata. 30t, Eulophia tricristata. 50t, Disa hamatopetala. 75t, Cynorchis glandulosa. 1k, Aerangis kotschyana. 1.50k, Polystachya dendrobiiflora. 2k, Disa ornithantha. 4k, Cytorchis praetermissa.

1979, Jan. 2 Litho. *Perf. 13½*

No.	Type	Description	Unused	Used
327	A67	1t multicolored	.60	.30
328	A67	2t multicolored	.60	.30
329	A67	5t multicolored	.60	.30
330	A67	7t multicolored	.60	.50
331	A67	8t multicolored	.60	.30
332	A67	10t multicolored	.60	.30
333	A67	15t multicolored	.60	.40
334	A67	20t multicolored	.70	.55
335	A67	30t multicolored	1.50	.40
336	A67	50t multicolored	1.25	.60
337	A67	75t multicolored	2.50	*4.00*
338	A67	1k multicolored	2.25	1.75
339	A67	1.50k multicolored	3.00	*4.75*
340	A67	2k multicolored	4.00	2.75
341	A67	4k multicolored	9.00	8.50
		Nos. 327-341 (15)	28.40	25.70

Brachystegia Spiciformis A68

Trees: 10t, Widdringtonia nodiflora. 20t, Sandalwood. 40t, African mahogany.

1979, Jan. 21 *Perf. 14x13½*

No.	Type	Description	Unused	Used
342	A68	5t multicolored	.30	.25
343	A68	10t multicolored	.40	.35
344	A68	20t multicolored	.70	.75
345	A68	40t multicolored	1.00	*2.25*
a.		Souvenir sheet of 4, #342-345	3.00	3.00
		Nos. 342-345 (4)	2.40	3.60

National Tree Planting Day.

Railroad Bridge A69

Designs: 10t, Station and train. 20t, 40t, Train passing through man-made pass, diff.

1979, Feb. 17 Litho. *Perf. 14½*

No.	Type	Description	Unused	Used
346	A69	5t multicolored	.30	.25
347	A69	10t multicolored	.50	.35
348	A69	20t multicolored	.80	.75
349	A69	40t multicolored	1.40	*2.00*
a.		Souvenir sheet of 4, #346-349	5.75	5.75
		Nos. 346-349 (4)	3.00	3.35

Inauguration of Salima-Lilongwe Railroad.

Malawi Boy and IYC Emblem — A70

Designs: Malawi children and IYC emblem.

1979, July 10 Wmk. 357 *Perf. 14*

No.	Type	Description	Unused	Used
350	A70	5t multicolored	.25	.25
351	A70	10t multicolored	.25	.25
352	A70	20t multicolored	.35	.30
353	A70	40t multicolored	.55	.55
		Nos. 350-353 (4)	1.40	1.35

International Year of the Child.

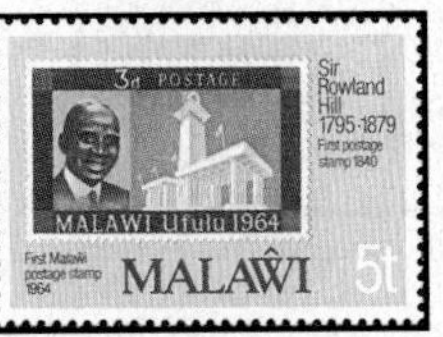

Malawi No. 1 A71

Stamps of Malawi: 10t, #2. 20t, #3. 40t, #4.

1979, Sept. 17 Litho. *Perf. 13½x14*

No.	Type	Description	Unused	Used
354	A71	5t multicolored	.25	.25
355	A71	10t multicolored	.25	.25
356	A71	20t multicolored	.25	.25
357	A71	40t multicolored	.25	.25
a.		Souvenir sheet of 4, #354-357	1.25	1.25
		Nos. 354-357 (4)	1.00	1.00

Sir Rowland Hill (1795-1879), originator of penny postage.

Christmas — A72

Designs: Landscapes.

1979, Nov. 15 Litho. *Perf. 13½x14*

No.	Type	Description	Unused	Used
358	A72	5t multicolored	.25	.25
359	A72	10t multicolored	.25	.25
360	A72	20t multicolored	.30	.30
361	A72	40t multicolored	.60	*2.00*
		Nos. 358-361 (4)	1.40	2.80

Limbe Rotary Club Emblem — A73

Malawi Rotary Club Emblems: 10t, Blantyre. 20t, Lilongwe. 40t, Rotary Intl.

1980, Feb. 23 Litho. *Perf. 13½*

No.	Type	Description	Unused	Used
362	A73	5t multicolored	.25	.25
363	A73	10t multicolored	.25	.25
364	A73	20t multicolored	.25	.25
365	A73	40t multicolored	.70	*2.00*
a.		Souvenir sheet of 4, #362-365	2.50	2.50
		Nos. 362-365 (4)	1.45	2.75

Rotary International, 75th anniversary.

Mangochi District Post Office, 1976, London 1980 Emblem — A74

London 1980 Emblem and: 10t, New Blantyre sorting office, 1979. 20t, Mail transfer hut, Walala. 1k, Nyasaland Post Office, Chiromo, 1891.

1980, May 6 Wmk. 357 *Perf. 14½*

No.	Type	Description	Unused	Used
366	A74	5t blue green & blk	.25	.25
367	A74	10t red & black	.25	.25
368	A74	20t dp violet & black	.25	.25
369	A74	1k dk blue & black	.40	.40
a.		Souvenir sheet of 4, #366-369	2.00	2.00
		Nos. 366-369 (4)	1.15	1.15

London 1980 International Stamp Exhibition, May 6-14.

Agate Nodule — A75

1980, Aug. 20 Litho. *Perf. 13½*

No.	Type	Description	Unused	Used
370	A75	5t shown	1.00	.25
371	A75	10t Sunstone	1.25	.25
372	A75	20t Smoky Quartz	2.50	.60
373	A75	1k Kyanite crystal	5.50	*7.50*
		Nos. 370-373 (4)	10.25	8.60

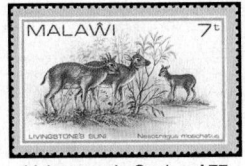

Elephants Drinking (Christmas) A76

1980, Nov. 10 Litho. *Perf. 13*

No.	Type	Description	Unused	Used
374	A76	5t shown	.50	.45
375	A76	10t Flowers	.45	.35
376	A76	20t Train	1.10	.90
377	A76	1k Bird	1.75	2.10
		Nos. 374-377 (4)	3.80	3.80

Livingstone's Suni — A77

10t, Blue duikers. 20t, African buffalo. 1k, Lichtenstein's hartebeests.

1981, Feb. 4 Litho. *Perf. 14½*

No.	Type	Description	Unused	Used
378	A77	7t shown	.25	.25
379	A77	10t multicolored	.30	.25
380	A77	20t multicolored	.50	.40
381	A77	1k multicolored	1.75	1.75
		Nos. 378-381 (4)	2.80	2.65

Standard A Earth Station A78

10t, Blantyre International Gateway Exchange. 20t, Standard B Earth Station. 1k, Satellite and earth.

1981, Apr. 24 Litho. *Perf. 14½*

No.	Type	Description	Unused	Used
382	A78	7t shown	.25	.25
383	A78	10t multicolored	.25	.25
384	A78	20t multicolored	.30	.25
385	A78	1k multicolored	1.50	*1.90*
a.		Souvenir sheet of 4, #382-385	2.75	2.75
		Nos. 382-385 (4)	2.30	2.65

International communications.

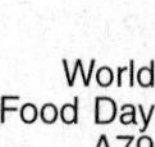

World Food Day A79

1981, Sept. 11 Litho. *Perf. 14*

386	A79	7t Corn	.25	.25
387	A79	10t Rice	.25	.25
388	A79	20t Finger millet	.50	.25
389	A79	1k Wheat	1.40	1.40
		Nos. 386-389 (4)	2.40	2.15

Holy Family, by Lippi A80

Christmas: 7t, Adoration of the Shepherds, by Murillo, vert. 20t, Adoration of the Shepherds, by Louis Le Nain. 1k, Virgin and Child, St. John the Baptist and Angel, by Paolo Morando, vert.

Perf. 13½x13, 13x13½

1981, Nov. 26 Litho.

390	A80	7t multicolored	.25	.25
391	A80	10t multicolored	.30	.25
392	A80	20t multicolored	.60	.55
393	A80	1k multicolored	1.50	1.50
		Nos. 390-393 (4)	2.65	2.55

Wildlife in Natl. Parks A81

1982, Mar. 15 Litho. *Perf. 14½x14*

394	A81	7t Impalas	.25	.25
395	A81	10t Lions	.45	.25
396	A81	20t Kudus	.75	.25
397	A81	1k Flamingos	3.00	3.00
		Nos. 394-397 (4)	4.45	3.75

Kamuzu Academy — A82

Designs: Academy views.

1982, July 1 Litho. *Perf. 14½*

398	A82	7t multicolored	.25	.25
399	A82	20t multicolored	.30	.25
400	A82	30t multicolored	.45	.40
401	A82	1k multicolored	1.50	1.50
		Nos. 398-401 (4)	2.50	2.40

1982 World Cup — A83

1982, Sept. *Perf. 14x14½*

402	A83	7t Players	1.10	1.00
403	A83	20t World Cup	2.00	2.00
404	A83	30t Stadium	2.50	2.50
		Nos. 402-404 (3)	5.60	5.50

Souvenir Sheet

405	A83	1k Emblem on field	2.50	2.50

Remembrance Day — A84

Designs: War Memorials.

1982, Nov. 5 *Perf. 14½*

406	A84	7t Blantyre	.25	.25
407	A84	20t Zomba	.25	.25
408	A84	30t Chichiri, badges	.30	.30
409	A84	1k Lilongwe	1.00	1.50
		Nos. 406-409 (4)	1.80	2.30

Commonwealth Day — A85

7t, Kwacha Intl. Conf. Ctr. 20t, Tea picking, Mulanje. 30t, Map. 1k, Pres. Banda, flag.

1983, Mar. 14 Wmk. 357 *Perf. 14*

410	A85	7t multicolored	.25	.25
411	A85	20t multicolored	.25	.25
412	A85	30t multicolored	.30	.25
413	A85	1k multicolored	.65	*.85*
		Nos. 410-413 (4)	1.45	1.60

The Miraculous Draught of Fishes, by Raphael (1483-1517) — A86

Designs: 7t, 20t, 30t, Details. 1k, Entire painting. 7t, 20t vert.

1983, Apr. 4 Litho. Wmk. 357

414	A86	7t multicolored	.40	.30
415	A86	20t multicolored	1.00	1.00
416	A86	30t multicolored	1.40	1.40
		Nos. 414-416 (3)	2.80	2.70

Souvenir Sheet

417	A86	1k multicolored	3.25	3.25

Fish Eagles — A87

Designs: a, Lakeside sentinel. b, Gull-like, far-carrying call. c, Diving on its fish prey. d, Prey captured. e, Feeding on its catch. Nos. 418a-418e in continuous design.

1983, July 11 Wmk. 357 *Perf. 14½*

418		Strip of 5	17.00	17.00
a.-e.		A87 30t multicolored	1.90	1.90

Manned Flight Bicentenary — A88

Kamuzu Intl. Airport.

1983, Aug. 31 Litho. *Perf. 14*

419	A88	7t multicolored	.25	.25
420	A88	20t multi, diff.	.45	.35
421	A88	30t multi, diff.	.60	.60
422	A88	1k multi, diff.	1.75	1.75
a.		Souvenir sheet of 4, #419-422	3.50	3.50
		Nos. 419-422 (4)	3.05	2.95

Christmas — A89

Local flowers: 7t, Clerodendium myricoides. 20t, Gloriosa superba. 30t, Gladiolus laxiflorus. 1k, Aframomum angustifolium.

1983, Nov. 1 Wmk. 357 *Perf. 14*

423	A89	7t multicolored	.60	.35
424	A89	20t multicolored	1.40	1.00
425	A89	30t multicolored	1.75	1.40
426	A89	1k multicolored	4.75	4.75
		Nos. 423-426 (4)	8.50	7.50

Aquarium Species, Lake Malawi A90

Designs: 1t, Melanochromis auratus. 2t, Haplochromis compressiceps. 5t, Labeotropheus fuelleborni. 7t, Pseudotropheus lombardoi. 8t, Gold pseudotropheus zebra. 10t, Trematocranus jacobfreibergi. 15t, Melanochromis crabro. 20t, Marbled pseadotropheus. 30t, Labidochromis caeruleus. 40t, Haplochromis venustus. 50t, Aulonacara of Thumbi. 75t, Melanochromis vermivorus. 1k, Pseudotropheus zebra. 2k, Trematocranus spp. 4k, Aulonacara of Mbenje.

Perf. 14½x14

1984, Feb. 2 Wmk. 373

Inscribed "1984" below design

427	A90	1t multicolored	.45	*1.00*
428	A90	2t multicolored	.45	*1.00*
429	A90	5t multicolored	.45	*1.00*
430	A90	7t multicolored	.45	.40
431	A90	8t multicolored	.45	.40
432	A90	10t multicolored	.45	.30
433	A90	15t multicolored	.45	.30
434	A90	20t multicolored	.55	.30
435	A90	30t multicolored	.65	.50
436	A90	40t multicolored	1.10	.65
437	A90	50t multicolored	2.75	2.50
438	A90	75t multicolored	4.00	4.00
439	A90	1k multicolored	4.50	4.50
440	A90	2k multicolored	6.50	6.50
441	A90	4k multicolored	9.25	9.25
		Nos. 427-441 (15)	32.45	32.60

Inscribed "1986" below design

1986

427a	A90	1t multicolored	1.75	*1.00*
430a	A90	7t multicolored	1.75	.40
431a	A90	8t multicolored	1.75	.40
432a	A90	10t multicolored	1.75	.30
433a	A90	15t multicolored	1.75	.30
434a	A90	20t multicolored	2.25	.30
435a	A90	30t multicolored	2.50	.50
436a	A90	40t multicolored	4.50	.65
		Nos. 427a-436a (8)	18.00	3.85

Nyika Red Hare A91

1984, Feb. 2 Wmk. 357 *Perf. 14*

442	A91	7t shown	.70	.25
443	A91	20t Sun squirrel	1.40	.45
444	A91	30t Hedgehog	1.90	1.00
445	A91	1k Genet	2.50	*3.75*
		Nos. 442-445 (4)	6.50	*5.45*

1984 Summer Olympics — A92

1984, June 1 Litho. *Perf. 14*

446	A92	7t Running	.25	.25
447	A92	20t Boxing	.60	.30
448	A92	30t Bicycling	.90	.90
449	A92	1k Long jump	1.60	1.60
a.		Souvenir sheet of 4, #446-449	4.50	4.50
		Nos. 446-449 (4)	3.35	3.05

Local Butterflies — A93

7t, Euphaedra neophron. 20t, Papilio dardanus. 30t, Antanartia schaeneia. 1k, Spindasis.

1984, Aug. 1 Photo. *Perf. 11½*

Granite Paper

450	A93	7t multicolored	1.25	.35
451	A93	20t multicolored	2.50	.50
452	A93	30t multicolored	3.25	1.25
453	A93	1k multicolored	5.50	*7.00*
		Nos. 450-453 (4)	12.50	9.10

Christmas — A94

Virgin and Child Paintings.

Wmk. 357

1984, Oct. 15 Litho. *Perf. 14½*

454	A94	7t Duccio	.75	.30
455	A94	20t Raphael	2.00	.40
456	A94	30t Lippi	2.50	1.25
457	A94	1k Wilton diptych	*5.25*	*8.00*
		Nos. 454-457 (4)	10.50	9.95

Fungi A94a

7t, Leucopaxillus gracillimus. 20t, Limacella guttata. 30t, Termitomyces eurhizles. 1k, Xerulina asprata.

1985, Jan. 23 *Perf. 14½x14*

458	A94a	7t multi	1.25	.45
459	A94a	20t multi	3.00	.55
460	A94a	30t multi	3.50	1.50
461	A94a	1k multi	7.00	*7.00*
		Nos. 458-461 (4)	14.75	*9.50*

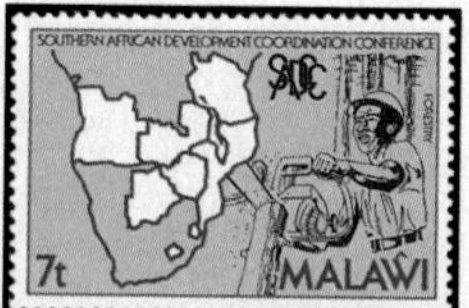

Southern African Development Coordination Conference — A95

1985, Apr. 1 Litho. *Perf. 14*

462	A95	7t Forestry	1.00	.35
463	A95	15t Communications	1.75	.40
464	A95	20t Transportation	4.00	1.50
465	A95	1k Fishing	6.50	6.50
		Nos. 462-465 (4)	13.25	8.75

Ships on Lake Malawi A96

1985, June 3 *Perf. 13½x13*

466	A96	7t Ufulu	1.00	.40
467	A96	15t Chauncy Maples	2.25	.40
468	A96	20t Mtendere	3.00	1.00
469	A96	1k Ilala	5.75	5.75
a.		Souvenir sheet of 4, #466-469, perf. 13x12	12.50	12.50
		Nos. 466-469 (4)	12.00	7.55

Audubon Birth Bicent. — A97

7t, Stierling's woodpecker. 15t, Lesser seed-cracker. 20t, Gunning's akalat. 1k, Boehm's bee-eater.

1985, Aug. 1 Litho. *Perf. 14*

470	A97	7t multicolored	1.50	.50
471	A97	15t multicolored	2.75	.50
472	A97	20t multicolored	3.00	1.00
473	A97	1k multicolored	5.25	5.25
a.		Souvenir sheet of 4, #470-473	12.50	12.50
		Nos. 470-473 (4)	12.50	7.25

Christmas — A98

Paintings: 7t, The Virgin of Humility, by Jaime Serra. 15t, Adoration of the Magi, by Stefano da Zevio. 20t, Madonna and Child, by Gerard van Honthorst. 1k, Virgin of Zbraslav, by a Master of Vissi Brod.

Perf. 11½x12

1985, Oct. 14 Unwmk.

474	A98	7t multicolored	.45	.30
475	A98	15t multicolored	1.10	.35
476	A98	20t multicolored	1.50	.55
477	A98	1k multicolored	4.00	*4.75*
		Nos. 474-477 (4)	7.05	5.95

Halley's Comet — A99

8t, Earth, comet and Giotto trajectories. 15t, Comet over Earth. 20t, Over Malawi. 1k, Giotto probe.

1986, Feb. 10 Wmk. 357 *Perf. 14½*

478	A99	8t multi	1.00	.35
479	A99	15t multi	1.10	.35
480	A99	20t multi	1.75	.45
481	A99	1k multi	*3.25*	*5.50*
		Nos. 478-481 (4)	7.10	6.65

1986 World Cup Soccer Championships, Mexico — A100

Various soccer plays.

Perf. 12x11½

1986, May 26 Unwmk.

Granite Paper

482	A100	8t multicolored	1.00	.30
483	A100	15t multicolored	1.50	.35
484	A100	20t multicolored	2.00	.85
485	A100	1k multicolored	5.00	5.50
a.		Souvenir sheet of 4, #482-485	14.00	14.00
		Nos. 482-485 (4)	9.50	7.00

Natl. Independence, 20th Anniv. — A101

1986, June 30 Litho. *Perf. 14*

486	A101	8t Pres. Banda	2.25	2.25
487	A101	15t Natl. flag	1.25	.25
488	A101	20t Natl. crest	1.40	.35
489	A101	1k Natl. airline	4.75	5.25
		Nos. 486-489 (4)	9.65	8.10

Christmas — A102

Paintings: 8t, Virgin and Child, by Botticelli (1445-1510). 15t, Adoration of the Shepherds, by Guido Reni (1575-1642). 20t, Madonna of the Veil, by Carlo Dolci (1616-86). 1k, Adoration of the Magi, by Jean Bourdichon.

1986, Dec. 15 Litho. *Perf. 11½*

490	A102	8t multicolored	.75	.25
491	A102	15t multicolored	1.25	.25
492	A102	20t multicolored	2.00	.50
493	A102	1k multicolored	*5.25*	*8.00*
		Nos. 490-493 (4)	9.25	9.00

World Wildlife Fund A103

Bugeranus carunculatus.

1987, Jan. 30 Wmk. 357 *Perf. 14½*

494	A103	8t Wattled crane	2.75	.45
495	A103	15t Two cranes	4.00	.60
496	A103	20t Nesting	4.75	.90
497	A103	75t Crane in water	8.75	8.75
		Nos. 494-497 (4)	20.25	10.70

1988, Oct. Wmk. 373

494a	A103	8t	7.75	1.75
495a	A103	15t	11.00	3.25
496a	A103	20t	12.00	3.75
497a	A103	75t	16.50	15.00
		Nos. 494a-497a (4)	47.25	23.75

British Steam Locomotives — A104

10t, Shamrock No. 2, 1902. 25t, D Class No. 8, 1914. 30t, Thistle No. 1, 1902. 1k, Kitson No. 6, 1903.

1987, May 25 Litho. *Perf. 14x13½*

498	A104	10t multi	3.25	.45
499	A104	25t multi	4.50	.60
500	A104	30t multi	5.00	1.00
501	A104	1k multi	9.00	9.00
		Nos. 498-501 (4)	21.75	11.05

Hippopotamus A105

10t, Feeding. 25t, Swimming, roaring. 30t, Mother and young swimming. 1k, At rest, egret.

1987, Aug. 24 Photo. *Perf. 12½*

Granite Paper

502	A105	10t multi	2.00	.35
503	A105	25t multi	3.75	.50
504	A105	30t multi	3.75	.85
505	A105	1k multi	9.50	8.75
a.		Souvenir sheet of 4, #502-505	19.00	19.00
		Nos. 502-505 (4)	19.00	10.45

Wild Flowers — A106

10t, Stathmostelma spectabile. 25t, Pentanisia schweinfurthii. 30t, Chironia krebsii. 1k, Ochna macrocalyx.

Unwmk.

1987, Oct. 19 Litho. *Perf. 14*

506	A106	10t multicolored	1.25	.25
507	A106	25t multicolored	2.50	.35
508	A106	30t multicolored	3.00	.70
509	A106	1k multicolored	5.00	5.00
		Nos. 506-509 (4)	11.75	6.30

Locally Carved and Staunton Chessmen A107

1988, Feb. 8 Wmk. 384 *Perf. 14½*

510	A107	15t Knights	2.00	.30
511	A107	35t Bishops	3.00	.90
512	A107	50t Rooks	3.50	1.75
513	A107	2k Queens	9.25	9.25
		Nos. 510-513 (4)	17.75	12.20

1988 Summer Olympics, Seoul — A108

1988, June 13 Unwmk. *Perf. 14*

514	A108	15t High jump	.60	.25
515	A108	35t Javelin	.90	.40
516	A108	50t Women's tennis	1.25	.70
517	A108	2k Shot put	2.75	2.75
a.		Souvenir sheet of 4, #514-517	6.50	6.50
		Nos. 514-517 (4)	5.50	4.10

Birds — A109

Designs: 1t, Eastern fores scrub-warbler. 2t, Yellow-throated warbler. 5t, Moustached green tinkerbird. 7t, Waller's chestnut-wing starling. 8t, Oriole finch. 10t, No. 533A, Starred robin. 15t, Bar-tailed trogon. 20t, Green twinspot. 30t, Gray cuckoo shrike. 40t, Black-fronted bush shrike. 50t, White-tailed crested flycatcher. 75t, Green barbet. 1k, Cinnamon dove. 2k, Silvery-cheeked hornbill. 4k, Crowned eagle. No. 533, Red and blue sunbird.

Perf. 11½x12, 15x14½ (#533)

1988-94 Photo.

Granite Paper (1t-4k)

518	A109	1t multicolored	.75	.60
519	A109	2t multicolored	.75	.60
520	A109	5t multicolored	.75	.60
521	A109	7t multicolored	.75	.60
522	A109	8t multicolored	.75	.60
523	A109	10t multicolored	1.90	1.00
524	A109	15t multicolored	.75	.25
525	A109	20t multicolored	.75	.25
526	A109	30t multicolored	.75	.25
527	A109	40t multicolored	.80	.40
528	A109	50t multicolored	1.90	1.00
529	A109	75t multicolored	1.40	1.00
530	A109	1k multicolored	1.90	1.10
531	A109	2k multicolored	3.00	2.00
532	A109	4k multicolored	6.50	3.75
533	A109	10k multicolored	16.00	9.75
533A	A109	10k multicolored	13.00	5.00
		Nos. 518-533A (17)	52.40	28.75

Issue dates: 10k, Oct. 3, No. 533A, 1994; others, July 25.

For surcharges, see Nos. 840-841.

Common Design Types pictured following the introduction.

Lloyds of London, 300th Anniv.

Common Design Type

15t, Royal Exchange, 1844. 35t, Opening of the Nkula Falls hydroelectric power station, horiz. 50t, Air Malawi passenger jet, horiz. 2k, Cruise ship Queen Elizabeth (Seawise University) on fire, Hong Kong, 1972.

Wmk. 373

1988, Oct. 24 Litho. *Perf. 14*

534	CD341	15t multicolored	.50	.30
535	CD341	35t multicolored	1.00	.50
536	CD341	50t multicolored	3.25	.80
537	CD341	2k multicolored	6.25	6.25
		Nos. 534-537 (4)	11.00	7.85

Christmas — A110

Paintings: 15t, Madonna in the Church, by Jan Van Eyck (d. 1441). 35t, Virgin, Infant Jesus and St. Anne, by Leonardo da Vinci. 50t, Virgin and Angels, by Cimabue (c. 1240-1302). 2k, Virgin and Child, by Alesso Baldovinetti (c. 1425-1499).

1988, Nov. 28 Unwmk. *Perf. 14*

538	A110	15t multicolored	.90	.30
539	A110	35t multicolored	1.60	.40
540	A110	50t multicolored	2.00	.90
541	A110	2k multicolored	4.75	4.75
		Nos. 538-541 (4)	9.25	6.35

Angling Soc. of Malawi, 50th Anniv. A111

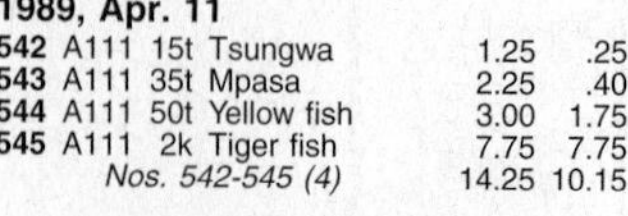

1989, Apr. 11

542 A111 15t Tsungwa 1.25 .25
543 A111 35t Mpasa 2.25 .40
544 A111 50t Yellow fish 3.00 1.75
545 A111 2k Tiger fish 7.75 7.75
Nos. 542-545 (4) 14.25 10.15

Natl. Independence, 25th Anniv. — A112

15t, Independence Arch. 35t, Grain silos. 50t, Capital Hill. 2k, Reserve Bank Headquarters.

1989, June 26

546 A112 15t multi 1.25 .30
547 A112 35t multi 2.75 .50
548 A112 50t multi 3.75 1.75
549 A112 2k multi 8.75 8.75
Nos. 546-549 (4) 16.50 11.30

African Development Bank, 25th Anniv. — A113

15t, Blantyre Digital Telex Exchange. 40t, Dzalanyama steer. 50t, Mikolongwe heifer. 2k, Zebu bull.

1989, Oct. 30

550 A113 15t multi 1.25 .30
551 A113 40t multi 2.25 .50
552 A113 50t multi 2.75 1.75
553 A113 2k multi 7.25 7.25
Nos. 550-553 (4) 13.50 9.80

Cooperation with the UN, 25th Anniv. — A114

40t, House, diff. 50t, Thatched dwelling, house. 2k, Tea Plantation.

1989, Dec. 1 *Perf. 14*

554 A114 15t shown 1.25 .30
555 A114 40t multi 2.25 .45
556 A114 50t multi 3.00 1.75
557 A114 2k multi 7.00 7.00
Nos. 554-557 (4) 13.50 9.50

Rural Housing Program.

Christmas A115

Designs: 15t, St. Michael and All Angels Church. 40t, Limbe Cathedral. 50t, Nkhoma CCAP Church. 2k, Likoma Is. Cathedral.

1989, Dec. 15

558 A115 15t multicolored 1.25 .30
559 A115 40t multicolored 2.25 .45
560 A115 50t multicolored 3.00 1.75
561 A115 2k multicolored 7.00 7.00
Nos. 558-561 (4) 13.50 9.50

Classic Cars A116

15t, Ford Sedan, 1915. 40t, Two-seater Ford, 1915. 50t, Ford, 1915. 2k, Chevrolet Luxury Bus, 1930.

Perf. 14x13½

1990, Apr. 2 **Litho.** **Unwmk.**

562 A116 15t multi 1.50 .40
563 A116 40t multi 3.00 1.00
564 A116 50t multi 3.75 2.00
565 A116 2k multi 9.00 9.00
a. Souvenir sheet of 4, #562-565, perf. 13x12 26.00 26.00
Nos. 562-565 (4) 17.25 12.40

World Cup Soccer Championships, Italy — A117

1990, June 14 **Litho.** *Perf. 14*

566 A117 15t shown 1.25 .30
567 A117 40t Two players 2.75 .75
568 A117 50t Shot on goal 3.75 2.00
569 A117 2k World Cup Trophy 9.00 9.00
a. Souvenir sheet of 4, #566-569 17.00 17.00
Nos. 566-569 (4) 16.75 12.05

SADCC, 10th Anniv. A118

1990, Aug. 24 **Litho.** *Perf. 14*

570 A118 15t Map 1.25 .40
571 A118 40t Chambo 2.25 .55
572 A118 50t Cedar trees 7.25 2.00
573 A118 2k Nyala 9.00 9.00
a. Souvenir sheet of 4, #570-573 16.00 16.00
Nos. 570-573 (4) 19.75 11.95

Christmas — A119

Paintings by Raphael: 15t, Virgin and Child. 40t, The Transfiguration, detail. 50t, St. Catherine of Alexandrie. 2k, The Transfiguration.

1990, Nov. 26 *Perf. 13½x14*

574 A119 15t multicolored 1.25 .40
575 A119 40t multicolored 2.50 .60
576 A119 50t multicolored 3.50 2.00
577 A119 2k multicolored 8.75 8.75
a. Souvenir sheet of 4, #574-577, perf. 12x13 18.00 18.00
Nos. 574-577 (4) 16.00 11.75

Orchids — A120

15t, Aerangis kotschyana. 40t, Angraecum eburneum. 50t, Aerangis luteo alba. 2k, Cyrtorchis arcuata.

1990, Dec. 7

578 A120 15t multi 1.75 .40
579 A120 40t multi 3.50 1.00
580 A120 50t multi 3.75 2.00
581 A120 2k multi 11.50 11.50
a. Souvenir sheet of 4, #578-581, perf. 12x13 21.00 21.00
Nos. 578-581 (4) 20.50 14.90

Wild Animals A121

1991, Apr. 23 **Litho.** *Perf. 14x13½*

582 A121 20t Buffalo 1.50 .40
583 A121 60t Cheetah 3.50 1.50
584 A121 75t Greater kudu 3.50 1.50
585 A121 2k Black rhinoceros 13.00 10.00
a. Souvenir sheet of 4, #582-585, perf. 13x12 22.50 22.50
Nos. 582-585 (4) 21.50 13.40

Malawi Postal Services, Cent. A122

20t, Chiromo Post Office, 1891. 60t, Mail exchange hut, Walala. 75t, Mangochi Post Office. 2k, Standard A Earth station, 1981.

1991, July 2 *Perf. 14x13½*

586 A122 20t multicolored 1.75 .40
587 A122 60t multicolored 2.50 1.00
588 A122 75t multicolored 2.75 1.25
589 A122 2k multicolored 9.00 7.50
a. Souvenir sheet of 4, #586-589, perf. 13x12 17.00 17.00
Nos. 586-589 (4) 16.00 10.15

Insects — A123

20t, Red locust. 60t, Weevil. 75t, Cotton stainer bug. 2k, Pollen beetle.

1991, Sept. 21 *Perf. 13½x14*

590 A123 20t multi 1.75 .40
591 A123 60t multi 3.50 1.50
592 A123 75t multi 3.50 1.75
593 A123 2k multi 9.00 7.50
Nos. 590-593 (4) 17.75 11.15

Christmas — A124

20t, Christ Child in manger. 60t, Adoration of the Magi. 75t, Nativity. 2k, Virgin and Child.

1991, Nov. 26 **Litho.** *Perf. 13½x14*

594 A124 20t multi .90 .35
595 A124 60t multi 2.75 .60
596 A124 75t multi 3.25 1.00
597 A124 2k multi 7.50 7.50
Nos. 594-597 (4) 14.40 9.45

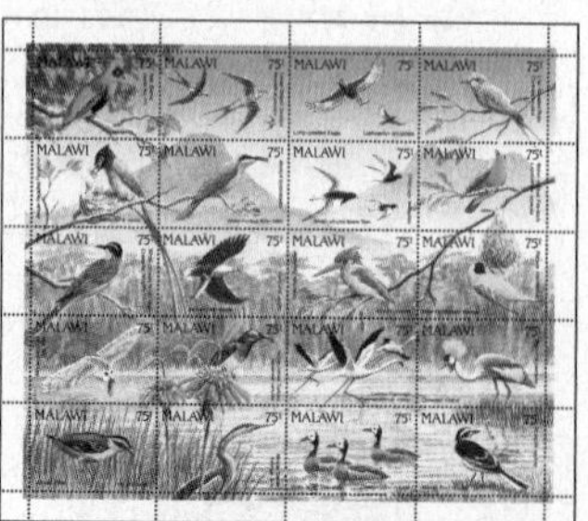

Birds — A125

Designs: a, Red bishop. b, Lesser striped swallow. c, Long-crested eagle. d, Lilac-breasted roller. e, African paradise flycatcher. f, White-fronted bee-eater. g, White-winged black tern. h, Brown-backed fire-finch. i, White-browed robin-chat. j, African fish eagle. k, Malachite kingfisher. l, Cabani's masked weaver. m, African barn owl. n, Yellow-bellied sunbird. o, Lesser flamingo. p, Crowned crane. q, African pitta. r, African darter. s, White-faced tree duck. t, African pied wagtail.

1992, Apr. 7 **Litho.** *Perf. 14*

598 A125 75t Sheet of 20, #a.-t. 60.00 60.00

1992 Summer Olympics, Barcelona — A126

1992, July 28 **Litho.** *Perf. 13½*

600 A126 20t Long jump 1.40 .35
601 A126 60t High jump 2.00 .80
602 A126 75t Javelin 2.50 1.10
603 A126 2k Running 5.00 5.00
a. Souvenir sheet of 4, #600-603 13.00 13.00
Nos. 600-603 (4) 10.90 7.25

Christmas — A127

Details from paintings: 20t, Angel from The Annunciation, by Philippe de Champaigne. 75t, Virgin and Child, by Bernardino Luini. 95t, Virgin and Child, by Sassoferrato. 2k, Mary from The Annunciation, by Champaigne.

1992, Nov. 9 **Litho.** *Perf. 14*

604 A127 20t multicolored .80 .25
605 A127 75t multicolored 1.90 .50
606 A127 95t multicolored 2.40 .80
607 A127 2k multicolored 5.75 5.50
Nos. 604-607 (4) 10.85 7.05

Intl. Space Year A128

Designs: 20t, Voyager II, Saturn. 75t, Center of a galaxy. 95t, Kanjedza II ground station. 2k, Communication satellite.

1992, Dec. 7 **Litho.** *Perf. 13½*

608 A128 20t multicolored 1.00 .35
609 A128 75t multicolored 2.25 .85
610 A128 95t multicolored 2.50 1.00
611 A128 2k multicolored 5.50 5.00
Nos. 608-611 (4) 11.25 7.20

Fruit — A129

20t, Strychnos spinosa. 75t, Adansonia digitata. 95t, Ximenia caffra. 2k, Uapaca kirkiana.

1993, Mar. 21 Litho. *Perf. 13½x14*

612	A129	20t multi	1.00	.30
613	A129	75t multi	2.50	1.00
614	A129	95t multi	2.75	1.10
615	A129	2k multi	4.75	4.75
		Nos. 612-615 (4)	11.00	7.15

Butterflies A130

20t, Apaturopsis cleocharis. 75t, Euryphura achlys. 95t, Cooksonia aliciae. 2k, Charaxes protoclea azota.

1993, June 28 Litho. *Perf. 13*

616	A130	20t multi	1.25	.40
617	A130	75t multi	2.75	1.00
618	A130	95t multi	3.25	1.60
619	A130	2k multi	4.75	4.50
		Nos. 616-619 (4)	12.00	7.50

A131

Dinosaurs — A132

Designs: No. 623a, Tyrannosaurus Rex. b, Dilophosaurus. c, Brachiosaurus. d, Gallimimus. e, Triceratops. f, Velociraptor.

1993, Dec. 30 Litho. *Perf. 13*

620	A131	20t Kentrosaurus	1.10	.75
621	A131	75t Stegosaurus	2.50	2.25
622	A131	95t Sauropod	3.00	2.50
		Nos. 620-622 (3)	6.60	5.50

Miniature Sheet

623	A132	2k Sheet of 6, #a.-f.	21.00	21.00

Christmas — A133

1993, Nov. 30 Photo. *Perf. 11½*
Granite Paper

624	A133	20t Holy family	.45	.45
625	A133	75t Shepherds	.55	.45
626	A133	95t Wise men	.70	.70
627	A133	2k Adoration of the magi	2.00	2.25
		Nos. 624-627 (4)	3.70	3.85

Fish of Lake Malawi — A134

Designs: 20t, Pseudotropheus socolofi. 75t, Melanochromis auratus. 95t, Pseudotropheus lombardoi. 1k, Labeotropheus trewavasae. 2k, Pseudotropheus zebra. 4k, Pseudotropheus elongatus.

1994, Mar. 21 Litho. *Perf. 14x15*

628	A134	20t multicolored	.45	.35
629	A134	75t multicolored	1.10	.45
630	A134	95t multicolored	1.25	.55
631	A134	1k multicolored	1.25	.90
632	A134	2k multicolored	2.50	2.25
633	A134	4k multicolored	4.25	3.75
		Nos. 628-633 (6)	10.80	8.25

Ships of Lake Malawi — A135

1994, Oct. 19 Litho. *Perf. 13x13½*

634	A135	20t Ilala	.70	.55
635	A135	75t MV Ufulu	1.10	.55
636	A135	95t The Pioneer	1.40	.65
637	A135	2k Dove	2.25	2.25
		Nos. 634-637 (4)	5.45	4.00

Souvenir Sheet

638	A135	5k Monteith	8.50	8.50

Christmas — A136

Details or entire paintings: 20t, Virgin and Child, by Durer, vert. 75t, Magi Present Gifts to Infant Jesus, Franco-Flemish Book of Hours, vert. 95t, The Nativity, by Fra Filippo Lippi. 2k, Nativity with Magi, by Rogier van der Weyden.

1994, Nov. 30 Litho. *Perf. 14½*

639	A136	20t multicolored	.55	.55
640	A136	75t multicolored	.65	.55
641	A136	95t multicolored	.80	.55
642	A136	2k multicolored	2.40	2.75
		Nos. 639-642 (4)	4.40	4.40

Pres. Bakili Muluzi — A137

1995, Apr. 10 Litho. *Perf. 11½x12*

643	A137	40t red & multi	.45	.45
644	A137	1.40k green & multi	.45	.45
645	A137	1.80k blue & multi	.55	.55
646	A137	2k brn org & multi	.80	.80
		Nos. 643-646 (4)	2.25	2.25

Establishment of COMESA (Common Market for Eastern & Southern African States).

Christmas A138

40t, Pre-schoolers. 1.40k, Dispensing medicine. 1.80k, Water supply. 2k, Voluntary return.

1995, Nov. 13 Litho. *Perf. 11½*
Granite Paper

647	A138	40t multi	.70	.70
648	A138	1.40k multi	.70	.70
649	A138	1.80k multi	.90	.90
650	A138	2k multi	1.25	1.25
		Nos. 647-650 (4)	3.55	3.55

Butterflies A139

1996, Dec. 5 Photo. *Perf. 11½*
Granite Paper

651	A139	60t Precis tugela	.60	.60
652	A139	3k Papilo pelodorus	1.40	.75
653	A139	4k Acrea acrita	1.50	.90
654	A139	10k Malantis leda	3.25	3.00
		Nos. 651-654 (4)	6.75	5.25

Christmas — A140

Designs: 10t, Instructor, children raising hands. 20t, Children enacting nativity scene. 30t, Children standing with hands clasped. 60t, Mother and child.

1996, Dec. 12 Granite Paper

655	A140	10t multicolored	.90	.90
656	A140	20t multicolored	.90	.90
657	A140	30t multicolored	1.10	.90
658	A140	60t multicolored	2.25	1.75
		Nos. 655-658 (4)	5.15	4.45

UN, 50th Anniv. A141

40t, Telecommunications & training. 1.40k, Clean water is essential for health. 1.80k, Protecting the environment, Mt. Mulanje. 2k, Food security.

1995, Oct. 30 Litho. *Perf. 11½*

659	A141	40t multicolored	.90	.90
660	A141	1.40k multicolored	.90	.90
661	A141	1.80k multicolored	1.10	1.10
662	A141	2k multicolored	1.10	1.10
a.		Souvenir sheet, #659-662	4.75	4.75
		Nos. 659-662 (4)	4.00	4.00

Paul Harris (1868-1947), Founder of Rotary, Intl. — A142

Rotary, Intl. emblem and: 60t, Map of Malawi. 3k, Eagle. 4.40k, Leopard.

1997, Oct. 6 Litho. *Perf. 11½*

663	A142	60t multicolored	.65	.65
664	A142	3k multicolored	1.10	1.10
665	A142	4.40k multicolored	1.60	1.60
666	A142	5k shown	1.75	1.75
		Nos. 663-666 (4)	5.10	5.10

UNICEF, 50th Anniv. A143

Designs: 60t, Care and protection. 3k, Education. 4.40k, Nutrition. 5k, Immunization.

1997, Oct. 31 Litho. *Perf. 11¾x11½*

667	A143	60t multi	.90	.90
668	A143	3k multi	.90	.90
669	A143	4.40k multi	1.50	1.50
670	A143	5k multi	1.90	1.90
		Nos. 667-670 (4)	5.20	5.20

A144

Christmas: 60t, Holy Night, by Carlo Maratta. 3k, The Nativity, by Bernardino Luini. 4.40k, Adoration of the Magi, by Luini. 5k, Holy Family.

1997, Dec. 15 *Perf. 11¾*

671	A144	60t multi	1.00	1.00
672	A144	3k multi	1.00	1.00
673	A144	4.40k multi	1.60	1.60
674	A144	5k multi	2.10	2.10
		Nos. 671-674 (4)	5.70	5.70

A145

Diana, Princess of Wales (1961-97): Various portraits.

1998, Nov. 30 Litho. *Perf. 14½*

675	A145	60t multicolored	.40	.40
676	A145	6k multicolored	.50	.50
677	A145	7k multicolored	.55	.55
678	A145	8k multicolored	.65	.65
a.		Souvenir sheet, Nos. 675-678	2.50	2.50
		Nos. 675-678 (4)	2.10	2.10

Tourism A146

60t, Tattooed Rock, Mwalawamphini, Cape Maclear, vert. 6k, War Memorial Tower, Zomba, vert. 7k, Mtengatenga Postal hut, Walala. 8k, Original P.I.M. Church, Chiradzulu.

1998, Dec. 2 Litho. *Perf. 13*

679	A146	60t multicolored	.60	.60
680	A146	6k multicolored	.70	.70
681	A146	7k multicolored	.85	.85
682	A146	8k multicolored	1.00	1.00
		Nos. 679-682 (4)	3.15	3.15

Universal Declaration of Human Rights, 50th Anniv. A147

Basic rights: 60t, Voting. 6k, Education. 7k, Equal justice. 8k, Owning property.

1998, Dec. 10

683	A147	60t multicolored	.60	.60
684	A147	6k multicolored	.70	.70
685	A147	7k multicolored	.85	.85
686	A147	8k multicolored	1.00	1.00
		Nos. 683-686 (4)	3.15	3.15

Christmas — A148

Design: Madonna and Child.

1998, Dec. 15 Photo. *Perf. 11¾*

Granite Paper

687	A148	60t multi	—	—
688	A148	6k multi	—	—
689	A148	7k Angel	—	—
690	A148	8k multi	—	—

Christmas — A149

60t, Madonna & Child. 6k, Nativity. 7k, Adoration of the Magi. 8k, Flight into Egypt.

1999, Dec. 13 Photo. *Perf. 11¾*

691	A149	60t multi	.90	.90
692	A149	6k multi	.90	.90
693	A149	7k multi	1.10	1.10
694	A149	8k multi	1.40	1.40
		Nos. 691-694 (4)	4.30	4.30

Southern African Development Community — A150

60t, Map of Africa. 6k, Malambe fruit juice bottles. 7k, Fishing resources research boat R/V Ndunduma. 8k, Locomotive.

Perf. 13¼x13½, 13½x13¼

2000, Feb. 22 Litho.

695	A150	60t multi, vert.	.75	.75
696	A150	6k multi, vert.	.75	.75
697	A150	7k multi	1.00	1.00
698	A150	8k multi	1.25	1.25
		Nos. 695-698 (4)	3.75	3.75

Modern British Commonwealth, 50th Anniv. — A151

African musical instruments: 60t, Ng'oma. 6k, Kaligo. 7k, Kalimba. 8k, Chisekese.

2000, Feb. 22 *Perf. 13¼x13½*

699	A151	60t multi	.75	.75
700	A151	6k multi	.75	.75
701	A151	7k multi	1.00	1.00
702	A151	8k multi	1.25	1.25
		Nos. 699-702 (4)	3.75	3.75

Christmas — A152

Designs: 5k, Madonna and Child. 18k, Nativity. 20k, Madonna and Child, diff.

2000, Dec. 12 Photo. *Perf. 11¾*

703-705	A152	Set of 3	3.25	3.25

Butterflies — A153

Designs: 1k, Euxanthe wakefieldi. 2k, Psuedacraea boisdurali. 4k, Catacroptera cloanthe. 5k, Myrina silenus ficedula. 10k, Cymothoe zombana. 20k, Charaxes castor. 50k, Charaxes pythoduras ventersi. 100k, Iolaus lalos.

2002 ? Litho. *Perf. 14½x13¾*

706	A153	1k multi	.35	.35
707	A153	2k multi	.35	.35
708	A153	4k multi	.35	.35
709	A153	5k multi	.35	.35
710	A153	10k multi	.35	.35
711	A153	20k multi	.80	.80
712	A153	50k multi	2.40	2.40
713	A153	100k multi	4.50	4.50
		Nos. 706-713 (8)	9.45	9.45

Worldwide Fund for Nature (WWF) A154

Kobus vardonii: a, Male. b, Two males butting heads. c, Male and female. d, Herd.

Perf. 13¼x13½

2003, Nov. 10 Litho.

714	Strip of 4	10.00	10.00
a.-d.	A154 50k Any single	1.25	1.25
e.	Souvenir sheet, 2 #714	20.00	20.00

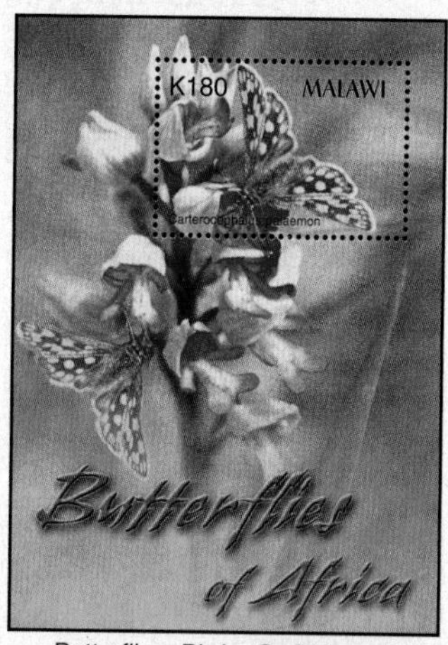

Butterflies, Birds, Orchids and Mushrooms — A155

No. 715, 50k — Butterflies: a, Bebearia octogramma. b, Charaxes nobilis. c, Cymothoe beckeri. d, Salamis anteva. e, Charaxes xiphares. f, Bebearia arcadius Fabricius.

No. 716, 50k, vert. — Birds: a, Upupa epops. b, Psittacus erithacus. c, Terathopus ecaudatus. d, Polemaetus bellicosus. e, Agapornis personatus. f, Scotopelia peli.

No. 717, 50k, vert. — Orchids: a, Angraecum eburneum. b, Ancistrochilus rothschildianus. c, Angraecum infundibulare. d, Ansellia africana. e, Disa veitchii. f, Angraecum compactum.

No. 718, 50k — Mushrooms: a, Pleurotus ostreatus. b, Macrolepiota procera. c, Amanita vaginata. d, Cantharellus tubaeformis. e, Hydnum repandum. f, Trametes versicolor.

No. 719, 180k, Carterocephalus palaemon. No. 720, 180k, Ardea cinerea. No. 721, 180k, Aerangis kotschyana. No. 722, 180k, Auricularia auricula, vert.

Perf. 13¼x13½, 13½x13¼

2003, Nov. 10

Sheets of 6, #a-f

715-718	A155	Set of 4	22.50	22.50

Souvenir Sheets

719-722	A155	Set of 4	13.50	13.50

Tour de France Bicycle Race, Cent. (in 2003) — A156

No. 723: a, Joop Zoetemelk, 1980. b, Bernard Hinault, 1981. c, Hinault, 1982. d, Laurent Fignon, 1983.

180k, Miguel Indurain, 1991-95.

2004, Feb. 6 *Perf. 13¼*

723	A156	75k Sheet of 4, #a-d	5.75	5.75

Souvenir Sheet

724	A156	180k multi	3.50	3.50

Powered Flight, Cent. (in 2003) — A157

No. 725: a, Vickers Vimy. b, D.H. 9A. c, Messerschmidt Bf. d, Mitsubishi A6M3.

180k, Fiat CR-2.

2004, Feb. 6 *Perf. 14*

725	A157	75k Sheet of 4, #a-d	5.75	5.75

Souvenir Sheet

726	A157	180k multi	3.50	3.50

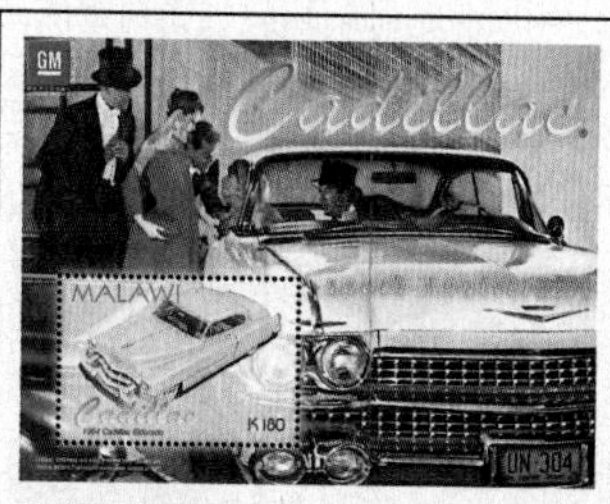

General Motors Automobiles — A158

No. 727, 75k — Cadillacs: a, 1959 Eldorado. b, 1962 Series 62. c, 1961 Sedan De Ville. d, 1930 V-16.

No. 728, 75k — Corvettes: a, 1965 convertible. b, 1965 Stingray. c, 1979. d, 1998.

No. 729, 180k, 1954 Cadillac Eldorado. No. 730, 180k, 1998 Corvette, diff.

2004, Feb. 6 Litho. *Perf. 14*

Sheets of 4, #a-d

727-728	A158	Set of 2	11.50	11.50

Souvenir Sheets

729-730	A158	Set of 2	6.75	6.75

The following items inscribed "Malawi" have been declared "illegal" by Malawi postal officials:

Souvenir sheets of three 80k stamps depicting Birds of prey; cats; locomotives; Ferrari Formula 1 cars.

A sheetlet of eight hexagonal 15k depicting the national birds of South African Postal Operators Association (SAPOA) countries was produced in limited quantities.

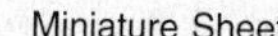

Miniature Sheet

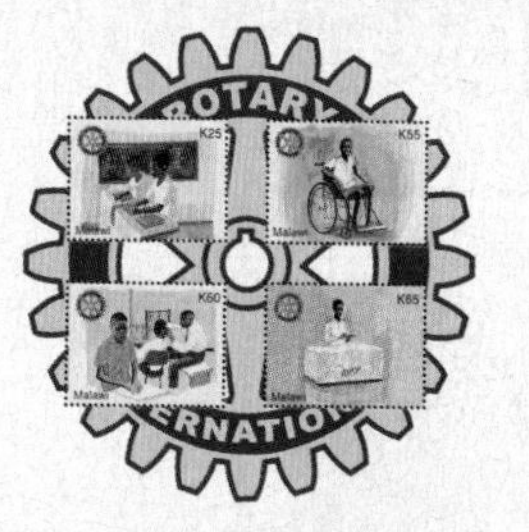

Rotary International, Cent. — A159

No. 731: a, 25k, Boys in classroom. b, 55k, Boy in wheelchair. c, 60k, Doctor examining patient. d, 65k, Nurse monitoring baby in incubator.

2005, July 25 Litho. *Perf. 13¼*

731	A159	Sheet of 4, #a-d	3.50	3.50

Butterflies — A161

Design: 5k, Myrina silenus ficedula. 10k, Cymothoe zombana. 20k, Charaxes castor. 40k, Papilio pelodorus, 50k, Charaxes pythoduras ventersi, 65k, Papilio pelodorus, 75k, Acrita acrita. 100k, Iolaus lalos. 105k, Acrea acrita. 110k, Euxanthe wakefieldi. 115k, Pseudacraea boisdurali.

2007 Litho. *Perf. 13¼x12¾*

733	A161	5k multi	—	—
734	A161	10k multi	—	—
735	A161	20k multi	—	—
736	A161	40k multi	—	—
736A	A161	50k multi	—	—
737	A161	65k multi	—	—
738	A161	75k multi	—	—
739	A161	100k multi	—	—
740	A161	105k multi	—	—
741	A161	110k multi	—	—
742	A161	115k multi	—	—

Compare with Type A153.

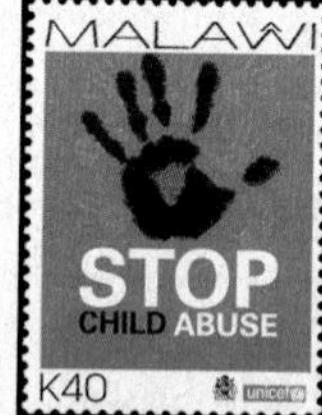

Stop Child Abuse — A162

2008, Nov. 19 Litho. *Perf. 13x13¼*

744	A162	40k multi	—

Endangered Animals — A163

No. 745: a, Black rhinoceros. b, Sable antelope. c, Zebra. d, African buffalo.

325k, Roan antelope.

2009, Sept. 30 *Perf. 11½x12*

745	A163	65k Sheet of 4, #a-d	3.75	3.75

Souvenir Sheet

Perf. 11½x11¼

746	A163	325k multi	4.75	4.75

Hippopotamus Amphibius — A164

No. 747 — Hippopotamus: a, Head, facing right. b, Reclining. c, Standing. d, Pair in water.
325k, Hippopotamus, vert.

2009, Sept. 30 ***Perf. 11½x12***
747 A164 105k Sheet of 4, #a-d 6.00 6.00

Souvenir Sheet
Perf. 11¼x11½

748 A164 325k multi 4.75 4.75

A165

Wildlife — A166

No. 749: a, Lion. b, Elephant shrew. c, Black-backed jackal. d, Reedbuck. e, African elephant. f, Warthog.
325k, Leopard.

2009, Sept. 30 ***Perf. 11½x11¼***
749 A165 110k Sheet of 6, #a-f 9.50 9.50

Souvenir Sheet

750 A166 325k multi 4.75 4.75

Worldwide Fund for Nature (WWF) A167

No. 751 — Lilian's lovebirds: a, Six birds on branches. b, Seven birds in flight. c, Two birds on branch, four in flight. d, Birds on ground and in flight.

2009, Sept. 30 ***Perf. 13¼***
751 Strip of 4 10.00 10.00
a.-d. A167 115k Any single 2.00 2.00
e. Sheet of 8, 2 each #751a-751d 20.00 20.00

Numerous items inscribed "Malawi" have been declared illegal by Malawi postal officials, incuding items with dates of 2007 and 2008 having topics of:
Rugby World Cup, Nelson Mandela, Mahatma Gandhi, Dalai Lama, and Pope John Paul II, Coral, Horses, Minerals, Birds, Bees, Exotic fish, Owls, Dinosaurs, Minerals and Scouts, Space, Automobiles, Mushrooms, Internet and Basketball stars.
Malawi postal officials have also declared "illegal" many other items with dates from 2005-2012 having a variety of topics.

Miniature Sheet

National Animals — A168

No. 752: a, Nyala (Malawi). b, Nyala (Zimbabwe). c, Burchell's zebra (Botswana). d, Oryx (Namibia). e, Buffalo (Zambia).

Litho. With Foil Application

2010, July 7 ***Perf. 13¾***
752 A168 55k Sheet of 5, #a-e *3.75 3.75*

See Botswana No. 838, Namibia Nos. 1141-1142, Zambia Nos. 1097-1101, Zimbabwe Nos. 1064-1068.

Miniature Sheet

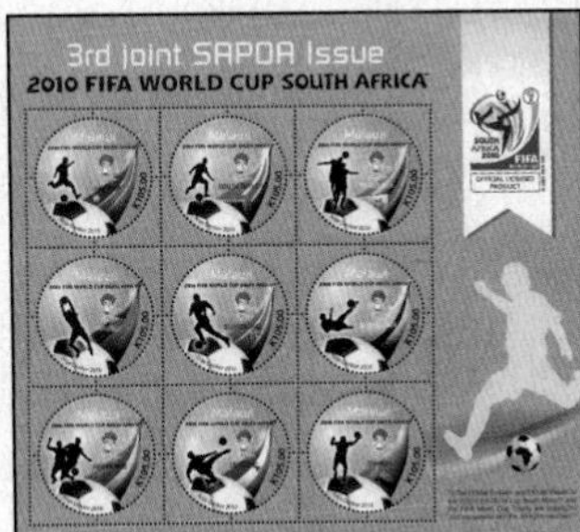

2010 World Cup Soccer Championships, South Africa — A169

No. 753 — Soccer players, ball, 2010 World Cup mascot and flag of: a, Namibia. b, South Africa. c, Zimbabwe. d, Malawi. e, Swaziland. f, Botswana. g, Mauritius. h, Lesotho. i, Zambia.

2010, Dec. 20 **Litho.** ***Perf. 13¾***
753 A169 105k Sheet of 9, #a-i 12.50 12.50

See Botswana Nos. 896-905, Lesotho No. , Mauritius No. , Namibia No. 1188, South Africa No. 1403, Swaziland Nos. 794-803, Zambia Nos. 1115-1118, and Zimbabwe Nos. 1112-1121.

Christmas A170

Various creche figures with bottom panel color of: No. 754, 65k, Red. No. 755, 65k, Blue violet. No. 756, 65k, Claret. No. 757, 65k, Green.

2010, Dec. 20 ***Perf. 13x13¼***
754-757 A170 Set of 4 3.50 3.50

Partnership Between Malawi and European Union, 35th Anniv. (in 2010) — A171

Flags of Malawi and European Union and: No. 758, 65k, Partnership projects. No. 759, 65k, Family, 35th anniversary emblem, vert.

2011, Jan. 18 ***Perf. 14***
758-759 A171 Set of 2 1.75 1.75
759a Souvenir sheet of 2, #758-759 1.75 1.75

Big Game Animals A172

Designs: 80k, Buffalo. 100k, Leopard. 135k, Black rhinoceros. 140k, Elephant. 145k, Lion.

2011, Nov. 3 ***Perf. 14x13¼***
760-764 A172 Set of 5 7.50 7.50
764a Souvenir sheet of 5, #760-764 7.50 7.50

Christmas A173

Designs: 80k, Angels proclaiming Gospel to shepherds. 100k, Shepherds lauding Jesus. 135k, Wise men following the star. 140k, Wise men giving Jesus gifts. 145k, Simeon blessing baby Jesus.

2011, Dec. 16 ***Perf. 13¼x14***
765-769 A173 Set of 5 7.25 7.25
769a Souvenir sheet of 5, #765-769 7.25 7.25

Pan-African Tsetse and Trypasonomiasis Eradication Campaign — A174

Stamps with white frames: No. 770, 65k, Man, tsetse fly, zebu, map of Malawi, campaign emblem. No. 771, 105k, Campaign emblem. No. 772, 110k, Tsetse flies, map of Malawi, campaign emblem. No. 773, 115k, Tsetse fly, map of Malawi, campaign emblem.
No. 774: a, 65k, Like No. 770, dull brown frame. b, 105k, Like No. 771, orange frame. c, 110k, Like No. 772, blue frame. d, 115k, Like No. 773, brown violet frame.

2012, Jan. 25 ***Perf. 14***
770-773 A174 Set of 4 5.00 5.00

Souvenir Sheet

774 A174 Sheet of 4, #a-d 5.00 5.00

Campaign Against AIDS — A175

Inscriptions: 80k, Stop AIDS keep the promise (red AIDS ribbon, map of Malawi). 100k, Male involvement (man and woman wearing AIDS ribbons). 135k, HTC (man, woman and doctor). 140k, Stop AIDS keep the promise (man and woman wearing AIDS ribbons). 145k, PMTCT (pregnant woman and nurse).

2012, Sept. 5 ***Perf. 13¼x12¾***
775-779 A175 Set of 5 4.50 4.50

One hundred sheetlets of five stamps inscribed "Standard Postage" were created and given to bulk purchasers of Nos. 775-779. The sheet margin is inscribed "Not For Sale" and the individual stamps on the sheet were not valid for postage.

Dances A176

Designs: 165k, Vimbuza. 260k, Uyeni. 270k, Tchopa. 280k, Masewe. 290k, Gule wa Mkulu.

2012, July **Litho.** ***Perf. 14***
780-784 A176 Set of 5 9.50 9.50
784a Souvenir sheet of 5, #780-784 9.50 9.50

Lake Malawi A177

Designs: 100k, MV Mtendere. 265k, Sunrise on Lake Malawi. 420k, Otter Point, Cape Maclear. 430k, Sunset on Lake Malawi. 450k, Fish eagle poised for a kill. 480k, Kayakers on Lake Malawi. 500k, Satellite map of Lake Malawi. 840k, Cichlids in Lake Malawi. 860k, Fish eagle catching fish. 900k, Lizard Island.

2014, Apr. 25 **Litho.** ***Perf. 14½x14***
785-794 A177 Set of 10 30.00 30.00
794a Souvenir sheet of 10, #785-794 30.00 30.00

Independence, 50th Anniv. — A178

Flag and: 330k, Independence Ark. 520k, Hastings Kamuzu Banda, first president. 560k, Corn silos. 600k, Parliament. 670k, Zebras.

2014, Oct. 21 **Litho.** ***Perf. 13x13½***
795 A178 330k multi 2.10 2.10
a. Booklet pane of 1 2.10 —
796 A178 520k multi 3.25 3.25
a. Booklet pane of 1 3.25 —
797 A178 560k multi 3.50 3.50
a. Booklet pane of 1 3.50 —
798 A178 600k multi 3.75 3.75
a. Booklet pane of 1 3.75 —
799 A178 670k multi 4.25 4.25
a. Booklet pane of 1 4.25 —
Complete booklet, #795a, 796a, 797a, 798a, 799a 17.00
b. Souvenir sheet of 5, #795-799 17.00 17.00
Nos. 795-799 (5) 16.85 16.85

Christmas A179

Designs: 330k, Christmas tree, candles, bells, street lights. 520k, Christmas tree, gifts. 560k, Christmas tree with star, snow in background. 600k, Undecorated Christmas tree. 670k, Christmast tree with star, tree branches in background.

2014 Litho. *Perf. 14½x14*

800-804 A179 Set of 5 11.00 11.00
804a Souvenir sheet of 5, #800-804 11.00 11.00

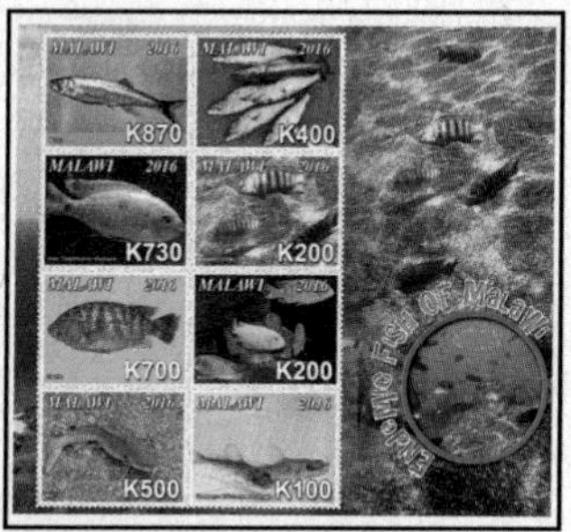

Fish — A180

No. 805: a, 100k, Kampango catfish. b, 200k, Four cichlids. c, 200k, Three striped cichlids. d, 400k, Butter fish. e, 500k, Mud fish. f, 700k, Chambo. g, 730k, Copadichromis chrysonotus. h, 870k, Mpasa.

No. 806: a, One cichlid facing backwards. b, Yellow cichlid facing left.

No. 807, 350k, Sanjika. No. 808, 350k, Blue Malawi cichlid. No. 809, 350k, Tilapia. No. 810, 730k, Metriaclima callainos.

2016, Apr. 6 Litho. *Perf. 13x13¼*

805 A180 Sheet of 8, #a-h 11.00 11.00

Souvenir Sheets

806 A180 350k Sheet of 2, #a-b 2.10 2.10
807-810 A180 Set of 4 5.25 5.25

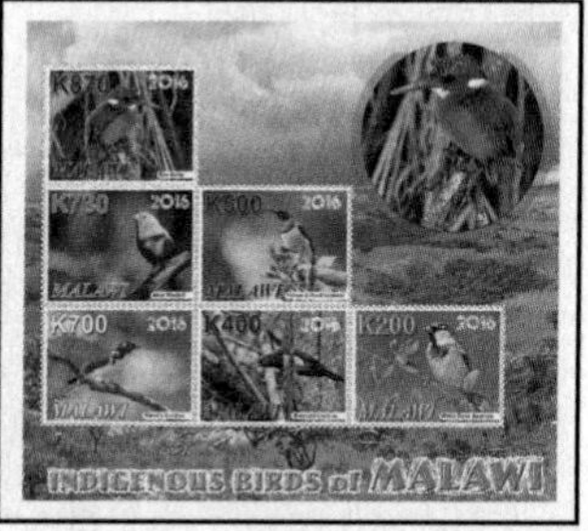

A181

Birds — A182

No. 811: a, 200k, White dove sparrow. b, 400k, Emerald cuckoo. c, 500k, Yellow-bellied sunbird. d, 700k, Klaas's cuckoo. e, 730k, Blue waxbill. f, 870k, Bee-eater.

No. 812, 350k, Collared sunbird. No. 813, 350k, Bee-eater, diff. No. 814, 350k, African yellow white-eye. No. 815, 350k, Bohm's bee-eater. No. 816, 350k, White dove sparrow, diff. No. 817, 350k, Klaas's cuckoo. No. 818, 350k, Yellow-bellied sunbird.

2016, May 27 Litho. *Perf. 13x13¼*

811 A181 Sheet of 6, #a-f 9.75 9.75

Souvenir Sheets

Perf. 13¼x13

812-818 A182 Set of 7 7.00 7.00

Wild Fruits — A183

No. 819: a, 200k, Ximenia caffra. b, 400k, Strychnos spinosa. c, 500k, Azanza garckeana. d, 700k, Flacourtia indica. e, 730k, Ziziphus mauritiana. f, 870k, Vitex doniana.

No. 820, 350k, Maboque fruta (Strychnos spinosa). No. 821, 350k, Vitex doniana, diff. No. 822, 350k, Baobab fruit. No. 823, 350k, Indian jujubes. No. 824, 350k, Flacourtia indica, diff. No. 825, 350k, Masukus.

2016, July 6 Litho. *Perf. 13x13¼*

819 A183 Sheet of 6, #a-f 9.50 9.50

Souvenir Sheets

820-825 A183 Set of 6 6.00 6.00

Endangered Animals — A184

No. 826: a, 100k, Syncerus caffer. b, 200k, Hippopotami. c, 400k, Rhinoceroses. d, 700k, Eyes of Panthera pardus. e, 700k, Head of Panthera pardus. f, 730k, Loxodonta africana. g, 870k, Panthera leo.

No. 827, 350k, Syncerus caffer, diff. No. 828, 350k, Hippopotamus. No. 829, 350k, Rhinoceros. No. 830, 350k, Eyes of Panthera pardus. No. 831, 350k, Loxodonta africana, diff. No. 832, 350k,Head of Panthera leo. No. 833, 350k, Zebras.

2016, Aug. 6 Litho. *Perf. 13x13¼*

826 A184 Sheet of 7, #a-g 10.50 10.50

Souvenir Sheets

827-833 A184 Set of 7 6.75 6.75

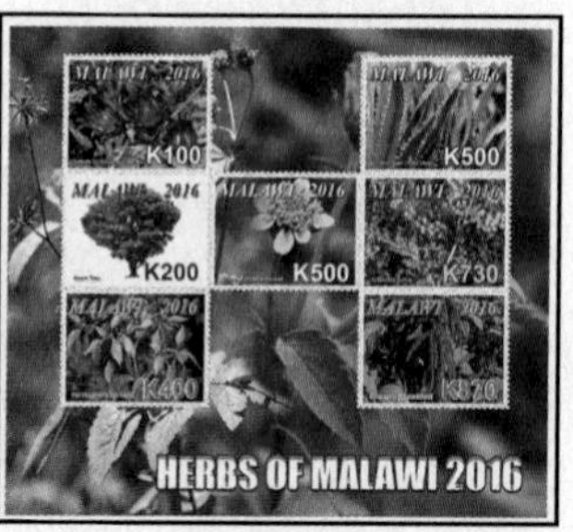

Herbs — A185

No. 834: a, 100k, Hibiscus sabdariffa. b, 200k, Neem tree. c, 400k, Bird's eye chilis. d, 500k, Bidens pilosa. e, 500k, Aloe vera. f, 730k, Artemisia annua. g, 870k, Amaranthus.

No. 835, 350k, Bidens pilosa, diff. No. 836, 350k, Silver artemisia. No. 837, 350k, Moringa. No. 838, 350k, Bird's eye chilis, diff. No. 839, 730k, Amaranthus, diff.

2016, Oct. 9 Litho. *Perf. 13x13¼*

834 A185 Sheet of 7, #a-g 9.25 9.25

Souvenir Sheets

835-839 A185 Set of 5 6.00 6.00

Nos. 521, 529 Surcharged

Methods and Perfs. As Before

2016, Nov. 7

840 A109 520k on 7t #521 1.50 1.50
841 A109 815k on 75t #529 2.25 2.25

POSTAGE DUE STAMPS

D1

Wmk. 357

1967, Sept. 1 Litho. *Perf. 11½*

J1 D1 1p deep lilac rose .25 *4.50*
J2 D1 2p sepia .25 *4.50*
J3 D1 4p lilac .25 *5.00*
J4 D1 6p dark blue .35 *5.50*
J5 D1 8p emerald .50 *6.00*
J6 D1 1sh black .60 *6.00*
Nos. J1-J6 (6) 2.20 *31.50*

Values in Decimal Currency

1971, Feb. 15 Size: 18x23mm

J7 D1 2t sepia .30 *4.25*
J8 D1 4t lilac .45 *4.25*
J9 D1 6t dark blue .75 *4.50*
J10 D1 8t green 1.00 *4.50*
J11 D1 10t black 1.25 *4.50*
Nos. J7-J11 (5) 3.75 *22.00*

Type of 1971 Redrawn

1975 Wmk. 357 *Perf. 14*

Size: 17x21mm

J12 D1 2t brown 1.75 *4.00*

No. J12 has accent mark over "W."

1977-78 Litho. Unwmk. *Perf. 14*

Size: 18x21mm

J13 D1 2t sepia 9.00 4.50
J14 D1 4t rose lilac 9.00 4.50
J15 D1 8t brt green ('78) 4.00 *4.50*
J16 D1 10t black 9.00 5.25
Nos. J13-J16 (4) 31.00 18.75

1982 Wmk. 357, Sideways

J13a D1 2t .60 *4.00*
J14a D1 4t .60 *4.00*
J16a D1 10t .60 *4.00*
Nos. J13a-J16a (3) 1.80 *12.00*

1989 Litho. Unwmk. *Perf. 15x14*

Size: 18x20½mm

J13b D1 2t 3.75 *5.50*
J14b D1 4t 3.75 *5.50*
J15a D1 8t 3.75 *5.50*
J16b D1 10t 3.75 *5.50*
Nos. J13b-J16b (4) 15.00 *22.00*

MALAYA

mə-'lā-ə

Federated Malay States

LOCATION — Malay peninsula
GOVT. — British Protectorate
AREA — 27,585 sq. mi.
CAPITAL — Kuala Lumpur

The Federated Malay States consisted of the sultanates of Negri Sembilan, Pahang, Perak and Selangor.

Stamps of the Federated Malay States replaced those of the individual states and were used until 1935, when individual issues were resumed.

100 Cents = 1 Dollar

Catalogue values for unused stamps in this country are for Never Hinged items, beginning with Scott 80 in the regular postage section, Scott J20 in the postage due section, Scott 128 in Johore, Scott 55 in Kedah, Scott 44 in Kelantan, Scott 1 in Malacca, Scott 36 in Negri Sembilan, Scott 44 in Pahang, Scott 1 in Penang, Scott 99 in Perak, Scott 1 in Perlis, Scott 74 in Selangor, and Scott 47 in Trengganu.

Watermarks

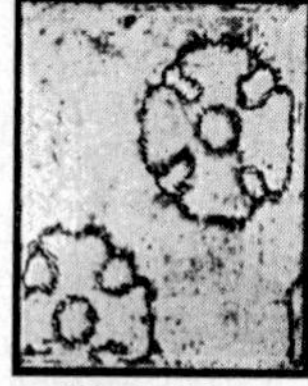

Wmk. 47 — Multiple Rosettes

Wmk. 71 — Rosette

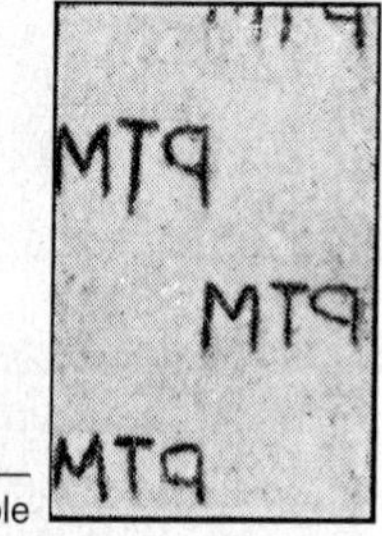

Wmk. 338 — PTM Multiple

(PTM stands for Persekutuan Tanah Melayu, or Federation of Malaya.)

Stamps of Straits Settlements overprinted "BMA MALAYA" are listed in Straits Settlements.

Stamps and Type of Negri Sembilan Overprinted in Black

1900 Wmk. 2 *Perf. 14*

1 A2 1c lilac & green 3.50 *13.50*
2 A2 2c lilac & brown 35.00 *77.50*
3 A2 3c lilac & black 3.25 *7.75*
4 A2 5c lilac & olive 85.00 *200.00*
5 A2 10c lilac & org 17.50 *57.50*
6 A2 20c green & olive 100.00 *135.00*
7 A2 25c grn & car rose 300.00 *425.00*
8 A2 50c green & black 110.00 *175.00*
Nos. 1-8 (8) 654.25 *1,091.*

Overprinted on Perak Nos. 51, 53, 57-58, 60-61

1900

9 A9 5c lilac & olive 32.50 *77.50*
10 A9 10c lilac & org 90.00 *80.00*

Wmk. 1

11 A10 $1 green & lt grn 210.00 *275.00*
12 A10 $2 green & car rose 200.00 *325.00*
13 A10 $5 green & ultra 575.00 *800.00*
Revenue cancel *75.00*
13A A10 $25 green & org *16,000.*
Revenue cancel *575.00*
Nos. 9-13 (5) 1,108. *1,558.*

No. 10 with bar omitted is an essay.

Elephants and Howdah — A3

1900 **Typo.**

14 A3 $1 green & lt green 200. *200.*
15 A3 $2 grn & car rose 190. *210.*
16 A3 $5 green & ultra 475. 500.
Revenue cancel 25.
17 A3 $25 grn & orange 4,900. 1,950.
Revenue cancel *125.*
Nos. 14-17 (4) 5,765. 2,860.

High values with revenue cancellations are plentiful and inexpensive.

Tiger — A4

Stamps of type A4 are watermarked sideways.

1901 **Wmk. 2**

18a A4 1c green & gray 6.00 1.25
19b A4 3c brn & gray brn 11.00 .25
20a A4 4c carmine & gray 12.50 8.25
21 A4 5c scar & grn, *yel* 3.00 3.75
22a A4 8c ultra & gray 26.00 9.50
23a A4 10c violet & gray 90.00 17.50
24 A4 20c black & gray vio 26.00 17.50
25b A4 50c brn org & gray brn 110.00 60.00
Nos. 18a-25b (8) 284.50 118.00

1904-10 **Wmk. 3**

26a A4 1c grn & gray brown 50.00 .85
27 A4 3c brown & gray 77.50 1.25
28 A4 4c rose & black 8.25 1.00
29 A4 5c scar & grn, *yel* 13.00 3.25
30c A4 8c ultra & gray brn ('07) 11.00 6.25
31c A4 10c claret & black 42.50 .75
32 A4 20c blk & gray vio ('05) 24.00 1.50
33b A4 50c orange & gray ('06) 72.50 18.00

The 1c and 4c are on ordinary paper, the other values on both ordinary and chalky papers. The least expensive varieties are shown. For comprehensive listing, see *Scott Classic Specialized Catalogue.*

Chalky Paper

34 A3 $1 green & lt green ('07) 110.00 57.50
35 A3 $2 green & car rose ('06) 120.00 140.00
36 A3 $5 grn & ultra ('06) 325.00 *160.00*
Revenue cancellation 25.00
37 A3 $25 grn & org ('10) 2,000. 900.00
Revenue cancellation 75.00
Nos. 26a-37 (12) 2,854. 1,290.

High values with revenue cancellations are plentiful and inexpensive.

1906-22 **Ordinary Paper**

Two dies for Nos. 38 and 44:
I — Thick line under "Malay."
II — Thin line under "Malay."

38 A4 1c dull grn, die II 16.00 .25
b. Die I 27.50 .55
39 A4 1c brown ('19) 3.00 1.25
40 A4 2c green ('19) 2.50 .55
41 A4 3c brown 10.50 .25
42 A4 3c carmine ('09) 5.00 .25
43 A4 3c dp gray ('19) 2.50 .25
44 A4 4c scar, die II 2.25 .25
b. Die I ('19) 3.75 5.50
45 A4 6c orange ('19) 3.25 *4.00*
46 A4 8c ultra ('09) 16.00 1.40
47 A4 10c ultra ('19) 9.00 2.25
48 A4 35c red, *yellow* 7.50 *17.50*
Nos. 38-48 (11) 77.50 28.20

1922-32 **Wmk. 4** **Ordinary Paper**

49 A4 1c brown ('22) 2.25 4.75
50 A4 1c black ('23) .85 .25
51 A4 2c dk brown ('25) 14.00 *15.00*
52 A4 2c green ('26) 3.00 .25
53 A4 3c dp gray ('23) 2.50 *7.50*
54 A4 3c green ('24) 2.75 2.00
55 A4 3c brown ('27) 5.00 .50
56 A4 4c scar (II) ('23) 4.00 .60
57 A4 4c orange ('26) 1.50 .25
c. Unwatermarked *475.00* *300.00*
58 A4 5c vio, *yel* ('22) 1.25 .25
59 A4 5c dk brown ('32) 3.50 .25
60 A4 6c orange ('22) 1.00 .55
61 A4 6c scarlet ('26) 1.50 .25
62 A4 10c ultra ('23) 1.75 *8.50*
63 A4 10c ultra & blk ('23) 2.50 .80
64 A4 10c vio, *yel,* chalky paper ('31) 6.00 .55
65 A4 12c ultra ('22) 1.75 .25

Chalky Paper

66 A4 20c blk & vio ('23) 5.00 2.75
a. Ordinary paper 72.50 5.25
67 A4 25c red vio & ol vio ('29) 3.50 3.00
68 A4 30c yel & dl vio ('29) 4.00 *5.00*
69 A4 35c red, *yel,* ordinary paper ('28) 6.00 *27.50*
70 A4 35c dk vio & car ('31) 17.00 15.00
71 A4 50c org & blk ('24) 17.00 *20.00*
72 A4 50c blk, *bl grn* ('31) 5.50 2.50
73 A3 $1 gray grn & yel grn ('26) 24.00 *100.00*
a. $1 green & blue green 24.00 *100.00*
74 A3 $2 grn & car ('26) 42.50 *95.00*
75 A3 $5 grn & ultra ('25) 210.00 *280.00*
76 A3 $25 grn & org ('28) 2,250. *2,500.*
Revenue cancel 175.00
Nos. 49-75 (27) 389.60 *593.25*

1931-34

77 A4 $1 red & blk, *blue* 15.00 5.25
78 A4 $2 car & green, *yel* ('34) 6.50 50.00
79 A4 $5 car & green, *emer* ('34) 350.00 *280.00*
Nos. 77-79 (3) 371.50 *335.25*

FEDERATION OF MALAYA

GOVT. — Sovereign state in British Commonwealth of Nations
AREA — 50,700 sq. mi.
POP. — 7,139,000 (est. 1961)
CAPITAL — Kuala Lumpur

The Federation comprised the nine states of Johore, Pahang, Negri Sembilan, Selangor, Perak, Kedah, Perlis, Kelantan and Trengganu and the settlements of Penang and Malacca.

Malaya joined the Federation of Malaysia in 1963.

100 Sen (Cents) = 1 Dollar (1957)

Catalogue values for unused stamps in this section are for Never Hinged items.

The Peace Issue of 1946 8c stamp inscribed "MALAYAN UNION" was not issued.

Rubber Tapping — A5

Map of Federation — A6

Designs: 12c, Federation coat of arms. 25c, Tin dredge and flag.

Perf. 13x12½, 12½
Engr., Litho.

1957, May 5 **Wmk. 314**

80 A5 6c blue, red & yel 1.00 .30
a. Yellow omitted 85.00
81 A5 12c car & multi 1.75 1.10
82 A5 25c multicolored 3.75 .40
83 A6 30c dp claret & red org 1.50 .30
Nos. 80-83 (4) 8.00 2.10

Chief Minister Tunku Abdul Rahman and People of Various Races — A7

Perf. 12½

1957, Aug. 31 **Wmk. 4** **Engr.**

84 A7 10c brown .80 .35

Independence Day, Aug. 31.

United Nations Emblem — A8

Design: 30c, UN emblem, vert.

Perf. 13½, 12½

1958, Mar. 5 **Wmk. 314**

85 A8 12c rose red .45 *1.00*
86 A8 30c plum .65 *1.00*

Conf. of the Economic Commission for Asia and the Far East (ECAFE), Kuala Lumpur, Mar. 5-15.

Merdeka Stadium and Flag — A9

Tuanku Abdul Rahman, Paramount Ruler of Malaya — A10

Perf. 13½x14½, 14½x13½

1958, Aug. 31 **Photo.** **Wmk. 314**

87 A9 10c multicolored .30 .30
88 A10 30c multicolored .60 *.90*

1st anniv. of the Independence of the Federation of Malaya.

A11

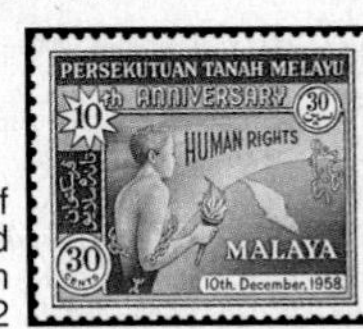

Torch of Freedom and Broken Chain — A12

Perf. 12½x13, 13x12½

1958, Dec. 10 **Litho.** **Wmk. 314**

89 A11 10c multicolored .25 .25

Photo.

90 A12 30c green .70 .70

10th anniv. of the signing of the Universal Declaration of Human Rights.

Mace and People — A13

Perf. 12½x13½

1959, Sept. 12 **Photo.** **Unwmk.**

91 A13 4c rose red .30 .30
92 A13 10c violet .30 .30
93 A13 25c yellow green .60 .40
Nos. 91-93 (3) 1.20 1.00

1st Federal Parliament of Malaya, inauguration.

WRY Emblem A14

Design: 30c, Similar to 12c, vert.

Perf. 13½, 13

1960, Apr. 7 **Engr.** **Wmk. 314**

94 A14 12c lilac .30 *.80*
95 A14 30c dark green .30 .30

World Refugee Year, 7/1/59-6/30/60.

Rubber Tree Seedling on Map of Malaya — A15

Perf. 13x13½

1960, Sept. 19 **Litho.** **Unwmk.**

96 A15 6s red brn, grn & blk .25 *1.25*
97 A15 30s ultra, yel grn & blk .60 *.75*

15th meeting of the Intl. Rubber Study Group and the Natural Rubber Research Conference, Kuala Lumpur, Sept. 26-Oct. 1.

Tuanku Syed Putra — A16

Perf. 13½x14½

1961, Jan. 4 **Photo.** **Wmk. 314**

98 A16 10s blue & black .30 .30

Installation of Tuanku Syed Putra of Perlis as Paramount Ruler (Yang di-Pertuan Agong.)

Colombo Plan Emblem — A17

1961, Oct. 30 **Unwmk.** ***Perf. 13½***

99 A17 12s rose pink & black .55 *3.25*
100 A17 25s brt yellow & black 1.10 *2.00*
101 A17 30s brt blue & black .90 *1.00*
Nos. 99-101 (3) 2.55 *6.25*

13th meeting of the Consultative Committee for Technical Co-operation in South and South East Asia, Kuala Lumpur, Oct. 30-Nov. 18.

Malaria Eradication Emblem — A18

Wmk. PTM Multiple (338)

1962, Apr. 7 *Perf. 14x14½*

102 A18 25s orange brown	.35	*.60*
103 A18 30s dull violet	.35	.30
104 A18 50s ultramarine	.60	*.80*
Nos. 102-104 (3)	1.30	*1.70*

WHO drive to eradicate malaria.

Palmyra Leaf A19

1962, July 21 **Photo.** *Perf. 13½*

105 A19 10s violet & gldn brown	.35	.35
106 A19 20s bluish grn & gldn brn	1.00	*1.25*
107 A19 50s car rose & gldn brn	2.25	2.25
Nos. 105-107 (3)	3.60	3.85

National Language Month. Watermark inverted on alternating stamps.

Children and their Future Shadows — A20

1962, Oct. 1 **Wmk. 338** *Perf. 13½*

108 A20 10s bright rose lilac	.25	.25
109 A20 25s ocher	.70	*1.25*
110 A20 30s bright green	3.00	.25
Nos. 108-110 (3)	3.95	1.75

Free primary education introduced Jan. 1962.

Forms of Food Production and Ears of Wheat — A21

1963, Mar. 21 **Unwmk.** *Perf. 11½*

Granite Paper

111 A21 25s lt ol grn & lilac rose	3.00	*4.00*
112 A21 30s dk car & lilac rose	3.25	1.75
113 A21 50s ultra & lilac rose	3.25	*4.00*
Nos. 111-113 (3)	9.50	9.75

FAO "Freedom from Hunger" campaign.

Cameron Highlands Dam and Pylon — A22

1963, June 26 **Wmk. 338** *Perf. 14*

114 A22 20s purple & brt green	.80	.25
115 A22 30s ultra & brt green	1.25	*1.50*

Opening of the Cameron Highlands hydroelectric plant.

Check listings for individual states for additional stamps inscribed "Malaya."

POSTAGE DUE STAMPS

D1

Perf. 14½x14

1924-26 **Typo.** **Wmk. 4**

J1 D1 1c violet	4.75	*50.00*
J2 D1 2c black	2.25	8.75
J3 D1 4c green ('26)	3.25	*8.00*
J4 D1 8c red	6.00	*47.50*
J5 D1 10c orange	10.00	*17.50*
J6 D1 12c ultramarine	10.00	*27.50*
Nos. J1-J6 (6)	36.25	*159.25*

D2

1936-38 *Perf. 14½x14*

J7 D2 1c dk violet ('38)	17.50	1.10
J8 D2 4c yellow green	40.00	1.40
J9 D2 8c scarlet	20.00	5.00
J10 D2 10c yel orange	25.00	.50
J11 D2 12c blue violet	40.00	*17.50*
J12 D2 50c black ('38)	30.00	*8.00*
Nos. J7-J12 (6)	172.50	*33.50*

Nos. J7-J12 were also used in Straits Settlements.

For overprints see Nos. NJ1-NJ20, Malacca Nos. NJ1-NJ6.

1945-49

J13 D2 1c reddish violet	5.00	2.25
J14 D2 3c yel green	10.00	6.00
J15 D2 5c org scarlet	6.00	*3.50*
J16 D2 8c yel org ('49)	13.00	*16.00*
J17 D2 9c yel orange	40.00	*50.00*
J18 D2 15c blue vio	110.00	35.00
J19 D2 20c dk blue ('48)	10.00	*10.00*
Nos. J13-J19 (7)	194.00	*122.75*

For surcharge see No. J34.

Catalogue values for unused stamps in this section, from this point to the end of the section, are for Never Hinged items.

1951-54 **Wmk. 4** *Perf. 14*

J20 D2 1c dull violet ('52)	.70	1.75
J21 D2 2c dk gray ('53)	1.25	2.25
J22 D2 3c green ('52)	37.50	20.00
J23 D2 4c dk brown ('53)	.70	7.00
J24 D2 5c vermilion	50.00	13.00
J25 D2 8c yel orange	2.50	8.00
J26 D2 12c magenta ('54)	1.25	6.50
J27 D2 20c deep blue	8.00	6.75
Nos. J20-J27 (8)	101.90	65.25

Nos. J13-J27 were used throughout the Federation and in Singapore, later in Malaysia.

1957-63 **Ordinary Paper** *Perf. 12½*

J21a D2 2c ('60)	4.50	*24.00*
b. 2c, chalky paper ('62)	1.75	*16.00*
J23a D2 4c ('60)	3.50	*25.00*
b. 4c, chalky paper ('62)	1.00	*20.00*
J26a D2 12c, chalky paper ('62)	5.00	*32.50*
J27a D2 20c	8.00	*25.00*
b. 20c, chalky paper ('63)	10.00	*50.00*
Nos. J21a-J27a (4)	21.00	*106.50*

1965 **Wmk. 314** *Perf. 12*

J28 D2 1c plum	1.50	*16.00*
J29 D2 2c bluish black	1.10	*22.50*
J30 D2 4c brown	1.75	*16.00*
J31 D2 8c yel orange	2.50	*22.50*
J32 D2 12c magenta	6.50	*40.00*
J33 D2 20c dark blue	10.00	*50.00*
Nos. J28-J33 (6)	23.35	*167.00*

Nos. J28-J33 were used in Malaysia.

1964, Apr. 14 *Perf. 12½*

J28a D2 1c	.50	*19.00*
J29a D2 2c	1.75	*16.00*
J30a D2 4c	1.00	*16.00*
J32a D2 12c	2.25	*22.50*
J33a D2 20c	3.00	*37.50*
Nos. J28a-J33a (5)	8.50	*111.00*

No. J16 Surcharged

1965, Jan. **Wmk. 4**

J34 D2 10c on 8c yel orange	.60	*3.00*

OCCUPATION STAMPS

Issued Under Japanese Occupation

Malayan Fruit and Fronds OS1

Tin Dredging OS2

Monument to Japanese War Dead — OS3

1943 **Unwmk.** **Litho.** *Perf. 12½*

N30 OS1 2c emerald	1.00	.25
a. Rouletted	2.25	2.25
b. Imperf., pair	6.50	6.50
N31 OS2 4c rose red	3.00	.25
a. Rouletted	2.25	2.25
b. Imperf., pair	6.50	6.50
N32 OS3 8c dull blue	.50	.25
Nos. N30-N32 (3)	4.50	.75

Malayan Plowman — OS4

1943, Sept. 1

N33 OS4 8c violet	11.00	3.50
N34 OS4 15c carmine red	8.00	3.50

Publicity for Postal Savings which had reached a $10,000,000 total in Malaya.

Rubber Tapping OS5

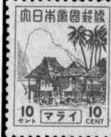

Seaside Houses OS6

Japanese Shrine, Singapore OS7

Sago Palms OS8

Johore Bahru and Strait of Johore OS9

Malay Mosque, Kuala Lumpur OS10

1943, Oct. 1

N35 OS5 1c gray green	1.75	.70
N36 OS5 3c olive gray	1.00	.25
N37 OS6 10c red brown	1.25	.25
N38 OS7 15c violet	1.75	*5.00*
N39 OS8 30c olive green	1.50	.50
N40 OS9 50c blue	5.00	5.00
N41 OS10 70c dull blue	27.50	16.00
Nos. N35-N41 (7)	39.75	27.70

Rice Planting and Map of Malaysia — OS11

1944, Feb. 15

N42 OS11 8c carmine	17.50	4.00
N43 OS11 15c violet	5.00	4.00

Issued on the anniversary of the fall of Singapore to commemorate the "Birth of New Malaya".

OCCUPATION POSTAGE DUE STAMPS

Stamps and Type of Postage Due Stamps of 1936-38 Handstamped in Black, Red or Brown

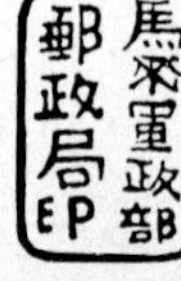

No. NJ7

1942 **Wmk. 4** *Perf. 14½x14*

NJ1 D2 1c violet	14.00	*35.00*
a. Brown overprint	190.00	*225.00*
b. Red overprint	200.00	250.00
NJ2 D2 3c yellow green	87.50	*97.50*
a. Red overprint	450.00	*475.00*
NJ3 D2 4c yellow green	95.00	60.00
a. Brown overprint	220.00	250.00
b. Red overprint	67.50	60.00
NJ4 D2 8c red	190.00	150.00
a. Brown overprint	375.00	375.00
b. Red overprint	275.00	175.00
NJ5 D2 10c yellow orange	40.00	*65.00*
a. Brown overprint	110.00	*140.00*
b. Red overprint	475.00	475.00
NJ6 D2 12c blue violet	27.50	*60.00*
a. Red overprint	475.00	460.00
NJ7 D2 50c black	82.50	*125.00*
a. Red overprint	750.00	*825.00*
Nos. NJ1-NJ7 (7)	536.50	592.50

Overprinted in Black

1942

NJ8 D2 1c violet	3.50	*10.50*
NJ9 D2 3c yel green	27.50	*35.00*
NJ10 D2 4c yel green	25.00	*12.50*
NJ11 D2 8c red	37.50	*27.50*
NJ12 D2 10c yel orange	2.00	*17.00*
NJ13 D2 12c blue violet	2.00	*50.00*
Nos. NJ8-NJ13 (6)	97.50	152.50

The 9c and 15c with this overprint were not regularly issued.

Postage Due Stamps of 1936-45 Overprinted

1943

NJ14 D2 1c reddish vio	2.25	*5.00*
NJ15 D2 3c yel green	2.25	*5.00*
NJ15A D2 4c yel green	70.00	52.50
NJ16 D2 5c scarlet	1.50	*5.00*
NJ17 D2 9c yel orange	.90	*8.50*
NJ18 D2 10c yel orange	2.25	*9.00*
NJ19 D2 12c blue violet	2.25	*25.00*
NJ20 D2 15c blue violet	2.25	*10.00*
Nos. NJ14-NJ20 (8)	83.65	120.00

No. NJ15A is said to have been extensively forged.

ISSUED UNDER THAI OCCUPATION

For use in Kedah, Kelantan, Perlis and Trengganu

War Memorial — OS1

Perf. 12½

1943, Dec. Unwmk. Litho.

2N1 OS1 1c pale yellow 35.00 *37.50*
2N2 OS1 2c buff 14.00 *24.00*
a. Imperf., pair 1,100.
2N3 OS1 3c pale green 22.50 *45.00*
a. Imperf., pair
2N4 OS1 4c dull lilac 16.00 *32.50*
2N5 OS1 8c rose 16.00 *24.00*
2N6 OS1 15c lt blue 45.00 *72.50*
Nos. 2N1-2N6 (6) 148.50 *235.50*

Perf. 12½x11

2N2b OS1 2c buff 20.00 24.00
2N3b OS1 3c pale green 30.00 45.00
2N4b OS1 4c dull lilac 20.00 37.50
2N5b OS1 8c rose 20.00 24.00
2N6b OS1 15c lt blue 45.00 72.50
Nos. 2N2b-2N6b (5) 135.00 203.00

These stamps, in cent denominations, were for use only in the four Malayan states ceded to Thailand by the Japanese. The states reverted to British rule in September 1945.

JOHORE

jə-'hōr

LOCATION — At the extreme south of the Malay Peninsula. Linked to Singapore by a causeway.
AREA — 7,330 sq. mi.
POP. — 1,009,649 (1960)
CAPITAL — Johore Bahru

Stamps of the Straits Settlements Overprinted in Black

Overprinted

1876 Wmk. 1 *Perf. 14*

1 A2 2c brown *21,500.* 7,000.
b. Double overprint —

Overprinted

Overprint 13 to 14mm Wide

1884-86 Wmk. 2

1A A2 2c rose 225.00 *225.00*
c. Double overprint 1,100.

No. 2d

Without Period

Overprint 16¾x2mm ("H" & "E" wide)

2 A2 2c rose 3,200. 800.
a. Double overprint 2,500.

Overprinted

Overprint 11x2½mm

3 A2 2c rose ('86) 130.00 *140.00*

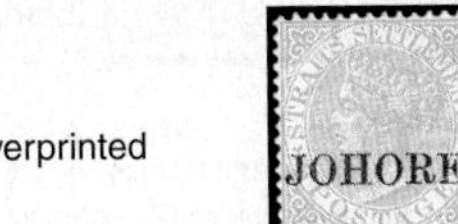

Overprinted

Overprint 17½x2¾mm

4 A2 2c rose ('85) *9,000.* —

Overprinted

Overprint 12½ to 15x2¾mm

5 A2 2c rose 25.00 *22.50*

Overprinted

Overprint 9x2½mm

7 A2 2c rose ('86) 80.00 65.00
a. Double overprint 850.00

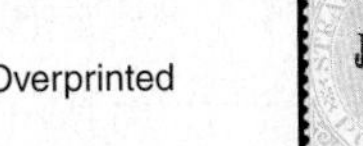

Overprinted

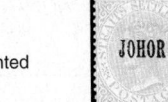

Overprint 9x3mm

8 A2 2c rose ('86) 72.50 67.50

Overprinted

Overprint 14 to 15x3mm

9 A2 2c rose 25.00 12.50

Tall "J" 3½mm high

10 A2 2c rose 300.00 200.00

Overprinted

1888 With Period

11 A2 2c rose 225.00 75.00
b. Double overprint 950.00

Overprinted

Overprint 12½ to 13x2½mm

1890-91

12 A2 2c rose 27.50 27.00

Overprint 12x2¾mm

13 A2 2c rose ('91) *10,500.*

Surcharged in Black

a

b

c

d

1891

14 A3(a) 2c on 24c green 47.50 *62.50*
15 A3(b) 2c on 24c green 150.00 160.00
16 A3(c) 2c on 24c green 30.00 45.00
a. "CENST" 1,000. 525.00
17 A3(d) 2c on 24c green 140.00 150.00
Nos. 14-17 (4) 367.50 417.50

Sultan Abubakar — A5

1891-94 Typo. Unwmk.

18 A5 1c lilac & vio ('94) 1.00 .60
19 A5 2c lilac & yellow .75 *1.75*
20 A5 3c lilac & car rose ('94) .75 .60
21 A5 4c lilac & black 3.25 *22.50*
22 A5 5c lilac & green 8.50 *22.50*
23 A5 6c lilac & blue 9.50 *22.50*
24 A5 $1 green & car rose 90.00 *190.00*
Nos. 18-24 (7) 113.75 *260.45*

For surcharges and overprints see Nos. 26-36.

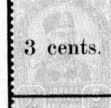

Stamps of 1892-94 Surcharged in Black

1894

26 A5 3c on 4c lilac & blk 3.00 .65
a. No period after "Cents" 125.00 85.00
27 A5 3c on 5c lilac & grn 2.40 4.25
a. No period after "Cents" 275.00 175.00
28 A5 3c on 6c lilac & bl 4.00 7.50
a. No period after "Cents" 210.00 240.00
29 A5 3c on $1 green & car 14.50 85.00
a. No period after "Cents" 500.00 900.00
Nos. 26-29 (4) 23.90 97.40

Coronation of Sultan Ibrahim
Stamps of 1892-94 Overprinted

Overprinted "KEMAHKOTAAN"

1896

30 A5 1c lilac & violet .60 1.25
31 A5 2c lilac & yellow .60 1.25
32 A5 3c lilac & car rose .65 1.25
33 A5 4c lilac & black 1.00 3.00
34 A5 5c lilac & green 6.00 8.00
35 A5 6c lilac & blue 4.00 *7.00*
36 A5 $1 green & car rose 70.00 135.00
Nos. 30-36 (7) 82.85 156.75

Overprinted "KETAHKOTAAN"

30a A5 1c 5.00 *6.00*
31a A5 2c 6.50 *8.50*
32a A5 3c 14.50 *20.00*
33a A5 4c 3.50 *21.00*
34a A5 5c 4.25 *8.50*
35a A5 6c 9.00 *20.00*
36a A5 $1 42.50 *190.00*
Nos. 30a-36a (7) 85.25 *274.00*

Sultan Ibrahim — A7

1896-99 Typo. Wmk. 71

37 A7 1c green 1.00 3.50
38 A7 2c green & blue .60 1.40
39 A7 3c green & vio 6.00 3.75
40 A7 4c green & car rose 1.25 3.75
41 A7 4c yel & red ('99) 1.75 2.50
42 A7 5c green & brn 2.40 5.00
43 A7 6c green & yel 2.40 7.50
44 A7 10c green & black 8.50 *55.00*
45 A7 25c green & vio 10.00 *50.00*
46 A7 50c grn & car rose 19.00 *52.50*
47 A7 $1 lilac & green 37.50 *85.00*
48 A7 $2 lilac & car rose 55.00 *100.00*
49 A7 $3 lilac & blue 50.00 *140.00*
50 A7 $4 lilac & brn 52.50 *100.00*
51 A7 $5 lilac & orange 100.00 *150.00*
Nos. 37-51 (15) 347.90 *759.90*

On Nos. 44-46 the numerals are on white tablets. Numerals of Nos. 48-51 are on tablets of solid color.

Stamps of 1896-1926 with revenue cancellations sell for a fraction of those used postally.

For surcharges see Nos. 52-58.

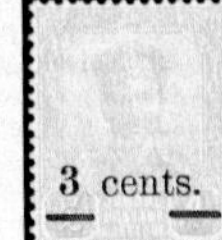

Nos. 40-41 Surcharged in Black

1903

52 A7 3c on 4c yel & red .80 1.25
a. Without bars 4.00 *27.50*
53 A7 10c on 4c grn & car rose 3.00 14.50
a. Without bars 27.50 *85.00*

Bars on Nos. 52-53 were handruled with pen and ink.

Surcharged

54 A7 50c on $3 lilac & blue 35.00 *87.50*

Surcharged

55 A7 $1 on $2 lilac & car rose 75.00 *140.00*
a. Inverted "e" in "one" 2,000.

Surcharged

1904

56 A7 10c on 4c yel & red 25.00 42.50
a. Double surcharge *8,750.*
57 A7 10c on 4c grn & car rose 10.50 *72.50*
58 A7 50c on $5 lil & org 80.00 175.00
Nos. 56-58 (3) 115.50 290.00

Sultan Ibrahim — A8

The 10c, 21c, 25c, 50c, and $10 to $500 denominations of type A8 show the numerals on white tablets. The numerals of the 8c, 30c, 40c, and $2 to $5 demoninations are shown on tablets of solid colors.

1904-10 Typo. Wmk. 71
Ordinary Paper

59 A8 1c violet & green 2.00 .40
a. Chalky paper ('09) 18.00 12.50
60 A8 2c violet & brn org 3.00 4.25
a. Chalky paper ('10) 20.00 *22.50*
61 A8 3c violet & black 5.00 .60
62 A8 4c violet & red 9.25 4.50
63 A8 5c violet & ol grn 2.50 3.00
64 A8 8c violet & blue 4.25 *17.50*
65 A8 10c violet & black 52.50 11.50
a. Chalky paper ('10) 120.00 82.50
66 A8 25c violet & green 8.50 *42.50*
67 A8 50c violet & red 47.50 17.50
68 A8 $1 green & vio 19.00 *72.50*
69 A8 $2 green & car 32.50 *62.50*
70 A8 $3 green & blue 45.00 *87.50*
71 A8 $4 green & brn 45.00 *125.00*
72 A8 $5 green & org 65.00 *100.00*
73 A8 $10 green & blk 125.00 *210.00*
74 A8 $50 green & blue *425.00* *575.00*
75 A8 $100 green & scar *625.00* *1,000.*
Revenue cancel 60.00
Nos. 59-73 (15) 466.00 *759.25*

Nos. 74 and 75 were theoretically available for postage but were mostly used for revenue purposes.
For surcharge see No. 86.

1912-19 Wmk. 47 Chalky Paper

76 A8 1c violet & green 1.25 .25
77 A8 2c violet & orange 6.00 1.00
78 A8 3c violet & black 10.00 .70
79 A8 4c violet & red 30.00 1.00
80 A8 5c violet & ol grn 10.00 2.75
81 A8 8c violet & blue 4.50 *14.00*
82 A8 10c violet & black 60.00 3.00
83 A8 25c violet & green 27.50 *55.00*
84 A8 50c violet & red ('19) 77.50 *145.00*
85 A8 $1 green & vio ('18) 120.00 *125.00*
Nos. 76-85 (10) 346.75 *347.70*

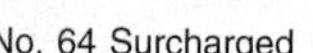

No. 64 Surcharged

1912 Wmk. 71

86 A8 3c on 8c vio & blue 15.00 *11.50*
a. "T" of "CENTS" omitted 1,750.

1918-20 Typo. Wmk. 3
Chalky Paper

87 A8 2c violet & orange 1.00 7.75
88 A8 2c violet & grn ('19) 1.00 5.50
89 A8 4c violet & red 1.75 .70
90 A8 5c vio & olive grn ('20) 2.00 15.00
91 A8 10c violet & blue 2.00 1.75
92 A8 21c violet & orange ('19) 3.00 3.25
93 A8 25c vio & grn ('20) 9.00 45.00
94 A8 50c vio & red ('19) 25.00 67.50
95 A8 $1 grn & red vio 15.00 77.50
96 A8 $2 green & scar 27.50 67.50
97 A8 $3 green & blue 75.00 145.00
98 A8 $4 green & brn 90.00 210.00
99 A8 $5 green & org 145.00 240.00
100 A8 $10 green & blk 450.00 625.00
Nos. 87-100 (14) 847.25 1,511.
Set, ovptd. "SPECIMEN" 750.00

1921-40 Wmk. 4

101 A8 1c violet & black .30 .25
102 A8 2c vio & brn ('24) 1.25 4.25
103 A8 2c green & dk grn ('28) .75 .40
104 A8 3c green ('25) 2.25 6.25
105 A8 3c dull vio & brn ('28) 1.40 1.50
106 A8 4c vio & red 2.50 .25
107 A8 5c vio & ol grn .50 .25
108 A8 6c vio & red brn .50 .50
109 A8 10c vio & blue 20.00 37.50
110 A8 10c vio & yel ('22) .50 .25
111 A8 12c vio & blue 1.25 1.60
111A A8 12c ultra ('40) 57.50 4.00
112 A8 21c dull vio & org ('28) 2.75 3.50
113 A8 25c vio & green 5.50 1.25
114 A8 30c dull vio & org ('36) 9.50 15.00
115 A8 40c dull vio & brn ('36) 10.50 15.00
116 A8 50c violet & red 3.75 1.60
117 A8 $1 grn & red vio 3.75 1.25
118 A8 $2 grn & red 10.00 5.00
119 A8 $3 grn & blue 85.00 105.00
120 A8 $4 grn & brn ('26) 110.00 190.00
121 A8 $5 grn & org 67.50 52.50
122 A8 $10 grn & blk 325.00 450.00
123 A8 $50 grn & ultra 1,450.
Revenue cancel 110.00
124 A8 $100 grn & red 2,000.
Revenue cancel 160.00
125 A8 $500 ultra & org brn ('26) *23,000.*
Revenue cancel 325.00
Nos. 101-122 (23) 721.95 *897.10*

Nos. 123, 124 and 125 were available for postage but were probably used only fiscally.

Sultan Ibrahim, Sultana — A9

1935, May 15 Engr. *Perf. 12½*

126 A9 8c grn & vio 6.75 3.50
Never hinged 10.00

Sultan Ibrahim — A10

1940, Feb. *Perf. 13½*

127 A10 8c blue & blk 26.00 1.35
Never hinged 40.00

Catalogue values for unused stamps in this section, from this point to the end of the section, are for Never Hinged items.

Silver Wedding Issue
Common Design Types
Inscribed: "Malaya Johore"
Perf. 14x14½

1948, Dec. 1 Wmk. 4 Photo.

128 CD304 10c purple .25 .75

Perf. 11½x11
Engr.; Name Typo.

129 CD305 $5 green 29.00 52.50

Common Design Types
Pictured following the introduction.

Sultan Ibrahim — A11

1949-55 Wmk. 4 Typo. *Perf. 18*

130 A11 1c black .75 .25
131 A11 2c orange .40 .30
132 A11 3c green 2.50 1.10
133 A11 4c chocolate 2.00 .25
134 A11 5c rose vio ('52) 3.00 .30
135 A11 6c gray 2.00 .25
a. Wmk. 4a (error) *3,250.* *2,150.*
136 A11 8c rose red 5.50 1.40
137 A11 8c green ('52) 10.00 2.25
138 A11 10c plum 1.50 .25
a. Imperf., pair *5,000.*
139 A11 12c rose red ('52) 11.00 9.00
140 A11 15c ultra 5.00 .45
141 A11 20c dk grn & blk 3.75 1.25
142 A11 20c ultra ('52) 2.00 .30
143 A11 25c org & rose lil 4.00 .25
144 A11 30c plum & rose red ('55) 3.25 2.75
145 A11 35c dk vio & rose red ('52) 12.00 2.25
146 A11 40c dk vio & rose red 8.50 18.00
147 A11 50c ultra & blk 5.50 .30
148 A11 $1 vio brn & ultra 13.00 2.50
149 A11 $2 rose red & emer 32.50 13.50
150 A11 $5 choc & emer 52.50 17.50
Nos. 130-150 (21) 180.65 74.40

UPU Issue
Common Design Types
Inscribed: "Malaya-Johore"
Engr.; Name Typo. on 15c, 25c

1949, Oct. 10 *Perf. 13½, 11x11½*

151 CD306 10c rose violet .30 .40
152 CD307 15c indigo 2.00 1.25
153 CD308 25c orange .80 3.50
154 CD309 50c slate 1.60 3.75
Nos. 151-154 (4) 4.70 8.90

Coronation Issue
Common Design Type

1953, June 2 Engr. *Perf. 13½x13*

155 CD312 10c magenta & black 1.40 .30

Sultan Ibrahim A12

1955, Nov. 1 Wmk. 4 *Perf. 14*

156 A12 10c carmine lake .35 .35

Sultan Ibrahim's Diamond Jubilee.

Sultan Ismail and Johore State Crest Seal — A13

Perf. 11½

1960, Feb. 10 Unwmk. Photo.
Granite Paper

157 A13 10c multicolored .35 .35

Coronation of Sultan Ismail.

Types of Kedah 1957 with Portrait of Sultan Ismail

1960 Wmk. 314 Engr. *Perf. 13*

158 A8 1c black .25 *.50*
159 A8 2c red orange .25 *1.25*
160 A8 4c dark brown .25 .25
161 A8 5c dk car rose .25 .25
162 A8 8c dark green 2.25 *3.50*
163 A7 10c violet brown .35 .25
164 A7 20c blue 2.25 1.00
165 A7 50c ultra & black .60 .30
166 A8 $1 plum & ultra 4.50 *6.00*
167 A8 $2 red & green 15.00 *22.50*
168 A8 $5 ol, grn & brn 35.00 *42.50*
Nos. 158-168 (11) 60.95 *78.30*

Starting in 1965, issues of Johore are listed with Malaysia.

POSTAGE DUE STAMPS

D1

Perf. 12½

1938, Jan. 1 Typo. Wmk. 4

J1 D1 1c rose red 22.50 *50.00*
J2 D1 4c green 45.00 *45.00*
J3 D1 8c dull yellow 50.00 *160.00*
J4 D1 10c bister brown 50.00 *57.50*
J5 D1 12c rose violet 60.00 *140.00*
Nos. J1-J5 (5) 227.50 *452.50*

OCCUPATION POSTAGE DUE STAMPS

Issued under Japanese Occupation

Johore Nos. J1-J5 Overprinted in Black, Brown or Red

1942 Wmk. 4 *Perf. 12½*

NJ1 D1 1c rose red 52.50 85.00
NJ2 D1 4c green 82.50 95.00
NJ3 D1 8c dull yellow 145.00 150.00
NJ4 D1 10c bister brown 52.50 72.50
NJ5 D1 12c rose violet 105.00 115.00
Nos. NJ1-NJ5 (5) 437.50 517.50

Johore Nos. J1-J5 Overprinted in Black

1943

NJ6 D1 1c rose red 10.00 *35.00*
NJ7 D1 4c green 8.00 *40.00*
NJ8 D1 8c dull yellow 10.00 *42.50*
NJ9 D1 10c bister brown 9.50 *50.00*
NJ10 D1 12c rose violet 11.00 *70.00*
Nos. NJ6-NJ10 (5) 48.50 *237.50*

Nos. NJ6-NJ10 exist with second character sideways. See Scott Classic Specialized catalogue for listings.

KEDAH

'ke-də

LOCATION — On the west coast of the Malay Peninsula.
AREA — 3,660 sq. mi.
POP. — 752,706 (1960)
CAPITAL — Alor Star

Sheaf of Rice — A1

Native Plowing — A2

Council Chamber — A3

1912-21 Engr. Wmk. 3 *Perf. 14*

1 A1 1c green & black .70 .30
2 A1 1c brown ('19) .75 .60
3 A1 2c green ('19) .60 .35
4 A1 3c car & black 5.00 .35
5 A1 3c dk violet ('19) .75 4.00
6 A1 4c slate & car 12.00 .30
7 A1 4c scarlet ('19) 5.50 1.00
8 A1 5c org brown & grn 2.75 *3.50*
9 A1 8c ultra & blk 4.25 *4.00*
10 A2 10c black brn & bl 2.75 1.25
11 A2 20c yel grn & blk 12.50 5.00
12 A2 21c red vio & vio ('19) 6.25 *70.00*
13 A2 25c red vio & bl ('21) 2.10 *37.50*
14 A2 30c car & black 3.50 *12.00*
15 A2 40c lilac & blk 4.00 *22.50*
16 A2 50c dull bl & brn 10.00 *14.00*
17 A3 $1 scar & blk, *yel* 17.50 *24.00*
18 A3 $2 dk brn & dk grn 25.00 *95.00*
19 A3 $3 dk bl & blk, *bl* 135.00 *190.00*
20 A3 $5 car & black 135.00 *200.00*
Nos. 1-20 (20) 385.90 *685.65*

There are two types of No. 7, one printed from separate plates for frame and center, the other printed from a single plate.
Overprints are listed after No. 45.

Stamps of 1912 Surcharged

1919

21 A3 50c on $2 dk brn & dk grn 80.00 *90.00*
a. "C" of ovpt. inserted by hand 1,450. 1,650.
22 A3 $1 on $3 dk bl & blk, *blue* 22.50 *110.00*

1921-36 Wmk. 4

Two types of 1c:
I — The 1's have rounded corners, small top serif. Small letters "c."
II — The 1's have square-cut corners, large top serif. Large letters "c."

Two types of 2c:
I — The 2's have oval drops. Letters "c" are fairly thick and rounded.
II — The 2's have round drops. Letters "c" thin and slightly larger.

23 A1 1c brown 1.50 .25
24 A1 1c blk (I) ('22) 1.00 .25
a. 1c black (II) ('39) 170.00 5.00
25 A1 2c green (I) 1.50 .25
a. 2c green (II) ('40) 350.00 8.00
26 A1 3c dk violet 1.00 .80
27 A1 3c green ('22) 2.75 1.00
28 A1 4c carmine 7.50 .25
29 A1 4c dull vio ('26) 1.50 .25
30 A1 5c yellow ('22) 3.00 .25
31 A1 6c scarlet ('26) 2.50 .80
32 A1 8c gray ('36) 22.50 .25
33 A2 10c blk brn & bl 3.25 1.00
34 A2 12c dk ultra & blk ('26) 10.00 5.00
35 A2 20c green & blk 8.00 3.00
36 A2 21c red vio & vio 3.25 *17.50*
37 A2 25c red vio & bl 3.25 *9.00*
38 A2 30c red & blk ('22) 4.00 *11.00*
39 A2 35c claret ('26) 22.50 *45.00*
40 A2 40c red vio & blk 8.00 *65.00*
41 A2 50c dp blue & brn 4.75 *27.50*
42 A3 $1 scar & blk, *yel* ('24) 80.00 85.00
43 A3 $2 brn & green 17.50 *125.00*
44 A3 $3 dk bl & blk, *bl* 80.00 *110.00*
45 A3 $5 car & black 115.00 *200.00*
Nos. 23-45 (23) 404.25 *708.35*

For overprints see Nos. N1-N6.

Stamps of 1912-21 Overprinted in Black: "MALAYA-BORNEO EXHIBITION." in Three Lines

1922 **Wmk. 3**
3a A1 2c green 5.00 *27.50*
12a A2 21c red vio & vio 45.00 *95.00*
13a A2 25c red vio & blue 47.50 *110.00*
b. Inverted overprint 1,625.
16a A2 50c dull blue & brn 50.00 *125.00*

Wmk. 4
23a A1 1c brown 7.50 *30.00*
26a A1 3c dark violet 5.50 *50.00*
28a A1 4c carmine 6.00 *25.00*
33a A2 10c blk brn & blue 14.50 *50.00*
Nos. 3a-33a (8) 181.00 *512.50*

Industrial fair at Singapore, Mar. 31-Apr. 15, 1922.
On Nos. 12a, 13a and 16a, "BORNEO" exists both 14mm and 15mm wide.

Sultan of Kedah, Sir Abdul Hamid Halim Shah — A4

1937, July **Wmk. 4** ***Perf. 12½***
46 A4 10c sepia & ultra 4.00 2.25
47 A4 12c gray vio & blk 42.50 *5.50*
48 A4 25c brn vio & ultra 10.00 *5.50*
49 A4 30c dp car & yel grn 10.00 *11.50*
50 A4 40c brn vio & blk 5.00 *16.00*
51 A4 50c dp blue & sepia 10.00 *5.50*
52 A4 $1 dk green & blk 4.00 *11.00*
53 A4 $2 dk brn & yel grn 90.00 *85.00*
54 A4 $5 dp car & black 27.50 *170.00*
Nos. 46-54 (9) 203.00 *312.25*
Set, never hinged 315.00

For overprints see Nos. N7-N15.

Catalogue values for unused stamps in this section, from this point to the end of the section, are for Never Hinged items.

Silver Wedding Issue
Common Design Types
Inscribed: "Malaya Kedah"

1948, Dec. 1 **Photo.** ***Perf. 14x14½***
55 CD304 10c purple .25 .25

Perf. 11½x11
Engraved; Name Typographed
56 CD305 $5 rose car 35.00 50.00

UPU Issue
Common Design Types
Inscribed: "Malaya-Kedah"

Engr.; Name Typo. on 15c, 25c
1949, Oct. 10 ***Perf. 13½, 11x11½***
57 CD306 10c rose violet .25 1.25
58 CD307 15c indigo 2.25 1.75
59 CD308 25c orange .80 3.00
60 CD309 50c slate 1.50 6.00
Nos. 57-60 (4) 4.80 12.00

Sheaf of Rice
A5

Sultan Tungku Badlishah
A6

1950-55 **Wmk. 4** **Typo.** ***Perf. 18***
61 A5 1c black .70 .30
62 A5 2c orange .50 .25
63 A5 3c green 2.00 1.00
64 A5 4c chocolate .75 .25
65 A5 5c rose vio ('52) 5.50 3.00
66 A5 6c gray .70 .25
67 A5 8c rose red 3.75 *5.00*
68 A5 8c green ('52) 5.50 3.00
69 A5 10c plum .70 .25
70 A5 12c rose red ('52) 5.50 3.00
71 A5 15c ultramarine 5.00 .70
72 A5 20c dk green & blk 5.00 3.00
73 A5 20c ultra ('52) 2.50 .35
74 A6 25c org & rose lilac 1.50 .50
75 A6 30c plum & rose red ('55) 6.00 1.50
76 A6 35c dk vio & rose red ('52) 6.25 2.00
77 A6 40c dk vio & rose red 7.50 *10.00*
78 A6 50c ultra & black 6.00 .35
79 A6 $1 vio brown & ultra 7.00 *8.00*
80 A6 $2 rose red & emer 30.00 *45.00*
81 A6 $5 choc & emerald 67.50 *90.00*
Nos. 61-81 (21) 169.85 *177.70*

Coronation Issue
Common Design Type

1953, June 2 **Engr.** ***Perf. 13½x13***
82 CD312 10c magenta & black 2.25 .60

Fishing Craft — A7

Weaving and Sultan — A8

Portrait of Sultan Tungku Badlishah and: 1c, Copra. 2c, Pineapples. 4c, Rice field. 5c, Mosque. 8c, East Coast Railway. 10c, Tiger. 50c, Aborigines with blowpipes. $1, Government offices. $2, Bersilat.

Perf. 13x12½, 12½x13
1957 **Engr.** **Wmk. 314**
83 A8 1c black .35 *.60*
84 A8 2c red orange .50 *1.75*
85 A8 4c dark brown .35 *1.00*
86 A8 5c dk car rose .35 .75
87 A8 8c dark green 3.00 *10.00*
88 A7 10c chocolate 1.00 .50
89 A7 20c blue 3.50 3.25

Perf. 12½, 13½ ($1)
90 A7 50c ultra & black 3.25 *4.25*
91 A8 $1 plum & ultra 9.00 *15.00*
92 A8 $2 red & green 32.50 *45.00*
Revenue cancel .20
93 A8 $5 ol grn & brown 55.00 47.50
Revenue cancel .35
Nos. 83-93 (11) 108.80 129.60

See Nos. 95-105.

Sultan Abdul Halim — A9

Perf. 14x14½
1959, Feb. 20 **Photo.** **Wmk. 314**
94 A9 10c ultra, red & yellow .80 .30

Installation of the Sultan of Kedah, Abdul Halim.

Types of 1957

Designs as before with portrait of Sultan Abdul Halim.

Perf. 13x12½, 12½x13, 12½, 13½
1959-62 **Engr.** **Wmk. 314**
95 A8 1c black .25 .85
96 A8 2c red orange .25 2.00
97 A8 4c dark brown .25 .85
98 A8 5c dk car rose .25 .30
99 A8 8c dark green 4.00 4.00
100 A7 10c chocolate 1.00 .30
101 A7 20c blue 1.00 1.00
102 A7 50c ultra & blk, perf. 12½x13 ('60) .35 1.75
a. Perf. 12½ .35 .60
103 A8 $1 plum & ultra 2.50 *3.00*
104 A8 $2 red & green 15.00 *22.50*
105 A8 $5 ol grn & brn, perf. 13x12½ ('62) 35.00 19.00
a. Perf. 12½ 20.00 *22.50*
Nos. 95-105 (11) 59.85 55.55

Starting in 1965, issues of Kedah are listed with Malaysia.

OCCUPATION STAMPS

Issued Under Japanese Occupation

Stamps of Kedah 1922-36, Overprinted in Red or Black

1942, May 13 **Wmk. 4** ***Perf. 14***
N1 A1 1c black (R) 9.50 15.00
N2 A1 2c green (R) 35.00 45.00
N3 A1 4c dull violet (R) 9.50 4.00
N4 A1 5c yellow (R) 5.50 7.50
a. Black overprint 300.00 325.00
N5 A1 6c scarlet (Bk) 6.00 25.00
N6 A1 8c gray (R) 7.00 5.00

Nos. 46 to 54 Overprinted in Red

Perf. 12½
N7 A4 10c sepia & ultra 18.00 20.00
N8 A4 12c gray vio & blk 42.50 60.00
N9 A4 25c brn vio & ultra 16.00 27.50
a. Black overprint 450.00 350.00
N10 A4 30c dp car & yel grn 75.00 85.00
N11 A4 40c brn vio & blk 42.50 50.00
N12 A4 50c dp blue & sep 42.50 50.00
N13 A4 $1 dk grn & blk 160.00 160.00
a. Inverted overprint 875.00 1,000.
N14 A4 $2 dk brn & yel green 210.00 190.00
N15 A4 $5 dp car & blk 90.00 125.00
a. Black overprint 1,600. 1,400.
Nos. N1-N15 (15) 769.00 869.00

KELANTAN

kə-ˈlan-ˌtan

LOCATION — On the eastern coast of the Malay Peninsula.
AREA — 5,750 sq. mi.
POP. — 545,620 (1960)
CAPITAL — Kota Bharu

Symbols of Government — A1

1911-15 **Typo.** **Wmk. 3** ***Perf. 14***
Ordinary Paper
1 A1 1c gray green 8.00 1.25
a. 1c green 7.25 .35
2 A1 3c rose red 5.00 .25
3 A1 4c black & red 1.90 .25
4 A1 5c grn & red, *yel* 12.00 1.25
5 A1 8c ultramarine 6.25 1.25
6 A1 10c black & violet 35.00 .90

Chalky Paper
7 A1 30c violet & red 12.50 3.00
8 A1 50c black & org 10.00 3.00
9 A1 $1 green & emer 55.00 45.00
10 A1 $1 grn & brn ('15) 75.00 2.40
11 A1 $2 grn & car rose 1.90 *3.75*
12 A1 $5 green & ultra 4.75 4.00
13 A1 $25 green & org 55.00 *110.00*
Nos. 1-13 (13) 282.30 *176.30*

For overprints see listings after No. 26. For surcharges see Nos. N20-N22.

1921-28 **Wmk. 4**
Ordinary Paper
14 A1 1c green 5.00 .75
15 A1 1c black ('23) 1.00 .60
16 A1 2c brown 7.50 4.75
17 A1 2c green ('26) 5.50 .60
18 A1 3c brown ('27) 5.00 1.50
19 A1 4c black & red 3.50 .25
20 A1 5c grn & red, *yel* 1.75 .25
21 A1 6c claret 3.50 2.00
22 A1 6c rose red ('28) 5.00 5.00
23 A1 10c black & violet 3.00 .25

Chalky Paper
24 A1 30c dull vio & red ('26) 5.00 *6.00*
25 A1 50c black & orange 7.25 *52.50*
26 A1 $1 green & brown 35.00 *90.00*
Nos. 14-26 (13) 88.00 *164.45*

Stamps of 1911-21 Overprinted in Black in Three Lines

1922 **Wmk. 3**
3a A1 4c black & red 7.00 *50.00*
4a A1 5c green & red, *yel* 7.50 *50.00*
7a A1 30c violet & red 8.00 *80.00*
8a A1 50c black & orange 11.00 *90.00*
10a A1 $1 green & brown 35.00 *125.00*
11a A1 $2 green & car rose 95.00 *275.00*
12a A1 $5 green & ultra 275.00 *525.00*

Wmk. 4
14a A1 1c green 4.00 *55.00*
23a A1 10c black & violet 7.50 *75.00*
Nos. 3a-23a (9) 450.00 1,325.

Industrial fair at Singapore. Mar. 31-Apr. 15, 1922.

Sultan Ismail — A2

Size: 21½x30mm

1928-33 **Engr.** ***Perf. 12***
27 A2 $1 ultramarine 17.50 *85.00*

Perf. 14
28 A2 $1 blue ('33) 75.00 *47.50*

Sultan Ismail — A2a

Size: 22½x34½mm

1937-40 ***Perf. 12***
29 A2a 1c yel & ol green 1.75 .65
30 A2a 2c deep green 5.50 .25
31 A2a 4c brick red 5.50 1.00
32 A2a 5c red brown 3.00 .25
33 A2a 6c car lake 16.00 *12.50*
34 A2a 8c gray green 3.00 .25
35 A2a 10c dark violet 22.50 3.50
36 A2a 12c deep blue 5.50 *8.50*
37 A2a 25c vio & red org 6.00 *4.75*
38 A2a 30c scar & dk vio 40.00 27.50
39 A2a 40c blue grn & org 7.00 *45.00*
40 A2a 50c org & ol grn 55.00 10.00

41 A2a $1 dp grn & dk violet 40.00 16.00
42 A2a $2 red & red brn ('40) 250.00 *275.00*
43 A2a $5 rose lake & org ('40) 550.00 *950.00*
Nos. 29-43 (15) 1,011. *1,355.*
Set, never hinged 1,525.

For overprints see Nos. N1-N19.

Catalogue values for unused stamps in this section, from this point to the end of the section, are for Never Hinged items.

Common Design Types pictured following the introduction.

Silver Wedding Issue
Common Design Types
Inscribed: "Malaya Kelantan"

Perf. 14x14½
1948, Dec. 1 Wmk. 4 Photo.
44 CD304 10c purple .75 *2.75*

Perf. 11½x11
Engraved; Name Typographed
45 CD305 $5 rose car 35.00 *60.00*

UPU Issue
Common Design Types
Inscribed: "Malaya-Kelantan"

Engr.; Name Typo. on 15c, 25c
1949, Oct. 10 *Perf. 13½, 11x11½*
46 CD306 10c rose violet .40 .40
47 CD307 15c indigo 2.25 2.75
48 CD308 25c orange .60 6.50
49 CD309 50c slate 1.00 3.00
Nos. 46-49 (4) 4.25 12.65

Sultan Ibrahim — A3

Perf. 18
1951, July 11 Wmk. 4 Typo.
50 A3 1c black .50 .40
51 A3 2c orange 1.20 .40
52 A3 3c green 6.75 1.75
53 A3 4c chocolate 2.00 .30
54 A3 6c gray .80 .30
55 A3 8c rose red 6.00 4.50
56 A3 10c plum .75 .30
57 A3 15c ultramarine 9.00 .80
58 A3 20c dk green & blk 7.50 15.00
59 A3 25c orange & plum 2.25 .80
60 A3 40c vio brn & rose red 17.50 27.50
61 A3 50c dp ultra & blk 8.00 .60
62 A3 $1 vio brown & ultra 10.00 16.50
63 A3 $2 rose red & emer 47.50 70.00
64 A3 $5 choc & emer 72.50 82.50

1952-55
65 A3 5c rose violet 1.50 .50
66 A3 8c green 7.50 2.25
67 A3 12c rose red 7.50 4.00
68 A3 20c ultramarine 2.00 .25
69 A3 30c plum & rose red ('55) 1.60 6.50
70 A3 35c dk vio & rose red 2.50 1.75
Nos. 50-70 (21) 214.85 236.90

Compare with Pahang A8, Perak A16, Selangor A15, Trengganu A5.

Coronation Issue
Common Design Type

1953, June 2 Engr. *Perf. 13½x13*
71 CD312 10c magenta & black 1.60 1.60

Aborigines with Blowpipes A4

Government Offices and Sultan A5

Portrait of Sultan Ibrahim and: 1c, Copra. 2c, Pineapples. 4c, Rice field. 5c, Mosque. 8c, East Coast Railway. 10c, Tiger. 20c, Fishing craft. 50c, Aborigines with blowpipes. $1, Government Offices and Sultan. $2, Bersilat. $5, Weaving.

Perf. 13x12½, 12½x13, 13½ ($1)
1957-63 Engr. Wmk. 314
72 A5 1c black .25 .45
73 A5 2c red orange .90 1.50
74 A5 4c dark brown .45 .25
75 A5 5c dk car rose .45 .25
76 A5 8c dark green 2.25 3.25
77 A4 10c chocolate 3.00 .25
78 A4 20c blue 2.50 .45
79 A4 50c ultra & blk ('60) 1.00 .60
a. Perf 12½ 1.00 1.25
80 A5 $1 plum & ultra 8.00 2.00
81 A5 $2 red & grn ('63) 15.00 *32.50*
a. Perf. 12½ 19.00 *9.00*
82 A5 $5 ol grn & brn ('63) 27.50 *37.50*
a. Perf. 12½ 24.00 *14.00*
Nos. 72-82 (11) 61.30 *79.00*

Sultan Yahya Petra — A6

1961, July 17 Photo. *Perf. 14½x14*
83 A6 10s multicolored .55 1.00

Installation of Sultan Yahya Petra.

Types of 1957 with Portrait of Sultan Yahya Petra
Designs as before.

Perf. 13x12½, 12½x13
1961-62 Engr. Wmk. 338
84 A5 1c black .25 *2.75*
85 A5 2c red orange .60 *3.00*
86 A5 4c dark brown 1.75 *2.00*
87 A5 5c dk car rose 1.75 .60
88 A5 8c dark green 14.00 *15.00*
89 A4 10c violet brown ('61) 1.75 .40
90 A4 20c blue 10.00 2.50
Nos. 84-90 (7) 30.10 26.25

Starting in 1965, issues of Kelantan are listed with Malaysia.

OCCUPATION STAMPS

Issued Under Japanese Occupation

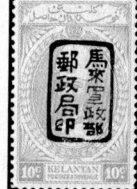

Kelantan No. 35 Handstamped in Black

1942 Wmk. 4 *Perf. 12*
N1 A2a 10c dark violet 400.00 500.00

Some authorities believe No. N1 was not regularly issued.

Kelantan Nos. 29-40 Surcharged in Black or Red and Handstamped with Oval Seal "a" in Red

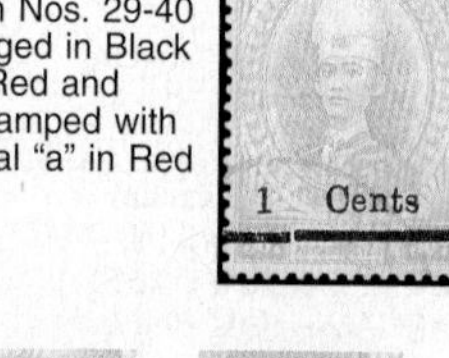

Sunakawa-a

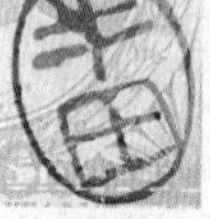
Handa-b

1942
N2 1c on 50c org & ol green 225.00 150.00
a. With "b" seal 160.00 200.00
N3 2c on 40c bl grn & orange 300.00 200.00
a. With "b" seal 160.00 200.00
N4 5c on 12c dp bl (R) 200.00 200.00
N5 8c on 5c red brn (R) 175.00 100.00
a. With "b" seal (R) 110.00 175.00
N6 10c on 6c car lake 475.00 500.00
a. With "b" seal 120.00 200.00
N7 12c on 8c gray green (R) 60.00 140.00
N8 30c on 4c brick red 2,500. 2,250.
N9 40c on 2c dp grn (R) 70.00 100.00
N10 50c on 1c yel & ol green 1,800. 1,500.

Kelantan Nos. 29-40, 19-20, 22 Surcharged in Black or Red and Handstamped with Oval Seal "b" in Red

N10A 1c on 50c org & ol green 350.00 200.00
N11 2c on 40c bl grn & orange 900.00 350.00
N11A 4c on 30c scar & dark vio 2,500. 1,400.
N12 5c on 12c dp bl (R) 350.00 200.00
N13 6c on 25c vio & red org 375.00 200.00
N14 8c on 5c red brown (R) 500.00 150.00
N15 10c on 6c car lake 100.00 125.00
N16 12c on 8c gray grn (R) 225.00 375.00
a. Seal omitted 70.00 120.00
N17 25c on 10c dk vio 1,600. 1,500.
N17A 30c on 4c brick red 2,500. 2,250.
N18 40c on 2c dp grn (R) 70.00 100.00
N19 50c on 1c yel & ol green 1,800. 1,500.

Perf. 14
N20 $1 on 4c blk & red (R) 60.00 85.00
N21 $2 on 5c grn & red, *yel* 60.00 85.00
N22 $5 on 6c rose red 60.00 85.00

Examples of Nos. N2-N22 without handstamped seal are from the remainder stocks sent to Singapore after Kelantan was ceded to Thailand. Some authorities believe stamps without seals were used before June 1942.

ISSUED UNDER THAI OCCUPATION

OS1

1943, Nov. 15 *Perf. 11*
2N1 OS1 1c violet & black *240.00 375.00*
2N2 OS1 2c violet & black *300.00 300.00*
2N3 OS1 4c violet & black *300.00 375.00*
2N4 OS1 8c violet & black *300.00 300.00*
2N5 OS1 10c violet & black *450.00 550.00*
Nos. 2N1-2N5 (5) *1,590. 1,900.*

Stamps with centers in red are revenues.

MALACCA

mə-ˈla-kə

Melaka

LOCATION — On the west coast of the Malay peninsula.
AREA — 640 sq. mi.
POP. — 318,110 (1960)
CAPITAL — Malacca

Catalogue values for unused stamps in this section are for Never Hinged items.

Common Design Types pictured following the introduction.

Silver Wedding Issue
Common Design Types
Inscribed: "Malaya Malacca"

Perf. 14x14½
1948, Dec. 1 Wmk. 4 Photo.
1 CD304 10c purple .40 *2.25*

Engraved; Name Typographed
Perf. 11½x11
2 CD305 $5 lt brown 35.00 *47.50*

Type of Straits Settlements, 1937-41, Inscribed "Malacca"

Perf. 18
1949, Mar. 1 Wmk. 4 Typo.
3 A29 1c black .40 *.85*
4 A29 2c orange 1.00 .60
5 A29 3c green .40 *2.25*
6 A29 4c chocolate .40 .25
7 A29 6c gray .90 *1.10*
8 A29 8c rose red .90 *7.50*
9 A29 10c plum .40 .25
10 A29 15c ultramarine 3.50 .85
11 A29 20c dk green & blk .60 *7.00*
12 A29 25c org & rose lil .60 .85
13 A29 40c dk vio & rose red 1.50 *13.00*
14 A29 50c ultra & black 1.50 1.50
15 A29 $1 vio brn & ultra 15.00 *26.00*
16 A29 $2 rose red & emer 27.50 27.50
17 A29 $5 choc & emer 60.00 50.00
Nos. 3-17 (15) 114.60 *139.50*

See Nos. 22-26.

UPU Issue
Common Design Types
Inscribed: "Malaya-Malacca"

Engr.; Name Typo. on 15c, 25c
Perf. 13½, 11x11½
1949, Oct. 10 Wmk. 4
18 CD306 10c rose violet .35 *.55*
19 CD307 15c indigo 2.40 *2.75*
20 CD308 25c orange .50 *8.50*
21 CD309 50c slate 1.00 *5.50*
Nos. 18-21 (4) 4.25 *17.30*

Type of Straits Settlements, 1937-41, Inscribed "Malacca"

1952, Sept. 1 Wmk. 4 *Perf. 18*
22 A29 5c rose violet 1.25 *1.75*
23 A29 8c green 6.00 *5.25*
24 A29 12c rose red 6.00 *9.50*
25 A29 20c ultramarine 7.50 3.00
26 A29 35c dk vio & rose red 6.00 *3.75*
Nos. 22-26 (5) 26.75 *23.25*

Coronation Issue
Common Design Type

1953, June 2 Engr. *Perf. 13½x13*
27 CD312 10c magenta & black 1.10 *1.50*

Queen Elizabeth II — A1

1954-55 Wmk. 4 Typo. *Perf. 18*
29 A1 1c black .25 .75
30 A1 2c orange .40 1.25
31 A1 4c chocolate 1.50 .25
32 A1 5c rose violet .40 2.75
33 A1 6c gray .25 .40
34 A1 8c green .55 3.00
35 A1 10c plum 2.00 .25
36 A1 12c rose red .40 3.25
37 A1 20c ultramarine .25 1.25
38 A1 25c orange & plum .25 1.75
39 A1 30c plum & rose red ('55) .25 *.40*
40 A1 35c vio brn & rose red .25 *1.50*
41 A1 50c ultra & black 4.00 2.75
42 A1 $1 vio brn & ultra 7.50 *12.00*
43 A1 $2 rose red & grn 29.00 *45.00*
44 A1 $5 choc & emerald 29.00 *47.50*
Nos. 29-44 (16) 76.25 124.05

Types of Kedah with Portrait of Queen Elizabeth II

Perf. 13x12½, 12½x13

1957 Engr. Wmk. 314

45 A8 1c black .25 *.55*
46 A8 2c red orange .25 *.55*
47 A8 4c dark brown .50 .25
48 A8 5c dark car rose .50 .25
49 A8 8c dark green 2.25 *3.00*
50 A7 10c chocolate .45 .25
51 A7 20c blue 2.50 1.00

Perf. 12½, 13½ ($1)

52 A7 50c ultra & black 1.00 1.00
53 A8 $1 plum & ultra 6.00 4.75
54 A8 $2 red & green 20.00 *27.50*
55 A8 $5 olive grn & brn 22.50 *47.50*
Nos. 45-55 (11) 56.20 86.60

Types of Kedah, 1957, With Melaka Tree and Mouse Deer Replacing Portrait of Queen Elizabeth II

Perf. 13x12½, 12½x13, 13½ ($1)

1960, Mar. 15 Engr. Wmk. 314

56 A8 1c black .25 *.50*
57 A8 2c red orange .25 *.70*
58 A8 4c dark brown .25 .25
59 A8 5c dark car rose .25 .25
60 A8 8c dark green 3.50 *3.75*
61 A7 10c violet brown .45 .25
62 A7 20c blue 2.25 1.00
63 A7 50c ultra & black 1.25 1.00
64 A8 $1 plum & ultra 5.00 3.25
65 A8 $2 red & green 7.50 *15.00*
66 A8 $5 ol grn & brn 14.00 *17.50*
Nos. 56-66 (11) 34.95 43.45

Starting in 1965, issues of Malacca (Melaka) are listed with Malaysia.

OCCUPATION STAMPS

Issued Under Japanese Occupation

Stamps of Straits Settlements, 1937-41 Handstamped in Carmine

The handstamp covers four stamps. Values are for single stamps. Blocks of four showing complete handstamp sell for six times the price of singles.

1942 Wmk. 4 *Perf. 14*

N1 A29 1c black 125.00 90.00
N2 A29 2c brown orange 75.00 75.00
N3 A29 3c green 80.00 90.00
N4 A29 5c brown 175.00 175.00
N5 A29 8c gray 300.00 150.00
N6 A29 10c dull violet 125.00 125.00
N7 A29 12c ultramarine 140.00 140.00
N8 A29 15c ultramarine 100.00 125.00
N9 A29 30c org & vio *3,500.* —
N10 A29 40c dk vio & rose red 700.00 700.00
N11 A29 50c blk, *emerald* 1,100. 1,100.
N12 A29 $1 red & blk, *bl* 1,350. 1,250.
N13 A29 $2 rose red & gray grn *3,500.* —
N14 A29 $5 grn & red, *grn* *3,500.* —

Some authorities believe Nos. N9, N13, and N14 were not regularly issued.

OCCUPATION POSTAGE DUE STAMPS

Malaya Postage Due Stamps and Type of 1936-38, Handstamped Like Nos. N1-N14 in Carmine

1942 Wmk. 4 *Perf. 14½x14*

NJ1 D2 1c violet *250.00 225.00*
NJ2 D2 4c yel green *275.00 275.00*
NJ3 D2 8c red *3,500. 2,250.*
NJ4 D2 10c yel orange *550.00 525.00*
NJ5 D2 12c blue violet *800.00 725.00*
NJ6 D2 50c black *3,000. 2,000.*
Nos. NJ1-NJ6 (6) 8,375. 6,000.

Pricing note above No. N1 also applies to Nos. NJ1-NJ6.

NEGRI SEMBILAN

'ne-grē səm-'bē-lən

LOCATION — South of Selangor on the west coast of the Malay Peninsula, bordering on Pahang on the east and Johore on the south.
AREA — 2,580 sq. mi.
POP. — 401,742 (1960)
CAPITAL — Seremban

Stamps of the Straits Settlements Overprinted in Black

1891 Wmk. 2 *Perf. 14*

Overprint 14½ to 15mm Wide

1 A2 2c rose 3.50 *16.50*

Tiger — A1

1891-94 Typo.

2 A1 1c green ('93) 4.00 1.25
3 A1 2c rose 4.00 *15.00*
4 A1 5c blue ('94) 35.00 *47.50*
Nos. 2-4 (3) 43.00 *63.75*

Tiger Head — A2

1895-99

5 A2 1c lilac & green 25.00 11.50
6 A2 2c lilac & brown 42.50 *140.00*
7 A2 3c lilac & car rose 18.00 3.00
8 A2 5c lilac & olive 15.00 16.00
9 A2 8c lilac & blue 35.00 22.50
10 A2 10c lilac & orange 32.50 17.00
11 A2 15c green & vio 50.00 *90.00*
12 A2 20c grn & ol ('99) 80.00 *45.00*
13 A2 25c grn & car rose 85.00 *110.00*
14 A2 50c green & black 90.00 80.00
Nos. 5-14 (10) 473.00 *535.00*

For surcharges see Nos. 15-16, 19-20; Federated Malay States Nos. 1-8.

Stamps of 1891-99 Surcharged

1899 Blue-green Surcharge

15 A2 4c on 8c lil & blue 13.50 5.00
a. Double surcharge 3,000. 2,500.
b. Pair, one without surcharge 10,000. 5,750.
c. Double surcharge, 1 green, 1 red 1,000. 1,100.

Black Surcharge

16 A2 4c on 8c lil & blue 1,400. *1,500.*

Surcharge on No. 16 is thinner and sharper than on No. 15.

Same Surcharge and Bar in Black

17 A1 4c on 1c green 3.50 *25.00*
18 A1 4c on 5c blue 1.50 *17.00*
19 A2 4c on 3c lil & car rose 6.00 *27.50*
a. Double surcharge 2,750. 1,200.
b. Pair, one without surcharge *15,000. 7,000.*
c. Bar omitted 1,000. 800.00
g. Inverted surcharge 2,500. 1,650.

Bar at bottom on Nos. 17-18, at top on No. 19.

No. 11 Surcharged in Black

1900

20 A2 1c on 15c grn & vio 125.00 *350.00*
a. Inverted period 500.00 *1,350.*

Arms of Negri Sembilan — A4

1935-41 Typo. Wmk. 4

21 A4 1c black ('36) 1.40 .25
22 A4 2c dp green ('36) 1.40 .25
22A A4 2c brown org ('41) 4.00 *75.00*
22B A4 3c green ('41) 40.00 *11.00*
23 A4 4c brown orange 2.00 .25
24 A4 5c chocolate 2.00 .25
25 A4 6c rose red 17.50 2.75
25A A4 6c gray ('41) 5.00 *140.00*
26 A4 8c gray 2.00 .40
27 A4 10c dull vio ('36) 1.40 .25
28 A4 12c ultra ('36) 3.25 .75
28A A4 15c ultra ('41) 11.00 *75.00*
29 A4 25c rose red & dull vio ('36) 2.00 1.00
30 A4 30c org & dull vio ('36) 3.50 2.50
31 A4 40c dull vio & car 3.50 *3.00*
32 A4 50c blk, *emer* ('36) 6.50 2.25
33 A4 $1 red & blk, *bl* ('36) 5.00 7.00
34 A4 $2 rose red & grn ('36) 60.00 22.50
35 A4 $5 brn red & grn, *emer* ('36) 40.00 *135.00*
Nos. 21-35 (19) 211.45 *479.40*
Set, never hinged 375.00

For overprints see Nos. N1-N31.

Catalogue values for unused stamps in this section, from this point to the end of the section, are for Never Hinged items.

Common Design Types pictured following the introduction.

Silver Wedding Issue

Common Design Types

Inscribed: "Malaya Negri Sembilan"

1948, Dec. 1 Photo. *Perf. 14x14½*

36 CD304 10c purple .60 .70

Perf. 11½x11

Engraved; Name Typographed

37 CD305 $5 green 27.50 37.50

Arms of Negri Sembilan — A5

1949-55 Wmk. 4 Typo. *Perf. 18*

38 A5 1c black 1.25 .25
39 A5 2c orange 1.00 .25
40 A5 3c green .60 .45
41 A5 4c chocolate .30 .25
42 A5 5c rose violet 1.00 .45
43 A5 6c gray 2.25 .25
44 A5 8c rose red .80 .95
45 A5 8c green 5.50 2.25
46 A5 10c plum .40 .25
47 A5 12c rose red 5.50 3.25
48 A5 15c ultramarine 4.25 .45
49 A5 20c dk green & blk 2.25 2.00
50 A5 20c ultramarine 2.00 .35
51 A5 25c org & rose lilac 1.00 .35
52 A5 30c plum & rose red ('55) 2.00 2.75
53 A5 35c dk vio & rose red 1.50 3.75
54 A5 40c dk vio & rose red 4.75 *6.00*
55 A5 50c ultra & black 5.00 .45
56 A5 $1 vio brn & ultra 6.00 2.25
57 A5 $2 rose red & emer 18.00 27.50
58 A5 $5 choc & emerald 60.00 75.00
Nos. 38-58 (21) 125.35 129.45

UPU Issue

Common Design Types

Inscribed: "Malaya-Negri Sembilan"

Engr.; Name Typo. on 15c, 25c

1949, Oct. 10 *Perf. 13½, 11x11½*

59 CD306 10c rose violet .25 .25
60 CD307 15c indigo 1.40 3.50
61 CD308 25c orange .75 3.00
62 CD309 50c slate 1.10 4.00
Nos. 59-62 (4) 3.50 10.75

Coronation Issue

Common Design Type

1953, June 2 Engr. *Perf. 13½x13*

63 CD312 10c magenta & black 1.40 .65

Types of Kedah with Arms of Negri Sembilan

Perf. 13x12½, 12½x13, 13½ ($1)

1957-63 Engr. Wmk. 314

64 A8 1c black .25 .25
65 A8 2c red orange .25 .25
66 A8 4c dark brown .25 .25
67 A8 5c dk car rose .25 .25
68 A8 8c dark green 2.00 *1.60*
69 A7 10c chocolate 2.00 *.25*
70 A7 20c blue 1.00 *.25*
71 A7 50c ultra & blk ('60) .60 *.25*
a. Perf. 12½ 1.75 *1.50*
72 A8 $1 plum & ultra 4.50 *2.25*
73 A8 $2 red & grn ('63) 20.00 *32.50*
a. Perf. 12½ 15.00 *20.00*
74 A8 $5 ol grn & brn ('62) 27.50 25.00
a. Perf. 12½ 20.00 *26.00*
Nos. 64-74 (11) 58.60 63.10

Negri Sembilan State Crest and Tuanku Munawir A6

1961, Apr. 17 Unwmk. *Perf. 14x13*

75 A6 10s blue & multi .45 *.70*

Installation of Tuanku Munawir as ruler (Yang di-Pertuan Besar) of Negri Sembilan.

Starting in 1965, issues of Negri (Negeri) Sembilan are listed with Malaysia.

OCCUPATION STAMPS

Issued under Japanese Occupation

Stamps and Type of Negri Sembilan, 1935-41, Handstamped in Red, Black, Brown or Violet

1942 Wmk. 4 *Perf. 14*

N1 A4 1c black 25.00 16.00
N2 A4 2c brown org 16.00 17.50
N3 A4 3c green 21.00 21.00
N4 A4 5c chocolate 29.00 27.50
N5 A4 6c rose red 600.00 600.00
N6 A4 6c gray 150.00 150.00
N7 A4 8c gray 87.50 87.50
N8 A4 8c rose red 55.00 47.50
N9 A4 10c dark violet 110.00 110.00
N10 A4 12c ultramarine 900.00 900.00
N11 A4 15c ultramarine 20.00 11.00
N12 A4 25c rose red & dk vio 35.00 40.00
N13 A4 30c org & dk vio 175.00 190.00
N14 A4 40c dk vio & car 750.00 750.00
N15 A4 $1 red & blk, *bl* 140.00 140.00
N16 A4 $5 brn red & grn, *emerald* 325.00 350.00

The 8c rose red is not known to have been issued without overprint.

Some authorities believe Nos. N5 and N7 were not regularly issued.

Stamps of Negri Sembilan, 1935-41, Overprinted in Black

N17 A4 1c black 1.40 1.40
a. Inverted overprint 17.00 27.50
b. Dbl. ovpt., one invtd. 47.50 *67.50*
N18 A4 2c brown orange 1.60 1.40
N19 A4 3c green 1.40 1.00
N20 A4 5c chocolate .90 .90

N21 A4 6c gray 2.00 2.00
a. Inverted overprint *1,000.*
N22 A4 8c rose red 2.75 2.75
N23 A4 10c dk violet 5.50 5.50
N24 A4 15c ultramarine 8.00 4.75
N25 A4 25c rose red & dk vio 2.00 *6.75*
N26 A4 30c org & dk vio 4.00 *5.00*
N27 A4 $1 red & blk, *bl* 140.00 175.00
Nos. N17-N27 (11) 169.55 206.45

The 8c rose red is not known to have been issued without overprint.

Negri Sembilan, Nos. 21, 24 and 29, Overprinted or Surcharged in Black

a

b

c

1943
N28 A4 1c black .65 .65
a. Inverted overprint 17.00 24.00
N29 A4 2c on 5c choc .55 .65
N30 A4 6c on 5c choc .65 .90
a. "6 cts." inverted 350.00 *400.00*
N31 A4 25c rose red & dk violet 2.00 2.75
Nos. N28-N31 (4) 3.85 4.95

The Japanese characters read: "Japanese Postal Service."

PAHANG

pə-'haŋ

LOCATION — On the east coast of the Malay Peninsula, bordering Johore on the south, Perak and Selangor on the west, and Trengganu on the north.
AREA — 13,820 sq. mi.
POP. — 338,210 (1960)
CAPITAL — Kuala Lipis

Stamps of the Straits Settlements Overprinted in Black

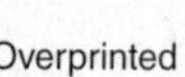
Overprinted

Overprint 16x2¾mm

1889 **Wmk. 2** ***Perf. 14***
1 A2 2c rose 165.00 60.00
2 A3 8c orange 1,800. 2,000.
3 A7 10c slate 225.00 300.00

Overprinted

Overprint 12½x2mm
4 A2 2c rose 15.00 *15.00*

Overprinted

1890 **Overprint 15x2½mm**
5 A2 2c rose 12,750. 3,250.

Overprinted

Overprint 16x2¾mm
6 A2 2c rose 135.00 16.00

Surcharged in Black

a

b

c

d

1891
7 A3 (a) 2c on 24c green 1,200. *1,300.*
8 A3 (b) 2c on 24c green 450.00 *475.00*
9 A3 (c) 2c on 24c green 275.00 *300.00*
10 A3 (d) 2c on 24c green 1,200. *1,300.*
Nos. 7-10 (4) 3,125. 3,375.

A5

1892-95 **Typo.**
11 A5 1c green 5.00 4.00
12 A5 2c rose 5.50 4.00
13 A5 5c blue 12.50 *47.50*
Nos. 11-13 (3) 23.00 *55.50*

For surcharges see Nos. 21-22.

A6

1895-99
14 A6 3c lilac & car rose 10.75 3.75
14A A6 4c lil & car rose ('99) 20.00 19.50
15 A6 5c lilac & olive 55.00 *25.00*
Nos. 14-15 (3) 85.75 *48.25*

For surcharge see No. 28.

Stamps of Perak, 1895-99, Overprinted

1898-99
16 A9 10c lilac & orange 27.50 *32.50*
17 A9 25c green & car rose 95.00 *190.00*
18 A9 50c green & black 500.00 *575.00*
18A A9 50c lilac & black 300.00 425.00

Overprinted

Wmk. 1
19 A10 $1 green & lt grn 425. 700.
20 A10 $5 green & ultra 1,700. 3,250.
Nos. 16-20 (6) 3,048. 5,173.

No. 13 Cut in Half Diagonally & Srchd. in Red & Initials "JFO" in ms.

1897, Aug. 2 **Wmk. 2**
Red Surcharge
21 A5 2c on half of 5c blue *1,750.* *450.*
a. Black surcharge *10,750.* *3,500.*
22 A5 3c on half of 5c blue *1,750.* *450.*
a. Black surcharge *10,750.* *3,500.*
d. Se-tenant pair, #21, 22 *5,500.* *1,200.*

Perak No. 52 Surcharged

1898
25 A9 4c on 8c lilac & blue 4.50 6.50
b. Inverted surcharge *3,250.* 1,500.

Surcharged on pieces of White Paper

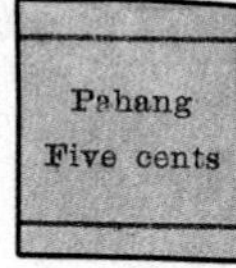

1898 **Without Gum** ***Imperf.***
26 4c black *5,250.*
27 5c black *3,250.*

Pahang No. 15 Surcharged

1899 ***Perf. 14***
28 A6 4c on 5c lilac & olive 25.00 *75.00*

Sultan Abu Bakar — A7

1935-41 **Typo.** **Wmk. 4** ***Perf. 14***
29 A7 1c black ('36) .25 .25
30 A7 2c dp green ('36) 1.40 .25
30A A7 3c green ('41) 10.00 *19.00*
31 A7 4c brown orange .70 .25
32 A7 5c chocolate .70 .25
33 A7 6c rose red ('36) 12.00 *3.50*
34 A7 8c gray 2.00 .25
34A A7 8c rose red ('41) 3.00 *60.00*
35 A7 10c dk violet ('36) 1.75 .25
36 A7 12c ultra ('36) 2.10 2.00
36A A7 15c ultra ('41) 14.00 *65.00*
37 A7 25c rose red & pale vio ('36) 3.00 1.50
38 A7 30c org & dk vio ('36) 1.50 1.25
39 A7 40c dk vio & car 1.25 2.40
40 A7 50c black, *emer* ('36) 2.50 2.00
41 A7 $1 red & blk, *blue* ('36) 2.50 8.00
42 A7 $2 rose red & green ('36) 15.00 *50.00*
43 A7 $5 brn red & grn, *emer* ('36) 6.00 *87.50*
Nos. 29-43 (18) 79.65 *303.65*

The 3c was printed on both ordinary and chalky paper; the 15c only on ordinary paper; other values only on chalky paper.

Values for Nos. 34A used and 36A used are for stamps with legible postmarks dated in 1941.

A 2c brown orange and 6c gray, type A7, exist, but are not known to have been regularly issued.

For overprints see Nos. N1-N21.

Catalogue values for unused stamps in this section, from this point to the end of the section, are for Never Hinged items.

Common Design Types pictured following the introduction.

Silver Wedding Issue
Common Design Types
Inscribed: "Malaya Pahang"
Perf. 14x14½

1948, Dec. 1 **Photo.** **Wmk. 4**
44 CD304 10c purple .50 .55
Perf. 11½x11
Engraved; Name Typopgraphed
45 CD305 $5 green 27.50 37.50

UPU Issue
Common Design Types
Inscribed: "Malaya-Pahang"
Engr.; Name Typo. on 15c, 25c

1949, Oct. 10 ***Perf. 13½, 11x11½***
46 CD306 10c rose violet .30 .25
47 CD307 15c indigo 1.10 1.50
48 CD308 25c orange .60 *2.50*
49 CD309 50c slate 1.00 3.00
Nos. 46-49 (4) 3.00 7.25

Sultan Abu Bakar — A8

Perf. 18
1950, June 1 **Wmk. 4** **Typo.**
50 A8 1c black .30 .30
51 A8 2c orange .30 .30
52 A8 3c green .30 .80
53 A8 4c chocolate 2.25 .35
54 A8 6c gray .50 .35
55 A8 8c rose red .50 *2.00*
56 A8 10c plum .30 .30
57 A8 15c ultramarine .75 .35
58 A8 20c dk green & blk 1.00 *3.00*
59 A8 25c org & rose lilac .50 .30
60 A8 40c dk vio & rose red 2.25 *8.50*
61 A8 50c dp ultra & black 1.50 .35
62 A8 $1 vio brn & ultra 3.50 3.50
63 A8 $2 rose red & emer 16.00 30.00
64 A8 $5 choc & emer 65.00 *90.00*

1952-55
65 A8 5c rose violet .50 *.70*
66 A8 8c green 1.25 1.10
67 A8 12c rose red 1.50 1.25
68 A8 20c ultramarine 2.50 .30
69 A8 30c plum & rose red ('55) 2.75 .50
70 A8 35c dk vio & rose red 1.00 .35
Nos. 50-70 (21) 104.45 *144.60*

Coronation Issue
Common Design Type

1953, June 2 **Engr.** ***Perf. 13½x13***
71 CD312 10c magenta & black 2.25 .25

Types of Kedah with Portrait of Sultan Abu Bakar
Perf. 13x12½, 12½x13, 13½ ($1)

1957-62 **Engr.** **Wmk. 314**
72 A8 1c black .25 .25
73 A8 2c red orange .25 .25
74 A8 4c dark brown .25 .25
75 A8 5c dark car rose .25 .25
76 A8 8c dark green 2.25 2.25
77 A7 10c chocolate 1.25 .25
78 A7 20c blue 2.75 .25
79 A7 50c ultra & blk ('60) 1.00 .25
a. Perf. 12½ .60 *1.00*
80 A8 $1 plum & ultra 10.00 2.75
81 A8 $2 red & green ('62) 9.00 *22.50*
a. Perf. 12½ 7.50 *11.00*
82 A8 $5 ol grn & brn ('60) 15.00 *24.00*
a. Perf. 12½ 14.00 *17.50*
Nos. 72-82 (11) 42.25 53.25

Starting in 1965, issues of Pahang are listed with Malaysia.

OCCUPATION STAMPS

Issued under Japanese Occupation

Stamps of Pahang, 1935-41, Handstamped in Black, Red, Brown or Violet

1942	Wmk. 4		*Perf. 14*	
N1	A7	1c black	60.00	55.00
N1A	A7	3c green	625.00	350.00
N2	A7	5c chocolate	22.50	14.50
N3	A7	8c rose red	30.00	9.00
N3A	A7	8c gray	1,650.	1,100.
N4	A7	10c dk violet	575.00	225.00
N5	A7	12c ultramarine	3,000.	2,900.
N6	A7	15c ultramarine	190.00	130.00
N7	A7	25c rose red & pale vio	29.00	30.00
N8	A7	30c org & dk vio	22.50	35.00
N9	A7	40c dk vio & car	32.50	40.00
N10	A7	50c blk, *emerald*	1,875.	1,900.
N11	A7	$1 red & blk, *bl*	350.00	350.00
N12	A7	$5 brown red & grn, *emer*	875.00	1,000.

Stamps of Pahang, 1935-41, Overprinted in Black

N13	A7	1c black	3.50	5.00
N14	A7	5c chocolate	2.00	2.00
N15	A7	8c rose red	40.00	3.75
N16	A7	10c violet brown	20.00	11.00
N17	A7	12c ultramarine	4.75	27.50
N18	A7	25c rose red & pale vio	9.50	*42.50*
N19	A7	30c org & dk vio	4.00	*20.00*
		Nos. N13-N19 (7)	83.75	*111.75*

Pahang No. 32 Overprinted and Surcharged in Black

e

f

1943

N20	A7(e) 6c on 5c chocolate	1.40	1.40
N21	A7(f) 6c on 5c chocolate	2.50	3.00

The Japanese characters read: "Japanese Postal Service."

PENANG

pə-naŋ

LOCATION — An island off the west coast of the Malay Peninsula, plus a coastal strip called Province Wellesley.
AREA — 400 sq. mi.
POP. — 616,254 (1960)
CAPITAL — Georgetown

Catalogue values for unused stamps in this section are for Never Hinged items.

Common Design Types pictured following the introduction.

Silver Wedding Issue
Common Design Types
Inscribed: "Malaya Penang"

Perf. 14x14½

1948, Dec. 1	Wmk. 4		Photo.	
1	CD304	10c purple	.50	.30

Perf. 11½x11

Engraved; Name Typographed

2	CD305	$5 lt brown	40.00	37.50

Type of Straits Settlements, 1937-41, Inscribed "Penang"

1949-52			*Perf. 18*	
3	A29	1c black	1.50	.30
4	A29	2c orange	1.50	.30
5	A29	3c green	.60	1.25
6	A29	4c chocolate	.50	.25
7	A29	5c rose vio ('52)	4.25	4.00
8	A29	6c gray	1.50	.30
9	A29	8c rose red	1.25	*5.00*
10	A29	8c green ('52)	4.00	3.00
11	A29	10c plum	.50	.25
12	A29	12c rose red ('52)	4.50	9.00
13	A29	15c ultramarine	2.00	.40
14	A29	20c dk grn & blk	2.75	1.50
15	A29	20c ultra ('52)	3.25	1.50
16	A29	25c org & rose lilac	3.00	1.25
17	A29	35c dk vio & rose red ('52)	3.25	1.50
18	A29	40c dk vio & rose red	4.25	*15.00*
19	A29	50c ultra & black	5.50	.30
20	A29	$1 vio brn & ultra	20.00	3.00
21	A29	$2 rose red & emer	26.00	2.50
22	A29	$5 choc & emer	52.50	3.75
		Nos. 3-22 (20)	142.60	*54.35*

UPU Issue
Common Design Types
Inscribed: "Malaya-Penang"

Engr.; Name Typo. on 15c, 25c

1949, Oct. 10		*Perf. 13½, 11x11½*		
23	CD306	10c rose violet	.25	.25
24	CD307	15c indigo	2.50	*3.75*
25	CD308	25c orange	.60	*3.75*
26	CD309	50c slate	1.75	*4.00*
		Nos. 23-26 (4)	5.10	11.75

Coronation Issue
Common Design Type

1953, June 2	Engr.	*Perf. 13½x13*		
27	CD312	10c magenta & black	1.75	.30

Type of Malacca, 1954

1954-55	Wmk. 4	Typo.	*Perf. 18*	
29	A1	1c black	.25	.85
30	A1	2c orange	.60	.40
31	A1	4c chocolate	1.25	.25
32	A1	5c rose violet	2.25	4.25
33	A1	6c gray	.25	1.00
34	A1	8c green	.30	*4.00*
35	A1	10c plum	.25	.25
36	A1	12c rose red	.35	4.00
37	A1	20c ultramarine	.60	.25
38	A1	25c orange & plum	.40	.25
39	A1	30c plum & rose red ('55)	.40	.25
40	A1	35c vio brn & rose red	.80	.95
41	A1	50c ultra & black	.65	.25
42	A1	$1 vio brn & ultra	2.75	.35
43	A1	$2 rose red & grn	15.00	4.25
44	A1	$5 choc & emerald	47.50	4.25
		Nos. 29-44 (16)	73.60	25.80

Types of Kedah with Portrait of Queen Elizabeth II

Perf. 13x12½, 12½x13

1957	Engr.		Wmk. 314	
45	A8	1c black	.30	1.50
46	A8	2c red orange	.30	1.25
47	A8	4c dark brown	.30	.25
48	A8	5c dk car rose	.30	.50
49	A8	8c dark green	2.50	2.75
50	A7	10c chocolate	.40	.25
51	A7	20c blue	1.00	.60

Perf. 12½, 13½ ($1)

52	A7	50c ultra & black	1.75	.85
53	A8	$1 plum & ultra	8.50	1.00
54	A8	$2 red & green	22.50	18.00
55	A8	$5 ol green & brown	27.50	15.00
		Nos. 45-55 (11)	65.35	41.95

Types of Kedah, 1957 with Penang State Crest and Areca-nut Palm Replacing Portrait of Elizabeth II

Perf. 13x12½, 12½x13, 13½ ($1)

1960, Mar. 15	Engr.		Wmk. 314	
56	A8	1c black	.25	*1.75*
57	A8	2c red orange	.25	*1.75*
58	A8	4c dark brown	.25	.25
59	A8	5c dk car rose	.25	.25
60	A8	8c dark green	3.00	*5.25*
61	A7	10c violet brown	.35	.25
62	A7	20c blue	.55	.25
63	A7	50c ultra & black	.35	.25
64	A8	$1 plum & ultra	7.50	1.90
65	A8	$2 red & green	8.00	7.25
		Revenue cancel		.20
66	A8	$5 ol green & brown	14.00	9.50
		Nos. 56-66 (11)	34.75	28.65

Starting in 1965, issues of Penang (Pulau Pinang) are listed with Malaysia.

OCCUPATION STAMPS

Issued under Japanese Occupation

Stamps of Straits Settlements, 1937-41, Overprinted in Red or Black

1942	Wmk. 4		*Perf. 14*	
N1	A29	1c black (R)	10.00	4.00
	a.	Inverted overprint	725.00	725.00
	b.	Double overprint	350.00	350.00
N2	A29	2c brown orange	12.00	5.25
	a.	Inverted overprint	180.00	
	b.	Double overprint	675.00	
N3	A29	3c green (R)	10.00	*10.00*
	a.	Double overprint, one inverted	475.00	
N4	A29	5c brown (R)	4.75	10.00
	a.	Double overprint	675.00	525.00
	b.	"N PPON" for "NIPPON"	220.00	
N5	A29	8c gray (R)	3.00	1.60
	a.	Double overprint, one inverted	625.00	
	b.	"N PPON" for "NIPPON"	75.00	70.00
N6	A29	10c dull vio (R)	2.00	2.50
	a.	Double overprint	500.00	500.00
	b.	Double overprint, one inverted	450.00	450.00
N7	A29	12c ultra (R)	5.75	*25.00*
	a.	Double overprint	500.00	
	b.	Double overprint, one inverted	750.00	725.00
	c.	"N PPON" for "NIPPON"	575.00	
N8	A29	15c ultra (R)	2.00	5.00
	a.	Inverted overprint	450.00	450.00
	b.	Double overprint	675.00	675.00
	c.	"N PPON" for "NIPPON"	120.00	150.00
N9	A29	40c dk vio & rose red	9.00	*25.00*
N10	A29	50c black, *emer* (R)	5.25	*42.50*
N11	A29	$1 red & blk, *bl*	14.00	*55.00*
	a.	Inverted overprint	*1,400.*	
N12	A29	$2 rose red & gray grn	70.00	*120.00*
N13	A29	$5 grn & red, *grn*	900.00	950.00
		Nos. N1-N13 (13)	1,048.	1,256.

Stamps of Straits Settlements Handstamped Okugawa Seal in Red

1942	Wmk. 4		*Perf. 14*	
N14	A29	1c black	14.00	18.00
N15	A29	2c brown orange	27.50	30.00
N16	A29	3c green	23.00	30.00
N17	A29	5c brown	35.00	42.50
N18	A29	8c gray	42.50	55.00
N19	A29	10c dull violet	57.50	60.00
N20	A29	12c ultramarine	55.00	60.00
N21	A29	15c ultramarine	65.00	65.00
N22	A29	40c dk vio & rose red	125.00	130.00
N23	A29	50c blk, *emerald*	230.00	260.00
N24	A29	$1 red & blk, *bl*	325.00	350.00
N25	A29	$2 rose red & gray grn	1,000.	850.00
N26	A29	$5 grn & red, *grn*	*3,500.*	*1,800.*
		Nos. N14-N26 (13)	5,500.	3,751.

Uchibori Seal Handstamped in Red

N14a	A29	1c	215.00	180.00
N15a	A29	2c	215.00	150.00
N16a	A29	3c	130.00	130.00
N17a	A29	5c	*3,750.*	*3,750.*
N18a	A29	8c	130.00	130.00
N19a	A29	10c	240.00	240.00
N20a	A29	12c	150.00	165.00
N21a	A29	15c	170.00	175.00
		Nos. N14a-N21a (8)	5,000.	4,920.

PERAK

ˈper-ə-ˌak

LOCATION — On the west coast of the Malay Peninsula.
AREA — 7,980 sq. mi.
POP. — 1,327,120 (1960)
CAPITAL — Taiping

Straits Settlements No. 10 Handstamped in Black

1878	Wmk. 1	*Perf. 14*	
1	A2 2c brown	2,250.	2,300.

Overprinted

Overprint 17x3½mm Wide

1880-81			
2	A2 2c brown	50.00	*90.00*

Overprinted

Overprint 12 to 13½mm wide

3	A2 2c brown ('81)	200.00	*200.00*

Same Overprint on Straits Settlements Nos. 40, 41a

1883		Wmk. 2	
4	A2 2c brown	26.50	*90.00*
a.	Double overprint	750.00	
5	A2 2c rose	50.00	*70.00*
c.	Double overprint	775.00	

Overprinted

Overprint 14 to 15½mm Wide

6	A2 2c rose	5.50	4.00
a.	Inverted overprint	475.00	600.00
b.	Double overprint	700.00	700.00

For surcharge, see No. 19E

Overprinted

Overprint 12¾ to 14mm Wide

1886-90			
7	A2 2c rose	2.50	*8.00*
a.	"FERAK" corrected by pen	450.00	*650.00*

Overprinted

Overprint 10x1¾mm

8	A2 2c rose	30.00	*62.50*

1891

Overprint 13mm long

9	A2 2c bright rose	*3,900.*	

Overprinted

Overprint 12-12½x2¾mm

10	A2 2c rose	15.50	*57.50*
a.	Double overprint	1,650.	

Overprinted

Overprint 10½-10¾x2½mm

11	A2	2c rose	225.00	*230.00*

Overprinted

Overprint 13x2¾mm

11A	A2	2c rose	3,750.	

Straits Settlements Nos. 11, 41a, 42 Surcharged in Black or Blue

q r

s t

12	A2(q)	2c on 4c rose, as #3 ('83)	750.00	350.00
13	A2(t)	1c on 2c rose	350.00	150.00
a.		Without period after "CENT" ('90)	—	300.00
14	A2(r)	1c on 2c rose	75.00	92.50
a.		Without period after "PERAK"	850.00	850.00
b.		Double surcharge	1,250.	
15	A2(s)	1c on 2c rose (Bl)	75.00	85.00
15A	A2(s)	1c on 2c rose (Bk)	2,150.	1,600.

In type "r" PERAK is 11½ to 14mm wide.

Surcharged in Black

16	A2	1c on 2c rose	210.00	210.00
a.		Double surcharge	*2,000.*	2,000.

Surcharged

18	A2	1c on 2c rose	*3,250.*	*3,500.*
b.		Double surcharge, one inverted		

Surcharged

18A	A2	1c on 2c rose	1,750.	1,000.

Surcharged

19	A2	1c on 2c rose	4.25	*20.00*
a.		Double surcharge, one inverted		
b.		Inverted surcharge		
c.		"One" inverted		*3,750.*
d.		Double surcharge		*1,400.*

No. 6 surcharged "1 CENT" in Italic Serifed Capital Letters

1886

19E	A2	1c on 2c rose	*4,750.*	*3,750.*

Straits Settlements No. 41a Surcharged

u v

w x

y z

h

1889-90

20	A2(u)	1c on 2c rose	4.00	*10.00*
a.		Italic Roman "K" in "PERAK"	37.50	*57.50*
b.		Double surcharge	*1,400.*	
21	A2(v)	1c on 2c rose	800.00	*975.00*
23	A2(w)	1c on 2c rose	27.50	*55.00*
a.		"PREAK"	900.00	*1,100.*
24	A2(x)	1c on 2c rose	150.00	*175.00*
25	A2(y)	1c on 2c rose	17.50	*27.50*
26	A2(z)	1c on 2c rose	18.00	*27.50*
27	A2(h)	1c on 2c rose	37.50	*57.50*

Straits Settlements Nos. 41a, 48, 54 Surcharged in Black

a b

c d

e f

g

1891 **Wmk. 2**

28	A2(a)	1c on 2c rose	2.75	15.00
a.		Bar omitted	215.00	
29	A2(a)	1c on 6c violet	60.00	42.50
30	A3(b)	2c on 24c green	32.50	16.50
31	A2(c)	1c on 2c rose	9.75	52.50
a.		Bar omitted	*1,000.*	
32	A2(d)	1c on 2c rose	2.75	20.00
a.		Bar omitted	450.00	
33	A2(d)	1c on 6c violet	110.00	95.00
34	A3(d)	2c on 24c green	85.00	42.50
35	A2(e)	1c on 2c rose	9.75	50.00
a.		Bar omitted	*1,000.*	
36	A2(e)	1c on 6c violet	210.00	210.00
37	A3(e)	2c on 24c green	140.00	80.00
38	A2(f)	1c on 6c violet	210.00	200.00
39	A3(f)	2c on 24c green	140.00	95.00
40	A2(g)	1c on 6c violet	210.00	200.00
41	A3(g)	2c on 24c green	140.00	95.00
		Nos. 28-41 (14)	1,363.	1,214.

A7

1892-95 **Typo.** ***Perf. 14***

42	A7	1c green	2.40	.45
43	A7	2c rose	1.80	.45
44	A7	2c orange ('95)	1.10	*9.50*
45	A7	5c blue	3.50	8.00
		Nos. 42-45 (4)	8.80	*18.40*

For overprint see No. O10.

Type of 1892 Surcharged in Black

1895

46	A7	3c on 5c rose	4.25	5.50

A9 A10

1895-99 **Wmk. 2** ***Perf. 14***

47	A9	1c lilac & green	3.25	.60
48	A9	2c lilac & brown	3.50	.60
49	A9	3c lilac & car rose	4.50	.60
50	A9	4c lil & car rose ('99)	20.00	7.50
51	A9	5c lilac & olive	12.00	.80
52	A9	8c lilac & blue	50.00	.75
53	A9	10c lilac & orange	17.00	.65
54	A9	25c grn & car rose ('96)	225.00	14.00
55	A9	50c lilac & black	52.50	52.50
56	A9	50c grn & blk ('99)	240.00	190.00

Wmk. 1

57	A10	$1 green & lt grn	325.00	225.00
58	A10	$2 grn & car rose ('96)	450.00	375.00
59	A10	$3 green & ol ('96)	650.00	575.00
60	A10	$5 green & ultra	675.00	625.00
61	A10	$25 grn & org ('96)	11,000.	4,500.
		Nos. 47-57 (11)	952.75	493.00

For surcharges and overprint see Nos. 62-68, O11, Malaya Nos. 9-13A.

Stamps of 1895-99 Surcharged in Black

i k

m

n

1900 **Wmk. 2**

62	A9(i)	1c on 2c lilac & brown	1.00	2.75
63	A9(k)	1c on 4c lilac & car rose	1.00	17.50
a.		Double surcharge	1,350.	
64	A9(i)	1c on 5c lilac & ol	3.25	22.50
65	A9(i)	3c on 8c lilac & blue	13.50	19.00
a.		No period after "Cent"	225.00	*325.00*
b.		Double surcharge	550.00	625.00
66	A9(i)	3c on 50c green & black	6.00	12.50
a.		No period after "Cent"	150.00	*240.00*

Wmk. 1

67	A10(m)	3c on $1 grn & lt green	60.00	*160.00*
a.		Double surcharge	1,650.	
b.		A10(n) Thin "t" in "Cent."	325.00	*550.00*
c.		As "b," double surcharge	3,000.	
68	A10(m)	3c on $2 grn & car rose	52.50	*90.00*
		Nos. 62-68 (7)	137.25	*324.25*

Sultan Iskandar — A14

1935-37 **Typo.** **Wmk. 4**

Chalky Paper

69	A14	1c black ('36)	3.50	.25
70	A14	2c dp green ('36)	3.50	.25
71	A14	4c brown orange	3.50	.25
72	A14	5c chocolate	.80	.25
73	A14	6c rose red ('37)	12.50	6.50
74	A14	8c gray	1.00	.25
75	A14	10c dk vio ('36)	1.00	.25
76	A14	12c ultra ('36)	4.75	1.00
77	A14	25c rose red & pale vio ('36)	3.50	1.00
78	A14	30c org & dark vio ('36)	5.00	1.50
79	A14	40c dk vio & car	8.00	8.00
80	A14	50c blk, *emer* ('36)	10.00	1.75
81	A14	$1 red & blk, *bl* ('36)	3.00	1.40
82	A14	$2 rose red & green ('36)	45.00	8.00
83	A14	$5 brn red & grn, *emer* ('36)	175.00	37.50
		Nos. 69-83 (15)	280.05	68.15
		Set, never hinged	200.00	

Sultan Iskandar — A15

1938-41

84	A15	1c black ('39)	7.00	.25
85	A15	2c dp green ('39)	4.50	.25
85A	A15	2c brn org, thin, striated paper ('41)	1.75	*25.00*
85B	A15	3c green ('41)	1.50	18.00
a.		Ordinary paper	5.50	10.50
86	A15	4c brn org ('39)	20.00	.25
87	A15	5c choc ('39)	3.50	.25
88	A15	6c rose red ('39)	14.00	.25
89	A15	8c gray	16.00	.25
89A	A15	8c rose red, thin, striated paper ('41)	.55	*95.00*
90	A15	10c dk violet	18.00	.25
91	A15	12c ultra, ordinary paper	13.00	2.00
91A	A15	15c ultra ('41)	2.25	*20.00*
92	A15	25c rose red & pale vio ('39)	27.50	4.00
93	A15	30c org & dk vio, chalky paper	5.00	3.00
94	A15	40c dk vio & rose red	27.50	3.00

95 A15 50c blk, *emerald* 17.50 1.25
96 A15 $1 red & blk, *bl* ('40) 75.00 32.50
97 A15 $2 rose red & grn ('40) 100.00 85.00
98 A15 $5 red, *emer* ('40) 160.00 *525.00*
Nos. 84-98 (19) 514.55 *815.50*
Set, never hinged 1,325.
Never hinged 575.00

For overprints see Nos. N1-N40.

Catalogue values for unused stamps in this section, from this point to the end of the section, are for Never Hinged items.

Common Design Types pictured following the introduction.

Silver Wedding Issue
Common Design Types
Inscribed: "Malaya Perak"

1948, Dec. 1 Photo. *Perf. 14x14½*
99 CD304 10c purple .30 .25

Perf. 11½x11
Engraved; Name Typographed
100 CD305 $5 green 27.50 37.50

UPU Issue
Common Design Types
Inscribed: "Malaya-Perak"
Engr.; Name Typo. on 15c, 25c
Perf. 13½, 11x11½

1949, Oct. 10 Wmk. 4
101 CD306 10c rose violet .25 .25
102 CD307 15c indigo 1.50 2.00
103 CD308 25c orange .40 5.00
104 CD309 50c slate 1.50 3.50
Nos. 101-104 (4) 3.65 10.75

Sultan Yussuf Izuddin Shah — A16

1950, Aug. 17 Typo. *Perf. 18*
105 A16 1c black .25 .40
106 A16 2c orange .25 .40
107 A16 3c green 3.00 1.40
108 A16 4c chocolate .75 .40
109 A16 6c gray .40 .40
110 A16 8c rose red 1.60 2.25
111 A16 10c plum .25 .40
112 A16 15c ultramarine 1.10 .50
113 A16 20c dk grn & blk 1.60 .75
114 A16 25c org & plum .90 .30
115 A16 40c vio brn & rose red 5.00 7.00
116 A16 50c dp ultra & blk 5.00 .30
117 A16 $1 vio brn & ultra 7.00 1.10
118 A16 $2 rose red & emer 17.00 7.50
119 A16 $5 choc & emerald 42.50 22.50

1952-55
120 A16 5c rose violet .50 2.00
121 A16 8c green 1.40 1.25
122 A16 12c rose red 1.40 5.00
123 A16 20c ultramarine 1.10 .30
124 A16 30c plum & rose red ('55) 2.25 .30
125 A16 35c dk vio & rose red 1.40 .40
Nos. 105-125 (21) 94.65 54.85

Coronation Issue
Common Design Type

1953 Engr. *Perf. 13½x13*
126 CD312 10c magenta & black 1.60 .25

Types of Kedah with Portrait of Sultan Yussuf Izuddin Shah
Perf. 13x12½, 12½x13, 13½ ($1)

1957-61 Engr. Wmk. 314
127 A8 1c black .25 .30
128 A8 2c red orange .45 1.00
129 A8 4c dark brown .25 .25
130 A8 5c dk car rose .25 .25
131 A8 8c dark green 2.50 4.00
132 A7 10c chocolate 2.25 .25
133 A7 20c blue 2.25 .25
134 A7 50c ultra & blk ('60) .45 .25
a. Perf. 12½ .60 1.00
135 A8 $1 plum & ultra 7.50 .50
136 A8 $2 red & grn ('61) 7.00 4.25
a. Perf. 12½ 5.00 5.00
137 A8 $5 ol grn & brn ('60) 14.00 9.00
a. Perf. 12½ 15.00 13.00
Nos. 127-137 (11) 37.15 20.30

Starting with 1963, issues of Perak are listed with Malaysia.

OFFICIAL STAMPS

Stamps and Types of Straits Settlements Overprinted in Black

1890 Wmk. 1 *Perf. 14*
O1 A3 12c blue 325.00 400.00
O2 A3 24c green 775.00 *900.00*

Wmk. 2
O3 A2 2c rose 10.00 10.00
a. No period after "S" 100.00 125.00
b. Double overprint 1,100. 1,100.
O4 A2 4c brown 37.50 40.00
a. No period after "S" 210.00 *275.00*
O5 A2 6c violet 45.00 60.00
O6 A3 8c orange 55.00 67.50
O7 A7 10c slate 80.00 80.00
O8 A3 12c vio brown 275.00 350.00
O9 A3 24c green 225.00 *240.00*

P.G.S. stands for Perak Government Service.

Perak No. 45 Overprinted

1894
O10 A7 5c blue 140.00 1.25
a. Inverted overprint 1,750. 525.00

Same Overprint on No. 51

1897
O11 A9 5c lilac & olive 3.50 .60
a. Double overprint 750.00 450.00

OCCUPATION STAMPS

Issued under Japanese Occupation

Stamps of Perak, 1938-41, Handstamped in Black, Red, Brown or Violet

1942 Wmk. 4 *Perf. 14*
N1 A15 1c black 75.00 50.00
N2 A15 2c brn orange 40.00 21.00
N3 A15 3c green 35.00 37.50
N4 A15 5c chocolate 12.50 11.00
N5 A15 8c gray 125.00 65.00
N6 A15 8c rose red 50.00 50.00
N7 A15 10c dk violet 27.50 27.50
N8 A15 12c ultramarine 300.00 275.00
N9 A15 15c ultramarine 25.00 35.00
N10 A15 25c rose red & pale vio 27.50 30.00
N11 A15 30c org & dk vio 35.00 40.00
N12 A15 40c dk vio & rose red 900.00 425.00
N13 A15 50c blk, *emer* 60.00 *60.00*
N14 A15 $1 red & blk, *bl* 675.00 450.00
N15 A15 $2 rose red & grn *5,750.* *6,000.*
N16 A15 $5 red, *emer* 650.00

Some authorities claim No. N6 was not regularly issued. This overprint also exists on No. 85

Stamps of Perak, 1938-41, Overprinted in Black

N16A A15 1c black *150.00*
N17 A15 2c brn org 4.50 4.50
a. Inverted overprint 75.00 75.00
N18 A15 3c green 1.50 1.60
a. Inverted overprint 27.50 *30.00*
N18B A15 5c chocolate *135.00*
N19 A15 8c rose red 1.50 .55
a. Inverted overprint 4.50 *10.00*
b. Dbl. ovpt., one invtd. 250.00 *275.00*
c. Pair, one without ovpt. 500.00
N20 A15 10c dk violet 22.50 9.50
N21 A15 15c ultramarine 16.00 6.00
N21A A15 30c org & dk vio *140.00*
N22 A15 50c blk, *emerald* 4.00 *8.00*
N23 A15 $1 red & blk, *bl* 625.00 *675.00*
N24 A15 $5 red, *emerald* 100.00 100.00
a. Inverted overprint 350.00 *425.00*

Some authorities claim Nos. N16A, N18B and N21A were not regularly issued.

Overprinted on Perak No. 87 and Surcharged in Black "2 Cents"
N25 A15 2c on 5c chocolate 2.00 5.00

Perak Nos. 84 and 89A Overprinted in Black

N26 A15 1c black 7.00 *11.00*
a. Inverted overprint 20.00 *47.50*
N27 A15 8c rose red 12.50 3.75
a. Inverted overprint 13.50 *27.50*

Overprinted on Perak No. 87 and Surcharged in Black "2 Cents"
N28 A15 2c on 5c chocolate 2.75 *6.50*
a. Inverted overprint 17.50 *50.00*
b. As "a," "2 Cents" omitted 52.50 *75.00*

Stamps of Perak, 1938-41, Overprinted or Surcharged in Black

n

No. N31

No. N32

1943
N29 A15 1c black 1.25 1.75
N30 A15 2c brn orange 35.00 35.00
N31 A15 2c on 5c choc 1.00 1.00
a. "2 Cents" inverted 35.00 40.00
b. Entire surcharge inverted 40.00 45.00
N32 A15 2c on 5c choc 1.40 1.40
a. Vertical characters invtd. 35.00 40.00
b. Entire surcharge inverted 35.00 40.00
N33 A15 3c green 37.50 37.50
N34 A15 5c chocolate 1.00 1.00
a. Inverted overprint 50.00 60.00
N35 A15 8c gray 35.00 35.00
N36 A15 8c rose red 1.25 3.50
a. Inverted overprint 35.00 40.00
N37 A15 10c dk violet 1.25 1.50
N38 A15 30c org & dk vio 5.50 10.00
N39 A15 50c blk, *emerald* 5.50 32.50
N40 A15 $5 red, *emerald* 90.00 175.00
Nos. N29-N40 (12) 215.65 335.15

No. N34 was also used in the Shan States of Burma. The Japanese characters read: "Japanese Postal Service."

Some authorities claim Nos. N30, N33 and N35 were not regularly issued.

PERLIS

'per-ləs

LOCATION — On the west coast of the Malay peninsula, adjoining Siam and Kedah.
AREA — 310 sq. mi.
POP. — 97,645 (1960)
CAPITAL — Kangar

Catalogue values for unused stamps in this section are for Never Hinged items.

Common Design Types pictured following the introduction.

Silver Wedding Issue
Common Design Types
Inscribed: "Malaya Perlis"
Perf. 14x14½

1948, Dec. 1 Photo. Wmk. 4
1 CD304 10c purple 1.00 *3.00*

Engraved; Name Typographed
Perf. 11½x11
2 CD305 $5 lt brown 32.50 *55.00*

UPU Issue
Common Design Types
Inscribed: "Malaya-Perlis"
Engr.; Name Typo. on 15c, 25c

1949, Oct. 10 *Perf. 13½, 11x11½*
3 CD306 10c rose violet .40 *2.00*
4 CD307 15c indigo 1.40 *4.50*
5 CD308 25c orange .65 *3.50*
6 CD309 50c slate 1.50 *4.25*
Nos. 3-6 (4) 3.95 14.25

Raja Syed Putra — A1

Perf. 18

1951, Mar. 26 Wmk. 4 Typo.
7 A1 1c black .25 *1.00*
8 A1 2c orange .75 .70
9 A1 3c green 1.75 *5.25*
10 A1 4c chocolate 1.75 1.50
11 A1 6c gray 1.50 2.50
12 A1 8c rose red 3.75 7.50
13 A1 10c plum 1.25 .50
14 A1 15c ultramarine 5.00 8.50
15 A1 20c dk green & blk 4.50 11.50
16 A1 25c org & rose lilac 2.25 3.75
17 A1 40c dk vio & rose red 5.00 *29.00*
18 A1 50c ultra & black 4.75 *7.00*
19 A1 $1 vio brn & ultra 10.00 *27.50*
20 A1 $2 rose red & emer 20.00 *60.00*
21 A1 $5 choc & emerald 70.00 *125.00*

1952-55
22 A1 5c rose violet .75 *3.75*
23 A1 8c green 2.75 *4.50*
24 A1 12c rose red 2.00 *6.25*
25 A1 20c ultramarine 1.25 1.75
26 A1 30c plum & rose red ('55) 2.75 *15.00*
27 A1 35c dk vio & rose red 3.00 *8.50*
Nos. 7-27 (21) 145.00 330.95

Coronation Issue
Common Design Type

1953, June 2 Engr. *Perf. 13½x13*
28 CD312 10c magenta & black 1.75 *4.00*

Types of Kedah with Portrait of Raja Syed Putra
Perf. 13x12½, 12½x13, 12½ ($2, $5), 13½ ($1)

1957-62 Engr. Wmk. 314
29 A8 1c black .25 *.40*
30 A8 2c red orange .25 *.40*
31 A8 4c dark brown .25 .25
32 A8 5c dk car rose .25 .25
33 A8 8c dark green 2.50 2.25
34 A7 10c chocolate 1.50 *3.00*
35 A7 20c blue 3.50 *5.00*
36 A7 50c ultra & blk ('62) 3.50 *4.75*
a. Perf. 12½ 1.50 *4.00*
37 A8 $1 plum & ultra 10.00 *14.00*
38 A8 $2 red & green 10.00 *10.00*
39 A8 $5 ol green & brown 15.00 *13.00*
Nos. 29-39 (11) 47.00 *53.30*

Starting in 1965, issues of Perlis are listed with Malaysia.

SELANGOR

sə-'laŋ-ər

LOCATION — South of Perak on the west coast of the Malay Peninsula.
AREA — 3,160 sq. mi.
POP. — 1,012,891 (1960)
CAPITAL — Kuala Lumpur

Stamps of the Straits Settlements Overprinted

Handstamped in Black or Red

1878 Wmk. 1 *Perf. 14*

1 A2 2c brown (Bk) —

Wmk. 2 *Perf.*

2 A2 2c brown (R) 600.00

The authenticity of Nos. 1-2 is questioned.

Overprinted in Black

1882

3 A2 2c brown — 3,300.

Overprinted

Overprint 16 to 16¾mm Wide

1881 Wmk. 1

5 A2 2c brown 140.00 140.00
  a. Double overprint

Overprint 16 to 17mm Wide

1882-83 Wmk. 2

"S" wide, all other letters narrow

6 A2 2c brown 200.00 160.00
7 A2 2c rose 160.00 125.00

Overprinted

Overprint 14¼x3mm

8 A2 2c rose 11.50 *24.00*
  a. Double overprint 975.00 850.00

Overprinted

Overprint 14½ to 15½mm Wide

1886-89

9 A2 2c rose 42.50 *55.00*

Overprinted

Overprint 16½x1¾mm

9A A2 2c rose 67.50 72.50
  b. Double overprint 1,000.

Overprinted

Overprint 15½ to 17mm Wide

With Period

10 A2 2c rose 140.00 90.00

Without Period

11 A2 2c rose 14.50 3.25

Same Overprint, but Vertically

12 A2 2c rose 22.50 *37.50*

Overprinted

12A A2 2c rose 150.00 3.75

Overprinted

Overprint 17mm Wide

13 A2 2c rose 1,700. *1,850.*

Overprinted

14 A2 2c rose 400.00 175.00

Overprinted Vertically

1889

15 A2 2c rose 725.00 40.00

Overprinted Vertically

Overprint 19 to 20¾mm Wide

16 A2 2c rose 325.00 95.00

Similar Overprint, but Diagonally

17 A2 2c rose 3,000.

Overprinted Vertically

18 A2 2c rose 90.00 6.75

Same Overprint Horizontally

18A A2 2c rose *4,500.*

Surcharged in Black

a b c d

e

1891

19 A3 (a) 2c on 24c green 40.00 *75.00*
20 A3 (b) 2c on 24c green 225.00 *275.00*
21 A3 (c) 2c on 24c green 225.00 *250.00*
22 A3 (d) 2c on 24c green 125.00 *150.00*
23 A3 (e) 2c on 24c green 225.00 *275.00*
  Nos. 19-23 (5) 840.00 1,025.

No. 22a occurred ijn the first printing in one position (R. 8/3) in the sheet.

A6

1891-95 Typo. Wmk. 2

24 A6 1c green 1.75 .30
25 A6 2c rose 4.00 1.25
26 A6 2c orange ('95) 3.00 1.00
27 A6 5c blue 27.50 5.25
  Nos. 24-27 (4) 36.25 7.80

Type of 1891 Surcharged

1894

28 A6 3c on 5c rose 5.00 .70

A8

A9

1895-99 Wmk. 2 *Perf. 14*

29 A8 3c lilac & car rose 7.00 .35
30 A8 5c lilac & olive 8.50 .35
31 A8 8c lilac & blue 55.00 8.50
32 A8 10c lilac & orange 13.50 2.50
33 A8 25c grn & car rose 90.00 60.00
34 A8 50c lilac & black 80.00 29.00
35 A8 50c green & black 475.00 140.00

Wmk. 1

36 A9 $1 green & lt grn 65.00 150.00
37 A9 $2 grn & car rose 250.00 300.00
38 A9 $3 green & olive 600.00 500.00
39 A9 $5 green & ultra 300.00 400.00
40 A9 $10 grn & brn vio 800.00 1,000.
41 A9 $25 green & org 4,000. 4,000.
  Nos. 29-39, Ovpt. "SPECIMEN" 450.00

High values with revenue cancellations are plentiful and inexpensive.

Surcharged in Black

1900 Wmk. 2

42 A8 1c on 5c lilac & olive 75.00 *125.00*
43 A8 1c on 50c grn & blk 3.50 29.00
  a. Surcharge reading "cent One cent." 3,500.
44 A8 3c on 50c grn & blk 6.00 *26.00*
  Nos. 42-44 (3) 84.50 *180.00*

Mosque at Klang
A12

Sultan Sulaiman
A13

1935-41 Typo. Wmk. 4 *Perf. 14*

45 A12 1c black ('36) .30 .25
46 A12 2c dp green ('36) .55 .25
46A A12 2c org brn ('41) 2.25 1.25
46B A12 3c green ('41) 1.25 *8.00*
47 A12 4c orange brown .30 .25
48 A12 5c chocolate .70 .25
49 A12 6c rose red ('37) 4.00 .25
50 A12 8c gray .35 .25
51 A12 10c dk violet ('36) .35 .25
52 A12 12c ultra ('36) .90 .25
52A A12 15c ultra ('41) 7.00 *35.00*
53 A12 25c rose red & pale vio ('36) .60 *.80*
54 A12 30c org & dk vio ('36) .60 *1.10*
55 A12 40c dk vio & car 1.50 1.25
56 A12 50c blk, *emer* ('36) 1.00 .50
57 A13 $1 red & black, *blue* ('36) 6.00 1.10
58 A13 $2 rose red & green ('36) 17.50 9.50
59 A13 $5 brn red & grn, *emer* ('36) 55.00 *30.00*
  Nos. 45-59 (18) 100.15 *90.50*
  Set, never hinged 170.00

Nos. 46A-46B were printed on both ordinary and chalky paper; 15c only on ordinary paper; other values only on chalky paper.

An 8c rose red was prepared but not issued.

For overprints see Nos. N1-N15, N18A-N24, N26-N39.

Sultan Hisam-ud-Din Alam Shah — A14

1941

72 A14 $1 red & blk, *blue* 11.50 7.00
73 A14 $2 car & green 30.00 *40.00*
  Set, never hinged 70.00

A $5 stamp of type A14, issued during the Japanese occupation with different overprints (Nos. N18, N25A, N42), also exists without overprint. The unoverprinted stamp was not issued. Value $125.

For overprints see Nos. N16-N17, N24A, N25, N40-N41.

Catalogue values for unused stamps in this section, from this point to the end of the section, are for Never Hinged items.

Common Design Types pictured following the introduction.

Silver Wedding Issue

Common Design Types

Inscribed: "Malaya Selangor"

Perf. 14x14½

1948, Dec. 1 Photo. Wmk. 4

74 CD304 10c purple .25 *.30*

Perf. 11½x11

Engraved; Name Typographed

75 CD305 $5 green 30.00 25.00

UPU Issue

Common Design Types

Inscribed: "Malaya-Selangor"

Engr.; Name Typo. on Nos. 77 & 78

1949, Oct. 10 *Perf. 13½, 11x11½*

76 CD306 10c rose violet .40 .30
77 CD307 15c indigo 2.50 2.50
78 CD308 25c orange .50 *4.50*
79 CD309 50c slate 1.50 *5.00*
  Nos. 76-79 (4) 4.90 12.30

Sultan Hisam-ud-Din Alam Shah — A15

1949, Sept. 12 Typo. *Perf. 18*

80 A15 1c black .25 .60
81 A15 2c orange .30 1.50
82 A15 3c green 4.00 2.00
83 A15 4c chocolate .50 .35
84 A15 6c gray .35 .35
85 A15 8c rose red 2.00 1.25
86 A15 10c plum .25 .25
87 A15 15c ultramarine 8.00 .35
88 A15 20c dk grn & black 5.00 .50
89 A15 25c orange & rose lil 2.00 .35
90 A15 40c dk vio & rose red 11.00 8.00
91 A15 50c ultra & black 3.50 .35
92 A15 $1 vio brn & ultra 4.00 .60
93 A15 $2 rose red & emer 15.00 1.10
94 A15 $5 choc & emerald 55.00 3.00

1952-55

95 A15 5c rose violet 1.00 2.75
96 A15 8c green 1.00 1.75
97 A15 12c rose red 1.25 3.50
98 A15 20c ultramarine 1.25 .35
99 A15 30c plum & rose red ('55) 2.25 2.25
100 A15 35c dk vio & rose red 1.50 1.50
Nos. 80-100 (21) 119.40 32.65

Coronation Issue
Common Design Type

1953, June 2 Engr. *Perf. 13½x13*

101 CD312 10c magenta & black 1.75 .25

A16

Sultan Hisam-ud-Din Alam Shah — A17

Designs as in Kelantan, 1957.

Perf. 13x12½, 12½x13, 13½ ($1)

1957-60 Engr. Wmk. 314

102 A17 1c black .25 *2.50*
103 A17 2c red orange .50 *1.00*
104 A17 4c dark brown .25 .25
105 A17 5c dark car rose .25 .25
106 A17 8c dark green 3.00 *4.00*
107 A16 10c chocolate 2.50 .25
108 A16 20c blue 3.25 .25
109 A16 50c ultra & blk ('60) 1.00 .25
a. Perf. 12½ .40 .25
110 A17 $1 plum & ultra 4.50 .25
111 A17 $2 red & grn ('60) 5.50 3.00
a. Perf. 12½ 4.00 3.00
112 A17 $5 ol grn & brn ('60) 12.00 2.40
a. Perf. 12½ 12.00 3.00
Nos. 102-112 (11) 33.00 14.40

See Nos. 114-120.

Sultan Salahuddin Abdul Aziz Shah — A18

1961, June 28 Photo. *Perf. 14½x14*

113 A18 10s multicolored .30 .25

Sultan Salahuddin Abdul Aziz Shah, installation.

Types of 1957 with Portrait of Sultan Salahuddin Abdul Aziz Shah

Designs as before.

Perf. 13x12½, 12½x13

1961-62 Engr. Wmk. 338

114 A17 1c black .40 *2.75*
115 A17 2c red orange .40 *3.00*
116 A17 4c dark brown 1.00 .25
117 A17 5c dark car rose 1.00 .25
118 A17 8c dark green 4.75 *6.00*
119 A16 10c vio brown ('61) .90 .25
120 A16 20c blue 8.00 1.50
Nos. 114-120 (7) 16.45 14.00

Starting in 1965, issues of Selangor are listed with Malaysia.

OCCUPATION STAMPS

Issued under Japanese Occupation

Stamps of Selangor 1935-41 Handstamped Vertically or Horizontally in Black, Red, Brown or Violet

1942, Apr. 3 Wmk. 4 *Perf. 14*

N1 A12 1c black 15.00 21.00
N2 A12 2c deep green 2,300. 1,500.
N3 A12 2c orange brown 55.00 55.00
N4 A12 3c green 35.00 17.00
N5 A12 5c chocolate 10.00 10.00
N6 A12 6c rose red 200.00 200.00
N7 A12 8c gray 27.50 27.50
N8 A12 10c dark violet 22.50 27.50
N9 A12 12c ultramarine 47.50 47.50
N10 A12 15c ultramarine 17.00 20.00
N11 A12 25c rose red & pale vio 80.00 95.00
N12 A12 30c org & dk vio 15.00 30.00
N13 A12 40c dk vio & car 100.00 140.00
N14 A12 50c blk, *emerald* 40.00 47.50
N15 A13 $5 brn red & grn, *emer* 275.00 275.00

Some authorities believe No. N15 was not issued regularly.

Handstamped Vertically on Stamps and Type of Selangor 1941 in Black or Red

N16 A14 $1 red & blk, *bl* 67.50 80.00
N17 A14 $2 car & green 80.00 110.00
N18 A14 $5 brn red & grn, *emer* 110.00 110.00

Stamps and Type of Selangor, 1935-41, Overprinted in Black

1942, May

N18A A12 1c black 110.00 110.00
N19 A12 3c green 1.00 1.00
N19A A12 5c chocolate 110.00 110.00
N20 A12 10c dark violet 35.00 35.00
N21 A12 12c ultramarine 2.75 5.00
N22 A12 15c ultramarine 5.50 4.00
N23 A12 30c org & dk vio 35.00 35.00
N24 A12 40c dk vio & car 4.00 4.00
N24A A14 $1 red & blk, *bl* 35.00 35.00
N25 A14 $2 car & green 24.00 30.00
N25A A14 $5 red & grn, *emer* 55.00 55.00
Nos. N18A-N25A (11) 417.25 424.00

Overprint is horizontal on $1, $2, $5.

On Nos. N18A and N19 the overprint is known reading up, instead of down.

Some authorities claim Nos. N18A, N19A, N20, N23, N24A and N25A were not regularly issued.

Selangor No. 46B Overprinted in Black

1942, Dec.

N26 A12 3c green 400.00 400.00

Stamps and Type of Selangor, 1935-41, Ovptd. or Srchd. in Black or Red

i

k

l

m

1943

N27 A12(i) 1c black 1.40 1.40
N28 A12(k) 1c black (R) .90 .90
N29 A12(l) 2c on 5c choc (R) .90 .90
N30 A12(i) 3c green 1.00 1.00
N31 A12(l) 3c on 5c choc .65 1.00
N32 A12(k) 5c choc (R) .65 1.00
N33 A12(l) 6c on 5c choc .25 *.90*
N34 A12(m) 6c on 5c choc .25 *1.00*
N35 A12(i) 12c ultra 1.40 1.60
N36 A12(i) 15c ultra 6.75 10.00
N37 A12(k) 15c ultra 13.50 13.50
N38 A12(m) $1 on 10c dk vio .50 *1.40*
N39 A12(m) $1.50 on 30c org & dk vio .50 *1.40*
N40 A14(i) $1 red & blk, *blue* 6.75 8.50
N41 A14(i) $2 car & grn 24.00 24.00
N42 A14(i) $5 brn red & grn, *emer* 50.00 55.00
Nos. N27-N42 (16) 109.40 123.50

The "i" overprint is vertical on Nos. N40-N42 and is also found reading in the opposite direction on Nos. N30, N35 and N36.

The overprint reads: "Japanese Postal Service."

Singapore is listed following Sierra Leone.

SUNGEI UJONG

'suŋ·ə ü-‚juŋ

Formerly a nonfederated native state on the Malay Peninsula, which in 1895 was consolidated with the Federated State of Negri Sembilan.

Stamps of the Straits Settlements Overprinted in Black

Overprinted

1878 Wmk. 1 *Perf. 14*

2 A2 2c brown 3,600. 3,900.

Overprinted

4 A2 2c brown 400.00
5 A2 4c rose *1,950.* 2,000.

No. 5 is no longer recognized by some experts.

Overprinted

1882-83 Wmk. 2

6 A2 2c brown 375.00 —
7 A2 4c rose 4,250. 4,800.

This overprint on the 2c brown, wmk. 1, is probably a trial printing.

Overprinted

11 A2 2c brown 325.00 *400.00*

Overprinted

1881-84

14 A2 2c brown 1,200. 750.00
15 A2 2c rose 140.00 140.00
a. "Ujong" printed sideways
b. "Sungei" printed twice
16 A2 4c brown 325.00 425.00
17 A3 8c orange 2,250. 1,700.
18 A7 10c slate 725.00 625.00

Overprinted

19 A2 2c brown 57.50 *160.00*

Overprinted

1885-90 Without Period

20 A2 2c rose 45.00 *77.50*

With Period

21 A2 2c rose 125.00 90.00
a. "UNJOG" 5,750. 4,000.

Overprinted

22 A2 2c rose 95.00 110.00
a. Double overprint 775.00 775.00

Overprinted

23 A2 2c rose 125.00 *150.00*

Overprinted

24 A2 2c rose 30.00 *47.50*
a. Double overprint

Overprinted

25 A2 2c rose 110.00 *125.00*

Overprinted

26 A2 2c rose 175.00 175.00
c. Double overprint

Overprinted

Overprint 14-16x3mm

26A A2 2c rose 12.00 16.00

Overprinted

26B A2 2c rose 50.00 21.00

Stamp of 1883-91 Surcharged

a

b

c

d

1891

27 A3 (a) 2c on 24c green 240. *275.*
28 A3 (b) 2c on 24c green 1,100. *1,200.*
29 A3 (c) 2c on 24c green 425. *500.*
30 A3 (d) 2c on 24c green 1,100. *1,200.*
Nos. 27-30 (4) 2,865. 3,175.

On Nos. 27-28, SUNGEI is 14½mm, UJONG 12¾x2½mm.

A3

1891-94 Typo. *Perf. 14*

31 A3 2c rose 40.00 35.00
32 A3 2c orange ('94) 2.25 5.50
33 A3 5c blue ('93) 6.50 7.75
Nos. 31-33 (3) 48.75 48.25

Type of 1891 Surcharged in Black

1894

34 A3 1c on 5c green 1.40 .90
35 A3 3c on 5c rose 3.25 *6.00*

A4

1895

36 A4 3c lilac & car rose 15.00 4.75

Stamps of Sungei Ujong were superseded by those of Negri Sembilan in 1895.

TRENGGANU

treŋ'gä-ˌnü

LOCATION — On the eastern coast of the Malay Peninsula.
AREA — 5,050 sq. mi.
POP. — 302,171 (1960)
CAPITAL — Kuala Trengganu

Sultan Zenalabidin
A1 A2

1910-19 Typo. Wmk. 3 *Perf. 14*

Ordinary Paper

1a A1 1c blue green 2.10 1.25
2 A1 2c red vio & brn ('15) 1.25 1.10
3 A1 3c rose red 2.75 2.75
4 A1 4c brn orange 4.25 *6.75*
5 A1 4c grn & org brn ('15) 2.50 *5.75*
6 A1 4c scarlet ('19) 1.50 *2.10*
7 A1 5c gray 1.75 *4.50*
8 A1 5c choc & gray ('15) 3.00 2.40
9 A1 8c ultramarine 1.75 11.00
10 A1 10c red & grn, *yel* ('15) 1.75 2.75

Chalky Paper

11a A1 10c violet, *pale yel* 4.00 9.00
12 A1 20c red vio & vio 4.25 *5.75*
13 A1 25c dl vio & grn ('15) 9.75 *42.50*
14 A1 30c blk & dl vio ('15) 8.50 *65.00*
15 A1 50c blk & sep, *grn* 5.75 *11.50*
16 A1 $1 red & blk, *blue* 22.50 *29.00*
17 A1 $3 red & grn, *grn* ('15) 225.00 *500.00*
18 A2 $5 lil & blue grn 225.00 *675.00*
19 A2 $25 green & car 1,800. *2,750.*
Revenue Cancel 300.00
Nos. 1a-19 (19) 2,327. 4,128.

On No. 19 the numerals and Arabic inscriptions at top, left and right are in color on a colorless background.

Overprints are listed after No. 41. For surcharges see Nos. B1-B4.

Sultan Badaru'l-alam
A3 A4

1921-38 Wmk. 4 *Perf. 14*

Chalky Paper

20 A3 1c black ('25) 2.75 1.75
21 A3 2c deep green 1.75 2.40
22 A3 3c dp grn ('25) 3.00 1.10
23 A3 3c lt brn ('38) 32.50 *22.50*
24 A3 4c rose red 2.40 2.00
25 A3 5c choc & gray 3.25 8.00
26 A3 5c vio, *yel* ('25) 2.75 2.00
27 A3 6c orange ('24) 6.00 .85
28 A3 8c gray ('38) 42.50 9.50
29 A3 10c ultramarine 3.25 1.50
30 A3 12c ultra ('25) 7.00 *7.25*
31 A3 20c org & dl vio 3.50 *2.40*
32 A3 25c dk vio & grn 3.75 *5.00*
33 A3 30c blk & dl vio 5.50 6.00
34 A3 35c red, *yel* ('25) 7.75 *12.50*
35 A3 50c car & green 11.50 5.25
36 A3 $1 ultra & vio, *bl* ('29) 15.00 6.00
37 A3 $3 red & green, *emer* ('25) 87.50 *240.00*
38 A4 $5 red & grn, *yel* ('38) 500.00 *2,800.*
39 A4 $25 blue & lil 750.00 *1,250.*
40 A4 $50 org & green 1,850. *3,200.*
41 A4 $100 red & green 6,500. *9,500.*
Nos. 20-37 (18) 241.65 *336.00*

On Nos. 39 to 41 the numerals and Arabic inscriptions at top, left and right are in color on a colorless background.

A 2c orange, 6c gray, 8c rose red and 15c ultramarine, type A3, exist, but are not known to have been regularly issued.

For surcharges and overprints see Nos. 45-46, N1-N60.

Stamps of 1910-21 Overprinted in Black

1922, Mar. Wmk. 3

8a A1 5c chocolate & gray 4.75 *37.50*
10a A1 10c red & green, *yel* 4.75 *37.50*
12a A1 20c red vio & violet 4.25 *50.00*
13a A1 25c dull vio & green 4.25 *50.00*
14a A1 30c black & dull vio 4.25 *50.00*
15a A1 50c blk & sepia, *grn* 4.25 *50.00*
16a A1 $1 red & blk, *blue* 20.00 *95.00*
17a A1 $3 red & grn, *green* 210.00 *575.00*
18a A2 $5 lil & blue green 300.00 *575.00*

Wmk. 4

21a A3 2c deep green 2.75 *47.50*
24a A3 4c rose red 7.75 *47.50*
Nos. 8a-24a (11) 567.00 *1,615.*

Industrial fair at Singapore, Mar. 31-Apr. 15.

1921 Wmk. 3 Chalky Paper

42 A3 $1 ultra & vio, *bl* 20.00 *40.00*
43 A3 $3 red & grn, *emer* 140.00 *160.00*
44 A4 $5 red & green, *yel* 140.00 *150.00*
Nos. 42-44 (3) 300.00 *350.00*

Types of 1921-25 Surcharged in Black

1941, May 1 Wmk. 4 *Perf. 13½x14*

45 A3 2c on 5c magenta, *yel* 5.50 *6.50*
46 A3 8c on 10c lt ultra 9.50 *6.50*

For overprints see Nos. N30-N33, N46-N47, N59-N60.

Catalogue values for unused stamps in this section, from this point to the end of the section, are for Never Hinged items.

Common Design Types pictured following the introduction.

Silver Wedding Issue
Common Design Types
Inscribed: "Malaya Trengganu"

1948, Dec. 1 Photo. *Perf. 14x14½*

47 CD304 10c purple .25 .25

Engraved; Name Typographed
Perf. 11½x11

48 CD305 $5 rose car 35.00 62.50

UPU Issue
Common Design Types
Inscribed: "Malaya-Trengganu"
Engr.; Name Typo. on 15c, 25c
Perf. 13½, 11x11½

1949, Oct. 10 Wmk. 4

49 CD306 10c rose violet .65 .65
50 CD307 15c indigo .80 2.10
51 CD308 25c orange 1.40 3.50
52 CD309 50c slate 2.10 3.50
Nos. 49-52 (4) 4.95 9.75

Sultan Ismail Nasiruddin Shah — A5

1949, Dec. 27 Typo. *Perf. 18*

53 A5 1c black .40 .45
54 A5 2c orange .40 .50
55 A5 3c green 1.25 1.50
56 A5 4c chocolate .60 .50
57 A5 6c gray 1.25 1.25
58 A5 8c rose red 1.60 1.90
59 A5 10c plum .60 .50
60 A5 15c ultramarine 1.75 1.60
61 A5 20c dk grn & black 2.40 5.00
62 A5 25c org & rose lilac 2.25 3.25
63 A5 40c dk vio & rose red 4.50 27.50
64 A5 50c dp ultra & black 2.75 2.75
65 A5 $1 vio brn & ultra 5.50 10.00
66 A5 $2 rose red & emer 30.00 24.50
67 A5 $5 choc & emerald 80.00 67.50

1952-55

68 A5 5c rose violet .40 .50
69 A5 8c green 1.60 3.25
70 A5 12c rose red 1.60 *6.75*
71 A5 20c ultramarine 1.60 1.50
72 A5 30c plum & rose red ('55) 3.00 6.75
73 A5 35c dk vio & rose red 3.50 6.75
Nos. 53-73 (21) 146.95 174.20

Coronation Issue
Common Design Type

1953, June 2 Engr. *Perf. 13½x13*

74 CD312 10c magenta & blk 1.50 1.00

Types of Kedah with Portrait of Sultan Ismail
Perf. 13x12½, 12½x13, 13½ ($1), 12½ ($2)

1957-63 Engr. Wmk. 314

75 A8 1c black .30 .50
76 A8 2c red orange 1.00 .50
77 A8 4c dark brown .30 .50
78 A8 5c dark car rose .30 .50
79 A8 8c dark green 9.00 .50
80 A7 10c chocolate .40 .50
81 A7 20c blue .85 .60
82 A7 50c blue & blk .40 2.40
a. Perf. 12½ .50 2.25
83 A8 $1 plum & ultra 9.50 9.50
84 A8 $2 red & green 18.00 12.00
85 A8 $5 ol grn & brn, perf. 12½ 27.50 25.00
a. Perf. 13x12½ 32.50 30.00
Nos. 75-85 (11) 67.55 52.50

Issued: 20c, No. 85, 6/26/57; 2c, 50c, $1, 7/25/57; 10c, 8/4/57; 1c, 4c, 5c, 8c, $2, 8/21/57; No. 82a, 5/17/60; No. 85a, 8/13/63.

Starting in 1965, issues of Trengganu are listed with Malaysia.

SEMI-POSTAL STAMPS

Nos. 3, 4 and 9 Surcharged

1917, Oct. Wmk. 3 *Perf. 14*

B1 A1 3c + 2c rose red 1.50 *8.00*
a. "CSOSS" 65.00 *100.00*
b. Comma after "2c" 4.00 *10.50*
c. Pair, one without surcharge 2,900. 2,900.
B2 A1 4c + 2c brn org 2.25 *12.50*
a. "CSOSS" 275.00 *275.00*
b. Comma after "2c" 16.00 *42.50*
B3 A1 8c + 2c ultra 3.50 *24.00*
a. "CSOSS" 175.00 *210.00*
b. Comma after "2c" 13.00 *45.00*
Nos. B1-B3 (3) 7.25 *44.50*

Same Surcharge on No. 5

1918

B4 A1 4c + 2c grn & org brn 4.25 *11.50*
a. Pair, one without surcharge *2,300.*

POSTAGE DUE STAMPS

D1

Perf. 14

1937, Aug. 10 Typo. Wmk. 4

J1 D1 1c rose red 8.25 *65.00*
J2 D1 4c green 9.00 *72.50*
J3 D1 8c lemon 47.50 *400.00*
J4 D1 10c light brown 92.50 *115.00*
Nos. J1-J4 (4) 157.25 *652.50*
Set, never hinged 275.00

For overprints see Nos. NJ1-NJ4.

OCCUPATION STAMPS

Issued under Japanese Occupation

No. N6

No. N17A

Stamps of Trengganu, 1921-38, Handstamped in Black or Brown

1942 **Wmk. 4** *Perf. 14*

N1 A3 1c black 110.00 110.00
N2 A3 2c deep green 190.00 275.00
N3 A3 3c lt brown 140.00 110.00
N4 A3 4c rose red 275.00 190.00
N5 A3 5c violet, *yel* 17.50 19.00
N6 A3 6c orange 13.50 20.00
N7 A3 8c gray 17.50 25.00
N8 A3 10c ultramarine 13.50 27.50
N9 A3 12c ultramarine 15.00 25.00
N10 A3 20c org & dl vio 15.00 22.50
N11 A3 25c dk vio & grn 13.50 27.50
N12 A3 30c blk & dl vio 13.50 25.00
N13 A3 35c red, *yel* 22.50 27.50
N14 A3 50c car & grn 125.00 95.00
N15 A3 $1 ultra & vio, *blue* 5,750. *5,750.*
N16 A3 $3 red & grn, *emerald* 125.00 140.00
N17 A4 $5 red & grn, *yellow* 240.00 240.00
N17A A4 $25 blue & lil 1,500.
N17B A4 $50 org & grn *8,800.*
N17C A4 $100 red & grn 950.00

Handstamped in Red

N18 A3 1c black 275.00 225.00
N19 A3 2c dp green 140.00 160.00
N20 A3 5c violet, *yel* 35.00 20.00
N21 A3 6c orange 20.00 20.00
N22 A3 8c gray 275.00 240.00
N23 A3 10c ultramarine 275.00 275.00
N24 A3 12c ultramarine 55.00 55.00
N25 A3 20c org & dl vio 35.00 35.00
N26 A3 25c dk vio & grn 40.00 40.00
N27 A3 30c blk & dl vio 35.00 35.00
N28 A3 35c red, *yellow* 35.00 20.00
N29 A3 $3 red & grn, *emerald* 100.00 40.00
N29A A3 $25 blue & lil 500.00 500.00

Handstamped on Nos. 45 and 46 in Black or Red

N30 A3 2c on 5c (Bk) 140.00 140.00
N31 A3 2c on 5c (R) 100.00 100.00
N32 A3 8c on 10c (Bk) 25.00 35.00
N33 A3 8c on 10c (R) 35.00 40.00

Stamps of Trengganu, 1921-38, Overprinted in Black

1942

N34 A3 1c black 15.00 17.00
N35 A3 2c deep green 100.00 *140.00*
N36 A3 3c light brown 16.00 29.00
N37 A3 4c rose red 15.00 20.00
N38 A3 5c violet, *yel* 10.00 20.00
N39 A3 6c orange 10.00 17.00
N40 A3 8c gray 67.50 20.00
N41 A3 12c ultramarine 10.00 13.50
N42 A3 20c org & dl vio 13.50 25.00
N43 A3 25c dk vio & grn 13.50 17.00
N44 A3 30c blk & dl vio 13.50 20.00
N45 A3 $3 red & grn, *emer* 100.00 140.00

Overprinted on Nos. 45 and 46 in Black

N46 A3 2c on 5c mag, *yel* 13.50 17.00
N47 A3 8c on 10c lt ultra 11.50 20.00
Nos. N34-N47 (14) 409.00 *515.50*

Stamps of Trengganu, 1921-38, Overprinted in Black

1943

N48 A3 1c black 13.50 19.00
N49 A3 2c deep green 13.50 27.50
N50 A3 5c violet, *yel* 11.50 27.50
N51 A3 6c orange 15.00 27.50
N52 A3 8c gray 95.00 67.50
N53 A3 10c ultramarine 100.00 175.00
N54 A3 12c ultramarine 19.00 *35.00*
N55 A3 20c org & dl vio 20.00 *35.00*
N56 A3 25c dl vio & grn 19.00 *35.00*
N57 A3 30c blk & dl vio 20.00 *35.00*
N58 A3 35c red, *yellow* 20.00 *40.00*

Overprinted on Nos. 45 and 46 in Black

N59 A3 2c on 5c mag, *yel* 11.00 *35.00*
N60 A3 8c on 10c lt ultra 27.50 *25.00*
Nos. N48-N60 (13) 385.00 *584.00*

The Japanese characters read: "Japanese Postal Service."

OCCUPATION POSTAGE DUE STAMPS

Trengganu Nos. J1-J4 Handstamped in Black or Brown

1942 **Wmk. 4** *Perf. 14*

NJ1 D1 1c rose red 67.50 *95.00*
NJ2 D1 4c green 125.00 *125.00*
NJ3 D1 8c lemon 25.00 *67.50*
NJ4 D1 10c light brown 25.00 *50.00*
Nos. NJ1-NJ4 (4) 242.50 *337.50*

The handstamp reads: "Seal of Post Office of Malayan Military Department."

MALAYSIA

mə-ˈlā-zh(ē-)ə

LOCATION — Malay peninsula and northwestern Borneo
GOVT. — Federation within the British Commonwealth
AREA — 127,317 sq. mi.
POP. — 21,376,066 (1999 est.)
CAPITAL — Putrajaya (administrative); Kuala Lumpur (financial)

The Federation of Malaysia was formed Sept. 16, 1963, by a merger of the former Federation of Malaya, Singapore, Sarawak, and North Borneo (renamed Sabah), totaling 14 states. Singapore withdrew in 1965.

Sabah and Sarawak, having different rates than mainland Malaysia, continued to issue their own stamps after joining the federation. The system of individual state issues was extended to Perak in Oct. 1963, and to the 10 other members in Nov. 1965.

100 Cents (Sen) = 1 Dollar (Ringgit)

Catalogue values for all unused stamps in this country are for Never Hinged items.

Watermarks

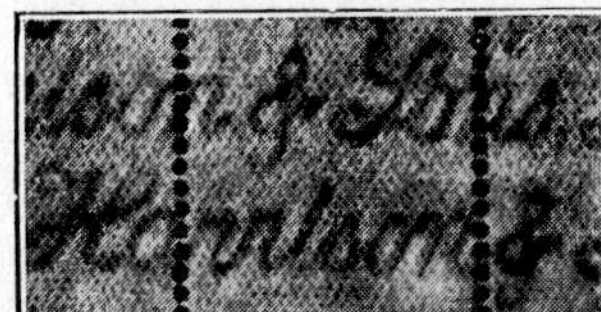
Wmk. 233 — "Harrison & Sons, London" in Script

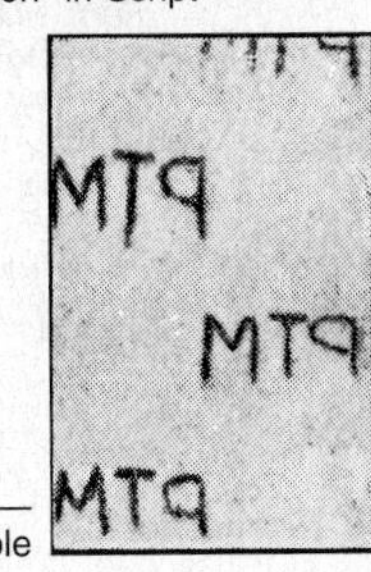

Wmk. 338 — PTM Multiple

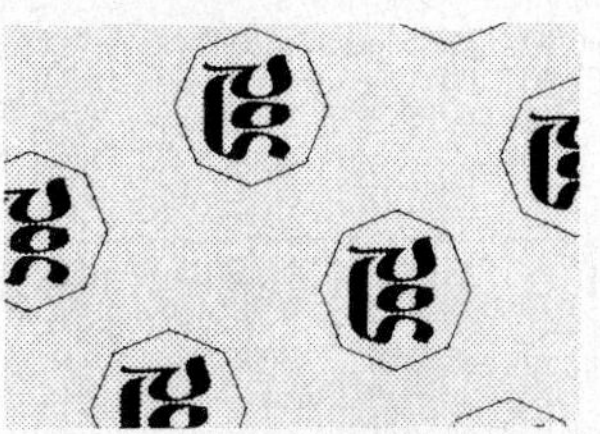
Wmk. 378 — Multiple POS in Octagonal Frame

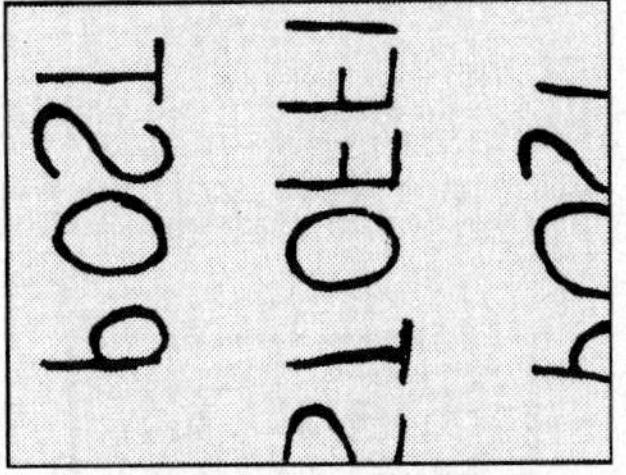
Wmk. 380 — "POST OFFICE"

Wmk. 388 — Multiple "SPM"

Map of Malaysia and 14-point Star — A1

Wmk. PTM Multiple (338)

1963, Sept. 16 **Photo.** *Perf. 14*

1 A1 10s violet & yellow 1.60 .25
a. Yellow omitted 525.00
2 A1 12s green & yellow 1.50 .60
3 A1 50s dk red brown & yel 1.50 .25
Nos. 1-3 (3) 4.60 1.10

Formation of the Federation of Malaysia.

Orchids — A2

1963, Oct. 3 **Unwmk.** *Perf. 13x14*

4 A2 6s red & multi 1.25 1.25
5 A2 25s black & multi 1.50 .75

4th World Orchid Conf., Singapore, Oct. 8-11.

Parliament and Commonwealth Parliamentary Association Emblem — A4

1963, Nov. 4 *Perf. 13½*

7 A4 20s dk car rose & gold 1.00 .40
8 A4 30s dk green & gold 1.75 .25

9th Commonwealth Parliamentary Assoc. Conf.

Globe, Torch, Snake and Hands — A5

1964, Oct. 10 **Photo.** *Perf. 14x13*

9 A5 25s Prus grn, red & blk .25 .25
10 A5 30s lt violet, red & blk .25 .25
11 A5 50s dull yellow, red & blk .35 .25
Nos. 9-11 (3) .85 .75

Eleanor Roosevelt, 1884-1962.

ITU Emblem and Radar Tower — A6

1965, May 17 **Photo.** *Perf. 11½*

Granite Paper

12 A6 2c violet, blk & org .70 *1.75*
13 A6 25c brown, blk & org 2.00 .60
14 A6 50c emerald, blk & brn 2.50 .30
Nos. 12-14 (3) 5.20 2.65

Cent. of the ITU.

National Mosque, Kuala Lumpur — A7

1965, Aug. 27 **Wmk. 338** *Perf. 14½*

15 A7 6c dark car rose .25 .25
16 A7 15c dark red brown .25 .25
17 A7 20c Prussian green .35 .30
Nos. 15-17 (3) .85 .80

Natl. Mosque at Kuala Lumpur, opening.

Control Tower and Airport — A8

1965, Aug. 30 *Perf. 14½x14*

18 A8 15c blue, blk & grn .35 .25
a. Green omitted 40.00
19 A8 30c brt pink, blk & grn .75 .30

Intl. Airport at Kuala Lumpur, opening.

Crested Wood Partridge — A9

Birds: 30c, Fairy bluebird. 50c, Blacknaped oriole. 75c, Rhinoceros hornbill. $1, Zebra dove. $2, Argus pheasant. $5, Indian paradise flycatcher. $10, Banded pitta.

1965, Sept. 9 **Photo.** *Perf. 14½*

20 A9 25c orange & multi .65 .25
21 A9 30c tan & multi .75 .25
a. Blue omitted 375.00
b. Yellow omitted 550.00
22 A9 50c rose & multi 1.40 .25
a. Yellow omitted 300.00
b. Imperf. pair 200.00
c. Scarlet omitted 120.00
23 A9 75c yel grn & multi 1.40 .25
24 A9 $1 ultra & multi 1.75 .25
25 A9 $2 maroon & multi 7.00 .35
a. Imperf. pair 200.00
26 A9 $5 dk grn & multi 16.00 2.00
27 A9 $10 brt red & multi 40.00 7.00
a. Imperf. pair 275.00
Nos. 20-27 (8) 68.95 10.60

Soccer and Sepak Raga (Ball Game) — A10

1965, Dec. 14 Unwmk. *Perf. 13*

28 A10 25c shown .35 *1.10*
29 A10 30c Runner .40 .25
30 A10 50c Diver .55 .30
Nos. 28-30 (3) 1.30 1.65

3rd South East Asia Peninsular Games, Kuala Lumpur, Dec. 14-21.

National Monument, Kuala Lumpur — A11

1966, Feb. 8 Wmk. 338 *Perf. 13½*

31 A11 10c yellow & multi .25 .25
a. Blue omitted 225.00
32 A11 20c ultra & multi 1.25 .45

The National Monument by US sculptor Felix W. de Weldon commemorates the struggle of the people of Malaysia for peace and for freedom from communism.

Tuanku Ismail Nasiruddin — A12

1966, Apr. 11 Unwmk. *Perf. 13½*

33 A12 15c yellow & black .25 .25
34 A12 50c blue & black .35 .35

Installation of Tuanku Ismail Nasiruddin of Trengganu as Paramount Ruler (Yang di-Pertuan Agong).

Penang Free School — A13

Design: 50c, like 20c with Malayan inscription and school crest added.

Perf. 13x12½

1966, Oct. 21 Photo. Wmk. 338

35 A13 20c multicolored .40 .30
36 A13 50c multicolored 1.15 .40

Penang Free School, 150th anniversary.

Mechanized Plowing and Palms — A14

No. 38, Rural health nurse, mother and child, dispensary. No. 39, Communication: train, plane, ship, cars and radio tower. No. 40, School children. No. 41, Dam and rice fields.

1966, Dec. 1 Unwmk. *Perf. 13*

37 A14 15c bister brn & multi .35 .25
38 A14 15c blue & multi .35 .25
39 A14 15c crimson & multi 2.00 .30
40 A14 15c ol green & multi .35 .25
41 A14 15c yellow & multi .35 .25
Nos. 37-41 (5) 3.40 1.30

Malaysia's First Development Plan.

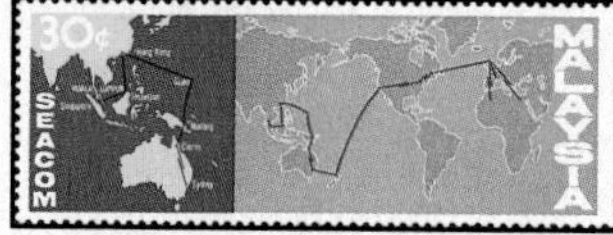

Maps Showing International and South East Asia Telephone Links — A15

1967, Mar. 30 Photo. *Perf. 13*

42 A15 30c multicolored 1.00 .50
43 A15 75c multicolored 3.75 *4.25*

Completion of the Hong Kong-Malaysia link of the South East Asia Commonwealth Cable, SEACOM.

Hibiscus and Rulers of Independent Malaysia — A16

1967, Aug. 31 Wmk. 338 *Perf. 14*

44 A16 15c yellow & multi .30 .25
45 A16 50c blue & multi 1.25 .80

10th anniversary of independence.

Arms of Sarawak and Council Mace — A17

1967, Sept. 8 Photo.

46 A17 15c yel green & multi .25 .25
47 A17 50c multicolored .35 .50

Representative Council of Sarawak, cent.

Straits Settlements No. 13 and Malaysia No. 20 — A18

30c, Straits Settlements #15, Malaysia #21. 50c, Straits Settlements #17, Malaysia #22.

1967, Dec. 2 Unwmk. *Perf. 11½*

48 A18 25c brt blue & multi 1.25 *2.50*
a. Horiz. tête-bêe pair 3.50 *7.50*
49 A18 30c dull green & multi 1.50 *2.25*
a. Horiz. tête-bêe pair 4.25 *6.50*
50 A18 50c yellow & multi 2.00 *3.00*
a. Horiz. tête-bêe pair 6.00 *8.00*
Nos. 48-50 (3) 4.75 *7.75*

Cent. of the Malaysian (Straits Settlements) postage stamps.

Tapped Rubber Tree and Molecular Unit — A20

Tapped Rubber Tree and: 30c, Rubber packed for shipment. 50c, Rubber tires for Vickers VC 10 plane.

Wmk. 338

1968, Aug. 29 Litho. *Perf. 12*

53 A20 25c brick red, blk & org .30 .25
54 A20 30c yellow, black & org .40 .30
55 A20 50c ultra, black & org .50 .30
Nos. 53-55 (3) 1.20 .85

Natural Rubber Conference, Kuala Lumpur.

Olympic Rings, Mexican Hat and Cloth — A21

75c, Olympic rings & Malaysian batik cloth.

1968, Oct. 12 Wmk. 338 *Perf. 12*

56 A21 30c rose red & multi .30 .25
57 A21 75c ocher & multi .60 .35

19th Olympic Games, Mexico City, 10/12-27.

Tunku Abdul Rahman Putra Al-Haj — A22

Various portraits of Prime Minister Tunku Abdul Rahman Putra Al-Haj with woven pandanus patterns as background. 50c is horiz.

Perf. 13½

1969, Feb. 8 Photo. Unwmk.

58 A22 15c gold & multi .35 .25
59 A22 20c gold & multi .55 1.25
60 A22 50c gold & multi .65 .30
Nos. 58-60 (3) 1.55 1.80

Issued for Solidarity Week, 1969.

Malaysian Girl Holding Sheaves of Rice — A23

1969, Dec. 8 Wmk. 338 *Perf. 13½*

61 A23 15c silver & multi .30 .25
62 A23 75c gold & multi 1.10 1.40

International Rice Year.

Kuantan Radar Station — A24

Intelsat III Orbiting Earth A25

Perf. 14x13

1970, Apr. 6 Photo. Unwmk.

63 A24 15c multicolored .80 .25
a. Tête-bêe pair 2.00 *3.00*
64 A25 30c multicolored 1.25 *2.25*
65 A25 30c gold & multi 1.40 *2.25*
Nos. 63-65 (3) 3.45 *4.75*

Satellite Communications Earth Station at Kuantan, Pahang, Malaysia.

No. 63 was printed tete beche (50 pairs) in sheet of 100 (10x10).

Blue-branded King Crow — A26

Butterflies: 30c, Saturn. 50c, Common Nawab. 75c, Great Mormon. $1, Orange albatross. $2, Raja Brooke's birdwing. $5, Centaur oakblue. $10, Royal Assyrian.

1970, Aug. 31 Litho. *Perf. 13x13½*

66 A26 25c multicolored 1.00 .25
67 A26 30c multicolored 1.50 .25
68 A26 50c multicolored 1.75 .25
69 A26 75c multicolored 2.00 .25
70 A26 $1 multicolored 2.75 .25
71 A26 $2 multicolored 3.50 .25
72 A26 $5 multicolored 5.25 2.25
73 A26 $10 multicolored 14.00 4.00
Nos. 66-73 (8) 31.75 7.75

ILO Emblem — A27

1970, Sept. 7 *Perf. 14½x13½*

74 A27 30c gray & blue .25 .25
75 A27 75c rose & blue .30 .30

50th anniv. of the ILO.

UN Emblem and Doves — A28

Designs: 25c, Doves in elliptical arrangement. 30c, Doves arranged diagonally.

1970, Oct. 24 Litho. *Perf. 13x12½*

76 A28 25c lt brown, blk & yel .35 .30
77 A28 30c lt blue, yel & black .35 .30
78 A28 50c lt ol green & black .40 .55
Nos. 76-78 (3) 1.10 1.15

25th anniversary of the United Nations.

Sultan Abdul Halim — A29

Perf. 14½x14

1971, Feb. 20 Photo. Unwmk.

79 A29 10c yellow, blk & gold .40 .35
80 A29 15c purple, blk & gold .40 .35
81 A29 50c blue, blk & gold .65 1.50
Nos. 79-81 (3) 1.45 2.20

Installation of Sultan Abdul Halim of Kedah as Paramount Ruler.

Bank Building and Crescent A30

1971, May 15 Photo. *Perf. 14*

82 A30 25c silver & black 2.50 2.00
83 A30 50c gold & brown 4.00 1.50

Opening of Main office of the Negara Malaysia Bank. Nos. 82-83 have circular perforations around vignette set within a white square of paper, perf. on 4 sides.

Malaysian Parliament — A31

Malaysian Parliament, Kuala Lumpur — A32

1971, Sept. 13 Litho. *Perf. 13½*

84	A31	25c multicolored	1.50	.50

Perf. 12½x13

85	A32	75c multicolored	3.50	1.75

17th Commonwealth Parliamentary Conference, Kuala Lumpur.

Malaysian Festival — A33

1971, Sept. 18 *Perf. 14½*

86	A33	Strip of 3	6.25	5.50
a.		30c Dancing couple	1.75	.75
b.		30c Dragon	1.75	.75
c.		30c Flags and stage horse	1.75	.75

Visit ASEAN (Association of South East Asian Nations) Year.

Elephant and Tiger — A34

Children's Drawings: No. 88, Cat and kittens. No. 89, Sun, flower and chick. No. 90, Monkey, elephant and lion in jungle. No. 91, Butterfly and flowers.

1971, Oct. 2 *Perf. 12½*

Size: 35x28mm

87	A34	15c pale yellow & multi	2.50	.60
88	A34	15c pale yellow & multi	2.50	.60

Size: 21x28mm

89	A34	15c pale yellow & multi	2.50	.60

Size: 35x28mm

90	A34	15c pale yellow & multi	2.50	.60
91	A34	15c pale yellow & multi	2.50	.60
a.		Strip of 5, #87-91	14.00	13.00

25th anniv. of UNICEF.

Track and Field — A35

30c, Sepak Raga (a ball game). 50c, Hockey.

1971, Dec. 11 *Perf. 14½*

92	A35	25c orange & multi	1.00	.40
93	A35	30c violet & multi	1.25	.50
94	A35	50c green & multi	1.50	.95
		Nos. 92-94 (3)	3.75	1.85

6th South East Asia Peninsular Games. Kuala Lumpur, Dec. 11-18.

South East Asian Tourist Attractions — A36

Designs include stylized map.

1972, Jan. 31 Litho. *Perf. 14½*

95	A36	Strip of 3	8.50	8.50
a.		30c Flag at left	2.00	1.00
b.		30c High rise building	2.00	1.00
c.		30c Horse & rider	2.00	1.00

Pacific Area Tourist Assoc. Conference.

Secretariat Building — A37

50c, Kuala Lumpur Secretariat Building by night.

1972, Feb. 1 *Perf. 14½x14*

96	A37	25c lt blue & multi	1.10	1.25
97	A37	50c black & multi	2.75	1.25

Achievement of city status by Kuala Lumpur.

Social Security Emblem — A38

1973, July 2 Litho. *Perf. 14½x13½*

98	A38	10c orange & multi	.25	.25
99	A38	15c yellow & multi	.25	.25
100	A38	50c gray & multi	.50	1.40
		Nos. 98-100 (3)	1.00	1.90

Introduction of Social Security System.

WHO Emblem — A39

Design: 30c, WHO emblem, horiz.

1973, Aug. 1 *Perf. 13x12½, 12½x13*

101	A39	30c yellow & multi	.60	.25
102	A39	75c blue & multi	1.30	2.50

25th anniv. of World Health Org.

Flag of Malaysia, Fireworks, Hibiscus — A40

1973, Aug. 31 Litho. *Perf. 14½*

103	A40	10c olive & multi	.50	.30
104	A40	15c brown & multi	.55	.30
105	A40	50c gray & multi	2.10	1.60
		Nos. 103-105 (3)	3.15	2.20

10th anniversary of independence.

INTERPOL and Malaysian Police Emblems A41

Design: 75c, "50" with INTERPOL and Malaysian police emblems.

1973, Sept. 15 *Perf. 12½*

106	A41	25c brown org & multi	1.00	.45
107	A41	75c deep violet & multi	2.50	2.00

50th anniv. of the Intl. Criminal Police Organization (INTERPOL).

MAS Emblem and Plane A42

1973, Oct. 1 Litho. *Perf. 14½*

108	A42	15c green & multi	.25	.25
109	A42	30c blue & multi	.60	.55
110	A42	50c brown & multi	1.40	1.60
		Nos. 108-110 (3)	2.25	2.40

Inauguration of Malaysian Airline System.

View of Kuala Lumpur — A43

1974, Feb. 1 Litho. *Perf. 12½x13*

111	A43	25c multicolored	.80	.75
112	A43	50c multicolored	1.60	1.75

Establishment of Kuala Lumpur as a Federal Territory.

Development Bank Emblem and Projects — A44

1974, Apr. 25 Litho. *Perf. 13½*

113	A44	30c gray & multi	.55	.45
114	A44	75c bister & multi	.90	1.75

7th annual meeting of the Board of Governors of the Asian Development Bank.

Map of Malaysia and Scout Emblem — A45

Scout Saluting, Malaysian and Scout Flags — A46

Design: 50c, Malaysian Scout emblem.

Perf. 14x13½, 13x13½ (15c)

1974, Aug. 1 Litho.

115	A45	10c multicolored	.55	.90
116	A46	15c multicolored	.90	.25
117	A45	50c multicolored	2.50	2.75
		Nos. 115-117 (3)	3.95	3.90

Malaysian Boy Scout Jamboree.

Power Installations, NEB Emblem — A47

National Electricity Board Building A48

Perf. 14x14½, 13½x14½

1974, Sept. 1 Litho.

118	A47	30c multicolored	.65	.45
119	A48	75c multicolored	1.10	2.25

National Electricity Board, 25th anniversary.

"100," UPU and P.O. Emblems A49

1974, Oct. 9 Litho. *Perf. 14½x13½*

120	A49	25c olive, red & yel	.35	.35
121	A49	30c blue, red & yel	.35	.35
122	A49	75c ocher, red & yel	.75	1.60
		Nos. 120-122 (3)	1.45	2.30

Centenary of Universal Postal Union.

Gravel Pump Tin Mine A50

Designs: 20c, Open cast mine. 50c, Silver tin ingot and tin dredge.

1974, Oct. 31 Litho. *Perf. 14*

123	A50	15c silver & multi	1.50	.30
124	A50	20c silver & multi	2.00	2.00
125	A50	50c silver & multi	5.00	5.00
		Nos. 123-125 (3)	8.50	7.30

4th World Tin Conference, Kuala Lumpur.

Hockey, Cup and Emblem A51

1975, Mar. 1 Litho. *Perf. 14*

126	A51	30c yellow & multi	1.25	.50
127	A51	75c blue & multi	2.75	2.00

Third World Cup Hockey Tournament, Kuala Lumpur, Mar. 1-15.

Trade Union Emblem and Workers — A52

1975, May 1 Litho. *Perf. 14x14½*

128	A52	20c orange & multi	.25	.25
129	A52	25c lt green & multi	.35	.25
130	A52	30c ultra & multi	.50	.50
		Nos. 128-130 (3)	1.10	1.00

Malaysian Trade Union Cong., 25th anniv.

National Women's Organization Emblem and Heads — A53

1975, Aug. 25 Litho. *Perf. 14*

131 A53 10c emerald & multi .45 .30
132 A53 15c lilac rose & multi .45 .30
133 A53 50c blue & multi 1.40 2.00
Nos. 131-133 (3) 2.30 2.60

International Women's Year.

Ubudiah Mosque, Perak — A54

b, Zahir Mosque, Kedah. c, National Mosque, Kuala Lumpur. d, Sultan Abu Bakar Mosque, Johore. e, Kuching State Mosque, Sarawak.

1975, Sept. 22 Litho. *Perf. 14½x14*

134 Strip of 5 14.50 9.50
a.-e. A54 15c single stamp 2.40 .40

Koran reading competition 1975, Malaysia.

Rubber Plantation and Emblem A55

Designs: 30c, "50" in form of latex cup and tire with emblem. 75c, Six test tubes showing various aspects of natural rubber.

1975, Oct. 22 Litho. *Perf. 14x14½*

135 A55 10c gold & multi .45 .30
136 A55 30c gold & multi 1.25 .60
137 A55 75c gold & multi 3.00 2.00
Nos. 135-137 (3) 4.70 2.90

Rubber Research Institute of Malaysia, 50th anniversary.

Butterflies — A55a

No. 137A, Hebomoia glaucippe aturia. No. 137B, Precis orithya wallacei.

Coil Stamps

1976, Feb. 6 *Perf. 14*

137A A55a 10c multicolored *3.50 7.00*
137B A55a 15c multicolored *3.50 7.00*

Scrub Typhus — A56

Designs: 25c, Malaria (microscope, blood cells, slides). $1, Beri-beri (grain and men).

1976, Feb. 6 Litho. *Perf. 14*

138 A56 20c red orange & multi .70 .30
139 A56 25c ultra & multi .85 .30
140 A56 $1 yellow & multi 1.60 2.25
Nos. 138-140 (3) 3.15 2.85

Institute for Medical Research, Kuala Lumpur, 75th anniversary.

Sultan Jahya Petra — A57

Perf. 14½x13½

1976, Feb. 28 Photo.

141 A57 10c yel, black & bis .35 .25
142 A57 15c lilac, black & bis .30 .25
143 A57 50c blue, black & bis 2.75 2.25
Nos. 141-143 (3) 3.40 2.75

Installation of Sultan Jahya Petra of Kelantan as Paramount Ruler (Yang di-Pertuan Agong).

Council and Administrative Buildings — A58

1976, Aug. 17 Litho. *Perf. 12½*

144 A58 15c orange & black .45 .25
145 A58 20c brt red lilac & black .55 .35
146 A58 50c blue & black 1.00 1.25
Nos. 144-146 (3) 2.00 1.85

Opening of the State Council Complex and Administrative Building, Sarawak.

Provident Fund Building A59

Provident Fund Emblems — A60

50c, Provident Fund Building at night.

Perf. 13½x14½, 14½ (A60)

1976, Oct. 18 Litho.

147 A59 10c blue & multi .50 .35
148 A60 25c gray & multi .45 .60
149 A59 50c violet & multi .65 1.25
Nos. 147-149 (3) 1.60 2.20

Employees' Provident Fund, 25th anniv.

Rehabilitation of the Blind — A61

75c, Blind man casting large shadow.

1976, Nov. 20 *Perf. 13½x14½*

150 A61 10c multicolored .50 .30
151 A61 75c multicolored 1.50 2.25

25th anniv. of the Malaysian Assoc. for the Blind.

Abdul Razak and Crowd — A62

Designs: b, Abdul Razak in cap and gown at lectern. c, Abdul Razak pointing to new roads and bridges on map. d, New constitution. e, Abdul Razak addressing Association of South-east Asian Countries.

1977, Jan. 14 Photo. *Perf. 14x14½*

152 Strip of 5 8.00 8.00
a.-e. A62 15c single stamp 1.00 .35

Prime Minister Tun Haji Abdul Razak bi Dato Hussein (1922-1976).

FELDA Housing Development A63

Design: 30c, View of oil palm settlement area and FELDA emblem.

1977, July 7 Litho. *Perf. 13½x14½*

153 A63 15c multicolored .55 .30
154 A63 30c multicolored .90 1.75

Federal Land Development Authority (FELDA), 21st anniversary.

ASEAN, 10th Anniv. — A64

75c, Flags of ASEAN members: Malaysia, Philippines, Singapore, Thailand and Indonesia.

1977, Aug. 8 Litho. *Perf. 13½x14½*

155 A64 10c multicolored .50 .25
156 A64 75c multicolored 1.00 .90

SEA Games Emblems A65

Designs: 20c, Ball, symbolic of 9 participating nations. 75c, Running.

Perf. 13½x14½

1977, Nov. 19 Litho.

157 A65 10c multicolored .30 .25
158 A65 20c multicolored .30 .25
159 A65 75c multicolored .75 1.60
Nos. 157-159 (3) 1.35 2.10

9th South East Asia Games, Kuala Lumpur.

Bank Emblem A66

1978, Mar. 15 Litho. *Perf. 14*

160 A66 30c multicolored .40 .25
161 A66 75c multicolored .60 .80

2nd annual meeting of Islamic Development Bank Governors, Kuala Lumpur, Mar. 1978.

Government Building A67

Designs: Views of Shah Alam.

1978, Dec. 7 Litho. *Perf. 13½x14½*

162 A67 10c multicolored .25 .25
163 A67 30c multicolored .30 .25
164 A67 75c multicolored .85 1.75
Nos. 162-164 (3) 1.40 2.25

Inauguration of Shah Alam as state capital of Selangor.

Mobile Post Office in Village — A68

Designs: 25c, General Post Office, Kuala Lumpur. 50c, Motorcyclist, rural mail delivery.

1978, July 10 *Perf. 13*

165 A68 10c multicolored 1.10 .40
166 A68 25c multicolored 1.25 1.75
167 A68 50c multicolored 1.50 2.75
Nos. 165-167 (3) 3.85 4.90

4th Conf. of Commonwealth Postal Administrators.

Jamboree Emblem A69

Bees and Honeycomb A70

1978, July 26 Litho. *Perf. 13½*

168 A69 15c multicolored 1.00 .30
169 A70 $1 multicolored 3.75 3.00

4th Boy Scout Jamboree, Sarawak.

Globe, Crest and WHO Emblem A71

1978, Sept. 30 *Perf. 13½x14½*

170 A71 15c blue, red & black .45 .35
171 A71 30c green, red & black .65 .45
172 A71 50c pink, red & black 1.00 .80
Nos. 170-172 (3) 2.10 1.60

Global eradication of smallpox.

Dome of the Rock A72

1978, Aug. 21 Litho. *Perf. 12½*

173 A72 15c red & multi 1.00 .35
174 A72 30c blue & multi 2.50 2.50

For Palestinian fighters and their families.

Tiger — A73

Designs: 40c, Cobego. 50c, Chevrotain. 75c, Pangolin. $1, Leatherback turtle. $2, Tapir. $5, Gaur. $10, Orangutan, vert.

Perf. 15x14½, 14½x15

1979, Jan. 4 Litho. Wmk. 378

175 A73 30c multicolored .50 .25
176 A73 40c multicolored .55 .25
177 A73 50c multicolored .90 .25
178 A73 75c multicolored 1.00 .25
179 A73 $1 multicolored 1.25 .25
180 A73 $2 multicolored 2.00 .75
181 A73 $5 multicolored 5.75 2.00
182 A73 $10 multicolored 10.00 3.00
Nos. 175-182 (8) 21.95 7.00

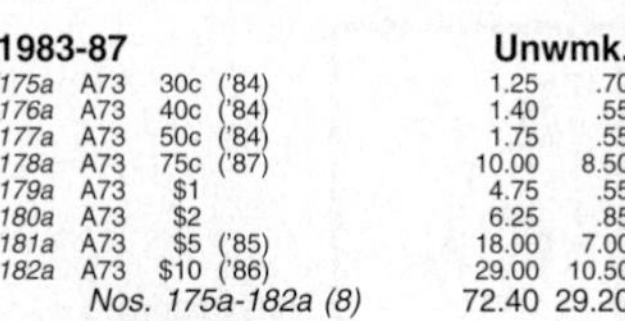

1983-87 **Unwmk.**

175a	A73	30c ('84)	1.25	.70
176a	A73	40c ('84)	1.40	.55
177a	A73	50c ('84)	1.75	.55
178a	A73	75c ('87)	10.00	8.50
179a	A73	$1	4.75	.55
180a	A73	$2	6.25	.85
181a	A73	$5 ('85)	18.00	7.00
182a	A73	$10 ('86)	29.00	10.50
		Nos. 175a-182a (8)	72.40	29.20

Central Bank of Malaysia — A74

10c, Central Bank of Malaysia & emblem.

Perf. 13½

1979, Jan. 26 **Litho.** **Unwmk.**

183	A74	10c multicolored, horiz.	.30	.30
184	A74	75c multicolored	1.10	1.40

Central Bank of Malaysia, 20th anniv.

Year of the Child Emblem — A75

Intl. Year of the Child: 15c, Children of the world, globe and ICY emblem. $1, Children at play, ICY emblem.

1979, Feb. 24 ***Perf. 14***

185	A75	10c multicolored	.50	.25
186	A75	15c multicolored	.40	.25
187	A75	$1 multicolored	3.25	3.50
		Nos. 185-187 (3)	4.15	4.00

Symbolic Rubber Plant — A76

Designs: 10c, Symbolic palm. 75c, Symbolic rubber products.

1978, Nov. 28 **Litho.** ***Perf. 13***

188	A76	10c brt green & gold	.25	.25
189	A76	20c multicolored	.45	.25
190	A76	75c brt green & gold	.60	.90
		Nos. 188-190 (3)	1.30	1.40

Centenary of rubber production (in 1977).

Rafflesia Hasseltii A77

Flowers: 2c, Pterocarpus indicus. 5c, Lagerstroemia speciosa. 10c, Durio zibethinus. 15c, Hibiscus. 20c, Rhododendron scortechinii. 25c, Phaeomeria speciosa.

Perf. 15x14½

1979, Apr. 30 **Wmk. 378**

191	A77	1c multicolored	.25	.25
192	A77	2c multicolored	.25	.25
193	A77	5c multicolored	.25	.25
a.		Unwmkd. ('84)		
194	A77	10c multicolored	.25	.25
a.		White flowers, unwmkd. ('84)	.25	.25
195	A77	15c multicolored	.25	.25
a.		15c yel & multi, unwmkd. ('83)	.25	.25
196	A77	20c multicolored	.30	.25
a.		20c greenish & multi, unwmkd. ('83)	.25	.25
197	A77	25c multicolored	.35	.25
a.		Unwmkd. ('85)	5.00	
		Nos. 191-197 (7)	1.90	1.75

Temengor Hydroelectric Dam — A78

Designs: 25c, 50c, Dam and river, diff.

Perf. 13½x14½

1979, Sept. 19 **Litho.** **Unwmk.**

198	A78	15c multicolored	.30	.30
199	A78	25c multicolored	.70	.50
200	A78	50c multicolored	1.00	1.25
		Nos. 198-200 (3)	2.00	2.05

"TELECOM 79" — A79

Telecom Emblem and: 15c, Telephone receiver and globes. 50c, Modes of communication.

1979, Sept. 20 ***Perf. 13½***

Size: 34x25mm

201	A79	10c multicolored	.35	.50
202	A79	15c multicolored	.25	.25

Perf. 14

Size: 39x28mm

203	A79	50c multicolored	.85	2.25
		Nos. 201-203 (3)	1.45	3.00

3rd World Telecommunications Exhibition, Geneva, Sept. 20-26.

Haji Ahmad Shah — A80

1980, July 10 **Litho.** ***Perf. 14½***

204	A80	10c multicolored	.25	.40
205	A80	15c multicolored	.25	.25
206	A80	50c multicolored	.70	2.00
		Nos. 204-206 (3)	1.20	2.65

Installation of Sultan Haji Ahmad Shah of Pahang as Paramount Ruler (Yang di-Pertuan Agong).

Pahang-Sarawak Cable — A81

Designs: 15c, Dial with views of Kuantan and Kuching. 50c, Telephone and maps.

1980, Aug. 31 **Litho.** ***Perf. 13½***

207	A81	10c shown	.25	.35
208	A81	15c multicolored	.25	.25
209	A81	50c multicolored	.35	1.75
		Nos. 207-209 (3)	.85	2.35

National University of Malaysia, 10th Anniversary A82

15c, Jalan Pantai Baru campus. 75c, Great Hall & Tun Haji Abdul Razak (1st chancellor).

1980, Sept. 2 **Litho.** ***Perf. 13½***

210	A82	10c shown	.25	.25
211	A82	15c multicolored	.25	.25
212	A82	75c multicolored	.50	2.75
		Nos. 210-212 (3)	1.00	3.25

Hegira (Pilgrimage Year) — A83

1980, Nov. 9

213	A83	15c multicolored	.30	.25
214	A83	50c multicolored	.45	1.25

International Year of the Disabled — A84

10c, Child learning to walk. 15c, Seamstress. 75c, Athlete.

1981, Feb. 14 **Litho.** ***Perf. 13½***

215	A84	10c multicolored	.50	.25
216	A84	15c multicolored	.55	.25
217	A84	75c multicolored	1.50	3.25
		Nos. 215-217 (3)	2.55	3.75

Sultan Mahmud of Trengganu — A85

1981, Mar. 21 **Litho.** ***Perf. 14½***

218	A85	10c multicolored	.25	.25
219	A85	15c multicolored	.25	.25
220	A85	50c multicolored	.90	.30
		Nos. 218-220 (3)	1.40	.80

Industrial Training Seminar A86

Designs: Various workers.

1981, May 2 **Litho.** ***Perf. 13½***

221	A86	10c multicolored	.35	.25
222	A86	15c multicolored	.25	.25
223	A86	30c multicolored	.35	.25
224	A86	75c multicolored	.60	2.00
		Nos. 221-224 (4)	1.55	2.75

World Energy Conference, 25th anniv. — A87

10c, "25". 15c, Sources of Energy. 75c, Non-renewable energy.

1981, June 17 **Litho.** ***Perf. 13½***

225	A87	10c multicolored	.40	.30
226	A87	15c multicolored	.35	.30
227	A87	75c multicolored	1.75	3.25
		Nos. 225-227 (3)	2.50	3.85

Centenary of Sabah — A88

15c, Views, 1881 and 1981. 80c, Traditional and modern farming.

1981, Aug. 31 **Litho.** ***Perf. 12***

228	A88	15c multicolored	.60	.30
229	A88	80c multicolored	3.00	4.00

Rain Tree A89

50c, Simber tree, vert. 80c, Borneo camphor-wood, vert.

1981, Dec. 16 **Litho.** ***Perf. 14***

230	A89	15c shown	.50	.25
231	A89	50c multicolored	1.50	1.25
232	A89	80c multicolored	3.00	4.00
		Nos. 230-232 (3)	5.00	5.50

Scouting Year and Jamboree, Apr. 9- 16 A90

1982, Apr. 10 **Litho.** ***Perf. 13½x13***

233	A90	15c Jamboree emblem	.40	.30
234	A90	50c Flag, emblem	1.00	.75
235	A90	80c Emblems, knot	1.75	4.00
		Nos. 233-235 (3)	3.15	5.05

15th Anniv. of Assoc. of South East Asian Nations (ASEAN) A91

1982, Aug. 8 **Litho.** ***Perf. 14***

236	A91	15c Meeting Center	.50	.25
237	A91	$1 Flags	2.00	3.25

Dome of the Rock, Jerusalem A92

1982, Aug. 21 ***Perf. 13½***

238	A92	15c multicolored	1.50	.35
239	A92	$1 multicolored	4.50	*5.25*

For the freedom of Palestine.

25th Anniv. of Independence — A93

10c, Kuala Lumpur. 15c, Independence celebration. 50c, Parade. 80c, Independence ceremony.

1982, Aug. 31 **Litho.** ***Perf. 14***

240	A93	10c multicolored	.25	.25
241	A93	15c multicolored	.25	.25
242	A93	50c multicolored	.40	.40
243	A93	80c multicolored	.70	*2.50*
a.		Souvenir sheet of 4, #240-243	15.00	15.00
b.		Souvenir sheet of 4, #240-243	10.00	10.00
		Nos. 240-243 (4)	1.60	3.40

No. 243a has a narrow silver frame around the center vignette of the 10c value. This frame was removed for the second printing, No. 243b.

Traditional Games — A94

1982, Oct. 30 *Perf. 13½*
244 A94 10c Shadow play 1.00 .35
245 A94 15c Cross top 1.00 .35
246 A94 75c Kite flying 2.75 4.25
Nos. 244-246 (3) 4.75 4.95

Handicrafts — A95

1982, Nov. 26 Litho. *Perf. 13x13½*
247 A95 10c Sabah hats .40 .45
248 A95 15c Gold-threaded cloth .40 .45
249 A95 75c Sarawak pottery 1.90 3.25
Nos. 247-249 (3) 2.70 4.15

Commonwealth Day — A96

15c, Flag. 20c, Seri Paduka Baginda. 40c, Oil palm refinery. $1, Globe.

1983, Mar. 14 Litho. *Perf. 14*
250 A96 15c multicolored .30 .25
251 A96 20c multicolored .30 .25
252 A96 40c multicolored .45 .40
253 A96 $1 multicolored .70 2.25
Nos. 250-253 (4) 1.75 3.15

First Shipment of Natural Gas, Bintulu, Sarawak — A97

15c, Bintulu Port Authority emblem. 20c, LNG Tanker Tenaga Satu. $1, Gas plant.

1983, Jan. 22 Litho. *Perf. 12*
254 A97 15c multi 1.10 .35
a. Perf. 13½ *30.00* 3.25
255 A97 20c multi 1.40 1.00
a. Perf. 13½ *35.00* 3.50
256 A97 $1 multi 4.50 6.25
a. Perf. 13½ *60.00* 12.50
Nos. 254-256 (3) 7.00 7.60
Nos. 254a-256a (3) 125.00 19.25

Freshwater Fish — A98

No. 257a, Tilapia nilotica. No. 257b, Cyprinus carpio. No. 258a, Puntius goniotus. No. 258b, Ctenopharyngodon idellus.

1983, June 15 *Perf. 12x12½*
257 Pair 6.00 3.00
a. A98 20c multicolored 1.50 .35
b. A98 20c multicolored 1.50 .35
c. As #257, perf. 13½x14 11.00 11.00
258 Pair 7.00 3.50
a. A98 40c multicolored 1.75 .40
b. A98 40c multicolored 1.75 .40
c. As #258, perf. 13½x14 11.50 11.50

Opening of East-West Highway — A99

15c, Lower Sungei Pergau Bridge. 20c, Sungei Perak Reservoir Bridge. $1, Map.

1983, July 1 *Perf. 14x13½*
259 A99 15c multicolored .75 .25
260 A99 20c multicolored 1.00 .60
261 A99 $1 multicolored 4.50 *6.25*
Nos. 259-261 (3) 6.25 7.10

Armed Forces, 50th Anniv. — A100

Designs: 15c, Royal Malaysian Aircraft. 20c, Navy vessel firing missile. 40c, Battle at Pasir Panjang. 80c, Trooping of the Royal colors.

1983, Sept. 16 Litho. *Perf. 13½*
262 A100 15c multicolored 1.25 .25
263 A100 20c multicolored 1.50 .45
264 A100 40c multicolored 2.25 2.25
265 A100 80c multicolored 3.00 *4.75*
a. Souvenir sheet of 4, #262-265 12.00 12.00
Nos. 262-265 (4) 8.00 7.70

Helmeted Hornbill — A101

20c, Wrinkled Hornbill. 50c, White crested Hornbill. $1, Rhinoceros Hornbill.

1983, Oct. 26 Litho. *Perf. 13½*
266 A101 15c shown 1.00 .25
267 A101 20c multicolored 1.25 .50
268 A101 50c multicolored 2.50 2.50
269 A101 $1 multicolored 3.75 *5.00*
Nos. 266-269 (4) 8.50 8.25

25th Anniv. of Begara Bank A102

Branch offices.

1984, Jan. 26 Litho. *Perf. 13½x14*
270 A102 20c Ipoh 1.25 .35
271 A102 $1 Alor Setar 2.25 3.25

10th Anniv. of Federal Territory A103

Views of Kuala Lumpur. 20c, 40c vert.

Perf. 14x13½, 13½x14
1984, Feb. 1 **Litho.**
272 A103 20c multicolored 1.00 .50
273 A103 40c multicolored 1.40 1.25
274 A103 80c multicolored 4.00 6.00
Nos. 272-274 (3) 6.40 7.75

Labuan Federal Territory — A104

20c, Development symbols, map, arms. $1, Flag, map.

1984, Apr. 16 Litho. *Perf. 13½x14*
275 A104 20c multicolored 1.50 .40
276 A104 $1 multicolored 4.75 5.25

Traditional Weapons — A105

No. 277, Keris Semenanjung. No. 278, Keris Pekakak. No. 279, Keris Jawa. No. 280, Tumbuk Lada.

1984, May 30 *Perf. 13x14*
277 A105 40c multicolored 1.10 1.10
278 A105 40c multicolored 1.10 1.10
279 A105 40c multicolored 1.10 1.10
280 A105 40c multicolored 1.10 1.10
a. Block of 4, #277-280 6.00 *7.00*

Asia-Pacific Broadcasting Union, 20th Anniv. — A106

1984, June 23 *Perf. 14x14½*
281 A106 20c Map, waves 1.50 .40
282 A106 $1 "20" 2.50 4.25

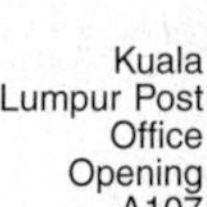
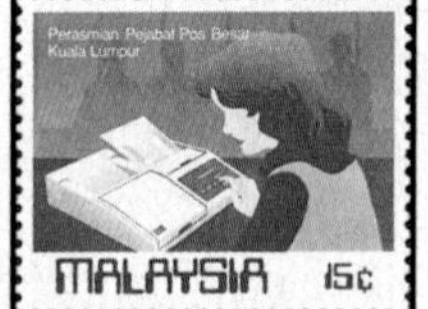

Kuala Lumpur Post Office Opening A107

15c, Facsimile transmission. 20c, Building. $1, Mail bag conveyor.

1984, Oct. 29 *Perf. 12x11½*
283 A107 15c multicolored .80 .35
284 A107 20c multicolored .80 .35
285 A107 $1 multicolored 2.00 4.00
Nos. 283-285 (3) 3.60 4.70

Installation of Sultan of Johore as 8th Paramount Ruler of Malaysia — A108

Sultan Mahmood, Arms A109

1984, Nov. 15 Litho. *Perf. 12*
286 A108 15c multicolored 1.00 .40
287 A108 20c multicolored 1.00 .35
288 A109 40c multicolored 1.40 .90
289 A109 80c multicolored 2.40 4.25
Nos. 286-289 (4) 5.80 5.90

Malaysian Hibiscus — A110

10c, White hibiscus. 20c, Red hibiscus. 40c, Pink hibiscus. $1, Orange hibiscus.

1984, Dec. 12 Litho. *Perf. 13½*
290 A110 10c multi 1.00 .40
291 A110 20c multi 1.00 .35
292 A110 40c multi 2.00 2.00
293 A110 $1 multi 3.25 5.00
Nos. 290-293 (4) 7.25 7.75

Parliament, 25th Anniv. — A111

20c, Badge, vert. $1, Parliament, Kuala Lumpur.

Perf. 13½x14, 14x13½
1985, Mar. 30 **Litho.**
294 A111 20c multi .80 .30
295 A111 $1 multi 1.75 3.00

Protected Wildlife A112

10c, Prionodon linsang. 40c, Nycticebus coucang, vert. $1, Petaurista elegans, vert.

1985, Apr. 25 *Perf. 14*
296 A112 10c multicolored 1.50 .55
297 A112 40c multicolored 1.75 1.25
298 A112 $1 multicolored 4.50 6.00
Nos. 296-298 (3) 7.75 7.80

Intl. Youth Year — A113

20c, Youth solidarity. $1, Participation in natl. development.

1985, May 15 *Perf. 13*
299 A113 20c multicolored 1.10 .40
300 A113 $1 multicolored 4.00 5.00

Malaya Railways Centenary A114

Locomotives: 15c, Steam engine, 1885. 20c, Diesel-electric, 1957. $1, Diesel, 1963.

80c, Train leaving Kuala Lumpur Station, 1938.

1985, June 1 *Perf. 13*
301 A114 15c multicolored 2.00 .50
302 A114 20c multicolored 2.10 .50
303 A114 $1 multicolored 5.25 6.25
Nos. 301-303 (3) 9.35 7.25

Souvenir Sheet

Perf. 14x13

304 A114 80c multi 10.50 11.00

No. 304 contains one stamp 48x32mm.

Proton Saga
A115

1985, July 9 ***Perf. 14***

305	A115 20c multicolored	1.25	.30
306	A115 40c multicolored	1.75	.80
307	A115 $1 multicolored	3.75	5.75
	Nos. 305-307 (3)	6.75	6.85

Inauguration of natl. automotive industry.

Sultan Salahuddin Abdul Aziz, Selangor Coat of Arms
A116

1985, Sept. 5 ***Perf. 13***

308	A116 15c multicolored	.70	.60
309	A116 20c multicolored	.80	.60
310	A116 $1 multicolored	3.75	6.00
	Nos. 308-310 (3)	5.25	7.20

25th anniv. of coronation.

Penang Bridge Opening
A117

1985, Sept. 15 Litho. ***Perf. 13½x13***

311	A117 20c shown	1.40	.45
312	A117 40c Bridge, map	2.75	.75

Size: 44x28mm

Perf. 12½

313	A117 $1 Map	4.00	5.25
	Nos. 311-313 (3)	8.15	6.45

Natl. Oil Industry
A118

15c, Offshore rig, vert. 20c, 1st refinery. $1, Map of oil and gas fields.

1985, Nov. 4 ***Perf. 12½***

314	A118 15c multi	1.40	.45
315	A118 20c multi	1.40	.45
316	A118 $1 multi	5.00	5.25
	Nos. 314-316 (3)	7.80	6.15

Coronation of Paduka Seri, Sultan of Perak
A119

1985, Dec. 9 ***Perf. 14***

317	A119 15c lt blue & multi	.55	.40
318	A119 20c lilac & multi	.80	.40
319	A119 $1 gold & multi	3.75	6.00
	Nos. 317-319 (3)	5.10	6.80

Birds
A120

No. 320, Lophura ignita, vert. No. 321, Pavo malacense, vert. No. 322, Lophura bulweri. No. 323, Argusianus argus.

Wmk. 388

1986, Mar. 11 Litho. ***Perf. 13¼***

320	A120 20c multicolored	2.50	.40
a.	Perf. 12	4.75	1.25
321	A120 20c multicolored	2.50	.40
a.	Pair, #320-321	5.00	1.50
b.	Perf. 12	7.50	2.00
c.	Pair, #320a, 321b	12.50	8.25
322	A120 40c multicolored	4.00	.50
a.	Perf. 12	8.25	1.50
323	A120 40c multicolored	5.00	.50
a.	Pair, #322-323	9.00	1.90
b.	Perf. 12	7.25	1.50
c.	Pair, #322a, 323b	15.50	11.50
	Nos. 320-323 (4)	14.00	1.80

PATA '86, Pacific Area Travel Assoc. Conference, Persidangan — A121

No. 324: a, Two women dancing. b, Woman in red. c, Man and woman.

No. 325: a, Woman in gold. b, Woman holding fan. c, Woman in violet.

Perf. 15x14½

1986, Apr. 14 Litho. Unwmk.

324	Strip of 3	3.00	3.25
a.-c.	A121 20c any single	.75	1.00
325	Strip of 3	4.00	4.00
a.-c.	A121 40c any single	1.00	1.25

Malaysia Games
A122

Games Emblem — A123

Flags — A124

Wmk. 388

1986, Apr. 14 Litho. ***Perf. 12***

326	A122 20c multicolored	1.60	.50
327	A123 40c multicolored	4.50	2.00
328	A124 $1 multicolored	6.00	6.50
	Nos. 326-328 (3)	12.10	9.00

Nephelium Lappaceum
A125

Averrhoa Carambola
A126

No. 330, Ananas comosus. No. 331, Durio zibethinus. No. 332, Garcinia mangostana. No. 332C, Musa sapientum. No. 334, Musa sapientum. No. 335, Mangifera odorata. No. 336, Carica papaya.

Litho. (#329-332), Photo. (#333-336)

Perf. 12 (#329-332)

1986-2000 Wmk. 388

329	A125 40c shown	.40	.25
a.	Perf. 13½x14	.75	
330	A125 50c multi	.60	.25
a.	Perf. 13½x14	.75	
331	A125 80c multi	.95	.35
a.	Perf. 13½x14	1.25	
332	A125 $1 multi	1.00	.35
a.	Perf. 13½x14	1.25	

Perf. 13½x14

332C	A125 $5 multi ('00)	1.75	.80

Perf. 13½

Wmk. 233

333	A126 $2 shown	2.00	.65
334	A126 $5 multi	4.00	1.10
335	A126 $10 multi	6.75	3.75
336	A126 $20 multi	12.00	5.50
	Nos. 329-336 (9)	29.45	13.00

No. 332C issued 2000; balance of set issued 6/5/86.

Two additional stamps were issued in this set. The editors would like to examine any examples.

Compare with Nos. 766A-766H.

Natl. Assoc. for the Prevention of Drug Abuse, 10th Anniv.
A127

1986, June 26 Wmk. 388 ***Perf. 13***

337	A127 20c Skull	1.10	.50
338	A127 40c Dove	1.75	.80
339	A127 $1 Addict, vert.	5.50	4.25
	Nos. 337-339 (3)	8.35	5.55

Malaysian Airlines Kuala Lumpur-Los Angeles Inaugural Flight — A128

20c, Flight routes map. 40c, MAS emblem, new route. $1, Emblem, stops.

1986, July 31 ***Perf. 14x13½***

340	A128 20c multi	2.25	.50
341	A128 40c multi	2.75	.70
342	A128 $1 multi	6.00	4.25
	Nos. 340-342 (3)	11.00	5.45

Industrial Productivity
A129

20c, Construction, vert. 40c, Industry. $1, Automobile factory.

1986, Nov. 3 Litho. ***Perf. 14***

343	A129 20c multi	.80	.40
344	A129 40c multi	1.75	1.00
345	A129 $1 multi	4.75	5.75
	Nos. 343-345 (3)	7.30	7.15

Historic Buildings
A130

15c, Istana Lama Seri Menanti, Negri Sembilan. 20c, Istana Kenangan, Perak. 40c, Bangunan Stadthuys, Malacca. $1, Istana Kuching, Sarawak.

1986, Dec. 20 ***Perf. 13***

346	A130 15c multicolored	.90	.30
347	A130 20c multicolored	.90	.30
348	A130 40c multicolored	2.00	.70
349	A130 $1 multicolored	3.00	4.50
	Nos. 346-349 (4)	6.80	5.80

See design A146.

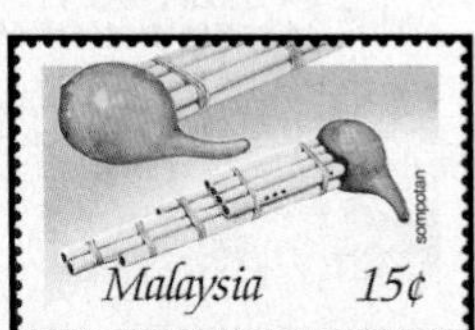

Folk Music Instruments — A131

1987, Mar. 7 Litho. ***Perf. 12***

350	A131 15c Sompotan	1.00	.65
351	A131 20c Sapih	1.00	.65
352	A131 50c Serunai, vert.	2.40	.65
353	A131 80c Rebab, vert.	4.00	2.25
	Nos. 350-353 (4)	8.40	4.20

Intl. Year of Shelter for the Homeless — A132

20c, Model village. $1, Symbols of family, shelter.

1987, Apr. 6 Litho. ***Perf. 12***

354	A132 20c multi	.80	.30
355	A132 $1 multi	4.00	1.50

UN Anti-Drug Campaign and Congress, Vienna
A133

No. 356, Health boy, family, rainbow. No. 357, Holding drugs. No. 358, Child warding off drugs. No. 359, Drugs, damaged body in capsule.

1987, June 8 Litho. ***Perf. 13½x13***

356	20c multi	.75	.75
357	20c multi	.75	.75
a.	A133 Pair, #356-357	3.00	3.00
358	40c multi	1.75	.75
359	40c multi	1.75	.75
a.	A133 Pair, #358-359	7.00	3.00
	Nos. 356-359 (4)	5.00	3.00

Nos. 357a, 359a have continuous designs.

Kenyir Hydroelectric Power Station Inauguration — A134

1987, July 13 ***Perf. 12***

360	A134 20c Power facility, dam	1.60	.40
361	A134 $1 Side view	3.50	1.75

33rd Commonwealth Parliamentary Conference — A135

20c, Maces, parliament. $1, Parliament, maces, diff.

1987, Sept. 1 Litho. ***Perf. 12***

362	A135 20c multi	.55	.25
363	A135 $1 multi	1.50	1.10

Transportation and Communications Decade in Asia and the Pacific (1985-94) — A136

Designs: 15c, Satellites, Earth, satellite dish. 20c, Car, diesel train, Kuala Lumpur Station. 40c, MISC container ship. $1, Malaysia Airlines jet, Kuala Lumpur Airport.

1987, Oct. 26 ***Perf. 13½x13***

364 A136 15c multicolored 1.25 .60
365 A136 20c multicolored 1.25 .70
366 A136 40c multicolored 2.25 1.25
367 A136 $1 multicolored 4.25 6.00
Nos. 364-367 (4) 9.00 8.55

Protected Wildcats A137

1987, Nov. 14

368 A137 15c Felis temminckii 2.50 .50
369 A137 20c Felis planiceps 3.00 .75
370 A137 40c Felis marmorata 4.00 1.75
371 A137 $1 Neofelis nebulosa 8.00 7.50
Nos. 368-371 (4) 17.50 10.50

ASEAN, 20th Anniv. A138

1987, Dec. 14 **Litho.** ***Perf. 13***

372 A138 20c "20," flags .35 .25
373 A138 $1 Flags, Earth 1.60 1.50

Opening of Sultan Salahuddin Abdul Aziz Shah Mosque, Selangor A139

Dome, minarets and: 15c, Arches. 20c, Sultan Abdul Aziz Shah, Selangor crest. $1, Interior, vert.

1988, Mar. 11 **Litho.** ***Perf. 12***

374 A139 15c multicolored .50 .35
375 A139 20c multicolored .50 .35
376 A139 $1 multicolored 1.40 2.25
Nos. 374-376 (3) 2.40 2.95

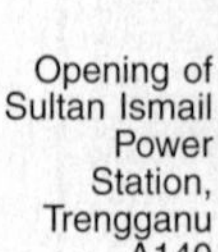

Opening of Sultan Ismail Power Station, Trengganu A140

1988, Apr. 4 ***Perf. 13***

377 A140 20c shown .40 .30
378 A140 $1 Station, diff. 2.00 1.25

Wildlife Protection — A141

Birds: No. 379, Hypothymis azurea. No. 380, Dicaeum cruentatum. No. 381, Aethopyga siparaja. No. 382, Cymbirhynchus macr-orhynchos.

1988, June 30 **Litho.** ***Perf. 13***

379 20c multicolored .70 .70
380 20c multicolored .70 .70
a. A141 Pair, #379-380 3.75 3.75
381 50c multicolored 1.40 1.40
382 50c multicolored 1.40 1.40
a. A141 Pair, #381-382 6.50 6.50
Nos. 379-382 (4) 4.20 4.20

A142

Independence of Sabah and Sarawak, 25th Anniv. — A143

1988, Aug. 31 **Litho.** ***Perf. 13x13½***

383 A142 20c Sabah .65 .70
384 A142 20c Sarawak .65 .70
a. Pair, #383-384 1.40 1.50
385 A143 $1 State and natl. symbols 2.25 3.25
Nos. 383-385 (3) 3.55 4.65

Nudibranchs A144

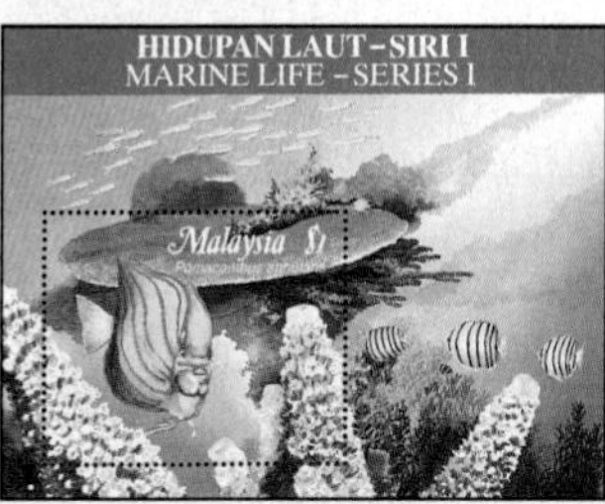

Marine Life — A145

No. 386: a, Glossodoris atromarginata. b, Phyllidia ocellata. c, Chromodoris annae. d, Flabellina macassarana. e, Fryeria ruppelli.
No. 387, Pomacanthus annularis.

1988, Dec. 17 **Litho.** ***Perf. 12***

386 Strip of 5 7.00 7.00
a.-e. A144 20c any single .75 .25

Souvenir Sheet

Perf. 14

387 A145 $1 multicolored 5.25 5.25

No. 387 contains one stamp 50x40mm.

Historic Buildings, Malacca A146

No. 388, Perisytiharan Kemerdekaan Memorial. No. 389, Istana Kesultanan. $1, Porta da Santiago.

Perf. 13½x13, 13x13½

1989, Apr. 15 **Litho.**

388 A146 20c multicolored .50 .35
389 A146 20c multicolored .50 .35
390 A146 $1 multicolored, vert. 1.90 1.50
Nos. 388-390 (3) 2.90 2.20

See design A130.

Crustaceans A147

No. 391, Tetralia nigrolineata. No. 392, Neopetrolisthes maculatus. No. 393, Periclimenes holthuisi. No. 394, Synalpheus neomeris.

Wmk. 388

1989, June 29 **Litho.** ***Perf. 12***

391 A147 20c multicolored .50 .50
392 A147 20c multicolored .50 .50
a. Pair, #391-392 1.60 1.60
393 A147 40c multicolored .90 .90
394 A147 40c multicolored .90 .90
a. Pair, #393-394 2.75 2.75
Nos. 391-394 (4) 2.80 2.80

7th Natl. Scout Jamboree A148

10c, Map, badges. 20c, Scout salute, natl. flag. 80c, Camping out.

1989, July 26 ***Perf. 13½x13, 13x13½***

395 A148 10c multicolored .50 .45
396 A148 20c multicolored .50 .45
397 A148 80c multicolored 2.50 3.00
Nos. 395-397 (3) 3.50 3.90

Nos. 395-396 vert.

15th SEA Games, Kuala Lumpur — A149

Designs: 10c, Cycling, horiz. 20c, Track events, horiz. 50c, Swimming. $1, Torchbearer, stadium and flags.

Perf. 13½x13, 13x13½

1989, Aug. 20 **Litho.** **Wmk. 388**

398 A149 10c multicolored .40 .60
399 A149 20c multicolored .40 .50
400 A149 50c multicolored 1.25 .80
401 A149 $1 multicolored 2.10 3.50
Nos. 398-401 (4) 4.15 5.40

Installation of Sultan Azlan as Supreme Ruler — A150

1989, Sept. 18 ***Perf. 13x13½***

402 A150 20c multicolored .35 .25
403 A150 40c multicolored .60 .30
404 A150 $1 multicolored 1.40 2.25
Nos. 402-404 (3) 2.35 2.80

Commonwealth Heads of Government Meeting — A151

1989, Oct. 18 ***Perf. 13½x13, 13x13½***

405 A151 20c Conference center .40 .30
406 A151 50c Folk dancers, vert. .80 .60
407 A151 $1 Map, flag 1.60 2.50
Nos. 405-407 (3) 2.80 3.40

Malaysia Airlines Inaugural Non-stop Flight to London, Dec. 2 A152

No. 408, Passenger jet, Malaysian clock tower, Big Ben. No. 409, Passenger jet, Malaysian skyscraper, Westminster Palace. $1, Map, passenger jet.

1989, Dec. 2 **Wmk. 388** ***Perf. 13***

408 A152 20c shown 2.00 2.00
409 A152 20c multicolored 2.00 2.00
a. Pair, #408-409 4.50 4.50
410 A152 $1 multicolored 5.50 5.50
Nos. 408-410 (3) 9.50 9.50

National Park, 50th Anniv. — A153

1989, Dec. 28 ***Perf. 13x13½***

411 A153 20c Map, sloth 1.60 .40
412 A153 $1 Crested arguses 4.50 4.50

Visit Malaysia.

Visit Malaysia Year — A154

20c, Map. 50c, Drummers. $1, Yachts, scuba divers.

1990, Jan. 11 ***Perf. 12***

413 A154 20c multicolored .60 .50
414 A154 50c multicolored 1.40 1.10
415 A154 $1 multicolored 2.25 3.25
Nos. 413-415 (3) 4.25 4.85

Wildflowers A155

15c, Dillenia suffruticosa. 20c, Mimosa pudica. 50c, Ipomoea carnea. $1, Nymphaea pubescens.

1990, Mar. 12

416 A155 15c multicolored .30 .30
417 A155 20c multicolored .30 .30
418 A155 50c multicolored .80 .80
419 A155 $1 multicolored 1.20 2.25
Nos. 416-419 (4) 2.60 3.65

Kuala Lumpur A156

Wmk. 388

1990, May 14 Litho. *Perf. 12*

420 A156 20c Flag, rainbow, vert. .40 .40
421 A156 40c shown .70 .50
422 A156 $1 Cityscape 1.50 2.75
Nos. 420-422 (3) 2.60 3.65

South-South Consultation and Cooperation Conference — A157

1990, June 1 *Perf. 13*

423 A157 20c shown .45 .35
424 A157 80c Emblem 1.75 2.25

Alor Setar, 250th Anniv. A158

40c, Musicians, vert. $1, Government bldg., vert.

1990, June 2 *Perf. 12*

425 A158 20c shown .40 .30
426 A158 40c multicolored .70 .35
427 A158 $1 multicolored 1.50 3.00
Nos. 425-427 (3) 2.60 3.65

Intl. Literacy Year A159

20c, Letters, sign language. 40c, People reading. $1, Globe, pen nib, vert.

1990, Sept. 8 *Perf. 12*

428 A159 20c multicolored .50 .35
a. Perf. 13 17.50
429 A159 40c multicolored 1.00 .40
430 A159 $1 multicolored 2.00 3.00
Nos. 428-430 (3) 3.50 3.75

Turtles A160

15c, Dermochelys coriacea. 20c, Chelonia mydas. 40c, Eretmochelys imbricata. $1, Lepidochelys olivacea.

1990, Nov. 17

431 A160 15c multicolored 1.25 .30
432 A160 20c multicolored 1.25 .30
433 A160 40c multicolored 1.50 .65
434 A160 $1 multicolored 3.25 3.75
Nos. 431-434 (4) 7.25 5.00

MARA (Council of Indigenous People), 25th Anniv. A161

1991, Apr. 25

435 A161 20c Construction .30 .30
436 A161 40c Education .50 .35
437 A161 $1 Banking & industry .70 2.00
Nos. 435-437 (3) 1.50 2.65

Wasps — A162

Designs: 15c, Eustenogaster calyptodoma. 20c, Vespa affinis indonensis. 50c, Sceliphorn javanum. $1, Ampulex compressa.

1991, July 29

438 A162 15c multicolored .40 .40
439 A162 20c multicolored .40 .40
440 A162 50c multicolored .90 .50
441 A162 $1 multicolored 1.90 2.10
a. Souvenir sheet of 4, #438-441, perf. 14½x14 5.50 5.50
Nos. 438-441 (4) 3.60 3.40

Prime Ministers — A163

No. 442, Tunku Abdul Rahman Putra Al-Haj (1903-90). No. 443, Tun Hussein Onn (1922-90). No. 444, Tun Abdul Razak Hussein (1922-76).

1991, Aug. 30

442 A163 $1 multicolored .90 1.00
443 A163 $1 multicolored .90 1.00
444 A163 $1 multicolored .90 1.00
Nos. 442-444 (3) 2.70 3.00

Historic Buildings A164

Designs: 15c, Istana Maziah, Trengganu. 20c, Istana Besar, Johore. 40c, Istana Bandar, Kuala Langat, Selangor. $1, Istana Jahar, Kelantan.

1991, Nov. 7

445 A164 15c multicolored .35 .30
446 A164 20c multicolored .35 .30
447 A164 40c multicolored .55 .40
448 A164 $1 multicolored 1.40 2.25
Nos. 445-448 (4) 2.65 3.25

Sarawak Museum, Cent. A165

Museum buildings, fabric pattern and: 30c, Brass lamp. $1, Vase.

1991, Dec. 21

449 A165 30c multicolored .40 .30
450 A165 $1 multicolored 1.40 2.00

Malaysian Postal Service — A166

Designs: No. 451a, Postman on bicycle. b, Postman on motorcycle. c, Mail truck. d, Mail truck, diff., oil tank. e, Globe, airplane.

1992, Jan. 1

451 A166 30c Strip of 5, #a.-e. 3.50 3.50

Malaysian Tropical Forests A167

Designs: 20c, Hill Dipterocarp Forest, Dyera costulata. 50c, Mangrove Swamp Forest, Rhizophora apiculata. $1, Lowland Dipterocarp Forest, Neobalanocarpus heimii.

1992, Mar. 23

452 A167 20c multicolored .35 .35
453 A167 50c multicolored .80 .50
454 A167 $1 multicolored 1.10 2.25
Nos. 452-454 (3) 2.25 3.10

Installation of Yang di-Pertuan Besar of Negri Sembilan, Silver Jubilee A168

1992, Apr. 18

455 A168 30c Portrait, arms .35 .25
456 A168 $1 Building 1.25 2.00

1992 Thomas Cup Champions in Badminton — A169

1992, July 25 *Perf. 12*

457 A169 $1 Cup, flag .90 1.20
458 A169 $1 Players .90 1.20

Souvenir Sheet

459 A169 $2 multicolored 2.50 2.50

No. 459 contains one 75x28mm stamp.

ASEAN, 25th Anniv. A170

1992, Aug. 8

460 A170 30c shown .55 .40
461 A170 50c Flora 1.00 .60
462 A170 $1 Architecture 1.60 2.00
Nos. 460-462 (3) 3.15 3.00

Postage Stamps in Malaysia, 125th Annv. A171

No. 463, Straits Settlements #1, Malaya #84. No. 464, Straits Settlements #2, Malaysia #2. No. 465, Straits Settlements #11, Malaysia #421. No. 466, Straits Settlements #14, Malaysia #467. No. 467, Flag, simulated stamp.

1992, Sept. 1

463 A171 30c multicolored .60 .25
464 A171 30c multicolored .60 .25
a. Pair #463-464 1.75 1.75
465 A171 50c multicolored 1.00 .25
466 A171 50c multicolored 1.00 .25
a. Pair #465-466 2.25 2.25
Nos. 463-466 (4) 3.20 1.00

Souvenir Sheet

467 A171 $2 multicolored 2.75 2.75

Kuala Lumpur '92.

A173

Coral — A174

No. 471: a, Acropora. b, Dendronephthya. c, Dendrophyllia. d, Sinularia. e, Melithaea.
No. 472, Subergorgia.

1992, Dec. 21

471 A173 30c Strip of 5, #a.-e. 5.00 5.00

Souvenir Sheet

472 A174 $2 multicolored 4.50 5.00

16th Asian-Pacific Dental Congress A175

Children from various countries: No. 473, 4 girls. No. 474, 4 girls, 1 holding koala.
Dentists, flags of: No. 475, Japan, Malaysia, South Korea. No. 476, New Zealand, Thailand, People's Republic of China, Indonesia.

1993, Apr. 24

473 A175 30c multicolored .60 .60
474 A175 30c multicolored .60 .60
a. Pair, #473-474 1.50 1.50
475 A175 50c multicolored .90 .90
476 A175 $1 multicolored 1.75 1.75
a. Pair, #475-476 3.50 3.50
Nos. 473-476 (4) 3.85 3.85

A176

30c, Fairway, vert. 50c, Old, new club houses, vert. $1, Sand trap.

1993, June 24

477 A176 30c multicolored .80 .55
478 A176 50c multicolored 1.50 .70
479 A176 $1 multicolored 2.40 3.00
Nos. 477-479 (3) 4.70 4.25

Royal Selangor Golf Club, cent.

Wildflowers A177

20c, Alpinia rafflesiana. 30c, Achasma megalocheilos. 50c, Zingiber spectabile. $1, Costus speciosus.

1993, Aug. 2

480 A177 20c multicolored .65 .50
481 A177 30c multicolored .65 .50
482 A177 50c multicolored 1.75 .65
483 A177 $1 multicolored 2.25 3.00
Nos. 480-483 (4) 5.30 4.65

14th Commonwealth Forestry Conference — A178

30c, Globe, forest. 50c, Hand holding trees. $1, Trees under dome, vert.

1993, Sept. 13

484 A178 30c multicolored .60 .50
485 A178 50c multicolored 1.10 .60
486 A178 $1 multicolored 1.60 2.25
Nos. 484-486 (3) 3.30 3.35

Nos. 484-486 with Bangkok '93 Emblem Added

Wmk. 388

1993, Oct. 1 Litho. *Perf. 12*

486A A178 30c multicolored *4.50 4.00*
486B A178 50c multicolored *5.50 5.00*
486C A178 $1 multicolored *10.00 8.50*
Nos. 486A-486C (3) 20.00 17.50

Kingfishers — A179

1993, Oct. 23

487 30c Halcyon smyrnensis 1.00 1.00
488 30c Alcedo meninting 1.00 1.00
a. A179 Pair, #487-488 2.50 2.50
489 50c Halcyon concreta 1.60 1.60
490 50c Ceyx erithacus 1.60 1.60
a. A179 Pair, #489-490 4.00 4.00
Nos. 487-490 (4) 5.20 5.20

A180

30c, SME MD3-160 airplane. 50c, Eagle X-TS airplane. $1, Patrol boat KD Kasturi. $2, Map of Malaysia.

1993, Dec. 7

491 A180 30c multicolored .60 .40
492 A180 50c multicolored 1.25 .70
493 A180 $1 multicolored 1.75 2.25
Nos. 491-493 (3) 3.60 3.35

Souvenir Sheet

494 A180 $2 multicolored 3.00 3.00

Langkawi Intl. Maritime and Aerospace Exhibition (LIMA '93).

Visit Malaysia Year — A181

1994, Jan. 1

495 A181 20c Jeriau Waterfalls .40 .40
496 A181 30c Flowers .50 .45
497 A181 50c Marine life 1.00 .60
498 A181 $1 Wildlife 1.50 2.00
Nos. 495-498 (4) 3.40 3.45

See Nos. 527A-527D.

Kuala Lumpur Natl. Planetarium A182

Designs: 30c, Exterior. 50c, Interior displays. $1, Theater auditorium.

1994, Feb. 7

499 A182 30c multicolored .50 .40
500 A182 50c multicolored .90 .65
501 A182 $1 multicolored 1.75 2.25
Nos. 499-501 (3) 3.15 3.30

Orchids — A183

Designs: 20c, Spathoglottis aurea. 30c, Paphiopedilum barbatum. 50c, Bulbophyllum lobbii. $1, Aerides odorata. $2, Grammatophyllum speciosum.

1994, Feb. 17

502 A183 20c multicolored .55 .35
503 A183 30c multicolored .55 .40
504 A183 50c multicolored .90 .70
505 A183 $1 multicolored 1.60 2.25
Nos. 502-505 (4) 3.60 3.70

Souvenir Sheet

506 A183 $2 multicolored 3.75 3.75

Hong Kong '94 (No. 506).

A184

1994, June 17

507 A184 20c Decorative bowl .35 .30
508 A184 30c Celestial sphere .40 .30
509 A184 50c Dinar coins .55 .55
510 A184 $1 Decorative tile 1.10 1.25
Nos. 507-510 (4) 2.40 2.40

World Islamic Civilization Festival '94. See Nos. 528-531.

Veterinary Services, Cent. — A185

1994, July 26

511 A185 30c shown .60 .40
512 A185 50c Meat processing .80 .60
513 A185 $1 Cattle, laboratory 1.60 2.00
Nos. 511-513 (3) 3.00 3.00

Electrification, Cent. — A186

1994, Sept. 3

514 A186 30c Laying cable .55 .40
515 A186 30c Lighted city .55 .40
a. Pair, #514-515 1.40 1.40
516 A186 $1 Futuristic city 1.40 1.75
Nos. 514-516 (3) 2.50 2.55

North-South Expressway A187

1994, Sept. 8

517 A187 30c shown .40 .30
518 A187 50c Interchange .55 .45
519 A187 $1 Bridge 1.25 1.60
Nos. 517-519 (3) 2.20 2.35

A188

1994, Sept. 22

520 A188 30c pink & multi .45 .30
521 A188 50c yellow & multi .60 .40
522 A188 $1 green & multi 1.10 1.60
Nos. 520-522 (3) 2.15 2.30

Installation of 10th Yang Di-Pertuan Agong (Head of State).

A189

Wmk. 388

1994, Oct. 29 Litho. *Perf. 12*

523 A189 $1 shown 1.25 1.25
524 A189 $1 Mascot 1.25 1.25
a. Pair, #523-524 + label 2.75 3.25

1998 Commonwealth Games, Kuala Lumpur.

Official Opening of Natl. Library Building A190

1994, Dec. 16

525 A190 30c Library building .45 .35
526 A190 50c Computer terminal .60 .45
527 A190 $1 Manuscript 1.25 1.00
Nos. 525-527 (3) 2.30 1.80

Nos. 495-498 with Added Inscription

Wmk. 388

1994, Nov. 8 Litho. *Perf. 12*

527A A181 20c multicolored .75 .85
527B A181 30c multicolored 1.25 .95
527C A181 50c multicolored 1.75 1.50
527D A181 $1 multicolored 3.00 2.75
Nos. 527A-527D (4) 6.75 6.05

Nos. 507-510 with Added Inscription

Wmk. 388

1994, Aug. 16 Litho. *Perf. 12*

528 A184 20c multicolored 1.40 1.40
529 A184 30c multicolored 1.10 1.10
530 A184 50c multicolored 2.75 2.75
531 A184 $1 multicolored 5.50 5.50
Nos. 528-531 (4) 10.75 10.75

A191

1994, Nov. 10 Unwmk. *Perf. 14½*

532 A191 30c shown .65 .35
533 A191 $1 Building complex 1.30 1.50

Memorial to Tunku Abdul Rahman Putra Al-Haj (1903-1990), former Prime Minister.

Fungi — A192

1995, Jan. 18 *Perf. 14½x14*

534 A192 20c Bracket fungus .65 .30
535 A192 30c Cup fungus .70 .30
536 A192 50c Veil fungus 1.10 .40
537 A192 $1 Coral fungus 2.25 2.75
Nos. 534-537 (4) 4.70 3.75

Neofelis Nebulosa A193

1995, Apr. 18 Wmk. 373 *Perf. 13½*

538 A193 20c shown .35 .30
539 A193 30c With young .55 .40
540 A193 50c With mouth open .90 .75
541 A193 $1 Lying on rock 1.75 2.00
a. Strip of 4, #538-541 5.00 5.00

Nos. 538-541 were issued in sheets of 16 stamps.

World Wildlife Fund.

Marine Life — A194

1995, Apr. 10 Wmk. 388 *Perf. 12*

Booklet Stamps

542 A194 20c Feather stars .90 .90
543 A194 20c Sea fans .90 .90
a. Pair, #542-543 2.00 2.00
b. Booklet pane, 5 each #542-543 9.75 9.75
Complete booklet, #543b 10.00
544 A194 30c Soft coral 1.20 1.20
545 A194 30c Cup coral 1.20 1.20
a. Pair, #544-545 2.60 2.60
b. Booklet pane, 5 each #544-545 13.00 13.00
Complete booklet, #543b 14.00
Nos. 542-545 (4) 4.20 4.20

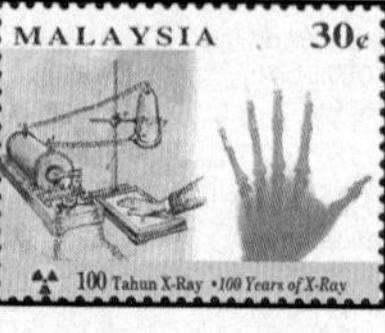

X-Ray, Cent. A195

No. 546, Early machine x-raying hand. No. 547, CAT scan machine. $1, Chest x-ray.

1995, May 29

546 A195 30c multicolored .55 .70
547 A195 30c multicolored .55 .70
a. Pair, #546-547 1.25 1.60
548 A195 $1 multicolored 1.50 1.75
Nos. 546-548 (3) 2.60 3.15

1998 Commonwealth Games, Kuala Lumpur — A196

Various sporting events: No. 549, Badminton, cricket, shooting, tennis, weight lifting, hurdles, field hockey. No. 550, Cycling, lawn bowling, boxing, basketball, rugby, gymnastics.

Wmk. 388

1995, Sept. 10 Litho. *Perf. 14*

549	A196	$1 multicolored	2.25	2.25
550	A196	$1 multicolored	2.25	2.25
a.		Pair, #549-550 + label	5.00	5.00

Traditional Weapons A197

1995, Sept. 1 Litho. *Perf. 14*

551	A197	20c Jemblah	.30	.25
552	A197	30c Keris panjang	.30	.25
553	A197	50c Kerambit	.45	.35
554	A197	$1 Keris sundang	.90	1.50
		Nos. 551-554 (4)	1.95	2.35

Souvenir Sheet

555	A197	$2 Lading terus	3.50	3.50

Singapore '95.

UN, 50th Anniv. A198

1995, Oct. 24 *Perf. 13½*

556	A198	30c shown	.40	.30
557	A198	$1 UN emblem	1.10	1.25

Intl. Assoc. of Travel Agents (IATA), 50th Anniv. — A199

Jet, globe and: No. 558, Historic buildings. No. 559, Sydney Opera House, Great Wall of China. No. 560, Eiffel Tower, Tower Bridge. No. 561, Hollywood Walk of Fame, Latin American pyramid.

1995, Oct. 30 *Perf. 14*

558		30c multicolored	.65	.65
559		30c multicolored	.65	.65
a.	A199	Pair, #558-559	1.75	1.75
560		50c multicolored	.90	.90
561		50c multicolored	.90	.90
a.	A199	Pair, #560-561	2.25	2.25
		Nos. 558-561 (4)	3.10	3.10

Turtles A200

No. 562, Chelonia mydas. No. 563, Dermochelys coriacea.

Perf. 14x14½

1995, Sept. 26 Litho. Wmk. 388

Booklet Stamps

562	A200	30c multi	2.00	1.25
563	A200	30c multi	2.00	1.25
a.		Booklet pane, 5 each #562-563	22.00	16.00
		Complete booklet, #563a	24.00	

Proton Cars, 10th Anniv. — A201

No. 564, 1985 Saga 1.5. No. 565, 1992 Iswara 1.5 aeroback. No. 566, 1992, Iswara 1.5 sedan. No. 567, 1993 Wira 1.6 sedan. No. 568, 1993 Wira 1.6 aeroback. No. 569, 1994 Rally. No. 570, 1994 Satria 1.6. No. 571, 1995 Perdana 2.0. No. 572, 1995 Wira 1.6 aeroback. No. 573, 1995 Wira 1.8 sedan.

1995, Dec. Litho. *Perf. 14*

Booklet Stamps

564	A201	30c multicolored	1.00	1.00
565	A201	30c multicolored	1.00	1.00
566	A201	30c multicolored	1.00	1.00
567	A201	30c multicolored	1.00	1.00
568	A201	30c multicolored	1.00	1.00
569	A201	30c multicolored	1.00	1.00
570	A201	30c multicolored	1.00	1.00
571	A201	30c multicolored	1.00	1.00
572	A201	30c multicolored	1.00	1.00
573	A201	30c multicolored	1.00	1.00
a.		Booklet pane, Nos. 564-573	10.00	10.00
		Complete booklet, No. 573a	10.00	

A202

Malaysia East Asia Satellite: 30c, Ariane 4 being launched. 50c, Satellite in Earth orbit over East Asia. $1, Satellite Control Center, Langkawai.
$5, Satellite entering orbit, horiz.

1996, Jan. 13 *Perf. 13½*

574	A202	30c multicolored	.40	.30
575	A202	50c multicolored	.60	.50
576	A202	$1 multicolored	1.10	1.60
		Nos. 574-576 (3)	2.10	2.40

Souvenir Sheet

Perf. 14

577	A202	$5 multicolored	7.25	7.25

No. 577 contains a holographic image. Soaking in water may affect the hologram.

Pitcher Plants — A203

No. 578, Nepenthes sanguinea. No. 579, Nepenthes macfarlanei. No. 580, Nepenthes rajah. No. 581, Nepenthes lowii.

Perf. 13½, 14½x14 (#580-581)

1996, Apr. 16 Litho. Wmk. 388

578	A203	30c multicolored	.30	.30
579	A203	30c multicolored	.30	.30
a.		Pair, Nos. 578-579	.75	.90
580	A203	50c multicolored	.45	.40
581	A203	50c multicolored	.45	.40
a.		Pair, Nos. 580-581	1.20	1.40
		Nos. 578-581 (4)	1.50	1.40

Birds of Prey A204

Designs: 20c, Haliastur indus. 30c, Spilornis cheela. 50c, Haliaeetus leucogaster. $1, Spizaetus cirrhatus.
$2, Spizaetus alboniger, vert.

Wmk. 388

1996, May 18 Litho. *Perf. 14*

582	A204	20c multicolored	.40	.40
583	A204	30c multicolored	.45	.45
584	A204	50c multicolored	.65	.65
585	A204	$1 multicolored	1.50	2.00
		Nos. 582-585 (4)	3.00	3.50

Souvenir Sheet

586	A204	$2 multicolored	4.50	4.50

CHINA '96 (No. 586).

Intl. Day Against Drug Abuse and Illicit Drug Trafficking A205

Designs: No. 587, Family, drugs burning. No. 588, Various sporting activities, marajuana plants. $1, Family, rainbow.

Wmk. 388

1996, June 26 Litho. *Perf. 14*

587	A205	30c multicolored	.40	.30
588	A205	30c multicolored	.40	.30
a.		Pair, #587-588	1.00	1.25
589	A205	$1 multicolored	1.75	1.75
		Nos. 587-589 (3)	2.55	2.35

Butterflies — A206

No. 590, Graphium sarpedon. No. 591, Melanocyma faunula. No. 592, Delias hyparete. No. 593, Trogonoptera brookiana. No. 594, Terinos terpander.

1996, Sept. 27 Litho. *Perf. 14½x14*

Booklet Stamps

590	A206	30c multicolored	1.75	1.25
591	A206	30c multicolored	1.75	1.25
592	A206	30c multicolored	1.75	1.25
593	A206	30c multicolored	1.75	1.25
594	A206	30c multicolored	1.75	1.25
a.		Pane of 10, 2 each #590-594	17.50	17.50
		Nos. 590-594 (5)	8.75	6.25

Kuala Lumpur Tower A207

30c, Artist's impression. 50c, Tower head diagram. $1, Tower head, city at night.
$2, Kuala Lumpur Tower, vert.

Perf. 13½

1996, Oct. 1 Litho. Unwmk.

595	A207	30c multicolored	.35	.25
596	A207	50c multicolored	.50	.30
597	A207	$1 multicolored	1.10	1.40
		Nos. 595-597 (3)	1.95	1.95

Souvenir Sheet

598	A207	$2 multicolored	2.50	2.50
a.		With added inscription in sheet margin	2.50	2.50

No. 598a inscribed with TAIPEI '96 emblem, issued 10/16/96.

14th Conference of Confederation of Asian and Pacific Accountants — A208

1996, Oct. 7 *Perf. 13½x14*

599	A208	30c CAPA logo	.50	.40
600	A208	$1 Globe	1.10	1.25

Natl. Science Center A209

30c, Model of molecular structure. 50c, Model of atom, Science Center. $1, Natl. Science Center.

Unwmk.

1996, Nov. 29 Litho. *Perf. 14*

601	A209	30c multicolored	.45	.35
602	A209	50c multicolored	.60	.40
603	A209	$1 multicolored	1.10	1.25
		Nos. 601-603 (3)	2.15	2.00

Souvenir Sheet

Stamp Week — A210

Wildlife: a, 20c, Nycticebus coucang. b, 30c, Callosciurus prevostil. c, 50c, Attacus atlas. d, $1, Hylobates lar. e, $1, Buceros rhinoceros. f, $2, Hemigalus derbyanus.

1996, Dec. 2

604	A210	Sheet of 6, #a.-f.	4.25	4.25

No. 604d is 30x60mm. Nos. 605e-605f are 60x30mm.

Birds — A211

Designs: 20c, Muscicapella hodgsoni. 30c, Leiothrix argentauris. 50c, Dicaeum celibicum. $1, Aethopyga mystacalis.

Perf. 13½x14

1997, Jan. 4 Litho. Unwmk.

605	A211	20c multicolored	.35	.35
606	A211	30c multicolored	.45	.35
607	A211	50c multicolored	.65	.40
608	A211	$1 multicolored	1.40	1.60
		Nos. 605-608 (4)	2.85	2.70

16th Commonwealth Games, Kuala Lumpur '98 — A212

1996, Dec. 21 *Perf. 12*

609	A212	30c Running	.45	.25
610	A212	30c Hurdles	.45	.25
a.		Pair, #609-610	1.10	.90
611	A212	50c High jump	.75	.35
612	A212	50c Javelin	.75	.35
a.		Pair, #611-612	1.75	1.50
		Nos. 609-612 (4)	2.40	1.20

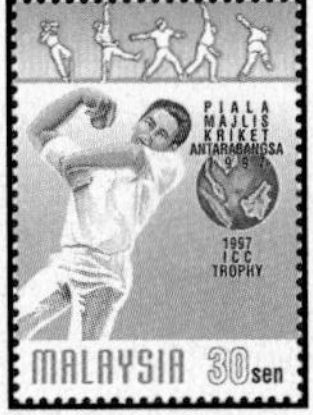

Intl. Cricket Cup Champions A213

1997, Mar. 24 Litho. *Perf. 14*

No.	Type	Description	Unused	Used
613	A213	30c shown	.35	.35
614	A213	50c Batsman	.50	.50
615	A213	$1 Wicket keeper	1.25	1.50
		Nos. 613-615 (3)	2.10	2.35

Aviation in Malaysia, 50th Anniv. A214

Designs: 30c, Jet, world map. 50c, Jet approaching Kuala Lumpur. $1, Airplane tailfins of four Malaysian airlines.

Perf. 14, 13½ (#617)

1997, Apr. 2 Wmk. 388

No.	Type	Description	Unused	Used
616	A214	30c multicolored	.55	.40
617	A214	50c multicolored	.95	.75
618	A214	$1 multicolored	2.00	2.25
a.		Perf. 13½	4.00	2.00
		Nos. 616-618 (3)	3.50	3.40

A215

Light Rail Transit System: No. 620, Two trains, one on bridge, Kuala Lumpur skyline.

Perf. 14x14½

1997, Mar. 1 Litho. Unwmk.

Booklet Stamps

No.	Type	Description	Unused	Used
619	A215	30c shown	1.60	.80
620	A215	30c multicolored	1.60	.80
a.		Booklet pane, 5 each #619-620	16.00	16.00
		Complete booklet, #620a	16.00	

Highland Flowers — A216

No. 621, Schima wallichi. No. 622, Aeschynanthus longicalyx. No. 623. Aeschynanthus speciosa. No. 624, Phyllagathis tuberculata. No. 625, Didymocarpus quinquevulnerus.

Booklet Stamps

1997, May 7 *Perf. 14½x14*

No.	Type	Description	Unused	Used
621	A216	30c multicolored	.70	.70
622	A216	30c multicolored	.70	.70
623	A216	30c multicolored	.70	.70
624	A216	30c multicolored	.70	.70
625	A216	30c multicolored	.70	.70
a.		Booklet pane, 2 each #621-625	7.50	7.50
		Complete booklet, #625a	8.00	
		Nos. 621-625 (5)	3.50	3.50

Ruler's Council, Cent. A217

Unwmk.

1997, July 31 Litho. *Perf. 14*

No.	Type	Description	Unused	Used
626	A217	30c Photo, 1897	.35	.30
627	A217	50c Emblem, arms	.55	.40
628	A217	$1 Emblem	.90	1.40
		Nos. 626-628 (3)	1.80	2.10

ASEAN, 30th Anniv. A218

50c, "30," emblem. $1, Emblem, color bars.

1997, Aug. 8 Wmk. 388 *Perf. 13½*

No.	Type	Description	Unused	Used
629	A218	30c shown	.65	.40
630	A218	50c multicolored	.85	.50
631	A218	$1 multicolored	1.50	1.75
		Nos. 629-631 (3)	3.00	2.65

A219

Coral: 20c, Tubastrea. 30c, Melithaea. 50c, Aulostomus chinensis. $1, Symphillia.

1997, Aug. 23 Unwmk. *Perf. 14½*

No.	Type	Description	Unused	Used
632	A219	20c multicolored	.30	.30
633	A219	30c multicolored	.30	.30
634	A219	50c multicolored	.40	.35
635	A219	$1 multicolored	1.10	1.25
		Nos. 632-635 (4)	2.10	2.20

A220

1997, Aug. 25 *Perf. 13x13½*

Booklet Stamps

No.	Type	Description	Unused	Used
636	A220	30c Career women	.70	.40
637	A220	30c Family	.70	.40
a.		Booklet pane, 5 each #636-637	7.00	7.00
		Complete booklet, #637a	7.00	

20th Intl. Conf. of Pan-Pacific and Southeast Asia Women's Assoc., Kuala Lumpur.

9th World Youth Soccer Championships A221

30c, Mascot. 50c, Soccer ball, players, flag. $1, Map of Malaysia, silhouettes of players, soccer ball.

Perf. 13½x13

1997, June 16 Unwmk.

No.	Type	Description	Unused	Used
638	A221	30c multicolored	.30	.30
639	A221	50c multicolored	.45	.40

Perf. 13x12½

No.	Type	Description	Unused	Used
640	A221	$1 multicolored	1.00	1.40
		Nos. 638-640 (3)	1.75	2.10

Souvenir Sheet

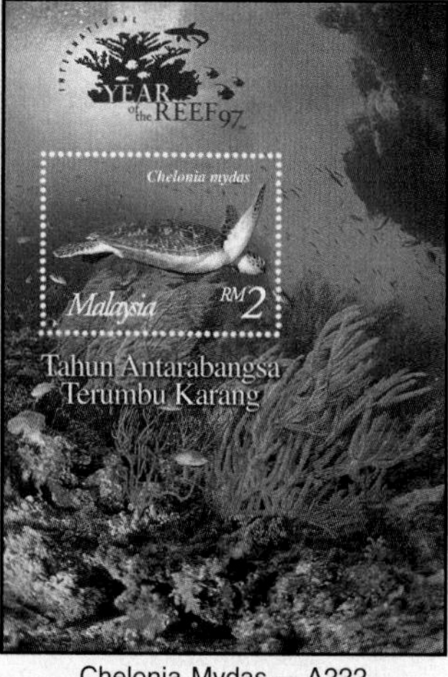

Chelonia Mydas — A222

1997, Aug. 23 Litho. *Perf. 14½*

No.	Type	Description	Unused	Used
641	A222	$2 multicolored	3.00	3.25

Year of the Coral Reef.

7th Summit Level of the Group of 15 — A223

$1, Emblem, natl. flags of member nations.

Perf. 12, 13½ (#643)

1997, Nov. 3 Litho. Unwmk.

No.	Type	Description	Unused	Used
642	A223	30c shown	.30	.30
643	A223	$1 multicolored	1.25	1.25

Stamp Week A224

Protected wildlife: a, 20c, Tomistoma schlegelli. b, 30c, Tarsius bancanus, vert. c, 50c, Cervus unicolor, vert. d, $2, Rollulus rouloul. e, $2, Scleropages formosus.

1997, Dec. 1 *Perf. 14½*

No.	Type	Description	Unused	Used
644	A224	Sheet of 5, #a.-e.	3.25	3.25

Philately in Malaysia, 50th Anniv. — A225

Malpex '97: a, 20c, Straits Settlements #7. b, 30c, #605-608. c, 50c, #604. d, $1, Early cover from Straits Settlements.

1997, Sept. 9 *Perf. 12½*

No.	Type	Description	Unused	Used
645	A225	Sheet of 4, #a.-d.	3.25	3.25
e.		Ovptd. in sheet margin in gold	2.00	2.00

No. 645e is inscribed in sheet margin with INDEPEX '97 exhibition emblem.

Rare Fruit — A226

20c, Bouea macrophylla. 30c, Sandoricum koetjape. 50c, Nephelium ramboutan-ake. $1, Garcinia atroviridis.

1998, Jan. 10 *Perf. 13½*

No.	Type	Description	Unused	Used
646	A226	20c multicolored	.25	.25
647	A226	30c multicolored	.30	.30
648	A226	50c multicolored	.40	.30
649	A226	$1 multicolored	.75	1.25
		Nos. 646-649 (4)	1.70	2.10

Kuala Lumpur '98 Games A227

1998, Feb. 23 *Perf. 12*

No.	Type	Description	Unused	Used
650	A227	30c Field hockey	.60	.60
651	A227	30c Women's netball	.60	.60
a.		Pair, #650-651 + label	1.40	1.40
652	A227	50c Cricket	.85	.85
653	A227	50c Rugby	.85	.85
a.		Pair, #652-653 + label	1.90	1.90
		Nos. 650-653 (4)	2.90	2.90

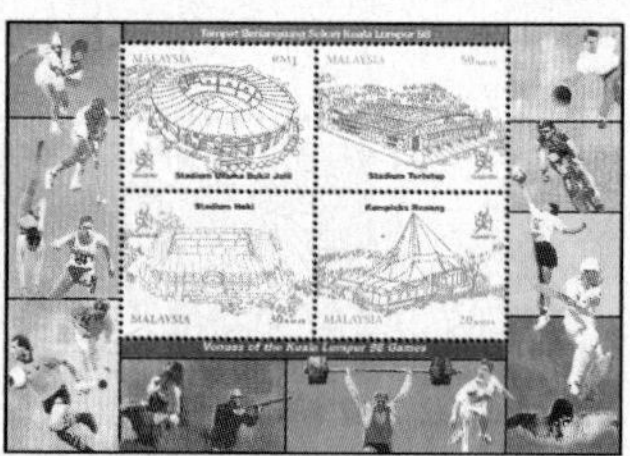

Kuala Lumpur '98 Games — A228

Stadiums for the venues: a, 1r, Utama Bukit Jalil. b, 50c, Tertutup. c, 30c, Hoki. d, 20c, Renang Complex.

Wmk. 388

1998, Feb. 23 Litho. *Perf. 13⅓*

No.	Type	Description	Unused	Used
654	A228	Sheet of 4, #a.-d.	2.50	2.50

Early Coins A229

Coin's region, date: 20c, Trengganu, 1793-1808. 30c, Kedah, 1661-87. 50c, Johore, 1597-1615. $1, Kelantan, 1400-1780.

Wmk. 388

1998, Apr. 11 Litho. *Perf. 13½*

No.	Type	Description	Unused	Used
655	A229	20c multicolored	.30	.30
a.		Perf. 14¼	3.00	.25
656	A229	30c multicolored	.40	.30
657	A229	50c multicolored	.45	.30
a.		Perf. 14¼	4.25	.35
658	A229	$1 multicolored	.70	1.10
		Nos. 655-658 (4)	1.85	2.00

Kuala Lumpur International Airport — A230

Designs: 30c, Tower, tramway, airplanes. 50c, Tower, airplanes at terminal. $1, Tower, airplane in air, airport below.
$2, Tower, globe overhead.

1998, June 27 *Perf. 12*

659 A230 30c multicolored .35 .30
a. Perf. 12½ 5.00
660 A230 50c multicolored .65 .30
661 A230 $1 multicolored 1.00 1.75
a. Perf. 12½ 6.00 3.75
Nos. 659-661 (3) 2.00 2.35

Souvenir Sheet

Perf. 14

662 A230 $2 multicolored 2.50 2.75

No. 662 contains one 26x36mm stamp.

Malaysian Red Crescent Society, 50th Anniv. — A231

30c, Rescue boat. $1, Mobile rescue unit.

1998, May 8 *Perf. 13½*

663 A231 30c multicolored .45 .40
a. Perf. 14¼ 2.75 2.75
664 A231 $1 multicolored 1.25 .60
a. Perf. 14¼ 2.75 2.75

Watermark on No. 664a is inverted. No. 664a also exists with watermark upright. Value $10.

Medicinal Plants — A234

20c, Solanum torvum. 30c, Tinospora crispa. 50c, Jatropha podagrica. $1, Hibiscus rosa-sinensis.

Wmk. 388

1998, July 18 Litho. *Perf. 13¾*

671 A234 20c multicolored .25 .25
672 A234 30c multicolored .30 .30

Perf. 14¼

673 A234 50c multicolored .40 .30
674 A234 $1 multicolored .60 1.25
Nos. 671-674 (4) 1.55 2.10

1998 Commonwealth Games, Kuala Lumpur — A235

a, 20c, Weight lifting. b, 20c, Badminton. c, 30c, Field hockey goalie. d, 30c, Field hockey. e, 20c, Netball. f, 20c, Shooting. g, 30c, Cycling. h, 30c, Lawn bowling. i, 50c, Gymnastics. j, 50c, Cricket. k, $1, Swimming. l, $1, Squash. m, 50c, Rugby. n, 50c, Running. o, $1, Boxing. p, $1, Bowling.

Perf. 14½x15

1998, Sept. 11 Litho. Wmk. 388

675 A235 Sheet of 16, #a.-p. 7.00 7.50

Modernization of Rail Transport — A236

Designs: 30c, Putra-LRT, 1998. 50c, Star-LRT, 1996. $1, KTM Commuter, 1995.

1998, Oct. 3 *Perf. 13¾, 14¼*

676 A236 30c multicolored .30 .30
a. Perf. 14¼ 3.25
677 A236 50c multicolored .55 .35
a. Perf. 14¼ 1.25 .30
678 A236 $1 multicolored (Perf. 14¼) 1.10 1.25
Nos. 676-678 (3) 1.95 1.90

1998 APEC (Asia-Pacific Economic Cooperation) Conference A237

Design: $1, Petronas Towers, people working with computers, office workers.

1998, Nov. 14 *Perf. 13½*

679 A237 30c shown 2.25 .35
a. Perf. 14½ .70 .35
680 A237 $1 multicolored .85 1.10
a. Perf. 14½ 3.75 3.75

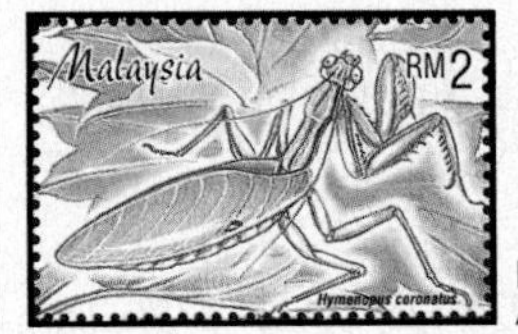

Insects A238

Designs: a, 20c, Xylotrupes gideon, vert. b, 30c, Pomponia imperatoria, vert. c, 50c, Phyllium pulchrifolium, vert. d, $2, Hymenopus coronatus. e, $2, Macrolyristes corporalis.

Wmk. 388

1998, Nov. 28 Litho. *Perf. 12½*

681 A238 Sheet of 5, #a.-e. 3.25 3.75

Stamp Week.
Nos. 681a-681c are each 30x40mm.

Gold Medal Winners at 16th Commonwealth Games — A238a

No. 681F: h, 30c, Air rifle. i, 30c, 48kg boxing. j, 30c, 50km walk. k, 30c, 69kg clean and jerk weight lifting. l, 50c, Men's doubles, bowling. m, 50c, Men's singles, bowling. n, 50c, Men's doubles, badminton. o, 50c, Men's singles, badminton. p, $1, Rhythmic gymnastics (64x26mm).
$2, Team photograph.

Perf. 13¾x14

1998, Dec. 12 Litho. Wmk. 388

681F A238a Sheet of 9, #h.-p., + 2 labels 10.00 10.00

Souvenir Sheet

681G A238a $2 multi 4.25 4.25

No. 681G contains one 128x80mm stamp.

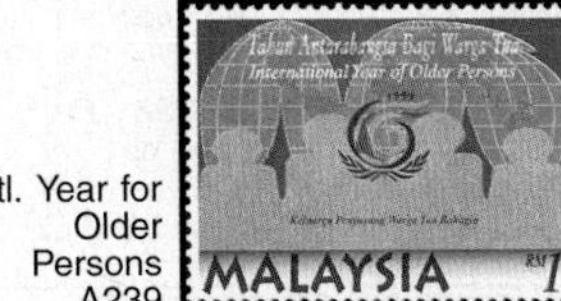

Intl. Year for Older Persons A239

No. 683, World map, people, diff.

Wmk. 388

1999, Jan. 28 Litho. *Perf. 14*

682 A239 $1 shown .85 1.00
683 A239 $1 multicolored .85 1.00

Fruit — A240

Designs: 20c, Syzgium malaccense. 30c, Garcinia prainiana. 50c, Mangifera caesia. $1, Salacca glabrescens.

1999, Feb. 27 *Perf. 12*

684 A240 20c multicolored .25 .25
685 A240 30c multicolored .30 .25
686 A240 50c multicolored .40 .30
687 A240 $1 multicolored .70 1.00
a. Strip of 4, #684-687 1.75 1.75
Nos. 684-687 (4) 1.65 1.80

Domestic Cats — A241

Designs: 30c, Kucing Malaysia. 50c, Siamese. $1, Abyssinian.
No. 691: a, British shorthair. b, Scottish fold. No. 692: a, Birman. b. Persian.

1999, Apr. 1 Litho. *Perf. 12*

688 A241 30c multicolored .35 .30
689 A241 50c multicolored .55 .30
690 A241 $1 multicolored .80 1.00
Nos. 688-690 (3) 1.70 1.60

Sheets of 2

691 A241 $1 #a.-b. 1.30 1.30
692 A241 $1 #a.-b. 1.30 1.30

Protected Mammals A242

Wmk. 388

1999, May 28 Litho. *Perf. 12*

693 A242 20c Rhinoceros .35 .45
694 A242 30c Panther .25 .45
695 A242 50c Bear .40 .55
696 A242 1r Elephant .80 1.10
697 A242 2r Orangutan 1.50 1.75
a. Strip of 5, #693-697 3.75 3.75
b. Souvenir sheet, #697 2.25 2.25

Nos. 693-697 were issued in sheet containing 4 each. No. 697b is a continuous design.

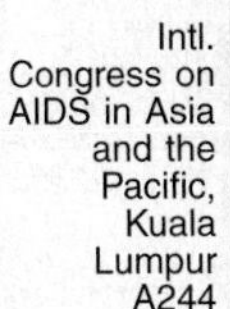

Intl. Congress on AIDS in Asia and the Pacific, Kuala Lumpur A244

Perf. 14, 13½ (#700, 701)

1999, June 19 Litho. Wmk. 388

699 A244 30c shown .35 .35
700 A244 50c Emblems, hearts .50 .40
701 A244 1r Emblem as heart .90 1.25
Nos. 699-701 (3) 1.75 2.00

P. Ramlee (1929-73), Actor, Director — A245

Designs: 20c, Wearing chain around neck. 30c, Wearing bow tie. 50c, Holding gun. No. 705, Behind camera.
No. 706: a, Wearing cap. b, With hands in air. c, Holding microphone. d, Wearing army uniform.
No. 707, Wearing patterned hat. No. 708, Wearing plaid shirt.

Perf. 13½x13¾

1999, July 24 Litho. Wmk. 388

702 A245 20c multicolored .40 .40
703 A245 30c multicolored .50 .40
704 A245 50c multicolored .75 .50
705 A245 $1 multicolored 1.30 1.50
a. Perf. 14¼ 1.10 1.30
Nos. 702-705 (4) 2.95 2.80

Strip of 4

706 A245 30c #a.-d. 3.50 3.50

Souvenir Sheets

Perf. 14¼

707 A245 $1 multicolored 10.00 10.00
708 A245 $1 multicolored 10.00 10.00

No. 706 printed in sheets of 16 stamps.

Water Plants and Fish — A246

No. 709, Monochoria hastata. No. 710, Trichopsis vittatus. No. 711, Limnocharis flava. No. 712, Betta imbellis. No. 713, Nymphaea pubescens. No. 714, Trichogaster trichopterus. No. 715, Ipomea aquatica. No. 716, Helostoma temmincki. No. 717, Eichhornia crassipes. No. 718, Sphaerichthys osphronemoides.

Perf. 13¾x14

1999, July 31 Litho. Wmk. 388

709 A246 10c multi .40 .40
710 A246 10c multi .40 .40
a. Pair, #709-710 .90 .90
711 A246 15c multi .40 .40
712 A246 15c multi .40 .40
a. Pair, #711-712 .90 .90
713 A246 25c multi .40 .40
714 A246 25c multi .40 .40
a. Pair, #713-714 1.00 1.00
715 A246 50c multi .50 .50
716 A246 50c multi .50 .50
a. Pair, #715-716 1.50 1.50
717 A246 50c multi .50 .50
718 A246 50c multi .50 .50
a. Pair, #717-718 1.50 1.50
b. Block of 10 with bottom row of perforations perf 14½ 4.50 4.50
Nos. 709-718 (10) 4.40 4.40

Trees — A247

Designs: No. 719, Dryobalanops aromatica. No. 720, Alstonia angustiloba. No. 721, Fagraea fragrans. No. 722, Lagerstroemia floribunda. No. 723, Elateriospermum tapos.

Perf. 14x13½

1999, Aug. 14 Litho. Wmk. 388

719 A247 30c multicolored .60 .60
720 A247 30c multicolored .60 .60
721 A247 30c multicolored .60 .60
722 A247 30c multicolored .60 .60
723 A247 30c multicolored .60 .60
a. Strip of 5, #719-723 3.00 3.00
Complete bklt., 4 ea #719-723 12.00

Petronas Towers — A248

Designs: 30c, Daytime view. 50c, Architectural drawing. $1, Nighttime view.
$5, Hologram.

Perf. 14x14¼

1999, Aug. 30 Litho. Unwmk.

724	A248 30c multicolored	.35	.30
725	A248 50c multicolored	.45	.40
726	A248 $1 multicolored	.90	1.10
	Nos. 724-726 (3)	1.70	1.80

Souvenir Sheet

Perf. 14½x14¼

727	A248 $5 multicolored	5.00	5.00

No. 727 contains one 30x50mm stamp with a holographic image. Soaking in water may affect hologram. No. 727 exists imperf.

Taiping, 125th Anniv. A249

Designs: 20c, Rickshaw, Peace Hotel. 30c, Automobile, building. 50c, Train, train station. $1, Airplanes, airport building.
$2, Building, horse-drawn carriage.

Unwmk.

1999, Sept. 1 Litho. *Perf. 12*

728	A249 20c multi	.45	.45
729	A249 30c multi	.45	.45
730	A249 50c multi	.55	.45
731	A249 $1 multi	1.10	1.50
	Nos. 728-731 (4)	2.55	2.85

Souvenir Sheet

732	A249 $2 multi	5.00	5.00

Tenaga Nasional, 50th Anniv. A250

Designs: 30c, Power station at night. 50c, High tension wire towers, control room. No. 735, Kuala Lumpur at night.
No. 736, Van, vert. No. 737, High tension wire towers, vert.

Perf. 14¼x14½

1999, Sept. 9 Litho. Unwmk.

733	A250 30c multicolored	.40	.30
734	A250 50c multicolored	.55	.35
735	A250 $1 multicolored	1.05	1.50
	Nos. 733-735 (3)	2.00	2.15

Souvenir Sheets

Perf. 13½x13¾

736	A250 $1 multicolored	1.00	1.25
737	A250 $1 multicolored	1.00	1.25

National Theater — A251

Various performers and views of building.

1999 Litho. Wmk. 388 *Perf. 12¼*

Panel Colors

738	A251 30c red	.35	.30
739	A251 50c green	.45	.40
740	A251 $1 violet	.80	1.10
	Nos. 738-740 (3)	1.60	1.80

Installation of 11th Yang Di-Pertuan Agong (Head of State) A252

Tuanku Salehuddin Abdul Aziz Shah ibni al-Marhum Hisamuddin Alam Shah and: 30c, Flag. 50c, Old building. $1, Modern building.
No. 744: a, Purple background. b, Yellow background. c, Blue background.

Perf. 13¾x13½

1999, Sept. 23 Litho. Wmk. 388

741	A252 30c multicolored	.30	.25

Perf. 14¼

742	A252 50c multicolored	.40	.30
743	A252 $1 multicolored	.80	1.00

Perf. 14x13¾

744	A252 30c Strip of 3, #a.-c.	2.00	2.40
	Nos. 741-744 (4)	3.50	3.95

Size of Nos. 744a-744c: 24x30mm.

21st World Road Congress — A253

Unwmk.

1999, Oct. 3 Litho. *Perf. 12*

745	A253 30c Entrance ramp	.30	.30
746	A253 50c Bridge	.45	.35
747	A253 $1 Interchange	.90	1.10
	Nos. 745-747 (3)	1.65	1.75

A254

1999 Malaysia Grand Prix — A255

Racing helmets and: 20c, Canopy over track's stands. 30c, Stands. 50c, Car on track. $1, side view of car.
No. 752: a, 20c, Stands b, 30c, Race control building. c, 50c, Pits. d, $1, Track.

Unwmk.

1999, Oct. 16 Litho. *Perf. 12*

748	A254 20c multi	.40	.35
749	A254 30c multi	.40	.35
750	A254 50c multi	.50	.45
751	A254 $1 multi	.90	1.10
	Nos. 748-751 (4)	2.20	2.25

Perf. 12½

752	A255 Strip or block of 4, #a.-d.	2.50	2.75

No. 752 printed in sheets of 16 stamps.

UPU, 125th Anniv. A256

Designs: 20c, Computer, envelopes. 30c, Globe, stamps. 50c, World map, airplane. $1, Malaysian Post Office emblem.

Perf. 13¾x13½

1999, Dec. 18 Litho. Wmk. 388

753	A256 20c multi	.40	.40
754	A256 30c multi	.40	.40

Perf. 14¼

755	A256 50c multi	.50	.50
756	A256 $1 multi	.90	1.30
	Nos. 753-756 (4)	2.20	2.60

Sultan of Pahang, 25th Anniv. of Reign — A257

Sultan and: a, Flowers. b, Butterfly, flower, highway. c, Divers, beach. d, Automobile plant. e, Palace.

Wmk. 388

1999, Oct. 23 Litho. *Perf. 14¼*

757	A257 30c Strip of 5, #a.-e.	2.50	2.50

Malaysia '99 World Cup Golf Tournament — A258

20c, World Cup. 30c, Ball on tee. 50c, Fairway and green. $1, Clubhouse and flag.

Perf. 14x13¾ Syncopated

1999, Nov. 18

758	A258 20c multi	.40	.40
759	A258 30c multi	.40	.40
760	A258 50c multi	.45	.45
761	A258 $1 multi	.90	1.25
a.	Sheet, 5 each #758-761	10.00	10.00
	Nos. 758-761 (4)	2.15	2.50

Flowers — A259

No. 762: a, Strelitzia augusta. b, Heliconia rostrata. c, Heliconia psittacorum (yellow petals). d, Heliconia stricta. e, Musa violescens. f, Strelitzia reginae. g, Heliconia colgantea. h, Heliconia psittacorum (pink and blue petals). i, Heliconia latispatha. j, Phaeomeria speciosa.

1999, Nov. 29 Wmk. 388 *Perf. 12¼*

762	A259 30c Block or strip of 10, #a.-j.	5.00	5.00
k.	Sheet, 2 blocks #762	10.00	10.00

Millennium — A260

Stamp number in parentheses.
No. 763: a, Vine, bird (1). b, Pottery, waterfall (2). c, Frog, forest (3). d, People and machine, cultivated land (4). e, Fish, boat and lighthouse (5). f, Chevrotain, house (6). g, Elephant, forest (7). h, Dagger, ship (8). i, Clock tower, archway (9). j, Boat with sail, palm trees (10).
No. 764: a, Man with musical instrument, native people (11). b, Lantern and nautilus shell, native people (12). c, Doctor and patient, native people (13). d, Badminton player, native people (14). e, Dancer, native women (15). f, Motorcycle, automobile and highway (16). g, Butterfly, race car, airplane and tower (17). h, Train, satellite and city buildings (18). i, Computer operator, mosque (19). j, Truck, ship (20).
No. 765, $1, Sailing ship, horiz. No. 766, $1, Airplane, horiz.

1999-2000 *Perf. 12¾x12½*

763	A260 30c Block of 10, #a.-j.	5.50	5.00
k.	Sheet, 2 #763	11.00	11.00
764	A260 30c Block or strip of 10, #a.-j.	5.50	5.00
k.	Sheet, 2 #764 blocks	11.00	11.00

Perf. 12½x12¾

Wmk. 388

765-766	A260 Set of 2	5.50	5.50

Issued: No. 763, 12/31/99; No. 764, 1/1/00. No. 765, 12/31/99; No. 766, 1/1/00.

Fruit Type of 1986 Redrawn With "Sen" Instead of "C" and "RM" Instead of "$"

Perf. 13¾x14

2002-04 Litho. Wmk. 388

766A	A125 40sen Like #329	*6.00*	*6.00*
766B	A125 50sen Like #330	*6.00*	*6.00*
766D	A125 1r Like #332 ('04)	—	—
766E	A126 2r Like #333 ('04)	—	—
766G	A126 10r Like #335	*6.00*	*6.00*
766H	A126 20r Like #336	*6.00*	*6.00*

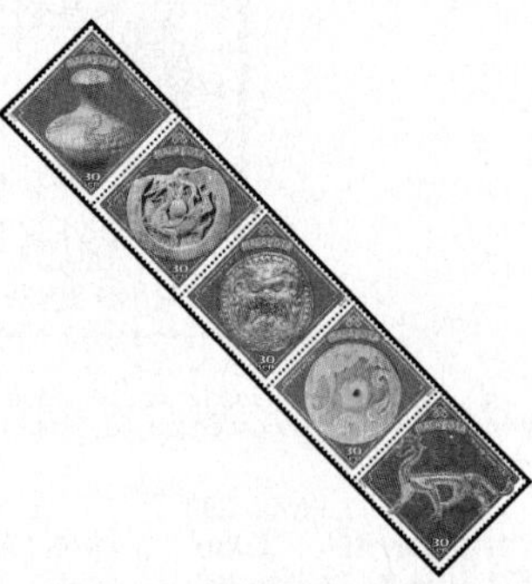
New Year 2000 (Year of the Dragon) — A261

No. 767 — Artifacts depicting dragons from: a, New stone age. b, 100 B.C. c, 800. d, 200 B.C. e, 700.
No. 768 — Fish: a, Osteoglossum bicirrhosum. b, Scleropages leichardti. c, Scleropages formosus (Prussian blue background). d, Osteoglossum ferreirai. e, Scleropages formosus (bister background).
No. 768G, Dragon on boat prow (square orientation). No. 768H, Dragon in parade (square orientation).

Wmk. 388

2000, Jan. 6 Litho. *Perf. 13¼*

767	A261 30c Strip of 5, #a.-e.	2.25	2.25
f.	Sheet, 4 #767	9.00	9.00
768	A261 30c Strip of 5, #a.-e.	2.25	2.25
f.	Sheet, 4 #768	9.00	9.00

Souvenir Sheets

768G	A261 $1 multi	1.50	1.50
768H	A261 $1 multi	1.50	1.50

Dawei 2000 World Team Table Tennis Championships — A262

30c, Paddles, globe. 50c, Tiger mascot playing table tennis. No. 771, Paddles, ball.
No. 772: a, Mascot, table and net. b, Paddles and table.

2000, Feb. 19 *Perf. 13½*

769	A262 30c multi	.35	.35
770	A262 50c multi	.35	.35
771	A262 $1 multi	.85	.95
	Nos. 769-771 (3)	1.55	1.65

Souvenir Sheet
Perf. 14¼

772 A262 $1 Sheet, #a.-b. 1.75 1.75

Souvenir Sheets

Millennium — A263

No. 773, Man, sailboat.
No. 774: a, Mt. Everest climbers with Malaysian flag. b, People with backpacks. c, Parachutist, people with flag, automobile.

2000, Feb. 26 Wmk. 388 *Perf. 12*
773 A263 50c Sheet of 1 .80 .80
774 A263 50c Sheet of 3, #a.-c. 2.50 2.50

2nd Global Knowledge Conference — A264

No. 775: a, Finger pointing. b, Eye, globe.
No. 776: a, Head facing right. b, Head facing left.

2000, Mar. 7 *Perf. 13½*
775 A264 30c Pair, a.-b., + central label .90 .90
Perf. 14x14¼
776 A264 50c Pair, a.-b., + central label 1.30 1.30

Islamic Arts Museum, Kuala Lumpur — A265

20c, Inverted dome. 30c, Main dome. No. 778A, Like No. 778 but with central design element entirely in gold. 50c, Ottoman panel. $1, Art of the mosque.

Perf. 13¾x13½ Syncopated
2000, Apr. 6 Wmk. 388
777 A265 20c multi .40 .40
778 A265 30c multi .40 .40
778A A265 30c multi .40 .40
779 A265 50c multi .50 .40
780 A265 $1 multi 1.00 1.40
Nos. 777-780 (5) 2.70 3.00

Boats — A266

No. 781: a, Perahu Buatan Barat. b, Perahu Payang (red and blue). c, Perahu Burung. d, Perahu Payang (red, white and green).

Perf. 14x13½
2000, Apr. 15 Litho. Wmk. 388
781 A266 Block of 4 2.00 2.00
a.-d. 30c Any single .30 .30
e. Booklet pane, 5 each #a-d 10.50
Complete booklet, #781e 10.50

Unit Trust Investment Week — A267

30c, Emblem, women with flags. 50c, People, Kuala Lumpur skyline. $1, People, globe.

Perf. 13½x13¾
2000, Apr. 20 Litho. Unwmk.
782 A267 30c multi .45 .45
783 A267 50c multi .60 .45
784 A267 $1 multi 1.10 1.40
Nos. 782-784 (3) 2.15 2.30

Thomas and Uber Cup Badminton Championships — A268

No. 785: a, Male player. b, Flags, Thomas Cup (with handles). c, Mascot. d, Flags, Uber Cup. e, Female player.
$1, Thomas Cup, vert.

Perf. 12½x12¾
2000, May 11 Wmk. 388
785 Horiz. strip of 5 2.00 2.00
a.-e. A268 30c Any single .30 .30

Souvenir Sheet
Perf. 12¾x12½x12x12½
786 A268 $1 multi 2.00 2.25

No. 785 printed in sheets of 10 strips and ten labels.

Children's Games — A269

No. 787: a, Hopscotch. b, Tarik Upih. c, Kite flying. d, Marbles. e, Hoops and sticks.

2000, June 24 *Perf. 13½x13¾*
787 Horiz. strip of 5 3.75 3.75
a.-e. A269 30c Any single .50 .50
f. Miniature sheet, 4 #787 16.50 16.00

Islamic Conference of Foreign Ministers, 27th Session A270

No. 788: a, Red globe, electronic circuitry. b, Blue globe, Islamic design. c, Emblem, flower, butterfly. d, Green globe, Islamic design, diff. e, Purple globe, pens.

2000, June 26 *Perf. 13¾x13½*
788 Horiz. strip of 5 2.00 2.00
a.-e. A270 30c Any single .25 .25

National Census A271

No. 789: a, Family, map. b, Family in house, appliances. c, People on pie chart. d, Map, diplomas, mortarboard, workers. e, Male and female symbols.

2000, July 5 *Perf. 14¼*
789 Horiz. strip of 5 2.25 2.25
a.-e. A271 30c Any single .25 .25

Birds — A272

Designs: 20c, Polyplectron inopinatum. 30c, Rheinardia ocellata. 50c, Argisianus argus. $1, Lophura erythropthalma.
$2, Rheinardia ocellata, diff.

2000, July 22 *Perf. 13x13¼*
790 A272 20c multi .55 .55
791 A272 30c multi .55 .55
a. Sheet of 20 20.00
792 A272 50c multi .70 .55
793 A272 $1 multi 1.50 1.50
Nos. 790-793 (4) 3.30 3.15

Souvenir Sheet
Perf. 13¾x14
794 A272 $2 multi 3.00 3.00

No. 794 contains one 32x27mm stamp.

A273

Intl. Union of Forestry Research World Congress — A274

No. 795: a, Shorea macrophylla. b, Dyera costulata. c, Alstonia angustiloba. d, Hopea odorata. e, Adenanthera pavonina.
No. 796 — Trees, 10c: a, Fagraea fragrans. b, Dryobalanops aromatica. c, Terminalia catappa. d, Samanea saman. e, Dracontomelon dao.
No. 797 — Leaves, 15c: a, Heritiera javanica. b, Johannesteijsmannia altifrons. c, Macaranga gigantea. d, Licuala grandis. e, Endospermum diadenum.
No. 798 — Tree barks, 25c: a, Pterocymbium javanicum. b, Dryobalanops aromatica. c, Dipterocarpus costulatus. d, Shorea leprosula. e, Ochanostachys amentacea.
No. 799 — Fauna, 50c: a, Muscicapa indigo. b, Nycticebus coucang. c, Felis marmorata. d, Cyprinus carpio. e, Trimerisurus wagleri.
Illustration A274 reduced.

Wmk. 388
2000, Aug. 7 Litho. *Perf. 12*
795 Horiz. strip of 5 3.75 3.75
a.-e. A273 30c Any single .70 .70
f. Sheet of 4 each #a-e 15.00 15.00

Sheets of 5, #a-e, + label
796-799 A274 Set of 4 8.00 8.00

Medical Research Institute, Cent. A275

Designs: 30c, Institute in 1901, Brugia malayi, Beri-beri. 50c, Institute in 1953, Clostridium bifermentans malaysia, Anophelese campestris. $1, Institute in 1976, chromatograph of DNA sequence, Eurycoma longifolia.

Perf. 13¾x13½, 14¼ (50c, $1, $2)
2000, Aug. 24 Unwmk.
800-802 A275 Set of 3 2.25 1.25

Souvenir Sheet
Wmk. 388
803 A275 $2 Molecular model 2.40 2.40

Protected Mammals A276

Designs: 20c, Cynogale bennettii (mouth open). No. 805, 30c, Cynogale bennettii (mouth closed). 50c, Arctictis binturong. $1, Arctictis binturong, diff.
No. 808: a, Hemigalus hosei. b, Paradoxurus hermaphroditus. c, Paguma larvata. d, Viverra tangalunga. e, Arctogalidia trivirgata.
No. 809: a, Hemigalus derbyanus. b, Prionodon linsang.

2000, Aug. 26 Wmk. 388 *Perf. 13¼*
804-807 A276 Set of 4 1.10 .55
808 Horiz. strip of 5 1.50 1.50
a.-e. A276 30c Any single .25 .25

Souvenir Sheet
809 A276 $1 Sheet of 2, #a-b 2.75 2.75

Rural and Industrial Development Authority, Trust Council for Indiginous People, 50th Anniv. — A277

Designs: 30c, Gear wheels. 50c, Compass, stethoscope. $1, Computer mouse and diskette.

2000, Sept. 14 *Perf. 14¼*
810-812 A277 Set of 3 2.25 2.25
810a Sheet of 20 2.50 2.50

Children's Games — A278

No. 813, 20c: a, Gasing. b, Baling tin.
No. 814, 30c: a, Letup-letup. b, Sepak raga.

Perf. 14¼, 13¾x13½ (#814)
2000, Sept. 16
Horiz. Pairs, #a-b
813-814 A278 Set of 2 2.10 1.25

World Heart Day — A279

No. 815: a, People walking, cyclist. b, People jumping rope, playing with hula hoop and ball. c, Boy flying kite, children playing soccer. d, People exercising. e, Man gardening.

2000, Sept. 24 *Perf. 12¼*
815 Horiz. strip of 5 2.10 1.25
a.-e. A279 30c Any single .25 .25

Rhododendrons — A280

No. 816: a, Brookeanum. b, Jasminiflorum. c, Scortechinii. d, Paucifiorum.
No. 817: a, Crassifloium. b, Longiflorum. c, Javanicum. d, Variolosum. e, Acuminatum. f, Praetervisum. g, Himantodes. h, Maxwellii. i, Erocoides. j, Fallacinum.
$1, Malayanum.

2000, Oct. 9

816 A280 30c Block of 4, #a-d 1.40 .80
817 A280 30c Block of 10, #a-j 3.00 1.50

Souvenir Sheet

818 A280 $1 multi 1.60 1.60

A281

Dragonflies and Damselflies A282

No. 819: a, Vestalis gracilis. b, Crocothemis s. servilia male. c, Trithemis auraora. d, Pseudothemis jorina. e, Diplacodes nebulosa. f, Crocothemis s. servilia female. g, Neurobasis c. chinensis male. h, Burmagomphus divaricatus. i, Ictinogomphus d. melanops. j, Orthetrum testaceum. k, Trithemis festiva. l, Brachythemis contaminata. m, Neurobasis c. chinensis female. n, Neurothemis fluctuans. o, Acisoma panorpoides. p, Orthetrum s. sabina. q, Rhyothemis p. phyllis. r, Rhyothemis obsolescens. s, Neurothemis t. tulia. t, Lathrecista a. asiatica. u, Aethriamanta gracilis. v, Diplacodes trivialis. w, Neurothemis fulvia. x, Rhyothemis triangularis. y, Orthetrum glaucum.
No. 820: a, Neurobasis c. chinensis. b, Aristocypha fenestrella (with blue sky). c, Vestalis gracilis. d, Nannophya pymaea. e, Aristocypha fenestrella (no sky). f, Rhyothemis p. phyllis. g, Crocothemis s. servilia. h, Euphaea ochracea male. i, Euphaea ochracea female. j, Ceriagrion cerinorubellum.

2000, Nov. 25 ***Perf. 14¼x13¾ Sync.***

819 Sheet of 25 11.50 11.50
a.-y. A281 (30c) Any single .30 .30

Booklet Stamps

Perf. 13½x14 Syncopated

820 Block of 10 5.25 5.25
a.-j. A282 30c Any single .30 .30
k. Booklet pane, 2 #820 10.50
Booklet, #820k 10.50

Quails and Partridges A283

Designs: 30c, Coturnix chinensis. 50c, Arborophila campbelli. $1, Turnix suscitator.

No. 824: a, Arborophila charltonii. b, Haematortyx sanguiniceps.

Wmk. 388, Unwmkd. (#822-823)

Perf. 13¾x13½, 14¼ (30c)

2001, Jan. 22 **Litho.**

821-823 A283 Set of 3 3.50 3.50

Souvenir Sheet

Perf. 14¼x14¼x13¾x14¼

824 A283 $2 Sheet of 2, #a-b 4.75 4.75

Creation of Putrajaya Federal Territory A284

Designs: 30c, Perdana Putra Building (Prime Minister's office building). $1, Perdana Putra Building, highway, government office buildings.

Perf. 13¾x13½, 14¼ ($1)

2001, Feb. 1 **Litho.** **Wmk. 388**

825-826 A284 Set of 2 3.25 1.60

Sabah and Sarawak Beads — A285

No. 827: a, Pinakol. b, Mareik Empang. c, Glass beads. d, Orot.

Wmk. 388

2001, Feb. 17 **Litho.** ***Perf. 13¾***

827 A285 30c Block of 4, #a-d 2.40 1.25

Flowers — A286

Designs: 30c, Cananga odorata. 50c, Mimusops elengi. $1, Mesua ferrea.
$2, Michelia champaca.

2001, Mar. 27 ***Perf. 13¾, 14¼ ($1)***

828-830 A286 Set of 3 3.25 1.60

Souvenir Sheet

Perf. 13¾x14¼x13¾x13¾

831 A286 $2 multi 3.25 3.25

Cutltural Items — A287

No. 832, 30c: a, Sireh Junjung. b, Penggendong Anak.
No. 833, 50c: a, Jebak Puyuh. b, Bekas Bara.

2001, June 11 ***Perf. 13¾***

Horiz. pairs, #a-b

832-833 A287 Set of 2 2.75 1.25

Automobiles A288

No. 834: a, 1995 Perodua Kancil. b, 1995 Proton Tiara. c, 1995 Perodua Rusa. d, 1997 Proton Putra. e, 1999 Inokom Permas. f, 1999 Perodua Kembara. g, 2000 Proton GTi. h, 2000 TD2000. i, 2000 Perodua Kenari. j, 2000 Proton Waja.

2001, July 9

834 Block of 10 6.25 2.75
a.-j. A288 30c Any single .30 .30
Booklet, #834 6.25

Bantams — A289

Designs: 30c, Ayam Serama. 50c, Ayam Kapan. $1, Ayam Serama and chicks.
$3, Ayam Hutan, horiz.

Perf. 12¾x12½, 12 (50c)

2001, Aug. 1

835-837 A289 Set of 3 2.75 1.25

Souvenir Sheet

Perf. 12½

838 A289 $3 multi 5.25 5.25
a. As #838, with PhilaNippon '01 Emblem in margin — —

No. 838 contains one 45x35mm stamp.

21st South East Asia Games — A290

Designs: 20c, Diving. 30c, Gymnastics. 50c, Bowling. $1, Weight lifting. $2, Cycling.
$5, Running.

2001, Sept. 8 ***Perf. 13½x13¾***

839-843 A290 Set of 5 4.75 2.25

Souvenir Sheet

844 A290 $5 multi 6.75 6.75

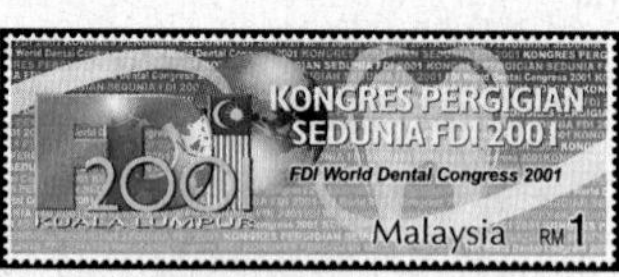
2001 World Dental Federation Congress — A291

2001, Sept. 27 ***Perf. 14¼***

845 A291 $1 multi 2.10 1.00

Employees' Provident Fund, 50th Anniv. A292

Designs: 30c, Headquarters. 50c, Bar graph. $1, Emblem, man and woman.

Perf. 14¼, 13¾x13½ ($1)

2001, Oct. 1

846-848 A292 Set of 3 2.75 1.25

Forestry Dept., Cent. — A293

Designs: 30c, Satellite, map, trees. 50c, Trees, leaf. $1, Seedlings and forest.

2001, Nov. 10 ***Perf. 14¼***

849-851 A293 Set of 3 2.75 2.00

Stamp Week A294

Marine life: 20c, Tridacna gigas. 30c, Hippocampus sp. 50c, Oreaster occidentalis. $1, Cassis cornuta.
$3, Dugong dugon.

2001, Nov. 10 ***Perf. 13¾x13½***

852-855 A294 Set of 4 3.00 1.75

Souvenir Sheet

Perf. 14¼

856 A294 $3 multi 3.25 3.25

No. 856 exists imperf. with a slightly larger, numbered margin. Value $5.

2002 KL Field Hockey World Cup — A295

Designs: 30c, Player with ball. 50c, Goaltender. $1, Player with ball, diff.
$3, Player, stadium playing field.

Perf. 13½x13¾

2002, Jan. 2 **Wmk. 388**

857-859 A295 Set of 3 3.00 1.75

Souvenir Sheet

Perf. 12¾x12½x12x12½

860 A295 $3 multi 3.25 3.25

No. 860 exists imperf. with a numbered margin.

Flowers — A296

Designs: 30c, Couroupita guianensii. No. 862, $1, Camellia nitidissima. No. 863, $1, Couroupita guianensis, diff.
No. 864: a, Schima brevifolia, horiz. b, Schima brevifolia.

2002, Feb. 5 **Wmk. 380** ***Perf. 12¾***

861-863 A296 Set of 3 2.75 1.40

Souvenir Sheet

864 A296 $2 Sheet of 2, #a-b 3.25 3.25

See People's Republic of China No. 3180.

Snakes — A297

Designs: No. 865, 30c, Gonyophis margaritatus. No. 866, 30c, Python reticulatus. 50c, Bungarus candidus. $1, Maticora bivirgata.
No. 869: a, Ophiophagus hannah (brown). b, Ophiophagus hannah (black and white striped).

2002, Mar. 5 Wmk. 388 *Perf. 14¼*
865-868 A297 Set of 4 3.75 1.75

Souvenir Sheet
Perf. 13¼
869 A297 $2 Sheet of 2, #a-b 4.00 4.00

Nos. 865-868 were each printed in sheets of 20 + 5 labels. No. 869 exists imperf. Value $5.

Express Rail Link A298

Designs: 30c, Kuala Lumpur Central Station.
No. 871: a, Train and station. b, Train, airplane and control tower.
No. 872: a, Train with red violet stripe, train with red stripe. b, Yellow and blue train, train with blue, orange and red stripes.
$2, Train with red violet stripe.

2002, Apr. 13 Wmk. 388 *Perf. 12*
870 A298 30c multi 1.00 1.00
871 A298 50c Horiz. pair, #a-b 2.75 1.25

Souvenir Sheets
Perf. 12½x12¾
872 A298 $1 Sheet of 2, #a-b 2.75 2.75
Perf. 12½x12¾x12½x12
873 A298 $2 multi 2.75 2.75

17th World Orchid Congress — A299

No. 874: a, Paraphalenopsis labukensis. b, Renanthera bella.
50c, Paphiopedilum sanderianum.
No. 876: a, Coelogyne pandurata. b, Phalaenopsis amabilis.
$5, Cleisocentron merillianum.

2002, Apr. 24 Wmk. 380 *Perf. 12¾*
874 A299 30c Horiz. pair, #a-b 1.40 .80
875 A299 50c multi 1.10 .80
876 A299 $1 Horiz. pair, #a-b 3.50 1.25
Nos. 874-876 (3) 6.00 2.85

Souvenir Sheet
Perf. 13
Unwmk.
877 A299 $5 multi 7.00 7.00

No. 877 contains one 45x40mm stamp and exists imperf.

Installation of 12th Yang Di-Pertuan Agong — A300

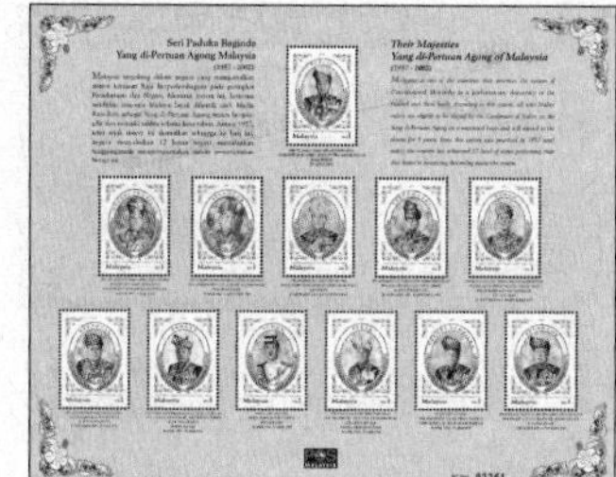
Yang Di-Pertuan Agongs — A301

Background colors: 30c, Green. 50c, Red violet. $1, Yellow.
No. 881 — Ordinal number of Yang Di-Pertuan Agong: a, 1st. b, 2nd. c, 3rd. d, 4th. e, 5th. f, 6th. g, 7th. h, 8th. i, 9th. j, 10th. k, 11th. l, 12th.

2002, Apr. 25 Wmk. 380 *Perf. 12¾*
878-880 A300 Set of 3 3.50 3.50

Miniature Sheet
881 A301 $1 Sheet of 12, #a-l 5.25 5.25

Aquatic Plants A302

Designs: 30c, Cryptocoryne purpurea. 50c, Barclaya kunstleri.
No. 884: a, Neptunia oleracea. b, Monochoria hastata.
No. 885: a, $1, Eichhornia crassipes, vert. b, $2, Nymphaea pubescens.

Perf. 12, 12½x12¾ (#884)
2002, May 11 Wmk. 388
882 A302 30c multi .60 .60
883 A302 50c multi 1.00 .60
884 A302 $1 Horiz. pair, #a-b 3.50 3.25
Nos. 882-884 (3) 5.10 4.45

Souvenir Sheet
Perf. 12¾x12½x12x12½, 12 (#885b)
885 A302 Sheet of 2, #a-b 7.00 7.00

Tropical Birds — A303

No. 886, 30c: a, Dryocopus javensis. b, Oriolus chinensis.
No. 887, $1: a, Anthreptes rhodolaema. b, Irena puella.
$5, Dicaeum trigonostigma.

2002, June 27 *Perf. 12¾x12½*
Horiz. Pairs, #a-b
886-887 A303 Set of 2 6.00 3.00

Souvenir Sheet
Perf. 12¾x12½x12x12½
888 A303 $5 multi 7.75 7.75

No. 888 contains one 60x40mm stamp.
See Singapore Nos. 1014-1017.

Islands and Beaches — A304

No. 889, 30c: a, Pulau Sibu, Johore. b, Pulau Perhentian, Trengganu.
No. 890, 50c: a, Pulau Manukan, Sabah. b, Pulau Tioman, Pahang.
No. 891, $1: a, Pulau Singa Besar, Kedah. b, Pulau Pangkor, Perak.
No. 892: a, Batu Ferringhi, Penang. b, Port Dickson, Negri Sembilan.

Wmk. 380
2002, July 31 Litho. *Perf. 12¾*
Horiz. Pairs, #a-b
889-891 A304 Set of 3 6.50 3.25

Souvenir Sheet
892 A304 $1 Sheet of 2, #a-b 4.25 2.00

Malaysian Unity — A305

No. 893: a, Musicians. b, Children at play.
50c, Seven people (80x29mm).
$2, People pulling rope.

Wmk. 380
2002, Aug. 24 Litho. *Perf. 12¾*
893 A305 30c Horiz. pair, #a-b 1.40 .80
894 A305 50c multi 1.00 .80

Souvenir Sheet
895 A305 $2 multi 3.00 1.50

Zainal Abidin bin Ahmad (1895-1973), Academic — A306

Abidin bin Ahmad: 30c, And blackboard.
No. 897: a, And typewriter. b, And building.
$1, In library, vert.

Perf. 13½x13¼
2002, Sept. 17 Wmk. 388
896 A306 30c multi .75 .75
897 A306 50c Horiz. pair, #a-b 2.00 1.40

Souvenir Sheet
Perf. 13¼x13½
898 A306 $1 multi 2.75 1.40

Clothing — A307

Designs: No. 899, 30c, Green blouse. No. 900, 30c, Red blouse. No. 901, 50c, Yellow blouse. No. 902, 50c, Red blouse, diff.
$2, Blouse and skirt.

Perf. 12¾ (30c), 12¾x13¼ (50c)
2002, Nov. 2
899-902 A307 Set of 4 3.50 1.60

Souvenir Sheet
903 A307 $2 multi 3.50 1.60

No. 903 contains one 35x70mm stamp.

Sultan Idris University, 80th Anniv. A308

Designs: 30c, Suluh Budiman Building.
No. 905: a, Tadahan Selatan. b, Chancellory Building.

2002, Nov. 29 *Perf. 12x12x13½x12*
904 A308 30c multi .70 .70
a. Perf. 12 .30 .30

Perf. 12
905 A308 50c Horiz. pair, #a-b 2.60 1.10
c. As "a," perf. 12x12x13½x12 .40 .25
d. As "b," perf. 12x12x13½x12 .40 .25
e. Pair, #905c-905d .85 .40
f. As "a," perf. 13½ — —
g. As "b," perf. 13½ — —

Wild and Tame Animals — A309

No. 906, 30c: a, Felis bengalensis. b, Felis catus.
No. 907, $1: a, Cacatua sulphurea. b, Ketupa ketupu.
No. 908, $1: a, Ratufa affinis. b, Oryctolagus cuniculus.
No. 909, $1, horiz.: a, Carassius auratus. b, Diodon liturosus.

2002, Dec. 17 *Perf. 12½*
Horiz. pairs, #a-b
906-907 A309 Set of 2 5.50 2.75

Souvenir Sheets of 2, #a-b
Perf. 13½x12x13¼x13½, 13½x13½x12x13¼ (#909)
908-909 A309 Set of 2 6.50 3.25

Stamp Week.

Endangered Animals — A310

Southern serow: 30c, Head.
No. 911: a, Serow laying down. b, Serow walking.

2003, Jan. 25 *Perf. 12¾x12½*
910 A310 30c multi .75 .75
911 A310 50c Horiz. pair, #a-b 2.25 1.00

13th Conference of Heads of State or Government of Non-Aligned Countries — A311

No. 912, 30c — Malaysian flag, world map, conference emblem and: a, Doves, years of previous conferences (1961-1979). b, Hands, years of conferences (1983-2003).
No. 913, 50c — Globe, conference emblem and: a, Map of Malaysia. b, Dove, "2003," Malaysian flag.

2003, Feb. 6 *Perf. 12½x12¾*
Horiz. pairs, #a-b
912-913 A311 Set of 2 3.00 1.50

Roses — A312

Designs: No. 914, Pink Rosa hybrida. No. 915, Red Rosa hybrida.
No. 916: a, Yellow Rosa hybrida. b, Floribunda.
No. 917: a, 1r, Floribunda miniature (29x40mm). b, 2r, Rosa centifolia (29x81mm).

Wmk. 380
2003, Feb. 22 Litho. *Perf. 13¾*
914 A312 30c shown .60 .50
915 A312 30c multi .60 .50
916 A312 50c Horiz. pair, #a-b 1.75 1.00
Nos. 914-916 (3) 2.95 2.00

Souvenir Sheet

Perf. 12¾

917 A312 Sheet of 2, #a-b 3.25 1.60

Nos. 914-917 are impregnated with a rose scent.

Tunku Abdul Rahman Putra Al-Haj (1903-90), Prime Minister — A313

Designs: 30c, Wearing brown hat. 50c, Wearing suit and tie.
No. 920: a, Wearing dark robe. b, Wearing light robe.
No. 921, With arm raised.

Perf. 12¾x12½

2003, Mar. 4 **Wmk. 388**

918 A313 30c multi .50 .50
919 A313 50c multi .60 .50
920 A313 $1 Horiz. pair, #a-b 2.75 1.40
Nos. 918-920 (3) 3.85 2.40

Souvenir Sheet

Perf. 13½

921 A313 $1 multi 2.50 1.25

Fighting Fish A314

Designs: 30c, Red and blue Betta splendens. No. 923, Yellow Betta splendens.
No. 924: a, Blue Betta splendens. b, Red Betta splendens.
No. 925: a, Betta imbellis. b, Betta coccina.

Perf. 12½x12¾, 13½x13¼ (#923)

2003, Apr. 26

922 A314 30c multi .65 .55
923 A314 50c multi .80 .55
924 A314 $1 Horiz. pair, #a-b 3.50 1.75
Nos. 922-924 (3) 4.95 2.85

Souvenir Sheet

Perf. 13½x13¾ Syncopated

925 A314 50c Sheet of 2, #a-b 3.00 1.40

No. 925 contains two 33x28mm stamps.

Clock Towers — A315

Designs: No. 926, 30c, Malacca, 1650. No. 927, 30c, Penang, 1897. No. 928, 30c, Sungai Petani, 1936. No. 929, 30c, Teluk Intan, 1885. No. 930, 30c, Sarawak State Council Monument, 1967.
No. 931: a, Sultan Abdul Samad Building, 1897. b, Taiping Clock Tower, Perak, 1881.

2003, May 24 ***Perf. 12¾x12½***

926-930 A315 Set of 5 2.75 1.25
930a Booklet pane, 2 each #926-930 6.00 —
Complete booklet, #930a 6.00

Souvenir Sheet

Perf. 12x12½x12¾x12½

931 A315 $1 Sheet of 2, #a-b 2.75 1.50

Beaches and Islands — A316

No. 932, 30c: a, Beach, Ligitan Island, Sabah. b, Map of Ligitan Island.
No. 933, 50c: a, Beach, Sipadan Island, Sabah. b, Map of Sipadan Island.
No. 934, vert.: a, Aerial view of Sipadan Island. b, Map of Ligitan Island.

Litho. (#932a-934a), Litho. & Embossed (#932b-934b)

2003, June 28 Wmk. 380 ***Perf. 13¼***

Horiz. Pairs, #a-b

932-933 A316 Set of 2 2.75 1.25

Souvenir Sheet

Perf. 12¾

934 A316 50c Sheet of 2, #a-b 2.75 1.25

Independence, 46th Anniv. — A317

Designs: 30c, Flag and clock tower. No. 936, $1, Flag (59x40mm).
No. 937, Tunku Abdul Rahman Putra in motorcade, horiz.

2003, Aug. 19 Litho. ***Perf. 12¾***

935-936 A317 Set of 2 2.75 1.25

Souvenir Sheet

937 A317 $1 black 2.75 1.25

No. 937 contains one 59x40mm stamp.

Motorcycles and Scooters Made in Malaysia A318

Designs: 30c, Modenas Jaguh 175.
No. 939: a, Modenas Kriss 2. b, Modenas Kriss SG.
No. 940: a, Modenas Karisma 125. b, Modenas Kriss 1.
No. 941, $1: a, Comel Turbulence RG125. b, Comel Cyclone GP150.
No. 942, $1: a, MZ 125SM. b, MZ Perintis 1205 Classic.
No. 943, $1: a, Caviga Momos 125R. b, Nitro NE150 Windstar.
No. 944, $1: a, Demak Adventurer. b, Demak Beetle.

2003, Aug. 27 ***Perf. 12¾***

938 A318 30c multi .75 .75
939 A318 50c Horiz. pair, #a-b 2.00 .85
940 A318 50c Horiz. pair, #a-b 2.00 .85
Nos. 938-940 (3) 4.75 2.45

Souvenir Sheets of 2, #a-b

941-944 A318 Set of 4 8.25 4.00

See Nos. 950-952.

10th Islamic Summit Conference — A319

No. 945, 30c: a, Putrajaya Convention Center. b, Arabic text.
No. 946, 50c: a, Mosque at left, field of flag. b, Mosque at right, flag stripes.

2003, Oct. 3 ***Perf. 12¾***

Horiz. Pairs, #a-b

945-946 A319 Set of 2 3.00 1.50

50th World Children's Day — A320

Designs: 20c, World map, children in ring.
No. 948: a, Family, house, car, flag. b, Children with kite, graduate, man at computer, rocket, airplane.
No. 949: a, Text. b, Book, school, flag, kite, rainbow, soccer ball, automobile and flower.

Perf. 13½x13¼

2003, Oct. 11 **Wmk. 388**

947 A320 20c multi .75 .75
a. Perf. 12½x12¾ .30 .30

Perf. 12

948 A320 30c Horiz. pair, #a-b 1.75 1.10
c. As "a," perf. 12½x12¾ .35 .35
d. As "b," perf. 12½x12¾ .35 .35
949 A320 30c Horiz. pair, #a-b 1.75 1.10
c. As "a," perf. 12½x12¾ .35 .35
d. As "b" perf. 12½x12¾ .35 .35
e. Booklet pane 2 each #947a, 948c, 948d, 949c, 949d 2.75 —
Complete booklet, #949e 2.75

Nos. 938-940 with Bangkok 2003 Emblem Added at Upper Right

Wmk. 380

2003, Oct. 4 Litho. ***Perf. 12¾***

950 A318 30c Like #938 .70 .50
951 A318 50c Like #939, horiz. pair, #a-b 1.75 .85
952 A318 50c Like #940, horiz. pair, #a-b 1.75 .85
Nos. 950-952 (3) 4.20 2.20

Monkeys — A321

Designs: No. 953, Red leaf monkey, tail above branch. No. 954, Red leaf monkey, tail below branch.
No. 955: a, Proboscis monkey sitting on branch. b, Proboscis monkey reaching for branch.

2003, Dec. 16

953 A321 30c multi .60 .60
954 A321 30c multi .60 .60
955 A321 50c Horiz. pair, #a-b 1.75 1.75
Nos. 953-955 (3) 2.95 2.95

Lighthouses A322

Designs: No. 956, 30c, Muka Head Lighthouse. No. 957, 30c, One Fathom Bank Lighthouse. No. 958, 30c, Althingsburg Lighthouse. No. 959, 30c, Pulau Undan Lighthouse.
$1, Tanjung Tuan Lighthouse.

Perf. 12¾x12½

2004, Jan. 31 **Wmk. 388**

956-959 A322 Set of 4 3.00 1.40

Souvenir Sheet

Perf. 13½

960 A322 $1 multi 3.00 1.40

Convention on Biological Diversity — A323

Designs; 30c, Flora and fauna. No. 962, 50c, DNA molecule, leaf, laboratory equipment, model showing human organs. No. 963, 50c, Convention emblem, world map.

2004, Feb. 9 Wmk. 380 ***Perf. 12¾***

961-963 A323 Set of 3 3.00 1.50

Commonwealth Tourism Ministers' Meeting — A324

Emblem and: 30c, World map, city skyline, golf ball. 50c, World map, rocky shoreline. $1, Malaysian tourist attractions, vert.

2004, Mar. 19

964-966 A324 Set of 3 3.25 1.60

National Service Program — A325

Designs: 30c, Emblem. 50c, Emblem, people on ropes. $1, Emblem, people with flag. $2, Emblem, man saluting.

2004, May 22 Wmk. 380 ***Perf. 12¾***

967-969 A325 Set of 3 3.25 1.60

Souvenir Sheet

Perf. 13½

Wmk. 388

970 A325 $2 multi 3.25 1.60

Malaysia - People's Republic of China Diplomatic Relations, 30th Anniv. — A326

No. 971, 30c: a, Malaysian flag, ship. b, Chinese flag, ship.
No. 972, $1: a, Ship, handshake. b, Flags, ship, world map.
$2, Malaysian and Chinese buildings, horiz.

Perf. 12¾x12½

2004, May 31 **Wmk. 388**

Horiz. pairs, #a-b

971-972 A326 Set of 2 3.25 1.60

Souvenir Sheet

973 A326 $2 multi 2.75 1.40
a. World Stamp Championship emblem added in margin in blue and black 2.75 1.40

No. 973 contains one 60x40mm stamp.
No. 973a issued 8/28.

Mammals — A327

No. 974, 30c: a, Bos javanicus. b, Bos gaurus.
No. 975, $1: a, Panthera tigris. b, Elephas maximusp.
$2, Tapirus indicus, vert.

Perf. 13½x13¼

2004, June 14 Wmk. 388

Horiz. pairs, #a-b

974-975 A327 Set of 2 5.00 2.50

Souvenir Sheet

Perf. 12¾

Wmk. 380

976 A327 $2 multi 3.00 1.50

See Nos. 1041-1045.

Multimedia Super Corridor A328

Emblem and: 30c, MSC Building, flags. 50c, Globe, Petronas Towers, binary code. $1, Hand with identity card, people using computers, butterfly, cross-section of brain.
$2, Map of Multimedia Super Corridor, vert.

Horizontal Pairs

2004, July 11 Wmk. 380 *Perf. 12¾*

977-979 A328 Set of 3 1.75 .85

Souvenir Sheet

Perf. 12¾x12½

Wmk. 388

980 A328 $2 multi 2.50 1.25

Ports A329

No. 981: a, Johore. b, Kota Kinabalu.
No. 982: a, Kuantan. b, Penang.
$1, Bintulu. $2, Northport.

12, 13½ (#983)

2004, July 24 Wmk. 388

981 A329 30c Horiz. pair, #a-b 1.20 .80
982 A329 50c Horiz. pair, #a-b 1.75 1.75
983 A329 $1 multi 1.75 1.75
Nos. 981-983 (3) 4.70 4.30

Souvenir Sheet

984 A329 $2 multi 2.75 1.40

Transportation — A330

Designs: 30c, Trishaw. 50c, Rickshaw. $1, Padi horse.
$2, Bullock cart, vert.

Perf. 12, 13½x13¼ (1r)

2004, Aug. 18 Litho. Wmk. 388

985-987 A330 Set of 3 2.10 1.00

Souvenir Sheet

Perf. 14

988 A330 $2 multi 2.75 1.40
a. Kuala Lumpur Stamp Show emblem in sheet margin 2.75 1.40

No. 988 contains one 40x50mm stamp and exists imperf.
No. 988a issued 9/3/04.

Matang Mangroves, Perak, Cent. — A331

No. 989, 30c: a, Monkey on mangrove tree root. b, Insect on plant.
No. 990, $1: a, Boat, shells. b, Birds, tree.
$2, Young trees.

2004, Oct. 4 Wmk. 380 *Perf. 12¾*

Horiz. pairs, #a-b

989-990 A331 Set of 2 4.00 2.00

Souvenir Sheet

991 A331 $2 multi 2.25 1.10

Marine Life A332

Designs: 30c, Humpback whale. 50c, Octopus. $1, Bottlenose dolphin.
$2, Thornback ray.

Wmk. 380

2004, Oct. 9 Litho. *Perf. 12¾*

992-994 A332 Set of 3 2.75 1.40

Souvenir Sheet

995 A332 $2 multi 2.25 1.10
a. Stamp Week emblem in sheet margin 2.25 1.10

Medicinal Plants A333

Designs: 30c, Eurycoma longifolia. 50c, Labisia pumila.
No. 998: a, Pithecellobium bubalinum benth. b, Alleurites moluccana.
$2, Ficus deltoidea jack.

Wmk. 380

2004, Dec. 11 Litho. *Perf. 12¾*

996 A333 30c multi .40 .25
997 A333 50c multi .60 .30
998 A333 $1 Horiz. pair, #a-b 2.10 1.00
Nos. 996-998 (3) 3.10 1.55

Souvenir Sheet

999 A333 $2 multi 2.50 1.25

Rare Rhododendrons A334

Designs: No. 1000, 30c, Rhododendron nervulosum. No. 1001, 30c, Rhododendron stenophyllum. 50c, Rhododendron rugosum. $1, Rhododendron stapfianum.
$2, Rhododendron lowii, horiz.

2005, Jan. 11 Wmk. 380 *Perf. 12¾*

1000-1003 A334 Set of 4 3.50 1.75

Souvenir Sheet

1004 A334 $2 multi 2.50 1.25

Fifth Minister's Forum on Infrastructure Development in the Asia-Pacific Region, Kuala Lumpur — A335

Emblems and: 30c, Kuala Lumpur skyline. 50c, Train and buildings. $1, Train station and airplane.

2005, Jan. 24 Wmk. 388 *Perf. 12*

1005-1007 A335 Set of 3 3.00 1.50

Birds A336

Designs: 30c, Crested honey buzzard. 50c, Purple heron. $1, Lesser crested tern.
$2, Dunlin.

2005, Feb. 3 Wmk. 388 *Perf. 13½*

1008-1010 A336 Set of 3 3.00 1.50

Souvenir Sheet

1011 A336 $2 multi 3.00 1.50
a. Like #1011, with Pacific Explorer World Stamp Expo emblem in margin 3.00 1.50

No. 1011a issued 4/21.

Proton Gen-2 Automobile A337

2005, Feb. 7 Wmk. 388 *Perf. 13½*

Color of Automobile

1012 A337 30c beige .40 .25
a. Perf. 12 .40 .25
b. Booklet pane, 10 #1012a 4.00 —
Complete booklet, #1012b 4.00
1013 A337 50c bright blue .60 .30
1014 A337 $1 red 1.75 .85
Nos. 1012-1014 (3) 2.75 1.40

Souvenir Sheet

1015 A337 $2 dark blue, vert. 2.00 1.00

Dances A338

Designs: 30c, Bharata Natyam and Kathak. 50c, Kipas and Payaung. $1, Zapin and Asyik.
$2, Datun Julud and Sumazau.

2005, Apr. 9 Wmk. 388 *Perf. 12*

1016 A338 30c multi .35 .25
a. Perf. 13½ .35 .25
1017 A338 50c multi .50 .25
1018 A338 $1 multi 1.00 .50
Nos. 1016-1018 (3) 1.85 1.00

Souvenir Sheet

Perf. 13½

1019 A338 $2 multi 2.25 1.10

Songkets A339

Designs: 30c, Pucuk Rebung Gigi Yu. 50c, Bunga Bertabur Pecah Lapan.
No. 1022: a, Pucuk Rebung Gigi Yu dan Bunga Kayoban. b, Teluk Berantai Bunga Pecah Empat.
$2, Potong Wajik Bertabur.

Perf. 12¾x12½

2005, Apr. 29 Wmk. 388

1020 A339 30c multi .30 .25
1021 A339 50c multi .50 .25
1022 A339 $1 Horiz. pair, #a-b 1.60 .80
Nos. 1020-1022 (3) 2.40 1.30

Souvenir Sheet

1023 A339 $2 multi 2.00 1.00

Birds — A340

Designs: 20c, Spotted dove. 30c, Ochraceous bulbul. 40c, Long-tailed parakeet. 50c, White-rumped shama. 75c, Olive-backed sunbird. $1, Green-winged pigeon. $2, Banded pitta. $5, Imperial pigeon.

2005, May 14 *Perf. 13½x14*

1024 A340 20c multi .35 .25
1025 A340 30c multi .40 .25
1026 A340 40c multi .50 .25
1027 A340 50c multi .60 .30
1028 A340 75c multi .80 .40
1029 A340 $1 multi .90 .45
1030 A340 $2 multi 1.75 .85
1031 A340 $5 multi 3.25 1.60
Nos. 1024-1031 (8) 8.55 4.35

University of Malaysia, Cent. A341

Designs: 30c, Dewan Tunku Canselor. 50c, Perpustakaan. No. 1034, Pusat Perubatan.
No. 1035: a, Rimba Ilmu. b, Koleksi Muzium Seni Asia.

2005, June 9 Wmk. 388 *Perf. 12*

1032 A341 30c multi .30 .25
a. Perf. 13½ .30 .25
b. Booklet pane, 10 #1032a 3.00 —
Complete booklet, #1032b 3.00
1033 A341 50c multi .50 .25

Perf. 13½

1034 A341 $1 multi .90 .45
Nos. 1032-1034 (3) 1.70 .95

Souvenir Sheet

Perf. 12½

1035 A341 $1 Sheet of 2, #a-b 1.60 .80

Malaysia — China Relations, 600th Anniv. — A342

Designs: No. 1036, 30c, Chinese chop. No. 1037, 30c, Ship. 50c, Malaysian and Chinese men talking. $1, Decorated plate.
$2, Ornament and coin.

Perf. 12¾x12½

2005, July 21 Litho. Wmk. 388

1036-1039 A342 Set of 4 1.75 .85

Souvenir Sheet

1040 A342 $2 multi 1.50 .75

Mammals Type of 2004

Endangered mammals: No. 1041, 30c, Malay weasel. No. 1042, 30c, Yellow-throated marten. 50c, Hairy-nosed otter. $1, Large spotted civet.
$2, Long-tailed porcupine, vert.

Perf. 13½, 12 (50c, $1)

2005, July 27

1041-1044 A327 Set of 4 2.50 1.25
1042a Perf. 12 .40 .25

Souvenir Sheet
Perf. 12¾x12½

1045 A327 $2 multi 2.00 1.00
a. As #1045, with Taipei 2005 emblem in sheet margin 2.00 1.00

No. 1045a issued 8/19.

Water Transport A343

Designs: 30c, Perahu kotak. 50c, Sampan. $1, Rakit buluh.
$2, Perahu batang, vert.

2005, Aug. 9 ***Perf. 13½***
1046-1048 A343 Set of 3 1.75 .85

Souvenir Sheet
Perf. 14x13½

1049 A343 $2 multi 2.00 1.00

No. 1049 contains one 40x55mm stamp.

Malay College, Kuala Kangsar, Cent. A344

Designs: 30c, School building. No. 1051, 50c, Tree. No. 1052, 50c, Prep school.
No. 1053, vert.: a, Sultan Idris Murshidul 'Adzam Shah. b, Sultan Alaiddin Sulaiman Shah. c, Yam Tuan Tuanku Muhamad Shah. d, Sultan Ahmad Al-Mu'adzam Shah.

2005, Aug. 30 ***Perf. 13½***
1050-1052 A344 Set of 3 1.50 .75

Souvenir Sheet
Perf. 12x11¾

1053 A344 50c Sheet of 4, #a-d 1.60 .80

No. 1053 contains four 22x51mm stamps.

Reptiles A345

Designs: No. 1054, 30c, Varanus rudicollis. No. 1055, 30c, Varanus dumerilii. 50c, Gonocephalus grandis. $1, Crocodylus porosus.
$2, Draco quinquefasciatus, vert.

2005, Sept. 28 ***Perf. 13½***
1054-1057 A345 Set of 4 2.50 1.25

Souvenir Sheet
Perf. 14x13½

1058 A345 $2 multi 1.75 .85

No. 1058 contains one 40x50mm stamp.

Kites A346

Designs: 30c, Wau Jala Budi. 50c, Wau Bulan. $1, Wau Kucing.
$2, Wau Merak.

2005, Oct. 10 ***Perf. 13½, 12 ($1)***
1059-1061 A346 Set of 3 2.00 1.00
1060a Perf. 12 .40 .25

Souvenir Sheet

1062 A346 $2 multi 1.60 .80

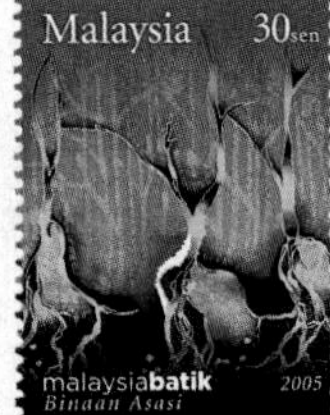

Batik — A347

Designs: 30c, Binaan Asasi. 50c, Pesona Sutera. $1, Malaysia Bersatu.
$2, Penyatuan.

2005, Dec. 2 ***Perf. 12¾x12½***
1063-1065 A347 Set of 3 1.40 .70

Souvenir Sheet

1066 A347 $2 multi 1.40 .70

11th ASEAN Summit, Kuala Lumpur A348

Emblem and: 30c, Flags of participating nations. 50c, Motto. $1, Aerial view of Kuala Lumpur.

2005, Dec. 12 ***Perf. 12½x12¾***
1067-1069 A348 Set of 3 1.40 .70

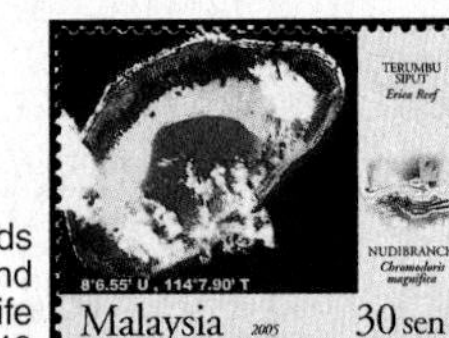

Islands and Marine Life A349

Designs: No. 1070, 30c, Erica Reef, Nudibranch. No. 1071, 30c, Mariveles Reef, Sea cucumber. No. 1072, $1, Swallow Island, Sea star. No. 1073, $1, Investigator Reef, bivalve.
$2, Erica Reef, Mariveles Reef, Swallow Island, Investigator Reef, and Ubi Reef.

Perf. 12½x12¾, 13½ ($1)
2005, Dec. 22
1070-1073 A349 Set of 4 2.00 1.00

Souvenir Sheet
Perf. 14

1074 A349 $2 multi 2.25 1.10

No. 1074 contains one 50x40mm stamp.

Ducks A350

Designs: No. 1075, 30c, Anas crecca. No. 1076, 30c, Cairina scutulata. No. 1077, 50c, Anas acuta. No. 1078, 50c, Anas clypeata.
$2, Phalacrocorax carbo.

Perf. 13½x13¼
2006, Jan. 26 **Litho.** **Wmk. 388**
1075-1078 A350 Set of 4 2.50 1.25
1076a Perf. 12 .40 .25

Souvenir Sheet

1079 A350 $2 multi 2.75 1.40

Negara Audit Institute, Cent. A351

Designs: 30c, Building. No. 1081, 50c, Documents. No. 1082, 50c, Emblems.

2006, Feb. 14 ***Perf. 12½x12¾***
1080-1082 A351 Set of 3 1.25 .60

Fruits — A352

Designs: 30c, Artocarpus sericicarpus. 50c, Phyllanthus acidus. No. 1085, $1, Garcinia hombroniana.
No. 1086, $1: a, Lepisanthes alata. b, Baccaurea polyneura.

Perf. 13¾x13½ Syncopated
2006, Mar. 28
1083-1085 A352 Set of 3 1.60 .80

Souvenir Sheet
Perf. 13¾ Syncopated

1086 A352 $1 Sheet of 2, #a-b 1.60 .80

Mountains — A353

No. 1087, 30c: a, Mt. Kinabalu and orchid. b, Gunung Ledang (Mt. Ophir) and flower.
No. 1088, 50c: a, Mt. Jerai and orchid. b, Mt. Mulu.
$2, Mt. Tahan.

Litho. & Embossed
Perf. 13½x13¼
2006, Apr. 26 **Wmk. 388**
Horiz. Pairs, #a-b
1087-1088 A353 Set of 2 2.50 1.25

Souvenir Sheet
Perf. 14
Litho.

1088C A353 $2 multi 1.60 .80

No. 1088C contains one 50x40mm stamp.

Fish A354

Designs: 30c, Leptobarbus hoevenii. No. 1090, 50c, Hampala macrolepidota. No. 1091, 50c, Pangasius sp. $1, Probarbus jullieni.
$5, Clarias batrachus, Mystus nemurus.

Perf. 12½x12¾
2006, May 25 **Litho.** **Wmk. 388**
1089-1092 A354 Set of 4 2.50 1.25

Souvenir Sheet
Litho. With Hologram Applied
Perf. 13¼

1093 A354 $5 multi 3.50 1.75

No. 1093 contains one 70x33mm stamp.

Dewan Bahasa Dan Pustaka (Malay Language Governing Board), 50th Anniv. A355

Designs: No. 1094, 50c, Emblem and leaf. No. 1095, 50c, Anniversary emblem and people reading. $1, Emblem, books and electronic devices.

2006. June 22 ***Perf. 12½x12¾***
1094-1096 A355 Set of 3 1.90 .95

Federal Land Development Authority, 50th Anniv. — A356

Designs: 30c, Palm plantation, fruit. 50c, Buildings. $1, Globe and buildings.

2006, July 7 **Litho.** ***Perf. 12½x12¾***
1097-1099 A356 Set of 3 1.75 .85

Sultan Azlan Shah Gallery A357

Designs: 30c, Gallery emblem, sword and sheath. 50c, Gallery building. $1, Gallery emblem, headdress.

2006, July 18 ***Perf. 12***
1100-1102 A357 Set of 3 1.75 .85

Festivals A358

Designs: 30c, Eid al-Fitr. 50c, Tahun Baru Cina (Chinese New Year). No. 1105, $1, Deepavali.
No. 1106, $1, vert.: a, Tadau Kaamatan. b, Pesta Gawai.

2006, Aug. 15 ***Perf. 12***
1103-1105 A358 Set of 3 1.75 .85

Souvenir Sheet
Perf. 12½

1106 A358 $1 Sheet of 2, #a-b 1.60 .80

Men's and Women's Traditional Costumes A359

Designs: No. 1107, 50c, Malaysian (blue green background). No. 1108, 50c, Indian (orange background). No. 1109, 50c, Chinese (red background).
No. 1110, $1, vert.: a, Iban (blue background). b, Kadazan (tan background).

2006, Aug. 29 ***Perf. 12¾x12½***
1107-1109 A359 Set of 3 1.75 .85

Souvenir Sheet
Perf. 13¼x13½

1110 A359 $1 Sheet of 2, #a-b 2.00 1.00

Semi-aquatic Animals — A360

Designs: 30c, Periophthalmodon schlosseri. 50c, Pagurus bernhardus. No. 1113, $1, Cuora amboinensis.
No. 1114, $1, vert.: a, Polypedates leucomystax. b, Varanus salvator. c, Cynogale bennettii. d, Xenochrophis trianguliger.

Perf. 13½x13¼

2006, Oct. 9 Litho. Wmk. 388

1111-1113 A360 Set of 3 2.00 1.00

Souvenir Sheet

Perf. 13¾x14¼ Syncopated

1114 A360 $1 Sheet of 4, #a-d 2.75 1.40

Stamp Week. No. 1114 contains four 29x34mm stamps.

18th Intl. Federation of Gynecology and Obstetrics Congress A361

"FIGO" and: 30c, Woman and tree leaves. No. 1116, 50c, Map, woman's torso. No. 1117, 50c, Map, fetus.

2006, Nov. 6 *Perf. 12½x12¾*

1115-1117 A361 Set of 3 1.75 .85

2006 Far East & South Pacific Games for the Disabled, Kuala Lumpur — A362

Designs: 30c, Wheelchair racing. 50c, Swimming. $1, Wheelchair tennis. $2, Wheelchair basketball.

2006, Nov. 25 *Perf. 12¾x12½*

1118-1120 A362 Set of 3 2.00 1.00

Souvenir Sheet

Perf. 13½

1121 A362 $2 multi 2.50 1.25

ASEAN Dialogue with People's Republic of China, 15th Anniv. A363

Designs: 30c, ASEAN emblem, Chinese flag, map with flags. 50c, Great Wall of China, flasks, port, highway, ASEAN emblem and Chinese flag. $1, Bow with ASEAN emblem and Chinese flag.

Perf. 12, 13½x13¼ ($1)

2006, Nov. 30

1122-1124 A363 Set of 3 2.00 2.00

25th General Assembly of World Veterans Federation, Kuala Lumpur A364

Emblem and: 30c, Map. 50c, "25," Kuala Lumpur buildings. $1, Malaysian flag, sculpture of soldiers.

Perf. 13½x13¼, 12 (50c)

2006, Dec. 4 Litho. Wmk. 388

1125 A364 30c multi .40 .25
1126 A364 50c multi .60 .30
1127 A364 $1 multi 1.10 .55
a. Perf. 12 1.10 .55
Nos. 1125-1127 (3) 2.10 1.10

South Pole Expedition A365

Designs: 30c, Mountains, sled, tent. 50c, Man on skis pulling sled. $1, Man on skis pulling sled with parasail.

2006, Dec. 28 *Perf. 13½x13¼*

1128-1130 A365 Set of 3 2.50 1.25

Marine Life — A373

Designs: No. 1139, Leaf scorpionfish. No. 1140, Orange-striped triggerfish.

No. 1141: a, Chambered nautilus. b, Spotted boxfish.

Perf. 13½x13¼

2007, Feb. 6 Litho. Wmk. 388

1139 A373 50c multi .70 .35
a. Perf. 12 .70 .35
1140 A373 50c multi .70 .35
a. Perf. 12 .70 .35

Souvenir Sheet

1141 A373 $1 Sheet of 2, #a-b 2.25 1.10

Dated 2006. See Brunei Nos. 588-590.

Tourism — A374

No. 1142: a, Hornbill, forest and flower. b, Diver and coral reef.

No. 1143: a, Buildings. b, Handicrafts.

No. 1144: a, Woman with red dress, with arms raised. b, Woman with red dress holding fan. c, Woman with blue dress. d, Woman with black dress. e, Woman with red and black dress with geometric patterns. f, Satay, Ketupat dan Aie Sirap. g, Yee Sang. h, Banana leaf rice dan Teh Tarik. i, Hinava. j, Manok Pansuh.

$2, Flag and buildings, vert.

2007, Mar. 19 *Perf. 13½x13¼*

1142 A374 30c Horiz. pair, #a-b .75 .35

Perf. 12

1143 A374 50c Horiz. pair, #a-b 1.50 .75

Booklet Stamps

Perf. 13½x13¼

1144 A374 30c Booklet pane of 10, #a-j 3.00 1.50
Compete booklet, #1144 3.00

Souvenir Sheet

Perf. 13¼x13½

1145 A374 $2 multi 2.00 1.00

No. 1145 contains one 30x50mm stamp.

Installation of 13th Yang Di-Pertuan Agong — A375

13th Yang Di-Pertuan Agong and background colors of: 30c, Yellow. 50c, Green. $1, Purple.

2007, Apr. 26 *Perf. 12½*

1146-1148 A375 Set of 3 2.00 1.00

Amphibians A376

Designs: 30c, Pedostibes hosii. No. 1150, 50c, Megophrys nasuta. No. 1151, 50c, Nyctixalus pictus.

$1, Rana laterimaculata.

2007, May 3 *Perf. 12*

1149-1151 A376 Set of 3 2.00 1.00

Souvenir Sheet

Perf. 13¼

1152 A376 $1 multi 1.40 .70

No. 1152 contains one 35x33mm stamp.

Airplanes A377

Designs: 30c, Shorts SC-7 Skyvan. No. 1154, 50c, GAF N22 Nomad. No. 1155, 50c, De Havilland Canada DHC 7-110.

No. 1156: a, Airspeed Consul. b, Douglas DC-3.

2007, May 24 *Perf. 12*

1153-1155 A377 Set of 3 1.60 .80

Souvenir Sheet

Perf. 13½x13¼

1156 A377 $1 Sheet of 2, #a-b 1.75 .85

Clock Towers — A378

Designs: 30c, J. W. W. Birch Clock Tower, 1917. 50c, Atkinson Clock Tower, 1905. $1, Alor Setar Clock Tower, 1912.

Perf. 13¼x14x13¼x13½

2007, June 6

1157-1159 A378 Set of 3 2.00 1.00

Children's Folk Tales A379

Designs: Nos. 1160a, 1161a, Bawang Putah Bawang Merah. Nos. 1160b, 1161b, Badang. Nos. 1160c, 1162a, Sang Kancil Dengan Buaya. Nos. 1160d, 1162b, Sang Kancil Menolong Kerbau. No. 1160e, Mat Jenin.

$5, Si Tanggang.

Perf. 13½x13¼

2007, June 26 Litho. Wmk. 388

1160 Horiz. strip of 5 2.00 2.00
a.-e. A379 30c Any single .40 .30
f. Booklet pane, 2 each #1160a-1160e 4.00 —
Complete booklet, #1160f 4.00
1161 Horiz. pair 1.25 .60
a.-b. A379 50c Any single .60 .30
1162 Horiz. pair 1.25 .60
a.-b. A379 50c Any single .60 .30

Souvenir Sheet

Litho. With Foil Application

Perf. 14

1163 A379 $5 multi 4.00 2.00

No. 1163 contains one 50x38mm stamp.

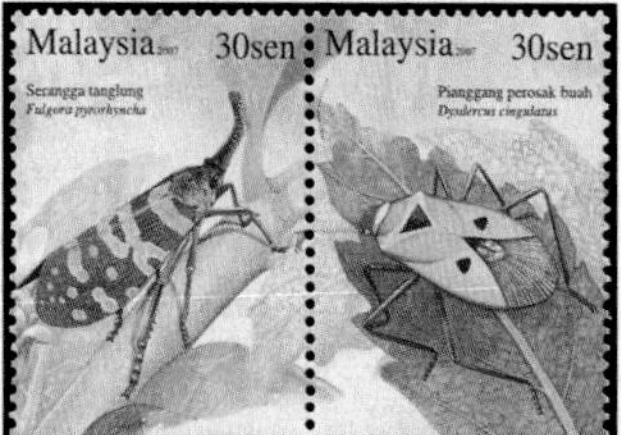

Insects — A380

No. 1164, 30c: a, Fulgora pyrorhyncha. b, Dysdercus cingulatus.

No. 1165, 50c: a, Valanga nigricornis. b, Rhaphipodus hopei.

$5, Antheraea helferi, horiz.

2007, July 7 *Perf. 12¾x12½*

Horiz. Pairs, #a-b

1164-1165 A380 Set of 2 1.75 .85

Souvenir Sheet

Perf. 14

1166 A380 $5 multi 4.00 2.00

No. 1166 contains one 50x38mm stamp.

Police Force, 200th Anniv. A381

Designs: 30c, Police and building. No. 1168, 50c, Police near jeep and in river, policeman wearing shorts. No. 1169, 50c, Police officers, cars, motorcycles, building and computer operator.

2007, July 24 *Perf. 13½x13¼*

1167-1169 A381 Set of 3 1.75 .85

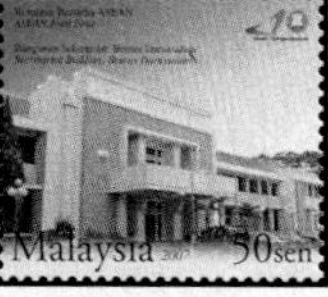

Association of South East Asian Nations (ASEAN), 40th Anniv. — A382

No. 1170: a, Secretariat Building, Bandar Seri Begawan, Brunei. b, National Museum of Cambodia. c, Fatahillah Museum, Jakarta, Indonesia. d, Typical house, Laos. e, Malayan Railway Headquarters Building, Kuala Lumpur. f, Yangon Post Office, Myanmar (Burma). g, Malacañang Palace, Philippines. h, National Museum of Singapore. i, Vimanmek Mansion, Bangkok, Thailand. j, Presidential Palace, Hanoi, Viet Nam.

2007, Aug. 8 *Perf. 13¾x14¼*

1170 Block of 10 5.00 5.00
a.-j. A382 50c Any single .50 .50

See Brunei No. 607, Burma No. 370, Cambodia No. 2339, Indonesia Nos. 2120-2121, Laos Nos. 1717-1718, Philippines Nos. 3103-3105, Singapore No. 1265, Thailand No. 2315, Viet Nam Nos. 3302-3311.

Malaysian Independence, 50th Anniv. — A383

No. 1171 — Anniversary emblem, flag and: a, Dato' Onn Jaafar. b, Tunku Abdul Rahman Putra Al-Haj. c, Tun Abdul Razak. d, Tun Tan Cheng Lock. e, Tun V. T. Sambantahan.

No. 1172 — Anniversary emblem and: a, Tunku Abdul Rahman Putra Al-Haj, buildings, people, flag, statue. b, Petronas Twin Towers, government building, automobile and bridge.

No. 1173: a, Tunku Abdul Rahman Putra Al-Haj signing declaration of independence and anniversary emblem. b, Anniversary emblem.

$5, Flag.

2007, Aug. 31 *Perf. 13½x13¼*

1171 Horiz. strip of 5 2.00 2.00
a.-e. A383 30c any single .40 .40
1172 Horiz. pair .80 .80
a.-b. A383 30c any single .40 .40
1173 Horiz. pair 1.00 1.00
a.-b. A383 50c any single .50 .50

Souvenir Sheet

Perf. 13¼

1174 A383 $5 multi 4.00 2.00

No. 1174 contains one 70x33mm stamp and has foil application in margin.

Petronas Twin Towers, Kuala Lumpur, 2007 Recipient of Aga Khan Award for Architecture A384

2007, Sept. 4 ***Perf. 13¼x13½***

1175 A384 50c multi 3.00 1.50

National and State Arms — A385

No. 1176: a, Malaysia. b, Kedah. c, Negri Sembilan. d, Pahang. e, Kelantan. f, Johore. g, Perak. h, Perlis. i. Selangor. j, Trengganu. k, Sarawak. l, Penang. m, Sabah. n, Malacca.

2007, Sept. 25 ***Perf. 13¾x14***

1176 Block of 14 5.75 4.25
a.-n. A385 50c Any single .40 .30

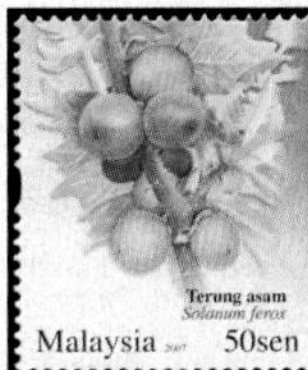

Vegetables A386

Designs: No. 1177, 50c, Solanum ferox. No. 1178, 50c, Etlingera elatior. No. 1179, 50c, Momordica charantia.

No. 1180: a, Luffa aegyptiaca. b, Psophocarpus tetragonolobus. c, Sesbania grandiflora. d, Solanum torvum.

Perf. 13¾x13½ Syncopated

2007, Nov. 26

1177-1179 A386 Set of 3 1.40 .70

Souvenir Sheet

Perf. 13¾x14 Syncopated

1180 A386 $1 Sheet of 4, #a-d 2.75 1.40

Kuala Lumpur Equestrian Grand Prix — A387

Horses: 30c, Oldenburger. No. 1182, 50c, Dutch Warmblood. No. 1183, 50c, Hanonverian.

2007, Dec. 13 ***Perf. 13½***

1181-1183 A387 Set of 3 1.50 .75

Bridges — A388

Designs: 30c, Merdeka Bridge, Kedah. No. 1185, 50c, Kota Bridge, Selangor. No. 1186, 50c, Victoria Bridge, Perak. $1, Sungai Segamat Bridge, Johore.

Perf. 13¾x13¼

2008, Feb. 28 **Litho.** **Wmk. 388**

1184-1187 A388 Set of 4 2.00 1.00

Nocturnal Animals A389

Designs: No. 1188, 30c, Mydaus javanensis. No. 1189, 30c, Echinosorex gymnurus. 50c, Catopuma temnickii. $1, Pteropas vampyrus.

No. 1192: a, $2, Tarsius bancanus (30x40mm). b, $3, Nycticebus coucang (60x40mm).

2008, Mar. 13 ***Perf. 13½x13¼***

1188-1191 A389 Set of 4 1.75 .85

Souvenir Sheet

Perf. 12¾x12½

1192 A389 Sheet of 2, #a-b 3.75 1.75
c. As #1192, imperf. 3.75 1.75

Butterflies A390

No. 1193: a, Smaller wood nymph. b, Malaysian lacewing.

50c, Malay red harlequin. $1, Glorious begum.

No. 1195A, Common rose. No. 1195B, Blue glassy tiger. No. 1195C, Green dragontail.

$5, Five-bar swordtail.

2008, Apr. 24 ***Perf. 13½x13¼***

1193 A390 30c Horiz. pair, #a-b .40 .30
d. As #1193, perf. 12 .40 .30
e. As #1193a, perf. 12 .40 .30
f. As #1193b, perf. 12 .40 .30
1194 A390 50c multi .40 .30
1195 A390 $1 multi .65 .40
Nos. 1193-1195 (3) 1.45 1.00

Booklet Stamps

1195A A390 30c multi .40 .25
1195B A390 30c multi .40 .25
1195C A390 30c multi .40 .25
d. Booklet pane, 2 each #1193a-1193b, 1195A-1195C 3.00 —
Complete booklet, #1195Cd 3.00
Nos. 1195A-1195C (3) 1.20 .75

Souvenir Sheet

Perf. 14

1196 A390 $5 multi 3.75 1.75

No. 1196 contains one 50x38mm stamp and has die cut slits in the sheet margin.

St. John Ambulance in Malaysia, Cent. A391

Centenary emblem and: 30c, Emergency ambulance service. 50c, First aid. $1, Cardiopulmonary resuscitation.

2008, May 22 ***Perf. 13½x13¼***

1197-1199 A391 Set of 3 2.75 1.40

A392

Cultural Items — A393

2008, June 10 ***Perf. 13½x13¼***

1200 A392 30c Batu Giling .30 .25
1201 A392 50c Supu .45 .45

Perf. 13¼x13¾

1202 A393 50c Kukur Kelapa .45 .45
Nos. 1200-1202 (3) 1.20 1.15

Intl. Dragon Boat Federation Club Crew World Championships — A394

Designs: 30c, Boats 6 and 3. 50c, Boats 5 and 2. $1, Boats 4 and 1.

$2, Boat 5.

Perf. 13½x13¼

2008, Aug. 1 **Litho.** **Wmk. 388**

1203-1205 A394 Set of 3 1.75 .85

Souvenir Sheet

1206 A394 $2 multi 1.60 .80
a. Imperf. 1.60 .80

No. 1206 contains one 80x30mm stamp.

Malaysian Scouting Association, Cent. — A395

Centenary emblem, scouting emblems and: 30c, Scouts reading map, Lord Robert Baden-Powell. No. 1208, 50c, Scout water activities. No. 1209, 50c, Scouts on monkey bridge.

2008, Aug. 14 ***Perf. 13½x13¼***

1207-1209 A395 Set of 3 1.50 .75

Art A396

Designs: 30c, Semangat Ledang, by Syed Ahmad Jamal. 50c, Musim Buah, by Chuah Thean Teng, vert. $1, Pago-pago, by Latiff Mohidin.

2008, Aug. 28 ***Perf. 12½x12¾***

1210 A396 30c multi .35 .25

Perf. 12¾x12½

1211 A396 50c multi .60 .30

Size:35x35mm

Perf. 13¼

1212 A396 $1 multi .80 .50
Nos. 1210-1212 (3) 1.75 1.05

Miniature Sheet

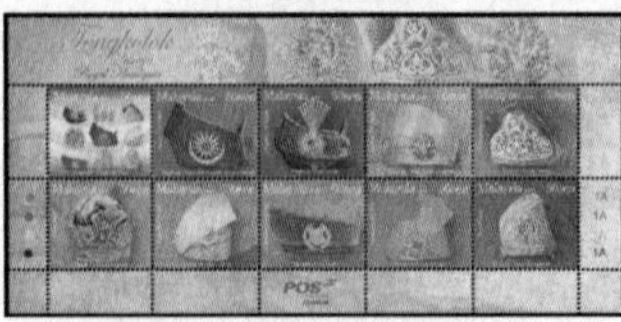

Royal Headgear — A397

No. 1213 — Headgear for: a, Leaders of Eight states and Yang Di-Pertuan Agong. b, Yang Di-Pertuan Agong. c, Sultan of Kedah. d, Yang Di-Pertuan Agong of Negri Sembilan. e, Sultan of Pahang. f, Sultan of Kelantan. g, Sultan of Perak. h, Raja of Perlis. i, Sultan of Selangor. j, Sultan of Trengganu.

2008, Sept. 16 ***Perf. 13¾x14***

1213 A397 50c Sheet of 10, #a-j 5.50 2.75

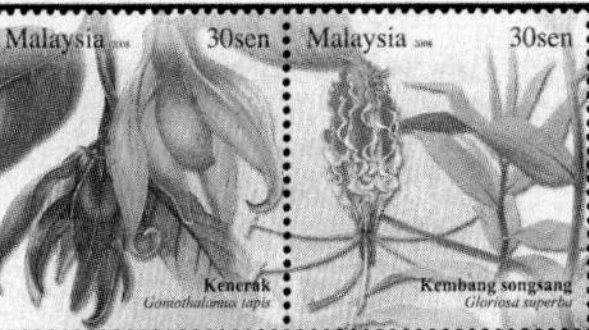

Flowers — A398

No. 1214, 30c: a, Goniothalamus tapis. b, Gloriosa superba.

No. 1215, 50c: a, Quisqualis indica. b, Michelia figo.

$5, Epiphyllum oxypetalum, vert.

Wmk. 388

2008, Oct. 9 **Litho.** ***Perf. 13¼***

Horiz. Pairs, #a-b

1214-1215 A398 Set of 2 2.25 1.10

Souvenir Sheet

Perf. 14

1216 A398 $5 multi 3.75 1.90

No. 1216 contains one 39x50mm stamp.

National Space Program — A399

Designs: 30c, Soyuz-TMA II rocket on launch pad. No. 1218, 50c, Malaysian astronaut. No. 1219, 50c, Intl. Space Station.

No. 1220: a, Rocket lifting off from launch pad. b, Rocket above Earth.

2008, Oct. 21 ***Perf. 13¼x13¾***

1217-1219 A399 Set of 3 1.60 .80

Souvenir Sheet

1220 A399 $1 Sheet of 2, #a-b 1.75 .85

Shells — A400

Designs: No. 1221, 30c, Burnt murex. No. 1222, 30c, Horned helmet. No. 1223, 50c, Triton's trumpet. No. 1224, 50c, Frog shell.

$2, Venus comb murex.

2008, Nov. 11 ***Perf. 11¾***

1221-1224 A400 Set of 4 2.00 1.00

Souvenir Sheet

Perf. 12¾x12½

1224A A400 $2 multi 2.00 1.00
b. Imperf. 2.00 1.00

No. 1224A contains one 60x40mm stamp.

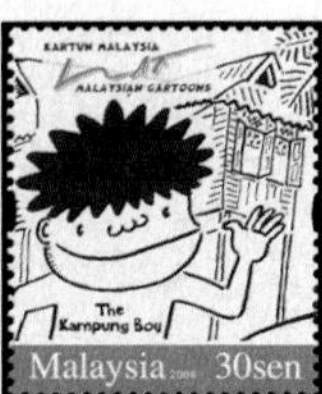

The Kampung Boy, Cartoons by Lat — A401

Designs: Nos. 1225a, 1226a, The Kampung Boy (29x33mm). Nos. 1225b, 1226b, Permainan Anak Kampung (58x33mm). Nos. 1225c, 1226c, Guru Sekolah Yang Garang (58x33mm). Nos. 1225d, 1226d, Town Boy (29x33mm). No. 1225e, Kampung Boy drawing picture (29x33mm).

$5, Malaysian daily life (60x40mm).

Perf. 13¾x14 Syncopated

2008, Dec. 1

1225 Horiz. strip of 5 1.50 1.50
a.-e. A401 30c Any single .30 .30
Complete booklet, 2 #1225 3.00
1226 Horiz. strip of 4 2.25 2.25
a.-d. A401 50c Any single .30 .30

Souvenir Sheet

Perf. 12¾x12½

1227 A401 $5 silver & blk 3.75 1.90

Schools — A402

Designs: No. 1228, 50c, SMK Convent Bukit Nanas, Kuala Lumpur. No. 1229, 50c, SMK St. Thomas, Kuching, Sarawak. No. 1230, 50c, SMK Victoria (Victoria Institution), Kuala Lumpur. No. 1231, 50c, SM All Saints, Kota Kinabalu, Sabah.

2008, Dec. 16 ***Perf. 13½x13¼***

1228-1231 A402 Set of 4 2.25 1.10

Birds A403

Designs: 30c, Polyplectron malacense. No. 1233, 50c, Mycteria cinerea. No. 1234, 50c, Myiophonus robinsoni.
$5, Aceros subruficollis.

Perf. 13½x13¼

2009, Jan. 21 Litho. Wmk. 388

1232-1234 A403 Set of 3 2.00 1.00

Souvenir Sheet

Perf. 12

Litho. & Embossed

1235 A403 $5 multi 4.00 2.00
a. With China 2009 World Stamp Exhibition emblem in sheet margin 4.00 2.00

Nos. 1235 and 1235a each contain one 45x35mm stamp.

Traditional Wedding Costumes A404

No. 1236: a, Bajau. b, Orang Ulu. c, Indian. d, Chinese. e, Malayan.
No. 1237: a, Malayan, diff. b, Chinese, diff. c, Indian, diff. d, Orang Ulu, diff. e, Bajau, diff.

Perf. 13¼x13½

2009, Mar. 23 Litho.

1236 Horiz. strip of 5 1.50 1.50
a.-e. A404 30c Any single .30 .30
Complete booklet, 2 each #1236a-1236e 3.00
1237 Horiz. strip of 5 2.50 2.50
a.-e. A404 50c Any single .50 .50

UNESCO World Heritage Sites — A405

No. 1238, 50c: a, Taman Negara Mulu, Sarawak, and tarsier. b, Taman Kinabalu, Sabah, and bird.
No. 1239, 50c: a, Town Square, Banda Hilir, Malacca, and door. b, Old City Hall, George Town, Penang, and windows.
No. 1240, 50c: a, Building, Banda Hilir, Malacca. b, Lenticular cloud over Taman Kinabalu, Sabah. c, Buildings, George Town, Penang. d, Cave, Taman Negara Mulu.

2009, Apr. 9 ***Perf. 13½x13¼***

Horiz. Pairs, #a-b

1238-1239 A405 Set of 2 1.25 .60

Perf. 14x13½

1240 A405 50c Sheet of 4, #a-d 1.25 .60

No. 1240 contains four 60x25mm stamps.

Engineering Projects of the Past and Present — A406

No. 1241, 30c — Transportation and port: a, Past. b, Present.
No. 1242, 30c — Telecommunication and power: a, Past. b, Present.
No. 1243, 50c — Road, bridge and dam: a, Past. b, Present.

Perf. 12½x12¾

2009, Apr. 20 Wmk. 388

Horiz. Pairs, #a-b

1241-1243 A406 Set of 3 2.50 1.25

Palm Trees — A407

Designs: No. 1244, 50c, Licuala grandis. No. 1245, 50c, Caryota mitis. No. 1246, 50c, Livistona saribus.
$3, Livistona endauensis and Johannesteijsmannia altifrons.

2009, May 19 Unwmk. ***Perf. 13¼***

1244-1246 A407 Set of 3 1.50 .75

Souvenir Sheet

Perf. 12

1247 A407 $3 multi 2.25 1.10

No. 1247 contains one 70x50mm L-shaped stamp.

Nature Conservation — A408

Inscriptions: 30c, Clean Water. No. 1249, 50c, Go Green. No. 1250, 50c, Fresh Air.

Perf. 13¾x13½

2009, June 18 Unwmk.

1248-1250 A408 Set of 3 1.75 .85

Miniature Sheet

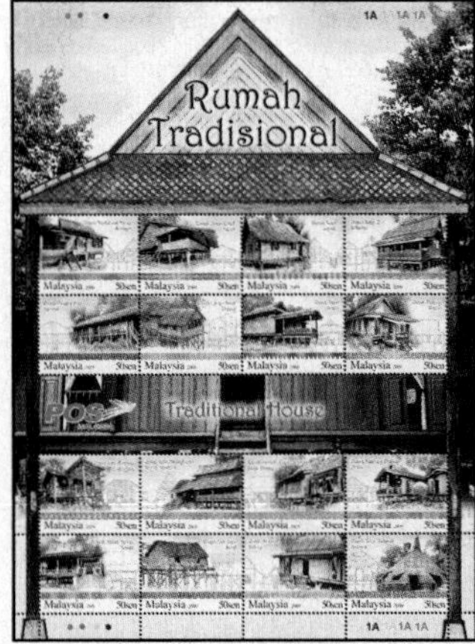

Traditional Houses — A409

No. 1251 Inscriptions: a, Rumah Traditional Melayu, Selangor. b, Rumah Dusun Lotud, Sabah. c, Rumah Kutai, Perak. d, Rumah Tiang 12, Kelantan. e, Rumah Panjang Iban, Sarawak. f, Rumah Orang Semai, Pahang. g, Rumah Limas, Johor. h, Rumah Panjang, Kedah. i, Rumah Limas Bungkus, Terengganu. j, Rumah Adat Minangkabau, Negeri Sembilan. k, Rumah Serambi Gajah Menyusu, Pulau Pinang. l, Rumah Bumbung Panjang, Perlis. m, Rumah Melayu Melaka, Melaka. n, Rumah Laut Bajau, Sabah. o, Rumah Serambi, Pahang. p, Rumah Ketua Bidayuh, Sarawak.

Perf. 12½x12¾

2009, July 9 Wmk. 388

1251 A409 50c Sheet of 16, #a-p 6.00 3.00

Tubers A410

Designs: No. 1252, 30c, Manihot esculenta crantz. No. 1253, 30c, Ipomoea batatas. No. 1254, 50c, Dioscorea alata. No. 1255, 50c, Pachyrrhizus erosus.
$3, Colocasia esculenta.

Perf. 13¼

2009, July 23 Litho. Unwmk.

1252-1255 A410 Set of 4 1.50 .75

Souvenir Sheet

Perf. 13¼ Syncopated

1256 A410 $3 multi 2.25 1.10

No. 1256 contains one 45x45mm stamp.

"Malaysia is Number 1" — A411

"1" and: Nos. 1257, 1260, Map of Malaysia. Nos. 1258, 1261, People in ring around Malaysian flag in heart. Nos. 1259, 1262, Lightbulb, seven people. No. 1263, Computer, Kuala Lumpur skyline, gauge, dish antenna, microscope, man at chart, woman with clipboard. No. 1264, Flower, people, gavel, building, traditional hat.
$5, Eight people around "1."

Perf. 13¾x14 Syncopated

2009, Aug. 31 Wmk. 388

1257 A411 30c multi .40 .30
1258 A411 30c multi .40 .30
1259 A411 30c multi .40 .30
Nos. 1257-1259 (3) 1.20 .90

Booklet Stamps

Perf. 13¾x13½ Syncopated

1260 A411 30c multi .40 .30
1261 A411 30c multi .40 .30
1262 A411 30c multi .40 .30
1263 A411 30c multi .40 .30
1264 A411 30c multi .40 .30
a. Booklet pane of 10, 2 each #1260-1264 4.00 —
Complete booklet, #1264a 4.00
Nos. 1260-1264 (5) 2.00 1.50

Souvenir Sheet

Perf. 13¼x13½

1265 A411 $5 multi 3.75 1.90

No. 1265 contains one 30x40mm stamp that has a clear holographic coating.

First Malaysian Submarine — A412

Submarine, flag of Malaysia and Navy crest with denomination at: 30c, LR. No. 1267, 50c, UR. No. 1268, 50c, LR.

2009, Sept. 3 ***Perf. 13½x13¼***

1266-1268 A412 Set of 3 1.50 .75

Energy Efficient Buildings — A413

Designs: 30c, Green Energy Office Building, Bangi. 50c, Low Energy Office Building, Putrajaya. $1, Diamond Building, Putrajaya.

2009, Sept. 9 ***Perf. 13¼x13½***

1269-1271 A413 Set of 3 1.75 .85
1270a Perf. 14 .40 .40
1271a Perf. 14 .75 .35

Declaration of the Rights of the Child, 20th Anniv. A414

No. 1272: a, Girl with pinwheel. b, Boy drinking. c, Boy carrying backpack. d, Girl under umbrella.

2009, Oct. 9 Litho. ***Perf. 13½***

1272 A414 30c Block of 4, #a-d 1.50 .75

Litho. & Embossed

1273 A414 $1 shown 1.00 .50

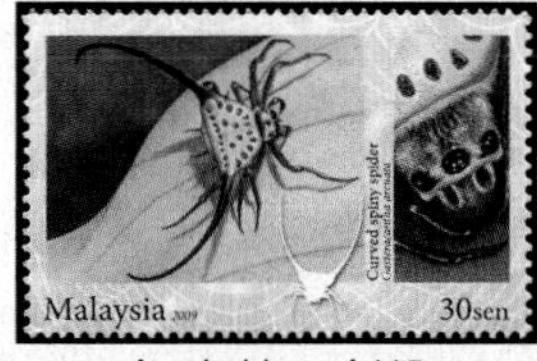

Arachnids — A415

Designs: No. 1274, 30c, Curved spiny spider. No. 1275, 30c, Fighting spider. 50c, St. Andrew's cross spider. $1, Golden orb-web spider.
$5, Black scorpion.

Perf. 13¾x13½

2009, Dec. 7 Litho. Wmk. 388

1274-1277 A415 Set of 4 2.00 1.00

Souvenir Sheet

Litho. & Embossed

Perf. 13¾x13

1278 A415 $5 multi 3.00 1.50

No. 1278 contains one 64x32mm hexagonal stamp.

Malaysian Currency A416

No. 1279, 50c — 1990 10 sen coin (orange ring): a, Obverse (with date). b, Reverse.
No. 1280, 50c — 1990 20 sen coin (green ring): a, Obverse (with date). b, Reverse.
No. 1281, 50c — 1990 50 sen coin (blue ring): a, Obverse (with date). b, Reverse.
$5, 50 ringgit banknote, horiz.

Perf. 13¼

2010, Jan. 18 Litho. Unwmk.

Vertical Pairs, #a-b

1279-1281 A416 Set of 3 1.75 .85

Souvenir Sheet

Litho. With Foil Application

Perf. 14x13½

1282 A416 $5 multi 3.00 1.50

No. 1282 contains one 50x40mm stamp.

A416a

Flag in "1" — A416b

2010 Litho. Wmk. 388 *Perf. 13¾*

Stamp and Label Separated By Perforations

1282A A416a 30c multi + label *13.50 13.50*

Stamp and Label Not Separated By Perforations

Perf. 14¼

1282B A416b 30c multi *18.00 18.00*
1282C A416b 60c multi *24.00 24.00*
Nos. 1282A-1282C (3) 55.50 55.50

Issued: No. 1282A, 2/4; No. 1282B, May. Labels could be personalized. No. 1282A was issued in sheets of 20 + 20 labels that sold for $6. No. 1282B was issued in sheets of 20 that sold for $19. No. 1282C was issued in sheets of 10 that sold for $19.

New Year 2010 (Year of the Tiger) — A417

No. 1283: a, Korean tiger. b, Malayan tiger.

Perf. 13½x14

2010, Feb. 23 Litho. Wmk. 388

1283 A417 50c Horiz. pair, #a-b .60 .30

Ferns — A418

No. 1284: a, Helminthostachys zeylanica. b, Stenochlaena palustris. c, Platycerium coronarium. d, Dicraopteris linearis. e, Diplazium esculentum.
$3, Asplenium nidus, Matonia pectinata, Dipteris conjugata, horiz.

Perf. 13¼x13½

2010, Mar. 10 Litho. Wmk. 388

1284 Horiz. strip of 5 1.50 .75
a.-e. A418 50c Any single .30 .25

Souvenir Sheet

Perf. 14

1285 A418 $3 multi 1.90 .95

No. 1285 contains one 100x45mm stamp.

A419

Local Markets — A420

No. 1286, 30c: a, Woman with vegetables at Kelantan market. b, Kelantan market.
No. 1287, 50c: a, Fruit at market, Sabah. b, Handicrafts at market, Sabah.
No. 1288 — Market in Sarawak: a, $1, Woman and vegetables. b, $2, Woman and man with potted plants.
No. 1289 — Market in Kedah: a, $1, Man looking at textiles, pile of baskets. b, $2, Man and woman shopping.

2010, Mar. 23 *Perf. 13¼*

Horiz. Pairs, #a-b

1286-1287 A419 Set of 2 1.00 .50

Souvenir Sheets

Perf. 13¼x13½

Sheets of 2, #a-b

1288-1289 A420 Set of 2 3.75 1.90

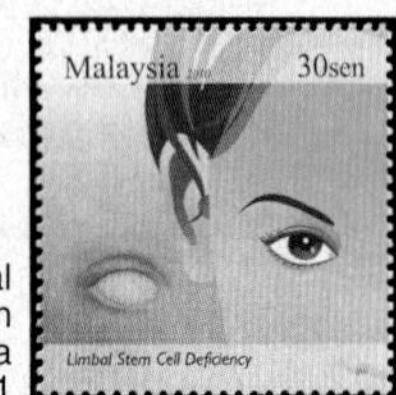

Medical Excellence in Malaysia A421

Designs: 30c, Limbal stem cell deficiency. 50c, Premaxilla retractor. $1, Arm transplant.

2010, Apr. 26 *Perf. 13¼*

1290-1292 A421 Set of 3 1.25 .60

Fireflies A422

Designs: No. 1293, 30c, Pteroptyx bearni. No. 1294, 30c, Pteroptyx valida. No. 1295, 50c, Lychnuris sp. No. 1296, 50c, Diaphanes sp.
$5, Pteroptyx tener.

2010, May 10 Litho. *Perf. 12¼*

1293-1296 A422 Set of 4 1.00 .50

Souvenir Sheet

Litho. With Hologram

Perf. 12¾x12½

1297 A422 $5 multi 3.00 1.50

No. 1297 contains one 60x40mm stamp.

Malaysian Railways — A423

No. 1298: a, Commuter train. b, ETS train. 50c, Blue Tiger. $1, 56 Class train.
No. 1301, 20 Class train. No. 1302, Commuter and ETS trains. No. 1303, Blue Tiger. No. 1304, 56 Class train. No. 1305, FMSR Class T train.
$3, FMSR Class T train, vert.

2010, June 22 Litho. *Perf. 12*

1298 A423 30c Horiz. pair, #a-b .40 .25

Size: 70x25mm

1299 A423 50c multi .35 .25
1300 A423 $1 multi .65 .30
Nos. 1298-1300 (3) 1.40 .80

Booklet Stamps

1301 A423 30c multi .25 .25
1302 A423 30c multi .25 .25
1303 A423 30c multi .25 .25
1304 A423 30c multi .25 .25
1305 A423 30c multi .25 .25
a. Vert. strip of 5, #1301-1305 1.00 1.00
b. Booklet pane of 10, 2 each #1301-1305 2.00 —
Complete booklet, #1305b 2.00

Souvenir Sheet

Perf. 13½

1306 A423 $3 multi 1.90 .95
a. As #1306, with Bangkok 2010 emblem in margin 1.90 .95
b. As #1306, with PhilaNippon '11 emblem in margin 2.00 1.00

No. 1306 contains one 30x50mm stamp.

Flowers — A424

Designs: 30c, Nelumbium nelumbo. 50c, Hydrangea macrophylla. 60c, Bougainvillea. 70c, Hippeastrum reticulatum. 80c, Hibiscus rosa-sinensis. 90c, Ipomoea indica. $1, Canna orientalis. $2, Allamanda cathartica.

2010, July 1 *Perf. 14x13¾*

1307 A424 30c multi .25 .25
1308 A424 50c multi .30 .25
1309 A424 60c multi .40 .25
1310 A424 70c multi .45 .25
1311 A424 80c multi .50 .25
1312 A424 90c multi .55 .30
1313 A424 $1 multi .65 .30
1314 A424 $2 multi 1.25 .60
Nos. 1307-1314 (8) 4.35 2.45

Threatened Habitats — A425

Habitats: 60c, Forest. 70c, Marine. 80c, River.

Perf. 13¾x14 Syncopated

2010, July 15

1315-1317 A425 Set of 3 1.40 .70

Grand Knight of Valor Award — A426

Grand Knight of Valor Award and: 60c, Soldiers, tank. 70c, People, Kuala Lumpur skyline. 80c, Soldiers, building.

2010, July 30 *Perf. 12¾x12½*

1318-1320 A426 Set of 3 1.40 .70

Miniature Sheets

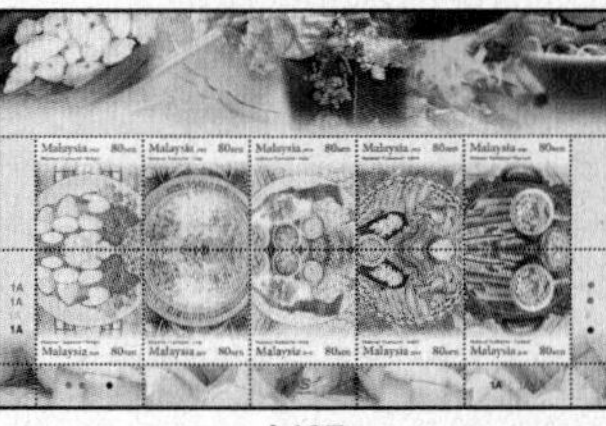

A427

Traditional Festive Food — A428

Nos. 1321 and 1322 — Various foods of people of: a, Malaysia, text at top. b, Malaysia, text at bottom. c, China, text at top. d, China, text at bottom. e, India, text at top. f, India, text at bottom. g, Sabah, text at top. h, Sabah, text at bottom. i, Sarawak, text at top, j, Sarawak, text at bottom. Foods on Nos. 1321 and 1322 are different.
No. 1323: a, Chinese foods. b, Indian foods. c, Malaysian foods.

2010, Aug. 10 *Perf. 13¼*

1321 A427 Sheet of 10 5.25 2.60
a.-j. 80c Any single .50 .25

Booklet Stamps

1322 A427 Booklet pane of 10 4.00 —
a.-j. 60c Any single .40 .25

Souvenir Sheet

1323 A428 Sheet of 3 2.00 1.00
a.-c. $1 Any single .65 .30

Life of Aboriginal People — A429

Designs: 60c. Women holding ketuk buluh (musical instruments). 70c, Man shooting with blowpipe. 80c, Man carving figures.

2010, Sept. 27 Wmk. 388

1324-1326 A429 Set of 3 1.40 .70

Old Post Offices — A430

No. 1327: a, Jalan Kelang Lama Post Office, Kuala Lumpur. b, Layang-Layang Post Office. c, Jalan Raja Post Office. d, Temangan Post Office. e, Merlimau Post Office. f, Seremban General Post Office. g, Fraser Hill (Bukit Fraser) Post Office. h, Kuala Kangsar Post Office. i, Kaki Bukit Post Office. j, Jalan Bagan Luar Post Office. k, Kudat Post Office. l, Kuching General Post Office. m, Kajang Post Office. n, Kuala Terengganu Post Office. o, Kuala Lumpur General Post Office, flag of Federal Territory. p, Johor Bahru General Post Office, flag of Johore. q, Sungai Petani Post Office, flag of Kedah. r, Rantau Panjang Post Office, flag of Kelantan. s, Alor Gajah Post Office, flag of Malacca. t, Bandar Baru Serting Post Office, flag of Negri Sembilan. u, Ringlet Post Office, flag of Pahang. v, Tronoh Post Office, flag of Perak. w, Kangar Post Office, flag of Perlis. x, Bukit Mertajam Post Office, flag of Penang. y, Kota Kinabalu General Post Office, flag of Sabah. z, Sarikei Post Office, flag of Sarawak. aa, Bukit Rotan Post Office, flag of Selangor. ab, Jerteh Post Office, flag of Trengganu.

Perf. 13¾x13½ Syncopated

2010, Oct. 9

1327 Sheet of 28 11.00 11.00
a.-ab. A430 60c Any single .35 .25

"Malaysia is Number 1" — A431

Handcrafted products, "Malaysia is Number 1" emblem and: No. 1328, 30c, Computer mouse, satellite dish. No. 1329, 30c, Astronaut and spaceship. No. 1330, 50c, Buildings. No. 1331, 50c, Robot.

2010, Nov. 10 ***Perf. 13¼x13½***

1328-1331 A431 Set of 4 1.10 .55

Children's Games — A432

No. 1332, 60c: a, Batu Seremban. b, Congkak.

No. 1333, 60c: a, Galah Panjang. b, Kondakondi.

No. 1334, 60c: a, Perang-perang. b, Telefon Tin.

$5, Main Bayang-bayang.

Litho. With Glitter Affixed

Perf. 13¾x14¼

2010, Dec. 13 **Unwmk.**

Self-Adhesive

Horiz. Pairs, #a-b

1332-1334 A432 Set of 3 2.40 1.25

Souvenir Sheet

Die Cut Perf. 13½x13¼

1335 A432 $5 multi 3.25 1.60

No. 1335 contains one 75x50mm stamp.

Pets — A433

Child and: 60c, Rabbit. 80c, Cat. $1, Dog.

No. 1339, $5, Rabbit. No. 1340, $5, Rabbit, with Indipex 2011 emblem.

2011 Litho. Wmk. 388 ***Perf. 13¼***

1336-1338 A433 Set of 3 1.60 .80

Souvenir Sheets

1339 A433 $5 multi 3.25 1.60
1340 A433 $5 multi 3.50 1.75

Issued: Nos. 1336-1339, 1/18; No. 1340, 2/18. Indipex 2011 World Philatelic Exhibition (No. 1340).

Highlands Tourism — A434

Designs: 50c, Funicular railroad, Bukit Bendera. 60c, Tea picker, Cameron Highlands. 90c, Cable car and station, Mat Cincang Mountain, Langkawi. $1, Cabbage patch, Kundasang.

2011, Feb. 21 ***Perf. 13½x13¼***

1341-1344 A434 Set of 4 2.00 1.00

Malaysia, Winners of 2010 Suzuki Cup — A435

Designs: No. 1345, 60c, Medal and emblem of Malaysian soccer team. No. 1346, 60c, Suzuki Cup and tournament emblem, vert. (30x50mm).

Perf. 13¼, 13¼x13½ (#1346)

2011, Feb. 28

1345-1346 A435 Set of 2 .80 .40

Spices A436

Designs: No. 1347, 60c, Cinnamon. 90c, Star anise. $1, Cardamom.

No. 1350, 60c: a, Fennel seed, text at top. b, Fennel seed, text at bottom. c, Turmeric, text at top. d, Turmeric, text at bottom. e, Chili peppers, text at top. f, Chili peppers, text at bottom. g, Coriander, text at top. h, Coriander, text at bottom. i, White pepper, text at top. j, White pepper, text at bottom.

No. 1351: a, $1, Various spice on stone, spice crushing roller. b, $2, Various spices on stone.

2011, Mar. 28 ***Perf. 13¼***

1347-1349 A436 Set of 3 1.75 .85
1350 Booklet pane of 10 4.00 —
a.-j. A436 60c Any single .40 .25
Complete booklet, #1350 4.00

Souvenir Sheet

Perf. 14x13¼

1351 A436 Sheet of 2, #a-b 2.00 1.00

No. 1351 contains two 50x60mm stamps.

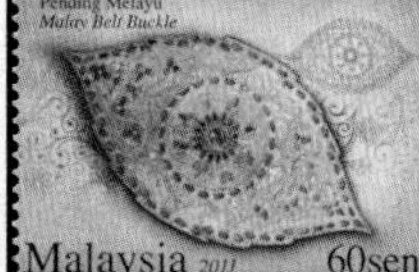

National Heritage Artifacts A437

No. 1352: a, Malay belt buckle. b, Gold coin showing deer. c, Sireh set (betel containers) of Sultan Abdul Samad of Selangor. d, Gold coin of Sultan Muzaffar Shah of Johore. e, Arch of sitting Buddha.

No. 1353: a, Royal Trengganu tobacco box. b, Gold Coin of Sultan Alau'uddin Riayat Shah. c, Dong S'on bell. d, Gold coin of Sultan Zainal Abidin II of Trengganu. e, Statue of Avalokitesvara.

2011, Apr. 11 ***Perf. 12½x12¾***

1352 Horiz. strip of 5 2.00 1.00
a.-e. A437 60c Any single .40 .25
1353 Horiz. strip of 5 2.00 1.00
a.-e. A437 60c Any single .40 .25

Personalized Stamps — A438

No. 1354: a, Bunga Raya. b, Durian. c, Handicraft. d, Wau Bulan.

2011, Apr. 28 ***Perf. 13¾x14***

1354 Block of 4 1.40 .70
a.-b. A438 35c Either single .25 .25
c.-d. A438 65c Either single .45 .25

No. 1354 printed in sheets containing two blocks of 4. The right halves of Nos. 1354a and 1354c and the left halves of Nos. 1354b and 1354d could be personalized. Images showing silver handicrafts are generic images. Compare with No. B1.

Virtues — A439

No. 1355 — Inscriptions in black: a, Love. b, Hardworking. c, Courteous. d, Mutual respect. e, Independent. f, Awareness. g, Kind hearted. h, Thankful ("Thank you" in green in 7 different languages). i, Living in harmony. j, Integrity.

2011, June 13 ***Perf. 12¾x12½***

1355 Block of 10 4.00 2.00
a.-j. A439 60c Any single .40 .25
k. As "h," "Thank you" in green in 8 different languages .40 .25
l. Block of 10, #1355a-1355g, 1355i-1355k 4.00 2.00

Issued: Nos. 1355k, 1355l, 7/18.

Aviation in Malaysia, Cent. A440

Designs: 60c, Early monoplane. 80c, Airport control tower, passenger airplane and fuel truck. $1, Airport terminal, jets.

Perf. 12½x12¾

2011, July 7 Litho. Wmk. 388

1356-1358 A440 Set of 3 1.60 .80

Miniature Sheet

Royal Palaces — A441

No. 1359 — Palace, arms and map of: a, Kuala Lumpur. b, Negri Sembilan. c, Selangor. d, Perlis. e, Trengganu. f, Kedah. g, Kelantan. h, Pahang. i, Johore. k, Perak.

2011, July 18 ***Perf. 14½x14¼***

1359 A441 Sheet of 10 7.00 3.50
a.-j. $1 Any single .70 .35

Miniature Sheet

Friendship Between Indonesia and Malaysia — A442

No. 1360: a, National Monument, Malaysia. b, Proclamation Monument, Indonesia. c, 1959 Malaya and North Borneo $1 banknote. d, 1945 5-sen Indonesia banknote. e, Malaya #84. f, Indonesia #1LM1. g, Gallus gallus. h, Gallus varius.

2011, Aug. 8 ***Perf. 12½x12¾***

1360 A442 Sheet of 8 5.00 2.40
a.-h. 90c Any single .60 .30

See Indonesia Nos. 2284-2285.

Art — A443

Designs: 60c, Datuk Bajau Horseman, North Borneo, by Mohd Hoessein Enas, 1963. 90c, Ayam Jantan, sculpture by Anthony Lau, 1963, horiz. $1, Flag, by Nik Zainal Abidin Nik Salleh, 1970, horiz.

Perf. 12¾x12½, 12½x12¾

2011, Sept. 19

1361-1363 A443 Set of 3 1.60 .80

Mailboxes A444

No. 1364 — Mailbox, building and postal service emblem with inscription at bottom: a, Bukit Bendera, Pulau Pinang. b, Bukit Fraser, Pahang. c, Melaka Bandaraya Bersejarah. d,

Seremban, Negeri Sembilan. e, Pejabat Pos Besar, Kuala Lumpur.

Litho. & Embossed
Perf. 13½x14

2011, Oct. 10 **Wmk. 388**

1364	Horiz. strip of 5	3.25	1.60
a.-e.	A444 $1 Any single	.65	.30

Mailboxes A445

Mailbox, buildings and inscription at LL: No. 1365, Bukit Bendera, Pulau Pinang. No. 1366, Bukit Fraser, Pahang. No. 1367, Melaka Bandaraya Bersejarah. No. 1368, Seremban, Negeri Sembilan. No. 1369, Pejabat Pos Besar, Kuala Lumpur.

Serpentine Die Cut 13x12¾

2011, Oct. 10 **Litho.** **Unwmk.**

Booklet Stamps
Self-Adhesive

1365	A445 60c multi	.40	.25
1366	A445 60c multi	.40	.25
1367	A445 60c multi	.40	.25
1368	A445 60c multi	.40	.25
1369	A445 60c multi	.40	.25
a.	Booklet pane of 10, 2 each #1365-1369	4.00	
	Nos. 1365-1369 (5)	2.00	1.25

Tunnel Construction — A446

No. 1370, 60c: a, Tunneling through. b, TBM after breakthrough.
No. 1371, 60c: a, Tunnel breakthrough. b, Construction gantry.
No. 1372, 60c: a, Road tunnel. b, Schematic cross-section.
No. 1373, vert.: a, Vignettes of Nos. 1370a, 1371a, 1371b. b, Vignettes of Nos. 1370b, 1372a, 1372b.

Perf. 13¼x14¼ Syncopated

2011, Nov. 21 **Litho.** **Unwmk.**

Vert. Pairs, #a-b

1370-1372	A446 Set of 3	2.40	1.25

Souvenir Sheet
Self-Adhesive
Litho. With Three-Dimensional Plastic Affixed
Serpentine Die Cut 12x12¾

1373	A446 Sheet of 2	3.25	1.60
a.	$2 multi	1.25	.60
b.	$3 multi	2.00	1.00

No. 1373 contains two 35x40mm stamps.

Regalia — A447

Designs: 60c, Crown (Gandik diraja). 80c, Belt buckle (Pending diraja). 90c, Throne (Singgahsana).

Wmk. 388

2011, Dec. 12 **Litho.** *Perf. 14*

1374-1376	A447 Set of 3	1.50	.75

Women Creating Textiles A448

Dragon on Robe — A449

No. 1377: a, Cindai. b, Songket. c, Pua Kumbu. d, Ci Xiu. e, Rangkit.

Wmk. 388

2012, Jan. 12 **Litho.** *Perf. 12*

1377	Horiz. strip of 5	2.00	1.00
a.-e.	A448 60c Any single	.40	.25

Souvenir Sheets
Variable Perfs. 13½-14

1378	A449 $3 multi	2.00	1.00
a.	With Indonesia 2012 World Stamp Championships emblem in sheet margin, perf. 13½	2.00	1.00

Litho. With Foil Application

1379	A449 $5 gold & multi	3.50	1.75
a.	With Indonesia 2012 World Stamp Championships emblem in sheet margin, variable perfs. 13¼-13½	3.50	1.75

Yes to Life, No to Drugs Campaign — A450

No. 1380: a, Family. b, Children at play.

Perf. 13¾x13

2012, Feb. 27 **Litho.** **Wmk. 388**

1380	A450 60c Horiz. pair, #a-b	.80	.40
1381	A450 $1 shown	.70	.35

Malaysian Antarctic Research Program A451

Design: 60c, Map of Antarctica, flag of Malaysia, scientist, emblem.
No. 1383: a, World map, emblem. b, Penguins, bacteria, scientist, emblem (70x35mm).

2012, Mar. 8 **Wmk. 388** *Perf. 13¼*

1382	A451 60c multi	.40	.25
1383	A451 90c Horiz. pair, #a-b	1.25	.60

Marine Life A452

Designs: No. 1384, Red-spotted coral crab. No. 1385, Leopard moray eel. No. 1386, Mandarinfish. No. 1387, Blue sea star.
$5, Green sea turtle, Robust ghostpipefish, Thorny seahorse.

2012, Mar. 21 *Perf. 12*

1384	A452 60c multi	.40	.25
1385	A452 60c multi	.40	.25
a.	Perf. 13½	.40	.25
1386	A452 60c multi	.40	.25
a.	Perf. 13½	.40	.25
1387	A452 60c multi	.40	.25
a.	Perf. 13½	.40	.25
	Nos. 1384-1387 (4)	1.60	1.00

Souvenir Sheet
Perf. 12½

1388	A452 $5 multi	3.25	1.60

No. 1388 contains one 90x35mm stamp.

Installation of 14th Yang Di-Pertuan Agong A453

Designs: 60c, 14th Yang Di-Pertuan Agong, yellow green frame. 80c, 14th Yang Di-Pertuan Agong and wife, horiz. $1, 14th Yang Di-Pertuan Agong, red frame.
No. 1392: a, Malaysia #79. b, 14th Yang Di-Pertuan Agong, gold frame.

Wmk. 388

2012, Apr. 11 **Litho.** *Perf. 14*

1389-1391	A453 Set of 3	1.60	.80

Souvenir Sheet
Litho. With Foil Application

1392	Sheet of 2	3.25	1.60
a.	A453 $2 multi	1.25	.60
b.	A453 $3 multi	2.00	1.00
c.	As #1392, with added emblem in gold in sheet margin	3.25	1.60

Issued: No. 1392c, 1/1/13. No. 1392c has added emblem similar to a circular cancel inscribed "100 Tahun Setem Kedah & 125 Tahun Perkhidmatan Pos Di Kedah" and "Pameran Setem."

Aromatic Plants A454

Designs: 60c, Polygonum minus. $1, Mentha piperita.
$5, Kaffir lime, vert.

Perf. 14¾x14 Syncopated

2012, May 24 **Litho.**

1393-1394	A454 Set of 2	1.00	.50

Souvenir Sheet
Perf. 14x14¾ Syncopated

1395	A454 $5 multi	3.25	1.60

No. 1395 is impregnated with a lime scent.

2012 World Gas Conference, Kuala Lumpur — A455

Inscriptions: No. 1396, 60c, Securing Gas Supply. No. 1397, 60c, Enhancing Gas Demand. No. 1398, 60c, A Sustainable Future. No. 1399, 60c, Foundation For Growth.

2012, June 4 **Wmk. 388** *Perf. 12½*

1396-1399	A455 Set of 4	1.50	.75

Miniature Sheet

Yang Di-Pertuan Agongs — A456

No. 1400 — Photograph and Roman numeral of Yang Di-Pertuan Agong: a, XI. b, XII. c, XIII. d, X. e, I. f, IX. g, II. h. VIII. i. III. j, VII. k, VI. l, V. m, IV. n, XIV. Nos. 1400a-1400m are 35x35mm, No. 1400n is 70x70mm.

Litho. With Foil Application

2012, June 21 **Wmk. 388** *Perf. 13¼*

1400	A456 Sheet of 14 + 2 labels	12.00	6.00
a.-m.	$1 Any single	.65	.30
n.	$5 multi	3.25	1.60

Traditional Occupations — A457

No. 1401: a, Tukang seni kertas (artist decorating lanterns). b, Tukang tilik (men with bird and cage).
No. 1402: a, Penjaja satay (satay griller). b, Penjaja nasi kandar (man carrying pot and baskets).
No. 1403: a, Penjaja lemang (woman stirring pot). b, Penjaja manisan (confection vender with bicycle). c, Tukang ubat tradisional (food vendor on mat). d, Penjaja pasembor (juice vendor on bicycle). e, Tukang dobi (laundry men).

2012, June 21 **Litho.** **Wmk. 388**

1401	A457 Horiz. pair	1.00	.50
a.-b.	80c Either single	.50	.25
1402	A457 Horiz. pair	1.30	.65
a.-b.	$1 Either single	.65	.30

Booklet Stamps

1403	A457 Horiz. strip of 5	2.00	1.25
a.-e.	60c Any single	.40	.25
f.	Booklet pane of 10, 2 each #1403a-1403e	4.00	—
	Complete booklet, #1403f	4.00	

Coins — A458

Designs: No. 1404, 60c, Obverse of 5-cent coin (lilac background). No. 1405, 60c, Reverse of 5-cent coin (no numeral on coin, lilac background). No. 1406, 60c, Obverse of 10-cent coin (light blue background). No. 1407, 60c, Reverse of 10-cent coin (no numeral on coin, light blue background). No. 1408, 60c, Obverse of 20-cent coin (light green background). No. 1409, 60c, Reverse of 20-cent coin (no numeral on coin, light green background). No. 1410, 60c, Obverse of 50-cent coin (pink background). No. 1411, 60c, Reverse of 50-cent coin (no numeral on coin, pink background).

Litho. & Embossed With Foil Application

2012, July 16 **Unwmk.** *Perf. 14*

1404-1411	A458 Set of 8	3.25	1.60

Souvenir Sheets

Banknotes — A459

No. 1412: a, 1-ringgit banknote. b, 50-ringgit banknote. c, 20-ringgit banknote.
No. 1413: a, 100-ringit banknote. b, 5-ringit banknote. d, 10-ringgit banknote.

Litho. With Foil Application
Perf. 14x13¼

2012, July 16 **Unwmk.**
1412 A459 Sheet of 3 9.75 5.00
a.-c. $5 Any single 3.25 1.60
1413 A459 Sheet of 3 9.75 5.00
a.-c. $5 Any single 3.25 1.60

National Unity — A460

Inscriptions below "Perpaduan": No. 1414, 60c, Bahasa. No. 1415, 60c, Gotong-Royong. No. 1416, 60c, Sukan. No. 1417, 60c, Tarian.

Perf. 13¼x13½

2012, Aug. 30 **Litho.** **Wmk. 388**
1414-1417 A460 Set of 4 1.60 .80

British Royalty A461

Designs: No. 1418, $1.50, Malaya Selangor #101. No. 1419, $1.50, Duke and Duchess of Cambridge.
No. 1420: a, Like No. 1418. b, Like No. 1419.

2012, Sept. 13 ***Perf. 14***
1418-1419 A461 Set of 2 2.00 1.00

Souvenir Sheet

1420 Sheet of 2 3.25 1.60
a.-b. A461 $2.50 Either single 1.60 .80
c. As No. 1420, with Thailand 2013 World Stamp Exhibition emblem in sheet margin 3.25 1.60

Reign of Queen Elizabeth II, 60th anniv. (Nos. 1418, 1420a), Wedding of Prince William and Catherine Middleton (Nos. 1419, 1420b).
Issued: No. 1420c, 8/2/13.

Festivals — A462

Inscriptions: No. 1421, 60c, Hari Raya Aidiladha (Eid ul-Adha). No. 1422, 60c, Perayaan Kuih Bulan (Chinese mid-autumn festival). No. 1423, 60c, Pesta Kaul (Kaul Festival). No. 1424, 60c, Regatta Lepa. No. 1425, 60c, Thaipusam.

Litho. With Foil Application
Perf. 13½x14

2012, Sept. 27 **Unwmk.**
1421-1425 A462 Set of 5 2.00 1.00

Malacca, 750th Anniv. — A463

Anniversary emblem and: 50c, Tokong Cheng Hoon Teng (Cheng Hoon Teng Temple). 90c, Masjid Kampong Hulu (Kampong Hulu Mosque).
750c, Muzium Yang Di-Pertua Negeri Malaka (Malacca Governor's Museum).

Wmk. 388

2012, Oct. 7 **Litho.** ***Perf. 12***
1426-1427 A463 Set of 2 .95 .45

Souvenir Sheet
Litho. With Foil Application
Perf. 13¼

1428 A463 750c multi 5.00 2.50

No. 1428 contains one 70x35mm stamp. See No. 1496.

World Post Day A464

Malaysian Postal Service and Universal Postal Union emblems: 60c, Postman with bicycle, 1950. 80c, Postman on scooter, 1970. No. 1431, $1, Postman on scooter, 1990.
No. 1432: a, $1, Postman holding scooter, emblems. b, $2, Five postmen (90x35mm).

Perf. 12½, 12½x12½x12x12½ (#1432b)

2012, Oct. 22 **Litho.**
1429-1431 A464 Set of 3 1.60 .80

Souvenir Sheet

1432 Sheet of 2 2.00 1.00
a. A464 $1 multi .65 .30
b. A464 $2 multi 1.30 .65

A465

Greetings Stamps — A466

No. 1433 — Inscription: a, Flora & Fauna / Malaysia. b, Bendera Malaysia / Malaysian Flag. c, Batik / Malaysia. d, Latarlangit Malaysia / Malaysian Skyline.
No. 1434 — Inscription: a, Bendera Malaysia / Malaysian Flag (flag in circle). b, Perayaan / Celebration. c, Tulus Ikhlas / Yours Sincerely. d, Salam / Greetings.

Perf. 13½x13¼

2012, Nov. 5 **Wmk. 388**
1433 A465 Block or vert. strip of 4 1.60 .80
a.-d. 60c Any single .40 .25
1434 A466 Block or vert. strip of 4 1.60 .80
a.-d. 60c Any single .40 .25

Children's Hobbies — A467

No. 1435, 60c: a, Girl baking cookies. b, Girl collecting stamps.
No. 1436, 60c: a, Boy playing soccer. b, Robot fishing.
No. 1437, 60c: a, Boy playing drums. b, Boy with camera.
$5, Children reading letters.

Perf. 13½x13¼

2012, Nov. 19 **Litho.** **Unwmk.**
Horiz. Pairs, #a-b

1435-1437 A467 Set of 3 2.40 1.25

Souvenir Sheet
Litho. With Foil Application
Perf. 12
Wmk. 388

1438 A467 $5 multi 3.25 1.60

No. 1438 contains one 70x45mm stamp.

Postal History of Kedah — A468

Designs: No. 1439, 90c, Malaya-Kedah #1. No. 1440, 90c, Malaya-Kedah #16. No. 1441, 90c, Malaya-Kedah #20.
$3, Kedah cancel on postal card from Siam, vert.

Perf. 14 Syncopated

2012, Dec. 20 **Litho.** **Wmk. 388**
1439-1441 A468 Set of 3 1.75 .90

Souvenir Sheet
Perf. 14¼

1442 A468 $3 multi 2.00 1.00

Postage stamps of Kedah, 100th anniv. No. 1442 contains one 28x38mm stamp.

Woodpeckers A469

Designs: 60c, Banded woodpecker. 80c, Common flameback woodpecker. $1, Lesser yellownape woodpecker.
$5, White-bellied woodpecker, horiz.

2013, Jan. 13 ***Perf. 13¼x13½***
1443-1445 A469 Set of 3 1.60 .80

Souvenir Sheet
Perf. 13¾x13½

1446 A469 $5 multi 3.25 1.60

No. 1446 contains one 64x48mm stamp.

Exotic Pets — A470

Designs: 60c, African pygmy hedgehog. 80c, Green iguana. $1, Sugar glider.
$3, $5, Royal python.

Perf. 13¼x13½

2013, Feb. 5 **Litho.** **Wmk. 388**
1447-1449 A470 Set of 3 1.60 .80
1447a Perf. 12 .40 .25

Souvenir Sheets

1450 A470 $3 multi 2.00 1.00

Litho. With Foil Application

1451 A470 $5 multi 3.25 1.60

Nos. 1450-1451 each contain one 30x50mm stamp.

National Unity — A471

No. 1452, 60c — Map of Malaysia, "1" and various people with inscription: a, Semangat Kasin Sayang. b, Semangat Keprihatinan.
No. 1453, 60c — Map of Malaysia, "1" and various people with inscription: a, Semangat Kerjasama. b, Semangat Kemasyarakatan.

Wmk. 388

2013, Mar. 26 **Litho.** ***Perf. 13¼***
Horiz. Pairs, #a-b

1452-1453 A471 Set of 2 1.60 .80

Lighthouses — A472

Designs: 50c, Pulau Rimau Lighthouse, Penang. No. 1455, 60c, Fort Cornwallis Lighthouse, Penang. No. 1456, 60c, Pulau Angsa Lighthouse, Selangor.
$5, One Fathom Bank Lighthouse, Selangor, vert.

Perf. 13½x13¼

2013, Apr. 30 **Litho.** **Unwmk.**
Granite Paper

1454-1456 A472 Set of 3 1.25 .60

Souvenir Sheet
Perf. 13¼x13½

1457 A472 $5 multi 3.25 1.60

Miniature Sheets

Malaysian Forests — A473

No. 1458 — Royal Belum Forest: a, Gould's frogmouth. b, Helmeted hornbill. c, Rafflesia azlanii. d, Trevesia burckii. e, Trilobite larvae.
No. 1459 — Maliau Basin Forest: a, Borneo pygmy elephant (30x40mm). b, Maliau Waterfall (50x40mm). c, Nepenthes veitchii (30x40mm). d, Dead leaf mantis (30x40mm). e, Violin beetle (30x40mm).

No. 1460 — Taman Negara Forest: a, Asian bearcat (30x40mm). b, Berkoh Cascade (30x40mm). c, Heteropoda davidbowie (30x40mm). d, Malayan peacock pheasant (50x40mm). e, Bioluminescent mushrooms (30x40mm).

Serpentine Die Cut 12¾

2013, May 13 Litho. Unwmk.

Self-Adhesive

1458	A473	Sheet of 5	3.25	
a.-e.		$1 Any single	.65	.30
1459	A473	Sheet of 5	3.25	
a.-e.		$1 Any single	.65	.30
1460	A473	Sheet of 5	3.25	
a.-e.		$1 Any single	.65	.30
		Nos. 1458-1460 (3)	9.75	

Marine Life — A474

No. 1461, 60c: a, Sea anemone. b, Soft coral.

No. 1462, 60c: Feather stars. b, Sea pen.

$5, Table coral.

Perf. 13½x13¼

2013, June 28 Litho. Unwmk.

Horiz. Pairs, #a-b

1461-1462	A474	Set of 2	1.50	.75

Souvenir Sheet

1463	A474	$5 multi	3.25	1.60

No. 1463 contains one 75x26mm stamp.

Salad Ingredients A475

No. 1464, 60c: a, Centella asiatica. b, Parkia speciosa.

No. 1465, 60c: a, Psophocarpus tetragonolobus. b, Annacardium occidentale.

Wmk. 388

2013, July 25 Litho. *Perf. 13¼*

Vert. Pairs, #a-b

1464-1465	A475	Set of 2	1.50	.75

Third Tri-Nation Stamp Exhibition — A476

Exhibition emblem, buildings and flags of Malaysia, Singapore and Thailand with: 90c, Flat flags. $2, Flags blowing in wind.

$3, Exhibition emblem, Hibiscus rosa-sinensis, Vanda Miss Joaquim, Cassia fistula.

Unwmk.

2013, Aug. 23 Litho. *Perf. 14*

1466-1467	A476	Set of 2	1.75	.90

Souvenir Sheet

Self-Adhesive

Die Cut Perf. 12

1468	A476	$3 multi	1.90	.95

No. 1468 contains one 54x38mm triangular stamp.

Museums — A477

No. 1469: a, Chimney Museum, Labuan. b, Sungai Lembing Museum, Pahang. c, Adat Museum (Tradition Museum), Jelebu, Negri Sembilan. d, Tekstil Negara Museum (Natl. Textile Museum), Kuala Lumpur.

No. 1470: a, Perak Museum, Taiping, Perak. b, Negara Museum (Natl. Museum), Kuala Lumpur. c, Lembah Bujang Archaeological Museum, Kedah. d, Galeria Perdana, Langkawi, Kedah. e, Kota Kayang Museum, Perlis. f, Labuan Museum, Labuan.

Perf. 14x14¼ Syncopated

2013, Aug. 31 Litho. Unwmk.

1469		Horiz. strip of 4	1.60	.80
a.-d.	A477	60c Any single	.40	.25
1470		Block of 6	2.40	1.25
a.-f.	A477	60c Any single	.40	.25

The right part of Nos. 1469a-1469d and 1470a-1470f has a rectangle of thermochromic ink, which, when warmed, reveals an item from the museum shown. See Nos. 1494-1495 for stamps dated "2014" without thermochromic ink.

Formation of the Federation of Malaysia, 50th Anniv. — A478

Perf. 13½x13¼

2013, Sept. 16 Litho. Wmk. 388

1471	A478	60c multi	.40	.25

A479

A480

Art by Diasbled Children — A481

Litho. & Thermography

2013, Oct. 22 Unwmk. *Perf. 13¼*

Granite Paper

1472	A479	60c multi	.40	.25
1473	A480	60c multi	.40	.25
1474	A481	60c multi	.40	.25
		Nos. 1472-1474 (3)	1.20	.75

Fruit — A482

Designs: 60c, Passiflora edulis. 80c, Annona squamosa. $1.20, Cynometra cauliflora.

Perf. 13¼x13½

2013, Oct. 28 Litho. Wmk. 388

1475-1477	A482	Set of 3	1.60	.80

RHB Bank, Cent. — A483

No. 1478: a, First bank branch building, Old Market Square, Kuala Lumpur. b, First automatic teller machine. c, Launch of Kwong Yik Bank Headquarters. d, RHB Bank Headquarters.

Litho. With Foil Application

2013, Nov. 23 Unwmk. *Perf. 14¼*

Granite Paper

1478	A483	60c Block of 4, #a-d	1.50	.75

Baba-Nyonya (Peranakan Chinese) Heritage — A484

No. 1479, 60c: a, Nyonyaware. b, Nyonya beaded slippers.

No. 1480, 80c: a, Malacca Peranakan townhouse. b, Baba and Nyonya wedding attire.

$5, Nyonya Kebaya emboridery.

Unwmk.

2013, Nov. 29 Litho. *Perf. 14*

Horiz. Pairs, #a-b

1479-1480	A484	Set of 2	1.75	.85

Souvenir Sheet

1481	A484	$5 multi	3.25	1.60

No. 1481 contains one 50x60mm stamp with laser-cut holes in the vignette.

Endangered Cats — A485

No. 1482: a, Panthera pardus with spotted fur. b, Panthera pardus with black fur.

No. 1483, Neofelis nebulosa. No. 1484, Neofelis diardi.

$3, Panthera tigris jacksoni, vert.

Perf. 13½x13¼

2013, Dec. 23 Litho. Wmk. 388

1482		Horiz. pair	.80	.40
a.-b.	A485	60c Either single	.40	.25
1483	A485	80c multi	.50	.25
1484	A485	80c multi	.50	.25
		Nos. 1482-1484 (3)	1.80	.90

Souvenir Sheet

Perf. 13¼x13½

1485	A485	$3 multi	1.90	.95
a.		As No. 1485, with Four Nations Stamp Show emblem in sheet margin	1.90	.95

Issued: No. 1485a, 5/27/14.

New Year 2014 (Year of the Horse) — A486

No. 1486, 50c — Inscription: a, Sukan Polo. b, Unit Berkuda DBKL.

No. 1487, 80c — Inscription: a, Unit Berkuda PSP PDRM. b, Unit Berkuda Kor Armor Diraja.

$3, Horse and rider, white background. $5, Horse and rider, gold background.

Perf. 13x13¼

2014, Jan. 27 Litho. Unwmk.

Horiz. Pairs, #a-b

1486-1487	A486	Set of 2	1.60	.80

Souvenir Sheets

1488-1489	A486	Set of 2	4.75	2.40

Roses — A487

Designs: 60c, White hybrid tea roses. 70c, Yellow Grandiflora roses. $1.20, Pink English roses.

$5, Hybrid tea roses.

Unwmk.

2014, Feb. 14 Litho. *Perf. 13*

1490-1492	A487	Set of 3	1.60	.80

Souvenir Sheet

Perf.

1493	A487	$5 multi	3.25	1.60

No. 1493 contains one 52x50mm heart-shaped stamp and is impregnated with a rose scent.

Museums Type of 2013 Without Thermochromic Ink

No. 1494: a, Chimney Museum, Labuan. b, Sungai Lembing Museum, Pahang. c, Adat Museum (Tradition Museum), Jelebu, Negri Sembilan. d, Tekstil Negara Museum (Natl. Textile Museum), Kuala Lumpur.

No. 1495: a, Perak Museum, Taiping, Perak. b, Negara Museum (Natl. Museum), Kuala Lumpur. c, Lembah Bujang Archaeological Museum, Kedah. d, Galeria Perdana, Langkawi, Kedah. e, Kota Kayang Museum, Perlis. f, Labuan Museum, Labuan.

Perf. 14¼ Syncopated

2014, Mar. 13 Litho. Unwmk.

Dated "2014"

1494		Horiz. strip of 4	1.60	.80
a.-d.	A477	60c Any single	.40	.25
1495		Block of 6	2.40	1.25
a.-f.	A477	60c Any single	.40	.25

Nos. 1494a-1494d and 1495a-1495f lack the thermographic ink present on Nos. 1469a-1469d and 1470a-1470f that covers an item from the museum. Stamps with thermographic ink are dated "2013" only.

No. 1427 Redrawn With Added Emblem

Wmk. 388

2014, May 24 Litho. *Perf. 12*

1496 A463 90c multi .55 .30

The emblem added to No. 1496 is inscribed "Melaka and Jogja City of Museums 2014" and is to the right of the flag emblem on No. 1427.

Opening of World Scout Bureau, Kuala Lumpur — A488

Scouting trefoil and: 30c, Display at World Scout Bureau. 50c, Malaysian scouting emblem, trefoil made of Scouts. 60c, Malaysian scouting emblem, buildings.

Perf. 13½x13¼

2014, June 18 Litho. Wmk. 388

1497-1499 A488 Set of 3 .90 .45

Opening of Kuala Lumpur International Airport 2 — A489

Inscriptions: No. 1500, 80c, Main Terminal Building. No. 1501, 80c, Skybridge. No. 1502, 80c, Departure Hall. No. 1503, 80c, Gateway@klia2.

$5, Aerial view of airport.

Perf. 14¼x14

2014, June 24 Litho. Unwmk.

1500-1503 A489 Set of 4 2.00 1.00

Souvenir Sheet

1504 A489 $5 multi 3.25 1.60

Fruit — A490

Designs: 60c, Artocarpus heterophyllus. 80c, Durio zibethinus. $1.20, Cucumis melo. $1.40, Averrhoa carambola.

Wmk. 388

2014, July 17 Litho. *Perf. 13¼*

1505-1508 A490 Set of 4 2.50 1.25

Independence, 57th Anniv. — A491

Perf. 13½x13¼

2014, Aug. 31 Litho. Wmk. 388

1509 A491 60c multi .40 .25

Local Foods of Malaysia and Hong Kong — A492

Flower and: No. 1510, $1.40, Nasi lemak. No. 1511, $1.40, Satay. No. 1512, $1.40, Egg waffle. No. 1513, $1.40, Poon choi.

Unwmk.

2014, Oct. 19 Litho. *Perf. 14*

1510-1513 A492 Set of 4 3.50 1.75

1513a Souvenir sheet of 4, #1510-1513 3.50 1.75

See Hong Kong Nos. 1683-1686.

Folk Tales — A493

No. 1514, 60c: a, Tun Kudu. b, Tun Fatimah.
No. 1515, 60c: a, Mahsuri. b, Merong Maha Wangsa.
No. 1516, 60c: a, Hang Tuah. b, Tun Teja.

Perf. 13½x13¼

2014, Oct. 27 Litho. Wmk. 388

Horiz. Pairs, #a-b

1514-1516 A493 Set of 3 2.25 1.10

Souvenir Sheet

2014 World Youth Stamp Exhibition, Kuala Lumpur — A494

Litho. With Foil Application

2014, Nov. 5 Wmk. 388 *Perf. 14*

1517 A494 $5 multi 3.00 1.50

A495

A496

A497

A498

A499

A500

2014 World Youth Stamp Exhibition, Kuala Lumpur — A501

No. 1518: a, $1, India #6 on cover, two India #5 on cover (40x60mm). b, $2, Three India #2, two India #4 on cover (40x30mm).
No. 1519: a, $2, Pongo pygmaeus. b, $3, Panthera tigris jacksoni.
No. 1520: a, $2, Hibiscus rosa-sinensis (30x50mm). b, $3, Rafflesia arnoldii (60x50mm).
No. 1521, India #7, two India #6 on cover. No. 1522, Sultan Abdul Samad Building, Kuala Lumpur. No. 1523, Mak Yong dancer. No. 1524, The Princess of Gunung Ledang.

Litho., Litho. with Foil Application (#1520, 1524)

Perf. 13½, 14 (#1520b)

2014, Dec. 1 Wmk. 388

1518 A495 Sheet of 2, #a-b 1.75 .85
1519 A496 Sheet of 2, #a-b 3.00 1.50
1520 A497 Sheet of 2, #a-b 3.00 1.50

Souvenir Sheets

1521 A498 $3 multi 1.75 .85
1522 A499 $5 multi 3.00 1.50
1523 A500 $5 multi 3.00 1.50
1524 A501 $5 multi 3.00 1.50
Nos. 1518-1524 (7) 18.50 9.20

Sultan Abdul Halim Mu'adzam Bridge, Penang — A502

Bridge: No. 1525, $1.20, At night. No. 1526, $1.20, In daylight.

Perf. 13¼x13½

2014, Dec. 31 Litho. Wmk. 388

1525-1526 A502 Set of 2 1.40 .70

Medicinal Plants — A503

Designs: 60c, Orthosiphon stamineus. 70c, Hibiscus sabdariffa. 80c, Andrographis paniculata.

$3, Clinacanthus nutans.

Perf. 13¼x13½

2015, Jan. 20 Litho. Wmk. 388

1527-1529 A503 Set of 3 1.25 .60

Souvenir Sheet

Perf. 14

1530 A503 $3 multi 1.75 .85

No. 1530 contains one 40x50mm stamp.

Malaysian Chairmanship of ASEAN — A504

Emblem, flags of ASEAN countries and and: 60c, Handshake, people. 80c, Upraised hands. $1.20, Stylized hand holding plant.

Perf. 13¼x13½

2015, Jan. 27 Litho. Wmk. 388

1531 A504 60c multi .35 .25
a. Perf. 13¼x14 .35 .25
1532 A504 80c multi .45 .25
a. Perf. 13¼x14 .45 .25
1533 A504 $1.20 multi .70 .35
a. Perf. 13¼x14 .70 .35
Nos. 1531-1533 (3) 1.50 .85

Farm Animals A505

Designs: 60c, Anser cygnoides. 80c, Bubalus bubalis. $1.20, Gallus domesticus.

$3, Capra aegagrus hircus, denomination at UR, vert.

$15, Like $3, denomination at LR, vert.

Perf. 13x13¼

2015, Feb. 16 Litho. Unwmk.

1534-1536 A505 Set of 3 1.50 .75

Souvenir Sheets

Perf. 14¼x14½

1537 A505 $3 multi 1.75 .85

Self-Adhesive
On Wood Veneer
Die Cut Perf. 6¾

1538 A505 $15 brown & red 8.25 4.25

No. 1537 contains one 48x66mm stamp. No. 1538 contains one 45x60mm stamp.

International Cooperative Project on Giant Panda Conservation A506

Flags of Malaysia and People's Republic of China and panda named: No. 1539, 70c, Liang Liang. No. 1540, 70c, Xing Xing.

No. 1541: a, Liang Liang, diff. b, Xing Xing, diff.

Perf. 13¼x13

2015, Feb. 25 Litho. Unwmk.

1539-1540 A506 Set of 2 .80 .40

Souvenir Sheet
On Flocked Granite Paper With Ripples
Perf. 13½x13¼

1541 A506 $4 Sheet of 2, #a-b 4.50 2.25

No. 1541 contains two 28x45mm stamps.

Endangered Marine Life — A507

Designs: 60c, Anoxypristis cuspidata. 80c, Balaenoptera musculus. $1.40, Orcinus orca. $5, Megaptera novaeangliae.

Perf. 13½x13¼

2015, Apr. 13 Litho. Unwmk.

1542-1544 A507 Set of 3 1.60 .80

Litho. With Foil Application
Souvenir Sheet
Perf. 14¼

1545 A507 $5 multi 3.00 1.50

No. 1545 contains one 45x38mm octagonal stamp.

Souvenir Sheet

Penny Black, 175th Anniv. — A508

Wmk. 388

2015, Apr. 30 Litho. *Perf. 14*

1546 A508 $3 multi 1.75 .85

International Telecommunication Union, 150th Anniv. — A509

150th anniv. emblem and: 60c, Telephones. 70c, Television, radio, microphone and antenna. 80c, Satellite, satellite dish, cell phone, map of Asia and Australia.

Wmk. 388

2015, May 17 Litho. *Perf. 13¼*

1547-1549 A509 Set of 3 1.25 .60

Marine Life — A510

Designs: No. 1550, 60c, Phyllorhiza punctata. No. 1551, 60c, Hypselodoris bullockii. No. 1552, $1.20, Trapezia areolata. No. 1553, $1.20, Hymenocera picta.

Perf. 13¼x13½

2015, June 8 Litho. Unwmk.

1550-1553 A510 Set of 4 1.90 .95

See Thailand Nos. 2857-2860.

Birds — A511

Designs: 60c, Nycticorax nycticorax. 70c, Butorides striatus. 80c, Ardea cinerea, horiz. $5, Ixobrychus cinnamomeus, horiz.

Perf. 13¼x13½, 13½x13¼

2015, June 25 Litho. Unwmk.

1554-1556 A511 Set of 3 1.10 .55

Souvenir Sheet
Perf. 14¼

1557 A511 $5 multi 2.75 1.40

No. 1557 contains one 50x40mm stamp.

Pearls — A512

Designs: 60c, Circle South Sea pearls. 70c, Baroque South Sea pearls. 80c, Drop South Sea pearls.

$5, Round South Sea pearl.

Perf. 14x14¼

2015, July 29 Litho. Unwmk.

1558-1560 A512 Set of 3 1.10 .55

Souvenir Sheet
Litho. & Embossed With Foil Application
Perf.

1561 A512 $5 multi 2.60 1.25

No. 1561 contains one 38mm diameter stamp.

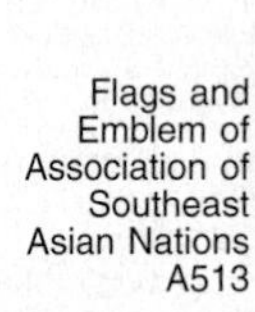

Flags and Emblem of Association of Southeast Asian Nations A513

Wmk. 388

2015, Aug. 8 Litho. *Perf. 13¼*

1562 A513 50c multi .25 .25

See Brunei No. 656, Burma Nos. 417-418, Cambodia No. , Indonesia No. 2428, Laos No. , Philippines No. 3619, Singapore No. 1742, Thailand No. 2875, Viet Nam No. 3529.

Mosques A514

Designs: 70c, Zahir Mosque, Alor Setar, Kedah. 80c, Kota Kinabalu City Mosque. $1, National Mosque.

Perf. 13½x13¼

2015, Aug. 27 Litho. Unwmk.

1563-1565 A514 Set of 3 1.25 .60

Malaysia Day — A515

No. 1566, 60c: a, Musicians and dancers (60x25mm). b, Emblem (30x25mm).

No. 1567, 70c: a, Malaysians at play (60x25mm). b, People holding Malaysian flag (30x25mm).

$3, Heart, people holding flagpole bearing Malaysian flag.

Perf. 14x13½

2015, Sept. 15 Litho. Wmk. 388

Horiz. pairs, #a-b

1566-1567 A515 Set of 2 1.25 .60

Souvenir Sheet
Perf. 13¼x14

1568 A515 $3 multi 1.40 .70

No. 1568 contains one 70x45mm stamp.

World Post Day — A516

Wmk. 388

2015, Oct. 9 Litho. *Perf. 13¼*

1569 A516 60c multi .30 .25

Stamp Week — A517

Wmk. 388

2015, Oct. 27 Litho. *Perf. 13¼*

1570 A517 60c multi .30 .25

Islands — A518

No. 1571: a, Pulau Tenggol, Trengganu. b, Pulau Tinggi, Johore.

No. 1572: a, Pulau Sembilang, Pahang. b, Pulau Satang, Sarawak.

$3, Pulau Mataking, Sabah.

Unwmk.

2015, Nov. 17 Litho. *Perf. 14*

1571 Horiz. pair .70 .35
a.-b. A518 70c Either single .35 .25
1572 Horiz. pair .80 .40
a.-b. A518 80c Either single .40 .25

Souvenir Sheet

1573 A518 $3 multi 1.40 .70

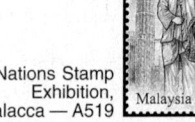

Four Nations Stamp Exhibition, Malacca — A519

Traditional clothing of men and women from: No. 1574, 60c, Malaysia. No. 1575, 60c, Singapore. No. 1576, 60c, Indonesia. No. 1577, 60c, Thailand.

$3, Show emblem, men and women from Malaysia, Singapore, Indonesia and Thailand.

Perf. 14x13¾

2015, Dec. 4 Litho. Wmk. 388

1574-1577 A519 Set of 4 1.10 .55

Souvenir Sheet
Imperf

1578 A519 $3 multi 1.40 .70

No. 1578 contains one 80x80mm diamond-shaped stamp.

Locomotives — A520

Designs: 60c, Hitachi Diesel hydraulic locomotive. 70c, Railbus. 80c, Diesel multiple unit. $5, Vulcan steam locomotive, vert.

Unwmk.

2015, Dec. 28 Litho. *Perf. 13*

1579-1581 A520 Set of 3 1.00 .50

Souvenir Sheet
Perf. 14x13¾ Syncopated

1582 A520 $5 multi 2.40 1.25
a. As No. 1582, with Thailand 2016 Intl. Stamp Exhibition emblem added 2.50 1.25

No. 1582 contains one 40x55mm stamp.

Primates — A521

Designs: 60c, Macaque. 70c, Silvered leaf monkeys. 80c, White-handed gibbons.

$3, Agile gibbon.

Perf. 13¼

2016, Jan. 26 Litho. Unwmk.

1583-1585 A521 Set of 3 1.00 .50

Souvenir Sheet

1587 A521 $3 multi 1.50 .75

Traditional Dances — A522

Dance: No. 1588, 60c, Cempaka Sari. No. 1589, 60c, Reben. No. 1590, 60c, Odissi. No. 1591, 60c, Magunatip. No. 1592, 60c, Rejang Be'uh.

Perf. 13½x14

2016, Feb. 3 Litho. Wmk. 388

1588-1592 A522 Set of 5 1.50 .75

Flowers A523

No. 1593 — Bread flowers: a, No insects on flower. b, Insects on flowers.

No. 1594 — Yellow saracas: a, Butterfly on flower at UR. b, Butterfly on flower at left.

No. 1595 — Cannonball flowers: a, Bee at right. b, Bee at left.

$5, Cape jasmine, vert.

Perf. 14¼x14

2016, Mar. 7 Litho. Unwmk.

1593 A523 70c Vert. pair, #a-b .75 .40
1594 A523 80c Vert. pair, #a-b .85 .40
1595 A523 80c Vert. pair, #a-b .85 .40
Nos. 1593-1595 (3) 2.45 1.20

Souvenir Sheet

Perf. 14¼

1596 A523 $5 multi 2.60 1.40

No. 1596 contains one 40x70mm stamp and is impregnated with a jasmine scent..

Writers — A524

Designs: No. 1597, 80c, Arena Wati (1925-2009). No. 1598, 80c, Tongkat Warrant (1929-2001). No. 1599, 80c, Keris Mas (1922-92).

Perf. 13½

2016, Apr. 29 Litho. Unwmk.

1597-1599 A524 Set of 3 1.25 .60

River Watercraft — A525

Designs: 70c, Longboat. 80c, Express boat. 90c, Ferry boat.

$3, Raft, vert.

Perf. 14x13½

2016, May 26 Litho. Unwmk.

1600-1602 A525 Set of 3 1.25 .60

Souvenir Sheet

1603 A525 $3 multi 1.50 .75

No. 1603 contains one 40x60mm stamp.

Tamil Calligraphy A526

Chinese Calligraphy A527

Arabic Calligraphy A528

Design: $5, Tamil, Chinese and Arabic calligraphy, horiz.

Unwmk.

2016, June 28 Litho. ***Perf. 14***

1604 A526 70c multi .35 .25
1605 A527 80c multi .40 .25
1606 A528 90c multi .45 .25
Nos. 1604-1606 (3) 1.20 .75

Souvenir Sheet

Perf. 14x14¼

1607 A528 $5 multi 2.50 1.25

No. 1607 contains one 60x45mm stamp.

Flag and Tourist Attractions of Kedah — A529

Flag and Tourist Attractions of Kelantan — A530

No. 1608: a, Muzium Padi (Rice Museum), Menara Alor Setar (Alor Setar Tower). b, Lembah Bujang, Candi Bendang Dalam.

No. 1609: a, Kampung Kraftangan dan Muzium Kraf (Craft Museum), Songket. b, Wau Bulan (moon kite).

No. 1610, vert.: a, Flag of Kedah, Pulau Langkawi. b, Flag of Kelantan, Pantai Bisikan Bayu (beach), Perahu Kolek (Kolek boat)

Perf. 14x13¼

2016, July 27 Litho. Unwmk.

1608 A529 80c Horiz. pair, #a-b .80 .40
1609 A530 80c Horiz. pair, #a-b .80 .40

Souvenir Sheet

Perf. 13¼x14

1610 A530 $2 Sheet of 2, #a-b 2.00 1.00

No. 1610 contains two 30x50mm stamps.

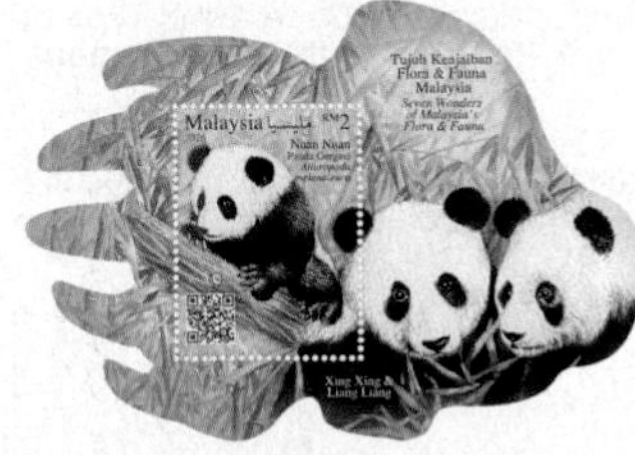

A531

Flora and Fauna — A532

Designs: $2, Giant panda Nuan Nuan.

No. 1612: a, 30c, Tragulus kanchil. b, 50c, Meliponula ferruginea. c, 50c, Piper sarmentosum. d, 60c, Polyplectron malacense. e, 60c, Rana erythraea. f, 70c, Amyda cartilaginea. g, 80c, Tor tambroides.

Perf. 13¼x14

2016, Aug. 23 Litho. Unwmk.

Souvenir Sheet

1611 A531 $2 multi 1.00 .50
a. Imperf. 1.00 .50

Miniature Sheet

Self-Adhesive

Die Cut Perf. 12

1612 A532 Sheet of 7, #a-g 2.00 1.00

Battles A533

Designs: No. 1613, 60c, Kota Malawati, Selangor. No. 1614, 60c, Kota Mat Salleh, Sabah. No. 1615, 80c, Kota Libau Rentap, Sarawak. No. 1616, 80c, Bukit Kepong, Johore.

$3, Kota Bharu, Kelantan, vert.

Perf. 14x13¼

2016, Sept. 15 Litho. Unwmk.

1613-1616 A533 Set of 4 1.40 .70

Souvenir Sheet

Perf. 13¼x14

1617 A533 $3 multi 1.50 .75

No. 1617 contains one 40x50mm stamp.

International Stamps — A534

Inscriptions: 10c, Festivals. 20c, Local fruits. 50c, Wildlife. $1, Unity. $2, Places of worship. $5, Our nation. $10, Flora. $20, Handicrafts.

Perf. 14x13¾

2016, Oct. 1 Litho. Wmk. 388

1618 A534 10c multi .25 .25
1619 A534 20c multi .25 .25
1620 A534 50c multi .25 .25
1621 A534 $1 multi .50 .25
1622 A534 $2 multi 1.00 .50
1623 A534 $5 multi 2.40 1.25
1624 A534 $10 multi 5.00 2.50
1625 A534 $20 multi 9.75 5.00
Nos. 1618-1625 (8) 19.40 10.25

Postal Workers — A535

Postal worker: 60c, On horse. 70c, In boat. 80c, On bicycle.

$3, Postal worker at table, vert.

Unwmk.

2016, Oct. 9 Litho. ***Perf. 14***

1626-1628 A535 Set of 3 1.00 .50

Souvenir Sheet

1629 A535 $3 multi 1.50 .75

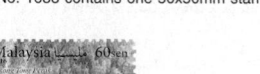

Penang Free School, 200th Anniv. A536

Crest and various views of school: 70c, 80c, 90c.

$5, Crest and ribbon.

Unwmk.

2016, Oct. 21 Litho. ***Perf. 14***

1630-1632 A536 Set of 3 1.25 .60

Souvenir Sheet

Litho. With Foil Application

Perf. 14¼x14

1633 A536 $5 gold & multi 2.40 1.25

No. 1633 contains one 50x50mm stamp.

Houses of Worship — A537

Designs: No. 1634, 60c, Tokong Tong Perak. No. 1635, 60c, Gurdwara Sahib Shapha, Kuala Lumpur. No. 1636, 60c, Kuil Sri Kandaswamy, Kuala Lumpur. No. 1637, 60c, St. Francis Xavier Church, Malacca. No. 1638, 60c, Masjid Kapitan Keling, Penang

Perf. 13¼

2016, Nov. 21 Litho. Unwmk.

1634-1638 A537 Set of 5 1.40 .70

Girl Guides Association of Malaysia, Cent. — A538

Designs: No. 1639, 85c, Girl Guides and badges. No. 1640, 85c, Girl Guides camping. No. 1641, 85c, Girl Guide, salute and knot.

Perf. 13¼x13½

2016, Dec. 9 Litho. Unwmk.

1639-1641 A538 Set of 3 1.25 .60

End of Term of 14th Yang di-Pertuan Agong — A539

Sultan Abdul Halim of Kedah: 85c With people and building. 95c, Reviewing soldiers. $1.05, With attendants, reviewing soldiers.

$3, Sultan Abdul Halim in automobile, vert.

Perf. 13¾x13½

2016, Dec. 14 Litho. Wmk. 388

1642-1644 A539 Set of 3 1.25 .65

Souvenir Sheet

Perf. 13½x13¼

1645 A539 $3 multi 1.40 .70

No. 1645 contains one 40x60mm stamp.

Gold Medalists at 2016 Paralympics, Rio de Janeiro — A540

Perf. 14¼x14

2016, Dec. 20 Litho. Unwmk.
1646 A540 95c multi .45 .25

New Year 2017 (Year of the Rooster) A541

Designs: 85c, Two roosters. 95c, Rooster, hen and chicks. $1.05, Two roosters, diff. $3, $8, Rooster and Chinese inscription, vert.

Perf. 14¼x14

2017, Jan. 10 Litho. Unwmk.
1647-1649 A541 Set of 3 1.40 .70

Souvenir Sheets

Perf. 14¼

1650 A541 $3 multi 1.40 .70
1651 A541 $8 multi 3.75 1.90

Nos. 1650-1651 each contain one 38x45 octagonal stamp.

SEMI-POSTAL STAMPS

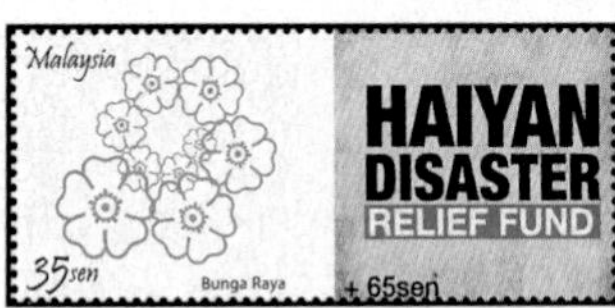

Typhoon Haiyan Disaster Relief Fund — SP1

No. B1: a, Bunga Raya. b, Durian. c, Handicraft. d, Wau Bulan.

Perf. 13¾x14

2013, Nov. 14 Litho. Wmk. 388
B1 Sheet of 8, #B1a, B1b, B1e, B1f, 2 each #B1c, B1d 6.25 6.25
a.-b. SP1 35c+65c Either single .75 .75
c.-d. SP1 65c+35c Either single .75 .75
e. As "a," perf. 13¾x14x14¼x14 .75 .75
f. As "b," perf. 13¾x14x14¼x14 .75 .75

No. B1 sold for $10.

POSTAGE DUE STAMPS

Until 1966 Malaysia used postage due stamps of the Malayan Postal Union. See listings under Malaya.

D1

Wmk. 338 Upright

1966, Aug. 15 Litho. *Perf. 14½x14*
J1 D1 1c pink .25 4.00
J2 D1 2c slate .60 2.25
J3 D1 4c lt yellow green 1.00 8.00
J4 D1 8c bright green 2.10 14.00
J5 D1 10c ultramarine 1.50 2.25
J6 D1 12c purple 1.10 4.00
J7 D1 20c brown 1.75 4.00
J8 D1 50c olive bister 3.50 7.00
Nos. J1-J8 (8) 11.80 45.50

Wmk. 338 Sideways

1972, May 23
J4a D1 8c bright green 7.75 22.50
J5a D1 10c ultramarine 7.75 15.00
J7a D1 20c brown 10.50 15.00
J8a D1 50c olive bister 11.50 20.00
Nos. J4a-J8a (4) 37.50 72.50

1980-86 Litho. Unwmk.
J9 D1 2c slate .35 3.00
J10 D1 8c bright green .60 6.00
J11 D1 10c blue .60 2.75
J11A D1 12c maroon ('86) 14.00 18.00
J12 D1 20c brown .80 3.25
J13 D1 50c olive bister 1.25 3.75
Nos. J9-J13 (6) *17.60 36.75*

D2

1986, Sept. 15 Litho. *Perf. 12x11½*
J14 D2 5c brt rose & lil rose .25 1.10
J15 D2 10c black & gray .25 .50
J16 D2 20c deep org & yel org .40 .65
J17 D2 50c blue grn & lt bl grn .60 .90
J18 D2 $1 brt blue & lt ultra 1.10 2.00
Nos. J14-J18 (5) 2.60 5.15
211 A2250c multi .25 .25

JOHORE

Vanda Hookeriana and Sultan Ismail — A14

Orchids: 2c, Arundina graminifolia. 5c, Paphiopedilum niveum. 6c, Spathoglottis plicata. 10c, Arachnis flosaeris. 15c, Rhyncostylis retusa. 20c, Phalaenopsis violacea.

Wmk. 338

1965, Nov. 15 Photo. *Perf. 14½*

Flowers in Natural Colors

169 A14 1c blk & lt grnsh bl .25 .25
a. Black omitted 375.00
b. Watermark sideways ('70) 1.60 6.00
170 A14 2c black, red & gray .25 .80
171 A14 5c black & Prus bl .25 .25
a. Yellow omitted 110.00
172 A14 6c black & lt lil .40 .25
173 A14 10c black & lt ultra .40 .25
a. Watermark sideways ('70) 3.00 2.50
174 A14 15c blk, lil rose & grn 1.50 .35
175 A14 20c black & brown 1.50 .65
a. Purple omitted 300.00
Nos. 169-175 (7) 4.55 2.80

Malayan Jezebel and Sultan Ismail — A15

Butterflies: 2c, Black-veined tiger. 5c, Clipper. 6c, Lime butterfly. 10c, Great orange tip. 15c, Blue pansy. 20c, Wanderer.

Perf. 13½x13

1971, Feb. 1 Litho. Unwmk.
176 A15 1c multicolored .50 1.75
177 A15 2c multicolored 1.40 2.50
178 A15 5c multicolored 1.75 .40
179 A15 6c multicolored 1.75 2.50
180 A15 10c multicolored 1.75 .55
181 A15 15c multicolored 1.75 .50
182 A15 20c multicolored 1.75 1.00
Nos. 176-182 (7) 10.65 9.20

1977 Photo.
176a A15 1c 3.00 3.50
177a A15 2c 3.00 *5.25*
178a A15 5c 3.00 .70
180a A15 10c 4.50 .35
181a A15 15c 9.25 .35
182a A15 20c 11.50 1.00
Nos. 176a-182a (6) 34.25 11.15

Differentiating the lithograph and photogravure printings of the Butterflies issues:

Denominations and inscriptions have straight edges on the lithographed printings and broken edges on the photogravure printings.

Background colors and portrait show prominent screen dots on the lithographed stamps, but these features appear almost solid on the photogravure stamps except under high magnification.

Rafflesia Hasseltii and Sultan Ismail — A16

Flowers: 2c, Pterocarpus indicus. 5c, Lagerstroemia speciosa. 10c, Durio zibethinus. 15c, Hibiscus. 20c, Rhododendron scortechinii. 25c, Phaeomeria speciosa.

Wmk. 378

1979, Apr. 30 Litho. *Perf. 14½*
183 A16 1c multicolored .25 .75
184 A16 2c multicolored .25 .75
185 A16 5c multicolored .25 .50
186 A16 10c multicolored .25 .25
187 A16 15c multicolored .25 .25
188 A16 20c multicolored .25 .25
189 A16 25c multicolored .40 .25
Nos. 183-189 (7) 1.90 3.00

1984 "Johor" in round type
185a A16 5c 1.10 1.40
186a A16 10c 1.10 1.40
187a A16 15c .75 .25
188a A16 20c 1.25 .55
Nos. 185a-188a (4) 4.20 3.60

Agriculture, State Arms and Sultan Mahmood Iskandar Al-Haj, Regent — A19

Wmk. 388

1986, Oct. 25 Litho. *Perf. 12*
190 A19 1c Coffea liberica .35 .35
191 A19 2c Cocos nucifera .35 .35
192 A19 5c Theobroma cacao .35 .35
193 A19 10c Piper nigrum .35 .35
194 A19 15c Hevea brasiliensis .35 .35
195 A19 20c Elaeis guineensis .35 .35
196 A19 30c Oryza sativa .50 .50
Nos. 190-196 (7) 2.60 2.60

1994-99?
192a A19 5c Perf. 14 3.25 .25
192b A19 5c Perf. 15x14½ ('95) 1.75
192c A19 5c Perf. 14x14½ ('98) 19.00
193a A19 10c Perf. 14x13 3.25 .25
193b A19 10c Perf. 14x14½ ('96) 4.25 .25
193c A19 10c Perf. 15x14½ ('99) 12.50
195a A19 20c Perf. 14 2.00 .25
195b A19 20c Perf. 15x14½ 1.60
195c A19 20c Perf. 14x14½ ('96) 14.50 .40
196a A19 30c Perf. 14 3.25 .25
196b A19 30c Perf. 15x14½ 13.50 1.00
196c A19 30c Perf. 14x14½ 3.75

Agriculture and State Arms Type of 1986 Redrawn With Denominations in "Sen"

Perf. 14x13¾

2002 Litho. Wmk. 388
196D A19 30sen Oryza sativa —
e. Perf. 15x14½ —

Flowers, Arms and Sultan Mahmood Iskandar Ibni Al-Marhum Sultan Ismail — A20

Designs: 5c, Nelumbium nelumbo. 10c, Hydrangea macrophylla. 20c, Hippeastrum reticulatum. 30c, Bougainvillea. 40c, Ipomoea indica. 50c, Hibiscus rosa-sinensis.

Perf. 14¾x14½

2007, Dec. 31 Litho. Wmk. 388
197 A20 5c multi .35 .25
a. Perf. 14x13¾ .35 .25
198 A20 10c multi .35 .25
a. Perf. 14x13¾ .35 .25

Perf. 14x13¾

199 A20 20c multi .35 .25
200 A20 30c multi .35 .25
201 A20 40c multi .35 .25
202 A20 50c multi .45 .25
a. Souvenir sheet of 6, #197a, 198a, 199-202 2.25 1.10
Nos. 197-202 (6) 2.20 1.50

Coronation of Sultan Ibrahim A21

Various photographs of Sultan Ibrahim in uniform: 60c, 80c, $1.
$5. Sultan Ismail and Raja Zarith Sofiah.

Unwmk.

2015, Mar. 23 Litho. *Perf. 13*
203-205 A21 Set of 3 1.40 .70

Souvenir Sheet

206 A21 $5 multi 2.75 1.40

Flowers, Arms and Sultan Ibrahim — A22

Designs: 10c, Nelumbium nelumbo. 20c, Hydrangea macrophylla. 30c, Hippeastrum reticulatum. 40c, Bougainvillea. 50c, Ipomoea indica. 60c, Hibiscus rosa-sinensis.

Perf. 14x13¾

2016, Feb. 25 Litho. Wmk. 388
207 A22 10c multi .25 .25
208 A22 20c multi .25 .25
209 A22 30c multi .25 .25
210 A22 40c multi .25 .25
211 A22 50c multi .25 .25
212 A22 60c multi .30 .25
a. Souvenir sheet of 6, #207-212 1.10 .55
Nos. 207-212 (6) 1.55 1.50

KEDAH

Orchid Type of Johore, 1965, with Portrait of Sultan Abdul Halim

Wmk. 338

1965, Nov. 15 Photo. *Perf. 14½*

Flowers in Natural Colors

106 A14 1c blk & lt grnsh bl .30 1.25
a. Black omitted 250.00
b. Watermark sideways ('70) 2.50 5.25
107 A14 2c black, red & gray .30 1.50
108 A14 5c black & Prus bl .30 .30
109 A14 6c black & lt lil .30 .50
110 A14 10c black & lt ultra .50 .30
a. Watermark sideways ('70) 1.50 4.00
111 A14 15c blk, lil rose & grn 1.75 .30
112 A14 20c black & brown 2.00 .90
Nos. 106-112 (7) 5.45 5.05

Butterfly Type of Johore, 1971, with Portrait of Sultan Abdul Halim

Perf. 13½x13

1971, Feb. 1 Litho. Unwmk.
113 A15 1c multicolored .35 1.50
114 A15 2c multicolored .45 1.50
115 A15 5c multicolored 1.10 .30
116 A15 6c multicolored 1.10 *1.75*
117 A15 10c multicolored 1.10 .30
118 A15 15c multicolored 1.10 .30
119 A15 20c multicolored 1.40 .60
Nos. 113-119 (7) 6.60 6.25

1977 Photo. Same Designs

114a	A15	2c	*22.50*	*17.00*
115a	A15	5c	5.00	1.25
117a	A15	10c	11.00	.75
118a	A15	15c	3.50	.50
119a	A15	20c	5.00	2.25
		Nos. 114a-119a (5)	47.00	21.75

For differentiating the lithograph and photogravure printings of the Butterflies issues, see notes after Johore No. 182a.

Flower Type of Johore, 1979, with Portrait of Sultan Abdul Halim

Wmk. 378

1979, Apr. 30 Litho. *Perf. 14½*

120	A16	1c multicolored	.25	.80
121	A16	2c multicolored	.25	.80
122	A16	5c multicolored	.25	.50
123	A16	10c multicolored	.25	.25
a.		Unwmkd. ('85)	*22.00*	*3.25*
124	A16	15c multicolored	.25	.25
a.		Unwmkd. ('84)	1.00	1.00
125	A16	20c multicolored	.35	.25
a.		Pale yellow flowers ('84)	.35	.25
126	A16	25c multicolored	.40	.25
		Nos. 120-126 (7)	2.00	3.10

25th Anniv. of Installation of Sultan Abdul Halim — A10

20c, Portrait, vert. 40c, View from Mt. Gunung Jerai. 50c, Rice fields, Mt. Gunung Jerai.

1983, July 15 Litho. *Perf. 13½*

127	A10	20c multi	1.10	.35
128	A10	40c multi	2.25	2.25
129	A10	50c multi	3.00	4.75
		Nos. 127-129 (3)	6.35	7.35

Agriculture and State Arms Type of Johore with Sultan Abdul Halim

Wmk. 388

1986, Oct. 25 Litho. *Perf. 12*

130	A19	1c multicolored	.30	.30
131	A19	2c multicolored	.30	.30
132	A19	5c multicolored	.30	.30
133	A19	10c multicolored	.30	.30
134	A19	15c multicolored	.30	.30
135	A19	20c multicolored	.30	.30
136	A19	30c multicolored	.30	.30
		Nos. 130-136 (7)	2.10	2.10

1986?

132a	A19	5c	Perf. 15x14½	4.25	.40
132b	A19	5c	Perf. 14	1.25	.25
133a	A19	10c	Perf. 14	3.00	.30
133b	A19	10c	Perf. 14x13¾, unwmk.	8.50	
135a	A19	20c	Perf. 14	1.00	.25
135b	A19	20c	Perf. 15x14½		—
136a	A19	30c	Perf. 14x14½	2.25	.25
136b	A19	30c	Perf. 14x13½	3.00	.25
136c	A19	30c	Perf. 15x14½	3.00	.25

Flowers and Arms Type of Johore of 2007 With Portrait of Sultan Abdul Halim

Perf. 14x13¾

2007, Dec. 31 Litho. Wmk. 388

137	A20	5c multi	.30	.25
138	A20	10c multi	.30	.25
139	A20	20c multi	.30	.25
140	A20	30c multi	.35	.25
141	A20	40c multi	.50	.25
142	A20	50c multi	.65	.30
a.		Souvenir sheet of 6, #137-142	2.25	1.10
		Nos. 137-142 (6)	2.40	1.55

Reign of Sultan Abdul Halim, 50th Anniv. A11

Sultan and: 30c, Buildings, farm field. 50c, Buildings. $1, Buildings and anniversary emblem.

Perf. 13½x13¼x12x13¼

2008, July 15

143-145	A11	Set of 3	1.10	1.10

KELANTAN

Orchid Type of Johore, 1965, with Portrait of Sultan Yahya Petra

Wmk. 338

1965, Nov. 15 Photo. *Perf. 14½*

Flowers in Natural Colors

91	A14	1c blk & lt grnsh bl	.35	1.10
a.		Watermark sideways ('70)	1.40	7.50
92	A14	2c black, red & gray	.25	1.50
93	A14	5c black & Prus bl	.25	.25
94	A14	6c black & lt lil	.80	2.00
95	A14	10c black & lt ultra	.40	.25
a.		Watermark sideways ('70)	4.25	4.75
96	A14	15c blk, lil rose & grn	1.75	.25
97	A14	20c black & brown	1.75	1.50
		Nos. 91-97 (7)	5.55	6.85

Butterfly Type of Johore, 1971, with Portrait of Sultan Yahya Petra

Perf. 13½x13

1971, Feb. 1 Litho. Unwmk.

98	A15	1c multicolored	.30	2.00
99	A15	2c multicolored	.30	2.00
100	A15	5c multicolored	1.25	.50
101	A15	6c multicolored	1.25	2.25
102	A15	10c multicolored	1.40	.25
103	A15	15c multicolored	2.00	.25
104	A15	20c multicolored	2.50	1.25
		Nos. 98-104 (7)	9.00	8.50

1977 Photo.

98a	A15	1c	1.25	*4.25*
100a	A15	5c	7.75	3.50
102a	A15	10c	8.50	3.00
103a	A15	15c	16.00	1.10
		Nos. 98a-103a (4)	33.50	11.85

For differentiating the lithograph and photogravure printings of the Butterflies issues, see notes after Johore No. 182a.

Flower Type of Johore, 1979, with Portrait of Sultan Yahya Petra

Wmk. 378

1979, Apr. 30 Litho. *Perf. 14½*

105	A16	1c multicolored	.25	.90
106	A16	2c multicolored	.25	.90
107	A16	5c multicolored	.25	.70
a.		Unwmkd. ('86)	.75	1.25
108	A16	10c multicolored	.25	.25
a.		White flowers ('84)	.30	.25
109	A16	15c multicolored	.25	.25
110	A16	20c multicolored	.25	.25
a.		Pale yellow flowers ('84)	.35	.25
111	A16	25c multicolored	.45	.55
		Nos. 105-111 (7)	1.95	3.80

Sultan Tengku Ismail Petra, Installation — A7

1980, Mar. 30 Litho. *Perf. 14½*

112	A7	10c multicolored	.35	.65
113	A7	15c multicolored	.50	.35
114	A7	50c multicolored	1.25	2.50
		Nos. 112-114 (3)	2.10	3.50

Agriculture and State Arms Type of Johore with Sultan Ismail Petra

Wmk. 388

1986, Oct. 25 Litho. *Perf. 12*

115	A19	1c multicolored	.30	.30
116	A19	2c multicolored	.30	.30
117	A19	5c multicolored	.30	.30
118	A19	10c multicolored	.30	.30
119	A19	15c multicolored	.30	.30
120	A19	20c multicolored	.30	.30
121	A19	30c multicolored	.30	.30
		Nos. 115-121 (7)	2.10	2.10

1986?

116a	A19	2c	Perf. 15x14½	3.00	.50
118a	A19	10c	Perf. 14	3.00	.50
120a	A19	20c	Perf. 14	3.25	.50
121a	A19	30c	Perf. 14	1.00	.25
121b	A19	30c	Perf. 14x14½		—

Reign of Sultan Tengku Ismail Petra, 25th Anniv. A8

Sultan and various buildings: 30c, 50c, $1.

Perf. 13½, 12 (50c)

2004, Feb. 29 Litho. Wmk. 388

122-124	A8	Set of 3	.95	.45

Flowers and Arms Type of Johore of 2007 With Portrait of Sultan Ismail Petra

Perf. 14x13¾

2007, Dec. 31 Litho. Wmk. 388

125	A20	5c multi	.30	.25
126	A20	10c multi	.30	.25
127	A20	20c multi	.30	.25
128	A20	30c multi	.35	.25
129	A20	40c multi	.50	.25
130	A20	50c multi	.65	.30
a.		Souvenir sheet of 6, #125-130	2.25	1.10
		Nos. 125-130 (6)	2.40	1.55

MALACCA

(Melaka)

Orchid Type of Johore, 1965, with State Crest

Wmk. 338

1965, Nov. 15 Photo. *Perf. 14½*

Flowers in Natural Colors

67	A14	1c blk & lt grnsh blue	.25	1.50
a.		Watermark sideways ('70)	1.50	7.50
68	A14	2c blk, red & gray	.25	1.25
69	A14	5c black & Prus bl	.25	.25
70	A14	6c black & lt lilac	.40	.90
71	A14	10c black & lt ultra	.30	.25
a.		Watermark sideways ('70)	6.25	7.00
72	A14	15c blk, lil rose & grn	1.75	.30
73	A14	20c black & brown	2.50	.95
		Nos. 67-73 (7)	5.70	5.40

Butterfly Type of Johore, 1971, with State Crest

Perf. 13½x13

1971, Feb. 1 Litho. Unwmk.

74	A15	1c multicolored	.60	2.00
75	A15	2c multicolored	1.00	2.00
76	A15	5c multicolored	1.50	.90
77	A15	6c multicolored	1.50	2.75
78	A15	10c multicolored	1.50	.65
79	A15	15c multicolored	2.75	.60
80	A15	20c multicolored	2.75	2.25
		Nos. 74-80 (7)	11.60	11.15

1977 Photo.

74a	A15	1c	6.00	*9.00*
76a	A15	5c	2.75	2.25
78a	A15	10c	7.00	2.25
79a	A15	15c	17.50	.75
80a	A15	20c	6.50	4.25
		Nos. 74a-80a (5)	39.75	18.50

For differentiating the lithograph and photogravure printings of the Butterflies issues, see notes after Johore No. 182a.

Flower Type of Johore, 1979, with State Crest

Wmk. 378

1979, Apr. 30 Litho. *Perf. 14½*

81	A16	1c multicolored	.25	1.10
82	A16	2c multicolored	.25	1.10
83	A16	5c multicolored	.25	.90
84	A16	10c multicolored	.25	.30
85	A16	15c multicolored	.25	.25
86	A16	20c multicolored	.35	.25
87	A16	25c multicolored	.45	.70
		Nos. 81-87 (7)	2.05	4.60

1983-86 Unwmk.

84a	A16	10c ('85)	1.25	2.75
85a	A16	15c ('86)	.65	.50
86a	A16	20c	.65	1.10
		Nos. 84a-86a (3)	2.55	

Agriculture and State Arms Type of Johore

Wmk. 388

1986, Oct. 25 Litho. *Perf. 12*

88	A19	1c multicolored	.30	.30
89	A19	2c multicolored	.30	.30
90	A19	5c multicolored	.30	.30
91	A19	10c multicolored	.30	.30
92	A19	15c multicolored	.30	.30
93	A19	20c multicolored	.30	.30
94	A19	30c multicolored	.40	.30
		Nos. 88-94 (7)	2.20	2.10

1986? Litho.

90a	A19	5c	Perf. 14	1.25	.25
91a	A19	10c	Perf. 14x13¾	1.00	.25
91b	A19	10c	Perf. 15x14½	1.75	.25
93a	A19	20c	Perf. 14	1.00	.25
94a	A19	30c	Perf. 14	4.50	.25
94b	A19	30c	Perf. 15x14½	6.25	.35

Flowers and Arms Type of Johore of 2007

Perf. 14x13¾, 14¾x14½ (20c)

2007, Dec. 31 Litho. Wmk. 388

95	A20	5c multi	.25	.25
96	A20	10c multi	.25	.25
97	A20	20c multi	.25	.25
a.		Perf. 14x13¾	.25	.25
98	A20	30c multi	.40	.25
99	A20	40c multi	.50	.30
100	A20	50c multi	.65	.35
a.		Souvenir sheet of 6, #95, 96, 97a, 98-100	2.25	1.10
		Nos. 95-100 (6)	2.30	1.65

NEGRI SEMBILAN

(Negeri Sembilan)

Orchid Type of Johore, 1965, with State Crest

Wmk. 338

1965, Nov. 15 Photo. *Perf. 14½*

Flowers in Natural Colors

76	A14	1c blk & lt grnsh blue	.25	1.50
a.		Watermark sideways ('70)	3.25	6.00
77	A14	2c black, red & gray	.25	1.50
78	A14	5c black & Prus blue	.50	.25
79	A14	6c black & lt lilac	.50	.60
80	A14	10c black & lt ultra	.50	.25
81	A14	15c blk, lil rose & grn	1.00	.25
82	A14	20c black & brown	1.50	.90
		Nos. 76-82 (7)	4.50	5.25

Tuanku Ja'afar and Crest of Negri Sembilan — A7

1968, Apr. 8 Photo. *Perf. 13½*

83	A7	15c brt blue & multi	.25	.60
84	A7	50c yellow & multi	.40	1.25

Installation of Tuanku Ja'afar ibni Al-Marhum as ruler (Yang di-Pertuan Besar) of Negri Sembilan.

Butterfly Type of Johore, 1971, with State Crest

Perf. 13½x13

1971, Feb. 1 Litho. Unwmk.

85	A15	1c multicolored	.40	1.75
86	A15	2c multicolored	.60	1.75
87	A15	5c multicolored	.90	.30
88	A15	6c multicolored	1.00	1.75
89	A15	10c multicolored	1.25	.30
90	A15	15c multicolored	2.00	.30
91	A15	20c multicolored	2.00	.45
		Nos. 85-91 (7)	8.15	6.60

1977 Photo.

86a	A15	2c	2.25	4.50
87a	A15	5c	2.25	1.50
89a	A15	10c	11.00	1.25
90a	A15	15c	17.50	.50
91a	A15	20c	5.50	2.00
		Nos. 86a-91a (5)	38.50	9.75

For differentiating the lithograph and photogravure printings of the Butterflies issues, see notes after Johore No. 182a.

Flower Type of Johore, 1979, with State Crest

Wmk. 378

1979, Apr. 30 Litho. *Perf. 14½*

92	A16	1c multicolored	.25	1.10
93	A16	2c multicolored	.25	1.10
94	A16	5c multicolored	.25	.30
a.		Unwmkd. ('85)	1.00	1.60
95	A16	10c multicolored	.25	.25
a.		White flowers ('84)	.25	.25
96	A16	15c multicolored	.35	.25
a.		Unwmkd. ('84)	.75	.75
97	A16	20c multicolored	.35	.25
a.		Pale yellow flowers ('84)	.35	.25
98	A16	25c multicolored	.45	.25
		Nos. 92-98 (7)	2.15	3.50

Agriculture and State Arms Type of Johore

Wmk. 388

1986, Oct. 25 Litho. *Perf. 12*

99	A19	1c multicolored	.30	.30
100	A19	2c multicolored	.30	.30
101	A19	5c multicolored	.30	.30
102	A19	10c multicolored	.30	.30
103	A19	15c multicolored	.30	.30
104	A19	20c multicolored	.40	.30
105	A19	30c multicolored	.30	.30
		Nos. 99-105 (7)	2.20	2.10

1986? **Litho.**

101a A19 5c Perf. 14 1.25 .25
102a A19 10c Perf. 14 1.00 .25
102b A19 10c Perf. 15x14½ 8.25 .35
104a A19 20c Perf. 14x13¼ 2.50 .25
104b A19 20c Perf. 15x14½ —
105a A19 30c Perf. 14 3.50 .25
105b A19 30c Perf. 14x14½ 5.25 .25

Royal Heritage of Negri Sembilan — A8

Designs: 30c, Eight long keris. 50c, Audience Hall. $1, Tuanku Ja'afar Ibni Al-Marhum Tuanku Abdul Rahman, ruler of Negri Sembilan
$2, Tuanku Ja'afar and wife.

Perf. 12¾x12½

2007, Aug. 2 **Litho.** **Wmk. 388**

106-108 A8 Set of 3 1.10 .55

Souvenir Sheet

109 A8 $2 multi 1.25 .60

Flowers and Arms Type of Johore of 2007 With Portrait of Tuanku Jaafar Ibni Al-Marhum Tuanku Abdul Rahman

Perf. 14x13¾, 14¾x14½ (30c)

2007, Dec. 31 **Litho.** **Wmk. 388**

110 A20 5c multi .25 .25
111 A20 10c multi .25 .25
112 A20 20c multi .25 .25
113 A20 30c multi .40 .25
114 A20 40c multi .50 .30
a. Perf. 14¾x14½ .50 .30
115 A20 50c multi .65 .35
a. Perf. 14¾x14½ .65 .40
Nos. 110-115 (6) 2.30 1.65

Installation of Tuanku Muhriz Ibni Al-Mahrum Tuanku Munawir — A9

Tuanku Muhriz: 30c, Wearing white headdress. 50c, Wearing black hat. $1, With wife, Tuanku Aishah Rohani, horiz. (58x34mm)

Perf. 13¾x14 Syncopated

2009, Oct. 26 **Litho.** **Wmk. 388**

116-118 A9 Set of 3 1.10 .55

Flowers and Arms Type of Johore of 2007 with Portrait of Tuanku Muhriz Ibni Al-Mahrum Tuanku Munawir

Designs as before.

Perf. 14x13¾

2009, Nov. 24 **Litho.** **Wmk. 388**

119 Sheet of 6 .95 .45
a. A20 5c multi .25 .25
b. A20 10c multi .25 .25
c. A20 20c multi .25 .25
d. A20 30c multi .25 .25
e. A20 40c multi .25 .25
f. A20 50c multi .30 .25

Tuanku Muhriz's headdress extends well to the left of his ear on Nos. 119a-119f, much like that seen in illustration A9. The headdress of Tuanku Jaafar on Nos. 110-115 does not extend to the left past his ear.

PAHANG

Orchid Type of Johore, 1965, with Portrait of Sultan Abu Bakar

Wmk. 338

1965, Nov. 15 **Photo.** ***Perf. 14½***

Flowers in Natural Colors

83 A14 1c blk & lt grnsh bl .25 1.10
a. Watermark sideways ('70) 2.25 6.50
84 A14 2c black, red & gray .25 1.10
a. Unwmkd. ('85)
85 A14 5c black & Prus bl .35 .25
86 A14 6c black & lt lil .40 1.10
87 A14 10c black & lt ultra .30 .25
a. Watermark sideways ('70) 1.50 3.25
88 A14 15c blk, lil rose & grn 1.25 .25
89 A14 20c black & brown 1.75 .40
Nos. 83-89 (7) 4.55 4.45

Butterfly Type of Johore, 1971, Portrait of Sultan Abu Bakar

Perf. 13½x13

1971, Feb. 1 **Litho.** **Unwmk.**

90 A15 1c multicolored .30 1.50
91 A15 2c multicolored .40 1.75
92 A15 5c multicolored .80 .40
93 A15 6c multicolored 1.25 2.00
94 A15 10c multicolored 1.25 .30
95 A15 15c multicolored 2.00 .30
96 A15 20c multicolored 2.25 .45
Nos. 90-96 (7) 8.25 6.70

In 1973 booklet panes of 4 of the 5c, 10c, 15c were made from sheets.

Sultan Haji Ahmad Shah — A9

1975, May 8 **Litho.** ***Perf. 14x14½***

97 A9 10c lilac, gold & black .45 1.10
98 A9 15c yellow, green & black .80 .30
99 A9 50c ultra, dk blue & black 2.00 4.00
Nos. 97-99 (3) 3.25 5.40

Installation of Sultan Haji Ahmad Shah as ruler of Pahang.

Black-veined Tiger and Sultan Haji Ahmad Shah — A18

1977-78

100 A18 2c multi ('78) *65.00 60.00*
101 A18 5c multicolored .85 1.10
102 A18 10c multi ('78) 1.25 .85
103 A18 15c multi ('78) 1.75 1.00
104 A18 20c multi ('78) 4.50 2.50
Nos. 100-104 (5) 73.35 65.45

Flower Type of Johore, 1979, with Portrait of Sultan Haji Ahmad Shah

Wmk. 378

1979, Apr. 30 **Litho.** ***Perf. 14½***

105 A16 1c multicolored .25 .90
106 A16 2c multicolored .25 .90
107 A16 5c multicolored .25 .25
a. 5c brt rose pink & yel flowers ('84) .25 .25
108 A16 10c multicolored .25 .25
a. Unwmkd. ('85) 1.25 1.50
109 A16 15c multicolored .25 .25
110 A16 20c multicolored .30 .25
a. Unwmkd. ('84) 1.00 .30
111 A16 25c multicolored .45 .40
Nos. 105-111 (7) 2.00 3.20

Agriculture and State Arms Type of Johore with Sultan Haji Ahmad Shah

Wmk. 388

1986, Oct. 25 **Litho.** ***Perf. 12***

112 A19 1c multicolored .30 .30
113 A19 2c multicolored .30 .35
114 A19 5c multicolored .30 .30
115 A19 10c multicolored .30 .30
116 A19 15c multicolored .30 .30
117 A19 20c multicolored .30 .30
118 A19 30c multicolored .45 .30
Nos. 112-118 (7) 2.25 2.15

1986?

112a A19 1c Perf. 13½x14 6.50 .35
114a A19 5c Perf. 14x13¾ —
115a A19 10c Perf. 15x14½ 8.50 .50
115b A19 10c Perf. 14x13½ 1.75 .40
117a A19 20c Perf. 14 1.00 .25
117b A19 20c Perf. 15x14½ —
118a A19 30c Perf. 14 3.00 .25
118b A19 30c Perf. 15x14½ 6.50 .50

Flowers and Arms Type of Johore of 2007 With Portrait of Sultan Haji Ahmad Shah

Perf. 14x13¾

2007, Dec. 31 **Litho.** **Wmk. 388**

119 A20 5c multi .25 .25
120 A20 10c multi .25 .25
121 A20 20c multi .25 .25
122 A20 30c multi .40 .25
123 A20 40c multi .50 .25
124 A20 50c multi .65 .35
a. Souvenir sheet of 6, #119-124 2.25 1.10
Nos. 119-124 (6) 2.30 1.60

Pahang Royalty and Regalia A19

Regalia and: 60c, Sultan Haji Ahmad Shah, Sultana Hajjah Kalson. 80c, Sultan in uniform. $1, Sultan in robe.

Wmk. 388

2010, Oct. 24 **Litho.** ***Perf. 14***

125-127 A19 Set of 3 1.60 .80

Reign of Sultan Haji Ahmad Shah, 40th Anniv. A20

Wmk. 388

2014, Dec. 23 **Litho.** ***Perf. 14***

128 A20 60c multi .35 .25

PENANG

(Pulau Pinang)

Orchid Type of Johore, 1965, with State Crest

Wmk. 338

1965, Nov. 15 **Photo.** ***Perf. 14½***

Orchids in Natural Colors

67 A14 1c black & lt grnsh bl .25 1.10
a. Watermark sideways ('70) 1.75 5.50
68 A14 2c black, red & gray .25 1.10
69 A14 5c black & Prus blue .40 .25
a. Prussian blue omitted *750.00*
b. Yellow omitted *75.00*
70 A14 6c black & lt lilac .50 1.10
71 A14 10c black & lt ultra .30 .25
a. Watermark sideways ('70) 7.25 3.75
72 A14 15c black, lil rose & grn 1.10 .25
73 A14 20c black & brown 1.60 .40
Nos. 67-73 (7) 4.40 4.45

Butterfly Type of Johore, 1971, with State Crest

Perf. 13½x13

1971, Feb. 1 **Litho.** **Unwmk.**

74 A15 1c multicolored .40 1.75
75 A15 2c multicolored .60 1.75
76 A15 5c multicolored 1.25 .30
77 A15 6c multicolored 1.25 1.75
78 A15 10c multicolored 1.40 .25
79 A15 15c multicolored 1.50 .25
80 A15 20c multicolored 1.75 .50
Nos. 74-80 (7) 8.15 6.55

1977 **Photo.**

74a A15 1c 6.00 7.00
76a A15 5c 3.50 .50
78a A15 10c 6.00 .50
79a A15 15c 18.00 .50
80a A15 20c 8.25 .90
Nos. 74a-80a (5) 41.75 9.40

For differentiating the lithograph and photogravure printings of the Butterflies issues, see notes after Johore No. 182a.

Flower Type of Johore, 1979, with State Crest

Wmk. 378

1979, Apr. 30 **Litho.** ***Perf. 14½***

81 A16 1c multicolored .25 .90
82 A16 2c multicolored .25 .90
83 A16 5c multicolored .25 .30
84 A16 10c multicolored .25 .25
85 A16 15c multicolored .25 .25
86 A16 20c multicolored .30 .25
87 A16 25c multicolored .40 .25
Nos. 81-87 (7) 1.95 3.10

1984-85 **Unwmk.**

83a A16 5c .40 .40
84a A16 10c ('85) 5.75 2.25
85a A16 15c .65 .35
86a A16 20c .90 .35

The State arms are larger on Nos. 83a-86a.

Agriculture and State Arms Type of Johore

Wmk. 388

1986, Oct. 25 **Litho.** ***Perf. 12***

88 A19 1c multicolored .30 .30
89 A19 2c multicolored .30 .30
90 A19 5c multicolored .30 .30
91 A19 10c multicolored .30 .30
92 A19 15c multicolored .30 .30
93 A19 20c multicolored .30 .30
94 A19 30c multicolored .30 .30
Nos. 88-94 (7) 2.10 2.10

1986?

90a A19 5c Perf. 14x13¾ 2.50 .25
90b A19 5c Perf. 15x14½ 2.50 .25
91a A19 10c Perf. 14 1.00 .25
91b A19 10c Perf. 14x14½ 3.00 .25
91c A19 10c Perf. 15x14½ 2.50 .25
93a A19 20c Perf. 14 1.00 .25
93b A19 20c Perf. 14x14½ 4.00 .25
93c A19 20c Perf. 15x14½ 4.00 .25
94a A19 30c Perf. 14 1.00 .25
94b A19 30c Perf. 14x14½ 2.50 .25
94c A19 30c Perf. 15x14½ 2.50 .25

Flowers and Arms Type of Johore of 2007

Perf. 14x13¾

2007, Dec. 31 **Litho.** **Wmk. 388**

95 A20 5c multi .25 .25
96 A20 10c multi .25 .25
97 A20 20c multi .25 .25
98 A20 30c multi .40 .25
99 A20 40c multi .50 .30
100 A20 50c multi .65 .35
a. Souvenir sheet of 6, #95-100 2.25 1.10
Nos. 95-100 (6) 2.30 1.65

PERAK

Sultan Idris Shah — A17

Wmk. 338

1963, Oct. 26 **Photo.** ***Perf. 14***

138 A17 10c yel, blk, blue & brn .35 .25

Installation of Idris Shah as Sultan of Perak.

Orchid Type of Johore, 1965, with Portrait of Sultan Idris Shah

1965, Nov. 15 **Wmk. 338** ***Perf. 14½***

Flowers in Natural Colors

139 A14 1c blk & lt grnsh bl .25 .40
a. Watermark sideways ('70) 2.50 6.50
140 A14 2c black, red & gray .25 .60
141 A14 5c black & Prus blue .30 .25
a. Yellow omitted 80.00
142 A14 6c black & lt lilac .30 .30
143 A14 10c black & lt ultra .30 .25
a. Watermark sideways ('70) 7.50 3.75
144 A14 15c blk, lil rose & grn .80 .25
a. Lilac rose omitted *900.00*
145 A14 20c black & brown 1.25 .25
Nos. 139-145 (7) 3.45 2.30

Butterfly Type of Johore, 1971, with Portrait of Sultan Idris Shah

Perf. 13½x13

1971, Feb. 1 **Litho.** **Unwmk.**

146 A15 1c multicolored .35 1.75
147 A15 2c multicolored .90 1.75
148 A15 5c multicolored 1.10 .25

149 A15 6c multicolored 1.10 1.75
150 A15 10c multicolored 1.25 .25
151 A15 15c multicolored 1.25 .35
152 A15 20c multicolored 1.75 .35
Nos. 146-152 (7) 7.70 6.45

In 1973 booklet panes of 4 of the 5c, 10c, 15c were made from sheets.

1977 Photo.

146a A15 1c 1.75 3.50
148b A15 5c 4.00 .65
150b A15 10c 3.25 .75
151b A15 15c 11.00 .50
152a A15 20c 4.50 1.40
Nos. 146a-152a (5) 24.50 6.80

For differentiating the lithograph and photogravure printings of the Butterflies issues, see notes after Johore No. 182a.

Flower Type of Johore, 1979, with Portrait of Sultan Idris Shah

Wmk. 378

1979, Apr. 30 Litho. *Perf. 14½*

153 A16 1c multicolored .25 .75
154 A16 2c multicolored .25 .75
155 A16 5c multicolored .25 .25
a. Brt rose pink & yel flowers ('84) .25 .25
156 A16 10c multicolored .25 .25
a. White flowers ('84) .25 .25
157 A16 15c multicolored .30 .25
a. Unwmkd. ('85) 1.00 .25
158 A16 20c multicolored .35 .25
a. Unwmkd. ('84) .90 .40
159 A16 25c multicolored .45 .25
Nos. 153-159 (7) 2.10 2.75

Agriculture and State Arms Type of Johore with Tun Azlan Shah, Raja

Wmk. 388

1986, Oct. 25 Litho. *Perf. 12*

160 A19 1c multicolored .25 .25
161 A19 2c multicolored .25 .30
162 A19 5c multicolored .25 .25
163 A19 10c multicolored .25 .25
164 A19 15c multicolored .25 .25
165 A19 20c multicolored .25 .25
166 A19 30c multicolored .35 .25
Nos. 160-166 (7) 1.85 1.80

1986?

161a A19 2c Perf. 14x14½ 3.00 .30
162a A19 5c Perf. 14 3.00 .25
162b A19 5c Perf. 15x14½ 4.00 .25
163a A19 10c Perf. 14x13¼ 1.00 .25
165a A19 20c Perf. 14 1.50 .25
165b A19 20c Perf. 14x14½ 4.00 .35
165c A19 20c Perf. 14¾x14½ 2.75 .45
166a A19 30c Perf. 14x14½ 3.50 .35
166b A19 30c Perf. 15x14½ 7.50 1.00
166c A19 30c Perf. 14x13½ 6.00 .35

Flowers and Arms Type of Johore of 2007 With Portrait of Sultan Azlan Shah

Perf. 14x13¾

2007, Dec. 31 Litho. Wmk. 388

167 A20 5c multi .25 .25
168 A20 10c multi .25 .25
169 A20 20c multi .25 .25
170 A20 30c multi .40 .25
171 A20 40c multi .50 .30
172 A20 50c multi .65 .35
a. Souvenir sheet of 6, #167-172 2.25 1.10
Nos. 167-172 (6) 2.30 1.65

Reign of Sultan Azlan Shah, 25th Anniv. — A18

Sultan and: 30c, Sultana Tuanku Bainun. 50c, Mosque. $1, Sultana, diff.

Perf. 13½x13¼

2009, Feb. 3 Litho. Wmk. 388

173-175 A18 Set of 3 1.00 .50

Installation of Sultan Nazrin Muizzuddin Shah — A19

Designs: 60s, Sultan Nazrin. 80s, Sultan Nazrin and Raja Zara. $1.20, Sultan Nazrin, diff.
$5, Sultan Nazrin and Raja Zara, diff.

Perf. 13¼x13½

2015, May 6 Litho. Unwmk.

176-178 A19 Set of 3 1.50 .75

Souvenir Sheet

179 A19 $5 multi 3.00 1.50

No. 179 contains one 42x70mm stamp.

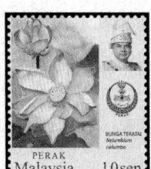

Flowers, Arms and Sultan Nazrin Muizzuddin Shah — A20

Designs: 10c, Nelumbium nelumbo. 20c, Hydrangea macrophylla. 30c, Hippeastrum reticulatum. 40c, Bougainvillea. 50c, Ipomoea indica. 60c, Hibiscus rosa-sinensis.

Perf. 14x13¾

2016, Mar. 21 Litho. Wmk. 388

180 A20 10c multi .25 .25
181 A20 20c multi .25 .25
182 A20 30c multi .25 .25
183 A20 40c multi .25 .25
184 A20 50c multi .25 .25
185 A20 60c multi .30 .25
a. Souvenir sheet of 6, #180-185, imperf. 1.10 .55
Nos. 180-185 (6) 1.55 1.50

PERLIS

Orchid Type of Johore, 1965, with Portrait of Regent Yang Teramat Mulia

Wmk. 338

1965, Nov. 15 Photo. *Perf. 14½*

Flowers in Natural Colors

40 A14 1c black & lt grnsh bl .30 .90
41 A14 2c black, red & gray .35 1.25
42 A14 5c black & Prus blue .30 .30
43 A14 6c black & lt lilac .60 1.25
44 A14 10c black & ultra .85 .35
45 A14 15c blk, lil rose & grn 1.25 .50
46 A14 20c black & brown 1.25 1.60
Nos. 40-46 (7) 4.90 6.15

Butterfly Type of Johore, 1971, with Portrait of Sultan Syed Putra

Perf. 13½x13

1971, Feb. 1 Litho. Unwmk.

47 A15 1c multicolored .25 1.10
48 A15 2c multicolored .30 1.75
49 A15 5c multicolored 1.10 1.10
50 A15 6c multicolored 1.25 2.75
51 A15 10c multicolored 1.75 1.10
52 A15 15c multicolored 1.75 .50
53 A15 20c multicolored 1.75 2.25
Nos. 47-53 (7) 8.15 10.55

In 1973 booklet panes of 4 of the 5c, 10c, 15c were made from sheets.

1977 Photo.

51b A15 10c 190.00 9.50
52b A15 15c 5.50 2.75
53a A15 20c 175.00 32.50
Nos. 51b-53a (3) 370.50 44.75

For differentiating the lithograph and photogravure printings of the Butterflies issues, see notes after Johore No. 182a.

Sultan Syed Putra — A2

1971, Mar. 28 Litho. *Perf. 13½x13*

54 A2 10c silver, yel & black .30 2.00
55 A2 15c silver, blue & blk .35 .65
56 A2 50c silver, lt vio & blk .90 4.00
Nos. 54-56 (3) 1.55 6.65

25th anniversary of the installation of Syed Putra as Raja of Perlis. Sold throughout Malaysia on Mar. 28, then only in Perlis.

Flower Type of Johore, 1979, with Portrait of Sultan Syed Putra

Wmk. 378

1979, Apr. 30 Litho. *Perf. 14½*

57 A16 1c multicolored .25 .90
58 A16 2c multicolored .25 .90
59 A16 5c multicolored .25 .90
60 A16 10c multicolored .25 .25
61 A16 15c multicolored .25 .25
62 A16 20c multicolored .30 .25
a. Unwmk. ('85) 1.75 1.75
63 A16 25c multicolored .45 .75
Nos. 57-63 (7) 2.00 4.20

Agriculture and State Arms Type of Johore with Tuanku Syed Putra, Raja

Wmk. 388

1986, Oct. 25 Litho. *Perf. 12*

64 A19 1c multicolored .30 .45
65 A19 2c multicolored .30 .45
66 A19 5c multicolored .30 .30
67 A19 10c multicolored .30 .30
68 A19 15c multicolored .30 .30
69 A19 20c multicolored .30 .30
70 A19 30c multicolored .40 .30
Nos. 64-70 (7) 2.20 2.40

1986?

67a A19 10c Perf. 15x14½ 4.25 .45
70a A19 30c Perf. 14 5.25 .25
70b A19 30c Perf. 15x14½ 14.50

Reign of Tuanku Syed Putra Jamalullail, Raja of Perlis, 50th Anniv. A3

30c, Industry and produce. $1, Palace.

Wmk. 388

1995, Dec. 4 Litho. *Perf. 14*

71 A3 30c green & multi .80 .80
72 A3 $1 blue & multi 2.40 2.40

Installation of Raja Tuanku Syed Sirajuddin Putra Jamalullail — A4

Denomination color: 30c, Blue. 50c, Green. $1, Purple.
$2, Raja and wife, horiz.

Perf. 13½x13¾

2001, May 7 Litho. Wmk. 388

73-75 A4 Set of 3 .95 .45

Souvenir Sheet

Perf. 14¼x13½x13¾x13½

76 A4 $2 multi 1.10 1.10

Flowers and Arms Type of Johore of 2007 With Portrait of Raja Tuanku Syed Sirajuddin Putra Jamalullail

Perf. 14x13¾

2007, Dec. 31 Litho. Wmk. 388

77 A20 5c multi .25 .25
78 A20 10c multi .25 .25
79 A20 20c multi .25 .25
80 A20 30c multi .40 .25
81 A20 40c multi .50 .30
82 A20 50c multi .65 .35
a. Souvenir sheet of 6, #77-82 2.25 1.10
Nos. 77-82 (6) 2.30 1.65

SABAH

North Borneo Nos. 280-295 Overprinted

On 1c-75c

On $1-$10

Perf. 13x12½, 12½x13

1964, July 1 Engr. Wmk. 314

1 A92 1c lt red brn & grn .25 .35
2 A92 4c orange & olive .25 .45
3 A92 5c violet & sepia .25 .35
4 A92 6c bluish grn & sl 1.10 .35
5 A92 10c rose red & lt grn 2.00 .35
6 A92 12c dull green & brn .25 .35
7 A92 20c ultra & blue grn 4.25 .35
8 A92 25c rose red & gray .90 .80
9 A92 30c gray ol & sepia .40 .30
10 A92 35c redsh brn & stl bl .40 .30
11 A92 50c brn org & blue grn .40 .30
12 A92 75c red vio & sl blue 3.75 .90
13 A93 $1 yel green & brn 9.50 1.75
14 A93 $2 slate & brown 15.00 3.00
15 A93 $5 brown vio & grn 17.00 13.00
16 A93 $10 blue & carmine 17.00 29.00
Nos. 1-16 (16) 72.70 51.90

Orchid Type of Johore, 1965, with State Crest

Wmk. 338

1965, Nov. 15 Photo. *Perf. 14½*

Flowers in Natural Colors

17 A14 1c black & lt grnsh bl .30 1.10
18 A14 2c black, red & gray .30 1.50
19 A14 5c black & Prus bl .45 .25
20 A14 6c black & lt lilac .45 1.25
21 A14 10c black & lt ultra .40 .25
a. Watermark sideways ('70) 5.50 5.50
22 A14 15c black, lil rose & grn 2.00 .30
23 A14 20c black & brown 3.00 .70
Nos. 17-23 (7) 6.90 5.35

Butterfly Type of Johore, 1971, with State Crest

Perf. 13½x13

1971, Feb. 1 Litho. Unwmk.

24 A15 1c multicolored .60 2.25
25 A15 2c multicolored .70 2.25
26 A15 5c multicolored .70 .40
27 A15 6c multicolored .90 1.75
28 A15 10c multicolored 1.00 .25
29 A15 15c multicolored 1.25 .25
30 A15 20c multicolored 1.30 1.10
Nos. 24-30 (7) 6.45 8.25

In 1973 booklet panes of 4 of the 5c, 10c, 15c were made from sheets.

1977 Photo.

24a A15 1c 1.75 4.25
25a A15 2c 1.75 4.25
26b A15 5c 10.00 2.25
28b A15 10c 2.00 1.00
29b A15 15c 2.50 .30
30a A15 20c 225.00 10.00
Nos. 24a-29b (5) 18.00 12.05

For differentiating the lithograph and photogravure printings of the Butterflies issues, see notes after Johore No. 182a.

Flower Type of Johore, 1979, with State Crest

Wmk. 378

1979, Apr. 30 Litho. *Perf. 14½*

32 A16 1c multicolored .35 1.50
33 A16 2c multicolored .35 1.50
34 A16 5c multicolored .35 .45
35 A16 10c multicolored .35 .35
36 A16 15c multicolored .50 .35

37 A16 20c multicolored .60 .35
38 A16 25c multicolored .75 .35
Nos. 32-38 (7) 3.25 4.85

1983-85 Unwmk.
35a A16 10c ('85) 5.50 7.25
36a A16 15c 2.75 .90
37a A16 20c 17.00 1.75

Agriculture and State Arms Type of Johore

Wmk. 388

1986, Oct. 25 Litho. *Perf. 12*
39 A19 1c multicolored .30 .30
40 A19 2c multicolored .30 .25
41 A19 5c multicolored .30 .25
42 A19 10c multicolored .30 .25
43 A19 15c multicolored .30 .25
44 A19 20c multicolored .30 .25
45 A19 30c multicolored .35 .25
Nos. 39-45 (7) 2.15 1.80

1986?
40a A19 2c Perf. 15x14½ 3.25 .35
42a A19 10c Perf. 14x13¾ — —
45a A19 30c Perf. 14 1.00 .25
45b A19 30c Perf. 15x14½ 4.75 .30

Flowers and Arms Type of Johore of 2007

Perf. 14x13¾

2007, Dec. 31 Litho. Wmk. 388
46 A20 5c multi .25 .25
47 A20 10c multi .25 .25
48 A20 20c multi .25 .25
49 A20 30c multi .40 .25
50 A20 40c multi .50 .30
51 A20 50c multi .65 .35
a. Souvenir sheet of 6, #46-51 2.25 1.10
Nos. 46-51 (6) 2.30 1.65

SARAWAK

Types of Sarawak of 1955-57

Perf. 11x11½, 11½x11

1964-65 Engr. Wmk. 314
215 A23 1c green .25 *1.00*
216 A23 2c red orange 1.00 *13.50*
217 A24 6c green blue 7.00 *5.25*
218 A24 10c dark green 2.25 1.40
219 A24 12c purple 3.75 *12.00*
220 A24 15c ultra 1.50 *17.50*
221 A24 20c brown & olive 1.00 *2.00*
222 A24 25c brt grn & brn 4.25 *6.00*
Nos. 215-222 (8) 21.00 *58.65*

Issued: 20c, 6/9/64; 2c, 15c, 8/17/65; others, 9/9/64.

Orchid Type of Johore (Malaysia), 1965, with State Crest

Wmk. 338

1965, Nov. 15 Photo. *Perf. 14½*

Flowers in Natural Colors

228 A14 1c black & lt grnsh bl .25 *1.25*
229 A14 2c black, red & gray .30 *2.50*
230 A14 5c black & Prus blue 1.50 .25
231 A14 6c black & lt lilac .90 *2.25*
232 A14 10c black & lt ultra 1.25 .25
233 A14 15c black, lil rose & grn 1.75 .25
234 A14 20c black & brown 2.50 .55
Nos. 228-234 (7) 8.45 7.30

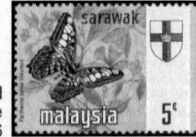

Clipper and State Crest — A26

1c, Delias ninus. 2c, Danaus melanippus. 5c, Parthenos sylvia. 6c, Papilio demoleus. 10c, Hebomnia glaucippe. 15c, Precis orithya. 20c, Valeria valeria.

Perf. 13½x13

1971, Feb. 1 Litho. Unwmk.
235 A26 1c multicolored .85 *2.25*
236 A26 2c multicolored .95 *2.25*
237 A26 5c multicolored 2.00 .25
a. Booklet pane of 4 ('73) 9.00
238 A26 6c multicolored 2.00 *3.00*
239 A26 10c multicolored 2.00 .25
a. Booklet pane of 4 ('73) 9.00
240 A26 15c multicolored 3.00 .25
a. Booklet pane of 4 ('73) 13.00
241 A26 20c multicolored 3.00 1.50
Nos. 235-241 (7) 13.80 9.75

Clipper and New State Crest — A27

Changed Colors, Designs as Before

1977-78 Photo. Unwmk.
242 A27 1c multi ('78) 8.50 *15.00*
243 A27 2c multi ('78) 20.00 *16.00*
244 A27 5c multicolored 2.50 2.00
245 A27 10c multicolored 1.50 .80
246 A27 15c multicolored 3.00 .30
247 A27 20c multi ('78) 7.00 5.75
Nos. 242-247 (6) 42.50 39.85

Flower Type of Johore, 1979, with State Crest

1979, Apr. 30 Wmk. 47 *Perf. 14½*
248 A16 1c multicolored .25 .40
249 A16 2c multicolored .25 .40
250 A16 5c multicolored .25 .50
251 A16 10c multicolored .30 .25
252 A16 15c multicolored .30 .25
253 A16 20c multicolored .60 .25
254 A16 25c multicolored .90 .70
Nos. 248-254 (7) 2.85 2.75

1983-86 Unwmk.
250a A16 5c ('86) 1.00 1.25
251a A16 10c ('85) 1.00 1.10
253a A16 20c 1.00 1.10
Nos. 250a-253a (3) 3.00 3.45

Agriculture and State Arms Type of Johore Shield Divided into 3 Parts of Different Colors

Wmk. 388

1986, Oct. 25 Litho. *Perf. 12*
255 A19 1c multicolored .25 .25
256 A19 2c multicolored .25 .25
257 A19 5c multicolored .30 .25
258 A19 10c multicolored .40 .25
259 A19 15c multicolored .55 .25
260 A19 20c multicolored .55 .25
261 A19 30c multicolored 1.00 .25
Nos. 255-261 (7) 3.30 1.75

Agriculture and Arms Type of Johore

Yellow Shield Divided by Diagonal Bands of Black and Red

1986-96 Litho. Wmk. 388 *Perf. 12*
262 A19 1c multicolored .25 .25
263 A19 2c multicolored .25 .25
a. Perf. 15x14½ 3.00
264 A19 5c multicolored .25 .25
a. Perf 14 ('96) .90 .25
265 A19 10c multicolored .25 .25
a. Perf. 14 ('95) 2.00
b. Perf. 15x14½ ('95) 2.00
c. Perf. 14x14½ ('96) 4.50 .35
266 A19 15c multicolored .25 .25
267 A19 20c multicolored .30 .25
268 A19 30c multicolored .40 .25
a. Perf. 14 ('94) 1.75 .25
b. Perf. 15x14½ ('94) 4.00 .35
c. Perf. 14x14½ ('94) 4.25 .45
Nos. 262-268 (7) 1.95 1.75

Flowers and Arms Type of Johore of 2007

Perf. 14x13¾

2007, Dec. 31 Litho. Wmk. 388
269 A20 5c multi .25 .25
270 A20 10c multi .30 .25
271 A20 20c multi .35 .25
272 A20 30c multi .50 .25
273 A20 40c multi .60 .30
274 A20 50c multi .75 .35
a. Souvenir sheet of 6, #269-274 3.00 2.50
Nos. 269-274 (6) 2.75 1.65

SELANGOR

Orchid Type of Johore, 1965, with Portrait of Sultan Salahuddin Abdul Aziz Shah

Wmk. 338

1965, Nov. 15 Photo. *Perf. 14½*

Flowers in Natural Colors

121 A14 1c blk & lt grnsh bl .25 .25
a. Watermark sideways ('70) 1.60 7.25
122 A14 2c black, red & gray .30 1.50
a. Rose carmine omitted
123 A14 5c black & Prus blue .35 .25
124 A14 6c black & lt lilac .35 .25
125 A14 10c black & lt ultra .35 .25
a. Watermark sideways ('70) 5.25 1.75
126 A14 15c blk, lil rose & grn 1.25 .25
127 A14 20c black & brown 2.25 .25
a. Watermark sideways ('70) 9.25 9.50
Nos. 121-127 (7) 5.10 3.00

Butterfly Type of Johore, 1971, with Portrait of Sultan Salahuddin Abdul Aziz Shah

Perf. 13½x13

1971, Feb. 1 Litho. Unwmk.
128 A15 1c multicolored .65 1.75
129 A15 2c multicolored 1.25 1.75
130 A15 5c multicolored 1.25 .30
131 A15 6c multicolored 1.25 1.75
132 A15 10c multicolored 1.60 .30
133 A15 15c multicolored 1.25 .30
134 A15 20c multicolored 1.25 .40
Nos. 128-134 (7) 8.50 6.55

In 1973 booklet panes of 4 of the 5c, 10c, 15c were made from sheets.

1977 Photo.
128a A15 1c .80 4.25
130b A15 5c 3.75 1.50
132b A15 10c 7.75 1.50
133b A15 15c 9.00 .40
134a A15 20c 4.50 1.25
Nos. 128a-134a (5) 25.80 8.90

For differentiating the lithograph and photogravure printings of the Butterflies issues, see notes after Johore No. 182a.

Flower Type of Johore, 1979, with Portrait of Sultan Salahuddin Abdul Aziz Shah

Wmk. 378

1979, Apr. 30 Litho. *Perf. 14½*
135 A16 1c multicolored .25 .90
136 A16 2c multicolored .25 .90
137 A16 5c multicolored .25 .25
a. brt rose pink & yel flowers ('84) .65 .80
138 A16 10c multicolored .25 .25
a. Unwmkd. ('85) .85 1.00
139 A16 15c multicolored .25 .25
a. Unwmkd. ('84) .85 .85
140 A16 20c multicolored .30 .25
a. pale yellow flowers ('84) 1.00 .50
141 A16 25c multicolored .40 .25
Nos. 135-141 (7) 1.95 3.05

Agriculture and State Arms Type of Johore with Sultan Salahuddin Abdul Aziz Shah

Wmk. 388

1986, Oct. 25 Litho. *Perf. 12*
142 A19 1c multicolored .30 .30
143 A19 2c multicolored .30 .30
144 A19 5c multicolored .30 .25
145 A19 10c multicolored .30 .25
146 A19 15c multicolored .30 .25
147 A19 20c multicolored .30 .25
148 A19 30c multicolored .35 .25
Nos. 142-148 (7) 2.15 1.85

1986?
144a A19 5c Perf. 14x14½ 13.00
144b A19 5c Perf. 15x14½ 4.25 .25
144c A19 5c Perf. 14x13½ .90 .25
145a A19 10c Perf. 14 3.25 .25
145b A19 10c Perf. 15x14½ 1.50 .25
147a A19 20c Perf. 14 1.00 .25
147b A19 20c Perf. 14x14½ — —
148a A19 30c Perf. 14 1.00 .25
148b A19 30c Perf. 14x14½ 8.50 .25
148c A19 30c Perf. 15x14½ 5.00 .25

Coronation of Sultan Sharafuddin Idris Shah — A19

Designs: 30c, Wearing yellow hat. 50c, Wearing naval uniform. 1r, Wearing crown.

Perf. 12 (30c), 12¾x12½

2003, Mar. 8 Litho. Wmk. 388
149-151 A19 Set of 3 .95 .45

Flowers and Arms Type of Johore of 2007 With Portrait of Sultan Sharafuddin Idris Shah

Perf. 14¾x14½

2007, Dec. 31 Litho. Wmk. 388
152 A20 5c multi .25 .25
a. Perf. 14x13¾ .25 .25
153 A20 10c multi .25 .25
a. Perf. 14x13¾ .25 .25

Perf. 14x13¾

154 A20 20c multi .25 .25
155 A20 30c multi .40 .25
156 A20 40c multi .50 .30
157 A20 50c multi .65 .35
a. Souvenir sheet of 6, #152a, 153a, 154-157 2.25 1.10
Nos. 152-157 (6) 2.30 1.65

TRENGGANU

Orchid Type of Johore, 1965, with Portrait of Sultan Ismail

Wmk. 338

1965, Nov. 15 Photo. *Perf. 14½*

Flowers in Natural Colors

86 A14 1c black & lt grnsh bl .25 1.75
87 A14 2c black, red & gray .30 1.75
88 A14 5c black & Prus blue .35 .60
89 A14 6c black & lt lilac .40 1.75
90 A14 10c black & lt ultra .35 .25
91 A14 15c blk, lil rose & grn 1.40 .25
92 A14 20c black & brown 1.50 1.25
Nos. 86-92 (7) 4.55 7.60

Tuanku Ismail Nasiruddin — A6

Perf. 14½x13½

1970, Dec. 16 Photo. Unwmk.
93 A6 10c multicolored .90 2.25
94 A6 15c brt yellow multi .70 1.10
95 A6 50c dp plum & multi 1.10 2.75
Nos. 93-95 (3) 2.70 6.10

Installation of Tuanku Ismail Nasiruddin Shah as Sultan of Trengganu, 25th anniv.

Butterfly Type of Johore, 1971, with Portrait of Sultan Ismail Nasiruddin

Perf. 13½x13

1971, Feb. 1 Litho. Unwmk.
96 A15 1c multicolored .35 2.25
97 A15 2c multicolored .70 2.25
98 A15 5c multicolored .90 1.10
99 A15 6c multicolored 1.50 2.50
100 A15 10c multicolored 1.75 .60
101 A15 15c multicolored 2.25 .30
102 A15 20c multicolored 2.25 2.00
Nos. 96-102 (7) 9.70 11.00

In 1973 booklet panes of 4 of the 5c, 10c, 15c were made from sheets.

1977 Photo.
98b A15 5c *24.00* *9.50*
100b A15 10c *8.25* *3.75*
101b A15 15c *5.25* *1.50*
Nos. 98b-101b (3) *37.50* *14.75*

For differentiating the lithograph and photogravure printings of the Butterflies issues, see notes after Johore No. 182a.

Flower Type of Johore, 1979, with Portrait of Sultan Ismail Nasiruddin

Wmk. 378

1979, Apr. 30 Litho. *Perf. 14½*
103 A16 1c multicolored .25 1.10
104 A16 2c multicolored .25 1.10
105 A16 5c multicolored .25 .50
106 A16 10c multicolored .25 .25
107 A16 15c multicolored .30 .25
108 A16 20c multicolored .35 .25
109 A16 25c multicolored .45 .40
Nos. 103-109 (7) 2.10 3.85

1983-86 Unwmk.
106a A16 10c ('86) 13.50 4.25
107a A16 15c ('85) .90 1.25
108a A16 20c 3.00 3.25
109a A16 25c Pale salmon flowers .90 1.10
Nos. 106a-109a (4) 18.30

The portrait and State arms are smaller.

Agriculture and State Arms Type of Johore with Sultan Mahmud Al Marhum

Wmk. 388

1986, Oct. 25 Litho. *Perf. 12*

110 A19 1c multicolored .30 .30
111 A19 2c multicolored .30 .30
112 A19 5c multicolored .30 .30
113 A19 10c multicolored .30 .30
114 A19 15c multicolored .30 .30
115 A19 20c multicolored .30 .30
116 A19 30c multicolored .40 .30
Nos. 110-116 (7) 2.20 2.10

1986?

110a A19 1c Perf. 13½x14 4.25 .35
115a A19 20c Perf. 14 7.25 .25
116a A19 30c Perf. 14 7.25 .30
116b A19 30c Perf. 14x14½ —

Installation of HRH Sultan Mizan Zainal Abidin A7

Sultan Abidin and: 30c, Istana Maziah. 50c, Istana Maziah, 1903. $1, Masjid Tengku Tengah Zaharah.

Wmk. 388

1999, Mar. 4 Litho. *Perf. 14¼*

117 A7 30c multicolored .50 .25

Perf. 14½

118 A7 50c multicolored .75 .50

Perf. 13¾

119 A7 $1 multicolored 1.40 2.50
Nos. 117-119 (3) 2.65 3.25

Flowers and Arms Type of Johore of 2007 With Portrait of Sultan Mizan Zainal Abidin

Perf. 14x13¾

2007, Dec. 31 Litho. Wmk. 388

120 A20 5c multi .25 .25
121 A20 10c multi .25 .25
122 A20 20c multi .25 .25
123 A20 30c multi .40 .25
124 A20 40c multi .50 .30
125 A20 50c multi .65 .35
a. Souvenir sheet of 6, #120-125 2.25 1.10
Nos. 121-125 (5) 2.05 1.40

WILAYAH PERSEKUTUAN

Agriculture and State Arms Type of Johore

Wmk. 388

1986, Oct. 25 Litho. *Perf. 12*

1 A19 1c multicolored .25 .25
2 A19 2c multicolored .25 .25
3 A19 5c multicolored .25 .25
4 A19 10c multicolored .25 .25
5 A19 15c multicolored .25 .25
6 A19 20c multicolored .25 .25
7 A19 30c multicolored .40 .25
Nos. 1-7 (7) 1.90 1.75

1986?

3a A19 5c Perf. 14 3.00
3b A19 5c Perf. 15x14½ 7.50
4a A19 10c Perf. 14 3.00
4b A19 10c Perf. 14x14½ 7.50
4c A19 10c Perf. 14¾x14½ — —
6a A19 20c Perf. 14 1.00 —
6b A19 20c Perf. 15x14½ —
7a A19 30c Perf. 14 1.00
7b A19 30c Perf. 15x14½ 4.00
7c A19 30c Perf. 14x14½ —

Agriculture and State Arms Type of Johore of 1986 Redrawn With "Sen" Instead of "C"

Designs as before.

Perf. 14x14¾

2002 ? Litho. Wmk. 388

10 A19 5sen multi — —

Perf. 14x14¾

11 A19 10sen multi — —
a. Perf. 14x13¾ —

Perf. 14x13¾

13 A19 20sen multi —
a. Perf. 14¾x14½ —

Perf. 14¾x14½

14 A19 30sen multi —
a. Perf. 14x13¾ —

Additional stamps were released in this set and also for other states. The editors would like to examine any examples.

Flowers and Arms Type of Johore of 2007

2007, Dec. 31 Litho. *Perf. 14x13¾*

15 A20 5c multi .25 .25
a. Perf. 14¾x14½ .25 .25
16 A20 10c multi .25 .25
17 A20 20c multi .25 .25
18 A20 30c multi .40 .25
19 A20 40c multi .50 .30
20 A20 50c multi .65 .35
a. Souvenir sheet of 6, #15-20 2.25 1.10
Nos. 15-20 (6) 2.30 1.65

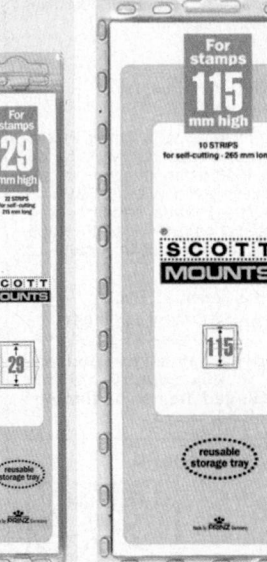

MALDIVE ISLANDS

'mol-ˌdiv 'i-ləndz

LOCATION — A group of 2,000 islands in the Indian Ocean about 400 miles southwest of Ceylon.
GOVT. — Republic
AREA — 115 sq. mi.
POP. — 300,220 (1999 est.)
CAPITAL — Male

Maldive Islands was a British Protectorate, first as a dependency of Ceylon, then from 1948 as an independent sultanate, except for a year (1953) as a republic. The islands became completely independent on July 26, 1965, and became a republic again on November 11, 1968.

100 Cents = 1 Rupee
100 Larees = 1 Rufiyaa (1951)

Catalogue values for unused stamps in this country are for Never Hinged items, beginning with Scott 20.

Watermarks

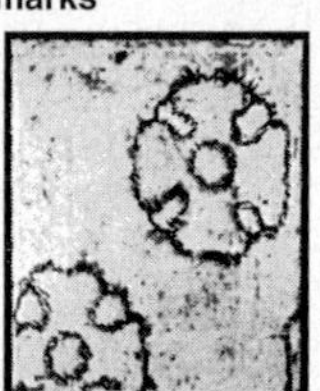

Wmk. 47 — Multiple Rosette

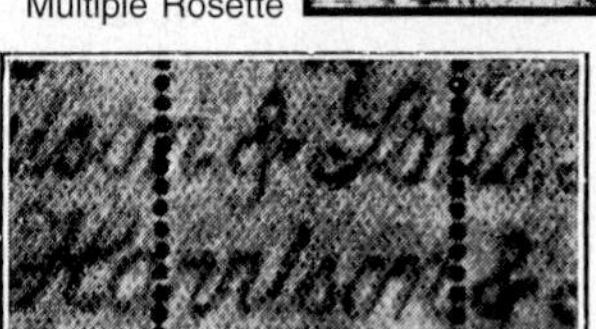

Wmk. 233 — "Harrison & Sons, London" in Script

Stamps of Ceylon, 1904-05, Overprinted

1906, Sept. 9 Wmk. 3 *Perf. 14*

1	A36	2c orange brown	17.50	*35.00*
2	A37	3c green	28.00	*40.00*
3	A37	4c yellow & blue	40.00	*62.50*
4	A38	5c dull lilac	4.00	*4.50*
5	A40	15c ultramarine	80.00	*125.00*
6	A40	25c bister	90.00	*160.00*
		Nos. 1-6 (6)	259.50	*427.00*

Minaret of Juma Mosque, near Male — A1

1909 Engr. Wmk. 47

7	A1	2c orange brown	2.25	*4.50*
a.		Perf 13½x14	2.50	.90
8	A1	3c green	.50	.70
9	A1	5c red violet	.50	.35
10	A1	10c carmine	7.50	.80
		Nos. 7-10 (4)	10.75	6.35

Type of 1909 Issue Redrawn

Perf. 14½x14

1933 Photo. Wmk. 233

11	A1	2c gray	2.00	*1.90*
12	A1	3c yellow brown	.55	*2.00*
13	A1	5c brown lake	42.50	7.50
14	A1	6c brown red	1.10	*4.25*
15	A1	10c green	.65	.40
16	A1	15c gray black	6.50	*21.00*
17	A1	25c red brown	6.50	*21.00*
18	A1	50c red violet	6.50	*26.00*
19	A1	1r blue black	11.00	21.00
		Nos. 11-19 (9)	77.30	105.05

On the 6c, 15c, 25c and 50c, the right hand panel carries only the word "CENTS."

Nos. 11-19 exist with watermark vert. or horiz. The 5c with vert. watermark sells for twice the price of the horiz. watermark.

Catalogue values for unused stamps in this section, from this point to the end of the section, are for Never Hinged items.

Palm Tree and Seascape — A2

Unwmk.

1950, Dec. 24 Engr. *Perf. 13*

20	A2	2 l olive green	4.50	*5.50*
21	A2	3 l deep blue	17.00	3.00
22	A2	5 l dp blue green	17.00	3.00
23	A2	6 l red brown	1.25	1.75
24	A2	10 l red	1.25	1.00
25	A2	15 l orange	1.25	1.00
26	A2	25 l rose violet	1.25	*4.00*
27	A2	50 l violet blue	1.50	*6.00*
28	A2	1r dark brown	14.00	*40.00*
		Nos. 20-28 (9)	59.00	65.25

Maldive Fish — A3

1952

29	A3	3 l shown	1.75	.75
30	A3	5 l Urns	.90	2.00

Harbor of Male — A4

Fort and Governor's Palace — A5

Perf. 13½ (A4), 11½x11 (A5)

1956 Engr. Unwmk.

31	A4	2 l lilac	.25	.25
32	A4	3 l gray green	.25	.25
33	A4	5 l reddish brown	.25	.25
34	A4	6 l blue violet	.25	.25
35	A4	10 l light green	.25	.25
36	A4	15 l brown	.25	.25
37	A4	25 l rose red	.25	.25
38	A4	50 l orange	.25	.25
39	A5	1r light green	.40	.30
40	A5	5r ultramarine	1.00	.65
41	A5	10r magenta	2.10	1.25
		Nos. 31-41 (11)	5.50	4.20

Bicyclists and Olympic Emblem — A6

Design: 25 l, 50 l, 1r, Basketball, vert.

Perf. 11½x11, 11x11½

1960, Aug. 20 Engr.

42	A6	2 l rose violet & green	.25	.25
43	A6	3 l grnsh gray & plum	.25	.25
44	A6	5 l vio brn & dk blue	.25	.25
45	A6	10 l brt green & brn	.25	.25
46	A6	15 l brown & blue	.25	.25
47	A6	25 l rose red & olive	.25	.25
48	A6	50 l orange & dk vio	.25	.35
49	A6	1r brt green & plum	.40	.75
		Nos. 42-49 (8)	2.15	2.60

17th Olympic Games, Rome, 8/25-9/11.

World Refugee Year Emblem A7

1960, Oct. 15 *Perf. 11½x11*

50	A7	2 l orange, vio & grn	.25	.25
51	A7	3 l green, brn & red	.25	.25
52	A7	5 l sepia, grn & red	.25	.25
53	A7	10 l dull pur, grn & red	.25	.25
54	A7	15 l gray grn, pur & red	.25	.25
55	A7	25 l redsh brn, ultra & olive	.25	.25
56	A7	50 l rose, olive & blue	.25	.25
57	A7	1r gray, car rose & vio	.35	.50
		Nos. 50-57 (8)	2.10	2.25

WRY, July 1, 1959-June 30, 1960.

Tomb of Sultan — A8

Designs: 3 l, Custom house. 5 l, Cowry shells. 6 l, Old royal palace. 10 l, Road to Minaret, Juma Mosque, Male. 15 l, Council house. 25 l, Government secretariat. 50 l, Prime minister's office. 1r, Tomb and sailboats. 5r, Tomb by the sea. 10r, Port.

1960, Oct. 15 *Perf. 11½x11*

Various Frames

58	A8	2 l lilac	.25	.25
59	A8	3 l green	.25	.25
60	A8	5 l brown orange	3.50	3.50
61	A8	6 l bright blue	.25	.25
62	A8	10 l carmine rose	.25	.25
63	A8	15 l sepia	.25	.25
64	A8	25 l dull violet	.25	.25
65	A8	50 l slate	.25	.25
66	A8	1r orange	.25	.25
67	A8	5r dark blue	8.00	.55
68	A8	10r dull green	12.50	2.10
		Nos. 58-68 (11)	26.00	8.15

Stamps in 25r, 50r and 100r denominations were also issued, but primarily for revenue purposes. Value for the three stamps, $350.

Coconuts — A9

Map of Male Showing Population Distribution A10

Perf. 14x14½, 14½x14

1961, Apr. 20 Photo. Unwmk.

Coconuts in Ocher

69	A9	2 l green	.25	.25
70	A9	3 l ultramarine	.25	.25
71	A9	5 l lilac rose	.25	.25
72	A9	10 l red orange	.25	.25
73	A9	15 l black	.25	.25
74	A10	25 l multicolored	.25	.25
75	A10	50 l multicolored	.25	.25
76	A10	1r multicolored	.50	.70
		Nos. 69-76 (8)	2.25	2.45

Pigeon and 5c Stamp of 1906 A11

Designs: 10 l, 15 l, 20 l, Post horn and 3c stamp of 1906. 25 l, 50 l, 1r, Laurel branch and 2c stamp of 1906.

1961, Sept. 9 *Perf. 14½x14*

77	A11	2 l violet blue & mar	.25	.25
78	A11	3 l violet blue & mar	.25	.25
79	A11	5 l violet blue & mar	.25	.25
80	A11	6 l violet blue & mar	.25	.25
81	A11	10 l maroon & green	.25	.25
82	A11	15 l maroon & green	.25	.25
83	A11	20 l maroon & green	.25	.25
84	A11	25 l green, mar & blk	.25	.25
85	A11	50 l green, mar & blk	.25	.25
86	A11	1r green, mar & blk	.35	.35
a.		Souvenir sheet of 4	2.40	3.00
		Nos. 77-86 (10)	2.60	2.60

55th anniv. of the 1st postage stamps of the Maldive Islands.

No. 86a contains 4 No. 86, with simulated perforations.

Malaria Eradication Emblem — A12

1962, Apr. 7 Engr. *Perf. 13½x13*

87	A12	2 l orange brown	.25	.25
88	A12	3 l green	.25	.25
89	A12	5 l blue	.25	.25
90	A12	10 l vermilion	.25	.25
91	A12	15 l black	.25	.25
92	A12	25 l dark blue	.25	.25
93	A12	50 l green	.25	.35
94	A12	1r purple	.35	.45
		Nos. 87-94 (8)	2.10	2.30

WHO drive to eradicate malaria.

Children and Map of Far East and Americas A13

UNICEF, 15th Anniv.: 25 l, 50 l, 1r, 5r, Children and Map of Africa, Europe and Asia.

Perf. 14½x14

1962, Sept. 9 Photo. Unwmk.

Children in Multicolor

95	A13	2 l sepia	.25	.25
96	A13	6 l violet	.25	.25
97	A13	10 l dark green	.25	.25
98	A13	15 l ultramarine	.25	.25
99	A13	25 l blue	.25	.25
100	A13	50 l bright green	.25	.25
101	A13	1r rose claret	.25	.25
102	A13	5r emerald	.50	.90
		Nos. 95-102 (8)	2.25	2.65

Sultan Mohamed Farid Didi — A14

1962, Nov. 29 *Perf. 14x14½*

Portrait in Orange Brown and Sepia

103	A14	3 l bluish green	.25	.25
104	A14	5 l slate	.25	.25
105	A14	10 l blue	.35	.35
106	A14	20 l olive	.35	.35
107	A14	50 l dk carmine rose	.35	.35
108	A14	1r dark purple	.45	.45
		Nos. 103-108 (6)	2.00	2.00

9th anniv. of the enthronement of Sultan Mohamed Farid Didi.

Regal Angelfish, Sultan's Crest and Skin Diver — A15

Tropical Fish: 10 l, 25 l, Moorish idol. 50 l, Diadem squirrelfish. 1r, Surgeonfish. 5r, Orange butterflyfish.

1963, Feb. 2 *Perf. 13½*

109	A15	2 l multicolored	.25	.25
110	A15	3 l multicolored	.25	.25
111	A15	5 l multicolored	.25	.25
112	A15	10 l multicolored	.35	.35
113	A15	25 l multicolored	.75	.75
114	A15	50 l multicolored	1.25	.70
115	A15	1r multicolored	1.50	.75
116	A15	5r multicolored	6.00	6.00
		Nos. 109-116 (8)	10.60	9.30

Fish in Net — A16

Design: 5 l, 10 l, 50 l, Wheat emblem and hand holding rice, vert.

1963, Mar. 21 **Photo.** *Perf. 12*

117	A16	2 l green & lt brown	.35	.35
118	A16	5 l dull rose & lt brn	.55	.55
119	A16	7 l grnsh blue & lt brn	.75	.75
120	A16	10 l blue & lt brown	.85	.85
121	A16	25 l brn red & lt brn	2.75	2.75
122	A16	50 l violet & lt brown	4.00	4.00
123	A16	1r rose cl & lt brn	6.50	6.50
		Nos. 117-123 (7)	15.75	15.75

FAO "Freedom from Hunger" campaign.

Centenary Emblem A17

1963, Oct. **Unwmk.** *Perf. 14x14½*

124	A17	2 l dull purple & red	.25	.25
125	A17	15 l slate green & red	.90	.90
126	A17	50 l brown & red	1.60	1.60
127	A17	1r dk blue & red	2.25	1.75
128	A17	4r dk ol grn & red	4.50	4.50
		Nos. 124-128 (5)	9.50	9.00

Centenary of the International Red Cross.

Scout Emblem and Knot — A18

1963, Dec. 7 **Unwmk.** *Perf. 13½*

129	A18	2 l purple & dp green	.25	.25
130	A18	3 l brown & dp green	.25	.25
131	A18	25 l dk blue & dp green	.25	.25
132	A18	1r dp car & dp grn	.50	.50
		Nos. 129-132 (4)	1.25	1.25

11th Boy Scout Jamboree, Marathon, Aug. 1963. Printed in sheets of 12 (3x4) with ornamental borders and inscriptions.

Mosque at Male — A19

Wmk. 314

1964, Aug. 10 **Engr.** *Perf. 11½*

133	A19	2 l rose violet	.25	.25
134	A19	3 l green	.25	.25
135	A19	10 l carmine rose	.25	.25
136	A19	40 l black brown	.30	.30
137	A19	60 l blue	.45	.45
138	A19	85 l orange brown	.60	.60
		Nos. 133-138 (6)	2.10	2.10

Conversion of the Maldive Islanders to Mohammedanism in 1733 (1153 by Islamic calendar).

Shot Put and Maldive Arms A20

15 l, 25 l, 50 l, 1r, Runner, Maldive arms.

Perf. 14x13½

1964, Oct. 6 **Litho.** **Wmk. 314**

139	A20	2 l grnsh bl & dull vio	.25	.25
140	A20	3 l red brn & maroon	.25	.25
141	A20	5 l dk green & gray	.25	.25
142	A20	10 l plum & indigo	.25	.25
143	A20	15 l bis brn & dk brn	.30	.30
144	A20	25 l dk bl & bluish blk	.55	.40
145	A20	50 l olive & black	.85	.45
146	A20	1r gray & dk purple	1.25	.75
a.		Souvenir sheet of 3	2.50	4.00
		Nos. 139-146 (8)	3.95	2.90

18th Olympic Games, Tokyo, Oct. 10-25. No. 146a contains 3 imperf. stamps similar to Nos. 144-146.

General Electric Observation Communication Satellite — A21

Perf. 14½

1965, July 1 **Photo.** **Unwmk.**

147	A21	5 l dark blue	.25	.25
148	A21	10 l brown	.25	.25
149	A21	25 l green	.50	.50
150	A21	1r magenta	1.00	1.00
		Nos. 147-150 (4)	2.00	2.00

Quiet Sun Year, 1964-65. Printed in sheets of 9 (3x3) with ornamental borders and inscriptions.

Queen Nefertari Holding Sistrum and Papyrus — A22

Designs: 3 l, 10 l, 25 l, 1r, Ramses II.

1965, Sept. 1 **Litho.** **Wmk. 314**

151	A22	2 l dull bl grn & mar	.25	.25
152	A22	3 l lake & green	.25	.25
153	A22	5 l green & lake	.25	.25
154	A22	10 l dk blue & ocher	.30	.25
155	A22	15 l redsh brn & ind	.55	.25
156	A22	25 l dull lil & indigo	.80	.25
157	A22	50 l green & brown	1.00	.40
158	A22	1r brown & green	1.40	.50
		Nos. 151-158 (8)	4.80	2.40

UNESCO world campaign to save historic monuments in Nubia.

John F. Kennedy and Doves A23

Design: 1r, 2r, President Kennedy and hands holding olive branches.

Unwmk.

1965, Oct. 1 **Photo.** *Perf. 12*

159	A23	2 l slate & brt pink	.25	.25
160	A23	5 l brown & brt pink	.25	.25
161	A23	25 l blue blk & brt pink	.25	.25
162	A23	1r red lil, yel & grn	.25	.25
163	A23	2r sl green, yel & grn	.45	.45
a.		Souvenir sheet of 4	2.75	3.25
		Nos. 159-163 (5)	1.45	1.45

No. 163a contains 4 imperf. stamps similar to No. 163.

UN Flag — A24

1965, Nov. 24 **Photo.** *Perf. 12*

Flag in Aquamarine

164	A24	3 l red brown	.25	.25
165	A24	10 l violet	.30	.25
166	A24	1r dark olive brown	.90	.35
		Nos. 164-166 (3)	1.45	.85

20th anniversary of the United Nations.

ICY Emblem A25

1965, Dec. 20 **Photo.** *Perf. 12*

167	A25	5 l bister & dk brn	.25	.25
168	A25	15 l dull vio & dk brn	.35	.25
169	A25	50 l olive & dk brn	.75	.30
170	A25	1r orange & dk brn	1.40	1.40
171	A25	2r blue & dk brn	1.75	3.50
a.		Souvenir sheet of 3	6.50	6.50
		Nos. 167-171 (5)	4.50	5.70

Intl. Cooperation Year. No. 171a contains three imperf. stamps with simulated perforation similar to Nos. 169-171.

Sea Shells A26

A27

Coat of Arms and: 2 l, 10 l, 30 l, No. 181, Conus alicus and cymatium maldiviensis (shells). 5 l, 10r, Conus litteratus and distorsia reticulata (shells). 7 l, No. 182, 2r, India-rubber vine flowers. 15 l, 50 l, 5r, Crab plover and gull. 3 l, 20 l, 1.50r, Reinwardtia trigynia.

1966, June 1 **Unwmk.** *Perf. 12*

172	A26	2 l multicolored	.25	1.10
173	A27	3 l multicolored	.25	1.10
174	A26	5 l multicolored	.25	.25
175	A27	7 l multicolored	.25	.25
176	A26	10 l multicolored	.85	.25
177	A26	15 l multicolored	3.25	.30
178	A27	20 l multicolored	.70	.30
179	A26	30 l multicolored	2.40	.35
180	A26	50 l multicolored	5.25	.50
181	A26	1r multicolored	3.50	.60
182	A27	1r multicolored	3.50	.60
183	A27	1.50r multicolored	3.25	3.25
184	A27	2r multicolored	4.50	3.75
185	A26	5r multicolored	20.00	15.00
186	A26	10r multicolored	20.00	20.00
		Nos. 172-186 (15)	68.20	47.60

Flag A28

1966, July 26 *Perf. 14x14½*

187	A28	10 l grnsh blue, red & grn	3.25	.65
188	A28	1r ocher, brn, red & grn	7.00	1.50

1st anniv. of full independence from Great Britain.

Luna 9 on Moon — A29

Designs: 25 l, 1r, 5r, Gemini 6 and 7, rendezvous in space. 2r, Gemini spaceship as seen from second Gemini spaceship.

1966, Nov. 1 **Litho.** *Perf. 15x14*

189	A29	10 l gray bl, lt brn & ultramarine	.25	.25
190	A29	25 l car rose & green	.30	.25
191	A29	50 l green & dp org	.55	.25
192	A29	1r org brn & grnsh bl	.90	.40
193	A29	2r violet & green	1.20	.60
194	A29	5r Prus blue & pink	1.75	1.60
a.		Souvenir sheet of 3	6.75	6.25
		Nos. 189-194 (6)	4.95	3.35

Rendezvous in space of Gemini 6 and 7 (US), Dec. 4, 1965, and the soft landing on Moon by Luna 9 (USSR), Feb. 3, 1966. No. 194a contains 3 imperf. stamps similar to Nos. 192-194 with simulated perforations.

UNESCO Emblem, Owl and Book — A30

20th anniv. of UNESCO: 3 l, 1r, Microscope, globe and communication waves. 5 l, 5r, Palette, violin and mask.

1966, Nov. 15 **Litho.** *Perf. 15x14*

195	A30	2 l green & multi	.40	.40
196	A30	3 l lt violet & multi	.40	.40
197	A30	5 l orange & multi	.75	.40
198	A30	50 l rose & multi	7.00	.75
199	A30	1r citron & multi	8.00	1.25
200	A30	5r multicolored	22.00	20.00
		Nos. 195-200 (6)	38.55	23.20

Winston Churchill and Coffin on Gun Carriage — A31

10 l, 25 l, 1r, Churchill and catafalque.

1967, Jan. 1 *Perf. 14½x13½*

201	A31	2 l ol grn, red & dk blue	.40	.45
202	A31	10 l Prus grn, red & dk blue	2.75	.35
203	A31	15 l grn, red & dk bl	3.50	.35
204	A31	25 l vio, red & dk bl	5.00	.40
205	A31	1r brn, red & dk bl	13.00	1.25
206	A31	2.50r brn lake, red & dk blue	30.00	17.50
		Nos. 201-206 (6)	54.65	20.30

Sir Winston Spencer Churchill (1874-1965), statesman and World War II leader.

Soccer and Jules Rimet Cup — A32

Designs: 3 l, 5 l, 25 l, 50 l, 1r, Various scenes from soccer and Jules Rimet Cup. 2r, British flag, Games' emblem and Big Ben Tower, London.

Perf. 14x13½

1967, Mar. 22 Photo. Unwmk.

207 A32 2 l ver & multi .35 .55
208 A32 3 l olive & multi .35 .55
209 A32 5 l brt purple & multi .35 .55
210 A32 25 l brt green & multi 1.25 .35
211 A32 50 l orange & multi 1.90 .35
212 A32 1r brt blue & multi 3.25 .75
213 A32 2r brown & multi 5.75 3.75
a. Souvenir sheet of 3 13.50 12.50
Nos. 207-213 (7) 13.20 6.85

England's victory in the World Soccer Cup Championship. No. 213a contains 3 imperf. stamps similar to Nos. 211-213.

Clown Butterflyfish — A33

Tropical Fish: 3 l, 1r, Four-saddled puffer. 5 l, Indo-Pacific blue trunkfish. 6 l, Striped triggerfish. 50 l, 2r, Blue angelfish.

1967, May 1 Photo. *Perf. 14*

214 A33 2 l brt violet & multi .30 .45
215 A33 3 l emerald & multi .30 .45
216 A33 5 l org brn & multi .30 .25
217 A33 6 l brt blue & multi .30 .25
218 A33 50 l olive & multi 3.50 .40
219 A33 1r rose red & multi 6.50 .80
220 A33 2r orange & multi 12.00 9.00
Nos. 214-220 (7) 23.20 11.60

Plane at Hulule Airport — A34

Designs: 5 l, 15 l, 50 l, 10r, Plane over administration building, Hulule Airport.

1967, July 26 *Perf. 14x13½*

221 A34 2 l citron & lil .25 .40
222 A34 5 l violet & green .45 .25
223 A34 10 l lt green & lilac .55 .25
224 A34 15 l yel bister & grn .90 .25
225 A34 30 l sky blue & vio bl 1.60 .25
226 A34 50 l brt pink & brn 2.25 .30
227 A34 5r org & vio blue 5.50 5.00
228 A34 10r lt ultra & dp brn 7.25 8.50
Nos. 221-228 (8) 18.75 15.20

For overprints see Nos. 235-242.
Higher denominations, primarily for revenue use, also were issued.

Man and Music Pavilion and EXPO '67 Emblem — A35

Designs: 5 l, 50 l, 2r, Man and his Community Pavilion and EXPO '67 emblem.

Perf. 14x13½

1967, Oct. 1 Photo. Unwmk.

EXPO '67 Emblem in Gold

229 A35 2 l ol gray, ol & brt rose .25 .25
230 A35 5 l ultra, grnsh blue & brn .25 .25
231 A35 10 l brn red, lt grn & red org .25 .25
232 A35 50 l brn, grnsh blue & org .45 .25
233 A35 1r vio, grn & rose lil .85 .45
234 A35 2r dk grn, emer & red brn 1.75 1.10
a. Souvenir sheet of 2 5.25 5.25
Nos. 229-234 (6) 3.80 2.55

EXPO '67 Intl. Exhibition, Montreal, Apr. 28-Oct. 27. No. 234a contains 2 imperf. stamps similar to Nos. 233-234 with simulated perforations.

Nos. 221-228 Overprinted in Gold: "International Tourist Year 1967"

1967, Dec. 1 Photo. *Perf. 14x13½*

235 A34 2 l citron & lilac .30 .35
236 A34 5 l violet & green .30 .30
237 A34 10 l lt green & lilac .30 .30
238 A34 15 l yel bister & grn .30 .30
239 A34 30 l sky blue & vio bl .35 .30
240 A34 50 l brt pink & brn .65 .35
241 A34 5r org & vio blue 4.00 4.00
242 A34 10r lt ultra & dp brn 5.50 5.50
Nos. 235-242 (8) 11.70 11.40

The overprint is in 3 lines on the 2 l, 10 l, 30 l, 5r; one line on the 5 l, 15 l, 50 l, 10r.

Lord Baden-Powell, Wolf Cubs, Campfire and Flag Signals — A36

Boy Scouts: 3 l, 1r, Lord Baden-Powell, Boy Scout saluting and drummer.

1968, Jan. 1 Litho. *Perf. 14x14½*

243 A36 2 l yel, brown & green .25 .25
244 A36 3 l lt bl, ultra & rose car .25 .25
245 A36 25 l dp org, red brn & vio blue 1.60 .40
246 A36 1r yel grn, grn & red brn 3.50 1.60
Nos. 243-246 (4) 5.60 2.50

Sheets of 12 (4x3) with decorative border.
For overprints see Nos. 278-281.

French Satellites D-1 and A-1 — A37

3 l, 25 l, Luna 10, USSR. 7 l, 1r, Orbiter & Mariner, US. 10 l, 2r, Edward White, Virgil Grissom & Roger Chaffee, US. 5r, Astronaut V. M. Komarov, USSR.

1968, Jan. 27 Photo. *Perf. 14*

247 A37 2 l dp ultra & brt pink .25 .25
248 A37 3 l dk ol bis & vio .25 .25
249 A37 7 l rose car & ol .30 .25
250 A37 10 l blk, gray & dk bl .30 .25
251 A37 25 l purple & brt grn .30 .25
252 A37 50 l brown org & blue .50 .25
253 A37 1r dk sl grn & vio brn 1.10 .30
254 A37 2r blk, bl & dk brn 1.75 1.00
a. Souvenir sheet of 2 5.25 5.75
255 A37 5r blk, tan & lil rose 4.25 2.50
Nos. 247-255 (9) 9.00 5.30

International achievements in space and to honor American and Russian astronauts, who gave their lives during space explorations in 1967. No. 254a contains 2 imperf. stamps similar to Nos. 253-254.

Shot Put — A38

Design: 6 l, 15 l, 2.50r, Discus.

1968, Feb. Litho. *Perf. 14½*

256 A38 2 l emerald & multi .25 .25
257 A38 6 l dull yel & multi .25 .25
258 A38 10 l multicolored .25 .25
259 A38 15 l orange & multi .25 .25
260 A38 1r blue & multi .60 .30
261 A38 2.50r rose & multi 1.40 1.40
Nos. 256-261 (6) 3.00 2.70

19th Olympic Games, Mexico City, 10/12-27.

View of the Lagoon Near Venice, by Richard P. Bonington — A39

Seascapes: 1r, Ulysses Deriding Polyphemus (detail), by Joseph M. W. Turner. 2r, Sailboat at Argenteuil, by Claude Monet. 5r, Fishing Boats at Saintes-Maries, by Vincent Van Gogh.

1968, Apr. 1 Photo. *Perf. 14*

262 A39 50 l ultra & multi 1.10 .30
263 A39 1r dk green & multi 1.60 .40
264 A39 2r multicolored 2.75 1.75
265 A39 5r multicolored 7.50 4.50
Nos. 262-265 (4) 12.95 6.95

Montgolfier Balloon, 1783, and Zeppelin LZ-130, 1928 — A40

History of Aviation: 3 l, 1r, Douglas DC-3, 1933, and Boeing 707, 1958. 5 l, 50 l, Lilienthal's glider, 1892, and Wright brothers' plane, 1905. 7 l, 2r, British-French Concorde and Supersonic Boeing 733, 1968.

1968, June 1 Photo. *Perf. 14x13*

266 A40 2 l yel grn, ultra & bis brn .25 .35
267 A40 3 l org brn, greenish bl & lil .25 .35
268 A40 5 l grnsh bl, sl grn & lilac .30 .25
269 A40 7 l org, cl & ultra 1.10 .50
270 A40 10 l rose lil, bl & brn .65 .30
271 A40 50 l ol, sl grn & mag 2.10 .35
272 A40 1r ver, blue & emer 3.50 .75
273 A40 2r ultra, ol & brn vio 17.50 11.00
Nos. 266-273 (8) 25.65 13.85

Issued in sheets of 12.

WHO Headquarters, Geneva — A41

1968, July 15 Litho. *Perf. 14½x13*

274 A41 10 l grnsh bl, bl grn & vio 1.00 .25
275 A41 25 l org, ocher & green 1.50 .25
276 A41 1r emer, brt grn & brown 4.00 .70
277 A41 2r rose lil, dp rose lil & dk blue 6.50 4.75
Nos. 274-277 (4) 13.00 5.95

20th anniv. of WHO.

Nos. 243-246 Overprinted "International / Boy Scout Jamboree, / Farragut Park, Idaho, / U.S.A. / August 1-9, 1967"

1968, Aug. 1 *Perf. 14x14½*

278 A36 2 l multicolored .25 .45
279 A36 3 l multicolored .25 .45
280 A36 25 l multicolored 1.50 .45
281 A36 1r multicolored 4.50 1.90
Nos. 278-281 (4) 6.50 3.25

1st anniv. of the Intl. Boy Scout Jamboree in Farragut State Park, ID.

Marine Snail Shells — A42

2 l, 50 l, Common curlew & redshank. 1r, Angel wings (clam shell) & marine snail shell.

1968, Sept. 24 Photo. *Perf. 14x13*

282 A42 2 l ultra & multi .45 .70
283 A42 10 l brown & multi 1.10 .30
284 A42 25 l multicolored 1.60 .30
285 A42 50 l multicolored 8.25 1.25
286 A42 1r multicolored 4.00 1.25
287 A42 2r multicolored 5.00 6.00
Nos. 282-287 (6) 20.40 9.80

Discus A43

50 l, Runner. 1r, Bicycling. 2r, Basketball.

1968, Oct. 12 *Perf. 14*

288 A43 10 l ultra & multi .30 .35
289 A43 50 l multicolored .55 .35
290 A43 1r plum & multi 3.00 .60
291 A43 2r violet & multi 3.50 2.25
Nos. 288-291 (4) 7.35 3.55

19th Olympic Games, Mexico City, 10/12-27.
For overprints see Nos. 302-303.

Republic

Dhow A44

Republic Day: 1r, Coat of arms, map and flag of Maldive Islands.

Perf. 14x14½

1968, Nov. 11 Unwmk.

292 A44 10 l yel grn, ultra & dk brn 1.50 .35
293 A44 1r ultra, red & emerald 3.50 1.10

The Thinker, by Auguste Rodin — A45

Rodin Sculptures and UNESCO Emblem: 10 l, Hands. 1.50r, Sister and Brother. 2.50r, The Prodigal Son.

1969, Apr. 10 Photo. *Perf. 13½*

294 A45 6 l emerald & multi .40 .40
295 A45 10 l multicolored .45 .45
296 A45 1.50r brt blue & multi 2.00 2.00
297 A45 2.50r multicolored 2.75 2.75
a. Souvenir sheet of 2 8.50 8.50
Nos. 294-297 (4) 5.60 5.60

Intl. Human Rights Year and honoring UNESCO.

No. 297a contains 2 imperf. stamps similar to Nos. 296-297.

Astronaut Gathering Rock Samples on Moon A46

Designs: 6 l, Lunar landing module. 1.50r, Astronaut on steps of module. 2.50r, Astronaut with television camera.

1969, Sept. 25 Litho. *Perf. 14*

298 A46 6 l multicolored .45 .25
299 A46 10 l multicolored .45 .25
300 A46 1.50r multicolored 1.75 1.40
301 A46 2.50r multicolored 2.50 2.25
a. Souvenir sheet of 4 3.75 3.75
Nos. 298-301 (4) 5.15 4.15

Man's 1st moon landing. See note after US No. C76.

Exist imperf.

No. 301a contains stamps similar to Nos. 298-301, with designs transposed on 10 l and 2.50r. Simulated perfs.

For overprints see Nos. 343-345.

Nos. 289-290 Overprinted: "REPUBLIC OF MALDIVES" and Commemorative Inscriptions

Designs: 50 l, overprinted "Gold Medal Winner / Mohamed Gammoudi / 5000m. run / Tunisia." 1r, overprinted "Gold Medal Winner / P. Trentin—Cycling / France."

1969, Dec. 10 Photo. *Perf. 14*

302 A43 50 l multicolored .50 .60
303 A43 1r multicolored 1.25 1.10

Columbia Daumon Victoria, 1899 — A47

Automobiles (pre-1908): 5 l, 50 l, Duryea Phaeton, 1902. 7 l, 1r, Packard S.24, 1906. 10 l, 2r, Autocar Runabout, 1907. 25 l, like 2 l.

1970, Feb. 1 Litho. *Perf. 12*

304 A47 2 l multicolored .25 .25
305 A47 5 l brt pink & multi .25 .25
306 A47 7 l ultra & multi .30 .25
307 A47 10 l ver & multi .35 .25
308 A47 25 l ocher & multi .90 .30
309 A47 50 l olive & multi 1.75 .40
310 A47 1r orange & multi 3.00 .70
311 A47 2r multicolored 4.00 4.50
a. Souvenir sheet of 2, #310-311, perf. 11½ 6.50 6.50
Nos. 304-311 (8) 10.80 6.90

Exist imperf.

Orange Butterflyfish — A48

Fish: 5 l, Spotted triggerfish. 25 l, Spotfin turkeyfish. 50 l, Forceps fish. 1r, Imperial angelfish. 2r, Regal angelfish.

1970, Mar. 1 Litho. *Perf. 10½*

312 A48 2 l blue & multi .35 .60
313 A48 5 l orange & multi .55 .60
314 A48 25 l emerald & multi 1.40 .60
315 A48 50 l brt pink & multi 2.10 .95
316 A48 1r lt vio bl & multi 2.75 1.40
317 A48 2r olive & multi 4.50 4.00
Nos. 312-317 (6) 11.65 8.15

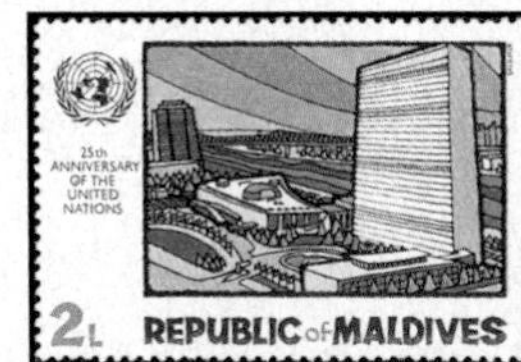

UN Headquarters, New York and UN Emblem — A49

25th anniv. of the UN: 10 l, Surgeons, nurse and WHO emblem. 25 l, Student, performer, musician and UNESCO emblem. 50 l, Children reading and playing, and UNICEF emblem. 1r, Lamb, cock, fish, grain and FAO emblem. 2r, Miner and ILO emblem.

1970, June 26 Litho. *Perf. 13½*

318 A49 2 l multicolored .25 .25
319 A49 10 l multicolored .75 .25
320 A49 25 l multicolored 1.60 .25
321 A49 50 l multicolored 1.90 .30
322 A49 1r multicolored 2.25 .75
323 A49 2r multicolored 4.50 2.00
Nos. 318-323 (6) 11.25 3.80

IMCO Emblem, Buoy and Ship — A50

Design: 1r, Lighthouse and ship.

1970, July 26 Litho. *Perf. 13½*

324 A50 50 l multicolored .60 .35
325 A50 1r multicolored 4.00 .90

10th anniv. of the Intergovernmental Maritime Consultative Organization (IMCO).

EXPO Emblem and Australian Pavilion — A51

EXPO Emblem and: 3 l, West German pavilion. 10 l, US pavilion. 25 l, British pavilion. 50 l, Russian pavilion. 1r, Japanese pavilion.

1970, Aug. 1 *Perf. 13½x14*

326 A51 2 l green & multi .25 .25
327 A51 3 l violet & multi .25 .25
328 A51 10 l brown & multi .50 .25
329 A51 25 l multicolored .95 .25
330 A51 50 l claret & multi 1.25 .35
331 A51 1r ultra & multi 1.90 .70
Nos. 326-331 (6) 5.10 2.05

EXPO '70 International Exhibition, Osaka, Japan, Mar. 15-Sept. 13, 1970.

Guitar Player, by Watteau — A52

Paintings: 7 l, Guitar Player in Spanish Costume, by Edouard Manet. 50 l, Guitar-playing Clown, by Antoine Watteau. 1r, Mandolin Player and Singers, by Lorenzo Costa (inscribed Ercole Roberti). 2.50r, Guitar Player and Lady, by Watteau. 5r, Mandolin Player, by Frans Hals.

1970, Aug. 1 Litho. *Perf. 14*

332 A52 3 l gray & multi .25 .25
333 A52 7 l yellow & multi .25 .25
334 A52 50 l multicolored .45 .45
335 A52 1r multicolored .85 .85
336 A52 2.50r multicolored 2.10 2.10
337 A52 5r multicolored 3.50 3.50
a. Souvenir sheet of 2 8.00 8.00
Nos. 332-337 (6) 7.40 7.40

No. 337a contains 2 stamps similar to Nos. 336-337 but rouletted 13 and printed se-tenant.

Education Year Emblem and Adult Education — A53

Education Year Emblem and: 10 l, Teacher training. 25 l, Geography class. 50 l, Classroom. 1r, Instruction by television.

1970, Sept. 7 Litho. *Perf. 14*

338 A53 5 l multicolored .45 .25
339 A53 10 l multicolored .45 .25
340 A53 25 l multicolored .75 .25
341 A53 50 l multicolored 1.00 .40
342 A53 1r multicolored 2.50 .80
Nos. 338-342 (5) 5.15 1.95

Issued for International Education Year.

Nos. 299-301 Overprinted in Silver: "Philympia / London 1970"

1970, Sept. 18

343 A46 10 l multicolored .30 .30
344 A46 1.50r multicolored .85 .85
345 A46 2.50r multicolored 1.25 1.25
Nos. 343-345 (3) 2.40 2.40

Issued to commemorate Philympia 1970, London Philatelic Exhibition, Sept. 18-26.

This overprint was also applied to No. 301a. Value $9.

Soccer Play, Rimet Cup — A54

Various Soccer Scenes, and Rimet Cup.

1970 Litho. *Perf. 13½*

346 A54 3 l emerald & multi .25 .25
347 A54 6 l rose lilac & multi .30 .25
348 A54 7 l dp orange & multi .30 .25
349 A54 25 l blue & multi 1.00 .25
350 A54 1r olive & multi 3.50 1.00
Nos. 346-350 (5) 5.35 2.00

Jules Rimet 9th World Soccer Championships, Mexico City, May 30-June 21.

Boy Holding UNICEF Flag — A55

UNICEF, 25th. Anniv.: 10 l, 2r, Girl holding balloon with UNICEF emblem.

1971, Apr. 1 Litho. *Perf. 12*

351 A55 5 l pink & multi .25 .25
352 A55 10 l lt blue & multi .25 .25
353 A55 1r yellow & multi 1.75 .70
354 A55 2r pale lilac & multi 3.00 2.00
Nos. 351-354 (4) 5.25 3.20

Astronauts Swigert, Lovell and Haise — A56

Safe return of Apollo 13: 20 l, Spacecraft and landing module. 1r, Capsule and boat in Pacific Ocean.

1971, Apr. 27 *Perf. 14*

355 A56 5 l dull purple & multi .25 .25
356 A56 20 l multicolored .50 .25
357 A56 1r brt blue & multi 1.10 .70
Nos. 355-357 (3) 1.85 1.20

Flowers Symbolizing Races and World — A57

1971, May 3

358 A57 10 l multicolored .30 .30
359 A57 25 l gray & multi .35 .30

Intl. year against racial discrimination.

Mother and Child, by Auguste Renoir A58

Mother and Child Paintings by: 7 l, Rembrandt. 10 l, Titian. 20 l, Degas. 25 l, Berthe Morisot. 1r, Rubens. 3r, Renoir.

1971, Sept. Litho. *Perf. 12*

360 A58 5 l multicolored .25 .25
361 A58 7 l multicolored .25 .25
362 A58 10 l multicolored .35 .25

363 A58 20 l multicolored .90 .25
364 A58 25 l multicolored 1.00 .25
365 A58 1r multicolored 3.00 .70
366 A58 3r multicolored 5.50 4.00
Nos. 360-366 (7) 11.25 5.95

Capt. Alan B. Shepard, Jr. — A59

10 l, Maj. Stuart A. Roosa. 1.50r, Com. Edgar D. Mitchell. 5r, Apollo 14 shoulder patch.

1971, Nov. 11 Photo. *Perf. 12½*
367 A59 6 l dp green & multi .40 .30
368 A59 10 l claret & multi .50 .30
369 A59 1.50r ultra & multi 3.50 3.25
370 A59 5r multicolored 10.00 7.50
Nos. 367-370 (4) 14.40 11.35

Apollo 14 US moon landing mission, 1/31-2/9.

Ballerina, by Degas A60

Paintings: 10 l, Dancing Couple, by Auguste Renoir. 2r, Spanish Dancer, by Edouard Manet. 5r, Ballerinas, by Degas. 10r, Moulin Rouge, by Henri Toulouse-Lautrec.

1971, Nov. 19 Litho. *Perf. 14*
371 A60 5 l plum & multi .25 .25
372 A60 10 l green & multi .25 .25
373 A60 2r org brn & multi 2.50 2.10
374 A60 5r dk blue & multi 4.25 3.50
375 A60 10r multicolored 6.50 5.50
Nos. 371-375 (5) 13.75 11.60

Nos. 371-375 Overprinted Vertically: "ROYAL VISIT 1972"

1972, Mar. 13 Litho. *Perf. 14*
376 A60 5 l plum & multi .25 .25
377 A60 10 l green & multi .25 .25
378 A60 2r org brn & multi 3.75 3.00
379 A60 5r dk blue & multi 6.75 6.75
380 A60 10r multicolored 7.50 7.50
Nos. 376-380 (5) 18.50 17.75

Visit of Elizabeth II and Prince Philip.

Book Year Emblem A61

1972, May 1 *Perf. 13x13½*
381 A61 25 l orange & multi .30 .25
382 A61 5r multicolored 1.90 1.75

International Book Year.

National Costume of Scotland A62

National Costumes: 15 l, Netherlands. 25 l, Norway. 50 l, Hungary. 1r, Austria. 2r, Spain.

1972, May 15 *Perf. 12*
383 A62 10 l gray & multi .60 .25
384 A62 15 l lt brown & multi .70 .25
385 A62 25 l multicolored 1.00 .25
386 A62 50 l lt brown & multi 2.00 .45
387 A62 1r gray & multi 2.50 .75
388 A62 2r lt olive & multi 4.50 3.00
Nos. 383-388 (6) 11.30 4.95

Stegosaurus — A63

Designs: Prehistoric reptiles.

1972, May 31 *Perf. 14*
389 A63 2 l shown .25 .50
390 A63 7 l Edaphosaurus .25 .45
391 A63 25 l Diplodocus .45 .45
392 A63 50 l Triceratops 1.00 .75
393 A63 2r Pteranodon 3.75 2.00
394 A63 5r Tyrannosaurus 15.00 9.50
Nos. 389-394 (6) 20.70 13.65

Set exists imperf.

A souvenir sheet has two stamps similar to Nos. 393-394 with simulated perforations. It was not regularly issued. Value, $50.

Sapporo '72 Emblem, Cross Country Skiing A64

1972, June Litho. *Perf. 14*
395 A64 3 l shown .25 .25
396 A64 6 l Bobsledding .25 .25
397 A64 15 l Speed skating .25 .25
398 A64 50 l Ski jump .90 .40
399 A64 1r Figure skating 1.50 .50
400 A64 2.50r Ice hockey 5.00 3.00
Nos. 395-400 (6) 8.15 4.65

11th Winter Olympic Games, Sapporo, Japan, Feb. 3-13.
Exists imperf. Value, set $15.

Boy Scout Saluting — A65

Scout: 15 l, with signal flags. 50 l, Bugler. 1r, Drummer.

1972, Aug. 1
401 A65 10 l Prus green & multi .55 .25
402 A65 15 l dk red & multi .80 .25
403 A65 50 l dp green & multi 2.60 1.10
404 A65 1r purple & multi 4.00 1.75
Nos. 401-404 (4) 7.95 3.35

13th International Boy Scout Jamboree, Asagiri Plain, Japan, Aug. 2-11, 1971.
Exists imperf. Value, set $17.50.

Olympic Emblems, Bicycling — A66

1972, Oct. Litho. *Perf. 14½x14*
405 A66 5 l shown .25 .25
406 A66 10 l Running .25 .25
407 A66 25 l Wrestling .25 .25
408 A66 50 l Hurdles, women's .30 .30
409 A66 2r Boxing 1.25 1.10
410 A66 5r Volleyball 3.50 3.00
Nos. 405-410 (6) 5.80 5.15

Souvenir Sheet
Perf. 15

411 Sheet of 2 5.00 5.00
a. A66 3r like 50 l 2.00 2.00
b. A66 4r like 10 l 2.50 2.50

20th Olympic Games, Munich, 8/26-9/11.
Nos. 405-410 exist imperf. Value, set $15.
For overprints see Nos. 417-419.

Globe, Environment Emblem — A67

1972, Nov. 15 Litho. *Perf. 14½*
412 A67 2 l violet & multi .25 .25
413 A67 3 l brown & multi .25 .25
414 A67 15 l blue & multi .30 .30
415 A67 50 l red & multi .70 .60
416 A67 2.50r green & multi 2.75 2.50
Nos. 412-416 (5) 4.25 3.90

UN Conference on Human Environment, Stockholm, June 5-16.
Nos. 412-416 exist imperf.

No. 409 Overprinted

No. 410 Overprinted

No. 411a Overprinted

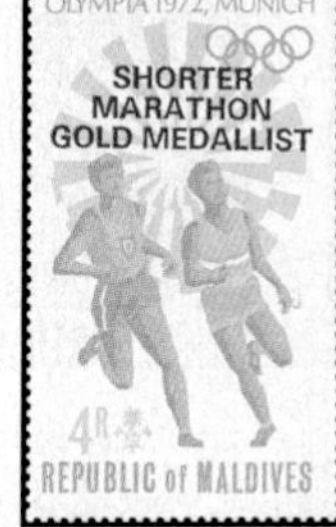

No. 411b Overprinted

1973, Feb. Litho. *Perf. 14½x14*
417 A66(a) 2r multicolored 3.00 1.75
418 A66(b) 5r multicolored 4.50 3.00

Souvenir Sheet

419 Sheet of 2 7.50 7.50
a. A66(c) 3r multicolored 2.75 2.75
b. A66(d) 4r multicolored 3.00 3.00

Gold medal winners in 20th Olympic Games: Viatschesiav Lemechev, USSR, middleweight boxing; Japanese team, volleyball. Annelie Ehrhardt, Germany, 100m. hurdles; Frank Shorter, US, marathon.
No. 419 exists imperf. Value, $20.

Flowers, by Vincent Van Gogh — A68

Paintings of flowers by: 2 l, 3 l, 1r, 5r, Auguste Renoir (each different). 50 l, 2r, Ambrosius Bosschaert. 3r, Van Gogh.

1973, Feb. *Perf. 13½*
420 A68 1 l blue & multi .25 .25
421 A68 2 l tan & multi .25 .25
422 A68 3 l lilac & multi .30 .25
423 A68 50 l ultra & multi .45 .25
424 A68 1r emerald & multi 1.10 .45
425 A68 5r magenta & multi 2.50 4.75
Nos. 420-425 (6) 4.85 6.20

Souvenir Sheet
Perf. 15

426 Sheet of 2 7.50 *7.50*
a. A68 2r black & multi 2.00 *2.25*
b. A68 3r black & multi 2.50 *2.75*

Nos. 420-426 exist imperf.

Scouts Treating Injured Lamb A69

Designs: 2 l, 1r, Lifesaving. 3 l, 5r, Agricultural training. 4 l, 2r, Carpentry. 5 l, Leapfrog.

1973, Aug. Litho. *Perf. 14½*
427 A69 1 l black & multi .25 .25
428 A69 2 l black & multi .25 .25
429 A69 3 l black & multi .25 .25
430 A69 4 l black & multi .25 .25
431 A69 5 l black & multi .25 .25
432 A69 1r black & multi 2.10 .60

433 A69 2r black & multi 4.00 3.75
434 A69 3r black & multi 5.00 5.00
Nos. 427-434 (8) 12.35 10.60

Souvenir Sheet

435 A69 5r black & multi 8.00 *8.00*

24th Boy Scout World Conference (1st in Africa), Nairobi, Kenya, July 16-21.
Exist imperf. Values: set, $25; souvenir sheet, $35.
For overprints see Nos. 571-574.

Herschel's Marlin A70

Fish and Ships: 2 l, 4r, Skipjack tuna. 3 l, Bluefin tuna. 5 l, 2.50r, Dolphinfish. 60 l, 75 l, Red snapper. 1.50r, Yellow crescent tail. 3r, Plectropoma maculatum. 5r, Like 1 l. 10r, Spanish mackerel.

1973, Aug. *Perf. 14½*

Size: 38½x24mm

436 A70 1 l lt green & multi .25 .25
437 A70 2 l dull org & multi .25 .25
438 A70 3 l brt red & multi .25 .25
439 A70 5 l multicolored .25 .25

Size: 28x22mm

440 A70 60 l yellow & multi .30 .30
441 A70 75 l purple & multi .75 .40

Size: 38½x24mm

442 A70 1.50r violet & multi 1.00 .75
443 A70 2.50r blue & multi 1.75 1.50
444 A70 3r multicolored 2.00 2.00
445 A70 10r orange & multi 6.00 5.00
Nos. 436-445 (10) 12.80 10.95

Souvenir Sheet

Perf. 15

446 Sheet of 2 17.50 17.50
a. A70 4r carmine & multi 5.50 5.50
b. A70 5r bright green & multi 6.50 6.50

Nos. 436-445 exist imperf.

Goldenfronted Leafbird — A71

2 l, 3r, Fruit bat. 3 l, 50 l, Indian starred tortoise. 4 l, 5r, Kallima inachus (butterfly).

1973, Oct. **Litho.** *Perf. 14½*

447 A71 1 l brt pink & multi .25 .25
448 A71 2 l brt blue & multi .25 .25
449 A71 3 l ver & multi .25 .25
450 A71 4 l citron & multi .25 .25
451 A71 50 l emerald & multi .40 .40
452 A71 2r lt violet & multi 3.25 3.25
453 A71 3r multicolored 4.50 3.00
Nos. 447-453 (7) 9.15 7.65

Souvenir Sheet

454 A71 5r yellow & multi 17.50 17.50

Lantana Camara — A72

Native Flowers: 2 l, Nerium oleander. 3 l, 2r, Rosa polyantha. 4 l, Hibiscus manihot. 5 l, Bougainvillea glabra. 10 l, 3r, Plumera alba. 50 l, Poinsettia pulcherrima. 5r, Ononis natrix.

1973, Dec. 19 **Litho.** *Perf. 14*

455 A72 1 l ultra & multi .25 .25
456 A72 2 l dp orange & multi .25 .25
457 A72 3 l emerald & multi .25 .25
458 A72 4 l blue grn & multi .25 .25
459 A72 5 l lemon & multi .25 .25
460 A72 10 l lilac & multi .25 .25
461 A72 50 l yel grn & multi .25 .25
462 A72 5r red & multi 2.75 2.75
Nos. 455-462 (8) 4.50 4.50

Souvenir Sheet

463 Sheet of 2 4.50 4.50
a. A72 2r lilac & multi 1.25 1.50
b. A72 3r blue & multi 2.00 2.25

Tiros Weather Satellite A73

Designs: 2 l, 10r, Nimbus satellite. 3 l, 3r, Nomad weather ("weater") station. 4 l, A.P.T. instant weather picture (radar). 5 l, Richard's electrical wind speed recorder. 2r, like 1 l.

1974, Jan. 10 *Perf. 14½*

464 A73 1 l olive & multi .25 .25
465 A73 2 l multicolored .25 .25
466 A73 3 l brt blue & multi .25 .25
467 A73 4 l ocher & multi .25 .25
468 A73 5 l ocher & multi .25 .25
469 A73 2r ultra & multi 2.50 2.25
470 A73 3r orange & multi 3.25 2.75
Nos. 464-470 (7) 7.00 6.25

Souvenir Sheet

471 A73 10r lilac & multi 8.00 8.00

World Meteorological Cooperation, cent.

Apollo Spacecraft, John F. Kennedy — A74

Designs: 2 l, 3r, Mercury spacecraft and John Glenn. 3 l, Vostok 1 and Yuri Gagarin. 4 l, Vostok 6 and Valentina Tereshkova. 5 l, Soyuz 11 and Salyut spacecrafts. 2r, Skylab. 10r, Like 1 l.

1974, Feb. 1 **Litho.** *Perf. 14½*

472 A74 1 l multicolored .25 .25
473 A74 2 l multicolored .25 .25
474 A74 3 l multicolored .25 .25
475 A74 4 l multicolored .25 .25
476 A74 5 l multicolored .25 .25
477 A74 2r multicolored 3.00 2.75
478 A74 3r multicolored 3.75 3.25
Nos. 472-478 (7) 8.00 7.25

Souvenir Sheet

479 A74 10r multicolored 12.00 *12.00*

Space explorations of US and USSR.
Exist imperf. Values: set, $20; souvenir sheet, $70.

Skylab and Copernicus — A75

Copernicus, Various Portraits and: 2 l, 1.50r, Futuristic orbiting station. 3 l, 5r, Futuristic flight station. 4 l, Mariner 2 on flight to Venus. 5 l, Mariner 4 on flight to Mars. 25 l, like 1 l. 10r, Copernicus Orbiting Observatory.

1974, Apr. 10 **Litho.** *Perf. 14½*

480 A75 1 l multicolored .25 .25
481 A75 2 l multicolored .25 .25
482 A75 3 l multicolored .25 .25
483 A75 4 l multicolored .25 .25
484 A75 5 l multicolored .25 .25
485 A75 25 l multicolored .60 .60
486 A75 1.50r multicolored 2.25 2.00
487 A75 5r multicolored 5.75 5.25
Nos. 480-487 (8) 9.85 9.10

Souvenir Sheet

488 A75 10r multicolored 15.00 *15.00*

Exist imperf. Values: set, $17.50; souvenir sheet, $50.

"Motherhood," by Picasso — A76

Picasso Paintings: 2 l, Harlequin and his Companion. 3 l, Pierrot Sitting. 20 l, 2r, Three Musicians. 75 l, L'Aficionada. 3r, 5r, Still life.

1974, May *Perf. 14*

489 A76 1 l multicolored .25 .25
490 A76 2 l multicolored .25 .25
491 A76 3 l multicolored .25 .25
492 A76 20 l multicolored .35 .30
493 A76 75 l multicolored .50 .30
494 A76 5r multicolored 4.75 3.50
Nos. 489-494 (6) 6.35 4.85

Souvenir Sheet

495 Sheet of 2 7.50 7.50
a. A76 2r multicolored 2.10 2.10
b. A76 3r multicolored 3.25 3.25

Pablo Picasso (1881-1973), painter.

UPU Emblem, Old and New Trains A77

UPU Emblem and: 2 l, 2.50r, Old and new ships. 3 l, Zeppelin and jet. 1.50r, Mail coach and truck. 4r, 5r, Like 1 l.

1974, May **Litho.** *Perf. 14½, 13½*

496 A77 1 l lt green & multi .25 .25
497 A77 2 l yellow & multi .25 .25
498 A77 3 l rose & multi .25 .25
499 A77 1.50r yel green & multi .75 .75
500 A77 2.50r blue & multi 1.25 1.25
501 A77 5r ocher & multi 3.50 3.50
Nos. 496-501 (6) 6.25 6.25

Souvenir Sheet

502 A77 4r ver & multi 5.50 5.50

UPU cent. Exist imperf. Values: set, $10; souvenir sheet, $22.50.
Nos. 496-501 were printed in sheets of 50, perf. 14½, and also in sheets of 5 plus label, perf. 13½. The label shows UPU emblem, post horn, globe and carrier pigeon. Value, set of 6 sheets, $30.

Capricorn A78

Designs: Zodiac signs and constellations.

1974, July 3

503 A78 1 l shown .25 .25
504 A78 2 l Aquarius .25 .25
505 A78 3 l Pisces .25 .25
506 A78 4 l Aries .25 .25
507 A78 5 l Taurus .25 .25
508 A78 6 l Gemini .25 .25
509 A78 7 l Cancer .25 .25
510 A78 10 l Leo .30 .30
511 A78 15 l Virgo .30 .30
512 A78 20 l Libra .30 .30
513 A78 25 l Scorpio .30 .30
514 A78 5r Sagittarius 8.50 8.50
Nos. 503-514 (12) 11.45 11.45

Souvenir Sheet

515 A78 10r Sun 22.50 22.50

Stamp size of 10r: 50x37mm.

Soccer and Games' Emblem — A79

Various soccer scenes & games' emblem.

1974, July 31 **Litho.** *Perf. 14½*

516 A79 1 l brown & multi .25 .25
517 A79 2 l green & multi .25 .25
518 A79 3 l ultra & multi .25 .25
519 A79 4 l red & multi .25 .25
520 A79 75 l lt blue & multi .45 .40
521 A79 4r olive & multi 2.00 2.00
522 A79 5r lilac & multi 4.00 2.00
Nos. 516-522 (7) 7.45 5.40

Souvenir Sheet

523 A79 10r rose & multi 8.00 8.00

World Cup Soccer Championship, Munich, June 13-July 7. Exist imperf. Values: set, $14; souvenir sheet, $12.

Churchill and WWII Plane A80

Churchill: 2 l, As pilot. 3 l, First Lord of the Admiralty and battleship. 4 l, 10r, Aircraft carrier. 5 l, RAF fighters. 60 l, Anti-aircraft unit. 75 l, Tank. 5r, Seaplane.

1974, Nov. 30 **Litho.** *Perf. 14½*

524 A80 1 l multicolored .25 .25
525 A80 2 l multicolored .25 .25
526 A80 3 l multicolored .25 .25
527 A80 4 l multicolored .25 .25
528 A80 5 l multicolored .25 .25
529 A80 60 l multicolored 2.40 1.25
530 A80 75 l multicolored 3.00 1.25
531 A80 5r multicolored 11.00 11.00
Nos. 524-531 (8) 17.65 14.75

Souvenir Sheet

532 A80 10r multicolored 17.50 17.50

Sir Winston Churchill (1874-1965). Exist imperf. Values: set, $17.50; souvenir sheet, $20.

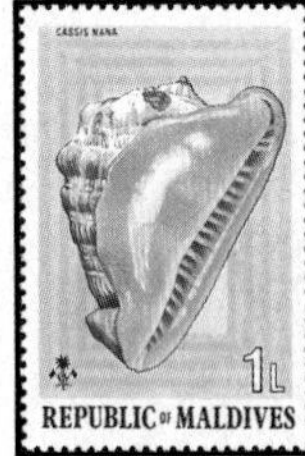

Cassis Nana — A81

Cypraea Diliculum — A82

2 l, Murex triremus. 3 l, Harpa major. 4 l, Lambis chiragra. 5 l, Conus pennaceus. 75 l, Clanculus pharaonis. 5r, Chicoreus ramosus.

1975, Jan. 25 *Perf. 14½, 14 (A82)*

533 A81 1 l shown .25 .25
534 A81 2 l multicolored .25 .25
535 A81 3 l multicolored .25 .25
536 A81 4 l multicolored .30 .25
537 A81 5 l multicolored .35 .30
538 A82 60 l shown 2.25 2.25
539 A82 75 l multicolored 2.75 2.75
540 A81 5r multicolored 7.50 7.50
Nos. 533-540 (8) 13.90 13.80

Souvenir Sheet

Perf. 13½

541 Sheet of 2 12.50 12.50
a. A81 2r like 3 l 3.75 3.75
b. A81 3r like 2 l 4.75 4.75

Sea shells, including cowries.

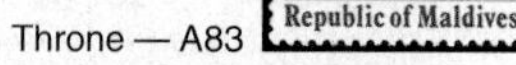

Throne — A83

Eid-Miskith Mosque — A84

Designs: 10 l, Ornamental candlesticks (dul-lisa). 25 l, Tree-shaped lamp. 60 l, Royal umbrellas. 3r, Tomb of Al-Hafiz Abu-al Barakath al-Barubari.

1975, Feb. 22 Litho. *Perf. 14*

No.	Type	Description	Unused	Used
542	A83	1 l multicolored	.25	.25
543	A83	10 l multicolored	.25	.25
544	A83	25 l multicolored	.25	.25
545	A83	60 l multicolored	.25	.25
546	A84	75 l multicolored	.35	.25
547	A84	3r multicolored	1.40	1.25
		Nos. 542-547 (6)	2.75	2.50

Historic relics and monuments.

Tropical Fruit — A85

1975, Mar. Litho. *Perf. 14½*

No.	Type	Description	Unused	Used
548	A85	2 l Guava	.25	.25
549	A85	4 l Maldive mulberry	.25	.25
550	A85	5 l Mountain apples	.25	.25
551	A85	10 l Bananas	.25	.25
552	A85	20 l Mangoes	.25	.25
553	A85	50 l Papaya	.70	.60
554	A85	1r Pomegranates	1.20	.65
555	A85	5r Coconut	6.00	5.50
		Nos. 548-555 (8)	9.15	8.00

Souvenir Sheet

Perf. 13½

No.	Type	Description	Unused	Used
556		Sheet of 2	10.00	*10.00*
a.	A85	2r like 10 l	2.75	*3.25*
b.	A85	3r like 2 l	3.25	*3.75*

Phyllangia — A86

Corals, sea urchins and starfish: 2 l, Madrepora oculata. 3 l, Acropora gravida. 4 l, Stylotella. 5 l, Acropora cervicornis. 60 l, Strongylocentrotus pupuratus. 75 l, Pisaster ochraceus. 5r, Marthasterias glacialis.

1975, June 6 Litho. *Perf. 14½*

No.	Type	Description	Unused	Used
557	A86	1 l shown	.25	.25
558	A86	2 l multicolored	.25	.25
559	A86	3 l multicolored	.25	.25
560	A86	4 l multicolored	.25	.25
561	A86	5 l multicolored	.25	.25
562	A86	60 l multicolored	.60	.25
563	A86	75 l multicolored	.90	.25
564	A86	5r multicolored	4.25	3.00
		Nos. 557-564 (8)	7.00	4.75

Souvenir Sheet

Imperf

No.	Type	Description	Unused	Used
565	A86	4r shown	11.00	11.00

"10," Clock Tower and Customs House A87

"10" and: 5 l, Government offices. 7 l, North Eastern waterfront, Male. 15 l, Mosque and Minaret. 10r, Sultan Park and Museum.

1975, July 26 Litho. *Perf. 14½*

No.	Type	Description	Unused	Used
566	A87	4 l salmon & multi	.25	.25
567	A87	5 l lt blue & multi	.25	.25
568	A87	7 l bister & multi	.25	.25
569	A87	15 l lilac & multi	.25	.25
570	A87	10r lt green & multi	3.25	*6.00*
		Nos. 566-570 (5)	4.25	*7.00*

10th anniversary of independence.

Nos. 432-435 Overprinted

Overprint reads: "14th Boy Scout Jamboree / July 29-Aug. 7, 1975"

1975, July 26 Litho. *Perf. 14½*

No.	Type	Description	Unused	Used
571	A69	1r multicolored	.55	.55
572	A69	2r multicolored	1.40	.90
573	A69	3r multicolored	2.25	1.75
		Nos. 571-573 (3)	4.20	3.20

Souvenir Sheet

No.	Type	Description	Unused	Used
574	A69	5r multicolored	7.50	7.50

Nordjamb 75, 14th World Boy Scout Jamboree, Lillehammer, Norway, July 29-Aug. 7.

Madura-Prau Bedang — A88

Sailing ships, except 5r: 2 l, Ganges patile. 3 l, Indian palla, vert. 4 l, "Odhi," vert. 5 l, Maldivian schooner. 25 l, Cutty Sark. 1r, 10r, Maldivian baggala, vert. 5r, Freighter Maldive Courage.

1975, July 26 *Perf. 14½*

No.	Type	Description	Unused	Used
575	A88	1 l multicolored	.25	.25
576	A88	2 l multicolored	.25	.25
577	A88	3 l multicolored	.25	.25
578	A88	4 l multicolored	.25	.25
579	A88	5 l multicolored	.25	.25
580	A88	25 l multicolored	.65	.30
581	A88	1r multicolored	1.00	.60
582	A88	5r multicolored	3.00	*3.00*
		Nos. 575-582 (8)	5.90	5.15

Souvenir Sheet

Perf. 13½

No.	Type	Description	Unused	Used
583	A88	10r multicolored	10.00	*10.00*

Butterflies A89

1 l, Brahmaea Wallichii. 2 l, Teoinopalpus imperialis. 3 l, Cethosia biblis. 4 l, Hestia jasonia. 5 l, Apatura. 25 l, Kallima horsfieldi. 1.50r, Hebomoia leucippe. 5r, Papilio memnon.

1975, Sept. 7 Litho. *Perf. 14½*

No.	Type	Description	Unused	Used
584	A89	1 l shown	.25	.25
585	A89	2 l multicolored	.25	.25
586	A89	3 l multicolored	.25	.25
587	A89	4 l multicolored	.25	.25
588	A89	5 l multicolored	.25	.25
589	A89	25 l multicolored	.65	.40
590	A89	1.50r multicolored	2.75	2.75
591	A89	5r multicolored	8.50	7.00
		Nos. 584-591 (8)	13.15	11.40

Souvenir Sheet

Perf. 13½

No.	Type	Description	Unused	Used
592	A89	10r like 25 l	20.00	20.00

Dying Slave by Michelangelo A90

Works by Michelangelo: 2 l, 4 l, 1r, 5r, paintings from Sistine Chapel. 3 l, Apollo. 5 l, Bacchus. 2r, 10r, David.

1975, Oct. 9 Litho. *Perf. 14½*

No.	Type	Description	Unused	Used
593	A90	1 l blue & multi	.25	.25
594	A90	2 l multicolored	.25	.25
595	A90	3 l red & multi	.25	.25
596	A90	4 l multicolored	.25	.25
597	A90	5 l emerald & multi	.25	.25
598	A90	1r multicolored	1.00	1.00
599	A90	2r red & multi	1.75	1.75
600	A90	5r multicolored	3.50	3.50
		Nos. 593-600 (8)	7.50	7.50

Souvenir Sheet

Perf. 13½

No.	Type	Description	Unused	Used
601	A90	10r multicolored	6.50	*6.50*

Michelangelo Buonarotti (1475-1564), Italian sculptor, painter and architect.

Cup and Vase — A91

Designs: 4 l, Boxes. 50 l, Vase with lid. 75 l, Bowls with covers. 1r, Worker finishing vases.

1975, Dec. Litho. *Perf. 14*

No.	Type	Description	Unused	Used
602	A91	2 l ultra & multi	.25	.25
603	A91	4 l rose & multi	.25	.25
604	A91	50 l multicolored	.25	.25
605	A91	75 l blue & multi	.35	.35
606	A91	1r multicolored	.65	.45
		Nos. 602-606 (5)	1.75	1.55

Maldivian lacquer ware.

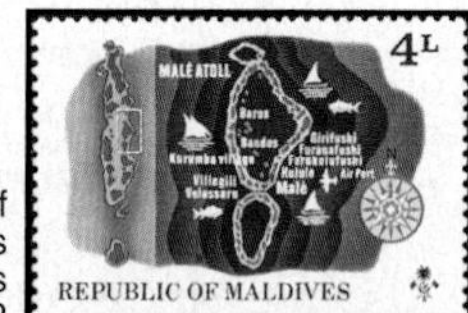

Map of Islands and Atolls A92

Designs: 5 l, Yacht at anchor. 7 l, Sailboats. 15 l, Deep-sea divers and corals. 3r, Hulule Airport. 10r, Cruising yachts.

1975, Dec. 25 Litho. *Perf. 14*

No.	Type	Description	Unused	Used
607	A92	4 l multicolored	.25	.25
608	A92	5 l multicolored	.25	.25
609	A92	7 l multicolored	.25	.25
610	A92	15 l multicolored	.30	.25
611	A92	3r multicolored	2.25	2.25
612	A92	10r multicolored	6.50	6.50
		Nos. 607-612 (6)	9.80	9.75

Tourist publicity.

Cross-country Skiing — A93

Winter Olympic Games' Emblem and: 2 l, Speed skating. 3 l, Figure skating, pair. 4 l, Bobsled. 5 l, Ski jump. 25 l, Figure skating, woman. 1.15r, Slalom. 4r, Ice hockey. 10r, Skiing.

1976, Jan. 10 Litho. *Perf. 14½*

No.	Type	Description	Unused	Used
613	A93	1 l multicolored	.25	.25
614	A93	2 l multicolored	.25	.25
615	A93	3 l multicolored	.25	.25
616	A93	4 l multicolored	.25	.25
617	A93	5 l multicolored	.25	.25
618	A93	25 l multicolored	.25	.25
619	A93	1.15r multicolored	.90	.90
620	A93	4r multicolored	1.50	1.50
		Nos. 613-620 (8)	3.90	3.90

Souvenir Sheet

Perf. 13½

No.	Type	Description	Unused	Used
621	A93	10r multicolored	7.00	*7.00*

12th Winter Olympic Games, Innsbruck, Austria, Feb. 4-15. Exist imperf. Values: set, $7; souvenir sheet, $14.

Gen. Burgoyne, by Joshua Reynolds — A94

Paintings: 2 l, John Hancock, by John S. Copley. 3 l, Death of Gen. Montgomery, by John Trumbull, horiz. 4 l, Paul Revere, by Copley. 5 l, Battle of Bunker Hill, by Trumbull, horiz. 2r, Crossing of the Delaware, by Thomas Sully, horiz. 3r, Samuel Adams, by Copley. 5r, Surrender of Cornwallis, by Trumbull, horiz. 10r, Washington at Dorchester Heights, by Gilbert Stuart.

1976, Feb. 15 *Perf. 14½*

No.	Type	Description	Unused	Used
622	A94	1 l multicolored	.25	.25
623	A94	2 l multicolored	.25	.25
624	A94	3 l multicolored	.25	.25
625	A94	4 l multicolored	.25	.25
626	A94	5 l multicolored	.25	.25
627	A94	2r multicolored	2.00	2.00
628	A94	3r multicolored	2.25	2.25
629	A94	5r multicolored	2.50	2.50
		Nos. 622-629 (8)	8.00	8.00

Souvenir Sheet

Perf. 13½

No.	Type	Description	Unused	Used
630	A94	10r multicolored	15.00	15.00

American Bicentennial. Nos. 622-629 exist imperf, same value as perf.

For overprints see Nos. 639-642.

Thomas Alva Edison A95

Designs: 2 l, Alexander Graham Bell and his telephone. 3 l, Telephones of 1919, 1937 and 1972. 10 l, Cable tunnel. 20 l, Equalizer circuit assembly. 1r, Ships laying underwater cable. 4r, Telephones of 1876, 1890 and 1879 Edison telephone. 10r, Intelsat IV-A over earth station.

1976, Mar. 10 Litho. *Perf. 14½*

No.	Type	Description	Unused	Used
631	A95	1 l multicolored	.25	.25
632	A95	2 l multicolored	.25	.25
633	A95	3 l multicolored	.25	.25
634	A95	10 l multicolored	.25	.25
635	A95	20 l multicolored	.25	.25
636	A95	1r multicolored	.65	.65
637	A95	10r multicolored	5.50	5.50
		Nos. 631-637 (7)	7.40	7.40

Souvenir Sheet

Perf. 13½

No.	Type	Description	Unused	Used
638	A95	4r multicolored	7.50	*7.50*

Centenary of first telephone call by Alexander Graham Bell, Mar. 10, 1876. Exist imperf. Values: set, $14; souvenir sheet, $15.

Nos. 627-630 Overprinted in Silver or Black

Overprint reads MAY 29TH-JUNE 6TH "INTERPHIL" 1976

1976, May 29 Litho. *Perf. 14½*

No.	Type	Description	Unused	Used
639	A94	2r multicolored (S)	1.50	1.50
640	A94	3r multicolored (S)	2.00	2.00
641	A94	5r multicolored (B)	2.50	2.50
		Nos. 639-641 (3)	6.00	6.00

Souvenir Sheet

Perf. 13½

642	A94	10r multicolored (S)	10.00	10.00

Interphil 76 Intl. Philatelic Exhibition, Philadelphia, Pa., May 29-June 6. Overprint on 3r and 10r vertical. Same overprint in one horizontal silver line in margin of No. 642.

Wrestling — A96

Olympic Rings and: 2 l, Shot put. 3 l, Hurdles. 4 l, Hockey. 5 l, Women running. 6 l, Javelin. 1.50r, Discus. 5r, Volleyball. 10r, Hammer throw.

1976, June 1 *Perf. 14½*

643	A96	1 l multicolored	.25	.25
644	A96	2 l multicolored	.25	.25
645	A96	3 l salmon & multi	.25	.25
646	A96	4 l multicolored	.25	.25
647	A96	5 l pink & multi	.25	.25
648	A96	6 l multicolored	.25	.25
649	A96	1.50r bister & multi	1.25	1.25
650	A96	5r lilac & multi	3.00	4.25
		Nos. 643-650 (8)	5.75	7.00

Souvenir Sheet

Perf. 13½

651	A96	10r lemon & multi	7.50	*7.50*

21st Olympic Games, Montreal, Canada, July 17-Aug. 1.

Bonavist Beans — A97

Designs: 4 l, 20 l, Beans. 10 l, Eggplant. 50 l, Cucumber. 75 l, 2r, Snake gourd. 1r, Balsam pear.

1976-77 **Litho.** *Perf. 14*

652	A97	2 l green & multi	.25	.25
653	A97	4 l lt blue & multi	.55	.55
654	A97	10 l ocher & multi	.55	.55
655	A97	20 l blue & multi ('77)	.55	.55
656	A97	50 l multicolored	.70	.70
657	A97	75 l bister & multi	.90	.90
658	A97	1r lilac & multi	1.30	1.30
659	A97	2r bis & multi ('77)	2.40	2.40
		Nos. 652-659 (8)	7.20	7.20

1976 stamps issued July 26.

Viking I and Mars A98

Design: 20r, Landing craft on Mars.

1976, Dec. 2 **Litho.** *Perf. 14*

660	A98	5r multicolored	2.00	2.00

Souvenir Sheet

661	A98	20r multicolored	10.00	*10.00*

Viking I US Mars Mission.

Coronation Ceremony — A99

Designs: 2 l, Elizabeth II and Prince Philip. 3 l, Queen, Prince Philip, Princes Edward and Andrew. 1.15r, Queen in procession. 3r, State coach. 4r, Queen, Prince Philip, Princess Anne and Prince Charles. 10r, Queen and Prince Charles.

1977, Feb. 6 *Perf. 14x13½, 12*

662	A99	1 l multicolored	.40	.40
663	A99	2 l multicolored	.40	.40
664	A99	3 l multicolored	.40	.40
665	A99	1.15r multicolored	.60	.60
666	A99	3r multicolored	1.25	*1.50*
667	A99	4r multicolored	1.25	*1.60*
		Nos. 662-667 (6)	4.30	*4.90*

Souvenir Sheet

668	A99	10r multicolored	5.00	5.00

25th anniv. of the reign of Elizabeth II.

Nos. 662-667 were printed in sheets of 40 (4x10), perf. 14x13½, and sheets of 5 plus label, perf. 12, in changed colors.

Nos. 662-668 exist imperf. Value, set $12.50.

Beethoven in Bonn, 1785 — A100

Designs: 2 l, Moonlight Sonata and portrait, 1801. 3 l, Goethe and Beethoven, Teplitz, 1811. 4 l, Beethoven, 1815, and his string instruments. 5 l, Beethoven House, Heiligenstadt, 1817. 25 l, Composer's hands, gold medal. 2r, Missa Solemnis, portrait, 1823. 4r, Piano, room where Beethoven died, death mask. 5r, Portrait, 1825, hearing aids.

1977, Mar. 26 **Litho.** *Perf. 14*

669	A100	1 l multicolored	.25	.25
670	A100	2 l multicolored	.25	.25
671	A100	3 l multicolored	.35	.35
672	A100	4 l multicolored	.35	.35
673	A100	5 l multicolored	.35	.35
674	A100	25 l multicolored	1.50	.25
675	A100	2r multicolored	4.00	3.50
676	A100	5r multicolored	6.50	6.50
		Nos. 669-676 (8)	13.55	11.80

Souvenir Sheet

677	A100	4r multicolored	8.50	*8.50*

Ludwig van Beethoven (1770-1827), composer, 150th death anniversary.

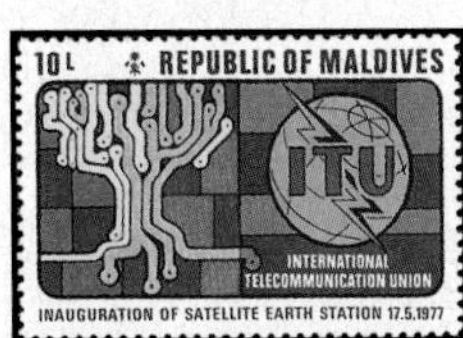

Electronic Tree and ITU Emblem A101

90 l, Central Telegraph Office, Maldives. 5r, Intelsat IV over map. 10r, Parabolic antenna, satellite communications earth station.

1977, May 17 **Litho.** *Perf. 14*

678	A101	10 l multicolored	.25	.25
679	A101	90 l multicolored	.50	.50
680	A101	10r multicolored	3.50	3.50
		Nos. 678-680 (3)	4.25	4.25

Souvenir Sheet

681	A101	5r multicolored	4.50	4.50

Inauguration of Satellite Earth Station and for World Telecommunications Day.

Portrait by Gainsborough A102

Paintings: 2 l, 5 l, 10r, Rubens. 3 l, 95 l, 5r, Titian. 4 l, 1r, Gainsborough.

1977, May 20

682	A102	1 l multicolored	.25	.25
683	A102	2 l multicolored	.25	.25
684	A102	3 l multicolored	.25	.25
685	A102	4 l multicolored	.25	.25
686	A102	5 l multicolored	.25	.25
687	A102	95 l multicolored	.80	.60
688	A102	1r multicolored	.80	.65
689	A102	10r multicolored	4.00	*6.00*
		Nos. 682-689 (8)	6.85	*8.50*

Souvenir Sheet

690	A102	5r multicolored	4.00	*4.00*

Birth annivs. of Thomas Gainsborough; Peter Paul Rubens; Titian.

Lesser Frigate Birds — A103

Birds: 2 l, Crab plovers. 3 l, Long-tailed tropic bird. 4 l, Wedge-tailed shearwater. 5 l, Gray heron. 20 l, White tern. 95 l, Cattle egret. 1.25r, Blacknaped terns. 5r, Pheasant coucals. 10r, Striated herons.

1977, July 26 **Litho.** *Perf. 14½*

691	A103	1 l multicolored	.25	.25
692	A103	2 l multicolored	.25	.25
693	A103	3 l multicolored	.25	.25
694	A103	4 l multicolored	.25	.25
695	A103	5 l multicolored	.25	.25
696	A103	20 l multicolored	.90	.30
697	A103	95 l multicolored	2.25	1.60
698	A103	1.25r multicolored	2.50	2.50
699	A103	5r multicolored	6.50	6.50
		Nos. 691-699 (9)	13.40	12.15

Souvenir Sheet

700	A103	10r multicolored	25.00	25.00

Charles A. Lindbergh — A104

Designs: 2 l, Lindbergh and Spirit of St. Louis. 3 l, Mohawk plane, horiz. 4 l, Lebaudy I airship, 1902, horiz. 5 l, Count Ferdinand von Zeppelin, and Zeppelin in Pernambuco. 1r, Los Angeles, U. S. Navy airship, 1924, horiz. 3r, Henry Ford and Lindbergh, 1942. 5r, Spirit of St. Louis, Statue of Liberty and Eiffel Tower, horiz. 7.50r, German naval airship over battleship, horiz. 10r, Vickers airship, 1917.

Perf. 13x13½, 13½x13

1977, Oct. 31 **Litho.**

701	A104	1 l multicolored	.25	.25
702	A104	2 l multicolored	.25	.25
703	A104	3 l multicolored	.25	.25
704	A104	4 l multicolored	.25	.25
705	A104	5 l multicolored	.25	.25
706	A104	1r multicolored	.60	.30
707	A104	3r multicolored	1.40	1.60
708	A104	10r multicolored	3.25	*5.25*
		Nos. 701-708 (8)	6.50	*8.40*

Souvenir Sheet

709		Sheet of 2	12.50	12.50
a.		A104 5r multicolored	3.75	3.75
b.		A104 7.50r multicolored	4.75	4.75

Charles A. Lindbergh's solo transatlantic flight from New York to Paris, 50th anniv., and 75th anniv. of first navigable airship.

Boat Building A105

Maldivian Occupations: 15 l, High sea fishing. 20 l, Cadjan weaving. 90 l, Mat weaving. 2r, Lacemaking, vert.

1977, Dec. 12

710	A105	6 l multicolored	.85	.85
711	A105	15 l multicolored	1.50	1.50
712	A105	20 l multicolored	1.75	1.75
713	A105	90 l multicolored	4.00	4.00
714	A105	2r multicolored	5.50	5.00
		Nos. 710-714 (5)	13.60	13.10

Rheumatic Heart — A106

X-Ray Pictures: 50 l, Shoulder. 2r, Hand. 3r, Knee.

1978, Feb. 9 *Perf. 14*

715	A106	1 l multicolored	.25	.25
716	A106	50 l multicolored	.40	.25
717	A106	2r multicolored	.75	.75
718	A106	3r multicolored	.85	.85
		Nos. 715-718 (4)	2.25	2.10

World Rheumatism Year.

Otto Lilienthal's Glider, 1890 — A107

Designs: 2 l, Chanute's glider, 1896. 3 l, Wright brothers testing glider, 1900. 4 l, A. V. Roe's plane with paper-covered wings, 1908. 5 l, Wilbur Wright showing his plane to King Alfonso of Spain, 1909. 10 l, Roe's second biplane. 20 l, Alexander Graham Bell and Wright brothers in Washington D.C., 1910. 95 l, Clifton Hadley's triplane, 1910. 5r, British B.E.2 planes, Upavon Field, 1914. 10r, Wilbur Wright flying first motorized plane, 1903.

1978, Feb. 27 **Litho.** *Perf. 13x13½*

719	A107	1 l multicolored	.25	.35
720	A107	2 l multicolored	.25	.35
721	A107	3 l multicolored	.25	.35
722	A107	4 l multicolored	.25	.35
723	A107	5 l multicolored	.25	.35
724	A107	10 l multicolored	.80	.40
725	A107	20 l multicolored	2.00	.40
726	A107	95 l multicolored	5.00	2.25
727	A107	5r multicolored	11.50	11.50
		Nos. 719-727 (9)	20.55	16.30

Souvenir Sheet

Perf. 14

728	A107	10r multicolored	12.50	*12.50*

75th anniversary of first motorized airplane.

Edward Jenner, Vaccination Discoverer A108

Designs: 15 l, Foundling Hospital, London, where children were first inoculated, 1743, horiz. 50 l, Newgate Prison, London, where first experiments were carried out, 1721.

1978, Mar. 15 *Perf. 14*

729	A108	15 l multicolored	.65	.30
730	A108	50 l multicolored	1.50	.65
731	A108	2r multicolored	2.75	2.75
		Nos. 729-731 (3)	4.90	3.70

World eradication of smallpox.

TV with Maldives Broadcasting Symbol — A109

Designs: 25 l, Circuit pattern. 1.50r, Station control panel, horiz.

1978, Mar. 29

732	A109	15 l multicolored	.55	.55
733	A109	25 l multicolored	.80	.80
734	A109	1.50r multicolored	2.25	2.25
		Nos. 732-734 (3)	3.60	3.60

Inauguration of Maldive Islands television.

Sailing Ship — A110

Ships: 1 l, Phoenician. 2 l, Two-master. 5 l, Freighter Maldive Trader. 1r, Trading schooner. 1.25r, 4r, Sailing boat. 3r, Barque Bangala. (1 l, 2 l, 5 l, 1.25r, 4r, horiz.)

1978, Apr. 27 Litho. *Perf. 14½*

735	A110	1 l multicolored	.25	.25
736	A110	2 l multicolored	.25	.25
737	A110	3 l multicolored	.25	.25
738	A110	5 l multicolored	.25	.25
739	A110	1r multicolored	.50	.50
740	A110	1.25r multicolored	1.00	1.00
741	A110	3r multicolored	1.50	1.50
742	A110	4r multicolored	1.75	1.75
a.		Souvenir sheet of 2	3.25	3.25
		Nos. 735-742 (8)	5.75	5.75

No. 742a contains No. 742 and a 1r stamp in the design of No. 736.

The Ampulla — A111

Designs: 2 l, Scepter with dove. 3 l, Orb with cross. 1.15r, St. Edward's crown. 2r, Scepter with cross. 5r, Queen Elizabeth II. 10r, Anointing spoon.

1978, May 15 *Perf. 14*

743	A111	1 l multicolored	.25	.25
744	A111	2 l multicolored	.25	.25
745	A111	3 l multicolored	.25	.25
746	A111	1.15r multicolored	.25	.25
747	A111	2r multicolored	.30	.30
748	A111	5r multicolored	.60	.60
		Nos. 743-748 (6)	1.90	1.90

Souvenir Sheet

749	A111	10r multicolored	2.00	2.00

Coronation of Elizabeth II, 25th anniv.

Nos. 743-748 were printed in sheets of 40 and in sheets of 3 + label, in changed colors. Labels show coronation regalia.

Capt. James Cook — A112

Designs: 2 l, Kamehameha I statue, Honolulu. 3 l, "Endeavour" and boat. 25 l, Capt. Cook and route of his 3rd voyage. 75 l, "Discovery" and "Resolution," map of Hawaiian Islands, horiz. 1.50r, Capt. Cook's first meeting with Hawaiians, horiz. 5r, "Endeavour." 10r, Capt. Cook's death, horiz.

1978, July 15 Litho. *Perf. 14½*

750	A112	1 l multicolored	.25	.25
751	A112	2 l multicolored	.25	.25
752	A112	3 l multicolored	.25	.25
753	A112	25 l multicolored	.50	.35
754	A112	75 l multicolored	1.25	1.25
755	A112	1.50r multicolored	1.75	1.75
756	A112	10r multicolored	6.50	*6.50*
		Nos. 750-756 (7)	10.75	*10.60*

Souvenir Sheet

757	A112	5r multicolored	14.00	*14.00*

Schizophrys Aspera — A113

Maldivian Crabs and Lobster: 2 l, Atergatis floridus. 3 l, Percnon planissimum. 90 l, Portunus granulatus. 1r, Carpilius maculatus. No. 763, Huenia proteus. No. 765, Panulirus longipes, vert. 25r, Etisus laevimanus.

1978, Aug. 30 Litho. *Perf. 14*

758	A113	1 l multicolored	.25	.25
759	A113	2 l multicolored	.25	.25
760	A113	3 l multicolored	.25	.25
761	A113	90 l multicolored	.60	.40
762	A113	1r multicolored	.60	.40
763	A113	2r multicolored	1.00	*1.00*
764	A113	25r multicolored	5.50	*5.50*
		Nos. 758-764 (7)	8.45	*8.05*

Souvenir Sheet

765	A113	2r multicolored	2.75	2.75

Four Apostles, by Dürer — A114

Paintings by Albrecht Dürer (1471-1528): 20 l, Self-portrait, age 27. 55 l, Virgin and Child with Pear. 1r, Rhinoceros, horiz. 1.80r, Hare. 3r, The Great Piece of Turf. 10r, Columbine.

1978, Oct. 28 Litho. *Perf. 14*

766	A114	10 l multicolored	.25	.25
767	A114	20 l multicolored	.25	.25
768	A114	55 l multicolored	.25	.25
769	A114	1r multicolored	.30	.30
770	A114	1.80r multicolored	.60	.60
771	A114	3r multicolored	.90	.90
		Nos. 766-771 (6)	2.55	2.55

Souvenir Sheet

772	A114	10r multicolored	4.00	4.00

Palms and Fishing Boat A115

Designs: 5 l, Montessori School. 10 l, TV tower and ITU emblem, vert. 25 l, Island with beach. 50 l, Boeing 737 over island. 95 l, Walk along the beach. 1.25r, Fishing boat at dawn. 2r, Presidential residence. 3r, Fishermen preparing nets. 5r, Afeefuddin Mosque.

1978, Nov. 11 Litho. *Perf. 14½*

773	A115	1 l multicolored	.25	.25
774	A115	5 l multicolored	.25	.25
775	A115	10 l multicolored	.25	.25
776	A115	25 l multicolored	.25	.25
777	A115	50 l multicolored	.25	.25
778	A115	95 l multicolored	.30	.25
779	A115	1.25r multicolored	.50	.50
780	A115	2r multicolored	.65	1.10
781	A115	5r multicolored	1.25	2.25
		Nos. 773-781 (9)	3.95	5.35

Souvenir Sheet

782	A115	3r multicolored	2.50	2.50

10th anniversary of Republic.

Human Rights Emblem A116

1978, Dec. 10 *Perf. 14*

783	A116	30 l multicolored	.25	.25
784	A116	90 l multicolored	.40	.50
785	A116	1.80r multicolored	.65	1.00
		Nos. 783-785 (3)	1.30	1.75

Universal Declaration of Human Rights, 30th anniversary.

Rare Spotted Cowrie — A117

Sea Shells: 2 l, Imperial cone. 3 l, Green turban. 10 l, Giant spider conch. 1r, Leucodon cowrie. 1.80r, Fig cone. 3r, Glory of the sea. 5r, Top vase.

1979, Jan. Litho. *Perf. 14*

786	A117	1 l multicolored	.25	.25
787	A117	2 l multicolored	.25	.25
788	A117	3 l multicolored	.25	.25
789	A117	10 l multicolored	.45	.25
790	A117	1r multicolored	2.00	.40
791	A117	1.80r multicolored	3.00	2.50
792	A117	3r multicolored	4.50	3.75
		Nos. 786-792 (7)	10.70	7.65

Souvenir Sheet

793	A117	5r multicolored	14.00	14.00

Bellman Delivering Mail — A118

Designs: 2 l, Royal mail coach, 1840, horiz. 3 l, First London letter box, 1855. 1.55r, Great Britain No. 1 and post horn. 5r, Maldive Islands No. 5 and carrier pigeon. 10r, Rowland Hill.

1979, Feb. 28 Litho. *Perf. 14*

794	A118	1 l multicolored	.25	.25
795	A118	2 l multicolored	.25	.25
796	A118	3 l multicolored	.25	.25
797	A118	1.55r multicolored	.45	.45
798	A118	5r multicolored	.80	.80
		Nos. 794-798 (5)	2.00	2.00

Souvenir Sheet

799	A118	10r multicolored	2.00	2.00

Sir Rowland Hill (1795-1879), originator of penny postage.

Nos. 794-798 were also each issued in sheetlets of 5 stamps and 1 label, perf. 12 with changed colors. Values: set, $1.50; set of sheetlets, $9.

For overprints see Nos. 853-855.

Girl with Teddy Bear — A119

IYC Emblem, Boy and: 1.25r, Model boat. 2r, Rocket launcher. 3r, Blimp. 5r, Train.

1979, May 10 Litho. *Perf. 14*

800	A119	5 l multicolored	.25	.25
801	A119	1.25r multicolored	.40	.40
802	A119	2r multicolored	.50	.50
803	A119	3r multicolored	.65	.65
		Nos. 800-803 (4)	1.80	1.80

Souvenir Sheet

804	A119	5r multicolored	1.25	1.25

International Year of the Child.

White Feathers, by Matisse A120

Paintings by Henri Matisse (1869-1954): 25 l, Joy of Life. 30 l, Eggplants. 1.50r, Harmony in Red. 4r, Water Pitcher. 5r, Still-life.

1979, Aug. 20 Litho. *Perf. 14*

805	A120	20 l multicolored	.25	.25
806	A120	25 l multicolored	.25	.25
807	A120	30 l multicolored	.25	.25
808	A120	1.50r multicolored	.45	.45
809	A120	5r multicolored	.75	.75
		Nos. 805-809 (5)	1.95	1.95

Souvenir Sheet

810	A120	4r multicolored	4.00	4.00

Sari and Mosque — A121

National Costumes: 75 l, Sashed apron dress. Male Harbor. 90 l, Serape with necklace, radar station. 95 l, Flowered dress, mosque and minaret.

1979, Aug. 22 Litho. *Perf. 14*

811	A121	50 l multicolored	.25	.25
812	A121	75 l multicolored	.25	.25
813	A121	90 l multicolored	.30	.30
814	A121	95 l multicolored	.35	.35
		Nos. 811-814 (4)	1.15	1.15

Maldive Wildflowers A122

1 l, Gloriosa Superba. 3 l, Hibiscus. 50 l, Barringtonia asiatica. 1r, Abutilon indicum. 5r, Guettarda speciosa.

4r, Pandanus odoratissimus.

1979, Oct. 29 Litho. *Perf. 14*

815	A122	1 l shown	.25	.25
816	A122	3 l multicolored	.25	.25
817	A122	50 l multicolored	.25	.25
818	A122	1r multicolored	.40	.40
819	A122	5r multicolored	1.00	1.00
		Nos. 815-819 (5)	2.15	2.15

Souvenir Sheet

820	A122	4r multicolored	1.75	1.75

Handicraft Exhibition A123

10 l, Jar and cup. 1.30r, Tortoise-shell jewelry. 2r, Wooden boxes.

5r, Bracelets, necklace.

1979, Nov. 11

821 A123 5 l shown .25 .25
822 A123 10 l multicolored .25 .25
823 A123 1.30r multicolored .45 .45
824 A123 2r multicolored .60 .60
Nos. 821-824 (4) 1.55 1.55

Souvenir Sheet

825 A123 5r multicolored 1.25 1.25

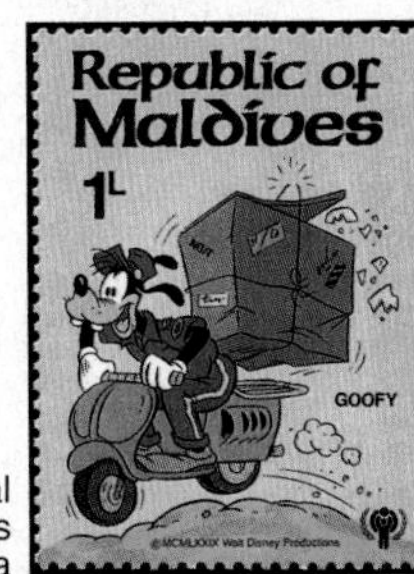

Postal Scenes A123a

1 l, Goofy delivering package. 2 l, Mickey at mailbox. 3 l, Goofy buried in letters. 4 l, Minnie Mouse, Pluto. 5 l, Mickey Mouse on skates. 10 l, Donald Duck at mailbox. 15 l, Chip and Dale carrying letter. 1.50r, Donald Duck on unicycle. 4r, Pluto at mailbox. 5r, Donald Duck wheeling crate.

1979, Dec. Litho. *Perf. 11*

826 A123a 1 l multicolored .25 .25
827 A123a 2 l multicolored .25 .25
828 A123a 3 l multicolored .25 .25
829 A123a 4 l multicolored .25 .25
830 A123a 5 l multicolored .25 .25
831 A123a 10 l multicolored .25 .25
832 A123a 15 l multicolored .25 .25
833 A123a 1.50r multicolored .75 .75
834 A123a 5r multicolored 2.25 *2.25*
Nos. 826-834 (9) 4.75 *4.75*

Souvenir Sheet

835 A123a 4r multicolored 5.50 5.50

National Day A124

Designs: 5 l, Post Ramadan dancing. 15 l, Festival of Eeduu. 95 l, Sultan's ceremonial band. 2r, Music festival. 5r, Sword dance.

1980, Jan. 19 Litho. *Perf. 14*

836 A124 5 l multicolored .25 .25
837 A124 15 l multicolored .25 .25
838 A124 95 l multicolored .35 .35
839 A124 2r multicolored .60 .60
Nos. 836-839 (4) 1.45 1.45

Souvenir Sheet

840 A124 5r multicolored 2.00 2.00

Leatherback Turtle — A125

1980, Feb. 17 Litho. *Perf. 14*

841 A125 1 l shown .25 .25
842 A125 2 l Flatback turtle .25 .25
843 A125 5 l Hawksbill turtle .25 .25
844 A125 10 l Loggerhead turtle .25 .25
845 A125 75 l Olive ridley .50 .50
846 A125 10r Atlantic ridley 3.00 3.00
Nos. 841-846 (6) 4.50 4.50

Souvenir Sheet

847 A125 4r Green turtle 2.00 2.00

Paul Harris in Rotary Emblem — A126

1980, Mar. Litho. *Perf. 14*

848 A126 75 l shown .45 .45
849 A126 90 l Family .50 .50
850 A126 1r Grain .50 .50
851 A126 10r Caduceus 2.75 2.75
Nos. 848-851 (4) 4.20 4.20

Souvenir Sheet

852 A126 5r Anniversary emblem 1.75 1.75

Rotary International, 75th anniversary.

Nos. 797-799 Overprinted "LONDON 1980"

1980, May 6 Litho. *Perf. 14*

853 A118 1.55r multicolored 2.00 1.75
854 A118 5r multicolored 4.00 4.00

Souvenir Sheet

855 A118 10r multicolored 7.00 7.00

London 1980 International Stamp Exhibition, May 6-14. Sheet margin overprinted "Earls Court—London 6-14 May 1980."

Swimming, Moscow '80 Emblem — A127

1980, June 4 Litho. *Perf. 14*

856 A127 10 l shown .25 .25
857 A127 50 l Sprinting .25 .25
858 A127 3r Shot put .75 .75
859 A127 4r High jump 1.00 1.00
Nos. 856-859 (4) 2.25 2.25

Souvenir Sheet

860 A127 5r Weight lifting 1.25 1.25

22nd Summer Olympic Games, Moscow, July 19-Aug. 3.

White-tailed Tropic Bird — A128

95 l, Sooty tern. 1r, Brown noddy. 1.55r, Eurasian curlew. 2r, Wilson's petrel. 4r, Caspian tern.
5r, Red-footed & brown boobies.

1980, July 10 Litho. *Perf. 14*

861 A128 75 l shown .30 .25
862 A128 95 l multi .30 .30
863 A128 1r multi .40 .30
864 A128 1.55r multi .55 .55
865 A128 2r multi .65 .65
866 A128 4r multi 1.20 1.20
Nos. 861-866 (6) 3.40 3.25

Souvenir Sheet

867 A128 5r multi 8.00 8.00

Seal of Sultan Ibrahim II (1720-1750) — A129

Sultans' Seals: 2 l, Mohamed Imadudeen II (1704-1720). 5 l, Mohamed Bin Haji Ali (1692-1701). 1r, Kuda Mohamed Rasgefaanu (1687-1691). 2r, Ibrahim Iskander I (1648-1687). 3r, Ibrahim Iskander, second seal.

1980, July 26

868 A129 1 l violet brn & blk .25 .25
869 A129 2 l violet brn & blk .25 .25
870 A129 5 l violet brn & blk .25 .25
871 A129 1r violet brn & blk .40 .40
872 A129 2r violet brn & blk .50 .50
Nos. 868-872 (5) 1.65 1.65

Souvenir Sheet

873 A129 3r violet brn & blk .85 .85

Queen Mother Elizabeth, 80th Birthday A130

1980, Sept. 29 *Perf. 14*

874 A130 4r multicolored 1.25 1.25

Souvenir Sheet
Perf. 12

875 A130 5r multicolored 1.60 1.60

Munnaaru Tower A131

10 l, Hukuru Miskiiy Mosque. 30 l, Medhuziyaaraiy Shrine. 55 l, Koran verses on wooden tablets. 90 l, Mother teaching son.
2r, Map and arms of Maldives.

1980, Nov. 9 Litho. *Perf. 15*

876 A131 5 l shown .25 .25
877 A131 10 l multicolored .25 .25
878 A131 30 l multicolored .25 .25
879 A131 55 l multicolored .30 .30
880 A131 90 l multicolored .45 .45
Nos. 876-880 (5) 1.50 1.50

Souvenir Sheet

881 A131 2r multicolored .80 1.00

Hegira (Pilgrimage Year).

Malaria Eradication Control — A132

1980, Nov. 30 *Perf. 14*

882 A132 15 l shown .30 .30
883 A132 25 l Balanced diet .30 .30
884 A132 1.50r Oral hygiene 1.00 1.00
885 A132 5r Clinic visit 3.25 3.25
Nos. 882-885 (4) 4.85 4.85

Souvenir Sheet

886 A132 4r like #885 1.50 1.50

World Health Day. No. 886 shows design of No. 885 in changed colors.

The Cheshire Cat — A133

Designs: Scenes from Walt Disney's Alice in Wonderland. 5r, vert.

1980, Dec. 22 *Perf. 11*

887 A133 1 l multicolored .25 .25
888 A133 2 l multicolored .25 .25
889 A133 3 l multicolored .25 .25
890 A133 4 l multicolored .25 .25
891 A133 5 l multicolored .25 .25
892 A133 10 l multicolored .25 .25
893 A133 15 l multicolored .25 .25
894 A133 2.50r multicolored 2.25 2.25
895 A133 4r multicolored 2.50 2.50
Nos. 887-895 (9) 6.50 6.50

Souvenir Sheet

896 A133 5r multicolored 5.00 *5.00*

Ridley Turtle A134

1980, Dec. 29 Litho. *Perf. 14*

897 A134 90 l shown 2.25 .60
898 A134 1.25r Angel flake fish 2.75 1.25
899 A134 2r Spiny lobster 3.25 1.75
Nos. 897-899 (3) 8.25 3.60

Souvenir Sheet

900 A134 4r Fish 3.50 3.50

Tomb of Ghaazee Muhammad Thakurufaan — A135

National Day (Furniture and Palace of Muhammad Thakurufaan): 20 l, Hanging lamp, 16th century, vert. 30 l, Chair, vert. 95 l, Utheem Palace. 10r, Couch, vert.

1981, Jan. 7 *Perf. 15*

901 A135 10 l multicolored .25 .25
902 A135 20 l multicolored .25 .25
903 A135 30 l multicolored .25 .25
904 A135 95 l multicolored .60 .30
905 A135 10r multicolored 2.75 2.75
Nos. 901-905 (5) 4.10 3.80

Common Design Types pictured following the introduction.

Royal Wedding Issue
Common Design Type

1r, Couple. 2r, Buckingham Palace. 5r, Charles.
10r, Royal state coach.

1981, June 22 Litho. *Perf. 14*

906 CD331a 1r multi .25 .25
907 CD331a 2r multi .25 .25
908 CD331a 5r multi .30 .30
Nos. 906-908 (3) .80 .80

Souvenir Sheet

909 CD331 10r multi .75 .75

Nos. 906-908 also printed in sheets of 5 plus label, perf. 12, in changed colors. Value, set $1.

Majlis Chamber, 1932 A136

50th Anniv. of Citizens' Majlis (Grievance Rights); 1r, Sultan Muhammed Shamsuddin III (instituted system, 1932), vert. 4r, Constitution, 1932.

1981, June 27 *Perf. 15*

910 A136 95 l multicolored .30 .30
911 A136 1r multicolored .35 .35

Souvenir Sheet

912 A136 4r multicolored 2.50 2.50

Self-portrait with Palette, by Picasso (1881-1973)
A137

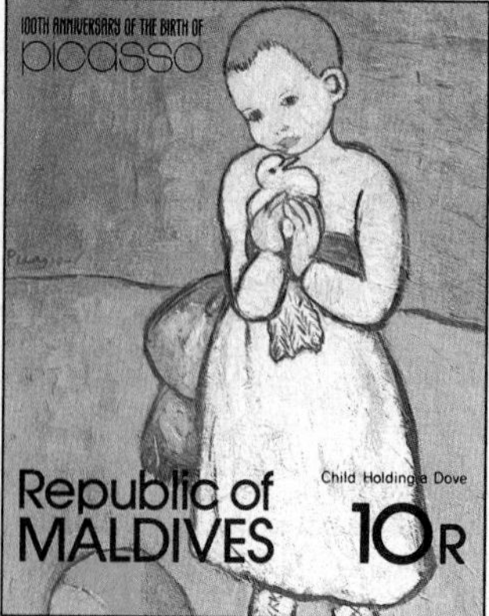

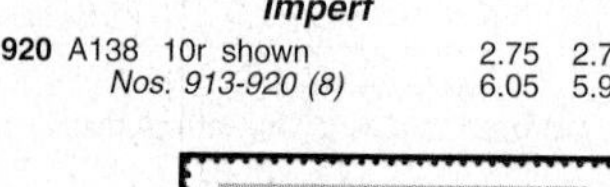

Child Holding a Dove — A138

1981, Aug. 26 Litho. *Perf. 14*

913 A137 5 l shown .25 .25

914 A137 10 l Woman in Blue .25 .25

915 A137 25 l Boy with a Pipe .30 .25

916 A137 30 l Card Player .30 .25

917 A137 90 l Sailor .40 .40

918 A137 3r Self-portrait .80 .80

919 A137 5r Harlequin 1.00 1.00

Imperf

920 A138 10r shown 2.75 2.75

Nos. 913-920 (8) 6.05 5.95

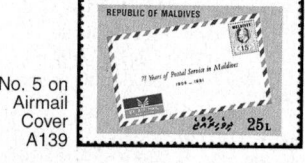

No. 5 on Airmail Cover
A139

1981, Sept. 9 Litho. *Perf. 14*

921 A139 25 l multicolored .25 .25

922 A139 75 l multicolored .25 .25

923 A139 5r multicolored .70 *1.00*

Nos. 921-923 (3) 1.20 1.50

Postal service, 75th anniv.

Hulule Intl. Airport Opening
A140

5 l, Jet taking off. 20 l, Passengers leaving jet. 1.80r, Refueling.
5r, Terminal.

1981, Nov. 11

924 A140 5 l multicolored .25 .25

925 A140 20 l multicolored .25 .25

926 A140 1.80r multicolored 1.00 1.00

927 A140 4r shown 1.20 *2.00*

Nos. 924-927 (4) 2.70 *3.50*

Souvenir Sheet

928 A140 5r multicolored 2.50 2.50

Intl. Year of the Disabled — A141

2 l, Homer. 5 l, Cervantes. 1r, Beethoven. 5r, Van Gogh.
4r, Helen Keller, Anne Sullivan.

1981, Nov. 18 Litho. *Perf. 14½*

929 A141 2 l multi .25 .25

930 A141 5 l multi .25 .25

931 A141 1r multi 2.00 2.00

932 A141 5r multi 3.50 *4.25*

Nos. 929-932 (4) 6.00 *6.75*

Souvenir Sheet

933 A141 4r multi 3.50 *3.50*

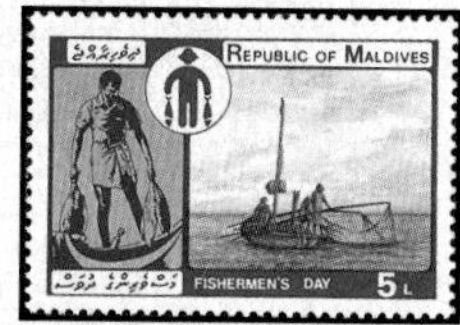

Decade for Women — A142

1981, Nov. 25 *Perf. 14*

934 A142 20 l Preparing fish .25 .25

935 A142 90 l 16th cent. woman .25 .25

936 A142 1r Tending yam crop .30 .30

937 A142 2r Making coir rope .55 .55

Nos. 934-937 (4) 1.35 1.35

Fishermen's Day — A143

5 l, Collecting bait. 15 l, Fishing boats. 90 l, Fisherman holding catch. 1.30r, Sorting fish.
3r, Loading fish for export.

1981, Dec. 10

938 A143 5 l multi .45 .25

939 A143 15 l multi .85 .25

940 A143 90 l multi 1.50 .60

941 A143 1.30r multi 2.10 1.00

Nos. 938-941 (4) 4.90 2.10

Souvenir Sheet

942 A143 3r multi 1.75 1.75

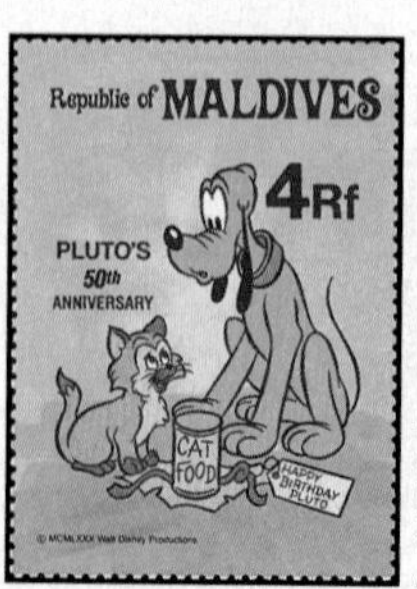

World Food Day
A144

1981, Dec. 30 Litho. *Perf. 14*

943 A144 10 l Breadfruit .35 .25

944 A144 25 l Hen, chicks .80 .25

945 A144 30 l Corn .80 .25

946 A144 75 l Skipjack tuna 2.25 .45

947 A144 1r Pumpkins 2.75 .60

948 A144 2r Coconuts 3.25 2.25

Nos. 943-948 (6) 10.20 4.05

Souvenir Sheet

949 A144 5r Eggplants 2.50 2.50

50th Anniv. of Walt Disney's Pluto (1980)
A145

4r, Scene from Chain Gang, 1930.
6r, The Pointer, 1939.

1982, Mar. 29 Litho. *Perf. 13½x14*

950 A145 4r multi 2.25 2.25

Souvenir Sheet

951 A145 6r multi 3.25 3.25

Princess Diana Issue

Common Design Type

1982, July 15 Litho. *Perf. 14½x14*

952 CD332 95 l Balmoral .50 .25

953 CD332 3r Honeymoon 1.25 .65

954 CD332 5r Diana 1.75 1.00

Nos. 952-954 (3) 3.50 1.90

Souvenir Sheet

955 CD332 8r Diana, diff. 2.00 2.00

Nos. 952-954 also issued in sheetlets of 5 plus label.

Nos. 952-955 and the sheetlets of 5 eixst imperf. Value: 952-954, $9.

For overprints and surcharges see Nos. 966-969, 1050, 1052, 1054, 1056.

Scouting Year
A146

1982, Aug. 9 Litho. *Perf. 14*

956 A146 1.30r Saluting .40 .40

957 A146 1.80r Fire building .50 .50

958 A146 4r Lifesaving 1.10 1.10

959 A146 5r Map reading 1.50 1.50

Nos. 956-959 (4) 3.50 3.50

Souvenir Sheet

960 A146 10r Flag, emblem 2.50 2.50

1982 World Cup — A147

Various soccer players.

1982, Oct. 4 Litho. *Perf. 14*

961 A147 90 l multicolored 1.25 .60

962 A147 1.50r multicolored 1.75 1.10

963 A147 3r multicolored 2.50 1.75

964 A147 5r multicolored 2.75 2.50

Nos. 961-964 (4) 8.25 5.95

Souvenir Sheet

965 A147 10r multicolored 4.50 4.50

Nos. 952-955 Overprinted: "ROYAL BABY/21.6.82"

1982, Oct. 18 *Perf. 14½x14*

966 CD332 95 l multicolored .50 .50

967 CD332 3r multicolored .75 .75

968 CD332 5r multicolored 1.00 1.00

Nos. 966-968 (3) 2.25 2.25

Souvenir Sheet

969 CD332 8r multicolored 3.50 3.50

Birth of Prince William of Wales, June 21. Nos. 966-968 also issued in sheetlets of 5 + label.

Nos. 966-969 and the sheetlets of 5 exists imperf. Value: 966-968, $7.50

For surcharges see Nos. 1051, 1053, 1055, 1057.

TB Bacillus Cent. — A148

5 l, Koch isolating bacillus. 15 l, Slide, microscope. 95 l, Koch, 1905. 3r, Koch, book illus. plates.
5r, Koch in lab.

1982, Nov. 22 *Perf. 14½*

970 A148 5 l multi .25 .25

971 A148 15 l multi .25 .25

972 A148 95 l multi .55 .45

973 A148 3r multi 1.00 1.00

Nos. 970-973 (4) 2.05 1.95

Souvenir Sheet

974 A148 5r multi 1.25 1.25

Natl. Education — A149

Designs: 90 l, Basic education scheme, 1980-85. 95 l, Formal primary education. 1.30r, Teacher training. 2.50r, Educational materials production. 6r, Thanna typewriter.

1982, Nov. 15

975 A149 90 l multicolored .25 .25

976 A149 95 l multicolored .25 .25

977 A149 1.30r multicolored .25 .25

978 A149 2.50r multicolored .45 .45

Nos. 975-978 (4) 1.20 1.20

Souvenir Sheet

979 A149 6r multicolored 1.25 1.25

Manned Flight Bicentenary — A150

90 l, Blohm & Voss Ha-139. 1.45r, Macchi Castoldi MC-72. 4r, Boeing F4B-3. 5r, Le France.
10r, Nadar's Le Geant.

1983, July 28 Litho. *Perf. 14*

980 A150 90 l multi 2.25 .75

981 A150 1.45r multi 2.75 1.75

982 A150 4r multi 4.50 3.25

983 A150 5r multi 4.50 3.50

Nos. 980-983 (4) 14.00 9.25

Souvenir Sheet

984 A150 10r multi 3.25 3.25

For overprints see Nos. 1020-1022.

Roughtooth Dolphin — A151

40 l, Indopacific humpback dolphin. 4r, Finless porpoise. 6r, Pygmy sperm whale.
5r, Striped dolphins.

1983, Sept. 6 Litho. *Perf. 14*

985 A151 30 l shown .75 .75

986 A151 40 l multi .75 .75

987 A151 4r multi 4.00 4.00

988 A151 6r multi 9.50 9.50

Nos. 985-988 (4) 15.00 15.00

Souvenir Sheet

989 A151 5r multi 5.50 5.50

Classic Cars
A152

5 l, Curved Dash Oldsmobile, 1902. 30 l, Aston Martin Tourer, 1932. 40 l, Lamborghini Miura, 1966. 1r, Mercedes-Benz 300sl, 1954. 1.45r, Stutz Bearcat, 1913. 5r, Lotus Elite, 1958.
10r, Grand Prix Sunbeam, 1924.

1983, Aug. 15 Litho. *Perf. 14½x15*

990 A152 5 l multi .25 .25

991 A152 30 l multi .60 .40

992 A152 40 l multi .60 .45

993 A152 1r multi 1.00 .75

994 A152 1.45r multi 1.25 1.25

995 A152 5r multi 2.00 2.00

Nos. 990-995 (6) 5.70 5.10

Souvenir Sheet

996 A152 10r multi 6.50 6.50

World Communications Year — A153

50 l, Dish antenna. 1r, Mail transport. 2r, Ship-to-shore communications. 10r, Land-air communications. 20r, Telephone calls.

1983, Oct. 9 *Perf. 14*

997 A153 50 l multicolored .30 .30
998 A153 1r multicolored .60 .60
999 A153 2r multicolored 1.10 1.10
1000 A153 10r multicolored 5.50 5.50
Nos. 997-1000 (4) 7.50 7.50

Souvenir Sheet

1001 A153 20r multicolored 4.50 4.50

Raphael, 500th Birth Anniv. — A154

90 l, La Donna Gravida. 3r, Jeanne of Aragon. 4r, The Woman with the Unicorn. 6r, La Muta.
10r, The Knights Dream.

1983, Oct. 25 Litho. *Perf. 13½x14*

1002 A154 90 l multi .45 .45
1003 A154 3r multi 1.00 1.00
1004 A154 4r multi 1.50 1.50
1005 A154 6r multi 2.00 2.00
Nos. 1002-1005 (4) 4.95 4.95

Souvenir Sheet

1006 A154 10r multi 3.00 3.00

Intl. Palestinian Solidarity Day — A155

Various refugees, mosque.

1983, Nov. 29 Litho. *Perf. 14*

1007 A155 4r multicolored 1.75 1.75
1008 A155 5r multicolored 2.25 2.25
1009 A155 6r multicolored 2.75 2.75
Nos. 1007-1009 (3) 6.75 6.75

Natl. Development Programs — A156

7 l, Education. 10 l, Health care. 5r, Food production. 6r, Fishing industry.
10r, Inter-atoll transportation.

1983, Dec. 10 Litho. *Perf. 13½x14*

1010 A156 7 l multi .25 .25
1011 A156 10 l multi .50 .25
1012 A156 5r multi 1.50 1.25
1013 A156 6r multi 2.25 1.50
Nos. 1010-1013 (4) 4.50 3.25

Souvenir Sheet

1014 A156 10r multi 2.25 2.25

A157

1984, Feb. *Perf. 14*

1015 A157 50 l Baseball .25 .25
1016 A157 1.55r Swimming .70 .70
1017 A157 3r Judo 1.25 1.25
1018 A157 4r Shot put 1.75 1.75
Nos. 1015-1018 (4) 3.95 3.95

Souvenir Sheet

1019 A157 10r Handball 2.75 2.75

23rd Olympic Games, Los Angeles, 7/28-8/12.
For overprints see Nos. 1090-1094.

Nos. 982-984 Overprinted

Overprint reads "19th UPU/CONGRESS HAMBURG"

1984 Litho. *Perf. 14*

1020 A150 4r multicolored 1.75 1.40
1021 A150 5r multicolored 1.75 1.60

Souvenir Sheet

1022 A150 10r multicolored 2.75 2.75

Tourism — A158

7 l, Island resorts. 15 l, Cruising. 20 l, Snorkelling. 2r, Wind surfing. 4r, Scuba diving. 6r, Night fishing. 8r, Big game fishing. 10r, Nature (turtle).

1984, Sept. 21 Litho. *Perf. 14½*

1023 A158 7 l multi .45 .45
1024 A158 15 l multi .45 .45
1025 A158 20 l multi .45 .45
1026 A158 2r multi 1.10 1.10
1027 A158 4r multi 2.25 2.25
1028 A158 6r multi 3.50 3.50
1029 A158 8r multi 4.50 4.50
1030 A158 10r multi 5.50 5.50
Nos. 1023-1030 (8) 18.20 18.20

50th Anniv. of Donald Duck — A160

Scenes from various cartoons and movies.

1984, Nov. Litho. *Perf. 14*

1040 A160 3 l multi .25 .25
1041 A160 4 l multi .25 .25
1042 A160 5 l multi .25 .25
1043 A160 10 l multi .25 .25
1044 A160 15 l multi .25 .25
1045 A160 25 l multi .25 .25
1045A A160 5r multi, perf. 12x12½ 2.25 2.25
1046 A160 8r multi 2.50 2.50
1047 A160 10r multi 3.00 3.00
Nos. 1040-1047 (9) 9.25 9.25

Souvenir Sheets

1048 A160 15r multi 5.00 5.00
1049 A160 15r multi 5.00 5.00

Nos. 952-955, 966-969 Surcharged

1984, July Litho. *Perf. 14½x14*

1050 CD332 1.45r on 95 l #952 *2.50 2.00*
1051 CD332 1.45r on 95 l #966 *2.50 2.00*
1052 CD332 1.45r on 3r #953 *2.50 2.00*
1053 CD332 1.45r on 3r #967 *2.50 2.00*
1054 CD332 1.45r on 5r #954 *2.50 2.00*
1055 CD332 1.45r on 5r #968 *2.50 2.00*
Nos. 1050-1055 (6) 15.00 12.00

Souvenir Sheet

1056 CD332 1.45r on 8r #955 *2.50 2.00*
1057 CD332 1.45r on 8r #969 *2.50 2.00*

Namibia Day A161

1984, Aug. 26 *Perf. 15*

1058 A161 6r Breaking chain 1.25 1.25
1059 A161 8r Family, rising sun 1.25 1.25

Souvenir Sheet

1060 A161 10r Map, sun 2.25 2.25

Ausipex '84 A162

5r, Frangipani. 10r, Cooktown orchid.
15r, Sun orchids.

1984, Sept. 21

1061 A162 5r multi 2.25 1.75
1062 A162 10r multi 4.75 3.75

Souvenir Sheet

1063 A162 15r multi 10.00 10.00

150th Birth Anniv. of Edgar Degas — A163

75 l, Portrait of Edmond Duranty. 2r, Portrait of James Tissot. 5r, Portrait of Achille Degas. 10r, Lady with Chrysanthemums.
15r, Self-Portrait.

1984, Oct. Litho. *Perf. 14*

1064 A163 75 l multi .25 .25
1065 A163 2r multi .50 .50
1066 A163 5r multi 1.00 1.00
1067 A163 10r multi 1.75 1.75
Nos. 1064-1067 (4) 3.50 3.50

Souvenir Sheet

1068 A163 15r multi 3.50 3.50

Opening of Islamic Center A164

2r, Mosque. 5r, Mosque, minaret, vert.

1984, Nov. 11 Litho. *Perf. 15*

1069 A164 2r multi .50 .50
1070 A164 5r multi 1.10 1.10

40th Anniv., International Civil Aviation Organization — A165

7 l, Boeing 737. 4r, Lockheed L-1011. 6r, McDonnell Douglas DC-10. 8r, Lockheed L-1011.
15r, Shorts SC7 Skyvan.

1984, Nov. 19 Litho. *Perf. 14*

1071 A165 7 l multi .35 .35
1072 A165 4r multi 2.40 2.00
1073 A165 6r multi 3.25 3.25
1074 A165 8r multi 4.00 4.00
Nos. 1071-1074 (4) 10.00 9.60

Souvenir Sheet

1075 A165 15r multi 4.00 4.00

450th Anniv. of the Death of Correggio — A166

5r, Detail from The Day. 10r, Detail from The Night.
15r, Portrait of a Man.

1984, Dec. 10 Litho. *Perf. 14*

1076 A166 5r multi 1.00 1.00
1077 A166 10r multi 1.60 1.60

Souvenir Sheet

1078 A166 15r multi 3.75 3.75

John J. Audubon A167

Illustrations from Audubon's Birds of America: 3r, Flesh-footed shearwater, vert. 3.50r, Little grebe. 4r, Great cormorant, vert. 4.50r, White-faced storm petrel.
15r, Red-necked phalarope.

1985, Mar. 9 Litho. *Perf. 14*

1079 A167 3r multi 1.75 .80
1080 A167 3.50r multi 2.00 .90
1081 A167 4r multi 2.00 1.00
1082 A167 4.50r multi 2.00 1.10
Nos. 1079-1082 (4) 7.75 3.80

Souvenir Sheet

1083 A167 15r multi 5.00 5.00

See Nos. 1195-1204.

Natl. Security Services — A168

15 l, Drill. 20 l, Combat training. 1r, Fire fighting. 2r, Coast guard. No. 1088, Parade, vert.
No. 1089, Badge, cannon.

1985, June 6 Litho. *Perf. 14*

1084 A168 15 l multi .50 .25
1085 A168 20 l multi .50 .25
1086 A168 1r multi 2.00 .40
1087 A168 2r multi 2.50 .90
1088 A168 10r multi 3.25 *3.25*
Nos. 1084-1088 (5) 8.75 5.05

Souvenir Sheet

1089 A168 10r multi 2.75 2.75

Nos. 1015-1019 Overprinted

Overprint includes Country or "Gold Medalist," Winner and Nation in 3 Lines

50 l, Japan. 1.55r, Theresa Andrews. 3r, Frank Wieneke. 4r, Claudia Loch.
10r, US.

1985, July 17

1090 A157 50 l multi .30 .25
1091 A157 1.55r multi .55 .55
1092 A157 3r multi 1.10 1.10
1093 A157 4r multi 1.25 1.25
Nos. 1090-1093 (4) 3.20 3.15

Souvenir Sheet

1094 A157 10r multi 2.00 2.00

Queen Mother, 85th Birthday — A169

1r, Wearing tiara. 4r, At Middlesex Hospital, horiz. 7r, Wearing fur stole.
15r, With Prince of Wales.

1985-86 *Perf. 14, 12 (1r, 4r, 10r)*

1095 A169 1r multi .45 .45
1096 A169 3r like 1r .55 .55
1097 A169 4r multi .65 .65
1098 A169 5r like 4r .90 .90
1099 A169 7r multi 1.10 1.10
1100 A169 10r like 7r 1.75 1.75
Nos. 1095-1100 (6) 5.40 5.40

Souvenir Sheet

1101 A169 15r multi 3.50 3.50

Issued: 1r, 4r, 10r, 1/4/86; 3r, 5r, 7r, 15r, 8/20/85. Nos. 1095, 1097, 1100 printed in sheets of 5 + label.

Johann Sebastian Bach, Composer — A170

Portrait, Invention No. 1 in C Major and: 15 l, Lira da Braccio. 2r, Tenor oboe. 4r, Serpent. 10r, Table organ.

1985, Sept. 3 *Perf. 14*

1102 A170 15 l multi .25 .25
1103 A170 2r multi .65 .65
1104 A170 4r multi .90 .90
1105 A170 10r multi 1.75 1.75
Nos. 1102-1105 (4) 3.55 3.55

Souvenir Sheet

1106 A170 15r Portrait 3.25 3.25

Ships A171

3 l, Masodi. 5 l, Naalu Baththeli. 10 l, Addu Odi. 2.60r, Masdhoni, 2nd generation. 2.70r, Masdhoni. 3r, Baththeli Dhoni. 5r, Inter 1. 10r, Yacht Dhoni.

1985, Sept. 23

1107 A171 3 l multi .25 .25
1108 A171 5 l multi .25 .25
1109 A171 10 l multi .25 .25
1110 A171 2.60r multi 1.75 1.75
1111 A171 2.70r multi 1.75 1.75
1112 A171 3r multi 2.00 1.75
1113 A171 5r multi 3.00 3.00
1114 A171 10r multi 4.50 4.50
Nos. 1107-1114 (8) 13.75 13.50

For surcharge, see No. 1493B.

World Tourism Org., 10th Anniv. A172

1985, Oct. 2

1115 A172 6r Wind surfing 2.50 2.50
1116 A172 8r Scuba diving 3.00 3.00

Souvenir Sheet

1117 A172 15r Kuda Hithi Resort 5.00 5.00

Maldives Admission to UN, 20th Anniv. — A173

15r, Flags, UN building.

1985, Oct. 24

1118 A173 20 l shown .25 .25
1119 A173 15r multi 2.75 2.75

UN 40th Anniv., Intl. Peace Year A174

15 l, UN Building. 2r, IPY emblem. 4r, Security Council. 10r, Lion, lamb.
15r, UN Building, diff.

1985, Oct. 24 **Litho.** *Perf. 14*

1120 A174 15 l multi .25 .25
1121 A174 2r multi .65 .65
1122 A174 4r multi .90 .90
1123 A174 10r multi 1.25 1.25
Nos. 1120-1123 (4) 3.05 3.05

Souvenir Sheet

1124 A174 15r multi 2.50 2.50

Nos. 1120-1121, 1123-1124, vert.

Intl. Youth Year A175

90 l, Culture. 6r, Games. 10r, Community service, vert.
15r, Youth camp, vert.

1985, Nov. 20 *Perf. 15*

1125 A175 90 l multi .35 .35
1126 A175 6r multi 1.00 1.00
1127 A175 10r multi 1.25 *1.25*
Nos. 1125-1127 (3) 2.60 2.60

Souvenir Sheet

1128 A175 15r multi 2.50 2.50

Summit Nations Flags, Dedication by Pres. Maumoon — A176

1985, Dec. 8 *Perf. 14*

1129 A176 3r multicolored 2.25 2.25

South Asian Regional Cooperation, SARC, 1st Summit, Dec. 7-8, 1985.

Tuna A177

1985, Dec. 10

1130 A177 25 l Frigate .45 .45
1131 A177 75 l Little tuna .75 .75
1132 A177 3r Dogtooth 2.00 1.00
1133 A177 5r Yellowfin 2.25 1.25
Nos. 1130-1133 (4) 5.45 3.45

Souvenir Sheet

1134 A177 15r Skipjack 4.50 4.50

Fisherman's Day.

Mark Twain, American Novelist A178

Disney characters and Twain quotes.

1985, Dec. 21

1135 A178 2 l multicolored .25 .25
1136 A178 3 l multicolored .25 .25
1137 A178 4 l multicolored .25 .25
1138 A178 20 l multicolored .25 .25
1139 A178 4r multicolored 1.25 1.25
1140 A178 13r multicolored 1.75 1.75
Nos. 1135-1140 (6) 4.00 4.00

Souvenir Sheet

1141 A178 15r multicolored 6.50 6.50

Intl. Youth Year. 4r issued in sheet of 8.

The Brothers Grimm — A179

Disney characters in Doctor Knowall.

1985, Dec. 21

1142 A179 1 l multicolored .25 .25
1143 A179 5 l multicolored .25 .25
1144 A179 10 l multicolored .25 .25
1145 A179 15 l multicolored .25 .25
1146 A179 3r multicolored 1.00 1.00
1147 A179 14r multicolored 5.00 5.00
Nos. 1142-1147 (6) 7.00 7.00

Souvenir Sheet

1148 A179 15r multicolored 6.50 6.50

3r issued in sheets of 8.

World Disarmament Day — A180

1986, Feb. 10 *Perf. 14½x14*

1149 A180 1.50r shown — —
1150 A180 10r Dove — —

Halley's Comet A181

Designs: 20 l, NASA space telescope. 1.50r, Giotto space probe. 2r, Plant-A probe, Japan. 4r, Edmond Halley, Stonehenge. 5r, Vega probe, USSR. 15r, Comet over Male.

1986, Apr. 29

1151 A181 20 l multicolored .50 .50
1152 A181 1.50r multicolored 1.25 1.25
1153 A181 2r multicolored 1.25 1.25
1154 A181 4r multicolored 2.00 2.00
1155 A181 5r multicolored 2.00 2.00
Nos. 1151-1155 (5) 7.00 7.00

Souvenir Sheet

1156 A181 15r multicolored 6.50 6.50

See Nos. 1210-1215.

Statue of Liberty, Cent. A182

Detail of statue and: 50 l, Walter Gropius (1883-1969), architect. 70 l, John Lennon (1940-1980), musician. 1r, George Balanchine (1904-1983), choreographer. 10r, Franz Werfel (1890-1945), writer. 15r, Close-up of statue, vert.

1986, May 5

1157 A182 50 l multicolored .40 .40
1158 A182 70 l multicolored 1.90 1.25
1159 A182 1r multicolored 2.00 1.25
1160 A182 10r multicolored 4.00 4.00
Nos. 1157-1160 (4) 8.30 6.90

Souvenir Sheet

1161 A182 15r multicolored 7.50 7.50

AMERIPEX '86 — A183

US stamps and Disney portrayals of American legends: 3 l, #1317, Johnny Appleseed. 4 l, #1122, Paul Bunyan. 5 l, #1381, Casey at the Bat. 10 l, #. 1548, Tales of Sleepy Hollow. 15 l, #922, John Henry. 20 l, #1061, Windwagon Smith. 13r, #1409, Mike Fink. 14r, #993, Casey Jones. No. 1170, Remember the Alamo, #1330. No. 1171, Pocahontas, #328-330.

1986, May 22 *Perf. 11*

1162 A183 3 l multicolored .25 .25
1163 A183 4 l multicolored .25 .25
1164 A183 5 l multicolored .25 .25
1165 A183 10 l multicolored .25 .25
1166 A183 15 l multicolored .25 .25
1167 A183 20 l multicolored .25 .25
1168 A183 13r multicolored 7.00 7.00
1169 A183 14r multicolored 8.00 8.00
Nos. 1162-1169 (8) 16.50 16.50

Souvenir Sheets

Perf. 14

1170 A183 15r multicolored 6.50 6.50
1171 A183 15r multicolored 6.50 6.50

Queen Elizabeth II, 60th Birthday

Common Design Type

1r, Girl Guides' rally, 1938. 2r, Canada visit, 1985. 12r, At Sandringham, 1970.
15r, Royal Lodge, 1940.

1986, May 29 *Perf. 14*

1172 CD339 1r multicolored .25 .25
1173 CD339 2r multicolored .50 .50
1174 CD339 12r multicolored 2.00 2.00
Nos. 1172-1174 (3) 2.75 2.75

Souvenir Sheet

1175 CD339 15r multicolored 3.50 3.50

For overprints see Nos. 1288-1291.

1986 World Cup Soccer Championships, Mexico — A184

Various soccer plays.

1986, June 18 **Litho.** *Perf. 14*

1176 A184 15 l multicolored .75 .30
1177 A184 2r multicolored 2.50 1.75
1178 A184 4r multicolored 4.00 3.50
1179 A184 10r multicolored 7.50 7.50
Nos. 1176-1179 (4) 14.75 13.05

Souvenir Sheet

1180 A184 15r multicolored 5.50 5.50

For overprints see Nos. 1205-1209.

Royal Wedding Issue, 1986
Common Design Type

Designs: 10 l, Prince Andrew and Sarah Ferguson. 2r, Andrew. 12r, Andrew on ship's deck in uniform. 15r, Couple, diff.

1986, July 23

1181	CD340	10 l multi	.25	.25
1182	CD340	2r multi	.70	.70
1183	CD340	12r multi	3.00	3.00
		Nos. 1181-1183 (3)	3.95	3.95

Souvenir Sheet

1184	CD340	15r multi	4.50	4.50

Marine Life A185

Designs: 50 l, Sea fan, moorish idol. 90 l, Regal angelfish. 1r, Anemone fish. 2r, Stinging coral, tiger cowrie. 3r, Emperor angelfish, staghorn coral. 4r, Black-naped tern. 5r, Fiddler crab, staghorn coral. 10r, Hawksbill turtle. No. 1193, Trumpet fish. No. 1194, Long-nosed butterflyfish.

1986, Sept. 22 Litho. *Perf. 15*

1185	A185	50 l multicolored	1.50	.40
1186	A185	90 l multicolored	2.00	.55
1187	A185	1r multicolored	2.00	.55
1188	A185	2r multicolored	2.50	1.50
1189	A185	3r multicolored	2.50	2.00
1190	A185	4r multicolored	2.75	2.75
1191	A185	5r multicolored	2.50	2.50
1192	A185	10r multicolored	3.00	3.00
		Nos. 1185-1192 (8)	18.75	13.25

Souvenir Sheets

1193	A185	15r multicolored	6.00	6.00
1194	A185	15r multicolored	6.00	6.00

Nos. 1185-1187 and 1189 show the World Wildlife Fund emblem.

Audubon Type of 1985

Birds: 3 l, Little blue heron. 4 l, White-tailed kite, vert. 5 l, Greater shearwater. 10 l, Magnificent frigatebird, vert. 15 l, Eared grebe, vert. 20 l, Common merganser, vert. 13r, Great-footed hawk. 14r, Greater prairie chicken. No. 1203, White-fronted goose. No. 1204, Northern fulmar, vert.

1986, Oct. 9 Litho. *Perf. 14*

1195	A167	3 l multicolored	.40	.40
1196	A167	4 l multicolored	.40	.40
1197	A167	5 l multicolored	.40	.40
1198	A167	10 l multicolored	.45	.45
1199	A167	15 l multicolored	.90	.90
1200	A167	20 l multicolored	.95	.95
1201	A167	13r multicolored	5.75	5.75
1202	A167	14r multicolored	5.75	5.75
		Nos. 1195-1202 (8)	15.00	15.00

Souvenir Sheets

1203	A167	15r multicolored	11.00	11.00
1204	A167	15r multicolored	11.00	11.00

Nos. 1197, 1199-1201 printed se-tenant with labels picturing a horned puffin, gray kingbird, downy woodpecker and water pipit, respectively.

Nos. 1176-1180 Overprinted in Gold

Overprint reads "WINNERS / Argentina 3 / W. Germany 2"

1986, Oct. 25

1205	A184	15 l multicolored	.40	.30
1206	A184	2r multicolored	1.25	1.10
1207	A184	4r multicolored	2.00	2.00
1208	A184	10r multicolored	2.75	2.75
		Nos. 1205-1208 (4)	6.40	6.15

Souvenir Sheet

1209	A184	15r multicolored	3.75	3.75

Nos. 1151-1156 Overprinted with Halley's Comet Symbol in Silver

1986, Oct. 30

1210	A181	20 l multicolored	.65	.40
1211	A181	1.50r multicolored	1.25	1.25
1212	A181	2r multicolored	1.50	1.50
1213	A181	4r multicolored	2.00	2.00
1214	A181	5r multicolored	2.00	2.00
		Nos. 1210-1214 (5)	7.40	7.15

Souvenir Sheet

1215	A181	15r multicolored	6.00	6.00

UNESCO, 40th Anniv. — A186

1986, Nov. 4 *Perf. 15*

1216	A186	1r Aviation	.75	.30
1217	A186	2r Boat-building	.90	.90
1218	A186	3r Education	1.00	1.00
1219	A186	5r Research	1.50	1.50
		Nos. 1216-1219 (4)	4.15	3.70

Souvenir Sheet

1220	A186	15r Ocean exploration	2.75	2.75

Mushrooms — A187

Designs: 15 l, Hypholoma fasciculare. 50 l, Kuehneromyces mutabilis, vert. 1r, Amanita muscaria, vert. 2r, Agaricus campestris. 3r, Amanita pantherina, vert. 4r, Coprinus comatus vert. 5r, Pholiota spectabilis. 10r, Pluteus cervinus. No. 1229, Armillaria mellea. No. 1230, Stropharia aeruginosa.

1986, Dec. 31 Litho. *Perf. 15*

1221	A187	15 l multicolored	.75	.25
1222	A187	50 l multicolored	1.60	.45
1223	A187	1r multicolored	1.75	.60
1224	A187	2r multicolored	2.00	1.50
1225	A187	3r multicolored	2.00	1.75
1226	A187	4r multicolored	2.00	2.00
1227	A187	5r multicolored	2.00	2.00
1228	A187	10r multicolored	3.00	3.00
		Nos. 1221-1228 (8)	15.10	11.55

Souvenir Sheets

1229	A187	15r multicolored	6.50	6.50
1230	A187	15r multicolored	6.50	6.50

Flowers — A188

1987, Jan. 29 Litho. *Perf. 15*

1231	A188	10 l Ixora	.25	.25
1232	A188	20 l Frangipani	.25	.25
1233	A188	50 l Crinum	.25	.25
1235	A188	2r Pink rose	.90	.90
1236	A188	4r Flamboyant	1.75	1.75
1238	A188	10r Ground orchid	4.75	4.75
		Nos. 1231-1238 (6)	8.15	8.15

Souvenir Sheet

1239	A188	15r Gardenia	2.75	2.75
1240	A188	15r Oleander	2.75	2.75

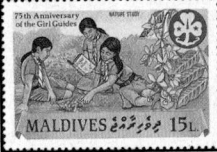

Indigenous Trees and Plants — A190

A191

America's Cup — A192

Butterflies — A193

Scientists — A194

Disney Characters, Space Exploration — A195

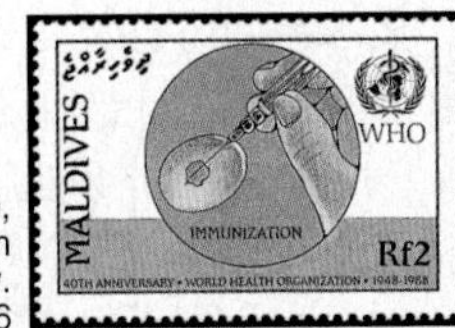

WHO, 40th Anniv. A196

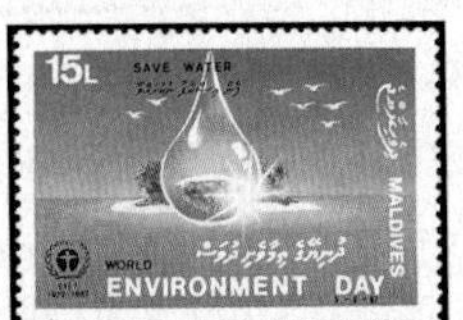

World Environment Day — A197

Girl Guides, 75th Anniv. (in 1985) A189

1987, Apr. 4 Litho. *Perf. 15*

1241	A189	15 l Nature study	.25	.25
1242	A189	2r Guides, rabbits	.65	.65
1243	A189	4r Bird-watching	2.10	2.10
1244	A189	12r Lady Baden-Powell, flag	2.40	2.40
		Nos. 1241-1244 (4)	5.40	5.40

Souvenir Sheet

1245	A189	15r Sailing	2.50	2.50

50 l, Thespesia populnea, vert. 1r, Cocos nucifera, vert. 2r, Calophyllum mophyllum, vert. 3r, Xyanthosoma indica. 5r, Ipomoea batatas. 7r, Artocarpus altilis, vert.
15r, Cocos nucifera, diff., vert.

1987, Apr. 22 Litho. *Perf. 14*

1246	A190	50 l multi	.25	.25
1247	A190	1r multi	.25	.25
1248	A190	2r multi	.40	.40
1249	A190	3r multi	.60	.60
1250	A190	5r multi	1.00	1.00
1251	A190	7r multi	1.25	1.25
		Nos. 1246-1251 (6)	3.75	3.75

Souvenir Sheet

1252	A190	15r multi	2.75	2.75

15 l, Intrepid, 1970. 1r, France II, 1974. 2r, Gretel, 1962. 12r, Volunteer, 1887.
15r, Defender Vs. Valkyrie III, 1895.

1987, May 4 Litho. *Perf. 15*

1253	A191	15 l multi	.25	.25
1254	A191	1r multi	.25	.25
1255	A191	2r multi	.40	.40
1256	A191	12r multi	2.25	2.25
		Nos. 1253-1256 (4)	3.15	3.15

Souvenir Sheet

1257	A192	15r multi	2.75	2.75

15 l, Precis octavia. 20 l, Pachliopta hector. 50 l, Teinopalpus imperialis. 1r, Kallima horsfieldi. 2r, Cethosia biblis. 4r, Hestia jasonia. 7r, Papilio memnon. 10r, Meneris tulbaghia.
No. 1266, Acraea violae acraeinae. No. 1267, Hebomoia leucippe.

1987, Dec. 16 Litho. *Perf. 15*

1258	A193	15 l multi	.50	.50
1259	A193	20 l multi	.50	.50
1260	A193	50 l multi	.75	.40
1261	A193	1r multi	1.00	.45
1262	A193	2r multi	1.50	1.25
1263	A193	4r multi	2.25	2.25
1264	A193	7r multi	2.75	2.75
1265	A193	10r multi	3.25	3.25
		Nos. 1258-1265 (8)	12.50	11.35

Souvenir Sheets

1266	A193	15r multi	4.50	4.50
1267	A193	15r multi	4.50	4.50

Designs: 1.50r, Sir Isaac Newton using prism to demonstrate his Theory of Light, horiz. 3r, Euclid (c. 300 B.C.), mathematician. 4r, Gregor Johann Mendel (1822-1884), botanist; father of genetics. 5r, Galileo, 1st man to observe 4 moons of Jupiter, horiz. 15r, Apollo spacecraft orbiting the moon.

1988, Jan. 10 *Perf. 14*

1268	A194	1.50r multicolored	1.25	1.00
1269	A194	3r multicolored	1.75	1.75
1270	A194	4r multicolored	1.75	1.75
1271	A194	5r multicolored	3.00	3.00
		Nos. 1268-1271 (4)	7.75	7.50

Souvenir Sheet

1272	A194	15r multicolored	5.75	5.75

3 l, Weather satellite. 4 l, Navigation satellite. 5 l, Communication satellite. 10 l, Moon rover. 20 l, Space shuttle. 13r, Space docking. 14r, Voyager 2.
No. 1280, 1st Man on Moon. No. 1281, Space station colony.

1988, Feb. 15

1273	A195	3 l multi	.25	.25
1274	A195	4 l multi	.25	.25
1275	A195	5 l multi	.25	.25
1276	A195	10 l multi	.25	.25
1277	A195	20 l multi	.25	.25
1278	A195	13r multi	5.00	5.00
1279	A195	14r multi	5.00	5.00
		Nos. 1273-1279 (7)	11.25	11.25

Souvenir Sheets

1280	A195	15r multi	6.25	6.25
1281	A195	15r multi	6.25	6.25

Nos. 1276-1278 and 1281 vert.

1988, Apr. 7 Litho. *Perf. 14*

1282	A196	2r Immunization	.45	.45
1283	A196	4r Clean water	.80	.80

For overprints see Nos. 1307-1308.

1988, May 9 *Perf. 15*
1284 A197 15 l Save water .25 .25
1285 A197 75 l Protect the reef .25 .25
1286 A197 2r Conserve nature .85 .85
Nos. 1284-1286 (3) 1.35 1.35

Souvenir Sheet

1287 A197 15r Banyan tree, vert. 4.00 4.00

Nos. 1172-1175 Overprinted in Gold

Overprint reads "40th WEDDING ANNIVERSARY/ H.M. QUEEN ELIZABETH II/ H.R.H. THE DUKE OF EDINBURGH"

1988, July 7 **Litho.** *Perf. 14*
1288 CD339 1r multicolored .50 .25
1289 CD339 2r multicolored .75 .55
1290 CD339 12r multicolored 3.00 3.00
Nos. 1288-1290 (3) 4.25 3.80

Souvenir Sheet

1291 CD339 15r multicolored 4.50 4.50

Transportation and Communication Decade for Asia and the Pacific — A198

Globe and: 2r, Postal communications. 3r, Earth satellite telecommunications technology. 5r, Space telecommunications technology. 10r, Automobile, aircraft and ship.

1988, May 31 **Litho.** *Perf. 14*
1292 A198 2r multicolored 1.25 1.25
1293 A198 3r multicolored 1.75 1.75
1294 A198 5r multicolored 2.75 2.75
1295 A198 10r multicolored 5.50 5.50
Nos. 1292-1295 (4) 11.25 11.25

For overprints, see Nos. 1344-1345.

1988 Summer Olympics, Seoul — A199

15 l, Discus. 2r, 100-Meter sprint. 4r, Gymnastics, horiz. 12r, Steeplechase, horiz. 20r, Tennis, horiz.

1988, July 16
1296 A199 15 l multi .25 .25
1297 A199 2r multi .40 .40
1298 A199 4r multi .75 .75
1299 A199 12r multi 2.25 2.25
Nos. 1296-1299 (4) 3.65 3.65

Souvenir Sheet

1300 A199 20r multi 4.25 4.25

For overprints see Nos. 1311-1315.

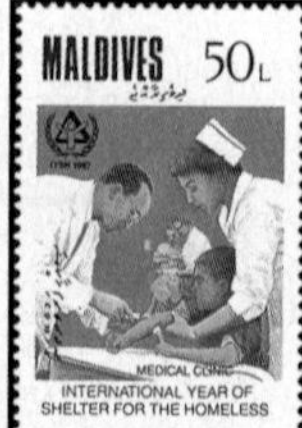

Intl. Year of Shelter for the Homeless — A200

1988, July 20
1301 A200 50 l Medical clinic .35 .35
1302 A200 3r Prefab housing 1.10 1.10

Souvenir Sheet

1303 A200 15r Construction site 2.00 2.00

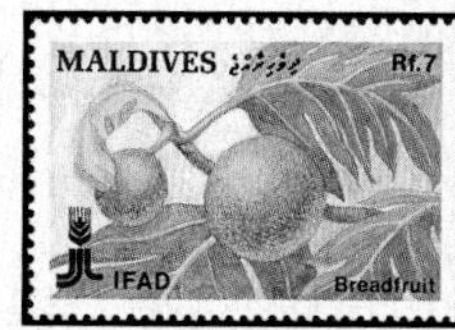

Intl. Fund for Agricultural Development (IFAD), 10th Anniv. — A201

7r, Breadfruit. 10r, Mango, vert. 15r, Coconut palm, yellowtail tuna.

1988, July 30
1304 A201 7r multi 1.00 1.00
1305 A201 10r multi 1.50 1.50

Souvenir Sheet

1306 A201 15r multi 2.75 2.75

Nos. 1282-1283 Ovptd.

1988, Dec. 1 **Litho.** *Perf. 14*
1307 A196 2r multicolored .35 .35
1308 A196 4r multicolored .65 .65

Intl. Day for the Fight Against Aids.

John F. Kennedy (1917-1963), 35th US President — A202

Space achievements: a, Apollo launch. b, 1st Man on the Moon. c, Earth and astronaut driving moon rover. d, Space module and Kennedy. 15r, Kennedy addressing the nation.

1989, Feb. 19
1309 A202 Strip of 4 9.00 9.00
a.-d. 5r any single 2.00 2.00

Souvenir Sheet

1310 A202 15r multicolored 4.00 4.00

No. 1296 Overprinted

No. 1297 Overprinted

No. 1298 Overprinted

No. 1299 Overprinted

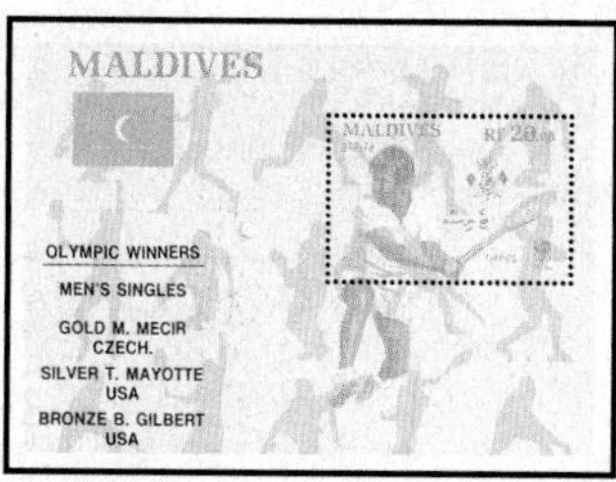

No. 1300 Overprinted

1989, Apr. 29 **Litho.** *Perf. 14*
1311 A199 15 l multicolored .25 .25
1312 A199 2r multicolored .65 .65
1313 A199 4r multicolored 1.40 1.40
1314 A199 12r multicolored 4.00 4.00
Nos. 1311-1314 (4) 6.30 6.30

Souvenir Sheet

1315 A199 20r multi 6.50 6.50

Paintings by Titian (b. 1489) A203

Designs: 15 l, Portrait of Benedetto Varchi, c. 1540. 1r, Portrait of a Young Man in a Fur, 1515. 2r, King Francis I of France, 1538. 5r, Portrait of Pietro Aretino, 1545. 15r, The Bravo, c. 1520. 20r, The Concert, 1512. No. 1322, An Allegory of Prudence, c. 1565. No. 1323, Portrait of Francesco Maria Della Rovere.

1989, May 15 **Litho.** *Perf. 13½x14*
1316 A203 15 l multicolored .25 .25
1317 A203 1r multicolored .25 .25
1318 A203 2r multicolored .50 .50
1319 A203 5r multicolored 1.25 1.25
1320 A203 15r multicolored 4.00 4.00
1321 A203 20r multicolored 4.00 4.00
Nos. 1316-1321 (6) 10.25 10.25

Souvenir Sheets

1322 A203 20r multicolored 4.25 4.25
1323 A203 20r multicolored 4.25 4.25

"Thirty-six Views of Mt. Fuji" — A204

Prints by Hokusai (1760-1849): 15 l, Fuji from Hodogaya. 50 l, Fuji from Lake Kawaguchi. 1r, Fuji from Owari. 2r, Fuji from Tsukudajima in Edo. 4r, Fuji from a Teahouse at Yoshida. 6r, Fuji from Tagonoura. 10r, Fuji from Mishima-goe. 12r, Fuji from the Sumida River in Edo. No. 1332, Fuji from Fukagawa in Edo. No. 1333, Fuji from Inume Pass.

1989 *Perf. 14*
1324 A204 15 l multicolored .25 .25
1325 A204 50 l multicolored .25 .25
1326 A204 1r multicolored .25 .25
1327 A204 2r multicolored .50 .40
1328 A204 4r multicolored .80 .80
1329 A204 6r multicolored 1.00 1.00
1330 A204 10r multicolored 2.25 2.25
1331 A204 12r multicolored 2.25 2.25
Nos. 1324-1331 (8) 7.55 7.45

Souvenir Sheets

1332 A204 18r multicolored 4.25 4.25
1333 A204 18r multicolored 4.25 4.25

Hirohito (1901-1989) and enthronement of Akihito as emperor of Japan.
Issue dates: No. 1332, 10/16, others, 9/2.

Tropical Fish A205

Designs: 20 l, Clown triggerfish. 50 l, Blue surgeonfish. 1r, Bluestripe snapper. 2r, Oriental sweetlips. 3r, Wrasse. 8r, Treadfin butterflyfish. 10r, Bicolor parrotfish. 12r, Saber squirrelfish.
No. 1342, Butterfly perch. No. 1343, Semicircle angelfish.

1989, Oct. 16 **Litho.** *Perf. 14*
1334 A205 20 l multicolored .25 .25
1335 A205 50 l multicolored .40 .25
1336 A205 1r multicolored .50 .30
1337 A205 2r multicolored .70 .70
1338 A205 3r multicolored .90 .90
1339 A205 8r multicolored 1.60 1.60
1340 A205 10r multicolored 2.00 2.00
1341 A205 12r multicolored 2.00 2.00
Nos. 1334-1341 (8) 8.35 8.00

Souvenir Sheet

1342 A205 15r multicolored 6.50 6.50
1343 A205 15r multicolored 6.50 6.50

Nos. 1293-1294 Overprinted in Silver

Overprint reads "ASIA-PACIFIC / TELECOMMUNITY / 10 YEARS"

1989, July 5 **Litho.** *Perf. 14*
1344 A198 3r multicolored 1.25 1.25
1345 A198 5r multicolored 2.25 2.25

World Stamp Expo '89 Emblem, Disney Characters and Japanese Automobiles — A206

Designs: 15 l, 1907 Takuri Type 3. 50 l, 1917 Mitsubishi Model A. 1r, 1935 Datsun Roadstar. 2r, 1940 Mazda. 4r, 1959 Nissan Bluebird 310. 6r, 1958 Subaru 360. 10r, 1966 Honda 5800. 12r, 1966 Daihatsu Fellow. No. 1354, 1981 Isuzu Trooper II. No. 1355, 1985 Toyota Supra.

1989, Nov. 17 **Litho.** *Perf. 14x13½*
1346 A206 15 l multicolored .25 .25
1347 A206 50 l multicolored .40 .30
1348 A206 1r multicolored .70 .50
1349 A206 2r multicolored 1.00 .75
1350 A206 4r multicolored 1.50 1.25
1351 A206 6r multicolored 1.75 1.75
1352 A206 10r multicolored 3.25 3.25
1353 A206 12r multicolored 3.75 3.75
Nos. 1346-1353 (8) 12.60 11.80

Souvenir Sheets

1354 A206 20r multicolored 5.50 5.50
1355 A206 20r multicolored 5.50 5.50

Souvenir Sheet

The Marine Corps War Memorial, Arlington, VA — A207

1989, Nov. 17 Litho. *Perf. 14*

1356	A207	8r multicolored	2.75	2.75

World Stamp Expo '89.

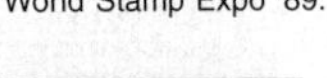

1st Moon Landing, 20th Anniv. A208

Designs: 1r, *Eagle* lunar module. 2r, Aldrin taking soil samples. 6r, Solar wind experiment. 10r, Nixon, astronauts.

18r, Armstrong descending ladder.

1989, Nov. 24 *Perf. 14*

1357	A208	1r multicolored	.30	.30
1358	A208	2r multicolored	.50	.50
1359	A208	6r multicolored	1.25	1.25
1360	A208	10r multicolored	2.00	2.00
		Nos. 1357-1360 (4)	4.05	4.05

Souvenir Sheet

1361	A208	18r multicolored	7.50	7.50

Railway Pioneers — A209

Designs: 10 l, Sir William Cornelius Van Horne (1843-1915), chairman of Canadian Pacific Railway, map and locomotive, 1894. 25 l, Matthew Murray, built rack locomotives for Middleton Colliery. 50 l, Louis Favre (1826-1879), built the St. Gotthard (spiral) Tunnel, 1881. 2r, George Stephenson (1781-1848), locomotive, 1825. 6r, Richard Trevithick (1771-1833), builder of 1st rail locomotive, 1804. 8r, George Nagelmackers, Orient Express dining car, 1869. 10r, William Jessop, Surrey horse-drawn cart on rails, 1770. 12r, Isambard Kingdom Brunel (1806-1859), chief engineer of Great Western Railway, introduced broad gauge, 1830's. No. 1370, George Pullman (1831-1897), *Pioneer* passenger car. No. 1371, Rudolf Diesel (1858-1913), inventor of the diesel engine, 1892, and diesel train.

1989, Dec. 26 Litho. *Perf. 14*

1362	A209	10 l multicolored	.25	.25
1363	A209	25 l multicolored	.35	.25
1364	A209	50 l multicolored	.40	.25
1365	A209	2r multicolored	.75	.55
1366	A209	6r multicolored	1.50	1.50
1367	A209	8r multicolored	1.75	1.75
1368	A209	10r multicolored	2.50	2.50
1369	A209	12r multicolored	3.00	3.00
		Nos. 1362-1369 (8)	10.50	10.05

Souvenir Sheets

1370	A209	18r multicolored	5.00	5.00
1371	A209	18r multicolored	5.00	5.00

Anniversaries and Events (in 1989) — A210

Designs: 20 l, Flag of India, Jawaharlal Nehru, Mahatma Gandhi. 50 l, Syringe, opium poppies, vert. 1r, William Shakespeare, birthplace, Stratford-on-Avon. 2r, Flag of France, storming of the Bastille, Paris, 1789, vert. 3r, Concorde jet, flags of France, Britain. 8r, George Washington, Mount Vernon estate, Virginia. 10r, Capt. William Bligh, the *Bounty*. 12r, Ships in port. No. 1380, 1st Televised baseball game, 1939, vert. No. 1381, Franz von Taxis (1458-1517), vert.

1990, Feb. 15 Litho. *Perf. 14*

1372	A210	20 l multicolored	.25	.25
1373	A210	50 l multicolored	.25	.25
1374	A210	1r multicolored	.60	.60
1375	A210	2r multicolored	1.10	1.10
1376	A210	3r multicolored	1.75	1.75
1377	A210	8r multicolored	5.50	5.50
1378	A210	10r multicolored	7.00	7.00
1379	A210	12r multicolored	8.50	8.50
		Nos. 1372-1379 (8)	24.95	24.95

Souvenir Sheets

1380	A210	18r multicolored	7.00	7.00
1381	A210	18r multicolored	7.00	7.00

Birth cent. of Nehru (20 l); SAARC Year for Combatting Drug Abuse (50 l); 425th birth anniv. of Shakespeare (1r); French Revolution, bicent. (2r); first test flight of the Concorde supersonic jet, 20th anniv. (3r); American presidency, bicent. (8r); Mutiny on the *Bounty*, bicent. (10r); Hamburg, 800th anniv. (12r); 1st televised baseball game, 50th anniv. (No. 1380); and European postal communications, 500th anniv. (No. 1381).

Johann von Taxis was the first postmaster of Thurn & Taxis in 1489, not Franz, who is credited on No. 1381.

Natl. Independence, 25th Anniv. — A211

Designs: 20 l, Bodu Thakurufaanu Memorial Center, Utheemu. 25 l, Islamic Center, Male. 50 l, Natl. flag, UN, Islamic Conf., Commonwealth and SAARC emblems. 2r, Muleeaage, Male. 5r, Natl. Security Service, Maldives. 10r, Natl. crest, emblem of the Citizens' Majlis (parliament).

1990, Jan. 1 Litho. *Perf. 14*

1382	A211	20 l multicolored	.25	.25
1383	A211	25 l multicolored	.25	.25
1384	A211	50 l multicolored	.25	.25
1385	A211	2r multicolored	.30	.30
1386	A211	5r multicolored	.90	.90
		Nos. 1382-1386 (5)	1.95	1.95

Souvenir Sheet

1387	A211	10r multicolored	4.25	4.25

French Revolution, Bicent. (in 1989) A212

Paintings: 15 l, *Louis XVI in Coronation Robes*, by Duplessis. 50 l, *Monsieur Lavoisier and His Wife*, by David. 1r, *Madame Pastoret*, by David. 2r, *Oath of Lafayette at the Festival of Federation*, by David. 4r, *Madame Trudaine*, by David. 6r, *Chenard Celebrating the Liberation of Savoy*, by Boilly. 10r, *An Officer Swears Allegiance to the Constitution*, artist unknown. 12r, *Self-portrait*, by David. No. 1396, *The Tennis Court Oath, June 20, 1789*, by David, horiz. No. 1397, *Jean-Jacques Rousseau and the Symbols of the Revolution*, by Jeaurat.

1990, Jan. 11 Litho. *Perf. 14*

1388	A212	15 l multicolored	.25	.25
1389	A212	50 l multicolored	.45	.25
1390	A212	1r multicolored	.65	.35
1391	A212	2r multicolored	1.00	.70
1392	A212	4r multicolored	1.75	1.50
1393	A212	6r multicolored	2.40	2.40
1394	A212	10r multicolored	4.00	4.00
1395	A212	12r multicolored	4.00	4.00
		Nos. 1388-1395 (8)	14.50	13.45

Souvenir Sheets

1396	A212	20r multicolored	6.50	6.50
1397	A212	20r multicolored	6.50	6.50

Stamp World London '90 — A213

Walt Disney characters demonstrating sports popular in Britain: 15 l, Rugby. 50 l, Curling. 1r, Polo. 2r, Soccer. 4r, Cricket. 6r, Horse racing, Ascot. 10r, Tennis. 12r, Lawn bowling.

No. 1406, Fox hunting. No. 1407, Golf, St. Andrews, Scotland.

1990 Litho. *Perf. 14x13½*

1398	A213	15 l multicolored	.30	.25
1399	A213	50 l multicolored	.45	.25
1400	A213	1r multicolored	.65	.40
1401	A213	2r multicolored	.90	.75
1402	A213	4r multicolored	1.75	1.50
1403	A213	6r multicolored	2.25	2.00
1404	A213	10r multicolored	3.50	3.50
1405	A213	12r multicolored	3.50	3.50
		Nos. 1398-1405 (8)	13.30	12.15

Souvenir Sheets

1406	A213	20r multicolored	7.50	7.50
1407	A213	20r multicolored	7.50	7.50

Penny Black, 150th Anniv. A214

1990, May 3 Litho. *Perf. 15x14*

1408	A214	8r Silhouettes	2.25	2.25
1409	A214	12r Silhouettes, diff.	2.50	2.50

Souvenir Sheet

1410	A214	18r Penny Black	5.00	5.00

Queen Mother 90th Birthday
A215 A216

No. 1413, As Lady Bowes-Lyon, diff.
No. 1414, On Wedding Day, diff.

1990, July 8 *Perf. 14*

1411	A215	6r shown	1.00	1.00
1412	A216	6r shown	1.00	1.00
1413	A215	6r multi	1.00	1.00
		Nos. 1411-1413 (3)	3.00	3.00

Souvenir Sheet

1414	A216	18r multi	3.00	3.00

Nos. 1411-1413 printed in sheets of 9.

A217

A218

A219

Islamic Heritage Year A220

1990, July 22 Litho. *Perf. 14*

1415	A217	1r blue & black	.35	.35
1416	A218	1r blue & black	.35	.35
1417	A218	1r Building, diff.	.35	.35
1418	A219	2r blue & black	.45	.45
1419	A220	2r blue & black	.45	.45
1420	A219	2r Building, diff.	.45	.45
a.		Block of 6, #1415-1420	2.50	2.50

Great Crested Tern A221

Design: 25 l, Great Crested Tern. 50 l, Koel. 1r, White tern. 3.50r, Cinnamon bittern. 6r, Sooty tern. 8r, Audubon's shearwater. 12r, Brown noddy. 15r, Lesser frigatebird.

No. 1429, White-tailed tropicbird. No. 1430, Grey heron.

1990, Aug. 9 Litho. *Perf. 14*

1421	A221	25 l multicolored	.25	.25
1422	A221	50 l multicolored	.25	.25
1423	A221	1r multicolored	.35	.35
1424	A221	3.50r multicolored	.90	.90
1425	A221	6r multicolored	1.40	1.40
1426	A221	8r multicolored	1.60	1.60
1427	A221	12r multicolored	2.50	2.50
1428	A221	15r multicolored	2.75	2.75
		Nos. 1421-1428 (8)	10.00	10.00

Souvenir Sheets

1429	A221	18r multicolored	4.50	4.50
1430	A221	18r multicolored	4.50	4.50

World War II Milestones — A222

Designs: 15 l, US Marines repulse Japanese invasion of Wake Island, Dec. 11, 1941. 25 l, Gen. Stilwell begins offensive in Burma, Mar. 4, 1944. 50 l, US begins offensive in Normandy, July 3, 1944. 1r, US forces secure Saipan, July 9, 1944. 2.50r, D-Day, June 6, 1944. 3.50r, Allied forces land in Norway, Apr. 14, 1940. 4r, Adm. Mountbatten named Chief of Combined Operations, Mar. 18, 1942. 6r, Gen. MacArthur accepts Japanese surrender, Sept. 2, 1945. 10r, Potsdam Conference, July 16, 1945. 12r, Allied invade Sicily, July 10, 1943. 18r, Atlantic convoys.

1990, Aug. 9 Litho. *Perf. 14*

1431	A222	15 l multicolored	.25	.25
1432	A222	25 l multicolored	.30	.25
1433	A222	50 l multicolored	.40	.25

1434	A222	1r multicolored	.55	.40
1435	A222	2.50r multicolored	.90	.80
1436	A222	3.50r multicolored	1.10	1.10
1437	A222	4r multicolored	1.40	1.40
1438	A222	6r multicolored	2.75	2.75
1439	A222	10r multicolored	2.75	2.75
1440	A222	12r multicolored	3.00	3.00
		Nos. 1431-1440 (10)	13.40	12.95

Souvenir Sheet

1441	A222	18r multicolored	5.50	5.50

A223

5th SAARC Summit — A224

Designs: 75 l, Satellite communications. 3.50r, Flags.
20r, Map.

1990, Nov. 21 Litho. *Perf. 14*

1442	A223	75 l multicolored	.30	.30
1443	A223	3.50r multicolored	1.75	1.50

Souvenir Sheet

1444	A224	20r multicolored	5.50	5.50

Flowers — A225

Designs: 20l, Spathoglottis plicata. 75 l, Hippeastrum puniceum. 2r, Tecoma stans. 3.50r, Catharanthus roseus. 10r, Ixora coccinea. 12r, Clitoria ternatea. 15r, Caesalpinia pulcherrima.

No. 1452, Rosa sp. No. 1453, Plumeria obtusa. No. 1454, Jasminum grandiflorum. No. 1455, Hibiscus tiliaceous.

1990, Dec. 9 Litho. *Perf. 14*

1445	A225	20 l multicolored	.25	.25
1446	A225	75 l multicolored	.25	.25
1447	A225	2r multicolored	.65	.65
1448	A225	3.50r multicolored	1.10	1.10
1449	A225	10r multicolored	3.25	3.25
1450	A225	12r multicolored	4.00	4.00
1451	A225	15r multicolored	4.75	4.75
		Nos. 1445-1451 (7)	14.25	14.25

Souvenir Sheets

1452	A225	20r multicolored	3.50	3.50
1453	A225	20r multicolored	3.50	3.50
1454	A225	20r multicolored	3.50	3.50
1455	A225	20r multicolored	3.50	3.50

Expo '90, Intl. Garden and Greenery Exposition, Osaka, Japan.
2r, 3.50r, 10r, 12r are horiz.

Bonsai — A226

Designs: 20 l, Winged Euonymus. 50 l, Japanese black pine. 1r, Japanese five needle pine. 3.50r, Flowering quince. 5r, Chinese elm. 8r, Japanese persimmon. 10r, Japanese wisteria. 12r, Satsuki azalea.

No. 1464, Sargent juniper. No. 1465, Trident maple.

1990-91

1456	A226	20 l multicolored	.25	.25
1457	A226	50 l multicolored	.25	.25
1458	A226	1r multicolored	.30	.30
1459	A226	3.50r multicolored	1.25	1.25
1460	A226	5r multicolored	1.50	1.50
1461	A226	8r multicolored	2.50	2.50
1462	A226	10r multicolored	3.00	3.00
1463	A226	12r multicolored	3.75	3.75
		Nos. 1456-1463 (8)	12.80	12.80

Souvenir Sheets

1464	A226	20r multicolored	6.00	6.00
1465	A226	20r multicolored	6.00	6.00

Expo '90, Intl. Garden and Greenery Exposition, Osaka, Japan.
Issued: 50 l, 1r, 8r, 10r, No. 1464, 12/9/90; 20 l, 3.50r, 5r, 12r, No. 1465, 1/29/91.

Aesop's Fables — A227

Walt Disney characters: 15 l, Tortoise and the Hare. 50 l, Town Mouse and Country Mouse. 1r, Fox and the Crow. 3.50r, Travellers and the Bear. 4r, Fox and the Lion. 6r, Mice and the Cat. 10r, Fox and the Goat. 12r, Dog in the Manger.

No. 1474, Miller, his Son and the Ass, vert. No. 1475, Miser's Gold, vert.

1990, Dec. 11 Litho. *Perf. 14*

1466	A227	15 l multicolored	.25	.25
1467	A227	50 l multicolored	.25	.25
1468	A227	1r multicolored	.35	.35
1469	A227	3.50r multicolored	1.25	1.25
1470	A227	4r multicolored	1.50	1.50
1471	A227	6r multicolored	2.00	2.00
1472	A227	10r multicolored	3.50	3.50
1473	A227	12r multicolored	4.00	4.00
		Nos. 1466-1473 (8)	13.10	13.10

Souvenir Sheets

1474	A227	20r multicolored	6.50	6.50
1475	A227	20r multicolored	6.50	6.50

Intl. Literacy Year.

A228

Steam Locomotives: 20 l, "31" Class, East African Railways. 50 l, Mikado, Sudan Railways. 1r, Beyer-Garratt GM Class, South African Railways. 3r, "7th" Class, Rhodesia Railways. 5r, Central Pacific 229. 8r, Reading 415. 10r, Porter Narrow-guage. 12r, Great Northern 515.

No. 1484, American Standard 315. No. 1485, East African Railways 5950.

1990, Dec. 15

1476	A228	20 l multicolored	.25	.25
1477	A228	50 l multicolored	.25	.25
1478	A228	1r multicolored	.40	.40
1479	A228	3r multicolored	1.25	1.25
1480	A228	5r multicolored	2.00	2.00
1481	A228	8r multicolored	3.25	3.25
1482	A228	10r multicolored	4.00	4.00
1483	A228	12r multicolored	4.75	4.75
		Nos. 1476-1483 (8)	16.15	16.15

Souvenir Sheets

1484	A228	20r multicolored	8.25	8.25
1485	A228	20r multicolored	8.25	8.25

A229

Various players from participating countries: 1r, Holland. 2.50r, England. 3.50r, Argentina. 5r, Brazil. 7r, Italy. 10r, Russia, 15r, West Germany.

No. 1490, Austria. No. 1491, South Korea. No. 1492, Italy (dk blue shirt). No. 1493, Argentina (blue & white shirt).

1990, Dec. 27

1486	A229	1r multicolored	.40	.40
1487	A229	2.50r multicolored	1.00	1.00
1487A	A229	3.50r multicolored	1.60	1.60
1488	A229	5r multicolored	2.10	2.10
1488A	A229	7r multicolored	2.75	2.75
1489	A229	10r multicolored	4.25	4.25
1489A	A229	15r multicolored	6.25	6.25
		Nos. 1486-1489A (7)	18.35	18.35

Souvenir Sheets

1490	A229	18r multicolored	4.50	4.50
1491	A229	18r multicolored	4.50	4.50
1492	A229	20r multicolored	4.50	4.50
1493	A229	20r multicolored	4.50	4.50

World Cup Soccer Championships, Italy.

No. 1111 Surcharged

Methods and Perfs As Before

1990

1493B	A171	3.50r on 2.70r #1111	—

An additional stamp was issued in this set. The editors would like to examine any examples.

Peter Paul Rubens (1577-1640), Painter — A230

Entire works or details from paintings by Rubens: 20 l, Summer. 50 l, Landscape with Rainbow. 1r, Wreckage of Aeneas. 2.50r, Chateau de Steen. 3.50r, Landscape with Herd of Cows. 7r, Ruins of Palantine. 10r, Landscape with Peasants and Cows. 12r, Wagon Fording a Stream.

No. 1502, Landscape with a Sunset. No. 1503, Peasants with Cattle by a Stream in a Woody Landscape. No. 1504, Shepherd with his Flock in a Wooded Landscape. No. 1505, Stuck Wagon.

1991, Feb. 7 Litho. *Perf. 14x13½*

1494	A230	20 l multicolored	.25	.25
1495	A230	50 l multicolored	.25	.25
1496	A230	1r multicolored	.35	.35
1497	A230	2.50r multicolored	.80	.80
1498	A230	3.50r multicolored	1.10	1.10
1499	A230	7r multicolored	2.10	2.10
1500	A230	10r multicolored	3.25	3.25
1501	A230	12r multicolored	3.75	3.75
		Nos. 1494-1501 (8)	11.85	11.85

Souvenir Sheets

1502-1505	A230	20r each	4.75	4.75

First Marathon Run, 490 B.C. — A231

Events and anniversaries (in 1990): 1r, Anthony Fokker (1890-1939), aircraft builder. 3.50r, Launch of first commercial satellite, 25th anniv. 7r, East, West German foreign ministers sign re-unification documents, Oct. 3, 1990, horiz. 8r, Magna Carta, 775th anniv. 10r, Dwight D. Eisenhower. 12r, Winston Churchill. 15r, Pres. Reagan destroying Berlin Wall, horiz. No. 1514, Brandenburg Gate, horiz. No. 1515, Battle of Britain, 50th anniv., horiz.

1991, Mar. 11 *Perf. 14*

1506	A231	50 l multicolored	.45	.25
1507	A231	1r multicolored	1.00	.45
1508	A231	3.50r multicolored	1.50	1.50
1509	A231	7r multicolored	1.75	1.75
1510	A231	8r multicolored	2.50	2.50
1511	A231	10r multicolored	2.25	2.25
1512	A231	12r multicolored	5.00	4.00
1513	A231	15r multicolored	3.00	3.00
		Nos. 1506-1513 (8)	17.45	15.70

Souvenir Sheets

1514	A231	20r multicolored	7.00	7.00
1515	A231	20r multicolored	7.00	7.00

Global Warming A232

1991, Apr. 10

1516	A232	3.50r Dhoni	2.00	1.25
1517	A232	7r Freighter	3.50	3.50

Year of the Girl Child — A233

1991, Apr. 14

1518	A233	7r multicolored	2.25	2.25

Year of the Child A234

Children's drawings: 3.50r, Beach scene. 5r, City scene. 10r, Visualizing fruit. 25r, Scuba diver.

1991, May 10

1519	A234	3.50r multicolored	1.25	1.25
1520	A234	5r multicolored	1.90	1.90
1521	A234	10r multicolored	3.75	3.75
1522	A234	25r multicolored	8.50	8.50
		Nos. 1519-1522 (4)	15.40	15.40

Paintings by Vincent Van Gogh — A235

Designs: 15 l, Japanese Vase with Roses and Anemones, vert. 20 l, Still Life: Red Poppies and Daisies, vert. 2r, Vincent's Bedroom in Arles. 3.50r, The Mulberry Tree. 7r, Blossoming Chestnut Branches. 10r, Morning: Peasant Couple Going to Work. 12r, Still Life: Pink Roses. 15r, Child with Orange, vert. No. 1531, Courtyard of the Hospital at Arles. No. 1532, Houses in Auvers, vert.

1991, June 6 Litho. *Perf. 13½*

1523	A235	15 l multicolored	.30	.30
1524	A235	20 l multicolored	.30	.30
1525	A235	2r multicolored	.75	.75
1526	A235	3.50r multicolored	1.40	1.40
1527	A235	7r multicolored	2.75	2.75
1528	A235	10r multicolored	4.00	4.00
1529	A235	12r multicolored	4.50	4.50
1530	A235	15r multicolored	5.75	5.75
		Nos. 1523-1530 (8)	19.75	19.75

Sizes: 100x75mm, 75x100mm

Imperf

1531	A235	25r multicolored	7.00	7.00
1532	A235	25r multicolored	7.00	7.00

Royal Family Birthday, Anniversary

Common Design Type

1r, 3.50r, 7r, 15r, No. 1542, Charles and Diana, 10th wedding anniversary. 2r, 5r, 8r, 12r, Queen Elizabeth II, 65th birthday.

No. 1541, Elizabeth, Philip. No. 1542, Charles, Diana, sons.

1991, July 4 Litho. *Perf. 14*

1533	CD347	1r multi	.30	.30
1534	CD347	2r multi	.60	.60
1535	CD347	3.50r multi	1.10	1.10
1536	CD347	5r multi	1.50	1.50
1537	CD347	7r multi	2.10	2.10
1538	CD347	8r multi	2.50	2.50
1539	CD347	12r multi	3.75	3.75
1540	CD347	15r multi	4.25	4.25
		Nos. 1533-1540 (8)	16.10	16.10

Souvenir Sheets

1541	CD347	25r multi	5.75	5.75
1542	CD347	25r multi	6.25	6.25

Hummel Figurines — A236

Designs: 10 l, No. 1552a, Child painting. 25 l, No. 1552b, Boy reading at table. 50 l, No. 1552c, Boy with back pack. 2r, No. 1551a, School Girl. 3.50r, No. 1551b, The Bookworm (boy sitting and reading). 8r, No. 1551c, Little Brother's Lesson. 10r, No. 1551d, School Girls. 25r, No. 1552d, Three school boys.

1991, July 25 Litho. *Perf. 14*

1543	A236	10 l multicolored	.25	.25
1544	A236	25 l multicolored	.25	.25
1545	A236	50 l multicolored	.30	.25
1546	A236	2r multicolored	.60	.60
1547	A236	3.50r multicolored	1.00	1.00
1548	A236	8r multicolored	2.25	2.25
1549	A236	10r multicolored	2.25	2.25
1550	A236	25r multicolored	4.75	4.75
		Nos. 1543-1550 (8)	11.65	11.60

Souvenir Sheets

1551	A236	5r Sheet of 4, #a.-d.	3.50	3.50
1552	A236	8r Sheet of 4, #a.-d.	5.50	5.50

Japanese Steam Locomotives — A237

1991, Aug. 25 Litho. *Perf. 14*

1553	A237	15 l C 57, vert.	.50	.25
1554	A237	25 l Series 6250	.75	.30
1555	A237	1r D 51, vert.	1.25	.40
1556	A237	3.50r Series 8620	2.00	1.25
1557	A237	5r Class 10	2.25	1.75
1558	A237	7r C 61, vert.	2.50	2.50
1559	A237	10r Series 9600	2.50	2.50
1560	A237	12r D 52	2.75	2.75
		Nos. 1553-1560 (8)	14.50	11.70

Souvenir Sheets

1561	A237	20r Class 1080	4.00	4.00
1562	A237	20r C 56	4.00	4.00

Phila Nippon '91.

Butterflies A238

10 l, Blue salamis. 25 l, Mountain beauty. 50 l, Lucerne blue. 2r, Monarch. 3.50r, Common rose. 5r, Black witch. 8r, Oriental swallowtail. 10r, Gaudy commodore.

No. 1571, Pearl crescent. No. 1572, Friar.

1991, Dec. 2 Litho. *Perf. 14*

1563	A238	10 l multi	.40	.40
1564	A238	25 l multi	.55	.55
1565	A238	50 l multi	.75	.75
1566	A238	2r multi	1.25	1.25
1567	A238	3.50r multi	1.75	1.75
1568	A238	5r multi	2.00	2.00
1569	A238	8r multi	2.50	2.50
1570	A238	10r multi	2.50	2.50
		Nos. 1563-1570 (8)	11.70	11.70

Souvenir Sheets

1571	A238	20r multi	5.00	5.00
1572	A238	20r multi	5.00	5.00

No. 1570 inscribed "guady."

Japanese Space Program A239

Designs: 15 l, H-11 Launch Vehicle. 20 l, H-II Orbiting plane. 2r, Geosynchronous satellite 5. 3.50r, Marine observation satellite-1. 7r, Communications satellite 3. 10r, Broadcasting satellite-2. 12r, H-1 Launch Vehicle, vert. 15r, Space flier unit, space shuttle. No. 1581, Katsura tracking and data acquisition station. No. 1582, M-3S II Launch vehicle, vert.

1991, Dec. 11

1573	A239	15 l multicolored	.50	.30
1574	A239	20 l multicolored	.50	.30
1575	A239	2r multicolored	1.25	.75
1576	A239	3.50r multicolored	1.60	1.40
1577	A239	7r multicolored	2.40	2.40
1578	A239	10r multicolored	2.75	2.75
1579	A239	12r multicolored	3.00	3.00
1580	A239	15r multicolored	3.00	3.00
		Nos. 1573-1580 (8)	15.00	13.90

Souvenir Sheets

1581	A239	20r multicolored	6.50	6.50
1582	A239	20r multicolored	6.50	6.50

Miniature Sheet

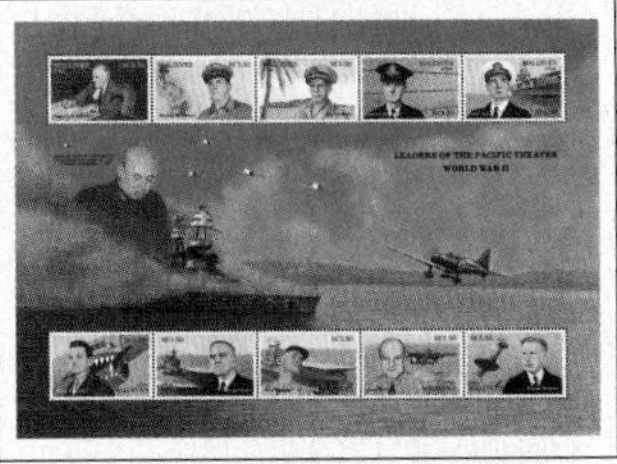

World War II Leaders of the Pacific Theater — A240

a, Franklin D. Roosevelt. b, Douglas MacArthur. c, Chester Nimitz. d, Jonathan Wainwright. e, Ernest King. f, Claire Chennault. g, William Halsey. h, Marc Mitscher. i, James Doolittle. j, Raymond Spruance.

1991, Dec. 30 Litho. *Perf. 14½x15*

1583	A240	3.50r Sheet of 10, #a.-j.	16.00	16.00

Grand Prix Race Cars A241

Designs: 20 l, Williams FW-07. 50 l, Brabham BT50 BMW Turbo. 1r, Williams FW-11 Honda. 3.50r, Ferrari 312 T3. 5r, Lotus Honda 99T. 7r, Benetton Ford B188. 10r, Tyrrell P34 Six-wheeler. 21r, Renault RE-30B Turbo. No. 1592, Ferrari F189. No. 1593, Brabham BT50 BMW Turbo, diff.

1991, Dec. 28 Litho. *Perf. 14*

1584	A241	20 l multicolored	.25	.25
1585	A241	50 l multicolored	.45	.30
1586	A241	1r multicolored	.60	.40
1587	A241	3.50r multicolored	1.25	1.25
1588	A241	5r multicolored	1.75	1.75
1589	A241	7r multicolored	2.00	2.00
1590	A241	10r multicolored	2.25	2.25
1591	A241	21r multicolored	4.00	4.00
		Nos. 1584-1591 (8)	12.55	12.20

Souvenir Sheets

1592	A241	25r multicolored	7.75	7.75
1593	A241	25r multicolored	7.75	7.75

Miniature Sheet

Enzo Ferrari (1898-1988) — A242

Ferrari Race cars: a, 1957 Testa Rossa. b, 1966 275GTB. c, 1951 "Aspirarta." d, Testarossa. f, 1958 Dino 246. g, 1952 Type 375. h, Mansell's Formula One. i, 1975 312T.

1991, Dec. 28

1594	A242	5r Sheet of 9, #a.-i.	16.00	16.00

17th World Scout Jamboree A243

Designs: 10r, Scouts diving on reef. 11r, Hand making scout sign, emblem, vert. 18r, Lord Robert Baden-Powell, vert. 20r, Czechoslovakian scout (local) stamp, vert.

1991, Dec. 30

1595	A243	10r multicolored	2.50	2.50
1596	A243	11r multicolored	2.50	2.50

Souvenir Sheets

1597	A243	18r multicolored	3.00	3.00
1598	A243	20r multicolored	3.00	3.00

Wolfgang Amadeus Mozart, Death Bicent. A244

Portrait of Mozart and: 50 l, Schwarzenberg Palace. 1r, Spa at Baden. 2r, Royal Palace, Berlin. 5r, Viennese Masonic seal. 7r, St. Marx. No. 1604, Josephsplatz, Vienna.

1991, Dec. 30

1599	A244	50 l multicolored	.25	.25
1600	A244	1r multicolored	.25	.25
1601	A244	2r multicolored	.55	.55
1602	A244	5r multicolored	1.25	1.25
1603	A244	7r multicolored	1.75	1.75
1604	A244	20r multicolored	5.00	5.00
		Nos. 1599-1604 (6)	9.05	9.05

Souvenir Sheet

1605	A244	20r Bust of Mozart, vert.	4.00	4.00

Brandenburg Gate, Bicent. — A245

Designs: 20 l, Flag. 1.75 l, Man embracing child, Berlin wall. 4r, Soldiers behind barricade, demonstrator. 15r, World War I Iron Cross. No. 1610, Helmet. No. 1611, 1939 helmet. No. 1612, Studded helmet.

1991, Dec. 30

1606	A245	20 l multicolored	.25	.25
1607	A245	1.75r multicolored	.45	.45
1608	A245	4r multicolored	1.00	1.00
1609	A245	15r multicolored	3.25	3.25
		Nos. 1606-1609 (4)	4.95	4.95

Souvenir Sheets

1610	A245	18r multicolored	3.50	3.50
1611	A245	18r multicolored	3.50	3.50
1612	A245	18r multicolored	3.50	3.50

Anniversaries and Events — A246

Designs: No. 1613, Otto Lilienthal, glider No. 16. No. 1614, "D-Day," Normandy 1944, Charles de Gaulle. 7r, Front of locomotive, vert. 8r, Kurt Schwitters, artist and Landesmuseum. 9r, Map, man in Swiss costume. 10r, Charles de Gaulle in Madagascar, 1958. 12r, Steam locomotive. 15r, Portrait of Charles de Gaulle, vert. 20r, Locomotive and coal car.

1991, Dec. 30 Litho. *Perf. 14*

1613	A246	6r multicolored	2.25	2.25
1614	A246	6r multicolored	1.75	1.75
1615	A246	7r multicolored	2.00	2.00
1616	A246	8r multicolored	2.25	2.25
1617	A246	9r multicolored	2.50	2.50
1618	A246	10r multicolored	2.75	2.75
1619	A246	12r multicolored	3.25	3.25
		Nos. 1613-1619 (7)	16.75	16.75

Souvenir Sheets

1620	A246	15r multicolored	3.50	3.50
1621	A246	20r multicolored	4.00	4.00

First glider flight, cent. (No. 1613). Charles de Gaulle, birth cent. in 1990 (Nos. 1614, 1618, & 1620). Trans-Siberian Railway, cent. (Nos. 1615, 1619 & 1621). Hanover, 750th anniv. (#1616). Swiss Confederation, 700th anniv. (No. 1617).

No. 1621 contains one 58x43mm stamp.

Birds — A247

Designs: 10 l, Numenius phaeopus. 25 l, Egretta alba. 50 l, Ardea cinerea. 2r, Phalacrocorax aristotelis. 3.50r, Sterna dougallii. 5r, Tringa nebularia. 6.50r+50 l, Neophron percnopterus. 8r, Upupa epops. 10r, Elanus caeruleus. 25r, Eudocimus ruber. 30r, Falco peregrinus. 40r, Milvus migrans. 50r, Pluvialis squatarola.

Perf. 14½, 13 (6.50r+50 l, 30r, 40r)

1992-94

1624	A247	10 l multi	.30	.30
1625	A247	25 l multi	.30	.30
1626	A247	50 l multi	.30	.30
1627	A247	2r multi	.70	.70
1628	A247	3.50r multi	1.25	1.25
1629	A247	5r multi	1.75	1.75
1630	A247	6.50r +50 l multi	2.00	2.00
1631	A247	8r multi	2.75	2.75
1632	A247	10r multi	3.50	3.50
1633	A247	25r multi	5.50	5.50
1634	A247	30r multi	7.00	7.00
1635	A247	40r multi	10.00	10.00
1636	A247	50r multi	12.50	12.50
		Nos. 1624-1636 (13)	47.85	47.85

Issued: 10 l, 25 l, 50 l, 2r, 3.50r, 5r, 8r, 10r, 25r, 2/17/92; 6.50r+50 l, 30r, 11/93; 40r, 1994(?).

See No. 2323.

Queen Elizabeth II's Accession to the Throne, 40th Anniv.

Common Design Type

No. 1641, Queen, palm trees. No. 1642, Queen, boat.

1992, Feb. 6 *Perf. 14*

1637	CD348	1r multicolored	.30	.30
1638	CD348	3.50r multicolored	1.00	1.00
1639	CD348	7r multicolored	2.00	2.00
1640	CD348	10r multicolored	2.75	2.75
		Nos. 1637-1640 (4)	6.05	6.05

Souvenir Sheets

1641	CD348	18r multicolored	5.75	5.75
1642	CD348	18r multicolored	5.75	5.75

This set differs from the common design in that the Queen's portrait and local view are separated by a curved line rather than with a cypher outline.

Disney Characters on World Tour A248

Designs: 25 l, Mickey on Flying Carpet Airways. 50 l, Goofy at Big Ben, London. 1r, Mickey in Holland. 2r, Pluto eating pasta, Italy. 3r, Mickey, Donald do sombero stomp in Mexico. 3.50r, Mickey, Goofy, and Donald form Miki Tiki, Polynesia. 5r, Goofy's Alpine antics, Austria. 7r, Mickey Maus, Germany. 10r, Donald as Samurai Duck. 12r, Mickey in Russia. 15r, Mickey's Oom-pah Band in Germany. No. 1654, Mickey, globe. No. 1655, Donald in Ireland chasing leprechaun with pot of gold at end of rainbow, horiz. No. 1655A, Pluto, kangaroo with joey, Australia.

1992, Feb. 4 *Perf. 13x13½*

1643	A248	25 l multi	.25	.25
1644	A248	50 l multi	.25	.25
1645	A248	1r multi	.35	.35
1646	A248	2r multi	.65	.65
1647	A248	3r multi	.90	.90
1648	A248	3.50r multi	.90	.90
1649	A248	5r multi	1.25	1.25
1650	A248	7r multi	1.50	1.50
1651	A248	10r multi	2.00	2.00
1652	A248	12r multi	2.50	2.50
1653	A248	15r multi	2.50	2.50
		Nos. 1643-1653 (11)	13.05	13.05

Souvenir Sheets

1654	A248	25r multi	5.00	5.00
1655	A248	25r multi	4.00	4.00
1655A	A248	25r multi	4.00	4.00

While the rest of the set has the same issue date as Nos. 1644-1645, 1647, 1653-1654, their dollar value was lower when they were released.

Fish A249

Designs: 7 l, Blue surgeonfish. 20 l, Bigeye. 50 l, Yellowfin tuna. 1r, two-spot red snapper. 3.50r, Sabre squirrelfish. 5r, Picasso triggerfish. 8r, Bennet's butterflyfish. 10r, Parrotfish. 12r, Grouper. 15r, Skpjack tuna. No. 1666, Clownfish. No. 1667, Sweetlips. No. 1667A, Treadfin butterflyfish. No. 1667B, Clown triggerfish.

1992, Mar. 23 **Litho.** *Perf. 14*

1656	A249	7 l multicolored	.30	.30
1657	A249	20 l multicolored	.30	.30
1658	A249	50 l multicolored	.30	.30
1659	A249	1r multicolored	.30	.30
1660	A249	3.50r multicolored	1.00	1.00
1661	A249	5r multicolored	1.40	1.40
1662	A249	8r multicolored	2.25	2.25
1663	A249	10r multicolored	2.50	2.50
1664	A249	12r multicolored	3.00	3.00
1665	A249	15r multicolored	3.50	3.50
		Nos. 1656-1665 (10)	14.85	14.85

Souvenir Sheets

1666	A249	20r multicolored	3.25	3.25
1667	A249	20r multicolored	3.25	3.25
1667A	A249	20r multicolored	3.25	3.25
1667B	A249	20r multicolored	3.25	3.25

World Columbian Stamp Expo '92, Chicago A250

Walt Disney characters in Chicago: 1r, Mickey as Indian with Jean Baptiste Pointe du Sable, founder of Chicago. 3.50r, Donald at old Chicago post office, 1831. 7r, Donald in old Fort Dearborn. 15r, Goofy, mastodon at Museum of Science and Industry. 25r, Minnie and Mickey at Ferris wheel midway, Columbian Exposition, 1893, horiz.

1992, Apr. 15 *Perf. 13½x14*

1668	A250	1r multicolored	.30	.30
1669	A250	3.50r multicolored	1.10	1.10
1670	A250	7r multicolored	2.10	2.10
1671	A250	15r multicolored	4.25	4.25
		Nos. 1668-1671 (4)	7.75	7.75

Souvenir Sheet

Perf. 14x13½

1672	A250	25r multicolored	5.50	5.50

No. 1671 identifies Field Museum as Museum of Science and Industry.

Granada '92 — A251

Disney characters in old Alhambra, Granada: 2r, Minnie in Court of Lions. 5r, Goofy bathing in Lions Fountain. 8r, Mickey walking near Gate of Justice. 12r, Donald Duck serenading Daisy in Vermilion Towers. No. 1682, Goofy and Mickey outside Towers of the Alhambra.

1992, Apr. 15 *Perf. 13½x14*

1678	A251	2r multicolored	.90	.60
1679	A251	5r multicolored	1.75	1.75
1680	A251	8r multicolored	2.25	2.25
1681	A251	12r multicolored	2.75	2.75
		Nos. 1678-1681 (4)	7.65	7.35

Souvenir Sheet

1682	A251	25r multicolored	5.50	5.50

A252

Flowers of the World — A253

1992, Apr. 26 **Litho.** *Perf. 14½*

1688	A252	25 l United States	.25	.25
1689	A252	50 l Australia	.25	.25
1690	A252	2r England	.70	.70
1691	A252	3.50r Brazil	1.25	1.25
1692	A252	5r Holland	1.75	1.75
1693	A252	8r France	2.75	2.75
1694	A252	10r Japan	3.25	3.25
1695	A252	15r Africa	4.75	4.75
		Nos. 1688-1695 (8)	14.95	14.95

Souvenir Sheets

Perf. 14

1696	A253	25r org, yel & red vio flowers	5.00	5.00
1696A	A253	25r red, pink & yel flowers	5.00	5.00

No. 1696 contains one 57x43mm stamp. No. 1696A contains one 57x34mm stamp.

Natl. Security Service, Cent. A254

3.50r, Coast Guard. 5r, Infantry. 10r, Aakoatey. 15r, Fire department.
20r, Sultan in procession.

1992, Apr. 21 *Perf. 14*

1697	A254	3.50r multi	1.25	1.25
1698	A254	5r multi	2.25	2.25
1699	A254	10r multi	4.75	4.75
1700	A254	15r multi	7.00	7.00
		Nos. 1697-1700 (4)	15.25	15.25

Souvenir Sheet

1701	A254	20r multi	7.00	7.00

A255

Mushrooms: 10 l, Laetiporus sulphureus. 25 l, Coprinus atramentarius. 50 l, Gandoderma lucidum. 3.50r, Russula aurata. 5r, Polyporus umbellatus. 8r, Suillus grevillei. 10r, Clavaria zollingeri. No. 1709, Boletus edulis. No. 1710, Trametes cinnabarina. No. 1711, Marasmius oreades.

1992, May 14 **Litho.** *Perf. 14*

1702	A255	10 l multicolored	.25	.25
1703	A255	25 l multicolored	.25	.25
1704	A255	50 l multicolored	.25	.25
1705	A255	3.50r multicolored	1.00	1.00
1706	A255	5r multicolored	1.25	1.25
1707	A255	8r multicolored	2.25	2.25
1708	A255	10r multicolored	2.50	2.50
1709	A255	25r multicolored	6.50	6.50
		Nos. 1702-1709 (8)	14.25	14.25

Souvenir Sheets

1710	A255	25r multicolored	6.75	6.75
1711	A255	25r multicolored	6.75	6.75

A256

10 l, Hurdles. 1r, Boxing. 3.50r, Women's running. 5r, Discus. 7r, Basketball. 10r, Race walking. 12r, Rhythmic gymnastics. 20r, Fencing.

No. 1720, Olympic flame. No. 1721, Olympic rings, flags.

1992, June 1

1712	A256	10 l multi	.25	.25
1713	A256	1r multi	.25	.25
1714	A256	3.50r multi	.90	.90
1715	A256	5r multi	1.25	1.25
1716	A256	7r multi	1.75	1.75
1717	A256	10r multi	2.50	2.50
1718	A256	12r multi	3.00	3.00
1719	A256	20r multi	5.00	5.00
		Nos. 1712-1719 (8)	14.90	14.90

Souvenir Sheets

1720	A256	25r multi	5.00	5.00
1721	A256	25r multi	5.00	5.00

1992 Summer Olympics, Barcelona.

A256a

1992 Winter Olympics, Albertville: 5r, Two-man bobsled. 8r, Free-style ski jump. 10r, Women's cross-country skiing. No. 1725, Women's slalom skiing, horiz. No. 1726, Men's figure skating.

1992, June 1 **Litho.** *Perf. 14*

1722	A256a	5r multicolored	1.00	1.00
1723	A256a	8r multicolored	1.60	1.60
1724	A256a	10r multicolored	2.00	2.00
		Nos. 1722-1724 (3)	4.60	4.60

Souvenir Sheets

1725	A256a	25r multicolored	4.75	4.75
1726	A256a	25r multicolored	4.75	4.75

Dinosaurs — A257

Designs: 5 l, Deinonychus. 10 l, Styracosaurus. 25 l, Mamenchisaurus. 50 l, Stenonychosaurus. 1r, Parasaurolophus. 1.25r, Scelidosaurus. 1.75r, Tyrannosaurus. 2r, Stegosaurus. 3.50r, Iguanodon. 4r, Anatosaurus. 5r, Monoclonius. 7r, Tenontosaurus. 8r, Brachiosaurus. 10r, Euoplocephalus. 25r, Triceratops. 50r, Apatosaurus.

No. 1743, Iguanodon, allosaurus. No. 1744, Hadrosaur. No. 1745, Tyrannosaurus, triceratops. No. 1746, Brachiosaurus, iguanodons.

1992, Sept. 15 **Litho.** *Perf. 14*

1727	A257	5 l multicolored	.25	.25
1728	A257	10 l multicolored	.25	.25
1729	A257	25 l multicolored	.25	.25
1730	A257	50 l multicolored	.25	.25
1731	A257	1r multicolored	.25	.25
1732	A257	1.25r multicolored	.30	.30
1733	A257	1.75r multicolored	.40	.40
1734	A257	2r multicolored	.45	.45
1735	A257	3.50r multicolored	.80	.80
1736	A257	4r multicolored	.90	.90
1737	A257	5r multicolored	1.10	1.10
1738	A257	7r multicolored	1.60	1.60
1739	A257	8r multicolored	1.90	1.90
1740	A257	10r multicolored	2.25	2.25
1741	A257	25r multicolored	5.75	5.75
1742	A257	50r multicolored	11.50	11.50
		Nos. 1727-1742 (16)	28.20	28.20

Souvenir Sheets

1743	A257	25r multicolored	5.00	5.00
1744	A257	25r multicolored	5.00	5.00
1745	A257	25r multicolored	5.00	5.00
1746	A257	25r multicolored	5.00	5.00

Genoa '92.

1992 Summer Olympics, Barcelona A258

10 l, Pole vault, vert.. 25 l, Pommel horse. 50 l, Shot put, vert. 1r, Horizontal bar. 2r, Triple jump. 3.50r, Table tennis, vert. 7r, Wrestling. 9r, Baseball, vert. 12r, Swimming.
25r, Decathlon (high jump).

1992, June 1 **Litho.** *Perf. 14*

1747	A258	10 l multicolored	.25	.25
1748	A258	25 l multicolored	.25	.25
1749	A258	50 l multicolored	.25	.25
1750	A258	1r multicolored	.25	.25

1751 A258 2r multicolored .50 .50
1752 A258 3.50r multicolored .90 .90
1753 A258 7r multicolored 1.90 1.90
1754 A258 9r multicolored 2.10 2.10
1755 A258 12r multicolored 3.00 3.00
Nos. 1747-1755 (9) 9.40 9.40

Souvenir Sheet

1756 A258 25r multicolored 9.00 9.00

Souvenir Sheets

Mysteries of the Universe — A259

No. 1757, Loch Ness monster. No. 1758, Explosion of the Hindenburg. No. 1759, Crystal skulls. No. 1760, Black holes. No. 1761, UFO over Washington State. No. 1762, UFO near Columbus, Ohio. No. 1763, Explosion at Chernobyl, 1986. No. 1764, Crop circles of Great Britain. No. 1765, Ghosts of English castles and mansions. No. 1766, Drawings of Plain of Nasca, Peru, vert. No. 1767, Stonehenge, England, vert. No. 1768, Bust of Plato, the disappearance of Atlantis. No. 1769, Footprint of Yeti (abominable snowman), vert. No. 1770, Pyramids of Giza. No. 1771, Bermuda Triangle. No. 1772, The Mary Celeste, vert.

1992, Oct. 28

1757-1772 A259 25r Set of 16 105.00 105.00

1994 World Cup Soccer Championships, US — A260

Players of 1990 German team: 10 l, Jurgen Klinsmann. 25 l, Pierre Littbarski. 50 l, Lothar Matthaus. 1r, Rudi Voller. 2r, Thomas Hassler. 3.50r, Thomas Berthold. 4r, Jurgen Kohler. 5r, Berti Vogts, trainer. 6r, Bodo Illgner. 7r, Klaus Augenthaler. 8r, Franz Beckenbauer, coach. 10r, Andreas Brehme. 12r, Guido Buchwald.

No. 1786, Team members, horiz. No. 1787, Unidentified player in action, horiz.

1992, Aug. 10 Litho. *Perf. 14*

1773 A260 10 l multicolored .25 .25
1774 A260 25 l multicolored .25 .25
1775 A260 50 l multicolored .25 .25
1776 A260 1r multicolored .25 .25
1777 A260 2r multicolored .60 .60
1778 A260 3.50r multicolored 1.00 1.00
1779 A260 4r multicolored 1.10 1.10
1780 A260 5r multicolored 1.50 1.50
1781 A260 6r multicolored 1.75 1.75
1782 A260 7r multicolored 2.00 2.00
1783 A260 8r multicolored 2.25 2.25
1784 A260 10r multicolored 3.00 3.00
1785 A260 12r multicolored 3.50 3.50
Nos. 1773-1785 (13) 17.70 17.70

Souvenir Sheets

1786 A260 35r multicolored 6.50 6.50
1787 A260 35r multicolored 6.50 6.50

Souvenir Sheet

New York Public Library — A261

1992, Oct. 28 Litho. *Perf. 14*

1788 A261 20r multicolored 7.50 7.50

Postage Stamp Mega Event '92, New York City.

Walt Disney's Goofy, 60th Anniv. — A262

Scenes from Disney cartoon films: 10 l, Father's Weekend, 1953. 50 l, Symphony Hour, 1942. 75 l, Frank Duck Brings 'Em Back Alive, 1946. 1r, Crazy with the Heat, 1947. 2r, The Big Wash, 1948. 3.50r, How to Ride a Horse, 1950. 5r, Two Gun Goofy, 1952. 8r, Saludos Amigos, 1943, vert. 10r, How to Be a Detective, 1952. 12r, For Whom the Bulls Toil, 1953. 15r, Double Dribble, 1946, vert.

No. 1801, Mickey and the Beanstalk, 1947. No. 1802, Double Dribble, 1946, vert., diff. No. 1803, The Goofy Success Story, 1955.

Perf. 14x13½, 13½x14

1992, Dec. 7 Litho.

1789 A262 10 l multicolored .25 .25
1791 A262 50 l multicolored .25 .25
1792 A262 75 l multicolored .25 .25
1793 A262 1r multicolored .25 .25
1794 A262 2r multicolored .50 .50
1795 A262 3.50r multicolored .90 .90
1796 A262 5r multicolored 1.25 1.25
1797 A262 8r multicolored 2.00 2.00
1798 A262 10r multicolored 2.25 2.25
1799 A262 12r multicolored 2.75 2.75
1800 A262 15r multicolored 3.50 3.50
Nos. 1789-1800 (11) 14.15 14.15

Souvenir Sheets

1801 A262 20r multicolored 4.25 4.25
1802 A262 20r multicolored 4.25 4.25
1803 A262 20r multicolored 4.25 4.25

A number has been reserved for an additional value in this set.

A263

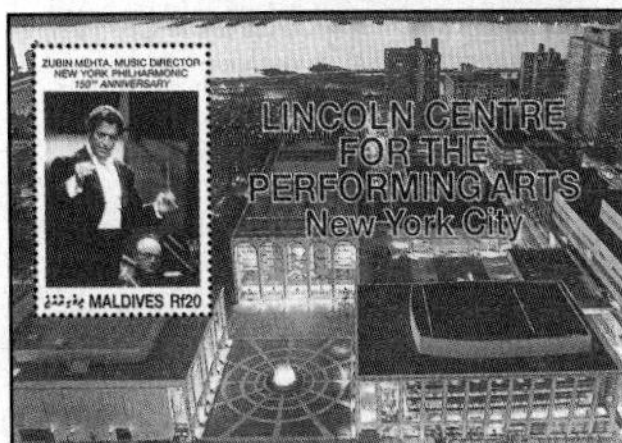

Anniversaries and Events — A264

Designs: 1r, Zeppelin on bombing raid over London during World War I. No. 1805, German, French flags, Konrad Adenauer, Charles de Gaulle. No. 1806, Radio telescope. No. 1807, Columbus studying globe. No. 1808, Indian rhinoceros. 7r, WHO, ICN, and FAO emblems. 8r, Green sea turtle. No. 1822, Scarlet macaw. No. 1811, Lion's Intl. emblem and Melvin Jones, founder. No. 1812, Yacht America, first America's Cup winner, 1851. 12r, Columbus claiming San Salvador for Spain. No. 1814, Voyager 1 approaching Saturn. No. 1815, NATO flag, airplanes, Adenauer. 20r, Graf Zeppelin over New York City. No. 1817, Landsat satellite. No. 1818, Count Zeppelin. No. 1819, Santa Maria. No. 1820, Konrad Adenauer. No. 1821, Zubin Mehta, music director, NY Philharmonic, vert. No. 1823, Friedrich Schmiedl (b. 1902), rocket mail pioneer.

1992-93 Litho. *Perf. 14*

1804 A263 1r multicolored .30 .30
1805 A263 3.50r multicolored .90 .90
1806 A263 3.50r multicolored .70 .70
1807 A263 6r multicolored 1.50 1.50
1808 A263 6r multicolored 1.25 1.25
1809 A263 7r multicolored 1.40 1.40
1810 A263 8r multicolored 1.60 1.60
1811 A263 10r multicolored 1.75 1.75
1812 A263 10r multicolored 1.75 1.75
1813 A263 12r multicolored 2.75 2.75
1814 A263 15r multicolored 2.75 2.75
1815 A263 15r multicolored 3.75 3.75
1816 A263 20r multicolored 5.50 5.50
Nos. 1804-1816 (13) 25.90 25.90

Souvenir Sheets

1817 A263 20r multicolored 6.00 6.00
1818 A263 20r multicolored 6.25 6.25
1819 A263 20r multicolored 6.25 6.25
1820 A263 20r multicolored 6.00 6.00
1821 A264 20r multicolored 6.75 6.75
1822 A263 20r multicolored 6.00 4.60
1823 A263 25r multicolored 6.50 6.50
Nos. 1817-1823 (7) 43.75 42.35

Count Zeppelin, 75th anniv. of death (Nos. 1804, 1816, 1818). Konrad Adenauer, 25th anniv. of death (Nos. 1805, 1815, 1820). Intl. Space Year (Nos. 1806, 1814, 1817). Columbus' discovery of America, 500th anniversary (Nos. 1807, 1813, 1819). Earth Summit, Rio de Janeiro (Nos. 1808, 1810, 1822). Intl. Conference on Nutrition, Rome (No. 1809). Lions Intl., 75th anniversary (No. 1811). America's Cup yacht race (No. 1812). New York Philharmonic, 150th anniv. (No. 1821).

No. 1823 contains one 27x35mm stamp.

Issue dates: Nos. 1805, 1808, 1810, 1815, 1820, 1822, Jan. 1993. Others, Nov. 1992.

Miniature Sheet

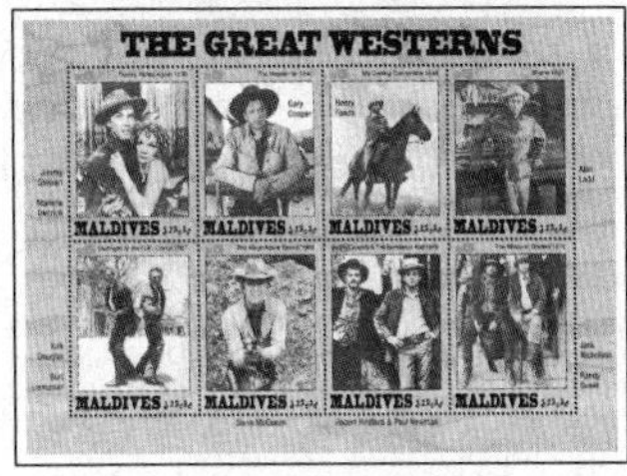

Western Films — A265

Actors and film: No. 1824a, Jimmy Stewart and Marlene Dietrich, Destry Rides Again, 1939. b, Gary Cooper, The Westerner, 1940. c, Henry Fonda, My Darling Clementine, 1940. d, Alan Ladd, Shane, 1953. e, Kirk Douglas and Burt Lancaster, Gunfight at the O.K. Coral, 1957. f, Steve McQueen, The Magnificent Seven, 1960. g, Robert Redford and Paul Newman, Butch Cassidy & The Sundance Kid, 1969. h, Jack Nicholson and Randy Quaid, The Missouri Breaks, 1976.

No. 1825, Clint Eastwood, Pale Rider. No. 1826, John Wayne, The Searchers, 1956.

1992-93 Litho. *Perf. 13½x14*

1824 A265 5r Sheet of 8, #a.-h. 11.00 11.00

Souvenir Sheets

1825 A265 20r multicolored 5.25 5.25
1826 A265 20r multicolored 5.25 5.25

Issued: Nos. 1824-1825, 1992; No. 1826, 1/1993.

Miniature Sheet

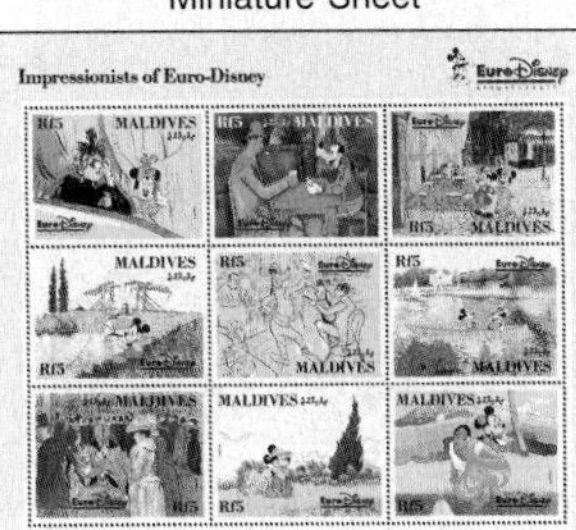

Opening of Euro Disney Resort, Paris — A266

Disney characters in paintings by French impressionists — No. 1827: a, Minnie on theater balcony. b, Goofy playing cards. c, Mickey and Minnie walking by outdoor cafe. d, Mickey fishing. e, Goofy dancing to music of harp player. f, Mickey and Minnie in boat. g, Minnie on dance floor. h, Mickey strolling through country. i, Minnie standing behind Polynesian woman.

1992, Dec. *Perf. 14x13½*

1827 A266 5r Sheet of 9, #a.-i. 15.00 15.00

Souvenir Sheets

1828 A266 20r Goofy 3.75 3.75
1829 A266 20r Minnie 3.75 3.75
1830 A266 20r Mickey 3.75 3.75

Perf. 13½x14

1831 A266 20r Donald Duck, vert. 3.75 3.75

SAARC Year of the Environment — A267

Designs: 25 l, Waterfall, drought area. 50 l, Clean, polluted beaches. 5r, Clean, polluted ocean. 10r, Clean island with vegetation, island polluted with trees dying.

1992, Dec. 30 Litho. *Perf. 14*

1832 A267 25 l multicolored .25 .25
1833 A267 50 l multicolored .25 .25
1834 A267 5r multicolored .90 .90
1835 A267 10r multicolored 1.75 1.75
Nos. 1832-1835 (4) 3.15 3.15

Elvis Presley (1935-1977) A268

a, Portrait. b, With guitar. c, With microphone.

1993, Jan. 7

1836 A268 3.50r Strip of 3, #a.-c. 2.75 2.75

A set of 4 stamps commemorating South Asia Tourism year, formerly listed as Nos. 1837-1840, were prepared but not issued.

Miniature Sheets

Madame Seriziat — A270

Louvre Museum, Bicent.

Details or entire paintings, by Jacques-Louis David (1748-1825):

No. 1841: b, Pierre Seriziat. c, Madame de Verninac. d, Madame Recamier. e, Self-portrait. f, General Bonaparte. g-h, The Lictors Returning to Brutus the Bodies of his Sons (left, right).

Paintings by Jean-Baptiste-Camille Corot (1796-1875)

No. 1842: a, Self-portrait. b, The Woman in Blue. c, The Jeweled Woman. d, Young Girl in her Dressing Room. e, Haydee. f, Chartres Cathedral. g, The Belfry at Douai. h, The Bridge at Mantes.

Paintings by Jean-Honore Fragonard (1732-1806):

No. 1843: a, The Study. b, Denis Diderot. c, Marie-Madeleine Guimard. d, The Inspiration. e, Tivoli Cascades. f, The Music Lesson. g, The Bolt. h, Blindman's Buff.

No. 1844, The Gardens of the Villa D'Este, Tivoli, by Jean-Baptiste-Camille Corot, horiz.

No. 1845, Young Tiger Playing with its Mother, by Delacroix.

1993, Jan. 7 Litho. *Perf. 12*

Sheets of 8

1841 A270 8r #a.-h. + label 11.00 11.00
1842 A270 8r #a.-h. + label 11.00 11.00
1843 A270 8r #a.-h. + label 11.00 11.00

Souvenir Sheets

Perf. 14½

1844 A270 20r multicolored 6.00 6.00
1845 A270 20r multicolored 6.00 6.00

Nos. 1844-1845 contains one 88x55mm stamp.

Miniature Sheet

Coronation of Queen Elizabeth II, 40th Anniv. — A271

Designs: a, 3.50r, Official coronation photograph. b, 5r, St. Edward's crown. c, 10r, Dignitaries viewing ceremony. d, 10r, Queen, Prince Philip examining banknote.

1993, June 2 *Perf. 13½x14*

1846 A271 Sheet, 2 ea #a.-d. 13.00 13.00

A number has been reserved for an additional value in this set.

Shells — A272

Designs: 7 l, Precious wentletrap. 15 l, Purple sea snail. 50 l, Arabian cowrie. 3.50r, Major harp. 4r, Royal paper bubble. 5r, Sieve cowrie. 6r, Episcopal miter. 7r, Camp pitar-venus. 8r, Eyed auger. 10r, Onyx cowrie. 12r, Map cowrie. 20r, Caltrop murex.

No. 1856, Scorpion spider conch. No. 1857, Black striped triton. No. 1857A, Bull's-mouth helmet.

1993, July 15 **Litho.** *Perf. 14*

1848 A272 7 l multicolored .30 .30
1849 A272 15 l multicolored .30 .30
1850 A272 50 l multicolored .30 .30
1850A A272 3.50r multicolored 1.00 1.00
1850B A272 4r multicolored 1.10 1.10
1851 A272 5r multicolored 1.40 1.40
1852 A272 6r multicolored 1.75 1.75
1852A A272 7r multicolored 1.90 1.90
1853 A272 8r multicolored 2.25 2.25
1854 A272 10r multicolored 2.75 2.75
1854A A272 12r multicolored 3.25 3.25
1855 A272 20r multicolored 5.75 5.75
Nos. 1848-1855 (12) 22.05 22.05

Souvenir Sheets

1856 A272 25r multicolored 8.00 8.00
1857 A272 25r multicolored 8.00 8.00
1857A A272 25r multicolored 8.00 8.00

Endangered Animals — A273

7 l, Sifaka lemur. 10 l, Snow leopard. 15 l, Numbat. 25 l, Gorilla. 2r, Koalas. 3.50r, Cheetah. 5r, Yellow-footed rock wallaby. 7r, Orangutan. 8r, Black lemur. 10r, Black rhinoceros. 15r, Humpback whale. 20r, Mauritius parakeet.

No. 1866, Asian elephant. No. 1867, Tiger. No. 1867A, Giant panda.

1993, July 20 **Litho.** *Perf. 14*

1857B A273 7 l multicolored .30 .30
1858 A273 10 l multicolored .30 .30
1859 A273 15 l multicolored .30 .30
1859A A273 25 l multicolored .30 .30
1860 A273 2r multicolored .65 .65
1860A A273 3.50r multicolored 1.10 1.40
1861 A273 5r multicolored 1.50 1.50
1862 A273 7r multicolored 2.10 2.10
1863 A273 8r multicolored 2.40 2.40
1864 A273 10r multicolored 3.00 3.00
1865 A273 15r multicolored 4.25 4.25
1865A A273 20r multicolored 5.50 5.50
Nos. 1857B-1865A (12) 21.70 22.00

Souvenir Sheets

1866 A273 25r multicolored 8.00 8.00
1867 A273 25r multicolored 8.00 8.00
1867A A273 25r multicolored 8.00 8.00

Miniature Sheets

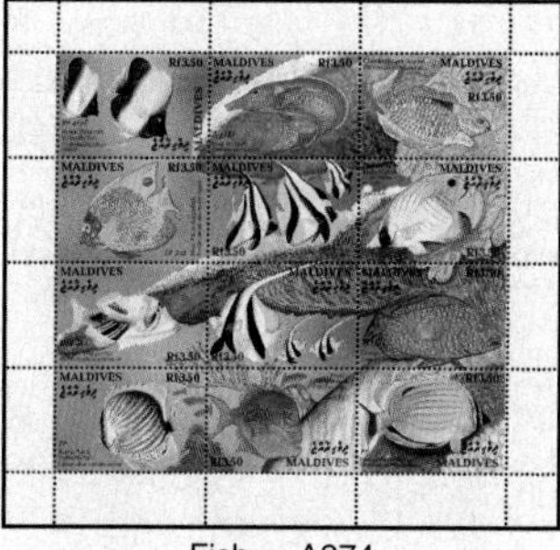

Fish — A274

No. 1868: b, Black pyramid butterflyfish. c, Bird wrasse. d, Checkerboard wrasse. e, Blue face angelfish. f, Bannerfish. g, Threadfin butterflyfish. h, Picasso triggerfish. i, Pennantfish. j, Grouper. k, Black back butterflyfish. l, Redfin triggerfish. m, Redfin butterflyfish.

No. 1868A: n, Yellow goatfish. o, Emperor angelfish. p, Madagascar butterflyfish. q, Empress angelfish. r, Longnose butterfly. s, Racoon butterflyfish. t, Harlequin filefish. u, Wedgetailed triggerfish. v, Clark's anemonefish. w, Clown triggerfish. x, Zebra lionfish. y, Maldive clownfish.

No. 1869, Goldbelly anemone, vert. No. 1869A, Klein's butterflyfish, vert.

1993, June 30 *Perf. 14x13½*

Sheets of 12

1868 A274 3.50r #b.-m. 10.00 10.00
1868A A274 3.50r #n.-y. 10.00 10.00

Souvenir Sheets

Perf. 12x13

1869 A274 25r multicolored 6.00 6.00
1869A A274 25r multicolored 6.00 6.00

Miniature Sheets

Birds — A275

No. 1870: a, Pallid harrier. b, Cattle egret. c, Koel (b). d, Tree pipit. e, Short-ear owl. f, European kestrel. g, Yellow wagtail. h, Common heron. i, Black bittern. j, Common snipe. k, Little egret. l, Little stint.

No. 1871: a, Gull-billed tern. b, Long-tailed tropicbird (a). c, Frigate bird. d, Wilson's petrel. e, White tern. f, Brown booby. g, Marsh harrier. h, Common noddy. i, Little heron. j, Turnstone. k, Curlew. l, Crab plover.

No. 1872, Caspian tern, horiz. No. 1873, Audubon's shearwater, horiz.

1993, July 5 *Perf. 13½x14*

1870 A275 3.50r Sheet of 12, #a.-l. 9.50 9.50
1871 A275 3.50r Sheet of 12, #a.-l. 9.50 9.50

Souvenir Sheet

Perf. 13x12

1872 A275 25r multicolored 6.00 6.00
1873 A275 25r multicolored 6.00 6.00

No. 1871 is horiz.

Year of Productivity
A276 A277

1993, July 25 *Perf. 14*

1874 A276 7r multicolored 1.40 1.40
1875 A277 10r multicolored 2.10 2.10

A278

Picasso (1881-1973): 3.50r, Still Life with Pitcher and Apples, 1919. 5r, Bowls and Jug, 1908. 10r, Bowls of Fruit and Loaves, 1908. 20r, Green Still Life, 1914, horiz.

1993, Oct. 11 **Litho.** *Perf. 14*

1876 A278 3.50r multicolored .80 .80
1877 A278 5r multicolored 1.10 1.10
1878 A278 10r multicolored 2.25 2.25
Nos. 1876-1878 (3) 4.15 4.15

Souvenir Sheet

1879 A278 20r multicolored 5.00 5.00

A279

Copernicus (1473-1543): 3.50r, Early astronomical instrument. 15r, Astronaut wearing Manned Maneuvering Unit. 20r, Copernicus.

1993, Oct. 11

1880 A279 3.50r multicolored .90 .90
1881 A279 15r multicolored 4.00 4.00

Souvenir Sheet

1882 A279 20r multicolored 5.00 5.00

Royal Wedding of Crown Prince Naruhito, Princess Masako — A280

3.50r, Crown Prince Naruhito. 10r, Princess Masako, horiz. 25r, Princess Masako.

1993, Oct. 11

1883 A280 3.50r multicolored .65 .65
1884 A280 10r multicolored 2.00 2.00

Souvenir Sheet

1885 A280 25r multicolored 6.00 6.00

1994 Winter Olympics, Lillehammer, Norway — A281

8r, Marina Kiehl, gold medalist, women's downhill, 1988. 15r, Vegard Ulvang, gold medalist, cross-country skiing, 1992. 25r, Soviet ice hockey goalie, 1980.

1993, Oct. 11

1886 A281 8r multicolored 1.75 1.75
1887 A281 15r multicolored 3.50 3.50

Souvenir Sheet

1888 A281 25r multicolored 6.00 6.00

Polska '93 — A282

Fine arts: 3.50r, Zolte Roze, by Menasze Seidenbeutel, 1932. 5r, Cracow Historical Museum. 8r, Apples and Curtain, by Waclaw Borowski. 25r, Seascape, by Roman Sielski, 1931, horiz.

1993, Oct. 11 **Litho.** *Perf. 14*

1889 A282 3.50r multicolored .85 .85
1890 A282 5r multicolored 1.10 1.10
1891 A282 8r multicolored 1.90 1.90
Nos. 1889-1891 (3) 3.85 3.85

Souvenir Sheet

1892 A282 25r multicolored 5.00 5.00

Butterflies A283

7 l, Commander. 20 l, Blue tiger. 25 l, Centaur oakblue. 50 l, Common banded peacock. 5r, Glad-eye bushbrown. 6.50r + 50 l, Common tree nymph. 7r, Lemon emigrant. 10r, Blue pansy. 12r, Painted lady. 15r, Blue mormon. 18r, Tamil yeoman. 20r, Crimson rose.

No. 1905, Common imperial, vert. No. 1906, Great orange tip, vert. No. 1907, Black prince, vert.

1993, Oct. 25

1893 A283 7 l multi .25 .25
1894 A283 20 l multi .25 .25
1895 A283 25 l multi .25 .25
1896 A283 50 l multi .25 .25
1897 A283 5r multi 1.40 1.40
1898 A283 6.50r + 50 l multi 2.00 2.00
1899 A283 7r multi 2.00 2.00
1900 A283 10r multi 2.75 2.75
1901 A283 12r multi 3.50 3.50
1902 A283 15r multi 4.25 4.25
1903 A283 18r multi 5.00 5.00
1904 A283 20r multi 5.50 5.50
Nos. 1893-1904 (12) 27.40 27.40

Souvenir Sheets

1905 A283 25r multi 7.50 7.50
1906 A283 25r multi 7.50 7.50
1907 A283 25r multi 7.50 7.50

Aviation Anniversaries — A284

Designs: 3.50r, Zeppelin on bombing raid caught in British search lights, vert. 5r, Homing pigeon. 10r, Dr. Hugo Eckener, vert. 15r, Airmal service medal, Jim Edgerton's Jenny, mail truck. 20r, USS Macon approaching mooring mast, vert.
Each 25r: No. 1913, Blanchard's balloon, 1793, vert. No. 1914, Santos-Dumont's flight around Eiffel Tower, 1901, vert.

1993, Nov. 22 Litho. *Perf. 14*

1908-1912	A284	Set of 5	14.00	14.00

Souvenir Sheets

1913-1914	A284	Set of 2	9.50	9.50

Dr. Hugo Eckener, 125th birth anniv. (3.50r, 10r, 20r, No. 1913).

Miniature Sheets

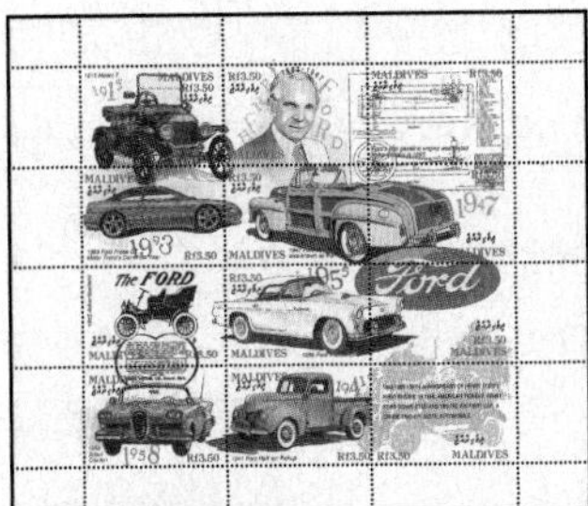

First Ford Engine, First Benz Four-Wheeled Car, Cent. — A285

No. 1915: a, 1915 Model T (b, d-e). b, Henry Ford (e). c, Drawing of 1st Ford engine (b, e-f). d, 1993 Ford Probe GT (e). e, 1947 Ford Sportsman, front (f). f, As "f," rear (e). g, 1915 Ford advertisement (j). h, 1955 Ford Thunderbird (g, i). i, Ford emblem (f, h). j, 1958 Edsel Citation. k, 1941 Ford half-ton pickup. l, Model T.
No. 1916: a, 1937 Daimler-Benz Straight 8 (b). b, Karl Benz (e). c, Mercedes-Benz advertisement (f). d, 1929 Mercedes 38-250SS (e). e, 1893 Benz Viktoria (f, h). f, Mercedes star emblem (i). g, WWI Mercedes engine. h, 1957 Mercedes-Benz 300SL Gullwing (g). i, 1993 Mercedes Benz SL coupe/roadster (h). j, 1906 Benz 4-cylinder car (k). k, Early Benz advertisement. l, Benz Viktoria, 1893.
No. 1917, 1933 Ford Model Y. No. 1918, 1955 Mercedes 300S.

1993, Nov. 22

1915	A285	3.50r Sheet of 12, #a.-l.	12.00	12.00
1916	A285	3.50r Sheet of 12, #a.-l.	12.00	12.00

Souvenir Sheets

1917	A285	25r multi	6.00	6.00
1918	A285	25r multi	6.00	6.00

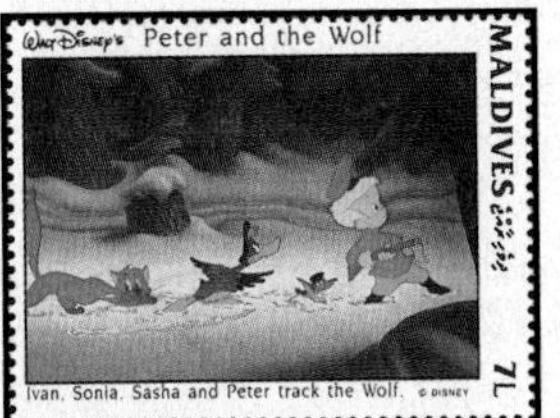

Peter and the Wolf — A286

Characters and scenes from Disney animated film: 7 l, 15 l, 20 l, 25 l, 50 l, 1r.
Nos. 1925a-1925i: Part 1.
Nos. 1926a-1926i: Part 2.

1993, Dec. 20

1919-1924	A286	Set of 6	1.00	1.00

Miniature Sheets of 9

1925	A286	3.50r #a.-i.	7.50	7.50
1926	A286	3.50r #a.-i.	7.50	7.50

Souvenir Sheets

1927	A286	25r Sonia	5.00	5.00
1928	A286	25r Ivan	5.00	5.00

Fine Art — A287

Paintings by Rembrandt: 50 l, Girl with a Broom. No. 1931, 3.50r, Young Girl at half-open Door. 5r, The Prophetess Hannah (Rembrandt's Mother). 7r, Woman with a Pink Flower. 12r, Lucretia. No. 1939, 15r, Lady with an Ostich Feather Fan.
Paintings by Matisse: 2r, Girl with Tulips (Jeanne Vaderin). No. 1932, 3.50r. Portrait of Greta Moll. 6.50r, The Idol. 9r, Mme. Matisse in Japanese Robe. 10r, Portrait of MMe Matisse (The Green Line). No. 1940, 15r, The Woman with the Hat.
Each 25r: No. 1941, Married Couple with 3 Children (A Family Group), by Rembrandt, horiz. No. 1942, The Painter's Family, by Matisse. No. 1942A: The Music Makers, by Rembrandt.

1994, Jan. 11 Litho. *Perf. 13*

1929-1940	A287	Set of 12	21.00	21.00

Souvenir Sheets

1941-1942A	A287	Set of 3	21.00	21.00

No. 1942A issued Feb. 2.

1994 World Cup Soccer US — A288

Players, country: 7 l, Windischmann, US; Giannini, Italy. 20 l, Carnevale, Gascoigne. 25 l, Platt & teammates, England. 3.50r, Koeman, Holland; Klinsmann, Germany. 5r, Quinn, Ireland; Maldini, Italy. 7r, Lineker, England. 15r, Hassan, Egypt; Moran, Ireland. 18r, Canniggia, Argentina.
Each 25r: No. 1951, Conejo, Costa Rica; Mozer, Brazil, horiz. No. 1952, Armstrong & Balboa, US; Ogris, Austria.

1994, Jan. 11 *Perf. 14*

1943-1950	A288	Set of 8	13.00	13.00

Souvenir Sheets

1951-1952	A288	Set of 2	12.50	12.50

A289

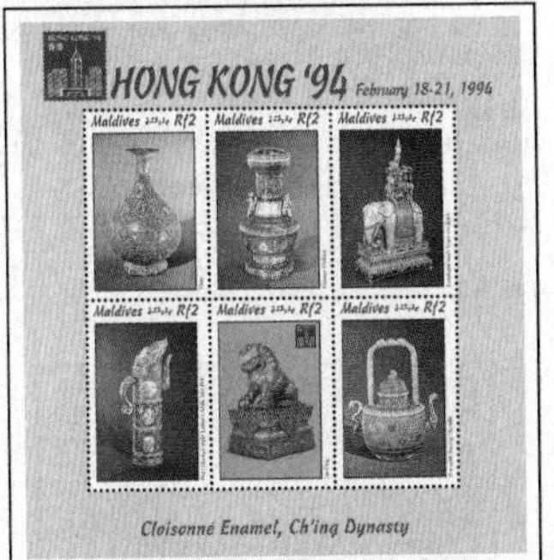

Hong Kong '94 — A290

Stamps, Moon-Lantern Festival, Hong Kong: No. 1953, Hong Kong #416, girls, lanterns. No. 1954, Lanterns, #660.
Cloisonne Enamel, Qing Dynasty: No. 1955a, Vase. b, Flower holder. c, Elephant with vase on back. d, Pot (Tibetan-style lama's milk-tea pot. e, Fo-dog. f, Pot with swing handle.

1994, Feb. 18 Litho. *Perf. 14*

1953	A289	4r multicolored	.80	.80
1954	A289	4r multicolored	.80	.80
a.		Pair, #1953-1954	1.60	1.60

Miniature Sheet

1955	A290	2r Sheet of 6, #a.-f.	6.75	6.75

Nos. 1953-1954 issued in sheets of 5 pairs. No. 1954a is a continuous design.
New Year 1994 (Year of the Dog) (No. 1955e).

Sierra Club, Cent. A290a

Various animals, each 6.50r:
Nos. 1956a-1956b, Prairie dog. c.-e, Woodland caribou. f, Galapagos penguin.
No. 1957, vert: a, Humpback whale. b.-c, Ocelot. d, Snow monkey. e, Prairie dog. f, Golden lion tamarin.
No. 1958: a.-b, Golden lion tamarin. c.-d, Humpback whale. e, Bengal tiger. f, Ocelot. g.-h, Snow monkey.
No. 1959, vert: a.-b, Galapagos penguin. c.-d, Bengal tiger. e.-g, Philippine tarsier. h, Sierra Club centennial emblem.

1994, May 20 Litho. *Perf. 14*

Miniature Sheets of 6, #a-f

1956-1957	A290a	Set of 2	20.00	20.00

Miniature Sheets of 8, #a-h

1958-1959	A290a	Set of 2	24.00	24.00

Dome of the Rock, Jerusalem — A291

1994, June 10 *Perf. 13½*

1960	A291	8r multicolored	1.60	1.60

A292

Designs: 25 l, Elasmosaurus. 50 l, Dilophosaurus. 1r, Avimimus. 5r, Chasmosaurus. 8r, Edmontonia. 10r, Anatosaurus. 15r, Velociraptor. 20r, Spinosaurus.
No. 1969, each 3r: a, Dimorphodon. b, Megalosaurus. c, Kuehneosaurus. d, Dryosaurus. e, Kentrosaurus. f, Baraposaurus (c). g, Tenontosaurus. h, Elaphrosaurus (i). i, Maiasaura. j, Huayangosaurus. k, Rutiodon. l, Pianitzkysaurus.
No. 1970, each 3r: a, Quetzalcoatlus. b, Daspletosaurus. c, Pleurocoelus. d, Baryonyx. e, Pentaceratops. f, Kritosaurus. g, Microvenator (h). h, Nodosaurus. i, Montanaceratops. j, Dromiceiomimus. k, Dryptosaurus. l, Parkosaurus.
Each 25r: No. 1971, Gallimimus. No. 1972, Plateosaurus, vert.

1994, June 20 *Perf. 14*

1961-1968	A292	Set of 8	17.00	17.00

Miniature Sheets of 12, #a-l

1969-1970	A292	Set of 2	20.00	20.00

Souvenir Sheets

1971-1972	A292	Set of 2	10.00	10.00

Nos. 1969-1970 are continuous design.

Locomotives A293

Designs: 25 l, 2-6-6-0 Mallet, Indonesia, horiz. 50 l, C62, Japan, horiz. 1r, D51, Japan. 5r, 4-6-0 Steam, India. 8r, Class 485 electric, Japan, horiz. 10r, Class WP Pacific, India. 15r, "People" class RM 4-6-2, China. 20r, C57, Japan, horiz.
No. 1981: a, W Class 0-6-2, India. b, C53 Class, Indonesia. c, C-10, Japan. d, Hanomag 4-8-0, India. e, Hakari bullet train, Japan. f, C-55, Japan.
Each 25r: No. 1982, 4-4-0, Indonesia. No. 1983, Series 8620, Japan.

1994, July 4

1973-1980	A293	Set of 8	12.00	12.00

Miniature Sheet of 6

1981	A293	6.50r +50 l, #a.-f.	8.00	8.00

Souvenir Sheets

1982-1983	A293	Set of 2	11.00	11.00

Domestic Cats — A294

Designs: 7 l, Japanese bobtail, horiz. 20 l, Siamese. 25 l, Persian longhair, horiz. 50 l, Somali. 3.50r, Oriental shorthair, horiz. 5r, Burmese, horiz. 7r, Bombay, horiz. 10r, Turkish van. 12r, Javanese. 15r, Singapura, horiz. 18r, Turkish angora. 20r, Egyptian mau.
Each 25r: No. 1996, Birman. No. 1997, Korat. No. 1998, Abyssinian.

1994, July 11

1984-1995	A294	Set of 12	20.00	20.00

Souvenir Sheets

1996-1998	A294	Set of 3	16.50	16.50

Miniature Sheets of 6

1994 World Cup Soccer Championships, US — A295

No. 1999: a, 10 l, Franco Baresi, Italy, Stuart McCall, Scotland. b, 25 l, McCarthy, Great Britain, Lineker, Ireland. c, 50 l, J. Helt, Denmark, R. Gordillo, Spain. d, 5r, Martin Vasquez, Spain, Enzo Scifo, Belgium. e, 10r, Emblem. f, 12r, Tomas Brolin, Sweden, Gordon Durie, Scotland.
No. 2000, vert.: a, Bebeto, Brazil. b, Lothar Matthaus, Great Britain. c, Diego Maradona, Argentina. d, Stephane Chapuisat, Switzerland. e, George Hagi, Romania. f, Carlos Valderrama, Colombia.
No. 2001, Hossam Hassan, 2nd Egyptian player.

1994, Aug. 4 Litho. *Perf. 14*

1999	A295	Sheet of 6, #a.-f.	5.50	5.50
2000	A295	6.50r Sheet of 6, #a.-f.	7.50	7.50

Souvenir Sheet

2001	A295	10r multicolored	4.00	4.00

D-Day, 50th Anniv. A296

Designs: 2r, Amphibious DUKW approaches Utah Beach. 4r, Landing craft tank, Sword Beach. 18r, Landing craft infantry damaged at Omaha Beach.

No. 2006, Canadian commandos, Juno Beach.

1994, Aug. 8

2003-2005 A296 Set of 3 4.50 4.50

Souvenir Sheet

2006 A296 25r multicolored 5.75 5.75

A297

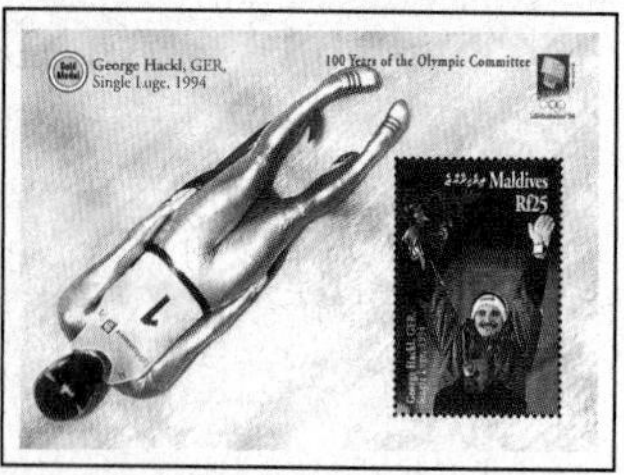

Intl. Olympic Committee, Cent. — A298

Designs: 7r, Linford Christie, Great Britain, track 1988. 12r, Koji Gushiken, Japan, gymnastics, 1984.

25r, George Hackl, Germany, single luge, 1994.

1994, Aug. 8

2007 A297 7r multicolored 1.25 1.25
2008 A297 12r multicolored 2.25 2.25

Souvenir Sheet

2009 A298 25r multicolored 5.50 5.50

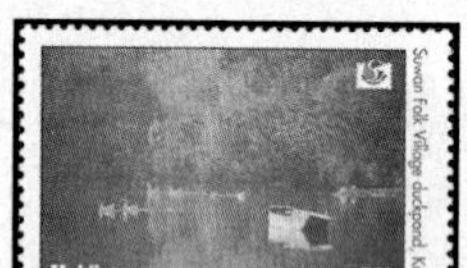

A299

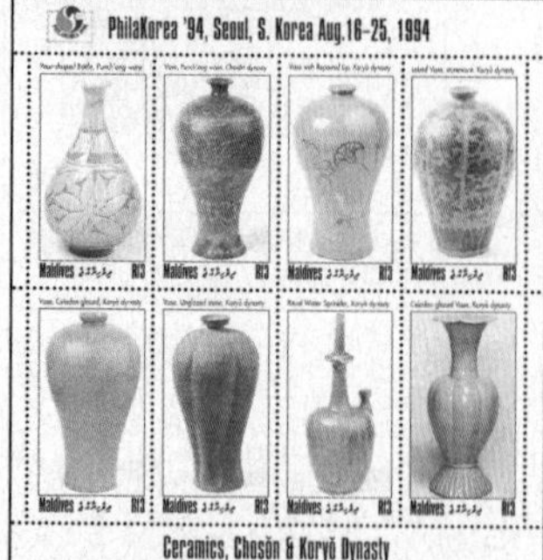

PHILAKOREA '94 — A300

Designs: 50 l, Suwan Folk Village duck pond. 3.50r, Youngduson Park. 20r, Ploughing, Hahoe Village, Andong region.

Ceramics, Choson & Koryo Dynasties: No. 2013a, Pear-shaped bottle. b, Vase. c, Vase with repaired lip. d, Labed vase, stoneware. e, Vase, celadon-glazed. f, Vase, unglazed stone. g, Ritual water sprinkler. h, Celadon-glazed vase.

25r, Hunting (detail from eight-panel screen, Choson Dynasty), vert.

1994, Aug. 8 ***Perf. 14, 13½ (#2013)***

2010-2012 A299 Set of 3 5.25 5.25

Miniature Sheet of 8

2013 A300 3r #a.-h. 5.25 5.25

Souvenir Sheet

2014 A299 25r multicolored 5.50 5.50

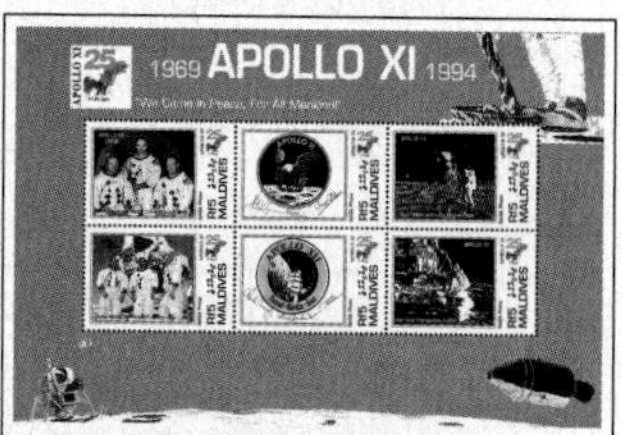

First Manned Moon Landing, 25th Anniv. — A301

No. 2015, each 5r: a, Apollo 11 crew. b, Apollo 11 patch, signatures of crew. c, "Buzz" Aldrin, lunar module, Eagle. d, Apollo 12 crew. e, Apollo 12 patch, signatures of crew. f, Alan Bean transporting ALSEP.

No. 2016, each 5r: a, Apollo 16 crew. b, Apollo 16 patch, signatures of crew. c, John Young gives a "Navy salute." d, Apollo 17 crew. e, Apollo 17 patch, signatures of crew. f, Night launch of Apollo 17.

25r, Launch at Baikonur.

1994, Aug. 8 ***Perf. 14***

Miniature Sheets of 6, #a-f

2015-2016 A301 Set of 2 14.00 14.00

Souvenir Sheet

2017 A301 25r multicolored 5.50 5.50

UN Development Plan — A302

1r, Woman, baby, undernourished man, city on island. 8r, Island native, case worker, island, ship.

1994 **Litho.** ***Perf. 14***

2018 A302 1r multicolored .25 .25
2019 A302 8r multicolored 2.00 2.00

Miniature Sheet of 12

Space Exploration — A304

No. 2020: a, Voyager 2. b, Sputnik. c, Apollo-Soyuz. d, Apollo 10 descent. e, Apollo 11 mission insignia. f, Hubble space telescope. g, Buzz Aldrin. h, RCA lunar cam. i, Lunar rover. j, Jim Irwin. k, Apollo 12 lunar module. l, Lunar soil extraction.

Each 25r: No. 2021, David Scott in open hatch of Apollo 9 command module. No. 2022, Alan Shepard, Jr. waving salute from moon, Apollo 14, horiz.

1994, Aug. 8 **Litho.** ***Perf. 14***

2020 A304 5r #a.-l. 17.50 17.50

Souvenir Sheets

2021-2022 A304 Set of 2 14.00 14.00

Aminiya School, 50th Anniv. A305

15 l, Discipline. 50 l, Arts. 1r, Emblem, hand holding book, vert. 8r, Girls carrying books, vert. 10r, Sports. 11r, Girls cheering, vert. 13r, Science.

1994, Nov. 28

2023-2029 A305 Set of 7 8.75 8.75

ICAO, 50th Anniv. A306

Designs: 50 l, Boeing 747. 1r, De Havilland Comet 4. 2r, Male Intl. Airport, Maldives. 3r, Lockheed 1649 Super Star. 8r, European Airbus. 10r, Dornier Do228. 25r, Concorde.

1994, Dec. 31

2030-2035 A306 Set of 6 8.50 8.50

Souvenir Sheet

2036 A306 25r multicolored 5.75 5.75

Miniature Sheets of 9

Water Birds — A307

Designs: No. 2037a, Northern pintail (b, d). b, Comb duck (c). c, Ruddy duck. d, Garganey (a, e, g, h). e, Lesser whistling duck (b, c, f). f, Green winged teal. g, Fulvous whistling duck. h, Northern shoveler (e). i, Cotton pygmy goose (h).

No. 2038, vert.: a, Pochard (b). b, Mallard (c, e, f). c, Wigeon. d, Northern shoveler (e, g). e, Northern pintail (h). f, Garganey (e, i). g, Tufted duck. h, Ferruginous duck (i). i, Red-crested pochard.

Each 25r: No. 2039, Cotton pygmy goose, vert. No. 2040, Garganey, diff.

1995, Feb. 27 **Litho.** ***Perf. 14***

2037 A307 5r #a.-i. 8.25 8.25
2038 A307 6.50r + 50 l #a.-i. 11.50 11.50

Souvenir Sheets

2039-2040 A307 Set of 2 11.00 11.00

Monuments of the World — A308

Designs: 7 l, Taj Mahal. 10 l, Washington Monument. 15 l, Mt. Rushmore Memorial. 25 l, Arc de Triomphe, vert. 50 l, Sphinx, vert. 5r, El Castillo Monument of the Toltec, Chichen Itza, Yucatan, Mexico. 8r, Toltec monument, Tula, Mexico, vert. 12r, Victory Column, Berlin, vert.

Each 25r: No. 2049, Moai statues, Easter Island. No. 2050, Stonehenge.

1995, Feb. 28

2041-2048 A308 Set of 8 6.00 6.00

Souvenir Sheets

2049-2050 A308 Set of 2 9.00 9.00

No. 2049 contains one 43x57mm stamp, No. 2050 one 85x28mm stamp.

Donald Duck, 60th Birthday (in 1994) — A309

Scenes from "Donald and the Wheel:" 3 l, Racing chariot. 4 l, Standing on log. 5 l, Operating steam locomotive. 10 l, Looking at cave drawing, vert. 20 l, Sitting in "junked" car, vert. 25 l, Listening to phonograph. 5r, Climbing on mammoth. 20r, Pushing old car.

Disney Duck family orchestra, vert, each 5r: No. 2059a, Donald Duck, saxophone. b, Moby Duck, violin. c, Feathry Duck, banjo. d, Daisy Duck, harp. e, Gladstone Gander, clarinet. f, Dewey, Louie, Huey, oboe. g, Gus Goose, flute. h, Ludwig von Drake, trombone.

Donald Duck family portraits, vert, each 5r: No. 2060a, Daisy. b, Donald. c, Grandma. d, Gus Goose. e, Gyro Gearloose, f, Huey, Dewey, Louie. g, Ludwig von Drake. h, Scrooge McDuck.

Each 25r: No. 2061, Dixieland band, vert. No. 2062, Donald conducting symphony orchestra. No. 2063, Donald being photographed, vert. No. 2064, Huey, Dewey, Louie in family portrait.

Perf. 13½x13, 13x13½

1995, Mar. 22 **Litho.**

2051-2058 A309 Set of 8 6.50 6.50

Miniature Sheets of 8, #a-h

2059-2060 A309 Set of 2 17.00 17.00

Souvenir Sheets

2061-2064 A309 Set of 4 18.00 18.00

EID Greetings — A310

1r, Mosque. 1r, Rose. 8r, Hibiscus. 10r, Orchids.

1995, May 1 **Litho.** ***Perf. 14***

2065-2068 A310 Set of 4 4.25 4.25

Whales, Dolphins, & Porpoises A311

Nos. 2069-2072: 1r, Killer whale. 2r, Bottlenose dolphin. 8r, Humpback whale. 10r, Common dolphin.

No. 2073, each 3r: a, Hourglass dolphin. b, Bottlenose dolphin. c, Dusky dolphin. d, Spectacled porpoise. e, Fraser's dolphin. f, Commerson's dolphin. g, Spinner dolphin. h, Dalls dolphin. i, Spotted dolphin. j, Indus river dolphin. k, Hector's dolphin. l, Amazon river dolphin.

No. 2074, each 3r: a, Right whale (d). b, Killer whale (a). c, Humpback whale (f). d, Beluga. e, Narwhale. f, Blue whale (e, g). g, Bowhead whale (h, k). h, Fin whale (d, e, g). i, Pilot whale. j, Grey whale. k, Sperm whale (l). l, Goosebeaked whale.

Each 25r: No. 2075, Hourglass dolphin. No. 2076, Sperm whale.

1995, May 16

2069-2072 A311 Set of 4 4.00 4.00

Miniature Sheets of 12, #a-l

2073-2074 A311 Set of 2 15.50 15.50

Souvenir Sheets

2075-2076 A311 Set of 2 12.00 12.00

Singapore '95.

UN, 50th Anniv. A311a

Designs: 30 l, Emblem, security of small states. 8r, Women in development. 11r, Peace keeping, peace making operations. 13r, Disarmament.

1995, July 6 **Litho.** ***Perf. 14***

2076A-2076D A311a Set of 4 5.75 5.75

UN, 50th Anniv. — A312

No. 2077: a, 6.50r+50 l, Child, dove flying left. b, 8r, Earth from space. c, 10r, Child, Dove flying right.
25r, UN emblem, dove.

1995, July 6 Litho. *Perf. 14*
2077 A312 Strip of 3, #a.-c. 4.50 4.50

Souvenir Sheet

2078 A312 25r multicolored 4.50 4.50

No. 2077 is a continuous design.

A312a

7r, Food for all. 8r, Dolphin-friendly fishing.

1995 Litho. *Perf. 14*
2078A A312a 7r multi 1.25 1.25
2078B A312a 8r multi 1.40 1.40

FAO, 50th Anniv. — A313

No. 2079: a, 6.50r+50 l, Child eating. b, 8r, FAO emblem. c, 10r, Mother, child.
25r, Food emblem, child, horiz.

1995, July 6
2079 A313 Strip of 3, #a.-c. 6.00 6.00

Souvenir Sheet

2080 A313 25r multicolored 6.00 6.00

1995 Boy Scout Jamboree, Holland — A314

No. 2081: a, 10r, Natl. flag, scouts, tents. b, 12r, Scout cooking. c, 15r, Scouts sitting before tents.
25r, Scout playing flute, camp at night, vert.

1995, July 6
2081 A314 Strip of 3, #a.-c. 6.75 6.75

Souvenir Sheet

2082 A314 25r multicolored 4.50 4.50

No. 2081 is a continuous design.

Queen Mother, 95th Birthday — A315

No. 2083: a, Drawing. b, Blue print dress, pearls. c, Formal portrait. d, Blue outfit.
25r, Pale violet hat, violet & blue dress.

1995, July 6 *Perf. 13½x14*
2083 A315 5r Block or strip of 4, #a.-d. 4.00 4.00

Souvenir Sheet

2084 A315 25r multicolored 5.75 5.75

No. 2083 was issued in sheets of 2.
Sheets of Nos. 2083-2084 exist overprinted in margin with black frame and text "In Memoriam 1900-2002."

Natl. Library, 50th Anniv. A316

Designs: 2r, Boys seated at library table. 8r, Two people standing, two at table.
10r, Library entrance.

1995, July 12 *Perf. 14*
2085 A316 2r multicolored .30 .30
2086 A316 8r multicolored 1.25 1.25

Size: 100x70mm

Imperf

2087 A316 10r multicolored 1.60 1.60

Miniature Sheets of 6 or 8

End of World War II, 50th Anniv. — A317

No. 2088: a, 203mm Red Army howitzer. b, Ruins of Hitler's residence, Berchtesgaden. c, Operation Manna, Allies drop food to starving Dutch. d, Soviet IL-1 fighter. e, Inmates, British troops burn last hut at Belsen. f, Last V1 Buzz Bomb launched against London. g, US 3rd Armored Division passes through ruins of Cologne. h, Gutted Reichstag, May 7, 1946.
No. 2089: a, Grumman F6F-3 Hellcat. b, F4-U1 attacking with rockets. c, Douglas Dauntless. d, Guadalcanal, Aug. 7, 1942. e, US Marines in Alligator landing craft. f, US Infantry landing craft.
Each 25r: No. 2090, Allied soldiers with smiling faces. No. 2091, Corsair fighters.

1995, July 6 Litho. *Perf. 14*
2088 A317 5r #a.-h. + label 7.25 7.25
2089 A317 6.50r +50 l #a.-f. + label 9.00 9.00

Souvenir Sheets

2090-2091 A317 Set of 2 10.00 10.00

Turtles A318

Hawksbill turtle: No. 2092a, Crawling. b, Two in water. c, One crawling out of water. d, Swimming.
No. 2093: a, Spur-thighed tortoise. b, Aldabra turtle. c, Loggerhead turtle. d, Olive ridley. e, Leatherback turtle. f, Green turtle. g, Atlantic ridley. h, Hawsbill turtle.
25r, Chelonia mydas.

1995, Aug. 22
2092 A318 10r Strip of 4, #a.-d. 10.00 10.00

Miniature Sheet of 8

2093 A318 3r #a.-h. 10.00 10.00

Souvenir Sheet

2094 A318 25r multicolored 13.00 13.00

World Wildlife Fund (No. 2092). No. 2092 was printed in sheets of 12 stamps.

Fourth World Conference on Women, Beijing — A318a

Designs: 30 l, Woman at computer. 1r, Woman high jumping. 8r, Women dancing. 11r, Woman pilot.

1995, Aug. 24 Litho. *Perf. 12¼*
2094A-2094D A318a Set of 4 — —

Miniature Sheets

Singapore '95 — A319

Mushrooms, butterflies, each 2r: No. 2095a, Russula aurata, papilio demodocus. b, Kallimoides rumia, lepista saeva. c, Lapista nuda, hypolimnas salmacis. d, Precis octavia, boletus subtomentosus.
No. 2096: a, 5r, Gyroporus castaneus, hypolimnas salmacis. b, 8r, Papilio dardanus, Gomphidius glutinosus. c, 10r, Russula olivacea, precis octavia. d, 12r, Prepona praeneste, boletus edulis.
Each 25r: No. 2097, Hypolimnas salmacis, boletus rhodoxanthus, vert. No. 2098, Amanita muscaria, kallimoides rumia, vert.

1995, Oct. 18 Litho. *Perf. 14*
2095 A319 Sheet of 4, #a.-d. 2.00 2.00
2096 A319 Sheet of 4, #a.-d. 10.00 10.00

Souvenir Sheets

2097-2098 A319 Set of 2 10.00 10.00

Flowers A320

Designs: 1r, Ballade tulip. 3r, White mallow. 5r, Regale trumpet lily. 7r, Lilactime dahlia. 8r, Blue ideal iris. 10r, Red crown imperial.
No. 2105, a, Dendrobium waipahu beauty. b, Brassocattleya Jean Murray "Allan Christenson." c, Cymbidium Fort George "Lewes." d, Paphiopedilum malipoense. e, Cycnoches chlorochilon. f, Rhyncholaelia digbgana. g, Lycaste deppei. h, Masdevallia constricta. i, Paphiopedilum Clair de Lune "Edgard Van Belle."
Each 25r: No. 2106, Psychopsis krameriana. No. 2107, Cockleshell orchid.

1995, Dec. 4 Litho. *Perf. 14*
2099-2104 A320 Set of 6 7.25 7.25

Miniature Sheet

2105 A320 5r Sheet of 9, #a.-i. 9.25 9.25

Souvenir Sheets

2106-2107 A320 Set of 2 9.00 9.00

Miniature Sheet

Elvis Presley (1935-77) — A321

Various portraits.

1995, Dec. 8 *Perf. 13½x14*
2108 A321 5r Sheet of 9, #a.-i. 8.00 8.00

Souvenir Sheet

Perf. 14x13½

2109 A321 25r multi, horiz. 4.50 4.50

Miniature Sheets

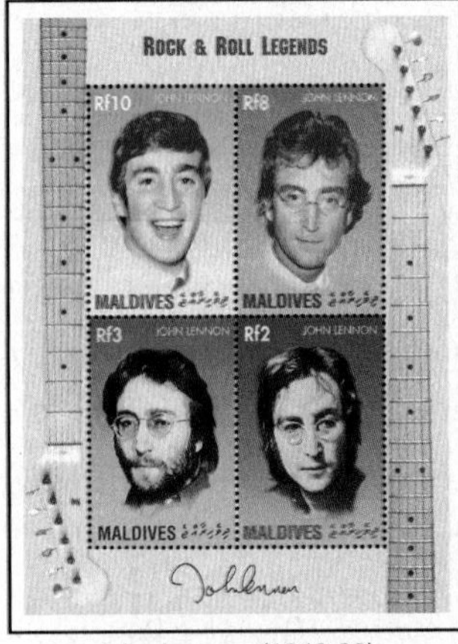

John Lennon (1940-80), Entertainer — A322

No. 2110, Various portraits.
No. 2111: a, 10r, As young man. b, 8r, Younger man with glasses. c, 3r, With beard. d, 2r, Older picture without beard.
No. 2112, Standing at microphone.

1995, Dec. 8
2110 A322 5r Sheet of 6, #a.-f. 9.00
2111 A322 Sheet of 4, #a.-d. 7.00

Souvenir Sheet

2112 A322 25r multicolored

Nobel Prize Fund Established, Cent. — A323

Recipients: No. 2113, each 5r: a, Bernardo A. Houssay, medicine, 1947. b, Paul H. Müller, medicine, 1948. c, Walter R. Hess, medicine, 1949. d, Sir MacFarlane Burnet, medicine, 1960. e, Baruch S. Blumberg, medicine, 1976. f, Daniel Nathans, medicine, 1978. g, Glenn T. Seaborg, chemistry, 1951. h, Ilya Prigogine, chemistry, 1977. i, Kenichi Fukui, chemistry, 1981.

No. 2114, each 5r: a, Johannes Van Der Waals, physics, 1910. b, Charles Edouard Guillaume, physics, 1920. c, Sir James Chadwick, physics, 1935. d, Willem Einthoven, medicine, 1924. e, Henrik Dam, medicine, 1943. f, Sir Alexander Fleming, medicine, 1945. g, Hermann J. Muller, medicine, 1946. h, Rodney R. Porter, medicine, 1972. i, Werner Arber, medicine, 1978.

No. 2115, each 5r: a, Dag Hammarskjold, peace, 1961. b, Alva R. Myrdal, peace, 1982. c, Archbishop Desmond M. Tutu, peace, 1984. d, Rudolf C. Eucken, literature, 1908. e, Aleksandr Solzhenitsyn, literature, 1970. f, Gabriel Garcia Márquez, literature, 1982. g, Chen N. Yang, physics, 1957. h, Karl A. Müller, physics, 1987. i, Melvin Schwartz, physics, 1988.

No. 2116, each 5r: a, Niels Bohr, physics, 1922. b, Ben R. Mottelson, physics, 1975. c, Patrick White, literature, 1973. d, Elias Canetti, literature, 1981. e, Theodor Kocher, medicine, 1909. f, August Krogh, medicine, 1920. g, William P. Murphy, medicine, 1934. h, John H. Northrop, chemistry, 1946. i, Luis F. Leloir, chemistry, 1970.

No. 2117, each 5r: a, Carl Spitteler, literatue, 1919. b, Henri Bergson, literature, 1927. c, Johannes V. Jensen, literature, 1944. d, Antoine-Henri Becquerel, physics, 1903. e, Sir William H. Bragg, physics, 1915. f, Sir William L. Bragg, physics, 1915. g, Fredrik Bajer, peace, 1908. h, Léon Bourgeois, peace, 1920. i, Karl Branting, peace, 1921.

No. 2118, each 5r: a, Robert A. Millikan, physics, 1923. b, Louis V. de Broglie, physics, 1929. c, Ernest Walton, physics, 1951. d, Richard Willstätter, chemistry, 1915. e, Lars Onsager, chemistry, 1968. f, Gerhard Herzberg, chemistry, 1971. g, William B. Yeats, literature, 1923. h, George B. Shaw, literature, 1925. i, Eugene O'Neill, literature, 1936.

Each 25r: No. 2119, Eisaku Sato, peace, 1974. No. 2120, Robert Koch, medicine, 1905. No. 2121, Otto Wallach, chemistry, 1910. No. 2122, Konrad Bloch, medicine, 1964. No. 2123, Samuel Beckett, literature, 1969. No. 2124, Hideki Yukawa, physics, 1949.

1995, Dec. 28 Litho. *Perf. 14*

Miniature Sheets of 9, #a-i

2113-2118 A323 Set of 6 48.00 48.00

Souvenir Sheets

2119-2124 A323 Set of 6 24.00 24.00

1996 Summer Olympics, Atlanta A324

... 1r, Rhythmic gymnastics, Tokyo, ...hery, Moscow, 1980. 5r, Diving, ... 7r, High jump, London, ... field, Berlin, 1936. 12r, ...28.

... 1976. b, Decathlon. c, ..., 1980. d, Fencing. e, Olympic medal. f, Equestrian. g, Sydney, 2000. h, Track and field. i, Seoul, 1988.

Each 25r: No. 2132, Olympic torch, vert. No. 2133, Olympic flame, vert.

1996, Jan. 25 Litho. *Perf. 14*

2125-2130 A324 Set of 6 7.75 7.75

Miniature Sheet

2131 A324 5r Sheet of 9, #a.-i. 9.00 9.00

Souvenir Sheets

2132-2133 A324 Set of 2 10.50 10.50

Paintings from Metropolitan Museum of Art — A325

No. 2134, each 4r: a, Self-portrait, by Degas. b, Andromache & Astyanax, by Prud'hon. c, René Grenier, by Toulouse-Lautrec. d, The Banks of the Biévre Near Bicetre, by Rousseau. e, The Repast of the Lion, by Rousseau. f, Portrait Yves Gobillard-Morisot, by Degas. g, Sunflowers, by Van Gogh. h, The Singer in Green, by Degas.

No. 2135, each 4r: a, Still Life, by Fantin-Latour. b, Portrait of a Lady in Gray, by Degas. c, Apples & Grapes, by Monet. d, The Englishman, by Toulouse-Lautrec. e, Cypresses, by Van Gogh. f, Flowers in Chinese Vase, by Redon. g, The Gardener, by Seurat. h, Large Sunflowers I, by Nolde.

By Manet: No. 2136, each 4r: a, The Spanish Singer. b, Young Man in Costume of Majo. c, Mademoisselle Victorine. d, Boating. e, Peonies. f, Woman with a Parrot. g, George Moore. h, The Monet Family in Their Garden.

No. 2137, each 4r7: a, Goldfish, by Matisse. b, Spanish Woman: Harmony in Blue, by Matisse. c, Nasturtiums & the "Dance" II, by Matisse. d, The House Behind Trees, by Braque. e, Mâda Primavesi, by Klimt. f, Head of a Woman, by Picasso. g, Woman in White, by Picasso. h, Harlequin, by Picasso.

Each 25r: No. 2138, Northeaster, by Homer. No. 2139, The Fortune Teller, by Georges de la Tour. No. 2140, Santi (Sanzio), Ritratto di Andrea Navagero E Agostino Beazzano, by Raphael. No. 2141, Portrait of a Woman, by Rubens.

1996, Apr. 22 Litho. *Perf. 13½x14*

Sheets of 8, #a-h + label

2134-2137 A325 Set of 4 35.00 35.00

Souvenir Sheets

Perf. 14

2138-2141 A325 Set of 4 22.50 22.50

Nos. 2138-2141 each contain one 85x57mm stamp.

Nos. 2140-2141 are not in the Metropolitan Museum.

Nos. 2134-2141 exist imperf. Value, set $100.

Disney Characters Visit China — A326

No. 2142, each 2r: a, Mickey at the Great Wall. b, Pluto's encounter in the Temple Garden. c, Minnie saves the pandas. d, Mickey sails with the junks. e, Goofy at the grottoes. f, Donald, Daisy at the marble boat.

No. 2143, each 2r: a, Mickey leads terra cotta statues. b, Goofy's masks. c, Traditional fishing with Donald, Goofy. d, Mickey, Minnie in dragon boat. e, Donald at Peking Opera. f, Mickey, Minnie, in Chinese Garden.

No. 2144, vert: a, Mickey, Minnie snowballing at ice pagoda. b, Donald, Mickey fly Chinese kites. c, Goofy plays anyiwu. d, Mickey, Goofy, origami. e, Donald, Mickey in dragon dance.

No. 2145, 5r, Mickey viewing Guilin. No. 2146, 7r, Mickey, Minnie at Moon Festival. No. 2147, 8r, Donald enjoying traditional Chinese food.

1996, May 10 *Perf. 14x13½, 13½x14*

Sheets of 6, #a-f

2142-2143 A326 Set of 2 11.50 11.50

Sheet of 5, #a-e

2144 A326 3r #a.-e. + label 6.00 6.00

Souvenir Sheets

2145 A326 5r multicolored 2.00 2.00
2146 A326 7r multicolored 2.50 2.50
2147 A326 8r multicolored 3.00 3.00

CHINA '96, 9th Asian Intl. Philatelic Exhibition.

1996 Summer Olympic Games, Atlanta A327

Gold medalists: 1r, Stella Walsh, 100-meters, 1932. 3r, Emil Zatopek, 10,000-meters, 1952, vert. 10r, Olga Fikotova, discus throw, 1956. 12r, Joan Benoit, women's marathon, 1984.

No. 2152: a, Ethel Catherwood, high jump, 1928. b, Mildred "Babe" Didrikson, javelin, 1932. c, Francina (Fanny) Blankers-Koen, hurdles, 1948. d, Tamara Press, shot put, 1960. e, Lia Manoliu, discus, 1968. f, Rosa Mota, women's marathon, 1988.

Gold medalists in weight lifting, vert: No. 2153a, Yanko Rusev, lightweight, 1980. b, Peter Baczako, middle heavyweight, 1980. c, Leonid Taranenko, heavyweight, 1980. d, Aleksandr Kurlovich, heavyweight, 1988. e, Assen Zlatev, middleweight, 1980. f, Zeng Guoqiang, flyweight, 1984. g, Yurik Vardanyan, heavyweight, 1980. h, Sultan Rakhmanov, super heavyweight, 1980. i, Vassily Alexeev, super heavyweight, 1972.

Each 25r: No. 2154, Irena Szewinska, gold medal winner, 400-meters, 1976. No. 2155, Naim Suleymanoglu, gold medal winner, weight lifting, 1988, vert.

1996, May 27 Litho. *Perf. 14*

2148-2151 A327 Set of 4 5.75 5.75

Miniature Sheets

2152 A327 5r Sheet of 6, #a.-f. 6.50 6.50
2153 A327 5r Sheet of 9, #a.-i. 9.50 9.50

Souvenir Sheets

2154-2155 A327 Set of 2 11.00 11.00

Olymphilex '96 (No. 2155).

Queen Elizabeth II, 70th Birthday — A329

Designs: a, Portrait. b, As younger woman wearing hat, pearls. c, Younger picture seated at desk.

25r, On balcony with Queen Mother.

1996, June 21 Litho. *Perf. 13½x14*

2164 A329 8r Strip of 3, #a.-c. 5.50 5.50

Souvenir Sheet

2165 A329 25r multicolored 6.25 6.25

No. 2164 was issued in sheets of 9 stamps.

UNICEF, 50th Anniv. — A330

Designs: 5r (No. 2166), 7r (No. 2167), 7r (No. 2167A), girl, blue margin, 10r (No. 2168), Girls of different races.

25r, Baby girl.

1996, July 10 *Perf. 14*

2166-2168 A330 Set of 4 4.50 4.50

Souvenir Sheet

2169 A330 25r multicolored 4.50 4.50

Butterflies — A331

No. 2170, vert: a, Cymothoe cocccinata. b, Morpho rhetenor. c, Callicore lidwina (b, d). d, Heliconius erato.

No. 2171: a, Epiphora albida. b, Satyrus dryas. c, Satyrus lena. d, Papilio tynderaeus. e, Urota Suraka. f, Satyrus nercis.

No. 2172, vert: a, Spicebush swallowtail. b, Giant swallowtail. c, Lime swallowtail caterpillar (b). d, Painted beauty (c). e, Monarch caterpillar. f, Monarch (e, g). g, Monarch caterpillar & pupa. h, Harris' checkerspot.

Each 25r: No. 2173, Heliconius cydno, vert. No. 2174, Zebra, vert.

1996, July 10

2170 A331 7r Strip of 4, #a.-d. 5.25 5.25
2171 A331 7r Sheet of 6, #a.-f. 8.00 8.00
2172 A331 7r Sheet of 8, #a.-h. 11.00 11.00

Souvenir Sheets

2173-2174 A331 Set of 2 11.00 11.00

No. 2170 was issued in sheets of 8 stamps.

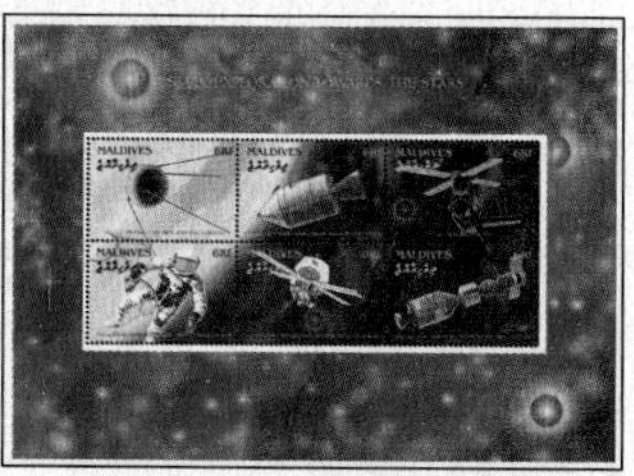
Space Exploration — A332

Designs: No. 2175a, Sputnik I, 1957. b, Apollo 11 Command Module returns to earth, 1969. c, Skylab, 1973. d, Edward White, 1st US astronaut to walk in space, 1965. e, Mariner 9, 1st artificial satellite of Mars, 1971. f, Apollo and Soviet Soyuz dock together, 1975.

25r, Apollo 8 being launched, 1968, vert.

1996, July 10 *Perf. 14*

2175 A332 6r Sheet of 6, #a.-f. 6.50 6.50

Souvenir Sheet

2176 A332 25r multicolored 5.25 5.25

Trains A333

No. 2177, each 3r: a, Electric container train, Germany. b, John Blenkinsop's rack locomotive. c, DB Diesel electric, West Germany. d, Timothy Hackworth's "Royal George," 1827. e, Robert Stephenson (1803-59). f, Trevithick's "New Castle" locomotive. g, Deltic locomotives, British Rail. h, Stockton No. 5, 1826. i, Passenger shuttle, English Channel Tunnel.

No. 2178, each 3r: a, Southern Pacific's "Daylight," San Francisco, US, 1952. b, Timothy Hackworth's "Sans Pareil." c, Chicago & North Western, US. d, Richard Trevithick's "Pen-Y-Darran" locomotive. e, Isambard Kingdom Brunel (1806-59). f, Great Western engine of 1838. g, Passenger train, Canada. h, Mohawk & Hudson Railroad "Experiment," 1832. i, "The ICE," Germany.

No. 2179, each 3r: a, F4 OPH Diesel locomotives, US. b, Stephenson's "Experiment." c, Indian Pacific Intercontinental, Australia. d, George Stephenson's engine, 1815. e, George Stephenson (1781-1848). f, Stephenson's "Rocket," 1829. g, British Rail 125 HST. h, First rail passenger coach, "Experiment," 1825. i, TOFAC, US.

Each 25r: No. 2180, Tom Thumb, 1830. No. 2181, The DeWitt Clinton, 1831. No. 2182, The General, 1855.

1996, Sept. 2 Litho. *Perf. 14*

Sheets of 9, #a-i

2177-2179 A333 Set of 3 24.00 24.00

Souvenir Sheets

2180-2182 A333 Set of 3 16.00 16.00

Fauna A334

Endangered animals:
No. 2183, each 5r: a, Shoebill stork. b, Red-billed hornbill. c, Hippopotamus. d, Gorilla. e, Lion. f, Gray-crowned crane.
No. 2184, each 5r: a, Giant panda. b, Indian elephant. c, Arrow poison frog. d, Mandrill. e, Snow leopard. f, California condor.
Wildlife:
No. 2185, vert, each 5r: a, Yellow baboon. b, Zebra duiker. c, Yellow-backed duiker. d, Pygmy hippopotamus. e, Large-spotted genet. f, African spoonbill. g, White-faced whistling duck. h, Helmeted gunieafowl.
No. 2186, vert, each 5r: a, Bongo. b, Bushback. c, Namaqua dove. d, Hoopoe. e, African fish eagle. f, Egyptian goose. g, Saddle-billed stork. h, Blue-breasted kingfisher.
Each 25r: No. 2187, Tiger, vert. No. 2188, Leopard.

1996, Sept. 9 Sheet of 6

2183-2184 A334 Set of 2 20.00 20.00

Sheet of 8

2185-2186 A334 Set of 2 26.50 26.50

Souvenir Sheets

2187-2188 A334 Set of 2 12.00 12.00

Motion Pictures, Cent. — A335

Progressive scenes from "Pluto and the Flypaper, each 4r:": Nos. 2189a-2189h, Scenes 1-8. No. 2191a-2191i, Scenes 9-17.
Progressive scenes from "Mickey Mouse in The Little Whirlwind, each 4r:" Nos. 2190a-2190h, Scenes 1-8. Nos. 2192a-2192i, Scenes 9-17.
Each 25r: No. 2193, Scene from "Pluto and the Flypaper." No. 2194, Scene from "Mickey Mouse in The Little Whirlwind."

1996, Dec. 2 Litho. *Perf. 13½x14*

Sheets of 8, #a-h, + Label

2189-2190 A335 Set of 2 25.00 25.00

Sheets of 9, #a-i

2191-2192 A335 Set of 2 27.50 27.50

Souvenir Sheets

2193-2194 A335 Set of 2 18.50 18.50

Fauna A336

Designs: a, Saguinus oedipus. b, Bison bonasus. c, Panthera tigris. d, Tetrao urogallus. e, Ailuropoda melanoleuca. f, Trogonoptera brookiana. g, Castor canadensis. h, Leiopelma hamiltoni. i, Trichechus manatus latirostris.
25r, Pan troglodytes.

1996 Litho. *Perf. 14*

2195 A336 7r Sheet of 9, #a.-i. 12.50 12.50

Souvenir Sheet

2196 A336 25r multicolored 5.00 5.00

Turtle Preservation — A336a

1996 ? Litho. *Perf. 12¾*

2196A Horiz. strip of 3 — —
b. A336a 1r Turtle's head — —
c. A336a 7r Turtle's plastron — —
d. A336a 8r Two turtles — —

Hong Kong '97 — A337

Chinese motifs inside letters: No. 2197a, "H." b, "O." c, "N." d, "G" (birds). e, "K." f, "O," diff. g, "N." h, "G" (junk).
25r, "Hong Kong."

1997, Feb. 12 Litho. *Perf. 14*

2197 A337 5r Sheet of 8, #a.-h. 8.50 8.50

Souvenir Sheet

2198 A337 25r multicolored 5.25 5.25

No. 2198 contains one 77x39mm stamp.

Birds — A338

a, Gymnogyps californianus. b, Larus audouinii. c, Fratercula artica. d, Pharomachrus mocinno. e, Amazona vittata. f, Paradisaea minor. g, Nipponia nippon. h, Falco punctatus. i, Strigops habroptilus.
25r, Campephilus principalis.

1997, Feb. 12

2199 A338 5r Sheet of 9, #a.-i. 10.50 10.50

Souvenir Sheet

2200 A338 25r multicolored 6.25 6.25

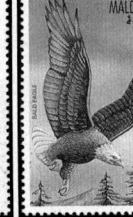

Eagles

A339 A340

Designs: 1r, Crowned solitary eagle. 2r, African hawk eagle, horiz. 3r, Lesser spotted eagle. 5r, Steller's sea eagle. 8r, Spanish imperial eagle, horiz. 10r, Harpy eagle. 12r, Crested serpent eagle, horiz.
Bald eagles: No. 2208: a, Wings upward in flight. b, Looking backward on limb. c, Up close, head left. d, Up close, head right. e, On limb. f, In flight.
No. 2209, American bald eagle, horiz. No. 2210, Bald eagle.

1997, Mar. 20 Litho. *Perf. 14*

2201-2207 A339 Set of 7 8.00 8.00
2208 A340 5r Sheet of 6, #a.-f. 6.00 6.00

Souvenir Sheets

2209 A339 25r multicolored 4.75 4.75
2210 A340 25r multicolored 4.75 4.75

Automobiles — A341

No. 2211, each 5r: a, 1911 Blitzer Benz, Germany. b, 1917 Datsun, Japan. c, 1929 Auburn 8-120, US. d, 1996 Mercedes-Benz C280, Germany. e, Suzuki UR-1, Japan. f, Chrysler Atlantic, US.
No. 2212, each 5r: a, 1961 Mercedes-Benz 190SL, Germany. b, 1916 Kwaishinha DAT, Japan. c, 20/25 Rolls-Royce Roadster, England. d, 1997 Mercedes-Benz SLK, Germany. e, 1996 Toyota Camry, Japan. f, 1959 Jaguar MK2, England.
Each 25r: No. 2213, 1939 VW built by Dr. Porsche. No. 2214, Mazda RX-01.

1997, Mar. 27 Sheets of 6, #a-f

2211-2212 A341 Set of 2 11.50 11.50

Souvenir Sheets

2213-2214 A341 Set of 2 9.50 9.50

1998 Winter Olympics, Nagano — A342

Medalists: 2r, Ye Qiaobo, 1992 speed skating. 3r, Leonhard Stock, 1980 downhill. 8r, Bjorn Daehlie, 1992 cross-country skiing. 12r, Wolfgang Hoppe, 1984 bobsledding.
No. 2219: a, Herma Von Szabo-Planck, 1924 figure skating. b, Katarina Witt, 1988 figure skating. c, Natalia Bestemianova, Andrei Bukin, 1988 ice dancing. d, Jayne Torvill, Christopher Dean, 1984 ice dancing.
Each 25r: No. 2220, Sonja Henie, 1924 figure skating. No. 2221, Andree Joly, Pierre Brunet, 1932 figure skating.

1997, Mar. 13 Litho. *Perf. 14*

2215-2218 A342 Set of 4 5.25 5.25
2219 A342 5r Block of 4, #a.-d. 4.25 4.25

Souvenir Sheets

2220-2221 A342 Set of 2 11.00 11.00

No. 2219 was issued in sheets of 8 stamps.

Ships A343

Designs: 1r, SS Patris II, 1926, Greece. 2r, MV Infanta Beatriz, 1928, Spain. 8r, SS Stavangerjord, 1918, Norway. 12r, MV Baloeran, 1929, Holland.
No. 2226, each 3r: a, SS Vasilefs Constantinos, 1914, Greece. b, SS Cunene, 1911, Portugal. c, MV Selandia, 1912, Denmark. d, SS President Harding, 1921, US. e, MV Ulster Monarch, 1929, Great Britain. f, SS Matsonia, 1913, US. g, SS France, 1911, France. h, SS Campania, 1893, Great Britain. i, SS Klipfontein, 1922, Holland.
No. 2227, each 3r: a, MV Eridan, 1929, France. b, SS Mount Clinton, 1921, US. c, SS Infanta Isabel, 1912, Spain. d, SS Suwa Maru, 1914, Japan. e, SS Yorkshire, 1920, Great Britain. f, MV Highland Chieftan, 1929, Great Britain. g, MV Sardinia, 1920, Norway. h, SS San Guglielmo, 1911, Italy. i, SS Avila, 1927, Great Britain.
Each 25r: No. 2228, SS Mauritania, 1907, Great Britain. No. 2229, SS United States, 1952, US. No. 2230, SS Queen Mary, 1930, Great Britain. No. 2231, Royal Yacht Brittania sailing into Hong Kong harbor.

1997, Apr. 1

2222-2225 A343 Set of 4 6.00 6.00

Sheets of 9, #a-i

2226-2227 A343 Set of 2 12.50 12.50

Souvenir Sheets

2228-2231 A343 Set of 4 22.00 22.00

No. 2231 contains one 57x42mm stamp.

UNESCO, 50th Anniv. — A344

1r, Prayer wheels, Lhasa, vert. 2r, Roman ruins, Temple of Diana, Portugal. 3r, Cathedral of Santa Maria Hildesheim, Germany. 7r, Monument of Nubia at Abu Simbel, Egypt, vert. 8r, Entrance to Port of Mandraki, Rhodes, Greece. 10r, Nature Reserve of Scandola, France. 12r, Temple on the Lake, China.
No. 2232, vert, each 5r: a, Virunga Natl. Park, Zaire. b, Valley of Mai Nature Reserve, Seychelles. c, Kandy, Sri Lanka. d, Taj Mahal, India. e, Istanbul, Turkey. f, Sana'a, Yemen. g, Blenheim Palace, Oxfordshire, England. h, Grand Canyon Natl. Park, US.
No. 2233, vert, each 5r: a, Gondar, Ethiopia. b, Bwindi Natl. Park, Uganda. c, Bemaraha Nature Reserve, Madagascar. d, Buddhist ruins of Takht-i-Bahi, Pakistan. e, Anuradhapura, Sri Lanka. f, Cairo, Egypt. g, Ruins at Petra, Jordan. h, Natl. Park of Ujung Kulon, Indonesia.
Sites in China, vert: No. 2234, each 5r: a-f, Mount Taishan. g-h, Terracotta warriors.
Sites in Japan: No. 2235, each 8r: a-e, Horyu-Ji.
No. 2236, each 8r: a, Monastery of Agios Stefanos Meteora, Greece. b, Taj Mahal, India. c, Cistercian Abbey of Fontenay, France. d, Yakushima, Japan. e, Cloisters of the Convent, San Gonzalo, Portugal.
No. 2237, each 8r: a, Olympic Natl. Park, US. b, Nahanni Waterfalls, Canada. c, Los Glaciares Natl. Park, Argentina. d, Bonfin Salvador Church, Brazil. e, Convent of the Companions of Jesus, Morelia, Mexico.
Each 25r: No. 2238, Temple, Chengde, China. No. 2239, Serengeti Natl. Park, Tanzania. No. 2240, Anuradhapura, Sri Lanka. No. 2241, Monument to Fatehpur Sikri, India.

1997, Apr. 7

2231A-2231G A344 Set of 7 5.75 5.75

Sheets of 8, #a-h, + Label

2232-2234 A344 Set of 3 22.00 22.00

Sheets of 5, #a-e, + Label

2235-2237 A344 Set of 3 22.00 22.00

Souvenir Sheets

2238-2241 A344 Set of 4 18.00 18.00

Queen Elizabeth II, Prince Philip, 50th Wedding Anniv. A345

No. 2242: a, Queen. b, Royal Arms. c, Queen, Prince seated on thrones. d, Queen, Prince holding baby. e, Buckingham Palace. f, Prince.
25r, Queen wearing crown.

1997, June 12 Litho. *Perf. 14*

2242 A345 5r Sheet of 6, #a.-f. 7.75 7.75

Souvenir Sheet

2243 A345 25r multicolored 5.50 5.50

Paintings by Hiroshige (1797-1858) A346

No. 2244: a, Dawn at Kanda Myojin Shrine. b, Kiyomizu Hall & Shinobazu Pond at Ueno. c, Ueno Yamashita. d, Moon Pine, Ueno. e, Flower Pavilion, Dango Slope, Sendagi. f, Shitaya Hirokoji.

Each 25r: No. 2245, Seido and Kanda River from Shohei Bridge. No. 2246, Hilltop View, Yushima Tenjin Shrine.

1997, June 12 ***Perf. 13½x14***
2244 A346 8r Sheet of 6, #a.-f. 8.50 8.50

Souvenir Sheets

2245-2246 A346 Set of 2 9.00 9.00

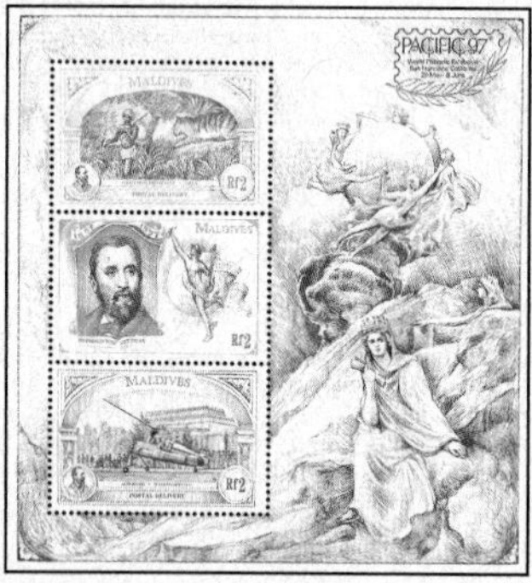

Heinrich von Stephan (1831-97) — A347

a, Early mail messenger, India. b, Von Stephan, UPU emblem. c, Autogiro, Washington DC.

1997, June 12 ***Perf. 14***
2247 A347 2r Sheet of 3, #a.-c. 3.25 3.25

PACIFIC 97.

A number has been reserved for a souvenir sheet with this set.

South Asian Assoc. for Regional Cooperation (SAARC) Summit — A348

1997, May 12 **Litho.** ***Perf. 13***
2249 A348 3r shown .60 .60
2250 A348 5r Flags, "SAARC" 1.10 1.10

A349

Birds: 30 l, Anous stolidus. 1r, Spectacled owl. 2r, Buffy fish owl. 3r, Peregrine falcon. 5r, Golden eagle. 8r, Bateleur. No. 2257, 10r, Crested caracara. No. 2258, 10r, Childonias hybrida. 15r, Sula sula.

No. 2260: a, Rueppell's parrot. b, Blue-headed parrot. c, St. Vincent parrot. d, Gray parrot. e, Masked lovebird. f, Sun parakeet.

Each 25r: No. 2261, Secretary bird. No. 2262, Bald eagle.

1997 ***Perf. 14***
2251-2259 A349 Set of 9 9.75 9.75
2260 A349 7r Sheet of 6, #a.-f. 8.25 8.25

Souvenir Sheets

2261-2262 A349 Set of 2 11.50 11.50

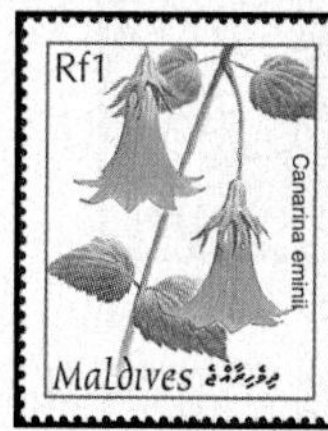

A350

Flowers: 1r, Canarina eminii. 2r, Delphinium macrocentron. 3r, Leucadendron discolor. 5r, Nymphaea caerulea. 7r, Rosa multiflora. 8r, Bulbophyllum barbigerum. 12r, Hibiscus vitifolius.

No. 2270, horiz: a, Acacia seyal. b, Gloriosa superba. c, Gnidia subcordata. d, Platycelphium voense. e, Aspilia mossambicensis. f, Adenium obesum.

Each 25r: No. 2271, Aerangis rhodosticta, horiz. No. 2272, Dichrostachys cinerea, horiz.

1997, June 24 **Litho.** ***Perf. 14½x14***
2263-2269 A350 Set of 6 7.50 7.50

Perf. 14x14½
2270 A350 8r Sheet of 6, #a.-f. 12.00 12.00

Souvenir Sheets

2271-2272 A350 Set of 2 18.00 18.00

No. 2267 is 16x20mm.

A351

Dinosaurs A352

5r, Archaeopteryx. 8r, Mosasaurus. 12r, Deinonychus. 15r, Triceratops.

No. 2277, each 7r: a, Diplodocus (b, c, d, e, f). b. Tyrannosaurus rex (c, e, f). c, Pteranodon. d, Montanaceratops. e, Dromaeosaurus (d). f, Oviraptor (e).

No. 2278, each 7r: a, Euoplocephalus. b, Compsognathus. c, Herrerasaurus. d, Styracosaurus. e, Baryonyx. f, Lesothosaurus.

No. 2279, each 7r: a, Triceratops. b, Pachycephalosaurus. c, Iguanodon. d, Tyrannosaurus. e, Corythosaurus. f, Stegosaurus.

No. 2280, each 7r: a, Troodon (d). b, Brachosaurus (c). c, Saltasaurus (a, b, d, e, f). d, Oviraptor. e, Parasaurolophus (f). f, Psittacosaurus.

No. 2281, Tyrannosaurus rex. No. 2282, Archaeopteryx.

1997, Nov. 20 **Litho.** ***Perf. 14***
2273-2276 A351 Set of 4 7.25 7.25

Sheets of 6, #a-f

2277 A351 7r #a.-f. 7.50 7.50
2278-2280 A352 Set of 3 22.50 22.50

Souvenir Sheets

2281 A351 25r multicolored 11.50 11.50
2282 A352 25r multicolored 11.50 11.50

1998 World Cup Soccer Championships, France — A353

Past winners: 1r, Brazil, 1994. 2r, West Germany, 1954. 3r, Argentina, 1986. 7r, Argentina, 1978. 8r, England, 1966. 10r, Brazil, 1970.

Various scenes from 1966 finals, England v. West Germany, each 3r: Nos. 2289a-2289h.

Italian tournament winners, each 3r: No. 2290: a, Paulo Rossi, Italy, 1982. b, Zoff & Gentile, Italy, 1982. c, Angelo Schiavio, Italy. d, 1934 team. e, 1934 team entering stadium. f, 1982 team. g, San Paolo Stadium, Italy. h, 1938 team.

Brazilian teams, players, each 3r: No. 2291: a, 1958 team pictue. b, Luis Bellini, 1958. c, 1962 team. d, Carlos Alberto, 1970. e, Mauro, 1962. f, 1970 team. g, Dunga, 1994. h, 1994 team.

Each 25r: No. 2292, Klinsmann, Germany. No. 2293, Ronaldo, Brazil, vert. No. 2294, Schmeichel, Denmark, vert.

Perf. 14x13½, 13½x14

1997, Dec. 10 **Litho.**
2283-2288 A353 Set of 6 5.75 5.75

Sheets of 8 + Label

2289-2291 A353 Set of 3 13.50 13.50

Souvenir Sheets

2292-2294 A353 Set of 3 15.50 15.50

Diana, Princess of Wales (1961-97) — A354

Various portraits, color of sheet margin, each 7r: No. 2295, Pale pink. No. 2296, Pale yellow. No. 2297, Pale blue.

Each 25r: No. 2298, Diana on ski lift. No. 2299, In polka dot dress. No. 2300, Wearing lei.

1998, Feb. 9 **Litho.** ***Perf. 13½***

Sheets of 6, #a-f

2295-2297 A354 Set of 3 20.00 20.00

Souvenir Sheets

2298-2300 A354 Set of 3 13.50 13.50

John F. Kennedy (1917-63) A355

Various portraits.

1998 **Litho.** ***Perf. 13½x14***
2301 A355 5r Sheet of 9, #a.-i. 8.50 8.50

Nelson Mandela, Pres. of South Africa — A356

1998 ***Perf. 14***
2302 A356 4r multicolored 1.60 1.60

Classic Airplanes A357

No. 2303: a, Yakovlev Yak 18. b, Beechcraft Bonanza. c, Piper Cub. d, Tupolev Tu-95. e, Lockheed C-130 Hercules. f, Piper PA-28 Cherokee. g, Mikoyan-Gurevich MiG-21. h, Pilatus PC-6 Turbo Porter. i, Antonov An-2.

25r, KC-135E.

1998
2303 A357 5r Sheet of 9, #a.-i. 8.50 8.50

Souvenir Sheet

2304 A357 25r multicolored 4.50 4.50

No. 2304 contains one 85x28mm stamp.

Cats A358

Designs, vert: 5r, White American shorthair. 8r, Sphinx. 10r, Tabby American shorthair. 12r, Scottish fold.

No. 2309, each 7r: a, American curl, Maine coon (d). b, Maine coon (a, d, e). c, Siberian (f). d, Somali. e, European Burmese (d). f, Nebelung.

No. 2310, each 7r: a, Bicolor British shorthair (b). b, Manx. c, Tabby American shorthair (b, e, f). d, Silver tabby Persian (e). e, Oriental white. f, Norwegian forest cat (e).

Each 30r: No. 2311, Snowshoe, vert. No. 2312, Norwegian forest cat, vert.

1998, June 1 **Litho.** ***Perf. 14***
2305-2308 A358 Set of 4 6.00 6.00

Sheets of 6, #a-f

2309-2310 A358 Set of 2 14.00 14.00

Souvenir Sheets

2311-2312 A358 Set of 2 11.00 11.00

Airplanes A359

Designs: 2r, Boeing 737 HS. 7r, Boeing 727. 8r, Boeing 747, 1970. 10r, Boeing 737.

No. 2317, each 5r: a, FSW Fighter. b, V-Jet II. c, Pilatus PC-12. d, Citation Exel. e, Stutz Bearcat (stamp actually shows Pitts S-2S Special). f, Cessna T-37 (B). g, Peregrine business jet. h, Beech Baron 53.

No. 2318, each 5r: a, CL-215. b, P-3 Orion. c, Yak 54. d, Cessna float plane. e, CL-215 Amphibian. f, CL-215 SAR Amphibian. g, Twin Otter. h, Rockwell Quail.

Each 25r: No. 2319, Falcon Jet. No. 2320, Beechcraft Model 18.

1998, Aug. 10 **Litho.** ***Perf. 14***
2313-2316 A359 Set of 4 4.75 4.75

Sheets of 8, #a-h

2317-2318 A359 Set of 2 14.50 14.50

Souvenir Sheets

2319-2320 A359 Set of 2 10.00 10.00

The Titanic A360

No. 2321: a, Capt. Edward J. Smith's cap. b, Deck chair. c, Fifth Officer Harold Lowe's coat button. d, Lifeboat. e, Steering wheel. f, Lifejacket.

25r, Newpaper picture of the Titanic at sea.

1998, Sept. 27 **Litho.** ***Perf. 14***
2321 A360 7r Sheet of 6, #a.-f. 8.75 8.75

Souvenir Sheet

2322 A360 25r multicolored 5.25 5.25

Bird Type of 1992

1998, Oct. 26 **Litho.** ***Perf. 14½***
2323 A247 100r Anas clypeata 14.00 14.00

IFAD, 20th Anniv. — A361

Designs: 1r, Papaya tree. 5r, Fruits. 7r, Fishermen on boat. 8r, Coconut tree. 10r, Vegetables.

1998, Nov. 30 Litho. *Perf. 14*
2324-2328 A361 Set of 5 5.50 5.50

Ferrari Automobiles — A361a

No. 2328A: c, 250 TR. d, 1957 250 GT TDF. e, 250 GT.
25r, 365 GTC 2+2.

1998, Dec. 15 Litho. *Perf. 14*
2328A A361a 10r Sheet of 3, #c-e 5.25 5.25

Souvenir Sheet

Perf. 13¾x14¼

2328B A361a 25r multi 4.25 4.25

No. 2328A contains three 39x25mm stamps.

1998 World Scout Jamboree, Chile — A362

a, Robert Baden-Powell inspecting Scouts, Amesbury, c. 1909. b, Lord, Lady Baden-Powell, children, South Africa Tour, 1927. c, Robert Baden-Powell pins merit badges on Chicago Scouts, 1926.

1998, Dec. 15
2329 A362 12r Sheet of 3, #a.-c. 6.75 6.75

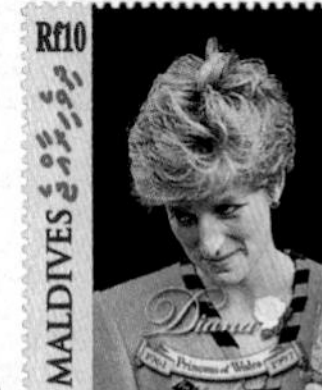
A363

Diana, Princess of Wales (1961-97) — A364

No. 2330: a, Inscription panel at left. b, Panel at right.

1998, Dec. 15 *Perf. 14½x14*
2330 A363 10r Horiz. pair, #a-b 3.75 3.75

Size: 95x56mm

Litho. & Embossed

Die Cut Perf. 7½

2331 A364 50r shown
2332 A364 50r Rose, Diana

No. 2330 was issued in sheets of 3 pairs.

Fish A365

Designs: No. 2333, 50 l, Threadfin butterfly fish. No. 2334, 50 l, Queen angelfish. 1r, Oriental sweetlips. No. 2336, 7r, Bandit angelfish. No. 2337, 7r, Achilles tang. 8r, Red-headed butterfly fish. 50r, Blue striped butterfly fish.

No. 2340: a, Mandarinfish. b, Copper-banded butterfly fish. c, Harlequin tuskfish. d, Yellow-tailed demoiselle. e, Wimplefish. f, Red emperor snapper. g, Clown triggerfish. h, Common clown. i, Regal tang.

No. 2341: a, Emperor angelfish. b, Common squirrelfish. c, Lemonpeel angelfish. d, Powderblue surgeon. e, Moorish idol. f, Bicolor cherub. g, Scribbled angelfish. h, Two-banded anemonefish. i, Yellow tang.

Each 25r: No. 2342, Porkfish. No. 2343, Long-nosed butterfly fish.

1998, Dec. 10 Litho. *Perf. 14*
2333-2339 A365 Set of 7 13.50 13.50
2340 A365 3r Sheet of 9, #a.-i. 4.75 4.75
2341 A365 5r Sheet of 9, #a.-i. 8.25 8.25

Souvenir Sheets

2342-2343 A365 Set of 2 9.00 9.00

Intl. Year of the Ocean A366

Marine life: No. 2344, Skipjack tuna.

No. 2345: a, 25 l, Triton. b, 50 l, Napoleon wrasse. c, 1r, Whale shark. d, 3r, Gray reef shark. e, 7r, Blue whale.

No. 2346: a, Harp seal. b, Killer whale. c, Sea otter. d, Beluga. e, Narwhal. f, Walrus. g, Sea lion. h, Humpback salmon. i, Emperor penguin.

No. 2347: a, Ocean sunfish. b, Opalescent squid. c, Electric eel. d, Corded neptune.

Each 25r: No. 2348, Horseshoe crab. No. 2349, Blue whale. No. 2350, Triton, diff.

1999, Apr. 1 Litho. *Perf. 14*
2344 A366 7r multicolored 1.25 1.25

Sheets of 6, 9, 4

2345 A366 #a.-e. + 1 #2344 3.50 3.50
2346 A366 5r #a.-i. 8.00 8.00
2347 A366 8r #a.-d. 5.75 5.75

Souvenir Sheets

2348-2350 A366 Set of 3 13.50 13.50

No. 2344 was issued in sheets of 6.
No. 2350 incorrectly inscribed Coral Reef.

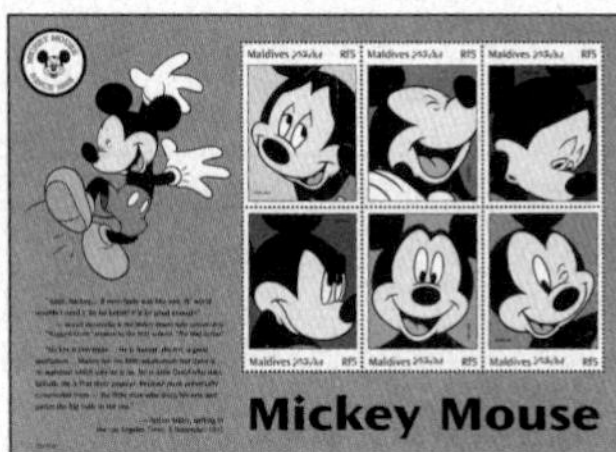
Mickey Mouse, 70th Anniv. (in 1998) — A367

No. 2351, each 5r: Various pictures of Mickey Mouse.

No. 2352, each 5r: Various pictures of Minnie Mouse.

No. 2353, each 7r: Various pictures of Donald Duck.

No. 2354, each 7r: Various pictures of Daisy Duck.

No. 2355, each 7r: Various pictures of Goofy.

No. 2356, each 7r: Various pictures of Pluto.

Each 25r: No. 2357, Minnie sipping drink. No. 2358, Minnie looking backward. No. 2359, Mickey grabbing Donald's hand, horiz. No. 2360, Minnie wearing pearls. No. 2361, Mickey with hand on head. No. 2362, Mickey after throwing ball.

Perf. 13½x14, 14x13½ (#2359)

1999, May 27 Litho.

Sheets of 6, #a-f

2351-2352 A367 Set of 2 12.00 12.00
2353-2356 A367 Set of 4 30.00 30.00

Souvenir Sheets

2357-2362 A367 Set of 6 25.00 25.00

Stamp in No. 2358 is printed se-tenant with label.

Sheets similar to Nos. 2351-2352 with "5Rs" denomination and Nos. 2353-2356 with "25Rs" exist. Value, set of 6 sheets, $195.

Butterflies A368

50 l, Great orange tip. 1r, Large green aporandria. 2r, Common mormon. 3r, African migrant. 5r, Common pierrot. 10r, Giant redeye.

No. 2369, vert, each 7r: a, Common red flash. b, Burmese lascar. c, Common peirrot. d, Baron. e, Leaf blue. f, Great orange tip.

No. 2370, vert, each 7r: a, Crimson tip. b, Tawny rajah. c, Leafwing butterfly. d, Great egg-fly. e, Blue admiral. f, African migrant.

Each 25r: No. 2371, Crimson tip. No. 2372, Large oak blue.

1999, June 8 Litho. *Perf. 14*
2363-2368 A368 Set of 6 3.75 3.75

Sheets of 6, #a-f

2369-2370 A368 Set of 2 15.00 15.00

Souvenir Sheets

2371-2372 A368 Set of 2 10.00 10.00

Dinosaurs A369

Designs: 1r, Scelidosaurus. 3r, Yansudaurus. 5r, Ornitholestes. 8r, Astrodon.

No. 2377, vert, each 7r: a, Anchisaurus. b, Pterenodon. c, Barosaurus. d, Iguanodon. e, Archaeopteryx. f, Ceratosaurus.

No. 2378, each 7r: a, Stegosaurus. b, Corythosaurus. c, Celiosaurus. d, Avimimus. e, Styracosaurus. f, Massospondylus.

No. 2379, vert, each 7r: a, Dimorphodon. b, Rhamphorhynchus. c, Allosaurus. d, Leaellynasaura. e, Troodon. f, Syntarsus.

Each 25r: No. 2380, Brachiosaurus. No. 2381, Megalosaurus.

1999, June 22
2373-2376 A369 Set of 4 3.25 3.25

Sheets of 6, #a-f

2377-2379 A369 Set of 3 24.50 24.50

Souvenir Sheets

2380-2381 A369 Set of 2 10.00 10.00

Marine Environment Wildlife — A370

30 l, Broderip's cowrie. 1r, Fairy tern. 3r, Darker Maldivian green heron. 7r, Blackflag sandperch. 8r, Coral hind. 10r, Olive ridley turtle.

No. 2388, each 5r: a, Brown booby. b, Red-tailed tropicbird. c, Sooty tern. d, Striped dolphin. e, Long-snouted spinner dolphin. f, Crab plover. g, Hawksbill turtle. h, Indo-Pacific sergeant. i, Yellowfin tuna.

No. 2389, each 5r: a, Manta ray. b, Green turtle. c, Pan-tropical spotted dolphin. d, Moorish idols. e, Threadfin anthias. f, Goldbar wrasse. g, Palette surgeonfish. h, Three spot angelfish. i, Oriental sweetlips.

Each 25r: No. 2390, Cinnamon bittern. No. 2391, Blue-faced angelfish.

1999, Oct. 26 Litho. *Perf. 14*
2382-2387 A370 Set of 6 6.00 6.00

Sheets of 9, #a-i

2388-2389 A370 Set of 2 16.50 16.50

Souvenir Sheets

2390-2391 A370 Set of 2 9.50 9.50

Trains A371

Designs: 50 l, 2-2-2 locomotive, Egypt. 1r, Le Shuttle, France. 2r, 4-4-0 Gowan & Marx, US. 3r, TGV, France. 5r, Ae 6/6 electric locomotive, Switzerland. 8r, Stephenson's Long-boilered 2-4-0 locomotive, Great Britain. 10r, The Philadelphia, Austria. 15r. E class, Great Britain.

No. 2400, each 7r: a, Stephenson's Long-boilered locomotive, diff. b, 4-2-2 Cornwall, Great Britain. c, First locomotive, Germany. d, Great Western, Great Britain. e, Standard Stephenson 2-4-0, France. f, 2-2-2 Meteor, Great Britain.

No. 2401, each 7r: a, Type 4 class 4t, Great Britain. b, 1500 horsepower Diesel-electric locomotive, Malaysia. c, Co-Co 7000 Class, France. d, Diesel-hydraulic passenger locomotive, Thailand. e, Diesel-hydraulic locomotive, Burma. f, Hikari, Japan.

Each 25r: No. 2402, 2-2-2, Passenger locomotive, France. No. 2403, King Arthur class, Great Britain.

1999, Oct. 26
2392-2399 A371 Set of 8 7.50 7.50

Sheets of 6, #a-f

2400-2401 A371 Set of 2 14.50 14.50

Souvenir Sheets

2402-2403 A371 Set of 2 10.00 10.00

A372

Queen Mother (b. 1900) — A373

No. 2404: a, With King George VI, 1936. b, In 1941. c, In 1960. d, In 1981.
25r, At Order of the Garter Service.

Gold Frames

1999, Dec. 1 Litho. *Perf. 14*
2404 A372 7r Sheet of 4, #a.-d., + label 6.00 6.00

Souvenir Sheet

Perf. 13¾

2405 A372 25r multi 6.00 6.00

Litho. & Embossed

Die Cut Perf. 8¾

Without Gum

2406 A373 50r gold & multi

No. 2405 contains one 38x51mm stamp.
See Nos. 2605-2606.

Hokusai Paintings — A374

No. 2407, each 7r: a, A Coastal view. b, Bath House by a Lake. c, Drawings (horse). d, Drawings (two birds). e, Evening Cool at Ryogoku. f, Girls Boating.

No. 2408, each 7r: a, Haunted House. b, Juniso Shrine at Yotsuya. c, Drawings (one bird). d, Drawings (two people). e, Lover in the Snow. f, Mountain Tea House.
Each 25r: No. 2409, Girls Gathering Spring Herbs, vert. No. 2410, Scene in the Yoshiwara, vert.

1999, Dec. 23 ***Perf. 13¾***
Sheets of 6, #a.-f.

2407-2408 A374 Set of 2 17.00 17.00

Souvenir Sheets

2409-2410 A374 Set of 2 10.00 10.00

IBRA '99, Nuremberg — A375

Trains (as described): 12r, Drache, 1848. 15r, Der Adler, 1833.

1999, Dec. 23 ***Perf. 14x14½***

2411-2412 A375 Set of 2 6.00 6.00

The illustrations of the two stamps were switched.

Souvenir Sheets

PhilexFrance '99 — A376

Trains: No. 2413, Standard Stephenson 2-4-0, 1837. No. 2414, Long-boilered Stephenson, 1841.

1999, Dec. 23 ***Perf. 13¾***

2413-2414 A376 25r each 8.00 8.00

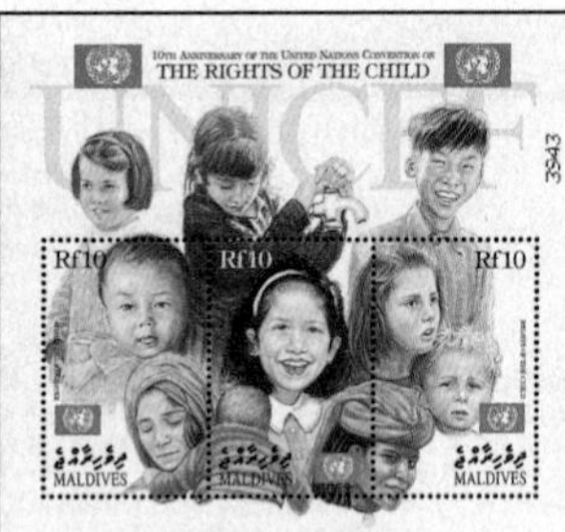

Rights of the Child — A377

No. 2415: a, Black denomination in UL. b, White denomination in UL. c, Black denomination in UR.
25r, Peter Ustinov, UNICEF goodwill ambassador.

1999, Dec. 23 ***Perf. 14***

2415 A377 10r Sheet of 3, #a.-c. 6.25 6.25

Souvenir Sheet

2416 A377 25r multi 4.50 4.50

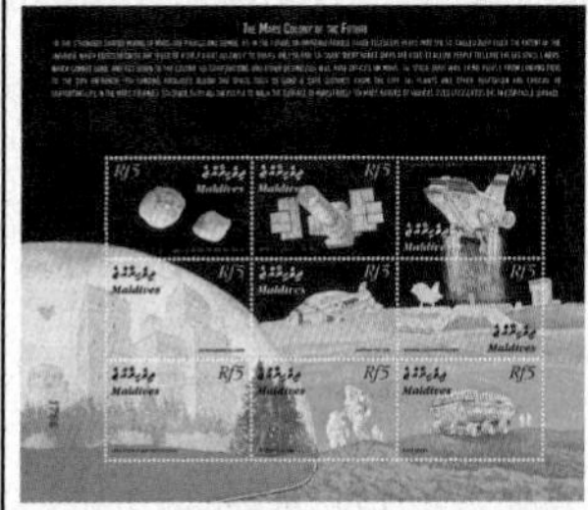

Mars Colony of the Future — A378

No. 2417, each 5r: a, Phobos and Deimos. b, Improved Hubble Telescope. c, Passenger shuttle. d, Skyscrapers. e, Taxi cab. f, Landing facilities. g, Vegetation. h, Walking on Mars. i, Mars rover.
No. 2418, each 5r: a, Russian Phobos 25. b, Earth and moon. c, Space shuttle. d, Lighthouse. e, Excursion space liner. f, Inner-city shuttle. g, Viking lander. h, Air and water purification plants. i, Life in a Mars city.
Each 25r: No. 2419, Mars, vert. No. 2420, Astronaut, vert.

2000, Jan. 24 **Litho.** ***Perf. 14***
Sheets of 9, #a.-i.

2417-2418 A378 Set of 2 18.00 18.00

Souvenir Sheets

2419-2420 A378 Set of 2 10.00 10.00

Millennium — A379

Highlights of 1750-1800: a, American Declaration of Independence, 1776. b, Hot air balloon flight by Montgolfier brothers, 1783. c, French Revolution begins with storming of the Bastille, 1789. d, James Watt patents steam engine, 1769. e, Wolfgang Amadeus Mozart born, 1756. f, Ts'ao Hsueh-ch'in publishes "Dream of the Red Chamber," 1791. g, Napoleon conquers Egypt, 1798. h, Catherine the Great becomes Empress of Russia, 1762. i, Joseph Priestley discovers oxygen, 1774. j, Benjamin Franklin publishes studies on electricity, 1751. k, Edward Jenner develops vaccination against smallpox, 1796. l, French and Indian War, 1754. m, Jean Honoré Fragonard paints "The Swing," c. 1766. n, Ludwig van Beethoven born, 1770. o, Louis marries Marie Antoinette, 1770. p, Capt. James Cook explores in South Pacific, discovers east coast of Australia, 1770 (60x40mm). q, Luigi Galvani experiments with electricity on nerves and muscles, c. 1780.

2000, Feb. 1 ***Perf. 12¾x12½***

2421 A379 3r Sheet of 17, #a.-q., + label 10.00 10.00

Destination 2000 Tourism Campaign — A380

Designs: a, Yellow flowers. b, School of fish. c, Airplane, boat prow. d, White flowers. e, Lionfish. f, Windsurfers.

2000, Feb. 1 ***Perf. 13¾***

2422 A380 7r Sheet of 6, #a.-f. 9.00 9.00

Solar Eclipse, Aug. 11, 1999 — A381

No. 2423 (Sky background), each 7r: a, First contact. b, Second contact. c, Totality. d, Third contact. e, Fourth contact. f, Observatory.
No. 2424 (Outer space background), each 7r: a, First contact. b, Second contact. c, Totality. d, Third contact. e, Fourth contact. f, Solar and heliospheric observatory.

2000, Mar. 8 **Litho.** ***Perf. 14***
Sheets of 6, #a.-f.

2423-2424 A381 Set of 2 14.50 14.50

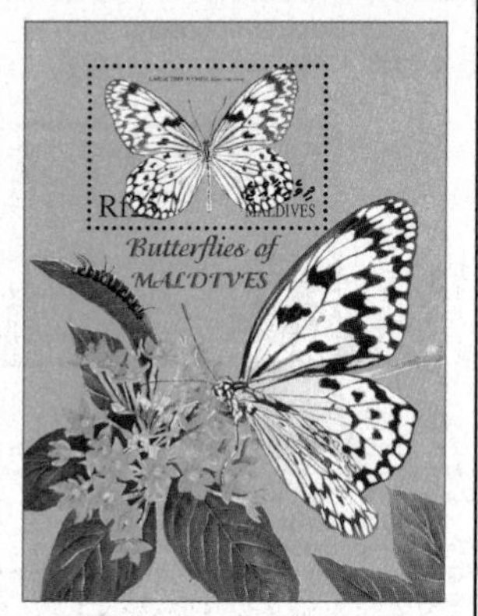

Butterflies — A382

No. 2425, each 5r: a, Red lacewing. b, Large oak blue. c, Yellow coster. d, Great orange tip. e, Common pierrot. f, Cruiser. g, Hedge blue. h, Great egg-fly. i, Common tiger.
No. 2426, each 5r: a, Common wall. b, Koh-i-noor. c, Indian red admiral. d, Tawny rajah. e, Blue triangle. f, Orange albatross. g, Common rose swallowtail. h, Jeweled nawab. i, Striped blue crow.
Each 25r: No. 2427, Large tree nymph. No. 2428, Blue pansy.

2000, Apr. 10 **Litho.** ***Perf. 13¼x13½***
Sheets of 9, #a-i

2425-2426 A382 Set of 2 18.00 18.00

Souvenir Sheets

2427-2428 A382 Set of 2 10.00 10.00

Paintings of Anthony Van Dyck — A383

No. 2429, each 5r: a, Martin Rijckaert. b, Frans Snyders. c, Quentin Simons. d, Lucas van Uffel, 1622. e, Nicolaes Rockox. f, Nicholas Lanier.
No. 2430, each 5r: a, Inigo Jones. b, Lucas van Uffel, (actually detail from John, Count of Nassau-Sieger and his Family) c. 1622-25. c, Margaretha de Vos, Wife of Frans Snyders. d, Peter Breughel the Younger. e, Cornelis van der Geest. f, Francois Langlois as a Savoyard.
No. 2431, each 5r: a, Portrait of a Family. b, Earl and Countess of Denby and Their Daughter. c, Family Portrait. d, A Genoese Nobleman with his Children. e, Thomas Howard, Earl of Arundel, and His Grandson. f, The Woman in Gold (Battonia Balbi with her Children).
Each 25r: No. 2432, John, Count of Nassau-Siegen, and His Family. No. 2433, The Lomellini Family. No. 2434, Lucas and Cornelis de Wael. No. 2435, The Painter Jan de Wael and His Wife Gertrude de Jode. No. 2436, Sir Kenelm and Lady Digby with Their Two Eldest Sons. No. 2437, Sir Philip Herbert, 4th Earl of Pembroke, and His Family.

2000, May 1 ***Perf. 13¾***
Sheets of 6, #a-f

2429-2431 A383 Set of 3 42.50 42.50

Souvenir Sheets

2432-2437 A383 Set of 6 26.00 26.00

Trains A384

Designs: 5r, Shinkansen, Japan. 8r, Super Azusa, Japan. No. 2440, 10r, Spacia, Japan. 15r, Nozomi, Japan.
No. 2442, each 10r: a, 1909 Shanghai-Nanking Railway 4-6-2. b, 1910 Shanghai-Nanking Railway 4-2-2. c, 1914 Manchurian Railway 4-6-2. d, 1934 Chinese National Railway Hankow Line 4-8-4. e, 1949 Chinese National Railway 2-8-2. f, 1949 Chinese National Railway 2-10-0.
No. 2443, each 10r: a, 1856 East Indian Railway "Fawn" 2-2-2. b, 1893 East Indian Railway 4-4-0. c, 1909 Bengal-Nagpur Railway 4-4-2. d, 11924 Great Peninsular Railway 4-6-0. e, 1932 North Western Railway 4-6-2. f, 1949 Indian National Railway 4-6-2.
Each 25r: No. 2444, Chinese National Railways Class JS 2-8-2. No. 2445, Indian National Railway Class WP 4-6-2.

2000, June 8 **Litho.** ***Perf. 14***

2438-2441 A384 Set of 4 6.50 6.50

Sheets of 6, #a-f

2442-2443 A384 Set of 2 20.00 20.00

Souvenir Sheets

2444-2445 A384 Set of 2 10.00 10.00

The Stamp Show 2000, London (Nos. 2442-2445). Nos. 2444-2445 each contain one 57x42mm stamp.

Millennium A385

Designs: 10 l, Republic Monument. 30 l, Bodu Thakurufaanu Memorial Center. 1r, Health services. No. 2449, 7r, Hukuru Miskiiy. No. 2450, 7r, Male Intl. Airport. 10r, Educational development.
No. 2452, 25r, People's Majlis. No. 2453, 25r, Economic development. No. 2454, 25r, Islamic Center.

2000, Aug. 31 **Litho.** ***Perf. 14***

2446-2451 A385 Set of 6 6.25 6.25

Souvenir Sheets
Perf. 13¼

2452-2454 A385 Set of 3 13.50 13.50

Souvenir Sheets

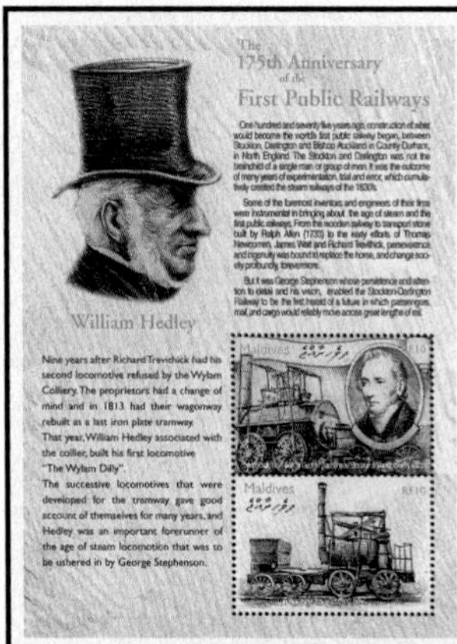

First Public Railways, 175th Anniv. — A386

No. 2455: a, Locomotion No. 1, George Stephenson. b, William Hedley's Puffing Billy.

2000, Sept. 13 *Perf. 14*

2455 A386 10r Sheet of 2, #a-b 4.75 4.75

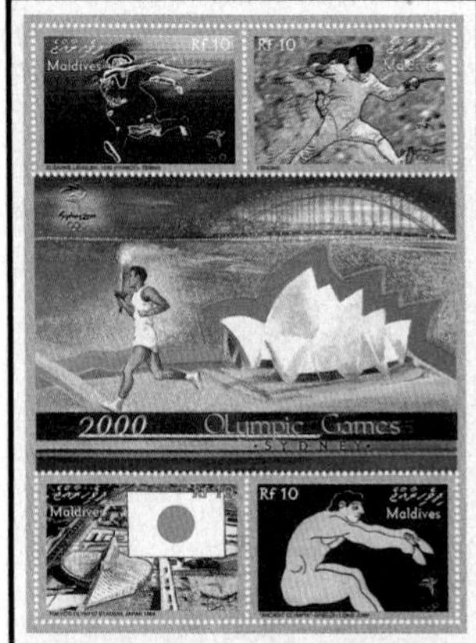

2000 Summer Olympics, Sydney — A387

No. 2456: a, Suzanne Lenglen. b, Fencing. c, Olympic Stadium, Tokyo, and Japanese flag. d, Ancient Greek long jumper.

2000, Sept. 13

2456 A387 10r Sheet of 4, #a-d 7.75 7.75

First Zeppelin Flight, Cent. — A388

No. 2457, horiz.: a, Graf Zeppelin. b, Graf Zeppelin II. c, LZ-9.

2000, Sept. 13 *Perf. 14*

2457 A388 13r Sheet of 3, #a-c 7.00 7.00

Souvenir Sheet

Perf. 13¾

2458 A388 25r LZ-88 6.25 6.25

No. 2457 contains three 39x25mm stamps.

Apollo-Soyuz Mission, 25th Anniv. — A389

No. 2459, vert.: a, Apollo 18 and Soyuz 19. b, Soyuz 19. c, Apollo 18.

2000, Sept. 13 *Perf. 14*

2459 A389 13r Sheet of 3, #a-c 6.75 6.75

Souvenir Sheet

2460 A389 25r Soyuz 19 5.50 5.50

Orchids — A390

Designs: 50 l, Dendrobium crepidatum. 1r, Eulophia guineensis. 2.50r, Cymbidium finlaysonianum. 3.50r, Paphiopedilum druryi.

No. 2465, 10r: a, Aerides odorata. b, Dendrobium chrysotoxum. c, Dendrobium anosmum. d, Calypso bulbosa. e, Paphiopedilum fairrieanum. f, Cynorkis fastigiata.

No. 2466, 10r: a, Angraecum germinyanum. b, Phalaenopsis amabilis. c, Thrixspermum cantipeda. d, Phaius tankervilleae. e, Rhynchostylis gigantea. f, Papilionanthe teres.

No. 2467, 25r, Cymbidium dayanum. No. 2468, 25r, Spathoglottis plicata.

2000, Sept. 13

2461-2464 A390 Set of 4 1.25 1.25

Sheets of 6, #a-f

2465-2466 A390 Set of 2 22.00 22.00

Souvenir Sheets

2467-2468 A390 Set of 2 10.00 10.00

Birds A391

Designs: 15 l, White tern. 25 l, Brown booby. 30 l, White-collared kingfisher, vert. 1r, Black-winged stilt, vert.

No. 2473, 10r: a, Great frigatebird. b, Common noddy. c, Common tern. d, Sula sula. e, Sooty tern. f, Phaeton leturus.

No. 2474, 10r, vert.: a, White-collared kingfisher. b, Island thrush. c, Red-tailed tropicbird. d, Peregrine falcon. e, Night heron. f, Great egret.

No. 2475, 13r: a, Ringed plover. b, Turnstone. c, Thicknee. d, Black-bellied plover. e, Crab plover. f, Curlew.

No. 2476, 25r, Great cormorant, vert. No. 2477, 25r, Cattle egret, vert.

2000, Sept. 13 *Perf. 13¾*

2469-2472 A391 Set of 4 2.50 2.50

Sheets of 6, #a-f

2473-2475 A391 Set of 3 32.50 32.50

Souvenir Sheets

2476-2477 A391 Set of 2 10.00 10.00

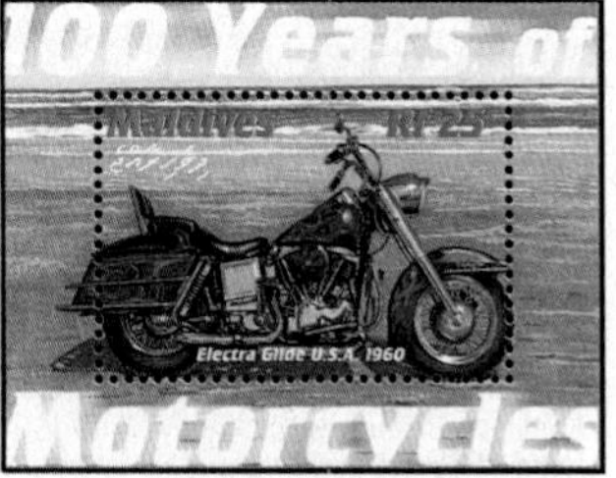

Motorcycles — A392

No. 2478, 7r: a, 1907 Matchless. b, 1966 Manch 4 1200 TTS. c, 1957 Lambretta LD-150. d, 1990 Yamaha XJP 1200. e, 1885 Daimler. f, 1950-60 John Player Norton.

No. 2479, 7r: a, 1969 Honda CB 750. b, 1913 Harley-Davidson. c, 1925 Bohmerland. d, 1910 American Indian. e, 1993 Triumph Trophy 1200. f, 1928, Moto Guzzi 500S.

No. 2480, 25r, 1960 Electra Glide. No. 2481, 25r, 1950 Harley-Davidson.

2000, Oct. 30 *Perf. 13¼x13½*

Sheets of 6, #a-f

2478-2479 A392 Set of 2 17.00 17.00

Souvenir Sheets

2480-2481 A392 Set of 2 10.00 10.00

A393

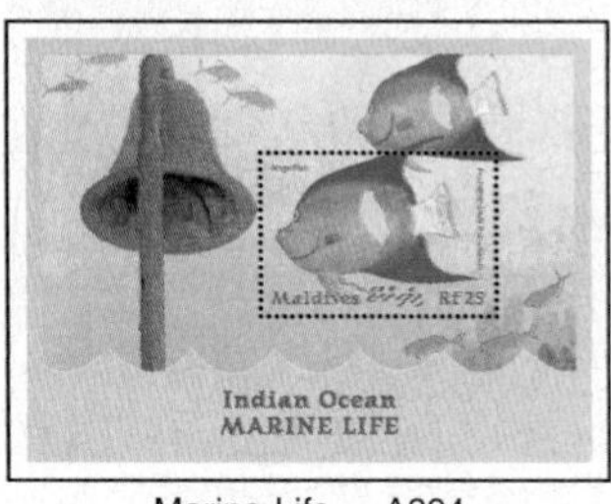

Marine Life — A394

No. 2482: a, Longnosed filefish. b, Hawaiian squirrelfish. c, Freckled hawkfish. d, McCosker's flasher wrasse. e, Pygoplites diacanthus. f, Paraeentzopyge venusta.

No. 2483, 5r: a, Chaetodon lunula. b, Stethojulis albovittata. c, Green turtle. d, Jobfish. e, Damsel fish. f, Chaetodon meyeri. g, Cirrhilabrus exquistus. h, Anemonefish.

No. 2484, 5r: a, Coris aygula. b, Snapper. c, Sea bass. d, Chaetodon bennetti. e, Pelagic snapper. f, Cardinalfish. g, Thalassoma hardwicke. h, Surgeonfish.

No. 2485, 5r: a, Grouper. b, Pygoplites diacanthus. c, Forcipiger flavissimus. d, Goatfish. e, Trumpet fish. f, Anthias. g, Centropyge bispinosus. h, Sweetlips.

No. 2486, 25r, H. aberrans. No. 2487, 25r, Angelfish. No. 2488, 25r, Moray eel. No. 2489, 25r, Spiny butterflyfish.

2000, Nov. 15 Litho. *Perf. 14*

2482 A393 5r Sheet of 6, #a-f 5.50 5.50

Sheets of 8, #a-h

2483-2485 A394 Set of 3 21.00 21.00

Souvenir Sheets

2486 A393 25r multi 4.25 4.25

2487-2489 A394 Set of 3 13.00 13.00

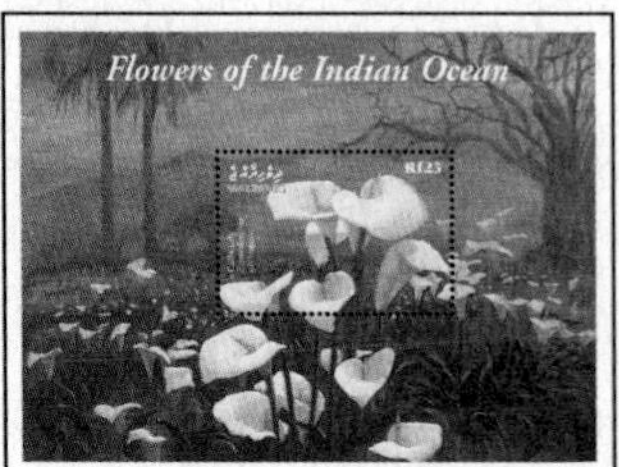

Flowers — A395

No. 2490, 5r: a, Corn lily. b, Clivia. c, Red hot poker. d, Crown of thorns. e, Cape daisy. f, Geranium.

No. 2491, 5r, horiz.: a, Fringed hibiscus. b, Erica vestita. c, Bird-of-paradise. d, Peacock orchid. e, Mesembryanthemums. f, African violets.

No. 2492, 25r, Gladiolus. No. 2493, 25r, Calla lily, horiz.

2000, Nov. 15

Sheets of 6, #a-f

2490-2491 A395 Set of 2 14.00 14.00

Souvenir Sheets

2492-2493 A395 Set of 2 10.00 10.00

Airplanes, Automobiles and Trains — A396

Designs: 2.50r, Papyrus, vert. 3r, Hiawatha. 12r, Supermarine SGB. 13r, MLX01.

No. 2498, 5r: a, Thrust SSC. b, Curtiss R3C-2. c, Rocket. d, BB-9004. e, Mallard. f, TGV.

No. 2499, 5r: a, Lockheed XP-80. b, Mikoyan MiG-23. c, Tempest. d, Bluebird. e, Blue Flame. f, Thrust 2.

No. 2500, 25r, Bell X-1. No. 2501, 25r, Lockheed SR-71 Blackbird, vert.

2000, Nov. 29

2494-2497 A396 Set of 4 5.25 5.25

Sheets of 6, #a-f

2498-2499 A396 Set of 2 10.00 10.00

Souvenir Sheets

2500-2501 A396 Set of 2 8.50 8.50

Paintings from the Prado — A397

No. 2502, 7r: a, The Nobleman with the Golden Chain, by Tintoretto. b, Triumphal Arch, by Domenichino. c, Don Garcia de Medici, by Bronzino. d, Micer Marsilio from Micer Marsilio and His Wife, by Lorenzo Lotto. e, La Infanta Maria Antoinetta Fernanda, by Jacopo Amigoni. f, Wife from Micer Marsilio and his Wife.

No. 2503, 7r: a, Two women with headdresses. b, Woman in red. c, Men. d, The Duke of Lerma on Horseback, by Rubens. e, The Death of Seneca, by the Workshop of Rubens. f, Marie de Medici by Rubens. a-c from Achilles Amongst the Daughters of Lycomedes, by Peter Paul Rubens and Anthony Van Dyck.

No. 2504, 7r: a, Self-portrait, by Albrecht Dürer. b, A Woman and Her Daughter, by Adriaen van Cronenburgh. c, Portrait of a man, by Dürer. d, Woman and children. e, Artemisia, by Rembrandt. f, The Artist. d, f from The Artist and His Family, by Jacob Jordaens.

No. 2505, 7r: a, The Painter Andrea Sacchi, by Carlo Maratta. b, Two men. c, Charles Cecil Roberts, by Pompeo Girolamo Batoni. d, Francesco Albani, by Sacchi. e, Three men. f, William Hamilton, by Batoni. b, e from The Turkish Ambassador to the Court of Naples, by Giuseppe Bonito

No. 2506, 7r: a, The Marquesa of Villafranca, by Francisco de Goya. b, Maria Ruthven, by Van Dyck. c, Cardinal-Infante Ferdinand, by Van Dyck. d, Frederik Hendrik, Prince of Orange, by Van Dyck. e, Van Dyck from Self-portrait with Endymion Porter. f, Porter from Self-portrait with Endymion Porter.

No. 2507, 7r: a, Philip V, by Hyacinthe Rigaud. b, Louis XIV, by Rigaud. c, Don Luis, Prince of Asturias, by Michel-Ange Houasse.

d, Duke Carlo Emanuele II of Savoy with His Wife and Son, by Charles Dauphin. e, Kitchen Maid by Charles-François Hutin. f, Hurdy-gurdy Player, by Georges de La Tour.

No. 2508, 25r, Elizabeth of Valois, by Sofonisba Anguisciola. No. 2509, 25r, Camilla Gonzaga, Countess of San Segundo with Her Three Children, by Parmigianino. No. 2510, 25r, The Turkish Ambassador to the Court of Naples. No. 2511, 25r, Duke Carlo Emanuele of Savoy with His Wife and Son. No. 2512, 25r, The Artist and His Family, horiz. No. 2513, 25r, The Devotion of Rudolf I, by Rubens and Jan Wildens, horiz.

Perf. 12x12¼, 12¼x12

2000, Nov. 29

Sheets of 6, #a-f

2502-2507 A397 Set of 6 42.50 42.50

Souvenir Sheets

2508-2513 A397 Set of 6 26.00 26.00

España 2000 Intl. Philatelic Exhibition.

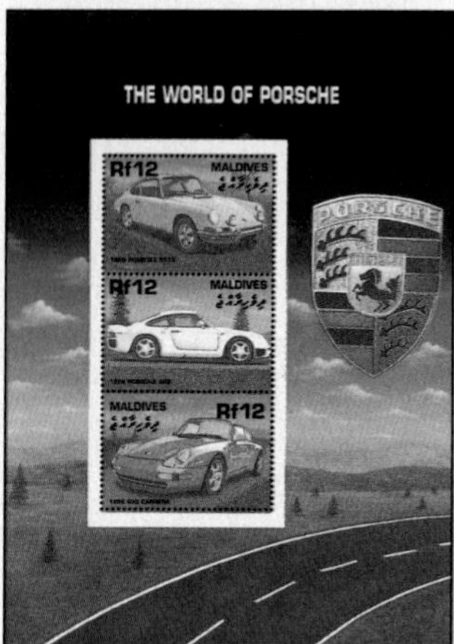

Porsche Automobiles — A398

No. 2514, 12r: a, 1966 911S. b, 1988 959. c, 1995 993 Carrera.

No. 2515, 12r: a, 1963 356 SC. b, 1975 911 Turbo. c, Unidentified.

2000, Nov. 30 Litho. ***Perf. 14***

Sheets of 3, #a-c

2514-2515 A398 Set of 2 12.50 12.50

Souvenir Sheet

2516 A398 25r 2000 Boxter 4.25 4.25

No. 2516 contains one 56x42mm stamp.

Mushrooms A399

Designs: 30 l, Cortinarius collinitus. 50 l, Russula ochroleuca. 2r, Lepiota acutesquamosa. 3r, Hebeloma radicosum. 13r, Amanita echinocephala. 15r, Collybia iocephala.

No. 2523, 7r: a, Tricholoma aurantium. b, Pholiota spectabilis. c, Russula caerulea. d, Amanita phalloides. e, Mycena strobilinoides. f, Boletus satanas.

No. 2524, 7r: a, Amanita muscaria. b, Mycena lilacifolia. c, Coprinus comatus. d, Morchella crassipes. e, Russula nigricans. f, Lepiota procera.

No. 2525, 25r, Tricholoma aurantium, diff. No. 2526, 25r, Lepiota procera, diff.

2001, Jan. 2

2517-2522 A399 Set of 6 5.75 5.75

Sheets of 6, #a-f

2523-2524 A399 Set of 2 14.50 14.50

Souvenir Sheets

2525-2526 A399 Set of 2 8.50 8.50

Battle of Britain, 60th Anniv. — A400

No. 2527, 5r: a, German commanders look across the English Channel. b, The armorers make ready. c, The German attack begins. d, Germany bombs the British coast. e, Germany bombs British cities. f, Luftwaffe sets St. Paul's Cathedral ablaze. g, Aerial dogfight. h, A British Spitfire is shot down.

No. 2528, 5r: a, Leaders of Great Britain. b, British pilots prepare to confront the Luftwaffe. c, RAF planes take off. d, British aircraft meet the enemy. e, Luftwaffe meets tough resistance. f, Dogfight above English Channel. g, German planes fall short of their objective. h Many German planes are shot down.

No. 2529, 25r, Hawker Hurricane. No. 2530, 25r, Messerschmitt ME 109.

2001, Jan. 2 ***Perf. 14***

Sheets of 8, #a-h

2527-2528 A400 Set of 2 14.50 14.50

Souvenir Sheets

2529-2530 A400 Set of 2 8.50 8.50

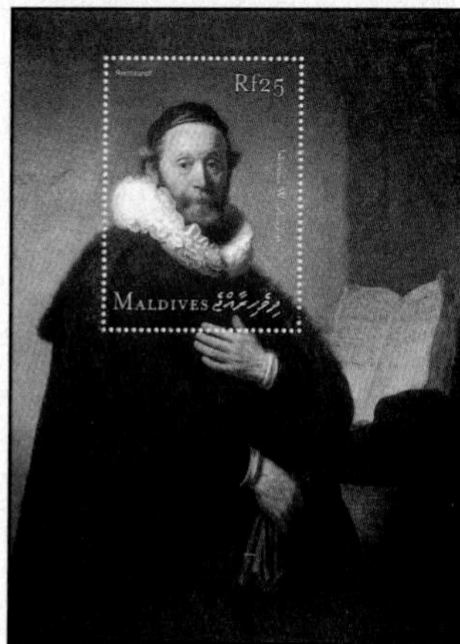

Rijksmuseum, Amsterdam, Bicent. (in 2000) — A401

No. 2531, 7r: a, Donkey's head and rider from Donkey Riding on the Beach, by Isaac Lazarus Israels. b, The Paternal Admonition, by Gerard Terborch, the Younger. c, The Sick Woman, by Jan Havicksz Steen. d, Girls with red hats from Donkey Riding on the Beach. e, Pompeius Occo, by Dirck Jacobsz. f, Woman With a Child in a Pantry, by Pieter de Hooch.

No. 2532, 7r: a, The Holy Kinship, by Geertgen tot Sint Jans. b, Sir Thomas Gresham, by Anthonis Mor. c, Self-portrait as St. Paul, by Rembrandt. d, Cleopatra's Banquet, by Gerard Lairesse. e, Still Life With Flowers in a Glass, by Jan Brueghel, the Elder. f, Portrait of a Man, Possibly Nicolaes Hasselaer, by Frans Hals.

No. 2533, 7r: a, Rembrandt's Mother, by Gerard Dou. b, Portrait of a Girl Dressed in Blue, by Jan Cornelisz Verspronck. c, Old Woman at Prayer, by Nicolaes Maes. d, Feeding the Hungry from The Seven Works of Charity, by the Master of Alkmaar. e, The Threatened Swan, by Jan Asselyn. f, The Daydreamer, by Maes.

No. 2534, 7r: a, Woman seated in doorway, from The Little Street, by Jan Vermeer. b, Two women from The Love Letter, by Vermeer. c, Woman in Blue Reading a Letter, by Vermeer. d, Woman and pillar from The Love Letter. e, The Milkmaid, by Vermeer. f, Arched doorway, from The Little Street.

No. 2535, 25r, Johannes Wtenbogaert, by Rembrandt. No. 2536, 25r, The Staalmeesters (The Syndics), by Rembrandt. No. 2537, 25r, The Night Watch, by Rembrandt. No. 2538, 25r, Shipwreck on a Rocky Coast, by Wijnandus Johannes Joseph Nuyen, horiz.

2001, Jan. 15 ***Perf. 13¾***

Sheets of 6, #a-f

2531-2534 A401 Set of 4 30.00 30.00

Souvenir Sheets

2535-2538 A401 Set of 4 17.00 17.00

Ill-fated Ships — A402

No. 2539, 5r: a, Milton Iatrides, 1970. b, Cyclops, 1918. c, Marine Sulphur Queen, 1963. d, Rosalie, 1840. e, Mary Celeste, 1872. f, Atlanta, 1880.

No. 2540, 5r: a, Windfall, 1962. b, Kobenhavn, 1928. c, Pearl, 1874. d, HMS Bulwark, 1914. e, Patriot, 1812. f, Lusitania, 1915.

No. 2541, 25r, La Boussole and L'Astrolabe, 1789. No. 2542, 25r, Titanic, 1912.

2001, Feb. 12 ***Perf. 14***

Sheets of 6, #a-f

2539-2540 A402 Set of 2 10.00 10.00

Souvenir Sheets

2541-2542 A402 Set of 2 8.50 8.50

Flower Type of 1997

2001, Mar. 1 ***Perf. 14¾x14***

Size: 16x20mm

2543 A350 10r Like #2267 1.75 1.75

Islam in Maldive Islands, 848th Anniv. — A403

No. 2544: a, Dharumavantha Rasgefaanu Mosque. b, Plaque of Hukurumiskiiy. c, Learning the Holy Koran. d, Institute of Islamic Studies. e, Center for the Holy Koran. f, Islamic Center.

25r, Medhu Ziyaarath.

2001, July 9 Litho. ***Perf. 13¾***

2544 A403 10r Sheet of 6, #a-f 10.00 10.00

Souvenir Sheet

2545 A403 25r multi 4.25 4.25

Fish — A404

Designs: No. 2546, 10r, Pterois miles. No. 2547, 10r, Pomacanthus imperator.

2001, July 16 ***Perf. 14x14¾***

2546-2547 A404 Set of 2 3.50 3.50

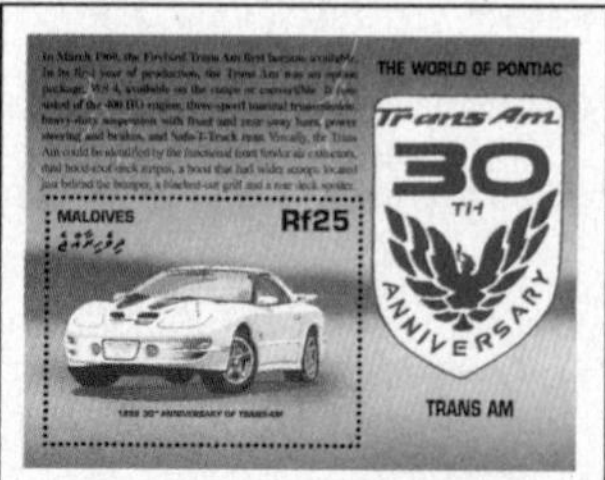

Pontiac Trans-Am Automobiles — A405

No. 2548, 12r: a, 1970. b, 1989. c, 1994.

No. 2549, 12r: a, 1976. b, 1988. c, 1988 Coupe.

2001 ***Perf. 14***

Sheets of 3, #a-c

2548-2549 A405 Set of 2 12.50 12.50

Souvenir Sheet

Perf. 14¼

2550 A405 25r 1999 4.25 4.25

Nos. 2548-2549 each contain three 42x28mm stamps.

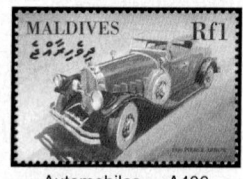

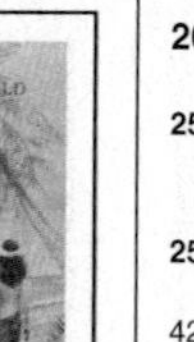

Automobiles — A406

Designs: 1r, 1930 Pierce-Arrow. 2r, 1938 Mercedes-Benz 540K. 8r, 1934 Duesenberg J. 10r, 1931 Bugatti Royale.

No. 2555, 7r: a, 1931 Auburn convertible sedan. b, 1931 Mercedes SSKL. c, 1929 Packard roadster. d, 1940 Chevrolet. e, 1915 Mercer. f, 1941 Packard sedan.

No. 2556, 7r: a, 1932 Chevrolet roadster. b, 1929 Cadillac Fleetwood roadster. c, 1928 Bentley Speed Six. d, 1930 Cadillac Fleetwood. e, 1936 Ford convertible. f, 1929 Hudson Phaeton.

No. 2557, 25r, 1930 Cord Brougham. No. 2558, 25r, 1931 Rolls-Royce P-1.

2001 ***Perf. 14***

2551-2554 A406 Set of 4 3.50 3.50

Sheets of 6, #a-f

2555-2556 A406 Set of 2 14.50 14.50

Souvenir Sheets

2557-2558 A406 Set of 2 8.50 8.50

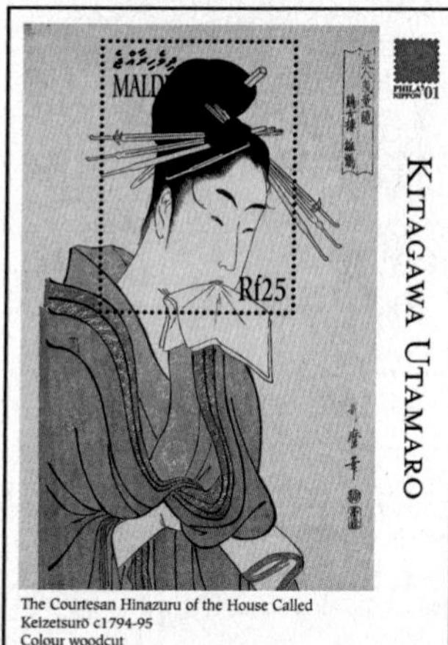

Phila Nippon '01, Japan — A407

No. 2559, 7r (28x42mm) — Prints of women by Utamaro: a, Reed Blind, Model Young Women Woven in Mist. b, Woman with Parasol. c, High-ranked Courtesan, Five Shades of Ink in the Northern Quarter. d, Comparison of Beauties of the Southern Quarter. e, The Barber.

No. 2560, 7r — Actors by Shunsho Katsukawa: a, Danjuro Ichikawa V (black kimono, 28x85mm). b, Danjuro Ichikawa V (arm raised, 28x85mm). c, Danjuro Ichikawa V (arms crossed on chest, 28x85mm). d, Danjuro Ichikawa V (wrapped in kimono, 28x85mm). e, Tomoeman Otani I and Mitsugaro Bando I (56x85mm).

No. 2561, 25r, The Courtesan Hinazuru of the House Called Keizetsuro, by Utamaro. No. 2562, 25r, Jomyo Tsutsui and the Priest Ichirai on the Uji Bridge, by Kiyomasu Torii.

2001, July 18 Litho. ***Perf. 14***

Sheets of 5, #a-e

2559-2560 A407 Set of 2 12.00 12.00

Souvenir Sheets

Perf. 13¾

2561-2562 A407 Set of 2 8.50 8.50

Giuseppe Verdi (1813-1901), Opera Composer — A408

No. 2563: a, Alfred Piccaver. b, Rigoletto costume, Heinrich. c, Rigoletto costume, Cologne. d, Cornell MacNeil.
25r, Matteo Manuguerra.

2001, Aug. 26 *Perf. 14*
2563 A408 10r Sheet of 4, #a-d 6.75 6.75

Souvenir Sheet

2564 A408 25r multi 4.25 4.25

Mao Zedong (1893-1976) — A409

No. 2565: a, Red background. b, Blue background. c, Gray background.
25r, Wearing cap.

2001, Aug. 26 *Perf. 13¾*
2565 A409 15r Sheet of 3, #a-c 7.75 7.75

Souvenir Sheet

2566 A409 25r multi 4.25 4.25

Queen Victoria (1819-1901) — A410

No. 2567: a, Earring at right. b, Earring at left. c, As old woman. d, In black dress.
25r, With hand on chin.

2001, Aug. 26 *Perf. 14*
2567 A410 10r Sheet of 4, #a-d 6.75 6.75

Souvenir Sheet

2568 A410 25r multi 4.25 4.25

Queen Elizabeth II, 75th Birthday — A411

No. 2569: a, Without hat. b, Wearing large crown. c, Wearing tiara. d, Wearing red uniform. e, Wearing black cape and hat. f, Wearing tan hat.
25r, Wearing crown, diff.

2001, Aug. 26
2569 A411 7r Sheet of 6, #a-f 7.25 7.25

Souvenir Sheet

2570 A411 25r multi 4.25 4.25

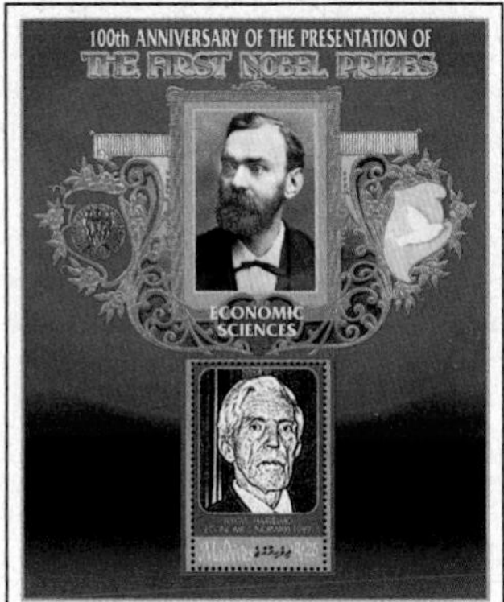

Nobel Prizes, Cent. — A412

No. 2571 — Economics laureates: a, Simon Kuznets, 1971. b, Wassily Leontief, 1973. c, Lawrence R. Klein, 1980. d, Friedrich A. von Hayek, 1974. e, Leonid V. Kantorovich, 1975.
No. 2572, 7r — Peace laureates: a, Ernesto T. Moneta, 1907. b, Albert J. Luthuli, 1960. c, Henri Dunant, 1901. d, Charles Albert Gobat, 1902. e, Sean MacBride, 1974. f, Elie Ducommun, 1902.
No. 2573, 7r — Peace laureates: a, Adolfo Pérez Esquivel, 1980. b, Mikhail S. Gorbachev, 1990. c, Betty Williams, 1976. d, Alfonso Garcia Robles, 1982. e, Paul D'Estournelles de Constant, 1909. f, Louis Renault, 1907.
No. 2574, 25r, Trygve Haavelmo, Economics, 1989. No. 2575, 25r, Vicente Aleixandre, Literature, 1977. No. 2576, 25r, Octavio Paz, Literature, 1990.

2001, Sept. 29 **Litho.** *Perf. 14*
2571 A412 7r Sheet of 5, #a-e 6.00 6.00

Sheets of 6, #a-f

2572-2573 A412 Set of 2 14.50 14.50

Souvenir Sheets

2574-2576 A412 Set of 3 13.00 13.00

Mercedes-Benz Automobiles, Cent. — A413

Designs: 2.50r, 1939 W165 Grand Prix. 5r, 1928 460 Nürburg Sport Roadster. 8r, 1928 Boattail Speedster. 15r, 1909 Blitzen Benz.
No. 2581, 7r: a, 1927 680S. b, 1934 150. c, 1936 540K Roadster. d, 1933 770 Grosser Mercedes. e, 1958 220SE. f, 1990 500SL.
No. 2582, 7r: a, 1933 290. b, 1927 Model S. c, 1953 300SL Coupe. d, 1911 Benz Victoria. e, 1968 280SL. f, 1937 W125 Grand Prix.
No. 2583, 25r, 1931 370S. No. 2584, 25r, 1955 300SLR.

2001, Oct. 30 **Litho.** *Perf. 14*
2577-2580 A413 Set of 4 5.25 5.25

Sheets of 6, #a-f

2581-2582 A413 Set of 2 14.50 14.50

Souvenir Sheets

2583-2584 A413 Set of 2 8.50 8.50

2002 World Cup Soccer Championships, Japan and Korea — A414

World Cup Trophy and: 1r, Eusebio, Portugal, Portuguese flag. 3r, Johan Cruyff, Netherlands, Netherlands flag. 7r, French player and flag. 10r, Japanese player and flag. 12r, Seoul World Cup Stadium, horiz. 15r, 1930 World Cup poster.
25r, Gerd Müller's winning goal for West Germany, 1974, vert.

2001, Nov. 28
2585-2590 A414 Set of 6 8.25 8.25

Souvenir Sheet

2591 A414 25r multi 4.25 4.25

No. 2591 contains one 42x56mm stamp.

Princess Diana (1961-97) — A415

No. 2592: a, Pink rose. b, White rose. c, Yellow rose. d, Beige rose.
25r, Wearing pearl necklace.

2001, Dec. 26
2592 A415 10r Sheet of 4, #a-d 6.75 6.75

Souvenir Sheet

2593 A415 25r multi 4.25 4.25

New Year 2002 (Year of the Horse) — A416

No. 2594 — Paintings by Xu Beihong: a, Running Horse (painting 45mm tall). b, Standing Horse. c, Running Horse (painting 49mm tall). d, Horse (painting 44mm tall). e, Horse (painting 48mm tall).
15r, Horse, horiz.

2001, Dec. 26 *Perf. 14*
2594 A416 5r Sheet of 5, #a-e 5.50 5.50

Souvenir Sheet
Perf. 14x14½

2595 A416 15r multi 2.60 2.60

No. 2594 contains five 31x63mm stamps.

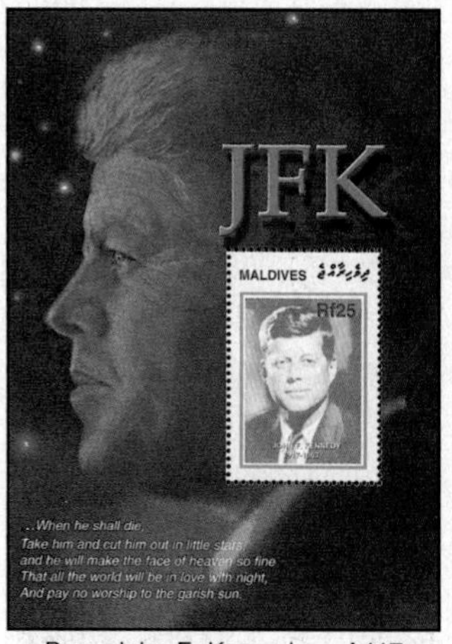

Pres. John F. Kennedy — A417

No. 2596, 5r: a, At Dexter, 1927. b, At Harvard, 1935. c, In Navy, 1943. d, At wedding, 1953. e, With brother Robert, 1956. f, At Presidential inauguration, 1961.
No. 2597, 5r: a, With Nikita Khrushchev, 1961. b, With Harold Macmillan. c, With Charles de Gaulle, 1961. d, With Jawaharlal Nehru, 1962. e, With Konrad Adenauer, 1963. f, With Dr. Martin Luther King, Jr., 1963.
No. 2598, 25r, Portrait. No. 2599, 25r, With wife, 1961.

2001, Dec. 26 *Perf. 14*

Sheets of 6, #a-f

2596-2597 A417 Set of 2 13.00 13.00

Souvenir Sheets

2598-2599 A417 Set of 2 8.50 8.50

Moths — A418

No. 2600, 7r: a, Cymothoe lucasi. b, Milionia grandis. c, Ornithoptera eroesus. d, Hyantis hodeva. e, Ammobiota festiva. f, Blue salamis.
No. 2601, 7r: a, Zygaena occitanica. b, Campyloes desgodinsi. c, Bhutanitis thaidina. d, Six-tailed helicopsis. e, Parnassius charltonius. f, Acraea ecucogiap.
No. 2602: a, Papilio dardanus. b, Baomisa hieroglyphica. c, Troides prattorum. d, Funonia rhadama.
No. 2603, 25r, Hypolera cassotis. No. 2604, 25r, Euphydryas maturna, vert.

2001, Dec. 26 **Litho.**

Sheets of 6, #a-f

2600-2601 A418 Set of 2 14.50 14.50
2602 A418 10r Sheet of 4, #a-d 6.75 6.75

Souvenir Sheets

2603-2604 A418 Set of 2 8.50 8.50

Queen Mother Type of 1999 Redrawn

No. 2605: a, With King George VI, 1936. b, In 1941. c, In 1960. d, In 1981.
25r, At Order of the Garter Service.

2001, Dec. ***Perf. 14***

Yellow Orange Frames

2605 A372 7r Sheet of 4, #a-d, + label 4.75 4.75

Souvenir Sheet

Perf. 13¾

2606 A372 25r multi 4.25 4.25

Queen Mother's 101st birthday. No. 2606 contains one 38x51mm stamp slightly darker than that found on No. 2405. Sheet margins of Nos. 2605-2606 lack embossing and gold arms and frames found on Nos. 2404-2405.

Reign of Queen Elizabeth II, 50th Anniv. — A419

No. 2607: a, With Princess Margaret. b, Wearing white hat. c, Wearing tiara. d, Holding flowers.
25r, At coronation.

2002, Feb. 6 **Litho.** ***Perf. 14¼***

2607 A419 10r Sheet of 4, #a-d 7.75 7.75

Souvenir Sheet

2608 A419 25r multi 4.25 4.25

Cats — A420

Designs: 3r, Havana brown. 5r, American wirehair. 8r, Norwegian forest cat. 10r, Seal point Siamese.

No. 2613, 7r: a, British blue. b, Red mackerel Manx. c, Scottish fold. d, Somali. e, Balinese. f, Exotic shorthair.

No. 2614, 7r, horiz.: a, Persian. b, Exotic shorthair, diff. c, Ragdoll. d, Manx. e, Tonkinese. f, Scottish fold, diff.

25r, Blue mackerel tabby Cornish rex.

2002, Apr. 8 ***Perf. 14***

2609-2612 A420 Set of 4 4.75 4.75

Sheets of 6, #a-f

2613-2614 A420 Set of 2 14.50 14.50

Souvenir Sheet

2615 A420 25r multi 4.25 4.25

Birds A421

Designs: 1r, Swinhoe's snipe. 2r, Oriental honey buzzard. 3r, Asian koel. No. 2619, 5r, Red-throated pipet. No. 2620, 7r, Short-eared owl. 10r, Eurasian spoonbill. 12r, Pied wheatear. 15r, Oriental pratincole.

No. 2624, 5r: a, Lesser noddy. b, Roseate tern. c, Frigate minor. d, Saunder's tern. e, White-bellied storm petrel. f, Red-footed booby.

No. 2625, 5r: a, Cattle egret. b, Barn swallow. c, Osprey. d, Little heron. e, Ruddy turnstone. f, Sooty tern.

No. 2626, 7r: a, Rose-ringed parakeet. b, Common swift. c, Lesser kestrel. d, Golden oriole. e, Asian paradise flycatcher. f, Indian roller.

No. 2627, 7r: a, Pallid harrier. b, Gray heron. c, Blue-tailed bee-eater. d, White-breasted water hen. e, Cotton pygmy goose. f, Maldivian pond heron.

No. 2628, 25r, White-tailed tropicbird. No. 2629, 25r, Greater flamingo. No. 2630, 25r, Cinnamon bittern. No. 2631, 25r, White tern.

2002, Apr. 8

2616-2623 A421 Set of 8 10.00 10.00

Sheets of 6, #a-f

2624-2627 A421 Set of 4 27.50 27.50

Souvenir Sheets

2628-2631 A421 Set of 4 17.00 17.00

Prehistoric Animals — A422

No. 2632, 7r: a, Sivatherium. b, Flat-headed peccary. c, Shasta ground sloth. d, Harlan's ground sloth. e, European woolly rhinoceros. f, Dwarf pronghorn.

No. 2633, 7r: a, Macrauchenia. b, Gyptodon. c, Nesodon. d, Imperial tapir. e, Short-faced bear. f, Mammoth.

No. 2634, 25r, Saber-toothed cat. No. 2635, 25r, Woolly mammoth, vert.

2002, May 21 **Sheets of 6, #a-f**

2632-2633 A422 Set of 2 15.00 15.00

Souvenir Sheets

2634-2635 A422 Set of 2 8.50 8.50

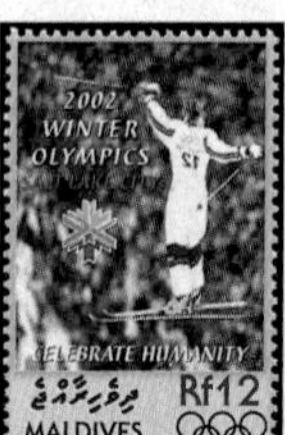

2002 Winter Olympics, Salt Lake City — A423

Designs: No. 2636, 12r, Freestyle skiing. No. 2637, 12r, Downhill skiing.

2002, July 11 **Litho.** ***Perf. 13½x13¼***

2636-2637 A423 Set of 2 4.50 4.50
a. Souvenir sheet, #2636-2637 4.50 4.50

Intl. Year of Mountains — A424

No. 2638: a, Mt. Ama Dablam, Nepal. b, Mt. Clements, US. c, Mt. Artesonraju, Peru. d, Mt. Cholatse, Nepal.
25r, Balloon and Mt. Jefferson, US.

2002, July 11 ***Perf. 14***

2638 A424 15r Sheet of 4, #a-d 10.50 10.50

Souvenir Sheet

2639 A424 25r multi 4.25 4.25

20th World Scout Jamboree, Thailand — A425

No. 2640, vert.: a, Temple. b, Thailand Scout. c, Merit badges.
25r, Mountain climbing merit badge.

2002, July 11

2640 A425 15r Sheet of 3, #a-c 7.75 7.75

Souvenir Sheet

2641 A425 25r multi 4.25 4.25

Souvenir Sheet

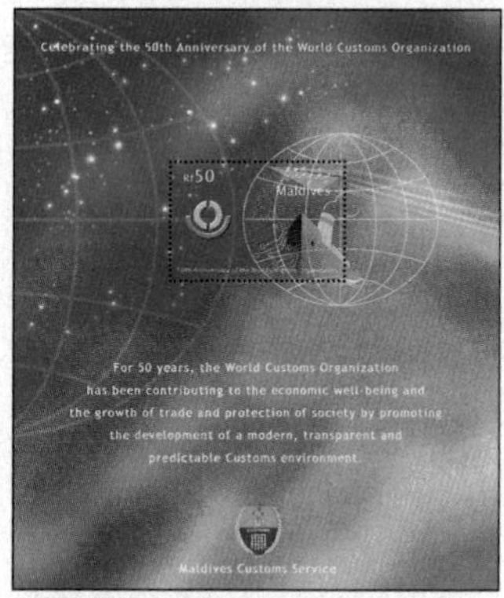

World Customs Organization, 50th Anniv. — A426

2002, Aug. 12 ***Perf. 13¾***

2642 A426 50r multi 8.50 8.50

Elvis Presley (1935-77) A427

2002, Oct. 7

2643 A427 5r multi 1.25 1.25

Printed in sheets of 9.

Flowers and Butterflies — A428

No. 2644, 7r — Flowers: a, Morning glory. b, Wedding bell anemone. c, Barrett Browning narcissus. d, Persian jewel nigella. e, Whirligig pink osteospermum. f, Brown lasso iris.

No. 2645, 7r — Orchids: a, Laelia gouldiana. b, Cattleya Louise Georgiana. c, Laeliocattleya Christopher Gubler. d, Miltoniopsis Bert Field Crimson Glow. e, Lemboglossum bictoniense. f, Derosara Divine Victor.

No. 2646, 7r — Butterflies: a, Morpho menelus. b, Small postman. c, Hewitson's blue hairstreak. d, Green swallowtail. e, Cairns birdwing. f, Queen.

No. 2647, 25r, Little pink beauty aster. No. 2648, 25r, Angraecum veitchii, vert. No. 2649, 25r, Cymothoe lurida butterfly.

2002, Nov. 4 **Litho.** ***Perf. 14***

Sheets of 6, #a-f

2644-2646 A428 Set of 3 22.50 22.50

Souvenir Sheets

2647-2649 A428 Set of 3 12.00 12.00

2002 World Cup Soccer Championships, Japan and Korea — A429

No. 2650, 7r: a, Torsten Frings sliding. b, Roberto Carlos. c, Frings kicking. d, Ronaldo pointing. e, Oliver Neuville. f, Ronaldo with ball.

No. 2651, 7r: a, Eul Yong Lee, Alpay Ozalan. b, Myung Bo Hong, Hakan Sukur. c, Emre Belozoglu, Chong Gug Song. d, Ergun Penbe, Chong Gug Song. e, Ergun Penbe, Ki Hyeon Seol. f, Chong Gug Song, Hakan Unsal.

No. 2652, 15r: a, Cafu and Neuville. b, Hands holding World Cup.

No. 2653, 15r: a, Dietmar Hamann. b, Cafu holding World Cup.

No. 2654, 15r: a, Ilhan Mansiz. b, Young Pyo Lee.

No. 2655, 15r: a, Hakan Sukur. b, Sang Chul Yoo.

2002, Nov. 12 ***Perf. 13½***

Sheets of 6, #a-f

2650-2651 A429 Set of 2 13.50 13.50

Souvenir Sheets of 2, #a-b

2652-2655 A429 Set of 4 19.00 19.00

Teddy Bears, Cent. — A430

No. 2656: a, Hairdresser. b, Construction worker. c, Gardener. d, Chef.

No. 2657, 12r: a, Mother. b, Sister and brother. c, Father.

No. 2658, 12r: a, Nurse. b, Doctor. c, Dentist.

No. 2659, 30r, Soccer player. No. 2660, 30r, Golfer. No. 2661, 30r, Snow boarder.

2002, Nov. 18 ***Perf. 14***

2656 A430 8r Sheet of 4, #a-d 5.00 5.00

Sheets of 3, #a-c

2657-2658 A430 Set of 2 11.50 11.50

Souvenir Sheets

2659-2661 A430 Set of 3 14.00 14.00

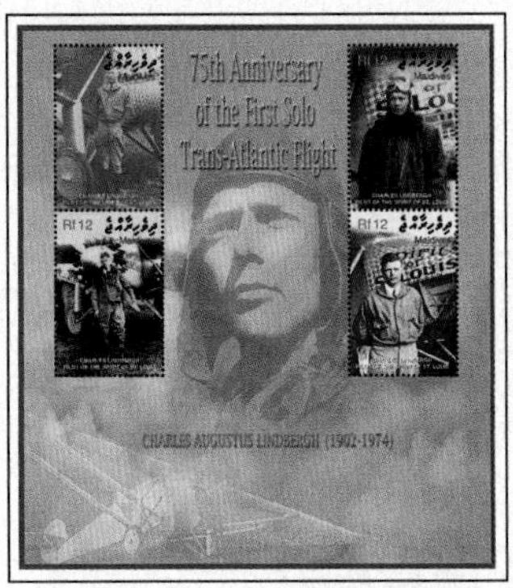

First Non-Stop Solo Transatlantic Flight, 75th Anniv. — A430a

No. 2661A, 12r — Various photos of Charles Lindbergh and Spirit of St. Louis: c, Blue. d, Brown. e, Gray. f, Red violet.

No. 2661B, 12r: g, Donald Hall, designer of Spirit of St. Louis. h, Charles Lindbergh. i, Lindbergh, Spirit of St. Louis (Lindbergh distorted). j, Lindbergh, Hall and President Mahoney of Ryan Aircraft.

2002, Dec. 2 Litho. *Perf. 14*

2661A	A430a	12r Sheet of 4, #c-f	7.50	7.50
2661B	A430a	12r Sheet of 4, #g-j	7.50	7.50

Princess Diana (1961-97)
A431 A432

2002, Dec. 2

2662	A431	12r multi	1.90	1.90
2663	A432	12r multi	1.90	1.90

Nos. 2662-2663 were each printed in sheets of 4.

Pres. John F. Kennedy (1917-63) — A432a

No. 2663A: b, With father Joseph P., and brother Joseph, Jr. c, At age 11. d, Inspecting Boston waterfront, 1951. e, As Navy Ensign, 1941. f, With sister Kathleen in London, 1939. g, With Eleanor Roosevelt, 1951.

2002, Dec. 2 Litho. *Perf. 14*

2663A	A432a	7r Sheet of 6, #b-g	7.25	7.25

Pres. Ronald Reagan — A433

Designs: No. 2664, Green background. No. 2665, Blue background.

No. 2666: a, Wearing brown suit. b, Wearing black suit with red tie.

2002, Dec. 2

2664	A433	12r multi	1.90	1.90
2665	A433	12r multi	1.90	1.90
a.		Horiz. pair, #2664-2665	4.00	4.00
2666	A433	12r Horiz. pair, #a-b	4.00	4.00
		Nos. 2664-2666 (3)	7.80	7.80

Nos. 2664-2665 were printed in sheets containing two of each stamp. No. 2666 was printed in sheets containing two pairs.

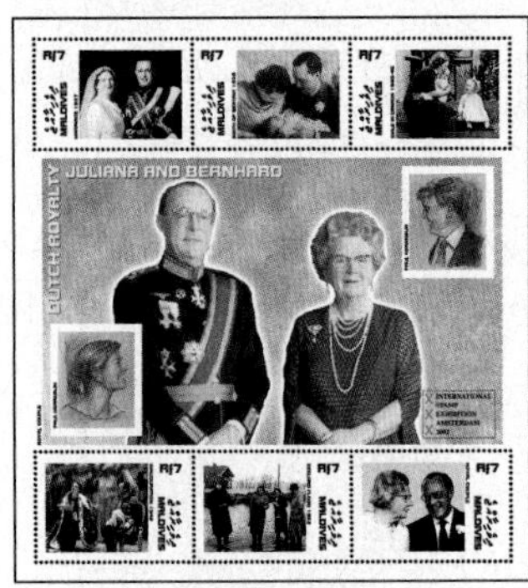

Amphilex 2002 Intl. Stamp Exhibition, Amsterdam — A434

No. 2667, 7r — Life of Queen Mother Juliana and Prince Bernhard: a, Wedding, 1937. b, Birth of Princess Beatrix, 1938. c, Exile in Canada, 1940-45. d, Installation of Juliana as queen, 1948. e, Zeeland flood, 1953. f, Royal couple.

No. 2668, 7r — Portraits depicting Queen Beatrix by: a, Pauline Hille. b, John Klinkenberg. c, Beatrice Filius. d, Will Kellermann. e, Graswinckel. f, Marjolijn Spreeuwenberg.

2002, Dec. 8 *Perf. 14*

Sheets of 6, #a-f

2667-2668	A434	Set of 2	13.50	13.50

Fish A435

Birds and Sharks — A436

Designs: 10 l, Flame basslet. 15 l, Teardrop butterflyfish. 20 l, Hamburg damselfish. 25 l, Bridled tern. 50 l, Blue-lined surgeonfish. 1r, Common tern. 2r, Common noddy. No. 2676, Yellow-breasted wrasse. No. 2677, Blue shark. 4r, Harlequin filefish. 5r, Orangespine unicornfish. 10r, Emperor angelfish. 12r, Bullseye. 20r, Scalloped hammerhead shark.

Perf. 14 (A435), 10¾x13 (25 l, 1r, 2r), 13¼x14 (#2677, 20r)

2002, Dec. 24

2669	A435	10 l multi	.25	.25
2670	A435	15 l multi	.25	.25
2671	A435	20 l multi	.25	.25
2672	A436	25 l multi	.25	.25
2673	A435	50 l multi	.25	.25
2674	A436	1r multi	.25	.25
2675	A436	2r multi	.30	.30
2676	A435	2.50r multi	.40	.40
2677	A436	2.50r multi	.40	.40
2678	A435	4r multi	.60	.60
2679	A435	5r multi	.75	.75
2680	A435	10r multi	1.50	1.50
2681	A435	12r multi	1.90	1.90
2682	A436	20r multi	3.00	3.00
		Nos. 2669-2682 (14)	10.35	10.35

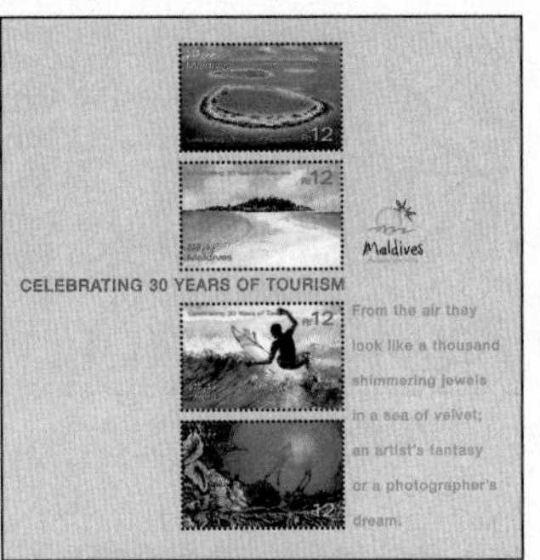

Tourism, 30th Anniv. — A437

No. 2683: a, Atolls. b, Sand spit. c, Surfer. d, Underwater scene.

2002, Dec. 25 *Perf. 13½*

2683	A437	12r Sheet of 4, #a-d	7.50	7.50

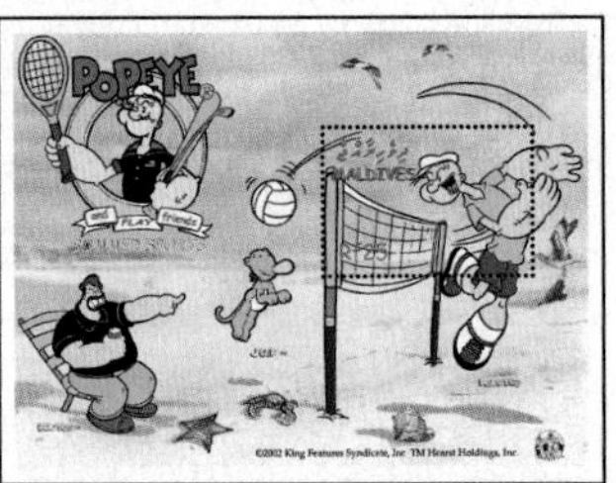

Popeye — A438

No. 2684, vert: a, Diving. b, Surfing. c, Sailboarding. d, Baseball. e, Hurdles. f, Tennis.

25r, Volleyball.

2003, Jan. 27 *Perf. 14*

2684	A438	7r Sheet of 6, #a-f	6.50	6.50

Souvenir Sheet

2685	A438	25r multi	4.00	4.00

National Museum, 50th Anniv. A439

Various museum items: 3r, 3.50r, 6.50r, 22r.

2003, Jan. 31 Litho.

2686-2689	A439	Set of 4	5.50	5.50

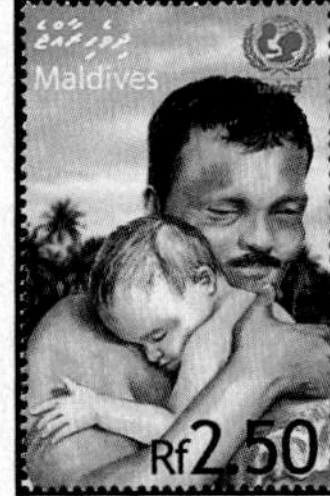

UNICEF — A440

Designs: 2.50r, Father and child. 5r, Mother kissing child. 20r, Child learning to walk.

2003, Jan. 31 *Perf. 15x14*

2690-2692	A440	Set of 3	4.50	4.50

Shells — A441

Designs: No. 2693, 10r, Sundial shell. No. 2694, 10r, Cardita clam. No. 2695, 10r, Corn shell. No. 2696, 10r, Cowrie shell.

2003, Mar. 25 Litho. *Perf. 13¼*

2693-2696	A441	Set of 4	7.00	7.00

Astronauts Killed in Space Shuttle Columbia Accident — A442

No. 2697: a, Mission Specialist 1 David M. Brown. b, Commander Rick D. Husband. c, Mission Specialist 4 Laurel Blair Salton Clark. d, Mission Specialist 4 Kalpana Chawla. e, Payload Commander Michael P. Anderson. f, Pilot William C. McCool. g, Payload Specialist 4 Ilan Ramon.

2003, Apr. 7 *Perf. 13½x13¼*

2697	A442	7r Sheet of 7, #a-g	7.75	7.75

Coronation of Queen Elizabeth II, 50th Anniv. — A443

No. 2698: a, Wearing hat. b, Wearing crown. c, Wearing tiara.

25r, Wearing tiara, diff.

2003, May 26 *Perf. 14*

2698	A443	15r Sheet of 3, #a-c	6.00	6.00

Souvenir Sheet

2699	A443	25r multi	4.00	4.00

Prince William, 21st Birthday — A444

No. 2700: a, As toddler. b, Wearing red and blue tie. c, Wearing tie with blue squares.

25r, As toddler, wearing cap.

2003, May 26

2700	A444	15r Sheet of 3, #a-c	6.00	6.00

Souvenir Sheet

2701	A444	25r multi	4.00	4.00

Paintings by Albrecht Dürer (1471-1528) A445

Designs: 3r, Drummer and Piper from wing of the Jabach Altarpiece. 5r, Portrait of a Young Man. 7r, Wire-drawing Mill, horiz. 10r, Innsbruck from the North, horiz.

No. 2706: a, Portrait of Jacob Muffel. b, Portrait of Hieronymus Holzschuher. c, Portrait of Johannes Kleberger. d, Self-portrait.

25r, The Weiden Mill, horiz.

2003, June 17 ***Perf. 14¼***

2702-2705 A445	Set of 4		4.50	4.50
2706 A445	12r Sheet of 4, #a-d		6.50	6.50

Souvenir Sheet

2707 A445	25r multi	4.00	4.00

Japanese Art — A446

Designs: 2r, Detail from The Actor Sojuro Nakamura as Mitsukuni, by Yoshitaki Utagawa. 5r, Detail from The Actor Sojuro Nakamura as Mitsukuni, by Yoshitaki Utagawa, diff. 7r, The Ghost of Koheiji Kohada, by Hokuei Shunkosai. 15r, Ariwara no Narihira as Seigen, by Kunisada Utagawa.

No. 2712: a, The Ghost of Mitsumune Shikibunojo, by Kunisada Utagawa. b, Fuwa Bansakui, by Yoshitoshi Tsukioka. c, The Lantern Ghost of Oiwa, by Shunkosai. d, The Greedy Hag, by Tsukioka.

25r, The Spirit of Sogoro Sakura Haunting Koszuke Hotta.

2003, June 17

2708-2711 A446	Set of 4	4.75	4.75
2712 A446	10r Sheet of 4, #a-d	5.25	5.25

Souvenir Sheet

2713 A446	25r multi	4.00	4.00

Paintings by Joan Miró (1893-1983) — A447

Designs: 3r, Untitled painting, 1934. 5r, Hirondelle Amour. 10r, Two Women. 15r, Women Listening to Music.

No. 2718: a, Woman and Birds. b, Nocturne. c, Morning Star. d, The Escape Ladder.

No. 2719, 25r, Rhythmic Personages, vert. No. 2720, 25r, Women Encircled by the Flight of a Bird, vert.

2003, June 17 ***Perf. 14¼***

2714-2717 A447	Set of 4	5.25	5.25
2718 A447	12r Sheet of 4, #a-d	6.50	6.50

Size: 83x104mm

Imperf

2719-2720 A447	Set of 2	7.00	7.00

Tour de France Bicycle Race, Cent. — A448

No. 2721, 10r: a, Maurice Garin, 1903. b, Henri Cornet, 1904. c, Louis Trousselier, 1905. d, René Pottier, 1906.

No. 2722, 10r: a, Lucien Petit-Breton on Bicycle, 1907. b, Head of Petit-Breton, 1907. c, François Faber, 1909. d, Octave Lapize, 1910.

No. 2723, 10r: a, Eddy Merckx, 1974. b, Bernard Thévenet, 1975. c, Lucien Van Impe, 1976. d, Thévenet, 1977.

No. 2724, 25r, Bernard Hinault, 1979. No. 2725, 25r, Henri Desgranges. No. 2726, 25r, Le Réveil Matin Cafe, Montgeron, France.

2003, July 3 ***Perf. 13¼***

Sheets of 4, #a-d

2721-2723 A448	Set of 3	17.50	17.50

Souvenir Sheets

2724-2726 A448	Set of 3	10.00	10.00

Powered Flight, Cent. — A449

No. 2727, 10r — Alberto Santos-Dumont's: a, Airship No. 1. b, Airship No. 4, c, Airship with 14bis airplane. d, Airship No. 16.

No. 2728, 10r: a, Santos Dumont with Demoiselle airplane. b, Demoiselle airplane. c, Voisin-Farman No. 1 biplane. d, Gold Bug, built by Glenn Curtiss.

No. 2729, 25r, Santos-Dumont's Airship No. 6. No. 2730, 25r, Santos-Dumont's 14bis Airplane.

2003, July 14 ***Perf. 14***

Sheets of 4, #a-d

2727-2728 A449	Set of 2	12.50	12.50

Souvenir Sheets

2729-2730 A449	Set of 2	8.00	8.00

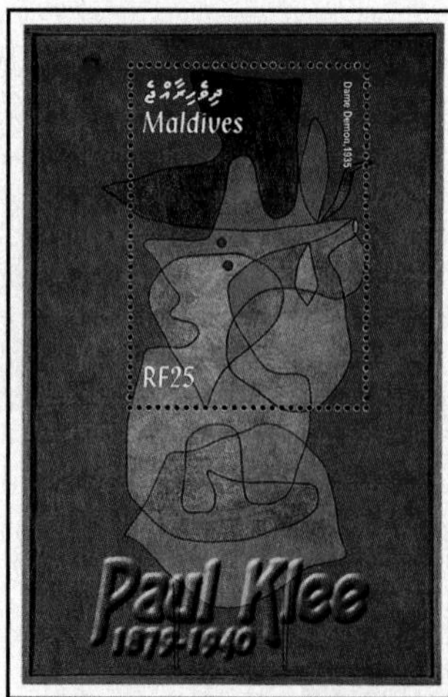

Paintings of Paul Klee (1879-1940) — A450

No. 2731, horiz.: a, Near Taormina, Scirocco. b, Small Town Among the Rocks. c, Still Life with Props. d, North Room.

25r, Dame Demon.

2003, Dec. 4 ***Perf. 13½***

2731 A450	10r Sheet of 4, #a-d	6.25	6.25

Souvenir Sheet

2732 A450	25r multi	4.00	4.00

Maumoon Abdul Gayoom, 25th Anniv. as President — A451

Litho. & Embossed

2003 ***Die Cut Perf. 8***

Without Gum

2733 A451	200r gold & multi	32.50	32.50

Norman Rockwell (1894-1978) — A452

No. 2734 — Four Seasons Calendar: Man and Boy, 1948: a, Winter (ice skating). b, Spring (resting amidst flowers). c, Summer (fishing). d, Autumn (raking leaves).

25r, Illustration for Hallmark Cards, 1937.

2003, Dec. 4 **Litho.** ***Perf. 13¼***

2734 A452	10r Sheet of 4, #a-d	6.25	6.25

Imperf

2735 A452	25r shown	4.00	4.00

No. 2734 contains four 38x50mm stamps.

Intl. Year of Fresh Water — A453

No. 2736: a, Ari Atoll. b, Fresh water for all. c, Desalination plant, Malé.

25r, Community rain water tank.

2003, Dec. 22 ***Perf. 14***

2736 A453	15r Sheet of 3, #a-c	6.00	6.00

Souvenir Sheet

2737 A453	25r multi	4.00	4.00

Fish A454

Designs: 1r, Clown triggerfish. 7r, Sixspot grouper. 10r, Long-nosed butterflyfish. 15r, Longfin bannerfish.

No. 2742: a, Goldtail demoiselle. b, Queen coris. c, Eight-banded butterflyfish. d, Meyer's butterflyfish. e, Exquisite butterflyfish. f, Yellowstripe snapper. g, Yellowback anthias. h, Black-spotted moray. i, Clown anemonefish.

No. 2743: a, Bluestreak cleaner wrasse. b, Threeband demoiselle. c, Palette surgeonfish. d, Emperor snapper. e, Bicolor angelfish. f, Picasso triggerfish.

25r, Chevron butterflyfish.

2003, Dec. 22

2738-2741 A454	Set of 4	5.25	5.25
2742 A454	4r Sheet of 9, #a-i	5.75	5.75
2743 A454	7r Sheet of 6, #a-f	6.75	6.75

Souvenir Sheet

2744 A454	25r multi	4.00	4.00

Nos. 2738-2741 were each printed in sheets of four.

Butterflies — A455

Designs: 3r, Yamfly. 5r, Striped blue crow. 8r, Indian red admiral. 15r, Great eggfly.

No. 2749, horiz.: a, Blue triangle. b, Monarch. c, Broad-bordered grass yellow. d, Red lacewing. e, African migrant. f, Plain tiger.

25r, Beak butterfly.

2003, Dec. 22

2745-2748 A455	Set of 4	5.25	5.25
2749 A455	7r Sheet of 6, #a-f	7.25	7.25

Souvenir Sheet

2750 A455	25r multi	4.25	4.25

Birds A456

Designs: 15 l, Great frigatebird. 20 l, Ruddy turnstone. 25 l, Hoopoe. 1r, Cattle egret.

No. 2755: a, Red-billed tropicbird. b, Red-footed booby. c, Common tern. d, Caspian tern. e, Common curlew. f, Black-bellied plover.

25r, Gray heron.

2003, Dec. 22

2751-2754 A456	Set of 4	6.50	6.50
2755 A456	7r Sheet of 6, #a-f	7.25	7.25

Souvenir Sheet

2756 A456	25r multi	4.25	4.25

Paintings by Pablo Picasso (1881-1973) — A457

No. 2757: a, Portrait of Jaime Sabartés, 1901. b, Portrait of the Artist's Wife (Olga), 1923. c, Portrait of Olga, 1923. d, Portrait of Jaime Sabartés, 1904.

30r, The Tragedy, 1903.

2003, Dec. 4 Litho. *Perf. 13¼*
2757 A457 10r Sheet of 4, #a-d 6.25 6.25

Imperf

2758 A457 30r multi 4.75 4.75

No. 2757 contains four 37x50mm stamps.

Flowers — A458

Designs: 30 l, Coelogyne asperata. 75 l, Calanthe rosea. 2r, Eria javanica. 10r, Spathoglottis affinis.
No. 2763, horiz.: a, Bird of paradise. b, Flamingo flower. c, Red ginger. d, Cooktown orchid. e, Vanda tricolor. f, Chinese hibiscus.
25r, Morning glory.

2003, Dec. 22 *Perf. 14*
2759-2762 A458 Set of 4 2.50 2.50
2763 A458 7r Sheet of 6, #a-f 6.75 6.75

Souvenir Sheet

2764 A458 25r multi 4.00 4.00

FIFA (Fédération Internationale de Football Association) Cent. — A459

World Cup winning teams: No. 2765, 5r, Germany, 1974. No. 2766, 5r, Argentina, 1978. No. 2767, 5r, Italy, 1982. No. 2768, 5r, Argentina, 1986. No. 2769, 5r, Germany, 1990. No. 2770, 5r, Brazil, 1994. No. 2771, 5r, France, 1998. No. 2772, 5r, Brazil, 2002.

2004, Mar. 8 *Perf. 13½*
2765-2772 A459 Set of 8 7.00 7.00

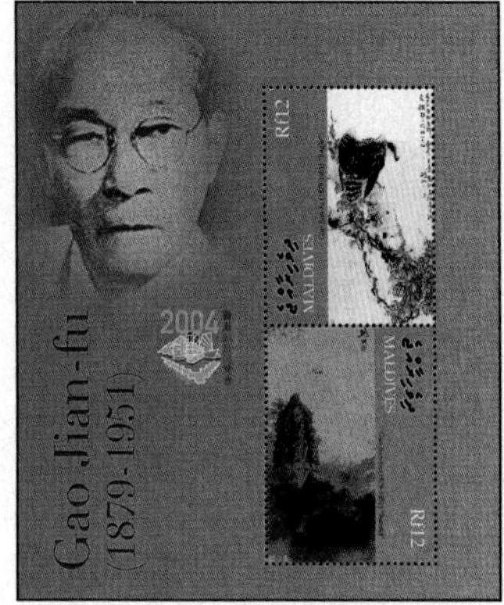

Paintings by Gao Jian-fu (1879-1951) — A460

No. 2773: a, Landscape. b, Moon Night. c, Fox. d, Spider web. e, Woman with mirror. f, Man sitting on ground.
No. 2774: a, Eagle. b, Sunset.

2004, Mar. 8 *Perf. 13¼*
2773 A460 7r Sheet of 6, #a-f 5.75 5.75
2774 A460 12r Sheet of 2, #a-b 3.25 3.25

2004 Hong Kong Stamp Expo.

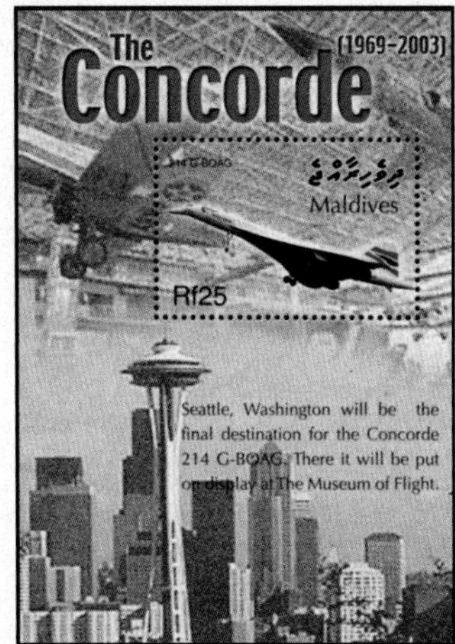

Cessation of Concorde Flights — A461

No. 2775: a, F-BVFD, Rio de Janeiro. b, F-BVFC, New York. c, F-BTSD, Honolulu. d, F-BTSD, Lisbon. e, F-BVFA, Washington. f, F-BVFD, Dakar, Senegal. g, G-BOAC, Singapore. h, G-BOAA, Sydney. i, G-BOAD, Hong Kong. j, G-BOAD, Amsterdam. k, G-BOAE, Tokyo. l, G-BOAF, Madrid.
No. 2776, 25r, 214 G-BOAG, Museum of Flight, Seattle. No. 2777, 25r, 214 G-BOAG, horizon. No. 2778, 25r, 204 G-BOAC, British flag.

2004, Mar. 8 *Perf. 13¼x13½*
2775 A461 1r Sheet of 12, #a-l 1.60 1.60

Souvenir Sheets

2776-2778 A461 Set of 3 10.00 10.00

Paintings in the Hermitage, St. Petersburg, Russia A462

Designs: 1r, Self-portrait, by Anthony van Dyck. 3r, Self-portrait, by Michael Sweerts. 7r, Anna Dalkeith, Countess of Morton, by van Dyck. 12r, Lady Anna Kirk, by van Dyck.
No. 2783: a, Portrait of Prince Alexander Kurakin, by Marie-Louise-Elisabeth Vigée-Lebrun. b, Portrait of a Lady in Waiting to the Infanta Isabella, by Peter Paul Rubens. c, Portrait of a Lady in Blue, by Thomas Gainsborough. d, The Actor Pierre Jéliolte in the Role of Apollo, by Louis Tocqué.
No. 2784, 25r, The Stolen Kiss, by Jean-Honoré Fragonard, horiz. No. 2785, 25r, A Scene from Corneille's Tragedy "La Comte d'Essex," by Nicolas Lancret, horiz.

2004, Mar. 29 *Perf. 14¼*
2779-2782 A462 Set of 4 4.00 4.00
2783 A462 10r Sheet of 4, #a-d 5.25 5.25

Souvenir Sheets

2784-2785 A462 Set of 2 6.75 6.75

D-Day, 60th Anniv. — A463

No. 2786, 6r: a, Gen. Dwight Eisenhower. b, Field Marshal Guenther von Kluge. c, Air Marshal Sir Trafford Leigh-Mallory. d, Field Marshal Walter Model. e, Field Marshal Gerd von Rundstedt. f, Sir Arthur Tedder.
No. 2787, 6r: a, Maj. Gen. Clarence Huebner. b, Brig. Gen. Anthony McAuliffe. c, Maj. Gen. Leonard Gerow. d, Gen. Adolf Galland. e, Brig. Gen. W. M. Hoge. f, Maj. Gen. Sir Percy Hobart.
No. 2788, 6r: a, Rear Admiral Kirk. b, Field Marshal Erwin Rommel. c, Gen. George Marshall. d, Gen. Jan Smuts. e, Gen. Lt. Gunther Blumentritt. f. Maj. Gen. J. Lawton Collins.
No. 2789, 6r: a, Winston Churchill. b, Adm. Sir Bertram Ramsay. c, Gen. Lt. Dietrich Kraiss. d, Maj. Gen. Richard Gale. e, Gen. George Patton. f, Maj. Gen. Maxwell Taylor.
No. 2790, 6r, horiz.: a, Lt. Gen. Omar Bradley. b, Rear Admiral Hall. c, Maj. Gen. Huebner, diff. d, Adm. Karl Dönitz. e, Rear Admiral Wilkes. f, Capt. Chauncey Camp.
No. 2791, 30r, Gen. Henry Arnold. No. 2792, 30r, Rear Adm. Donald Moon. No. 2793, 30r, Lt. Gen. Sir Frederick Morgan. No. 2794, 30r, Gen. Sir Bernard Montgomery. No. 2795, 30r, Rear Adm. Carlton Bryant, horiz.

Perf. 13½x13¼, 13¼x13½

2004, May 19 Sheets of 6, #a-f
2786-2790 A463 Set of 5 28.00 28.00

Souvenir Sheets

2791-2795 A463 Set of 5 24.00 24.00

Paintings by Paul Cézanne (1839-1906) — A464

No. 2796, horiz.: a, Still Life with Peppermint Bottle and Blue Rug. b, House in Provence. c. Le Château Noir. d, Basket of Apples.
25r, Boy in a Red Waistcoat Leaning on his Elbow.

2004, July 6 *Perf. 13¼*
2796 A464 10r Sheet of 4, #a-d 6.25 6.25

Imperf

2797 A464 25r multi 4.00 4.00

No. 2796 contains four 50x37mm stamps.

Paintings by Henri Rousseau (1844-1910) — A465

No. 2798, horiz.: a, Nègre Attaqué par un Jaguar. b, Paysage Exotique. c. La Cascade. d, Le Repas du Lion.
25r, Le Rêve.

2004, July 6 *Perf. 13¼*
2798 A465 10r Sheet of 4, #a-d 6.25 6.25

Imperf

2799 A465 25r multi 4.00 4.00

No. 2798 contains four 50x37mm stamps.

Paintings by Henri Matisse (1869-1954) — A466

No. 2800, horiz.: a, Conversation. b, Still Life with a Blue Tablecloth. c. Seville Still Life II. d, Woman Before an Aquarium.
25r, Interior at Nice.

2004, July 6 *Perf. 13¼*
2800 A466 10r Sheet of 4, #a-d 6.25 6.25

Imperf

2801 A466 25r multi 4.00 4.00

No. 2800 contains four 50x37mm stamps.

Steam Locomotives, 200th Anniv. — A467

No. 2802, 12r: a, Planet Class 2-2-0. b, American 4-4-0. c, Newmar. d, Class 500 4-6-0.

No. 2803, 12r: a, Firefly Class 2-2-2. b, French "Single." c, Medoc Class 2-4-0. d, German 4-4-0.

No. 2804, 12r: a, Adler 2-2-2. b, Beuth 2-2-2. c, Northumbrian 0-2-2. d, Class 4-6-2.

No. 2805, 12r: a, Woodburning Beyer Garratt 4-8-2+2-8-4. b, Double headed train over Kaaiman River, Africa. c, Garratt 4-8-2+2-8-4. d, Class 15 Garratt.

No. 2806, 12r: a, East African Railways Garratt. b, Rhodesian Railways 12th Class. c, Class 2-6-2. d, Class 19D 4-8-2.

No. 2807, 12r: a, Evening Star. b, Britannia. c, The George Stephenson. d, Sudan Railways 310 2-8-2.

No. 2808, 30r, Claud Hamilton Class 4-4-0. No. 2809, 30r, Class P8 4-6-0. No. 2810, 30r, Vauxhall 2-2-0. No. 2811, 30r, American, diff. No. 2812, 30r, The Lord Nelson. No. 2813, 30r, Flying Scotsman.

2004, July 6 ***Perf. 13¼x13½***

Sheets of 4, #a-d

2802-2807 A467 Set of 6 45.00 45.00

Souvenir Sheets

2808-2813 A467 Set of 6 28.00 28.00

Jules Verne (1828-1905), Writer — A468

No. 2814, 12r: a, Archipelago on Fire. b, Clovis Dardentor. c, The Golden Volcano. d, Le Superbe Orénoque.

No. 2815, 12r — Michael Strogoff, Courier of the Czar: a, People (pink background). b, People in grass (green background). c, People (blue background). d, Animal and head in grass (green background).

No. 2816, 12r — Family Without a Name: a, Woman. b, Soldier. c, Crowd. d, Soldiers and Indian with guns.

No. 2817, 12r — César Cascabel: a, Men pushing train car (blue green background). b, Man (brown background). c, Crevasse (blue green background). d, Crowd and sign (pink background).

No. 2818, 12r — The Lighthouse at the End of the World: a, Men on ship. b, Man with arm extended. c, Rocks. d, Fisherman with hat.

No. 2819, 25r, The Survivors of the Chancellor. No. 2820, 25r, Keraban the Inflexible. No. 2821, 25r, Family Without a Name, diff. No. 2822, 25r, César Cascabel, diff. No. 2823, 25r, The Lighthouse at the End of the World, diff.

2004, July 29 ***Perf. 13¼x13½***

Sheets of 4, #a-d

2814-2818 A468 Set of 5 37.00 37.00

Souvenir Sheets

2819-2823 A468 Set of 5 19.00 19.00

Marilyn Monroe — A469

2004, Aug. 16 ***Perf. 13½x13¼***

2824 A469 7r multi 1.25 1.25

Printed in sheets of 6.

George Herman "Babe" Ruth (1895-1948), Baseball Player — A470

No. 2826: a, Swinging bat. b, Wearing cap, striped uniform. c, Holding two bats. d, Profile of Ruth.

2004

2825 A470 3r shown .55 .55

2826 A470 10r Sheet of 4, #a-d 6.25 6.25

No. 2825 printed in sheets of 16. World Series, 100th anniv.

Paintings by Salvador Dali (1904-89) — A471

No. 2827: a, The Endless Enigma. b, The Persistence of Memory. c, Soft Construction with Boiled Beans — Premonition of Civil War. d, Still Life — Fast Moving.

25r, Figure on the Rocks.

2004, July 6 **Litho.** ***Perf. 13½***

2827 A471 10r Sheet of 4, #a-d 6.25 6.25

Imperf

2828 A471 25r multi 4.00 4.00

No. 2827 contains four 50x37mm stamps.

2004 Summer Olympics, Athens A472

Designs: 2r, Gold medal, 1904 St. Louis Olympics. 5r, Krater depicting Olympic athletes. 7r, Count Jean de Beaumont, Intl. Olympic Committee member. 12r, Pommel horse, horiz.

2004, Sept. 30 ***Perf. 14¼***

2829-2832 A472 Set of 4 4.25 4.25

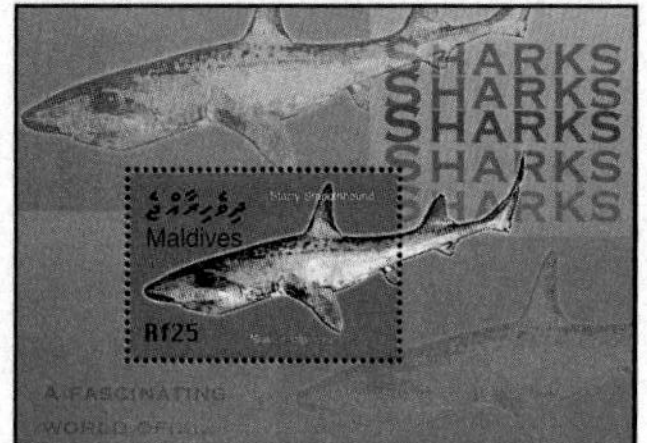

Sharks — A473

No. 2833: a, Silvertip shark. b, Silky shark. c, Great white shark. d, Gray reef shark.

$25, Starry smoothhound shark.

2004, Nov. 4

2833 A473 10r Sheet of 4, #a-d 6.25 6.25

Souvenir Sheet

2834 A473 25r multi 4.00 4.00

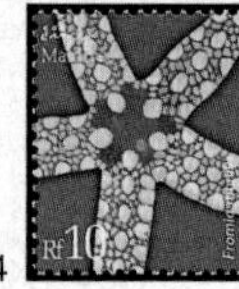

Starfish — A474

Designs: No. 2835, 10r, Fromia monilis (green background). No. 2836, 10r, Linckia laevigata. No. 2837, 10r, Nardoa novaecalidoniae. No. 2838, 10r, Fromia monilis (red background).

2004, Nov. 4 ***Perf. 15x14***

2835-2838 A474 Set of 4 6.25 6.25

Worldwide Fund for Nature (WWF) — A475

No. 2839 — Eurypegasus draconis and: a, Country name at LL, denomination at LR. b, Country name at UL, denomination at LR, dark background. c, Country name at LR, denomination at UL. d, Country name at UL, denomination at LR, light background.

2004, Dec. 15 **Litho.** ***Perf. 14***

2839 A475 7r Block of 4, #a-d 4.50 4.50

e. Miniature sheet, 2 each #2839a-2839d 9.00 9.00

Butterflies — A476

No. 2840, horiz.: a, Red lacewing. b, Amesia sanguiflua. c, Pericallia galactina. d, Limenitis dudu dudu.

25r, Lime butterfly.

2004, Dec. 15

2840 A476 10r Sheet of 4, #a-d 6.25 6.25

Souvenir Sheet

2841 A476 25r multi 4.00 4.00

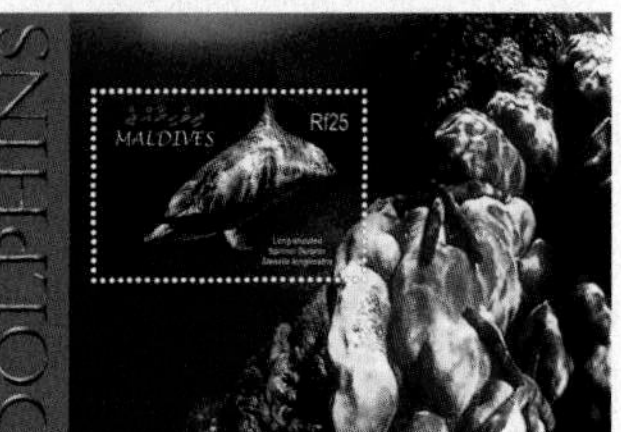

Dolphins — A477

No. 2842: a, Striped dolphin. b, Amazon River dolphin. c, Bottlenose dolphin. d, Spinner dolphin.

25r, Long-snouted spinner dolphin.

2004, Dec. 15 **Litho.** ***Perf. 14***

2842 A477 10r Sheet of 4, #a-d 6.25 6.25

Souvenir Sheet

2843 A477 25r multi 4.00 4.00

Reptiles and Amphibians — A478

No. 2844, horiz.: a, Eyelash pit viper. b, Basilisk lizard. c, Calico snake. d, Maki frog.

25r, Naja melanoleuca.

2004, Dec. 15

2844 A478 10r Sheet of 4, #a-d 6.25 6.25

Souvenir Sheet

2845 A478 25r multi 4.00 4.00

Mushrooms — A479

No. 2846, horiz.: a, Parrot mushroom. b, Hygrocybe miniata. c, Aleuria aurantia. d, Thaxterogaster porphyreum.

25r, Galerina autumnalis.

2004, Dec. 15

2846 A479 10r Sheet of 4, #a-d 6.25 6.25

Souvenir Sheet

2847 A479 25r multi 4.00 4.00

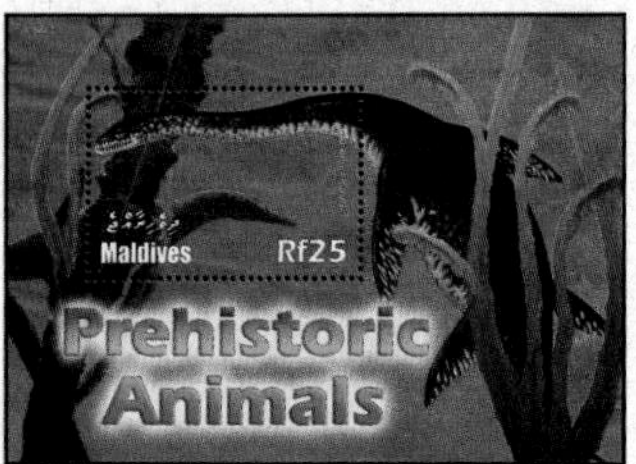

Prehistoric Animals — A480

No. 2848, 10r: a, Macroplata. b, Ichthyosaurus. c, Shonisaurus. d, Archelon.

No. 2849, 10r, vert.: a, Albertosaurus. b, Iguanodon. c, Deinonychus, name at right. d, Baryonyx.
No. 2850, 10r, vert.: a, Deinonychus, name at left. b, Styracosaurus. c, Ornitholestes. d, Euoplocephalus.
No. 2851, 10r, vert.: a, Pterodactylus. b, Cearadactylus. c, Pterosaur. d, Sordes.
No. 2852, 25r, Muraeonosaurus. No. 2853, 25r, Styracosaurus, diff. No. 2854, 25r, Leptoceratops. No. 2855, 25r, Archaeopteryx.

2004, Dec. 15 *Perf. 14*

Sheets of 4, #a-d

2848-2851 A480 Set of 4 25.00 25.00

Souvenir Sheets

2852-2855 A480 Set of 4 16.00 16.00

Souvenir Sheet

Deng Xiaoping (1904-97), Chinese Leader — A481

2005, Jan. 26

2856 A481 25r multi 4.00 4.00

2004 European Soccer Championships, Portugal — A482

No. 2857, vert.: a, Jupp Derwall. b, René Vandereycke. c, Horst Hrubesch. d, Stadio Olimpico.
25r, 1980 Germany team.

2005, Jan. 26 *Perf. 14*

2857 A482 12r Sheet of 4, #a-d 7.50 7.50

Souvenir Sheet

2858 A482 25r multi 4.00 4.00

No. 2857 contains four 28x42mm stamps.

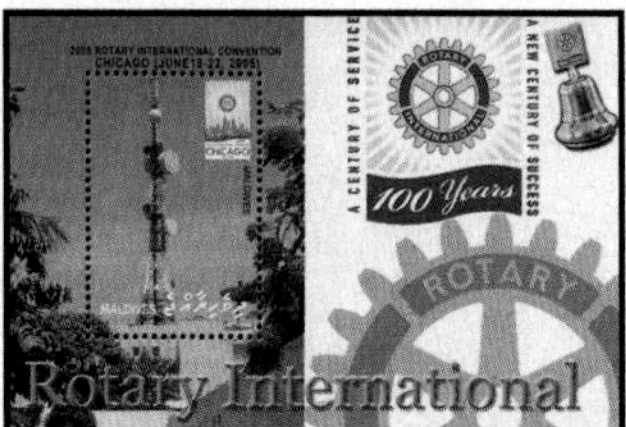

Rotary International, Cent. — A483

No. 2859 — Chicago skyline: a, Part of Sears Tower at R. b, Sears Tower at L. c, CNA Tower (red brick building) at L.
25r, Telecommunications tower.

2005, July 12 **Litho.** *Perf. 12¾*

2859 A483 15r Sheet of 3, #a-c 7.00 7.00

Souvenir Sheet

2860 A483 25r multi 4.00 4.00

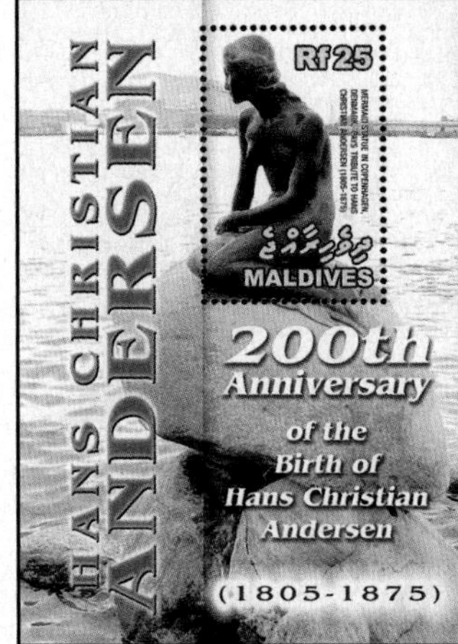

Hans Christian Andersen (1805-75), Author — A484

No. 2861: a, Statue of Andersen wearing hat. b, Photograph of Andersen. c, Statue of Andersen without hat.
25r, Little Mermaid Statue, Copenhagen.

2005, Sept. 20

2861 A484 15r Sheet of 3, #a-c 7.00 7.00

Souvenir Sheet

2862 A484 25r multi 4.00 4.00

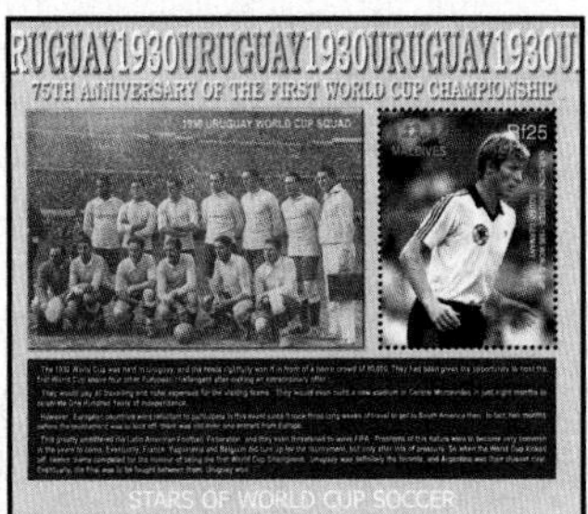

World Cup Soccer Championships, 75th Anniv. — A485

No. 2863: a, Oscar. b, Karl-Heinz Rummenigge. c, Oliver Kahn.
25r, Karlheinz Forster.

2005, Sept. 20 *Perf. 13¼*

2863 A485 15r Sheet of 3, #a-c 7.00 7.00

Souvenir Sheet

Perf. 12¼x12

2864 A485 25r multi 4.00 4.00

Battle of Trafalgar, Bicent. — A486

No. 2865, vert.: a, Admiral Cuthbert Collingwood. b, Napoleon Bonaparte. c, Admiral Horatio Nelson. d, Capt. Thomas Masterman Hardy.
25r, Ships at battle.

2005, Sept. 20 *Perf. 12¾*

2865 A486 10r Sheet of 4, #a-d 7.00 7.00

Souvenir Sheet

2866 A486 25r multi 4.25 4.25

Albert Einstein (1879-1955), Physicist — A487

No. 2867, horiz. — Portraits of Einstein in: a, Red brown (denomination at R). b, Pink & blue (denomination at L). c, Green & pink (denomination at R). d, Brown (denomination at L).
25r, Einstein, diff.

2005, Sept. 20

2867 A487 15r Sheet of 4, #a-d 6.25 6.25

Souvenir Sheet

2868 A487 25r multi 4.00 4.00

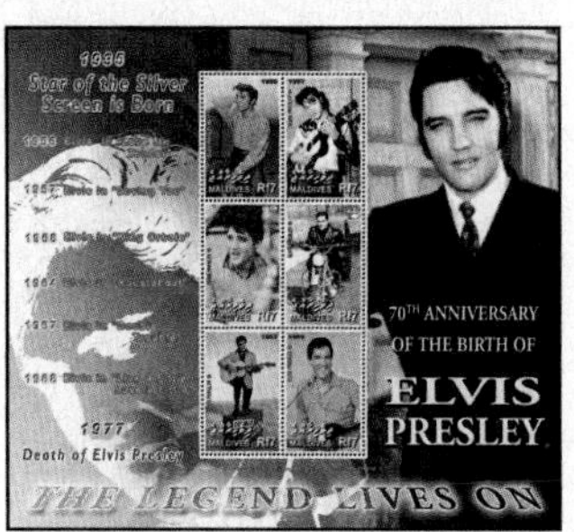

Elvis Presley (1935-77) — A488

No. 2869, 7r — Photographs of Presley from: a, 1956 (sepia). b, 1957. c, 1958. d, 1964. e, 1967. f, 1968.
No. 2870, 7r — Photographs of Presley from: a, 1956 (black and white). b, 1960. c, 1962. d, 1969. e, 1973. f, 1975.

2005, Nov. 15 *Perf. 13¾x13¼*

Sheets of 6, #a-f

2869-2870 A488 Set of 2 13.00 13.00

Elvis Presley (1935-77) — A489

Lihto. & Embossed

2006, Jan. 17 *Die Cut Perf 7½*

Without Gum

2871 A489 85r gold & multi 13.50 13.50

Miniature Sheets

Children's Drawings — A490

No. 2872, 10r — Sea Life: a, Bubbles, by Raquel Bobolia. b, Bubble Fish, by Sarah Bowen. c, Lipfish, by Elsa Fleisher. d, Flounder, by Erica Malchowski.
No. 2873, 10r — Birds: a, Purple Bird, by Anna Badger. b, Parrots, by Nick Abrams. c, Pretty Bird, by Jessie Abrams. d, Royal Parrot, by Ashley Mondfrans.
No. 2874, 10r — Flowers: a, Orange Sunflower, by Brett Walker. b, Red Flower, by Jessica Shutt. c, Flower Pot, by Nick Abrams. d, Blue Flower Vase, by Trevor Nielsen.

2006, Jan. 24 **Litho.** *Perf. 13¼*

Sheets of 4, #a-d

2872-2874 A490 Set of 3 19.00 19.00

Skates and Rays — A491

Designs: 20 l, Himantura uamak. 1r, Manta birostris. 2r, Taeniura lymma. 20r, Aetobatus narinari.

2006, Feb. 27 *Perf. 13¾x14¼*

2875-2878 A491 Set of 4 4.00 4.00

Souvenir Sheet

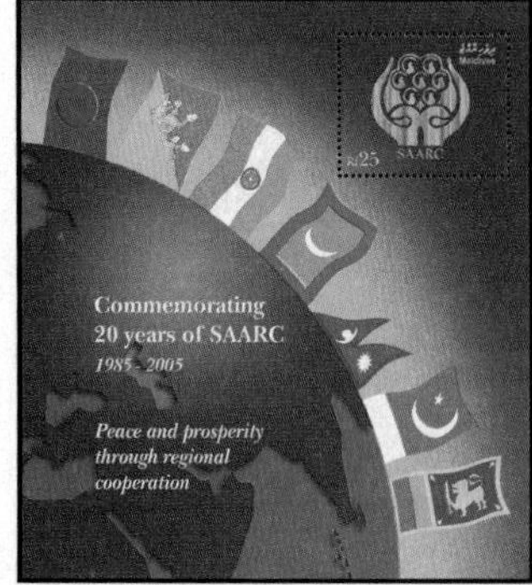

South Asian Association for Regional Cooperation, 20th Anniv. — A492

2006, Mar. 9 *Perf. 13¼*

2879 A492 25r multi 4.00 4.00

2006 Winter Olympics, Turin — A493

Designs: 7r, Norway #B52. 8r, Poster for 1952 Oslo Winter Olympics, vert. 10r, Poster for 1936 Garmisch-Partenkirchen Winter Olympics, vert. 12r, Germany #B79, vert.

2006, May 9 *Perf. 14¼*

2880-2883 A493 Set of 4 5.75 5.75

Miniature Sheet

Wolfgang Amadeus Mozart (1756-91), Composer — A494

No. 2884: a, Portrait in oval frame. b, Mozart looking left. c, Mozart as child. d, Bust.

2006, June 29 *Perf. 12¾*

2884 A494 12r Sheet of 4, #a-d 7.50 7.50

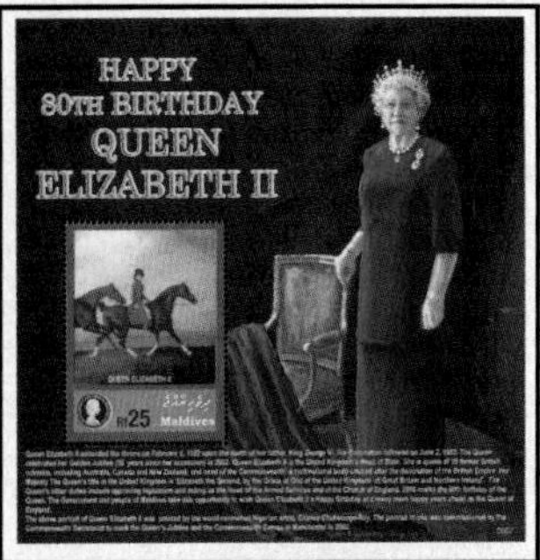

Queen Elizabeth II, 80th Birthday — A495

No. 2885 — Queen and: a, Pres. John F. Kennedy. b, Pres. Ronald Reagan. c, Pres. Gerald R. Ford. d, Pres. George W. Bush.
25r, Portrait of Queen on horse by Chinwe Chukwuogo-Roy.

2006 *Perf. 14¼*
2885 A495 15r Sheet of 4, #a-d 9.50 9.50

Souvenir Sheet

2886 A495 25r multi 4.00 4.00

Souvenir Sheet

Maldive Islands Postal Service, Cent. — A496

2006, Nov. 1 Litho. *Perf. 12½*
2887 A496 12r multi 1.90 1.90

Souvenir Sheet

Ludwig Durr (1878-1956), Zeppelin Engineer — A497

No. 2888 — Durr and: a, Zeppelin over Frankfurt. b, Balloons and Festhalle, Frankfurt. c, Hindenburg.

2006, Nov. 15 *Perf. 13¼*
2888 A497 15r Sheet of 3, #a-c 7.00 7.00

Fish — A498

Designs: No. 2889, 10r, Dascyllus aruanus. No. 2890, 10r, Balistoides conspicillum. No. 2891, 10r, Pomacanthus imperator. No. 2892, 10r, Chaetodon meyeri.

2006, Nov. 1 Litho. *Perf. 12¾*
2889-2892 A498 Set of 4 6.25 6.25

Miniature Sheet

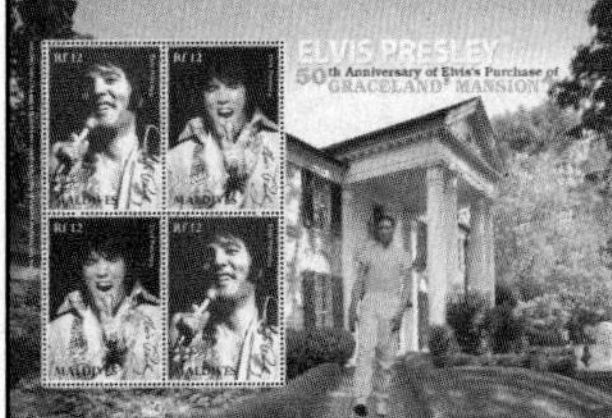

Elvis Presley (1935-77) — A499

No. 2893 — Presley with: a, Microphone at left, denomination in pink. b, Microphone at center, denomination in white. c, Microphone at center, denomination in light blue. d, Microphone at left, denomination in light green.

2006, Nov. 15 *Perf. 13¼*
2893 A499 12r Sheet of 4, #a-d 7.50 7.50

Space Achievements — A500

No. 2894: a, R-7 missile (Sputnik 1 launcher). b, Sputnik 1. c, Inside Sputnik 1. d, Sputnik 2. e, Map of Earth showing Sputnik 1 orbits. f, Sputnik 3.
No. 2895, 12r: a, Calipso satellite. b, Cloud-Sat satellite. c, Aqua satellite. d, Aura satellite.
No. 2896, 12r: a, Nucleus of Halley's Comet. b, Halley's Comet. c, Giotto Space Probe. d, Close-up image of Halley's Comet taken by Giotto.
No. 2897, 25r, Apollo spacecraft. No. 2898, 25r, Giotto. No. 2899, 25r, Stardust satellite.

2006, Nov. 15 *Perf. 13¼*
2894 A500 8r Sheet of 6, #a-f 7.50 7.50

Sheets of 4, #a-d

2895-2896 A500 Set of 2 15.00 15.00

Souvenir Sheets

2897-2899 A500 Set of 3 12.00 12.00

Nos. 2894-2899 exist imperf. Value, set $75.

Birds A501

Designs: 1r, Bar-tailed godwit. 2r, Black-headed gull. No. 2902, 10r, Masked booby, vert. 20r, Kentish plover.
No. 2904, 10r: a, Common swifts. b, Sooty tern. c, Yellow wagtail. d, House sparrow.
No. 2905, 10r: a, Tufted duck. b, Caspian tern. c, Southern giant petrel. d, Glossy ibis.
No. 2906, 30r, Purple herons. No. 2907, 30r, Osprey, vert. No. 2908, 30r, Golden-throated barbet, vert.

2007, Feb. 8 *Perf. 14*
2900-2903 A501 Set of 4 5.25 5.25

Sheets of 4, #a-d

2904-2905 A501 Set of 2 12.50 12.50

Souvenir Sheets

2906-2908 A501 Set of 3 14.00 14.00

Fish A502

Designs: 1r, Ragged-finned lionfish. 2r, Vlaming's unicornfish. No. 2911, 10r, White-spotted grouper. 20r, Maldive anemonefish.
No. 2913, 10r: a, Bicolor parrotfish. b, Blue-barred parrotfish. c, Bullethead parrotfish. d, Dusky parrotfish.
No. 2914, 10r: a, Imperial angelfish. b, Clown triggerfish. c, Black-saddled coral trout. d, Slender grouper.
No. 2915, 30r, Shadow soldierfish. No. 2916, 30r, Picasso triggerfish. No. 2917, 30r, Blue-faced angelfish.

2007, Feb. 8
2909-2912 A502 Set of 4 5.25 5.25

Sheets of 4, #a-d

2913-2914 A502 Set of 2 12.50 12.50

Souvenir Sheets

2915-2917 A502 Set of 3 14.00 14.00

Flowers A503

Designs: 1r, Ranunculus eschscholtzii. 2r, Ratibida columnaris. No. 2920, 10r, Mentzelia laevicaulis. 20r, Clintonia unifloria.
No. 2922, 10r: a, Machaeranthera tanacetifolia. b, Aquilegia coerulea. c, Gentiana detonsa. d, Linum perenne.
No. 2923, 10r: a, Ipomopsis aggregata. b, Rosa woodsii. c, Lewisia rediviva. d, Penstemon rydbergii.
No. 2924, 30r, Ipomoea purpurea. No. 2925, 30r, Encelia farinosa. No. 2926, 30r, Epilobium angustifolium.

2007, Feb. 8
2918-2921 A503 Set of 4 5.25 5.25

Sheets of 4, #a-d

2922-2923 A503 Set of 2 12.50 12.50

Souvenir Sheets

2924-2926 A503 Set of 3 14.00 14.00

Orchids — A504

Designs: 1r, Dendrobium formosum. 2r, Bulbophyllum Elizabeth Ann. No. 2929, 10r, Dendrobium bigibbum. 20r, Spathoglottis gracilis.
No. 2931, 10r: a, Bulbophyllum lasiochilum. b, Phaius Microburst. c, Coelogyne mooreana. d, Bulbophyllum nasseri.
No. 2932, 10r: a, Cymbidium erythrostylum. b, Phaius humboldtii x Phaius tuberculosis. c, Dendrobium farmeri. d, Dendrobium junceum.
No. 2933, 30r, Coelogyne cristata, horiz. No. 2934, 30r, Bulbophyllum graveolens, horiz. No. 2935, 30r, Dendrobium crocatum.

2007, Feb. 8
2927-2930 A504 Set of 4 5.25 5.25

Sheets of 4, #a-d

2931-2932 A504 Set of 2 12.50 12.50

Souvenir Sheets

2933-2935 A504 Set of 3 14.00 14.00

Scouting, Cent. A505

2007, Feb. 21 *Perf. 13¼*

Color of Denomination

2936 A505 15r purple 2.40 2.40

Souvenir Sheet

2937 A505 25r blue 4.00 4.00

No. 2936 was printed in sheets of 3.

Intl. Polar Year — A506

No. 2938 — King penguins with background color of: a, Light blue. b, Lilac. c, Yellow green. d, Blue green. e, Red violet. f, Green.
25r, African penguin with party hat.

2007, May 1 Litho. *Perf. 13¼*
2938 A506 12r Sheet of 6, #a-f 11.50 11.50

Souvenir Sheet

2939 A506 25r multi 4.00 4.00

Miniature Sheet

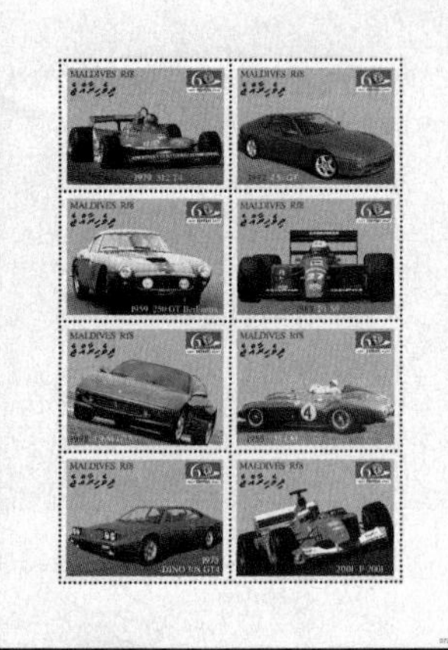

Ferrari Automobiles, 60th Anniv. — A507

No. 2940: a, 1979 312 T4. b, 1992 456 GT. c, 1959 250 GT Berlinetta. d, 1989 F1 89. e, 1998 456M GTA. f, 1955 735 LM. g, 1973 Dino 308 GT4. h, 2001 F 2001.

2007, Aug. 12
2940 A507 8r Sheet of 8, #a-h 10.00 10.00

Princess Diana (1961-97) — A508

No. 2941 — Diana with white hat and: a, Gray jacket, close-up. b, Green dress, close-up. c, White striped jacket, close-up. d, Green dress. e, White striped jacket. f, Gray jacket.
25r, Black and white jacket.

2007, Aug. 12
2941 A508 8r Sheet of 6, #a-f 7.50 7.50

Souvenir Sheet

2942 A508 25r multi 4.00 4.00

Fish — A509

Designs: 10 l, Chaetodon triangulum. 50 l, Chaetodon kleinii. 12r, Chaetodon trifasciatus. 15r, Chaetodon madagascariensis. 20r, Chaetodon lunula.

2007, Oct. 9 Litho. ***Perf. 13¼***
2943-2947 A509 Set of 5 7.50 7.50

2008 Summer Olympics, Beijing — A510

No. 2948: a, Rie Mastenbroek, swimming gold medalist, 1936. b, Poster for 1936 Summer Olympics. c, Jesse Owens, long jump gold medalist, 1936. d, Jack Beresford, rowing gold medalist, 1936.

2008, Jan. 8 Litho. ***Perf. 13¼***
2948 Horiz. strip of 4 4.50 4.50
a.-d. A510 7r Any single 1.10 1.10
e. Souvenir sheet, #2948a-2948d 4.50 4.50

Miniature Sheet

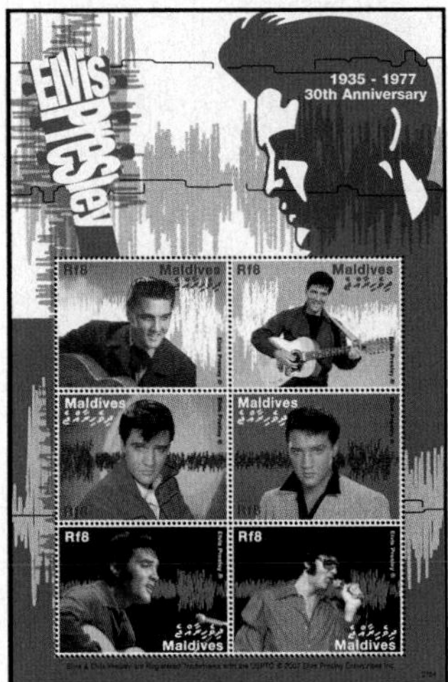

Elvis Presley (1935-77) — A511

No. 2949 — Presley wearing: a, Brown jacket. b, Blue shirt, holding guitar. c, Red jacket and white shirt. d, Gray jacket and black shirt. e, Blue shirt, holding guitar behind microphone. f, Red shirt, holding microphone.

2008, Jan. 8 Litho. ***Perf. 13¼***
2949 A511 8r Sheet of 6, #a-f 7.50 7.50

America's Cup Yachting Championships — A512

No. 2950 — Various yachts with panel colors of: a, Yellow orange. b, Red. c, Dark blue. d, Blue green.

2008, Jan. 8
2950 Strip of 4 9.25 9.25
a. A512 10r multi 1.60 1.60
b. A512 12r multi 1.90 1.90
c. A512 15r multi 2.40 2.40
d. A512 20r multi 3.25 3.25

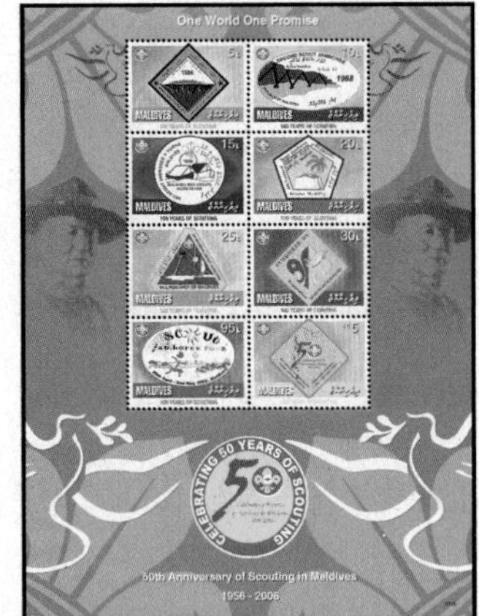

Scouting In Maldive Islands, 50th Anniv. — A513

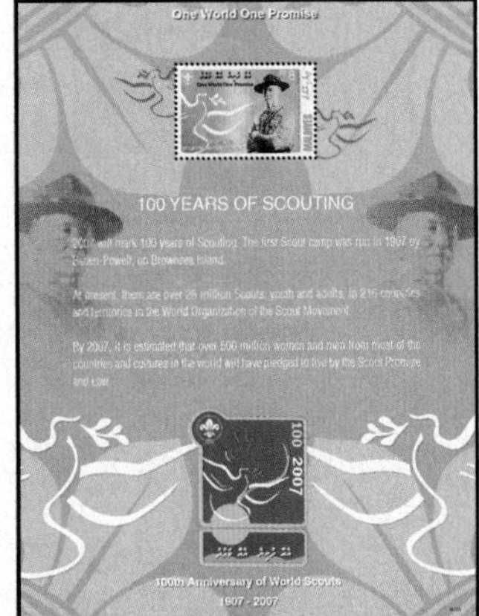

Scouting, Cent. (in 2007) — A514

No. 2951 — Emblems of national jamborees from: a, 5 l, 1986. b, 10 l, 1988. c, 15 l, 1990. d, 20 l, 1992. e, 25 l, 1995. f, 30 l, 1998. g, 95 l, 2002. h, 5r, 2007.

2008, Feb. 19
2951 A513 Sheet of 8, #a-h 1.10 1.10

Souvenir Sheet

2952 A514 8r multi 1.25 1.25

Miniature Sheet

Intl. Day for the Preservation of the Ozone Layer — A515

No. 2953 — Various "Save the Ozone Layer" posters by Maldivian students: a, 5r. b, 12r. c, 15r. d, 18r.

2008, Sept. 10 Litho. ***Perf. 12½***
2953 A515 Sheet of 4, #a-d 8.00 8.00

Miniature Sheet

Elvis Presley (1935-77) — A516

No. 2954 — Presley: a, Playing guitar. b, With hand in foreground at right. c, Singing, with legs shown. d, Facing right, holding microphone. e, Singing, with microphone at left. f, Beside car, wearing hat.

2008, Sept. 11 ***Perf. 13¼***
2954 A516 8r Sheet of 6, #a-f 7.50 7.50

Miniature Sheet

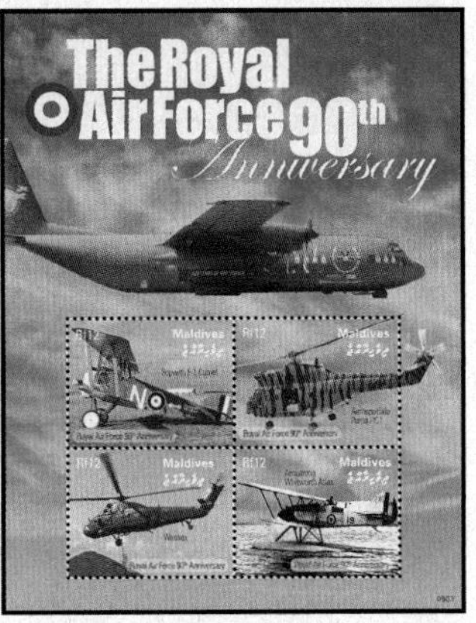

Royal Air Force, 90th Anniv. — A517

No. 2955: a, Sopwith F-1 Camel. b, Aerospatiale Puma HC1 helicopter. c, Wessex helicopter. d, Armstrong Whitworth Atlas.

2008, Sept. 11 ***Perf. 11½***
2955 A517 12r Sheet of 4, #a-d 7.50 7.50

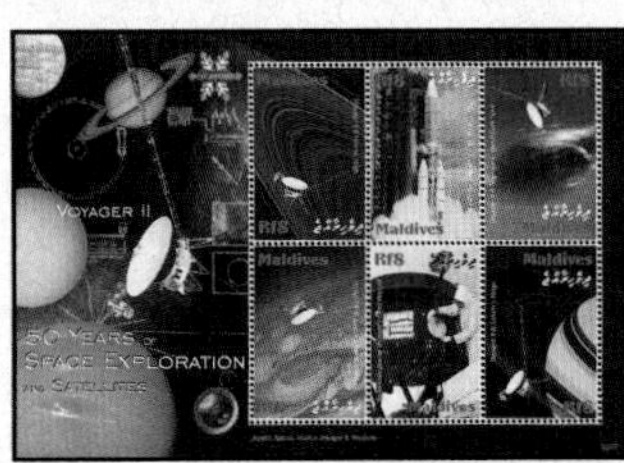

A518

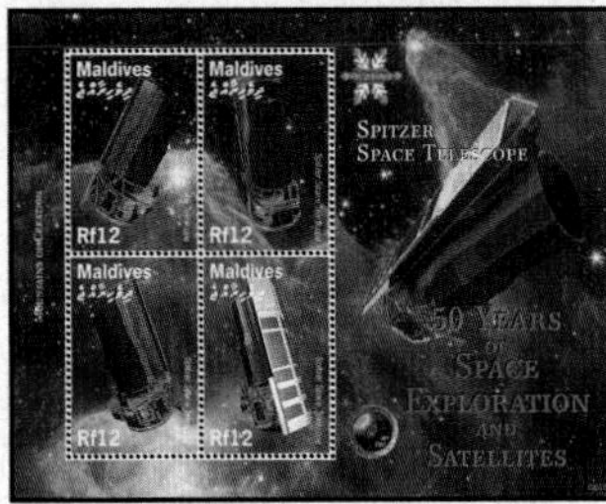

Space Exploration, 50th Anniv. (in 2007) — A519

No. 2956: a, Voyager 2 and rings of Uranus. b, Titan 3E Centaur rocket launching Voyager 2. c, Voyager 2 and Neptune's Great Dark Spot. d, Voyager 2 and Jupiter's Great Red Spot. e, Technician placing gold record into Voyager 2. f, Voyager 2 and rings of Saturn.

No. 2957, 12r — Spitzer Space Telescope: a, Top of telescope pointing to UR corner. b, Top of telescope pointing to top margin. c, Top of telescope pointing to UL corner. d, Solar panels of telescope shown.

No. 2958, 12r — Sputnik 1: a, With black background, denomination at LL. b, With orange background. c, And technician. d, With Moon in background.

No. 2959, 12r — Explorer 1: a, Atop Juno 1 rocket. b, With Earth in background. c, With clouds in background. d, And Dr. James Van Allen.

No. 2960, 12r — Vanguard 1: a, With Earth at top. b, And technicians. c, And rocket. d, With Earth at bottom.

2008, Sept. 11 ***Perf. 13¼***
2956 A518 8r Sheet of 6, #a-f 7.50 7.50

Sheets of 4, #a-d

2957-2960 A519 Set of 4 30.00 30.00

Miniature Sheets

End of World War I, 90th Anniv. — A520

No. 2961, 12r: a, Soldiers in trench. b, Two soldiers resting in trench. c, Two soldiers aiming guns in trench. d, Soldier carrying wounded soldier.

No. 2962, 12r, horiz.: a, Soldiers on motorcycles. b, Soldiers moving up hill. c, Tank. d, Two soldiers in machine gun nest.

Perf. 11¼x11½, 11½x11¼
2008, Nov. 11 Litho.

Sheets of 4, #a-d

2961-2962 A520 Set of 2 15.00 15.00

Inauguration of U.S. Pres. Barack Obama — A521

No. 2963, 10r, vert.: a, Pres. Obama waving. b, Obama with dark blue striped tie, facing right. c, First Lady Michelle Obama. d, Obama with red striped tie. e, Michelle Obama clapping. f, Obama with light blue tie.

30r, Couple.

2009, Jan. 20 ***Perf. 11¼x11½***
2963 A521 10r Sheet of 6, #a-f 9.50 9.50

Souvenir Sheet

Perf. 13¼

2964 A521 30r multi 4.75 4.75

No. 2963 contains six 30x40mm stamps.

Miniature Sheet

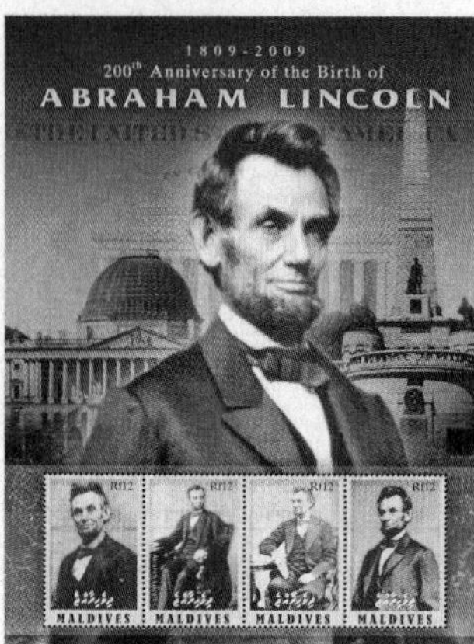

U.S. Pres. Abraham Lincoln (1809-65) — A522

No. 2965 — Reverse of U.S. $5 banknote and Lincoln: a, Standing, no suit buttons visible. b, Seated, with hand on arm of chair. c, Seated, holding paper. d, Standing, with suit buttons visible.

2009, Feb. 12 ***Perf. 13¼***
2965 A522 12r Sheet of 4, #a-d 7.50 7.50

Fish A523

Designs: No. 2966, 12r, Black-saddled coral grouper. No. 2967, 12r, Peacock hind. No. 2968, 12r, Four-saddle grouper. No. 2969, 12r, Six-blotch hind.

2009, Sept. 24 **Litho.** ***Perf. 13¼***
2966-2969 A523 Set of 4 7.50 7.50

Miniature Sheet

Visit of Prince Harry to New York — A524

No. 2970: a, At official naming of the British Garden. b, At World Trade Center site. c, Head of Prince Harry. d, Playing polo.

2009, Sept. 29 ***Perf. 11½***
2970 A524 12r Sheet of 4, #a-d 7.50 7.50

Miniature Sheets

A525

Star Trek Characters — A526

No. 2971: a, Fleet crew. b, Lt. Uhura. c, Mr. Spock. d, Dr. McCoy.
No. 2972: a, Scotty. b, Dr. McCoy, diff. c, Captain Kirk. d, Mr. Spock, diff.

2009, Sept. 29 ***Perf. 13¼***
2971 A525 12r Sheet of 4, #a-d 7.50 7.50
2972 A526 12r Sheet of 4, #a-d 7.50 7.50

Miniature Sheet

Marilyn Monroe (1926-62), Actress — A527

No. 2973: a, Face. b, In car. c, Wearing patterned blouse, in room. d, With hand near chin.

2009, Oct. 21 ***Perf. 12½x12¾***
2973 A527 16r Sheet of 4, #a-d 10.00 10.00

Whales — A528

Designs: 10 l, Beluga whale. No. 2975, 12r, Hector's beaked whale. 16r, Beaked whale. 18r, Baird's beaked whale.
No. 2978, 12r, horiz.: a, Dwarf sperm whale. b, Pygmy sperm whale. c, Baird's beaked whale, diff. d, Sperm whale. e, Shepherd's beaked whale. f, Cuvier's beaked whale.

2009, Oct. 21 ***Perf. 12½***
2974-2977 A528 Set of 4 7.25 7.25
2978 A528 12r Sheet of 6, #a-f 11.50 11.50

Butterflies A529

Designs: 10 l, Crimson rose. 16r, Common Mormon. 18r, Common jay. 20r, Common tiger.
No. 2983, horiz.: a, Small salmon Arab. b, Lemon pansy. c, Tamil yeoman. d, Dark blue tiger.
No. 2984: a, Common jezebel. b, Common gull.

2009, Oct. 21 ***Perf. 12½***
2979-2982 A529 Set of 4 8.50 8.50

Perf. 12

2983 A529 12r Sheet of 4, #a-d 7.50 7.50

Souvenir Sheet

2984 A529 15r Sheet of 2, #a-b 4.75 4.75

Chinese Aviation, Cent. — A530

No. 2985 — Airplanes: a, Y-5. b, Y-7. c, Y-8. d, Y-12
25r, MA60.

2009, Nov. 12 **Litho.** ***Perf. 14¼***
2985 A530 9r Sheet of 4, #a-d 5.75 5.75

Souvenir Sheet

2986 A530 25r multi 4.00 4.00

Aeropex 2009, Beijing. No. 2985 contains four 42x28mm stamps.

Worldwide Fund for Nature (WWF) — A531

No. 2987 — Melon-headed whale: a, Pod of whales underwater. b, Pod of whales at surface, swimming right. c, Whale. d, Pod of whales at surface, swimming left.

2009, Nov. 18 ***Perf. 13¼***
2987 Block or strip of 4 5.00 5.00
a.-d. A531 8r Any single 1.25 1.25
e. Sheet of 8, 2 each #2987a-2987d 10.00 10.00

First Man on the Moon, 40th Anniv. — A532

No. 2988, vert.: a, Apollo 11 Command and Service Modules. b, Apollo 11 Command, Service and Lunar Modules. c, Neil Armstrong. d, Apollo 11 Lunar Module.
30r, Crew of Apollo 11.

2009, July 20 **Litho.** ***Perf. 13¼***
2988 A532 12r Sheet of 4, #a-d 7.50 7.50

Souvenir Sheet

2989 A532 30r multi 4.75 4.75

Intl. Year of Astronomy.

Miniature Sheets

A533

Mushrooms — A534

No. 2990: a, Copelandia bispora. b, Copelandia cyanescens. c, Psilocybe semilanceata. d, Volvariella volvacea.
No. 2991: Various unnamed mushrooms.

2009, Nov. 18 ***Perf. 11½***
2990 A533 8r Sheet of 4, #a-d 5.00 5.00
2991 A534 8r Sheet of 6, #a-f 7.50 7.50

Flowers — A535

No. 2992: a, Nelumbo nucifera. b, Rosa bracteata. c, Freycinetia cumingiata. d, Thespesia lampas. e, Plumeria champa. f, Plumeria cubensis.
No. 2993: a, Lagerstroemia speciosa. b, Plumeria alba.
No. 2994: a, Plumeria rubra. b, Hibiscus tiliaceus.

2009, Dec. 9
2992 A535 10r Sheet of 6, #a-f 9.50 9.50

Souvenir Sheets

2993 A535 15r Sheet of 2, #a-b 4.75 4.75
2994 A535 15r Sheet of 2, #a-b 4.75 4.75

Souvenir Sheet

New Year 2010 (Year of the Tiger) — A536

No. 2995: a, Chinese characters. b, Tiger.

2010, Jan. 4 **Litho.** ***Perf. 12***
2995 A536 25r Sheet of 2, #a-b 8.00 8.00

Shells — A537

Designs: 10 l, Conus abbas. 12r, Conus amadis. 16r, Conus bengalensis. 18r, Pinctada margaritifera.
No. 3000: a, Harpa costata. b, Phalium fimbria. c, Zoila friendii friendii. d, Cyprae leucodon tenuidon.

2010, June 22 ***Perf. 11¼x11½***
2996-2999 A537 Set of 4 7.25 7.25

Perf. 12x11½

3000 A537 15r Sheet of 4, #a-d 9.50 9.50

Miniature Sheets

Election of Pres. John F. Kennedy, 50th Anniv. — A538

No. 3001, 15r: a, Pres. Kennedy at lectern. b, Pulitzer Prize medal. c, Civil Rights Act of 1964. d, Peace Corps emblem.
No. 3002, 15r: a, Vice-president Lyndon B. Johnson. b, Pres. Kennedy. c, Brochures for 1960 presidential election. d, Campaign placard.

2010, June 22 ***Perf. 13¼***

Sheets of 4, #a-d

3001-3002 A538 Set of 2 19.00 19.00

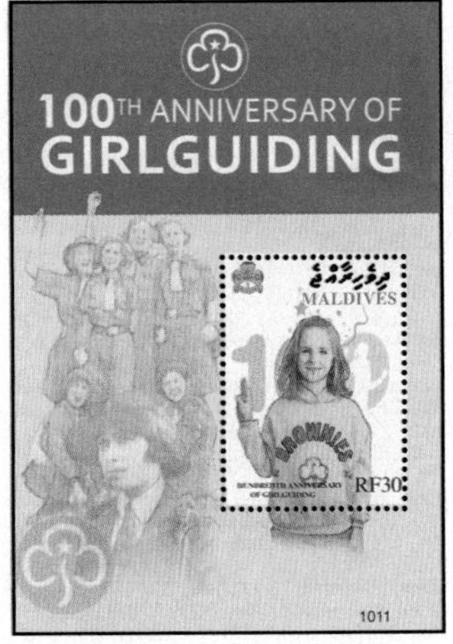

Girl Guides, Cent. — A539

No. 3003, horiz.: a, Three Girl Guides. b, Two Girl Guides, "100." c, Girl Guide climbing rock. d, Two Girl Guides jumping.
30r, Brownie.

2010, June 22 ***Perf. 13x13¼***

3003 A539 16r Sheet of 4, #a-d 10.00 10.00

Souvenir Sheet

Perf. 13¼x13

3004 A539 30r multi 4.75 4.75

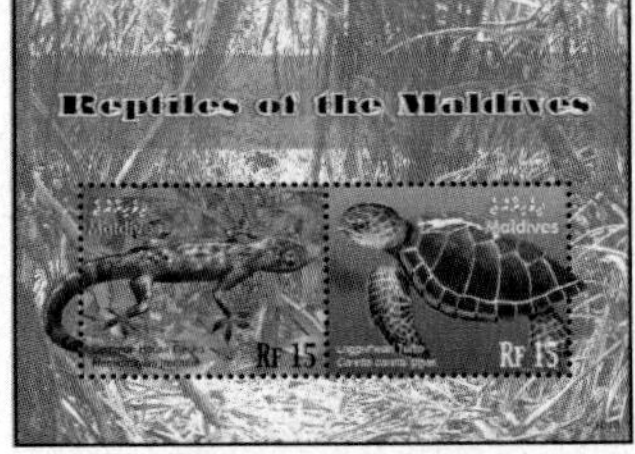

Reptiles — A540

No. 3005: a, Olive ridley turtle. b, Blood sucker lizard. c, Indian wolf snake. d, Green turtle.
No. 3006: a, Common house gecko. b, Loggerhead turtle.

2010, June 22 ***Perf. 11½***

3005 A540 15r Sheet of 4, #a-d 9.50 9.50

Souvenir Sheet

Perf. 11½x12

3006 A540 15r Sheet of 2, #a-b 4.75 4.75

Birds — A541

No. 3007, horiz.: a, White-tailed tropicbird. b, Common tern. c, Bar-tailed godwit. d, Crab plover. e, Whimbrel. f, Black-winged stilt.
30r, Asian koel.

2010, June 22 ***Perf. 11½x12***

3007 A541 8r Sheet of 6, #a-f 7.50 7.50

Souvenir Sheet

Perf. 11¼x11½

3008 A541 30r multi 4.75 4.75

Souvenir Sheets

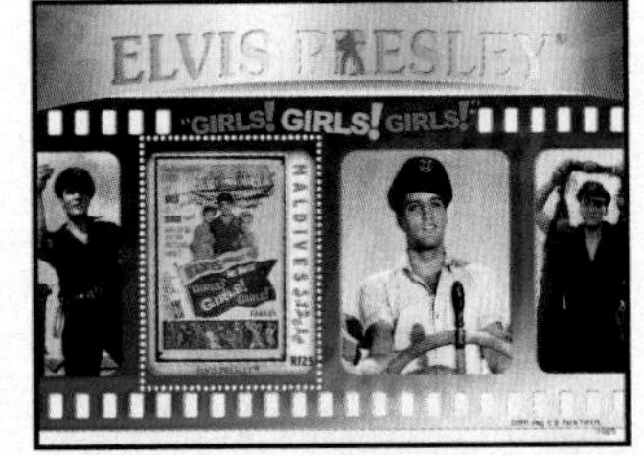

A542

A543

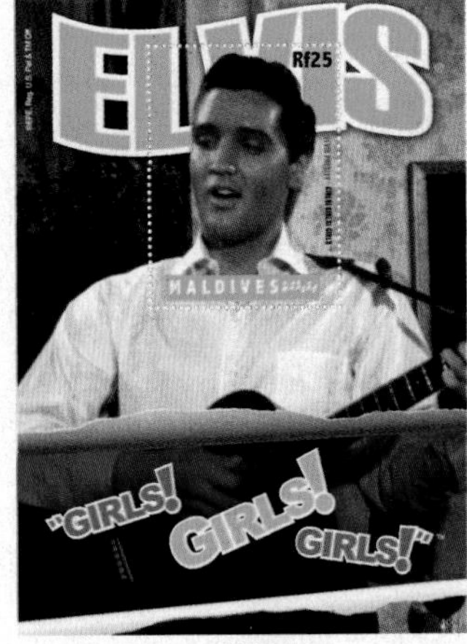

A544

Elvis Presley (1935-77) — A545

2010, June 22 ***Perf. 13½***

3009 A542 25r multi 4.00 4.00
3010 A543 25r multi 4.00 4.00
3011 A544 25r multi 4.00 4.00
3012 A545 25r multi 4.00 4.00
Nos. 3009-3012 (4) 16.00 16.00

Muhammad Ali's Boxing Gold Medal in 1960 Summer Olympics, 50th Anniv. — A596

No. 3013 — Ali: a, Black-and-white photo. b, Sepia photo.
No. 3014 — Silhouette of Ali and photo of Ali: a, Wearing gold medal, country name at top. b, Throwing punch, country name at top. c, As "b," country name at bottom. d, As "a," country name at bottom.

2010, June 22 Litho. ***Perf. 12x11½***

3013 A596 15r Vert. pair, #a-b 4.75 4.75
3014 A596 15r Sheet of 4, #a-d 9.50 9.50

Souvenir Sheet

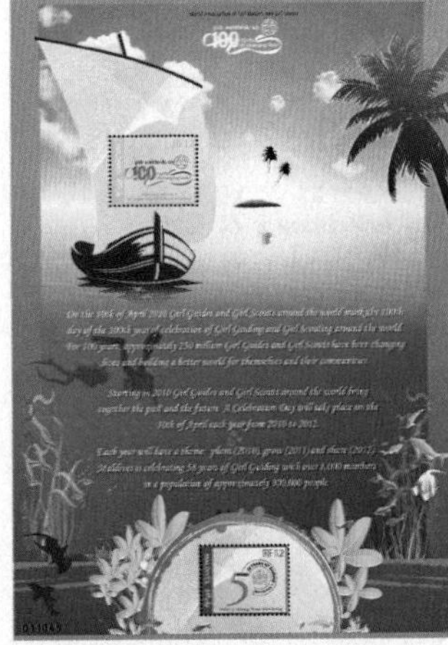

Girl Guides, Cent. — A597

No. 3015: a, Girl Guides emblem and centenary text. b, Maldives Girl Guides 50th anniversary emblem.

2010, June 22 ***Perf. 11¾x12¼***

3015 A597 12r Sheet of 2, #a-b 3.75 3.75

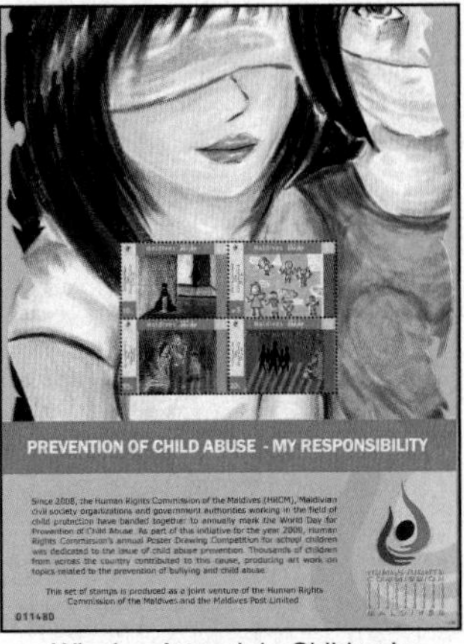

Winning Artwork in Children's Prevention of Child Abuse Stamp Design Contest — A598

No. 3016 — Art by: a, 10 l, Aishath Shamha Nizam. b, 20 l, Shaulaan Shafeeq. c, 95 l, Sameen Moosa. d, 5r, Zaha Mohamed Ziyad.
No. 3017, vert. — Art by: a, 25 l, Emau Ahmed Saleem. b, 50 l, Rishwan Naseem. c, 1r, Ahmed Nafiu. d, 2r, Sam'aan Abdul Raheem. e, 3r, Ummu Haanee Hussain. f, 4r, Fathimath Shaufa Easa. g, 6r, Hussain Hazim. h, 7r, Fathimath Afaaf Bushree.

2010, June 22 ***Perf. 13¼***

3016 A598 Sheet of 4, #a-d 1.00 1.00
3017 A598 Sheet of 8, #a-h 3.75 3.75

Miniature Sheet

Chinese Zodiac Animals — A599

No. 3018: a, Rat. b, Ox. c, Tiger. d, Rabbit. e, Dragon. f, Snake. g, Horse. h, Ram. i, Monkey. j, Rooster. k, Dog. l, Pig.

2010, Jan. 4

3018 A599 3r Sheet of 12, #a-l 5.75 5.75

Souvenir Sheet

New Year 2010 (Year of the Rabbit) — A600

2010, June 22 ***Perf. 12***

3019 A600 19r Sheet of 2 6.00 6.00
a. Single stamp 3.00 3.00

Diplomatic Relations Between the Maldive Islands and People's Republic of China, 40th Anniv. — A601

No. 3020: a, Dhoni. b, Treasure boat of Admiral Zheng He. c, Lacquerware. d, Hornless dragon vase. e, Hawksbill turtle. f, Chinese sturgeon.

2012 Litho. *Perf. 12*

3020 A601 40r Block of 6, #a-f 31.00 31.00
g. Souvenir sheet of 6, #3020a-3020f 31.00 31.00

Worldwide Fund for Nature (WWF) A602

Amaurornis phoenicurus: Nos. 3021a, 3022d, Single bird in flight. Nos. 3021b, 3022a, Single bird at water's edge. Nos. 3021c, 3022b, Two birds. Nos. 3021d, 3022c, Adult bird and chicks.

70r, Amaurornis phoenicurus and flower.

2013, Sept. 30 Litho. *Perf. 13x13¼*

Stamp Size: 40x30mm

3021 Horiz. strip of 4 12.00 12.00
a.-d. A602 22r Any single 3.00 3.00
e. Souvenir sheet of 8, 2 each #3021a-3021d, + central label 24.00 24.00

Miniature Sheet

Stamp Size: 47x37mm

Perf. 13¼

3022 A602 22r Sheet of 4, #a-d 12.00 12.00

Souvenir Sheet

3023 A602 70r multi 9.25 9.25

Wildlife of the Indian Ocean — A603

No. 3024, 20r — Seals: a, Arctocephalus pusillus. b, Arctocephalus forsteri. c, Neophoca cinerea. d, Arctocephalus tropicalis.

No. 3025, 20r — Dugong dugon: a, Three dugongs facing right. b, One dugong facing left. c, One dugong facing right. d, Three dugongs facing left.

No. 3026, 20r — Whales: a, Caperea marginata. b, Indopacetus pacificus. c, Balaenoptera edeni. d, Balaenoptera physalus.

No. 3027, 20r — Starfish: a, Fromia indica, Pentaceraster cumingi. b, Astropecten aranciacus, Asterias rubens. c, Protoreaster linckii, Choriaster granulatus. d, Two Protoreaster nodosus.

No. 3028, 22r — Dolphins: a, Tursiops truncatus above water, facing right. b, Tursiops truncatus above water, facing left. c, Tursiops truncatus underwater, facing right. d, Tursiops aduncus.

No. 3029, 22r — Birds: a, Sula leucogaster. b, Fregata ariel. c, Sula sula. d, Puffinus carneipes.

No. 3030, 22r — Fish: a, Nemateleotris decora. b, Forcipiger flavissimus. c, Odonus niger. d, Oxycirrhites typus.

No. 3031, 22r — Shells: a, Phalium areola. b, Cypraea cribraria. c, Conus vexillum. d, Strombus sinuatus.

No. 3032, 22r — Turtles: a, Caretta caretta. b, Dermochelys coriacea. c, Eretmochelys imbricata. d, Chelonia mydas.

No. 3033, 60r, Neophoca cinerea, diff. No. 3034, 60r, Dugong dugon facing left, diff. No. 3035, 60r, Balaenoptera musculus. No. 3036, 60r, Iconaster longimanus, Fromia monilis. No. 3037, 70r, Tursiops truncatus, diff. No. 3038, 70r, Pelecanus onocrotalus. No. 3039, 70r, Chaetodon auriga. No. 3040, 70r, Melo aethiopicus. No. 3041, 70r, Dermochelys coriacea, diff.

2013, Sept. 30 Litho. *Perf. 13¼*

Sheets of 4, #a-d

3024-3032 A603 Set of 9 100.00 100.00

Souvenir Sheets

3033-3041 A603 Set of 9 77.50 77.50

Fauna and Flora — A604

No. 3042, 20r — Fruit bats: a, Pteropus giganteus ariel, bat in flight at left. b, Pteropus giganteus ariel, bat hanging at left. c, Pteropus hypomelanus maris, bat hanging at left. d, Pteropus hypomelanus maris, bat flying at left.

No. 3043, 20r — Protected marine species: a, Rhincodon typus. b, Chelonia mydas. c, Charonia variegata. d, Cheilinus undulatus.

No. 3044, 20r — Water birds: a, Pelecanus onocrotalus. b, Gallinago stenura. c, Anous stolida. d, Anas clypeata.

No. 3045, 20r — Lizards: a, Hemidactylus frenatus, climbing. b, Calotes versicolor, facing left. c, Calotes versicolor, facing right. d, Hemidactylus frenatus, with eggs.

No. 3046, 20r — Crocdylus porosus: a, Crocodile at left with head turning right, crocodile at right with open mouth. b, Crocodile at left with head turning right and with mouth open, crocodile at right facing forward. c, Crocodile at left with head turning left, crocodile at right with mouth open. d, Crocodiles at left and right facing forward.

No. 3047, 22r — Orchids: a, Orchis mascula. b, Cattleya coccinea. c, Dendrobium crumenatum. d, Phalaenopsis cultivar.

No. 3048, 22r — Asio flammeus: a, Owl at left flying to left. b, Owl at left flying to right. c, Owl at left flying to right, vine in background. d, Owl at left flying over water to left.

No. 3049, 22r — Birds of prey: a, Asio flammeus, bird at left on branch. b, Falco subbuteo. c, Buteo buteo. d, Circus aeruginosus.

No. 3050, 22r — Tropical butterflies: a, Sasakia charonda. b, Graphium sarpedon luctatius. c, Evenus regalis. d, Godyris duilia.

No. 3051, 22r — Fish: a, Chaetodon benetti. b, Manata birostris. c, Carcharhinus amblyrhynchos. d, Zanclus cornutus.

No. 3052, 60r, Pteropus giganteus ariel, diff. No. 3053, 60r, Myrichthys colubrinus. No. 3054, 60r, Philomachus pugnax. No. 3055, 60r, Calotes versicolor, diff. No. 3056, 70r, Crocodylus porosus, diff. No. 3057, 70r, Orchis mascula, diff. No. 3058, 70r, Asio flammeus, diff. No. 3059, 70r, Pandion haliaetus. No. 3060, 70r, Vindula dejone erotella. No. 3061, 70r, Juvenile Pomacanthus imperator.

2013, Oct. 25 Litho. *Perf. 13¼*

Sheets of 4, #a-d

3042-3051 A604 Set of 10 110.00 110.00

Souvenir Sheets

3052-3061 A604 Set of 10 85.00 85.00

Mohandas K. Gandhi (1869-1948), Indian Independence Leader — A605

No. 3062 — Gandhi and: a, Lotus flower. b, Salt marchers, Indian flag. c, Women, Indian flag. d, Peacock.

70r, Gandhi, Jawaharlal Nehru, tiger, vert.

Litho. With Three-Dimensional Plastic Affixed

2013, Nov. 18 *Perf. 13¼*

3062 A605 22r Sheet of 4, #a-d 11.50 11.50

Souvenir Sheet

3063 A605 70r multi 9.25 9.25

No. 3063 contains one 51x66mm stamp.

Famous People — A606

No. 3064, 20r — Marilyn Monroe (1926-62), actress: a, With skirt rising at right. b, With hand touching hair at right. c, In chair at right. d, Holding open umbrella at right.

No. 3065, 20r — Pierre de Coubertin (1863-1937), founder of modern Olympics, and: a, Swimmer. b, Runner. c, Cyclist. d, Fencers.

No. 3066, 20r — Brazilian 2013 Confederations Cup soccer players: a, Marcelo. b, Fred. c, Hulk. d, David Luiz.

No. 3067, 20r — Bobby Fischer (1943-2008), chess player, and: a, King and rook. b, Pawn and knight. c, King and pawn. d, Queen.

No. 3068, 20r — Birth of Prince George of Cambridge: a, Duchess of Cambridge holding Prince George at left, Duke and Duchess of Cambridge with Prince George at right. b, Duke and Duchess of Cambridge with Prince George at left, Prince Charles and Princess Diana with Prince William at right. c, Duke and Duchess of Cambridge with Prince George at left, Prince George at right. d, Duke of Cambridge holding Prince George at left, Duke and Duchess of Cambridge with Prince George at right.

No. 3069, 22r — Valentina Tereshkova, first woman in space: a, With Yuri Gagarin (1934-68), cosmonaut. b, And Vostok 6. c, With medical technician, at right. d, Holding pen, at right.

No. 3070, 22r — 95th birthday of Nelson Mandela (1918-2013), President of South Africa: a, Mandela and Dalai Lama. b, Mandela and Pope John Paul II (1920-2005). c, Mandela and Kofi Annan. d, Mandela and Princess Diana (1961-97).

No. 3071, 22r — Elvis Presley (1935-77): a, Holding microphone at right. b, Without hat at left, playing guitar at right. c, Wearing hat at left, playing guitar at right. d, Holding guitar at right.

No. 3072, 22r — Paintings by Pablo Picasso (1881-1973): a, Bottle of Vieux Marc, Glass, Guitar and Newspaper, 1913. b, Study for a Head Crying, 1937, Jacqueline with Crossed Hands, 1954. c, A Boy with a Pipe, 1905, Two Acrobats with a Dog, 1905. d, Houses on the Hill Horta de Ebro, 1909.

No. 3073, 60r, Monroe, vert. No. 3074, 60r, Coubertin and Olympic torch, vert. No. 3075, 60r, Neymar, vert. No. 3076, 60r, Fischer examining chess board, vert. No. 3077, 60r, Duke and Duchess of Cambridge with Prince George, vert. No. 3078, 70r, Tereshkova and Vostok 6 rocket, vert. No. 3079, 70r, Mandela, vert. No. 3080, 70r, Presley, vert. No. 3081, 70r, Head of a Woman, by Picasso, vert.

2013, Nov. 18 Litho. *Perf. 13¼*

Sheets of 4, #a-d

3064-3072 A606 Set of 9 100.00 100.00

Souvenir Sheets

3073-3081 A606 Set of 9 75.00 75.00

Brasiliana 2013 Intl. Philatelic Exhibition (Nos. 3066, 3075). Nos. 3073-3081 each contain one 51x66 mm stamp.

Transportation and Space — A607

No. 3082, 20r — Yuri Gagarin (1934-68), cosmonaut, and: a, Vostok 1 capsule in space. b, Vostok 1 capsule and booster in space. c, Vostok 1 rocket and emblem. d, Vostok 1 capsule on Earth.

No. 3083, 20r — Steam trains: a, Jenny Lind. b, Thompson L1 Class. c, GWR Iron Duke Class. d, Eureka.

No. 3084, 20r — Rescue boats: a, Koos van Messel KNRM, Netherlands. b, RS 103 Dagfinn Paust, Norway. c, AMF Pauanui, New Zealand. d, Autonomous Rescue and Recovery Craft in North Sea.

No. 3085, 20r — History of the automobile: a, 1955 Abarth A Coupe Boano. b, 1950 Volkswagen Beetle. c, 1927 Mercedes-Benz 600 Cabriolet. d, 1953 Fiat BV Demon Rouge.

No. 3086, 20r — Formula 1 race cars: a, McLaren-Mercedes MP4-24. b, Force India VJM06. c, Williams FW35. d, Ferrari F60.

No. 3087, 22r — Concorde: a, Air France Concode. b, Braniff Concorde. c, Aerospatiale BAC Concorde. d, Singapore Airlines Concorde.

No. 3088, 22r — Fire engines: a, 1970 Seagraves pumper. b, 1999 LTI ALF 75 Quint. c, 1950 Dennis F7. d, 2001 E-One 75-foot Quint.

No. 3089, 22r — Seaplanes: a, Short S-25 Sandringham 4. b, De Havilland Canada DHC-2 Beaver. c, Republic RC-3 Seabee. d, Grumman HU-16B Albatross.

No. 3090, 22r — High-speed trains: a, Frecciarossa 1000. b, Javelin. c, Acela Express. d, HSR-350x.

No. 3091, 22r — Space tourism: a, SpaceShipOne. b, EADS Astrium. c, Armadillo Aerospace. d, XCOR Aerospace.

No. 3092, 60r, Gagarin and Vostok 1, diff. No. 3093, 60r, Best Friend of Charleston. No. 3094, 60r, SK Hermann Marwede, Germany. No. 3095, 60r, 1886 Benz Patent Motorwagen. No. 3096, 60r, Renault R28 race car. No. 3097, 70r, British Airways Concorde. No. 3098, 70r, 1987 Sutphen 100-foot Platform Quint fire engine. No. 3099, 70r, Rans S-7 Courier. No. 3100, 70r, Eurostar. No. 3101, 70r, SpaceX Dragon.

2013, Dec. 2 Litho. *Perf. 13¼*

Sheets of 4, #a-d

3082-3091 A607 Set of 10 110.00 110.00

Souvenir Sheets

3092-3101 A607 Set of 10 85.00 85.00

Famous People — A608

No. 3102, 20r — Race car and Ayrton Senna (1960-94), driver: a, With hand on chin, wearing red racing suit with shoulder patch. b, Hands not visible, wearing red racing suit with shoulder patch. c, Hands not visible, wearing racing suit, no shoulder patch visible. d, With hand on chin, wearing white shirt.

No. 3103, 20r — Giacomo Puccini (1858-1924), composer, and scene from opera: a, Madame Butterfly. b, Tosca. c, Turandot. d, Turandot (Sarasota Opera production).

No. 3104, 20r — Nelson Mandela (1918-2013), President of South Africa: a, Behind microphone. b, With Dalai Lama. c, With Fidel Castro. d, Behind lectern.

No. 3105, 20r — Charles Lindbergh (1902-74), aviator: a, Lindbergh and airplane facing left. b, Nose of airplane, airplane over ocean. c, Airplane, map of Lindbergh's transatlantic flight. d, Lindbergh and nose of The Spirit of St. Louis.

No. 3106, 20r — Paintings by Salvador Dalí (1904-89): a, Swans Reflecting Elephants, 1937. b, The Persistence of Memory, 1931. c, The Enigma of My Desire, 1929. d, Weaning of Furniture Nutrition, 1934.

No. 3107, 22r — Bette Davis (1908-89), actress: a, On telephone at right. b, Wearing green dress at right. c, Wearing dress with shoulder straps at right. d, Wearing white dress and flower garland in hair at right.

No. 3108, 22r — Frida Kahlo (1907-54), painter, and: a, Roots, 1943. b, The Wounded Deer, 1946. c, The Dream (The Bed), 1940. d, My Dress Hangs There, 1933.

No. 3109, 22r — Marie Curie (1867-1934), chemist: a, Alone in laboratory at left. b, Radiation warning sign and atom at left. c, Molecular diagrams at left. d, With husband, Pierre, in laboratory at left.

No. 3110, 22r — Christoph Willibald Gluck (1714-87), composer, and: a, Echo and Narcissus, painting by John William Waterhouse. b, Harp. c, Violin. d, The Death of Alcestis, painting by Pierre Peyron.

No. 3111, 22r — Charlie Chaplin (1889-1977), actor, and: a, Paulette Goddard, in scene from *Modern Times,* 1936. b, Billy Armstrong, in scene from *His New Job,* 1915. c, Baby, in scene from *The Great Dictator,* 1940. d, Martha Raye, in scene from *Monsieur Verdoux,* 1947.

No. 3112, 60r, Senna and race car, diff. No. 3113, 60r, Puccini and poster for Madame Butterfly. No. 3114, 60r, Mandela, diff. No. 3115, 60r, Lindbergh and airplane, diff. No. 3116, 60r, Sleep, painting by Dalí, 1937. No. 3117, 70r, Davis, diff. No. 3118, 70r, The Love Embrace of the Universe, the Earth (Mexico), Myself, Diego and Señor Xolotl, painting by Kahlo, 1949. No. 3119, 70r, Curie, diff. No. 3120, 70r, Gluck and title page of libretto of *Iphigénie en Tauride.* No. 3121, 70r, Chaplin and Virginia Cherrill, in scene from *City Lights,* 1931.

2014, Feb. 20 Litho. *Perf. 13¼*

Sheets of 4, #a-d

3102-3111 A608 Set of 10 110.00 110.00

Souvenir Sheets

3112-3121 A608 Set of 10 85.00 85.00

Impressionist Paintings — A609

No. 3122, 20r — Paintings by Mary Cassatt: a, At the Theater. b, Portrait of Alexander J. Cassatt and His Son Robert Kelso Cassatt. c, Mother and Child. d, The Banjo Lesson.

No. 3123, 20r — Paintings by Edgar Degas: a, The Cafe Concert (The Song of the Dog). b, The Ballet Class. c, The Belleli Family. d, Edmondo and Therese Morbilli.

No. 3124, 20r — Paintings by Edouard Manet: a, Railway. b, Argenteuil. c, Tarring the Boat. d, The Rest, Portrait of Berthe Morisot.

No. 3125, 20r — Paintings by Berthe Morisot: a, Eugene Manet with His Daughter at Bougival. b, Paule Gobillard Painting. c, Dahlias. d, The Mother and Sister of the Artist.

No. 3126, 20r — Paintings by Camille Pissarro: a, L'Hermitage à Pontoise. b, Apple Picking. c, The Effect of Snow at Monfoucault. d, Coteau de l'Hermitage, Pontoise.

No. 3127, 22r — Paintings by Paul Cézanne: a, The Card Players. b, Maison Maria with a View of Chateau Noir. c, Still Life, Drapery, Pitcher and Fruit Bowl. d, Lady in Blue.

No. 3128, 22r — Paintings by Armand Guillaumin: a, Madame Guillaumin Reading. b, Cottages in a Landscape. c, Windmills in Holland. d, Vase of Chrysanthemums.

No. 3129, 22r — Paintings by Claude Monet: a, The Beach at Etretat. b, Springtime. c, Camille Monet and a Child in the Artist's Garden at Argenteuil. d, Entrance to the Port of Trouville.

No. 3130, 22r — Paintings by Pierre-Auguste Renoir: a, The Clearing. b, Dance in the Country. c, The Seine at Asnieres (The Skiff). d, Still Life with a Pomegranate.

No. 3131, 22r — Paintings by American Impressionists: a, Portrait of Miss Dora Wheeler, by William Merritt Chase. b, Morning Light, by Childe Hassam. c, The House in Giverny, by Frederick Carl Frieseke. d, Fireside Dreams, by Julian Alden Weir.

No. 3132, 60r, Children Playing on the Beach, by Cassatt. No. 3133, 60r, Orchestra of the Opera, by Degas. No. 3134, 60r, The Grand Canal of Venice (Blue Venice), by Manet. No. 3135, 60r, Peasant Girl Among Tulips, by Morisot. No. 3136, 60r, White Frost (Woman Breaking Wood), by Pissarro. No. 3137, 70r, The Seine at Bercy, by Cézanne. No. 3138, 70r, Moulin Bouchardon, Crozant, by Guillaumin. No. 3139, 70r, The boardwalk on the Beach at Trouville, by Monet. No. 3140, 70r, Two Sisters (On the Terrace), by Renoir. No. 3141, 70r, Gloucester Harbor Sun, by Willard Metcalf.

2014, Mar. 5 Litho. *Perf. 13¼*

Sheets of 4, #a-d

3122-3131 A609 Set of 10 110.00 110.00

Souvenir Sheets

3132-3141 A609 Set of 10 85.00 85.00

Fauna of the Indian Ocean Area — A610

No. 3142, 20r — Sharks: a, Alopias vulpinus. b, Galeocerdo cuvier. c, Carcharhinus limbatus. d, Squalus acanthias.

No. 3143, 20r — Octopi: a, Octopus cyanea. b, Octopus vulgaris. c, Octopus ornatus. d, Octopus kaurna.

No. 3144, 20r — Crustaceans: a, Carpilius convexus. b, Lysmata amboinensis. c, Panulirus ornatus. d, Hoplophrys oatesi.

No. 3145, 20r — Frogs: a, Mantidactylus madecassus. b, Sooglossus thomasseti. c, Litoria maini. d, Dyscophus antongilii.

No. 3146, 20r — Reptiles: a, Calotes versicolor. b, Varanus komodoensis. c, Lycodon aulicus. d, Dermochelys coriacea.

No. 3147, 22r — Owls: a, Phodilus badius. b, Strix leptogrammica. c, Aegolius funereus. d, Bubo zeylonensis.

No. 3148, 22r — Birds of prey: a, Asio flammeus. b, Circus macrourus. c, Pernis ptilorhyncus. d, Falco amurensis.

No. 3149, 22r — Butterflies: a, Euploea mulciber. b, Papilio clytia. c, Danaus genutia. d, Graphium agamemnon.

No. 3150, 22r — Deep water creatures: a, Serpula. b, Anoplogaster cornuta. c, Argyropelecus hemigymnus. d, Bathynomus giganteus.

No. 3151, 22r — Jellyfish: a, Atolla wyvillei. b, Chironex fleckeri. c, Carybdea sivickisi. d, Mastigias papua.

No. 3152, 60r, Isurus oxyrinchus. No. 3153, 60r, Octopus kaurma, diff. No. 3154, 60r, Periclimenes imperator. No. 3155, 60r, Mantella expectata. No. 3156, 60r, Caretta caretta. No. 3157, 70r, Tyto alba. No. 3158, 70r, Falco naumanni. No. 3159, 70r, Chrysiridia rhipheus. No. 3160, 70r, Chaunacidae. No. 3161, 70r, Chrysaora quinquecirrha.

2014, Apr. 1 Litho. *Perf. 13¼*

Sheets of 4, #a-d

3142-3151 A610 Set of 10 110.00 110.00

Souvenir Sheets

3152-3161 A610 Set of 10 85.00 85.00

Painting by He Xiangning (1878-1972) — A611

2014, May 7 Litho. *Perf. 13¼*

3162 A611 22r multi 3.00 3.00

No. 3162 was printed in sheets of 4.

Miniature Sheet

E. Marinella Necktie Company, Naples, Cent. — A612

No. 3163: a, Storefront, vert. b, 100th anniv. emblem, vert. c, Painting of Naples. d, 100th anniv. emblem, signature of E. Marinella, denomination in olive brown. e, 100th anniv. emblem, signature of E. Marinella, denomination in dull yellow.

Perf. 13¼x13 (vert. stamps), 13x13¼

2014, May 7 Litho.

3163 A612 20r Sheet of 5, #a-e 13.00 13.00

A613

No. 3164, 20r — Marriage of Joe DiMaggio and Marilyn Monroe, 60th anniv.: a, DiMaggio swinging bat at left, Monroe at right. b, Couple at left, DiMaggio at right. c, Monroe at left, DiMaggio at right. d, DiMaggio at left, Monroe holding bat at right.

No. 3165, 20r — Red List of endangered animals, 50th anniv.: a, Spizaetus bartelsi. b, Leontopithecus rosalia. c, Hippocampus capensis. d, Capra falconeri.

No. 3166, 20r — Channel Tunnel, 20th anniv.: a, Eurostar Class 373. b, British Rail Class 92. c, ICE 3 M. d, Eurotunnel Class 9.

No. 3167, 20r — Paintings by Wassily Kandinsky (1866-1944): a, Color Study: Squares with Concentric Circles. b, Black Frame. c, The Last Judgment. d, Improvisation 19.

No. 3168, 20r — Start of World War I, cent.: a, Emperor Wilhelm II of Germany (1859-1941), Mark I tank. b, Two Fokker E.III airplanes. c, Soldier wearing gas mask, map. d, Marshal Joseph Joffre (1852-1931), trench-digging machine.

No. 3169, 22r — Battle of the Bulge, 70th anniv.: a, American flag, soldiers in trench. b, Airplane above German tanks. c, Soldier watching comrades march through snow. d, Soldiers and tanks.

No. 3170, 22r — Paintings by Henri Matisse (1869-1954): a, Still Life with Apples on a Pink Tablecloth. b, Dishes and Fruit. c, Small Odalisque in Purple Robe. d, Still Life with Sleeper.

No. 3171, 22r — Renault automobiles: a, 1931 Renault Primaquatre KZ 6. b, 2013 Renault Twizy RS F1 Concept. c, 2014 Renault KWID Concept. d, 1961 Renault Alpine A110.

No. 3172, 22r — Two images of Elvis Presley (1935-77): a, Holding guitar. b, Blue Moon of Kentucky cover at right. c, 45rpm record at right. d, Elvis 75: Good Rockin' Tonight image at right.

No. 3173, 60r, Monroe and DiMaggio, diff. No. 3174, 60r, Abronia graminea. No. 3175, 60r, Two Eurostar Class 373 trains. No. 3176, 60r, Composition IV, by Kandinsky. No. 3177, 60r, Soldier wearing goggles and face mask, Joseph Gallieni (1849-1916), military governor of Paris. No. 3178, 70r, Gen. Dwight D. Eisenhower (1890-1969), map of battle. No. 3179, 70r, Lemons and Saxifrages, by Matisse. No. 3180, 70r, 1922 Renault NN Torpedo. No. 3181, 70r, Presley and his first 45rpm record.

2014, May 7 Litho. *Perf. 13¼*

Sheets of 4, #a-d

3164-3172 A613 Set of 9 97.50 97.50

Souvenir Sheets

3173-3181 A613 Set of 9 75.00 75.00

Souvenir Sheets

A614

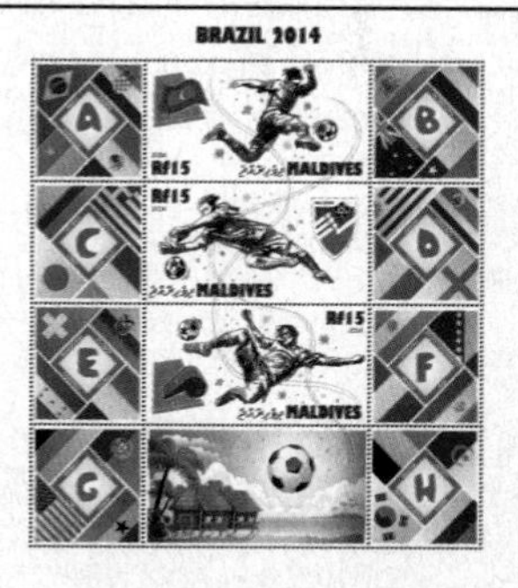

2014 World Cup Soccer Championships, Brazil — A615

No. 3182 — Various soccer players and: a, Emblem at UL. b, Mascot at UR. c, "2014 FIFA World Cup Brazil" at LL.

No. 3183 — Various soccer players and: a, Soccer field and Maldive Islands flag at UL. b, Emblem of Soccer Association of Maldives at UR. c, Soccer field and whistle at LL.

2014, July 3 Litho. *Perf. 12¾x13¼*

3182 A614 15r Sheet of 3, #a-c, + 9 labels 6.00 6.00

3183 A615 15r Sheet of 3, #a-c, + 9 labels 6.00 6.00

Chess and Sports — A616

No. 3184, 20r — Chess players: a, Garry Kasparov. b, Viswanathan Anand. c, Vladimir Kramnik. d, Levon Aronian.

No. 3185, 20r — Cricket players: a, Ian Botham. b, Sachin Tendulkar. c, Sir Vivian Richards. d, Kapil Dev.

No. 3186, 20r — Judokas: a, Ilias Iliadis. b, Udo Quellmalz. c, Ole Bischof. d, Kosei Inoue.

No. 3187, 20r — 2014 Winter Olympics, Sochi, Russia: a, Figure skating. b, Ski jumping. c, Luge. d, Ice hockey.

No. 3188, 20r — Rally racing: a, Citroen DS3 WRC. b, Mitsubishi Lancer Evolution VII. c, Citroen C4 WRC. d, Subaru Impreza.

No. 3189, 22r — Golfers: a, Greg Norman. b, Jack Nicklaus. c, Vijay Singh. d, Phil Mickelson.

No. 3190, 22r — Table tennis players: a, Jan-Ove Waldner. b, Liu Guoliang. c, Zhang Jike. d, Deng Yaping.

No. 3191, 22r — Horse racing: a, Three horses running right. b, Two steeplechase horses. c, Four horses running left. d, Three steeplechase horses.

No. 3192, 22r — First heavyweight championship of Muhammad Ali, 50th anniv.: a, Full color image of Ali at left, black-and-white image of Ali and opponent at UR, denomination at UL. b, Ali and opponent, denomination at UR. c, Ali and opponent, denomination at UL. d, Full color image of Ali at right, dimmed color image of Ali and opponent at left, denomination at UR.

No. 3193, 60r, Magnus Carlsen. No. 3194, 60r, Sir Donald Bradman (1908-2001). No. 3195, 60r, Teddy Riner. No. 3196, 60r, Cross-country skiing. No. 3197, 60r, Ford Focus RS. No. 3198, 70r, Tiger Woods. No. 3199, 70r, Li Xianxia. No. 3200, 70r, Race horses and starting gate. No. 3201, 70r, Ali, referee, knocked-out opponent.

2014, July 3 Litho. *Perf. 13¼*

Sheets of 4, #a-d

3184-3192 A616 Set of 9 100.00 100.00

Souvenir Sheets

3193-3201 A616 Set of 9 75.00 75.00

Paintings by Flemish Artists — A617

No. 3202, 20r — Paintings by Peter Paul Rubens (1577-1640): a, Samson and Delilah. b, Drunken Silenus. c, The Entombment. d, Satyr and Girl.

No. 3203, 20r — Paintings by Quentin Matsys (1466-1530): a, Madonna and Child with the Lamb. b, Portrait of a Woman. c, Portrait of Erasmus of Rotterdam. d, Ill-matched Lovers.

No. 3204, 20r — Paintings by Dieric Bouts (1410-75): a, Mater Dolorosa. b, Lamentation. c, The Meeting of Abraham and Melchizedek. d, The Execution of the Innocent Man.

No. 3205, 20r — Paintings by Pieter Brueghel, the Elder (1525-69) and the Younger (1564-1638): a, Parable of the Blind, by the Elder. b, The Adoration of the Magi, by the Younger. c, The Spring, by the Younger. d, The Fight Between Carnival and Lent, by the Elder.

No. 3206, 22r — Paintings by Rogier van der Weyden (1400-64): a, Group of Men. b, Portrait of a Lady. c, Saints Margaret and Apollonia. d, The Magdalene Reading.

No. 3207, 22r — Paintings by Jan van Eyck (1385-1441): a, St. Jerome. b, The Soldiers of Christ. c, The Ince Hall Madonna. d, Stigmatization of St. Francis.

No. 3208, 22r — Paintings by Sir Anthony van Dyck (1599-1641): a, Crowning with Thorns. b, Blessed Joseph Hermann. c, Rubens Mourning His Wife. d, Portrait of the Three Eldest Children of Charles I.

No. 3209, 22r — Paintings by Frans Hals, the Elder (1582-1666): a, Fisher Boy. b, Shrovetide Revelers. c, Officers and Sergeants of the St. Hadrian Civic Guard. d, Fisher Girl.

No. 3210, 22r — Paintings by Hans Memling (1430-94): a, Mystic Marriage of St. Catherine. b, Virgin and Child Enthroned with Two Angels. c, Annunciation. d, The Nativity (left wing of triptych of the Adoration of the Magi).

No. 3211, 60r, Night Scene, by Rubens. No. 3212, 60r, The Moneylender and His Wife, by Matsys. No. 3213, 60r, Adoration of the Magi (middle panel of The Pearl of Brabant triptych), by Bouts. No. 3214, 60r, Hunters in the Snow, by Brueghel the Elder. No. 3215, 70r, Virgin and Child by van der Weyden. No. 3216, 70r, The Arnolfini Wedding, by van Eyck. No. 3217, 70r, Saint Rosalie Interceding for the Plague-stricken of Palermo, by van Dyck. No. 3218, 70r, Young Man with a Skull, by Hals. No. 3219, 70r, Christ Surrounded by Musician Angels, by Memling.

2014, July 3 Litho. *Perf. 13¼*

Sheets of 4, #a-d

3202-3210 A617 Set of 9 100.00 100.00

Souvenir Sheets

3211-3219 A617 Set of 9 77.50 77.50

A618

No. 3220, 20r — Cassini Mission to Saturn, 10th anniv.: a, Cassini-Huygens probe and Saturn, antenna at left. b, Solar system. c, Cassini-Huygens probe above Saturn. d, Cassini-Huygens probe, antenna at right.

No. 3221, 20r — Galileo Galilei (1564-1642), astonomer, with: a, Telescope, sun and planets. b, Cardinals, telescope, planets. c, Assistants, balance, satellite, planets. d, Hubble Space Telescope.

No. 3222, 20r — Awarding of Nobel Peace Prize to Dr. Martin Luther King, Jr., 50th anniv.: a, King and microphones. b, King and Pres. John F. Kennedy. c, King holding Nobel medal. d, King with hands together.

No. 3223, 20r — Hermitage Museum, St. Petersburg, Russia, 250th anniv.: a, Card Game, by Theodor Rombouts. b, Cleopatra's Feast, by Jacob Jordaens. c, Lesson of Singing, by Jan Josef Horemans II. d, Continence of Scipio, by Pompeo Batoni.

No. 3224, 20r — German players at 2014 World Cup Soccer Championships, Brazil: a, Mario Götze. b, Manuel Neuer. c, Thomas Müller. d, Miroslav Klose.

No. 3225, 22r — Circumnavigation of Graf Zeppelin, 85th anniv.: a, U. S. Capitol, LZ-127 Graf Zeppelin. b, Ferdinand von Zeppelin, New York City. c, Hugo Eckener and LZ-127 Graf Zeppelin. d, LZ-127 Graf Zeppelin and mountain.

No. 3226, 22r — King Felipe VI of Spain and: a, Crowd and flagbearer. b, Picture of King as child. c, Queen Letizia and crowd at palace. d, Parents, King Juan Carlos and Queen Sofia.

No. 3227, 22r — Deng Xiaoping (1904-97), Paramount leader of People's Republic of China, and: a, Mao Zedong (1893-1976), chairman of Chinese Communist Party. b, Baling River Bridge, dove, flag of People's Republic of China. c, CRH380A, statue of Mao Zedong, flag of People's Republic of China. d, Chinese buildings.

No. 3228, 22r — Third Intl. Conference on Small Island Developing States: a, Woman wearing headdress. b, Red Cross worker feeding infant. c, Two children. d, Samoan prime minister Tuilaepa Lupesoliai Sailele Malielegaoi, solar panels, wind generators.

No. 3229, 22r — 17th Asian Games, Incheon, South Korea: a, Boxing, Northeast Asia Trade Tower, Incheon. b, Weight lifting, Incheon buildings. c, Cycling, Incheon Munhak Stadium. d, Sailboarding, Incheon Bridge.

No. 3230, 60r, Cassini-Huygens probe, Saturn, diff. No. 3231, 60r, Galileo looking through telescope, space probe. No. 3232, 60r, King, Nobel medal, diff. No. 3233, 60r, Jephthah's Daughter, by Pieter van Lint. No. 3234, 60r, Klose, diff. No. 3235, 70r, LZ-127 Graf Zeppelin. No. 3236, 70r, King Felipe VI of Spain, flag of Spain, Royal Palace, Madrid. No. 3237, 70r, Deng Xiaoping, rocket, Great Wall of China. No. 3238, 70r, Chinese diplomat Wu Hongbo, beach scene, smokestacks, polar bear. No. 3239, 70r, Stylized archer, gymnast, tennis player.

Litho., Litho. With Foil Application (#3224, 3234)

2014, Oct. 7 *Perf. 13¼*

Sheets of 4, #a-d

3220-3229 A618 Set of 10 110.00 110.00

Souvenir Sheets

3230-3239 A618 Set of 10 85.00 85.00

A619

No. 3240, 20r — Cats: a, Siberian cat. b, Head of Abyssinian cat. c, Abyssinian cat. d, Sphynx.

No. 3241, 20r — Dolphins: a, Stenella frontalis. b, Delphinus delphis. c, Cephalorhynchus hectori. d, Lagenorhynchus obliquidens.

No. 3242, 20r — Butterflies: a, Lycaena virgaureae. b, Polygonia interrogationis. c, Heliconius cydno. d, Morpho peleides.

No. 3243, 20r — Turtles: a, Chelonoidis nigra. b, Chelonia mydas, Latin name at LR. c, Podocnemis expansa. d, Chelonia mydas, Latin name at UR.

No. 3244, 20r — Mushrooms: a, Cantharellus cibarius. b, Kuehneromyces mutabilis. c, Macrolepiota procera. d, Boletus badius.

No. 3245, 22r — Dogs: a, Nova Scotia duck tolling retriever. b, Belgian shepherd jumping. c, Belgian shepherd running. d, Boxer.

No. 3246, 22r — Dinosaurs: a, Tylosaurus, Pteranodon. b, Cryolophosaurus. c, Tyrannosaurus rex. d, Kentrosaurus.

No. 3247, 22r — Orchids: a, Brassolaeliocattleya "Taiwan Queen." b, Paphiopedilum cultivar. c, Encyclia cultivar. d, Phalaenopsis cultivar.

No. 3248, 22r — Minerals: a, Turquoise. b, Desert rose. c, Marcasite. d, Elbaite.

No. 3249, 22r — Lighthouses: a, Peggy's Cove Lighthouse, Nova Scotia, Canada. b, Ploumanac'h Lighthouse, France. c, Hornby Lighthouse, Australia. d, Brant Point Lighthouse, Massachusetts.

No. 3250, 60r, British shorthair cat. No. 3251, 60r, Lagenorhynchus obliquidens, diff. No. 3252, 60r, Aporia crataegi. No. 3253, 60r, Chelonia mydas, diff. No. 3254, 60r, Boletus edulis. No. 3255, 70r, Russian wolfhounds. No. 3256, 70r, Nanotyrannus. No. 3257, 70r, Paphiopedilum callosum. No. 3258, 70r, Copper sulphate. No. 3259, 70r, Portland Head Lighthouse, Maine.

2014, Oct. 14 Litho. *Perf. 13¼*

Sheets of 4, #a-d

3240-3249 A619 Set of 10 110.00 110.00

Souvenir Sheets

3250-3259 A619 Set of 10 85.00 85.00

Nos. 3247 and 3257 are impregnated with an orchid scent.

Birds — A620

No. 3260, 20r — Pelecanus onocrotalus (pelican): a, With green fish entering mouth. b, With fish in mouth, wings spread. c, Two birds. d, With orange fish entering mouth.

No. 3261, 20r — Songbirds: a, Anthus trivialis. b, Acridotheres tristis, Cethosia biblis butterfly. c, Corvus splendens, Parantica aglea. d, Motacilla cinerea.

No. 3262, 20r — Pigeons and fruit: a, Columba livia, Mangifera indica. b, Columba livia, Cocos nucifera. c, Streptopelia orientalis, Passiflora edulis. d, Streptopelia turtur, Musa acuminata.

No. 3263, 20r — Water birds and corals: a, Fulica atra, Dendrophyllia sp. b, Gallinula chloropus, Plerogyra sinuosa. c, Amaurornis phoenicurus, Acropora robusta. d, Gallicrex cinerea, Trachyphyllia geoffroyi.

No. 3264, 20r — Wading birds and insects: a, Ardea cinerea, Delias eucharis. b, Ardeola grayii, Enallagma maldivensis. c, Phalacrocorax fuscicollis, Anoplolepsis gracilipes. d, Platalea leucorodia, Glyphodes, bivitralis.

No. 3265, 22r — Birds of prey: a, Falco subbuteo. b, Falco amurensis. c, Falco tinnunculus. d, Falco naumanni.

No. 3266, 22r — Seabirds and shells: a, Calonectris leucomelas, Melo aethiopica. b, Oceanites oceanicus, Acrosterigma dupuchensis. c, Puffinus lherminieri, Casmaria ponderosa ponderosa. d, Puffinus pacificus, Harpa major.

No. 3267, 22r — Bee-eaters and orchids: a, Merops apiaster, Cattleya labiata. b, Merops apiaster, Vanda tricolor. c, Merops apiaster, Cymbidium dayanum. d, Merops apiaster, Vanda denisoniana.

No. 3268, 22r — Owls and mushrooms: a, Asio flammeus, Lactarius indigo. b, Asio flammeus, Ganoderma lucidum. c, Asio flammeus, Coprinopsis atramentaria. d, Asio flammeus, Leucocoprinus birnbaumii.

No. 3269, 22r — Terns and lighthouses: a, Sterna dougallii, Pemaquid Lighthouse, Maine. b, Sterna hirundo, Portland Head Lighthouse, Maine. c, Hydroprogne, caspia, Cape Neddick Lighthouse, Maine. d, Onychoprion fuscata, Cloch Lighthouse, Scotland.

No. 3270, 60r, Pelecanus onocrotalus, diff. No. 3271, 60r, Passer domesticus. No. 3272, 60r, Streptopelia orientalis, Carica papaya. No. 3273, 60r, Gallinula chloropus, Acropora sp. No. 3274, 60r, Bulbulcus ibis, Darna furva. No. 3275, 70r, Circus pygargus. No. 3276, 70r, Bulweria bulwerii, Tridacna gigas. No. 3277, 70r, Merops apiaster, Cymbidium hybrid. No. 3278, 70r, Asio flammeus, Psilocybe aztecorum. No. 3279, 70r, Hydroprogne caspia, Heceta Head Lighthouse, Oregon.

2014, Dec. 15 Litho. *Perf. 13¼*

Sheets of 4, #a-d

3260-3269 A620 Set of 10 110.00 110.00

Souvenir Sheets

3270-3279 A620 Set of 10 85.00 85.00

MALI

'mä-lē

(Federation of Mali)

LOCATION — West Africa
GOVT. — Republic within French Community
AREA — 482,077 sq. mi.
POP. — 5,862,000 (est.)
CAPITAL — Dakar and Bamako

The Federation of Mali, founded Jan. 17, 1959, consisted of the Republic of Senegal and the French Sudan. It broke up in June, 1960. See Senegal.

100 Centimes = 1 Franc

Catalogue values for all unused stamps in this country are for Never Hinged items.

Flag and Map of Mali
A1

Unwmk.

1959, Nov. 7 Engr. *Perf. 13*

1 A1 25fr grn, car & dp claret 1.00 .50

Founding of the Federation of Mali.

Imperforates

Most Mali stamps exist imperforate in issued and trial colors, and also in small presentation sheets in issued colors.

Parrotfish
A2

Fish: 10fr, Triggerfish. 15fr, Psetta. 20fr, Blepharis crinitus. 25fr, Butterflyfish. 30fr, Surgeonfish. 85fr, Dentex.

1960, Mar. 5

Fish in Natural Colors

2 A2 5fr olive .40 .25
3 A2 10fr brt grnsh blue .40 .25
4 A2 15fr dark blue .45 .25
5 A2 20fr gray green .65 .35
6 A2 25fr slate green 1.10 .55
7 A2 30fr dark blue 1.50 .90
8 A2 85fr dark green 3.50 2.00
Nos. 2-8 (7) 8.00 4.55

For overprints see Nos. 10-12.

Common Design Types pictured following the introduction.

C.C.T.A. Issue

Common Design Type

1960, May 21 *Perf. 13*

9 CD106 25fr lt violet & magenta 1.20 .50

REPUBLIC OF MALI

GOVT. — Republic
AREA — 463,500 sq. mi.
POP. — 10,429,124 (1999 est.)
CAPITAL — Bamako

The Republic of Mali, formerly the French Sudan, proclaimed its independence on June 20, 1960, when the Federation of Mali ceased to exist.

Nos. 5-6 and 8 Ovptd.

Unwmk.

1961, Jan. 15 Engr. *Perf. 13*

Fish in Natural Colors

10 A2 20fr gray green 1.25 .65
11 A2 25fr slate green 2.00 .65
12 A2 85fr dark green 3.25 1.60
Nos. 10-12 (3) 6.50 2.90

Pres. Mamadou Konate — A3

Design: 25fr, Pres. Modibo Keita.

1961, Mar. 18

13 A3 20fr green & baclk .30 .25
14 A3 25fr maroon & black .45 .25

For miniature sheet see No. C11a.

Reading Class, Bullock Team and Factory — A4

1961, Sept. 22 Unwmk. *Perf. 13*

15 A4 25fr multi .75 .40

First anniversary of Independence.

Shepherd and Sheep
A5

Designs: 1fr, 10fr, 40fr, Cattle. 2fr, 15fr, 50fr, Mali Arts Museum. 3fr, 20fr, 60fr, Plowing. 4fr, 25fr, 85fr, Harvester.

Unwmk.

1961, Dec. 24 Engr. *Perf. 13*

16 A5 50c car rose, blk & dk grn .25 .25
17 A5 1fr grn, bl & bister .25 .25
18 A5 2fr ultra, grn & org red .25 .25
19 A5 3fr bl, grn & brn .25 .25
20 A5 4fr bl grn, indigo & bis .25 .25
21 A5 5fr bl, olive & maroon .25 .25
22 A5 10fr ol blk, bl & sepia .25 .25
23 A5 15fr ultra, grn & bis brn .25 .25
24 A5 20fr bl, grn & org red .35 .25
25 A5 25fr dk bl & yel grn .45 .25
26 A5 30fr vio, grn & dk brn .60 .30
27 A5 40fr sl grn, bl & org red 1.10 .30
28 A5 50fr ultra, grn & rose car .55 .30
29 A5 60fr blue, green & brown 1.25 .30
30 A5 85fr bl, bis & dk red brn 1.90 .45
Nos. 16-30 (15) 8.20 4.15

King Mohammed V of Morocco and Map of Africa — A6

1962, Jan. 4 Photo. *Perf. 12*

31 A6 25fr multicolored .30 .25
32 A6 50fr multicolored .55 .25

1st anniv. of the conference of African heads of state at Casablanca.

Patrice Lumumba
A7

1962, Feb. 12 Unwmk. *Perf. 12*

33 A7 25fr choc & brn org .35 .25
34 A7 100fr choc & emerald 1.00 .45

Issued in memory of Patrice Lumumba, Premier of the Congo (Democratic) Republic.

Pegasus and UPU Monument, Bern — A8

1962, Apr. 21 *Perf. 12½x12*

35 A8 85fr red brn, yel & brt grn 1.50 .75

1st anniv. of Mali's admission to the UPU.

Map of Africa and Post Horn — A8a

1962, Apr. 23 *Perf. 13½x13*

36 A8a 25fr dk red brn & dp grn .35 .25
37 A8a 85fr dp green & org 1.10 .40

Establishment of African Postal Union.

Sansanding Dam — A9

Cotton Plant
A10

1962, Oct. 27 Photo. *Perf. 12*

38 A9 25fr dk gray, ultra & grn .35 .25
39 A10 45fr multicolored 1.25 .40

Telstar, Earth and Television Set — A10a

1962, Nov. 24 Engr. *Perf. 13*

40 A10a 45fr dk car, vio & brn 1.00 .45
41 A10a 55fr green, vio & ol 1.20 .55

1st television connection of the US and Europe through the Telstar satellite, 7/11-12.

Bull, Chemical Equipment, Chicks — A11

1963, Feb. 23 Unwmk. *Perf. 13*

42 A11 25fr red brn & grnsh bl .50 .25

Sotuba Zootechnical Institute. See No. C15.

Tractor
A12

1963, Mar. 21 Engr.

43 A12 25fr vio bl, dk brn & blk .55 .25
44 A12 45fr bl grn, red brn & grn 1.00 .30

FAO "Freedom from Hunger" campaign.

High Altitude Balloon and WMO Emblem
A13

1963, June 12 Photo. *Perf. 12½*

Green Emblem; Yellow and Black Balloon

45 A13 25fr ultra .35 .25
46 A13 45fr carmine rose .70 .35
47 A13 60fr red brown .90 .45
Nos. 45-47 (3) 1.95 1.05

Studies of the atmosphere.

Winners, 800-meter Race — A14

20fr, Acrobatic dancers. 85fr, Soccer.

1963, Aug. 10 Unwmk. *Perf. 12*

48 A14 5fr multi .25 .25
49 A14 10fr multi .25 .25
50 A14 20fr multi, horiz. .60 .25
51 A14 85fr multi, horiz. 1.75 .75
Nos. 48-51 (4) 2.85 1.50

Issued to publicize Youth Week.

Centenary Emblem — A15

1963, Sept. 1 ***Perf. 13½x13***
Emblem in Gray, Yellow and Red

52 A15 5fr lt ol grn & blk .25 .25
53 A15 10fr yellow & blk .35 .25
54 A15 85fr red & blk 1.30 .75
Nos. 52-54 (3) 1.90 1.25

Centenary of the International Red Cross.

Kaempferia Aethiopica — A16

Tropical plants: 70fr, Bombax costatum. 100fr, Adenium Honghel.

1963, Dec. 23 **Unwmk.** ***Perf. 13***
55 A16 30fr multicolored .55 .25
56 A16 70fr multicolored 1.40 .45
57 A16 100fr multicolored 3.50 .60
Nos. 55-57 (3) 5.45 1.30

Plane Spraying, Locust and Village A17

Designs (each inscribed "O.I.C.M.A."): 5fr, Head of locust and map of Africa, vert. 10fr, Locust in flight over map of Mali, vert.

1964, June 15 **Engr.** ***Perf. 13***
58 A17 5fr org brn, dl cl & grn .35 .25
59 A17 10fr org brn, ol & bl grn .75 .30
60 A17 20fr bis, org brn & yel grn 1.25 .50
Nos. 58-60 (3) 2.35 1.05

Anti-locust campaign.

Soccer Player and Tokyo Stadium — A18

Designs (stadium in background): 10fr, Boxer, vert. 15fr, Runner, vert. 85fr, Hurdler.

1964, June 27 **Unwmk.**
61 A18 5fr red, brt grn & dk pur .25 .25
62 A18 10fr blk, dl bl & org brn .30 .25
63 A18 15fr violet & dk red .45 .25
64 A18 85fr vio, dk brn & sl grn 2.10 1.25
a. Min. sheet of 4, #61-64 4.00 3.00
Nos. 61-64 (4) 3.10 2.00

18th Olympic Games, Tokyo, Oct. 10-25.

IQSY Emblem and Eclipse of Sun — A19

1964, July 27 **Engr.** ***Perf. 13***
65 A19 45fr multicolored .90 .40

International Quiet Sun Year, 1964-65.

Map of Viet Nam — A20

1964, Nov. 2 **Photo.** ***Perf. 12x12½***
66 A20 30fr multicolored .60 .25

Issued to publicize the solidarity of the workers of Mali and those of South Viet Nam.

Defassa Waterbuck — A21

Designs: 5fr, Cape buffalo, horiz. 10fr, Scimitar-horned oryx. 30fr, Leopard, horiz. 90fr, Giraffe.

1965, Apr. 5 **Engr.**
67 A21 1fr choc, brt bl & grn .25 .25
68 A21 5fr grn, ocher & choc .25 .25
69 A21 10fr grn, brt pink & bis brn .45 .25
70 A21 30fr dk red, grn & choc .90 .35
71 A21 90fr bis brn, sl & yel grn 2.25 .75
Nos. 67-71 (5) 4.10 1.85

Abraham Lincoln — A22

1965, Apr. 15 **Photo.** ***Perf. 13x12½***
72 A22 45fr black & multi .75 .50
73 A22 55fr dp green & multi .85 .60

Centenary of the death of Lincoln.

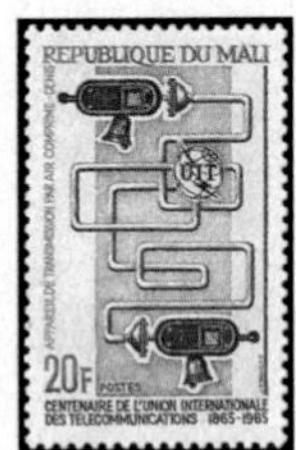
Denis Compressed Air Transmitter — A23

Designs: 30fr, Hughes telegraph system, horiz. 50fr, Lescurre heliograph.

1965, May 17 **Engr.** ***Perf. 13***
74 A23 20fr orange, blk & bl .35 .25
75 A23 30fr org, ocher & sl grn .60 .30
76 A23 50fr org, dk brn & sl grn 1.10 .50
Nos. 74-76 (3) 2.05 1.05

Centenary of the ITU.

Mother and infants — A24

Designs: 5fr, Mobile X-ray Unit and Lungs. 25fr, Examination of patient at Marchoux Institute and slide. 45fr, Biology laboratory.

1965, July 5 **Unwmk.** ***Perf. 13***
77 A24 5fr lake, red & vio .25 .25
78 A24 10fr brn ol, red & sl grn .30 .25
79 A24 25fr dk brn, red & grn .50 .25
80 A24 45fr dk brn, red & sl grn 1.00 .50
Nos. 77-80 (4) 2.05 1.25

Issued to publicize the Health Service.

Swimmer A25

1965, July 19 **Engr.**
81 A25 5fr shown .25 .25
82 A25 15fr Judo .80 .30

1st African Games, Brazzaville, July 18-25.

Globe, Vase, Quill, Trumpet A26

55fr, Mask, palette and microphones. 90fr, Dancers, mask and printed cloth.

1966, Apr. 4 **Engr.** ***Perf. 13***
83 A26 30fr black, red & ocher .45 .25
84 A26 55fr car rose, emer & blk .90 .30
85 A26 90fr ultra, org & dk brn 1.25 .45
Nos. 83-85 (3) 2.60 1.00

International Negro Arts Festival, Dakar, Senegal, Apr. 1-24.

WHO Headquarters, Geneva — A27

1966, May 3 **Photo.** ***Perf. 12½x13***
86 A27 30fr org yel, bl & ol grn .60 .25
87 A27 45fr org yel, bl & dl red .75 .30

Inauguration of the WHO Headquarters.

Fishermen with Nets — A28

River Fishing: 4fr, 60fr, Group fishing with large net. 20fr, 85fr, Commercial fishing boats.

1966, May 30 **Engr.** ***Perf. 13***
88 A28 3fr ultra & brn .25 .25
89 A28 4fr Prus bl & org brn .25 .25
90 A28 20fr dk brn, ultra & grn .45 .25
91 A28 25fr dk brn, bl & brt grn .60 .25
92 A28 60fr mag, brn & brt grn .90 .30
93 A28 85fr dk pur, dl bl & grn 1.25 .60
Nos. 88-93 (6) 3.70 1.90

Initiation of Pioneers A29

Design: 25fr, Dance and Pioneer emblem.

1966, July 25 **Engr.** ***Perf. 13***
94 A29 5fr multicolored .25 .25
95 A29 25fr multicolored .75 .25

Issued to honor the pioneers of Mali.

Inoculation of Zebu A30

1967, Jan. 16 **Photo.** ***Perf. 12½x13***
96 A30 10fr dp grn, yel grn & brn .30 .25
97 A30 30fr Prus bl, bl & brn .90 .30

Campaign against cattle plague.

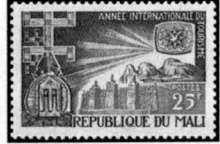

View of Timbuktu and Tourist Year Emblem A31

1967, May 15 **Engr.** ***Perf. 13***
98 A31 25fr Prus bl, red lil & org .60 .25

International Tourist Year, 1967.

Ugada Grandicollis A32

Insects: 5fr, Chelorrhina polyphemus, vert. 50fr, Phymateus cinctus.

1967, Aug. 14 **Engr.** ***Perf. 13***
99 A32 5fr brt bl, sl grn & brn .60 .25
100 A32 15fr sl grn, dk brn & red 1.00 .35
101 A32 50fr sl grn, dk brn & dp org 2.75 .75
Nos. 99-101 (3) 4.35 1.35

Teacher and Adult Class A33

1967, Sept. 8 **Photo.** ***Perf. 12½x13***
102 A33 50fr black, grn & car .85 .25

International Literacy Day, Sept. 8.

Europafrica Issue

Birds, New Buildings and Map A34

1967, Sept. 18 ***Perf. 12½x12***
103 A34 45fr multicolored 1.00 .35

Lions Emblem and Crocodile — A35

1967, Oct. 16 **Photo.** ***Perf. 13x12½***
104 A35 90fr yellow & multi 1.40 .75

50th anniversary of Lions International.

Water Cycle and UNESCO Emblem A36

1967, Nov. 15 Photo. *Perf. 13*
105 A36 25fr multicolored .60 .25

Hydrological Decade (UNESCO), 1965-74.

WHO Emblem A37

1968, Apr. 8 Engr. *Perf. 13*
106 A37 90fr sl grn, dk car rose & bl 1.20 .40

20th anniv. of the World Health Organization.

Linked Hearts and People A38

1968, Apr. 28 Engr. *Perf. 13*
107 A38 50fr sl grn, red & vio bl .65 .25

International Day of Sister Communities.

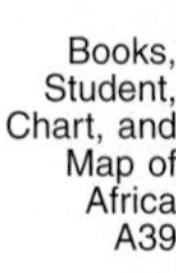

Books, Student, Chart, and Map of Africa A39

1968, Aug. 12 Engr. *Perf. 13*
108 A39 100fr carmine, ol & blk 1.00 .40

10th anniv. of the Intl. Assoc. for the Development of Libraries and Archives in Africa.

Michaux bicycle, 1861 A40

Designs: 2fr, Draisienne, 1809. 5fr, De Dion-Bouton automobile, 1894, horiz. 45fr, Panhard & Levassor automobile, 1914, horiz.

1968, Aug. 12
109 A40 2fr grn, olive & magenta .35 .25
110 A40 5fr lemon, indigo & red .65 .25
111 A40 10fr brt grn, indigo & brn 1.10 .25
112 A40 45fr ocher, gray grn & blk 2.00 .30
Nos. 109-112,C60-C61 (6) 7.70 2.05

Tourist Emblem with Map of Africa and Dove A41

1969, May 12 Photo. *Perf. 12½x13*
113 A41 50fr lt ultra, grn & red .60 .25

Year of African Tourism.

ILO Emblem and "OIT" A42

1969, May 12 Engr. *Perf. 13*
114 A42 50fr vio, slate grn & brt bl .45 .25
115 A42 60fr slate, red & ol brn .75 .25

Intl. Labor Organization, 50th anniv.

Panhard, 1897, and Citroen 24, 1969 — A43

30fr, Citroen, 1923, Citroen DS 21, 1969.

1969, May 30 Engr. *Perf. 13*
116 A43 25fr blk, maroon & lemon 1.00 .25
117 A43 30fr blk, brt grn & dk grn 1.25 .25
Nos. 116-117,C71-C72 (4) 6.10 1.45

Play Blocks A44

Toys: 10fr, Mule on wheels. 15fr, Ducks. 20fr, Racing car and track.

1969 Photo. *Perf. 12½x13*
118 A44 5fr red, gray & yel .25 .25
119 A44 10fr red, yel & olive .25 .25
120 A44 15fr red, salmon & yel grn .30 .25
121 A44 20fr red, indigo & org .35 .25
Nos. 118-121 (4) 1.15 1.00

Intl. Toy Fair in Nuremberg, Germany.

Ram A45

1969, Aug. 18 Engr. *Perf. 13*
122 A45 1fr shown .25 .25
123 A45 2fr Goat .25 .25
124 A45 10fr Donkey .30 .25
125 A45 35fr Horse .90 .30
126 A45 90fr Dromedaries 1.40 .50
Nos. 122-126 (5) 3.10 1.55

Development Bank Issue
Common Design Type

1969, Sept. 10
127 CD130 50fr brt lil, grn & ocher .35 .25
128 CD130 90fr ol brn, grn & ocher .65 .25

Boy Being Vaccinated A46

1969, Nov. 10 Engr. *Perf. 13*
129 A46 50fr brn, indigo & brt grn .75 .25

Campaign against smallbox and measles.

ASECNA Issue
Common Design Type

1969, Dec. 12 Engr. *Perf. 13*
130 CD132 100fr dark slate green .90 .40

African and Japanese Women A47

150fr, Flags and maps of Mali and Japan.

1970, Apr. 13 Engr. *Perf. 13*
131 A47 100fr brown, bl & ocher .90 .40
132 A47 150fr dk red, yel grn & org 1.25 .50

Issued to publicize EXPO '70 International Exhibition, Osaka, Japan, Mar. 15-Sept. 13.

Satellite Telecommunications, Map of Africa and ITU Emblem — A48

1970, May 17 Engr. *Perf. 13*
133 A48 90fr car rose & brn .90 .40

World Telecommunications Day.

UPU Headquarters Issue
Common Design Type

1970, May 20 Engr. *Perf. 13*
134 CD133 50fr dk red, bl grn & ol .45 .25
135 CD133 60fr red lil, ultra & red brn .60 .25

Post Office, Bamako A49

Public Buildings: 40fr, Chamber of Commerce, Bamako. 60fr, Public Works Ministry, Bamako. 80fr, City Hall, Segou.

1970, Nov. 23 Engr. *Perf. 13*
136 A49 30fr brn, brt grn & olive .35 .25
137 A49 40fr brn, sl grn & dp claret .45 .25
138 A49 60fr brn red, sl grn & gray .60 .30
139 A49 80fr brn, brt grn & emer .85 .40
Nos. 136-139 (4) 2.25 1.20

Gallet 030T, 1882 A50

Old Steam Locomotives: 40fr, Felou 030T, 1882. 50fr, Bechevel 230T, 1882. 80fr, Type 231, 1930. 100fr, Type 141, 1930.

1970, Dec. 14 Engr. *Perf. 13*
140 A50 20fr brt grn, dk car & blk 1.75 .55
141 A50 40fr blk, dk grn & ocher 2.25 .65
142 A50 50fr bis brn, bl grn & blk 3.00 .90
143 A50 80fr car rose, blk & bl grn 4.25 1.10
144 A50 100fr ocher, bl grn & blk 7.00 1.75
Nos. 140-144 (5) 18.25 4.95

Scout Sounding Retreat — A51

Boy Scouts: 5fr, Crossing river, horiz. 100fr, Canoeing, horiz.

Perf. 13x12½, 12½x13
1970, Dec. 28 Litho.
145 A51 5fr multicolored .25 .25
146 A51 30fr multicolored .50 .25
147 A51 100fr multicolored 1.25 .40
Nos. 145-147 (3) 2.00 .90

Bambara Mask, San — A52

Designs: 25fr, Dogon mask, Bandiagara. 50fr, Kanaga ideogram. 80fr, Bambara ideogram.

1971, Jan. 25 Photo. *Perf. 12x12½*
148 A52 20fr orange & multi .25 .25
149 A52 25fr brt green & multi .35 .25
150 A52 50fr dk purple & multi .60 .25
151 A52 80fr blue & multi .90 .25
Nos. 148-151 (4) 2.10 1.00

Boy, Medical and Scientific Symbols A53

1971, Mar. 22 Engr. *Perf. 13*
152 A53 100fr dp car, ocher & grn 1.20 .50

B.C.G. inoculation (Bacillus-Calmette-Guerin) against tuberculosis, 50th anniv.

Boy Scouts, Mt. Fuji, Japanese Print — A54

1971, Apr. 19
153 A54 80fr lt ultra, dp plum & brt grn .75 .30

13th Boy Scout World Jamboree, Asagiri Plain, Japan, Aug. 2-10.

UNICEF Emblem, Hands and Rose A55

60fr, UNICEF emblem, women & children, vert.

1971, May 24 Engr. *Perf. 13*
154 A55 50fr brn org, car & dk brn .45 .25
155 A55 60fr vio bl, grn & red brn .60 .25

25th anniv. of UNICEF.

Mali Farmer — A56

Costumes of Mali: 10fr, Mali farm woman. 15fr, Tuareg. 60fr, Embroidered robe, Grand Boubou. 80fr, Ceremonial robe, woman.

1971, June 14 Photo. *Perf. 13*

156 A56 5fr gray & multi .25 .25
157 A56 10fr vio bl & multi .30 .25
158 A56 15fr yellow & multi .35 .25
159 A56 60fr gray & multi .60 .25
160 A56 80fr tan & multi .85 .30
Nos. 156-160 (5) 2.35 1.30

Map of Africa with Communications Network — A57

1971, Aug. 16 Photo. *Perf. 13*

161 A57 50fr bl, vio bl & org .50 .25

Pan-African telecommunications system.

Hibiscus A58

Flowers: 50fr, Poinsettia. 60fr, Adenium obesum. 80fr, Dogbane. 100fr, Satanocrater berhautii.

1971, Oct. 4 Litho. *Perf. 14x13½*

162 A58 20fr multicolored .45 .25
163 A58 50fr multicolored .90 .30
164 A58 60fr multicolored 1.20 .35
165 A58 80fr multicolored 1.50 .45
166 A58 100fr multicolored 2.00 .55
Nos. 162-166 (5) 6.05 1.90

For surcharge see No. 204.

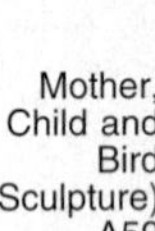

Mother, Child and Bird (Sculpture) A59

1971, Dec. 27 Engr. *Perf. 13x12½*

167 A59 70fr mag, sepia & bl grn .75 .25

Natl. Institute of Social Security, 15th anniv.

ITU Emblem A60

1972, May 17 Photo. *Perf. 13x13½*

168 A60 70fr blue, maroon & blk .75 .25

4th World Telecommunications Day.

Clay Funerary Statuette — A61

Mali Art: 40fr, Female torso, wood. 50fr, Masked figure, painted stone. 100fr, Animals and men, wrought iron.

1972, May 29 *Perf. 12½x13*

169 A61 30fr org red & multi .30 .25
170 A61 40fr yellow & multi .45 .25
171 A61 50fr red & multi .60 .25
172 A61 100fr lt green & multi 1.20 .40
Nos. 169-172 (4) 2.55 1.15

Morse and Telegraph A62

1972, June 5 Engr. *Perf. 13*

173 A62 80fr red, emer & choc .75 .35

Centenary of the death of Samuel F. B. Morse (1791-1872), inventor of the telegraph.

Weather Balloon over Africa — A63

1972, July 10 Photo. *Perf. 12½x13*

174 A63 130fr multicolored 1.50 .60

12th World Meteorology Day.

Folk Dances — A64

10fr, Sarakolé Dance, Kayes. 20fr, LaGomba, Bamako. 50fr, Hunters' dance, Bougouni. 70fr, Koré Duga, Ségou. 80fr, Kanaga, Sanga. 120fr, Targui, Timbuktu.

1972, Aug. 21 Photo. *Perf. 13*

175 A64 10fr shown .30 .25
176 A64 20fr multi .45 .25
177 A64 50fr multi .60 .25
178 A64 70fr multi .75 .30
179 A64 80fr multi .95 .35
180 A64 120fr multi 1.40 .45
Nos. 175-180 (6) 4.45 1.85

People, Book, Pencil — A65

1972, Sept. 8 Typo. *Perf. 12½x13*

181 A65 80fr black & yel grn .75 .25

World Literacy Day, Sept. 8.

"Edison Classique," Mali Instruments A66

1972, Sept. 18 Engr. *Perf. 13*

182 A66 100fr multicolored 1.00 .40

First Anthology of Music of Mali.

Aries — A67

Signs of the Zodiac: No. 184, Taurus. No. 185, Gemini. No. 186, Cancer. No. 187, Leo. No. 188, Virgo. No. 189, Libra. No. 190, Scorpio. No. 191, Sagittarius. No. 192, Capricorn. No. 193, Aquarius. No. 194, Pisces.

1972, Oct. 23 Engr. *Perf. 11*

183 A67 15fr lilac & bis brn .25 .25
184 A67 15fr bister brn & blk .25 .25
a. Pair #183-184 .50 .40
185 A67 35fr maroon & indigo .55 .25
186 A67 35fr emerald & mar .55 .25
a. Pair ,#185-186 1.25 .40
187 A67 40fr blue & red brn .60 .25
188 A67 40fr dk pur & red brn .60 .25
a. Pair, #187-188 1.40 .40
189 A67 45fr dk blue & mar .65 .30
190 A67 45fr maroon & brt grn .65 .30
a. Pair, #189-180 1.50 .60
191 A67 65fr dk violet & ind .90 .35
192 A67 65fr dk vio & gray ol .90 .35
a. Pair, #191-192 2.00 .70
193 A67 90fr brt pink & ind 1.40 .60
194 A67 90fr brt pink & grn 1.40 .60
a. Pair, #193-194 3.00 1.25
Nos. 183-194 (12) 8.70 4.00

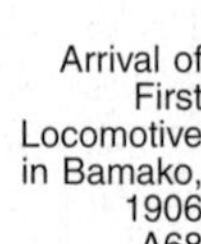

Arrival of First Locomotive in Bamako, 1906 A68

Designs (Locomotives): 30fr, Thies-Bamako, 1920. 60fr, Thies-Bamako, 1927. 120fr, Two Alsthom BB, 1947.

1972, Dec. 11 Engr. *Perf. 13*

195 A68 10fr ind, brn & sl grn 1.90 .60
196 A68 30fr sl grn, ind & brn 3.75 1.25
197 A68 60fr sl grn, ind & brn 5.50 1.75
198 A68 120fr sl grn & choc 7.50 2.50
Nos. 195-198 (4) 18.65 6.10

2nd African Games, Lagos, Nigeria, Jan. 7-18 — A69

1973, Jan. 15 Photo. *Perf. 12½*

199 A69 70fr High jump .50 .25
200 A69 270fr Discus 1.25 .60
201 A69 280fr Soccer 1.40 .85
Nos. 199-201 (3) 3.15 1.70

INTERPOL Emblem and Headquarters — A70

1973, Feb. 28 Photo. *Perf. 13*

202 A70 80fr multi .90 .25

50th anniversary of International Criminal Police Organization (INTERPOL).

Blind Man and Disabled Boy — A71

1973, Apr. 24 Engr. *Perf. 12½x13*

203 A71 70fr dk car, brick red & blk .60 .25

Help for the handicapped.

No. 166 Surcharged with New Value, 2 Bars, and Overprinted

Overprint reads "SECHERESSE / SOLIDARITE AFRICAINE".

1973, Aug. 16 Litho. *Perf. 13½*

204 A58 200fr on 100fr multi 1.75 .75

African solidarity in drought emergency.

Cora — A72

Musical Instruments: 10fr, Balafon, horiz. 15fr, Djembe. 20fr, Guitar. 25fr, N'Djarka. 30fr, M'Bolon. 35fr, Dozo N'Goni. 40fr, N'Tamani.

Perf. 12½x13, 13x12½

1973, Dec. 10 Engr.

205 A72 5fr mar, dk grn & brn .30 .25
206 A72 10fr bl & choc .35 .25
207 A72 15fr brn, dk red & yel .45 .25
208 A72 20fr mar & brn ol .55 .25
209 A72 25fr org, yel & blk .60 .25
210 A72 30fr vio bl & blk .65 .25
211 A72 35fr dk red & brn .75 .35
212 A72 40fr dk red & choc .85 .35
Nos. 205-212 (8) 4.50 2.20

Farmer with Newspaper, Corn — A73

1974, Mar. 11 Engr. *Perf. 12½x13*

213 A73 70fr multi .60 .25

"Kibaru," rural newspaper, 2nd anniv.

Soccer, Goalkeeper, Symbolic Globe and Net — A74

280fr, Games' emblem, soccer and ball.

1974, May 6 Engr. *Perf. 13*

214 A74 270fr multi 1.10 .60
215 A74 280fr multi 1.90 .90

World Cup Soccer Championships, Munich, June 13-July 7.
For surcharges see Nos. 219-220.

Old and New Ships, UPU Emblem — A75

90fr, Old and new planes, UPU emblem. 270fr, Old and new trains, UPU emblem.

1974, June 2 Engr. *Perf. 12½x13*

216 A75 80fr brn & multir .45 .25
217 A75 90fr ultra & multi .65 .35
218 A75 270fr lt grn & multi 1.90 .85
Nos. 216-218 (3) 3.00 1.45

Centenary of Universal Postal Union.
For surcharges see Nos. 229-230.

Nos. 214-215 Surcharged and Overprinted in Black or Red

Overprint reads "R.F.A. 2 / HOLLANDE 1".

1974, Aug. 28 Engr. *Perf. 13*

219 A74 300fr on 270fr multi 2.10 1.00
220 A74 330fr on 280fr multi (R) 2.40 1.10

World Cup Soccer Championship, 1974, victory of German Federal Republic.

Artisans of Mali — A76

1974, Sept. 16 Photo. *Perf. 12½x13*

221 A76 50fr Weaver .45 .25
222 A76 60fr Potter .55 .25
223 A76 70fr Smiths .60 .25
224 A76 80fr Sculptor .70 .30
Nos. 221-224 (4) 2.30 1.05

Niger River near Gao — A77

Landscapes: 20fr, The Hand of Fatma (rock formation), vert. 40fr, Gouina Waterfall. 70fr, Dogon houses, vert.

Perf. 13x12½, 12½x13

1974, Sept. 23

225 A77 10fr multi .25 .25
226 A77 20fr multi .25 .25
227 A77 40fr multi .45 .25
228 A77 70fr multi .65 .30
Nos. 225-228 (4) 1.60 1.05

Nos. 216 and 218 Surcharged and Overprinted in Black or Red

Overprint reads "9 OCTOBRE 1974".

1974, Oct. 9 Engr. *Perf. 13*

229 A75 250fr on 80fr multi 1.60 .80
230 A75 300fr on 270fr multi (R) 2.10 1.00

UPU Day.

Mao Tse-tung, Flags, Great Wall — A78

1974, Oct. 21 Engr. *Perf. 13*

231 A78 100fr multi 2.75 .65

People's Republic of China, 25th anniv.

Artisans and Lions Emblem — A79

100fr, View of Samanko and Lions emblem.

1975, Feb. 3 Photo. *Perf. 13*

232 A79 90fr red & multi .80 .25
233 A79 100fr blue & multi 1.00 .30

5th anniv. of lepers' rehabilitation village, Samanko, sponsored by Lions Intl.
For surcharges see Nos. 303-304.

Fish — A80

Designs: 60fr, Tetrodon Fahaka. 70fr, Malopterurus electricus. 80fr, Citharinus latus. 90fr, Hydrocyon forskali. 110fr, Lates niloticus.

1975, May 12 Engr. *Perf. 13*

234 A80 60fr shown 1.10 .30
235 A80 70fr multicolored 1.25 .35
236 A80 80fr multicolored 1.50 .40
237 A80 90fr multicolored 1.75 .45
238 A80 110fr multicolored 2.25 .50
Nos. 234-238 (5) 7.85 2.00

See Nos. 256-260.

Woman and IWY Emblem — A81

1975, June 9 Engr. *Perf. 13*

239 A81 150fr red & grn 1.00 .35

International Women's Year 1975.

Morris "Oxford," 1913 A82

Automobiles: 130fr, Franklin "E," 1907. 190fr, Daimler, 1900. 230fr, Panhard & Levassor, 1895.

1975, June 16

240 A82 90fr blk, ol & lil .70 .30
241 A82 130fr vio bl, gray & red 1.10 .40
242 A82 190fr bl, grn & indigo 1.60 .55
243 A82 230fr red, ultra & brn ol 1.80 .55
Nos. 240-243 (4) 5.20 1.80

Carthaginian Tristater, 500 B.C. — A83

Ancient Coins: 170fr, Decadrachma, Syracuse, 413 B.C. 190fr, Acanthe tetradrachma, 400 B.C. 260fr, Didrachma, Eritrea, 480-445 B.C.

1975, Oct. 13 Engr. *Perf. 13*

244 A83 130fr bl, cl & blk .70 .25
245 A83 170fr emer, brn & blk 1.00 .50
246 A83 190fr grn, red & blk 1.40 .70
247 A83 260fr dp bl, org & blk 2.00 1.00
Nos. 244-247 (4) 5.10 2.45

UN Emblem and "ONU" — A84

1975, Nov. 10 Engr. *Perf. 13*

248 A84 200fr emer & brt bl 1.10 .45

30th anniversary of UN.

A. G. Bell, Waves, Satellite, Telephone — A85

1976, Mar. 8 Litho. *Perf. 12x12½*

249 A85 180fr brn, ultra & ocher 1.10 .40

Centenary of first telephone call by Alexander Graham Bell, Mar. 10, 1876.

Chameleon A86

1976, Mar. 31 Litho. *Perf. 12½*

250 A86 20fr shown .35 .25
251 A86 30fr Lizard .50 .25
252 A86 40fr Tortoise .70 .25
253 A86 90fr Python 1.60 .50
254 A86 120fr Crocodile 2.00 .60
Nos. 250-254 (5) 5.15 1.85

Konrad Adenauer and Cologne Cathedral — A87

1976, Apr. 26 Engr. *Perf. 13*

255 A87 180fr mag & dk brn 1.20 .50

Konrad Adenauer (1876-1967), German Chancellor.

Fish Type of 1975

100fr, Heterotis niloticus. 120fr, Synodontis budgetti. 130fr, Heterobranchus bidorsalis. 150fr, Tilapia monodi. 220fr, Alestes macrolepidotus.

1976, June 28 Engr. *Perf. 13*

256 A80 100fr multi .75 .25
257 A80 120fr multi 1.00 .25
258 A80 130fr multi 1.10 .30
259 A80 150fr multi 1.20 .40
260 A80 220fr multi 1.75 .50
Nos. 256-260 (5) 5.80 1.70

Page from Children's Book — A88

1976, July 19

261 A88 130fr red & multi .75 .35

Books for children.

"Le Roi de l'Air" — A89

1976, July 26 Litho. *Perf. 12½x13*

262 A89 120fr multi 1.25 .45

First lottery, sponsored by L'Essor newspaper.

"Do not overload scaffold" — A90

1976, Aug. 16 Litho. *Perf. 13*

263 A90 120fr multi .60 .25

National Insurance Institute, 20th anniv.

Letters, UPU and UN Emblems — A91

1976, Oct. 4 **Engr.** ***Perf. 13***
264 A91 120fr lil, org & grn .75 .35

UN Postal Administration, 25th anniv.

Moto-Guzzi 254, Italy — A92

Motorcycles: 120fr, BMW 900, Germany. 130fr, Honda-Egli, Japan. 140fr, Motobecane LT-3, France.

1976, Oct. 18 **Engr.** ***Perf. 13***
265 A92 90fr multi 1.00 .25
266 A92 120fr multi 1.25 .30
267 A92 130fr multi 1.25 .40
268 A92 140fr multi 1.50 .40
Nos. 265-268 (4) 5.00 1.35

Fishing Boat, Muscat — A93

180fr, Coaster, Cochin China. 190fr, Fireboat, Dunkirk, 1878. 200fr, Nile river boat.

1976, Dec. 6 **Engr.** ***Perf. 13***
269 A93 160fr multi .80 .30
270 A93 180fr multi .90 .30
271 A93 190fr multi 1.00 .35
272 A93 200fr multi 1.00 .45
Nos. 269-272 (4) 3.70 1.40

Indigo Finch A94

Birds: 25fr, Yellow-breasted barbet. 30fr, Vitelline masked weaver. 40fr, Bee-eater. 50fr, Senegal parrot.

1977, Apr. 18 **Photo.** ***Perf. 13***
273 A94 15fr multi .50 .25
274 A94 25fr multi .90 .25
275 A94 30fr multi 1.10 .25
276 A94 40fr multi 1.40 .30
277 A94 50fr multi 1.80 .35
Nos. 273-277 (5) 5.70 1.40

See Nos. 298-302.

Braille Statue, Script and Reading Hands — A95

1977, Apr. 25 **Engr.** ***Perf. 13***
278 A95 200fr multi 1.25 .55

Louis Braille (1809-1852), inventor of the reading and writing system for the blind.

Electronic Tree, ITU Emblem — A96

1977, May 17 **Photo.**
279 A96 120fr dk brn & org .50 .25

World Telecommunications Day.

Dragonfly A97

Insects: 10fr, Praying mantis. 20fr, Tropical wasp. 35fr, Cockchafer. 60fr, Flying stag beetle.

1977, June 15 **Photo.** ***Perf. 13x12½***
280 A97 5fr multi .35 .25
281 A97 10fr multi .50 .25
282 A97 20fr multi .60 .25
283 A97 35fr multi 1.00 .25
284 A97 60fr multi 1.25 .30
Nos. 280-284 (5) 3.70 1.30

Knight and Rook A98

Chess Pieces: 130fr, Bishop and pawn, vert. 300fr, Queen and King.

1977, June 27 **Engr.** ***Perf. 13***
285 A98 120fr multi 1.50 .45
286 A98 130fr multi 1.60 .55
287 A98 300fr multi 3.50 1.25
Nos. 285-287 (3) 6.60 2.25

Europafrica Issue

Symbolic Ship, White and Brown Persons — A99

1977, July 18 **Litho.** ***Perf. 13***
288 A99 400fr multi 2.00 .80

Horse, by Leonardo da Vinci A100

Drawings by Leonardo da Vinci: 300fr, Head of Young Woman. 500fr, Self-portrait.

1977, Sept. 5 **Engr.** ***Perf. 13***
289 A100 200fr dk brn & blk 1.25 .65
290 A100 300fr dk brn & ol 1.75 .65
291 A100 500fr dk brn & red 2.40 1.10
Nos. 289-291 (3) 5.40 2.40

Hotel de l'Amitié, Bamako — A101

1977, Oct. 15 **Litho.** ***Perf. 13x12½***
292 A101 120fr multi .60 .25

Opening of the Hotel de l'Amitié, Oct. 15.

Dome of the Rock Jerusalem A102

1977, Oct. 17 ***Perf. 12½***
293 A102 120fr multi .55 .25
294 A102 180fr multi .85 .40

Palestinian fighters and their families.

Black Man, Chains and UN Emblem A103

130fr, Statue of Liberty, people & UN emblem. 180fr, Black children & horse behind fence.

1978, Mar. 13 **Engr.** ***Perf. 13***
295 A103 120fr multi .55 .25
296 A103 130fr multi .60 .25
297 A103 180fr multi .90 .35
Nos. 295-297 (3) 2.05 .85

International Year against Apartheid.

Bird Type of 1977

Birds: 20fr, Granatine bengala. 30fr, Lagonosticta vinacea. 50fr, Lagonosticta. 70fr, Turtle dove. 80fr, Buffalo weaver.

1978, Apr. 10 **Litho.** ***Perf. 13***
298 A94 20fr multi .65 .25
299 A94 30fr multi .90 .25
300 A94 50fr multi 1.10 .30
301 A94 70fr multi 1.50 .40
302 A94 80fr multi 2.00 .50
Nos. 298-302 (5) 6.15 1.70

Nos. 232-233 Surcharged with New Value, Bar and Overprinted

Overprint reads "XXe ANNIVERSAIRE DU LIONS CLUB DE BAMAKO 1958-1978".

1978, May 8 **Photo.**
303 A79 120fr on 90fr multi .70 .25
304 A79 130fr on 100fr multi .80 .25

20th anniversary of Bamako Lions Club.

Wall and Desert — A105

1978, May 18 **Litho.** ***Perf. 13***
306 A105 200fr multi 1.00 .40

Hammamet Conference for reclamation of the desert.

Mahatma Gandhi and Roses — A106

1978, May 29 **Engr.**
307 A106 140fr blk, brn & red 1.50 .30

Mohandas K. Gandhi (1869-1948), Hindu spiritual leader.

Dermestes — A107

Insects: 25fr, Ground beetle. 90fr, Cricket. 120fr, Ladybird. 140fr, Goliath beetle.

1978, June 12 **Photo.** ***Perf. 13***
308 A107 15fr multi .55 .25
309 A107 25fr multi .70 .25
310 A107 90fr multi 1.20 .25
311 A107 120fr multi 1.20 .30
312 A107 140fr multi 1.50 .35
Nos. 308-312 (5) 5.15 1.40

Bridge — A108

Design: 100fr, Dominoes, vert.

1978, June 26 **Engr.**
313 A108 100fr multi .75 .25
314 A108 130fr multi 1.00 .30

Aristotle — A109

1978, Oct. 16 Engr. *Perf. 13*

315 A109 200fr multi 1.20 .35

Aristotle (384-322 B.C.), Greek philosopher.

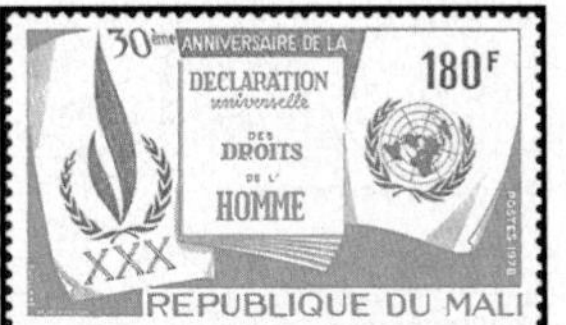
Human Rights and UN Emblems — A110

1978, Dec. 11 Engr. *Perf. 13*

316 A110 180fr red, bl & brn 1.25 .25

Universal Declaration of Human Rights, 30th anniversary.

Manatee — A111

Endangered Wildlife: 120fr, Chimpanzee. 130fr, Damaliscus antelope. 180fr, Oryx. 200fr, Derby's eland.

1979, Apr. 23 Litho. *Perf. 12½*

317 A111 100fr multi .75 .25
318 A111 120fr multi .90 .25
319 A111 130fr multi 1.00 .25
320 A111 180fr multi 1.40 .35
321 A111 200fr multi 1.50 .35
Nos. 317-321 (5) 5.55 1.45

Boy Praying and IYC Emblem — A112

IYC emblem and: 200fr, Girl and Boy Scout holding bird. 300fr, IYC emblem, boys with calf.

1979, May 7 Engr. *Perf. 13*

322 A112 120fr multi .60 .25
323 A112 200fr multi .90 .35
324 A112 300fr multi 1.50 .50
Nos. 322-324 (3) 3.00 1.10

International Year of the Child.

Judo and Notre Dame, Paris — A113

1979, May 14 Engr. *Perf. 13*

325 A113 200fr multi 1.40 .45

World Judo Championship, Paris.

Telecommunica-tions — A114

1979, May 17 Litho.

326 A114 120fr multi .60 .25

11th Telecommunications Day.

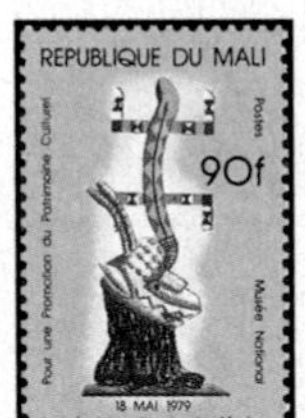
Wood Carving — A115

Sculptures from National Museum: 120fr, Ancestral figures. 130fr, Animal heads, and kneeling woman.

1979, May 18 *Perf. 13x12½*

327 A115 90fr multi .45 .25
328 A115 120fr multi .60 .25
329 A115 130fr multi .75 .30
Nos. 327-329 (3) 1.80 .80

International Museums Day.

Rowland Hill and Mali No. 15 — A116

130fr, Zeppelin & Saxony #1. 180fr, Concorde & France #3. 200fr, Stagecoach & US #2. 300fr, UPU emblem & Penny Black.

1979, May 21 Engr. *Perf. 13*

330 A116 120fr multi .55 .25
331 A116 130fr multi .55 .25
332 A116 180fr multi .75 .30
333 A116 200fr multi .85 .30
334 A116 300fr multi 1.50 .55
Nos. 330-334 (5) 4.20 1.65

Sir Rowland Hill (1795-1879), originator of penny postage.

Cora Players — A117

1979, June 4 Litho. *Perf. 13*

335 A117 200fr multi 1.50 .50

Adenium Obesum and Sankore Mosque — A118

Design: 300fr, Satellite, mounted messenger, globe and letter, vert.

1979, June 8 Photo.

336 A118 120fr multi 1.50 .75

Engr.

337 A118 300fr multi 2.60 1.60

Philexafrique II, Libreville, Gabon, June 8-17. Nos. 336, 337 printed in sheets of 10 and 5 labels showing exhibition emblem.

Map of Mali — A119

Design: 300fr, Men planting trees.

1979, June 18 Litho. *Perf. 13x12½*

338 A119 200fr multi 1.00 .40
339 A119 300fr multi 1.60 .70

Operation Green Sahel.

Lemons — A120

1979, June 25 *Perf. 12½x13*

340 A120 10fr shown .25 .25
341 A120 60fr Pineapple .45 .25
342 A120 100fr Papayas .75 .25
343 A120 120fr Soursops .85 .25
344 A120 130fr Mangoes 1.00 .25
Nos. 340-344 (5) 3.30 1.25

Sigmund Freud — A121

1979, Sept. 17 Engr. *Perf. 13*

345 A121 300fr vio bl & sepia 1.50 .60

Sigmund Freud (1856-1939), founder of psychoanalysis.

Timbuktu, Man and Camel A122

Design: 130fr, Caillié, Map of Sahara.

1979, Sept. 27 *Perf. 13x12½*

346 A122 120fr multi .75 .30
347 A122 130fr multi .85 .35

René Caillié (1799-1838), French explorer, 180th birth anniversary.

Eurema Brigitta A123

120fr, Papilio pylades. 130fr, Melanitis leda satyridae. 180fr, Gonimbrasia belina occidentalis. 200fr, Bunaea alcinoe.

1979, Oct. 15 Litho. *Perf. 13*

348 A123 100fr shown 1.10 .25
349 A123 120fr multi 1.25 .30
350 A123 130fr multi 1.40 .35
351 A123 180fr multi 2.00 .45
352 A123 200fr multi 2.25 .50
Nos. 348-352 (5) 8.00 1.85

Greyhound A124

Designs: Dogs.

1979, Nov. 12 Litho. *Perf. 12½*

353 A124 20fr multi .65 .25
354 A124 50fr multi .80 .25
355 A124 70fr multi .95 .25
356 A124 80fr multi 1.20 .25
357 A124 90fr multi 1.40 .30
Nos. 353-357 (5) 5.00 1.30

Wild Donkey — A125

1980, Feb. 4 Litho. *Perf. 13x13½*

358 A125 90fr shown .80 .25
359 A125 120fr Addax 1.00 .25
360 A125 130fr Cheetahs 1.15 .30
361 A125 140fr Mouflon 1.25 .35
362 A125 180fr Buffalo 1.80 .35
Nos. 358-362 (5) 6.00 1.50

Photovoltaic Cell Pumping Station, Koni — A126

Solar Energy Utilization: 100fr, Sun shields, Dire. 120fr, Solar stove, Bamako. 130fr, Heliodynamic solar energy generating station, Dire.

1980, Mar. 10 Litho. *Perf. 13*

363 A126 90fr multi .45 .25
364 A126 100fr multi .55 .25
365 A126 120fr multi .60 .25
366 A126 130fr multi .75 .25
Nos. 363-366 (4) 2.35 1.00

For surcharge see No. 511.

Horse Breeding, Mopti A127

1980, Mar. 17

367 A127 100fr shown .80 .25
368 A127 120fr Nioro .90 .25
369 A127 130fr Koro 1.00 .25
370 A127 180fr Coastal zone 1.25 .30
371 A127 200fr Banamba 1.25 .55
Nos. 367-371 (5) 5.20 1.60

Alexander Fleming (Discoverer of Penicillin) A128

1980, May 5 Engr. *Perf. 13*

372 A128 200fr multi 1.25 .50

Avicenna and Medical Instruments A129

Design: 180fr, Avicenna as teacher (12th century manuscript illustration)

1980, May 12 *Perf. 13x12½*

373	A129 120fr multi	.65	.25
374	A129 180fr multi	.85	.35

Avicenna (980-1037), Arab physician and philosopher, 1000th birth anniversary.

Pilgrim at Mecca — A130

130fr, Praying hands, stars, Mecca. 180fr, Pilgrims, camels, horiz.

1980, May 26 **Litho.** *Perf. 13*

375	A130 120fr shown	.55	.25
376	A130 130fr multi	.55	.25
377	A130 180fr multi	.80	.30
	Nos. 375-377 (3)	1.90	.80

Hegira, 1500th Anniversary.

Guavas — A131

1980, June 9

378	A131 90fr shown	.55	.25
379	A131 120fr Cashews	.60	.25
380	A131 130fr Oranges	.70	.25
381	A131 140fr Bananas	.90	.25
382	A131 180fr Grapefruit	1.00	.30
	Nos. 378-382 (5)	3.75	1.30

League of Nations, 60th Anniversary A132

1980, June 23 **Engr.** *Perf. 13*

383	A132 200fr multi	.75	.30

Festival Emblem, Mask, Xylophone A133

1980, July 5 **Litho.** *Perf. 12½*

384	A133 120fr multi	.60	.25

6th Biennial Arts and Cultural Festival, Bamako, July 5-15.

Sun Rising over Map of Africa — A134

1980, July 7 **Engr.** *Perf. 13*

385	A134 300fr multi	1.10	.45

Afro-Asian Bandung Conference, 25th anniversary.

Market Place, Conference Emblem A135

120fr, View of Mali, vert.

1980, Sept. 15 **Litho.** *Perf. 13*

386	A135 120fr multi	.55	.25
387	A135 180fr shown	.85	.30

World Tourism Conf., Manila, Sept. 27.

Hydro-electric Dam and Power Station — A136

20th Anniversary of Independence: 120fr, Pres. Traore, flag of Mali, National Assembly building. 130fr, Independence monument, Bamako, Political Party badge, vert.

1980, Sept. 15 *Perf. 13x12½*

388	A136 100fr multi	.45	.25
389	A136 120fr multi	.60	.25
390	A136 130fr multi	.75	.30
	Nos. 388-390 (3)	1.80	.80

Utetheisa Pulchella A137

60fr, Mylothis chloris pieridae. 70fr, Hypolimnas mishippus. 80fr, Papilio demodocus.

1980, Oct. 6 *Perf. 13½*

391	A137 50fr shown	.85	.25
392	A137 60fr multi	1.05	.25
393	A137 70fr multi	1.25	.30
394	A137 80fr multi	1.40	.35
	Nos. 391-394,C402 (5)	8.30	2.15

Fight Against Cigarette Smoking — A138

1980, Oct. 13 **Litho.** *Perf. 12½x12*

395	A138 200fr multi	1.10	.45

European-African Economic Convention — A139

1980, Oct. 20 *Perf. 12½*

396	A139 300fr multi	1.90	.60

Agricultural Map of West Africa A140

West African Economic Council, 5th anniversary (Economic Maps): 120fr, Transportation. 130fr, Industry. 140fr, Communications.

1980, Nov. 5 *Perf. 13½x13*

397	A140 100fr multi	.50	.25
398	A140 120fr multi	.55	.25
399	A140 130fr multi	.65	.25
400	A140 140fr multi	.70	.30
	Nos. 397-400 (4)	2.40	1.05

African Postal Union, 5th Anniv. — A141

1980, Dec. 24 **Photo.** *Perf. 13½*

401	A141 130fr multi	.75	.30

Senuofo Fertility Statue — A142

Designs: Fertility statues.

1981, Jan. 12 **Litho.** *Perf. 13*

402	A142 60fr Nomo dogon	.30	.25
403	A142 70fr shown	.40	.25
404	A142 90fr Bamanan	.55	.25
405	A142 100fr Spirit	.60	.25
406	A142 120fr Dogon	.95	.25
	Nos. 402-406 (5)	2.80	1.25

Mambi Sidibe — A143

Philosophers: 130fr, Amadou Hampate.

1981, Feb. 16 *Perf. 12½x13*

407	A143 120fr shown	.60	.25
408	A143 130fr multi	.60	.25

Hegira (Pilgrimage Year) — A144

1981, Feb. 23 *Perf. 13*

409	A144 120fr multi	.55	.25
410	A144 180fr multi	1.00	.35

Cattle Breeds A145

20fr, Kaarta zebu. 30fr, Peul du Macina zebu. 40fr, Maure zebu. 80fr, Touareg zebu. 100fr, N'Dama cow.

1981, Mar. 9 *Perf. 12½*

411	A145 20fr multi	.50	.25
412	A145 30fr multi	.65	.25
413	A145 40fr multi	.80	.25
414	A145 80fr multi	1.20	.25
415	A145 100fr multi	1.25	.30
	Nos. 411-415 (5)	4.40	1.30

See Nos. 433-437.

Flowers — A146

Designs: 50fr, Crinum de Moore. 100fr, Double Rose Hibiscus. 120fr, Pervenche. 130fr, Frangipani. 180fr, Orgueil de Chine.

1981, Mar. 16

416	A146 50fr multi	.30	.25
417	A146 100fr multi	.65	.25
418	A146 120fr multi	.80	.25
419	A146 130fr multi	1.00	.25
420	A146 180fr multi	1.25	.45
	Nos. 416-420 (5)	4.00	1.45

See Nos. 442-446.

Wrench Operated by Artificial Hand A147

Perf. 13x12½, 12x13

1981, May 4 **Engr.**

421	A147 100fr Heads, vert.	.55	.25
422	A147 120fr shown	.60	.25

Intl. Year of the Disabled.

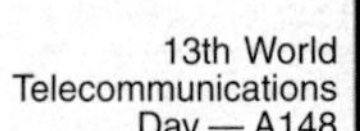
13th World Telecommunications Day — A148

1981, May 17 **Litho.** *Perf. 13x12½*

423	A148 130fr multi	.75	.25

Pierre Curie, Lab Equipment A149

1981, May 25 **Engr.**

424 A149 180fr multi 1.25 .50

Curie (1859-1906), discoverer of radium.

Scouts at Water Hole — A150

1981, June 8 **Litho.** ***Perf. 13***

425 A150 110fr shown 1.25 .30
426 A150 160fr Sending signals 1.75 .45
427 A150 300fr Salute, vert. 3.00 .70
Nos. 425-427 (3) 6.00 1.45

Souvenir Sheet

428 A150 500fr Lord Baden-Powell 6.00 4.00

4th African Scouting Conf., Abidjan, June.

Nos. 425-428 Overprinted in Red in 2 or 3 Lines

Overprint reads "DAKAR 8 AOUT 1981/28e CONFERENCE MONDIALE DU SCOUTISME".

1981, June 29

429 A150 110fr multi 1.10 .30
430 A150 160fr multi 1.50 .45
431 A150 300fr multi 3.00 .70
Nos. 429-431 (3) 5.60 1.45

Souvenir Sheet

432 A150 500fr multi 6.50 4.00

28th World Scouting Conf., Dakar, Aug. 8.

Various Goats

1981, Sept. 14 **Litho.** ***Perf. 13x13½***

433 A150a 10fr Maure .25 .25
434 A150a 25fr Peul .30 .25
435 A150a 140fr Sahel 1.10 .25
436 A150a 180fr Tuareg 1.40 .30
437 A150a 200fr Djallonke 1.60 .35
Nos. 433-437 (5) 4.65 1.40

World UPU Day — A151

1981, Oct. 9 **Engr.** ***Perf. 13***

438 A151 400fr multi 2.25 .70

World Food Day — A152

1981, Oct. 16

439 A152 200fr multi 1.10 .40

Europafrica Economic Convention — A153

1981, Nov. 23 **Engr.** ***Perf. 13***

440 A153 700fr multi 3.00 1.05

60th Anniv. of Tuberculosis Inoculation — A154

1981, Dec. 7 ***Perf. 13x12½***

441 A154 200fr multi 1.10 .45

Flower Type of 1981

1982, Jan. 18 **Litho.** ***Perf. 13***

442 A146 170fr White water lilies .85 .25
443 A146 180fr Red kapok bush .90 .25
444 A146 200fr Purple mimosa 1.10 .30
445 A146 220fr Pobego lilies 1.10 .40
446 A146 270fr Satan's chalices 1.40 .50
Nos. 442-446 (5) 5.35 1.70

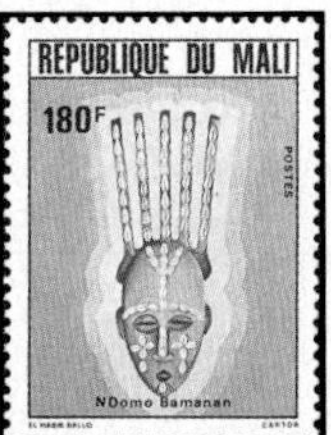

Ceremonial Mask — A155

Designs: Various masks.

1982, Feb. 22 **Litho.** ***Perf. 12½***

447 A155 5fr multi .25 .25
448 A155 35fr multi .25 .25
449 A155 180fr multi .90 .30
450 A155 200fr multi 1.00 .35
451 A155 250fr multi 1.20 .35
Nos. 447-451 (5) 3.60 1.50

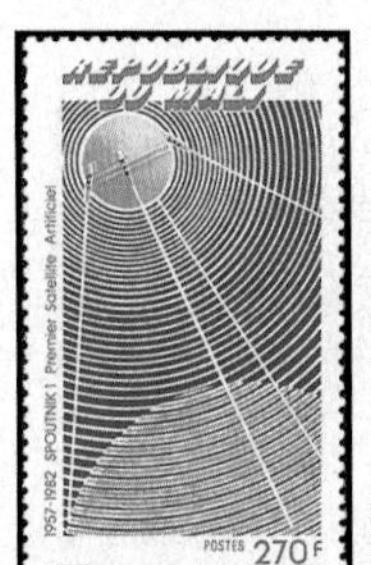

25th Anniv. of Sputnik I Flight — A156

1982, Mar. 29 **Litho.** ***Perf. 13***

452 A156 270fr multi 1.40 .50

Fight Against Polio — A157

1982, May 3

453 A157 180fr multi .90 .35

Lions Intl. and Day of the Blind A158

1982, May 10 **Engr.**

454 A158 260fr multi 1.40 .30

"Good Friends" Hairstyle — A159

Designs: Various hairstyles.

1982, May 24 **Litho.**

455 A159 140fr multi .45 .25
456 A159 150fr multi .60 .25
457 A159 160fr multi .75 .30
458 A159 180fr multi 1.10 .35
459 A159 270fr multi 1.75 .60
Nos. 455-459 (5) 4.65 1.75

Zebu A160

Designs: Various breeds of zebu.

1982, July 5 ***Perf. 12½***

460 A160 10fr multi .30 .25
461 A160 60fr multi .60 .25
462 A160 110fr multi .90 .25
463 A160 180fr multi 1.40 .35
464 A160 200fr multi 1.50 .40
Nos. 460-464 (5) 4.70 1.50

Wind Surfing (New Olympic Class) — A161

Designs: Various wind surfers.

1982, Nov. 22 **Litho.** ***Perf. 12½x13***

465 A161 200fr multi .90 .35
466 A161 270fr multi 1.25 .50
467 A161 300fr multi 1.40 .60
Nos. 465-467 (3) 3.55 1.45

Pres. John F. Kennedy — A162

800fr, Martin Luther King.

1983, Apr. 4 **Engr.** ***Perf. 13***

468 A162 800fr brown & red 3.25 1.25
469 A162 800fr brn, blue & pur 3.25 1.25

Oua Traditional Hairstyle — A163

1983, Apr. 25 **Litho.**

470 A163 180fr shown 1.00 .25
471 A163 200fr Nation 1.10 .25
472 A163 270fr Rond point 1.40 .35
473 A163 300fr Naamu-Naamu 1.50 .40
474 A163 500fr Bamba-Bamba 2.60 .70
Nos. 470-474 (5) 7.60 1.95

World Communications Year — A164

1983, May 17 **Litho.** ***Perf. 13***

475 A164 180fr multi 1.00 .40

Bicent. of Lavoisier's Water Analysis — A165

1983, May 27 **Engr.** ***Perf. 13***

476 A165 300fr multi 1.40 .50

Musicians — A166

200fr, Banzoumana Sissoko. 300fr, Batourou Sekou Kouyate.

1983, June 13 **Litho.** ***Perf. 13x13½***

477 A166 200fr multi .90 .25
478 A166 300fr multi 1.20 .35

Nicephore Niepce, Photography Pioneer, (1765-1833) A167

400fr, Portrait, early camera.

1983, July 4 **Engr.** ***Perf. 13***
479 A167 400fr multi 1.75 .45

2nd Pan African Youth Festival — A168

Palestinian Solidarity A169

1983, Aug. 22 **Litho.** ***Perf. 12½***
480 A168 240fr multi 1.10 .30
481 A169 270fr multi 1.20 .40

14th World UPU Day — A170

1983, Oct. 10 **Engr.** ***Perf. 12½***
482 A170 240fr multi 1.25 .35

For surcharge see No. 500.

Sahel Goat A171

1984, Jan. 30 **Litho.** ***Perf. 13***
483 A171 20fr shown .25 .25
484 A171 30fr Billy goat .35 .25
485 A171 50fr Billy goat, diff. .65 .25
486 A171 240fr Kaarta goat 1.60 .30
487 A171 350fr Southern goats 2.25 .45
Nos. 483-487 (5) 5.10 1.50

For surcharges see Nos. 497-499, 501-502.

Rural Development A172

5fr, Crop disease prevention. 90fr, Carpenters, horiz. 100fr, Tapestry weaving, horiz. 135fr, Metal workers, horiz.

1984, June 1 **Litho.** ***Perf. 13***
488 A172 5fr multi .25 .25
489 A172 90fr multi .75 .25
490 A172 100fr multi .75 .30
491 A172 135fr multi 1.00 .45
Nos. 488-491 (4) 2.75 1.25

Fragrant Trees — A173

515fr, Borassus flabelifer. 1225fr, Vitelaria paradoxa.

1984, June 1
492 A173 515fr multi 4.00 1.90
493 A173 1225fr multi 9.50 4.25

For surcharge see No. 583.

UN Infant Survival Campaign — A174

1984, June 12 **Engr.**
494 A174 120fr Child, hearts 1.10 .40
495 A174 135fr Children 1.25 .45

1984 UPU Congress — A175

135fr, Anchor, UPU emblem, view of Hamburg.

1984, June 18
496 A175 135fr multicolored 1.25 .40

Nos. 482-487 Surcharged

1984
497 A171 10fr on 20fr #483 .25 .25
498 A171 15fr on 30fr #484 .25 .25
499 A171 25fr on 50fr #485 .40 .25
500 A170 120fr on 240fr #482 1.50 .30
501 A171 120fr on 240fr #486 1.60 .30
502 A171 175fr on 350fr #487 2.25 .50
Nos. 497-502 (6) 6.25 1.85

West African Economic Community, CEAO, 10th Anniv. A176

1984, Oct. 22 **Litho.** ***Perf. 13½***
503 A176 350fr multi 2.75 1.50

For surcharge see No. 588.

Prehistoric Animals A177

10fr, Dimetrodon. 25fr, Iguanodon, vert. 30fr, Archaeopteryx, vert.

1984, Nov. 5 **Litho.** ***Perf. 12½***
504 A177 10fr multi .25 .25
505 A177 25fr multi .40 .25
506 A177 30fr multi .50 .25
507 A177 120fr Like 10fr 2.00 .40
508 A177 175fr Like 25fr 3.00 .60
509 A177 350fr Like 30fr 5.50 1.50
510 A177 470fr Triceratops 7.50 2.50
Nos. 504-510 (7) 19.15 5.75

For surcharges see Nos. 579, 593.

No. 366 Overprinted "Aide au Sahel 84" and Surcharged

1984 **Litho.** ***Perf. 13***
511 A126 470fr on 130fr 3.75 2.25

Issued to publicize drought relief efforts.

Mali Horses A178

90fr, Modern horse. 135fr, Horse from Beledougou. 190fr, Horse from Nara. 530fr, Horse from Trait.

1985, Jan. 21 **Litho.** ***Perf. 13½***
512 A178 90fr multi .90 .35
513 A178 135fr multi 1.20 .45
514 A178 190fr multi 1.75 .70
515 A178 530fr multi 5.00 1.90
Nos. 512-515 (4) 8.85 3.40

For surcharges see Nos. 586, 591.

Fungi — A179

120fr, Clitocybe nebularis. 200fr, Lepiota cortinarius. 485fr, Agavicus semotus. 525fr, Lepiota procera.

1985, Jan. 28 **Litho.** ***Perf. 12½***
516 A179 120fr multi 1.40 .90
517 A179 200fr multi 2.10 1.00
518 A179 485fr multi 5.25 1.75
519 A179 525fr multi 5.50 1.75
Nos. 516-519 (4) 14.25 5.40

For surcharges see Nos. 589-590.

Health — A180

Designs: 120fr, 32nd World Leprosy Day, Emile Marchoux (1862-1943), Marchoux Institute, 150th anniv. 135fr, Lions Intl., Samanko Convalescence Village, 15th anniv. 470fr, Anti-polio campaign, research facility, victim.

1985, Feb. 18 **Litho.** ***Perf. 13***
520 A180 120fr multi .90 .40
521 A180 135fr multi 1.10 .45
522 A180 470fr multi 3.25 1.75
Nos. 520-522 (3) 5.25 2.60

For surcharges see Nos. 580, 584. No. 522 is airmail.

Cultural and Technical Cooperation Agency, 15th Anniv. — A181

1985, Mar. 20
523 A181 540fr brn & brt bl grn 4.50 1.75

Intl. Youth Year A182

Youth activities: 120fr, Natl. Pioneers Movement emblem. 190fr, Agricultural production. 500fr, Sports.

1985, May 13 ***Perf. 12½x13***
524 A182 120fr multi 1.00 .45
525 A182 190fr multi 1.75 .70
526 A182 500fr multi 4.50 1.75
Nos. 524-526 (3) 7.25 2.90

For surcharge see No. 587.

PHILEXAFRICA '85, Lome, Togo — A183

No. 527, Education, telecommunications. No. 528, Road, dam, computers.

1985, June 24 ***Perf. 13***
527 A183 250fr multi 2.25 1.50
528 A183 250fr multi 2.25 1.50
a. Pair, #527-528 + label 5.50 4.50
Nos. 527-528,C517-C518 (4) 8.50 5.50

Nos. 527-528 show the UPU emblem.

Cats A184

1986, Feb. 15 **Litho.** ***Perf. 13½***
529 A184 150fr Gray 1.50 .55
530 A184 200fr White 2.25 .85
531 A184 300fr Tabby 3.00 1.10
Nos. 529-531 (3) 6.75 2.50

For surcharge see No. 582.

Fight Against Apartheid — A185

120fr, Map, broken chain.

1986, Feb. 24 ***Perf. 13***
532 A185 100fr shown 1.00 .35
533 A185 120fr multi 1.10 .45

Telecommunications and Agriculture — A186

1986, May 17 Litho. *Perf. 13*

534 A186 200fr multi 1.50 .70

1986 World Cup Soccer Championships, Mexico — A187

Various soccer plays.

1986, May 24 Litho. *Perf. 12½*

535 A187 160fr multi 1.20 .50
536 A187 225fr multi 2.00 .75

Souvenir Sheet

537 A187 500fr multi 3.75 2.75

For overprints surcharges see No. 539-541, 585.

James Watt (1736-1819), Inventor, and Steam Engine — A188

1986, May 26 *Perf. 12½x12*

538 A188 110fr multi 1.10 .40

For surcharge see No. 581.

Nos. 535-537 Ovptd. "ARGENTINE 3 / R.F.A. 2" in Red

1986, July 30 Litho. *Perf. 12½*

539 A187 160fr multi 1.50 .70
540 A187 225fr multi 2.25 .90

Souvenir Sheet

541 A187 500fr multi 4.50 3.00

World Wildlife Fund — A189

Derby's Eland, Taurotragus derbianus.

1986, Aug. 11 Litho. *Perf. 13*

542 A189 5fr Adult head 1.20 .25
543 A189 20fr Adult in brush 2.25 .25
544 A189 25fr Adult walking 2.25 .25
545 A189 200fr Calf suckling 17.50 3.50
Nos. 542-545 (4) 23.20 4.25

Henry Ford (1863-1947), Auto Manufacturer, Inventor of Mass Production — A190

150fr, Model A, 1903. 200fr, Model T, 1923. 225fr, Thunderbird, 1968. 300fr, Lincoln Continental, 1963.

1987, Feb. 16 Litho. *Perf. 13*

546 A190 150fr multi 1.40 .50
547 A190 200fr multi 2.00 1.00
548 A190 225fr multi 2.25 1.10
549 A190 300fr multi 2.25 1.25
Nos. 546-549 (4) 7.90 3.85

Bees A191

100fr, Apis florea, Asia. 150fr, Apis dorsata, Asia. 175fr, Apis adansonii, Africa. 200fr, Apis mellifica, worldwide.

1987, May 11 Litho. *Perf. 13½*

550 A191 100fr multi 1.10 .55
551 A191 150fr multi 1.40 .65
552 A191 175fr multi 1.75 .85
553 A191 200fr multi 2.10 1.00
Nos. 550-553 (4) 6.35 3.05

Lions Club Activities — A192

1988, Jan. 13 Litho. *Perf. 12½*

554 A192 200fr multi 1.50 .85

World Health Organization, 40th Anniv. — A193

1988, Feb. 22 Litho. *Perf. 12½x12*

555 A193 150fr multi 1.25 .55

For surcharge see No. 557.

John F. Kennedy (1917-1963), 35th US President A194

1988, June 6 Litho. *Perf. 13*

556 A194 640fr multi 5.25 2.50

For surcharge see No. 592.

No. 555 Surcharged in Dark Red

1988, June 13 *Perf. 12½x12*

557 A193 300fr on 150fr multi 2.60 1.60

Mali Mission Hospital in Mopti and World Medicine organization.

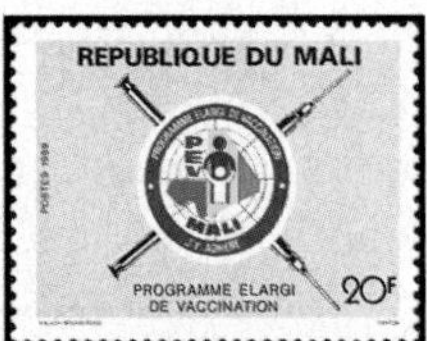

Organization of African Unity, 25th Anniv. — A194a

1988, June 27 Litho. *Perf. 12½*

558 A194a 400fr multi 3.00 1.75

Universal Immunization Campaign — A195

30fr, Inoculating woman. 50fr, Emblem, needles, diff. 175fr, Inoculating boy.

1989, May 2 Litho. *Perf. 13½*

559 A195 20fr shown .25 .25
560 A195 30fr multi .30 .25
561 A195 50fr multi .45 .25
562 A195 175fr multi 1.50 .80
Nos. 559-562 (4) 2.50 1.55

Intl. Law Institute of the French-Speaking Nations — A196

1989, May 15 *Perf. 12½*

563 A196 150fr multi 1.40 .70
564 A196 200fr multi 1.75 .90

World Post Day — A197

1989, Oct. 9 Litho. *Perf. 13*

565 A197 625fr multicolored 5.50 2.50

For surcharge see No. 594.

Visit of Pope John Paul II — A198

1990, Jan. 28 Litho. *Perf. 13x12½*

566 A198 200fr multicolored 2.00 .75

Multinational Postal School, 20th Anniv. — A199

1990, May 31 Litho. *Perf. 12½*

567 A199 150fr multicolored 1.40 .65

Independence, 30th Anniv. — A200

1990, Sept. 20 Litho. *Perf. 13x12½*

568 A200 400fr multicolored 3.75 1.90

Intl. Literacy Year A201

1990, Sept. 24 Litho. *Perf. 13½*

569 A201 150fr grn & multi 1.25 .65
570 A201 200fr org & multi 2.00 .90

A202

Lions Intl. Water Project, 6th anniv.: No. 572, Rotary Club fight against polio, 30th anniv.

1991, Feb. 25 Litho. *Perf. 13x12½*

571 A202 200fr multicolored 2.00 1.00
572 A202 200fr multicolored 2.00 1.00

Tribal Dances of Mali — A203

1991, Apr. 29 Litho. *Perf. 12½*

573 A203 50fr Takamba .50 .30
574 A203 100fr Mandiani .90 .60
575 A203 150fr Kono 1.40 .90
576 A203 200fr Songho 1.90 1.10
Nos. 573-576 (4) 4.70 2.90

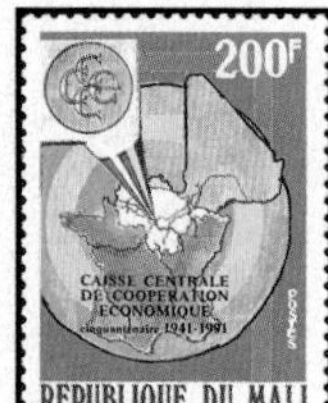

A204

1991, Dec. 2 Litho. *Perf. 12½*
577 A204 200fr multicolored 2.00 1.00

Central Fund for Economic Cooperation, 50th anniv.

A205

1992, Mar. 26 Litho. *Perf. 12½*
578 A205 150fr multicolored 1.40 .75

National Women's Movement.

Stamps of 1984-89 Srchd. in Black or Black & Silver

1992, June Litho. *Perfs. as Before*
579 A177 25fr on 470fr #510 — —
580 A180 25fr on 470fr #522 — —
581 A188 30fr on 110fr #538 — —
582 A184 50fr on 300fr #531 — —
583 A173 50fr on 1225fr #493 — —
584 A180 150fr on 135fr #521 (Bk & S) — —
585 A187 150fr on 160fr #535 — —
586 A178 150fr on 190fr #514 — —
587 A182 150fr on 190fr #525 — —
588 A176 150fr on 350fr #503 — —
589 A179 150fr on 485fr #518 — —
590 A179 150fr on 525fr #519 — —
591 A178 150fr on 530fr #515 — —
592 A194 200fr on 640fr #556 — —
593 A177 240fr on 350fr #509 — —
594 A197 240fr on 625fr #565 — —

No. 580 is airmail. Size and location of surcharge varies. No. 585 also overprinted "Euro '92."

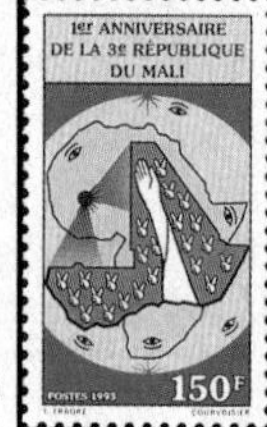

New Constitution, 1st Anniv. — A205a

1993, Jan. 12 Litho. *Perf. 11½x12*
594A A205a 150fr multi *25.00*
594B A205a 225fr multi *35.00*

Martyr's Day, 2nd Anniv. — A206

1993, Mar. 26 Litho. *Perf. 11½*
595 A206 150fr blue & multi *30.00 30.00*
596 A206 160fr yellow & multi *30.00 30.00*

Rotary Intl. and World Health Organization (WHO) — A206a

Designs: 150fr, Polio victims, Rotary emblem. 200fr, WHO emblem, pregnant woman receiving vaccination.

1993, Apr. 16 Litho. *Perf. 14*
596A A206a 150fr multi *25.00*
596B A206a 200fr multi *35.00*

Lions Club in Mali, 35th Anniv. A207

1993, Dec. 20 Litho. *Perf. 14½*
597 A207 200fr blue & multi *30.00 30.00*
598 A207 225fr red & multi *30.00 30.00*

Monument, Liberty Place — A207a

1993, Dec. 20 Photo. *Perf. 11¾*
Granite Paper
598A A207a 20fr multi — —
598B A207a 25fr multi — —
598C A207a 50fr multi — —
598D A207a 100fr multi — —
598E A207a 110fr multi — —
598F A207a 150fr multi — —
598G A207a 200fr multi — —
598H A207a 225fr multi — —
598I A207a 240fr multi — —
598J A207a 260fr multi — —
Nos. 598A-598J (10) *125.00*

1994 Winter Olympics, Lillehammer A208

150fr, Pairs figure skating. 200fr, Giant slalom. 225fr, Ski jumping. 750fr, Speed skating. 2000fr, Downhill skiing.

1994, Feb. 12 Litho. *Perf. 13*
599 A208 150fr multi .90 .50
600 A208 200fr multi 1.25 .75
601 A208 225fr multi 1.75 1.00
602 A208 750fr multi 3.00 1.75
Nos. 599-602 (4) 6.90 4.00

Souvenir Sheet
603 A208 2000fr multi 8.00 8.00

No. 603 contains one 36x36mm stamp.
For overprints see Nos. 671-676.

1994 World Cup Soccer Championships, US — A209

Designs: 200fr, Juan Schiaffino, Uruguay. 240fr, Diego Maradona, Argentina. 260fr, Paolo Rossi, Italy. 1000fr, Franz Beckenbauer, Germany. 2000fr, Just Fontaine, France.

1994, Mar. 15 Litho. *Perf. 13*
604 A209 200fr multicolored .90 .90
605 A209 240fr multicolored 1.40 .80
606 A209 260fr multicolored 1.60 .90
607 A209 1000fr multicolored 5.00 2.75
Nos. 604-607 (4) 8.90 5.35

Souvenir Sheet
608 A209 2000fr multicolored 8.00 8.00

For overprints see Nos. 677-681.

Miniature Sheet

Dinosaurs — A210

a, 5fr, Scaphonyx. b, 10fr, Cynognathus. c, 15fr, Lesothosaurus. d, 20fr, Scutellosaurus. e, 25fr, Ceratosaurus. f, 30fr, Dilophosaurus. g, 40fr, Dryosaurus. h, 50fr, Heterodontosaurus. i, 60fr, Anatosaurus. j, 70fr, Saurornithoides. k, 80fr, Avimimus. l, 90fr, Saltasaurus. m, 300fr, Dromaeosaurus. n, 400fr, Tsintaosaurus. o, 600fr, Velociraptor. p, 700fr, Ouranosaurus.
2000fr, Daspletosaurus, iguanodon.

1994, Mar. 28
609 A210 Sheet of 16, #a.-p. 13.00 10.00

Souvenir Sheet
610 A210 2000fr multi 10.00 10.00

Insects A211

Designs: 40fr, Sternuera castanea, vert. 50fr, Eudicella gralli. 100fr, Homoderus mellyi, vert. 200fr, Kraussaria angulifera.

1994, Mar. 30 Litho. *Perf. 13*
611 A211 40fr multicolored .40 .25
612 A211 50fr multicolored .70 .35
613 A211 100fr multicolored 1.10 .60
614 A211 200fr multicolored 2.00 1.00
Nos. 611-614 (4) 4.20 2.20

Vaccination Campaign Against Measles — A212

1994, Apr. 7 Litho. *Perf. 13½*
615 A212 150fr black & green .90 .50
616 A212 200fr black & blue 1.60 .90

Birds A213

25fr, Pigeons. 30fr, Turkeys. 150fr, Crowned cranes, vert. 200fr, Chickens, vert.

1994, Apr. 25
617 A213 25fr multi .30 .25
618 A213 30fr multi .30 .25
619 A213 150fr multi 1.40 .70
620 A213 200fr multi 1.50 .80
Nos. 617-620 (4) 3.50 2.00

Intl. Year of the Family — A213a

1994, May 2
620A A213a 220fr multicolored 1.25 .60

Jazz Musicians A214

200fr, Ella Fitzgerald. 225fr, Lionel Hampton. 240fr, Sarah Vaughan. 300fr, Count Basie. 400fr, Duke Ellington. 600fr, Miles Davis.
1500fr, Louis Armstrong.

1994, May 23 Litho. *Perf. 13*
621 A214 200fr multi .80 .60
622 A214 225fr multi 1.00 .80
623 A214 240fr multi 1.25 .95
624 A214 300fr multi 1.75 1.40
625 A214 400fr multi 2.25 1.75
626 A214 600fr multi 3.00 2.25
Nos. 621-626 (6) 10.05 7.75

Souvenir Sheet
627 A214 1500fr multi 8.00 8.00

No. 627 contains one 45x45mm stamp.

Ancient Art — A215

Nos. 628-647: 15fr, Venus of Brassempoury, vert. 25fr, Petroglyphs, Tanum, vert. 45fr, Prehistoric cave drawings, vert. 50fr, Cave paintaings, Lascaux. 55fr, Tomb of Amonherkhopeshef, vert. 65fr, God Anubis and the pharaoh. 75fr, Sphinx. 85fr, Bust of Nefertiti, vert. 95fr, Statue of Shibum, vert. 100fr, Standard of Ur. 130fr, Mesopotamian bull's head harp, vert. 135fr, Mesopotamian scroll. 140fr, Assyrian dignitary, vert. 180fr, Enameled horse, Babylon. 190fr, Assyrian carving of hunters, vert. 200fr, Mona Lisa of Nimrud, vert. 225fr, Carthaginian coin. 250fr,

Phoenician sphinx, vert. 275fr, Persian archer, vert. 280fr, Ceramic and glass mask, vert.

1994, Aug. 24 Litho. *Perf. 13½*
628-647 A215 Set of 20 15.00 15.00

D-Day Landings, Normandy, 50th Anniv. — A216

Villiers-Bocage, June 12: No. 648a, Explosion, men being killed. b, Tank firing. c, Tank, men with weapons.

Beaumont-Sur-Sarthe, June 6: No. 649a, Explosion, airplanes. b, British airplanes, tanks. c, German tanks, soldier firing machine gun.

Utah Beach, June 6: No. 650a, Explosion, bow of landing craft. b, Stern of landing craft, soldiers. c, Landing craft filled with troops.

Aerial battle: No. 651a, British planes dropping bombs. b, British, German planes. c, British, German planes, explosion.

Sainte-Mere-Eglise, June 5: No. 652a, German troops firing on paratroopers. b, Church tower. c, Paratroopers, German troops.

1994, June 6 Strips of 3
648 A216 200fr #a.-c. 3.25 2.00
649 A216 300fr #a.-c. 4.00 2.50
650 A216 300fr #a.-c. 4.00 2.50
651 A216 400fr #a.-c. 5.25 3.50
652 A216 400fr #a.-c. 5.25 3.50
Nos. 648-652 (5) 21.75 14.00

Nos. 648-652 are each continuous designs. Nos. 648b, 649b, 650b, 651b, 652b are each 30x47mm.

Orchids, Vegetables, & Mushrooms A217

Orchids: 25fr, Disa kewensis. 50fr, Angraecum eburneum. 100fr, Ansellia africana.

Vegetables: 140fr, Sorghum. 150fr, Onions. 190fr, Corn.

Mushrooms: 200fr, Lepiota (clitocybe) nebularis. 225fr, Macrolepiota (lepiota) procera. 500fr, Lepiota aspera.

1994, Sept. 12
653 A217 25fr multicolored .25 .25
654 A217 50fr multicolored .35 .25
655 A217 100fr multicolored .65 .35
a. Souvenir sheet of 3, #653-655 11.00 7.50
656 A217 140fr multicolored .70 .40
657 A217 150fr multicolored .80 .45
658 A217 190fr multicolored 1.00 .60
a. Souvenir sheet of 3, #656-658 11.00 7.50
659 A217 200fr multicolored 1.10 .65
660 A217 225fr multicolored 1.25 .75
661 A217 500fr multicolored 2.75 1.50
a. Souvenir sheet of 3, #659-661 11.00 7.50
Nos. 653-661 (9) 8.85 5.20

Moths, Butterflies & Insects A218

Designs: 20fr, Polyptychus roseus. 30fr, Elymniopsis bammakoo. 40fr, Deilephila nerii. 150fr, Utetheisa pulchella. 180fr, Charaxes jasius. 200fr, Mylothris chloris.

Insects: 225fr, Goliath beetle. 240fr, Locust. 350fr, Praying mantis.

1994, Sept. 12
662 A218 20fr multicolored .25 .25
663 A218 30fr multicolored .25 .25
664 A218 40fr multicolored .25 .25
665 A218 150fr multicolored .90 .50
666 A218 180fr multicolored 1.00 .55
667 A218 200fr multicolored 1.00 .60
a. Souv. sheet of 6, #662-667 22.50 12.50
668 A218 225fr multicolored 1.10 .65
669 A218 240fr multicolored 1.25 .70
670 A218 350fr multicolored 1.60 .90
a. Souv. sheet of 3, #668-670 11.00 6.50
Nos. 662-670 (9) 7.60 4.65

Nos. 599-603 Ovptd. in Silver or Gold with Name of Olympic Medalist, Country

Overprints in silver: No. 671a, "Y. GORDEYEVA / S. GRINKOV / RUSSIE." No. 671b, "O. GRISHCHUK / Y. PLATOV / RUSSIE." No. 672a, "D. COMPAGNONI / ITALIE." No. 672b, "M. WASMEIER / ALLEMAGNE." No. 673a, "E. BREDESEN /NORVEGE." No. 673b, "J. WEISSFLOG / ALLEMAGNE." No. 674a, "B. BLAIR, U.S.A." No. 674b, "J.O. KOSS / NORVEGE."

Overprint in gold: No. 675, "L. KJUS / NORVEGE." No. 676, "P. WIBERG / SUEDE."

1994, Sept. 12 Litho. *Perf. 13*
671 A208 150fr Pair, #a.-b. 1.75 1.00
672 A208 200fr Pair, #a.-b. 2.75 1.50
673 A208 225fr Pair, #a.-b. 3.50 2.00
674 A208 750fr Pair, #a.-b. 10.00 5.50
Nos. 671-674 (4) 18.00 10.00

Souvenir Sheet
675 A208 2000fr multicolored 8.00 6.00
676 A208 2000fr multicolored 8.00 6.00

Nos. 604-608 Ovptd. in Metallic Red

1994, Sept. 15 Litho. *Perf. 13*
677 A209 200fr multicolored .90 .50
678 A209 240fr multicolored 1.25 .70
679 A209 260fr multicolored 1.40 .80
680 A209 1000fr multicolored 5.25 3.00
Nos. 677-680 (4) 8.80 5.00

Souvenir Sheet
681 A209 2000fr multicolored 8.00 6.00

Intl. Olympic Committee, Cent. — A218a

1994, June 23 Litho. *Perf. 13½*
681A A218a 150fr multicolored 1.10 .60
681B A218a 200fr multicolored 1.60 .90

Exist in imperf souvenir sheets of 1.

Intl. Olympic Committee, Cent. — A219

Pierre de Coubertin and: 225fr, Woman carrying flame, vert. 240fr, Olympic rings, vert. 300fr, Torch bearer. 500fr, Gold medal of Olympic rings.

600fr, Flame, statue of flag bearer.

1994, June 23 *Perf. 13½*
682 A219 225fr multicolored .90 .55
683 A219 240fr multicolored 1.00 .65
684 A219 300fr multicolored 1.60 1.00
685 A219 500fr multicolored 2.75 1.75
Nos. 682-685 (4) 6.25 3.95

Souvenir Sheet
686 A219 600fr multicolored 3.50 2.25

Anniversaries & Events A220

Designs: 150fr, Ernst Julius Opik, Galileo probe, impact of comet on Jupiter. 200fr, Clyde Tombaugh, probe moving toward Pluto. 500fr, Intl. Red Cross, Henri Dunant. 650fr, Crew of Apollo 11, 1st manned moon landing. 700fr, Lions Intl., Rotary Intl. 800fr, Gary Kasparov chess champion.

1995, Apr. 10 Litho. *Perf. 13½*
687 A220 150fr multicolored .50 .30
688 A220 200fr multicolored .80 .45
689 A220 500fr multicolored 2.25 1.25
690 A220 650fr multicolored 2.50 1.50
691 A220 700fr multicolored 2.75 1.75
692 A220 800fr multicolored 3.25 1.90
Nos. 687-692 (6) 12.05 7.15

Nos. 687-692 exist in souvenir sheets of 1.

Motion Picture, Cent. — A221

Movie star, movie: 100fr, Kirk Douglas, Spartacus. 150fr, Elizabeth Taylor, Cleopatra. 200fr, Clint Eastwood, Sierra Torrid. 225fr, Marilyn Monroe, The River of No Return. 500fr, Arnold Schwarzenegger, Conan the Barbarian. 1000fr, Elvis Presley, Loving You. 1500fr, Charlton Heston, The Ten Commandments.

1994, May 23 Litho. *Perf. 13½*
693-698 A221 Set of 6 16.00 8.75

Souvenir Sheet
699 A221 1500fr multicolored 8.25 5.00

No. 695 is airmail.

Fight Against AIDS A222

Designs: 150fr, Woman, man holding condoms. 225fr, Nurse with AIDS patient, researcher looking into microscope.

1994, June 30
700 A222 150fr multicolored 1.10 .60
701 A222 225fr multicolored 1.60 .90

Tourism A223

Designs: 150fr, Traditional buildings, statue, vert. 200fr, Sphinx, pyramids, ruins.

1994, Dec. 5
702 A223 150fr multicolored 1.10 .60
703 A223 200fr multicolored 1.60 .90

1996 Summer Olympics, Atlanta — A224

Designs: 25fr, Reiner Klimke, dressage. 50fr, Kristin Otto, swimming. 100fr, Hans-Gunther Winkler, equestrian. 150fr, Birgit Fischer-Schmidt, kayak. 200fr, Nicole Uphoff, dressage, vert. 225fr, Renate Stecher, track, vert. 230fr, Michael Gross, swimming. 240fr, Karin Janz, gymnastics. 550fr, Anja Fichtel, fencing, vert. 700fr, Heide Rosendahl-Ecker, track, vert.

1995, Mar. 27
704-713 A224 Set of 10 12.50 8.00

Dated 1994.

Rotary Intl., 90th Anniv. — A225

1000fr, Paul Harris, logo. 1500fr, 1905, 1995 Logos.

1995, Oct. 18 Litho. *Perf. 14*
714 A225 1000fr multi 6.50 4.00

Souvenir Sheet
715 A225 1500fr multi 8.00 5.00

Miniature Sheets

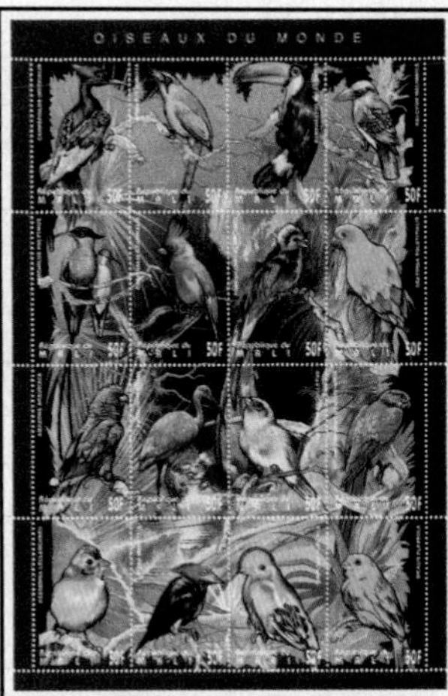

Birds, Butterflies — A226

No. 716: a, Campephilus imperialis. b, Momotus momota. c, Ramphastos sulfuratus. d, Halcyon malimbica. e, Trochilus polytmus. f, Cardinalis cardinalis. g, Pharomachrus mocinno. h, Aratinga solstitialis. i, Amazona arausiaca. j, Eudocimus ruber. k, Carduelis cucullatus. l, Anodorhynchus hyacinthinus. m, Passerina leclancherii. n, Pipra mentalis. o, Rupicola rupicola. p, Sicalis flaveola.

No. 717: a, Capito niger. b, Chloroceryle amazona. c, Tersina virdis. d, Momotus momota. e, Campephilus menaloleucos. f, Leistes militaris. g, Sarcoramphus papa. h, Pilherodius pileatus. i, Tityra cayana. j, Tangara chilensis. k, Amazona ochrocephala. l, Saltator maximus. m, Paroaria dominicana. n, Egretta tricolor. o, Piaya melanogaster. p, Thamnophilus doliatus.

No. 718: a, Paradise whydah (g). b, Red-necked francolin. c, Whale-headed stork (i). d, Ruff (j). e, Marabou stork (k). f, White pelican. g, Western curlew. h, Scarlet ibis. i, Great crested crebe. j, White spoonbill. k, African jacana. l, African pygmy goose.

No. 719: a, Ruby-throated hummingbird. b, Grape shoemaker, blue morpho butterflies. c, Northern hobby. d, Cuvier toucan (g). e, Black-necked red cotinga (h). f, Green-winged

macaws (i). g, Flamingo (j). h, Malachite kingfisher. i, Bushy-crested hornbill (l). j, Purple swamphen (k). k, Striped body (j, l). l, Painted lady butterfly.
Each 1000fr: No. 720, Topaza pella. No. 721, Sporophila lineola.

1995, Oct. 20 Litho. *Perf. 14*
Sheets of 16 & 12

716 A226 50fr #a.-p. 6.50 4.00
717 A226 100fr #a.-p. 11.00 6.75
718 A226 150fr #a.-l. 12.00 7.25
719 A226 200fr #a.-l. 16.00 9.25
Nos. 716-719 (4) 45.50 27.25

Souvenir Sheets

720-721 A226 Set of 2 12.00 7.50

John Lennon (1940-80) A227

1995 Litho. *Perf. 14*
722 A227 150fr multicolored 1.25 .70

No. 722 was issued in sheets of 16.

Miniature Sheets

Motion Pictures, Cent. — A228

Western actors: No. 723:a, Justus D. Barnes (misidentified as George Barnes). b, William S. Hart. c, Tom Mix. d, Wallace Beery. e, Gary Cooper. f, John Wayne.
Actresses and their directors: No. 724: a, Marlene Dietrich, Josef Von Sternberg. b, Jean Harlow, George Cukor. c, Mary Astor, John Huston (Houston on stamp). d, Ingrid Bergman, Alfred Hitchcock. e, Claudette Colbert, Cecil B. DeMille. f, Marilyn Monroe, Billy Wilder.
Musicals and their stars: No. 725: a, Singin' in the Rain, Gene Kelly. b, The Bandwagon, Anne Miller, Ray Bolger. c, Cabaret, Liza Minnelli, Joel Grey. d, The Sound of Music, Julie Andrews. e, Top Hat, Ginger Rogers, Fred Astaire. f, Saturday Night Fever, John Travolta.
Each 1000fr: No. 726, Robert Redford as the Sundance Kid. No. 727, Liv Ullman, actress, Ingmar Bergman, director. No. 728, Judy Garland in the Wizard of Oz.

1995, Dec. 8 Litho. *Perf. 13½x14*
Sheets of 6

723 A228 150fr #a.-f. 5.25 3.50
724 A228 200fr #a.-f. 7.25 4.50
725 A228 240fr #a.-f. 9.00 5.50
Nos. 723-725 (3) 21.50 13.50

Souvenir Sheets

726-728 A228 Set of 3 16.00 10.00

Nos. 723-728 have various styles of lettering.

Miniature Sheet

Stars of Rock and Roll — A229

No. 729: a, Connie Francis. b, The Ronettes. c, Janis Joplin. d, Debbie Harry of Blondie. e, Cyndi Lauper. f, Carly Simon.

No. 730, Bette Midler.

1995, Dec. 8
729 A229 225fr Sheet of 6, #a.-f. 8.00 5.00

Souvenir Sheet

730 A229 1000fr multicolored 5.25 3.50

Traditional Cooking Utensils A230

5fr, Canaris, vert. 50fr, Mortier, calebasse, vert. 150fr, Fourneau. 200fr, Vans, vert. 500fr, Vans.

1995, Nov. 20 Litho. *Perf. 14*
731-734 A230 Set of 4 2.75 1.75

Souvenir Sheet

735 A230 500fr multicolored 3.00 2.00

18th World Scout Jamboree, Holland — A231

Scout examining butterfly or mushroom: 150fr, Saturnia pyri. 225fr, Gonepteryx rhamni. 240fr, Myrina silenus. 500fr, Clitocybe nebularis. 650fr, Agaricus semotus. 725fr, Lepiota procera.
1500fr, Morpho cypris.

1995, Aug. 1 Litho. *Perf. 13½*
736-741 A231 Set of 6 11.50 5.75

Souvenir Sheet

742 A231 1500fr multicolored 9.25 5.00

Nos. 736-741 exist in souvenir sheets of 1.

UN, 50th Anniv. A232

Designs: 20fr, 170fr, UN emblem, scales of justice, doves, vert. 225fr, 240fr, Doves, UN emblem, four men of different races.

1995, Oct. 24 Litho. *Perf. 13*
743 A232 20fr light blue & multi .25 .25
744 A232 170fr light grn & multi .80 .60
745 A232 225fr light pur & multi 1.10 .70
746 A232 240fr light org & multi 1.25 .95
Nos. 743-746 (4) 3.40 2.50

Ayrton Senna (1960-94), F-1 Race Car Driver — A233

1000fr, Jerry Garcia (1942-95), entertainer.

1995 *Perf. 13½*
747 A233 500fr multicolored 2.25 1.25
748 A233 1000fr multicolored 4.50 2.50

Nos. 747-748 exist in souvenir sheets of one.

A234

150fr, Charles de Gaulle. 200fr, De Gaulle, liberation of Paris. 240fr, Enzo Ferrari. 650fr, 1945-49 Greenland Expeditions of Paul Emile Victor. 725fr, Paul Harris. 740fr, Michael Schumacher.

1995
749 A234 150fr multicolored .70 .35
750 A234 200fr multicolored .90 .50
751 A234 240fr multicolored 1.10 .60
752 A234 650fr multicolored 3.00 1.75
753 A234 725fr multicolored 3.25 1.80
754 A234 740fr multicolored 3.50 1.90
Nos. 749-754 (6) 12.45 6.90

Nos. 749-754 exist in souvenir sheets of 1.

A235

Designs: 150fr, Second election party emblems, horiz. 200fr, Pres. Alpha Oumar Konare. 225fr, First election party emblems, horiz. 240fr, Natl. flag, map, party representations.

1995 Litho. *Perf. 13½*
755 A235 150fr multicolored .65 .35
756 A235 200fr multicolored .80 .45
757 A235 225fr multicolored .90 .50
758 A235 240fr multicolored .95 .55
Nos. 755-758 (4) 3.30 1.85

Second Presidential elections.

A236

Economic Community of West African States (ECOWAS): 150fr, Regional integration, horiz. 200fr, Cooperation. 220fr, Prospect of creating one currency, horiz. 225fr, Peace and security, horiz.

1995
759 A236 150fr multicolored .70 .35
760 A236 200fr multicolored .90 .45
761 A236 220fr multicolored 1.00 .50
762 A236 225fr multicolored 1.00 .50
Nos. 759-762 (4) 3.60 1.80

Mushrooms — A237

Genus Russula: No. 763: a, Emetica. b, Laurocerasi. c, Rosacea. d, Occidentalis. e, Fragilis. f, Mariae. g, Eeruginea. h, Compacta.
Genus Boletus: No. 764: a, Felleus. b, Elagans. c, Castaneus. d, Edulis. e, Aereus. f, Granulatus. g, Cavipes. h, Badius.
Genus Lactarius: No. 765: a, Deliciosus. b, Luculentus. c, Pseudomucidus. d, Scrobiculatus. e, Deceptivus. f, Indigo. g, Peckii. h, Lignyotus.
Genus Amanita: No. 766a, Caesarea. b, Muscaria. c, Solitaria. d, Verna. e, Malleata. f. Phalloides. g, Citrina. h, Pantherina.
Each 1000fr: No. 767, Coprinus atramentarius. No. 768, Panaeolus subbalteatus.

1996, Mar. 15 Litho. *Perf. 14*
763 A237 25fr Sheet of 8, #a.-h. 1.60 .95
764 A237 150fr Sheet of 8, #a.-h. 9.00 5.50
765 A237 200fr Sheet of 8, #a.-h. 12.00 7.25
766 A237 225fr Sheet of 8, #a.-h. 14.00 8.25

Souvenir Sheets

767-768 A237 Set of 2 14.00 9.00

Sites in Beijing — A238

No. 769: a, Bridge, Gateway to Hall of Supreme Harmony. b, Temple of Heaven. c, Great Wall. d, Hall of Supreme Harmony. e, Courtyard, Gate of Heavenly Purity, f, Younghe Gong Temple. g, Lang Ru Ting, Bridge of Seventeen Arches. h, Meridian Gate (Wu Men). i, Corner Tower.
Each 500fr: No. 770, Pagoda, vert. No. 771, Li Peng.

1996, May 13
769 A238 100fr Sheet of 9, #a.-i. 7.50 4.75

Souvenir Sheets

770-771 A238 Set of 2 7.00 4.75

No. 771 contains one 47x72mm stamp. CHINA '96 (Nos. 769, 771).

Trains A239

Historic: No. 772: a, "Novelty," 1829. b, Premiere class Liverpool & Manchester Line, 1830. c, William Norris, 1843. d, Trevithick, 1808. e, Robert Stephenson "Rocket," 1829. f, "Puffing Billy," William Hedley, 1813.
No. 773: a, Subway Train, London. b, San Francisco cable car. c, Japanese monorail. d, Pantograph car, Stockholm. e, Double-decker tram, Hong Kong. f, Sacre-Coeur Cog Train, Montmartre, France.
No. 774: a, Docklands Light Railway, London. b, British Railway's high-speed diesel train. c, Japanese Bullet Train. d, Germany Inter-City Electric high speed train. e, French TGV high-speed electric train. f, German "Wuppertal" monorail.
Trains of China: No. 775: a, RM Class Pacific. b, Manchurian steam engine. c, SY Class 2-8-2, Tangshan. d, SL Class 4-6-2 Pacific. e, Chengtu-Kunming steam. f, Lanchow passenger train.
Each 500fr: No. 776, Rheingold Express, 1925. No. 777, Matterhorn cable car, vert. No. 778, Superchief, best long-distance diesel, US. No. 779, Shanghai-Nanking Railway.

1996, July 29
772 A239 180fr Sheet of 6, #a.-f. 8.00 5.00
773 A239 250fr Sheet of 6, #a.-f. 12.00 7.00
774 A239 310fr Sheet of 6, #a.-f. 14.00 8.50
775 A239 320fr Sheet of 6, #a.-f. 15.00 9.00

Souvenir Sheets

776-779 A239 Set of 4 13.00 10.00

Nos. 776-779 each contain one 57x43mm stamp.

Express Mail Service, 10th Anniv. A240

Designs: 30fr, Man with package, vert. 40fr, Bird holding package, letter, vert. 90fr, World map, woman with letter holding telephone receiver. 320fr, 320fr, Mail van, hands holding letters, map.

1996, Sept. 1 Litho. *Perf. 14*

780	A240	30fr multicolored	.25	.25
781	A240	40fr multicolored	.30	.25
782	A240	90fr multicolored	.55	.30
783	A240	320fr multicolored	1.75	1.00
		Nos. 780-783 (4)	2.85	1.80

Queen Elizabeth II, 70th Birthday — A241

Designs: a, Portrait. b, Wearing blue & red hat. c, Portrait as young woman.
1000fr, Portrait as young girl.

1996, Sept. 9 *Perf. 13½x14*

784 A241 370fr Strip of 3, #a.-c. 4.75 2.50

Souvenir Sheet

785 A241 1000fr multicolored 4.75 2.50

No. 784 was issued in sheets of 9 stamps.

Nanking Bridge — A242

1996 Litho. *Perf. 13½*

786 A242 270fr multicolored 2.50 1.25

Mosques A243

1996

787	A243	250fr Djenne	3.50	2.25
788	A243	310fr Sankore	4.50	2.75

Pandas, Dogs, and Cats — A244

Panda, vert: No. 789: a, Climbing on branch. b, On bare limb. c. Closer view. d, Lying in branch with leaves.
Dogs, cats: No. 790: a, Azawakh. b, Basenji. c, Javanais. d, Abyssin.

1996

789	A244	150fr Sheet of 4, #a.-d.	3.25	1.75
790	A244	310fr Sheet of 4, #a.-d.	6.00	3.50

Nos. 789a-789d are 39x42mm.

Marilyn Monroe (1926-62) — A245

Various portraits.

1996

791 A245 320fr Sheet of 9, #a.-i. 14.00 8.00

Souvenir Sheet

792 A245 2000fr multicolored 9.50 5.50

No. 792 contains one 42x60mm stamp.

Entertainers — A246

No. 793: a, Frank Sinatra. b, Johnny Mathis. c, Dean Martin. d, Bing Crosby. e, Sammy Davis, Jr. f, Elvis Presley. g, Paul Anka. h, Tony Bennett. i, Nat "King" Cole.
No. 794, Various portraits of John Lennon.

1996 Sheets of 9

793	A246	250fr #a.-i.	10.00	5.50
794	A246	310fr #a.-i.	12.50	7.00

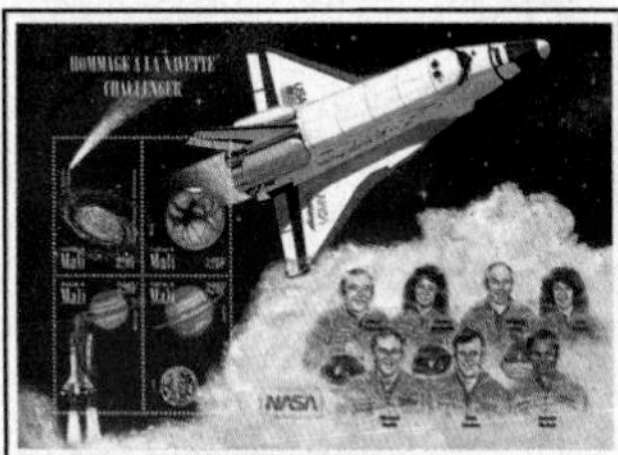
U.S. Space Shuttle, Challenger — A247

Designs: a, Halley's Comet, Andromeda Galaxy. b, Mars. c, Challenger, Saturn. d, Moon, Jupiter.
1000fr, Shuttle Challenger.

1996, Oct. 14 *Perf. 14*

795 A247 320fr Sheet of 4, #a.-d. 5.75 3.50

Souvenir Sheet

796 A247 1000fr multicolored 5.25 3.50

No. 796 contains one 85x29mm stamp.

Mickey's ABC's A248

Disney characters in various scenes with: No. 797: a, "MICKEY." b, "A." c, "B." d, "C." e, "D." f, "E." g, "F." h, "G." i, "H."
No. 798: a, "I." b, "J." c, "K." d, "L." e, "M." f, "N." g, "O." h, "P." i, "Q."
No. 799: a, "R." b, "S." c, "T." d, "U." e, "V." f, "W." g, "X." h, "Y." i, "Z."
Each 1000fr: No. 800, Mouse child holding "DE MICKEY" sign, horiz. No. 801, Mouse children with various letters.

1996, Oct. 15 Litho. *Perf. 13½x14*

797	A248	50fr Sheet of 9, #a.-i.	2.25	1.50
798	A248	100fr Sheet of 9, #a.-i.	4.50	2.75
799	A248	200fr Sheet of 9, #a.-i.	9.00	5.50

Souvenir Sheets

800-801 A248 Set of 2 10.50 6.75

Sites in Beijing A249

No. 802, Hall of Supreme Harmony. No. 803, Great Wall. No. 804, Hall of Prayers for Good Harvests, Temple of Heaven.

1996 *Perf. 13½*

802	A249	180fr multicolored	1.75	1.00
803	A249	180fr multicolored	1.75	1.00
804	A249	180fr multicolored	1.75	1.00
		Nos. 802-804 (3)	5.25	3.00

Cotton Production A250

Designs: 20fr, Cotton plant, vert. 25fr, People working in cotton fields. 50fr, Holding plant, vert. 310fr, Dumping cotton into cart.

1996 *Perf. 13½*

805	A250	20fr multicolored	.25	.25
806	A250	25fr multicolored	.25	.25
807	A250	50fr multicolored	.25	.25
808	A250	310fr multicolored	1.40	.70
		Nos. 805-808 (4)	2.15	1.45

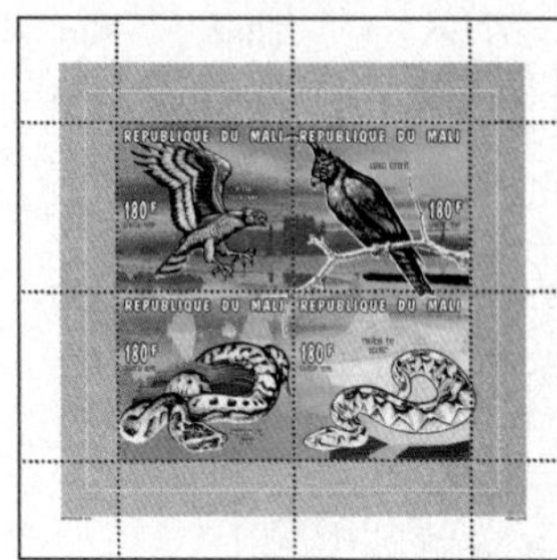
Birds and Snakes — A251

a, Crowned eagle in flight. b, Tufted eagle. c, Python. d, Gabon viper.
Songbirds: No. 810: a, Choucador splendide. b, Astrid ondulé. c, Martin chasseur. d, Coucou didric.
Butterfies: No. 811a, Salamis parhassus. b, Charaxes bohemani. c, Coeliades forestan. d, Mimacrea marshalli.

1996

809	A251	180fr Sheet of 4, #a.-d.	3.25	1.90
810	A251	250fr Sheet of 4, #a.-d.	4.50	2.75
811	A251	320fr Sheet of 4, #a.-d.	5.75	3.50

Third World — A252

Design: 250fr, Hot air balloon in flight.

1996

812	A252	180fr shown	2.50	1.40
813	A252	250fr multicolored	3.00	1.75

A253

1996

814	A253	180fr green & multi	1.00	.50
815	A253	250fr bister & multi	1.50	.75

Death of Abdoul Karim Camara (Cabral), 16th anniv.

A254

Dogs: No. 816, Airedale terrier. No. 817, Briard. No. 818, Schnauzer. No. 819, Chow chow.
Cats: No. 820, Turkish van. NO. 821, Sphynx. No. 822, Korat. No. 823, American curl.
Dogs, horiz.: No. 824: a, Basset hound. b, Dachshund. c, Brittany spaniel. d, Saint Bernard. e, Bernese mountain. f, Irish setter. g, Gordon setter. h, Poodle. i, Pointer.
Cats, horiz: No. 825: a, Scottish fold. b, Javanese. c, Norwegian forest. d, American shorthair. e, Turkish angora. f, British shorthair. g, Egyptian mau. h, Maine coon. i, Burmese.
Each 1000fr: No. 826, Newfoundland. No. 827, Flame point Himalayan Persian.

1997, Jan. 10 Litho. *Perf. 14*

816-819 A254 100fr Set of 4	2.50	1.25
820-823 A254 150fr Set of 4	3.25	1.10
824 A254 150fr Sheet of 9, #a.-i.	7.50	3.75
825 A254 180fr Sheet of 9, #a.-i.	8.50	4.25

Souvenir Sheets

826-827 A254 Set of 2 11.00 6.75

Environmental Protection A255

Fauna: No. 828: a, Dolphin. b, Okapi, c, Rhea. d, Black rhinocrhinoceros. e, Malayan tapir. f, Galapagos tortoise. g, Walrus. h, Gray wolf. i, Giraffe.
1000fr, Koala.

1997, Feb. 3

828 A255 250fr Sheet of 9, #a.-i. 11.50 8.50

Souvenir Sheet

829 A255 1000fr multicolored 5.00 3.75

Ships — A256

Warships: No. 830: a, Bellerophon, England, 1867. b, Chen Yuan, China 1882. c, Hiei, Japan, 1877. d, Kaiser, Austria, 1862. e, King Wilhelm, Germany, 1869. f, Re D'Italia, Italy, 1864.
Paddle steamers: No. 831: a, Arctic, US, 1849. b, Washington, France, 1847. c, Esploratore, Italy, 1863. d, Fuad, Turkey, 1864. e, Hope, Confederate States of America, 1864. f, Britannia, England, 1840.
Each 1000fr: No. 832, Arabia, England, 1851. No. 833, Northumberland, England, 1867.

1996, Dec. 20 Litho. *Perf. 14*

830 A256 250fr Sheet of 6, #a.-f. 4.50 3.50
831 A256 320fr Sheet of 6, #a.-f. 8.50 4.25

Souvenir Sheets

832-833 A256 Set of 2 10.00 7.25

Wildlife — A257

Designs: a, Hippotragus niger. b, Damaliscus hunter. c, G. demidovii. d, Chimpanzee.

1996 Litho. *Perf. 13½*

834 A257 250fr Sheet of 4, #a.-d. 5.00 2.50

UNESCO, 50th anniv.

Red Cross — A258

Dogs: a, Rottweiler. b, Newfoundland. c, German shepherd. d, Bobtail (English sheepdog).

1996

835 A258 250fr Sheet of 4, #a.-d. 4.25 2.10

African Education Year — A259

100fr, Student with book, map, vert. 150fr, Classroom. 180fr, Families watching video program on farming techniques. 250fr, African people being educated, map, vert.

1996, Apr. 4 *Perf. 14*

836 A259 100fr multicolored	.45	.45
837 A259 150fr multicolored	.65	.65
838 A259 180fr multicolored	.80	.80
839 A259 250fr multicolored	1.10	1.10
Nos. 836-839 (4)	3.00	3.00

Nos. 836-839 were not available until March 1997.

Folk Dances — A260

1996 *Perf. 13½*

840 A260 150fr Dounouba	.65	.65
841 A260 170fr Gomba	.75	.75
842 A260 225fr Sandia	1.40	1.40
843 A260 230fr Sabar	1.50	1.50
Nos. 840-843 (4)	4.30	4.30

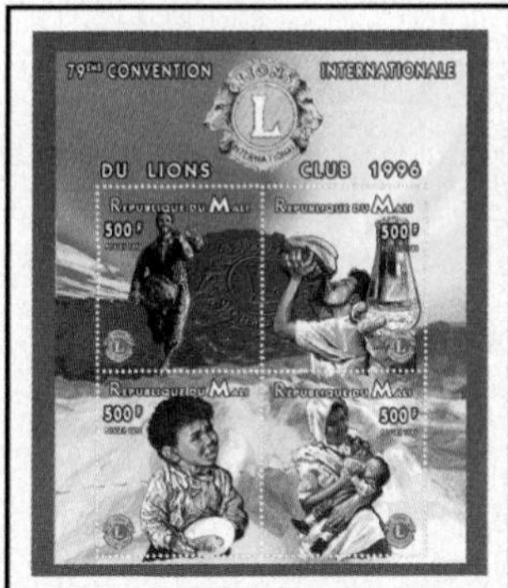

Service Organizations — A261

No. 844: a, Man carrying bags. b, Man drinking water. c, Child holding bowl of food. d, Mother feeding infant.

No. 845: a, Girl with food. b, Man holding rice bowl. c, Woman holding bowl of food. d, Child opening box of food.

1996

844 A261 500fr Sheet of 4, #a.-d. 8.50 4.25
845 A261 650fr Sheet of 4, #a.-d. 11.50 5.75

79th Lions Intl. Convention (No. 844). 91st Rotary Intl. Convention (No. 845).

City of Canton, 2210th Anniv. — A262

Designs: a, Statue of goats. b, Seal. c, Boat. d, Fruits, tea pot. e, Buildings. f, Dragon.

1996

846 A262 50fr Sheet of 6, #a.-f. 1.40 .80

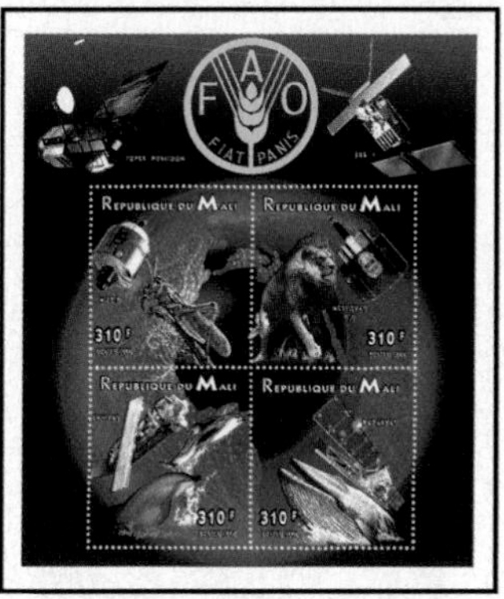

FAO, 50th Anniv. — A264

Space satellite, fauna: a, MOP.2, grasshopper. b, Meteosat P.2, lion. c, Envisat, dolphins. d, Radar satellite, whale.

1996 Litho. *Perf. 13½*

847 A264 310fr Sheet of 4, #a.-d. 5.00 2.50

Artifacts from Natl. Museum — A265

1996

848 A265 5fr Kara	.25	.25
849 A265 10fr Hambe	.25	.25
850 A265 180fr Pinge	.80	.45
851 A265 250fr Merenkun	1.10	.60
Nos. 848-851 (4)	2.40	1.55

Nos. 848-851 exist in souvenir sheets of 1.

1998 Winter Olympics, Nagano A266

250fr, Speed skating. 310fr, Slalom skiing. 750fr, Figure skating. 900fr, Hockey.
2000fr, Downhill skiing.

1996

852 A266 250fr multicolored	1.25	.65
853 A266 310fr multicolored	1.50	.85
854 A266 750fr multicolored	3.50	1.90
855 A266 900fr multicolored	4.00	2.25
Nos. 852-855 (4)	10.25	5.65

Souvenir Sheet

856 A266 2000fr multicolored 10.00 5.50

Fauna, Mushrooms — A267

a, Ploceus ocularis. b, Hemiolaus coecolus. c, Hebeloma radicosum. d, Sparassus dufouri simon.

1996

857 A267 750fr Sheet of 4, #a.-d. 13.00 7.25

New Year 1997 (Year of the Ox) — A268

1997

858 A268 500fr shown 2.25 1.25

Size: 53x35mm

859 A268 500fr Black porcelain ox 2.25 1.25

Nos. 858-859 exist in souvenir sheets of 1.

Butterflies A269

No. 860, Black-lined eggar. No. 861, Common opae. No. 862, Veined tiger. No. 863, The basker.
No. 864: a, Natal barred blue. b, Common grass blue. c, Fire grid. d, Mocker swallowtail. e, Azure hairstreak. f, Mother-of-pearl butterfly. g, Boisduval's false asraea. h, Pirate butterfly. i, African moon moth.
No. 865, vert.: a, Striped policeman. b, Mountain sandman. c, Brown-veined white. d, Bowker's widow. e, Foxy charaxes. f, Pirate. g, African clouded yellow. h, Garden inspector.
Each 1000fr: No. 866, Plain tiger. No. 867, Beautiful tiger. No. 868, African clouded yellow, vert. No. 869, Zebra white, vert.

1997, Jan. 27 *Perf. 14*

860-863 A269 180fr Set of 4 3.50 2.00
864 A269 150fr Sheet of 9, #a.-i. 6.25 3.50
865 A259 210fr Sheet of 8, #a.-h. 9.50 5.25

Souvenir Sheets

866-869 A269 Set of 4 24.00 14.00

Disney Characters A270

Greetings stamps: 25fr, Goofy, Bon Voyage. 50fr, Mickey, Happy New Year. 100fr, Goofy, Happy Birthday. 150fr, Donald writing. 180fr, Minnie writing. 250fr, Mickey, Minnie, anniversary. 310fr, Mickey, Minnie going on vacation. 320fr, Mickey, Minnie kissing.

Each 1500fr: No. 878, Daisy Duck, horiz. No. 879, Huey, Dewey, Louie throwing school books in air, horiz.

1997, Mar. 1 *Perf. 13½x14*

870-877 A270 Set of 8 7.00 4.00

Souvenir Sheets

878-879 A270 Set of 2 12.50 8.25

Bridges — A271

1997 **Litho.** *Perf. 14*

880	A271 100fr Mahina	.50	.25
881	A271 150fr Selingue Dam	.80	.45
882	A271 180fr King Fahd	1.00	.55
883	A271 250fr Martyrs	1.50	.85
	Nos. 880-883 (4)	3.80	2.10

Dated 1996.

1998 World Cup Soccer Championships, France — A272

Various action scenes.

1997 *Perf. 13½*

884	A272 180fr multicolored	1.00	.55
885	A272 250fr multicolored	1.25	.65
886	A272 320fr multicolored	1.50	.85
887	A272 1060fr multicolored	4.50	2.50
	Nos. 884-887 (4)	8.25	4.55

Souvenir Sheet

888 A272 2000fr multicolored 9.00 4.75

Dated 1996. No. 888 contains one 36x42mm stamp.

Formula I Race Car Drivers — A273

Designs: a, Michael Schumacher. b, Damon Hill. c, Jacques Villeneuve. d, Gerhard Berger.

1996 **Litho.** *Perf. 13½*

889 A273 650fr Sheet of 4, #a.-d. 13.00 6.00

John F. Kennedy (1917-63) — A274

Various portraits.

1997

890 A274 390fr Sheet of 9, #a.-i. 17.50 8.75

John Lennon (1940-80) — A275

Various portraits.

1997

891 A275 250fr Sheet of 9, #a.-i. 11.50 5.25

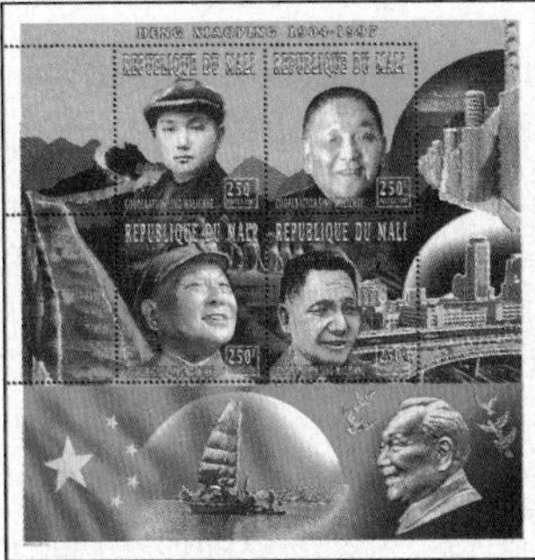

Deng Xiaoping (1904-97), Chinese Leader — A276

Designs: a, As young man. b, Without hat. c, With hat. d, As middle-aged man.

250fr, Being kissed by child.

1997 *Perf. 13½*

892 A276 250fr Sheet of 4, #a.-d. 5.50 2.50

Souvenir Sheet

Perf. 13x13½

893 A276 250fr multicolored 5.00 2.25

No. 893 contains 69x50mm stamp.

Elvis Presley, 20th Death Anniv. — A277

No. 894, Various portraits. No. 895, Portrait, Elvis on motorcycle.

1997 **Litho.** *Perf. 13½*

894 A277 310fr Sheet of 9, #a.-i. 13.00 7.00

Souvenir Sheet

895 A277 2000fr multicolored 10.00 5.50

No. 895 contains one 42x51mm stamp.

Marine Life A278

No. 896: a, Chaetodon auriga. b, Balistoides conspicillum. c, Forcipiger longirostris. d, Chelmon rostratus. e, Plectorhinchus diagrammus. f, Stegastes leucostictus. g, Chaetodon kleinii. h, Synchiropus splendidus. i, Platax orbicularis.

No. 897: a, Amphiprion percula. b, Holacanthus ciliaris. c, Chaetodon reticulatus. d, Pomacanthus imperator. e, Heniochus acuminatus. f, Lienardella fasciata. g, Zanclus cornutus. h, Scarus guacamaia. i, Lutjanus sebae.

No. 898: a, Tursiops truncatus. b, Phaethon lepturus. c, Istiophorus platypterus. d, Sphyma zygaena. e, Reinhardtius hippoglossoides. f, Manta birostris. g, Thunnus albacares. h, Himantolophus groenlandicus. i, Tridacna gigas.

No. 899: a, Cypselurus heterurus. b, Sailboat. c, Delphinus delphis. d, Cacharodon carcharias. e, Orcinus orca (b, f). f, Salmo salar. g, Conger conger. h, Pomatomus saltatrix. i, Sphyraena barracuda.

Each 1000r: No. 900, Balaenoptera musculus. No. 901, Megaptera novaeangliae, vert.

1997, Mar. 2 **Litho.** *Perf. 14*

896	A278 150fr Sheet of 9, #a.-i.	7.50	7.50
897	A278 180fr Sheet of 9, #a.-i	8.00	8.00
898	A278 250fr Sheet of 9, #a.-i.	12.00	12.00
899	A278 310fr Sheet of 9, #a.-i.	15.00	15.00

Souvenir Sheets

900-901 A278 Set of 2 10.00 10.00

Transportation — A279

Cyclists: No. 902: a, Rudolph Lewis, 1912. b, Jacques Anquetil, 4-time Tour de France winner. c, Miguel Indurain, hour record holder.

Sailing ships: No. 903: a, Lightning, by Donald McKay, 1856. b, Olivier de Kersauson, winner of Jules Verne trophy. c. Lockheed Sea Shadow, US.

Motorcycles, cyclists: No. 904: a, Coventry Eagle-Jap 998cm3. b, Michael Doohan, Honda 500 NSRV4. c, Harley-Davidson, Heritage Softail classic FLSTC.

Airships: No. 905: a, "Gifford," steam-powered dirigible, 1852. b, Count Ferdinand von Zeppelin, Zeppelin NT LZ N07. c, Nobile N1, "Norge," 1926.

Trains: No. 906: a, Locomotive G 4/5 2-8-0, Switzerland. b, W.V. Siemens, ICE train, Germany. c, Maglev HSST-5, Japan.

Race cars: No. 907: a, 1949 Ferrari Type 166/MM. b, Michael Schumacher, F1 310B Ferrari. c, Ferrari F50.

Sled dogs: No. 908: a, Eskimo. b, Alaskan malamute. c, Siberian husky.

Aircraft: No. 909: a, Wright Brothers' first flight at Kitty Hawk. b, Andre Turcat, Concorde. c, X34 space vehicle.

1997 **Litho.** *Perf. 13½*

902	A279 180fr Strip of 3, #a.-c.	2.50	1.25
903	A279 250fr Strip of 3, #a.-c.	3.25	1.75
904	A279 320fr Strip of 3, #a.-c.	4.25	2.50
905	A279 370fr Strip of 3, #a.-c.	4.75	2.75
906	A279 460fr Strip of 3, #a.-c.	6.00	3.00
907	A279 490fr Strip of 3, #a.-c.	6.75	3.50
908	A279 530fr Strip of 3, #a.-c.	7.50	3.75
909	A279 750fr Strip of 3, #a.-c.	10.00	5.00

Movie Stars — A281

Designs: a, John Wayne. b, Frank Sinatra. c, Rita Hayworth. d, Sammy Davis, Jr. e, Marilyn Monroe. f, Eddie Murphy. g, Elizabeth Taylor. h, James Dean. i, Robert Mitchum.

1997

910 A281 320fr Sheet of 9, #a.-i. 13.00 6.50

A282

A283

Diana, Princess of Wales (1961-97) — A284

Designs: No. 911, Various close-up portraits. No. 912, Pictures of various times in Diana's life.

Each 1500fr: No. 913, In pink dress with Pres. Clinton (in margin). No. 914, Wearing strapless evening dress. No. 915, Wearing hat and veil. No. 916, In blue dress with Nelson Mandela (in margin).

1997 Litho. *Perf. 13½*

911 A282 250fr Sheet of 9, #a.-i. 10.00 5.00
912 A283 370fr Sheet of 9, #a.-i. 15.00 7.50

Souvenir Sheets

913-916 A284 Set of 4 24.00 14.50

Mars Pathfinder — A285

No. 917 — Dr. Cheick M. Diarra with: a, blue & multi background. b, green & multi background. c, Part of Mars in background. d, violet black & multi background.

No. 917E: f, Like #917a. g, Like #917b. h, Like #917c, i, Like #917d.

1997

917 A285 180fr Sheet of 4, #a.-d. 4.50 2.50
917E A285 320fr Sheet of 4, #f-i 6.75 3.50

Crested Porcupine — A286

World Wildlife Fund: a, Two adults. b, One adult crawling right. c, Mother with young. d, Adult with quills raised.

1998

918 A286 250fr Block of 4, #a.-d. 6.75 3.00

Churches A287

5fr, Kita Basilica. 10fr, San Cathedral. 150fr, Bamako Cathedral. 370fr, Mandiakuy Church.

1997 Litho. *Perf. 13½*

919 A287 5fr multi .25 .25
920 A287 10fr multi .25 .25
921 A287 150fr multi .70 .35
922 A287 370fr multi 2.00 .85
Nos. 919-922 (4) 3.20 1.70

Pieces from Natl. Museum — A288

20fr, Bamanan. 25fr, Dogon couple. 250fr, Tasmasheq. 310fr, Oil lamp, Boo.

1997

923 A288 20fr multicolored .25 .25
924 A288 25fr multicolored .25 .25
925 A288 250fr multicolored 1.40 .60
926 A288 310fr multicolored 1.75 .75
Nos. 923-926 (4) 3.65 1.85

Cotton Industry — A289

30fr, Spools of threads. 50fr, Clothing. 180fr, Towels. 320fr, Textile production.

1997

927 A289 30fr multi .25 .25
928 A289 50fr multi .25 .25
929 A289 180fr multi 1.25 .50
930 A289 320fr multi 1.75 .75
Nos. 927-930 (4) 3.50 1.75

"Star Wars" Motion Pictures — A290

Various scenes from: No. 931, "The Return of the Jedi." No. 932, "Star Wars." No. 933: "The Empire Strikes Back."

1997 Litho. *Perf. 13½*

Sheets of 9

931 A290 180fr #a.-i. 7.50 7.50
932 A290 310fr #a.-i. 12.00 12.00
933 A290 320fr #a.-i. 13.00 13.00

Wild Animals — A291

Lions Intl. — No. 934: a, Lion. b, Cheetah standing. c, Cheetah lying down. d, Leopard.

Rotary Intl. — No. 935: a, Giraffe. b, Addax. c, Kob. d, Okapi.

1997

934 A291 310fr Sheet of 4, #a.-d. 5.50 2.75
935 A291 320fr Sheet of 4, #a.-d. 6.75 3.50

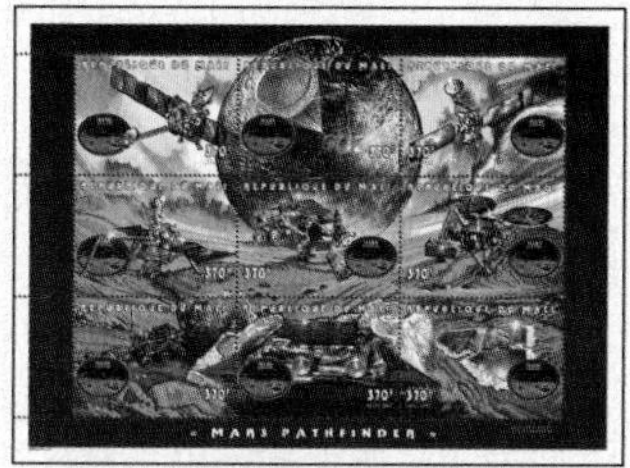

Mars Pathfinder — A292

Insignia and various scenes of Pathfinder mission.

1997

936 A292 370fr Sheet of 9, #a.-i. 16.00 8.00

Cats — A293

No. 937: a, Sphynx. b, Siberian brown tabby. c, Somali creme. d, Java cream point. 1500fr, Chartreux.

1997 Litho. *Perf. 13½*

937 A293 530fr Sheet of 4, #a.-d. 10.00 5.00

Souvenir Sheet

938 A293 1500fr multicolored 7.00 3.50

No. 938 contains one 36x42mm stamp.

Scouts and Birds A294

1997 Color of Bird

939 A294 180fr yellow & black 1.00 .50
940 A294 490fr black & white 3.00 1.50
941 A294 530fr gray & yel org 3.25 1.60
Nos. 939-941 (3) 7.25 3.60

Souvenir Sheets

942 A294 Sheet of 3, #a.-c. + 3 labels 10.00 5.00
943 A294 1500fr multicolored 7.00 7.00

No. 942 sold for 2200fr. Nos. 942a-942c have the same designs and denominations as Nos. 939-941 but have continuous background showing portion of scouting emblem.

No. 943 contains 42x50mm stamp.

1997

Various mushrooms, scout: 250fr, Frying mushrooms. 320fr, Grilling mushrooms. 1060fr, Gathering mushrooms, placing in bag.

944 A294 250fr multicolored 1.40 .70
945 A294 320fr multicolored 1.75 .85
946 A294 1060fr multicolored 5.50 2.75
Nos. 944-946 (3) 8.65 4.30

Souvenir Sheet

947 A294 Sheet of 3, #a.-c. + 3 labels 11.00 5.50

No. 947 sold for 2600fr. Nos. 947a-947c have the same designs and denominations as Nos. 944-946 but have continuous background showing portion of scouting emblem. A number has been reserved for an additional souvenir sheet with this set.

1998

Various minerals, scout: 150fr, Looking at minerals with magnifying glass. 750fr, Reading book. 900fr, Using chisel.

949 A294 150fr multicolored .75 .40
950 A294 750fr multicolored 4.25 2.25
951 A294 900fr multicolored 5.00 2.50
Nos. 949-951 (3) 10.00 5.15

Souvenir Sheet

952 A294 Sheet of 3, #a.-c. + 3 labels 12.00 6.00

No. 952 sold for 2800fr. Nos. 952a-952c have the same designs and denominations as Nos. 949-951 but have continuous background showing portion of scouting emblem.

1998 Litho. *Perf. 13½*

Various butterflies, scout: 310fr, Photographing butterfly. 430fr, Using book to identify butterfly. 460fr, Holding and looking at butterfly.

954 A294 310fr multicolored 1.60 .80
955 A294 430fr multicolored 2.00 1.30
956 A294 460fr multicolored 3.00 1.50
Nos. 954-956 (3) 6.60 3.60

Souvenir Sheet

957 A294 Sheet of 3, #a.-c. + 3 labels 10.00 5.00

No. 957 sold for 2200fr. Nos. 957a-957c have same designs and denominations as Nos. 954-956 but have continuous background showing portion of scouting emblem. A number has been reserved for an additional souvenir sheet with this set.

Flame of Peace, Timbuktu — A295

1997

959 A295 180fr yellow & multi 3.00 1.50
960 A295 250fr dull red & multi 4.00 2.00

Dated 1996.

Pan-African Postal Union, 18th anniv. — A296

1998

961 A296 250fr Addax 1.60 .80

Local Views — A297

5fr, Mosque, Mopti. 10fr, Fertility doll, Mopti. 15fr, Fishermen. 20fr, Woman carrying bowls on head, Macina. 25fr, Friendship Hotel. 30fr, Sikasso Hill. 40fr, Camel caravan, Azalai. 50fr, Women's hair style, Kayes. 60fr, Old Dogon man. 70fr, Shepherd. 80fr, Playing musical instrument, Wassoulou. 90fr, Crest, Ciwara Bamanan.

1998

962 A297 5fr multi .25 .25
963 A297 10fr multi, vert. .25 .25
964 A297 15fr multi .25 .25
965 A297 20fr multi, vert. .25 .25
966 A297 25fr multi, vert. .30 .30
967 A297 30fr multi, vert. .30 .30
968 A297 40fr multi, vert. .30 .30
969 A297 50fr multi, vert. .30 .30
970 A297 60fr multi, vert. .40 .40
971 A297 70fr multi, vert. .40 .40
972 A297 80fr multi, vert. .40 .40
973 A297 90fr multi, vert. .40 .40
Nos. 962-973 (12) 3.80 3.80

Travels of Pope John Paul II — A298

No. 974: a, Looking at book with Fidel Castro, Cuba. b, Walking with Castro, Cuba. c, With girl, Castro, Cuba. d, With boy, Nigeria. e, With three nuns, Cuba. f, Reading inscription on monument, Cuba. g, Holding crucifix, blessing child, Nigeria. h, Standing before monument, Nigeria. i, Giving blessing, people in traditional costumes, Nigeria.
Nos. 975a, 975c, 975d, 975e, 975f, 975g, 975i: Various portraits of Mother Teresa with Pope John Paul II. No. 975b, Pope John Paul II. No. 975h, Mother Teresa.

1998 Litho. *Perf. 13½*
Sheets of 9

974 A298 310fr #a.-i. 12.00 6.00
975 A298 320fr #a.-i. 12.00 6.00

Animal Type of 1997

Dogs — No. 976: a, Dachshund. b, Persian hound. c, Chihuahua. d, Pug.
1500fr, Dalmatian.

1998 Litho. *Perf. 13½*
976 A293 390fr Sheet of 4, #a.-d. 6.50 3.25

Souvenir Sheet

977 A293 1500fr multicolored 7.00 3.50

No. 977 contains one 36x42mm stamp.

Entertainers — A299

No. 978, Various portraits of James Dean.
No. 979, opera singers: a, Placido Domingo. b, Luciano Pavarotti. c, Jose Carreras. d, Andrea Bocelli. e, Maria Callas. f, Jose Van Dam. g, Renata Tebaldi. h, Montserrat Caballe. i, Kiri Te Kanawa.
No. 980, actresses: a, Audrey Hepburn. b, Greta Garbo. c, Elizabeth Taylor. d, Grace Kelly. e, Jean Harlow. f, Ava Gardner. g, Lana Turner. h, Marilyn Monroe. i, Vivien Leigh.

1998 Litho. *Perf. 13½*
Sheets of 9

978 A299 250fr #a.-i. 10.00 5.00
979 A299 310fr #a.-i. 14.00 7.00
980 A299 320fr #a.-i. 14.00 7.00

Chess Masters — A300

Portraits: a, Adolf Anderssen, 1818-79. b, Wilhelm Steinitz, 1836-1900. c, Emmanuel Lasker, 1868-1941. d, Alexandre Alekhine, 1892-1946. e, Tigran Petrosian, 1929-84. f, Boris Spassky, 1937. g, Bobby Fischer, 1943-2008. h, Garry Kasparov, 1963. i, Anatoli Karpov, 1951.

1998
981 A300 370fr Sheet of 9, #a.-i. 16.00 8.00

Eric Tabarly (1931-98), French Sailor — A301

Designs: a, Portrait. b, Tabarly at helm, yachts Pen Duick, Pen Duick VI. c, Tabarly, Charles de Gaulle.

1998
982 A301 390fr Sheet of 3, #a.-c. 5.00 2.50

No. 982b is 60x50mm.

France, 1998 World Cup Soccer Champions — A302

No. 983: a, Laurent Blanc. b, Lilian Thuram. c, David Trezeguet.
No. 984: a, Marcel Desailly. b, Fabien Barthez. c, Christian Karembeu.
No. 985: a, Didier Deschamps. b, Emmanuel Petit. c, Bixente Lizarazu.
No. 986: a, Youri Djorkaeff. b, Zinedine Zidane. c, Aime Jacquet.
2000fr, Team picture.

1998 Litho. *Perf. 13½*
Sheets of 3

983 A302 250fr #a.-c. 4.50 2.25
984 A302 370fr #a.-c. 6.00 3.00
985 A302 390fr #a.-c. 6.75 3.50
986 A302 750fr #a.-c. 11.50 5.75

Souvenir Sheet

987 A302 2000fr multicolored 11.00 11.00

No. 987 contains one 57x51mm stamp.

Jacques-Yves Cousteau (1910-97), Underwater Explorer, Environmentalist — A303

No. 988: a, Cousteau, ship Calypso. b, Divers, underwater submersibles. c, Diver looking into submarine habitat, man playing chess.
No. 989: a, Portrait, Cousteau with Pres. John F. Kennedy. b, Divers retrieving amphora. c, Hard hat diver, Cousteau wearing early aqualung.

1998 Sheets of 3

988 A303 460fr #a.-c. 7.25 3.75
989 A303 490fr #a.-c. 8.25 4.25

Nos. 988b, 989b are each 60x51mm.

History of Chess — A304

Chess pieces, boards — No. 990: a, India, 18th cent. b, Italy, 1700. c, Siam, 18th cent. d, France, 1880. e, Austria, 1872. f, Germany, 1925. g, Yugoslavia, 20th cent. h, China, 20th cent. i, Russia, 20th cent.
No. 991, Albert V of Bavaria playing chess with his wife, Anne of Austria. No. 992, Arabian chess. No. 993, Japanese chess. No. 994, Nefertari, Ramses II playing chess.

1998 Litho. *Perf. 13½*
990 A304 370fr Sheet of 9, #a.-i. 16.00 8.00

Souvenir Sheets

991-994 A304 1500fr each 8.00 4.00

Nos. 991-994 each contain one 57x51mm stamp.

Pope John Paul II — A305

No. 995: Various portraits of John Paul II portrayed with events, popes depicting papal history.

Pope John Paul II, famous cathedrals —No. 996: a, Chartres. b, Santiago de Compostela. c, St. Sophie, Novgorod, Russia. d, St. Peter's Basilica, Vatican City. e, Our Lady of Peace Basilica, Yamoussoukro, Ivory Coast. f, Milan.
Pope John Paul II, famous cathedrals — No. 997: a, Sacred Family, Barcelona. b, Saint Sophie, Kiev. c, Notre Dame, Lausanne. d, Cathedral of Mexico. e, Cathedral of Cologne. f, Burgos Cathedral.

1998 Litho. *Perf. 13½*
Sheets of 6 or 9

995 A305 250fr #a.-i. 9.00 4.50
996 A305 370fr #a.-f. 8.00 4.00
997 A305 750fr #a.-f. 17.50 8.75

Granaries A306

1998 Litho. *Perf. 13½*

998 A306 25fr Sénoufo, vert. .25 .25
999 A306 180fr Sarakolé .80 .40
1000 A306 310fr Minianka, vert. 1.60 .80
1001 A306 320fr Boo, vert. 1.60 .80
Nos. 998-1001 (4) 4.25 2.25

Trees A307

100fr, Tamarindus indica. 150fr, Adansonia digitata. 180fr, Acacia senegal. 310fr, Parkia biglobosa.

1998

1002 A307 100fr multicolored .60 .30
1003 A307 150fr multicolored .80 .40
1004 A307 180fr multicolored .90 .45
1005 A307 310fr multicolored 1.60 .80
Nos. 1002-1005 (4) 3.90 1.95

National Museum Pieces — A308

1998

1006 A308 50fr Bamanan .25 .25
1007 A308 150fr Dogon .65 .35
1008 A308 250fr Bamanan, diff. 1.25 .65
1009 A308 320fr Minianka 1.60 .80
Nos. 1006-1009 (4) 3.75 2.05

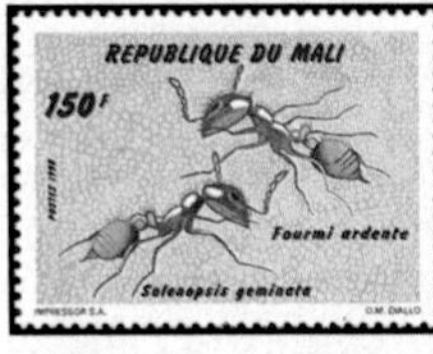

Ants A309

150fr, Solenopsis geminata. 180fr, Camponotus pennsylvanicus. 250fr, Monorium minimum. 310fr, Lasius niger.

1998

1010 A309 150fr multi .60 .30
1011 A309 180fr multi, vert. .80 .40
1012 A309 250fr multi 1.25 .60
1013 A309 310fr multi 1.50 .75
Nos. 1010-1013 (4) 4.15 2.05

Baladji Cisse (1924-77), Boxer — A309a

150fr, Cisse boxing. 250fr, In green jacket.

1999, May 12 Litho. *Perf. 13½*

1013A	A309a 150fr multi		—	—
1013B	A309a 250fr multi		—	—

World Teachers' Day A310

Various views of teachers working.

1999 Litho. *Perf. 13½*

1014	A310 150fr multi, vert.	.70	.35
1015	A310 250fr multi, vert.	1.25	.65
1016	A310 370fr multi, vert.	1.75	.80
1017	A310 390fr multi	1.90	.95
	Nos. 1014-1017 (4)	5.60	2.75

Fight Against Poverty A311

150fr, Agriculture. 180fr, Labor projects. 750fr, Food, vert. 1000fr, Potable water.

1999 Litho. *Perf. 13¼*

1018	A311 150fr multi	.80	.40
1019	A311 180fr multi	1.00	.50
1020	A311 750fr multi	3.75	1.80
1021	A311 1000fr multi	4.75	2.50
	Nos. 1018-1021 (4)	10.30	5.20

UPU, 125th Anniv. A312

UPU emblem and: 150fr, Airplane, train, boat. 250fr, Stick figures with letters. 310fr, Eagles, antelopes with letters. 320fr, Eagle with letter on mud structure, vert.

1999

1022	A312 150fr multi	.70	.35
1023	A312 250fr multi	1.25	.65
1024	A312 310fr multi	1.50	.75
1025	A312 320fr multi	1.60	.80
	Nos. 1022-1025 (4)	5.05	2.55

Flora and Fauna — A313

No. 1026 — Reptiles: a, Pseudonaja textilis. b, Litoria chloris. c, Imantodes inornata. d, Pyton arboricole. e, Pachydactylus bibroni. f, Trimeresurus wagleri.

No. 1027 — Orchids: a, Epidendrum ellipticum. b, Oncidium macranthum. c, Miltoniopsis roezlii. d, Oncidium barbatum. e, Miltonia warscewiczii. f, Lockhartia oerstedii.

No. 1028 — Birds: a, Amandava subflava. b, Ploceus bojeri. c, Lagonosticta senegala. d, Uraeginthus bengalus. e, Monticola saxatilis. f, Saxicola torquata.

No. 1028G — Birds: h, Tyto alba. i, Pernis apivorus. j, Bubo africanus. k, Gypaetus barbatus meridionalis. l, Strix aluco. m, Milvus migrans.

No. 1029 — Butterflies: a, Cymothoe hypatha. b, Cymothoe sangaris. c, Top view, Charaxes fournierae. d, Male Catopsilia thauruma. e, Bottom view, Charaxes fournierae. f, Female Catopsilia thauruma.

No. 1030 — Mushrooms: a, Amanita muscaria. b, Amanita spissa. c, Helvella acetabulum. d, Pleurotus ostreatus. e, Phallus duplicatus. f, Cortinarius salor.

1999 Sheets of 6

1026	A313 350fr #a.-f.	10.00	5.00
1027	A313 390fr #a.-f.	11.00	5.50
1028	A313 430fr #a.-f.	12.00	6.00
1028G	A313 460fr #h-m	14.00	7.00
1029	A313 490fr #a.-f.	15.00	7.50
1030	A313 530fr #a.-f.	16.00	8.00
	Nos. 1026-1030 (6)	78.00	39.00

Rocks, Dinosaurs and Volcanoes — A314

No. 1031 — Dinosaurs and rocks: a, Edmontonia, Ensisheim meteorite. b, Iguanodon, Saint-Mesmin meteorite. c, Allosaurus, Pallasite meteorite. d, Troodon, Lunar meteorite. e, Lesothosaurus, rock from Bouvant. f, Carnotaurus, Axtell meteorite. g, Deinonychus, Orgueil meteorite. h, Dilophosaurus, rock from Douar Mghila. i. Psittacosaurus, L'Aigle meteorite.

No. 1032 — Volcanic eruptions and rocks: a, Popocatepetl, 1519, Peekskill meteorite. b, Santorin, 1645, Tamentit meteorite. c, Mt. Pelee, 1902, Ouallen meteorite. d, Herculaneum during Vesuvius eruption, 79, Chinguetti meteorite. e, Krakatoa, 1883, Pultush meteorite. f, Soufriere, 1979, rock from Sienne. g, Mt. St. Helens, 1980, Allende meteorite. h, Kilauea, 1984, Parnallee meteorite. i, Mt. Etna, 1986, Tamentit meteorite.

1500fr, Pompeii during Vesuvius eruption, 79.

1999 Sheets of 9 *Perf. 13¼*

1031	A314 250fr #a.-i.	11.00	5.50
1032	A314 310fr #a.-i.	15.00	7.50

Souvenir Sheet

Perf. 13½

1033	A314 1500fr multi	7.50	3.75

No. 1033 contains one 39x56mm stamp.

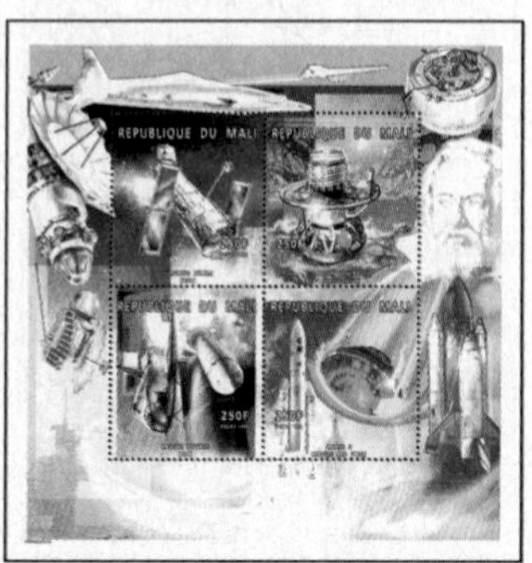

Space — A315

No. 1034: a, Hubble Space Telescope. b, Venera 12. c, Space shuttle. d, Ariane 5.

No. 1035: a, Apollo-Soyuz mission. b, Carl Sagan, Viking 1. c, Voyager 1. d, Giotto probe, Edmond Halley.

No. 1036: a, Frank Borman, Apollo 8. b, Neil Armstrong, Apollo 11. c, Luna 16 and Lunokhod 2. d, Surveyor 3.

No. 1037: a, Konstantin Tsiolkovsky. b, Robert H. Goddard. c, Hermann Oberth. d, Theodor von Kármán.

No. 1038: a, Laika, Sputnik 2. b, Yuri Gagarin, Vostok 1. c, Edward White, Gemini 4. d, John Glenn, Friendship 7.

No. 1039: a, Apollo 15 Lunar Rover. b, Pioneer 10. c, Skylab. d, Mariner 10.

1999 Sheets of 4 *Perf. 13¼*

1034	A315 250fr #a.-d.	5.50	2.75
1035	A315 310fr #a.-d.	6.00	3.00
1036	A315 320fr #a-d	6.50	3.25
1037	A315 500fr #a-d	11.00	5.50
1038	A315 750fr #a-d	15.00	7.50
1039	A315 900fr #a-d	18.00	9.00
	Nos. 1034-1039 (6)	62.00	31.00

The Malian government declared that sheets of 9 stamps containing 100, 150, 200, 250, 300, 350, 400, 450 and 500fr stamps with the following topics are "illegal": Trains, Chess, Prehistoric Animals, Ferdinand Magellan, Christopher Columbus, Mushrooms, Computers, Wolves, Minerals, International Red Cross, Composers, Horses, and Wild Animals (tiger, lion, eagle, etc.)

I Love Lucy — A318

No. 1045: a, Lucy showing Fred open handcuffs. b, Lucy touching reclining Ricky while handcuffed. c, Fred watching Ricky glare at Lucy. d, Handcuffed Lucy and Ricky trying to go in opposite directions. e, Handcuffed Lucy and Ricky seated. f, Lucy and Ricky handcuffed on bed. g, Lucy trying to get off bed while handcuffed to Ricky. h, Handcuffed Ricky with hand between legs. i, Ricky with arm draped over Lucy.

No. 1046, 1000fr, Fred examining handcuffs on Lucy and Ricky. No. 1047, 1000fr, Lucy and Ricky looking down.

1999, May 20 Litho. *Perf. 13¼*

1045	A318 320fr Sheet of 9, #a-i	16.00	16.00

Souvenir Sheets

1046-1047	A318 Set of 2	12.00	12.00

Garfield the Cat — A319

No. 1048: a, With eyes half shut, pink background. b, With eyes open, pink background. c, Touching chin. d, With eyes open and open mouth. e, Showing tongue. f, With eyes open, showing teeth. g, With eyes open, blue background. h, With eyes half shut, blue background. i, Odie.

1000fr, As mailman.

1999, May 20 Litho. *Perf. 13¼*

1048	A319 250fr Sheet of 9, #a-i	12.50	6.25

Souvenir Sheet

1049	A319 1000fr multi	5.50	2.75

No. 1049 contains one 36x42mm stamp.

Miniature Sheet

Millennium — A320

No. 1051: a, Jules Verne, Scene from "20,000 Leagues Under the Sea," 1905. b, Commander William R. Anderson, USS Nautilus, map of Arctic region showing underwater voyage across North Pole, 1958. c, Discovery of tomb of King Tutankhamun, 1922. d, Transatlantic flight of Charles A. Lindbergh, 1927.

No. 1052: a, Marilyn Monroe (1926-62), actress. b, The Beatles, 1962. c, Neil Armstrong, first man on the Moon, 1969. d, Elvis Presley (1935-77).

No. 1053: a, Mohandas Gandhi, Independence of India, 1947. b, Jean Monnet (1888-1979), map of Europe, euro symbol, 1951 meeting of European Coal and Steel Community. c, Pres. John F. Kennedy (1917-63). d, First heart transplant by Dr. Christiaan Barnard, 1967.

No. 1056: a, Mother Teresa holding Nobel diploma, dove. b, Princess Diana, rose, dove. c, Pope John Paul II. d, Fall of the Berlin Wall, doves.

1999, July 2 Litho. *Perf. 13¼*

1051	A320 310fr Sheet of 4, #a-d	—	—
1052	A320 320fr Sheet of 4, #a-d	—	—
1053	A320 390fr Sheet of 4, #a-d	—	—
1056	A320 490fr Sheet of 4, #a-d	—	—

Four additional sheets exist in this set. The editors would like to examine any these sheets.

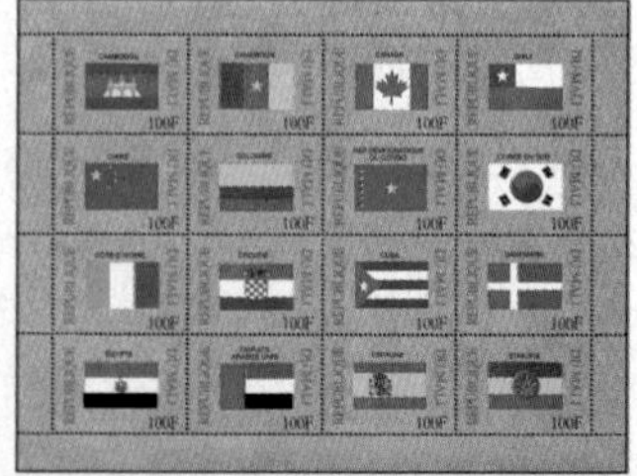

Flags of the World — A321

No. 1058: a, Myanmar. b, Namibia. c, Nepal. d, Niger. e, Nigeria. f, Norway. g, Uganda. h, Pakistan. i, Netherlands. j, Peru. k, Philippines. l, Poland. m, New Zealand. n, Portugal. o, North Korea. p, Romania.

No. 1059: a, Russia. b, Rwanda. c, Singapore. d, Slovakia. e, Sudan. f, Sri Lanka. g, Sweden. h, Switzerland. i, Syria. j, Tanzania. k, Czech Republic. l, Thailand. m, Somalia. n, Tunisia. o, Turkey. p, Ukraine.

No. 1060: a, Finland. b, France. c, Great Britain. d, Greece. e, Guinea. f, Hungary. g, India. h, Indonesia. i, Iran. j, Iraq. k, Ireland. l, Iceland. m, Israel. n, Italy. o, Libya. p, Japan.

No. 1061: a, Cambodia. b, Cameroun. c, Canada. d, Chile. e, People's Republic of China. f, Colombia. g, Democratic Republic of the Congo. h, South Korea. i, Ivory Coast. j, Croatia. k, Cuba. l, Denmark. m, Egypt. n, United Arab Emirates. o, Spain. p, Ethiopia.

No. 1062: a, Afghanistan. b, South Africa. c, Albania. d, Algeria. e, Germany. f, United States. g, Angola. h, Saudi Arabia. i, Argentina. j, Australia. k, Austria. l, Bangladesh. m, Belgium. n, Bolivia. o, Brazil. p, Bulgaria.

No. 1063: a, Jordan. b, Kenya. c, Kuwait. d, Laos. e, Lebanon. f, Lithuania. g, Luxembourg. h, Madagascar. i, Malaysia. j, Mali. k, Viet Nam. l, Morocco. m, Mauritius. n, Mexico. o, Monaco. p, Mongolia.

1999, Aug. 2 Litho. *Perf. 13¼*

1058 A321 20fr Sheet of 16, #a-p — —
1059 A321 25fr Sheet of 16, #a-p — —
1060 A321 50fr Sheet of 16, #a-p — —
1061 A321 100fr Sheet of 16, #a-p 5.00 2.50
q. Cameroun, flag with green star — —
r. Sheet of 16, #1061a, 1061c-1061q — —
1062 A321 100fr Sheet of 16, #a-p — —
1063 A321 100fr Sheet of 16, #a-p — —

No. 1061b has a Cameroun flag with a yellow star.

Two additional sheets exist in this set. The editors would like to examine them.

Sikasso Cathedral — A322

No. 1065: a, Photograph. b, Drawing.

1999, Dec. 25 Litho. *Perf. 13¼*

1065 A322 150fr Horiz. pair, #a-b 1.75 .85

Christianity, 2000th Anniv. — A323

No. 1066, 100fr: a, St. Louis. b, Construction of Amiens Cathedral, 13th cent. c, Joan of Arc. d, Pope John Paul II.

No. 1067, 180fr: a, Jesus Christ. b, Persecution of Christians by Nero. c, St. Peter. d, Charlemagne.

1999, Dec. 25 Sheets of 4, #a-d

1066-1067 A323 Set of 2 6.00 3.00

Religious Paintings — A324

No. 1068, 250fr: a, Heller Madonna, by Albrecht Dürer. b, Virgin and Child, by Dürer. c, Madonna with Sts. Francis and Liberale, by Giorgione. d, Virgin and Child, by Giorgione.

No. 1069, 310fr: a, Virgin and Child, by Fra Filippo Lippi. b, Virgin and Child with Two Angels, by Lippi. c, Virgin and Sleeping Child, by Andrea Mantegna. d, Madonna of Victory, by Mantegna.

No. 1070, 320fr: a, Virgin and Child, by Hugo van der Goes. b, Virgin and Child and landscape, by van der Goes. c, Madonna and Child with St. Peter and a Martyred Saint, by Paolo Veronese. d, Adoration of the Magi, by Veronese.

No. 1071, 370fr: a, Madonna and Child Between St. Peter and St. Sebastian, by Giovanni Bellini. b, Madonna and Child with Cherubim, by Bellini. c, Madonna and Child with Two Angels, by Sandro Botticelli. d, Bardi Madonna, by Botticelli.

No. 1072, 390fr: a, Rest During the Flight to Egypt, with St. Francis, by Corregio. b, The Night, by Corregio. c, Senigallia Madonna, by Piero della Francesca. d, Virgin and Child and Four Angels, by della Francesca.

No. 1073, 750fr: a, Virgin and Child (rectangular), by Quentin Massys. b, Virgin and Child (curved top) by Massys. c, Madonna and Saint Sixtus, by Raphael. d, Madonna of the Duke of Alba, by Raphael.

1999, Dec. 25 Sheets of 4, #a-d

1068-1073 A324 Set of 6 50.00 25.00

2000 Summer Olympics, Sydney — A325

No. 1074, 150fr — Equestrian events: a, Show jumping. b, Military jumping. c, Dressage, horse facing left. d, Dressage, horse facing right.

No. 1075, 460fr — Tennis: a, Woman with green trim on dress. b, Man with red trim on shirt. c, Woman, diff. d, Man, diff.

No. 1076, 530fr — Table tennis: a, Green and red shirt and shorts. b, White shirt, red shorts. c, White and red shirt, black shorts. d, Yellow and green shirt, black shorts.

No. 1077, 750fr — Basketball: a, Red and yellow uniform. b, Green uniform. c, White and red uniform. d, Yellow and green uniform.

1000fr, Hurdler, horse and rider, horiz.

2000, June 30 Sheets of 4, #a-d

1074-1077 A325 Set of 4 57.50 30.00

Souvenir Sheet

1078 A325 1000fr multi 7.50 3.75

No. 1078 contains one 57x51mm stamp.

2002 World Cup Soccer Championships, Japan and Korea — A326

No. 1079, 150fr: a, Pedro Cea. b, Schiavo. c, Luigi Colaussi. d, Juan Schiaffino.

No. 1080, 250fr: a, Fritz Walter. b, Pelé. c, Amarildo. d, Bobby Moore.

No. 1081, 320fr: a, Jairzinho. b, Franz Beckenbauer. c, Mario Kempes. d, Paolo Rossi.

No. 1082, 750fr: a, Diego Maradona. b, Jurgen Klinsmann. c, Romario. d, Zinedine Zidane.

2000, June 30 Sheets of 4, #a-d

1079-1082 A326 Set of 4 42.50 22.50

Fauna, Mushrooms and Prehistoric Animals — A327

No. 1083, 150fr — Birds: a, Ganga de Liechtenstein. b, Guepier à gorge blanche. c, Moineau domestique. d, Euplecte de feu. e, Irrisor namaquois. f, Pique-boeuf à bec jaune.

No. 1084, 180fr — Dogs: a, Dalmatian. b, Hungarian Kuvasz. c, Swedish shepherd. d, Ibiza dog. e, Golden retriever. f, Dachshund.

No. 1085, 250fr — Cats: a, White cat with orange eyes. b, Somali. c, Himalayan blue tortie point. d, Korat. e, Bombay. f, La Perm.

No. 1086, 310fr — Butterflies: a, Paralethe dendrophilis. b, Papilio ophidicephalus. c, Kallima jacksoni. d, Hypolimnas antevorta. e, Papilio nobilis. f, Euxanthe wakefieldi.

No. 1087, 320fr — Butterflies: a, Euxanthe eurinome. b, Euryphura chalcis. c, Dira mintha. d, Euphaedra zaddachi. e, Euphaedra neophron. f, Euxanthe tiberius.

No. 1088, 370fr — Mushrooms: a, Volvariella acystidiata. b, Leucopricus birnbaumii. c, Cystoderma elegans. d, Leucoprinus elaidis. e, Leucoprinus discoideus. f, Leucoagaricus carminescens.

No. 1089, 370fr — Birds: a, Pririt du cap. b, Petit duc scops. c, Ouette d'Egypte. d, Rollier d'Europe. e, Promerops du cap. f, Sauteur du cap.

No. 1090, 390fr — Mushrooms: a, Volvariella parvispora. b, Volvariella surrecta. c, Lentinus similis. d, Leucoagaricus holosericeus. e, Leucoagaricus pepinus. f, Agrocybe elegantior.

No. 1091, 460fr — Prehistoric animals: a, Psittacosaurus. b, Phororhacos. c, Coelophysis. d, Saurornithoides. e, Acanthopholis. f, Varannosaurus.

No. 1092, 490fr — Prehistoric animals: a, Dromiceiomimus. b, Placodus. c, Ceratosaurus. d, Heterodontosaurus. e, Diatryma. f, Ouranosaurus.

2000, Sept. 25 Sheets of 6, #a-f

1083-1092 A327 Set of 10 145.00 75.00

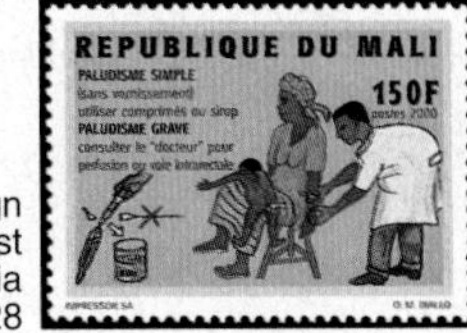

Campaign Against Malaria A328

Designs: No. 1093, 150fr, Doctor, mother and child. No. 1094, 150fr, Man with briefcase, man with crutch, syringe. No. 1095, 150fr, Doctor, syringe. 430fr, Mother, child, syringe, quinine tablets.

2000

1093-1096 A328 Set of 4 4.00 2.00

Intl. Volunteers Year (in 2001) — A329

2000

1097 A329 250fr multi 1.00 .50

Independence, 40th Anniv. — A330

Designs: 20fr, Provincial map. 375fr, Flag-raising ceremony, front and back of 50-franc banknote, vert.

2001 Litho. *Perf. 13*

1099 A330 20fr multi — —
1100 A330 375fr multi — —

An additional stamp was issued in this set. The editors would like to examine it.

Senegal River Regional Organization — A331

2001 Litho. *Perf. 12¾*

1101 A331 30fr multi, dated "2004" — —
1102 A331 100fr multi — —
a. Dated "2003" — —
1103 A331 5000fr multi, dated "2002" — —

A332

A333

Perf. 13¼ (A332), 13x12¾ (A333)

2002 Litho.

1104 A332 195fr multi — —
1105 A333 255fr multi — —
1106 A332 385fr multi — —
1107 A333 395fr multi —
1108 A333 565fr multi —
1109 A332 975fr multi —

23rd African Cup Soccer Tournament. Dated "2001."

Bobo Mask — A334

Dogon Mask — A335

Sénoufo Sanctuary Door — A336

Bamanan Fertility Statue — A337

2001-04 Litho. *Perf. 12¾*

1110	A334	5fr multi	—	—
1111	A335	10fr multi	—	—
a.		Dated "2004"	—	—
1112	A336	25fr multi	—	—
a.		Dated "2004"		—
1113	A334	40fr multi		—
1114	A335	75fr multi	—	—
a.		Dated "2004"	—	—
1115	A334	195fr multi	—	—
1116	A335	195fr multi	1.00	.50
a.		Dated "2005"	—	—
1117	A334	235fr multi	—	—
1118	A335	255fr multi	—	—
1119	A337	255fr multi	1.40	.70
1120	A335	325fr multi	—	—
1121	A336	385fr multi	—	—
1122	A336	400fr multi		—
1123	A337	500fr multi	—	—
1124	A337	1000fr multi		—

Issued: Nos. 1115, 1117, 1118, 1120, 1121-1123, 2001; Nos. 1110, 1111-1114, 2002. Nos. 1116, 1119, 2003. No. 1124, 2004.

A338

AIDS Prevention A339

2002, Jan. 10 Litho. *Perf. 12¾*

1125	A338	195fr multi		—
1127	A338	225fr multi	—	—
1128	A339	225fr multi	—	—
1129	A338	385fr multi		—
1130	A339	385fr multi		—

An additional stamp was issued in this set. The editors would like to examine any example of it.

Songhoi Woman's Hairstyle — A340

Peulh Woman — A341

Badiangara Cliffs A342

Perf. 12¾, 13x12¾ (#1131)

2003, Mar. 7 Litho.

1131	A340	50fr multi	.25	.25
1132	A341	385fr multi	2.25	2.25
a.		Dated "2004"		—
1133	A342	485fr multi	2.75	2.75

Balaphone Festival A343

2003, Mar. 7 Litho. *Perf. 12¾*

1134	A343	565fr multi	3.50	3.50

Men Drinking Tea in Desert — A344

2005, Aug. 18 Litho. *Perf. 12¾*

1135	A344	10fr multi		—

See No. 1147.

Djenné Fair — A345

2005, Aug. 18 Litho. *Perf. 12¾*

1136	A345	20fr multi	.50	.50

Map of Africa, Water Drop, Lions International Emblem — A346

2005, Aug. 18 Litho. *Perf. 12¾*

1137	A346	465fr multi	4.50	4.50

World Summit on the Information Society, Tunis A347

2005, Aug. 18 Litho. *Perf. 12¾x13*

1138	A347	195fr multi		—
1139	A347	255fr multi		—
1140	A347	385fr multi		—

23rd Summit of Heads of State of Africa and France
A348 A349

2005, Aug. 18 Litho. *Perf. 13x12¾*

1141	A348	195fr multi		—
1142	A349	195fr multi		—

Three additional stamps were issued in this set. The editors would like to examine any examples.

23rd Summit of Heads of State of Africa and France Type of 2005

2005, Aug. 18 Litho. *Perf. 13x12¾*

1146	A349	385fr multi		—

Three additional stamps exist in this set. The editors would like to examine any examples.

Men Drinking Tea in Desert Type of 2005

2007 Litho. *Perf. 12¾*

1147	A344	20fr multi		—

Mother Nursing Baby — A350

2009 Litho. *Perf. 13x12¾*

1149	A350	195fr multi		—

An additional stamp was issued in this set. The editors would like to examine any example.

Independence, 50th Anniv. — A351

50th anniversary emblem with: 5fr, Pale yellow background, orange yellow top panel, green bottom panel. 10fr, White background, orange yellow top panel, red bottom panel. 20fr, White background, orange yellow top and bottom panels. 25fr, Pale yellow background, green top panel, red bottom panel. 40fr, Light blue background, red top panel, orange yellow bottom panel. 100fr, Light blue background, red top panel, green bottom panel. 195fr, White background, red top and bottom panels. 565fr, White background, green top and bottom panels.

2010 Litho. *Perf. 13*

1151-1158	A351	Set of 8	11.50	11.50

Independence, 50th Anniv. — A352

Denomination color: 195fr, Green. 485fr, Red.

2010 Litho. *Perf. 13*

1159-1160	A352	Set of 2	8.00	8.00

SEMI-POSTAL STAMPS

Anti-Malaria Issue

Common Design Type

Perf. 12½x12

1962, Apr. 7 Engr. Unwmk.

B1	CD108	25fr + 5fr pale vio bl	1.25	.60

Algerian Family — SP1

1962, Dec. 24 Photo. *Perf. 12x12½*

B2	SP1	25fr + 5fr multi	.70	.30

Issued for the national campaign to show the solidarity of the peoples of Mali and Algeria.

AIR POST STAMPS

Federation

Composite View of St. Louis, Senegal — AP1

Unwmk.

1959, Dec. 11 Engr. *Perf. 13*

C1	AP1	85fr multi	2.10	1.00

Founding of St. Louis, Senegal, tercentenary, and opening of the 6th meeting of the executive council of the French Community.

Birds — AP2

100fr, Amethyst starling. 200fr, Bateleur eagle, horiz. 500fr, Barbary shrike.

Perf. 12½x13, 13x12½

1960, Feb. 13 **Photo.**

C2 AP2 100fr multi 3.00 1.50
C3 AP2 200fr multi 7.00 2.50
C4 AP2 500fr multi 20.00 11.50
Nos. C2-C4 (3) 30.00 15.50

Republic
Nos. C2-C4 Overprinted or Surcharged

1960, Dec. 18

C5 AP2 100fr multi 4.50 1.75
C6 AP2 200fr multi 6.75 3.00
C7 AP2 300fr on 500fr multi 10.00 6.00
C8 AP2 500fr multi 16.50 9.00
Nos. C5-C8 (4) 37.75 19.75

Pres. Modibo Keita — AP3

Designs: 200fr, Mamadou Konate.

1961, Mar. 18 **Engr.** ***Perf. 13***

C9 AP3 200fr claret & gray brn 3.00 .95
C10 AP3 300fr grn & blk 4.50 1.25

Flag, Map, UN Emblem — AP4

1961, Mar. 18

C11 AP4 100fr multicolored 1.75 .75
a. Min. sheet of 3, #13, 14, C11 2.75 2.75

Proclamation of independence and admission to UN.

Sankore Mosque, Timbuktu — AP5

200fr, View of Timbuktu. 500fr, Bamako & arms.

1961, Apr. 15 **Unwmk.** ***Perf. 13***

C12 AP5 100fr Prus bl, red brn & gray 2.25 .60
C13 AP5 200fr grn, brn & red 4.50 1.75
C14 AP5 500fr red brn, Prus bl & dk grn 11.00 3.25
Nos. C12-C14 (3) 17.75 5.60

Inauguration of Timbuktu airport and Air Mali.

Bull, Chemical Equipment and Chicks — AP6

1963, Feb. 23 **Engr.**

C15 AP6 200fr bis, mar & grnsh bl 4.25 1.50

Sotuba Zootechnical Institute.

Air Ambulance — AP7

Designs: 55fr, National Line plane loading. 100fr, Intl. Line Vickers Viscount in flight.

1963, Nov. 2 **Unwmk.** ***Perf. 13***

C16 AP7 25fr dk bl, emer & red brn .35 .25
C17 AP7 55fr bis, bl & red brn 1.00 .35
C18 AP7 100fr dk bl, red brn & yel grn 1.75 .70
Nos. C16-C18 (3) 3.10 1.30

Issued to publicize Air Mali.

Crowned Crane and Giant Tortoise — AP8

1963, Nov. 23 **Unwmk.** ***Perf. 13***

C19 AP8 25fr sepia, org & ver 1.25 .60
C20 AP8 200fr multi 5.25 2.25

Animal protection.

UN Emblem, Flag, Doves — AP9

1963, Dec. 10 **Engr.**

C21 AP9 50fr lt grn, yel & red 1.20 .50

15th anniversary of the Universal Declaration of Human Rights.

Cleopatra and Ptolemy at Kôm Ombo — AP10

1964, Mar. 9 **Unwmk.** ***Perf. 12***

C22 AP10 25fr dp claret & bister .75 .35
C23 AP10 55fr dp claret & lt ol grn 1.50 .75

UNESCO world campaign to save historic monuments in Nubia.

Pres. John F. Kennedy — AP11

1964, Oct. 26 **Photo.** ***Perf. 12½***

C24 AP11 100fr sl, red brn & blk 2.25 1.25
a. Souv. sheet of 4 7.50 6.00

Touracos — AP12

200fr, Abyssinian ground hornbills, vert. 300fr, Egyptian vultures, vert. 500fr, Goliath herons.

1965, Feb. 15 **Engr.** ***Perf. 13***

C25 AP12 100fr grn, dk bl & red 2.25 .90
C26 AP12 200fr blk, red & brt bl 7.00 1.40
C27 AP12 300fr blk, sl grn & yel 10.50 2.50
C28 AP12 500fr sl grn, dk brn & claret 16.00 4.00
Nos. C25-C28 (4) 35.75 8.80

UN Headquarters, New York, and ICY Emblem — AP13

1965, Mar. 15 **Unwmk.** ***Perf. 13***

C29 AP13 55fr bis, dk bl & vio brn 1.10 .40

International Cooperation Year.

Pope John XXIII AP14

Perf. 12½x13

1965, Sept. 14 **Photo.** **Unwmk.**

C30 AP14 100fr multi 2.10 1.00

Winston Churchill — AP15

1965, Oct. 11 **Engr.** ***Perf. 13***

C31 AP15 100fr brn & indigo 2.10 1.00

Dr. Albert Schweitzer and Sick Child — AP16

1965, Dec. 20 **Photo.** ***Perf. 12½***

C32 AP16 100fr multi 2.25 1.00
a. Souv. sheet of 4 9.00 9.00

Major Edward H. White and Gemini 4 — AP17

No. C34, Lt. Col. Alexei A. Leonov. 300fr, Gordon Cooper, Charles Conrad, Alexei Leonov & Pavel Belyayev, Parthenon, Athens, & vase, vert.

1966, Jan. 10

C33 AP17 100fr vio, yel, lt bl & blk 1.50 1.00
C34 AP17 100fr bl, red, yel & blk 1.50 1.00
C35 AP17 300fr multi 4.50 2.50
Nos. C33-C35 (3) 7.50 4.50

Achievements in space research and 16th Intl. Astronautical Congress, Athens, Sept. 12-18, 1965.

Papal Arms and UN Emblem — AP18

1966, July 11 **Engr.** ***Perf. 13***

C36 AP18 200fr brt bl, grnsh bl & grn 3.00 1.50

Visit of Pope Paul VI to the UN, NYC, Oct. 4, 1965.

People and UNESCO Emblem — AP19

1966, Sept. 5 **Engr.** ***Perf. 13***

C37 AP19 100fr dk car rose, sl grn & ultra 2.10 1.25

20th anniv. of UNESCO.

Soccer Players, Ball, Globe, and Jules Rimet Cup — AP20

1966, Oct. 31 **Photo.** ***Perf. 13***

C38 AP20 100fr multi 2.25 1.25

8th International Soccer Championship Games, Wembley, England, July 11-30.

Crab and Mt. Fuji — AP21

1966, Nov. 30 Photo. *Perf. 13*

C39 AP21 100fr multi 1.75 .75

9th Intl. Anticancer Cong., Tokyo, Oct. 23-29.

UNICEF Emblem and Children — AP22

1966, Dec. 10 Engr.

C40 AP22 45fr dp bl, bis brn & red lil .90 .40

20th anniv. of UNICEF.

Land Cruisers in Hoggar Mountain Pass — AP23

1967, Mar. 20 Engr. *Perf. 13*

C41 AP23 200fr multi 5.25 2.25

"Black Cruise 1924," which crossed Africa from Beni-Abbes, Algeria to the Indian Ocean and on to Tananarive, Madagascar, Oct. 28, 1924-June 26, 1925.

Diamant Rocket and Francesco de Lana's 1650 Flying Boat — AP24

Designs: 100fr, A-1 satellite and rocket launching adapted from Jules Verne. 200fr, D-1 satellite and Leonardo da Vinci's bird-borne flying machine.

1967, Apr. 17 Engr. *Perf. 13*

C42 AP24 50fr brt bl, pur & grn .75 .25

C43 AP24 100fr dk Prus bl, dk car & lil 1.50 .50

C44 AP24 200fr sl bl, ol & pur 3.00 1.00

Nos. C42-C44 (3) 5.25 1.75

Honoring French achievements in space.

Amelia Earhart and Map of Mali — AP25

1967, May 29 Photo. *Perf. 13*

C45 AP25 500fr bl & multi 8.00 3.00

Amelia Earhart's stop at Gao, West Africa, 30th anniv.

Paul as Harlequin, by Picasso AP26

Picasso Paintings: 50fr, Bird Cage. 250fr, The Flutes of Pan.

1967, June 16 *Perf. 12½*

C46 AP26 50fr multi 1.00 .40

C47 AP26 100fr multi 2.10 .75

C48 AP26 250fr multi 4.50 1.60

Nos. C46-C48 (3) 7.60 2.75

See Nos. C56, C58, C82.

Jamboree Emblem, Scout Knots and Badges — AP27

Design: 100fr, Scout with portable radio transmitter, tents and Jamboree badge.

1967, July 10 Engr. *Perf. 13*

C49 AP27 70fr dk car, emer & bl grn .90 .25

C50 AP27 100fr dk car lake, sl grn & blk 1.25 .30

a. Strip of 2, #C49-C50 + label 3.00 1.75

12th Boy Scout World Jamboree, Farragut State Park, Idaho, Aug. 1-9.

Head of Horse, by Toulouse-Lautrec — AP28

300fr, Cob-drawn gig, by Toulouse-Lautrec.

Perf. 12x12½, 12½x12

1967, Dec. 11 Photo.

C51 AP28 100fr multi 2.50 1.00

C52 AP28 300fr multi, vert. 6.00 2.00

See Nos. C66-C67.

Grenoble AP29

Design: 150fr, Bobsled course on Huez Alp.

1968, Jan. 8 Engr. *Perf. 13*

C53 AP29 50fr bl, yel brn & grn .75 .25

C54 AP29 150fr brn, vio bl & stl bl 1.90 .75

10th Winter Olympic Games, Grenoble, France, Feb. 6-18.

Painting Type of 1967 and

Roses and Anemones, by Van Gogh — AP30

Paintings: 150fr, Peonies in Vase, by Edouard Manet. 300fr, Bouquet, by Delacroix. 500fr, Daisies in Vase, by Jean François Millet, horiz.

Perf. 13, 12½x12, 12x12½

1968, June 24 Photo.

C55 AP30 50fr multi .75 .50

C56 AP26 150fr grn & multi 1.90 .65

C57 AP30 300fr grn & multi 3.75 1.40

C58 AP26 500fr car & multi 5.50 2.00

Nos. C55-C58 (4) 11.90 4.55

Martin Luther King, Jr. — AP31

1968, July 22 *Perf. 12½*

C59 AP31 100fr rose lil, sal pink & blk 1.20 .40

Bicycle Type of Regular Issue

Designs: 50fr, Bicyclette, 1918. 100fr, Mercedes Benz, 1927, horiz.

1968, Aug. 12 Engr. *Perf. 13*

C60 A40 50fr gray, dk grn & brick red 1.10 .30

C61 A40 100fr lemon, indigo & car 2.50 .70

Long Jumper and Satellite — AP32

100fr, Soccer goalkeeper and satellite.

1968, Nov. 25 Photo. *Perf. 12½*

C62 AP32 100fr multi, horiz. 1.00 .60

C63 AP32 150fr multi 2.00 .80

19th Olympic Games, Mexico City, 10/12-27.

PHILEXAFRIQUE Issue

Editorial Department, by François Marius Granet — AP33

1968, Dec. 23 Photo. *Perf. 12½x12*

C64 AP33 200fr multi 3.00 1.75

Issued to publicize PHILEXAFRIQUE Philatelic Exhibition in Abidjan, Feb. 14-23. Printed with alternating light green label.

See Nos. C85-C87, C110-C112, C205-C207, C216-C217.

2nd PHILEXAFRIQUE Issue

Common Design Type

100fr, French Sudan #64, sculpture.

1969, Feb. 14 Engr. *Perf. 13*

C65 CD128 100fr pur & multi 1.75 1.00

Painting Type of 1967

Paintings: 150fr, Napoleon as First Consul, by Antoine Jean Gros, vert. 250fr, Bivouac at Austerlitz, by Louis François Lejeune.

Perf. 12½x12, 12x12½

1969, Feb. 25 Photo.

C66 AP28 150fr multi 3.00 1.25

C67 AP28 250fr multi 4.50 1.75

Napoleon Bonaparte (1769-1821).

Montgolfier's Balloon — AP34

Designs: 150fr, Ferber 5, experimental biplane. 300fr, Concorde.

1969, Mar. 10 Photo. *Perf. 13*

C68 AP34 50fr multi .60 .30

C69 AP34 150fr multi 1.90 .60

C70 AP34 300fr multi 3.75 1.40

a. Strip of 3, #C68-C70 7.50 4.50

1st flight of the prototype Concorde plane at Toulouse, France, Mar. 1, 1969.

For overprints see Nos. C78-C80.

Auto Type of Regular Issue

55fr, Renault, 1898, Renault 16, 1969. 90fr, Peugeot, 1893, Peugeot 404, 1969.

1969, May 30 Engr. *Perf. 13*

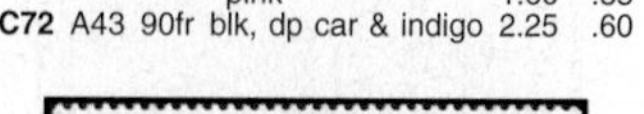

C71 A43 55fr rose car, blk & brt pink 1.60 .35

C72 A43 90fr blk, dp car & indigo 2.25 .60

Ronald Clarke, Australia, 10,000-meter Run, 1965 — AP35

World Records: 90fr, Yanis Lusis, USSR, Javelin, 1968. 120fr, Yoshinobu Miyake, Japan, weight lifting, 1967. 140fr, Randy Matson, US, shot put, 1968. 150fr, Kipchoge Keino, Kenya, 3,000-meter run, 1965.

1969, June 23 Engr. *Perf. 13*

C73 AP35 60fr bl & ol brn .35 .25
C74 AP35 90fr car rose & red brn .55 .30
C75 AP35 120fr emer & gray ol .80 .45
C76 AP35 140fr gray & brn .85 .50
C77 AP35 150fr red org & blk 1.00 .60
Nos. C73-C77 (5) 3.55 2.10

Issued to honor sports world records.

Nos. C68-C70 Overprinted in Red

Overprint includes Lunar Landing Module and "L'HOMME SUR LA LUNE / JUILLET 1969 / APOLLO 11".

1969, July 25 Photo. *Perf. 13*

C78 AP34 50fr multi .90 .60
C79 AP34 150fr multi 2.25 1.25
C80 AP34 300fr multi 3.50 2.00
a. Strip of 3, #C78-C80 9.00 4.50

Man's 1st landing on moon, July 20, 1969. US astronauts Neil A. Armstrong and Col. Edwin E. Aldrin, Jr., with Lieut. Col. Michael Collins piloting Apollo 11.

Apollo 8, Moon and Earth — AP35a

Embossed on Gold Foil

1969, July 24 *Die-cut perf 10½*

C81 AP35a 2000fr gold 20.00 20.00

US Apollo 8 mission, the 1st men in orbit around the moon, Dec. 21-27, 1968.

Painting Type of 1967

500fr, Mona Lisa, by Leonardo da Vinci.

1969, Oct. 20 Photo. *Perf. 12½*

C82 AP26 500fr multi 5.50 3.25

Mahatma Gandhi — AP36

1969, Nov. 24 Engr. *Perf. 13*

C83 AP36 150fr brt bl, ol brn & red brn 3.00 .70

Map of West Africa, Post Horns and Lightning Bolts — AP37

1970, Feb. 23 Photo. *Perf. 12½*

C84 AP37 100fr multi .85 .40

11th anniversary of the West African Postal Union (CAPTEAO).

Painting Type of 1968

Paintings: 100fr, Madonna and Child, from Rogier van der Weyden school. 150fr, Nativity, by the master of Flemalle. 250fr, Madonna and Child with St. John, from the Dutch School.

1970, Mar. 2

C85 AP33 100fr multi .85 .40
C86 AP33 150fr multi 1.25 .80
C87 AP33 250fr multi 2.75 1.40
Nos. C85-C87 (3) 4.85 2.60

Roosevelt AP38

1970, Mar. 30 Photo. *Perf. 12½*

C88 AP38 500fr red, lt ultra & blk 3.75 2.50

Pres. Franklin D. Roosevelt (1882-1945).

Lenin — AP39

1970, Apr. 22

C89 AP39 300fr pink, grn & blk 3.00 1.25

Jules Verne and Firing of Moon Rockets — AP40

150fr, Jules Verne, rockets, landing modules & moon. 300fr, Jules Verne & splashdown.

1970, May 4

C90 AP40 50fr multi .80 .30
C91 AP40 150fr multi 2.00 .80
C92 AP40 300fr multi 3.50 1.60
Nos. C90-C92 (3) 6.30 2.70

Nos. C90-C92 Overprinted in Red or Blue

Overprint reads "APOLLO XIII / EPOPEE SPATIALE / 11-17 AVRIL 1970".

1970, June Photo. *Perf. 12½*

C93 AP40 50fr multi (Bl) .50 .25
C94 AP40 150fr multi (R) 1.50 .80
C95 AP40 300fr multi (Bl) 3.00 1.60
Nos. C93-C95 (3) 5.00 2.65

Flight and safe return of Apollo 13, Apr. 11-13, 1970.

Intelsat III — AP41

Telecommunications Through Space: 200fr, Molniya I satellite. 300fr, Radar. 500fr, "Project Symphony" (various satellites).

1970, July 13 Engr. *Perf. 13*

C96 AP41 100fr gray, brt bl & org .70 .40
C97 AP41 200fr bl, gray & red lil 1.40 .55
C98 AP41 300fr org, dk brn & gray 2.25 1.60
C99 AP41 500fr dk brn, sl & grnsh bl 3.50 2.50
Nos. C96-C99 (4) 7.85 5.05

For surcharges see Nos. C108-C109.

Auguste and Louis Lumière, Jean Harlow and Marilyn Monroe AP42

1970, July 27 Photo. *Perf. 12½x12*

C100 AP42 250fr multi 4.50 2.00

Issued to honor Auguste Lumière (1862-1954), and his brother Louis Jean Lumière (1864-1948), inventors of the Lumière process of color photography and of a motion picture camera.

Soccer — AP43

1970, Sept. 7 Engr. *Perf. 13*

C101 AP43 80fr bl, dp car & brn ol .75 .30
C102 AP43 200fr dp car, bl grn & ol brn 2.00 .80

9th World Soccer Championships for the Jules Rimet Cup, Mexico City, May 30-June 21, 1970.

Rotary Emblem, Map of Mali and Ceremonial Antelope Heads — AP44

1970, Sept. 21 Photo. *Perf. 12½*

C103 AP44 200fr multi 2.25 1.25

Issued to honor Rotary International.

Men Holding UN Emblem, and Doves — AP45

1970, Oct. 5 Engr. *Perf. 13*

C104 AP45 100fr dk pur, red brn & dk bl .90 .50

25th anniversary of the United Nations.

Koran Page, Baghdad, 11th Century AP46

Moslem Art: 200fr, Tree, and lion killing deer, mosaic, Jordan, c. 730, horiz. 250fr, Scribe, miniature, Baghdad, 1287.

1970, Oct. 26 Photo. *Perf. 12½x12*

C105 AP46 50fr multi .75 .30
C106 AP46 200fr multi 1.50 .65
C107 AP46 250fr multi 2.25 .95
Nos. C105-C107 (3) 4.50 1.90

Nos. C97-C98 Surcharged and Overprinted

Overprint reads "LUNA 16 / PREMIERS PRELEVEMENTS AUTOMATIQUES / SUR LA LUNE / SEPTEMBRE 1970".

1970, Nov. 9 Engr. *Perf. 13*

C108 AP41 150fr on 200fr multi 1.00 .65
C109 AP41 250fr on 300fr multi 1.75 .95

Unmanned moon probe of the Russian space ship Luna 16, Sept. 12-24.

Painting Type of 1968

100fr, Nativity, Antwerp School, c. 1530. 250fr, Adoration of the Shepherds, by Hans Memling. 300fr, Adoration of the Kings, Flemish School, 17th cent.

1970, Dec. 1 Photo. *Perf. 12½x12*

C110 AP33 100fr brown & multi .80 .40
C111 AP33 250fr brown & multi 1.75 .95
C112 AP33 300fr brown & multi 2.50 1.25
Nos. C110-C112 (3) 5.05 2.60

Christmas 1970.

Gamal Abdel Nasser — AP47

Embossed on Gold Foil

1970, Nov. 25 *Perf. 12½*

C113 AP47 1000fr gold 9.00 9.00

In memory of Gamal Abdel Nasser (1918-1970), President of Egypt.

Charles de Gaulle AP48

Embossed on Gold Foil

1971, Feb. 8 *Die-cut Perf. 10*

C114 AP48 2000fr gold, red & dp ultra 60.00 60.00

In memory of Gen. Charles de Gaulle (1890-1970), President of France.

Alfred Nobel — AP49

1971, Feb. 22 Engr. *Perf. 13*
C115 AP49 300fr multi 3.00 1.00

Alfred Nobel (1833-1896), inventor of dynamite, sponsor of Nobel Prize.

Tennis, Davis Cup — AP50

Designs: 150fr, Derby at Epsom, horiz. 200fr, Racing yacht, America's Cup.

1971, Mar. 8
C116 AP50 100fr bl, lil & slate 1.40 .60
C117 AP50 150fr brn, brt grn & ol 2.00 .90
C118 AP50 200fr brt bl, ol & brn 2.75 1.25
Nos. C116-C118 (3) 6.15 2.75

The Arabian Nights — AP51

Designs: 180fr, Ali Baba and the 40 Thieves. 200fr, Aladdin's Lamp.

1971, Apr. 5 Photo. *Perf. 13*
C119 AP51 120fr gold & multi 1.50 .60
C120 AP51 180fr gold & multi 2.00 .90
C121 AP51 200fr gold & multi 2.50 1.00
Nos. C119-C121 (3) 6.00 2.50

Olympic Rings and Sports — AP52

1971, June 28 Photo. *Perf. 12½*
C122 AP52 80fr ultra, yel grn & brt mag .75 .30

Pre-Olympic Year.

Mariner 4 — AP53

Design: 300fr, Venera 5 in space.

1971, Sept. 13 Engr. *Perf. 13*
C123 AP53 200fr multi 1.40 .70
C124 AP53 300fr multi 2.10 .95

Space explorations of US Mariner 4 (200fr); and USSR Venera 5 (300fr).

Santa Maria, 1492 — AP54

Famous Ships: 150fr, Mayflower, 1620. 200fr, Potemkin, 1905. 250fr, Normandie, 1935.

1971, Sept. 27
C125 AP54 100fr brn, bluish grn & pur 1.00 .40
C126 AP54 150fr sl grn, brn & pur 1.60 .70
C127 AP54 200fr car, bl & dk ol 2.10 .80
C128 AP54 250fr blk, bl & red 2.75 1.00
Nos. C125-C128 (4) 7.45 2.90

Symbols of Justice and Maps — AP55

1971, Oct. 18
C129 AP55 160fr mar, ocher & dk brn 1.20 .50

25th anniversary of the International Court of Justice in The Hague, Netherlands.

Statue of Zeus, by Phidias — AP56

The Seven Wonders of the Ancient World: 80fr, Cheops Pyramid and Sphinx. 100fr, Temple of Artemis, Ephesus, horiz. 130fr, Lighthouse at Alexandria. 150fr, Hanging Gardens of Babylon, horiz. 270fr, Mausoleum of Halicarnassus. 280fr, Colossus of Rhodes.

1971, Dec. 13
C130 AP56 70fr ind, dk red & pink .60 .25
C131 AP56 80fr brn, bl & blk .75 .25
C132 AP56 100fr org, ind & pur .90 .30
C133 AP56 130fr rose lil, blk & grnsh bl 1.10 .40
C134 AP56 150fr brn, brt grn & bl 1.25 .50
C135 AP56 270fr sl, brn & plum 2.10 .70
C136 AP56 280fr sl lil & ol 2.25 .80
Nos. C130-C136 (7) 8.95 3.20

Nat "King" Cole — AP57

Famous American Black Musicians: 150fr, Erroll Garner. 270fr, Louis Armstrong.

1971, Dec. 6 Photo. *Perf. 13x12½*
C137 AP57 130fr blk, brn & yel 2.25 .40
C138 AP57 150fr blk, bl & yel 2.60 .50
C139 AP57 270fr blk, rose car & yel 4.25 .70
Nos. C137-C139 (3) 9.10 1.60

Slalom and Japanese Child AP58

200fr, Ice hockey & character from Noh play.

1972, Jan. 10 Engr. *Perf. 13*
C140 AP58 150fr multicolored 1.10 .50
C141 AP58 200fr multicolored 1.50 .70
a. Souv. sheet of 2, #C140-C141 3.00 3.00

11th Winter Olympic Games, Sapporo, Japan, Feb. 3-13.

Santa Maria della Salute, by Ippolito Caffi — AP59

Paintings of Venice, by Ippolito Caffi: 270fr, Rialto Bridge. 280fr, St. Mark's Square, vert.

1972, Feb. 21 Photo. *Perf. 13*
C142 AP59 130fr gold & multi 1.00 .45
C143 AP59 270fr gold & multi 1.50 .70
C144 AP59 280fr gold & multi 1.75 .75
Nos. C142-C144 (3) 4.25 1.90

UNESCO campaign to save Venice.

Hands of 4 Races Holding Scout Flag — AP60

1972, Mar. 27 Engr. *Perf. 13*
C145 AP60 200fr dk red, ocher & ol gray 1.75 .60

World Boy Scout Seminar, Cotonou, Dahomey, March, 1972.

"Your Heart is your Health" — AP61

1972, Apr. 7 Engr. *Perf. 13*
C146 AP61 150fr brt bl & red 1.50 .50

World Health Day.

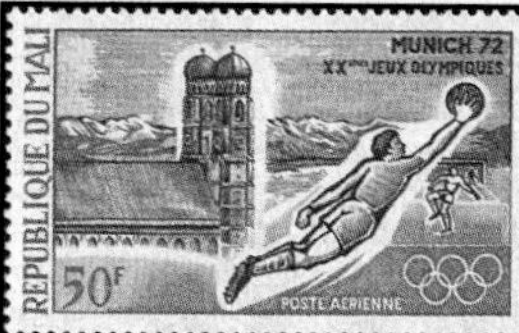

Soccer Player and Frauenkirche, Munich — AP62

Designs (Sport and Munich Landmarks): 150fr, Judo and TV Tower, vert. 200fr, Steeplechase and Propylaeum, vert. 300fr, Runner and Church of the Theatines.

1972, Apr. 17
C147 AP62 50fr ocher, dk bl & grn .40 .25
C148 AP62 150fr dk bl, ocher & grn 1.00 .45
C149 AP62 200fr grn, dk bl & ocher 1.10 .60
C150 AP62 300fr dk bl, grn & ocher 1.75 .75
a. Min. sheet of 4, #C147-C150 4.50 4.50
Nos. C147-C150 (4) 4.25 2.05

20th Olympic Games, Munich, 8/26-9/10.
For overprints see Nos. C165-C166, C168.

Apollo 15, Lunar Rover, Landing Module — AP63

Design: 250fr, Cugnot's steam wagon and Montgolfier's Balloon.

1972, Apr. 27
C151 AP63 150fr multicolored 1.50 .80
C152 AP63 250fr multicolored 3.00 1.50

Development of transportation.

Cinderella AP64

Fairy Tales: 80fr, Puss in Boots. 150fr, Sleeping Beauty.

1972, June 19 Engr. *Perf. 13x12½*
C153 AP64 70fr multicolored 1.10 .30
C154 AP64 80fr multicolored 1.25 .35
C155 AP64 150fr multicolored 2.00 .60
Nos. C153-C155 (3) 4.35 1.25

Charles Perrault (1628-1703), French writer.

Astronauts and Lunar Rover on Moon — AP65

1972, July 24 Engr. *Perf. 13*
C156 AP65 500fr multicolored 3.00 1.40

US Apollo 16 moon mission, Apr. 15-27.

Book Year Emblem — AP66

1972, Aug. 7 Litho. *Perf. 12½*
C157 AP66 80fr bl, gold & grn 1.50 .60

International Book Year 1972.

Bamako Rotary Emblem with Crocodiles AP67

1972, Oct. 9 Engr. *Perf. 13*
C158 AP67 170fr dk brn, red & ultra 1.50 .60

10th anniv. of the Bamako Rotary Club.

Hurdler, Olympic Rings, Melbourne Cathedral, Kangaroo — AP68

Designs (Olympic Rings and): 70fr, Boxing, Helsinki Railroad Station, arms of Finland, vert. 140fr, Running, Colosseum, Roman wolf. 150fr, Weight lifting, Tokyo stadium, phoenix, vert. 170fr, Swimming, University Library, Mexico City; Aztec sculpture. 210fr, Javelin, Munich Stadium, Arms of Munich. Stamps inscribed with name of gold medal winner of event shown.

1972, Nov. 13 Engr. *Perf. 13*
C159 AP68 70fr red, ocher & ind .40 .25
C160 AP68 90fr red brn, bl & sl .45 .25
C161 AP68 140fr brn, brt grn & ol gray .75 .30
C162 AP68 150fr dk car, emer & gray ol .85 .35
C163 AP68 170fr red lil, brn & Prus bl 1.00 .40
C164 AP68 210fr ultra, emer & brick red 1.10 .50
Nos. C159-C164 (6) 4.55 2.05

Retrospective of Olympic Games 1952-1972.
For overprint see No. C167.

Nos. C148-C150, C164 Overprinted

a. JUDO / RUSKA / 2 MEDAILLES D'OR
b. STEEPLE / KEINO / MEDAILLE D'OR
c. MEDAILLE D'OR / 90m. 48
d. 100m.-200m. / BORZOV / 2 MEDAILLES D'OR

1972, Nov. 27 Engr. *Perf. 13*
C165 AP62 150fr multi (a) .90 .40
C166 AP62 200fr multi (b) 1.20 .50
C167 AP68 210fr multi (c) 1.40 .55
C168 AP62 300fr multi (d) 1.90 .70
Nos. C165-C168 (4) 5.40 2.15

Gold medal winners in 20th Olympic Games: Wim Ruska, Netherlands, heavyweight judo (No. C165); Kipchoge Keino, Kenya, 3000m. steeplechase (No. C166); Klaus Wolfermann, Germany, javelin (No. C167); Valery Borzov, USSR, 100m., 200m. race (No. C168).

Emperor Haile Selassie AP69

1972, Dec. 26 Photo. *Perf. 12½*
C169 AP69 70fr grn & multi .60 .25

80th birthday of Emperor Haile Selassie of Ethiopia.

Plane, Balloon, Route Timbuktu to Bamako — AP70

300fr, Balloon, jet & route Timbuktu to Bamako.

1972, Dec. 29 *Perf. 13½*
C170 AP70 200fr multi 1.10 .50
C171 AP70 300fr bl & multi 1.90 .80

First postal balloon flight in Mali.

Bishop of 14th Century European Chess Set — AP71

Design: 200fr, Knight (elephant), from 18th century Indian set.

1973, Feb. 19 Engr. *Perf. 13*
C172 AP71 100fr dk car, bl & ind 1.50 .60
C173 AP71 200fr blk, red & brn 3.00 1.25

World Chess Championship, Reykjavik, Iceland, July-Sept., 1972.

Postal Union Emblem, Letter and Dove AP72

1973, Mar. 9 Photo. *Perf. 11½x11*
C174 AP72 70fr bl, blk & org .60 .25

10th anniv. (in 1971) of African Postal Union. This stamp was to be issued Dec. 8, 1971. It was offered by the agency on Mar. 9, 1973. Copies were sold in Mali as early as July or August, 1972.

No. C20, Collector's Hand and Philatelic Background AP73

1973, Mar. 12 Engr. *Perf. 13*
C175 AP73 70fr multi 1.50 .50

Stamp Day, 1973.

Astronauts and Lunar Rover on Moon AP74

1973, Mar. 26
C176 AP74 250fr bl, indigo & bis 2.25 1.00

Souvenir Sheet

C177 AP74 350fr choc, vio bl & ultra 2.50 1.60

Apollo 17 US moon mission, 12/7-19/72.

Nicolaus Copernicus — AP75

1973, Apr. 9 Engr. *Perf. 13*
C178 AP75 300fr brt bl & mag 2.75 1.25

500th anniversary of the birth of Nicolaus Copernicus (1473-1543), Polish astronomer.

Dr. Armauer G. Hansen and Leprosy Bacillus — AP76

1973, May 7 Engr. *Perf. 13*
C179 AP76 200fr blk, yel grn & red 1.90 .85

Centenary of the discovery of the Hansen bacillus, the cause of leprosy.

Bentley and Alfa Romeo, 1930 — AP77

Designs: 100fr, Jaguar and Talbot, 1953. 200fr, Matra and Porsche, 1972.

1973, May 21 Engr. *Perf. 13*
C180 AP77 50fr bl, org & grn .45 .25
C181 AP77 100fr grn, ultra & car .80 .30
C182 AP77 200fr ind, grn & car 2.00 .60
Nos. C180-C182 (3) 3.25 1.15

50th anniversary of the 24-hour automobile race at Le Mans, France.

Camp Fire, Fleur-de-Lis AP78

Designs (Fleur-de-Lis and): 70fr, Scouts saluting flag, vert. 80fr, Scouts with flags. 130fr, Lord Baden-Powell, vert. 270fr, Round dance and map of Africa.

1973, June 4
C183 AP78 50fr dk red, ultra & choc .35 .25
C184 AP78 70fr sl grn, dk brn & red .50 .25
C185 AP78 80fr mag, sl grn & ol .55 .25
C186 AP78 130fr brn, ultra & sl grn .90 .40
C187 AP78 270fr mag, gray & vio bl 1.75 .60
Nos. C183-C187 (5) 4.05 1.75

Mali Boy and Girl Scouts and International Scouts Congress.
For surcharges see Nos. C222-C223.

Swimming, US and "Africa" Flags — AP79

80fr, Discus, javelin, vert. 330fr, Runners.

1973, July 30 Engr. *Perf. 13*
C188 AP79 70fr red, sl grn & bl .45 .25
C189 AP79 80fr vio bl, dk ol & red .55 .25
C190 AP79 330fr red & vio bl 2.10 .80
Nos. C188-C190 (3) 3.10 1.30

First African-United States sports meet.

Head and City Hall, Brussels AP80

1973, Sept. 17 Engr. *Perf. 13*
C191 AP80 70fr brt ultra, ol & vio .60 .25

Africa Weeks, Brussels, Sept. 15-30, 1973.

Perseus, by Benvenuto Cellini — AP81

Famous Sculptures: 150fr, Pietá, by Michelangelo. 250fr, Victory of Samothrace, Greek 1st century B.C.

1973, Sept. 24
C192 AP81 100fr dk car & sl grn .90 .30
C193 AP81 150fr dk car & dp cl 1.40 .50
C194 AP81 250fr dk car & dk ol 2.25 .80
Nos. C192-C194 (3) 4.55 1.60

Stephenson's Rocket and Buddicom Engine — AP82

Locomotives: 150fr, Union Pacific, 1890, and Santa Fe, 1940. 200fr, Mistral and Tokaido, 1970.

1973, Oct. 8 Engr. *Perf. 13*
C195 AP82 100fr brn, bl & blk 1.00 .40
C196 AP82 150fr red, brt ultra & dk car 1.40 .70
C197 AP82 200fr ocher, bl & ind 2.10 .90
Nos. C195-C197 (3) 4.50 2.00

Apollo XI on Moon AP83

75fr, Landing capsule, Apollo XIII. 100fr, Astronauts & equipment on moon, Apollo XIV. 280fr, Rover, landing module % astronauts on moon, Apollo XV. 300fr, Lift-off from moon, Apollo XVII.

1973, Oct. 25

C198	AP83	50fr vio, org & sl grn	.30	.25
C199	AP83	75fr slate, red & bl	.45	.25
C200	AP83	100fr slate, bl & ol brn	.60	.30
C201	AP83	280fr vio bl, red & sl grn	1.50	.55
C202	AP83	300fr slate, red & sl grn	1.60	.80
		Nos. C198-C202 (5)	4.45	2.15

Apollo US moon missions.

For surcharges see Nos. C224-C225.

Pablo Picasso — AP84

1973, Nov. 7 Litho. *Perf. 12½*

C203	AP84	500fr multi	4.25	2.00

Pablo Picasso (1881-1973), painter.

John F. Kennedy — AP85

1973, Nov. 12

C204	AP85	500fr gold, brt rose lil & blk	3.50	1.75

Painting Type of 1968

100fr, Annunciation, by Vittore Carpaccio, horiz. 200fr, Virgin of St. Simon, by Federico Barocci. 250fr, Flight into Egypt, by Andrea Solario.

Perf. 13x12½, 12½x12, 12½x13

1973, Nov. 30 Litho.

C205	AP33	100fr blk & multi	.75	.25
C206	AP33	200fr blk & multi	1.25	.60
C207	AP33	250fr blk & multi	1.75	.80
		Nos. C205-C207 (3)	3.75	1.65

Christmas 1973.

Soccer Player and Ball — AP86

250fr, Goalkeeper & ball. 500fr, Frauenkirche, Munich, Arms of Munich & soccer ball, horiz.

1973, Dec. 3 Engr. *Perf. 13*

C208	AP86	150fr emer, ol brn & red	1.10	.50
C209	AP86	250fr emer, vio bl & ol brn	1.90	.70

Souvenir Sheet

C210	AP86	500fr bl & multi	4.00	4.00

World Soccer Cup, Munich.

Musicians, Mosaic from Pompeii — AP87

Designs (Mosaics from Pompeii): 250fr, Alexander the Great in battle, vert. 350fr, Bacchants, vert.

1974, Jan. 21 Engr. *Perf. 13*

C211	AP87	150fr sl bl, ol & rose	1.10	.30
C212	AP87	250fr mag, ol & ocher	1.50	.50
C213	AP87	350fr ol, dp brn & ocher	1.90	.70
		Nos. C211-C213 (3)	4.50	1.50

Winston Churchill — AP88

1974, Mar. 18 Engr. *Perf. 13*

C214	AP88	500fr black	3.00	1.25

Chess Game — AP89

1974, Mar. 25 Engr. *Perf. 13*

C215	AP89	250fr multi	4.50	1.75

21st Chess Olympic Games, Nice 1974.

Painting Type of 1968

Paintings: 400fr, Crucifixion, Alsatian School, c. 1380, vert. 500fr, Burial of Christ, by Titian.

Perf. 12½x13, 13x12½

1974, Apr. 12 Photo.

C216	AP33	400fr multi	2.10	.90
C217	AP33	500fr multi	2.90	1.25

Easter 1974.

Lenin — AP90

1974, Apr. 22 Engr. *Perf. 13*

C218	AP90	150fr vio bl & lake	2.00	.60

50th anniversary of the death of Lenin.

Women's Steeplechase — AP91

1974, May 20 Engr. *Perf. 13*

C219	AP91	130fr bl, lil & brn	1.60	.60

World Horsewomen's Championship, La Baule, France, June 30-July 7.

Skylab Docking in Space — AP92

250fr, Skylab over globe with Africa.

1974, July 1 Engr. *Perf. 13*

C220	AP92	200fr bl, sl & org	1.10	.50
C221	AP92	250fr lil, sl & org	1.90	.70

Skylab's flight over Africa, 1974.

Nos. C184-C185 Surcharged in Violet Blue

(a)

(b)

1974, July 8 Engr. *Perf. 13*

C222	AP78	130fr on 70fr (a)	1.20	.50
C223	AP78	170fr on 80fr (b)	1.50	.60

11th Pan-Arab Jamboree and Pan-Arab Congress, Batrun, Lebanon, Aug. 1974.

Nos. C200-C201 Surcharged in Red

(c)

(d)

1974, July 15

C224	AP83	130fr on 100fr (c)	.75	.40
C225	AP83	300fr on 280fr (d)	2.25	1.25

First manned moon landing, July 20, 1969, and first step on moon, July 21, 1969.

1906 and 1939 Locomotives — AP93

Locomotives: 120fr, Baldwin, 1870, and Pacific, 1920. 210fr, Al., 1925, and Buddicom, 1847. 330fr, Hudson, 1938, and La Gironde, 1839.

1974, Oct. 7 Engr. *Perf. 13*

C226	AP93	90fr dk car & multi	.90	.40
C227	AP93	120fr ocher & multi	1.30	.50
C228	AP93	210fr org & multi	2.00	.70
C229	AP93	330fr grn & multi	3.00	1.10
		Nos. C226-C229 (4)	7.20	2.70

Skier, Winter Sports and Olympic Rings AP94

1974, Oct. 7

C230	AP94	300fr multi	2.10	.80

Holy Family, by Hans Memling AP95

310fr, Virgin & Child, Bourgogne School. 400fr, Adoration of the Kings, by Martin Schongauer.

1974, Nov. 4 Photo. *Perf. 12½*

C231	AP95	290fr multi	1.60	.60
C232	AP95	310fr multi	1.90	.70
C233	AP95	400fr multi	2.50	1.10
		Nos. C231-C233 (3)	6.00	2.40

Christmas 1974.

See Nos. C238-C240, C267-C269.

Raoul Follereau — AP96

1974, Nov. 18 Engr. *Perf. 13*
C234 AP96 200fr brt bl 2.25 .85

Raoul Follereau (1903-1977), apostle to the lepers and educator of the blind. See No. C468.

Europafrica Issue

Train, Jet, Cogwheel, Grain, Maps of Africa and Europe — AP97

1974, Dec. 27 Engr. *Perf. 13*
C235 AP97 100fr brn, grn & indigo .75 .30
C236 AP97 110fr ocher, vio bl & pur 1.00 .40

Painting Type of 1974

Designs: 200fr, Christ at Emmaus, by Philipe de Champaigne, horiz. 300fr, Christ at Emmaus, by Paolo Veronese, horiz. 500fr, Christ in Majesty, Limoges, 13th century.

Perf. 13x12½, 12½x13
1975, Mar. 24 Litho.
C238 AP95 200fr multi 1.60 .50
C239 AP95 300fr multi 1.90 .70
C240 AP95 500fr multi 2.50 1.25
Nos. C238-C240 (3) 6.00 2.45

Easter 1975.

"Voyage to the Center of the Earth" — AP99

Jules Verne's Stories: 170fr, "From Earth to Moon" and Verne's portrait. 190fr, "20,000 Leagues under the Sea." 220fr, "A Floating City."

1975, Apr. 7 Engr. *Perf. 13*
C241 AP99 100fr multi .60 .25
C242 AP99 170fr multi 1.00 .45
C243 AP99 190fr multi 1.10 .50
C244 AP99 220fr multi 1.40 .55
Nos. C241-C244 (4) 4.10 1.75

Dawn, by Michelangelo — AP100

Design: 500fr, Moses, by Michelangelo.

1975, Apr. 28 Photo. *Perf. 13*
C245 AP100 400fr multi 2.25 .90
C246 AP100 500fr multi 3.00 1.25

Michelangelo Buonarroti (1475-1564), Italian sculptor, painter and architect.

Astronaut on Moon — AP101

Designs: 300fr, Constellations Virgo and Capricorn. 370fr, Statue of Liberty, Kremlin, Soyuz and Apollo spacecraft.

1975, May 19 Engr. *Perf. 13*
C247 AP101 290fr multi 1.10 .60
C248 AP101 300fr multi 1.10 .60
C249 AP101 370fr multi 1.90 .90
Nos. C247-C249 (3) 4.10 2.10

Soviet-American space cooperation.
For overprints see Nos. C264-C266.

Boy Scout, Globe, Nordjamb 75 Emblem AP103

150fr, Boy Scout giving Scout sign. 290fr, Scouts around campfire.

1975, June 23 Engr. *Perf. 13*
C251 AP103 100fr claret, brn & bl .60 .25
C252 AP103 150fr red, brn & grn .90 .30
C253 AP103 290fr bl, grn & claret 1.60 .65
Nos. C251-C253 (3) 3.10 1.20

Nordjamb 75, 14th Boy Scout Jamboree, Lillehammer, Norway, July 29-Aug. 7.

Battle Scene and Marquis de Lafayette — AP104

300fr, Battle scene & George Washington. 370fr, Battle of Chesapeake Bay & Count de Grasse.

1975, July 7 Engr. *Perf. 13*
C254 AP104 290fr lt bl & indigo 1.50 .60
C255 AP104 300fr lt bl & indigo 1.50 .60
C256 AP104 370fr lt bl & indigo 2.25 .90
a. Strip of 3, #C254-C256 6.00 3.50

Bicentenary of the American Revolution. No. C256a has continuous design.

Schweitzer, Bach and Score AP105

Designs: No. C257, Albert Einstein (1879-1955), theoretical physicist. No. No. C258, André-Marie Ampère (1775-1836), French physicist. 100fr, Clément Ader (1841-1925), French aviation pioneer. No. C260, Dr. Albert Schweitzer (1875-1965), Medical missionary and musician. No. C261, Sir Alexander Fleming (1881-1955), British bacteriologist, discoverer of penicillin.

1975 Engr. *Perf. 13*
C257 AP105 90fr multi .90 .40
C258 AP105 90fr pur, org & bister .90 .40
C259 AP105 100fr bl, red & lilac .90 .40
C260 AP105 150fr grn, bl & dk grn 1.10 .60
C261 AP105 150fr lil, bl & brick red 1.10 .45
Nos. C257-C261 (5) 4.90 2.25

Issued: No. C257, 5/26; No. C258, 9/23; 100fr, 12/8; No. C260, 1/14; No. C261, 7/21.
For surcharge see No. C358.

Olympic Rings and Globe — AP106

400fr, Montreal Olympic Games' emblem.

1975, Oct.
C262 AP106 350fr pur & bl 1.90 .75
C263 AP106 400fr blue 2.25 .85

Pre-Olympic Year 1975.

Nos. C247-C249 Overprinted: "ARRIMAGE / 17 Juil. 1975"

1975, Oct. 20 Engr. *Perf. 13*
C264 AP101 290fr multi 1.60 .60
C265 AP101 300fr multi 1.75 .65
C266 AP101 370fr multi 2.50 1.00
Nos. C264-C266 (3) 5.85 2.25

Apollo-Soyuz link-up in space, July 17, 1975.

Painting Type of 1974

Designs: 290fr, Visitation, by Ghirlandaio. 300fr, Nativity, Fra Filippo Lippi school. 370fr, Adoration of the Kings, by Velazquez.

1975, Nov. 24 Litho. *Perf. 12½x13*
C267 AP95 290fr multi 1.50 .60
C268 AP95 300fr multi 1.75 .70
C269 AP95 370fr multi 2.40 1.10
Nos. C267-C269 (3) 5.65 2.40

Christmas 1975.

Concorde — AP107

1976, Jan. 12 Litho. *Perf. 13*
C270 AP107 500fr multi 3.75 1.50

Concorde supersonic jet, first commercial flight, Jan. 21, 1976.
For overprint see No. C315.

AP108

1976, Feb. 16 Litho. *Perf. 13*
C271 AP108 120fr Figure skating .60 .25
C272 AP108 420fr Ski jump 2.00 .70
C273 AP108 430fr Slalom 2.00 .70
Nos. C271-C273 (3) 4.60 1.65

12th Winter Olympic Games, Innsbruck, Austria, Feb. 4-15.

AP109

Eye examination, WHO emblem.

1976, Apr. 5 Litho. *Perf. 12½*
C274 AP109 130fr multi .75 .25

World Health Day: "Foresight prevents blindness."

Space Ship with Solar Batteries — AP110

Design: 300fr, Astronaut working on orbital space station, vert.

1976, May 10 Engr. *Perf. 13*
C275 AP110 300fr org, dk & lt bl 1.50 .60
C276 AP110 400fr mag, dk bl & org 2.25 .90

Futuristic space achievements.

American Eagle, Flag and Liberty Bell — AP111

Designs: 400fr, Revolutionary War naval battle and American eagle. 440fr, Indians on horseback and American eagle, vert.

1976, May 24 Litho. *Perf. 12½*
C277 AP111 100fr multi .60 .25
C278 AP111 400fr multi 2.25 .75
C279 AP111 440fr multi 2.40 .80
Nos. C277-C279 (3) 5.25 1.80

American Bicentennial. Nos. C278-C279 also for Interphil 76, International Philatelic Exhibition, Philadelphia, Pa, May 29-June 6.

Running AP112

Designs (Olympic Rings and): 250fr, Swimming. 300fr, Field ball. 440fr, Soccer.

1976, June 7 Engr. *Perf. 13*
C280 AP112 200fr red brn & blk .90 .30
C281 AP112 250fr multi 1.25 .40
C282 AP112 300fr multi 1.75 .50
C283 AP112 440fr multi 2.25 .75
Nos. C280-C283 (4) 6.15 1.95

21st Olympic Games, Montreal, Canada, July 17-Aug. 1.

Cub Scout and Leader — AP113

Designs: 180fr, Scouts tending sick animal, horiz. 200fr, Night hike.

1976, June 14 Engr. *Perf. 13*

C284 AP113 140fr ultra & red brn .75 .35
C285 AP113 180fr dk brn & multi 1.10 .45
C286 AP113 200fr brn org & vio bl 1.20 .50
Nos. C284-C286 (3) 3.05 1.30

First African Boy Scout Jamboree, Nigeria.

Mohenjo-Daro, Bull from Wall Relief — AP114

Design: 500fr, Man's head, animals, wall and UNESCO emblem.

1976, Sept. 6 Engr. *Perf. 13*

C287 AP114 400fr blk, bl & pur 1.90 .60
C288 AP114 500fr dk red, bl & grn 2.60 1.10

UNESCO campaign to save Mohenjo-Daro excavations.

Europafrica Issue

Freighter, Plane, Map of Europe and Africa — AP115

1976, Sept. 20

C289 AP115 200fr vio brn & bl 1.50 .70

Nativity, by Taddeo Gaddi — AP116

Paintings: 300fr, Adoration of the Kings, by Hans Memling. 320fr, Nativity, by Carlo Crivelli.

1976, Nov. 8 Litho. *Perf. 13x12½*

C290 AP116 280fr multi 1.50 .50
C291 AP116 300fr multi 1.80 .60
C292 AP116 320fr multi 1.75 .75
Nos. C290-C292 (3) 5.05 1.85

Christmas 1976.

Viking Flying to Mars — AP117

1000fr, Viking landing craft on Mars.

1976, Dec. 8 Engr. *Perf. 13*

C293 AP117 500fr red, brn & bl 2.25 1.25
C294 AP117 1000fr multi 3.75 1.75
a. Miniature sheet of 2 7.50 3.50

Operation Viking, US Mars mission, No. C294a contains 2 stamps similar to Nos. C293-C294 in changed colors.

Pres. Giscard d'Estaing, Village and Bambara Antelope — AP118

1977, Feb. 13 Photo. *Perf. 13*

C295 AP118 430fr multi 2.75 .90

Visit of Pres. Valéry Giscard d'Estaing of France, Feb. 13-15.

Elizabeth II and Prince Philip — AP119

Designs: 200fr, Charles de Gaulle. vert. 250fr, Queen Wilhelmina, vert. 300fr, King Baudouin and Queen Fabiola. 480fr, Coronation of Queen Elizabeth II, vert.

1977, Mar. 21 Litho. *Perf. 12*

C296 AP119 180fr multi .90 .45
C297 AP119 200fr multi 1.00 .45
C298 AP119 250fr multi 1.25 .55
C299 AP119 300fr multi 1.50 .65
C300 AP119 480fr multi 2.40 1.00
Nos. C296-C300 (5) 7.05 3.10

Personalities involved in de-colonization.

Newton, Rocket and Apple — AP120

1977, May 7 Engr. *Perf. 13*

C301 AP120 400fr grn, brn & red 2.50 .90

Isaac Newton (1643-1727), natural philosopher and mathematician, 250th death anniversary.

Charles Lindbergh and Spirit of St. Louis — AP121

430fr, Spirit of St. Louis flying over clouds.

1977, Apr. 4 Litho. *Perf. 12*

C302 AP121 420fr org & pur 2.25 .80
C303 AP121 430fr multi 2.25 .80

Charles A. Lindbergh's solo transatlantic flight from New York to Paris, 50th anniversary.

Sassenage Castle, Grenoble — AP122

1977, May 21 Litho. *Perf. 12½*

C304 AP122 300fr multi 1.50 .60

Intl. French Language Council, 10th anniv.

Zeppelin No. 1, 1900 — AP123

Designs: 130fr, Graf Zeppelin, 1924. 350fr, Hindenburg aflame at Lakehurst, NJ, 1937. 500fr, Ferdinand von Zeppelin and Graf Zeppelin.

1977, May 30 Engr. *Perf. 13*

C305 AP123 120fr multi .60 .25
C306 AP123 130fr multi .75 .25
C307 AP123 350fr multi 2.00 .65
C308 AP123 500fr multi 2.75 .75
Nos. C305-C308 (4) 6.10 1.90

History of the Zeppelin.

Martin Luther King, American and Swedish Flags — AP124

Design: 600fr, Henri Dunant, Red Cross, Swiss and Swedish flags.

1977, July 4 Engr. *Perf. 13*

C309 AP124 600fr multi 2.00 .70
C310 AP124 700fr multi 2.50 .75

Nobel Peace Prize recipients.

Soccer — AP125

Designs: 200fr, 3 soccer players, vert. 420fr, 3 soccer players.

1977, Oct. 3 Engr. *Perf. 13*

C311 AP125 180fr multi .60 .30
C312 AP125 200fr multi .75 .35
C313 AP125 420fr multi 1.60 .75
Nos. C311-C313 (3) 2.95 1.40

World Soccer Cup Elimination Games.

Mao Tse-tung and COMATEX Hall, Bamako — AP126

1977, Nov. 7 Engr. *Perf. 13*

C314 AP126 300fr dull red 3.75 .90

Chairman Mao Tse-tung (1893-1976).

No. C270 Overprinted in Violet Blue: "PARIS NEW-YORK 22.11.77"

1977, Nov. 22 Litho. *Perf. 13*

C315 AP107 500fr multi 9.00 5.50

Concorde, first commerical transatlantic flight, Paris to New York.

Virgin and Child, by Rubens AP127

Rubens Paintings: 400fr, Adoration of the Kings. 600fr, Detail from Adoration of the Kings, horiz.

1977, Dec. 5 *Perf. 12½x12, 12x12½*

C316 AP127 400fr gold & multi 1.40 .60
C317 AP127 500fr gold & multi 1.75 .80
C318 AP127 600fr gold & multi 2.40 1.00
Nos. C316-C318 (3) 5.55 2.40

Christmas 1977, and 400th birth anniversary of Peter Paul Rubens (1577-1640).

Battle of the Amazons, by Rubens — AP128

Rubens Paintings: 300fr, Return from the fields. 500fr, Hercules fighting the Nemean Lion, vert.

Perf. 12x12½, 12½x12

1978, Jan. 16 Litho.

C319 AP128 200fr multi .85 .30
C320 AP128 300fr multi 1.25 .50
C321 AP128 500fr multi 2.10 .80
Nos. C319-C321 (3) 4.20 1.60

Peter Paul Rubens, 400th birth anniversary.

Schubert Composing "Winterreise" — AP129

Design: 300fr, Schubert and score, vert.

1978, Feb. 13

C322 AP129 300fr multi 1.25 .50
C323 AP129 420fr multi 2.00 .70

Franz Schubert (1797-1828), Austrian composer.

Capt. Cook Receiving Hawaiian Delegation — AP130

Design: 300fr, Cook landing on Hawaii. Designs after sketches by John Weber.

1978, Feb. 27 Engr. *Perf. 13*

C324 AP130 200fr multi 1.10 .40
C325 AP130 300fr multi 1.90 .55

Capt. James Cook (1728-1779), bicentenary of his arrival in Hawaii.

Soccer — AP131

250fr, One player. 300fr, Two players, horiz.

1978, Mar. 20

C326 AP131 150fr multi 1.10 .30
C327 AP131 250fr multi 1.75 .50
a. "REPUPLIQUE" 3.00 .90
C328 AP131 300fr multi 2.25 .60
a. Min. sheet of 3, #C326-C328 + label 6.00 4.00
b. As "a," #C326, C327a, C328 9.00 6.00
Nos. C326-C328 (3) 5.10 1.40

World Soccer Cup Championships, Argentina, 1978, June 1-25.
Nos. C327 and C328a were issued in July to correct the spelling error.
For overprints see Nos. C338-C340.

Jesus with Crown of Thorns, by Dürer AP132

430fr, Resurrection, by Albrecht Dürer.

1978, Mar. 28

C329 AP132 420fr multi 2.50 .60
C330 AP132 430fr multi 2.75 .60

Easter 1978. See Nos. C359-C361.

Citroen, C3-Trefle, 1922 — AP133

Citroen Cars: 130fr, Croisiere Noire, 1924, tractor. 180fr, B14G, 1927. 200fr, "11" Tractor Avant, 1934.

1978, Apr. 24 Engr. *Perf. 13*

C331 AP133 120fr multi 1.00 .25
C332 AP133 130fr multi 1.10 .25
C333 AP133 180fr multi 1.40 .40
C334 AP133 200fr multi 1.50 .45
Nos. C331-C334 (4) 5.00 1.35

Andre Citroen (1878-1935), automobile designer and manufacturer.

UPU Emblem, World Map, Country Names — AP133a

Design: 130fr, UPU emblem, globe and names of member countries.

1978, May 15

C334A AP133a 120fr multi .70 .25
C335 AP133a 130fr red, grn & emer .85 .25

Centenary of Congress of Paris where General Postal Union became the Universal Postal Union.

Europafrica Issue

Zebra, Miniature by Mansur, Jehangir School, 1620 — AP134

Design: 100fr, Ostrich Incubating Eggs, Syrian Manuscript, 14th Century.

1978, July 24 Litho. *Perf. 13x12½*

C336 AP134 100fr multi 1.50 .60
C337 AP134 110fr multi 1.50 .60

Nos. C326-C328a Overprinted in Black

(a)

(c)

b. 2e HOLLANDE

1978, Aug. 7 Engr. *Perf. 13*

C338 AP131 150fr multi (a) .85 .35
C339 AP131 250fr multi (b) 1.25 .50
C340 AP131 300fr multi (c) 1.50 .60
a. Souvenir sheet of 3 5.00 2.50
Nos. C338-C340 (3) 3.60 1.45

Winners, World Soccer Cup Championship, Argentina. Overprints on No. C340a are green including label overprint: FINALE / ARGENTINA 3 HOLLANDE 1.

Elizabeth II in Coronation Robes AP135

Design: 500fr, Coronation coach.

1978, Sept. 18 Litho. *Perf. 12½x12*

C341 AP135 500fr multi 1.60 .65
C342 AP135 1000fr multi 3.25 1.50

Coronation of Queen Elizabeth II, 25th anniv.

US No. C3a and Douglas DC-3 AP136

History of Aviation: 100fr, Belgium No. 252 and Stampe SV-4. 120fr, France No. C48 and Ader's plane No. 3. 130fr, Germany No. C2 and Junker Ju-52. 320fr, Japan No. C25 and Mitsubishi A-6M "Zero."

1978, Oct. 16 Engr. *Perf. 13*

C343 AP136 80fr multi .35 .25
C344 AP136 100fr multi .45 .25
C345 AP136 120fr multi .55 .25
C346 AP136 130fr multi .60 .25
C347 AP136 320fr multi 1.50 .55
Nos. C343-C347 (5) 3.45 1.55

Annunciation, by Dürer — AP137

Etchings by Dürer: 430fr, Virgin and Child. 500fr, Adoration of the Kings.

1978, Nov. 6

C348 AP137 420fr blk & rose car 1.40 .50
C349 AP137 430fr ol grn & brn 1.50 .60
C350 AP137 500fr blk & red 2.00 .70
Nos. C348-C350 (3) 4.90 1.80

Christmas 1978 and 450th death anniversary of Albrecht Dürer (1471-1528), German painter.

Rocket and Trajectory Around Moon — AP138

Design: 300fr, Spaceship circling moon.

1978, Nov. 20 Engr. *Perf. 13*

C351 AP138 200fr multi 1.25 .60
C352 AP138 300fr multi 1.25 .70
a. Pair, #C351-C352 + label 3.00 2.00

10th anniversary of 1st flight around moon.

Ader's Plane and Concorde — AP139

Designs: 130fr, Wright Flyer A and Concorde. 200fr, Spirit of St. Louis and Concorde.

1979, Jan. 25 Litho. *Perf. 13*

C353 AP139 120fr multi .60 .25
C354 AP139 130fr multi .75 .30
C355 AP139 200fr multi 1.40 .55
Nos. C353-C355 (3) 2.75 1.10

1st supersonic commercial flight, 3rd anniv.
For surcharges see Nos. C529-C531.

Philexafrique II-Essen Issue
Common Design Types

Designs: No. C356, Dromedary and Mali No. C26. No. C357, Bird and Lubeck No. 1.

1979, Jan. 29 Litho. *Perf. 13x12½*

C356 CD138 200fr multi 2.25 1.00
C357 CD139 200fr multi 2.25 1.00
a. Pair, #C356-C357 + label 5.00 3.00

No. C257 Surcharged

1979, Mar. 26 Engr. *Perf. 13*

C358 AP105 130fr on 90fr multi 1.25 .50

Albert Einstein (1879-1955).

Easter Type of 1978

Dürer Etchings: 400fr, Jesus Carrying Cross. 430fr, Crucified Christ. 480fr, Pietà.

1979, Apr. 9

C359 AP132 400fr bl & blk 1.90 .70
C360 AP132 430fr red & blk 2.10 .75
C361 AP132 480fr ultra & blk 2.40 .85
Nos. C359-C361 (3) 6.40 2.30

Easter 1979.

Basketball and Cathedral, Moscow AP140

430fr, Soccer and St. Basil's Cathedral.

1979, Apr. 17 Litho. *Perf. 13*

C362 AP140 420fr multi 1.75 .80
C363 AP140 430fr multi 1.75 .80

Pre-Olympic Year.

Mali #C92, Apollo Spacecraft AP141

Design: 500fr, Mali No. C176, lift-off.

1979, Oct. 22 Litho. *Perf. 12½x13*
C364 AP141 430fr multi 1.75 .70
C365 AP141 500fr multi 2.00 .80

Apollo 11 moon landing, 10th anniversary.

Capt. Cook, Ship, Kerguelen Island — AP142

Design: 480fr, Capt. Cook, Ship, Hawaii.

1979, Oct. 29 *Perf. 13x12½*
C366 AP142 300fr multi 1.40 .60
C367 AP142 480fr multi 2.00 .85

Capt. James Cook (1728-1779).

David Janowski (1868-1927), Chess Pieces — AP143

Chess Pieces and Grand Masters: 140fr, Alexander Alekhine (1892-1946). 200fr, W. Schlage. 300fr, Effim D. Bogoljubow (1889-1952).

1979, Nov. 30 Engr. *Perf. 13*
C368 AP143 100fr red & brn .85 .25
C369 AP143 140fr multi 1.20 .25
C370 AP143 200fr multi 1.60 .40
C371 AP143 300fr multi 2.50 .55
Nos. C368-C371 (4) 6.15 1.45

For overprints see Nos. C441-C442.

Adoration of the Kings, by Dürer AP144

Christmas 1979: 400fr, 500fr, Adoration of the Kings by Dürer, diff.

1979, Dec. 10 *Perf. 13x13½*
C372 AP144 300fr brn org & brn 1.40 .50
C373 AP144 400fr bl & brn 1.90 .70
C374 AP144 500fr dk grn & brn 2.40 .90
Nos. C372-C374 (3) 5.70 2.10

Jet, Map of Africa AP145

1979, Dec. 27 Litho. *Perf. 12½*
C375 AP145 120fr multi .75 .30

ASECNA (Air Safety Board), 20th anniv.

Train, Globe, Rotary Emblem AP146

Rotary Intl., 75th Anniv.: 250fr, Jet. 430fr, Bamako Club emblem, meeting hall.

1980, Jan. 28 Litho. *Perf. 12½*
C376 AP146 220fr multi 1.10 .40
C377 AP146 250fr multi 1.10 .40
C378 AP146 430fr multi 2.00 .70
Nos. C376-C378 (3) 4.20 1.50

Speed Skating, Lake Placid '80 Emblem, Snowflake AP147

1980, Feb. 11 *Perf. 13*
C379 AP147 200fr shown .90 .25
C380 AP147 300fr Ski jump 1.25 .50
a. Souvenir sheet of 2 3.00 2.00

13th Winter Olympic Games, Lake Placid, NY, Feb. 12-24. No. C380a contains Nos. C379-C380 in changed colors.

Stephenson's Rocket, Mali No. 196 — AP148

Liverpool-Manchester Railroad, 150th Anniversary: 300fr, Stephenson's Rocket, Mali No. 142.

1980, Feb. 25 Engr.
C381 AP148 200fr multi 1.00 .25
C382 AP148 300fr multi 1.50 .50

Equestrian, Moscow '80 Emblem — AP149

1980, Mar. 10 Engr. *Perf. 13*
C383 AP149 200fr shown .85 .30
C384 AP149 300fr Yachting 1.20 .50
C385 AP149 400fr Soccer 1.90 .70
a. Souvenir sheet of 3, #C383-C385 4.50 4.50
Nos. C383-C385 (3) 3.95 1.50

22nd Summer Olympic Games, Moscow, July 19-Aug. 3.
For overprints see Nos. C399-C401.

Jesus Carrying Cross, by Maurice Denis AP150

Easter: 500fr, Jesus before Pilate, by Dürer.

1980, Mar. 31
C386 AP150 480fr brn & org red 2.25 .80
C387 AP150 500fr org red & brn 2.25 .80

Kepler, Copernicus and Solar System Diagram — AP151

200fr, Kepler & diagram of earth's orbit.

1980, Apr. 7 Engr. *Perf. 13*
C388 AP151 200fr multi, vert. 1.00 .30
C389 AP151 300fr multi 1.50 .50

Discovery of Pluto, 50th Anniversary — AP152

1980, Apr. 21
C390 AP152 420fr multi 1.75 .75

Lunokhod I, Russian Flag — AP153

Design: 500fr, Apollo and Soyuz spacecraft, flags of US and Russia.

1980, Apr. 28
C391 AP153 480fr multi 1.90 .70
C392 AP153 500fr multi 1.90 .70

Lunokhod I, 10th anniversary; Apollo-Soyuz space test program, 5th anniversary.

Rochambeau, French Fleet Landing at Newport, R.I. — AP154

French Cooperation in American Revolution: 430fr, Rochambeau and George Washington, eagle.

1980, June 16 Engr. *Perf. 13*
C393 AP154 420fr multi 1.90 .75
C394 AP154 430fr multi 1.90 .75

Jet Flying Around Earth — AP155

Designs: No. C396, Ship, people, attack. No. C397, Astronaut on moon. No. C398, Space craft, scientists, moon. Nos. C395-C396 from "Around the World in 80 Days;" Nos. C397-C398 from "From Earth to Moon."

1980, June 30 Engr. *Perf. 11*
C395 AP155 100fr multi + label .80 .25
C396 AP155 100fr multi + label .80 .25
C397 AP155 150fr multi + label 1.10 .30
C398 AP155 150fr multi + label 1.10 .30
Nos. C395-C398 (4) 3.80 1.10

Jules Verne (1828-1905), French science fiction writer. Nos. C395-C398 each printed se-tenant with label showing various space scenes.

Nos. C383-C385a Overprinted

200fr — CONCOURS COMPLET/ INDIVIDUEL/ROMAN (It.)/ BLINOV (Urss) /SALNIKOV (Urss)
300fr — FINN/RECHARDT (Fin.)/ MAYRHOFER (Autr.)/ BALACHOV (Urss)
400fr — TCHECOSLOVAQUIE/ ALLEMAGNE DE L'EST/URSS

1980, Sept. 8 Engr. *Perf. 13*
C399 AP149 200fr multi .85 .30
C400 AP149 300fr multi 1.25 .50
C401 AP149 400fr multi 1.90 .75
a. Souvenir sheet of 3 4.25 4.25
Nos. C399-C401 (3) 4.00 1.55

Butterfly Type of 1980

1980, Oct. 6 Litho. *Perf. 13x12½*
Size: 48x36mm
C402 A137 420fr *Denaus chrysippus* 3.75 1.00

Charles De Gaulle, Map and Colors of France — AP156

1980, Nov. 9 Litho. *Perf. 13½x13*
C403 AP156 420fr shown 3.00 .90
C404 AP156 430fr De Gaulle, cross 3.00 .90

Charles De Gaulle, 10th anniv. of death.

Mali No. 140, Amtrak Train — AP157

Mali Stamps and Trains: 120fr, No. 195, Tokaido, Japan, vert. 200fr, No. 144, Rembrandt, Germany. 480fr, No. 143, TGV-001 France, vert.

1980, Nov. 17 Engr. *Perf. 13*
C405 AP157 120fr multi .60 .25
C406 AP157 130fr multi .70 .25
C407 AP157 200fr multi 1.00 .40
C408 AP157 480fr multi 2.40 .90
Nos. C405-C408 (4) 4.70 1.80

For overprint see No. C425.

Holy Family, by Lorenzo Lotto — AP158

Christmas 1980 (Paintings): 400fr, Flight to Egypt, by Rembrandt, vert. 500fr, Christmas Night, by Gauguin.

1980, Dec. 1 Litho. ***Perf. 13x12½***
C409 AP158 300fr multi 1.40 .55
C410 AP158 400fr multi 1.75 .70
C411 AP158 500fr multi 2.10 .80
Nos. C409-C411 (3) 5.25 2.05

Self-portrait, by Picasso — AP159

1981, Jan. 26 Litho. ***Perf. 12½x13***
C412 AP159 1000fr multi 5.50 2.00

Pablo Picasso (1881-1973).

Soccer Players — AP160

Designs: Soccer players.

1981, Feb. 28 ***Perf. 13***
C413 AP160 100fr multi .55 .25
C414 AP160 200fr multi 1.00 .35
C415 AP160 300fr multi 1.50 .50
Nos. C413-C415 (3) 3.05 1.10

Souvenir Sheet

C416 AP160 600fr multi 3.25 1.75

World Cup Soccer preliminary games.

Mozart and Instruments — AP161

225th Birth Anniversary of Wolfgang Amadeus Mozart: 430fr, Mozart and instruments, diff.

1981, Mar. 30 Litho. ***Perf. 13***
C417 AP161 420fr multi 2.00 .70
C418 AP161 430fr multi 2.00 .70

Jesus Falls on the Way to Calvary, by Raphael AP162

Easter 1981: 600fr, Ecce Homo, by Rembrandt.

1981, Apr. 6 ***Perf. 12½x13***
C419 AP162 500fr multi 2.10 .80
C420 AP162 600fr multi 2.50 .90

Alan B. Shepard AP163

Exploration of Saturn — AP164

Space Anniversaries: No. C422, Yuri Gagarin's flight, 1961. 430fr, Uranus discovery bicentennial, horiz.

1981, Apr. 21 Litho. ***Perf. 13***
C421 AP163 200fr multi .90 .30
C422 AP163 200fr multi .90 .30
C423 AP164 380fr multi 1.60 .55
C424 AP163 430fr multi 1.75 .65
Nos. C421-C424 (4) 5.15 1.80

No. C408 Overprinted

Overprint reads "26 fevrier 1981 Record du monde de/vitesse-380 km/h.".

1981, June 15 Engr.
C425 AP157 480fr multi 2.75 .90

New railroad speed record.

US No. 233, Columbus and His Fleet — AP165

475th Death Anniversary of Christopher Columbus (Santa Maria and): 200fr, Spain No. 418, vert. 260fr, Spain No. 421, vert. 300fr, US No. 232.

1981, June 22
C426 AP165 180fr multi .90 .30
C427 AP165 200fr multi 1.00 .35
C428 AP165 260fr multi 1.50 .55
C429 AP165 300fr multi 1.75 .65
Nos. C426-C429 (4) 5.15 1.85

Columbia Space Shuttle — AP166

Designs: Space shuttle.

1981, July 6 Litho. ***Perf. 13***
C430 AP166 200fr multi .90 .30
C431 AP166 500fr multi 2.25 .90
C432 AP166 600fr multi 2.75 1.00
Nos. C430-C432 (3) 5.90 2.20

Souvenir Sheet
Perf. 12

C433 AP166 700fr multi 4.00 2.00

For overprint see No. C440.

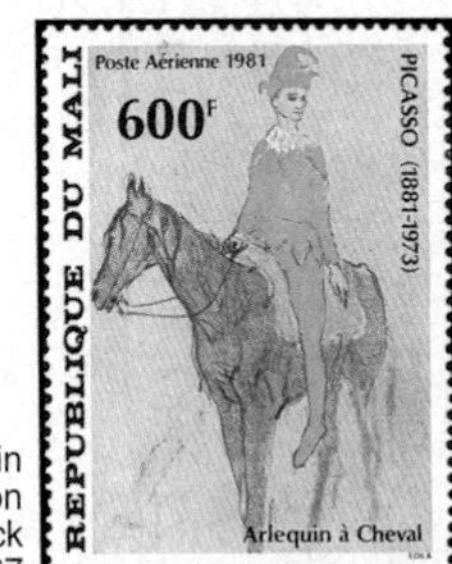
Harlequin on Horseback AP167

Picasso Birth Cent.: 750fr, Child Holding a Dove.

1981, July 15 ***Perf. 12½x13***
C434 AP167 600fr multi 3.50 1.00
C435 AP167 750fr multi 4.00 1.10

Prince Charles and Lady Diana, St. Paul's Cathedral AP168

1981, July 20 ***Perf. 12½***
C436 AP168 500fr shown 1.75 .70
C437 AP168 700fr Couple, coach 2.50 1.00

Royal wedding.

Christmas 1981 AP169

Designs: Virgin and Child paintings.

1981, Nov. 9 Litho. ***Perf. 12½x13***
C438 AP169 500fr Grunewald 2.25 .70
C439 AP169 700fr Correggio 3.00 1.00

See Nos. C451-C452, C464-C466, C475-C477, C488-C489, C511.

No. C433 Overprinted In Blue

Overprint reads "JOE ENGLE / RICHARD TRULY / 2 eme VOL SPATIAL".

1981, Nov. 12 Litho. ***Perf. 12***
C440 AP166 700fr multi 4.00 1.50

Nos. C369, C371 Overprinted with Winners' Names and Dates

1981, Dec. Engr. ***Perf. 13***
C441 AP143 140fr multi 1.00 .35
C442 AP143 300fr multi 2.25 .60

Lewis Carroll (1832-1908) — AP170

Designs: Scenes from Alice in Wonderland.

1982, Jan. 30 Litho. ***Perf. 12½***
C443 AP170 110fr multi 2.50 .60
C444 AP170 130fr multi 2.50 .80
C445 AP170 140fr multi 2.50 1.00
Nos. C443-C445 (3) 7.50 2.40

AP171

Portrait, by Gilbert Stuart.

1982, Feb. 8 ***Perf. 13***
C446 AP171 700fr multi 3.00 1.10

George Washington's Birth, 250th anniv. Incorrectly inscribed "Stuart Gilbert."

AP172

1982 World Cup: Various soccer players.

1982, Mar. 15 Litho. ***Perf. 13***
C447 AP172 220fr multi .90 .30
C448 AP172 420fr multi 1.60 .50
C449 AP172 500fr multi 1.75 .75
Nos. C447-C449 (3) 4.25 1.55

Souvenir Sheet
Perf. 12½

C450 AP172 680fr multi 3.75 2.00

For overprints see Nos. C458-C461.

Art Type of 1981

Paintings: 680fr, Transfiguration, by Fra Angelico. 1000fr, Pieta, by Bellini, horiz.

Perf. 12½x13, 13x12½
1982, Apr. 19 Litho.
C451 AP169 680fr multi 2.50 1.75
C452 AP169 1000fr multi 3.25 1.25

Mali No. O30, France No. 1985 — AP174

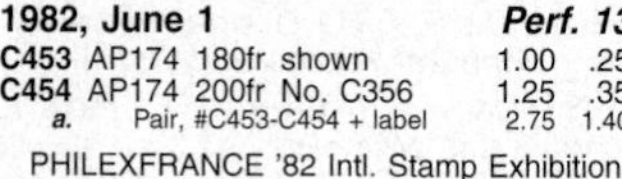

1982, June 1 ***Perf. 13***
C453 AP174 180fr shown 1.00 .25
C454 AP174 200fr No. C356 1.25 .35
a. Pair, #C453-C454 + label 2.75 1.40

PHILEXFRANCE '82 Intl. Stamp Exhibition, Paris, June 11-21.

Fire Engine, France, 1850 — AP175

Designs: French fire engines.

1982, June 14
C455 AP175 180fr shown 1.00 .25
C456 AP175 200fr 1921 1.00 .30
C457 AP175 270fr 1982 1.50 .45
Nos. C455-C457 (3) 3.50 1.00

Nos. C447-C450 Overprinted with Finalists' and Scores in Brown, Black, Blue or Red

1982, Aug. 16 **Litho.** ***Perf. 13***
C458 AP172 220fr multi (Brn) 1.10 .25
C459 AP172 420fr multi 1.50 .55
C460 AP172 500fr multi (Bl) 1.90 .75
Nos. C458-C460 (3) 4.50 1.55

Souvenir Sheet

Perf. 12½

C461 AP172 680fr multi (R) 3.00 1.75

Italy's victory in 1982 World Cup.

Scouting Year — AP176

300fr, Tent, Baden-Powell. 500fr, Salute, emblem.

1982 ***Perf. 12½***
C462 AP176 300fr multi 1.10 .45
C463 AP176 500fr multi 1.90 .80

Art Type of 1981

Boy with Cherries, by Edouard Manet (1832-83).

1982, Oct. 28 **Litho.** ***Perf. 12½x13***
C464 AP169 680fr multi 3.75 1.25

Art Type of 1981

Madonna and Child Paintings.

1982, Nov. 10
C465 AP169 500fr Titian 1.90 .75
C466 AP169 1000fr Bellini 3.75 1.25

Johann von Goethe (1749-1832), Poet — AP179

1982, Dec. 13 **Engr.** ***Perf. 13***
C467 AP179 500fr multi 2.75 .85

Follereau Type of 1974

1983, Jan. 24
C468 AP96 200fr dk brn 1.10 .35

Vostok VI, 20th Anniv. — AP180

400fr, Valentina Tereshkova.

1983, Feb. 14 **Litho.** ***Perf. 12½***
C469 AP180 400fr multi 1.75 .60

Manned Flight, 200th Anniv. — AP181

500fr, Eagle transatlantic balloon. 700fr, Montgolfiere.

1983, Feb. 28 ***Perf. 13***
C470 AP181 500fr multi 2.50 .75
C471 AP181 700fr multi 3.50 1.10

Pre-Olympic Year — AP182

1983, Mar. 14 **Litho.** ***Perf. 13***
C472 AP182 180fr Soccer .75 .25
C473 AP182 270fr Hurdles 1.10 .45
C474 AP182 300fr Wind surfing 1.50 .55
Nos. C472-C474 (3) 3.35 1.25

Art Type of 1981

Raphael paintings.

1983, Mar. 28 ***Perf. 12½x13***
C475 AP169 400fr Transfiguration 1.60 .60
C476 AP169 600fr Deposition 2.40 .85

Art Type of 1981

Design: Family of Acrobats with Monkey, by Picasso (1881-1973).

1983, Apr. 30 **Litho.** ***Perf. 12½x13***
C477 AP169 680fr multi 3.25 1.25

Lions Intl. — AP185

1983, May 9 ***Perf. 12½***
C478 Pair 12.00 6.50
a. AP185 700fr shown 3.00 1.10
b. AP185 700fr Rotary Intl. 3.00 1.10

Challenger Spacecraft AP186

1983, July 29 **Litho.** ***Perf. 13***
C479 AP186 1000fr multi 3.75 1.25

Printed se-tenant with orange red label showing astronaut Sally Ride.

Paris-Dakar Auto Race — AP187

240fr, Mercedes, 1914. 270fr, SSK, 1929. 500fr, W196, 1954.
1000fr, Mercedes van.

1983, Sept. 5 **Litho.** ***Perf. 12½***
C480 AP187 240fr multi 1.20 .35
C481 AP187 270fr multi 1.40 .45
C482 AP187 500fr multi 2.75 .75
Nos. C480-C482 (3) 5.35 1.55

Souvenir Sheet

C483 AP187 1000fr multi 6.50 2.00

For surcharge see No. C506.

Chess Game — AP188

300fr, Pawn, bishop. 420fr, Knight, castle. 500fr, King, Queen.
700fr, Various chess pieces.

1983, Oct. 24 **Engr.** ***Perf. 13***
C484 AP188 300fr multi 2.00 .40
C485 AP188 420fr multi 2.40 .70
C486 AP188 500fr multi 3.25 .80
Nos. C484-C486 (3) 7.65 1.90

Souvenir Sheet

C487 AP188 700fr multi 5.00 1.75

Art Type of 1981

Raphael Paintings: 700fr, Canigiani Madonna. 800fr, Madonna with Lamb.

1983, Nov. 7 **Litho.** ***Perf. 12½x13***
C488 AP169 700fr multi 2.50 .90
C489 AP169 800fr multi 3.00 1.00

Portrait of Leopold Zborowski, by Amedeo Modigliani (1884-1920) — AP190

1984, Feb. 13 **Litho.** ***Perf. 12½x13***
C490 AP190 700fr multi 4.00 1.25

Abraham Lincoln — AP191

1984, Feb. 27 ***Perf. 12½***
C491 AP191 400fr Henri Dunant 1.60 .50
C492 AP191 540fr shown 2.00 .60

Duke Ellington AP192

1984, Mar. 12 ***Perf. 13½x13***
C493 AP192 470fr Sidney Bechet 3.50 .90
C494 AP192 500fr shown 4.25 .90

Glider — AP193

1984, Mar. 26
C495 AP193 270fr shown 1.40 .35
C496 AP193 350fr Hang glider 1.60 .55

1984 Summer Olympics — AP194

1984, Apr. 9 ***Perf. 13***
C497 AP194 265fr Weight lifting 1.40 .35
C498 AP194 440fr Equestrian 2.10 .55
C499 AP194 500fr Hurdles 2.50 .60

Souvenir Sheet

Perf. 12½

C500 AP194 700fr Yachting 4.50 1.75

For surcharges see Nos. C507-C510.

Easter 1984 — AP195

Paintings; 940fr, Crucifixion, by Rubens, vert. 970fr, Resurrection, by Mantegna.

1984, Apr. 24 **Engr.**
C501 AP195 940fr multi 5.25 1.25
C502 AP195 970fr multi 5.25 1.25

Gottlieb Daimler Birth Sesquicentenary — AP196

350fr, Mercedes Simplex. 470fr, Mercedes-Benz 370-S. 485fr, 500-SEC.

1984, June 1 **Engr.** ***Perf. 13***
C503 AP196 350fr multi 3.00 1.00
C504 AP196 470fr multi 4.25 1.25
C505 AP196 485fr multi 4.25 1.25
Nos. C503-C505 (3) 11.50 3.50

No. C480 Overprinted and Surcharged

1984 **Litho.** ***Perf. 12½***
C506 AP187 120fr on 240fr #C480 1.40 .40

Nos. C497-C500 Overprinted and Surcharged

1984, Oct. **Litho.** ***Perf. 13***
C507 AP194 135fr on 265fr .90 .50
C508 AP194 220fr on 440fr 1.50 1.00
C509 AP194 250fr on 500fr 2.10 1.25
Nos. C507-C509 (3) 4.50 2.75

Souvenir Sheet

C510 AP194 350fr on 700fr 4.50 3.00

Overprints refer to the winners of the events depicted.

Art Type of 1981

Painting: Virgin and Child, by Lorenzo Lotto.

1984, Nov. 20 **Litho.** ***Perf. 12½x13***
C511 AP169 500fr multi 4.25 2.00

Audubon Birth Bicentenary — AP198

1985, Apr. 15 **Litho.** ***Perf. 13***
C512 AP198 180fr Kingfisher 1.40 .70
C513 AP198 300fr Bustard, vert. 2.50 1.25
C514 AP198 470fr Ostrich, vert. 4.25 2.00
C515 AP198 540fr Buzzard 5.25 2.10
Nos. C512-C515 (4) 13.40 6.05

For surcharge see No. C560, C562, C567.

ASECNA Airlines, 25th Anniv. — AP199

1985, June 10 ***Perf. 12½***
C516 AP199 700fr multi 5.25 2.50

For surcharge see No. C559.

PHILEXAFRICA Type of 1985

No. C517, Boy Scouts, lion. No. C518, Satellite communications.

1985, June 24 ***Perf. 13***
C517 A183 200fr multi 2.00 1.25
C518 A183 200fr multi 2.00 1.25
a. Pair, #C517-C518 + label 5.75 3.00

Halley's Comet — AP200

1986, Mar. 24 **Litho.** ***Perf. 12½***
C519 AP200 300fr multi 2.50 1.10

For surcharge see No. C558.

Statue of Liberty, Cent. — AP201

1986, Apr. 7 ***Perf. 13***
C520 AP201 600fr multi 5.25 2.25

Gottlieb Daimler Motorcycle — AP202

1986, Apr. 14
C521 AP202 400fr multi 3.00 1.40

1st Internal combustion automotive engine, cent.

Paul Robeson (1898-1976), American Actor, Singer — AP203

500fr, Portrait, Show Boat.

1986, May 10
C522 AP203 500fr multi 5.00 1.75

Karl Eberth (1835-1926), Bacteriologist, and Typhoid Bacilli — AP204

1986, June 7 **Litho.** ***Perf. 12x12½***
C523 AP204 550fr multi 4.50 2.50

World Chess Championships AP205

1986, June 16 ***Perf. 12½***
C524 AP205 400fr Chessmen 3.25 1.40
C525 AP205 500fr Knight 5.00 1.75

Disappearance of Jean Mermoz, 50th Anniv. — AP206

Mermoz and: 150fr, Latecoere-300 seaplane. 600fr, Cams 53 Oiseau Tango, seaplane. 625fr, Flight map, Le Comte de La Vaulx aircraft.

1986, Aug. 18 **Litho.** ***Perf. 13***
C526 AP206 150fr multi 1.50 .50
C527 AP206 600fr multi 4.50 1.75
C528 AP206 625fr multi 4.50 2.00
Nos. C526-C528 (3) 10.50 4.25

Nos. C353-C355 Surcharged New Value and Overprinted

Overprint reads "1986-10e Anniversaire du ler Vol/Commercial Supersonique".

1986, Sept. 29
C529 AP139 175fr on 120fr 1.50 .60
C530 AP139 225fr on 130fr 1.75 .80
C531 AP139 300fr on 200fr 2.75 1.00
Nos. C529-C531 (3) 6.00 2.40

Hansen, Leprosy Bacillus, Follereau and Lepers — AP207

1987, Jan. 26 **Litho.** ***Perf. 13***
C532 AP207 500fr multi 4.25 1.60

Gerhard Hansen (1841-1912), Norwegian physician who discovered the leprosy bacillus (1869); Raoul Follereau (1903-1977), philanthropist.

Konrad Adenauer (1876-1967), West German Chancellor AP208

1987, Mar. 9 **Litho.** ***Perf. 13***
C533 AP208 625fr org, buff & blk 5.75 2.25

Pre-Olympics Year — AP209

Buddha and: 400fr, Runners. 500fr, Soccer players.

1987, Apr. 6 **Engr.**
C534 AP209 400fr blk & red brn 3.50 1.40
C535 AP209 500fr lil rose, ol grn & ol 4.50 1.75

25th Summer Olympics, Seoul, 1988.

Al Jolson in The Jazz Singer — AP210

1987, Apr. 20
C536 AP210 550fr dk red brn & car rose 7.00 2.25

Sound films, 60th anniv.

Albert John Luthuli (1899-1967), 1960 Nobel Peace Prize Winner — AP211

1987, May 26 **Engr.** ***Perf. 13***
C537 AP211 400fr multi 3.25 1.10

Service Organizations AP212

1987, June 8 **Litho.** ***Perf. 13***
C538 AP212 500fr Rotary Int'l. 4.00 1.60
C539 AP212 500fr Lions Int'l. 4.00 1.60

Coubertin, Ancient Greek Runners, Contemporary Athletes — AP213

400fr, 5-ring emblem, stadium.

1988, Feb. 14 **Litho.** ***Perf. 13***
C540 AP213 240fr shown 2.00 .80
C541 AP213 400fr multi 3.50 1.40

125th birth anniv. of Baron Pierre de Coubertin (1863-1937), French educator and sportsman who promulgated revival of the Olympic Games; 1988 Summer Olympics, Seoul.

For surcharge see No. C565

Harlequin, by Pablo Picasso (1881-1973) — AP214

1988, Apr. 4 Litho. *Perf. 13*
C542 AP214 600fr multi 5.50 2.00

For surcharge see No. C563.

1st Scheduled Transatlantic Flight of the Concorde (London-New York), 15th Anniv. — AP215

1988, May 2 *Perf. 13*
C543 AP215 500fr multi 4.50 2.00

Home Improvement for a Verdant Mali — AP216

10fr, Furnace, tree, field.

1989, Feb. 6 Litho. *Perf. 12½*
C544 AP216 5fr shown .25 .25
C545 AP216 10fr multi .25 .25
C546 AP216 25fr like 5fr .30 .25
C547 AP216 100fr like 10fr 1.00 .45
Nos. C544-C547 (4) 1.80 1.20

1st Man on the Moon, 20th Anniv. — AP217

1989, Mar. 13 Engr. *Perf. 13*
C548 AP217 300fr multi. 2.50 1.00
C549 AP217 500fr multi, vert. 4.25 1.60

For surcharges see Nos. C561, C564.

French Revolution, Bicent. AP218

400fr, Women's march on Versailles. 600fr, Storming of the Bastille.

1989, July 3 Engr. *Perf. 13*
C550 AP218 400fr multi 4.00 1.40
C551 AP218 600fr multi 5.50 1.90

For surcharges see Nos. C566, C568.

World Cup Soccer Championships, Italy — AP219

1990, June 4 Litho. *Perf. 13*
C552 AP219 200fr multi 1.90 .70
C553 AP219 225fr multi, diff. 2.10 .80

Souvenir Sheet

C554 AP219 500fr like #C552 4.75 2.50

No. C552-C554 Overprinted in Red

1990, Aug. 13
C555 AP219 200fr on #C552 1.90 .85
C556 AP219 225fr on #C553 2.10 .85

Souvenir Sheet

C557 AP219 500fr on #C554 4.75 2.75

Nos. C512-C513, C515-C516, C519, C541-C542, C548-C551 Surcharged Like Nos. 579-594

1992, June *Perfs. as Before*

Printing Methods as Before

C558 AP200 20fr on 300fr — —
C559 AP199 20fr on 700fr — —
C560 AP198 30fr on 180fr *20.00* —
C561 AP217 30fr on 500fr — —
C562 AP198 100fr on 540fr *20.00* —
C563 AP214 100fr on 600fr — —
C564 AP217 150fr on 300fr — —
C565 AP213 150fr on 400fr — —
C566 AP218 150fr on 400fr — —
C567 AP198 200fr on 300fr *20.00* —
C568 AP218 240fr on 600fr — —
Nos. C558-C568 (11) 60.00

Size and location of surcharge varies. No. C565 also overprinted "BARCELONE 92."

POSTAGE DUE STAMPS

Bambara Headpiece — D1

Perf. 14x13½

1961, Mar. 18 Engr. Unwmk.
J1 D1 1fr black .25 .25
J2 D1 2fr bright ultra .25 .25
J3 D1 5fr red lilac .30 .25
J4 D1 10fr orange .50 .25
J5 D1 20fr bright green .75 .25
J6 D1 25fr red brown .95 .30
Nos. J1-J6 (6) 3.00 1.55

Polyptychus Roseus — D2

No. J8, Deilephila Nerii. No. J9, Gynanisa maja. No. J10, Bunaea alcinoe. No. J11, Teracolus eris. No. J12, Colotis antevippe. No. J13, Charaxes epijasius. No. J14, Manatha microcera. No. J15, Hypokopelates otraeda. No. J16, Lipaphnaeus leonina. No. J17, Gonimbrasia hecate. No. J18, Lobounaea christyi. No. J19, Hypolimnas misippus. No. J20, Catopsilia florella.

1964, June 1 Photo. *Perf. 11*

Butterflies and Moths in Natural Colors

J7 1fr olive green .30 .25
J8 1fr org & brn .30 .25
a. D2 Pair, #J7-J8 .60 .25
J9 2fr emer & brn .40 .25
J10 2fr emer & brn .40 .25
a. D2 Pair, #J9-J10 .80 .25
J11 3fr rose lil & brn .40 .25
J12 3fr rose lil & brn .40 .25
a. D2 Pair, #J11-J12 .80 .25
J13 5fr blk & rose .40 .25
J14 5fr green .40 .25
a. D2 Pair, #J13-J14 .80 .25
J15 10fr yel, org & blk .85 .35
J16 10fr blue .85 .35
a. D2 Pair, #J15-J16 1.75 .70
J17 20fr lt bl & brn 1.60 .70
J18 20fr lt bl & brn 1.60 .70
a. D2 Pair, #J17-J18 3.25 1.40
J19 25fr grn & yel 2.25 1.00
J20 25fr dp grn & blk 2.25 1.00
a. D2 Pair, #J19-J20 4.50 2.00
Nos. J7-J20 (14) 12.40 6.10

Nos. J7-J20 Surcharged

1984 Photo. *Perf. 11*
J21 5fr on 1fr #J7 .30 .25
J22 5fr on 1fr #J8 .30 .25
a. D2 Pair, #J21-J22 .60 .25
J23 10fr on 2fr #J9 .30 .25
J24 10fr on 2fr #J10 .30 .25
a. D2 Pair, #J23-J24 .60 .25
J25 15fr on 3fr #J11 .30 .25
J26 15fr on 3fr #J12 .30 .25
a. D2 Pair, #J25-J26 .60 .25
J27 25fr on 5fr #J13 .40 .25
J28 25fr on 5fr #J14 .40 .25
a. Pair, #J27-J28 .80 .25
J29 50fr on 10fr #J15 .70 .30
J30 50fr on 10fr #J16 .70 .30
a. D2 Pair, #J29-J30 1.40 .60
J31 100fr on 20fr #J17 1.60 .70
J32 100fr on 20fr #J18 1.60 .70
a. D2 Pair, #J31-J32 3.25 1.40
J33 125fr on 25fr #J19 2.00 .85
J34 125fr on 25fr #J20 2.00 .85
a. Pair, #J33-J34 4.00 1.75
Nos. J21-J34 (14) 11.20 5.70

OFFICIAL STAMPS

Dogon Mask — O1

Perf. 14x13½

1961, Mar. 18 Engr. Unwmk.
O1 O1 1fr gray .30 .25
O2 O1 2fr red orange .30 .25
O3 O1 3fr black .30 .25
O4 O1 5fr light blue .30 .25
O5 O1 10fr bister brown .35 .25
O6 O1 25fr brt ultra .75 .25
O7 O1 30fr car rose .90 .25
O8 O1 50fr Prus green 1.00 .25
O9 O1 85fr red brown 1.50 .65
O10 O1 100fr emerald 1.50 .65
O11 O1 200fr red lilac 3.75 1.25
Nos. O1-O11 (11) 10.95 4.55

Mali Coat of Arms — O2

National Colors and Arms in Multicolor, Background in Light Green

1964, June 1 Photo. *Perf. 12½*
O12 O2 1fr green .30 .25
O13 O2 2fr light vio .30 .25
O14 O2 3fr gray .30 .25
O15 O2 5fr lilac rose .30 .25
O16 O2 10fr bright blue .30 .25
O17 O2 25fr ocher .35 .25
O18 O2 30fr dark green .50 .25
O19 O2 50fr orange .75 .25
O20 O2 85fr dark brown .80 .60
O21 O2 100fr red 1.00 .60
O22 O2 200fr dk vio bl 1.80 .75
Nos. O12-O22 (11) 6.70 3.95

City Coats of Arms — O3

1981, Sept. Photo. *Perf. 12½x13*
O23 O3 5fr Gao .30 .25
O24 O3 15fr Timbuktu .35 .25
O25 O3 50fr Mopti .45 .25
O26 O3 180fr Segou 1.00 .25
O27 O3 200fr Sikasso 1.25 .35
O28 O3 680fr Koulikoro 3.25 .90
O29 O3 700fr Kayes 3.75 1.10
O30 O3 1000fr Bamako 5.00 1.40
Nos. O23-O30 (8) 15.35 4.75

Nos. O23-O30 Surcharged

1984 Photo. *Perf. 12½x13*
O31 O3 15fr on 5fr .30 .25
O32 O3 50fr on 15fr .55 .25
O33 O3 120fr on 50fr .95 .25
O34 O3 295fr on 180fr 2.50 .60
O35 O3 470fr on 200fr 3.50 .85
O36 O3 515fr on 680fr 3.75 1.00
O37 O3 845fr on 700fr 6.00 1.75
O38 O3 1225fr on 1000fr 10.00 2.25
Nos. O31-O38 (8) 27.55 7.20

MALTA

'mol-tə

LOCATION — A group of islands in the Mediterranean Sea off the coast of Sicily
GOVT. — Republic within the British Commonwealth
AREA — 122 sq. mi.
POP. — 376,513 (1998)
CAPITAL — Valletta

The former colony includes the islands of Malta, Gozo, and Comino. It became a republic Dec. 13, 1974.

4 Farthings = 1 Penny
12 Pence = 1 Shilling
20 Shillings = 1 Pound
10 Mils = 1 Cent (1972)
100 Cents = 1 Pound (1972)
100 Cents = 1 Euro (2008)

Catalogue values for unused stamps in this country are for Never Hinged items, beginning with Scott 206 in the regular postage section, Scott B1 in the semi-postal section, Scott C2 in the air post section, and Scott J21 in the postage due section.

Watermark

Wmk. 354 — Maltese Cross, Multiple

Values for unused stamps are for examples with original gum as defined in the catalogue introduction. Very fine examples of Nos. 1-7 will have perforations touching the frameline on one or more sides due to the narrow spacing of the stamps on the plate. Stamps with perfs clear of the frameline are scarce and will command higher prices.

Queen Victoria — A1

1860-61 Unwmk. Typo. *Perf. 14*
1 A1 ½p buff ('63) 900.00 425.00
2 A1 ½p buff, *bluish* 1,400. 700.00
a. Imperf. (single) *12,000.*

1863-80 Wmk. 1
3 A1 ½p yellow buff ('75) 90.00 70.00
a. ½p buff 130.00 80.00
b. ½p brown orange ('67) 450.00 120.00
c. ½p orange yellow ('80) 300.00 130.00
4 A1 ½p golden yel (aniline) ('74) 350.00 400.00

1865 *Perf. 12½*
5 A1 ½p buff 175.00 120.00
a. ½p yellow buff 425.00 190.00

1878 *Perf. 14x12½*
6 A1 ½p buff 210.00 110.00
a. Perf. 12½x14 —

No. 6a unused is believed to be unique. It has a small fault.

1882 Wmk. 2 *Perf. 14*
7 A1 ½p reddish orange ('84) 21.00 *57.50*

A2

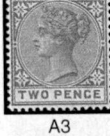

A3

Queen Victoria — A4

1885, Jan. 1
8 A1 ½p green 6.00 .60
9 A2 1p car rose 14.50 .40
a. 1p rose 100.00 30.00
10 A3 2p gray 11.00 2.25
11 A4 2½p ultramarine 55.00 1.25
a. 2½p bright ultramarine 55.00 1.25
b. 2½p dull blue 70.00 3.25
12 A3 4p brown 13.00 3.50
a. Imperf., pair *6,000. 6,000.*
13 A3 1sh violet 60.00 22.50
Nos. 8-13 (6) 159.50 30.50

For surcharge see No. 20.

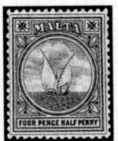

Queen Victoria within Maltese Cross — A5

1886 Wmk. 1
14 A5 5sh rose 125.00 95.00

Gozo Fishing Boat — A6

Ancient Galley — A7

1899, Feb. 4 Engr. Wmk. 2
15 A6 4½p black brown 28.00 17.50
16 A7 5p brown red 50.00 21.00

See Nos. 42-45.

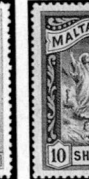

"Malta" — A8

St. Paul after Shipwreck — A9

1899 Wmk. 1
17 A8 2sh6p olive gray 47.50 17.50
18 A9 10sh blue black 110.00 75.00

See No. 64. For overprint see No. 85.

Valletta Harbor — A10

1901, Jan. 1 Wmk. 2
19 A10 1f red brown 1.75 .55

See Nos. 28-29.

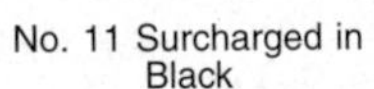

No. 11 Surcharged in Black

1902, July 4
20 A4 1p on 2½p dull blue 1.75 2.25
a. "Pnney" 35.00 *65.00*
b. Double surcharge *17,500. 4,500.*

King Edward VII — A12

1903-04 Typo.
21 A12 ½p dark green 11.00 1.00
22 A12 1p car & black 17.50 .50
23 A12 2p gray & red vio 32.50 7.00
24 A12 2½p ultra & brn vio 35.00 5.25
25 A12 3p red vio & gray 2.25 .60
26 A12 4p brown & blk ('04) 30.00 21.00
27 A12 1sh violet & gray 32.50 9.50
Nos. 21-27 (7) 160.75 44.85

1904-11 Wmk. 3
28 A10 1f red brown ('05) 10.00 2.75
29 A10 1f dk brown ('10) 9.00 .25
30 A12 ½p green 6.00 .35
31 A12 1p car & blk ('05) 27.50 .25
32 A12 1p carmine ('07) 4.00 .25
33 A12 2p gray & red vio ('05) 16.50 4.00
34 A12 2p gray ('11) 6.00 6.50
35 A12 2½p ultra & brn vio 37.50 .70
36 A12 2½p ultra ('11) 6.50 4.50
37 A12 4p brn & blk ('06) 13.00 9.00
38 A12 4p scar & blk, *yel* ('11) 4.75 5.50
39 A12 1sh violet & gray 57.50 2.40
40 A12 1sh blk, *grn* ('11) 8.75 4.50
41 A12 5sh scar & grn, *yel* ('11) 75.00 87.50

Engr.
42 A6 4½p black brn ('05) 45.00 7.00
43 A6 4½p orange ('11) 5.25 5.00
44 A7 5p red ('04) 45.00 9.00
45 A7 5p ol green ('10) 5.25 4.50
Nos. 28-45 (18) 382.50 153.95

A13

A15

King George V — A16

1914-21 Ordinary Paper Typo.
49 A13 ¼p brown 1.60 .25
50 A13 ½p green 3.25 .35
51 A13 1p scarlet ('15) 2.75 .45
a. 1p carmine ('14) 1.75 .25
52 A13 2p gray ('15) 16.00 8.25
53 A13 2½p ultramarine 2.75 .70

Chalky Paper
54 A15 3p vio, *yel* 3.00 *22.00*
58 A13 6p dull vio & red vio 13.00 *23.00*
59 A15 1sh black, *green* 14.00 *47.50*
a. 1sh black, *bl grn, ol back* 22.50 *35.00*
b. 1sh black, *emerald* ('21) 47.50 *97.50*
c. As "b," olive back 13.00 *32.50*
60 A16 2sh ultra & dl vio, *bl* 57.50 40.00
61 A16 5sh scar & grn, *yel* 105.00 *115.00*

Surface-colored Paper
62 A15 1sh blk, *grn* ('14) 17.50 *47.50*
Nos. 49-54,58-62 (11) 236.35 305.00

See Nos. 66-68, 70-72. For overprints see Nos. 77-82, 84.

Valletta Harbor — A17

1915 Ordinary Paper Engr.
63 A17 4p black 17.50 7.75

St. Paul — A18

1919
64 A8 2sh6p olive green 82.50 *95.00*
65 A18 10sh black 3,500. *4,750.*
Revenue cancel 100.00

For overprint see No. 83.

George V — A19

1921-22 Typo. Wmk. 4

Ordinary Paper
66 A13 ¼p brown 6.50 *45.00*
67 A13 ½p green 7.00 *37.50*
68 A13 1p rose red 7.75 3.00
69 A19 2p gray 11.00 2.00
70 A13 2½p ultramarine 7.75 *52.50*

Chalky Paper
71 A13 6p dull vio & red vio 37.50 *90.00*
72 A16 2sh ultra & dull vio, *bl* 75.00 *240.00*

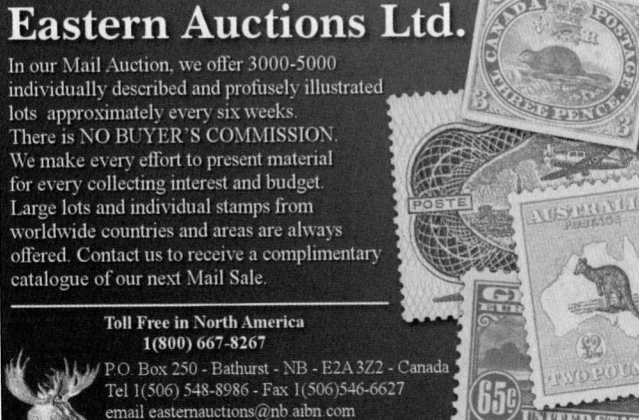

Engr.
Ordinary Paper

73 A18 10sh black 400.00 *850.00*
Nos. 66-73 (8) 552.50 1,320.

For overprints and surcharge see Nos. 86-93, 97.

Stamps of 1914-19 Overprinted in Red or Black

1922 Ordinary Paper Wmk. 3
Overprint 21mm

77 A13 ½p green 2.50 *4.00*
78 A13 2½p ultra 20.00 *50.00*

Chalky Paper

79 A15 3p violet, *yel* 5.00 *30.00*
80 A13 6p dull lil & red vio 6.50 *40.00*
81 A15 1sh black, *emer* 6.50 *30.00*

Overprint 28mm

82 A16 2sh ultra & dull vio, *bl* (R) 275.00 *525.00*

Ordinary Paper

83 A8 2sh6p olive grn 35.00 *60.00*

Chalky Paper

84 A16 5sh scar & grn, *yel* 65.00 *110.00*
Nos. 77-84 (8) 415.50 *849.00*

Wmk. 1
Ordinary Paper

85 A9 10sh blue black (R) 225.00 *400.00*

Same Overprint on Stamps of 1921

1922 Ordinary Paper Wmk. 4
Overprint 21mm

86 A13 ¼p brown .35 *.80*
87 A13 ½p green 5.50 *14.50*
88 A13 1p rose red 1.10 .25
89 A19 2p gray 5.50 .55
90 A13 2½p ultramarine 1.25 *2.25*

Chalky Paper

91 A13 6p dull vio & red vio 27.50 *60.00*

Overprint 28mm

92 A16 2sh ultra & dull vio, *bl* (R) 55.00 *100.00*

Ordinary Paper

93 A18 10sh black (R) 160.00 *275.00*
Nos. 86-93 (8) 256.20 *453.35*

No. 69 Surcharged

1922, Apr. 15

97 A19 1f on 2p gray .90 .50

"Malta" — A20

Britannia and Malta — A21

1922-26 Chalky Paper Typo.

98 A20 ¼p brown 3.00 .70
99 A20 ½p green 3.00 .25
100 A20 1p buff & plum 6.50 .25
101 A20 1p violet ('24) 4.75 .90
102 A20 1½p org brn ('23) 6.00 .25
103 A20 2p ol brn & turq 3.50 1.40
104 A20 2½p ultra ('26) 6.00 *20.00*
105 A20 3p ultramarine 6.50 3.25
a. 3p blue 8.50 3.75
106 A20 3p blk, *yel* ('26) 5.25 *27.50*
107 A20 4p yel & ultra 3.25 *6.00*
108 A20 6p ol grn & vio 7.00 5.00
109 A21 1sh ol brn & blue 15.00 4.75
110 A21 2sh ultra & ol brn 15.00 *24.00*
111 A21 2sh6p blk & red vio 14.50 *17.50*
112 A21 5sh ultra & org 24.00 *55.00*
113 A21 10sh ol brn & gray 70.00 *175.00*

Engr.
Ordinary Paper

114 A20 £1 car red & blk ('25) 125.00 *500.00*
a. £1 rose car & blk ('22) 165.00 *375.00*
Nos. 98-114 (17) 318.25 *841.75*

No. 114a has watermark sideways.

For overprints and surcharges see Nos. 115-129.

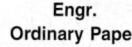

No. 105 Surcharged

1925, Dec.

115 A20 2½p on 3p ultramarine 2.00 *6.50*

Stamps of 1922-26 Overprinted

1926

116 A20 ¼p brown 1.10 *8.25*
117 A20 ½p green .80 .25
118 A20 1p violet 1.10 .25
119 A20 1½p orange brown 1.40 .70
120 A20 2p ol brn & turq .85 *2.25*
121 A20 2½p ultramarine 1.40 *1.60*
122 A20 3p black, *yel* .85 .90
a. Inverted overprint 200.00 *550.00*
123 A20 4p yel & ultra 25.00 *42.50*
124 A20 6p ol grn & vio 3.25 *8.25*
125 A21 1sh ol brn & bl 6.25 *25.00*
126 A21 2sh ultra & ol brown 60.00 *160.00*
127 A21 2sh6p blk & red vio 20.00 *55.00*
128 A21 5sh ultra & org 11.00 *55.00*
129 A21 10sh ol brn & gray 8.50 *24.00*
Nos. 116-129 (14) 141.50 383.95

George V — A22

Valletta Harbor — A23

St. Publius — A24

Notabile (Mdina) — A25

Gozo Fishing Boat — A26

Statue of Neptune — A27

Ruins at Mnaidra — A28

St. Paul — A29

1926-27 Typo. Perf. 14½x14

131 A22 ¼p brown .90 .25
132 A22 ½p green .70 .25
133 A22 1p red 3.50 1.60
134 A22 1½p orange brn 2.25 .25
135 A22 2p gray 5.25 *18.00*
136 A22 2½p blue 4.50 2.25
137 A22 3p dark violet 5.00 *6.00*
138 A22 4p org red & blk 3.75 *20.00*
139 A22 4½p yel buff & vio 4.00 *6.50*
140 A22 6p red & violet 5.00 *9.00*

Engr. Perf. 12½
Inscribed: "Postage"

141 A23 1sh black 7.50 *12.00*
142 A24 1sh6p green & blk 9.00 *24.00*
143 A25 2sh dp vio & blk 9.50 *30.00*
144 A26 2sh6p ver & black 23.00 *60.00*
145 A27 3sh blue & blk 23.00 *50.00*
146 A28 5sh green & blk 26.00 *82.50*
147 A29 10sh car & blk 70.00 *120.00*
Nos. 131-147 (17) 202.85 *442.60*

See Nos. 167-183. For overprints see Nos. 148-166.

Stamps and Type of 1926-27 Overprinted in Black

1928 Perf. 14½x14

148 A22 ¼p brown 1.75 .25
149 A22 ½p green 1.75 .25
150 A22 1p red 2.00 *3.75*
151 A22 1p orange brown 5.25 .25
152 A22 1½p yel brown 2.75 1.00
153 A22 1½p red 5.00 .25
154 A22 2p gray 5.00 *10.50*
155 A22 2½p blue 2.25 .25
156 A22 3p dark violet 2.25 1.00
157 A22 4p org red & blk 2.25 2.00
158 A22 4½p yel & violet 2.50 1.10
159 A22 6p red & violet 2.50 1.75

Overprinted in Red

Perf. 12½

160 A23 1sh black 6.25 3.00
161 A24 1sh6p green & blk 14.50 *12.00*
162 A25 2sh dp vio & blk 30.00 *75.00*
163 A26 2sh6p ver & black 20.00 *26.00*
164 A27 3sh ultra & blk 25.00 *35.00*
165 A28 5sh yel grn & blk 42.50 *75.00*
166 A29 10sh car rose & black 75.00 *110.00*
Nos. 148-166 (19) 248.50 358.35

Issued: Nos. 151, 153, Dec. 5; others, Oct. 1.

Types of 1926-27 Issue
Inscribed: "Postage & Revenue"

1930, Oct. 20 Typo. Perf. 14½x14

167 A22 ¼p brown .70 .25
168 A22 ½p green .70 .25
169 A22 1p yel brown .70 .25
170 A22 1½p red .80 .25
171 A22 2p gray 1.40 .60
172 A22 2½p blue 2.25 .25
173 A22 3p dark violet 1.75 .25
174 A22 4p org red & blk 1.40 *7.50*
175 A22 4½p yel & violet 3.75 1.40
176 A22 6p red & violet 3.25 2.50

Engr. Perf. 12½

177 A23 1sh black 11.00 *25.00*
178 A24 1sh6p green & blk 9.75 *32.50*
179 A25 2sh dp vio & blk 14.50 *30.00*
180 A26 2sh6p ver & black 20.00 *65.00*
181 A27 3sh ultra & blk 55.00 *65.00*
182 A28 5sh yel grn & blk 60.00 *80.00*
183 A29 10sh car rose & blk 120.00 *200.00*
Nos. 167-183 (17) 306.95 *511.00*

Common Design Types pictured following the introduction.

Silver Jubilee Issue
Common Design Type

1935, May 6 Perf. 11x12

184 CD301 ½p green & blk .50 .70
185 CD301 2½p ultra & brn 2.00 *4.00*
186 CD301 6p ol grn & lt bl 5.50 *6.50*
187 CD301 1sh brn vio & ind 14.00 22.50
Nos. 184-187 (4) 22.00 33.70
Set, never hinged 40.00

Coronation Issue
Common Design Type

1937, May 12 Wmk. 4 Perf. 13½x14

188 CD302 ½p deep green .25 .25
189 CD302 1½p carmine .50 .60
190 CD302 2½p bright ultra .50 .75
Nos. 188-190 (3) 1.25 1.60
Set, never hinged 2.25

Valletta Harbor — A30

Fort St. Angelo — A31

Verdala Palace — A32

Neolithic Ruins — A33

Victoria and Citadel, Gozo — A34

De l'Isle Adam Entering Mdina — A35

St. John's Co-Cathedral A36

Mnaidra Temple — A37

Statue of Antonio Manoel de Vilhena — A38

Woman in Faldetta — A39

St. Publius — A40

Mdina Cathedral A41

Statue of Neptune — A42

Palace Square — A43

St. Paul — A44

1938-43 Wmk. 4 *Perf. 12½*

191	A30	1f	brown	.25	.35
192	A31	½p	green	2.75	.30
192A	A31	½p	chnt ('43)	.35	.30
193	A32	1p	chestnut	4.25	.35
193A	A32	1p	grn ('43)	.40	.25
194	A33	1½p	rose red	2.25	.30
194A	A33	1½p	dk gray ('43)	.25	.25
195	A34	2p	dark gray	2.25	1.75
195A	A34	2p	rose red ('43)	.35	.25
196	A35	2½p	blue	4.50	1.25
196A	A35	2½p	violet ('43)	.40	.25
197	A36	3p	violet	3.00	.80
197A	A36	3p	blue ('43)	.30	.25
198	A37	4½p	ocher & ol green	.30	.30
199	A38	6p	rose red & ol green	1.75	.30
200	A39	1sh	black	1.75	.55
201	A40	1sh6p	sage grn & black	5.00	4.00
202	A41	2sh	dk bl & lt grn	3.25	*7.50*
203	A42	2sh6p	rose red & black	5.50	*6.00*
204	A43	5sh	bl grn & blk	3.50	*9.00*
205	A44	10sh	dp rose & blk	11.50	11.50
			Nos. 191-205 (21)	53.85	45.80
			Set, never hinged	75.00	

See No. 236a. For overprints see Nos. 208-222.

Catalogue values for unused stamps in this section, from this point to the end of the section, are for Never Hinged items.

Peace Issue

Common Design Type
Inscribed: "Malta" and Crosses

Perf. 13½x14

1946, Dec. 3 Engr. Wmk. 4

206	CD303	1p	bright green	.25	.25
207	CD303	3p	dark ultra	.40	1.75

Stamps of 1938-43 Overprinted in Black or Carmine

a

1948, Nov. 25 *Perf. 12½*

208	A30	1f	brown	.30	.25
209	A31	½p	chestnut	.30	.25
210	A32	1p	green	.30	.25
211	A33	1½p	dk gray (C)	1.25	.25
212	A34	2p	rose red	1.25	.25
213	A35	2½p	violet (C)	.80	.25
214	A36	3p	blue (C)	3.00	.25
215	A37	4½p	ocher & ol grn	2.75	1.00
216	A38	6p	rose red & ol green	3.25	.30
217	A39	1sh	black	3.75	.45
218	A40	1sh6p	sage grn & blk	2.50	.50
219	A41	2sh	dk bl & lt grn (C)	6.00	2.50
220	A42	2sh6p	rose red & blk	14.00	2.50
221	A43	5sh	bl grn & blk (C)	26.00	3.50
222	A44	10sh	dp rose & blk	26.00	25.00
			Nos. 208-222 (15)	91.45	37.50

The overprint is smaller on No. 208. It reads from lower left to upper right on Nos. 209 and 221.

See Nos. 235-240.

Silver Wedding Issue

Common Design Types
Inscribed: "Malta" and Crosses

1949, Jan. 4 Photo. *Perf. 14x14½*

223	CD304	1p	dark green	.55	.25

Perf. 11½x11

Engr.

224	CD305	£1	dark blue	40.00	45.00

UPU Issue

Common Design Types
Inscribed: "Malta" and Crosses

Perf. 13½, 11x11½

1949, Oct. 10 Engr. Wmk. 4

225	CD306	2½p	violet	.30	.25
226	CD307	3p	indigo	3.00	1.10
227	CD308	6p	dp carmine	.60	1.00
228	CD309	1sh	slate	.60	*2.50*
			Nos. 225-228 (4)	4.50	4.85

Princess Elizabeth — A45

1950, Dec. 1 Engr. *Perf. 12x11½*

229	A45	1p	emerald	.25	.25
230	A45	3p	bright blue	.25	.25
231	A45	1sh	gray black	.90	*2.00*
			Nos. 229-231 (3)	1.40	2.50

Visit of Princess Elizabeth.

Madonna and Child — A46

1951, July 12

232	A46	1p	green	.25	.25
233	A46	3p	purple	.55	.25
234	A46	1sh	slate black	1.60	1.40
			Nos. 232-234 (3)	2.40	1.90

700th anniv. of the presentation of the scapular to St. Simon Stock.

Types of 1938-43 Overprinted Type "a" in Red or Black

1953, Jan. 8 Wmk. 4 *Perf. 12½*

235	A32	1p	gray (R)	.85	.25
236	A33	1½p	green	.40	.25
a.			Overprint omitted		*18,000.*
237	A34	2p	ocher	.40	.25
238	A35	2½p	rose red	.75	*1.50*
239	A36	3p	violet (R)	.75	.25
240	A37	4½p	ultra & ol grn (R)	.75	*.90*
			Nos. 235-240 (6)	3.90	3.40

Coronation Issue

Common Design Type
Inscribed: "Malta" and Crosses

1953, June 3 Engr. *Perf. 13½x13*

241	CD312	1½p	dk green black	.50	.25

Type of 1938-43 with Portrait of Queen Elizabeth II Inscribed: "Royal Visit 1954."

1954, May 3 *Perf. 12½*

242	A36	3p	violet	.35	.25

Visit of Elizabeth II and the Duke of Edinburgh, 1954.

Central Altarpiece, Collegiate Parish Church, Cospicua — A47

Perf. 14½x13½

1954, Sept. 8 Photo. Wmk. 4

243	A47	1½p	bright green	.25	.25
244	A47	3p	ultramarine	.25	.25
245	A47	1sh	gray black	.30	.25
			Nos. 243-245 (3)	.80	.75

Cent. of the promulgation of the Dogma of the Immaculate Conception.

Monument of the Great Siege, 1565 — A48

Auberge de Castille — A49

Designs: ¼p, Wignacourt Aqueduct Horse-trough. 1p, Victory Church. 1½p, War Memorial. 2p, Mosta Dome. 3p, King's Scroll. 4½p, Roosevelt's Scroll. 6p, Neolithic Temples at Tarxien. 8p, Vedette. 1sh, Mdina Gate. 1sh6p, Les Gavroches. 2sh, Monument of Christ the King. 2sh6p, Monument of Nicolas Cottoner. 5sh, Raymond Perellos Monument. 10sh, St. Paul. £1, Baptism of Christ.

1956-57 Engr. *Perf. 11½*

246	A48	¼p	violet	.25	.25
247	A48	½p	yel orange	.45	.25
248	A48	1p	black	1.00	.25
249	A48	1½p	brt green	.30	.25
250	A48	2p	brown	2.00	.25
251	A49	2½p	orange brown	1.75	.35
252	A48	3p	rose red	1.25	.25
253	A48	4½p	blue	2.25	.75
254	A49	6p	slate blue	.65	.25
255	A48	8p	olive bister	3.25	1.00
256	A48	1sh	purple	1.10	.30
257	A48	1sh6p	Prus green	12.00	.40
258	A48	2sh	olive green	11.00	3.00

Perf. 13½x13

259	A48	2sh6p	cop brown	8.50	2.50
260	A48	5sh	emerald	13.50	3.00
261	A48	10sh	dk carmine	34.00	14.00
262	A48	£1	yel brn ('57)	34.00	29.00
			Nos. 246-262 (17)	127.25	56.05

See Nos. 296-297.

First George Cross Issue

Symbol of Malta's War Effort — A50

Searchlights over Malta — A51

Design: 1sh, Bombed houses.

Perf. 14x14½, 14½x14

1957, Apr. 15 Photo.

Cross in Silver

263	A50	1½p	green	.25	.25
264	A51	3p	bright red	.25	.25
265	A50	1sh	dark red brown	.25	.25
			Nos. 263-265 (3)	.75	.75

Award of the George Cross to Malta for its war effort.

See Nos. 269-274.

Symbols of Architecture — A52

Designs: 3p, Symbols of Industry, vert. 1sh, Symbols of electronics and chemistry and Technical School, Paola.

Perf. 14½x14, 14x14½

1958, Feb. 15 Wmk. 314

266	A52	1½p	dp green & blk	.25	.25
267	A52	3p	rose red, blk & gray	.25	.25
268	A52	1sh	gray, blk & lilac	.25	.25
			Nos. 266-268 (3)	.75	.75

Technical education on Malta.

Second George Cross Issue

Types of 1957

1½p, Bombed-out family & searchlights. 3p, Convoy entering harbor. 1sh, Searchlight battery.

1958, Apr. 15 *Perf. 14½x14, 14x14½*

Cross in Silver

269	A51	1½p	black & brt green	.25	.25
270	A50	3p	black & vermilion	.25	.25
271	A51	1sh	black & brt lilac	.25	.25
			Nos. 269-271 (3)	.75	.75

Third George Cross Issue

Types of 1957

Designs: 1½p, Air Raid Precautions Organization helping wounded. 3p, Allegory of Malta. 1sh, Mother and child during air raid.

1959, Apr. 15 *Perf. 14x14½, 14½x14*

272	A50	1½p	gold, green & black	.25	.25
273	A51	3p	gold, lilac & black	.25	.25
274	A50	1sh	gold, gray & black	.80	1.25
			Nos. 272-274 (3)	1.30	1.75

St. Paul's Shipwreck, Painting in St. Paul's Church, Valletta — A53

Statue of St. Paul, St. Paul's Grotto, Rabat — A54

Designs: 3p, Consecration of St. Publius. 6p, St. Paul leaving Malta; painting, St. Paul's Church, Valletta. 1sh, Angel holding tablet with quotations from Acts of the Apostles. 2sh6p, St. Paul and St. Paul's Bay islets.

Wmk. 314

1960, Feb. 9 Photo. *Perf. 13*
275 A53 1½p bister, brt bl & gold .25 .25
a. Gold dates & crosses omitted *75.00 110.00*
276 A53 3p lt blue, red lil & gold .30 .25
277 A53 6p car, gray & gold .25 .25

Perf. 14x14½
278 A54 8p black & gold .40 *.65*
279 A54 1sh brt cl & gold .35 .25
280 A54 2sh6p brt grnsh bl & gold 1.25 *2.25*
a. Gold omitted 1,800. *700.00*
Nos. 275-280 (6) 2.80 *3.90*

19th centenary of St. Paul's shipwreck on Malta.

Stamp of 1860 — A55

Perf. 13x13½
1960, Dec. 1 Engr. Wmk. 314
281 A55 1½p multi .25 .25
282 A55 3p multi .35 .25
283 A55 6p multi .50 1.00
Nos. 281-283 (3) 1.10 1.50

Centenary of Malta's first postage stamp.

Fourth George Cross Issue

George Cross A56

Background designs: 3p, Sun and water. 1sh, Maltese crosses.

1961, Apr. 15 Photo. *Perf. 14½x14*
284 A56 1½p gray, bister & buff .25 .25
285 A56 3p ol gray, lt & dk grnsh blue .30 .25
286 A56 1sh ol green, vio & lil .70 2.25
Nos. 284-286 (3) 1.25 2.75

19th anniv. of the award of the George Cross to Malta.

Madonna Damascena — A57

Designs: 3p, Great Siege Monument by Antonio Sciortino. 6p, Grand Master La Valette (1557-1568). 1sh, Assault on Fort Elmo (old map).

Perf. 12½x12
1962, Sept. 7 Wmk. 314
287 A57 2p ultramarine .25 .25
288 A57 3p dark red .25 .25
289 A57 6p olive green .25 .25
290 A57 1sh rose lake .25 .40
Nos. 287-290 (4) 1.00 1.15

Great Siege of 1565 in which the knights of the Order of St. John and the Maltese Christians defeated the Turks.

Freedom from Hunger Issue
Common Design Type

1963, June 4 *Perf. 14x14½*
291 CD314 1sh6p sepia 2.00 2.00

Red Cross Centenary Issue
Common Design Type

1963, Sept. 2 Litho. *Perf. 13*
292 CD315 2p black & red .25 .25
293 CD315 1sh6p ultra & red 2.25 *4.50*

Type of 1956

Designs as before.

1963-64 Engr. *Perf. 11½*
296 A48 1p black .70 .50
297 A48 2p brown ('64) 2.10 *3.50*

David Bruce and Themistocles Zammit — A58

1sh6p, Goat and laboratory equipment.

Perf. 14x13½
1964, Apr. 14 Photo. Wmk. 314
298 A58 2p dl grn, blk & brn .25 .25
a. Black omitted *450.00*
299 A58 1sh6p rose lake & blk .90 *1.25*

Anti-Brucellosis (Malta fever) Congress of the UN FAO, Valletta, June 8-13.

Nicola Cottoner Attending Sick Man and Congress Emblem — A59

6p, Statue of St. Luke & St. Luke's Hospital. 1sh6p, Sacra Infermeria, Valletta.

Perf. 13½x14
1964, Sept. 5 Wmk. 354
300 A59 2p multicolored .25 .25
301 A59 6p multicolored .50 .55
302 A59 1sh6p multicolored 1.10 *1.75*
Nos. 300-302 (3) 1.85 2.55

1st European Cong. of Catholic Physicians, Malta, Sept. 6-10.

Independent State

Dove, Maltese Cross and British Crown — A60

Dove, Maltese Cross and: 3p, 1sh6p, Pope's tiara. 6p, 2sh6p, UN Emblem.

Perf. 14½x13½
1964, Sept. 21 Photo.
Gold and
303 A60 2p ol brn & red .35 .25
304 A60 3p dk red brn & red .40 .25
305 A60 6p sl blue & red .65 .25
306 A60 1sh ultra & red .75 .30
307 A60 1sh6p bl blk & red 2.00 1.00
308 A60 2sh6p vio bl & red 2.25 *3.00*
Nos. 303-308 (6) 6.40 5.05

Malta's independence.

Nativity — A61

Perf. 13x13½
1964, Nov. 3 Wmk. 354
309 A61 2p magenta & gold .25 .25
310 A61 4p ultra & gold .25 .25
311 A61 8p dp green & gold .45 .45
Nos. 309-311 (3) .95 .95

Cippus, Phoenician and Greek Inscriptions — A62

British Arms, Armory, Valletta A63

Designs (History of Malta): ½p, Neolithic (sculpture of sleeping woman). 1½p, Roman (sculpture). 2p, Proto-Christian (lamp, Roman temple, Chrismon). 2½p, Saracen (tomb, 12th cent.). 3p, Siculo Norman (arch, Palazzo Gatto-Murina, Notabile). 4p, Knights of Malta (lamp base, cross, and armor of knights). 4½p, Maltese navy (16th cent. galleons). 5p, Fortifications. 6p, French occupation (Cathedral of Notabile, cap, fasces). 10p, Naval Arsenal. 1sh, Maltese Corps of the British Army (insignia). 1sh3p, International Eucharistic Congress, 1913 (angels adoring Eucharist and map of Malta). 1sh6p, Self Government, 1921 (Knights of Malta Hall, present assembly seat). 2sh, Civic Council, Gozo (Statue of Livia, Gozo City Hall). 2sh6p, State of Malta (seated woman and George Cross). 3sh, Independence (doves, UN emblem, British crown, and Pope's tiara).

5sh, "HAFMED," (headquarters and insigne of Allied Forces, Mediterranean). 10sh, Map of Mediterranean. £1, Catholicism (Sts. Paul, Publius and Agatha).

Perf. 14x14½, 14½ (A63)
1965-70 Photo. Wmk. 354
312 A62 ½p violet & yel .25 .25
a. ½p double 10.00
b. ½p double, one inverted 2,250.
c. ½p omitted 85.00
313 A62 1p multi .25 .25
a. Booklet pane of 6 ('70) .85
314 A62 1½p multi .30 .25
315 A62 2p multi .25 .25
a. Gold omitted 26.00
b. Booklet pane of 6 ('70) 1.10
c. Imperf. pair 275.00
316 A62 2½p multi .25 .25
a. Gold ("SARACENIC") omitted 55.00
317 A62 3p multi .25 .25
a. Imperf., pair 300.00
b. Gold (windows) omitted 100.00
c. Pair, value omitted on one 1,100.
d. Silver ("MALTA") omitted 26.00
e. Silver ("MALTA") double 400.00
318 A62 4p multi 1.25 .25
a. Black (arms shading) omitted 70.00
b. Silver ("KNIGHTS OF MALTA") omitted 45.00
c. Silver ("MALTA") omitted 120.00
d. Imperf. pair 175.00
319 A62 4½p multi 1.25 .75
c. Silver ("MALTA") omitted 1,800.
319A A62 5p multi ('70) .30 .25
b. Booklet pane of 6 ('71) 1.75
320 A62 6p multi .30 .25
a. Black omitted 110.00
b. Silver ("MALTA") omitted 55.00
321 A63 8p multi .70 .25
321A A63 10p multi ('70) .50 *1.50*
322 A63 1sh multi .30 .25
323 A63 1sh3p multi 1.75 1.25
a. Imperf. pair 400.00
324 A63 1sh6p multi .60 .25
a. Queen's head omitted *375.00*
325 A63 2sh multi .70 .45
a. Gold date (1964) omitted *200.00*
326 A63 2sh6p multi .75 .50
327 A63 3sh multi 1.40 .60
328 A63 5sh multi 3.00 1.00
329 A63 10sh multi 2.50 *4.50*
a. Gold center emblem omitted *400.00*
330 A63 £1 multi 3.00 *4.75*
a. Pink (shading on figures) omitted 32.00
Nos. 312-330 (21) 19.85 18.30

Issued: 5p, 10p, 8/1/70; others 1/7/65.
For surcharges see Nos. 447-449, 521.

Dante, by Raphael — A64

1965, July 7 Unwmk. *Perf. 14*
331 A64 2p dark blue .25 .25
332 A64 6p olive green .25 .25
333 A64 2sh chocolate .95 *1.25*
Nos. 331-333 (3) 1.45 1.75

700th birth anniv. of Dante Alighieri.

Turkish Encampment and Fort St. Michael A65

Blockading Turkish Armada — A66

Designs: 3p, Knights and Turks in battle. 8p, Arrival of relief force. 1sh, Trophy, arms of Grandmaster Jean de La Valette. 1sh6p, Allegory of Victory, mural by Calabrese from St. John's Co-Cathedral. 2sh6p, Great Siege victory medal; Jean de La Valette on obverse, David slaying Goliath on reverse.

Perf. 14½x14, 13
1965, Sept. 1 Photo. Wmk. 354
334 A65 2p multicolored .25 .25
a. Flag (red) omitted *425.00*
335 A65 3p multicolored .25 .25
336 A66 6p multicolored .35 .25
a. Black omitted *375.00*
b. Gold omitted *375.00*
337 A65 8p multicolored .80 *.90*
a. Gold (flag & dates) omitted *180.00*
338 A66 1sh multicolored .40 .25
339 A65 1sh6p multicolored .90 .35
340 A65 2sh6p multicolored 1.75 *3.00*
Nos. 334-340 (7) 4.70 *5.25*

Great Siege (Turks against Malta), 4th cent.

The Three Wise Men A67

Perf. 11x11½
1965, Oct. 7 Photo. Wmk. 354
341 A67 1p dk purple & red .25 .25
342 A67 4p dk pur & blue .30 .30
343 A67 1sh3p dk pur & dp mag .35 .35
Nos. 341-343 (3) .90 .90

Winston Churchill, Map and Cross of Malta — A68

Winston Churchill: 3p, 1sh6p, Warships in Valletta Harbor and George Cross.

1966, Jan. 24 *Perf. 14½x14*
344 A68 2p blk, gold & red .25 .25
345 A68 3p dk grn, gold & blk .25 .25
a. Gold omitted 375.00
346 A68 1sh dp cl, gold & red .30 .25
a. Gold omitted 300.00
347 A68 1sh6p dk bl, gold & vio .45 *1.00*
Nos. 344-347 (4) 1.25 1.75

Grand Master Jean Parisot de la Valette — A69

3p, Pope St. Pius V. 6p, Map of Valletta. 1sh, Francesco Laparelli, Italian architect. 2sh6p, Girolamo Cassar, Maltese architect.

1966, Mar. 28 **Unwmk.** *Perf. 12*
348 A69 2p gold & multi .25 .25
349 A69 3p gold & multi .25 .25
a. Gold omitted 600.00
350 A69 6p gold & multi .25 .25
351 A69 1sh gold & multi .25 .25
352 A69 2sh6p gold & multi .30 .50
Nos. 348-352 (5) 1.30 1.50

400th anniversary of Valletta.

Kennedy — A70

Perf. 15x14
1966, May 28 **Photo.** **Wmk. 354**
353 A70 3p ol gray, blk & gold .25 .25
a. Gold omitted 300.00
354 A70 1sh6p dull bl, blk & gold .25 .25

President John F. Kennedy (1917-1963).

Trade Fair — A71

1966, June 16 *Perf. 13x13½*
355 A71 2p multicolored .25 .25
356 A71 8p gray & multi .25 .25
357 A71 2sh6p tan & multi .30 .90
Nos. 355-357 (3) .80 1.40

The 10th Malta Trade Fair.

Nativity — A72

1966, Oct. 7 **Photo.** **Wmk. 354**
358 A72 1p multicolored .25 .25
359 A72 4p multicolored .25 .25
360 A72 1sh3p multicolored .25 .25
Nos. 358-360 (3) .75 .75

George Cross — A73

1967, Mar. 1 *Perf. 14½x14*
361 A73 2p multicolored .25 .25
362 A73 4p multicolored .25 .25
363 A73 3sh slate & multi .25 .25
Nos. 361-363 (3) .75 .75

25th anniv. of the award of the George Cross to Malta and Gozo for the war effort.

Crucifixion of St. Peter — A74

Keys, Tiara, Bible, Cross and Sword — A75

Design: 3sh, Beheading of St. Paul.

Perf. 14½, 13½x14
1967, June 28 **Photo.** **Wmk. 354**
364 A74 2p black & brn orange .25 .25
365 A75 8p blk, gold & lt ol grn .25 .25
366 A74 3sh black & brt blue .25 .25
Nos. 364-366 (3) .75 .75

1900th anniv. of the martyrdom of the Apostles Peter and Paul.

St. Catherine of Siena by Melchior Gafá — A76

Sculptures by Gafá: 4p, St. Thomas from Villanova. 1sh6p, Christ's baptism. 2sh6p, St. John the Baptist.

1967, Aug. 1 *Perf. 13½*
367 A76 2p black, gold, buff & ultra .25 .25
368 A76 4p gold, buff, blk & grn .25 .25
369 A76 1sh6p gold, buff, blk & org brown .25 .25
370 A76 2sh6p black, gold, buff & dp car .25 .25
Nos. 367-370 (4) 1.00 1.00

Melchior Gafá (1635-67), Maltese sculptor.

Ruins of Megalithic Temples, Tarxien — A77

Designs: 6p, Facade of Palazzo Falzon, Notabile. 1sh, Facade of Old Parish Church, Birkirkara. 3sh, Entrance to Auberge de Castille.

1967, Sept. 12 **Photo.** *Perf. 14½*
371 A77 2p gold, Prus bl & blk .25 .25
372 A77 6p org brn, blk, gray & gold .25 .25
373 A77 1sh gold, ol, ind & blk .25 .25
374 A77 3sh dk car, rose, blk, gray & gold .25 .25
Nos. 371-374 (4) 1.00 1.00

Issued to publicize the 15th Congress of the History of Architecture, Malta, Sept. 12-16.

Nativity — A78

Design: 1sh4p, Angels facing left.

1967, Oct. 20 *Perf. 13½x14*
375 1p slate, gold & red .25 .25
a. Red omitted (stars) 120.00
376 8p slate, gold & red .25 .25
377 1sh4p slate, gold & red .25 .25
a. A78 Triptych, #375-377 .65 .65
Nos. 375-377 (3) .75 .75

Sheets of Nos. 375-377 were arranged in 2 ways: sheets containing 60 stamps of the same denomination arranged tête bêche, and sheets containing 20 triptychs.

Arms of Malta — A80

Designs: 4p, Queen Elizabeth II in the robes of the Order of St. Michael and St. George, vert. 3sh, Queen and map of Malta.

Perf. 14½x14, 14x14½
1967, Nov. 13 **Photo.** **Wmk. 354**
378 A80 2p slate & multi .25 .25
a. Grey-brown omitted 150.00
379 A80 4p dp claret, blk & gold .25 .25
380 A80 3sh black & gold .25 .30
Nos. 378-380 (3) .75 .80

Visit of Queen Elizabeth II, Nov. 14-17.

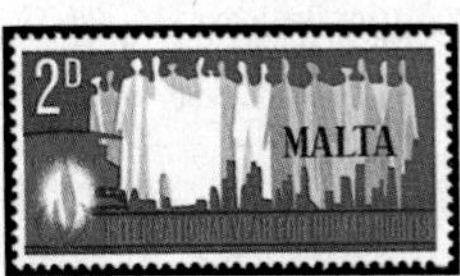

Human Rights Flame and People — A81

1968, May 2 **Photo.** *Perf. 14½*
Size: 40x19mm
381 A81 2p sepia, dp car, blk & gold .25 .25

Perf. 12x12½
Size: 24x24mm
382 A81 6p gray, dk blue, blk & gold .25 .25

Perf. 14½
Size: 40x19mm
383 A81 2sh gray, grnsh blue, blk & gold .25 .25
Nos. 381-383 (3) .75 .75

International Human Rights Year.

Fair Emblem — A82

Perf. 14x14½
1968, June 1 **Photo.** **Wmk. 354**
384 A82 4p black & multi .25 .25
385 A82 8p Prus blue & multi .25 .25
386 A82 3sh dp claret & multi .25 .25
Nos. 384-386 (3) .75 .75

12th Malta Intl. Trade Fair, July 1-15.

La Valette in Battle Dress — A83

La Valette's Tomb, Church of St. John, Valletta — A84

Designs: 1p, Arms of Order of St. John of Jerusalem and La Valette's arms, horiz. 2sh6p, Putti bearing shield with date of La Valette's death, and map of Malta.

Perf. 13x14, 14x13
1968, Aug. 1 **Photo.** **Wmk. 354**
387 A83 1p black & multi .25 .25
388 A83 8p dull blue & multi .25 .25
389 A84 1sh6p blue grn & multi .25 .25
390 A83 2sh6p dp claret & multi .25 .25
Nos. 387-390 (4) 1.00 1.00

400th anniv. of the death of Grand Master Jean de La Valette (1494-1568).

Star of Bethlehem, Shepherds and Angel A85

8p, Nativity. 1sh4p, The Three Wise Men.

Perf. 14½x14
1968, Oct. 3 **Wmk. 354**
391 A85 1p multicolored .25 .25
392 A85 8p gray & multi .25 .25
393 A85 1sh4p tan & multi .25 .25
Nos. 391-393 (3) .75 .75

Christmas. Printed in sheets of 60 with alternate rows inverted.

"Agriculture" — A86

1sh, Greek medal and FAO emblem. 2sh6p, Woman symbolizing soil care.

1968, Oct. 21 **Photo.** *Perf. 12½x12*
394 A86 4p ultra & multi .25 .25
395 A86 1sh gray & multi .25 .25
396 A86 2sh6p multicolored .25 .25
Nos. 394-396 (3) .75 .75

6th Regional Congress for Europe of the FAO, Malta, Oct. 28-31.

Mahatma Gandhi — A87

Perf. 12x12½
1969, Mar. 24 **Photo.** **Wmk. 354**
397 A87 1sh6p gold, blk & sepia .75 .75

Birth cent. of Mohandas K. Gandhi (1869-1948), leader in India's struggle for independence.

ILO Emblem A88

1969, May 26 *Perf. 13½x14½*

398	A88	2p indigo, blue grn & gold	.25	.25
399	A88	6p brn blk, red brn & gold	.25	.25

50th anniv. of the ILO.

Sea Bed, UN Emblem and Dove — A89

Designs: 2p, Robert Samut, bar of music and coat of arms. 10p, Map of Malta and homing birds. 2sh, Grand Master Pinto and arms of Malta University.

1969, July 26 **Photo.** *Perf. 13½*

400	A89	2p vio blk, blk, gold & red	.25	.25
401	A89	5p gray, Prus blue, gold & blk	.25	.25
402	A89	10p olive, blk & gold	.25	.25
403	A89	2sh dk olive, blk, red & gold	.25	.25
		Nos. 400-403 (4)	1.00	1.00

Cent. of the birth of Robert Samut, composer of Natl. Anthem (2p); UN resolution on peaceful uses of the sea bed (5p); convention of Maltese emigrants (10p), Aug. 3-16; bicent. of the founding of Malta University (2sh).

June 17, 1919, Uprising Monument A90

"Tourism" A91

Designs: 5p, Maltese flag and 5 doves, horiz. 1sh6p, Dove and emblems of Malta, UN and Council of Euorpe. 2sh6p, Dove and symbols of trade and industry.

Perf. 13x12½

1969, Sept. 20 **Photo.** **Wmk. 354**

404	A90	2p black, gray, buff & gold	.25	.25
405	A91	5p gray, blk, red & gold	.25	.25
406	A91	10p gold, Prus blue, gray & blk	.25	.25
407	A91	1sh6p gold, olive & multi	.25	.25
408	A91	2sh6p gold, brn ol, gray & blk	.25	.50
		Nos. 404-408 (5)	1.25	1.50

Fifth anniversary of independence.

St. John the Baptist in Robe of Knight of Malta A92

Mortar and Jars from Infirmary — A93

Designs: 1p, The Beheading of St. John By Caravaggio. 5p, Interior of St. John's Co-Cathedral. 6p, Allegory depicting functions of the Order. 8p, St. Jerome, by Caravaggio. 1sh6p, St. Gerard Receiving Godfrey de Bouillon, 1093, by Antoine de Favray. 2sh, Sacred vestments.

Perf. 14x13 (1p, 8p); 13½x14 (2p, 6p, 1sh6p); 13½ (5p) 12x12½ (10p, 2sh)

1970, Mar. 21 **Photo.** **Wmk. 354**

409	A92	1p black & multi	.25	.25
410	A92	2p black & multi	.25	.25
411	A92	5p black & multi	.25	.25
412	A92	6p black & multi	.25	.25
413	A92	8p black & multi	.25	.50
414	A93	10p black & multi	.25	.25
415	A92	1sh6p black & multi	.25	.40
416	A93	2sh black & multi	.25	.55
		Nos. 409-416 (8)	2.00	2.70

13th Council of Europe Art Exhibition in honor of the Order of St. John in Malta, Apr. 2-July 1.

Sizes: 1p, 8p, 54x38mm; 2p, 6p, 44x30mm; 5p, 37x37mm; 10p, 2sh, 60x19mm; 1sh6p, 44x33mm.

EXPO '70 Emblem — A94

1970, May 29 *Perf. 15*

417	A94	2p gold & multi	.25	.25
418	A94	5p gold & multi	.25	.25
419	A94	3sh gold & multi	.25	.25
		Nos. 417-419 (3)	.75	.75

Issued to publicize EXPO '70 International Exhibition, Osaka, Japan, Mar. 15-Sept. 13.

UN Emblem, Dove, Scales and Symbolic Figure — A95

Perf. 14x14½

1970, Sept. 30 **Litho.** **Wmk. 354**

420	A95	2p brown & multi	.25	.25
421	A95	5p purple & multi	.25	.25
422	A95	2sh6p vio blue & multi	.25	.25
		Nos. 420-422 (3)	.75	.75

25th anniversary of the United Nations.

Books and Quill — A96

Dun Karm, Books and Pens — A97

Perf. 13x14

1971, Mar. 20 **Litho.** **Wmk. 354**

423	A96	1sh6p multicolored	.25	.25
424	A97	2sh black & multi	.25	.25

No. 423 issued in memory of Canon Gian Pietro Francesco Agius Sultana (De Soldanis; 1712-1770), historian and writer; No. 424 for the centenary of the birth of Mgr. Karm Psaila (Dun Karm, 1871-1961), Maltese poet.

Europa Issue, 1971

Common Design Type

1971, May 3 *Perf. 13½x14½*

Size: 32x22mm

425	CD14	2p olive, org & blk	.25	.25
426	CD14	5p ver, org & black	.25	.25
427	CD14	1sh6p gray, org & blk	*.30*	*.30*
		Nos. 425-427 (3)	*.80*	*.80*

St. Joseph, by Giuseppe Cali — A98

Design: 5p, 1sh6p, Statue of Our Lady of Victory. 10p, Like 2p.

Perf. 13x13½

1971, July 24 **Litho.** **Wmk. 354**

428	A98	2p dk blue & multi	.25	.25
429	A98	5p gray & multi	.25	.25
430	A98	10p multicolored	.25	.25
431	A98	1sh6p multicolored	.25	.45
		Nos. 428-431 (4)	1.00	1.20

Centenary (in 1970) of the proclamation of St. Joseph as patron of the Universal Church (2p, 10p), and 50th anniversary of the coronation of the statue of Our Lady of Victory in Senglea, Malta.

Blue Rock Thrush — A99

Design: 2p, 1sh6p, Thistle, vert.

Perf. 14x14½, 14½x14

1971, Sept. 18

432	A99	2p multicolored	.25	.25
433	A99	5p bister & multi	.25	.25
434	A99	10p orange & multi	.30	.30
435	A99	1sh6p bister & multi	.35	1.00
		Nos. 432-435 (4)	1.15	1.80

Heart and WHO Emblem A100

1972, Mar. 20 *Perf. 14*

436	A100	2p yel green & multi	.25	.25
437	A100	10p lilac & multi	.25	.25
438	A100	2sh6p lt blue & multi	.30	.75
		Nos. 436-438 (3)	.80	1.25

World Health Day, Apr. 7.

Coin Showing Mnara (Lampstand) — A101

Decimal Currency Coins: 2m, Maltese Cross. 3m, Bee and honeycomb. 1c, George Cross. 2c, Penthesilea. 5c, Altar, Megalithic Period. 10c, Grandmaster's Barge, 18th century. 50c, Great Siege Monument, by Antonio Sciortino.

Perf. 14 (16x21mm), 2m, 3m, 2c; Perf. 14½x14 (21x26mm), 5m, 1c, 5c

1972, May 16

439	A101	2m rose red & multi	.25	.25
440	A101	3m pink & multi	.25	.25
441	A101	5m lilac & multi	.25	.25
442	A101	1c multicolored	.25	.25
443	A101	2c orange & multi	.25	.25
444	A101	5c multicolored	.25	.25

Perf. 13½

Size: 27x35mm

445	A101	10c yellow & multi	.25	.25
446	A101	50c multicolored	1.10	1.10
		Nos. 439-446 (8)	2.85	2.85

Coins to mark introduction of decimal currency.

Nos. 319A, 321 and 323 Surcharged with New Value and 2 Bars

Perf. 14x14½, 14½

1972, Sept. 30 **Photo.** **Wmk. 354**

447	A62	1c3m on 5p multi	.25	.25
448	A63	3c on 8p multi	.25	.25
449	A63	5c on 1sh3p multi	.25	.25
		Nos. 447-449 (3)	.75	.75

Europa Issue 1972

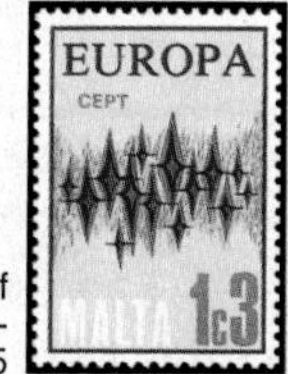

Sparkles, Symbolic of Communications — CD15

1972, Nov. 11 **Litho.** *Perf. 13x13½*

450	CD15	1c3m yellow & multi	.25	.25
451	CD15	3c multicolored	.25	.25
452	CD15	5c pink & multi	*.25*	*.30*
453	CD15	7c5m multicolored	*.30*	*.60*
		Nos. 450-453 (4)	1.05	1.40

Issued in sheets of 10 plus 2 labels (4x3). Labels are in top row.

Archaeology — A103

1973, Mar. 31 **Litho.** *Perf. 13½*

Size: 22x24mm

454	A103	2m shown	.25	.25
455	A103	4m History (knights)	.25	.25
456	A103	5m Folklore	.25	.25
457	A103	8m Industry	.25	.25
458	A103	1c Fishing	.25	.25
459	A103	1c3m Pottery	.25	.25
460	A103	2c Agriculture	.25	.25
461	A103	3c Sport	.25	.25
462	A103	4c Marina	.25	.25
463	A103	5c Fiesta	.25	.25
464	A103	7c5m Regatta	.25	.25
465	A103	10c Charity (St. Martin)	.25	.25
466	A103	50c Education	1.75	.50
467	A103	£1 Religion	2.50	2.00

Perf. 13½x14

Size: 32x27mm

468	A103	£2 Arms of Malta	7.75	*12.50*
		Nos. 454-468 (15)	15.00	18.00

Europa Issue 1973

Common Design Type

1973, June 2 **Unwmk.** *Perf. 14*

Size: 36½x19½mm

469	CD16	3c multicolored	.25	.25
470	CD16	5c multicolored	*.25*	*.35*
471	CD16	7c5m dk bl & multi	*.40*	*.60*
		Nos. 469-471 (3)	.90	1.20

Woman with Grain, FAO Emblem — A104

7c5m, Mother and child, WHO emblem. 10c, Two heads, Human Rights flame.

1973, Oct. 6 **Wmk. 354** *Perf. 13½*

472	A104	1c3m yel grn, blk & gold	.25	.25
473	A104	7c5m ultra, blk & gold	.25	.40
474	A104	10c claret, blk & gold	.30	.50
		Nos. 472-474 (3)	.80	1.15

World Food Program, 10th anniv.; WHO, 25th anniv.; Universal Declaration of Human Rights, 25th anniv.

Girolamo Cassar, Architect — A105

3c, Giuseppe Barth, opthalmologist. 5c, Nicolo' Isouard, composer. 7c5m, John Borg, botanist. 10c, Antonio Sciortino, sculptor.

1974, Jan. 12 Litho. *Perf. 14*

475 A105 1c3m slate green & gold .25 .25
476 A105 3c indigo & gold .25 .25
477 A105 5c olive gray & gold .25 .25
478 A105 7c5m slate blue & gold .25 .30
479 A105 10c brn vio & gold .25 .45
Nos. 475-479 (5) 1.25 1.50

Prominent Maltese.

Statue of Goddess, 3rd Millenium B.C. A106

Europa (CEPT Emblem and): 3c, Carved door, Cathedral, Mdina, 11th cent, vert. 5c, Silver monstrance, 1689. 7c5m, "Vettina" (statue of nude woman), by Antonio Sciortino (1879-1947), vert.

1974, July 13 *Perf. 13½x14, 14x13½*

480 A106 1c3m gray blue, blk & gold .25 .25
481 A106 3c ol brn, blk & gold .25 .25
482 A106 5c lilac, blk & gold *.25 .40*
483 A106 7c5m dull grn, blk & gold *.40 .90*
Nos. 480-483 (4) 1.15 1.80

Heinrich von Stephan, Coach and Train, UPU Emblem A107

UPU Emblem, von Stephan and: 5c, Paddle steamer and ocean liner. 7c5m, Balloon and jet. 50c, UPU Congress Building, Lausanne, and UPU Headquarters, Bern.

Wmk. 354

1974, Sept. Litho. *Perf. 13½*

484 A107 1c3m multicolored .30 .25
485 A107 5c multicolored .30 .30
486 A107 7c5m multicolored .40 .40
487 A107 50c multicolored 1.10 1.10
a. Souvenir sheet of 4, #484-487 5.25 *7.00*
Nos. 484-487 (4) 2.10 2.05

Centenary of Universal Postal Union.

President, Prime Minister, Minister of Justice at Microphone — A108

1c3m, President, Prime Minister, Speaker at Swearing-in ceremony. 5c, Flag of Malta.

1975, Mar. 31 *Perf. 14*

488 A108 1c3m red & multi .25 .25
489 A108 5c gray, red & black .25 .25
490 A108 25c red & multi .60 *1.00*
Nos. 488-490 (3) 1.10 1.50

Proclamation of the Republic, Dec. 13, 1974.

IWY Emblem, Mother and Child A109

Designs: 3c, 20c, Secretary (woman in public life), IWY emblem. 5c, Like 1c3m.

Wmk. 354

1975, May 30 Litho. *Perf. 13*

491 A109 1c3m violet & gold .25 .25
492 A109 3c blue gray & gold .25 .25
493 A109 5c olive & gold .25 .25
494 A109 20c red brown & gold 1.25 *2.50*
Nos. 491-494 (4) 2.00 3.25

International Women's Year.

Allegory of Malta, by Francesco de Mura — A110

Europa: 15c, Judith and Holofernes, by Valentin de Boulogne.

1975, July 15 Litho. *Perf. 14*

495 A110 5c multicolored *.30 .30*
496 A110 15c multicolored *.80 .80*

Floor Plan of Ggantija Complex, 3000 B.C. — A111

Designs: 3c, View of Mdina. 5c, Typical Maltese town. 25c, Fort St. Angelo.

1975, Sept. 16 *Perf. 14*

497 A111 1c3m black & org .25 .25
498 A111 3c org, pur & black .25 .25
499 A111 5c gray, black & org .40 .25
500 A111 25c org, tan & black 1.25 *2.75*
Nos. 497-500 (4) 2.15 3.50

European Architectural Heritage Year.

"Right to Work" — A112

Designs: 5c, Protection of the Environment (Landscape). 25c, Maltese flags.

1975, Dec. 12 Litho. Wmk. 354

501 A112 1c3m multicolored .25 .25
502 A112 5c multicolored .25 .25
503 A112 25c multicolored .70 *1.00*
Nos. 501-503 (3) 1.20 1.50

First anniversary of Malta Republic.

Republic Coat of Arms — A113

Perf. 13½x14

1976, Jan. 28 Litho. Wmk. 354

504 A113 £2 black & multi 8.00 *13.00*

Feast of Sts. Peter and Paul — A114

Designs: 1c3m, "Festa" (flags and fireworks), vert. 7c5m, Carnival. 10c, Good Friday (Christ carrying cross), vert.

1976, Feb. 26 Litho. *Perf. 14*

505 A114 1c3m multicolored .25 .25
506 A114 5c multicolored .25 .25
507 A114 7c5m multicolored .35 *.60*
508 A114 10c multicolored .55 *1.25*
Nos. 505-508 (4) 1.40 2.35

Maltese folk festivals.

Water Polo, Olympic Rings A115

Olympic Rings and: 5c, Yachting. 30c, Running.

1976, Apr. 28 Litho. *Perf. 13½x14*

509 A115 1c7m sl green & red .25 .25
510 A115 5c dp blue & red .25 .25
511 A115 30c sepia & red .90 *1.40*
Nos. 509-511 (3) 1.40 1.90

21st Olympic Games, Montreal, Canada, July 17-Aug. 1.

Europa A116

1976, July 8 Litho. Wmk. 354

512 A116 7c Lace-making *.35 .35*
513 A116 15c Stone carving *.65 .65*

Grandmaster Nicola Cotoner, Founder — A117

5c, Dissected arm & hand. 7c, Dr. Fra Giuseppe Zammit, 1st professor. 11c, School & balustrade.

1976, Sept. 14 Litho. *Perf. 13½*

514 A117 2c multicolored .25 .25
515 A117 5c multicolored .25 .25
516 A117 7c multicolored .25 .25
517 A117 11c multicolored .35 *.65*
Nos. 514-517 (4) 1.10 1.40

School of Anatomy and Surgery, Valletta, 300th anniversary.

Armor of Grand Master Jean de La Valette — A118

Suits of Armor: 7c, Grand Master Aloph de Wignacourt. 11c, Grand Commander Jean Jacques de Verdelin.

1977, Jan. 20 Litho. Wmk. 354

518 A118 2c green & multi .25 .25
519 A118 7c brown & multi .25 .25
520 A118 11c ultra & multi .30 *.50*
Nos. 518-520 (3) .80 1.00

No. 318 Surcharged with New Value and Bar

1977, Mar. 24 Photo. *Perf. 14x14½*

521 A62 1c7m on 4p multi .40 .25

Annunciation, Tapestry after Rubens — A119

Crucifixion — A120

Tapestries after Designs by Rubens: 7c, The Four Evangelists. 11c, Nativity. 20c, Adoration of the Kings.

Flemish tapestries commissioned for St. John's Co-Cathedral, Valletta.

Wmk. 354

1977, Mar. 30 Litho. *Perf. 14*

522 A119 2c multicolored .25 .25
523 A119 7c multicolored .30 .25
524 A120 11c multicolored .40 .45
525 A120 20c multicolored .70 *1.00*

1978, Jan. 26

Flemish Tapestries: 2c, Jesus' Entry into Jerusalem, by unknown painter. 7c, Last Supper, by Nicholas Poussin. 11c, Crucifixion, by Rubens. 25c, Resurrection, by Rubens.

526 A120 2c multicolored .25 .25
527 A120 7c multicolored .35 .25
528 A120 11c multicolored .45 .35
529 A120 25c multicolored .80 .80

1979, Jan. 24

Tapestries after Designs by Rubens (Triumph of): 2c, Catholic Church. 7c, Charity. 11c, Faith. 25c, Truth.

530 A119 2c multicolored .25 .25
531 A119 7c multicolored .40 .25
532 A119 11c multicolored .45 .40
533 A119 25c multicolored .90 .90
Nos. 522-533 (12) 5.50 5.40

Consecration of St. John's Co-Cathedral, Valetta, 400th anniv. (Nos. 522-533). Peter Paul Rubens (1577-1640; Nos. 522-525).

See Nos. 567-569.

Malta Map, Telecommunication — A121

Designs: 1c, 6c, Map of Italy, Sicily, Malta and North Africa, telecommunication tower and waves, vert. 17c, like 8c.

Perf. 14x13½, 13½x14

1977, May 17 Litho. Wmk. 354

535 A121 1c green, red & blk .25 .25
536 A121 6c multicolored .25 .25
537 A121 8c multicolored .30 .30
538 A121 17c purple, red & blk .50 .50
Nos. 535-538 (4) 1.30 1.30

World Telecommunication Day.

View of Ta' L-Isperanza — A122

Europa: 20c, Harbor, Is-Salini.

1977, July Litho. *Perf. 13½*

539 A122 7c multicolored *.30 .25*
540 A122 20c multicolored *.50 .90*

Issued in sheets of 10.

Help Given Handicapped Worker — A123

7c, Stonemason & shipbuilder. 20c, Mother holding dead son, & Service to the Republic order, horiz. Sculptures from Workers' Monument.

1977, Oct. 12 Litho. Wmk. 354

541 A123 2c red brown & brn .25 .25
542 A123 7c brown & dk brn .25 .25
543 A123 20c multicolored .55 .55
Nos. 541-543 (3) 1.05 1.05

Tribute to Maltese workers.

Lady on Horseback and Soldier, by Dürer — A124

Dürer Engravings: 8c, Bagpiper. 17c, Madonna with Long-tailed Monkey.

1978, Mar. 7 ***Perf. 14***

544 A124 1c7m dk blue, blk & red .25 .25
545 A124 8c gray, blk & red .25 .25
546 A124 17c dk grn, blk & red .45 .45
Nos. 544-546 (3) .95 .95

Albrecht Dürer (1471-1528), German painter and engraver.

Grand Master Nicola Cotoner Monument — A125

Europa: 25c, Grand Master Ramon Perellos monument, by Giusepe Mazzuoli. The monument on 7c is believed to be the work of Giovanni Batista Foggini.

1978, Apr. 26 ***Perf. 14x13½***

547 A125 7c multicolored *.25 .25*
548 A125 25c multicolored *.75 .90*

Goalkeeper — A126

Argentina '78 Emblem and: 11c, 15c, different soccer scenes.

Perf. 14x13½

1978, June 6 Litho. Wmk. 354

549 A126 2c multicolored .25 .25
550 A126 11c multicolored .25 .25
551 A126 15c multicolored .50 .50
a. Souvenir sheet of 3, #549-551 2.00 *2.50*
Nos. 549-551 (3) 1.00 1.00

11th World Cup Soccer Championship, Argentina, June 1-25.

Fishing Boat — A127

Designs: 5c, 17c Changing of colors. 7c, 20c, British soldier and oranges. 8c, like 2c.

1979, Mar. 31 ***Perf. 14***

552 A127 2c claret & multi .25 .25
553 A127 5c claret & multi .25 .25
554 A127 7c claret & multi .25 .25
555 A127 8c dk blue & multi .30 .30
556 A127 17c dk blue & multi .35 .35
557 A127 20c dk blue & multi .40 .40
Nos. 552-557 (6) 1.80 1.80

End of military agreement between Malta and Great Britain.

Maltese Speronara and AirMalta Fuselage — A128

Europa: 25c, Coastal watch tower and radio link tower.

1979, May 9

558 A128 7c multicolored *.25 .25*
559 A128 25c multicolored *.90 .90*

Children and Globe — A129

Designs: 7c, Children flying kites. 11c, Children in a circle holding hands.

1979, June 13 ***Perf. 14x13½, 14***

Size: 20x38mm

560 A129 2c multicolored .25 .25

Size: 27x33mm

561 A129 7c multicolored .25 .25
562 A129 11c multicolored .25 .25
Nos. 560-562 (3) .75 .75

International Year of the Child.

Loggerhead Turtle — A130

Marine Life: 2c, Gibbula nivosa. 7c, Dolphinfish. 25c, Noble pen shell.

1979, Oct. 10 Litho. ***Perf. 13½***

563 A130 2c multicolored .25 .25
564 A130 5c multicolored .25 .25
565 A130 7c multicolored .25 .25
566 A130 25c multicolored .75 *1.25*
Nos. 563-566 (4) 1.50 2.00

Tapestry Types of 1977-79

Tapestries after Designs by Rubens: 2c, The Institution of Corpus Domini. 8c, The Destruction of Idolatry. 50c, Portrait of Grand Master Perellos, vert.

1980, Jan. 30 Wmk. 354 ***Perf. 14***

567 A120 2c multicolored .25 .25
568 A120 8c multicolored .30 .30

Souvenir Sheet

569 A119 50c multicolored 1.50 1.50

Victoria Citadel, Gozo A131

Monument Restoration (UNESCO Emblem and): 2c5m, Hal Saflieni Catacombs, Paola, 2500 B.C., vert. 6c, Vilhena Palace, Mdina, 18th century, vert. 12c, St. Elmo Fort, Valletta, 16th century.

1980, Feb. 15

570 A131 2c5m multicolored .25 .25
571 A131 6c multicolored .25 .25
572 A131 8c multicolored .25 .25
573 A131 12c multicolored .35 .35
Nos. 570-573 (4) 1.10 1.10

Don Gorg Preca (1880-1962), Founder of Soc. of Christian Doctrine — A132

1980, Apr. 12 Litho. ***Perf. 14x13½***

574 A132 2c5m gray violet .30 .30

Ruzar Briffa (1906-1963), Poet, by Vincent Apap — A133

Europa (Vincent Apap Sculpture): 30c, Mikiel Anton Vassalli (1764-1829), freedom fighter and scholar.

1980, Apr. 29 ***Perf. 13½x14***

575 A133 8c slate grn & dp bis *.25 .25*
576 A133 30c brown red & olive *.70 1.10*

Chess Pieces A134

Designs: Chess pieces. 30c, vert.

1980, Nov. Litho. ***Perf. 14***

577 A134 2c5m multicolored .25 .25
578 A134 8c multicolored .45 .45
579 A134 30c multicolored .75 *1.50*
Nos. 577-579 (3) 1.45 2.20

Chess Olympiad, Valletta, Nov. 20-Dec. 8.

Barn Owl — A135

1981, Jan. 20 Wmk. 354 ***Perf. 13½***

580 A135 3c shown .30 .30
581 A135 8c Sardinian warbler .50 .50
582 A135 12c Woodchat shrike .60 .60
583 A135 23c Stormy petrel 1.00 *1.75*
Nos. 580-583 (4) 2.40 3.15

Europa Issue

Climbing the Gostra (Greasy Pole) — A136

1981, Apr. 28 Litho. ***Perf. 14***

584 A136 8c Horse race *.30 .30*
585 A136 30c shown *.75 1.00*

25th Intl. Fair of Malta, Naxxar, July 1-15 — A137

1981, June 12 ***Perf. 13½***

586 A137 4c multicolored .25 .25
587 A137 25c multicolored .75 .75

Disabled Artist — A138

1981, July 17 Litho. ***Perf. 13½***

588 A138 3c shown .25 .25
589 A138 35c Boy on crutches .85 .85

Intl. Year of the Disabled.

World Food Day — A139

1981, Oct. 16 Litho. ***Perf. 14***

590 A139 8c multicolored .25 .25
591 A139 23c multicolored .90 .90

Men Hauling Building Stone — A140

1981, Oct. 31 Wmk. 354 ***Perf. 14***

592 A140 5m shown .25 .25
593 A140 1c Growing cotton .25 .25
594 A140 2c Ship building .50 .25
595 A140 3c Minting coins .30 .25
596 A140 5c Artistic achievements .30 .25
597 A140 6c Fishing .90 .25
598 A140 7c Farming .30 *.80*
599 A140 8c Quarrying .85 .35
600 A140 10c Grape pressing .35 *.40*
601 A140 12c Ship repairing 1.50 1.50
602 A140 15c Energy .70 *1.00*
603 A140 20c Communications .75 .75
604 A140 25c Factories 1.00 *1.40*
605 A140 50c Water drilling 2.75 2.50
606 A140 £1 Sea transport 4.50 *5.25*
607 A140 £3 Air transport 10.00 *15.00*
Nos. 592-607 (16) 25.20 30.45

Shipbuilding and Repairing, Tarznar Shipyards — A141

1982, Jan. 29 Litho. ***Perf. 13½x14***

608 A141 3c Assembly sheds .25 .25
609 A141 8c Ships in dry dock .35 .35
610 A141 13c Tanker .65 .65
611 A141 27c Tanker, diff. 1.25 1.25
Nos. 608-611 (4) 2.50 2.50

Man and Home for the Elderly A142

1982, Mar. 16 Litho. *Perf. 14*
612 A142 8c shown .35 .35
613 A142 30c Woman, hospital 1.50 1.50

Europa Issue

Redemption of the Islands, 1428 — A143

30c, Declaration of Rights, 1802.

1982, Apr. 29 Litho. *Perf. 14*
614 A143 8c shown *.30 .30*
615 A143 30c multicolored *1.10 1.40*

1982 World Cup — A144

Designs: Various soccer players.

1982, June 11 Litho. *Perf. 14*
616 A144 3c multicolored .25 .25
617 A144 12c multicolored .60 .60
618 A144 15c multicolored .80 .80
a. Souvenir sheet of 3, #616-618 4.25 4.25
Nos. 616-618 (3) 1.65 1.65

Brigantine — A145

1982, Nov. 13 Litho.
619 A145 3c shown .40 .40
619A A145 8c Tartana .75 .75
619B A145 12c Xebec .90 .90
619C A145 20c Speronara 1.60 1.60
Nos. 619-619C (4) 3.65 3.65

See Nos. 637-640, 670-673, 686-689, 703-706.

Malta Railway Centenary — A146

3c, Manning Wardle, 1883. 13c, Black Hawthorn, 1884. 27c, Beyer Peacock, 1895.

1983, Jan. 21 Wmk. 354 *Perf. 14*
620 A146 3c multicolored .50 .25
621 A146 13c multicolored 1.00 1.00
622 A146 27c multicolored 2.25 *3.25*
Nos. 620-622 (3) 3.75 4.50

Commonwealth Day — A147

1983, Mar. 14
623 A147 8c Map .35 .35
624 A147 12c Transportation .40 .40
625 A147 15c Beach, vert. .45 .45
626 A147 23c Industry, vert. .60 *1.00*
Nos. 623-626 (4) 1.80 2.20

Europa Issue

Megalithic Temples, Ggantija — A148

Wmk. 354

1983, May 5 Litho. *Perf. 14*
627 A148 8c shown *.30 .30*
628 A148 30c Fort St. Angelo *1.20 1.20*

World Communications Year — A149

Perf. 13½x14

1983, July 14 Litho. Wmk. 354
629 A149 3c Dish antennas .25 .25
630 A149 7c Ships .40 .40
631 A149 13c Trucks .85 .85
632 A149 20c Games emblem 1.40 *2.25*
Nos. 629-632 (4) 2.90 3.75

25th anniv. of Intl. Maritime Org. (7c); 30th anniv. of Customs Cooperation Council (13c); 9th Mediterranean Games, Casablanca, 9/3-17 (20c).

Monsignor Giuseppe De Piro (1877-1933), Founder of Missionary Society of St. Paul — A150

1983, Sept. 1 Litho. *Perf. 14*
633 A150 3c multicolored .40 .40

40th Anniv. of General Workers' Union — A151

1983, Oct. 5 Litho. *Perf. 14x13½*
634 A151 3c Founding rally .25 .25
635 A151 8c Family, workers .40 .40
636 A151 27c Headquarters 1.40 1.40
Nos. 634-636 (3) 2.05 2.05

Ships Type of 1982

1983, Nov. 17 Litho. *Perf. 14x13½*
637 A145 2c Strangier, 1813 .35 .35
638 A145 12c Tigre 1839 .90 .90
639 A145 13c La Speranza, 1844 1.00 1.00
640 A145 20c Wignacourt 1844 1.40 *2.75*
Nos. 637-640 (4) 3.65 5.00

Europa (1959-1984) A152

1984, Apr. 27 Wmk. 354 *Perf. 14*
641 A152 8c multicolored *.35 .35*
642 A152 30c multicolored *1.25 1.25*

Police Force, 170th Anniv. — A153

3c, Officer, 1880. 8c, Mounted policeman. 11c, Officer on motorcycle. 25c, Traffic duty, firemen.

1984, June 14 Litho. *Perf. 14x13½*
643 A153 3c multi .70 .70
644 A153 8c multi 1.25 1.25
645 A153 11c multi 1.50 1.50
646 A153 25c multi 2.25 2.25
Nos. 643-646 (4) 5.70 5.70

1984 Summer Olympics — A154

1984, July 26 Litho. *Perf. 13½x14*
647 A154 7c Running .35 .35
648 A154 12c Gymnastics .60 .60
649 A154 23c Swimming .95 .95
Nos. 647-649 (3) 1.90 1.90

10th Anniv. of Republic — A155

1984, Dec. 12 Litho. Wmk. 354
650 A155 3c Dove on map .35 .35
651 A155 8c Fortress .75 .75
652 A155 30c Hands 2.40 *4.50*
Nos. 650-652 (3) 3.50 5.60

Malta Post Office Cent. — A156

1985, Jan. 2 Litho. *Perf. 14*
653 A156 3c No. 8 .40 .45
654 A156 8c No. 9 .65 .60
655 A156 12c No. 11 .90 .90
656 A156 20c No. 12 1.40 *3.00*
a. Souvenir sheet of 4, #653-656 3.75 3.75
Nos. 653-656 (4) 3.35 4.95

International Youth Year — A157

13c, Three youths, vert. 27c, Female holding flame.

1985, Mar. 7 *Perf. 14x13½, 13½x14*
657 A157 2c shown .25 .25
658 A157 13c multi .70 .70
659 A157 27c multi 1.25 1.25
Nos. 657-659 (3) 2.20 2.20

European Music Year — A158

Europa: 8c, Nicolo Baldacchino (1895-1971), tenor. 30c, Francesco Azopardi (1748-1809), composer.

1985, Apr. 25 Litho. *Perf. 14*
660 A158 8c multicolored *1.00 1.00*
661 A158 30c multicolored *3.00 3.00*

Guzeppi Bajada and Manwel Attard, Martyrs A159

7c, Karmnu Abela, Wenzu Dyer. 35c, June 7 Uprising Memorial Monument, vert.

1985, June 7 *Perf. 14x14½, 14½x14*
662 A159 3c multicolored .30 .30
663 A159 7c multicolored .55 .55
664 A159 35c multicolored 1.60 1.60
Nos. 662-664 (3) 2.45 2.45

June 7 Uprising, 66th anniv.

UN, 40th Anniv. A160

1985, July 26 *Perf. 13½x14*
665 A160 4c Stylized birds .25 .25
666 A160 11c Arrows .60 *1.00*
667 A160 31c Human figures 1.60 *3.00*
Nos. 665-667 (3) 2.45 *4.25*

Famous Men — A161

Portraits: 8c, George Mitrovich (1794-1885), politician and author, novel frontispiece, The Cause of the People of Malta Now Before Parliament. 12c, Pietru Caxaru (1438-1485), scholar, manuscript.

1985, Oct. 3 *Perf. 14*
668 A161 8c multicolored .85 .35
669 A161 12c multicolored 1.30 *2.25*

Ships Type of 1982

3c, Scotia paddle steamer, 1844. 7c, Tagliaferro, 1882. 15c, Gleneagles, 1885. 23c, L'Isle Adam, 1886.

1985, Nov. 27
670 A145 3c multi .85 .25
671 A145 7c multi 1.25 .75
672 A145 15c multi 1.75 *2.50*
673 A145 23c multi 3.00 *3.50*
Nos. 670-673 (4) 6.85 7.00

Intl. Peace Year A162

8c, John XXIII Peace Laboratory. 11c, Unity. 27c, Peaceful coexistence.

Perf. 14x14½, 13½x14 (#675)

1986, Jan. 28 Litho. Wmk. 354

674 A162 8c multi 1.25 .40
675 A162 11c multi 1.50 1.50
676 A162 27c multi 2.50 *4.50*
Nos. 674-676 (3) 5.25 6.40

Size of No. 675: 43x27mm.

Europa Issue

Butterflies A163

35c, Earth, air, fire and water.

1986, Apr. 3 ***Perf. 14½x14***

677 A163 8c shown *.75 .75*
678 A163 35c multi *3.00 3.00*

1986 World Cup Soccer Championships, Mexico — A164

3c, Heading the ball. 7c, Goalie catching ball. 23c, Dribbling.

1986, May 30 Wmk. 354 ***Perf. 14***

679 A164 3c multi .60 .25
680 A164 7c multi 1.25 .70
681 A164 23c multi 3.25 5.50
a. Souvenir sheet of 3, #679-681 6.50 6.50
Nos. 679-681 (3) 5.10 6.45

Philanthropists A165

Designs: 2c, Fra Diegu (1831-1902). 3c, Adelaide Cini (1838-1885). 8c, Alfonso Maria Galea (1861-1941). 27c, Vincenzo Bugeja (1820-1890).

1986, Aug. 28 ***Perf. 14½x14***

682 A165 2c multicolored .60 .30
683 A165 3c multicolored .70 .30
684 A165 8c multicolored 1.25 .60
685 A165 27c multicolored 3.50 *5.75*
Nos. 682-685 (4) 6.05 6.95

Ships Type of 1982

1986, Nov. 19 Wmk. 354 ***Perf. 14***

686 A145 7c San Paul 1.00 1.00
687 A145 10c Knight of Malta 1.25 1.25
688 A145 12c Valetta City 1.50 1.50
689 A145 20c Saver 2.25 2.25
Nos. 686-689 (4) 6.00 6.00

Malta Ornithological Society, 25th Anniv. — A166

3c, Erithacus rubecula. 8c, Falco peregrinus. 13c, Upupa epops. 23c, Calonectris diomedea.

1987, Jan. 26 Litho. ***Perf. 14***

690 A166 3c multi 1.00 .55
691 A166 8c multi 2.00 1.00
692 A166 13c multi 2.75 *3.75*
693 A166 23c multi 3.25 *5.50*
Nos. 690-693 (4) 9.00 *10.80*

Nos. 691-692 vert.

Europa Issue

Limestone Buildings A167

8c, Aquasun Lido. 35c, St. Joseph's Church, Manikata.

1987, Apr. 15 Litho. ***Perf. 14½x14***

694 A167 8c multi *.50 .50*
695 A167 35c multi *2.90 2.90*

Military Uniforms — A168

Uniforms of the Order of St. John of Jerusalem (1530-1798): 3c, Soldier, 16th cent. 7c, Officer, 16th cent. 10c, Flag bearer, 18th cent. 27c, General of the galleys, 18th cent.

1987, June 10 Wmk. 354 ***Perf. 14***

696 A168 3c multi .65 .65
697 A168 7c multi 1.40 1.40
698 A168 10c multi 1.50 1.50
699 A168 27c multi 3.00 3.00
Nos. 696-699 (4) 6.55 6.55

See Nos. 723-726, 739-742, 764-767, 774-777.

European Environment Year — A169

Anniversaries and events: 8c, Esperanto movement, cent. 23s, Intl. Year of Shelter for the Homeless.

Perf. 14½x14

1987, Aug. 18 Wmk. 354

700 A169 5c shown 1.25 .50
701 A169 8c multicolored 2.00 .60
702 A169 23c multicolored 3.00 3.00
Nos. 700-702 (3) 6.25 4.10

Ships Type of 1982

1987, Oct. 16 Litho. ***Perf. 14***

703 A145 2c Medina, 1969 .60 .60
704 A145 11c Rabat, 1974 1.75 1.75
705 A145 13c Ghawdex, 1979 2.00 2.00
706 A145 20c Pinto, 1987 2.50 2.50
Nos. 703-706 (4) 6.85 6.85

A170

Designs: 8c, Dr. Arvid Pardo, representative to UN from Malta who proposed the resolution. 12c, UN emblem.

Wmk. 354

1987, Dec. 18 Litho. ***Perf. 14½***

707 A170 8c multicolored 1.25 1.25
708 A170 12c multicolored 2.25 2.25

Souvenir Sheet

Perf. 13x13½

709 Sheet of 2 3.75 3.75
a. A170 8c multicolored 1.25 1.25
b. A170 12c multicolored 2.00 2.00

UN resolution for peaceful use of marine resources, 20th anniv. Nos. 709a-709b printed in a continuous design.

Nazju Falzon (1813-1865), Clergyman A171

Famous men: 3c, Monsignor Sidor Formosa (1851-1931), benefactor of the poor. 4c, Sir Luigi Preziosi (1888-1965), opthalmologist who developed an operation for the treatment of glaucoma. 10c, Father Anastasju Cuschieri (1876-1962), theologian, poet. 25c, Monsignor Pietru Pawl Saydon (1895-1971), translator, commentator on scripture.

Perf. 14½x14

1988, Jan. 23 Wmk. 354

710 A171 2c shown .35 .35
711 A171 3c multicolored .35 .35
712 A171 4c multicolored .60 .60
713 A171 10c multicolored .80 .80
714 A171 25c multicolored 2.00 2.00
Nos. 710-714 (5) 4.10 4.10

Anniversaries and Events — A172

10c, Statue of youth and St. John Bosco in the chapel at St. Patrick's School, Sliema. 12c, Assumption of Our Lady, main altarpiece at Ta' Pinu Sanctuary, Gozo, completed in 1619 by Amodeo Bartolomeo Perugino. 14c, Christ the King monument at the Mall, Floriana, by Antonio Sciortino (1879-1947).

1988, Mar. 5 Litho. ***Perf. 14***

715 A172 10c multicolored 1.00 1.00
716 A172 12c multicolored 1.25 1.25
717 A172 14c multicolored 1.50 1.50
Nos. 715-717 (3) 3.75 3.75

St. John Bosco (1815-88), educator (10c); Marian Year (12c); Intl. Eucharistic Congress, Malta, Apr. 24-28, 1913, 75th anniv. (14c).

Land, Sea and Air Transportation A173

Europa (Transport and communication): 35c, Telecommunications.

1988, Apr. 9 ***Perf. 14***

718 A173 10c multicolored *.65 .65*
719 A173 35c multicolored *2.40 2.40*

Intl. Anniversaries and Events A174

Globe picturing hemispheres and: 4c, Red Cross, Red Crescent emblems. 18c, Symbolic design dividing world into north and south regions. 19c, Caduceus, EKG readout.

1988, May 25 Litho. ***Perf. 14***

720 A174 4c multicolored .60 .50
721 A174 18c multicolored 1.50 *2.50*
722 A174 19c multicolored 1.50 *2.50*
Nos. 720-722 (3) 3.60 *5.50*

Intl. Red Cross and Red Crescent Organizations, 125th annivs. (4c); European Public Campaign on North-South Interdependence and Solidarity (18c); WHO, 40th anniv. (19c).

Military Uniforms Type of 1987

Designs: 3c, Light Infantry private, 1800. 4c, Coast Artillery gunner, 1802. 10c, Ist Maltese Provincial Battalion field officer, 1805. 25c, Royal Malta Regiment subaltern, 1809.

1988, July 23 Litho. Wmk. 354

723 A168 3c multicolored .35 .35
724 A168 4c multicolored .40 .40
725 A168 10c multicolored 1.25 1.25
726 A168 25c multicolored 2.50 2.50
Nos. 723-726 (4) 4.50 4.50

A175

Perf. 14x13½

1988, Sept. 17 Wmk. 354

727 A175 4c Running .30 .30
728 A175 10c Women's diving .70 .70
729 A175 35c Basketball 2.00 2.00
Nos. 727-729 (3) 3.00 3.00

1988 Summer Olympics, Seoul.

A176

1989, Jan. 28 Litho. ***Perf. 13½***

730 A176 2c Commonwealth .30 .30
731 A176 3c Council of Europe .30 .30
732 A176 4c United Nations .35 .35
733 A176 10c Labor .80 .80
734 A176 12c Justice .90 .90

Size: 41x32mm

Perf. 14

735 A176 25c Liberty 1.90 *3.00*
Nos. 730-735 (6) 4.55 5.65

Natl. independence, 25th anniv.

New Natl. Emblem — A177

1989, Mar. 25 *Perf. 14*
736 A177 £1 multicolored 4.25 3.50

Children's Toys — A178

Europa.

1989, May 6
737 A178 10c Kite *.75 .75*
738 A178 35c Dolls *2.75 2.75*

Military Uniforms Type of 1987

3c, Officer of the Maltese Veterans, 1815. 4c, Subaltern of the Royal Malta Fencibles, 1839. 10c, Militia private, 1856. 25c, Royal Malta Fencibles Artillery colonel, 1875.

1989, June 24 Litho. Wmk. 354
739 A168 3c multicolored .45 .45
740 A168 4c multicolored .50 .50
741 A168 10c multicolored 1.50 1.50
742 A168 25c multicolored 2.75 2.75
Nos. 739-742 (4) 5.20 5.20

Anniversaries and Events — A179

1989, Oct. 17 Litho. Wmk. 354
743 A179 3c multicolored .40 .40
744 A179 4c multi, diff. .45 .45
745 A179 10c multi, diff. 1.00 1.00
746 A179 14c multi, diff. 1.25 1.25
747 A179 25c multi, diff. 2.00 *3.25*
Nos. 743-747 (5) 5.10 6.35

UN Declaration on Social Progress and Development, 20th anniv. (3c); signing of the European Social Charter by Malta (4c); Council of Europe, 40th anniv. (10c); Natl. Teachers' Union, 70th anniv. (14c); assembly of the Knights of the Sovereign Military Order of Malta (25c).

Pres. Bush, Map and Gen.-Sec. Gorbachev — A180

1989, Dec. 2 Litho. Wmk. 354
748 A180 10c chalky blue, org & brn 1.50 1.50

US-Soviet summit, Malta, Dec. 2-3.

Europa 1990 — A181

Post offices: 10c, Auberge d'Italie, Valletta, 1574, vert. 35c, Branch P.O., Zebbug, 1987.

1990, Feb. 9
749 A181 10c multicolored *.65 .65*
750 A181 35c multicolored *2.40 2.40*

Anniversaries & Events — A182

1990, Apr. 7
751 A182 3c multi, vert. .40 .40
752 A182 4c shown .50 .50
753 A182 19c multicolored 2.00 2.00
754 A182 20c multi, vert. 2.00 2.00
Nos. 751-754 (4) 4.90 4.90

UNESCO World Literacy Year (3c); subjection of Malta to Count Roger the Norman and subsequent rulers of Sicily, 900th anniv. (4c); 25th anniv. of Malta's membership in the ITU (19c); and 20th Congress of the Union of European Soccer Associations, Malta (20c).

British Poets and Novelists — A183

4c, Samuel Taylor Coleridge. 10c, Lord Byron. 12c, Sir Walter Scott. 25c, William Makepeace Thackeray.

1990, May 3 *Perf. 13½*
755 A183 4c multi .40 .40
756 A183 10c multi .95 .95
757 A183 12c multi 1.25 1.25
758 A183 25c multi 2.25 2.25
Nos. 755-758 (4) 4.85 4.85

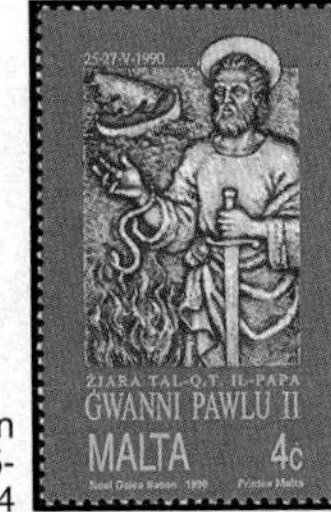

Visit of Pope John Paul II, May 25-27 — A184

1990, May 25 *Perf. 14*
759 A184 4c St. Paul .30 .30
760 A184 25c Pope John Paul II 2.00 2.00
a. Pair, #759-760 2.50 2.50

World Cup Soccer Championships, Italy — A185

Soccer ball &: 5c, flags. 10c, hands & goal net.

1990, June 8 Wmk. 354
761 A185 5c multicolored .40 .40
762 A185 10c multicolored .70 .70
763 A185 14c multicolored 1.10 1.10
a. Souvenir sheet of 3, #761-763 2.75 2.75
Nos. 761-763 (3) 2.20 2.20

Military Uniforms Type of 1987

Designs: 3c, Captain, Royal Malta Militia, 1889. 4c, Field Officer, Royal Malta Artillery, 1905. 10c, Laborer, Malta Labor Corps, 1915. 25c, Lieutenant, King's Own Malta Regiment of Militia, 1918.

1990, Aug. 25 *Perf. 14*
764 A168 3c multicolored .50 .50
765 A168 4c multicolored .85 .85
766 A168 10c multicolored 2.00 2.00
767 A168 25c multicolored 4.00 4.00
Nos. 764-767 (4) 7.35 7.35

Maltese Philatelic Society, 25th Anniv. A186

1991, Mar. 6 Litho. Wmk. 354
768 A186 10c multicolored 1.00 1.00

Europa — A187

10c, Eurostar. 35c, Ariane 4, space plane.

1991, Mar. 16
769 A187 10c multi *.70 .70*
770 A187 35c multi *2.40 2.40*

St. Ignatius of Loyola (1491-1556), Founder of Jesuit Order — A188

Designs: 4c, Marie Therese Pisani (1806-1865), Benedictine Nun, vert. 30c, St. John of the Cross (1542-1591), Christian mystic.

1991, Apr. 29 Litho. *Perf. 14*
771 A188 3c multicolored .30 .30
772 A188 4c multicolored .40 .40
773 A188 30c multicoloed 2.10 2.10
Nos. 771-773 (3) 2.80 2.80

Military Uniforms Type of 1987

Colors Officers: 3c, Royal Malta Fencibles, 1860. 10c, Royal Malta Regiment of Militia, 1903. 19c, King's Own Malta Regiment, 1968. 25c, Armed Forces of Malta, 1991.

Wmk. 354
1991, Sept. 23 Litho. *Perf. 14*
774 A168 3c multicolored .35 .35
775 A168 10c multicolored .75 .75
776 A168 19c multicolored 1.50 1.50
777 A168 25c multicolored 2.00 2.00
Nos. 774-777 (4) 4.60 4.60

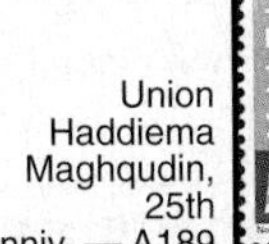

Union Haddiema Maghqudin, 25th Anniv. — A189

1991, Sept. 23 *Perf. 14x13½*
778 A189 4c multicolored .40 .40

Birds of Prey — A190

No. 779, Pernis apivorus. No. 780, Circus aeruginosus. No. 781, Falco eleonorae. No. 782, Falco naumanni.

1991, Oct. 3 *Perf. 14*
779 A190 4c multi *1.50 1.00*
780 A190 4c multi *1.50 1.00*
781 A190 10c multi *2.75 1.75*
782 A190 10c multi *2.75 1.75*
a. Strip of 4, #779-782 *10.00 10.00*
Nos. 779-782 (4) 8.50 5.50

World Wildlife Fund.

Tourism A191

Designs: 1c, Ta' Hagrat neolithic temples, Mgarr. 2c, Cottoner Gate. 3c, St. Michael's Bastion, Valletta. 4c, Spinola Palace, St. Julian's. 5c, Old church, Birkirkara. 10c, Wind surfing, Mellieha Bay. 12c, Boat anchored at Wied iz-Zurrieq. 14c, Mgarr Harbor, Gozo. 20c, Yacht Marina. 50c, Gozo Channel. £1, Statue of Arab Horses, by Sciortino. £2, Independence Monument, by Bonnici, vert.

1991, Dec. 9 *Perf. 13½*
783 A191 1c multicolored .30 *.50*
784 A191 2c multicolored .35 .35
785 A191 3c multicolored .35 .35
786 A191 4c multicolored .40 .25
787 A191 5c multicolored .45 .25
788 A191 10c multicolored .85 .25
789 A191 12c multicolored 1.00 .40
790 A191 14c multicolored 1.25 .45
791 A191 20c multicolored 1.75 .65
792 A191 50c multicolored 3.00 1.75
793 A191 £1 multicolored 5.00 3.25
794 A191 £2 multicolored 9.50 8.50
Nos. 783-794 (12) 24.20 16.95

Malta Intl. Airport A192

1992, Feb. 8 *Perf. 14*
795 A192 4c shown .60 .40
796 A192 10c Flags, airport 1.25 .75

Discovery of America, 500th Anniv. — A193

1992, Feb. 20 *Perf. 14x14½*
797 A193 10c Columbus' fleet *.65 .65*
798 A193 35c Columbus, map *2.25 2.25*

Europa.

George Cross, 1942 — A194

George Cross and: 4c, Royal Malta Artillery. 10c, Siege Bell. 50c, Santa Maria convoy entering Grand Harbor.

1992, Apr. 15 *Perf. 14*
799 A194 4c multicolored .80 .50
800 A194 10c multicolored 1.25 1.25
801 A194 50c multicolored 6.00 6.00
Nos. 799-801 (3) 8.05 7.75

1992 Summer Olympics, Barcelona — A195

1992, June 24

802	A195	3c Runners	.60	.60
803	A195	10c High jump	.90	.90
804	A195	30c Swimmer	2.25	2.25
		Nos. 802-804 (3)	3.75	3.75

Historic Buildings A196

Designs: 3c, Church of the Flight of the Holy Family into Egypt, vert. 4c, St. John's Co-Cathedral. 19c, Church of the Madonna del Pilar, vert. 25c, Auberge de Provence.

1992, July 5

805	A196	3c blk, gray & buff	.50	.50
806	A196	4c blk, salmon & buff	.60	.60
807	A196	19c blk, green & buff	2.00	2.00
808	A196	25c blk, pink & buff	2.75	2.75
		Nos. 805-808 (4)	5.85	5.85

University of Malta, 400th Anniv. — A197

4c, Early building, vert. 30c, Modern complex.

1992, Nov. 11

809	A197	4c multi	.65	.25
810	A197	30c multi	2.50	*4.00*

Lions Intl., 75th Anniv. — A198

4c, We serve. 50c, Sight first campaign.

1993, Feb. 4

811	A198	4c multi	.50	.50
812	A198	50c multi	3.50	3.50

Europa A199

Contemporary paintings by: 10c, Pawl Carbonaro, vert. 35c, Alfred Chircop.

1993, Apr. 7

813	A199	10c multicolored	*.75*	*.75*
814	A199	35c multicolored	*2.50*	*2.50*

5th Games of Small States of Europe A200

1993, May 4 *Perf. 13½x14*

815	A200	3c Torchbearer	.25	.25
816	A200	4c Cycling	1.25	1.25
817	A200	10c Tennis	1.40	1.40
818	A200	35c Sailing	2.00	2.00
a.		Souvenir sheet of 4, #815-818	5.50	5.0
		Nos. 815-818 (4)	4.90	4.90

Boy Scouts and Girl Guides of Malta — A201

3c, Leader bandaging girl. 4c, Bronze Cross. 10c, Scout at camp fire. 35c, Scout recieving Bronze Cross.

1993, July 21 *Perf. 14*

819	A201	3c multi	.50	.30
820	A201	4c multi	.50	.30
821	A201	10c multi	1.10	1.10
822	A201	35c multi	2.75	4.00
		Nos. 819-822 (4)	4.85	5.70

Girl Guides in Malta, 70th anniv. (No. 819). Award of Bronze Cross for Gallantry to Boy Scouts of Malta, 50th anniv. (Nos. 820-822).

A202

1993, Sept. 23 *Perf. 14½x14*

823	A202	5c Papilio machaon	.55	.55
824	A202	35c Vanessa atalanta	2.75	2.75

A203

1993, Oct. 5 *Perf. 13½*

825	A203	4c multicolored	.40	.40

General Worker's Union, 50th anniv.

Souvenir Sheet

Local Councils — A204

Designs showing various local coats of arms with denominations at: a, UL. b, UR. c, LL. d, LR.

1993, Nov. 20 *Perf. 14½*

826	A204	Sheet of 4	2.00	2.00
a.-d.		5c any single	.40	.40

Dental Assoc. of Malta, 50th Anniv. — A205

Design: 44c, Dental instrument, teeth.

1994, Feb. 12

827	A205	5c multicolored	.45	.45
828	A205	44c multicolored	3.75	3.75

Europa — A206

Designs: 14c, Sir Themistocles Zammit (1864-1935), discoverer of micro-organism causing undulant fever. 30c, Marble candelabrum, 2nd cent. B.C., Natl. Museum of Archaeology, Valletta.

1994, Mar. 29 *Perf. 14*

829	A206	14c multicolored	*1.00*	*1.00*
830	A206	30c multicolored	*2.25*	*2.25*

Anniversaries and Events — A207

1994, May 10

831	A207	5c shown	.45	.45
832	A207	9c Crosses	.85	.85
833	A207	14c Farm animals	1.10	1.10
834	A207	20c Factory worker	1.50	1.50
835	A207	25c Cathedral, vert.	2.00	2.00
		Nos. 831-835 (5)	5.90	5.90

Intl. Year of the Family (No. 831). Malta Red Cross Society, 3rd anniv. (No. 832). Agrarian Society, 150th anniv. (No. 833). ILO, 75th anniv. (No. 834). St. Paul's Anglican Cathedral, 150th anniv. (No. 835).

1994 World Cup Soccer Championships, U.S. — A208

1994, June 9

836	A208	5c shown	.50	.25
837	A208	14c Ball, net, map	1.10	1.00
838	A208	30c Ball, field, map	2.00	*4.00*
a.		Souvenir sheet of 3, #836-838	4.25	4.25
		Nos. 836-838 (3)	3.60	5.25

Aviation Anniversaries & Events — A209

Aircraft, related objects: 5c, Trophy, map, Twin Comanche. 14c, Airshow emblem, Phantom jet, demonstration team in silhouette, Alouette helicopter, flag. 20c, Emblem, Avro York, old terminal building, DeHavilland Dove. 25c, Emblem, DeHavilland Comet, new terminal, Airbus 320.

1994, July 2

839	A209	5c multicolored	.50	.50
840	A209	14c multicolored	1.50	1.50
841	A209	20c multicolored	1.75	1.75
842	A209	25c multicolored	2.10	2.10
		Nos. 839-842 (4)	5.85	5.85

Intl. Air Rally of Malta, 25th anniv. (No. 839). Malta Intl. Airshow (No. 840). ICAO, 50th anniv. (Nos. 841-842).

First Manned Moon Landing, 25th Anniv. — A210

1994, July 20

843	A210	14c multicolored	1.50	1.50

Christmas — A211

No. 845, Angel in pink. No. 846, Madonna & child. No. 847, Angel in green.

1994, Oct. 26

844	A211	5c shown	.35	.25

Size: 28x40mm

845	A211	9c +2c multi	.70	.70
846	A211	14c +3c multi	1.00	1.00
847	A211	20c +3c multi	1.25	*2.25*
		Nos. 844-847 (4)	3.30	4.20

Antique Maltese Silver — A212

Designs: 5c, Ewer, Vilhena period. 14c, Balsamina, Pinto period. 20c, Coffee pot, Pinto period. 25c, Sugar box, Pinto period.

Wmk. 354

1994, Dec. 12 **Litho.** *Perf. 14*

848	A212	5c multicolored	.60	.60
849	A212	14c multicolored	1.25	1.25
850	A212	20c multicolored	1.75	1.75
851	A212	25c multicolored	1.90	1.90
		Nos. 848-851 (4)	5.50	5.50

Anniversaries & Events — A213

1995, Feb. 27

852	A213	2c multicolored	.30	.30
853	A213	5c multicolored	.50	.50
854	A213	14c multicolored	.75	.75
855	A213	20c multicolored	1.25	1.25
856	A213	25c multicolored	1.75	1.75
		Nos. 852-856 (5)	4.55	4.55

Natl. Assoc. of Pensioners, 25th anniv. (No. 852). Natl. Youth Council of Malta, 10th anniv. (No. 853). 4th World Conf. on Women, Beijing (No. 854). Malta Memorial District Nursing Assoc., 50th anniv. (No. 855). Louis Pasteur (1822-95) (No. 856).

Peace & Freedom A214

Europa: 14c, Hand with olive twig, rainbow, vert. 30c, Doves.

1995, Mar. 29

857 A214 14c multicolored	*1.00*	*1.00*
858 A214 30c multicolored	*2.00*	*2.00*

50th Anniversaries — A215

Designs: 5c, End of World War II, ships, planes. 14c, Formation of UN, people joining hands. 35c, FAO, hands holding bowl of wheat, FAO emblem.

1995, Apr. 21

859 A215 5c multicolored	.35	.35
860 A215 14c multicolored	.75	.75
861 A215 35c multi, vert.	2.00	2.00
Nos. 859-861 (3)	3.10	3.10

Telecommunications & Electricity — A216

2c, Light bulb. 5c, Cable, binary numbers. 9c, Satellite dish. 14c, Sun's rays, trees. 20c, Telephone, satellite.

1995, June 15

862 A216 2c multi	.30	.30
863 A216 5c multi	.35	.35
864 A216 9c multi	.50	.50
865 A216 14c multi	.75	.75
866 A216 20c multi	1.00	1.00
Nos. 862-866 (5)	2.90	2.90

European Nature Conservation Year — A217

1995, July 24

867 A217 5c Ruins, Girna	.50	.50
868 A217 14c Podarcis filfolensis	1.75	1.75
869 A217 44c Pina halepensis	3.75	3.75
Nos. 867-869 (3)	6.00	6.00

Antique Clocks — A218

Designs: 1c, Pinto's turret clock. 5c, Michelangelo Sapiano, long case & smaller clock. 14c, Arlogg tal-lira (case) clock. 25c, Maltese sundials.

1995, Oct. 5

870 A218 1c multicolored	.30	.30
871 A218 5c multicolored	.50	.50
872 A218 14c multicolored	1.50	1.50
873 A218 25c multicolored	2.50	2.50
Nos. 870-873 (4)	4.80	4.80

Christmas — A219

Designs: 5c, Christmas Eve children's procession. 5c+2c, Children carrying manger. 14c+3c, Boy carrying manger, boy with lamp. 25c+3c, Boy with lamp, balcony.

Wmk. 354

1995, Nov. 15 Litho. *Perf. 14*

874 A219 5c multi	.30	.30

Size: 26x32mm

875 A219 5c +2c multi	.40	.40
876 A219 14c +3c multi	1.00	1.00
877 A219 25c +3c multi	1.75	1.75
Nos. 874-877 (4)	3.45	3.45

Surtax for child welfare organizations.

Child and Youth Welfare Organizations — A220

Silhouettes of youth, children, and: 5c, Maltese cross, Palace of the President. 14c, Fr. Nazzareno Camilleri, St. Patricks' School. 20c, St. Maria of St. Euphrasia Pelletier, convent building. 25c, Globe, children looking at pool.

1996, Feb. 29

878 A220 5c multicolored	.35	.35
879 A220 14c multicolored	.75	.75
880 A220 20c multicolored	1.25	1.25
881 A220 25c multicolored	1.50	1.50
Nos. 878-881 (4)	3.85	3.85

President's Award, 35th anniv. (No. 878). Fr. Camilleri, 90th death anniv. (No. 879). St. Maria, death bicent. (No. 880). UNICEF, 50th anniv. (No. 881).

Prehistoric Art — A221

Sculptures, pottery from 5000-2500BC: 5c, People, animals. 14c, Two people seated, one with missing head. 20c, Venus figure, vert. 35c, Pitcher, vert.

1996, Mar. 29

882 A221 5c multicolored	.40	.40
883 A221 14c multicolored	.90	.90
884 A221 20c multicolored	1.25	1.25
885 A221 35c multicolored	2.25	2.25
Nos. 882-885 (4)	4.80	4.80

Famous Women — A222

Europa: 14c, Mabel Strickland (1899-1988). 30c, Inez Soler (1910-1974).

1996, Apr. 24

886 A222 14c multicolored	*1.00*	*1.00*
887 A222 30c multicolored	*2.50*	*2.50*

Anniversaries and Events — A223

Designs: No. 888, UN, decade against drug abuse. No. 889, Malta Federation of Industry, 50th anniv. 14c, Self-government, 75th anniv. 44c, Guglielmo Marconi, radio, cent.

1996, June 5

888 A223 5c multicolored	.30	.30
889 A223 5c multicolored	.35	.35
890 A223 14c multicolored	1.00	1.00
891 A223 44c multicolored	2.25	2.25
Nos. 888-891 (4)	3.90	3.90

1996 Summer Olympic Games, Atlanta A224

1996, July 10

892 A224 2c Judo	.25	.25
893 A224 5c Running	.40	.40
894 A224 14c Swimming	1.25	1.25
895 A224 25c Shooting	2.00	2.00
Nos. 892-895 (4)	3.90	3.90

Paintings, by or of Giuseppe Calì — A225

Designs: 5c, Boy cutting wheat. 14c, Dog. 20c, Woman with hoe standing on hillside, vert. 25c, Portrait of Calì, by Dingli, vert.

1996, Aug. 22

896 A225 5c multicolored	.35	.35
897 A225 14c multicolored	.85	.85
898 A225 20c multicolored	1.00	1.00
899 A225 25c multicolored	1.10	1.10
Nos. 896-899 (4)	3.30	3.30

Buses A226

2c, Tal-Gallarija "Diamond Star" No. 1990. 5c, Stewart "Tom Mix" No. 434. 14c, Diamond T "Verdala" No. 1764. 30c, Front control No. 3495.

Wmk. 354

1996, Sept. 26 Litho. *Perf. 14*

900 A226 2c multicolored	.50	.50
901 A226 5c multicolored	.75	.75
902 A226 14c multicolored	1.50	1.50
903 A226 30c multicolored	2.10	2.10
Nos. 900-903 (4)	4.85	4.85

Christmas — A227

Stained glass windows: 5c+2c, Madonna and Child. 14c+3c, Angel flying right. 25c+3c, Angel flying left.

1996, Nov. 7

904 A227 5c shown	.45	.45

Size: 26x31mm

905 A227 5c +2c multi	.65	.65
906 A227 14c +3c multi	1.00	1.00
907 A227 25c +3c multi	1.40	1.40
Nos. 904-907 (4)	3.50	3.50

City Bicentennials A228

1997, Feb. 20

908 A228 6c Hompesch	.40	.40
909 A228 16c Ferdinand	1.00	1.00
910 A228 26c Beland	1.40	1.40
a. Souvenir Sheet of 3, #908-910	5.25	5.25
Nos. 908-910 (3)	2.80	2.80

Treasures of Malta — A229

2c, Suggetta. 6c, Suggetta, diff. 16c, Sedan chair, vert. 27c, Sedan chair, diff., vert.

1997, Apr. 11

911 A229 2c multi	.25	.25
912 A229 6c multi	.45	.45
913 A229 16c multi	1.10	1.10
914 A229 27c multi	1.50	1.50
Nos. 911-914 (4)	3.30	3.30

A230

Europa (Stories and Legends): 16c, Man carrying door, figure in front of house (Gahan). 35c, Woman kneeling in prayer, knight on white horse (St. Dimitri).

1997, May 5

915 A230 16c multicolored	*1.00*	*1.00*
916 A230 35c multicolored	*2.25*	*2.25*

A231

1997, July 10

917 A231 1c multicolored	.30	.30
918 A231 16c multicolored	1.20	1.20

Antonio Sciortino (1879-1947), sculptor.

Gozo Cathedral, 300th Anniv. — A232

1997, July 10

919 A232 6c multi .50 .50
920 A232 11c multi, diff. .80 .80

Joseph Calleia (1897-1975), Actor — A233

1997, July 10

921 A233 6c multicolored .50 .50
922 A233 22c multi, diff. 1.25 1.25

Pioneers of Education A234

Designs: 6c, Dr. Albert V. Laferla (1887-1943). 16c, Sister Emilie de Vialar (1797-1856). 19c, Msgr. Paolo Pullicino (1815-90). 26c, Msgr. Tommaso Gargallo (c. 1544-1614).

Wmk. 354

1997, Sept. 24 Litho. *Perf. 14*

923 A234 6c multicolored .40 .40
924 A234 16c multicolored .90 .90
925 A234 19c multicolored 1.10 1.10
926 A234 26c multicolored 1.25 1.25
Nos. 923-926 (4) 3.65 3.65

Christmas — A235

Designs: 6c, Nativity. 6c+2c, Madonna and Child, vert. 16c+3c, Joseph with donkey, vert. 26c+3c, Shepherd, sheep, vert.

1997, Nov. 12

927 A235 6c multi .40 .40
928 A235 6c +2c multi .50 .50
929 A235 16c +3c multi 1.10 1.10
930 A235 26c +3c multi 1.60 1.60
Nos. 927-930 (4) 3.60 3.60

Victoria Lines, Cent. A236

Designs: 2c, Fort, soldiers in front of wall. 16c, Soldiers with cannon, fort.

1997, Dec. 5

931 A236 2c multicolored .30 .30
932 A236 16c multicolored 1.00 1.00

Self-government, 50th Anniv. — A237

Designs: 6c, Man looking at paper, group of people. 37c, People in line waiting to vote.

1997, Dec. 5

933 A237 6c multicolored .40 .40
934 A237 37c multicolored 1.60 1.60

Treasures of Malta — A238

Designs: No. 935, Vest. No. 936, Portrait of a Woman, by Antoine de Favray (1706-98). No. 937, Portrait of Woman Holding Girl, by de Favray. No. 938, Early woman's costume.
26c, Valletta, city of culture.

1998, Feb. 26

935 A238 6c multicolored .40 .40
936 A238 6c multicolored .40 .40
937 A238 16c multicolored .85 .85
938 A238 16c multicolored .85 .85
Nos. 935-938 (4) 2.50 2.50

Souvenir Sheet

Perf. 13x13½

939 A238 26c multicolored 2.10 2.10

No. 939 contains one 39x48mm stamp.

French Occupation of Malta, Bicent. — A239

Designs: No. 940, Ferdinand von Hompesch, commander of Knights of St. John. No. 941, French fleet, map. No. 942, French coming ashore. No. 943, Napoleon Bonaparte.

Wmk. 239

1998, Mar. 28 Litho. *Perf. 14*

940 A239 6c multicolored .55 .55
941 A239 6c multicolored .55 .55
a. Pair, #940-941 1.25 1.25
942 A239 16c multicolored 1.10 1.10
943 A239 16c multicolored 1.10 1.10
a. Pair, #942-943 3.00 3.00
Nos. 940-943 (4) 3.30 3.30

National Festivals A240

Europa: 16c, 35c, Various boats at annual regatta.

Wmk. 354

1998, Apr. 22 Litho. *Perf. 14*

944 A240 16c multicolored *1.00 1.00*
945 A240 35c multicolored *2.25 2.25*

Intl. Year of the Ocean A241

Designs: 2c, Diver, dolphin, vert. 6c, Diver, hand holding sea urchin, vert. 16c, Diver, Jacques Cousteau (1910-97), deep sea explorer. 27c, Two divers.

Wmk. 354

1998, May 27 Litho. *Perf. 14*

946 A241 2c multicolored .40 .40
947 A241 6c multicolored .65 .65
948 A241 16c multicolored 1.60 1.60
949 A241 27c multicolored 2.00 2.00
Nos. 946-949 (4) 4.65 4.65

1998 World Cup Soccer Championship, France — A242

Various soccer plays, flags from participating teams.

1998, June 10

950 A242 6c multicolored .65 .65
951 A242 16c multicolored 1.25 1.25
952 A242 22c multicolored 2.25 2.25
a. Souvenir sheet, #950-952 4.50 4.50
Nos. 950-952 (3) 4.15 4.15

Anniversaries and Events — A243

1c, Intl. Maritime Organization, 50th anniv. 6c, Symbolic people, emblem, Universal Declaration of Human Rights. 11c, Cogs in wheels, Assoc. of General Retailers & Traders, 50th anniv. 19c, Roman god Mercury, Malta Chamber of Commerce, 150th anniv. 26c, Stylized planes, Air Malta, 25th anniv.

Wmk. 354

1998, Sept. 17 Litho. *Perf. 14*

953 A243 1c multicolored .30 .30
954 A243 6c multicolored .55 .55
955 A243 11c multicolored .95 .95
956 A243 19c multicolored 1.25 1.25
957 A243 26c multicolored 1.60 1.60
Nos. 953-957 (5) 4.65 4.65

Christmas A244

Paintings by Mattia Preti (1613-99): 6c, Rest on the Flight to Egypt. 6c+2c, Virgin and Child with Saints Anthony the Abbot and John the Baptist. 16c+3c, Virgin and Child with Saints Raphael, Nicholas and Gregory. 26c+3c, Virgin and Child with Saints John the Baptist and Nicholas.

Wmk. 354

1998, Nov. 19 Litho. *Perf. 14*

958 A244 6c multicolored .40 .40
959 A244 6c +2c multi .55 .55
960 A244 16c +3c multi 1.50 1.50
961 A244 26c +3c multi 1.90 1.90
Nos. 958-961 (4) 4.35 4.35

Knights Hospitaller, Order of St. John of Jerusalem, 900th Anniv. — A245

2c, Fort St. Angelo. 6c, Grandmaster L'Isle Adam, vert. 16c, Grandmaster La Valette, vert. 27c, Auberge de Castille.

Wmk. 354

1999, Feb. 26 Litho. *Perf. 14*

962 A245 2c multicolored .30 .30
963 A245 6c multicolored .60 .60
964 A245 16c multicolored 1.40 1.40
965 A245 27c multicolored 2.50 2.50
Nos. 962-965 (4) 4.80 4.80

Council of Europe, 50th Anniv. — A246

Designs: 6c, European Parliament in session. 16c, Human Rights Building.

1999, Apr. 6

966 A246 6c multicolored .55 .55
967 A246 16c multicolored 1.25 1.25

Nature Reserves — A247

Europa: 16c, Charadrius dubius, Ghadira Nature Reserve. 35c, Alcedo atthis, Simar Nature Reserve.

Unwmk.

1999, Apr. 6 Litho. *Perf. 14*

968 A247 16c multicolored *1.00 1.00*
969 A247 35c multicolored *2.25 2.25*

UPU, 125th Anniv. — A248

UPU emblem and: a, 6c, Sailing ship, Valletta Bastions, Marsamxett Harbor. b, 16c, IBRA '99 emblem, Nuremberg, Germany. c, 22c, Philexfrance emblem, Eiffel Tower, Paris. d, 27c, Beijing '99 emblem, Beijing. e, 37c, Australia '99 emblem, Melbourne.

1999, June 2 *Perf. 13¾x14*

970 A248 Strip of 5, #a.-e. 7.50 7.50

Tourism — A249

Sun shining and: 6c, Man, woman in boat, vert. 16c, Man taking picture of family posed with Knight of Malta, vert. 22c, Man basking in sun while frying egg on stomach. 27c, Girl with flowers, man pushing woman in horse-drawn carriage. 37c, Cave man among ruins pulling luggage, reading travel guide.

Perf. 14x13¾, 13¾x14

1999, June 16

971	A249	6c multicolored	1.00	1.00
972	A249	16c multicolored	1.40	1.40
973	A249	22c multicolored	1.50	1.50
974	A249	27c multicolored	1.60	1.60
975	A249	37c multicolored	2.00	2.00
		Nos. 971-975 (5)	7.50	7.50

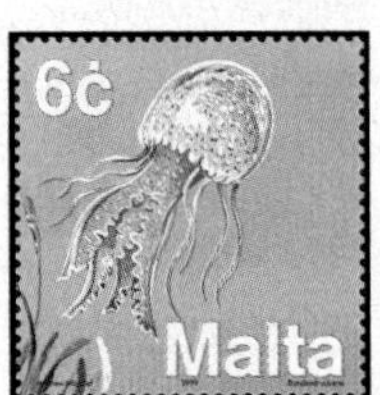

Marine Life — A250

No. 976: a, Pelagia noctiluca (jellyfish). b, Thalassoma pavo (fish with green stripes). c, Sepia officinalis (squid.) d, Sphaerechinus granularis (sea urchin). e, Epinephelus guaza (large fish). f, Diplodus vulgaris (fish with black stripes). g, Astroides calycularis (corals). h, Maia squinado (crab). i, Coris julis (fish with orange stripes). j, Octopus vulgaris (octopus). k, Charonia variegata (shell). l, Sparisoma cretense (red, green and blue fish). m, Hippocampus ramulosus (seahorse). n, Dardanus arrosor (hermit crab). o, Muraena helena (moray eel). p, Echinaster sepositus (starfish).

Perf. 13¾

1999, Aug. 25 Litho. Unwmk.

976		Sheet of 16	10.00	10.00
a.-p.		A250 6c Any single	.60	.60

Animal names are on sheet margin only.

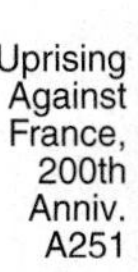

Uprising Against France, 200th Anniv. A251

No. 977, Father Mikiel Scerri. No. 978, Sculpture. No. 979, French Gen. Belgrand de Vaubois. No. 980, British Capt. Alexander Ball.

1999, Oct. 6 Litho. *Perf. 14*

977	A251	6c multicolored	.80	.80
978	A251	6c multicolored	.80	.80
a.		Pair, #977-978	2.25	2.25
979	A251	16c multicolored	1.40	1.40
980	A251	16c multicolored	1.40	1.40
a.		Pair, #979-980	3.75	3.75
		Nos. 977-980 (4)	4.40	4.40

Crowning of Painting of Our Lady of Mellieha, Cent. — A252

6c, Crowned Madonna, vert.

1999, Oct. 6

981	A252	35c shown	2.25	2.25

Souvenir Sheet

982	A252	6c multicolored	1.00	1.00

Flowers A253

Designs: 2c, Pancratium maritimum. 4c, Iris pseudopumila. 6c, Narcissus tazetta. 16c, Crocus longiflorus. 25c, Ornithogalum arabicum. 46c, Tulipa sylvestris.

1999, Oct. 20 Litho. *Perf. 13¾*

983	A253	2c multi	.25	.25
984	A253	4c multi	.25	.25
985	A253	6c multi	.25	.25
986	A253	16c multi	.65	.65
987	A253	25c multi	1.10	1.10
988	A253	46c multi	2.25	2.25
		Nos. 983-988 (6)	4.75	4.75

See Nos. 1022-1027, 1061-1066, 1102-1107, 1139-1140, 1213-1214.

Christmas A254

6c, Madonna & Child. 6c+3c, Carolers. 16c+3c, Santa Claus. 26c+3c, Tree, ornament.

1999, Nov. 27

989	A254	6c multi	.60	.60
990	A254	6c + 3c multi	.75	.75
991	A254	16c + 3c multi	1.50	1.50
992	A254	26c + 3c multi	2.00	2.00
		Nos. 989-992 (4)	4.85	4.85

Republic of Malta, 25th Anniv. — A255

6c, Legislative meeting room. 11c, Chambers of House of Representatives. 16c, Central Bank of Malta. 19c, Flags, aerial view of Valletta. 26c, Computer, airplane, port facilities.

1999, Dec. 10 Litho. *Perf. 14*

993	A255	6c multi	.40	.40
994	A255	11c multi	.60	.60
995	A255	16c multi	.80	.80
996	A255	19c multi	1.10	1.10
997	A255	26c multi	1.40	1.40
		Nos. 993-997 (5)	4.30	4.30

Greetings — A256

Designs: 3c, Gift, roses. 6c, Roses, letter, picture frame. 16c, Heart, tulips. 20c, Clock, champagne bottle, glass. 22c, Roses, wedding rings.

Unwmk.

2000, Feb. 9 Litho. *Perf. 14*

998	A256	3c multi	.35	.35
999	A256	6c multi	.55	.55
1000	A256	16c multi	1.00	1.00
1001	A256	20c multi	1.10	1.10
1002	A256	22c multi	1.40	1.40
		Nos. 998-1002 (5)	4.40	4.40

Malta in the 20th Century — A257

Designs: 6c, Cruise ship, small boat. 16c, Festival, musicians. 22c, Family walking, view of harbor. 27c, Farm family, Victoria Citadel, Gozo.

2000, Mar. 7 *Perf. 13¾x14*

1003	A257	6c multi	.50	.50
1004	A257	16c multi	1.00	1.00
1005	A257	22c multi	1.25	1.25
1006	A257	27c multi	1.75	1.75
		Nos. 1003-1006 (4)	4.50	4.50

Sports A258

Designs: 6c, Soccer players, trophy. 16c, Swimmer, sailboats. 26c, Judo, shooting, runners. 37c, Soccer players.

2000, Mar. 28 *Perf. 14*

1007	A258	6c multi	.55	.55
1008	A258	16c multi	1.00	1.00
1009	A258	26c multi	1.50	1.50
1010	A258	37c multi	1.75	1.75
		Nos. 1007-1010 (4)	4.80	4.80

Malta Soccer Assoc., cent. (6c); 2000 Summer Olympics, Sydney (16c, 26c); European Soccer Championships (37c).

Europa, 2000

Common Design Type

2000, May 9 *Perf. 14*

Color of Large "E"

1011	CD17	16c green	*1.10*	*1.10*
1012	CD17	46c blue	*3.25*	*3.25*

Air Transportation, Cent. — A259

No. 1013, D. H. 66 Hercules, 1928. No. 1014, Zeppelin LZ-127, 1933. No. 1015, Douglas DC-3 Dakota, 1949. No. 1016, Airbus A320.

2000, July 28

1013	A259	6c multi	.70	.70
1014	A259	6c multi	.70	.70
a.		Pair, #1013-1014	2.00	2.00
1015	A259	16c multi	1.40	1.40
1016	A259	16c multi	1.40	1.40
a.		Pair, #1015-1016	4.00	4.00
b.		Souvenir sheet, #1013-1016	4.75	4.75
		Nos. 1013-1016 (4)	4.20	4.20

Fireworks — A260

Denominations: 2c, 6c, 16c, 20c, 50c.

2000, July 19 Litho. *Perf. 13¾x14*

1017-1021	A260	Set of 5	6.25	6.25

Flower Type of 1999

Designs: 1c, Helichrysum melitense. 3c, Cistus creticus. 10c, Rosa sempervirens. 12c, Cynara cardunculus. 20c, Anacamptis pyramidalis. £2, Adonis microcarpa.

2000, Sept. 13 Litho. *Perf. 13¾*

1022	A253	1c multi	.25	.25
1023	A253	3c multi	.25	.25
1024	A253	10c multi	.60	.60
1025	A253	12c multi	.70	.70
1026	A253	20c multi	1.25	1.25
1027	A253	£2 multi	9.00	9.00
		Nos. 1022-1027 (6)	12.05	12.05

Stampin' the Future Children's Stamp Design Contest Winners A261

Artwork by: No. 1028, Bettina Paris. No. 1029, Roxana Caruana. No. 1030, Jean Paul Zammit. No. 1031, Chiara Borg.

2000, Oct. 18 *Perf. 14x13¾*

1028-1031	A261	6c Set of 4	2.00	2.00

See also Nos. 1250, B85.

Christmas — A262

Designs: 6c, Children, Holy Family. 6c+3c, Magi. 16c+3c, Christmas tree, Santa Claus, family. 26c, Christmas tree, church, family.

2000, Nov. 18 Litho. *Perf. 14*

1032-1035	A262	Set of 4	4.75	4.75
1035a		Souv. sheet, #1032-1035	4.75	4.75

Size of No. 1033: 23x27mm.

Carnival — A263

Various scenes and cartoon mascots at LL with: 6c, Horn. 11c, Guitar, vert. 16c, Drum, vert. 19c, Tambourine, vert. 27c, Flute.

No. 1041: a, 12c, Clowns (black and white photo), mascot with tambourine, b, 37c, Clowns (color photo), mascot with drum.

Perf. 13¾x14, 14x13¾

2001, Feb. 23 Litho.

1036-1040	A263	Set of 5	5.25	5.25

Souvenir Sheet

Perf. 13¾

1041	A263	Sheet of 2, #a-b	3.00	3.00

No. 1041 contains two 34x34mm stamps.

Lighthouses A264

Designs: 6c, Sant'Iermu. 16c, Gurdan. 22c, Delimara.

2001, Mar. 21 *Perf. 14x13¾*

1042-1044	A264	Set of 3	3.75	3.75

Paintings by Edward Caruana Dingli — A265

Denominations: 2c, 4c, 6c, 10c, 26c.

2001, Apr. 18

1045-1049	A265	Set of 5	4.00	4.00

Visit of Pope John Paul II A266

Designs: 6c, Nazju Falzon, Gorg Preca, and Adeodata Pisani, Maltese beatified by Pope. 16c, Pope, statue.
75c, Falzon, Preca, Pisani and Pope.

2001, May 4 *Perf. 14*
1050-1051 A266 Set of 2 3.00 3.00

Souvenir Sheet

1052 A266 75c multi 5.00 5.00

Europa A267

Designs: 16c, Discoglossus pictus. 46c, Sympetrum fonscolombii.

2001, May 23 Litho. *Perf. 14x14¼*
1053-1054 A267 Set of 2 *4.50 4.50*

Birds — A268

No. 1055: a, Larus cachinnans. b, Falco tinnunculus. c, Oriolus oriolus, d, Fringilla coelebs. e, Monticola solitarius. f, Merops apiaster. g, Hirundo rustica. h, Passer hispaniolensis. i, Sylvia conspicillata. j, Streptopelia turtur. k, Anas acuta. l, Ixobrychus minutus. m, Scolopax rusticola. n, Asio flammeus. o, Vanellus vanellus. p, Gallinula chloropus.

2001, June 22 Litho. *Perf. 13¾*
1055 A268 6c Sheet of 16, #a-p 11.50 11.50

Musical Instruments A269

Designs: 1c, Whistle flute. 3c, Reed pipe. 14c, Maltese bagpipe. 20c, Friction drum. 25c, Frame drum.

2001, Aug. 22 Litho. *Perf. 13¾*
1056-1060 A269 Set of 5 4.25 4.25

Flower Type of 1999

Designs: 5c, Papaver rhoeas. 11c, Silene colorata. 19c, Anthemis arvensis. 27c, Borago officinalis. 50c, Chrysanthemum coronarium. £1, Malva sylvestris.

2001, Sept. 19
1061-1066 A253 Set of 6 11.00 11.00

See No. 1269A.

Dogs A270

Designs: 6c, Kelb tal-Fenek. 16c, Kelb tal-Kacca. 19c, Maltese. 35c, Kelb tal-But.

2001, Oct. 20 Litho. *Perf. 14*
1067-1070 A270 Set of 4 5.25 5.25

Worldwide Fund for Nature (WWF) — A271

Seahorses: No. 1071, 6c, Hippocampus guttulatus. No. 1072, 6c, Hippocampus hippocampus. No. 1073, 16c, Hippocampus guttulatus, diff. No. 1074, 16c, Hippocampus hippocampus, diff.

2002 Litho. *Perf. 14¼x14*
1071-1074 A271 Set of 4 3.50 3.50

Antique Furniture — A272

Designs: 2c, Credenza. 4c, Bureau, vert. 11c, Table, vert. 26c, Armoire, vert. 60c, Credenza, diff.

2002, Mar. 27 Litho. *Perf. 14*
1075-1079 A272 Set of 5 6.00 6.00

Europa — A273

2002, May 9 Litho. *Perf. 14*
1080 A273 16c multi *1.50 1.50*

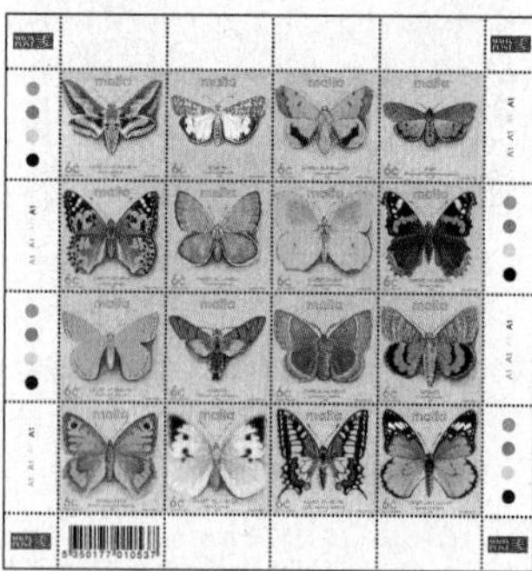

Butterflies and Moths — A274

No. 1081: a, Hyles sammuii. b, Utetheisa pulchella. c, Ophiusa tirhaca. d, Phragmatobia fulginosa melitensis. e, Vanessa cardui. f, Polyommatus icarus. g, Gonepteryx cleopatra. h, Vanessa atalanta. i, Eucrostes indigenata. j, Macroglossum stellatarum. k, Lasiocampa quercus. l, Catoeala elocata. m, Maniola jurtina hyperhispulla. n, Pieris brassicae. o, Papilio machaon melitensis. p, Danaus chrysippus.

2002, June *Perf. 13¾*
1081 A274 6c Sheet of 16, #a-p 7.25 7.25

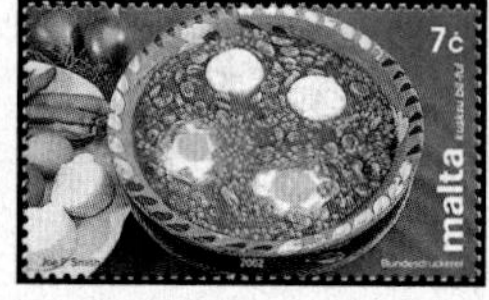

Maltese Cuisine A275

Designs: 7c, Kusksu bil-ful. 12c, Qaqocc mimli. 16c, Lampuki. 27c, Qaghqa tal-kavatelli. 75c, Stuffat tal-fenek.

2002, Aug. 13 Litho. *Perf. 14*
1082-1085 A275 Set of 4 5.25 5.25

Souvenir Sheet

1086 A275 75c multi 6.50 6.50

Succulent Plants — A276

Designs: 1c, Yavia cryptocarpa. 7c, Aztekium hintonii, vert. 28c, Pseudolithos migiurtinus. 37c, Pierrebraunia brauniorum, vert. 76c, Euphorbia turbiniformis.

2002, Sept. 25
1087-1091 A276 Set of 5 8.25 8.25

Famous Men — A277

Designs: 3c, Adrian Dingli (1817-1900), legislator. 7c, Oreste Kirkop (1923-98), opera singer. 15c, Father Athanasius Kircher (1602-80), vulcanologist. 35c, Father Saverio Cassar (1746-1805), Gozo Uprising leader. 50c, Emmanuele Vitale (1759-1802), commander in uprising against the French.

2002, Oct. 18 Litho. *Perf. 14*
1092-1096 A277 Set of 5 6.25 6.25

Christmas — A278

Designs: 7c, Mary and Joseph in donkey cart. 16c, Angels, Magi, Holy Family in bus. 22c, Holy Family and Angels on boat. 37c, Shepherds in field, Holy family in horse-drawn carriage. 75c, Angel, Magi, Holy Family and animals on galley.

2002, Nov. 20
1097-1101 A278 Set of 5 9.00 9.00

Flower Type of 1999

Designs: 7c, Vitex agnus-castus. 22c, Spartium junceum. 28c, Crataegus azalorus. 37c, Cercis siliquastrum. 45c, Myrtus communis. 76c, Pistacia lentiscus.

2003, Jan. 30 *Perf. 13¾*
1102 A253 7c multi .65 .65
1103 A253 22c multi 1.75 1.75
1104 A253 28c multi 1.90 1.90
1105 A253 37c multi 2.00 2.00
1106 A253 45c multi 2.25 2.25
1107 A253 76c multi 3.75 3.75
Nos. 1102-1107 (6) 12.30 12.30

Automobiles — A279

Designs: 2c, 1965 Vanden Plas Princess. 7c, 1948 Allard "M" Type. 10c, 1904 Cadillac Model B. 26c, 1936 Fiat Cinquecento Model A Topolino. 35c, 1965 Ford Anglia Super.

2003, Feb. 26 Litho. *Perf. 14*
1108-1112 A279 Set of 5 5.50 5.50

Military Architecture — A280

Designs: 1c, Fort St. Elmo. 4c, Rinella Battery. 11c, Fort St. Angelo. 16c, Reserve Post R15. 44c, Fort Tigné.

2003, Mar. 21 Litho. *Perf. 14*
1113-1117 A280 Set of 5 4.50 4.50

Martyrdom of St. George, 1700th Anniv. — A281

Various paintings depicting St. George: 3c, 7c, 14c, 19c, 27c.

2003, Apr. 23
1118-1122 A281 Set of 5 4.50 4.50

Europa — A282

Poster art: 16c, Cisk Beer. 46c, 1939 Carnival.

2003, May 9
1123-1124 A282 Set of 2 *3.75 3.75*

Games of Small European States A283

Designs: 25c, Track and field. 50c, Shooting. 75c, Volleyball. £3, Swimming.

2003, May 21 Litho. *Perf. 14x14¼*
1125-1128 A283 Set of 4 22.50 22.50

Coronation of Queen Elizabeth II, 50th Anniv. — A284

Queen Elizabeth II: 12c, With woman. 15c, Seated in limousine. 22c, With Prince Philip, reading book. 60c, With Prince Philip, receiving book from man.
£1, Queen and crowd of people.

2003, June 3
1129-1132 A284 Set of 4 6.00 6.00

Souvenir Sheet

1133 A284 £1 multi 6.75 6.75

Souvenir Sheet

Valletta Bastions — A285

2003, July 1 Litho. *Perf. 14x13¾*
1134 A285 £1.50 multi + 4 labels 11.00 11.00

Elton John concert, July 6, 2003.

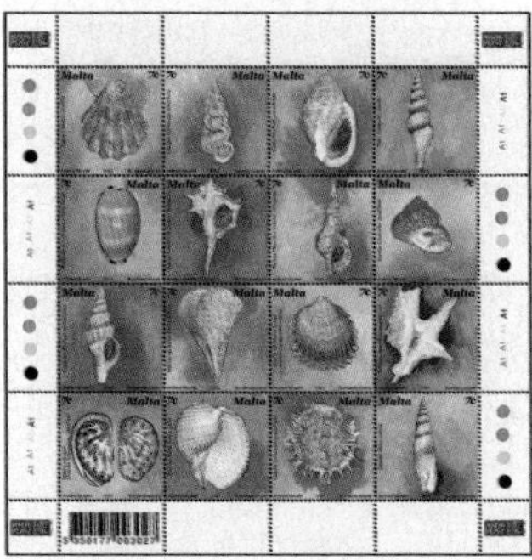

Shells — A286

No. 1135: a, Chlamys pesfelis. b, Gyroscala lamellosa. c, Phalium granulatum. d, Fusiturris similis. e, Luria lurida. f, Bolinus brandaris. g, Charonia tritonis variegata. h, Clanculus corallinus. i, Fusinus syracusanus. j, Pinna nobilis. k, Acanthocardia tuberculata. l, Aporrhais pespelcani. m, Haliotis tuberculata lamellosa. n, Tonna galea. o, Spondylus gaederopus. p, Mitra zonata.

2003, Aug. 20 Litho. *Perf. 13¾*
1135 A286 7c Sheet of 16, #a-p 7.50 7.50

Sailboats A287

Designs: 8c, Malta-Syracuse Race. 22c, Middle Sea Race, vert. 35c, Royal Malta Yacht Club, vert.

2003, Sept. 30 Litho. *Perf. 14*
1136-1138 A287 Set of 3 4.00 4.00

Flower Type of 1999

Designs: 7c, Vitex agnus-castus.16c, Crocus longiflorus.

Booklet Stamps
Size: 23x23mm

Serpentine Die Cut 12½ on 2 or 3 Sides

2003, Oct. 22 Self-Adhesive
1139 A253 7c multi .45 .45
a. Booklet pane of 12 5.50
1140 A253 16c multi 1.00 1.00
a. Booklet pane of 6 6.00

Windmills A288

Designs: 11c, Is-Sur ta'San Mikiel, Valletta. 27c, Ta'Kola, Xaghra, vert. 45c, Tax-Xarolla, Zurrieq, vert.

2003, Oct. 29 *Perf. 14*
1141-1143 A288 Set of 3 5.25 5.25

Christmas — A289

Designs: 7c, The Annunciation, vert. 16c, Holy Family, vert. 22c, Adoration of the Magi. 50c, Adoration of the Magi.

2003, Nov. 12
1144-1147 A289 Set of 4 6.75 6.75

Letter Boxes — A290

Boxes from era of: 1c, Queen Victoria. 16c, King Edward VII. 22c, King George V, King George VI. 37c, Queen Elizabeth II. 76c, Independent Malta (Malta Post).

2004, Mar. 12
1148-1152 A290 Set of 5 11.00 11.00

Cats — A291

Various cats with denominations and country name in: 7c, Golden brown. 27c, Dark brown. 28c, Lilac. 50c, Red brown. 60c, Green.

2004, Mar. 26 *Perf. 13¾*
1153-1157 A291 Set of 5 11.00 11.00

Souvenir Sheet

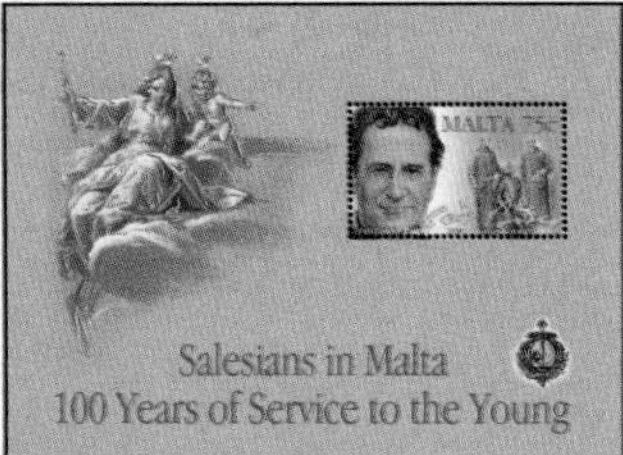

Salesians in Malta, Cent. — A292

2004, Apr. 7 *Perf. 14*
1158 A292 75c multi 4.50 4.50

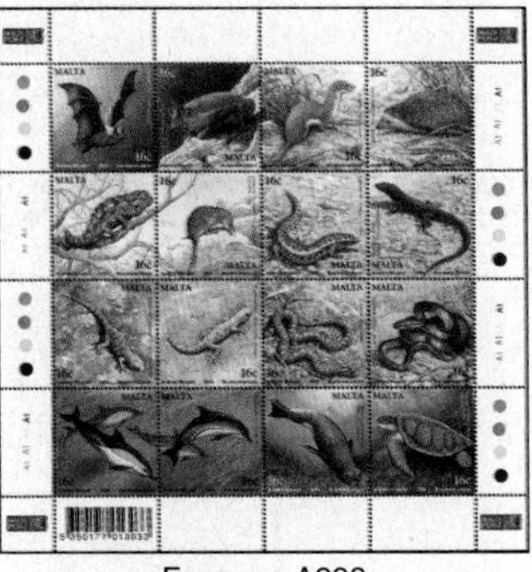

Fauna — A293

No. 1159: a, Pipistrellus pygmaeus. b, Myotis blythi punicus. c, Mustela nivalis. d, Atelerix algirus fallax. e, Chamaeleo chamaeleon. f, Crocidura sicula. g, Chalcides ocellatus. h, Podarcis filfolensis filfolensis. i, Tarentola mauritanica. j, Hemidactylus turcicus. k, Elaphe situla. l, Coluber viridiflavus. m, Delphinus delphis. n, Stenella coeruleoalba. o, Monachus monachus. p, Chelonia mydas.

2004, Apr. 21 *Perf. 13¾*
1159 A293 16c Sheet of 16, #a-p 15.00 15.00

Admission to European Union — A294

Stars, map of Europe and: 16c, Flags of newly-admitted countries. 28c, Officials signing treaty.

2004, May 1 *Perf. 14*
1160-1161 A294 Set of 2 2.75 2.75

Europa — A295

Designs: 16c, Youths jumping into water. 51c, People at archaeological site.

2004, May 19 *Perf. 13¾x14*
1162-1163 A295 Set of 2 *4.00 4.00*

Wayside Chapels A296

Designs: 3c, Lunzjata-Hal Milliere, Zurrieq. 7c, San Basilju, Mqabba. 39c, San Cir, Rabat. 48c, Santa Lucija, Mtarfa. 66c, Ta' Santa Marija, Kemmuna.

2004, June 16 Litho. *Perf. 14*
1164-1168 A296 Set of 5 11.00 11.00

Trams A297

Designs: 19c, Side view of tram. 37c, Tram and conductor (22x40mm). 50c, Ticket (22x40mm). 75c, Tram and archway.

Perf. 13¾, 14 (37c, 50c)

2004, July 14
1169-1172 A297 Set of 4 10.50 10.50

2004 Summer Olympics, Athens A298

Designs: 11c, Discus thrower. 16c, Doric column, olive wreath. 76c, Javelin thrower.

Perf. 14¼

2004, Aug. 13 Litho. Unwmk.
1173-1175 A298 Set of 3 6.00 6.00

Religious Festivals — A299

Designs: 5c, Ascension Day. 15c, St. Gregory's Day. 27c, Pilgrimage on First Sunday in Lent. 51c, St. Martin's Day, vert. £1, Feast of Sts. Peter and Paul, vert.

Perf. 14x14¼, 14¼x14

2004, Sept. 15 Wmk. 354
1176-1180 A299 Set of 5 12.00 12.00

Works of Art A300

Designs: 2c, Church of St. Mary, Attard. 20c, Mdina Cathedral organ, music by Benignon Zerafa, vert. 57c, Statue of St. Agatha, vert. 62c, Books, illustration for poem "The Turkish Galleon," by Gian Antonio Vassallo, vert.

72c, Icon of St. Paul, vert.

Perf. 14x14¼, 14¼x14

2004, Oct. 13 Litho. Wmk. 354
1181-1184 A300 Set of 4 11.00 11.00

Souvenir Sheet

1185 A300 72c multi 5.25 5.25

Christmas — A301

Various effigies of Infant Jesus: 7c, 16c, 22c, 50c. Nos. 1187-1189 vert.

Perf. 14x14¼, 14¼x14

2004, Nov. 10 Litho. Wmk. 354
1186-1189 A301 Set of 4 5.75 5.75

Historic Maps A302

Designs: 1c, Map of Malta by Abbé Jean Quintin, 1536. 12c, Map of Malta by Antonio Lafreri, 1551. 37c, Fresco map of Malta, by Matteo Perez d'Aleccio, 1565. £1.02, Map of Gozo, Comino, Cominotto and Marfa Peninsula, by Fr. Luigi Bartolo, 1745.

Wmk. 354

2005, Jan. 19 Litho. *Perf. 14*
1190-1193 A302 Set of 4 9.00 9.00

Rotary International, Cent. — A303

Rotary emblem and: 27c, Dar il-Kaptan Home, Mtarfa, woman, man. 76c, Map of Malta.

Perf. 14x14¼

2005, Feb. 23 Litho. Wmk. 354
1194-1195 A303 Set of 2 6.00 6.00

Hans Christian Andersen (1805-75), Author A304

Paper Cutting by Andersen, Scissors — A305

Designs: 60c, Pen, inkwell, illustration of duckling, manuscript handwritten by Andersen. 75c, Andersen's drawing of Casino dell'Orlogio, Rome, and boots.

Perf. 14x13¾

2005, Mar. 3 Litho. Wmk. 354

1196 A304	7c gray & black	.50	.50
1197 A305	22c blue & black	1.25	1.25
1198 A305	60c multi	3.50	3.50
1199 A305	75c multi	4.25	4.25
	Nos. 1196-1199 (4)	9.50	9.50

See Denmark Nos. 1323-1326.

Pope John Paul II (1920-2005) A306

2005, Apr. 15 *Perf. 14*
1200 A306 51c multi 4.25 4.25

Miniature Sheet

Insects — A307

No. 1201: a, Coccinella septempunctata. b, Chrysoperla carnea. c, Apis mellifera. d, Crocothermis erythraea. e, Anax imperator. f, Lampyris pallida. g, Henosepilachna elaterii. h, Forficula decipiens. i, Mantis religiosa. j, Eumenes lunulatus. k, Cerambyx cerdo. l, Gryllus bimaculatus. m, Xylocopa violacea. n, Cicada orni. o, Acrida ungarica. p, Oryctes nasicornis.

2005, Apr. 20 *Perf. 14¼*
1201 A307 16c Sheet of 16, #a-p 16.00 16.00

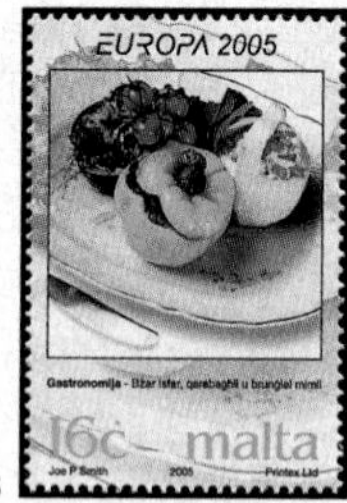

Europa — A308

Designs: 16c, Stuffed peppers, zucchini and eggplant. 51c, Fried rabbit in wine and garlic.

2005, May 9 *Perf. 14¼x14*
1202-1203 A308 Set of 2 *4.00 4.00*

Paintings Depicting St. Catherine — A309

Designs: No. 1204, 28c, The Beheading of St. Catherine, by unknown artist. No. 1205, 28c, The Martyrdom of St. Catherine, by Mattia Preti, vert. No. 1206, 45c, St. Catherine Disputing the Philosophers, by Francesco Zahra. No. 1207, 45c, Mystic Marriage, by Sahra, vert.

Perf. 14x14¼, 14¼x14

2005, June 15 Litho. Wmk. 354
1204-1207 A309 Set of 4 7.50 7.50

Famous People A310

Designs: 3c, Monsignor Michael Azzopardi (1910-87), religious educator. 19c, Egidio Lapira (1897-1970), dental surgeon. 20c, Petition of Guzeppi Callus (1505-61), doctor executed for taxation opposition. 46c, Hand and quill pen of Geronimo Matteo Abos (1715-60), composer. 76c, Gio Francesco Abela (1592-1655), historian, ambassador.

Wmk. 354

2005, July 13 Litho. *Perf. 14¼*
1208-1212 A310 Set of 5 8.25 8.25

Flower Type of 1999 Redrawn

Design: 7c, Vitex agnus-castus. 16c, Crocus longiflorus.

2005 Litho. *Perf. 14¼*

1213 A253	7c multi + label	.50	.50
1214 A253	16c multi + label	1.25	1.25

Nos. 1213-1214 have "2005" year date and "Printex Ltd" inscription at lower right. Additionally, No. 1213 has wider distance between denomination and country name than No. 1102, and No. 1214 has denomination and country name in a different font than No. 986. Nos. 1213-1214 were issued in sheets of 10 stamps and 10 labels. Labels could be personalized for an additional fee.

Horses and Mules at Work A311

Designs: 11c, Horse-drawn hearse. 15c, Mule pulling plow. 62c, Mule at grindstone. 66c, Horse pulling cart.

Perf. 14x14¼

2005, Aug. 19 Litho. Wmk. 354
1215-1218 A311 Set of 4 8.00 8.00

End of World War II, 60th Anniv. A312

Scenes from Battle of Malta: 2c, Civilians on food line. 5c, Royal Navy ships under attack. 25c, Anti-aircraft gunners. 51c, Aviators and planes. £1, Tanker "Ohio."

2005, Sept. 23
1219-1223 A312 Set of 5 11.00 11.00

Christmas — A313

Mosaics of paintings by Envin Cremona from National Sanctuary of Our Lady of Ta' Pinu, Gozo: 7c, Nativity. 16c, Annunciation, vert. 22c, Adoration of the Magi. 50c, Flight into Egypt (68x27mm).

Perf. 14¼, 13¾x14 (50c)

2005, Oct. 12 Litho. Wmk. 354
1224-1227 A313 Set of 4 5.75 5.75

Souvenir Sheets

Commonwealth Heads of Governments Meeting — A314

Flags of Malta, British Commonwealth and: 14c, Commonwealth Heads of Government flag. 28c, Doves. 37c, Maltese cross. 75c, People.

Perf. 14x14¼

2005, Nov. 23 Litho. Wmk. 354
1228-1231 A314 Set of 4 8.50 8.50

Souvenir Sheet

Europa Stamps, 50th Anniv. — A315

No. 1232: a, 5c, #677. b, 13c, #628. c, 23c, #540. d, 24c, #738.

2006, Jan. 3 *Perf. 13¾x14*
1232 A315 Sheet of 4, #a-d 4.50 4.50

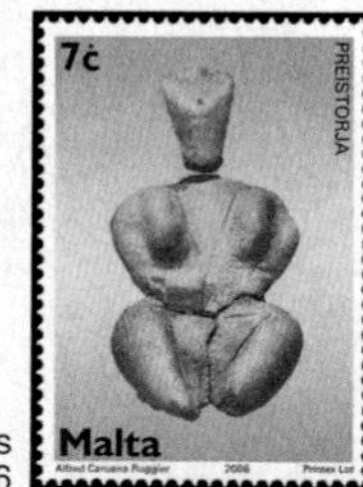

Ceramics A316

Designs: 7c, Neolithic terra-cotta female figurine. 16c, Roman terra-cotta head. 28c, Terra-cotta oil lamp holder. 37c, Sicilian maiolica plate. 60c, Stylized figure in traditional Maltese costume, by Ianni Bonnici.

Wmk. 354

2006, Feb. 25 Litho. *Perf. 14¼*
1233-1237 A316 Set of 5 8.00 8.00

Miniature Sheet

Pets — A317

No. 1238: a, Shetland pony. b, Chihuahua. c, Goldfish. d, Siamese cat. e, Siamese fighting fish. f, Ferret. g, Canary. h, Turtle. i, Chinchilla. j, Parakeet. k, Rabbit. l, Zebra finch. m, Pointer. n, Pigeon. o, Guinea pig. p, House cat.

Wmk. 354

2006, Mar. 14 Litho. *Perf. 14¼*

1238 A317	Sheet of 16	13.00	13.00
a.-h.	7c Any single	.35	.35
i.-p.	22c Any single	1.25	1.25

Traditional Holy Week Celebrations A318

Designs: 7c, Men carrying crosses. 15c, Men carrying crucifixion scene. 22c, Float. 27c, Men pulling statue of Jesus. 82c, Decorated altar.

2006, Apr. 12 *Perf. 14¼x14*
1239-1243 A318 Set of 5 7.50 7.50

Europa A319

Designs: 16c, Shown. 51c, Stick figures, diff. (28x41mm).

Perf. 14¼, 14¼x14 (51c)

2006, May 9
1244-1245 A319 Set of 2 3.50 3.50

2006 World Cup Soccer Championships, Germany A320

Designs: 7c, Bobby Charlton. 16c, Pelé. 27c, Franz Beckenbauer. 76c, Dino Zoff.

2006, June 2 *Perf. 14¼x14*
1246-1249 A320 Set of 4 7.00 7.00
1249a Souvenir sheet, #1246-1249 7.00 7.00

Stampin' The Future Type of 2000 Souvenir Sheet

2006, June 5 *Perf. 14*
1250 A261 £1.50 Like #1028 8.00 8.00

Ten percent of the sale went to the Rainforest Foundation.

Naval Vessels A321

Designs: 8c, Gran Carraca di Rodi. 29c, Guillaume Tell (HMS Malta). 51c, USS Constitution. 76c, HMS Dreadnought. £1, Slava and USS Belknap.

Wmk. 354

2006, Aug. 18 **Litho.** *Perf. 14¼*
1251-1255 A321 Set of 5 15.00 15.00

Greetings A322

Inscriptions: 8c, Happy Birthday. 16c, Happy Anniversary. 27c, Congratulations. 37c, Best Wishes.

2006, Sept. 18
1256-1259 A322 Set of 4 5.00 5.00

Castles and Towers A323

Designs: 7c, Wignacourt Tower. 16c, Verdala Castle. 27c, San Lucjan Tower. 37c, Kemmuna Tower. £1, Selmun Castle.

Perf. 14x14¼

2006, Sept. 29 **Litho.** **Wmk. 354**
1260-1264 A323 Set of 5 10.50 10.50

Christmas — A324

Designs: 8c, Paolino Vassallo (1856-1923), composer of "Inno per Natale," Nativity. 16c, Carmelo Pace (1906-93), composer of "They Heard the Angels," Magi on camels. 22c, Paul Nani (1906-86), composer of "Maltese Christmas," angels. 27c, Carlo Diacono (1876-1942), composer of "Notte di Natale," shepherds and angel.

50c, Wolfgang Amadeus Mozart (1756-91), composer of "Alma Dei Creatoris."

2006, Nov. 6 *Perf. 14¼*
1265-1268 A324 Set of 4 5.00 5.00

Souvenir Sheet

Perf. 13¾

1269 A324 50c multi 3.25 3.25

No. 1269 contains one 40x30mm stamp.

Flower Type of 1999 Redrawn

2006 **Litho.** **Wmk. 354** *Perf. 14¼*
1269A A253 1c Like #1022 .55 .55

No. 1269A has a "2006" year date and "Printex Ltd." inscription at lower right. Additionally, the country name has a different font than No. 1022, with the lines in the lettering being of equal thickness throughout the letter on No. 1269A. Other differences in the vignette exist.

Due to the scheduled conversion to the euro on Jan. 1, 2008, Nos. 1270-1274 and all stamps issued in 2007 will show denominations in pounds and the not-yet-circulating euros.

Crafts A325

Designs: 8c, Wrought iron window guard, blacksmith and anvil. 16c, Glass ornamental objects, glassblower. 22c, Filigree pendant, silversmith. 37c, Pottery, potter. 60c, Reed baskets, basket maker.

2006, Dec. 29 *Perf. 14¼*
1270-1274 A325 Set of 5 10.00 10.00

Sculptures from 3000-2500 B.C. — A326

Designs: 15c, Human head. 29c, Animals, horiz. 60c, Spirals, horiz. £1.50, Headless nude female.

Wmk. 354

2007, Feb. 28 **Litho.** *Perf. 14¼*
1275-1278 A326 Set of 4 15.00 15.00

Miniature Sheet

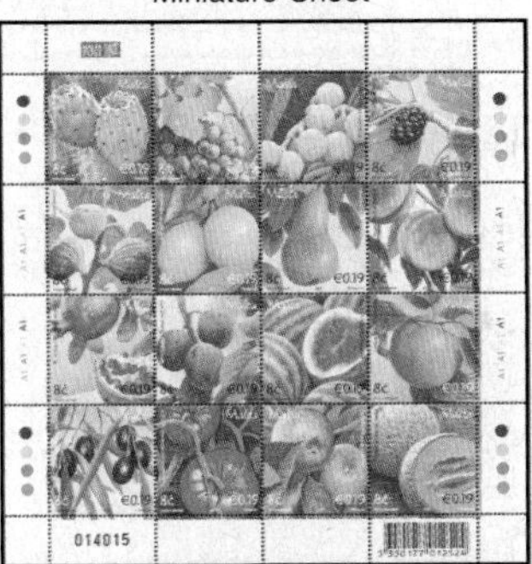

Fruit — A327

No. 1279: a, Opuntia ficus-indica (prickly pears). b, Viris vinifera (grapes). c, Eriobotrya japonica (loquats). d, Morus nigra (black mulberries). e, Ficus carica (figs). f, Citrus limonum (lemons). g, Pyrus communis (pear). h, Prunus persica (peaches). i, Punica granatum (pomegranates). j, Prunus salicina (plums). k, Citrullus vulgaris (watermelons). l, Citrus sinensis (orange). m, Olea europaea (olives). n, Lycopersicon esculentum (tomatoes). o, Malus domestica (apples). p, Cucumis melo (cantaloupe).

2007, Apr. 16
1279 A327 8c Sheet of 16, #a-p 8.00 8.00

Balconies A328

Designs: 8c, Wrought iron balcony. 22c, Stone balcony. 27c, Balustraded balcony, National Library. 29c, Closed wooden balcony. 46c, Art Deco balcony by Silvio Mercieca.

51c, Ornamented balcony, Hostel de Verdelin, Valletta, horiz.

Wmk. 354

2007, Apr. 28 **Litho.** *Perf. 14¼*
1280-1284 A328 Set of 5 8.50 8.50

Souvenir Sheet

Perf. 13¾

1285 A328 51c multi 3.25 3.25

No. 1285 contains one 37x28mm stamp.

Europa A329

Emblems of Scout Association of Malta, Scouting Centenary and: 16c, Lord Robert Baden-Powell. 51c, Maltese scouts at 1957 Jamboree.

2007, May 9 *Perf. 14¼*
1286-1287 A329 Set of 2 4.75 4.75

Canonization of St. George Preca (1880-1962) A330

Background color: 8c, Blue. £1, Orange.

Wmk. 354

2007, May 28 **Litho.** *Perf. 14¼*
1288-1289 A330 Set of 2 7.00 7.00

Toys — A331

Photographs of children and: 2c, Rocking horse, tricycle, car. 3c, Baby carriage, drums and tops. 16c, Boats, beach pails and shovel. 22c, Dolls. 50c, Truck, motorcycle and race car.

2007, July 11 *Perf. 14¼x14*
1290-1294 A331 Set of 5 7.00 7.00

Paintings by Caravaggio — A332

Designs: 5c, St. Jerome. 29c, The Beheading of St. John the Baptist (48x40mm). £2, The Beheading of St. John the Baptist, vert.

2007, July 20 *Perf. 14¼*
1295-1296 A332 Set of 2 2.25 2.25

Souvenir Sheet

1297 A332 £2 multi 16.00 16.00

Arrival of Caravaggio on Malta, 400th anniv. No. 1297 with an overprint in gold in the sheet margin marking the 400th anniv. of the death of Caravaggio was a limited edtition.

Motorcycles — A333

Designs: 1c, 1954 Royal Enfield. 16c, 1941 Matchless G3/L. 27c, 1903 Minerva. 50c, 1965 Triumph Speed Twin.

Perf. 14x14¼

2007, Sept. 12 **Litho.** **Wmk. 354**
1298-1301 A333 Set of 4 7.00 7.00

Greetings Stamps A334

2007, Sept. 28 *Perf. 14¼*

1302	A334 8c Hearts	.55	.55
a.	Sheet of 5 + 5 labels	13.50	13.50
1303	A334 8c Stars	.55	.55
a.	Sheet of 5 + 5 labels	13.50	13.50
1304	A334 8c Roses	.55	.55
a.	Sheet of 5 + 5 labels	13.50	13.50
1305	A334 8c Balloons	.55	.55
a.	Sheet of 5 + 5 labels	13.50	13.50
1306	A334 8c Champagne flutes	.55	.55
a.	Sheet of 5 + 5 labels	13.50	13.50
1307	A334 8c Teddy bears	.55	.55
a.	Sheet of 5 + 5 labels	13.50	13.50
	Nos. 1302-1307 (6)	3.30	3.30

Labels on Nos. 1302a-1307a were personalizable, with full sheets each selling for £2, with a minimum purchase of two sheets of any stamp.

Paintings by John Martin Borg A335

Designs: 11c, Mdina Skyline. 16c, Qrendi. 37c, Vittoriosa Waterfront. 46c, Mgarr Harbor, Gozo. 76c, Xlendi Bay, Gozo.

2007, Oct. 1 *Perf. 14¼*
1308-1312 A335 Set of 5 14.00 14.00

Fruit Type of 2007

Souvenir Sheet

2007, Oct. 18
1313 A327 75c Like #1279m 5.50 5.50

National Tree Planting Weekend. An unspecified portion of the proceeds of the sale went to the 34U Campaign.

Bands A336

Various bands: 4c, 15c, 21c, 22c, £1.

2007, Nov. 13
1314-1318 A336 Set of 5 11.00 11.00

Christmas A337

Maltese arms and nave paintings in St. Andrew's Church, Luqa, by Giuseppe Calì: 8c, Madonna and Child. 16c, Holy Family with Women and Young Girl. 21c, Infant Jesus and Young Girl.

2007, Nov. 20
1319-1321 A337 Set of 3 3.50 3.50

See Vatican City Nos. 1370-1372.

Youth Soccer Association, 25th Anniv. — A338

Society of Christian Doctrine Museum, Cent. — A339

Religious Figures — A340

Treaty of Rome, 50th Anniv. — A341

Designs: 16c, Monsignor Frangisk Bonnici (1852-1905), founder of St. Joseph Institute, Hamrun. 43c, Father Manwel Magri (1851-1907), ethnographer and archaeologist. 86c, Carolina Cauchi (1824-1907), founder of Dominican Sisters of Malta.

Wmk. 354

2007, Dec. 1 Litho. ***Perf. 14¼***
1322 A338 4m multi .25 .25
1323 A339 9c multi .60 .60
1324 A340 16c multi 1.10 1.10
1325 A340 43c multi 3.00 3.00
1326 A340 86c multi 6.00 6.00
Nos. 1322-1326 (5) 10.95 10.95

Souvenir Sheet

Perf. 13¾

1327 A341 76c multi 5.25 5.25

No. 1327 contains one 40x30mm stamp.

Souvenir Sheet

Obverse and Reverse of Maltese Pound Coin — A342

Wmk. 354

2007, Dec. 31 Litho. ***Perf. 14¼***
1328 A342 £1 multi 7.00 7.00

Last day of use of pound currency.

100 Cents = 1 Euro

Souvenir Sheet

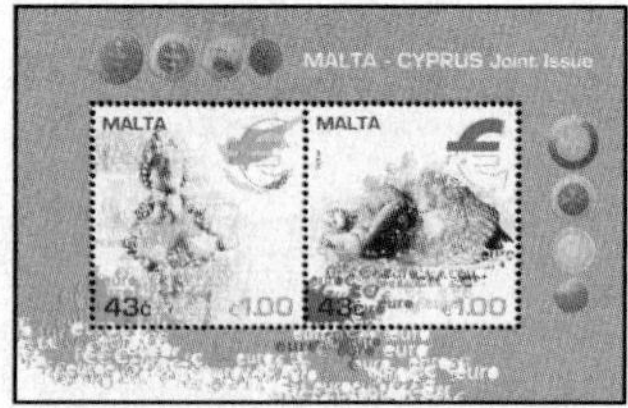
Introduction of Euro Currency — A343

No. 1329: a, Statue of Aphrodite, map of Cyprus. b, Sleeping Lady statue.

Wmk. 354

2008, Jan. 1 Litho. ***Perf. 14¼***
1329 A343 €1 Sheet of 2, #a-b 7.00 7.00

See Cyprus No. 1088.

Souvenir Sheet

Obverse and Reverse of Maltese Euro Coin — A344

2008, Jan. 1
1330 A344 €1 multi 5.00 5.00

Door Knockers A345

Various door knockers with background color of: 26c, Blue. 51c, Red. 63c, Brown. €1.77, Green.

2008, Mar. 5 ***Perf. 14¼x14***
1331-1334 A345 Set of 4 9.75 9.75

2008 Summer Olympics, Beijing — A346

Designs: 5c, Shooting. 12c, Swimming. €1.57, Running.

2008, Mar. 7 ***Perf. 14x14¼***
1335-1337 A346 Set of 3 5.50 5.50

Europa — A347

Mail room, postman with bicycle in: 37c, Sepia. €1.19, Black.

Wmk. 354

2008, May 9 Litho. ***Perf. 14¼***
1338-1339 A347 Set of 2 5.00 5.00

Birth of St. Paul, 2000th Anniv. — A348

Statues depicting St. Paul from: 19c, Conversion of St. Paul Church, Safi. 68c, St. Paul's Shipwreck Church, Munxar. €1.08, St. Paul's Shipwreck Church, Rabat.
€3, St. Paul's Shipwreck Church, Valletta.

2008, June 28
1340-1342 A348 Set of 3 6.25 6.25

Souvenir Sheet

1343 A348 €3 multi 9.50 9.50

Intl. Year of Planet Earth A349

Emblem and: 7c, Sand dune. 86c, Tree in field. €1, Earth. €1.77, Sea coast.

Wmk. 354

2008, Aug. 11 Litho. ***Perf. 14¼***
1344-1347 A349 Set of 4 11.00 11.00

Cruise Liners A350

Designs: 63c, MSC Musica. €1.16, M.S. Voyager of the Seas. €1.40, M. S. Westerdam. €3, RMS Queen Elizabeth 2.

Perf. 14x14¼

2008, Nov. 18 Litho. Wmk. 354
1348-1351 A350 Set of 4 20.00 20.00

Christmas — A351

Paintings: 19c, Madonna and Child with the Infant St. John the Baptist, by Francesco Trevisani. 26c, Nativity, by Master Alberto. 37c, Virgin and Child with the Infant St. John the Baptist, by Carlo Maratta.

2008, Nov. 27 ***Perf. 14¼***
1352-1354 A351 Set of 3 2.25 2.25

Mushrooms A352

Designs: 5c, Laetiorus sulphureus. 12c, Montagnea arenaria. 19c, Pleurotus eryngii. 26c, Inonotus indicus. €1.57, Suillus collinitus.

Wmk. 354

2009, Mar. 27 Litho. ***Perf. 14¼***
1355-1359 A352 Set of 5 8.00 8.00

Postal Transportation A353

Designs: 9c, Airplane. 35c, Motorcycles. €2.50, Bicycles. €3, Mail boat to Gozo.

2009, Apr. 28
1360-1363 A353 Set of 4 20.00 20.00

Introduction of Euro Currency, 10th Anniv. — A354

Wmk. 354

2009, Apr. 30 Litho. ***Perf. 14¼***
1364 A354 €2 multi 7.50 7.50

Europa — A355

Designs: 37c, Galileo Galilei, Sketch of Moon by Galileo, Lunar Module. €1.19, Telescope of William Lassell, M42 nebula.

2009, May 9 ***Perf. 14¼x14***
1365 A355 37c multi 1.10 1.10
a. Booklet pane of 5 6.00 —
Complete booklet, #1365a 6.00
1366 A355 €1.19 multi 3.50 3.50

Intl. Year of Astronomy.

13th Games of the Small States of Europe, Cyprus A356

Designs: 10c, Sailing. 19c, Judo. 37c, Shooting. 67c, Swimming. €1.77, Running.

2009, June 1 ***Perf. 14x14¼***
1367-1371 A356 Set of 5 9.75 9.75

Cruise Liners Type of 2008

Designs: 37c, MS Seabourn Pride. 68c, MS Brilliance of the Seas. 91c, Costa Magica and Costa Atlantica. €2, MS MSC Splendida.

2009, July 15
1372-1375 A350 Set of 4 12.50 12.50

Scenic Views A357

Designs: 2c, Mediterranean coast. 7c, Watchtower. 37c, Salt pans, Qbajjar, Gozo. €1.02, Ggantija Temple ruins.

Perf. 14x14¼
2009, Sept. 16 Litho. Wmk. 354
1376-1379 A357 Set of 4 6.00 6.00

Christmas A358

Designs: 19c, Mater Admirabilis, in the manner of Botticelli by unknown artist. 37c, Madonna and Child, by Corrado Giaquinto. 63c, Madonna and Child, by Follower of Simone Cantarini.

Perf. 14¼x14
2009, Nov. 30 Litho. Wmk. 354
1380-1382 A358 Set of 3 4.25 4.25

History of Malta A359

Inscriptions: 1c, Pleistocene Period. 2c, Early Temple Period. 5c, Late Temple Period. 7c, Bronze Period. 9c, Phoenician & Punic Period, vert. 10c, Roman Period. 19c, Byzantine Period, vert. 26c, Arab Period. 37c, Norman & Hohenstaufen Period, vert. 50c, Angevin & Aragaonese, vert. 51c, Knights of St. John. 63c, French Period. 68c, British Period, vert. 86c, Independence, vert. €1, Republic, vert. €1.08, E.U. Accession, vert. €5, Coat of arms, vert.

2009, Dec. 29 ***Perf. 14x14¼, 14¼x14***

1383	A359	1c	multi	.30	.30
1384	A359	2c	multi	.30	.30
1385	A359	5c	multi	.30	.30
1386	A359	7c	multi	.30	.30
1387	A359	9c	multi	.30	.30
1388	A359	10c	multi	.35	.35
1389	A359	19c	multi	.70	.70
1390	A359	26c	multi	.95	.95
1391	A359	37c	multi	1.40	1.40
1392	A359	50c	multi	1.50	1.50
1393	A359	51c	multi	1.75	1.75
1394	A359	63c	multi	2.00	2.00
1395	A359	68c	multi	2.25	2.25
1396	A359	86c	multi	3.00	3.00
1397	A359	€1	multi	3.50	3.50
1398	A359	€1.08	multi	3.75	3.75
1399	A359	€5	multi	13.00	13.00
a.	Souvenir sheet, #1383-1399			40.00	40.00
	Nos. 1383-1399 (17)			35.65	35.65

See Nos. 1443-1444.

Miniature Sheet

100-Ton Guns of Malta and Gibraltar — A360

No. 1400 — 100-ton gun from: a, Fort Rinella, Malta, 2010. b, Fort Rinella, 1882. c, Napier of Magdala Battery, Gibraltar, 1880. d, Napier of Magdala Battery, 2010.

Wmk. 354
2010, Feb. 19 Litho. ***Perf. 13¾***
1400 A360 75c Sheet of 4, #a-d 10.00 10.00

See Gibraltar No. 1221.

Balloons A361

Islands A362

Mortarboard and Diploma — A363

Wedding A364

Champagne Bottle, Bucket and Flutes — A365

Clock Tower and Fireworks A366

Hand Holding Trophy — A367

Map of Malta A368

Wmk. 354
2010, Mar. 17 Litho. ***Perf. 14¼***

1401	A361	19c	multi	.65	.65
1402	A362	19c	multi	.65	.65
1403	A363	19c	multi	.65	.65
1404	A364	19c	multi	.65	.65
1405	A365	19c	multi	.65	.65
1406	A366	19c	multi	.65	.65
1407	A367	19c	multi	.65	.65
1408	A368	37c	multi	1.25	1.25
	Nos. 1401-1408 (8)			5.80	5.80

Souvenir Sheet

Visit of Pope Benedict XVI to Malta — A369

2010, Mar. 17
1409 A369 €3 multi 10.00 10.00

Europa — A370

Characters from children's books: 37c, Putinu u Toninu, by Dr. Philip Farrugia Randon. €1.19, Meta l-Milied Ma Glex (When Christmas Didn't Come), by Clare Azzopardi.

2010, May 4

1410-1411	A370	Set of 2	4.00	4.00
1411a	Booklet pane of 5 #1411		6.00	—
	Complete booklet, #1411a		6.00	

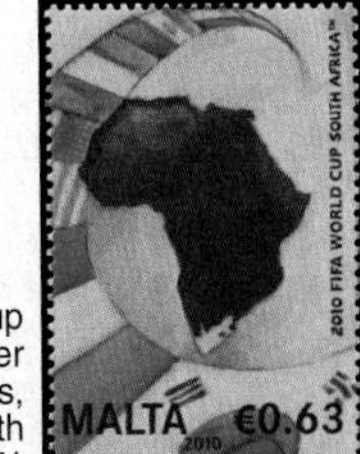

2010 World Cup Soccer Championships, South Africa — A371

Designs: 63c, Flags, map of Africa. €2.50, Mascot, flag and map of South Africa.

Wmk. 354
2010, June 11 Litho. ***Perf. 14¼***

1412-1413	A371	Set of 2	8.50	8.50
1413a	Souvenir sheet, #1412-1413		8.50	8.50

Intl. Year of Biodiversity — A372

Designs: 19c, Maltese wall lizard. 68c, Storm petrel, vert. 86c, Maltese pyramidal orchid, vert. €1.40, Freshwater crab.

Perf. 14x14¼, 14¼x14
2010, Sept. 23 Litho. Wmk. 354
1414-1417 A372 Set of 4 10.00 10.00

Coastline Features — A373

Designs: 37c, Azure Window, Gozo. 51c, Blue Grotto, Zurrieq, vert. 67c, Ta' Cenc Cliffs, Gozo, vert. €1.16, Filfla.

Perf. 14x14¼, 14¼x14
2010, Oct. 19 Litho. Wmk. 354
1418-1421 A373 Set of 4 8.50 8.50

Christmas — A374

Designs: 19c, The Adoration of the Magi, by the Studio of Valerio Castello. 37c, The Flight Into Egypt, attributed to Filippo Paladini. 63c, Madonna di Maggio, by Pierre Guillemin, vert.

Perf. 14x14¼, 14¼x14
2010, Nov. 9 Litho. Wmk. 354
1422-1424 A374 Set of 3 4.00 4.00

Compare with type A358.

Souvenir Sheet

First Malta Stamp, 150th Anniv. — A375

2010, Dec. 1 ***Perf. 14¼x14***
1425 A375 €2.80 multi 9.50 9.50

Maltese Landscape Paintings by Edward Said — A376

Designs: 19c, Valletta. 37c, Manoel Island. €1.57, Cittadella.

Perf. 14x14¼
2011, Mar. 9 Litho. Wmk. 354
1426-1428 A376 Set of 3 6.00 6.00

Miniature Sheet

Worldwide Fund for Nature (WWF), 50th Anniv. — A377

Various depictions of Chimaera monstrosa: a, 51c. b, 63c. c, 67c. d, 97c.

2011, Apr. 29 *Perf. 13¾*
1429 A377 Sheet of 4, #a-d 8.00 8.00

Europa — A378

Forest and: 37c, Butterfly and building. €1.19, Building.

2011, May 9 *Perf. 14¼x14*
1430-1431 A378 Set of 2 4.50 4.50

Intl. Year of Forests.

Miniature Sheets

Buses — A379

No. 1432: a, Reo bus on B'Kara route. b, Dodge T110L bus on Zabbar route. c, Leyland Comet bus on Zurrieq route. d, Ford V8 bus on Zebbug-Siggiewi route. e, Bedford SLD bus on Gudja-Ghaxaq route. f, Maltese Chassis Gozo Mail Bus. g, Federal Bus on Kalafrana route. h, Dodge T110L bus on Siggiewi route. i, Indiana bus on Rabat route. j, Austin CXD bus on Zetjun route.

No. 1433: a, Ford V8 bus on Sliema route. b, Commer Q4 bus on Lija route. c, Fordson BB bus on Mosta-Naxxar route. d, Thornycroft Sturdy ZE bus on Mellieha route. e, Bedford QL bus on Cospicua route. f, Magirus Deutz bus for all routes. g, Commer Q4 bus on Naxxar route. h, Bedford SB8 bus on Gozo route. i, Thames ET7 bus on B'Kara-St. Julians route. j, Bedford QL private hire bus.

2011, July 2 *Perf. 14x14¼*
1432 A379 20c Sheet of 10, #a-j 5.75 5.75
1433 A379 69c Sheet of 10, #a-j 19.50 19.50

Boats A380

Designs: 26c, Ferry M.V, Ta'Pinu. 37c, Ferry M.V. Jean De La Vallete. 67c, Patrol boat P23. 91c, Tugboat M.V. Spinola.

Perf. 14x14¼
2011, Aug. 10 **Litho.** **Wmk. 354**
1434-1437 A380 Set of 4 6.50 6.50

Souvenir Sheet

Fishing Boat at Mgarr — A381

2011, Sept. 15 *Perf. 13¾*
1438 A381 €2.07 multi 5.75 5.75

See Iceland No. 1245.

Christmas A382

Paintings: 20c, The Holy Family in an Interior, by Follower of Marcello Venusti. 37c, The Madonna and Child with Infant St. John the Baptist, by the Tuscan School. 63c, The Rest on the Flight to Egypt, attributed to Circle of Pieter van Mol.

2011, Nov. 15 **Wmk. 354** *Perf. 14¼*
1439-1441 A382 Set of 3 3.25 3.25

Souvenir Sheet

Malta No. 114 — A383

2011, Dec. 2
1442 A383 £4.16 multi 11.50 11.50

Malta Senate and Legislative Assembly, 90th anniv.

History of Malta Type of 2009

Inscriptions: 20c, Byzantine Period. 69c, British Period.

Perf. 14¼x14
2012, Mar. 7 **Litho.** **Wmk. 354**
1443 A359 20c multi .55 .55
1444 A359 69c multi 1.90 1.90

Paintings of Maltese Sites — A384

Designs: 20c, Marsalforn, by H. M. Bateman. 26c, Qala, by Bateman. 37c, Ghajnsielem, by Bateman, vert. 67c, Inquisitor's Palace, by Edward Lear. 97c, Gran Fontana, by Lear.

Wmk. 354
2012, Mar. 23 **Litho.** *Perf. 14¼*
1445-1449 A384 Set of 5 6.50 6.50

Wedding Rings A385

Mortarboard and Diploma — A386

Christmas Ornaments — A387

Comino Shoreline — A388

Auberge de Castille, Painting by Charles Frederick de Brocktorff — A389

St. John's Co-cathedral, Valletta — A390

Trophy — A391

Champagne Bottle and Flutes — A392

2012, Apr. 3

1450	A385	37c multi	1.00	1.00
1451	A386	37c multi	1.00	1.00
1452	A387	37c multi	1.00	1.00
1453	A388	37c multi	1.00	1.00
1454	A389	37c multi	1.00	1.00
1455	A390	37c multi	1.00	1.00
1456	A391	37c multi	1.00	1.00
1457	A392	37c multi	1.00	1.00
		Nos. 1450-1457 (8)	8.00	8.00

Souvenir Sheet

Awarding of George Cross to Malta, 70th Anniv. — A393

2012, Apr. 14
1458 A393 €4.16 multi 11.00 11.00

Europa — A394

No. 1459 — Grand Harbour: a, 37c. b, €1.19.

2012, May 9
1459 A394 Horiz. pair, #a-b 4.25 4.25

Souvenir Sheet

2012 Summer Olympics, London — A395

No. 1460 — 2012 Olympic Games: a, 37c, Emblem. b, €2.11, Mascot.

2012, July 27
1460 A395 Sheet of 2, #a-b 6.25 6.25

Ships Involved in Operation Pedestal — A396

No. 1461: a, S.S. Almeria Lykes. b, H.M.S. Amazon. c, H.M.S. Antelope. d, H.M.S. Ashanti. e, H.M.S. Badsworth. f, H.M.S. Bicester. g, H.M.S. Bramham. h, M.V. Brisbane Star.

No. 1462: a, R.F.A. Brown Ranger. b, H.M.S. Cairo. c, H.M.S. Charybdis. d, M.V. Clan Ferguson. e, H.M.S. Coltsfoot. f, H.M.S. Derwent. g, M.V. Deucalion. h, R.F.A. Dingledale.

No. 1463: a, M.V. Dorset. b, H.M.S. Eagle. c, M.V. Empire Hope. d, H.M.S. Eskimo. e, H.M.S. Foresight. f, H.M.S. Furious. g, H.M.S. Fury. h, H.M.S. Geranium.

No. 1464: a, M.V. Glenorchy. b, H.M.S. Hebe. c, H.M.S. Hythe. d, H.M.S. Icarus. e, H.M.S. Indomitable. f, H.M.S. Intrepid. g, H.M.S. Ithuriel. h, H.M.S. Jaunty.

No. 1465: a, H.M.S. Jonquil. b, H.M.S. Kenya. c, H.M.S. Keppel. d, H.M.S. Laforey. e, H.M.S. Ledbury. f, H.M.S. Lightning. g, H.M.S. Lookout. h, H.M.S. Malcolm.

No. 1466: a, H.M.S. Manchester. b, H.M.S. Matchless. c, M.V. Melbourne Star. d, H.M.S. Nelson. e, H.M.S. Nigeria. f, S.S. Ohio. g, H.M.S. Pathfinder. h, H.M.S. Penn.

No. 1467: a, H.M.S. Phoebe. b, M.V. Port Chalmers. c, H.M.S. Quentin. d, M.V. Rochester Castle. e, H.M.S. Rodney. f, H.M.S. Rye. g, H.M.S. Salvonia. h, S.S. Santa Elisa.

No. 1468: a, H.M.S. Sirius. b, H.M.S. Somali. c, H.M.S. Speedy. d, H.M.S. Spirea. e, H.M.S. Tartar. f, H.M.S. Una. g, H.M.S. Utmost. h, H.M.S. Vansittart.

No. 1469: a, H.M.S. Venomous. b, H.M.S. Victorious. c, H.M.S. Vidette. d, S.S. Waimarama. e, M.V. Wairangi. f, H.M.S. Westcott. g, H.M.S. Wilton. h, H.M.S. Wishart.

No. 1470: a, H.M.S. Wolverine. b, H.M.S. Wrestler. c, H.M.S. Zetland. d, H.M.S. P.34. e, H.M.S. P.42. f, H.M.S. P.44. g, H.M.S. P.46. h, M.L. 321.

No. 1471: a, M.L. 126. b, M.L. 134. c, M.L. 135. d, M.L. 168. e, H.M.S. P.211. f, H.M.S. P.222. g, M.L. 459. h, M.L. 462.

2012, Aug. 10

1461	Sheet of 8, #a-h, + 2 labels	5.75	5.75
a.-h.	A396 26c Any single	.70	.70
1462	Sheet of 8, #a-h, + 2 labels	5.75	5.75
a.-h.	A396 26c Any single	.70	.70
1463	Sheet of 8, #a-h, + 2 labels	5.75	5.75
a.-h.	A396 26c Any single	.70	.70
1464	Sheet of 8, #a-h, + 2 labels	5.75	5.75
a.-h.	A396 26c Any single	.70	.70
1465	Sheet of 8, #a-h, + 2 labels	5.75	5.75
a.-h.	A396 26c Any single	.70	.70
1466	Sheet of 8, #a-h, + 2 labels	5.75	5.75
a.-h.	A396 26c Any single	.70	.70
1467	Sheet of 8, #a-h, + 2 labels	5.75	5.75
a.-h.	A396 26c Any single	.70	.70
1468	Sheet of 8, #a-h, + 2 labels	5.75	5.75
a.-h.	A396 26c Any single	.70	.70
1469	Sheet of 8, #a-h, + 2 labels	5.75	5.75
a.-h.	A396 26c Any single	.70	.70
1470	Sheet of 8, #a-h, + 2 labels	5.75	5.75
a.-h.	A396 26c Any single	.70	.70
1471	Sheet of 8, #a-h, + 2 labels	5.75	5.75
a.-h.	A396 26c Any single	.70	.70
	Nos. 1461-1471 (11)	63.25	63.25

Operation Pedestal, 70th anniv.

Historic Gates A397

Designs: 20c, Notre Dame Gate, Zabbar. 37c, Couvre Port Gate, Victoria, vert. 67c, Lunzjata Valley Gate, Victoria, vert. 69c, Fort Chambray Gate, Ghajnsielem.

2012, Sept. 26

1472-1475 A397 Set of 4 5.00 5.00

Christmas A398

Paintings: 20c, The Adoration of the Magi, by German Follower of Peter Paul Rubens. 37c, The Holy Family, by the Circle of Denys Calvaert. 63c, Holy Family, by the Dutch School.

2012, Oct. 31

1476-1478 A398 Set of 3 3.25 3.25

Souvenir Sheet

Blessed Gerard, by Antoine Favray — A399

2013, Feb. 15

1479 A399 €2.47 multi 6.50 6.50

Papal Bull of Pope Paschal II to Blessed Gerard concerning Hospital of St. John of Jerusalem, 900th anniv.

Souvenir Sheet

Paintings of Mattia Preti (1613-99) — A400

No. 1480: a, 97c, The Baptism of Christ (35x35mm). b, €1.87, Self-portrait (31x44mm).

2013, Feb. 23

1480 A400 Sheet of 2, #a-b 7.50 7.50

Fountains A401

Designs: 6c, Vilhena Fountain, Floriana. 32c, Triton Fountain, Floriana, horiz. €2.62, Spinola Fountain, Valletta.

Perf. 14¼x14, 14x14¼

2013, Mar. 27 **Wmk. 354**

1481-1483 A401 Set of 3 7.75 7.75

Europa A402

Postal vehicles: 37c, Ford Transit Mark 1 van. €1.19, Lambretta three-wheeled van.

2013, May 9 ***Perf. 14x13½***

1484-1485 A402 Set of 2 4.25 4.25

European Maritime Day — A403

Ocean liners: 26c, Riviera. 51c, Costa Deliziosa. 97c, MS Ryndam.

2013, May 20 ***Perf. 14x14¼***

1486-1488 A403 Set of 3 4.75 4.75

Mammals — A404

Designs: 37c, Wild rabbit. €2.25, Maltese ox.

2013, June 20

1489-1490 A404 Set of 2 7.00 7.00

Souvenir Sheet

Grand Harbor, Malta — A405

2013, Aug. 20 ***Perf. 13½x13¾***

1491 A405 €4.51 multi 12.00 12.00

See Curaçao No. 137.

Buses A406

Designs: 6c, Park Royal-Commer airport bus, 1940s. 10c, Thornycroft bus on Valletta-St. Julian's Route, c. 1903. 37c, Victoria Hire Service bus, c. 1925. 52c, Bedford SB Royal Armed Forces bus, 1950s. €1.16, Thames ET6 police bus, 1970s. €2.25, Magirus-Deutz O3500 bus.

2013, Aug. 27 ***Perf. 14x14¼***

1492-1497 A406 Set of 6 12.00 12.00

Souvenir Sheet

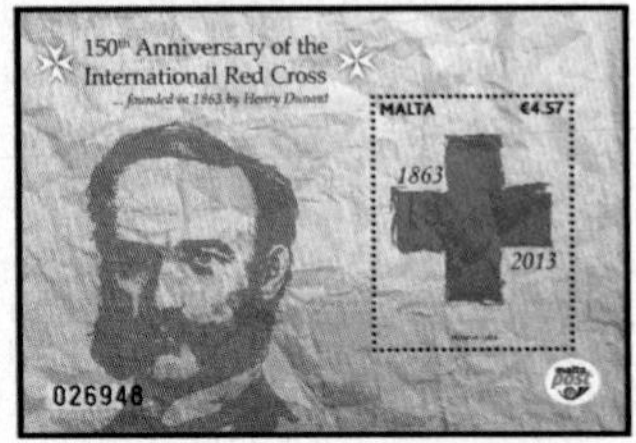

International Red Cross, 150th Anniv. — A407

Wmk. 354

2013, Oct. 29 **Litho.** ***Perf. 13¼***

1498 A407 €4.57 multi 12.50 12.50

Christmas A408

Details from creche scene from Jesus of Nazareth Institute, Zejtun: 26c, 37c, 63c.

No. 1502 — Entire creche scene showing: a, Combined designs of 37c and 63c stamps. b, Design of 26c stamp and other creche figures.

Perf. 13¾x14

2013, Nov. 18 **Litho.** **Wmk. 354**

1499-1501 A408 Set of 3 3.50 3.50

Souvenir Sheet

1502 A408 €1 Sheet of 2, #a-b 5.50 5.50

No. 1502 contains two 76x20mm stamps.

Fountains A409

Fountain at: 42c, Floriana. 59c, San Anton Gardens, Attard, horiz. €1.25, Kercem.

Wmk. 354

2014, Jan. 3 **Litho.** ***Perf. 14¼***

1503-1505 A409 Set of 3 6.25 6.25

Halls of the Knights Hospitaller, Acre, Israel and Valletta, Malta — A410

Wmk. 354

2014, Jan. 28 **Litho.** ***Perf. 13¾***

1506 A410 51c multi 1.40 1.40

See Israel No. 2000.

Watercraft A411

Designs: No. 1507, 26c, Police boat at Valletta. No. 1508, 26c, Police boat at Sliema Ferries. No. 1509, €1.55, HMS Alexander. No. 1510, €1.55, HMS London.

Wmk. 354

2014, Mar. 18 **Litho.** ***Perf. 14***

1507-1510 A411 Set of 4 10.00 10.00

Malta Police Force, 200th anniv. (Nos. 1507-1508); End of Military Facilities Agreement, 35th anniv. (Nos. 1509-1510).

Souvenir Sheet

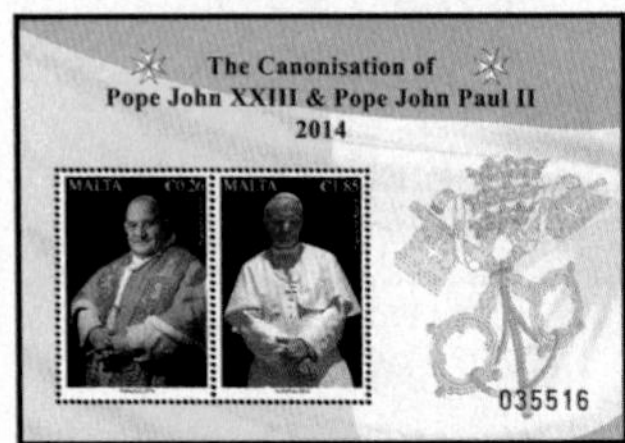

Canonization of Popes John XXIII and John Paul II — A412

No. 1511: a, 26c, Pope John XXIII (1881-1963). b, €1.85, Pope John Paul II (1920-2005).

Wmk. 354

2014, Apr. 26 Litho. *Perf. 14¼*
1511 A412 Sheet of 2, #a-b 6.00 6.00

Admission to the European Union, 10th Anniv. — A413

Wmk. 354

2014, Apr. 30 Litho. *Perf. 14¼*
1512 A413 59c multi 1.75 1.75

Europa — A414

Details from painting by Girolamo Gianni: 59c, Man playing Maltese bagpipe. €2.19, Man playing drum.

Wmk. 354

2014, May 9 Litho. *Perf. 13½*
1513-1514 A414 Set of 2 7.75 7.75

Souvenir Sheet

National Anniversaries — A415

No. 1515: a, 59c, #308 redrawn with "50th Anniversary 1964-2014" added (27x33mm). b, €3, #489 redrawn with "40th Anniversary 1974-2014" added (44x31mm).

Perf. 14, 14x14¼ (No. 1515c)

2014, May 15 Litho. Wmk. 354
1515 A415 Sheet of 2, #a-b 9.75 9.75

Souvenir Sheet

2014 World Cup Soccer Championships, Brazil — A416

No. 1516: a, 59c, Emblem. b, €1.55, Mascot.

Wmk. 354

2014, June 12 Litho. *Perf. 14¼*
1516 A416 Sheet of 2, #a-b 6.00 6.00

Flowers — A417

Designs: 26c, Gladiolus italicus. 59c, Verbascum sinuatum. €1.16, Orchis conica.

Perf. 14x13¾

2014, June 27 Litho. Wmk. 354
1517-1519 A417 Set of 3 5.50 5.50

See Nos. 1532-1534, 1555-1557, 1583-1585.

Euromed Postal Emblem and Mediterranean Sea — A418

Wmk. 354

2014, July 9 Litho. *Perf. 13¾*
1520 A418 €1.85 multi 5.00 5.00

Grand Masters of the Sovereign Military Order of Malta — A419

No. 1521: a, Philippe de Villiers de L'Isle-Adam. b, Pierino del Ponte. c, Didier de Saint-Jaille. d, Jean de Homedes. e, Claude de la Sengle. f, Jean de la Valette-Parisot. g, Pierre de Monte. h, Jean L'Evesque de la Cassière.

No. 1522: a, Hugues Loubenx de Verdala. b, Martin Garzez. c, Alof de Wignacourt. d, Luis Mendez de Vasconcellos. e, Antoine de Paule. f, Jean-Paul de Lascaris-Castellar. g, Martín de Redín. h, Annet de Clermont-Gessant. i, Raphael Cotoner. j, Nicolas Cotoner.

No. 1523: a, Gregorio Carafa. b, Adrien de Wignacourt. c, Ramon Perellos y Roccaful. d, Marc'Antonio Zondadari. e, Antonio Manoel de Vilhena. f, Raymond Despuig. g, Manuel Pinto de Fonseca. h, Francisco Ximenes de Texada. i, Emmanuel de Rohan-Polduc. j, Ferdinand von Hompesch zu Bolheim.

Wmk. 354

2014, Sept. 30 Litho. *Perf. 14¼*
1521 Sheet of 8 + 2 labels 5.25 5.25
a.-h. A419 26c Any single .65 .65
1522 Sheet of 10 6.50 6.50
a.-j. A419 26c Any single .65 .65
1523 Sheet of 10 6.50 6.50
a.-j. A419 26c Any single .65 .65
Nos. 1521-1523 (3) 18.25 18.25

World War I, Cent. A420

Poppy and: 10c, Bighi Hospital. 59c, Floriana Hospital. €2, HMHS Rewa.

Perf. 14x14¼

2014, Nov. 7 Litho. Wmk. 354
1524-1526 A420 Set of 3 6.75 6.75

Christmas A421

Actors in live Nativity scene in Ghajnsielem depicting: 26c, Holy Family. 59c, Adoration of the Magi, horiz. 63c, Shepherds, horiz. €1.16, Holy Family, diff.

Perf. 14¼x14, 14x14¼

2014, Nov. 17 Litho. Wmk. 354
1527-1530 A421 Set of 4 6.50 6.50

Malta and Yalta Conferences, 70th Anniv. — A422

No. 1531: a, Franklin D. Roosevelt and Winston Churchill meeting in Malta. b, Montgomery House, Floriana, Malta. c, Churchill, Roosevelt, Joseph Stalin and other officials at Yalta Conference.

Wmk. 354

2015, Feb. 4 Litho. *Perf. 14¼*
1531 Horiz. strip of 3 7.50 7.50
a.-c. A422 €1 Any single 2.50 2.50

Flowers Type of 2014

Designs: 26c, Tragopogon hybridus. 59c, Anemone coronaria. €1.16, Arisarum vulgare.

Perf. 14x13¾

2015, Feb. 14 Litho. Wmk. 354
1532-1534 A417 Set of 3 4.50 4.50

Aqueducts — A423

Designs: 42c, Fleur-de-lys Aqueduct. €1.55, Wignacourt Water Tower, Floriana, vert.

Wmk. 354

2015, Apr. 21 Litho. *Perf. 14¼*
1535-1536 A423 Set of 2 4.50 4.50

Souvenir Sheet

Gallipoli Campaign, Cent. — A424

Wmk. 354

2015, Apr. 25 Litho. *Perf. 13¾*
1537 A424 €3.59 multi 8.25 8.25

Penny Black, 175th Anniv. — A425

Wmk. 354

2015, May 2 Litho. *Perf. 13¾*
1538 A425 €1.21 multi 2.75 2.75

No. 1538 was printed in sheets of 3.

Europa — A426

Children playing with: 59c, Cart. €2.19, Hoop.

Wmk. 354

2015, May 9 Litho. *Perf. 13¾*
1539-1540 A426 Set of 2 6.25 6.25

Culture in Malta — A427

Designs: 26c, Feast of St. George, Victoria. 59c, Regatta, Grand Harbor. €1.16, Easter procession, Zebbug.

Wmk. 354

2015, June 16 Litho. *Perf. 14¼*
1541-1543 A427 Set of 3 4.50 4.50

Firilla A428

Wmk. 354

2015, July 9 Litho. *Perf. 13¾*
1544 A428 €3.59 multi 8.00 8.00

Ex-Voto Paintings — A429

Painting from: 51c, 1835. 82c, 1839. €1, 1843.

Wmk. 354

2015, July 29 Litho. *Perf. 14¼*
1545-1547 A429 Set of 3 5.25 5.25

St. John Bosco (1815-88) A430

Perf. 14¼x14

2015, Aug. 14 Litho. Wmk. 354

1548 A430 €2 multi 4.50 4.50

Souvenir Sheet

The Allegory of the Triumph of the Order, by Mattia Preti — A431

Wmk. 354

2015, Sept. 7 Litho. *Perf. 13¼*

1549 A431 €4.25 multi 9.50 9.50

Great Siege of Malta, 450th anniv.

Souvenir Sheet

United Nations, 70th Anniv. — A432

Wmk. 354

2015, Oct. 24 Litho. *Perf. 14¼*

1550 A432 €3.51 multi 7.75 7.75

Christmas A433

Woodcuts by Albrecht Dürer: 26c, The Flight into Egypt. 59c, The Nativity of the Lord. 63c, The Adoration of the Magi.

Wmk. 354

2015, Nov. 14 Litho. *Perf. 14¼*

1551-1553 A433 Set of 3 3.25 3.25

Souvenir Sheet

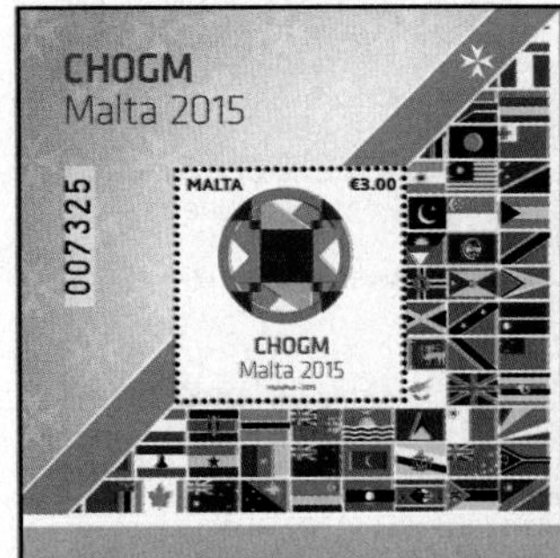

Commonwealth Heads of Government Meeting, Malta — A434

Wmk. 354

2015, Nov. 27 Litho. *Perf. 14¼*

1554 A434 €3 multi 6.50 6.50

Flowers Type of 2014

Designs: 26c, Asphodelus aestivus. 59c, Anacamptis pyramidalis. €1.16, Ophrys melitensis.

Perf. 14x13¾

2016, Jan. 22 Litho. Wmk. 354

1555-1557 A417 Set of 3 4.50 4.50

Souvenir Sheet

Valletta, 450th Anniv. — A435

Wmk. 354

2016, Mar. 28 Litho. *Perf. 14¼*

1558 A435 €4.25 multi 9.75 9.75

Miniature Sheet

Worldwide Fund for Nature (WWF) — A436

No. 1559 — Shearwater: a, Flying right. b, Flying left. c, One on water. d, Four on water.

Wmk. 354

2016, Apr. 15 Litho. *Perf. 14¼*

1559 A436 Sheet of 4 7.00 7.00

a.-d. 75c Any single 1.75 1.75

A437

Europa A438

Wmk. 354

2016, May 9 Litho. *Perf. 14¼*

1560 A437 59c multi 1.40 1.40

1561 A438 €2.19 multi 5.00 5.00

Think Green Issue.

Paintings by Nicholas P. Krasnoff (1869-1947) A439

Designs: No. 1562, €1, View from Vittoriosa Gate, Malta. No. 1563, €1, Dulber Palace, Crimea.

Wmk. 354

2016, May 24 Litho. *Perf. 14¼*

1562-1563 A439 Set of 2 4.50 4.50

See Russia No. 7725.

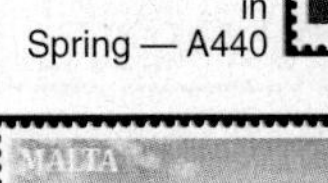

Woman in Traditional Costume, Citadella, Gozo in Spring — A440

Woman on Ghajn Tuffieha Beach in Summer A441

Woman and Verdala Palace in Autumn — A442

Woman and Ghar-id-Dud in Winter — A443

2016, June 21 Litho. *Perf. 14¼*

1564 A440 26c multi .60 .60

1565 A441 51c multi 1.25 1.25

1566 A442 59c multi 1.40 1.40

1567 A443 €2 multi 4.50 4.50

Nos. 1564-1567 (4) 7.75 7.75

Coryphaena Hippurus — A444

Wmk. 354

2016, July 9 Litho. *Perf. 14¼*

1568 A444 €3.59 multi 8.00 8.00

2016 Summer Olympics, Rio de Janeiro — A445

Designs: 42c, Shooting. 62c, Swimming. 90c Weight lifting. €1.55, Relay race.

Wmk. 354

2016, Aug. 5 Litho. *Perf. 14¼*

1569-1572 A445 Set of 4 8.00 8.00

Dominic Mintoff (1916-2012), Prime Minister — A446

Wmk. 354

2016, Aug. 6 Litho. *Perf. 14¼*

1573 A446 €3 multi 6.75 6.75

Souvenir Sheet

HMS Hastings in Valletta Grand Harbor, by Charles von Brocktorff — A447

Wmk. 354

2016, Sept. 15 Litho. *Perf. 13¼*

1574 A447 €3.59 multi 8.00 8.00

Balcony Corbels — A448

Various corbels with panel color of: 26c, Green. €1, Purple. €1.16, Red.

Wmk. 354

2016, Oct. 15 Litho. *Perf. 14¼*

1575-1577 A448 Set of 3 5.50 5.50

Souvenir Sheet

Fortifications in Malta and San Marino — A449

No. 1578: a, 59c, Citadella, Gozo, Malta. b, €3, First Tower, San Marino.

Wmk. 354

2016, Oct. 18 Litho. *Perf. 13¾*

1578 A449	Sheet of 2, #a-b	8.00	8.00

See San Marino No. 1975.

Christmas A450

Designs: 26c, Nativity. 59c, Star of Bethlehem over manger. 63c, Adoration of the Magi.

Wmk. 354

2016, Nov. 18 Litho. *Perf. 13¾*

1579-1581 A450	Set of 3	3.25	3.25

Souvenir Sheet

Maltese Presidency of the Council of the European Union — A451

Perf. 14¼x14

2017, Jan. 12 Litho. Wmk. 354

1582 A451	€3.59 multi	7.75	7.75

Flowers Type of 2014

Designs: 26c, Orchis collina. 42c, Ophrys lutea. €1.25, Serapias parviflora.

2017, Feb. 24 Litho. *Perf. 14x13¾*

1583-1585 A417	Set of 3	4.25	4.25

SEMI-POSTAL STAMPS

All semi-postal issues are for Christmas.

Catalogue values for unused stamps in this section are for Never Hinged items.

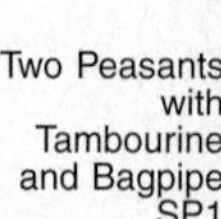

Two Peasants with Tambourine and Bagpipe SP1

Star of Bethlehem and: 5p+1p, Angels with Trumpet and Harp, Star of Bethlehem and Mdina Cathedral. 1sh6p+3p, Choir boys singing Christmas carols.

The background of the 3 stamps together shows the Cathedral of Mdina, Malta, and surrounding countryside.

Wmk. 354

1969, Nov. 8 Litho. *Perf. 12½*

B1	SP1 1p +1p multi	.25	.25
a.	Gold omitted	180.00	
B2	SP1 5p +1p multi	.25	.25
B3	SP1 1sh6p +3p multi	.25	*.45*
a.	Triptych, #B1-B3	.50	.50
	Nos. B1-B3 (3)	.75	.95

Nos. B1-B3 were printed each in sheets of 60, and in sheets containing 20 triptychs.

Christmas Eve Procession — SP2

10p+2p, Nativity & Cathedral. 1sh6p+3p, Adoration of the Shepherds & Mdina Cathedral.

1970, Nov. 7 Photo. *Perf. 14x13½*

B4	SP2 1p +½p multi	.25	.25
B5	SP2 10p +2p multi	.25	.25
B6	SP2 1sh6p +3p multi	.25	*.45*
	Nos. B4-B6 (3)	.75	*.95*

Surtax for child welfare organizations.

Angel — SP3

No. B8, Madonna & Child. No. B9, Shepherd.

1971, Nov. 8 *Perf. 14*

B7	SP3 1p +½p multi	.25	.25
B8	SP3 10p +2p multi	.25	.25
B9	SP3 1sh6p +3p multi	.25	.40
a.	Souv. sheet, #B7-B9, perf. 15	1.00	*1.25*
	Nos. B7-B9 (3)	.75	.90

1972, Dec. Litho. *Perf. 13½*

Designs: 3c+1c, Angel playing tambourine. 7c5m+1c5m, Angel singing.

B10	SP3 8m +2m dk gray & gold	.25	.25
B11	SP3 3c +1c dk purple & gold	.25	.25
B12	SP3 7c5m +1c5m slate & gold	.25	*.50*
a.	Souvenir sheet of 3, #B10-B12	2.50	*3.50*
	Nos. B10-B12 (3)	.75	1.00

1973, Nov. 10 Litho. *Perf. 13½*

8m+2m, Singers, organ pipes. 3c+1c, Virgin & Child with star. 7c5m+1c5m, Star, candles, buildings, tambourine.

B13	SP3 8m +2m multi	.25	.25
B14	SP3 3c +1c multi	.25	*.30*
B15	SP3 7c5m +1c5m multi	.45	*1.25*
a.	Souvenir sheet of 3, #B13-B15	6.00	*6.50*
	Nos. B13-B15 (3)	.95	*1.80*
	Nos. B7-B15 (9)	2.45	3.70

Star and Holy Family — SP4

Designs: 3c+1c, Star and two shepherds. 5c+1c, Star and three shepherds. 7c5m+1c5m, Star and Three Kings.

1974, Nov. 22 Litho. *Perf. 14*

B16	SP4 8m +2m multi	.25	.25
B17	SP4 3c +1c multi	.25	.25
B18	SP4 5c +1c multi	.25	.30
B19	SP4 7c5m +1c5m multi	.30	.45
	Nos. B16-B19 (4)	1.05	1.25

Nativity, by Maestro Alberto — SP5

8m+2m, Shepherds. 7c5m+1c5m, Three Kings.

1975, Nov. 4 *Perf. 13½*

Size: 24x23mm (#B20, B22); 49x23mm (#B21)

B20	SP5 8m +2m multi	.25	.25
B21	SP5 3c +1c multi	.45	*.60*
B22	SP5 7c5m +1c5m multi	.60	*1.50*
a.	Triptych, #B20-B22	3.50	*4.00*
	Nos. B20-B22 (3)	1.30	*2.35*

Printed singly and as triptychs. Surtax for child welfare.

SP6

Madonna and Saints, by Domenico di Michelino — SP7

Details of Painting: 5c+1c, Virgin & Child. 7c+1c5m, St. Christopher & Bishop.

1976, Nov. 23 Litho. *Perf. 13½*

B23	SP6 1c +5m multi	.25	.25
B24	SP6 5c +1c multi	.25	.25
B25	SP6 7c +1c5m multi	.40	*.65*

Perf. 13½x14

B26	SP7 10c +2c multi	1.60	*1.25*
	Nos. B23-B26 (4)	2.50	2.40

Nativity SP8

Crèche Figurines: 1c+5m, Annunciation to the Shepherds. 11c+1c5m, Shepherds.

Perf. 13½x14

1977, Nov. 16 Wmk. 354

B27	SP8 1c +5m multi	.25	.25
B28	SP8 7c +1c multi	.25	*.45*
B29	SP8 11c +1c5m multi	.30	*.70*
a.	Triptych, #B27-B29	1.25	1.25
	Nos. B27-B29 (3)	.80	1.40

Nos. B27-B29 printed singly and as triptychs. No. B29a is not a continuous picture. Surtax was for child welfare.

Christmas Decorations, People and Church — SP9

Designs: 5c+1c, Decorations and angels. 7c+1c5m, Decorations and carolers. 11c+3c, Combined designs of Nos. B30-B32.

1978, Nov. 9 Litho. *Perf. 14*

Size: 24x30mm

B30	SP9 1c +5m multi	.25	.25
B31	SP9 5c +1c multi	.25	.25
B32	SP9 7c +1c5m multi	.25	*.35*

Perf. 13½

Size: 58x22½mm

B33	SP9 11c +3c multi	.25	*.45*
	Nos. B30-B33 (4)	1.00	1.30

Nativity, by Giuseppe Cali — SP10

Designs (Cali Paintings): 5c+1c, 11c+3c, Flight into Egypt. 7c+1c5m, Nativity.

1979, Nov. 14 Litho. *Perf. 14x13½*

B34	SP10 1c +5m multi	.25	.25
B35	SP10 5c +1c multi	.25	.25
B36	SP10 7c +1c5m multi	.25	.25
B37	SP10 11c +3c multi	.35	*.50*
	Nos. B34-B37 (4)	1.10	1.25

Nativity, by Anton Inglott (1915-1945) — SP11

Details of Painting: 2c+5m, Annunciation. 6c+1c, Angel. 8c+1c5m, Holy Family.

1980, Oct. 7 Litho. *Perf. 14x13½*

Size: 20x47mm

B38	SP11 2c +5m multi	.25	.25
B39	SP11 6c +1c multi	.25	.25
B40	SP11 8c +1c5m multi	.25	.25

Perf. 14½x14

Size: 47x39mm

B41	SP11 12c +3c shown	.45	.45
	Nos. B38-B41 (4)	1.20	1.20

SP12

1981, Nov. 18 Wmk. 354 *Perf. 14*

B42	SP12 2c +1c Children, vert.	.25	.25
B43	SP12 8c +2c Procession	.35	.35
B44	SP12 20c +3c Service, vert.	.65	*1.00*
	Nos. B42-B44 (3)	1.25	1.60

SP13

Three Kings Following Star: 2c+1c, Star. 8c+2c, Three Kings. 20c+3c, Entire design.

1982, Oct. 8 Litho. *Perf. 13½*

B45	SP13 2c +1c multi	.25	.25
B46	SP13 8c +2c multi	.45	.45

Perf. 14

Size: 45x36mm

B47	SP13 20c +3c multi	.85	*1.25*
	Nos. B45-B47 (3)	1.55	1.95

SP14

Illuminated Manuscripts, Book of Hours, 15th Cent.: 2c+1c, Annunciation. 8c+2c, Nativity. 20c+3c, Three Kings bearing gifts. Surtax was for child welfare.

1983, Sept. 6 Litho. *Perf. 14*

B48	SP14	2c +1c multi	.25	.25
B49	SP14	8c +2c multi	.60	.60
B50	SP14	20c +3c multi	1.40	1.40
		Nos. B48-B50 (3)	2.25	2.25

SP15

Paintings by Peter-Paul Caruana, Church of Our Lady of Porto Salvo, Valletta, 1850: 2c+1c, Visitation, vert. 8c+2c, Epiphany. 20c+3c, Jesus Among the Doctors.

1984, Oct. 5 Litho. *Perf. 14*

B51	SP15	2c +1c multi	.35	.35
B52	SP15	8c +2c multi	.80	.80
B53	SP15	20c +3c multi	1.75	1.75
		Nos. B51-B53 (3)	2.90	2.90

SP16

No. B54, Adoration of the Magi. B55, Nativity. No. B56, Trumpeter Angels.

1985, Oct. 10 Litho. *Perf. 14*

B54	SP16	2c +1c multi	.40	.40
B55	SP16	8c +2c multi	.90	.90
B56	SP16	20c +3c multi	2.00	2.00
		Nos. B54-B56 (3)	3.30	3.30

Surtax for child welfare organizations.

SP17

Paintings by Giuseppe D'Arena (1633-1719): No. B57, The Nativity. No. B58, The Nativity, detail, vert. No. B59, The Epiphany.

1986, Oct. 10 Wmk. 354 *Perf. 14½*

B57	SP17	2c +1c multi	.85	*1.75*
B58	SP17	8c +2c multi	2.25	*3.25*
B59	SP17	20c +3c multi	3.00	*6.50*
		Nos. B57-B59 (3)	6.10	*11.50*

Surtax for child welfare organizations.

SP18

Illuminated text from choral books of the Veneranda Assemblea of St. John's Conventual Church, Valletta: No. B60, Mary's Visit to Elizabeth. No. B61, Nativity. No. B62, Adoration of the Magi.

1987, Nov. 6 Litho. *Perf. 14*

B60	SP18	2c +1c multi	.50	.50
B61	SP18	8c +2c multi	1.75	*2.50*
B62	SP18	20c +3c multi	3.25	*4.50*
		Nos. B60-B62 (3)	5.50	*7.50*

Surtax for child welfare organizations and the handicapped.

SP19

1988, Nov. 5 Litho. *Perf. 14½x14*

B63	SP19	3c +1c Shepherd	.35	.35
B64	SP19	10c +2c Nativity	.90	.90
B65	SP19	25c +3c Magi	1.75	*2.50*
		Nos. B63-B65 (3)	3.00	3.75

Surtax for child welfare organizations and the handicapped.

SP20

Various angels from frescoes by Mattia Preti in the vault of St. John's Co-Cathedral, Valletta, 1666.

1989, Nov. 11 *Perf. 14*

B66	SP20	3c +1c multi	.50	.50
B67	SP20	10c +2c multi	1.25	1.25
B68	SP20	20c +3c multi	2.00	*3.75*
		Nos. B66-B68 (3)	3.75	5.50

Surtax for child welfare organizations and the handicapped.

SP21

Creche figures — No. B69, Carrying water. No. B70, Nativity. No. B71, Shepherd.
No. B70 measures 41x27mm.

1990, Nov. 10

B69	SP21	3c +1c multi	.30	*.50*
B70	SP21	10c +2c multi	.85	*1.25*
B71	SP21	25c +3c multi	1.60	*2.50*
		Nos. B69-B71 (3)	2.75	*4.25*

Surtax for child welfare organizations.

SP22

No. B72, Wise men. No. B73, Mary, Joseph, Jesus. No. B74, Shepherds.

1991, Nov. 6

B72	SP22	3c +1c multi	.40	.40
B73	SP22	10c +2c multi	1.00	1.00
B74	SP22	25c +3c multi	2.50	2.50
		Nos. B72-B74 (3)	3.90	3.90

Surtax for child welfare organizations.

SP23

Paintings from dome spandrels of Mosta Parish Church by Giusepppe Cali (1846-1930): 3c+1c, Nativity scene. 10c+2c, Adoration of the Magi. 25c+3c, Christ among the Elders in the Temple.

1992, Oct. 22

B75	SP23	3c +1c multi	.40	.40
B76	SP23	10c +2c multi	1.60	1.60
B77	SP23	25c +3c multi	4.00	4.00
		Nos. B75-B77 (3)	6.00	6.00

Surtax for child welfare organizations.

SP24

Designs: 3c+1c, Christ Child in manger. 10c+2c, Christmas tree. 25c+3c, Star.

1993, Nov. 20

B78	SP24	3c +1c multi	.40	.40
B79	SP24	10c +2c multi	.90	.90
B80	SP24	25c +3c multi	1.90	1.90
		Nos. B78-B80 (3)	3.20	3.20

Beginning with No. 845, semi-postal stamps are included with the postage portion of the set.

Christmas — SP25

Children's art: 6c+2c, Man with net chasing star. 15c+2c, People, Chirstmas tree. 16c+2c, People hugging. 19c+3c, Woman with shopping bags.

2001, Nov. 29 Litho. *Perf. 14*

B81-B84	SP25	Set of 4	5.00	5.00

Stampin' the Future Type of 2000

Souvenir Sheet

Wmk. 354

2006, Dec. 22 Litho. *Perf. 14*

B85	A261	£1.50 + (16c) Like #1029	10.00	10.00

Surtax was for the Valletta YMCA.

AIR POST STAMPS

No. 140 Overprinted

Perf. 14½x14

1928, Apr. 1 Typo. Wmk. 4

C1	A22	6p red & violet	2.00	1.25
		Never hinged	4.50	

Catalogue values for unused stamps in this section, from this point to the end of the section, are for Never Hinged items.

Jet over Valletta AP1

Designs: 3c, 5c, 20c, 35c, Winged emblem. 7c5m, 25c, like 4c.

Wmk. 354

1974, Mar. Litho. *Perf. 13½*

Cross Emblem in Red and Blue

C2	AP1	3c ol brown & gold	.25	.25
C3	AP1	4c dk blue & gold	.25	.25
C4	AP1	5c dk vio bl & gold	.30	.30
C5	AP1	7c5m sl green & gold	.40	.40
C6	AP1	20c vio brn & gold	.50	.50
C7	AP1	25c slate & gold	.60	.50
C8	AP1	35c brown & gold	.70	1.00
		Nos. C2-C8 (7)	3.00	3.20

Jet and Megalithic Temple — AP2

Designs: 7c, 20c, Air Malta Boeing 720B approaching Malta. 11c, 75c, Jumbo jet landing at Luqa Airport. 17c, like 5c.

1978, Oct. 3 Litho. *Perf. 13½*

C9	AP2	5c multicolored	.30	.30
C10	AP2	7c multicolored	.35	.35
C11	AP2	11c multicolored	.40	.40
C12	AP2	17c multicolored	.50	.50
C13	AP2	20c multicolored	.75	.75
C14	AP2	75c multicolored	1.75	*2.40*
		Nos. C9-C14 (6)	4.05	4.70

Boeing 737, 1984 AP3

8c, Boeing 720B, 1974. 16c, Vickers Vanguard, 1964. 23c, Vickers Viscount, 1958. 27c, Douglas DC3 Dakota, 1948. 38c, AW Atlanta, 1936. 75c, Dornier Wal, 1929.

1984, Jan. 26 Wmk. 354 *Perf. 14*

C15	AP3	7c shown	.40	.40
C16	AP3	8c multi	.45	.45
C17	AP3	16c multi	.80	.80
C18	AP3	23c multi	1.00	1.00
C19	AP3	27c multi	1.25	1.25
C20	AP3	38c multi	2.00	2.00
C21	AP3	75c multi	2.50	2.50
		Nos. C15-C21 (7)	8.40	8.40

POSTAGE DUE STAMPS

D1

1925 Typeset Unwmk. *Imperf.*

J1	D1	½p black, *white*	1.25	8.00
J2	D1	1p black, *white*	3.00	3.50
J3	D1	1½p black, *white*	2.75	3.50
J4	D1	2p black, *white*	12.00	*21.00*
J5	D1	2½p black, *white*	2.50	2.50
a.		"2" of "½" omitted	1,000.	1,400.
J6	D1	3p black, *gray*	8.50	*15.00*
J7	D1	4p black, *orange*	4.50	*8.50*
J8	D1	6p black, *orange*	4.50	*22.50*
J9	D1	1sh black, *orange*	6.00	*25.00*
J10	D1	1sh6p black, *orange*	16.00	*62.50*
		Nos. J1-J10 (10)	61.00	*172.00*
		Set, never hinged	130.00	

These stamps were typeset in groups of 42. In each sheet there were four impressions of a group, two of them being inverted and making tete-beche pairs. Value set of tete-beche pairs $175.

Forged examples of No. J5a are known.

Maltese Cross — D2

Wmk. 4 Sideways

1925 Typo. Perf. 12

No.	Type	Denom.	Color	Unused	Used
J11	D2	½p	blue green	1.40	.70
J12	D2	1p	violet	1.40	.50
J13	D2	1½p	yellow brown	1.75	1.00
J14	D2	2p	gray	8.50	1.25
J15	D2	2½p	orange	2.25	1.25
J16	D2	3p	dark blue	4.50	1.25
J17	D2	4p	olive green	12.00	*16.00*
J18	D2	6p	claret	3.50	4.75
J19	D2	1sh	gray black	7.50	*14.00*
J20	D2	1sh6p	deep rose	9.00	*42.50*
			Nos. J11-J20 (10)	51.80	*83.20*
			Set, never hinged	85.00	

In 1953-57 six values (½p-2p, 3p, 4p) were reissued on chalky paper in slightly different colors.

Catalogue values for unused stamps in this section, from this point to the end of the section, are for Never Hinged items.

1966 Wmk. 314 Perf. 12

No.	Type	Denom.	Color	Unused	Used
J21	D2	2p	sepia	16.00	*24.00*

Wmk. 354 Sideways

1968 Perf. 12½

No.	Type	Denom.	Color	Unused	Used
J22	D2	½p	green	.30	.25
J23	D2	1p	rose violet	.25	.25
J24	D2	1½p	bister brn	.35	.30
J25	D2	2p	brown black	.65	.45
J26	D2	2½p	orange	.50	.50
J27	D2	3p	Prus blue	.60	.60
J28	D2	4p	olive	.95	.90
J29	D2	6p	purple	.80	*1.75*
J30	D2	1sh	black	.95	*1.50*
J31	D2	1sh6p	rose car	2.50	*5.00*
			Nos. J22-J31 (10)	7.85	11.50

1967, Nov. 9 Perf. 12

No.	Type	Denom.	Color	Unused	Used
J22a	D2	½p		4.25	*8.00*
J23a	D2	1p		4.50	*8.00*
J25a	D2	2p		7.00	*9.00*
J28a	D2	4p		50.00	*110.00*
			Nos. J22a-J28a (4)	65.75	*135.00*

Numeral — D3

Perf. 13x13½

1973, Apr. 28 Litho. Wmk. 354

No.	Type	Denom.	Color	Unused	Used
J32	D3	2m	brown	.25	.25
J33	D3	3m	brown orange	.25	.25
J34	D3	5m	carmine	.25	.25
J35	D3	1c	deep green	.25	.25
J36	D3	2c	black	.35	.30
J37	D3	3c	olive	.35	.30
J38	D3	5c	violet blue	.55	.50
J39	D3	10c	deep magenta	.75	*.90*
			Nos. J32-J39 (8)	3.00	3.00

Scroll — D4

Wmk. 354

1993, Jan. 4 Litho. Perf. 14

No.	Type	Denom.	Color	Unused	Used
J40	D4	1c	brt pink & lt pink	.25	.30
J41	D4	2c	brt blue & lt blue	.25	.35
J42	D4	5c	brt grn & lt grn	.30	.40
J43	D4	10c	org yel & brt yel	.50	.50
			Nos. J40-J43 (4)	1.30	1.55

WAR TAX STAMPS

Nos. 50, 25 Overprinted

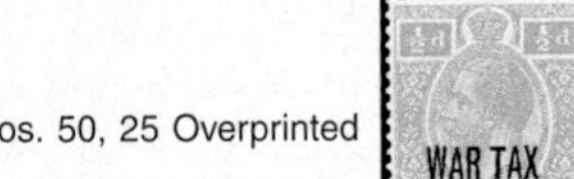

1918 Wmk. 3 Perf. 14

No.	Type	Denom.	Color	Unused	Used
MR1	A13	½p	green	2.25	.30

Wmk. 2

No.	Type	Denom.	Color	Unused	Used
MR2	A12	3p	red violet & gray	3.00	*15.00*

MANCHUKUO

'man-'chü-'kwō

LOCATION — Covering Manchuria, or China's three northeastern provinces —Fengtien, Kirin and Heilungkiang—plus Jehol province.
GOVT. — Independent state under Japanese influence
AREA — 503,013 sq. mi. (estimated)
POP. — 43,233,954 (est. 1940)
CAPITAL — Hsinking (Changchun)

Manchukuo was formed in 1932 with the assistance of Japan. In 1934 Henry Pu-yi, Chief Executive, was enthroned as Emperor Kang Teh. In 1945, when Japan surrendered to the Allies, the terms included the return of Manchukuo to China. The puppet state was dissolved.

100 Fen = 1 Yuan

Watermarks

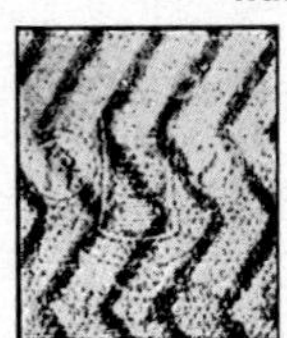

Wmk. 141 — Horizontal Zigzag Lines

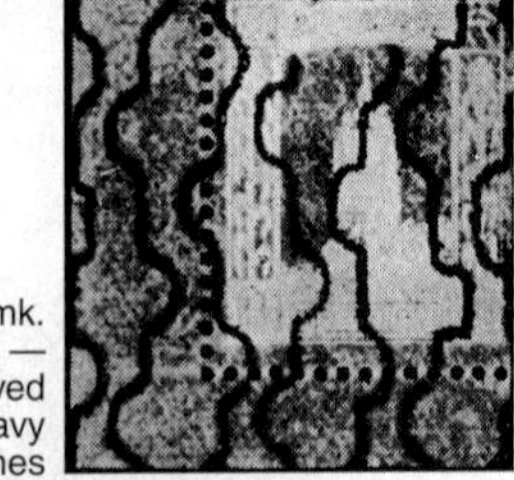

Wmk. 239 — Curved Wavy Lines

Wmk. 242 — Characters

Pagoda at Liaoyang A1

Chief Executive Henry Pu-yi A2

Five characters in top label.
Inscription reads "Manchu State Postal Administration."

Lithographed

Perf. 13x13½

1932, July 26 Unwmk.

White Paper

No.	Type	Denom.	Color	Unused	Used
1	A1	½f	gray brown	2.00	1.00
2	A1	1f	dull red	2.25	1.50
3	A1	1½f	lilac	7.00	7.00
4	A1	2f	slate	7.00	7.50
5	A1	3f	dull brown	9.50	9.50
6	A1	4f	olive green	3.50	.70
7	A1	5f	green	5.00	1.50
8	A1	6f	rose	12.00	5.50
9	A1	7f	gray	5.00	3.00
10	A1	8f	ocher	20.00	16.00
11	A1	10f	orange	7.50	1.50
12	A2	13f	dull brown	16.00	10.00
13	A2	15f	rose	22.50	5.00
14	A2	16f	turquoise grn	32.50	13.00
15	A2	20f	gray brown	12.00	4.00
16	A2	30f	orange	13.50	5.00
17	A2	50f	olive green	27.50	5.00
18	A2	1y	violet	45.00	17.50
			Nos. 1-18 (18)	249.75	114.20
			Set, never hinged	300.00	

A local provisional overprint of a horizontal line of four characters in red or black, reading "Chinese Postal Administration," was applied to Nos. 1-18 by followers of Gen. Su Ping-wen, who rebelled against the Manchukuo government in September, 1932. Many counterfeits exist.

See Nos. 23-31. For surcharges see Nos. 36, 59-61.

See note on local handstamps at end of the Manchukuo listings.

Flags, Map and Wreath — A3

Old State Council Building — A4

1933, Mar. 1 Perf. 12½

No.	Type	Denom.	Color	Unused	Used
19	A3	1f	orange	8.00	5.50
20	A4	2f	dull green	20.00	16.00
21	A3	4f	light red	7.00	5.50
22	A4	10f	deep blue	40.00	37.50
			Nos. 19-22 (4)	75.00	64.50
			Set, never hinged	110.00	

1st anniv. of the establishing of the State. Nos. 19-22 were printed in sheets of 100 with a special printing in sheets of 20.

Type of 1932

Perf. 13x13½

1934, Feb. Engr. Wmk. 239

Granite Paper

No.	Type	Denom.	Color	Unused	Used
23	A1	½f	dark brown	4.50	2.50
24	A1	1f	red brown	5.00	1.25
25	A1	1½f	dark violet	8.00	5.00
26	A1	2f	slate	10.00	3.50
27	A1	3f	brown	5.00	1.10
28	A1	4f	olive brown	40.00	7.50
29	A1	10f	deep orange	18.00	3.00
30	A2	15f	rose	900.00	325.00
31	A2	1y	violet	60.00	17.50
			Nos. 23-31 (9)	1,051.	366.35

For surcharge see No. 60.

Emperor's Palace — A5

Phoenix — A6

1934, Mar. 1 Perf. 12½

No.	Type	Denom.	Color	Unused	Used
32	A5	1½f	orange brown	7.00	5.50
33	A6	3f	carmine	6.50	4.50
34	A5	6f	green	20.00	12.50
35	A6	10f	dark blue	32.50	20.00
			Nos. 32-35 (4)	66.00	42.50
			Set, never hinged	100.00	

Enthronement of Emperor Kang Teh. Nos. 32-35 were printed in sheets of 100, with a special printing in sheets of 20.

No. 6 Surcharged in Black

Perf. 13x13½

1934 Unwmk. White Paper

No.	Type	Description	Unused	Used
36	A1	1f on 4f olive grn	7.00	5.00
		Never hinged	12.00	
a.		Brown surcharge	47.50	47.50
b.		Upper left character of surcharge omitted		
c.		Inverted surcharge	*1,000.*	*1,000.*

Pagoda at Liaoyang A7

Emperor Kang Teh A8

Six characters in top label instead of five as in 1932-34 issues.
Inscription reads "Manchu Empire Postal Administration."

Perf. 13x13½

1934-36 Wmk. 239 Engr.

Granite Paper

No.	Type	Denom.	Color	Unused	Used
37	A7	½f	brown	.80	.60
38	A7	1f	red brown	1.10	.60
39	A7	1½f	dk violet	1.50	1.00
a.			Booklet pane of 6	*200.00*	
41	A7	3f	brown ('35)	.90	.70
a.			Booklet pane of 6	*200.00*	
42	A7	5f	dk blue ('35)	14.00	4.00
43	A7	5f	gray ('36)	6.00	4.00
44	A7	6f	rose ('35)	5.00	1.75
45	A7	7f	dk gray ('36)	4.00	2.25
47	A7	9f	red orange ('35)	3.75	1.75
50	A8	15f	ver ('35)	4.00	1.75
51	A8	18f	Prus grn ('35)	32.50	8.00
52	A8	20f	dk brown ('35)	6.50	2.00
53	A8	30f	orange brn ('35)	7.00	2.00
54	A8	50f	ol grn ('35)	8.00	3.25
55	A8	1y	dk violet ('35)	30.00	9.00
a.		1y	violet	32.50	10.00
			Nos. 37-55 (15)	125.05	42.65
			Set, never hinged	155.00	

4f and 8f, type A7, were prepared but not issued. Values $45 and $15, respectively.

1935 Wmk. 242 Perf. 13x13½

No.	Type	Denom.	Color	Unused	Used
57	A7	10f	deep blue	13.00	2.50
58	A8	13f	light brown	16.00	8.00
			Set, never hinged	42.00	

Nos. 6 and 28 Surcharged in Black

1935 White Paper Unwmk.

No.	Type	Description	Unused	Used
59	A1	3f on 4f ol grn	70.00	60.00
		Never hinged	100.00	

1935 Granite Paper Wmk. 239

No.	Type	Description	Unused	Used
60	A1	3f on 4f olive brn	10.00	6.00
		Never hinged	17.50	

Similar Surcharge on No. 14

1935 White Paper Unwmk.

No.	Type	Description	Unused	Used
61	A2	3f on 16f turq grn	18.00	12.00
		Never hinged	24.00	
		Nos. 59-61 (3)	98.00	78.00

Orchid Crest of Manchukuo A9

Sacred White Mountains and Black Waters A10

1935, Jan. 1 Litho. Wmk. 141

Granite Paper

No.	Type	Denom.	Color	Unused	Used
62	A9	2f	green	6.50	3.50
63	A10	4f	dull ol grn	3.25	2.50
64	A9	8f	ocher	4.75	3.75
65	A10	12f	brown red	16.00	*20.00*
			Nos. 62-65 (4)	30.50	29.75
			Set, never hinged	44.00	

Nos. 62-65 exist imperforate.

1935 **Wmk. 242**
66 A9 2f yellow green 6.00 2.00
68 A9 8f ocher 8.00 8.00
70 A10 12f brown red 15.00 *20.00*
Nos. 66-70 (3) 29.00 30.00
Set, never hinged 40.00

Nos. 62-70 issued primarily to pay postage to China, but valid for any postal use.

See Nos. 75-78, 113, 115, 158. For surcharges see Nos. 101, 103-104, 106-109, People's Republic of China No. 2L19.

Mt. Fuji — A11

Phoenix — A12

Perf. 11, 12½ and Compound

1935, Apr. 1 **Engr.** **Wmk. 242**
71 A11 1½f dull green 3.75 3.00
72 A12 3f orange 4.00 3.75
a. 3f red orange 7.50 6.00
73 A11 6f dk carmine 8.00 7.00
a. Horiz. pair, imperf. btwn. *1,200.*
b. Perf. 11x12½ 50.00 40.00
74 A12 10f dark blue 10.00 8.50
a. Perf. 12½x11 85.00 60.00
b. Perf. 12½ 30.00 27.50
Nos. 71-74 (4) 25.75 22.25
Set, never hinged 35.00

Visit of the Emperor of Manchukuo to Tokyo.

Orchid Crest — A13

Types of A9 & A10 Redrawn and Engraved

1936 **Wmk. 242** ***Perf. 13x13½***
75 A13 2f lt green 1.50 1.00
76 A10 4f olive green 4.50 2.50
77 A13 8f ocher 5.00 2.50
78 A10 12f orange brn 47.50 32.50
Nos. 75-78 (4) 58.50 38.50
Set, never hinged 80.00

Unbroken lines of shading in the background of Nos. 76 and 78. Shading has been removed from right and left of the mountains. Nearly all lines have been removed from the lake. There are numerous other alterations in the design.

Issued primarily to pay postage to China, but valid for any postal use.

See No. 112. For surcharges see Nos. 102-106.

Wild Goose over Sea of Japan — A14

Communications Building at Hsinking — A15

Perf. 12x12½, 12½x12

1936, Jan. 26 **Wmk. 242**
79 A14 1½f black brown 4.50 3.00
80 A15 3f rose lilac 4.50 3.00
81 A14 6f carmine rose 9.00 8.00
82 A15 10f blue 14.00 10.00
Nos. 79-82 (4) 32.00 24.00
Set, never hinged 50.00

Postal convention with Japan.

New State Council Building A16

Carting Soybeans A17

North Mausoleum at Mukden A18

Summer Palace at Chengteh A19

1936-37 **Wmk. 242** ***Perf. 13x13½***
83 A16 ½f brown .75 .60
84 A16 1f red brown .75 .50
85 A16 1½f violet 7.00 5.00
a. Booklet pane of 6 *150.00*
86 A17 2f lt green ('37) 1.00 .50
a. Booklet pane of 6 *65.00*
87 A16 3f chocolate 1.25 .75
a. Booklet pane of 6 *375.00*
88 A18 4f lt ol grn ('37) 1.25 .75
a. Booklet pane of 6 *60.00*
89 A16 5f gray black 30.00 12.00
90 A17 6f carmine 1.25 .50
91 A18 7f brown blk 1.75 1.00
92 A18 9f red orange 2.25 1.25
93 A19 10f blue 2.50 .60
94 A18 12f dp orange ('37) 2.25 .50
95 A18 13f brown 42.50 37.50
96 A18 15f carmine 3.75 1.00
97 A17 20f dk brown 2.25 .90
98 A19 30f chestnut brn 2.25 .90
99 A17 50f olive green 2.75 1.25
100 A19 1y violet 6.00 1.75
Nos. 83-100 (18) 111.50 67.25
Set, never hinged 160.00

Nos. 83, 84, 86, 88 and 93 are known imperforate but were not regularly issued.

See Nos. 159-163. For overprints see Nos. 140-141, 148-151. For surcharges see People's Republic of China Nos. 2L1-2L2, 2L11-2L18, 2L20-2L37, 2L40-2L52.

a

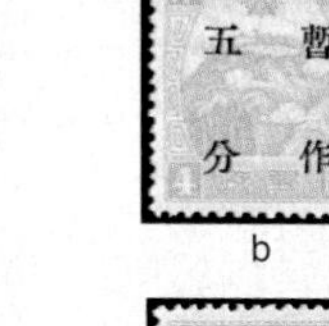

b

c

d

1937 **Surcharged on No. 66**
101 A9 (a) 2½f on 2f 4.00 3.50

Surcharged on Nos. 75, 76 and 78

102 A13 (a) 2½f on 2f 4.50 3.50
103 A10 (b) 5f on 4f 5.50 4.50
104 A10 (c) 13f on 12f 14.00 12.00

Surcharged in Black on Nos. 75, 76 and 70
Space between bottom characters of surcharge 4½mm

105 A13 (d) 2½f on 2f 3.25 3.00
a. Inverted surcharge *700.00* *850.00*
b. Vert. pair, one without surch. *200.00*
106 A10 (b) 5f on 4f 4.50 4.00
107 A10 (c) 13f on 12f 13.50 12.50

Surcharged on No. 70
Space between characters 6½mm

108 A10 (c) 13f on 12f 225.00 200.00

Same Surcharge on No. 63
Space between characters 4½mm
Wmk. 141

109 A10 (b) 5f on 4f 8.25 7.00
Nos. 101-109 (9) 282.50 250.00
Set, never hinged 390.00

Nos. 101-109 were issued primarily to pay postage to China, but were valid for any postal use.

Rising Sun over Manchurian Plain — A20

Composite Picture of Manchurian City — A21

Perf. 12½

1937, Mar. 1 **Litho.** **Unwmk.**
110 A20 1½f carmine rose 5.00 4.50
111 A21 3f blue green 4.00 3.50
Set, never hinged 12.00

5th anniv. of the founding of the State of Manchukuo.

Types of 1936
Perf. 13x13½

1937 **Wmk. 242** **Engr.**
112 A13 2½f dk violet 1.25 1.00
113 A10 5f black .65 .65
115 A10 13f dk red brown 2.25 1.00
Nos. 112-115 (3) 4.15 2.65
Set, never hinged 7.00

Issued primarily to pay postage to China, but were valid for any postal use.

Pouter Pigeon — A22

National Flag and Buildings — A23

Perf. 12x12½

1937, Sept. 16 **Unwmk.**
116 A22 2f dark violet 3.25 2.50
117 A23 4f rose carmine 3.50 2.50
118 A22 10f dark green 6.75 5.00
119 A23 20f dark blue 9.00 7.00
Nos. 116-119 (4) 22.50 17.00
Set, never hinged 29.00

Completion of the national capital, Hsinking, under the first Five-Year Construction Plan.

Map — A24

Dept. of Justice Building — A27

Japanese Residents' Association Building — A25

Postal Administration Building — A26

Perf. 12x12½, 13, 12½x13, 13x13½, 13½x13

1937, Dec. 1 **Litho.** **Unwmk.**
121 A24 2f dark carmine 2.00 1.75
122 A25 4f green 3.50 2.50
123 A25 8f orange 6.00 5.00
124 A26 10f blue 6.50 5.00
125 A27 12f lt violet 7.50 7.50
126 A26 20f lilac brown 11.00 8.00
Nos. 121-126 (6) 36.50 29.75
Set, never hinged 48.00

Issued in commemoration of the abolition of extraterritorial rights within Manchukuo.

Perf varieties exist on Nos. 122-126, lowest value listed, others about 25-35% higher.

New Year Greetings — A28

1937, Dec. 15 **Engr.** ***Perf. 12x12½***
127 A28 2f dk blue & red 3.00 2.00
Never hinged 4.00
a. Double impression of border *17.50*

Issued to pay postage on New Year's greeting cards.

Map and Cross — A29

Wmk. 242

1938, Oct. 15 **Litho.** ***Perf. 13***
128 A29 2f lake & scarlet 2.00 1.50
129 A29 4f slate grn & scar 2.00 1.50
Set, never hinged 6.00

Founding of the Red Cross Soc. in Manchukuo.

Network of State Railroads in Manchukuo A30

Express Train "Asia" A31

1939, Oct. 21
130 A30 2f dk org, blk & dp bl 2.50 1.75
131 A31 4f dp blue & indigo 2.50 1.75
Set, never hinged 7.00

Attainment of 10,000 kilometers in the railway mileage in Manchuria.

Stork Flying above Mast of Imperial Flagship — A32

1940 **Photo.** **Unwmk.**
132 A32 2f brt red violet 2.00 1.50
133 A32 4f brt green 2.00 1.50
Set, never hinged 6.00

Second visit of Emperor Kang Teh to Emperor Hirohito of Japan.

Census Taker and Map of Manchukuo
A33

Census Form
A34

1940, Sept. 10 Litho. Wmk. 242

134 A33 2f vio brn & org 1.50 1.50
135 A34 4f black & green 1.50 1.50
a. Double impression of green *100.00*
Set, never hinged 4.00

National census starting Oct. 1.

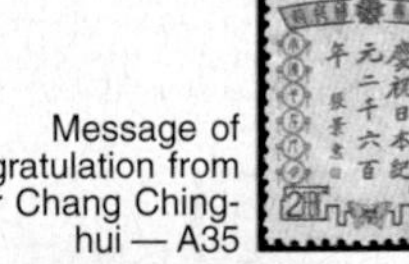

Message of Congratulation from Premier Chang Ching-hui — A35

Dragon Dance
A36

1940, Sept. 18 Engr. *Perf. 13x13½*

136 A35 2f carmine 1.25 1.25

Perf. 13½x13

137 A36 4f indigo 1.25 1.25
a. Imperf., pair 1,000.
Set, never hinged 3.50

2600th anniversary of the birth of the Japanese Empire.

Soldier — A37

Perf. 13x13½

1941, May 25 Photo. Unwmk.

138 A37 2f deep carmine 1.25 1.25
139 A37 4f bright ultra 1.25 1.25
Set, never hinged 3.50

Conscription Law, effective June 1, 1941.

Nos. 86 and 88 Overprinted in Red or Blue

Perf. 13x13½

1942, Feb. 16 Wmk. 242

140 A17 2f lt green (R) 1.25 1.25
141 A18 4f lt olive grn (Bl) 1.25 1.25
Set, never hinged 3.50

"Return of Singapore to East Asia, 9th year of Kang Teh."

Kengoku Shrine
A38

Map of Manchukuo
A39

Flag of Manchukuo
A40

Perf. 12x12½, 12½x12

1942, Mar. 1 Engr.

142 A38 2f carmine .90 .90
143 A38 4f lilac 1.00 .90
144 A39 10f red, *yel* 2.25 2.25
145 A40 20f indigo, *yel* 3.00 3.00
Nos. 142-145 (4) 7.15 7.05
Set, never hinged 10.00

"10th anniv. of Manchukuo, Mar. 1, 1942."

Allegory of National Harmony — A41

Women of Five Races, Dancing — A42

1942, Sept. 15

146 A41 3f orange 1.25 1.25
147 A42 6f light green 1.25 *2.00*
Set, never hinged 3.50

"10th anniv. of the founding of Manchukuo, Sept. 15, 1942."

Nos. 87 and 90 Overprinted in Green or Blue

1942, Dec. 8 *Perf. 13x13½*

148 A16 3f chocolate (G) 1.00 1.00
149 A17 6f carmine (Bl) 1.00 1.00
Set, never hinged 3.00

1st anniv. of the "Greater East Asia War."
The overprint reads "Asiatic Prosperity Began This Day December 8, 1941."

Nos. 87 and 90 Overprinted in Red or Blue

1943, May 1

150 A16 3f chocolate (R) 1.00 1.00
151 A17 6f carmine (Bl) 1.00 1.00
Set, never hinged 3.00

Proclamation of the labor service law.

Red Cross Nurse Carrying Stretcher — A43

1943, Oct. 1 Photo.

152 A43 6f green 1.25 1.25
Never hinged 2.00

5th anniv. of the founding of the Red Cross Society of Manchukuo, Oct. 1, 1938.

Smelting Furnace — A44

1943, Dec. 8 Unwmk. *Perf. 13*

153 A44 6f red brown 1.25 1.25
Never hinged 1.75

2nd anniv. of the "Greater East Asia War."

Chinese Characters
A45

Japanese Characters
A46

Perf. 13x13½

1944 Wmk. 242 Litho.

154 A45 10f rose .80 *1.25*
a. Imperf., vert. pair #154, 155 17.50
b. Vert. pair #154, 155 2.25 *2.50*
155 A46 10f rose .80 *5.00*
156 A45 40f gray green 3.75 4.00
a. Imperf., vert. pair #156, 157 60.00
b. 40f with 10f vignette, perf. *300.00 400.00*
c. 40f with 10f vignette, imperf. *450.00*
d. Vert. pair #156, 157 8.00 *14.00*
157 A46 40f gray green 3.75 *4.00*
Nos. 154-157 (4) 9.10 *14.25*
Set, never hinged 13.50

"Japan's Progress Is Manchukuo's Progress." Issued as propaganda for the close relationship of Japan and Manchukuo.
Frames of the 10f vignettes have rounded corners, those of the 40f vignettes have indented corners.

Types of 1935 and 1936-37

1944-45 Litho.

158 A10 5f gray black 1.25 *2.75*
a. Imperf., pair 12.00
159 A17 6f crimson rose 3.75 *5.00*
160 A19 10f light blue 6.50 *8.00*
161 A17 20f brown 2.50 *4.00*
162 A19 30f buff ('45) 2.75 *4.00*
163 A19 1y dull lilac 3.00 *3.75*
Nos. 158-163 (6) 19.75 *27.50*
Set, never hinged 29.00

For surcharges see People's Republic of China Nos. 2L1, 2L14, 2L19, 2L24, 2L27, 2L30-2L31, 2L35, 2L37, 2L49, 2L52.

"One Heart, One Soul" — A47

1945, May 2

164 A47 10f red 1.25 *3.50*
Never hinged 2.50
a. Imperf., pair *12.00 25.00*

Emperor's edict of May 2, 1935, 10th anniv.

AIR POST STAMPS

Sheep Grazing
AP1

Railroad Bridge
AP2

Wmk. Characters (242)

1936-37 Engr. *Perf. 13x13½*

Granite Paper

C1 AP1 18f green 16.00 18.00
C2 AP1 19f blue green ('37) 6.00 7.00
C3 AP2 38f blue 17.50 17.50
C4 AP2 39f deep blue ('37) 3.00 4.25
Nos. C1-C4 (4) 42.50 46.75
Set, never hinged 54.00

民中
國華

With the end of World War II and the collapse of Manchukuo, the Northeastern Provinces reverted to China. In many Manchurian towns and cities, the Manchukuo stamps were locally handstamped in ideograms: "Republic of China," "China Postal Service" or "Temporary Use for China." A typical example is shown above. Many of these local issues also were surcharged.

MARIANA ISLANDS

ˌmar-ē-ˈa-nə ˈī-ləndz

LOCATION — A group of 14 islands in the West Pacific Ocean, about 1500 miles east of the Philippines.
GOVT. — Possession of Spain, then of Germany
AREA — 246 sq. mi.
POP. — 44,025 (1935)
CAPITAL — Saipan

Until 1899 this group belonged to Spain but in that year all except Guam were ceded to Germany.

100 Centavos = 1 Peso
100 Pfennig = 1 Mark (1899)

Values for unused stamps are for examples with original gum as defined in the catalogue introduction. Very fine examples of Nos. 1-6 will have perforations touching or just cutting into the design. Stamps with perfs clear on all sides and well centered are rare and sell for substantially more.

Issued under Spanish Dominion

Philippines Stamps Hstmpd. Vert. in Blackish Violet Reading Up or Down

1899, Sept. Unwmk. *Perf. 14*

1	A39	2c dark blue green	800.	350.
2	A39	3c dark brown	500.	275.
3	A39	5c car rose	800.	275.
4	A39	6c dark blue	*5,000.*	2,500.
5	A39	8c gray brown	500.	175.
6	A39	15c dull ol grn	1,700.	900.

Overprint forgeries of Nos. 1-6 exist.
No. 4 was issued in a quantity of 50 stamps.

Issued under German Dominion

Values for Nos. 11-16 are for postally used examples in the correct period of use. Favor cancellations exist and are valued at 25 percent to 50 percent of the values shown here if used during the correct period. Expertization is recommended.

Stamps of Germany, 1889-90, Overprinted in Black at 56 degree Angle

1900, May Unwmk. *Perf. 13½x14½*

11	A9	3pf dark brown	12.00	*30.00*
12	A9	5pf green	16.00	*32.50*
13	A10	10pf carmine	20.00	*45.00*
14	A10	20pf ultra	25.00	*125.00*
15	A10	25pf orange	62.50	*160.00*
b.		Inverted overprint	*2,400.*	
16	A10	50pf red brn	65.00	*210.00*
		Nos. 11-16 (6)	200.50	*602.50*

Forged cancellations exist on Nos. 11-16, 17-29.

Stamps of Germany, 1889-90, Overprinted in Black at 48 degree Angle

1899, Nov. 18

11a	A9	3pf light brown	*2,000.*	*2,000.*
12a	A9	5pf green	*2,500.*	*1,700.*
13a	A10	10pf carmine	190.00	*200.00*
14a	A10	20pf ultra	190.00	*200.00*
15a	A10	25pf orange	*2,750.*	*2,750.*
16a	A10	50pf red brown	*2,750.*	*2,750.*

Kaiser's Yacht "Hohenzollern"
A4 A5

1901, Jan. Typo. *Perf. 14*

17	A4	3pf brown	1.10	*1.75*
18	A4	5pf green	1.10	*1.90*
19	A4	10pf carmine	1.10	*4.25*
20	A4	20pf ultra	1.25	*7.25*
21	A4	25pf org & blk, *yel*	1.75	*12.50*
22	A4	30pf org & blk, *sal*	1.75	*13.50*
23	A4	40pf lake & blk	1.75	*13.50*
24	A4	50pf pur & blk, *sal*	2.00	*15.00*
25	A4	80pf lake & blk, *rose*	2.50	*25.00*

Engr.
Perf. 14½x14

26	A5	1m carmine	4.00	*72.50*
27	A5	2m blue	5.50	*92.50*
28	A5	3m blk vio	8.00	*140.00*
29	A5	5m slate & car	140.00	*500.00*
		Nos. 17-29 (13)	171.80	*899.65*

Wmk. Lozenges (125)
1916-19 Typo. *Perf. 14*

30	A4	3pf brown ('19)	1.00

Engr.
Perf. 14½x14

31	A5	5m slate & carmine, 25x17 holes	30.00

Nos. 30 and 31 were never placed in use.

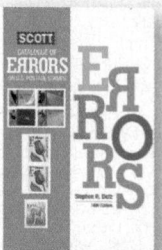

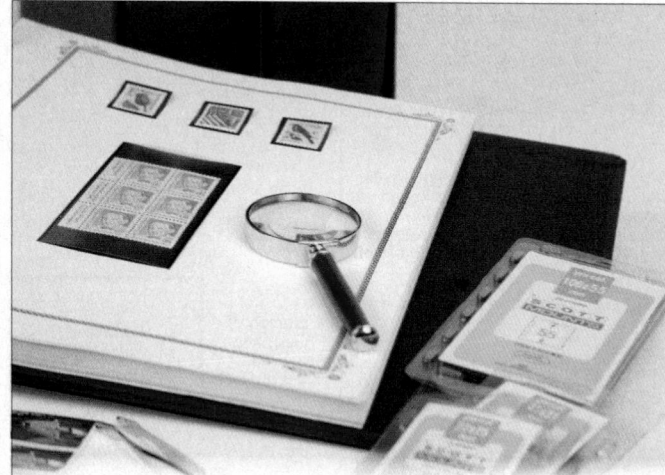

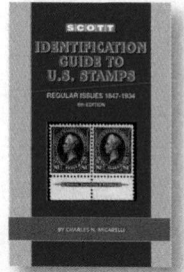

MARIENWERDER

mä-ˈrē-ən-ˌveˌəˌrd-ər

LOCATION — Northeastern Germany, bordering on Poland

GOVT. — A district of West Prussia

By the Versailles Treaty the greater portion of West Prussia was ceded to Poland but the district of Marienwerder was allowed a plebiscite which was held in 1920 and resulted in favor of Germany.

100 Pfennig = 1 Mark

Plebiscite Issues

Symbolical of Allied Supervision of the Plebiscite — A1

1920 Unwmk. Litho. *Perf. 11½*

1	A1	5pf green	.75	*2.25*
2	A1	10pf rose red	.75	*1.75*
3	A1	15pf gray	.75	*2.60*
4	A1	20pf brn org	.75	*1.75*
5	A1	25pf deep blue	.75	*2.25*
6	A1	30pf orange	.95	*2.25*
7	A1	40pf brown	.75	*2.75*
8	A1	50pf violet	.75	*2.00*
9	A1	60pf red brown	4.25	*3.75*
10	A1	75pf chocolate	.95	*2.00*
11	A1	1m brn & grn	.75	*2.00*
12	A1	2m dk vio	2.10	*4.50*
13	A1	3m red	5.00	*7.50*
14	A1	5m blue & rose	27.50	22.00
		Nos. 1-14 (14)	46.75	59.35
		Set, never hinged	130.00	

These stamps occasionally show parts of two papermakers' watermarks, consisting of the letters "O. B. M." with two stars before and after, or "P. & C. M."

Nos. 1-14 exist imperf.; value for set, $700. Nearly all exist part perf.

Stamps of Germany, 1905-19, Overprinted

1920 Wmk. 125 *Perf. 14, 14½*

24	A16	5pf green	15.00	*30.00*
a.		Inverted overprint	125.00	
		Never hinged	210.00	
b.		Double overprint, one inverted	450.00	*750.00*
		Never hinged	750.00	
26	A16	20pf bl vio	7.25	*27.50*
a.		Inverted overprint	62.50	*135.00*
		Never hinged	125.00	
b.		Double overprint	85.00	
		Never hinged	150.00	
28	A16	50pf vio & blk, *buff*	375.00	*850.00*
29	A16	75pf grn & blk	4.75	*8.75*
a.		Inverted overprint	62.50	*135.00*
		Never hinged	125.00	
30	A16	80pf lake & blk, *rose*	75.00	*120.00*
31	A17	1m car rose	85.00	*160.00*
a.		Inverted overprint	425.00	
		Never hinged	850.00	
		Nos. 24-31 (6)	562.00	*1,196.*
		Set, never hinged	1,200.	

Trial impressions were made in red, green and lilac, and with 2½mm instead of 3mm space between the lines of the overprint. These were printed on the 75pf and 80pf. The 1 mark was overprinted with the same words in 3 lines of large sans-serif capitals. All these are essays. Some were passed through the post, apparently with speculative intent.

Stamps of Germany, 1905-18, Surcharged

32	A22	1m on 2pf gray	30.00	*45.00*
33	A22	2m on 2½pf gray	15.00	*17.50*
a.		Inverted surcharge	55.00	*125.00*
		Never hinged	125.00	
34	A16	3m on 3pf brown	15.00	*17.50*
a.		Double surcharge	55.00	*125.00*
		Never hinged	125.00	
b.		Inverted surcharge	55.00	*120.00*
		Never hinged	120.00	
35	A22	5m on 7½pf org	15.00	*21.00*
a.		Inverted surcharge	55.00	*125.00*
		Never hinged	125.00	
b.		Double surcharge	55.00	*120.00*
		Never hinged	125.00	
		Nos. 32-35 (4)	75.00	*101.00*
		Set, never hinged	220.00	

There are two types of the letters "M," "C," "i" and "e" and of the numerals "2" and "5" in these surcharges.

Counterfeits exist of Nos. 24-35.

Stamps of Germany, 1920, Overprinted

1920, July *Perf. 15x14½*

36	A17	1m red	2.50	*7.25*
37	A17	1.25m green	3.25	*9.00*
38	A17	1.50m yellow brown	4.25	*9.75*
39	A21	2.50m lilac rose	2.50	*9.00*
		Nos. 36-39 (4)	12.50	*35.00*
		Set, never hinged	32.50	

A2

1920 Unwmk. *Perf. 11½*

40	A2	5pf green	4.00	1.60
41	A2	10pf rose red	4.00	1.60
42	A2	15pf gray	15.00	11.00
43	A2	20pf brn org	3.00	*1.60*
44	A2	25pf dp bl	15.00	*14.50*
45	A2	30pf orange	3.00	1.25
46	A2	40pf brown	3.00	*1.25*
47	A2	50pf violet	2.25	1.60
48	A2	60pf red brn	7.50	4.50
49	A2	75pf chocolate	7.50	4.50
50	A2	1m brn & grn	3.00	1.25
51	A2	2m dk vio	3.00	1.25
52	A2	3m light red	3.00	1.60
53	A2	5m blue & rose	4.00	2.25
		Nos. 40-53 (14)	77.25	49.75
		Set, never hinged	200.00	

MARSHALL ISLANDS

ˈmär-shəl ˈī-ləndz

LOCATION — Two chains of islands in the West Pacific Ocean, about 2,500 miles southeast of Tokyo

GOVT. — Republic

AREA — 70 sq. mi.

POP. — 65,507 (1999 est.)

CAPITAL — Dalap-Uliga-Darrit

The Marshall Islands were German possession from 1885 to 1914. Seized by Japan in 1914, the islands were taken by the US in WW II and became part of the US Trust Territory of the Pacific in 1947. By agreement with the USPS, the islands began issuing their own stamps in 1984, with the USPS continuing to carry the mail to and from the islands.

On Oct. 21, 1986 Marshall Islands became a Federation as a Sovereign State in Compact of Free Association with the US.

100 Pfennig = 1 Mark

100 Cents = 1 Dollar

Catalogue values for unused stamps in this country are for Never Hinged items, beginning with Scott 31 in the regular postage section, and Scott C1 in the airpost section.

Watermark

Wmk. 125 — Lozenges

Issued under German Dominion

A1

A2

Stamps of Germany Overprinted "Marschall-Inseln" in Black

1897 Unwmk. *Perf. 13½x14½*

1	A1	3pf dark brown	140.00	*725.00*
a.		3pf light yellowish brn	*4,250.*	*2,200.*
2	A1	5pf green	120.00	*550.00*
3	A1	10pf carmine	55.00	*150.00*
4	A2	20pf ultra	50.00	*150.00*
5	A2	25pf orange	140.00	*925.00*
6	A2	50pf red brown	140.00	*925.00*
		Nos. 1-6 (6)	645.00	3,425.

Nos. 5 and 6 were not placed in use, but canceled stamps exist.

A small quantity of the 3pf, 5pf, 10pf and 20pf were issued at Jaluit. These have yellowish, dull gum. Later overprintings of Nos. 1-6 were sold only at Berlin, and have white, smooth, shiny gum. No. 1a belongs to the Jaluit issue. For detailed listings, see the *Scott Specialized Catalogue of Stamps and Covers.*

Forged cancellations are found on almost all Marshall Islands stamps.

Overprinted "Marshall-Inseln"

1899-1900

7	A1	3pf dk brn ('00)	4.50	*5.50*
a.		3pf light brown	275.00	*775.00*
8	A1	5pf green	9.25	*12.50*
9	A2	10pf car ('00)	12.00	*15.00*
a.		Half used as 5pf on post-card		*8,000.*
10	A2	20pf ultra ('00)	17.00	*25.00*
11	A2	25pf orange	19.00	*42.50*
12	A2	50pf red brown	30.00	*47.50*
a.		Half used as 25pf on cover		*35,000.*
		Nos. 7-12 (6)	91.75	*148.00*

Values for Nos. 9a and 12a are for properly used items, addressed and sent to Germany.

Kaiser's Yacht "Hohenzollern"
A3 A4

1901 Unwmk. Typo. *Perf. 14*

13	A3	3pf brown	.65	1.75
14	A3	5pf green	.65	1.75
15	A3	10pf carmine	.65	*5.00*
16	A3	20pf ultra	.95	*9.25*
17	A3	25pf org & blk, *yel*	1.00	*16.00*
18	A3	30pf org & blk, *sal*	1.00	*16.00*
19	A3	40pf lake & blk	1.00	*16.00*
20	A3	50pf pur & blk, *sal*	1.40	*25.00*
21	A3	80pf lake & blk, *rose*	2.50	*35.00*

Engr.

Perf. 14½x14

22	A4	1m carmine	4.00	*85.00*
23	A4	2m blue	5.50	*120.00*
24	A4	3m blk vio	8.50	*200.00*
25	A4	5m slate & car	140.00	*500.00*
		Nos. 13-25 (13)	167.80	1,031.

Wmk. Lozenges (125)

1916 Typo. *Perf. 14*

26	A3	3pf brown	.85

Engr.

Perf. 14½x14

27	A4	5m slate & carmine, 25x17 holes	35.00

Nos. 26 and 27 were never placed in use.

The stamps of Marshall Islands overprinted "G. R. I." and new values in British currency were all used in New Britain and are listed among the issues for that country.

Two unauthorized issues appeared in 1979. The 1st, a set of five for the "Establishment of Government, May 1, 1979," consists of 8c, 15c, 21c, 31c and 75c labels. The 75c is about the size of a postcard. The 2nd, a set of four se-tenant blocks of four 10c labels for the Intl. Year of the Child. This set also exists imperf. and with specimen overprints.

Catalogue values for unused stamps in this section, from this point to the end of the section, are for Never Hinged items.

Inauguration of Postal Service — A5

No. 31, Outrigger canoe. No. 32, Fishnet. No. 33, Navigational stick chart. No. 34, Islet.

1984, May 2 Litho. *Perf. 14x13½*

31	A5	20c multicolored	.50	.50
32	A5	20c multicolored	.50	.50
33	A5	20c multicolored	.50	.50
34	A5	20c multicolored	.50	.50
a.		Block of 4, #31-34	2.00	2.00

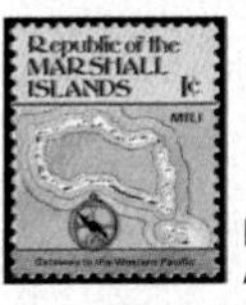

Mili Atoll, Astrolabe — A6

Maps and Navigational Instruments: 3c, Likiep, Azimuth compass. 5c, Ebon, 16th cent. compass. 10c, Jaluit, anchor buoys. 13c, Ailinginae, Nocturnal. 14c, Wotho Atoll, navigational stick chart. 20c, Kwajalein and Ebeye, stick chart. 22c, Eniwetok, 18th cent. lodestone storage case. 28c, Ailinglaplap, printed compass. 30c, Majuro, navigational stick-chart. 33c, Namu, stick chart. 37c, Rongelap, quadrant. 39c, Taka, map compass, 16th cent. sea chart. 44c, Ujelang, chronograph. 50c, Maloelap and Aur, nocturlabe. $1, Arno, 16th cent. sector compass.

1984-85 Litho. *Perf. 15x14*

35	A6	1c shown	.25	.25
36	A6	3c multicolored	.25	.25
37	A6	5c multicolored	.25	.25
38	A6	10c multicolored	.25	.25
39	A6	13c multicolored	.25	.25
a.		Booklet pane of 10	*8.00*	—
40	A6	14c multicolored	.30	.30
a.		Booklet pane of 10	*7.50*	—
41	A6	20c multicolored	.40	.40
a.		Booklet pane of 10	*10.00*	—
b.		Bklt. pane, 5 each 13c, 20c	*9.25*	—
42	A6	22c multicolored	.45	.45
a.		Booklet pane of 10	*9.50*	—
b.		Bklt. pane, 5 each 14c, 22c	*8.50*	—
43	A6	28c multicolored	.55	.55
44	A6	30c multicolored	.60	.60
45	A6	33c multicolored	.65	.65
46	A6	37c multicolored	.75	.75
47	A6	39c multicolored	.80	.80
48	A6	44c multicolored	.90	.90
49	A6	50c multicolored	1.00	1.00
49A	A6	$1 multicolored	2.00	2.00
		Nos. 35-49A (16)	9.65	9.65

Issued: 1c, 3c, 10c, 30c, $1, 6/12; 13c, 20c, 28c, 37c, 12/19/84; 14c, 22c, 33c, 39c, 44c, 50c, 6/5/85.

See Nos. 107-109.

No. 7 — A7

1984, June 19 *Perf. 14½x15*

50 A7 40c shown .60 .60
51 A7 40c No. 13 .60 .60
52 A7 40c No. 4 .60 .60
53 A7 40c No. 25 .60 .60
a. Block of 4, #50-53 2.40 2.40

Philatelic Salon, 19th UPU Congress, Hamburg, June 19-26.

Ausipex '84 — A8

Dolphins.

1984, Sept. 5 Litho. *Perf. 14*

54 A8 20c Common .40 .40
55 A8 20c Risso's .40 .40
56 A8 20c Spotter .40 .40
57 A8 20c Bottlenose .40 .40
a. Block of 4, #54-57 1.60 1.60

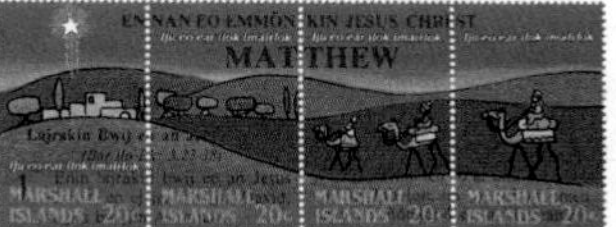

Christmas — A9

1984, Nov. 7 Litho. *Perf. 14*

58 A9 Strip of 4 2.25 2.25
a.-d. 20c any single .40 .40
e. Sheet of 16 9.00

Sheet background shows text from Marshallese New Testament, giving each stamp a different background.

Marshall Islands Constitution, 5th Anniv. — A10

1984, Dec. 19 Litho. *Perf. 14*

59 A10 20c Traditional chief .40 .40
60 A10 20c Amata Kabua .40 .40
61 A10 20c Chester Nimitz .40 .40
62 A10 20c Trygve Lie .40 .40
a. Block of 4, #59-62 1.60 1.60

Audubon Bicentenary — A11

1985, Feb. 15 Litho. *Perf. 14*

63 A11 22c Forked-tailed Petrel .60 .60
64 A11 22c Pectoral Sandpiper .60 .60
a. Pair, #63-64 1.20 1.20
Nos. 63-64,C1-C2 (4) 3.00 3.00

Sea Shells — A12

No. 65, Cymatium lotorium. No. 66, Chicoreus cornucervi. No. 67, Strombus aurisdanae. No. 68, Turbo marmoratus. No. 69, Chicoreus palmarosae.

1985, Apr. 17 Litho. *Perf. 14*

65 A12 22c multicolored .45 .45
66 A12 22c multicolored .45 .45
67 A12 22c multicolored .45 .45
68 A12 22c multicolored .45 .45
69 A12 22c multicolored .45 .45
a. Strip of 5, #65-69 2.25 2.25

See Nos. 119-123, 152-156, 216-220.

Decade for Women A13

1985, June 5 Litho. *Perf. 14*

70 A13 22c Native drum .40 .40
71 A13 22c Palm branches .40 .40
72 A13 22c Pounding stone .40 .40
73 A13 22c Ak bird .40 .40
a. Block of 4, #70-73 1.65 1.65

Reef and Lagoon Fish A14

No. 74, Acanthurus dussumieri. No. 75, Adioryx caudimaculatus. No. 76, Ostracion meleacaris. No. 77, Chaetodon ephippium.

1985, July 15 Litho. *Perf. 14*

74 A14 22c multicolored .45 .45
75 A14 22c multicolored .45 .45
76 A14 22c multicolored .45 .45
77 A14 22c multicolored .45 .45
a. Block of 4, #74-77 1.80 1.80

Intl. Youth Year A15

IYY and Alele Nautical Museum emblems and: No. 78, Marshallese youths and Peace Corps volunteers playing basketball. No. 79, Legend teller reciting local history, girl listening to recording. No. 80, Islander explaining navigational stick charts. No. 81, Jabwa stick dance.

1985, Aug. 31 Litho. *Perf. 14*

78 A15 22c multicolored .45 .45
79 A15 22c multicolored .45 .45
80 A15 22c multicolored .45 .45
81 A15 22c multicolored .45 .45
a. Block of 4, #78-81 1.80 1.80

1856 American Board of Commissions Stock Certificate for Foreign Missions — A16

Missionary ship Morning Star I: 22c, Launch, Jothan Stetson Shipyard, Chelsea, MA, Aug. 7, 1857. 33c, First voyage, Honolulu to the Marshalls, 1857. 44c, Marshall islanders pulling Morning Star I into Ebon Lagoon, 1857.

1985, Oct. 21 Litho. *Perf. 14*

82 A16 14c multicolored .25 .25
83 A16 22c multicolored .45 .45
84 A16 33c multicolored .65 .65
85 A16 44c multicolored .90 .90
Nos. 82-85 (4) 2.25 2.25

Christmas.

US Space Shuttle, Astro Telescope, Halley's Comet — A17

Comet tail and research spacecraft: No. 87, Planet A Space Probe, Japan. No. 88, Giotto spacecraft, European Space Agency. No. 89, INTERCOSMOS Project Vega spacecraft, Russia, France, etc. No. 90, US naval tracking ship, NASA observational aircraft, cameo portrait of Edmond Halley (1656-1742), astronomer. Se-tenant in continuous design.

1985, Nov. 21

86 A17 22c multicolored 1.00 1.00
87 A17 22c multicolored 1.00 1.00
88 A17 22c multicolored 1.00 1.00
89 A17 22c multicolored 1.00 1.00
90 A17 22c multicolored 1.00 1.00
a. Strip of 5, #86-90 5.00 5.00

Medicinal Plants A18

1985, Dec. 31 Litho. *Perf. 14*

91 A18 22c Sida fallax .45 .45
92 A18 22c Scaevola frutescens .45 .45
93 A18 22c Guettarda speciosa .45 .45
94 A18 22c Cassytha filiformis .45 .45
a. Block of 4, #91-94 1.90 1.90

Maps Type of 1984

$2, Wotje and Erikub, terrestrial globe, 1571. $5, Bikini, Stick chart. $10, Stick chart of the atolls.

1986-87 *Perf. 15x14, 14 ($10)*

107 A6 $2 multicolored 4.50 4.50
108 A6 $5 multicolored 9.50 9.50

Size: 31x31mm

109 A6 $10 multicolored 16.00 16.00
Nos. 107-109 (3) 30.00 30.00

Issued: $2, $5, 3/7/86; $10, 3/31/87.

Marine Invertebrates — A19

1986, Mar. 31 Litho. *Perf. 14½x14*

110 A19 14c Triton's trumpet 1.50 1.50
111 A19 14c Giant clam 1.50 1.50
112 A19 14c Small giant clam 1.50 1.50
113 A19 14c Coconut crab 1.50 1.50
a. Block of 4, #110-113 8.00 8.00

Souvenir Sheet

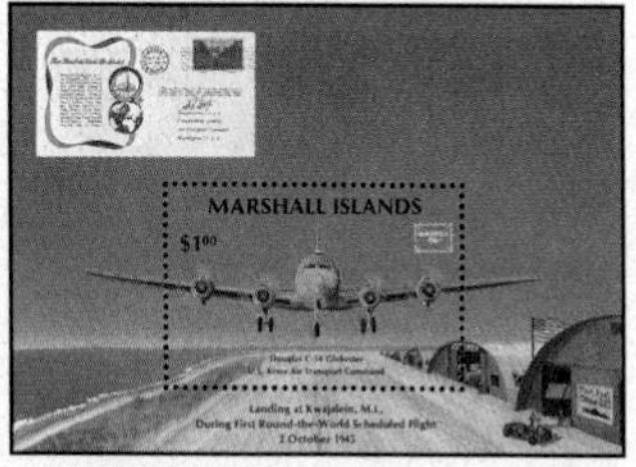

AMERIPEX '86, Chicago, May 22-June 1 — A20

Design: $1, Douglas C-54 Globester.

1986, May 22 Litho. *Perf. 14*

114 A20 $1 multicolored 2.75 2.75

1st Around-the-world scheduled flight, 40th anniv. No. 114 has multicolored margin continuing the design and picturing US Air Transport Command Base, Kwajalein Atoll and souvenir card.

See Nos. C3-C6.

Operation Crossroads, Atomic Bomb Tests, 40th Anniv. — A21

Designs: No. 115, King Juda, Bikinians sailing tibinal canoe. No. 116, USS Sumner, amphibious DUKW, advance landing. No. 117, Evacuating Bikinians. No. 118, Land reclamation, 1986.

1986, July 1 Litho. *Perf. 14*

115 A21 22c multicolored .45 .45
116 A21 22c multicolored .45 .45
117 A21 22c multicolored .45 .45
118 A21 22c multicolored .45 .45
a. Block of 4, #115-118 1.90 1.90

See No. C7.

Seashells Type of 1985

No. 119, Ramose murex. No. 120, Orange spider. No. 121, Red-mouth frog shell. No. 122, Laciniate conch. No. 123, Giant frog shell.

1986, Aug. 1 Litho. *Perf. 14*

119 A12 22c multicolored .45 .45
120 A12 22c multicolored .45 .45
121 A12 22c multicolored .45 .45
122 A12 22c multicolored .45 .45
123 A12 22c multicolored .45 .45
a. Strip of 5, #119-123 2.25 2.25

Game Fish A22

1986, Sept. 10 Litho.

124 A22 22c Blue marlin .40 .40
125 A22 22c Wahoo .40 .40
126 A22 22c Dolphin fish .40 .40
127 A22 22c Yellowfin tuna .40 .40
a. Block of 4, #124-127 1.60 1.60

Christmas, Intl. Peace Year — A23

1986, Oct. 28 Litho. *Perf. 14*

128 A23 22c United Nations UR .60 .60
129 A23 22c United Nations UL .60 .60
130 A23 22c United Nations LR .60 .60
131 A23 22c United Nations LL .60 .60
a. Block of 4, #128-131 2.50 2.50

See No. C8.

US Whaling Ships A24

No. 132, James Arnold, 1854. No. 133, General Scott, 1859. No. 134, Charles W. Morgan, 1865. No. 135, Lucretia, 1884.

1987, Feb. 20 Litho. *Perf. 14*

132 A24 22c multicolored .50 .50
133 A24 22c multicolored .50 .50
134 A24 22c multicolored .50 .50
135 A24 22c multicolored .50 .50
a. Block of 4, #132-135 2.00 2.00

Historic and Military Flights A25

Designs: No. 136, Charles Lindbergh commemorative medal, Spirit of St. Louis crossing the Atlantic, 1927. No. 137, Lindbergh flying in the Battle of the Marshalls, 1944. No. 138, William Bridgeman flying in the Battle of Kwajalein, 1944. No. 139, Bridgeman testing the Douglas Skyrocket, 1951. No. 140, John Glenn flying in the Battle of the Marshalls. No. 141, Glenn, the first American to orbit the Earth, 1962.

1987, Mar. 12 Litho. *Perf. 14½*

136 A25 33c multicolored .70 .70
137 A25 33c multicolored .70 .70
a. Pair, #136-137 1.40 1.40
138 A25 39c multicolored .75 .75
139 A25 39c multicolored .75 .75
a. Pair, #138-139 1.50 1.50
140 A25 44c multicolored .80 .80
141 A25 44c multicolored .80 .80
a. Pair, #140-141 1.60 1.60
Nos. 136-141 (6) 4.50 4.50

Souvenir Sheet

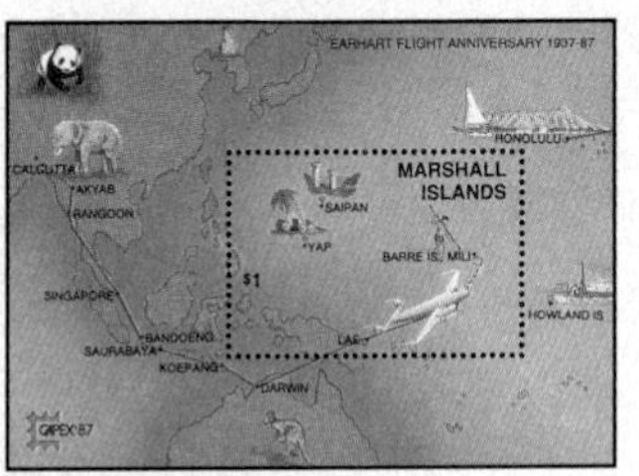

CAPEX '87 — A26

1987, June 15 Litho. *Perf. 14*

142 A26 $1 Map of flight 2.50 2.50

Amelia Earhart (1897-1937), American aviator who died during attempted round-the-world flight, 50th anniv. No. 142 has multicolored margin picturing Earhart's flight pattern from Calcutta, India, to the crash site near Barre Is., Marshall Is.

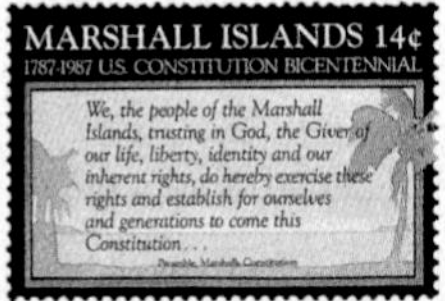

US Constitution Bicentennial — A27

Excerpts from the Marshall Islands and US Constitutions: No. 143, We,... Marshall. No. 144, National seals. No. 145, We,... United States. No. 146, All we have.... No. 147, Flags. No. 148, to establish.... No. 149, With this Constitution.... No. 150, Stick chart, Liberty Bell. No. 151, to promote....

1987, July 16 Litho. *Perf. 14*

143 A27 14c multicolored .30 .30
144 A27 14c multicolored .30 .30
145 A27 14c multicolored .30 .30
a. Triptych, #143-145 1.00 1.00
146 A27 22c multicolored .40 .40
147 A27 22c multicolored .40 .40
148 A27 22c multicolored .40 .40
a. Triptych, #146-148 1.25 1.25
149 A27 44c multicolored .80 .80
150 A27 44c multicolored .80 .80
151 A27 44c multicolored .80 .80
a. Triptych, #149-151 2.50 2.50
Nos. 143-151 (9) 4.50 4.50

Triptychs printed in continuous designs.

Seashells Type of 1985

No. 152, Magnificent cone. No. 153, Partridge tun. No. 154, Scorpion spider conch. No. 155, Hairy triton. No. 156, Chiragra spider conch.

1987, Sept. 1 Litho. *Perf. 14*

152 A12 22c multicolored .40 .40
153 A12 22c multicolored .40 .40
154 A12 22c multicolored .40 .40
155 A12 22c multicolored .40 .40
156 A12 22c multicolored .40 .40
a. Strip of 5, #152-156 2.00 2.00

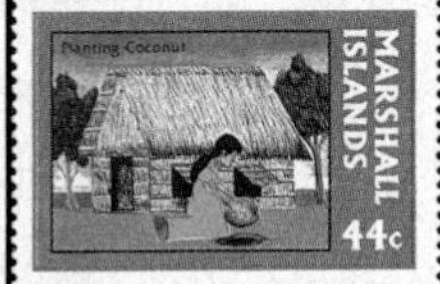

Copra Industry A28

Contest-winning crayon drawings by Amram Enox; design contest sponsored by the Tobular Copra Processing Co.

1987, Dec. 10 Litho. *Perf. 14*

157 A28 44c Planting coconut .65 .65
158 A28 44c Making copra .65 .65
159 A28 44c Bottling coconut oil .65 .65
a. Triptych, #157-159 2.00 2.00

Biblical Verses A29

1987, Dec. 10

160 A29 14c Matthew 2:1 .25 .25
161 A29 22c Luke 2:14 .40 .40
162 A29 33c Psalms 33:3 .60 .60
163 A29 44c Pslams 150:5 .75 .75
Nos. 160-163 (4) 2.00 2.00

Christmas.

Marine Birds A30

1988, Jan. 27

164 A30 44c Pacific reef herons .75 .75
165 A30 44c Bar-tailed godwit .75 .75
166 A30 44c Masked booby .75 .75
167 A30 44c Northern shoveler .75 .75
a. Block of 4, #164-167 3.00 3.00

Fish — A31

Designs: 1c, Damselfish. 3c, Blackface butterflyfish. 14c, Hawkfish. 15c, Balloonfish. 17c, Trunk fish. 22c, Lyretail wrasse. 25c, Parrotfish. 33c, White-spotted boxfish. 36c, Spotted boxfish. 39c, Surgeonfish. 44c, Long-snouted butterflyfish. 45c, Trumpetfish. 56c, Sharp-nosed puffer. $1, Seahorse. $2, Ghost pipefish. $5, Big-spotted triggerfish. $10, Blue jack.

Perf. 14½x14, 14 (#187)

1988-89 Litho.

168 A31 1c multicolored .25 .25
169 A31 3c multicolored .25 .25
170 A31 14c multicolored .25 .25
a. Booklet pane of 10 3.75 —
171 A31 15c multicolored .25 .25
a. Booklet pane of 10 4.50 —
172 A31 17c multicolored .30 .30
173 A31 22c multicolored .35 .35
a. Booklet pane of 10 5.00 —
b. Bklt. pane, 5 each 14c, 22c 5.00 —
174 A31 25c multicolored .35 .35
a. Booklet pane of 10 7.25 —
b. Bklt. pane, 5 each 15c, 25c 7.25 —
175 A31 33c multicolored .60 .60
176 A31 36c multicolored .65 .65
177 A31 39c multicolored .75 .75
178 A31 44c multicolored .80 .80
179 A31 45c multicolored .80 .80
180 A31 56c multicolored 1.00 1.00
181 A31 $1 multicolored 1.90 1.90
182 A31 $2 multicolored 3.50 3.50
183 A31 $5 multicolored 8.00 8.00
184 A31 $10 multi ('89) 16.00 16.00
Nos. 168-184 (17) 36.00 36.00

Issued: Nos. 170a, 173a, 173b, 3/31/88; 15c, 25c, 36c, 45c, 7/19/; Nos. 171a, 174a, 174b, 12/15; $10, 3/31/89; others, 3/17/88.

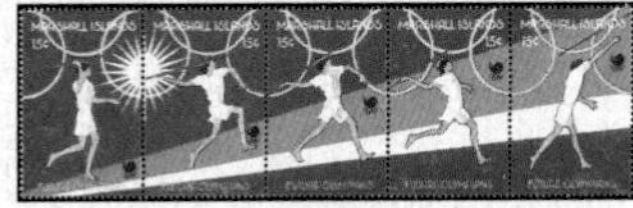

A32

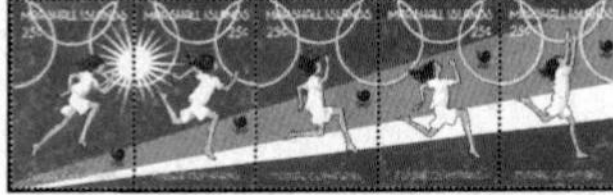

1988 Summer Olympics, Seoul — A33

Athletes in motion: 15c, Javelin thrower. 25c, Runner.

1988, June 30 Litho. *Perf. 14*

188 A32 15c Strip of 5, #a-e 1.65 1.65
189 A33 25c Strip of 5, #a-e 2.25 2.25

Souvenir Sheet

Pacific Voyages of Robert Louis Stevenson — A34

Stick chart of the Marshalls and: a, *Casco* sailing through the Golden Gate. b, At the Needles of Ua-Pu, Marquesas. c, *Equator* departing from Honolulu and Kaiulani, an Hawaiian princess. d, Chief's canoe, Majuro Lagoon. e, Bronze medallion, 1887, by Augustus St. Gaudens in the Tate Gallery, London. f, Outrigger canoe and S.S. *Janet Nicoll* in Majuro Lagoon. g, View of Apemama, Gilbert Is. h, Samoan outrigger canoe, Apia Harbor. i, Stevenson riding horse Jack at his estate, Vallima, Samoa.

1988, July 19 Litho. *Perf. 14*

190 A34 Sheet of 9 6.25 4.50
a.-i. 25c any single .50 .50

Robert Louis Stevenson (1850-1894), Scottish novelist, poet and essayist.

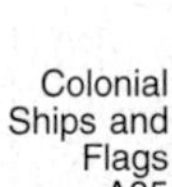

Colonial Ships and Flags A35

Designs: No. 191, Galleon *Santa Maria de La Victoria,* 1526, and Spanish "Ragged Cross" ensign in use from 1516 to 1785. No. 192, Transport ships *Charlotte* and *Scarborough,* 1788, and British red ensign, 1707-1800. No. 193, Schooner *Flying Fish,* sloop-of-war *Peacock,* 1841, and U.S. flag, 1837-1845. No. 194, Steamer *Planet,* 1909, and German flag, 1867-1919.

1988, Sept. 2 Litho. *Perf. 14*

191 A35 25c multicolored .50 .50
192 A35 25c multicolored .50 .50
193 A35 25c multicolored .50 .50
194 A35 25c multicolored .50 .50
a. Block of 4, #191-194 2.00 2.00

Christmas — A36

No. 195, Santa Claus riding in sleigh. No. 196, Reindeer, hut and palm trees. No. 197, Reindeer and palm trees. No. 198, Reindeer, palm tree, fish. No. 199, Reindeer and outrigger canoe.

1988, Nov. 7 Litho. *Perf. 14*

195 A36 25c multicolored .50 .50
196 A36 25c multicolored .50 .50
197 A36 25c multicolored .50 .50
198 A36 25c multicolored .50 .50
199 A36 25c multicolored .50 .50
a. Strip of 5, #195-199 2.50 2.50

No. 199a has a continuous design.

Tribute to John F. Kennedy — A37

No. 200, Nuclear threat diminished. No. 201, Signing the Test Ban Treaty. No. 202, Portrait. No. 203, US-USSR Hotline. No. 204, Peace Corps enactment.

1988, Nov. 22 Litho. *Perf. 14*

200 A37 25c multicolored .55 .55
201 A37 25c multicolored .55 .55
202 A37 25c multicolored .55 .55
203 A37 25c multicolored .55 .55
204 A37 25c multicolored .55 .55
a. Strip of 5, #200-204 2.75 2.75

No. 204a has a continuous design.

US Space Shuttle Program and Kwajalein — A38

No. 205, Launch of *Prime* from Vandenberg Air Force Base downrange to the Kwajalein Missile Range. No. 206, *Prime* X023A/SV-5D lifting body reentering atmosphere. No. 207, Parachute landing and craft recovery off Kwajalein Is. No. 208, Shuttle over island.

1988, Dec. 23 Litho. *Perf. 14*

205 25c multicolored .50 .50
206 25c multicolored .50 .50
207 25c multicolored .50 .50
208 25c multicolored .50 .50
a. A38 Strip of 4, #205-208 2.00 2.00

NASA 30th anniv. and 25th anniv. of the Project PRIME wind tunnel tests.

See No. C21.

Links to Japan A39

Designs: No. 209, Typhoon Monument, Majuro, 1918. No. 210, Seaplane base and railway depot, Djarrej Islet, c. 1940. No. 211, Fishing boats. No. 212, Japanese honeymooners scuba diving, 1988.

1989, Jan. 19 Litho. *Perf. 14*

209 A39 45c multicolored .75 .75
210 A39 45c multicolored .75 .75
211 A39 45c multicolored .75 .75
212 A39 45c multicolored .75 .75
a. Block of 4, #209-212 3.00 3.00

Links to Alaska A40

Paintings by Claire Fejes: No. 213, Island Woman. No. 214, Kotzebue, Alaska. No. 215, Marshallese Madonna.

1989, Mar. 31 Litho. *Perf. 14*

213 A40 45c multi .85 .85
214 A40 45c multi .85 .85
215 A40 45c multi .85 .85
a. Strip of 3, #213-215 2.55 2.55

Printed in sheets of 9.

Seashells Type of 1985

No. 216, Pontifical miter. No. 217, Tapestry turban. No. 218, Flame-mouthed helmet. No. 219, Prickly Pacific drupe. No. 220, Blood-mouthed conch.

1989, May 15 Litho. *Perf. 14*

216 A12 25c multi .50 .50
217 A12 25c multi .50 .50
218 A12 25c multi .50 .50
219 A12 25c multi .50 .50
220 A12 25c multi .50 .50
a. Strip of 5, #216-220 2.50 2.50

Souvenir Sheet

In Praise of Sovereigns, 1940, by Sanko Inoue — A41

1989, May 15 Litho. *Perf. 14*

221 A41 $1 multicolored 2.00 2.00

Hirohito (1901-89) and enthronement of Akihito as emperor of Japan.

Migrant Birds A42

No. 222, Wandering tattler. No. 223, Ruddy turnstone. No. 224, Pacific golden plover. No. 225, Sanderling.

1989, June 27 Litho. *Perf. 14*

222 A42 45c multi .85 .85
223 A42 45c multi .85 .85
224 A42 45c multi .85 .85
225 A42 45c multi .85 .85
a. Block of 4, #222-225 3.40 3.40

Postal History A43

PHILEXFRANCE '89 — A44

Designs: No. 226, Missionary ship *Morning Star V,* 1905, and Marshall Isls. #15 canceled. No. 227, Marshall Isls. #15-16 on registered letter, 1906. No. 228, *Prinz Eitel Friedrich,* 1914, and German sea post cancel. No. 229, Cruiser squadron led by SMS *Scharnhorst,* 1914, and German sea post cancel.

No. 230: a, SMS *Bussard* and German sea post cancel and Germany #32. b, US Type A924 and Marshall Isls. #34a on FDC. c, LST 119 FPO, 1944, US Navy cancel and pair of US #853. d, Mail boat, 1936, cancel and Japan #222. e, Majuro PO f, Marshall Isls. cancel, 1951, and four US #803.

No. 231, Germany #32 and Marshall Isls. cancel, 1889.

1989, July 7

226 A43 45c multicolored .80 .80
227 A43 45c multicolored .80 .80
228 A43 45c multicolored .80 .80
229 A43 45c multicolored .80 .80
a. Block of 4, #226-229 3.25 3.25

Souvenir Sheets

230 Sheet of 6 10.00 10.00
a.-f. A44 25c any single 1.50 1.50
231 A43 $1 multicolored 10.00 3.00

Nos. 230b and 230e are printed in a continuous design.

1st Moon Landing, 20th Anniv. A45

Apollo 11: No. 232, Liftoff. No. 233, Neil Armstrong. No. 234, Lunar module *Eagle.* No. 235, Michael Collins. No. 236, Raising the American flag on the Moon. No. 237, Buzz Aldrin. $1, 1st step on the Moon and "We came in peace for all mankind."

1989, Aug. 1 Litho. *Perf. 13½*

Booklet Stamps

232 A45 25c multicolored 1.25 1.25
233 A45 25c multicolored 1.25 1.25
234 A45 25c multicolored 1.25 1.25
235 A45 25c multicolored 1.25 1.25
236 A45 25c multicolored 1.25 1.25
237 A45 25c multicolored 1.25 1.25

Size: 75x32mm

238 A45 $1 multicolored 7.00 5.00
a. Booklet pane of 7, #232-238 15.00
Nos. 232-238 (7) 14.50 12.50

Decorative inscribed selvage separates No. 238 from Nos. 232-237 and surrounds it like a souvenir sheet margin. Selvage around Nos. 232-237 is plain.

World War II

A46

Anniversaries and events, 1939: No. 239, Invasion of Poland. No. 240, Sinking of HMS *Royal Oak.* No. 241, Invasion of Finland.

Battle of the River Plate: No. 242, HMS *Exeter,.* No. 243, HMS *Ajax,.* No. 244, *Admiral Graf Spee,.* No. 245, HMNZS *Achilles,.*

1989 Litho. *Perf. 13½*

239 A46 25c W1 (1-1) .60 .45
240 A46 45c W2 (1-1) 1.00 .75
241 A46 45c W3 (1-1) 1.00 .75
242 A46 45c W4 (4-1) .80 .75
243 A46 45c W4 (4-2) .80 .75
244 A46 45c W4 (4-3) .80 .75
245 A46 45c W4 (4-4) .80 .75
a. Block of 4, #242-245 3.25 3.00

Issued: No. 239, 9/1; No. 240, 10/13; No. 241, 11/30; No. 245a, 12/13.

A47

1940 — No. 246, Invasion of Denmark. No. 247, Invasion of Norway. No. 248, Katyn Forest Massacre. No. 249, Bombing of Rotterdam. No. 250, Invasion of Belgium. No. 251, Winston Churchill becomes prime minister of England. No. 252, Evacuation of the British Expeditionary Force at Dunkirk. No. 253, Evacuation at Dunkirk. No. 254, Occupation of Paris.

1990

246 A46 25c W5 (2-1) .60 .50
247 A46 25c W5 (2-2) .60 .50
a. Pair, #246-247 1.25 1.00
248 A47 25c W6 (1-1) .50 .50
249 A46 25c W8 (2-1) .50 .50
250 A46 25c W8 (2-2) .50 .50
a. Pair, #249-250 1.00 1.00
251 A46 45c W7 (1-1) 1.00 .90
252 A46 45c W9 (2-1) 1.00 .90
253 A46 45c W9 (2-2) 1.00 .90
a. Pair, #252-253 2.00 1.80
254 A47 45c W10 (1-1) 1.00 .90

Issued: No. 247a, 4/9; No. 248, 4/16; Nos. 249-251, 5/10; Nos. 252-253, 6/4; No. 254, 6/14.

1990

No. 255, Battle of Mers-el-Kebir, 1940. No. 256, Battles for the Burma Road, 1940-45.

US Destroyers for British bases: No. 257, HMS Georgetown (ex-USS Maddox). No. 258, HMS Banff (ex-USCGC Saranac). No. 259, HMS Buxton (ex-USS Edwards). No. 260, HMS Rockingham (ex-USS Swasey).

Battle of Britain: No. 261, Supermarine Spitfire Mark IA. No. 262, Hawker Hurricane Mark I. No. 263, Messerschmitt Bf109E. No. 264, Junkers JU87B-2. No. 265, Tripartite Pact Signed 1940.

255 A46 25c W11 (1-1) .60 .50
256 A47 25c W12 (1-1) .60 .50
257 A46 45c W13 (4-1) 1.00 .90
258 A46 45c W13 (4-2) 1.00 .90
259 A46 45c W13 (4-3) 1.00 .90
260 A46 45c W13 (4-4) 1.00 .90
a. Block of 4, #257-260 4.00 3.60
261 A46 45c W14 (4-1) 1.00 .90
262 A46 45c W14 (4-2) 1.00 .90
263 A46 45c W14 (4-3) 1.00 .90
264 A46 45c W14 (4-4) 1.00 .90
a. Block of 4, #261-264 4.00 3.60
265 A46 45c W15 1.10 .90

Issued: No. 255, 7/3; No. 256, 7/18; No. 260a, 9/9; No. 264a, 9/15; No. 265, 9/27.

1990-91

Designs: No. 266, Roosevelt elected to third term, 1940. Battle of Taranto: No. 267, HMS Illustrious. No. 268, Fairey Swordfish. No. 269, RM Andrea Doria. No. 270, RM Conte di Cavour.

Roosevelt's Four Freedoms Speech: No. 271, Freedom of Speech. No. 272, Freedom from Want. No. 273, Freedom of Worship. No. 274, Freedom From Fear. No. 275, Battle of Beda Fomm, Feb. 5-7, 1941.

Germany Invades the Balkans: No. 276, Invasion of Greece. No. 277, Invasion of Yugoslavia.

Sinking of the Bismarck: No. 278, HMS Prince of Wales. No. 279, HMS Hood. No. 280, Bismarck. No. 281, Fairey Swordfish. No. 282, German Invasion of Russia, 1941.

266 A47 25c W16 .60 .50
267 A46 25c W17 (4-1) .60 .50
268 A46 25c W17 (4-2) .60 .50
269 A46 25c W17 (4-3) .60 .50
270 A46 25c W17 (4-4) .60 .50
a. Block of 4, #266-270 2.50 2.00
271 A46 30c W18 (4-1) .65 .60
272 A46 30c W18 (4-2) .65 .60
273 A46 30c W18 (4-3) .65 .60
274 A46 30c W18 (4-4) .65 .60
a. Block of 4, #271-274 2.60 2.40
275 A46 30c Tanks, W19 .60 .60
276 A47 29c W20 (2-1) .60 .60
277 A47 29c W20 (2-2) .60 .60
a. Pair, #276-277 1.25 1.25
278 A46 50c W21 (4-1) 1.00 1.00
279 A46 50c W21 (4-2) 1.00 1.00
280 A46 50c W21 (4-3) 1.00 1.00
281 A46 50c W21 (4-4) 1.00 1.00
a. Block of 4, #278-281 4.00 4.00
282 A46 30c Tanks, W22 .60 .60

Issued: No. 266, 11/5/90; No. 270a, 11/11/90; No. 274a, 1/6/91; No. 275, 2/5/91; No. 277a, 4/6/91; No. 281a, 5/27/91; No. 282, 6/22/91.

1991

1941 — Declaration of the Atlantic Charter: No. 283, Pres. Roosevelt and USS Augusta. No. 284, Churchill and HMS Prince of Wales. No. 285, Siege of Moscow.

Sinking of USS Reuben James: No. 286, Reuben James hit by torpedo. No. 287, German U-562 submarine.

Japanese attack on Pearl Harbor: No. 288, American warplanes. No. 289, Japanese warplanes. No. 290, USS Arizona. No. 291, Japanese aircraft carrier Akagi.

283 A47 29c W23 (2-1) .60 .60
284 A47 29c W23 (2-2) .60 .60
a. Pair, #283-284 1.25 1.25
285 A46 29c W24 .60 .60
286 A46 30c W25 (2-1) .60 .60
287 A46 30c W25 (2-1) .60 .60
a. Pair, #286-287 1.25 1.25
288 A47 50c W26 (4-1) 1.00 1.00
a. Revised inscription 4.75 1.00
289 A47 50c W26 (4-2) 1.00 1.00
290 A47 50c W26 (4-3) 1.00 1.00
291 A47 50c W26 (4-4) 1.00 1.00
a. Block of 4, #288-291 4.00 4.00
b. Block of 4, #288a, 289-291 8.50 4.00

Inscriptions read "Peal" on No. 288 and "Pearl" on No. 288a.

Issued: No. 284a, 8/14; No. 285, 10/2; No. 287a, 10/31; No. 291a, 12/7.

1991-92

1941-42: No. 292, Japanese capture Guam. No. 293, Fall of Singapore.

First combat of the Flying Tigers: No. 294, Curtiss Tomahawk. No. 295, Mitsubishi Ki-21 on fire.

No. 296, Fall of Wake Island.

No. 297, Roosevelt and Churchill at Arcadia Conference. No. 298, Japanese tank entering Manila. No. 299, Japanese take Rabaul. No. 300, Battle of the Java Sea. No. 301, Rangoon falls to Japanese. No. 302, Japanese land on New Guinea. No. 303, MacArthur evacuated from Corregidor. No. 304, Raid on Saint-Nazaire. No. 305, Surrender of Bataan / Death

March. No. 306, Doolittle Raid on Tokyo. No. 307, Fall of Corregidor.

292 A47 29c W27 .60 .60
293 A46 29c W28 .60 .60
294 A46 50c W29 (2-1) 1.00 1.00
295 A46 50c W29 (2-2) 1.00 1.00
a. Pair, #294-295 2.00 2.00
296 A46 29c W30 .60 .60
297 A46 29c W31 .60 .60
298 A46 50c W32 1.00 1.00
299 A46 29c W33 .60 .60
300 A46 29c W34 .60 .60
301 A47 50c W35 1.00 1.00
302 A46 29c W36 .60 .60
303 A46 29c W37 .60 .60
304 A46 29c W38 .60 .60
305 A47 29c W39 .60 .60
306 A47 50c W40 1.00 1.00
307 A46 29c W41 .60 .60

Issued: Nos. 292-293, 12/10/91; No. 295a, 12/20/91; No. 296, 12/23/91; No. 297, 1/1/92; No. 298, 1/2/92; No. 299, 1/23/92; No. 300, 2/15/92; Nos. 301-302, 3/8/92; No. 303, 3/11/92; No. 304, 3/27/92; No. 305, 4/9/92; No. 306, 4/18/92; No. 307, 5/6/92.

1992

1942 — Battle of the Coral Sea: No. 308, USS Lexington. No. 309, Japanese Mitsubishi A6M2 Zeros. No. 310, Douglas SBD Dauntless dive bombers. No. 311, Japanese carrier Shoho.

Battle of Midway: No. 312, Japanese aircraft carrier Akagi. No. 313, U.S. Douglas SBD Dauntless dive bombers. No. 314, USS Yorktown. No. 315, Nakajima B5N2 Kate torpedo planes.

No. 316, Village of Lidice destroyed. No. 317, Fall of Sevastopol.

Convoy PQ17 destroyed: No. 318, British merchant ship in convoy. No. 319, German U-boats.

No. 320, Marines land on Guadalcanal. No. 323, Battle of Stalingrad. No. 324, Battle of Eastern Solomons.

No. 321, Battle of Savo Island. No. 322, Dieppe Raid. No. 325, Battle of Cape Esperance. No. 326, Battle of El Alamein.

Battle of Barents Sea: No. 327, HMS Sheffield. No. 328, Admiral Hipper.

308 A46 50c W42 (4-1) 1.00 1.00
a. Revised inscription 2.00 1.00
309 A46 50c W42 (4-2) 1.00 1.00
a. Revised inscription 2.00 1.00
310 A46 50c W42 (4-3) 1.00 1.00
a. Revised inscription 2.00 1.00
311 A46 50c W42 (4-4) 1.00 1.00
a. Block of 4, #308-311 4.00 4.00
b. Revised inscription 2.00 1.00
c. Block of 4, #308a-310a, 311b 8.50 4.00
312 A46 50c W43 (4-1) 1.00 1.00
313 A46 50c W43 (4-3) 1.00 1.00
314 A46 50c W43 (4-2) 1.00 1.00
315 A46 50c W43 (4-4) 1.00 1.00
a. Block of 4, #312-315 4.00 4.00
316 A46 29c W44 .60 .60
317 A47 29c W45 .60 .60
318 A46 29c W46 (2-1) .60 .60
319 A46 29c W46 (2-2) .60 .60
a. Pair, #318-319 1.25 1.25
320 A46 29c W47 .60 .60
321 A47 29c W48 .60 .60
322 A46 29c W49 .60 .60
323 A47 50c W50 1.25 1.00
324 A46 29c W51 .60 .60
325 A46 50c W52 1.25 1.00
326 A46 29c W53 .60 .60
327 A46 29c W54 (2-1) .60 .60
328 A46 29c W54 (2-2) .60 .60
a. Pair, #327-328 1.25 1.25

Inscription reads "U.S.S. Lexington/Grumman F4F-3 Wildcat" on No. 308a, "Japanese Aichi D3A1 Vals/Nakajima B5N2 Kate" on No. 309a, "U.S. Douglas TBD-1 Devastators" on No. 310a, "Japanese Carrier Shoho/Mitsubishi A6M2 Zeros" on No. 311b.

Issued: No. 311a, 5/8/92; No. 315a, 6/4; No. 316, 6/9/92; No. 317, 7/4; No. 319a, 7/5; No. 320, 8/7; #321, 8/9; Nos. 322-323, 8/19; No. 324, 8/24; No. 325, 10/11; No. 326, 10/23; No. 328a, 12/31.

Vertical pairs, Nos. 312-313 and Nos. 314-315 have continuous designs.

No. 310 incorrectly identifies Douglas TBD torpedo bombers.

1993 Litho. *Perf. 13½*

1943 — No. 329, Casablanca Conf. No. 330, Liberation of Kharkov.

Battle of Bismarck Sea: No. 331, Japanese A6M Zeroes, destroyer Arashio. No. 332, U.S. P38 Lightnings, Australian Beaufighter. No. 333, Japanese destroyer Shirayuki. No. 334, U.S. A-20 Havoc, B-25 Mitchell.

No. 335, Interception of Admiral Yamamoto.

Battle of Kursk: No. 336, German Tiger I. No. 337, Soviet T-34.

329 A46 29c W55 .65 .60
330 A46 29c W56 .65 .60
331 A46 50c W57 (4-1) 1.00 1.00
332 A46 50c W57 (4-2) 1.00 1.00
333 A46 50c W57 (4-3) 1.00 1.00
334 A46 50c W57 (4-4) 1.00 1.00
a. Block of 4, #331-334 4.00 4.00
335 A46 50c W58 1.00 1.00
336 A46 29c W59 (2-1) .85 .60
337 A46 29c W59 (2-2) .85 .60
a. Pair, #336-337 1.70 1.25
Nos. 239-337 (99) 78.50 74.05

Issued: No. 329, 1/14; No. 330, 2/16; No. 334a, 3/3; No. 335, 4/18; No. 337a, 7/5.

See Nos. 467-524, 562-563.

Christmas A57

Angels playing musical instruments.

1989, Oct. 25 *Perf. 13½*

341 A57 25c Horn .80 .80
342 A57 25c Singing carol .80 .80
343 A57 25c Lute .80 .80
344 A57 25c Lyre .80 .80
a. Block of 4, #341-344 3.25 3.25

Miniature Sheet

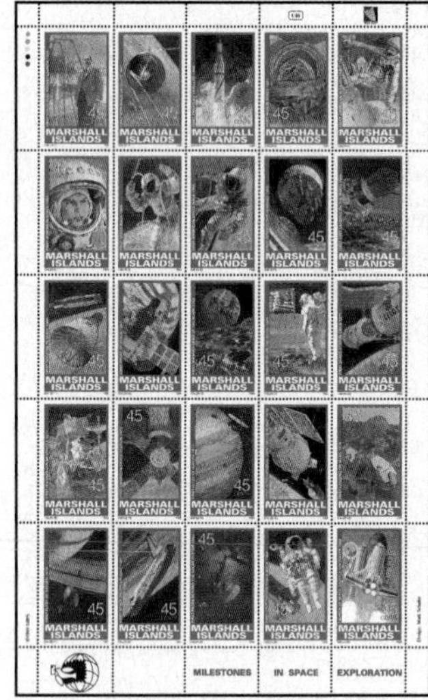

Milestones in Space Exploration — A58

Designs: a, Robert Goddard and 1st liquid fuel rocket launch, 1926. b, *Sputnik,* 1st man-made satellite, 1957. c, 1st American satellite, 1958. d, Yuri Gagarin, 1st man in space, 1961. e, John Glenn, 1st American to orbit Earth, 1962. f, Valentina Tereshkova, 1st woman in space, 1963. g, Aleksei Leonov, 1st space walk, 1965. h, Edward White, 1st American to walk in space, 1965. i, Gemini-Titan 6A, 1st rendezvous in space, 1965. j, 1st Soft landing on the Moon, 1966. k, Gemini 8, 1st docking in space, 1966. l, 1st probe of Venus, 1967. m, Apollo 8, 1st manned orbit of the Moon, 1968. n, Apollo 11, 1st man on the Moon, 1969. o, Soyuz 11, 1st space station crew, 1971. p, Apollo 15, 1st manned lunar vehicle, 1971. q, *Skylab 2,* 1st American manned space station, 1973. r, 1st Flyby of Jupiter, 1973. s, Apollo-Soyuz, 1st joint space flight, 1975. t, 1st Landing on Mars, 1976. u, 1st flyby of Saturn, 1979. v, *Columbia,* 1st space shuttle flight, 1981. w, 1st probe beyond the solar system, 1983. x, 1st untethered space walk, 1984. y, Launch of space shuttle *Discovery,* 1988.

1989, Nov. 24 Litho. *Perf. 13½*

345 A58 Sheet of 25 25.00 25.00
a.-y. 45c any single .90 .90

No. 345 contains World Stamp Expo '89 emblem on selvage.

Birds
A59 A59a

Designs: 1c, Black noddy. 5c, Red-tailed tropic bird. 10c, Sanderling. 12c, Black-naped tern. 15c, Wandering tattler. 20c, Bristle-thighed curlew. 23c, Northern shoveler. 25c, Brown noddy. 27c, Sooty tern. 29c, Wedge-tailed shearwater. 30c, Northern pintail. 35c, Pacific golden plover. 36c, Red footed booby. 40c, White tern. 50c, Great frigate bird. 52c, Great crested tern. 65c, Lesser sand plover. 75c, Little tern. $1, Pacific reef heron. $2, Masked booby.

1990-92 Litho. *Perf. 13½*

346 A59 1c multicolored .25 .25
347 A59 5c multicolored .25 .25
348 A59 10c multicolored .25 .25
349 A59 12c multicolored .25 .25
350 A59 15c multicolored .30 .30
351 A59 20c multicolored .40 .40
352 A59 23c multicolored .45 .45
353 A59 25c multicolored .50 .50
354 A59 27c multicolored .55 .55
355 A59 29c multicolored .60 .60
356 A59a 29c multicolored .60 .60
357 A59 30c multicolored .60 .60
358 A59 35c multicolored .70 .70
359 A59 36c multicolored .75 .75
360 A59 40c multicolored .80 .80
361 A59 50c multicolored 1.00 1.00
a. Min. sheet of 4 (#347, 350, 353, 361) 2.25 2.00
362 A59 52c multicolored 1.00 1.00
363 A59 65c multicolored 1.25 1.25
364 A59 75c multicolored 1.50 1.50
365 A59 $1 multicolored 2.00 2.00
365A A59 $2 multicolored 4.00 4.00
Nos. 346-365A (21) 18.00 18.00

No. 361a for ESSEN '90, Germany Apr. 19-22.

Issued: 5c, 15c, 25c, 50c, 3/8; 30c, 36c, 40c, $1, 10/11; No. 361a, 4/19; No. 355, 20c, 52c, 2/22/91; 27c, 3/8/91; 1c, 12c, 35c, $2, 11/6/91; No. 356, 2/3/92; 10c, 23c, 65c, 75c, 4/24/92.

See Nos. 430-433.

Children's Games A60

1990, Mar. 15

366 A60 25c Lodidean .80 .75
367 A60 25c Lejonjon .80 .75
368 A60 25c Etobobo .80 .75
369 A60 25c Didmakol .80 .75
a. Block of 4, #366-369 3.25 3.00

Penny Black, 150th Anniv. A61

Designs: No. 370, Penny Black, 1840. No. 371, Essay by James Chalmers. No. 372, Essay by Robert Sievier. No. 373, Essay by Charles Whiting. No. 374, Essay by George Dickinson. No. 375, Medal engraved by William Wyon to celebrate Queen Victoria's first visit to London. $1, Engraver Charles Heath, engraving for master die.

1990, Apr. 6 Booklet Stamps

370 A61 25c multicolored 1.00 1.00
371 A61 25c multicolored 1.00 1.00
372 A61 25c multicolored 1.00 1.00
373 A61 25c multicolored 1.00 1.00
374 A61 25c multicolored 1.00 1.00
375 A61 25c multicolored 1.00 1.00

Size: 73x31mm

376 A61 $1 multicolored 4.00 4.00
a. Booklet pane of 7, #370-376 10.00 —
Nos. 370-376 (7) 10.00 10.00

Decorative inscribed selvage picturing part of a Penny Black proof sheet separates No. 376 from Nos. 370-375 in pane and surrounds it like a souvenir sheet margin. Selvage around Nos. 370-375 is plain.

Endangered Wildlife — A62

Sea Turtles: No. 377, Pacific green turtle hatchlings entering ocean. No. 378, Pacific great turtle under water. No. 379, Hawksbill hatchling, eggs. No. 380, Hawksbill turtle in water.

1990, May 3

377 25c multicolored .80 .75
378 25c multicolored .80 .75
379 25c multicolored .80 .75
380 25c multicolored .80 .75
a. A62 Block of 4, #377-380 3.25 3.00

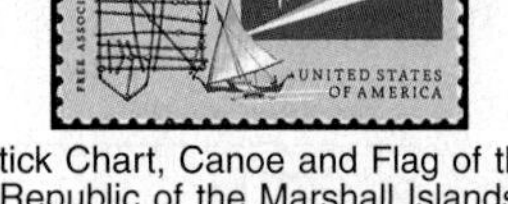

Stick Chart, Canoe and Flag of the Republic of the Marshall Islands A63

1990, Sept. 28 *Perf. 11x10½*

381 A63 25c multicolored .95 .60

See No. 615, US No. 2507, Micronesia Nos. 124-126.

German Reunification — A64

1990, Oct. 3 *Perf. 13½*

382 A64 45c multicolored 1.25 1.00

Christmas A65

No. 383, Canoe, stick chart. No. 384, Missionary preaching. No. 385, Sailors dancing. No. 386, Youths dancing.

1990, Oct. 25 Litho. *Perf. 13½*

383 A65 25c multi .75 .75
384 A65 25c multi .75 .75
385 A65 25c multi .75 .75
386 A65 25c multi .75 .75
a. Block of 4, #383-386 3.00 3.00

Breadfruit — A66

1990, Dec. 15 Litho. *Perf. 12x12½*

387	A66 25c Harvesting	.75	.75
388	A66 25c Peeling, slicing	.75	.75
389	A66 25c Preserving	.75	.75
390	A66 25c Kneading dough	.75	.75
a.	Block of 4, #387-390	3.00	3.00

US Space Shuttle Flights, 10th Anniv. — A67

No. 391, 747 ferry. No. 392, Orbital release of LDEF. No. 393, Lift-off. No. 394, Landing.

1991, Apr. 12 Litho. *Perf. 13½*

391	50c multi	.90	.90
392	50c multi	.90	.90
393	50c multi	.90	.90
394	50c multi	.90	.90
a.	A67 Block of 4, #391-394	3.75	3.75

Flowers — A68

No. 395, Ixora carolinensis. No. 396, Clerodendrum inerme. No. 397, Messerchmidia argentea. No. 398, Vigna marina.

1991, June 10 Litho. *Perf. 13½*

395	A68 52c multi	1.10	1.00
396	A68 52c multi	1.10	1.00
397	A68 52c multi	1.10	1.00
398	A68 52c multi	1.10	1.00
a.	Miniature sheet of 4, #395-398	4.75	4.00
b.	Block of 4, #395-398, without inscription	4.50	4.00

Phila Nippon '91 (No. 398a). Stamps from miniature sheets inscribed C53A.

Operation Desert Storm — A69

1991, July 4 Litho. *Perf. 13½*

399	A69 29c multicolored	.80	.60

Birds — A70

No. 400, Red-footed booby. No. 401, Great frigate bird (7-2). No. 402, Brown booby. No. 403, White tern. No. 404, Great frigate bird (7-5). No. 405, Black noddy. No. 406, White-tailed tropic bird.

1991, July 16 Booklet Stamps

400	A70 29c multi	1.25	.60
401	A70 29c multi	1.25	.60
402	A70 29c multi	1.25	.60
403	A70 29c multi	1.25	.60
404	A70 29c multi	1.25	.60
405	A70 29c multi	1.25	.60

Size: 75x33mm

406	A70 $1 multi	6.50	2.00
a.	Booklet pane of 7, #400-406	14.00	—
	Nos. 400-406 (7)	14.00	5.60

Decorative selvage separates No. 406 from Nos. 400-405 and surrounds it like a souvenir sheet margin.

Aircraft of Air Marshall Islands — A71

No. 407, Dornier 228. No. 408, Douglas DC-8. No. 409, Hawker Siddeley 748. No. 410, Saab 2000.

1991, Sept. 10 Litho. *Perf. 13½*

407	A71 12c multi	.25	.25
408	A71 29c multi	.65	.50
409	A71 50c multi	1.10	.85
410	A71 50c multi	1.10	.85
	Nos. 407-410 (4)	3.10	2.45

Admission to United Nations A72

1991, Sept. 24 Litho. *Perf. 11x10½*

411	A72 29c multicolored	.70	.65

Christmas — A73

1991, Oct. 25 *Perf. 13½*

412	A73 30c multicolored	.75	.75

Peace Corps in Marshall Islands, 25th Anniv. A74

1991, Nov. 26 Litho. *Perf. 11x10½*

413	A74 29c multicolored	.75	.60

Ships A75

No. 414, Bulk cargo carrier, Emlain. No. 415, Tanker, CSK Valiant. No. 416, Patrol boat, Ionmeto. No. 417, Freighter, Micro Pilot.

1992, Feb. 15 Litho. *Perf. 11x10½*

414	A75 29c multicolored	.80	.45
415	A75 29c multicolored	.80	.45
416	A75 29c multicolored	.80	.45
417	A75 29c multicolored	.80	.45
a.	Strip of 4, #414-417	3.25	2.00

Voyages of Discovery A76

Designs: No. 418, Traditional tipnol. No. 419, Reconstructed Santa Maria. No. 420, Constellation Argo Navis. No. 421, Marshallese sailor, tipnol. No. 422, Columbus, Santa Maria. No. 423, Astronaunt, Argo Navis. $1, Columbus, sailor, and astronaunt.

1992, May 23 Litho. *Perf. 13½*

Booklet Stamps

418	A76 50c multicolored	1.00	1.00
419	A76 50c multicolored	1.00	1.00
420	A76 50c multicolored	1.00	1.00
421	A76 50c multicolored	1.00	1.00
422	A76 50c multicolored	1.00	1.00
423	A76 50c multicolored	1.00	1.00

Size: 75x32mm

424	A76 $1 multicolored	4.00	2.00
a.	Booklet pane of 7, #418-424	10.00	—

Decorative selvage separates No. 424 from Nos. 418-423 and surrounds it like a souvenir sheet margin. See No. 1124.

Traditional Handicrafts — A77

1992, Sept. 9 Litho. *Perf. 13½*

425	A77 29c Basket weaving	.60	.60
426	A77 29c Canoe models	.60	.60
427	A77 29c Wood carving	.60	.60
428	A77 29c Fan making	.60	.60
a.	Strip of 4, #425-428	2.40	2.40

Christmas A78

1992, Oct. 29 Litho. *Perf. 11x10½*

429	A78 29c multicolored	.70	.60

Bird Type of 1990

9c, Whimbrel. 22c, Greater scaup. 28c, Sharp-tailed sandpiper. 45c, Common teal.

1992, Nov. 10 Litho. *Perf. 13½*

430	A59 9c multi	.25	.25
431	A59 22c multi	.45	.45
432	A59 28c multi	.55	.55
433	A59 45c multi	.90	.90
	Nos. 430-433 (4)	2.15	2.15

Reef Life — A79

1993, May 26 Litho. *Perf. 13½*

434	A79 50c Butterflyfish	1.40	1.00
435	A79 50c Soldierfish	1.40	1.00
436	A79 50c Damselfish	1.40	1.00
437	A79 50c Filefish	1.40	1.00
438	A79 50c Hawkfish	1.40	1.00
439	A79 50c Surgeonfish	1.40	1.00

Size: 75x33mm

440	A79 $1 Parrotfish	5.50	2.00
a.	Booklet pane of 7, #434-440	13.00	—
	Nos. 434-440 (7)	13.90	8.00

Decorative selvage separates No. 440 from Nos. 434-439 and surrounds it like a souvenir sheet margin. See No. 1103.

Ships A80

Marshallese Sailing Vessels — A81

Designs: 10c, Spanish galleon San Jeronimo. 14c, USCG Fisheries Patrol vessel Cape Corwin. 15c, British merchant ship Britannia. 19c, Island transport Micro Palm. 20c, Dutch ship Eendracht. 23c, Frigate HMS Cornwallis. 24c, U.S. naval schooner Dolphin. 29c, Missionary packet Morning Star. 30c, Russian brig Rurick. 32c, Spanish sailing ship Santa Maria de la Vittoria. 35c, German warship SMS Nautilus. 40c, British brig Nautilus. 45c, Japanese warships Nagara, Isuzu. 46c, Trading schooner Equator. 50c, Aircraft carrier USS Lexington CV-16. 52c, HMS Serpent. 55c, Whaling ship Potomac. 60c, Coast Guard cutter Assateague. 75c, British transport Scarborough. 78c, Whaler Charles W. Morgan. 95c, US steam vessel Tanager. $1, Walap, Eniwetok. $1, Barkentine hospital ship Tole Mour. $2, Walap, Jaluit. $2.90, Marshall Islands fishing vessels. $3, Schooner Victoria. $5, Tipnol, Ailuk. $10, Racing canoes.

Perf. 11x10½ (A80), 13½ (A81)

1993-95 Litho.

441	A80	10c multicolored	.25	.25
442	A80	14c multicolored	.30	.30
443	A80	15c multicolored	.30	.30
444	A80	19c multicolored	.40	.40
445	A80	20c multicolored	.40	.40
446	A80	23c multicolored	.45	.45
447	A80	24c multicolored	.50	.50
448	A80	29c multicolored	.60	.60
449	A80	30c multicolored	.60	.60
450	A80	32c multicolored	.65	.65
451	A80	35c multicolored	.70	.70
452	A80	40c multicolored	.80	.80
453	A80	45c multicolored	.90	.90
454	A80	46c multicolored	.95	.95
455	A80	50c multicolored	1.00	1.00
456	A80	52c multicolored	1.10	1.10
457	A80	55c multicolored	1.10	1.10
458	A80	60c multicolored	1.25	1.25
459	A80	75c multicolored	1.50	1.50
460	A80	78c multicolored	1.65	1.65
461	A80	95c multicolored	1.90	1.90
462	A80	$1 multicolored	2.00	2.00
463	A81	$1 multicolored	2.00	2.00
464	A81	$2 multicolored	4.00	4.00
465	A80	$2.90 multicolored	5.75	5.75
466	A80	$3 multicolored	6.00	6.00
466A	A81	$5 multicolored	10.00	10.00
466B	A81	$10 multicolored	20.00	20.00
		Nos. 441-466B (28)	67.05	67.05

Souvenir Sheet

Stamp Size: 46x26mm

466C	A81 Sheet of 4, #d.-g.	3.75	3.50

No. 466C contains 15c, 23c, 52c and 75c stamps. Inscription reads "Hong Kong '94 Stamp Exhibition" in Chinese on Nos. 466Cd, 466Cg, and in English on Nos. 466Ce-466Cf.

Issued: 15c, 24c, 29c, 50c, 6/24/93; 19c, 23c, 52c, 75c, 10/14/93; No. 463, 5/29/93; $2, 8/26. 10c, 30c, 35c, $2.90, 4/19/94; $5, 3/15/94; $10, 8/18/94; 20c, 40c, 45c, 55c, 9/23/94; No. 466C, 2/18/94; 14c, 46c, 95c, No. 462, 9/25/95; 32c, 60c, 78c, $3, 5/5/95.

See No. 605.

World War II Type of 1989

1943 — Invasion of Sicily: No. 467, Gen. George S. Patton, Jr. No. 468, Gen. Bernard L. Montgomery. No. 469, Americans landing at at Licata. No. 470, British landing south of Syracuse.

Allied bomber raids on Schweinfurt: No. 471, B-17F Flying Fortresses and Bf-109 fighter. No. 472, Liberation of Smolensk. No. 473, Landings at Bougainville. No. 474, Invasion of Tarawa, 1943. No. 475, Teheran Conference, 1943.

Battle of North Cape: No. 476, HMS Duke of York. No. 477, Scharnhorst.

1944 — \No. 478, Gen. Dwight D. Eisenhower, SHAEF Commander. No. 479, Invasion of Anzio. No. 480, Siege of Leningrad lifted. No. 481, U.S. liberates Marshall Islands. #482, Japanese defeated at Truk. No. 483, Big Week, US bombing of Germany.

1993-94 Litho. *Perf. 13½*

467	A46 52c W60 (4-1)	1.10	1.10
468	A46 52c W60 (4-2)	1.10	1.10
469	A46 52c W60 (4-3)	1.10	1.10
470	A46 52c W60 (4-4)	1.10	1.10
a.	Block of 4, #467-470	4.50	4.50
471	A46 50c W61	1.00	1.00
472	A47 29c W62	.60	.60
473	A46 29c W63	.60	.60
474	A46 50c W64	1.00	1.00
475	A47 52c W65	1.10	1.10
476	A46 29c W66 (2-1)	.60	.60
477	A46 29c W66 (2-2)	.60	.60
a.	Pair, #476-477	1.25	1.25
478	A46 29c W67	.60	.60
479	A46 50c W68	1.00	1.00
480	A46 52c W69	1.10	1.10
481	A46 29c W70	.60	.60
482	A47 29c W71	.60	.60
483	A46 52c W72	1.10	1.10
	Nos. 467-483 (17)	14.90	14.90

Issued: Nos. 467-470, 7/10/93; No. 471, 8/17/93; No. 472, 9/25/93; No. 473, 11/1/93; No. 474, 11/20/93; No. 475, 12/1/93; Nos. 476-477, 12/26/93; No. 478, 1/16/94; No. 479,

1/22/94; No. 480, 1/27/94; No. 481, 2/4/94; No. 482, 2/17/94; No. 483, 2/20/94.

1994 Litho. *Perf. 13½*

1944 — No. 484, Lt. Gen. Mark Clark, Rome falls to the Allies.

D-Day-Allied landings in Normandy: No. 485, Horsa gliders. No. 486, U.S. P-51B Mustangs, British Hurricanes. No. 487, German gun defenses. No. 488, Allied amphibious landing.

No. 489, V-1 flying bombs strike England. No. 490, U.S. Marines land on Saipan.

First Battle of the Philippine Sea: No. 491, Grumman F6F-3 Hellcat.

No. 492, U.S. liberates Guam. No. 493, Warsaw uprising. No. 494, Liberation of Paris. No. 495, U.S. Marines land on Peliliu. No. 496, MacArthur returns to the Philippines. No. 497, Battle of Leyte Gulf.

German battleship Tirpitz sunk: No. 498, Avro Lancaster. No. 499, Tirpitz.

Battle of the Bulge: No. 500, Infantry. No. 501, Armor. No. 502, Aviation. No. 503, Lt. Col. Creighton W. Abrams, Brig. Gen. Anthony C. McAuliffe.

484 A47 50c W73	1.00	1.00
485 A46 75c W74 (4-1)	1.60	1.50
a. Revised inscription	3.25	1.50
486 A46 75c W74 (4-2)	1.60	1.50
a. Revised inscription	3.25	1.50
487 A46 75c W74 (4-3)	1.60	1.50
a. Revised inscription	3.25	1.50
488 A46 75c W74 (4-4)	1.60	1.50
a. Block of 4, #485-488	6.50	6.00
b. Block of 4, #485a-487a, 488	12.00	6.00
489 A46 50c W75	1.00	1.00
490 A46 29c W76	.60	.60
491 A46 50c W77	1.00	1.00
492 A46 29c W78	.60	.60
493 A46 50c W79	1.00	1.00
494 A46 50c W80	1.00	1.00
495 A46 29c W81	.60	.60
496 A46 52c W82	1.00	1.00
497 A46 52c multicolored	1.00	1.00
498 A46 50c W84 (2-1)	1.00	1.00
499 A46 50c W84 (2-2)	1.00	1.00
a. Pair, #498-499	2.00	2.00
500 A47 50c W85 (4-1)	1.00	1.00
501 A47 50c W85 (4-2)	1.00	1.00
502 A47 50c W85 (4-3)	1.00	1.00
503 A47 50c W85 (4-4)	1.00	1.00
a. Block of 4, #500-503	5.00	4.00
Nos. 484-503 (20)	21.20	20.80

Inscription reads "Horsa Gliders, Parachute Troops" on #485a, "British Typhoon-1B, U.S. P51B Mustangs" on #486a, "German Gun Defenses, Pointe du Hoc" on #487a.

Issued: No. 484, 6/4; Nos. 485-488, 6/6; No. 489, 6/13; No. 490, 6/15; No. 491, 6/19; No. 492, 7/21; No. 493, 8/1; 494, 8/25; No. 495, 9/15; No. 496, 10/20; No. 497, 10/24; Nos. 498-499, 11/12; Nos. 500-503, 12/16.

1995 Litho. *Perf. 13½*

1945 — No. 504, Stalin, Churchill, Roosevelt, Yalta Conference. No. 505, Meissen porcelain, bombing of Dresden, 1945. No. 506, Iwo Jima invaded by US Marines.

No. 507, Remagen Bridge taken by US forces.

No. 508, Okinawa invaded by US forces. No. 509, Death of Franklin D. Roosevelt.

No. 510, US/USSR troops meet at Elbe River. No. 511, Russian troops capture Berlin. No. 512, Allies liberate concentration camps.

VE Day: No. 513, German surrender, Rheims. No. 514, Times Square, New York. No. 515, Victory Parade, Moscow. No. 516, Buckingham Palace, London.

UN Charter signed: No. 517, 563, U.S. Pres. Harry S Truman, Veteran's Memorial Hall, San Francisco.

No. 518, Potsdam Conference Convenes. No. 519, Churchill resigns. No. 520, B-29 Enola Gay drops atomic bomb on Hiroshima.

V-J Day: No. 521, Mt. Fuji, ships in Tokyo Bay. No. 522, USS Missouri. No. 523, Adm. Nimitz signs surrender document. No. 524, Japanese delegation.

504 A47 32c W86	.65	.65
505 A47 55c W87	1.10	1.10
506 A47 $1 W88	2.25	2.00
507 A47 32c W89	.65	.65
508 A47 55c W90	1.10	1.10
509 A46 50c W91	1.00	1.00
510 A46 32c W92	.65	.65
511 A46 60c W93	1.25	1.25
512 A46 55c W94	1.10	1.10
513 A46 75c W95 (4-1)	1.60	1.50
514 A46 75c W95 (4-2)	1.60	1.50
515 A46 75c W95 (4-3)	1.60	1.50
516 A46 75c W95 (4-4)	1.60	1.50
a. Block of 4, #513-516	6.50	6.00
517 A46 32c W96	.65	.65
518 A46 55c W97	1.10	1.10
519 A47 60c W98	1.25	1.25
520 A46 $1 W99	2.25	2.00
521 A46 75c W100 (4-1)	1.75	1.50
522 A46 75c W100 (4-2)	1.75	1.50
523 A46 75c W100 (4-3)	1.75	1.50
524 A46 75c W100 (4-4)	1.75	1.50
a. Block of 4, #521-524	7.25	6.00
Nos. 504-524 (21)	28.40	26.50

Issued: No. 504, 2/4/95; No. 505, 2/13/95; No. 506, 2/19/95; No. 507, 3/7/95; No. 508, 4/1/95; No. 509, 4/12/95; No. 516a, 5/8/95; No. 517, 6/26/95; No. 518, 7/7/95; No. 519, 7/26/95; No. 520, 8/6/95; No. 524a, 9/2/95.

Souvenir Sheets

No. 562a, like #303. No. 562b, like #496.

1994-95 *Imperf.*

562 Sheet of 2	2.00	2.00
a.-b. A46 50c any single	1.00	1.00
563 A46 $1 like #517	2.00	2.00

No. 563 contains one 80x50mm stamp with UN 50th anniv. emblem.

Issued: No. 562, 10/20/94; No. 563, 6/26/95.

Nos. 525-561, 564-566 are unassigned.

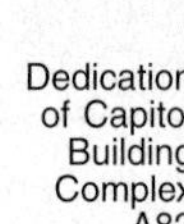

Dedication of Capitol Building Complex A82

Designs: No. 567, Capitol building. No. 568, Nitijela (parliament) building. No. 569, Natl. seal, vert. No. 570, Flag over complex, vert.

1993, Aug. 11 Litho. *Perf. 11x10½*

567 A82 29c multi (4-1)	.50	.50
568 A82 29c multi (4-2)	.50	.50
Perf. 10½x11		
569 A82 29c multi (4-3)	.50	.50
570 A82 29c multi (4-4)	.50	.50
Nos. 567-570 (4)	2.00	2.00

Souvenir Sheet

Christening of Mobil Super Tanker Eagle — A83

1993, Aug. 25 *Perf. 13½*

571 A83 50c multicolored .85 .85

Marshallese Life in 1800's — A84

No. 572, Woman, breadfruit (4-1). No. 573, Canoes, warrior (4-2). No. 574, Young chief (4-3). No. 575, Drummer, dancers (4-4).

1993, Sept. 15 Litho. *Perf. 13½*

572 A84 29c multi	.60	.60
573 A84 29c multi	.60	.60
574 A84 29c multi	.60	.60
575 A84 29c multi	.60	.60
a. Block of 4, #572-575	2.40	2.40

Christmas A85

1993, Oct. 25 Litho. *Perf. 13½*

576 A85 29c multicolored .60 .60

Souvenir Sheet

Constitution, 15th Anniv. — A86

1994, May 1 Litho. *Perf. 13½*

577 A86 $2.90 multicolored 4.50 4.50

Souvenir Sheet

Marshall Islands Postal Service, 10th Anniv. — A87

1994, May 2

578 A87 29c multicolored .60 .60

1994 World Cup Soccer Championships, U.S. — A88

Design: No. 580, Soccer players, diff.

1994, June 17 Litho. *Perf. 13½*

579 A88 50c red & multi (2-1)	1.60	1.00
580 A88 50c blue & multi (2-2)	1.60	1.00
a. Pair, #579-580	3.25	2.00

No. 580a has a continuous design.

Miniature Sheet

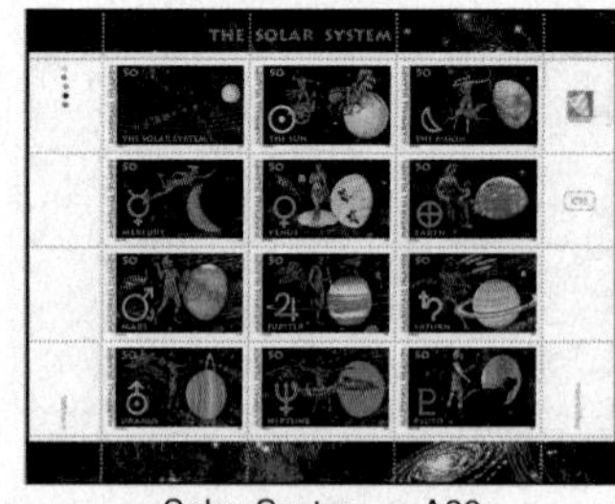

Solar System — A89

Mythological characters, symbols: a, Solar system. b, Sun. c, Moon. d, Mercury. e, Venus. f, Earth. g, Mars. h, Jupiter. i, Saturn. j, Uranus. k, Neptune. l, Pluto.

1994, July 20 Litho. *Perf. 13½*

582 A89 50c Sheet of 12, #a.-l. 12.00 12.00

First Manned Moon Landing, 25th Anniv. — A90

Designs: No. 583, First step onto Moon's surface. No. 584, Planting US flag on Moon. No. 585, Astronaut's salute to America, flag. No. 586, Astronaut stepping onto Moon, John F. Kennedy.

1994, July 20

583 A90 75c multi (4-1)	1.10	1.10
584 A90 75c multi (4-2)	1.10	1.10
585 A90 75c multi (4-3)	1.10	1.10
586 A90 75c multi (4-4)	1.10	1.10
a. Block of 4, #583-586	4.50	4.50
b. Souvenir sheet of 4, #583-586	4.50	4.50

Souvenir Sheet

Butterflies — A91

1994, Aug. 16 Litho. *Perf. 13½*

587 A91 Sheet of 3	3.75	3.75
a. 29c Meadow argus	.60	.60
b. 52c Brown awl	1.10	1.10
c. $1 Great eggfly	2.00	2.00

PHILAKOREA '94.

Christmas — A92

1994, Oct. 28 Litho. *Perf. 13½*

588 A92 29c multicolored .60 .60

Souvenir Sheet

New Year 1995 (Year of the Boar) — A93

1995, Jan. 2 Litho. *Perf. 13½*

589 A93 50c multicolored 1.00 1.00

Marine Life — A94

Designs: a, Meyer's butterflyfish, achilles tang, scuba diver. b, Scuba diver, moorish idols (a, d). c, Pacific green turtle, fairy basslets. d, Fairy basslets, emperor angelfish, orange-fin anemonefish.

1995, Mar. 20 Litho. *Perf. 13½*

590 Block of 4	4.50	4.50
a.-d. A94 55c Any single	1.10	1.10

See Nos. 614, 644.

John F. Kennedy (1917-63), 35th Pres. of US — A95

Designs: a, PT-109. b, Taking presidential oath. c, Peace Corps volunteers. d, US aircraft, naval vessels, Cuban Missile Crisis. e, Signing Nuclear Test Ban Treaty. f, Eternal flame, Arlington Natl. Cemetery.

1995, May 29 Litho. *Perf. 13½*

591 Strip of 6 5.25 5.25
a.-f. A95 55c Any single 1.00 1.00

Marilyn Monroe (1926-1962), Actress — A96

Various portraits with background color: a, red. b, green. c, orange. d, violet.

1995, June 1 Litho. *Perf. 13½*

592 A96 75c Block of 4, #a.-d. 5.75 5.75

No. 592 was issued in sheets of three blocks.

Cats — A97

Designs: a, Siamese, exotic shorthair. b, American shorthair, Persian. c, Maine coon, Burmese. d, Abyssinian, Himalayan.

1995, July 5 Litho. *Perf. 13½*

593 Block of 4 2.50 2.50
a.-d. A97 32c Any single .60 .60

Mir-Space Shuttle Docking & Apollo-Soyuz Link-Up — A98

a, Space station Mir. b, Space shuttle Atlantis. c, Apollo command module. d, Soyuz spacecraft.

1995, June 29 Litho. *Perf. 13½*

594 A98 75c Block of 4, #a.-d. 4.75 4.75

Nos. 594 is a continuous design.

Pacific Game Fish — A99

a, Pacific sailfish. b, Albacore. c, Wahoo. d, Pacific blue marlin. e, Yellowfin tuna. f, Giant trevally. g, Dolphin fish. h, Mako shark.

1995, Aug. 21 Litho. *Perf. 13½*

595 Block of 8 11.00 11.00
a.-h. A99 60c Any single 1.35 1.35

Island Legends — A100

Designs: a, Inedel's Magic Kite. b, Lijebake Rescues Her Granddaughter. c, Jebro's Mother Invents the Sail. d, Limajnon Escapes to the Moon.

1995, Aug. 25 Litho. *Perf. 13½*

596 Block of 4 + 4 labels 2.50 2.50
a.-d. A100 32c Any single .60 .60

See Nos. 612, 643.

Miniature Sheet

Singapore '95 World Stamp Exhibition — A101

Orchids: a, Paphiopedilum armeniacum. b, Masdevallia veitchiana. c, Cattleya francis. d, Cattleya x guatemalensis.

1995, Sept. 1 Litho. *Perf. 13½*

597 A101 32c Sheet of 4, #a.-d. 2.25 2.25

Souvenir Sheet

Intl. Stamp & Coin Expo, Beijing '95 — A102

1995, Sept. 12

598 A102 50c Suzhou Gardens .85 .85

Christmas A103

1995, Oct. 31 Litho. *Perf. 13½*

599 A103 32c multicolored .55 .55

Miniature Sheet

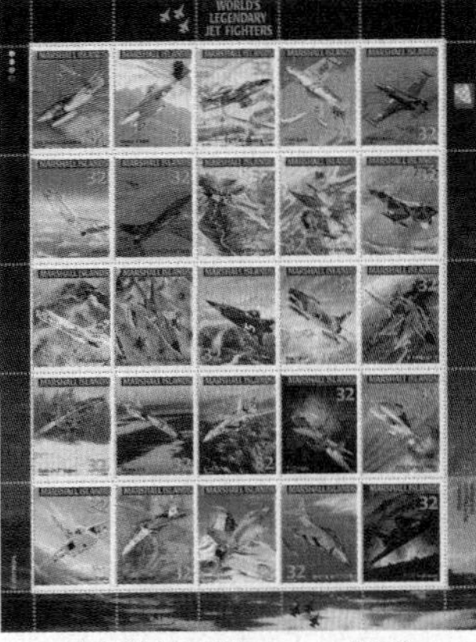

Jet Fighter Planes — A104

a, Me 262-1a Schwalbe. b, Meteor F.MK8. c, F-80 Shooting Star. d, F-86 Sabre. e, F9F-2 Panther. f, MiG-15. g, F-100 Super Sabre. h, F-102A Delta Dagger. i, F-104 Starfighter. j, MiG-21 MT. k, F8U Crusader. l, F-105 Thunderbird. m, Saab J35 Draken. n, Fiat G91Y. o, F-4 Phantom II. p, Saab JA37 Viggen. q, Mirage F1C. r, F-14 Tomcat. s, F-15 Eagle. t, F-16 Fighting Falcon. u, Tornado F.MK3. v, Sukhoi Su-27UB. w, Mirage 2000C. x, Sea Harrier FRS.MK1. y, F-117 Nighthawk.

1995, Nov. 10

600 A104 32c Sheet of 25, #a.-y. 16.00 16.00

No. 600 was sold in uncut sheets of 6 panes.

See Nos. 617, 641, 666, 708, 728.

Yitzhak Rabin (1922-95), Israeli Prime Minister — A105

1995, Nov. 10 Litho. *Perf. 14*

601 A105 32c multicolored .55 .55

No. 601 was issued in sheets of 8.

Souvenir Sheet

New Year 1996 (Year of the Rat) — A106

1996, Jan. 5 Litho. *Perf. 13½*

602 A106 50c multicolored .85 .85

Native Birds A107

Designs: a, Blue-gray noddy. b, Gray-backed tern. c, Masked booby. d, Black-footed albatross.

1996, Feb. 26 Litho. *Perf. 13½*

603 Block of 4 2.50 2.50
a.-d. A107 32c Any single .60 .60

Wild Cats — A108

a, Cheetah. b, Tiger. c, Lion. d, Jaguar.

1996, Mar. 8 Litho. *Perf. 13½*

604 Block of 4 3.75 3.75
a.-d. A108 55c Any single .90 .90

Sailing Ship Type of 1993

Miniature Sheet

Designs: a, like #443. b, like #447. c, like #448. d, like #455. e, like #444. f, like #446. g, like #456. h, like #459. i, like #441. j, like #449. k, like #451. l, like #465. m, Malmel outrigger sailing canoe. n, like #445. o, like #452. p, like #453. q, like #457. r, like #450. s, like #458. t, like #460. u, like #466. v, like #442. w, like #454. x, like #459A. y, like #462.

1996, Apr. 18 Litho. *Perf. 11x10½*

605 A80 32c Sheet of 25, #a.-y. 16.00 16.00

Olympic Games, Cent. — A109

First Olympic stamps, Greece: a, #119. b, #124. c, #123. d, #125.

1996, Apr. 27 Litho. *Perf. 12*

606 Block of 4 4.00 4.00
a.-d. A109 60c Any single .95 .95

Issued in sheets of 4. A small number were were overprinted in gold in the margin for Olymphilex '96.

Miniature Sheet

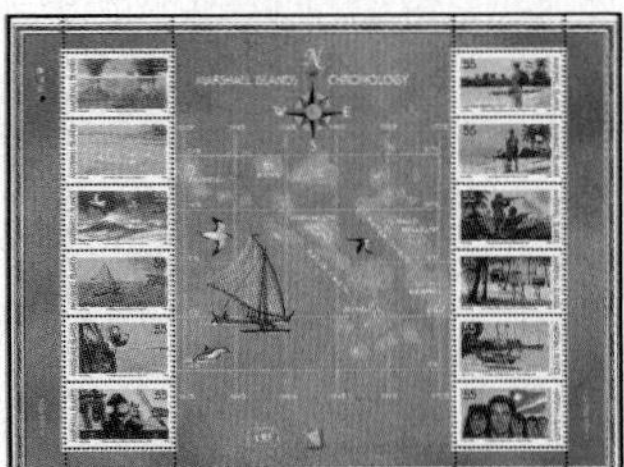

History of the Marshall Islands — A110

a, Undersea eruptions form island bases. b, Coral reefs grow. c, Storms bring birds & seeds. d, Early human inhabitants arrive. e, Seen by Spanish explorers, 1527. f, Capt. John Marshall, RN, charts islands, 1788. g, Islands become German protectorate, 1885. h, Japan seizes islands, 1914. i, US troops liberate islands, 1944. j, Bikiniatoll evacuated for nuclear testing, 1946. k, Islands become UN Trust Territory, 1947. l, Independence, 1986.

1996, May 2 Litho. *Perf. 13x12*

607 A110 55c Sheet of 12, #a.-l. 10.50 10.50

Elvis Presley's First #1 Hit, "Heartbreak Hotel," 40th Anniv. — A111

1996, May 5 ***Perf. 10½x11***
608 A111 32c multicolored .65 .65

Issued in sheets of 20.

Souvenir Sheet

China '96, 9th Asian Intl. Philatelic Exhibition — A112

Design: The Palance Museum, Shenyang.

1996, May 17 ***Perf. 13½***
609 A112 50c multicolored 1.00 1.00

James Dean (1931-55), Actor — A113

1996, June 1 Litho. ***Perf. 10½x11***
610 A113 32c multicolored .65 .65

No. 610 was issued in sheets of 20.

First Ford Automobile, Cent. — A114

Designs: a, 1896 Quadricycle. b, 1903 Model A Roadster. c, 1909 Model T Touring Car. d, 1929 Model A Station Wagon. e, 1955 Thunderbird. f, 1964½ Mustang convertible. g, 1995 Explorer. h, 1996 Taurus.

1996, June 4 Litho. ***Perf. 13½***
611 Sheet of 8 6.00 6.00
a.-h. A114 60c Any single .75 .75

Island Legends Type of 1995

Designs: a, Kijeek An Letao. b, Mennin Jobwodda. c, Wa Kone, Waan Letao. d, Kouj.

1996, July 19
612 Block of 4 + 4 labels 2.25 2.25
a.-d. A100 32c Any single .55 .55

Steam Locomotives — A115

Designs: a, Pennsylvania K4, U.S. b, "Big Boy," US. c, Mallard, Great Britain. d, RENFE Class 242, Spain. e, DB Class 01, Germany. f, FS Group 691, Italy. g, "Royal Hudson," Canada. h, Evening Star, Great Britain. i, SAR 520 Class, Australia. j, SNCF 232.U1, France. k, QJ "Advance Forward," China. l, C62 "Swallow," Japan.

1996, Aug. 23 Litho. ***Perf. 13½***
613 Sheet of 12 11.00 11.00
a.-l. A115 55c Any single .90 .90

Marine Life Type of 1995

Designs: a, like #590a. b, like #590b. c, like #590c. d, like #590d.

1996, Oct. 21 Litho. ***Perf. 13½***
614 Block of 4 1.75 1.75
a.-d. A94 32c Any single .40 .40

Taipei '96, 10th Asian Intl. Philatelic Exhibition. Nos. 614a-614b have Chinese inscription, Nos. 614c-614d English.

Stick Chart, Canoe and Flag of the Republic Type of 1990

1996, Oct. 21 ***Perf. 11x10½***
615 A63 $3 like No. 381 6.00 6.00

No. 615 inscribed "Free Association United States of America."

Angels from "Madonna and Child with Four Saints," by Rosso Fiorentino A116

1996, Oct. 31 Litho. ***Perf. 13½***
616 A116 32c multicolored .55 .55

Christmas.

Legendary Planes Type of 1995

Biplanes: a, JN-3 Jenny. b, SPAD XIII. c, Albatros D.III. d, DH-4 LIberty. e, Fokker Dr.1. f, F-1 Camel. g, Martin MB-2. h, MB-3A Tommy. i, Curtiss TS-1. j, P-1 Hawk. k, Boeing PW-9. l, Douglas 0-2H. m, LB-5 Pirate. n, 02U-1 Corsair. o, F8C Heldiver. p, Boeing F4B-4. q, J6B Gerfalcon. r, Martin BM. s, FF-1 Fifi. t, C.R. 32 Cricket. u, Polikarpov I-15 Gull. v, Mk.1 Swordfish. w, Aichi D1A2. x, Grumman F3F. y, SOC-3 Seagull.

1996, Nov. 1
617 A104 32c Sheet of 25, #a.-y. 16.00 16.00

Native Crafts A117

Designs: a, Fan making. b, Canoe models. c, Carving. d, Basketmaking.

1996, Nov. 7 Litho. ***Perf. 11x10½***
618 Block of 4 1.60 1.60
a.-d. A117 32c Any single .40 .40

See Nos. 629-630.

Souvenir Sheet

New Year 1997 (Year of the Ox) — A118

1997, Jan. 7 Litho. ***Perf. 13x13½***
619 A118 60c multicolored 1.25 1.25

Amata Kabua (1928-96), President of Marshall Islands — A119

1997, Jan. 27 Litho. ***Perf. 13½***
620 A119 32c multicolored .65 .65
621 A119 60c multicolored 1.25 1.25

No. 621 has vertical inscriptions in English.

Elvis Presley (1935-77) A120

Designs: a, "Rocking 50's." b, "Soaring 60's." c, "Sensational 70's."

1997, Jan. 8 Litho. ***Perf. 13½***
622 A120 32c Strip of 3, #a.-c. 2.00 2.00

Hong Kong '97 — A121

Hong Kong at sunrise, ships: No. 623: a, Walap. b, Junk.
Hong Kong at night, ships: No. 624: a, Canoe. b, Junk, diff.

1997, Feb. 12 ***Perf. 12***
623 Sheet of 2 + 3 labels 1.25 1.25
a.-b. A121 32c Any single .60 .60
624 Sheet of 2 + 3 labels 1.25 1.25
a.-b. A121 32c Any single .60 .60

Christianity in Marshall Islands, 140th Anniv. — A122

Apostles: No. 625: a, Andrew. b, Matthew. c, Philip. d, Simon. e, Thaddeus. f, Thomas. g, Bartholomew. h, John. i, James, the Lesser. j, James, the Greater. k, Paul. l, Peter.
$3, The Last Supper, by Peter Paul Rubens.

1997, Mar. 28 ***Perf. 13½***
625 Sheet of 12 14.50 14.50
a.-l. A122 60c Any single 1.20 1.20

Souvenir Sheet

Perf. 13x13½

626 A122 $3 multicolored 6.00 6.00

No. 626 contains one 80x50mm stamp.

First Decade of 20th Century — A123

Designs: a, Family of immigrants. b, Dowager Empress, Boxers, China. c, Photography for every man. d, Dr. Walter Reed, mosquito. e, Sigmund Freud. f, Marconi, wireless transmitter. g, Enrico Caruso, phonograph. h, Wright Brothers, Flyer. i, Einstein. j, HMS Dreadnought. k, San Francisco earthquake, 1906. l, Gandhi, non-violent protestors. m, Picasso. n, Dawn of the automobile age. o, Man, camels, oil derrick amid sand dunes.

1997, Apr. 15 Litho. ***Perf. 13½***
627 Sheet of 15 18.00 18.00
a.-o. A123 60c Any single 1.10 1.10

See Nos. 646, 654, 657, 679, 702, 711, 723, 726 and 730.

Deng Xiaoping (1904-97), Chinese Leader — A124

1997, Apr. 21
628 A124 60c multicolored 1.25 1.25

Crafts Type of 1996

Designs: Nos. 629a, 630a, Fan making. Nos. 629b, 630b, Canoe models. Nos. 629c, 630c, Wood carving. Nos. 629d, 630d, Basket making.

1997, May 29 Litho. ***Perf. 11x10½***

Self-Adhesive

629 Block of 4 2.50 2.50
a.-d. A117 32c Any single .60 .60

Serpentine Die Cut Perf. 11

Self-Adhesive

630 Strip of 4 2.50 2.50
a.-d. A117 32c Any single .60 .60

No. 629 was issued in sheets of 20 stamps. No. 630 was issued in sheets of 16 stamps. Die cutting does not extend through backing paper on No. 630.

Marshall Islands Stamps, Cent., US Stamps, 150th Anniv. A126

1997, May 29 Litho. ***Perf. 13½***

Booklet Stamps

631 A126 50c No. 1 1.00 1.00
632 A126 50c No. 2 1.00 1.00
633 A126 50c No. 3 1.00 1.00
634 A126 50c No. 4 1.00 1.00
635 A126 50c No. 5 1.00 1.00
636 A126 50c No. 6 1.00 1.00
a. Booklet pane, #631-636 6.00

Size: 75x32mm

637 A126 $1 US Nos. 1 & 2 2.00 2.00
a. Booklet pane of 1 2.00
Complete booklet, #636a, #637a 8.00

PACIFIC 97.

Bristle-thighed Curlew — A127

World Wildlife Fund: a, Walking right. b, On tree branch. c, Standing with mouth open. d, In flight.

1997, June 6
638 Block or strip of 4 4.00 4.00
a.-d. A127 16c Any single 1.00 1.00

Souvenir Sheet

Bank of China, Hong Kong — A128

1997, July 1 Litho. *Perf. 13½*
639 A128 50c multicolored 1.00 1.00

Canoes A129

Designs: a, Pacific Arts Festival canoe, Walap of Enewetak. b, Large Voyaging canoe, Walap of Jaluit. c. Racing canoe. d, Sailing canoe, Tipnol of Ailuk.

1997, July 10 Litho. *Perf. 13½*
640 Block or strip of 4 2.50 2.50
a.-d. A129 32c Any single .60 .60

See No. 1111.

Legendary Aircraft Type of 1995

Designs: a, C-54 Skymaster. b, B-36 Peacemaker. c, F-86 Sabre. d, B-47 Stratojet. e, C-124 Globemaster II. f, C-121 Constellation. g, B-52 Stratofortress. h, F-100 Super Sabre. i, F-104 Starfighter. j, C-130 Hercules. k, F-105 Thunderchief. l, KC-135 Stratotanker. m, B-58 Hustler. n, F-4 Phanton II. o, T-38 Talon. p, C-141 Star Lifter. q, F-111 Aardvark. r, SR-71 "Blackbird." s, C-5 Galaxy. t, A-10 Thunderbolt II. u, F-15 Eagle. v, F-16 Fighting Falcon. w, F-117 Nighthawk. x, B-2 Spirit. y, C-17 Globemaster III.

1997, July 19
641 A104 32c Sheet of 25, #a.-y. 16.00 16.00

USS Constitution, Bicent. — A130

1997, July 21
642 A130 32c multicolored .65 .65

Island Legends Type of 1995

Designs: a, The Large Pool of Mejit. b, The Beautiful Woman of Kwajalein. c, Sharks and Lowakalle Reef. d, The Demon of Adrie.

1997, Aug. 15 Litho. *Perf. 13½*
643 Block of 4 +4 labels 2.50 2.50
a.-d. A100 32c Any single .60 .60

Marine Life Type of 1995

Designs: a, Watanabe's angelfish, gray reef shark. b, Raccoon butterflyfish. c, Flame angelfish. d, Square-spot fairy basslets.

1997, Aug. 21
644 Block of 4 4.75 4.75
a.-d. A94 60c Any single 1.10 1.10

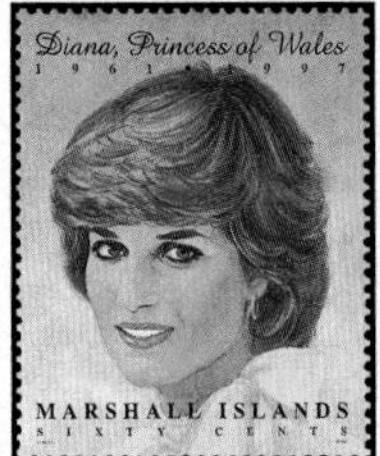

Diana, Princess of Wales (1961-97) A131

Various portraits, background color: a, violet. b, blue. c, yellow orange.

1997, Sept. 30 Litho. *Perf. 13½*
645 Strip of 3 3.75 3.75
a.-c. A131 60c Any single 1.25 1.25

No. 645 printed in sheets with two vertical strips flanking three horizontal strips.

Events of the 20th Century Type

1910-19: a, Women mobilize for equal rights. b, Ernest Rutherford, model of atom. c, Sun Yat-sen. d, Sinking of the Titanic. e, Igor Stravinsky, The Rite of Spring. f, Ford begins assembly line production of autos. g, Archduke Franz Ferdinand, wife Sophie. h, German U-boat sinks Lusitania. i, Soldiers in trenches at Battle of Verdun. j, Patrick Pearse proclaims Irish Republic. k, Jews praying at Wailing Wall. l, Cruiser Aurora. m, Baron Manfred von Richtofen. n, German revolutionary troops, 1918. o, Negotiators write Treaty of Versailles.

1997, Oct. 15 Litho. *Perf. 13½*
646 Sheet of 15 18.00 18.00
a.-o. A123 60c Any single 1.20 1.20

Christmas A132

Cherubs from Sistine Madonna, by Raphael: No. 647, With hand under chin. No. 648, With arms folded under chin.

1997, Oct. 25
647 A132 32c multicolored .60 .60
648 A132 32c multicolored .60 .60
a. Pair, #647-648 1.25 1.25

US State-Named Warships — A133

Designs: a.-z., aa.-ax.: USS Alabama-USS Wyoming in alphabetical order. USS Honolulu shown for Hawaii.

1997, Nov. 1
649 Sheet of 50 20.00 20.00
a.-ax. A133 20c Any single .40 .40

Souvenir Sheet

Shanghai 97, Intl. Stamp and Coin Expo — A134

Treasure ship, Ming Dynasty.

1997, Nov. 19 Litho. *Perf. 13x13½*
650 A134 50c multicolored 1.00 1.00

Souvenir Sheet

New Year 1998 (Year of the Tiger) — A135

1998, Jan. 2 Litho. *Perf. 13x13½*
651 A135 60c multicolored 1.25 1.25

Elvis Presley's 1968 Television Special A136

Scenes from special: a, shown. b, Red background. c, Elvis in white suit.

1998, Jan. 8 *Perf. 13½*
652 Strip of 3 1.75 1.75
a.-c. A136 32c Any single .55 .55

Sea Shells A137

a, Chicoreus brunneus. b, Cypraea aurantium. c, Lambis chiragra. d, Tridanca squamosa.

1998, Feb. 13 Litho. *Perf. 13½*
653 Strip of 4 2.50 2.50
a.-d. A137 32c Any single .60 .60

Latin name on No. 653d is spelled incorrectly. See No. 1110.

Events of the 20th Century Type

1920-29: a, Radio broadcasting reaches the world. b, Quest for peace lurches forward. c, Architects reshape the world. d, Funerary mask of King Tutankhamen. e, USSR emerges as a Communist State. f, Nations emerge from Ottoman Empire, Kemal Ataturk. g, Arrival of the Jazz Age. h, Age of the rocket launched, Robert Goddard. i, Talkies arrive at the movie theater. j, Scourge of Fascism arrives. k, Man's universe expands. l, Penicillin launches antibiotic revolution. m, First glimmers of television. n, Aviation shrinks the world, Graf Zeppelin. o, World suffers economic depression.

1998, Mar. 16 Litho. *Perf. 13½*
654 Sheet of 15 18.00 18.00
a.-o. A123 60c Any single 1.20 1.20

Canoes of the Pacific — A138

a, Pahi Sailing canoe, Tuamotu Archipelago. b, Maori war canoe, New Zealand. c, Wa'a Kaukahi fishing canoe, Hawaii. d, Amatasi sailing canoe, Samoa. e, Ndrua sailing canoe, Fiji. f, Tongiaki voyaging canoe, Tonga. g, Tipairua traveling canoe, Tahiti. h, Walap sailing canoe, Marshall Islands.

1998, May 21 Litho. *Perf. 13½*
655 A138 32c Sheet of 8, #a.-h. 5.00 5.00

See Nos. 690-698.

Berlin Airlift, 50th Anniv. — A139

Designs: a, Douglas C-54/R4D-5. b, Avro York. c, Watching the flights of freedom. d, Berliners welcoming supplies.

1998, June 26 Litho. *Perf. 13½*
656 A139 60c Block of 4, #a.-d. 4.75 4.75

Events of the 20th Century Type

1930-39: a, Economic depression engulfs the world. b, Scientists split the atom. c, Stalin's terror reigns in Soviet Union. d, Fascism becomes rampant. e, Engineers harness nature (Dneproges Dam). f, Streamlined design symbolizes bright future. g, Passengers travel airways in comfort. h, Artists protest the scourges of war. i, Media create indelible memories. j, Japanese agression arouses world opinion. k, Era of appeasement. l, Inventions pave way to future. m, Persecution of Jews portends holocaust. n, World War II begins in Europe. o, Movies cheer audiences.

1998, July 15
657 Sheet of 15 17.50 17.50
a.-o. A123 60c Any single 1.10 1.10

Czar Nicholas II — A140

No. 658, Coronation Czar Nicholas II, 1896. No. 659, Russo-Japanese War and the Cruiser Varyag, 1904-05. No. 660, Czar's Manifesto, 1905. No. 661, Peasant sower, Rasputin, 1905. No. 662, Czar with soldiers at the front, 1915. No. 663, Ipateva House, Ekaterinburg, 1917. $3, Family portrait.

1998, July 17 *Perf. 13½*

Booklet Stamps

658 A140 60c multicolored 1.25 1.25
659 A140 60c multicolored 1.25 1.25
660 A140 60c multicolored 1.25 1.25
661 A140 60c multicolored 1.25 1.25
662 A140 60c multicolored 1.25 1.25
663 A140 60c multicolored 1.25 1.25

Size: 60x54mm

Perf. 13½ at Top

664 A140 $3 multicolored 6.00 6.00
a. Booklet pane, #658-664 13.50
Complete booklet, #664a 13.50

George Herman "Babe" Ruth (1895-1948) A141

1998, Aug. 16 Litho. *Perf. 13½*
665 A141 32c multicolored .65 .65

Legendary Aircraft Type of 1995

US Navy aircraft: a, NC-4. b, PBY-5 Catalina. c, TBD Devastator. d, SB2U Vindicator. e, F4F Wildcat. f, OS2U Kingfisher. g, SBD Dauntless. h, F4U Corsair. i, SB2C Helldiver. j, PV-Ventura. k, TBM Avenger. l, F6F Hellcat. m, PB4Y-2 Privateer. n, A-1J Skyraider. o, F2H Banshee. p, F9F-2B Panther. q, P5M Marlin. r, F-8 Crusader. s, F-4 Phantom II. t, A-6 Intruder. u, P-3 Orion. v, A-7 Corsair II. w, A-4 Skyhawk. x, S-3 Viking. y, F/A-18 Hornet.

1998, Aug. 28
666 A104 32c Sheet of 25, #a.-y. 16.00 16.00

Chevrolet Automobiles — A142

Designs: a, 1912 Classic Six. b, 1931 Sports Roadster. c, 1941 Special Deluxe. d, 1955 Cameo Carrier Fleetside. e, 1957 Corvette. f, 1957 Bel Air. g, 1967 Camaro. h, 1970 Chevelle SS 454.

1998, Sept. 1
667 Sheet of 8 9.50 9.50
a.-h. A142 60c Any single 1.15 1.15

Marshallese Language and Alphabet — A143

Letter, example of Marshallese word beginning with letter: a, "A," Amata Kabua, first president. b, "A," Aj, to weave. c, "B," butterfly. d, "D," beautiful lady. e, "E," fish. f, "I," Rainbow. g, "J," mat. h, "K," house of government. i, "L," stars. j, "L," Tropicbird. k, "M," breadfruit. l, "M," Arrowroot plant. m, "N," Coconut tree. n, "N," Ocean wave. o, "N," shark tooth. p, "O," Fish net. q, "O," Tattoo. r, "O," Lionfish. s, "P," Visitor's hut. t, "R," Whale. u, "T," outrigger canoe. v, "U," Fire. w, "U," Dorsal fin of whale. x, "W," Woven sail.

1998, Sept. 14
668 Sheet of 24 16.00 16.00
a.-x. A143 33c Any single .65 .65

New Buildings in Marshall Islands — A144

a, Trust Company of the Marshall Islands, 1998. b, Embassy of the People's Republic of China, 1996. c, Outrigger Marshall Islands Resort, 1996.

1998, Oct. 12
669 Strip of 3 2.00 2.00
a.-c. A144 33c Any single .65 .65

Christmas A145

1998, Oct. 26
670 A145 32c Midnight angel .65 .65

John Glenn's Return to Space A146

No. 671, Friendship 7 launch, 1962. No. 672, Glenn in spacesuit, 1962. No. 673, Mercury capsule in space, 1962. No. 674, Shuttle Discovery Launch, 1998. No. 675, Astronaut and US Senator Glenn, 1998. No. 676, Shuttle Discovery in space, 1998.
$3, US #1193, astrological drawings.

1998, Oct. 29 **Booklet Stamps**
671 A146 60c multicolored 1.25 1.25
672 A146 60c multicolored 1.25 1.25
673 A146 60c multicolored 1.25 1.25
674 A146 60c multicolored 1.25 1.25
675 A146 60c multicolored 1.25 1.25
676 A146 60c multicolored 1.25 1.25

Size: 75x32mm

677 A146 $3 multicolored 6.00 6.00
a. Booklet pane, #671-677 13.50
Complete booklet, #677a 13.50

Souvenir Sheet

Antonov An-124 Delivering Drought Relief Supplies — A147

1998, Nov. 3 **Litho.** ***Perf. 13½***
678 A147 $3.20 multicolored 6.50 6.50

Events of the 20th Century Type

1940-49: a, Aviation assumes strategic importance. b, State of war becomes global. c, Missiles announce new age of warfare. d, Music raises spirits. e, Determined peoples fight for survival. f, The Holocaust. g, Mankind faces Atomic Age. h, War's end brings hope. i, Computer age dawns. j, Nations unite for peace. k, World demands justice from war criminals. l, A time for rebuilding. m, Transistor opens door to miniaturization. n, World divided by cold war. o, New China is proclaimed.

1998, Nov. 16 **Litho.** ***Perf. 13½***
679 Sheet of 15 17.50 17.50
a.-o. A123 60c Any single 1.15 1.15

Warships — A148

Designs: a, Trireme Galley. b, Trireme Romano. c, Viking Longship. d, Ming Treasure ship. e, The Mary Rose. f, Nuestra Señora del Rosario. g, Korean Turtle ship. h, Brederode. i, Galera Veneziana. j, Santisima Trinidad. k, Ville de Paris. l, HMS Victory. m, Bonhomme Richard. n, USS Constellation. o, USS Hartford. p, Fijian Ndrua. q, HMS Dreadnought. r, HMAS Australia. s, HMS Dorsetshire. t, Graf Spee. u, Yamato. v, USS Tautog. w, Bismarck. x, USS Hornet. y, USS Missouri.

1998, Dec. 1
680 A148 33c Sheet of 25, #a.-y. 16.00 16.00

Souvenir Sheet

New Year 1999 (Year of the Rabbit) — A149

1999, Jan. 2 **Litho.** ***Perf. 13x13½***
681 A149 60c multicolored 1.25 1.25

Birds — A150

1c, Lesser golden plover. 3c, Siberian tattler. 20c, Brown noddy. 22c, Common fairy tern. 33c, Micronesian pigeon. 55c, Long-tailed cuckoo. $1, Christmas shearwater. $10, Eurasian tree sparrow.

1999, Jan. 9 ***Perf. 13½***
682 A150 1c multicolored .25 .25
683 A150 3c multicolored .25 .25
684 A150 20c multicolored .40 .40
685 A150 22c multicolored .45 .45
686 A150 33c multicolored .65 .65
687 A150 55c multicolored 1.10 1.10
688 A150 $1 multicolored 2.00 2.00
689 A150 $10 multicolored 15.00 15.00
Nos. 682-689 (8) 20.10 20.10

See Nos. 714-721.

Canoes of the Pacific Type

Designs: a, like #655a. b, like #655b. c, like #655c. d, like #655f. e, like #655e. f, like #655d. g, like #655g. h, like #655h.

1999, Jan. 25 **Litho.** ***Perf. 13½***
690 A138 33c Sheet of 8, #a.-h. 5.25 5.25

Self-Adhesive

Size: 40x25mm

Perf. 11x10½

691 A138 33c like #690a .65 .65
692 A138 33c like #690b .65 .65
693 A138 33c like #690c .65 .65
694 A138 33c like #690d .65 .65
695 A138 33c like #690e .65 .65
696 A138 33c like #690f .65 .65
697 A138 33c like #690g .65 .65
698 A138 33c like #690h .65 .65
a. Block of 10, #691-697, 3 #698 6.50

Issued in sheets of 20.

Great American Indian Chiefs — A151

Designs: a, Tecumseh. b, Powhatan. c, Hiawatha. d, Dull knife. e, Sequoyah. f, Sitting Bull. g, Cochise. h, Red Cloud. i, Geronimo. j, Chief Joseph. k, Pontiac. l, Crazy Horse.

1999, Feb. 1 ***Perf. 13½***
699 Sheet of 12 14.50 14.50
a.-l. A151 60c Any single 1.15 1.15

National Flag A152

1999, Feb. 5 ***Perf. 14***
700 A152 33c multicolored .65 .65

Flowers of the Pacific A153

Designs: a, Plumeria. b, Vanda. c, Ilima. d, Tiare. e, White ginger. f, Hibiscus.

1999, Feb. 18 ***Perf. 13½***
701 Block of 6 4.00 4.00
a.-f. A153 33c Any single .65 .65

Events of the 20th Century Type

1950-59: a, World enters age of television. b, Cold war battles erupt. c, Vaccines conquer scourge of polio. d, U.S., USSR engage in arms race. e, Science begins to unravel genetic code. f, Conquests reach unconquered heights. g, Pageantry reassures commonwealth. h, Rock 'n' roll reshapes music beat. i, Suns sets on Colonial Empires. j, World condemns racial discrimination. k, Unrest challenges Communism's march. l, Vision of European Union takes form. m, Space race opens space age. n, Jets shrink time and distance. o, Microchip presages computer revolution.

1999, Mar. 15
702 Sheet of 15 18.00 18.00
a.-o. A123 60c Any single 1.20 1.20

Souvenir Sheet

HMAS Australia — A154

1999, Mar. 19
703 A154 $1.20 multicolored 2.50 2.50

Australia '99, World Stamp Expo.

Elvis Presley — A155

1999, Apr. 6 **Litho.** ***Perf. 13½***
704 A155 33c multicolored .65 .65

IBRA '99 World Stamp Exhibition, Nuremberg, Germany A156

Designs: a, #25. b. #24. c. #23. d, #22.

1999, Apr. 27 **Litho.** ***Perf. 13½***
705 Sheet of 4 4.75 4.75
a.-d. A156 60c Any single 1.15 1.15

Marshall Islands Constitution, 20th Anniv. — A157

Design: 33c, Constitution Committee.

1999, May 1 Litho. *Perf. 13½*
706 A157 33c multicolored .65 .65

Marshall Islands Postal Service, 15th Anniv. — A158

Portions of No. 607 and, clockwise: a, #572, 644, 689, 597d (b). b, #668c, 595c, 655h, 597a. c, #381, 570, 574, 668d. d, #597b, 643b, 621.

1999, May 2
707 A158 33c Block of 4, #a.-d. 2.50 2.50

Legendary Aircraft Type of 1995

a, Martin B-10B. b, Northrop A-17A Nomad. c, Douglas B-18 Bolo. d, Boeing B-17F Flying Fortress. e, Douglas A-20 Havoc. f, North American B-25B Mitchell. g, Consolidated B-24D Liberator. h, North American P-51B Mustang. i, Martin B-26 Marauder. j, Douglas A-26B Invader. k, Bell P-59 Airacomet. l, Boeing KC-97 Stratofreighter. m, Douglas A-1J Skyraider. n, Lockheed P2V-7 Neptune. o, North American B-45 Tornado. p, Boeing B-50 Superfortress. q, North American AJ-2 Savage. r, Grumman F9F Cougar. s, Douglas A-3 Skywarrior. t, Martin B-57E Canberra. u, Douglas EB-66 Destroyer. v, Grumman E-2A Hawkeye. w, Northrop F-5E Tiger II. x, McDonnell Douglas AV-8B Harrier II. y, Rockwell B-1B Lancer.

1999, June 1
708 A104 33c Sheet of 25, #a.-y. 16.00 16.00

Souvenir Sheet

PhilexFrance 99 — A159

Design: $1, Astronaut, lunar rover.

1999, July 2 Litho. *Perf. 13½*
709 A159 $1 multicolored 2.00 2.00

Souvenir Sheet

Tanker Alrehab — A160

1999, July 15 Litho. *Perf. 13x13½*
710 A160 60c multi 1.25 1.25

Events of the 20th Century Type

1960-69: a, Invention of the laser. b, Pill revolutionizes family planning. c, Gagarin becomes the Columbus of the cosmos. d, Communism advertizes failures. e, Planet Earth endangered. f, Superpowers totter on precipice of war. g, Spirit of ecumenism renews Christianity. h, Railways achieve record speeds. i, Cultural Revolution stuns China. j, Arab-Israeli War unsettles Middle East. k, Organ transplants repair human body. l, America engulfed in Vietnam War. m, Political assassinations shock world. n, Supersonic travel becomes a reality. o, Mankind leaps from Earth to Moon.

1999, July 15 *Perf. 13½*
711 Sheet of 15 18.00 18.00
a.-o. A123 60c Any single 1.20 1.20

First Manned Moon Landing, 30th Anniv. — A161

Designs: a, Saluting astronaut, Earth. b, Flag. c, Astronaut.

1999, July 20
712 A161 33c Sheet of 3, #a.-c. 2.00 2.00

Ships — A162

Designs: a, Galleon Los Reyes, Spain, 1568. b, Frigate Dolphin, Great Britain, 1767. c, Bark Scarborough, Great Britain, 1788. d, Brig Rurick, Russia, 1817.

1999, Aug. 26
713 A162 33c Block of 4, #a.-d. 2.75 2.75

See No. 1112.

Bird Type of 1999

Designs: 5c, Black-tailed godwit. 40c, Franklin's gull. 45c, Rufous-necked stint. 75c, Kermadec petrel. $1.20, Purple-capped fruit dove. $2, Mongolian plover. $3.20, Cattle egret. $5, Dunlin.

1999, Sept. 16 Litho. *Perf. 13½*

714	A150	5c multi	.25	.25
715	A150	40c multi	.80	.80
716	A150	45c multi	.90	.90
717	A150	75c multi	1.50	1.50
718	A150	$1.20 multi	2.40	2.40
719	A150	$2 multi	4.00	4.00
720	A150	$3.20 multi	6.50	6.50
721	A150	$5 multi	10.00	10.00
		Nos. 714-721 (8)	26.35	26.35

Christmas A163

1999, Oct. 26 Litho. *Perf. 13½*
722 A163 33c multi .65 .65

Events of the 20th Century Type

1970-79: a, Jumbo jets enter transatlantic service. b, China advances on world stage. c, Terrorists range the world. d, Space stations orbit earth. e, Oil crisis strangles world. f, China unearths underground army. g, Reign of death devastates Cambodia. h, Superpowers proclaim era of détente. i, America celebrates bicentennial. j, Personal computers reach markets. k, Diagnostic tools revolutionize medicine. l, Automobiles transport millions. m, Prospect of peace in Middle East. n, Compact disc revolutionizes recording. o, Islam's prophets resurgent.

1999, Nov. 15
723 Sheet of 15 18.00 18.00
a.-o. A123 60c Any single 1.20 1.20

Millennium — A164

Earth and inscriptions: No. 724, "December 31, 1999." No. 725, "January 1, 2000."

1999, Dec. 31 Litho. *Perf. 13½*
724 33c multi .65 .65
725 33c multi .65 .65
a. A164 Pair, #724-725 1.30 1.30

Events of the 20th Century Type

1980-89: a, People unite in freedom's quest. b, Mankind confronts new diseases. c, Royal romance captivates the world. d, Information age begins. e, Armed conflicts upset peace. f, Cell phone revolutionizes communication. g, Every man a movie maker. h, Space exploration makes headlines. i, Disaster alerts public to nuclear risks. j, Perestroika signals change. k, Technology of war advances. l, Terrorism claims innocent victims. m, World's oceans endangered. n, Eys of the world on Tiananmen. o, Events signal "end of history."

2000, Jan. 15
726 Sheet of 15 18.00 18.00
a.-o. A123 60c Any single 1.20 1.20

Souvenir Sheet

New Year 2000 (Year of the Dragon) — A165

2000, Jan. 20 *Perf. 13x13½*
727 A165 60c multi 1.25 1.25

Legendary Aircraft Type of 1995

Designs: a, P-26 Peashooter. b, N2S-1 Kaydet. c, P-35A. d, P-36A Hawk. e, P-40B Warhawk. f, P-38 Lightning. g, P-39D Airacobra. h, C-46 Commando. i, P-47D Thunderbolt. j, P-61B Black Widow. k, B-29 Superfortress. l, F7F-3N Tigercat. m, F8F-2 Bearcat. n, F-82, Twin Mustang. o, F-84G Thunderjet. p, FJ-1 Fury. q, C-119C Flying Boxcar. r, F3D-2 Skynight. s, F-89D Scorpion. t, F-94B Starfire. u, F4D Skyray. v, F3H-2 Demon. w, RF-101A/C Voodoo. x, U-2F Dragon Lady. y, OV-10 Bronco.

2000, Feb. 10 *Perf. 13½*
728 A104 33c Sheet of 25, #a.-y. 16.00 16.00

Roses — A166

Rose varieties: a, Masquerade. b, Tuscany Superb. c, Frau Dagmar Hastrup. d, Ivory Fashion. e, Charles De Mills. f, Peace.

2000, Feb. 23
729 Block of 6 4.00 4.00
a.-f. A166 33c Any single .65 .65

Events of the 20th Century Type

1990-99: a, Free markets and trade reshape world economy. b, Coalition expels Iraq from Kuwait. c, South Africans freed from apartheid. d, WWW revolutionizes information superhighway. e, Era of Soviet power ends. f, A lasting peace in Middle East is promised. g, Engineering triumphs alter landscape. h, Ethnic conflicts stun world. i, Athletes celebrate peaceful world competition. j, Scientists probe secrets of life. k, Hong Kong and Macao return to China. l, Space exploration captivates millions. m, World mourns global heroines. n, Architecture shows confidence in the future. o, World population soars to new record.

2000, Mar. 15 Litho. *Perf. 13½*
730 Sheet of 15 18.00 18.00
a.-o. A123 60c Any single 1.20 1.20

Pandas — A167

a, Adult seated. b, Adult, seated, facing away, & cub. c, Adult holding cub. d, Two adults. e, Adult climbing. f, Adult & cub seated.

2000, Mar. 31 *Perf. 11¾*
731 A167 33c Block of 6, #a-f 4.00 4.00

American Presidents — A168

No. 732: a, 1c, George Washington. b, 2c, John Adams. c, 3c, Thomas Jefferson. d, 4c, James Madison. e, 5c, James Monroe. f, 6c, John Quincy Adams.

No. 733: a, 7c, Andrew Jackson. b, 8c, Martin Van Buren. c, 9c, William Henry Harrison. d, 10c, John Tyler. e, 11c, James K. Polk. f, 12c, Zachary Taylor.

No. 734: a, 13c, Millard Fillmore. b, 14c, Franklin Pierce. c, 15c, James Buchanan. d, 16c, Abraham Lincoln. e, 17c, Andrew Johnson. f, 18c, Ulysses S. Grant.

No. 735: a, 19c, Rutherford B. Hayes. b, 20c, James A. Garfield. c, 21c, Chester A. Arthur. d, 22c, Grover Cleveland. e, 23c, Benjamin Harrison. f, 24c, White House.

No. 736: a, 25c, William McKinley. b, 26c, Theodore Roosevelt. c, 27c, William H. Taft. d, 28c, Woodrow Wilson. e, 29c, Warren G. Harding. f, 30c, Calvin Coolidge.

No. 737: a, 31c, Herbert C. Hoover. b, 32c, Franklin D. Roosevelt. c, 33c, Harry S Truman. d, 34c, Dwight D. Eisenhower. e, 35c, John F. Kennedy. f, 36c, Lyndon B. Johnson.

No. 738: a, 37c, Richard M. Nixon. b, 38c, Gerald R. Ford. c, 39c, James E. Carter. d, 40c, Ronald W. Reagan. e, 41c, George H. W. Bush. f, 42c, William J. Clinton.

2000, Apr. 18 ***Perf. 13½***

732 A168 Sheet of 6, #a-f .45 .45
733 A168 Sheet of 6, #a-f 1.25 1.25
734 A168 Sheet of 6, #a-f 1.90 1.90
735 A168 Sheet of 6, #a-f 2.60 2.60
736 A168 Sheet of 6, #a-f 3.25 3.25
737 A168 Sheet of 6, #a-f 4.00 4.00
738 A168 Sheet of 6, #a-f 4.75 4.75
Nos. 732-738 (7) 18.20 18.20

First Zeppelin Flight, Cent. — A169

Designs: a, Original Zeppelin, 1900. b, Graf Zeppelin I, 1928. c, Hindenburg, 1936. d, Graf Zeppelin II, 1937.

2000, May 11 ***Perf. 13½***

739 A169 33c Block of 4, #a-d 2.75 2.75

Sir Winston Churchill — A170

No. 740, War correspondent in South Africa, 1899-1900. No. 741, Engagement and marriage to Clementine Hozier, 1908. No. 742, Young statesman, 1900-14. No. 743, Writer and academic, 1898-1960. No. 744, First Lord of the Admiralty, 1939-40. No. 745, Prime Minister, 1940-45. $1, Appointed knight, Nobel Prize for Literature, 1946-65.

2000, June 16 **Litho.** ***Perf. 13½***

Booklet Stamps

740 A170 60c multi 1.25 1.25
741 A170 60c multi 1.25 1.25
742 A170 60c multi 1.25 1.25
743 A170 60c multi 1.25 1.25
744 A170 60c multi 1.25 1.25
745 A170 60c multi 1.25 1.25

Size: 87x67mm

Perf. 13½ at Top

746 A170 $1 multi 2.00 2.00
a. Booklet pane, #740-746 9.50
Booklet, #746a 9.50

US Military, 225th Anniv. A171

No. 747: a, Army. b, Navy, c, Marines.

2000, June 22 ***Perf. 13½***

747 Horiz. strip of 3 2.00 2.00
a.-c. A171 33c Any single .65 .65

National Government — A172

No. 748: a, National seal. b, Nitijela, horiz. c, National flag. d, Capitol buildijng, horiz.

2000, July 4 **Litho.** ***Perf. 13½***

748 A172 33c Block of 4, #a-d 2.75 2.75

Ships — A173

No. 749: a, Half Moon. b, La Grande Hermine. c, Golden Hind. d, Mathew. e, Victoria. f, Sao Gabriel.

2000, July 20

749 A173 60c Block of 6, #a-f 7.25 7.25

Queen Mother, 100th Birthday — A174

No. 750: a, As child. b, As young wife. c, As Queen. d, As Queen Mother.

2000, Aug. 4

750 A174 60c Block of 4, #a-d 5.00 5.00

Compare with No. 810.

Reef Life A175

No. 751: a, Green sea turtle. b, Blue-girdled angelfish. c, Clown triggerfish. d, Harlequin tuskfish. e, Lined butterflyfish. f, White-bonnet anemonefish. g, Longnose filefish. h, Emperor angelfish.

2000, Aug. 24

751 Sheet of 8 5.50 5.50
a.-h. A175 33c Any single .65 .65

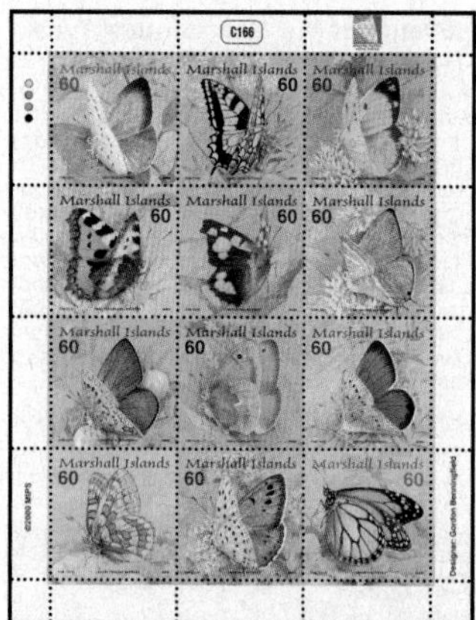

Butterflies — A176

No. 752: a, Holly blue. b, Swallowtail. c, Clouded yellow. d, Small tortoiseshell. e, Nettle tree. f, Long-tailed blue. g, Cranberry blue. h, Small heath. i, Pontic blue. j, Lapland fritillary k, Large blue. l, Monarch.

2000, Sept. 14 ***Perf. 11¾***

752 A176 60c Sheet of 12, #a-l 14.50 14.50

See also Nos. 776, 798, 821, 876.

Reunification of Germany, 10th Anniv. — A177

2000, Oct. 3 ***Perf. 13½***

753 A177 33c multi .65 .65

Submarines — A178

No. 754: a, USS S-44, 1925. b, USS Gato, 1941. c, USS Wyoming, 1996. d, USS Cheyenne, 1997.

2000, Oct. 12

754 A178 33c Block of 4, #a.-d. 2.75 2.75

Christmas — A179

2000, Oct. 26 ***Perf. 10¼x11¼***

755 A179 33c multi .65 .65

Sun Yat-sen — A180

No. 756: a, As youth in Cuiheng village, 1866. b, As student in Honolulu and Hong Kong, 1879. c, As President of Tong Meng Hui, 1905. d, Revolution, 1911. e, President of the Republic of China, 1912. f, Principles of Democracy. g, Sun Yat-sen Memorial, Nanjing and Great Wall of China (87x62mm).

2000, Nov. 12 **Litho.** ***Perf. 13½***

756 Booklet pane of 7 9.50
a.-f. A180 60c Any single 1.25 1.25
g. A180 $1 multi, perf. 13½ at top 2.00 2.00
Booklet, #756 9.50

Souvenir Sheet

New Year 2001 (Year of the Snake) — A181

2001, Jan. 2 **Litho.** ***Perf. 13x13¾***

757 A181 80c multi 1.60 1.60

Flowers of the Month — A182

2001 **Stamp + label** ***Perf. 11¾***

758 A182 34c Carnations .70 .70
759 A182 34c Violets .70 .70
760 A182 34c Jonquil .70 .70
761 A182 34c Sweet pea .70 .70
762 A182 34c Lily of the valley .70 .70
763 A182 34c Rose .70 .70
764 A182 34c Larkspur .70 .70
765 A182 34c Poppy .70 .70
766 A182 34c Aster .70 .70
767 A182 34c Marigold .70 .70
768 A182 34c Chrysanthemum .70 .70
769 A182 34c Poinsettia .70 .70
Nos. 758-769 (12) 8.40 8.40

Issued: No. 758, 1/5; No. 759, 2/1; No. 760, 3/1; No. 761, 4/3; No. 762, 5/1; No. 763, 6/1; No. 764, 7/3; No. 765, 8/1; No. 766, 9/5; No. 767, 10/1; No. 768, 11/1; No. 769, 12/1.

Sailing Canoes A183

Walaps of: $5, Jaluit. $10, Eniwetok.

2001, Jan. 19 **Engr.** ***Perf. 12¼***

770 A183 $5 green 10.00 10.00
771 A183 $10 blue 20.00 20.00

Famous People — A184

Designs: 34c, Pres. Amata Kabua. 55c, Robert Reimers, entrepreneur. 80c, Leonard Hacker, S. J., humanitarian. $1, Dwight Heine, educator.

2001, Jan. 22 **Litho.** ***Perf. 10¼x11¼***

772 A184 34c multi .70 .70
773 A184 55c multi 1.10 1.10
774 A184 80c multi 1.60 1.60
775 A184 $1 multi 2.00 2.00
Nos. 772-775 (4) 5.40 5.40

See Nos. 784, 817-819.

Butterflies Type of 2000

No. 776: a, Red admiral. b, Moroccan orange tip. c, Silver-studded blue. d, Marbled white. e, False Apollo. f, Ringlet. g, Map. h, Fenton's wood white. i, Grecian copper. j, Pale

Arctic clouded yellow. k, Great banded grey-ling. l, Cardinal.

2001, Feb. 22 *Perf. 11¾*
776 A176 80c Sheet of 12, #a-l 20.00 20.00

Fairy Tales A185

No. 777: a, Tom Thumb. b, Three Little Pigs. c, Gulliver's Travels. d, Cinderella. e, Gallant John. f, Ugly Duckling. g, Fisher and the Goldfish.

2001, Mar. 22 **Litho.** *Perf. 13½*
777 Vert. strip of 7 5.00 5.00
a.-g. A185 34c Any single .70 .70

Watercraft Racing — A186

No. 778: a, Canoeing. b, Windsurfing. c, Cruising yachts. d, Sailing dinghy.

2001, Apr. 6
778 A186 34c Block of 4, #a-d 2.75 2.75

Manned Spaceflight, 40th Anniv. A187

No. 779: a, Yuri A. Gagarin. b, Alan B. Shepard, Jr. c, Virgil I. Grissom. d, Gherman S. Titov.

2001, Apr. 12
779 Block of 4 + 4 labels 6.50 6.50
a.-d. A187 80c Any single 1.60 1.60

Stamp Day — A188

2001, May 2
780 A188 34c multi .70 .70
a. Tete-beche pair 1.40 1.40

American Achievements in Space — A189

No. 781: a, First U.S. astronaut in space, 1962. b, First US space walk, 1965. c, First man on the Moon, 1969. d, First space shuttle, 1977.

2001, May 15
781 A189 80c Block of 4, #a-d 6.50 6.50

Marine Life — A190

No. 782: a, Longnose butterflyfish, star puffer, starfish. b, Nautilus. c, Raccoon butterflyfish. d, Porkfish, grouper.

2001, June 7
782 A190 34c Block of 4, #a-d 2.75 2.75

Sports — A191

No. 783: a, Basketball. b, Bowling. c, Table tennis. d, Kayaking.

2001, June 26 *Perf. 11¾*
783 A191 34c Block of 4, #a-d 2.75 2.75

Famous People Type of 2001

Design: 57c, Atlan Anien, legislator.

2001, July 9 *Perf. 10¼x11¼*
784 A184 57c multi 1.10 1.10

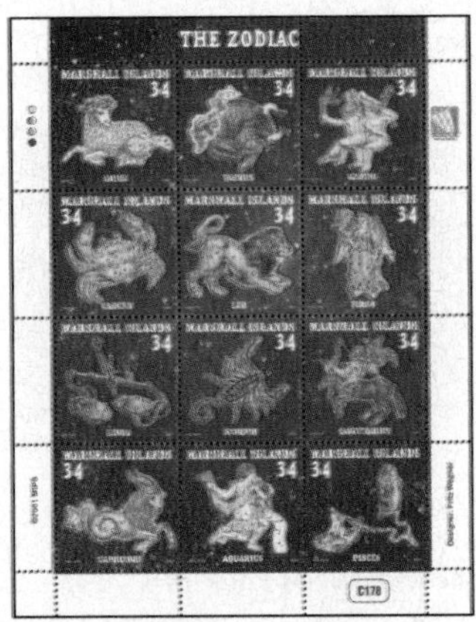

Zodiac Signs — A192

No. 785: a, Aries. b, Taurus. c, Gemini. d, Cancer. e, Leo. f, Virgo. g, Libra. h, Scorpio. i, Sagittarius. j, Capricorn. k, Aquarius. l, Pisces.

2001, July 17 *Perf. 11¾*
785 A192 34c Sheet of 12, #a-l 8.25 8.25

Phila Nippon '01 — A193

No. 786: a, Black Cat, by Tan Axi. b, Brown Cat, by Tan Axi. c, Cliffs, by Wang Xinhai. d, Boat and Bridge, by Li Yan. e, Rooster, by Wang Xinlan. f, Great Wall, by Liu Zhong. g, Crane, by Wang Lynn. h, Baboon With Basket, by Wang Yani. i, Baboon in Tree, by Wang Yani. j, Umbrella, by Sun Yuan. k, Baboon With Fruit, by Wang Yani. l, Baboon on Ox, by Wang Yani.

2001, Aug. 1 **Litho.** *Perf. 11¾*
786 A193 80c Sheet of 12, #a-l 20.00 20.00

US Naval Heroes in WWII Pacific Theater — A194

No. 787: a, Adm. Raymond A. Spruance. b, Adm. Arleigh A. Burke. c, Adm. Ernest A. King. d, Adm. Richmond K. Turner. e, Adm. Marc A. Mitscher. f, Adm. Chester W. Nimitz. g, Lt. Edward H. O'Hare. h, Adm. William F. Halsey, Jr. i, The Sullivan Brothers.

2001, Aug. 24 *Perf. 13½*
787 A194 80c Sheet of 9, #a-i 14.50 14.50

Classic Cars — A195

No. 788: a, 1916 Stutz Bearcat. b, 1909 Stanley Steamer. c, 1934 Citroen 7CV. d, 1910 Rolls-Royce Silver Ghost. e, 1927 Daimler. f, 1935 Hispano-Suiza Type 68V-12. g, 1928 Lancia Lambda V4. h, 1927 Volvo OV4.

2001, Sept. 11
788 A195 34c Block of 8, #a-h 5.50 5.50

See also Nos. 796, 809, 823, 828, 865.

Remembrance of Victims of Sept. 11, 2001 Terrorist Attacks — A196

No. 789: a, U.S. flag, "Blessed are those. . ." b, Statue of Liberty, "United we stand. . ." c, U.S. flag, "An attack on freedom. . ." d, U.S. flag, "In the great struggle. . ." e, Statue of Freedom, "We go forward. . ." f, U.S. flag, "In the face of terrorism. . ." g, American people (75x32mm)

2001, Oct. 11 **Litho.** *Perf. 13½*
789 Booklet pane of 7 6.25 —
a.-f. A196 34c Any single .70 .70
g. A196 $1 multi 2.00 2.00
Booklet, #789 6.25

Christmas A197

No. 790: a, Angel on high. b, Adoration of the Magi. c, Nativity scene. d, Adoration of the shepherds.

2001, Oct. 26
790 Strip of 4 2.80 2.80
a.-d. A197 34c Any single .70 .70

Airplanes — A198

No. 791: a, Supermarine Sea Eagle. b, Gloster Sea Gladiator. c, DHC-6 Twin Otter. d, Shorts 330. e, Sandringham Flying Boat. f, De Havilland DHC-7. g, Beech Duke B60. h, Fokker Friendship F27. i, Consolidated B-24J Liberator. j, Vickers 953C Merchantman.

Perf. 11¼x10¼
2001, Nov. 13 **Litho.**
791 A198 80c Block of 10, #a-j 16.00 16.00

Souvenir Sheet

New Year 2002 (Year of the Horse) — A199

2002, Jan. 2 *Perf. 13x13½*
792 A199 80c multi 1.60 1.60

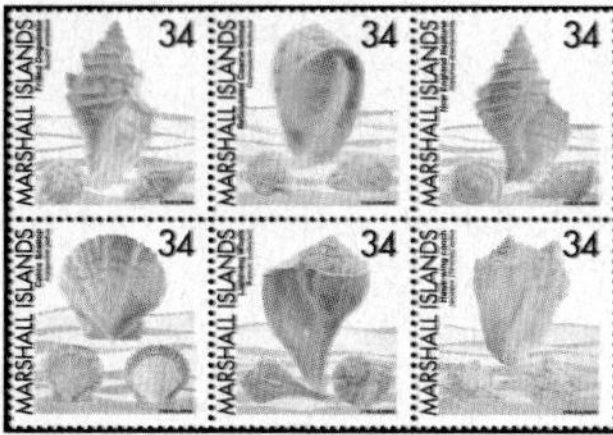

Shells — A200

No. 793: a, Frilled dogwinkle. b, Reticulated cowrie-helmet. c, New England neptune. d, Calico scallop. e, Lightning whelk. f, Hawk-wing conch.

2002, Jan. 22 ***Perf. 11¾***
793 A200 34c Block of 6, #a-f 4.25 4.25

Souvenir Sheet

Reign of Queen Elizabeth II, 50th Anniv. — A201

2002, Feb. 6 Litho. ***Perf. 13x13½***
794 A201 80c multi 1.60 1.60

United We Stand — A202

2002, Feb. 11 ***Perf. 13½***
795 A202 34c multi .70 .70

Classic Cars Type of 2001

No. 796: a, 1909 Le Zebre. b, 1886 Hammel. c, 1902 Wolseley. d, 1899 Eysink. e, 1903 Dansk. f, 1907 Spyker. g, 1913 Fiat Model Zero. h, 1902 Weber.

2002, Feb. 26
796 A195 34c Block of 8, #a-h 5.50 5.50

Corals — A203

No. 797: a, Mixed. b, Chalice. c, Elkhorn. d, Finger.

2002, Mar. 13
797 A203 34c Block of 4, #a-d 2.75 2.75

Butterflies Type of 2000

No. 798: a, Grayling. b, Eastern festoon. c, Speckled wood. d, Cranberry fritillary. e, Bath white. f, Meadow brown. g, Two-tailed pasha. h, Scarce swallowtail. i, Dusky grizzled skipper. j, Provençal short-tailed blue. k, Dryal. l, Comma.

2002, Mar. 25 ***Perf. 11¾***
798 A176 80c Sheet of 12, #a-l 20.00 20.00

Horses in Art — A204

No. 799: a, Horses, by Giorgio de Chirico. b, Tartar Envoys Give Horse to Qianlong, by Father Giuseppe Castiglione. c, Gathering Seaweed, by Anton Mauve. d, Mares and Foals, by George Stubbs. e, A Mare and Her Foal in a Spring Meadow, by Wilson Hepple. f, Horse with Child and a Dog, by Natale Attanasio. g, The Horse, by Waterhouse Hawkins. h, Attendants and a Horse, by Edgar Degas. i, Mares and Foals in a Landscape, by Stubbs. j, The Horse, by Guglielmo Ciardi. k, Little Blue Horse, by Franz Marc. l, Sketch for the Set of "Fire Bird," by Pavel Kuznetsov.

80c, Emperor Qianlong Leaving for his Summer Residence, by Castiglione.

2002, Apr. 15 Litho. ***Perf. 13½***
799 A204 34c Sheet of 12, #a-l 8.25 8.25

Souvenir Sheet

Perf. 13x13½

800 A204 80c multi 1.60 1.60

No. 800 contains one 80x50mm stamp.

Miniature Sheet

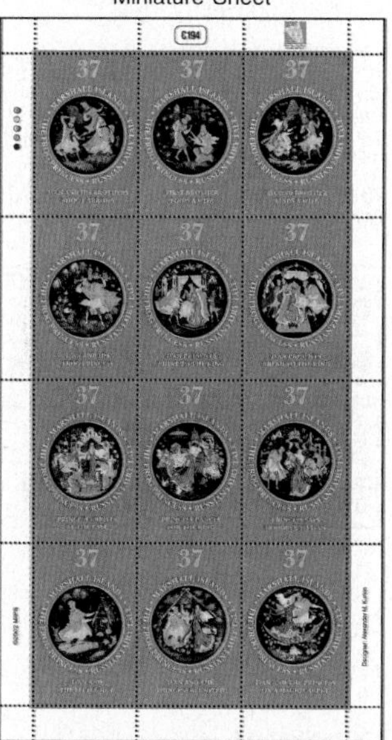

Russian Fairy Tale, "The Frog Princess" — A205

No. 801: a, Ivan and his brothers shoot arrows. b, First brother finds a wife. c, Second brother finds a wife. d, Ivan and his Frog Princess. e, Ivan presents shirt to the king. f, Ivan presents bread to the king. g, Princess arrives at the ball. h, Princess dances for the king. i, Princess says goodbye to ivan. j, Ivan and the little hut. k, Ivan and the Princess reunited. l, Ivan and the Princess on a magic carpet.

2002, Apr. 26 Litho. ***Perf. 12½x12¼***
801 A205 37c Sheet of 12, #a-l 9.00 9.00

Carousel Figures — A206

No. 802: a, Armored horse and rabbit. b, Zebra and camel. c, Horse, reindeer and angel. d, Horse, frog and tiger.

2002, May 13 Litho. ***Perf. 13½***
802 A206 80c Block of 4, #a-d 6.50 6.50

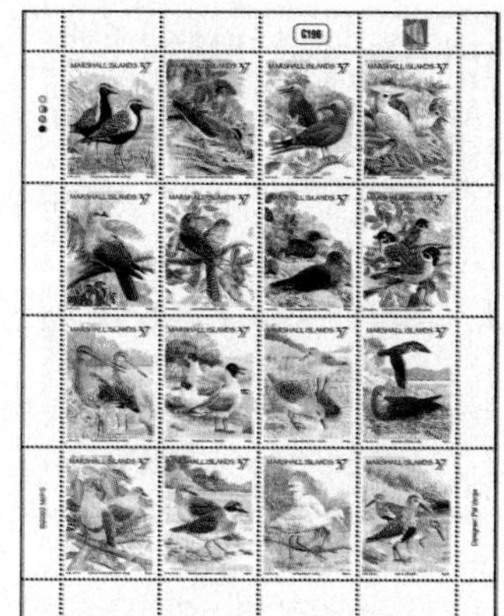

Birds — A207

No. 803: a, Lesser golden plover. b, Siberian tattler. c, Brown noddy. d, Common fairy tern. e, Micronesian pigeon. f, Long-tailed cuckoo. g, Christmas shearwater. h, Eurasian tree sparrow. i, Black-tailed godwit. j, Franklin's gull. k, Rufous-necked stint. l, Kermadec petrel. m, Purple-capped fruit dove. n, Mongolian plover. o, Cattle egret. p, Dunlin.

2002, May 29
803 A207 37c Sheet of 16, #a-p 12.00 12.00

Benjamin Franklin (1706-90) — A208

No. 804: a, Inventor. b, Scholar.

2002, June 10 Litho. ***Perf. 13½***
804 A208 80c Horiz. pair, #a-b 3.25 3.25

Sea Turtles — A209

No. 805: a, Loggerhead. b, Leatherback. c, Hawksbill. d, Green.

2002, June 25
805 A209 37c Block of 4, #a-d 3.00 3.00

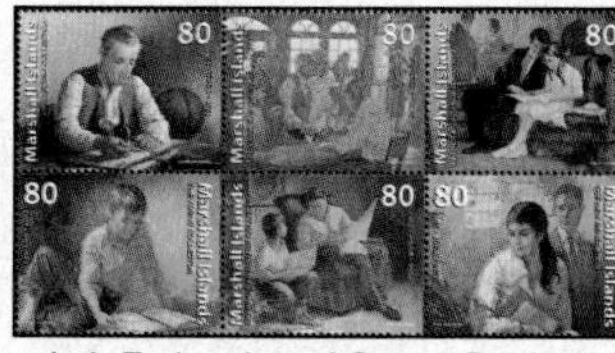

Intl. Federation of Stamp Dealers' Associations, 50th Anniv. — A210

No. 806: a, Stamp collector. b, First day of issue. c, Father and daughter collectors. d, Young collector. e, Sharing Dad's stamp collection. f, The new generation.

2002, July 2
806 A210 80c Block of 6, #a-f 9.75 9.75

US Navy Ships — A211

No. 807: a, USS Hartford. b, Bon Homme Richard. c, Prince de Neufchatel. d, USS Ohio. e, USS Onkahye. f, USS Oneida.

2002, July 18
807 A211 37c Block of 6, #a-f 4.50 4.50

See No. 827.

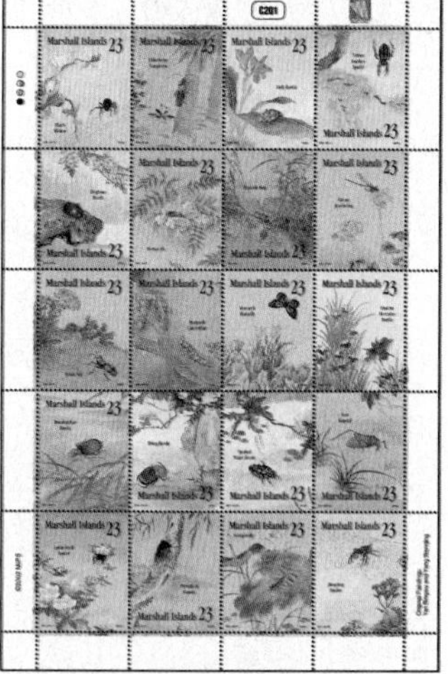

Insects and Spiders — A212

No. 808: a, Black widow spider. b, Elderberry longhorn. c, Ladybug. d, Yellow garden spider. e, Dogbane beetle. f, Flower fly. g, Assassin bug. h, Ebony jewelwing. i, Velvet ant. j, Monarch caterpillar. k, Monarch butterfly. l, Eastern Hercules beetle. m, Bombardier beetle. n, Dung beetle. o, Spotted water beetle. p, True katydid. q, Spiny-back spider. r, Periodical cicada. s, Scorpionfly. t, Jumping spider.

2002, Aug. 2 Litho. ***Perf. 13½***
808 A212 23c Sheet of 20, #a-t 9.25 9.25

Classic Cars Type of 2001

No. 809: a, 1934 Hotchkiss. b, 1909 De Dion Bouton. c, 1922 Renault. d, 1927 Amilcar Surbaisse. e, 1943 Austin. f, 1913 Peugeot Bebe. g, 1927 O.M. Type 665 Superba. h, 1922 Elizalde Tipo 20C.

2002, Aug. 15
809 A195 80c Block of 8, #a-h 13.00 13.00

Queen Mother Type of 2000 Redrawn

No. 810: a, As child. b, As young wife. c, As Queen. d, As Queen Mother.

2002, Aug. 30
810 A174 80c Block of 4, #a-d 6.50 6.50

Queen Mother Elizabeth (1900-2002).

Souvenir Sheet

Regal Princess — A213

2002, Sept. 10 ***Perf. 13¼x13¾***
811 A213 80c multi 1.60 1.60

World War I Heroes — A214

No. 812: a, Adm. William S. Sims. b, Gen. William E. Mitchell. c, Cpl. Freddie Stowers. d, Maj. Gen. Smedley D. Butler. e, Capt. Edward V. Rickenbacker. f, Sgt. Alvin C. York. g, Maj. Gen. John A. Lejeune. h, Gen. John J. Pershing.

2002, Sept. 23 ***Perf. 13½***
812 A214 80c Block of 8, #a-h 13.00 13.00

Christmas — A215

Snowman cookies with denomination in: a, Green. b, Red.

2002, Oct. 26 Litho. ***Perf. 13½***
813 A215 37c Horiz. pair, #a-b 1.50 1.50

Souvenir Sheet

New Year 2003 (Year of the Ram) — A216

2003, Jan. 2 Litho. ***Perf. 13x13¾***
814 A216 80c multi 1.60 1.60

UN Membership, 12th Anniv. — A217

2003, Jan. 29 ***Perf. 11¼x10¼***
815 A217 60c multi 1.25 1.25

Folktales — A218

No. 816: a, Inedel's Magic Kite. b, Lijebake Rescues Her Granddaughter. c, Jebro's Mother Invents the Sail. d, Limajnon Escapes to the Moon.

2003, Jan. 29 ***Perf. 13½***
816 A218 50c Block of 4, #a-d, + 4 labels 4.00 4.00

Famous People Type of 2001

Designs: 37c, Oscar deBrum (1929-2002), first Chief Secretary. $3.85, Senator Tipne Philippo (1933-2000). $13.65, Senator Henchi Balos (1946-2000).

Perf. 10¼x11¼
2003, Mar. 25 Litho.

817	A184	37c multi	.75	.75
818	A184	$3.85 multi	7.75	7.75
819	A184	$13.65 multi	25.00	25.00
		Nos. 817-819 (3)	33.50	33.50

The denomination of No. 819 was printed in a thermographic ink that changes color when warmed.

Marshallese Culture — A219

No. 820: a, Lagajimi, c. 1870s, by Franz Hernsheim (21x38mm). b, Old-style house with attic-like roof space (46x38mm). c, Tidal lake on Jabwor (46x38mm). d, Kabua, c. 1870s, by Hernsheim (21x38mm). e, Children in mat dresses (21x38mm). f, Jaluit pass, c. 1870s, by Hernsheim (46x38mm). g, Traditional Canoe c. 1870s, by Hernsheim (46x38mm). h, Man in fishing attire (21x38mm).

2003, Mar. 25 ***Perf. 13½***
820 A219 37c Block of 8, #a-h 6.00 6.00

See No. 824.

Butterflies Type of 2000

No. 821: a, False grayling. b, Green hairstreak. c, Purple-shot copper. d, Black-veined white. e, Arctic grayling. f, Greek clouded yellow. g, American painted lady. h, Wall brown. i, Polar fritillary. j, Mountain clouded yellow. k, Camberwell beauty. l, Large white.

2003, May 2 Litho. ***Perf. 11¾***
821 A176 80c Sheet of 12, #a-l 20.00 20.00

Powered Flight, Cent. — A220

No. 822: a, 1903 Wright Flyer. b, Curtiss JN-3 "Jenny." c, Douglas World Cruiser. d, "Spirit of St. Louis." e, Lockheed Vega. f, Boeing 314 Clipper. g, Douglas C-47 Skytrain. h, Boeing B-50 Superfortress. i, Antonov An-225 Mriya. j, B-2 Spirit.

2003, June 10 ***Perf. 13½***
822 A220 37c Block of 10, #a-j 7.50 7.50

Classic Cars Type of 2001

No. 823: a, 1927 Alfa Romeo RLSS. b, 1912 Austro-Daimler Prince Henry. c, 1923 Mors 14/20 HP Tourer. d, 1926 AC Tourer. e, 1903 Scania, 1897 Vabis. f, 1914 Graf und Stift. g, 1919 Pic-Pic. h, 1911 Hispano-Suiza-Alfonso XIII.

2003, July 10 Litho. ***Perf. 13½***
823 A195 37c Block of 8, #a-h 6.00 6.00

Marshallese Culture Type of 2003

No. 824: a, Kabua's Daughter on Pandanus, c. 1906, by Augustin Krämer (21x38mm). b, Traditional walap (46x38mm). c, Jabwor, Jaluit Atoll (46x38mm). d, Traditional and Modern Dress, by Augustin Erdland (21x38mm). e, Nemedj, c. 1905, by Krämer (21x38mm). f, Typhoon of 1905, by Josef Schmidlin (46x38mm). g, Marshallese Kor Kor, c. 1905, by Richard Deeken (46x38mm). h, Marshallese Grandfather, by Erdland (21x38mm).

2003, Aug. 7 ***Perf. 13½x13¼***
824 A219 37c Block of 8, #a-h 6.00 6.00

Christmas Ornaments — A221

No. 825: a, Snowman. b, Jack-in-the-box. c, Toy soldier. d, Reindeer.

2003, Oct. 24 ***Perf. 13½***
825 A221 37c Block of 4, #a-d 3.00 3.00

Souvenir Sheet

New Year 2004 (Year of the Monkey) — A222

2004, Jan. 4 Litho. ***Perf. 13x13¾***
826 A222 $1 multi 2.00 2.00

Ship Type of 2002

No. 827: a, Bonhomme Richard. b, HMS Resolution, denomination at UR. c, HMS Resolution, denomination at UL.

2004, Feb. 14 ***Perf. 13½***
827 A211 37c Horiz. strip of 3, #a-c 2.25 2.25

Classic Cars Type of 2001

No. 828: a, 1906 Wolseley-Siddeley. b, 1901 Mors. c, 1908 Hutton. d, 1907 Metallurgique. e, 1902 Benz. f, 1900 Cudell. g, 1906 Peugeot. h, Mercedes 60.

2004, Mar. 15 ***Perf. 13½***
828 A195 37c Block of 8, #a-h 6.00 6.00

Greetings — A223

No. 829: a, Thank you! b, Congratulations. c, Happy birthday. d, Best wishes. e, Get well soon. f, Loye you, Dad. g, Love you, Mom. h, Best wishes, Get well soon, Love you, Mom, Congratulations, Love you, Dad, Happy birthday, Thank you.

2004, Apr. 15 Litho. ***Perf. 13½***
829 A223 37c Sheet of 8, #a-h 6.00 6.00

Marshall Islands Postal Service, 20th Anniv. — A224

Messenger and canoe with background colors of: 37c, Prussian blue. 60c, Brown. $2.30, Purple.

2004, May 2
830-832 A224 Set of 3 6.75 6.75

No. 832 printed in sheets of 8 stamps + 8 adjacent certified mail etiquettes. Value is for set with No. 832 with attached etiquette.

Lewis and Clark Expedition, Bicent. — A225

No. 833 — Inscriptions: a, The saga begins. b, Westward bound. c, Endless bison.

2004, May 14
833 Horiz. strip of 3 2.25 2.25
a.-c. A225 37c Any single .75 .75

See Nos. 840, 845, 855, 867, 871, 885.

D-Day, 60th Anniv. — A226

No. 834: a, Horsa gliders and parachute troops. b, British Typhoon 1B and US P-51B Mustangs. c, German defenses and Pointe du Hoc. d, Allied amphibious landing.

2004, June 6 Litho. ***Perf. 13½***
834 A226 37c Block of 4, #a-d 3.00 3.00

Marine Life — A227

No. 835: a, Chambered nautilus, map cowrie, fish, coral, trumpet triton (2-1). b, Marlin spike, fish, coral, turban shell, Toulerei's cowrie (2-2).

2004, July 1
835 A227 37c Horiz. pair, #a-b 1.50 1.50

Pres. Ronald Reagan (1911-2004) A228

2004, July 4
836 A228 60c multi 1.25 1.25

First Manned Moon Landing, 35th Anniv. — A229

No. 837: a, Astronaut floating in space (4-1). b, Astronaut in space (4-2). c, Astronaut floating in orbit (4-3). d, Astronaut and Jupiter (4-4).

2004, July 20
837 A229 37c Block of 4, #a-d 3.00 3.00

Festival of Arts — A230

No. 838: a, Woman showing fan making. b, Woman making baskets. c, Men carving. d, Children making canoe models. e, White ginger. f, Vanda. g, Tiare. h, Hibiscus. i, Breadfruit. j, Tattooed warrior. k, Young chiefs. l, Drummers and dancers.

2004, July 22
838 A230 37c Sheet of 12, #a-l 9.00 9.00

Aircraft — A231

No. 839: a, 1903 Wright Flyer. b, Blériot XI. c, Curtiss Golden Flyer. d, Curtiss Flying Boat. e, Deperdussin Racer. f, Sikorsky Il'ya Muromets. g, Fokker E1. h, Junkers J1. i, S.E. 5A. j, Handley Page O/400. k, Fokker D VII. l, Junkers F13. m, Lockheed Vega. n, M-130 Pan Am Clipper. o, Messerschmitt BF 109. p, Spitfire. q, Junkers Ju-88. r, A6M Zero. s, Ilyushin Il-2. t, Heinkel He-178. u, C-47 Skytrain. v, Piper Cub. w, Avro Lancaster. x, B-17F Flying Fortress. y, Messerschmitt Me-262. z, B-29 Superfortress. aa, P-51 Mustang. ab, Yak-9. ac, Bell Model 47 helicopter. ad, Bell X-1. ae, Beechcraft Bonanza. af, AN-225 Mriya. ag, B-47 Stratojet. ah, MiG-15. ai, Saab J35 Draken. aj, B-52 Stratofortress. ak, Boeing 367-80. al, U-2. am, C-130 Hercules. an, F-4 Phantom II. ao, North American X-15. ap, Sikorsky S-61 (HH-3E). aq, Learjet 23. ar, SR-71 Blackbird. as, Boeing 747. at, Concorde. au, Airbus A300. av, MiG-29. aw, F-117A Nighthawk. ax, F/A-22 Raptor.

Perf. 10¼x11¼

2004, Aug. 12 **Litho.**
839 Sheet of 50 23.00 23.00
a.-ax. A231 23c Any single .45 .45

Lewis and Clark Type of 2004

No. 840 — Inscriptions: a, First Fourth of July. b, Death of Sgt. Charles Floyd. c, Setting the prairie on fire.

2004, Aug. 24 ***Perf. 13½***
840 Horiz. strip of 3 2.25 2.25
a.-c. A225 37c Any single .75 .75

John Wayne (1907-79), Actor — A232

2004, Sept. 9 ***Perf. 10¼x11¼***
841 A232 37c multi .75 .75

Miniature Sheet

23rd UPU Congress, Bucharest, Romania — A233

No. 842: a, Great Britain #1. b, Romania #1. c, Marshall Islands #1. d, Marshall Islands #31.

2004, Sept. 15 **Litho.** ***Perf. 13½***
842 A233 $1 Sheet of 4, #a-d 8.00 8.00

Miniature Sheet

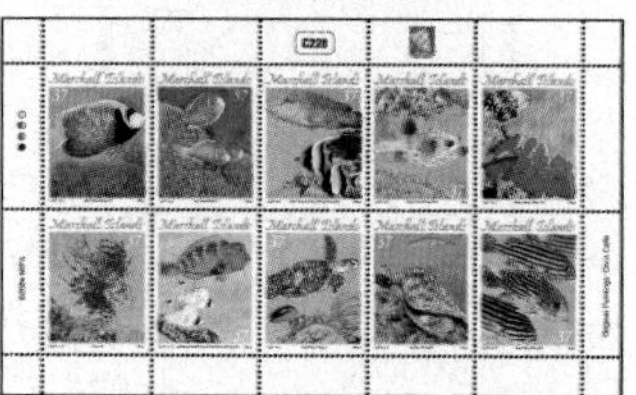

Marine Life — A234

No. 843: a, Emperor angelfish. b, Pink anemonefish. c, Humphead wrasse, Moorish idol. d, Black-spotted puffer. e, Snowflake moray eel. f, Lionfish. g, Bumphead parrotfish, threadfin butterflyfish. h, Hawksbill turtle. i, Triton's trumpet. j, Oriental sweetlips.

2004, Oct. 1
843 A234 37c Sheet of 10, #a-j 7.50 7.50

Miniature Sheet

Christmas — A235

No. 844: a, Angel with bells. b, God Almighty. c, Appears the Star of Bethlehem. d, Three Wise Men. e, Procession of the poor people. f, Pastors with sheep. g, Flight to Egypt. h, Holy Family. i, Animals adoring Jesus.

2004, Oct. 27
844 A235 37c Sheet of 9, #a-i 6.75 6.75

Lewis and Clark Type of 2004

No. 845 — Inscriptions: a, The interpreters. b, Sacred bison calling. c, Teton Sioux rob men.

2004, Nov. 22
845 Horiz. strip of 3 2.25 2.25
a.-c. A225 37c Any single .75 .75

Battle of the Bulge, 60th Anniv. — A236

No. 846: a, Infantry. b, Armor. c, Aviation. d, Lt. Col. Creighton Abrams and Brig. Gen. Anthony McAuliffe.

2004, Dec. 1
846 A236 37c Block of 4, #a-d 3.00 3.00

United States Presidents — A237

No. 847: a, 1c, George Washington. b, 2c, John Adams. c, 3c, Thomas Jefferson. d, 4c, James Madison. e, 5c, James Monroe. f, 6c, John Quincy Adams. g, 7c, Andrew Jackson. h, 8c, Martin Van Buren. i, 9c, William Henry Harrison. j, 10c, John Tyler. k, 11c, James K. Polk. l, 12c, Zachary Taylor. m, 13c, Millard Fillmore. n, 14c, Franklin Pierce. o, 15c, James Buchanan. p, 16c, Abraham Lincoln. q, 17c, Andrew Johnson. r, 18c, Ulysses S. Grant. s, 19c, Rutherford B. Hayes. t, 20c, James A. Garfield. u, 21c, Chester A. Arthur. v, 22c, Grover Cleveland. w, 23c, Benjamin Harrison. x, 24c, Grover Cleveland. y, 25c, William McKinley. z, 26c, Theodore Roosevelt. aa, 27c, William Howard Taft. ab, 28c, Woodrow Wilson. ac, 29c, Warren G. Harding. ad, 30c, Calvin Coolidge. ae, 31c, Herbert Hoover. af, 32c, Franklin D. Roosevelt. ag, 33c, Harry S Truman. ah, 34c, Dwight D. Eisenhower. ai, 35c, John F. Kennedy. aj, 36c, Lyndon B. Johnson. ak, 37c, Richard M. Nixon. al, 38c, Gerald R. Ford. am, 39c, Jimmy Carter. an, 40c, Ronald W. Reagan. ao, 41c, George H. W. Bush. ap, 42c, William J. Clinton. aq, 43c, George W. Bush. ar, 60c, White House. as, $1, White House.

2005, Jan. 20 **Litho.** ***Perf. 13½***
847 A237 Sheet of 45, #a-as 31.00 31.00

No. 847 sold for $15.49.

Souvenir Sheet

New Year 2005 (Year of the Rooster) — A238

2005, Feb. 9 **Litho.** ***Perf. 13x13½***
848 A238 $1 multi 2.00 2.00

Rotary International, Cent. — A239

2005, Feb. 23 ***Perf. 13½***
849 A239 37c multi .75 .75

Hibiscus Varieties — A240

Designs: 37c, Burgundy Blush. 60c, Fiesta. 80c, June's Joy. $1, Norman Lee.

Perf. 10¼x11¼

2005, Mar. 15 **Litho.**

850 A240 37c multi .75 .75
851 A240 60c multi 1.25 1.25
852 A240 80c multi 1.60 1.60
853 A240 $1 multi 2.00 2.00
Nos. 850-853 (4) 5.60 5.60

See Nos. 860-863, 878-881.

Hans Christian Andersen (1805-75), Author — A241

No. 854: a, The Princess and the Pea. b, Thumbelina. c, The Little Mermaid. d, The Emperor's New Suit.

2005, Apr. 2 ***Perf. 13½***

854 A241 37c Block of 4, #a-d 3.00 3.00

Lewis and Clark Type of 2004

No. 855 — Inscriptions: a, First grizzly confrontation. b, Lewis reaching the Great Falls. c, Sacajawea and her brother reunite.

2005, Apr. 29

855 Horiz. strip of 3 2.25 2.25
a.-c. A225 37c Any single .75 .75

American First Day Cover Society, 50th Anniv. — A242

No. 856: a, George W. Linn first day cover for US No. 610 (Harding Memorial stamp). b, First day cover for Marshall Islands Nos. 31-34. c, First day cover of US No. C76 with Moon Landing cancel. d, First day cover for Marshall Islands No. 856.

2005, May 2

856 A242 37c Block of 4, #a-d 3.00 3.00

V-E Day, 60th Anniv. — A243

No. 857: a, German surrender, Reims, France. b, Times Square, New York. c, Victory parade, Moscow. d, Royal family and Winston Churchill, Buckingham Palace, London.

2005, May 9

857 A243 37c Block of 4, #a-d 3.00 3.00

Pope John Paul II (1920-2005) — A244

No. 858: a, Wearing red cape, with arm raised. b, Wearing green vestments. c, Close-up. d, Holding crucifix, wearing red vestments. e, Wearing miter.

2005, May 18 **Litho.** ***Perf. 13½***

858 Vert. strip of 5 3.75 3.75
a.-e. A244 37c Any single .75 .75

Exists imperf. Vertical strip of 5, value $250.

United Nations, 60th Anniv. — A245

2005, June 26

859 A245 Horiz. pair 2.40 2.40
a. 37c Six people .75 .75
b. 80c Seven people 1.60 1.60

Hibiscus Varieties Type of 2005

Designs: 1c, Margaret Okano. 24c, Cameo Queen. 39c, Madonna. $4, Estrella Red.

2005, July 13 ***Perf. 10¼x11¼***

860 A240 1c multi .25 .25
861 A240 24c multi .50 .50
862 A240 39c multi .80 .80
863 A240 $4 multi 8.00 8.00
Nos. 860-863 (4) 9.55 9.55

Space Shuttles A246

No. 864: a, Columbia. b, Discovery. c, Endeavour. d, Challenger. e, Atlantis.

2005, July 26 ***Perf. 13½***

864 Horiz. strip of 5 3.75 3.75
a.-e. A246 37c Any single .75 .75

Classic Cars Type of 2001

No. 865: a, 1925 Excelsior (8-1). b, 1912 Adler K (8-2). c, 1920 Thulin (8-3). d, 1913 Palladium (8-4). e, 1926 Minerva (8-5). f, 1922 Elizalde (8-6). g, 1911 Rolls-Royce Silver Ghost (8-7). h, 1931 Invicta (8-8).

2005, Aug. 4

865 Block of 8 6.00 6.00
a.-h. A195 37c Any single .75 .75

No. 865b is incorrectly inscribed "1926 Minerva."

V-J Day, 60th Anniv. — A247

No. 866: a, Fujiyama and Tokyo Bay. b, USS Missouri. c, US contingent. d, Japanese delegation.

2005, Sept. 2

866 A247 37c Block of 4, #a-d 3.00 3.00

Lewis & Clark Type of 2004

No. 867 — Inscriptions: a, Crossing the Bitterroots. b, Peace agreement. c, Ocean in view.

2005, Sept. 22

867 Horiz. strip of 3 2.25 2.25
a.-c. A225 37c Any single .75 .75

Battle of Trafalgar, Bicent. — A248

No. 868 — Fighting ships: a, Trireme galley. b, Trireme Romano. c, Viking longship. d, Ming treasure ship. e, Mary Rose. f, Nuestra Senora del Rosario. g, Korean turtle ship. h, Brederode. i, Galera Veneziana. j, Santisima Trinidad. k, Ville de Paris. l, HMS Victory. m, Bonhomme Richard. n, USS Constellation. o, USS Hartford. p, Fijian ndrua. q, HMS Dreadnought. r, HMAS Australia. s, HMS Dorsetshire. t, Admiral Graf Spee. u, Yamato. v, USS Tautog. w, Bismarck. x, USS Hornet. y, USS Missouri.

$2, HMS Victory, diff.

Illustration reduced.

2005, Oct. 21 **Litho.** ***Perf. 13½***

868 A248 37c Sheet of 25, #a-y 18.50 18.50

Souvenir Sheet

Imperf

869 A248 $2 multi 4.00 4.00

No. 868 contains twenty-five 40x31mm stamps.

Christmas — A249

No. 870 — Angels with: a, Lute. b, Harp, horn and lute. c, Horn. d, Harp.

2005, Nov. 1 ***Perf. 13½***

870 A249 37c Block of 4, #a-d 3.00 3.00

Lewis & Clark Type of 2004

No. 871 — Inscriptions: a, First vote allowed to all. b, Leaving Fort Clatsop. c, At Pompey's Pillar.

2005, Nov. 24

871 Horiz. strip of 3 2.25 2.25
a.-c. A225 37c Any single .75 .75

Marshallese Culture A250

No. 872 — Photographs: a, First Catholic Church on Jabwor, Jaluit Atoll, by Josef Schmidlin. b, Women on Jaluit Atoll, by Richard Deeken. c, Canoes in Jaluit Harbor, by Deeken. d, Nelu and His Wife Ledagoba, by Augustin Kramer. e, An Old Man from Ebon Atoll, by Augustin Erdland.

2005, Dec. 1

872 Horiz. strip of 5 3.75 3.75
a.-e. A250 37c Any single .75 .75

See also Nos. 886, 901, 929, 950, 973.

Miniature Sheet

Benjamin Franklin (1706-90), Statesman — A251

No. 873 — Franklin: a, Painting by J. S. Duplessis. b, Painting by David K. Stone. c, Painting by Mason Chamberlain. d, Painting by John Trumbull. e, Sculpture, by James Earle Fraser. f, Painting by David Martin. g, Painting by Benjamin West. h, Painting by J. B. Greuze. i, Painting by C. N. Cochin.

2006, Jan. 17 ***Perf. 13½***

873 A251 48c Sheet of 9, #a-i 8.75 8.75

Souvenir Sheet

New Year 2006 (Year of the Dog) — A252

2006, Jan. 27 ***Perf. 13¼x13½***

874 A252 $1 multi 2.00 2.00

Love — A253

2006, Feb. 14 **Litho.** ***Perf. 13½***

875 A253 39c multi .80 .80

Butterflies Type of 2000

No. 876: a, Peacock. b, Southern comma. c, Pale clouded yellow. d, Common blue. e, Wood white. f, Baltic grayling. g, Purple emperor. h, Silky ringlet. i, Peak white. j, Idas blue. k, Cleopatra. l, Chequered skipper.

2006, Mar. 20 ***Perf. 11¾***

876 A176 84c Sheet of 12, #a-l 21.00 21.00

First Spaceflight by Yuri Gagarin, 45th Anniv. — A254

2006, Apr. 12 **Litho.** ***Perf. 11¾***

877 A254 39c multi .80 .80

Hibiscus Varieties Type of 2005

Designs: 10c, Butterscotch Sundae. 63c, Magic Moments. 84c, Joanne Boulin. $4.05, Capsicum Red.

2006, May 2 ***Perf. 10¼x11¼***

878 A240 10c multi .25 .25
879 A240 63c multi 1.25 1.25
880 A240 84c multi 1.75 1.75
881 A240 $4.05 multi 8.25 8.25
Nos. 878-881 (4) 11.50 11.50

Miniature Sheet

Washington 2006 World Philiatelic Exhibition — A255

No. 882 — Designs of the United States 1922-25 definitive issue inscribed "Marshall Islands Postage": a, ½c, Nathan Hale. b, 1c, Benjamin Franklin. c, 1 ½c, Warren G. Harding. d, 2c, George Washington. e, 3c, Abraham Lincoln. f, 4c, Martha Washington. g, 5c, Theodore Roosevelt. h, 6c, James A. Garfield. i, 7c, William McKinley. j, 8c, Ulysses S. Grant. k, 9c, Thomas Jefferson. l, 10c, James Monroe. m, 11c, Rutherford B. Hayes. n, 12c, Grover Cleveland. o, 14c, American Indian chief. p, 15c, Statue of Liberty. q, 20c, Golden Gate, horiz. r, 25c, Niagara Falls, horiz. s, 30c, Buffalo, horiz. t, 50c, Arlington Amphitheater, horiz.

2006, May 27 Litho. *Perf. 13½*

882 A255 Sheet of 20, #a-t 4.75 4.75
u. Souvenir sheet, #882o, 882s, imperf. .90 .90

Sharks — A256

No. 883: a, Gray reef shark. b, Silvertip shark. c, Blacktip reef shark. d, Whitetip reef shark.

2006, June 16 *Perf. 13½*

883 A256 39c Block of 4, #a-d 3.25 3.25

Miniature Sheet

Operations Crossroads, 60th Anniv. — A257

No. 884: a, Evacuation of Bikinians. b, Navy preparations. c, "Able" bomb blast. d, "Baker" bomb blast. e, Ghost fleet. f, Effects on the Bikinians.

2006, July 1 Litho. *Perf. 13½*

884 A257 39c Sheet of 6, #a-f, + 6 labels 4.75 4.75

Lewis and Clark Type of 2004

No. 885 — Inscriptions: a, Leaving Sacagawea and Charbonneau. b, Return to St. Louis.

2006, Aug. 24

885 Horiz. pair 1.60 1.60
a.-b. A225 39c Either single .80 .80

Marshallese Culture Type of 2005

No. 886 — Photographs: a, Harbor Front of Jabwor, Jaluit Atoll, by L. Sander. b, Irooj with Family, Jabwor, Jaluit Atoll, by Richard Deeken. c, Traditional Voyaging Canoe at Jaluit Atoll, by Sander. d, Mission Sisters and Girls Doing Laundry, Jaluit, by Hildegard von Bunsen. e, Traditional House on Mile Atoll, by Hans Seidel.

2006, Sept. 22 Litho. *Perf. 13½*

886 Horiz. strip of 5 4.00 4.00
a.-e. A250 39c Any single .80 .80

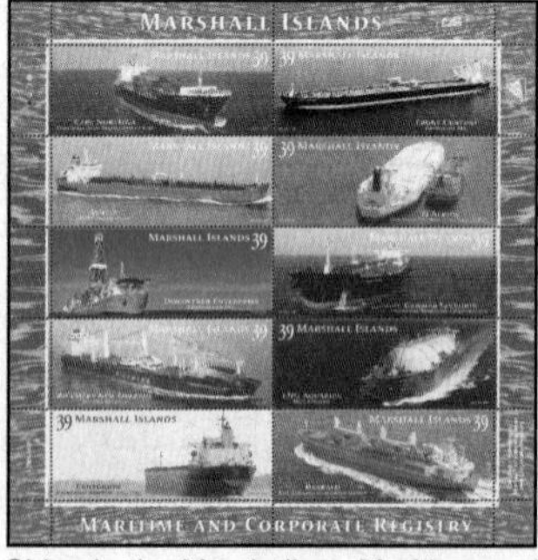

Ships in the Marshallese Maritime and Corporate Registry — A258

No. 887: a, Cape Norviega. b, Front Century. c, Ashley. d, TI Africa. e, Discoverer Enterprise. f, Genmar Spyridon. g, Rickmers New Orleans. h, LNG Aquarius. i, Centurion. j, Barkald.

2006, Oct. 9

887 A258 39c Sheet of 10, #a-j 8.00 8.00

Christmas A259

2006, Nov. 1

888 A259 39c multi .80 .80

Greetings — A260

No. 889: a, "Happy Birthday." b, "Congratulations." c, "Thank You." d, "Best Wishes."

2007, Jan. 16 *Perf. 11¾*

889 A260 39c Block of 4, #a-d 3.25 3.25

Souvenir Sheet

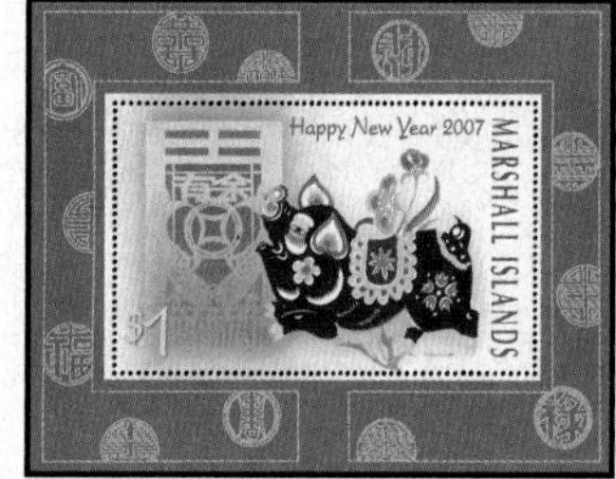

New Year 2007 (Year of the Pig) — A261

2007, Feb. 19 Litho. *Perf. 13x13½*

890 A261 $1 multi 2.00 2.00

Trains — A262

No. 891: a, Art Deco train. b, Pennsylvania. c, Santa Fe Chief. d, Hiawatha. e, 20th Century Limited. f, Daylight.

2007, Mar. 26 *Perf. 13½*

891 A262 39c Block of 6, #a-f 4.75 4.75

Dolphins — A263

No. 892: a, Spotter dolphins. b, Bottlenose dolphins. c, Risso's dolphin. d, Common dolphin.

2007, Apr. 9

892 A263 39c Block of 4, #a-d 3.25 3.25

Fish A264

Designs: 26c, Achilles tang. 41c, Regal angelfish. 52c, Saddled butterflyfish. 61c, Tinker's butterflyfish.

Perf. 10¼x11¼

2007, June 12 Litho.

893 A264 26c multi .55 .55
894 A264 41c multi .85 .85
895 A264 52c multi 1.10 1.10
896 A264 61c multi 1.25 1.25
Nos. 893-896 (4) 3.75 3.75

Miniature Sheet

Space Age, 50th Anniv. — A265

No. 897: a, First man in space. b, First man-made satellite. c, First men on the Moon. d, First docking in space. e, First woman in space. f, First manned lunar vehicle. g, First space walk. h, First landing on Mars. i, First probe of Venus. j, First American in orbit.

2007, June 12 *Perf. 13½*

897 A265 41c Sheet of 10, #a-j 8.25 8.25

Scouting, Cent. — A266

No. 898 — Inscriptions: a, Helping others. b, Physically strong. c, Mentally awake. d, Fun and adventure.

2007, June 25

898 A266 41c Block of 4, #a-d 3.50 3.50

Purple Heart, 225th Anniv. — A267

2007, July 30 Litho. *Perf. 13½*

899 A267 41c multi .85 .85

Miniature Sheet

United States Air Force, 60th Anniv. — A268

No. 900: a, C-54 Skymaster. b, B-36 Peacemaker. c, F-86 Sabre. d, B-47 Stratojet. e, C-124 Globemaster II. f, C-121 Constellation. g, B-52 Stratofortress. h, F-100 Super Sabre. i, F-104 Starfighter. j, C-130 Hercules. k, F-105 Thunderchief. l, KC-135 Stratotanker. m, B-58 Hustler. n, F-4 Phantom II. o, T-38 Talon. p, C-141 Starlifter. q, F-111 Aardvark. r, SR-71 Blackbird. s, C-5 Galaxy. t, A-10 Thunderbolt II. u, F-15 Eagle. v, F-16 Fighting Falcon. w, F-117 Nighthawk. x, B-2 Spirit. y, C-17 Globemaster III.

2007, Aug. 7

900 A268 41c Sheet of 25, #a-y 21.00 21.00

Marshallese Culture Type of 2005

No. 901 — Photographs by J. Debrum: a, Lonkwon Getting Fish from His Trap. b, Alele Style of Fishing at Bilarek. c, Portrait of Lanju and Family. d, Outrigger with Sail. e, Lien and Litublan Collecting Shells.

2007, Sept. 18 Litho. *Perf. 13½*

901 Horiz. strip of 5 4.25 4.25
a.-e. A250 41c Any single .85 .85

Miniature Sheet

Marshall Islands Yacht Registry — A269

No. 902 — Registered yachts: a, Domani. b, Excellence III. c, Aquasition. d, Perfect Symmetry 5. e, Happy Days. f, Mystique. g, Halcyon Days. h, Man of Steel. i, Marathon. j, Sinbad.

2007, Oct. 8

902 A269 41c Sheet of 10, #a-j 8.25 8.25

Christmas — A270

No. 903 — Santa Claus: a, Reading list. b, Standing by fireplace. c, Holding gift. d, Waving from sleigh.

2007, Dec. 12

903 A270 41c Block of 4, #a-d 3.50 3.50

Miniature Sheet

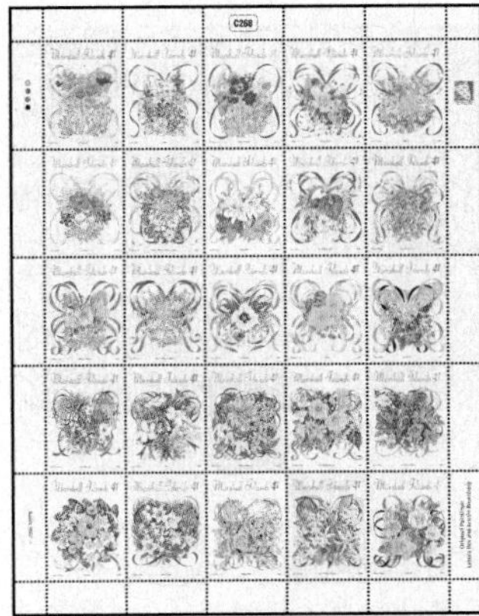

Flower Bouquets — A271

No. 904 — Various bouquets with country name at bottom: a, Scotland. b, Jersey. c, Gibraltar. d, Dominica. e, Canada. f, Cyprus. g, Turks and Caicos Islands. h, Bahamas. i, Montserrat. j, Cayman Islands. k, Bangladesh. l, Falkland Islands. m, Grenada. n, Nevis. o, Jamaica. p, Australia. q, Fiji. r, New Hebrides. s, Pitcairn Islands. t, Cook Islands. u, Tonga. v, Seychelles. w, Zimbabwe. x, Christmas Island. y, Antigua.

2008, Jan. 15 Litho. *Perf. 13½*

904 A271 41c Sheet of 25, #a-y 20.50 20.50

See No. 934.

Miniature Sheet

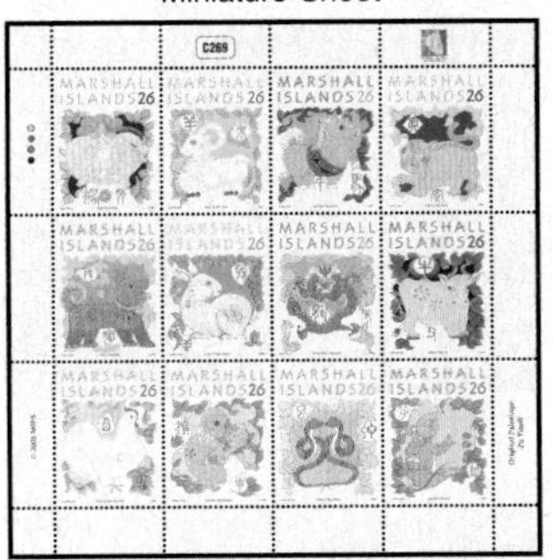

Chinese New Year Animals and Characters — A272

No. 905: a, Pig. b, Ram. c, Horse. d, Tiger. e, Dog. f, Rabbit. g, Dragon. h, Ox. i, Rooster. j, Monkey. k, Snake. l, Rat.

2008, Feb. 7

905 A272 26c Sheet of 12, #a-l 6.25 6.25

United States Lighthouses — A273

No. 906: a, St. Augustine Lighthouse, Florida. b, Old Cape Henry Lighthouse, Virginia. c, Cape Lookout Lighthouse, North Carolina. d, Tybee Island Lighthouse, Georgia. e, Morris Island Lighthouse, South Carolina. f, Hillsboro Inlet Lighthouse, Florida.

2008, Mar. 6 Litho. *Perf. 13½*

906 A273 41c Block of 6, #a-f 5.00 5.00

Miniature Sheet

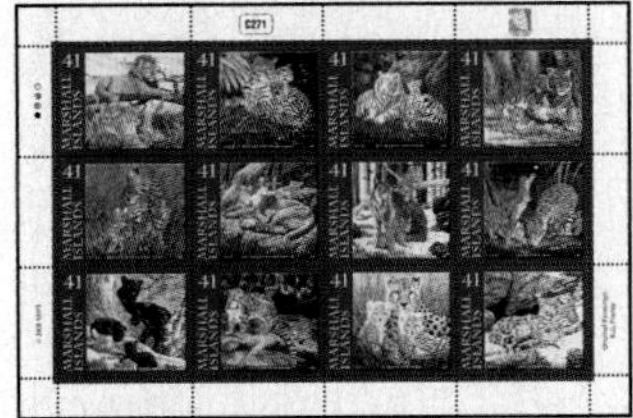

Wild Cats — A274

No. 907: a, Lion family at rest. b, Ocelot mother with cub sitting in grass. c, White Siberian tiger mother with cubs. d, Mother tiger with cubs lying in grass. e, Serval mother with cubs sitting in tall grass. f, North American cougar mother with cubs. g, Lynx mother with cubs. h, Jaguar with cubs at stream. i, Black panther mother with cubs. j, Clouded leopard mother with cubs. k, Cheetah with cubs lying in grass. l, Snow leopard with cubs.

2008, Mar. 26 Litho. *Perf. 13½*

907 A274 41c Sheet of 12, #a-l 10.00 10.00

Miniature Sheet

Sailing Ships — A275

No. 908: a, H.M.S. Victory. b, La Grande Hermine. c, U.S.S. Constitution. d, Fram. e, Tovarisch I. f, Ark and Dove. g, Rainbow. h, Great Republic. i, H.M.S. Resolution. j, La Dauphine. k, Kreuzenshtern. l, Golden Hind.

2008, Apr. 2

908 A275 41c Sheet of 12, #a-l 10.00 10.00

Miniature Sheet

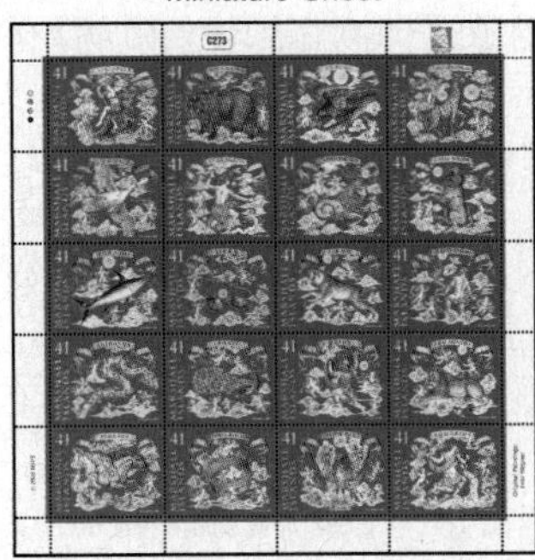

Constellations — A276

No. 909: a, Cassiopeia. b, Ursa Major. c, Corvus. d, Camelopardalis. e, Cygnus. f, Andromeda. g, Capricornus. h, Canis Major. i, Dorado. j, Libra. k, Lynx. l, Serpentarius. m, Eridanus. n, Pavo. o, Orion. p, Leo Minor. q, Pegasus. r, Corona Borealis. s, Phoenix. t, Aquarius.

2008, Apr. 29 Litho. *Perf. 13½*

909 A276 41c Sheet of 20, #a-t 16.50 16.50

See Nos. 945, 964.

Miniature Sheet

US Marine Corps — A277

No. 910: a, US liberates Marshall Islands. b, John Lejeune. c, Holland Smith. d, Smedley D. Butler. e, Daniel J. Daly. f, Lewis "Chesty" Puller. g, John Basilone. h, Alexander Vandegrift. i, Gregory "Pappy" Boyington. j, Marines raising flag on Iwo Jima.

2008, May 12

910 A277 42c Sheet of 10, #a-j 8.50 8.50

Tropical Fish A278

Designs: 1c, Banded butterflyfish. 3c, Damselfish. 5c, Pink skunk clownfish. 27c, Copperband butterflyfish. 42c, Threadfin butterflyfish. 60c, Beau Gregory damselfish. 61c, Porkfish. 63c, Goatfish. 94c, Common longnose butterflyfish. $1, Royal gramma. $4.80, Longfin bannerfish. $5, Blue-striped blenny. $16.50, Emperor butterflyfish.

2008 Litho. *Perf. 11¼x10¼*

No.	Type	Value	Unused	Used
911	A278	1c multi	.25	.25
912	A278	3c multi	.25	.25
913	A278	5c multi	.25	.25
914	A278	27c multi	.55	.55
915	A278	42c multi	.85	.85
916	A278	60c multi	1.25	1.25
917	A278	61c multi	1.25	1.25
918	A278	63c multi	1.25	1.25
919	A278	94c multi	1.90	1.90
920	A278	$1 multi	2.00	2.00
921	A278	$4.80 multi	9.75	9.75
922	A278	$5 multi	10.00	10.00
923	A278	$16.50 multi	33.00	33.00
	Nos. 911-923 (13)		62.55	62.55

Issued: Nos. 914, 915, 6/24; Nos. 919, 921, 923, 5/12. Nos. 911-913, 916-918, 920, 922, 9/9.

Miniature Sheet

Birds — A279

No. 924: a, Blue-gray tanager. b, St. Vincent parrot. c, Green-throated carib. d, Yellow oriole. e, Blue-hooded euphonia. f, Crested honeycreeper. g, Purple-capped fruit dove. h, Green magpie. i, Bay-headed tanager. j, Bananaquit. k, Cardinal honeyeater. l, Toco toucan. m, Cattle egret. n, Ringed kingfisher. o, Red-necked parrot. p, Purple gallinule. q, Copper-rumped hummingbird. r, Micronesian pigeon. s, Painted bunting. t, Black-naped oriole. u, Channel-billed toucan. v, Saddle-billed stork. w, Blood pheasant. x, Gray-crowned crane. y, Little blue heron.

2008, June 3 Litho. *Perf. 13½*

924 A279 42c Sheet of 25, #a-y 21.00 21.00

Miniature Sheet

Dinosaurs — A280

No. 925: a, Camarasaurus. b, Allosaurus. c, Parasaurolophus. d, Ornithomimus. e, Goniopholis. f, Camptosaurus. g, Edmontia. h, Ceratosaurus. i, Stegosaurus. j, Einiosaurus. k, Brachiosaurus. l, Corythosaurus.

2008, June 19
925 A280 42c Sheet of 12, #a-l 10.50 10.50

Miniature Sheet

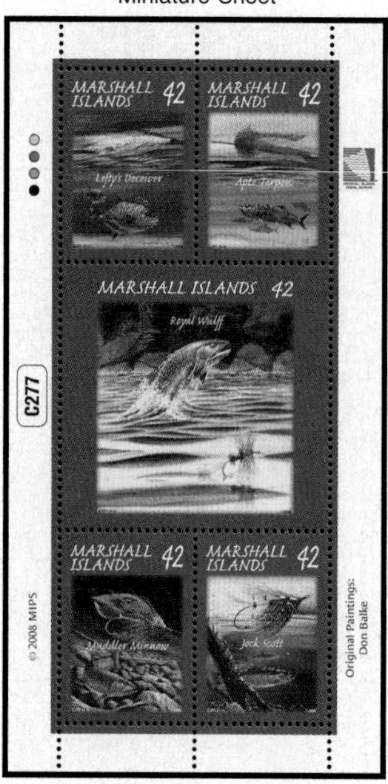

Fishing Flies — A281

No. 926: a, Lefty's Deceiver (25x35mm). b, Apte Tarpon (25x35mm). c, Royal Wulff (50x48mm). d, Muddler Minnow (25x35mm). e, Jock Scott (25x35mm).

2008, July 20
926 A281 42c Sheet of 5, #a-e 4.25 4.25

Miniature Sheet

Personalities of the Wild West — A282

No. 927: a, Wild Bill Hickok. b, Jim Bridger. c, Geronimo. d, Charles Goodnight. e, Chief Joseph. f, Kit Carson. g, Jim Beckwourth. h, Wyatt Earp. i, Bat Masterson. j, Bill Pickett. k, Bill Tilghman. l, Annie Oakley. m, Buffalo Bill Cody. n, Nellie Cashman. o, Sacagawea. p, John Fremont.

2008, Aug. 14
927 A282 42c Sheet of 16, #a-p 13.50 13.50

Endangered Species — A283

No. 928: a, Blue whale. b, Amazonian manatee. c, Hawaiian monk seal. d, Green turtle. e, Giant clam. f, Killer whale.

2008, Aug. 19 Litho. *Perf. 13½*
928 A283 42c Block of 6, #a-f 5.25 5.25

Marshallese Culture Type of 2005

No. 929, vert. — Photographs by J. Debrum: a, Lokeinlik Wearing Traditional Mat for Men. b, Limekto Weaving Hat from Kimej. c, Unfinished Outrigger. d, Young Boys in Mejit. e, Lonkoon with Fish Trap.

2008, Sept. 15 Litho. *Perf. 13½*
929 Horiz. strip of 5 4.25 4.25
a.-e. A250 42c Any single .85 .85

Miniature Sheet

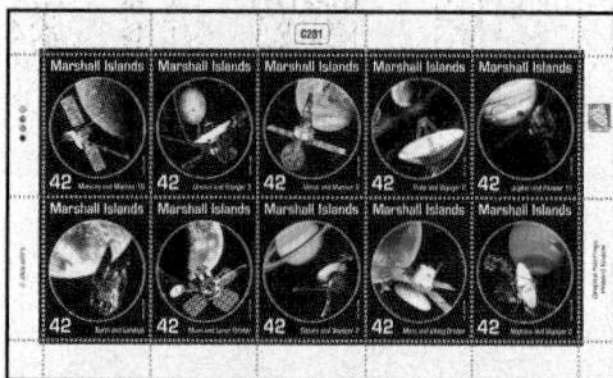

Spacecraft and the Solar System — A284

No. 930: a, Mercury, Mariner 10. b, Uranus, Voyager 2. c, Venus, Mariner 2. d, Pluto, Voyager 2. e, Jupiter, Pioneer 11. f, Earth, Landsat. g, Moon, Lunar Orbiter. h, Saturn, Voyager 2. i, Mars, Viking Orbiter. j, Neptune, Voyager 2.

2008, Oct. 1
930 A284 42c Sheet of 10, #a-j 8.50 8.50

Miniature Sheet

Christmas — A285

No. 931 — Song titles under ornament: a, Silent Night. b, We Three Kings. c, Deck the Halls. d, Hark, the Herald Angels Sing. e, O Little Town of Bethlehem. f, Joy to the World. g, Jingle Bells. h, O Come All Ye Faithful.

2008, Oct. 15 Litho. *Perf. 13½*
931 A285 42c Sheet of 8, #a-h 6.75 6.75

Owls — A286

No. 932: a, Barn owl. b, Barred owl. c, Burrowing owl. d, Snowy owl. e, Great horned owl. f, Spotted owl.

2008, Nov. 5
932 A286 42c Block of 6, #a-f 5.25 5.25

Souvenir Sheet

First United States Airmail Stamp, 90th Anniv. — A287

2008, Dec. 10 *Perf. 13x13½*
933 A287 $1 multi 2.00 2.00

Flower Bouquets Type of 2008

Miniature Sheet

No. 934 — Various bouquets with country name at bottom: a, Isle of Man. b, St. Lucia. c, Grenada. d, Bermuda. e, Anguilla. f, Barbados. g, Belize. h, St. Kitts. i, Hong Kong. j, British Virgin Islands. k, St. Vincent. l, Tristan da Cunha. m, St. Helena. n, British Antarctic Territory. o, St. Vincent and the Grenadines. p, New Zealand. q, Papua New Guinea. r, Western Samoa. s, Solomon Islands. t, Brunei. u, Swaziland. v, Botswana. w, Maldives. x, Ghana. y, Sierra Leone.

2009, Mar. 31 Litho. *Perf. 13½*
934 A271 42c Sheet of 25, #a-y 21.00 21.00

Pres. Abraham Lincoln (1809-65) — A288

No. 935 — Lincoln and: a, "Honesty." b, "Equality." c, "Unity." d, "Liberty."

2009, Apr. 7 Litho. *Perf. 13½*
935 A288 $1 Block of 4, #a-d 8.00 8.00

Arctic Explorers — A289

No. 936: a, Elisha Kent Kane, ships. b, Robert E. Peary, Matthew A. Henson, dog sled. c, Vilhjalmur Stefansson, ship, dog sled. d, Adolphus Washington Greely, ship.

2009, Apr. 14
936 A289 42c Block of 4, #a-d 3.50 3.50

Peary Expedition to North Pole, cent.

Miniature Sheet

Famous American Indians — A290

No. 937: a, Black Hawk. b, Colorow. c, Looking Glass. d, Dull Knife. e, Mangas Coloradas. f, Red Cloud. g, Little Raven. h, Black Kettle. i, Standing Bear. j, Little Crow. k, Seattle. l, Washakie.

2009, Apr. 21 Litho. *Perf. 13½*
937 A290 44c Sheet of 12, #a-l 11.00 11.00

See Nos. 960, 987.

Miniature Sheet

US Military Heroes of the Air — A291

No. 938: a, Richard I. Bong. b, Charles "Chuck" Yeager. c, Lauris Norstad. d, William "Billy" Mitchell. e, Curtis E. LeMay. f, Edward Henry O'Hare. g, Claire L. Chennault. h, George C. Kenney. i, James "Jimmy" Doolittle. j, Paul W. Tibbets, Jr. k, Benjamin O. Davis, Jr. l, Carl "Tooey" Spaatz. m, Ira C. Eaker. n, Edward "Eddie" Rickenbacker. o, Henry "Hap" Arnold. p, Map of Marshall Islands, birds, outrigger canoe, dolphin.

2009, Apr. 28
938 A291 44c Sheet of 16, #a-p 14.50 14.50

Souvenir Sheet

Marshall Islands Postal Service, 25th Anniv. — A292

2009, May 2 Litho. *Perf. 13x13½*
939 A292 44c multi .90 .90

Marine Life A293

Designs: 28c, Masked butterflyfish. 44c, Queen angelfish. 88c, Clownfish. 98c, Starfish. $1.22, Orca whale.

2009, May 11 Litho. ***Perf. 11¼x10¼***

940	A293	28c multi	.60	.60
941	A293	44c multi	.90	.90
942	A293	88c multi	1.75	1.75
943	A293	98c multi	2.00	2.00
944	A293	$1.22 multi	2.50	2.50
		Nos. 940-944 (5)	7.75	7.75

See No. 965.

Constellations Type of 2008
Miniature Sheet

No. 945: a, Antinous. b, Aquila. c, Cancer. d, Canis Major. e, Leo. f, Ara. g, Sextans Uraniae. h, Cepheus. i, Apus. j, Indus. k, Ursa Minor. l, Grus. m, Centaurus. n, Cetus. o, Piscis Volans. p, Lupus. q, Equuleus. r, Draco. s, Boötes. t, Scorpius.

2009, June 1 ***Perf. 13½***
945 A276 44c Sheet of 20, #a-t 18.00 18.00

2005-09 Rose Varieties of the Year — A294

No. 946: a, Summertime, 2005. b, Champagne Moment, 2006. c, Tickled Pink, 2007. d, Sweet Haze, 2008. e, Lucky!, 2009.

2009, June 18
946 Horiz. strip of 5 4.50 4.50
a.-e. A294 44c Any single .90 .90

Hot Air Balloons A295

No. 947: a, Montgolfier's balloon. b, Intrepid. c, Explorer II. d, Double Eagle. e, Contemporary balloons.

2009, July 13
947 Horiz. strip of 5 4.50 4.50
a.-e. A295 44c Any single .90 .90

July 22, 2009 Solar Eclipse — A296

No. 948 — Eclipse phases: a, Beginning (shown). b, Totality and near-totality. c, Ending.

2009, July 22
948 Horiz. strip of 3 2.75 2.75
a.-c. A296 44c Any single .90 .90

Steam Locomotives — A297

No. 949: a, Samson. b, Best Friend of Charleston. c, John Bull. d, Gowan & Marx. e, Stourbridge Lion. f, Brother Jonathan.

2009, Aug. 6 Litho. ***Perf. 13½***
949 A297 44c Block of 6, #a-f 5.50 5.50

Marshallese Culture Type of 2005

No. 950 — Photographs by J. Debrum: a, Making Arrowroot Lagoonside. b, Boats in Lagoon, One Capsized for Repair. c, Family Portrait in Front of Wooden Home with Pandanus Roof. d, Man Carrying Fish Trap. e, Portrait of New Year and LemeLali Weaving Baskets.

2009, Sept. 1 Litho. ***Perf. 13½***
950 Horiz. strip of 5 4.50 4.50
a.-e. A250 44c Any single .90 .90

Eagles — A298

No. 951: a, Philippine eagle. b, Tawny eagle. c, Martial eagle. d, Bald eagle. e, African fish eagle. f, Bataleur eagle. g, Golden eagle. h, Harpy eagle.

2009, Sept. 14 Litho. ***Perf. 13½***
951 A298 44c Block of 8, #a-h 7.25 7.25

Dogs — A299

No. 952: a, Beagle and Boston terrier. b, Chesapeake Bay retriever and Cocker spaniel. c, Alaskan malamute and Collie. d, Water spaniel and Basset hound. e, Coonhound and Foxhound.

No. 953, horiz.: a, Old English sheepdog. b, Irish setter. c, Welsh springer spaniel. d, West Highland terrier.

2009, Oct. 5 Litho. ***Perf. 13½***
952 Horiz. strip of 5 4.50 4.50
a.-e. A299 44c Any single .90 .90
953 Sheet of 4 8.00 8.00
a.-d. A299 98c Any single 2.00 2.00

Christmas A300

No. 954: a, Chili wreath. b, Christmas wreath. c, Traditional wreath. d, Tropical wreath. e, Colonial wreath.

2009, Oct. 15 Litho. ***Perf. 13½***
954 Horiz. strip of 5 4.50 4.50
a.-e. A300 44c Any single .90 .90

Miniature Sheet

Endangered Species — A301

No. 955: a, Giant anteater. b, Caracal. c, Wild yak. d, Giant panda. e, Black-footed ferret. f, Black rhinoceros. g, Golden lion tamarin. h, African elephant. i, Persian fallow deer. j, Polar bear. k, Ocelot. l, Gorilla.

2009, Nov. 2 Litho. ***Perf. 13½***
955 A301 44c Sheet of 12, #a-l 11.00 11.00

Prehistoric Animals — A302

No. 956: a, Mastodons on prairie. b, Eohippus. c, Woolly mammoth. d, Saber-toothed cat. e, Mastodons in marsh.

2009, Nov. 24
956 Horiz. strip of 5 4.50 4.50
a.-e. A302 44c Any single .90 .90

Shells — A303

No. 957: a, Paper nautilus. b, Giant tun. c, Pilgrim's scallop. d, Gibbula magus.

2009, Dec. 8
957 A303 44c Block of 4, #a-d 3.75 3.75

Miniature Sheet

Signs of the Zodiac — A304

No. 958: a, Aquarius. b, Pisces. c, Aries. d, Taurus. e, Gemini. f, Cancer. g, Leo. h, Virgo. i, Libra. j, Scorpio. k, Sagittarius. l, Capricorn.

2010, Jan. 5 ***Perf. 11¾***
958 A304 44c Sheet of 12, #a-l 11.00 11.00

Miniature Sheet

Waterfowl — A305

No. 959: a, European wigeon. b, Tufted ducks. c, Mallards. d, Gadwall. e, Snow geese. f, Pintail ducks. g, Northern shoveler. h, Canvasback ducks.

2010, Feb. 10 Litho. ***Perf. 11¾***
959 A305 44c Sheet of 8, #a-h 7.25 7.25

Famous American Indians Type of 2009
Miniature Sheet

No. 960: a, Osceola. b, Lone Wolf. c, Menawa. d, Wabasha. e, Captain Jack. f, Quanah Parker. g, Ouray. h, Mannelito. i, Cochise. j, Satanta. k, Massasoit. l, Red Eagle.

2010, Mar. 4 Litho. ***Perf. 13½***
960 A290 44c Sheet of 12, #a-l 11.00 11.00

Boy Scouts of America, Cent. — A306

No. 961 — Background color: a, Olive green. b, Red. c, Yellow bister. d, Blue.

2010, Mar. 18 Litho. ***Perf. 13½***
961 A306 44c Block of 4, #a-d 3.75 3.75

Shells — A307

No. 962: a, Paper nautilus. b, Giant tun. c, Pilgrim's scallop. d, Gibbula magus.

2010, Mar. 29 Litho. ***Perf. 13½***
962 A307 98c Block of 4, #a-d 8.00 8.00

See Nos. 971-972.

Astronomers A308

No. 963: a, Nicolaus Copernicus. b, Johannes Kepler. c, Galileo Galilei. d, Sir Isaac Newton. e, Sir William Herschel.

2010, Apr. 7
963 Horiz. strip of 5 4.50 4.50
a.-e. A308 44c Any single .90 .90

No. 963e is incorrectly inscribed "Hirschel."

Constellations Type of 2008

No. 964: a, Columba. b, Virgo. c, Argo Navis. d, Tucana (Toucan). e, Aries. f, Coma Berenices. g, Delphinus. h, Perseus. i, Taurus. j, Monoceros. k, Gemini. l, Vulpecula. m, Lepus. n, Auriga. o, Pisces. p, Sagittarius. q, Crater. r, Lyra. s, Hercules. t, Canes Venatici.

2010, June 1
964 A276 44c Sheet of 20, #a-t 18.00 18.00

Fish Type of 2009

2010, June 1 ***Perf. 11¼x10¼***
965 A293 28c Mandarin goby .60 .60

Marshallese Alphabet — A309

No. 966 — Letters and Marshallese words: a, "A," Amata (first name of first Marshallese president). b, "A with macron," Aj (to weave). c, "B," Babbub (butterfly). d, "D," Deo (beautiful young lady). e, "E," Ek (fish). f, "I," Iokwe (rainbow). g, "J," Jaki (mat). h, "K," Imon Kien (house of government). i, "L," Loktanur (star Capella). j, "L with cedilla," Lokwajek (red-tailed tropic bird). k, "M," Ma (breadfruit). l, "M with cedilla," Makmok (arrowroot plant). m, "N," Ni (coconut tree). n, "N with cedilla," No (ocean wave). o, "N with macron," Niin-pako (shark tooth). p, "O," Ok (fish net). q, "O with cedilla," Eo (tattoo). r, "O with macron," Oo (lionfish). s, "P," Pejak (visitor's hut). t, "R," Raj (whale). u, "T," Tipnol (outrigger sailing canoe). v, "U," Urur (fire). w, "U with macron," Ulin-raj (dorsal fin of whale). x, "W," Wojla (woven pandanus leaf sail).

2010, June 16 Litho. ***Perf. 13½***
966 Sheet of 24 22.00 22.00
a.-x. A309 44c Any single .90 .90

Miniature Sheet

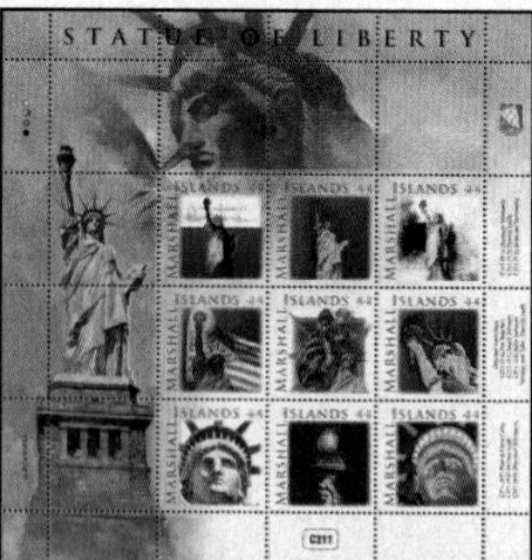

Statue of Liberty — A310

No. 967 — Statue of Liberty: a, Red clouds and water (9-1). b, Blue background (9-2). c, Brown and gray clouds (9-3). d, American flag (9-4). e, Frederic Bartholdi (9-5). f, Blue background, diff. (9-6). g, White background around head (9-7). h, Torch (9-8). i, Brown background around head (9-9).

2010, June 17 ***Perf. 11¾***
967 A310 44c Sheet of 9, #a-i, + 7 labels 8.25 8.25

Miniature Sheet

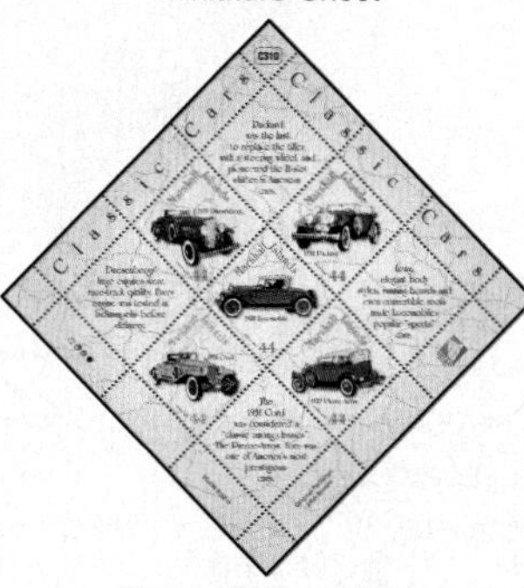

Classic Cars — A311

No. 968: a, 1935 Duesenberg. b, 1932 Packard. c, 1928 Locomobile. d, 1931 Cord. e, 1929 Pierce Arrow.

2010, July 7
968 A311 44c Sheet of 5, #a-e, + 4 labels 4.50 4.50

Carousel Horses — A312

No. 969 — Various carousel horses numberd: a, (6-1). b, (6-2). c, (6-3). d, (6-4). e, (6-5). f, (6-6).

2010, Aug. 12 ***Perf. 13½***
969 A312 44c Block of 6, #a-f 5.50 5.50

US Warships of World War II — A313

No. 970: a, USS Nevada. b, USS Missouri. c, USS Wisconsin. d, USS Oregon. e, USS Massachusetts. f, USS North Carolina. g, USS Texas. h, USS Idaho. i, USS New Jersey. j, USS Colorado. k, USS South Dakota. l, USS New Mexico. m, USS Washington. n, USS Iowa. o, USS Alabama.

2010, Sept. 2 ***Perf. 13½***
970 Sheet of 15 13.50 13.50
a.-o. A313 44c Any single .90 .90

Shells Type of 2010

Designs: 28c, Pilgrim's scallop. 98c, Gibbula magus.

2010, Sept. 20
971 A307 28c multi .60 .60
972 A307 98c multi 2.00 2.00

Marshallese Culture Type of 2005

No. 973 — Photographs by L. Debrum: a, Church Buildings in Likiep. b, Ijuran Ready to Launch. c, Group of People, One Man Holding Fish Net. d, Lejek with Fish Trap on Korkor in Likiep. e, Landscape with Outrigger and Sailboat.

2010, Sept.14 ***Perf. 13½***
973 Horiz. strip of 5 4.50 4.50
a.-e. A250 44c Any single .90 .90

Christmas — A314

No. 974 — Various depictions of Santa Claus numbered: a, (4-1). b, (4-2). c, (4-3). d, (4-4).

2010, Oct. 18
974 Horiz. strip of 4 3.75 3.75
a.-d. A314 44c Any single .90 .90

Miniature Sheet

Pres. John F. Kennedy (1917-63) — A315

No. 975 — Various portraits of Kennedy numbered: a, (6-1). b, (6-2). c, (6-3). d, (6-4). e, (6-5). f, (6-6).

2010, Nov. 3
975 A315 44c Sheet of 6, #a-f, + 6 labels 5.50 5.50

Miniature Sheet

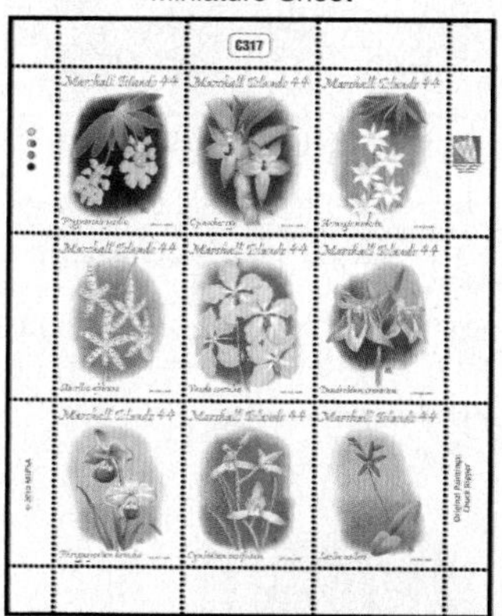
Orchids — A316

No. 976: a, Psygmorchis purilla. b, Cycnoches spp. c, Aerangis modesta. d, Ansellia africana. e, Vanda coerulea. f, Dendrobium cruentum. g, Phragmipedium korachii. h, Cymbdium ensifolium. i, Laelia milleri.

2010, Nov. 17
976 A316 44c Sheet of 9, #a-i 8.00 8.00

Miniature Sheet

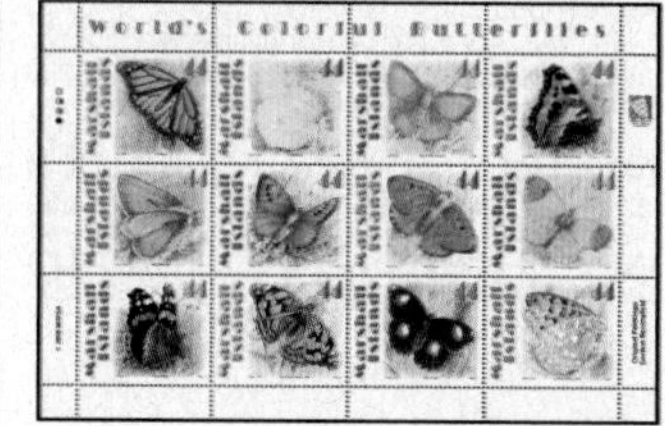

Butterflies — A317

No. 977: a, Monarch. b, Brimstone. c, Blue-spot hairstreak. d, Small tortoiseshell. e, Small skipper. f, Large blue. g, Large copper. h, Eastern orange-tip. i, Red admiral. j, American painted lady. k, Great eggfly. l, Dark green fritillary.

2010, Dec. 8
977 A317 44c Sheet of 12, #a-l 11.00 11.00

Tulips A318

No. 978 — Inscriptions: a, Yellow tulip. b, Tulips. c, Purple tulips. d, Red and black tulips. e, Yellow and orange tulips. f, Red tulips.

2011, Jan. 11
978 Block of 6 5.50 5.50
a.-f. A318 44c Any single .90 .90

Miniature Sheet

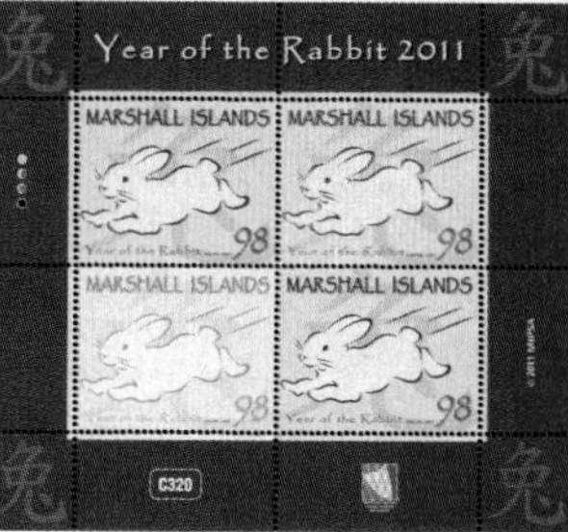

New Year 2011 (Year of the Rabbit) — A319

No. 979 — Rabbit in: a, Blue. b, Red violet. c, Bister. d, Green.

2011, Feb. 3
979 A319 98c Sheet of 4, #a-d 8.00 8.00

Pres. Ronald Reagan (1911-2004) A320

No. 980 — Inscription: a, Early years. b, Movie actor. c, Governor of California. d, 40th President. e, Elder statesman/late years.

2011, Feb. 6
980 Horiz. strip of 5 4.50 4.50
a.-e. A320 44c Any single .90 .90

Firsts in Flight A321

No. 981 — Inscription: a, Centennial of first airmail flight. b, First airmail service in America. c, First U.S. coast-to-coast airmail service. d, First permanent U.S. transcontinental airmail service. e, First international airmail service.

2011, Feb. 18
981 Horiz. strip of 5 4.50 4.50
a.-e. A321 44c Any single .90 .90

See Nos. 988, 994, 1004, 1012.

Turtles
A322

Designs: 1c, Green turtle. 2c, Loggerhead turtle. 5c, Leatherback turtle. $10, Hawksbill turtle.

Perf. 11¼x10¼

2011, Feb. 22 **Litho.**

982	A322	1c multi	.25	.25
983	A322	2c multi	.25	.25
984	A322	5c multi	.25	.25
985	A322	$10 multi	20.00	20.00
	Nos. 982-985 (4)		20.75	20.75

Corals and Fish — A323

No. 986 — Inscriptions: a, Flora & fauna of the Pacific Ocean. b, Chalice coral. c, Elkhorn coral. d, Brain coral. e, Finger coral.

2011, Mar. 10 ***Perf. 13½***

986 Horiz. strip of 5 3.00 3.00
a.-e. A323 29c Any single .60 .60

Famous American Indians Type of 2009

No. 987: a, Pontiac. b, Barboncito. c, Geronimo. d, Victorio. e, Sitting Bull. f, Cornplanter. g, Uncas. h, Little Wolf. i, Crazy Horse. j, Gall. k, Joseph. l, Tecumseh.

2011, Mar. 22

987 A290 44c Sheet of 12, #a-l 11.00 11.00

Firsts in Flight Type of 2011

No. 988 — Inscriptions: a, First manned flight. b, First manned flight of semi-controlled airship. c, First powered aircraft leaves the ground. d, First manned flight of powered, controlled airship. e, First controlled powered flight.

2011, Apr. 12

988 Horiz. strip of 5 4.50 4.50
a.-e. A321 44c Any single .90 .90

First Man in Space, 50th Anniv. A324

No. 989: a, Rocket launch, Yuri Gagarin on medal. b, Gagarin wearing space helmet, spacecraft, Earth. c, Monument, Apollo and Soyuz spacecraft docked, medal.

2011, Apr. 12

989 Strip of 3 6.00 6.00
a.-c. A324 $1 Any single 2.00 2.00

Printed in sheets containing three strips and seven labels.

Miniature Sheet

Wedding of Prince William and Catherine Middleton — A325

No. 990 — Various flowers numbered: a, 15-1. b, 15-2. c, 15-3. d, 15-4. e, 15-5. f, 15-6. g, 15-7. h, 15-8. i, 15-9. j, 15-10. k, 15-11. l, 15-12. m, 15-13. n, 15-14. o,15-15.

2011, Apr. 29

990 A325 44c Sheet of 15, #a-o 13.50 13.50

Miniature Sheet

Apostles of Jesus — A326

No. 991: a, Andrew. b, Philip. c, Simon. d, James the Lesser. e, Paul. f, Matthew. g, James the Greater. h, Thaddeus. i, Peter. j, John. k, Bartholomew. l, Thomas.

2011, May 2

991 A326 44c Sheet of 12, #a-l 11.00 11.00

Miniature Sheet

Garden Life — A327

No. 992: a, Great eggfly butterfly. b, Passionflower. c, Ladybug. d, Emperor dragonfly. e, Sweet white violet. f, Magpie moth. g, Bluets. h, Katydid. i, Painted lady butterfly. j, Bumblebee. k, Stag beetle. l, Large tortoiseshell butterfly.

2011, May 28

992 A327 44c Sheet of 12, #a-l 11.00 11.00

Miniature Sheet

Antarctic Treaty, 50th Anniv. — A328

No. 993: a, Penguin and ship (6-1). b, Emperor penguin and juvenile (6-2). c, Penguin and ship (6-3). d, Two penguins on iceberg (6-4). e, King penguin mother and baby (6-5). f, King penguin mothers with babies (6-6). g, Penguin and ship (6-7). h, Two adult Emperor penguins and juvenile (6-8). i, Penguin and ship (6-9).

2011, June 23

993 A328 98c Sheet of 9, #a-i, + 7 labels 18.00 18.00

Firsts in Flight Type of 2011

No. 994 — Inscriptions: a, First flight to land on a ship. b, First non-stop North American coast-to-coast flight. c, First non-stop transatlantic flight. d, First round-the-world flight. e, First flight over the North Pole.

2011, July 7

994 Horiz. strip of 5 4.50 4.50
a.-e. A321 44c Any single .90 .90

Outrigger Canoes — A329

Plumeria Flowers — A330

Marshall Islands Flag — A331

Coconut Palm Trees and Coconuts — A332

Micronesian Pigeons — A333

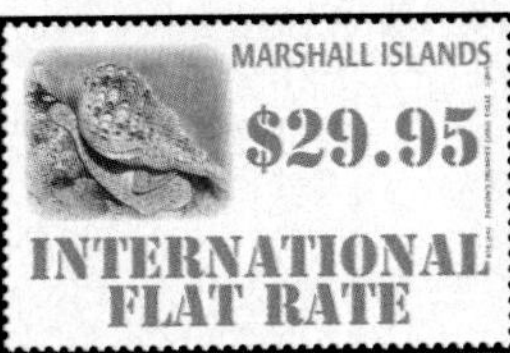

Triton's Trumpet — A334

2011, July 7

995	A329	$4.95 multi	10.00	10.00
996	A330	$10.95 multi	22.00	22.00
997	A331	$13.95 multi	28.00	28.00
998	A332	$14.95 multi	30.00	30.00
999	A333	$18.30 multi	37.00	37.00
1000	A334	$29.95 multi	60.00	60.00
	Nos. 995-1000 (6)		187.00	187.00

Miniature Sheet

End of Space Shuttle Missions — A335

No. 1001 — Space Shuttle: a, And schematic diagrams. b, Lifting off. c, And eagle. d, In orbit. e, On approach for landing. f, Lifting off, U.S. flag in background. g, And planets.

2011, July 21

1001 A335 44c Sheet of 7, #a-g, + 8 labels 6.25 6.25

The label on No. 1001 with the names of the Challenger astronauts has the name of "Judith Resnik" misspelled as "Judith Resuik." The sheet was reprinted later in 2011 with the corrected spelling.

Marshallese Culture Type of 2005

No. 1002 — Photographs by L. Debrum: a, Celebration of Alfonso Capelle's Kemen. b, Three Women Making Pandanus Thatch. c, Men Spearfishing on Reef Oceaside of Likiep. d, Men in Boathouse Grinding Arrowroot. e, The Boat Vilma Being Launched at Likiep.

2011, July 22

1002 Horiz. strip of 5 4.50 4.50
a.-e. A250 44c Any single .90 .90

Miniature Sheet

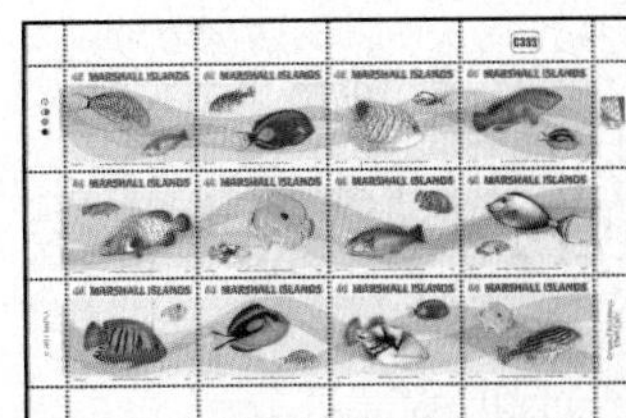

Fish — A336

No. 1003: a, Blue-banded surgeonfish, Bleeker's parrotfish. b, Achilles tang, Oriental sweetlips. c, Regal angelfish, Orangespine unicornfish. d, Coral grouper, Palette surgeonfish. e, Peacock grouper, Coral grouper. f, Bennett's butterflyfish, Picassofish. g, Bleeker's parrotfish, Flame angelfish. h, Orangespine unicornfish, Peacock grouper. i, Flame angelfish, Regal angelfish. j, Palette surgeonfish, Blue-banded surgeonfish. k, Picassofish, Achilles tang. l, Oriental sweetlips, Bennett's butterflyfish.

2011, Aug. 11

1003 A336 44c Sheet of 12, #a-l 11.00 11.00

Firsts in Flight Type of 2011

No. 1004 — Inscriptions: a, First turbojet flight. b, First jet fighter flight. c, First jet passenger service. d, First Transatlantic jet passenger service. e, First supersonic commercial aircraft.

2011, Aug. 21

1004 Horiz. strip of 5 4.50 4.50
a.-e. A321 44c Any single .90 .90

National Buildings and Symbols A337

Designs: No. 1005, 64c, Capitol Building. No. 1006, 64c, Nitijela Building. No. 1007, 64c, National seal, vert. No. 1008, 64c, National flag, vert.

Perf. 11¼x10¼, 10¼x11¼

2011, Aug. 31 **Litho.**

1005-1008 A337 Set of 4 5.25 5.25

Souvenir Sheet

Marshall Islands No. 411 — A338

2011, Sept. 17 **Litho.** *Perf. 13½*

1009 A338 $4.95 multi 10.00 10.00

Admission to the United Nations, 20th anniv.

Miniature Sheet

Christmas — A339

No. 1010: a, 10c, Christmas shopping. b, 20c, Cutting Christmas tree. c, 30c, Putting wreath on door. d, 40c, Caroling in cathedral at Christmas. e, 50c, Bringing home the tree. f, 60c, A winter sleigh ride. g, 70c, Arrival in sleigh at church. h, 80c, A pause in the sleigh ride. i, 90c, Christmas caroling outside church. j, $1, Sleigh ride to get Christmas tree. k, $1.10, Western Christmas. l, $1.20, Christmas caroling.

2011, Oct. 13

1010 A339 Sheet of 12, #a-l 16.00 16.00

Souvenir Sheet

Compact of Free Association, 25th Anniv. — A340

No. 1011: a, Marshall Islands national seal. b, Walap sailing. c, Marshall Islands flag.

2011, Oct. 21

1011 A340 98c Sheet of 3, #a-c, + 3 labels 6.00 6.00

Firsts in Flight Type of 2011

No. 1012 — Inscriptions: a, First man to fly faster than sound. b, First man in space. c, First astronaut in space. d, First man to walk in space. e, First man on the Moon.

2011, Nov. 4

1012 Horiz. strip of 5 4.50 4.50
a.-e. A321 44c Any single .90 .90

Hanukkah — A341

No. 1013 — Various menorahs on: a, Day 1. b, Day 2. c, Day 3. d, Day 4. e, Day 5. f, Day 6. g, Day 7. h, Day 8.

2011, Nov. 20 **Litho.** *Perf. 13½*

1013 A341 44c Block of 8, #a-h 7.25 7.25

Miniature Sheet

American Entry Into World War II, 70th Anniv. — A342

No. 1014 — Inscriptions: a, Burma Road, 717-mile lifeline to China. b, Roosevelt calls for America's first peacetime draft. c, U.S must become "Great Arsenal" to save democracy. d, Lend-Lease Act, aid to our allies. e, Roosevelt, Churchill draft 8 peace aims, joint steps believed changed at parley. f, U.S. Destroyer Reuben James sunk by German U-boat. g, Civil defense mobilizes the U.S.A. h, Kaiser launches Liberty ships. i, War! Oahu bombed by Japanese planes. j, Congress declares war on Japan, 1500 killed in attack on Hawaii.

2011, Dec. 7

1014 A342 44c Sheet of 10, #a-j, + 10 labels 9.00 9.00

See Nos. 1035, 1065, 1089, 1123.

Miniature Sheet

Stained Glass Windows — A343

No. 1015 — Stained glass windows of: a, Cathedral of Santa Maria del Fiore, Florence, Italy (9-1). b, Nidaros Cathedral, Trondheim, Norway (9-2). c, Canterbury Cathedral, Canterbury, England (9-3). d, Notre Dame Cathedral, Tournai, Belgium (9-4). e, Cathedral of Monaco (9-5). f, St. John's Church, Gouda, Netherlands (9-6). g, St. Florin's Cathedral, Vaduz, Liechtenstein (9-7). h, St. Mary the Crowned Cathedral, Gibraltar (9-8). i, Parish Church of St. Saviour, Jersey (9-9).

2011, Dec. 9

1015 A343 44c Sheet of 9, #a-i 8.00 8.00

Miniature Sheet

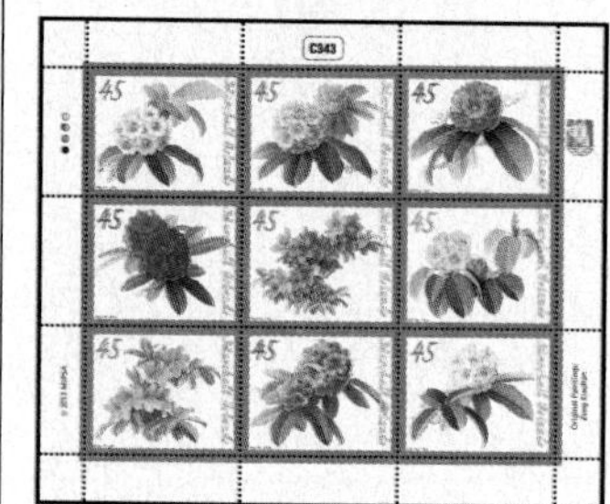
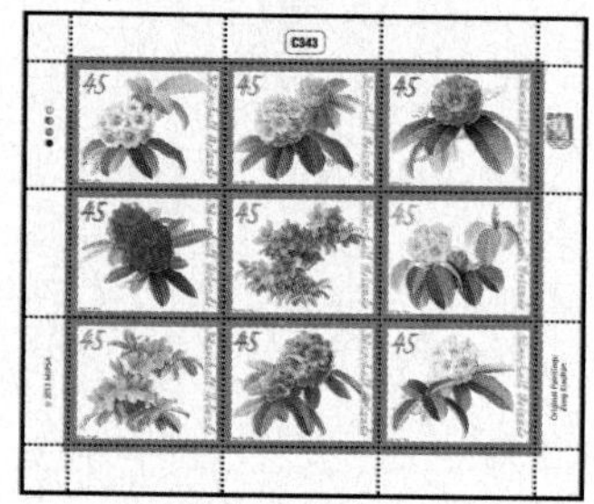

Rhododendrons — A344

No. 1016 — Various rhododendrons numbered: a, (9-1). b, (9-2). c, (9-3). d, (9-4). e, (9-5). f, (9-6). g, (9-7). h, (9-8). i, (9-9).

2012, Jan. 10

1016 A344 45c Sheet of 9, #a-i 8.25 8.25

Marine Life — A345

2012, Jan. 22

1017 A345 45c multi .90 .90

Miniature Sheet

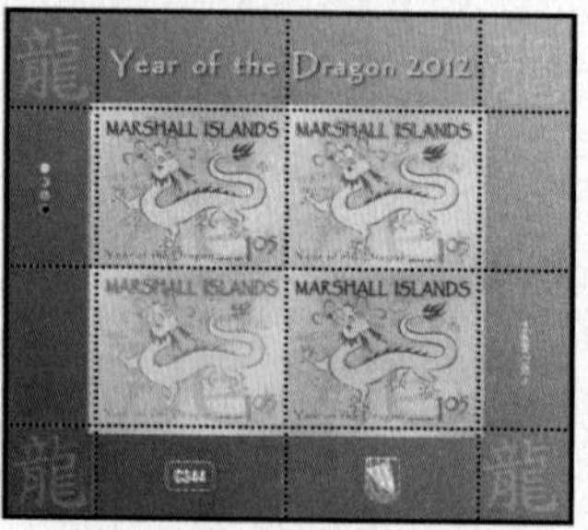

New Year 2012 (Year of the Dragon) — A346

No. 1018 — Background color: a, Blue. b, Pink. c, Yellow green. d, Green.

2012, Jan. 23

1018 A346 $1.05 Sheet of 4, #a-d 8.50 8.50

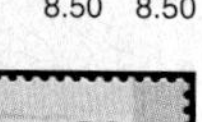

Whales A347

No. 1019: a, Right whales. b, Killer whales. c, Gervais's whales. d, Blue whales.

2012, Feb. 20 *Perf. 13½*

1019 Horiz. strip of 4 2.60 2.60
a.-d. A347 32c Any single .65 .65

Chuuk War Canoe — A348

Cymbidium Orchid — A349

Arrival of Early Inhabitants — A350

Mandarinfish — A351

Hibiscus Rosa-sinensis — A352

Seahorses — A353

2012, Feb. 27

1020	A348	$5.15 multi	10.00	10.00
1021	A349	$11.35 multi	22.50	22.50
1022	A350	$15.45 multi	31.00	31.00
1023	A351	$16.95 multi	34.00	34.00
1024	A352	$18.95 multi	37.50	37.50
1025	A353	$38 multi	75.00	75.00
	Nos. 1020-1025 (6)		210.00	210.00

Compare No. 1020 with No. 1042.

Miniature Sheet

Reign of Queen Elizabeth II, 60th Anniv. — A354

No. 1026 — Stamps of Great Britain depicting Queen Elizabeth II: a, #MH206 (10p). b, #MH211 (20p). c, #MH219 (30p). d, #MH266 (40p). e, #MH385 (50p). f, #MH397 (60p).

2012, Feb. 6
1026 A354 $1.05 Sheet of 6, #a-f 13.00 13.00

Birds A355

Designs: 85c, Black-footed albatross. $1.05, Red-tailed tropic bird.

2012, Feb. 27 ***Perf. 11¼x10¼***
1027 A355 85c multi 1.75 1.75
1028 A355 $1.05 multi 2.10 2.10

Chinese Terra Cotta Warriors — A356

No. 1029: a, General figure (6-1). b, Kneeling shooter (6-2). c, Armor warriors (6-3). d, Arrow shooter (6-4). e, General figure (6-5). f, Heavy armor (6-6).

2012, Mar. 15 ***Perf. 13½***
1029 A356 45c Block of 6, #a-f 5.50 5.50

Inuits — A357

No. 1030: a, Inuits enjoy a hot drink in their igloo. b, Inuit crafts and sculptures. c, Inuit drummers and dancers. d, Inuit men fishing with harpoons. e, Inuit family in skin tent. f, Inuit hunting.

2012, Mar. 26
1030 A357 45c Block of 6, #a-f 5.50 5.50

Creation of Tobolar Coconut Twine and Rope A358

No. 1031: a, Husking the ripe coconuts after they come off the tree. b, Soaking the husks in sea water under mat and stones. c, Pounding the husks to separate the twine from the meat. d, Making twine and rope from the husk fibers.

2012, Apr. 8
1031 Horiz. strip of 4 3.75 3.75
a.-d. A358 45c Any single .90 .90

Miniature Sheet

Scientists — A359

No. 1032: a, Charles Darwin. b, William Harvey. c, Robert Boyle. d, Johannes Kepler. e, Thomas Edison. f, André-Marie Ampère. g, Michael Faraday. h, Jöns Jacob Berzelius. i, James Watt. j, Galileo Galilei. k, Andreas Vesalius. l, Antoine Lavoisier. m, Dmitry Mendeleyev. n, Carl Gauss. o, Isaac Newton. p, Gregor Mendel. q, John Dalton. r, Carl Linnaeus. s, Robert Fulton. t, William Thomson, Baron Kelvin.

2012, Apr. 23 ***Perf. 13½***
1032 A359 45c Sheet of 20, #a-t 18.00 18.00

Miniature Sheet

Clouds — A360

No. 1033: a, Altocumulus undulatus. b, Altostratus translucidus. c, Cirrostratus fibratus. d, Cumulus congestus. e, Cumulonimbus incus. f, Cirrus radiatus. g, Cirrocumulus undulatus. h, Cumulonimbus with tornado. i, Cumulus humilis. j, Cumulonimbus mammatus. k, Stratus opacus. l, Altocumulus castellanus. m, Altocumulus stratiformis. n, Altocumulus lenticularis. o, Stratocumulus undulatus.

2012, May 10
1033 A360 45c Sheet of 15, #a-o 13.50 13.50

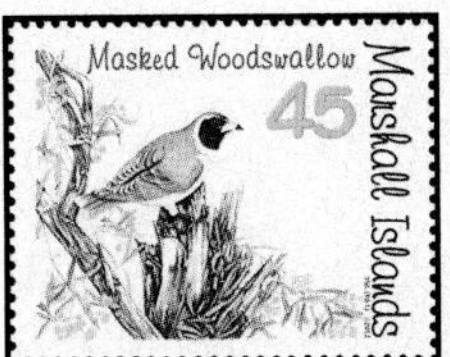

Birds A361

No. 1034: a, Masked woodswallow. b, Golden-shouldered parrot. c, Regent bowerbird. d, King parrot. e, Rainbow pitta. f, Rainbow bee-eaters on branch. g, White-tailed kingfisher. h, Spotted catbird. i, Rainbow bee-eater in flight. j, Western magpie.

2012, June 18
1034 Block of 10 9.00 9.00
a.-j. A361 45c Any single .90 .90

World War II Type of 2011

Miniature Sheet

No. 1035 — Inscriptions: a, Tokyo bombed! b, Roosevelt praises U.S. rationing effort. c, U.S. wins great naval battle in Coral Sea. d, Corregidor surrenders under land attack after withstanding 300 raids from the air. e, Japanese make landings in Aleutian Islands; U.S. warships attack Attu Island, defeat Japs. f, Codebreaking: Turning the tide in the Pacific. g, Jap fleet smashed by U.S., 2 carriers sunk at Midway. h, Women in the war: "Rosie the Riveter." i, Marines gain hold on Solomon Islands; ships and planes wage fights. j, American forces land in French Africa.

2012, July 3
1035 A342 45c Sheet of 10, #a-j, + 10 labels 9.00 9.00

Miniature Sheet

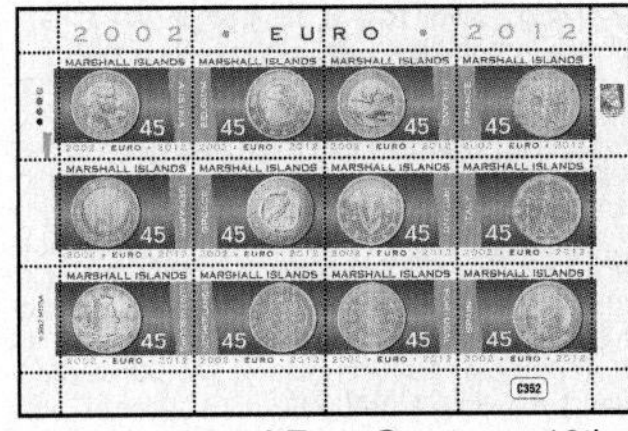

Introduction of Euro Currency, 10th Anniv. — A362

No. 1036 — 1-euro coins of: a, Austria. b, Belgium. c, Finland. d, France. e, Germany. f, Greece. g, Ireland. h, Italy. i, Luxembourg. j, Netherlands. k, Portugal. l, Spain.

2012, July 16
1036 A362 45c Sheet of 12, #a-l 11.00 11.00

Miniature Sheet

American Civil War, 150th Anniv. — A363

No. 1037 — U.S. stamps commemorating Civil War centennial: a, #1178 (Fort Sumter, 34x25mm). b, #1179 (Battle of Shiloh, 34x25mm). c, #1180 (Battle of Gettysburg, 34x25mm). d, #1181 (Battle of the Wilderness, 34x25mm). d, #1182 (Surrender at Appomattox, 48x50mm).

2012, July 25
1037 A363 45c Sheet of 5, #a-e 4.50 4.50

American Indian Dances — A364

No. 1038: a, Traditional Dance. b, Raven Dance. c, Fancy Dance. d, Hoop Dance. e, Grass Dance. f, Butterfly Dance.

2012, Aug. 16
1038 A364 45c Block of 6, #a-f 5.50 5.50

Souvenir Sheet

USS Constitution and HMS Guerrière — A365

2012, Aug. 20
1039 A365 $4.95 multi + 4 labels 10.00 10.00

War of 1812, bicent.

Miniature Sheet

Christmas — A366

No. 1040 — Items from carol *The Twelve Days of Christmas*: a, Partridge in a pear tree (12-1). b, Two turtle doves (12-2). c, Three French hens (12-3). d, Four calling birds (12-4). e, Five golden rings (12-5). f, Six geese a-layiing (12-6). g, Seven swans a-swimming (12-7). h, Eight maids a-milking (12-8). i, Nine drummers drumming (12-9). j, Ten pipers piping (12-10). k, Eleven ladies dancing (12-11). l, Twelve lords a-leaping (12-12).

2012, Sept. 28
1040 A366 45c Sheet of 12, #a-l 11.00 11.00

Locomotives of the Fifty States — A367

No. 1041 — Steam locomotive from: a, Alabama. b, Alaska. c, Arizona. d, Arkansas. e, California. f, Colorado. g, Connecticut. h, Delaware. i, Florida. j, Georgia. k, Hawaii. l, Idaho. m, Illinois. n, Indiana. o, Iowa. p, Kansas. q, Kentucky. r, Louisiana. s, Maine. t, Maryland. u, Massachusetts. v, Michigan. w, Minnesota. x, Mississippi. y, Missouri. z, Montana. aa, Nebraska. ab, Nevada. ac, New Hampshire. ad, New Jersey. ae, New Mexico. af, New York. ag, North Carolina. ah, North Dakota. ai, Ohio. aj, Oklahoma. ak, Oregon. al, Pennsylvania. am, Rhode Island. an, South Carolina. ao, South Dakota. ap, Tennessee. aq, Texas. ar, Utah. as, Vermont. at, Virginia. au, Washington. av, West Virginia. aw, Wisconsin. ax, Wyoming.

2012, Nov. 3
1041 Sheet of 50 45.00 45.00
a.-ax. A367 45c Any single .90 .90

Chuuk War Canoe A368

2012, Nov. 8 ***Perf. 11¼x10¼***
1042 A368 $5.15 multi 10.00 10.00

Compare No. 1042 and No. 1020.

Birds — A369

No. 1043: a, Great hornbill. b, Peregrine falcon. c, Bald eagle. d, Channel-billed toucan. e, Secretary bird. f, Black-bellied bustard. g, Toco toucan. h, Hyacinth macaw. i, Burrowing owl. j, Bald ibis.

2013, Jan. 10 ***Perf. 13½***
1043 A369 45c Sheet of 10, #a-j 9.00 9.00

See Nos. 1056-1058.

Australia, 225th Anniv. A370

No. 1044 — Stars and: a, Australian settler and land claim. b, Tennis racket, coin showing King George V. c, Sydney Harbour Bridge, Sydney Opera House. d, Cricket player. e, Clipper ship, Southern Cross constellation. f, Clipper ship, sextant markings. g, Australian Parliament, Aboriginal drawings. h, William Shakespeare. i, British Parliament, London. j, Queen Elizabeth II, British coat of arms.

2013, Jan. 25
1044 Sheet of 10 9.50 9.50
a.-j. A370 46c Any single .95 .95

Inscription on No. 1044b is incorrect.

Marine Life — A371

Designs: 33c, Raccoon butterflyfish. 46c, Dolphins. $1.10, Long-nosed butterflyfish, horiz. $5.60, Tiger shark, horiz. $12.35, Star puffer, horiz. $16.85, Nassau grouper, horiz. $19.95, Starfish, horiz. $23.95, Porkfish, horiz. $44.95, Grouper, horiz.

2013, Jan. 28 ***Perf. 10¼x11¼***
1045 A371 33c multi .70 .70
1046 A371 46c multi .95 .95

Perf. 11¼x10¼
1047 A371 $1.10 multi 2.25 2.25
1048 A371 $5.60 multi 11.50 11.50
1049 A371 $12.35 multi 25.00 25.00
1050 A371 $16.85 multi 34.00 34.00
1051 A371 $19.95 multi 40.00 40.00
1052 A371 $23.95 multi 47.50 47.50
1053 A371 $44.95 multi 90.00 90.00

Miniature Sheet

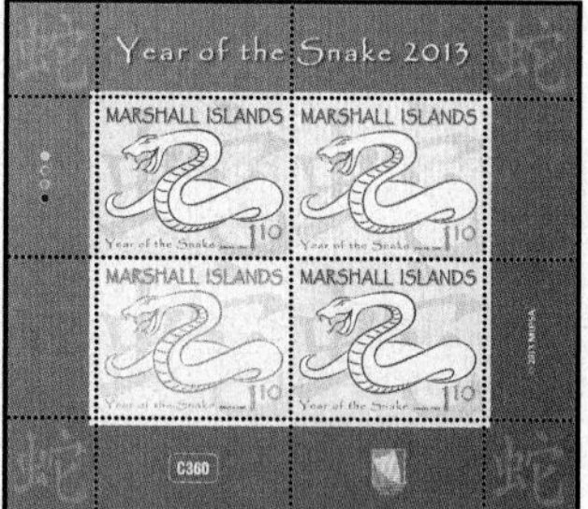
New Year 2013 (Year of the Snake) — A372

No. 1054 — Color of snake: a, Blue (4-1). b, Red Brown (4-2). c, Yellow brown (4-3). d, Green (4-4).

2013, Feb. 10 ***Perf. 13½***
1054 A372 $1.10 Sheet of 4, #a-d 9.00 9.00

Camellias — A373

No. 1055 — Number and color of camellias: a, One white (8-1). b, Two red and white (8-2). c, Three pink (8-3). d, One pink (8-4). e, Three dark pink (8-5). f, Two pink (8-6). g, One red (8-7). h, Three pink (8-8).

2013, Feb. 22
1055 A373 46c Block of 8, #a-h 7.50 7.50

Birds Type of 2013
Miniature Sheets

No. 1056: a, Hadada ibis. b, White-face whistling duck. c, Scarlet ibises. d, Fulvous tree duck. e, Knob-billed goose. f, Egyptian goose. g, Baikal teal. h, Humboldt penguins. i, Whooping cranes. j, Red-breasted goose.

No. 1057: a, Caribbean flamingos. b, Dalmatian pelicans. c, Piping plovers. d, Coscoroba swans. e, Hawaiian goose. f, Brown pelican. g, Jabiru. h, King penguins. i, White spoonbill. j, Blue cranes.

No. 1058: a, Golden conure. b, Major Mitchell's cockatoos. c, Eastern bluebirds. d, Giant scops owl. e, Thick-billed parrot. f, Blue-crowned pigeon. g, American kestrels. h, White-breasted silver-eyes. i, St. Lucia amazon. j, California condors.

2013 ***Perf. 13½***
1056 A369 46c Sheet of 10, #a-j 9.50 9.50
1057 A369 46c Sheet of 10, #a-j 9.50 9.50
1058 A369 46c Sheet of 10, #a-j 9.50 9.50

Issued: No. 1056, 3/9; No. 1057, 5/16; No. 1058, 10/3.

Cats — A374

No. 1059: a, Four cats, pink flower (6-5). b, Three cats, blue flower, butterflies (6-6). c, Three cats, pink flowers, basket (6-1). d, Three cats looking at grasshopper on basket (6-2). e, Three cats, red and yellow flowers (6-3). f, Three cats, two hummingbirds (6-4).

2013, Mar. 27 **Litho.** ***Perf. 13½***
1059 Horiz. strip of 6 4.25 4.25
a.-f. A374 33c Any single .70 .70

Medals — A375

No. 1060 — Inscription below medal: a, George Washington. b, John Adams. c, Thomas Jefferson. d, James Madison. e, James Monroe. f, John Quincy Adams. g, Andrew Jackson. h, Martin Van Buren. i, William H. Harrison. j, John Tyler. k, James K. Polk. l, Zachary Taylor. m, Millard Fillmore. n, Franklin Pierce. o, James Buchanan. p, Abraham Lincoln. q, Andrew Johnson. r, Ulysses S. Grant. s, Rutherford B. Hayes. t, James Garfield. u, Chester Arthur. v, Grover Cleveland. w, Benjamin Harrison. x, Peace and Friendship. y, William McKinley. z, Theodore Roosevelt. aa, William H. Taft. ab, Woodrow Wilson. ac, Warren G. Harding. ad, Calvin Coolidge. ae, Herbert Hoover. af, Franklin Delano Roosevelt. ag, Harry S. Truman. ah, Dwight D. Eisenhower. ai, John F. Kennedy. aj, Lyndon B. Johnson. ak, Richard Milhous Nixon. al, Rerald R. Ford. am, Jimmy Carter. an, Ronald Reagan. ao, Geroge Bush. ap, William Jefferson Clinton. aq, George W. Bush. ar, Presidential Seal. as, The White House.

2013, Apr. 9
1060 Sheet of 45 43.00 43.00
a.-as. A375 46c Any single .95 .95

Souvenir Sheet

"Ich Bin Ein Berliner" Speech, by Pres. John F. Kennedy, 50th Anniv. — A376

2013, June 29 ***Perf. 13¼x13½***
1061 A376 $2 multi 4.00 4.00

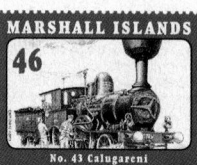

British Steam Locomotives A377

No. 1062: a, No. 43 Calugareni. b, Beyer Peacock 2-6-4T. c, Adam Brown. d, Baldwin 4-6-0. e, 15A Class Garratt. f, Enterprise 1845. g, Grahamstown. h, Flying Scotsman. i, Black Hawthorn. j, LNER "Mallard" 4-6-2.

2013, July 3 ***Perf. 13½***
1062 Sheet of 10 9.50 9.50
a.-j. A377 46c Any single .95 .95

Indian Headdresses A378

No. 1063 — Inscription: a, Cheyenne Headress. b, Flathead Headress. c, American Indian Headress. d, Shoshone Headress. e, Assiniboine Headress.

2013, Aug. 8
1063 Horiz. strip of 5 4.75 4.75
a.-e. A378 46c Any single .95 .95

"Headdress" is spelled incorrectly on Nos. 1063a-1063e.

Miniature Sheet

Landmark Events in American Civil Rights Movement — A379

No. 1064: a, Executive Order 9981, 1948. b, Brown v. Board of Education, 1954. c, Montgomery bus boycott, 1955. d, Little Rock Nine, 1957. e, Lunch counter sit-ins, 1960. f, Freedom Riders, 1961. g, Dr. Martin Luther King's "I Have a Dream" speech, 1963. h, Civil Rights Act, 1964. i, Selma March, 1965. j, Voting Rights Act, 1964.

2013, Aug. 28
1064 A379 46c Sheet of 10, #a-j 9.50 9.50

World War II Type of 2011
Miniature Sheet

No. 1065 — Inscriptions: a, Tenth Fleet: Overcoming the U-boat menace. b, U.S. Medical Service saving lives on the front lines. c, Allies invade Sicily: Patton's Seventh Army drives on Palermo. d, B-24 Liberators bomb Ploesti Oilfields. e, V-Mail — Letters from around the globe. f, Allied forces land at Salerno. g, Back the attack. h, Willie and Joe: A classic portrait of the American GI. i, Gold Star — Remembering those who died for a just cause — Freedom. j, U.S. Marines land on Tarawa Atoll.

2013, Sept. 9 ***Perf. 13½***
1065 A342 46c Sheet of 10, #a-j, + 10 labels 9.50 9.50

Traditional Marshallese Children's Games — A380

No. 1066: a, Etobobo (4-1). b, Lejonjon (4-2). c, Lodidean (4-3). d, Didmakol (4-4).

2013, Sept. 27
1066 Horiz. strip of 4 4.00 4.00
a.-d. A380 46c Any single .95 .95

Miniature Sheet

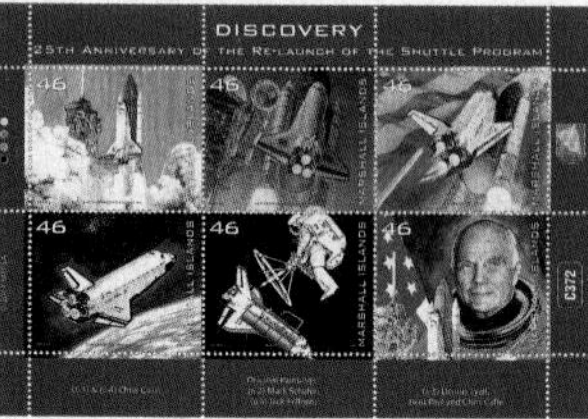
Restarting of Space Shuttle Program, 25th Anniv. — A381

No. 1067: a, Launch of Space Shuttle Discovery mission STS-95 (6-1). b, Launch, diff. (6-2). c, Space Shuttle Discoverey and U.S. flag (6-3). d, Space Shuttle Discovery in orbit (6-4). e, Astronaut working outside of Space Shuttle Discovery (6-5). f, U.S. flag, Space Shuttle Discovery on launch pad, Astronaut John Glenn (6-6).

2013, Sept. 29
1067 A381 46c Sheet of 6, #a-f 5.75 5.75

World War II Aircraft — A382

No. 1068: a, F4U Corsair. b, C-46 Commando. c, A6M Zero. d, B-29 Superfortress. e, Bf 109. f, Ju 88. g, P-38 Lightning. h, A-26 Invader. i, B-17 Flying Fortress. j, P-51 Mustang. k, Il-2. l, P-40 Warhawk. m, C-47 Skytrain. n, B-24 Liberator. o, Spitfire. p, B-25 Mitchell. q, PBY Catalina. r, B-26 Marauder. s, TBM-1C Avenger. t, Lancaster. u, Yak-9. v, F6F Hellcat. w, C54 Skymaster. x, PB4Y-2 Privateer. y, P-47 Thunderbolt.

2013, Oct. 14
1068 A382 Sheet of 25 24.00 24.00
a.-y. 46c Any single .95 .95

Christmas — A383

No. 1069: a, Annunciation (6-1). b, Journey to Bethlehem (6-2). c, Holy Family (6-3). d, Angel and shepherds (6-4). e, Magi (6-5). f, Nativity (6-6).

2013, Oct. 31 Litho. *Perf. 13½*
1069 A383 46c Block of 6, #a-f 5.75 5.75

Miniature Sheet

Gettysburg Address, 150th Anniv. — A384

No. 1070 — Soldiers and: a, U.S. Pres. Abraham Lincoln, U.S. flag (34x25mm). b, Confederate States Pres. Jefferson Davis, Confederate flag (34x25mm). c, Gen. Ulysses S. Grant, U.S. flag (34x25mm). d, Gen. Robert E. Lee, Confederate flag (34x25mm). e, U.S. and Confederate flags (48x50mm).

2013, Nov. 19 Litho. *Perf. 13½*
1070 A384 46c Sheet of 5, #a-e 4.75 4.75

Souvenir Sheet

Declaration of Thanksgiving Day as U.S. Federal Holiday, 150th Anniv. — A385

Perf. 13¼x13¾
2013, Nov. 28 Litho.
1071 A385 $2 multi 4.00 4.00

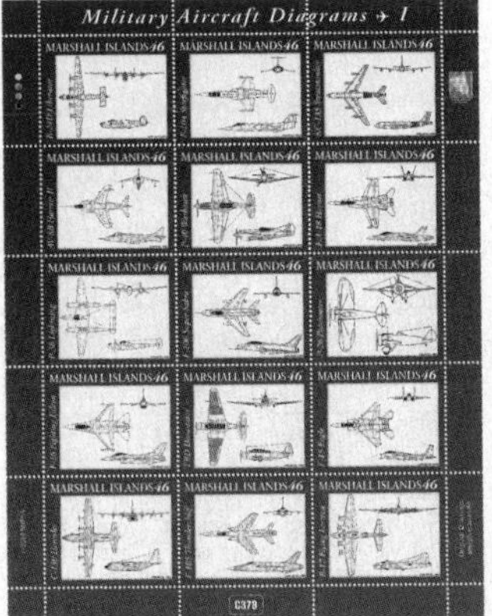

Military Aircraft Diagrams — A386

No. 1072: a, B-24D Liberator. b, F-104 Starfighter. c, KC-135 Stratotanker. d, AV-8B Harrier II. e, P40-Warhawk. f, F/A-18 Hornet. g, P-38 Lightning. h, F-100 Super Sabre. i, P-26 Peashooter. j, F-16 Fighting Falcon. k, TBD Devastator. l, F-15 Eagle. m, C-130 Hercules. n, F-105 Thunderchief. o, B-17 Flying Fortress.

2014, Jan. 12 Litho. *Perf. 13½*
1072 A386 46c Sheet of 15, #a-o 14.00 14.00

See Nos. 1082, 1098.

Souvenir Sheet

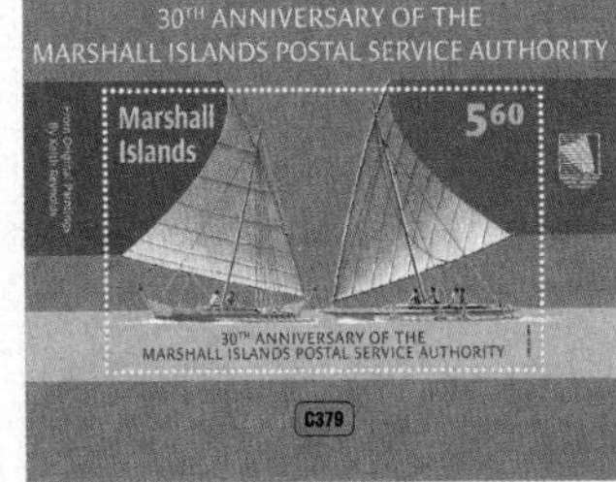

Marshall Islands Postal Service Authority, 30th Anniv. — A387

2014, Jan. 22 Litho. *Perf. 13¼x13½*
1073 A387 $5.60 multi 11.50 11.50

Shells A388

Reticulated helmet, New England neptune and Calico scallop shells, with largest being: 34c, Reticulated helmet. 49c, New England neptune. $1.15, Calico scallop.

2014, Jan. 26 Litho. *Perf. 11¼x10¼*

1074	A388	34c multi	.70	.70
1075	A388	49c multi	1.00	1.00
1076	A388	$1.15 multi	2.40	2.40
		Nos. 1074-1076 (3)	4.10	4.10

See Nos. 1083-1084, 1090-1094.

Miniature Sheet

New Year 2014 (Year of the Horse) — A389

No. 1077 — Color of horse: a, Blue (4-1). b, Red brown (4-2). c, Golden brown (4-3). d, Green (4-4).

2014, Jan. 31 Litho. *Perf. 13½*
1077 A389 $1.15 Sheet of 4, #a-d 9.25 9.25

Insects — A390

No. 1078: a, Garden insects, red panels (10-1). b, Checkered beetle (10-2). c, Lacewing (10-3). d, Red admiral butterfly (10-4). e, Honey bee (10-5). f, Leaf skeletonizer (10-6). g, Drone fly (10-7). h, Bumblebee (10-8). i, Lamellicorn beetle (10-9). j, Garden insects, blue panels (10-10).

2014, Mar. 1 Litho. *Perf. 13½*
1078 Block of 10 10.00 10.00
a.-j. A390 49c Any single 1.00 1.00

Castles in Great Britain — A391

No. 1079: a, Carrickfergus Castle, Northern Ireland (4-1). b, Windsor Castle, England (4-2). c, Caernarfon Castle, Wales (4-3). d, Edinburgh Castle, Scotland (4-4).

2014, Mar. 15 Litho. *Perf. 13½*
1079 Horiz. strip of 4 9.75 9.75
a.-d. A391 $1.15 Any single 2.40 2.40

Miniature Sheet

Historical Flags of the United States — A392

No. 1080: a, Continental flag (15-1). b, Bennington flag (15-2). c, Forster flag (15-3). d, Sons of Liberty flag (15-4). e, Brandywine flag (15-5). f, Pierre L'Enfant flag (15-6). g, Indian Peace flag (15-7). h, Star Spangled Banner (15-8). i, Great Star flag (15-9). j, Fort Sumter flag (15-10). k, Centennial flag (15-11). l, 29-star flag (15-12). m, 38-star flag (15-13). n, 48-star flag (15-14). o, 50-star flag (15-15).

2014, Apr. 4 Litho. *Perf. 13½*
1080 A392 49c Sheet of 15, #a-o, + 9 labels 15.00 15.00

Miniature Sheet

Traditional Costumes of European Countries — A393

No. 1081: a, Switzerland (20-1). b, Monaco (20-2). c, Luxembourg (20-3). d, Spain (20-4). e, Belgium (20-5). f, Denmark (20-6). g, Italy (20-7). h, Ireland (20-8). i, Norway (20-9). j, Great Britain (20-10). k, Portugal (20-11). l, Turkey (20-12). m, France (20-13). n, Sweden (20-14). o, Iceland (20-15). p, Germany (20-16). q, Netherlands (20-17). r, Greece (20-18). s, Liechtenstein (20-19). t, Finland (20-20).

2014, May 10 Litho. *Perf. 13½*
1081 A393 49c Sheet of 20, #a-t 20.00 20.00

Military Aircraft Diagrams Type of 2014

Miniature Sheet

No. 1082: a, F-80 Shooting Star. b, SR-71 Blackbird. c, U-2. d, F-86 Sabre. e, F-14 Tomcat. f, F6F Hellcat. g, P-47 Thunderbolt. h, F-117 Nighthawk. i, C-5 Galaxy. j, B-52 Stratofortress. k, F-4 Phantom II. l, P-51 Mustang. m, SBD Dauntless. n, B-1 Lancer. o, PBY-5 Catalina.

2014, June 2 Litho. *Perf. 13½*
1082 A386 49c Sheet of 15, #a-o 15.00 15.00

Shells Type of 2014

Various shells with largest being: 4c, Hawk-winged conch. $19.99, Frilled dogwinkle.

Perf. 11¼x10¼
2014, June 16 Litho.
1083 A388 4c multi .25 .25
1084 A388 $19.99 multi 40.00 40.00

Trees — A394

No. 1085: a, White willow (6-1). b, Poplar (6-2). c, Oak (6-3). d, Birch (6-4). e, Maple (6-5). f, Larch (6-6).

2014, July 7 Litho. *Perf. 13½*
1085 A394 49c Block of 6, #a-f 6.00 6.00

Souvenir Sheet

Opening of Panama Canal, Cent. — A395

2014, Aug. 15 Litho. *Perf. 13x13½*
1086 A395 $5.60 multi 11.50 11.50

Miniature Sheet

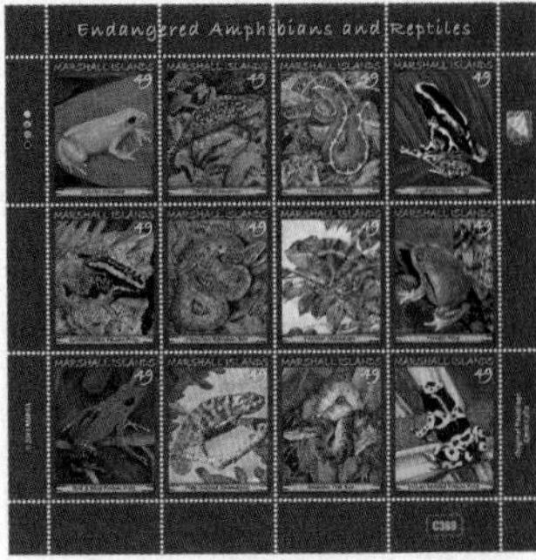

Amphibians and Reptiles — A396

No. 1087: a, Golden mantella frog (12-1). b, Carpet chameleon (12-2). c, Emerald tree boa (12-3). d, Dyeing poison dart frog (12-4). e, Golfodulcean poison frog (12-5). f, Peruvian rainbow boa (12-6). g, Panther chameleon (12-7). h, Tomato frog (12-8). i, Red & blue poison frog (12-9). j, Flap-necked chameleon (12-10). k, Amazon tree boa (12-11). l, Yellow-banded poison dart frog (12-12).

2014, Aug. 21 Litho. *Perf. 13½*
1087 A396 49c Sheet of 12, #a-l 12.00 12.00

Souvenir Sheet

Writing of "The Star-Spangled Banner," 200th Anniv. — A397

2014, Sept. 3 Litho. ***Perf. 13x13½***

1088 A397 $5.60 multi 11.50 11.50

World War II Type of 2011

Miniature Sheet

No. 1089 — Inscriptions: a, Allied Forces retake New Guinea. b, 2,000 U.S. planes attack Berlin and 2 aircraft plants near city. c, Invasion is on! d, Airborne units spearhead ground attacks. e, Submarine warfare cripple Japan's shipping routes. f, Paris and Rome liberated by Allies. g, Operation Forager. h, Red Ball Express speeds vital supplies to allies. i, Battle for Leyte Gulf. j, Battle of the Bulge.

2014, Sept. 15 Litho. ***Perf. 13½***

1089 A342 49c Sheet of 10, #a-j, + 10 labels 10.00 10.00

Shells Type of 2014

Various shells.

Perf. 11¼x10¼

2014, Sept. 18 Litho.

1090	A388	$5.75 multi	11.50	11.50
1091	A388	$5.95 multi	12.00	12.00
1092	A388	$6.10 multi	12.50	12.50
1093	A388	$12.65 multi	25.50	25.50
1094	A388	$17.90 multi	36.00	36.00
		Nos. 1090-1094 (5)	97.50	97.50

Movie Monsters — A398

No. 1095: a, Count Dracula holding candle (10-1). b, Frankenstein's Monster near stairway (10-2). c, Phantom of the Opera without mask (10-3). d, The Mummy carrying woman (10-4). e, The Wolf Man crouching (10-5). f, Count Dracula at open window (10-6). g, Frankenstein's Monster in laboratory (10-7). h, Phantom of the Opera wearing mask (10-8). i, The Mummy and skull (10-9). j, The Wolf Man and wolf (10-10).

2014, Oct. 14 Litho. ***Perf. 13½***

1095 A398 49c Block of 10, #a-j 10.00 10.00

Christmas — A399

No. 1096: a, Singing angels (6-1). b, Shepherd with flock (6-2). c, Three Kings following star (6-3). d, Three Kings at manger (6-4). e, Mary and Baby Jesus (6-5). f, White doves (6-6).

2014, Oct. 10 Litho. ***Perf. 13½***

1096 A399 49c Block of 6, #a-f 6.00 6.00

Seahorses — A400

No. 1097: a, Horned seahorse (4-1). b, Lined seahorse (4-2). c, Lined seahorse, diff. (4-3). d, Lined seahorse, diff. (4-4).

2014, Oct. 20 Litho. ***Perf. 13½***

1097 Horiz. strip of 4 4.00 4.00
a.-d. A400 49c Any single 1.00 1.00

Military Aircraft Diagrams Type of 2014

Miniature Sheet

No. 1098: a, Fokker D VII. b, J35 Draaken. c, Bf 109. d, Yak 9. e, MiG 29. f, A-10 Thunderbolt II. g, Me 262. h, B-2 Spirit. i, Spitfire. j, B-29 Superfortress. k, X-15. l, Lancaster. m, A6M Zero. n, F/A 22. o, J1 Monoplane.

2014, Oct. 28 Litho. ***Perf. 13½***

1098 A386 49c Sheet of 15, #a-o 15.00 15.00

A401

A402

A403

Space Adventure for Children A404

2014, Nov. 7 Litho. ***Perf. 13½***

1099	Strip of 4	4.00	4.00
a.	A401 49c multi	1.00	1.00
b.	A402 49c multi	1.00	1.00
c.	A403 49c multi	1.00	1.00
d.	A404 49c multi	1.00	1.00

Flowers A405

No. 1100: a, Six flowers including thistle at LL (10-1). b, Lily (10-2). c, Iris (10-3). d, Thistles (10-4). e, Rose (10-5). f, Pansy (10-6). g, Strawberries and blossom (10-7). h, Tulip (10-8). i, Three pansies (10-9). j, Five flowers and strawberry at bottom center (10-10).

2014, Nov. 18 Litho. ***Perf. 13½***

1100 Block of 10 10.00 10.00
a.-j. A405 49c Any single 1.00 1.00

Greetings — A406

No. 1101: a, Happy birthday. b, Thinking of you. c, Love. d, Thank you. e, Best wishes. f, Congratulations.

2015, Jan. 5 Litho. ***Perf. 13½***

1101 A406 49c Block of 6, #a-f 6.00 6.00

Dinosaur Skeletons A407

No. 1102: a, Triceratops. b, Stegosaurus. c, Protoceratops. d, Tyrannosaurus.

2015, Jan. 15 Litho. ***Perf. 13½***

1102 Horiz. strip of 4 2.80 2.80
a.-d. A407 34c Any single .70 .70

Reef Life Type of 1993

Miniature Sheet

No. 1103: a, Butterflyfish. b, Soldierfish. c, Damselfish. d, Filefish. e, Hawkfish. f, Surgeonfish. g, Parrotfish (75x33mm).

2015, Jan. 28 Litho. ***Perf. 13½***

1103	Sheet of 7	17.00	17.00
a.-f.	A79 $1 Any single	2.00	2.00
g.	A79 $2.50 multi	5.00	5.00

Berries — A408

No. 1104: a, Blueberries. b, Raspberries. c, Blackberries, raspberries, strawberries and blueberries. d, Strawberries. e, Blackberries.

2015, Feb. 14 Litho. ***Perf. 13½***

1104 Horiz. strip of 5 5.00 5.00
a.-e. A408 49c Any single 1.00 1.00

Miniature Sheet

New Year 2015 (Year of the Ram) — A409

No. 1105 — Color of ram: a, Blue (4-1). b, Red brown (4-2). c, Yellow brown (4-3). d, Green (4-4).

2015, Feb. 19 Litho. ***Perf. 13½***

1105 A409 $1.15 Sheet of 4, #a-d 9.25 9.25

Rays A410

Designs: 7c, Manta rays. 22c, Spotted eagle rays. 35c, Spotted eagle rays, diff. $1.20, Southern stingray.

Perf. 11¼x10¼

2015, Feb. 23 Litho.

1106	A410	7c multi	.25	.25
1107	A410	22c multi	.45	.45
1108	A410	35c multi	.70	.70
1109	A410	$1.20 multi	2.40	2.40
		Nos. 1106-1109 (4)	3.80	3.80

Seashells Type of 1998 Redrawn

No. 1110: a, Chicoreus brunneus. b, Cypraea aurantium. c, Lambis chiragra. d, Tridacna squamosa.

2014, Feb. 26 Litho. ***Perf. 13½***

Stamps With White Frames

1110 Horiz. strip of 4 4.00 4.00
a.-d. A137 49c Any single 1.00 1.00

Canoes Type of 1997 Redrawn

No. 1111: a, Pacific Arts Festival canoe Walap of Enewetak. b, Large voyaging canoe Walap of Jaluit. c, Racing canoe Kôr Kôr. d, Sailing canoe Tipnol of Ailuk.

2014, Mar. 10 Litho. ***Perf. 13½***

Stamps With White Frames

1111 Vert. strip of 4 4.00 4.00
a.-d. A129 49c Any single 1.00 1.00

Ships Type of 1999

No. 1112: a, Galleon Los Reyes, Spain, 1568. b, Frigate Dolphin, Great Britain, 1767. c, Bark Scarborough, Great Britain, 1788. d, Brig Rurik, Russia, 1817.

2015, Mar. 18 Litho. ***Perf. 13½***

Stamps With Tan Frames

1112 A162 49c Horiz. strip of 4, #a-d 4.00 4.00

Miniature Sheet

Marine Life — A411

No. 1113: a, Blue tang. b, Loggerhead turtle. c, Hammerhead shark. d, Commerson's dolphin. e, Humpback whale. f, Seahorse. g, Peale's porpoise. h, Sea anemone. i, Bowhead whale. j, Flying gurnard. k, Spotted trunkfish. l, Foureye butterflyfish. m, Bottlenose dolphin. n, Blue whale. o, Blue shark.

2015, Apr. 13 Litho. ***Perf. 13½***

1113 A411 49c Sheet of 15, #a-o 15.00 15.00

Souvenir Sheet

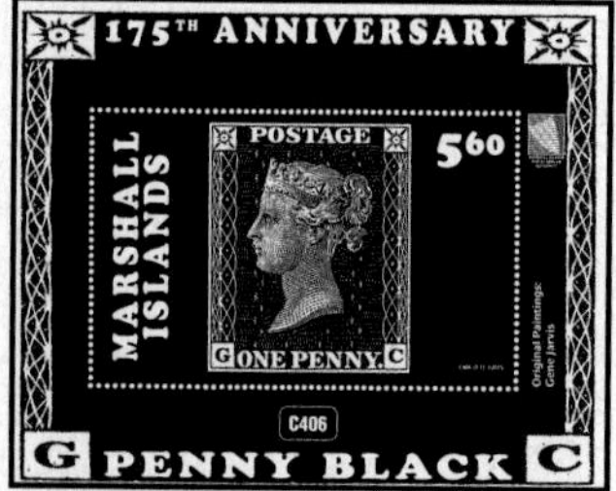

Penny Black, 175th Anniv. — A412

2015, May 1 Litho. ***Perf. 13¼x13½***

1114 A412 $5.60 black 11.50 11.50

Souvenir Sheet

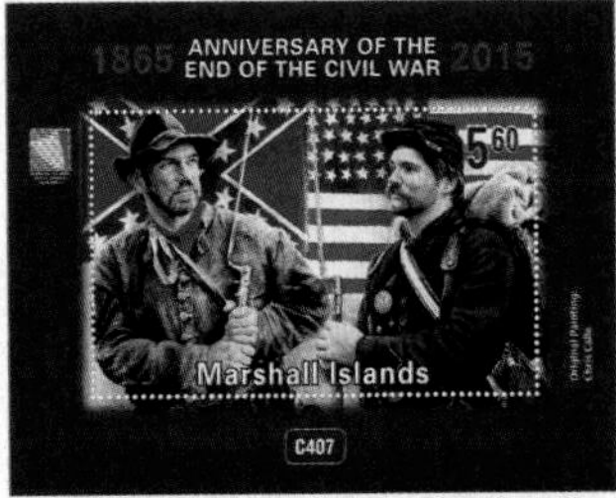

End of American Civil War, 150th Anniv. — A413

2015, May 1 Litho. Perf. 13¼x13½
1115 A413 $5.60 multi 11.50 11.50

Miniature Sheet

Postal Relics — A414

No. 1116 — Mailboxes and other postal-related items from: a, Sweden. b, Germany. c, Australia. d, Canada. e, Great Britain. f, Switzerland. g, France. h, United States. i, Austria. j, Japan. k, Brazil. l, China.

2015, June 5 Litho. Perf. 13½
1116 A414 49c Sheet of 12, #a-l 12.00 12.00

Miniature Sheet

Birds — A415

No. 1117: a, Red-billed hornbill. b, Great black-backed gull. c, Barn owl. d, Eastern white pelican. e, Sea eagle. f, Tibetan eared pheasant. g, Hermit ibis. h, Common heron. i, Bearded vulture. j, Kingfisher. k, White-breasted cormorant. l, White egret. m, Broad-winged hawk. n, Greater flamingo. o, Peregrine falcon.

2015, July 7 Litho. Perf. 13½
1117 A415 49c Sheet of 15, #a-o 15.00 15.00

Souvenir Sheet

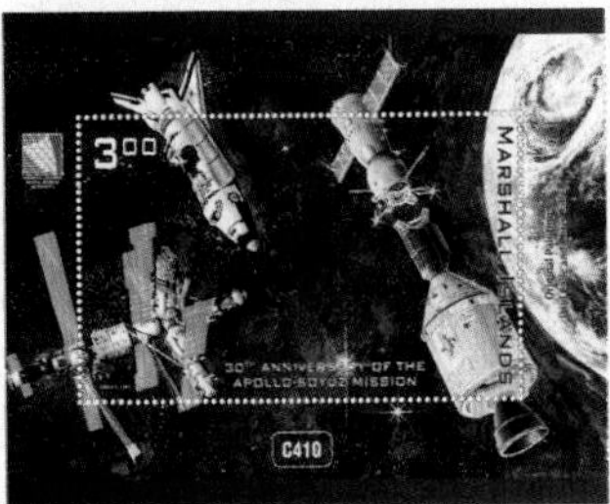

Apollo-Soyuz Space Mission, 40th Anniv. — A416

2015, July 17 Litho. Perf. 13x13½
1118 A416 $3 multi 6.00 6.00
a. Inscribed "40th Anniversary" 6.00 6.00

No. 1118 is incorrectly inscribed "30th anniversary."

National Buildings and Symbols A417

Designs: No. 1119, Capitol Building. No. 1120, Nitijela (Legislature Building). No. 1121, National seal and Nitijela, vert. No. 1122, National flag and Nitijela, vert.

2015, Aug. 3 Litho. Perf. 11¼x10¼
1119 A417 $1.20 multi 2.40 2.40
1120 A417 $1.20 multi 2.40 2.40

Perf. 10¼x11¼
1121 A417 $1.20 multi 2.40 2.40
1122 A417 $1.20 multi 2.40 2.40
Nos. 1119-1122 (4) 9.60 9.60

World War II Type of 2011

No. 1123 — Inscriptions: a, Marines take Suribachi, chief point on Iwo. b, MacArthur back in Luzon. c, Marines land on Okinawa, push forward from beachhead. d, U.S. and Russian soldiers link-up at Elbe River. e, Allied forces liberate concentration camps. f, The war in Europe is ended. g, War uproots millions, Europe filled with refugees. h, First atomic bomb dropped on Japan. i, War over, Japan surrenders unconditionally. j, The war is ended! U.S. troops return home.

2015, Aug. 22 Litho. Perf. 13½
1123 A342 49c Sheet of 10, #a-j, + 10 labels 10.00 10.00

Voyages of Discovery Type of 1992 Redrawn

No. 1124: a, Traditional tipnol (39x32m). b, Reconstructed Santa Maria (39x32mm). c, Constellation Argo Navis (39x32mm). d, Marshallese sailor, tipnol (39x32mm). e, Christopher Columbus, Santa Maria (39x32mm). f, Astronaut, Argo Navis (39x32mm). g, Columbus, sailor, and astronaut (75x32mm).

Perf. 13¼x13½

2015, Sept. 11 Litho.
1124 Sheet of 7 17.00 17.00
a.-f. A76 $1 Any single 2.00 2.00
g. A76 $2.50 multi 5.00 5.00

Souvenir Sheet

German Reunification, 25th Anniv. — A418

2015, Oct. 3 Litho. Perf. 13¼x13¾
1125 A418 $5.60 multi 11.50 11.50

Mammals A419

No. 1126: a, Snow leopard (15-1). b, Pampas deer (15-2). c, Musk ox (15-3). d, Maned wolf (15-4). e, Okapi (15-5). f, Chinese yellow bull (15-6). g, Chinese porcupine (15-7). h, Arabian oryx (15-8). i, Clawless otter (15-9). j, Siberian tiger (15-10). k, Bridled nail-tailed wallaby (15-11). l, Jaguar (15-12). m, Hairy-nosed wombat (15-13). n, Chimpanzee (15-14). o, Polar bear (15-15).

2015, Oct. 9 Litho. Perf. 13½
1126 Sheet of 15 15.00 15.00
a.-o. A419 49c Any single 1.00 1.00

Miniature Sheets

Christmas — A420

No. 1127, vert. — Four identical snowflakes in various sizes with stamp numbered: a, (10-1). b, (10-2). c, (10-3). d, (10-4). e, (10-5). f, (10-6). g, (10-7). h, (10-8). i, (10-9). j, (10-10).

No. 1128 — Five different snowflakes with stamp numbered: a, (4-1). b, (4-2). c, (4-3). d, (4-4).

2015, Oct. 20 Litho. Perf. 13½
1127 A420 49c Sheet of 10, #a-j 10.00 10.00
1128 A420 $1.20 Sheet of 4, #a-d 9.75 9.75

Legends — A421

No. 1129: a, Kijeek An Letao (8-1). b, Mennin Jobwodda (8-2). c, Wa Koñe, Waan Letao (8-3). d, Kouj (8-4). e, The Large Pool of Mejit (8-5). f, The Beautiful Woman of Kwajalein (8-6). g, Sharks and Lowakalle Reef (8-7). h, The Demon of Adrie (8-8).

2015, Nov. 5 Litho. Perf. 13½
1129 A421 49c Block of 8, #a-h 8.00 8.00

Miniature Sheet

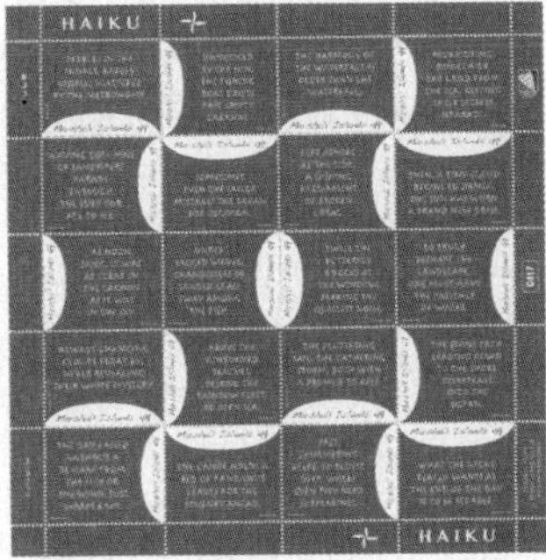

Haiku — A422

No. 1130: a, Pebbles in the shoals, barely visible, scattered by the metronome (20-1). b, Unnoticed by the sun, the fishing boat drifts past empty cabanas (20-2). c, The harmony of the waterfall is older than the waterfall (20-3). d, Murmuring dunes hide the land from the sea, keeping their secrets separate (20-4). e, Waving columns of sandpipers parade through the surf for all to see (20-5). f, Sometiimes even the sailor mistakes the ocean for oblivion (20-6). g, Left ashore by the tide, a shining parliament of broken coral (20-7). h, Then, a tiny cloud begins to dance. The sun has worn a brand new dress (20-8). i, As noon sang, it was clear in the lagoon as it was in the sky (20-9). j, Under jagged waves, chandeliers of sanded glass sway among the fish (20-10). k, Twice the butterfly knocks at the window, making the quietest noise (20-11). l, To truly reshape the landscape, one must have the patience of water (20-12). m, Always-changing clouds float by, never revealing their white mystery (20-13). n, Above the sunburned beaches, beyond the rainbow fleet to open sea (20-14). o, The fluttering sail, the gathering storm, both with a promise to keep (20-15). p, The stone path leading down to the shore disappears into the ocean (20-16). q, The day passed without a remark from the sun or the wind. Just warm rain. (20-17). r, The canoe holds a bed of pandanus leaves for the journey ahead (20-18). s, Past shimmering reefs, to bluest deep, where even fish need submarines (20-19). t, What the night really wants at the end of the day is to be set free (20-20).

2016, Jan. 5 Litho. Perf. 13½
1130 A422 49c Sheet of 20, #a-t 20.00 20.00

See No. 1151.

Souvenir Sheet

First Commercial Flight of the Concorde, 40th Anniv. — A423

2016, Jan. 21 Litho. Perf. 13x13½
1131 A423 $4 multi 8.00 8.00

Miniature Sheet

New Year 2016 (Year of the Monkey) — A424

No. 1132 — Color of monkey: a, Deep violet (4-1). b, Red brown (4-2). c, Yellow brown (4-3). d, Green (4-4).

2016, Feb. 8 Litho. Perf. 13½
1132 A424 $1.20 Sheet of 4, #a-d 9.75 9.75

Miniature Sheet

Wildlife — A425

No. 1133: a, Starfish (10-1). b, Common dolphins (10-2). c, Blue whales (10-3). d, Megapode (10-4). e, Leatherback turtle (10-5). f, Doves (10-6). g, Hawksbill turtle (10-7). h, Goruper (10-8). i, Manta rays (10-9). j, Tuna (10-10).

2016, Mar. 3 Litho. Perf. 13½
1133 A425 49c Sheet of 10, #a-j 10.00 10.00

Miniature Sheets

Seals of the States of the Union — A426

No. 1134: a, Delaware (10-1). b, Pennsylvania (10-2). c, New Jersey (10-3). d, Georgia (10-4). e, Connecticut (10-5). f, Massachusetts (10-6). g, Maryland (10-7). h, South Carolina (10-8). i, New Hampshire (10-9). j, Virginia (10-10).

No. 1135: a, New York (10-1). b, North Carolina (10-2). c, Rhode Island (10-3). d, Vermont (10-4). e, Kentucky (10-5). f, Tennessee

(10-6). g, Ohio (10-7). h, Louisiana (10-8). i, Indiana (10-9). j, Mississippi (10-10).

No. 1136: a, Illinois (10-1). b, Alabama (10-2). c, Maine (10-3). d, Missouri (10-4). e, Arkansas (10-5). f, Michigan (10-6). g, Florida (10-7). h, Texas (10-8). i, Iowa (10-9). j, Wisconsin (10-10).

No. 1137: a, California (10-1). b, Minnesota (10-2). c, Oregon (10-3). d, Kansas (10-4). e, West Virginia (10-5). f, Nevada (10-6). g, Nebraska (10-7). h, Colorado (10-8). i, North Dakota (10-9). j, South Dakota (10-10).

No. 1138: a, Montana (10-1). b, Washington (10-2). c, Idaho (10-3). d, Wyoming (10-4). e, Utah (10-5). f, Oklahoma (10-6). g, New Mexico (10-7). h, Arizona (10-8). i, Alaska (10-9). j, Hawaii (10-10).

2016 Litho. *Perf. 11¾*

1134 A426 49c Sheet of 10, #a-j 10.00 10.00
1135 A426 49c Sheet of 10, #a-j 10.00 10.00
1136 A426 49c Sheet of 10, #a-j 10.00 10.00
1137 A426 49c Sheet of 10, #a-j 10.00 10.00
1138 A426 49c Sheet of 10, #a-j 10.00 10.00
Nos. 1134-1138 (5) 50.00 50.00

Issued: No. 1134, 4/4; No. 1135, 5/12; No. 1136, 5/24; No. 1137, 6/8; No. 1138, 9/2.

Miniature Sheet

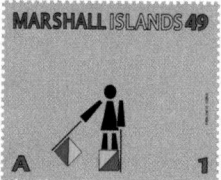

Queen Elizabeth II, 90th Birthday — A427

No. 1139 — Hat color: a, Blue (6-1). b, Yellow (6-2). c, Peach (6-3). d, Red violet (6-4). e, Purple (6-5). f, Green gray (6-6).

2016, Apr. 21 Litho. *Perf. 13½*

1139 A427 90c Sheet of 6, #a-f 11.00 11.00

Semaphore Symbols — A428

No. 1140 — Flag position for: a, "A" and "1" (30-1). b, "B" and "2" (30-2). c, "C" and "3" (30-3). d, "D" and "4" (30-4). e, "E" and "5" (30-5). f, "F" and "6" (30-6). g, "G" and "7" (30-7). h, "H" and "8" (30-8). i, "I" and "9" (30-9). j, "J" (30-10). k, "K" and "0" (30-11). l, "L" (30-12). m, "M" (30-13). n, "N" (30-14). o, "O" (30-15). p, "P" (30-16). q, "Q" (30-17). r, "R" (30-18). s, "S" (30-19). t, "T" (30-20). u, "U" (30-21). v, "V" (30-22). w, "W" (30-23). x, "X" (30-24). y, "Y" (30-25). z, "Z" (30-26). aa, Numeric (30-27). ab, Attention (30-28). ac, Cancel (30-29). ad, Space (30-30).

2016, July 5 Litho. *Perf. 13½*

1140 Sheet of 30 30.00 30.00
a.-ad. A428 49c Any single 1.00 1.00

Miniature Sheet

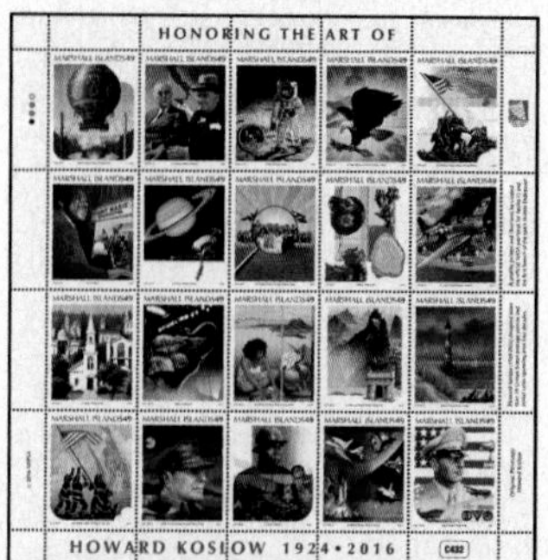

Paintings by Howard Koslow (1924-2016), Stamp Designer — A429

No. 1141: a, Montgolfier Hot Air Balloon (20-1). b, Roosevelt and Churchill (20-2). c, Astronaut on Moon (20-3). d, To the Heroes of Desert Storm-Eagle (20-4). e, Marines Raising Flag on Mt. Suribachi (20-5). f, Count Basie (20-6). g, Saturn with Voyager 2 (20-7). h, 15th Anniversary of RMI Constitution (20-8). i, Various Minerals (20-9). j, U.S. Liberates Marshall Islands (20-10). k, Freedom of Worship (20-11). l, Circus Elephant (20-12). m, Woman Kneading Breadfruit Dough (20-13). n, China Folk Houses/View of Village (20-14). o, Morris Island Lighthouse (20-15). p, Firemen Raising the American Flag (20-16). q, MacArthur Evacuated from Corregidor (20-17). r, Freddie Stowers (20-18). s, Montage of U.S. Space Vehicles (20-19). t, James "Jimmy" Doolittle (20-20).

2016, July 20 Litho. *Perf. 13½*

1141 A429 49c Sheet of 20, #a-t 20.00 20.00

Peace Doves — A430

No. 1142: a, Three doves, Swords into Plowshares statue (6-1). b, Four doves, Japanese Peace Bell (6-2). c, Dove and Earth II (6-3). d, Hands Releasing Dove (6-4). e, Dove and Earth (6-5). f, Peace Dove with Horse and Rider (6-6).

2016, Aug. 5 Litho. *Perf. 13½*

1142 A430 49c Block of 6, #a-f 6.00 6.00

Souvenir Sheet

Marshall Islands Constitution Committee — A431

2016, Sept. 16 Litho. *Perf. 13x13½*

1143 A431 98c multi 2.00 2.00

Souvenir Sheet

Marshall Islands Sovereignty, 30th Anniv. — A432

2016, Oct. 21 Litho. *Perf. 13x13½*

1144 A432 $3 multi 6.00 6.00

Miniature Sheets

Christmas — A433

No. 1145 — Ornaments shaped like: a, Star (10-1). b, Gingerbread man (10-2). c, Mitten (10-3). d, Christmas tree (10-4). e, Candy cane (10-5). f, Wreath (10-6). g, Gift (10-7). h, Santa Claus (10-8). i, Christmas stocking (10-9). j, Poinsettia (10-10).

No. 1146, horiz. — Ornaments shaped like: a, Christmas tree (4-1). b, Christmas stocking (4-2). c, Candy cane (4-3). d, Gift (4-4).

2016, Nov. 3 Litho. *Perf. 13½*

1145 A433 49c Sheet of 10, #a-j 10.00 10.00
1146 A433 $1.20 Sheet of 4, #a-d 9.75 9.75

Souvenir Sheet

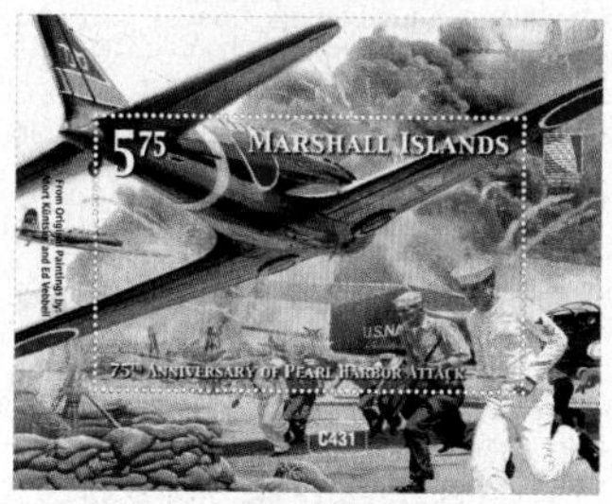

Attack on Pearl Harbor, 75th Anniv. — A434

2016, Dec. 7 Litho. *Perf. 13x13½*

1147 A434 $5.75 multi 11.50 11.50

Miniature Sheet

United States National Park Service, Cent. — A435

No. 1148 — National Parks: a, Denali (10-1). b, Crater Lake (10-2). c, Haleakala (10-3). d, Yellowstone (10-4). e, Glacier (10-5). f, Everglades (10-6). g, Grand Canyon (10-7). h, Great Smoky Mountains (10-8). i, Yosemite (10-9). j, Isle Royale (10-10).

2016, Dec. 15 Litho. *Perf. 13½*

1148 A435 49c Sheet of 10, #a-j 10.00 10.00

Miniature Sheet

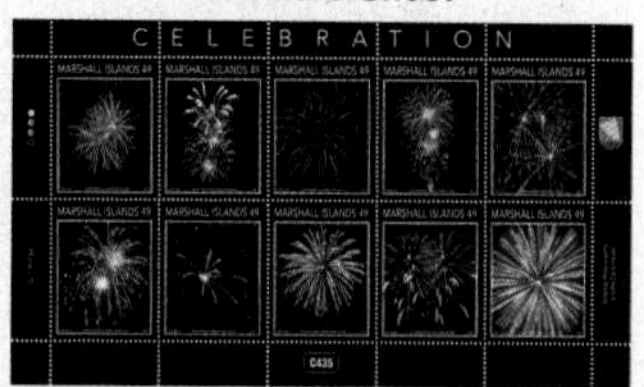

Fireworks — A436

No. 1149 — Various fireworks displays numbered: a, (10-1). b, (10-2). c, (10-3). d, (10-4). e, (10-5). f, (10-6). g, (10-7). h, (10-8). i, (10-9). j, (10-10).

2017, Jan. 2 Litho. *Perf. 13½*

1149 A436 49c Sheet of 10, #a-j 10.00 10.00

Miniature Sheet

New Year 2017 (Year of the Rooster) — A437

No. 1150 — Color of rooster: a, Greenish blue (4-1). b, Chestnut (4-2). c, Ochre (4-3). d, Deep blue green (4-4).

2017, Jan. 28 Litho. *Perf. 13½*

1150 A437 $1.20 Sheet of 4, #a-d 9.75 9.75

Haiku Type of 2016

Miniature Sheet

No. 1151: a, Because of how light works, everything we see is only reflection (20-1). b, All that remained when the moon broke the clouds was the rabbit's silhouette (20-2). c, The grass has every intention of reaching all the way to the sky (20-3). d, The mountain lake was so still that either bird could have been the real one (20-4). e, As the great river bends, it is not the water that turns but the land (20-5). f, Whatever happens, the sparrows still wing their way every afternoon (20-6). g, The chief dreamed only of the great eagle, who dreamed only of the clouds (20-7). h, From the planets to the humble bees, such divine choreography (20-8). i, The first leaf from the tree is the most tentative, and yet the most brave (20-9). j, There is an endless joy which transcends the finite pain of living things (20-10). k, Imperceptible, the moments between moments make all the difference (20-11). l, The sound of the leaves and the sound of the ocean are from the same song (20-12). m, A subtle madness compels the moon to challenge the sun for the night (20-13). n, Rejoice in small things, let them fill you, as starlight fills the mountain sky (20-14). o, Even clouds holding nothing tend to appear at the right time and place (20-15). p, The fleeting thought which preceded morning flight was known but to the bird (20-16). q, If one could chart the path of but a single cloud, one would know all things (20-17). r, Consider the red leaf, and how it is every color except red (20-18). s, Between two branches, the space where a blackbird once was, or might have been (20-19). t, Each ending has two beginnings: the one before and the one after (20-20).

2017, Feb. 22 Litho. *Perf. 13½*

Red Brown Stamps

1151 A422 49c Sheet of 20, #a-t 20.00 20.00

SEMI-POSTAL STAMPS

Operation Crossroads, Nuclear Testing at Bikini Atoll, 50th Anniv. — SP1

Designs: a, Evacuation of Bikinians. b, Navy preparations. c, Able. d, Baker. e, Ghost fleet. f, Effects on Bikinians.

1996, July 1 Litho. *Perf. 13½*

B1 SP1 32c +8c #a.-f. + 6 labels 4.75 4.75

Surtax for the benefit of the people of Bikini.

AIR POST STAMPS

Audubon Type of 1985

1985, Feb. 15 Litho. *Perf. 14*

C1 A11 44c Booby Gannet, vert. .90 .90
C2 A11 44c Esquimaux Curlew, vert. .90 .90
a. Pair, #C1-C2 1.80 1.80

AMERIPEX Type of 1986

Designs: No. C3, Consolidated PBY-5A Catalina Amphibian. No. C4, Grumman SA-16 Albatross. No. C5, McDonnell Douglas DC-6B Super Cloudmaster. No. C6, Boeing 727-100.

1986, May 22 Litho. *Perf. 14*

C3 A20 44c multicolored .85 .85
C4 A20 44c multicolored .85 .85
C5 A20 44c multicolored .85 .85
C6 A20 44c multicolored .85 .85
a. Block of 4, #C3-C6 3.50 3.50

Operation Crossroads Type of 1986
Souvenir Sheet

1986, July 1 Litho. *Perf. 14*

C7 A21 44c USS Saratoga *4.00 4.00*

Statue of Liberty Cent., Intl. Peace Year — AP1

1986, Oct. 28 Litho.

C8 AP1 44c multicolored 1.00 .95

Natl. Girl Scout Movement, 20th Anniv. — AP2

No. C9, Community service. No. C10, Salute. No. C11, Health care. No. C12, Learning skills.

1986, Dec. 8 Litho.

C9 AP2 44c multicolored .75 .75
C10 AP2 44c multicolored .75 .75
C11 AP2 44c multicolored .75 .75
C12 AP2 44c multicolored .75 .75
a. Block of 4, #C9-C12 3.00 3.00

Girl Scout Movement in the US, 75th anniv. (1912-1987).

Marine Birds AP3

No. C13, Wedge-tailed shearwater. No. C14, Red-footed booby. No. C15, Red-tailed tropic-bird. No. C16, Great frigatebird.

1987, Jan. 12 Litho. *Perf. 14*

C13 AP3 44c multicolored .75 .75
C14 AP3 44c multicolored .75 .75
C15 AP3 44c multicolored .75 .75
C16 AP3 44c multicolored .75 .75
a. Block of 4, #C13-C16 3.00 3.00

CAPEX '87 AP4

Last flight of Amelia Earhart: No. C17, Take-off at Lae, New Guinea, July 2, 1937. No. C18, USCG Itasca cutter at Howland Is. No. C19, Purported crash landing of the Electra at Mili Atoll. No. C20, Recovery of the Electra by the Koshu, a Japanese survey ship.

1987, June 15 Litho. *Perf. 14*

C17 AP4 44c multicolored .75 .75
C18 AP4 44c multicolored .75 .75
C19 AP4 44c multicolored .75 .75
C20 AP4 44c multicolored .75 .75
a. Block of 4, #C17-C20 3.00 3.00

Space Shuttle Type of 1988

Design: 45c, Astronaut, shuttle over Rongelap.

1988, Dec. 23 Litho. *Perf. 14*

C21 A38 45c multicolored .85 .85

Aircraft — AP5

12c, Dornier Do228. 36c, Boeing 737. 39c, Hawker Siddeley 748. 45c, Boeing 727.

1989, Apr. 24 Litho. *Perf. 14x14½*

C22 AP5 12c multi .25 .25
a. Booklet pane of 10 3.00 —
C23 AP5 36c multi .75 .75
a. Booklet pane of 10 8.00 —
C24 AP5 39c multi .90 .90
a. Booklet pane of 10 9.00 —
C25 AP5 45c multi 1.00 1.00
a. Booklet pane of 10 10.00 —
b. Bklt. pane, 5 each 36c, 45c 8.75 —
Nos. C22-C25 (4) 2.90 2.90

MARTINIQUE

ˌmär-tən-ˈēk

LOCATION — Island in the West Indies, southeast of Puerto Rico
GOVT. — French Colony
AREA — 385 sq. mi.
POP. — 261,595 (1946)
CAPITAL — Fort-de-France

Formerly a French colony, Martinique became an integral part of the Republic, acquiring the same status as the departments in metropolitan France, under a law effective Jan. 1, 1947.

100 Centimes = 1 Franc

Catalogue values for unused stamps in this country are for Never Hinged items, beginning with Scott 196 in the regular postage section, Scott C1 in the air-post section, and Scott J37 in the postage due section.

See France Nos. 1278 and 1508 for stamps inscribed "Martinique."

Stamps of French Colonies 1881-86 Surcharged in Black

Nos. 1, 7

No. 2

No. 3

No. 4

Nos. 5-6, 8

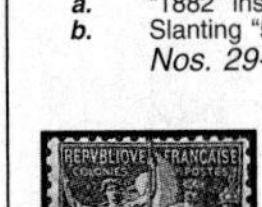

Nos. 9-20

1886-91 Unwmk. *Perf. 14x13½*

1 A9 5 on 20c 65.00 55.00
a. Double surcharge *750.00 750.00*
2 A9 5c on 20c *15,000. 15,000.*
3 A9 15c on 20c ('87) 275.00 240.00
a. Inverted surcharge *2,350. 2,500.*
4 A9 15c on 20c ('87) 100.00 100.00
a. Inverted surcharge *1,500. 1,500.*
b. Se-tenant pair, #3-4 475.00 425.00
c. Se-tenant pair, #3a-4a *4,750. 4,750.*
5 A9 01 on 20c ('88) 20.00 19.00
a. Inverted surcharge *350.00 350.00*
6 A9 05 on 20c 16.00 13.00
7 A9 15 on 20c ('88) 200.00 180.00
c. Inverted surcharge *700.00 750.00*
8 A9 015 on 20c ('87) 60.00 *65.00*
a. Inverted surcharge *875.00 825.00*
9 A9 01c on 2c ('88) 4.75 3.25
a. Double surcharge *475.00 475.00*
10 A9 01c on 4c ('88) 15.00 4.75
11 A9 05c on 4c ('88) 1,500. 1,375.
12 A9 05c on 10c ('90) 120.00 72.50
a. Slanting "5" *300.00 240.00*
13 A9 05c on 20c ('88) 28.00 20.00
a. Slanting "5" *150.00 120.00*
b. Inverted surcharge *425.00 375.00*
14 A9 05c on 30c ('91) 35.00 28.00
a. Slanting "5" *160.00 150.00*
15 A9 05c on 35c ('91) 20.00 16.00
a. Slanting "5" *160.00 150.00*
b. Inverted surcharge *325.00 300.00*
16 A9 05c on 40c ('91) 65.00 47.50
a. Slanting "5" *260.00 165.00*
17 A9 15c on 4c ('88) *12,000. 11,000.*
18 A9 15c on 20c ('87) 150.00 120.00
a. Slanting "5" *500.00 425.00*
b. Double surcharge *700.00 700.00*
19 A9 15c on 25c ('90) 32.50 20.00
a. Slanting "5" *150.00 130.00*
b. Inverted surcharge *325.00 275.00*
c. Double surcharge 450.00 450.00
20 A9 15c on 75c ('91) 210.00 175.00
a. Slanting "5" *550.00 450.00*

French Colonies No. 47 Surcharged

1891

21 A9 01c on 2c brn, *buff* 11.00 11.00

French Colonies Nos. J5-J9 Surcharged

1891-92 Black Surcharge *Imperf.*

22 D1 05c on 5c blk ('92) 17.50 17.00
a. Slanting "5" *72.50 65.00*
23 D1 05c on 15c blk 16.00 16.00
b. Slanting "5" *72.50 65.00*
24 D1 15c on 20c blk 20.00 16.00
a. Inverted surcharge *300.00 300.00*
b. Double surcharge *300.00 300.00*
25 D1 15c on 30c blk 20.00 16.00
a. Inverted surcharge *300.00 300.00*
b. Slanting "5" *80.00 72.50*
Nos. 22-25 (4) 73.50 65.00

Red Surcharge

26 D1 05c on 10c blk 14.50 11.00
a. Inverted surcharge *300.00 300.00*
27 D1 05c on 15c blk 16.00 16.00
28 D1 15c on 20c blk 52.50 45.00
a. Inverted surcharge *450.00 450.00*
Nos. 26-28 (3) 83.00 72.00

French Colonies No. 54 Surcharged in Black

j

k

1892 *Perf. 14x13½*

29 A9 (j) 05c on 25c 65.00 65.00
a. Slanting "5" *300.00 300.00*
30 A9 (j) 15c on 25c 36.00 36.00
a. Slanting "5" *275.00 275.00*
31 A9 (k) 05c on 25c 65.00 65.00
a. "1882" instead of "1892" *675.00 600.00*
b. "95" instead of "05" *850.00 800.00*
c. Slanting "5" *300.00 300.00*
32 A9 (k) 15c on 25c 32.50 32.50
a. "1882" instead of "1892" *600.00 600.00*
b. Slanting "5" *160.00 160.00*
Nos. 29-32 (4) 198.50 198.50

Navigation and Commerce — A15

1892-1906 Typo. *Perf. 14x13½*
"MARTINIQUE" Colony in Carmine or Blue

33 A15 1c blk, *lil bl* 1.50 1.40
a. "MARTINIQUE" in blue 1,000. 1,000.
b. "MARTINIQUE" omitted 5,500.
34 A15 2c brn, *buff* 1.75 1.40
35 A15 4c claret, *lav* 2.00 1.50
36 A15 5c grn, *grnsh* 2.40 1.50
37 A15 5c yel grn ('99) 3.50 1.10
38 A15 10c blk, *lav* 11.00 2.00
39 A15 10c red ('99) 5.25 1.50
40 A15 15c blue, quadrille paper 42.50 8.00
41 A15 15c gray ('99) 13.50 2.10
42 A15 20c red, *grn* 20.00 10.00
43 A15 25c blk, *rose* 24.00 3.25
44 A15 25c blue ('99) 16.00 14.50
45 A15 30c brn, *bis* 36.00 19.00
46 A15 35c blk, *yel* ('06) 16.00 9.50
47 A15 40c red, *straw* 36.00 19.00
48 A15 50c car, *rose* 40.00 24.00
49 A15 50c brn, *az* ('99) 42.50 32.50
50 A15 75c dp vio, *org* 32.50 20.00
51 A15 1fr brnz grn, *straw* 32.50 21.00
52 A15 2fr vio, *rose* ('04) 92.50 75.00
53 A15 5fr lil, *lav* ('03) 110.00 95.00
Nos. 33-53 (21) 581.40 363.25

Perf. 13½x14 stamps are counterfeits.
For surcharges see Nos. 54-61, 101-104.

Stamps of 1892-1903 Surcharged in Black

1904

54 A15 10c on 30c brn, *bis* 14.50 14.50
a. Double surcharge 525.00 525.00
b. Inverted surcharge 1,600. 1,600.
55 A15 10c on 5fr lil, *lav* 16.00 16.00

Surcharged

56 A15 10c on 30c brn, *bis* 24.00 24.00
57 A15 10c on 40c red, *straw* 24.00 24.00
a. Double surcharge 600.00 600.00
58 A15 10c on 50c car, *rose* 28.00 28.00
59 A15 10c on 75c dp vio, *org* 20.00 20.00
60 A15 10c on 1fr brnz grn, *straw* 24.00 24.00
a. Double surcharge 350.00 350.00
61 A15 10c on 5fr lil, *lav* 200.00 200.00
Nos. 54-61 (8) 350.50 350.50

Martinique Woman — A16

Girl Bearing Pineapple in Cane Field — A18

View of Fort-de-France — A17

1908-30 **Typo.**

62 A16 1c red brn & brn .25 .25
63 A16 2c ol grn & brn .30 .25
64 A16 4c vio brn & brn .30 .30
65 A16 5c grn & brn 1.10 .40
66 A16 5c org & brn ('22) .50 .40
67 A16 10c car & brn 1.10 .50
68 A16 10c bl grn & grn ('22) .55 .40
69 A16 10c brn vio & rose ('25) .55 .40
70 A16 15c brn vio & rose ('17) .65 .40
71 A16 15c bl grn & gray grn ('25) .50 .40
72 A16 15c dp bl & red org ('28) 1.60 1.60
73 A16 20c vio & brn 1.40 1.10
74 A17 25c bl & brn 2.25 1.10
75 A17 25c org & brn ('22) .90 .55
76 A17 30c brn org & brn 2.25 1.10
77 A17 30c dl red & brn ('22) .75 .65
78 A17 30c rose & ver ('24) .55 .55
79 A17 30c ol brn & brn ('25) .55 .55
80 A17 30c sl bl & bl grn ('27) 1.60 1.60
81 A17 35c vio & brn .90 .65
 a. White chalky paper 4.50 2.75
82 A17 40c gray grn & brn .90 .65
83 A17 45c dk brn & brn .90 .65
 a. White chalky paper 2.00 1.60
84 A17 50c rose & brn 2.25 1.10
85 A17 50c bl & brn ('22) 1.40 1.30
86 A17 50c org & grn ('25) .90 .40
87 A17 60c dk bl & lil rose ('25) .75 .75
88 A17 65c vio & ol brn ('27) 2.00 2.00
89 A17 75c slate & brn 1.40 1.10
90 A17 75c ind & dk bl ('25) .90 .90
91 A17 75c org brn & lt bl ('27) 2.75 2.75
92 A17 90c brn red & brt red ('30) 5.50 5.50
93 A18 1fr dl bl & brn 1.20 1.00
94 A18 1fr dk bl ('25) 1.00 .90
95 A18 1fr ver & ol grn ('27) 2.75 2.75
96 A18 1.10fr vio & dk brn ('28) 3.75 *4.50*
97 A18 1.50fr ind & ultra ('30) 5.50 5.50
98 A18 2fr gray & brn 4.50 2.00
99 A18 3fr red vio ('30) 9.50 9.50
100 A18 5fr org red & brn 10.50 8.00
 Nos. 62-100 (39) 76.90 64.40

For surcharges see Nos. 105-128, B1.

Nos. 41, 43, 47 and 53 Surcharged in Carmine or Black

Spacing between figures of surcharge 1.5mm (5c), 2mm (10c)

1912, Aug.

101 A15 5c on 15c gray (C) 1.00 1.00
102 A15 5c on 25c blk, *rose* (C) 1.50 1.50
103 A15 10c on 40c red, *straw* 2.40 2.40
104 A15 10c on 5fr lil, *lav* 3.00 3.00
 Nos. 101-104 (4) 7.90 7.90

Two spacings between the surcharged numerals are found on Nos. 101 to 104. For detailed listings, see the *Scott Classic Specialized Catalogue of Stamps and Covers.*

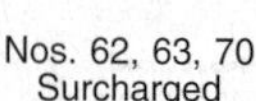

Nos. 62, 63, 70 Surcharged

1920, June 15

105 A16 5c on 1c 2.10 2.10
 a. Double surcharge 45.00 45.00
 b. Inverted surcharge 32.50 32.50
106 A16 10c on 2c 2.10 2.10
 a. Double surcharge 130.00
 b. Inverted surcharge 45.00 45.00
 c. Double surcharge, one inverted 95.00
107 A16 25c on 15c 2.25 2.25
 a. Double surcharge 55.00 55.00
 b. Inverted surcharge 55.00 55.00
 c. Double surcharge, one inverted 100.00
 d. Pair, one stamp without surcharge 160.00 160.00
 Nos. 105-107 (3) 6.45 6.45

No. 70 Surcharged in Various Colors

1922, Dec.

108 A16 1c on 15c (Bk) .50 .50
 a. Double surcharge 190.00 190.00
109 A16 2c on 15c (Bl) .50 .50
110 A16 5c on 15c (R) .65 .65
 a. Imperf., pair 260.00
 Nos. 108-110 (3) 1.65 1.65

Types of 1908-30 Surcharged

1923-25

111 A17 60c on 75c bl & rose .65 .65
112 A17 65c on 45c ol brn & brn ('25) 1.45 1.45
113 A17 85c on 75c blk & brn (R) ('25) 1.75 1.75
 Nos. 111-113 (3) 3.85 3.85

Nos. 63, 73, 76-77, 84-85 Surcharged in Brown

Surcharge is horiz. on Nos. 114-115, vert. reading up on Nos. 116, 119 and down on Nos. 117-118.

1924, Feb. 14

114 A16 1c on 2c 3.25 3.25
 a. Double surcharge 550.00 550.00
 b. Inverted surcharge 100.00 100.00
115 A16 5c on 20c 4.00 4.00
 a. Inverted surcharge 100.00 100.00
116 A17 15c on 30c (#76) 16.00 16.00
 a. Surcharge reading down 57.50 57.50
117 A17 15c on 30c (#77) 22.50 22.50
 a. Surcharge reading up 67.50 67.50
118 A17 25c on 50c (#84) 325.00 350.00
119 A17 25c on 50c (#85) 10.50 10.50
 a. Double surcharge 400.00 400.00
 b. Surcharge reading down 47.50
 Nos. 114-119 (6) 381.25 406.25

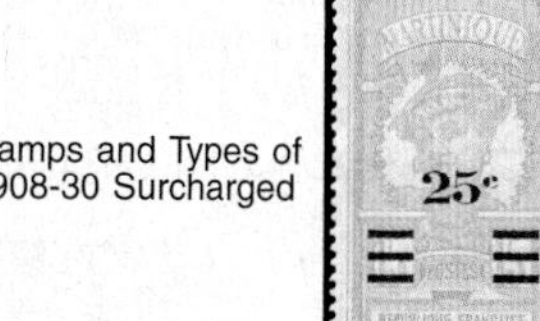

Stamps and Types of 1908-30 Surcharged

1924-27

120 A16 25c on 15c brn vio & rose ('25) .55 .55
121 A18 25c on 2fr gray & brn .50 .50
122 A18 25c on 5fr org red & brn (Bl) 2.10 1.75
123 A17 90c on 75c brn red & red ('27) 3.75 2.75
124 A18 1.25fr on 1fr dk bl ('26) 1.10 1.00
125 A18 1.50fr on 1fr dk bl & ultra ('27) 2.00 1.10
126 A18 3fr on 5fr dl red & grn ('27) 3.00 3.00
127 A18 10fr on 5fr dl grn & dp red ('27) 12.00 12.00
128 A18 20fr on 5fr org brn & red vio ('27) 18.50 17.50
 Nos. 120-128 (9) 43.50 40.15

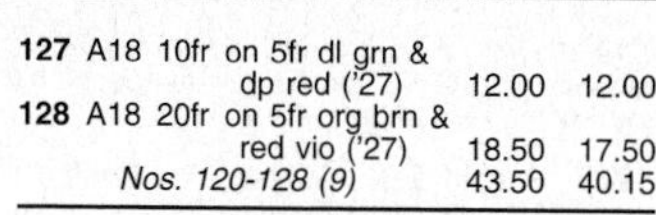

Common Design Types pictured following the introduction.

Colonial Exposition Issue

Common Design Types

1931, Apr. 13 **Engr.** ***Perf. 12½***

Name of Country in Black

129 CD70 40c deep green 5.25 5.25
130 CD71 50c violet 5.25 5.25
131 CD72 90c red orange 5.25 5.25
132 CD73 1.50fr dull blue 5.25 5.25
 Nos. 129-132 (4) 21.00 21.00

Village of Basse-Pointe — A19

Government Palace, Fort-de-France — A20

Martinique Women A21

1933-40 **Photo.** ***Perf. 13½***

133 A19 1c red, *pink* .25 .25
134 A20 2c dull blue .25 .25
135 A20 3c sepia ('40) .35 .35
136 A19 4c olive grn .25 .25
137 A20 5c dp rose .35 .35
138 A19 10c blk, *pink* .35 .35
139 A20 15c blk, *org* .35 .35
140 A21 20c org brn .35 .35
141 A19 25c brn vio .35 .35
142 A20 30c green .50 .50
143 A20 30c lt ultra ('40) .40 .40
144 A21 35c dl grn ('38) 1.00 .90
145 A21 40c olive brn .65 .50
146 A20 45c dk brn 2.00 1.90
147 A20 45c grn ('40) .65 .65
148 A20 50c red .50 .30
149 A19 55c brn red ('38) 1.30 1.00
150 A19 60c lt bl ('40) .95 .95
151 A21 65c red, *grn* .50 .50
152 A21 70c brt red vio ('40) .75 .75
153 A19 75c dk brn 1.10 .90
154 A20 80c vio ('38) .75 .65
155 A19 90c carmine 1.90 1.75
156 A19 90c brt red vio ('39) .95 .95
157 A20 1fr blk, *grn* 1.90 1.40
158 A20 1fr rose red ('38) .75 .65
159 A21 1.25fr dk vio .80 .80
160 A21 1.25fr dp rose ('39) .75 .75
161 A19 1.40fr lt ultra ('40) .80 .80
162 A20 1.50fr dp bl .65 .55
163 A20 1.60fr chnt ('40) .80 .80
164 A21 1.75fr ol grn 9.50 5.25
165 A21 1.75fr dp bl ('38) .75 .75
166 A19 2fr dk bl,*grn* .50 .40
167 A21 2.25fr blue ('39) .75 .75
168 A19 2.50fr sepia ('40) .95 .95
169 A21 3fr brn vio .65 .60
170 A21 5fr red, *pink* 1.30 1.10
171 A19 10fr dk bl, *bl* 1.10 .80
172 A20 20fr red, *yel* 1.35 .95
 Nos. 133-172 (40) 40.05 32.75

For surcharges see Nos. 190-195.
For type A20 without "RF," see Nos. 189A-189E.

Landing of Bélain d'Esnambuc — A22

Freed Slaves Paying Homage to Victor Schoelcher A23

1935, Oct. 22 **Engr.** ***Perf. 13***

173 A22 40c blk brn 3.25 3.25
174 A22 50c dl red 3.25 3.25
175 A22 1.50fr ultra 12.00 12.00
176 A23 1.75fr lil rose 12.00 12.00
177 A23 5fr brown 12.00 12.00
 a. 5fr ultramarine (error) 950.00
178 A23 10fr blue grn 9.50 9.50
 Nos. 173-178 (6) 52.00 52.00

Tercentenary of French possessions in the West Indies.

Colonial Arts Exhibition Issue

Common Design Type

Souvenir Sheet

1937 ***Imperf.***

179 CD74 3fr brt grn 8.75 *10.50*
 a. "MARTINIQUE" omitted 3,100.
 b. Inscriptions inverted 2,200.

Paris International Exposition Issue

Common Design Types

1937, Apr. 15 ***Perf. 13***

180 CD74 20c dp vio 2.10 2.10
181 CD75 30c dk grn 1.75 1.75
182 CD76 40c car rose 1.75 1.75
183 CD77 50c dk brn & blk 1.60 1.60
184 CD78 90c red 2.00 2.00
185 CD79 1.50fr ultra 2.00 2.00
 Nos. 180-185 (6) 11.20 11.20

New York World's Fair Issue

Common Design Type

1939, May 10 ***Perf. 12½x12***

186 CD82 1.25fr car lake 1.10 1.10
187 CD82 2.25fr ultra 1.25 1.25

View of Fort-de-France and Marshal Pétain — A23a

1941 **Engr.** ***Perf. 12½x12***

188 A23a 1fr dull lilac .80
189 A23a 2.50fr blue .80

Nos. 188-189 were issued by the Vichy government in France, but were not placed on sale in Martinique.

For surcharges, see Nos. B10A-B10B.

Types of 1933-40 without "RF"

1942-44 **Photo.** ***Perf. 13½***

189A A20 3c sepia .50
189B A20 15c blk, *org* .55
189C A20 30c yel green .55
189D A20 50c red 1.40
189E A20 1.50fr dp bl .65
 Nos. 189A-189E (5) 3.65

Nos. 189A-189E were issued by the Vichy government in France, but were not placed on sale in Martinique.

Nos. 134, 135, 136 and 151 Surcharged in Red, Black or Blue

1945 ***Perf. 13½, 13x13½***

190 A20 1fr on 2c dl bl (R) .65 .65
191 A19 2fr on 4c ol grn .65 .65
192 A20 3fr on 2c dl bl (R) .80 .80
193 A21 5fr on 65c red, *grn* 1.40 1.40
194 A21 10fr on 65c red, *grn* 1.50 1.50
195 A20 20fr on 3c sepia (Bl) 1.50 1.50
 Nos. 190-195 (6) 6.50 6.50

Catalogue values for unused stamps in this section, from this point to the end of the section, are for Never Hinged items.

Eboue Issue
Common Design Type

1945 Engr. *Perf. 13*

196 CD91	2fr black	.75	.55
197 CD91	25fr Prussian green	1.30	1.00

Victor Schoelcher and View of Town of Schoelcher A24

1945 Unwmk. Litho. *Perf. 11½*

198 A24	10c dp bl vio & ultra	.35	.25
199 A24	30c dk org brn & lt org brn	.35	.25
200 A24	40c grnsh bl & pale bl	.40	.35
201 A24	50c car brn & rose lil	.40	.35
202 A24	60c org yel & yel	.40	.35
203 A24	70c brn & pale brn	.40	.35
204 A24	80c lt bl grn & pale grn	.40	.35
205 A24	1fr bl & lt bl	.40	.35
206 A24	1.20fr rose vio & rose lil	.40	.35
207 A24	1.50fr red org & org	.40	.35
208 A24	2fr blk & gray	.40	.35
209 A24	2.40fr red & pink	1.75	1.00
210 A24	3fr pink & pale pink	.75	.50
211 A24	4fr ultra & lt ultra	.95	.50
212 A24	4.50fr yel grn & lt grn	1.10	.50
213 A24	5fr org brn & lt org brn	.95	.50
214 A24	10fr dk vio & lil	1.10	.65
215 A24	15fr rose car & lil rose	1.50	.75
216 A24	20fr ol grn & lt ol grn	2.25	1.25
	Nos. 198-216 (19)	14.65	9.30

Martinique Girl A25

Mountains A30

Cliffs A26

Gathering Sugar Cane A27

Mount Pelée A28

Tropical Fruit — A29

1947, June 2 Engr. *Perf. 13*

217 A25	10c red brown	.50	.25
218 A25	30c deep blue	.50	.40
219 A25	50c olive brown	.50	.40
220 A26	60c dark green	.55	.50
221 A26	1fr red brown	.55	.35
222 A26	1.50fr purple	.60	.50
223 A27	2fr blue green	1.10	.75
224 A27	2.50fr blk brn	1.10	.65
225 A27	3fr deep blue	1.10	.65
226 A28	4fr dk brown	1.00	.65
227 A28	5fr dark green	1.10	.65
228 A28	6fr lilac rose	1.00	.65
229 A29	10fr indigo	1.75	1.25
230 A29	15fr red brown	1.90	1.25
231 A29	20fr blk brown	2.50	1.50
232 A30	25fr violet	2.50	1.60
233 A30	40fr blue green	3.00	2.00
	Nos. 217-233 (17)	21.25	14.00

SEMI-POSTAL STAMPS

Regular Issue of 1908 Surcharged in Red

Perf. 13½x14

1915, May 15 Unwmk.

B1 A16	10c + 5c car & brn	2.75	2.00
	Never hinged	4.00	

Curie Issue
Common Design Type

1938, Oct. 24 *Perf. 13*

B2 CD80	1.75fr + 50c brt ultra	13.00	13.00
	Never hinged	17.50	

French Revolution Issue
Common Design Type

Photo.; Name & Value Typo. in Black

1939, July 5

B3 CD83	45c + 25c grn	10.50	10.50
	Never hinged	15.00	
B4 CD83	70c + 30c brn	10.50	10.50
	Never hinged	15.00	
B5 CD83	90c + 35c red org	10.50	10.50
	Never hinged	15.00	
B6 CD83	1.25fr + 1fr rose pink	10.50	10.50
	Never hinged	15.00	
B7 CD83	2.25fr + 2fr blue	10.50	10.50
	Never hinged	15.00	
	Nos. B3-B7 (5)	52.50	52.50

Common Design Type and

Colonial Infantry with Machine Gun SP1

Naval Rifleman SP2

1941 Photo. *Perf. 13½*

B8 SP1	1fr + 1fr red	1.25
B9 CD86	1.50fr + 3fr maroon	1.40
B10 SP2	2.50fr + 1fr blue	1.40
	Nos. B8-B10 (3)	4.05

Nos. B8-B10 were issued by the Vichy government in France, but were not placed on sale in Martinique.

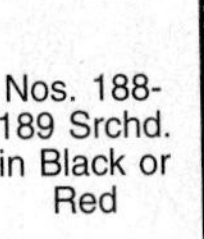

Nos. 188-189 Srchd. in Black or Red

1944 Engr. *Perf. 12½x12*

B10A	50c + 1.50fr on 2.50fr blue (R)	.95
B10B	+ 2.50fr on 1fr dull lilac	1.00

Colonial Development Fund.

Nos. B10A-B10B were issued by the Vichy government in France, but were not placed on sale in Martinique.

Red Cross Issue
Common Design Type

1944 *Perf. 14½x14*

B11 CD90	5fr + 20fr dark purple	1.20	1.20

The surtax was for the French Red Cross and national relief.

AIR POST STAMPS

Catalogue values for unused stamps in this section are for Never Hinged items.

Common Design Type

1945 Unwmk. Photo. *Perf. 14½x14*

C1 CD87	50fr dark green	1.25	.80
C2 CD87	100fr plum	1.75	.80

Two other values, 8.50fr orange and 18fr red brown, were prepared but not issued. Value, $210 each.

Victory Issue
Common Design Type

1946, May 8 Engr. *Perf. 12½*

C3 CD92	8fr indigo	1.30	1.00

European victory of the Allied Nations in WWII.

Chad to Rhine Issue
Common Design Types

1946, June 6

C4 CD93	5fr orange	1.00	.90
C5 CD94	10fr slate grn	1.40	1.10
C6 CD95	15fr carmine	1.40	1.20
C7 CD96	20fr chocolate	1.40	1.20
C8 CD97	25fr deep blue	1.75	1.40
C9 CD98	50fr gray blk	1.90	1.50
	Nos. C4-C9 (6)	8.85	7.30

Seaplane and Beach Scene — AP1

Plane over Tropic Shore — AP2

Albatross — AP3

1947, June 2 *Perf. 13*

C10 AP1	50fr dk brn vio	6.50	2.75
C11 AP2	100fr dk bl grn	8.00	3.75
C12 AP3	200fr violet	45.00	25.00
	Nos. C10-C12 (3)	59.50	31.50

AIR POST SEMI-POSTAL STAMPS

Nurse with Mother & Child — SPAP1

Unwmk.

1942, June 22 Engr. *Perf. 13*

CB1 SPAP1	1.50fr + 3.50fr green	.90
CB2 SPAP1	2fr + 6fr brn & red	.90

Native children's welfare fund.

Nos. CB1-CB2 were issued by the Vichy government in France, but were not placed on sale in Martinique.

Colonial Education Fund
Common Design Type

1942, June 22

CB3 CD86a	1.20fr + 1.80fr blue & red	1.00

No. CB3 was issued by the Vichy government in France, but was not placed on sale in Martinique.

POSTAGE DUE STAMPS

The set of 14 French Colonies postage due stamps (Nos. J1-J14) overprinted "MARTINIQUE" diagonally in red in 1887 was not an official issue.

Postage Due Stamps of France, 1893-1926 Overprinted

1927, Oct. 10 *Perf. 14x13½*

J15 D2	5c light blue	1.75	1.75
J16 D2	10c brown	2.10	2.00
J17 D2	20c olive green	2.10	2.00
J18 D2	25c rose	2.75	2.60
J19 D2	30c red	3.75	3.50
J20 D2	45c green	5.25	5.00
J21 D2	50c brn violet	6.50	6.00
J22 D2	60c blue green	6.50	6.00
J23 D2	1fr red brown	8.75	8.25
J24 D2	2fr bright vio	12.00	11.00
J25 D2	3fr magenta	13.00	12.00
	Nos. J15-J25 (11)	64.45	60.10

Tropical Fruit — D3

1933, Feb. 15 Photo. *Perf. 13½*

J26 D3	5c dk bl, *green*	.50	.50
J27 D3	10c orange brown	.50	.50
J28 D3	20c dk blue	.95	.95
J29 D3	25c red, *pink*	1.40	1.40
J30 D3	30c dk vio	1.40	1.40
J31 D3	45c red, *yel*	1.10	1.10
J32 D3	50c dk brn	1.75	1.75
J33 D3	60c dl grn	1.75	1.75
J34 D3	1fr blk, *org*	1.75	1.75
J35 D3	2fr dp rose	1.75	1.75
J36 D3	3fr dk blue, *bl*	1.75	1.75
	Nos. J26-J36 (11)	14.60	14.60

Type of 1933 Without "RF"

1943

J36A D3 10c orange brown .35
J36B D3 20c dk blue .35
J36C D3 25c red, *pink* .50
J36D D3 30c dk vio .50
Nos. J36A-J36D (4) 1.70

Nos. J36A-J36D were issued by the Vichy government in France, but were not placed on sale in Martinique.

Catalogue values for unused stamps in this section, from this point to the end of the section, are for Never Hinged items.

Map — D4

1947, June 2 Engr. *Perf. 14x13*

J37 D4 10c ultra .40 .30
J38 D4 30c brt bl grn .40 .30
J39 D4 50c slate gray .40 .30
J40 D4 1fr org red .40 .30
J41 D4 2fr dk vio brn .90 .75
J42 D4 3fr lilac rose .95 .80
J43 D4 4fr dk brn .95 .95
J44 D4 5fr red 1.20 .95
J45 D4 10fr black 2.10 1.60
J46 D4 20fr olive grn 2.40 1.75
Nos. J37-J46 (10) 10.10 8.00

PARCEL POST STAMP

Postage Due Stamp of French Colonies Surcharged in Black

1903, Oct. Unwmk. *Imperf.*

Q1 D1 5fr on 60c brn, *buff* 550.00 *675.00*
a. Inverted surcharge 875.00 *950.00*

MAURITANIA

mor-ə-ta-nē-ə

LOCATION — Northwestern Africa, bordering on the Atlantic Ocean
GOVT. — Republic
AREA — 398,000 sq. mi.
POP. — 2,581,738 (1999 est.)
CAPITAL — Nouakchott

The Islamic Republic of Mauritania was proclaimed Nov. 28, 1958.

Stamps of French West Africa were used in the period between the issues of the colony and the republic.

100 Centimes = 1 Franc
Ouguiya ("um") (1973)

Catalogue values for unused stamps in this country are for Never Hinged items, beginning with Scott 114 in the regular postage section, Scott B9 in the semi-postal section, Scott C6 in the air-post section, Scott J19 in the postage due section, and Scott O1 in the official section.

See French West Africa No. 65 for additional stamp inscribed "Mauritanie" and "Afrique Occidentale Francaise."

General Louis Faidherbe A1

Oil Palms — A2

Dr. Noel Eugène Ballay A3

Perf. 14x13½

1906-07 Typo. Unwmk.

"Mauritanie" in Red or Blue

1 A1 1c slate .70 .70
2 A1 2c chocolate 2.10 2.10
3 A1 4c choc, *gray bl* 2.75 2.75
4 A1 5c green 1.40 1.40
5 A1 10c carmine (B) 14.00 7.00
7 A2 20c black, *azure* 27.50 17.50
8 A2 25c blue, *pnksh* 10.00 7.00
9 A2 30c choc, *pnksh* 105.00 62.50
10 A2 35c black, *yellow* 10.00 7.00
11 A2 40c car, *az* (B) 10.00 10.00
12 A2 45c choc, *grnsh* ('07) 10.00 10.00
13 A2 50c deep violet 10.00 7.00
14 A2 75c blue, *org* 10.00 10.00
15 A3 1fr black, *azure* 27.50 27.50
16 A3 2fr blue, *pink* 55.00 55.00
17 A3 5fr car, *straw* (B) 140.00 150.00
Nos. 1-17 (16) 435.95 377.45

Crossing Desert A4

1913-38

18 A4 1c brn vio & brn .30 *.55*
19 A4 2c black & blue .30 *.55*
20 A4 4c violet & blk .30 *.55*
21 A4 5c yel grn & bl grn 1.00 .70
a. Chalky paper 2.10 1.40
22 A4 5c brn vio & rose ('22) .35 .35
23 A4 10c rose & red org 2.50 1.75
a. Chalky paper 3.50 2.50
24 A4 10c yel grn & bl grn ('22) .35 .70
25 A4 10c lil rose, *bluish* ('25) .70 1.00
26 A4 15c dk brn & blk ('17) .70 .70
a. Chalky paper 1.00 1.00
27 A4 20c bis brn & org .70 .70
28 A4 25c blue & vio 1.40 1.00
29 A4 25c grn & rose ('22) .35 .35
30 A4 30c bl grn & rose 1.40 1.50
31 A4 30c rose & red org ('22) 1.75 *2.10*
32 A4 30c black & yel ('26) .35 .35
33 A4 30c bl grn & yel grn ('28) 1.40 1.40
34 A4 35c brown & vio .70 .75
35 A4 35c dp grn & lt grn ('38) 1.40 1.40
36 A4 40c gray & bl grn 2.75 2.50
37 A4 45c org & bis brn 1.40 *1.75*
38 A4 50c brn vio & rose 1.00 *1.40*
39 A4 50c dk bl & ultra ('22) .70 *.70*
40 A4 50c gray grn & dp bl ('26) .35 .70
41 A4 60c vio, *pnksh* ('25) .70 *1.00*
42 A4 65c yel brn & lt bl ('26) 1.00 *1.75*
43 A4 75c ultra & brown 1.00 1.40
44 A4 85c myr grn & lt brn ('26) 1.40 *1.75*
45 A4 90c brn red & rose ('30) 2.10 2.10
46 A4 1fr rose & black 1.00 *1.40*
47 A4 1.10fr vio & ver ('28) 10.00 *14.00*
48 A4 1.25fr dk bl & blk brn ('33) 2.10 2.50
49 A4 1.50fr lt bl & dp bl ('30) 1.40 *1.40*
50 A4 1.75fr bl grn & brn red ('33) 2.10 2.50
51 A4 1.75fr dk bl & ultra ('38) 2.10 2.10
52 A4 2fr red org & vio 1.75 *2.10*
53 A4 3fr red violet ('30) 2.10 2.10
54 A4 5fr violet & blue 3.00 *3.75*
Nos. 18-54 (37) 53.90 63.30

Stamp and Type of 1913-38 Srchd.

1922-25

55 A4 60c on 75c violet, *pnksh* 1.00 *1.40*
56 A4 65c on 15c dk brn & blk ('25) 1.75 *2.10*
57 A4 85c on 75c ultra & brn ('25) 1.75 *2.10*
Nos. 55-57 (3) 4.50 *5.60*

Type of 1913-38 Srchd.

1924-27

58 A4 25c on 2fr red org & vio 1.00 1.40
59 A4 90c on 75c brn red & cer ('27) 2.10 *2.75*
60 A4 1.25fr on 1fr dk bl & ultra ('26) .70 *.70*
61 A4 1.50fr on 1fr bl & dp bl ('27) 1.40 *1.75*
62 A4 3fr on 5fr ol brn & red vio ('27) 7.00 7.00
63 A4 10fr on 5fr mag & bl grn ('27) 7.00 7.75
64 A4 20fr on 5fr bl vio & dp org ('27) 7.00 *8.00*
Nos. 58-64 (7) 26.20 *29.35*

Common Design Types pictured following the introduction.

Colonial Exposition Issue

Common Design Types

Engr.; Name of Country Typo. in Black

1931, Apr. 13 *Perf. 12½*

65 CD70 40c deep green 7.00 7.00
66 CD71 50c violet 5.00 5.00
67 CD72 90c red orange 5.00 5.00
68 CD73 1.50fr dull blue 5.00 5.00
Nos. 65-68 (4) 22.00 22.00

Paris International Exposition Issue

Common Design Types

1937, Apr. 15 *Perf. 13*

69 CD74 20c deep violet 1.75 1.75
70 CD75 30c dark green 1.75 1.75
71 CD76 40c carmine rose 2.10 2.10
72 CD77 50c dk brn & blk 1.40 1.40
73 CD78 90c red 1.40 1.40
74 CD79 1.50fr ultra 2.10 2.10
Nos. 69-74 (6) 10.50 10.50

Colonial Arts Exhibition Issue

Common Design Type

Souvenir Sheet

1937 *Imperf.*

75 CD76 3fr dark blue 10.00 *14.00*

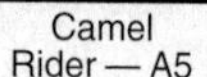

Camel Rider — A5

Mauri Couple — A8

Mauris on Camels A6

Family Before Tent — A7

1938-40 *Perf. 13*

76 A5 2c violet blk .25 .25
77 A5 3c dp ultra .25 .25
78 A5 4c rose violet .30 .30
79 A5 5c orange red .30 .30
80 A5 10c brown car .35 .35
81 A5 15c dk violet .35 .35
82 A6 20c red .35 .35
83 A6 25c deep ultra .35 .35
84 A6 30c deep brown .25 .25
85 A6 35c Prus green .35 .70
86 A6 40c rose car ('40) .35 .35
87 A6 45c Prus grn ('40) .35 .35
88 A6 50c purple .35 .50
89 A7 55c rose violet .70 1.00
90 A7 60c violet ('40) .35 .35
91 A7 65c deep green .70 1.00
92 A7 70c red ('40) .70 .70
93 A7 80c deep blue 1.40 1.40
94 A7 90c rose violet ('39) .70 .70
95 A7 1fr red 2.75 2.10
96 A7 1fr dp green ('40) .70 1.00
97 A7 1.25fr rose car ('39) 1.40 1.40
98 A7 1.40fr dp blue ('40) .70 .70
99 A7 1.50fr violet .70 1.00
99A A7 1.50fr red brn ('40) 125.00
100 A7 1.60fr black brn ('40) 1.75 1.75
101 A8 1.75fr deep ultra 1.40 *1.40*
102 A8 2fr rose violet .35 *1.00*
103 A8 2.25fr dull ultra ('39) .70 .70
104 A8 2.50fr black brn ('40) 1.40 1.40
105 A8 3fr deep green .35 *.90*
106 A8 5fr scarlet .70 *1.00*
107 A8 10fr deep brown 1.75 *1.90*
108 A8 20fr brown car 2.10 *2.25*
Nos. 76-108 (34) 150.45 28.30

Nos. 91 and 109 surcharged with new values are listed under French West Africa.

For surcharges see Nos. B9-B12.

Caillie Issue

Common Design Type

1939, Apr. 5 Engr. *Perf. 12½x12*

109 CD81 90c org brn & org .35 *1.00*
110 CD81 2fr brt violet .35 *1.40*
111 CD81 2.25fr ultra & dk bl .35 *1.40*
Nos. 109-111 (3) 1.05 3.80

New York World's Fair Issue

Common Design Type

1939, May 10

112 CD82 1.25fr carmine lake .70 1.40
113 CD82 2.25fr ultra .70 1.40

Catalogue values for unused stamps in this section, from this point to the end of the section, are for Never Hinged items.

Caravan and Marshal Pétain A9

1941

114 A9 1fr green .80 *1.25*
115 A9 2.50fr deep blue .80 *1.25*

For surcharges, see Nos. B15A-B15B.

Types of 1938-40 Without "RF"

1943-44

115A A5 10c brown car .70
115B A5 15c dk violet 1.40
115C A6 40c rose car 1.75
115D A6 50c purple 1.75
115E A7 60c violet 1.75
115F A7 1fr dp green 1.75
Nos. 115A-115F (6) 9.10

Nos. 115A-115F were issued by the Vichy government in France, but were not placed on sale in Mauritania.

Islamic Republic

Camel and Hands Raising Flag — A10

Unwmk.

1960, Jan. 20 Engr. *Perf. 13*
116 A10 25fr multi, *pink* .60 .35

Issued to commemorate the proclamation of the Islamic Republic of Mauritania.

> Imperforates
> Most Mauritania stamps from 1960 onward exist imperforate in issued and trial colors, and also in small presentation sheets in issued colors.

C.C.T.A. Issue
Common Design Type

1960, May 16
117 CD106 25fr bluish grn & ultra .75 .40

Flag and Map — A11

1960, Dec. 15 Engr. *Perf. 13*
118 A11 25fr org brn, emer & sepia .60 .30

Proclamation of independence, Nov. 28, 1960.

Pastoral Well — A12

Spotted Hyena A13

Ore Train and Camel Riders A14

Scimitar-horned Oryx — A15

Designs: 50c, 1fr, Well. 2fr, Date harvesting. 3fr, Aoudad. 4fr, Fennecs. 5fr, Millet harvesting. 10fr, Shoemaker. 15fr, Fishing boats. 20fr, Nomad school. 25fr, 30fr, Seated dance. No. 130, Religious student. 60fr, Metalworker.

1960-62 Unwmk. *Perf. 13*
119 A12 50c mag, yel & brn ('61) .25 .25
120 A12 1fr brn, yel brn & grn .25 .25
121 A12 2fr dk brn, bl & grn .25 .25
122 A13 3fr bl grn, red brn & gray ('61) .40 .25
123 A13 4fr yel grn & ocher ('61) .40 .25
124 A12 5fr red, dk brn & yel brn .35 .25
125 A14 10fr dk bl & org .40 .25
126 A14 15fr ver, dk brn, grn & bl .50 .25
127 A14 20fr grn, sl grn & red brn .50 .25
128 A12 25fr ultra & gray grn ('61) .65 .25
129 A12 30fr lil, bis & indigo .65 .25
130 A12 50fr org brn & grn 1.10 .40
131 A14 50fr red brn, bl & ol ('62) 3.00 .80
132 A12 60fr grn, cl & pur 2.00 .40
133 A15 85fr bl, brn & blk ('61) 4.75 1.90
Nos. 119-133 (15) 15.45 6.25

An overprint, "Jeux Olympiques / Rome 1960 / Tokyo 1964," the 5-ring Olympic emblem and a 75fr surcharge were applied to Nos. 126-127 in 1962. Two overprint types, varying in size. Values, set: small overprint, $20; large overprint, $22.50.

An overprint, "Aide aux Rèfugiès" with uprooted oak emblem, was applied in 1962 to No. 132 and to pink-paper printings of Nos. 129-130. Two types: type 1, 26 leaves on tree; type 2, 37 leaves on tree. Values, set: type 1, $24; type 2, $8.

Other overprints, applied to airmail stamps, are noted after No. C16.

1963, July 6

Designs: 50c, Striped hyena. 1.50fr, Cheetah. 2fr, Guinea baboons. 5fr, Dromedaries. 10fr, Leopard. 15fr, Bongo antelopes. 20fr, Aardvark. 25fr, Patas monkeys. 30fr, Crested porcupine. 50fr, Dorcas gazelle. 60fr, Common chameleon.

134 A15 50c sl grn, blk & org brn .25 .25
135 A13 1fr ultra, blk & yel .25 .25
136 A15 1.50fr ol grn, brn & bis .35 .25
137 A13 2fr dk brn, grn & dp org .30 .25
138 A15 5fr brn, ultra & bis .35 .25
139 A13 10fr blk & bis .75 .25
140 A13 15fr vio bl & red brn .75 .25
141 A13 20fr dk red brn, dk bl & bis .85 .30
142 A15 25fr brt grn, red brn & ol bis 1.25 .30
143 A13 30fr dk brn, dk bl & ol bis 2.40 .30
144 A15 50fr grn, ocher & brn 3.00 .90
145 A13 60fr dk bl, emer & ocher 3.75 1.25
Nos. 134-145 (12) 14.25 4.80

UN Headquarters, New York, and View of Nouakchott — A15a

1962, June 1 Engr. *Perf. 13*
167 A15a 15fr blk, ultra & cop red .30 .30
168 A15a 25fr cop red, sl grn & ultra .45 .35
169 A15a 85fr dk bl, dl pur & cop red 1.25 1.10
Nos. 167-169 (3) 2.00 1.75

Mauritania's admission to the UN.

African-Malagasy Union Issue
Common Design Type

1962, Sept. 8 Photo. *Perf. 12½x12*
170 CD110 30fr multi .75 .50

Organization Emblem and View of Nouakchott — A16

1962, Oct. 15 *Perf. 12½*
171 A16 30fr dk red brn, ultra & brt grn .70 .50

8th Conf. of the Organization to Fight Endemic Diseases, Nouakchott, Oct. 15-18.

Map, Mechanized and Manual Farm Work — A17

1962, Nov. 28 Engr. *Perf. 13*
172 A17 30fr blk, grn & vio brn .75 .40

2nd anniversary of independence.

People in European and Mauritanian Clothes — A18

1962, Dec. 24 Unwmk.
173 A18 25fr multicolored .40 .25

First anniversary of Congress for Unity.

Weather and WMO Symbols — A20

1964, Mar. 23 Unwmk. *Perf. 13*
175 A20 85fr dk brn, dk bl & org 1.50 .85

UN 4th World Meteorological Day, Mar. 23.

IQSY Emblem A21

1964, July 3 Engr.
176 A21 25fr dk bl, red & grn .60 .45

International Quiet Sun Year, 1964-65.

Striped Mullet A22

Designs: 5fr, Mauritanian lobster, vert. 10fr, Royal lobster, vert. 60fr, Maigre fish.

1964, Oct. 5 Engr. *Perf. 13*
177 A22 1fr org brn, dk bl & grn .40 .25
178 A22 5fr org brn, sl grn & choc .50 .25
179 A22 10fr dk bl, bis & sl grn .80 .25
180 A22 60fr dk brn, dp grn & dl bl 3.00 .80
Nos. 177-180 (4) 4.70 1.55

Cooperation Issue
Common Design Type

1964, Nov. 7 Unwmk. *Perf. 13*
181 CD119 25fr mag, sl grn & dk brn .60 .35

Water Lilies A23

Tropical Plants: 10fr, Acacia. 20fr, Adenium obesum. 45fr, Caralluma retrospiciens.

1965, Jan. 11 Engr. *Perf. 13*
182 A23 5fr multi .25 .25
183 A23 10fr multi, vert. .25 .25
184 A23 20fr multi .55 .25
185 A23 45fr multi, vert. 1.00 .50
Nos. 182-185 (4) 2.05 1.25

Hardine A24

Musical Instruments: 8fr, Tobol (drums). 25fr, Tidinit (stringed instruments). 40fr, Musicians.

1965, Mar. 8 *Perf. 13*
186 A24 2fr red brn, brt bl & sep .25 .25
187 A24 8fr red brn, red & brn .40 .25
188 A24 25fr red brn, emer & blk .65 .25
189 A24 40fr vio bl, plum & blk 1.00 .35
Nos. 186-189 (4) 2.30 1.10

Abraham Lincoln (1809-1865) — A25

1965, Apr. 23 Photo. *Perf. 13x12½*
190 A25 50fr lt ultra & multi .80 .40

Palms at Adrar A26

Designs: 4fr, Chinguetti mosque, vert. 15fr, Clay pit and donkeys. 60fr, Decorated door, Oualata.

1965, June 14 Engr. *Perf. 13*
191 A26 1fr brn, bl & grn .25 .25
192 A26 4fr dk red, bl & brn .25 .25
193 A26 15fr multi .35 .25
194 A26 60fr grn, dk brn & red brn 1.10 .55
Nos. 191-194 (4) 1.95 1.30

Issued for tourist publicity.

Tea Service in Inlaid Box — A27

7fr, Tobacco pouch and pipe, vert. 25fr, Dagger, vert. 50fr, Mederdra ornamental chest.

1965, Sept. 13 Unwmk. *Perf. 13*
195 A27 3fr gray, choc & ocher .25 .25
196 A27 7fr red lil, Prus bl & org .25 .25
197 A27 25fr blk, org red & brn .50 .25
198 A27 50fr brt grn, brn org & mar 1.00 .40
Nos. 195-198 (4) 2.00 1.15

Choum Railroad Tunnel — A28

10fr, Nouakchott wharf, ships & anchor, horiz. 30fr, as 5fr. 85fr, Nouakchott hospital & caduceus, horiz.

1965, Oct. 18 Engr. *Perf. 13*

199 A28 5fr dk brn & brt grn .25 .25
200 A28 10fr dk vio bl, brn red & Prus bl .25 .25
201 A28 30fr brn red, red & red brn .70 .25
202 A28 85fr dp bl, rose cl & lil 1.30 .65
Nos. 199-202 (4) 2.50 1.40

Sculptured Heads A29

Designs: 30fr, "Music and Dance." 60fr, Movie camera and huts.

1966, Apr. Engr. *Perf. 13*

203 A29 10fr brt grn, blk & brn .25 .25
204 A29 30fr brt bl, red lil & blk .50 .25
205 A29 60fr red, org & dk brn 1.00 .45
Nos. 203-205 (3) 1.75 .95

Intl. Negro Arts Festival, Dakar, Senegal, Apr. 1-24.

Mimosa — A30

Flowers: 15fr, Schouwia purpurea. 20fr, Ipomea asarifolia. 25fr, Grewia bicolor. 30fr, Pancratium trianthum. 60fr, Blepharis linariifolia.

1966, Aug. 8 Photo. *Perf. 13x12½*

Flowers in Natural Colors

206 A30 10fr dl bl & dk bl .40 .25
207 A30 15fr dk brn & buff .50 .35
208 A30 20fr grnsh bl & lt bl .60 .40
209 A30 25fr brn & buff .80 .50
210 A30 30fr lil & vio 1.20 .65
211 A30 60fr grn & pale grn 1.60 1.00
Nos. 206-211 (6) 5.10 3.15

Myrina Silenus — A31

Various Butterflies.

1966, Oct. 3 Photo. *Perf. 12x12½*

212 A31 5fr buff & multi 1.10 .30
213 A31 30fr bl grn & multi 3.50 .45
214 A31 45fr yel grn & multi 4.75 .65
215 A31 60fr dl bl & multi 6.75 1.10
Nos. 212-215 (4) 16.10 2.50

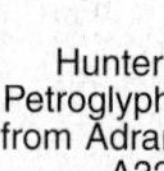

Hunter, Petroglyph from Adrar A32

Designs: 3fr, Two men fighting, petroglyph from Tenses (Adrar). 30fr, Copper jug, Le Mreyer (Adrar). 50fr, Camel caravan.

1966, Oct. 24 Engr. *Perf. 13*

216 A32 2fr dk brn & brn org .30 .25
217 A32 3fr bl & brn org .80 .25
218 A32 30fr sl grn & dk red 1.40 .30
219 A32 50fr mag, sl grn & brn 2.40 .70
Nos. 216-219 (4) 4.90 1.50

Issued for tourist publicity.

UNESCO, 20th Anniv. A33

1966, Dec. 5 Litho. *Perf. 12½x13*

220 A33 30fr multi .60 .40

Plaza of Three Cultures, Mexico City — A34

Olympic Village, Grenoble A35

Designs: 40fr, Olympic torch and skating rink. 100fr, Olympic Stadium, Mexico City.

1967, Mar. 11 Engr. *Perf. 13*

221 A34 20fr dl bl, brn & sl grn .50 .25
222 A35 30fr dl bl, brn & grn .60 .40
223 A34 40fr brt bl, dk brn & sep 1.00 .55
224 A35 100fr brn, emer & blk 1.75 1.00
Nos. 221-224 (4) 3.85 2.20

Nos. 221 and 224 commemorate the 19th Olympic Games, Mexico City; Nos. 222 and 223, the 10th Winter Olympic Games, Grenoble.

Trees — A36

1967, May 15 Engr. *Perf. 13*

225 A36 10fr Prosopis .45 .25
226 A36 15fr Jujube .60 .25
227 A36 20fr Date palm .70 .25
228 A36 25fr Peltophorum .80 .30
229 A36 30fr Baobob 1.10 .35
Nos. 225-229 (5) 3.65 1.40

1967 Jamboree Emblem and Campsite — A37

Design: 90fr, 1967 Jamboree emblem and Mauritanian Boy Scouts, horiz.

1967, June 5

230 A37 60fr brn, ultra & slate grn .95 .35
231 A37 90fr dl red, bl & slate grn 1.40 .50

12th Boy Scout World Jamboree, Farragut State Park, Idaho, Aug. 1-9.

Weavers A38

10fr, Embroiderer, vert. 20fr, Nurse, mother & infant. 30fr, Laundress, vert. 50fr, Seamstresses.

1967, July 3 Engr. *Perf. 13*

232 A38 5fr plum, blk & cl .25 .25
233 A38 10fr plum, brt grn & blk .25 .25
234 A38 20fr brt bl, plum & blk .50 .25
235 A38 30fr dk bl, brn & blk .60 .30
236 A38 50fr plum, sl & blk 1.00 .30
Nos. 232-236 (5) 2.60 1.35

Progress made by working women.

Cattle and Hypodermic Syringe — A39

1967, Aug. 21 Engr. *Perf. 13*

237 A39 30fr sl grn, brt bl & rose cl .80 .35

Campaign against cattle plague.

Monetary Union Issue

Common Design Type

1967, Nov. 4 Engr. *Perf. 13*

238 CD125 30fr gray & orange .45 .25

Fruit — A40

1967, Dec. 4 Engr. *Perf. 13*

239 A40 1fr Doom palm .35 .25
240 A40 2fr Bito, horiz. .40 .25
241 A40 3fr Baobob .50 .25
242 A40 4fr Jujube, horiz. .60 .25
243 A40 5fr Daye .75 .40
Nos. 239-243 (5) 2.60 1.40

For surcharges see Nos. 323-327.

Human Rights Flame — A41

1968, Jan. 8 Photo. *Perf. 13x12½*

244 A41 30fr brt grn, blk & yel .60 .25
245 A41 50fr brn org, blk & yel .75 .35

International Human Rights Year.

Nouakchott Mosque A42

45fr, Amogjar Pass. 90fr, Cavaliers' Towers.

1968, Apr. 1 Photo. *Perf. 12½x13*

246 A42 30fr multi .35 .25
247 A42 45fr multi .50 .25
248 A42 90fr multi .85 .50
Nos. 246-248 (3) 1.70 1.00

For surcharges see Nos. 332-333.

UPU Building, Bern, Globe and Map of Africa A43

1968, June 3 Engr. *Perf. 13*

249 A43 30fr ver, ultra & olive .60 .25

Mauritania's admission to the UPU.

Symbolic Water Cycle A44

1968, June 24

250 A44 90fr car, lake, grn & sl grn .75 .40

Hydrological Decade (UNESCO), 1965-74.

Land Yacht Racing — A45

40fr, Three land yachts racing, horiz. 60fr, Crew changing wheel of land yacht.

1968, Oct. 7 Engr. *Perf. 13*

251 A45 30fr ultra, org & ocher .55 .25
252 A45 40fr ultra, dp org & plum .70 .30
253 A45 60fr brt grn, dp org & ocher 1.10 .60
Nos. 251-253 (3) 2.35 1.15

Donkey and Foal — A46

Domestic Animals: 10fr, Ewe and lamb. 15fr, Camel and calf. 30fr, Mare and foal. 50fr, Cow and calf. 90fr, Goat and kid.

1968, Dec. 16 Photo. *Perf. 13*

254 A46 5fr ocher & multi .30 .25
255 A46 10fr multi .40 .25
256 A46 15fr multi .45 .25
257 A46 30fr multi .85 .30
258 A46 50fr pur & multi 1.25 .40
259 A46 90fr multi 2.40 .60
Nos. 254-259 (6) 5.65 2.05

For surcharge see No. 303.

ILO Emblem and Map — A47

1969, Apr. 14 Photo. *Perf. 13x12½*

260 A47 50fr dk & lt bl, pur & org .60 .30

ILO, 50th anniversary.

Desert Monitor — A48

Reptiles: 10fr, Horned viper. 30fr, Common spitting cobra. 60fr, Rock python. 85fr, African crocodile.

1969, May 5 Photo. *Perf. 13x12½*

261 A48 5fr brn, pink & yel .40 .25
262 A48 10fr brn, lt grn & yel .70 .30
263 A48 30fr dk brn, pink & yel 1.75 .50
264 A48 60fr dk brn, lt bl & yel 3.00 1.40
265 A48 85fr dk brn, yel & red 5.50 1.75
Nos. 261-265 (5) 11.35 4.20

Lady Beetle Eating Noxious Insects A49

1969, May 26 Engr. *Perf. 13*

266 A49 30fr indigo, grn & mar 1.50 .70

Natural protection of date palms.

Development Bank Issue
Common Design Type

1969, Sept. 10 Engr. *Perf. 13*

267 CD130 30fr Prus bl, grn & ocher .60 .25

Pendant — A50

Design: 20fr, Rahla headdress, horiz.

1969, Oct. 13 Engr. *Perf. 13*

268 A50 10fr dk brn, lil & brn .25 .25
269 A50 20fr blk, Prus bl & mag .50 .25

For surcharges see Nos. 309-310.

Desalination Plant A51

Designs: 15fr, Fishing harbor, Nouadhibou. 30fr, Meat refrigeration plant, Kaedi.

1969, Dec. 1 Engr. *Perf. 13*

270 A51 10fr brt rose lil, dk bl & red brn .25 .25
271 A51 15fr dk car, blk & dp bl .25 .25
272 A51 30fr blk, dk bl & rose brn .40 .25
Nos. 270-272 (3) .90 .75

Issued to publicize economic progress.

Lenin (1870-1924) — A52

1970, Feb. 16 Photo. *Perf. 12x12½*

273 A52 30fr car, lt bl & blk 1.40 .40

Sternocera Interrupta — A53

Insects: 10fr, Anoplocnemis curvipes. 20fr, Julodis aequinoctialis. 30fr, Thermophilum sexmaculatum marginatum. 40fr, Plocaederus denticornis.

1970, Mar. 16 Engr. *Perf. 13*

274 A53 5fr red brn, buff & blk .40 .25
275 A53 10fr red brn, yel & brn .65 .25
276 A53 20fr red brn, lil & dk ol .85 .30
277 A53 30fr red brn, grn & vio 1.40 .45
278 A53 40fr red brn, lt bl & brn 2.25 .85
Nos. 274-278 (5) 5.55 2.10

For surcharges see Nos. 311-315.

Soccer Players and Hemispheres — A54

Hemispheres & various views of soccer play.

1970, May 11 Engr. *Perf. 13*

279 A54 25fr bl, vio bl & dk brn .45 .25
280 A54 30fr vio bl, brn & ol brn .45 .25
281 A54 70fr brt pink, mar & dk brn .90 .50
282 A54 150fr brn red, grn & dk brn 2.10 .75
Nos. 279-282 (4) 3.90 1.75

9th World Soccer Championships for the Jules Rimet Cup, Mexico City, 5/29-6/21.

UPU Headquarters Issue
Common Design Type

1970, May 20 Engr. *Perf. 13*

283 CD133 30fr grn, dk brn & red brn .60 .30

Woman Wearing "Boubou" — A55

Various Traditional Costumes: 30fr, 70fr, Men. 40fr, 50fr, Women.

1970, Sept. 21 Engr. *Perf. 12½x13*

284 A55 10fr red brn & org .25 .25
285 A55 30fr ol, red brn & ind .60 .25
286 A55 40fr red brn, plum & dk brn .85 .35
287 A55 50fr dk brn & brt bl 1.20 .45
288 A55 70fr bl, brn & dk brn 1.50 .65
Nos. 284-288 (5) 4.40 1.95

People of Various Races — A55a

Design: 40fr, Outstretched hands, vert.

1971, Mar. 22 Engr. *Perf. 13*

288A A55a 30fr brn vio, ol & brt bl .60 .25
288B A55a 40fr brn red, bl & blk .80 .35

Intl. year against racial discrimination.

Gen. Charles de Gaulle (1890-1970), President of France — A56

Design: 100fr, De Gaulle as President.

1971, June 18 Photo. *Perf. 13*

289 A56 40fr gold, blk & grnsh bl 2.00 .75
290 A56 100fr lt bl, gold & blk 4.50 1.50
a. Souvenir sheet of 2, #289-290 6.50 6.50

Iron Ore Freight Train of Miferma Mines — A57

1971, Nov. 8 Photo. *Perf. 12½x12*

291 35fr ore cars 1.75 .65
292 100fr engines 4.00 1.60
a. A57 Pair, #291-292 7.50 7.50

UNICEF Emblem and Child A59

1971, Dec. 11 Litho. *Perf. 13½*

293 A59 35fr lt ultra, blk & brn .50 .25

UNICEF, 25th anniv.

Samuel F. B. Morse and Telegraph — A60

Designs: 40fr, Relay satellite over globes. 75fr, Alexander Graham Bell.

1972, May 17 Engr. *Perf. 13*

294 A60 35fr lilac, indigo & vio .55 .25
295 A60 40fr bl, ocher & choc .60 .25
296 A60 75fr grn, ol grn & Prus bl .90 .45
Nos. 294-296 (3) 2.05 .95

4th World Telecommunications Day.
For surcharge see No. 343.

Fossil Spirifer Shell — A61

1972, July 31 Litho. *Perf. 12½*

297 A61 25fr shown 2.25 .90
298 A61 75fr Phacops rana 4.00 1.25

Fossil shells.
For surcharges see Nos. 306, 308.

West African Monetary Union Issue
Common Design Type

1972, Nov. 2 Engr. *Perf. 13*

299 CD136 35fr brn, yel grn & gray .75 .25

Mediterranean Monk Seal and Pup — A63

1973, Feb. 28 Litho. *Perf. 13*

300 A63 40fr multi 2.00 .80

See No. C130. For surcharges see Nos. 307, C145.

Food Program Symbols and Emblem A64

1973, Apr. 30 Photo. *Perf. 12x12½*

301 A64 35fr gray bl & multi .45 .25

World Food Program, 10th anniversary.

UPU Monument and Globe A65

1973, May 28 Engr. *Perf. 13*

302 A65 100fr grn, ocher & bl 1.60 .75

Universal Postal Union Day.

Currency Change to Ouguiya ("um")
No. 258 Surcharged with New Value, 2 Bars, and Overprinted: "SECHERESSE / SOLIDARITE / AFRICAINE"

1973, Aug. 16 Photo. *Perf. 13*

303 A46 20um on 50fr multi .90 .40

African solidarity in drought emergency.

African Postal Union Issue
Common Design Type

1973, Sept. 12 Engr. *Perf. 13*

304 CD137 20um org, brn & ocher 1.10 .40

INTERPOL Emblem, Detective, Criminal, Fingerprint A66

1973, Sept. 24

305 A66 15um brn, ver & vio .90 .50

50th anniv. of Intl. Criminal Police Org.

Nos. 297-298, 300 and 268-269 Surcharged with New Value and Two Bars in Ultramarine, Red or Black

1973-74 Litho. *Perf. 12½*

306 A61 5um on 25fr (U) ('74) 2.50 .40
307 A63 8um on 40fr (R) .95 .40
308 A61 15um on 75fr (U) ('74) 7.00 1.75

Engr.
Perf. 13

309 A50 27um on 10fr (B) ('74) 1.60 .75
310 A50 28um on 20fr (R) ('74) 1.75 .90
Nos. 306-310 (5) 13.80 4.20

Nos. 274-278 Surcharged in Violet Blue or Red

1974, July 29 Engr. *Perf. 13*

311 A53 5um on 5fr (VB) 1.25 .60
312 A53 7um on 10fr (VB) 1.10 .40
313 A53 8um on 20fr (VB) 1.25 .45
314 A53 10um on 30fr (R) 1.75 .50
315 A53 20um on 40fr (VB) 3.50 1.40
Nos. 311-315 (5) 8.85 3.35

UPU Emblem and Globes — A67

1974, Aug. 5 Photo. *Perf. 13*

316 A67 30um multi 2.10 .80
317 A67 50um multi 3.50 1.40

Centenary of Universal Postal Union.
For overprints see Nos. 321-322.

5-Ouguiya Coin and Bank Note — A68

Designs: 8um, 10-ouguiya coin. 20um, 20-ouguiya coin. Each design includes picture of different bank note.

1974, Aug. 12 Engr.

318 A68 7um blk, ultra & grn .60 .25
319 A68 8um blk, sl grn & mag .70 .25
320 A68 20um blk, red & bl 1.40 .55
Nos. 318-320 (3) 2.70 1.05

First anniversary of currency reform.

Nos. 316-317 Overprinted in Red: "9 OCTOBRE / 100 ANS D'UNION POSTALE / INTERNATIONALE"

1974, Oct. 9 Photo. *Perf. 13*

321 A67 30um multi 2.25 1.00
322 A67 50um multi 4.00 1.50

Centenary of Universal Postal Union.

Nos. 239-243 Srchd. in Black or Violet Blue

1975, Feb. 14 Engr. *Perf. 13*

323 A40 1um on 5fr multi (B) .30 .25
324 A40 2um on 4fr multi (VB) .30 .25
325 A40 3um on 2fr multi (B) .35 .25
326 A40 10um on 1fr multi (B) .95 .25
327 A40 12um on 3fr multi (VB) 1.10 .30
Nos. 323-327 (5) 3.00 1.30

Hunters, Rock Carvings — A69

Rock Carvings from Zemmour Cave: 5um, Ostrich. 10um, Elephant, horiz.

1975, May 26 Engr. *Perf. 13*

328 A69 4um lt brn & car 1.00 .25
329 A69 5um red lil 1.25 .30
330 A69 10um blue 1.90 .45
Nos. 328-330 (3) 4.15 1.00

Europafrica Issue

White and Black Men, Map of Europe and Africa — A70

1975, July 7 Engr. *Perf. 13*

331 A70 40um dk brn & red 2.10 .80

Nos. 247-248 Surcharged in Red or Black

1975, Aug. 25 Photo. *Perf. 12½x13*

332 A42 15um on 45fr (R) 1.25 .50
333 A42 25um on 90fr 2.00 .80

African solidarity in drought emergency.

Map of Africa with Mauritania, Akjoujt Blast Furnace, Camel — A71

Design: 12um, Snim emblem, furnace, dump truck, excavator.

1975, Sept. 22 Engr. *Perf. 13*

334 A71 10um brt bl, choc & org .90 .30
335 A71 12um brt bl & multi 1.00 .40

Mining and industry: Somima (Société Minière de Mauritanie) and Snim (Société Nationale Industrielle et Minière).

Fair Emblem — A72

1975, Oct. 5 Litho. *Perf. 12*

336 A72 10um multi .60 .30

National Nouakchott Fair, Nov. 28-Dec. 7.

Commemorative Medal — A73

Design: 12um, Map of Mauritania, vert.

1975, Nov. 28 Litho. *Perf. 12*

337 A73 10um sil & multi 1.00 .35
338 A73 12um grn, yel & grn 1.00 .35

15th anniversary of independence.

Docked Space Ships and Astronauts — A74

Docked Space Ships and: 10um, Soyuz rocket launch.

1975, Dec. 29 Litho. *Perf. 14*

339 A74 8um multi .70 .25
340 A74 10um multi .85 .25
Nos. 339-340,C156-C158 (5) 7.15 2.65

Apollo Soyuz space test project, Russo-American cooperation, launched July 15, link-up July 17, 1975.

French Legion Infantryman A75

Uniform: 10um, Green Mountain Boy.

1976, Jan. 26 *Perf. 13½x14*

341 A75 8um multi .80 .25
342 A75 10um multi 1.00 .25
Nos. 341-342,C160-C162 (5) 7.30 2.75

American Bicentennial.

No. 296 Surcharged

1976, Mar. 1 Engr. *Perf. 13*

343 A60 12um on 75fr multi .70 .30

Arab Labor Charter, 10th anniversary.

Map of Mauritania with Spanish Sahara Incorporated — A76

1976, Mar. 15 Litho. *Perf. 13x12½*

344 A76 10um grn & multi .80 .30

Reunified Mauritania, Feb. 29, 1976.

LZ-4 over Hangar — A77

75th anniv. of the Zeppelin: 10um, Dr. Hugo Eckener and "Schwaben" (LZ-10). 12um, "Hansa" (LZ-13) over Heligoland. 20um, "Bodensee" (LZ-120) and Dr. Ludwig Dürr.

1976, June 28 Litho. *Perf. 11*

345 A77 5um multi .25 .25
346 A77 10um multi .60 .25
347 A77 12um multi .75 .30
348 A77 20um multi 1.25 .40
Nos. 345-348,C167-C168 (6) 9.35 3.85

Mohenjo-Daro — A78

1976, Sept. 6 Litho. *Perf. 12*

349 A78 15um multi 1.10 .40

UNESCO campaign to save Mohenjo-Daro excavations, Pakistan.

A. G. Bell, Telephone and Satellite — A79

1976, Oct. 11 Engr. *Perf. 13*

350 A79 10um bl, car & red .80 .25

Centenary of first telephone call by Alexander Graham Bell, Mar. 10, 1876.

Mohammed Ali Jinnah (1876-1948), Governor General of Pakistan — A80

1976, Dec. 25 Litho. *Perf. 13*

351 A80 10um multi .60 .30

NASA Control Room, Houston — A81

Design: 12um, Viking components, vert.

1977, Feb. 28 *Perf. 14*

352 A81 10um multi .60 .25
353 A81 12um multi .75 .25
Nos. 352-353,C173-C175 (5) 7.60 2.15

Viking Mars project.
For surcharge and overprints see Nos. 425-426, C192-C195.

Jackals A82

Designs: 5um, Wild rabbits. 12um, Wart-hogs. 14um, Lions. 15um, Elephants.

1977, Mar. 14 Litho. *Perf. 12½*

354 A82 5um multi .40 .25
355 A82 10um multi 1.00 .40
356 A82 12um multi 1.40 .50
357 A82 14um multi 1.50 .60
358 A82 15um multi 3.00 .90
Nos. 354-358 (5) 7.30 2.65

For surcharge see No. 577.

Irene and Frederic Joliot-Curie, Chemistry — A83

Nobel prize winners: 15um, Emil A. von Bering, medicine.

1977, Apr. 29 Litho. *Perf. 14*

359 A83 12um multi	1.10	.25
360 A83 15um multi	.90	.25
Nos. 359-360,C177-C179 (5)	9.05	2.10

APU Emblem, Member's Flags — A84

1977, May 30 Photo. *Perf. 13*

361 A84 12um multi	.65	.40

Arab Postal Union, 25th anniversary.

Oil Lamp A85

Tegdaoust Pottery: 2um, 4-handled pot. 5um, Large jar. 12um, Jug with filter.

1977, June 13 Engr. *Perf. 13*

362 A85 1um multi	.25	.25
363 A85 2um multi	.25	.25
364 A85 5um multi	.30	.25
365 A85 12um multi	.80	.30
Nos. 362-365 (4)	1.60	1.05

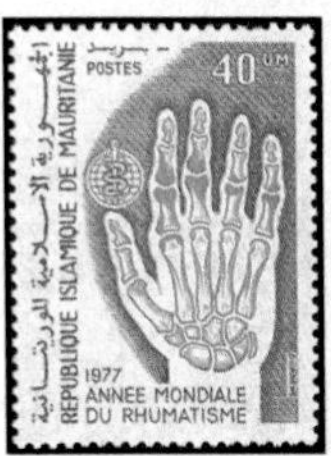
X-ray of Hand — A86

1977, June 27 Engr. *Perf. 12½x13*

366 A86 40um multi	2.50	1.25

World Rheumatism Year.

Charles Lindbergh and "Spirit of St. Louis" — A87

History of aviation: 14um, Clement Ader and "Eole!" 15um, Louis Bleriot over channel. 55um, Italo Balbo and seaplanes. 60um, Concorde. 100um, Charles Lindbergh and "Spirit of St. Louis."

1977, Sept. 19

367 A87 12um multi	.65	.25
368 A87 14um multi	.70	.25
369 A87 15um multi	.85	.30
370 A87 55um multi	3.00	.70
371 A87 60um multi	3.50	.75
Nos. 367-371 (5)	8.70	2.25

Souvenir Sheet

372 A87 100um multi	6.00	1.50

Dome of the Rock, Jerusalem — A88

1977, Oct. 31 Litho. *Perf. 12½*

373 A88 12um multi	.65	.25
374 A88 14um multi	.85	.40

Palestinian fighters and their families.

Soccer and Emblems — A89

Emblems and: 14um, Alf Ramsey and stadium. 15um, Players and goalkeeper.

1977, Dec. 19 Litho. *Perf. 13½*

375 A89 12um multi	.55	.25
376 A89 14um multi	.65	.25
377 A89 15um multi	.80	.25
Nos. 375-377,C182-C183 (5)	7.25	2.05

Elimination Games for World Cup Soccer Championship, Argentina, 1978.
For overprints see Nos. 399-401, C187-C189.

Helen Fourment and her Children, by Rubens A90

Paintings by Peter Paul Rubens (1577-1640): 14um, Knight in armor. 67um, Three Burghers. 69um, Landscape, horiz. 100um, Rubens with wife and son.

1977, Dec. 26

378 A90 12um multi	.65	.25
379 A90 14um multi	.80	.35
380 A90 67um multi	3.25	.70
381 A90 69um multi	3.50	.85
Nos. 378-381 (4)	8.20	2.15

Souvenir Sheet

382 A90 100um gold & multi	5.50	1.50

Sable Antelope and Wildlife Fund Emblem — A91

Endangered Animals: 12um, Gazelles, vert. 14um, Manatee. 55um, Aoudad, vert. 60um, Elephant. 100um, Ostrich, vert.

1978, Feb. 28 Litho. *Perf. 13½x14*

383 A91 5um multi	*.80*	*.30*
384 A91 12um multi	*1.60*	*.40*
385 A91 14um multi	*1.75*	*.60*
386 A91 55um multi	*6.00*	*1.75*
387 A91 60um multi	*7.00*	*2.00*
388 A91 100um multi	*9.00*	*3.25*
Nos. 383-388 (6)	*26.15*	*8.30*

Nouakchott-Nema Road — A91a

1978, June 19 Litho. *Perf. 13*

388A A91a 12um multicolored	*11.00*	8.50
388B A91a 14um multicolored	*12.50*	9.00

Soccer and Games' Emblem — A92

14um, Rimet Cup. 20um, Soccer ball & F.I.F.A. flag. 50um, Soccer ball & Rimet Cup, horiz.

1978, June 26 Photo. *Perf. 13*

389 A92 12um multi	.60	.25
390 A92 14um multi	.70	.30
391 A92 20um multi	1.10	.30
Nos. 389-391 (3)	2.40	.85

Souvenir Sheet

392 A92 50um multi	2.50	1.00

11th World Cup Soccer Championship, Argentina, June 1-25.

Raoul Follereau and St. George Slaying Dragon — A93

1978, Sept. 4 Engr. *Perf. 13*

393 A93 12um brn & dp grn	1.50	.60

25th anniversary of the Raoul Follereau Anti-Leprosy Foundation.

Anti-Apartheid Emblem, Fenced-in People — A94

Design: 30um, Anti-Apartheid emblem and free people, vert.

1978, Oct. 9

394 A94 25um bl, red & brn	1.25	.65
395 A94 30um grn, bl & brn	1.75	.85

Anti-Apartheid Year.

Charles de Gaulle A95

14um, King Baudouin. 55um, Queen Elizabeth II.

1978, Oct. 16 Litho. *Perf. 12½x12*

396 A95 12um multi	1.10	.40
397 A95 14um multi	1.10	.40
398 A95 55um multi	2.50	1.00
Nos. 396-398 (3)	4.70	1.80

Rulers who helped in de-colonization. No. 398 also commemorates 25th anniversary of coronation of Queen Elizabeth II.

Nos. 375-377 Overprinted in Arabic and French in Silver: "ARGENTINE- / PAYS BAS 3-1"

1978, Dec. 11 Litho. *Perf. 13½*

399 A89 12um multi	.60	.25
400 A89 14um multi	.65	.30
401 A89 15um multi	.90	.50
Nos. 399-401,C187-C188 (5)	7.25	3.90

Argentina's victory in World Cup Soccer Championship 1978.

View of Nouakchott — A96

1978, Dec. 18 Litho. *Perf. 12*

402 A96 12um multi	.65	.30

20th anniversary of Nouakchott.

Flame Emblem — A97

1978, Dec. 26 *Perf. 12½*

403 A97 55um ultra & red	2.50	1.25

Universal Declaration of Human Rights, 30th anniv.

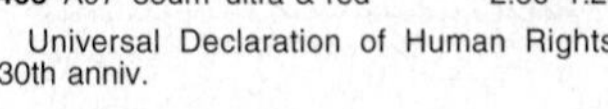

Leather Key Holder — A98

Leather Craft: 7um, Toothbrush case. 10um, Knife holder.

1979, Feb. 5 Litho. *Perf. 13½x14*

404 A98 5um multi	.35	.25
405 A98 7um multi	.45	.25
406 A98 10um multi	.65	.30
Nos. 404-406 (3)	1.45	.80

Farmers at Market, by Dürer — A99

Engravings by Albrecht Durer (1471-1528): 14um, Young Peasant and Wife. 55um, Mercenary with flag. 60um, St. George Slaying Dragon. 100um, Mercenaries, horiz.

Litho.; Red Foil Embossed

1979, May 3 *Perf. 13½x14*

407 A99 12um blk, *buff* .60 .25
408 A99 14um blk, *buff* 1.00 .25
409 A99 55um blk, *buff* 2.40 .80
410 A99 60um blk, *buff* 3.00 .95
Nos. 407-410 (4) 7.00 2.25

Souvenir Sheet

Perf. 14x13½

411 A99 100um blk, *buff* 5.00 3.50

Buddha, Borobudur Temple and UNESCO Emblem — A100

UNESCO Emblem and: 14um, Hunter on horseback, Carthage. 55um, Caryatid, Acropolis.

1979, May 14 **Photo.** *Perf. 12½*

412 A100 12um multi .70 .35
413 A100 14um multi .90 .40
414 A100 55um multi 2.75 1.25
Nos. 412-414 (3) 4.35 2.00

Preservation of art treasures with help from UNESCO.

Paddle Steamer Sirius, Rowland Hill — A101

Sir Rowland Hill (1795-1879), originator of penny postage, and: 14um, Paddle steamer Great Republic. 55um, S.S. Mauritania. 60um, M.S. Stirling Castle. 100um, Mauritania No. 8.

1979, June 4 **Litho.** *Perf. 13½x14*

415 A101 12um multi .55 .25
416 A101 14um multi .70 .25
417 A101 55um multi 2.40 .55
418 A101 60um multi 2.90 .70
Nos. 415-418 (4) 6.55 1.75

Souvenir Sheet

419 A101 100um multi 5.00 1.25

Embossed Leather Cushion — A102

30um, Satellite, jet, ship, globe & UPU emblem.

1979, June 8 **Litho.** *Perf. 12½*

420 A102 12um multi 1.10 .50

Engr.

Perf. 13

421 A102 30um multi, vert. 3.00 1.40

Philexafrique II, Libreville, Gabon, June 8-17. Nos. 420, 421 each printed in sheets of 10 and 5 labels showing exhibition emblem.

Mother and Children, IYC Emblem — A103

1979, Oct. 2 **Litho.** *Perf. 12½*

422 A103 12um multi .55 .25
423 A103 14um multi .70 .35
424 A103 40um multi 2.00 .90
Nos. 422-424 (3) 3.25 1.50

International Year of the Child

Nos. 352-353 Overprinted in Silver: "ALUNISSAGE / APOLLO XI / JUILLET 1969" and Emblem

1979, Oct. 24 **Litho.** *Perf. 14*

425 A81 10um multi .60 .30
426 A81 12um multi .60 .30
Nos. 425-426,C192-C194 (5) 7.20 3.35

Apollo 11 moon landing, 10th anniversary.

Runner, Moscow '80 Emblem A104

Moscow '80 Emblem and: 14um, 55um, 100um, Running, diff. 60um, Hurdles.

1979, Oct. 26 **Litho.** *Perf. 13½*

427 A104 12um multi .55 .25
428 A104 14um multi .75 .25
429 A104 55um multi 2.10 .50
430 A104 60um multi 2.50 .60
Nos. 427-430 (4) 5.90 1.60

Souvenir Sheet

431 A104 100um multi 4.75 1.25

Pre-Olympic Year.

Scomberesox Saurus Walbaum — A104a

1979, Nov. 12 **Photo.** *Perf. 14*

431A A104a 1um shown .75 .30
431B A104a 5um Trigla lucerna .75 .30

A 20m denomination (Xiphias gladius) also exists. Value $250.

Ice Hockey, Lake Placid '80 Emblem — A105

Various ice hockey plays.

1979, Dec. 6 **Litho.** *Perf. 14½*

432 A105 10um multi .50 .25
433 A105 12um multi .65 .25
434 A105 14um multi .65 .30
435 A105 55um multi 2.40 .55
436 A105 60um multi 2.50 .65
437 A105 100um multi 4.25 1.10
Nos. 432-437 (6) 10.95 3.10

13th Winter Olympic Games. Lake Placid, NY, Feb. 12-24, 1980.

For overprints see Nos. 440-445.

Arab Achievements — A106

1980, Mar. 22 **Litho.** *Perf. 13*

438 A106 12um multi .70 .35
439 A106 15um multi .80 .35

Nos. 432-437 Overprinted:

a. Médaille / de bronze / SUÈDE
b. MÉDAILLE / DE BRONZE / SUÈDE
c. Médaille / d'argent / U.R.S.S.
d. MÉDAILLE / D'ARGENT/ U.R.S.S.
e. MÉDAILLE / D'OR / ÉTATS-UNIS
f. Médaille / d'or / ÉTATS-UNIS

1980, June 14 **Litho.** *Perf. 14½*

440 A105(a) 10um multi .55 .25
441 A105(b) 12um multi .60 .25
442 A105(c) 14um multi .60 .35
443 A105(d) 55um multi 2.40 .85
444 A105(e) 60um multi 2.50 .95
445 A105(f) 100um multi 4.25 1.50
Nos. 440-445 (6) 10.90 4.15

Equestrian, Olympic Rings — A107

Designs: Equestrian scenes. 10um, 20um, 70um, 100um, vert.

1980, June **Litho.** *Perf. 14*

446 A107 10um multi .45 .25
447 A107 20um multi .85 .25
448 A107 50um multi 2.40 .50
449 A107 70um multi 3.25 .70
Nos. 446-449 (4) 6.95 1.70

Souvenir Sheet

450 A107 100um multi 5.50 1.75

22nd Summer Olympic Games, Moscow, July 19-Aug. 3.

For overprints see Nos. 464-468.

Armed Forces Day — A108

1980, July 9 *Perf. 13x12½*

451 A108 12um multi .60 .25
452 A108 14um multi .65 .30

World Red Cross Day — A109

1980, June 14 *Perf. 13*

453 A109 20um multi 12.00 —

Pilgrimage to Mecca — A110

Design: 50um, Mosque, outside view.

1980

454 A110 10um multi .90 .35
455 A110 50um multi 2.75 1.40

Man with Turban, by Rembrandt A111

Rembrandt Paintings: 10um, Self-portrait. 20um, His mother. 70um, His son Titus reading. 100um, Polish knight, horiz.

1980, July **Litho.** *Perf. 12½*

456 A111 10um multi .60 .25
457 A111 20um multi 1.00 .30
458 A111 50um multi 2.60 .50
459 A111 70um multi 3.00 .80
Nos. 456-459 (4) 7.20 1.85

Souvenir Sheet

460 A111 100um multi 5.50 1.50

Tea Time A112

1980, Mar. 11 **Litho.** *Perf. 12½*

460A A112 1um multi .40 .25
461 A112 5um multi .60 .25
462 A112 12um multi 1.00 .30
Nos. 460A-462 (3) 2.00 .80

Arbor Day — A113

1980, Aug. 29

463 A113 12um multi 1.10 .40

Nos. 446-450 Overprinted with Winner and Country

1980, Oct. Litho. *Perf. 14*

464 A107 10um multi .45 .25
465 A107 20um multi .85 .30
466 A107 50um multi 2.25 .60
467 A107 70um multi 3.00 .80
Nos. 464-467 (4) 6.55 1.95

Souvenir Sheet

468 A107 100um multi 4.75 2.50

Mastodont Locomotive, 1850 — A114

Various locomotives: 12um, Iron ore train. 14um, Chicago-Milwaukee line, 1900. 20um, Bury, 1837. 67um, Reseau North line, 1870. 100um, Potsdam, 1840.

1980, Nov. *Perf. 12½*

469 A114 10um shown .70 .25
470 A114 12um multi .85 .30
471 A114 14um multi 1.10 .40
472 A114 20um multi 1.50 .50
473 A114 67um multi 5.00 .70
474 A114 100um multi 7.50 1.10
Nos. 469-474 (6) 16.65 3.25

20th Anniversary of Independence — A115

1980, Nov. 27 *Perf. 13*

475 A115 12um multi .55 .25
476 A115 15um multi .60 .30

El Haram Mosque — A116

12um, Medina Mosque. 14um, Chinguetti Mosque.

1981, Apr. 13 Litho. *Perf. 12½*

477 A116 2um shown .25 .25
478 A116 12um multi .60 .30
479 A116 14um multi .80 .30
Nos. 477-479 (3) 1.65 .85

Hegira, 1500th anniversary.

Prince Charles and Lady Diana, Coach — A117

Designs: Coaches.

1981, July 8 Litho. *Perf. 14½*

480 A117 14um multi .60 .25
481 A117 18um multi .75 .25
482 A117 77um multi 2.75 .90
Nos. 480-482 (3) 4.10 1.40

Souvenir Sheet

483 A117 100um multi 4.50 1.10

Royal wedding.
For overprints see Nos. 518-521.

Intl. Year of the Disabled A119

1981, June 29 Litho. *Perf. 13x13½*

486 A119 12um multi .80 .40

Battle of Yorktown Bicentenary (American Revolution) — A120

14um, George Washington, vert. 18um, Admiral de Grasse, vert. 63um, Surrender of Cornwallis. 81um, Battle of Chesapeake Bay.

1981, Oct. 5 *Perf. 12½*

487 A120 14um multi .55 .25
488 A120 18um multi .80 .30
489 A120 63um multi 2.50 1.00
490 A120 81um multi 3.50 1.50
Nos. 487-490 (4) 7.35 3.05

475th Death Anniv. of Christopher Columbus (1451-1506) — A121

1981, Oct. 5

491 A121 19um Pinta 1.10 .40
492 A121 55um Santa Maria 3.25 1.10

World Food Day — A122

1981, Oct. 16 *Perf. 13*

493 A122 19um multi .80 .40

Kemal Ataturk Birth Cent. — A123

1981, Oct. 29 *Perf. 12½*

494 A123 63um multi 2.50 1.25

Scouting Year — A124

Designs: Boating scenes. 92um vert.

1982, Jan. 20 Litho. *Perf. 12½*

495 A124 14um multi .70 .25
496 A124 19um multi 1.00 .25
497 A124 22um multi 1.10 .25
498 A124 92um multi 4.25 .85
Nos. 495-498 (4) 7.05 1.60

Souvenir Sheet

Perf. 13

499 A124 100um Baden-Powell, scout 5.00 1.25

75th Anniv. of Grand Prix — A125

Winners and their Cars: 7um, Deusenberg, 1921. 12um, Alfa Romeo, 1932. 14um, Juan Fangio, 1949. 18um, Renault, 1979. 19um, Niki Lauda, 1974.
100um, Race.

1982, Jan. 23 *Perf. 13½*

500 A125 7um multi .60 .25
501 A125 12um multi .85 .25
502 A125 14um multi .95 .25
503 A125 18um multi 1.10 .25
504 A125 19um multi 1.25 .30
Nos. 500-504 (5) 4.75 1.30

Souvenir Sheet

505 A125 100um multi 6.00 1.75

Birds of the Arguin Bank A126

1981, Dec. 17 Photo. *Perf. 13*

506 A126 2um White pelicans 1.00 .25
507 A126 18um Pink flamingoes 3.75 .75

Battle of Karameh A127

14um, Hand holding tattered flag.

1982, Dec. 19 Litho.

508 A127 14um multi .80 .35

Deluth Turtle — A128

Designs: Sea turtles.

1981, Dec. 21 Photo. *Perf. 14x13½*

509 A128 1um shown 1.50 .25
510 A128 3um Green turtle 2.00 .25
511 A128 4um Shell turtle 2.50 .35
Nos. 509-511 (3) 6.00 .85

APU, 30th Anniv. — A129

1982, May 14 Litho. *Perf. 13*

512 A129 14um org & brn .65 .30

A130

1982, May 17 Photo. *Perf. 13½x13*

513 A130 21um multi .85 .40

14th World Telecommunications Day.

A131

1982, June 7 Litho. *Perf. 12½*

514 A131 14um grnsh bl .65 .30

UN Conf. on Human Environment, 10th anniv.

21st Birthday of Princess Diana of Wales — A132

Portraits.

1982, July *Perf. 14x13½*

515 A132 21um multi .75 .40
516 A132 77um multi 2.50 .85

Souvenir Sheet

517 A132 100um multi 3.75 1.50

Nos. 480-483 Overprinted in Blue: "NAISSANCE ROYALE 1982"

1982, Aug. 2 *Perf. 14½*

518 A117 14um multi .50 .30
519 A117 18um multi .70 .35
520 A117 77um multi 2.50 1.25
Nos. 518-520 (3) 3.70 1.90

Souvenir Sheet

521 A117 100um multi 3.50 1.50

Birth of Prince William of Wales, June 21.

Agricultrual Development — A132a

Designs: 14um, Cattle and camels at watering hole, Hodh el Gharbi. 18um, Irrigation system, Gorgol.

1982, Dec. 13 Litho. *Perf. 14½*
521A A132a 14um multi 5.00 2.00
521B A132a 18um multi 7.00 2.50

Manned Flight Bicentenary A133

14um, Montgolfiere balloon, 1783, vert. 18um, Hydrogen balloon, 1783. 19um, Zeppelin, vert. 55um, Nieuport plane. 63um, Concorde. 77um, Apollo II, vert.

1982, Dec. 29 Litho. *Perf. 14*
522 A133 14um multi .95 .25
523 A133 18um multi .95 .25
524 A133 19um multi .95 .35
525 A133 55um multi 2.50 .50
526 A133 63um multi 2.75 .60
527 A133 77um multi 3.00 .70
Nos. 522-527 (6) 11.10 2.65

Preservation of Ancient Cities — A134

14um, City Wall, Ouadane. 18um, Chinguetti. 24um, Staircase, panels, Qualata. 30um, Ruins, Tichitt.

1983, Feb. 16 Litho. *Perf. 14x14½*
528 A134 14um multi .70 .25
529 A134 18um multi .80 .30
530 A134 24um multi 1.00 .50
531 A134 30um multi 1.60 .70
Nos. 528-531 (4) 4.10 1.75

World Communications Year — A135

1983, June 21 Litho. *Perf. 13*
532 A135 14um multi .70 .30

30th Anniv. of Customs Cooperation Council — A136

1983, June 25
533 A136 14um multi .70 .30

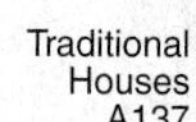

Traditional Houses A137

1983, June 14 Photo. *Perf. 13½*
534 A137 14um Peule *2.25* .35
535 A137 18um Toucouleur *3.00* .50
536 A137 19um Tent *3.25* .55
Nos. 534-536 (3) *8.50* 1.40

Ancient Manuscript Page — A138

5um, Ornamental scrollwork. 7um, Sheath.

1983, June 15 Photo. *Perf. 12½x13*
537 A138 2um shown .30 .25
538 A138 5um multi .50 .25
539 A138 7um multi .65 .25
Nos. 537-539 (3) 1.45 .75

Manned Flight Bicentenary — A139

Early Fliers and their Balloons or Dirigibles: 10um, F. Pilatre de Rozier, vert. 14um, John Wise, vert. 25um, Charles Renard. No. 543, Henri Julliot.
No. 544, Joseph Montgolfier.

1983, Oct. 17 Litho. *Perf. 13½*
540 A139 10um multi .70 .25
541 A139 14um multi .85 .25
542 A139 25um multi 1.75 .30
543 A139 100um multi 5.50 1.10
Nos. 540-543 (4) 8.80 1.90

Souvenir Sheet

544 A139 100um multi 6.00 1.25

No. 544 contains one stamp 47x37mm. Nos. 543-544 airmail.

Mortar — A140

Various prehistoric grinding implements.

1983, Dec. 28 Litho. *Perf. 13*
545 A140 10um multi .85 .35
546 A140 14um multi 1.40 .45
547 A140 18um multi 1.90 .75
Nos. 545-547 (3) 4.15 1.55

Pre-Olympics — A141

1983, Dec. 31 Litho. *Perf. 13½*
548 A141 1um Basketball .25 .25
549 A141 20um Wrestling .85 .40
550 A141 50um Equestrian 2.00 .70
551 A141 77um Running 3.50 .95
Nos. 548-551 (4) 6.60 2.30

Souvenir Sheet

552 A141 100um Soccer 4.75 1.25

No. 552 contains one stamp 41x36mm. Nos. 551-552 airmail.

Scouting Year — A142

Artemis, by Rembrandt — A142a

Events & Annivs.: 5um, Flag, Baden-Powell. 14um, Johann Wolfgang von Goethe. 25um, Virgin and Child, by Peter Paul Rubens.

1984, Jan. 24
553 A142 5um multicolored 1.00 .50
553A A142 14um multicolored 1.00 .50
553B A142 25um multicolored 1.50 .50
Nos. 553-553B (3) 3.50 1.50

Souvenir Sheet

553C A142a 100um multicolored 4.25 1.50

No. 553C is airmail and contains one 42x51mm stamp.

Sand Rose A143

1984, Mar. Litho. *Perf. 14*
554 A143 21um multi *15.00* 1.50

Inscribed 1982.

Anniversaries and Events — A145

10um, Albrecht Durer (1471-1528). 12um, Apollo XI, 15th anniv. 50um, Chess.

1984, Apr. 26
555 A145 10um multi .70 .25
556 A145 12um multi .85 .35
557 A145 50um multi 2.75 1.25
Nos. 555-557 (3) 4.30 1.85

1984, Apr. 16 Litho. *Perf. 13½*

Designs: 77um, Prince Charles, Princess Diana. 100um, Prince Charles, Princess Diana, vert.

557A A145 77um multi 3.75 1.90

Miniature Sheet

557B A145 100um multi 5.50 3.50

Nos. 557A-557B airmail.

Fishing Industry A146

1984
558 A146 1um Tuna .40 .25
559 A146 2um Mackerel .40 .25
560 A146 5um Haddock .55 .25
561 A146 14um Black chinchard 1.40 .50
562 A146 18um Boat building 1.75 .60
Nos. 558-562 (5) 4.50 1.85

Nouakchott Olympic Complex A148

1984, Sept. 26 Litho. *Perf. 13½*
569 A148 14um multi 1.00 .40

Infant Survival Campaign A149

1984, Sept. 26 Litho. *Perf. 12½*
570 A149 1um Feeding by glass .30 .25
571 A149 4um Breastfeeding .30 .25
572 A149 10um Vaccinating .90 .25
573 A149 14um Weighing 1.10 .30
Nos. 570-573 (4) 2.60 1.05

Pilgrimage to Mecca — A150

1984, Oct. 3 Litho. *Perf. 13*
574 A150 14um Tents, mosque .70 .40
575 A150 18um Tents, courtyard 1.25 .60

10th Anniv., West African Union — A151

14um, Map of member nations.

1984, Nov. Litho. *Perf. 13*
576 A151 14um multi .85 .40

No. 355 Overprinted "Aide au Sahel 84" and Surcharged

1984 Litho. *Perf. 12½*
577 A82 18um on 10um 1.25 .50

Issued to publicize drought relief efforts.

Technical & Cultural Cooperation Agency, 15th Anniv. — A152

1985, Mar. 20 Litho. *Perf. 12½*
578 A152 18um Profiles, emblem 1.00 .45

League of Arab States, 40th Anniv. — A153

1985, May 7 *Perf. 13*
579 A153 14um brt yel grn & blk .75 .40

German Railways 150th Anniv. — A154

Anniversaries and events: 12um, Adler, 1st German locomotive, 1835. 18um, Series 10, 1956, last Fed. German Railways locomotive. 44um, European Music Year, Johann Sebastian Bach, composer, and Angels Making Music, unattributed painting. 77um, George Frideric Handel. 90um, Statue of Liberty, cent., vert. 100um, Queen Mother, 85th birthday, vert.

1985, Sept.
580 A154 12um multi .65 .25
581 A154 18um multi 1.00 .45
582 A154 44um multi 2.00 1.10
583 A154 77um multi 3.50 1.90
584 A154 90um multi 4.00 2.25
Nos. 580-584 (5) 11.15 5.95

Souvenir Sheet

585 A154 100um multi 4.75 2.25

World Food Day — A155

1985, Oct. 16 *Perf. 13x12½*
586 A155 18um multi .70 .40

UN Food and Agriculture Org., 40th anniv.

Fight Against Drought A156

1985, Apr. 10 Litho. *Perf. 13*
586A A156 10um Tree planting .50 .30
587 A156 14um Antelope .70 .35
588 A156 18um Oasis .90 .50

Fight Against Desert Encroachment — A157

10um, Grain harvest, vert. 14um, Brush fire. 18um, Planting brush.

1985
589 A157 10um multi .55 .30
590 A157 14um multi 2.00 .75
591 A157 18um multi 2.00 .75
Nos. 589-591 (3) 4.55 1.80

Natl. Independence, 25th Anniv. — A158

1985, Nov. 27 *Perf. 15x14½*
592 A158 18um multi 1.00 .40

Intl. Youth Year A159

1986, Feb. 13 Litho. *Perf. 13*
593 A159 18um Development .80 .40
594 A159 22um Participation 1.00 .50
595 A159 25um Peace, vert. 1.40 .60
Nos. 593-595 (3) 3.20 1.50

Toujounine Satellite Station — A160

1986, May 22 Litho. *Perf. 12½*
596 A160 25um multi 1.25 .60

World Wildlife Fund — A161

Monk seal (Monachus monachus).

1986, June 12 *Perf. 13*
597 A161 2um multi *1.50* .35
598 A161 5um multi *2.40* .60
599 A161 10um multi *3.75* 1.00
600 A161 18um multi *6.75* 2.00
Nos. 597-600 (4) *14.40* 3.95

Souvenir Sheet

601 A161 50um multi *15.00* 5.00

Weaving — A162

1986, July 20 Litho. *Perf. 12½*
602 A162 18um multi .80 .40

Sabra and Chatila Massacre, 4th Anniv. — A163

1986, Oct. 18
603 A163 22um multi .90 .40

A164

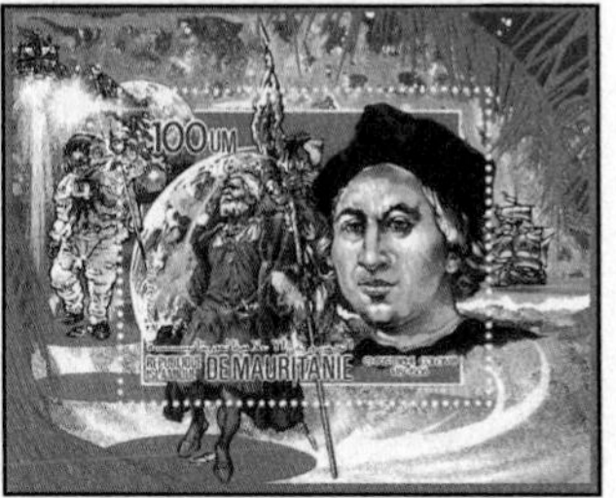

Christopher Columbus — A165

Indians, maps on globe and: 2um, Santa Maria. 22um, Nina. 35um, Pinta. 150um, Columbus.

1986, Oct. 14 Litho. *Perf. 13½*
604 A164 2um multi .25 .25
605 A164 22um multi .80 .35
606 A164 35um multi 1.25 .55
607 A164 150um multi 5.50 2.25
Nos. 604-607 (4) 7.80 3.40

Souvenir Sheet

608 A165 100um Columbus, Earth 4.50 4.00

Nos. 607-608 are airmail.

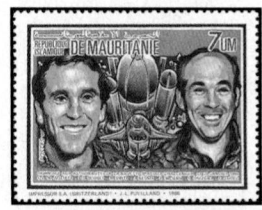

US Space Shuttle Challenger Explosion, Jan. 28, 1986 — A166

Crew members and: 7um, Space shuttle. 22um, Canadarm. 32um, Sky, moon. 43um, Memorial emblem.

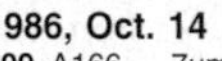

1986, Oct. 14
609 A166 7um multi .25 .25
610 A166 22um multi .80 .30
611 A166 32um multi 1.25 .50
612 A166 43um multi 1.75 .65
Nos. 609-612 (4) 4.05 1.70

Souvenir Sheet

613 A166 100um Crew, lift-off 4.00 1.50

Nos. 612-613 are airmail.

Fish A167

1986, Oct. 16 *Perf. 13*
614 A167 4um Dorade .50 .25
615 A167 98um Truite de mer 7.50 2.25

See Nos. 631-633.

Birds A168

1986, Oct. 16
616 A168 22um Spatule blanche 2.50 .60
617 A168 32um Sterne bridee 3.00 .80

See Nos. 634-635.

World Food Day A169

1986, Nov. 6 *Perf. 12½*
618 A169 22um multi 1.00 .40

A170

Halley's Comet — A171

Space probes and portraits: 5um, J.H. Dort, Giotto probe. 18um, Sir William Huggins (1824-1910), English astronomer, and launch of Giotto on Ariane rocket. 26um, E.J. Opik, Giotto and Vega. 80um, F.L. Whipple, Planet-A. 100um, Edmond Halley, Giotto.

1986, Oct. 14 Litho. *Perf. 13½*

619 A170 5um multi .25 .25
620 A170 18um multi .60 .25
621 A170 26um multi 1.00 .40
622 A170 80um multi 3.25 1.25
Nos. 619-622 (4) 5.10 2.15

Souvenir Sheet

623 A171 100um multi 4.00 2.00

Nos. 622-623 are airmail.

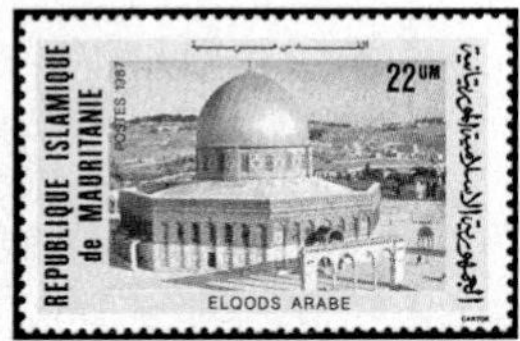

Jerusalem Day — A172

22um, Dome of the Rock.

1987, May 21 Litho. *Perf. 13½*

624 A172 22um multi 1.00 .40

Cordoue Mosque, 1200th Anniv. A173

1987, Sept. 5 Litho. *Perf. 13½*

625 A173 30um multi 1.50 .55

Literacy Campaign A174

18um, Classroom. 22um, Family reading, vert.

1987, Sept. 12

626 A174 18um multi .70 .40
627 A174 22um multi .90 .60

World Health Day — A175

1987, Oct. 1 *Perf. 13*

628 A175 18um multi .80 .40

Natl. Population Census A176

1988, Aug. 21 Litho. *Perf. 13½*

629 A176 20um multi .80 .40

WHO, 40th Anniv. — A177

1988, Sept. 19 *Perf. 13*

630 A177 30um multi 1.25 .50

Fish Type of 1986

1um, Rascasse blanche. 7um, Baliste. 15um, Bonite a ventre raye.

1988, Sept. 10 Litho. *Perf. 13*

631 A167 1um multi .60 .25
632 A167 7um multi 1.90 .35
633 A167 15um multi 2.75 .75
Nos. 631-633 (3) 5.25 1.35

Bird Type of 1986

1988, Sept. 15

634 A168 18um Grand cormorant 1.40 .60
635 A168 80um Royal tern 6.00 2.75

Arab Scouting Movement, 75th Anniv. — A178

1988, Sept. 29 Litho. *Perf. 13*

636 A178 35um multi 1.60 .60

1st Municipal Elections — A179

20um, Men casting ballots. 24um, Woman casting ballot.

1988, Nov. 22 *Perf. 13½*

637 A179 20um multi .65 .30
638 A179 24um multi 1.00 .40

Organization of African Unity, 25th Anniv. (in 1988) — A180

1988, Dec. 7 Litho. *Perf. 13*

639 A180 40um multi 1.25 .65

Intl. Fund for Agricultural Development, 10th Anniv. (in 1988) — A181

1988, Dec. 15

640 A181 35um multi 1.75 .70

Autonomy of Nouakchott (Amitie) Port, 1st Anniv. — A182

1988, Dec. 20 Litho. *Perf. 13*

641 A182 24um multi 1.40 .60

A183

1989, July 7 Litho. *Perf. 13*

642 A183 35um multi 1.60 .60

French Revolution bicent., PHILEXFRANCE '89.

A184

1989, July 17

643 A184 20um multi .90 .40

1990 World Cup Soccer Championships, Italy.

Pilgrimage to Mecca A185

1989, Aug. 26 Litho. *Perf. 13½*

644 A185 20um Mosque .90 .40

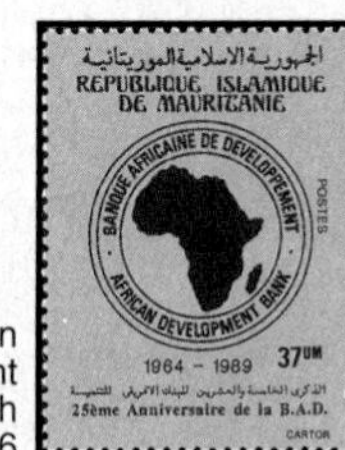

African Development Bank, 25th Anniv. — A186

1989, Sept. 2

645 A186 37um lt vio & blk 1.25 .60

Tapestry — A187

1989, Oct. 1 *Perf. 13*

646 A187 50um multicolored 2.25 .85

Locusts, Moths and Ladybugs A188

No. 647, Heliothis armigera. No. 648, Locust. No. 649, Aphis gossypii. No. 650, Agrotis ypsilon. No. 651, Chilo. No. 652, Two locusts, egg case. No. 653, Locusts emerging. No. 654, Plitella xylostella. No. 655, Henosepilachna elaterii. No. 656, Locust flying. No. 657, Trichoplusia ni. No. 658, Locust, diff.

1989, Dec. 29

647 A188 2um multi .25 .25
648 A188 5um multi .50 .25
649 A188 6um multi .25 .25
650 A188 10um multi .50 .25
651 A188 20um multi .95 .35
652 A188 20um multi 1.00 .35
653 A188 24um multi 1.10 .40
654 A188 24um multi 1.10 .40
655 A188 30um multi 1.60 .50
656 A188 40um multi 2.25 .70
657 A188 42um multi 2.00 .70
658 A188 88um multi 5.50 1.40
Nos. 647-658 (12) 17.00 5.80

For surcharge see No. 737.

Revolt — A189

1989, Dec. 8 Litho. *Perf. 13*

659 A189 35um multicolored 1.60 .70

2nd Anniv. of the Palestinian Uprising and 1st anniv. of the declaration of a Palestinian State.

Maghreb Arab Union, 1st Anniv. — A190

1990, Feb. 17 Litho. ***Perf. 13½***

660	A190	50um multicolored	1.75	.80

Mineral Resources A191

1990, July 27 ***Perf. 11½***

661	A191	60um multicolored	2.75	1.60

Intl. Literacy Year — A192

1990, July 27

662	A192	60um multicolored	1.75	1.00

1992 Summer Olympics, Barcelona A193

5um, Equestrian. 50um, Archery. 60um, Hammer throw. 75um, Field hockey. 90um, Handball. 220um, Table tennis.
150um, Runner.

Litho. & Typo.

1990, Sept. 2 ***Perf. 13½***

663	A193	5um multi	.25	.25
664	A193	50um multi	1.90	.75
665	A193	60um multi	2.00	1.25
666	A193	75um multi	2.75	1.25
667	A193	90um multi	3.50	1.50
668	A193	220um multi	8.50	3.25
		Nos. 663-668 (6)	18.90	8.25

Souvenir Sheet

669	A193	150um multi	6.25	2.50

Nos. 668-669 airmail.

A194

1990, July 27 ***Perf. 11½***

670	A194	50um multicolored	2.00	.75

Multinational Postal School, 20th anniv.

A195

1990, Nov. 21 Litho. ***Perf. 11½***

671	A195	85um multicolored	3.75	1.60

Declaration of the Palestinian State, 2nd anniv.

1992 Winter Olympics, Albertville A196

60um, Downhill skiing. 75um, Cross-country skiing. 90um, Ice hockey. 220um, Pairs figure skating.
150um, Slalom skiing.

1990, Dec. 10 Litho. ***Perf. 13½***

672	A196	60um multi	1.75	.75
673	A196	75um multi	2.00	.90
674	A196	90um multi	2.75	1.10
675	A196	220um multi	6.25	2.75
		Nos. 672-675 (4)	12.75	5.50

Souvenir Sheet

676	A196	150um multi	5.00	2.50

Nos. 675-676 are airmail.

Release of Nelson Mandela A197

1990, Dec. 10

677	A197	85um multicolored	3.75	1.90

Return of Senegalese Refugees — A198

50um, Cooking at encampment. 75um, Women sewing. 85um, Drawing water.

1990, Dec. 10

678	A198	50um multi	2.00	1.00
679	A198	75um multi	3.00	1.60
680	A198	85um multi	3.50	1.75
		Nos. 678-680 (3)	8.50	4.35

Boy Scouts Observing Nature — A199

Scout: 5um, Picking mushrooms. 50um, Holding mushroom. 60um, Drawing butterfly. 75um, Feeding butterfly. 90um, Photographing butterfly. 220um, Drying mushrooms. No. 687, Using microscope.

1991, Jan. 16 Litho. ***Perf. 13½***

681	A199	5um multicolored	.40	.25
682	A199	50um multicolored	2.40	.95
683	A199	60um multicolored	2.25	1.10
684	A199	75um multicolored	2.50	1.00
685	A199	90um multicolored	2.50	1.10
686	A199	220um multicolored	5.75	2.75
		Nos. 681-686 (6)	15.80	7.15

Souvenir Sheet

687	A199	150um multicolored	6.00	4.00

Nos. 684 and 687 are airmail. Nos. 683-685 exist in souvenir sheets of 1.

Independence, 30th Anniv. — A200

50um, Satellite dish antennae. 60um, Container ship. 100um, Harvesting rice.

1991, Mar. 5

688	A200	50um multi	1.90	1.00
689	A200	60um multi	2.25	1.40
690	A200	100um multi	3.75	1.90
		Nos. 688-690 (3)	7.90	4.30

World Meteorology Day — A201

1991, Mar. 23 ***Perf. 14x15***

691	A201	100um multicolored	3.75	2.10

World Population Day — A202

1991, July 27 Litho. ***Perf. 13½***

692	A202	90um multicolored	3.50	1.75

Domesticated Animals — A203

1991 Litho. ***Perf. 13½***

693	A203	50um Cats	2.25	1.00
693A	A203	60um Dog	2.75	1.60

Campaign Against Blindness A204

1991, Nov. 10 Litho. ***Perf. 13½***

694	A204	50um multicolored	2.00	1.00

Doctors Without Borders, 20th Anniv. A205

1991 Litho. ***Perf. 13½***

695	A205	60um multicolored	2.50	1.25

Installation of Central Electric Service (in 1989) A206

1991, Dec. 29 Litho. ***Perf. 13½***

696	A206	50um multicolored	2.50	1.00

Mineral Exploration, M'Haoudat A207

60um, Desert landscape.

1993 Litho. ***Perf. 13½***

697	A207	50um shown	2.10	1.00
698	A207	60um multi	2.50	1.40

1994 Winter Olympics, Lillehammer A208

10um, Bobsled. 50um, Luge. 60um, Figure skating. 80um, Downhill skiing. 220um, Cross-country skiing.
150um, Downhill skiing, diff.

1993

699	A208	10um multi	.40	.25
700	A208	50um multi	1.75	1.25
701	A208	60um multi	2.10	1.25
702	A208	80um multi	2.75	1.75
703	A208	220um multi	7.75	4.50
		Nos. 699-703 (5)	14.75	8.80

Souvenir Sheet

704	A208	150um multi	5.75	3.25

No. 704 is airmail.
No. 700 exists dated "1998."

Intifada, 6th Anniv. — A209

Design: 60um, Palestinian children, horiz.

1993

705	A209	50um multicolored	2.10	1.00
706	A209	60um multicolored	2.50	1.40

First Multiparty Presidential Elections, 1st Anniv. A209a

Design: 60um, Line at polling place.

1993 **Litho.** ***Perf. 13½***
706B A209a 60um multi *25.00* —

An additional stamp was issued in this set. The editors would like to examine any example.

Caravans — A210

1993
707 A210 50um blue & multi 1.90 1.00
708 A210 60um violet & multi 2.25 1.40

Hut A210a

1994 **Litho.** ***Perf. 13¼x13½***
708A A210a 50um Hut, diff. — —
708B A210a 60um multi — —
708C A210a 80um Hut, diff. —
Set of 3 80.00

1994 World Cup Soccer Championships, U.S. — A211

Designs: 10um, Soldier Field. 50um, Foxboro Stadium. 60um, Robert F. Kennedy Stadium. 90um, Stanford Stadium. 220um, Giants Stadium. 150um, Rose Bowl.

1994, Feb. 10 **Litho.** ***Perf. 13***
709 A211 10um multicolored .35 .25
710 A211 50um multicolored 1.60 1.05
711 A211 60um multicolored 1.90 1.25
712 A211 90um multicolored 2.75 1.75
713 A211 220um multicolored 7.00 4.50
Nos. 709-713 (5) 13.60 8.80

Souvenir Sheet

714 A211 150um multicolored 5.75 3.25

Birds of Banc d'Arguin National Park — A211a

Designs: 10 um, Gulls, horiz. 30um, Various birds. 40um, Terns. 50um, Sandpipers.

1994 **Litho.** ***Perf. 13½***
714A A211a 10um lt blue & multi — —
714B A211a 30um lt blue & multi — —
714C A211a 40um lt blue & multi — —
714D A211a 50um lt blue & multi — —

UN, 50th Anniv. A212

1995 **Litho.** ***Perf. 11½***
715 A212 60um Emblem, #167 1.50 .75

FAO, 50th Anniv. A213

1995
716 A213 50um Working in field 1.00 .70
717 A213 60um With fishing boat 1.25 .85
718 A213 90um Planting garden 1.90 1.25
Nos. 716-718 (3) 4.15 2.80

Traditional Handicrafts — A214

1995, Aug. 14 **Litho.** ***Perf. 12***
719 A214 50um Weaving rug — —
Perf. 11½x12
720 A214 60um Kettle — —

1996 Summer Olympics, Atlanta — A216

Design: 20um, Sprinters crouching at starting line. 40um, Five Runners. 50um, Runners.

1996, July 19 **Litho.** ***Perf. 11¾***
725 A216 20um pink & multi — —
727 A216 40um blue & multi — —
728 A216 50um yel & multi — —

An additional stamp was issued in this set. The editors would like to examine any example.

Traditional Games A218

Design: 90um, Women and sticks.

1996, Oct. 25 **Litho.** ***Perf. 11¾***
733 A218 90um multi — —

Two additional stamps were issued in this set. The editors would like to examine any examples.

French Pres. Jacques Chirac, Mauritanian Pres. Maaouya Ould Sid Ahmed Taya — A219

1997 **Litho.** ***Perf. 13¼x13***
735A A219 60um multi — —

State visit of Chirac to Mauritania.

Universal Declaration of Human Rights, 50th Anniv. A220

1998 **Litho.** ***Perf. 13x13¼***
736 A220 60um multi — —

The editors suspect that other stamps were issued in this set and would like to examine any examples.

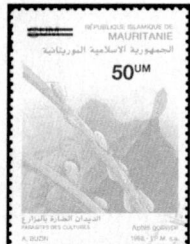

No. 649 Surcharged

2000 **Method and Perf. As Before**
737 A188 50um on 6um #649 — —

Independence, 40th Anniv. — A221

2000 **Litho.** ***Perf. 13¼***
738 A221 50um multi — —

Education A222

Designs: 50um, Man with tablet, woman at computer. 60um, Open-air class. 90um, Reading class. 100um, Mathematics class.

2000
739-742 A222 Set of 4 — —

Mauritanian postal officials have declared as "illegal" the following items:

Sheets of 9 stamps with 60um denominations depicting Famous actresses (2 different). Classic actresses, Marilyn Monroe, Elvis Presley, The Beatles, Queen, Walt Disney, The Simpsons, Teddy bears.

Sheets of 6 stamps with 80um denominations depicting Birds and Scout emblem (15 different).

Sheets of 6 stamps with 60um denominations depicting Trains (5 different), Penguins and Rotary emblem (2 different), Cats and Rotary emblem (2 different), Elephants and Rotary emblem (2 different), Polar bears and Rotary emblem (2 different), Lighthouses and Rotary emblem (2 different), Firearms and Rotary emblem, Firearms and Scout emblem, Pope John Paul II, Harry Potter, Scooby-Doo.

Sheets of 4 stamps depicting various sports of the Sydney Olympics (2 different).

Souvenir sheet depicting Various sports of the Sydney Olympics.

Se-tenant sets of 4 stamps depicting sports of the Sydney Olympics (2 different).

Flora, Fauna and Mushrooms — A223

No. 743: a, Chelonia mydas. b, Octopus vulgaris. c, Coelacanth.
No. 744: a, Lepiota aspera. b, Lactarius camphoratus. c, Clitocybe gibba.
No. 745: a, Harpa costata. b, Voluta lapponica. c, Tellina variegata.
No. 746: a, Akhal-Teke horse. b, Arabian horse. c, Lipizzaner horse.
No. 747: a, Tibetan dog, Balinese cat. b, Shetland sheepdog, Ragdoll cat. c, Cao de Serra de Aires sheepdog, Abyssinian cat.
No. 748: a, Acraea igati. b, Mylotris humbolti. c, Mylotris ngaziya.
No. 749: a, Zosterops maderaspatana. b, Otus rutilus. c, Nelicurvitus nelicourvi.
No. 750: a, Maxillaria tenuifolia. b, Crotalaria. c, Maxillaria marginata.
No. 751, Russula virescens. No. 752, Black Russian cat.

2000, Nov, 5 **Litho.** ***Perf. 13½***
743 Horiz. strip of 3 1.60 1.60
a.-c. A223 50um Any single .50 .50
744 Horiz. strip of 3 1.60 1.60
a.-c. A223 50um Any single .50 .50
745 Horiz. strip of 3 1.75 1.75
a.-c. A223 60um Any single .55 .55
746 Horiz. strip of 3 2.75 2.75
a.-c. A223 90um Any single .90 .90
747 Horiz. strip of 3 3.00 3.00
a.-c. A223 100um Any single 1.00 1.00
748 Horiz. strip of 3 6.00 6.00
a.-c. A223 200um Any single 2.00 2.00
749 Horiz. strip of 3 7.00 7.00
a.-c. A223 220um Any single 2.25 2.25
750 Horiz. strip of 3 2.75 2.75
a. A223 60um multi .60 .60
b. A223 90um multi .90 .90
c. A223 100um multi 1.00 1.00
Nos. 743-750 (8) 26.45 26.45

Souvenir Sheets

751 A223 300um multi 4.75 4.75
752 A223 300um multi 4.75 4.75

Nos. 746-749 exist in souvenir sheets containing one strip of 3 with light blue frames. No. 750 exists imperf.

2002 World Cup Soccer Championships, Japan and Korea — A224

No. 753: a, Zinedine Zidane. b, Christian Vieri. c, Alessandro del Piero. d, Lilian Thuram.

No. 754: a, Oliver Bierhoff. b, Jürgen Klinsmann. c, Edgar Davids. d, Dennis Bergkamp.
300um, Jules Rimet Cup, soccer players, horiz.

2000

753 Horiz. strip of 4 14.00 14.00
a.-d. A224 90um Any single 3.00 3.00
754 Horiz. strip of 4 14.00 14.00
a.-d. A224 100um Any single 3.00 3.00

Souvenir Sheet

755 A224 300um multi 4.00 4.00

No. 755 contains one 57x51mm stamp. Souvenir sheets of 4 stamps exist with Nos. 753a-753d and 754a-754d with colored stamp frames.

Theodore Monod (1902-2000), Naturalist A225

2003, Jan. 1 ***Perf. 13¼x13***
756 A225 370um multi 3.50 2.50

Trains A226

Designs: 100um, Freight train for minerals. 370um, Passenger train. 440um, Desert train.

2003, Jan. 1 ***Perf. 13x13¼***
757-759 A226 Set of 3 10.00 10.00

Tourist Attractions A227

Designs: 100um, Sailboats, Banc d'Arguin. 220um, Ben Amera. 370um, Desert warthogs, Diawling Park. 440fr, Palms, Tergit, vert.

2003, Jan. 1 ***Perf. 13x13¼, 13¼x13***
760-763 A227 Set of 4 12.00 7.00

Handicrafts A228

Designs: 100um, Wooden chest. 220um, Pipes. 310um, Teapot. 370um, Beads.

2003, Jan. 1 ***Perf. 13x13¼***
764-767 A228 Set of 4 10.00 6.00

Historic Towns A229

Designs: 100um, Mosque, Chinguetti. 220um, Mosque, Ouadane. 660um, Wall design, Oualata. 880um, Mosque, Tichitt.

2003, Jan. 1
768-771 A229 Set of 4 18.00 12.00

Promotion of Books and Reading A230

Open book and: 100um, Stack of books, chair. 220um, Camel. 280um, Tower. 370um, Man, construction equipment.

2003, Jan. 1 **Litho.** ***Perf. 13***
772-775 A230 Set of 4 12.50 6.00

Diplomatic Relations Between Mauritania and People's Republic of China, 40th Anniv. A231

Flags and: 100um, Ships and crane. 370um, Ship and crane, vert.

Perf. 13x13¼, 13¼x13
2005, July 19 **Litho.**
776-777 A231 Set of 2 6.25 6.25

Independence, 45th Anniv. — A232

Denominations: 100um, 370um.

2005, Nov. 16 ***Perf. 13***
778-779 A232 Set of 2 5.00 5.00

World Summit on the Information Society, Tunis A233

Denominations: 100um, 370um.

2005, Nov. 16
780-781 A233 Set of 2 5.00 5.00

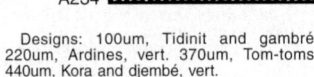

Musical Instruments A234

Designs: 100um, Tidinit and gambré. 220um, Ardines, vert. 370um, Tom-toms. 440um, Kora and djembé, vert.

2005, Nov. 28
782-785 A234 Set of 4 13.00 13.00

Flora A235

Designs: 100um, Acacia tree. 220um, Euphorbia, vert. 370um, Jujube tree. 440um, Baobab tree, vert.

2005, Nov. 28
786-789 A235 Set of 4 13.00 13.00

Fauna A236

Designs: 100um, Starred lizard. 220um, Horned viper, vert. 370um, Lizard. 440um, Scorpion, vert.

2005, Nov. 28
790-793 A236 Set of 4 13.00 13.00

Tourism A237

Designs: 100um, People, fish and dolphins in water. 220um, Hodh El Gharbi. 370um, Adrar. 440um, Tiris Zemour.

2005, Nov. 28
794-797 A237 Set of 4 13.00 13.00

Jewelry A238

Designs: 100um, Necklaces. 220um, Khalkhal bracelets. 370um, Strings of beads. 440fr, Bracelets.

2008 **Litho.** ***Perf. 13***
798-801 A238 Set of 4 17.00 17.00

Exploitation of Natural Resources — A239

Designs: 100um, Zouerate iron mine. 280um, Chinguitti oil platform, vert. 310um, Akjoujt copper mine. 370um, Taziast gold mine, vert.

2008
802-805 A239 Set of 4 17.00 17.00

Animals A240

Designs: 100um, Birds. 220um, Dolphins. 370um, Seal. 440um, Sea turtle.

2009 **Litho.** ***Perf. 13***
806-809 A240 Set of 4 13.50 13.50

Saddles A241

Saddle for: 100um, Horse. 220um, Cow. 370um, Ass. 440um, Camel.

2009
810-813 A241 Set of 4 13.50 13.50

Gear for Nomads A242

Designs: 100um, Rifle holster. 150um, Tassoufra. 220um, Powder horns. 370um, Palanquin, vert. 440um, Prayer rug.

2009
814-818 A242 Set of 5 16.50 16.50

Necklaces A243

Designs: 100um, Ebony necklace. 150um, Agate necklace. 220um, Amber necklace. 370um, Traditional necklace. 440um, Stone necklace.

2010 ***Perf. 13¼***
819-823 A243 Set of 5 12.00 12.00

Independence, 50th Anniv. — A244

2010 ***Perf. 13***
824 A244 370um multi 7.50 7.50

Fish A245

Designs: 100um, Daisy stingray (pastenague marguerite). 220um, Guitar fish (raie guitare). 370um, Spinner shark (requin tisserand).

2011
825-827 A245 Set of 3 7.00 7.00

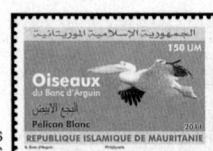

Birds A246

Designs: 150um, Great white pelican (pélican blanc). 220um, Dimorphic egret (aigrette dimorphe). 370um, Little stint (bécasseau minute). 440um, Caspian tern (sterne caspienne).

2011 **Litho.** ***Perf. 13***
828-831 A246 Set of 4 *45.00 45.00*

Mammals A247

Designs: 100um, Hyena. 370um, Fennec.

2011 **Litho.** ***Perf. 13***
832-833 A247 Set of 2 5.00 5.00

2012 Festival of Old Towns, Ouadane — A248

Designs: 100um, Town. 370um, Festival emblem and names of host towns.

2012
834-835 A248 Set of 2 6.00 5.00

Marine Life A249

Designs: 100um, King mackerel (Maquereau bonite). 150um, Butterfish (Lippe). 220um, Red-banded sea bream (Pagre rayé). 280um, Blue-spotted sea bream (Merou à points bleus). No. 840, 370um, Dogfish (Chien de mer). No. 841, 370um, Cuttlefish (Seiche commune). 440um, Round sardinella (Sardinelle ronde).

2013 **Litho.** ***Perf. 12¾x13***
836-842 A249 Set of 7 — —

Nouadhibou Free Zone, 1st Anniv. — A251

2014 **Litho.** ***Perf. 12¾***
844 A251 370um multi 2.60 2.60

Marine Life A252

Designs: No. 845, 100um, Threadfin (petit capitaine). No. 846, 100um, Sea trout (truite de mer). 220um, Black mullet (mulet noir). 280um, Atlantic horse mackerel (chinchard d'europe). No. 849, 370um, Zebra sea bream (sar tambour). No. 850, 370um, Pink shrimp (crevette rose). 440um, Red mullet (rouget barbet).

2014 **Litho.** ***Perf. 12¾***
845-851 A252 Set of 7 *22.50 22.50*

Festival of Old Towns A253

2014 **Litho.** ***Perf. 12¾***
852 A253 370um multi 2.60 2.60

SEMI-POSTAL STAMPS

Nos. 23 and 26 Surcharged in Red

1915-18 **Unwmk.** ***Perf. 14x13½***
B1 A4 10c + 5c rose & red org 1.75 *2.10*
a. Double surcharge 225.00
B2 A4 15c + 5c dk brn & blk ('18) 1.75 *2.10*
a. Double surcharge 190.00
b. Inverted surcharge 150.00

Curie Issue
Common Design Type

1938, Oct. 24 ***Perf. 13***
B3 CD80 1.75fr + 50c brt ultra 7.75 7.75

French Revolution Issue
Common Design Type

Photo.; Name and Value Typographed in Black

1939, July 5 **Unwmk.**
B4 CD83 45c + 25c grn 8.50 8.50
B5 CD83 70c + 30c brn 8.50 8.50
B6 CD83 90c + 35c red org 8.50 8.50
B7 CD83 1.25fr + 1fr rose pink 8.50 8.50
B8 CD83 2.25fr + 2fr bl 8.50 8.50
Nos. B4-B8 (5) 42.50 42.50

Catalogue values for unused stamps in this section, from this point to the end of the section, are for Never Hinged items.

Stamps of 1938 Surcharge in Red or Black

1941
B9 A6 50c + 1fr pur (R) 7.00 3.50
B10 A7 80c + 2fr dp bl (R) 14.00 7.00
B11 A7 1.50fr + 2fr vio (R) 14.00 10.00
B12 A8 2fr + 3fr rose vio (Bk) 14.00 10.00
Nos. B9-B12 (4) 49.00 30.50

Common Design Type and

Moorish Goumier SP1

White Goumier — SP2

1941 **Photo.** ***Perf. 13½***
B13 SP1 1fr + 1fr red 1.00
B14 CD86 1.50fr + 3fr claret 1.00
B15 SP2 2.50fr + 1fr blue 1.00
Nos. B13-B15 (3) 3.00

Nos. B13-B15 were issued by the Vichy government in France, but were not placed on sale in Mauritania.

Nos. 114-115 Surcharged in Black or Red

1944 **Engr.** ***Perf. 12½x12***
B15A 50c + 1.50fr on 2.50fr deep blue (R) .80
B15B + 2.50fr on 1fr green .80

Colonial Development Fund.

Nos. B15A-B15B were issued by the Vichy government in France, but were not placed on sale in Mauritania.

Islamic Republic Anti-Malaria Issue
Common Design Type

1962, Apr. 7 **Engr.** ***Perf. 12½x12***
B16 CD108 25fr + 5f light olive grn .80 .80

Freedom from Hunger Issue
Common Design Type

1963, Mar. 21 **Unwmk.** ***Perf. 13***
B17 CD112 25fr + 5fr multi .80 .80

Nurse Tending Infant SP3

1972, May 8 **Photo.** ***Perf. 12½x13***
B18 SP3 35fr + 5fr grn, red & brn 1.50 1.50

Surtax was for Mauritania Red Crescent Society.

AIR POST STAMPS

Common Design Type
Perf. 12½x12

1940, Feb. 8 **Engr.** **Unwmk.**
C1 CD85 1.90fr ultra .35 .35
C2 CD85 2.90fr dk red .35 .35
C3 CD85 4.50fr dk gray grn .70 .70
C4 CD85 4.90fr yel bister .70 .70
C5 CD85 6.90fr deep org 1.40 1.40
Nos. C1-C5 (5) 3.50 3.50

Catalogue values for unused stamps in this section, from this point to the end of the section, are for Never Hinged items.

Common Design Types

1942
C6 CD88 50c car & bl .35
C7 CD88 1fr brn & blk .35
C8 CD88 2fr dk grn & red brn .70
C9 CD88 3fr dk bl & scar .70
C10 CD88 5fr vio & brn red 1.00

Frame Engraved, Center Typo.

C11 CD89 10fr ultra, ind & hn 1.40
a. Center inverted *1,400.*
C12 CD89 20fr rose car, mag & buff 1.75
a. Center inverted *1,400.*
C13 CD89 50fr yel grn, dl grn & org 3.50 *3.25*
Nos. C6-C13 (8) 9.75

There is doubt whether Nos. C6-C12 were officially placed in use.

No. C11 exists with violet-blue center. Value $300.

Islamic Republic

Flamingoes AP1

Designs: 200fr, African spoonbills. 500fr, Slender-billed gull, horiz.

Unwmk.

1961, June 30 **Engr.** ***Perf. 13***
C14 AP1 100fr red org, brn & ultra 3.75 2.00
C15 AP1 200fr red org, sep & sl grn 5.75 3.50
C16 AP1 500fr red org, gray & bl 17.00 8.00
Nos. C14-C16 (3) 26.50 13.50

An overprint, "Europa / CECA / MIFERMA," was applied in carmine to No. C16 in 1962. Two types exist: type 1, no box around "MIFERMA"; box surrounding "MIFERMA". Values: type 1, $35; type 2, $16.

The anti-malaria emblem, including slogan "Le Monde contre le Paludisme," was overprinted on Nos. C14-C15 in 1962. Two types of overprint: type 1, double lines of latitude and longitude on globe; type single lines of latitude and longitude on globe. Values: type 1, $27.50; type 2: $8.

Air Afrique Issue
Common Design Type

1962, Feb. 17
C17 CD107 100fr sl grn, choc & bis 2.50 1.25

UN Headquarters, New York; View of Nouakchott — AP2

1962, Oct. 27 **Engr.** ***Perf. 13***
C18 AP2 100fr bluish grn, dk bl & org brn 1.50 1.00

Mauritania's admission to the UN.

Plane, Nouakchott Airport — AP3

1963, May 3 **Unwmk.** ***Perf. 13***
C19 AP3 500fr dp bl, gldn brn & slate grn 11.00 4.00

Miferma Open-pit Mine at Zouerate — AP4

Design: 200fr, Ore transport at Port Etienne.

1963, June **Photo.** ***Perf. 13x12***
C20 AP4 100fr multi 1.90 .55
C21 AP4 200fr multi 4.75 1.25

African Postal Union Issue
Common Design Type

1963, Sept. 8 **Unwmk.** ***Perf. 12½***
C22 CD114 85fr blk brn, ocher & red 1.50 .60

Globe and Telstar — AP5

Design: 150fr, Relay satellite and stars.

1963, Oct. 7 Engr. *Perf. 13*
C23 AP5 50fr yel grn, pur & red brn .75 .40
C24 AP5 150fr red brn & sl grn 2.50 1.40

Communication through space.

Tiros Satellite and Emblem of WMO — AP6

1963, Nov. 4
C25 AP6 200fr ultra, brn & grn 4.00 1.75

Space research for meteorology and navigation.

1963 Air Afrique Issue
Common Design Type

1963, Nov. 19 Photo. *Perf. 13x12*
C26 CD115 25fr multi .70 .25

UN Emblem, Doves and Sun — AP7

1963, Dec. 10 Engr. *Perf. 13*
C27 AP7 100fr vio, brn, & dk bl 1.75 .90

Universal Declaration of Human Rights, 15th anniv.

Europafrica Issue

Symbols of Agriculture and Industry — AP8

1964, Jan. 6 Photo.
C28 AP8 50fr multi 1.40 .90

Signing of economic agreement between the European Economic Community and the African and Malgache Union at Yaoundé, Cameroun, July 20, 1963.

Lichtenstein's Sand Grouse — AP9

Birds: 200fr, Long-tailed cormorant. 500fr, Chanting goshawk.

1964, Feb. 3 Engr. *Perf. 13*
C29 AP9 100fr ocher, ol & dk brn 3.25 1.10
C30 AP9 200fr blk, dk bl & brn 5.00 1.90
C31 AP9 500fr rose red, grn & sl 15.00 5.75
Nos. C29-C31 (3) 23.25 8.75

Isis, Temple at Philae and Trajan's Kiosk — AP10

1964, Mar. 8 Unwmk. *Perf. 13*
C32 AP10 10fr red brn, Prus bl & blk .50 .25
C33 AP10 25fr red brn, ind & Prus bl .80 .40
C34 AP10 60fr blk brn, Prus bl & red brn 1.60 .75
Nos. C32-C34 (3) 2.90 1.40

UNESCO world campaign to save historic monuments in Nubia.

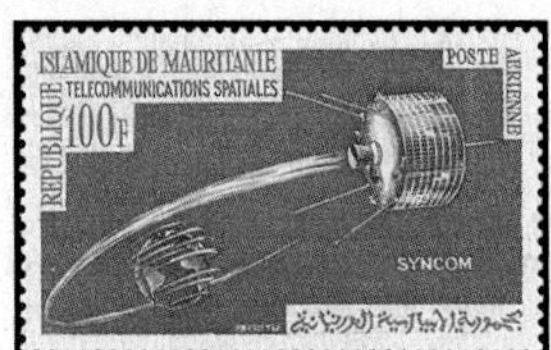

Syncom Satellite, Globe — AP11

1964, May 4 Engr.
C35 AP11 100fr red, red brn & ultra 1.50 .75

Issued to publicize space communications.

Horse Race on Bowl — AP12

Sport Designs from Ancient Pottery: 50fr, Runner, vert. 85fr, Wrestlers, vert. 100fr, Charioteer.

1964, Sept. 27 Unwmk. *Perf. 13*
C36 AP12 15fr ol bis & choc .45 .30
C37 AP12 50fr bl & org brn 1.10 .55
C38 AP12 85fr crim & brn 1.90 1.10
C39 AP12 100fr emer & dk red brn 2.40 1.40
a. Min. sheet of 4, #C36-C39 7.25 7.25
Nos. C36-C39 (4) 5.85 3.35

18th Olympic Games, Tokyo, Oct. 10-25.

Pres. John F. Kennedy (1917-1963) AP13

1964, Dec. 7 Photo. *Perf. 12½*
C40 AP13 100fr red brn, bl grn & dk brn 1.50 1.50
a. Souv. sheet of 4 7.00 7.00

ITU Emblem, Induction Telegraph and Relay Satellite — AP14

1965, May 17 Engr. *Perf. 13*
C41 AP14 250fr multi 4.75 3.00

ITU, centenary.

Fight Against Cancer — AP15

1965, July 19 Unwmk. *Perf. 13*
C42 AP15 100fr bis, Prus bl & red 1.45 .70

Issued to publicize the fight against cancer.

Winston Churchill — AP16

1965, Dec. 6 Photo. *Perf. 13*
C43 AP16 200fr multi 2.75 1.40

Sir Winston Spencer Churchill (1874-1965), statesman and WWII leader.

Diamant Rocket Ascending AP17

French achievements in space: 60fr, Satellite A-1 and earth, horiz. 90fr, Scout rocket and satellite FR-1, horiz.

1966, Feb. 7 Engr. *Perf. 13*
C44 AP17 30fr dp bl, red & grn .50 .30
C45 AP17 60fr mar, Prus grn & bl 1.10 .55
C46 AP17 90fr dp bl, rose cl & vio 1.60 .80
Nos. C44-C46 (3) 3.20 1.65

Dr. Albert Schweitzer and Clinic — AP18

1966, Feb. 21 Photo. *Perf. 12½*
C47 AP18 50fr multi 1.50 .65

Schweitzer (1875-1965), medical missionary to Gabon, theologian and musician.

Thomas P. Stafford, Walter M. Schirra and Gemini 6 — AP19

Designs: 100fr, Frank A. Borman, James A. Lovell, Jr., and Gemini 7. 200fr, Pavel Belyayev, Alexei Leonov, Voskhod 2.

1966, Mar. 7 Photo. *Perf. 12½*
C48 AP19 50fr multi .70 .30
C49 AP19 100fr multi 1.50 .55
C50 AP19 200fr multi 2.50 1.25
Nos. C48-C50 (3) 4.70 2.10

Issued to honor achievements in space.

Map of Africa and Dove — AP20

1966, May 9 Photo. *Perf. 13*
C51 AP20 100fr red brn, sl & yel grn 1.00 .50

Organization for African Unity.

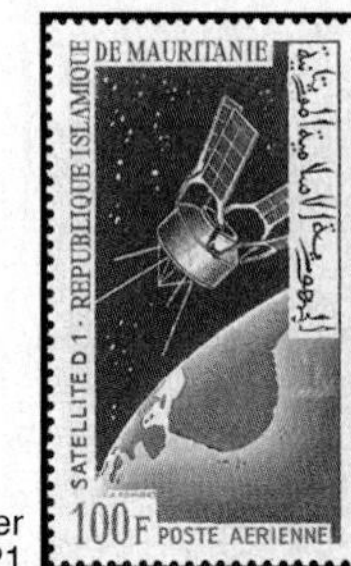

D-1 Satellite over Earth — AP21

1966, June 6 Engr.
C52 AP21 100fr bl, dk pur & ocher 1.50 .80

Launching of the D-1 satellite at Hammaguir, Algeria, Feb. 17, 1966.

Bréguet 14 — AP22

Planes: 100fr, Goliath Farman, and camel caravan. 150fr, Couzinet "Arc-en-Ciel." 200fr, Latécoère 28 hydroplane.

1966, July 4 Engr. *Perf. 13*

C53 AP22 50fr sl bl, dl grn & ol bis 1.00 .30
C54 AP22 100fr brt bl, dk grn & dk red brn 2.10 .50
C55 AP22 150fr dl brn, Prus bl & saph 3.00 .80
C56 AP22 200fr dk red brn, bl & ind 4.25 1.25
Nos. C53-C56 (4) 10.35 2.85

Air Afrique Issue
Common Design Type

1966, Aug. 31 Photo. *Perf. 13*

C57 CD123 30fr red, blk & gray .80 .30

"The Raft of the Medusa," by Théodore Géricault — AP23

1966, Sept. 5 Photo. *Perf. 12½*

C58 AP23 500fr multi 11.50 7.00

Sinking of the frigate "Medusa" off Mauritania, July 2, 1816.

Symbols of Agriculture and Industry — AP24

1966, Nov. 7 Photo. *Perf. 13x12*

C59 AP24 50fr multi 1.00 .40

Third anniversary, economic agreement between the European Economic Community and the African and Malgache Union.

Crowned Crane — AP25

1967, Apr. 3 *Perf. 12½x13*

C60 AP25 100fr shown 2.40 .85
C61 AP25 200fr Common egret 4.50 1.25
C62 AP25 500fr Ostrich 12.00 4.75
Nos. C60-C62 (3) 18.90 6.85

For surcharge see No. C129.

Eye, Globe and Rockets — AP26

1967, May 2 Engr. *Perf. 13*

C63 AP26 250fr brn, Prus bl & blk 4.00 1.40

EXPO '67 Intl. Exhibition, Montreal, Apr. 28-Oct. 27.

Emblem of Atomic Energy Commission AP27

1967, Aug. 7 Engr. *Perf. 13*

C64 AP27 200fr dk red, brt grn & ultra 2.75 1.25

International Atomic Energy Commission.

African Postal Union Issue
Common Design Type

1967, Sept. 9 Engr. *Perf. 13*

C65 CD124 100fr brn org, vio brn & brt grn 1.25 .60

Francesca da Rimini, by Ingres AP28

Paintings by and of Ingres: 100fr, Young man's torso. 150fr, "The Iliad" (seated woman). 200fr, Ingres in his Studio, by Alaux. 250fr, "The Odyssey" (seated woman).

1967-68 Photo. *Perf. 12½*

C66 AP28 90fr multi 1.75 .60
C67 AP28 100fr multi ('68) 1.75 .70
C68 AP28 150fr multi ('68) 2.50 1.05
C69 AP28 200fr multi 3.00 1.10
C70 AP28 250fr multi ('68) 4.25 1.75
Nos. C66-C70 (5) 13.25 5.20

Jean Dominique Ingres (1780-1867), French painter.

Issued: 90fr, 200fr, 10/2/67; others, 9/2/68.

See No. C79.

Konrad Adenauer AP29

1968, Feb. 5 Photo. *Perf. 12½*

C71 AP29 100fr org brn, lt bl & blk 1.50 .70
a. Souv. sheet of 4 7.50 6.00

Adenauer (1876-1967), chancellor of West Germany (1949-63).

Gymnast AP30

Sports: 20fr, Slalom, horiz. 50fr, Ski jump. 100fr, Hurdling, horiz.

1968, Mar. 4 Engr. *Perf. 13*

C72 AP30 20fr plum, blk & bl .35 .25
C73 AP30 30fr dl pur, brt grn & brn .45 .25
C74 AP30 50fr Prus bl, bis & bl grn .65 .30
C75 AP30 100fr brn, grn & ver 1.40 .45
Nos. C72-C75 (4) 2.85 1.25

1968 Olympic Games.

WHO Emblem, Man and Insects — AP31

1968, May 2 Engr. *Perf. 13*

C76 AP31 150fr red lil, dp bl & org red 1.90 .80

WHO, 20th anniversary.

Martin Luther King — AP32

Design: No. C78, Mahatma Gandhi.

1968, Nov. 4 Photo. *Perf. 12½*

C77 AP32 50fr sl bl, cit & blk 1.00 .30
C78 AP32 50fr sl bl, lt bl & blk 1.00 .30
a. Souv. sheet of 4, 2 each #C77-C78 4.25 4.25

Issued to honor two apostles of peace.

PHILEXAFRIQUE Issue
Painting Type of 1967

Design: 100fr, The Surprise Letter, by Charles Antoine Coypel.

1968, Dec. 9 Photo. *Perf. 12½*

C79 AP28 100fr multi 3.00 1.50

PHILEXAFRIQUE, Phil. Exhib., Abidjan, Feb. 14-23. Printed with alternating brown red label.

2nd PHILEXAFRIQUE Issue
Common Design Type

50fr, Mauritania #89 & family on jungle trail.

1969, Feb. 14 Engr. *Perf. 13*

C80 CD128 50fr sl grn, vio brn & red brn 1.90 .75

Napoleon Installed in Council of State, by Louis Charles Couder AP33

Paintings: 50fr, Napoleon at Council of the 500, by F. Bouchot. 250fr, Farewell at Fontainebleau, by Horace Vernet.

1969, Feb. 24 Photo. *Perf. 12½*

C81 AP33 50fr pur & multi 2.00 .90
C82 AP33 90fr multi 2.50 1.40
C83 AP33 250fr multi 6.75 3.25
Nos. C81-C83 (3) 11.25 5.55

Napoleon Bonaparte (1769-1821).

Camel, Gazelles, and Tourist Year Emblem — AP34

1969, June 9 Engr. *Perf. 13*

C84 AP34 50fr org, dk brn & lt bl 1.00 .50

Year of African Tourism.

Dancers and Temple Ruins, Baalbek — AP35

1969, June 16

C85 AP35 100fr Prus bl, ol brn & rose car 1.40 .55

International Baalbek Festival, Lebanon.

Apollo 8 and Moon Surface — AP36

Embossed on Gold Foil

1969 *Die-cut Perf. 10*

C86 AP36 1000fr gold 20.00 20.00

Man's first flight around the moon, Dec. 21-28, 1968 (US astronauts Col. Frank Borman, Capt. James Lovell and Maj. William Anders).

Mamo Wolde, Ethiopia, Marathon AP37

Designs: 70fr, Bob Beamon, US, broad jump. 150fr, Vera Caslavska, Czechoslovakia, gymnastics.

1969, July 7 Engr. *Perf. 13*
C87 AP37 30fr multi .40 .25
C88 AP37 70fr multi .70 .40
C89 AP37 150fr multi 1.90 .90
Nos. C87-C89 (3) 3.00 1.55

Issued to honor gold medal winners in the 19th Olympic Games, Mexico City.

Map of London-Istanbul Route — AP38

London to Sydney automobile rally: 20fr, Map showing Ankara to Teheran route, and compass rose. 50fr, Map showing Kandahar to Bombay route, arms of Afghanistan and elephant. 70fr, Map of Australia with Perth to Sydney route, and kangaroo.

1969, Aug. 14 Engr. *Perf. 13*
C90 AP38 10fr multicolored .25 .25
C91 AP38 20fr multicolored .45 .25
C92 AP38 50fr multicolored .75 .30
C93 AP38 70fr multicolored 1.10 .40
a. Min. sheet of 4, #C90-C93 3.00 3.00
Nos. C90-C93 (4) 2.55 1.20

Palette with World Map, Geisha and EXPO '70 Emblem — AP39

EXPO '70 Emblem and: 75fr, Fan & fireworks. 150fr, Stylized bird, map of Japan & boat.

1970, June 15 Photo. *Perf. 12½*
C94 AP39 50fr multi .70 .25
C95 AP39 75fr multi 1.00 .40
C96 AP39 150fr multi 1.75 .80
Nos. C94-C96 (3) 3.45 1.45

Issued to publicize EXPO '70 International Exhibition, Osaka, Japan, Mar. 15-Sept. 13.

UN Emblem, Balloon, Rocket, Farm Woman, Tractor, Old and New Record Players — AP40

1970, June 22 Engr. *Perf. 13*
C97 AP40 100fr ultra, dk brn & grn 1.20 .55

25th anniversary of the United Nations.

Elliott See (1927-1966), American Astronaut AP41

No. C99, Vladimir Komarov (1927-67). No. C100, Yuri Gagarin (1934-68). No. C101, Virgil Grissom (1926-67). No. C102, Edward White (1930-67). No. C103, Roger Chaffee (1935-67).

1970 Engr. *Perf. 13*
Portrait in Brown
C98 AP41 150fr gray & brt bl 1.75 .80
C99 AP41 150fr gray & org 1.75 .80
C100 AP41 150fr gray & org 1.75 .80
a. Souv. sheet of 3, #C98-C100 5.50 5.50
C101 AP41 150fr ultra & grnsh bl 1.75 .80
C102 AP41 150fr ultra & org 1.75 .80
C103 AP41 150fr ultra & grnsh bl 1.75 .80
a. Souv. sheet of 3, #C101-C103 5.50 5.50
Nos. C98-C103 (6) 10.50 4.80

American and Russian astronauts who died in space explorations.

Apollo 13 Capsule with Parachutes AP42

Gold Embossed

1970, Aug. 17 *Perf. 12½*
C104 AP42 500fr gold, crim & bl 7.00 7.00

Safe return of Apollo 13 crew.

Parliament, Nouakchott, and Coat of Arms — AP43

1970, Nov. 28 Photo. *Perf. 12½*
C105 AP43 100fr multi 1.25 .50

10th anniversary of Independence.

Hercules Wrestling Antaeus — AP44

1971, Mar. 8 Engr. *Perf. 13*
C106 AP44 100fr red lil, brn & ultra 1.90 .85

Pre-Olympic Year. Design from a vase decoration by Euphronius.

Gamal Abdel Nasser (1918-1970), President of U.A.R. — AP46

1971, May 10 Photo. *Perf. 12½*
C109 AP46 100fr gold & multi 1.00 .45

Boy Scout, Emblem and Map of Mauritania AP47

1971, Aug. 16 Photo. *Perf. 12½*
C110 AP47 35fr yel & multi .55 .25
C111 AP47 40fr pink & multi .60 .25
C112 AP47 100fr multi 1.50 .45
Nos. C110-C112 (3) 2.65 .95

13th Boy Scout World Jamboree, Asagiri Plain, Japan, Aug. 2-10.

African Postal Union Issue
Common Design Type

Design: 100fr, Women musicians and UAMPT building, Brazzaville, Congo.

1971, Nov. 13 Photo. *Perf. 13x13½*
C113 CD135 100fr bl & multi 1.20 .65

Letter and Postal Emblem AP48

1971, Dec. 2 *Perf. 13*
C114 AP48 35fr bis & multi .65 .30

10th anniversary of African Postal Union.

Mosul Monarch, from Book of Songs, c. 1218 AP49

Designs from Mohammedan Miniatures: 40fr, Prince holding audience, Egypt, 1334. 100fr, Pilgrim caravan, from "Maquamat," Baghdad, 1237.

1972, Jan. 10 Photo. *Perf. 13*
C115 AP49 35fr gold & multi .50 .25
C116 AP49 40fr gray & multi .65 .30
C117 AP49 100fr buff & multi 1.75 .60
Nos. C115-C117 (3) 2.90 1.15

For surcharges see Nos. C140, C143-C144.

Grand Canal, by Canaletto — AP50

Designs: 45fr, Venice Harbor, by Carlevaris, vert. 250fr, Santa Maria della Salute, by Canaletto.

1972, Feb. 14
C118 AP50 45fr gold & multi .75 .30
C119 AP50 100fr gold & multi 1.90 .70
C120 AP50 250fr gold & multi 4.00 1.10
Nos. C118-C120 (3) 6.65 2.10

UNESCO campaign to save Venice.

Hurdles and Olympic Rings — AP51

1972, Apr. 27 Engr. *Perf. 13*
C121 AP51 75fr org, vio brn & blk .75 .25
C122 AP51 100fr Prus bl, vio brn & brn 1.10 .40
C123 AP51 200fr lake, vio brn & blk 2.40 .60
a. Min. sheet of 3, #C121-C123 6.00 6.00
Nos. C121-C123 (3) 4.25 1.25

20th Olympic Games, Munich, Aug. 26-Sept. 11.
For overprints see Nos. C126-C128.

Luna 17 on Moon — AP52

75fr, Luna 16 take-off from moon, vert.

1972, Oct. 9
C124 AP52 75fr vio bl, bis & grn .80 .25
C125 AP52 100fr dl pur, sl & ol bis 1.10 .40

Russian moon missions, Luna 16, Sept. 12-14, 1970; and Luna 17, Nov. 10-17, 1970.

Nos. C121-C123 Overprinted in Violet Blue or Red:

a. 110m HAIES / MILBURN MEDAILLE D'OR
b. 400m HAIES / AKII-BUA MEDAILLE D'OR
c. 3.000m STEEPLE / KEINO MEDAILLE D'OR

1972, Oct. 16
C126 AP51(a) 75fr multi (VB) .90 .40
C127 AP51(b) 100fr multi (R) 1.10 .55
C128 AP51(c) 200fr multi (VB) 2.50 1.05
Nos. C126-C128 (3) 4.50 2.00

Gold medal winners in 20th Olympic Games: Rod Milburn, US, John Akii-Bua, Uganda, and Kipchoge Keino, Kenya.

No. C62 Surcharged with New Value, Two Bars and: "Apollo XVII / December 1972"

1973, Jan. 29 Photo. *Perf. 12½x13*
C129 AP25 250fr on 500fr multi 3.50 1.40

Apollo 17 moon mission, Dec. 7-19, 1972.

Seal Type of Regular Issue

1973, Feb. 28 Litho. *Perf. 13*
C130 A63 135fr Seal's head 4.50 1.90

For surcharge see No. C145.

Lion Eating Caiman, by Delacroix — AP53

Painting: 250fr, Lion Eating Boar, by Delacroix.

1973, Mar. 26 Photo. *Perf. 13x12½*
C131 AP53 100fr blk & multi 2.00 .90
C132 AP53 250fr blk & multi 4.50 2.25

For surcharges see Nos. C148-C149.

Villagers Observing Solar Eclipse — AP54

40fr, Rocket take-off & Concord, vert. 140fr, Scientists with telescopes observing eclipse.

1973, June 20 Engr. *Perf. 13*

C133	AP54	35fr grn & pur	.50 .25
C134	AP54	40fr ultra, pur & scar	.55 .30
C135	AP54	140fr scar & pur	2.00 .80
a.		Souvenir sheet of 3	3.75 3.75
		Nos. C133-C135 (3)	3.05 1.35

Solar eclipse, June 30, 1973. No. C135a contains 3 stamps similar to Nos. C133-C135 in changed colors (35fr, 140fr in magenta and violet blue; 40fr in magenta, violet blue and orange).

For surcharges see Nos. C141-C142, C146.

Soccer AP55

1973, Dec. 24 Photo. *Perf. 13*

C136	AP55	7um multi	.55 .25
C137	AP55	8um multi	.55 .25
C138	AP55	20um multi	1.90 .60
		Nos. C136-C138 (3)	3.00 1.10

Souvenir Sheet

C139	AP55	30um multi	1.75 1.75

World Soccer Cup, Munich, 1974.

Nos. C115-C117, C130 and C133-C135 Surcharged with New Value and Two Bars in Red, Black or Ultramarine

1973-74 Photo., Litho. or Engr.

C140	AP49	7um on 35fr (R) ('74)	.50 .25
C141	AP54	7um on 35fr (B)	.60 .25
C142	AP54	8um on 40fr (B)	.60 .25
C143	AP49	8um on 40fr (U) ('74)	.50 .25
C144	AP49	20um on 100fr (R) ('74)	1.75 .70
C145	A63	27um on 135fr (R)	2.50 .80
C146	AP54	28um on 140fr (B)	2.00 .80
		Nos. C140-C146 (7)	8.45 3.30

Winston Churchill (1874-1965) AP56

1974, June 3 Engr. *Perf. 13*

C147	AP56	40um blk, brn & hn brn	2.00 1.00

Nos. C131-C132 Surcharged with New Value and Two Bars in Red

1974, July 15 Photo. *Perf. 13x12½*

C148	AP53	20um on 100fr multi	1.50 .70
C149	AP53	50um on 250fr multi	4.00 1.80

Lenin (1870-1924) AP57

1974, Sept. 16 Engr. *Perf. 13*

C150	AP57	40um slate grn & red	3.50 1.25

Women, IWY Emblem AP58

40um, Woman's head and IWY emblems.

1975, June 16 Engr. *Perf. 13*

C151	AP58	12um multi	.60 .25
C152	AP58	40um dk brn, lt brn & bl	2.25 .90

International Women's Year.

Albert Schweitzer and Patients Arriving — AP59

1975, Aug. 4 Engr. *Perf. 13*

C153	AP59	60um multi	3.25 1.60

Schweitzer (1875-1965), medical missionary.

Javelin and Olympic Emblem — AP60

52um, Running and Olympic emblem.

1975, Nov. 17 Engr. *Perf. 13*

C154	AP60	50um sl grn, red & ol	2.50 1.40
C155	AP60	52um car, ocher & ultra	2.50 1.40

Pre-Olympic Year 1975.

Apollo Soyuz Type, 1975

Docked Space Ships and: 20um, Apollo rocket launch. 50um, Handshake in linked-up cabin. 60um, Apollo splash-down. 100um, Astronauts and Cosmonauts.

1975, Dec. 29 Litho. *Perf. 14*

C156	A74	20um multi	.90 .40
C157	A74	50um multi	2.10 .75
C158	A74	60um multi	2.60 1.00
		Nos. C156-C158 (3)	6.00 2.15

Souvenir Sheet

C159	A74	100um multi	4.00 1.75

American Bicentennial Type, 1976

Uniforms: 20um, French Hussar officer. 50um, 3rd Continental Artillery officer. 60um, French infantry regiment grenadier. 100um, American infantryman.

1976, Jan. 26

C160	A75	20um multi	.75 .35
C161	A75	50um multi	2.00 .90
C162	A75	60um multi	2.75 1.00
		Nos. C160-C162 (3)	5.50 1.75

Souvenir Sheet

C163	A75	100um multi	4.50 1.60

Running and Olympic Rings AP61

12um, High jump. 52um, Fencing.

1976, June 14 Engr. *Perf. 13*

C164	AP61	10um pur, grn & brn	.80 .25
C165	AP61	12um pur, grn & brn	1.00 .40
C166	AP61	52um pur, grn & brn	3.50 1.50
		Nos. C164-C166 (3)	5.30 2.15

21st Olympic Games, Montreal, Canada, July 17-Aug. 1.

Zeppelin Type, 1976

Designs: 50um, "Graf Zeppelin" (LZ-127) over US Capitol. 60um, "Hindenburg" (LZ-130) over Swiss Alps. 100um, "Führersland" (LZ-129) over 1936 Olympic stadium.

1976, June 28 Litho. *Perf. 11*

C167	A77	50um multi	2.75 1.25
C168	A77	60um multi	3.75 1.40

Souvenir Sheet

C169	A77	100um multi	6.00 1.00

Marabou Storks — AP62

African Birds: 50um, Sacred ibis, vert. 200um, Long-crested eagles, vert.

1976, Sept. 20 Litho. *Perf. 13½*

C170	AP62	50um multi	3.50 1.10
C171	AP62	100um multi	6.50 1.90
C172	AP62	200um multi	13.00 4.00
		Nos. C170-C172 (3)	23.00 7.00

Viking Type, 1977

Designs: 20um, Viking orbiter in flight to Mars. 50um, Viking "B" in descent to Mars. 60um, Various phases of descent. 100um, Viking lander using probe.

1977, Feb. 28 *Perf. 14*

C173	A81	20um multi	1.00 .25
C174	A81	50um multi	2.50 .60
C175	A81	60um multi	2.75 .80
		Nos. C173-C175 (3)	6.50 1.40

Souvenir Sheet

C176	A81	100um multi	5.00 1.00

For surcharge & overprints see #C192-C195.

Nobel Prize Type, 1977

14um, George Bernard Shaw, literature. 55um, Thomas Mann, literature. 60um, Intl. Red Cross Society, peace. 100um, George C. Marshall, peace.

1977, Apr. 29 Litho. *Perf. 14*

C177	A83	14um multi	.80 .25
C178	A83	55um multi	2.75 .60
C179	A83	60um multi	3.50 .75
		Nos. C177-C179 (3)	8.50 1.40

Souvenir Sheet

C180	A83	100um multi	7.00 2.00

Holy Kaaba — AP63

1977, July 25 Litho. *Perf. 12½*

C181	AP63	12um multi	1.75 .50

Pilgrimage to Mecca.

Soccer Type of 1977

50um, Soccer ball. 60um, Eusebio Ferreira. 100um, Players holding pennants.

1977, Dec. 19 Litho. *Perf. 13½*

C182	A89	50um multi	2.50 .55
C183	A89	60um multi	2.75 .75

Souvenir Sheet

C184	A89	100um multi	4.50 1.40

For overprints see Nos. C187-C189.

Franco-African Co-operation — AP63a

1978, June 7 Embossed *Perf. 10½*

C184A	AP63a	250um silver	10.00 10.00
C184B	AP63a	500um gold	25.00 25.00

Philexafrique II — Essen Issue

Common Design Types

No. C185, Hyena and Mauritania #C60. No. C186, Wading bird and Hamburg #1.

1978, Nov. 1 Litho. *Perf. 12½*

C185	CD138	20um multi	1.75 1.10
C186	CD139	20um multi	1.75 1.10
a.		Pair #C185-C186 + label	4.50 4.00

Nos. C182-C184 Overprinted in Arabic and French in Silver: "ARGENTINE- / PAYS BAS 3-1"

1978, Dec. 11 Litho. *Perf. 13½*

C187	A89	50um multi	2.10 1.25
C188	A89	60um multi	3.00 1.60

Souvenir Sheet

C189	A89	100um multi	5.00 5.00

Argentina's victory in World Cup Soccer Championship 1978.

Flyer A and Prototype Plane — AP64

Design: 40um, Flyer A and supersonic jet.

1979, Jan. 29 Engr. *Perf. 13*

C190	AP64	15um multi	1.10 .35
C191	AP64	40um multi	2.50 1.00

75th anniversary of first powered flight.

Nos. C173-C176 Overprinted and Surcharged in Silver: "ALUNISSAGE / APOLLO XI / JUILLET 1969" and Emblem

1979, Oct. 24 Litho. *Perf. 14*

C192 A81 14um on 20um multi .75 .30
C193 A81 50um multi 2.50 1.05
C194 A81 60um multi 2.75 1.40
Nos. C192-C194 (3) 6.00 2.45

Souvenir Sheet

C195 A81 100um multi 5.00 5.00

Apollo 11 moon landing, 10th anniversary.

Soccer Players — AP65

Designs: Various soccer scenes.

1980, Sept. 29 Litho. *Perf. 12½*

C196 AP65 10um multi .40 .25
C197 AP65 12um multi .50 .25
C198 AP65 14um multi .50 .25
C199 AP65 20um multi .90 .30
C200 AP65 67um multi 2.50 .70
Nos. C196-C200 (5) 4.80 1.75

Souvenir Sheet

C201 AP65 100um multi 4.50 1.25

World Soccer Cup 1982.
For overprints see Nos. C212-C217.

Flight of Columbia Space Shuttle — AP66

Designs: Views of Columbia space shuttle.

1981, Apr. 27 Litho. *Perf. 12½*

C202 AP66 12um multi .60 .25
C203 AP66 20um multi 1.00 .25
C204 AP66 50um multi 2.25 .60
C205 AP66 70um multi 3.25 .80
Nos. C202-C205 (4) 7.10 1.90

Souvenir Sheet

C206 AP66 100um multi 5.00 1.40

Dinard Landscape, by Pablo Picasso — AP67

Picasso Birth Centenary: 12um, Harlequin, vert. 20um, Vase of Flowers, vert. 50um, Three Women at the Well. 100um, Picnic.

1981, June 29 Litho. *Perf. 12½*

C207 AP67 12um multi .70 .25
C208 AP67 20um multi 1.10 .30
C209 AP67 50um multi 2.50 .70
C210 AP67 70um multi 3.50 .95
C211 AP67 100um multi 5.00 1.40
Nos. C207-C211 (5) 12.80 3.60

Nos. C196-C201 Overprinted in Red with Finalists and Score on 1 or 2 Lines

1982, Sept. 18 Litho. *Perf. 12½*

C212 AP65 10um multi .40 .25
C213 AP65 12um multi .50 .25
C214 AP65 14um multi .50 .30
C215 AP65 20um multi .90 .30
C216 AP65 67um multi 2.50 .75
Nos. C212-C216 (5) 4.80 1.85

Souvenir Sheet

C217 AP65 100um multi 4.50 1.25

Italy's victory in 1982 World Cup.

25th Anniv. of Intl. Maritime Org. — AP68

1983, June 18 Litho. *Perf. 12½x13*

C218 AP68 18um multi .85 .40

Paul Harris, Rotary Founder AP69

1984, Jan. 20 Litho. *Perf. 13½*

C219 AP69 100um multi 4.75 1.10

1984 Summer Olympics — AP70

14um, Running, horiz. 18um, Shot put. 19um, Hurdles. 44um, Javelin. 77um, High jump.
100um, Steeplechase.

1984, July 15 Litho. *Perf. 14*

C223 AP70 14um multi .60 .30
C224 AP70 18um multi .75 .40
C225 AP70 19um multi .85 .40
C226 AP70 44um multi 1.75 1.00
C227 AP70 77um multi 3.75 1.90
Nos. C223-C227 (5) 7.70 4.00

Souvenir Sheet

C228 AP70 100um multi 6.00 2.50

Olympics Winners — AP71

14um, Van den Berg, sailboard, Netherlands. 18um, Coutts, Finn sailing, N.Z. 19um, 470 class, Spain. 44um, Soling, US.
100um, Sailing, US.

1984, Dec. 20 Litho. *Perf. 13*

C229 AP71 14um multi .85 .30
C230 AP71 18um multi 1.00 .45
C231 AP71 19um multi 1.10 .50
C232 AP71 44um multi 2.50 1.10
Nos. C229-C232 (4) 5.45 2.35

Souvenir Sheet

C233 AP71 100um multi 5.75 3.50

PHILEXAFRICA '85, Lome, Togo — AP72

No. C234, Youths, map, IYY emblem. No. C235, Oil refinery, Nouadhibou.

1985, May 23 Litho. *Perf. 13*

C234 AP72 40um multi .60 .45
C235 AP72 40um multi 1.75 1.20
a. Pair, #C234-C235 + label 3.25 3.25

Exists with two labels showing map of Africa or Lome '85 emblem.

1985, Nov. 12 *Perf. 13x12½*

C236 AP72 50um Iron mine, train 2.50 1.00
C237 AP72 50um Boy reading, herding sheep 2.50 1.00
a. Pair, #C236-C237 + label 6.00 6.00

Audubon Birth Bicentenary AP73

14um, Passeriformes thraupidae. 18um, Larus philadelphia. 19um, Cyanocitta cristata. 44um, Rhyncops nigra.
100um, Anhinga anhinga.

1985, Aug. 14

C238 AP73 14um multi .80 .30
C239 AP73 18um multi 1.00 .30
C240 AP73 19um multi 1.25 .40
C241 AP73 44um multi 2.75 .80
Nos. C238-C241 (4) 5.80 1.80

Souvenir Sheet

C242 AP73 100um multi 8.00 5.00

1st South Atlantic Crossing, 55th Anniv. — AP74

18um, Comte de Vaux, 1930. 50um, Flight reenactment, 1985.

1986, May 19 Litho. *Perf. 13*

C243 AP74 18um multi .65 .35
C244 AP74 50um multi 1.75 1.00
a. Pair, #C243-C244 + label 3.25 3.25

1986 World Cup Soccer Championships, Mexico — AP75

Various soccer plays.

1986, June 19 Litho. *Perf. 13*

C245 AP75 8um No. 279 .30 .25
C246 AP75 18um No. 280 .75 .35
C247 AP75 22um No. 281 .95 .40
C248 AP75 25um No. 282 1.10 .45
C249 AP75 40um Soccer cup 1.75 .80
Nos. C245-C249 (5) 4.85 2.25

Souvenir Sheet

C250 AP75 100um multi 4.75 3.00

Air Africa, 25th Anniv. — AP76

1986, Oct. 6 Litho. *Perf. 13*

C251 AP76 26um multi .90 .45

1988 Summer Olympics, Seoul — AP77

1987, Aug. 13 Litho. *Perf. 13*

C252 AP77 30um Boxing 1.25 .50
C253 AP77 40um Judo 1.60 .65
C254 AP77 50um Fencing 1.90 .85
C255 AP77 75um Wrestling 3.25 1.25
Nos. C252-C255 (4) 8.00 3.25

Souvenir Sheet

C256 AP77 150um Judo, diff. 6.00 2.75

1988 Winter Olympics, Calgary — AP78

30um, Women's slalom. 40um, Speed skating. 50um, Ice hockey. 75um, Women's downhill skiing.
150um, Men's cross-country skiing.

1987, Sept.

C257 AP78 30um multi 1.25 .50
C258 AP78 40um multi 1.60 .65
C259 AP78 50um multi 1.90 .85
C260 AP78 75um multi 3.25 1.25
Nos. C257-C260 (4) 8.00 3.25

Souvenir Sheet

C261 AP78 150um multi 6.00 2.75

For overprints see Nos. C267-C271.

1988 Summer Olympics, Seoul AP79

1988, Sept. 17 Litho. *Perf. 13*

C262 AP79 20um Hammer throw .85 .35
C263 AP79 24um Discus .90 .40
C264 AP79 30um Shot put 1.25 .50
C265 AP79 150um Javelin 5.75 2.25
Nos. C262-C265 (4) 8.75 3.50

Souvenir Sheet

C266 AP79 170um Javelin, diff. 6.50 2.75

Nos. C257-C261 Overprinted "Medaille d'or" in Red or Bright Blue and:

a. "Vreni Schneider (Suisse)"
b. "1500 m / Andre Hoffman (R.D.A.)"
c. "U.R.S.S."
d. "Marina Kiehl (R.F.A.)"
e. "15 km / Mikhail Deviatiarov (U.R.S.S.)"

1988, Sept. 18

C267	AP78(a)	30um multi	1.25	.50
C268	AP78(b)	40um multi (BB)	1.75	.65
C269	AP78(c)	50um multi	2.00	.90
C270	AP78(d)	75um multi	3.50	1.40
		Nos. C267-C270 (4)	8.50	3.45

Souvenir Sheet

C271	AP78(e)	150um multi	6.50	3.50

World Cup Soccer Championships, Italy — AP80

Map of Italy and various soccer plays.

1990 Litho. *Perf. 13*

C272	AP80	50um multicolored	2.00	.65
C273	AP80	60um multicolored	2.00	.85
C274	AP80	70um multicolored	2.50	.95
C275	AP80	90um multicolored	3.50	1.25
C276	AP80	150um multicolored	7.50	2.75
		Nos. C272-C276 (5)	17.50	6.45

AIR POST SEMI-POSTAL STAMPS

Maternity Hospital, Dakar — SPAP1

Dispensary, Mopti — SPAP2

Nurse Weighing Baby — SPAP3

Unwmk.

1942, June 22 Engr. *Perf. 13*

CB1	SPAP1	1.50fr + 3.50fr green	.80	5.50
CB2	SPAP2	2fr + 6fr brown	.80	5.50
CB3	SPAP3	3fr + 9fr carmine	.80	5.50
		Nos. CB1-CB3 (3)	2.40	16.50

Native children's welfare fund.

Colonial Education Fund

Common Design Type

1942, June 22

CB4	CD86a	1.20fr + 1.80fr bl & red	.80	5.50

POSTAGE DUE STAMPS

D1

Perf. 14x13½

1906-07 Unwmk. Typo.

J1	D1	5c grn, *grnsh*	3.50	3.50
J2	D1	10c red brn	5.00	5.00
J3	D1	15c dk bl	10.00	7.00
J4	D1	20c blk, *yellow*	12.00	10.00
J5	D1	30c red, *straw*	14.00	11.00
J6	D1	50c violet	20.00	19.00
J7	D1	60c blk, *buff*	16.00	14.00
J8	D1	1fr blk, *pinkish*	26.00	20.00
		Nos. J1-J8 (8)	106.50	89.50

Issue dates: 20c, 1906; others 1907.

Regular postage stamps canceled "T" in a triangle were used for postage due.

D2

1914

J9	D2	5c green	.25	*.35*
J10	D2	10c rose	.30	*.50*
J11	D2	15c gray	.35	*.70*
J12	D2	20c brown	.35	*.70*
J13	D2	30c blue	.70	*1.00*
J14	D2	50c black	1.75	*1.75*
J15	D2	60c orange	1.40	*1.40*
J16	D2	1fr violet	1.40	*1.40*
		Nos. J9-J16 (8)	6.50	*7.80*

Type of 1914 Issue Surcharged

1927, Oct. 10

J17	D2	2fr on 1fr lil rose	3.50	3.50
a.		Period after "F" omitted	14.00	*15.00*
J18	D2	3fr on 1fr org brn	3.50	*4.25*

Catalogue values for unused stamps in this section, from this point to the end of the section, are for Never Hinged items.

Islamic Republic

Oualata Motif — D3

Perf. 14x13½

1961, July 1 Typo. Unwmk.

Denominations in Black

J19	D3	1fr plum & org yel	.25	.25
J20	D3	2fr red & gray	.25	.25
J21	D3	5fr mar & pink	.25	.25
J22	D3	10fr dk grn & grn	.30	.25
J23	D3	15fr ol & brn org	.30	.25
J24	D3	20fr red brn & lt blue	.50	.25
J25	D3	25fr grn & vermilion	.75	.50
		Nos. J19-J25 (7)	2.60	2.00

Vulture (Ruppell's Griffon) — D4

Birds: No. J27, Eurasian crane. No. J28, Pink-backed pelican. No. J29, Garganey teal. No. J30, European golden oriole. No. J31, Variable sunbird. No. J32, Shoveler ducks. No. J33, Great snipe. No. J34, Vulturine guinea fowl. No. J35, Black stork. No. J36, Gray heron. No. J37, White stork. No. J38, Red-legged partridge. No. J39, Paradise whydah. No. J40, Sandpiper (little stint). No. J41, Sudan bustard.

1963, Sept. 7 Engr. *Perf. 11*

J26	D4	50c blk, yel org & red	.25	.25
J27	D4	50c blk, yel org & red	.25	.25
a.		Pair, #J26-J27	.50	.50
J28	D4	1fr blk, red & yel	.25	.25
J29	D4	1fr blk, red & yel	.25	.25
a.		Pair, #J28-J29	.60	.60
J30	D4	2fr blk, bl grn & yel	.25	.25
J31	D4	2fr blk, bl grn & yel	.25	.25
a.		Pair, #J30-J31	.80	.80
J32	D4	5fr blk, grn & red brn	.35	.35
J33	D4	5fr blk, grn & red brn	.35	.35
a.		Pair, #J32-J33	1.25	1.25
J34	D4	10fr blk, red & tan	.70	.70
J35	D4	10fr blk, red & tan	.70	.70
a.		Pair, #J34-J35	2.50	2.50
J36	D4	15fr blk, emer & red	.75	.75
J37	D4	15fr blk, emer & red	.75	.75
a.		Pair, #J36-J37	2.75	2.75
J38	D4	20fr blk, yel grn & red	1.00	1.00
J39	D4	20fr blk, yel grn & red	1.00	1.00
a.		Pair, #J38-J39	3.25	3.25
J40	D4	25fr blk, yel grn & brn	1.50	1.50
J41	D4	25fr blk, yel grn & brn	1.50	1.50
a.		Pair, #J40-J41	4.50	4.50
		Nos. J26-J41 (16)	10.10	10.10
		Nos. J27a-J41a (8)	16.15	16.15

Ornament D5

1976, May 10 Litho. *Perf. 12½x13*

J42	D5	1um buff & multi	.25	.25
J43	D5	3um buff & multi	.25	.25
J44	D5	10um buff & multi	.45	.45
J45	D5	12um buff & multi	.55	.55
J46	D5	20um buff & multi	.95	.95
		Nos. J42-J46 (5)	2.45	2.45

OFFICIAL STAMPS

Catalogue values for unused stamps in this section are for Never Hinged items.

Islamic Republic

Cross of Trarza — O1

Perf. 14x13½

1961, July 1 Typo. Unwmk.

O1	O1	1fr vio & lilac	.25	.25
O2	O1	3fr red & slate	.25	.25
O3	O1	5fr grn & brown	.25	.25
O4	O1	10fr grn & vio bl	.25	.25
O5	O1	15fr blue & org	.35	.25
O6	O1	20fr sl grn & emer	.45	.25
O7	O1	25fr red org & mar	.50	.30
O8	O1	30fr maroon & grn	.60	.40
O9	O1	50fr dk red & dk brn	1.25	.50
O10	O1	100fr orange & blue	1.90	.90
O11	O1	200fr grn & red org	3.75	1.75
		Nos. O1-O11 (11)	9.80	5.35

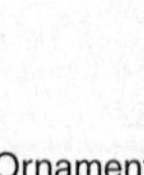

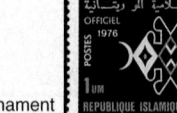

Ornament O2

1976, May 3 Litho. *Perf. 12½x13*

O12	O2	1um black & multi	.25	.25
O13	O2	2um black & multi	.25	.25
O14	O2	5um black & multi	.25	.25
O15	O2	10um black & multi	.50	.25
O16	O2	12um black & multi	.70	.30
O17	O2	40um black & multi	2.50	.90
O18	O2	50um black & multi	3.00	1.25
		Nos. O12-O18 (7)	7.45	3.45

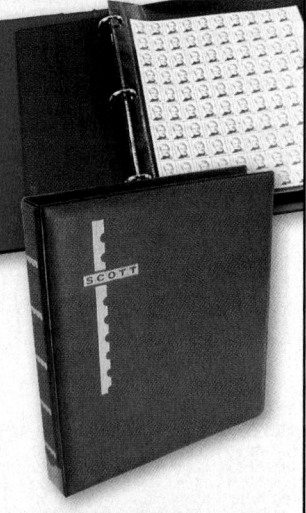

MAURITIUS

mo-ˈri-sh͵ē-͵əs

LOCATION — Island in the Indian Ocean about 550 miles east of Madagascar
GOVT. — Republic
AREA — 720 sq. mi.
POP. — 1,182,212 (1999 est.)
CAPITAL — Port Louis

12 Pence = 1 Shilling
100 Cents = 1 Rupee (1878)

The British Crown Colony of Mauritius was granted self-government in 1967 and became an independent state on March 12, 1968.

Nos. 1-6, 14-17 unused are valued without gum.

Nos. 3a-8, 14-15 are printed on fragile paper with natural irregularities which might be mistaken for faults.

Very fine examples of Nos. 22-58 will have perforations touching the design on one or more sides. Examples with perfs clear on four sides are scarce and will sell for more. Inferior examples will sell for much reduced prices.

Catalogue values for unused stamps in this country are for Never Hinged items, beginning with Scott 223 in the regular postage section, Scott J1 in the postage due section.

Queen Victoria — A1

1847 Unwmk. Engr. *Imperf.*

1 A1 1p orange *1,250,000.* 1,250,000.
2 A1 2p dark blue 1,700,000.

Nos. 1 and 2 were engraved and printed in Port Louis. There is but one type of each value. The initials "J. B." on the bust are those of the engraver, J. Barnard.

All unused examples of the 2p are in museums. There is one unused example of the 1p in private hands. There are two used examples of the 1p in private hands, both of which have small faults and are valued thus.

Queen Victoria — A2

Earliest Impressions

1848 Thick Yellowish Paper

3 A2 1p orange *65,000.* *18,000.*
4 A2 2p dark blue *62,500.* *24,500.*
d. "PENOE" *125,000.* *42,500.*

Early Impressions

Yellowish White Paper

3a A2 1p orange *32,500.* *7,250.*
4a A2 2p blue *35,000.* *8,500.*
e. "PENOE" *65,000.* *16,000.*

Bluish Paper

5 A2 1p orange *32,500.* *7,250.*
6 A2 2p blue *35,000.* *8,500.*
c. "PENOE" *65,000.* *16,000.*

Intermediate Impressions

Yellowish White Paper

3b A2 1p red orange *21,500.* 2,850.
4b A2 2p blue *22,500.* 3,600.
f. "PENOE" *40,000.* *7,500.*

Bluish Paper

5a A2 1p red orange *21,500.* 2,900.
6a A2 2p blue *22,500.* 3,750.
d. "PENOE" *40,000.* *7,500.*
f. Double impression —

Worn Impressions

Yellowish White Paper

3c A2 1p orange red 7,500. 900.
d. 1p brownish red 7,500. 900.
4c A2 2p blue 9,250. 1,600.
g. "PENOE" *12,500.* 3,000.

Bluish Paper

5b A2 1p orange red 7,000. 850.
c. 1p brownish red 7,000. 850.
d. Double impression
6b A2 2p blue 9,500. 1,500.
e. "PENOE" *12,500.* 3,000.

Latest Impressions

Yellowish or Grayish Paper

3e A2 1p orange red 6,000. 750.
f. 1p brownish red 6,000. 750.
4h A2 2p blue 7,500. 1,100.
i. "PENOE" *14,000.* 2,100.

Bluish Paper

5e A2 1p orange red 6,000. 750.
f. 1p brownish red 6,000. 750.
6g A2 2p blue 7,500. 1,100.
h. "PENOE" 14,000. 2,000.

These stamps were printed in sheets of twelve, four rows of three, and each position differs in details. The "PENOE" error is the most pronounced variety on the plates and is from position 7.

The stamps were in use until 1859. Earliest impressions, Nos. 3-4, show the full background of diagonal and vertical lines with the diagonal lines predominant. Early impressions, Nos. 3a-4a, 5-6, show the full background with the vertical lines predominating. As the plate became worn the vertical lines disappeared, giving the intermediate impressions, Nos. 3b-4b, 5a-6a.

Worn impressions, Nos. 3c-4c, 5b-6b, have little background remaining, and latest impressions, Nos. 3e-4h, 5e-6g, have also lost details of the frame and head. The paper of the early impressions is usually rather thick, that of the worn impressions rather thin. Expect natural fibrous inclusions in the paper of all impressions.

"Britannia" — A3

1849-58

7 A3 red brown, *blue* 26.00
8 A3 blue ('58) 10.00

Nos. 7-8 were never placed in use.

1858-59

9 A3 (4p) green, *bluish* 550.00 225.00
10 A3 (6p) red 60.00 *125.00*
11 A3 (9p) magenta ('59) 850.00 225.00

No. 11 was re-issued in Nov. 1862, as a 1p stamp (No. 11a). When used as such it is always canceled "B53." Price so used, $200.

"Britannia" — A4

1858 Black Surcharge

12 A4 4p green, *bluish* 1,650. 525.00

Queen Victoria — A5

1859, Mar. Early Impressions

14 A5 2p blue, *grayish* 16,500. 3,000.
a. 2p deep blue, *grayish* 18,500. 3,500.
14B A5 2p blue, *bluish* 16,500. 3,000.
c. Intermediate impression 9,000. 1,300.
d. Worn impression 4,500. 850.00

Type A5 was engraved by Lapirot, in Port Louis, and was printed locally. There were twelve varieties in the sheet.

Early impressions have clear and distinct background lines. In the intermediate impressions, the lines are somewhat blurred, and white patches appear. In the worn impressions, the background lines are discontinuous, with many white patches. Analogous wear is also obvious in the background of the inscriptions on all four sides. Values depend on the state of wear. One should expect natural fibrous inclusions in the paper on all printings.

A6

1859, Oct.

15 A6 2p blue, *bluish* *210,000.* 11,000.

No. 15 was printed from the plate of the 1848 issue after it had been entirely re-engraved by Sherwin. It is commonly known as the "fillet head." The plate of the 1p, 1848, was also re-engraved but was never put in use.

A7

1859, Dec. Litho. Laid Paper

16 A7 1p vermilion *9,000.* 1,350.
a. 1p deep red *15,000.* 2,350.
b. 1p red *11,250.* 1,675.
17 A7 2p pale blue *5,000.* 850.
a. 2p slate blue *9,250.* 1,250.
b. 2p blue 5,000. 950.

Lithographed locally by Dardenne.

"Britannia" — A8

1859 Wove Paper Engr. *Imperf.*

18 A8 6p blue 800.00 57.50
19 A8 1sh vermilion 3,150. 65.00

1861

20 A8 6p gray violet 37.50 *110.00*
21 A8 1sh green 675.00 160.00

1862 *Perf. 14 to 16*

22 A8 6p slate 37.50 *110.00*
a. Horiz. pair, imperf between *8,500.*
23 A8 1sh deep green 2,750. 350.00

Values for Nos. 22-23 are for examples with perfs. touching the design.

Following the change in currency in 1878, a number of issues denominated in sterling were overprinted "CANCELLED" in serifed type and sold as remainders.

A9

1860-63 Typo. *Perf. 14*

24 A9 1p brown lilac 400.00 42.50
25 A9 2p blue 425.00 60.00
26 A9 4p rose 425.00 42.50
27 A9 6p green ('62) 1,050. 175.00
28 A9 6p lilac ('63) 425.00 125.00
29 A9 9p dull lilac 190.00 42.50
30 A9 1sh buff ('62) 400.00 100.00
31 A9 1sh green ('63) 900.00 200.00

For surcharges see Nos. 43-45.

1863-72 Wmk. 1

32 A9 1p lilac brown 85.00 17.00
a. 1p bister brown 150.00 17.00
b. 1p brown 110.00 13.00
33 A9 2p blue 100.00 13.00
a. Imperf., pair 1,850. 2,350.
34 A9 3p vermilion 90.00 21.00
35 A9 4p rose 100.00 4.00
36 A9 6p lilac ('64) 425.00 45.00
37 A9 6p blue grn ('65) 235.00 7.00
a. 6p yellow green ('65) 300.00 17.00
38 A9 9p green ('72) 190.00 *375.00*
39 A9 1sh org yel ('64) 365.00 29.00
a. 1sh yellow 285.00 13.50
40 A9 1sh blue ('70) 140.00 29.00
41 A9 5sh red violet 260.00 60.00
a. 5sh bright violet 325.00 60.00
Nos. 32-41 (10) 1,990. 600.00

For surcharges see Nos. 48-49, 51-58, 87.

A10

1872

42 A10 10p claret 375.00 57.50

For surcharges see Nos. 46-47.

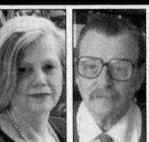

No. 29 Surcharged in Black or Red

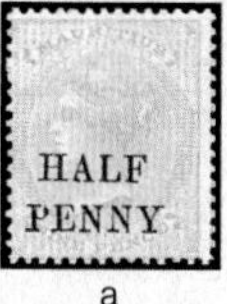

a

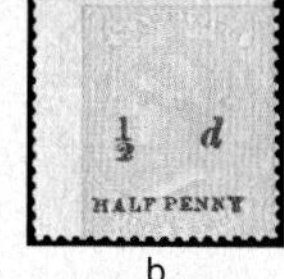

b

1876 **Unwmk.**

43 A9(a) ½p on 9p 24.00 24.00
a. Inverted surcharge *800.00*
b. Double surcharge *2,350.*
44 A9(b) ½p on 9p *5,000.*
45 A9(b) ½p on 9p (R) *3,400.*

Nos. 44 and 45 were never placed in use. No. 45 is valued with perfs cutting into the design.

Stamps of 1863-72 Surcharged in Black

c

d

1876-77 **Wmk. 1**

46 A10(a) ½p on 10p claret 4.75 *29.00*
47 A10(c) ½p on 10p cl ('77) 12.00 *50.00*
48 A9(d) 1p on 4p rose ('77) 25.00 27.50
49 A9(d) 1sh on 5sh red vio ('77) 350.00 125.00
a. 1sh on 5sh violet ('77) 340.00 160.00
Nos. 46-49 (4) 391.75 *231.50*

A16

1878 **Black Surcharge**

50 A16 2c claret 17.50 12.50

Stamps and Type of 1863-72 Surcharged in Black — e

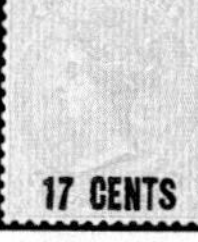

51 A9 4c on 1p bister brn 27.50 10.00
52 A9 8c on 2p blue 90.00 4.25
53 A9 13c on 3p org red 26.00 52.50
54 A9 17c on 4p rose 200.00 4.50
55 A9 25c on 6p sl blue 275.00 8.00
56 A9 38c on 9p violet 50.00 *100.00*
57 A9 50c on 1sh green 100.00 5.75
58 A9 2r50c on 5sh violet 22.50 *26.00*
Nos. 50-58 (9) 808.50 *223.50*

For surcharge see No. 87.

A18

A19

A20

A21

A22 A23

A24

A25

A26

1879-80 **Wmk. 1**

59 A18 2c red brn ('80) 55.00 27.50
60 A19 4c orange 72.50 4.25
61 A20 8c blue ('80) 40.00 4.50
62 A21 13c slate ('80) 180.00 325.00
63 A22 17c rose ('80) 95.00 10.00
64 A23 25c bister 475.00 18.00
65 A24 38c violet ('80) 200.00 375.00
66 A25 50c green ('80) 6.50 5.50
67 A26 2r50c brn vio ('80) 57.50 *85.00*
Nos. 59-67 (9) 1,182. 854.75

Nos. 59-67 are known imperforate.
For surcharges & overprints see Nos. 76-78, 83-86, 122-123.

1882-93 **Wmk. 2**

68 A18 1c violet ('93) 2.50 .55
69 A18 2c red brown 40.00 7.00
70 A18 2c green ('85) 4.75 .75
71 A19 4c orange 95.00 7.00
72 A19 4c rose ('85) 5.50 1.25
73 A20 8c blue ('91) 5.00 1.80
74 A23 25c bister ('83) 14.00 4.00
75 A25 50c dp orange ('87) 45.00 20.00
Nos. 68-75 (8) 211.75 42.35

For surcharges and overprint see Nos. 88-89, 121.

Nos. 63 and Type of 1882 Surcharged in Black

f

g

1883 **Wmk. 1**

Surcharge Measures 14x3½mm

76 A22(f) 16c on 17c rose 180.00 60.00
a. Double surcharge 2,900.

Surcharge Measures 15½x3½mm

77 A22(f) 16c on 17c rose 190.00 60.00
a. Double surcharge 3,150.

Surcharge Measures 15½x2¾mm

78 A22(f) 16c on 17c rose *375.00* *140.00*

Wmk. 2

79 A22(g) 16c on 17c rose 115.00 2.40
Nos. 76-79 (4) *860.00* *262.40*

Queen Victoria — A29

1885-94

80 A29 15c orange brown ('92) 9.00 1.50
81 A29 15c blue ('94) 10.00 1.50
82 A29 16c orange brown 9.50 2.75
Nos. 80-82 (3) 28.50 5.75

For surcharges see Nos. 90, 116.

Various Stamps Surcharged in Black or Red

h

j

1885-87 **Wmk. 1**

83 A24(h) 2c on 38c violet 170.00 47.50
a. Inverted surcharge 1,250. 1,000.
b. Double surcharge 1,350.
c. Without bar 275.00
84 A21(j) 2c on 13c sl (R) ('87) 80.00 *130.00*
a. Inverted surcharge 260.00 *300.00*
b. Double surcharge *975.00* 850.00
c. As "b," one on back *1,000.*
d. Double surcharge, both inverted *1,750.*

k

l

1891

85 A22(k) 2c on 17c rose 145.00 *155.00*
a. Inverted surcharge 575.00 575.00
b. Double surcharge 950.00 950.00
86 A24(k) 2c on 38c vio 11.50 16.00
a. Double surcharge 240.00 *260.00*
b. Dbl. surch., one invtd. 260.00 *300.00*
c. Inverted surcharge 1,250. —
87 A9(e+l) 2c on 38c on 9p vio 15.00 6.75
a. Double surcharge 850.00 850.00
b. Inverted surcharge 625.00 —
c. Dbl. surch., one invtd. 200.00 *225.00*

Wmk. 2

88 A19(k) 2c on 4c rose 2.50 1.00
a. Double surcharge 95.00 90.00
b. Inverted surcharge 90.00 —
c. Dbl. surch., one invtd. 95.00 90.00
Nos. 85-88 (4) 174.00 178.75

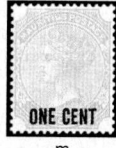

m

n

1893, Jan.

89 A18(m) 1c on 2c violet 2.75 1.75
90 A29(n) 1c on 16c org brown 3.25 *4.50*

Coat of Arms — A38

1895-1904 **Wmk. 2**

91 A38 1c lilac & ultra .90 1.80
92 A38 1c gray blk & blk .60 .25
93 A38 2c lilac & orange 7.50 .60
94 A38 2c dull lil & vio 1.00 .25
95 A38 3c lilac .85 .60
96 A38 3c grn & scar, *yel* 4.50 1.50
97 A38 4c lilac & green 6.00 .60
98 A38 4c dull lil & car, *yel* 3.00 .50
99 A38 4c gray grn & pur 3.00 *2.40*
100 A38 4c blk & car, *blue* 18.00 .75
101 A38 5c lilac & vio, *buff* 12.00 *100.00*
102 A38 5c lilac & blk, *buff* 3.00 3.00
103 A38 6c grn & rose 5.75 5.00
104 A38 6c vio & scar, *red* 4.75 1.00
105 A38 8c gray grn & blk, *buff* 4.50 *15.00*
106 A38 12c black & car rose 3.00 *3.00*
107 A38 15c grn & org 30.00 *10.00*
108 A38 15c blk & ultra, *blue* 65.00 1.50
109 A38 18c gray grn & ultra 22.50 4.25
110 A38 25c grn & car, *grn*, chalky paper 6.00 *27.50*
111 A38 50c green, *yel* 20.00 *80.00*
Nos. 91-111 (21) 221.85 *259.50*

The 25c is on both ordinary and chalky paper. Ornaments in lower panel omitted on Nos. 106-111.

Year of issue: Nos. 103, 107, 1899; Nos. 92, 94, 98, 1900; Nos. 96, 99, 101-102, 104-106, 110-111, 1902; Nos. 100, 108, 1904; others, 1895.

See Nos. 128-135. For surcharges and overprints see Nos. 113, 114, 117-120.

Diamond Jubilee Issue

Arms A39

1898, May 23 **Wmk. 46**

112 A39 36c brown org & ultra 13.50 *27.50*

60th year of Queen Victoria's reign.
For surcharges see Nos. 114 and 127.

No. 109 Surcharged in Red

1899 **Wmk. 2**

113 A38 6c on 18c 1.40 1.25
a. Inverted surcharge 725.00 340.00

No. 112 Surcharged in Blue

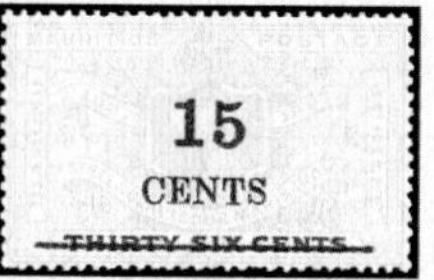

Wmk. 46

114 A39 15c on 36c 3.50 2.10
a. Without bar 500.00

Admiral Mahe de La Bourdonnais A40

1899, Dec. **Engr.** **Wmk. 1**

115 A40 15c ultra 30.00 5.00

Birth bicent. of Admiral Mahe de La Bourdonnais, governor of Mauritius, 1734-46.

No. 82 Surcharged in Black

1900 **Wmk. 2**

116 A29 4c on 16c orange brown 17.50 27.50

No. 109 Surcharged in Black — r

1902

117 A38 12c on 18c grn & ultra 3.50 *11.00*

Preceding Issues Overprinted in Black

1902

118 A38 4c lilac & car, *yel* 1.50 .30
119 A38 6c green & rose 1.50 *3.25*
120 A38 15c green & org 6.25 1.35
121 A23 25c bister 8.00 3.25

Wmk. 1

122 A25 50c green 20.00 6.25
123 A26 2r50c brown violet 135.00 *225.00*
Nos. 118-123 (6) 172.25 239.40

Coat of Arms — A41

1902 **Wmk. 1**

124 A41 1r blk & car rose 62.50 60.00

Wmk. 2 Sideways

125 A41 2r50c grn & blk, *bl* 40.00 *160.00*
126 A41 5r blk & car, *red* 110.00 *180.00*
Nos. 124-126 (3) 212.50 400.00

No. 112 Surcharged type "r" but with longer bar

1902 **Wmk. 46**

127 A39 12c on 36c 2.40 1.50
a. Inverted surcharge 775.00 525.00

Arms Type of 1895-1904

1904-07 **Wmk. 3** **Chalky Paper**

128 A38 1c gray blk & black ('07) 8.75 5.00
129 A38 2c dl lil & vio ('05) 35.00 3.00
130 A38 3c grn & scar, *yel* 22.50 13.00
131 A38 4c blk & car, *blue* 16.00 .25
132 A38 6c vio & scar, *red* ('06) 14.00 .35
133 A38 15c blk & ultra, *bl* 4.50 .40
135 A38 50c green, *yel* 3.00 *7.00*
136 A41 1r black & car rose ('07) 50.00 *65.00*
Nos. 128-136 (8) 153.75 *94.00*

The 2c, 4c, 6c also exist on ordinary paper.
Ornaments in lower panel omitted on 15c and 50c.

Arms — A42

Edward VII — A43

1910 **Wmk. 3** **Ordinary Paper**

137 A42 1c black 3.25 .30
138 A42 2c brown 3.00 .25
139 A42 3c green 3.25 .25
140 A42 4c ol grn & rose 4.00 .25
141 A43 5c gray & rose 3.00 *3.25*
142 A42 6c carmine 5.25 .25
143 A42 8c brn org 3.25 *1.60*
144 A43 12c gray 3.75 *3.00*
145 A42 15c ultramarine 21.00 .25

Chalky Paper

146 A43 25c blk & scar, *yel* 2.25 *13.00*
147 A43 50c dull vio & blk 2.60 *20.00*
148 A43 1r blk, *green* 17.75 *13.00*
149 A43 2r50c blk & car, *bl* 27.50 *75.00*
150 A43 5r grn & car, *yel* 42.50 *100.00*
151 A43 10r grn & car, *grn* 165.00 *250.00*
Nos. 137-151 (15) 307.35 *480.40*

Numerals of 12c, 25c and 10r of type A43 are in color on plain tablet.
See Nos. 161-178.

King George V — A44

For description of dies I and II see "Dies of British Colonial Stamps" in table of contents.
Numeral tablet of 5c, 50c, 1r, 2.50r and 5r of type A44 has lined background with colorless denomination.

Die I

1912-22 **Wmk. 3** **Ordinary Paper**

152 A44 5c gray & rose 3.00 *4.50*
153 A44 12c gray 8.00 1.10

Chalky Paper

154 A44 25c blk & red, *yel* .45 1.50
a. 25c gray black & red, *yellow*, Die II 1.10 *25.00*
155 A44 50c dull vio & blk 52.50 *125.00*
156 A44 1r black, *emerald*, die II 2.50 *8.00*
a. 1r black, *emer*, olive back, die I ('21) 11.50 *60.00*
b. 1r blk, *bl grn*, olive back, die I 6.75 *21.00*
157 A44 2r50c blk & red, *bl* 42.50 *75.00*
158 A44 5r grn & red, *yel* 115.00 *175.00*
a. Die II ('22) 115.00 *200.00*
159 A44 10r grn & red, *emer*, die II ('21) 47.50 *180.00*
a. 10r grn & red, *bl grn*, olive back, die I 1,150.
b. 10r green & red, *emer*, die I 85.00 *200.00*
c. 10r grn & red, *emer*, olive back, die I 145.00 *210.00*
d. 10r grn & red, *grn*, die I 105.00 *210.00*

Surface-colored Paper

160 A44 25c blk & red, *yel* ('16) 2.75 *21.00*
Nos. 152-160 (9) 274.20 *591.10*

1921-26 **Wmk. 4** **Ordinary Paper**

161 A42 1c black 1.10 1.10
162 A42 2c brown 1.10 .25
163 A42 2c violet, *yel* ('25) 3.50 2.00
164 A42 3c green ('25) 3.50 3.50
165 A42 4c ol grn & rose 1.60 *2.00*
166 A42 4c green 1.10 .25
167 A42 4c brown ('25) 4.50 2.50
168 A42 6c rose red 13.50 7.25
169 A42 6c violet 1.35 .25
170 A42 8c brown org ('25) 2.50 *24.00*
171 A42 10c gray ('22) 2.25 *3.75*
172 A42 10c rose red ('25) 12.00 6.75
173 A42 12c rose red 1.70 1.60
174 A42 12c gray ('25) 1.90 *5.00*
175 A42 15c ultramarine 6.00 5.50
176 A42 15c dull blue ('25) 1.60 .25
177 A42 20c ultra ('22) 2.25 .90
178 A42 20c dull vio ('25) 9.50 *16.00*
Nos. 161-178 (18) 70.95 *82.85*

Ornaments in lower panel omitted on Nos. 171-178.
For surcharges see Nos. 201-203.

Die II

1922-34 **Ordinary Paper**

179 A44 1c black 2.40 *3.00*
180 A44 2c brown 1.10 .25
181 A44 3c green 2.10 .45
182 A44 4c olive grn & red ('27) 3.25 .30
a. Die I ('32) 18.00 *62.50*
183 A44 4c green, die I ('33) 13.50 *.50*
184 A44 5c gray & car 1.10 .25
a. Die I ('32) 10.00 6.50
185 A44 6c olive brn ('28) 5.50 .65
186 A44 8c orange 2.10 *15.50*
187 A44 10c rose red ('26) 4.25 .25
a. Die I ('32) 15.50 *16.75*
188 A44 12c gray, small "c" ('22) 5.00 *23.00*
189 A44 12c gray, "c" larger & thinner ('34) 17.50 .25
190 A44 12c rose red .70 *3.75*
191 A44 15c dk blue ('28) 4.75 .25
192 A44 20c dull vio 4.75 .45
193 A44 20c dk blue ('34) 28.00 .45
a. Die I ('27) 11.00 2.60
194 A44 25c black & red, *yel* 1.10 .25
a. Die I ('32) 7.25 *67.50*

Chalky Paper

195 A44 50c dull vio & blk 8.00 3.75
196 A44 1r blk, *emerald* 6.75 .55
a. Die I ('32) 25.00 *62.50*
197 A44 2r50c blk & red, *bl* 22.00 19.00
198 A44 5r green & red, *yel* 47.50 *95.00*
199 A44 10r green & red, *emer* ('28) 145.00 *340.00*
Nos. 179-199 (21) 326.35 *507.85*

A45

1924

200 A45 50r lilac & green 1,000. *2,750.*

Nos. 166, 173, 177 Surcharged

1925

201 A42 3c on 4c green 8.00 *6.25*
202 A42 10c on 12c rose red .50 *1.60*
203 A42 15c on 20c ultra .65 1.75
Nos. 201-203 (3) 9.15 9.60

Common Design Types pictured following the introduction.

Silver Jubilee Issue
Common Design Type

1935, May 6 **Engr.** ***Perf. 13½x14***

204 CD301 5c gray black & ultra .60 .25
205 CD301 12c indigo & green 5.50 .25
206 CD301 20c blue & brown 6.50 .25
207 CD301 1r brt vio & indigo 35.00 *57.50*
Nos. 204-207 (4) 47.60 58.25
Set, never hinged 60.00

Coronation Issue
Common Design Type

1937, May 12 **Wmk. 4** ***Perf. 13½x14***

208 CD302 5c dark purple .30 .25
209 CD302 12c carmine .50 2.40
210 CD302 20c bright ultra 1.25 1.10
Nos. 208-210 (3) 2.05 3.75
Set, never hinged 3.25

King George VI — A46

1938-43 **Typo.** ***Perf. 14***

211 A46 2c gray ('43) .25 .25
a. Perf. 15x14 ('43) .70 .25
212 A46 3c rose vio & car ('43) 1.50 2.15
213 A46 4c green ('43) 3.25 *2.15*
214 A46 5c violet ('43) 2.10 .25
a. Perf. 15x14 ('43) 40.00 .25
215 A46 10c carmine ('43) 1.90 .25
a. Perf. 15x14 ('43) 25.00 2.50
216 A46 12c sal pink ('43) .70 .25
a. Perf. 15x14 ('43) 40.00 1.35
217 A46 20c blue ('43) .70 .25
218 A46 25c maroon ('43) 6.00 .25
219 A46 1r brn blk ('43) 14.00 2.00
220 A46 2.50r pale vio ('43) 25.00 26.00
221 A46 5r ol grn ('43) 21.00 42.50
222 A46 10r rose vio ('43) 9.75 *42.50*
Nos. 211-222 (12) 86.15 118.80
Set, never hinged 127.00

Nos. 218-222 exist on both chalky and ordinary papers. Values above are for stamps on ordinary paper. For detailed listings, see *Scott Classic Specialized Catalogue of Stamps & Covers.*

Catalogue values for unused stamps in this section, from this point to the end of the section, are for Never Hinged items.

Peace Issue
Common Design Type
Perf. 13½x14

1946, Nov. 20 **Engr.** **Wmk. 4**

223 CD303 5c lilac .25 .80
224 CD303 20c deep blue .25 .25

"Post Office" Stamp of 1847 — A47

1948, Mar. 22 ***Perf. 11½***

225 A47 5c red vio & orange .25 .55
226 A47 12c green & orange .25 .25
227 A47 20c blue & dp blue .25 .25
228 A47 1r lt red brn & dp blue .35 .35
Nos. 225-228 (4) 1.10 1.40

Cent. of the 1st Mauritius postage stamps.

Silver Wedding Issue
Common Design Types

1948, Oct. 25 **Photo.** ***Perf. 14x14½***

229 CD304 5c violet .25 .25

Perf. 11½x11
Engraved; Name Typographed

230 CD305 10r lilac rose 17.50 45.00

UPU Issue
Common Design Types
Engr.; Name Typo. on 20c, 35c
Perf. 13½, 11x11½

1949, Oct. 10 **Wmk. 4**

231 CD306 12c rose carmine .65 2.10
232 CD307 20c indigo 2.40 2.75
233 CD308 35c rose violet .65 1.60
234 CD309 1r sepia .65 .25
Nos. 231-234 (4) 4.35 6.70

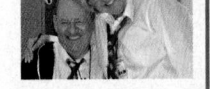

Sugar Factory — A48

Aloe Plant — A49

Designs: 2c, Grand Port. 4c, Tamarind Falls. 5c, Rempart Mountain. 10c, Transporting cane. 12c, Map and dodo. 20c, "Paul et Virginie." 25c, Statue of Mahe La Bourdonnais. 35c, Government House. 50c, Pieter Both Mountain. 1r, Sambar. 2.50r, Port Louis. 5r, Beach scene. 10r, Arms.

Perf. 13½x14½, 14½x13½

1950, July 1 **Photo.**
235 A48 1c red violet .25 .55
236 A48 2c cerise .25 .25
237 A49 3c yel green .70 *4.50*
238 A49 4c green .25 *3.25*
239 A48 5c greenish blue .25 .25
240 A48 10c red .30 *.80*
241 A48 12c olive green 1.60 *3.25*
242 A49 20c brt ultra 1.10 .25
243 A49 25c vio brown 2.15 .45
244 A48 35c rose violet .45 .25
245 A49 50c emerald 3.00 .55
246 A48 1r sepia 10.00 .25
247 A48 2.50r orange 22.00 17.50
248 A48 5r red brown 23.00 17.50
249 A48 10r gray blue 18.00 *37.50*
Nos. 235-249 (15) 83.30 87.10

Coronation Issue
Common Design Type

1953, June 2 **Engr.** ***Perf. 13½x13***
250 CD312 10c dk green & black 1.00 .25

Sugar Factory — A50

Tamarind Falls — A51

Designs: 2c, Grand Port. 3c, Aloe plant. 5c, Rempart Mountain. 15c, Museum, Mahebourg. 20c, Statue of Mahe La Bourdonnais. 25c, "Paul et Virginie." 35c, Government House. 50c, Pieter Both Mountain. 60c, Map and dodo. 1r, Sambar. 2.50r, Port Louis. 5r, Beach scene. 10r, Arms.

Perf. 13½x14½, 14½x13½

1953-54 **Photo.** **Wmk. 4**
251 A50 2c rose car ('54) .30 .25
252 A51 3c yel green ('54) .35 .25
253 A50 4c red violet .30 *.60*
254 A50 5c grnsh blue ('54) .30 .25
255 A51 10c dk green .30 .25
256 A50 15c scarlet .30 .25
257 A51 20c violet brown .30 .25
a. Imperf., pair
258 A51 25c brt ultra 1.60 .25
259 A50 35c rose vio ('54) .30 .25
260 A51 50c emerald .75 .75
261 A50 60c gray grn ('54) 12.00 .25
262 A50 1r sepia .35 .25
a. Imperf., pair
263 A50 2.50r orange ('54) 16.00 9.25
264 A50 5r red brn ('54) 16.00 9.25
265 A50 10r gray blue ('54) 16.00 1.25
Nos. 251-265 (15) 65.15 23.60

See Nos. 273-275.

King George III and Queen Elizabeth II — A52

Wmk. 314

1961, Jan. 11 **Litho.** ***Perf. 13½***
266 A52 10c dk red & dk brown .25 .25
267 A52 20c lt blue & dk blue .25 .25
268 A52 35c org yel & brown .30 .30
269 A52 1r yel green & dk brn .60 .60
Nos. 266-269 (4) 1.40 1.40

Sesquicentenary of postal service under British administration.

Freedom from Hunger Issue
Common Design Type

1963, June 4 **Photo.** ***Perf. 14x14½***
270 CD314 60c lilac .50 .50

Red Cross Centenary Issue
Common Design Type

1963, Sept. 2 **Litho.** ***Perf. 13***
271 CD315 10c black & red .25 .25
272 CD315 60c ultra & red .65 .65

Types of 1953-54

Perf. 14½x13½, 13½x14½

1963-64 **Photo.** **Wmk. 314**
273 A51 10c dark green ('64) .50 .30
274 A50 60c gray green ('64) 2.75 .30
275 A50 2.50r orange 9.75 *11.00*
Nos. 273-275 (3) 13.00 11.60

Gray White-Eye — A53

Birds of Mauritius: 3c, Rodriguez fody. 4c, Olive white-eye. 5c, Mauritius paradise flycatcher. 10c, Mauritius fody. 15c, Rose-ringed parakeet. 20c, Cuckoo shrike. 25c, Mauritian kestrel. 35c, Pink pigeon. 50c, Mauritius olivaceous bulbul. 60c, Mauritius blue pigeon. 1r, Dodo. 2.50r, Rodriguez solitaire. 5r, Van den Broeck's red rail. 10r, Broad-billed Mauritian parrot.

Wmk. 314

1965, Mar. 16 **Photo.** ***Perf. 14½***
Birds in Natural Colors
276 A53 2c brt yel & brn .50 .30
a. Gray (leg, etc.) omitted 210.00
277 A53 3c brn & dk brn 1.00 .30
a. Black (eye, beak) omitted 210.00
278 A53 4c dl rose lil & blk .35 .30
a. Rose lilac omitted 55.00
279 A53 5c gray & ultra 3.25 .30
a. Wmkd. sideways ('66) .25 .25
280 A53 10c dl grn & dk brn .35 .30
281 A53 15c lt gray & dk brn 2.10 .30
a. Carmine (beak) omitted 160.00
282 A53 20c pale yel & dk brown 2.10 .30
283 A53 25c gray & brown 2.10 .30
284 A53 35c vio bl & blk 2.75 .30
a. Wmkd. sideways ('67) .40 .35
285 A53 50c pale yel & blk .50 .50
286 A53 60c pale cit & brn .60 .30
287 A53 1r lt yel grn & blk 5.50 .30
a. Pale gray (ground) omitted 250.00
b. Pale orange omitted 175.00
288 A53 2.50r pale grn & brn 4.75 6.00
289 A53 5r pale blue & blk 14.00 9.00
290 A53 10r pale grn & ultra 26.00 22.50
Nos. 276-290 (15) 65.85 41.30

On No. 278 the background was printed in two colors. The rose lilac tint is omitted on No. 278a.

See Nos. 327-332. For overprints see Nos. 306-320.

ITU Issue
Common Design Type

Perf. 11x11½

1965, May 17 **Litho.** **Wmk. 314**
291 CD317 10c dp org & apple grn .30 .25
292 CD317 60c yellow & violet .90 .40

Intl. Cooperation Year Issue
Common Design Type

1965, Oct. 25 ***Perf. 14½***
293 CD318 10c lt green & claret .25 .25
294 CD318 60c lt violet & green .45 .45

Churchill Memorial Issue
Common Design Type

1966, Jan. 24 **Photo.** ***Perf. 14***
Design in Black, Gold and Carmine Rose
295 CD319 2c brt blue .40 .40
296 CD319 10c green .40 .40
297 CD319 60c brown 1.00 1.00
298 CD319 1r violet 2.25 2.25
Nos. 295-298 (4) 4.05 4.05

UNESCO Anniversary Issue
Common Design Type

1966, Dec. 1 **Litho.** ***Perf. 14***
299 CD323 5c "Education" .35 .35
300 CD323 10c "Science" .35 .35
301 CD323 60c "Culture" 1.40 .80
Nos. 299-301 (3) 2.10 1.50

Red-Tailed Tropic Bird — A54

Birds of Mauritius: 10c, Rodriguez bush warbler. 60c, Newton's parakeet. 1r, Mauritius swiftlet.

1967, Sept. 1 **Photo.** ***Perf. 14½***
302 A54 2c lt ultra & multi .40 .40
303 A54 10c emerald & multi .40 .40
304 A54 60c salmon & multi 1.25 1.25
305 A54 1r yellow & multi 2.40 2.40
Nos. 302-305 (4) 4.45 4.45

Attainment of self-government, Sept. 1, 1967.

Bird Issue of 1965-67 and Type Overprinted: "SELF GOVERNMENT 1967"

1967, Dec. 1 **Photo.** **Wmk. 314**
306 A53 2c multicolored .25 .25
307 A53 3c multicolored .25 .25
308 A53 4c multicolored .25 .25
309 A53 5c multicolored .25 .25
310 A53 10c multicolored .25 .25
311 A53 15c multicolored .25 .25
312 A53 20c multicolored .25 .25
313 A53 25c multicolored .25 .25
314 A53 35c multicolored .25 .25
315 A53 50c multicolored .40 .25
316 A53 60c multicolored .45 .30
317 A53 1r multicolored .75 .45
318 A53 2.50r multicolored 2.10 2.25
319 A53 5r multicolored 4.25 4.25
320 A53 10r multicolored 8.00 8.50
Nos. 306-320 (15) 18.20 18.25

5c, 10c, 35c watermarked sideways.

Independent State

Flag of Mauritius — A55

Designs: 3c, 20c, 1r, Dodo emerging from egg and coat of arms.

Perf. 13½x13

1968, Mar. 12 **Litho.** **Unwmk.**
321 A55 2c brt violet & multi .25 .25
322 A55 3c red brown & multi .25 .25
323 A55 15c brown & multi .25 .25
324 A55 20c multicolored .50 .25
325 A55 60c dk green & multi .65 .40
326 A55 1r brt violet & multi 1.00 .65
Nos. 321-326 (6) 2.90 2.05

Independence of Mauritius.

Bird Type of 1965 in Changed Background Colors

Wmk. 314

1968, July 12 **Photo.** ***Perf. 14½***
Birds in Natural Colors
327 A53 2c lemon & brown .30 .25
328 A53 3c ultra & dk brown .30 .25
329 A53 15c tan & dk brown .90 .25
330 A53 20c dull yel & dk brn 1.40 .25
331 A53 60c pink & black 3.50 2.50
332 A53 1r rose lilac & black 5.50 4.50
Nos. 327-332 (6) 11.90 8.00

Domingue Rescuing Paul and Virginie — A56

Designs: 15c, Paul and Virginie crossing river, vert. 50c, La Bourdonnais visiting Madame de 1a Tour. 60c, Paul and Virginie, vert. 1r, Departure of Virginie for Europe. 2.50r, Bernardin de St. Pierre, vert. The designs are from old prints illustrating "Paul et Virginie."

Perf. 13½

1968, Dec. 2 **Unwmk.** **Litho.**
333 A56 2c multicolored .25 .25
334 A56 15c multicolored .25 .25
335 A56 50c multicolored .30 .30
336 A56 60c multicolored .40 .40
337 A56 1r multicolored .65 .65
338 A56 2.50r multicolored 1.75 1.75
Nos. 333-338 (6) 3.60 3.60

Bicent. of the visit of Bernardin de St. Pierre (1737-1814), author of "Paul et Virginie."

Batardé Fish A57

Marine Life: 3c, Red reef crab. 4c, Episcopal miter shell. 5c, Bourse fish. 10c, Starfish. 15c, Sea urchin. 20c, Fiddler crab. 25c, Spiny shrimp. 30c, Single and double harp shells. 35c, Argonaut shell. 40c, Nudibranch (sea-slug). 50c, Violet and orange spider shells. 60c, Blue marlin. 75c, Conus clytospira. 1r, Dorad. 2.50r, Spiny lobster. 5r, Sacré chien rouge fish. 10r, Moonfish.

Wmk. 314 Sideways (#339-344, 351-352), others Upright

1969, Mar. 12 **Photo.** ***Perf. 14***
339 A57 2c pink & multi .30 .30
340 A57 3c yellow & multi .30 .30
341 A57 4c multicolored .30 .30
342 A57 5c lt blue & multi .30 .30
343 A57 10c salmon & multi .30 .30
344 A57 15c pale blue & multi .30 .30
345 A57 20c pale gray & multi .30 .30
346 A57 25c multicolored .30 .30
347 A57 30c multicolored .30 .40
348 A57 35c multicolored .30 .40
349 A57 40c tan & multi .40 .50
350 A57 50c lt vio & multi .50 .60
351 A57 60c ultra & multi .70 .75
352 A57 75c lemon & multi .85 .85
353 A57 1r cream & multi .90 1.10
354 A57 2.50r lt vio & multi 3.75 4.75
355 A57 5r multicolored 7.75 10.00
356 A57 10r multicolored 13.50 17.50
Nos. 339-356 (18) 31.35 39.25

For overprints see Nos. 368-369.

Wmk. 314 Upright (#339a-344a, 351a-352a), others Sideways

1972-74
339a A57 2c multi ('74) 1.00 1.00
340a A57 3c multi ('74) 1.00 1.00
341a A57 4c multi ('74) 1.00 1.00
342a A57 5c multi ('74) 1.00 1.00
343a A57 10c multicolored 1.00 1.00
344a A57 15c multi ('74) 1.00 1.00
345a A57 20c multicolored 1.00 1.00
346a A57 25c multi ('73) 1.00 1.00
347a A57 30c multicolored 1.25 1.00
348a A57 35c multicolored 1.50 1.25
349a A57 40c multicolored 1.50 1.50
350a A57 50c multi ('73) 1.50 1.50
351a A57 60c multi ('74) 2.00 1.50
352a A57 75c multicolored 2.50 2.00
353a A57 1r multicolored 3.00 2.50

354a	A57	2.50r multi ('73)	7.50	7.00
355a	A57	5r multi ('73)	15.00	12.50
356a	A57	10r multicolored	29.00	25.00
		Nos. 339a-356a (18)	72.75	63.75

1975-77 Wmk. 373

339b	A57	2c multi ('77)	.75	.75
340b	A57	3c multi ('77)	.75	.75
341b	A57	4c multi ('77)	.75	.75
342b	A57	5c multicolored	.75	.75
344b	A57	15c multicolored	.75	.75
345b	A57	20c multi ('76)	.75	.75
346b	A57	25c multicolored	.95	.75
347b	A57	30c multicolored	1.10	.95
348b	A57	35c multi ('76)	1.10	.95
349b	A57	40c multi ('76)	1.10	1.10
350b	A57	50c multi ('76)	1.50	1.10
351b	A57	60c multi ('77)	1.90	1.50
352b	A57	75c multi ('77)	1.90	1.90
353b	A57	1r multi ('76)	3.00	2.75
354b	A57	2.50r multi ('77)	12.50	7.50
355b	A57	5r multicolored	21.00	16.00
356b	A57	10r multicolored	50.00	32.50
		Nos. 339b-356b (17)	100.55	71.50

Gandhi as Law Student in London A58

Portraits of Gandhi: 15c, as stretcher bearer during Zulu rebellion. 50c, as member of non-violent movement in South Africa (Satyagrahi). 60c, wearing Indian garment at No. 10 Downing Street, London. 1r, wearing turban in Mauritius, 1901. 2.50r, as old man.

1969, July 1 Litho. *Perf. 13½*

357	A58	2c dull org & multi	.30	.30
358	A58	15c brt blue & multi	.30	.30
359	A58	50c multicolored	.30	.30
360	A58	60c brick red & multi	.40	.40
361	A58	1r multicolored	.75	.75
362	A58	2.50r olive & multi	1.90	1.90
a.		Souvenir sheet of 6, #357-362	7.50	7.50
		Nos. 357-362 (6)	3.95	3.95

Mohandas K. Gandhi (1869-1948), leader in India's struggle for independence.

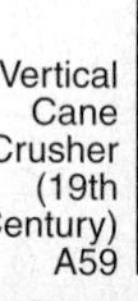

Vertical Cane Crusher (19th Century) A59

Dr. Charles Telfair (1778-1833) A60

Designs: 15c, The Frangourinier, 18th century cane crusher. 60c, Beau Rivage sugar factory, 1867, painting by Numa Desjardin. 1r, Mon Desert-Alma sugar factory, 1969.

Perf. 11x11½, 11½x11

1969, Dec. 22 Photo. Wmk. 314

363	A59	2c multicolored	.25	.25
364	A59	15c multicolored	.25	.25
365	A59	60c multicolored	.25	.25
366	A59	1r multicolored	.30	.30
367	A60	2.50r multicolored	.60	.60
a.		Souvenir sheet of 5	2.75	2.75
		Nos. 363-367 (5)	1.65	1.65

150th anniv. of Telfair's improvements of the sugar industry.

No. 367a contains one each of Nos. 363-367. The 2.50r in the sheet is imperf., the others are perf. 11x11½.

Nos. 351 and 353 Overprinted: "EXPO '70 / OSAKA"

1970, Apr. 7 *Perf. 14*

368	A57	60c ultra & multi	.25	.25
369	A57	1r cream & multi	.40	.40

EXPO '70 Intl. Exhib., Osaka, Japan, Mar. 15-Sept. 13.

Lufthansa Plane over Mauritius — A61

25c, Brabant Hotel, Morne Beach, horiz.

1970, May 2 Litho. *Perf. 14*

370	A61	25c multicolored	.25	.25
371	A61	50c multicolored	.40	.40

Lufthansa's inaugural flight from Mauritius to Frankfurt, Germany, May 2, 1970.

Lenin as Student, by V. Tsigal — A62

Design: 75c, Bust of Lenin.

1970, May 15 Photo. *Perf. 12x11½*

372	A62	15c dk slate blue & sil	.25	.25
373	A62	75c dk brown & gold	.65	.65

Birth cent. of Lenin (1870-1924), Russian communist leader.

UN Emblem and Symbols of UN Activities — A63

1970, Oct. 24 Litho. *Perf. 14*

374	A63	10c blue black & multi	.25	.25
375	A63	60c blue black & multi	.40	.40

25th anniversary of the United Nations.

Mauritius No. 2, and Post Office before 1870 A64

Designs: 15c, General Post Office Building, 1870-1970. 50c, Mauritius mail coach, 1870. 75c, Port Louis harbor, 1970. 2.50r, Arrival of Pierre André de Suffren de St. Tropez in Port Louis harbor, 1783.

1970, Oct. 15 Litho. *Perf. 14*

376	A64	5c multicolored	.25	.25
377	A64	15c multicolored	.25	.25
378	A64	50c multicolored	.25	.25
379	A64	75c multicolored	.30	.30
380	A64	2.50r multicolored	1.00	1.00
a.		Souvenir sheet of 5	5.00	5.00
		Nos. 376-380 (5)	2.05	2.05

Centenary of the General Post Office and to show the improvements of Port Louis harbor. No. 380a contains one each of Nos. 376-380 and a label showing map of Mauritius.

Waterfall A65

15c, Trois Mamelles Mountains. 60c, Beach scene with sailboats. 2.50r, Marine life.

1971, Apr. 12 Litho. *Perf. 14*

381	A65	10c multicolored	.25	.25
382	A65	15c multicolored	.25	.25
383	A65	60c multicolored	.40	.40
384	A65	2.50r multicolored	1.90	1.90
		Nos. 381-384 (4)	2.80	2.80

Tourist publicity. Each stamp has a different 6-line message printed in black on back.

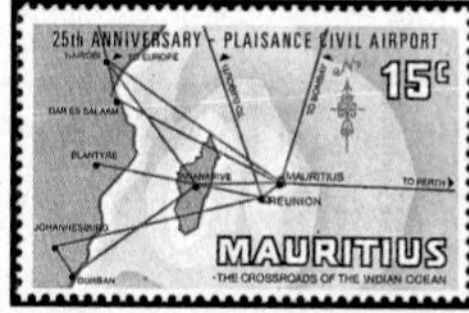

Mauritius at Crossroads of Indian Ocean — A66

60c, Plane at Plaisance Airport. 1r, Stewardesses on plane ramp. 2.50r, Roland Garros' airplane, Choisy Airfield, 1937.

1971, Oct. 23 Wmk. 314 *Perf. 14½*

385	A66	15c multicolored	.25	.25
386	A66	60c multicolored	.55	.55
387	A66	1r multicolored	.65	.65
388	A66	2.50r multicolored	2.75	2.75
		Nos. 385-388 (4)	4.20	4.20

25th anniversary of Plaisance Civil Airport.

Princess Margaret Orthopedic Center — A67

75c, Operating room, National Hospital.

1971, Nov. 2 *Perf. 14x14½*

389	A67	10c multicolored	.25	.25
390	A67	75c multicolored	.30	.30

3rd Commonwealth Medical Conf., Nov. 1971.

Elizabeth II and Prince Philip — A68

Design: 2.50r, Queen Elizabeth II, vert.

1972, Mar. Litho. *Perf. 14½*

391	A68	15c brown & multi	.30	.30
392	A68	2.50r ultra & multi	2.75	2.75

Visit of Elizabeth II and Prince Philip.

Port Louis Theater and Masks A69

Design: 1r, Interior view and masks of Comedy and Tragedy.

1972, June 26

393	A69	10c brown & multi	.25	.25
394	A69	1r multicolored	.45	.45

Sesquicentennial of Port Louis Theater.

Pirate Dhow Entering Tamarind River A70

60c, Treasure chest, vert. 1r, Lememe and brig Hirondelle, vert. 2.50r, Robert Surcouf.

Perf. 14x14½, 14½x14

1972, Nov. 17 Litho.

395	A70	15c shown	.30	.30
396	A70	60c multi	.85	.85
397	A70	1r multi	2.00	2.00
398	A70	2.50r multi	7.00	7.00
		Nos. 395-398 (4)	10.15	10.15

Pirates and privateers.

Mauritius University — A71

60c, Tea development plant. 1r, Bank of Mauritius.

1973, Apr. 10 *Perf. 14½*

399	A71	15c green & multi	.25	.25
400	A71	60c yellow & multi	.25	.25
401	A71	1r red & multi	.30	.30
		Nos. 399-401 (3)	.80	.80

5th anniversary of independence.

OCAM Emblem A72

Design: 2.50r, Handshake, map of Africa; inscriptions in French, vert.

1973, Apr. 25

402	A72	10c multicolored	.25	.25
403	A72	2.50r lt blue & multi	.60	.60

Conference of the Organisation Commune Africaine, Malgache et Mauricienne (OCAM), Mauritius, Apr. 25-May 6.

WHO Emblem A73

Perf. 14½x14

1973, Nov. 20 Wmk. 314

404	A73	1r green & multi	.40	.40

25th anniv. of WHO.

Meteorological Station, Vacoas — A74

1973, Nov. 27

405	A74	75c multicolored	.40	.40

Cent. of intl. meteorological cooperation.

Surcouf and Capture of the "Kent" A75

1974, Mar. 21 Litho. *Perf. 14½x14*

406	A75	60c sepia & multi	1.25	1.25

Bicentenary of the birth of Robert Surcouf (1773-1827), French privateer.

Philibert Commerson & Bougainvillaea A76

1974, Apr. 18 *Perf. 14*

407 A76 2.50r slate grn & multi	.70	.70

Philibert Commerson (1727-1773), French physician and naturalist.

FAO Emblem, Woman Milking Cow A77

1974, Oct. 23 *Perf. 14½*

408 A77 60c multicolored	.35	.35

8th FAO Regional Conference, Aug. 1-17.

Mail Train and UPU Emblem A78

Design: 1r, New General Post Office Building, Port Louis, and UPU emblem.

1974, Dec. 4 **Litho.** *Perf. 14½*

409 A78 15c multicolored	.30	.30
410 A78 1r multicolored	.80	.80

Centenary of Universal Postal Union.

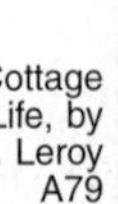

Cottage Life, by F. Leroy A79

Paintings: 60c, Milk Seller, by A. Richard, vert. 1r, Entrance to Port Louis Market, by Thuillier. 2.50r, Washerwomen, by Max Boullé, vert.

1975, Mar. 6 **Wmk. 373**

411 A79 15c multicolored	.25	.25
412 A79 60c multicolored	.40	.40
413 A79 1r multicolored	.65	.65
414 A79 2.50r multicolored	1.50	1.50
Nos. 411-414 (4)	2.80	2.80

Artistic views of life on Mauritius.

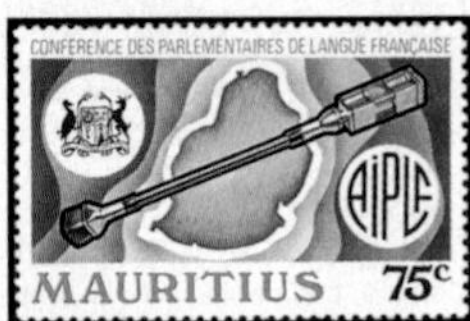

Mace, Map and Arms of Mauritius, Association Emblem — A80

1975, Nov. 21 **Litho.** **Wmk. 373**

415 A80 75c multicolored	.60	.60

French-speaking Parliamentary Association, conf.

Woman and Aladdin's Lamp A81

1975, Dec. 5 *Perf. 14½*

416 A81 2.50r multicolored	.75	.75

International Women's Year.

Parched Land A82

Drought in Africa: 60c, Map of Africa, carcass and desert, vert.

1976, Feb. 26 **Litho.** **Wmk. 373**

417 A82 50c vermilion & multi	.25	.25
418 A82 60c blue & multi	.30	.30

Pierre Loti, 1953-1970 — A83

Mail Carriers: 15c, Secunder, 1907. 50c, Hindoostan, 1842. 60c, St. Geran, 1740. 2.50r, Maen, 1638.

1976, July 2 **Litho.** **Wmk. 373**

419 A83 10c multicolored	.65	.65
420 A83 15c multicolored	.65	.65
421 A83 50c multicolored	.95	.95
422 A83 60c multicolored	1.25	1.25
423 A83 2.50r multicolored	5.50	5.50
a. Souvenir sheet of 5, #419-423	13.50	13.50
Nos. 419-423 (5)	9.00	9.00

Flame, and "Hindi Carried Across the Sea" A84

Designs: 75c, like 10c. 1.20r, Flame and tablet with Hindi inscription.

1976, Aug. 28 *Perf. 14½x14*

424 A84 10c multicolored	.25	.25
425 A84 75c lt blue & multi	.25	.25
426 A84 1.20r multicolored	.35	.35
Nos. 424-426 (3)	.85	.85

2nd World Hindi Convention.

Commonwealth Emblem, Map of Mauritius — A85

2.50r, Commonwealth emblem twice.

1976, Sept. 22 **Litho.** *Perf. 14x14½*

427 A85 1r multicolored	.40	.40
428 A85 2.50r multicolored	.90	.90

22nd Commonwealth Parliamentary Association Conference, Mauritius, Sept. 17-30.

King Priest and Steatite Pectoral — A86

Designs: 1r, House with well, and goblet. 2.50r, Terracotta goddess and necklace.

1976, Dec. 15 **Wmk. 373** *Perf. 14*

429 A86 60c multicolored	.35	.35
430 A86 1r multicolored	.75	.75
431 A86 2.50r multicolored	1.75	1.75
Nos. 429-431 (3)	2.85	2.85

UNESCO campaign to save Mohenjo-Daro excavations.

Sega Dance A87

1977, Jan. 20 **Litho.** *Perf. 13*

432 A87 1r multicolored	.50	.50

2nd World Black and African Festival, Lagos, Nigeria, Jan. 15-Feb. 12.

Elizabeth II at Mauritius Legislative Assembly — A88

Designs: 75c, Queen holding scepter and orb. 5r, Presentation of scepter and orb.

1977, Feb. 7 *Perf. 14½x14*

433 A88 50c multicolored	.25	.25
434 A88 75c multicolored	.25	.25
435 A88 5r multicolored	1.10	1.10
Nos. 433-435 (3)	1.60	1.60

25th anniv. of the reign of Elizabeth II.

Hugonia Tomentosa — A89

Flowers: 1r, Oehna mauritiana, vert. 1.50r, Dombeya acuntangula. 5r, Trochetia blackburniana, vert.

1977, Sept. 22 **Wmk. 373** *Perf. 14*

436 A89 20c multicolored	.25	.25
437 A89 1r multicolored	.40	.40
438 A89 1.50r multicolored	.60	.60
439 A89 5r multicolored	1.75	1.75
a. Souvenir sheet of 4, #436-439	5.00	5.00
Nos. 436-439 (4)	3.00	3.00

Twin Otter of Air Mauritius — A90

Designs: 50c, Air Mauritius emblem (red-tailed tropic bird) and Twin Otter. 75c, Piper Navajo and Boeing 747. 5r, Air Mauritius Boeing 707 in flight.

1977, Oct. 31 **Litho.** *Perf. 14½*

440 A90 25c multicolored	.60	.60
441 A90 50c multicolored	.90	.90
442 A90 75c multicolored	1.00	1.00
443 A90 5r multicolored	5.50	5.50
a. Souvenir sheet of 4, #440-443	12.00	12.00
Nos. 440-443 (4)	8.00	8.00

Air Mauritius International Inaugural Flight.

Mauritius, Portuguese Map, 1519 — A91

Dutch Occupation, 1638-1710 — A92

Designs: 20c, Mauritius, map by Van Keulen, c. 1700. 25c, 1st settlement of Rodrigues, 1708. 35c, Proclamation, arrival of French settlers, 1715. 50c, Construction of Port Louis, c. 1736. 60c, Pierre Poivre and nutmeg tree. 70c, Map by Belin, 1763. 75c, First coin minted in Mauritius, 1810. 90c, Naval battle of Grand Port, 1810. 1r, Landing of the British, Nov. 1810. 1.20r, Government House, c. 1840. 1.25r, Invitation with No. 1 and ball of Lady Gomm, 1847. 1.50r, Indian immigration in Mauritius, 1835. 2r, Champ de Mars race course, c. 1870. 3r, Place D'Armes, c. 1880. 5r, Postal card commemorating visit of Prince and Princess of Wales, 1901. 10r, Curepipe College, 1914. 15r, Raising flag of Mauritius, 1968. 25r, Raman Osman, first Governor General and Seewoosagur Ramgoolan, first Prime Minister.

1978, Mar. 12 **Wmk. 373** *Perf. 13½*

444 A91 10c multicolored	.25	.25
445 A92 15c multicolored	.25	.25
446 A92 20c multicolored	.25	.25
447 A91 25c multicolored	.25	.25
448 A91 35c multicolored	.25	.25
b. Perf. 14½, "1986"	.25	.25
449 A92 50c multicolored	.25	.25
450 A91 60c multicolored	.35	.35
451 A92 70c multicolored	.40	.35
452 A91 75c multicolored	.45	.40
453 A92 90c multicolored	.45	.40
454 A92 1r multicolored	.45	.45
455 A92 1.20r multicolored	.45	.45
456 A91 1.25r multicolored	.45	.45
457 A92 1.50r multicolored	.55	.60
458 A92 2r multicolored	.75	.80
459 A92 3r multicolored	1.10	1.25
460 A92 5r multicolored	1.90	2.00
461 A92 10r multicolored	3.75	4.00
462 A91 15r multicolored	5.25	6.00
463 A92 25r multicolored	8.75	9.75
Nos. 444-463 (20)	26.55	28.75

Nos. 448, 452, 456, 458 reprinted inscribed 1983; Nos. 444, 447-449, 452, 454, 456, 460 reprinted inscribed 1985.

1985-89 **Wmk. 384** *Perf. 14½*

446a A92 20c "1987"	.25	.25
447a A91 25c "1987"	.25	.25
448a A91 35c ('85)	.25	.25
449a A92 50c ('85)	.25	.25
452a A91 75c ('85)	.25	.25
458a A92 2r "1987"	.25	.25
459a A92 3r "1989"	.40	.40
460a A92 5r "1989"	.70	.70
463a A92 25r "1989"	3.45	3.45
Nos. 446a-463a (9)	6.05	6.05

Issued: 20c, 25c, 2r, 1/11/87; 3r-25r, 1/19/89.

Nos. 449a and 458a reprinted inscribed 1989.

Elizabeth II Coronation Anniv. Issue
Common Design Types
Souvenir Sheet

1978, Apr. 21 **Unwmk.** *Perf. 15*

464 Sheet of 6	2.75	2.75
a. CD326 3r Antelope of Bohun	.50	.50
b. CD327 3r Elizabeth II	.50	.50
c. CD328 3r Dodo	.50	.50

No. 464 contains 2 se-tenant strips of Nos. 464a-464c, separated by horizontal gutter with commemorative and descriptive inscriptions and showing central part of coronation procession with coach.

Dr. Fleming, WWI Casualty, Bacteria — A93

1r, Microscope & 1st mold growth, 1928. 1.50r, Penicillium notatum, close-up. 5r, Alexander Fleming & nurse administering penicillin.

Wmk. 373

1978, Aug. 3 Litho. *Perf. 13½*

465	A93	20c multicolored	.80	.80
466	A93	1r multicolored	1.60	1.60
467	A93	1.50r multicolored	2.75	2.75
468	A93	5r multicolored	3.75	3.75
a.		Souvenir sheet of 4, #465-468	11.00	11.00
		Nos. 465-468 (4)	8.90	8.90

Discovery of penicillin by Dr. Alexander Fleming, 50th anniversary.

Citrus Butterfly — A94

Wildlife Protection (Wildlife Fund Emblem and): 1r, Geckos. 1.50r, Flying foxes. 5r, Mauritius kestrels.

1978, Sept. 21 *Perf. 13½x14*

469	A94	20c multicolored	*4.00*	*2.50*
470	A94	1r multicolored	*3.50*	*2.50*
471	A94	1.50r multicolored	*3.50*	*2.50*
472	A94	5r multicolored	*18.50*	*5.00*
a.		Souvenir sheet of 4, #469-472	*110.00*	*80.00*
		Nos. 469-472 (4)	*29.50*	*12.50*

Le Reduit — A95

15c, Ornate table. 3r, Reduit gardens.

1978, Dec. 21 *Perf. 14½x14*

473	A95	15c multicolored	.25	.25
474	A95	75c multicolored	.30	.30
475	A95	3r multicolored	1.00	1.00
		Nos. 473-475 (3)	1.55	1.55

Reconstruction of Chateau Le Reduit, 200th anniversary.

Whitcomb, 1949 — A96

Locomotives: 1r, Sir William, 1922. 1.50r, Kitson, 1930. 2r, Garratt, 1927.

1979, Feb. 1 *Perf. 14½*

476	A96	20c multicolored	.25	.25
477	A96	1r multicolored	.50	.50
478	A96	1.50r multicolored	.95	.95
479	A96	2r multicolored	1.25	1.25
a.		Souvenir sheet of 4, #476-479	5.25	5.25
		Nos. 476-479 (4)	2.95	2.95

Father Laval and Crucifix — A97

Designs: 1.50r, Jacques Desire Laval. 5r, Father Laval's sarcophagus, horiz.

1979, Apr. 30 Wmk. 373 *Perf. 14*

480	A97	20c multicolored	.25	.25
481	A97	1.50r multicolored	.30	.30
482	A97	5r multicolored	1.00	1.00
a.		Souvenir sheet of 3, #480-482	3.75	3.75
		Nos. 480-482 (3)	1.55	1.55

Beatification of Father Laval (1803-1864), physician and missionary.

Souvenir Booklet

10th Anniv. of Apollo 11 Moon Landing — A98

Imperf. x Roulette 5

1979, July 20 Litho.

Self-adhesive

483	A98	Booklet of 9	8.00
a.		20c Astronaut and Lunar Module	.20
b.		3r Neil Armstrong on moon	.90
c.		5r Astronaut walking on moon	3.75
d.		Bklt. pane of 3 (20c, 5r, 3r)	5.00
e.		Bklt. pane of 6 (3 each 20c, 3r)	3.50

No. 483 contains 2 panes printed on peelable paper backing showing map of moon (d) and details of uniform and spacecraft (e).

Rowland Hill and Great Britain No. 23 — A99

Rowland Hill and: 2r, Mauritius No. 261. 3r, Mauritius No. 2. 5r, Mauritius No. 1.

1979, Aug. 29 *Perf. 14½*

484	A99	25c multicolored	.25	.25
485	A99	2r multicolored	.50	.50
486	A99	5r multicolored	1.25	1.25
		Nos. 484-486 (3)	2.00	2.00

Souvenir Sheet

Perf. 14½

487	A99	3r multicolored	1.75	1.75

Sir Rowland Hill (1795-1879), originator of penny postage. No. 487 contains one stamp.

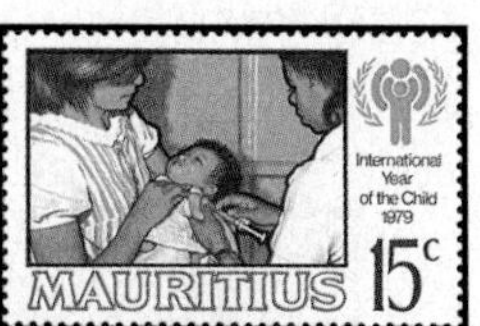

Infant Vaccination — A100

IYC Emblem and: 25c, Children playing. 1r, Coat of arms, vert. 1.50r, Children in laboratory. 3r, Teacher and student working lathe.

Wmk. 373

1979, Oct. 11 Litho. *Perf. 14*

488	A100	15c multicolored	.25	.25
489	A100	25c multicolored	.25	.25
490	A100	1r multicolored	.25	.25
491	A100	1.50r multicolored	.35	.35
492	A100	3r multicolored	.70	.70
		Nos. 488-492 (5)	1.80	1.80

International Year of the Child.

Lienard Obelisk — A101

Designs: 25c, Poivre Avenue, 1r, Pandanus. 2r, Giant water lilies, 5r, Mon Plaisir.

1980, Jan. 24 *Perf. 14x14½*

493	A101	20c multicolored	.25	.25
494	A101	25c multicolored	.25	.25
495	A101	1r multicolored	.25	.25
496	A101	2r multicolored	.40	.40
497	A101	5r multicolored	1.00	1.00
a.		Souvenir sheet of 5, #493-497	4.25	4.25
		Nos. 493-497 (5)	2.15	2.15

Pamplemousses Botanical Gardens.

"Emirne," 19th Century, London 1980 Emblem — A102

1r, Boissevain, 1930's. 2r, La Boudeuse, 18th cent. 5r, Sea Breeze, 19th cent.

1980, May 6 Litho. *Perf. 14½*

498	A102	25c shown	.25	.25
499	A102	1r multi	.50	.50
500	A102	2r multi	1.00	1.00
501	A102	5r multi	2.25	2.25
		Nos. 498-501 (4)	4.00	4.00

London 80 Intl. Stamp Exhib., May 6-14.

Helen Keller Reading Braille — A103

25c, Blind men weaving baskets. 1r, Teacher and deaf girl. 5r, Keller graduating college.

1980, June 27 Litho. *Perf. 14½*

502	A103	25c multicolored	.25	.25
503	A103	1r multicolored	.50	.50
504	A103	2.50r shown	1.25	1.25
505	A103	5r multicolored	2.00	2.00
		Nos. 502-505 (4)	4.00	4.00

Helen Keller (1880-1968), blind and deaf writer and lecturer.

Prime Minister Seewoosagur Ramgoolan, 80th Birthday — A104

Litho.; Gold Embossed

1980, Sept. 18 *Perf. 13½*

506	A104	15r multicolored	2.00	2.00

Mauritius Institute, Centenary — A105

2r, Rare Veda copy. 2.50r, Rare cone. 5r, Landscape, by Henri Harpignies.

1980, Oct. 1 Litho. *Perf. 13*

507	A105	25c shown	.25	.25
508	A105	2r multicolored	.50	.50
509	A105	2.50r multicolored	.60	.60
510	A105	5r multicolored	1.25	1.25
		Nos. 507-510 (4)	2.60	2.60

Hibiscus Liliiflorus — A106

2r, Erythrospermum monticolum. 2.50r, Chasalia boryana. 5r, Hibiscus columnaris.

1981, Jan. 15 Litho. *Perf. 14*

511	A106	25c shown	.25	.25
512	A106	2r multicolored	.70	.70
513	A106	2.50r multicolored	.90	.90
514	A106	5r multicolored	1.75	1.75
		Nos. 511-514 (4)	3.60	3.60

Arms of Curepipe — A107

City coats of arms: 25c, Beau-Bassin / Rose Hill. 2r, Quatre-Bornes. 2.50r, Vacoas/ Phoenix. 5r, Port Louis.

Perf. 13½x13

1981, Apr. 10 Litho. Wmk. 373

515	A107	25c multicolored	.25	.25
516	A107	1.50r shown	.30	.30
517	A107	2r multicolored	.40	.40
518	A107	2.50r multicolored	.50	.50
519	A107	5r multicolored	1.00	1.00
a.		Souv. sheet of 5, #515-519, perf. 14	3.25	3.25
		Nos. 515-519 (5)	2.45	2.45

Royal Wedding Issue

Common Design Type

1981, July 22 Litho. *Perf. 14*

520	CD331	25c Bouquet	.25	.25
521	CD331	2.50r Charles	.50	.50
522	CD331	10r Couple	2.00	2.00
		Nos. 520-522 (3)	2.75	2.75

Emmanuel Anquetil and Guy Rozemont — A108

Famous Men: 25c, Remy Ollier, Sookdeo Bissoondoyal. 1.25r, Maurice Cure, Barthelemy Ohsan. 1.50r, Guy Forget, Renganaden Seeneevassen. 2r, Abdul Razak Mohamed, Jules Koenig. 2.50r, Abdoollatiff Mahomed Osman, Dazzi Rama. 5r, Thomas Lewis.

1981, Aug. 13 *Perf. 14½*

523	A108	20c black & red	.25	.25
524	A108	25c black & yellow	.25	.25
525	A108	1.25r black & green	.35	.35

526 A108 1.50r black & vermilion .40 .40
527 A108 2r black & ultra .55 .55
528 A108 2.50r black & red brn .65 .65
529 A108 5r black & blue grn 1.40 1.40
Nos. 523-529 (7) 3.85 3.85

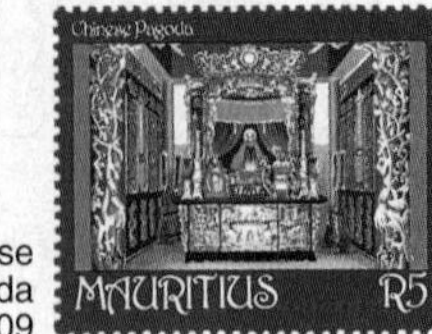

Chinese Pagoda A109

20c, Tamil Women. 2r, Swami Sivananda, vert.

1981, Sept. 16 *Perf. 13½*
530 A109 20c multicolored .25 .25
531 A109 2r multicolored .75 .75
532 A109 5r shown 1.90 1.90
Nos. 530-532 (3) 2.90 2.90

World Tamil Culture Conference, 1980 (20c).

A110

25c, Pottery making. 1.25r, Dog grooming. 5r, Hiking. 10r, Duke of Edinburgh.

1981, Oct. 26 **Litho.** *Perf. 14*
533 A110 25c multicolored .25 .25
534 A110 1.25r multicolored .25 .25
535 A110 5r multicolored .75 .75
536 A110 10r multicolored 1.50 1.50
Nos. 533-536 (4) 2.75 2.75

Duke of Edinburgh's Awards, 25th anniv.

Hegira, 1,500th Anniv. — A111

25c, Holy Ka'aba, Mecca. 2r, Prophet's Mosque. 5r, Holy Ka'aba, Prophet's Mosque.

1981, Nov. 26 **Wmk. 373** *Perf. 14½*
537 A111 25c multicolored .30 .30
538 A111 2r multicolored .80 .80
539 A111 5r multicolored 1.90 1.90
Nos. 537-539 (3) 3.00 3.00

Scouting Year — A112

1982, Feb. 25 **Litho.** *Perf. 14x14½*
540 A112 25c Emblem .25 .25
541 A112 2r Baden-Powell .60 .60
542 A112 5r Grand howl, sign 1.40 1.40
543 A112 10r Scouts, mountain 2.75 2.75
Nos. 540-543 (4) 5.00 5.00

Darwin Death Centenary — A113

1982, Apr. 19 **Litho.** *Perf. 14*
544 A113 25c Portrait .25 .25
545 A113 2r Telescope .45 .45
546 A113 2.50r Riding elephant .55 .55
547 A113 10r The Beagle 2.25 2.25
Nos. 544-547 (4) 3.50 3.50

Princess Diana Issue
Common Design Type

1982, July 1 **Litho.** *Perf. 13*
548 CD333 25c Arms .25 .25
549 CD333 2.50r Diana .75 .75
550 CD333 5r Wedding 1.50 1.50
551 CD333 10r Portrait 3.00 3.00
Nos. 548-551 (4) 5.50 5.50

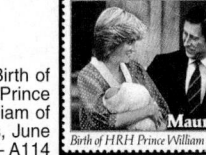

Birth of Prince William of Wales, June 21 — A114

1982, Sept. 22 **Litho.** *Perf. 14½*
552 A114 2.50r multicolored 1.10 1.10

Issued in sheets of 9.

TB Bacillus Centenary — A115

25c, Aphloia theiformis. 1.25r, Central Market, Port Louis. 2r, Gaertnera psychotrioides. 5r, Selaginella deliquescens. 10r, Koch.

1982, Dec. 15 *Perf. 14*
553 A115 25c multicolored .25 .25
554 A115 1.25r multicolored .55 .55
555 A115 2r multicolored .85 .85
556 A115 5r multicolored 1.25 1.25
557 A115 10r multicolored 3.75 3.75
Nos. 553-557 (5) 6.65 6.65

A116

25c, Flag, arms. 2.50r, Satellite view. 5r, Sugar cane harvest. 10r, Port Louis Harbor.

1983, Mar. 14 *Perf. 13x13½*
558 A116 25c multi .25 .25
559 A116 2.50r multi .40 .40
560 A116 5r multi .85 .85
561 A116 10r multi 1.75 1.75
Nos. 558-561 (4) 3.25 3.25

Commonwealth Day.

World Communications Year — A117

25c, Antique telephone, vert. 1.25r, Early telegraph apparatus. 2r, Earth satellite station, vert. 10r, 1st hot air balloon in Mauritius, 1784.

1983, June 24 **Wmk. 373** *Perf. 14*
562 A117 25c multi .25 .25
563 A117 1.25r multi .35 .35
564 A117 2r multi .50 .50
565 A117 10r multi 2.40 2.40
Nos. 562-565 (4) 3.50 3.50

Namibia Day — A118

25c, Map. 2.50r, Breaking chains. 5r, Family, village. 10r, Diamond mining.

1983, Aug. 26
566 A118 25c multi .70 .70
567 A118 2.50r multi 1.60 1.60
568 A118 5r multi 3.25 3.25
569 A118 10r multi 6.00 6.00
Nos. 566-569 (4) 11.55 11.55

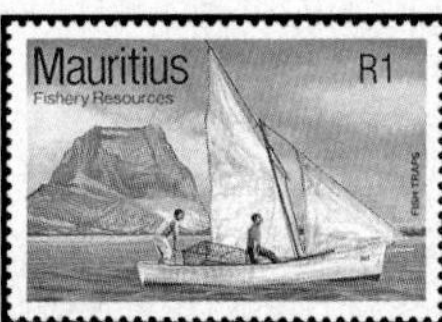

Fishery Resources — A119

1983, Oct. 7
570 A119 25c Fish trap, vert. .25 .25
571 A119 1r Fishermen in boat .40 .40
572 A119 5r Game fishing, vert. 1.75 1.75
573 A119 10r Octopus drying 3.75 3.75
Nos. 570-573 (4) 6.15 6.15

Swami Dayananda, Death Centenary — A120

35c, Last meeting with father. 2r, Receiving instruction. 5r, Demonstrating strength. 10r, Religious gathering.

1983, Nov. 3 **Litho.** **Wmk. 373**
574 A120 25c shown .25 .25
575 A120 35c multi .25 .25
576 A120 2r multi .30 .30
577 A120 5r multi .80 .80
578 A120 10r multi 1.75 1.75
Nos. 574-578 (5) 3.35 3.35

Adolf von Plevitz (1837-1893), Social Reformer A121

1.25r, Government school. 5r, Addressing Commission of Enquiry. 10r, Indian field workers.

1983, Dec. 8
579 A121 25c shown .30 .30
580 A121 1.25r multi .65 .65
581 A121 5r multi 1.10 1.10
582 A121 10r multi 2.50 2.50
Nos. 579-582 (4) 4.55 4.55

Mauritius Kestrels A122

25c, Courtship chase. 2r, Side view, vert. 2.50r, Fledgling. 10r, Bird, diff., vert.

1984, Mar. 26 **Wmk. 373** *Perf. 14*
583 A122 25c multi .40 .40
584 A122 2r multi 2.40 2.40
585 A122 2.50r multi 2.75 2.75
586 A122 10r multi 12.00 12.00
Nos. 583-586 (4) 17.55 17.55

Lloyd's List Issue
Common Design Type

25c, Tayeb, Port Lewis. 1r, Taher. 5r, East Indiaman Triton. 10r, Astor.

1984, May 23 **Litho.** *Perf. 14½x14*
587 CD335 25c multi .35 .35
588 CD335 1r multi .70 .70
589 CD335 5r multi 2.40 2.40
590 CD335 10r multi 5.50 5.50
Nos. 587-590 (4) 8.95 8.95

Palm Trees — A123

25c, Blue latan. 50c, Hyophorbe vaughanii. 2.50r, Tectiphiala ferox. 5r, Round Isld. bottle-palm. 10r, Hyophorbe amaricaulis.

1984, July 23 **Litho.** *Perf. 14*
591 A123 25c multi .30 .30
592 A123 50c multi .30 .30
593 A123 2.50r multi 1.40 1.40
594 A123 5r multi 2.75 2.75
595 A123 10r multi 5.75 5.75
Nos. 591-595 (5) 10.50 10.50

Slave Sale — A124

25c, Woman. 2r, Family, horiz. 10r, Immigrant arrival, horiz.

1984, Aug. *Perf. 14½*
596 A124 25c brn ochre & brn pur .30 .30
597 A124 1r ochre & brn pur .95 .95
598 A124 2r mar & brn pur 1.50 1.50
599 A124 10r brown purple 7.50 7.50
Nos. 596-599 (4) 10.25 10.25

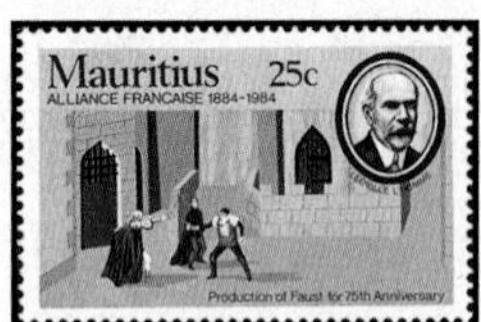

Alliance Francaise Centenary — A125

25c, Production of Faust, 1959. 1.25r, Award ceremony. 5r, Headquarters. 10r, Lion Mountain.

1984, Sept. 10 *Perf. 14½*
600 A125 25c multi .25 .25
601 A125 1.25r multi .65 .65
602 A125 5r multi 2.10 2.10
603 A125 10r multi 4.50 4.50
Nos. 600-603 (4) 7.50 7.50

Queen Mother 85th Birthday

Common Design Type

25c, Portrait, 1926. 2r, With Princess Margaret. 5r, On Clarence House balcony. 10r, Holding Prince Henry.

15r, On Royal Barge, reopening Stratford Canal, 1964.

Perf. 14½x14

1985, June 7 Wmk. 384

604 CD336 25c multi .25 .25
605 CD336 2r multi .55 .55
606 CD336 5r multi 1.50 1.50
607 CD336 10r multi 2.75 2.75
Nos. 604-607 (4) 5.05 5.05

Souvenir Sheet

608 CD336 15r multi 6.75 6.75

2nd Annual Indian Ocean Islands Games — A126

1985, Aug. 24 Wmk. 373 *Perf. 14½*

609 A126 25c High jump .35 .35
610 A126 50c Javelin .75 .75
611 A126 1.25r Cycling 4.75 4.75
612 A126 10r Wind surfing 8.25 8.25
Nos. 609-612 (4) 14.10 14.10

Pink Pigeon — A127

25c, Adult and young. 2r, Nest site display. 2.50r, Nesting. 5r, Preening.

1985, Sept. 2 Wmk. 384 *Perf. 14*

613 A127 25c multi *6.25* *1.25*
614 A127 2r multi *11.00* *2.75*
615 A127 2.50r multi *12.50* *4.25*
616 A127 5r multi *20.00* *6.00*
Nos. 613-616 (4) *49.75* *14.25*

World Wildlife Fund.

World Tourism Org., 10th Anniv. A128

25c, Patates Caverns. 35c, Colored Earth, Chamarel. 5r, Serpent Island. 10r, Coin de Mire Island.

1985, Sept. 20 *Perf. 14½*

617 A128 25c multi .60 .60
618 A128 35c multi .60 .60
619 A128 5r multi 2.75 2.75
620 A128 10r multi 11.00 11.00
Nos. 617-620 (4) 14.95 14.95

Port Louis, 250th Anniv. A129

25c, Old Town Hall. 1r, Al-Aqsa Mosque. 2.50r, Tamil-speaking Indians, settlement. 10r, Port Louis Harbor.

1985, Nov. 22 *Perf. 13½*

621 A129 25c multi .30 .30
622 A129 1r multi .90 .90
623 A129 2.50r multi 1.75 1.75
624 A129 10r multi 6.50 6.50
Nos. 621-624 (4) 9.45 9.45

Halley's Comet A130

25c, Halley, map. 1.25r, Newton's telescope, 1682 sighting. 3r, Mauritius from space. 10r, Giotto space probe.

1986, Feb. 21 Wmk. 384 *Perf. 14*

625 A130 25c multi .55 .55
626 A130 1.25r multi .75 .75
627 A130 3r multi 1.50 1.50
628 A130 10r multi 5.00 5.00
Nos. 625-628 (4) 7.80 7.80

Queen Elizabeth II 60th Birthday

Common Design Type

Designs: 25c, In uniform, Grenadier Guards, 1942. 75c, Investiture of the Prince of Wales, 1969. 2r, State visit with Prince Philip. 3r, State visit to Germany, 1978. 15r, Visiting Crown Agents' offices, 1983.

1986, Apr. 21 Litho. *Perf. 14½x14*

629 CD337 25c scar, black & sil .25 .25
630 CD337 75c ultra & multi .25 .25
631 CD337 2r green & multi .40 .40
632 CD337 3r violet & multi .55 .55
633 CD337 15r rose vio & multi 2.25 2.25
Nos. 629-633 (5) 3.70 3.70

Intl. Events — A131

Designs: 25c, World Food Day, FAO emblem, corn. 1r, African Regional Industrial Property Organization, 10th anniv., ARIPO emblem. 1.25r, Intl. Peace Year, IPY emblem. 10r, 1986 World Cup Soccer Championships, Athlete, MFA.

1986, July 25 Litho. *Perf. 14*

634 A131 25c multi .30 .30
635 A131 1r multi .65 .65
636 A131 1.25r multi .95 .95
637 A131 10r multi 7.25 7.25
Nos. 634-637 (4) 9.15 9.15

Orchids — A132

25c, Cryptopus elatus. 2r, Jumellea recta. 2.50r, Angraecum mauritianum. 10r, Bulbophyllum longiflorum.

1986, Oct. 3 Litho. *Perf. 14½*

638 A132 25c multi .65 .65
639 A132 2r multi 1.10 1.10
640 A132 2.50r multi 1.75 1.75
641 A132 10r multi 6.50 6.50
Nos. 638-641 (4) 10.00 10.00

Bridges A133

25c, Hesketh Bell. 50c, Sir Colville Deverell. 2.50r, Cavendish. 5r, Tamarin. 10r, Grand River North West.

1987, May 22 Wmk. 373

642 A133 25c multi .25 .25
643 A133 50c multi .60 .60
644 A133 2.50r multi 1.50 1.50
645 A133 5r multi 3.00 3.00
646 A133 10r multi 6.00 6.00
Nos. 642-646 (5) 11.35 11.35

The Bar, Bicent. A134

25c, Port Louis Supreme Court. 1r, Flacq District Court. 1.25r, Statue of Justice. 10r, Barristers, 1787-1987.

Perf. 14x14½

1987, June 2 Wmk. 384

647 A134 25c multi .25 .25
648 A134 1r multi .50 .50
649 A134 1.25r multi .55 .55
650 A134 10r multi 3.25 3.25
Nos. 647-650 (4) 4.55 4.55

Intl. Festival of the Sea — A135

25c, Dodo mascot, vert. 1.50r, Sailboats. 3r, Water-skier. 5r, Tall ship Svanen, vert.

1987, Sept. 5 Wmk. 373

651 A135 25c multi .75 .75
652 A135 1.50r multi 1.75 1.75
653 A135 3r multi 2.75 2.75
654 A135 5r multi 4.75 4.75
Nos. 651-654 (4) 10.00 10.00

Industrialization — A136

1987, Oct. 30 *Perf. 14*

655 A136 20c Toy .30 .30
656 A136 35c Spinning .30 .30
657 A136 50c Rattan .30 .30
658 A136 2.50r Optical .95 .95
659 A136 10r Stone carving 3.25 3.25
Nos. 655-659 (5) 5.10 5.10

Art & Architecture A137

Designs: 25c, Maison Ouvriere, Intl. Year of Shelter for the Homeless emblem. 1r, Paul et Virginie, a lithograph. 1.25r, Chateau Rosney. 2r, Old Farmhouse, Boulle. 5r, Three Peaks, watercolor.

1988, June 29 Wmk. 384 *Perf. 14½*

660 A137 25c multicolored .25 .25
661 A137 1r gray & black .40 .40
662 A137 1.25r multicolored .50 .50
663 A137 2r multicolored .60 .60
664 A137 5r multicolored 1.60 1.60
Nos. 660-664 (5) 3.35 3.35

Natl. Independence, 20th Anniv. — A138

Designs: 25c, University of Mauritius. 75c, Calisthenics at sunset in stadium. 2.50r, Runners, Sir Maurice Rault Stadium. 5r, Air Mauritius jet at gate, Sir Seewoosagur Ramgoolam Intl. Airport. 10r, Gov.-Gen. Veerasamy Ringadoo and Prime Minister Anerood Jugnauth.

1988, Mar. 11 Wmk. 373 *Perf. 14*

665 A138 25c multicolored .25 .25
666 A138 75c multicolored .25 .25
667 A138 2.50r multicolored .90 .90
668 A138 5r multicolored 1.60 1.60
669 A138 10r multicolored 3.25 3.25
Nos. 665-669 (5) 6.25 6.25

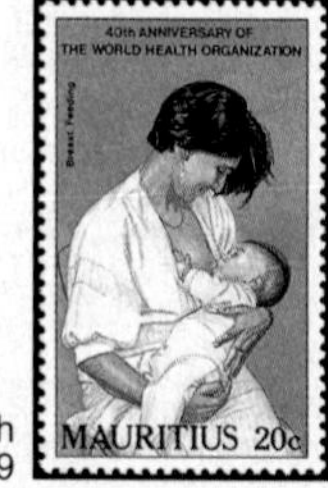

WHO, 40th Anniv. — A139

1988, July 1 Wmk. 373 *Perf. 13½*

670 A139 20c Breast-feeding .30 .30
671 A139 2r Immunization .90 .90
672 A139 3r Nutrition 1.75 1.75
673 A139 10r Emblem 5.00 5.00
Nos. 670-673 (4) 7.95 7.95

Mauritius Commercial Bank, Ltd., 150th Anniv. A140

25c, Bank, 1981, vert. 1r, Bank, 1897. 1.25r, Coat of arms, vert. 25r, 15-Dollar bank note, 1838.

1988, Sept. 1 Wmk. 373 *Perf. 14*

674 A140 25c multi .30 .30
675 A140 1r multi .40 .40
676 A140 1.25r multi .50 .50
677 A140 25r multi 8.00 8.00
Nos. 674-677 (4) 9.20 9.20

1988 Summer Olympics, Seoul A141

1988, Oct. 1

678 A141 25c shown .25 .25
679 A141 35c Wrestling .35 .35
680 A141 1.50r Running .65 .65
681 A141 10r Swimming 4.00 4.00
Nos. 678-681 (4) 5.25 5.25

Environmental Protection — A142

15c, Tropical reef. 30c, Greenshank. 50c, Round Island, vert. 75c, Bassin Blanc. 1r, Mangrove, vert. 1.50r, Whimbrel. 2r, Le Morne. 3r, Fish. 4r, Fern tree, vert. 5r, Riviere du Poste Estuary. 6r, Ecological scenery, vert. 10r, Phelsuma ornata, vert. 15r, Benares surf. 25r, Migratory birds, vert.

Wmk. 384 (20c, 40c, 50c, 1r, 10r), 373 (Others)

1989-97 Litho. *Perf. 14*

682 A142 15c multi .35 .35
a. Dated "1994" .35 .35
b. Dated "1995" .35 .35
683 A142 20c like #682 .35 .35
684 A142 30c multi .40 .40
a. Wmk. 384 .35 .35
b. As No. 684, dated "1995" .40 .40
685 A142 40c shown .35 .35
a. Wmk. 373 .35 .35
b. As a, dated "1994 .35 .35
c. As a, dated "1997 .35 .35
686 A142 50c multi .35 .35
687 A142 60c like #686 .35 .35
a. Dated "1997" .35 .35
688 A142 75c multi .35 .35
689 A142 1r multi .35 .35
a. Dated "1998" .35 .35
690 A142 1.50r multi .40 .40
691 A142 2r multi .40 .40

692 A142 3r multi .75 .75
693 A142 4r multi 1.00 1.00
a. Dated "1994" 1.00 1.00
b. Dated "1998" 1.00 1.00
694 A142 5r multi 1.00 1.00
a. Dated "1998" 1.00 1.00
695 A142 6r multi 1.50 1.50
a. Dated "1998" 1.50 1.50
696 A142 10r multi 2.40 2.40
a. Wmk. 373 ('97) 2.40 2.40
b. As a, dated "1995" 2.40 2.40
c. As a, dated "1997" 2.40 2.40
d. As a, dated "1998" 2.40 2.40
697 A142 15r multi 3.25 3.25
a. Wmk. 384 3.00 3.00
b. As No. 697, dated "1998" 3.25 3.25
698 A142 25r multi 5.50 5.50
a. Wmk. 384 ('96) 5.25 5.25
b. As a, dated "1997" 5.25 5.25
c. As No. 698, dated "1998" 5.50 5.50
Nos. 682-698 (17) 19.05 19.05

Issued: 40c, 3r-10r, 3/11/89; No. 685a, 2/19/91; 50c, 75c, 2r, 5r, 15r, 10/4/91; 20c, 60c, 3/96; others, 11/22/90.

For surcharge see No. 781.

A143

French Revolution, Bicent.: 30c, La Tour Sumeire, Place Du Theatre Municipal. 1r, Salle De Spectacle Du Jardin. 8r, Le Comte De Malartic. 15r, Anniv. emblem.

1989, July 14 **Wmk. 373**
702 A143 30c multicolored .25 .25
703 A143 1r multicolored .25 .25
704 A143 8r multicolored 2.00 2.00
705 A143 15r multicolored 3.75 3.75
Nos. 702-705 (4) 6.25 6.25

A144

Visit of Pope John Paul II: 30c, Cardinal Jean Margeot. 40c, Pope welcoming Prime Minister Aneerood Jugnauth to the Vatican, 1988. 3r, Mother Mary Magdalene of the Cross (1810-1889) and Filles des Marie Chapel, Port Louis, 1864. 6r, St. Francis of Assisi Church, 1756, Pamplemousses. 10r, Pope John Paul II.

1989, Oct. 13 ***Perf. 14x13½***
706 A144 30c multicolored .30 .30
707 A144 40c multicolored 1.00 1.00
708 A144 3r multicolored 2.00 2.00
709 A144 6r multicolored 4.25 4.25
710 A144 10r multicolored 6.75 6.75
Nos. 706-710 (5) 14.30 14.30

Jawaharlal Nehru, 1st Prime Minister of India — A145

Designs: 1.50r, Nehru and Indira, Rajiv and Sanjay Gandhi. 3r, With Mahatma Gandhi. 4r, With Nasser and Tito. 10r, With children.

1989, Oct. 13 **Wmk. 384** ***Perf. 14***
711 A145 40c shown 1.25 1.25
712 A145 1.50r multicolored 1.50 1.50
713 A145 3r multicolored 3.00 3.00
714 A145 4r multicolored 3.75 3.75
715 A145 10r multicolored 9.00 9.00
Nos. 711-715 (5) 18.50 18.50

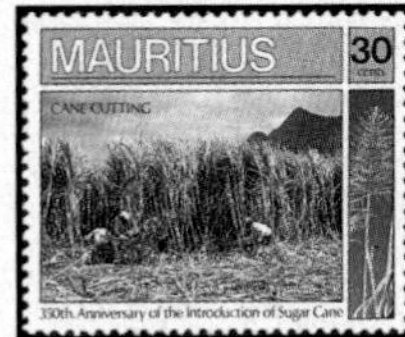

Sugar Cane Industry, 350th Anniv. A146

30c, Cutting cane. 40c, Refinery, 1867. 1r, Mechanically loading cane. 25r, Modern refinery.

Perf. 13½x14

1990, Jan. 10 **Litho.** **Wmk. 384**
716 A146 30c multi .30 .30
717 A146 40c multi .30 .30
718 A146 1r multi .75 .75
719 A146 25r multi 12.00 12.00
Nos. 716-719 (4) 13.35 13.35

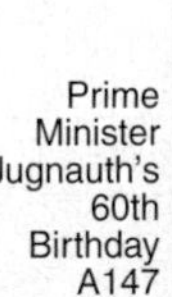

Prime Minister Jugnauth's 60th Birthday A147

Jugnauth: 35c, And symbols of the industrial estate. 40c, At his desk. 1.50r, And stock exchange emblem. 4r, And Gov.-Gen. Ramgoolam. 10r, And Pope John Paul II, map.

Wmk. 373

1990, Mar. 29 **Litho.** ***Perf. 14***
720 A147 35c multicolored .35 .35
721 A147 40c multicolored .35 .35
722 A147 1.50r multicolored 1.60 1.60
723 A147 4r multicolored 3.50 3.50
724 A147 10r multicolored 8.75 8.75
Nos. 720-724 (5) 14.55 14.55

Mauritian Television, 25th Anniv. A148

Anniversaries and Events: 30c, Death of Desjardins, naturalist, 150th anniversary, vert. 6r, Line barracks, 250th anniversary, vert. 8r, Municipality of Curepipe, centenary.

1990, July 5
725 A148 30c lt orange & multi .50 .50
726 A148 35c pink & multi .50 .50
727 A148 6r lt blue & multi 5.25 5.25
728 A148 8r lt green & multi 6.50 6.50
Nos. 725-728 (4) 12.75 12.75

Intl. Literacy Year A149

1r, Blind girl printing braille. 3r, Globe, open book. 10r, Open book, world map.

Wmk. 373

1990, Sept. 28 **Litho.** ***Perf. 14***
729 A149 30c shown .35 .35
730 A149 1r multi 1.40 1.40
731 A149 3r multi 2.50 2.50
732 A149 10r multi 8.75 8.75
Nos. 729-732 (4) 13.00 13.00

Elizabeth & Philip, Birthdays
Common Design Types
Wmk. 384

1991, June 17 **Litho.** ***Perf. 14½***
733 CD345 8r multicolored 1.75 1.75
734 CD346 8r multicolored 1.75 1.75
a. Pair, #733-734 + label 3.75 3.75

Port Louis, City Incorporation, 25th Anniv. — A150

Anniversaries and Events: 4r, Col. Draper, 150th death anniv., vert. 6r, Joseph Barnard, engraver of first Mauritius stamps, 175th birth anniv., vert. 10r, Spitfire, Mauritius' contribution to Allied war effort, 1939-1945.

Wmk. 373

1991, Aug. 18 **Litho.** ***Perf. 14***
735 A150 40c multicolored .30 .30
736 A150 4r multicolored 2.10 2.10
737 A150 6r multicolored 3.25 3.25
738 A150 10r multicolored 5.25 5.25
Nos. 735-738 (4) 10.90 10.90

Phila Nippon '91 — A151

Butterflies: 40c, Euploea euphon. 3r, Hypolimnas misippus, female. 8r, Papilio manlius. 10r, Hypolimnas misippus, male.

Perf. 14x14½

1991, Nov. 15 **Litho.** **Wmk. 373**
739 A151 40c multicolored .90 .90
740 A151 3r multicolored 2.00 2.00
741 A151 8r multicolored 4.75 4.75
742 A151 10r multicolored 5.50 5.50
Nos. 739-742 (4) 13.15 13.15

Flora and Fauna From Mauritius A152

Designs: 40c, Chelonia mydas, Tromelin. 1r, Ibis, Agalega. 2r, Takamaka flowers, Chagos Archipelago. 15r, Lambis violacea, St. Brandon.

1991, Dec. 13 ***Perf. 14***
743 A152 40c multicolored .75 .75
744 A152 1r multicolored 1.25 1.25
745 A152 2r multicolored 1.60 1.60
746 A152 15r multicolored 9.50 9.50
Nos. 743-746 (4) 13.10 13.10

Republic

Proclamation of the Republic of Mauritius — A153

40c, President. 4r, Prime Minister. 8r, Mauritian children. 10r, President's flag.

1992, Mar. 12
747 A153 40c multi .30 .30
748 A153 4r multi 1.40 1.40
749 A153 8r multi 3.00 3.00
750 A153 10r multi 3.50 3.50
Nos. 747-750 (4) 8.20 8.20

8th African Track and Field Championships A154

Designs: 40c, Games mascot, Tricolo. 4r, Sir Anerood Jugnauth Stadium, horiz. 5r, High jumper, horiz. 6r, Torch, emblem of games.

1992, June 25 ***Perf. 13½***
751 A154 40c multicolored .25 .25
752 A154 4r multicolored .85 .85
753 A154 5r multicolored 1.25 1.25
754 A154 6r multicolored 1.50 1.50
Nos. 751-754 (4) 3.85 3.85

Anniversaries and Events — A155

Designs: 40c, Flower, vert. 1r, Swami Krishnanandji Maharaj, vert. 2r, Boy and dog. 3r, Building, flags. 15r, Radio telescope antennae.

1992, Aug. 13
755 A155 40c multicolored .25 .25
756 A155 1r multicolored .60 .60
757 A155 2r multicolored .95 .95
758 A155 3r multicolored 1.50 1.50
759 A155 15r multicolored 6.50 6.50
Nos. 755-759 (5) 9.80 9.80

Fleurir Maurice, 25th anniv. (No. 755). 25th anniv. of Swami Maharaj's arrival (No. 756). Humane education (No. 757). Indian Ocean Commission, 10th anniv. (No. 758). Inauguration of radio telescope project (No. 759).

Bank of Mauritius, Silver Jubilee A156

Designs: 40c, Bank of Mauritius building, vert. 4r, Dodo gold bullion coin. 8r, First bank note issues. 15r, Foreign exchange reserves 1967-1992.

Perf. 14½x14, 14x14½

1992, Oct. 29 **Litho.** **Wmk. 373**
760 A156 40c multicolored .30 .30
761 A156 4r multicolored 1.60 1.60
762 A156 8r multicolored 3.50 3.50
763 A156 15r multicolored 5.75 5.75
Nos. 760-763 (4) 11.15 11.15

National Day, 25th Anniv. — A157

30c, Housing development. 40c, Computer showing gross domestic product. 3r, Flag in shape of map of Mauritius. 4r, Ballot box. 15r, Medal for Grand Commander of the Order of the Star & Key of the Indian Ocean.

1993, Mar. 12 ***Perf. 15x14***
764 A157 30c multicolored .25 .25
765 A157 40c multicolored .25 .25
766 A157 3r multicolored .55 .55
767 A157 4r multicolored .80 .80
768 A157 15r multicolored 2.75 2.75
Nos. 764-768 (5) 4.60 4.60

Air Mauritius Ltd., 25th Anniv. A158

40c, Bell 206B Jet Ranger. 3r, Boeing 747SP. 4r, ATR 42. 10r, Boeing 767-200ER.

1993, June 14 *Perf. 14*

769 A158 40c multicolored .85 .85
770 A158 3r multicolored 1.50 1.50
771 A158 4r multicolored 2.00 2.00
772 A158 10r multicolored 4.75 4.75
a. Souvenir sheet of 4, #769-772 11.50 11.50
Nos. 769-772 (4) 9.10 9.10

5th Francophone Summit — A159

Designs: 1r, 1715 Act of French Seizure of Mauritius, 1810 Act of Surrender. 5r, Signs. 6r, Page from Napoleonic Code. 7r, French publications.

1993, Oct. 16

773 A159 1r multicolored .25 .25
774 A159 5r multicolored 2.50 2.50
775 A159 6r multicolored 3.00 3.00
776 A159 7r multicolored 3.50 3.50
Nos. 773-776 (4) 9.25 9.25

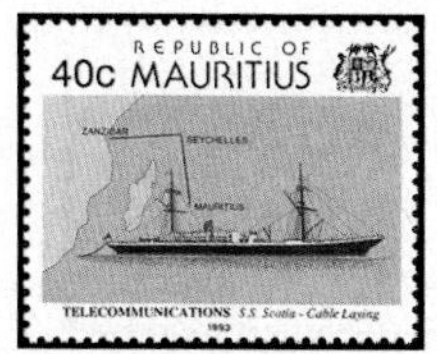

Telecommunications — A160

Designs: 40c, SS Scotia, cable laying. 3r, Morse code, Morse key. 4r, Signal mountain station. 8r, Communications satellite.

1993, Nov. 25 *Perf. 13*

777 A160 40c multicolored .65 .65
778 A160 3r multicolored 1.10 1.10
779 A160 4r multicolored 1.75 1.75
780 A160 8r multicolored 3.50 3.50
Nos. 777-780 (4) 7.00 7.00

No. 686 Surcharged

1993, Sept. 15 **Litho.** *Perf. 14*

781 A142 40c on 75c multi 2.00 2.00

Mammals — A161

Wmk. 384

1994, Mar. 9 **Litho.** *Perf. 14½*

782 A161 40c Mongoose .30 .30
783 A161 2r Hare 1.25 1.25
784 A161 8r Monkey 4.00 4.00
785 A161 10r Tenrec 4.50 4.50
Nos. 782-785 (4) 10.05 10.05

Anniversaries and Events — A162

40c, Dr. E. Brown-Sequard (1817-94). 4r, Silhouettes of family. 8r, World Cup trophy, US map. 10r, Control Tower, SSR Intl. Airport.

Wmk. 373

1994, June 16 **Litho.** *Perf. 14*

786 A162 40c multicolored .25 .25
787 A162 4r multicolored .75 .75
788 A162 8r multicolored 1.60 1.60
789 A162 10r multicolored 2.00 2.00
Nos. 786-789 (4) 4.60 4.60

Intl. Year of the Family (No. 787). 1994 World Cup Soccer Championships, US (No. 788). ICAO, 50th anniv. (No. 789).

Wreck of the St. Geran, 250th Anniv. A163

Wmk. 384

1994, Aug. 18 **Litho.** *Perf. 14*

790 A163 40c Leaving L'Orient .35 .35
791 A163 5r In rough seas 1.50 1.50
792 A163 6r Ship's bell 1.75 1.75
793 A163 10r Relics from ship 3.00 3.00
Nos. 790-793 (4) 6.60 6.60

Souvenir Sheet

794 A163 15r St. Geran, vert. 9.00 9.00

Children's Paintings of Leisure Activities — A164

Designs: 30c, "Ring Around the Rosey." 40c, Playing with balls, jump rope. 8r, Water sports. 10r, "Blindman's Buff."

Wmk. 373

1994, Oct. 25 **Litho.** *Perf. 13½*

795 A164 30c multicolored .25 .25
796 A164 40c multicolored .25 .25
797 A164 8r multicolored 1.50 1.50
798 A164 10r multicolored 1.90 1.90
Nos. 795-798 (4) 3.90 3.90

Spices — A165

Perf. 13x14

1995, Mar. 10 **Litho.** **Wmk. 373**

799 A165 40c Nutmeg .30 .30
800 A165 4r Coriander .85 .85
801 A165 5r Cloves 1.25 1.25
802 A165 10r Cardamon 2.40 2.40
Nos. 799-802 (4) 4.80 4.80

End of World War II

Common Design Type

Designs: No. 803, HMS Mauritius. No. 804, Mauritian servicemen, map of North Africa. No. 805, Catalina, Tombeau Bay.

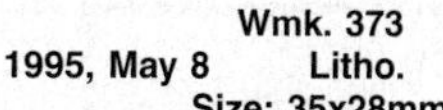

Wmk. 373

1995, May 8 **Litho.** *Perf. 14*

Size: 35x28mm

803 CD351 5r multicolored 2.50 2.50
804 CD351 5r multicolored 2.50 2.50
805 CD351 5r multicolored 2.50 2.50
Nos. 803-805 (3) 7.50 7.50

Anniversaries & Events — A166

1995, May 8

806 A166 40c multicolored .25 .25
807 A166 4r multicolored 1.25 1.25
808 A166 10r multicolored 2.75 2.75
Nos. 806-808 (3) 4.25 4.25

Construction of Mare Longue Reservoir, 50th anniv. (No. 806). Construction of Mahebourg-Curepipe Road, bicent. (No. 807). Great fire of Port Louis, cent. (No. 808).

Lighthouses A167

Designs: 30c, Ile Plate. 40c, Pointe aux Caves. 8r, Ile aux Fouquets. 10r, Pointe aux Canonniers.

Perf. 13x14

1995, Aug. 28 **Litho.** **Wmk. 373**

809 A167 30c multi 1.00 1.00
810 A167 40c multi 1.00 1.00
811 A167 8r multi 4.75 4.75
812 A167 10r multi 6.00 6.00
a. Souvenir sheet of 4, #809-812 15.00 15.00
Nos. 809-812 (4) 12.75 12.75

UN, 50th Anniv.

Common Design Type

Designs: 40c, Silhouettes of children under UNICEF umbrella. 4r, ILO contruction site. 8r, WMO satellite view of hurricane. 10r, Bread, grain representing FAO.

Wmk. 373

1995, Oct. 24 **Litho.** *Perf. 14*

813 CD353 40c multicolored .25 .25
814 CD353 4r multicolored .65 .65
815 CD353 8r multicolored 1.40 1.40
816 CD353 10r multicolored 1.60 1.60
Nos. 813-816 (4) 3.90 3.90

A168

1995, Dec. 8 **Litho.** *Perf. 13*

817 A168 60c pink & multi .25 .25
818 A168 4r blue & multi .55 .55
819 A168 8r yellow & multi 1.25 1.25
820 A168 10r green & multi 1.40 1.40
Nos. 817-820 (4) 3.45 3.45

Common Market for Eastern and Southern Africa (COMESA).

Snails A169

Designs: 60c, Pachystyla bicolor. 4r, Gonidomus pagodus. 5r, Harmogenanina implicata. 10r, Tropidophora eugeniae.

Wmk. 373

1996, Mar. 11 **Litho.** *Perf. 13*

821 A169 60c multicolored .35 .35
822 A169 4r multicolored 1.00 1.00
823 A169 5r multicolored 1.25 1.25
824 A169 10r multicolored 2.50 2.50
Nos. 821-824 (4) 5.10 5.10

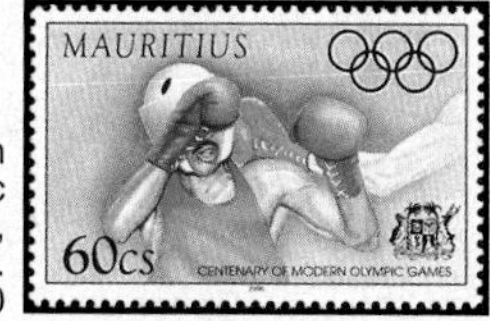

Modern Olympic Games, Cent. A170

Wmk. 384

1996, June 26 **Litho.** *Perf. 13½*

825 A170 60c Boxing .30 .30
826 A170 4r Badminton .75 .75
827 A170 5r Basketball .95 .95
828 A170 10r Table tennis 2.00 2.00
Nos. 825-828 (4) 4.00 4.00

Ships A171

Wmk. 373

1996, Sept. 30 **Litho.** *Perf. 14*

829 A171 60c SS Zambezia .30 .30
830 A171 4r MV Sir Jules .80 .80
831 A171 5r MV Mauritius 1.00 1.00
832 A171 10r MS Mauritius Pride 2.10 2.10
a. Souvenir sheet of 4, #829-832 5.00 5.00
Nos. 829-832 (4) 4.20 4.20

Post Office Ordinance, 150th Anniv. — A172

60c, Pillar box. 4r, Early handstamp cancel. 5r, Mobile post office. 10r, Carriole.

Wmk. 384

1996, Dec. 2 **Litho.** *Perf. 13½*

833 A172 60c multi .30 .30
834 A172 4r multi 1.10 1.10
835 A172 5r multi 1.50 1.50
836 A172 10r multi 3.00 3.00
Nos. 833-836 (4) 5.90 5.90

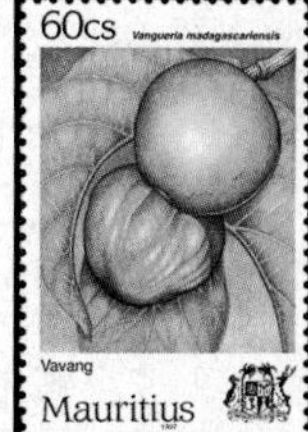

Fruit — A173

Designs: 60c, Vangueria madgascariensis. 4r, Mimusops coriacea. 5r, Syzgium jambos. 10r, Diospyros digyna.

Perf. 14x13½

1997, Mar. 10 **Litho.** **Wmk. 373**

837 A173 60c multicolored .25 .25
838 A173 4r multicolored .50 .50
839 A173 5r multicolored .65 .65
840 A173 10r multicolored 1.40 1.40
Nos. 837-840 (4) 2.80 2.80

Anniversaries and Events — A174

Designs: 60c, Ile de France, Mahé de La Bourdonnais. 1r, Exploration, La Perouse. 4r, Lady Gomm's Ball, Sir William Maynard Gomm. 6r, Skeleton of the Dodo, George Clark. 10r, Professor Brian Abel-Smith.

Wmk. 373

1997, June 9 Litho. *Perf. 13½*

841 A174 60c multicolored .45 .45
842 A174 1r multicolored .45 .45
843 A174 4r multicolored .85 .85
844 A174 6r multicolored 1.25 1.25
845 A174 10r multicolored 2.00 2.00
Nos. 841-845 (5) 5.00 5.00

First Postage Stamps of Mauritius, 150th Anniv. A175

Stamps: 60c, #1. 4r, #2. 5r, #2, #1, gold background. 10r, #1, #2, silver background. 20r, #2, #1 on "The Bordeaux Cover."

Wmk. 373

1997, Sept. 22 Litho. *Perf. 13½*

846 A175 60c multicolored .40 .40
847 A175 4r multicolored 1.25 1.25
a. Sheet of 12, 7 #846, 5 #847 6.75 6.75
848 A175 5r multicolored 1.50 1.50
849 A175 10r multicolored 3.25 3.25
Nos. 846-849 (4) 6.40 6.40

Souvenir Sheet

850 A175 20r multicolored 5.75 5.75

Booklet Panes and Booklets

846a Booklet pane of 10 3.50
Complete booklet, #846a 3.50
847b Booklet pane of 10 11.00
Complete booklet, #847b 11.00
848a Booklet pane of 10 14.50
Complete booklet, #848a 14.50
849a Booklet pane of 10 30.00
Complete booklet, #849a 30.00

Local Occupations — A176

Wmk. 373

1997, Dec. 1 Litho. *Perf. 14½*

851 A176 60c Wheelwright .40 .40
852 A176 4r Washerman .70 .70
853 A176 5r Shipwright .90 .90
854 A176 15r Quarryman 2.75 2.75
Nos. 851-854 (4) 4.75 4.75

Geckos A177

Designs: 1r, Phelsuma guentheri. 6r, Nactus serpensinsula. 7r, Nactus coindemirensis. 8r, Phelsuma edwardnewtonii.

Wmk. 373

1998, Mar. 11 Litho. *Perf. 13½*

855 A177 1r multicolored .40 .40
856 A177 6r multicolored 1.25 1.25
857 A177 7r multicolored 1.50 1.50
858 A177 8r multicolored 1.75 1.75
Nos. 855-858 (4) 4.90 4.90

Inland Transportation — A178

40c, Railroad. 5r, Truck. 6r, Bus, bicycles, cars. 10r, Boat.

Wmk. 373

1998, June 15 Litho. *Perf. 13½*

859 A178 40c multi .60 .60
860 A178 5r multi 1.25 1.25
861 A178 6r multi 1.60 1.60
862 A178 10r multi 2.50 2.50
Nos. 859-862 (4) 5.95 5.95

Dutch Landing, 400th Anniv. A179

50c, Maurits van Nassau, landing scene. 1r, Otaheite sugar cane, Frederik Hendrik Fort. 7r, Dutch map, 1670. 8r, Landing fleet.
25r, Ships of landing fleet.

Wmk. 373

1998, Sept. 18 Litho. *Perf. 13½*

863 A179 50c multicolored .35 .35
864 A179 1r multicolored .35 .35
865 A179 7r multicolored 1.75 1.75
866 A179 8r multicolored 2.25 2.25
Nos. 863-866 (4) 4.70 4.70

Souvenir Sheet

867 A179 25r multicolored 5.50 5.50

State Visit of South African Pres. Nelson Mandela — A180

1998, Sept. 10 Litho. *Perf. 14*

868 A180 25r multicolored 3.25 3.25

Waterfalls — A181

1r, Balfour Falls. 5r, Rochester Falls. 6r, GRSE Falls, vert. 10r, 500-Foot Falls, vert.

1998 Litho. Wmk. 384 *Perf. 13½*

869 A181 1r multicolored .50 .50
870 A181 5r multicolored 1.00 1.00
871 A181 6r multicolored 1.40 1.40
872 A181 10r multicolored 2.10 2.10
Nos. 869-872 (4) 5.00 5.00

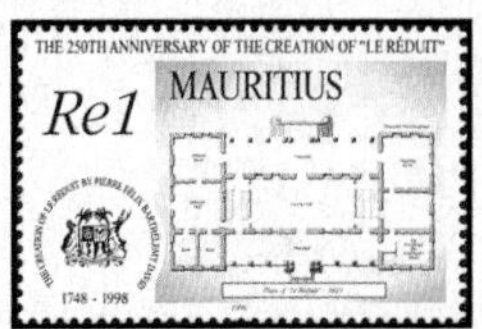

Creation of Presidential Residence "Le Réduit," 250th Anniv. — A182

Designs: 1r, Drawing of floor plan, 1823. 4r, Exterior view, by P.A.F. Thuillier, 1814. 5r, "Le Réduit," by Hassen Edun, 1998. 15r, Commemorative monument, 1998.

1998 Litho. Wmk. 373 *Perf. 14½*

873 A182 1r multicolored .40 .40
874 A182 4r multicolored .70 .70
875 A182 5r multicolored .90 .90
876 A182 15r multicolored 2.50 2.50
Nos. 873-876 (4) 4.50 4.50

Admiral Mahé de la Bourdonnais, 300th Birth Anniv. — A183

Wmk. 373

1999, Feb. 11 Litho. *Perf. 13*

877 A183 7r No. 115 1.75 1.75

Native Flowers A184

Designs: 1r, Clerodendron laciniatum. 2r, Senecio lemarckianus. 5r, Cylindrocline commersonii. 9r, Psiadia pollicina.

1999, Mar. 10 *Perf. 13½*

878 A184 1r multicolored .40 .40
879 A184 2r multicolored .40 .40
880 A184 5r multicolored .70 .70
881 A184 9r multicolored 1.25 1.25
Nos. 878-881 (4) 2.75 2.75

Paintings — A185

Designs: 1r, "The Washerwomen," by Hervé Masson. 3r, "The Casino," by Gaetan de Rosnay. 4r, "The Four Elements," by Andrée Poilly. 6r, "Coming out of Mass," by Xavier Le Juge de Segrais.

1999, June 18 *Perf. 14x15*

882 A185 1r multicolored .50 .50
883 A185 3r multicolored .60 .60
884 A185 4r multicolored .70 .70
885 A185 6r multicolored 1.10 1.10
Nos. 882-885 (4) 2.90 2.90

Old Sugar Mill Chimneys — A186

Wmk. 384

1999, Sept. 17 Litho. *Perf. 14¼*

886 A186 1r Alma .40 .40
887 A186 2r Antoinette .60 .60
888 A186 5r Belle Mare .90 .90
889 A186 7r Grande Rosalie 1.00 1.00
a. Souvenir sheet of 4, #886-889, Wmk. 373 3.25 3.25
Nos. 886-889 (4) 2.90 2.90

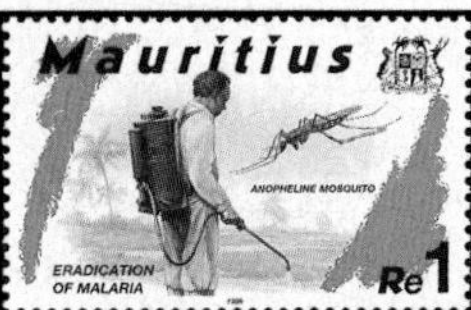

Achievements in the 20th Century — A187

Designs: 1r, Eradication of malaria. 2r, Emancipation of women. 5r, International Conference Center. 9r, Special sugars.

Perf. 13¼x13

1999, Dec. 7 Litho. Wmk. 373

890 A187 1r multi .40 .40
891 A187 2r multi .60 .60
892 A187 5r multi 1.10 1.10
893 A187 9r multi 2.00 2.00
Nos. 890-893 (4) 4.10 4.10

Chamber of Commerce & Industry, 150th Anniv. — A188

1r, Emblem. 2r, Computer chip. 7r, Francis Channell, 1st sec. 15r, Louis Léchelle, 1st pres.

2000, Jan. 25 Litho. *Perf. 13¼*

894 A188 1r multi .40 .40
895 A188 2r multi .60 .60
896 A188 7r multi 1.10 1.10
897 A188 15r multi 2.10 2.10
Nos. 894-897 (4) 4.20 4.20

Insects A189

Designs: 1r, Cratopus striga. 2r, Cratopus armatus. 3r, Cratopus chrysochlorus. 15r, Cratopus nigrogranatus.

Wmk. 373

2000, Mar. 29 Litho. *Perf. 14¼*

898 A189 1r multi .40 .40
899 A189 2r multi .40 .40
900 A189 3r multi .50 .50
901 A189 15r multi 2.40 2.40
a. Souvenir sheet of 4, #898-901 4.00 4.00
Nos. 898-901 (4) 3.70 3.70

2000 Summer Olympics, Sydney — A190

Wmk. 373

2000, June 28 Litho. *Perf. 14½*

902 A190 1r Handball .40 .40
903 A190 2r Archery .60 .60
904 A190 5r Sailing .80 .80
905 A190 15r Judo 2.40 2.40
Nos. 902-905 (4) 4.20 4.20

Sir Seewoosagur Ramgoolam, Birth Cent. — A191

Designs: 1r, Ramgoolam with Mother Teresa. 2r, As elected member of legislative council, vert. 5r, As student, 1926, vert. 15r, As Prime Minister, 1968, vert.

Perf. 13¼x13, 13x13¼

2000, Sept. 18 Litho. Wmk. 373

906-909 A191 Set of 4 4.25 4.25

Fish A192

Designs: 50c, Scarus ghobban. 1r, Cephalopholis sonnerati. 2r, Naso brevirostris. 3r, Lethrinus nebulosus. 4r, Centropyge debelius. 5r, Amphiprion chrysogaster. 6r, Forcipiger flavissimus. 7r, Acanthurus leucosternon. 8r, Pterois volitans. 10r, Siderea grisea. 15r, Carcharhinus wheeleri. 25r, Istiophorus platypterus.

Perf. 14½x14¼

2000, Oct. 9 Litho. Wmk. 373

910	A192	50c multi	.40	.40
911	A192	1r multi	.40	.40
912	A192	2r multi	.40	.40
913	A192	3r multi	.40	.40
914	A192	4r multi	.50	.50
915	A192	5r multi	.60	.60
916	A192	6r multi	.75	.75
917	A192	7r multi	.80	.80
918	A192	8r multi	1.00	1.00
919	A192	10r multi	1.10	1.10
a.		Souvenir sheet, #914, 917-919	3.50	3.50
b.		As #919, perf. 13½ ('08)	.75	.75
920	A192	15r multi	1.90	1.90
a.		Souvenir sheet, #913, 915-916, 920	3.50	3.50
921	A192	25r multi	2.75	2.75
a.		Souvenir sheet, #910-912, 921	3.50	3.50
		Nos. 910-921 (12)	11.00	11.00

No. 919b issued 5/28/08.

Famous People — A193

Designs: 1r, Affan Tank Wen (1842-1900). 5r, Alphonse Ravaton (1900-92), musician. 7r, Dr. Idrice Goumany (1859-89). 9r, Anjalay Coopen (d. 1943), martyr.

Perf. 14¼x14½

2000, Dec. 13 Wmk. 373

922-925 A193 Set of 4 3.75 3.75

Textile Industry A194

Designs: 1r, Finished sweater. 3r, Computer-aided machinery. 6r, T-shirt folder. 10r, Embroidery machine.

2001, Jan. 10 *Perf. 14½x14¼*

926-929 A194 Set of 4 3.25 3.25

End of Slavery and Indentured Labor, 166th Anniv. — A195

2001, Feb. 1 *Perf. 14x13½*

930 A195 7r multi 2.00 2.00

Trees A196

Designs: 1r, Foetida mauritana. 3r, Diospyros tessellaria. 5r, Sideroxylon puberulum. 15r, Gastonia mauritana.

2001, Mar. 21 Wmk. 373 *Perf. 13½*

931-934 A196 Set of 4 5.00 5.00

Expedition of Nicholas Baudin, Bicent. — A197

Designs: 1r, Ships Géographe and Naturaliste. 4r, Baudin and map of itinerary. 6r, Phedina borbonica. 10r, Napoleon Bonaparte and account of expedition, vert.

Wmk. 373

2001, June 13 Litho. *Perf. 14¼*

935-938 A197 Set of 4 4.00 4.00

20th Century Achievements — A198

Designs: 2r, Hotel School of Mauritius. 3r, Steel bar milling. 6r, Solar energy, Agalega. 10r, Indian Ocean Rim Association for Regional Cooperation.

Wmk. 373

2001, Sept. 12 Litho. *Perf. 13½*

939-942 A198 Set of 4 3.50 3.50

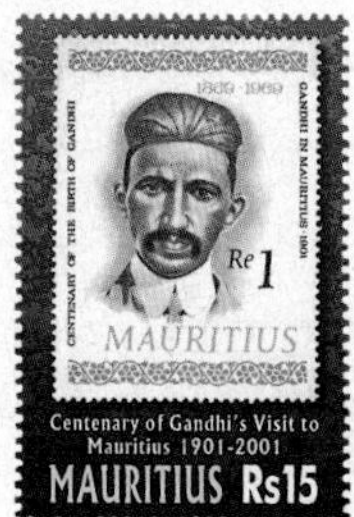

Mahatma Gandhi's Visit to Mauritius, Cent. — A199

2001, Oct. 2 *Perf. 14¾x14*

943 A199 15r No. 361 3.00 3.00

Copra Industry A200

Designs: 1r, Dehusking of coconuts, vert. 5r, Deshelling of coconuts. 6r, Drying copra. 10r, Oil extraction, vert.

2001, Dec. 5 *Perf. 13½*

944-947 A200 Set of 4 4.75 4.75

Republic, 10th Anniv. A201

Designs: 1r, Port development. 4r, Financial services. 5r, Water storage. 9r, Road development.

Perf. 13½x13¾

2002, Mar. 12 Litho. Wmk. 373

948-951 A201 Set of 4 4.00 4.00

Cicadas — A202

Designs: 1r, Abricta brunnea. 6r, Fractuosella darwini. 7r, Distantada thomaseti. 8r, Dinarobia claudeae.

Wmk. 373

2002, June 12 Litho. *Perf. 13½*

952-955 A202 Set of 4 3.50 3.50

a. Souvenir sheet, #952-955 4.00 4.00

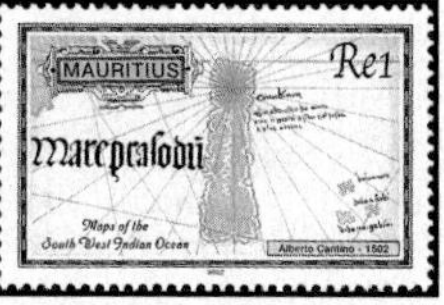

Maps of the Southwest Indian Ocean — A203

Maps by: 1r, Alberto Cantino, 1502. 3r, Jorge Reinel, 1520. 4r, Diogo Ribeiro, 1529. 10r, Gerard Mercator, 1569.

2002, Sept. 18

956-959 A203 Set of 4 5.00 5.00

Constellations A204

Designs: 1r, Orion. 7r, Sagittarius. 8r, Scorpius. 9r, Crux.

Perf. 14¼x14½

2002, Dec. 18 Litho. Wmk. 373

960-963 A204 Set of 4 4.00 4.00

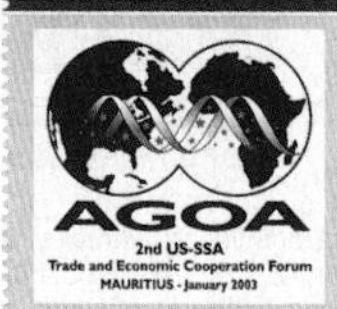

2nd U.S. — Sub-Saharan Africa Trade and Economic Forum — A205

Panel color: 1r, Violet blue. 25r, Red.

2003, Jan. *Perf. 14¼*

964-965 A205 Set of 2 3.25 3.25

Worldwide Fund for Nature (WWF) — A206

Echo parakeet: 1r, Chick. 2r, Fledgling. 5r, Female. 15r, Male.

Wmk. 373

2003, Mar. 19 Litho. *Perf. 13½*

966-969 A206 Set of 4 4.00 4.00

Flowers — A207

Designs: 1r, Trochetia boutoniana. 4r, Trochetia uniflora. 7r, Trochetia triflora. 9r, Trochetia parviflora.

Wmk. 373

2003, June 18 Litho. *Perf. 13½*

970-973 A207 Set of 4 3.75 3.75

Anniversaries and Events — A208

Designs: 2r, Sixth Indian Ocean Games, Mauritius. 6r, Mauritius Chamber of Agriculture, 150th anniv. 9r, Visit of Abbé de la Caille, 250th anniv. 10r, Mauritius Sugar Industry Research Institute, 50th anniv.

2003, Aug. 20

974-977 A208 Set of 4 5.75 5.75

Fortresses — A209

Designs: 2r, Batterie de la Pointe du Diable. 5r, Donjon St. Louis. 6r, Martello tower. 12r, Fort Adelaide,

2003, Dec. 10

978-981 A209 Set of 4 4.00 4.00

Indian Ocean Commission, 20th Anniv. — A210

Wmk. 373

2004, Feb. 16 Litho. *Perf. 13½*

982 A210 10r multi 2.25 2.25

Mountains — A211

Designs: 2r, Le Pouce. 7r, Corps de Garde. 8r, Le Chat et La Souris. 25r, Piton du Milieu.

2004, Mar. 11 *Perf. 14½x14¼*

983-986 A211 Set of 4 6.50 6.50

Traditional Trades — A212

Designs: 2r, Tinsmith. 7r, Cobbler. 9r, Blacksmith. 15r, Basket weaver.

Wmk. 373

2004, June 30 Litho. *Perf. 13½*
987-990 A212 Set of 4 5.00 5.00

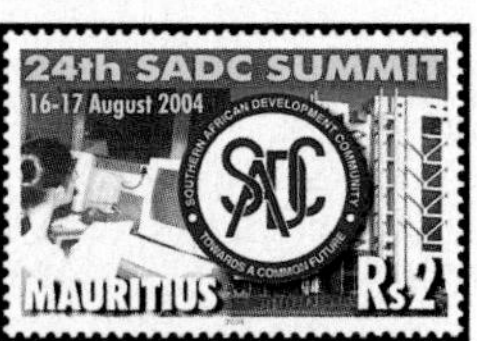

24th Southern Africa Development Community Summit — A213

Emblem, woman at computer, building and panel in: 2r, Gray. 50r, Red.

Wmk. 373

2004, Aug. 16 Litho. *Perf. 13½*
991-992 A213 Set of 2 7.50 7.50

Rodrigues Regional Assembly — A214

Designs: 2r, Plaine Corail Airport. 7r, Ecotourism. 8r, Agricultural products. 10r, Coat of arms.

Wmk. 373

2004, Oct. 12 Litho. *Perf. 13½*
993-996 A214 Set of 4 5.50 5.50

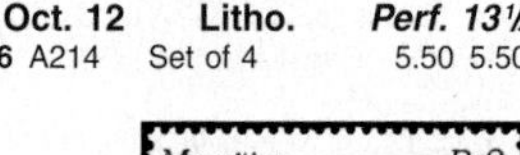

Anthurium Andreanum Varieties A215

Designs: 2r, Acropolis. 8r, Tropical. 10r, Paradisio. 25r, Fantasia.

2004, Dec. 1 *Perf. 13¼*
997-1000 A215 Set of 4 7.00 7.00

Round Island Flora and Fauna A216

Designs: 2r, Juvenile keel scale boa. 8r, Hurricane palm. 9r, Round Island petrel. 25r, Mazambron.

Wmk. 373

2005, Mar. 18 Litho. *Perf. 13¼*
1001-1004 A216 Set of 4 7.00 7.00

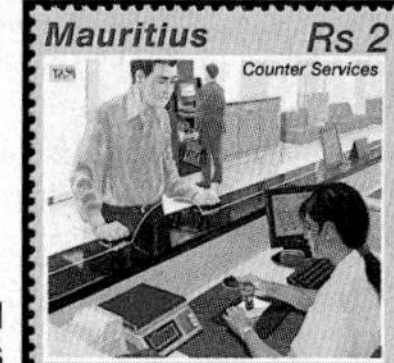

Postal Services A217

Designs: 2r, Counter services. 7r, Mail sorting. 8r, Mail distribution. 10r, Mail transfer.

Wmk. 373

2005, July 14 Litho. *Perf. 13¼*
1005-1008 A217 Set of 4 4.00 4.00

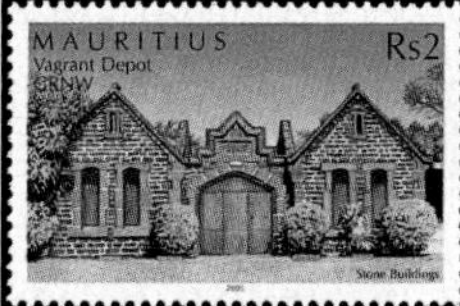

Stone Buildings — A218

Designs: 2r, Vagrant Depot, Grand River North West. 7r, Postal Museum, Port Louis. 16r, Carnegie Library, Curepipe.

Wmk. 373

2005, Oct. 9 Litho. *Perf. 13½*
1009-1011 A218 Set of 3 3.75 3.75

Ship Models — A219

Designs: 7r, 100-gun ship. 8r, Sampan. 9r, Roman galley. 16r, Drakkar.
25r, Drakkar, horiz.

Perf. 13¾x13½

2005, Dec. 20 Litho.
1012-1015 A219 Set of 4 6.00 6.00

Souvenir Sheet

Perf. 13½x13¾

1016 A219 25r multi 4.25 4.25

Mahebourg, Bicent. — A220

Designs: 2r, Market. 7r, Regattas. 8r, Le Lavoir. No. 1020, 16r, Pointe des Régates.

No. 1021, vert.: a, 16r, Mahé de la Bourdonnais. b, 16r, Gen. Charles Decaen.

Wmk. 373

2006, Feb. 4 Litho. *Perf. 13½*
1017-1020 A220 Set of 4 5.00 5.00

Souvenir Sheet

1021 A220 16r Sheet of 2, #a-b 5.25 5.25

Professor Basdeo Bissoondoyal (1906-91), Educator — A221

Wmk. 373

2006, Apr. 15 Litho. *Perf. 13¾*
1022 A221 10r multi 1.10 1.10

Ecological History — A222

Designs: 2r, Biological control of locusts with introduction of mynah birds, 1763. 8r, Fish repopulation with artificial reefs, 1980. 10r, Erosion control with terraces in Rodrigues, 1958. 25r, First captive breeding of giant tortoises, 1881.

2006, June 5 *Perf. 13½*
1023-1026 A222 Set of 4 5.50 5.50

Crabs — A223

Designs: 2r, Tourloulou crab. 7r, Land crab. 8s, Freshwater crab. 25r, Coconut crab.

Wmk. 373

2006, Oct. 9 Litho. *Perf. 13¼*
1027-1030 A223 Set of 4 4.50 4.50

Traditional Children's Activities — A224

Designs: 5r, Sapsiwaye. 10r, Marbles, horiz. 15r, Hop Scotch, horiz. 25r, Kite flying.

Perf. 13¾x13½, 13½x13¾

2006, Dec. 7
1031-1034 A224 Set of 4 3.50 3.50

Corals A225

Designs: 3r, Rodrigues endemic coral. 5r, Soft coral. 10r, Chagos coral. 15r, Head coral. 22r, Table coral. 25r, Tube coral.

Wmk. 373

2007, Apr. 30 Litho. *Perf. 13½*
1035-1040 A225 Set of 6 5.25 5.25

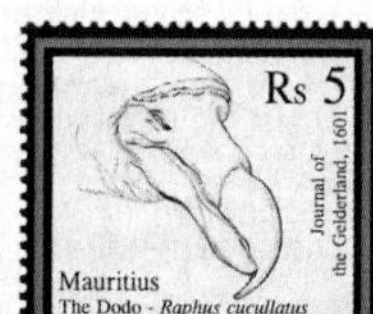

Drawings of Dodo Birds — A226

Drawing: 5r, From Journal of the Gelderland, 1601. 10r, By Adrian van de Venne, 1626. 15r, Published by Harrison, 1798. No. 1044, 25r, By J. W. Frohawk, 1905.

No. 1045, By Julian Pender Hume, 2001, vert.

Wmk. 373

2007, June 25 Litho. *Perf. 13½*
1041-1044 A226 Set of 4 3.50 3.50

Souvenir Sheet

Perf. 13x13¼

1045 A226 25r multi 1.60 1.60

No. 1045 contains one 28x45mm stamp.

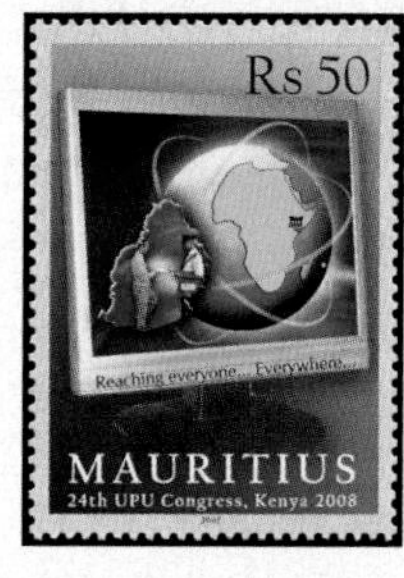

24th UPU Congress, Nairobi A227

Wmk. 373

2007, Oct. 9 Litho. *Perf. 13¼*
1046 A227 50r multi 3.50 3.50

Due to political unrest in Kenya, the UPU Congress was moved to Geneva, Switzerland.

Anniversaries — A228

Designs: 5r, Ministerial System, 50th anniv. 10r, Arrival in Mauritius of Manilall Doctor, cent., vert. 15r, Scouting, cent., vert. 25r, First meteorological observatory in Mauritius, 175th anniv.

2007, Dec. 4 *Perf. 13½*
1047-1050 A228 Set of 4 3.75 3.75

Ministerial System, 50th Anniv. (With Corrected Photograph) — A229

2007, Dec. 4 Litho. *Perf. 13½*
1051 A229 5r multi .35 .35

The photo in the LR corner on No. 1051 differs from the photo in the LR corner on No. 1047.

Authors Who Mentioned Mauritius — A230

Author and work: 5r, Bernardin de St. Pierre (1737-1814), Paul et Virginie. 10r, Alexandre Dumas (père) (1802-70), Georges. 15r, Charles Baudelaire (1821-67), A une Dame Creole. 22r, Mark Twain (1835-1910), Following the Equator. 25r, Joesph Conrad (1857-1924), A Smile of Fortune.

Wmk. 406

2008, Dec. 8 Litho. *Perf. 13½*
1052-1056 A230 Set of 5 4.75 4.75

Flowers — A231

Designs: 3r, Myonima obovata. 4r, Cylindrocline lorencei. 5r, Crinum mauritianum. 6r, Elaeocarpus bojeri. 7r, Bremeria landia. 8r, Distephanus populifolius. 9r, Gaertnera longifolia. 10r, Dombeya acutangula. 15r, Aphloia theiformis. 22r, Barleria observatrix. 25r, Roussea simplex. 50r, Hibiscus fragilis.

Wmk. 406

2009, Apr. 9 Litho. *Perf. 13½*

1057 A231 3r multi	.25	.25
a. Dated "2016"	.25	.25
1058 A231 4r multi	.25	.25
1059 A231 5r multi	.30	.30
1060 A231 6r multi	.35	.35
1061 A231 7r multi	.45	.45
a. Dated "2010"	.50	.50
b. Dated "2015"	.40	.40
1062 A231 8r multi	.50	.50
a. Dated "2010"	.55	.55
b. Dated "2016"	.45	.45
1063 A231 9r multi	.55	.55
1064 A231 10r multi	.60	.60
1065 A231 15r multi	.90	.90
a. Dated "2010"	1.00	1.00
1066 A231 22r multi	1.40	1.40
1067 A231 25r multi	1.50	1.50
a. Dated "2010"	1.75	1.75
b. Dated "2016"	1.40	1.40
1068 A231 50r multi	3.00	3.00
Nos. 1057-1068 (12)	10.05	10.05

Issued: Nos. 1057a, 1062b, 1067b, 6/1/16.

Extinct Mauritian Giant Tortoises — A232

Designs: 5r, Cylindraspis peltastes. 10r, Cylindraspis vosmaeri, vert. 15r, Cylindraspis inepta. 25r, Cylindraspis triserrata, vert. 50r, Cylindraspis peltastes, diff.

Wmk. 406

2009, July 16 Litho. *Perf. 13½*

1069-1072 A232 Set of 4 3.50 3.50

Souvenir Sheet

1073 A232 50r multi 3.25 3.25

New Mauritius Travel Slogan — A233

No. 1074 — New slogan on: a, Yellow background. b, Mountain background.

Perf. 13½x13

2009, Oct. 9 Litho. Wmk. 406

1074 A233 7r Vert. pair, #a-b .95 .95

Chinese Chamber of Commerce, Cent. (in 2008) — A234

Dr. Kissoonsingh Hazareesingh, Historian, Birth Cent. — A235

Capture of Rodrigues Island by British, Bicent. — A236

Teeluckpersad Callychurn, Postmaster General, Birth Cent. — A237

Wmk. 406

2009, Nov. 30 Litho. *Perf. 13½*

1075 A234 7r multi	.50	.50
1076 A235 14r multi	1.00	1.00
1077 A236 20r multi	1.40	1.40
1078 A237 21r multi	1.50	1.50
Nos. 1075-1078 (4)	4.40	4.40

Muhammad al-Idrisi (c.1100-c.1165), Geographer and Cartographer A238

Wmk. 406

2010, Aug. 2 Litho. *Perf. 13½*

1079 A238 27r multi 1.90 1.90

Mauritius No. 2 — A239

2010, Aug. 20

1080 A239 30r multi 2.00 2.00

Expo 2010, Shanghai.

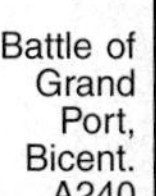

Battle of Grand Port, Bicent. A240

Designs: 14r, Battle scene. 21r, Ile de la Passe.

2010, Aug. 20

1081-1082 A240 Set of 2 2.25 2.25

Sir Seewoosagur Ramgoolam (1900-85), Prime Minister — A241

Litho. & Embossed With Foil Application

2010, Sept. 18 Wmk. 406

1083 A241 100r multi 6.75 6.75

British Conquest of Isle de France, Bicent. — A242

Designs: 2r, Capitulation document. 7r, British landing on Isle de France, horiz.

Wmk. 406

2010, Dec. 3 Litho. *Perf. 13½*

1084-1085 A242 Set of 2 .60 .60

UNESCO World Heritage Sites — A244

Designs: 7r, Steps, Aapravasi Ghat. 14r, Mountain, Le Morne, horiz. 15r, Monument, Le Morne, horiz. 25r, Hospital kitchen, Aapravasi Ghat.

Wmk. 406

2011, Apr. 11 Litho. *Perf. 13½*

1087-1090 A244	Set of 4	4.50	4.50
1090a	Souvenir sheet of 4, #1087-1090	4.50	4.50

19th Century Census Form A245

Sir Moilin Jean Ah Chuen (1911-91), Politician — A246

Dr. Maurice Curé (1886-1977), Co-Founder of Labor Party — A247

Médine Sugar Estates, Cent. A248

2011, June 30

1091 A245 7r multi	.50	.50
1092 A246 14r multi	1.00	1.00
1093 A247 21r multi	1.50	1.50
1094 A248 25r multi	1.75	1.75
Nos. 1091-1094 (4)	4.75	4.75

Observation of Transit of Venus From Rodrigues by Alexandre Guy Pingré — A249

Intl. Year of Chemistry — A250

Intl. Year of Forests A251

2011, Sept. 8

1095 A249 11r multi	.80	.80
1096 A250 12r multi	.85	.85
1097 A251 17r multi	1.25	1.25
Nos. 1095-1097 (3)	2.90	2.90

HIV and AIDS Awareness A252

Post Office in Rodrigues, 150th Anniv. — A253

2011, Oct. 9

1098 A252 7r multi	.50	.50
1099 A253 21r multi	1.50	1.50

Tea Industry — A254

Designs: 7r, Tea flushes. 8r, Tea pickers, horiz. 15r, Loose tea on saucer, spoon, tea bags, horiz. 25r, Tea pot and cup.

2011, Dec. 19
1100-1103 A254 Set of 4 3.75 3.75

Law Day A255

Designs: 7r, Grand Port District Court. 8r, Interior of Court of Justice. 15r, Sir Michel Rivalland, 1967-70 Chief Justice, vert. 20r, Gavel.

2012, Apr. 4 ***Perf. 13¼***
1104-1107 A255 Set of 4 3.50 3.50

Mauritius postal officials have declared sheets of four and six 9r stamps depicting Michael Jackson as "illegal."

Mauritius Turf Club, 200th Anniv. — A256

Designs: 7r, Horse race. 10r, Aerial view of Champ de Mars Race Track. 14r, Grandstand, 1917. 21r, Emblem of Mauritius Turf Club, vert. 50r, Jockey on horse in paddock.

2012, June 25 ***Perf. 13½***
1108-1111 A256 Set of 4 3.50 3.50

Souvenir Sheet

1112 A256 50r multi 3.25 3.25

Customs Department — A257

Designs: 7r, Old and new Custom Houses. 8r, Customs officer scanning packages. 20r, Dog sniffing packages, vert. 25r, Customs officers on boat.

2012, Sept. 10
1113-1116 A257 Set of 4 4.00 4.00

Intl. Year of Cooperatives — A258

Diplomatic Relations Between Mauritius and People's Republic of China, 40th Anniv. — A259

Scouting in Mauritius, Cent. — A260

2012, Oct. 9

1117 A258 6r multi	.40	.40
1118 A259 14r multi	.90	.90
1119 A260 21r multi	1.40	1.40
Nos. 1117-1119 (3)	2.70	2.70

Famous Men — A261

Designs: 6r, Marcel Cabon (1912-72), musician. 10r, Goolam Mahomed Dawjee Atchia, newspaper publisher.

2012, Nov. 9
1120-1121 A261 Set of 2 1.10 1.10

Methods of Mail Conveyance — A262

Early Mauritius Stamps — A263

No. 1122: a, Foot messenger, 1772. b, Packet mail landing, 1915. c, Express letter messenger, 1930. d, Inland mail arrival, 1935. e, Delivery of mail bags by van, 2012.

No. 1123: a, Mauritius #1 and copper plate cliché. b, Mauritius #2 and copper plate cliché.

2012, Dec. 21 ***Perf. 12½x13***

1122 Horiz. strip of 5	2.25	2.25
a.-e. A262 7r Any single	.45	.45

Souvenir Sheet

Perf. 13½

1123 A263 25r Sheet of 2, #a-b, + label 3.25 3.25

Postal services in Mauritius, 240th anniv.

Sites and Monuments — A264

Designs: 5r, Belle Mare Prison. 9r, Bel Ombre Château. 10r, IBL Building, Bowen Square. 18r, Le Batelage.

Wmk. 406

2013, Apr. 18 **Litho.** ***Perf. 13½***
1124-1127 A264 Set of 4 2.75 2.75

Intl. Red Cross, 150th Anniv. — A265

2013, May 30
1128 A265 3r multi .25 .25

63rd FIFA Congress, Mauritius — A266

2013, May 30
1129 A266 18r multi 1.25 1.25

Renewable Energy — A267

Designs: 2r, Solar energy. 6r, Wind energy.

2013, May 30
1130-1131 A267 Set of 2 .55 .55

Flora and Fauna — A268

Designs: 3r, Hurricane palm. 10r, Oeoniella polystachys orchid. 18w, Mascarene swallow.

Wmk. 406

2013, Aug. 30 **Litho.** ***Perf. 13½***
1132-1134 A268 Set of 3 2.00 2.00

Famous Men — A269

Designs: 9r, Hervé Masson (1919-90), painter. 26r, Prof. Stanley Alexander de Smith (1922-74), Constitiutional Commissioner of Mauritius.

Wmk. 406

2013, Dec. 11 **Litho.** ***Perf. 13½***
1135-1136 A269 Set of 2 2.40 2.40

Flora and Fauna A270

Designs: 7r, Dragonfly. 14r, Roussette de Rodrigues. 25r, Pignon d'Inde, vert.

Wmk. 406

2014, Mar. 28 **Litho.** ***Perf. 13½***
1137-1139 A270 Set of 3 3.00 3.00

Father Jacques-Désiré Laval (1803-64), Missionary — A271

Children's Office Ombudsperson, 10th Anniv. — A272

Arrival in Mauritius of Rev. Jean Joseph Lebrun as Missionary, 200th Anniv. — A273

Introduction of Mobile Telephones in Mauritius, 25th Anniv. — A274

Wmk. 406

2014, May 28 **Litho.** ***Perf. 13½***

1140 A271 8r multi	.55	.55
1141 A272 14r multi	.95	.95
1142 A273 15r multi	1.00	1.00
1143 A274 25r multi	1.60	1.60
Nos. 1140-1143 (4)	4.10	4.10

Green Turtle A275

Unwmk.

2014, Oct. 9 Litho. *Perf. 14*
1144 A275 14r multi .90 .90

See Comoro Islands No. , France No. 4695, French Southern and Antarctic Territories No. 511, Malagasy Republic No. 1637, Seychelles No. 904.

Disaster Risk Reduction — A276

Wmk. 406

2015, June 29 Litho. *Perf. 13½*
1145 A276 17r multi .95 .95

Ninth Indian Ocean Games, Réunion A277

Wmk. 406

2015, Aug. 1 Litho. *Perf. 13½*
1146 A277 17r multi .95 .95

Landing of French on Mauritius, 300th Anniv. — A278

Perf. 13¼

2015, Sept. 25 Litho. Unwmk.
1147 A278 17r multi .95 .95

See France No. 4874.

National Archives, 200th Anniv. — A279

Perf. 13x13½

2015, Dec. 7 Litho. Wmk. 406
1148 A279 10r multi .55 .55

United Nations Sustainable Development Goals — A280

Wmk. 406

2016, May 9 Litho. *Perf. 13½*
1149 A280 27r multi 1.60 1.60

Freshwater Fauna — A281

Designs: 1r, Giant mottled eel. 10r, Water scorpion. 18r, Nile tilapia. 32r, Freshwater shrimp.

Wmk. 406

2016, June 6 Litho. *Perf. 13½*
1150-1153 A281 Set of 4 3.50 3.50

Maritime Air Squadron's New Dornier MPCG 04 — A282

Wmk. 406

2016, July 13 Litho. *Perf. 13½*
1154 A282 11r multi .65 .65

Nature Walks — A283

Designs: 2r, Powder Mills Nature Walk. 20r, Sophie Nature Walk.

Wmk. 406

2016, Sept. 15 Litho. *Perf. 13½*
1155-1156 A283 Set of 2 1.25 1.25

Flowers — A284

Designs: 11r, Bacopa monnieri. 13r, Ludwigia octovalvis. 16r, Nelumbo nucifera. 31r, Nelumbo nucifera, diff.

Wmk. 406

2016, Oct. 18 Litho. *Perf. 13½*
1157-1160 A284 Set of 4 4.00 4.00

World Diabetes Day — A285

2016, Nov. 14 Litho. *Perf. 13½*
1161 A285 10r multi .55 .55

SPECIAL DELIVERY STAMPS

SD1

1903 Wmk. 1 *Perf. 14*

Red Surcharge

E1 SD1 15c on 15c ultra 14.50 37.50

SD2

SD3

EXPRESS DELIVERY (INLAND) 15 c

New Setting with Smaller "15c" without period — SD3a

1904

E2 SD2 15c on 15c ultra 62.50 95.00
- *a.* "INLAND" inverted 3,400.
- *b.* Inverted "A" in "INLAND" 1,700. 1,250.

E3 SD3 15c on 15c ultra 9.00 3.75
- *a.* Double surcharge, both inverted 1,875. 1,900.
- *b.* Inverted surcharge 1,250. 800.00
- *c.* Vert. pair, imperf between *6,250.*

E3F SD3a 15c on 15c ultra 840.00 800.00
- *g.* Inverted surcharge 1,775.
- *h.* Double surcharge 3,750.
- *i.* Double surcharge, both inverted — 5,500.
- *j.* "c" omitted 2,750.

To make No. E2 the word "INLAND" was printed on No. E1. For Nos. E3 and E3F, new settings of the surcharge were made with different spacing between the words.

SD4

SD5

E4 SD4 15c green & red 18.00 6.25
- *a.* Double surcharge 800.00 800.00
- *b.* Inverted surcharge 1,000. 900.00
- *c.* "LNIAND." —
- *d.* As "c," double surcharge *900.00* 800.00

E5 SD5 18c green & black 3.00 32.50
- *a.* Exclamation point (!) instead of "I" in "FOREIGN" 800.00

POSTAGE DUE STAMPS

Catalogue values for unused stamps in this section are for Never Hinged items.

Numeral — D1

Perf. 14½x14

1933-54 Typo. Wmk. 4

J1	D1	2c black	1.50	.60
J2	D1	4c violet	.60	.80
J3	D1	6c red	.70	*.95*
J4	D1	10c green	.85	*2.40*
J5	D1	20c ultramarine	.75	*2.60*
J6	D1	50c dp red lilac ('54)	.65	*19.00*
J7	D1	1r orange ('54)	.85	*19.00*
		Nos. J1-J7 (7)	5.90	*45.35*

1966-68 Wmk. 314 *Perf. 14*

J8	D1	2c black ('67)	2.75	3.75

Perf. 14½14

J9	D1	4c rose violet ('68)	1.90	8.50
J10	D1	6c dp orange ('68)	7.00	27.50
J11	D1	10c yel green ('67)	.35	2.10
J12	D1	20c ultramarine	2.40	5.75
J13	D1	50c dp red lilac ('68)	.80	13.00
		Nos. J8-J13 (6)	15.20	60.60

Nos. 445-446, 450, 455, 457, 462 Surcharged "POSTAGE/ DUE" and New Value

Wmk. 373

1982, Oct. 25 Litho. *Perf. 13½*

J14	A92	10c on 15c multi	.25	.25
J15	A92	20c on 20c multi	.25	.60
J16	A91	50c on 60c multi	.35	.35
J17	A92	1r on 1.20r multi	.45	.35
J18	A92	1.50r on 1.50r multi	.60	.85
J19	A91	5r on 15r multi	1.10	2.50
		Nos. J14-J19 (6)	3.00	4.90

MAYOTTE

mä-ˈyät

LOCATION — One of the Comoro Islands situated in the Mozambique Channel midway between Madagascar and Mozambique (Africa)
GOVT. — French Colony
AREA — 144 sq. mi.
POP. — 149,336 (1999 est.)
CAPITAL — Mamoutzou
See Comoro Islands.

100 Centimes = 1 Franc
100 Cents = 1 Euro (2002)

Stamps of Mayotte were replaced successively by those of Madagascar, Comoro Islands and France. Individual issues were resumed in 1997.

See France No. 2271 for French stamp inscribed "Mayotte."

Catalogue values for unused stamps in this country are for Never Hinged items, beginning with Scott 75 in the regular postage section, and Scott C1 in the airpost section.

Navigation and Commerce — A1

Perf. 14x13½

1892-1907 Typo. Unwmk.
Name of Colony in Blue or Carmine

1	A1	1c blk, *lil bl*	1.40	.90
2	A1	2c brn, *buff*	1.90	1.40
a.		Name double	575.00	500.00
3	A1	4c claret, *lav*	2.40	1.75
4	A1	5c grn, *grnsh*	4.75	3.25
5	A1	10c blk, *lavender*	9.00	4.75
6	A1	10c red ('00)	75.00	52.50
7	A1	15c blue, quadrille paper	17.50	10.50
8	A1	15c gray ('00)	140.00	110.00
9	A1	20c red, *grn*	13.50	10.50
10	A1	25c blk, *rose*	14.50	9.75
11	A1	25c blue ('00)	16.00	13.50
12	A1	30c brn, *bis*	22.00	16.00
13	A1	35c blk, *yel* ('00)	11.00	8.00
14	A1	40c red, *straw*	22.50	16.00
15	A1	45c blk, *gray grn* ('07)	21.00	20.00
16	A1	50c carmine, *rose*	32.00	22.50
17	A1	50c brn, *az* ('00)	30.00	30.00
18	A1	75c dp vio, *org*	30.00	21.00
19	A1	1fr brnz grn, *straw*	32.00	22.50
20	A1	5fr red lil, *lav* ('99)	135.00	130.00
		Nos. 1-20 (20)	631.45	504.80

Perf. 13½x14 stamps are counterfeits.

Issues of 1892-1907 Surcharged in Black or Carmine

1912

22	A1	5c on 2c brn, *buff*	3.25	*4.00*
23	A1	5c on 4c cl, *lav* (C)	2.00	2.00
24	A1	5c on 15c bl (C)	2.00	2.00
25	A1	5c on 20c red, *grn*	2.00	*2.40*
26	A1	5c on 25c blk, *rose* (C)	1.60	1.60
a.		Double surcharge	360.00	
b.		Pair, one stamp without surcharge	1,000.	
27	A1	5c on 30c brn, *bis* (C)	2.00	2.00
28	A1	10c on 40c red, *straw*	2.00	*2.40*
a.		Double surcharge	360.00	
29	A1	10c on 45c blk, *gray grn* (C)	2.00	2.00
a.		Double surcharge	360.00	*325.00*
30	A1	10c on 50c car, *rose*	4.50	*5.00*
31	A1	10c on 75c dp vio, *org*	3.50	*4.25*
32	A1	10c on 1fr brnz grn, *straw*	3.50	*4.25*
		Nos. 22-32 (11)	28.35	*31.90*

Two spacings between the surcharged numerals are found on Nos. 22-32. For detailed listings, see the *Scott Classic Specialized Catalogue of Stamps and Covers.*

Nos. 22-32 were available for use in Madagascar and the entire Comoro archipelago.

Catalogue values for unused stamps in this section, from this point to the end of the section, are for Never Hinged items.

Marianne Type of France Overprinted

1997, Jan. 2 Engr. *Perf. 13*
Design A1161

75	10c on #2179	.25	*.30*
76	20c on #2180	.25	*.30*
77	50c on #2181	.25	*.30*
78	1fr on #2182	.55	.55
79	2fr on #2333	1.10	1.10
80	(2.50fr) on #2340	1.25	1.25
81	2.70fr on #2335	1.50	1.50
82	3.80fr on #2337	2.00	2.00
83	5fr on #2194	2.75	2.75
84	10fr on #2195	5.50	5.50
	Nos. 75-84 (10)	15.40	15.55

Ylang Ylang — A5

1997, Jan. 2 Litho. *Perf. 13½x13*
85 A5 2.70fr multicolored 1.50 1.50

Coat of Arms — A6

1997, Jan. 2 *Perf. 13x13½*
86 A6 3fr multicolored 1.60 1.60
a. Sheet of 4 7.25 7.25

No. 86a issued 6/19/99 for Philex France 99.

Le Banga — A7

1997, May 31 Litho. *Perf. 13*
87 A7 3.80fr multicolored 1.90 1.90

Dzen Dzé Musical Instrument A8

Photo. & Engr.
1997, May 31 *Perf. 12½*
88 A8 5.20fr multicolored 2.50 2.50

Lemur A9

1997, Aug. 30 Engr. *Perf. 12*
89 A9 3fr red & dk brown 1.60 1.60

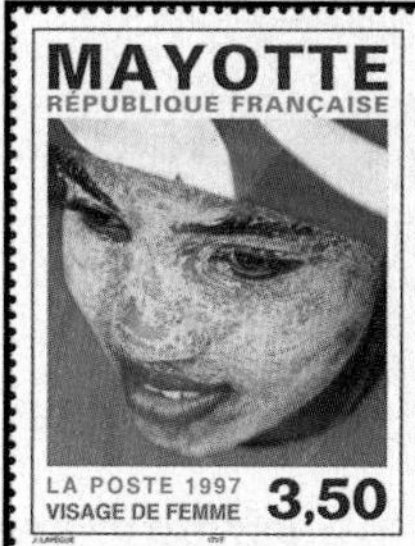

Face of a Woman A10

1997, Aug. 30 Litho. *Perf. 13*
90 A10 3.50fr multicolored 1.75 1.75

Marine Life — A11

1997, Nov. 29 Litho. *Perf. 13*
91 A11 3fr multicolored 1.60 1.60

Longoni Port — A12

1998, Jan. 31 Litho. *Perf. 13*
92 A12 2.70fr multicolored 1.40 1.40

Chelonia Mydas — A13

1998, Jan. 31
93 A13 3fr multicolored 1.75 1.75

Family Planning — A14

1998, Apr. 1 Litho. *Perf. 13¼x13*
94 A14 1fr multicolored .75 .75

France Nos. 2594, 2595 and 2597 Overprinted "MAYOTTE"

1997, Aug. 18 Engr. *Perf. 13*
95 A1409 2.70fr brt grn (#2594) — —
96 A1409 (3fr) red (#2495) — —
97 A1409 3.80fr blue (#2497) — —

France No. 2604 Ovptd. "MAYOTTE"
Die Cut x Serpentine Die Cut 7
1998, Apr. 15 Engr.
Self-Adhesive

104 A1409 (3fr) red 1.40 1.40
a. Booklet pane of 10 14.00

No. 104a is a complete booklet, the peelable backing serves as a booklet cover.

Children's Carnival A15

1998, May 30 Litho. *Perf. 13*
105 A15 3fr multicolored 1.50 1.50

Ferry, "Salama Djema II" — A16

1998, May 30
106 A16 3.80fr multicolored 1.75 1.75

Mosque of Tsingoni A17

1998, Sept. 5 Litho. *Perf. 13*
107 A17 3fr multicolored 1.50 1.50

Mariama Salim — A18

Photo. & Engr.
1998, Oct. 3 *Perf. 13*
108 A18 2.70fr multicolored 1.25 1.25

Traditional Fishing, Djarifa — A19

1998, Nov. 7 **Litho.** ***Perf. 13***
109 A19 2fr multicolored 1.25 1.25

Pomacanthus — A20

1998, Nov. 7
110 A20 3fr multicolored 1.50 1.50

See Nos. 121-124.

Agricultural Tools — A21

1998, Dec. 19 **Litho.** ***Perf. 13***
111 A21 3fr multicolored 1.50 1.50

France Nos. 2589-2593, 2601, 2603 Ovptd. "MAYOTTE"

1999, Jan. 1 **Engr.** ***Perf. 13***

112	A1409	10c brn (#2589)	.25	.25
113	A1409	20c brt bl grn (#2590)	.30	.30
114	A1409	50c purple (#2591)	.50	.50
115	A1409	1fr brt orange (#2592)	.65	.65
116	A1409	2fr brt blue (#2593)	1.00	1.00
117	A1409	5fr brt grn bl (#2601)	2.25	2.25
118	A1409	10fr violet (#2603)	4.75	4.75
		Nos. 112-118 (7)	9.70	9.70

Map of Mayotte A22

1999, Feb. 6 ***Perf. 12x13***
119 A22 3fr multicolored 1.50 1.50

Combani Dam A23

1999, Feb. 6 **Litho.** ***Perf. 13***
120 A23 8fr multicolored 3.50 3.50

Fish Type of 1998

Designs: 2.70fr, Cephalopholis miniatus, vert. 3fr, Pterois volitans. 5.20fr, Pygoplites diacanthus. 10fr, Acanthurus leucosternon.

Perf. 13¼x13, 13x13¼

1999, Apr. 3 **Litho.**

121	A20	2.70fr multicolored	1.25	1.25
122	A20	3fr multicolored	1.40	1.40
123	A20	5.20fr multicolored	2.50	2.50
124	A20	10fr multicolored	4.25	4.25
		Nos. 121-124 (4)	9.40	9.40

France No. 2691 Ovptd. "MAYOTTE"

1999, May 25 **Engr.** ***Perf. 13***
125 A1470 3fr red & blue 1.25 1.25

Founga — A24

Photo. & Engr.

1999, June 5 ***Perf. 13***
126 A24 5.40fr multicolored 2.50 2.50

Baobab Tree — A25

1999, June 5 **Litho.** ***Perf. 13x13½***
127 A25 8fr multicolored 3.50 3.50

Dzaoudzi Prefecture A26

1999, Sept. 25 **Litho.** ***Perf. 13x13¼***
128 A26 3fr multicolored 1.40 1.40

Souvenir Sheet

Pirogues — A27

Designs: a, Pirogues on beach, shown. b, Pirogues, vert. c, Pirogues, close-up.

1999, Sept. 25 ***Perf. 13***
129 A27 5fr Sheet of 3, #a.-c. 10.50 10.50

Vanilla A28

1999, Nov. 6 **Litho.** ***Perf. 13***
130 A28 4.50fr multi 1.75 1.75

Soulou Waterfalls — A29

1999, Dec. 11 ***Perf. 13½x13***
131 A29 10fr multi 4.00 4.00

Year 2000 A30

1999, Dec. 11 ***Perf. 13***
132 A30 3fr multi 1.25 1.25

Indian Ocean Boat — A31

2000, Feb. 5 **Litho.** ***Perf. 13x13¼***
133 A31 3fr multi 1.25 1.25

Whales A32

2000, Feb. 5 **Litho.** ***Perf. 13x13¼***
134 A32 5.20fr multi 2.50 2.50

Inner Wheel Rotary District — A33

2000, Mar. 24 ***Perf. 13¼x13***
135 A33 5.20fr multi 2.50 2.50

Lagoon A34

2000, Apr. 29 **Litho.** ***Perf. 13x13¼***
136 A34 3fr multi 1.40 1.40

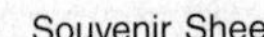
Souvenir Sheet

Mahoraise Women — A35

Woman in: a, 3fr, red. b, 5.20fr, white.

2000, Apr. 29 ***Perf. 13¼x13***
137 A35 Sheet of 2, #a-b 5.00 5.00

Tire Race A36

2000, June 24 ***Perf. 13x13¼***
138 A36 3fr multi 1.40 1.40

Tomb of Sultan Andriantsouli — A37

2000, June 24
139 A37 5.40fr multi 2.10 2.10

Souvenir Sheet

Sea Shells — A38

No. 140: a, Cassis cornuta. b, Charonia tritonis. c, Cyraecassis rufa. d, Cyprae mauritania, Cyprae tigris.

2000, Sept. 23 **Litho.** ***Perf. 13x13½***
140 A38 3fr Sheet of 4, #a-d 8.00 8.00

Zéna M'Déré (1917-99), Politician A39

2000, Oct. 27 ***Perf. 13***
141 A39 3fr multi 1.40 1.40

Ylang Distillery A40

2000, Nov. 25 Litho. ***Perf. 13x13½***
142 A40 2.70fr multi 1.40 1.40

New Hospital — A41

2000, Nov. 25 ***Perf. 13½x13***
143 A41 10fr multi 4.50 4.50

Map of Mayotte — A42

2001, Jan. 1 Litho. ***Perf. 13***
144 A42 2.70fr grn & blk 1.25 1.25
145 A42 (3fr) red & blk 1.25 1.25

Breastfeeding A43

2001, Jan. 27 ***Perf. 13¼x13***
146 A43 3fr multi 1.60 1.60

Return of Pilgrims to Mecca A44

2001, Mar. 10 ***Perf. 13x13¼***
147 A44 2.70fr multi 1.40 1.40

Bush Taxi — A45

2001, Mar. 10 ***Perf. 13***
148 A45 3fr multi 1.40 1.40

Soccer — A46

2001, May 26 Litho. ***Perf. 13¼x13***
149 A46 3fr multi 1.40 1.40

Fish Type of 1998

Design: Pajama fish (gaterin, plectorhinchus orientalis).

2001, May 26 ***Perf. 13x13¼***
150 A20 10fr multi 5.00 5.00

Foreign Legion Detachment in Mayotte, 25th Anniv. — A47

2001, Apr. 30 Litho. ***Perf. 13***
151 A47 5.20fr multi 2.75 2.75

Souvenir Sheet

Flying Foxes — A48

No. 152: a, 3fr, Hanging from branch. b, 5.20fr, In flight.

2001, July 7 Litho. ***Perf. 13x13½***
152 A48 Sheet of 2, #a-b 6.50 6.50

Adapted Military Service Group, 1st Anniv. A49

2001, Sept. 1 Litho. ***Perf. 13x13½***
153 A49 3fr multi 1.40 1.40

Flowers A50

Designs: 3fr, Shown. 5.40fr, Fruits.

2001, Sept. 22 ***Perf. 13***
154-155 A50 Set of 2 4.00 4.00

Lake Dziani Dzaha — A51

2001, Nov. 17
156 A51 5.20fr multi 2.40 2.40

Mayotte Post Office A52

2001, Nov. 17
157 A52 10fr multi 5.00 5.00

100 Cents = 1 Euro (€)

Arms — A53

2002, Jan. 1 Litho. ***Perf. 13x13½***
158 A53 46c multi 1.75 1.75

France Nos. 2835, 2849-2863 Overprinted

2002, Jan. 1 Engr. ***Perf. 13***

159	A1583	1c	yellow	.25	.25
160	A1583	2c	brown	.25	.25
161	A1583	5c	brt bl grn	.30	.30
162	A1583	10c	purple	.40	.40
163	A1583	20c	brt org	.70	.70
164	A1583	41c	brt green	1.25	1.25
165	A1409	(46c)	red	1.40	1.40
166	A1583	50c	dk blue	1.50	1.50
167	A1583	53c	apple grn	1.60	1.60
168	A1583	58c	blue	1.75	1.75
169	A1583	64c	dark org	2.00	2.00
170	A1583	67c	brt blue	2.10	2.10
171	A1583	69c	brt pink	2.25	2.25
172	A1583	€1	Prus blue	3.00	3.00
173	A1583	€1.02	dk green	3.00	3.00
174	A1583	€2	violet	6.00	6.00
	Nos. 159-174 (16)			27.75	27.75

Athletics — A54

2002, Mar. 23 Litho. ***Perf. 13***
175 A54 41c multi 1.50 1.50

Kawéni Mangrove Swamp — A55

2002, Mar. 25
176 A55 €1.52 multi 5.00 5.00

Mayotte Communes, 25th Anniv. — A56

2002, June 3 Litho. ***Perf. 13¼x13***
177 A56 46c multi 1.60 1.60

Salt Drying — A57

2002, June 3 ***Perf. 13x13¼***
178 A57 79c multi 3.00 3.00

2002 Census — A58

2002, July 29 Litho. ***Perf. 13¼x13***
179 A58 46c multi 1.75 1.75

Abandoned Sugar Processing Equipment — A59

2002, Sept. 21 Litho. ***Perf. 13***
180 A59 82c multi 2.75 2.75

Miniature Sheet

Birds — A60

No. 181: a, Souimanga. b, Drongo. c, Oiseau-lunette. d, Foudy.

2002, Sept. 21 ***Perf. 13x13¼***
181 A60 46c Sheet of 4, #a-d 8.50 8.50

Mt. Choungui — A61

2002, Nov. 16 Litho. ***Perf. 13¼x13***
182 A61 46c multi 1.75 1.75

Breadfruit — A62

2002, Nov. 16
183 A62 €1.22 multi 4.00 4.00

Vanilla and Ylang Museum A63

2003, Jan. 1 Litho. ***Perf. 13x13½***
184 A63 46c multi 2.00 2.00

Banana Tree — A64

2003, Feb. 1 ***Perf. 13½x13***
185 A64 79c multi 2.75 2.75

Holiday Face Decorations A65

2003, Apr. 5 Litho. ***Perf. 13***
186 A65 46c multi 1.75 1.75

Swordfish — A66

2003, Apr. 5
187 A66 79c multi 3.00 3.00

Gecko — A67

2003, June 14 Litho. ***Perf. 13***
188 A67 50c multi 2.00 2.00

Mraha Game — A68

2003, June 14 Engr. ***Perf. 13x12½***
189 A68 €1.52 claret & brown 5.50 5.50

Mtzamboro College A69

2003, Sept. 6 Litho. ***Perf. 13x13¼***
190 A69 45c multi 1.75 1.75

Ziyara de Pole — A70

2003, Sept. 6 ***Perf. 13¼x13***
191 A70 82c multi 3.00 3.00

Basketball — A71

2003, Nov. 15 Litho. ***Perf. 13¼x13***
192 A71 50c multi 1.75 1.75

Wadaha A72

2004, Jan. 3 ***Perf. 13***
193 A72 50c multi 1.75 1.75

Map Type of 2001 Inscribed "RF" and With Euro Denominations Only

2004

194	A42	1c yel & blk	.25	.25
195	A42	2c gray & blk	.25	.25
196	A42	5c greenish bl & blk	.30	.30
197	A42	10c red vio & blk	.30	.30
198	A42	20c org & blk	.50	.50
199	A42	45c green & black	1.25	1.25
200	A42	50c dk bl & blk	1.25	1.25
201	A42	€1 Prus bl & blk	2.40	2.40
202	A42	€2 violet & blk	5.00	5.00
		Nos. 194-202 (9)	11.50	11.50

Issued: 1c, 2c, 50c, €2, 3/10; 5c, 10c, 20c, €1, 4/17; 45c, 7/17.

Sada Bay — A73

2004, Apr. 3 Litho. ***Perf. 13***
203 A73 90c multi 2.75 2.75

Souvenir Sheet

Butterflies — A74

No. 204: a, Junonia rhadama. b, Papilio demodocus. c, Acraea ranavalona. d, Danaus chrysippus.

2004, Apr. 3 ***Perf. 13x13¼***
204 A74 50c Sheet of 4, #a-d 7.00 7.00

Papaya and Papaya Tree A75

2004, June 12 Litho. ***Perf. 13x13¼***
205 A75 50c multi 1.75 1.75

Gold Jewelry A76

2004, June 12 Litho. ***Perf. 13***
206 A76 €2.40 multi 7.50 7.50

Kwalé River Bridge A77

2004, Sept. 25 Litho. ***Perf. 13x13¼***
207 A77 50c multi 1.75 1.75

Maki and Young A78

2004, Sept. 25 ***Perf. 13***
208 A78 75c multi 2.50 2.50

Woman Cooking Food A79

2004, Nov. 13 ***Perf. 13x13¼***
209 A79 45c multi 1.50 1.50

Domino Players — A80

2004, Nov. 13 ***Perf. 13***
210 A80 75c multi 2.50 2.50

Ylang-ylang Trees — A81

2005, Jan. 3 Litho. ***Perf. 13***
211 A81 50c multi 2.00 2.00

Traditional Women's Clothing A82

2005, Mar. 14 Litho. ***Perf. 13***
212 A82 53c multi 2.00 2.00

Breadfruit and Tree — A83

2005, Mar. 14 ***Perf. 13¼x13***
213 A83 64c multi 2.00 2.00

Rotary International, Cent. — A84

2005, May 13 ***Perf. 13***
214 A84 90c multi 2.75 2.75

Souvenir Sheet

Marine Mammals — A85

No. 215: a, Humpback whale (Baleine à bosse). b, Dolphins. c, Sperm whale (grand cachalot). d, Dugongs.

2005, May 13 ***Perf. 13x13¼***
215 A85 53c Sheet of 4, #a-d 8.00 8.00

Stick Figure Drawings A86

2005, July 4 ***Perf. 13***
216 A86 48c multi 1.75 1.75

Mamoudzou — A87

2005, Sept. 10 Litho. ***Perf. 13***
217 A87 48c multi 1.50 1.50

Fisherman in Pirogue A88

2005, Sept. 10
218 A88 75c multi 2.25 2.25

Blacksmith A89

2005, Nov. 12 Litho. ***Perf. 13x13¼***
219 A89 53c multi 1.75 1.75

Tam-tam Boeuf Celebration — A90

2005, Nov. 12 ***Perf. 13***
220 A90 53c multi 1.75 1.75

Woman Grating Coconuts A91

2006, Jan. 14 Litho. ***Perf. 13x13¼***
221 A91 53c multi 1.75 1.75

Moya Beach — A92

2006, Mar. 18 Litho. ***Perf. 13***
222 A92 48c multi 1.75 1.75

Souvenir Sheet

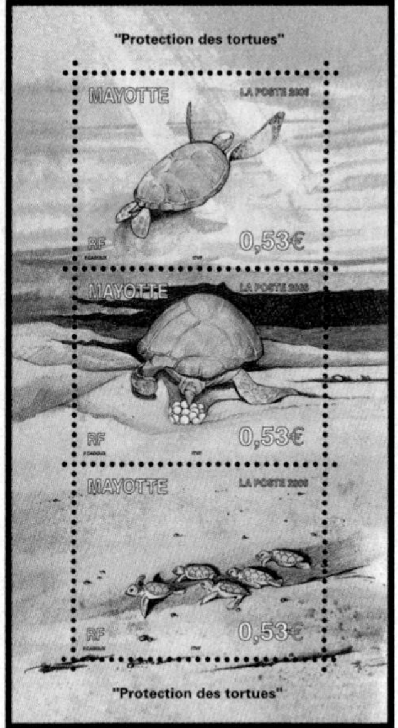

Turtle Protection — A93

No. 223: a, Turtle swimming. b, Turtle laying eggs. c, Hatchlings.

2006, Mar. 18 ***Perf. 13x13¼***
223 A93 53c Sheet of 3, #a-c 7.50 7.50

Farmer's Market — A94

Ferries — A95

2006, May 15 Litho. ***Perf. 13x12¾***
224 A94 53c multi 1.50 1.50
225 A95 €1.07 multi 3.50 3.50

Aloe Mayottensis A96

2006, July 3 Litho. ***Perf. 13¼x13***
226 A96 53c multi 1.75 1.75

Frangipani Shrub and Flowers A97

2006, Sept. 9 ***Perf. 13x13¼***
227 A97 53c multi 1.75 1.75

Moulidi Dance — A98

2006, Sept. 9 ***Perf. 13***
228 A98 75c multi 2.75 2.75

Tropic Birds A99

2006, Nov. 18 Litho. ***Perf. 13***
229 A99 54c multi 2.00 2.00

Resumption of Stamp Issues, 10th Anniv. — A100

2007, Jan. 20 Litho. ***Perf. 13½x13***
230 A100 54c multi 1.75 1.75

Phanelopsis Orchid — A101

2007, Jan. 20 ***Perf. 13x13½***
231 A101 54c multi 2.00 2.00

Audit Office, Bicent. A102

2007, Mar. 17 Engr. ***Perf. 13¼***
232 A102 54c multi 1.75 1.75

Phyllostachys Edulis — A103

2007, Mar. 19 Litho. *Perf. 13¼x13*
233 A103 €1.01 multi 4.00 4.00

Traditional House A104

2007, May 14 *Perf. 13x13¼*
234 A104 54c multi 1.75 1.75

General Council, 30th Anniv. — A105

2007, May 12 Litho. *Perf. 13¼x13*
235 A105 54c multi 2.00 2.00

Souvenir Sheet

Corals — A106

No. 236: a, Corail corne d'elan. b, Gorgone eventail. c, Corail corne de cerf. d, Cerveau de Neptune.

2007, June 16 *Perf. 13x13¼*
236 A106 54c Sheet of 4, #a-d 9.00 9.00

Mangos and Mango Tree A107

2007, Sept. 17 Litho. *Perf. 13x13¼*
237 A107 54c multi 1.75 1.75

Chameleon — A108

2007, Sept. 17
238 A108 54c multi 1.75 1.75

Beach Grill and Shelter — A109

2007, Nov. 10 *Perf. 13*
239 A109 54c multi 1.75 1.75

N'Gouja Beach — A110

2007, Nov. 10 *Perf. 13x13¼*
240 A110 54c multi 2.00 2.00

Zebu A111

2008, Jan. 28 Litho. *Perf. 13x13½*
241 A111 54c multi 1.75 1.75

Coconuts and Coconut Palm — A112

2008, Jan. 28 *Perf. 13x13¼*
242 A112 54c multi 1.75 1.75

Miniature Sheet

Spices — A113

No. 243: a, Cinnamon (cannelle). b, Nutmeg (muscade). c, Turmeric (curcuma). d, Ginger (gingembre).

2008, Mar. 22 Litho. *Perf. 13x13¼*
243 A113 55c Sheet of 4, #a-d 7.75 7.75

Hibiscus — A114

2008, May 26 *Perf. 13¼x13*
244 A114 55c multi 2.00 2.00

Wedding Ceremony A115

2008, May 26 *Perf. 13*
245 A115 55c multi 2.00 2.00

Younoussa Bamana (1935-2007), Politician — A116

2008, June 23 Litho. *Perf. 13¼x13*
246 A116 55c multi 1.90 1.90

M'Biwi Dance A117

2008, Sept. 22 Litho. *Perf. 13x13¼*
247 A117 55c multi 1.75 1.75

Embroidery — A118

2008, Nov. 10 Litho. *Perf. 13x13¼*
248 A118 55c multi 1.75 1.75

Mamoudzou Town Hall — A119

2008, Dec. 8 *Perf. 13*
249 A119 55c multi 1.75 1.75

Longoni Power Station — A120

2009, Jan. 12
250 A120 55c multi 1.75 1.75

Cardinals A121

2009, Jan. 12 Litho. *Perf. 13*
251 A121 55c multi 2.00 2.00

Tamarind Tree and Fruit A122

2009, Mar. 9 *Perf. 13x13¼*
252 A122 56c multi 1.75 1.75

Fishing by Kerosene Lantern — A123

2009, Mar. 9 *Perf. 13*
253 A123 56c multi 1.75 1.75

Miniature Sheet

Citrus Fruits — A124

No. 254: a, Oranges. b, Grapefruit (pamplemousse). c, Lemons (citron). d, Kaffir limes (combava).

2009, May 18 *Perf. 13x13¼*
254 A124 56c Sheet of 4, #a-d 7.75 7.75

Souvenir Sheet

Les Quatres Freres — A125

No. 255: a, Close-up view (blue sky). b, Distant view (yellow sky).

2009, June 29 Litho. *Perf. 13x13¼*
255 A125 56c Sheet of 2, #a-b 4.00 4.00

Jasmine Flowers
A126

2009, Sept. 21 Litho. *Perf. 13*
256 A126 56c multi 2.00 2.00

Gaboussi Player
A127

2009, Nov. 16 *Perf. 13x13¼*
257 A127 56c multi 1.75 1.75

Welcome to Travelers
A128

2010, Jan. 11 Litho. *Perf. 13*
258 A128 56c multi 1.75 1.75

Basket Weaver — A129

2010, Mar. 8 Litho. *Perf. 13*
259 A129 56c multi 1.75 1.75

Governor's House — A130

2010, Mar. 8
260 A130 56c multi 1.75 1.75

Sparrow Hawk
A131

2010, May 17 Engr. *Perf. 13¼*
261 A131 56c multi 1.40 1.40

Platycerium Alcicorne
A132

2010, May 17 Litho. *Perf. 13¼*
262 A132 56c multi 1.40 1.40

Decorated Book Rest
A133

2010, July 5 Engr. *Perf. 12¼*
263 A133 58c multi 1.50 1.50

Customs Department Building — A134

2010, July 30 Litho. *Perf. 13x13½*
264 A134 58c multi 1.50 1.50

Chigoma Dance — A135

2010, Sept. 13
265 A135 95c multi 2.60 2.60

Mail Carrier on All-Terrain Vehicle — A136

2010, Nov. 8 *Perf. 13¼x13*
266 A136 58c multi 1.60 1.60

Miniature Sheet

Women's Hairstyles — A137

No. 267 — Various hairstyles of women wearing: a, Lilac clothing, woman facing right. b, Yellow brown clothing. c, Red clothing. d, Lilac clothing, woman facing left.

2011, Jan. 17 *Perf. 13½x13*
267 A137 58c Sheet of 4, #a-d 6.50 6.50

Grand Mosque of Mtsapéré
A138

2011, Feb. 14 *Perf. 13¼x13*
268 A138 58c multi 1.75 1.75

Woman Carrying Laundry
A139

2011, Mar. 14 *Perf. 13*
269 A139 58c multi 1.75 1.75

Bee-eaters
A140

2011, Mar. 14
270 A140 58c multi 1.75 1.75

Mayotte's Association With France, 170th Anniv. — A141

2011, Apr. 4 Engr. *Perf. 13x12¼*
271 A141 58c brown 1.75 1.75

White Sand Island
A142

2011, May 16 Litho. *Perf. 13x13¼*
272 A142 58c multi 1.75 1.75

Kingfisher
A143

2011, May 16 *Perf. 13¼x13*
273 A143 58c multi 1.75 1.75

Kapok Tree — A144

2011, June 20
274 A144 58c multi 1.75 1.75

Mtzamboro Island Oranges and Orange Tree — A145

2011, June 20
275 A145 58c multi 1.75 1.75

Majlis Ceremony — A146

2011, June 20 *Perf. 13*
276 A146 58c multi 1.75 1.75

Skin Divers — A147

2011, July 4 Litho. *Perf. 13¼x13*
277 A147 60c multi 1.75 1.75

Karehani Lake — A148

2011, July 4
278 A148 60c multi 1.75 1.75

Marketplace — A149

2011, Sept. 5 *Perf. 13x13½*
279 A149 60c multi 1.75 1.75

Flycatchers — A150

2011, Sept. 5
280 A150 60c multi 1.75 1.75

Indian Ocean Philatelic Show A151

2011, Sept. 19 *Perf. 13*
281 A151 60c multi 1.75 1.75

Change of Mayotte's Political Status — A152

2011, Sept. 1
282 A152 60c multi 1.75 1.75

The Overseas Collectivity of Mayotte became France's 101st department on Mar. 31, 2011.

Pottery — A153

2011, Oct. 3 *Perf. 13¼x13*
283 A153 60c multi 1.75 1.75

Aquaculture — A154

2011, Nov. 14 *Perf. 13x13¼*
284 A154 60c multi 1.60 1.60

Padza of Dapani A155

2011, Nov. 14
285 A155 60c multi 1.60 1.60

Fishermen Returning with Catch A156

2011, Dec. 5 *Perf. 13*
286 A156 60c multi 1.60 1.60

Northern Islets A157

2011, Dec. 12 *Perf. 13x13¼*
287 A157 60c multi 1.60 1.60

Ship Marion Dufresne in Mamoudzou Lagoon — A158

2011, Dec. 31 *Perf. 13*
288 A158 60c multi 1.60 1.60

See French Southern & Antarctic Territories No. 453.

Mayotte began to use the postage stamps of France as of Jan. 1, 2012.

AIR POST STAMPS

Catalogue values for unused stamps in this section are for Never Hinged items.

Opening of New Air Terminal — AP1

1997, Mar. 1 Engr. *Perf. 13x12½*
C1 AP1 20fr multicolored 11.00 11.00

First Mayotte-Réunion Flight, 20th Anniv. — AP2

Photo. & Engr.
1997, Nov. 29 *Perf. 13x12½*
C2 AP2 5fr multicolored 3.00 3.00

Pique-boeuf Bird, Zebu — AP3

1998, Apr. 1 Litho. *Perf. 13*
C3 AP3 30fr multicolored 13.00 13.00

Deba Religious Festival — AP4

1999, Nov. 6 Litho. *Perf. 13*
C4 AP4 10fr multicolored 5.00 5.00

Dzaoudzi Aero Club — AP5

2001, July 7 Litho. *Perf. 13*
C5 AP5 20fr multi 9.50 9.50

Dzaoudzi Rock — AP6

2003, Nov. 15 Litho. *Perf. 13*
C6 AP6 €1.50 multi 5.00 5.00

MEMEL

'mā-məl

LOCATION — In northern Europe, bordering on the Baltic Sea
GOVT. — Special commission (see below)
AREA — 1099 sq. mi.
POP. — 151,960

Following World War I this territory was detached from Germany and by Treaty of Versailles assigned to the government of a commission of the Allied and Associated Powers (not the League of Nations), which administered it until January, 1923, when it was forcibly occupied by Lithuania. In 1924 Memel became incorporated as a semi-autonomous district of Lithuania with the approval of the Allied Powers and the League of Nations.

100 Pfennig = 1 Mark
100 Centu = 1 Litas (1923)

Excellent counterfeits of all Memel stamps exist.

Stamps of Germany, 1905-20, Overprinted

Wmk. Lozenges (125)
1920, Aug. 1 *Perf. 14, 14½*

1	A16	5pf green	1.50	*15.00*
2	A16	10pf car rose	1.90	*9.00*
3	A16	10pf orange	.30	*3.25*
4	A22	15pf violet brown	2.60	*12.00*
5	A16	20pf blue violet	1.10	*5.25*
6	A16	30pf org & blk, *buff*	1.25	*8.25*
7	A16	30pf dull blue	.40	*3.25*
8	A16	40pf lake & blk	.25	*3.25*
9	A16	50pf pur & blk, *buff*	.30	*3.25*
10	A16	60pf olive green	1.50	*6.00*
11	A16	75pf grn & blk	2.60	*22.50*
12	A16	80pf blue violet	1.35	*9.75*

Overprinted

13	A17	1m car rose	.30	*3.25*
14	A17	1.25m green	13.00	*50.00*
15	A17	1.50m yel brn	4.50	*30.00*
16	A21	2m blue	7.50	*13.50*
17	A21	2.50m red lilac	11.50	*60.00*
		Nos. 1-17 (17)	51.85	*257.50*

Stamps of France, Surcharged in Black

On A22

On A18

1920 Unwmk. *Perf. 14x13½*

18	A22	5pf on 5c green	.75	*3.25*
19	A22	10pf on 10c red	.60	*2.60*
20	A22	20pf on 25c blue	1.10	*3.75*
21	A22	30pf on 30c org	.75	*3.25*
22	A22	40pf on 20c red brn	1.10	*3.25*
23	A22	50pf on 35c vio	.30	*3.25*
24	A18	60pf on 40c red & pale bl	.40	*3.75*
25	A18	80pf on 45c grn & bl	1.10	*4.50*
26	A18	1m on 50c brn & lav	.50	*3.75*
27	A18	1m 25pf on 60c vio & ultra	1.20	*9.00*
28	A18	2m on 1fr cl & ol grn	.60	*3.50*
29	A18	3m on 5fr bl & buff	22.50	*67.50*
		Nos. 18-29 (12)	30.90	*111.35*

For stamps with additional surcharges and overprints see Nos. 43-49, C1-C4.

French Stamps of 1900-20 Surcharged like Nos. 24 to 29 in Red or Black

On A18

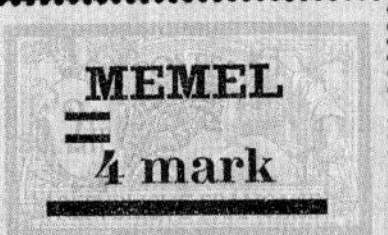

Type I

Type II

1920-21 Unwmk. *Perf. 14x13½*

30	A18	3m on 2fr org & pale bl	22.50	*67.50*
31	A18	4m on 2fr org & pale bl (I) (Bk)	.45	*3.75*
a.		Type II	.45	*3.75*

32 A18 10m on 5fr bl & buff 3.00 *15.00*
33 A18 20m on 5fr bl & buff 37.50 *150.00*
Nos. 30-33 (4) 63.45 *236.25*

For stamps with additional overprints see Nos. C5, C19.

New Value with Initial Capital

1921

39 A18 60Pf on 40c red & pale bl 4.50 *19.00*
40 A18 3M on 60c vio & ultra 2.25 *7.50*
41 A18 10M on 5fr bl & buff 2.25 *8.25*
42 A18 20M on 45c grn & bl 4.50 *26.00*
Nos. 39-42 (4) 13.50 *60.75*

The surcharged value on No. 40 is in italics. For stamps with additional overprints see Nos. C6-C7, C18.

Stamps of 1920 Surcharged with Large Numerals in Dark Blue or Red

No. 43

No. 49

1921-22

43 A22 15pf on 10pf on 10c .40 *1.90*
a. Inverted surcharge 55.00 *225.00*
44 A22 15pf on 20pf on 25c .40 *3.00*
a. Inverted surcharge 55.00
45 A22 15pf on 50pf on 35c (R) .40 *3.00*
a. Inverted surcharge 55.00
46 A22 60pf on 40pf on 20c .40 *1.90*
a. Inverted surcharge 55.00 *225.00*
47 A18 75pf on 60pf on 40c .75 *3.75*
48 A18 1.25m on 1m on 50c .60 *3.00*
49 A18 5.00m on 2m on 1fr .90 *4.50*
a. Inverted surcharge 150.00 *525.00*
Nos. 43-49 (7) 3.85 *21.05*

Stamps of France Surcharged in Black or Red

On A20, A22

1922

50 A22 5pf on 5c org .25 *1.35*
51 A22 10pf on 10c red .75 *5.25*
52 A22 10pf on 10c grn .25 *1.35*
53 A22 15pf on 10c grn .25 *1.35*
54 A22 20pf on 20c red brn 7.50 *37.50*
55 A22 20pf on 25c bl 7.50 *37.50*
56 A22 25pf on 5c org .25 *1.35*
57 A22 30pf on 30c red 1.10 *5.25*
58 A22 35pf on 35c vio .25 *.75*
59 A20 50pf on 50c dl bl .25 *1.35*
60 A20 75pf on 15c grn .30 *.75*
61 A22 75pf on 35c vio .30 *1.35*
62 A22 1m on 25c blue .30 *.75*
63 A22 1¼m on 30c red .25 *.75*
64 A22 3m on 5c org .40 *5.00*
65 A20 6m on 15c grn (R) .75 *5.00*
66 A22 8m on 30c red .75 *13.00*

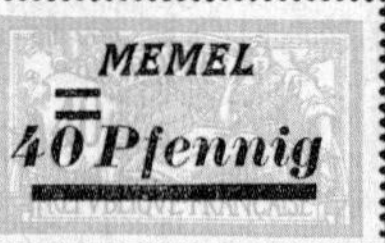
On A18

67 A18 40pf on 40c red & pale bl .25 *1.35*
68 A18 80pf on 45c grn & bl .30 *1.35*
69 A18 1m on 40c red & pale bl .30 *2.25*
70 A18 1.25m on 60c vio & ultra (R) .30 *2.25*
71 A18 1.50m on 45c grn & bl (R) .30 *2.25*
72 A18 2m on 45c grn & bl .75 *2.60*
73 A18 2m on 1fr cl & ol grn .30 *2.25*
74 A18 2¼m on 40c red & pale bl .25 *.75*
75 A18 2½m on 60c vio & ultra .75 *2.50*
76 A18 3m on 60c vio & ultra (R) 1.10 *5.25*
77 A18 4m on 45c grn & bl .25 *.75*
78 A18 5m on 1fr cl & ol grn .30 *3.00*
79 A18 6m on 60c vio & ultra .25 *.75*
80 A18 6m on 2fr org & pale bl .30 *3.00*
81 A18 9m on 1fr cl & ol grn .25 *.75*
82 A18 9m on 5fr bl & buff (R) .40 *3.00*
83 A18 10m on 45c grn & bl (R) .75 *5.00*
84 A18 12m on 40c red & pale bl .40 *2.25*
85 A18 20m on 40c red & pale bl .75 *5.00*
86 A18 20m on 2fr org & pale bl .25 *2.00*
87 A18 30m on 60c vio & ultra .75 *5.00*
88 A18 30m on 5fr dk bl & buff 2.60 *19.00*
89 A18 40m on 1fr cl & ol grn .75 *6.50*
90 A18 50m on 2fr org & pale bl 7.50 *45.00*
91 A18 80m on 2fr org & pale bl (R) .75 *6.50*
92 A18 100m on 5fr bl & buff 1.10 *12.00*
Nos. 50-92 (43) 43.35 *261.90*

A 500m on 5fr dark blue and buff was prepared, but not officially issued. Value: unused $800; never hinged $2,000.

For stamps with additional surcharges and overprints see Nos. 93-99, C8-C17, C20-C29.

Nos. 52, 54, 67, 59 Surcharged "Mark"

1922-23

93 A22 10m on 10pf on 10c .75 *7.00*
a. Double surcharge 100.00 *500.00*
94 A22 20m on 20pf on 20c .40 *4.50*
95 A18 40m on 40pf on 40c ('23) .75 *5.00*
96 A20 50m on 50pf on 50c 2.25 *14.50*
Nos. 93-96 (4) 4.15 *31.00*

Nos. 72, 61, 70 Srchd. in Red or Black

1922-23

97 A18 10m on 2m on 45c 1.90 *13.00*
98 A22 25m on 1m on 25c 1.90 *13.00*
99 A18 80m on 1.25m on 60c (Bk) ('23) 1.10 *7.00*
Nos. 97-99 (3) 4.90 *33.00*

For No. 99 with additional surcharges see Nos. N28-N30.

AIR POST STAMPS

Nos. 24-26, 28, 31, 39-40 Ovptd. in Dark Blue

1921, July 6 Unwmk. *Perf. 14x13½*

C1 A18 60pf on 40c 30.00 *150.00*
C2 A18 80pf on 45c 3.75 *13.00*
C3 A18 1m on 50c 4.00 *13.00*
C4 A18 2m on 1fr 4.50 *13.50*
a. "Flugpost" inverted 150.00 *375.00*
C5 A18 4m on 2fr (I) 3.75 *19.00*
a. Type II 75.00 *260.00*
b. Pair, type I and type II 100.00

New Value with Initial Capital

C6 A18 60Pf on 40c 3.75 *17.00*
a. "Flugpost" inverted 150.00 *375.00*
C7 A18 3M on 60c 2.60 *17.00*
a. "Flugpost" inverted 260.00 *600.00*
Nos. C1-C7 (7) 52.35 *242.50*

The surcharged value on No. C7 is in italics.

Nos. 67-71, 73, 76, 78, 80, 82 Ovptd. in Dark Blue

1922, May 12

C8 A18 40pf on 40c .40 *3.75*
C9 A18 80pf on 45c .40 *3.75*
C10 A18 1m on 40c .40 *3.75*
C11 A18 1.25m on 60c .75 *6.00*
C12 A18 1.50m on 45c .75 *6.00*
C13 A18 2m on 1fr .75 *6.00*
C14 A18 3m on 60c .75 *6.00*
C15 A18 5m on 1fr 1.10 *6.00*
C16 A18 6m on 2fr 1.10 *6.00*
C17 A18 9m on 5fr 1.10 *6.00*

Same Overprint On Nos. 40, 31

C18 A18 3m on 60c 120.00 *1,050.*
C19 A18 4m on 2fr .75 *6.00*
Nos. C8-C17,C19 (11) 8.25 *59.25*

Nos. 67, 69-71, 73, 76, 78, 80, 82 Ovptd. in Black or Red

1922, Oct. 17

C20 A18 40pf on 40c 1.25 *15.00*
C21 A18 1m on 40c 1.25 *15.00*
C22 A18 1.25m on 60c (R) 1.25 *15.00*
C23 A18 1.50m on 45c (R) 1.25 *15.00*
C24 A18 2m on 1fr 1.25 *15.00*
C25 A18 3m on 60c (R) 1.25 *15.00*
C26 A18 4m on 2fr 1.25 *15.00*
C27 A18 5m on 1fr 1.25 *15.00*
C28 A18 6m on 2fr 1.25 *15.00*
C29 A18 9m on 5fr (R) 1.25 *15.00*
Nos. C20-C29 (10) 12.50 *150.00*

No. C26 is not known without the "FLUGPOST" overprint.

OCCUPATION STAMPS

Issued under Lithuanian Occupation

Surcharged in Various Colors on Unissued Official Stamps of Lithuania Similar to Type O4

On Nos. N1-N6

On Nos. N7-N11

Memel Printing

1923 Unwmk. Litho. *Perf. 11*

N1 O4 10m on 5c bl (Bk) 1.00 *10.00*
a. Double overprint 35.00 *230.00*
b. "Memel" and bars omitted 7.00 *52.50*
N2 O4 25m on 5c bl (R) 1.00 *10.00*
a. Double overprint 35.00 *230.00*
N3 O4 50m on 25c red (Bk) 1.00 *10.00*
a. Double overprint 35.00 *230.00*
N4 O4 100m on 25c red (G) 1.00 *10.00*
a. Double overprint 35.00 *230.00*
N5 O4 400m on 1 l brn (R) 1.30 *13.00*
a. Double overprint 35.00 *230.00*
N6 O4 500m on 1 l brn (Bl) 1.30 *13.00*
a. Double overprint 35.00 *230.00*
Nos. N1-N6 (6) 6.60 *66.00*

Kaunas Printing

Black Surcharge

N7 O4 10m on 5c blue .70 *6.00*
N8 O4 25m on 5c blue .70 *6.00*
N9 O4 50m on 25c red .70 *6.00*
N10 O4 100m on 25c red .80 *6.00*
N11 O4 400m on 1 l brn 1.30 *9.25*
Nos. N7-N11 (5) 4.20 *33.25*

No. N8 has the value in "Markes," others of the group have it in "Markiu."

For additional surcharge see No. N87.

Surcharged in Various Colors on Unissued Official Stamps of Lithuania Similar to Type O4

1923

N12 O4 10m on 5c bl (R) 1.30 *8.00*
a. "Markes" instead of "Markiu" 13.00 *92.50*
N13 O4 20m on 5c bl (R) 1.30 *8.00*
N14 O4 25m on 25c red (Bl) 1.30 *10.50*
N15 O4 50m on 25c red (Bl) 2.60 *10.50*
a. Inverted surcharge 32.50 *130.00*
N16 O4 100m on 1 l brn (Bk) 2.60 *15.00*
a. Inverted surcharge 32.50 130.00
N17 O4 200m on 1 l brn (Bk) 4.00 *17.00*
Nos. N12-N17 (6) 13.10 *69.00*

No. N14 has the value in "Markes," others of the group have it in "Markiu."

"Vytis"
O4 O5

1923, Mar.

N18 O4 10m lt brown .35 *5.50*
N19 O4 20m yellow .35 *5.50*
N20 O4 25m orange .35 *7.00*
N21 O4 40m violet .35 *5.50*
N22 O4 50m yellow grn 1.00 *12.00*
N23 O5 100m carmine .45 *6.00*
N24 O5 300m olive grn 5.00 *120.00*
N25 O5 400m olive brn .45 *6.00*
N26 O5 500m lilac 5.00 *120.00*
N27 O5 1000m blue .85 *10.00*
Nos. N18-N27 (10) 14.15 *297.50*

No. N20 has the value in "Markes."

For surcharges see Nos. N44-N69, N88-N114.

No. 99 Surcharged in Green

1923, Apr. 13

N28 A18 100m on No. 99 3.00 *60.00*
a. Inverted overprint 70.00
N29 A18 400m on No. 99 4.00 *60.00*
a. Inverted overprint 70.00
N30 A18 500m on No. 99 3.00 *60.00*
a. Inverted overprint 70.00
Nos. N28-N30 (3) 10.00 180.00

The normal position of the green surcharge is sideways, up-reading, with the top at the left. Inverted varieties are reversed, with the overprint down-reading.

Ship — O7

Seal — O8

Lighthouse — O9

1923, Apr. 12 Litho.

N31 O7 40m olive grn 3.75 *32.50*
N32 O7 50m brown 3.75 *32.50*
N33 O7 80m green 3.75 *32.50*
N34 O7 100m red 3.75 *32.50*
N35 O8 200m deep blue 3.75 *32.50*
N36 O8 300m brown 3.75 *32.50*
N37 O8 400m lilac 3.75 *32.50*
N38 O8 500m orange 3.75 *32.50*
N39 O8 600m olive grn 3.75 *32.50*
N40 O9 800m deep blue 3.75 *32.50*
N41 O9 1000m lilac 3.75 *32.50*
N42 O9 2000m red 3.75 *32.50*
N43 O9 3000m green 3.75 *32.50*
Nos. N31-N43 (13) 48.75 *422.50*

Union of Memel with Lithuania. Forgeries exist.

For surcharges see Nos. N70-N86.

Nos. N20, N24, N26 Surcharged in Various Colors

1923 **Thin Figures**

No.	Type	Description	Unused	Used
N44	O5	2c on 300m (R)	5.25	*13.00*
a.		Double surcharge	70.00	*325.00*
N45	O5	3c on 300m (R)	6.00	*17.00*
a.		Double surcharge	145.00	*400.00*
N46	O4	10c on 25m (Bk)	6.00	*13.00*
a.		Double surcharge	70.00	*325.00*
b.		Inverted surcharge	92.50	*260.00*
N47	O4	15c on 25m (Bk)	6.00	*13.00*
N48	O5	20c on 500m (Bl)	9.25	*26.00*
N49	O5	30c on 500m (Bk)	7.25	*13.00*
a.		Double surcharge		
N50	O5	50c on 500m (G)	11.00	*26.00*
a.		Inverted surcharge	52.50	*200.00*
b.		Double surcharge	130.00	*600.00*
		Nos. N44-N50 (7)	50.75	*121.00*

Nos. N19, N21-N27 Surcharged

No.	Type	Description	Unused	Used
N51	O4	2c on 20m yellow	3.25	*13.00*
N52	O4	2c on 50c yel grn	3.25	*13.00*
a.		Double surcharge	50.00	*260.00*
b.		Vert. pair, imperf between	70.00	*300.00*
N53	O4	3c on 40m violet	5.50	*12.00*
a.		Double surcharge	57.50	*260.00*
N54	O5	3c on 300m ol grn	3.25	*10.00*
a.		Double surcharge	130.00	*450.00*
N55	O5	5c on 100m carmine	8.00	*10.00*
N56	O5	5c on 300m ol grn (R)	3.25	*17.00*
a.		Double surcharge	92.50	*325.00*
N57	O5	10c on 400m ol brn	17.00	*20.00*
N58	O5	30c on 500m lilac	5.25	*22.50*
a.		Double surcharge	92.50	*325.00*
b.		Inverted surcharge	100.00	*360.00*
N59	O5	1 l on 1000m blue	22.50	*65.00*
a.		Double surcharge	130.00	*460.00*
		Nos. N51-N59 (9)	71.25	*182.50*

There are several types of the numerals in these surcharges. Nos. N56 and N58 have "CENT" in short, thick letters, as on Nos. N44 to N50.

Nos. N18-N23, N25, N27 Surcharged

Thick Figures

No.	Type	Description	Unused	Used
N60	O4	2c on 10m lt brn	5.25	*65.00*
N61	O4	2c on 20m yellow	17.00	*120.00*
N62	O4	2c on 50m yel grn	6.50	*80.00*
N63	O4	3c on 10m lt brn	17.00	*110.00*
a.		Double surcharge	130.00	*525.00*
N64	O4	3c on 40m violet	20.00	*190.00*
N65	O5	5c on 100m car	10.00	*32.50*
a.		Double surcharge	92.50	*300.00*
N66	O5	10c on 400m ol brn	130.00	*550.00*
N67	O4	15c on 25m orange	130.00	*550.00*
N68	O5	50c on 1000m blue	5.25	*10.00*
a.		Double surcharge	92.50	*300.00*
N69	O5	1 l on 1000m blue	6.50	*20.00*
a.		Double surcharge	92.50	*300.00*
		Nos. N60-N69 (10)	347.50	*1,728.*

No. N69 is surcharged like type "b" in the following group.

Nos. N31-N43 Surcharged

a

b

No.	Type	Description	Unused	Used
N70	O7(a)	15c on 40m ol grn	4.25	*26.00*
N71	O7(a)	30c on 50m brown	4.25	*20.00*
a.		Double surcharge	52.50	*230.00*
N72	O7(a)	30c on 80m green	4.25	*32.50*
N73	O7(a)	30c on 100m red	4.25	*13.00*
N74	O8(a)	50c on 200m dp blue	4.25	*26.00*
N75	O8(a)	50c on 300m brn	4.25	*13.00*
a.		Double surcharge	52.50	*230.00*
b.		Inverted surcharge	52.50	*230.00*
N76	O8(a)	50c on 400m lilac	4.25	*22.50*
a.		Inverted surcharge	60.00	*260.00*
N77	O8(a)	50c on 500m org	4.25	*13.00*
a.		Double surcharge	52.50	*230.00*
N78	O8(b)	1 l on 600m ol grn	4.25	*30.00*
N79	O9(b)	1 l on 800m dp blue	5.00	*30.00*
N80	O9(b)	1 l on 1000m lil	4.50	*30.00*
N81	O9(b)	1 l on 2000m red	5.00	*30.00*
N82	O9(b)	1 l on 3000m grn	5.00	*30.00*
		Nos. N70-N82 (13)	57.75	*316.00*

These stamps are said to have been issued to commemorate the institution of autonomous government.

Nos. N32, N34, N36, N38 Surcharged in Green

1923

No.	Type	Description	Unused	Used
N83	O7	15c on 50m brn	165.	*1,650.*
a.		Thick numerals in surcharge	*1,000.*	*4,000.*
N84	O7	25c on 100m red	70.	*1,000.*
a.		Thick numerals in surcharge	*1,000.*	*2,600.*
N85	O8	30c on 300m brn	130.	*1,050.*
a.		Thick numerals in surcharge	*800.*	*3,000.*
N86	O8	60c on 500m org	80.	*1,000.*
a.		Thick numerals in surcharge	*525.*	*2,000.*

Surcharges on Nos. N83-N86 are of two types, differing in width of numerals. Values are for stamps with narrow numerals, as illustrated. Stamps with wide numerals sell for two to four times as much. For detailed listing see the *Scott Classic Specialized Catalogue of Stamps & Covers.*

Nos. N8, N10-N11, N3 Surcharged in Red or Green

No.	Type	Description	Unused	Used
N87	O4	10c on 25m on 5c bl (R)	26.00	*100.00*
N88	O4	15c on 100m on 25c red (G)	32.50	*300.00*
a.		Inverted surcharge	325.00	*1,850.*
N89	O4	30c on 400m on 1 l brn (R)	6.50	*40.00*
N90	O4	60c on 50m on 25c red (G)	32.50	*260.00*
		Nos. N87-N90 (4)	97.50	*700.00*

Nos. N18-N22 Surcharged in Green or Red

No.	Type	Description	Unused	Used
N91	O4	15c on 10m	26.00	*200.00*
N92	O4	15c on 20m	2.60	*26.00*
N93	O4	15c on 25m	5.50	*52.50*
N94	O4	15c on 40m	1.65	*26.00*
N95	O4	15c on 50m (R)	2.40	*30.00*
a.		Inverted surcharge	50.00	
N96	O4	25c on 10m	9.25	*100.00*
N97	O4	25c on 20m	2.40	*26.00*
a.		Double surcharge	160.00	
N98	O4	25c on 25m	4.50	*40.00*
N99	O4	25c on 40m	4.00	*40.00*
a.		Inverted surcharge	50.00	
N100	O4	25c on 50m (R)	2.40	*20.00*
a.		Inverted surcharge	50.00	
N101	O4	30c on 10m	26.00	*200.00*
N102	O4	30c on 20m	4.00	*32.50*
N103	O4	30c on 25m	4.50	*52.50*
N104	O4	30c on 40m	3.25	*20.00*
N105	O4	30c on 50m (R)	2.60	*20.00*
a.		Inverted surcharge	50.00	
		Nos. N91-N105 (15)	101.05	*885.50*

Nos. N23, N25, N27 Surcharged in Green or Red

No.	Type	Description	Unused	Used
N106	O5	15c on 100m	2.40	*20.00*
a.		Inverted surcharge	50.00	
N107	O5	15c on 400m	2.00	*17.00*
N108	O5	15c on 1000m (R)	52.50	*400.00*
a.		Inverted surcharge	165.00	*700.00*
N109	O5	25c on 100m	2.00	*20.00*
N110	O5	25c on 400m	2.00	*20.00*
a.		Double surcharge	100.00	
N111	O5	25c on 1000m (R)	52.50	*400.00*
a.		Inverted surcharge	165.00	*700.00*
N112	O5	30c on 100m	2.60	*20.00*
a.		Inverted surcharge	50.00	
N113	O5	30c on 400m	2.60	*20.00*
N114	O5	30c on 1000m (R)	52.50	*400.00*
a.		Inverted surcharge	165.00	*700.00*
		Nos. N106-N114 (9)	171.10	*1,317.*

Nos. N96 to N100 and N109 to N111 are surcharged "Centai," the others "Centu."

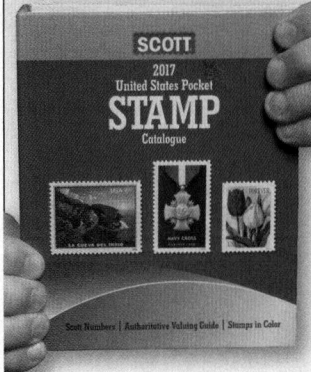

MESOPOTAMIA

ˌme-sə̦-pə-ˈtā-mē-ə

LOCATION — In Western Asia, bounded on the north by Syria and Turkey, on the east by Persia, on the south by Saudi Arabia and on the west by Trans-Jordan.
GOVT. — A former Turkish Province
AREA — 143,250 (1918) sq. mi.
POP. — 2,849,282 (1920)
CAPITAL — Baghdad

During World War I this territory was occupied by Great Britain. It was recognized as an independent state and placed under British Mandate but in 1932 the Mandate was terminated and the country admitted to membership in the League of Nations as the Kingdom of Iraq. Postage stamps of Iraq are now in use.

16 Annas = 1 Rupee

Watermark

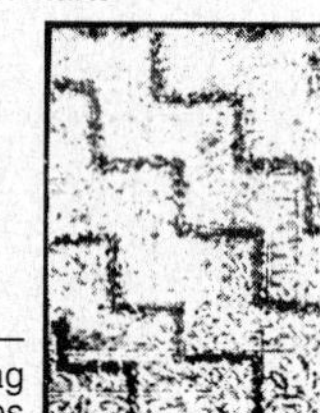

Wmk. 48 — Diagonal Zigzag Lines

Issued under British Occupation

Baghdad Issue

Stamps of Turkey 1901-16 Surcharged

Turkey No. 254 Surcharged

Turkey No. 256 Surcharged

Turkey No. 258 Surcharged

Turkey No. 259 Surcharged

Turkey No. 260 Surcharged

The surcharges were printed from slugs which were arranged to fit the various shapes of the stamps.

1917 **Unwmk.** ***Perf. 12, 13½***

N1 ¼a on 2pa red lil 400.00 425.00
a. "IN BRITISH" omitted *17,500.*
N2 ¼a on 5pa vio brown 300.00 325.00
a. "¼ An" omitted *20,000.*
N3 ½a on 10pa green 1,450. *1,750.*
N4 1a on 20pa red 1,000. *1,100.*
a. "BAGHDAD" double 2,600.
N5 2a on 1pi blue 450.00 *500.00*
Nos. N1-N5 (5) 3,600. 4,100.

On Turkey No. 249

N6 A22 2a on 1pi ultra 1,150. *1,375.*
a. "IN BRITISH" omitted *17,500.*

Turkey No. 251 Surcharged

N7 A23 ½a on 10pa green 3,250. 3,500.

On Turkey Nos. 272-273

N8 A29 1a on 20pa red 675. *750.*
a. "OCCUPATION" omitted *20,000.*
b. "BAGHDAD" double 2,600.
N9 A30 2a on 1pi blue 5,250. *8,500.*

On Turkey Nos. 346-348

N10 A41 ½a on 10pa car, perf 12½ 1,000. *1,200.*
a. Perf 13½ 2,100. *2,400.*
N11 A41 1a on 20pa ultra, perf 13½ 2,650. 3,250.
a. "1 An" omitted *18,500.*
b. Perf 12½ *14,000.* 350.00
N12 A41 2a on 1pi vio & black, perf 13½ 325.00 *200.00*
a. "BAGHDAD" omitted *20,000.*
b. Perf 12½ *650.00* *700.00*

On Turkey Nos. 297, 300

N13 A17 ¼a on 5pa purple *20,000.*
N14 A17 2a on 1pi blue 450. 500.
a. "OCCUPATION" omitted 17,500.

On Turkey No. 306

N15 A18 1a on 20pa car 1,000. *1,150.*
a. Value omitted *17,500.*

On Turkey Nos. 329-331

N16 A22 ½a on 10pa bl grn 300.00 350.00
N17 A22 1a on 20pa car rose 1,000. *1,000.*
a. "1 An" omitted *10,000.* *7,500.*
b. With additional "Behie" *11,000.* *10,500.*
N18 A22 2a on 1pi ultra 325.00 350.00
a. "BAGHDAD" omitted —

On Turkey No. 337

N19 A22 1a on 20pa car rose *9,000.* *11,750.*

On Turkey No. P125

N20 A17 1a on 20pa car —

On Turkey Nos. B1, B8

Inscription in crescent is obliterated by another crescent handstamped in violet black on Nos. N21-N27.

N21 A18 ½a on 10pa dull grn 325.00 *375.00*
a. "OCCUPATION" omitted *16,000.*
N22 A21 1a on 20pa car rose 1,000. *1,100.*

On Turkey No. B29

N23 A21 2a on 1pi ultra 3,750. *4,000.*

On Turkey Nos. B33-B34

N24 A22 1a on 20pa car rose 325.00 *375.00*
N25 A22 2a on 1pi ultra 450.00 *500.00*
a. "OCCUPATION" omitted *17,500.*
b. "BAGHDAD" omitted *16,500.*

On Turkey No. B42

N26 A41 ½a on 10pa car, perf 12½ 450.00 *500.00*
a. "BAGHDAD" double —
b. Perf 13½ 900.00 *1,000.*

On Turkey No. B38

N27 A11 1a on 10pa on 20pa vio brn 500.00 550.00
a. "OCCUPATION" omitted — *17,500.*

Iraq Issue

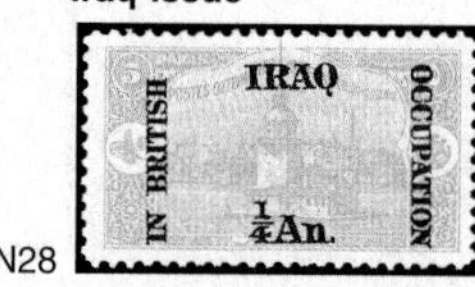

N28

N29

N30

N31

N32

N33

N34

N35

N36

N37

N38

N39

N40

N41

Turkey Nos. 256, 258-269 Surcharged

1918-20 ***Perf. 12***

N28 ¼a on 5pa vio brn .55 *1.10*
N29 ½a on 10pa grn 1.00 .25
N30 1a on 20pa red .55 .25
N31 1½a on 5pa vio brn 16.50 .75
N32 2½a on 1pi blue 1.50 1.50
a. Inverted surcharge *11,500.*
N33 3a on 1½pi car & black 1.60 .25
a. Double surcharge, red & blk *4,500.* *5,500.*
N34 4a on 1¾pi slate & red brn 1.60 .30
a. Center inverted *37,500.*

N35 6a on 2pi grn & black 2.50 2.00
N36 8a on 2½pi org & ol grn 3.75 2.25
N37 12a on 5pi dl vio 2.00 6.50
N38 1r on 10pi red brown 2.75 1.50
N39 2r on 25pi ol grn 12.50 3.25
N40 5r on 50pi car 30.00 32.50
N41 10r on 100pi dp blue 100.00 18.50
Nos. N28-N41 (14) 176.80 70.90

See #N50-N53. For overprints see #NO1-NO21.

Mosul Issue

A13

A14

A15

A16

A17

A18

A19

1919 **Unwmk.** ***Perf. 11½, 12***
N42 A13 ½a on 1pi grn & brn red 2.40 2.10
N43 A14 1a on 20pa *rose* 1.50 1.90
a. "POSTAGE" omitted
N44 A15 1a on 20pa *rose* 4.50 4.50
a. Double surcharge 725.00

Turkish word at right of tughra ("reshad") is large on No. N43, small on No. N44.

Wmk. Turkish Characters
Perf. 12½
N45 A16 2½a on 1pi vio & yel 1.60 1.60
N46 A17 3a on 20pa grn & yel 90.00 *125.00*

Wmk. 48
N47 A17 3a on 20pa green 1.75 *4.25*
N48 A18 4a on 1pi dull vio 3.50 3.75
a. Double surcharge 1,250.
b. "4" omitted 2,000.
c. As "b," double surcharge
N49 A19 8a on 10pa claret 4.25 *5.50*
a. Double surcharge *750.00* *875.00*
b. Inverted surcharge *900.00* *1,000.*
c. 8a on 1pi dull violet *3,500.*
Nos. N42-N49 (8) 109.50 148.60

Value for No. 49c is for a stamp with the perfs cutting into the design.

Iraq Issue
Types of 1918-20 Issue

1921 **Wmk. 4** ***Perf. 12***
N50 A28 ½a on 10pa green 7.50 2.50
N51 A26 1½a on 5pa dp brn 5.00 1.35
N52 A37 2r on 25pi ol grn 37.50 14.00
Nos. N50-N52 (3) 50.00 17.85

Type of 1918-20 without "Reshad"
1922 **Unwmk.**
N53 A36 1r on 10pi red brn 350.00 27.50

"Reshad" is the small Turkish word at right of the tughra in circle at top center.
For overprint see No. NO22.

OFFICIAL STAMPS

Nos. N29-N41 Overprinted

1920 **Unwmk.** ***Perf. 12***
NO1 A28 ½a on 10pa grn 25.00 2.00
NO2 A29 1a on 20pa red 8.00 1.00
NO3 A26 1½a on 5pa vio brown 60.00 3.00
NO4 A30 2½a on 1pi blue 8.00 8.00
NO5 A31 3a on 1½pi car & black 27.50 1.00
NO6 A32 4a on 1¾pi sl & red brn 55.00 4.75
NO7 A33 6a on 2pi grn & black 42.50 10.00
NO8 A34 8a on 2½pi org & ol grn 55.00 6.00
NO9 A35 12a on 5pi dull vio 32.50 24.00
NO10 A36 1r on 10pi red brown 47.50 12.00
NO11 A37 2r on 25pi ol green 45.00 22.50
NO12 A38 5r on 50pi car 85.00 65.00
NO13 A39 10r on 100pi dp blue 125.00 *160.00*
Nos. NO1-NO13 (13) 616.00 319.25

Same Overprint on Types of Regular Issue of 1918-20
1921-22 **Wmk. 4**
NO14 A28 ½a on 10pa grn 1.10 1.10
NO15 A29 1a on 20pa red 11.50 1.10
NO16 A26 1½a on 5pa dp brn 3.00 1.25
NO17 A32 4a on 1¾pi gray & red brn 2.25 *3.25*
NO18 A33 6a on 2pi grn & black 42.50 *175.00*
NO19 A34 8a on 2½pi org & yel grn 3.50 2.25
NO20 A35 12a on 5pi dl vio 42.50 *95.00*
NO21 A37 2r on 25pi ol grn 125.00 *165.00*
Nos. NO14-NO21 (8) 231.35 *443.95*

Same Overprint on No. N53
1922 **Unwmk.**
NO22 A36 1r on 10pi red brn 50.00 7.50

MEXICO

'mek-si-ˌkō

LOCATION — Extreme southern part of the North American continent, south of the United States
GOVT. — Republic
AREA — 759,529 sq. mi.
POP. — 100,294,036 (1999 est.)
CAPITAL — Mexico, D.F

8 Reales = 1 Peso
100 Centavos = 1 Peso

Catalogue values for unused stamps in this country are for Never Hinged items, beginning with Scott 792 in the regular postage section, Scott C143 in the airpost section, Scott E8 in the special delivery section, and Scott G4 in the insured letter section.

District Overprints

Nos. 1-149 are overprinted with names of various districts, and sometimes also with district numbers and year dates. Some of the district overprints are rare and command high prices. Values given for Nos. 1-149 are for the more common district overprints.

Watermarks

Wmk. 150 — PAPEL SELLADO in Sheet

Wmk. 151 — R. P. S. in the Sheet (R.P.S. stands for "Renta Papel Sellado")

Wmk. 152 — "CORREOS E U M" on Every Horizontal Line of Ten Stamps

Wmk. 153 — "R M" Interlaced

Wmk. 154 — Eagle and R M

Wmk. 155 — SERVICIO POSTAL DE LOS ESTADOS UNIDOS MEXICANOS

Wmk. 156 — CORREOS MEXICO

Wmk. 248 — SECRETARIA DE HACIENDA MEXICO

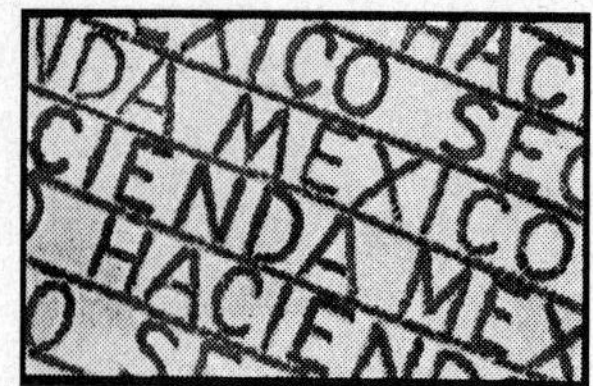

Wmk. 260 — Lines and SECRETARIA DE HACIENDA MEXICO

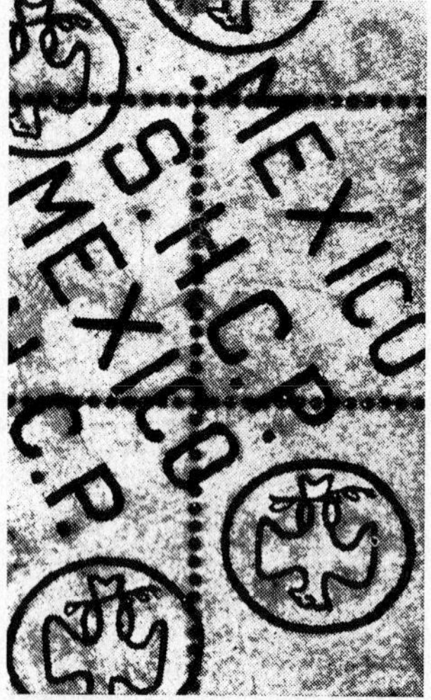

Wmk. 272 — "S. H. C. P. MEXICO" and Eagle in Circle

Wmk. 279 — GOBIERNO MEXICANO and Eagle in Circle

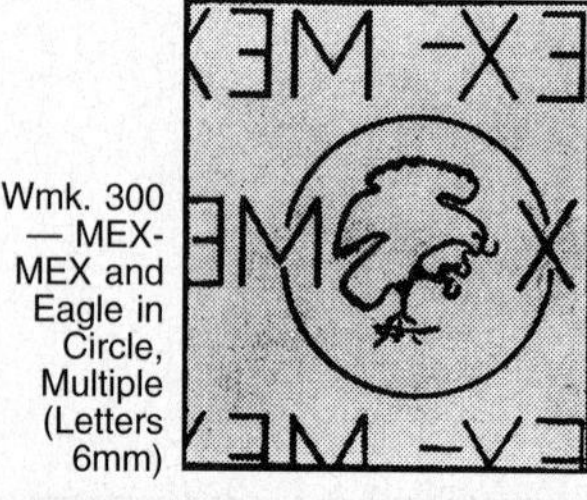

Wmk. 300 — MEX-MEX and Eagle in Circle, Multiple (Letters 6mm)

Wmk. 350 — MEX and Eagle in Circle, Multiple. Letters 8-9mm

Miguel Hidalgo y Costilla — A1

Handstamped with District Name

1856 Unwmk. Engr. *Imperf.*

1 A1 ½r blue 50.00 45.00
b. Without overprint 45.00 50.00
2 A1 1r yellow 30.00 5.50
b. Half used as ½r on cover *10,000.*
c. Without overprint 25.00 30.00
d. 1r green (error)
3 A1 2r yellow grn 27.50 5.50
a. 2r blue green 275.00 45.00
b. 2r emerald 250.00 55.00
c. Half used as 1r on cover 600.00
d. Without overprint 40.00 22.50
e. As "a," without overprint 250.00 45.00
f. As "b," without overprint 75.00
g. Printed on both sides (yel green) 300.00
4 A1 4r red 175.00 110.00
a. Half used as 2r on cover 250.00
b. Quarter used as 1r on cover 700.00
c. Without overprint 140.00 *160.00*
d. Three quarters used as 3r on cover *12,000.*
5 A1 8r red lilac 350.00 200.00
a. 8r violet 300.00 200.00
b. Without overprint 225.00 225.00
c. Eighth used as 1r on cover *17,500.*
d. Quarter used as 2r on cover 225.00
e. Half used as 4r on cover 900.00
Nos. 1-5 (5) 632.50 366.00

The 1r and 2r were printed in sheets of 60 with wide spacing between stamps, and in sheets of 190 or 200 with narrow spacing.

No. 3a can be distinguished from the other 2r stamps by the horizontal grain of the paper. The plate for No. 3b has framelines.

All values, except the 1r, have been reprinted, some of them several times. The reprints usually show signs of wear and the impressions are often smudgy. The paper is usually thicker than that of the originals. Reprints are usually on very white paper. Reprints are found with and without overprints and with cancellations made both from the original handstamps and from forged ones.

Counterfeits exist.

See Nos. 6-12. For overprints see Nos. 35-45.

1861

6 A1 ½r black, *buff* 50.00 45.00
a. Without overprint 34.00 62.50
7 A1 1r black, *green* 20.00 5.50
a. Impression of 2r on back 750.00
b. Without overprint 5.00 22.50
d. As "b," blk, *pink* (error) 8,000 *9,000.*
f. Double impression 150.00
8 A1 2r black, *pink* 15.00 6.50
a. Impression of 1r on back 2,000.
b. Half used as 1r on cover 750.00
c. Without overprint 3.50 22.50
d. Printed on both sides 2,250.
e. Double impression 100.00
f. As "e," without overprint —
9 A1 4r black, *yellow* 200.00 100.00
a. Half used as 2r on cover 190.00
b. Without overprint 50.00 100.00
c. Quarter used as 1r on cover 700.00
d. Three-quarters used as 3r on cover *35,000.*
10 A1 4r dull rose, *yel* 200.00 80.00
a. Half used as 2r on cover *950.00*
b. Without overprint 110.00 140.00
c. Printed on both sides *9,000.*
d. Quarter used as 1r on cover *10,000.*
11 A1 8r black, *red brn* 375.00 250.00
a. ⅛ used as 1R on cover front *11,000.*
b. Quarter used as 2r on cover 250.00
c. Half used as 4r on cover 750.00
d. Without overprint 110.00 225.00
e. Three quarters used as 6r on cover *45,000.*
12 A1 8r grn, *red brn* 500.00 240.00
a. Half used as 4r on cover 30,000.
b. Without overprint 150.00 200.00
c. Quarter used as 2r on cover 40,000.
d. Printed on both sides *12,500.* *12,500.*
Nos. 6-12 (7) 1,360. 727.00

Nos. 6, 9, 10, 11 and 12 have been reprinted. Most reprints of the ½r, 4r and 8r are on vertically grained paper. Originals are on horizontally grained paper. The original ½r stamps are much worn but the reprints are unworn. The paper of the 4r is too deep and rich in color and No. 10 is printed in too bright red.

Reprints of the 8r can only be told by experts. All these reprints are found in fancy colors and with overprints and cancellations as in the 1856 issue.

Counterfeits exist.

Hidalgo — A3

With District Name

1864 *Perf. 12*

14 A3 1r red *750.* *3,000.*
a. Without District Name .75
15 A3 2r blue *1,100.* *1,750.*
a. Without District Name .75
16 A3 4r brown *1,250.* *2,400.*
a. Without District Name 1.25
b. Vert. pair, imperf. between
17 A3 1p black *3,250.* —
a. Without District Name 2.00

Nos. 14 to 17 were issued with district overprints of Saltillo or Monterrey on the toned paper of 1864. Overprints on the 1867 white paper are fraudulent. Counterfeits and counterfeit cancellations are plentiful. The 1r red with "½" surcharge is bogus.

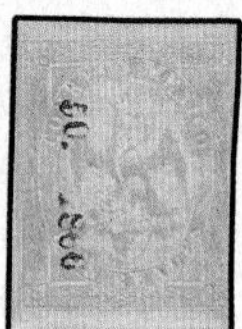
Coat of Arms — A4

Overprint of District Name, etc.

Five types of overprints:

I — District name only.

II — District name, consignment number and "1864" in large figures.

III — District name, number and "1864" in small figures.

IV — District name, number and "1865."

V — District name, number and "1866."

1864-66 *Imperf.*

18 A4 3c brn (IV, V) 1,300. *3,250.*
a. Without overprint 700.00
b. Laid paper *4,500.* *6,000.*
19 A4 ½r brown (I) 400.00 250.00
a. Type II 2,200. 2,250.
b. Without overprint 200.00 *650.00*
20 A4 ½r lilac (IV) 60.00 55.00
a. Type III 140.00 75.00
b. Type II 200.00 200.00
c. Type V *3,000.*
d. ½r gray (V) 70.00 80.00
e. Without overprint 5.75
f. ½r gray lilac 250.00 100.00
21 A4 1r blue (IV, V) 15.00 9.00
a. Type III 80.00 40.00
b. Without overprint 2.50
c. Half used as ½r on cover *10,000.*
22 A4 1r ultra (I, II) 120.00 30.00
a. Type III 90.00 40.00
b. Without overprint 160.00 150.00
c. Half used as ½r on cover *7,250.*
23 A4 2r org (III, IV, V) 10.00 6.00
a. Type II 20.00 10.00
b. Type I 50.00 10.00
c. 2r dp org, without ovpt., early plate 175.00 65.00
d. Without ovpt., late plate 2.00
e. Half used as 1r on cover *6,000.*
24 A4 4r grn (III, IV, V) 100.00 50.00
a. Types I, II 160.00 77.50
b. 4r dk grn, without ovpt. 4.75 *1,700.*
d. Half used as 2r on cover *700.00*
25 A4 8r red (IV, V) 150.00 90.00
a. Types II, III 175.00 125.00
b. Type I 400.00 175.00
c. 8r dk red, without ovpt. 7.00 *575.00*
f. Quarter used as 2r on cover *15,000.*
g. Three-quarters used as 6r on cover

The 2r printings from the early plates are 25½mm high; those from the late plate, 24½mm.

Varieties listed as "Without overprint" in unused condition are remainders.

Besides the overprints of district name, number and date, Nos. 18-34 often received, in the district offices, additional overprints of numbers and sometimes year dates. Stamps with these "sub-consignment numbers" sell for more than stamps without them.

Genuine examples of No. 20c should bear Mexico district name overprint, together with consignment numbers 1-1866 or 17-1866. Gray lilac stamps of other consignments are examples of No. 20f.

Value unused for No. 18 is for an example without gum. Examples with original gum sell for more. Examples of No. 18a on laid paper are forgeries.

No. 25g does not exist on full cover.

Faked quarterlings and bisects of 1856-64 are plentiful.

The 3c has been reprinted from a die on which the words "TRES CENTAVOS," the outlines of the serpent and some of the background lines have been retouched.

Emperor Maximilian — A5

Overprinted with District Name, Number and Date 1866 or 866; also with Number and Date only, or with Name only

1866 Litho.

26 A5 7c lilac gray 65.00 125.00
a. 7c deep gray 85.00 140.00
27 A5 13c blue 35.00 35.00
a. Half used as 7c on cover —
b. 13c cobalt blue 25.00 25.00
c. Without overprint 2,500.
28 A5 25c buff 12.50 9.00
a. Half used as 13c on cover —
b. Without overprint 2,500.
29 A5 25c orange 12.00 12.00
a. 25c red orange 20.00 27.50
b. 25c red brown 85.00 47.50
c. 25c brown *110.00* 85.00
30 A5 50c green 25.00 30.00
Nos. 26-30 (5) 149.50 211.00

Litho. printings have round period after value numerals.

Overprinted with District Name, Number and Date 866 or 867; also with Number and Date only

Engr.

31 A5 7c lilac 450.00 *5,500.*
a. Without overprint 3.50
32 A5 13c blue 12.00 12.00
a. Without overprint 1.25
33 A5 25c orange brown 12.00 11.00
a. Without overprint 1.25
34 A5 50c green 700.00 70.00
a. Without overprint 2.50

See "sub-consignment" note after No. 25.

Engraved printings have square period after value numerals.

Varieties listed as "Without overprint" in unused condition are remainders.

1867

35 A1 ½r blk, *buff* 2,500. *5,000.*
36 A1 1r blk, *green* 60.00 10.00
37 A1 2r blk, *pink* 22.50 5.00
a. Printed on both sides 140.00
38 A1 4r red, *yel* 625.00 50.00
a. Printed on both sides 175.00
39 A1 4r red *6,000.* *3,250.*
40 A1 8r blk, *red brn* 3,500. 275.00
41 A1 8r grn, *red brn* *4,000.*

Dangerous counterfeits exist of the "Mexico" overprint.

Examples of No. 38 with yellow removed are offered as No. 39.

Same Overprint
Thin Gray Blue Paper
Wmk. 151

42 A1 ½r gray 275.00 190.00
a. Without overprint 175.00 175.00
43 A1 1r blue 400.00 65.00
b. Without overprint 300.00 125.00
44 A1 2r green 200.00 30.00
a. Printed on both sides 6,000. 3,500.
b. Without overprint 300.00 50.00
45 A1 4r rose 3,000. 75.00
a. Without overprint *5,000.* 225.00

Most examples of Nos. 42-45 do not show the watermark. Values are for such stamps. Examples showing the watermark sell for more.

Reprints of the ½r and 4r exist on watermarked paper. Reprints of ½r and 8r also exist in gray on thick grayish wove paper, unwatermarked.

Hidalgo — A6

Thin Figures of Value, without Period after Numerals

Overprinted with District Name, Number and Abbreviated Date

1868 Unwmk. Litho. *Imperf.*

46 A6 6c blk, *buff* 40.00 20.00
47 A6 12c blk, *green* 45.00 20.00
a. Period after "12" 65.00 55.00
48 A6 25c bl, *pink* 75.00 20.00
a. Without overprint 125.00
49 A6 50c blk, *yellow* 600.00 60.00
50 A6 100c blk, *brown* 775.00 140.00
a. Half used as 50c on cover 3,000.
51 A6 100c brn, *brn* 1,750. 500.00

Perf.

52 A6 6c blk, *buff* 35.00 35.00
a. Without overprint 150.00
b. Period after "6" 100.00 75.00
53 A6 12c blk, *green* 35.00 12.00
a. Period after "12" 85.00 30.00
b. Very thick paper 50.00 25.00
c. Without overprint 110.00
54 A6 25c blue, *pink* 55.00 10.00
b. Without overprint 150.00
55 A6 50c blk, *yellow* 325.00 45.00
a. Half used as 50c on cover 3,000.
56 A6 100c blk, *brown* 375.00 110.00
c. Without overprint 350.00
57 A6 100c brn, *brn* 1,000. 375.00
a. Printed on both sides 1,250. 1,000.

Four kinds of perforation are found in the 1868 issue: serrate, square, pin and regular. The narrow spacing between stamps was inadequate for some of these perforation types.

Thick Figures of Value, with Period after Numerals

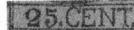

Overprinted with District Name, Number and Abbreviated Date

58 A6 6c blk, *buff* 9.50 4.50
59 A6 12c blk, *green* 4.25 1.25
a. Very thick paper 10.00
c. 12c black, *buff* (error) 575.00 575.00
d. Printed on both sides 3,000.
e. No period after "12" —
61 A6 25c blue, *pink* 8.00 1.25
a. No period after "25" 90.00
c. Very thick paper 25.00 6.00
d. "85" for "25" 75.00 50.00
e. "35" for "25" 75.00
f. Printed on both sides —
62 A6 50c blk, *yellow* 125.00 15.00
a. No period after "50" 225.00 35.00
b. 50c blue, *lt pink* (error) 3,000. 2,000.
c. Half used as 25c on cover 1,000.
d. Very thick paper 50.00
e. "30" for "50" 750.00 750.00
64 A6 100c blk, *brown* 150.00 90.00
a. No period after "100" 175.00 100.00
b. Very thick paper 75.00
c. Quarter used as 25c on cover 2,000.
d. Bisect used on cover as 50c 4,000.
Nos. 58-64 (5) 296.75 112.00

Perf.

65 A6 6c blk, *buff* 40.00 20.00
a. Very thick paper 60.00 35.00
66 A6 12c blk, *green* 5.50 5.50
a. Very thick paper 20.00 15.00
b. 12c black, *buff* (error) 575.00 575.00
c. No period after "12" —
68 A6 25c blue, *pink* 20.00 2.50
a. No period after "25" 80.00 80.00
c. Thick paper 30.00 15.00
d. "85" for "25" 80.00 40.00
69 A6 50c blk, *yellow* 200.00 25.00
a. No period after "50" 200.00 30.00
b. 50c blue, *lt pink* (error) 2,500. 1,500.
c. Thick paper 60.00
70 A6 100c blk, *brown* 200.00 60.00
a. No period after "100" 200.00 65.00
b. Very thick paper 80.00
Nos. 65-70 (5) 465.50 113.00

Postal forgeries of Nos. 58-70 were printed from original plates with district name overprints forged. These include the pelure paper varieties and some thick paper varieties. The "Anotado" handstamp was applied to some of the confiscated forgeries and they were issued, including Nos. 73a and 78a.

Stamps of 1868 Handstamped

Overprinted with District Name, Number and Abbreviated Date Thick Figures with Period

1872 *Imperf.*

71 A6 6c blk, *buff* 650.00 675.00
72 A6 12c blk, *green* 85.00 75.00
73 A6 25c bl, *pink* 40.00 45.00
a. Pelure paper 55.00 65.00
b. "85" for "25" 125.00
74 A6 50c blk, *yellow* 850.00 475.00
a. No period after "50" 900.00 475.00
75 A6 100c blk, *brown* 1,250. 1,000.
a. No period after "100" 1,100.

Perf.

76 A6 6c blk, *buff* 750.00
77 A6 12c blk, *green* 90.00 80.00
78 A6 25c blue, *pink* 35.00 42.50
a. Pelure paper 65.00 90.00
79 A6 50c blk, *yellow* 850.00 600.00
a. No period after "50" 550.00
80 A6 100c blk, *brown* 1,200.

Counterfeit "Anotado" overprints abound. Genuine cancellations other than Mexico City or of the Diligencias de Puebla are unknown. It is recommended that these be purchased accompanied by certificates of authenticity from competent experts.

The stamps of the 1872 issue are found perforated with square holes, pin-perf. 13, 14 or 15, and with serrate perforation.

Counterfeits of the 1868 6c, 12c buff, 50c and 100c (both colors) from new plates have clear, sharp impressions and more facial shading lines than the originals. These counterfeits are found perf. and imperf., with thick and thin numerals, and with the "Anotado" overprint.

Hidalgo — A8

Moiré on White Back Overprinted with District Name, Number and Abbreviated Date White Wove Paper

1872 Litho. Wmk. 150 *Imperf.*

81 A8 6c green 325.00 275.00
82 A8 12c blue 250.00 125.00
a. Laid paper 2,000. 350.00
83 A8 25c red 400.00 125.00
a. Laid paper 2,000. 350.00
84 A8 50c yellow 2,000. 850.00
a. 50c blue (error) 3,000.
b. Laid paper 4,000.
c. As "a," without ovpt. 130.00
86 A8 100c gray lilac 1,000. 650.00
Nos. 81-86 (5) 3,975. 2,025.

Wmk. "LA + F"

81a A8 6c green 2,000. 1,000.
82b A8 12c blue 450.00 325.00
83b A8 25c red 575.00 575.00
c. Without overprint 500.00
84d A8 50c yellow 3,500. 2,000.
86a A8 100c gray lilac 4,000. 1,500.

1872 Wmk. 150 *Pin-perf.*

87 A8 6c green 2,500. 2,000.
88 A8 12c blue 475.00 175.00
89 A8 25c red 550.00 275.00
b. Laid paper 1,000.
90 A8 50c yellow 1,500. 950.00
a. 50c blue (error) *1,000.* *1,250.*
b. As "a," without overprint 200.00
92 A8 100c gray lilac 1,200. 1,200.
Nos. 87-92 (5) 6,225. 4,600.

Wmk. "LA + F"

87a A8 6c green 2,500. 2,000.
88a A8 12c blue 450.00 *400.00*
89a A8 25c red 950.00 350.00
90c A8 50c yellow 4,000. 2,500.
92a A8 100c gray lilac 3,600. 2,750.

The watermark "LA+F" stands for La Croix Frères, the paper manufacturers, and is in double-lined block capitals 13mm high. A single stamp will show only part of this watermark.

Values for Nos. 87-92a are for examples with visible perfs on all sides.

1872 Unwmk. *Imperf.*

93 A8 6c green 12.50 12.50
a. Without moiré on back, without overprint 60.00 65.00
b. Vertically laid paper 3,000. 1,300.
c. Bottom label retouched 100.00 90.00
d. Very thick paper 37.50 37.50
94 A8 12c blue 2.00 1.75
a. Without moiré on back, without overprint 30.00 35.00
b. Vertically laid paper 350.00 210.00
c. Thin gray bl paper of 1867 (Wmk 151) 2,000.
95 A8 25c red 8.50 2.00
a. Without moiré on back, without overprint 30.00 35.00
b. Vertically laid paper 450.00 500.00
c. Thin gray bl paper of 1867 (Wmk 151) 1,500.
96 A8 50c yellow 140.00 35.00
a. 50c orange 140.00 35.00
b. Without moiré on back, without overprint 50.00 70.00
c. Vertically laid paper 2,000.
d. 50c blue (error) 650.00
e. As "d," without overprint 45.00
f. As "e," without moiré on back 65.00
g. Half used as 25c on cover *5,000.*
98 A8 100c gray lilac 90.00 50.00
a. 100c lilac 100.00 42.50
b. Without moiré on back, without overprint 50.00 110.00
c. Vertically laid paper 1,250.
Nos. 93-98 (5) 253.00 101.25

Counterfeits of these stamps are 24½mm high instead of 24mm. The printing is sharper and more uniform than the genuine. Forged district names and consignment numbers exist.

Pin-perf. and Serrate Perf.

99 A8 6c green 90.00 75.00
100 A8 12c blue 3.50 3.00
a. Vertically laid paper 350.00
b. Horiz. pair, imperf. vert. 100.00 100.00
c. Vert. pair, imperf. between 150.00
101 A8 25c red 3.25 1.50
a. Vertically laid paper 500.00
b. Horiz. pair, imperf. vert. 100.00 100.00
102 A8 50c yellow 175.00 50.00
a. 50c orange 160.00 50.00
b. 50c blue (error) 475.00 500.00
c. As "b," without overprint 45.00
104 A8 100c lilac 150.00 80.00
a. 100c gray lilac 125.00 80.00
Nos. 99-104 (5) 421.75 209.50

Values for Nos. 99-104a are for examples with visible perfs on all sides.

Hidalgo
A9 A10

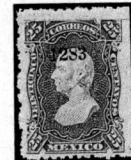

A11 A12

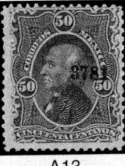

A13 A14

Overprinted with District Name and Number and Date; also with Number and Date only Thick Wove Paper, Some Showing Vertical Ribbing

1874-80 Unwmk. Engr. *Perf. 12*

105 A9 4c org ('80) 12.50 12.00
a. Vert. pair, imperf. btwn. 60.00
b. Without overprint 6.50 12.50
c. Half used as 2c on cover 1,000.
106 A10 5c brown 4.50 3.00
a. Horizontally laid paper 100.00 55.00
b. Imperf., pair 60.00
c. Horiz. pair, imperf. btwn. 50.00 300.00
d. Vert. pair, imperf. btwn. 110.00 110.00
e. Without overprint 37.50 37.50
f. As "a," wmkd. "LACROIX" 1,750. 1,000.
107 A11 10c black 2.00 1.25
a. Horizontally laid paper 2.50 2.50
b. Horiz. pair, imperf. btwn. 75.00 75.00
c. Without overprint 35.00 27.50
d. Half used as 5c on cover 2,000.
e. Imperf., pair
f. As "a," wmkd. "LACROIX" 350.00 250.00
108 A11 10c org ('78) 2.00 1.25
a. 10c yellow bister 7.50 4.25
b. Imperf., pair
c. Without overprint 55.00 55.00
d. Half used as 5c on cover 100.00
109 A12 25c blue .85 .70
b. Horizontally laid paper 2.25 1.75
c. Imperf., pair 50.00 25.00
d. Without overprint 35.00 20.00
e. Horiz. pair, imperf. btwn. 125.00
f. As "b," horiz. pair, imperf. vert. 200.00
g. As "b," wmkd. "LACROIX" 300.00 250.00
h. Printed on both sides 1,500.
i. Half used as 10c on cover 2,000.
110 A13 50c green 13.00 13.00
a. Without overprint 50.00
b. Half used as 25c on cover 2,500.
111 A14 100c carmine 18.00 15.00
a. Imperf., pair 200.00 200.00
b. Without overprint 50.00
c. Quarterf used as 25c on cover 3,000.
Nos. 105-111 (7) 52.85 46.20

The "LACROIX" watermark is spelled out "LACROIX FRERES" in 2 lines of block capitals without serifs once to a sheet of horiz. laid paper. 6-12 stamps may have a portion of the wmk.

1875-77 Wmk. 150

112 A10 5c brown 110.00 70.00
113 A11 10c black 110.00 70.00
114 A12 25c blue 110.00 70.00
115 A13 50c green 650.00 450.00
116 A14 100c carmine 600.00 400.00
Nos. 112-116 (5) 1,580. 1,060.

1881 Unwmk. Thin Wove Paper

117 A9 4c orange 70.00 70.00
a. Without overprint 20.00 20.00
118 A10 5c brown 10.00 6.50
a. Without overprint .50 20.00
b. As "a," vert. pair, imperf. horiz. 1,000.
119 A11 10c orange 6.00 3.50
a. Imperf., pair
b. Vert. pair, imperf. horiz.
c. Without overprint .75 4.50
d. Vert. pair, imperf. btwn.
e. Half used as 5c on cover 1,500.
120 A12 25c blue 4.00 2.25
a. Imperf., pair 100.00
b. Without overprint .50 8.00
c. Double impression 65.00
d. Printed on both sides *1,500.*
121 A13 50c green 45.00 40.00
a. Without overprint 4.00 30.00
122 A14 100c carmine 50.00 50.00
a. Without overprint 6.00 300.00

The stamps of 1874-81 are found with number and date wide apart, close together or omitted, and in various colors.

The thin paper is fragile and easily damaged. Values for Nos. 117-122 are for undamaged, fine examples.

Benito Juárez — A15

Overprinted with District Name and Number and Date; also with Number and Date only
Thick Wove Paper, Some Showing Vertical Ribbing

1879 *Perf. 12*

123 A15 1c brown 4.00 4.00
a. Without overprint 75.00 140.00
b. 1c gray 20.00 15.00
124 A15 2c dk violet 4.00 4.50
a. Without overprint 75.00 150.00
b. Printed on both sides
c. 2c dark gray 20.00 14.00
125 A15 5c orange 2.25 1.50
a. Without overprint 75.00 90.00
b. Double impression *500.00*
126 A15 10c blue 3.00 2.50
a. Without overprint 75.00 150.00
b. 10c ultra 160.00 160.00
127 A15 25c rose 8.00 30.00
a. Without overprint 1.75 150.00
128 A15 50c green 15.00 50.00
a. Without overprint 1.25 150.00
b. Printed on both sides 165.00
129 A15 85c violet 20.00 250.00
a. Without overprint 2.50
130 A15 100c black 25.00 75.00
a. Without overprint 3.00 150.00
Nos. 123-130 (8) 81.25 417.50

Used values for Nos. 127-130 are for stamps with postal cancellations. Pen cancelled examples are worth the same as unused stamps.

Forged cancellations on Nos. 127-130 are plentiful.

1882 **Thin Wove Paper**

131 A15 1c brown 40.00 37.50
a. Without overprint 125.00
132 A15 2c dk violet 27.50 24.00
a. 2c slate 47.50 50.00
b. Without overprint 110.00
c. Half used as 1c on cover
133 A15 5c orange 9.00 6.00
a. Without overprint 1.25
b. Half used as 2c on cover
c. As "a," vert. pair, imperf. btwn.
134 A15 10c blue 9.00 6.00
a. Without overprint 1.25
b. Half used as 5c on cover
135 A15 10c brown 9.00
a. Imperf., pair 3.00
136 A15 12c brown 7.50 8.00
a. Without overprint 2.50 22.50
b. Imperf., pair 75.00
c. Half used as 6c on cover
137 A15 18c orange brn 9.00 15.00
a. Horiz. pair, imperf. btwn. 100.00
b. Without overprint 2.25 18.00
138 A15 24c violet 9.00 11.00
a. Without overprint 2.25 17.50
139 A15 25c rose 45.00 250.00
a. Without overprint 4.50
140 A15 25c orange brn 5.50
141 A15 50c green 45.00 75.00
a. Without overprint 6.25
142 A15 50c yellow 80.00 350.00
a. Without overprint 150.00
143 A15 85c red violet 55.00
144 A15 100c black 75.00 *250.00*
a. Without overprint 5.00
b. Vert. pair, imperf. btwn. 165.00 165.00
145 A15 100c orange 95.00 400.00
a. Without overprint 175.00
Nos. 131-145 (15) 520.50 1,433.

No. 135, 140 and 143 exist only without overprint. They were never placed in use.

Used values for Nos. 139, 141, 142, 144 and 145 are for postally used stamps. Forged cancellations are plentiful. Pen cancelled examples are worth the same as unused stamps.

See note on thin paper after No. 122.

A16

Overprinted with District Name, Number and Abbreviated Date

1882-83

146 A16 2c green 11.00 8.00
a. Without overprint 27.50 20.00
147 A16 3c car lake 11.00 8.00
a. Without overprint 5.25 8.50
148 A16 6c blue ('83) 30.00 40.00
a. Without overprint 30.00 50.00
149 A16 6c ultra 6.00 8.50
a. Without overprint 3.50 6.00
b. As "a," imperf pair 50.00
Nos. 146-149 (4) 58.00 64.50

See note on thin paper after No. 122.

Hidalgo — A17

1884 **Wove or Laid Paper** *Perf. 12*

150 A17 1c green 4.00 .75
a. Imperf., pair 125.00
b. 1c blue (error) 600.00 475.00
151 A17 2c green 6.75 2.00
a. Imperf., pair 200.00 225.00
b. Half used as 1c on cover
152 A17 3c green 12.50 2.00
a. Imperf., pair 200.00 250.00
b. Horiz. pair, imperf. vert. 225.00 250.00
153 A17 4c green 16.00 2.00
a. Imperf., pair 200.00 250.00
b. Half used as 2c on cover 400.00
c. Horiz. pair, imperf. btwn. 200.00 250.00
154 A17 5c green 17.50 1.50
a. Imperf., pair 200.00 250.00
c. Horiz. pair, imperf. btwn. 250.00
d. Vert. pair, imperf. btwn. 275.00
155 A17 6c green 15.00 1.50
a. Imperf., pair 200.00 250.00
156 A17 10c green 16.00 .75
a. Imperf., pair 125.00 150.00
157 A17 12c green 30.00 3.50
a. Vert. pair, imperf. between 250.00 350.00
b. Half used as 6c on cover 300.00
158 A17 20c green 90.00 2.50
a. Diagonal half used as 10c on cover 300.00
b. Imperf., pair 350.00 350.00
159 A17 25c green 150.00 5.00
a. Imperf., pair 300.00 300.00
160 A17 50c green .60 *5.00*
a. Imperf., pair 150.00 150.00
b. Horiz. pair, imperf. btwn. 300.00
c. Double impression 200.00 200.00
161 A17 1p blue .60 *11.00*
a. Imperf., pair 250.00 250.00
b. Vert. pair, imperf. between 100.00
c. 1p with 1c printed on back 300.00
d. Horiz. pair, imperf. btwn. 250.00
162 A17 2p blue .60 *22.50*
a. Imperf., pair 175.00 200.00
163 A17 5p blue 350.00 300.00
164 A17 10p blue 500.00 225.00
Nos. 150-162 (13) 359.55 *60.00*

Imperforate varieties should be purchased in pairs or larger. Single imperforates are usually trimmed perforated stamps.

Beware of examples of No. 150 that have been chemically changed to resemble No. 150b.

Bisects were not officially authorized. Nos. 155 and 160 exist as bisects on piece.

Forged cancels on Nos. 161-162 are plentiful.

Some values exist perf. 11.

See Nos. 165-173, 230-231.

1885

165 A17 1c pale green 35.00 7.00
166 A17 2c carmine 25.00 3.50
a. Diagonal half used as 1c on cover 350.00
167 A17 3c orange brn 25.00 6.00
a. Imperf., pair 250.00 250.00
b. Horiz. pair, imperf. btwn. 300.00
168 A17 4c red orange 42.50 19.00
169 A17 5c ultra 27.50 3.50
170 A17 6c dk brown 32.50 6.00
a. Half used as 3c on cover 350.00
171 A17 10c orange 27.50 1.50
a. 10c yellow 30.00 1.50
b. Horiz. pair, imperf. btwn. 250.00 250.00
c. Imperf., pair 300.00
172 A17 12c olive brn 57.50 9.00
a. Printed on both sides 300.00
173 A17 25c grnsh blue 225.00 22.50
Nos. 165-173 (9) 497.50 78.00

Numeral of Value — A18

1886 *Perf. 12*

174 A18 1c yellow green 2.25 .75
a. 1c blue grn 5.50 4.50
b. Horiz. pair, imperf. btwn. 200.00 200.00
c. Perf. 11 45.00 45.00
175 A18 2c carmine 2.60 .90
a. Horiz. pair, imperf. btwn. 80.00 75.00
b. Vert. pair, imperf. between 200.00 200.00
c. Perf. 11 45.00 45.00
d. Half used as 1c on cover 100.00
176 A18 3c lilac 12.00 7.50
177 A18 4c lilac 18.00 5.25
a. Perf. 11 50.00 *55.00*
b. Horiz. pair, imperf. btwn. 450.00
178 A18 5c ultra 2.25 1.00
a. 5c blue 2.25 .75
179 A18 6c lilac 30.00 7.50
180 A18 10c lilac 22.50 1.10
a. Perf. 11 125.00
181 A18 12c lilac 25.00 14.00
182 A18 20c lilac 190.00 110.00
183 A18 25c lilac 75.00 19.00
Nos. 174-183 (10) 379.60 167.00

Nos. 175, 191, 194B, 196, 202 exist with blue or black surcharge "Vale 1 Cvo." These were made by the Colima postmaster.

1887

184 A18 3c scarlet 1.90 .60
a. Imperf., pair 75.00
185 A18 4c scarlet 7.50 2.25
a. Imperf., pair 500.00
b. Horiz. pair, imperf. btwn. 400.00
186 A18 6c scarlet 12.50 2.25
a. Horiz. pair, imperf. btwn. 200.00
187 A18 10c scarlet 2.75 .60
a. Imperf., pair 75.00
b. Horiz. pair, imperf. btwn. 200.00
188 A18 20c scarlet 18.00 1.50
a. Horiz. pair, imperf. btwn. 275.00
b. Vert. pair, imperf. btwn. 350.00
189 A18 25c scarlet 15.00 4.00
Nos. 184-189 (6) 57.65 11.20

Perf. 6

190 A18 1c blue grn 45.00 45.00
191 A18 2c brown car 22.50 42.00
192 A18 5c ultra 15.00 4.50
a. 5c blue 15.00 4.50
193 A18 10c lilac 15.00 4.25
193A A18 10c brown lilac 15.00 3.00
194 A18 10c scarlet 35.00 15.00

Perf. 6x12

194A A18 1c blue grn 62.50 42.50
194B A18 2c brown car 85.00 75.00
194C A18 3c scarlet 300.00 350.00
194D A18 5c ultra 60.00 45.00
194E A18 10c lilac 90.00 75.00
194F A18 10c scarlet 80.00 60.00
194G A18 10c brown lilac 90.00 75.00

Many shades exist.

Paper with colored ruled lines on face or reverse of stamp

1887 *Perf. 12*

195 A18 1c green 75.00 45.00
196 A18 2c brown car 190.00 47.50
198 A18 5c ultra 110.00 30.00
199 A18 10c scarlet 110.00 25.00

Perf. 6

201 A18 1c green 60.00 20.00
202 A18 2c brown car 60.00 24.00
204 A18 5c ultra 50.00 12.00
205 A18 10c brown lil 42.50 10.00
206 A18 10c scarlet 250.00 40.00
Nos. 201-206 (5) 462.50 106.00

Perf. 6x12

207 A18 1c green 225.00 140.00
208 A18 2c brown car 325.00 140.00
209 A18 5c ultra 225.00 140.00
210 A18 10c brown lil 290.00 135.00
211 A18 10c scarlet 350.00 225.00
Nos. 207-211 (5) 1,415. 780.00

1890-95 **Wmk. 152** *Perf. 11 & 12*
Wove or Laid Paper

212 A18 1c yellow grn .75 .35
a. 1c blue green .75 .35
b. Horiz. pair, imperf. btwn. 125.00 125.00
c. Laid paper 2.50 2.50
d. Horiz. pair, imperf. vert. 125.00 125.00
213 A18 2c carmine 1.50 .75
a. 2c brown car 1.25 1.00
b. Vert. pair, imperf. btwn. 150.00
c. Imperf., pair 200.00
214 A18 3c vermilion 1.00 .60
b. Horiz. pair, imperf. btwn. 200.00
215 A18 4c vermilion 3.25 2.10
a. Horiz. pair, imperf. btwn. 200.00
216 A18 5c ultra .60 .50
a. 5c dull blue 1.00 .50
217 A18 6c vermilion 3.75 2.75
a. Horiz. pair, imperf. btwn. 300.00
218 A18 10c vermilion .50 .35
b. Horiz. or vert. pair, imperf. btwn. 175.00 175.00
c. Vert. pair, imperf. horiz. 175.00
d. Imperf., pair 200.00
219 A18 12c ver ('95) 14.00 18.00
a. Horiz. pair, imperf. btwn. 450.00
220 A18 20c vermilion 3.50 1.50
220A A18 20c dk violet 160.00 *190.00*
221 A18 25c vermilion 5.00 2.50
Nos. 212-220,221 (10) 33.85 29.40

No. 219 has been reprinted in slightly darker shade than the original.

1892

222 A18 3c orange 4.00 2.00
223 A18 4c orange 4.25 3.00
224 A18 6c orange 5.75 2.00
225 A18 10c orange 27.50 2.00
226 A18 20c orange 50.00 6.00
227 A18 25c orange 16.00 4.50
Nos. 222-227 (6) 107.50 19.50

1892

228 A18 5p carmine 1,250. 900.
229 A18 10p carmine 1,900. 1,250.
230 A17 5p blue green 3,500. 1,200.
231 A17 10p blue green *7,000.* *2,700.*

1894 *Perf. 5½, 6*

232 A18 1c yellow grn 3.00 3.00
233 A18 3c vermilion 9.00 9.00
234 A18 4c vermilion 40.00 37.50
235 A18 5c ultra 12.50 5.00
236 A18 10c vermilion 7.50 3.00
236A A18 20c vermilion 110.00 110.00
237 A18 25c vermilion 62.50 62.50
Nos. 232-237 (7) 244.50 230.00

Perf. 5½x11, 11x5½, Compound and Irregular

238 A18 1c yellow grn 7.00 7.00
238A A18 2c brown car 16.00 16.00
238B A18 3c vermilion 47.50 32.50
238C A18 4c vermilion 55.00 55.00
239 A18 5c ultra 17.50 12.50
a. 5c blue 12.50 12.50
239C A18 6c vermilion 75.00 75.00
240 A18 10c vermilion 20.00 7.00
240A A18 20c vermilion 200.00 200.00
241 A18 25c vermilion 62.50 62.50
Nos. 238-241 (9) 500.50 467.50

The stamps of the 1890 to 1895 issues are also to be found unwatermarked, as part of the sheet frequently escaped the watermark.

Letter Carrier — A20

Mounted Courier with Pack Mule — A21

Statue of Cuauhtémoc A22

Mail Coach A23

Mail Train — A24

Regular or Pin Perf. 12

1895 **Wmk. 152**
Wove or Laid Paper

242 A20 1c green 3.00 .75
a. Vert. pair, imperf. horiz. 175.00
d. Watermarked sideway ('97) 125.00 15.00
243 A20 2c carmine 3.75 1.00
a. Half used as 1c on cover 250.00
c. Watermarked sideways ('97) 80.00 10.00
244 A20 3c orange brown 3.75 1.00
a. Vert. pair, imperf. horiz. 250.00
d. Watermarked sideways ('97) 125.00 10.00
e. Horiz. or vert. pair, imperf. between 300.00
246 A21 4c orange 12.50 1.50
a. 4c orange red 7.50 1.25
247 A22 5c ultra 7.00 .35
a. Imperf., pair 175.00 200.00
b. Horiz. or vert. pair, imperf. between 175.00 200.00
e. Half used as 2c on cover 400.00
f. Watermarked sideways ('97) 15.00 5.00
248 A23 10c lilac rose 4.50 1.00
a. Horiz. or vert. pair, imperf. between 250.00
b. Half used as 5c on cover 250.00
249 A21 12c olive brown 50.00 12.50
251 A23 15c brt blue 27.50 3.00
b. Watermarked sideways ('97) 100.00
c. Imperf., pair 300.00
252 A23 20c brown rose 32.50 3.00
b. Half used as 10c on cover 200.00
c. Watermarked sideways ('97) 1,000. 750.00
253 A23 50c purple 70.00 16.00
254 A24 1p brown 90.00 35.00
a. Watermarked sideways ('97) 750.00 *900.00*

255	A24	5p	scarlet	300.00	190.00
256	A24	10p	deep blue	650.00	350.00
			Nos. 242-256 (13)	1,255.	615.10

No. 248 exists in perf. 11.

Nos. 242d, 243c, 244d, 247f, 251b, 252c and 254a was a special printing, made in Jan. 1897. The watermark is sideways, the grain of the paper is horizontal (rather than vertical, as appears on Nos. 242-256), and the design is somewhat shorter than the other stamps in this series. The sideways orientation of the watermark is the most easily identifiable feature of this printing.

Important: For unwatermarked examples of Nos. 242-256, see the footnote after No. 291.

Perf. 6

242b	A20	1c	green	60.00	35.00
243b	A20	2c	carmine	125.00	60.00
244b	A20	3c	orange brown	90.00	50.00
247c	A22	5c	ultra	90.00	50.00
248c	A23	10c	lilac rose	125.00	55.00
249a	A21	12c	olive brown	100.00	50.00

Perf. 6x12, 12x6 & Compound or Irregular

242c	A20	1c	green	30.00	20.00
244c	A20	3c	orange brown	35.00	20.00
246b	A21	4c	orange	75.00	50.00
247d	A22	5c	ultra	75.00	50.00
248d	A23	10c	lilac rose	35.00	20.00
249b	A21	12c	olive brown	50.00	25.00
251a	A23	15c	brt blue	60.00	40.00
252a	A23	20c	brown rose	100.00	70.00
253b	A23	50c	purple	150.00	100.00

See Nos. 257-291. For overprints see Nos. O10-O48A.

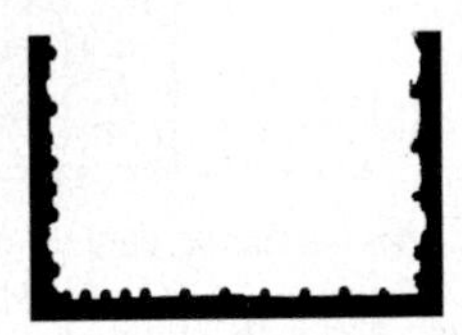

"Irregular" Perfs.

Some stamps perf. 6x12, 12x6, 5½x11 and 11x5½ have both perf. 6 and 12 or perf. 5½ and 11 on one or more sides of the stamp. These are known as irregular perfs.

1896-97 Wmk. 153 *Perf. 12*

257	A20	1c	green	14.00	1.25
c.			Imperf., pair		250.00
258	A20	2c	carmine	17.50	1.50
a.			Horiz. pair, imperf. vert.		
259	A20	3c	orange brn	20.00	1.50
c.			Horiz. pair, imperf. between		300.00
260	A21	4c	orange	32.50	1.75
c.			4c deep orange	30.00	6.00
261	A22	5c	ultra	9.00	1.25
a.			Imperf., pair	200.00	200.00
b.			Vert. pair, imperf. btwn.	200.00	
262	A21	12c	olive brn	160.00	80.00
263	A23	15c	brt blue	200.00	13.00
264	A23	20c	brown rose	750.00	275.00
265	A23	50c	purple	175.00	110.00
266	A24	1p	brown	300.00	250.00
267	A24	5p	scarlet	800.00	600.00
268	A24	10p	dp blue	900.00	525.00
			Nos. 257-268 (12)	3,378.	1,860.

Perf. 6

257a	A20	1c	green	35.00	25.00
259a	A20	3c	orange brown	35.00	20.00
260a	A21	4c	orange	40.00	25.00
261c	A22	5c	ultra	110.00	70.00
263a	A23	15c	bright blue	75.00	35.00

Perf. 6x12, 12x6 and Compound or Irregular

257b	A20	1c	green	25.00	20.00
258b	A20	2c	carmine	50.00	25.00
259b	A20	3c	orange brown	40.00	20.00
260b	A21	4c	orange	45.00	20.00
261d	A22	5c	ultra	40.00	20.00
262a	A21	12c	olive brown	125.00	80.00
263b	A23	15c	bright blue	250.00	125.00
264a	A23	20c	brown rose		
265a	A23	50c	purple		

1897-98 Wmk. 154 *Perf. 12*

269	A20	1c	green	20.00	3.00
270	A20	2c	scarlet	35.00	4.50
c.			Horiz. pair, imperf. btwn.		250.00
271	A21	4c	orange	52.50	3.75
a.			Horizontal pair, imperf. vertical	—	
272	A22	5c	ultra	50.00	3.75
a.			Imperf., pair	85.00	
273	A21	12c	olive brown	200.00	45.00
275	A23	15c	brt blue	275.00	85.00
276	A23	20c	brown rose	175.00	15.00
c.			Horiz. pair, imperf. btwn.		300.00
277	A23	50c	purple	375.00	75.00
278	A24	1p	brown	425.00	200.00
278A	A24	5p	scarlet	—	*4,000.*
			Nos. 269-278 (9)	1,608.	435.00

Perf. 6

269a	A20	1c	green	45.00	25.00
270a	A20	2c	scarlet	45.00	25.00
272b	A22	5c	ultra	60.00	25.00
273a	A21	12c	olive brown	110.00	60.00
276a	A23	20c	brown rose		*650.00*

Perf. 6x12, 12x6 and Compound or Irregular

269b	A20	1c	green	25.00	15.00
270b	A20	2c	scarlet	30.00	22.50
271b	A21	4c	orange	65.00	12.50
272c	A22	5c	ultra	50.00	15.00
273b	A21	12c	olive brown	125.00	65.00
275a	A23	15c	bright blue	125.00	65.00
276b	A23	20c	brown rose	240.00	30.00
277a	A23	50c	purple	125.00	50.00

1898 Unwmk. *Perf. 12*

279	A20	1c	green	3.00	.50
a.			Horiz. pair, imperf. vert	300.00	
b.			Imperf., pair	250.00	
280	A20	2c	scarlet	6.25	.75
a.			2c green (error)	*475.00*	
281	A20	3c	orange brn	6.00	.75
a.			Imperf., pair	250.00	250.00
b.			Pair, imperf. between	80.00	80.00
282	A21	4c	orange	30.00	3.00
b.			4c deep orange	37.50	7.00
c.			Imperf., pair		300.00
283	A22	5c	ultra	2.00	.50
a.			Imperf., pair	200.00	200.00
b.			Pair, imperf. between	200.00	
284	A23	10c	lilac rose	550.00	175.00
285	A21	12c	olive brn	80.00	27.50
a.			Imperf., pair	200.00	
286	A23	15c	brt blue	175.00	8.00
287	A23	20c	brown rose	35.00	3.00
a.			Imperf., pair	250.00	
288	A23	50c	purple	150.00	42.50
289	A24	1p	brown	175.00	80.00
290	A24	5p	carmine rose	550.00	425.00
291	A24	10p	deep blue	800.00	575.00
			Nos. 279-291 (13)	2,562.	1,342.

Warning: Sheets of Nos. 242-256 (watermarked "CORREOS E U M") have a column of stamps without watermarks, because the watermark did not fit the sheet size. As a result, be careful not to confuse unwatermarked examples of Nos. 242-256 with Nos. 279-291. This is especially important for No. 284. Nos. 242-256 and the watermarked 1895-97 overprinted Officials, Nos. O10-O39, have a vertical grain or mesh to the paper. Nos. 279-291 and the unwatermarked 1898 overprinted Officials, Nos. O40-O48B, have a horizontal grain or mesh to the paper. Be careful not to confuse unwatermarked examples of Nos. O10-O39 with Nos. O40-O48B.

Perf. 6

279c	A20	1c	green	85.00	35.00
280b	A20	2c	scarlet	75.00	30.00
281c	A20	3c	orange brown	50.00	35.00
283c	A22	5c	ultra	65.00	30.00
287b	A23	20c	brown rose	125.00	75.00
291a	A24	10p	deep blue		

Perf. 6x12, 12x6 and Compound or Irregular

279d	A20	1c	green	25.00	20.00
280c	A20	2c	scarlet	25.00	20.00
281d	A20	3c	orange brown	30.00	20.00
282a	A21	4c	orange	40.00	25.00
283d	A22	5c	ultra	20.00	10.00
284a	A23	10c	lilac rose	125.00	85.00
285b	A21	12c	olive brown	90.00	60.00
286a	A23	15c	bright blue	75.00	50.00
287c	A23	20c	brown rose	100.00	50.00
288a	A23	50c	purple	575.00	575.00

Forgeries of the 6 and 6x12 perforations of 1895-98 are plentiful.

Coat of Arms
A25 A26

A27

A28

A29

A30

A31

Juanacatlán Falls — A32

View of Mt. Popocatépetl A33

Cathedral, Mexico, D. F. — A34

1899, Nov. 1 Wmk. 155 *Perf. 14, 15*

294	A25	1c	green	1.90	.35
295	A26	2c	vermilion	4.50	.35
296	A27	3c	orange brn	3.00	.35
297	A28	5c	dark blue	4.75	.35
298	A29	10c	violet & org	6.00	.35
299	A30	15c	lav & claret	8.00	.35
300	A31	20c	rose & dk bl	9.00	.40
301	A32	50c	red lil & blk	35.00	2.25
a.			50c lilac & black	42.50	2.25
302	A33	1p	blue & blk	80.00	3.50
303	A34	5p	carmine & blk	275.00	12.00
			Nos. 294-303 (10)	427.15	20.25
			Set, never hinged	1,500.	

See Nos. 304-305, 307-309. For overprints see Nos. 420-422, 439-450, 452-454, 482-483, 515-516, 539, 550, O49-O60, O62-O66, O68-O74, O101.

A35

1903

304	A25	1c	violet	1.50	.35
305	A26	2c	green	2.00	.35
306	A35	4c	carmine	5.00	.45
307	A28	5c	orange	1.25	.35
308	A29	10c	blue & org	5.00	.35
309	A32	50c	carmine & blk	75.00	6.50
			Nos. 304-309 (6)	89.75	8.35
			Set, never hinged	350.00	

For overprints see Nos. 451, O61, O67.

Independence Issue

Josefa Ortiz — A36

Leona Vicario — A37

López Rayón — A38

Juan Aldama — A39

Miguel Hidalgo — A40

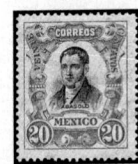

Ignacio Allende — A41

Epigmenio González A42

Mariano Abasolo A43

Declaration of Independence A44

Mass on the Mount of Crosses A45

Capture of Granaditas A46

1910 *Perf. 14*

310	A36	1c	dull violet	.35	.35
311	A37	2c	green	.35	.35
312	A38	3c	orange brn	.60	.35
313	A39	4c	carmine	2.50	.45
314	A40	5c	orange	.35	.35
315	A41	10c	blue & org	1.50	.35
316	A42	15c	gray bl & cl	8.00	.50
317	A43	20c	red & bl	5.00	.40
318	A44	50c	red brn & blk	12.00	1.60
319	A45	1p	blue & blk	15.00	2.00
320	A46	5p	car & blk	57.50	16.50
			Nos. 310-320 (11)	103.15	23.20
			Set, never hinged	325.00	

Independence of Mexico from Spain, cent.

For overprints and surcharges see Nos. 370-380, 423-433, 455-465, 484-494, 517-538, 540-549, 551-558, 577-590, O75-O85, O102-O112, O191-O192, O195, RA13, Merida 1.

CIVIL WAR ISSUES

During the 1913-16 Civil War, provisional issues with various handstamped overprints were circulated in limited areas.

Sonora

A47

Seal

Typeset in a row of five varieties. Two impressions placed tête bêche (foot to foot) constitute a sheet. The settings show various wrong font and defective letters, "!" for "1" in

"1913," etc. The paper occasionally has a manufacturer's watermark.

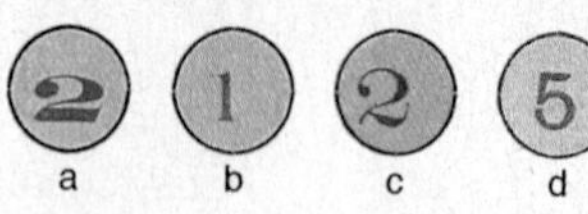

a b c d

Four Types of the Numerals.
a — Wide, heavy-faced numerals.
b — Narrow Roman numerals.
c — Wide Roman numerals.
d — Gothic or sans-serif numerals.

Nos. 321-346 Issued Without Gum
Embossed "CONSTITUCIONAL"

1913 Typeset Unwmk. *Perf. 12*
321 A47 (a) 5c blk & red *4,250.* 800.00
a. "CENTAVOB" *4,750.* *850.00*

Colorless Roulette
322 A47(b) 1c blk & red 22.00 25.00
a. With green seal *1,500.* *1,250.*
323 A47(a) 2c blk & red 18.00 15.00
a. With green seal *2,000.* *2,000.*
324 A47(c) 2c blk & red 87.50 72.50
a. With green seal *5,000.* *5,000.*
325 A47(a) 3c blk & red 97.50 77.50
a. With green seal *750.00* *750.00*
326 A47(a) 5c blk & red 190.00 77.50
a. "CENTAVOB" 200.00 50.00
327 A47(d) 5c blk & red 1,200. 350.00
a. With green seal *1,000.*
328 A47(b) 10c blk & red 35.00 *37.50*

Black Roulette
329 A47(d) 5c blk & red 300.00 140.00
a. "MARO" 87.50 52.50

Stamps are known with the embossing double or omitted.

The varieties with green seal are from a few sheets embossed "Constitucional" which were in stock at the time the green seal control was adopted.

Nos. 322-329 are known with papermakers' watermark ("Peerless Mills" or "Yukon Aurora").

No. 339

Without Embossing
With Green Seal
Colorless Roulette
336 A47(b) 1c blk & red 15.00 10.00
337 A47(a) 3c blk & red 14.50 9.00
a. Imperf. *350.00*
338 A47(a) 5c blk & red 750.00 250.00
a. "CENTAVOB" *800.00* 275.00
339 A47(b) 10c blk & red 8.00 7.50

Colored Roulette
340 A47(d) 5c brnsh blk & red 25.00 6.00
a. 5c lilac brown & red 75.00 22.50
b. Double seal *1,250.*
c. Red printing omitted *1,000.*

Nos. 336-340 are known with papermaker's watermark ("Peerless Mills" or "Yukon Aurora").

1913-14 *Black Roulette*
With Green Seal
341 A47(a) 1c black & red 4.00 4.00
b. "erano" ('14) 100.00 60.00
342 A47(d) 2c black & red 4.50 4.00
a. "erano" ('14) 30.00 35.00
343 A47(a) 3c black & red 4.75 4.00
a. "CENTAVO" 25.00 25.00
b. "erano" ('14) 35.00 35.00
344 A47(d) 5c black & red 4.75 4.00
b. Heavy black penetrating roulette 2.75 1.75
c. As "b," "MARO" 10.50 5.00
d. Without green seal *2,250.*
Nos. 341-344 (4) 18.00 16.00

Stamps without seal are unfinished remainders.

On Nos. 341-344 the rouletting cuts the paper slightly or not at all. On Nos. 344b-344c the rouletting is heavy, cutting deeply into the paper.

1914
345 A47(a) 5c black & red 5.00 5.00
346 A47(b) 10c black & red 4.25 5.00

Coat of Arms — A49

Revenue Stamps Used for Postage
1913 Litho. *Rouletted 14, 14x7*
347 A49 1c yellow grn 2.00 *2.50*
a. With coupon 7.00 6.00
348 A49 2c violet 3.50 *4.00*
a. With coupon 17.50 14.50
349 A49 5c brown .60 *.75*
a. With coupon 2.00 1.50
350 A49 10c claret 2.50 *3.50*
a. With coupon 15.00 12.00
351 A49 20c gray grn 3.00 *3.50*
a. With coupon 20.00 18.00
352 A49 50c ultra 11.00 *16.00*
a. With coupon 60.00 47.50
353 A49 1p orange 45.00 *55.00*
a. With coupon 175.00 120.00
Nos. 347-353 (7) 67.60 85.25
Set, never hinged 275.00

For a short time these stamps (called "Ejercitos") were used for postage with coupon attached. Later this was required to be removed unless they were to be used for revenue. Stamps overprinted with district names are revenues. Values above 1p were used for revenue. Imperfs exist of all values, but were not issued.

Many examples do not have gum because of a flood.

Use of typeset Sonora revenue stamps for postage was not authorized or allowed.

Coat of Arms
A50 A51

5c (A50): "CINCO CENTAVOS" 14x2mm
1914 *Rouletted 9½x14*
354 A50 1c deep blue .45 .45
355 A50 2c yellow grn .60 .35
a. 2c green 3.00 1.75
356 A50 4c blue vio 11.00 2.50
a. Horiz. pair, imperf. btwn. 250.00
357 A50 5c gray grn 11.00 3.00
a. Horiz. pair imperf. btwn. 250.00
358 A50 10c red .45 .45
359 A50 20c yellow brn .60 .60
a. 20c deep brown 2.25 2.25
b. Horiz. pair, imperf. btwn. 250.00
360 A50 50c claret 2.50 3.50
a. Horiz. pair, imperf. btwn. 250.00
361 A50 1p brt violet 14.00 16.00
a. Horiz. pair, imperf. btwn. 250.00
Nos. 354-361 (8) 40.60 26.85
Set, never hinged 175.00

Nos. 354-361 (called "Transitorios") exist imperf. but were not regularly issued.

Many examples do not have gum because of a flood.

See Note after No. 465.

See No. 369. For overprints see Nos. 362-368, 559-565.

Overprinted in Black

1914
362 A50 1c deep blue 200.00 175.00
a. "1912" for "1914" *2,000.*
363 A50 2c yellow green 225.00 200.00
364 A50 4c blue violet 250.00 300.00
365 A50 5c gray green 35.00 50.00
a. Horiz. pair, imperf. btwn. 550.00
366 A50 10c red 150.00 150.00
a. "1912" for "1914" *2,000.*
367 A50 20c yellow brn *2,500.* *2,500.*
a. "1912" for "1914" *7,000.*
368 A50 50c claret *3,500.* *3,500.*

Values are for stamps with design close to, or just touching, the perfs.

Excellent counterfeits of this overprint exist.

Redrawn
"CINCO CENTAVOS" 16x2½mm
1914 *Perf. 12*
369 A51 5c gray green 1.00 .35

Imperfs are printers' waste.

Regular Issue of 1910 Overprinted in Violet, Magenta, Black or Green

1914 Wmk. 155 *Perf. 14*
370 A36 1c dull violet 1.50 .60
371 A37 2c green 3.00 1.25
372 A38 3c orange brn 3.00 1.25
373 A39 4c carmine 5.00 2.00
374 A40 5c orange 1.00 .35
375 A41 10c blue & org 6.00 2.00
376 A42 15c gray bl & cl 10.00 3.00
377 A43 20c red & blue 20.00 6.00
378 A44 50c red brn & blk 25.00 8.00
379 A45 1p blue & blk 55.00 11.00
380 A46 5p carmine & blk 190.00 160.00
Nos. 370-380 (11) 319.50 195.45
Set, never hinged 1,000.

Overprinted On Postage Due Stamps of 1908
381 D1 1c blue 27.50 *30.00*
382 D1 2c blue 27.50 *30.00*
383 D1 4c blue 27.50 *30.00*
384 D1 5c blue 27.50 *30.00*
385 D1 10c blue 27.50 *30.00*
Nos. 381-385 (5) 137.50 150.00
Set, never hinged 375.00

This overprint is found double, inverted, sideways and in pairs with and without the overprint.

There are two or more types of this overprint.

The Postage Due Stamps and similar groups of them which follow were issued and used as regular postage stamps.

Values are for stamps where the overprint is clear enough to be expertised.

Counterfeits abound.

A52

1914 Unwmk. Litho. *Perf. 12*
386 A52 1c pale blue .35 .50
387 A52 2c light green .35 .45
388 A52 3c orange .50 .50
389 A52 5c deep rose .50 .35
390 A52 10c rose .70 .85
391 A52 15c rose lilac 1.20 1.75
392 A52 50c yellow 2.00 2.50
a. 50c ocher 1.75
393 A52 1p violet 8.50 12.00
Nos. 386-393 (8) 14.10 18.90
Set, never hinged 50.00

Nos. 386-393, are known imperforate.

This set is usually called the Denver Issue because it was printed there.

See Note after No. 465.

For overprints and surcharges see Nos. 566-573, 591-592.

A53

Revenue Stamps Used for Postage
1914, July *Perf. 12*
393A A53 1c rose 40.00
393B A53 2c lt green 35.00
393C A53 3c lt orange 75.00
393D A53 5c red 15.00
393E A53 10c gray green 70.00
393F A53 25c blue 150.00
Nos. 393A-393F (6) 385.00

Nos. 393A-393F were used in the northeast. Values are for examples with postal cancellations.

Unused examples are to be considered as revenues.

Pres. Madero

Stamps in this design, featuring Pres. Madero, within a frame very similar to that of the Denver Issue (Nos. 386-393), were ordered in 1915 by Francisco Villa, to be used by the Constitutionalist government. Five values (1c green, 2c brown, 3c carmine, 5c blue, and 10c yellow) were printed by Ellis Brothers & Co., El Paso, Texas. By the time of the stamps' arrival in Mexico City, the Constitutionalist regime had fallen, and the new Conventionist government returned them to the printer, who later sold the unissued stamps within the philatelic market. Value, set $10.

Background as A55 — A54

Nos. 394-413 Issued Without Gum
1914 *Imperf.*
Values and Inscriptions in Black
Inscribed "SONORA"
394 A54 1c blue & red .35 .35
a. Double seal
b. Without seal 20.00
395 A54 2c green & org .35 .35
a. Without seal 100.00
396 A54 5c yellow & grn .35 .35
a. 5c orange & green 1.50 1.25
b. Without seal *300.00*
397 A54 10c lt bl & red 3.50 1.75
a. 10c blue & red 40.00 15.00
398 A54 20c yellow & grn 1.75 2.00
399 A54 20c orange & bl 15.00 17.50
400 A54 50c green & org 1.25 1.25
Nos. 394-400 (7) 22.55 23.55

Shades. Stamps of type A54 are usually termed the "Coach Seal Issue."

Inscribed "DISTRITO SUR DE LA BAJA CAL"
401 A54 1c yellow & blue 2.00 *30.00*
a. Without seal 50.00
402 A54 2c gray & ol grn 2.50 *25.00*
403 A54 5c olive & rose 2.00 *20.00*
a. Without seal 50.00
404 A54 10c pale red & dl vio 2.00 *20.00*
a. Without seal 50.00
Nos. 401-404 (4) 8.50 95.00

Counterfeit cancellations exist.

A55

Inscribed "SONORA"
405 A55 1c blue & red 6.00
a. Without seal 50.00
406 A55 2c green & org .50
407 A55 5c yellow & grn .50 *2.50*
a. Without seal 75.00
408 A55 10c blue & red .50 *2.50*
409 A55 20c yellow & grn 75.00 *15.00*
a. Without seal 95.00
b. Double seal *80.00*
Nos. 405-409 (5) *82.50* *20.00*

With "PLATA" added to the inscription
410 A55 1c blue & red 1.00
a. "PLATA" inverted 60.00
b. Pair, one without "PLATA" 15.00
411 A55 10c blue & red 1.00
412 A55 20c yellow & grn 2.50
a. "PLATA" double 50.00
413 A55 50c gray grn & org 1.75
a. Without seal 1.00
b. As "a," "P" of "PLATA" missing 150.00
Nos. 410-413 (4) 6.25

Stamps of type A55 are termed the "Anvil Seal Issue".

Nos. 410-413 were not placed in use.

Oaxaca

Coat of Arms — A56

5c:
Type I — Thick numerals, 2mm wide.
Type II — Thin numerals, 1½mm wide.

Perf. 8½ to 14

1915 **Typo.** **Unwmk.**

414 A56 1c dull violet 2.00 1.25
415 A56 2c emerald 3.00 2.25
a. Inverted numeral 30.00
e. Numeral omitted 35.00
416 A56 3c red brown 4.00 3.50
b. Inverted numeral 30.00
417 A56 5c org (type I) 77.50 77.50
a. Tête bêche pair 175.00 175.00
418 A56 5c org (type II) .50 .75
a. Types I and II in pair 70.00
419 A56 10c blue & car 4.00 4.00
Nos. 414-419 (6) 91.00 89.25
Set, never hinged 275.00

Many printing errors, imperfs and part perfs exist. Mostly these are printers' waste, private reprints or counterfeits.

Nos. 414-419 printed on backs of post office receipt forms.

Regular Issues of 1899-1910 Overprinted in Black

1914 **Wmk. 155** ***Perf. 14***

On Issues of 1899-1903

420 A28 5c orange
421 A30 15c lav & claret 250.00 250.00
Never hinged 700.00
422 A31 20c rose & dk bl *1,000.* 500.00

Counterfeits exist.

The listing of No. 420 is being re-evaluated. The Catalogue Editors would appreciate any information on the stamp.

On Issue of 1910

423 A36 1c dull violet .35 .35
424 A37 2c green .35 .35
425 A38 3c orange brown .40 .40
426 A39 4c carmine .50 .50
427 A40 5c orange .35 .35
428 A41 10c blue & orange .35 .35
429 A42 15c gray bl & claret .70 .60
430 A43 20c red & blue .75 .70

Overprinted

431 A44 50c red brn & blk 1.75 1.50
432 A45 1p blue & blk 8.00 5.50
433 A46 5p carmine & blk 42.50 32.50
Nos. 423-433 (11) 56.00 43.10
Set, never hinged 170.00

In the first setting of the overprint on 1c to 20c, the variety "GONSTITUCIONALISTA" occurs 4 times in each sheet of 100. In the second setting it occurs on the last stamp in each row of 10.

The overprint exists reading downward on Nos. 423-430; inverted on Nos. 431-433; double on Nos. 423-425, 427.

See Note after No. 465.

For overprints see Nos. 528-538.

Postage Due Stamps of 1908 Overprinted

434 D1 1c blue 4.75 5.00
435 D1 2c blue 6.00 5.00
436 D1 4c blue 25.00 25.00
437 D1 5c blue 25.00 25.00
438 D1 10c blue 5.50 5.00
a. Double overprint
Nos. 434-438 (5) 66.25 65.00
Set, never hinged 200.00

Preceding Issues Overprinted

This is usually called the "Villa" monogram. Counterfeits abound.

1915 **On Issue of 1899**

439 A25 1c green *210.00*
440 A26 2c vermilion *210.00*
441 A27 3c orange brn *175.00*
442 A28 5c dark blue *210.00*
443 A29 10c violet & org *210.00*
444 A30 15c lav & claret *750.00* 750.00
445 A31 20c rose & bl *1,000.* —
446 A32 50c red lil & blk *500.00* —
447 A33 1p blue & blk *500.00*
448 A34 5p car & blk *750.00* —
Nos. 439-448 (10) *4,515.*

On Issue of 1903

449 A25 1c violet *200.00*
450 A26 2c green *200.00*
451 A35 4c carmine *200.00*
452 A28 5c orange 45.00
a. Inverted overprint *75.00*
453 A29 10c blue & org *750.00* —
454 A32 50c car & blk — —
Nos. 449-453 (5) *1,395.*

In Sept. 1915 Postmaster Hinojosa ordered a special printing of Nos. 439-454 (as valued) for sale to collectors. Earlier a small quantity of Nos. 444-445, 448 and 452-454 was regularly issued. They are hard to distinguish and sell for much more. Counterfeits abound.

On Issue of 1910

455 A36 1c dull violet .85 1.00
456 A37 2c green .40 .60
457 A38 3c orange brown .60 .75
458 A39 4c carmine 4.00 4.50
459 A40 5c orange .35 .35
460 A41 10c blue & orange 7.00 7.50
461 A42 15c gray bl & cl 3.00 4.00
462 A43 20c red & blue 5.50 7.00
463 A44 50c red brn & blk 13.00 14.00
464 A45 1p blue & blk 17.00 20.00
465 A46 5p carmine & blk *150.00*
Nos. 455-464 (10) 51.70 59.70
Nos. 455-464, never hinged 175.00

Nos. 455-465 are known with overprint inverted, double and other variations. Most were ordered by Postmaster General Hinojosa for philtelic purposes. They were sold at a premium. This applies to Nos. 354-361, 386-393, 431-433 with this monogram as well.

Overprinted On Postage Due Stamps of 1908

466 D1 1c blue 15.00 20.00
467 D1 2c blue 15.00 20.00
468 D1 4c blue 15.00 20.00
469 D1 5c blue 15.00 20.00
470 D1 10c blue 15.00 20.00
Nos. 466-470 (5) 75.00 100.00
Set, never hinged 225.00

Nos. 466 to 470 are known with inverted overprint. All other values of the 1899 and 1903 issues exist with this overprint. See note after No. 465.

Issues of 1899-1910 Overprinted

This is called the "Carranza" or small monogram. Counterfeits abound.

On Issues of 1899-1903

482 A28 5c orange 40.00 20.00
Never hinged 125.00
483 A30 15c lav & claret 200.00 80.00
Never hinged 650.00

On Issue of 1910

484 A36 1c dull violet .70 .70
485 A37 2c green .70 .60
486 A38 3c orange brn .75 .75
487 A39 4c carmine 2.00 2.00
488 A40 5c orange .35 .35
489 A41 10c blue & org 1.50 1.50
a. Double ovpt., one invtd. 25.00
490 A42 15c gray bl & cl 1.50 1.50
491 A43 20c red & blue 1.50 1.50
492 A44 50c red brn & blk 10.00 10.00
493 A45 1p blue & blk 15.00 15.00
494 A46 5p car & blk 150.00 *150.00*
Nos. 484-494 (11) 184.00 *183.90*
Set, never hinged 550.00

All values exist with inverted overprint; all but 5p with double overprint.

Overprinted On Postage Due Stamps of 1908

495 D1 1c blue 22.00 *25.00*
496 D1 2c blue 22.00 *25.00*
497 D1 4c blue 22.00 *25.00*
498 D1 5c blue 22.00 *25.00*
499 D1 10c blue 22.00 *25.00*
Nos. 495-499 (5) 110.00 125.00
Set, never hinged 325.00

Nos. 495-499 exist with inverted overprint.

It is stated that, in parts of Mexico occupied by the revolutionary forces, instructions were given to apply a distinguishing overprint to all stamps found in the post offices. This overprint was usually some arrangement or abbreviation of "Gobierno Constitucionalista". Such overprints as were specially authorized or were in general use in large sections of the country are listed. Numerous other handstamped overprints were used in one town or locality. They were essentially military faction control marks necessitated in most instances by the chaotic situation following the split between Villa and Carranza. The fact that some were often struck in a variety of colors and positions suggests the influence of philatelists.

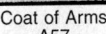

Coat of Arms A57

Statue of Cuauhtémoc A58

Ignacio Zaragoza A59

José María Morelos A60

Francisco Madero — A61

Benito Juárez — A62

1915 **Unwmk.** **Litho.** ***Rouletted 14***

500 A57 1c violet .25 .25
501 A58 2c green .25 .25
502 A59 3c brown .50 .25
503 A60 4c carmine .50 .25
504 A61 5c orange .75 .25
505 A62 10c ultra .35 .30
Nos. 500-505 (6) 2.60 1.55
Set, never hinged 4.00

Nos. 500-505 exists imperf.; some exist imperf. vertically or horizontally; some with rouletting and perforation combined. These probably were not regularly issued in these forms.

See Nos. 506-511. For overprints see Nos. O86-O97.

Map of Mexico — A63

Veracruz Lighthouse A64

Post Office, Mexico, D.F. — A65

TEN CENTAVOS:
Type I — Size 19½x24mm. Crossed lines on coat.
Type II — Size 19x23½mm. Diagonal lines only on coat.

1915-16 ***Perf. 12***

506 A57 1c violet .40 .25
507 A58 2c green .40 .30
508 A59 3c brown .50 .30
509 A60 4c carmine .50 .35
a. "CEATRO" 7.50 7.50
510 A61 5c orange .75 .35
511 A62 10c ultra, type I 1.00 .35
a. 10c ultra, type II .50 .25

Engr.

512 A63 40c slate .75 .35
513 A64 1p brown & blk 1.00 .75
a. Inverted center 200.00 275.00
514 A65 5p cl & ultra ('16) 12.00 4.00
a. Inverted center 450.00
Nos. 506-514 (9) 17.30 7.00
Set, never hinged 60.00

Nos. 507-508, 510-514, exist imperf; Nos. 513-514 imperf with inverted center. These varieties were not regularly issued.

See Nos. 626-628, 647. For overprints see Nos. O92-O100, O121-O123, O132-O133, O142-O144, O153-O154, O162-O164, O174, O188, O193, O207, O222.

Issues of 1899-1910 Overprinted in Blue, Red or Black

On Issues of 1899-1903

1916 **Wmk. 155** ***Perf. 14***

515 A28 5c orange (Bl) 125.00 175.00
Never hinged 400.00
516 A30 15c lav & cl (Bl) 775.00 775.00
Never hinged 2,250.

On Issue of 1910

517 A36 1c dull vio (R) 10.00 *10.00*
518 A37 2c green (R) .50 .35
519 A38 3c orange brn (Bl) .55 .40
a. Double overprint 500.00
520 A39 4c carmine (Bl) 6.00 *8.00*
521 A40 5c orange (Bl) .25 .25
a. Double overprint 75.00
522 A41 10c blue & org (R) 1.25 1.50
523 A42 15c gray bl & cl (Bk) 1.75 3.00
524 A43 20c red & bl (Bk) 1.75 3.00
525 A44 50c red brn & blk (R) 8.50 5.00
526 A45 1p blue & blk (R) 15.00 6.50
527 A46 5p car & blk (R) 175.00 175.00
Nos. 517-527 (11) 220.55 213.00
Nos. 517-527, never hinged 650.00

Nos. 519-524 exist with this overprint (called the "Corbata") reading downward and Nos. 525-527 with it inverted. Of these varieties only Nos. 519-521 were regularly issued.

On Nos. 423-430

528 A36 1c dull vio (R) 2.50 4.00
529 A37 2c green (R) .75 .60
530 A38 3c orange brn (Bl) .60 .60
531 A39 4c carmine (Bl) .60 .60
532 A40 5c orange (Bl) 1.00 .30
533 A41 10c blue & org (R) .75 .60
534 A42 15c gray bl & cl (Bk) .80 .80
535 A43 20c red & bl (Bk) .80 .80

On Nos. 431-433 in Red

536 A44 50c red brn & blk 7.50 6.00
537 A45 1p blue & blk 16.00 16.00
538 A46 5p carmine & blk 150.00 140.00
a. Tablet inverted 300.00
Nos. 528-538 (11) 181.30 170.30
Set, never hinged 550.00

Nos. 529 to 535 are known with the overprint reading downward and Nos. 536 to 538 with it inverted.

On No. 482

539 A28 5c orange (Bl) 400.00 *400.00*

On Nos. 484-494

540 A36 1c dull vio (R) 6.00 *6.00*
541 A37 2c green (R) .75 .75
a. Monogram inverted 100.00
542 A38 3c orange brn (Bl) .75 .75
543 A39 4c carmine (Bl) 8.50 *10.00*
544 A40 5c orange (Bl) 1.25 .35
545 A41 10c blue & org (R) 2.00 *2.50*
546 A42 15c gray bl & cl (Bk) 1.75 .75
a. Tablet double *750.00 750.00*
b. Monogram double *750.00*
547 A43 20c red & bl (Bk) 1.75 1.50
548 A44 50c red brn & blk (R) 9.00 *10.00*
a. Monogram inverted 75.00
b. Tablet inverted 85.00
549 A45 1p blue & blk (R) 13.00 14.00
a. Tablet double 200.00
b. Monogram inverted 70.00
Nos. 539-549 (11) 444.75 *446.60*
Set, never hinged 1,300.

Nos. 541-547 exist with overprint reading downward. A few 5p were overprinted for the Post Office collection.

On No. 452

550 A28 5c orange (Bl) 125.00 *125.00*

On Nos. 455-462

551 A36 1c dull vio (R) 11.00 *15.00*
552 A37 2c green (R) 1.50 .90
553 A38 3c org brn (Bl) 3.25 *4.50*
554 A39 4c carmine (Bl) 13.00 *15.00*
555 A40 5c orange (Bl) 4.50 *6.00*
556 A41 10c bl & org (R) 12.00 *14.00*
a. Monogram inverted *250.00*
557 A42 15c gray bl & cl (Bk) 12.00 *14.00*
a. Monogram inverted *250.00*
558 A43 20c red & bl (Bk) 12.00 *14.00*
a. Monogram inverted *250.00*
Nos. 550-558 (9) 194.25 *208.40*
Set, never hinged 650.00

Stamps of 50c, 1p and 5p were overprinted for the Post Office collection but were not regularly issued.

Issues of 1914 Overprinted

On "Transitorio" Issue

Rouletted 9½x14

Unwmk.

559 A50 1c dp blue (R) 24.00 24.00
Never hinged 75.00
560 A50 2c yellow grn (R) 12.00 18.00
Never hinged 27.50
561 A50 4c blue vio (R) 425.00 375.00
Never hinged 1,200.
562 A50 10c red (Bl) 2.00 6.00
Never hinged 4.00
a. Vertical overprint 125.00
563 A50 20c yellow brn (Bl) 3.00 6.00
Never hinged 7.50
564 A50 50c claret (Bl) 15.00 20.00
Never hinged 45.00
565 A50 1p violet (Bl) 24.00 24.00
Never hinged 100.00
a. Horiz. pair, imperf. btwn.
Nos. 559-565 (7) 505.00 473.00

Overprinted in Blue On "Denver" Issue

Perf. 12

566 A52 1c pale blue 3.75
567 A52 2c lt green 3.75
568 A52 3c orange .45 *5.00*
569 A52 5c deep rose .45 *5.00*
570 A52 10c rose .45 *5.00*
571 A52 15c rose lilac .45 *5.00*
572 A52 50c yellow 1.10 *15.00*
573 A52 1p violet 9.50 *25.00*
Nos. 566-573 (8) 19.90
Set, never hinged 65.00

Many of the foregoing stamps exist with the "G. P. DE M." overprint printed in other colors than those listed. These "trial color" stamps were not regularly on sale at post offices but were available for postage and used stamps are known.

There appears to have been speculation in Nos. 516, 517, 520, 528, 539, 540, 543, 566, and 567. A small quantity of each of these stamps was sold at post offices but subsequently they could be obtained only from officials or their agents at advanced prices.

Venustiano Carranza — A66

1916, June 1 Engr. *Perf. 12*

574 A66 10c blue 1.75 1.00
a. Imperf., pair 25.00
575 A66 10c lilac brown 15.00 15.00
a. Imperf., pair 50.00
Nos. 574-575, never hinged 32.50

Entry of Carranza into Mexico, D.F.

Stamps of type A66 with only horizontal lines in the background of the oval are essays.

Coat of Arms — A67

1916

576 A67 1c lilac .35 .25
Never hinged .80

Issue of 1910 Surcharged in Various Colors

This overprint is called the "Barril."

1916 Wmk. 155 *Perf. 14*

577 A36 5c on 1c dl vio (Br) .50 .50
a. Vertical surcharge 1.25 1.25
b. Double surcharge 150.00
578 A36 10c on 1c dl vio (Bl) .50 .50
a. Double surcharge 100.00
579 A40 20c on 5c org (Br) .50 .50
a. Double surcharge 90.00
580 A40 25c on 5c org (G) .40 .50
581 A37 60c on 2c grn (R) 27.50 20.00
Nos. 577-581 (5) 29.40 22.00
Set, never hinged 100.00

On Nos. 423-424, 427

582 A36 5c on 1c (Br) .50 .50
a. Double tablet, one vertical 100.00
b. Inverted tablet 250.00 250.00
583 A36 10c on 1c (Bl) 1.00 1.00
584 A40 25c on 5c (G) .50 .50
a. Inverted tablet 225.00 225.00
585 A37 60c on 2c (R) 650.00 *425.00*
Nos. 582-584, never hinged 4.50

No. 585 was not regularly issued.

The variety "GONSTITUCIONALISTA" is found on Nos. 582 to 585.

On No. 459

586 A40 25c on 5c org (G) .25 .25
Never hinged .70

On Nos. 484-485, 488

587 A36 5c on 1c (Br) 15.00 20.00
a. Vertical tablet 100.00 125.00
588 A36 10c on 1c (Bl) 5.00 7.50
589 A40 25c on 5c (G) 1.00 1.50
a. Inverted tablet 225.00
590 A37 60c on 2c (R) 650.00
Nos. 587-589, never hinged 60.00

No. 590 was not regularly issued.

Surcharged on "Denver" Issue of 1914

1916 Unwmk. *Perf. 12*

591 A52 60c on 1c pale bl (Br) 3.00 6.00
592 A52 60c on 2c lt grn (Br) 3.00 6.00
a. Inverted surcharge *1,250.*
Set, never hinged 18.00

Postage Due Stamps Surcharged Like Nos. 577-581

1916 Wmk. 155 *Perf. 14*

593 D1 5c on 1c blue (Br) 2.50
594 D1 10c on 2c blue (V) 2.50
595 D1 20c on 4c blue (Br) 2.50
596 D1 25c on 5c blue (G) 2.50
597 D1 60c on 10c blue (R) 1.50
598 D1 1p on 1c blue (C) 1.50
599 D1 1p on 2c blue (C) 1.50
600 D1 1p on 4c blue (C) .80 .80
601 D1 1p on 5c blue (C) 2.50
602 D1 1p on 10c blue (C) 2.50
Nos. 593-602 (10) 20.30
Set, never hinged 60.00

There are numerous "trial colors" and "essays" of the overprints and surcharges on Nos. 577 to 602. They were available for postage though not regularly issued.

Postage Due Stamps Surcharged

1916

603 D1 2.50p on 1c blue 1.25 1.25
604 D1 2.50p on 2c blue 10.00
605 D1 2.50p on 4c blue 10.00 250.00
606 D1 2.50p on 5c blue 10.00
607 D1 2.50p on 10c blue 10.00
a. Inverted surcharge *1,500.*
Nos. 603-607 (5) 41.25
Set, never hinged 125.00

Regular Issue

Ignacio Zaragoza A68

Ildefonso Vázquez A69

J. M. Pino Suárez A70

Jesús Carranza A71

Maclovio Herrera — A72

F. I. Madero — A73

Belisario Domínguez A74

Aquiles Serdán A75

Rouletted 14½

1917-20 Engr. Unwmk.

Thick Paper

608 A68 1c dull violet 2.00 1.00
Never hinged 4.00
609 A68 1c lilac gray ('20) 5.00 .75
Never hinged 9.50
a. 1c gray ('20) 5.00 5.00
610 A69 2c gray green 1.50 .50
Never hinged 3.00
611 A70 3c bister brn 1.50 1.00
Never hinged 3.00
612 A71 4c carmine 2.50 1.00
Never hinged 7.50
613 A72 5c ultra 2.50 .50
Never hinged 5.00
a. Horiz. pair, imperf. btwn. 75.00
b. Imperf., pair 35.00 75.00
614 A73 10c blue 4.00 .50
Never hinged 10.00
a. Without imprint 7.50 1.00
Never hinged 16.00
615 A74 20c brown rose 40.00 2.00
Never hinged 90.00
a. 20c rose 40.00 2.00
Never hinged 80.00
616 A75 30c gray brown 90.00 3.00
Never hinged 250.00
617 A75 30c gray blk ('20) 100.00 4.00
Never hinged 250.00
Nos. 608-617 (10) 249.00 14.25

Perf. 12

Thick or Medium Paper

618 A68 1c dull violet 35.00 25.00
Never hinged 100.00
619 A69 2c gray green 10.00 6.00
Never hinged 20.00
620 A70 3c bis brn ('17) 200.00 200.00
Never hinged 400.00
622 A72 5c ultra 5.00 .25
Never hinged 10.00
623 A73 10c blue ('17) 5.00 .25
Never hinged 10.00
a. Without imprint ('17) 20.00 15.00
Never hinged 40.00
624 A74 20c rose ('20) 140.00 3.00
Never hinged 350.00
625 A75 30c gray blk ('20) 140.00 2.00
Never hinged 350.00

Thin or Medium Paper

626 A63 40c violet 65.00 1.00
Never hinged 200.00
627 A64 1p blue & blk 50.00 1.50
Never hinged 150.00
a. With center of 5p 800.00
b. 1p bl & dark blue (error) 500.00 20.00
c. Vert. pair, imperf. btwn. 250.00
628 A65 5p green & blk 1.50 *10.00*
Never hinged 3.00
a. With violet or red control number 25.00 10.00
b. With center of 1p 800.00

The 1, 2, 3, 5 and 10c are known on thin paper perforated. It is stated they were printed for Postal Union and "specimen" purposes.

All values exist imperf; these are not known to have been regularly issued. Nos. 627a and 628b were not regularly issued.

All values except 3c have an imprint.

For overprints and surcharges see Nos. B1-B2, O113-O165.

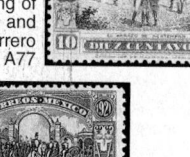

Meeting of Iturbide and Guerrero A77

Entering City of Mexico A78

1921

632 A77 10c blue & brn 25.00 3.00
Never hinged 82.50
a. Center inverted *40,000.*
633 A78 10p black brn & blk 22.50 *37.50*
Never hinged 75.00

Commemorating the meeting of Agustín de Iturbide and Vicente Guerrero and the entry into City of Mexico in 1821.

For overprint see No. O194.

"El Salto de Agua," Public Fountain A79

Pyramid of the Sun at Teotihuacán A80

Chapultepec Castle A81

Columbus Monument A82

Juárez Colonnade, Mexico, D. F.
A83

Monument to Josefa Ortiz de Dominguez
A84

Cuauhtémoc Monument — A85

1923	**Unwmk.**	***Rouletted 14½***		
634	A79	2c scarlet	2.00	.25
635	A80	3c bister brn	2.00	.25
636	A81	4c green	2.50	.75
637	A82	5c orange	5.00	.25
638	A83	10c brown	3.75	.25
639	A85	10c claret	3.50	.25
640	A84	20c dk blue	52.50	1.75
641	A85	30c dk green	52.50	2.00
		Nos. 634-641 (8)	123.75	5.75
		Set, never hinged	300.00	

See Nos. 642-646, 650-657, 688-692, 727A, 735A-736. For overprints see Nos. O166-O173, O178-O181, O183-O187, O196-O197, O199-O206, O210, O212-O214, O217-O222.

Communications Building — A87

Palace of Fine Arts (National Theater)
A88

Type I

Type II

Two types of 1p:
I — Eagle on palace dome.
II — Without eagle.

1923	**Wmk. 156**	***Perf. 12***		
642	A79	2c scarlet	10.00	10.00
643	A81	4c green	1.40	.30
644	A82	5c orange	10.00	7.00
645	A85	10c brown lake	12.50	6.00
646	A83	30c dark green	.95	.25
647	A63	40c violet	1.25	.25
648	A87	50c olive brn	1.00	.25
649	A88	1p red brn & bl (I)	1.00	1.00
a.		Type II	3.00	*10.00*
		Nos. 642-649 (8)	38.10	25.05
		Set, never hinged	90.00	

Most of Nos. 642-649 are known imperforate or part perforate but probably were not regularly issued.

For overprints see Nos. O175-O176, O189-O190, O208-O209, O223.

1923-34		***Rouletted 14½***		
650	A79	2c scarlet	.25	.25
651	A80	3c bis brn ('27)	.25	.25
652	A81	4c green	47.50	35.00
653	A82	4c green ('27)	.25	.25
654	A82	5c orange	.25	.25
655	A85	10c lake	.25	.25
656	A84	20c deep blue	.75	.30
657	A83	30c dk green ('34)	.75	.30
		Nos. 650-657 (8)	50.25	36.85
		Set, never hinged	125.00	

Nos. 650 to 657 inclusive exist imperforate.

Medallion
A90

Map of Americas
A91

Francisco García y Santos — A92

Post Office, Mexico, D. F. — A93

1926		***Perf. 12***		
658	A90	2c red	2.50	1.00
659	A91	4c green	2.50	1.00
660	A90	5c orange	2.50	.75
661	A91	10c brown red	4.00	1.00
662	A92	20c dk blue	4.00	1.25
663	A92	30c dk green	7.50	4.00
664	A92	40c violet	13.50	3.00
665	A93	1p brown & blue	27.50	10.00
a.		1p red & blue	37.50	15.00
		Nos. 658-665 (8)	64.00	22.00
		Set, never hinged	150.00	

Pan-American Postal Congress.

Nos. 658-665 were also printed in black, on unwatermarked paper, for presentation to delegates to the Universal Postal Congress at London in 1929. Remainders were overprinted in 1929 for use as airmail official stamps, and are listed as Nos. CO3-CO10.

For overprints see Nos. 667-674, 675A-682, CO3-CO10.

Benito Juárez — A94

1926		***Rouletted 14½***		
666	A94	8c orange	.30	.25
		Never hinged	.70	

For overprint see No. O182.

Nos. 658-665 Overprinted

1930		***Perf. 12***		
667	A90	2c red	4.00	2.25
a.		Reading down	15.00	15.00
668	A91	4c green	4.00	2.50
a.		Reading down	15.00	15.00
669	A90	5c orange	4.00	2.00
a.		Reading down	15.00	35.00
b.		Double overprint	75.00	*75.00*
670	A91	10c brown red	7.50	2.50
671	A92	20c dk blue	9.50	3.50
672	A92	30c dk green	8.50	4.00
a.		Reading down	10.00	12.00
673	A92	40c violet	12.50	8.50
a.		Reading down	47.50	50.00
674	A93	1p red brn & bl	11.00	7.00
a.		Double overprint	250.00	
b.		Triple overprint	200.00	
		Nos. 667-674 (8)	61.00	32.25
		Set, never hinged	150.00	

Overprint horizontal on 1p.

Arms of Puebla — A95

1931, May 1		**Engr.**		
675	A95	10c dk bl & dk brn	3.00	.50
		Never hinged	7.50	

400th anniversary of Puebla.

Nos. 658-665a Overprinted

1931				
676	A91	4c green	70.00	*75.00*
a.		Inverted overprint	*750.00*	
677	A90	5c orange	13.00	*17.00*
678	A91	10c brown red	13.00	*14.00*
679	A92	20c dk blue	13.00	*18.00*
680	A92	30c dk green	22.50	*25.00*
681	A92	40c violet	32.50	*35.00*
682	A93	1p brown & bl	30.00	*35.00*
a.		1p red & blue	42.50	*45.00*
		Nos. 676-682 (7)	194.00	219.00
		Set, never hinged	475.00	

Overprint horizontal on 1p.

Nos. 676 and 682 are not known to have been sold to the public through post offices.

Forgeries of overprint exist.

Bartolomé de las Casas — A96

1933, Mar. 3	**Engr.**	***Rouletted 14½***		
683	A96	15c dark blue	.30	.25
		Never hinged	.70	

For overprint see No. O215.

Emblem of Mexican Society of Geography and Statistics — A97

1933, Oct.		***Rouletted 14½***		
684	A97	2c deep green	1.50	.60
685	A97	5c dark brown	1.75	.50
686	A97	10c dark blue	.75	.25
687	A97	1p dark violet	100.00	65.00
		Nos. 684-687 (4)	104.00	66.35
		Set, never hinged	250.00	

XXI Intl. Congress of Statistics and the 1st centenary of the Mexican Society of Geography and Statistics.

Types of 1923 and PT1

1934		***Perf. 10½, 11 (4c)***		
687A	PT1	1c brown	1.00	.30
688	A79	2c scarlet	.35	.25
689	A82	4c green	.35	.25
690	A85	10c brown lake	.35	.25
691	A84	20c dark blue	.75	.75
692	A83	30c dk blue grn	1.00	1.25
		Nos. 687A-692 (6)	3.80	3.05
		Set, never hinged	9.00	

See 2nd note after Postal Tax stamp No. RA3.

Indian Archer — A99

Indian — A100

Woman Decorating Pottery
A101

Peon
A102

Potter
A103

Sculptor
A104

Craftsman
A105

Offering to the Gods
A106

Worshiper — A107

1934, Sept. 1	**Wmk. 156**	***Perf. 10½***		
698	A99	5c dk green	10.00	3.00
699	A100	10c brown lake	17.00	4.00
700	A101	20c ultra	30.00	20.00
701	A102	30c black	60.00	42.50
702	A103	40c black brn	37.50	25.00
703	A104	50c dull blue	175.00	160.00
704	A105	1p brn lake & blk	350.00	175.00
705	A106	5p brn blk & red brn	750.00	725.00
706	A107	10p brown & vio	2,000.	2,500.
a.		Unwatermarked	*3,250.*	
		Never hinged	5,000.	
		Nos. 698-706 (9)	3,430.	3,655.
		Set, never hinged	7,500.	

National University.

The design of the 1p is wider than the rest of the set. Values are for examples with perfs just touching the design.

See Nos. C54-C61, RA13B.

Yalalteca Indian — A108

Tehuana Indian — A109

Arch of the Revolution
A110

Tower of Los Remedios
A111

Cross of Palenque A112

Independence Monument A113

Independence Monument, Puebla A114

Monument to the Heroic Cadets A115

Stone of Tizoc — A116

Ruins of Mitla — A117

Coat of Arms A118

Charro A119

Imprint: "Oficina Impresora de Hacienda-Mexico"

1934-40 Wmk. 156 *Perf. 10½*
Size: 20x26mm

707 A108 1c orange .65 .25
a. Unwmkd. —
708 A109 2c green .65 .25
a. Unwmkd. 3.75 3.75
709 A110 4c carmine .90 .25
710 A111 5c olive brn .65 .25
a. Unwmkd. 400.00 350.00
711 A112 10c dk blue .80 .25
712 A112 10c violet ('35) 1.25 .25
a. Unwmkd. 200.00 40.00
713 A113 15c lt blue 4.00 .30
714 A114 20c gray green 1.90 .25
a. 20c olive green 2.00 .25
715 A114 20c ultra ('35) 1.40 .25
a. Unwmkd. 150.00
716 A115 30c lake .90 .25
a. Unwmkd. 350.00
716B A115 30c lt ultra ('40) 1.00 .25
717 A116 40c red brown 1.00 .25
718 A117 50c grnsh black .90 .25
a. Imperf., pair 110.00
b. Unwmkd. 375.00
719 A118 1p dk brn & org 2.50 .25
a. Imperf., pair 350.00
720 A119 5p org & vio 7.75 .75
Nos. 707-720 (15) 26.25 4.30
Set, never hinged 70.00

No. 718a was not regularly issued.
The existence of No. 707a has been questioned.
See Nos. 729-733, 733B, 735, 784-788, 795A-800A, 837-838, 840-841, 844, 846-851. For overprints see Nos. 728, O224-O232.

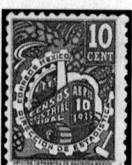

Tractor — A120

1935, Apr. 1 Wmk. 156 *Perf. 10½*
721 A120 10c violet 4.00 .50
Never hinged 9.00

Industrial census of Apr. 10, 1935.

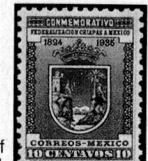

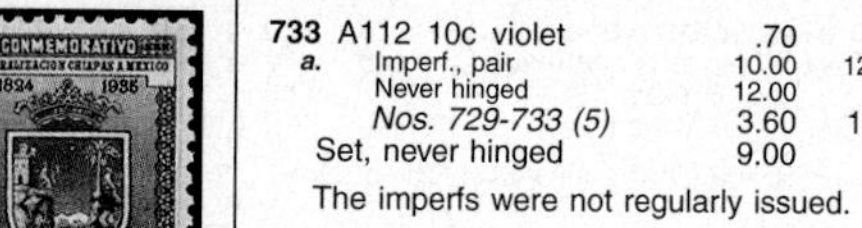
Arms of Chiapas — A121

1935, Sept. 14
722 A121 10c dark blue .50 .25
Never hinged 1.40
a. Unwmkd. 125.00 100.00

The 111th anniversary of the joining of the state of Chiapas with the federal republic of Mexico. See No. 734.

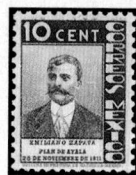

Emiliano Zapata — A122

1935, Nov. 20 Wmk. 156
723 A122 10c violet .75 .25
Never hinged 2.00

25th anniversary of the Plan of Ayala.

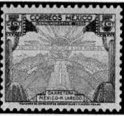

US and Mexico Joined by Highways A123

Matalote Bridge A124

View of Nuevo Laredo Highway — A125

1936 Wmk. 248 *Perf. 14*
725 A123 5c blue grn & rose .35 .25
726 A124 10c slate bl & blk .50 .25
727 A125 20c brn & dk grn 1.50 1.00
Nos. 725-727,C77-C79 (6) 3.60 2.50
Set, never hinged 8.50

Opening of the Mexico City - Nuevo Laredo Highway.

Monument Type of 1923

1936 Wmk. 248 Engr. *Perf. 10½*
727A A85 10c brown lake *2,500.* 650.00

No. 712 Overprinted in Green

1936, Dec. 15 Wmk. 156
728 A112 10c violet .60 .50
Never hinged 1.50

1st National Congress of Industrial Hygiene and Medicine.

Type of 1934
Redrawn size: 17½x21mm
Imprint: "Talleres de Imp. de Est. y Valores-Mexico"

1937 Photo. Wmk. 156 *Perf. 14*
729 A108 1c orange .60 .25
a. Imperf., pair 12.50 12.50
Never hinged 25.00
730 A109 2c dull green .60 .25
a. Imperf., pair 12.50 12.50
Never hinged 30.00
731 A110 4c carmine .90 .25
a. Imperf., pair 12.50 12.50
Never hinged 30.00
732 A111 5c olive brn .80 .25
a. Unwmkd. *300.00*
733 A112 10c violet .70 .25
a. Imperf., pair 10.00 12.50
Never hinged 12.00
Nos. 729-733 (5) 3.60 1.25
Set, never hinged 9.00

The imperfs were not regularly issued.

Types of 1934-35

1937 Wmk. 260 Size: 17½x21mm
733B A111 5c olive brown *4,000.* 250.00
Never hinged *6,000.*

1937 Engr. *Perf. 10½*
734 A121 10c dark blue 35.00 35.00
Never hinged 75.00

1937 Size: 20x26mm
735 A112 10c violet 350.00 55.00

Types of 1923

1934-37 Wmk. 260 *Perf. 10½*
735A A79 2c scarlet *6,000.*
735B A85 10c brown lake —

Forged perforations exist.
The listing of No. 735B is being re-evaluated. The Catalogue Editors would appreciate any information on the stamp.

Rouletted 14½
736 A85 10c claret *5,500. 175.00*

Blacksmith A126

Revolutionary Soldier A127

Revolutionary Envoy — A128

Wmk. 156

1938, Mar. 26 Photo. *Perf. 14*
737 A126 5c black & brn .80 .25
738 A127 10c red brown .35 .25
739 A128 20c maroon & org 6.00 1.00
Nos. 737-739,C82-C84 (6) 13.15 5.00
Set, never hinged 32.00

Plan of Guadalupe, 25th anniv.

Arch of the Revolution A129

Independence Monument A131

Design: 10c, National Theater.

1938, July 1
740 A129 5c bister brn 4.25 .60
741 A129 5c red brown 25.00 2.25
742 A129 10c orange 15.00 11.00
743 A129 10c chocolate 1.00 .25
744 A131 20c brown lake 6.00 4.00
745 A131 20c black 18.00 15.00
Nos. 740-745 (6) 69.25 33.10
Nos. 740-745,C85-C90 (12) 129.60 63.35
Set, never hinged 275.00

16th Intl. Congress of Planning & Housing.

Arch of the Revolution A132

1939, May 1
746 A132 10c Prus blue .65 .25
Nos. 746,C91-C93 (4) 4.75 3.00
Set, never hinged 11.00

New York World's Fair.

Indian — A133

1939, May 17
747 A133 10c red orange .45 .25
Nos. 747,C94-C96 (4) 5.55 2.80
Set, never hinged 13.00

Tulsa World Philatelic Convention.

Juan Zumárraga A134

First Printing Shop in Mexico, 1539 A135

Design: 10c, Antonio de Mendoza.

1939, Sept. 1 Engr. *Perf. 10½*
748 A134 2c brown blk .75 .25
749 A135 5c green .75 .25
750 A134 10c red brown .25 .25
Nos. 748-750,C97-C99 (6) 3.75 1.95
Set, never hinged 11.50

400th anniversary of printing in Mexico.

View of Taxco A137

Allegory of Agriculture A138

10c, Two hands holding symbols of commerce.

1939, Oct. 1 Photo. *Perf. 12x13*
751 A137 2c dark carmine 1.25 .25
752 A138 5c sl grn & gray grn .25 .25
753 A138 10c org brn & buff .25 .25
Nos. 751-753,C100-C102 (6) 6.25 2.00
Set, never hinged 14.00

Census Taking.

"Penny Black" of 1840 — A140

1940, May *Perf. 14*

754	A140	5c black & lemon	.90	.50
755	A140	10c dark violet	.25	.25
756	A140	20c lt blue & car	.25	.25
757	A140	1p gray & red org	7.00	4.00
758	A140	5p black & Prus bl	50.00	50.00
		Nos. 754-758,C103-C107 (10)	141.00	116.05
		Set, never hinged	340.00	

Postage stamp centenary.

Roadside Monument — A141

1940 **Wmk. 156**

759	A141	6c deep green	.50	.25
		Never hinged	1.25	

Opening of the highway between Mexico, D. F., and Guadalajara. See Nos. 789, 842.

Vasco de Quiroga — A142

Melchor Ocampo — A143

College Seal — A144

1940, July 15 **Engr.** *Perf. 10½*

760	A142	2c violet	1.30	.50
761	A143	5c copper red	.80	.25
762	A144	10c olive bister	.80	.30
	a.	Imperf., pair	150.00	
		Nos. 760-762,C108-C110 (6)	5.10	2.60
		Set, never hinged	11.00	

Founding of the National College of San Nicolas de Hidalgo, 400th anniv.

Coat of Arms of Campeche A145

1940, Aug. 7 **Photo.** *Perf. 12x13*

763	A145	10c bis brn & dk car	5.00	1.25
		Nos. 763,C111-C113 (4)	12.60	6.70
		Set, never hinged	30.00	

400th anniversary of the founding of Campeche.

Man at Helm A146

1940, Dec. 1

764	A146	2c red org & blk	1.60	.60
765	A146	5c peacock bl & red brn	8.00	3.50
766	A146	10c slate grn & dk brn	4.00	.85
		Nos. 764-766,C114-C116 (6)	21.00	9.45
		Set, never hinged	45.00	

Inauguration of Pres. Manuel Avila Camacho.

Alternated Perforations

Nos. 763-766, 774-779, 792-795, 801-804, 806-811, 813-818, C100-C102, C111-C116, C123-C128, C143-C162, C430-C431 have alternating small and large perforations.

Javelin Thrower — A147

1941, Nov. 4 *Perf. 14*

767	A147	10c dull yellow grn	5.00	.50

National Athletic Games of the Revolution, Nov. 4-20, 1941.

Serpent Columns, Chichén Itzá A148

Mayan Sculpture A149

Coat of Arms of Merída — A150

1942, June 30

768	A148	2c dk olive bis	1.40	.75
769	A149	5c deep orange	2.25	.60
770	A150	10c dark violet	1.60	.25
		Nos. 768-770,C117-C119 (6)	11.50	6.35

400th anniversary of the founding of Merida.

Independence Monument to Hidalgo — A151

Government Palace — A152

View of Guadalajara — A153

1942, Feb. 11 **Engr.** *Perf. 10x10½*

771	A151	2c bl vio & vio brn	.35	.30
772	A152	5c black & cop red	1.25	.50
773	A153	10c red org & ultra	1.25	.40
		Nos. 771-773,C120-C122 (6)	7.85	4.20

Founding of Guadalajara, 400th anniv.

No. 773 exists imperf on unwatermarked paper as a color proof.

Black Cloud in Orion A154

Designs: 5c, Total solar eclipse. 10c, Spiral galaxy in the "Hunting Dogs."

1942, Feb. 17 **Photo.** *Perf. 12x13*

774	A154	2c lt vio & indigo	10.00	3.00
775	A154	5c blue & indigo	15.00	2.00
776	A154	10c red org & indigo	15.00	.75
		Nos. 774-776,C123-C125 (6)	100.00	17.25

Astrophysics Congress and the inauguration of an observatory at Tonanzintla, Feb. 17, 1942.

"Mother Earth" A157

Sowing Wheat A158

Western Hemisphere Carrying a Torch — A159

1942, July 1

777	A157	2c chestnut	2.00	.40
778	A158	5c turq blue	3.50	1.10
779	A159	10c red orange	1.50	.55
		Nos. 777-779,C126-C128 (6)	12.90	5.50

2nd Inter-American Agricultural Conference.

Fuente Academy A160

1942, Nov. 16 *Perf. 14*

780	A160	10c grnsh black	2.50	.75

75th anniversary of Fuente Academy.

Las Monjas Church — A161

Generalissimo Ignacio José de Allende — A163

Design: 5c, San Miguel Church.

1943, May 11

781	A161	2c intense blue	1.00	.35
782	A161	5c deep brown	1.10	.30
783	A163	10c dull black	3.50	1.00
		Nos. 781-783,C129-C131 (6)	10.60	5.35

400th anniv. of the founding of San Miguel de Allende.

Types of 1937

1944 **Photo.** **Wmk. 272**

784	A108	1c orange	2.00	.25
785	A109	2c dull green	2.00	.25
786	A110	4c carmine	4.00	.25
787	A111	5c olive brown	4.00	.25
788	A112	10c violet	2.00	.25

Type of 1940

789	A141	6c green	2.00	.25
		Nos. 784-789 (6)	16.00	1.50

"Liberty" — A164

1944 **Photo.**

790	A164	12c violet brown	.35	.25

See No. 845.

Juan M. de Castorena — A165

1944, Oct. 12 **Engr.** *Perf. 10*

791	A165	12c dark brown	.60	.25

Third Book Fair. See No. C142.

Catalogue values for unused stamps in this section, from this point to the end of the section, are for Never Hinged items.

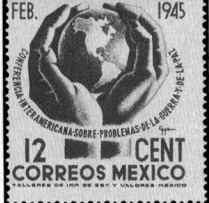

Hands Holding Globe Showing Western Hemisphere A166

1945, Feb. 27 **Photo.** *Perf. 12x13*

792	A166	12c dark carmine	.60	.25
793	A166	1p slate green	1.00	.25
794	A166	5p olive brown	5.75	4.50
795	A166	10p black	17.50	8.00
		Nos. 792-795,C143-C147 (9)	55.25	33.80

Inter-American Conf. held at Chapultepec, Feb. 1945.

Types of 1934-40

Wmk. 272

1945-46 Engr. *Perf. 10½*

795A	A113	15c lt grnsh bl ('46)	325.00	60.00
796	A114	20c gray grn	2.50	.25
797	A115	30c lt ultra	3.25	.25
798	A116	40c brown	2.50	.25
799	A117	50c grnsh blk	1.60	.25
800	A118	1p dk brn & org	7.00	.25
b.		Imperf., pair		
800A	A119	5p org & vio ('46)	17.00	6.00
		Nos. 795A-800A (7)	358.85	67.25

Theater of Peace, San Luis Potosi A167

1945, July 27 Photo. *Perf. 12x13*

801	A167	12c blk & vio brn	.45	.25
802	A167	1p blk & bl gray	.60	.40
803	A167	5p blk & brn lake	5.50	5.00
804	A167	10p blk & grnsh bl	17.00	12.00
		Nos. 801-804,C148-C152 (9)	51.65	35.50

Reconstruction of the Peace Theater (Teatro de la Paz), San Luis Potosi.

Fountain of Diana, the Huntress — A168

1945 *Perf. 14*

805	A168	3c violet blue	.55	.25

See No. 839.

Removing Blindfold A169

1945, Nov. 2 *Perf. 12x13*

806	A169	2c bluish grn	.40	.25
807	A169	6c orange	.40	.25
808	A169	12c ultra	.40	.25
809	A169	1p olive	.60	.25
810	A169	5p gray & pale rose	3.50	3.00
811	A169	10p bl & yel grn	27.50	20.00
		Nos. 806-811 (6)	32.80	24.00
		Nos. 806-811,C153-C157 (11)	68.30	56.05

Issued to publicize the national literacy campaign.

M. E. de Almanza — A170

1946 *Perf. 14*

812	A170	8c black	1.25	.25

Martines Enriquez de Almanza, founder of the Mexican posts. See No. 843.

Allegory of World Peace A171

1946, Apr. 10 *Perf. 12x13*

813	A171	2c dk olive bis	.35	.25
814	A171	6c red brown	.30	.25
815	A171	12c Prus green	.25	.25
816	A171	1p lt green	.60	.40
817	A171	5p dull red vio	5.50	5.00
818	A171	10p lt ultra	30.00	20.00
		Nos. 813-818 (6)	37.00	26.15
		Nos. 813-818,C158-C162 (11)	64.25	40.95

United Nations.

Arms of Zacatecas A173

Monument to Gen. Gonzalez Ortega A174

Ramón Lopez Velarde — A175

Francisco Garcia Salinas — A176

Wmk. 279

1946, Sept. 1 Photo. *Perf. 14*

820	A173	2c orange brn	.55	.25
821	A173	12c Prus blue	.25	.25

Engr.

Perf. 10x10½

822	A174	1p lilac rose	.70	.25
823	A175	5p red	5.50	3.00
824	A176	10p dk blue & blk	40.00	10.00
		Nos. 820-824 (5)	47.00	13.75
		Nos. 820-824,C163-C166 (9)	68.65	32.35

400th anniversary of the founding of the city of Zacatecas.

A177

1947 Photo. *Perf. 14*

825	A177	15c Postman	.25	.25
a.		Imperf., pair	110.00	

A178

10c, F. D. Roosevelt and Stamp of 1st Mexican Issue. 15c, Arms of Mexico and Stamp of 1st US Issue.

1947, May 16

826	A178	10c yellow brown	1.60	1.00
827	A178	15c green	.25	.25
		Nos. 826-827,C167-C169 (5)	4.60	2.40

Cent. Intl. Phil. Exhib., NYC, 5/17-25/47.

Justo Sierra — A180

Communications Building — A181

Perf. 10x10½, 10½x10

1947 Engr. Wmk. 279

828	A180	10p brown & dl grn	150.00	40.00
829	A181	20p dk green & lil	1.60	2.00

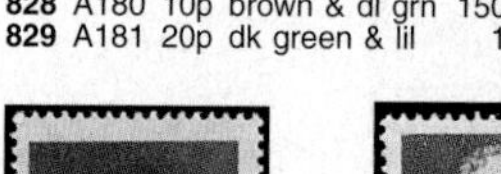

Cadet Juan Escutia — A182

Gen. Manuel Rincón — A186

Flag of San Blas Battalion — A188

Designs: 2c, Cadet Francisco Márquez. 5c, Cadet Fernando Montes de Oca. 10c, Cadet Juan Escutia. 15c, Cadet Agustin Melgar. 1p, Gen. Lucas Balderas.

1947, Sept. 8 Photo. *Perf. 14*

830	A182	2c brown black	.45	.25
831	A182	5c red orange	.30	.25
832	A182	10c dk brown	.25	.25
833	A182	15c dk Prus green	.25	.25
834	A186	30c dull olive grn	.35	.25

Engr.

Perf. 10x10½

835	A186	1p aqua	.45	.45
836	A188	5p dk blue & claret	1.90	1.90
		Nos. 830-836 (7)	3.95	3.60
		Nos. 830-836,C180-C184 (12)	7.30	6.60

Centenary of the battles of Chapultepec, Churubusco and Molino del Rey.

Types of 1934-46

1947-50 Wmk. 279 Photo. *Perf. 14*

837	A108	1c orange	1.00	.30
a.		Imperf., pair	150.00	
838	A109	2c dk green	.60	.25
839	A168	3c violet blue	.60	.25
840	A110	4c dull red	1.90	.25
841	A111	5c olive brown	2.50	.25
842	A141	6c deep green	.45	.25
a.		Imperf., pair	150.00	
843	A170	8c black	.35	.25
844	A112	10c violet	1.90	.25
845	A164	12c violet brn	12.00	.75

Types A108 to A112 are in the redrawn size of 1937.

Size: 19x25mm

Engr. *Perf. 10½*

846	A114	20c olive green	1.25	.25
a.		20c green	3.00	.30
847	A115	30c lt ultra	12.00	.40
848	A116	40c red brown	1.40	.25
849	A117	50c green	1.90	.25
a.		Imperf., pair	110.00	
850	A118	1p dk brn & org	45.00	9.00
851	A119	5p org & vio ('50)	35.00	11.00
		Nos. 837-851 (15)	117.85	23.95

A189

Designs: 3c, Modernistic church, Nuevo Leon. 5c, Modern building, Mexico City. 10c, Convent, Morelos. 15c, Benito Juarez. 20c, Puebla Cathedral. 30c, Indian dancer, Michoacan. 40c, Stone head, Tabasco. 50c, Carved head, Veracruz. 1p, Convent and carved head, Hidalgo. 5p, Galleon, arms of Campeche. 10p, Francisco I. Madero. 20p, Modern building, Mexico City.

1950-52 Wmk. 279 Photo. *Perf. 14*

856	A189	3c blue vio ('51)	.50	.25
857	A189	5c dk red brn	.75	.25
858	A189	10c dk green	3.50	.25
859	A189	15c dk green ('51)	1.75	.25
860	A189	20c blue violet	14.00	.25
861	A189	30c red	.50	.25
862	A189	40c red orange ('51)	1.00	.25
863	A189	50c blue	1.25	.25

Engr.

864	A189	1p dull brown	4.50	.25
865	A189	5p ultra & bl grn	7.00	4.00
866	A189	10p blk & dp ultra ('52)	7.00	7.00
867	A189	20p pur & grn ('52)	10.00	10.00
		Nos. 856-867 (12)	51.75	23.25

See Nos. 875-885, 909, 928-931, 943-952, 1003-1004, 1054-1055, 1072, 1076, 1081, 1090-1091, 1094-1102.

Highway Bridge A190

Symbolical of Construction in 1950 — A191

Perf. 10½x10, 10x10½

1950, May 5 Engr.

868	A190	15c purple	.60	.25
869	A191	20c deep blue	.40	.25
		Nos. 868-869,C199-C200 (4)	4.30	1.00

Completion of the International Highway between Ciudad Juarez and the Guatemala border.

Railroad Laborer — A192

Design: 20c, Map and locomotive.

Inscribed: "Ferrocarril del Sureste 1950"

1950, May 24 *Perf. 10x10½*

870	A192	15c chocolate	1.25	.25
871	A192	20c dp carmine	.45	.25
		Nos. 870-871,C201-C202 (4)	2.55	1.00

Opening of the Southeastern Railroad between Veracruz, Coatzocoalcos and Yucatan, 1950.

Postal Service — A193

1950, June 25 ***Perf. 10x10½***
872 A193 50c purple .40 .25
Nos. 872,C203-C204 (3) 1.25 .80

75th anniv. (in 1949) of the UPU.

Miguel Hidalgo y Costilla — A194

Wmk. 300

1953, May 8 **Photo.** ***Perf. 14***
873 A194 20c grnsh bl & dk brn 1.75 .25
Nos. 873,C206-C207 (3) 3.55 .75

Bicentenary of birth of Miguel Hidalgo y Costilla. See Nos. C206-C207.

Type of 1950-52

Designs as before.
Two types of 5p:
Type I — Imprint ½mm high and blurred.
Type II — Imprint ¾mm high and clear.

1954-67 **Photo.** ***Perf. 14***
875 A189 5c red brown .50 .25
876 A189 10c green, redrawn 2.50 .25
a. 10c dark green 2.50 .25
877 A189 15c dk green .40 .25
878 A189 20c bluish blk, white paper, colorless gum ('67) .60 .25
a. 20c dark blue 3.50 .25
879 A189 30c brown red .75 .25
a. 30c redsh brn .75 .25
880 A189 40c red orange 1.50 .25
881 A189 50c lt blue 1.00 .25

Engr.

882 A189 1p olive grn, perf. 11, vert. wmk. ('58) 12.00 .25
a. 1p olive grn, perf. 14 7.00 .25
b. olive brown 12.00 .25
883 A189 5p ultra & bl grn, I 7.00 1.00
a. Type II 500.00 7.00
884 A189 10p sl & dp ultra ('56) 9.00 5.00
a. 10p slate green & ultra 35.00 5.00
885 A189 20p purple & grn 11.00 9.00
a. 20p brn vio & yel grn 75.00 20.00
Nos. 875-885 (11) 46.25 17.00

Nos. 875-881 come only with watermark vertical, and in various shades. Watermark inverted on Nos. 884, 885.

On No. 876, imprint extends full width of stamp.

Vert. pairs, imperf. horiz. of Nos. 878, 880 are noted after No. 1004.

Aztec Messenger of the Sun — A195

1954, Mar. 6
886 A195 20c rose & bl gray 1.10 .25
Nos. 886,C222-C223 (3) 2.85 .85

7th Central American and Caribbean Games.

Symbolizing Adoption of National Anthem — A196

1954, Sept. 16 **Photo.**
887 A196 5c rose lil & dk bl .75 .25
888 A196 20c yel brn & brn vio .90 .25
889 A196 1p gray grn & cerise .65 .40
Nos. 887-889,C224-C226 (6) 3.40 1.65

Centenary of the adoption of Mexico's National Anthem.

Torch-Bearer and Stadium — A197

1955, Mar. 12 **Wmk. 300** ***Perf. 14***
890 A197 20c dk grn & red brn .85 .25
Nos. 890,C227-C228 (3) 2.35 .85

Second Pan American Games, 1955.

Aztec Designs A198

1956, Aug. 1
891 A198 5c "Motion" .50 .25
892 A198 10c Bird .50 .25
893 A198 30c Flowers .40 .25
894 A198 50c Corn .50 .25
895 A198 1p Deer .60 .25
896 A198 5p Man 2.25 2.25
a. Souv. sheet, #891-896, imperf. 75.00 75.00
Nos. 891-896,C229-C234 (12) 7.90 6.00

Centenary of Mexico's 1st postage stamps. No. 896a sold for 15p.

Stamp of 1856 A199

1956, Aug. 1
897 A199 30c brn & intense bl .75 .25

Cent. of 1st Mexican Stamp Intl. Philatelic Exhibition, Mexico City, Aug. 16, 1956.

Francisco Zarco — A200

Portraits: 25c, 45c, Guillermo Prieto. 60c, Ponciano Arriaga.

1956-63
897A A200 25c dk brown ('63) .75 .50
898 A200 45c dk blue green .35 .25
899 A200 60c red lilac .35 .35
900 A200 70c violet blue .40 .25
Nos. 897A-900,C236-C237A (7) 4.45 2.70

Centenary of the constitution (in 1957). See Nos. C289, 1075, 1092-1093.

"Mexico" — A201

Design: 1p, National Assembly.

1957, Aug. 31 **Photo.** ***Perf. 14***
901 A201 30c maroon & gold .50 .25
902 A201 1p pale brn & metallic grn .35 .25
Nos. 901-902,C239-C240 (4) 1.70 1.00

Constitution, centenary.

Mexican Eagle and Oil Derrick — A202

Design: 5p, Map of Mexico and refinery.

1958, Aug. 30 **Wmk. 300** ***Perf. 14***
903 A202 30c lt blue & blk .50 .25
904 A202 5p hn brn & Prus grn 6.00 4.00
Nos. 903-904,C243-C244 (4) 7.15 4.75

20th anniv. of the nationalization of Mexico's oil industry.

UNESCO Building and Eiffel Tower — A203

1959, Jan. 20
905 A203 30c dull lilac & blk .50 .25

UNESCO Headquarters opening, Paris, Nov. 9.

UN Headquarters, New York — A204

1959, Sept. 7 **Litho.** ***Perf. 14***
906 A204 30c org yel & bl .50 .25

Meeting of UNESCO.

Carranza — A205

1960, Jan. 15 **Photo.** **Wmk. 300**
907 A205 30c pale grn & plum .35 .25

Birth centenary of Pres. Venustiano Carranza. See No. C246.

Humboldt Statue — A206

1960, Mar. 16 **Wmk. 300** ***Perf. 14***
908 A206 40c bis brn & grn .35 .25

Cent. of the death (in 1859) of Alexander von Humboldt, German naturalist and geographer.

Type of 1950-52 Inscribed: "HOMENAJE AL COLECCIONISTA DEL TIMBRE DE MEXICO-JUNIO 1960"

1960, June 8 **Engr.** **Wmk. 300**
909 A189 10p lil, brn & grn 100.00 75.00

Visit of the Elmhurst (Ill.) Philatelic Society of Mexico Specialists to Mexico, 25th anniv. See No. C249.

Independence Bell & Monument
A207 A208

5p, Bell of Dolores and Miguel Hidalgo.

Wmk. 300

1960, Sept. 15 **Photo.** ***Perf. 14***
910 A207 30c grn & rose red 3.00 .25
911 A208 1p dl grn & dk brn .50 .25
912 A208 5p maroon & dk bl 5.00 5.00
Nos. 910-912,C250-C252 (6) 15.50 8.25

150th anniv. of Mexican independence. See US No. 1157.

Agricultural Reform A209

Symbols of Health Education — A210

Designs: 20c, Sailor and Soldier, 1960, and Fighter of 1910. 30c, Electrification. 1p, Political development (schools). 5p, Currency stability (Bank and money).

1960-61 **Photo.** ***Perf. 14***
913 A209 10c sl grn, blk & red org .75 .25
914 A210 15c grn & org brn 2.75 .50
915 A210 20c brt bl & lt brn ('61) 1.00 .25
916 A210 30c vio brn & sep .40 .25
917 A210 1p redsh brn & slate .50 .25
918 A210 5p maroon & gray 6.00 3.50
Nos. 913-918,C253-C256 (10) 18.80 8.80

50th anniversary (in 1960) of the Mexican Revolution.

Issued: No. 913, 11/20/60; No. 914, 916-918, 12/23/60; No. 915, 3/14/61.

Tunnel — A211

1961, Dec. 7 **Wmk. 300** ***Perf. 14***
919 A211 40c blk & brt grn .40 .25
Nos. 919,C258-C259 (3) 1.20 .75

Opening of the railroad from Chihuahua to the Pacific Ocean.

Microscope, Mosquito and Globe — A212

1962, Apr. 7
920 A212 40c dl bl & maroon .40 .25

WHO drive to eradicate malaria.

President Joao Goulart of Brazil — A213

Wmk. 300

1962, Apr. 11 Photo. *Perf. 14*
921 A213 40c brown olive 1.00 .25

Visit of Joao Goulart, president of Brazil, to Mexico.

Insurgent at Marker for Battle of Puebla — A214

1962, May 5
922 A214 40c sepia & dk grn .35 .25

Centenary of the Battle of May 5 at Puebla and the defeat of French forces by Gen. Ignacio Zaragoza. See No. C260.

Draftsman and Surveyor — A215

1962, June 11
923 A215 40c slate grn & dk bl .90 .25

25th anniversary of the National Polytechnic Institute. See No. C261.

Plumbline — A216

1962, June 21
924 A216 20c dp blue & blk 1.40 .25

Issued to publicize the importance of mental health.

"Space Needle" and Gear Wheels — A217

1962, July 6
925 A217 40c dk grn & gray .35 .25

"Century 21" International Exposition, Seattle, Wash., Apr. 21-Oct. 12.

Globe — A218

1962, Oct. 1 *Perf. 14*
926 A218 40c gray & brn .35 .25

1962 meeting of the Inter-American Economic and Social Council. See No. C263.

Pres. Alessandri of Chile — A219

1962, Dec. 20 Wmk. 300 *Perf. 14*
927 A219 20c olive black .75 .25

Visit of President Jorge Alessandri Rodriguez of Chile to Mexico, Dec. 17-20.

Type of 1950-52

Designs as before.

Wmk. 300, Vertical

1962-74 Photo. *Perf. 14*

928	A189	1p ol gray ('67)	1.25	.25
a.		1p green	4.00	.25
929	A189	5p dl bl & dk grn	3.50	.75
a.		5p bluish gray & dark green, white paper ('67)	3.50	.50
930	A189	10p gray & bl ('63)	8.50	5.00
a.		10p green & deep blue ('74)	8.50	5.50
931	A189	20p lil & blk ('63)	9.00	7.50
a.		Redrawn, white paper	10.00	10.00
		Nos. 928-931 (4)	22.25	13.50

No. 928 is on thick, luminescent paper. No. 929 is 20½mm high; No. 929a, 20¾mm. Nos. 931a and 1102 (unwmkd.) have more shading in sky and spots on first floor windows.

Pres. Betancourt of Venezuela — A220

1963, Feb. 23 Wmk. 300
932 A220 20c slate .70 .25

Visit of President Romulo Betancourt of Venezuela to Mexico.

Congress Emblem — A221

1963, Apr. 22 Wmk. 300 *Perf. 14*
933 A221 40c fawn & blk .60 .25

19th International Chamber of Commerce Congress. See No. C271.

Wheat Emblem — A222

1963, June 23 Wmk. 300 *Perf. 14*
934 A222 40c crim & dk bl .60 .25

FAO "Freedom from Hunger" campaign.

Mercado Mountains and Arms of Durango — A223

1963, July 13 Photo.
935 A223 20c dk bl & choc .60 .25

400th anniv. of the founding of Durango.

Belisario Dominguez — A224

1963, July 13 Photo.
936 A224 20c dk grn & ol gray .60 .25

Centenary of the birth of Belisario Dominguez, revolutionary leader.

Mexico. No. 897, depicting Mexico No. 1 — A225

1963, Oct. 9 Wmk. 350 *Perf. 14*
937 A225 1p int blue & brn 1.25 .75

77th Annual Convention of the American Philatelic Society, Mexico City, Oct. 7-13. See No. C274.

Tree of Life — A226

1963, Oct. 26 Wmk. 350 *Perf. 14*
938 A226 20c dl bl grn & car .40 .25

Intl. Red Cross, cent. See No. C277.

José Morelos — A227

1963, Nov. 9
939 A227 40c grn & dk sl grn .55 .25

150th anniv. of the 1st congress of Anahuac.

Pres. Victor Paz Estenssoro — A228

1963, Nov. 9 Wmk. 350 *Perf. 14*
940 A228 40c dk brn & dk red brn .60 .25

Visit of President Victor Paz Estenssoro of Bolivia.

Arms of Sinaloa University — A229

1963 Photo.
941 A229 40c slate grn & ol bister .60 .25

90th anniversary of the founding of the University of Sinaloa.

Diesel Train, Rail Cross Section and Globe A230

1963, Nov. 29 Photo.
942 A230 20c black & dk brn .90 .50

11th Pan-American Railroad Congress. See No. C279.

Type of 1950-52

Designs as before.

1963-66 Wmk. 350 Photo. *Perf. 14*

943	A189	5c red brn ('65)	.60	.25
944	A189	10c dk green ('64)	.65	.25
945	A189	15c dk green ('66)	.60	.25
946	A189	20c dark blue	.60	.25
948	A189	40c red orange	.70	.25
949	A189	50c blue ('64)	2.00	.25
950	A189	1p olive grn ('64)	4.00	.25
951	A189	5p dl bl & dk grn ('66)	100.00	30.00

952 A189 10p gray & Prus bl ('65) 35.00 25.00
Nos. 943-952 (9) 144.15 56.75

The 20c is redrawn; clouds almost eliminated and other slight variations.

"F.S.T.S.E." Emblem — A231

1964, Feb. 15
954 A231 20c red org & dk brn .40 .25

25th anniv. (in 1963) of the Civil Service Statute affecting federal employees.

Academy of Medicine Emblem — A232

1964, May 18 Wmk. 350 *Perf. 14*
955 A232 20c gold & blk .40 .25

National Academy of Medicine, cent.

José Rizal — A233

40c, Miguel Lopez de Legaspi, Spanish navigator.

1964, Nov. 10 Photo. *Perf. 14*
956 A233 20c dk bl & dp grn .50 .25
957 A233 40c dk bl & brt vio .60 .25
Nos. 956-957,C300-C301 (4) 6.10 1.85

Issued to honor 400 years of Mexican-Philippine friendship.

View of Zacatecas — A234

1964, Nov. 10 Wmk. 350
958 A234 40c slate grn & red .55 .25

50th anniv. of the capture of Zacatecas.

Col. Gregorio Mendez — A235

1964, Nov. 10
959 A235 40c grysh blk & dk brn .50 .25

Cent. of the Battle of Jahuactal, Tabasco.

Morelos Theater, Aguascalientes A236

1965, Jan. 9 Photo. *Perf. 14*
960 A236 20c dl cl & dk gray .35 .25

50th anniversary of the Aguascalientes Convention, Oct. 1-Nov. 9, 1914.

Andrés Manuel del Río A237

1965, Feb. 18 Wmk. 350 *Perf. 14*
961 A237 30c gray .40 .25

Bicentenary of the birth of Andrés Manuel del Rio, founder of the National School of Mining and discoverer of vanadium.

José Morelos and Constitution — A238

1965, Apr. 24 Photo. *Perf. 14*
962 A238 40c brt grn & dk red brn .45 .25

Sesquicentennial (in 1964) of the 1st Mexican constitution.

Trees — A239

1965, July 14 Wmk. 350 *Perf. 14*
963 A239 20c blue & green .30 .25

Issued to commemorate Tree Day, July 8.

ICY Emblem A240

1965, Sept. 13 Photo.
964 A240 40c olive gray & slate grn .30 .25

International Cooperation Year, 1965.

Athlete with Sling, Clay Figure A241

Design: 40c, Batter. Clay figures on 20c and 40c found in Colima, period 300-650 A.D.

1965, Dec. 17 Wmk. 350 *Perf. 14*
965 A241 20c olive & vio bl 3.25 .25
966 A241 40c pink & black 1.00 .25
Nos. 965-966,C309-C311 (5) 6.70 1.30

19th Olympic Games, Mexico, 1968.

José Morelos by Diego Rivera — A242

1965, Dec. 22
967 A242 20c lt vio bl & blk .40 .25

José Maria Morelos y Pavon (1765-1815), priest and patriot in 1810 revolution against Spain.

Emiliano Zapata — A243

20c, Corn, cotton, bamboo, wheat and cow.

1966, Jan. 10 Photo.
968 A243 20c carmine rose .35 .25
969 A243 40c black .45 .25

50th anniv. of the Agrarian Reform Law.

Mexican Postal Service Emblem — A244

1966, June 24 Wmk. 300 *Perf. 14*
970 A244 40c brt green & blk .40 .25
Nos. 970,C314-C315 (3) 1.00 .75

Congress of the Postal Union of the Americas and Spain, UPAE, Mexico City, June 24-July 23.

Bartolomé de Las Casas — A245

1966, Aug. 1 Photo. Wmk. 300
971 A245 20c black & buff .40 .25

400th anniv. of the death of Bartolomé de Las Casas (1474-1566), "Apostle of the Indies."

Mechanical Drawings and Cogwheels A246

1966, Aug. 15 Photo. *Perf. 14*
972 A246 20c gray & grn .30 .25

50th anniversary of the founding of the School of Mechanical and Electrical Engineering (ESIME).

FAO Emblem — A247

1966, Sept. 30 Wmk. 300 *Perf. 14*
973 A247 40c green .30 .25

FAO International Rice Year.

Wrestling, by Diego Rivera A248

20c, Running and Jumping.

1966, Oct. 15 Size: 35x21mm
974 A248 20c multicolored 1.25 .25
975 A248 40c shown 1.00 .25
a. Souvenir sheet 4.00 4.00
Nos. 974-975,C318-C320 (5) 5.70 1.55

Issued to publicize the 19th Olympic Games, Mexico City, D.F., 1968. No. 975a contains 2 imperf. stamps similar to Nos. 974-975 with simulated perforations. Sold for 90c.

First Page of Constitution — A249

Wmk. 300
1967, Feb. 5 Photo. *Perf. 14*
976 A249 40c black .50 .25

Constitution, 50th anniv. See No. C322.

Oil Refinery and Pyramid of the Sun — A250

1967, Apr. 2 Wmk. 300 *Perf. 14*
977 A250 40c lt bl & blk .35 .25

7th Intl. Oil Congress, Mexico City, Sept. 1967.

Nayarit Indian — A251

Wmk. 300
1967, May 1 Photo. *Perf. 14*
978 A251 20c pale grn & blk .30 .25

50th anniversary of Nayarit Statehood.

Degollado Theater, Guadalajara — A252

Wmk. 300
1967, June 12 Photo. *Perf. 14*
979 A252 40c pink & black .35 .25

Centenary of the founding of the Degollado Theater, Guadalajara.

Mexican Eagle over Imperial Crown — A253

Perf. 10x10½
1967, June 19 Litho. Wmk. 350
980 A253 20c black & ocher .30 .25

Centenary of the victory of the Mexican republican forces and of the execution of Emperor Maximilian I.

Canoeing A254

Designs: 40c, Basketball. 50c, Hockey. 80c, Bicycling. 2p, Fencing.

Wmk. 300
1967, Oct. 12 Photo. *Perf. 14*
981 A254 20c blue & blk .50 .25
982 A254 40c brick red & blk .50 .25
983 A254 50c brt yel grn & blk .50 .25
a. Souvenir sheet of 3, #981-983, imperf. 5.00 3.50
984 A254 80c brt pur & blk 1.25 .25
985 A254 2p orange & blk 2.25 .30
a. Souvenir sheet of 2, #984-985, imperf. 7.00 4.00
Nos. 981-985,C328-C331 (9) 8.75 2.95
Nos. 981-985 (5) 5.00 1.30

Issued to publicize the 19th Olympic Games, Mexico City, Oct. 12-27, 1968.

No. 983a sold for 1.50p; No. 985a sold for 3.50p. Both sheets are watermark 350.
See Nos. 990-995, C335-C338.

Artemio de Valle-Arizpe — A255

1967, Nov. 1 Photo.
986 A255 20c brown & slate .35 .30

Centenary of the Ateneo Fuente, a college at Saltillo, Coahuila.

Pedro Moreno — A256

1967, Nov. 18 Wmk. 300 *Perf. 14*
987 A256 40c blk & lt bl .35 .25

Moreno (1775-1817), revolutionary leader.

Gabino Barreda A257

Staircase, Palace of Mining A258

1968, Jan. 27 Photo. *Perf. 14*
988 A257 40c dk bl & rose claret .40 .25
989 A258 40c blk & bl gray .40 .25

Centenary of the founding of the National Preparatory and Engineering Schools.

Type of Olympic Issue, 1967

20c, Wrestling. 40c, Pentathlon. 50c, Water polo. 80c, Gymnastics. 1p, Boxing. 2p, Pistol shoot.

1968, Mar. 21 Wmk. 300 *Perf. 14*
990 A254 20c olive & blk .75 .25
991 A254 40c red lil & blk .75 .25
992 A254 50c brt green & blk .75 .25
a. Souvenir sheet of 3, #990-992, imperf. 7.00 4.00
993 A254 80c brt pink & blk 1.00 .25
994 A254 1p org brn & blk 4.00 3.50
995 A254 2p gray & blk 5.50 3.50
a. Souvenir sheet of 3, #993-995, imperf. 7.50 4.00
Nos. 990-995,C335-C338 (10) 15.45 9.90

19th Olympic Games, Mexico City, Oct. 12-27. No. 992a sold for 1.50p; No. 995a sold for 5p. Both sheets are watermark 350.

Map of Mexico, Peace Dove — A259

Symbols of Cultural Events A260

40c, University City Olympic stadium. 50c, Telecommunications tower. 2p, Sports Palace. 10p, Pyramid of the Sun, Teotihuacan, & Olympic torch.

Wmk. 350
1968, Oct. Photo. *Perf. 14*
996 A259 20c blue, yel & grn .75 .25
997 A259 40c multicolored .75 .25
998 A259 50c multicolored .75 .25
a. Souv. sheet of 3, #996-998, imperf. 20.00 10.00
999 A260 2p multicolored 4.00 .50
1000 A260 5p silver & blk 10.00 1.25
a. Souv. sheet of 2, #999-1000, imperf. 25.00 20.00
1001 A259 10p multicolored 7.50 2.00
Nos. 996-1001,C340-C344 (11) 32.35 8.40

19th Olympic Games, Mexico City, Oct. 12-27 (Nos. 996-1000). Arrival of the Olympic torch in Veracruz (No. 1001).
#998a sold for 1.50p. No. 1000a sold for 9p.
Issued: Nos.996-1000, 10/12; No. 1001, 10/6.

Arms of Veracruz — A261

1969, May 20 Wmk. 350 *Perf. 14*
1002 A261 40c multicolored .35 .25

450th anniv. of the founding of Veracruz.

Type of 1950-52
Coil Stamps
Perf. 11 Vert.
1969 Wmk. 300 Photo.
1003 A189 20c dk blue 4.00 2.00
1004 A189 40c red orange 5.00 3.00

Vert. pairs, imperf. horiz. may be from uncut rolls of coils.

Subway Train — A262

1969, Sept. 4 Wmk. 350 *Perf. 14*
1005 A262 40c multicolored .35 .25

Inauguration of Mexico City subway.

Honeycomb, Bee and ILO Emblem — A263

1969, Oct. 18 Photo. *Perf. 14*
1006 A263 40c multicolored .30 .25

50th anniversary of the ILO.

Gen. Allende, by Diego Rivera — A264

1969, Nov. 15 Wmk. 350 *Perf. 14*
1007 A264 40c multicolored .30 .25

Gen. Ignacio Allende Unzaga (1769-1811), hero of Mexican independence.

Tourist Issue

Pyramid of Niches at El Tajin, Veracruz, and Dancers Swinging from Pole A265

Anthropology Museum, Mexico City — A266

Deer Dance, Sonora — A267

Designs: No. 1010, View of Puerto Vallarta. No. 1011, Puebla Cathedral. No. 1012, Calle Belaunzaran. No. 1014, Ocotlan Cathedral, horiz.

1969-73 Photo. Wmk. 350
1008 A265 40c shown .45 .25
1009 A266 40c shown ('70) .45 .25
1010 A266 40c Jalisco ('70) .45 .25
1011 A266 40c Puebla ('70) .45 .25
1012 A266 40c Guanajuato ('70) .45 .25

Wmk. 300
1013 A267 40c shown ('73) .35 .25
1014 A267 40c Tlaxcala ('73) .35 .25
Nos. 1008-1014,C354-C358 (12) 6.35 3.15
Nos. 1008-1014 (7) 2.95 1.75

No. 1010 is inscribed "1970" below the design. Copies inscribed "1969" are from an earlier, unissued printing. Value $500.
Issued: No. 1008, 12/13/69; Nos. 1009-1012, 1/17/70; Nos. 1013-1014, 3/6/73.

Luminescence
Fluorescent stamps include Nos. 1013-1014, 1035, 1038, 1041, 1043-1045, 1047-1050, 1054-1059. (See Luminescence note over No. C527.)

"How Many, Who and What are We?" — A268

40c, "What, How & How Much do we produce?" (horse's head & symbols of agriculture).

1970, Jan. 26 Wmk. 350 *Perf. 14*
1024 A268 20c multicolored .30 .25
1025 A268 40c blue & multi .30 .25

Issued to publicize the 1970 census.

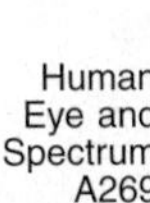
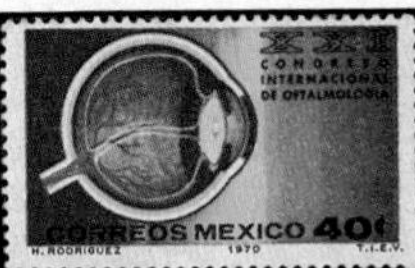

Human Eye and Spectrum A269

1970, Mar. 8 Photo. Wmk. 350

1026 A269 40c multicolored .30 .25

21st International Congress of Ophthalmology, Mexico City, Mar. 8-14.

Helmets of 1920 and 1970 A270

1970, Apr. 11 Wmk. 350 ***Perf. 14***

1027 A270 40c dk car rose, blk & lt brn .30 .25

50th anniversary of the Military College.

José Maria Pino Suarez — A271

1970, Apr. 25 Photo.

1028 A271 40c black & multi .30 .25

Centenary of the birth of José Maria Pino Suarez (1869-1913), lawyer, poet and Vice President of Mexico.

Coat of Arms of Celaya — A272

1970, Oct. 12 Photo. ***Perf. 14***

1029 A272 40c black & multi .30 .25

City of Celaya, 400th anniversary.

Eclipse of Sun — A273

1970, Nov. 27 Wmk. 350 ***Perf. 14***

1030 A273 40c black & gray .30 .25

Total eclipse of the sun, Mar. 7, 1970.

Spheres with Dates 1970-1770 A274

1971, June 26 Photo. ***Perf. 14***

1031 A274 40c emerald & blk .30 .25

Bicentenary of National Lottery.

Vasco de Quiroga, Mural by O'Gorman A275

1971, July 10 Photo.

1032 A275 40c multicolored .30 .25

500th anniversary of the birth of Vasco de Quiroga (1470-1565), Archbishop of Michoacan, founder of hospitals and schools.

Amado Nervo (1870-1919), Poet — A276

1971, Aug. 7 Wmk. 350 ***Perf. 14***

1033 A276 40c multicolored .30 .25

Waves and Transformer A277

1971, Oct. 8

1034 A277 40c blk, lt bl & lt grn .30 .25

50th anniversary of Mexican radio.

Pres. Lazaro Cardenas (1895-1970) — A278

1971, Oct. 19 Wmk. 300

1035 A278 40c blk & pale lil .30 .25

Keyboard and Lara's Signature A279

1971, Nov. 6 Wmk. 350

1036 A279 40c blk, buff & pale bl .30 .25

Agustin Lara (1900-70), composer.

Arms of Monterrey — A280

1971, Dec. 18

1037 A280 40c black & multi .30 .25

375th anniv. of the founding of Monterrey.

Cardiology Institute and WHO Emblems — A281

1972, Apr. 8 Wmk. 300

1038 A281 40c multicolored .30 .25

"Your heart is your health," World Health Day 1972. See No. C395.

Gaceta de Mexico, Jan. 1, 1722 A282

1972, June 24 Wmk. 350

1039 A282 40c multicolored .30 .25

250th anniv. of 1st Mexican newspaper.

Lions Intl. Emblem — A283

1972, June 28

1040 A283 40c black & multi .30 .25

55th Lions International Convention.

Sailing Ship Zaragoza — A284

1972, July 1

1041 A284 40c blue & multi .30 .25

75th anniv. of the Naval School of Veracruz.

Olive Tree and Branch — A285

1972, July 18 Wmk. 350 ***Perf. 14***

1042 A285 40c bl grn, ocher & blk .30 .25

a. 40c blue green, yellow & black 3.00 3.00

Centenary of Chilpancingo as capital of Guerrero State.

Margarita Maza de Juárez A286

Design: 40c, Benito Juárez, by Diego Rivera.

1972, Sept. 15 Photo. Wmk. 300

1043 A286 20c pink & multi .40 .25

1044 A286 40c dp yellow & multi .40 .25

Nos. 1043-1044,C403-C405 (5) 1.65 1.25

Benito Juárez (1806-1872), revolutionary leader and president of Mexico.

Emperor Justinian I, Mosaic A287

1972, Sept. 30 Wmk. 300

1045 A287 40c multicolored .65 .25

Mexican Bar Association, 50th anniv.

Caravel — A288

1972, Oct. 12 Wmk. 350

1046 A288 80c buff, pur & ocher .40 .25

Stamp Day of The Americas.

Olympic Emblems A289

1972, Dec. 9 Wmk. 300

1047 A289 40c multicolored 1.00 .25

20th Olympic Games, Munich, Aug. 26-Sept. 11. See Nos. C410-C411.

Library, Book Year Emblem — A290

1972, Dec. 16

1048 A290 40c black & multi .30 .25

International Book Year 1972.

Fish in Clean Water A291

1972, Dec. 16
1049 A291 40c blk & lt bl .40 .25

Anti-pollution campaign. See No. C412.

Metlac Railroad Bridge — A292

1973, Feb. 2 ***Perf. 14***
1050 A292 40c multicolored .85 .25

Centenary of Mexican railroads.

Cadet — A293

1973, Oct. 11 Photo. Wmk. 300
1051 A293 40c black & multi .45 .25

Sesquicentennial of Military College.

Madero, by Diego Rivera — A294

1973, Nov. 9 Wmk. 350 ***Perf. 14***
1052 A294 40c multicolored .30 .25

Pres. Francisco I. Madero (1873-1913).

Antonio Narro — A295

1973, Nov. 9 Photo.
1053 A295 40c steel gray .35 .25

50th anniversary of the Antonio Narro Agriculture School in Saltillo.

Type of 1950-52

Designs as before.

1973 Unwmk. ***Perf. 14***
1054 A189 20c blue violet 5.00 2.00
1055 A189 40c red orange 5.00 2.00

Fluorescent printing on back (or on front of 40c) consisting of network pattern and diagonal inscription.

Unsaturated Hydrocarbon Molecule — A296

Wmk. 300

1973, Dec. 7 Photo. ***Perf. 14***
1056 A296 40c blk, dk car & yel .30 .25

Pointing Hand Emblem of Foreign Trade Institute — A297

1974, Jan. 11 Photo. Wmk. 300
1057 A297 40c dk green & blk .30 .25

Export promotion.

A298

1974, Jan. 18 Litho. Wmk. 300
1058 A298 40c black .30 .25

EXMEX 73 Philatelic Exhibition, Cuernavaca, Apr. 7-15. See No. C424.

Manuel M. Ponce at Keyboard A299

1974, Jan. 18 Photo. Wmk. 300
1059 A299 40c gold & multi .30 .25

Manuel M. Ponce (1882-1948), composer.

Silver Statuette of Mexican Woman — A300

1974, Mar. 23 Photo. ***Perf. 14***
1060 A300 40c red & multi .30 .25

First World Silver Fair.

Mariano Azuela A301

1974, Apr. 26 Wmk. 300 ***Perf. 14***
1061 A301 40c multicolored .30 .25

Mariano Azuela (1873-1952), writer.

Dancing Dogs, Pre-Columbian A302

1974, Apr. 10
1062 A302 40c multicolored .30 .25

6th Traveling Dog Exhibition, Mexico City, Nov. 23-Dec. 1.

Aqueduct, Tepotzotlan — A303

1974, July 1 Photo. Wmk. 300
1063 A303 40c brt blue & blk .45 .25

National Engineers' Day, July 1.

Dr. Rodolfo Robles A304

1974, July 19 ***Perf. 14***
1064 A304 40c bister & grn .30 .25

25th anniv. of WHO (in 1973).

EXFILMEX 74 Emblem — A305

1974, July 26 ***Perf. 13x12***
1065 A305 40c buff, grn & blk .30 .25

EXFILMEX 74, 5th Inter-American Philatelic Exhibition honoring UPU cent, Mexico City, 10/26-11/3. See No. C429.

Demosthenes A306

1974, Aug. 2 Photo. ***Perf. 14***
1066 A306 20c green & brn .35 .25

2nd Spanish-American Cong. for Reading and Writing Studies, Mexico City, May 7-14.

Map of Chiapas and Head A307

1974, Sept. 14 Wmk. 300 ***Perf. 14***
1067 A307 20c black & grn .30 .25

Sesquicentenary of Chiapas statehood.

Law of 1824 — A308

1974, Oct. 11 Wmk. 300
1068 A308 40c gray & grn .30 .25

Sesquicentennial of the establishment of the Federal Republic of Mexico.

Sebastian Lerdo de Tejada — A309

1974, Oct. 11 Photo.
1069 A309 40c black & lt bl .30 .25

Centenary of restoration of the Senate.

UPU Monument, Bern A310

1974, Dec. 13 Wmk. 300 ***Perf. 14***
1070 A310 40c ultra & org brn .30 .25
Nos. 1070,C437-C438 (3) .80 .75

Cent. of UPU.

Types of 1950-56

Designs (as 1951-56 issues): 80c, Michoacan dance of the Moors. 2.30p, Guillermo Prieto. 3p, Modernistic church, Nuevo Leon. 50p, Benito Juarez.

1975 Photo. Wmk. 300 *Perf. 14*

1072	A189	80c green	.55	.25
1075	A200	2.30p dp violet bl	.85	.35
1076	A189	3p brick red	.85	.35
1081	A189	50p orange & grn	10.00	7.50
		Nos. 1072-1081 (4)	12.25	8.45

See No. 1097 for unwmkd. 3p with no shading under "Leon."

Gov. José Maria Mora — A312

1975, Feb. 21 Photo. Wmk. 300

1084	A312	20c yellow & multi	.30	.25

Sesquicentennial (in 1974) of establishment of the State of Mexico.

Merchants with Pre-Columbian Goods — A313

1975, Apr. 18 Photo. Unwmk.

1085	A313	80c multicolored	.30	.25

Centenary (in 1974) of the National Chamber of Commerce in Mexico City. Design from Florentine Codex.

Juan Aldama, by Diego Rivera A314

1975, June 6 *Perf. 14*

1086	A314	80c multicolored	.30	.25

Juan Aldama (1774-1811), officer and patriot, birth bicentenary.

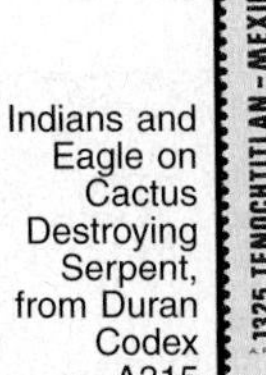
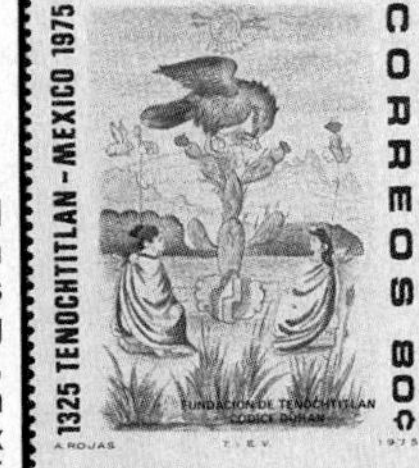
Indians and Eagle on Cactus Destroying Serpent, from Duran Codex A315

1975, Aug. 1 Photo. Unwmk.

1087	A315	80c multicolored	.30	.25

650th anniv. of Tenochtitlan (Mexico City). See No. C465.

Julián Carrillo — A316

1975, Sept. 12 Photo. Unwmk.

1088	A316	80c brt grn & red brn	.30	.25

Julián Carrillo (1875-1965), violinist and composer, birth centenary.

Academy Emblem — A317

1975, Sept. 13 *Perf. 14*

1089	A317	80c brown & ocher	.30	.25

Cent. of Mexican Academy of Languages.

Types of 1950-56

Designs (as 1950-56 issues): 80c, Indian dancer, Michoacan. 2p, Convent, Morelos.

1975-76 Photo. Unwmk.

1090	A189	40c orange	.35	.25
1091	A189	50c blue	.40	.25
1092	A200	60c red lilac	.50	.25
1093	A200	70c violet blue	.50	.25
1094	A189	80c green	.50	.25
1095	A189	1p olive green	.50	.25
1096	A189	2p scarlet	1.00	.50
1097	A189	3p brick red	1.00	.50
1099	A189	5p gray bl & grn	2.10	1.00
1101	A189	10p grn & dp ultra ('76)	5.00	2.00
1102	A189	20p lilac & blk ('76)	10.00	4.00
		Nos. 1090-1102 (11)	21.85	9.50

University of Guadalajara — A318

1975, Oct. 1 Photo. *Perf. 14*

1107	A318	80c multicolored	.30	.25

University of Guadalajara, 50th anniversary.

Road Workers — A319

1975, Oct. 17 Photo. Unwmk.

1108	A319	80c gray grn, grn & blk	.30	.25

50 years of road building for progress.

Pistons A320

Designs: Export Emblem and 5c, 6p, Steel pipes. 20c, Chemistry flasks. 40c, Cup of coffee. 80c, Meat cuts marked on steer. 1p, Electrical conductor. 2p, Abalone. 3p, Men's shoes. 4p, Tiles. 5p, Minerals. 7p, 8p, 9p, Overalls. 10p, Tequila. 15p, Honey. 20p, Wrought iron. 25p, Copper vase. 35p, 40p, No. 1133, 80p, Books. No. 1132, Jewelry. 100p, Strawberry. 200p, Citrus fruit. 300p, Motor vehicles. 400p, Circuit board. 500p, Cotton.

Some stamps have a gray burelage;

Type I — Burelage lines run lower left to upper right with arch towards lower right.

Type II — Burelage lines run lower left to upper right with arch towards upper left.

1975-87 Photo. Unwmk. *Perf. 14*

1109	A320	5c slate bl ('77)	1.00	.25
1110	A320	20c blk ('76)	.25	.25
1111	A320	40c dk brn ('76)	.90	.25
a.		40c claret brown ('81)	1.00	.25
1112	A320	50c slate, thin paper ('81)	.75	.25
a.		50c slate blue ('76)	.90	.25
b.		50c black ('83)	.60	.25
c.		50c dull blue ('75)	.90	.25
1113	A320	80c brt car ('76)	5.50	.25
a.		Perf. 11	.40	.25
b.		Perf. 11½x11	.75	.25
c.		As "a," thin paper ('81)	1.40	.75
d.		As "b," thin paper ('81)	.75	.75
1114	A320	1p vio bl & org ('78)	.90	.25
1115	A320	1p lt vio & org ('83)	1.50	.25
1116	A320	1p black & org ('84)	.25	.25
1117	A320	2p grn & brt bl ('81)	1.25	.25
a.		2p bl grn & dk bl ('76)	1.50	.25
1118	A320	3p red brown	2.75	.25
a.		3p brn, perf 11½x11 ('82)	3.00	.25
b.		Golden brn, thin paper ('81)	.60	.25
1119	A320	4p tan & dk brn ('80)	.25	.25
1120	A320	5p gray olive ('78)	2.25	.25
a.		Perf 11½x11 ('84)	.25	.25
1121	A320	6p brt org ('83)	.30	.25
a.		Perf 11½x11 ('83)	.30	.25
b.		Perf 11 ('84)	3.25	.25
1121C	A320	6p gray, perf. 11½x11 ('84)	.25	.25
1122	A320	7p Prus blue ('84)	.25	.25
a.		7p blue gray ('84)	5.00	.25
1123	A320	8p bis brn, perf 11½x11 ('84)	.25	.25
a.		Perf 11 ('84)	8.00	.25
1124	A320	9p dk bl ('84)	.25	.25
1125	A320	10p dk & lt grn ('78)	.35	.25
a.		Thin paper ('81)	.65	.30
b.		Dk ol grn & yel grn ('86)	2.00	.25
c.		Dk ol grn & brt ol grn ('87)	.30	.25
1126	A320	15p yel org & red brn ('84)	.30	.25
1127	A320	20p black ('78)	1.25	.25
1128	A320	20p dk gray ('84)	.25	.25
1129	A320	25p org brn ('84)	.40	.25
1130	A320	35p brt cer & yel ('84)	.25	.25
1131	A320	40p org brn & lt yel ('84)	.30	.25
1132	A320	50p gray, sil, brt vio & pur ('80)	6.00	.75
1133	A320	50p brt bl & lt yel ('83)	1.50	.25
1133A	A320	80p pink & gold ('85)	1.60	.35
1134	A320	100p scar & brt grn, I ('83)	1.50	.80
1135	A320	200p emer & yel grn, I ('83)	4.50	.50
a.		Emer & lemon, I ('87)	6.00	1.25
b.		Emer & yel grn, II ('83)	5.00	2.00
1136	A320	300p brt bl & red, I ('83)	4.00	2.00
a.		Type II ('87)	125.00	20.00
1137	A320	400p lem & red brn, I ('84)	3.00	.75
1138	A320	500p lt ol grn & yel org, I ('84)	4.00	.75
		Nos. 1109-1138 (32)	48.05	12.15

No. 1125b is 2mm wider than No. 1125. Size of No. 1125b: 37x21mm.

Nos. 1117, 1119, 1126, 1135 exist with one or more colors missing. These were not regularly issued.

See Nos. 1166-1176, 1465-1470A, 1491-1505, 1583-1603, 1763-1776, C486-C508, C594-C603.

Aguascalientes Cathedral — A323

1975, Nov. 28

1140	A323	50c bl grn & blk	.75	.25

400th anniversary of Aguascalientes.

Jaime Torres Bodet — A324

1975, Nov. 28

1141	A324	80c blue & brn	.30	.25

Jaime Torres Bodet (1920-1974), writer, director general of UNESCO (1958-1962).

Allegory, by José Clemente Orozco — A325

1975, Dec. 9 *Perf. 14*

1142	A325	80c multicolored	.30	.25

Sesquicentennial of Supreme Court.

The Death of Cuauhtemoc, by Chavez Morado — A326

1975, Dec. 12 Photo.

1143	A326	80c multicolored	.30	.25

450th anniv. of the death of Cuauhtemoc (1495?-1525), last Aztec emperor.

Netzahualcoyotl (Water God) — A327

1976, Jan. 9 Unwmk. *Perf. 14*

1144	A327	80c blue & vio bl	.30	.25

50th anniv. of Mexican irrigation projects.

Arch, Leon A328

1976, Jan. 20

1145	A328	80c dk brn & ocher	.30	.25

400th anniversary of León, Guanajuato.

Forest Fire A329

1976, July 8 Photo. *Perf. 14*
1146 A329 80c blk, grn & red .30 .25

Prevent fires!

Hat and Scout Emblem — A330

1976, Aug. 24 Photo. Unwmk.
1147 A330 80c olive & red brn .30 .25

Mexican Boy Scout Assoc., 50th anniv.

Exhibition Emblem — A331

1976, Sept. 2
1148 A331 80c black, red & grn .30 .25

Mexico Today and Tomorrow Exhibition.

New Building, Military College A332

1976, Sept. 13 *Perf. 14*
1149 A332 50c red brn & ocher .30 .25

Military College, new installations.

Dr. Ricardo Vertiz — A333

1976, Sept. 24 Photo. *Perf. 14*
1150 A333 80c blk & redsh brn .30 .25

Our Lady of Light Ophthalmological Hospital, centenary.

National Basilica of Guadeloupe — A334

1976, Oct. 12
1151 A334 50c black & ocher .30 .25

Inauguration of the new National Basilica of Our Lady of Guadeloupe.

"40" and Emblem A335

1976, Oct. 28 Photo. *Perf. 14*
1152 A335 80c blk, lt grn & car .30 .25

Natl. Polytechnic Institute, 40th anniv.

Blast Furnace A336

1976, Nov. 4
1153 A336 50c multicolored .30 .25

Inauguration of the Lazaro Cardenas Steel Mill, Las Truchas.

Saltillo Cathedral — A337

1977, July 25 Photo. *Perf. 14*
1154 A337 80c yel & dk brn .30 .25

400th anniversary of the founding of Saltillo.

Electrification A338

1977, Aug. 14 Photo. *Perf. 14*
1155 A338 80c multicolored .30 .25

40 years of Mexican development program.

Flags of Spain and Mexico A339

1977, Oct. 8 Photo. Wmk. 300
1156 A339 50c multicolored .30 .25
1157 A339 80c multicolored .30 .25
Nos. 1156-1157,C537-C539 (5) 1.45 1.25

Resumption of diplomatic relations with Spain.

Aquiles Serdan (1877-1910), Martyr of the Revolution — A340

1977, Nov. 18 Photo. *Perf. 14*
1158 A340 80c lt & dk grn & blk .30 .25

Poinsettia A341

1977, Dec. 2 Wmk. 300 *Perf. 14*
1159 A341 50c multicolored .30 .25

Christmas 1977.

Old and New Telephones — A342

1978, Mar. 15 Photo. *Perf. 14*
1160 A342 80c salmon & maroon .30 .25

Centenary of first telephone in Mexico.

Oil Derrick A343

1978, Mar. 18
1161 A343 80c dp org & mar .30 .25
Nos. 1161,C556-C557 (3) .85 .75

Nationalization of oil industry, 40th anniv.

Institute Emblem A344

1978, July 21 Photo. *Perf. 14*
1162 A344 80c blue & black .30 .25
Nos. 1162,C574-C575 (3) .90 .75

Pan-American Institute for Geography and History, 50th anniv.

Dahlias — A345

1978, Sept. 29 Photo. Wmk. 300
1163 A345 50c shown .30 .25
1164 A345 80c Frangipani .75 .25

See No. 1196.

Decorations and Candles — A346

1978, Nov. 22 Photo. *Perf. 14*
1165 A346 50c multicolored .30 .25

Christmas 1978.

Export Type of 1975

Designs as before. 50p, Jewelry.

1979-81 Photo. Wmk. 300 *Perf. 14*

1166	A320	20c black ('81)	.40	.25
1167	A320	50c slate blue	.25	.25
a.		50c bluish black	.30	.25
1168	A320	80c brt car, perf 11	1.00	.25
a.		Perf. 14	1.00	.25
1169	A320	1p ultra & org	.30	.25
1170	A320	2p brt grn & bl	.50	.25
1171	A320	3p dk brown	.60	.25
1172	A320	4p tan & dk brn ('80)	.75	.25
1173	A320	5p gray olive	1.00	.35
1174	A320	10p dk & lt green	2.75	.75
1175	A320	20p black	2.75	.75
1176	A320	50p gray, sil, brt vio & pur	6.75	2.50
		Nos. 1166-1176 (11)	17.05	6.10

A347

1979, Apr. 26 Wmk. 300 *Perf. 14*
1177 A347 80c multicolored .30 .25

Centenary of Hermosillo, Sonora.

Soccer Ball — A348

Designs: 80c, Aztec ball player. 1p, Wall painting showing athletes. 5p, Runners, horiz.

1979, June 15 Photo. Wmk. 300
1178 A348 50c blue & blk .30 .25
1179 A348 80c multicolored .30 .25
1180 A348 1p multicolored .30 .25
Nos. 1178-1180,C606-C607 (5) 1.50 1.25

Souvenir Sheet

Imperf

1181 A348 5p multicolored 3.50 3.50

Universiada '79, World Games, Mexico City, 9/79. No. 1181 has simulated perforations.

Josefa Ortiz de Dominguez, Wife of the Mayor of Queretaro (Miguel Dominguez), 150th Death Anniv. — A349

1979, July 6 *Perf. 14*
1182 A349 80c multicolored .30 .25

Allegory of National Culture, by Alfaro Siqueiros — A350

3p, Conquest of Energy, by Chavez Morado.

1979, July 10

1183 A350 80c multicolored .30 .25
1184 A350 3p multicolored .30 .25
Nos. 1183-1184,C609-C610 (4) 1.20 1.00

National University, 50th anniv. of autonomy.

Emiliano Zapata, by Diego Rivera — A351

1979, Aug. 8 **Photo.** ***Perf. 14***

1185 A351 80c multicolored .30 .25

Emiliano Zapata (1879-1919), revolutionist.

Soccer A352

Designs: 80c, Women's volleyball. 1p, Basketball. 5p, Fencing.

1979, Sept. 2

1186 A352 50c multicolored .30 .25
1187 A352 80c multicolored .30 .25
1188 A352 1p multicolored .30 .25
Nos. 1186-1188,C612-C613 (5) 1.50 1.25

Souvenir Sheet

Imperf

1189 A352 5p multicolored 2.25 2.25

Universiada '79 World University Games, Mexico City. No. 1189 has simulated perforations.

Tepoztlan, Morelos — A353

Tourism: No. 1191, Mexcaltitan, Nayarit.

1979, Sept. 28 **Photo.** ***Perf. 14***

1190 A353 80c multicolored .30 .25
1191 A353 80c multicolored .30 .25
Nos. 1190-1191,C615-C616 (4) 1.10 1.00

See Nos. 1274-1277, 1318-1321, 1513-1516.

Postmaster Martin de Olivares — A354

1979, Oct. 26 **Wmk. 300** ***Perf. 14***

1192 A354 80c multicolored .30 .25

Royal proclamation of mail service in the New World (New Spain), 400th anniversary. See Nos. C618-C620.

Shepherd and Sheep — A355

1979, Nov. 15

1193 A355 50c multicolored .30 .25

Christmas 1979. See No. C623.

Serpent, Mayan Temple A356

1980, Feb. 16 **Photo.** ***Perf. 14x14½***

1194 A356 80c multicolored .30 .25
Nos. 1194,C625-C626 (3) .90 .75

Pre-Hispanic monuments.

North American Turkey — A357

Tajetes Erecta — A358

Wmk. 300

1980, Mar. 8 **Photo.** ***Perf. 14***

1195 A357 80c multicolored .30 .25
1196 A358 80c multicolored .30 .25
Nos. 1195-1196,C632-C633 (4) 1.10 1.00

See Nos. 1163-1164, 1234-1237.

A359

Designs: 50c, China Poblana (woman's costume), Puebla. 80c, Jarocha, Veracruz.

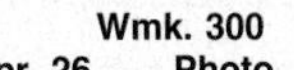

Wmk. 300

1980, Apr. 26 **Photo.** ***Perf. 14***

1197 A359 50c multicolored .30 .25
1198 A359 80c multicolored .30 .25
Nos. 1197-1198,C636 (3) .85 .75

See Nos. 1231-1233.

10th National Census — A360

1980, June 4

1200 A360 3p silver & blk .30 .25

Cuauhtemoc (Last Aztec Emperor), 1520, Matritense Codex — A361

Pre-Hispanic Art (Leaders): 1.60p, Nezahualcoyotl (1402-1472), governor of Tetzcoco, poet, Azcatitlan Codex. 5.50p, Eight Deer Tiger's Claw (1011-1063), 11th king of Mixtec, Nuttall Codex.

1980, June 21

1201 A361 80c multicolored .30 .25
1202 A361 1.60p multicolored .30 .25
1203 A361 5.50p multicolored .45 .25
Nos. 1201-1203 (3) 1.05 .75

See Nos. 1285-1287, 1510-1512.

Xipe (Aztec God of Medicine), Bourbon Codex A362

1980, June 29

1204 A362 1.60p multicolored .30 .25

22nd Intl. Biennial Cong. of the Intl. College of Surgeons, Mexico City, 6/29-7/4.

Moscow '80 Bronze Medal, Emblem, Misha, Olympic Rings — A363

1980, July 19 **Photo.** ***Perf. 14***

1205 A363 1.60p shown .30 .25
1206 A363 3p Silver medal .30 .25
1207 A363 5.50p Gold medal .40 .25
Nos. 1205-1207 (3) 1.00 .75

22nd Summer Olympic Games, Moscow, July 19-Aug. 3.

Ceremonial Vessel, Tenochtitlan Temple A364

Wmk. 300

1980, Aug. 23 **Photo.** ***Perf. 14***

1208 A364 80c shown .30 .25
1209 A364 1.60p Caracol .30 .25
1210 A364 5.50p Chacmool .30 .25
Nos. 1208-1210 (3) .90 .75

Pre-Columbian Art.

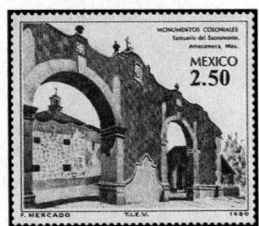

Sacromonte Sanctuary, Amecameca — A365

Colonial Monuments: No. 1212, St. Catherine's Convent, Patzcuaro. No. 1213, Basilica, Cuilapan, vert. No. 1214, Calvary Hermitage, Cuernavaca.

1980, Sept. 26 **Photo.** ***Perf. 14***

1211 A365 2.50p black .30 .25
1212 A365 2.50p black .30 .25
1213 A365 3p black .30 .25
1214 A365 3p black .30 .25
Nos. 1211-1214 (4) 1.20 1.00

See Nos. 1260-1263, 1303-1306, 1338-1341.

Quetzalcoatl (God) — A366

1980, Sept. 27

1215 A366 2.50p multicolored .30 .25

World Tourism Conf., Manila, Sept. 27.

Sinaloa Coat of Arms — A367

1980, Oct. 13

1216 A367 1.60p multicolored .30 .25

Sinaloa state sesquicentennial.

Straw Angel — A368

Christmas 1980: 1.60p, Poinsettias.

1980 Photo. *Perf. 14*
1217 A368 50c multicolored .30 .25
1218 A368 1.60p multicolored .30 .25

Issued: No. 1217, 11/15; No. 1218, 10/15.

Congress Emblem A369

1980, Dec. 1
1219 A369 1.60p multicolored .30 .25

4th International Civil Justice Congress.

Glass Vase and Animals A370

1p, Poncho. 3p, Wooden mask, 17th century.

1980, Dec. 13 Wmk. 300
1220 A370 50c shown .30 .25
1221 A370 1p multi .30 .25
1222 A370 3p multi .30 .25
Nos. 1220-1222 (3) .90 .75

See Nos. 1267-1269.

Simon Bolivar, by Paulin Guerin — A371

1980, Dec. 17
1223 A371 4p multicolored .40 .25

Simon Bolivar death sesquicentennial.

Vicente Guerrero — A372

1981, Feb. 14
1224 A372 80c multicolored .30 .25

Vicente Guerrero (1783-1831), statesman.

Valentin Gomez Farias — A373

1981, Feb. 14
1225 A373 80c brt grn & gray .30 .25

First Latin-American Table Tennis Cup — A374

Wmk. 300
1981, Feb. 27 Photo. *Perf. 14*
1226 A374 4p multicolored .40 .25

Jesus Gonzalez Ortega, Politician, Birth Cent. — A375

Wmk. 300
1981, Feb. 28 Photo. *Perf. 14*
1227 A375 80c brn & yel org .30 .25

Gabino Barreda (1818-1881), Physician — A376

1981, Mar. 10
1228 A376 80c multicolored .30 .25

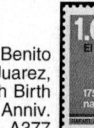

Benito Juarez, 175th Birth Anniv. A377

1981, Mar. 21
1229 A377 1.60p multicolored .30 .25

450th Anniv. of Puebla City — A378

1981, Apr. 16 Unwmk.
1230 A378 80c multicolored .30 .25
a. Wmk. 300 3.00 .25

Costume Type of 1980

50c, Purepecha, Michoacan. 80c, Charra, Jalisco. 1.60p, Mestiza, Yucatan.

1981, Apr. 25 Unwmk.
1231 A359 50c multi .30 .25
1232 A359 80c multi .30 .25
1233 A359 1.60p multi .30 .25
Nos. 1231-1233 (3) .90 .75

Flora and Fauna Types of 1980

No. 1234, Mimus polyglottos. No. 1235, Persea americana. No. 1236, Trogon mexicanus. No. 1237, Theobromo cacao.

Wmk. 300 (#1235), Unwmkd.
1981, May 30
1234 A357 80c multi .30 .25
1235 A358 80c multi .30 .25
1236 A357 1.60p multi .30 .25
1237 A358 1.60p multi .30 .25
Nos. 1234-1237 (4) 1.20 1.00

Workers' Strike, by David Alfaro Siqueiros — A379

Wmk. 300
1981, June 10 Photo. *Perf. 14*
1238 A379 1.60p multicolored .30 .25

Labor strike martyrs of Cananea, 75th anniv.

Intl. Year of the Disabled A380

1981, July 4 Unwmk. *Perf. 14*
1239 A380 4p multicolored .40 .25

450th Anniv. of Queretaro City — A381

1981, July 25 Unwmk.
1240 A381 80c multicolored .30 .25
a. Wmk. 300 3.00 .25

Alexander Fleming (1881-1955), Discoverer of Penicillin — A382

1981, Aug. 6 Unwmk.
1241 A382 5p blue & orange .40 .25

No. 1 A383

1981, Aug. 12
1242 A383 4p multicolored .30 .25
a. Wmk. 300 3.00 .25

125th anniv. of Mexican stamps.

St. Francis Xavier Clavijero, 250th Birth Anniv. — A384

1981, Sept. 9 Unwmk. *Perf. 14*
1243 A384 80c multicolored .30 .25

Union Congress Building Opening — A385

1981, Sept. 1
1244 A385 1.60p red & brt grn .30 .25

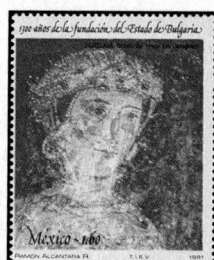

1300th Anniv. of Bulgarian State A386

1.60p, Desislava, mural, 1259. 4p, Thracian gold cup. 7p, Horseman.

1981, Sept. 19 Photo. *Perf. 14*
1245 A386 1.60p multi .30 .25
1246 A386 4p multi .30 .25
1247 A386 7p multi .50 .25
Nos. 1245-1247 (3) 1.10 .75

Pre-Hispanic Art — A387

1981, Sept. 26
1248 A387 80c Squatting diety .30 .25
1249 A387 1.60p Animal head .30 .25
1250 A387 4p Fish .40 .25
Nos. 1248-1250 (3) 1.00 .75

Pablo Picasso (1881-1973) — A388

1981, Oct. 5
1251 A388 5p lt ol grn & grn .40 .25

Christmas 1981 — A389

1981, Oct. 15
1252 A389 50c Shepherd .30 .25
1253 A389 1.60p Girl .30 .25

World Food Day A390

1981, Oct. 16
1254 A390 4p multicolored .30 .25

50th Death Anniv. of Thomas Edison A391

1981, Oct. 18
1255 A391 4p multicolored .30 .25

Intl. Meeting on Cooperation and Development — A392

1981, Oct. 22
1256 A392 4p multicolored .30 .25

Pan-American Railway Congress — A393

1981, Oct. 25 **Unwmk.**
1257 A393 1.60p multicolored .30 .25

50th Anniv. of Mexican Sound Movies A394

1981, Nov. 3 **Photo.** ***Perf. 14***
1258 A394 4p multicolored .30 .25

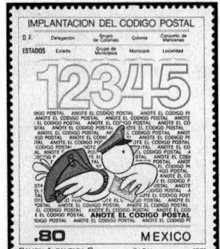

Inauguration of Zip Codes — A395

1981, Nov. 12
1259 A395 80c multicolored .30 .25

Colonial Monument Type of 1980

No. 1260, Mascarones House. No. 1261, La Merced Order Convent. No. 1262, Third Order Chapel, Texoco. No. 1263, Friar Tembleque Aqueduct, Otumba.

1981, Nov. 28
1260 A365 4p black .30 .25
1261 A365 4p black .30 .25
1262 A365 5p black .30 .25
1263 A365 5p black .30 .25
Nos. 1260-1263 (4) 1.20 1.00

Martyrs of Rio Blanco, 75th Anniv. A396

1982, Jan. 7 **Photo.** ***Perf. 14***
1264 A396 80c multicolored .30 .25

Death Sesquicentennial of Ignacio Lopez Rayon — A397

1982, Feb. 2
1265 A397 1.60p multicolored .30 .25

75th Anniv. of Postal Headquarters — A398

1982, Feb. 17
1266 A398 4p green & ocher .30 .25

Crafts Type of 1980

50c, Huichole art. 1p, Ceramic snail. 3p, Tiger mask, Madera.

1982, Mar. 6 **Photo.** ***Perf. 14***
1267 A370 50c multi .30 .25
1268 A370 1p multi .30 .25
1269 A370 3p multi .30 .25
Nos. 1267-1269 (3) .90 .75

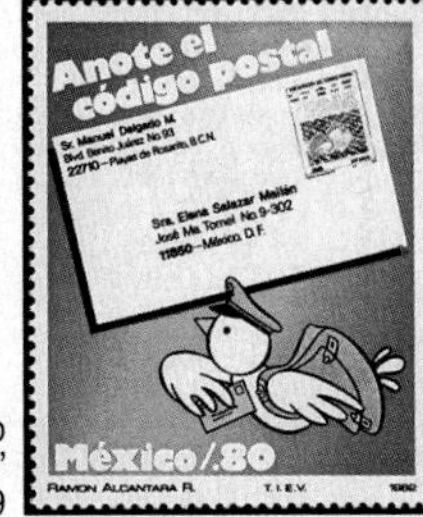

"Use Zip Codes" A399

1982, Mar. 20
1270 A399 80c multicolored .30 .25

TB Bacillus Centenary and World Health Day A400

1982, Apr. 7 **Photo.** ***Perf. 14***
1271 A400 4p multicolored .30 .25

50th Anniv. of Military Academy A401

1982, Apr. 15
1272 A401 80c multicolored .30 .25

Oaxaca City, 450th Anniv. — A402

1982, Apr. 25
1273 A402 1.60p multicolored .30 .25

Tourism Type of 1979

No. 1274, Basaseachic Cascade, Chihuahua. No. 1275, Silence Zone, Durango. No. 1276, Ruins, Maya city of Edzna, Campeche. No. 1277, Olmec sculpture, Tabasco.

1982, May 29 **Photo.** ***Perf. 14***
1274 A353 80c multicolored .30 .25
1275 A353 80c multicolored .30 .25
1276 A353 1.60p multicolored .30 .25
1277 A353 1.60p multicolored .30 .25
Nos. 1274-1277 (4) 1.20 1.00

1982 World Cup A403

Designs: Various soccer players.

1982, June 13
1278 A403 1.60p multicolored 1.00 .25
1279 A403 4p multicolored 1.00 .25
1280 A403 7p multicolored 1.00 .25
Nos. 1278-1280 (3) 3.00 .75

Turtles and Map A404

1982, July 3
1281 A404 1.60p shown 1.00 .25
1282 A404 4p Gray whales 2.00 .25

Gen. Vicente Guerrero (1783-1831) — A405

1982, Aug. 9 **Photo.** ***Perf. 14***
1283 A405 80c multicolored .30 .25

2nd UN Conference on Peaceful Uses of Outer Space, Vienna, Aug. 9-21 A406

1982, Aug. 14
1284 A406 4p multicolored .30 .25

Pre-Hispanic Art Type of 1980

Designs: 80c, Tariacuri, founder of Tarasco Kingdom, Chronicle of Michoacan, 16th cent. 1.60p, Acamapichtli, Aztec emperor, 1376-1396, Azcatitlan Codex. 4p, 10-Deer Tiger's Breastplate, wife of Lord 13-Eagle Tlaloc Copal Ball, 12th cent., Nuttal Mixtec Codex.

1982, Sept. 4
1285 A361 80c multicolored .30 .25
1286 A361 1.60p multicolored .30 .25
1287 A361 4p multicolored .30 .25
Nos. 1285-1287 (3) .90 .75

Papaya A407

1982, Sept. 18 **Unwmk.** ***Perf. 14***
1288 A407 80c shown .30 .25
1289 A407 1.60p Corn .30 .25

Florentine Codex Illustrations A408

1982, Oct. 2

1290	A408	80c Astrologer	.30	.25
1291	A408	1.60p School	.30	.25
1292	A408	4p Musicians	.30	.25
		Nos. 1290-1292 (3)	.90	.75

See Nos. 1520-1522.

Manuel Gamio (1883-1960) Anthropologist — A409

Scientists: No. 1294, Isaac Ochoterena (1855-1950), biologist. No. 1295, Angel Maria Garibay K. (1892-1976), philologist. No. 1296, Manuel Sandoval Vallarta (1899-), nuclear physicist. No. 1297, Guillermo Gonzalez Camarena (b. 1917), electronic engineer.

1982, Oct. 16 **Photo.** ***Perf. 14***

1293	A409	1.60p multicolored	.30	.25
1294	A409	1.60p multicolored	.30	.25
1295	A409	1.60p multicolored	.30	.25
1296	A409	1.60p multicolored	.30	.25
1297	A409	1.60p multicolored	.30	.25
a.		Strip of 5, #1293-1297	4.00	4.00

Natl. Archives Opening, Aug. 27 — A410

1982, Oct. 23 ***Perf. 14***

1298	A410	1.60p brt grn & blk	.30	.25

Christmas 1982 A411

1982, Oct. 30 ***Perf. 14***

1299	A411	50c Dove	.30	.25
1300	A411	1.60p Dove, diff.	.30	.25

Mexican Food System A412

1982, Nov. 13 **Photo.** ***Perf. 14***

1301	A412	1.60p multicolored	.30	.25

Opening of Revolutionary Museum, Chihuahua — A413

1982, Nov. 17 ***Perf. 14***

1302	A413	1.60p No. C232	.30	.25

Colonial Monument Type of 1980

Designs: 1.60p, College of Sts. Peter and Paul, Mexico City, 1576. 8p, Convent of Jesus Maria, Mexico City, 1603. 10p, Open Chapel, Tlalmanalco, 1585. 14p, Convent at Actopan, Hidalgo State, 1548.

1982, Nov. 27

1303	A365	1.60p black & gray	.30	.25
1304	A365	8p black & gray	.30	.25
1305	A365	10p black & gray	.30	.25
1306	A365	14p black & gray	.40	.25
a.		Vert. strip of 4, #1303-1306 + label	*15.00*	*15.00*
		Nos. 1303-1306 (4)	1.30	1.00

Alfonso Garcia Robles, 1982 Nobel Peace Prize Winner A414

1982, Dec. 10 **Unwmk.** ***Perf. 14***

1307	A414	1.60p gold & blk	.30	.25
1308	A414	14p multicolored	.30	.25

Jose Vasconcelos, Philosopher — A415

1982, Dec. 11 ***Perf. 14***

1309	A415	1.60p bl & blk	.30	.25

World Communications Year — A416

1983, Feb. 12 **Photo.** ***Perf. 14***

1310	A416	16p multicolored	.30	.25

First Philatelic Exposition of the Mexican Revolution A417

1983, Mar. 13 **Photo.** ***Perf. 14***

1311	A417	6p No. 326	.30	.25

25th Anniv. of Intl. Maritime Org. — A418

1983, Mar. 17

1312	A418	16p multicolored	.35	.25

Year of Constitutional Right to Health Protection — A419

1983, Apr. 7

1313	A419	6p red & olive	.30	.25

Society of Geography and Statistics Sesquicentennial — A420

1983, Apr. 18

1314	A420	6p Founder Gomez Farias	.30	.25

2nd World Youth Soccer Championships A421

1983, June 2 **Photo.** ***Perf. 14***

1315	A421	6p green & blk	.30	.25
1316	A421	13p red & blk	.35	.25
1317	A421	14p blue & blk	.35	.25
		Nos. 1315-1317 (3)	1.00	.75

Tourism Type of 1979

Designs: No. 1318, Federal Palace Building, Queretaro. No. 1319, Fountain, San Luis Potosi. 13p, Cable car, Zacatecas. 14p, Mayan stone head, Quintana Roo.

1983, June 24 **Photo.** ***Perf. 14***

1318	A353	6p multicolored	.25	.25
1319	A353	6p multicolored	.25	.25
1320	A353	13p multicolored	.35	.25
1321	A353	14p multicolored	.35	.25
a.		Vert. strip of 4, #1318-1321 + label	2.75	2.75
		Nos. 1318-1321 (4)	1.20	1.00

Simon Bolivar (1783-1830) — A422

1983, July 24

1322	A422	21p multicolored	.40	.25

Angela Peralta, Opera Singer (1845-1883) — A423

1983, Aug. 30 **Photo.** ***Perf. 14***

1323	A423	9p multicolored	.30	.25

Mexican Flora A424

1983, Sept. 23 **Photo.** ***Perf. 14***

1324	A424	9p Achras zapota	.30	.25
1325	A424	9p Agave atrovirens	.30	.25

Mexican Fauna A425

No. 1326, Boa constrictor imperator. No. 1327, Papilio machaon.

1983, Sept. 23 **Photo.** ***Perf. 14***

1326	A425	9p multi	2.00	.25
1327	A425	9p multi	2.00	.25

Christmas 1983 — A426

1983, Oct. 15 **Photo.** ***Perf. 14***

1328	A426	9p multicolored	.30	.25
1329	A426	20p multicolored	.30	.25

Integral Communications and Transportation Systems — A427

1983, Oct. 17 **Photo.** ***Perf. 14***

1330	A427	13p brt blue & blk	.30	.25

Carlos Chavez (1899-1978), Musician, Composer — A428

Contemporary Artists: No. 1332, Francisco Goitia (1882-1960), Painter. No. 1333, Salvador Diaz Miron (1853-1927), Lyrical Poet. No. 1334, Carlos Bracho (1899-1966), Sculptor. No. 1335, Fanny Anitua (1887-1968), Singer.

1983, Nov. 7 Photo. *Perf. 14*

1331	A428	9p brown & multi	.30	.25
1332	A428	9p brown & multi	.30	.25
1333	A428	9p brown & multi	.30	.25
1334	A428	9p brown & multi	.30	.25
1335	A428	9p brown & multi	.30	.25
a.		Horiz. strip of 5, #1331-1335	4.00	4.00

Jose Clemente Orozco (1883-1949), Painter — A429

1983, Nov. 23 Photo. *Perf. 14*

1336 A429 9p multicolored .30 .25

35th Anniv. of Human Rights Declaration A430

1983, Dec. 10 *Perf. 14*

1337 A430 20p multicolored .30 .25

Colonial Monument Type of 1980

9p, Convent Garden, Malinalco, 16th cent. 20p, Open Chapel, Cuernavaca Cathedral, Morelos. 21p, Tepeji del Rio Convent, Hidalgo. 24p, Atlatlahuacan Convent, Morelos.

1983, Dec. 16 Photo. *Perf. 14*

1338	A365	9p black & gray	.30	.25
1339	A365	20p black & gray	.40	.25
1340	A365	21p black & gray	.40	.25
1341	A365	24p black & gray	.40	.25
a.		Vert. strip of 4, #1338-1341 + label	4.00	4.00

Antonio Caso (1883-1946), Philosopher — A431

1983, Dec. 19 Granite Paper

1342 A431 9p multicolored .30 .25

Royal Mining Decree Bicentenary — A432

9p, Joaquin Velazquez Leon, reform author.

1983, Dec. 21

1343 A432 9p multi .30 .25

Postal Code Centenary A433

1984, Jan. 2 Photo. *Perf. 14*

1344 A433 12p Envelopes .35 .25

Fight Against Polio A434

1984, Apr. 7 Photo. *Perf. 14*

1345 A434 12p Children dancing .35 .25

Aquatic Birds — A435

12p, Muscovy duck. 20p, Black-bellied whistling tree duck.

1984, May 4 Photo. *Perf. 14*

1346	12p multi	.40	.25
1347	20p multi	.45	.25
a.	A435 Pair, #1346-1347 + label	3.50	3.50

World Dog Exposition, Mexico City A436

1984, May 27

1348 A436 12p multicolored 1.25 .25

Natl. Bank of Mexico Centenary — A437

1984, June 2

1349 A437 12p multicolored .35 .25

Forest Protection and Conservation — A438

1984, July 12 Photo. *Perf. 14*

1350 A438 20p Hands holding trees .40 .25

1984 Summer Olympics A439

1984, July 28

1351	A439	14p Shot put	1.00	.25
1352	A439	20p Equestrian	1.00	.25
1353	A439	23p Gymnastics	1.00	.25
1354	A439	24p Diving	1.00	.25
1355	A439	25p Boxing	1.00	.25
1356	A439	26p Fencing	1.00	.25

Size: 56x62mm

Imperf

1357	A439	40p Rings	3.50	1.50
		Nos. 1351-1357 (7)	9.50	3.00

Mexico-USSR Diplomatic Relations, 60th Anniv. — A440

1984, Aug. 4

1358 A440 23p Flags .40 .25

Intl. Population Conference, Aug. 5-14 — A441

20p, UN emblem, hand.

1984, Aug. 6

1359 A441 20p multicolored .40 .25

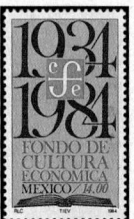

Economic Culture Fund, 50th Anniv. — A442

1984, Sept. 3

1360 A442 14p multicolored .35 .25

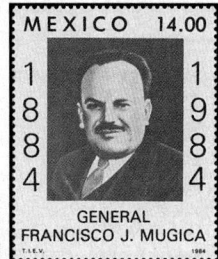

Gen Francisco J. Mugica A443

1984, Sept. 3

1361 A443 14p black & brown .35 .25

Red Cactus, by Sebastian A444

Airline Emblem A445

1984, Sept. 14 Photo. *Perf. 14*

1362	A444	14p multicolored	.30	.25
1363	A445	20p blk & org	.30	.25

Aeromexico (airline), 50th anniv.

Palace of Fine Arts, 50th Anniv. A446

1984, Sept. 29

1364 A446 14p multicolored .35 .25

275th Anniv. of Chihuahua City A447

14p, Cathedral exterior detail.

1984, Oct. 12

1365 A447 14p multicolored .35 .25

Coatzacoalcos Bridge Inauguration — A448

1984, Oct. 17 *Perf. 14*
1366 A448 14p Aerial view .35 .25

UN Disarmament Week — A449

1984, Oct. 24 Photo. *Perf. 14*
1367 A449 20p multicolored .30 .25

Christmas 1984 A450

14p, Toy train & tree. 20p, Pinata breaking, vert.

1984, Oct. 31 Photo. *Perf. 14*
1368 A450 14p multi .30 .25
1369 A450 20p multi .30 .25

Politician-Journalist Ignacio M. Altamirano (1834-1893) — A451

1984, Nov. 13 Photo. *Perf. 14*
1370 A451 14p blk & lt red brn .30 .25

State Audit Office, 160th Anniv. A452

1984, Nov. 16
1371 A452 14p multicolored .35 .25

1986 World Cup Soccer Championships, Mexico — A453

1984, Nov. 19
1372 A453 20p multicolored *1.75* .25
1373 A453 24p multicolored *2.25* .25
a. Pair, #1372-1373 + label *5.50 5.50*

Romulo Gallegos (1884-1969), Author and Former Pres. of Venezuela — A454

1984, Dec. 6
1374 A454 20p blue & gray .30 .25

State Registry Office, 125th Anniv. A455

1984, Dec. 13
1375 A455 24p slate blue .30 .25

Natl. Flag, 50th Anniv. A456

1985, Feb. 24
1376 A456 22p multicolored .50 .25

Johann Sebastian Bach — A457

1985, Mar. 21 Photo. *Perf. 14*
1377 A457 35p dl red brn, gold & blk .45 .25

Intl. Youth Year — A458

1985, Mar. 28 Photo. *Perf. 14*
1378 A458 35p rose vio, gold & blk .35 .25

Child Survival Campaign A459

1985, Apr. 7 Photo. *Perf. 14*
1379 A459 36p multicolored .45 .25

Mexican Mint, 450th Anniv. A460

1985, May 11 Photo. *Perf. 14*
1380 A460 35p 1st gold & copper coins .45 .25

Victor Hugo A461

1985, May 22 Photo. *Perf. 14*
1381 A461 35p slate .45 .25

MEXFIL '85 — A462

1985, June 9 Photo. *Perf. 14*
1382 A462 22p No. 5 .40 .40
1383 A462 35p No. 574 .40 .40
1384 A462 36p No. 1081 .40 .40
Nos. 1382-1384 (3) 1.20 1.20

Souvenir Sheet

1985, June 27 *Imperf.*
1385 A462 90p No. 111 on cover 3.50 2.50

Morelos Telecommunications Satellite Launch — A463

22p, Shuttle launch. 36p, Ground receiver. 90p, Modes of communication.

1985, June 17 *Perf. 14*
1386 A463 22p multi .25 .25
1387 A463 36p multi .25 .25
1388 A463 90p multi .50 .40
a. Strip of 3, #1386-1388 + 2 labels 4.00 4.00
Nos. 1386-1388 (3) 1.00 .90

Souvenir Sheet
Imperf
1389 A463 100p multicolored 3.50 3.00

Nos. 1386-1388 has continuous design. No. 1389 pictures uninscribed continuous design of Nos. 1386-1388.

9th World Forestry Congress, Mexico City, July 1-9 A464

1985, July 1 *Perf. 14*
1390 A464 22p Conifer .25 .25
1391 A464 35p Silk-cotton tree .25 .25
1392 A464 36p Mahogany .25 .25
a. Strip of 3, #1390-1392 + 2 labels 4.50 4.50
Nos. 1390-1392 (3) .75 .75

Martin Luis Guzman (1887-1977), Journalist, Politician — A465

Contemporary writers: No. 1394, Agustin Yanez (1904-1980), politician. No. 1395, Alfonso Reyes (1889-1959), diplomat. No. 1396, Jose Ruben Romero (1890-1952), diplomat. No. 1397, Artemio de Valle Arizpe (1888-1961), historian.

1985, July 19 *Perf. 14*
1393 A465 22p multicolored .25 .25
1394 A465 22p multicolored .25 .25
1395 A465 22p multicolored .25 .25
1396 A465 22p multicolored .25 .25
1397 A465 22p multicolored .25 .25
a. Strip of 5, #1393-1397 4.50 4.50
Nos. 1393-1397 (5) 1.25 1.25

Heroes of the Mexican Independence, 1810 — A466

1985, Sept. 15
1398 A466 22p Miguel Hidalgo .25 .25
1399 A466 35p Jose Morelos .25 .25
1400 A466 35p Ignacio Allende .25 .25
1401 A466 36p Leona Vicario .25 .25
1402 A466 110p Vicente Guerrero .75 .75
Nos. 1398-1402 (5) 1.75 1.75

Souvenir Sheet
Imperf
1403 A466 90p Bell, church 3.00 2.50

175th anniv. of independence from Spanish rule. No. 1403 contains one 56x49mm stamp.

University of Mexico, 75th Anniv. A467

No. 1404, San Ildefonso, 1910. No. 1405, University emblem. No. 1406, Rectory, 1985. No. 1407, 1st Rector Justo Sierra, crest, 1910. No. 1408, Crest, 1985.

1985, Sept. 22 Photo. *Perf. 14*

1404 A467 26p multi .25 .25
1405 A467 26p multi .25 .25
1406 A467 40p multi .25 .25
1407 A467 45p multi .25 .25
1408 A467 90p multi .50 .40
a. Strip of 5, #1404-1408 8.50 8.50
Nos. 1404-1408 (5) 1.50 1.40

Interamerican Development Bank, 25th Anniv. — A468

1985, Oct. 23 Photo. *Perf. 14*

1409 A468 26p multicolored .30 .25

UN Disarmament Week — A469

1985, Oct. 24 *Perf. 14*

1410 A469 36p Guns, doves .30 .25

UN, 40th Anniv. — A470

1985, Oct. 25 *Perf. 14*

1411 A470 26p Hand, dove .25 .25

Christmas 1985 A471

Children's drawings.

1985, Nov. 15 Photo. *Perf. 14*

1412 A471 26p multicolored .25 .25
1413 A471 35p multicolored .25 .25

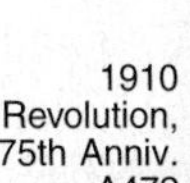

1910 Revolution, 75th Anniv. A472

26p, Soldadera. 35p, Francisco Villa. 40p, Emiliano Zapata. 45p, Venustiano Carranza. 110p, Francisco Madero. 90p, Liberty bell.

1985, Nov. 18 *Perf. 14*

1414 A472 26p multi .25 .25
1415 A472 35p multi .25 .25
1416 A472 40p multi .25 .25
1417 A472 45p multi .25 .25
1418 A472 110p multi .75 .25
Nos. 1414-1418 (5) 1.75 1.25

Souvenir Sheet

Imperf

1419 A472 90p multi 3.00 2.50

No. 1419 contains one 48x40mm stamp.

Astronaut, by Sebastian A473

The Watchman, by Federico Silva A474

Mexican Astronaut, Rodolfo Neri, by Cauduro — A475

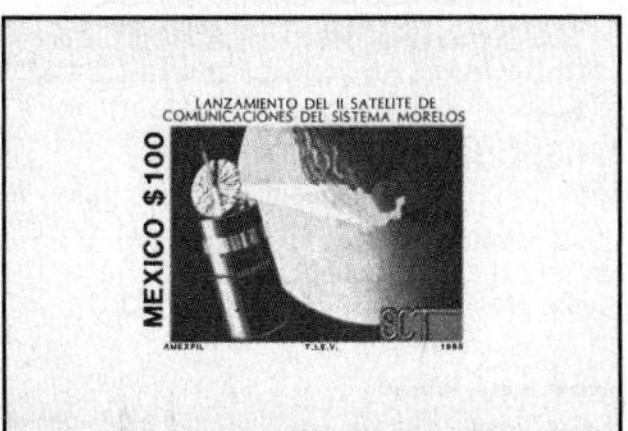

Morelos and Telecommunications Satellite Launch — A476

1985, Nov. 26 *Perf. 14*

1420 A473 26p multicolored .25 .25
1421 A474 35p multicolored .25 .25
1422 A475 45p multicolored .25 .25
Nos. 1420-1422 (3) .75 .75

Miniature Sheet

Imperf

1423 A476 100p multicolored 3.00 2.50

1986 World Cup Soccer Championships, Mexico — A477

1985, Dec. 15 Photo. *Perf. 14*

1424 A477 26p Olympic Stadium 1.50 .25
1425 A477 45p Aztec Stadium 2.00 .25

1st Free Textbook for Primary Education, 25th Anniv. — A478

1985, Dec. 16

1426 A478 26p Book cover .25 .25

Colonial Monuments A479

Landmarks in Mexico City: 26p, College of the Vizcainas, c. 1735. 35p, Palace of the Counts of Heras and Soto. 40p, Palace of the Counts of Calimaya, 16th cent. 45p, San Carlos Academy, 16th cent.

1985, Dec. 27 *Perf. 14*

1427 A479 26p grnsh blk & fawn .25 .25
1428 A479 35p grnsh blk & fawn .25 .25
1429 A479 40p grnsh blk & fawn .25 .25
1430 A479 45p grnsh blk & fawn .25 .25
a. Strip of 4, #1427-1430 + label 4.00 4.00
Nos. 1427-1430 (4) 1.00 1.00

Natl. Polytechnic Institute, 50th Anniv. A480

40p, Luis Enrique Erro Planetarium. 65p, School of Arts & Communications. 75p, Emblem, founders.

1986, Feb. 7 *Perf. 14*

1431 A480 40p multi .25 .25
1432 A480 65p multi .25 .25
1433 A480 75p multi .30 .25
a. Strip of 3, #1431-1433 + 2 labels 7.00 7.00
Nos. 1431-1433 (3) .80 .75

Fruit — A481

40p, Cucurbita pepo. 65p, Nopalea coccinellifera.

1986, Feb. 21 *Perf. 14*

1434 A481 40p multi .25 .25
1435 A481 65p multi .30 .25

World Health Day A482

1986, Apr. 7 Photo. *Perf. 14*

1436 A482 65p Doll .25 .25

Halley's Comet A483

1986, Apr. 25

1437 A483 90p multicolored .50 .25

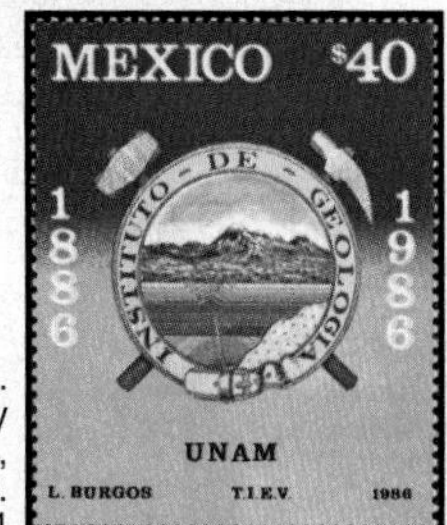

Natl. Geology Institute, Cent. A484

1986, May 26

1438 A484 40p multicolored .35 .25

1986 World Cup Soccer Championships — A485

Paintings by Angel Zarraga (1886-1946) and Sergio Guerrero Morales: 30p, Three Soccer Players with Cap. 40p, Portrait of Ramon Novaro. 65p, Dimanche. 70p, Portrait of Ernest Charles Gimpel. 90p, Three Soccer Players. 110p, Poster for 1986 championships, by Morales.

1986, May 31

1439 A485 30p multicolored .50 .25
1440 A485 40p multicolored .50 .25
1441 A485 65p multicolored .50 .25
1442 A485 70p multicolored .50 .25
1443 A485 90p multicolored .50 .30

Size: 120x91mm

Imperf

1444 A485 110p multicolored 6.00 3.00
Nos. 1439-1444 (6) 8.50 4.30

Independence War Heroes — A486

175th Death anniv. of: 40p, Ignacio Allende (1769-1811). 65p, Juan Aldama (1774-1811). 75p, Mariano Jimenez (1781-1811).

1986, June 26 Photo. *Perf. 14*

1445 A486 40p multicolored .35 .25
1446 A486 65p multicolored .35 .25
1447 A486 75p multicolored .35 .25
Nos. 1445-1447 (3) 1.05 .75

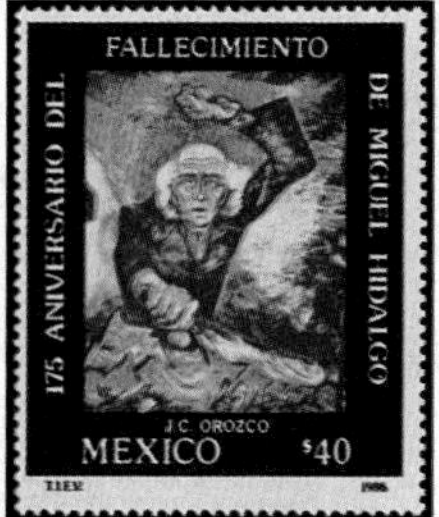
Miguel Hidalgo y Costilla (1753-1811), Mural by Jose Clemente Orozco — A487

1986, July 30 Photo. *Perf. 14*

1448 A487 40p multicolored .30 .25

Federal Tax Court, 50th Anniv. — A488

1986, Aug. 27 *Perf. 14*

1449 A488 40p gray, bl & blk .30 .25

Gen. Nicolas Bravo (1786-1854) — A489

1986, Sept. 10 *Perf. 14*

1450 A489 40p multicolored .40 .25

Paintings by Diego Rivera — A490

Designs: 50p, Paisaje Zapatista, 1915, vert. 80p, Desnudo con Alcatraces, 1944, vert. 110p, Sueno de una Tarde Dominical en la Alameda Central, 1947-48.

1986, Sept. 26 *Perf. 14*

1451 A490 50p multicolored .25 .25
1452 A490 80p multicolored .45 .25
1453 A490 110p multicolored .55 .35
Nos. 1451-1453 (3) 1.25 .85

See Nos. 1571-1573.

Guadalupe Victoria (1786-1843), 1st President — A491

1986, Sept. 29 *Perf. 14*

1454 A491 50p multicolored .30 .25

Natl. Storage Warehouse, 50th Anniv. — A492

1986, Oct. 3

1455 A492 40p multicolored .30 .25

Intl. Post Day A493

1986, Oct. 9 *Perf. 14*

1456 A493 120p multicolored .50 .25

Natl. Committee Commemorating the 500th Anniv. (1992) of the Meeting of Two Worlds — A494

1986, Oct. 12 *Perf. 14*

1457 A494 50p black & lake .30 .25

15th Pan American Highways Congress, Mexico City A495

80p, Palacio de Mineria.

1986, Oct. 17 Photo. *Perf. 14*

1458 A495 80p multicolored .40 .25

Franz Liszt, Composer, 175th Birth Anniv. — A496

1986, Oct. 22 *Perf. 14*

1459 A496 100p black & brown .45 .25

Intl. Peace Year A497

1986, Oct. 24

1460 A497 80p blk, bl & dk red .40 .25

Interment of Pino Suarez in the Rotunda of Illustrious Men — A498

1986, Nov. 6

1461 A498 50p multicolored .30 .25

Jose Maria Pino Suarez, vice-president of 1st revolutionary government, 1911.
See Nos. 1472, 1475, 1487, 1563.

Christmas — A499

Clay figurines from Tonala, Jalisco.

1986, Nov. 28

1462 A499 50p King .30 .25
1463 A499 80p Angel .30 .25

Diego Rivera (1886-1957), Painter — A500

1986, Dec. 8 Photo. *Perf. 14*

1464 A500 80p Self-portrait .30 .25

Export Type of 1975

Designs as before and: 60p, Men's shoes. 70p, Copperware. 80p, Denim overalls. 90p, Abalone. 100p, Cup of coffee.

1986-87 Unwmk. *Perf. 11½x11*

1465 A320 20p gray .25 .25

Perf. 14

1466 A320 40p pale grn & gold .35 .25

Perf. 11½x11

1467 A320 60p brown .50 .25
1468 A320 70p orange brn 1.50 .25
a. Perf. 14 1.60 .25

Perf. 14

1469 A320 80p blue .50 .25
1470 A320 90p green & blue .75 .25
1470A A320 100p brown ('88) .50 .25
b. 100p dark brown, perf. 11½x11 ('87) .75 .30
Nos. 1465-1470A (7) 4.35 1.75

Natl. Polio Vaccination Program, Jan. 24-Mar. 28 — A501

1987, Jan. 20 Photo. *Perf. 14*

1471 A501 50p Oral vaccine .30 .25

Rotunda of Illustrious Men Type of 1986

1987, Feb. 4

1472 A498 100p multicolored .40 .25

Jose Maria Iglesias (1823-1891), president in 1876.

Natl. Teachers' College, 100th Anniv. A503

1987, Feb. 24 *Perf. 14*

1473 A503 100p multicolored .50 .25

Exploration of Pima Indian Territory by Eusebio Francisco Kino, 300th Anniv. — A504

1987, Feb. 27 *Perf. 14*

1474 A504 100p multicolored .50 .25

Rotunda of Illustrious Men Type of 1986

100p, Pedro Sainz de Baranda.

1987, Mar. 20 Photo. *Perf. 14*

1475 A498 100p multi .40 .25

World Health Day, UN Child Survival Program A505

1987, Apr. 7

1476 A505 100p blue & slate blue .50 .25

Autonomous University of Puebla, 50th Anniv. — A506

1987, Apr. 23

1477 A506 200p multicolored .75 .50

Battle of Puebla, 125th Anniv. — A507

1987, May 5 Photo. *Perf. 14*

1478 A507 100p multicolored .40 .25

METROPOLIS '87 — A508

1987, May 19

1479 A508 310p gray blk, grn & red 1.25 .75

Cong. of metropolitan areas, Mexico City.

Handicrafts A509

100p, Lacquerware tray, Uruapan, Michoacan. 200p, Blanket, Santa Ana Chiautempan, Tlaxcala. 230p, Lidded jar, Puebla, Pue.

1987, May 29 Photo. *Perf. 14*

1480 A509 100p multicolored .30 .25
1481 A509 200p multicolored .60 .35
1482 A509 230p multicolored 1.00 .50
Nos. 1480-1482 (3) 1.90 1.10

Genaro Estrada, (1887-1937) Political Reformer — A510

1987, June 2

1483 A510 100p pale pink, blk & pale rose .30 .25

See Nos. 1509, 1568-1569.

Native Traders, 1961, Mural by P. O'Higgins — A511

1987, June 8

1484 A511 100p multicolored .30 .25

Nat'l. Bank of Int'l. Commerce, 50th anniv.

Publication of the 1st Shipbuilding Manual in the Americas, by Diego Garcia Palacio, 400th Anniv. — A512

1987, June 15

1485 A512 100p multicolored .30 .25

Nat'l. Food Program, 50th Anniv. A513

1987, June 22

1486 A513 100p multicolored .30 .25

Rotunda of Illustrious Men Type of 1986

1987, June 22

1487 A498 100p multicolored .30 .25

Leandro Valle (1833-1861), General.

Paintings by Saturnino Herran (1887-1918) — A514

1917 paintings: No. 1488, Self-portrait with Skull. No. 1489, The Offering. No. 1490, Creole Woman with Mantilla.

1987, July 9

1488 A514 100p black & red brn .35 .25
1489 A514 100p multicolored .35 .25
1490 A514 400p multicolored 1.10 .75
Nos. 1488-1490 (3) 1.80 1.25

Export Type of 1975

Designs: 10p, Meat cuts marked on steer. 20p, Bicycle. 50p, Tomatoes. 300p, Motor vehicle. 500p, Petroleum valves. 600p, Jewelry. 700p, Film. 800p, Construction materials. 900p, Pistons. 1,000p, Agricultural machinery. 2,000p, Wrought iron. 3,000p, Electric wiring. 4,000p, Honey. 5,000p, Cotton.

1987-88 Photo. Unwmk. *Perf. 14*

1491 A320 10p brt carmine .25 .25
1492 A320 20p black & org .25 .25
1493 A320 50p ver & yel grn .45 .25
1494 A320 300p chalky blue & scar, type I .45 .25
1495 A320 300p Prus blue & brt rose .55 .25
a. Thin paper 1.10 .25
b. Brt blue & brt rose .60 .25
1496 A320 500p dark gray & Prus blue .90 .25
1497 A320 600p multicolored 1.75 .30
a. Thin paper 1.50 .25
1498 A320 700p brt yel grn, dark red & blk 1.50 .75
a. Brt yel grn, lilac rose & blk 1.75 .85
1499 A320 800p dark red brn & golden brn 2.50 1.25
1500 A320 900p black 5.00 2.10

Wmk. 300
Granite Paper
Type I Burelage in Gray

1501 A320 1000p dk red & blk 6.00 1.10
1502 A320 2000p black 5.50 1.75
1503 A320 3000p gray blk & org 5.50 1.75
1504 A320 4000p yel org & red brn 5.00 2.50
1505 A320 5000p apple grn & org 6.50 3.25
Nos. 1491-1505 (15) 42.10 16.25

Issue years: 10p-50p, 1987; others, 1988.

A515

10th Pan American Games, Indianapolis — A516

Unwmk.

1987, Aug. 7 Photo. *Perf. 14*

1506 A515 100p multicolored .30 .25
1507 A516 200p blk, brt grn & dk red .30 .25

Federal Power Commission, 50th Anniv. — A517

1987, Aug. 14 Photo. *Perf. 14*

1508 A517 200p multicolored .40 .25

Art and Science Type of 1987

Design: J.E. Hernandez y Davalos (1827-1893), historian.

1987, Aug. 25 *Perf. 14*

1509 A510 100p buff, blk & dull red brn .30 .25

Pre-Hispanic Art Type of 1980

Designs: 100p, Xolotl (d. 1232), king of Amaquemecan. 200p, Nezahualpilli (1460-1516), king of Texcoco, conqueror. 400p, Motecuhzoma Ilhuicamina (Montezuma I d. 1469), emperor of Tenochtitlan (1440-1469).

1987, Aug. 31 *Perf. 14*

1510 A361 100p multicolored .30 .25
1511 A361 200p multicolored .50 .30
1512 A361 400p multicolored .90 .35
Nos. 1510-1512 (3) 1.70 .90

Tourism Type of 1979

Designs: 100p, Central Public Library, Mexico State. No. 1514, Patzcuaro Harbor, Michoacan. No. 1515, Garcia Caverns, Nuevo Leon. No. 1516, Beach resort, Mazatlan, Sinaloa.

1987 *Perf. 14*

1513 A353 100p multicolored .30 .25
1514 A353 150p multicolored .30 .25
1515 A353 150p multicolored .30 .25
1516 A353 150p multicolored .30 .25
Nos. 1513-1516 (4) 1.20 1.00

Issue dates: 100p, Sept. 11; others, Oct. 19.

Formula 1 Grand Prix Race, Oct. 18 — A518

1987, Sept. 11

1517 A518 100p multicolored .30 .25

13th Intl. Cartography Conference — A519

1987, Oct. 12

1518 A519 150p Map, 16th cent. .30 .25

Discovery of America, 500th Anniv. (in 1992) A520

Design: Santa Maria, emblem of the Discovery of America Festival to be held in 1992.

1987, Oct. 12 *Perf. 14*

1519 A520 150p multicolored 3.50 .25

For overprint see No. 1698.

Illuminated Codices Type of 1982

Mendocino Codex (c. 1541): No. 1520, Founding of Tenochtitlan by the Aztecs, 1324. No. 1521, Pre-Hispanic wedding. No. 1522, Montezuma's Council.

1987, Nov. 3

1520 A408 150p multicolored .35 .25
1521 A408 150p multicolored .35 .25
1522 A408 150p multicolored .35 .25
Nos. 1520-1522 (3) 1.05 .75

Christmas 1987 A521

1987, Nov. 6

1523 A521 150p brt pink .30 .25
1524 A521 150p dull blue .30 .25

World Post Day
A522

Documents: 150p, Ordinance for expediting mail by sea, 1777. 600p, Roster of correspondence transported by coach, 1857.

1987, Nov. 12

1525 A522 150p pale gray & slate gray .30 .25

Size: 129x102mm

Imperf

1526 A522 600p rose lake & yel bis 3.00 1.00

Meeting of Eight Latin American Presidents, 1st Anniv. — A523

500p, Flags, peace doves.

1987, Nov. 26 ***Perf. 14***

1527 A523 250p shown .40 .25
1528 A523 500p multi .60 .40

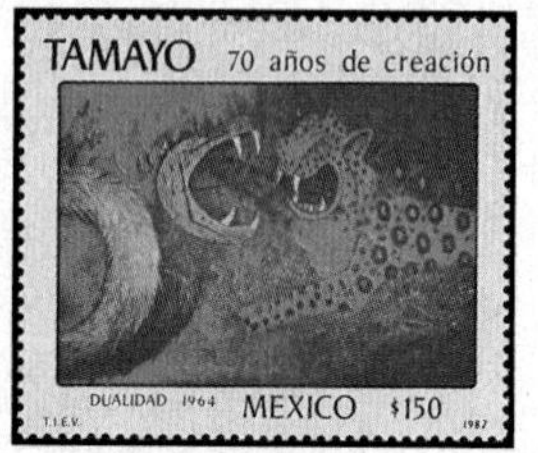

Dualidad 1964, by Rufino Tamayo (b. 1899) — A524

1987, Dec. 9

1529 A524 150p multicolored .35 .25

Nationalization of Mexican Railroads, 50th Anniv. — A525

1987, Dec. 15

1530 A525 150p Metlac Bridge 1.00 .25

Antonio Stradivarius (c. 1644-1737), Italian Violin Maker — A526

1987, Dec. 18 ***Perf. 14***

1531 A526 150p bluish lilac .40 .25

Constitutional Tribunal of the Supreme Court, Plenum Hall, Jan. 15 — A527

Design: Statue of Manuel Rejon, author of the Mexican constitution.

1988, Jan. 15 **Photo.** ***Perf. 14***

1532 A527 300p multicolored .50 .30

Fauna
A528

No. 1533, Ambystoma mexicanum. No. 1534, Trichechus manatus.

1988, Feb. 29 **Photo.** ***Perf. 14***

1533 A528 300p multi 1.00 .40
1534 A528 300p multi 1.00 .40

A529

Nationalization of the Petroleum Industry, 50th Anniv. — A530

No. 1536, PEMEX emblem, vert.

1988, Mar. 18

1535 A529 300p blue & blk .30 .25
1536 A530 300p multi .30 .25
1537 A530 500p shown .40 .35
Nos. 1535-1537 (3) 1.00 .85

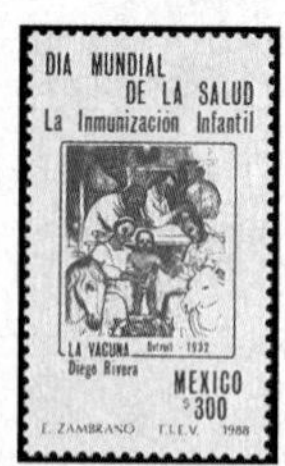

Vaccination, Detroit, 1932, Mural (detail) by Diego Rivera — A531

1988, Apr. 7

1538 A531 300p olive grn & henna brn .35 .25

World Health Day: child immunization.

The People in Pursuit of Health, 1953, by Diego Rivera — A532

1988, Apr. 7

1539 A532 300p multicolored .35 .25

World Health Organization, 40th anniv.

Vallejo in Repose (Large) — A533

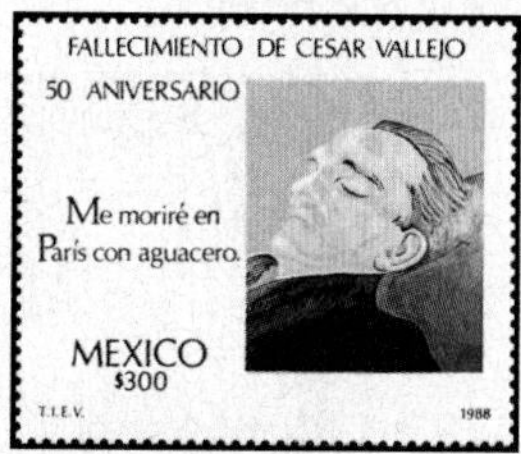

Vallejo in Repose (Small) — A534

1988, Apr. 15

1540 A533 300p shown .35 .25
1541 A533 300p Portrait, diff. (large) .35 .25
a. Pair, #1540-1541 + label 3.25 3.25
b. Bklt. pane of 4 (2 each #1540-1541) + label 250.00
1542 A534 300p shown .35 .25
1543 A534 300p As #1541 (small) .35 .25
a. Pair, #1542-1543 + label 3.25 3.25
Nos. 1540-1543 (4) 1.40 1.00

Cesar Vallejo (1892-1938), Peruvian poet. Stamps of the same type printed se-tenant in sheets of 20 stamps containing 10 pairs plus 5 labels between inscribed with various Vallejo quotes or commemorative text.

Issued: No. 1541b, 11/9/90. Label in No. 1541b is overprinted in red with Mexican Chicagopex '90 souvenir cancel, and had limited distribution.

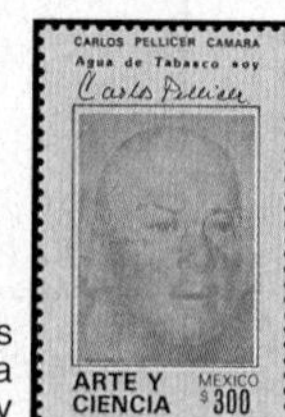

Sketch of Carlos Pellicer Camara (1897-1977), Poet, by Fontanelly — A535

1988, Apr. 23

1544 A535 300p pale vio, blk & sal .35 .25

MEPSIRREY '88 Philatelic Exhibition, Monterrey, May 27-29 — A536

No. 1545, Youth collectors. No. 1546, Handstamped cover. No. 1547, Alfa Planetarium.

1988, May 27

1545 A536 300p multicolored .35 .25
1546 A536 300p multicolored .35 .25
1547 A536 500p multicolored .55 .50
Nos. 1545-1547 (3) 1.25 1.00

Mexico-Elmhurst Philatelic Society Intl. (MEPSI).

1988 Formula I Grand Prix of Mexico — A537

Design: Layout of Hermanos Rodriguez race track, Mexico City, and car.

1988, May 28 **Photo.** ***Perf. 14***

1548 A537 500p multicolored .50 .35

A538

Birth Centenary of Ramon Lopez Velarde
A539

No. 1549, Drawing and watercolor art outlined in plaster. No. 1550, Ramon Lopez Velarde (1888-1921), Poet.

1988, June 15

1549 A538 300p multicolored .30 .25
1550 A539 300p multicolored .30 .25
a. Bklt. pane of 4 + label 250.00

Issue date: No. 1550a, Nov. 9, 1990. Label in No. 1550a is overprinted in red with Mexican Chicagopex '90 souvenir cancel, and had limited distribution.

University Military Pentathlon, 50th Anniv. — A540

1988, July 9 **Photo.** ***Perf. 14***

1551 A540 300p multicolored .30 .25

1st Mexico-Japan Friendship, Commerce and Navigation Treaty, Cent. — A541

1988, Aug. 16
1552 A541 500p multicolored .50 .35

Joint Oceanographic Assembly, Acapulco, Aug. 23-31 — A542

1988, Aug. 23
1553 A542 500p multicolored .50 .35

1988 Summer Olympics, Seoul — A543

700p, Emblems, Olympic flame.

1988, Aug. 31 Photo. *Perf. 14*
1554 A543 500p multicolored 1.00 .35

Size: 71x55mm

Imperf

1555 A543 700p multi 3.50 .60

World Boxing Council, 25th Anniv. A544

1988, Sept. 9
1556 A544 500p multi .50 .35

Intl. Red Cross and Red Crescent Organizations, 125th Annivs. — A545

1988, Sept. 23 Photo. *Perf. 14*
1557 A545 300p blk, gray & scar .30 .25

Jose Guadalupe Posada (1852-1913), Painter, Illustrator — A546

1988, Sept. 29
1558 A546 300p sil & blk .30 .25

World Wildlife Fund — A547

Various monarch butterflies, *Danaus plexippus:* No. 1560, Three adults. No. 1561, Larva, adult, pupa. No. 1562, Five adults.

1988, Sept. 30 *Perf. 14*
1559 A547 300p shown 3.00 .65
1560 A547 300p multi 3.00 .65
1561 A547 300p multi 3.00 .65
1562 A547 300p multi 3.00 .65
Nos. 1559-1562 (4) 12.00 2.60

Rotunda of Illustrious Men Type of 1986

Portrait and eternal flame: Manuel Sandoval Vallarta (1899-1977), physicist.

1988, Oct. 5
1563 A498 300p multi .30 .25

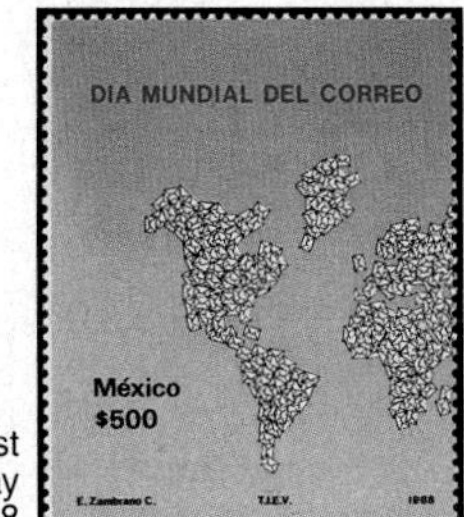

World Post Day A548

500p, World map. 700p, Envelope, doves, Earth.

1988, Oct. 9 *Perf. 14*
1564 A548 500p multi .50 .35

Size: 75x44mm

Imperf

1565 A548 700p multi 3.50 1.00

Discovery of America, 500th Anniv. (in 1992) — A549

Illuminations: Aztec painter Tlacuilo from the Mendocine Codex, 1541, and Dominican scribe from the Yanhuitlan Codex, 1541-50.

1988, Oct. 12 *Perf. 14*
1566 A549 500p multi .50 .35

World Food Day A550

1988, Oct. 16 *Perf. 14*
1567 A550 500p multi .50 .35

Art and Science Type of 1987

No. 1568, Alfonso Caso (1896-1970), educator, founder of the Natl. Museum of Anthropology. No. 1569, Vito Alessio Robles (1879-1957), historian.

1988, Oct. 24 *Perf. 14*
1568 A510 300p gray & blk .30 .25
1569 A510 300p pale yel, blk & red brn .30 .25

Act of Independence, 175th Anniv. — A551

1988, Nov. 9
1570 A551 300p claret brn & fawn .30 .25

Art Type of 1986

Paintings by Antonio M. Ruiz (1895-1964): No. 1571, *Parade,* 1936. No. 1572, *La Malinche,* 1939. No. 1573, *Self-portrait,* 1925, vert.

1988, Nov. 21 *Perf. 14*
1571 A490 300p multi .30 .25
1572 A490 300p multi .30 .25
1573 A490 300p multi .30 .25
Nos. 1571-1573 (3) .90 .75

Tempera and Oil Paintings by Jose Reyes (b. 1924) A552

1988, Nov. 25 *Perf. 14*
1574 A552 300p Feast .30 .25
1575 A552 300p Pinata, vert. .30 .25

Christmas.

Municipal Workers' Trade Union, 50th Anniv. A553

1988, Dec. 5 *Perf. 14*
1576 A553 300p pale bister & blk .30 .25

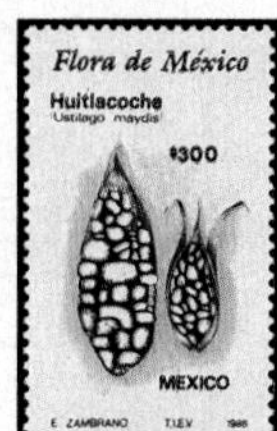

Flora — A554

No. 1577, Ustilago maydis. No. 1578, Mimosa tenuiflora.

1988, Dec. 20 *Perf. 14*
1577 A554 300p multi .30 .25
1578 A554 300p multi .30 .25

Exporta Type of 1975

Designs: 40p, 1400p, Chemistry flasks. 200p, Citrus fruit. 450p, Circuit board. 750p, Film. 950p, Pistons. 1000p, Agricultural machinery. 1100p, Minerals. 1300p, Strawberries. 1500p, Copper vase. 1600p, Steel pipes. 1700p, Tequila. 1900p, Abalone. 2000p, Wrought iron. 2100p, Bicycles. 2500p, Overalls. 5000p, Cotton.

Nos. 1588A, 1589, 1592, 1598A, 1599, 1601, 1603 have gray burelage Type I.

1988-92 Photo. Unwmk. *Perf. 14*

Design A320

1583 40p black .25 .25
1584 200p emer & brt yel .50 .25
a. Thin paper 1.10 .40
1585 450p yel bister & lil rose .75 .25
a. Thin paper 1.25 .40
1586 750p brt yel grn, dark red & dark gray 2.00 .40
1587 950p indigo 1.75 .60
a. Thin paper 2.25 .75
1588 1000p dark red & blk 1.10 .25
1588A 1000p dark red & blk, type 1 2.50 .25
1589 1100p dark gray, type I 1.75 .40
1590 1100p dark gray 2.25 .50
1591 1300p red & grn 2.25 .55
1592 1300p red & grn, type I 2.00 .55
a. Thin paper 3.00 .75
1593 1400p black 1.75 .50
1594 1500p tan 1.75 .60
a. 1500p orange brown 1.75 .60
1595 1600p red orange 1.60 .55
1596 1700p dk grn & yel grn 1.60 .60
1597 1900p bl grn & bl 1.75 .65
1598 2000p black 2.75 .75
1598A 2000p black, type 1 2.25 .25
1599 2100p black & orange, type I 4.00 .85
1600 2100p black & ver 7.50 1.00
1601 2500p dark blue, type I 4.00 1.00
1602 2500p slate blue 4.00 .90
1603 5000p apple grn & org, type I 4.50 1.90
Nos. 1583-1603 (23) 54.55 13.80

Issued: 40p, 1/5/88; 200p, 2/27/89; 450p, 2/10/89; No. 1585a, 950p, No. 1587a, 1589, 3/30/89; 1,000p, 1989; Nos. 1590, 1599, 1601, 1991; Nos. 1600, 1602, 5000p, 1992; others, 1990.

Graphic Arts Workshop, 50th Anniv. A555

1989, Feb. 9 Photo. *Perf. 14*
1604 A555 450p yel bis, red & blk .45 .35

Coat of Arms and *E Santo Domingo,* the Natl. Hymn — A556

1989, Feb. 27
1605 A556 450p multicolored .45 .35

Dominican Republic independence, 145th anniv.

Intl. Border and Territorial Waters Commission of Mexico and the US, Cent. — A557

1989, Mar. 1
1606 A557 1100p multi 1.25 .80

10th Intl. Book Fair A558

450p, UNAM School of Engineering.

1989, Mar. 4
1607 A558 450p multi .45 .35

Lyricists and Composers Soc., 25th Anniv. A559

1989, Mar. 17
1608 A559 450p multi .45 .35

World Day for the Fight Against AIDS — A560

1989, Apr. 7
1609 A560 450p multi .45 .35

Leona Vicario (1779-1842), Heroine of the Independence Movement — A561

1989, Apr. 20 **Photo.** *Perf. 14*
1610 A561 450p blk, sepia & golden brn .45 .35

Alfonso Reyes (1889-1959), Author, Educator — A562

1989, May 17
1611 A562 450p multi .45 .35

Formula 1 Grand Prix of Mexico — A563

1989, May 28 *Perf. 14*
1612 A563 450p multi .45 .35

14th Tourism Congress, Acapulco — A564

1989, June 11 *Perf. 14*
1613 A564 1100p multi 1.10 .80

14th Intl. Gerontology Congress, Mexico — A565

Statue: The god Huehueteotl as an old man bearing the weight of the world on his shoulders.

1989, June 18
1614 A565 450p multi .45 .35

Battle of Zacatecas, 75th Anniv. — A566

1989, June 23
1615 A566 450p black .45 .35

Baseball Hall of Fame of Mexico — A567

No. 1616, Umpire, catcher. No. 1617, Batter.

1989, June 25
1616 A567 550p multi 3.00 .45
1617 A567 550p multi 3.00 .45
a. Pair, #1616-1617 + label 15.00 15.00

No. 1617a has continuous design.

35th World Archery Championships, Lausanne, Switzerland, July 4-8 — A568

No. 1618, Bows and arrows. No. 1619, Arrows, target.

1989, July 2
1618 A568 650p multi 1.50 .50
1619 A568 650p multi 1.50 .50
a. Pair, #1618-1619 + label 15.00 15.00

No. 1619a has continuous design.

Tijuana, Cent. A569

1989, July 11 **Photo.** *Perf. 14*
1620 A569 1100p Municipal arms .90 .70

French Revolution, Bicent. A570

1989, July 14
1621 A570 1300p blue, blk & dark red 1.40 .80

Gen. Francisco Xavier Mina (1789-1817), Independence Hero — A571

1989, Sept. 7
1622 A571 450p green, blk & dark red .50 .30

Natl. Museum of Anthropology, Chapultepec, 25th Anniv. — A572

1989, Sept. 17 *Perf. 14*
1623 A572 450p multicolored .50 .30

7th Mexico City Marathon — A573

1989, Sept. 24
1624 A573 450p multicolored .50 .30

Printing in America, 450th Anniv. — A574

1989, Sept. 28
1625 A574 450p multicolored .50 .30

World Post Day A575

1989, Oct. 9 **Photo.** *Perf. 14*
1626 A575 1100p multicolored 1.10 .65

Sovereign Revolutionary Convention of Aguascalientes, 75th Anniv. — A576

1989, Oct. 10
1627 A576 450p multicolored .90 .25

Exploration and Colonization of the Americas by Europeans — A577

1989, Oct. 12
1628 A577 1300p multicolored 2.00 .75

America Issue — A578

UPAE emblem and symbols like those produced on art by pre-Columbian peoples.

1989, Oct. 12

1629 A578 450p shown .50 .25
1630 A578 450p multi, diff., vert. .50 .25

Natl. Tuberculosis Foundation, 50th Anniv. — A579

1989, Nov. 10

1631 A579 450p multicolored .35 .25

Mask of the Bat God, Zapoteca Culture, c. 200-300 A580

1989, Nov. 28

1632 A580 450p multicolored .50 .25

Serfin Commercial Bank of Mexico, 125th Anniv. A581

1989, Nov. 29

1633 A581 450p deep blue, gold & blk .50 .25

Pres. Adolfo Ruiz Cortines (1889-1973) — A582

1989, Dec. 3

1634 A582 450p multicolored .50 .25

Christmas A583

No. 1635, Candlelight vigil. No. 1636, Man sees star, vert.

1989, Dec. 11

1635 A583 450p multi .50 .25
1636 A583 450p multi .50 .25

Natl. Institute of Anthropology and Natural History, 50th Anniv. — A584

1989, Dec. 13

1637 A584 450p dark red, gold & black .60 .25

Nationalization of the Railway System in Mexico, 80th Anniv. — A585

1989

1638 A585 450p multicolored .70 .25

Issue dates for some 1990-1991 issues are based on First Day cancels. Original printings were small. Later printings, made in 1991, were distributed to the stamp trade and seem to be the ones used for "First Day Covers."

Tampico Bridge — A586

1990, Jan. 11 Photo. *Perf. 14*

1639 A586 600p gold, blk & red .80 .30

Eradication of Polio — A587

1990, Feb. 1

1640 A587 700p multicolored .70 .35

Natl. Census A588

1990, Mar. 12

1641 A588 700p lt grn & yel .75 .35

Mexican Philatelic Assoc., 10th Anniv. — A589

1990, Apr. 19

1642 A589 700p multicolored .75 .35

Natl. Archives, Bicentennial — A590

1990, Apr. 24

1643 A590 700p pale violet .75 .35

Intl. Conf. of Advertising Agencies — A591

1990, Apr. 27

1644 A591 700p multicolored .75 .35

Stamp World London '90 — A592

1990, May 3

1645 A592 700p multicolored .80 .35

First Postage Stamps, 150th Anniv. — A593

1990, May 6

1646 A593 700p lake, gold & blk .80 .35

15th Tourism Exposition — A594

1990, May 6

1647 A594 700p multicolored .75 .35

Visit of Pope John Paul II A595

1990, May 6

1648 A595 700p multicolored .80 .35

Health of Young Mothers A596

1990, May 10

1649 A596 700p multicolored .75 .35

Fight Against Smoking — A597

1990, May 31

1650 A597 700p multicolored .75 .35

World Environment Day — A598

1990, June 5

1651 A598 700p multicolored .75 .35

Formula 1 Grand Prix of Mexico — A599

1990, June 24

1652 A599 700p grn, red & blk .75 .35

Airport & Auxiliary Services, 25th Anniv. — A600

1990, June 25 Photo. *Perf. 14*

1653 A600 700p multicolored .70 .35

Fight Against Drugs — A601

1990, June 26

1654 A601 700p multicolored .75 .35

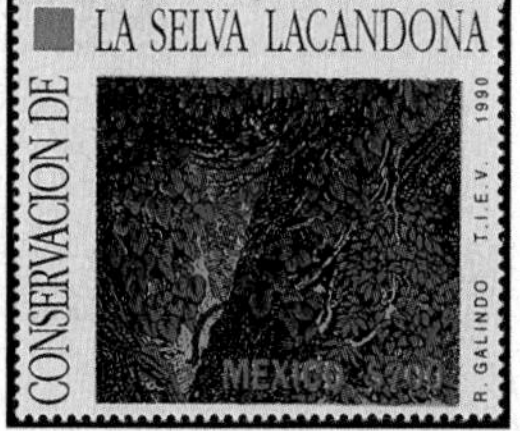

Protection of Rain Forests — A602

1990, July 6

1655 A602 700p multicolored .90 .35

Solidarity with Poor People — A603

1990, Aug. 8

1656 A603 700p multicolored .70 .35

Solidarity is a governmental social program of Pres. Salinas de Gortari. See No. 1704.

Oaxaca Cultural Heritage — A604

1990, Aug. 10

1657 A604 700p multicolored .75 .35

Nature Conservation — A605

1990, Aug. 21

1658 A605 700p blk, gray & org .85 .35

Mexican Institute of Petroleum, 25th Anniv. A606

1990, Aug. 23

1659 A606 700p black & blue .75 .35

8th Mexico City Marathon — A607

1990, Aug. 24

1660 A607 700p blk, red & grn .75 .35

University of Colima, 50th Anniv. A608

1990, Sept. 16

1661 A608 700p gray, bister, red & grn .70 .35

Mexico City Advisory Council, Founded in 1929 — A609

1990, Sept. 17

1662 A609 700p sil, yel, blk & org .70 .35

Nationalization of Electric Industry, 30th Anniv. — A610

1990, Sept. 27

1663 A610 700p gray, grn, red & blk .75 .35

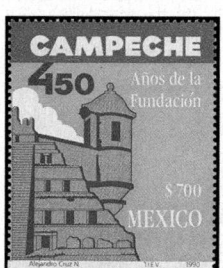

City of Campeche, 450th Anniv. A611

1990, Oct. 4

1664 A611 700p multicolored .70 .35

Silvestre Revueltas (1899-1940), Musician — A612

1990, Oct. 4

1665 A612 700p multicolored .60 .35

Plan of San Luis, 80th Anniv. A613

1990, Oct. 5

1666 A613 700p multicolored .60 .35

14th World Conference of Supreme Counselors — A614

1990, Oct. 8

1667 A614 1500p vio, sil, gold & grn 1.10 .80

Discovery of America, 498th Anniv. — A615

1990, Oct. 12

1668 A615 700p multicolored .50 .35

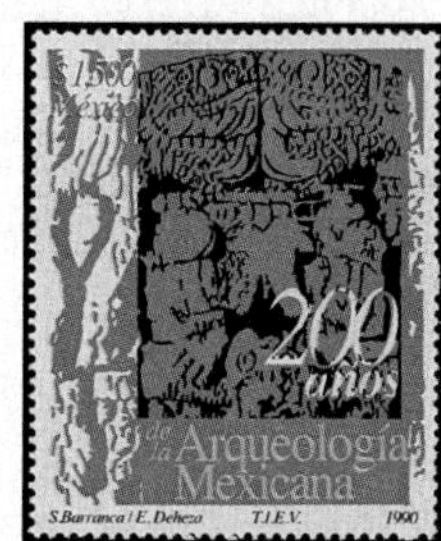

Mexican Archaeology, Bicentennial — A616

1990, Nov. 18

1669 A616 1500p multicolored 1.50 .80

16th Central American and Caribbean Games — A617

No. 1671, Mayan ball player. No. 1672, Mayan ball player, vert. No. 1673, Ball court, stone ring, vert.

1990, Nov. 20

1670	A617	750p shown	.75	.40
1671	A617	750p multi	.75	.40
1672	A617	750p multi	.75	.40
1673	A617	750p multi	.75	.40
a.		Strip of 4, #1670-1673	4.50	4.50
		Nos. 1670-1673 (4)	3.00	1.60

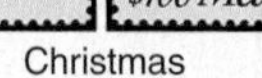

Christmas

A618 A619

1990, Dec. 3

1674 A618 700p Poinsettias .70 .35

1675 A619 700p Candles .70 .35

Mexican Canine Federation, 50th Anniv. A620

1990, Dec. 9
1676 A620 700p multicolored .80 .35

World Post Day A621

1990, Oct. 9 **Photo.** ***Perf. 14***
1677 A621 1500p multicolored 1.50 .80

America Issue A622

No. 1678, Flowers, galleon. No. 1679, Galleon, parrot.

1990, Oct. 12
1678 A622 700p multicolored .85 .35
1679 A622 700p multicolored .85 .35
a. Pair, #1678-1679 + blank label 2.75 2.75

No. 1679a has continuous design.

Mexican Brewing Industry, Cent. — A623

1990, Nov. 8 ***Perf. 14***
1680 A623 700p multicolored .75 .35

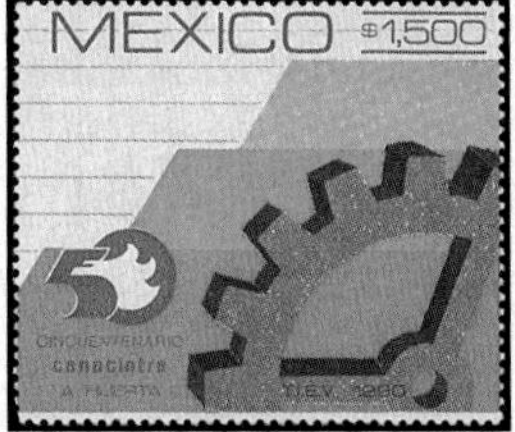

National Chamber of Industrial Development, 50th Anniv. — A624

1990, Dec. 5 ***Perf. 14***
1681 A624 1500p multicolored 1.40 .80

Naval Secretariat, 50th Anniv. A625

1991, Jan. 4 **Photo.** ***Perf. 14***
1682 A625 1000p bl, blk & gold .90 .50

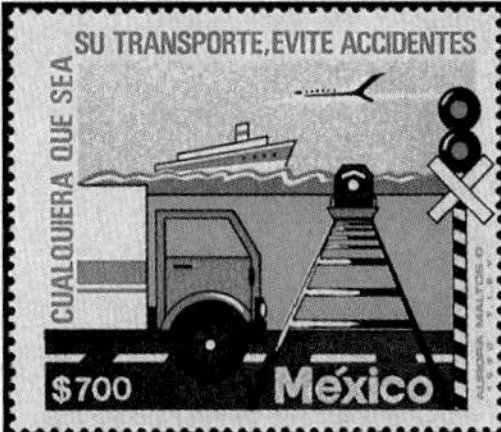

Prevent Transportation Accidents — A626

1991, Jan. 11 **Photo.** ***Perf. 14***
1683 A626 700p multicolored .75 .40

Natl. Consumers Institute, 15th Anniv. — A627

1991, Feb. 11
1684 A627 1000p multicolored .80 .55

Voter Registration A628

1991, Feb. 13 ***Perf. 14***
1685 A628 1000p org, blk & grn .80 .55

Olympic Basketball — A629

1991, Feb. 25 ***Perf. 14***
1686 A629 1000p black & yellow 1.00 .55

Campaign Against Polio — A630

1991, Mar. 8
1687 A630 1000p multicolored 1.25 .55

Nos. 1688-1691, 1697 with "NP" and Post Office eagle head logo or just the logo, are specimens.

Childrens' Day for Peace and Development — A631

Health and Family Life A632

1991, Apr. 16 ***Perf. 14***
1688 A631 1000p multicolored .95 .55
1689 A632 1000p multicolored .95 .55

Mining in Mexico, 500th Anniv. — A633

1991, Apr. 25 ***Perf. 14***
1690 A633 1000p multicolored .80 .55

Promotion of Breastfeeding — A634

1991, May 10 ***Perf. 14***
1691 A634 1000p multicolored .80 .55

16th Tourism Exposition — A635

1991, May 12 ***Perf. 14***
1692 A635 1000p brt grn & dk grn .85 .60

Rotary Intl. Convention A636

1991, June 2 ***Rouletted 6½***
1693 A636 1000p blue & gold .85 .60

Integrated Communications and Transportation Systems (SCT), Cent. — A637

Designs: No. 1695a, 1000p, Jet landing. b, 1500p, Airport control tower. c, 1000p, FAX machine. d, 1500p, Upper floors, SCT headquarters. e, 1000p, Communications van. f, 1500p, Satellite. g, 1000p, Satellite in orbit, earth. h, 1000p, Boxcars. i, 1500p, Locomotives. j, 1000p, People using telephones. k, 1500p, Lower floors, SCT headquarters. l, 1000p, Hillside road, left section, highway bridge. m, 1500p, Center section, highway bridge. n, 1000p, Right section of bridge. o, 1000p, Cranes loading cargo ship. p, 1500p, Bow of cargo ship. q, 1000p, Television camera. r, 1500p, Bus. s, 1000p, Truck. t, 1500p, Trailers passing through toll plaza. u, 1000p, Bridge construction. Continuous design.

1991, June 11 ***Rouletted 6½***
1694 A637 1000p gray & multi 1.00 .60
1695 A637 Block of 21, #a.-u. 50.00 *55.00*

Jaguar — A638

1991, June 12 ***Perf. 14***
1696 A638 1000p black & orange 2.00 .60

Conservation of the rain forests.

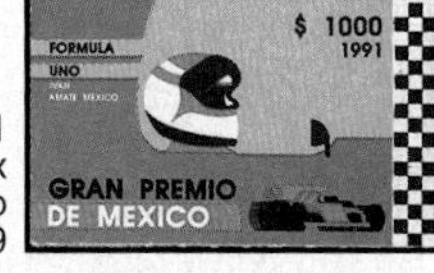

Formula 1 Grand Prix of Mexico A639

1991, June 16 **Litho.** ***Rouletted 6½***
1697 A639 1000p multicolored .85 .50

No. 1519 Ovptd. in Red

1991, June 14 **Photo.** ***Perf. 14***
1698 A520 150p multicolored *9.00 18.00*

No. 1698 was available in strips of 5 only in booklets with limited distribution, also containing a strip of 3 Scott No. 1693 and with 2 different booklet covers. Some quantities have recently been place in the marketplace. Value of No.1698 and complete booklets is currently speculative.

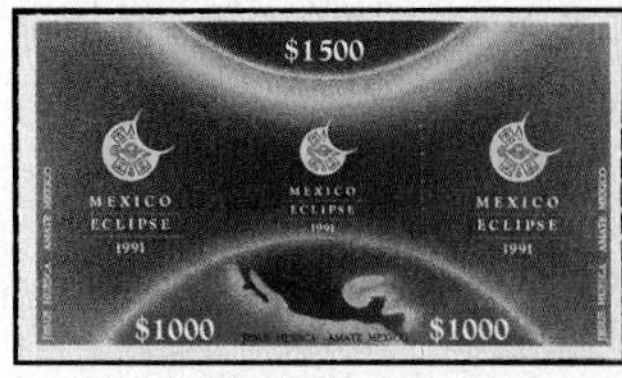

Total Solar Eclipse — A640

Designs: No. 1699a, 1000p, Denomination at lower right. b, Globe showing Mexico. c, 1000p, Denomination at lower left. Continuous design.

1991, July 5 ***Rouletted 6½***
1699 A640 Strip of 3, #a.-c. 6.50 5.00

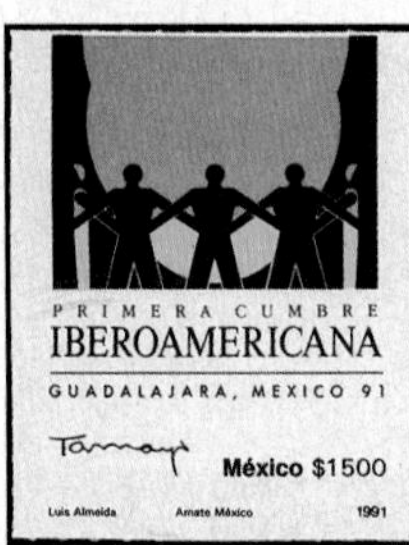

First Latin American Presidential Summit, Guadalajara A641

1991, July 18
1700 A641 1500p blk, org & yel 1.10 .80

Solidarity Bridge — A642

1991, July 31
1701 A642 2000p multicolored 1.75 1.25

Ninth Mexico City Marathon — A643

1991, Aug. 22
1702 A643 1000p multicolored .85 .60

Federal Tax Court, 55th Anniv. — A644

1991, Aug. 27
1703 A644 1000p blue & silver .85 .60

Solidarity Type of 1990 and

A645

1991 ***Perf. 14***
1704 A603 1000p multicolored .85 .60

Rouletted 6½
1705 A645 1000p multicolored .85 .60

Issued: No. 1704, 12/17; No. 1705, 9/9.

World Post Day — A646

1991, Oct. 9 ***Rouletted 6½***
1706 A646 1000p multicolored .85 .60

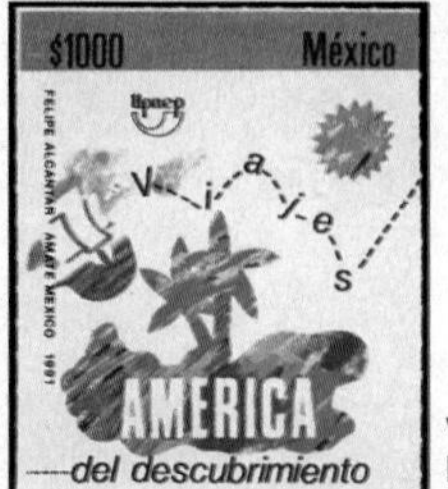

Voyages of Discovery A647

Discovery of America, 500th Anniv. (in 1992) A648

Design: No. 1708, Sailing ship, storm.

1991, Oct. 12
1707 A647 1000p multicolored 1.75 .60
1708 A647 1000p multicolored 1.75 .60
a. Pair, #1707-1708 4.00 1.25
1709 A648 1000p multicolored 2.50 .60
Nos. 1707-1709 (3) 6.00 1.80

No. 1708a has continuous design. Printed in sheets of 20+5 labels.

A649

Christmas A650

1991, Nov. 26
1710 A649 1000p multicolored .85 .60
1711 A650 1000p multicolored .85 .60

Carlos Merida, Birth Cent. A651

1991, Dec. 2 Photo. ***Rouletted 6½***
1712 A651 1000p multicolored .85 .60

Wolfgang Amadeus Mozart, Death Bicent. A652

1991, Dec. 5
1713 A652 1000p multicolored .85 .60

Self-sufficiency in Corn and Bean Production — A653

1991, Dec. 11 Photo. ***Rouletted 6½***
1714 A653 1000p multicolored .80 .55

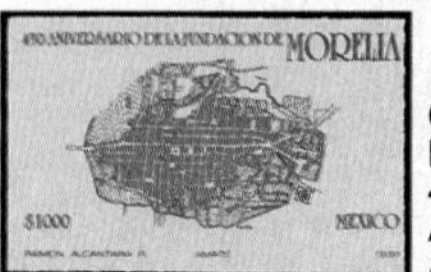

City of Morelia, 450th Anniv. A654

1991, Dec. 13
1715 A654 1000p multicolored .80 .55

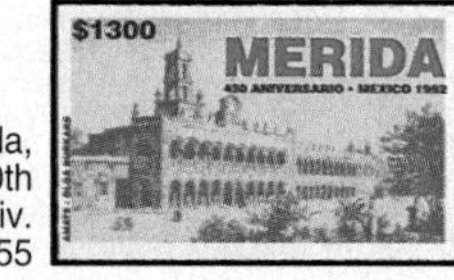

Merida, 450th Anniv. A655

1992, Jan. 6 Photo. ***Rouletted 6½***
1716 A655 1300p multicolored 1.10 .70

Engineering Education in Mexico, Bicent. A656

1992, Jan. 15
1717 A656 1300p blue & red 1.10 .70

1992 Summer Olympics, Barcelona A657

Design: No. 1719, Stylized Olympic Rings.

1992 Photo. ***Rouletted 6½***
1718 A657 2000p multicolored 1.50 1.00
1719 A657 2000p multicolored 1.50 .95

Issued: No. 1718, Feb. 10; No. 1719, Mar. 1.

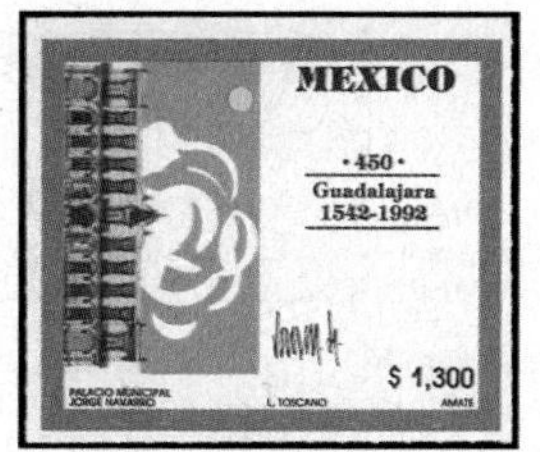

Guadalajara, 450th Anniv. — A658

No. 1720: a, 1300p, Coat of arms. b, 1300p, Municipal buildings. c, 1300p, Guadalajara Cathedral. d, 1900p, Allegory of the city's founding. e, 1900p, Anniversary emblem.

1992, Feb. 14
1720 A658 Strip of 5, #a.-e. 15.00 15.00

Healthy Child Development — A659

1992, Feb. 26
1721 A659 2000p multicolored 1.50 .95

Formula 1 Grand Prix of Mexico A660

1992, Mar. 22
1722 A660 1300p multicolored 1.00 .65

Introduction of the wheel and domesticated horses to America, 500th anniv.

Telecom '92 — A661

1992, Apr. 6
1723 A661 1300p multicolored 1.00 .65

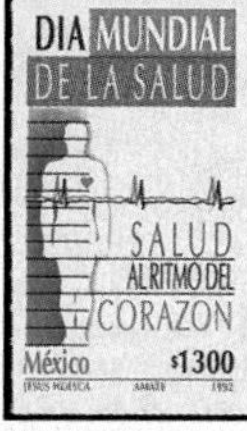

World Health Day — A662

1992, Apr. 7
1724 A662 1300p blk, red & bl 1.00 .65

War College, 60th Anniv. A663

1992, Apr. 15
1725 A663 1300p multicolored 1.00 .65

Discovery of America, 500th Anniv. A664

Paintings: No. 1726, Inspiration of Christopher Columbus, by Jose Maria Obregon. No. 1727, Meeting of the Races, by Jorge Gonzalez Camarena. No. 1728, Spanish, Indian and Mestizo, from the Natl. Historical Museum. No. 1729, Origin of the Sky, from Selden Codex. No. 1730, Quetzalcoatl and Tezcatlipoca, from Borbonico Codex. No. 1731, Human Culture by Camarena.

1992, Apr. 24 Litho. ***Perf. 14***
1726 A664 1300p multicolored 2.25 .65
1727 A664 1300p multicolored 2.25 .65
1728 A664 2000p multicolored 3.50 .95
1729 A664 2000p multicolored 3.50 .95
1730 A664 2000p multicolored 3.50 .95
Nos. 1726-1730 (5) 15.00 4.15

Size: 107x84mm

Imperf
1731 A664 7000p multicolored 20.00 4.50

Granada '92. For overprints see Nos. 1752-1757.

Natl. Medical Center in the 21st Cent. — A665

1992, Apr. 27 Photo. ***Rouletted 6½***
1732 A665 1300p multicolored 1.00 .65

Rights of the Child A666

1992, Apr. 30
1733 A666 1300p multicolored 1.00 .65

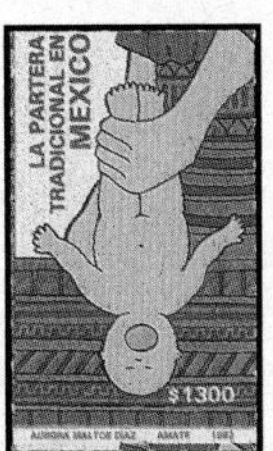

Midwives in Mexico — A667

1992, May 10

1734 A667 1300p multicolored 1.00 .65

Discovery of America, 500th Anniv. — A668

1992, May 22 Litho. *Imperf.*

1735 A668 7000p multicolored 9.00 3.75

World Columbian Stamp Expo, Chicago.

Notary College of Mexico, Mexico City, Bicent. A669

1992, June 18 Litho. *Rouletted 6½*

1736 A669 1300p multicolored 1.00 .70

Arbor Day — A670

1992, July 9 *Rouletted 5*

1737 A670 1300p multicolored 1.00 .70

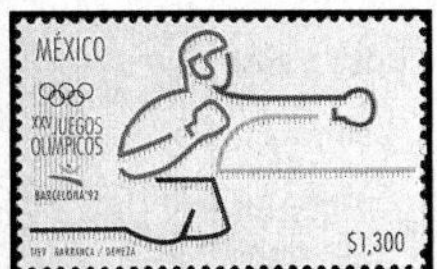

1992 Summer Olympics, Barcelona A671

1992, July 30 *Perf. 14*

1738	A671	1300p	Boxing	1.25	.70
1739	A671	1300p	Fencing	1.25	.70
1740	A671	1300p	High jump	1.25	.70
1741	A671	1300p	Gymnastics	1.25	.70
1742	A671	1300p	Shooting	1.25	.70
1743	A671	1900p	Swimming	2.50	1.00
1744	A671	1900p	Running	2.50	1.00
1745	A671	1900p	Rowing	2.50	1.00
1746	A671	1900p	Soccer	2.50	1.00
1747	A671	2000p	Equestrian	2.50	1.10
	Nos. 1738-1747 (10)			18.75	8.60

Souvenir Sheet

Perf. 10

1748 A671 7000p Torch bearer 15.00 8.00

10th Intl. Marathon of Mexico City — A672

1992, Aug. 26 Litho. *Rouletted 5*

1749 A672 1300p multicolored 1.00 .65

Solidarity, United for Progress — A673

1992, Sept. 8 *Perf. 10*

1750 A673 1300p multicolored 1.00 .65

Souvenir Sheet

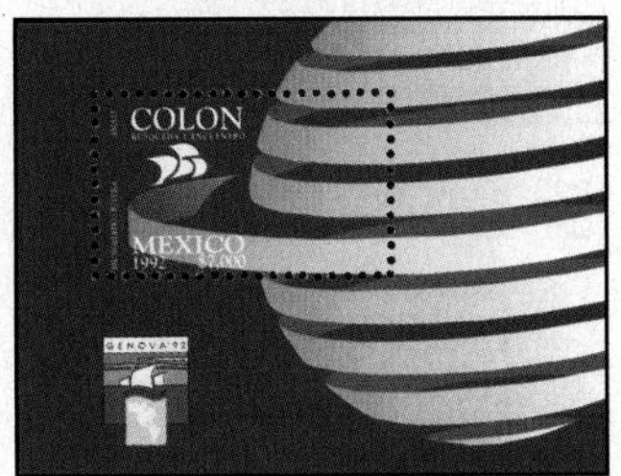

Discovery of America, 500th Anniv. — A674

1992, Sept. 18 *Perf. 10*

1751 A674 7000p multicolored 10.00 3.25

Genoa '92.

Nos. 1726-1731 Ovptd. with emblem of World Columbian Stamp Expo '92, Chicago

1992, Apr. 24 Litho. *Perf. 14*

1752	A664	1300p	on #1726	16.00	16.00
1753	A664	1300p	on #1727	16.00	16.00
1754	A664	2000p	on #1728	16.00	16.00
1755	A664	2000p	on #1729	16.00	16.00
1756	A664	2000p	on #1730	16.00	16.00
	Nos. 1752-1756 (5)			80.00	80.00

Size: 107x84mm

Imperf

1757 A664 7000p on #1731 85.00 85.00

Nos. 1752-1757 were produced in limited quantities and had limited distribution with no advance release information available.

Natl. Council of Radio and Television, 50th Anniv. A675

1992, Oct. 5 Litho. *Perf. 10*

1758 A675 1300p multicolored 1.00 .65

World Post Day A676

1992, Oct. 9 Litho. *Perf. 10*

1759 A676 1300p multicolored 1.00 .65

Communications System of the Americas — A677

1992, Oct. 12

1760 A677 2000p multicolored 2.00 1.00

Discovery of America, 500th Anniv. A678

Designs: No. 1761, Aztec calendar stone. No. 1762, Snake, fish, compass.

1992, Oct. 12

1761	A678	2000p	shown	2.00	1.00
1762	A678	2000p	multicolored	2.00	1.00
a.	Pair, #1761-1762			4.50	2.00

Exporta Type of 1975

Designs: 2200p, Cuts of meat marked on steer. 2800p, Chemistry flasks. 3600p, Pistons. 3900p, Petroleum valves. 4000p, Honey. 4800p, Tomatoes. 6000p, Citrus fruit. 7200p, Film.

1992 Photo. *Perf. 14*

1763	A320	2200p	red	1.60	.80
1764	A320	2800p	black	2.50	1.00
		With Gray Burelage			
1765	A320	3600p	blk, I	2.75	1.40
1766	A320	3900p	gray & bl, II	3.50	1.50
1767	A320	4000p	yel org & red brn, I	3.50	1.40
1768	A320	4800p	red & grn, I	4.00	1.75
1768A	A320	4800p	red & green, II	25.00	1.75
1769	A320	6000p	yel & grn, I	5.00	2.25
1770	A320	7200p	grn, red & blk, I	6.00	2.75
	Nos. 1763-1770 (9)			53.85	14.60

San Luis Potosi, 400th Anniv. A679

1992, Nov. 3 Litho. *Perf. 10*

1777 A679 1300p multicolored 1.00 .65

Values are for copies with perfs touching the design.

United for Conservation — A680

1992, Nov. 17

1778 A680 1300p multicolored 2.00 .65

Navy Day A681

1992, Nov. 23

1779 A681 1300p multicolored 1.00 .65

Values are for copies with perfs touching the design.

Christmas A682

1300p, Christmas tree, children, pinata, vert.

1992, Nov. 26

1780	A682	1300p	multicolored	1.00	.65
1781	A682	2000p	multicolored	2.00	1.00

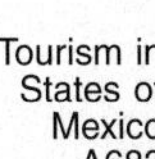

Tourism in States of Mexico A683

No. 1782, Campeche. No. 1783, Guanajuato. No. 1784, Guanajuato. No. 1785, Colima. No. 1786, Coahuila. No. 1787, Campeche. No. 1788, Colima. No. 1789, Chiapas. No. 1790, Michoacan, vert. No. 1791, Coahuila. No. 1792, Colima. No. 1793, Queretaro. No. 1794, Sinaloa. No. 1795, Yucatan. No. 1796, Sonora. No. 1797, Mexico. No. 1798, Zacatecas, vert. No. 1798A, Campeche. No. 1799, Sinaloa. No. 1800, Sinaloa. No. 1801, Yucatan. No. 1802, Yucatan. No. 1803, Chiapas. No. 1804, Mexico. No. 1805, Sonora.

1993-96 Photo. Unwmk. *Perf. 14*

1782	A683	90c	multi	1.25	.50
1783	A683	1p	multi	1.50	.60
1784	A683	1.10p	multi	1.75	.25
1785	A683	1.30p	multi	1.90	.70
1786	A683	1.80p	multi	1.40	.45
1787	A683	1.80p	multi	1.00	.40
1788	A683	1.80p	multi	1.00	.40
1789	A683	1.80p	multi	1.00	.30
1790	A683	1.90p	multi	3.00	1.10
1791	A683	2p	multi	2.75	1.10
1792	A683	2p	multi	2.75	.25
1793	A683	2.20p	multi	3.25	1.25
1794	A683	2.30p	multi	1.50	.35
1795	A683	2.40p	multi	1.75	.40
1796	A683	2.50p	multi	4.50	1.40
1797	A683	2.70p	multi	3.00	.60
1798	A683	2.80p	multi	4.75	1.50
1798A	A683	3p	multi	3.75	.30
1799	A683	3.40p	multi	3.75	.80
1800	A683	3.70p	multi	10.00	1.90
1801	A683	3.80p	multi	2.90	.85
1802	A683	4.40p	multi	6.75	2.40
1803	A683	4.80p	multi	7.75	2.50
1804	A683	6p	multi	10.00	3.25
1805	A683	6.50p	multi	5.00	1.50
	Nos. 1782-1805 (25)			87.95	25.05

A 2nd printing of No. 1797 exists. This printing appears crude, with missing and misregistered color dots.

Issued: 90c, 1p, 1.30p, 1.90p, No. 1791, 2.20p, 2.30p, 2.40p, 2.50p, 2.80p, 3.70p, 4.40p, 4.80p, 6p, 1993; 1.10p, 1.80p, 2.70p, 3.40p, 3.80p, 6.50p, 1995; No. 1792, 3p, 1996.

See Nos. 1960-1980, 2119, 2122-2140.

A685

A686

Designs: No. 1807, Doctor, child. No. 1808, Child's drawing, ball, blocks. No. 1809, Hands.

1993, Jan. 19 Litho. *Perf. 10*

1807 A685 1.30p multicolored .90 .65
1808 A685 1.30p multicolored 1.00 .75
1809 A685 1.30p multicolored 1.00 .75
1810 A686 1.50p multicolored 1.10 .85
Nos. 1807-1810 (4) 4.00 3.00

Mexican Social Security Institute, 50th anniv. Medical Services (No. 1807), Day Nursery Social Security Service (No. 1808), security and solidarity (No. 1809).

Issued: 1.50p, 1/19; No. 1807, 5/11; others, 12/7.

Mexican Society of Ophthalmolgists, Cent. — A687

1993, Feb. 16 Litho. *Perf. 10*

1811 A687 1.30p multicolored .95 .70

Children's Month — A688

1993, Feb. 23

1812 A688 1.30p multicolored .95 .70

Mexican Geography and Statistics Society, 160th Anniv. A689

1993, Apr. 19 Litho. *Perf. 10*

1813 A689 1.30p blue, blk & red .95 .70

Miguel Ramos Arizpe (1776-1843), Proponent of Mexican Federalism — A690

1993, Apr. 28

1814 A690 1.30p multicolored .95 .70

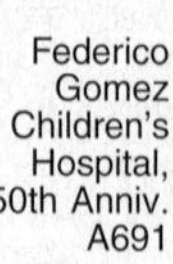

Federico Gomez Children's Hospital, 50th Anniv. A691

1993, Apr. 29

1815 A691 1.30p multicolored .95 .70

Health Begins at Home A692

1993, May 31

1816 A692 1.30p multicolored .95 .70

Upper Gulf of California, Nature Preserve A693

1993, June 10 Litho. *Perf. 10*

1817 A693 1.30p multicolored .95 .70

Mario Moreno (Cantinflas), Film Actor — A694

1993, June 24 Photo. *Perf. 14*

1818 A694 1.30p black & blue .95 .70

See Nos. 1847-1851.

Secretariat of Health, 50th Anniv. A695

Designs: No. 1819, Dr. Maximiliano Ruiz Castaneda. No. 1820, Dr. Bernardo Sepulveda Gutierrez. No. 1821, Dr. Ignacio Chavez Sanchez. No. 1822, Dr. Mario Salazar Mallen. No. 1823, Dr. Gustavo Baz Prada.

1993 Litho. *Perf. 10*

1819 A695 1.30p multicolored .95 .70
1820 A695 1.30p multicolored .95 .70
1821 A695 1.30p multicolored .95 .70
1822 A695 1.30p multicolored .95 .70
1823 A695 1.30p multicolored .95 .70
Nos. 1819-1823 (5) 4.75 3.50

Issued: No. 1819, 6/29; No. 1820, 7/26; No. 1821, 8/31; No. 1822, 9/23; No. 1823, 10/26.

First Postage Stamps of Brazil, 150th Anniv. A696

1993, July 30

1824 A696 2p multicolored 1.50 1.10

Runners — A697

1993, Aug. 25

1825 A697 1.30p multi .95 .70

11th Intl. Marathon of Mexico City.

A698

1.30p, Open book, lightning bolt. 2p, Buildings.

1993, Sept. 6

1826 1.30p multicolored .95 .70
1827 2p multicolored 1.40 1.00
a. A698 Pair, #1826-1827 2.50 2.00

Monterrey Institute of Technology and Higher Studies, 50th anniv.

Solidarity Week A699

1993, Sept. 6

1828 A699 1.30p multicolored .95 .70

Confederation of Mexican Chambers of Industry, 75th Anniv. — A700

1993, Sept. 13 Litho. *Perf. 10*

1829 A700 1.30p multicolored .95 .70

City of Torreon, Cent. — A701

1993, Sept. 15

1830 A701 1.30p multicolored .95 .70

Europalia '93 — A702

1993, Sept. 22

1831 A702 2p multicolored 1.50 1.10

World Post Day — A703

1993, Oct. 9

1832 A703 2p multicolored 1.50 1.10

A704

1993, Oct. 10

1833 A704 1.30p multicolored .95 .70

Guadalupe Victoria (1786-1843), first president of Mexico.

Natl. Civil Protection System — A705

1993, Oct. 13

1834 A705 1.30p multicolored .95 .70

Intl. Day for Reduction of Natural Disasters.

UN Decade for Intl. Law A706

1993, Oct. 19

1835 A706 2p multicolored 1.50 1.10

20th Natl. Wheelchair Games A707

1993, Oct. 21

1836 A707 1.30p multicolored .95 .70

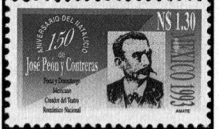

Jose Peon y Contreras, Poet, 150th Anniv. of Birth A708

1993, Oct. 22 Litho. *Perf. 10*

1837 A708 1.30p purple & black .95 .70

Endangered Species — A709

1993, Oct. 25 Litho. *Perf. 10*

1838 A709 2p Quetzal 2.50 1.10
1839 A709 2p Pavon, vert. 2.50 1.10

Christmas A710

Designs: No. 1840, Adoration of the Magi. No. 1841, Christmas trees, presents, vert.

1993, Nov. 26 Litho. *Perf. 10*
1840 A710 1.30p multicolored .95 .70
1841 A710 1.30p multicolored .95 .70

Solidarity A711

1993, Nov. 20
1842 A711 1.30p multicolored 1.00 .75

Natl. Preparatory School, 125th Anniv. — A712

1993, Dec. 2 Litho. *Perf. 10*
1843 A712 1.30p multicolored 1.00 .75

FSTSE, 55th Anniv. A713

1993, Dec. 6 Photo.
1844 A713 1.30p multicolored 1.00 .75

Mescala Bridge A714

1993, Dec. 7
1845 A714 1.30p multicolored 1.00 .75

Highway of the Sun A715

1993, Dec. 7
1846 A715 1.30p multicolored 1.00 .75

Film Actor Type of 1993

No. 1847, Pedro Armendariz. No. 1848, Pedro Infante. No. 1849, Jorge Negrete. No. 1850, Maria Felix. No. 1851, Dolores del Rio.

1993, Dec. 9 *Perf. 14*
1847 A694 1.30p black & light blue 1.00 .75
1848 A694 1.30p black & green 1.00 .75
1849 A694 1.30p black & purple 1.00 .75
1850 A694 1.30p black & orange 1.00 .75
1851 A694 1.30p black & rose 1.00 .75
Nos. 1847-1851 (5) 5.00 3.75

Secretariat of Education, 72nd Anniv. A716

Famous educators: No. 1852, Jose Vasconcelos. No. 1853, Rafael Ramirez Castaneda. No. 1854, Estefania Castaneda Nunez. No. 1855, Moises Saenz Garza. No. 1856, Rosaura Zapata Cano. No. 1857, Gregorio Torres Quintero. No. 1858, Lauro Aguirre Espinosa.

1994, Jan. 26 Litho. *Perf. 10*
1852 A716 1.30p multicolored 1.00 .75
1853 A716 1.30p multicolored 1.00 .75
1854 A716 1.30p multicolored 1.00 .75
1855 A716 1.30p multicolored 1.00 .75
1856 A716 1.30p multicolored 1.00 .75
1857 A716 1.30p multicolored 1.00 .75
1858 A716 1.30p multicolored 1.00 .75
Nos. 1852-1858 (7) 7.00 5.25

Emiliano Zapata, (1879-1919), Revolutionary — A717

1994, Apr. 10 Litho. *Perf. 10*
1859 A717 1.30p multicolored .95 .70

ILO, 75th Anniv. — A718

1994, Apr. 18 *Perf. 14*
1860 A718 2p multicolored 1.40 1.00

School Construction by CAPFCE, 50th Anniv. — A719

1994, Apr. 19
1861 A719 1.30p multicolored .90 .70

Children for Peace A720

1994, Apr. 28
1862 A720 1.30p multicolored .90 .70

Youth Services A721

1994, May 12 *Rouletted 12*
1863 A721 1.30p green & black .90 .70

United for Conservation — A722

1994, May 6 *Perf. 10*
1864 A722 1.30p multicolored 2.50 .70

Rouletting on many of the 1994 issues leaves individual stamps with rough, unattractive edges. Some examples are separated by scissors because of the difficulty in separating stamps.

The gum on many issues is poorly applied, often having a rough feel and appearance, due to air bubbles. Gum may not cover the entire back side.

Serial numbers are found on the back of some examples of No. 1896. These may appear on other stamps.

Francisco Zuniga — A723

1994, Apr. 26 *Rouletted 12*
1865 A723 1.30p multicolored .90 .70

A724

1994, May 16 Litho. *Rouletted 13*
1866 A724 2p multicolored 1.40 1.00

34th World Advertising Congress, Cancun.

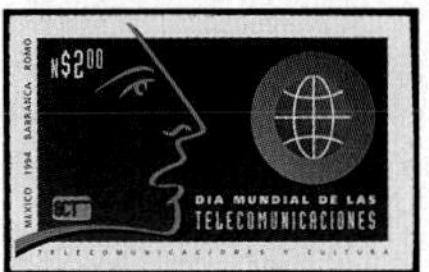
World Telecommunications Day — A725

1994, May 17 Litho. *Rouletted 13*
1867 A725 2p multicolored 1.40 .75

ANIERM (Natl. Assoc. of Importers & Exporters of the Republic of Mexico), 50th Anniv. A726

1994, May 17 *Rouletted 12½*
1868 A726 1.30p multicolored .90 .70

Yumka Natural Wildlife Center A727

1994, May 21 Litho. *Rouletted 13*
1869 A727 1.30p multicolored .90 .70

City of Zacatecas A728

1994, May 26 *Rouletted 12½*
1870 A728 1.30p multicolored .90 .70

Prevention of Mental Retardation — A729

1994, June 1 Litho. *Perf. 14*
1871 A729 1.30p multicolored .90 .70

Month of the Child.

Friendship Hospital — A730

1.30p, Mother and child.

1994, June 1 Litho. *Perf. 14*
1872 A730 1.30p multicolored .90 .70

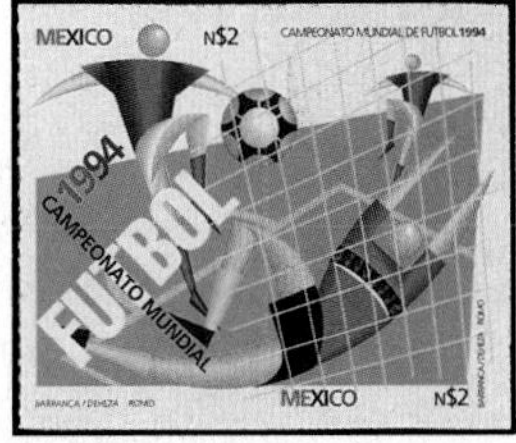
A731

Stylized soccer players: a, Kicking ball. b, Behind net.

1994, June 7 *Rouletted 13*
1873 A731 2p Pair, #a.-b. 3.25 2.25

1994 World Cup Soccer Championships, US.

Intl. Fish Fair, Vera Cruz — A732

1994, June 8
1874 A732 1.30p multicolored .90 .70

A733

Wildlife conservation: a, Silhouettes of ornamental songbirds (green). b, Silhouettes of cynegetic birds (blue). c, Silhouettes of fierce-looking wildlife (brown). d, Silhouettes of endangered wildlife (red). e, Perico frenteanaranjada. f, Calandria cola amarilla. g, Cardenal torito. h, Sastrecillo americano. i, Cenzontle norteno. j, Guajolote norteno. k, Paloma de ala blanca. l, Pato pijiji de ala blanca. m, Ganso blanco. n, Codorniz de gambel. o, Peregrin falcon. p, Jaguar. q, Jaguarundi. r, Mono saraguato. s, Lobo fino de guadalupe. t, Berrendo peninsular. u, Guacamaya roja. v, Mexican prairie dog. w, Mexican wolf. x, Manati.

1994, June 5 *Perf. 14*
1875 A733 1.30p Block of 24, #a.-x. + label 50.00 50.00

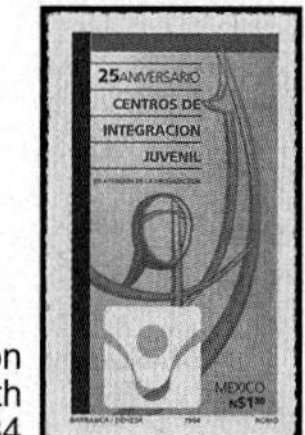

Juvenile Integration Centers, 25th Anniv. — A734

Rouletted 12½
1994, June 29 **Litho.**
1876 A734 1.30p multicolored .90 .70

Mexican-Canadian Diplomatic Relations, 50th Anniv. — A735

1994, July 1
1877 A735 2p multicolored 1.40 1.10

Natl. Population Council, 20th Anniv. A736

1994, July 15
1878 A736 1.30p multicolored .90 .70

Intl. Year of the Family — A737

1994, July 20
1879 A737 2p multicolored 1.40 1.00

Arbor Day — A738

Rouletted 12½
1994, Aug. 22 **Photo.**
1880 A738 1.30p multi .90 .70

12th Mexico City Marathon — A739

1994, July 27
1881 A739 1.30p multicolored .90 .70

Chapultepec Zoo — A740

1994, Aug. 1
1882 A740 1.30p Giant panda 1.25 .70

Metro System, 25th Anniv. — A741

1994, Sept. 5 *Perf. 13x13½*
1883 A741 1.30p multicolored .90 .70

A742

1994, Sept. 5
1884 A742 1.30p multicolored .90 .70

Economic Cultural Foundation, 60th Anniv..

A743

1994, Sept. 22
1885 A743 1.30p multicolored .90 .70

Don Adolfo Lopez Mateos, 25th Death Anniv.

Solidarity Week — A744

1994, Sept. 22
1886 A744 1.30p multicolored .90 .70

City University, 40th Anniv. A745

1994, Sept. 21 **Litho.** *Perf. 13½*
1887 A745 1.30p blue & yellow .90 .70

Opening of the Natl. Medical Center A746

1994, Oct. 3
1888 A746 1.30p multicolored .90 .70

Natl. Week of Patriot Symbols A747

1994, Sept. 16
1889 A747 1.30p multicolored .90 .70

Intl. Olympic Committee, Cent. — A748

1994, Sept. 29
1890 A748 2p multicolored 2.50 1.00

America Issue — A749

Mail delivery vehicles: a, bicycle. b, Railroad cycle.

1994, Oct. 12
1891 A749 2p Pair, #a.-b. 3.75 2.50

City of Salvatierra Guanajuato, 350th Anniv. — A750

1994, Sept. 12
1892 A750 1.30p multicolored .90 .70

Horses — A751

Designs: a, Saddled Aztec racer. b, Light brown quarter horse. c, Black quarter horse. d, Charro on horseback. e, Aztec racer. f, Chinaco riding galloping horse.

1994, Sept. 30 *Perf. 14*
1893 A751 1.30p Block of 6, #a.-f. 10.00 10.00

Issued in sheets of 3 No. 1893 + 7 labels.

Grandparents' Day — A752

1994, Oct. 15 *Perf. 13½*
1894 A752 1.30p multicolored .90 .70

Palace of Fine Arts, Mexico City, 60th Anniv. A753

1994, Sept. 29 **Litho.** *Perf. 13½*
1895 A753 1.30p multicolored .90 .70

Antoine de Saint-Exupery (1900-44), Writer — A754

1994, Oct. 6 *Rouletted 13*
1896 A754 2p multicolored 1.40 1.00

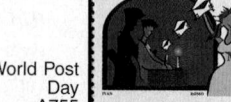

World Post Day A755

1994, Oct. 9 *Perf. 13½*
1897 A755 2p multicolored 1.40 1.00

Natl. Clean Water Program A756

1994, Oct. 17
1898 A756 1.30p multicolored .90 .70

Dr. Jose Luis Mora (1794-1850), Politician — A757

1994, Oct. 27
1899 A757 1.30p multicolored .90 .70

City Theater, Saltillo, 50th Anniv. A758

1994, Nov. 3
1900 A758 1.30p multicolored .90 .70

ICAO, 50th Anniv. A759

1994, Nov. 3
1901 A759 2p multicolored 1.40 1.00

Natl. Museum of Anthropology, 30th Anniv. — A760

1994, Nov. 8
1902 A760 1.30p multicolored .90 .70

Natl. Assoc. of Actors, 60th Anniv. — A761

1994, Nov. 9
1903 A761 1.30p multicolored .90 .70

Ignacio Allende (1769-1811), Independence Hero — A762

1994, Nov. 10
1904 A762 1.30p multicolored .90 .70

Natl. Museum of History, 50th Anniv. — A763

1994, Nov. 22 ***Perf. 14***
1905 A763 1.30p multicolored .90 .70

Coahuila Teachers' College, Cent. — A764

1994, Nov. 23 ***Perf. 13½***
1906 A764 1.30p multicolored .90 .70

Pumas UNAM Soccer Team, 40th Anniv. — A765

1994, Nov. 23
1907 A765 1.30p blue & gold .90 .70

Christmas A766

1994, Nov. 29
1908 A766 2p shown 1.40 1.00
1909 A766 2p Tree, vert. 1.40 1.00

Chalco Valley Solidarity A767

1994, Nov. 30
1910 A767 1.30p multicolored .90 .70

Sr. Juana Ines de la Cruz (1648-95), Writer — A768

1995, Apr. 17 **Litho.** ***Perf. 13½***
1911 A768 1.80p multicolored .75 .60

Wilhelm Roentgen (1845-1923), Discovery of the X-Ray, Cent. — A769

1995, May 8
1912 A769 2p multicolored .85 .65

Teachers' Day A770

1.80p, Ignacio M. Altamirano.

1995, May 15
1913 A770 1.80p multicolored .75 .60

World Telecommunications Day — A771

1995, May 17 ***Perf. 14x14½***
1914 A771 2.70p multicolored 1.10 .85

A772

1995, May 18 ***Perf. 13½***
1915 A772 1.80p multicolored .75 .60

Natl. Institute of Public Administration, 40th anniv.

A773

Jose Marti (1853-95), Cuban patriot.

1995, May 19 ***Perf. 14x14½***
1916 A773 2.70p multicolored 1.10 .85

A774

1.80p, Venustiano Carranza (1859-1920), politician, President of Mexico, 1917-20.

1995, May 23 ***Perf. 13½***
1917 A774 1.80p multicolored .75 .60

A775

1995, June 11
1918 A775 2.70p multicolored 1.10 .85

Tianguis Turistico, travel trade show, 20th anniv.

A776

a, Face becoming skull with pills, needle. b, Person as puppet. c, Faces behind bars.

1995, June 26
1919 A776 1.80p Strip of 3, #a.-c. 2.25 1.75

Intl. Day Against Illegal Drugs.

A777

1995, June 28
1920 A777 1.80p black .75 .60

Lazaro Cardenas (1895-1970), soldier, politician, President of Mexico, 1934-40.

Natl. School for the Blind, 125th Anniv. A778

1995, July 18 **Litho.** ***Perf. 13½***
1921 A778 1.30p sepia & black .45 .35

Migratory Wildlife A781

Designs: a, Danaus plexippus. b, Lasiurus cinereus. c, Anas acuta. d, Ceryle alcyon.

1995, Aug. 15 **Litho.** ***Perf. 13½***
1924 A781 2.70p Block or strip of 4, #a.-d. 8.00 8.00

See Canada Nos. 1563-1567.

13th Mexico City Marathon A782

1995, Aug. 22 **Litho.** ***Perf. 13½***
1925 A782 2.70p multicolored .95 .70

16th Congress of UPAEP — A783

1995, Sept. 15
1926 A783 2.70p multicolored .95 .70

Louis Pasteur (1822-95) — A784

1995, Sept. 26 *Perf. 14*
1927 A784 2.70p multicolored .95 .70

World Post Day — A785

1995, Oct. 9
1928 A785 2.70p multicolored .95 .70

World Food Day — A786

1995, Oct. 16 *Perf. 14x14½*
1929 A786 1.80p multicolored .85 .50

FAO, 50th Anniv. A787

1995, Oct. 16 *Perf. 14*
1930 A787 2.70p multicolored .95 .70

Plutarco Elias Calles (1877-1945), President of Mexico 1924-28 — A788

1995, Oct. 19 *Perf. 13½*
1931 A788 1.80p multicolored .85 .50

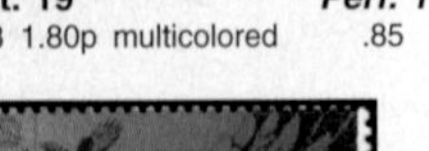

Birth of Cuauhtemoc, 500th Anniv. — A789

1995, Oct. 21
1932 A789 1.80p multicolored .85 .50

A790

National Symbols: 1.80p, Natl. flag, Constitution of Apatzingan, words of Natl. Anthem.

1995, Oct. 22
1933 A790 1.80p multicolored .85 .50

UN, 50th Anniv. — A791

1995, Oct. 24 Litho. *Perf. 14½x14*
1934 A791 2.70p multicolored .95 .70

Intl. Year of Travel A792

1995, Nov. 14 Litho. *Perf. 13½*
1935 A792 2.70p multicolored .85 .65

Viceregal Gallery of Art Painting, The Holy Family, by Andres de Conchas A793

1995, Nov. 16 *Perf. 14*
1936 A793 1.80p multicolored .75 .40

Famous Generals A794

Designs: No. 1937, Ignacio Zaragoza (1829-62). No. 1938, Sóstenes Rocha (1831-97). No. 1939, Felipe B. Berriozábal (1829-1900). No. 1940, Pedro María Anaya (1795-1854). No. 1941, Leandro Valle (1833-61). No. 1942, Santos Degollado (1811-61).

1995, Nov. 23 *Perf. 13½*
1937 A794 1.80p yel, blk & bister .75 .40
1938 A794 1.80p yel, blk & bister .75 .40
1939 A794 1.80p yel, blk & bister .75 .40
1940 A794 1.80p yel, blk & bister .75 .40
1941 A794 1.80p yel, blk & bister .75 .40
1942 A794 1.80p yel, blk & bister .75 .40
Nos. 1937-1942 (6) 4.50 2.40

Christmas A795

Children's paintings: 1.80p, Family celebrating Christmas inside house. 2.70p, Adoration of the Magi.

1995, Nov. 27
1943 A795 1.80p multicolored .55 .40
1944 A795 2.70p multicolored .85 .65
a. Pair, Nos. 1943-1944 1.40 1.10

Mexican Health Foundation, 10th Anniv. — A796

1995, Nov. 30 Litho. *Perf. 14*
1945 A796 1.80p multicolored .80 .45

Wildlife Conservation — A797

1995, Dec. 4 *Perf. 14*
1946 A797 1.80p Ocelot 2.00 .40

Motion Pictures, Cent. — A798

1995, Dec. 12
1947 A798 1.80p violet & black .75 .40

Natl. Library of Education A799

1995, Dec. 13 *Perf. 13½*
1948 A799 1.80p bl grn & yel .75 .40

A800

1995, Dec. 15
1949 A800 1.80p multicolored .75 .40

Natl. Arts and Sciences Awards, 50th anniv.

A801

Radio personalities: a, Pedro Vargas. b, Agustin Lara. c, Hermanas Aguila. d, Toña "La Negra." e, "Cri-Cri," (F. Gabilondo Soler). f, Emilio Tuero. g, Gonzalo Curiel. h, Lola Beltrán.

1995, Dec. 19 *Perf. 14*
1950 A801 1.80p Strip or block of 8, #a.-h. 10.00 10.00

Natl. Council of Science and Technology, 25th Anniv. A802

1995, Dec. 20 *Perf. 13½*
1951 A802 1.80p multicolored .75 .40

Plaza de Toros, Mexico City, 50th Anniv. A803

Matadors: 1.80p, Silverio Perez, Carlos Arruza, Manolo Martinez. 2.70p, Rodolfo Gaona, Fermin Espinosa "Armillita," Lorenzo Garza.

1996, Feb. 5 Litho. *Perf. 13½*
1952 1.80p multicolored .55 .40
1953 2.70p multicolored .85 .65
a. A803 Pair, Nos. 1952-1953 1.40 1.10

No. 1953a is a contiunuous design.

Mexican Aviation Day A804

Designs: a, 2.70p, Patrol jet. b, 2.70p, Jet landing, airport terminal. c, 1.80p, Fighter plane, Squadron 201 (1945), map. d, 1.80p, Commercial biplane (1921), commerical jet.

1996, Jan. 20 Litho. *Perf. 13½*
1954 A804 Strip or block of 4, #a.-d. 7.50 7.50

Dr. Alfonso Caso (1896-1970), Archaeologist — A805

1996, Feb. 1
1955 A805 1.80p multicolored .75 .40

Natl. Consumer Agency, 20th Anniv. A806

1996, Feb. 9 *Perf. 14*
1956 A806 1.80p multicolored .75 .40

Tourism Type of 1993
Denomination Shown As $

Nos. 1960, 1962, 1976, Colima. Nos. 1961, 1964, Chiapas. No. 1963, Guanajuato. Nos. 1965, 1975, Queretaro. Nos. 1966, 1970, 1980, Mexico. Nos. 1967, 1972, Campeche. No. 1968, Coahuila. Nos. 1969, 1978, Sinaloa. Nos. 1971, 1979, Sonora. No. 1973, Michoacan, vert. No. 1974, Yucatan. No. 1977, Zacatecas, vert.

1996-99 Photo. Unwmk. *Perf. 14*
Design A683

1960 1p multi ('97) 1.00 .25
1961 1.80p multi 1.00 .25
1962 2p multi 1.00 .25
1963 2p multi ('97) 1.00 .25
1964 2.30p multi ('97) 1.50 .30
1965 2.50p multi ('97) 1.50 .40
1966 2.70p multi 2.00 .35
1967 3p multi 2.00 .40
1968 3.10p multi ('97) 2.00 .35
1969 3.40p multi 2.50 .45
a. Pair, #1799, 1969 *125.00 125.00*

1970	3.50p multi ('97)	2.50	.60
1971	3.60p multi ('99)	2.50	.35
1972	3.70p multi ('98)	2.50	.35
1973	4p multi ('97)	3.00	.50
1974	4.40p multi ('97)	3.00	.50
1975	5p multi	3.00	.65
1976	5p multi ('98)	4.00	.50
1977	6p multi ('97)	4.00	.70
1978	6.50p multi ('98)	5.00	.65
1979	7p multi ('97)	6.00	.80
1980	8.50p multi ('97)	7.50	1.00
	Nos. 1960-1980 (21)	58.50	9.85

Denomination on Nos. 1782-1805 was shown as N$.

Two additional printings of the 3.50p appear crude with missing and mis-registered dots. One of these printings is perf 12.

Two additional printings of No. 1975 exist. These appear crude, with missing and mis-registered color dots. One of the reprints is perf 12.

Orthopedics Society, 50th Anniv. — A807

1996, Apr. 29 Litho. ***Perf. 13½***
1981 A807 1.80p multicolored .75 .40

Juan Rulfo (1917-86), Writer A808

1996, May 3
1982 A808 1.80p multicolored .75 .40

Natl. Polytechnical Institute, 60th Anniv. — A809

1996, May 21
1983 A809 1.80p multicolored .75 .40

A810

Stylized designs: a, 1.80p, Hands reaching toward one another. b, 1.80p, Person helping another out of hole. c, 2.70p, Two people.

1996, June 26 Litho. ***Perf. 13½***
1984 A810 Strip of 3, #a.-c. 3.00 3.00

Decade of United Nations Against Illegal Drug Abuse and Trafficking.

A811

1996 Summer Olympic Games, Atlanta: a, Women's gymnastics. b, Soccer. c, Marathon race. d, Hurdles. e, Equestrian show jumping.

1996, July 19 ***Perf. 14x14½***
1985 A811 Strip of 5, #a.-e. 6.00 6.00

Motion Pictures, Cent. A812

1996, Aug. 6 Litho. ***Perf. 13½***
Color of Film Cells
1986 A812 1.80p grn, ocher & vio .45 .35
1987 A812 1.80p pur, grn & red .45 .35
a. Pair, #1986-1987 2.25 2.25

Justice Dept., 60th Anniv. A813

1996, Aug. 18
1988 A813 1.80p multicolored .75 .35

14th Mexico City Marathon A814

1996, Aug. 20
1989 A814 2.70p multicolored .90 .50

City of Zacatecas, 450th Anniv. A815

1996, Sept. 8
1990 A815 1.80p multicolored .90 .35

Natl. Council to Promote Education, 25th Anniv. A816

1996, Sept. 17
1991 A816 1.80p multicolored .90 .35

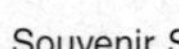

Souvenir Sheet

City of Monterrey, 400th Anniv. — A817

1996, Sept. 20
1992 A817 7.40p multicolored 4.50 4.50

Family Planning — A818

1996, Sept. 26
1993 A818 1.80p multicolored .90 .35

Independence, 175th Anniv. — A819

1996, Sept. 27
1994 A819 1.80p multicolored .90 .35

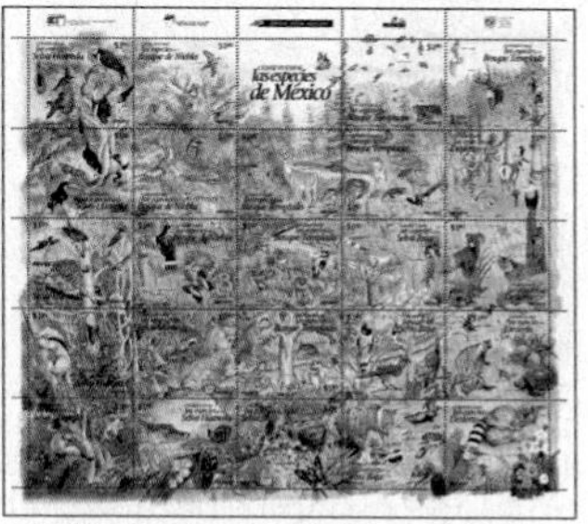

Endangered Species — A820

Designs show a wide variety of species, one from each stamp is: a, Aguila arpia. b, Tortola serrana. c, Monarch butterflies. d, Vernado bura. e, Guacamaya roja. f, Quetzal. g, Venado cola blanca. h, Puma. i, Coyote. j, Jaguar. k, Martucha. l, Woodpecker. m, Cuco canelo. n, Lince. o, Oso hormiguero. p, Ocelote. q, Encino. r, Chachalaca. s, Liebre. t, Tapir. u, Crocodile. v, Armadillo. w, Pecari. x, Cacomixtle.

1996, Oct. 2 Sheet of 24
1995 A820 1.80p #a.-x. + label 24.00 24.00

See US No. 3105.

World Post Day — A821

1996, Oct. 9
1996 A821 2.70p multicolored .90 .50

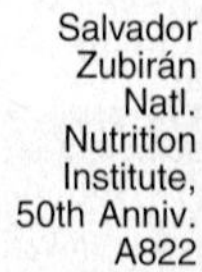

Salvador Zubirán Natl. Nutrition Institute, 50th Anniv. A822

1996, Oct. 12
1997 A822 1.80p multicolored .90 .35

Radio in Mexico, 75th Anniv. — A823

1996, Oct. 13
1998 A823 1.80p multicolored .90 .35

Paintings in Viceregal Gallery A824

Designs: a, 1.80p, Portrait of a Woman, by Baltasar de Echave Ibia. b, 2.70p, Archangel Michael, by Luis Juarez. c, 1.80p, Portrait of young Joaquín Manuel Fernández of Santa Cruz, by Nicolas Rodriguez Xuarez. d, 2.70p. The Virgin of the Apocalypse, by Miguel Cabrera. e, 1.80p, Portrait of Dona Maria Luisa Gonzaga Foncerrada y Labarrieta, by Jose Maria Vazquez.

1996, Oct. 14 ***Perf. 14***
1999 A824 Strip of 5, #a.-e. 4.75 4.75

World Food Day — A825

1996, Oct. 31 ***Perf. 13½***
2000 A825 2.70p multicolored .90 .50

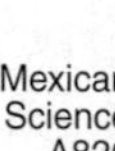

Mexican Science A826

1996, Sept. 2
2001 A826 1.80p multicolored .90 .35

Intl. Subway Conference A828

1996, Nov. 12 Litho. ***Perf. 13½***
2003 A828 2.70p multicolored .90 .50

Christmas A829

1p, Star pinata. 1.80p, Man carrying pinatas.

1996, Nov. 14 Litho. ***Perf. 13½***
2004 A829 1p multi .35 .25
2005 A829 1.80p multi .55 .30

Andres Henestrosa, Writer — A830

1996, Nov. 23 Litho. *Perf. 14*
2006 A830 1.80p multicolored .90 .30

Natl. Cancer Institute, 50th Anniv. A831

1996, Nov. 25 Litho. *Perf. 13½*
2007 A831 1.80p multicolored .90 .30

Paisano Program — A832

1996, Nov. 28 Litho. *Perf. 13½*
2008 A832 2.70p multicolored .90 .50

David Alfaro Siqueiros (1896-1974), Painter — A833

1996, Dec. 5 Litho. *Perf. 13½*
2009 A833 1.80p multicolored .90 .30

32nd Natl. Assembly of Surgeons A834

Dr. José Ma. Barceló de Villagrán

1996, Dec. 6 Litho. *Perf. 13½*
2010 A834 1.80p multicolored .90 .30

Wildlife Conservation — A835

1.80p, Black bear, cubs.

1996, Dec. 11 Litho. *Perf. 14*
2011 A835 1.80p multi 2.25 .75

UNICEF, 50th Anniv. A836

1996, Dec. 11 Litho. *Perf. 13½*
2012 A836 1.80p multicolored .90 .30

Palafoxiana Library, Puebla, 350th Anniv. — A837

1996, Dec. 17 Litho. *Perf. 13½*
2013 A837 1.80p multicolored .90 .30

Natl. Institute of Nuclear Research A838

1996, Dec. 19 Litho. *Perf. 13½*
2014 A838 1.80p multicolored .90 .30

A839

1996, Dec. 19 Litho. *Perf. 13½*
2015 A839 1.80p multicolored .90 .30

Intl. Day for Preservation of the Ozone Layer.

A840

1996, Dec. 20 Litho. *Perf. 13½*
2016 A840 1.80p multicolored .90 .30

30 year career of plastic arts sculptor Sebastian.

Mexican Diplomats A841

Design: Isidro Fabela (b. 1882), lawyer, and Genaro Estrada (1887-1977), journalist, politician.

1996, Oct. 24 Litho. *Perf. 13½*
2017 A841 1.80p multicolored .90 .30

Carlos Pellicer (1897-1977), Poet, Museum Founder — A842

1997, Jan. 16
2018 A842 2.30p multicolored 1.00 .40

Andres Eloy Blanco (1896-1955), Poet — A843

1997, Feb. 6 Litho. *Perf. 13½*
2019 A843 3.40p multicolored 1.40 .60

A844

1997, Feb. 10
2020 A844 3.40p multicolored 1.40 .60

UNESCO Intl. Summit on Education, Confederation of American Educators.

A845

1997, Feb. 14
2021 A845 3.40p multicolored 1.40 .60

Treaty of Tlatelolco prohibiting nuclear weapons in Latin America & Caribbean.

Souvenir Sheet

Mexican Central Post Office, 90th Anniv. — A846

1997, Feb. 20
2022 A846 7.40p multicolored 6.00 6.00

A847

Generals: No. 2023, Francisco L. Urquizo. No. 2024, Mariano Escobedo. No. 2025, Jacinto B. Trevino Gonzalez. No. 2026, Felipe Angeles. No. 2027, Candido Aguilar Vargas. No. 2028, Joaquin Amaro Dominguez.

1997, Mar. 5
2023 A847 2.30p multicolored .90 .40
2024 A847 2.30p multicolored .90 .40
2025 A847 2.30p multicolored .90 .40
2026 A847 2.30p multicolored .90 .40
2027 A847 2.30p multicolored .90 .40
2028 A847 2.30p multicolored .90 .40
Nos. 2023-2028 (6) 5.40 2.40

Intl. Women's Day — A848

1997, Mar. 8
2029 A848 2.30p multicolored .80 .40

1st Intl. Congress for Spanish Language A849

Painting: Allegory, "La Gramatica," by Juan Correa.

1997, Apr. 7 Litho. *Perf. 13½*
2030 A849 3.40p multicolored .90 .40

Dr. Ignacio Chávez, Pres. of Natl. Academy of Medicine, Birth Cent. A850

1997, Apr. 23
2031 A850 2.30p multicolored .80 .40

Mexican Constitution, 80th Anniv. — A851

2.30p, Venustiano Carranza.

1997, Apr. 29
2032 A851 2.30p multi .80 .40

First Edition of "Al Filo Del Agua," by Agustín Yáñez, 50th Anniv. A852

1997, May 9
2033 A852 2.30p multicolored .80 .40

Prof. Rafael Ramírez (1855-1959), Educator — A853

1997, May 15
2034 A853 2.30p green & gray .80 .40

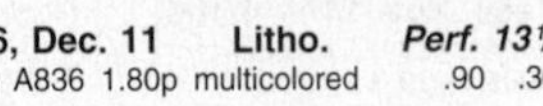

Japanese Emigration to Mexico, Cent. A854

1997, May 12

2035 A854 3.40p multicolored 1.75 .60

See Japan No. 2569.

A855

1997, May 31

2036 A855 2.30p multicolored .80 .40

Autonomous University of Baja California, 40th Anniv.

A856

Intl. Day to Stop Use of Illegal Drugs: a, 2.30p, Dove, clouds, sunlight. b, 3.40p, Man with one hand on bars, one hand raised toward sky. c, 3.40p, Dove in window behind bars.

1997, June 26

2037 A856 Strip of 3, #a.-c. + label 5.50 5.50

Sigmund Freud — A857

1997, June 28

2038 A857 2.30p multicolored .80 .40

Naval Military School, Cent. — A858

1997, July 1

2039 A858 2.30p multicolored .80 .40

Natl. Bank of Foreign Commerce, 60th Anniv. A859

1997, July 4 Litho. *Perf. 13½*

2040 A859 3.40p multicolored 1.25 .60

United for Conservation — A860

1997, July 16

2041 A860 2.30p Vaquita, calf 2.00 .90

Mexican College of Aviation Pilots, 50th Anniv. A861

1997, July 17

2042 A861 2.30p multicolored .90 .40

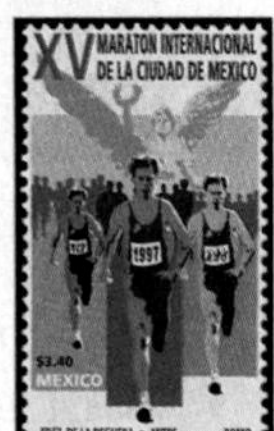

15th Mexico City Marathon — A862

1997, Aug. 6

2043 A862 3.40p multicolored 1.25 .60

Juarez Hospital of Mexico, 150th Anniv. A863

1997, Aug. 18

2044 A863 2.30p multicolored .90 .40

Battles of 1847 A864

No. 2045, Battle of Padierna. No. 2046, Battle of Churubusco. No. 2047, Battle of Molino del Rey. No. 2047A, Defense of the Castle of Chapultepec.

1997

2045	A864 2.30p multicolored	.90	.40
2046	A864 2.30p multicolored	.90	.40
2047	A864 2.30p multicolored	.90	.40
2047A	A864 2.30p multicolored	.90	.40
	Nos. 2045-2047A (4)	3.60	1.60

Issued: No. 2045, 8/19; No. 2046, 8/20; No. 2047, 9/8; No. 2047A, 9/13.

A865

1997, Sept. 3

2048 A865 2.30p multicolored .90 .40

Guillermo Prieto, poet, death cent.

A866

1997, Sept. 12 Litho. *Perf. 13½*

2049 A866 3.40p multicolored 1.25 .60

Battalion of St. Patrick, 150th anniv. See Ireland No. 1085.

A867

1997, Oct. 6

2050 A867 2.30p multicolored .90 .40

Reproductive health for adolescents month.

Stamp Day — A868

1997, Oct. 9

2051 A868 3.40p multi 1.25 .60

Heinrich von Stephan (1831-97) A869

1997, Oct. 9

2052 A869 3.40p multicolored 1.25 .60

Manuel Gómez Morin (1897-1949), Politician — A870

1997, Oct. 14

2053 A870 2.30p multicolored .90 .40

Dr. Manuel Gea González General Hospital, 50th Anniv. A871

1997, Oct. 14

2054 A871 2.30p multicolored .90 .40

Mexican Bar Assoc. College of Law, 75th Anniv. — A872

1997, Oct. 30

2055 A872 2.30p multicolored .90 .40

Christmas A873

Children with piñatas: No. 2056, By Ana R. Botello. No. 2057, By Adrián Laris.

1997, Nov. 19

2056 A873 2.30p multicolored .90 .40

2057 A873 2.30p multicolored .90 .40

New Law on Social Security — A874

1997, Dec. 10

2058 A874 2.30p multicolored .90 .40

Central University Hospital, Chihuahua, Cent. — A875

1997, Dec. 5 Litho. *Perf. 13½*

2059 A875 2.30p multicolored .90 .40

Dr. Mario Jose Molina Henriquez, 1995 Nobel Prize Recipient in Chemistry A876

1997, Dec. 8

2060 A876 3.40p multicolored 1.25 .55

Baking Industry Granary, 50th Anniv. A877

Baked goods and: a, Storage shelves. b, Man working at oven. c, Basic ingredients, man working with dough.

1997, Dec. 10
2061 A877 2.30p Vert. strip of 3, #a.-c. + label 4.00 4.00

A878

Modern Mexican art, by Jose Chavez Morado.

1997, Dec. 19
2062 A878 2.30p multicolored .90 .40

Cervantes Festival, Guanajuato, 45th anniv.

City of Loreto, 300th Anniv. — A879

1997, Dec. 20
2063 A879 2.30p multicolored .90 .40

Military School of Arms, 50th Anniv. A880

1998, Mar. 1 **Litho.** ***Perf. 13½***
2064 A880 2.30p multicolored .90 .40

Intl. Mother's Day A881

1998, Mar. 8
2065 A881 2.30p multicolored .90 .40

Cinco de Mayo — A882

1998, Apr. 16
2066 A882 3.50p multicolored 1.25 .60

See US No. 3203.

1998 World Cup Soccer Championships, France — A883

Eiffel Tower, national colors of France and Mexico and: No. 2067, Soccer player. No. 2068, Mexican Eagle mascot.

No. 2069: a, 8.60p, like #2067. b, 6.20p, like #2068.

1998
2067 A883 2.30p multicolored 1.50 1.50
2068 A883 2.30p multicolored 1.50 1.50

Souvenir Sheet

2069 A883 Sheet of 2, #a.-b. 8.00 8.00

Issued: No. 2067, 4/20; No. 2068, 5/11; No. 2069, 5/25. No. 2069 contains two 24x40mm stamps with a continuous design.

Justo Sierra, Educator, 150th Birth Anniv. — A884

1998, Apr. 23
2070 A884 2.30p multicolored .90 .40

Dr. Salvador Zubiran, Birth Cent. A885

1998, Apr. 24
2071 A885 2.30p multicolored .90 .40

Organization of American States, 50th Anniv. — A886

1998, Apr. 27
2072 A886 3.40p multicolored 1.00 .55

University of Puebla, 25th Anniv. A887

1998, May 6
2073 A887 2.30p multicolored .90 .40

Teacher's Day — A888

2.30p, Soledad Anaya Solorzano.

1998, May 15
2074 A888 2.30p multi .90 .40

State of Tamaulipas (New Santander), 250th Anniv. — A889

1998, May 31
2075 A889 2.30p multicolored .90 .40

Sports Lottery, 20th Anniv. A890

1998, June 2
2076 A890 2.30p multicolored .90 .40

Universal Declaration of Human Rights, 50th Anniv. A891

1998, June 5 **Litho.** ***Perf. 13½***
2077 A891 3.40p multicolored 1.00 .35

Federico García Lorca (1898-1936), Poet — A892

1998, June 5
2078 A892 3.40p multicolored 1.00 .35

Philippine Independence, Cent. — A893

3.40p, Mexican flag, sailing ship. 7.40p, Mexican, Philippine flags, sailing ship.

1998, June 3 **Litho.** ***Perf. 13½***
2079 A893 3.40p multicolored 1.00 .55

Souvenir Sheet

2080 A893 7.40p multicolored 4.75 4.75

See Philippines Nos. 2537-2539, Spain No. 2949.

Intl. Day Against Drugs — A894

1998, June 26
2081 A894 2.30p multicolored .90 .35

Chapultepec Zoological Park, 7th Anniv. — A895

Design: Alfonso L. Herrera, jaguar.

1998, July 6
2082 A895 2.30p multicolored .90 .35

Arbor Day — A896

1998, July 9
2083 A896 2.30p multicolored .90 .35

Opening of the Philatelic Museum, Oaxaca — A897

Designs: No. 2084, Convent of St. Peter and St. Paul, Teposcolula. No. 2085, Burnished vase with carving. No. 2086, San Bartolo Coyotepec, "El Camino," by Francisco Toledo. No. 2087, Golden breast plate from Tomb 7, Monte Alban.

1998, July 9
2084 A897 2.30p multicolored .90 .35
2085 A897 2.30p multicolored .90 .35
2086 A897 3.40p multicolored 1.75 .75
2087 A897 3.40p multicolored 1.75 .75
Nos. 2084-2087 (4) 5.30 2.20

Precinct in Natl. Palace Honoring Benito Juárez (1806-72) A898

1998, July 18 ***Perf. 14***
2088 A898 2.30p multicolored .90 .35

Santo Domingo Cultural Center, Oaxaca — A899

a, Entire complex. b, Portals of museum. c, Francisco da Burgoa Library. d, Ethnobotanical Garden.

1998, July 24 ***Perf. 13½***
2089 A899 2.30p Block of 4, #a.-d. 4.25 4.25

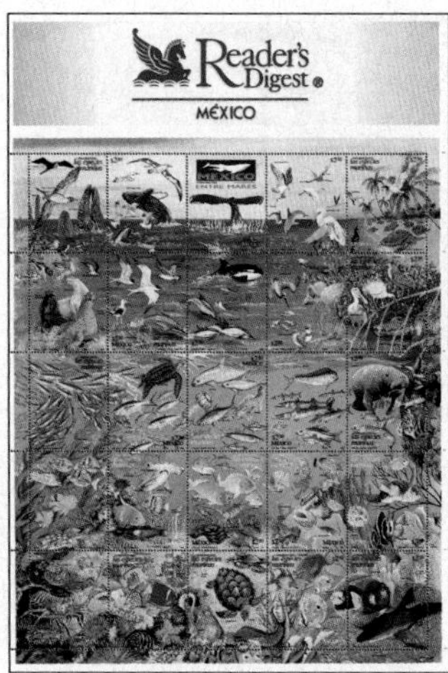

Marine Life — A900

a, Frigatebird, gray whale. b, Albatross. c, Whale's tail flukes. d, Dolphins, flamingos. e, Turtles. f, Sea lions. g, Elegant swallows, dolphin. h, Killer whale. i, Flamingos. j, Alligator. k, Sardines. l, Squid, loggerhead turtle. m, Bluefin tuna, jellyfish. n, Barracudas. o, Manatee. p, Garibaldi. q, Hammerhead shark. r, Huachinango, shrimp, ray. s, Octopus, mero. t, Blowfish, turtle. u, Crab, sandollars. v, Seahorse, angelfish. w, Crab, turtle, moray eel. x, Mariposa de cuatro ojos. y, Shark, coral.

1998, Aug. 14 **Sheet of 25**
2090 A900 2.30p #a.-y. 25.00 25.00

No. 2090 is a continuous design showing many different species of marine life, aquatic birds, and surrounding vegetation. Just a few species from each stamp are described in the above design note.

16th Mexico City Marathon A901

1998, Aug. 19 **Litho.** ***Perf. 13½***
2091 A901 3.40p multicolored 1.00 .55

World Tourism Day A902

1998, Sept. 25
2092 A902 3.40p multicolored 1.00 .55

Natl. Archives, 175th Anniv. A903

1998, Sept. 29 ***Perf. 14***
2093 A903 2.30p multicolored .90 .35

Interpol, 75th Anniv. — A904

1998, Oct. 1 ***Perf. 13½***
2094 A904 3.40p multicolored 1.00 .55

Reproductive Health Month — A905

1998, Oct. 5
2095 A905 2.30p multicolored .60 .35

Luis Nishizawa (b. 1918), Painter — A906

1998, Oct. 9
2096 A906 2.30p multicolored .60 .35

World Post Day A907

1998, Oct. 9
2097 A907 3.40p multicolored 1.00 .55

Heroic Military College, 175th Anniv. A908

1998, Oct. 11
2098 A908 2.30p multicolored .60 .35

District of Tamaulipas, 250th Anniv. A909

1998, Oct. 12
2099 A909 2.30p multicolored .60 .35

United for Conservation — A910

1998, Oct. 13
2100 A910 2.30p Aguila real .60 .35

World Food Day A911

1998, Oct. 16
2101 A911 3.40p multicolored 1.00 .55

Natl. Mexican Migration Week A912

1998, Oct. 19
2102 A912 2.30p multicolored .60 .35

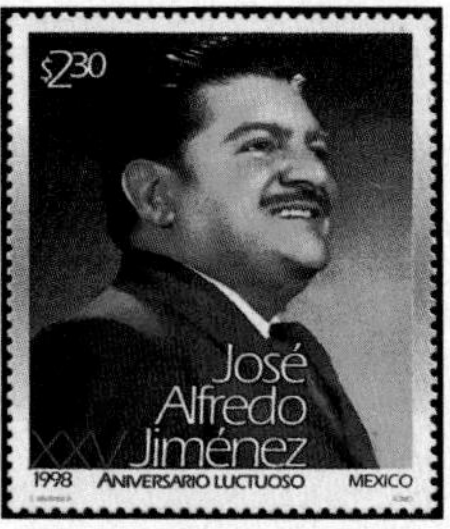

José Alfredo Jiménez (1926-72), Composer A913

1998, Nov. 11
2103 A913 2.30p multicolored .60 .35

College of Petroleum Engineers, 25th Anniv. — A914

1998, Nov. 11
2104 A914 3.40p multicolored 1.00 .55

Cultural and Economic Cooperation Between Mexico and France — A915

1998, Nov. 12
2105 A915 3.40p multicolored 1.00 .55

City of Colima, 475th Anniv. A916

1998, Nov. 16
2106 A916 2.30p multicolored .60 .35

Christmas A917

Children's drawings: 2.30p, Nativity scene. 3.40p, Pinata, candy, vert.

1998, Nov. 17 **Self-Adhesive**
2107 A917 2.30p multicolored .60 .35
2108 A917 3.40p multicolored 1.00 .55

Latin American Civil Aviation Commission, 25th Anniv. — A918

1998, Dec. 14 **Litho.** ***Perf. 13½***
2109 A918 3.40p multicolored 1.00 .55

Natl. Institute of Native People, 50th Anniv. A919

1998, Dec. 4
2110 A919 2.30p multicolored .60 .35

Federation of Govt. Workers, 60th Anniv. A920

1998, Dec. 7
2111 A920 2.30p multicolored .60 .35

State University of Sinaloa, 125th Anniv. — A921

1998, Dec. 18
2112 A921 2.30p multicolored .60 .35

Mexico's Natl. Program for Women A922

1999, Mar. 8 **Litho.** ***Perf. 13½***
2113 A922 4.20p multicolored 1.25 .45

A923

1999, Feb. 9
2114 A923 3p multicolored .90 .35

Carnaval '99, Veracruz.

A924

1999, Feb. 27

2115	3p Hammock	.65	.35
2116	4.20p Divers	.90	.45
a.	A924 Pair, #2115-2116	4.00	4.00

Acapulco, 200th Anniv.

Launching of SATMEX 5 — A925

1999, Feb. 9

2117 A925 3p multicolored .90 .35

Souvenir Sheet

Visit of Pope John Paul II — A926

1999, Jan. 22

2118 A926 10p multicolored 5.00 5.00

Tourism Type of 1993

Denomination Shown As $

Nos. 2119, 2122, 2126, 2136, Coahuila. Nos. 2120, 2123, Yucatan. Nos. 2121, 2139, 2139A, 2141A, Chiapas. No. 2124, Colima. Nos. 2125, 2131, 2134, 2141B, Michoacan, vert. No. 2127, Guanajuato. Nos. 2128, 2137, 2140, Zacatecas, vert. No. 2129, Mexico. No. 2130, Sonora. Nos. 2132, 2135, 2141C-2141D, Queretaro. Nos. 2133, 2138, Sinaloa. No. 2141, Campeche.

Unwmk.

1999-2001 Photo. *Perf. 14*

2119	A683	50c	multi	.75	.25
2120	A683	70c	multi	.75	.25
2121	A683	1.50p	multi	1.00	.25
2122	A683	2p	multi	1.00	.25
2123	A683	2.50p	multi	1.25	.25
2124	A683	2.60p	multi	2.00	.30
2125	A683	3p	multi	1.75	.30
2126	A683	3.60p	multi	1.75	.40
2127	A683	4.20p	multi	1.75	.45
2128	A683	4.20p	multi	3.00	.45
2129	A683	4.50p	multi	3.00	.50
2130	A683	4.90p	multi	3.00	.50
2131	A683	5.30p	multi	3.75	.55
2132	A683	5.90p	multi	3.50	.55
2133	A683	6p	multi	3.50	.70
2134	A683	6p	multi	4.00	.70
2135	A683	6.50p	multi	4.50	.70
2136	A683	7p	multi	4.50	.75
2137	A683	8p	multi	9.00	.85
2138	A683	8p	multi	4.75	.85
2139	A683	8.50p	multi	4.75	.90
2139A	A683	8.50p	denom. upright	5.50	1.10
2140	A683	8.50p	multi	4.75	.95
2141	A683	10p	multi	18.00	1.10
2141A	A683	10p	multi	7.50	1.10
2141B	A683	10.50p	multi	7.00	1.10
2141C	A683	11.50p	multi	8.50	1.25
2141D	A683	30p	multi	19.00	3.25
	Nos. 2119-2141D (28)			133.50	20.55

Issued: Nos. 2122, 2124, 2126, 2127, 2130-2133, 2137, 1999; No. 2120, 2000; Nos. 2119, 2121, 2123, 2125, 2128, 2129, 2134-2136, 2138-2141D, 2001.

The denomination of No. 2139 is in italics.

Natl. Commission to Distribute Free Textbooks, 40th Anniv. — A927

1999, Mar. 11 Litho. *Perf. 13½*

2142 A927 3p gold & multi 1.00 .35

See Nos. 2155-2156, 2172.

Natl. Population Commission, 25th Anniv. — A928

1999, Mar. 26

2143 A928 3p multicolored 1.00 .35

Souvenir Sheet

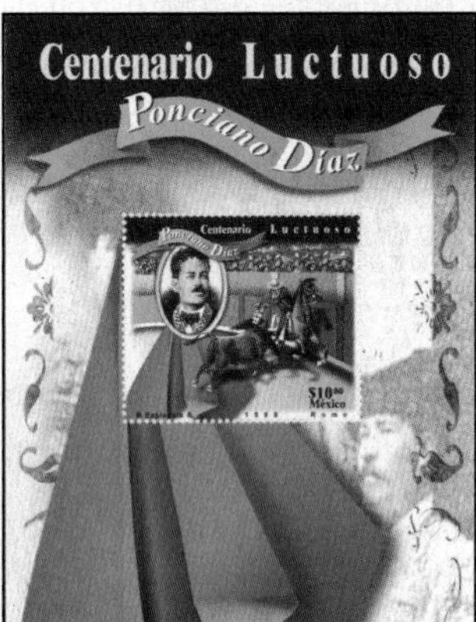

Ponciano Díaz Salinas (1856-99), Bullfighter — A929

Sheet Size: 95x240mm

1999, Apr. 17

2144 A929 10p sheet of 1 5.00 5.00

Ceniceros de Pérez (1908-68), Teacher A930

1999, May 15

2145 A930 3p multicolored .90 .35

Teacher's Day.

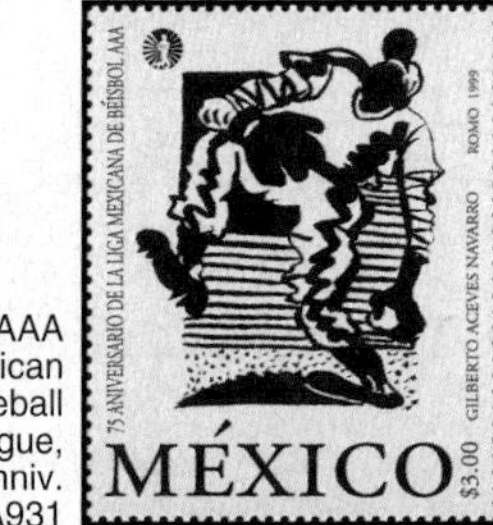

AAA Mexican Baseball League, 75th Anniv. A931

Designs: a, Skeleton pitcher, skeleton batter. b, Stylized pitcher. c, Pitcher lifting up large foot, sun. d, Catcher.

1999, May 31

2146 A931 3p Block of 4, #a.-d. 5.00 5.00

Also available in strip of 4 + label.

National Bank of Mexico, 115th Anniv. — A932

Designs: No. 2147, Old, new bank buildings. No. 2148, 10p bill.

1999, June 2

2147 A932 3p multicolored .90 .35
2148 A932 3p multicolored .90 .35

World Dog Show — A933

a, 4.20p, Chihuahua. b, 4.20p, Xoloitzcuintle. c, 3p, German shepherd. d, 3p, Rottweiler.

1999, June 2

2149 A933 Sheet of 4, #a.-d. 7.50 7.50

A934

Perf. 13¼x13½

1999, June 25 Litho.

2150 A934 4.20p multicolored 1.25 .45

Intl. Day Against Illegal Drugs.

National Bank, 65th Anniv. — A935

1999, July 2 Litho. *Perf. 13¼x13½*

2151 A935 3p multicolored .90 .35

Arbor Day A936

1999, July 26 *Perf. 13½x13¼*

2152 A936 3p multicolored .90 .35

Civil Register, 140th Anniv. A937

1999, July 27

2153 A937 3p multicolored .90 .35

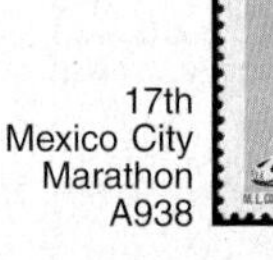

17th Mexico City Marathon A938

1999, Aug. 11

2154 A938 4.20p multicolored 1.75 .45

Free Textbook Type of 1999

Designs: No. 2155, Children, book, flag, cacti. No. 2156, "Tsuni tsame."

1999 Litho. *Perf. 13¼x13½*

2155 A927 3p green & multi .90 .35
2156 A927 3p orange & multi .90 .35

Issued: No. 2155, 8/23; No. 2156, 10/28.

Self-portrait, by Rufino Tamayo (1899-1991) — A939

1999, Aug. 28 *Perf. 13¼x13½*

2157 A939 3p multicolored .90 .35

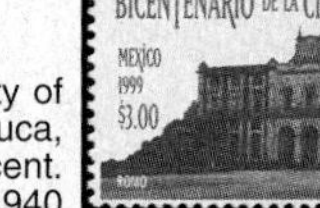

City of Toluca, Bicent. A940

1999, Sept. 12 *Perf. 13½x13¼*

2158 A940 3p copper & brown .90 .35

State of Mexico, 175th Anniv. A941

1999, Sept. 14

2159 A941 3p multicolored 1.00 .35

Union of Latin American Universities, 50th Anniv. — A942

1999, Sept. 22 *Perf. 13¼x13½*

2160 A942 4.20p multicolored 1.25 .45

Institute of Security & Social Services of State Workers, 40th Anniv. A943

1999, Oct. 1 *Perf. 13½x13¼*

2161 A943 3p multicolored 1.00 .35

State of Baja California Sur, 25th Anniv. A944

1999, Oct. 4

2162 A944 3p multicolored 1.00 .35

Family Planning, 25th Anniv. A945

1999, Oct. 4

2163 A945 3p multicolored 1.00 .35

Nature Conservation — A946

1999, Oct. 5
2164 A946 3p Harpy eagle 1.00 .35

State of Quintana Roo, 25th Anniv. — A947

1999, Oct. 8 Litho. *Perf. 13¼x13½*
2165 A947 3p multicolored 1.00 .35

UPU, 125th Anniv. — A948

1999, Oct. 9
2166 A948 4.20p multicolored 1.50 .45

World Post Day — A949

1999, Oct. 9
2167 A949 4.20p multicolored 1.50 .45

12th General Assembly of the Int'l Council on Monuments and Sites A950

1999, Oct. 17 *Perf. 13½x13¼*
2168 A950 4.20p multicolored 1.50 .45

Carlos Chavez (1899-1978) & Silvestre Revueltas (1899-1940), Composers — A951

1999, Oct. 21
2169 A951 3p multicolored 1.00 .35

Autonomous Metropolitan University, 25th Anniv. — A952

1999, Oct. 25 *Perf. 13¼x13½*
2170 A952 3p multicolored 1.00 .35

State of Guerrero, 150th Anniv. A953

1999, Oct. 27 Litho. *Perf. 13½x13¼*
2171 A953 3p multicolored 1.00 .35

Free Textbook Type of 1999

Design: "Ciencias Naturales."

Perf. 13¼x13½

1999, Nov. 12 Litho.
2172 A927 3p multi 1.00 .35

Christmas
A954 A955

1999, Nov. 29
2173 A954 3p multi 1.00 .35
2174 A955 4.20p multi 1.75 .45

Natl. Commission of Professional Education, 20th Anniv. — A956

1999, Dec. 1 *Perf. 13½x 13¼*
2175 A956 3p multi 1.00 .35

Scientific Voyage of Alexander von Humboldt to Americas, Bicent. A957

1999, Dec. 1
2176 A957 3p multi 1.00 .35

The 20th Century A958

Education: a, 3p, Natl. Autonomous University of Mexico. b, 3p, Justo Sierra, José Vasconcelos. c, 3p, Natl. Poytechnic Institute. d, 3p, Free text books. e, 4.20p, Reading programs.

Litho. & Embossed

1999, Dec. 15 *Perf. 14x14½*
2177 A958 Sheet of 5, #a.-e. 10.00 10.00

Nos. 2177c-2177d are 79x25mm, No. 2177e is oval-shaped and 39x49mm.
See Nos. 2180-2181, 2191-2196.

2000 Census — A959

2000, Jan. 24 Litho. *Perf. 13¼x13½*
2178 A959 3p multi 1.00 .35

International Women's Day — A960

2000, Mar. 8 Litho. *Perf. 13¼x13½*
2179 A960 4.20p multi 1.50 .45

The 20th Century Type of 1999

Building Democracy — No. 2180: a, 3p, Mexican presidents from Porfirio Díaz to Lázaro Cárdenas, Mexican Constitution. b, 3p, Pancho Villa, Emiliano Zapata. c, 3p, Mexican presidents from Manuel Avila Camacho to Gustavo Díaz Ordaz. d, 3p, Political figures, protestors, newspaper boy. e, 4.20p, Voter registration card, child at ballot box.
10p, People writing and at computers.

Litho. & Embossed

2000, Mar. 16 *Perf. 14x14½*
2180 A958 Sheet of 5, #a-e 10.00 10.00

Souvenir Sheet

Litho.

Perf. 13½

2181 A958 10p multi 7.50 7.50

Nos. 2180a and 2180b are 79x25mm, and No. 2180e is oval-shaped and 39x49mm.

Natl. Assoc. of Universities and Institutions of Higher Learning, 50th Anniv. A961

Perf. 13½x13¼

2000, Mar. 24 Litho.
2182 A961 3p multi 1.00 .35

25th Mexican Travel Trade Show, Acapulco A962

2000, Apr. 9
2183 A962 4.20p multi 1.50 .45

Discovery of Brazil, 500th Anniv. A963

2000, Apr. 22
2184 A963 4.20p multi 1.50 .45

Teacher's Day — A964

3p, Luis Alvarez Barret.

2000, May 15 *Perf. 13¼x13½*
2185 A964 3p multi 1.00 .35

Stampin' the Future Children's Stamp Design Contest Winners A965

Art by: 3p, Alejandro Guerra Millán. 4.20p, Carlos Hernández García.

2000, May 17 *Perf. 13½x13¼*
2186 A965 3p multi 1.00 .35
2187 A965 4.20p multi 1.50 .45

Fourth Meeting of Telecommunications Ministers and Information Industry Leaders — A966

2000, May 24
2188 A966 4.20p multi 1.50 .45

Intl. Day Against Illegal Drugs — A967

Perf. 13¼x13½

2000, June 26 Litho.
2189 A967 4.20p multi 1.50 .45

National Worker's Housing Fund Institute — A968

No. 2190, Sculptures: a, 3p, Pre-Hispanic building. b, 3p, Pre-Hispanic building with stairway. c, 10p, Pre-Hispanic natives in circle.

2000, June 27 ***Perf. 14¼x13½***
2190 A968 Sheet of 3, #a-c 7.00 7.00

The 20th Century Type of 1999

Cultural Idenity and Diversity — No. 2191: a, Xóchitl Incuícatl. b, Corre y se va. c, Tercera llamada. . . Cácado! d, Al Hablar como al guisar, su granito de sal. e, Children.

Health — No. 2192: a, Six men, certificate, man in tuberculosis prevention truck. b, Children on line. c, Nine men, posters. d, Poster showing tractor, health care. e, Modern medical equipment.

Art — No. 2193: a, El sello de la casa. b, Espíritu del siglo. c, La luz de México. d, Los nostros en que nos reconocemos. e, Building dome, artists and artwork.

Photography — No. 2194: a, Colchón enrollado, by Manuel Alvarez Bravo. b, Roses, by Tina Modotti. c, Four vertical photos, four horizontal photos. d, Two vertical photos, six horizontal photos. e, Three photos.

Commercial Development and Industrialization — No. 2195: a, Tractor. b, Truck cab. c, Store. d, Automobile. e, Globe.

Communications — No. 2196: a, Telephones and telegraph. b, Roads and bridges. c, Postal services. d, Railroads. e, Satellite, satellite dish, train.

Litho. & Embossed

2000 ***Perf. 14x14¼***

2191	Sheet of 5	10.00	10.00
a.-d.	A958 3p Any single	1.00	.30
e.	A958 4.20p multicolored	1.50	.45
2192	Sheet of 5	10.00	10.00
a.-d.	A958 3p Any single	1.00	.30
e.	A958 4.20p multicolored	1.50	.45
2193	Sheet of 5	10.00	10.00
a.-d.	A958 3p Any single	1.00	.30
e.	A958 4.20p multicolored	1.50	.45
2194	Sheet of 5	10.00	10.00
a.-d.	A958 3p Any single	1.00	.30
e.	A958 4.20p multicolored	1.50	.45
2195	Sheet of 5	10.00	10.00
a.-d.	A958 3p Any single	1.00	.30
e.	A958 4.20p multicolored	1.50	.45
2196	Sheet of 5	10.00	10.00
a.-d.	A958 3p Any single	1.00	.30
e.	A958 4.20p multicolored	1.50	.45
	Nos. 2191-2196 (6)	60.00	60.00

Issued: No. 2191, 7/18; No. 2192, 10/24; No. 2193, 11/10; No. 2194, 12/9; No. 2195, 12/20; No. 2196, 12/21.

Nos. 2191c-2196c, 2191d-2196d are 79x25mm and Nos. 2191e-2196e are oval shaped and 39x49mm.

Natl. Program for Development of Handicapped People, 5th Anniv. — A969

2000, Aug. 2 **Litho.** ***Perf. 13¼x13½***
2197 A969 3p multi 1.00 .35

Latin American Integration Association, 20th Anniv. — A970

2000, Aug. 11 ***Perf. 13½x13¼***
2198 A970 4.20p multi 1.50 .45

Restoration of the Senate, 125th Anniv. — A971

2000, Aug. 17 ***Perf. 13¼x13½***
2199 A971 3p multi 1.00 .35

Souvenir Sheet

Expo 2000, Hanover — A972

a, 1p, Mexican soul. b, 1p, Natl. mosaic. c, 1.80p, Future construction. d, 1.80p, Plaza pyramid. e, 2p, Creation of towns. f, 2p, Millennial construction. g, 3p, Naturea. h, 3p, Humanity. i, 3p, Technology. j, 3.60p, Expo 2000, Hanover. k, 4.20p, Emblem.

Litho. & Embossed

2000, Aug. 20 ***Perf. 14½x14***
2200 A972 Sheet of 11, #a-k 12.50 12.50

No. 2200k is oval shaped and 39x49mm.

Bank of Mexico, 75th Anniv. — A973

2000, Aug. 23 **Litho.** ***Perf.***
2201 A973 10p multi 5.00 5.00

Stamp is oval-shaped and 49x39mm.

18th Mexico City Marathon A974

2000, Aug. 24 ***Perf. 13½x13¼***
2202 A974 4.20p multi 1.50 .45

2000 Summer Olympics, Sydney A975

2000, Sept. 15
2203 A975 4.20p multi 1.50 .45

Paisano Program A976

2000, Sept. 21
2204 A976 4.20p multi 1.50 .45

2nd Intl. Memory of the World Conference A977

2000, Sept. 12
2205 A977 4.20p multi 1.50 .45

Women's Reproductive Health Month — A978

2000, Oct. 5 ***Perf. 13¼x13½***
2206 A978 3p multi 1.00 .35

Ciudad Victoria, 250th Anniv. A979

2000, Oct. 6 ***Perf. 13½x13¼***
2207 A979 3p multi 1.00 .35

World Post Day — A980

2000, Oct. 9 ***Perf. 13¼x13½***
2208 A980 4.20p multi 1.50 .45

Natl. Human Rights Commission, 10th Anniv. — A981

2000, Oct. 23 ***Perf. 13½x13¼***
2209 A981 3p multi 1.00 .35

World Meteorological Organization, 50th Anniv. — A982

2000, Oct. 27
2210 A982 3p multi 1.00 .35

Intl. Diabetes Federation, 50th Anniv. A983

2000, Nov. 6
2211 A983 4.20p multi 1.50 .45

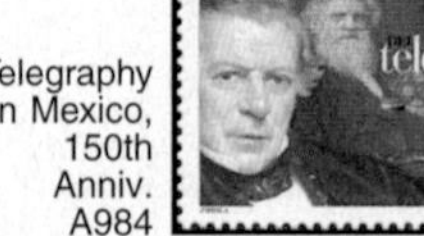

Telegraphy in Mexico, 150th Anniv. A984

2000, Nov. 11
2212 A984 3p multi 1.00 .35

Luis Buñuel (1900-83), Film Director A985

2000, Nov. 21
2213 A985 3p multi 1.00 .35

Electrical Research Institute, 25th Anniv. A986

2000, Nov. 25
2214 A986 3p multi 1.00 .35

Customs Administration, Cent. — A987

2000, Nov. 28
2215 A987 3p multi 1.00 .35

Christmas A988

2000, Nov. 29
2216 A988 3p shown 1.00 .35
2217 A988 4.20p Poinsettias 1.50 .45

Television in Mexico, 50th Anniv. A989

2000, Nov. 30
2218 A989 3p multi 1.00 .35

Souvenir Sheet

Postal Headquarters — A990

No. 2219: a, 3p, Adamo Boari (1863-1928), architect. b, 3p, Roofline. c, 3p, Gonzalo Garita y Frontera (1867-1922), engineer. d, 10p, Headquarters building.

Litho. & Embossed

2000, Nov. 30 ***Perf. 14¼x13½***
2219 A990 Sheet of 4, #a-d 9.00 9.00

Pre-Hispanic City of El Tajín — A991

Perf. 13½x13¼

2000, Dec. 14 **Litho.**

2220 A991 3p multi 1.00 .35

Nature Conservation — A992

2000, Dec. 15

2221 A992 3p Manatee 1.00 .35

Stamps inscribed 'Aquila Real / Unidos Para Conservacion' with white, yellow or gray backgrounds and 20c denominations have no postal validity.

Francisco Sarabia (1900-39), Aviator — A993

2000, Dec. 20 ***Perf. 13¼x13½***

2222 A993 3p multi 1.00 .35

Law Faculty of National Autonomous University of Mexico, 50th Anniv. A994

2001, Mar. 7 **Litho.** ***Perf. 13½x13¼***

2223 A994 3p multi 1.00 .30

Intl. Women's Day A995

2001, Mar. 8

2224 A995 4.20p multi 1.50 .45

National Cement Council, 53rd Anniv. A996

2001, Mar. 27

2225 A996 3p multi 1.00 .30

Teacher's Day A997

2001, May 15 ***Perf. 14***

2226 A997 3p José Vasconcelos 1.00 .30

World Refugee Day — A998

2001, June 20

2227 A998 4.20p multi 1.50 .45

Frida Kahlo (1907-54), Painter — A999

2001, June 21

2228 A999 4.20p multi 1.50 .45

Intl. Day Against Illegal Drugs — A1000

2001, June 26

2229 A1000 4.20p multi 1.50 .45

Mario de la Cueva, Educator, Cent. of Birth — A1001

2001, July 11 **Litho.** ***Perf. 14***

2230 A1001 3p multi 1.00 .30

Intl. Volunteers Year A1002

2001, July 25

2231 A1002 4.20p multi 1.50 .45

Souvenir Sheet

Rodolfo Morales (1925-2001), Painter — A1003

2001, Aug. 4 ***Perf. 14¼x13½***

2232 A1003 10p multi 4.50 4.50

Federal Fiscal and Administrative Justice Tribunal, 65th Anniv. — A1004

2001, Aug. 23 ***Perf. 14***

2233 A1004 3p multi 1.00 .30

University of Mexico, 450th Anniv. A1005

2001, Sept. 3

2234 A1005 3p multi 1.00 .30

Adela Formoso de Obregón Santcilia (1907-81), Woman's Rights Activist — A1006

2001, Sept. 6

2235 A1006 3p multi 1.00 .30

Daniel Cosío Villegas (1898-1976), Historian — A1007

2001, Sept. 6

2236 A1007 3p multi 1.00 .30

Mexican Pharmacies A1008

2001, Sept. 27 **Litho.** ***Perf. 14***

2237 A1008 3p multi 1.00 .30

Intl. Day of the Elderly A1009

2001, Oct. 1

2238 A1009 3p multi 1.00 .30

Year of Dialogue Among Civilizations — A1010

2001, Oct. 9

2239 A1010 3p multi 1.00 .30

World Post Day — A1011

2001, Oct. 9

2240 A1011 3p multi 1.00 .30

Women's Health Day — A1012

2001, Oct. 31

2241 A1012 3p multi 1.00 .30

Ophthalmology Institute, 25th Anniv. — A1013

2001, Nov. 23

2242 A1013 4.20p multi 1.50 .45

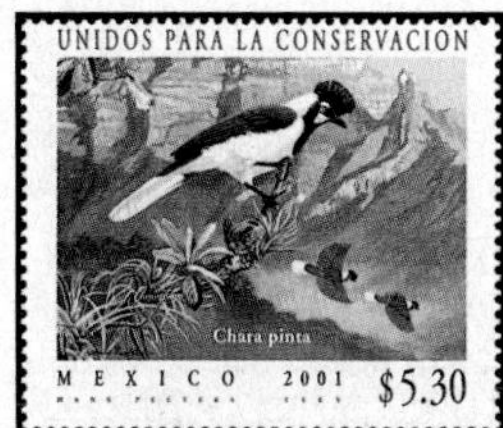

United for Conservation — A1014

2001, Nov. 26

2243 A1014 5.30p Chara pinta 2.50 .90

Christmas A1015

2001, Dec. 3

2244 A1015 3p shown 1.00 .30

2245 A1015 4.20p Candles 1.50 .45

Souvenir Sheet

Fund for Indigenous People's Health and Education — A1016

2001, Dec. 4 ***Perf. 13½x14¼***

2246 A1016 3p multi 1.50 1.50

Souvenir Sheet

National Scholarship Fund — A1017

2001, Dec. 4
2247 A1017 3p multi 1.50 1.50

Children's Protection — A1018

2001, Dec. 11 ***Perf. 14***
2248 A1018 3p multi 1.00 .30

World Food Day — A1019

2001, Dec. 17
2249 A1019 3p multi 1.00 .30

United For Conservation — A1020

2002, Jan. 24 Litho. *Perf. 14*
2250 A1020 6p Borrego cimarrón 2.50 .90

Manuel Alvarez Bravo, Photographer, Cent. of Birth — A1021

2002, Feb. 3
2251 A1021 6p gray & blk 2.25 .70

Mexico — People's Republic of China A1022

Designs: No. 2252, green panel at UL and brown panel at LL. No. 2252A, Like #2252, but with brown panel at UL, green panel at LL.

2002, Feb. 14 Litho. *Perf. 14*
2252 A1022 6p multi 2.00 .65
2252A A1022 6p multi 2.00 .65
b. Vert. pair, #2252-2252A 5.00 5.00

Conservation — A1023

Designs: 50c, Mangrove swamps. No. 2254, Rivers. No. 2255, Forests. 1.50p, No. 2267, Land mammals. No. 2257, Rain forests. No. 2258, Cacti. 4.50p, Birds. No. 2260, Sea turtles. No. 2261, Reptiles. No. 2262, Butterflies. No. 2263, Eagles. 7p, Reefs. 8.50p, 12p, Tropical forests. No. 2266, Marine mammals. No. 2268, Orchids. No. 2269, Cats. No. 2270, Oceans. No. 2271, Coastal birds. No. 2273, Deserts. No. 2274, Lakes and lagoons.

2002, Feb. 18 Litho. *Perf. 14*

2253	A1023	50c	multi	.25	.25
2254	A1023	1p	multi	.25	.25
2255	A1023	1p	multi	.35	.25
2256	A1023	1.50p	multi	.50	.25
2257	A1023	2p	multi	.70	.25
2258	A1023	2p	multi	.70	.25
2259	A1023	4.50p	multi	1.50	.50
2260	A1023	5p	multi	1.75	.55
2261	A1023	5p	multi	1.75	.55
2262	A1023	6p	multi	2.00	.65
2263	A1023	6p	multi	2.00	.65
2264	A1023	7p	multi	2.40	.75
2265	A1023	8.50p	multi	2.75	.95
2266	A1023	10p	multi	3.50	1.10
2267	A1023	10p	multi	3.50	1.10
2268	A1023	10.50p	multi	3.50	1.25
2269	A1023	10.50p	multi	3.50	1.25
2270	A1023	11.50p	multi	3.75	1.25
2271	A1023	11.50p	multi	3.75	1.25
2272	A1023	12p	multi	4.00	1.25
2273	A1023	30p	multi	10.00	3.25
2274	A1023	30p	multi	10.00	3.25
	Nos. 2253-2274 (22)			62.40	21.05

2003 ***Perf. 13x13¼***

2253a	A1023	50c	multi	.40	.25
2254a	A1023	1p	multi	1.10	.25
2255a	A1023	1p	multi	1.10	.25
2259a	A1023	4.50p	multi	3.50	.40
2260a	A1023	5p	multi	1.75	.45
2261a	A1023	5p	multi	1.75	.45
2262a	A1023	6p	multi	2.50	.55
2263a	A1023	6p	multi	2.00	.55
2264a	A1023	7p	multi	2.50	.65
2265a	A1023	8.50p	multi	3.75	.75
2266a	A1023	10p	multi	4.00	.90
2267a	A1023	10p	multi	4.25	.90
2268a	A1023	10.50p	multi	5.00	.95
2269a	A1023	10.50p	multi	4.25	.95
2270a	A1023	11.50p	multi	6.00	1.00
2271a	A1023	11.50p	multi	6.00	1.00
	Nos. 2253a-2271a (16)			49.85	10.25

See Nos. 2321-2330, 2362-2377, 2394-2436, 2452-2473.

2002 Winter Olympics, Salt Lake City A1024

2002, Feb. 20 Litho. *Perf. 14*
2275 A1024 8.50p multi 2.75 .95

Veracruz Port Modernization, Cent. — A1025

2002, Mar. 4
2276 A1025 6p multi 2.25 .70

Mexico — South Korea Diplomatic Relations, 40th Anniv. A1026

2002, Mar. 5
2277 A1026 8.50p multi 2.75 .95

Council for the Restoration of Historic Central Mexico City — A1027

2002, Mar. 7
2278 A1027 6p multi 2.25 .70

Natl. Women's Institute — A1028

2002, Mar. 8
2279 A1028 8.50p multi 2.75 .95

José Guadalupe Posada (1851-1913), Printmaker — A1029

2002, Mar. 18
2280 A1029 6p gold & black 2.25 .65

Justo Sierra Mendez (1848-1912), Writer — A1030

2002, May 15 Litho. *Perf. 14*
2281 A1030 6p multi 2.25 .65

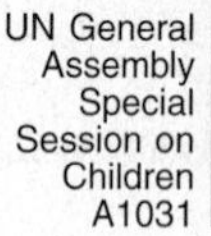

UN General Assembly Special Session on Children A1031

2002, May 27
2282 A1031 6p multi 2.25 .65

Discovery of the Tomb of Pakal, 50th Anniv. A1032

2002, June 14
2283 A1032 6p multi 2.25 .65

2002 World Cup Soccer Championships, Japan and Korea — A1033

2002, June 15
2284 A1033 8.50p multi 2.75 .85

Intl. Day Against Illegal Drugs — A1034

2002, June 26
2285 A1034 6p multi 2.25 .65

5th Mexico-Central American Summit — A1035

2002, June 27
2286 A1035 6p multi 2.25 .65

Intl. Year of Mountains A1036

2002, July 24 Litho. *Perf. 14*
2287 A1036 6p multi 2.25 .65

Intl. Day of Indigenous People A1037

2002, Aug. 9 ***Perf. 13x13¼***
2288 A1037 6p multi 2.25 .65

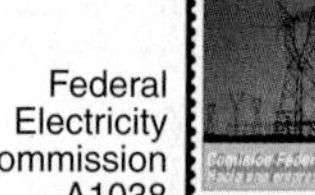

Federal Electricity Commission A1038

2002, Aug. 14 ***Perf. 14***
2289 A1038 6p multi 2.25 .65

Natl. Blood Donor Day — A1039

2002, Aug. 23 ***Perf. 13¼x13***
2290 A1039 6p multi 2.25 .65

Campaign Against Corruption A1040

2002, Sept. 12 Litho. *Perf. 13x13¼*
2291 A1040 6p multi 2.25 .60

Code of Ethics for Public Servants — A1041

2002, Sept. 12 ***Perf. 13¼x13***
2292 A1041 6p multi 2.25 .60

World Tourism Day A1042

2002, Sept. 27 ***Perf. 13x13¼***
2293 A1042 8.50p multi 2.75 .85

Natl. Organ Transplant and Donation Week — A1043

2002, Oct. 7 ***Perf. 13¼x13***
2294 A1043 6p multi 2.25 .60

World Post Day A1044

2002, Oct. 9 ***Perf. 13x13¼***
2295 A1044 8.50p multi 2.75 .85

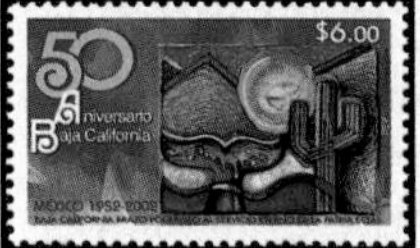
State of Baja California, 50th Anniv. A1045

2002, Nov. 1
2296 A1045 6p multi 2.25 .60

Luis Barragan (1902-88), Architect — A1046

2002, Nov. 7 ***Perf. 13¼x13***
2297 A1046 6p multi 2.25 .60

Renewal of Diplomatic Relations Between Mexico and Spain, 25th Anniv. A1047

2002, Nov. 19 ***Perf. 13x13¼***
2298 A1047 8.50p multi 2.75 .85

Mexico City Intl. Airport, 50th Anniv. — A1048

Details from mural "The Conquest of the Air by Man": a, Indian chief at left, Montgolfier balloon flight at right. b, Charles Lindbergh at left, parachutist at center. c, Wright Brothers at left, Mexico City at center.

2002, Nov. 19 ***Perf. 13¼x13***
2299 Horiz. strip of 3 7.50 7.50
a.-b. A1048 6p Either single 2.25 .60
c. A1048 8.50p multi 2.75 .85

Information Technology Development in Mexico, 75th Anniv. — A1049

2002, Nov. 21
2300 A1049 6p multi 1.75 .60

Anti-Violence Campaign — A1050

2002, Nov. 25 ***Perf. 13x13¼***
2301 A1050 8.50p multi 2.50 .85

Pan-American Health Organization, Cent. — A1051

2002, Dec. 2 ***Perf. 13¼x13***
2302 A1051 8.50p multi 1.75 .85

Acolmiztli Nezahualcóyotl (1402-72), Poet — A1052

2002, Dec. 10
2303 A1052 6p multi 1.75 .60

Christmas A1053

Children's art: 6p, Nativity, by Sara Elisa Miranda Alcaraz. 8.50p, Children with Nativity Scene, by Alejandro Ruíz Sampedro.

2002, Dec. 19 ***Perf. 13x13¼***
2304 A1053 6p multi 1.75 .60
2305 A1053 8.50p multi 2.50 .80

Powered Flight, Cent. A1054

2003, Mar. 6 Litho. ***Perf. 13x13¼***
2306 A1054 8.50p multi 2.50 .80

Iberoamerican University, 60th Anniv. — A1055

2003, Mar. 7 ***Perf. 13¼x13***
2307 A1055 6p multi 1.75 .55

Intl. Women's Day — A1056

2003, Mar. 8
2308 A1056 8.50p multi 2.50 .80

Mexicali, Cent. A1057

2003, Mar. 14 ***Perf. 13x13¼***
2309 A1057 6p multi 1.75 .55

Mexican Chamber of Industry and Construction, 50th Anniv. — A1058

2003, Mar. 26
2310 A1058 6p multi 1.75 .55

Federico Gomez Children's Hospital, 60th Anniv. A1059

2003, Apr. 30 Litho. ***Perf. 13x13¼***
2311 A1059 6p multi 1.75 .60

Miguel Hidalgo y Costilla (1753-1811), Independence Leader — A1060

2003, May 8 ***Perf. 13¼x13***
2312 A1060 6p multi 1.75 .60
a. Perf 14 *350.00 350.00*

Gregorio Torres Quintero (1866-1934), Educator — A1061

2003, May 15
2313 A1061 6p multi 1.75 .55
a. Perf. 14 *150.00* —

Natl. Astronomical Observatory, 125th Anniv. — A1062

2003, May 20 ***Perf. 13x13¼***
2314 A1062 6p multi 1.75 .55

World Day Against Tobacco — A1063

2003, May 30 ***Perf. 13¼x13***
2315 A1063 8.50p multi 2.50 .80

Inauguration of Satellite Internet Network — A1064

2003, June 5
2316 A1064 6p multi 1.75 .55

Intl. Day Against Illegal Drugs A1065

2003, June 26 Litho. ***Perf. 13x13¼***
2317 A1065 8.50p multi 2.50 .80

Mexican Baseball Hall of Fame, 30th Anniv. A1066

2003, July 21
2318 A1066 6p multi 1.75 .55

Xavier Villaurrutia (1903-51), Poet A1067

2003, July 24
2319 A1067 6p multi 1.75 .55

Veterinary Medicine Education in Mexico, 150th Anniv. A1068

2003, Aug. 16
2320 A1068 6p multi 1.75 .55

Conservation Type of 2002

Designs: 50c, Oceans. 1p, Reptiles. No. 2323, Land mammals. No. 2324, Rain forests. No. 2325, Coastal birds. 4.50p, Orchids. 6p, Rivers. 8.50p, Cacti. No. 2329, Lakes and lagoons. No. 2330, Sea turtles.

Perf. 13x13¼, 13½ (#2328)

2003-04 **Litho.**

2321	A1023	50c multi ('04)		.50	.25
2322	A1023	1p multi ('04)		.50	.25
2323	A1023	2.50p multi		1.25	.25
2324	A1023	2.50p multi		1.25	.25
2325	A1023	2.50p multi ('04)		1.25	.25
2326	A1023	4.50p multi ('04)		2.00	.40
2327	A1023	6p multi ('04)		2.75	.55
2328	A1023	8.50p multi ('04)		3.50	.75
2329	A1023	10.50p multi ('04)		4.00	.95
2330	A1023	10.50p multi ('04)		4.50	.95
	Nos. 2321-2330 (10)			21.50	4.85

National Pedagogical University, 25th Anniv. — A1069

2003, Aug. 29 **Litho.** *Perf. 13¼x13*
2331 A1069 6p multi 1.75 .55

Federico Silva Museum, San Luis Potosí A1070

2003, Sept. 18 *Perf. 13x13¼*
2332 A1070 6p multi 1.75 .55

National Organ and Tissue Donation Week A1071

2003, Sept. 26
2333 A1071 6p multi 1.75 .55

World Post Day — A1072

2003, Oct. 9 *Perf. 13¼x13*
2334 A1072 8.50p multi 2.25 .75

Woman Suffrage, 50th Anniv. — A1073

2003, Oct. 16
2335 A1073 6p multi 1.50 .55

Health Ministry, 60th Anniv. A1074

2003, Oct. 23 *Perf. 13x13¼*
2336 A1074 6p multi 1.50 .55

Juarez Theater, Cent. A1075

2003, Oct. 27
2337 A1075 6p multi 1.50 .55

Teaching of Law in the Americas, 450th Anniv. — A1076

2003, Nov. 4 *Perf. 13¼x13*
2338 A1076 8.50p multi 2.25 .80

Central Power and Light, Cent. A1077

2003, Nov. 18 **Litho.** *Perf. 13x13¼*
2339 A1077 6p multi 1.50 .55

Christmas A1078

Children's drawings of Nativity by: 6p, Valeria Báez. 8.50p, Octavio Alemán.

2003, Dec. 3
2340 A1078 6p multi 1.50 .55
2341 A1078 8.50p multi 2.25 .75

Children's Rights — A1079

2003, Dec. 5 *Perf. 13¼x13*
2342 A1079 6p multi 1.50 .55

Intl. Year of Fresh Water — A1080

2003, Dec. 11
2343 A1080 8.50p multi 2.25 .75

National Technical Education College, 25th Anniv. A1081

2003, Dec. 15 *Perf. 13x13¼*
2344 A1081 6p multi 1.50 .55

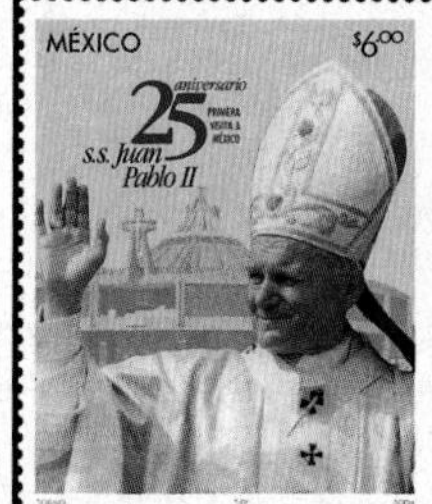

First Visit of Pope John Paul II to Mexico, 25th Anniv. A1082

2004, Jan. 28 **Litho.** *Perf. 13x13¼*
2345 A1082 6p multi 1.10 .55

Agustín Yáñez (1904-80), Novelist A1083

2004, May 4
2346 A1083 8.50p multi 1.50 .75

Enrique Aguilar González — A1084

2004, May 15 *Perf. 13¼x13*
2347 A1084 8.50p multi 1.50 .75

Teacher's Day.

Cable Television in Mexico, 50th Anniv. — A1085

2004, May 19
2348 A1085 6p multi 1.10 .55

Mexican Geological Society, Cent. A1086

2004, June 2 *Perf. 13x13¼*
2349 A1086 8.50p multi 1.50 .75

Intl. Day Against Illegal Drugs — A1087

2004, June 25 *Perf. 13¼x13*
2350 A1087 8.50p multi 1.50 .75

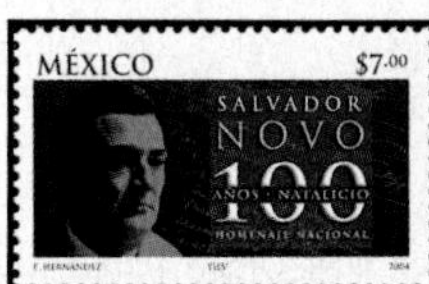

Salvador Novo (1904-74), Poet A1088

2004, July 30 *Perf. 13x13¼*
2351 A1088 7p multi 1.25 .60

Gilberto Owen (1905-52), Poet A1089

2004, Aug. 8 **Litho.** *Perf. 13x13¼*
2352 A1089 7p multi 1.25 .60

FIFA (Fédération Internationale de Football Association), Cent. — A1090

2004, Aug. 11
2353 A1090 11.50p multi 2.00 1.00

Mexican Cartooning — A1091

2004, Aug. 13 *Perf. 13¼x13*
2354 A1091 6p multi 1.00 .50

2004 Summer Olympics, Athens — A1092

2004, Aug. 13
2355 A1092 10.50p multi 1.90 .95

Celestino Gorostiza (1904-67), Writer A1093

2004, Aug. 16 Litho. ***Perf. 13x13¼***
2356 A1093 7p multi 1.25 .60

Fresnillo, 450th Anniv. — A1094

2004, Sept. 2 ***Perf. 13¼x13***
2357 A1094 7p multi 1.25 .60

Economic Culture Fund, 70th Anniv. A1095

2004, Sept. 6 ***Perf. 13x13¼***
2358 A1095 8.50p multi 1.50 .75

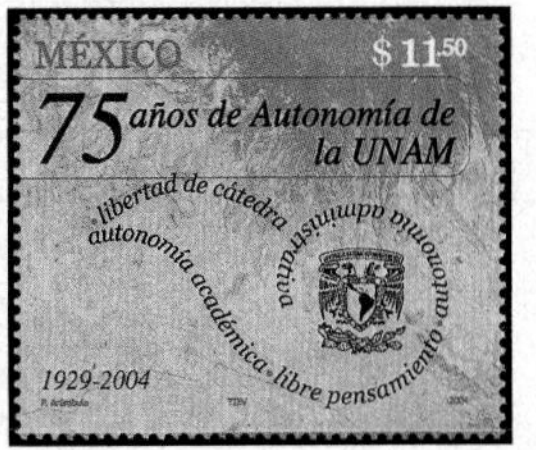

Autonomy of National Autonomous University of Mexico, 75th Anniv. — A1096

2004, Sept. 6 ***Perf. 13¼x13***
2359 A1096 11.50p multi 2.00 1.00

Autonomous University of Chihuahua, 50th Anniv. — A1097

2004, Sept. 8 ***Perf. 13x13¼***
2360 A1097 7p multi 1.25 .60

Palace of Fine Arts, 70th Anniv. A1098

2004, Sept. 29
2361 A1098 7p multi 1.25 .60

Conservation Type of 2002

Designs: 50c, Cats. No. 2363, Oceans. No. 2364, Rain forests. 2.50p, No. 2374, Reefs. 4.50p, Forests. 5p, No. 2370, Land mammals.

Nos. 2368, 2376, Reptiles. No. 2369, Birds. Nos. 2371, 2375, Deserts. No. 2372, Cacti. No. 2373, Tropical forests. No. 2377, Coastal birds.

2004 Litho. ***Perf. 13x13¼***

2362	A1023	50c multi	.45	.25
2363	A1023	1p multi	2.50	.25
2364	A1023	1p multi	.45	.25
2365	A1023	2.50p multi	1.25	.25
2366	A1023	4.50p multi	1.25	.40
2367	A1023	5p multi	1.90	.45
2368	A1023	6p multi	1.90	.55
2369	A1023	6p multi	1.75	.55
2370	A1023	6p multi	2.00	.55
2371	A1023	7p multi	2.00	.60
2372	A1023	7p multi	2.00	.60
2373	A1023	10p multi	3.50	.90
2374	A1023	10p multi	3.50	.90
2375	A1023	10.50p multi	3.50	.95
a.		Microprinting at top in black	4.25	1.00
2376	A1023	30p multi	8.00	2.25
2377	A1023	30p multi	8.00	2.25
		Nos. 2362-2377 (16)	43.95	11.95

Microprinting at top on No. 2375 is in gray.

State Workers' Institute of Social Services and Security — A1099

2004, Oct. 1 Litho. ***Perf. 13¼x13***
2378 A1099 6p multi 1.10 .55

Termination of Walled District of Campeche, 300th Anniv. — A1100

2004, Oct. 6 ***Perf. 13x13¼***
2379 A1100 6p multi 1.10 .55

National Anthem, 150th Anniv. A1101

2004, Oct. 8
2380 A1101 6.50p multi 1.25 .60

World Post Day A1102

2004, Oct. 11
2381 A1102 6p bright rose lilac 1.10 .55

Admission to UPU, 125th Anniv. A1103

2004, Oct. 29
2382 A1103 8.50p multi 1.50 .75

Channel 11 Television — A1104

2004, Nov. 10 ***Perf. 13¼x13***
2383 A1104 8.50p multi 1.50 .75

Superior Federation Audit, 180th Anniv. — A1105

2004, Nov. 16
2384 A1105 6.50p multi 1.25 .60

Health Secretary's Building, 75th Anniv. A1106

2004, Nov. 22 ***Perf. 13x13¼***
2385 A1106 8.50p multi 1.60 .80

Culture on the Radio — A1107

2004, Nov. 30 ***Perf. 13¼x13***
2386 A1107 6.50p multi 1.25 .60

Natl. Communications and Transportation Department Center, 50th Anniv. — A1108

2004, Nov. 30 ***Perf. 13¼x13***
2387 A1108 6.50p multi 1.25 .60

Souvenir Sheet
Perf. 14¼x14
2388 A1108 7.50p multi 1.40 .70

Town of General Escobedo, 400th Anniv. A1109

2004, Dec. 3 ***Perf. 13x13¼***
2389 A1109 8.50p multi 1.60 .80

Natl. Free Textbook Commission, 45th Anniv. — A1110

2004, Dec. 6
2390 A1110 10.50p multi 1.90 .95

A1111

Christmas — A1112

2004, Dec. 13 ***Perf. 13x13¼***
2391 A1111 7.50p multi 1.40 .70
Perf. 13¼x13
2392 A1112 10.50p multi 1.90 .95

Traffic Accident Prevention — A1113

2004, Dec. 17 Litho. ***Perf. 13¼x13***
2393 A1113 8.50p multi 1.60 .80

Conservation Type of 2002

Designs: Nos. 2394, 2404, Deserts. Nos. 2395, 2406, 2408, 2411, Orchids. Nos. 2396, 2410, 2419, 2435, Sea turtles. Nos. 2397, 2416, Birds. Nos. 2398, 2401, 2421, 2433, Marine mammals. Nos. 2399, 2425, Oceans. Nos. 2400, 2402, 2424, Cats. Nos. 2403, 2430, Rain forests. Nos. 2405, 2412, Eagles. Nos. 2407, 2415, Lakes and lagoons. Nos. 2409, 2436, Butterflies. Nos. 2413, 2423, Tropical forests. Nos. 2414, 2431, Rivers. Nos. 2417, 2429, Reefs. Nos. 2418, 2427, Forests. Nos. 2420, 2434, Coastal birds. No. 2422, Reptiles. Nos. 2426, 2428, Land mammals. No. 2432, Mangrove swamps.

2004-05 Litho. ***Perf. 13½x13¼***
Inscribed "ROMO" at Lower Right

2394	A1023	50c multi	.50	.25
2395	A1023	1p multi	.50	.25
2396	A1023	2.50p multi	1.00	.50
2397	A1023	6.50p multi	2.00	1.00
2398	A1023	6.50p multi	*150.00*	—
2399	A1023	7p multi	3.00	1.50
2400	A1023	7.50p multi	3.00	1.50
2401	A1023	8.50p multi	3.50	1.75
		Complete booklet, 6 #2401	21.00	
2402	A1023	10.50p multi	6.50	3.25
		Complete booklet, 6 #2402	39.00	
2403	A1023	13p multi	10.00	5.00

Inscribed "TIEV" at Lower Right
Perf. 13x13¼

2404	A1023	50c multi	.50	.25
2405	A1023	50c multi	.50	.25
2406	A1023	50p multi	.75	.40
2407	A1023	1p multi	.40	.25
2408	A1023	1p multi	.40	.25
a.		Perf. 14	1.75	.80
2409	A1023	2p multi	.80	.40
2410	A1023	2.50p multi	.90	.45

No.	Type	Value	Color	Unused	Used
2411	A1023	2.50p	multi	.90	.45
2412	A1023	2.50p	multi	1.00	.50
2413	A1023	5p	multi	1.75	.90
2414	A1023	5p	multi	1.75	.90
2415	A1023	5p	multi	1.75	.90
2416	A1023	6.50p	multi	1.75	.90
2417	A1023	6.50p	multi	1.75	.90
2418	A1023	6.50p	multi	1.75	.90
2419	A1023	6.50p	multi	2.00	1.00
2420	A1023	6.50p	multi	2.00	1.00
2421	A1023	6.50p	multi	1.75	.90
2422	A1023	6.50p	multi	1.75	.90
2423	A1023	7p	multi	1.75	.90
2424	A1023	7.50p	multi	2.25	1.10
2425	A1023	7.50p	multi	2.25	1.10
2426	A1023	7.50p	multi, denom in black	2.50	1.25
a.			Denomination in gray	9.00	4.50
2427	A1023	8.50p	multi	3.00	1.50
2428	A1023	10.50p	multi	4.00	2.00
2429	A1023	10.50p	multi	4.00	2.00
2430	A1023	13p	multi	5.50	2.75
2431	A1023	13p	multi	5.50	2.75
2432	A1023	13p	multi	5.50	2.75
2433	A1023	14.50p	multi	5.50	2.75
2434	A1023	14.50p	multi	5.50	2.75
2435	A1023	30.50p	multi	7.25	3.75
2436	A1023	30.50p	multi	7.25	3.75
			Nos. 2394-2436 (43)	265.90	58.50

Issued: Nos. 2401, 2402, 2004. Others, 2005. Colors are duller on stamps inscribed "TIEV" than those on similar stamps inscribed "ROMO."

Mexico General Hospital, Cent. — A1114

2005, Feb. 4 Litho. ***Perf. 13¼x13***
2437 A1114 6.50p multi 1.25 .60

Intl. Women's Day A1115

2005, Mar. 8 ***Perf. 13x13¼***
2438 A1115 6.50p multi 1.25 .60

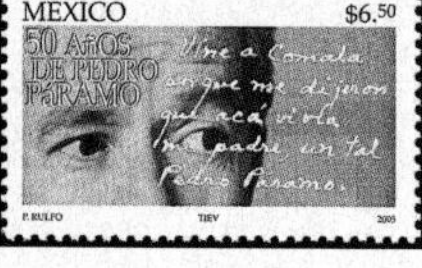

Publication of Pedro Paramo by Juan Rulfo, 50th Anniv. A1116

2005, Mar. 13
2439 A1116 6.50p multi 1.25 .60

Natl. University Games — A1117

2005, Apr. 18 ***Perf. 13¼x13***
2440 A1117 7.50p multi 1.40 .70

World Without Polio — A1118

2005, Apr. 29
2441 A1118 10.50p multi 1.90 .95

Eulalia Guzmán A1119

2005, May 15 ***Perf. 13x13¼***
2442 A1119 6.50p multi 1.25 .60

Teacher's Day.

Souvenir Sheet

Publication of Don Quixote, 400th Anniv. — A1120

No. 2443: a, 6.50p, Silhouette of Don Quixote. b, 10.50p, Crowd, horse and rider. c, 10.50p, Don Quixote.

2005, May 23 ***Perf. 13¼x13***
2443 A1120 Sheet of 3, #a-c 5.25 5.25

Intl. Year of Physics — A1121

2005, May 26
2444 A1121 7.50p multi 1.40 .70

Natl. Human Rights Commission — A1122

2005, June 5 ***Perf. 13x13¼***
2445 A1122 6.50p multi 1.25 .60

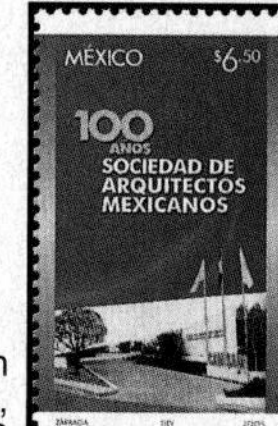

Society of Mexican Architects, Cent. — A1123

2005, June 8 ***Perf. 13¼x13***
2446 A1123 6.50p multi 1.25 .60

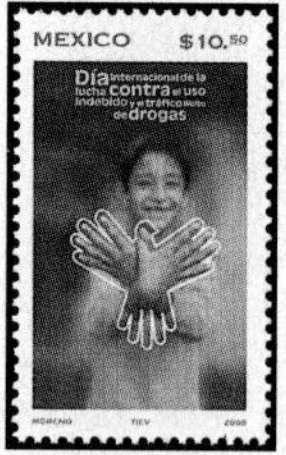

Intl. Day Against Illegal Drugs — A1124

2005, June 24
2447 A1124 10.50p multi 2.00 1.00

Baseball — A1125

2005, June 27
2448 A1125 7.50p multi 1.40 .70

Information Access and Transparency — A1126

2005, June 27
2449 A1126 6.50p multi 1.25 .60

Memin Pinguin, by Yolanda Vargas Dulche — A1127

Memin Pinguin: a, And comic book page. b, Holding flower. c, Holding open comic book. d, Wearing tuxedo. e, Holding closed book.

2005, June 28 ***Perf. 13***
2450 Horiz. strip of 5 *9.50 9.50*
a.-e. A1127 6.50p Any single *1.90 .95*

Multiple Self-portrait, by Juan O'Gorman (1905-82) — A1128

2005, June 29 ***Perf. 13¼x13***
2451 A1128 7.50p multi 1.40 .70

Conservation Type of 2002

Designs: No. 2452, Butterflies. Nos. 2453, 2473, Sea turtles. No. 2454, Coastal birds. Nos. 2456, 2463, Marine mammals. Nos. 2457, 2459, Rivers. Nos. 2458, 2462, 2466, Oceans. No. 2460, Lakes and lagoons. Nos. 2461, 2469, Cats. No. 2464, Reptiles. No. 2465, Mangrove swamps. No. 2467, Birds. No. 2468, Cacti. No. 2470, Reefs. No. 2471, Eagles. No. 2472, Tropical forests.

2005 Litho. ***Perf. 13x13¼***

Inscribed "TIEV" at Lower Right

No.	Type	Value	Color	Unused	Used
2452	A1023	50c	multi	.25	.25
2453	A1023	50c	multi	.25	.25
2454	A1023	1p	multi	.25	.25
2456	A1023	1p	multi	.25	.25
2457	A1023	2.50p	multi	.50	.25
2458	A1023	5p	multi	.95	.50
2459	A1023	6.50p	multi	1.25	.60
2460	A1023	6.50p	multi	1.25	.60
2461	A1023	6.50p	multi	1.25	.60
2462	A1023	7p	multi	1.40	.70
2463	A1023	7p	multi	1.40	.70
2464	A1023	7.50p	multi	1.40	.70
2465	A1023	7.50p	multi	1.40	.70
2466	A1023	10.50p	multi	2.00	1.00
2467	A1023	10.50p	multi	2.00	1.00
2468	A1023	13p	multi	2.50	1.25
2469	A1023	13p	multi	2.50	1.25
2470	A1023	13p	multi	2.50	1.25
2471	A1023	14.50p	multi	2.75	1.40
2472	A1023	30.50p	multi	5.75	2.75

Inscribed "ROMO" at Lower Right

Booklet Stamp

No.	Type	Value	Color	Unused	Used
2473	A1023	(15.75p)	multi	3.00	1.50
a.			Booklet pane of 4	12.00	—
			Complete booklet, 4 #2473	12.00	
			Nos. 2452-2473 (21)	34.80	17.75

See No. 2399 for 7p Oceans stamp with "ROMO" inscription. No. 2473 is inscribed "Porte mundial" at lower left.

Minerals — A1129

No. 2474: a, Silver. b, Argentite. c, Marcasite, quartz and galena. d, Allende meteorite. e, Gold. f, Galena. g, Pyrargyrite. h, Gypsum. i, Manganocalcite. j, Barite. k, Stephanite. l, Red calcite. m, Calcite. n, Asbestos. o, Valencianite. p, Livingstoneite. q, Beryl. r, Smithsonite. s, Fluorite. t, Amethyst quartz. u, Azurite. v, Hemimorphite. w, Apatite. x, Pyromorphite. y, Actinolite with talc.

2005, Aug. 3 ***Perf. 13¼x13***
2474 Sheet of 25 32.50 32.50
a.-y. A1129 6.50p Any single 1.25 .60

Ignacio L. Vallarta (1830-94), Chief Justice A1130

2005, Aug. 23 ***Perf. 13x13¼***
2475 A1130 7.50p multi 1.40 .70

Judicial Anniversaries — A1131

Designs: No. 2476, Federal Justice Council, 10th anniv. No. 2477, Supreme Court, 180th anniv. 10.50p, Supreme Justice Tribunal, 190th anniv.

2005, Aug. 23

2476 A1131 6.50p multi 1.25 .60
2477 A1131 6.50p multi 1.25 .60
2478 A1131 10.50p multi 2.00 1.00
a. Souvenir sheet, #2476-2478 4.50 4.50

Expo 2005, Aichi, Japan — A1132

2005, Sept. 15 *Perf. 13¼x13*

2479 A1132 13p multi 2.40 1.25

Federal District Superior Court, 150th Anniv. — A1133

No. 2480 — Buildings from: a, 1855. b, 2005. c, 1964.

2005, Oct. 6

2480 Horiz. strip of 3 4.00 4.00
a.-b. A1133 6.50p Either single 1.25 .60
c. A1133 7.50p multi 1.40 .70

World Post Day — A1134

2005, Oct. 10

2481 A1134 10.50p multi 2.00 1.00

United Nations Day A1135

2005, Oct. 24 *Perf. 13x13¼*

2482 A1135 10.50p multi 2.00 1.00

Jalisco Philatelic Organization, Cent. — A1136

2005, Oct. 27

2483 A1136 6.50p multi 1.25 .60

Lebanese in Mexico, 125th Anniv. — A1137

2005, Nov. 11 *Perf. 13¼x13*

2484 A1137 10.50p multi 2.00 1.00

Rodolfo Usigli (1905-79), Playwright — A1138

2005, Nov. 15

2485 A1138 7.50p multi 1.50 .75

San Juan de Ulua, Last Spanish Redoubt — A1139

2005, Nov. 23

2486 A1139 7.50p multi 1.50 .75

Gómez Palacio, Cent. — A1140

2005, Nov. 24

2487 A1140 6.50p multi 1.25 .60

Folk Art — A1141

Designs: 50c, Legged earthen pot. 1p, Lacquered wooden chest. 1.50p, Horn comb. 2p, Black clay jug. 2.50p, Paper bull. 5p, Silk shawl. No. 2494, Model. No. 2495, Glazed basin. No. 2496, Vase. No. 2497, Wooden mask. No. 2498, Tin rooster. 7p, Doll. 7.50p, Copper jar. 9p, Embroidered tablecloth. 10.50p, 11.50p, Woven basket. 13p, 13.50p, Silver pear. 14.50p, 15p, Amber marimba. 30.50p, Obsidian and opal turtle.

2005, Nov. 30 Litho. *Perf. 13¼x13*

2488 A1141 50c multi .25 .25
a. Dated "2006" .25 .25
b. Dated "2007" .25 .25
c. Dated "2008" .25 .25
d. Magenta panel, dated "2010" .25 .25
e. Dated "2011" .25 .25
f. Dated "2012" .25 .25
g. Dated "2013" .25 .25
h. Dated "2014" .25 .25
i. Dated "2015" .25 .25
j. Dated "2016" .25 .25

2489 A1141 1p multi .25 .25
a. Dated "2006" .25 .25
b. Dated "2007" .25 .25
c. Dated "2008" .25 .25
d. Dated "2010" .25 .25
e. Dated "2011" .25 .25
f. Dated "2012" .25 .25
g. Dated "2013" .25 .25
h. Dated "2014" .25 .25
i. Dated "2015" .25 .25
j. Dated "2016" .25 .25

2490 A1141 1.50p multi .30 .25
a. Dated "2006" .30 .25
b. Dated "2007" .30 .25
c. Dated "2008" .25 .25
d. Dated "2009" .25 .25
e. Dated "2010" .25 .25
f. Dated "2011" .25 .25
g. Dated "2012" .25 .25
h. Dated "2013" .25 .25
i. Dated "2014" .25 .25
j. Dated "2015" .25 .25
k. Dated "2016" .25 .25

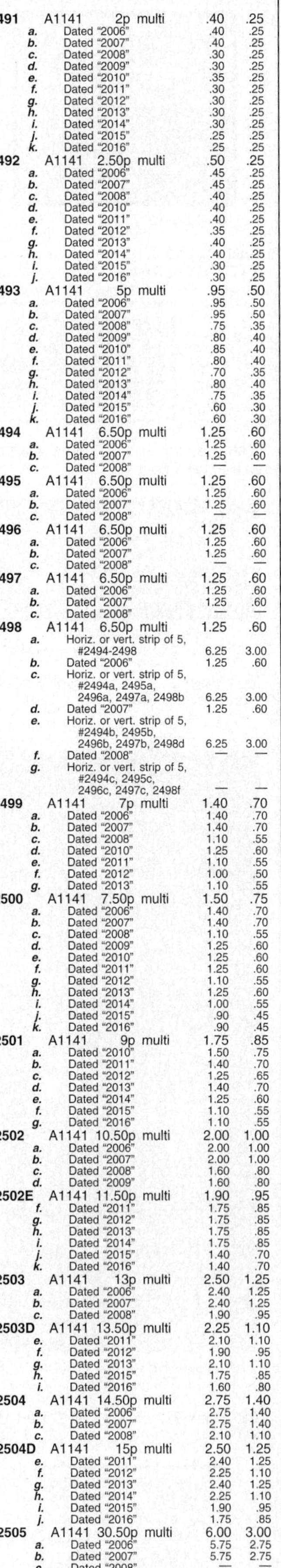

2491 A1141 2p multi .40 .25
a. Dated "2006" .40 .25
b. Dated "2007" .40 .25
c. Dated "2008" .30 .25
d. Dated "2009" .30 .25
e. Dated "2010" .35 .25
f. Dated "2011" .30 .25
g. Dated "2012" .30 .25
h. Dated "2013" .30 .25
i. Dated "2014" .30 .25
j. Dated "2015" .25 .25
k. Dated "2016" .25 .25

2492 A1141 2.50p multi .50 .25
a. Dated "2006" .45 .25
b. Dated "2007" .45 .25
c. Dated "2008" .40 .25
d. Dated "2010" .40 .25
e. Dated "2011" .40 .25
f. Dated "2012" .35 .25
g. Dated "2013" .40 .25
h. Dated "2014" .40 .25
i. Dated "2015" .30 .25
j. Dated "2016" .30 .25

2493 A1141 5p multi .95 .50
a. Dated "2006" .95 .50
b. Dated "2007" .95 .50
c. Dated "2008" .75 .35
d. Dated "2009" .80 .40
e. Dated "2010" .85 .40
f. Dated "2011" .80 .40
g. Dated "2012" .70 .35
h. Dated "2013" .80 .40
i. Dated "2014" .75 .35
j. Dated "2015" .60 .30
k. Dated "2016" .60 .30

2494 A1141 6.50p multi 1.25 .60
a. Dated "2006" 1.25 .60
b. Dated "2007" 1.25 .60
c. Dated "2008" — —

2495 A1141 6.50p multi 1.25 .60
a. Dated "2006" 1.25 .60
b. Dated "2007" 1.25 .60
c. Dated "2008" — —

2496 A1141 6.50p multi 1.25 .60
a. Dated "2006" 1.25 .60
b. Dated "2007" 1.25 .60
c. Dated "2008" — —

2497 A1141 6.50p multi 1.25 .60
a. Dated "2006" 1.25 .60
b. Dated "2007" 1.25 .60
c. Dated "2008" — —

2498 A1141 6.50p multi 1.25 .60
a. Horiz. or vert. strip of 5, #2494-2498 6.25 3.00
b. Dated "2006" 1.25 .60
c. Horiz. or vert. strip of 5, #2494a, 2495a, 2496a, 2497a, 2498b 6.25 3.00
d. Dated "2007" 1.25 .60
e. Horiz. or vert. strip of 5, #2494b, 2495b, 2496b, 2497b, 2498d 6.25 3.00
f. Dated "2008" — —
g. Horiz. or vert. strip of 5, #2494c, 2495c, 2496c, 2497c, 2498f — —

2499 A1141 7p multi 1.40 .70
a. Dated "2006" 1.40 .70
b. Dated "2007" 1.40 .70
c. Dated "2008" 1.10 .55
d. Dated "2010" 1.25 .60
e. Dated "2011" 1.10 .55
f. Dated "2012" 1.00 .50
g. Dated "2013" 1.10 .55

2500 A1141 7.50p multi 1.50 .75
a. Dated "2006" 1.40 .70
b. Dated "2007" 1.40 .70
c. Dated "2008" 1.10 .55
d. Dated "2009" 1.25 .60
e. Dated "2010" 1.25 .60
f. Dated "2011" 1.25 .60
g. Dated "2012" 1.10 .55
h. Dated "2013" 1.25 .60
i. Dated "2014" 1.00 .55
j. Dated "2015" .90 .45
k. Dated "2016" .90 .45

2501 A1141 9p multi 1.75 .85
a. Dated "2010" 1.50 .75
b. Dated "2011" 1.40 .70
c. Dated "2012" 1.25 .65
d. Dated "2013" 1.40 .70
e. Dated "2014" 1.25 .60
f. Dated "2015" 1.10 .55
g. Dated "2016" 1.10 .55

2502 A1141 10.50p multi 2.00 1.00
a. Dated "2006" 2.00 1.00
b. Dated "2007" 2.00 1.00
c. Dated "2008" 1.60 .80
d. Dated "2009" 1.60 .80

2502E A1141 11.50p multi 1.90 .95
f. Dated "2011" 1.75 .85
g. Dated "2012" 1.75 .85
h. Dated "2013" 1.75 .85
i. Dated "2014" 1.75 .85
j. Dated "2015" 1.40 .70
k. Dated "2016" 1.40 .70

2503 A1141 13p multi 2.50 1.25
a. Dated "2006" 2.40 1.25
b. Dated "2007" 2.40 1.25
c. Dated "2008" 1.90 .95

2503D A1141 13.50p multi 2.25 1.10
e. Dated "2011" 2.10 1.10
f. Dated "2012" 1.90 .95
g. Dated "2013" 2.10 1.10
h. Dated "2015" 1.75 .85
i. Dated "2016" 1.60 .80

2504 A1141 14.50p multi 2.75 1.40
a. Dated "2006" 2.75 1.40
b. Dated "2007" 2.75 1.40
c. Dated "2008" 2.10 1.10

2504D A1141 15p multi 2.50 1.25
e. Dated "2011" 2.40 1.25
f. Dated "2012" 2.25 1.10
g. Dated "2013" 2.40 1.25
h. Dated "2014" 2.25 1.10
i. Dated "2015" 1.90 .95
j. Dated "2016" 1.75 .85

2505 A1141 30.50p multi 6.00 3.00
a. Dated "2006" 5.75 2.75
b. Dated "2007" 5.75 2.75
c. Dated "2008" — —
d. Dated "2012" 4.50 2.25
e. Dated "2016" 3.50 1.75
Nos. 2488-2505 (21) 33.45 17.00

Nos. 2502E, 2503D and 2504D are dated "2010."

Christian Brothers in Mexico, Cent. — A1142

2005, Dec. 2 *Perf. 13¼x13*

2506 A1142 6.50p multi 1.25 .60

Jews in Mexico, Cent. — A1143

2005, Dec. 6

2507 A1143 7.50p multi 1.40 .70

Indigenous Popular Culture A1144

2005, Dec. 16 *Perf. 13x13¼*

2508 A1144 6.50p multi 1.25 .60

A1145

Christmas A1146

2005, Dec. 20

2509 A1145 6.50p multi 1.25 .60
2510 A1146 7.50p multi 1.40 .70

Souvenir Sheet

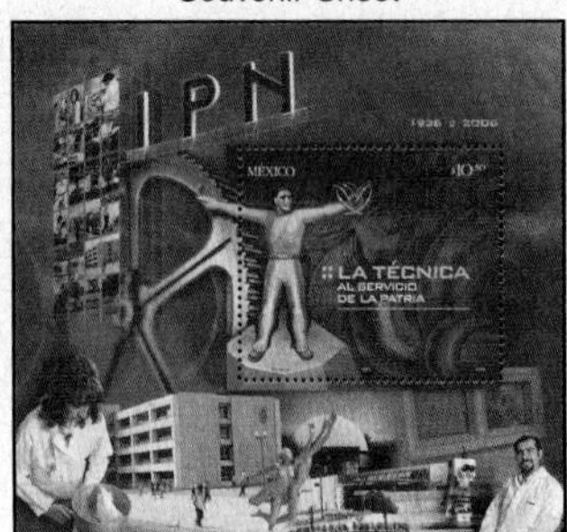

National Polytechnic Institute, 70th Anniv. — A1147

2006, Feb. 27 Litho. *Perf. 13¼x13*

2511 A1147 10.50p multi 2.00 1.00

Wolfgang Amadeus Mozart (1756-91), Composer — A1148

2006, Mar. 31

2512 A1148 7.50p multi 1.40 .70

Central Library of National Autonomous University of Mexico, 50th Anniv. — A1149

2006, Apr. 5

2513 A1149 6.50p multi 1.25 .60

Latin American Tower, 50th Anniv. A1150

2006, Apr. 26 *Perf. 13x13¼*

2514 6.50p multi 1.25 .60
2515 10.50p multi 2.00 1.00
a. A1150 Vert. pair, #2514-2515 3.25 1.60

Isidro Castillo Pérez, Educator — A1151

2006, May 15 *Perf. 13¼x13*

2516 A1151 6.50p multi 1.25 .60

Vasconcelos Library — A1152

2006, May 16

2517 A1152 6.50p multi 1.25 .60

Intl. Women's Day A1153

2006, May 31 *Perf. 13x13¼*

2518 A1153 6.50p multi 1.25 .60

2006 World Cup Soccer Championships, Germany — A1154

2006, June 9 *Perf. 13¼x13*

2519 A1154 13p multi 2.40 1.25

Souvenir Sheet

President Benito Juarez (1806-72) — A1155

2006, June 22 *Perf. 13x13¼*

2520 A1155 13p multi 2.40 1.25

Navy Qualification Center, 50th Anniv. — A1156

2006, Aug. 11 **Litho.**

2521 A1156 6.50p multi 1.25 .60

Popular Television Characters — A1157

No. 2522: a, El Chavo del Ocho and barrel. b, El Chapulín Colorado with arms crossed. c, El Chavo del Ocho, door and window d, El Chapulín Colorado with arms spread. e, El Chavo del Ocho holding suspenders.

2006, Aug. 21 *Perf. 13¼x13*

2522 Horiz. strip of 5 9.75 4.75
a. A1157 6.50p multi 1.25 .60
b. A1157 7.50p multi 1.40 .70
c. A1157 10.50p multi 1.90 .95
d. A1157 13p multi 2.40 1.25
e. A1157 14.50p multi 2.60 1.25

Intl. Year of Deserts and Desertification — A1158

2006, Sept. 20

2523 A1158 6.50p multi 1.25 .60

Souvenir Sheet

Dinosaurs — A1159

No. 2524: a, 6.50p, Muzzy (40x24mm). b, 7.50p, Sabinosaurus (40x48mm). c, 10.50p, Aramberri Monster (40x48mm).

2006, Sept. 29 *Perf. 13x13¼*

2524 A1159 Sheet of 3, #a-c 4.50 2.25

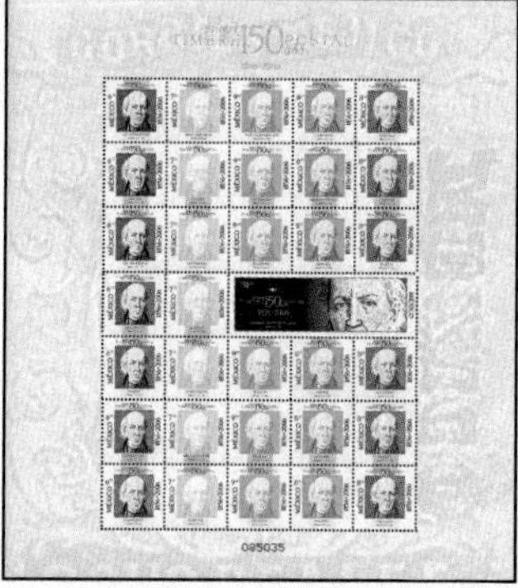
Engineering Institute of National Autonomous University of Mexico, 50th Anniv. — A1160

2006, Oct. 5 *Perf. 13¼x13*

2525 A1160 6.50p multi 1.25 .60

Miniature Sheet

First Mexican Stamps, 150th Anniv. — A1161

No. 2526 — Miguel Hidalgo y Costilla and inscription: a, Aguascalientes. b, Colima. c, Edo. de México. d, Michoacán. e, Nayarit. f, Quintana Roo. g, Tamaulipas. h, Baja California. i, Chiapas. j, Guanajuato. k, Morelos. l, Nuevo León. m, San Luis Potosí. n, Tlaxcala. o, Baja California Sur. p, Chihuahua. q, Guerrero. r, Oaxaca. s, Sinaloa. t, Veracruz. u, Campeche. v, Distrito Federal. w, Hidalgo. x, Puebla. y, Sonora. z, Yucatán. aa, Coahuila. ab, Durango. ac, Jalisco. ad, Querétaro. ae, Tabasco. af, Zacatecas. ag, Estados Unidos Mexicanos (70x22mm).

Litho., Litho. & Embossed (50p)

2006, Oct. 9

2526 A1161 Sheet of 33 65.00 65.00
a.-g. 6.50p Any single 1.25 .60
h.-n. 7.50p Any single 1.40 .70
o.-t. 9p Any single 1.75 .85
u.-z. 10.50p Any single 1.90 .95
aa.-af. 13p Any single 2.40 1.25
ag. 50p multi 9.25 4.75

World Post Day — A1162

2006, Oct. 9 **Litho.**

2527 A1162 13p multi 2.40 1.25

Popular Television Characters — A1163

Xavier López "Chabelo": 6.50p, Boy with ice cream cone. 10.50p, Man seated.

2006, Oct. 30

2528 6.50p multi 1.25 .60
2529 10.50p multi 2.00 1.00
a. A1163 Horiz. pair, #2528-2529 3.25 1.60

Letter Carrier's Day — A1164

2006, Nov. 10

2530 A1164 6.50p multi 1.25 .60

Transformation of the Autonomous Scientific and Literary Institute, Autonomous University of the State of Mexico, 50th Anniv. — A1165

2006, Nov. 17 *Perf. 13x13¼*
2531 A1165 10.50p multi 1.90 .95

"Children, The Future of Mexico" A1166

2006, Nov. 22
2532 A1166 10.50p multi + label 1.90 .95

Andrés Henestrosa, Writer, Cent. of Birth — A1167

2006, Nov. 23 *Perf. 13¼x13*
2533 A1167 9p multi 1.75 .85

Edmundo O'Gorman (1906-95), Historian A1168

2006, Nov. 28 *Perf. 13x13¼*
2534 A1168 10.50p multi 1.90 .95

Mexico in Intl. Telecommunications Union, Cent. — A1169

2006, Nov. 30 *Perf. 13¼x13*
2535 A1169 7p multi 1.40 .70

Christmas A1170

Children's art by: 7.50p, Ricardo Salas Pineda. 10.50p, Maria José Goytia.

2006, Dec. 6 **Litho.** *Perf. 13x13¼*
2536 7.50p multi 1.40 .70
2537 10.50p multi 2.00 1.00
a. A1170 Pair, #2536-2537 3.40 1.70

El Universal Newspaper, 90th Anniv. — A1171

2006, Dec. 22 *Perf. 13¼x13*
2538 A1171 10.50p multi + label 2.00 1.00

Teacher's Day — A1172

2007, May 15
2539 A1172 7.50p multi 1.40 .70

Frida Kahlo (1907-54), Painter A1173

2007, June 13 *Perf. 13x13¼*
2540 A1173 13p multi 2.40 1.25

Scouting, Cent. — A1174

Designs: 6.50p, Dove and compass. 10.50p, Centenary emblem, compass.

2007, June 30 *Perf. 13¼x13*
2541 6.50p multi 1.25 .60
2542 10.50p multi 2.00 1.00
a. A1174 Pair, #2541-2542 3.25 1.60

Miniature Sheet

Chichén Itzá — A1175

No. 2543: a, Pelota ring, Jaguar Temple, serpent head. b, Colonnade. c, Observatory. d, Castillo, jaguar head. e, Chac Mool.

2007, July 13
2543 A1175 Sheet of 5 + label 9.25 4.75
a.-b. 6.50p Either single 1.25 .60
c. 10.50p multi 1.90 .95
d.-e. 13p Either single 2.40 1.25

State of Colima, 150th Anniv. — A1176

2007, July 19
2544 A1176 10.50p multi 1.90 .95

Miniature Sheet

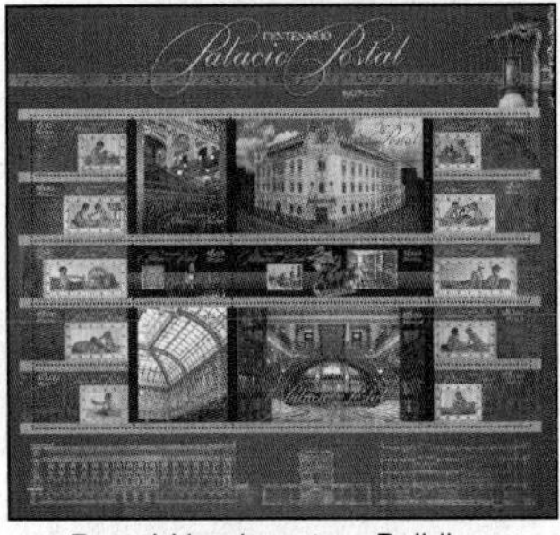

Postal Headquarters Building, Cent. — A1177

No. 2545: a, Nude boy writing (40x23mm). b, Nude boy touching item on pedestal (40x23mm). c, Two nude boys, chalice (40x23mm). d, Two nude boys, press (40x23mm). e, Boy, gear (40x23mm). f, Clock and machinery (40x23mm). g, Sculpture of UPU emblem, photographs (80x23mm). h, Mercury and caduceus (40x23mm). i, Two nude boys (40x23mm). j, Two nude boys, diff. (40x23mm). k, Seated nude boy with arms extended, holding bird (40x23mm). l, Seated nude boy holding bird (40x23mm). m, Stairway (40x48mm). n, Glass ceiling (40x48). o, Stairways (80x48mm). p, Building exterior (80x48mm).

2007, Aug. 1 *Perf. 13x13¼*
2545 A1177 Sheet of 16 35.00 35.00
a.-b. 5.50p Either single 1.00 .50
c.-g. 6.50p Any single 1.25 .60
h.-i. 9p Either single 1.75 .85
j. 10.50p multi 1.90 .95
k.-l. 13p Either single 2.40 1.25
m.-n. 14.50p Either single 2.75 1.40
o. 15.50p multi 3.00 1.50
p. 39.50p multi 7.25 3.50

Torreón, Cent. A1178

No. 2546: a, Locomotive, Torreón Station Museum. b, Bridge, church spires. c, Isauro Martínez Theater. d, Statue of Jesus Christ. e, Bilbao Dunes, Tower.

2007, Sept. 5
2546 Horiz. strip of 5 8.75 4.50
a. A1178 5p multi .90 .45
b.-c. A1178 6.50p Either single 1.25 .60
d.-e. A1178 14.50p Either single 2.60 1.25

Cultural Forum, Monterrey A1179

No. 2547: a, Dove and hand. b, Child and books. c, Children, windmill, hand picking orange. d, Woman and artist. e, Sculpture and figurines.

2007, Aug. 20 **Litho.** *Perf. 13x13¼*
2547 Horiz. strip of 5 9.00 4.50
a. A1179 7p multi 1.25 .60
b.-c. A1179 7.50p Either single 1.40 .70
d.-e. A1179 13p Either single 2.40 1.25

Central University City Campus of National Autonomous University of Mexico World Heritage Site — A1180

No. 2548: a, Olympic Stadium and artwork. b, University building, University Library. c, Rectory Building.

2007, Sept. 21
2548 Horiz. strip of 3 5.25 2.75
a. A1180 6.50p multi 1.25 .60
b. A1180 9p multi 1.60 .80
c. A1180 13p multi 2.40 1.25

University of Baja California, 50th Anniv. A1181

2007, Oct. 1
2549 A1181 7.50p multi 1.40 .70

Ozone Layer Protection A1182

No. 2550: a, Doves, tree, leaves. b, Doves, Earth in hands.

2007, Oct. 1
2550 A1182 Vert. pair 4.00 2.00
a. 7p multi 1.25 .60
b. 14.50p multi 2.75 1.40

St. Christopher, by Nicolás Rodríguez Juárez — A1183

2007, Oct. 3
2551 A1183 6.50p multi 1.25 .60

Autonomous University of Coahuila, 50th Anniv. — A1184

2007, Oct. 4 ***Perf. 13¼x13***
2552 A1184 7.50p multi 1.40 .70

World Post Day A1185

No. 2553 — Envelope with denomination in: a, Yellow. b, Black.

2007, Oct. 9 ***Perf. 13x13¼***
2553 A1185 Vert. pair 3.25 1.60
a. 7p multi 1.25 .60
b. 10.50p multi 2.00 1.00

Rights of People With Disabilities A1186

2007, Oct. 11
2554 A1186 6.50p multi 1.25 .60

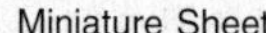

Miniature Sheet

Francisco Gabilondo Soler (1907-90), Composer of Children's Songs — A1187

No. 2555: a, Turtle, giraffe, peacock (Caminito de la Escuela). b, Dog, camel, mouse (Caminito de la Escuela). c, Duck and ducklings (La Patita). d, Girl and mouse (La Muñeca Fea). e, Cat with guitar (Gato de Barrio). f, King and cakes (Bombón I). g, Three pigs and cakes (Cochinitos Dormilones). h, Three pigs in bed (Cochinitos Dormilones). i, Old woman and cat (Di Por Que). j, Mouse in cowboy's clothes (El Ratón Vaquero). k, Boy eating watermelon (Negrito Sandía). l, Cricket holding stick (Cri-Cri). m, Soler. n, Cricket at music stand (Cri-Cri). o, Ant and fountain (El Chorrito).

2007, Oct. 11 ***Perf. 13¼x13***
2555 A1187 Sheet of 15 18.50 18.50
a.-b. 5p Either single .90 .45
c.-k. 6.50p Any single 1.25 .60
l.-n. 7p Any single 1.25 .60
o. 7.50p multi 1.40 .70

Degrees in Administration, 50th Anniv. — A1188

2007, Oct. 19 ***Perf. 13x13¼***
2556 A1188 7.50p multi 1.40 .70

Cuauhtemoc Sailing School — A1189

2007, Nov. 4 ***Perf. 13¼x13***
2557 A1189 7.50p multi 1.40 .70

A1190

A1191

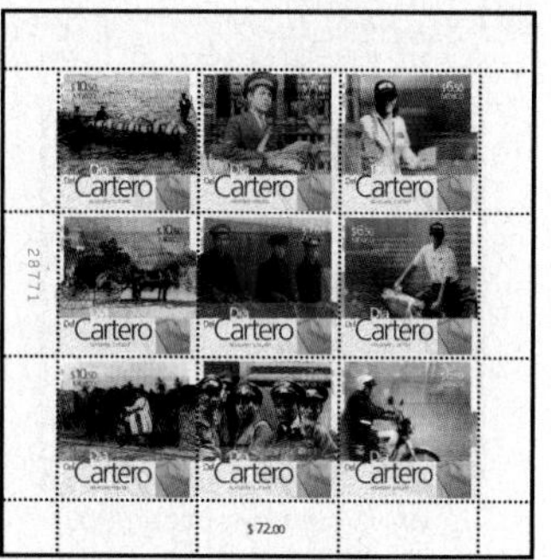

Letter Carrier's Day — A1192

No. 2559: a, Girl writing letter, letter carrier on bicycle. b, Girl mailing letter in mailbox. c, Letter carrier on bicycle. d, Letter carrier delivering letter.

No. 2560: a, Female letter carrier. b, Letter carrier on bicycle. c, Letter carrier on motorcycle. d, Letter carrier with mail bag. e, Three letter carriers. f, Five letter carriers. g, Letter carriers on rowboat. h, Horse-drawn carriage. i, Letter carrier and mail bag on railway hand car.

2007, Nov. 12 ***Perf. 13***
2558 A1190 10.50p multi 2.00 1.00
2559 A1191 Block of 4 5.00 2.50
a.-d. 6.50p Any single 1.25 .60
2560 A1192 Sheet of 9 13.50 13.50
a.-c. 6.50p Any single 1.25 .60
d.-f. 7p Any single 1.25 .60
g.-i. 10.50p Any single 2.00 1.00

Mountains — A1193

Designs: No. 2561, Mt. Minya Konka, People's Republic of China. No. 2562, Popocatépetl, Mexico.

2007, Nov. 22 Litho. ***Perf. 13¼x13***
2561 A1193 6.50p multi 1.25 .60
2562 A1193 6.50p multi 1.25 .60

See People's Republic of China Nos. 3635-3636.

Intl. Day Against Violence Towards Women — A1194

2007, Nov. 26
2563 A1194 7p multi 1.40 .70

Mariano Otero (1817-50), Judicial and Constitutional Reformer — A1195

2007, Nov. 27 ***Perf. 13x13¼***
2564 A1195 10.50p multi 2.00 1.00

Trials of Amparo, legal protection of individual constitutional guarantees in federal courts.

Miniature Sheet

Monte Albán Archaeological Site — A1196

No. 2565: a, Scribe of Cuilapan. b, Head with jaguar helmet. c, Building II, Cocijo urn. d, Building I, Central Plaza, Cocijo urn. e, Observatory, Southern Platform, Central Plaza.

2007, Dec. 11 ***Perf. 13¼x13***
2565 A1196 Sheet of 5 + label 9.50 4.75
a.-b. 6.50p Either single 1.25 .60
c. 10.50p multi 2.00 1.00
d.-e. 13p Either single 2.40 1.25

Christmas A1197

2007, Dec. 12 ***Perf. 13***
2566 Horiz. strip of 5 10.00 5.00
a. A1197 6.50p Candle 1.25 .60
b. A1197 7p Bell 1.40 .70
c. A1197 10.50p Angel 2.00 1.00
d. A1197 13.50p Magi 2.50 1.25
e. A1197 14.50p Holy Family 2.75 1.40

Miniature Sheet

Dogs — A1198

No. 2567: a, Two English bulldogs. b, Two rottweilers. c, Two boxers. d, Two beagles. e, Head of English Bulldog. f, Head of Rottweiler. g, Head of boxer. h, Head of beagle. i, English bulldog. j, Rottweiler. k, Boxer. l, Beagle.

2007, Dec. 14
2567 A1198 Sheet of 12 19.00 9.50
a.-d. 6.50p Any single 1.25 .60
e.-h. 7p Any single 1.40 .70
i.-l. 10.50p Any single 2.00 1.00

See Nos. 2762-2763.

Jesús García Corona (1883-1907), Heroic Railroad Engineer — A1199

2007, Dec. 17 ***Perf. 13¼x13***
2568 A1199 10.50p multi 2.00 1.00

Satélite Towers, Naucalpan, 50th Anniv. A1200

2007, Dec. 19 ***Perf. 13x13¼***
2569 A1200 6.50p multi 1.25 .60

El Cajón Dam — A1201

Aerial view of: 7p, Open spillway. 13p, Dam.

2007, Dec. 28 ***Perf. 13¼x13***
2570 A1201 7p multi 1.40 .70
2571 A1201 13p multi 2.40 1.25

Letter and Heart A1202

2008, Jan. 29 Litho. ***Perf. 13½x13¼***
2572 A1202 6.50p multi 1.25 .60

Mother's Day A1203

2008, May 2 ***Perf. 13x13¼***
2573 A1203 6.50p multi 1.25 .60

Pres. Miguel Alemán Valdés (1900-83) A1204

2008, May 14 ***Perf. 13x13¼***
2574 A1204 6.50p multi 1.25 .60

The Fruits, by Diego Rivera A1205

2008, May 15
2575 A1205 6.50p multi 1.25 .60

Teacher's Day.

Miniature Sheet

El Santo and El Hijo del Santo — A1206

No. 2576: a, El Santo wearing silver mask and robe. b, El Santo in ring. c, El Hijo del Santo with hands outstretched. d, El Santo with automobile. e, El Hijo del Santo in ring. f, El Hijo del Santo with arms crossed.

2008, June 17 ***Perf. 13***
2576 A1206 Sheet of 6 7.50 3.75
a.-f. 6.50p Any single 1.25 .60

El Santo (Rodolfo Guzmán Huerta, 1917-84), El Hijo del Santo (Jorge Guzmán), wrestling legends and film stars.

2008 Summer Olympics, Beijing A1207

Designs: No. 2577, Rowing. No. 2578, Weight lifting. No. 2579, Rhythmic gymnastics.

2008, Aug. 8 ***Perf. 13***
2577 A1207 6.50p multi 1.25 .60
2578 A1207 6.50p multi 1.25 .60
2579 A1207 6.50p multi 1.25 .60
Nos. 2577-2579 (3) 3.75 1.80

Electoral Justice — A1208

2008, Aug. 19 Litho. ***Perf. 13¼x13***
2580 A1208 6.50p multi 1.25 .60

Mexico Post Emblem — A1209

2008, Sept. 8
2581 A1209 6.50p multi 1.25 .60

Fight for Mexican Independence, Bicent. — A1210

Designs: No. 2582, Ignacio Allende (1769-1811), revolutionary leader. No. 2583, Josefa Ortíz de Dominguez (1768-1829), revolutionary leader. No. 2584, José María Morelos y Pavón (1765-1815), revolutionary leader. No. 2585, Battle of Monte de las Cruces, 1810, horiz. No. 2586, Battle of Alhóndiga de Granditas, 1810, horiz. No. 2587, Meeting of Miguel Hidalgo and Morelos, horiz. No. 2588, Querétaro Conspiracy, horiz. No. 2589, Francisco Primo de Verdad y Ramos (1760-1808), promoter of Mexican independence, horiz. No. 2590, Miguel Hidalgo and Cry of Independence. No. 2591, Crowd on Mexico City Alameda.

2008, Sept. 15 ***Perf. 13x13¼***
2582 A1210 6.50p multi 1.25 .60
2583 A1210 6.50p multi 1.25 .60
2584 A1210 6.50p multi 1.25 .60
a. Country name in black (pos. 6) — —

Perf. 13¼x13

2585 A1210 6.50p multi 1.25 .60

Size: 71x30mm

2586 A1210 6.50p multi 1.25 .60
2587 A1210 6.50p multi 1.25 .60
2588 A1210 6.50p multi 1.25 .60
2589 A1210 6.50p multi 1.25 .60
Nos. 2582-2589 (8) 10.00 4.80

Imperf

Size:80x80mm

2590 A1210 10.50p multi 1.90 .95
2591 A1210 10.50p multi 1.90 .95

See Nos. 2627-2636.

Miniature Sheet

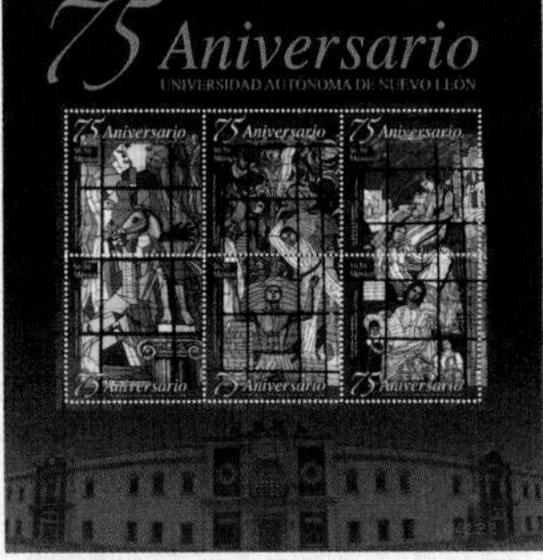

Autonomous University of Nuevo León, 75th Anniv. — A1211

No. 2592 — Stained-glass windows by Roberto Montenegro: a, Top of "La Historia." b, Top of "La Agricultura." c, Top of "La Ciencia y la Sabiduría." d, Bottom of "La Historia." e, Bottom of "La Agricultura." f, Bottom of "La Ciencia y la Sabiduría."

2008, Sept. 25 ***Perf. 13***
2592 A1211 Sheet of 6 7.50 7.50
a.-f. 6.50p Any single 1.25 .60

World Post Day A1212

2008, Oct. 9 ***Perf. 13x13¼***
2593 A1212 10.50p multi 1.60 .80

Flowers — A1213

No. 2594: a, Hylocereus undulatus. b, Curcubita pepo.

2008, Oct. 10 ***Perf. 13***
2594 A1213 Horiz. pair 2.00 1.00
a.-b. 6.50p Either single 1.00 .50

Juarez Autonomous University of Tabasco, 50th Anniv. — A1214

2008, Nov. 3 Litho. ***Perf. 13x13¼***
2595 A1214 6.50p multi 1.00 .50

Miniature Sheet

Letter Carrier's Day — A1215

No. 2596: a, Letter carrier with large shoulder pouch. b, Letter carrier on bicycle. c, Letter carrier on motorcycle with sidecar. d, Letter carrier on motor scooter. e, Postal service automobile. f, Postal truck. g, Letter carriers, bicycles and truck. h, Postal van, letter carrier on bicycle.

2008, Nov. 12 ***Perf. 13***
2596 A1215 Sheet of 8 7.75 7.75
a.-h. 6.50p Any single .95 .50

National Employment Service — A1216

2008, Nov. 19 *Perf. 13¼x13½*

2597 A1216 6.50p multi .95 .50

Mexican Revolution, Cent. (in 2011) A1217

Designs: No. 2598, José María Pino Suárez (1869-1913), politician. No. 2599, Aquiles Serdán (1876-1910), politician. No. 2600, Ricardo Flores Magón (1874-1922), anarchist, and Regeneración Newspaper. No. 2601, Mexican Liberal Party. No. 2602, Cananea Strike. No. 2603, Railway system. No. 2604, Rio Blanco Strike. No. 2605, Revolutionary Junta of Puebla.

No. 2606, Triumphal Entry of Francisco I. Madero. No. 2607, Tienda de raya (company store).

2008, Nov. 20 *Perf. 13x13¼*

2598 A1217 6.50p multi .95 .50
2599 A1217 6.50p multi .95 .50
2600 A1217 6.50p multi .95 .50

Size: 71x30mm

Perf. 13¼x13

2601 A1217 6.50p multi .95 .50
2602 A1217 6.50p multi .95 .50
2603 A1217 6.50p multi .95 .50
2604 A1217 6.50p multi .95 .50
2605 A1217 6.50p multi .95 .50
Nos. 2598-2605 (8) 7.60 4.00

Imperf

Size: 80x80mm

2606 A1217 10.50p multi 1.60 .80
2607 A1217 10.50p multi 1.60 .80

See Nos. 2647-2656.

Parque La Venta Archaeological Museum, La Venta — A1218

2008, Dec. 4 *Perf. 13*

2608 A1218 6.50p multi .95 .50

Christmas A1219

Designs: 6.50p, Adoration of the Shepherds, by Cristóbal de Villalpando. 10.50p, Adoration of the Magi, by unknown artist.

2008, Dec. 10 *Perf. 13x13¼*

2609 A1219 6.50p multi 1.00 .50
2610 A1219 10.50p multi 1.60 .80
a. Horiz. pair, #2609-2610 2.60 1.30

Dr. Gonzalo Aguirre Beltrán (1908-96), Anthropologist — A1220

2008, Dec. 16 *Perf. 13¼x13*

2611 A1220 6.50p multi .95 .50

Miniature Sheet

Palenque Archaeological Site — A1221

No. 2612: a, Mayan hieroglyphic cartouches, tomb, seated figure. b, Jade mask, skull mask, tablet. c, Palace and tower. d, Temple of the Sun, Temples 14 and 15. e, Temple of Inscriptions, incense holder.

2008, Dec. 19 **Litho.**

2612 A1221 Sheet of 5 + label 7.25 7.25
a.-b. 6.50p Either single .95 .50
c. 10.50p multi 1.50 .75
d.-e. 13p Either single 1.90 .95

Mexican Academy of Film Ariel Awards, 50th Anniv. — A1222

2008, Dec. 24 *Perf. 13¼x13*

2613 A1222 6.50p multi .95 .50

St. Valentine's Day — A1223

2009, Feb. 9 **Litho.** *Perf. 13x13¼*

2614 A1223 6.50p multi .90 .45

Veracruz Carnival A1224

2009, Feb. 18

2615 A1224 6.50p multi .90 .45

Miniature Sheet

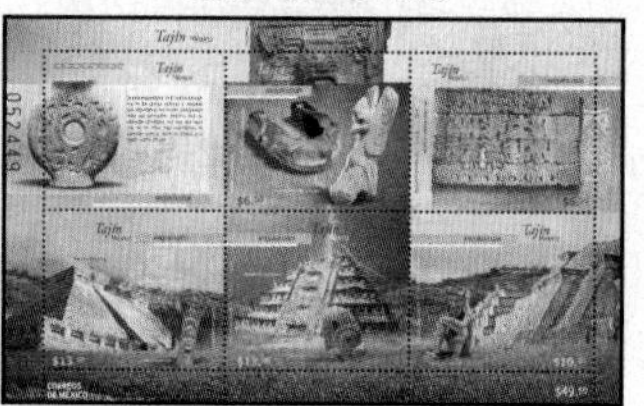

Tajín Archaeological Site — A1225

No. 2616: a, Yoke, eagle-shaped hatchet. b, Decorated panel. c, Terracotta pelota player and pelota pyramid. d, Pyramid, bird's head hatchet, lightning bolt. e, Temple, temple diagram, decorated handle.

2009, Mar. 21 *Perf. 13¼x13*

2616 A1225 Sheet of 5 + label 7.50 3.75
a.-b. 6.50p Either single .95 .50
c. 10.50p multi 1.60 .80
d.-e. 13p Either single 1.90 .95

Channel 11 Television, 50th Anniv. — A1226

2009, Mar. 27

2617 A1226 6.50p multi .95 .50

Teacher's Day A1227

2009, May 15 *Perf. 13x13¼*

2618 A1227 6.50p multi 1.00 .50

Miniature Sheet

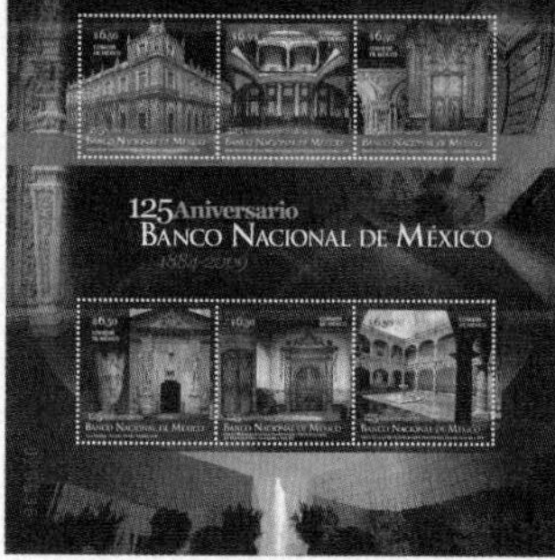

National Bank of Mexico, 125th Anniv. — A1228

No. 2619: a, Palacio de los Condes de San Mateo de Valparaiso, Mexico City. b, Main patio, Palacio de los Condes de San Mateo de Valparaiso. c, Column and main door, Palacio de Iturbide, Mexico City. d, Casa Montejo, Mérida. e, Doors, Casa del Mayorazgo de la Canal, San Miguel de Allende. f, Main patio, Palacio de los Condes del Valle de Súchil, Durango.

2009, June 2 *Perf. 13*

2619 A1228 Sheet of 6 6.00 3.00
a.-f. 6.50p Any single 1.00 .50

World Environment Day — A1229

2009, June 5 *Perf. 13¼x13*

2620 A1229 10.50p multi 1.60 .80

Aguascalientes Autonomous University — A1230

2009, June 19

2621 A1230 10.50p multi 1.60 .80

Gymnogyps Californianus — A1231

2009, July 27 *Perf. 13x13¼*

2622 A1231 10.50p multi 1.60 .80

Intl. Day of Indigenous People A1232

2009, Aug. 11

2623 A1232 6.50p multi 1.00 .50

The Country, by Jorge González Camarena — A1233

2009, Aug. 20 Litho. *Perf. 13¼x13*

2624 A1233 6.50p multi 1.00 .50

National Free Textbook Commission, 50th anniv.

Preservation of Polar Regions and Glaciers — A1234

Designs: 10.50p, Mts. Popocatépetl and Iztaccíhuatl. 13p, Mt. Citlaltépetl.

2009, Sept. 14 *Perf. 13*

2625 10.50p multi 1.60 .80
2626 13p multi 1.90 .95
a. A1234 Vert. pair, #2625-2626 3.50 1.75

Fight For Mexican Independence Type of 2008

Designs: No. 2627, Congress of Chilpancingo. No. 2628, Establishment of the Supreme Junta. No. 2629, Leona Vicario (1789-1842), supporter of independence movement, and husband, Andrés Quintana Roo (1787-1851), independence movement leader and politician. No. 2630, Execution of José María Morelos y Pavón, horiz. No. 2631, Capture of Miguel Hidalgo and insurgents, horiz. No. 2632, Execution of Hidalgo, horiz. No. 2633, Siege of Cuautla, horiz. No. 2634, Constitution of Apatzingán, horiz.

No. 2635, Map of campaign of Morelos, portraits of compatriots Hermenegildo Galeana, Mariano Matamoros, Pablo Galeana, and Nicolás Bravo. No. 2636, Abolition of slavery.

2009, Sept. 16 *Perf. 13x13¼*

2627 A1210 6.50p multi 1.00 .50
2628 A1210 6.50p multi 1.00 .50
2629 A1210 6.50p multi 1.00 .50

Perf. 13¼x13

2630 A1210 6.50p multi 1.00 .50
2631 A1210 6.50p multi 1.00 .50
2632 A1210 6.50p multi 1.00 .50

Size: 71x30mm

2633 A1210 6.50p multi 1.00 .50
2634 A1210 6.50p multi 1.00 .50
Nos. 2627-2634 (8) 8.00 4.00

Imperf

Size: 80x80mm

2635 A1210 10.50p multi 1.60 .80
2636 A1210 10.50p multi 1.60 .80

UNI Global Union Post and Logistics Conference, Mexico City — A1235

2009, Sept. 30 *Perf. 13x13¼*

2637 A1235 6.50p multi 1.00 .50

Autonomous University of San Luis Potosí Scientific and Literary Institute, 150th Anniv. — A1236

2009, Oct. 5 *Perf. 13¼x13*

2638 A1236 6.50p multi 1.00 .50

World Post Day A1237

2009, Oct. 9 *Perf. 13x13¼*

2639 A1237 10.50p multi 1.60 .80

City of Chihuahua, 300th Anniv. — A1238

2009, Oct. 12 *Perf. 13¼x13*

2640 A1238 6.50p multi 1.00 .50

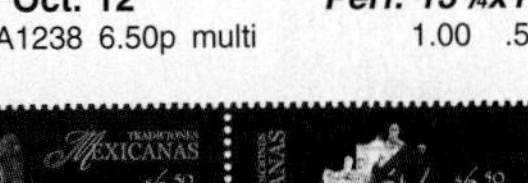

Day of the Dead (All Souls' Day) — A1239

Figurines: No. 2641, Woman honoring dead. No. 2642, Ferris wheel with skeleton riders.

2009, Nov. 2 *Perf. 13*

2641 6.50p multi 1.00 .50
2642 6.50p multi 1.00 .50
a. A1239 Horiz. pair, #2641-2642 2.00 1.00

Juan Bosch (1909-2001), President of Dominican Republic — A1240

2009, Nov. 4 *Perf. 13x13¼*

2643 A1240 10.50p multi 1.60 .80

Wilderness Areas A1241

No. 2644: a, El Carmen Mountains, Mexico. b, Nahanni National Park, Canada. c, Zion National Park, US. d, Kronotsky Reserve, Russia. e, Baviaanskloof Reserve, South Africa.

2009, Nov. 6 Litho. *Perf. 13*

2644 Horiz. strip of 5 8.50 4.25
a. A1241 6.50p multi 1.00 .50
b.-c. A1241 10.50p Either single 1.60 .80
d. A1241 13p multi 2.00 1.00
e. A1241 14.50p multi 2.25 1.10

Letter Carrier's Day — A1242

Letter carrier on: No. 2645, Bicycle. No. 2646, Motorcycle.

2009, Nov. 12 *Perf. 13*

2645 6.50p multi 1.00 .50
2646 6.50p multi 1.00 .50
a. A1242 Horiz. pair, #2645-2646 2.00 1.00

Mexican Revolution Type of 2008

Designs: No. 2647, Emiliano Zapata (1879-1919), General of Liberation Army of the South. No. 2648, Pres. Francisco I. Madero (1873-1913). No. 2649, Proclamation of the Plan of Ayala. No. 2650, Taking of Zacatecas, horiz. No. 2651, Women revolution fighters, horiz. No. 2652, Francisco "Pancho" Villa (1878-1923), General of the Division of the North, horiz. No. 2653, Railroads in the revolution, horiz. No. 2654, The "Ten Tragic Days," horiz.

No. 2655, Venustiano Carranza (1859-1920), revolution leader, and proclamation of Plan of Guadalupe. No. 2656, Revolutionaries, painting by David Alfaro Siqueiros.

2009, Nov. 20 *Perf. 13x13¼*

2647 A1217 6.50p multi 1.10 .55
2648 A1217 6.50p multi 1.10 .55
2649 A1217 6.50p multi 1.10 .55

Perf. 13¼x13

2650 A1217 6.50p multi 1.10 .55
2651 A1217 6.50p multi 1.10 .55

Size: 71x30mm

2652 A1217 6.50p multi 1.10 .55
2653 A1217 6.50p multi 1.10 .55
2654 A1217 6.50p multi 1.10 .55
Nos. 2647-2654 (8) 8.80 4.40

Imperf

Size: 80x80mm

2655 A1217 10.50p multi 1.75 .85
2656 A1217 10.50p multi 1.75 .85

Traffic Safety A1243

2009, Nov. 23 *Perf. 13¼x13*

2657 A1243 6.50p multi 1.10 .55

Jaíme Sabínes (1926-99), Poet — A1244

2009, Nov. 27 Litho.

2658 A1244 6.50p multi 1.10 .55

Federal Fiscal Auditor, 50th Anniv. — A1245

2009, Nov. 30

2659 A1245 6.50p multi 1.10 .55

Christmas
A1246 A1247

2009, Dec. 1 *Perf. 13¼x13*

2660 A1246 6.50p Melchior 1.10 .55
2661 A1246 6.50p Gaspar 1.10 .55
2662 A1246 6.50p Balthazar 1.10 .55
2663 A1247 6.50p Santa Claus 1.10 .55
Nos. 2660-2663 (4) 4.40 2.20

Oportunidades Human Development Program — A1248

2009, Dec. 15 *Perf. 13x13¼*

2664 A1248 6.50p multi 1.00 .50

Energy Conservation — A1249

No. 2665 — Children's drawings: a, Child connecting power cord from house to sun. b, Light bulbs in daytime and nighttime. c, Light bulb people in room.

2009, Dec. 16 *Perf. 13¼x13*

2665 Horiz. strip of 3 3.00 1.50
a.-c. A1249 6.50p Any single 1.00 .50

Paisano Program A1250

2009, Dec. 18 *Perf. 13x13¼*

2666 A1250 6.50p multi 1.00 .50

Pres. Venustiano Carranza (1859-1920) — A1251

2009, Dec. 21
2667 A1251 6.50p multi 1.00 .50

Aviation in Mexico, Cent. — A1252

2010, Jan. 8 Litho. ***Perf. 13¼x13***
2668 A1252 7p multi 1.10 .55

State Workers' Security and Social Services Institute, 50th Anniv. — A1253

2010, Jan. 19
2669 A1253 7p multi 1.10 .55

St. Valentine's Day — A1254

2010, Feb. 3
2670 A1254 7p multi 1.10 .55

New Year 2010 (Year of the Tiger) A1255

2010, Feb. 11 ***Perf. 13x13¼***
2671 A1255 7p multi 1.10 .55

Mexican Red Cross, Cent. A1256

2010, Feb. 21 ***Perf. 13***
2672 A1256 10.50p multi 1.75 .85

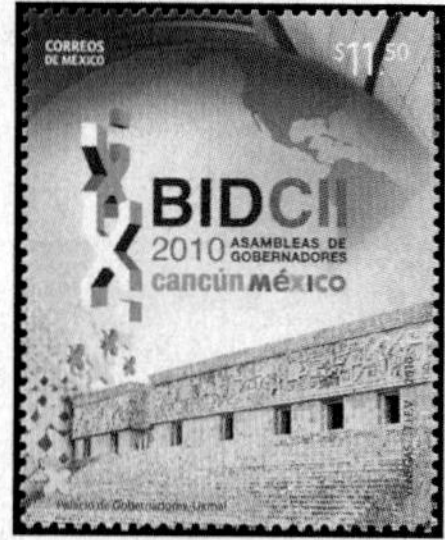

Inter-America Development Bank Assembly of Governors, Cancun — A1257

2010, Mar. 19 ***Perf. 13x13¼***
2673 A1257 11.50p multi 1.90 .95

Souvenir Sheet

Mexico City Red Devils Baseball Players — A1258

No. 2674: a, José Luis Sandoval. b, Miguel Ojeda. c, Roberto Saucedo.

2010, Apr. 11 ***Perf. 13***
2674 A1258 Sheet of 3 3.50 1.75
a.-c. 7p Any single 1.10 .55

Mother's Day A1259

2010, Apr. 23 ***Perf. 13x13¼***
2675 A1259 7p multi 1.10 .55

Teacher's Day A1260

2010, May 15
2676 A1260 7p multi 1.10 .55

2010 World Cup Soccer Championships, South Africa — A1261

No. 2677 — 2010 World Cup emblem and: a, Mexican team. b, Gerardo Torrado, Giovani Dos Santos. c, Andrés Guardado, Guillermo Ochoa.

2010, May 15 ***Perf. 13¼x13***
2677 Horiz. strip of 3 4.00 2.00
a.-b. A1261 7p Either single 1.10 .55
c. A1261 11.50p multi 1.75 .90

Intl. Mother Language Day — A1262

2010, May 21
2678 A1262 11.50p multi 1.75 .90

Pres. Adolfo López Mateos (1909-69) — A1263

2010, May 26
2679 A1263 7p multi 1.10 .55

Natl. Human Rights Commission — A1264

2010, June 7 **Litho.**
2680 A1264 7p multi 1.10 .55

Scouting in Mexico, 90th Anniv. A1265

2010, July 17 ***Perf. 13***
2681 A1265 7p multi 1.10 .55

Grandparent's Day — A1266

2010, Aug. 16
2682 A1266 7p multi 1.10 .55

Mexican Petroleum Institute — A1267

2010, Aug. 23 ***Perf. 13¼x13***
2683 A1267 7p multi 1.10 .55

Mexican Independence, Bicent. — A1268

Designs: No. 2684, Pres. Guadalupe Victoria (1789-1843). No. 2685, Pedro Moreno (1775-1817), revolutionary leader. No. 2686, Father Servando Teresa de Mier (1765-1827), politician. No. 2687, Xavier Mina (1789-1817), revolutionary leader. No. 2688, Vicente Guerrero (1783-1831), soldier and politician. No. 2689, Flag of the Army of the Three Guarantees. No. 2690, Gen. Manuel de Mier y Terán (1789-1832), Nicolás Bravo (1786-1854), soldier and politician, horiz. No. 2691, Ignacio López Rayón (1773-1832), leader of revolutionary government, Gen. Ramón Rayón (1775-1839), horiz. No. 2692, O'Donojú Conference, horiz.

No. 2693, Miguel Hidalgo y Costilla (1753-1811), revolutionary leader; Lieutenant Colonel Mariano Jiménez (1781-1811); Juan Aldama (1774-1811), soldier; Leona Vicario (1789-1842), revolution supporter; José María Morelos y Pavón (1765-1815), revolutionary leader; Ignacío Allende (1769-1811), revolutionary leader; Josefa Ortiz de Domínguez (1768-1829), revolution supporter; and Miguel Domínguez (1756-1830), revolutionary leader. No. 2694, Entrance into Mexico City of the Army of the Three Guarantees.

2010, Sept. 16 ***Perf. 13x13¼***
2684 A1268 7p multi 1.10 .55
2685 A1268 7p multi 1.10 .55
2686 A1268 7p multi 1.10 .55
2687 A1268 7p multi 1.10 .55
2688 A1268 7p multi 1.10 .55
2689 A1268 7p multi 1.10 .55

Perf. 13¼x13

2690 A1268 7p multi 1.10 .55
2691 A1268 7p multi 1.10 .55
2692 A1268 7p multi 1.10 .55
Nos. 2684-2692 (9) 9.90 4.95

Imperf

Size: 80x80mm

2693 A1268 11.50p multi 1.90 .95
2694 A1268 11.50p multi 1.90 .95

Miniature Sheet

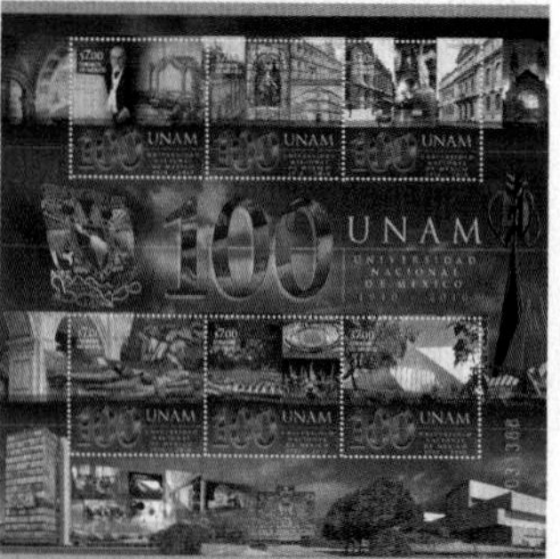

National University of Mexico, Cent. — A1269

No. 2695: a, University founder Justo Sierra, opening of National University. b, National Preparatory School, College of San Ildefonso. c, National School of Law, Academy of San Carlos, National School of Higher Studies. d, Murals by José Clemente Orozco and David Alfaro Siqueiros. e, National University of Mexico Symphonic Orchestra in Nezahualcoyotl Hall, Olympic Stadium, Dancers of National University of Mexico Choreographic Studio. f, University Museum of Contemporaneous Art.

2010, Sept. 21 Litho. ***Perf. 13***
2695 A1269 Sheet of 6 6.75 3.50
a.-f. 7p Any single 1.10 .55

Girl Guides of Mexico A1270

2010, Sept. 25
2696 A1270 7p multi 1.10 .55

Plenipotentiary Conference of the Intl. Telecommunications Union, Guadalajara — A1271

2010, Oct. 4 *Perf. 13¼x13*
2697 A1271 11.50p multi 1.90 .95

World Post Day A1272

2010, Oct. 9 *Perf. 13x13¼*
2698 A1272 11.50p multi 1.90 .95

Souvenir Sheet

Temples — A1273

No. 2699: a, Pyramid of the Sun, Teotihuacan, Mexico. b, Ateshgah, Baku, Azerbaijan.

2010, Oct. 12
2699 A1273 Sheet of 2 2.25 1.10
a.-b. 7p Either single 1.10 .55

See Azerbaijan No. 934.

National Center for Disaster Prevention, 20th Anniv. A1274

2010, Oct. 13
2700 A1274 7p multi 1.25 .60

All Souls' Day (Day of the Dead) — A1275

2010, Oct. 25
2701 A1275 7p multi 1.25 .60

A1276

Christmas A1277

Designs: No. 2702, Santa Claus, children, Christmas tree, toys.
No. 2703 — Red ribbon and: a, Holy Family and angel. b, Candle, children hitting piñata. c, Three Magi.

2010, Nov. 4 **Litho.** *Perf. 13*
2702 A1276 7p multi 1.25 .60
2703 Horiz. strip of 3 3.75 1.90
a.-c. A1277 7p Any single 1.25 .60

Letter Carrier's Day — A1278

Designs: 7p, Postman and old postal truck. 11.50p, Postman on motorcycle, row of postal trucks.

2010, Nov. 11
2704 7p multi 1.25 .60
2705 11.50p multi 1.90 .95
a. A1278 Horiz. pair, #2704-2705 3.25 1.60

Rodolfo Neri Vela, First Mexican in Space, 25th Anniv. A1279

Neri Vela and: No. 2706, Space equipment. No. 2707, Mexican flag, Space Shuttles.

2010, Nov. 16 *Perf. 13x13¼*
2706 7p multi 1.25 .60
2707 7p multi 1.25 .60
a. A1279 Vert. pair, #2706-2707 2.50 1.25

Palace of Fine Arts, Mexico City — A1280

2010, Nov. 19 *Perf. 13¼x13*
2708 A1280 7p multi 1.25 .60

Mexican Revolution, Cent. A1281

Designs: No. 2709, Pres. Venustiano Carranza (1859-1920), Carranza and crowd. No. 2710, Luis Cabrera (1876-1954), politician, and Agricultural Law. No. 2711, 1917 Constitution, detail of painting by Jorge González Camarena depicting Pres. Carranza and papers. No. 2712, 1917 Constitution, by Camarena, detail depicting Constitutional Congress and eagle. No. 2713, The Convention of Aguascalientes, detail of painting by Oswaldo Barra Cunningham, horiz. No. 2714, Battle of Celaya, horiz. No. 2715, Provisional Presidents Eulalio Gutiérrez (1881-1939), Roque González Garza (1885-1962), and Francisco Lagos Cházaro (1878-1932), Provisional Government one-peso banknote, horiz. No. 2716, Women fighters in the Mexican Revolution, horiz.
No. 2717, Revolution leaders Carranza, Francisco "Pancho" Villa (1878-1923), and Emiliano Zapata (1879-1919) on horseback. No. 2718, 1910 Revolution, detail of mural by Diego Rivera depicting revolution leaders.

2010, Nov. 20 *Perf. 13x13¼*
2709 A1281 7p multi 1.25 .60
2710 A1281 7p multi 1.25 .60
2711 A1281 7p multi 1.25 .60
2712 A1281 7p multi 1.25 .60

Perf. 13¼x13

2713 A1281 7p multi 1.25 .60
2714 A1281 7p multi 1.25 .60

Size: 71x30mm

2715 A1281 7p multi 1.25 .60
2716 A1281 7p multi 1.25 .60
Nos. 2709-2716 (8) 10.00 4.80

Imperf

Size: 80x80mm

2717 A1281 11.50p multi 1.90 .95
2718 A1281 11.50p multi 1.90 .95

Monumental Clock, Pachuca, Cent. — A1282

2010, Nov. 25 *Perf. 13*
2719 A1282 7p multi 1.25 .60

Campaign Against Violence Towards Women — A1283

2010, Dec. 1 *Perf. 13¼x13*
2720 A1283 11.50p multi 1.90 .95

2010 United Nations Climate Change Conference, Cancún — A1284

2010, Dec. 6 *Perf. 13x13¼*
2721 A1284 7p multi 1.25 .60

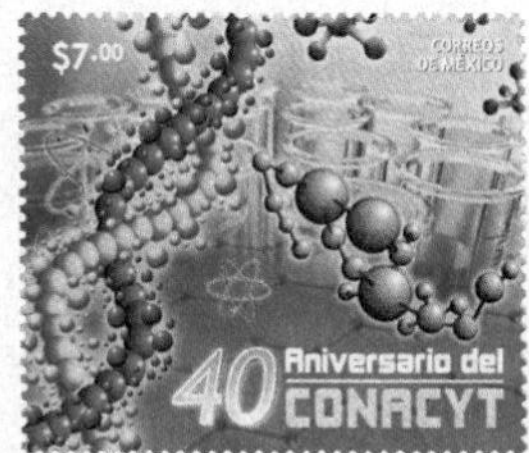
National Council of Science and Technology (CONACYT), 40th Anniv. — A1285

2010, Dec. 9 *Perf. 13¼x13*
2722 A1285 7p multi 1.25 .60

Awarding of Nobel Prize for Literature to Octavio Paz, 20th Anniv. — A1286

2010, Dec. 10 **Litho.**
2723 A1286 7p multi 1.25 .60

National Week of Small and Medium Enterprises — A1287

2010, Dec. 13
2724 A1287 7p multi 1.25 .60

Ardea Herodias — A1288

2010, Dec. 15
2725 A1288 11.50p multi 1.90 .95

Souvenir Sheet

Dances — A1289

No. 2726: a, Ballet Folklorico de Mexico de Amalia Hernandez. b, Kalbelia Dance, India.

2010, Dec. 15 ***Perf. 13***
2726 A1289 Sheet of 2 2.50 1.25
a.-b. 7p Either single 1.25 .60

See India Nos. 2473-2474.

Miniature Sheet

Teotihuacan Archaeological Site — A1290

No. 2727: a, Detail from mural, onyx carving. b, Columns from Quetzalpapalotl Palace, Sun sculpture. c, Censer and vessel. d, Pyramid of the Sun and mask. e, Pyramid of the Moon

2010, Dec. 16 ***Perf. 13¼x13***
2727 A1290 Sheet of 5 + label 9.00 4.50
a.-b. 7p Either single 1.25 .60
c. 11.50p multi 1.90 .95
d.-e. 13.50p Either single 2.25 1.10

Miniature Sheet

Orchids — A1291

No. 2728: a, Cypripedium irapeanum. b, Sobralia macrantha. c, Prosthechea lonophlebia. d, Laelia anceps subspecies dawsonii f. chilapensis. e, Trichocentrum oerstedii. f, Laelia rubescens.

2010, Dec. 17 ***Perf. 13***
2728 A1291 Sheet of 6 7.50 3.75
a.-f. 7p Any single 1.25 .60

Trust For Electrical Energy Conservation, 20th Anniv. — A1292

2010, Dec. 20 ***Perf. 13¼x13***
2729 A1292 7p multi 1.25 .60

A1293

Love A1294

2011, Jan. 31 ***Perf. 13***
2730 A1293 7p multi 1.25 .60
2731 A1294 7p multi 1.25 .60

Postal Union of the Americas, Spain and Portugal (UPAEP), Cent. A1295

2011, Mar. 23 **Litho.**
2732 A1295 13.50p multi 2.40 1.25

Mother's Day A1296

2011, Apr. 13
2733 A1296 7p multi 1.25 .60

National Seed Inspection and Certification Service, 50th Anniv. — A1297

No. 2734: a, Corn kernels, hands holding seed corn. b, Flowers, flower testers. c, Bananas, prickly pear fruit, flower, agave, avocado, citrus fruit, poinsettia, map of Mexico, corn cobs and kernels.

2011, Apr. 29 ***Perf. 13x13¼***
2734 Vert. strip of 3 3.75 1.90
a.-c. A1297 7p Any single 1.25 .60

Main Post Office, Mexico City — A1298

2011, May 4 **Litho.**
2735 A1298 7p multi 1.25 .60

Souvenir Sheet

Mil Mascaras (Man of a Thousand Masks), Professional Wrestler — A1299

No. 2736 — Mil Mascaras (Aaron Rodríguez Arellano) wearing: a, Yellow, black and red mask with red "M," and match scene c, Black and white mask with red "M" and cape, Mil Mascaras with outer masks. d, Yellow and black mask with red "M," Mil Mascaras leaping in ring.

2011, May 11 ***Perf. 13***
2736 A1299 Sheet of 3 3.75 1.90
a.-c. 7p Any single 1.25 .60

The Rural Teacher, by Diego Rivera — A1300

2011, May 15 ***Perf. 13¼x13***
2737 A1300 7p multi 1.25 .60

Teacher's Day.

Armillita (Fermín Espinosa, 1911-78), Matador A1301

2011, May 17 ***Perf. 13x13¼***
2738 A1301 7p multi 1.25 .60

Under-17 World Soccer Championships, Mexico — A1302

Tournament emblem, trophy, stadia and various soccer players.

2011, June 15 **Litho.** ***Perf. 13¼x13***
2739 Horiz. strip of 3 5.75 3.00
a. A1302 7p multi 1.25 .60
b. A1302 11.50p multi 2.00 1.00
c. A1302 13.50p multi 2.40 1.25

Grandparent's Day — A1303

2011, Aug. 3 ***Perf. 13***
2740 A1303 7p multi 1.25 .60

Intl. Year of Forests A1304

2011, Aug. 5 ***Perf. 13x13¼***
2741 A1304 11.50p multi 1.90 .95

Promotion of Philately A1305

2011, Aug. 8 ***Perf. 13***
2742 A1305 7p multi 1.25 .60

National Defense College, 30th Anniv. — A1306

2011, Aug. 12 *Perf. 13¼x13*
2743 A1306 7p multi 1.25 .60

Mario Moreno (Cantinflas) (1911-93), Film Actor A1307

Cantinflas: 7p, Photographs. 11.50p, Caricatures.

2011, Aug. 12 *Perf. 13x13¼*
2744 7p multi 1.25 .60
2745 11.50p multi 1.90 .95
a. A1307 Vert. pair, #2744-2745 3.25 1.60

Natl. Institute of Adult Education, 30th Anniv. — A1308

2011, Aug. 18 *Perf. 13¼x13*
2746 A1308 7p multi 1.10 .55

Sepomex (Mexican Postal Service), 25th Anniv. — A1309

2011, Aug. 22
2747 A1309 7p multi 1.10 .55

Law of Fiscal Justice, 75th Anniv. — A1310

2011, Aug. 24
2748 A1310 7p multi 1.10 .55

Mexico Tourism Year A1311

2011, Aug. 24 *Perf. 13x13¼*
2749 A1311 11.50p multi 1.75 .90

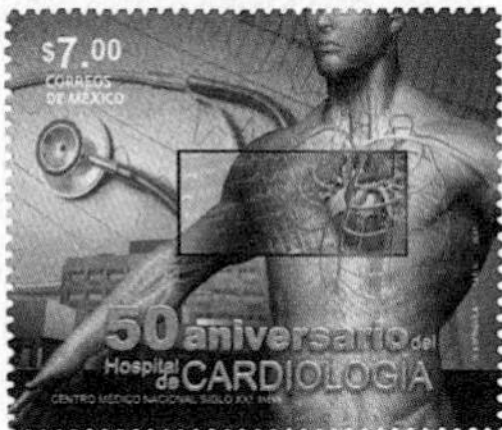
Cardiology Hospital, Mexico City, 50th Anniv. — A1312

2011, Sept. 13
2750 A1312 7p multi 1.10 .55

National System of Civil Protection, 25th Anniv. A1313

2011, Sept. 19 *Perf. 13x13¼*
2751 A1313 11.50p multi 1.75 .85

Souvenir Sheet

Highway Projects — A1314

No. 2752: a, Highway interchange north of Mexico City. b, Piedra Colorada Tunnel. c, Tex-capa Bridge.

2011, Sept. 26 *Perf. 13*
2752 A1314 Sheet of 3 5.00 2.50
a. 7p multi 1.10 .55
b. 11.50p multi 1.75 .85
c. 13.50p multi 2.10 1.10

World Post Day — A1315

2011, Oct. 7 *Perf. 13¼x13*
2753 A1315 11.50p multi 1.75 .85

Miniature Sheet

Secretary of Public Education, 90th Anniv. — A1316

No. 2754: a, First Secretary of Public Education José Vasconcelos in chair, man standing next to chair, cover of 1917 Mexican Constitution. b, Man reading to child, teacher in school. c, Building and murals. d, Child reading book, family, children in school. e, Scenes of school laboratories. f, Murals.

2011, Oct. 12 *Perf. 13*
2754 A1316 Sheet of 6 6.75 3.50
a.-f. 7p Any single 1.10 .55

2011 Pan American Games, Guadalajara — A1317

No. 2755 — Emblem and: a, Diamonds. b, Mascots. c, Agave plants.

2011, Oct. 14 *Perf. 13¼x13*
2755 Horiz. strip of 3 5.00 2.50
a. A1317 7p multi 1.10 .55
b. A1317 11.50p multi 1.75 .85
c. A1317 13.50p multi 2.00 1.00

National Polytechnic Institute Center for Research and Advanced Studies (CINVESTAV), 50th Anniv. — A1318

2011, Oct. 17 *Perf. 13x13¼*
2756 A1318 7p multi 1.10 .55

Miniature Sheet

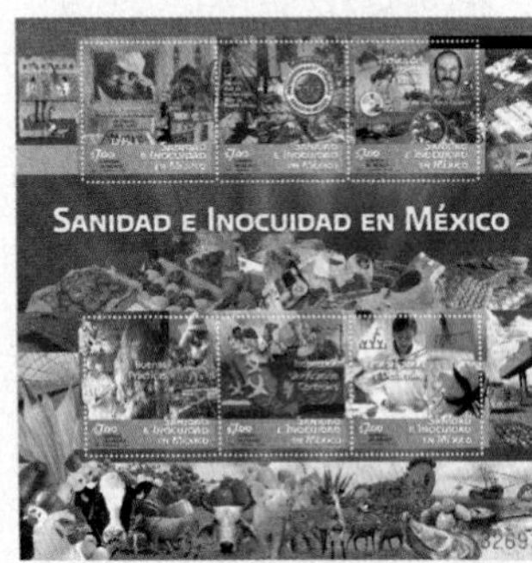
Agricultural and Food Safety in Mexico — A1319

No. 2757: a, Alfonso Luis Herrera López (1868-1942), biologist, insect specimens, micoscope. b, Cattle, packaged meats, butchers, emblem of Mexican food inspection agency (TIF). c, Dr. Dieter Enkerlin (1926-95), entomologist, and insects. d, Food workers using safe food handling practices. e, Map of Mexico, ship, airplane, birds, food inspectors, dog, shipping containers. f, Scientists in laboratory, insect, cotton plant.

2011, Oct. 18 *Perf. 13*
2757 A1319 Sheet of 6 6.75 3.50
a.-f. 7p Any single 1.10 .55

All Souls' Day (Day of the Dead) — A1320

2011, Oct. 25 *Perf. 13¼x13*
2758 A1320 7p multi 1.10 .55

National Council for Educational Development (CONAFE), 40th Anniv. — A1321

2011, Oct. 27 *Perf. 13x13¼*
2759 A1321 7p multi 1.10 .55

State Employees' Social Security and Social Services Institute of Zacatecas, 25th Anniv. — A1322

2011, Oct. 27 **Litho.**
2760 A1322 7p multi 1.10 .55

Letter Carrier's Day A1323

2011, Nov. 11
2761 A1323 7p multi 1.10 .55

Dogs Type of 2007

Designs: 7p, German shepherd (Pastor Alemán). 13.50p, English cocker spaniel (Cocker spaniel Inglés).

2011, Nov. 17 *Perf. 13*
2762 A1198 7p multi 1.10 .55
2763 A1198 13.50p multi 2.00 1.00

Christmas — A1324

Designs: No. 2764, Santa Claus, letters, silhouette of Santa's sleigh in front of Moon.
No. 2765, vert.: a, Children, Christmas piñata. b, Creche, candle, fruit and cup. c, Letters, Magi, Christmas gifts.

2011, Nov. 18 *Perf. 13¼x13*

2764	A1324 11.50p multi	1.75	.85
2765	Vert. strip of 3	4.75	2.25
a.	A1324 7p multi	1.10	.55
b.-c.	A1324 11.50p Either single	1.75	.85

Veracruz Delegation of Mexican Social Security Institute, 50th Anniv. A1326

2011, Nov. 30 *Perf. 13x13¼*

2766	A1326 7p multi	1.10	.55

Intl. Day for Elimination of Violence Toward Women — A1327

2011, Nov. 30 *Perf. 13¼x13*

2767	A1327 11.50p multi	1.75	.85

National Voluntary Action and Solidarity Prize A1328

2011, Dec. 7 *Perf. 13x13¼*

2768	A1328 11.50p multi	1.75	.85

Mexican Urban UNESCO World Heritage Sites — A1329

2011, Dec. 8 *Perf. 13¼x13*

2769	A1329 11.50p multi	1.75	.85

State Workers' Security and Social Services Institute, 50th Anniv. A1330

2011, Dec. 16 *Perf. 13x13¼*

2770	A1330 7p multi	1.10	.55

Diplomatic Relations Between Mexico and South Korea, 50th Anniv. — A1331

Designs: No. 2771, Adult gray whale, denomination at left. No. 2772, Juvenile gray whale, denomination at right.

2012, Jan. 26 Litho. *Perf. 13¼x13*

2771	13.50p multi	2.10	1.10
2772	13.50p multi	2.10	1.10
a.	A1331 Horiz. pair, #2771-2772	4.25	2.25

See South Korea No. 2377.

St. Valentine's Day — A1332

2012, Feb. 2 *Perf. 13*

2773	A1332 7p multi	1.10	.55

Intl. Women's Day A1333

2012, Mar. 8 *Perf. 13x13¼*

2774	A1333 11.50p multi	1.75	.90

World Down Syndrome Day — A1334

2012, Mar. 21 *Perf. 13¼x13*

2775	A1334 13.50p multi	2.10	1.10

National Bioethics Commission, 20th Anniv. — A1335

2012, Mar. 27 **Litho.**

2776	A1335 7p multi	1.10	.55

Campaign Against Human Trafficking A1336

2012, Mar. 29 *Perf. 13x13¼*

2777	A1336 7p multi	1.10	.55

Linares, 300th Anniv. — A1337

2012, Apr. 10 *Perf. 13¼x13*

2778	A1337 7p multi	1.10	.55

Mother's Day A1338

Designs: No. 2779, Mother receiving card and breakfast from two children. No. 2780, Mothers and children.

2012, Apr. 26 *Perf. 13*

2779	A1338 7p grn & multi	1.10	.55
2780	A1338 7p pink & multi	1.10	.55

Interior Stairway of Postal Palace (Main Post Office), Mexico City — A1339

2012, May 4 *Perf. 13x13¼*

2781	A1339 7p multi	1.00	.50

Souvenir Sheet

Battle of Puebla, 150th Anniv. — A1340

No. 2782: a, Map of Mexico, flags of France, Great Britain and Spain. b, General Ignacio Zaragoza, soldiers. c, Army of the East.

2012, May 5 *Perf. 13*

2782	A1340 Sheet of 3	3.00	1.50
a.-c.	7p Any single	1.00	.50

Teacher's Day A1341

2012, May 15 *Perf. 13x13¼*

2783	A1341 7p multi	1.00	.50

Traditional Foods of Mexico and Brazil A1342

Designs: No. 2784, Pozole. No. 2785, Milho e mandioca.

2012, June 1 Litho. *Perf. 13*

2784	13.50p multi	1.90	.95
2785	13.50p multi	1.90	.95
a.	A1342 Horiz. pair, #2784-2785	3.80	1.90

See Brazil No. 3217.

Mexican Wolves — A1343

2012, June 4 *Perf. 13¼x13*

2786	A1343 11.50p multi	1.75	.85

World Anti-Tobacco Day — A1344

2012, July 5 *Perf. 13¼x13*

2787	A1344 7p multi	1.10	.55

Escuela Libre de Derecho (Law School), Mexico City, Cent. — A1345

2012, July 24 **Litho.**

2788	A1345 7p multi	1.10	.55

Grandparent's Day — A1346

2012, Aug. 13 ***Perf. 13***
2789 A1346 7p multi 1.10 .55

Miniature Sheet

Federal Electricity Commission, 75th Anniv. — A1347

No. 2790: a, El Cajón Dam, Nayarit. b, Guaycora Solar Farm, Sonora. c, La Venta Wind Generators, Oaxaca. d, Lineman and electrical lines. e, National Energy Control Center. f, Transmission towers, Colima.

2012, Aug. 14 ***Perf. 13***
2790 A1347 Sheet of 6 6.75 3.50
a.-f. 7p Any single 1.10 .55

Mexican Petroleum Congress A1348

Designs: No. 2791, PEMEX Refinery, Ciudad Madera. No. 2792, PEMEX offshore oil platform.

2012, Sept. 9 ***Perf. 13x13¼***
2791 7p multi 1.10 .55
2792 7p multi 1.10 .55
a. A1348 Vert. pair, #2791-2792 2.20 1.10

40th Intl. Cervantes Festival, Guanajuato — A1349

2012, Sept. 25 ***Perf. 13¼x13***
2793 A1349 13.50p multi 2.10 1.10

National Polytechnic Institute Center for Research and Advanced Studies (CINVESTAV), Saltillo, 50th Anniv. — A1350

2012, Oct. 2
2794 A1350 7p multi 1.10 .55

University of Sonora, 70th Anniv. A1351

No. 2795: a, Rector's Building (denomination at UR). b, Stained-glass window depicting Don Quixote. c, University Library and Museum (denomination at UL).

2012, Oct. 2 ***Perf. 13x13¼***
2795 Horiz. strip of 3 3.50 1.75
a.-c. A1351 7p Any single 1.10 .55

World Post Day A1352

2012, Oct. 9 ***Perf. 13¼x13***
2796 A1352 11.50p multi 1.75 .90

Minaret, Agua Caliente — A1353

2012, Oct. 11
2797 A1353 11.50p multi 1.75 .90

School Counseling, 20th Anniv. A1354

2012, Oct. 15 ***Perf. 13x13¼***
2798 A1354 7p multi 1.10 .55

Sacred Art of the Viceroys — A1355

Paintings by unknown artists of crowned nuns: No. 2799, Sister María Engracia Josefa del Santísimo Rosario (holding candlestick with flowers). No. 2800, Sister from Order of the Immaculate Conception (with round breastplate).

2012, Oct. 25
2799 7p multi 1.10 .55
2800 7p multi 1.10 .55
a. A1355 Horiz. pair, #2799-2800 2.20 1.10

All Souls' Day (Day of the Dead) A1356

2012, Oct. 29 ***Perf. 13¼x13***
2801 A1356 7p multi 1.10 .55

Miniature Sheet

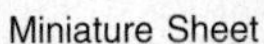

Tulum Archaeological Site — A1357

No. 2802: a, Interior of Temple of the Paintings. b, View of cliffs and the side of the Castillo. c, Front view of the Castillo. d, Temple of the Paintings. e, Building ruins and sculpture of Itzamná from corner of Temple of the Paintings.

2012, Oct. 31 **Litho.**
2802 A1357 Sheet of 5 + label 8.25 4.25
a.-b. 7p Either single 1.10 .55
c. 11.50p multi 1.75 .90
d.-e. 13.50p Either single 2.10 1.10

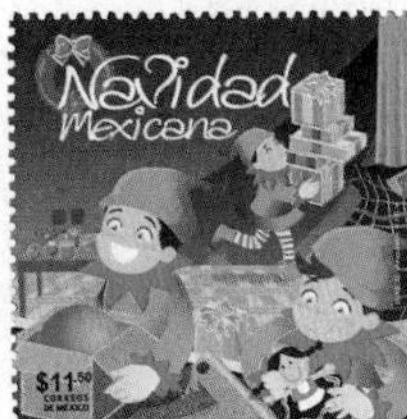

Christmas A1358

No. 2803: a, Elves packing toys in boxes. b, People celebrating Christmas. c, Magi on camels.

2012, Nov. 8 ***Perf. 13***
2803 Horiz. strip of 3 5.25 2.75
a.-c. A1358 11.50p Any single 1.75 .90

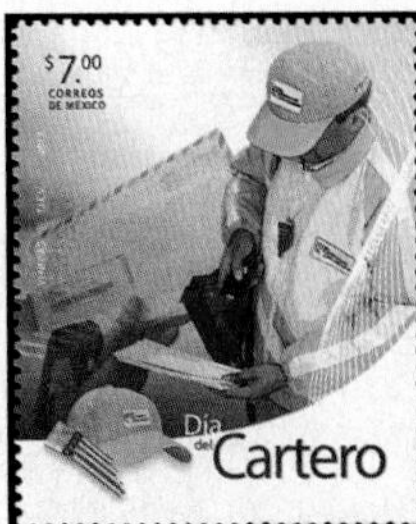

Letter Carrier's Day A1359

2012, Nov. 12 ***Perf. 13x13¼***
2804 A1359 7p multi 1.10 .55

Lebanese Center, Mexico City, 50th Anniv. — A1360

2012, Nov. 13 ***Perf. 13¼x13***
2805 A1360 13.50p multi 2.10 1.10

Public Housing Authority (FOVISSSTE), 40th Anniv. — A1361

2012, Nov. 28 ***Perf. 13x13¼***
2806 A1361 7p multi 1.10 .55

University of Guanajuato, 280th Anniv. — A1362

2012, Dec. 3 ***Perf. 13¼x13***
2807 A1362 7p multi 1.10 .55

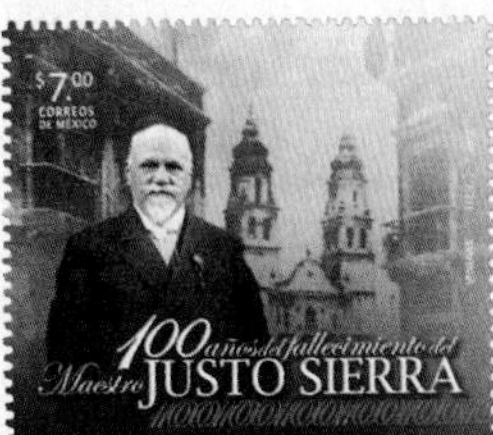

Justo Sierra (1848-1912), Writer — A1363

2012, Dec. 7 **Litho.**
2808 A1363 7p multi 1.10 .55

Sacred Mayan Canoe Crossing — A1364

No. 2809 — Rowers at: a, Rear of canoe. b, Center of canoe. c, Front of canoe.

2012, Dec. 21 *Perf. 13¼x13*

2809	Horiz. strip of 3	5.25	2.75
a.	A1364 7.50p multi	1.25	.60
b.	A1364 11.50p multi	1.90	.95
c.	A1364 13.50p multi	2.10	1.10

St. Valentine's Day A1365

2013, Feb. 8 *Perf. 13*

2810 A1365 7p multi 1.10 .55

President's Day — A1366

2013, Feb. 15 *Perf. 13¼x13*

2811 A1366 7p multi 1.10 .55

Iberoamericana University, Mexico City, 70th Anniv. — A1367

No. 2812: a, Statue and building. b, Buildings. c, Covered steps.

2013, Mar. 7 *Perf. 13x13¼*

2812	A1367 Horiz. strip of 3	3.30	1.65
a.-c.	7p Any single	1.10	.55

National Association of Supermarkets and Department Stores, 30th Anniv. — A1368

2013, Mar. 13 *Perf. 13¼x13*

2813 A1368 7p multi 1.25 .60

Intl. Mother Language Day — A1369

2013, Mar. 13

2814 A1369 11.50p multi 1.90 .95

Expropriation of Foreign-Owned Petroleum Rights and Facilities, 75th Anniv. — A1370

2013, Mar. 17 **Litho.**

2815 A1370 7p multi 1.25 .60

Guillermo Haro Barraza (1913-88), Astronomer A1371

2013, Mar. 21 *Perf. 13x13¼*

2816 A1371 7p multi 1.25 .60

Promulgation of Plan of Guadalupe, Cent. — A1372

2013, Mar. 26 *Perf. 13¼x13*

2817 A1372 7p multi 1.25 .60

Diplomatic Relations Between Mexico and Indonesia, 60th Anniv. — A1373

Designs: No. 2818, Neofelis diardi borneensis. No. 2819, Panthera onca.

2013, Apr. 6 *Perf. 13*

2818	15p multi	2.50	1.25
2819	15p multi	2.50	1.25
a.	A1373 Horiz. pair, #2818-2819	5.00	2.50

See Indonesia No. 2345.

Mexican Army, Cent. A1374

2013, Apr. 17 *Perf. 13x13¼*

2820 A1374 7p multi 1.25 .60

Federico Gómez Children's Hospital, Mexico City, 70th Anniv. — A1375

2013, Apr. 30 **Litho.** *Perf. 13¼x13*

2821 A1375 7p multi 1.25 .60

Children's Day — A1376

2013, Apr. 30 **Litho.** *Perf. 13¼x13*

2822 A1376 7p multi 1.25 .60

Mother's Day A1377

2013, May 10 **Litho.** *Perf. 13*

2823 A1377 11.50p multi 1.90 .95

Teacher's Day A1378

2013, May 15 **Litho.** *Perf. 13x13¼*

2824 A1378 7p multi 1.10 .55

Mexican Army, Cent. — A1379

2013, Aug. 13 **Litho.** *Perf. 13¼x13*

2825 A1379 7p multi 1.10 .55

Veterinary Education in Mexico, 160th Anniv. — A1380

2013, Aug. 16 **Litho.** *Perf. 13¼x13*

2826 A1380 7p multi 1.10 .55

Manuel Acuña (1849-73), Writer — A1381

2013, Aug. 27 **Litho.** *Perf. 13¼x13*

2827 A1381 7p multi 1.10 .55

Grandparent's Day — A1382

2013, Aug. 28 **Litho.** *Perf. 13*

2828 A1382 7p multi 1.10 .55

First Congress of Anáhuac, 200th Anniv. — A1383

2013, Sept. 5 **Litho.** *Perf. 13¼x13*

2829 A1383 7p multi 1.10 .55

Metropolitan Cathedral, Mexico City, 200th Anniv. — A1384

2013, Sept. 11 **Litho.** *Perf. 13x13¼*

2830 A1384 7p multi 1.10 .55

Confederation of Industrial Chambers of Mexico, 95th Anniv. — A1385

2013, Sept. 20 **Litho.** *Perf. 13¼x13*

2831 A1385 7p multi 1.10 .55

Miniature Sheet

Autonomous University of Nuevo León, 80th Anniv. — A1386

No. 2832: a, Las Informantes de Sahagún, by Federico Cantú (head at center top facing right). b, Las Informantes de Sahagún (head at center top facing left). c, Espejos Comunicantes, by Guillermo Ceniceros (compass rose at right). d, Espejos Comunicantes (heads at right). e, Einstein, by Sebastián Xavier Treviño (head of Albert Einstein). f, Einstein (faceless figure and geometric shapes).

2013, Sept. 25 Litho. ***Perf. 13***
2832 A1386 Sheet of 6 6.75 3.50
a.-f. 7p Any single 1.10 .55

World Post Day — A1387

2013, Oct. 9 Litho. ***Perf. 13¼x13***
2833 A1387 13.50p multi 2.10 1.10

Woman Suffrage in Mexico, 60th Anniv. A1388

2013, Oct. 11 Litho. ***Perf. 13x13¼***
2834 A1388 7p multi 1.10 .55

Secretary of Health, 70th Anniv. A1389

2013, Oct. 18 Litho. ***Perf. 13x13¼***
2835 A1389 7p multi 1.10 .55

All Souls' Day (Day of the Dead) — A1390

2013, Oct. 22 Litho. ***Imperf.***
2836 A1390 15p multi 2.25 1.10

Gran Café de la Parroquia Restaurant, Veracruz, 205th Anniv. A1391

2013, Oct. 23 Litho. ***Perf. 13x13¼***
2837 A1391 7p multi 1.10 .55

Bilateral Relations Between Mexico and South Africa, 20th Anniv. A1392

2013, Oct. 24 Litho. ***Perf. 13x13¼***
2838 A1392 15p multi 2.25 1.10

National Institute for Rural Development, 40th Anniv. — A1393

2013, Nov. 5 Litho. ***Perf. 13x13¼***
2839 A1393 7p multi 1.10 .55

Federal Conciliation and Arbitration Tribunal, 50th Anniv. A1394

2013, Nov. 8 Litho. ***Perf. 13x13¼***
2840 A1394 7p multi 1.10 .55

Letter Carrier's Day A1395

2013, Nov. 12 Litho. ***Perf. 13x13¼***
2841 A1395 7p multi 1.10 .55

Casino Español Restaurant, Mexico City, 150th Anniv. A1396

2013, Nov. 14 Litho. ***Perf. 13x13¼***
2842 A1396 13.50p multi 2.10 1.10

Mexican Army, Cent. — A1397

2013, Nov. 15 Litho. ***Perf. 13¼x13***
2843 A1397 7p multi 1.10 .55

Interior of Postal Palace (Main Post Office), Mexico City A1398

2013, Nov. 19 Litho. ***Perf. 13x13¼***
2844 A1398 7p multi 1.10 .55

San Matías Jalatlaco Temple, Former Convent of San Pablo, Historical Center of Oaxaca UNESCO World Heritage Site — A1399

2013, Nov. 21 Litho. ***Perf. 13¼x13***
2845 A1399 15p multi 2.40 1.25
a. Tete-beche pair 4.80 2.50

Migrant's Protection Program A1400

2013, Nov. 27 Litho. ***Perf. 13x13¼***
2846 A1400 7p multi 1.10 .55

Christmas — A1401

Poinsettia and: No. 2847, Magi. No. 2848, Santa Claus. 11.50p, Christmas tree. 13.50p, Holy Family.

2013, Nov. 28 Litho. ***Perf. 13***
2847 A1401 7p multi 1.10 .55
2848 A1401 7p multi 1.10 .55
2849 A1401 11.50p multi 1.75 .80
a. Pair, #2847, 2849 3.00 1.40
2850 A1401 13.50p multi 2.10 1.10
a. Pair, #2848, 2850 3.25 1.75
Nos. 2847-2850 (4) 6.05 3.00

Morelos State Autonomous University, 60th Anniv. — A1402

2013, Dec. 6 Litho. ***Perf. 13¼x13***
2851 A1402 7p multi 1.10 .55

National Education Worker's Union, 70th Anniv. A1403

2013, Dec. 7 Litho. ***Perf. 13x13¼***
2852 A1403 7p multi 1.10 .55

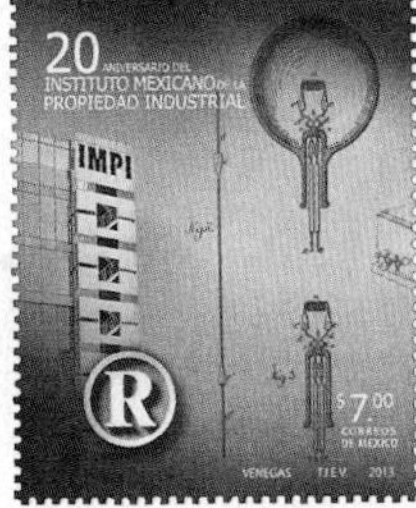

Mexican Institute of Industrial Property, 20th Anniv. A1404

2013, Dec. 12 Litho. ***Perf. 13x13¼***
2853 A1404 7p multi 1.10 .55

National Commission for Sports and Physical Culture, 25th Anniv. — A1405

2013, Dec. 13 Litho. ***Perf. 13¾x13***
2854 A1405 7p multi 1.10 .55

Paintings by Francisco Eppens (1913-90), Stamp Designer A1406

No. 2855: a, La Danza de la Media Luna, 1984. b, Alcatraces, 1988. c, Cactáceas, 1988. d, Guerrero Aguila y Guerrero Tiger, 1980. e, Caballos de Colores, 1985.

2013, Dec. 13 Litho. *Perf. 13x13¼*

2855	Horiz. strip of 5	8.50	4.50
a.-b.	A1406 7p Either single	1.10	.55
c.	A1406 11.50p multi	1.75	.90
d.	A1406 13.50p multi	2.10	1.10
e.	A1406 15p multi	2.40	1.25

Promotion of philately.

Industrial Labor Training Centers, 50th Anniv. A1407

2013, Dec. 17 Litho. *Perf. 13x13¼*
2856 A1407 7p multi 1.10 .55

Federal Police, 85th Anniv. A1408

2013, Dec. 19 Litho. *Perf. 13x13¼*
2857 A1408 7p multi 1.10 .55

Pipe Organs — A1409

No. 2858 — Organs in Oaxaca: a, Santa Maria Tiltepec Temple. b, San Jerónimo Tlacochahuaya Church. c, San Andrés Zautla Church. d, Santa María de la Natividad Tamazulapan. e, Santo Domingo Yanhuitlán Church. f, Oaxaca Cathedral.

2013, Dec. 20 Litho. *Perf. 13¼x13*

2858	Horiz. strip of 6	10.00	5.00
a.-b.	A1409 7p Either single	1.10	.55
c.-d.	A1409 11.50p Either single	1.75	.85
e.-f.	A1409 13.50p Either single	2.10	1.10

National Water Commission, 25th Anniv. — A1410

No. 2859: a, Weir at Los Mochis, Abelardo Rodríguez Dam, Rosales Canal. b, San Pedro Piedra Gorda Dam, San José I Dam. c, Francisco I. Madero Dam, "El Manantial," sculpture by José Sacal. d, Los Berros Water Purification Plant, La Principal Water Treatment Plant. e, Water tunnel, Atotonilco Water Treatment Plant.

2014, Jan. 16 Litho. *Perf. 13x13¼*

2859	Horiz. strip of 5	5.50	2.75
a.-e.	A1410 7p Any single	1.10	.55

St. Valentine's Day A1411

2014, Jan. 31 Litho. *Perf. 13*
2860 A1411 7p multi 1.10 .55

National Chamber of the Mexican Publishing Industry, 50th Anniv. — A1412

2014, Feb. 28 Litho. *Perf. 13¼x13*
2861 A1412 7p multi 1.10 .55

Octavio Paz (1914-98), 1990 Nobel Laureate in Literature A1413

2014, Mar. 20 Litho. *Perf. 13x13¼*
2862 A1413 7p multi 1.10 .55

National Fund for Tourism Development, 40th Anniv. — A1414

2014, Apr. 1 Litho. *Perf. 13¼x13*
2863 A1414 7p multi 1.10 .55

Second Battle of Torreón, Cent. — A1415

2014, Apr. 3 Litho. *Perf. 13¼x13*
2864 A1415 7p multi 1.10 .55

Mexican Pres. Adolfo López Mateos and French Pres. Charles de Gaulle A1416

2014, Apr. 11 Litho. *Perf. 13x13¼*
2865 A1416 13.50p multi 2.10 1.10

Visit of Pres. de Gaulle to Mexico, 50th anniv.

Miniature Sheet

American Occupation of Veracruz, Cent. — A1417

No. 2866: a, Veracruz citizens face the intervention. b, Naval Academy cadets. c, General Rubio Navarrete prepares to contain the American advance. d, Venustiano Carranza makes his triumphal entry into Mexico City. e, Cadet José Virgilio Uribe Robles, Lieutenant Luis Felipe José Azueta Abad. f, Naval Academy parade after the intervention.

2014, Apr. 21 Litho. *Perf. 13*

2866	A1417 Sheet of 6	6.75	3.50
a.-f.	7p Any single	1.10	.55

City of General Escobedo, 410th Anniv. A1418

2014, Apr. 25 Litho. *Perf. 13x13¼*
2867 A1418 7p multi 1.10 .55

Intl. Day of Intellectual Property A1419

2014, Apr. 28 Litho. *Perf. 13x13¼*
2868 A1419 15p multi 2.40 1.25

Children's Day A1420

2014, Apr. 30 Litho. *Perf. 13*
2869 A1420 7p multi 1.10 .55

City of Misantla, 450th Anniv. — A1421

2014, May 3 Litho. *Perf. 13¼x13*
2870 A1421 7p multi 1.10 .55

Mother's Day A1422

2014, May 9 Litho. *Perf. 13*
2871 A1422 11.50p multi 1.75 .90

National Fund for Workers Consumption (FONACOT), 40th Anniv. — A1423

2014, May 14 Litho. *Perf. 13¼x13*
2872 A1423 7p multi 1.10 .55

Autonomous University of the State of Mexico, 70th Anniv. — A1424

2014, May 14 Litho. *Perf. 13x13¼*
2873 A1424 7p multi 1.10 .55

Laura Mendez de Cuenca (1853-1928), Teacher and Writer — A1425

2014, May 15 Litho. *Perf. 13¼x13*
2874 A1425 7p multi 1.10 .55

Teacher's Day.

Mexican National Soccer Team — A1426

2014, May 27 Litho. *Perf. 13¼x13*
2875 A1426 7p multi 1.10 .55

Diplomatic Relations Between Mexico and Portugal, 150th Anniv. — A1427

Mexican and Portuguese flags with denomination color of: No. 2876, White. No. 2877, Black.

2014, June 6 **Litho.** ***Perf. 13***

2876 13.50p multi 2.10 1.10
2877 13.50p multi 2.10 1.10
a. A1427 Horiz. pair, #2876-2877 4.20 2.20

See Portugal Nos. 3605-3606.

Signing of the Treaties of Teoloyucan, Cent. A1428

2014, Aug. 13 **Litho.** ***Perf. 13x13¼***

2878 A1428 7p multi 1.10 .55

National Association of Engineering Schools, 50th Anniv. — A1429

2014, Aug. 22 **Litho.** ***Perf. 13¼x13***

2879 A1429 7p multi 1.10 .55

Firefighter's Day — A1430

2014, Aug. 22 **Litho.** ***Perf. 13¼x13***

2880 A1430 7p multi 1.10 .55

Technological Institute of Ciudad Juárez, 50th Anniv. — A1431

2014, Sept. 4 **Litho.** ***Perf. 13x13¼***

2881 A1431 7p multi 1.10 .55

Greetings — A1432

No. 2882: a, Graduates and diploma. b, Doves and stained-glass window. c, Flowers. d, Clown candle. e, Cupcakes.

2014, Sept. 5 **Litho.** ***Perf. 13¼x13***

2882 Horiz. strip of 5 7.00 3.50
a.-c. A1432 7p Any single 1.10 .55
d.-e. A1432 11.50p Either single 1.75 .85

National Bank of Mexico, 130th Anniv. A1433

2014, Sept. 9 **Litho.** ***Perf. 13***

2883 A1433 11.50p multi 1.75 .85

Veracruz University, 70th Anniv. — A1434

2014, Sept. 10 **Litho.** ***Perf. 13¼x13***

2884 A1434 7.50p multi 1.10 .55

Postal Palace (Main Post Office), Mexico City A1435

2014, Sept. 11 **Litho.** ***Perf. 13x13¼***

2885 A1435 7p multi 1.10 .55

La Jornada Newspaper, 30th Anniv. — A1436

2014, Sept. 18 **Litho.** ***Perf. 13¼x13***

2886 A1436 7p multi 1.10 .55

Palace of Fine Arts, 80th Anniv. A1437

2014, Sept. 29 **Litho.** ***Perf. 13x13¼***

2887 A1437 7p multi 1.10 .55

Resolution of Chamizal Border Dispute With United States, 50th Anniv. A1438

2014, Sept. 30 **Litho.** ***Perf. 13x13¼***

2888 A1438 11.50p multi 1.75 .85

Creation of State of Quintana Roo, 40th Anniv. A1439

2014, Oct. 1 **Litho.** ***Perf. 13x13¼***

2889 A1439 7p multi 1.10 .55

Autonomous Metropolitan University, 40th Anniv. — A1440

2014, Oct. 8 **Litho.** ***Perf. 13¼x13***

2890 A1440 7p multi 1.10 .55

World Post Day A1441

2014, Oct. 9 **Litho.** ***Perf. 13x13¼***

2891 A1441 13.50p multi 2.00 1.00

2014 Latin American Integration Association Expo, Montevideo, Uruguay A1442

2014, Oct. 10 **Litho.** ***Perf. 13x13¼***

2892 A1442 13.50p multi 2.00 1.00

Battle of Zacatecas, Cent. — A1443

2014, Oct. 14 **Litho.** ***Perf. 13¼x13***

2893 A1443 7p multi 1.10 .55

Institute of Epidemiological Diagnosis and Reference, 75th Anniv. — A1444

2014, Oct. 17 **Litho.** ***Perf. 13x13¼***

2894 A1444 7p multi 1.10 .55

Dated 2012.

Air Traffic Controller's Day — A1445

2014, Oct. 20 **Litho.** ***Perf. 13¼x13***

2895 A1445 7p multi 1.10 .55

Constitution of Apatzingán, 200th Anniv. — A1446

2014, Oct. 22 **Litho.** ***Perf. 13¼x13***

2896 A1446 7p multi 1.10 .55

Philips Mexico, 75th Anniv. A1447

2014, Oct. 22 **Litho.** ***Perf. 13x13¼***

2897 A1447 13.50p multi 2.00 1.00

Miniature Sheet

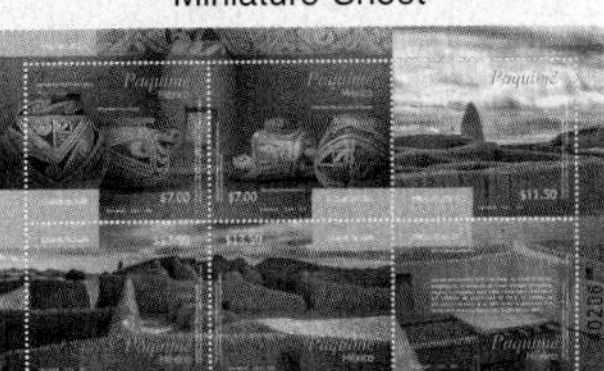

Paquimé Archaeological Site — A1448

No. 2898: a, Pottery, denomination at LR. b, Pottery, denomination at LL. c, Casa de los Cranéos. d, Casa de las Guacamayas, denomination at UR. e, Casa de las Guacamayas, denomination at UL.

2014, Oct. 25 **Litho.** ***Perf. 13¼x13***

2898 A1448 Sheet of 5 + label 8.00 4.00
a.-b. 7p Either single 1.10 .55
c. 11.50p multi 1.75 .85
d.-e. 13.50p Either single 2.00 1.00

All Souls' Day (Day of the Dead) A1449

2014, Oct. 29 **Litho.** ***Perf. 13¼x13***

2899 A1449 11.50p multi 1.75 .85

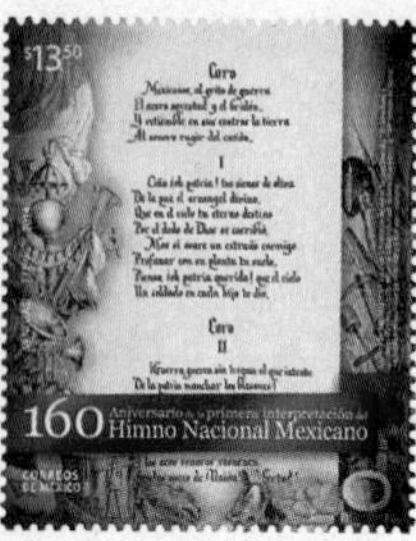

First Performance of Mexican National Anthem, 160th Anniv. — A1450

2014, Oct. 30 Litho. ***Perf. 13x13¼***
2900 A1450 13.50p multi 2.00 1.00

Inventor's Day — A1451

2014, Nov. 4 Litho. ***Perf. 13¼x13***
2901 A1451 7p multi 1.10 .55

Souvenir Sheet

Alberto Córdova Stadium, Autonomous University of Mexico State, 50th Anniv. — A1452

No. 2902: a, Aerial view of area, stadium in inset. b, Hill overlooking decorated stadium seats. c, Aerial view of stadium and other buildings.

2014, Nov. 5 Litho. ***Perf. 13x13¼***
2902 A1452 Sheet of 3 3.30 1.75
a.-c. 7p Any single 1.10 .55

Letter Carrier's Day — A1453

2014, Nov. 10 Litho. ***Perf. 13¼x13***
2903 A1453 7p multi 1.00 .50

Crabs — A1454

Designs: 13.50p, Isostichopus fuscus. 15p, Danielum ixbauchac.

2014, Nov. 18 Litho. ***Perf. 13¼x13***
2904 13.50p multi 1.90 .95
2905 15p multi 2.10 1.10
a. A1454 Horiz. pair, #2904-2905 4.00 2.10

Ciudad Madero Technological Institute, 60th Anniv. — A1455

2014, Nov. 19 Litho. ***Perf. 13¼x13***
2906 A1455 7p multi 1.00 .50

Intl. Year of Crystallography A1456

2014, Nov. 19 Litho. ***Perf. 13¼x13***
2907 A1456 13.50p multi 1.90 .95

Ministry of Health, 85th Anniv. — A1457

2014, Nov. 20 Litho. ***Perf. 13¼x13***
2908 A1457 7p multi 1.00 .50

World Food Day A1458

Designs: 7p, Shrimp boat, hand holding shrimp. 13.50p, Hand holding tilapia.

2014, Nov. 24 Litho. ***Perf. 13x13¼***
2909 7p multi 1.00 .50
2910 13.50p multi 1.90 .95
a. A1458 Pair, #2909-2910 3.00 1.50

Anáhuac University, 50th Anniv. A1459

No. 2911: a, Building and plaza. b, Commemorative pillar, building. c, Fountain.

2014, Nov. 26 Litho. ***Perf. 13x13¼***
2911 Horiz. strip of 3 3.00 1.50
a.-c. A1459 7p Any single 1.00 .50

Autonomous University of Chihuahua, 60th Anniv. — A1460

2014, Dec. 3 Litho. ***Perf. 13¼x13***
2912 A1460 11.50p multi 1.60 .80

Christmas — A1461

Designs: No. 2913, Magi. No. 2914, Santa Claus. 11.50p, Christmas tree. 13.50p, Holy Family, shepherd and lambs.

2014, Dec. 5 Litho. ***Perf. 13***
2913 A1461 7p multi .95 .45
2914 A1461 7p multi .95 .45
2915 A1461 11.50p multi 1.60 .80
a. Pair, #2913, 2915 2.60 1.25
2916 A1461 13.50p multi 1.90 .95
a. Pair, #2914, 2916 3.00 1.40
Nos. 2913-2916 (4) 5.40 2.65

General Eulalio Gutiérrez (1881-1939), Provisional President — A1462

2014, Dec. 8 Litho. ***Perf. 13x13¼***
2917 A1462 7p multi .95 .45

Sovereign Revolutionary Convention, cent.

Latin American Parliament, 50th Anniv. — A1463

2014, Dec. 9 Litho. ***Perf. 13¼x13***
2918 A1463 13.50p multi 1.90 .95

Fernando Hiriart Balderrama (1914-2005), Secretary of Energy, Mines and State Industry — A1464

2014, Dec. 10 Litho. ***Perf. 13x13¼***
2919 A1464 7p multi .95 .45

Taking of San Pedro, Cent. A1465

2014, Dec. 11 Litho. ***Perf. 13¼x13***
2920 A1465 7p multi .95 .45

National College of Professsional Technical Education, 35th Anniv. — A1466

2014, Dec. 11 Litho. ***Perf. 13¼x13***
2921 A1466 7p multi .95 .45

North American Free Trade Agreement, 20th Anniv. — A1467

2014, Dec. 18 Litho. ***Perf. 13¼x13***
2922 A1467 11.50p multi 1.60 .80

Diplomatic Relations Between Mexico and Iran, 50th Anniv. — A1468

2014, Dec. 18 Litho. ***Perf. 13¼x13***
2923 A1468 15p multi 2.10 1.10

See Iran No. 3131.

Philately and Postal Culture — A1469

2014, Dec. 19 Litho. *Perf. 13¼x13*
2924 A1469 7p multi .95 .45

St. Valentine's Day A1470

2015, Jan. 30 Litho. *Perf. 13*
2925 A1470 7p multi .95 .45

Postal Palace (Main Post Office), Mexico City A1471

2015, Feb. 17 Litho. *Perf. 13x13¼*
2926 A1471 13.50p multi 1.90 .95

First Supreme Court, 200th Anniv. A1472

2015, Mar. 7 Litho. *Perf. 13x13¼*
2927 A1472 7p multi .95 .45

National Livestock Convention, 80th Anniv. A1473

2015, Mar. 30 Litho. *Perf. 13x13¼*
2928 A1473 7p multi .95 .45

Battle of Celaya, Cent. A1474

2015, Apr. 15 Litho. *Perf. 13x13¼*
2929 A1474 7p multi .95 .45

National Public Administration Institute, 60th Anniv. — A1475

2015, Apr. 16 Litho. *Perf. 13x13¼*
2930 A1475 7p multi .95 .45

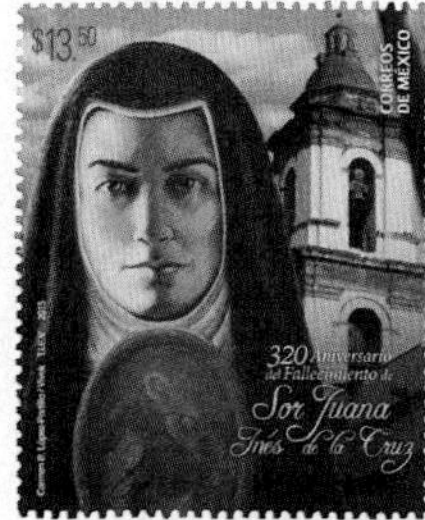

Sister Juana Inés de la Cruz (1651-95), Poet A1476

2015, Apr. 17 Litho. *Perf. 13x13¼*
2931 A1476 13.50p multi 1.75 .90

2015 Mexican Aerospace Fair, Santa Lucia — A1477

2015, Apr. 22 Litho. *Perf. 13¼x13*
2932 A1477 13.50p multi 1.75 .90

Children's Day A1478

2015, Apr. 30 Litho. *Perf. 13*
2933 A1478 7p multi .95 .45

Mother's Day A1479

2015, May 11 Litho. *Perf. 13*
2934 A1479 13.50p multi 1.75 .85

Dolores Correa Zapata (1853-1924), Teacher — A1480

2015, May 15 Litho. *Perf. 13¼x13*
2935 A1480 7p multi .90 .45

Teacher's Day.

Airports and Auxiliary Services, 50th Anniv. — A1481

2015, June 10 Litho. *Perf. 13¼x13*
2936 A1481 7p multi .90 .45

World Intellectual Property Day — A1482

2015, July 7 Litho. *Perf. 13¼x13*
2937 A1482 15p multi 1.90 .95

National Human Rights Commision, 25th Anniv. A1483

2015, July 9 Litho. *Perf. 13x13¼*
2938 A1483 7p multi .90 .45

Guelaguetza Festival — A1484

2015, July 10 Litho. *Perf. 13x13¼*
2939 A1484 13.50p multi 1.75 .85

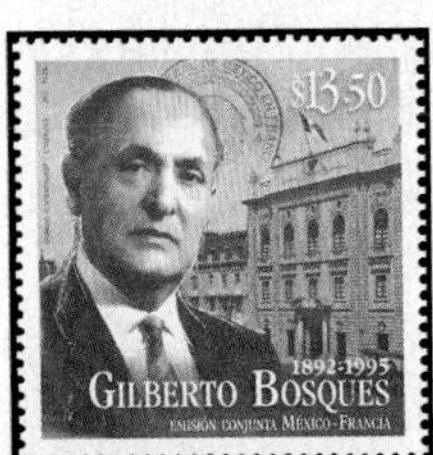

Gilberto Bosques (1892-1995), Mexican Diplomat Who Saved Jews In World War II — A1485

Bosques and: 7p, Notre Dame de la Garde Basilica, Marseilles and signed travel visa. 13.50p, Embassy, Mexican consular handstamp.

2015, July 16 Litho. *Perf. 13*
2940 A1485 7p multi .90 .45
2941 A1485 13.50p multi 1.75 .85
a. Horiz. pair, #2940-2941 2.75 1.40

See France Nos. 4839-4840.

Autonomous University of Campeche, 50th Anniv. — A1486

Designs: No. 2942, Painting. No. 2943, University building.

2015, Aug. 19 Litho. *Perf. 13¼x13*
2942 A1486 7p multi .85 .40
2943 A1486 7p multi .85 .40
a. Horiz. pair, #2942-2943 1.75 .80

Mexican Petroleum Institute, 50th Anniv. — A1487

2015, Aug. 24 Litho. *Perf. 13¼x13*
2944 A1487 7p multi .85 .40

University of the Americas, Puebla, 75th Anniv. — A1488

2015, Sept. 2 Litho. *Perf. 13¼x13*
2945 A1488 13.50p multi 1.60 .80

University of Colima, 75th Anniv. A1489

2015, Sept. 3 Litho. *Perf. 13x13¼*
2946 A1489 7p multi .85 .40

International Balloon Festival — A1490

2015, Sept. 10 Litho. *Perf. 13¼x13*
2947 A1490 11.50p multi 1.40 .70

Technological Institute of La Laguna, 50th Anniv. — A1491

2015, Sept. 25 Litho. *Perf. 13¼x13*
2948 A1491 7p multi .85 .40

Cacti A1492

Designs: 7p, Lophophora williamsii. 11.50p, Mammillaria mystax.

2015, Sept. 29 Litho. *Perf. 13*
2949 A1492 7p multi .85 .40
2950 A1492 11.50p multi 1.40 .70
a. Vert. pair, #2949-2950 2.25 1.10

José María Morelos (1765-1815), Priest and Patriot — A1493

2015, Sept. 30 Litho. *Perf. 13¼x13*
2951 A1493 7p multi .85 .40

Miniature Sheet

Xochicalco Archaeological Site — A1494

No. 2952: a, Plaza de la Estela and pillar. b, Observatory and sculpture. c, Temple of the Feathered Serpent. d, Arcaheological zone (denomination at UR). e, Archaeological zone and pelota goal (denomination at UL).

2015, Oct. 1 Litho. *Perf. 13¼x13*
2952 A1494 Sheet of 5 + label 6.50 3.25
a.-b. 7p Either single .85 .40
c. 11.50p multi 1.40 .70
d.-e. 13.50p Either single 1.60 .80

World Post Day A1495

2015, Oct. 9 Litho. *Perf. 13x13¼*
2953 A1495 7p multi .85 .40

Mexico City Red Devils Baseball Team, 75th Anniv. A1496

2015, Oct. 17 Litho. *Perf. 13x13¼*
2954 A1496 7.50p multi .90 .45
2954a Tete-beche pair 1.80 .90

Diplomatic Relations Between Mexico and Russia, 125th Anniv. — A1497

Designs: 7p, Saints Peter and Paul Cathedral, St. Petersburg, Russia. 13.50p, Chapultepec Castle, Mexico City.

2015, Oct. 19 Litho. *Perf. 13*
2955 7p multi .85 .40
2956 13.50p multi 1.75 .85
a. A1497 Horiz. pair, #2955-2956 2.60 1.25

See Russia No. 7685.

Cynomys Mexicanus A1498

2015, Oct. 22 Litho. *Perf. 13*
2957 A1498 13.50p multi 1.75 .85

Mexican Constitution — A1499

Designs: No. 2958, 1823 Plan for Constitution. No. 2959, 1824 Cosntitution.

2015, Oct. 28 Litho. *Perf. 13¼x13*
2958 7p multi .85 .40
2959 7p multi .85 .40
a. A1499 Horiz. pair, #2958-2959 1.70 .80

All Souls' Day (Day of the Dead) A1500

2015, Oct. 30 Litho. *Perf. 13x13¼*
2960 A1500 9p multi 1.10 .55

UNESCO International Hydrological Program, 50th Anniv. — A1501

2015, Nov. 10 Litho. *Perf. 13¼x13*
2961 A1501 13.50p multi 1.75 .85

Letter Carrier's Day A1502

2015, Nov. 11 Litho. *Perf. 13x13¼*
2962 A1502 7p multi .85 .40

Philately and Postal Culture — A1503

2015, Nov. 19 Litho. *Perf. 13¼x13*
2963 A1503 13.50p multi 1.75 .85

National Bank for Savings and Financial Services, 65th Anniv. A1504

2015, Nov. 23 Litho. *Perf. 13x13¼*
2964 A1504 7p multi .85 .40

Rock Paintings, Baja California A1505

2015, Nov. 23 Litho. *Perf. 13x13¼*
2965 A1505 13.50p multi 1.75 .85

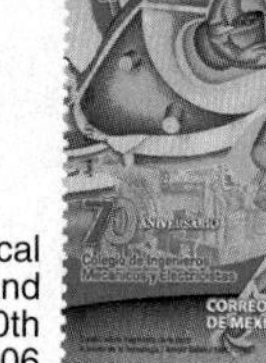

College of Mechanical Engineers and Electricians, 70th Anniv. — A1506

2015, Nov. 26 Litho. *Perf. 13¼x13*
2966 A1506 9p multi 1.10 .55

Mexican Acceptance of Treaty of the Meter, 125th Anniv. A1507

2015, Dec. 1 Litho. *Perf. 13x13¼*
2967 A1507 13.50p multi 1.75 .85

Christmas A1508

Designs: No. 2968, Magi and Star of Bethlehem. No. 2969, Santa Claus and Christmas tree. 11.50p, Piñata. 13.50p, Holy Family, angel, lamb, poinsettia.

2015, Dec. 1 Litho. *Perf. 13*
2968 A1508 7p multi .85 .40
2969 A1508 7p multi .85 .40
2970 A1508 11.50p multi 1.40 .70
a. Pair, #2968, 2970 2.25 1.10
2971 A1508 13.50p multi 1.75 .85
a. Pair, #2969, 2971 2.60 1.25
Nos. 2968-2971 (4) 4.85 2.35

National Council for Standardization and Certification of Labor Skills, 20th Anniv. — A1509

2015, Dec. 9 Litho. *Perf. 13x13¼*
2972 A1509 7p multi .80 .40

National Council for Science and Technology, 45th Anniv. — A1510

2015, Dec. 10 Litho. *Perf. 13¼x13*
2973 A1510 11.50p multi 1.40 .70

Fourth World Conference on Women and Beijing Declaration and Platform for Action, 20th Anniv. — A1511

2015, Dec. 18 Litho. *Perf. 13¼x13*
2974 A1511 13.50p multi 1.60 .80

Phocoena Sinus — A1512

No. 2975: a, Three vaquitas. b, Vaquita, aerial view of Baja California and Gulf of California. c, Two vaquitas.

2015, Dec. 21 Litho. *Perf. 13¼x13*
2975 Horiz. strip of 3 3.75 1.90
a. A1512 7.50p multi .90 .45
b.-c. A1512 11.50p Either single 1.40 .70

Reforms — A1513

Inscriptions at bottom: No. 2976, Reforma Hacendaria. No. 2977, Código Nacional de Procedimientos Penales. No. 2978, Pacto por México. No. 2979, En Materia de Disciplina Financiera de las Entidades Federativas y los Municipios. No. 2980, Reforma Anticorrupción. No. 2981, Nueva Ley de Amparo. No. 2982, Reforma en Materia de Transparencia. No. 2983, Reforma Educativa. No. 2984, Reforma Financiera. No. 2985, Reforma en Materia de Telecomunicaciones y Radiodifusión. No. 2986, Reforma Política-Electoral. No. 2987, Reforma Laboral. No. 2988, Reforma de Competencia Económica. No. 2989, Reforma Energética.

2015, Dec. 21 Litho. *Perf. 13¼x13*
2976 A1513 7p multi .80 .40
2977 A1513 7p multi .80 .40
2978 A1513 7p multi .80 .40
2979 A1513 7p multi .80 .40
2980 A1513 7p multi .80 .40
2981 A1513 7p multi .80 .40
2982 A1513 7p multi .80 .40

Size: 72x40mm

2983 A1513 7p multi .80 .40
2984 A1513 7p multi .80 .40
2985 A1513 7p multi .80 .40
2986 A1513 7p multi .80 .40
2987 A1513 7p multi .80 .40
2988 A1513 7p multi .80 .40
2989 A1513 7p multi .80 .40
Nos. 2976-2989 (14) 11.20 5.60

José María Morelos y Pavón (1765-1815), Priest and Leader in War of Independence — A1514

2015, Dec. 22 Litho. *Perf. 13x13¼*
2990 A1514 7p multi .80 .40

Adding of Value to Women in the History of Mexico A1515

2016, Jan. 21 Litho. *Perf. 13x13¼*
2991 A1515 7p multi .80 .40

End of International Year of Light — A1516

2016, Feb. 3 Litho. *Perf. 13¼x13*
2992 A1516 13.50p multi 1.50 .75

Chamber of Deputies, 1840 and 1857 Federal Constitution of the United Mexican States — A1517

2016, Feb. 5 Litho. *Perf. 13¼x13*
2993 A1517 9p multi 1.00 .50

St. Valentine's Day A1518

2016, Feb. 10 Litho. *Perf. 13*
2994 A1518 11.50p multi 1.40 .70

Visit of Pope Francis to Mexico — A1519

2016, Feb. 13 Litho. *Perf. 13¼x13*
2995 A1519 15p multi 1.75 .85

Postal Palace (Main Post Office), Mexico City — A1520

2016, Feb. 17 Litho. *Perf. 13¼x13*
2996 A1520 11.50p multi 1.40 .70

Autonomous University of the State of Mexico, 60th Anniv. — A1521

2016, Mar. 3 Litho. *Perf. 13x13¼*
2997 A1521 7p multi .80 .40

College of Civil Engineers of Mexico, 70th Anniv. A1522

2016, Mar. 8 Litho. *Perf. 13x13¼*
2998 A1522 11.50p multi 1.40 .70

World Intellectual Property Day — A1523

2016, Apr. 28 Litho. *Perf. 13¼x13*
2999 A1523 13.50p multi 1.60 .80

Children's Day — A1524

2016, Apr. 29 Litho. *Perf. 13¼x13*
3000 A1524 7p Doll .85 .40
3001 A1524 7p Top .85 .40
a. Horiz. pair, #3000-3001 1.70 .80

National Livestock Day — A1525

2016, May 6 Litho. *Perf. 13¼x13*
3002 A1525 7p multi .75 .40

Mother's Day A1526

2016, May 9 Litho. *Perf. 13*
3003 A1526 13.50p multi 1.50 .75

Communications and Transportation Secretariat, 125th Anniv. — A1527

2016, May 13 Litho. *Perf. 13x13¼*
3004 A1527 7p silver .75 .40

Jaime Torres Bodet (1902-74), Secretary of Public Education A1528

2016, May 15 Litho. *Perf. 13x13¼*
3005 A1528 7p multi .75 .40

Teacher's Day.

National Polytechnic Institute, 80th Anniv. — A1529

2016, May 20 Litho. *Perf. 13¼x13*
3006 A1529 7p multi .75 .40

University of Quintana Roo, 25th Anniv. — A1530

2016, May 24 Litho. *Perf. 13¼x13*
3007 A1530 11.50p multi 1.25 .60

Torre Latinoamericana, Mexico City, 60th Anniv. — A1531

2016, May 31 Litho. *Perf. 13¼x13*
3008 A1531 13.50p multi 1.50 .75

Supreme Court Building, 75th Anniv. A1532

2016, June 2 Litho. *Perf. 13x13¼*
3009 A1532 7p multi .80 .40

New Criminal Justice System — A1533

2016, June 17 Litho. *Perf. 13¼x13*
3010 A1533 7p multi .80 .40

Technological Institute of Saltillo, 65th Anniv. — A1534

2016, June 23 Litho. *Perf. 13¼x13*
3011 A1534 7.50p multi .85 .40

Clean and Safe Energy Industry — A1535

2016, July 27 Litho. *Perf. 13¼x13*
3012 A1535 9p multi .95 .45

First Mexican Stamps, 160th Anniv. — A1536

2016, Aug. 1 Litho. *Perf. 13¼x13*
3013 A1536 9p multi .95 .45

Promotion of Breastfeeding A1537

2016, Aug. 5 Litho. *Perf. 13¼x13*
3014 A1537 11.50p multi 1.25 .60

El Universal Newspaper, Cent. — A1538

2016, Aug. 15 Litho. *Perf. 13x13¼*
3015 A1538 13.50p multi 1.50 .75

Mexico Post, 30th Anniv. — A1539

2016, Aug. 19 Litho. *Perf. 13¼x13*
3016 A1539 7p multi .75 .35

School of Mechanical and Electrical Engineering, Mexico City, Cent. — A1540

2016, Aug. 23 Litho. *Perf. 13x13¼*
3017 A1540 9p multi .95 .50

Federal Institute of Telecommunications — A1541

2016, Sept. 9 Litho. *Perf. 13¼x13*
3018 A1541 7p multi .75 .35

National Institute for Adult Education, 35th Anniv. — A1542

2016, Sept. 26 Litho. *Perf. 13¼x13*
3019 A1542 7p multi .75 .35

State of Mexico Symphony Orchestra, 45th Anniv. A1543

2016, Sept. 27 Litho. *Perf. 13x13¼*
3020 A1543 7p multi .75 .35

Lozano Brothers Group, 50th Anniv. A1544

2016, Oct. 5 Litho. *Perf. 13x13¼*
3021 A1544 7p multi .75 .35

World Space Week A1545

2016, Oct. 6 Litho. *Perf. 13x13¼*
3022 A1545 11.50p multi 1.25 .60

Confederation of Mexican Workers, 80th Anniv. — A1546

2016, Oct. 7 Litho. *Perf. 13¼x13*
3023 A1546 7.50p multi .80 .40

World Post Day — A1547

2016, Oct. 10 Litho. *Perf. 13¼x13*
3024 A1547 13.50p multi 1.40 .70

Civilian Disaster Aid Plan, 50th Anniv. A1548

2016, Oct. 11 Litho. *Perf. 13x13¼*
3025 A1548 7p multi .75 .35

Engineering Institute of the National Autonomous University of Mexico, 60th Anniv. — A1549

2016, Oct. 11 Litho. *Perf. 13¼x13*
3026 A1549 9p multi .95 .45

Souvenir Sheet

Military Industry, Cent. — A1550

No. 3027: a, Pres. Venustiano Carranza (1859-1920), bullets, factory gate. b, Gun maker. c, Military vehicle.

2016, Oct. 18 Litho. *Perf. 13*
3027 A1550 Sheet of 3 2.25 1.10
a.-c. 7p Any single .75 .35

Miniature Sheet

Sharks — A1551

No. 3028: a, Prionace glauca. b, Sphyrna zygaena. c, Carcharodon carcharia. d, Carcharhinus falciformis.

2016, Oct. 20 Litho. *Perf. 13*
3028 A1551 Sheet of 12, 3 each #3028a-3028d 12.00 12.00
a.-b. 7p Either single .75 .35
c.-d. 11.50p Either single 1.25 .60

Diplomatic Relations Between Mexico and Jamaica, 50th Anniv. — A1552

Design: 7p, Papilio cresphontes. 11.50p, Danaus plexippus.

2016, Oct. 28 Litho. *Perf. 13*
3029 7p multicolored .75 .35
3030 11.50p multicolored 1.25 .60
a. A1552 Horiz. pair, #3029-3030 2.00 1.00

See Jamaica No. 1126.

All Souls' Day (Day of the Dead) — A1553

2016, Oct. 31 Litho. *Perf. 13¼x13*
3031 A1553 15p multi 1.60 .80

Letter Carrier's Day A1554

2016, Nov. 14 Litho. *Perf. 13x13¼*
3032 A1554 7p multi .70 .35

Rondalla de Saltillo Musical Group, 50th Anniv. A1555

2016, Nov. 22 Litho. *Perf. 13x13¼*
3033 A1555 7.50p multi .75 .35

Roberto Kobeh González, Former President of Council of Intl. Civil Aviation Organization — A1556

2016, Nov. 29 Litho. *Perf. 13¼x13*
3034 A1556 7p multi .70 .35

Jesús F. Contreras (1866-1902), Sculptor — A1557

2016, Nov. 30 Litho. *Perf. 13¼x13*
3035 A1557 11.50p multi 1.10 .55

Christmas — A1558

No. 3036: a, Magi creche figurines. b, Star of Bethlehem. c, Poinsettia. d, Holy Family creche figurines.

2016, Dec. 2 Litho. *Perf. 13*
3036 A1558 Block of 4 3.75 1.90
a.-b. 7p Either single .70 .35
c.-d. 11.50p Either single 1.10 .55

Battle of Juchitán, 150th Anniv. — A1559

2016, Dec. 7 Litho. *Perf. 13¼x13*
3037 A1559 13.50p multi 1.40 .70

Samalayuca Rock Paintings — A1560

2016, Dec. 9 Litho. *Perf. 13¼x13*
3038 A1560 13.50p multi 1.40 .70

Federal Consumer Attorney's Office, 40th Anniv. A1561

2016, Dec. 22 Litho. *Perf. 13x13¼*
3039 A1561 7p multi .70 .35

SEMI-POSTAL STAMPS

Nos. 622, 614 Surcharged in Red

1918, Dec. 25 Unwmk. *Perf. 12*
B1 A72 5c + 3c ultra 20.00 25.00

Rouletted 14½
B2 A73 10c + 5c blue 25.00 25.00
Set, never hinged 57.50

AIR POST STAMPS

Eagle AP1

Unwmk.
1922, Apr. 2 Engr. *Perf. 12*
C1 AP1 50c blue & red brn 67.50 50.00
Never hinged 160.00
a. 50c dark blue & claret ('29) 90.00 90.00
Never hinged 200.00

See Nos. C2-C3. For overprints and surcharges see Nos. C47-C48, CO1-CO2B, CO18-CO19, CO29.

1927, Oct. 13 Wmk. 156
C2 AP1 50c dk bl & red brn .75 .25
Never hinged 2.50
a. 50c dark blue & claret ('29) .75 .25
Never hinged 3.00
b. Vert. strip of 3, imperf. btwn. *7,500.*

The vignettes of Nos. C1a and C2a fluoresce a bright rose red under UV light.

1928
C3 AP1 25c brn car & gray brn .45 .25
C4 AP1 25c dk grn & gray brn .45 .25
Set, never hinged 2.50

On May 3, 1929, certain proofs or essays were sold at the post office in Mexico, D. F. They were printed in different colors from those of the regularly issued stamps. There were 7 varieties perf. and 2 imperf. and a total of 225 copies. They were sold with the understanding that they were for collections but the majority of them were used on air mail sent out that day.

Capt. Emilio Carranza and his Airplane "México Excelsior" AP2

1929, June 19
C5 AP2 5c ol grn & sepia 1.10 .65
C6 AP2 10c sep & brn red 1.25 .70
C7 AP2 15c vio & dk grn 3.00 1.25
C8 AP2 20c brown & blk 1.25 .75
C9 AP2 50c brn red & blk 7.50 5.00
C10 AP2 1p black & brn 15.00 10.00
Nos. C5-C10 (6) 29.10 18.35
Set, never hinged 75.00

1st anniv. of death of Carranza (1905-28).
For overprints see Nos. C29-C36, C40-C44.

Coat of Arms and Airplane AP3

1929-34 *Perf. 11½, 12*
C11 AP3 10c violet .35 .25
C12 AP3 15c carmine 1.35 .25
C13 AP3 20c brown olive 37.50 1.25
C14 AP3 30c gray black .25 .25
C15 AP3 35c blue green .35 .25
a. Imperf., pair 1,200.
C16 AP3 50c red brn ('34) 1.25 .65
C17 AP3 1p blk & dk bl 1.25 .65
C18 AP3 5p claret & dp bl 4.00 3.50
C19 AP3 10p vio & ol brn 6.00 7.00
Nos. C11-C19 (9) 52.30 14.05
Set, never hinged 130.00

1930-32 *Rouletted 13, 13½*
C20 AP3 5c lt blue ('32) .35 .25
C21 AP3 10c violet .35 .25
C22 AP3 15c carmine .35 .25
a. 15c rose carmine .40 .25
C23 AP3 20c brown olive 1.50 .25
a. 20c brown .50 .25
b. 20c yellow brown .50 .25
c. Horiz. pair, imperf. btwn.
C24 AP3 25c violet .95 .80
C25 AP3 50c red brown .90 .75
Nos. C20-C25 (6) 4.40 2.55
Set, never hinged 13.00

Trial impressions of No. C20 were printed in orange but were never sold at post offices.

See Nos. C62-C64, C75. For overprints and surcharges see Nos. C28, C38-C39, C46, C49-C50, CO17, CO20-CO28, CO30.

Plane over Plaza, Mexico City — AP4

1929, Dec. 10 Wmk. 156 *Perf. 12*
C26 AP4 20c black violet 1.25 1.00
C27 AP4 40c slate green 85.00 75.00
Set, never hinged 210.00

Aviation Week, Dec. 10-16.
For overprint see No. CO11.

No. C21 Overprinted in Red

1930, Apr. 20 *Rouletted 13, 13½*
C28 AP3 10c violet 2.00 1.25
Never hinged 5.50

National Tourism Congress at Mexico, D. F., Apr. 20-27, 1930.

Nos. C5 and C7 Overprinted

1930, Sept. 1 *Perf. 12*
C29 AP2 5c ol grn & sepia 5.50 4.50
a. Double overprint 225.00 *250.00*
C30 AP2 15c violet & dk grn 9.00 7.75
Set, never hinged 45.00

Nos. C5-C10 Overprinted

1930, Dec. 18
C31 AP2 5c ol grn & sepia 7.00 6.50
C32 AP2 10c sep & brn red 3.50 4.00
a. Double overprint 60.00 60.00
C33 AP2 15c vio & dk grn 7.50 7.00
C34 AP2 20c brown & blk 7.00 5.50
C35 AP2 50c brn red & blk 14.00 10.00
C36 AP2 1p black & brn 4.00 2.75
Nos. C31-C36 (6) 43.00 35.75
Set, never hinged 130.00

Plane over Flying Field AP5

1931, May 15 Engr. *Perf. 12*
C37 AP5 25c lake 4.00 4.50
Never hinged 11.00
a. Imperf., pair 80.00 72.50
Never hinged 175.00

Aeronautic Exhibition of the Aero Club of Mexico. Of the 25c, 15c paid air mail postage and 10c went to a fund to improve the Mexico City airport.
For surcharge see No. C45.

Nos. C13 and C23 Srchd. in Red

1931
C38 AP3 15c on 20c brn ol 32.50 35.00
Never hinged 80.00

Rouletted 13, 13½
C39 AP3 15c on 20c brn ol .30 .25
Never hinged 1.00
a. Inverted surcharge 150.00 *200.00*
b. Double surcharge 150.00 *200.00*
c. Pair, one without surcharge 350.00

Nos. C5 to C9 Overprinted

1932, July 13 *Perf. 12*
C40 AP2 5c ol grn & sep 6.00 5.00
a. Imperf., pair 60.00 60.00
C41 AP2 10c sep & brn red 5.00 3.00
a. Imperf., pair 60.00 60.00
C42 AP2 15c vio & bk grn 6.00 4.00
a. Imperf., pair 60.00 60.00
C43 AP2 20c brn & blk 5.00 2.75
a. Imperf., pair 60.00 60.00
C44 AP2 50c brn red & blk 35.00 35.00
a. Imperf., pair 60.00 60.00
Nos. C40-C44 (5) 57.00 49.75
Set, never hinged 170.00
Set, C40a-C44a never hinged 650.00

Death of Capt. Emilio Carranza, 4th anniv.

No. C37 Surcharged

1932
C45 AP5 20c on 25c lake .70 .30
Never hinged 2.50
a. Imperf., pair 72.50 72.50
Never hinged 150.00

No. C13 Surcharged

C46 AP3 30c on 20c brn ol 30.00 30.00
Never hinged 75.00

Similar Surcharge on Nos. C3 and C4

C47 AP1 40c on 25c (#C3) .90 .90
Never hinged 3.00
a. Inverted surcharge *11,000.*
C48 AP1 40c on 25c (#C4) 50.00 50.00
Never hinged 125.00

Surcharge on Nos. C23 and C24

Rouletted 13, 13½
C49 AP3 30c on 20c brn ol .35 .25
Never hinged 1.00
a. Inverted surcharge *2,750.*
C50 AP3 80c on 25c dl vio 1.75 1.25
Never hinged 5.00
Nos. C45-C50 (6) 83.70 82.70

Palace of Fine Arts AP6

1933, Oct. 1 Engr. *Perf. 12*

C51 AP6 20c dk red & dl vio 3.50 1.40
C52 AP6 30c dk brn & dl vio 7.00 6.00
C53 AP6 1p grnsh blk & dl vio 72.50 70.00
Nos. C51-C53 (3) 83.00 77.40
Set, never hinged 190.00

21st Intl. Cong. of Statistics and the cent. of the Mexican Soc. of Geography and Statistics.

National University Issue

Nevado de Toluca AP7

Pyramids of the Sun and Moon AP8

View of Ajusco AP9

Volcanoes Popocatepetl and Iztaccíhuatl — AP10

Bridge over Tepecayo AP11

Chapultepec Fortress — AP12

Orizaba Volcano (Citlaltépetl) AP13

Mexican Girl and Aztec Calendar Stone AP14

1934, Sept. 1 Wmk. 156 *Perf. 10½*

C54 AP7 20c orange 15.00 10.00
C55 AP8 30c red lilac & vio 20.00 20.00
C56 AP9 50c ol grn & bis brn 20.00 *25.00*
C57 AP10 75c blk & yel grn 25.00 *25.00*
C58 AP11 1p blk & pck bl 30.00 30.00
C59 AP12 5p bis brn & dk bl 225.00 *250.00*
C60 AP13 10p indigo & mar 550.00 525.00
C61 AP14 20p brn & brn lake 1,800. *1,800.*
Nos. C54-C61 (8) 2,685. 2,685.
Set, never hinged 4,750.

Type of 1929-34

1934-35 *Perf. 10½, 10½x10*

C62 AP3 20c olive green .35 .25
a. 20c slate 500.00 500.00
Never hinged 600.00
C63 AP3 30c slate .40 .40
C64 AP3 50c red brn ('35) 2.00 2.00
Nos. C62-C64 (3) 2.75 2.65
Set, never hinged 7.00

Symbols of Air Service AP15

Tláloc, God of Water (Quetzalcóatl Temple) — AP16

Orizaba Volcano (Citlaltépetl) AP17

"Eagle Man" AP18

Symbolical of Flight AP19

Aztec Bird-Man — AP20

Allegory of Flight and Pyramid of the Sun AP21

"Eagle Man" and Airplanes AP22

Natives Looking at Airplane and Orizaba Volcano — AP23

Imprint: "Oficina Impresora de Hacienda-Mexico"

Perf. 10½x10, 10x10½

1934-35 Wmk. 156

C65 AP15 5c black .45 .25
a. Imperf., pair
C66 AP16 10c red brown .90 .25
C67 AP17 15c gray green 1.25 .25
a. Imperf., pair *400.00*
C68 AP18 20c brown car 3.00 .25
a. 20c lake 4.00 .25
b. Imperf., pair
C69 AP19 30c brown olive .70 .25
C70 AP20 40c blue ('35) 1.25 .25
C71 AP21 50c green 2.50 .25
a. Imperf., pair 275.00
C72 AP22 1p gray grn & red brn 3.50 .25
C73 AP23 5p dk car & blk 7.25 .70
Nos. C65-C73 (9) 20.80 2.70
Set, never hinged 45.00

See Nos. C76A, C80, C81, C132-C140, C170-C177A. For overprint see No. C74.

No. C68 Overprinted in Violet

1935, Apr. 16

C74 AP18 20c lake *3,250. 4,000.*
Never hinged *6,000.*

Amelia Earhart's goodwill flight to Mexico. No. C74 with "Muestra" to left of "Mexico" was not issued for postage.

Arms-Plane Type of 1929-34

1935 Wmk. 248 *Perf. 10½x10*

C75 AP3 30c slate 3.00 *5.00*
Never hinged 5.00

Francisco I. Madero AP24

1935, Nov. 20 Wmk. 156

C76 AP24 20c scarlet .30 .25
Never hinged .75

Plan of San Luis, 25th anniv. See No. C76B.

Eagle Man Type of 1934-35

1936 Wmk. 260

C76A AP18 20c lake *4,500.* 60.00
Never hinged 7,500.

Madero Type of 1935

1936

C76B AP24 20c scarlet *12,500.*

Tasquillo Bridge AP25

Corona River Bridge AP26

Bridge on Nuevo Laredo Highway AP27

Wmk. 248

1936, July 1 Photo. *Perf. 14*

C77 AP25 10c slate bl & lt bl .35 .25
C78 AP26 20c dl vio & org .35 .25
C79 AP27 40c dk bl & dk grn .55 .50
Nos. C77-C79 (3) 1.25 .90
Set, never hinged 2.75

Opening of Nuevo Laredo Highway.

Eagle Man Type of 1934-35

Perf. 10½x10

1936, June 18 Engr. Unwmk.

C80 AP18 20c brown carmine 10.00 7.00
Never hinged 25.00

Imprint: "Talleres de Imp. de Est. y Valores-Mexico"

1937 Wmk. 156 Photo. *Perf. 14*

C81 AP18 20c rose red 1.25 .25
Never hinged 2.50
a. 20c brown carmine 1.50 .25
Never hinged 3.00
b. 20c dark carmine 2.00 .25
Never hinged 4.50
c. Imperf., pair 37.50 50.00
Never hinged 75.00

There are two sizes of watermark 156. No. C81c was not regularly issued.

Cavalryman AP28

Early Biplane over Mountains AP29

Venustiano Carranza on Horseback AP30

1938, Mar. 26

C82 AP28 20c org red & bl .50 .25
C83 AP29 40c bl & org red .75 *1.00*
C84 AP30 1p bl & bis brn 4.75 2.25
Nos. C82-C84 (3) 6.00 3.45
Set, never hinged 18.00

Plan of Guadalupe, 25th anniversary.

Reconstructed edifices of Chichén Itzá — AP31

Designs: Nos. C85, C86, The Zócalo and Cathedral, Mexico City. Nos. C89, C90, View of Acapulco.

1938, July 1

C85 AP31 20c carmine rose .35 .25
C86 AP31 20c purple 20.00 10.00
C87 AP31 40c brt green 10.00 5.00
C88 AP31 40c dark green 10.00 5.00
C89 AP31 1p light blue 10.00 5.00
C90 AP31 1p slate blue 10.00 5.00
Nos. C85-C90 (6) 60.35 30.25
Set, never hinged 130.00

16th Intl. Cong. of Planning & Housing.

Statue of José María Morelos — AP34

1939 Engr. *Perf. 10½*

C91 AP34 20c green .70 .50
Never hinged 1.00
C92 AP34 40c red violet 2.00 1.25
Never hinged 5.00
C93 AP34 1p vio brn & car 1.40 1.00
Never hinged 1.75
Nos. C91-C93 (3) 4.10 2.75
Set, never hinged 9.50

New York World's Fair. Released in New York May 2, in Mexico May 24.

Type of 1939 Overprinted in Cerise

1939, May 23
C93A AP34 20c blue & red 425.00 425.00
Never hinged 800.00

Issued for the flight of Francisco Sarabia from Mexico City to New York on May 25.

Statue of Pioneer Woman, Ponca City, OK — AP35

1939, May 17
C94 AP35 20c gray brown 1.00 .40
Never hinged 2.00
C95 AP35 40c slate green 2.50 1.25
Never hinged 7.00
C96 AP35 1p violet 1.60 .90
Never hinged 3.00
Nos. C94-C96 (3) 5.10 2.55
Set, never hinged 12.00

Tulsa World Philatelic Convention.

First Engraving Made in Mexico, 1544 — AP36

First Work of Legislation Printed in America, 1563 — AP37

Designs: 1p, Reproduction of oldest preserved Mexican printing.

1939, Sept. 7 **Wmk. 156**
C97 AP36 20c slate blue .25 .25
a. Unwmkd. 50.00 *25.00*
C98 AP37 40c slate green .65 .25
a. Imperf., pair *700.00*
C99 AP37 1p dk brn & car 1.10 .70
Nos. C97-C99 (3) 2.00 1.10
Set, never hinged 8.00

400th anniversary of printing in Mexico.

Alternated Perforations

Nos. 763-766, 774-779, 792-795, 801-804, 806-811, 813-818, C100-C102, C111-C116, C123-C128, C143-C162, C430-C431 have alternating small and large perforations.

Transportation — AP39

Designs: 40c, Finger counting and factory. 1p, "Seven Censuses."

Perf. 12x13, 13x12

1939, Oct. 2 **Photo.**
C100 AP39 20c dk bl & bl 1.00 .25
C101 AP39 40c red org & org .75 .25
C102 AP39 1p ind & vio bl 2.75 .75
Nos. C100-C102 (3) 4.50 1.20
Set, never hinged 10.00

National Census of 1939-40.

Penny Black Type of Regular Issue, 1940

1940, May ***Perf. 14***
C103 A140 5c blk & dk grn .65 .55
C104 A140 10c bis brn & dp bl .55 .25
C105 A140 20c car & bl vio .40 .25
C106 A140 1p car & choc 6.00 5.00
C107 A140 5p gray grn & red brn 75.00 55.00
Nos. C103-C107 (5) 82.60 61.00
Set, never hinged 200.00

Issue dates: 5c-1p, May 2; 5p, May 15.

Part of Original College at Pátzcuaro AP43

College at Morelia (18th Century) — AP44

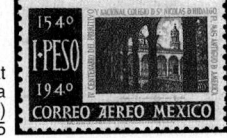

College at Morelia (1940) AP45

1940, July 15 **Engr.** ***Perf. 10½***
C108 AP43 20c brt green .45 .25
C109 AP44 40c orange .50 .30
C110 AP45 1p dp pur, red brn & org 1.25 1.00
Nos. C108-C110 (3) 2.20 1.50
Set, never hinged 5.00

400th anniv. of the founding of the National College of San Nicolas de Hidalgo.

Pirate Ship AP46

Designs: 40c, Castle of San Miguel. 1p, Temple of San Francisco.

Perf. 12x13, 13x12

1940, Aug. 7 **Photo.**
C111 AP46 20c red brn & bis brn 1.10 .70
C112 AP46 40c blk & sl grn 1.50 .75
C113 AP46 1p vio bl & blk 5.00 4.00
Nos. C111-C113 (3) 7.60 5.45
Set, never hinged 20.00

400th anniversary of Campeche.

Inauguration Type of Regular Issue, 1940

1940, Dec. 1 ***Perf. 12x13***
C114 A146 20c gray blk & red org 1.90 1.00
C115 A146 40c chnt brn & dk sl 2.00 1.50
C116 A146 1p brt vio bl & rose 3.50 2.00
Nos. C114-C116 (3) 7.40 4.50
Set, never hinged 20.00

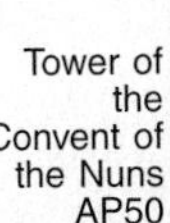

Tower of the Convent of the Nuns AP50

Casa de Montejo — AP51

1p, Campanile of Cathedral at Merída.

1942, Jan. 2 ***Perf. 14***
C117 AP50 20c Prus blue 1.50 .75
C118 AP51 40c grnsh blk (C) 2.25 2.00
a. Without overprint 7.50 7.50
C119 AP50 1p carmine 2.50 2.00
Nos. C117-C119 (3) 6.25 4.75

400th anniversary of Merída.

No. C118 bears the overprint "Servicio Aereo" in carmine.

Church of Zapopan AP53

Our Lady of Guadalupe Church AP54

Guadalajara Arms — AP55

1942, Feb. 11 **Engr.** ***Perf. 10½x10***
C120 AP53 20c green & blk 1.60 .75
C121 AP54 40c ol & yel grn 1.75 1.00
C122 AP55 1p purple & sepia 1.65 1.25
Nos. C120-C122 (3) 5.00 3.00

400th anniversary of Guadalajara.

Astrophysics Type of Regular Issue

Designs: 20c, Spiral Galaxy NGC 4594. 40c, Planetary Nebula in Lyra. 1p, Russell Diagrams.

1942, Feb. 17 **Photo.** ***Perf. 12x13***
C123 A154 20c dk grn & ind 20.00 3.00
C124 A154 40c car lake & ind 15.00 4.00
C125 A154 1p orange & blk 25.00 4.50
Nos. C123-C125 (3) 60.00 11.50

Corn AP59

1942, July 1
C126 AP59 20c shown 1.90 .70
C127 AP59 40c Coffee 1.50 .75
C128 AP59 1p Bananas 2.50 2.00
Nos. C126-C128 (3) 5.90 3.45

2nd Inter-American Agricultural Conf.

View of San Miguel de Allende AP62

Designs: 40c, Birthplace of Allende. 1p, Church of Our Lady of Health.

1943, May 18 ***Perf. 14***
C129 AP62 20c dk slate grn 1.00 .60
C130 AP62 40c purple 1.25 .60
C131 AP62 1p dp carmine 2.75 2.50
Nos. C129-C131 (3) 5.00 3.70

400th anniversary of the founding of San Miguel de Allende.

Types of 1934-35

1944 **Photo.** **Wmk. 272**
C132 AP18 20c brown carmine .75 .25

Perf. 10½x10

1944-46 **Engr.** **Wmk. 272**
C133 AP15 5c black .50 .25
C134 AP16 10c red brn ('45) 1.25 .25
C135 AP17 15c gray grn ('45) .85 .25
C136 AP19 30c brown ol ('45) 12.50 .75
C137 AP20 40c gray bl ('45) 1.10 .25
C138 AP21 50c green .85 .25
C139 AP22 1p gray grn & red brn ('45) 6.00 1.50
C140 AP23 5p dk car & blk ('46) 4.75 2.00
Nos. C133-C140 (8) 27.80 5.50

Symbol of Flight — AP65

1944 **Photo.** ***Perf. 14***
C141 AP65 25c chestnut brown .35 .25

See No. C185.

Microphone, Book and Camera — AP66

1944, Nov. 8 **Wmk. 272**
C142 AP66 25c dull slate grn .65 .25

Issued to commemorate the third Book Fair.

Catalogue values for unused stamps in this section, from this point to the end of the section, are for Never Hinged items.

Globe-in-Hands Type

1945, Feb. 27 ***Perf. 12x13***
C143 A166 25c red orange .40 .25
C144 A166 1p brt green .50 .30
C145 A166 5p indigo 2.50 2.00
C146 A166 10p brt rose 7.00 5.25
C147 A166 20p brt vio bl 20.00 13.00
Nos. C143-C147 (5) 29.75 20.75

Theater Type

1945, July 27
C148 A167 30c slate & ol .35 .25
C149 A167 1p slate & lil .50 .35
C150 A167 5p slate & blk 3.25 2.50
C151 A167 10p sl & lt ultra 6.00 4.25
C152 A167 20p blk & gray grn 18.00 10.50
Nos. C148-C152 (5) 26.35 17.80

Blindfold Type

1945, Nov. 21
C153 A169 30c slate green .25 .25
C154 A169 1p brown red .50 .30
C155 A169 5p red brn & pale bl 3.75 2.50

C156 A169 10p sl blk & pale lil 6.00 5.00
C157 A169 20p grn & lt brn 25.00 24.00
Nos. C153-C157 (5) 33.55 32.00

Torch, Laurel and Flag-decorated ONU — AP70

1946, Apr. 10
C158 AP70 30c chocolate .25 .25
C159 AP70 1p slate grn .50 .30
C160 AP70 5p chnt & dk grn 2.00 1.25
C161 AP70 10p dk brn & chnt 6.50 4.00
C162 AP70 20p sl grn & org red 18.00 9.00
Nos. C158-C162 (5) 25.15 14.75

Issued to honor the United Nations.

Father Margil de Jesus and Plane over Zacatecas AP71

Zacatecas scene and: 1p, Genaro Codina. 5p, Gen. Enrique Estrada. 10p, Fernando Villalpando.

Perf. 10½x10
1946, Sept. 13 Engr. Wmk. 279
C163 AP71 30c gray .25 .25
C164 AP71 1p brn & Prus grn .40 .35
C165 AP71 5p red & olive 3.00 3.00
C166 AP71 10p Prus grn & dk brn 18.00 15.00
Nos. C163-C166 (4) 21.60 18.55

400th anniversary of Zacatecas.

Franklin D. Roosevelt and Stamp of 1st Mexican Issue AP72

30c, Arms of Mexico & Stamp of 1st US Issue.

1947, May 16 Photo. *Perf. 14*
C167 AP72 25c lt violet bl .90 .50
C168 AP72 30c gray black .60 .25
a. Imperf., pair 325.00
C169 AP72 1p blue & carmine 1.25 .40
Nos. C167-C169 (3) 2.75 1.15

Centenary International Philatelic Exhibition, New York, May 17-25, 1947.

Type of 1934-35
Perf. 10½x10, 10x10½
1947 Engr. Wmk. 279
C170 AP15 5c black 1.50 .25
C171 AP16 10c red brown 3.00 .30
C172 AP17 15c olive grn 3.00 .30
C173 AP19 30c brown ol 2.00 .25
C174 AP20 40c blue gray 2.00 .25
C175 AP21 50c green 12.50 .30
a. Imperf., pair 450.00
C176 AP22 1p gray grn & red brn 3.50 .25
a. Imperf., pair 500.00
C177 AP23 5p red & blk 9.00 1.25
c. 5p dark car & black 200.00 3.00

Perf. 14
C177A AP18 20c brown car 2.75 .50
b. Imperf., pair 250.00
Nos. C170-C177A (9) 39.25 3.65

Emilio Carranza AP74

Douglas DC-4 AP75

1947, June 25 Engr. *Perf. 10½x10*
C178 AP74 10p red & dk brn 1.75 1.50
a. 10p dark carmine & brown 8.00
C179 AP75 20p bl & red brn 2.75 2.75

Cadet Vicente Suárez AP76

Chapultepec Castle — AP78

30c, Lieut. Juan de la Barrera. 1p, Gen. Pedro M. Anaya. 5p, Gen. Antonio de Leon.

1947, Sept. 8 Photo. *Perf. 14*
C180 AP76 25c dull violet .25 .25
C181 AP76 30c blue .25 .25

Engr.
Perf. 10x10½
C182 AP78 50c deep green .35 .25
C183 AP78 1p violet .50 .25
C184 AP78 5p aqua & brn 2.00 2.00
a. Imperf. pair 600.00
Nos. C180-C184 (5) 3.35 2.80

Centenary of the battles of Chapultepec, Churubusco and Molino del Rey.

Flight Symbol Type of 1944
1947 Wmk. 279 Photo. *Perf. 14*
C185 AP65 25c chestnut brown .50 .25
a. Imperf., pair 250.00

Puebla, Dance of the Half Moon AP81

Designs: 5c, Guerrero, Acapulco waterfront. 10c, Oaxaca, dance. 20c, Chiapas, musicians (Mayan). 25c, Michoacan, masks. 30c, Cuauhtemoc. 35c, Guerrero, view of Taxco. 40c, San Luis Potosi, head. 50c, Chiapas, bas-relief profile, Mayan culture. 80c, Mexico City University Stadium. 5p, Queretaro, architecture. 10p, Miguel Hidalgo. 20p, Modern building.

Two types of 20p:
Type I — Blue gray part 21¼mm wide. Child's figure touching left edge.
Type II — Blue gray part 21¾mm wide; "LQ" at lower left corner. Child's figure 1mm from left edge.

Imprint: "Talleres de Impresion de Estampillas y Valores-Mexico"
Perf. 10½x10
1950-52 Wmk. 279 Engr.
C186 AP81 5c aqua ('51) .50 .25
C187 AP81 10c brn org ('51) 2.75 .50
C188 AP81 20c carmine 1.25 .25
C189 AP81 25c redsh brown 1.25 .25
C190 AP81 30c olive bister .50 .25
C191 AP81 35c violet 2.75 .25
a. Retouched die 19.00 .30
b. As "a," imperf., pair 300.00
C192 AP81 40c dk gray bl ('51) 2.25 .25
a. Imperf., pair 300.00
C193 AP81 50c green 3.75 .25
C194 AP81 80c claret ('52) 2.25 .50
a. Imperf., pair 300.00
C195 AP81 1p blue gray 1.40 .25
C196 AP81 5p dk brn & org ('51) 5.00 1.00
a. Imperf., pair 1,800.
C197 AP81 10p blk & aqua ('52) 95.00 20.00
C198 AP81 20p car & bl gray, I ('52) 8.50 9.00
a. Type II 400.00 100.00
Nos. C186-C198 (13) 127.15 33.00

No. C191a: A patch of heavy shading has been added at right of "MEXICO;" lines in sky increased and strengthened. On Nos. C191, C191a, the top of the highest tower is even with the top of the "o" in "Guerrero," and has no frame line at right. No. C220C has frame line at right and tower top is even with "Arquitectura."

Many shades exist of Nos. C186-C198.

See Nos. C208-C221, C249, C265-C268, C285-C288, C290-C298, C347-C349, C422, C444, C446-C450, C471-C480.

Pres. Aleman and Highway Bridging Map of Mexico AP82

Design: 35c, Pres. Juarez and map.

1950, May 21 Engr.
C199 AP82 25c lilac rose 3.00 .25
C200 AP82 35c deep green .30 .25

Completion of the Intl. Highway between Ciudad Juarez and the Guatemala border.

Trains Crossing Isthmus of Tehuantepec — AP83

Design: 35c, Pres. Aleman and bridge.

1950, May 24
C201 AP83 25c green .50 .25
C202 AP83 35c ultra .35 .25

Opening of the Southeastern Railroad between Veracruz, Coatzocoalcos and Yucatan, 1950.

Aztec Courier, Plane, Train AP84

80c, Symbols of universal postal service.

1950, June 15
C203 AP84 25c red orange .35 .25
C204 AP84 80c blue .50 .30

75th anniv. (in 1949) of the UPU.

Miguel Hidalgo AP86

Design: 35c, Hidalgo and Mexican Flag.

Wmk. 300
1953, May 8 Photo. *Perf. 14*
C206 AP86 25c gray bl & dk red brn .90 .25
C207 AP86 35c slate green .90 .25
a. Wmk. 279 —

Bicentenary of birth of Miguel Hidalgo y Costilla (1753-1811), priest and revolutionist.

Type of 1950-52
Designs as before.

Imprint: "Talleres de Impresion de Estampillas y Valores-Mexico"
Wmk. 300, Horizontal
1953-56 Engr. *Perf. 10½x10*
C208 AP81 5c aqua .50 .25
C209 AP81 10c orange brn 5.50 3.50
a. 10c orange 11.50 2.50
C210 AP81 30c gray olive 18.00 10.00
C211 AP81 40c gray bl ('56) 18.00 1.50
C212 AP81 50c green 350.00 250.00
C213 AP81 80c claret 100.00 10.00
C214 AP81 1p blue gray 3.00 .30
C215 AP81 5p dk brn & org 2.75 .60
C216 AP81 10p black & aqua 6.25 1.25
C217 AP81 20p car & bl gray (II) ('56) 75.00 8.00
Nos. C208-C211,C213-C217 (9) 229.00 35.40

Printed in sheets of 30.

Type of 1950-52

Designs as in 1950-52. 2p, Guerrero, view of Taxco. 2.25p, Michoacan, masks.

Two types of 2p:
I — No dots after "Colonial". Frame line at right broken near top.
II — Three dots in a line after "Colonial". Right frame line unbroken.

Wmk. 300, Vertical
1955-65 *Perf. 11½x11*
Design AP81
C218 5c bluish grn ('56) .25 .25

Perf. 11
C219 10c orange brn ('60) .35 .25
a. Perf. 11½x11 1.10 .40
C220 20c carmine ('60) .35 .25
k. Perf. 11½x11 ('57) 1.60 .25
C220A 25c vio brn, perf. 11½x11 1.75 .25
C220B 30c olive gray ('60) .35 .25
l. Perf. 11½x11 .90 .25
C220C 35c dk vio, perf. 11½x11 .90 .25
C220D 40c slate bl ('60) .35 .25
m. Perf. 11½x11 10.00 .25
C220E 50c green, perf. 11½x11 .90 .25
n. Perf. 11 ('60) 1.10 .25
q. 50c yellow green 1.10 .25
C220F 80c claret ('60) 5.00 .70
o. Perf. 11½x11 5.00 .60
C220G 1p grn gray ('60) 1.10 .30
p. Perf. 11½x11 12.50 .30
C220H 2p dk org brn, II ('63) 1.10 .60
i. 2p lt org brn, perf. 11½x11 ('65) 150.00 40.00
j. 2p org brn, I, perf. 11 8.50 1.25
C221 2.25p maroon ('63) .65 .70
Nos. C218-C221 (12) 13.05 4.30

Printed in sheets of 45 and 50. Nos. C218-C221 have been re-engraved.

No. C218 has been redrawn and there are many differences. "CTS" measures 7mm; it is 5½mm on No. C208.

Nos. C208-C221 exist in various shades.

For No. C220C, see note after No. C198.

No. C220En was privately overprinted in red: "25vo Aniversario / Primer Cohete Internacional / Reynosa, Mexico-McAllen, U.S.A. / 1936-1961."

Mayan Ball Court and Player AP87

Design: 35c, Modern Stadium, Mexico.

1954, Mar. 6 Photo. *Perf. 14*
C222 AP87 25c brn & dk bl grn 1.00 .35
C223 AP87 35c dl sl grn & lil rose .75 .25

7th Central American & Caribbean Games.

Allegory AP88

1954, Sept. 15
C224 AP88 25c red brn & dp bl .50 .25
C225 AP88 35c dk bl & vio brn .30 .25
C226 AP88 80c blk & bl grn .30 .25
Nos. C224-C226 (3) 1.10 .70

Centenary of national anthem.

Aztec God Tezcatlipoca and Map — AP89

Design: 35c, Stadium and map.

1955, Mar. 12

C227 AP89 25c dk Prus grn & red brn .75 .30
C228 AP89 35c carmine & brn .75 .30

2nd Pan American Games, 1955.

Ornaments and Mask, Archeological Era — AP90

Designs: 10c, Virrey Enriquez de Almanza, bell tower and coach, colonial era. 50c, Jose Maria Morelos and cannon, heroic Mexico. 1p, Woman and child and horse back rider, revolutionary Mexico. 1.20p, Sombrero and Spurs, popular Mexico. 5p, Pointing hand and school, modern Mexico.

Perf. 11½x11

1956, Aug. 1 Engr. Wmk. 300

C229 AP90 5c black .40 .25
C230 AP90 10c lt blue .40 .25
C231 AP90 50c violet brn .30 .25
C232 AP90 1p blue gray .40 .25
C233 AP90 1.20p magenta .40 .25
C234 AP90 5p blue grn 1.25 1.25
a. Souv. sheet of 6, #C229-C234, perf. 10½x10 60.00 60.00
Nos. C229-C234 (6) 3.15 2.30

Centenary of Mexico's 1st postage stamps. No. C234a sold for 15 pesos.

Paricutín Volcano AP91

1956, Sept. 5 Photo. *Perf. 14*

C235 AP91 50c dk violet bl .50 .25

20th Intl. Geological Cong., Mexico City.

Valentin Gomez Farias and Melchor Ocampo AP92

1.20p, Leon Guzman and Ignacio Ramirez.

1956-63 Wmk. 300 *Perf. 14*

C236 AP92 15c intense blue .50 .25
C237 AP92 1.20p dk grn & pur .85 .35
b. Dark green omitted 110.00
c. Purple omitted 125.00
C237A AP92 2.75p purple ('63) 1.25 .75
Nos. C236-C237A (3) 2.60 1.30

Centenary of the constitution (in 1957). See Nos. C289, C445, C451, C471A.

Map AP93

1956, Dec. 1

C238 AP93 25c gray & dk bl .35 .25

4th Inter-American Regional Tourism Congress of the Gulf of Mexico and the Caribbean (in 1955).

Eagle Holding Scales AP94

1p, Allegorical figure writing the law.

1957, Aug. 31 Photo. *Perf. 14*

C239 AP94 50c metallic red brn & green .35 .25
C240 AP94 1p metallic lilac & ultra .50 .25

Centenary of 1857 Constitution.

Globe, Weights and Measure AP95

1957, Sept. 21

C241 AP95 50c metallic bl & blk .40 .25

Centenary of the adoption of the metric system in Mexico.

Death of Jesus Garcia AP96

1957, Nov. 7 Wmk. 300 *Perf. 14*

C242 AP96 50c car rose & dk vio .35 .25

50th anniversary of the death of Jesus Garcia, hero of Nacozari.

Oil Industry Symbols AP97

Design: 1p, Oil refinery at night.

1958, Aug. 30

C243 AP97 50c emerald & blk .25 .25
C244 AP97 1p car & bluish blk .40 .25

Nationalization of Mexico's oil industry, 20th anniv.

Independence Monument Figure — AP98

1958, Dec. 15 Engr. *Perf. 11*

C245 AP98 50c gray blue .35 .25

10th anniversary of the signing of the Universal Declaration of Human Rights.

Pres. Venustiano Carranza AP99

1960, Jan. 15 Photo. *Perf. 14*

C246 AP99 50c salmon & dk bl .35 .25

Centenary of the birth of President Venustiano Carranza.

Alberto Braniff's 1910 Plane, Douglas DC-7 and Mexican Airlines Map AP100

1960, May 15 Wmk. 300 *Perf. 14*

C247 AP100 50c lt brn & vio .50 .25
C248 AP100 1p lt brn & bl grn .40 .25

50th anniversary of Mexican aviation.

Type of 1950-52 inscribed: "HOMENAJE AL COLECCIONISTA DEL TIMBRE DE MEXICO-JUNIO 1960"

1960, June 8 Engr. *Perf. 10½x10*

C249 AP81 20p lil, brn & lt grn 100.00 100.00

See note below No. 909.

Flag AP101

Designs: 1.20p, Bell of Dolores and eagle. 5p, Dolores Church.

Wmk. 300

1960, Sept. 16 Photo. *Perf. 14*

C250 AP101 50c dp grn & brt red .40 .25
C251 AP101 1.20p grnsh bl & dk brn .60 .25
C252 AP101 5p sepia & green 6.00 2.25
Nos. C250-C252 (3) 7.00 2.70

150th anniversary of independence.

Aviation (Douglas DC-8 Airliner) AP102

Designs: 1p, Oil industry. 1.20p, Road development. 5p, Water power (dam).

1960, Nov. 20 Photo. *Perf. 14*

C253 AP102 50c gray bl & blk .40 .25
C254 AP102 1p dk grn & rose car .50 .25
C255 AP102 1.20p dk grn & sep .50 .30
C256 AP102 5p blue & lilac 6.00 3.00
Nos. C253-C256 (4) 7.40 3.75

50th anniversary of Mexican Revolution.

Count de Revillaggigedo AP103

1960, Dec. 23

C257 AP103 60c dk car & blk .60 .25

80th census and to honor Juan Vicente Güémez Pacheco de Padilla Horcasitas, Count de Revillagigedo, who conducted the 1st census in America, 1793.

Railroad Tracks and Map AP104

Design: 70c, Railroad bridge.

1961, Nov. Wmk. 300 *Perf. 14*

C258 AP104 60c chlky bl & dk grn .40 .25
C259 AP104 70c dk blue & gray .40 .25

Opening of the railroad from Chihuahua to the Pacific Ocean.

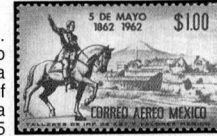

Gen. Ignacio Zaragoza and View of Puebla AP105

1962, May 5

C260 AP105 1p gray grn & slate grn .60 .25

Centenary of the Battle of May 5 at Puebla and the defeat of French forces by Gen. Ignacio Zaragoza.

Laboratory AP106

1962, June 11

C261 AP106 1p olive & vio bl .60 .25

National Polytechnic Institute, 25th anniv.

Pres. John F. Kennedy AP107

1962, June 29

C262 AP107 80c brt blue & car 1.75 .40

Commemorates visit of President John F. Kennedy to Mexico, June 29-30.

Globe AP108

1962, Oct. 20

C263 AP108 1.20p violet & dk brn .60 .25

Inter-American Economic and Social Council meeting.

Balloon over Mexico City, 1862 — AP109

1962, Dec. 21 Wmk. 300 *Perf. 14*

C264 AP109 80c lt blue & blk 1.60 .60

Cent. of the 1st Mexican balloon ascension by Joaquin de la Cantolla y Rico.

Type of 1950-52

Designs as before.

Two sizes of 80c:
I — 35½x20mm.
II — 37x20½mm.

Imprint: "Talleres de Imp. de Est. y Valores-Mexico"

Wmk. 300, Vertical

1962-72 Photo. *Perf. 14*

C265 AP81 80c cl, I ('63) 1.40 .30
a. Perf. 11½x11, size II ('63) 4.00 .35
b. Perf. 11, size II ('63) 3.50 .30
c. Perf. 11, size I ('72) 2.50 .25
C266 AP81 5p dk brn & yel org 4.00 1.00

C267 AP81 10p blk & lt grn ('63) 7.00 3.75
C268 AP81 20p car & bl gray 15.00 3.50
a. 20p carmine & aqua 17.00 4.75
Nos. C265-C268 (4) 27.40 8.55

Vert. pairs, imperf. horiz. of No. C265, perf. 11, may be from uncut rolls of No. C348.

ALALC Emblem AP110

1963, Feb. 15 **Wmk. 300**
C269 AP110 80c orange & dl pur 1.10 .30

2nd general session of the Latin American Free Trade Assoc. (ALALC), held in 1962.

Mexican Eagle and Refinery AP111

1963, Mar. 23
C270 AP111 80c red org & slate .60 .25

Nationalization of the oil industry, 25th anniv.

Polyconic Map AP112

1963, Apr. 22 **Photo.** ***Perf. 14***
C271 AP112 80c blue & blk .85 .30

19th Intl. Chamber of Commerce Congress.

EXMEX Emblem and Postmark AP113

1963, Oct. 9 **Wmk. 350** ***Perf. 14***
C274 AP113 5p rose red 2.75 1.75

77th Annual Convention of the American Philatelic Society, Mexico City, Oct. 7-13.

Marshal Tito AP114

1963, Oct. 15 **Wmk. 350** ***Perf. 14***
C275 AP114 2p dk grn & vio 2.00 .70

Visit of Marshal Tito of Yugoslavia.

Modern Architecture — AP115

1963, Oct. 19
C276 AP115 80c dk blue & gray .70 .25

Intl. Architects' Convention, Mexico City.

Dove AP116

1963, Oct. 26
C277 AP116 80c dl bl grn & car 1.25 .35

Centenary of the International Red Cross.

Don Quixote by José Guadalupe Posada AP117

1963, Nov. 9 **Engr.** ***Perf. 10½x10***
C278 AP117 1.20p black 1.75 .50

50th anniversary of the death of José Guadalupe Posada, satirical artist.

Horse-drawn Rail Coach, Old and New Trains — AP118

Wmk. 350
1963, Nov. 29 **Photo.** ***Perf. 14***
C279 AP118 1.20p violet bl & bl .90 .35

11th Pan-American Railroad Congress.

Eleanor Roosevelt, Flame and UN Emblem AP119

1964, Feb. 22 **Wmk. 350** ***Perf. 14***
C280 AP119 80c lt ultra & red .85 .25

15th anniversary (in 1963) of the Universal Declaration of Human Rights and to honor Eleanor Roosevelt.

Gen. Charles de Gaulle AP120

1964, Mar. 16 **Photo.**
C281 AP120 2p dl vio bl & brn 2.50 .80

Visit of President Charles de Gaulle of France to Mexico, Mar. 16-18.

Pres. John F. Kennedy and Pres. Adolfo López Mateos and Map AP121

1964, Apr. 11 **Photo.**
C282 AP121 80c vio bl & gray .85 .25

Ratification of the Chamizal Treaty, returning the Chamizal area of El Paso, Texas, to Mexico, July 18, 1963.

Queen Juliana AP122

1964, May 8 **Wmk. 350** ***Perf. 14***
C283 AP122 80c bister & vio bl 1.25 .25

Visit of Queen Juliana of the Netherlands.

Lt. José Azueta and Cadet Virgilio Uribe AP123

1964, June 18 **Wmk. 350** ***Perf. 14***
C284 AP123 40c dk brn & blk .55 .25

50th anniversary of the defense of Veracruz (against US Navy).

Types of 1950-62

Designs as before.

Perf. 11 (20c, 40c, 50c, 80c, 2p); 14
Photo.; Engr. (C296-C298)

1964-73 **Wmk. 350**

C285	AP81	20c	carmine ('71)	.75	1.25
C286	AP81	40c	gray bl ('71)	125.00	*100.00*
C287	AP81	50c	green ('71)	.50	.50
C288	AP81	80c	claret, I ('73)	.50	.50
C289	AP92	1.20p	dk grn & pur	6.50	2.50
C290	AP81	2p	red brn, II ('71)	1.75	1.40
C296	AP81	5p	brn & org ('66)	11.00	9.00
C297	AP81	10p	black & aqua	35.00	17.50
C298	AP81	20p	car & bl gray	55.00	40.00
	Nos. C285-C290,C296-C298 (9)			236.00	*172.65*

National Emblem, Cahill's Butterfly World Map, Sword and Scales of Justice AP124

1964, July 29 **Photo.**
C299 AP124 40c sepia & dp bl .60 .25

10th conference of the International Bar Association, Mexico City, July 27-31.

Galleon AP125

Map Showing 16th Century Voyages Between Mexico and Philippines — AP126

1964, Nov. 10 **Wmk. 350** ***Perf. 14***
C300 AP125 80c ultra & indigo 2.25 .35
C301 AP126 2.75p brt yel & blk 2.75 1.00

400 years of Mexican-Philippine friendship.

Netzahualcoyotl Dam, Grijalva River — AP127

1965, Feb. 19 **Photo.** ***Perf. 14***
C302 AP127 80c vio gray & dk brn .50 .25

Radio-electric Unit of San Benito, Chiapas — AP128

80c, Microwave tower, Villahermosa, Tabasco.

1965, June 19 **Wmk. 350** ***Perf. 14***
C303 AP128 80c lt bl & dk bl .65 .30
C304 AP128 1.20p dk grn & blk .70 .30

Centenary of the ITU.

Campfire, Tent and Scout Emblem AP129

1965, Sept. 27 **Photo.** ***Perf. 14***
C305 AP129 80c lt ultra & vio bl .65 .30

20th World Scout Conference, Mexico City, Sept. 27-Oct. 3.

King Baudouin, Queen Fabiola and Arms of Belgium AP130

1965, Oct. 18 **Wmk. 350** ***Perf. 14***
C306 AP130 2p slate grn & dl bl 1.00 .40

Visit of the King and Queen of Belgium.

Mayan Antiquities and Unisphere AP131

1965, Nov. 9 **Photo.**
C307 AP131 80c lemon & emer .50 .25

Issued for the NY World's Fair, 1964-65.

Dante by Raphael — AP132

Perf. 10x10½
1965, Nov. 23 **Wmk. 350** **Engr.**
C308 AP132 2p henna brown 1.25 .65

700th anniv. of the birth of Dante Alighieri.

Runner in Starting Position, Terra Cotta Found in Colima, 300-650 A.D.
AP133

Designs: 1.20p, Chin cultic disk, ball game scoring stone with ball player in center, Mayan culture, c. 500 A.D., found in Chiapas. 2p, Clay sculpture of ball court, players, spectators and temple. Pieces on 80c and 2p from 300-650 A.D.

1965, Dec. 17 Photo. *Perf. 14*
Size: 35x21mm

C309 AP133 80c orange & sl .80 .25
C310 AP133 1.20p bl & vio bl .90 .30
a. Souv. sheet of 4, #965-966, C309-C310, imperf. 3.50 3.50

Size: 43x36mm

C311 AP133 2p brt bl & dk brn .75 .25
a. Souv. sheet, imperf. 3.50 3.50
Nos. C309-C311 (3) 2.45 .80

19th Olympic Games, Mexico, 1968. No. C310a sold for 3.90p. No. C311a sold for 3p.
Nos. C310a and C311a have large watermark of national arms (diameter 54mm) and "SECRETARIA DE HACIENDA Y CREDITO PUBLICO." Issued without gum.

Ruben Dario — AP134

1966, Mar. 17 Wmk. 350 *Perf. 14*
C312 AP134 1.20p sepia .60 .35

Ruben Dario (pen name of Felix Ruben Garcia Sarmiento, 1867-1916), Nicaraguan poet, newspaper correspondent and diplomat.

Father Andres de Urdaneta and Compass Rose
AP135

Perf. 10½x10
1966, June 4 Engr. Wmk. 350
C313 AP135 2.75p bluish blk 1.25 .60

4th centenary of Father Urdaneta's return trip from the Philippines.

UPAE Type of Regular Issue

Designs: 80c, Pennant and post horn. 1.20p, Pennant and UPAE emblem, horiz.

Wmk. 300
1966, June 24 Photo. *Perf. 14*
C314 A244 80c magenta & blk .25 .25
C315 A244 1.20p lt ultra & blk .35 .25

U Thant and UN Emblem
AP136

1966, Aug. 24 Photo. Wmk. 300
C316 AP136 80c black & ultra .75 .25

Visit of U Thant, Secretary General of the UN.

AP137

1966, Aug. 26 *Perf. 14*
C317 AP137 80c green & red .25 .25

Issued to publicize the year of friendship between Mexico and Central America.

Olympic Type of Regular Issue

Designs by Diego Rivera: 80c, Obstacle race. 2.25p, Football. 2.75p, Lighting Olympic torch.

1966, Oct. 15 Wmk. 300 *Perf. 14*
Size: 57x21mm

C318 A248 80c org brn & blk .55 .25
C319 A248 2.25p green & blk .90 .35
C320 A248 2.75p dp pur & blk 2.00 .45
a. Souvenir sheet of 3 3.00 3.00
Nos. C318-C320 (3) 3.45 1.00

Issued to publicize the 19th Olympic Games, Mexico City, D.F., 1968. No. C320a contains 3 imperf. stamps similar to Nos. C318-C320 with simulated perforations. Sold for 8.70p.

UNESCO Emblem
AP138

Litho. & Engr.
1966, Nov. 4 *Perf. 11*
C321 AP138 80c blk, car, brt grn & org .50 .25
a. Perf. 10½ 5.00 2.00
b. Perf. 10½x11 25.00
c. Perf. 11x10½ 12.50 5.00

UNESCO 20th anniv. The 4th color varies from yellow to orange. A number of perforation varieties exist on the perf 11 stamps.

Venustiano Carranza — AP139

1967, Feb. 5 Photo. *Perf. 14*
C322 AP139 80c dk red brn & ocher .35 .25

Constitution, 50th anniv. Venustiano Carranza (1859-1920), was president of Mexico 1917-20.

Tiros Satellite over Earth — AP140

1967, Mar. 23 Photo. Wmk. 300
C323 AP140 80c blk & dk bl .50 .25

World Meteorological Day, Mar. 23.

Medical School Emblem — AP141

1967, July 10 Wmk. 300 *Perf. 14*
C324 AP141 80c black & ocher .35 .25

Mexican Military Medical School, 50th anniv.

Captain Horacio Ruiz Gaviño — AP142

Design: 2p, Biplane, horiz.

1967, July 17 Photo.
C325 AP142 80c black & brown .25 .25
C326 AP142 2p black & brown .45 .25

50th anniv. of the 1st Mexican airmail flight, from Pachuca to Mexico City, July 6, 1917.

Marco Polo and ITY Emblem — AP143

1967, Sept. 9 Wmk. 300 *Perf. 14*
C327 AP143 80c rose cl & blk .25 .25

Issued for International Tourist Year, 1967.

Olympic Games Type of Regular Issue, 1967

Designs: 80c, Diving. 1.20p, Runners. 2p, Weight lifters. 5p, Soccer.

1967, Oct. 12 Photo. *Perf. 14*
C328 A254 80c dp lil rose & blk .45 .25
C329 A254 1.20p brt grn & blk .45 .25
a. Souv. sheet of 2, #C328-C329, imperf. 5.50 3.75
C330 A254 2p yellow & blk 1.25 .40
C331 A254 5p olive & blk 1.60 .75
a. Souv. sheet of 2, #C330-C331, imperf. 7.50 4.00
Nos. C328-C331 (4) 3.75 1.55

No. C329a sold for 2.50p; No. C331a sold for 9p. Both sheets are watermark 350.

Heinrich Hertz and James Clerk Maxwell
AP144

1967, Nov. 15 Photo. Wmk. 300
C332 AP144 80c brt grn & blk .30 .25

2nd Intl. Telecommunications Plan Conf., Mexico City, Oct. 30-Nov. 15.

EFIMEX Emblem, Showing Official Stamp of 1884 — AP145

1968, Feb. 24 Wmk. 300 *Perf. 14*
C333 AP145 80c black & grn .45 .25
C334 AP145 2p black & ver .45 .25

EFIMEX '68, International Philatelic Exhibition, Mexico City, Nov. 1-9, 1968.

Olympic Games Type of Regular Issue, 1967

Designs: 80c, Sailing. 1p, Rowing. 2p, Volleyball. 5p, Equestrian.

1968, Mar. 21 Photo. *Perf. 14*
C335 A254 80c ultra & blk .25 .25
C336 A254 1p brt bl grn & blk .35 .25
a. Souv. sheet of 2, #C335-C336, imperf. 3.50 2.75
C337 A254 2p yellow & blk .70 .30
C338 A254 5p red brn & blk 1.40 1.10
a. Souv. sheet of 2, #C337-C338, imperf. 7.50 4.50
Nos. C335-C338 (4) 2.70 1.80

No. C336a sold for 2.40p; No. C338a sold for 9p. Both sheets are watermark 350.

Martin Luther King, Jr. — AP146

1968, June 8 Photo. Wmk. 300
C339 AP146 80c black & gray .35 .25

Rev. Dr. Martin Luther King, Jr. (1929-1968), American civil rights leader.

Olympic Types of Regular Issue, 1968

Designs: 80c, Peace dove and Olympic rings. 1p, Discobolus. 2p, Olympic medals. 5p, Symbols of Olympic sports events. 10p, Symbolic design for Mexican Olympic Games.

1968, Oct. 12 Wmk. 350 *Perf. 14*
C340 A259 80c green, lil & org .35 .25
C341 A259 1p green, bl & blk .45 .25
C342 A259 2p multicolored .90 .50
a. Souvenir sheet of 3, #C340-C342, imperf. 20.00 17.50
C343 A260 5p multicolored 4.00 1.40
C344 A260 10p black & multi 2.90 1.50
a. Souvenir sheet of 2, #C343-C344, imperf. 20.00 17.50
Nos. C340-C344 (5) 8.60 3.80

19th Olympic Games, Mexico City, Oct. 12-27. No. C342a sold for 5p. No. C344a sold for 20p.

Souvenir Sheet

EFIMEX Emblem — AP147

1968, Nov. 1 Photo. *Imperf.*
C345 AP147 5p black & ultra 3.50 2.50

EFIMEX '68 International philatelic exhibition, Mexico City, Nov. 1-9. No. C345 contains one stamp with simulated perforations.

Father Francisco Palóu (See footnote)
AP148

1969, July 16 Wmk. 350 *Perf. 14*
C346 AP148 80c multicolored .40 .25

Issued to honor Father Junipero Serra (1713-1784), Franciscan missionary, founder of San Diego, Calif. The portrait was intended to be that of Father Serra. By error the head of Father Palóu, his coworker, was taken from a painting (c. 1785) by Mariano Guerrero which also contains a Serra portrait.

Type of 1950-52 Redrawn
Imprint: "T.I.E.V."
Coil Stamps

Wmk. 300 Vert.

1969 Photo. *Perf. 11 Vert.*

C347 AP81 20c carmine 2.75 2.00

Imprint: "Talleres de Imp de Est y Valores-Mexico"

C348 AP81 80c claret 4.00 2.00

Imprint: "T.I.E.V."

C349 AP81 1p gray grn 4.00 2.25
Nos. C347-C349 (3) 10.75 6.25

Soccer Ball AP149

Design: 2p, Foot and soccer ball.

1969, Aug. 16 Wmk. 350 *Perf. 14*

C350 AP149 80c red & multi 1.25 .25
C351 AP149 2p green & multi 1.25 .25

9th World Soccer Championships for the Jules Rimet Cup, Mexico City, May 30-June 21, 1970.

Mahatma Gandhi — AP150

1969, Sept. 27 Photo. *Perf. 14*

C352 AP150 80c multicolored .30 .25

Mohandas K. Gandhi (1869-1948), leader in India's fight for independence.

Astronaut's Footprint — AP151

1969, Sept. 29 Photo.

C353 AP151 2p black .50 .25

Man's 1st landing on the moon, July 20, 1969. See note after US No. C76.

Tourist Issue

Type of Regular Issue, 1969-73 and

"Sound and Light" at Pyramid, Teotihuacan — AP152

Designs: No. C355, Acapulco Bay. No. C356, El Caracol Observatory, Yucatan. No. C357, Dancer with fruit basket, Oaxaca. No. C358, Sports fishing, Lower California, horiz.

1969-73 Wmk. 350 *Perf. 14*

C354 AP152 80c shown .90 .30
C355 AP152 80c multicolored .90 .30
C356 AP152 80c multicolored .90 .30

Wmk. 300

C357 A267 80c multicolored .35 .25
C358 A267 80c multicolored .35 .25
Nos. C354-C358 (5) 3.40 1.40

Issue dates: Nos. C354-C356, Nov. 1, 1969. Nos. C357-C358, Mar. 16, 1973.

Red Crosses AP154

1969, Nov. 8 Photo. Wmk. 350

C370 AP154 80c black & multi .35 .25
a. Red omitted 150.00

50th anniv. of the League of Red Cross Societies.

AP155

1969, Dec. 6 Wmk. 350 *Perf. 14*

C371 AP155 80c multicolored .35 .25

Installation of the ground station for communications by satellite at Tulancingo, Hidalgo.

AP156

Design: 80c, Soccer Ball, and Mexican Masks. 2p, Pre-Columbian sculptured heads and soccer ball.

1970, May 31 Wmk. 350 *Perf. 14*

C372 AP156 80c blue & multi 1.25 .25
C373 AP156 2p multicolored 1.25 .25

World Soccer Championships for the Jules Rimet Cup, Mexico City, May 30-June 21, 1970. The design of Nos. C372-C373 is continuous.

SPORTMEX '70 Emblem — AP157

1970, June 19 *Rouletted 13*

C374 AP157 2p gray & car 5.00 3.00

SPORTMEX '70 philatelic exposition devoted to sports, especially soccer, on stamps. Mexico City, June 19-28. The 2p stamp of No. C374 is imperf.

Ode to Joy and Beethoven's Signature AP158

1970, Sept. 26 Wmk. 350 *Perf. 14*

C375 AP158 2p multicolored .50 .25

200th anniversary of the birth of Ludwig van Beethoven (1770-1827), composer.

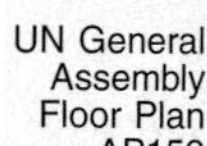

UN General Assembly Floor Plan AP159

1970, Oct. 24 Photo. *Perf. 14*

C376 AP159 80c multicolored .30 .25

25th anniversary of United Nations.

Isaac Newton AP160

1971, Feb. 27 Wmk. 350 *Perf. 14*

C377 AP160 2p shown .45 .25
C378 AP160 2p Galileo .45 .25
C379 AP160 2p Johannes Kepler .45 .25
Nos. C377-C379 (3) 1.35 .75

Mayan Warriors, Dresden Codex AP161

Designs: No. C381, Sister Juana, by Miguel Cabrera (1695-1768). No. C382, José Maria Velasco (1840-1912), self-portrait. No. C383, El Paricutin (volcano), by Gerardo Murillo ("Dr. Atl," 1875-1964). No. C384, Detail of mural, Man in Flames, by José Clemente Orozco (1883-1949).

Imprint includes "1971"

1971, Apr. 24 Photo. Wmk. 350

C380 AP161 80c multicolored .30 .25
C381 AP161 80c multicolored .30 .25
C382 AP161 80c multicolored .30 .25
C383 AP161 80c multicolored .30 .25
C384 AP161 80c multicolored .30 .25
Nos. C380-C384 (5) 1.50 1.25

Mexican art and science through the centuries. See Nos. C396-C400, C417-C421, C439-C443, C513-C517, C527-C531.

Stamps of Venezuela, Mexico and Colombia AP162

1971, May 22 Photo. Wmk. 350

C385 AP162 80c multicolored .35 .25

EXFILCA 70, 2nd Interamerican Philatelic Exhibition, Caracas, Venezuela, Nov. 27-Dec. 6, 1970.

Francisco Javier Clavijero AP163

1971, July 10 Wmk. 350 *Perf. 14*

C386 AP163 2p lt ol bis & dk brn .50 .25

Francisco Javier Clavijero (1731-1786), Jesuit and historian, whose remains were returned from Italy to Mexico in 1970.

Waves — AP164

1971, Aug. 7 Wmk. 350 *Perf. 14*

C387 AP164 80c multicolored .25 .25

3rd World Telecommunications Day, May 17.

Mariano Matamoros, by Diego Rivera — AP165

1971, Aug. 28 Photo.

C388 AP165 2p multicolored .45 .25

Bicentenary of the birth of Mariano Matamoros (1770-1814), priest and patriot.

Vicente Guerrero — AP166

1971, Sept. 27

C389 AP166 2p multicolored .40 .25

Vicente Guerrero (1783-1831), independence leader, president of Mexico. Painting by Juan O'Gorman.

Circles — AP167

1971, Nov. 4 Wmk. 300

C390 AP167 80c grnsh bl, dk bl & blk .30 .25

25th anniv. of UNESCO.

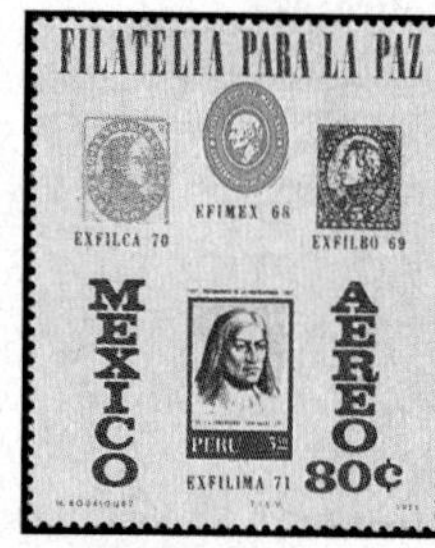

Stamps of Venezuela, Mexico, Colombia and Peru AP168

1971, Nov. 4

C391 AP168 80c multicolored .45 .25

EXFILIMA '71, 3rd Interamerican Philatelic Exhibition, Lima, Peru, Nov. 6-14.

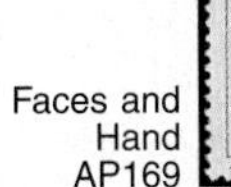

Faces and Hand AP169

1971, Nov. 29
C392 AP169 2p blk, dk bl & pink .45 .25

5th Congress of Psychiatry, Mexico City, Nov. 28-Dec. 4.

Ex Libris by Albrecht Dürer AP170

1971, Dec. 18
C393 AP170 2p blk & buff .65 .25

Albrecht Dürer (1471-1528), German painter and engraver.

Retort, Pulley and Burner — AP171

1972, Feb. 26 Wmk. 300 *Perf. 14*
C394 AP171 2p lilac, blk & yel .35 .25

Anniversary of the National Council on Science and Technology.

Scientists and WHO Emblem — AP172

1972, Apr. 8
C395 AP172 80c multicolored .25 .25

World Health Day 1972. Stamp shows Willem Einthoven and Frank Wilson.

Art and Science Type of 1971

Designs: No. C396, King Netzahuacoyotl (1402-1472) of Texcoco, art patron. No. C397, Juan Ruiz de Alarcon (c. 1580-1639), dramatist. No. C398, José Joaquin Fernandez de Lizardi (1776-1827), author. No. C399, Ramon Lopez Velarde (1888-1921), writer. No. C400, Enrique Gonzalez Martinez (1871-1952), poet.

Imprint includes "1972"

1972, Apr. 15 Wmk. 350

Black Inscriptions

C396 AP161 80c ocher 1.25 .25
C397 AP161 80c green 1.25 .25
C398 AP161 80c brown 1.25 .25
C399 AP161 80c carmine 1.25 .25
C400 AP161 80c gray blue 1.25 .25
Nos. C396-C400 (5) 6.25 1.25

Mexican art and science through the centuries.

Rotary Emblem AP173

1972, Apr. 15
C401 AP173 80c multicolored .30 .25

Rotary Intl. in Mexico, 50th anniv.

Tire Treads AP174

1972, May 11 Wmk. 300
C402 AP174 80c gray & blk .30 .25

74th Assembly of the International Tourism Alliance, Mexico City, May 8-11.

Benito Juárez AP175

Designs: 80c, Page of Civil Register. 1.20p, Juárez, by Pelegrin Clavé.

1972 Photo. *Perf. 14*
C403 AP175 80c gray bl & blk .25 .25
C404 AP175 1.20p multi .25 .25
C405 AP175 2p yellow & multi .35 .25
Nos. C403-C405 (3) .80 .60

Benito Juárez (1806-1872), revolutionary leader and president of Mexico.
Issue dates: 80c, 2p, July 18; 1.20p, Sept. 15.

Atom Symbol, Olive Branch — AP176

1972, Oct. 3 Photo. Wmk. 300
C406 AP176 2p gray, bl & blk .40 .25

16th Conference of the Atomic Energy Commission, Mexico City, Sept. 26.

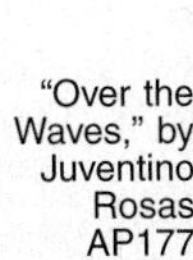

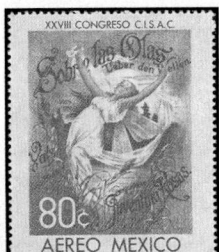

"Over the Waves," by Juventino Rosas AP177

1972, Oct. 16 *Perf. 14*
C407 AP177 80c olive bister .25 .25

28th Intl. Cong. of the Societies of Authors and Composers, Mexico City, Oct. 16-21.

Child with Doll, by Guerrero Galvan, UNICEF Emblem — AP178

1972, Nov. 4
C408 AP178 80c multicolored .75 .25

25th anniv. (in 1971) of UNICEF.

Pedro de Gante, by Rodriguez y Arangorti — AP179

1972, Nov. 22 *Perf. 14*
C409 AP179 2p multicolored .35 .25

Brother Pedro de Gante (Pedro Moor or van der Moere; 1480?-1572), Franciscan brother who founded first school in Mexico, and writer.

Olympic Games Type of Regular Issue, 1972

Designs: 80c, Olympic emblems and stylized soccer game. 2p, Olympic emblems, vert.

1972, Dec. 9 Photo. Wmk. 300
C410 A289 80c green & multi .35 .25
C411 A289 2p yel grn, blk & bl .65 .25

20th Olympic Games, Munich, Aug. 26-Sept. 11.

Anti-pollution Type of Regular Issue

80c, Bird sitting on ornamental capital, vert.

1972, Dec. 16
C412 A291 80c lt blue & blk .25 .25

Anti-pollution campaign.

Map of Americas with Tourists' Footprints — AP180

1972, Dec. 23
C413 AP180 80c black, yel & grn .25 .25

Tourism Year of the Americas.

Mexico #O1, Brazil #992, Colombia #130, Venezuela #22, Peru #C320 AP181

1973, Jan. 19 *Perf. 14*
C414 AP181 80c multicolored .25 .25

4th Interamerican Philatelic Exhibition, EXFILBRA 72, Rio de Janeiro, Brazil, Aug. 26-Sept. 2, 1972.

Aeolus, God of Winds — AP182

1973, Sept. 14 Photo. Wmk. 300
C415 AP182 80c brt pink, blk & bl .60 .25

Cent. of intl. meteorological cooperation.

Nicolaus Copernicus — AP183

Wmk. 300

1973, Oct. 10 Photo. *Perf. 14*
C416 AP183 80c slate green .30 .25

500th anniversary of the birth of Nicolaus Copernicus (1473-1543), Polish astronomer.

Art and Science Type of 1971

Designs: No. C417, Aztec calendar stone. No. C418, Carlos de Sigüenza y Gongora (1645-1700), mathematician, astronomer. No. C419, Francisco Diaz Covarrubias (1833-1889), topographer. No. C420, Joaquin Gallo (1882-1965), geographer, astronomer. No. C421, Luis Enrique Erro (1897-1955), founder of Tonanzintla Observatory.

Imprint includes "1973"

1973, Nov. 21 Wmk. 350
C417 AP161 80c car & sl grn .25 .25
C418 AP161 80c multicolored .25 .25
C419 AP161 80c multicolored .25 .25
C420 AP161 80c multicolored .25 .25
C421 AP161 80c multicolored .25 .25
Nos. C417-C421 (5) 1.25 1.25

Type of 1950-52

Design: Mexico City University Stadium.

Imprint: "Talleres de Imp. de Est. y Valores-Mexico"

1973 Unwmk. *Perf. 11*
C422 AP81 80c claret, I 3.00 .95

Fluorescent printing on front or back of stamps consisting of beehive pattern and diagonal inscription.

San Martin Monument — AP184

Wmk. 350

1973, Dec. 14 Photo. *Perf. 14*
C423 AP184 80c orange, indigo & yel .25 .25

Erection of a monument to San Martin in Mexico City, a gift of Argentina.

Palace of Cortes, Cuernavaca — AP185

Wmk. 300

1974, Feb. 22 Litho. *Perf. 14*

C424 AP185 80c black & multi .25 .25

EXMEX 73 Philatelic Exhibition, Cuernavaca, Apr. 7-15.

Gold Brooch, Mochica Culture AP186

1974, Mar. 6 Photo. Wmk. 300

C425 AP186 80c gold & multi .25 .25

Exhibition of Peruvian gold treasures, Mexico City, 1973-74.

Luggage — AP187

1974, Mar. 22 *Perf. 14*

C426 AP187 80c multicolored .25 .25

16th Convention of the Federation of Latin American Tourist Organizations (COTAL), Acapulco, May 1974.

CEPAL Emblem AP188

1974, Mar. 22

C427 AP188 80c black & multi .25 .25

a. Red omitted 100.00

25th anniversary (in 1973) of the Economic Commission for Latin America (CEPAL).

"The Enameled Casserole," by Picasso — AP189

1974, Mar. 29 Wmk. 300

C428 AP189 80c multicolored .35 .25

Pablo Ruiz Picasso (1881-1973), painter and sculptor.

EXFILMEX Type of 1974

1974, July 26 *Perf. 13x12*

C429 A305 80c buff, red brn & blk .25 .25

See note after No. 1065.

Biplane — AP190

Perf. 13x12

1974, Aug. 20 Photo. Wmk. 300

C430 AP190 80c shown .25 .25

C431 AP190 2p Jet plane .25 .25

50th anniversary of Mexican Airlines (MEXICANA).

Transmitter and Waves Circling Globe — AP191

1974, Oct. 4 Wmk. 300 *Perf. 14*

C432 AP191 2p multicolored .25 .25

First International Congress of Electric and Electronic Communications, Sept. 17-21.

Volleyball AP192

1974, Oct. 12 *Perf. 13x12*

C433 AP192 2p orange, bis & blk .25 .25

8th World Volleyball Championship. Perforation holes are of two sizes.

Souvenir Sheet

Mexico #O1, Colombia #130, Venezuela #22, Peru #C320, Brazil #992, Mexico #123 — AP193

Wmk. 300

1974, Oct. 26 Photo. *Imperf.*

C434 AP193 10p multicolored 3.50 1.50

EXFILMEX 74, 5th Inter-American Philatelic Exhibition, Mexico City, Oct. 26-Nov. 3.

Exists with red omitted.

Felipe Carrillo Puerto AP194

1974, Nov. 8 *Perf. 14*

C435 AP194 80c grn & gldn brn .25 .25

Birth centenary of Felipe Carrillo Puerto (1874-1924), politician and journalist.

Mask, Bat and Catcher's Mitt — AP195

1974, Nov. 29 Wmk. 350 *Perf. 14*

C436 AP195 80c multi .25 .25

Mexican Baseball League, 50th anniversary.

Man's Face, Mailbox, Colonial Period AP196

Design: 2p, Heinrich von Stephan, contemporary engraving.

1974, Dec. 13 Photo. Wmk. 300

C437 AP196 80c multicolored .25 .25

C438 AP196 2p green & ocher .25 .25

Centenary of Universal Postal Union.

Art and Science Type of 1971

Designs: No. C439, Mayan mural (8th century), Bonampak, Chiapas. No. C440, First musical score printed in Mexico, 1556. No. C441, Miguel Lerdo de Tejada (1869-1941), composer. No. C442, Silvestre Revueltas (1899-1940), composer (bronze bust). No. C443, Angela Peralta (1845-1883), singer.

Imprint includes "1974"

1974, Dec. 20 Wmk. 300

C439 AP161 80c multi .25 .25

C440 AP161 80c multi .25 .25

C441 AP161 80c multi .25 .25

C442 AP161 80c multi .25 .25

C443 AP161 80c multi .25 .25

Nos. C439-C443 (5) 1.25 1.25

Types of 1950-56

Designs (as 1950-56 issues): 40c, San Luis Potosi, head. 60c, Leon Guzman and Ignacio Ramirez. 1.60p, Chiapas, Mayan bas-relief. 1.90p, Guerrero, Acapulco waterfront. 4.30p, Oaxaca, dance. 5.20p, Guerrero, view of Taxco. 5.60p, Michoacan, masks. 50p, Valentin Gomez Farias and Melchor Ocampo.

Engraved (40c), Photogravure

Perf. 11 (40c, 1.60p), 14

1975 Wmk. 300

C444 AP81 40c bluish gray .35 .25

C445 AP92 60c yellow grn .90 .30

C446 AP81 1.60p red 3.00 .35

C447 AP81 1.90p rose red 3.00 .35

C448 AP81 4.30p ultra 1.00 .25

C449 AP81 5.20p purple 1.75 .40

C450 AP81 5.60p blue grn 2.25 .50

C451 AP92 50p dk bl & brick red 15.00 3.50

Nos. C444-C451 (8) 27.25 5.90

Women's Year Emblem — AP199

1975, Jan. 3 Wmk. 300 *Perf. 14*

C456 AP199 1.60p brt pink & blk .25 .25

International Women's Year 1975.

Declaration, UN Emblem, Mexican Flag AP200

1975, Feb. 7 Photo. Wmk. 300

C457 AP200 1.60p multi .25 .25

Declaration of Economic Rights and Duties of Nations.

Balsa Raft "Acali" — AP201

1975, Mar. 7 Wmk. 300 *Perf. 14*

C458 AP201 80c multicolored .25 .25

Trans-Atlantic voyage of the "Acali" from Canary Islands to Yucatan, May-Aug. 1973.

Dr. Miguel Jimenez, by I. Ramirez — AP202

1975, Mar. 24 Unwmk. *Perf. 14*

C459 AP202 2p multicolored .25 .25

Fifth World Gastroenterology Congress.

Miguel de Cervantes — AP203

1975, Apr. 26 Photo. Unwmk.

C460 AP203 1.60p bl blk & dk car .25 .25

Third International Cervantes Festival, Guanajuato, Apr. 26-May 11.

Four-reales Coin, 1535 — AP204

1975, May 2
C461 AP204 1.60p bl, gold & blk .25 .25

Intl. Numismatic Convention, Mexico City, Mar. 28-30, 1974.

Salvador Novo, by Roberto Montenegro — AP205

1975, May 9
C462 AP205 1.60p multi .25 .25

Salvador Novo (1904-1974), author.

Mural, Siqueiros — AP206

1975, May 16
C463 AP206 1.60p multi .25 .25

David Alfaro Siqueiros (1896-1974), painter.

UN and IWY Emblems AP207

1975, June 19
C464 AP207 1.60p ultra & pink .25 .25

International Women's Year World Conference, Mexico City, June 19-July 2.

Mexico City Coat of Arms AP208

Unwmk.
1975, Aug. 1 Photo. *Perf. 14*
C465 AP208 1.60p multi .25 .25

650th anniv. of Tenochtitlan (Mexico City).

Domingo F. Sarmiento — AP209

Unwmk.
1975, Aug. 9 Photo. *Perf. 14*
C466 AP209 1.60p brown & sl grn .25 .25

1st International Congress of Third World Educators, Acapulco, Aug. 5-9. Domingo Faustino Sarmiento (1811-1888), Argentinian statesman, writer and educator.

Teachers' Monument — AP210

1975, Aug. 9
C467 AP210 4.30p green & ocher .35 .25

Mexican-Lebanese friendship. The monument in Mexico City, by I Naffa al Rozzi, shows Cadmus, a mythical Phoenician, teaching the alphabet.

7th Pan American Games' Emblem AP211

1975, Aug. 29
C468 AP211 1.60p multi .25 .25

Pan American Games, Mexico City, Oct. 13-26.

Dr. Atl, Self-portrait AP212

Unwmk.
1975, Oct. 3 Photo. *Perf. 14*
C469 AP212 4.30p multi .35 .25

Geraldo Murillo ("Dr. Atl," 1875-1924), painter and writer, birth centenary.

Globe and Traffic Circle — AP213

1975, Oct. 17
C470 AP213 1.60p bl, blk & gray .25 .25

15th World Road Congress, Mexico City, Oct. 12-26.

Type of 1950-52

Designs: 40c, San Luis Potosi, head. 60c, Leon Guzman & Ignacio Ramirez. 80c, Mexico City University stadium. 1p, Puebla, Half Moon dance. 1.60p, Chiapas, Mayan bas-relief. 5p, Queretaro, architecture. 5.60p, Michoacan, masks. 10p, Miguel Hidalgo. 20p, Modern building.

Engraved (40c, 1p), Photogravure
Perf. 11 (40c, 80c, 1p, 1.60p), 14
1975-76 Unwmk.

C471 AP81 40c bluish gray .35 .35
C471A AP92 60c yel grn *1,200.*
C472 AP81 80c claret, II .60 .50
C473 AP81 1p grysh grn 1.00 .80
C474 AP81 1.60p red 1.75 1.00
C476 AP81 5p dk brn & org ('76) 1.50 1.00
a. 5p dark brown & red orange 2.00 2.00
C477 AP81 5.60p bluish grn ('76) 4.75 3.25
C479 AP81 10p blk & grn 4.00 2.50
C480 AP81 20p red & dl grn ('76) 7.50 4.00
Nos. C471,C472-C480 (8) 21.45 13.40

Bicycle and Export Emblem AP214

Designs: Export Emblem and 30c, Copper vase. 80c, Overalls. 1.90p, Oil valves. 2p, Books. 4p, Honey. 4.30p, Strawberry. 5p, Motor vehicles. 5.20p, Farm machinery. 5.60p, Cotton. 20p, Film. 50p, Cotton thread.

1975-82 Unwmk. Photo. *Perf. 14*

C486 AP214 30c copper ('76) .25 .25
C489 AP214 80c dull blue ('76) .25 .25
C491 AP214 1.60p black & org .35 .25
a. Thin paper ('81) 1.00 .25
C492 AP214 1.90p ver & dk grn .35 .25
C493 AP214 2p ultra & gold ('76) .65 .25
C495 AP214 4p yel bis & brn ('82) 1.25 .25
C496 AP214 4.30p brt pink & ol .50 .25
C497 AP214 5p dk bl & ocher ('76) 1.50 .25
C498 AP214 5.20p red & blk ('76) .75 .40
C499 AP214 5.60p yel grn & org ('76) .35 .25
C503 AP214 20p multi, thin paper ('81) 1.00 .25
C508 AP214 50p multi ('82) 4.00 2.00
Nos. C486-C508 (12) 11.20 4.90

See Nos. C594-C603.

Art and Science Type of 1971

Designs: No. C513, Title page of "Medical History of New Spain," by Francisco Hernandez, 1628. No. C514, Alfonso L. Herrera (1868-1942), biologist. No. C515, Title page, Aztec Herbal, 1552. No. C516, Arturo S. Rosenblueth (1900-1970). No. C517, Alfredo Augusto Duges (1826-1910) French-born naturalist.

Imprint includes "1975"
1975, Nov. 21 Unwmk. *Perf. 14*

C513 AP161 1.60p buff, red & blk .25 .25
C514 AP161 1.60p vio bl & multi .25 .25
C515 AP161 1.60p black & multi .25 .25
C516 AP161 1.60p gray & multi .25 .25
C517 AP161 1.60p green & multi .25 .25
a. Thin paper 400.00
Nos. C513-C517 (5) 1.25 1.25

Telephone — AP216

1976, Mar. 10 Photo.
C518 AP216 1.60p gray & blk .25 .25

Centenary of first telephone call by Alexander Graham Bell, Mar. 10, 1876.

60-peso Gold Coin, Oaxaca, 1917 — AP217

1976, Mar. 25 Photo. Unwmk.
C519 AP217 1.60p black, ocher & yel .25 .25

4th International Numismatic Convention, Mexico City, March 1976.

Rain God Tlaloc and Calles Dam AP218

1976, Mar. 29 *Perf. 14*
C520 AP218 1.60p vio brn & dk grn .25 .25

12th International Great Dams Congress, Mar. 29-Apr. 2.

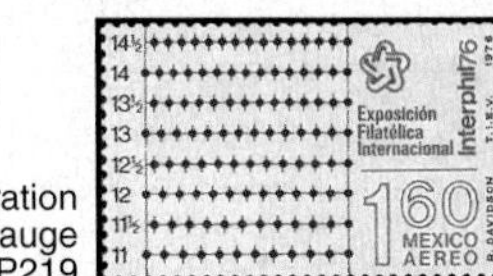

Perforation Gauge AP219

1976, May 7 Photo. Unwmk.
C521 AP219 1.60p blk, red & bl .25 .25

Interphil 76 International Philatelic Exhibition, Philadelphia, Pa., May 29-June 6.

Rainbow over City — AP220

1976, May 31 Unwmk. *Perf. 14*
C522 AP220 1.60p black & multi .25 .25

Habitat, UN Conf. on Human Settlements, Vancouver, Canada, May 31-June 11.

Liberty Bell — AP221

1976, July 4 Photo. *Perf. 14*
C523 AP221 1.60p ultra & red .25 .25

American Bicentennial.

"Peace" — AP222

Design: "Peace" written in Chinese, Japanese, Hebrew, Hindi and Arabic.

1976, Aug. 3 Photo. *Perf. 14*
C524 AP222 1.60p multi .25 .25

30th Intl. Cong. of Science and Humanities of Asia and North Africa, Mexico, Aug. 3-8.

Television Screen AP223

1976, Aug. 24 Photo. Unwmk.
C525 AP223 1.60p multi .25 .25

1st Latin-American Forum on Children's Television.

Luminescence

Fluorescent airmail stamps include Nos. C265, C265c, C288, C357-C358, C390-C415, C422-C423.

Airmail stamps issued on both ordinary and fluorescent paper include Nos. C220, C220D-C220E, C220G-C220H, C265b, C266-C268, C286.

Sky, Sun, Water and Earth AP224

1976, Nov. 8 Photo. *Perf. 14*
C526 AP224 1.60p multi .25 .25

World Conservation Day.

Art and Science Type of 1971

Designs: No. C527, Coatlicue, Mother of Earth, Aztec sculpture. No. C528, El Caballito, statue of Charles IV of Spain, by Manuel Tolsá. No. C529, Chief Tlahuicole, bronze statue by Manuel Vilar. No. C530, Today's God, Money, seated ceramic figure, by L. Ortiz Monasterio. No. C531, Signal, abstract sculpture by Angela Gurria.

Imprint includes "1976"

1976, Dec. 10 Photo. *Perf. 14*
C527 AP161 1.60p black & yel .25 .25
C528 AP161 1.60p blk & red brn .25 .25
C529 AP161 1.60p black & multi .25 .25
C530 AP161 1.60p car & multi .25 .25
C531 AP161 1.60p carmine & blk .25 .25
Nos. C527-C531 (5) 1.25 1.25

Score for El Pesebre by Casals AP225

1976, Dec. 29
C532 AP225 4.30p lt bl, blk & brn .35 .25

Pablo Casals (1876-1973), cellist and composer, birth centenary.

Mankind Destroyed by Nuclear Power AP226

1977, Feb. 14 Photo. *Perf. 14*
C533 AP226 1.60p multi .25 .25
a. Wmk. 300 50.00 40.00

10th anniv. of the Agreement of Tlatelolco, banning nuclear arms in Latin America.

Soccer AP227

Anniversary Emblem — AP228

1977, Aug. 23 Wmk. 300 *Perf. 14*
C534 AP227 1.60p multicolored .25 .25
C535 AP228 4.30p black, bl & yel .35 .25

Mexican Soccer Fed., 50th anniv.

Hands and Scales AP229

1977, Sept. 23 Photo. *Perf. 14*
C536 AP229 1.60p org, brn & blk .25 .25

Federal Council of Reconciliation and Arbitration, 50th anniversary.

Arms of Mexico and Spain AP230

1.90p, Maps of Mexico & Spain. 4.30p, Pres. José Lopez Portillo & King Juan Carlos.

1977, Oct. 8 *Perf. 14*
C537 AP230 1.60p dull bl & blk .25 .25
C538 AP230 1.90p lt grn & maroon .25 .25
C539 AP230 4.30p tan, grn & brn .35 .25
Nos. C537-C539 (3) .85 .60

Resumption of diplomatic relations with Spain.

Tlaloc, the Rain God — AP231

Wmk. 300

1977, Nov. 4 Photo. *Perf. 14*
C540 AP231 1.60p multi .25 .25

National Central Observatory, centenary.

Ludwig van Beethoven — AP232

1977, Nov. 10 Photo.
C541 AP232 1.60p brt grn & brn .25 .25
C542 AP232 4.30p lilac rose & bl .30 .25

Tractor and Dam AP233

1977, Nov. 25 Photo. *Perf. 14*
C543 AP233 1.60p multi .25 .25

United Nations Desertification Conference.

Mexico City-Cuernavaca Highway — AP234

1977, Nov. 30
C544 AP234 1.60p multi .25 .25

25th anniversary of first national highway.

Arms of Campeche — AP235

1977, Dec. 3
C545 AP235 1.60p multi .25 .25

200th anniv. of the naming of Campeche.

Congress Emblem AP236

1977, Dec. 9
C546 AP236 1.60p multi .25 .25

20th World Congress for Education, Hygiene and Recreation, July 18-24, 1977.

Freighter Navimex AP237

1977, Dec. 16
C547 AP237 1.60p multi .25 .25

60th anniv. of National Merchant Marine.

Mayan Dancer, Jaina — AP238

Pre-Columbian Sculptures: No. C549, Aztec dance god. No. C550, Snake dancer, bas-relief. No. C551, Monte Alban, bas-relief. No. C552, Totonaca figurine.

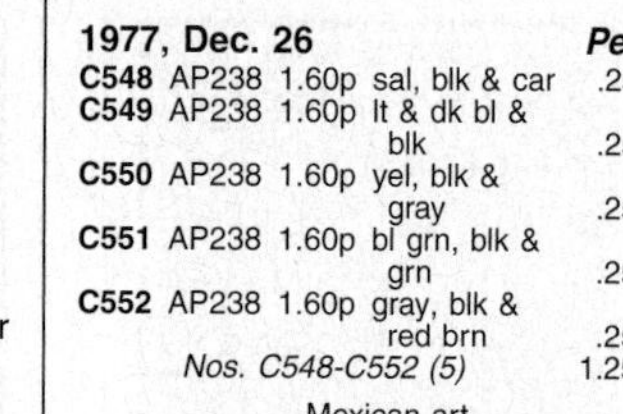

1977, Dec. 26 *Perf. 14*
C548 AP238 1.60p sal, blk & car .25 .25
C549 AP238 1.60p lt & dk bl & blk .25 .25
C550 AP238 1.60p yel, blk & gray .25 .25
C551 AP238 1.60p bl grn, blk & grn .25 .25
C552 AP238 1.60p gray, blk & red brn .25 .25
Nos. C548-C552 (5) 1.25 1.25

Mexican art.

Tumor Clinic, by David A. Siqueiros — AP239

4.30p, La Raza Medical Center, by Diego Rivera.

1978, Jan. 19 Photo. Wmk. 300
C553 AP239 1.60p multi .25 .25
C554 AP239 4.30p multi .30 .25

Mexican Social Security Institute, 35th anniv.

Moorish Fountain — AP240

1978, Mar. 1 Photo. *Perf. 14*
C555 AP240 1.60p multi .25 .25

Founding of Chiapa de Corzo, Chiapas, 450th anniv.

Oil Industry Type of 1978

Designs: 1.60p, Gen. Lazaro Cardenas. 4.30p, Offshore oil rig.

Wmk. 300

1978, Mar. 18 Photo. *Perf. 14*
C556 A343 1.60p brt bl & lil rose .25 .25
C557 A343 4.30p bl, brt bl & blk .30 .25

Oil industry nationalization, 40th anniv.

Arms of Diego de Mazariegos AP241

Wmk. 300

1978, Apr. 3 Photo. *Perf. 14*
C558 AP241 1.60p pink, blk & pur .25 .25

400th anniversary of the founding of San Cristobal de las Casas, Chiapas, by Diego de Mazariegos.

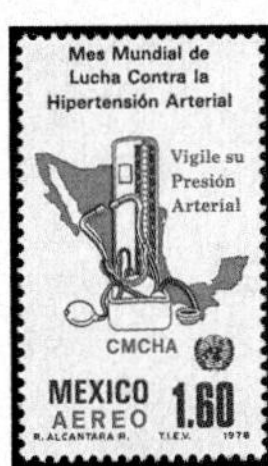

Blood Pressure Gauge, Map of Mexico AP242

Globe, Snake, Hand Holding Stethoscope AP243

1978, Apr. 7

C559 AP242 1.60p dk bl & car .25 .25
C560 AP243 4.30p org & dk bl .30 .25

Drive against hypertension and World Health Day.

X-ABC1 Plane AP244

1978, Apr. 15

C561 AP244 1.60p ultra & multi .25 .25
C562 AP244 4.30p ultra & multi .30 .25

1st Mexican airmail route, 50th anniv.

Globe, Cogwheel, UN Emblem — AP245

4.30p, Globe, flags, cogwheel, UN emblem.

1978, Apr. 21

C563 AP245 1.60p multi .25 .25
C564 AP245 4.30p multi .30 .25

World Conference on Technical Cooperation of Underdeveloped Countries.

Soccer — AP246

Designs: 1.90p, Goalkeeper catching ball. 4.30p, Soccer player.

Wmk. 300

1978, June 1 **Photo.** ***Perf. 14***

C565 AP246 1.60p multi .25 .25
C566 AP246 1.90p multi .25 .25
C567 AP246 4.30p multi .35 .25
Nos. C565-C567 (3) .85 .75

11th World Cup Soccer Championship, Argentina, June 1-25.

Francisco (Pancho) Villa AP247

1978, June 5

C568 AP247 1.60p multi .25 .25

Pancho Villa (1878-1923), revolutionary leader.

Mexico No. C6, Independence Monument, Washington Monument — AP248

1978, June 11

C569 AP248 1.60p ol gray & red .25 .25

50th anniversary of flight Mexico to Washington by Emilio Carranza (1905-1928).

Woman and Calendar Stone — AP249

Wmk. 300

1978, July 15 **Photo.** ***Perf. 14***

C570 AP249 1.60p rose, blk & brn .25 .25
C571 AP249 1.90p brt grn, blk & brn .25 .25
C572 AP249 4.30p org, blk & brn .35 .25
Nos. C570-C572 (3) .85 .75

Miss Universe contest, Acapulco, July 1978.

Alvaro Obregón AP250

1978, July 17

C573 AP250 1.60p multi .25 .25

Obregón (1880-1928), president of Mexico.

Geographical Institute Type of 1978

Institute emblem in different arrangements.

1978, July 21 **Photo.** **Wmk. 300**

C574 A344 1.60p emerald & blk .25 .25
C575 A344 4.30p ocher & blk .35 .25

Pan-American Institute for Geography and History, 50th anniversary.

Sun Rising over Ciudad Obregón AP251

1978, Aug. 4 ***Perf. 14***

C576 AP251 1.60p multi .25 .25

Founding of the city of Obregón, 50th anniv.

Mayan Figure, Castle and Pawn — AP252

1978, Aug. 19 **Photo.** ***Perf. 14***

C577 AP252 1.60p multi .25 .25
C578 AP252 4.30p multi .35 .25

World Youth Team Chess Championship, Ajedrez, Aug. 19-Sept. 7.

Aristotle (384-322 B.C.), Philosopher — AP253

Design: 4.30p, Statue of Aristotle.

1978, Aug. 25

C579 AP253 1.60p multi .25 .25
C580 AP253 4.30p multi .35 .25

Mule Deer — AP254

1978, Sept. 8 **Photo.** **Wmk. 300**

C581 AP254 1.60p shown .25 .25
C582 AP254 1.60p Ocelot .35 .25

Protected animals.

Man's Head, Dove, UN Emblem — AP255

4.30p, Woman's head, dove, UN emblem.

1978, Sept. 22 ***Perf. 14***

C583 AP255 1.60p ver, gray & blk .25 .25
C584 AP255 4.30p lil, gray & blk .35 .25

Anti-Apartheid Year.

Emblem — AP256

Wmk. 300

1978, Oct. 23 **Photo.** ***Perf. 14***

C585 AP256 1.60p multi .25 .25

13th Congress of International Union of Architects, Mexico City, Oct. 23-27.

Dr. Rafael Lucio (1819-1886) AP257

1978, Nov. 13 **Wmk. 350**

C586 AP257 1.60p yellow grn .25 .25

11th International Anti-Leprosy Congress.

Franz Schubert, "Death and the Maiden" — AP258

1978, Nov. 19 **Photo.** ***Perf. 14***

C587 AP258 4.30p brn, grn & blk .35 .25

Schubert (1797-1828), Austrian composer.

Children, Christmas Decorations AP259

Wmk. 350

1978, Nov. 22 **Photo.** ***Perf. 14***

C588 AP259 1.60p multi .25 .25

Christmas 1978.

Antonio Vivaldi — AP260

1978, Dec. 1

C589 AP260 4.30p multi .35 .25

Antonio Vivaldi (1675-1741), Italian violinist and composer.

Wright Brothers' Flyer AP261

Design: 4.30p, Flyer, different view.

1978, Dec. 17

C590 AP261 1.60p multi .25 .25
C591 AP261 4.30p multi .35 .25

75th anniversary of 1st powered flight.

Einstein and his Equation AP262

Wmk. 300

1979, Apr. 20 Photo. *Perf. 14*

C592 AP262 1.60p multi .25 .25

Albert Einstein (1879-1955), theoretical physicist.

Rowland Hill — AP263

1979, Apr. 27

C593 AP263 1.60p multi .25 .25

Sir Rowland Hill (1795-1879), originator of penny postage.

Export Type of 1975

Designs: Export Emblem and 50c, Circuit board. 1.60p, Bicycle. 1.90p, Oil valves. 2.50p, Tomato. 4p, Honey. 5p, Motor vehicles. 10p, Citrus fruit. 50p, Cotton thread.

1979-81 Photo. Wmk. 300

C594	AP214	50c	ocher & red brn	.35	.25
C596	AP214	1.60p	black & org	.35	.25
C597	AP214	1.90p	ver & dk grn ('81)	.50	.40
C599	AP214	2.50p	ver & grn	.35	.25
C600	AP214	4p	yel bis & brn ('81)	.35	.25
C601	AP214	5p	dk bl & dl org	4.50	.50
C602	AP214	10p	grn & yel grn ('81)	.90	.75
C603	AP214	50p	multicolored	6.00	1.50
			Nos. C594-C603 (8)	13.30	4.15

No. C600 exists with brown omitted.

Children, Child's Drawing — AP264

1979, May 16

C604 AP264 1.60p multi .25 .25

International Year of the Child.

Registered Letter from Mexico to Rome, 1880 — AP265

Wmk. 300

1979, June 7 Photo. *Perf. 14*

C605 AP265 1.60p multi .25 .25

MEPSIPEX '79, 3rd Intl. Exhibition of Elmhurst Philatelic Society, Mexico City, 6/7-10.

Sports Type of 1979

Designs: 1.60p, Games emblem. 4.30p, Symbolic flame and birds. 10p, Women gymnasts, horiz.

1979, June 15

C606 A348 1.60p multi .25 .25
C607 A348 4.30p multi .35 .25

Souvenir Sheet

Imperf

C608 A348 10p multi 2.00 2.00

No. C608 has simulated perforations.

University Type of 1979

Paintings: 1.60p, The Return of Quetzalcoatl, by Chavez Morado. 4.30p, Students Reaching for Culture, by Alfaro Siqueiros.

1979, July 10 *Perf. 14*

C609 A350 1.60p multi .25 .25
C610 A350 4.30p multi .35 .25

Messenger and UPU Emblem AP266

1979, July 27 Photo. Wmk. 300

C611 AP266 1.60p multi .25 .25

Cent. of Mexico's membership in UPU.

Sports Type of 1979

1979, Sept. 2 Wmk. 300 *Perf. 14*

C612 A352 1.60p Tennis .25 .25
C613 A352 5.50p Swimming .35 .25

Souvenir Sheet

Imperf

C614 A352 10p Various sports 1.75 1.75

Tourism Type of 1979

No. C615, Agua Azul Waterfall, Chiapas. No. C616, King Coliman statue, Colima.

Wmk. 300

1979, Sept. 28 Photo. *Perf. 14*

C615 A353 1.60p multi .25 .25
C616 A353 1.60p multi .25 .25

Graphic Design AP267

1979, Oct. 14 Photo. Wmk. 300

C617 AP267 1.60p multi .25 .25

ICSID, 11th Congress and Assembly of the Intl. Industrial Design Council, Oct. 1979.

Mail Service Type of 1979

Designs: 1.60p, Martin Enriquez de Almanza, Viceroy of New Spain. 5.50p, King Philip II of Spain. 10p, Sailing ship, horiz.

1979, Oct. 26

C618 A354 1.60p multi .25 .25
C619 A354 5.50p multi .35 .25

Souvenir Sheet

Imperf

C620 A354 10p multi 4.50 1.50

No. C620 contains stamp with simulated perfs.

Early Lamp — AP268

1979, Oct. 21 Wmk. 300

C621 AP268 1.60p multi .25 .25

Centenary of invention of electric light.

Union Emblem AP269

Wmk. 300

1979, Nov. 12 Photo. *Perf. 14*

C622 AP269 1.60p multi .25 .25

Latin American Universities Union, 8th general assembly.

Christmas Type of 1979

Design: 1.60p, Girl and Christmas tree.

1979, Nov. 15

C623 A355 1.60p multi .25 .25

Moon Symbol from Mexican Codex AP270

1979, Nov. 30

C624 AP270 2.50p multi .25 .25

Apollo 11 moon landing, 10th anniversary.

Monument Type of 1980

Stone Sculptures: 1.60p, Tlaloc, water god. 5.50p, Coyolxauqui, goddess.

1980, Feb. 16 Photo. *Perf. 14*

C625 A356 1.60p multi .25 .25
C626 A356 5.50p multi .35 .25

16th Century Church, Acolman AP271

16th Century Churches in: No. C628, Actopan Convent. No. C629, Tlayacapan. No. C630, Yanhuitlan. No. C631, Yuriria. No. C628 actually shows Tlayacapan; No. C629, Actopan convent (inscriptions reversed).

1980, Feb. 1

C627 AP271 1.60p multi .25 .25
C628 AP271 1.60p multi .25 .25
C629 AP271 1.60p multi .25 .25
C630 AP271 1.60p multi .25 .25
C631 AP271 1.60p multi .25 .25
Nos. C627-C631 (5) 1.25 1.25

Flora and Fauna Types of 1980

1980, Mar. 8 *Perf. 14*

C632 A357 1.60p Flamingo .25 .25
C633 A358 1.60p Vanilla plant .25 .25

Jules Verne AP272

Wmk. 300

1980, Mar. 24 Photo. *Perf. 14*

C634 AP272 5.50p blk & red brn .35 .25

Jules Verne (1828-1905) French science fiction writer.

Skeleton Smoking Cigar, UN Emblem AP273

1980, Apr. 7 *Perf. 14*

C635 AP273 1.60p multi .25 .25

World Health Day/Fight against cigarette smoking.

Costume Type

1.60p, Chiapaneca, Chiapas.

1980, Apr. 26 *Perf. 14*

C636 A359 1.60p multi .25 .25

Items inscribed "MEXICO" and "correo aereo" picturing Emiliano Zapata are not postage stamps.

AIR POST OFFICIAL STAMPS

Nos. C4 and C3 Overprinted in Black or Red

1929 Wmk. 156 *Perf. 12*

CO1	AP1	25c	dk grn & gray brn	4.50	3.25
	a.		Without period	20.00	20.00
CO2	AP1	25c	dk grn & gray brn (R)	4.00	*5.00*
	a.		Without period	21.00	21.00
CO2B	AP1	25c	brn car & gray brn	10.00	*12.50*
	c.		Without period	25.00	25.00
			Nos. CO1-CO2B (3)	18.50	20.75
			Set, never hinged	35.00	

Types of Regular Issue of 1926 Overprinted in Red

1929, Oct. 15 Unwmk.

CO3	A90	2c	black	75.00	*90.00*
CO4	A91	4c	black	75.00	*90.00*
CO5	A90	5c	black	75.00	*90.00*
CO6	A91	10c	black	75.00	*90.00*
CO7	A92	20c	black	75.00	*90.00*

CO8 A92 30c black 75.00 *90.00*
CO9 A92 40c black 75.00 *90.00*
Nos. CO3-CO9 (7) 525.00 630.00
Set, never hinged 1,100.

Horizontal Overprint

CO10 A93 1p black *2,250.* *2,250.*
Never hinged *4,000.*

Nos. CO3-CO9 also exist with overprint reading up.

No. C26 Overprinted in Black

1930 **Wmk. 156**

CO11 AP4 20c black violet 1.10 *1.75*
Never hinged 2.25
a. Without period 20.00 *20.00*
b. Inverted overprint 18.00 *18.00*
c. As "a," inverted overprint 210.00 210.00

No. CO11 with red overprint is believed not to have been issued for postal purposes.

Plane over Mexico City OA1

1930 **Engr.**

CO12 OA1 20c gray black 6.50 6.50
CO13 OA1 35c lt violet 1.10 *1.90*
CO14 OA1 40c ol brn & dp bl 1.25 *1.75*
CO15 OA1 70c vio & ol gray 1.50 *1.75*
Nos. CO12-CO15 (4) 10.35 *11.90*
Set, never hinged 23.50

No. CO12 Surcharged in Red

1931

CO16 OA1 15c on 20c .85 *1.40*
Never hinged 1.60
a. Inverted surcharge 140.00
b. Double surcharge 140.00

No. C20 Overprinted

1932 ***Rouletted 13, 13½***

CO17 AP3 5c light blue .80 *.90*
Never hinged 1.75

Air Post Stamps of 1927-32 Overprinted

On No. C1a

1932 **Unwmk.** ***Perf. 12***

CO18 AP1 50c dk bl & cl 1,000. 1,000.
Never hinged 2,000.

On Nos. C2, C2a
Wmk. 156

CO19 AP1 50c dk bl & red brn 1.25 *1.50*
Never hinged 2.25
a. 50c dark blue & claret 1.40 *1.60*

See note after No. C2.

On Nos. C11 and C12

1932 ***Perf. 12***

CO20 AP3 10c violet 22.50 *25.00*
Never hinged 45.00
CO21 AP3 15c carmine 350.00 *375.00*
Never hinged 700.00

On Nos. C21 to C23
Rouletted 13, 13½

CO22 AP3 10c violet .35 *.55*
CO23 AP3 15c carmine 1.40 *2.00*
CO24 AP3 20c brn olive 1.40 *2.00*

Nos. C20, C21 C23 and C25 Overprinted

1933-34 ***Rouletted 13½***

CO25 AP3 5c light blue .30 *.55*
CO26 AP3 10c violet ('34) .30 *.90*
CO27 AP3 20c brown olive .75 *1.25*
CO28 AP3 50c red brn ('34) 1.25 *1.90*

On No. C2
Perf. 12

CO29 AP1 50c dk bl & red brn 1.10 *2.00*
a. 50c dark blue & claret 1.60 *2.50*

On No. C11
Perf. 12

CO30 AP3 10c violet ('34) 140.00 *175.00*
a. Double overprint *325.00*

Forgeries exist.

SPECIAL DELIVERY STAMPS

Motorcycle Postman SD1

1919 **Unwmk.** **Engr.** ***Perf. 12***

E1 SD1 20c red & black 70.00 2.75

1923 **Wmk. 156**

E2 SD1 20c blk car & blk .30 .25

For overprint see No. E7

Messenger with Quipu — SD2

1934

E3 SD2 10c brn red & blue .30 .50

Indian Archer — SD3

Imprint: "Oficina Impresora de Hacienda Mexico."

1934 ***Perf. 10x10½***

E4 SD3 10c black violet 1.50 .50

See Nos. E5-E6, E8-E9.

Redrawn

Imprint: "Talleres de Imp. de Est. y Valores-Mexico."

1938-41 **Photo.** ***Perf. 14***

E5 SD3 10c slate violet .75 .25
a. Unwatermarked 50.00
E6 SD3 20c orange red ('41) .50 .25

Imperforate examples of No. E6 were not regularly issued.

No. E2 Overprinted "1940" in Violet

1940 **Engr.** ***Perf. 12***

E7 SD1 20c red & black .40 .25

Catalogue values for unused stamps in this section, from this point to the end of the section, are for Never Hinged items.

Redrawn Archer Type of 1941

1944-47 **Wmk. 272** **Photo.** ***Perf. 14***

E8 SD3 20c orange red 1.40 .25

Wmk. 279

E9 SD3 20c orange red ('47) 1.75 .25

Special Delivery Messenger SD4

Messengers' Hands Transferring Letter — SD5

1950-51 **Photo.** **Wmk. 279**

E10 SD4 25c bright red .35 .25
E11 SD5 60c dk bl grn ('51) 2.00 .95

Redrawn

1951

E12 SD4 25c bright red 40.00 5.00

Sharper Impression, heavier shading; motorcycle sidecar ½mm from "s" of "centavos;" imprint wider, beginning under "n" of "inmediata."

Second Redrawing

1952

E13 SD4 25c bright red 15.00 2.00

Design 35½mm wide (33mm on Nos. E10 and E12); finer lettering at left, and height of letters in imprint reduced 50 per cent; three distinct lines in tires.

Redrawn Type of 1951

1954 **Wmk. 300**

E14 SD4 25c red orange .45 .25

Type of 1951

1954

E15 SD5 60c dk blue grn .55 *1.10*

Hands and Pigeon SD6

Plane Circling Globe SD7

1956 **Wmk. 300** **Photo.** ***Perf. 14***

E16 SD6 35c red lilac .25 .25
E17 SD7 80c henna brown .35 *1.40*

1962

E18 SD6 50c green .80 .25
E19 SD7 1.20p dark purple 1.25 *1.40*

1964 **Wmk. 350**

E20 SD6 50c green .65 .25
E21 SD7 1.20p dk purple 1.40 1.00

1973 **Unwmk.**

E22 SD6 50c green 3.50 3.25

Fluorescent printing on front or back consists of beehive pattern and diagonal inscription.

1975 **Wmk. 300**

E23 SD6 2p orange .25 *1.00*
E24 SD7 5p vio bl 1.25 .90

1976 **Unwmk.**

E25 SD6 2p red org .25 .40
E26 SD7 5p dk vio bl .35 1.00

Watch SD8

1976 **Unwmk.** **Photo.** ***Perf. 14***

E27 SD8 2p org & blk .25 *1.00*

INSURED LETTER STAMPS

Insured Letters — IL1

Registered Mailbag — IL2

Safe — IL3

1935 **Engr.** **Wmk. 156** ***Perf. 10½***

G1 IL1 10c vermilion 1.75 .75
a. Perf. 10x10½
G2 IL2 50c dk bl 10.00 .60
G3 IL3 1p turq grn 1.25 .85
Nos. G1-G3 (3) 13.00 2.20

Nos. G1 and G4 were issued both with and without imprint.

Catalogue values for unused stamps in this section, from this point to the end of the section, are for Never Hinged items.

1944-45 **Wmk. 272** ***Perf. 10x10½***

G4 IL1 10c ver ('45) 12.50 1.50
G5 IL2 50c dk bl 2.00 .50
G6 IL3 1p turq grn 3.50 .65
Nos. G4-G6 (3) 18.00 2.65

1947 **Wmk. 279** ***Perf. 10x10½***

G7 IL1 10c vermilion 9.50 .85
G8 IL2 50c dark blue 12.00 1.50
G9 IL3 1p turq grn 4.00 1.00
Nos. G7-G9 (3) 25.50 3.35

Vault — IL4

1950-51 **Photo.** ***Perf. 14***

G10 IL4 20c blue 3.75 .45
G11 IL4 40c purple .40 .25
G12 IL4 1p yel grn ('51) 1.75 .50

No.	Design	Description	Unused	Used
G13	IL4	5p dk bl & gray grn ('51)	1.40	1.00
G14	IL4	10p car & ultra ('51)	4.00	4.00
		Nos. G10-G14 (5)	11.30	6.20

1954-71 Wmk. 300

No.	Design	Description	Unused	Used
G15	IL4	20c blue ('56)	.25	.25
G16	IL4	40c lt pur ('56)	.25	.25
G17	IL4	1p yel grn	.40	.25
a.		Size: 37x20¼mm ('71)	2.00	1.10
G18	IL4	5p bl & grn ('59)	1.25	1.00
G19	IL4	10p car & ultra ('63)	4.75	2.50
		Nos. G15-G19 (5)	6.90	4.25

No. G17 measures 35x19½mm. Vertical measurement excludes imprint.

1967 Wmk. 350 *Perf. 14*

No.	Design	Description	Unused	Used
G21	IL4	40c light purple	2.00	1.50
G22	IL4	1p yellow green	2.00	1.50

1975 Photo. Wmk. 300

No.	Design	Description	Unused	Used
G23	IL4	2p lilac rose	.40	.30
G24	IL4	20p orange & gray	3.25	3.00

Padlock — IL5

1976-81 Unwmk. Photo. *Perf. 14*

No.	Design	Description	Unused	Used
G25	IL5	40c black & blue	.30	.30
G26	IL5	1p black & blue	.30	.30
G26A	IL5	2p blk & bl ('81)	.35	.30
G27	IL5	5p black & blue	1.50	.50
G28	IL5	10p black & blue	1.50	.50
G28A	IL5	20p black & blue	2.25	.55
		Nos. G25-G28A (6)	6.20	2.45

1979 Photo. Wmk. 300

No.	Design	Description	Unused	Used
G29	IL5	40c black & blue	.90	.40
G30	IL5	1p black & blue	.90	.30
G31	IL5	5p black & blue	1.50	.45
G32	IL5	10p black & blue	4.00	.40
G33	IL5	20p black & blue	4.00	.75
		Nos. G29-G33 (5)	11.30	2.30

Perf. 14½x14

1983-86 Photo. Unwmk.

Size of Lock: 20x31mm

No.	Design	Description	Unused	Used
G36	IL5	5p black & blue	1.25	.40
G37	IL5	10p black & blue	1.00	.40
G38	IL5	20p black & blue	1.00	.40
G39	IL5	50p black & blue	2.50	.45
G40	IL5	100p blk & bl ('86)	5.00	3.00
		Nos. G36-G40 (5)	10.75	4.65

POSTAGE DUE STAMPS

D1

1908 Engr. Wmk. 155 *Perf. 14*

No.	Design	Description	Unused	Used
J1	D1	1c blue	1.00	*3.00*
J2	D1	2c blue	1.00	*3.00*
J3	D1	4c blue	1.00	*3.00*
J4	D1	5c blue	1.00	*3.00*
J5	D1	10c blue	1.00	*3.00*
		Nos. J1-J5 (5)	5.00	*15.00*

For overprints and surcharges see Nos. 381-385, 434-438, 466-470, 495-499, 593-607.

PORTE DE MAR STAMPS

These stamps were used to indicate the amount of cash to be paid to the captains of the mail steamers taking outgoing foreign mail.

PM2

1875 Unwmk. Litho. *Imperf.*

No.	Design	Description	Unused	Used
JX9	PM2	2c black	.60	*50.00*
a.		"5" added to make 25c	12.00	*100.00*
JX10	PM2	10c black	.80	*30.00*
JX11	PM2	12c black	.80	*50.00*
JX12	PM2	20c black	1.00	*50.00*
JX13	PM2	25c black	3.25	*50.00*
JX14	PM2	35c black	3.25	*60.00*
JX15	PM2	50c black	3.00	*60.00*
JX16	PM2	60c black	3.00	*75.00*
JX17	PM2	75c black	3.50	*75.00*
JX18	PM2	85c black	3.25	*100.00*
JX19	PM2	100c black	4.00	*100.00*
		Nos. JX9-JX19 (11)	26.45	700.00

Same, Numerals Larger

No.	Design	Description	Unused	Used
JX20	PM2	5c black	1.00	*50.00*
JX21	PM2	25c black	1.65	*50.00*
JX22	PM2	35c black	250.00	
JX23	PM2	50c black	1.00	*50.00*
JX24	PM2	60c black	125.00	
JX25	PM2	100c black	.60	*100.00*
		Nos. JX20-JX25 (6)	379.25	

In Nos. JX9-JX19 the figures of value are 7mm high and "CENTAVOS" is 7½mm long. On Nos. JX20-JX25 the figures of value are 8mm high and "CENTAVOS" is 9½mm long.

Nos. JX9-JX25 exist with overprints of district names.

Counterfeits exist of Nos. JX9-JX31.

PM3

1879

No.	Design	Description	Unused	Used
JX26	PM3	2c brown	.50	
JX27	PM3	5c yellow	.50	
JX28	PM3	10c red	.50	
JX29	PM3	25c blue	.50	
JX30	PM3	50c green	.50	
JX31	PM3	100c violet	.50	
		Nos. JX26-JX31 (6)	3.00	

Nos. JX26-JX31 were never put in use.

Nos. JX26-JX31 were printed on paper watermarked "ADMINISTRACION GENERAL DE CORREOS MEXICO." Aprroximately ¾ of the stamps do not show any of the watermark.

Stamps of this design were never issued. Examples appeared on the market in 1884. Value, set, $75. Value, full sheet $400.

All were printed in same sheet of 49 (7x7). Sheet consists of 14 of 10c; 7 each of 25c, 35c, 50c; 4 each of 60c, 85c; 3 each of 75c, 100c. There are four varieties of 10c, two of 25c, 35c and 50c.

OFFICIAL STAMPS

Hidalgo — O1

Wove or Laid Paper

1884-93 Unwmk. Engr. *Perf. 12*

No.	Design	Description	Unused	Used
O1	O1	red	1.40	1.00
a.		Vert. pair, imperf. betwn.	120.00	
O1B	O1	scarlet ('85)	1.40	1.00
O2	O1	olive brn ('87)	.90	.70
a.		Horiz. pair, imperf. betwn.	—	
b.		Blue ruled lines on paper		
O3	O1	orange ('88)	2.50	.90
a.		Vert. pair, imperf. betwn.	110.00	
b.		Perf. 11	15.00	12.00
O4	O1	blue grn ('93)	1.40	.80
a.		Imperf., pair	15.00	12.00
b.		Perf. 11	15.00	12.00
		Nos. O1-O4 (5)	7.60	4.40

Pin-perf. 6

No.	Design	Description	Unused	Used
O5	O1	olive brown ('87)	100.00	50.00

Wmk. "Correos E U M" on every Vertical Line of Ten Stamps (152)

1894 *Perf. 5½*

No.	Design	Description	Unused	Used
O6	O1	ultra	3.00	2.75
a.		Vert. pair, imperf. horiz.	35.00	
b.		Imperf., pair	45.00	

Perf. 11, 12

No.	Design	Description	Unused	Used
O7	O1	ultra	1.75	1.60

Perf. 5½x11, 11x5½

No.	Design	Description	Unused	Used
O9	O1	ultra	12.00	8.00
		Nos. O6-O9 (3)	16.75	12.35

Regular Issues with Handstamped Overprint in Black

1895 Wmk. 152 *Perf. 12*

No.	Design	Description	Unused	Used
O10	A20	1c green	17.50	6.00
O11	A20	2c carmine	20.00	6.00
O12	A20	3c orange brn	17.50	6.00
O13	A21	4c red orange	26.00	12.00
a.		4c orange	42.50	14.00
O14	A22	5c ultra	35.00	12.00
O15	A23	10c lilac rose	32.50	3.00
O16	A21	12c olive brn	70.00	30.00
O17	A23	15c brt blue	42.50	18.00
O18	A23	20c brown rose	42.50	18.00
O19	A23	50c purple	90.00	42.50
O20	A24	1p brown	200.00	90.00
O21	A24	5p scarlet	475.00	250.00
O22	A24	10p deep blue	750.00	500.00
		Nos. O10-O22 (13)	1,819.	993.50

Similar stamps with red overprint were not officially placed in use. Nos. O10-O22 have a vertical grain or mesh to the paper.

1896-97 Wmk. 153

Black Overprint

No.	Design	Description	Unused	Used
O23	A20	1c green	60.00	10.00
O24	A20	2c carmine	60.00	12.00
O25	A20	3c orange brn	60.00	12.00
O26	A21	4c red orange	60.00	12.00
a.		4c orange	75.00	22.50
O27	A22	5c ultra	60.00	12.00
O28	A21	12c olive brn	80.00	30.00
O29	A23	15c brt blue	100.00	30.00
O29A	A23	50c purple	650.00	650.00
		Nos. O23-O29A (8)	1,130.	768.00

Nos. O23-O29A have a vertical grain or mesh to the paper.

1897 Wmk. 154 Black Overprint

No.	Design	Description	Unused	Used
O30	A20	1c green	100.00	30.00
O31	A20	2c scarlet	90.00	35.00
O33	A21	4c orange	125.00	60.00
O34	A22	5c ultra	100.00	35.00
O35	A21	12c olive brn	125.00	42.50
O36	A23	15c brt blue	160.00	42.50
O37	A23	20c brown rose	110.00	18.00
O38	A23	50c purple	150.00	30.00
O39	A24	1p brown	375.00	125.00
		Nos. O30-O39 (9)	1,335.	418.00

Nos. O30-O39 have a vertical grain or mesh to the paper.

1898 Unwmk. Black Overprint

No.	Design	Description	Unused	Used
O40	A20	1c green	35.00	9.50
O41	A20	2c scarlet	35.00	9.50
O42	A20	3c orange brn	35.00	9.50
O43	A21	4c orange	60.00	12.00
O44	A22	5c ultra	60.00	20.00
O45	A23	10c lilac rose	—	—
O46	A21	12c olive brn	125.00	30.00
O47	A23	15c brt blue	125.00	30.00
O48	A23	20c brown rose	225.00	75.00
O48A	A23	50c purple	375.00	150.00
O48B	A24	10p deep blue	*5,500.*	*5,500.*
		Nos. O40-O48A (10)	1,075.	345.50

The existence of No. O45 has been questioned by specialists. The editors would like to see authenticated evidence of this stamp.

See note following No. 291.

Black Overprint

1900 Wmk. 155 *Perf. 14, 15*

No.	Design	Description	Unused	Used
O49	A25	1c green	37.50	2.50
O50	A26	2c vermilion	50.00	4.00
O51	A27	3c yellow brn	50.00	2.50
O52	A28	5c dark blue	50.00	4.50
O53	A29	10c violet & org	65.00	5.50
O54	A30	15c lavender & cl	65.00	5.50
O55	A31	20c rose & dk bl	75.00	2.50
O56	A32	50c red lil & blk	150.00	25.00
O57	A33	1p blue & blk	300.00	25.00
O58	A34	5p carmine & blk	575.00	75.00
		Nos. O49-O58 (10)	1,418.	152.00

1903 Black Overprint

No.	Design	Description	Unused	Used
O59	A25	1c violet	35.00	4.00
O60	A26	2c green	35.00	4.00
O61	A35	4c carmine	65.00	2.50
O62	A28	5c orange	65.00	13.00
O63	A29	10c blue & org	70.00	4.00
O64	A32	50c carmine & blk	200.00	25.00
		Nos. O59-O64 (6)	470.00	52.50

Regular Issues Overprinted

1910 On Issues of 1899-1903

No.	Design	Description	Unused	Used
O65	A26	2c green	175.00	6.50
O66	A27	3c orange brn	175.00	4.00
O67	A35	4c carmine	200.00	10.00
O68	A28	5c orange	225.00	50.00
O69	A29	10c blue & org	200.00	4.00
O70	A30	15c lav & claret	225.00	6.50
O71	A31	20c rose & dk bl	275.00	3.00
O72	A32	50c carmine & blk	375.00	35.00
O73	A33	1p blue & blk	575.00	125.00
O74	A34	5p carmine & blk	200.00	125.00
		Nos. O65-O74 (10)	2,625.	369.00

1911 On Issue of 1910

No.	Design	Description	Unused	Used
O75	A36	1c violet	5.00	5.00
O76	A37	2c green	3.75	2.25
O77	A38	3c orange brn	5.00	2.50
O78	A39	4c carmine	5.50	2.25
O79	A40	5c orange	12.50	7.00
O80	A41	10c blue & org	5.50	2.50
O81	A42	15c gray bl & cl	13.00	8.50
O82	A43	20c red & blue	10.00	2.50
O83	A44	50c red brn & blk	35.00	15.00
O84	A45	1p blue & blk	60.00	25.00
O85	A46	5p carmine & blk	300.00	125.00
		Nos. O75-O85 (11)	455.25	197.50

Nos. 500 to 505 Overprinted

1915 Unwmk. *Rouletted 14½*

No.	Design	Description	Unused	Used
O86	A57	1c violet	1.00	*2.00*
O87	A58	2c green	1.00	*2.00*
O88	A59	3c brown	1.25	*2.00*
O89	A60	4c carmine	1.00	*2.00*
O90	A61	5c orange	1.00	*2.00*
O91	A62	10c ultra	1.25	*2.00*
		Nos. O86-O91 (6)	6.50	12.00

All values are known with inverted overprint. All values exist imperforate and part perforate but were not regularly issued in these forms.

On Nos. 506 to 514

1915-16 *Perf. 12*

No.	Design	Description	Unused	Used
O92	A57	1c violet	1.50	*2.00*
O93	A58	2c green	1.50	*2.00*
O94	A59	3c brown	1.50	*2.00*
O95	A60	4c carmine	1.50	*2.00*
a.		"CEATRO"	21.00	*30.00*
O96	A61	5c orange	1.50	*2.00*
O97	A62	10c ultra, type II	1.50	*2.00*
a.		Double overprint	*475.00*	
O98	A63	40c slate	8.00	*14.50*
a.		Inverted overprint	24.00	*25.00*
b.		Double overprint	40.00	
O99	A64	1p brown & blk	10.00	*14.50*
a.		Inverted overprint	27.50	27.50
O100	A65	5p claret & ultra	60.00	*60.00*
a.		Inverted overprint	80.00	
		Nos. O92-O100 (9)	87.00	101.00

Nos. O98 and O99 exist imperforate but probably were not issued in that form.

Preceding Issues Overprinted in Red, Blue or Black

On No. O74

1916 **Wmk. 155**

O101 A34 5p carmine & blk 900.00

On Nos. O75 to O85

O102 A36 1c violet 6.50
O103 A37 2c green 1.25
O104 A38 3c orange brn (Bl) 1.75
O105 A39 4c carmine (Bl) 7.00
O106 A40 5c orange (Bl) 1.75
O107 A41 10c blue & org 1.75
O108 A42 15c gray bl & cl (Bk) 1.75
O109 A43 20c red & bl (Bk) 1.90
O110 A44 50c red brn & blk 200.00
O111 A45 1p blue & blk 11.00
O112 A46 5p carmine & blk *3,250.*
Nos. O102-O111 (10) 234.65

No. O102 with blue overprint is a trial color. Counterfeits exist of Nos. O110, O112.

Nos. 608, 610 to 612, 615 and 616 Overprinted Vertically in Red or Black

Thick Paper

1918 **Unwmk.** ***Rouletted 14½***

O113 A68 1c violet (R) 60.00 35.00
O114 A69 2c gray grn (R) 65.00 35.00
O115 A70 3c bis brn (R) 60.00 35.00
O116 A71 4c carmine (Bk) 60.00 35.00
O117 A74 20c rose (Bk) 125.00 90.00
O118 A75 30c gray brn (R) 190.00 175.00

On Nos. 622-623
Medium Paper
Perf. 12

O119 A72 5c ultra (R) 40.00 40.00
O120 A73 10c blue (R) 35.00 25.00
a. Double overprint 400.00 *400.00*
Nos. O113-O120 (8) 635.00 470.00

Overprinted Horizontally in Red

On Nos. 626-628
Thin Paper

O121 A63 40c violet (R) 35.00 27.50
O122 A64 1p bl & blk (R) 85.00 70.00
O123 A65 5p grn & blk (R) *575.00 600.00*
Nos. O121-O123 (3) *695.00 697.50*

Nos. 608 and 610 to 615 Ovptd. Vertically Up in Red or Black

Thick Paper

1919 ***Rouletted 14½***

O124 A68 1c dull vio (R) 6.00 6.00
a. "OFICIAN" 70.00 *80.00*
O125 A69 2c gray grn (R) 9.50 3.50
a. "OFICIAN" 70.00 *80.00*
O126 A70 3c bis brn (R) 14.00 6.00
a. "OFICIAN" 95.00 *100.00*
O127 A71 4c car (Bk) 29.00 13.00
c. "OFICIAN" —
O127A A72 5c ultra 200.00 125.00
b. "OFICIAN" *500.00*
O128 A73 10c blue (R) 9.50 2.50
a. "OFICIAN" 85.00 60.00
O129 A74 20c rose (Bk) 60.00 47.50
a. "OFICIAN" 140.00

On Nos. 618, 622
Perf. 12

O130 A68 1c dull violet (R) 47.50 47.50
a. "OFICIAN" 140.00 100.00
O131 A72 5c ultra (R) 47.50 22.50
a. "OFICIAN" 140.00 100.00

Overprinted Horizontally
On Nos. 626-627
Thin Paper

O132 A63 40c violet (R) 47.50 35.00
O133 A64 1p bl & blk (R) 60.00 50.00
Nos. O124-O133 (11) 530.50 358.50

Nos. 608 to 615 and 617 Ovptd. Vertically down in Black, Red or Blue

Size: 17½x3mm

1921 ***Rouletted 14½***

O134 A68 1c gray (Bk) 30.00 12.00
a. 1c dull violet (Bk) 17.00 7.00
O135 A69 2c gray grn (R) 5.00 3.00
O136 A70 3c bis brn (R) 8.50 4.50
O137 A71 4c carmine (Bk) 27.50 21.00
O138 A72 5c ultra (R) 25.00 12.00
O139 A73 10c bl, reading down (R) 32.50 12.00
a. Overprint reading up 60.00 60.00
O140 A74 20c rose (Bl) 47.50 27.50
O141 A75 30c gray blk (R) 25.00 25.00

Overprinted Horizontally
On Nos. 626-628
Perf. 12

O142 A63 40c violet (R) 32.50 32.50
O143 A64 1p bl & blk (R) 25.00 25.00
O144 A65 5p grn & blk (Bk) *600.00 600.00*
Nos. O134-O144 (11) *858.50 774.50*

Nos. 609 to 615 Overprinted Vertically Down in Black

1921-30 ***Rouletted 14½***

O145 A68 1c gray 5.00 2.50
a. 1c lilac gray 1.00 .70
O146 A69 2c gray green 1.75 .70
O147 A70 3c bister brn .80 .70
a. "OFICAL" 47.50 25.00
b. "OIFCIAL" 47.50 25.00
c. Double overprint 140.00
O148 A71 4c carmine 22.50 2.50
O149 A72 5c ultra 1.00 .70
O150 A73 10c blue 1.00 .70
a. "OIFCIAL" 50.00
O151 A74 20c brown rose 9.00 *9.50*
a. 20c rose 5.00 2.50

On No. 625
Perf. 12

O152 A75 30c gray black 7.25 2.50

Overprinted Horizontally
On Nos. 626, 628

O153 A63 40c violet 7.00 5.00
a. "OFICAL" 60.00 60.00
b. "OICIFAL" 60.00 60.00
c. Inverted overprint 90.00 *125.00*
O154 A65 5p grn & blk ('30) 375.00 *375.00*
Nos. O145-O154 (10) 430.30 *399.80*

Ovptd. Vertically Down in Red On Nos. 609, 610, 611, 613 and 614

1921-24 ***Rouletted 14½***

O155 A68 1c lilac 1.60 1.00
O156 A69 2c gray green 1.50 .90
O157 A70 3c bister brown 4.00 1.00
O158 A72 5c ultra 1.60 .80
O159 A73 10c blue 35.00 3.50
a. Double overprint

On Nos. 624-625
Perf. 12

O160 A74 20c rose 7.25 1.60
O161 A75 30c gray black 19.00 5.00

Overprinted Horizontally
On Nos. 626-628

O162 A63 40c violet 14.00 7.50
a. Vert. pair, imperf. btwn.
O163 A64 1p blue & blk 35.00 25.00
O164 A65 5p green & blk 300.00 *300.00*

Overprinted Vertically Down in Blue on No. 612
Rouletted 14½

O165 A71 4c carmine 7.00 3.50
Nos. O155-O165 (11) 425.95 *349.80*

Same Overprint Vertically Down in Red on Nos. 635 and 637

1926-27 ***Rouletted 14½***

O166 A80 3c bis brn, ovpt. horiz. 12.00 12.00
a. Period omitted 30.00 30.00
O167 A82 5c orange 27.50 *30.00*

Same Overprint Vertically Down in Blue or Red On Nos. 650, 651, 655 and 656
Wmk. 156

O168 A79 2c scarlet (Bl) 20.00 20.00
a. Overprint reading up 30.00 30.00
O169 A80 3c bis brn, ovpt. horiz. (R) 5.00 5.00
a. Inverted overprint 60.00
O170 A85 10c claret (Bl) 35.00 16.00
O171 A84 20c deep blue (R) 14.00 12.00
a. Overprint reading up 14.00 12.00

Overprinted Horizontally in Red
On Nos. 643, 646-649
Perf. 12

O172 A81 4c green 6.00 6.00
O173 A83 30c dk grn 6.00 6.00
O174 A63 40c violet 16.00 16.00
a. Inverted overprint 80.00
O175 A87 50c olive brn 1.50 1.50
a. 50c yellow brown 18.00 18.00
O176 A88 1p red brn & bl 15.00 15.00
Nos. O168-O176 (9) 118.50 97.50

Same Overprint Horizontally on No. 651, Vertically Up on Nos. 650, 653-656, 666, RA1

1927-31 ***Rouletted 14½***

O177 PT1 1c brown ('31) .70 *1.00*
O178 A79 2c scarlet .70 *1.00*
a. "OFICAIL" 30.00 30.00
b. Overprint reading down 1.50 *2.00*
O179 A80 3c bis brn 2.00 1.50
a. "OFICAIL" 40.00 30.00
O180 A82 4c green 1.50 1.00
a. "OFICAIL" 40.00 40.00
b. Overprint reading down 10.00 2.00
O181 A82 5c orange 4.00 3.00
a. Overprint reading down 4.00 2.50
O182 A94 8c orange 12.00 8.00
a. Overprint reading down 7.00 6.00
O183 A85 10c lake 2.00 2.00
a. Overprint reading down 2.00 2.00
O184 A84 20c dark blue 10.00 4.00
a. "OFICAIL" 40.00 40.00
b. Overprint reading down 20.00 20.00
Nos. O177-O184 (8) 32.90 21.50

Overprinted Vertically Up on #O186, Horizontally
On Nos. 643 and 645 to 649

1927-33 ***Perf. 12***

O185 A81 4c green 6.00 5.00
a. Inverted overprint 30.00 30.00
O186 A85 10c brown lake 55.00 45.00
O187 A83 30c dark green 1.40 1.00
a. Inverted overprint 30.00 30.00
b. Pair, tête bêche overprints 35.00 35.00
c. "OFICAIL" 35.00 35.00
O188 A63 40c violet 12.00 8.00
O189 A87 50c olive brn ('33) 3.25 *4.00*
O190 A88 1p red brn & bl 24.00 20.00
Nos. O185-O190 (6) 101.65 83.00

The overprint on No. O186 is vertical.

Nos. 320, 628, 633 Overprinted Horizontally

On Stamp No. 320

1927-28 **Wmk. 155** ***Perf. 14, 15***

O191 A46 5p car & blk (R) 175.00 *250.00*
O192 A46 5p car & blk (Bl) 175.00 *250.00*

Unwmk. ***Perf. 12***

O193 A65 5p grn & blk (Bk) 375.00 *500.00*
a. Inverted overprint — —
O194 A78 10p blk brn & blk (Bl) 200.00 *300.00*

No. 320 Overprinted Horizontally

Wmk. 155 ***Perf. 14***

O195 A46 5p carmine & blk 300.00

Nos. 650 and 655 Overprinted Horizontally

1928-29 **Wmk. 156** ***Rouletted 14½***

Size: 16x2½mm

O196 A79 2c dull red 18.00 12.00
O197 A85 10c rose lake 27.50 12.00

Nos. RA1, 650-651, 653-656 Overprinted

1932-33

O198 PT1 1c brown .70 *1.00*
O199 A79 2c dull red .80 *1.00*
O200 A80 3c bister brn 3.00 3.00
O201 A82 4c green 10.00 8.00
O202 A82 5c orange 12.00 8.00
O203 A85 10c rose lake 3.25 3.00
O204 A84 20c dark blue 15.00 10.00
a. Double overprint *200.00 90.00*
Nos. O198-O204 (7) 44.75 34.00

Nos. 651, 646-649 Overprinted Horizontally

1933 ***Rouletted 14½***

O205 A80 3c bister brn 3.00 3.00

Perf. 12

O206 A83 30c dk green 8.00 3.00
O207 A63 40c violet 15.00 6.00
O208 A87 50c olive brn 2.50 3.00
a. "OFICIAL OFICIAL" 50.00 50.00
O209 A88 1p red brn & bl, type I 3.00 3.00
a. Type II 2.75 *3.50*

Overprinted Vertically On No. 656
Rouletted 14½

O210 A84 20c dark blue 18.00 10.00
Nos. O205-O210 (6) 49.50 28.00

Nos. RA1, 651, 653, 654, 683 Overprinted Horizontally

1934-37 ***Rouletted 14½***

Size: 13x2mm

O211 PT1 1c brown 5.00 *6.00*
O212 A80 3c bister brn .70 .70
O213 A82 4c green 12.00 10.00
O214 A82 5c orange .70 .70
O215 A96 15c dk blue ('37) 1.00 1.00
Nos. O211-O215 (5) 19.40 18.40

See No. O217a.

Same Overprint on Nos. 687A-692

1934-37 ***Perf. 10½***

O216 PT1 1c brown ('37) 1.00 *1.25*
O217 A79 2c scarlet 1.00 *1.50*
a. On No. 650 (error) 350.00
b. Double overprint 275.00
O218 A82 4c green ('35) 1.40 1.60
O219 A85 10c brown lake 1.00 1.00
O220 A84 20c dk blue ('37) 1.25 1.25
O221 A83 30c dk bl grn ('37) 2.00 2.00

On Nos. 647 and 649
Perf. 12, 11½x12

O222	A63	40c violet	3.00	3.50
O223	A88	1p red brn & bl (I)	5.00	*6.00*
a.		Type II	4.00	4.00
		Nos. O216-O223 (8)	15.65	18.10

On Nos. 707 to 709, 712, 715, 716, 717, 718 and 719

O224	A108	1c orange	2.00	*4.00*
O225	A109	2c green	1.25	*2.00*
O226	A110	4c carmine	1.25	*1.40*
O227	A112	10c violet	1.25	*2.50*
O228	A114	20c ultra	1.60	*2.50*
O229	A115	30c lake	2.00	*4.00*
O230	A116	40c red brown	2.50	*4.00*
O231	A117	50c black	2.75	*2.75*
O232	A118	1p dk brn & org	8.00	*12.00*
		Nos. O224-O232 (9)	22.60	*35.15*

PARCEL POST STAMPS

Railroad Train PP1

1941 Photo. Wmk. 156 *Perf. 14*

Q1	PP1	10c brt rose	2.75	.35
Q2	PP1	20c dk vio bl	1.75	.35

1944-46 Wmk. 272

Q3	PP1	10c brt rose	1.75	1.00
Q4	PP1	20c dk vio bl ('46)	5.00	2.50

1947-49 Wmk. 279

Q5	PP1	10c brt rose	1.25	.60
Q6	PP1	20c dk vio bl ('49)	1.60	.60

Streamlined Locomotive PP2

1951

Q7	PP2	10c rose pink	5.00	.40
Q8	PP2	20c blue violet	4.00	.70

1954 Wmk. 300

Q9	PP2	10c rose pink	4.25	.60
Q10	PP2	20c blue violet	4.25	1.50

POSTAL TAX STAMPS

Morelos Monument — PT1

Rouletted 14½

1925 Engr. Wmk. 156

RA1	PT1	1c brown	.35	.25
a.		Imperf.	30.00	

1926 *Perf. 12*

RA2	PT1	1c brown	.75	*5.00*
a.		Booklet pane of 2	12.00	

1925 Unwmk. *Rouletted 14½*

RA3	PT1	1c brown	75.00	19.00

It was obligatory to add a stamp of type PT1 to the regular postage on every article of domestic mail matter. The money obtained from this source formed a fund to combat a plague of locusts.

In 1931, 1c stamps of type PT1 were discontinued as Postal Tax stamps. It was subsequently used for the payment of postage on drop letters (announcement cards and unsealed circulars) to be delivered in the city of cancellation. See No. 687A.

For overprints see Nos. O177, O198, O211, O216, RA4.

No. RA1 Overprinted in Red

1929 Wmk. 156

RA4	PT1	1c brown	.35	.25
a.		Overprint reading down	75.00	75.00

There were two settings of this overprint. They may be distinguished by the two lines being spaced 4mm or 6mm apart.

The money from sales of this stamp was devoted to child welfare work.

Mother and Child — PT3

1929 Litho. *Rouletted 13, 13½*

RA5	PT3	1c violet	.35	.25

PT4

1929 Size: 18x24½mm Unwmk.

RA6	PT4	2c deep green	.40	.25
RA7	PT4	5c brown	.40	.25
a.		Imperf., pair	60.00	60.00

For surcharges see Nos. RA10-RA11.

PT5

Two types of 1c:

Type I — Background lines continue through lettering of top inscription. Denomination circle hangs below second background line. Paper and gum white.

Type II — Background lines cut away behind some letters. Circle rests on second background line. Paper and gum yellowish.

1929 Size: 19x25¼mm

RA8	PT5	1c violet, type I	.35	.25
a.		Booklet pane of 4	10.00	
b.		Booklet pane of 2	18.00	
c.		Type II	.40	.25
d.		Imperf., pair	50.00	50.00
RA9	PT5	2c deep green	.65	.25
a.		Imperf., pair	12.00	

The use of these stamps, in addition to the regular postage, was compulsory. The money obtained from their sale was used for child welfare work.

For surcharge see No. RA12.

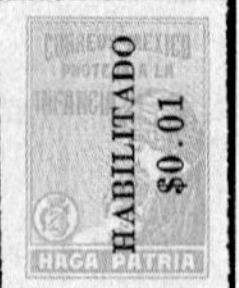

Nos. RA6, RA7, RA9 Surcharged

1930

RA10	PT4	1c on 2c dp grn	.75	.40
RA11	PT4	1c on 5c brown	1.00	.60
RA12	PT5	1c on 2c dp grn	2.00	1.00
		Nos. RA10-RA12 (3)	3.75	2.00

Used stamps exist with surcharge double or reading down.

No. 423 Overprinted

1931, Jan. 30 Wmk. 155 *Perf. 14*

RA13	A36	1c dull violet	.40	.40
a.		"PRO INFANCIA" double	50.00	

Indian Mother and Child — PT6

Wmk. 156

1934, Sept. 1 Engr. *Perf. 10½*

RA13B	PT6	1c dull orange	.30	.25

Mosquito Attacking Man — PT7

1939 Photo. Wmk. 156 *Perf. 14*

RA14	PT7	1c Prus blue	1.50	.25
a.		Imperf.	3.00	3.00

This stamp was obligatory on all mail, the money being used to aid in a drive against malaria.

See Nos. RA16, RA19.

Miguel Hidalgo y Costilla — PT8

1941

RA15	PT8	1c brt carmine	.45	.25

Type of 1939

1944 Wmk. 272 *Perf. 14*

RA16	PT7	1c Prus blue	1.00	.25

Learning Vowels — PT9

1946 Photo. Wmk. 279

RA17	PT9	1c black brown	.45	.25
a.		1c green black	1.00	1.00

1947 Wmk. 272

RA18	PT9	1c black brown	65.00	5.00

Type of 1939
Wmk. 279

RA19	PT7	1c Prus blue	3.50	.30

PROVISIONAL ISSUES

During the struggle led by Juarez to expel the Emperor Maximilian, installed June, 1864 by Napoleon III and French troops, a number of towns when free of Imperial forces issued provisional postage stamps. Maximilian was captured and executed June 19, 1867, but provisional issues continued current for a time pending re-establishment of Republican Government.

Campeche

A southern state in Mexico, comprising the western part of the Yucatan peninsula.

A1

White Paper
Numerals in Black

1876 Handstamped *Imperf.*

1	A1	5c gray blue & blue	*2,000.*	
2	A1	25c gray blue & blue	*1,100.*	
3	A1	50c gray blue & blue	*4,500.*	

The stamps printed in blue-black and blue on yellowish paper, formerly listed as issued in 1867, are now known to be an unofficial production of later years. They are reprints, but produced without official sanction.

Chiapas

A southern state in Mexico, bordering on Guatemala and the Pacific Ocean.

A1

1866 Typeset

1	A1	½r blk, *gray bl*	*2,000.*	*1,300.*
2	A1	1r blk, *lt grn*		*850.*
3	A1	2r blk, *rose*		*900.*
4	A1	4r blk, *lt buff*		*2,000.*
a.		Vertical half used as 2r on cover		*3,000.*
5	A1	8r blk, *rose*		*15,000.*
a.		Quarter used as 2r on cover		*4,000.*
b.		Half used as 4r on cover		*5,000.*

Chihuahua

A city of northern Mexico and capital of the State of Chihuahua.

A1

A2

1872 Handstamped

1	A1	12(c) black	*3,000.*	
2	A2	25(c) black	*3,000.*	

Cuautla

A town in the state of Morelos.

A1

1867 **Handstamped**
1 A1 (2r) black *7,000.*

All known examples on cover are uncanceled. Examples are known without the "73" inside the oval.

Cuernavaca

A city of Mexico, just south of the capital, and the capital of the State of Morelos.

A1

1867 **Handstamped**
1 A1 (1r) black *1,750.*
2 A1 (2r) black *40,000.*

No. 1 was canceled at Cuernavaca with the district name overprint. Supplies of overprinted stamps were sent to the Tetecala and Yquala sub-offices, where they were canceled with the usual local postmarks.

No. 2 was created by doubling the impression of the basic stamp and applying the district name overprint twice.

Unused examples of Nos. 1 and 2 do not exist.

Counterfeits exist.

Guadalajara

A city of Mexico and capital of the State of Jalisco.

A1

Dated "1867"
1st Printing
Medium Wove Paper

1867 **Handstamped** ***Imperf.***
1 A1 Medio r blk, *white* 350.00 250.00
2 A1 un r blk, *gray bl* 750.00 350.00
a. Overprinted "Cd. Guzman" *1,000.*
3 A1 un r blk, *dk bl* 450.00
4 A1 un r blk, *white* 250.00
a. Overprinted "Cd. Guzman" *750.00*
5 A1 2r blk, *dk grn* 250.00 21.00
a. Overprinted "Cd. Guzman" *500.00*
6 A1 2r blk, *white* 125.00
a. Overprinted "Cd. Guzman" *400.00*
b. Double print 250.00
7 A1 4r blk, *rose* 250.00 *300.00*
a. Half used as 2r on cover 500.00
b. Overprinted "Cd. Guzman" *900.00*
8 A1 4r blk, *white* 500.00
a. Half used as 2r on cover 2,500.
9 A1 un p blk, *lilac* 250.00 *300.00*

Serrate Perf.
10 A1 un r blk, *gray bl* *900.00*
11 A1 2r blk, *dk grn* 700.00
12 A1 4r blk, *rose* 350.00
12A A1 un p blk, *lilac* *1,750.*

2nd Printing
No Period after "2" or "4"
Thin Quadrille Paper
Imperf
13 A1 2r blk, *green* 30.00 20.00
a. Half used as 1r on cover 400.00

Serrate Perf.
14 A1 2r blk, *green* 225.00

Thin Laid Batonné Paper
Imperf
15 A1 2r blk, *green* 45.00 24.00

Serrate Perf.
16 A1 2r blk, *green* 225.00

3rd Printing
Capital "U" in "Un" on 1r, 1p
Period after "2" and "4"
Thin Wove Paper
Imperf
16A A1 Un r blk, *white* 125.00
17 A1 Un r blk, *blue* 90.00
17A A1 Un r blk, *lilac* 100.00
18 A1 2r blk, *rose* 50.00
18A A1 4r blk, *blue* 500.00 *1,000.*
18B A1 Un p blue 1,750.

Serrate Perf.
19 A1 Un r blk, *blue* 300.00
19A A1 2r blk, *rose* *750.00*
19B A1 4r blue *500.00*

Thin Quadrille Paper
Imperf
20 A1 2r blk, *rose* 42.50 42.50
21 A1 4r blk, *blue* 15.00 30.00
22 A1 4r blk, *white* 200.00
23 A1 Un p blk, *lilac* 15.00 60.00
24 A1 Un p blk, *rose* 65.00
24A A1 Un p blk, *white* 1,500.

Serrate Perf
24B A1 2r blk, *rose* *500.00*
25 A1 Un p blk, *lilac* 750.00 750.00
25A A1 Un p blk, *rose* 700.00 300.00

Thin Laid Batonné Paper
Imperf
26 A1 Un r blk, *green* 22.50 17.50
27 A1 2r blk, *rose* 27.50 22.50
27A A1 2r blk, *green* 47.50
28 A1 4r blk, *blue* 17.50 42.50
29 A1 4r blk, *white* 100.00
30 A1 Un p blk, *lilac* 30.00 52.50
31 A1 Un p blk, *rose* 65.00

Serrate Perf.
32 A1 Un r blk, *green* 300.00
33 A1 2r blk, *rose* 400.00 *200.00*
34 A1 4r blk, *blue* 425.00
34A A1 4r blk, *white* *1,750.*
34B A1 Un p blk, *lilac* 700.00

Thin Oblong Quadrille Paper
Imperf
35 A1 Un r blk, *blue* 250.00 22.50
35A A1 Un r blk, *white* 1,500.
36 A1 4r blk, *blue* 600.00

Serrate Perf.
37 A1 Un r blk, *blue* 300.00

4th Printing
Dated "1868"
Wove Paper

1868 ***Imperf.***
38 A1 2r blk, *lilac* 30.00 14.00
a. Half used as 1r on cover 500.00
39 A1 2r blk, *rose* 52.50 65.00

Serrate Perf.
40 A1 2r blk, *lilac* *300.00*
41 A1 2r blk, *rose* 750.00 300.00

Laid Batonné Paper
Imperf
42 A1 un r blk, *green* 12.50 12.50
43 A1 2r blk, *lilac* 12.50 12.50
a. Half used as 1r on cover 1,500.
43A A1 2r blk, *rose* 750.00

Serrate Perf.
44 A1 un r blk, *green* 250.00 200.00
44A A1 2r blk, *rose* 500.00

Quadrille Paper.
Imperf
45 A1 2r blk, *lilac* 25.00 14.00

Serrate Perf.
46 A1 2r blk, *lilac* 300.00 300.00

Laid Paper
Imperf
47 A1 un r blk, *green* 13.00 17.00
a. Watermarked "LA + F" *750.00* *1,000.*
b. "nu" instead of "un" 750.00
c. Dated "1863" 300.00
48 A1 2r blk, *lilac* 32.50 32.50
49 A1 2r blk, *rose* 37.50 37.50

Serrate Perf.
50 A1 un r blk, *green* 750.00 300.00
51 A1 2r blk, *rose* 475.00

Counterfeits of Nos. 1-51 abound.

Merida

A city of southeastern Mexico, capital of the State of Yucatan.

Mexico No. 521 Surcharged **25**

1916 **Wmk. 155** ***Perf. 14***
1 A40 25(c) on 5c org, on cover *500.00*

The G.P.DE.M. overprint reads down.

Authorities consider the Monterrey, Morelia and Patzcuaro stamps to be bogus.

Tlacotalpan

A village in the state of Veracruz.

A1

Handstamped Monogram, Value in Manuscript

1856, Oct.
1 A1 ½(r) black *30,000.*

Research suggests that this stamp was not an officially sanctioned issue, but was instead part of a postal fraud orchestrated by Tlacotalpan postmaster Angel Fernando and his assistant Ignacio Crespo to cover theft of funds in that post office. The initials IMC in the stamp are most likely those of Crespo.

REVOLUTIONARY ISSUES

SINALOA

A northern state in Mexico, bordering on the Pacific Ocean. Stamps were issued by a provisional government.

Coat of Arms — A1

1929 **Unwmk.** **Litho.** ***Perf. 12***
1 A1 10c blk, red & bl 5.00
a. Tête bêche pair 35.00
2 A1 20c blk, red & gray 5.00

Just as Nos. 1 and 2 were ready to be placed on sale the state was occupied by the Federal forces and the stamps could not be used. At a later date a few stamps were canceled by favor.

A recent find included a number of errors or printer's waste.

YUCATAN

A southeastern state of Mexico.

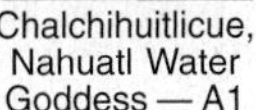

Chalchihuitlicue, Nahuatl Water Goddess — A1

"Casa de Monjas" — A2

Temple of the Tigers — A3

Without Gum

1924 **Unwmk.** **Litho.** ***Imperf.***
1 A1 5c violet 10.00 15.00
2 A2 10c carmine 40.00 50.00
3 A3 50c olive green 175.00

Perf. 12
4 A1 5c violet 50.00 60.00
5 A2 10c carmine 50.00 75.00
6 A3 50c olive green 200.00

Nos. 3 and 6 were not regularly issued.

MICRONESIA

ˌmī-krə-ˈnē-zhə

LOCATION — A group of over 600 islands in the West Pacific Ocean, north of the Equator.
GOVT. — Republic
AREA — 271 sq. miles
POP. — 131,500 (1999 est.)
CAPITAL — Palikir

These islands, also known as the Caroline Islands, were bought by Germany from Spain in 1899. Caroline Islands stamps issued as a German territory are listed in Vol. 2 of this Catalogue. Seized by Japan in 1914, they were taken by the US in WWII and became part of the US Trust Territory of the Pacific in 1947. By agreement with the USPS, the islands began issuing their own stamps in 1984, with the USPS continuing to carry the mail to and from the islands.

On Nov. 3, 1986 Micronesia became a Federation as a Sovereign State in Compact of Free Association with the US.

100 Cents = 1 Dollar

Catalogue values for all unused stamps in this country are for Never Hinged items.

Postal Service Inauguration — A1

1984, July 12 Litho. *Perf. 14*

1	A1 20c Yap		.45	.45
2	A1 20c Truk		.45	.45
3	A1 20c Pohnpei		.45	.45
4	A1 20c Kosrae		.45	.45
a.	Block of 4, #1-4		1.90	1.90

For surcharges see Nos. 48-51.

Fernandez de Quiros — A2

Men's House, Yap — A3

Designs: 1c, 19c, Pedro Fernandez de Quiros, Spanish explorer, first discovered Pohnpei, 1595. 2c, 20c, Louis Duperrey, French explorer. 3c, 30c, Fyodor Litke, Russian explorer. 4c, 37c, Dumont d'Urville. 10c, Sleeping Lady, Kosrae. 13c, Liduduhriap Waterfall, Pohnpei. 17c, Tonachau Peak, Truk. 50c, Devil mask, Truk. $1, Sokeh's Rock, Pohnpei. $2, Canoes, Kosrae. $5, Stone money, Yap.

1984, July 12 *Perf. 13½x13*

5	A2	1c Prussian blue	.25	.25
6	A2	2c deep claret	.25	.25
7	A2	3c dark blue	.25	.25
8	A2	4c green	.25	.25
9	A3	5c yellow brown	.25	.25
10	A3	10c dark violet	.25	.25
11	A3	13c dark blue	.25	.25
12	A3	17c brown lake	.25	.25
13	A2	19c dark violet	.30	.30
14	A2	20c olive green	.30	.30
15	A2	30c rose lake	.45	.45
16	A2	37c deep violet	.55	.55
17	A3	50c brown	.75	.75
18	A3	$1 olive	1.75	1.75
19	A3	$2 Prussian blue	3.50	3.50
20	A3	$5 brown lake	8.50	8.50
		Nos. 5-20 (16)	18.10	18.10

See Nos. 33, 36, 38.

Ausipex '84 A4

1984, Sept. 21 Litho. *Perf. 13½*

21	A4 20c Truk Post Office	.40	.40
	Nos. 21,C4-C6 (4)	3.00	3.00

Christmas A5

Child's drawing.

1984, Dec. 20

22	A5 20c Child in manger	.90	.90
	Nos. 22,C7-C9 (4)	3.55	3.55

Ships — A6

22c, U.S.S. Jamestown.

1985, Aug. 19

23	A6 22c multi	.55	.55
	Nos. 23,C10-C12 (4)	3.00	3.00

Christmas A7

22c, Lelu Protestant Church, Kosrae.

1985, Oct. 15 Litho. *Perf. 13½*

24	A7 22c multi	.75	.60
	Nos. 24,C13-C14 (3)	2.90	2.75

Audubon Birth Bicentenary — A8

1985, Oct. 30 *Perf. 14½*

25	A8 22c Noddy tern	.60	.60
26	A8 22c Turnstone	.60	.60
27	A8 22c Golden plover	.60	.60
28	A8 22c Black-bellied plover	.60	.60
a.	Block of 4, #25-28	2.60	2.60
	Nos. 25-28,C15 (5)	3.40	3.40

Types of 1984 and

Birds — A9

Tall Ship Senyavin A10

Natl. Seal A11

No. 31, Long-billed white-eye. No. 32, Truk monarch. No. 33, Liduduhriap Waterfall, Pohnpei. No. 35, Pohnpei mountain starling. No. 36, Tonachau Peak, Truk. No. 38, Sleeping Lady, Kosrae.

Perf. 13½ (A8a), 13½x13

1985-88 Litho.

31	A9	3c multi	.25	.25
32	A9	14c multi	.30	.30
33	A3	15c dark red	.30	.30
a.		Booklet pane of 10	6.00	—
34	A10	22c bright blue green	.35	.35
35	A9	22c multi	.45	.45
36	A3	25c ochre	.50	.50
a.		Booklet pane of 10	6.50	—
b.		Booklet pane, 5 15c + 5 25c	7.50	—
37	A10	36c ultramarine	.70	.70
38	A3	45c emerald	.90	.90
39	A11	$10 bright ultra	15.00	15.00
		Nos. 31-39,C34-C36 (12)	21.75	21.75

Issued: $10, 10/15; No. 34, 4/14/86; 3c, 14c, No. 35, 8/1/88; 15c, 25c, 36c, 45c, 9/1/88.

Nan Madol Ruins, Pohnpei A16

22c, Land of the Sacred Masonry.

1985, Dec. Litho. *Perf. 13½*

45	A16 22c multicolored	.60	.60
	Nos. 45,C16-C18 (4)	3.00	3.00

Intl. Peace Year — A17

1986, May 16

46	A17 22c multicolored	.65	.60

Nos. 1-4 Surcharged

1986, May 19 Litho. *Perf. 14*

48	Al 22c on 20c No. 1	.40	.40
49	A1 22c on 20c No. 2	.40	.40
50	A1 22c on 20c No. 3	.40	.40
51	A1 22c on 20c No. 4	.40	.40
a.	Block of 4, #48-51	1.75	1.75

AMERIPEX '86 A18

Bully Hayes (1829-1877), Buccaneer.

1986, May 22 *Perf. 13½*

52	A18 22c At ship's helm	.50	.50
	Nos. 52,C21-C24 (5)	4.00	4.00

First Passport A19

1986, Nov. 4 Litho. *Perf. 13½*

53	A19 22c multicolored	.60	.60

Christmas A20

Virgin and child paintings: 5c, Italy, 18th cent. 22c, Germany, 19th cent.

1986, Oct. 15 Litho. *Perf. 14½*

54	A20 5c multicolored	.25	.25
55	A20 22c multicolored	.75	.75
	Nos. 54-55,C26-C27 (4)	3.40	3.40

Anniversaries and Events — A21

22c, Intl. Year of Shelter for the Homeless. $1, CAPEX '87.

1987, June 13 Litho. *Perf. 14½*

56	A21 22c multicolored	.50	.50
	Nos. 56,C28-C30 (4)	3.20	3.20

Souvenir Sheet

57	A21 $1 multicolored	3.25	3.25

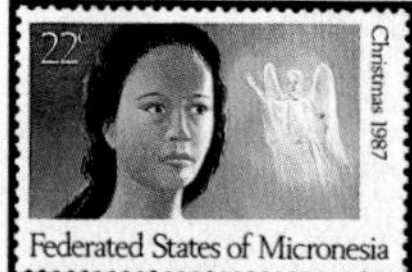

Christmas A22

22c, Archangel Gabriel appearing before Mary.

1987, Nov. 16 Litho. *Perf. 14½*

58	A22 22c multicolored	.60	.60
	Nos. 58,C31-C33 (4)	3.30	3.30

Colonial Eras — A23

1988, July 20 Litho. *Perf. 13x13½*

59	A23 22c German	.60	.60
60	A23 22c Spanish	.60	.60
61	A23 22c Japanese	.60	.60
62	A23 22c US Trust Territory	.60	.60
a.	Block of 4, #59-62	2.40	2.40
	Nos. 59-62,C37-C38 (6)	4.30	4.30

Printed se-tenant in sheets of 28 plus 4 center labels picturing flags of Spain (UL), Germany (UR), Japan (LL) and the US (LR).

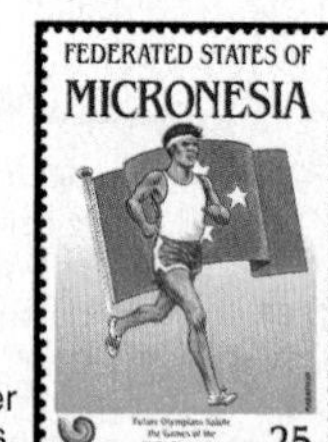

1988 Summer Olympics, Seoul — A24

1988, Sept. 1 Litho. *Perf. 14*

63	A24 25c Running	.50	.50
64	A24 25c Women's hurdles	.50	.50
a.	Pair, #63-64	1.00	1.00
65	A24 45c Basketball	.80	.80
66	A24 45c Women's volleyball	.80	.80
a.	Pair, #65-66	1.65	1.65
	Nos. 63-66 (4)	2.60	2.60

Christmas — A25

Children decorating tree: No. 67, Two girls, UL of tree. No. 68, Boy, girl, dove, UR of tree. No. 69, Boy, girl, LL of tree. No. 70, Boy, girl, LR of tree. Se-tenant in a continuous design.

1988, Oct. 28 Litho. *Perf. 14*

67	A25 25c multicolored	.45	.45
68	A25 25c multicolored	.45	.45
69	A25 25c multicolored	.45	.45
70	A25 25c multicolored	.45	.45
a.	Block of 4, #67-70	1.90	1.90

Miniature Sheet

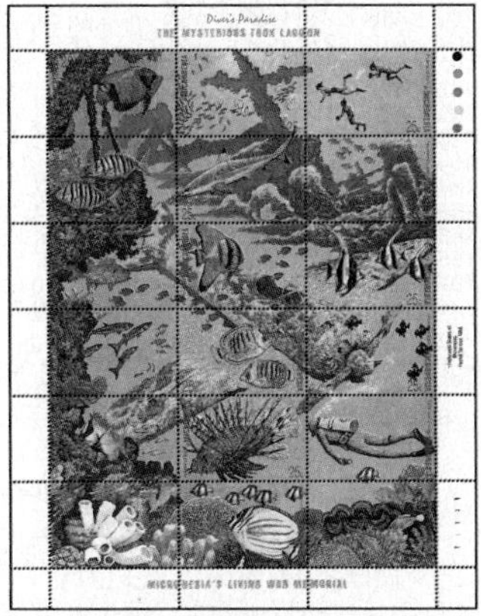

Truk Lagoon State Monument — A26

a, Sun and stars angelfish. b, School of fish. c, 3 divers. d, Goldenjack. e, Blacktip reef shark. f, 2 schools of fish. g, Squirrelfish. h, Batfish. i, Moorish idols. j, Barracudas. k, Spot banded butterflyfish. l, Three-spotted damselfish. m, Foxface. n, Lionfish. o, Diver. p, Coral. q, Butterflyfish. r, Bivalve, fish, coral.

1988, Dec. 19 Litho. *Perf. 14*

71	A26 Sheet of 18	9.50	9.50
a.-r.	25c any single	.50	.50

Mwarmwarms — A27

1989, Mar. 31 Litho. *Perf. 14*

72	A27 45c Plumeria	.65	.65
73	A27 45c Hibiscus	.65	.65
74	A27 45c Jasmine	.65	.65
75	A27 45c Bougainvillea	.65	.65
a.	Block of 4, #72-75	2.75	2.75

Souvenir Sheet

Pheasant and Chrysanthemum, 1830s, by Hiroshige (1797-1858) — A28

1989, May 15 Litho. *Perf. 14½*

76	A28 $1 multicolored	1.60	1.60

Hirohito (1901-1989), emperor of Japan.

Sharks A29

1989, July 7

77	A29 25c Whale	.40	.40
78	A29 25c Hammerhead	.40	.40
a.	Pair, #77-78	.80	.80
79	A29 45c Tiger, vert.	.75	.75
80	A29 45c Great white, vert.	.75	.75
a.	Pair, #79-80	1.50	1.50
	Nos. 77-80 (4)	2.30	2.30

Miniature Sheet

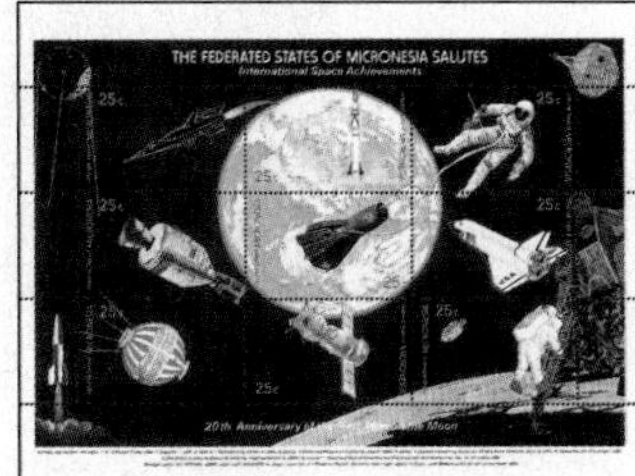

First Moon Landing, 20th Anniv. — A30

Space achievements: a, X-15 rocket plane, 1959. b, *Explorer 1* launched into orbit, 1958. c, Ed White, 1st American to walk in space, Gemini 4 mission, 1965. d, Apollo 18 command module, 1975. e. Gemini 4 capsule. f, Space shuttle *Challenger,* 1983-86. g, *San Marco 2,* satellite engineered by Italy. h, Soyuz 19 spacecraft, 1975. i, *Columbia* command module and Neil Armstrong taking man's first step onto the Moon during the Apollo 11 mission, 1969.

1989, July 20 Litho. *Perf. 14*

81	A30 Sheet of 9	5.25	4.50
a.-i.	25c any single	.50	.45

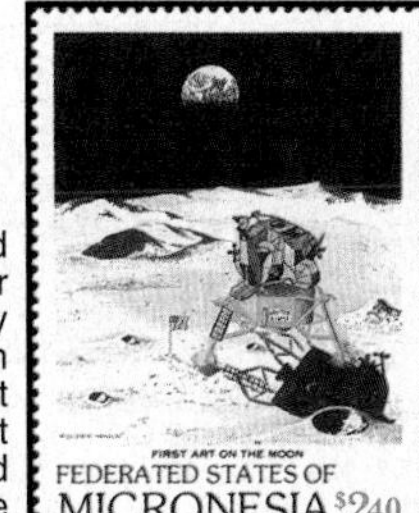

Earth and Lunar Module, by William Hanson, 1st Art Transported to the Moon — A31

1989, July 20 *Perf. 13½x14*

82	A31 $2.40 multicolored	4.50	4.00

First Moon landing, 20th anniv.

Seashells — A32

1c, Horse's hoof. 3c, Rare spotted cowrie. 15c, Commercial trochus. 20c, General cone. 25c, Triton's trumpet. 30c, Laciniated conch. 36c, Red-mouthed olive. 45c, Map cowrie. 50c, Textile cone. $1, Orange spider conch. $2, Golden cowrie. $5, Episcopal miter.

1989, Sept. 26 *Perf. 14*

83	A32 1c multi	.25	.25
84	A32 3c multi	.25	.25
85	A32 15c multi	.25	.25
a.	Booklet pane of 10	5.00	—
87	A32 20c multi	.30	.30
88	A32 25c multi	.40	.40
a.	Booklet pane of 10	7.50	—
b.	Booklet pane, 5 each 15c, 25c	7.50	—
90	A32 30c multi	.45	.45
91	A32 36c multi	.55	.55
93	A32 45c multi	.70	.70
95	A32 50c multi	.75	.75
100	A32 $1 multi	1.75	1.75
101	A32 $2 multi	3.50	3.50
102	A32 $5 multi	8.50	8.50
	Nos. 83-102 (12)	17.65	17.65

Booklet panes issued Sept. 14, 1990.

Miniature Sheet

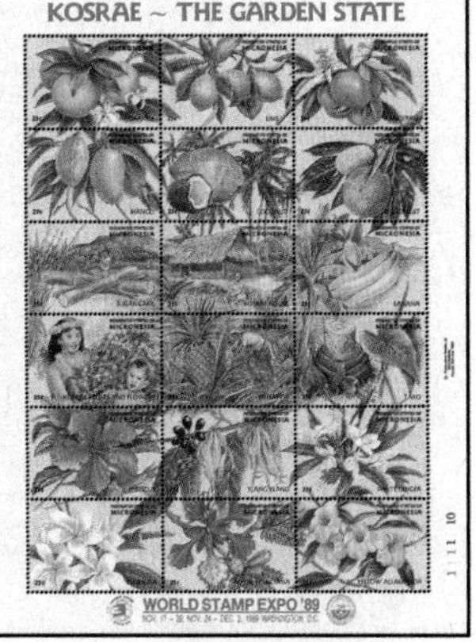

Fruits and Flowers Endemic to Kosrae — A33

Designs: a, Orange. b, Lime. c, Tangerine. d, Mango. e, Coconut. f, Breadfruit. g, Sugar cane. h, Thatched dwelling. i, Banana. j, Girl, boy. k, Pineapple picker. l, Taro. m, Hibiscus. n, Ylang ylang. o, White ginger. p, Plumeria. q, Royal poinciana. r, Yellow allamanda.

1989, Nov. 18 Litho. *Perf. 14*

103	A33 Sheet of 18	9.00	9.00
a.-r.	25c any single	.45	.45

Margin inscribed for World Stamp Expo '89.

Christmas — A34

1989, Dec. 14 Litho. *Perf. 14½*

104	A34 25c Heralding angel	.50	.50
105	A34 45c Three wise men	.90	.90

World Wildlife Fund A35

Micronesian kingfishers and pigeons.

1990, Feb. 19 Litho. *Perf. 14*

106	A35 10c Kingfisher (juvenile)	*.55*	*.55*
107	A35 15c Kingfisher (adult)	*1.25*	*1.25*
108	A35 20c Pigeon	*1.75*	*1.75*
109	A35 25c Pigeon, diff.	*2.50*	*2.50*
	Nos. 106-109 (4)	*6.05*	*6.05*

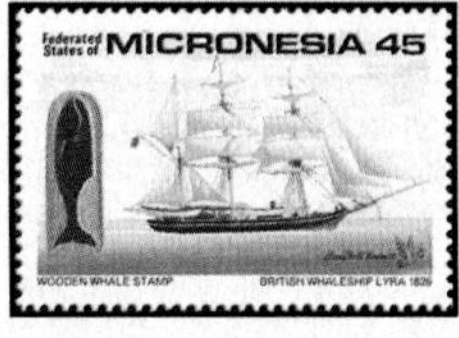

Stamp World London '90 — A36

Exhibition emblem, artifacts and whaling vessels: No. 110, Wooden whale stamp, *Lyra,* 1826. No. 111, Harpoons, *Prudent,* 1827. No. 112, Scrimshaw (whale), *Rhone,* 1851. No. 113, Scrimshaw on whale tooth, *Sussex,* 1843. $1, Whalers at kill.

1990, May 3 Litho. *Perf. 14*

110	A36 45c multicolored	.80	.80
111	A36 45c multicolored	.80	.80
112	A36 45c multicolored	.80	.80
113	A36 45c multicolored	.80	.80
a.	Block of 4, #110-113	3.25	3.25

Souvenir Sheet

114	A36 $1 multicolored	2.00	2.00

Souvenir Sheet

Penny Black, 150th Anniv. — A37

1990, May 6 *Perf. 14*

115	A37 $1 Great Britain No. 1	2.00	2.00

Main Building — A38

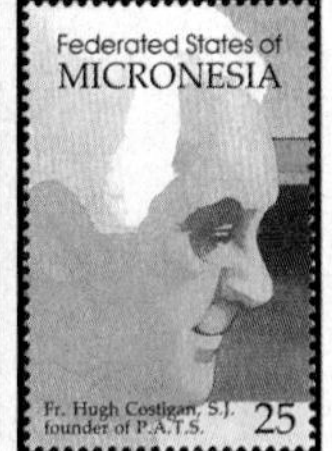

Fr. Hugh Costigan, School Founder — A39

Designs: No. 117, Fr. Costigan, students. No. 119, Fr. Costigan, Isaphu Samuel Hadley. No. 120, New York City Police Badge.

1990, July 31 Litho. *Perf. 14*

116	A38 25c multicolored	.50	.50
117	A38 25c multicolored	.50	.50
118	A39 25c multicolored	.50	.50
119	A39 25c multicolored	.50	.50
120	A38 25c multicolored	.50	.50
a.	Strip of 5, #116-120	2.50	2.50

Pohnpei Agriculture and Trade School, 25th anniversary. Printed in sheets of 15.

Souvenir Sheet

Expo '90, Intl. Garden and Greenery Exposition, Osaka, Japan — A40

1990, July 31 Litho. *Perf. 14*

121	A40 $1 multicolored	1.75	1.75

Loading Mail, Pohnpei Airport, 1990 A41

Pacifica Emblem and: 45c, Japanese mail boat, Truk Lagoon, 1940.

1990, Aug. 24

122	A41 25c multicolored	.50	.50
123	A41 45c multicolored	1.25	1.25

Canoe, Flag of Federated States of Micronesia A42

Designs: No. 124, Stick chart, canoe, flag of Marshall Islands. No. 125, Frigate bird, eagle, USS Constitution, flag of US.

1990, Sept. 28 ***Perf. 13½***

124 A42 25c multicolored .55 .55
125 A42 25c multicolored .55 .55
126 A42 25c multicolored .55 .55
a. Strip of 3, #124-126 1.75 1.75

Compact of Free Association with the US. Printed in sheets of 15. See No. 253, US No. 2506, Marshall Islands No. 381.

Moths A43

No. 127, Gracillariidae. No. 128, Yponomeatidae. No. 129 Cosmopterigidae, full moon. No. 130, Cosmopterigidae, ¾ moon.

1990, Nov. 10 **Litho.** ***Perf. 14***

127 A43 45c multi .80 .80
128 A43 45c multi .80 .80
129 A43 45c shown .80 .80
130 A43 45c multi .80 .80
a. Block of 4, #127-130 3.25 3.25

Miniature Sheet

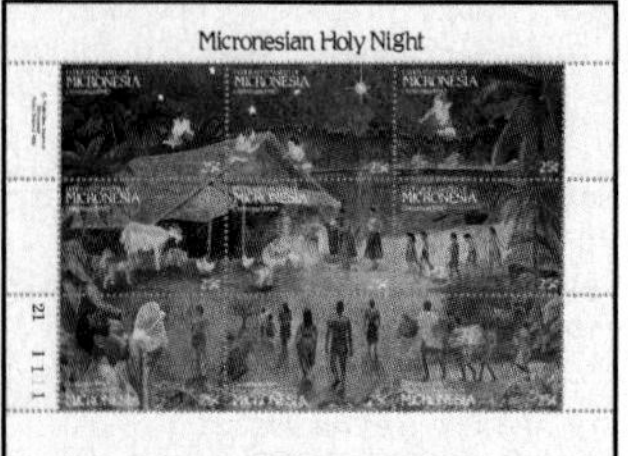

Christmas — A44

Designs: a, Cherub. b, Star of Bethlehem. c, Cherub blowing horn. d, Goats. e, Nativity scene. f, Children, outrigger canoe. g, Messenger blowing a conch shell. h, Family walking. i, People carrying bundles.

1990, Nov. 19 **Litho.** ***Perf. 14***

131 A44 Sheet of 9 4.50 4.50
a.-i. 25c any single .50 .50

Souvenir Sheets

New Capital of Micronesia — A45

1991, Jan. 15 **Litho.** ***Perf. 14x13½***

132 A45 Sheet of 2 1.40 1.40
a. 25c Executive Branch .50 .50
b. 45c Legislative, Judicial Branches .90 .90
133 A45 $1 New Capitol 2.00 2.00

Turtles — A46

1991, Mar. 14 **Litho.** ***Perf. 14***

134 A46 29c Hawksbill on beach 1.10 1.10
135 A46 29c Green 1.10 1.10
a. Pair, #134-135 2.25 2.25
136 A46 50c Hawksbill 1.40 1.40
137 A46 50c Leatherback 1.40 1.40
a. Pair, #136-137 2.75 2.75
Nos. 134-137 (4) 5.00 5.00

Operation Desert Storm A47

No. 138, Battleship Missouri. No. 139, Multiple launch rocket system. No. 140, F-14 Tomcat. No. 141, E-3 Sentry (AWACS). No. 142, Frigatebird, flag.

1991, July 30 **Litho.** ***Perf. 14***

138 A47 29c multicolored .60 .60
139 A47 29c multicolored .60 .60
140 A47 29c multicolored .60 .60
141 A47 29c multicolored .60 .60
a. Block or strip of 4, #138-141 2.40 2.40

Size: 51x38mm

142 A47 $2.90 multicolored 5.00 5.00
a. Souvenir sheet of 1 5.50 5.50
Nos. 138-142 (5) 7.40 7.40

Miniature Sheets

Phila Nippon '91 — A48

Ukiyo-e prints by Paul Jacoulet (1902-1960) — No. 143: a, Evening Flowers, Toloas, Truk, 1941. b, The Chief's Daughter, Mogomog, 1953. c, Yagourouh and Mio, Yap, 1938. No. 144a, Yap Beauty and Orchids, 1934. b, The Yellow-eyed Boys, Ohlol, 1940. c, Violet Flowers, Tomil, 1937. $1, First Love, Yap, 1937, horiz.

1991, Sept. **Litho.** ***Perf. 14***

143 A48 Sheet of 3 2.25 2.25
a.-c. 29c any single .75 .75
144 A48 Sheet of 3 3.50 3.50
a.-c. 50c any single 1.25 1.25

Souvenir Sheet

145 A48 $1 multicolored 2.40 2.40

Christmas — A49

Handicraft scenes: 29c, Nativity. 40c, Adoration of the Magi. 50c, Adoration of the Shepherds.

1991, Oct. 30 ***Perf. 14x13½***

146 A49 29c multicolored .50 .50
147 A49 40c multicolored .75 .75
148 A49 50c multicolored 1.00 1.00
Nos. 146-148 (3) 2.25 2.25

Pohnpei Rain Forest A50

Designs: a, Pohnpei fruit bat. b, Purple capped fruit-dove. c, Micronesian kingfisher. d, Birdnest fern. e, Island swiftlet. f, Long-billed white-eye. g, Brown noddy. h, Pohnpei lory. i, Pohnpei flycatcher. j, Caroline ground-dove. k, White-tailed tropicbird. l, Micronesian honeyeater. m, Ixora. n, Pohnpei fantail. o, Gray white-eye. p, Blue-faced parrotfinch. q, Cicadabird. r, Green skink.

1991, Nov. 18

149 Sheet of 18 13.00 13.00
a.-r. A50 29c any single .65 .65

Peace Corps — A51

Designs: a, Learning crop planting techniques. b, Education. c, John F. Kennedy. d, Public health nurses. e, Recreation.

1992, Apr. 10 **Litho.** ***Perf. 14***

150 A51 29c Strip of 5, #a.-e. 2.50 2.50

Printed in sheets of 15.

Discovery of America, 500th Anniv. — A52

Designs: a, Queen Isabella I. b, Santa Maria. c, Columbus.

1992, May 23 **Litho.** ***Perf. 13½***

151 Strip of 3 5.00 5.00
a.-c. A52 29c any single 1.65 1.65

Admission to the UN, First Anniv. A53

1992, Sept. 24 ***Perf. 11x10½***

152 A53 29c multicolored 1.50 1.50
153 A53 50c multicolored 2.25 2.25
a. Souvenir sheet of 2, #152-153 3.50 3.50

Christmas A54

1992, Dec. 4 ***Perf. 13½***

154 A54 29c multicolored 1.90 1.90

Pioneers of Flight — A55

a, Andrei N. Tupolev. b, John A. Macready. c, Edward V. Rickenbacker. d, Manfred von Richtofen. e, Hugh M. Trenchard. f, Glenn H. Curtiss. g, Charles E. Kingsford-Smith. h, Igor I. Sikorsky.

1993, Apr. 12

155 A55 29c Block of 8, #a.-h. 4.75 4.75

See Nos. 178, 191, 200, 210, 233, 238, 249.

Fish — A56

Designs: 10c, Bigscale soldierfish. 19c, Bennett's butterflyfish. 20c, Peacock grouper. 22c, Great barracuda. 25c, Coral grouper. 29c, Regal angelfish. 30c, Bleeker's parrotfish. 35c, Picassofish. 40c, Mandarinfish. 45c, Bluebanded surgeonfish. 50c, Orange-striped triggerfish. 52c, Palette surgeonfish. 75c, Oriental sweetlips. $1, Zebra moray. $2, Foxface rabbitfish. $2.90, Orangespine unicornfish.

1993-94 **Litho.** ***Perf. 13½***

156 A56 10c multicolored .25 .25
157 A56 19c multicolored .35 .35
158 A56 20c multicolored .35 .35
159 A56 22c multicolored .40 .40
160 A56 25c multicolored .45 .45
161 A56 29c multicolored .55 .55
162 A56 30c multicolored .55 .55
162A A56 35c multicolored .65 .65
163 A56 40c multicolored .70 .70
163A A56 45c multicolored .75 .75
164 A56 50c multicolored .90 .90
164A A56 52c multicolored 1.00 1.00
164B A56 75c multicolored 1.40 1.40
165 A56 $1 multicolored 1.75 1.75
166 A56 $2 multicolored 3.50 3.50
167 A56 $2.90 multicolored 5.50 5.50
Nos. 156-167 (16) 19.05 19.05

Issued: 19c, 29c, 50c, $1, 5/14/93; 22c, 30c, 40c, 45c, 8/26/93; 10c, 20c, 35c, $2.90, 5/20/94; 25c, 52c, 75c, $2, 8/5/94.

See Nos. 213-227, 250.

A57

Sailing Ships: a, Great Republic. b, Benjamin F. Packard. c, Stag Hound. d, Herald of the Morning. e, Rainbow. f, Flying Cloud. g, Lightning. h, Sea Witch. i, Columbia. j, New World. k, Young America. l, Courier.

1993, May 21 **Litho.** ***Perf. 13½***

168 A57 29c Sheet of 12, #a.-l. 15.00 15.00

A59

1993, July 4 **Litho.** ***Perf. 13½***

172 A59 29c multicolored .80 .80

Thomas Jefferson, 250th anniv. of birth.

Pacific Canoes — A60

1993, July 21 **Litho.** ***Perf. 13½***

173 A60 29c Yap .80 .80
174 A60 29c Kosrae .80 .80
175 A60 29c Pohnpei .80 .80
176 A60 29c Chuuk .80 .80
a. Block of 4, #173-176 3.25 3.25

Local Leaders — A61

Designs: a, Ambilos Iehsi, (1935-81), educator. b, Andrew Roboman (1905-92), Yap chief. c, Joab N. Sigrah (1932-88), first vice-speaker of Congress. d, Petrus Mailo (1902-71), Chuuk leader.

1993, Sept. 16 Litho. *Perf. 13½*
177 Strip of 4 2.50 2.50
a.-d. A61 29c any single .65 .65

See Nos. 204-207.

Pioneers of Flight Type of 1993

Designs: a, Hugh L. Dryden. b, Theodore von Karman. c, Otto Lilienthal. d, Thomas O.M. Sopwith. e, Lawrence B. Sperry. f, Alberto Santos-Dumont. g, Orville Wright. h, Wilbur Wright.

1993, Sept. 25 Litho. *Perf. 13½*
178 A55 50c Block of 8, #a.-h. 6.75 6.75

Tourist Attractions, Pohnpei — A62

1993, Oct. 5
179 A62 29c Kepirohi Falls .75 .75
180 A62 50c Spanish Wall 1.50 1.50

Souvenir Sheet

181 A62 $1 Sokehs Rock 2.00 2.00

No. 181 contains one 80x50mm stamp.
See Nos. 187-189.

Butterflies — A63

No. 182: a, Great eggfly female (typical). b, Great eggfly female (local variant).
No. 183: a, Monarch. b, Great eggfly male.

1993, Oct. 20 Litho. *Perf. 13½*
182 Pair 1.40 1.40
a.-b. A63 29c Any single .70 .70
183 Pair 2.00 2.00
a.-b. A63 50c Any single 1.00 1.00

See No. 190.

Christmas — A64

29c, We Three Kings. 50c, Silent Night, Holy Night.

1993, Nov. 11
184 A64 29c multicolored .75 .75
185 A64 50c multicolored 1.25 1.25

Miniature Sheet

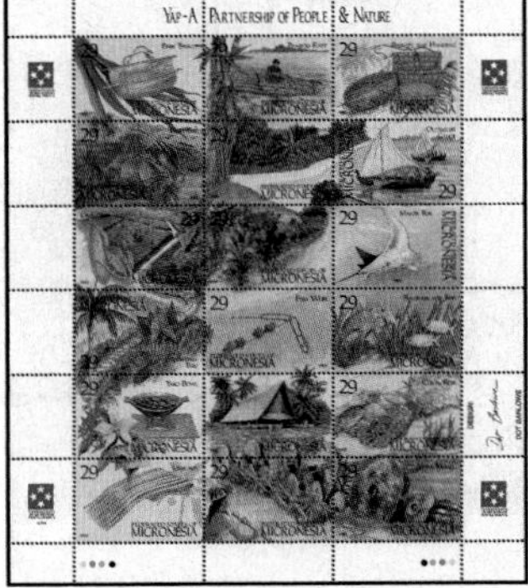

Yap Culture — A65

Designs: a, Baby basket. b, Bamboo raft. c, Baskets, handbag. d, Fruit bat. e, Forest. f, Outrigger canoe. g, Dioscorea yams. h, Mangroves. i, Manta ray. j, Cyrtosperma taro. k, Fish weir. l, Seagrass, fish. m, Taro bowl. n, Thatched house. o, Coral reef. p, Lavalava. q, Dance. r, Stone money.

1993, Dec. 15 Litho. *Perf. 13½x14*
186 A65 29c Sheet of 18, #a.-r. 12.50 12.50

Tourist Attractions Type of 1993

Sites on Kosrae: 29c, Sleeping Lady Mountain. 40c, Walung. 50c, Lelu Ruins.

1994, Feb. 11 Litho. *Perf. 13½*
187 A62 29c multicolored .55 .55
188 A62 40c multicolored .75 .75
189 A62 50c multicolored .95 .95
Nos. 187-189 (3) 2.25 2.25

Butterfly Type of 1993 with Added Inscription

Souvenir Sheet

a, 29c, like No. 182a. b, 29c, like No. 182b. c, 50c, like No. 183a. d, 50c, like No. 183b.

1994, Feb. 18
190 A63 Sheet of 4, #a.-d. 4.25 4.25

Inscription reads "Hong Kong '94 Stamp Exhibition" in Chinese on Nos. 190a, 190d, and in English on Nos. 190b-190c.
Inscriptions on Nos. 190a-190d are in black.

Pioneers of Flight Type of 1993

Designs: a, Edwin E. Aldrin, Jr. b, Neil A. Armstrong. c, Michael Collins. d, Wernher von Braun. e, Octave Chanute. f, T. Claude Ryan. g, Frank Whittle. h, Waldo D. Waterman.

1994, Mar. 4 Litho. *Perf. 13½*
191 A55 29c Block of 8, #a.-h. 5.75 5.75

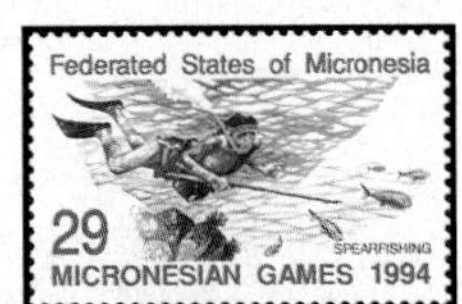

1994 Micronesian Games — A66

Designs: a, Spearfishing. b, Basketball. c, Coconut husking. d, Tree climbing.

1994, Mar. 26 *Perf. 13½x14*
192 Block of 4 2.75 2.75
a.-d. A66 29c any single .70 .70

Native Costumes — A67

a, Pohnpei. b, Kosrae. c, Chuuk. d, Yap.

1994, Mar. 31 *Perf. 13½*
193 Block of 4, #a.-d. 2.75 2.75
a.-d. A67 29c any single .70 .70

Constitution, 15th Anniv. — A68

1994, May 10 Litho. *Perf. 11x10½*
194 A68 29c multicolored 1.50 1.50

Flowers — A69

Designs: a, Fagraea berteriana. b, Pangium edule. c, Pittosporum ferrugineum. d, Sonneratia caseolaris.

1994, June 6 Litho. *Perf. 13½*
195 Strip of 4 2.75 2.75
a.-d. A69 29c any single .70 .70

1994 World Cup Soccer Championships, US — A70

Design: No. 197, Soccer players, diff.

1994, June 17 Litho. *Perf. 13½*
196 A70 50c red & multi 2.25 2.25
197 A70 50c blue & multi 2.25 2.25
a. Pair, #196-197 4.50 4.50

No. 197a has a continuous design.

Micronesian Postal Service, 10th Anniv. — A71

Stamps: a, #39, 45, 54 (c), 159, 189, 192 (b). b, #58 (d), 151, 161 (d), 176a, 183a (d). c, #4a, 137a, 184 (a), C12 (d), C39, C41. d, #161 (b), 183a (b), 183b, 193, C12, C40, C42.

1994, July 12 Litho. *Perf. 13½*
198 Block of 4 5.00 5.00
a.-d. A71 29c any single 1.25 1.25

No. 198 is a continuous design.

Souvenir Sheet

PHILAKOREA '94 — A72

Dinosaurs: a, 29c, Iguanodons (b). b, 52c, Coelurosaurs (c). c, $1, Camarasaurus.

1994, Aug. 16 Litho. *Perf. 13½*
199 A72 Sheet of 3, #a.-c. 5.25 5.25

Pioneers of Flight Type of 1993

a, William A. Bishop. b, Karel J. Bossart. c, Marcel Dassault. d, Geoffrey de Havilland. e, Yuri A. Gagarin. f, Alan B. Shepard, Jr. g, John H. Towers. h, Hermann J. Oberth.

1994, Sept. 20 Litho. *Perf. 13½*
200 A55 50c Block of 8, #a.-h. 6.75 6.75

Migratory Birds — A73

Designs: a, Oriental cuckoo. b, Long-tailed cuckoo. c, Short-eared owl. d, Dollarbird.

1994, Oct. 20 Litho. *Perf. 13½*
201 Block of 4 2.50 2.50
a.-d. A73 29c any single .65 .65

Christmas A74

1994, Nov. 2
202 A74 29c Doves .60 .60
203 A74 50c Angels 1.00 1.00

Local Leaders Type of 1993

Pioneers of island unification: No. 204, Johnny Moses (1900-91), Pohnpei. No. 205, Belarmino Hatheylul (1907-93), Yap. No. 206, Anton Ring Buas (1907-79), Chuuk. No. 207, Paliknoa Sigrah (King John) (1875-1957), Kosrae.

1994, Dec. 15 Litho. *Perf. 13½*
204 A61 32c multicolored .65 .65
205 A61 32c multicolored .65 .65
206 A61 32c multicolored .65 .65
207 A61 32c multicolored .65 .65
Nos. 204-207 (4) 2.60 2.60

Souvenir Sheet

New Year 1995 (Year of the Boar) — A75

1995, Jan. 2
208 A75 50c multicolored 1.00 1.00

Chuuk Lagoon A76

Underwater scenes: a, Photographer with light. b, Various species of fish, coral. c, Diver. d, Two gold fish.

1995, Feb. 6
209 Block of 4 2.50 2.50
a.-d. A76 32c any single .65 .65

Pioneers of Flight Type of 1993

Designs: a, Robert H. Goddard. b, Leroy R. Grumman. c, Hugo Junkers. d, James A. Lovell, Jr. e, Louis-Charles Breguet. f, Juan de la Cierva. g, Donald W. Douglas. h, Reginald J. Mitchell.

1995, Mar. 4 Litho. *Perf. 13½*
210 A55 32c Block of 8, #a.-h. 5.25 5.25

Dogs
A77

a, West Highland white terrier. b, Welsh springer spaniel. c, Irish setter. d, Old English sheepdog.

1995, Apr. 5 Litho. *Perf. 13½*
211 Block of 4 2.50 2.50
a.-d. A77 32c any single .65 .65

Fish Type of 1993

Designs: 23c, Yellow-fin tuna. 32c, Saddled butterflyfish. 46c, Achilles tang. 55c, Moorish idol. 60c, Skipjack tuna. 78c, Square-spot fairy basslet. 95c, Bluelined snapper. $3, Flame angelfish. $5, Cave grouper.

No. 227: a, like #157. b, like #161. c, like #164. d, like #165. e, like #159. f. like #162. g, like #163. h, like #163A. i, like #156. j, like #158. k, like #162A. l, like #167. m, like #217. n, like #160. o, like #164A. p, like #164B. q, like #166. r, like #214. s, like #218. t, like #222. u, like #225. v, like #213. w, like #219. x, like #223. y, like #226.

1996 Litho. *Perf. 13½*
213 A56 23c multicolored .45 .45
214 A56 32c multicolored .65 .65
217 A56 46c multicolored .95 .95
218 A56 55c multicolored 1.10 1.10
219 A56 60c multicolored 1.25 1.25
222 A56 78c multicolored 1.50 1.50
223 A56 95c multicolored 1.90 1.90
225 A56 $3 multicolored 6.00 6.00
226 A56 $5 multicolored 10.00 10.00
Nos. 213-226 (9) 23.80 23.80

Miniature Sheet

227 A56 32c Sheet of 25, #a.-y. 16.00 16.00

Issued: 32c, 55c, 78c, $3, 5/15/95. 23c, 60c, 95c, $5, 8/4/95; 46c, 4/10/96.

Hibiscus — A78

a, Tiliaceus. b, Huegelii. c, Trionum. d, Splendens.

1995, June 1 Litho. *Perf. 13½*
228 Strip of 4 2.50 2.50
a.-d. A78 32c any single .65 .65

No. 228 is a continuous design.

Souvenir Sheet

UN, 50th Anniv. — A79

1995, June 26 Litho. *Perf. 13½*
229 A79 $1 multicolored 2.00 2.00

Miniature Sheet

Singapore '95 — A80

Orchids: a, Paphiopedilum henrietta fujiwara. b, Thunia alba. c, Lycaste virginalis. d, Laeliocattleya prism palette.

1995, Sept. 1 Litho. *Perf. 13½*
230 Sheet of 4 2.60 2.60
a.-d. A80 32c any single .65 .65

End of World War II, 50th Anniv. — A81

US warships: a, USS Portland. b, USS Tillman. c, USS Soley. d, USS Hyman.

1995, Sept. 2
231 Block of 4 5.00 5.00
a.-d. A81 60c any single 1.25 1.25

Souvenir Sheet

Intl. Stamp & Coin Expo, Beijing '95 — A82

1995, Sept. 14
232 A82 50c Temple of Heaven 1.00 1.00

Pioneers of Flight Type of 1993

Designs: a, Hugh C.T. Dowding. b, William Mitchell. c, John K. Northrop. d, Frederick Handley Page. e, Frederick H. Rohr. f, Juan T. Trippe. g, Konstantin E. Tsiolkovsky. h. Ferdinand Graf von Zeppelin.

1995, Sept. 21 Litho. *Perf. 13½*
233 A55 60c Block of 8, #a.-h. 9.50 9.50

Christmas Poinsettias
A83

1995, Oct. 30 Litho. *Perf. 13½*
234 A83 32c gray & multi .65 .65
235 A83 60c bister & multi 1.25 1.25

Yitzhak Rabin (1922-95), Israeli Prime Minister — A84

1995, Nov. 30 Litho. *Perf. 13½*
236 A84 32c multicolored .65 .65

No. 236 was issued in sheets of 8.

Souvenir Sheet

New Year 1996 (Year of the Rat) — A85

1996, Jan. 5 Litho. *Perf. 13½*
237 A85 50c multicolored 1.00 1.00

Pioneers of Flight Type of 1993

Designs: a, James H. Doolittle. b, Claude Dornier. c, Ira C. Eaker. d, Jacob C.H. Ellehammer. e, Henry H. Arnold. f, Louis Blériot. g, William E. Boeing. h, Sydney Camm.

1996, Feb. 21 Litho. *Perf. 13½*
238 A55 32c Block of 8, #a.-h. 5.25 5.25

Tourism in Yap — A86

a, Meeting house. b, Stone money. c, Churu dancing. d, Traditional canoe.

1996, Mar. 13 Litho. *Perf. 13½*
239 Block of 4 2.50 2.50
a.-d. A86 32c any single .65 .65

Sea Stars
A87

Designs: a, Rhinoceros. b, Necklace c, Thick-skinned. d, Blue.

1996, Apr. 26 Litho. *Perf. 12*
240 Block of 4 4.50 4.50
a.-d. A87 55c any single 1.15 1.15

Olympic Games, Cent. — A88

First Olympic stamps, Greece: a, #120. b, #122. c, #121. d, #128.

1996, Apr. 27
241 Block of 4 4.75 4.75
a.-d. A88 60c any single 1.20 1.20

Souvenir Sheet

China '96, 9th Asian Intl. Philatelic Exhibition — A89

Design: The Tarrying Garden, Suzhou.

1996, May 15 *Perf. 13x13½*
242 A89 50c multicolored 1.00 1.00

Patrol Boats — A90

1996, May 3 Litho. *Perf. 13½*
243 A90 32c FSS Palikir .65 .65
244 A90 32c FSS Micronesia .65 .65
a. Pair, #243-244 1.30 1.30

No. 244a is a continuous design.

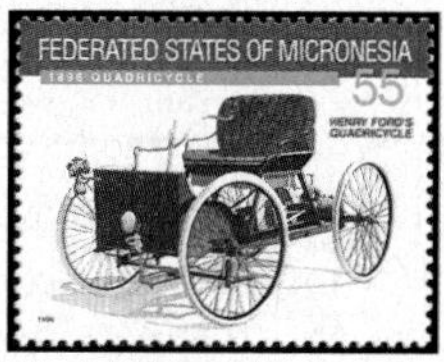
First Ford Automobile, Cent. — A91

a, 1896 Quadricycle. b, 1917 Model T truck. c, 1928 Model A Tudor Sedan. d, 1932 V-8 Sport Roadster. e, 1941 Lincoln Continental. f, 1953 F-100 Truck. g, 1958 Thunderbird convertible. h, 1996 Mercury Sable.

1996, June 4 *Perf. 13½*
245 Sheet of 8 8.75 8.75
a.-h. A91 55c any single 1.10 1.10

Officer Reza, Member of Natl. Police Drug Enforcement Unit — A93

1996, July 31 Litho. *Perf. 13½*
247 A93 32c multicolored .65 .65

Citrus Fruit — A94

a, Orange. b, Lime. c, Lemon. d, Tangerine.

1996, Aug. 24 Litho. *Perf. 13½*
248 Strip of 4 4.00 4.00
a.-d. A94 50c any single 1.00 1.00

Pioneers of Flight Type of 1993

Designs: a, Gianni Caproni. b, Henri Farman. c, Curtis E. LeMay. d, Grover Loening. e, Sergey P. Korolyov. f, Isaac M. Laddon. g, Glenn L. Martin. h, Alliott Verdon Roe.

1996, Sept. 18
249 A55 60c Block of 8, #a.-h. 12.50 12.50

Fish Type of 1993

Designs: a, like #157. b, like #165. c, like #162A. d, like #218.

1996, Oct. 21 Litho. *Perf. 13½*
250 A56 32c Block of 4, #a.-d. 2.50 2.50

Taipei '96, 10th Asian Intl. Philatelic Exhibition. Nos. 250a, 250d have English inscriptions. Nos. 250b-250c have Chinese inscriptions.

Magi Following Star to Bethlehem A95

1996, Oct. 30 Litho. *Perf. 13½*
251 A95 32c dark blue & multi .65 .65
252 A95 60c blue & multi 1.25 1.25

Christmas.

Canoe, Flag of Federated States of Micronesia Type of 1990

1996, Nov. 3 *Perf. 11x10½*
253 A42 $3 like #124 6.00 6.00

No. 253 inscribed "Free Association United States of America."

Deng Xiaoping (1904-97) — A96

Portraits: a, Wearing white-collared shirt. b, Looking left. c, Looking right. d, Wearing hat. $3, Looking left, diff.

1997 Litho. *Perf. 14*
254 Sheet of 4 4.75 4.75
a.-d. A96 60c any single 1.20 1.20

Souvenir Sheet

255 A96 $3 multicolored 6.00 6.00

Souvenir Sheet

Hong Kong — A97

1997
256 A97 $2 multicolored 4.00 4.00

New Year 1997 (Year of the Ox) — A98

1997 Litho. *Perf. 14*
257 A98 32c multicolored .65 .65

Souvenir Sheet

258 A98 $2 like #257 4.00 4.00

Return of Hong Kong to China A99

Flowers, Victoria Harbor: a, Melia azedarach. b, Sail from ship, Victoria Peak. c, Sail from ship, dendrobium chrysotoxum. d, Bauhinia blakeana. e, Cassia surattensis, Chinese junk. f, Junk, nelumbo nucifera.
$3, Strongylodon macrobatrys, pagoda.

1997, July 1
259 Sheet of 6 7.25 7.25
a.-f. A99 60c any single 1.20 1.20

Souvenir Sheet

260 A99 $3 multicolored 6.00 6.00

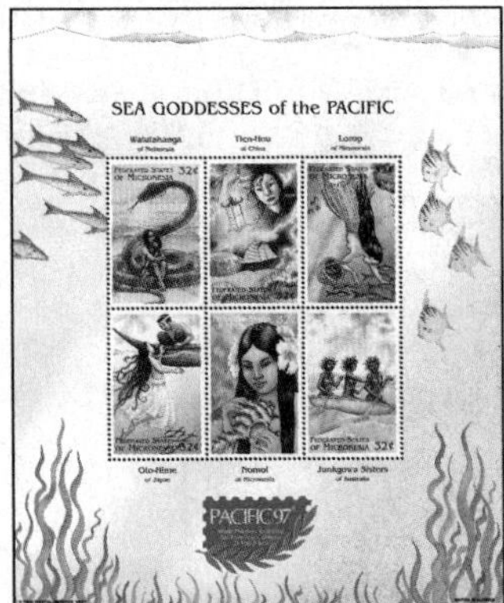

Sea Goddesses of the Pacific — A100

a, Giant serpent, woman holding child, Walutahanga of Melanesia. b, Sailing ship in storm, woman holding lantern, Tien-Hou of China. c, Woman swimming to bottom of sea gathering fish into basket, Lorop of Micronesia. d, Woman swimming to man in canoe, Oto-Hime of Japan. e, Woman holding seashell, Nomoi of Micronesia. f, Three women in canoe, Junkgowa sisters of Australia.

1997, May 29 Litho. *Perf. 14*
261 A100 32c Sheet of 6, #a.-f. 3.75 3.75

PACIFIC 97.

Paintings by Hiroshige (1797-1858) A101

Whirlpools at Naruto in Awa Province, 1857: No. 262: a, Sailboats in distance. b, Island of trees at left. c, Island of trees at right.
Tale of Genji: Viewing the Plum Blossoms, 1852: No. 263: a, Small evergreen trees in front of woman. b, Woman. c, Trees, house in distance with woman.
Snow on the Sumida River, 1847: No. 264: a, House, river. b, Two women under umbrella. c, Woman with folded umbrella.
Each $2: No. 265, Rapids in Bitchu Province, 1854. No. 266, Fuji from Satta Point, 1858.

1997, July 25 *Perf. 13½x14*
262 Sheet of 3 1.25 1.25
a.-c. A101 20c any single .40 .40
263 Sheet of 3 3.00 3.00
a.-c. A101 50c any single 1.00 1.00
264 Sheet of 3 3.50 3.50
a.-c. A101 60c any single 1.20 1.20

Souvenir Sheets

265-266 A101 Set of 2 8.00 8.00

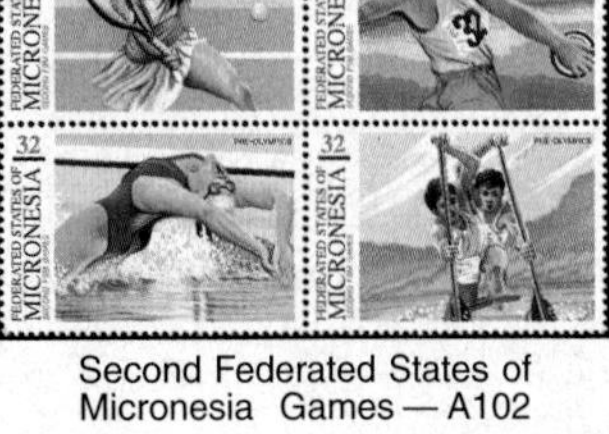

Second Federated States of Micronesia Games — A102

a, Tennis. b, Discus. c, Swimming. d, Canoeing.

1997, Aug. 15 Litho. *Perf. 14*
267 A102 32c Block of 4, #a.-d. 2.50 2.50

No. 267 was issued in sheets of 16 stamps.

Elvis Presley (1935-77) A103

Various portraits.

1997, Aug. 16
268 Sheet of 6 6.00 6.00
a.-f. A103 50c any single 1.00 1.00

Ocean Exploration A104

No. 269: a, Simon Lake, Argonaut, 1897. b, William Beebe, Bathysphere, 1934. c, Auguste Piccard, Bathyscaphe, 1954. d, Harold Edgerton, deep-sea camera, 1954. e, Jacques Piccard, Trieste, 1960. f, Edwin Link, Man-in-Sea Project, 1962. g, Melvin Fisher, search for treasure, 1971. h, Robert Ballard, Alvin, 1978. i, Sylvia Earle, Deep Rover, 1979.
Each $2: No. 270, C. Wyville Thomson, deep-sea dredge, vert. No. 271, Shinkai 6500 exploring bottom of sea, vert. No. 272, Jacques-Yves Cousteau, vert.

1997, Oct. 6 Litho. *Perf. 14*
269 Sheet of 9 4.25 4.25
a.-i. A104 32c any single .45 .45

Souvenir Sheets

270-272 A104 Set of 3 30.00 30.00

Diana, Princess of Wales (1961-97) A105

1997, Nov. 26 Litho. *Perf. 14*
273 A105 60c multicolored 1.25 1.25

No. 273 was issued in sheets of 6.

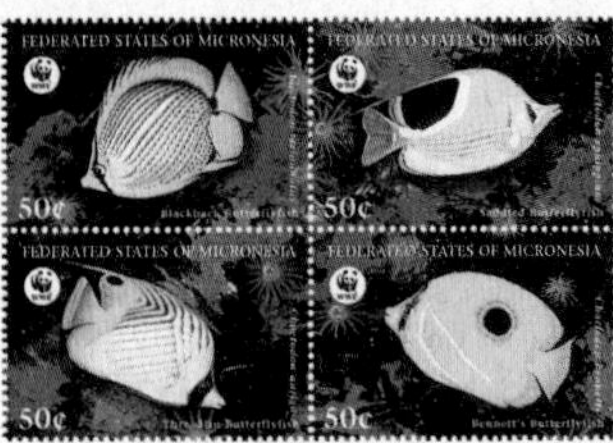

World Wildlife Fund — A106

Butterfly fish: a, Blackback. b, Saddled. c, Threadfin. d, Bennett's.

1997, Nov. 24 Litho. *Perf. 14*
274 A106 50c Block of 4, #a.-d. 8.00 8.00

No. 274 was issued in sheets of 16 stamps.

Christmas Paintings A107

Christ Glorified in the Court of Heaven, by Fra Angelico: No. 275, Angels playing musical instruments. No. 276, Choir of Angels.
A Choir of Angels, by Simon Marmion: No. 277, Two angels blowing long horns. No. 278, One angel blowing horn.

1997, Nov. 25
275 A107 32c multicolored .65 .65
276 A107 32c multicolored .65 .65
a. Horiz. pair, Nos. 275-276 1.30 1.30
277 A107 60c multicolored 1.25 1.25
278 A107 60c multicolored 1.25 1.25
a. Vert. pair, Nos. 277-278 2.50 2.50

Nos. 276a, 278a were each issued in sheets of 8 pairs.

Souvenir Sheets

New Year 1998 (Year of the Tiger) — A108

1998, Jan. 2 Litho. *Perf. 14*
279 A108 50c shown 1.00 1.00
280 A108 50c Chinese toy (face) 1.00 1.00

Souvenir Sheet

Micronesia's Admission to United Nations, 7th Anniv. — A109

1998, Feb. 13 *Perf. 13½*
281 A109 $1 multicolored 2.00 2.00

Winnie the Pooh — A110

No. 282: a, Rabbit. b, Owl. c, Eeyore. d, Kanga and Roo. e, Piglet. f, Tigger. g, Pooh. h, Christopher Robin.

Each $2: No. 283, Piglet, Pooh, and Tigger. No. 284, Rabbit and Pooh.

1998, Feb. 16 *Perf. 14x14½*

282 Sheet of 8 5.25 5.25
a.-h. A110 32c any single .65 .65

Souvenir Sheets

283-284 A110 Set of 2 8.00 8.00

1998 World Cup Soccer Championships, France — A111

Various soccer plays, color of foreground player's shirt & shorts — No. 285: a, White & black. b, Green & white. c, Yellow & blue, socks with colored stripes. d, Green & black. e, Yellow & black. f, Red & blue. g, Yellow & blue, plain socks. h, Red & white.

Each $2: No. 286, Red & blue. No. 287, Green, black & white.

1998, Mar. 20 Litho. *Perf. 13½*

285 Sheet of 8 5.00 5.00
a.-h. A111 32c any single .65 .65

Souvenir Sheets

286-287 A111 Set of 2 8.00 8.00

Souvenir Sheet

Micronesia's Recognition by Intl. Olympic Committee — A112

1998, Mar. 20

288 A112 $3 multicolored 6.00 6.00

Old Testament Bible Stories — A113

Adam and Eve — No. 289: a, Land of plenty. b, Adam, Eve before the fall. c, Serpent of temptation.

Joseph and his brethren — No. 290: a, Brothers plan to sell Joseph. b, Joseph in his many-colored coat. c, Ishmaelites take Joseph.

Rebekah — No. 291: a, Rebekah at the well. b, Abraham's servant Eliezer. c, Angel sent to prosper Eliezer's way.

Each $2: No. 292, Adam and Eve sent forth from Eden. No. 293, Joseph forgives his brothers. No. 294, Isaac takes Rebekah to wife.

1998, May 13 Litho. *Perf. 13½x14*

289 Sheet of 3 1.90 1.90
a.-c. A113 32c any single .65 .65
290 Sheet of 3 2.50 2.50
a.-c. A113 40c any single .85 .85
291 Sheet of 3 3.50 3.50
a.-c. A113 60c any single 1.20 1.20

Souvenir Sheets

292-294 A113 Set of 3 12.00 12.00

Israel '98.

Intl. Year of the Ocean A114

Deep sea research — No. 295: a, Marine observation satellite. b, Support vessel, Natsushima. c, Research vessel, Kaiyo. d, Deep sea anemone. e, Shinkai 2000. f, Deep tow. g, Tripod fish. h, Towed deep survey system. i, Black smokers.

Each $2: No. 296, Communications satellite. No. 297, Ocean observation buoy, vert. No. 298, Weather satellite.

1998, June 2 Litho. *Perf. 13*

295 Sheet of 9 5.75 5.75
a.-i. A114 32c any single .65 .65

Souvenir Sheets

296-298 A114 Set of 3 12.00 12.00

Native Birds — A115

No. 299: a, Kosrae white-eye. b, Chuuk monarch. c, Yap monarch. d, Pohnpei lory.

$3, Pohnpei mountain starling.

1998, June 30 *Perf. 14x14½*

299 A115 50c Block or strip of 4, #a.-d. 4.00 4.00

Souvenir Sheet

300 A115 $3 multicolored 6.00 6.00

No. 299 was issued in sheets of 16 stamps.

Fish — A116

Designs: 1c, White-tipped soldierfish. 2c, Red-breasted wrasse. 3c, Bicolor angelfish. 4c, Falco hawkfish. 5c, Convict tang. 10c, Square-spot fairy basslet. 13c, Orangeband surgeonfish. 15c, Multibarred goatfish. 17c, Masked rabbitfish. 20c, White-spotted surgeonfish. 22c, Blue-girdled angelfish. 32c, Wedge picassofish. 39c, Red parrotfish. 40c, Lemonpeel angelfish. 60c, Humphead wrasse. 78c, Sapphire damselfish. $1, Bluefin travally. $3, Whitespot hawkfish. $5, Spotted trunkfish. $10.75, Pinktail triggerfish.

1998 Litho. *Perf. 14½*

301	A116	1c multi	.25	.25
302	A116	2c multi	.25	.25
303	A116	3c multi	.25	.25
304	A116	4c multi	.25	.25
305	A116	5c multi	.25	.25
306	A116	10c multi	.25	.25
307	A116	13c multi	.25	.25
308	A116	15c multi	.30	.30
309	A116	17c multi	.35	.35
310	A116	20c multi	.40	.40
311	A116	22c multi	.45	.45
312	A116	32c multi	.65	.65
313	A116	39c multi	.75	.75
314	A116	40c multi	.80	.80
315	A116	60c multi	1.25	1.25
316	A116	78c multi	1.50	1.50
317	A116	$1 multi	1.90	1.90
318	A116	$3 multi	5.75	5.75
319	A116	$5 multi	10.00	10.00
319A	A116	$10.75 multi	21.00	21.00
	Nos. 301-319A (20)		46.85	46.85

Issued: $10.75, 9/8; others, 7/20.

See Nos. 328-333.

Fala, Franklin D. Roosevelt's Scottish Terrier — A117

Designs: a, Roosevelt's hand petting dog. b, Radio at right. c, Radio at left. d, In car with FDR. e, Presidential seal. f, Closeup of Fala looking left.

1998, Aug. 27 Litho. *Perf. 13½*

320 Sheet of 6 3.75 3.75
a.-f. A117 32c any single .65 .65

Christmas A118

Twentieth cent. art — No. 321: a, Eskimo Madonna, by Claire Fejes. b, Madonna, by Man Ray. c, Peasant Mother, by David Siquerios.

No. 322: a, Mother and Child, by Pablo Picasso. b, Gypsy Woman with Baby, by Amedeo Modigliani. c, Mother and Child, by José Orozco.

$2, Detail from The Family, by Marisol, horiz.

1998, Sept. 15 Litho. *Perf. 13½x14*

321 Sheet of 3 1.90 1.90
a.-c. A118 32c any single .65 .65
322 Sheet of 3 3.75 3.75
a.-c. A118 60c any single 1.25 1.25

Souvenir Sheet

Perf. 14x13½

323 A118 $2 multicolored 4.00 4.00

John Glenn's Return to Space — A119

Each 60c: No. 324: Various photos of Friendship 7 mission, 1962.

Each 60c: No. 325: Various photos of Discovery space shuttle mission, 1998.

Each $2: No. 326, Launch of Friendship 7. No. 327, Portrait of Glenn, 1998.

1998, Oct. 29 Litho. *Perf. 14*

Sheets of 8

324-325 Set of 2 19.00 19.00
a.-h. A119 60c any single 1.20 1.20

Souvenir Sheets

326-327 A119 Set of 2 8.00 8.00

Fish Type of 1993

Designs: 33c, Black jack. 50c, Whitecheek surgeonfish. 55c, Long-jawed squirrelfish. 77c, Onespot snapper. $3.20, Tan-faced parrotfish. $11.75, Yellow-faced angelfish.

1999 Litho. *Perf. 14½*

328	A116	33c multicolored	.65	.65
329	A116	50c multicolored	1.00	1.00
330	A116	55c multicolored	1.10	1.10
331	A116	77c multicolored	1.50	1.50
332	A116	$3.20 multicolored	6.50	6.50

Perf. 14

Size: 45x21mm

333	A116	$11.75 multicolored	22.50	22.50
	Nos. 328-333 (6)		33.25	33.25

Issued: $11.75, 3/31; others, 2/22.

Russian Space Exploration A120

No. 334: a, Sputnik 1, 1957. b, Leika in Sputnik 2, 1957. c, Luna 1, 1959. d, Luna 3, 1959. e, Yuri Gagarin in Vostok 1, 1961. f, Venera 1, 1961. g, Mars 1, 1962. h, Valentina Tereshkova in Vostok 6, 1963. i, Voskhod 1, 1964. j, Aleksei Leonov in Voskhod 2, 1965. k, Venera 3, 1966. l, Luna 10. m, Luna 9. n, Luna 16, 1970. o, Luna 17, 1970. p, Mars 3, 1971. q, Leonid Popov, Valeri Ryumin, Soyuz 35, 1980. r, Vega 1, 1985. s, Vega 1, Halley's Comet, 1986. t, Mir, 1986-98.

Each $2: No. 335, Russian Space Station, Mir, 1998. No. 336, Docking of USSR Soyuz 19 and Apollo 18, horiz.

1999, Mar. 15 *Perf. 14*

334 Sheet of 20 13.50 13.50
a.-t. A120 33c any single .70 .70

Souvenir Sheets

335-336 A120 Set of 2 8.00 8.00

See Nos. 344-346.

"Romance of the Three Kingdoms," by Lo Kuan-Chung A121

No. 337: a, Men, women conferring. b, Four men, one grabbing on clothes of another. c, Two men jousting. d, Four men looking down at one man. e, Man kneeling before another man in wheelchair.

No. 338: a, Mounted warriors approaching drawbridge. b, Warriors fighting in front of fire, banners. c, Warrior fighting off others, smoke. d, Man, woman kneeling before old man. e, Two men looking up at smoke coming from boiling pot.

No. 339, Three men in boat, raging fire.

1999, Mar. 19 Litho. *Perf. 13½*

Sheets of 5

337 A121 33c #a.-e. 3.25 3.25
338 A121 50c #a.-e. 5.00 5.00

Souvenir Sheet

339 A121 $2 multicolored 4.00 4.00

No. 339 contains one 52x79mm stamp.

IBRA '99, World Stamp Exhibition, Nuremberg, Germany — A122

Designs: No. 340, The Leipzig-Dresden Railway, Caroline Islands #4. No. 341, Göl-sdorf 4-4-0, Caroline Islands #16.
$2, Exhibition emblem, Caroline Islands #6, vert.

1999, Apr. 27 *Perf. 14x14½*
340 A122 55c multicolored 1.10 1.10
341 A122 55c multicolored 1.10 1.10

Souvenir Sheet

342 A122 $2 multicolored 4.00 4.00

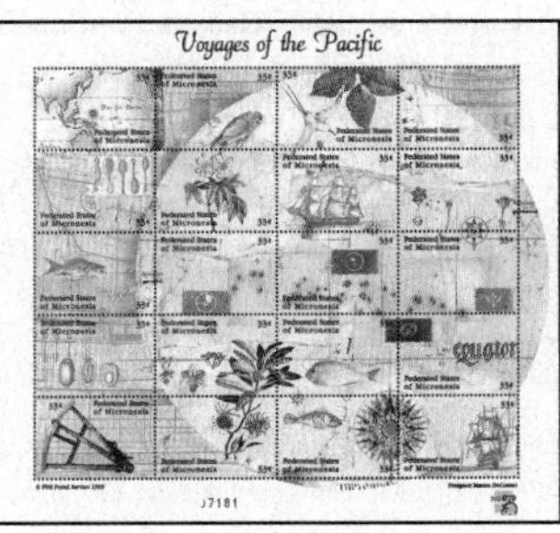

Voyages of the Pacific — A123

Designs: a, Map of Pacific Ocean. b, Parrot. c, Bird in flight, leaves. d, Map, ship's stern. e, Part of ship, various blocks. f, Flower. g, Sailing ship, side view. h, Three flowers, compass rose. i, Fish over ship's drawing. j, Map, flag LL. k, Map, flag UR. l, Map, flag LR. m, Three sections of coconut. n, Three flowers, plant. o, Fish. p, Flag, UL, "Equator." q, Sextant. r, Bottom of plant. s, Fish, compass rose. t, Sailing ship, bow on.

1999, Mar. 19 **Litho.** *Perf. 13½*
343 A123 33c Sheet of 20, #a.-t. 13.50 13.50

Space Achievements Type of 1999

US space achievements — No. 344: a, Explorer 1, 1958. b, OSO 1, 1962. c, Mariner 2 to Venus, 1962. d, Mariner 2, 1962. e, Apollo 8, 1968. f, First step onto moon, Apollo 11, 1969. g, First samples from moon, Apollo 11, 1969. h, Apollo 15, 1971. i, Mariner 9, 1971. j, Pioneer 10, 1973. k, Mariner 10, 1974. l, Viking 1, 1976. m, Pioneer 11, 1979. n, STS 1, 1981. o, Pioneer 10, 1983. p, Solar Maximum Mission, 1984. q, Cometary Explorer, 1985. r, Voyager 2, 1989. s, Gallileo to Gaspra, 1992. t, Sojourner, 1997.
Each $2: No. 345, International space station. No. 346, Shuttle mission to repair Hubble Telescope, 1993.

1999, Mar. 15 **Litho.** *Perf. 14*
344 A120 33c Sheet of 20, #a.-t. 13.50 13.50

Souvenir Sheets

345-346 A120 Set of 2 8.00 8.00

Illustrations on Nos. 344p and 344q are incorrect.

Earth Day — A124

Endangered, extinct, and prehistoric species — No. 347: a, Black rhinoceros. b, Cheetah. c, Jackass penguin. d, Blue whale. e, Red-headed woodpecker. f, African elephant. g, Aurochs. h, Dodo bird. i, Tasmanian wolf. j, Giant lemur. k, Quagga. l, Steller's sea cow. m, Pteranodon. n, Shonisaurus. o, Stegosaurus. p, Galliminus. q, Tyrannosaurus. r, Archelon. s, Brachiosaurus. t, Triceratops.
Each $2: No. 348, Moa. No. 349, Suchominus tenerensis, horiz.

1999
347 Sheet of 20 13.50 13.50
a.-t. A124 33c any single .70 .70

Souvenir Sheets

348-349 A124 Set of 2 8.00 8.00

Nos. 348-349 contain one 50x38mm and one 38x50mm stamp, respectively.

Paintings by Hokusai (1760-1849) A125

Details or entire paintings — No. 350, each 33c: a, Ghost of O-Iwa. b, Horse Drawings (head down). c, Abe Nakamaro. d, Ghost of Kasane. e, Horse Drawings (head up). f, The Ghost of Kiku and the Priest Mitazuki.
No. 351, each 33c: a, Belly Band Float. b, Drawing of Women (facing left). c, Swimmers. d, Eel Climb. e, Drawings of Women (facing right). f, Kimo Ga Imo Ni Naru.
Each $2: No. 352, Whaling off Goto. No. 353, Fishing by Torchlight.

1999, July 20 **Litho.** *Perf. 13¾x14*

Sheets of 6

350-351 Set of 2 8.00 8.00
a.-f. A125 33c any single .65 .65

Souvenir Sheets

352-353 A125 Set of 2 8.00 8.00

Flowers — A126

Various flowers making up a photomosaic of Princess Diana.

1999 **Litho.** *Perf. 13¼*
354 A126 50c Sheet of 8, #a.-h. 8.00 8.00

See No. 393, 403.

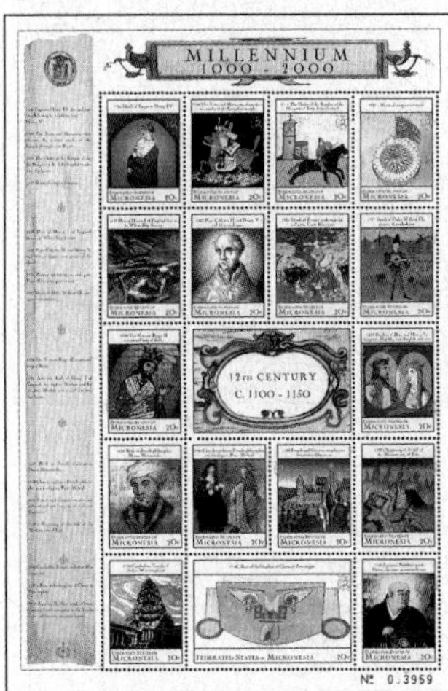

Millennium — A127

No. 355 — Highlights of the 12th Century: a, Death of Emperor Henry IV. b, Taira and Minamoto clans. c, Order of the Knights of the Hospital of St. John founded. d, Nautical compass invented. e, "White Ship" disaster. f, Pope Calixtus and Henry V end dispute. g, Death of Omar Khyyam. h, Death of Duke William IX. i, Roger II crowned King of Sicily. j, Stephen of Blois, Matilda. k, Birth of Maimonides. l, Church condemns Peter Abelard. m, Crusaders defeated at Damascus. n, Fall of city of Tula. o, Completion of Angkor Wat. p, Chimu culture flourishes (60x40mm). q, Honen becomes hermit.
No. 356 — Science and Technology of Ancient China: a, Well drilling. b, Chain pump. c, Magic lantern. d, Seismograph. e, Dial and pointer devices. f, Refined value of pi. g, Porcelain. h, Water mill. i, Stirrup. j, Tea. k, Umbrella. l, Brandy and whiskey. m, Printing. n, Paper money. o, Gunpowder. p, Arch bridge (60x40mm). q, Mercator map projection.

1999, Oct. 4 *Perf. 12¾x12½*

Sheets of 17

355 A127 20c #a.-q. + label 7.00 7.00
356 A127 33c #a.-q. + label 11.50 11.50

Inscriptions on Nos. 355g, 355o, and perhaps others, are incorrect or misspelled.
See No. 377.

Costumes — A128

Designs: a, French princess gown (head at R). b, As "a," (head at B). c, As "a," (bust). d, As "a," (umbrella). e, Scissors. f, Tools for fabric making. g, Micronesian wedding costume (head at R). h, As "g," (midriff). i, As "g," (feet). j, Japanese fabrics. k, Masai warrior costume (head at L). l, As "k," (head at R). m, African fabric details. n, Kabuki theater costume (head). o, As "n," (midriff). p, French Renaissance costume (head at B). q, Textile patterns. r, As "p," (head at R). s, Rulers. t, Iron.

1999, Nov. 22 *Perf. 14¾*
357 A128 33c Sheet of 20, #a.-t. 13.50 13.50

Vertical strips of 2, 3 or 5 have continuous designs.

Christmas A129

Paintings by Anthony Van Dyck: 33c, Holy Family with St. John. 60c, Madonna with Child. No. 360, The Virgin and Child with Two Donors (detail).
No. 361, The Adoration of the Shepherds.

1999, Dec. 1 **Litho.** *Perf. 13¾*
358 A129 33c multi .65 .65
359 A129 60c multi 1.25 1.25
360 A129 $2 multi 4.00 4.00
Nos. 358-360 (3) 5.90 5.90

Souvenir Sheet

361 A129 $2 multi 4.00 4.00

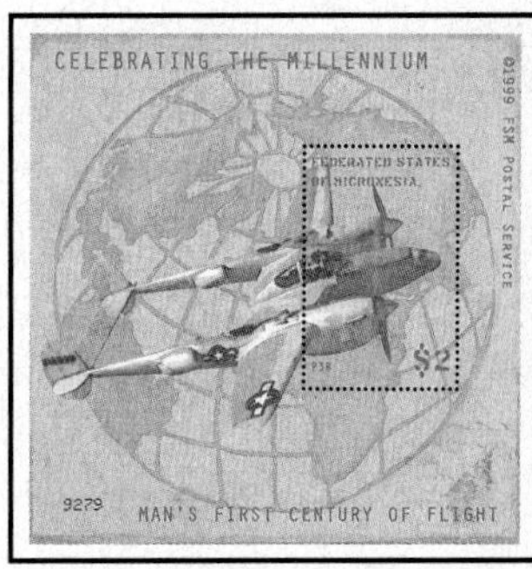

Millennium — A130

Airplanes — No. 362: a, Wright Flyer I. b, Blériot XI. c, Fokker D VII. d, Dornier Komet I. e, Ryan NYP. f, Mitsubishi A6M. g, Boeing B-29. h, Messerschmitt 262A. i, Bell X-1. j, MiG-19. k, Lockheed U-2. l, Boeing 707. m, Concorde. n, McDonnell Douglas DC-10. o, B-2.
No. 363, P38. No. 364, Dornier Do X.

1999, Dec. 9 *Perf. 14*
362 A130 33c Sheet of 15, #a.-o. 10.00 10.00

Souvenir Sheets

Perf. 13¾

363 A130 $2 multi 4.00 4.00
364 A130 $2 multi 4.00 4.00

No. 363 contains one 32x48mm stamp. No. 364 contains one 48x32mm stamp.

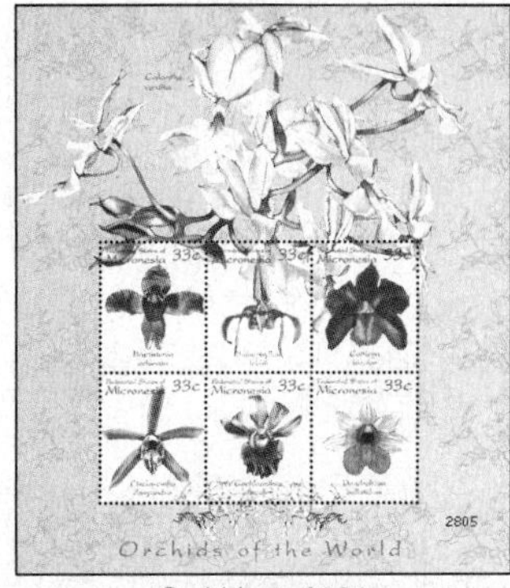

Orchids — A131

No. 365: a, Baptistonia echinata. b, Bulbophyllum lobbii. c, Cattleya bicolor. d, Cischweinfia dasyandra. e, Cochleanthes discolor. f, Dendrobium bellatulum.
No. 366: a, Esmeralda clarkei. b, Gomesa crispa. c, Masdevallia elephanticeps. d, Maxillaria variabilis. e, Mitoniopsis roezlii. f, Oncidium cavendishianum.
No. 367: a, Oncidium obryzatum. b, Oncidium phalaenopsis. c, Oncidium pulvinatum. d, Paphiopedilum armeniacum. e, Paphiopedilum dayanum. f, Paphiopedilum druryi.
No. 368, Paphiopedilum hirutissimum. No. 369, Licoglossum oerstedii.

2000, Jan. 5 *Perf. 14¼x14*

Sheets of 6

365 A131 33c #a.-f. 4.00 4.00
366 A131 33c #a.-f. 4.00 4.00
367 A131 33c #a.-f. 4.00 4.00

Souvenir Sheets

Perf. 14x14¼

368 A131 $1 multi 2.00 2.00
369 A131 $1 multi 2.00 2.00

Nos. 368-369 each contain one 31x53mm stamp.

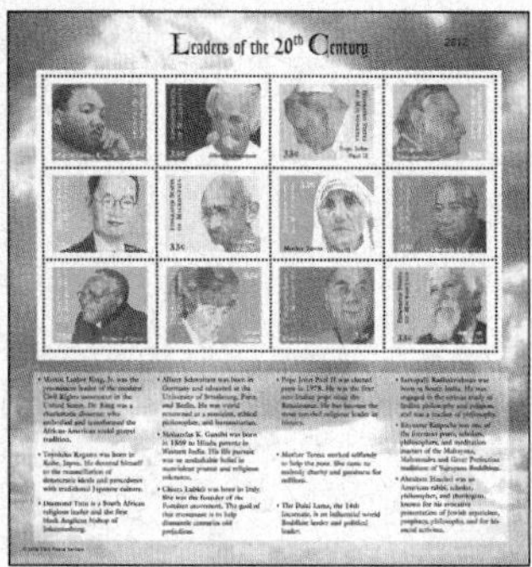
Leaders of the 20th Century — A132

Designs: a, Martin Luther King, Jr. b, Albert Schweitzer. c, Pope John Paul II. d, Sarvepalli Radhakrishnan. e, Toyohiko Kagawa. f, Mahatma Gandhi. g, Mother Teresa. h, Khyentse Rinpoche. i, Desmond Tutu. j, Chiara Lubich. k, 14th Dalai Lama. l, Abraham Heschel.

2000, Jan. 18 Litho. *Perf. 14¼*
370 A132 33c Sheet of 12, #a.-l. 8.00 8.00

Souvenir Sheet

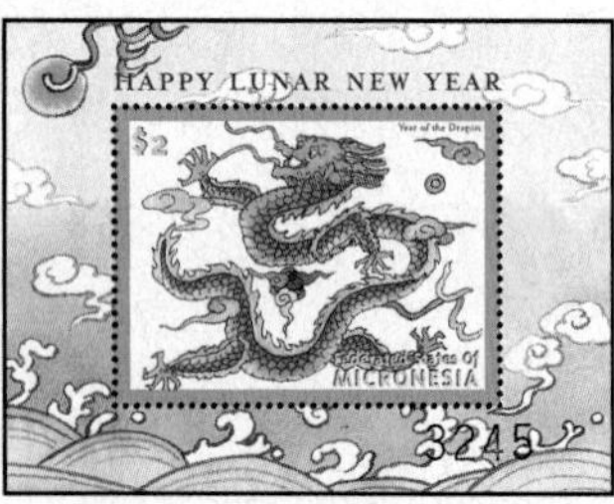
New Year 2000 (Year of the Dragon) — A133

2000, Feb. 5 *Perf. 13¾*
371 A133 $2 multi 4.00 4.00

Butterflies — A134

No. 372: a, Salamis parhassus. b, Morpho rhetenor. c, Danaus plexippus. d, Phyciodes actinote. e, Idea leucone. f, Actinote negra.

No. 373: a, Graphium sarpedon. b, Papilio machaon. c, Ornithoptera priamus. d, Ornithoptera chimaerea. e, Graphium antiphates. f, Pachliopta aristochiae.

Each $2: No. 374, Hamadryas amphinome, vert. No. 375, Colias croceus, vert. No. 376, Butterfly collector, vert.

2000, Feb. 28 Litho. *Perf. 14*
Sheets of 6
372 A134 20c #a.-f. 2.40 2.40
373 A134 55c #a.-f. 6.75 6.75

Souvenir Sheets
374-376 A134 Set of 3 12.00 12.00

Millennium Type of 1999

Highlights of the 1920s: a, Mahatma Gandhi leads non-violent reform in India. b, International Dada Fair in Berlin. c, American women win right to vote. d, Sacco and Vanzetti case. e, Hermann Rorshach develops inkblot test. f, Thomas J. Watson incorporates IBM. g, First successful commercial 35mm camera. h, Scopes "Monkey Trial." i, Charles Lindbergh makes first solo transatlantic flight. j, George Lemaitre develops "Big Bang" theory of cosmology. k, Chiang Kai-shek becomes generalissimo of China. l, Werner Heisenberg states "uncertainty principle" of physics. m, Alexander Fleming isolates Penicillium mold. n, Hirohito enthroned as Japanese emperor. o, Stock market crash starts Great Depression. p, First round-the-world flight (60x40mm). q, "All Quiet on the Western Front" published.

2000, Mar. 13 *Perf. 12¾x12½*
Sheet of 17
377 A127 20c #a.-q. + label 7.00 7.00

Inscriptions are incorrect or misspelled on Nos. 377a, 377f and 377m.

Millennium Type of 1999 with "Millennium 2000" Inscription
Perf. 13¼x13½

2000, Mar. 13 Litho.
378 A127 33c Like #356o .65 .65

Peacemakers — A135

a, Mikhail Gorbachev. b, Ending the Cold War. c, Ronald Reagan. d, Le Duc Tho. e, Resolving the conflict in Viet Nam. f, Henry Kissinger. g, Linus Pauling. h, Protest against nuclear weapons. i, Peter Benenson. j, Amnesty Intl. k, Mahatma Gandhi. l, Fasting for peace. m, Initiating the Peace Corps. n, John F. Kennedy. o, Praying for peace. p, The 14th Dalai Lama. q, The UN. r, Cordell Hull. s, F. W. De Klerk. t, Ending apartheid. u, Nelson Mandela. v, Franklin Roosevelt. w, Yalta Conference. x, Winston Churchill.

Illustration reduced.

2000, Mar. 28 *Perf. 14*
379 A135 33c Sheet of 24, #a-x 16.00 16.00

Philanthropists — A136

a, Andrew Carnegie. b, John D. Rockefeller. c, Henry Ford. d, Madam C. J. Walker. e, James B. Duke. f, Andrew Mellon. g, Charles F. Kettering. h, Robert W. Woodruff. i, Brooke Astor. j, Howard Hughes. k, Jesse H. Jones. l, Paul Mellon. m, J. Paul Getty. n, George Soros. o, Phyllis Wattis. p, Ted Turner.

2000, May 1 *Perf. 14¼x14½*
380 A136 33c Sheet of 16, #a-p 11.00 11.00

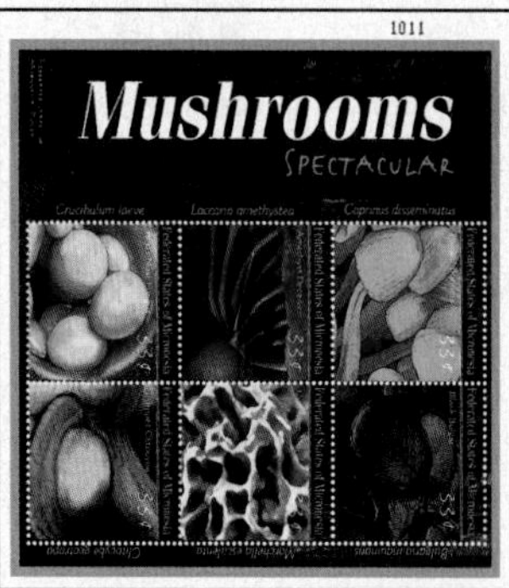
Mushrooms — A137

No. 381, each 33c: a, Fairies' bonnets. b, Black bulgar. c, Amethyst deceiver. d, Common morel. e, Bird's nest fungus. f, Trumpet clitocybe.

No. 382, each 33c: a, Bonnet mycena. b, Horse mushroom. c, Velvet boletus. d, Oyster. d, Aztec mandala. e, Fly agaric.

Each $2: No. 383, Magpie ink cap. No, 384, Brown birch bolete.

2000, May 15 *Perf. 13¾x14¼*
Sheets of 6, #a-f
381-382 A137 Set of 2 8.00 8.00

Souvenir Sheets
383-384 A137 Set of 2 8.00 8.00

Flowers of the Pacific — A138

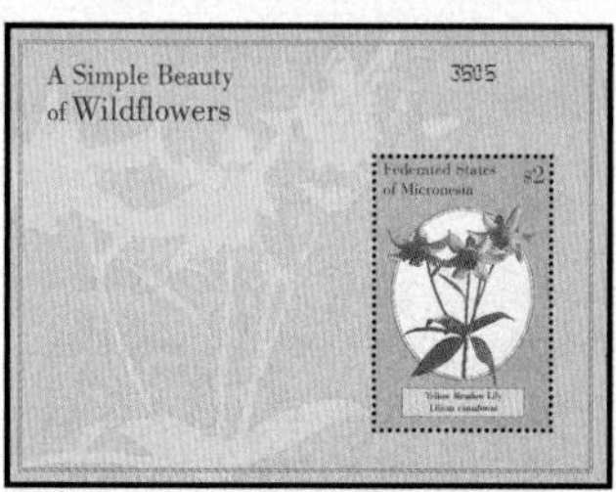
Wildflowers — A139

No. 385: a, Freycinetia arborea. b, Mount Cook lily. c, Sun orchid. d, Bossiaea ensata. e, Swamp hibiscus. f, Gardenia brighamii.

No. 386: a, Eleagant brodiaea. b, Skyrocket. c, Hedge bindweed. d, Woods' rose. e, Swamp rose. f, Wake robin.

No. 387, Black-eyed Susan. No. 388, Yellow meadow lily.

2000, May 29 *Perf. 14x13¾*
385 A138 33c Sheet of 6, #a-f 4.00 4.00
386 A139 33c Sheet of 6, #a-f 4.00 4.00

Souvenir Sheets
387 A138 $2 multi 4.00 4.00
388 A139 $2 multi 4.00 4.00

Souvenir Sheet

2000 Summer Olympics, Sydney — A140

No. 389: a, Henry Taylor. b, Cycling. c, Olympic Stadium, Munich and German flag. d, Ancient Greek wrestling.

2000, July 10 Litho. *Perf. 14*
389 A140 33c Sheet of 4, #a-d 2.75 2.75

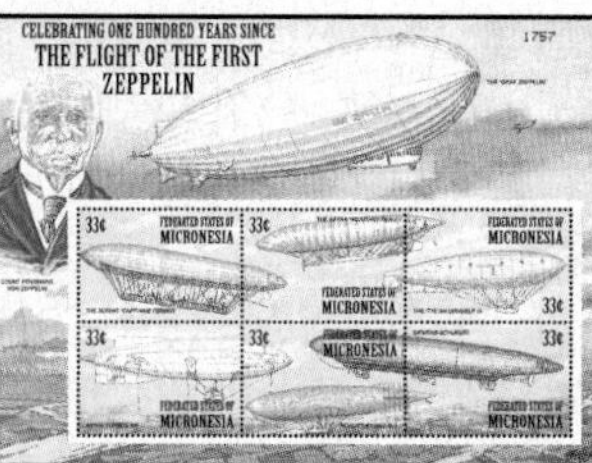
Zeppelins and Airships — A141

No. 390: a, Zodiac Capitaine Ferber. b, Astra Adjutant Reau. c, Italian dirigible IA. d, Astra-Torres XIV. e, Schuttle-Lanz SL3. f, Siemens-Schukert.

Each $2: No. 391, Graf Zeppelin. No. 392, Dupuy de Lome airship.

2000, Aug. 7 Litho. *Perf. 14*
390 A141 33c Sheet of 6, #a-f 4.00 4.00

Souvenir Sheets
391-392 A141 Set of 2 8.00 8.00

First Zeppelin flight, cent. (Nos. 390, 391).

Flower Photomosaic Type of 1999

Various flowers making up a photomosaic of the Queen Mother.

2000, Sept. 5 Litho. *Perf. 13¾*
393 A126 33c Sheet of 8, #a-h 5.25 5.25

Souvenir Sheet

2000 Summer Olympics, Sydney — A142

No. 394: a, 33c, Weight lifting. b, 33c, Basketball. c, $1, Weight lifting.

2000, Sept. 11 *Perf. 14*
394 A142 Sheet of 3, #a-c 3.50 3.50

Olymphilex 2000, Sydney.

Fish A143

Designs: No. 395, Rock beauty. No. 396, Bluestreak cleaner wrasse. No. 397, Chevroned butterflyfish (with frame). No. 398, Longfin bannerfish (with frame).

No. 399: a, Mandarinfish. b, Emperor snapper. c, Copper-banded butterflyfish. d, Chevroned butterflyfish (no frame). e, Lemonpeel angelfish. f, Harlequin tuskfish. g, Clown triggerfish. h, Coral hind. i, Longfin bannerfish (no frame).

No. 400: a, Six-spot grouper. b, Common jellyfish. c, Palette surgeonfish. d, Bicolor angelfish. e, Threadfin butterflyfish. f, Clown anemonefish. g, Three-banded demoiselle. h, Reef shark. i, Starfish.

No. 401, Long-nosed butterflyfish. No. 402, Emperor angelfish.

2000, Nov. 1
395-398 A143 33c Set of 4 2.60 2.60

Sheets of 9, #a-i
399-400 A143 33c Set of 2 12.00 12.00

Souvenir Sheets
401-402 A143 $2 Set of 2 8.00 8.00

Flower Photomosaic Type of 1999

Various photos with religious themes making up a photomosaic of Pope John Paul II.

2000, Nov. 1 Litho. *Perf. 13¾x14*
403 A126 50c Sheet of 8, #a-h 8.00 8.00

Christmas A144

Designs: 20c, The Holy Trinity, by Titian. 33c, The Adoration of the Magi, by Diego Velazquez. 60c, The Holy Nereus, by Peter Paul Rubens. $3.20, St. Gregory With Saints Around Him, by Rubens.

2000, Dec. 1 *Perf. 14¼*

404-407 A144 Set of 4 8.75 8.75

Dogs and Cats — A145

No. 408, 33c: a, Afghan hound. b, Yellow Labrador retriever. c, Greyhound. d, German shepherd. e, King Charles spaniel. f, Jack Russell terrier.

No. 409, 33c: a, Siamese. b, Mackerel tabby. c, British shorthair. d, Persian. e, Turkish angora. f, Calico.

No. 410, $2, Dog in field. No. 411, $2, Cat stalking bird.

2000, June 26 Litho. *Perf. 14*

Sheets of 6, #a-f

408-409 A145 Set of 2 8.00 8.00

Souvenir Sheets

410-411 A145 Set of 2 8.00 8.00

Souvenir Sheets

New Year 2001 (Year of the Snake) — A146

Designs: No. 412, 60c, Snake on ground. No. 413, 60c, Snake in bamboo, vert.

2001, Jan. 2

412-413 A146 Set of 2 2.40 2.40

Pokémon — A147

No. 414: a, Weepinbell. b, Snorlax. c, Seel. d, Hitmonchan. e, Jynx. f, Ponyta.

2001, Feb. 13 *Perf. 13¾*

414 A147 50c Sheet of 6, #a-f 6.00 6.00

Souvenir Sheet

415 A147 $2 Farfetch'd 4.00 4.00

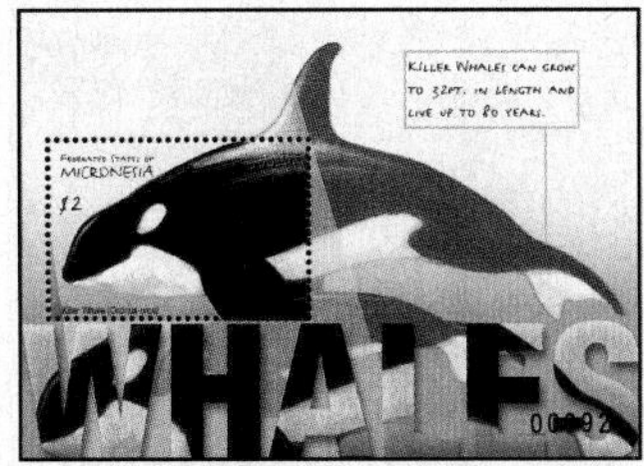
Whales — A148

No. 416, 50c: a, Fin. b, Right. c, Pygmy right. d, Humpback. e, Blue. f, Bowhead.

No. 417, 60c: a, True's beaked. b, Cuvier's beaked. c, Shepherd's beaked. d, Baird's beaked. e, Northern bottlenose. f, Pygmy sperm.

No. 418, $2, Killer. No. 419, $2, Sperm.

2001, Feb. 27 *Perf. 13¼x13¾*

Sheets of 6, #a-f

416-417 A148 Set of 2 13.50 13.50

Souvenir Sheets

418-419 A148 Set of 2 8.00 8.00

Ecology — A149

No. 420: a, Coral reef in peril. b, Galapagos Islands tortoise. c, Tasmanian tiger. d, Yanomani. e, Bird from Florida Keys. f, Eagle, Endangered species act.

No. 421: a, Pollution. b, Deforestation. c, Acid rain. d, Greenhouse effect.

No. 422, $2, Bird in flight. No. 423, Chimpanzee, vert.

Perf. 13¼x13¾, 13¾x13¼

2001, Feb. 27 Litho.

420 A149 34c Sheet of 6, #a-f 4.25 4.25
421 A149 60c Sheet of 4, #a-d 5.00 5.00

Souvenir Sheets

422-423 A149 $2 Set of 2 8.00 8.00

Fish Type of 1998

Designs: 11c, Yellow damselfish. 34c, Rainbow runner. 70c, Whitelined grouper. 80c, Purple queen anthias. $3.50, Eibl's angelfish. $12.25, Blue-spotted boxfish.

2001, Mar. 28 *Perf. 14½x14¾*

424	A116	11c multi	.25	.25
425	A116	34c multi	.70	.70
426	A116	70c multi	1.40	1.40
427	A116	80c multi	1.60	1.60
428	A116	$3.50 multi	7.00	7.00
429	A116	$12.25 multi	25.00	25.00
		Nos. 424-429 (6)	35.95	35.95

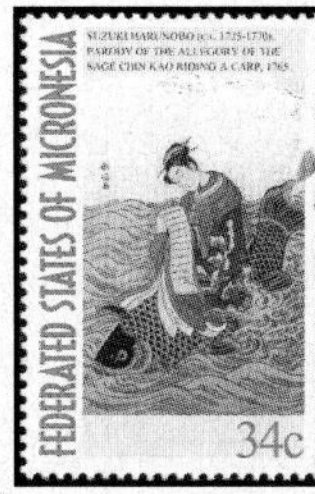
Japanese Art — A150

Designs: No. 430, 34c, Parody of the Allegory of the Sage Chin Kao Riding a Carp, by Suzuki Harunobu. No. 431, 34c, The Courtesan Hinazuru of the Choji-Ya, by Chokosai Eisho. No. 432, 34c, Girl Tying Her Hair Ribbon, by Torii Kiyomine. No. 433, 34c, The Iris Garden, by Kiyonaga Torii. No. 434, 34c, The Courtesan Mayuzumi of the Daimonji-Ya, by Shunsho Katsukawa. No. 435, 34c, Bath House Scene, by Toyokuni Utagawa.

No. 436 — Paintings by Utamaro: a, Dance of a Kamisha. b, The Courtesan Hinazura at the Keizetsuro. c, Toilet Scene. d, Applying Lip Rouge. e, Beauty Reading a Letter. f, The Geisha Kamekichi.

No. 437, $2, Allegory of Ariwara No Narihira, by Kikugawa Eizan, horiz. No. 438, $2, Girl Seated by a Brook, by Harunobu, horiz.

2001, Apr. 20 *Perf. 14*

430-435 A150 Set of 6 4.25 4.25
436 A150 34c Sheet of 6, #a-f 4.25 4.25

Imperf

Size: 118x88mm

437-438 A150 Set of 2 8.00 8.00

Phila Nippon '01, Japan (Nos. 436-438).

Toulouse-Lautrec Paintings — A151

No. 439: a, Oscar Wilde. b, Doctor Tapie in a Theater Corridor. c, Monsieur Delaporte.

$2, The Clowness Cha-U-Kao.

2001, May 15 *Perf. 13¾*

439 A151 60c Sheet of 3, #a-c 3.75 3.75

Souvenir Sheet

440 A151 $2 multi 4.00 4.00

Queen Victoria (1819-1901) — A152

Various portraits.

2001, May 15 *Perf. 14*

441 A152 60c Sheet of 6, #a-f 7.25 7.25

Souvenir Sheet

Perf. 13¾

442 A152 $2 shown 4.00 4.00

No. 441 contains six 28x42mm stamps.

Queen Elizabeth II, 75th Birthday — A153

No. 443: a, With necklace and brooch. b, Color photograph. c, As girl. d, As child. e, With dog. f, Facing left.

$2, Portrait in color.

2001, May 15 *Perf. 14*

443 A153 60c Sheet of 6, #a-f 7.25 7.25

Souvenir Sheet

444 A153 $2 multi 4.00 4.00

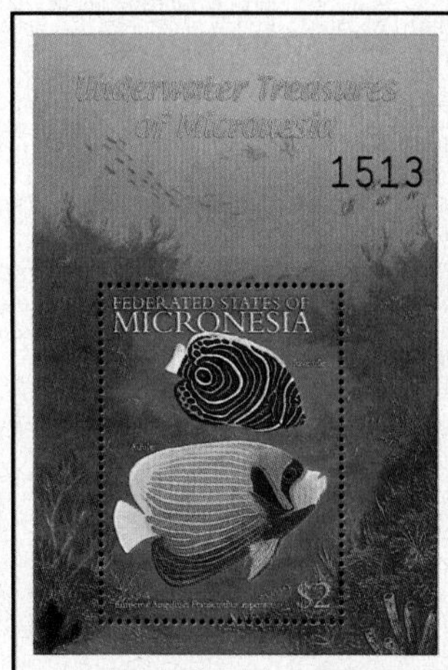
Marine Life — A154

No. 445, 60c, horiz.: a, Striped dolphin. b, Olive Ridley turtle. c, Goldrim tang. d, Blue shark. e, Picasso triggerfish. f, Polkadot grouper.

No. 446, 60c, horiz.: a, Loggerhead turtle. b, Striped marlin. c, Bicolor cherub. d, Clown wrasse. e, Clown triggerfish. f, Japanese tang.

No. 447, $2, Adult and juvenile emperor angelfish. No. 448, $2, Harlequin tuskfish, horiz.

2001, July 16 *Perf. 14*

Sheets of 6, #a-f

445-446 A154 Set of 2 14.50 14.50

Souvenir Sheets

Perf. 13¾

447-448 A154 Set of 2 8.00 8.00

Nos. 445-446 each contain six 42x28mm stamps.

Prehistoric Animals — A155

Designs: No. 449, 60c, Allosaurus (with frame). No. 450, 60c, Psittacosaurus. No. 451, 60c, Triceratops. No. 452, 60c, Archaeopteryx (with frame).

No. 453, 60c: a, Tyrannosaurus. b, Pteranodon. c, Brachiosaurus. d, Spinosaurus. e, Deinonychus. f, Teratosaurus.

No. 454, 60c: a, Parasaurolophus. b, Plateosaurus. c, Archaeopteryx (no frame). d, Allosaurus (no frame). e, Torosaurus. f, Euoplocephalus.

No. 455, $2, Tyrannosaurus. No. 456, $2, Parasaurolophus, horiz.

2001, Aug. 12 **Litho.** *Perf. 14*

449-452 A155 Set of 4 4.75 4.75

Sheets of 6, #a-f

453-454 A155 Set of 2 14.50 14.50

Souvenir Sheets

455-456 A155 Set of 2 8.00 8.00

Shells — A156

No. 457, 50c: a, Bat volute. b, Horned helmet. c, Troschel's murex. d, Lotorium triton. e, Orange-mouthed olive. f, Phos whelk.

No. 458, 50c, vert.: a, Oblique nutmeg. b, Imperial volute. c, Pontifical miter. d, Eburneus cone. e, Variegated sundial. f, Heart cockle.

No. 459, $2, Eyed auger. No. 460, $2, Geography cone.

2001, Oct. 15 **Litho.** *Perf. 14*

Sheets of 6, #a-f

457-458 A156 Set of 2 12.00 12.00

Souvenir Sheets

459-460 A156 Set of 2 8.00 8.00

On Nos. 485a-458f, the descriptions of the shells are transposed. Our descriptions are those of the stamps as they are printed.

Birds A157

Designs: 5c, Malleefowl. 22c, Corncrake. 23c, Hooded merganser. $2.10, Purple gallinule.

No. 465, 60c: a, Fairy wren. b, Golden-crowned kinglet warbler. c, Flame-tempered babbler. d, Golden-headed cisticola. e, White-browed babbler. f, White-breasted dipper.

No. 466, 60c: a, Logrunner. b, Eurasian treecreeper. c, Goldfinch. d, Rufous fantail. e, Orange-billed flowerpecker. f, American goldfinch.

No. 467, $2, Emperor bird of paradise. No. 468, $2, Yellow-eyed cuckooshrike, vert.

2001, Oct. 29 **Litho.** *Perf. 14*

461-464 A157 Set of 4 5.25 5.25

Sheets of 6, #a-f

465-466 A157 Set of 2 14.50 14.50

Souvenir Sheets

467-468 A157 Set of 2 8.00 8.00

Nobel Prizes, Cent. — A158

No. 469, 60c — Physiology or Medicine laureates: a, Alexis Carrel, 1912. b, Max Theiler, 1951. c, Niels Finsen, 1903. d, Philip S. Hench, 1950. e, Sune Bergström, 1982. f, John R. Vane, 1982.

No. 470, 60c — Laureates: a, Bengt Samuelsson, Physiology or Medicine, 1982. b, Johannes Fibiger, Physiology or Medicine, 1926. c, Theodore Richards, Chemistry, 1914. d, Tadeus Reichstein, Physiology or Medicine, 1950. e, Frederick Soddy, Chemistry, 1921. f, Albert Szent-Györgyi, 1937.

No. 471, $2, Irving Langmuir, Chemistry, 1932. No. 472, $2, Artturi Illmari Virtanen, Chemistry, 1945.

2001, Nov. 12 **Sheets of 6, #a-f**

469-470 A158 Set of 2 14.50 14.50

Souvenir Sheets

471-472 A158 Set of 2 8.00 8.00

Christmas A159

Santa Claus: 22c, On cat. 34c, Between Christmas trees. 60c, In sleigh. $1, On dog.

$2, Entering chimney, vert.

2001, Dec. 5

473-476 A159 Set of 4 4.50 4.50

Souvenir Sheet

477 A159 $2 multi 4.00 4.00

Attack on Pearl Harbor, 60th Anniv. — A160

No. 478, 60c: a, Rollover of USS Oklahoma. b, Japanese attack Wheeler Air Field. c, Japanese sailors loading bombs onto planes. d, Destroyer USS Ward sinks a Japanese submarine. e, USS Arizona sunk by Japanese bombs. f, Ewa Marine Base attacked by Japanese.

No. 479, 60c: a, Memorial poster showing attack. b, Japanese Prime Minister Hideki Tojo. c, Rescue at Bellows Field. d, Rescue of USS Arizona crew. e, Admiral Isoroku Yamamoto. f, Memorial poster showing soldier and flag.

No. 480, $2, USS Arizona Memorial. No. 481, $2, Pres. Franklin D. Roosevelt.

2001, Dec. 7 **Sheets of 6, #a-f**

478-479 A160 Set of 2 14.50 14.50

Souvenir Sheets

480-481 A160 Set of 2 8.00 8.00

Souvenir Sheet

New Year 2002 (Year of the Horse) — A161

Various horses.

2002, Jan. 24 *Perf. 13¾x13¼*

482 A161 60c Sheet of 5, #a-e 6.00 6.00

Reign of Queen Elizabeth II, 50th Anniv. — A162

No. 483: a, Queen wearing flowered dress. b, Prince Philip. c, Queen waving, holding flowers. d, Queen with children.

$2, Queen wearing scarf.

2002, Feb. 6 *Perf. 14¼*

483 A162 80c Sheet of 4, #a-d 6.50 6.50

Souvenir Sheet

484 A162 $2 multi 4.00 4.00

United We Stand — A163

2002, Feb. 20 *Perf. 13¾x13¼*

485 A163 $1 multi 2.00 2.00

Issued in sheets of 4.

2002 Winter Olympics, Salt Lake City — A164

Designs: No. 486, $1, Luge. No. 487, $1, Ice hockey.

2002, Mar. 18 *Perf. 14*

486-487 A164 Set of 2 4.00 4.00

487a Souvenir sheet, #486-487 4.00 4.00

Compare with Nos. 502-503.

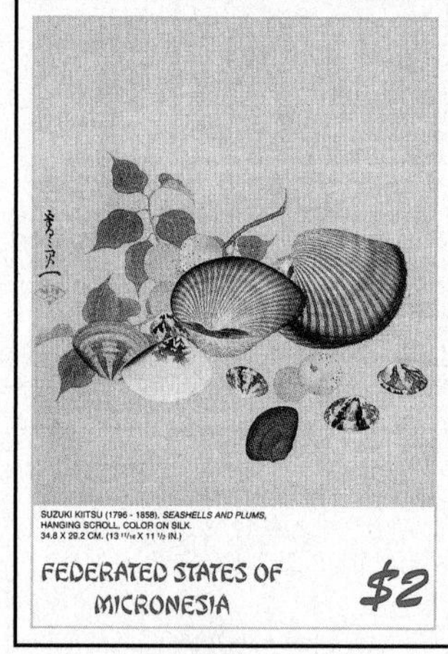

Japanese Art — A165

Birds and Flowers of the Twelve Months, by Hoitsu Sakai — No. 488, 60c: a, January. b, February. c, March. d, April. e, May. f, June.

No. 489, 60c: a, July. b, August. c, September. d, October. e, November. f, December.

No. 490, $2, Seashells and Plums by Kiitsu Suzuki. No. 491, Peacock and Peonies, by Rosetsu Nagasawa.

2002, Mar. 25 **Litho.** *Perf. 14x14¾*

Sheets of 6, #a-f

488-489 A165 Set of 2 14.50 14.50

Imperf

490-491 A165 Set of 2 8.00 8.00

Nos. 488-489 each contain six 77x26mm stamps.

Intl. Year of Mountains — A166

No. 492: a, Matterhorn, Switzerland. b, Maroonbells, U.S. c, Wetterhorn, Switzerland. d, Mt. Tsaranora, Africa.

$2, Cerro Fitzroy, South America.

2002, Mar. 30 *Perf. 14*

492 A166 80c Sheet of 4, #a-d 6.50 6.50

Souvenir Sheet

493 A166 $2 multi 4.00 4.00

Pres. John F. Kennedy (1917-63) — A167

No. 494: a, Dark blue background. b, Lilac background, name at left. c, Tan background, name at right. d, Light blue background.
$2, Purple background.

2002, Mar. 30
494 A167 60c Sheet of 4, #a-d 5.00 5.00

Souvenir Sheet

495 A167 $2 multi 4.00 4.00

Princess Diana (1961-97) — A168

No. 496: a, Wearing wedding veil. b, Wearing tiara and necklace. c, Wearing brimless hat. d, Wearing scarf. e, Hatless. f, Wearing tiara and large collar.
$2, Wearing hat with brim.

2002, Mar. 30
496 A168 60c Sheet of 6, #a-f 7.25 7.25

Souvenir Sheet

497 A168 $2 multi 4.00 4.00

Intl. Year of Ecotourism — A169

No. 498: a, Lizard. b, Canoes. c, Micronesian house. d, Three children in costume. e, Woman. f, Two dancers, house.
$2, Fishermen.

Perf. 13¼x13½

2002, June 17 **Litho.**
498 A169 80c Sheet of 6, #a-f 9.75 9.75

Souvenir Sheet

499 A169 $2 multi 4.00 4.00

20th World Scout Jamboree, Thailand — A170

No. 500: a, Thai temple. b, American scout insignia. c, Scout cap.
$2, Merit badges.

2002, June 17 *Perf. 13½x13¼*
500 A170 $1 Sheet of 3, #a-c 6.00 6.00

Souvenir Sheet

501 A170 $2 multi 4.00 4.00

Winter Olympics Type of 2002 Redrawn With White Panel Behind Olympic Rings

Designs: No. 502, $1, Luge. No. 503, $1, Ice hockey.

2002, July 15
502-503 A164 Set of 2 4.00 4.00
503a Souvenir sheet, #502-503 4.00 4.00

Xavier High School, 50th Anniv. A171

2002, July 31 *Perf. 13½x13¾*
504 A171 37c multi .75 .75

Queen Mother Elizabeth (1900-2002) — A172

No. 505, horiz.: a, At age 7. b, At wedding. c, At birth of Princess Elizabeth. d, At coronation of King George VI, 1937.
$2, As elderly lady.

2002, Aug. 12 *Perf. 14*
505 A172 80c Sheet of 4, #a-d 6.50 6.50

Souvenir Sheet

506 A172 $2 multi 4.00 4.00

Teddy Bears, Cent. — A173

No. 507: a, Burglar bear. b, White bear with heart. c, Blue bear with flowers. d, Brown bear with heart.

2002, Sept. 23 **Litho.** *Perf. 14*
507 A173 80c Sheet of 4, #a-d 6.50 6.50

Elvis Presley (1935-77) — A174

Presley with: a, Hand below guitar. b, Head on guitar. c, Hat. d, Checked shirt, no hat. e, Arms raised. f, Microphone.

2002, Oct. 7 *Perf. 13¾*
508 A174 37c Sheet of 6, #a-f 4.50 4.50

Christmas A175

Paintings: 21c, Madonna and Child, by Filippino Lippi, vert. 37c, Madonna and Child, by Giovanni Bellini, vert. 70c, Madonna and Child Between St. Stephen and St. Ladislaus, by Simone Martini. 80c, Holy Family, by Bronzino, vert. No. 513, $2, Holy Family, by Martini, vert.
No. 514, Sacred Conversation, by Bellini, vert.

2002, Nov. 4 *Perf. 14*
509-513 A175 Set of 5 8.25 8.25

Souvenir Sheet

Perf. 14x14¼

514 A175 $2 multi 4.00 4.00

Flora, Fauna and Mushrooms — A176

No. 515, 37c — Moths: a, White-lined sphinx. b, Tropical fruit-piercer. c, Coppery dysphania. d, Large agarista. e, Indian moon moth. f, Croker's frother.
No. 516, 55c — Mushrooms: a, Phellinus robustus. b, Purple coincap. c, Shaggy parasol. d, King bolete. e, Boletus crocipodius. f, Sharp-scaled parasol.
No. 517, 60c — Orchids: a, Eria javanica. b, Cymbidium finlaysonianum. c, Coelogyne asperata. d, Spathoglottis affinis. e, Vanda tricolor. f, Calanthe rosea.
No. 518, 60c — Butterflies: a, Meadow argus. b, Cairns birdwing. c, Large green-banded blue. d, Beak butterfly. e, Palmfly. f, Broad-bordered grass yellow.
No. 519, 80c — Insects and spiders: a, Stag beetle. b, Honeybee. c, Black widow spider. d, Mosquito. e, Black ant. f, Cicada.
No. 520, $2, Zodiac moth. No. 521, $2, Lepiota acutesquamosa mushroom. No. 522, $2, Dendrobium phalaenopsis orchid. No. 523, $2, Yamfly butterfly. No. 524, $2, Dragonfly, horiz.

2002, Dec. 16 *Perf. 14*

Sheets of 6, #a-f

515-519 A176 Set of 5 35.00 35.00

Souvenir Sheets

520-524 A176 Set of 5 20.00 20.00

Birds — A177

Designs: 3c, Greater flame-backed woodpecker. 5c, Red-tailed tropicbird. 21c, Hair-crested drongo. 22c, Pale white-eye. 23c, White-backed munia. 37c, Yap monarch. 60c, Eclectus parrot. 70c, Sulphur-crested cockatoo. 80c, Giant white-eye. $2, Green magpie. $3.85, Dollarbird. $5, Great frigatebird. $13.65, Micronesian pigeon.

2002, Dec. 30 *Perf. 14¼x14*
525 A177 3c multi .25 .25
526 A177 5c multi .25 .25
527 A177 21c multi .40 .40
528 A177 22c multi .45 .45
529 A177 23c multi .45 .45
530 A177 37c multi .75 .75
531 A177 60c multi 1.25 1.25
532 A177 70c multi 1.40 1.40
533 A177 80c multi 1.60 1.60
534 A177 $2 multi 4.00 4.00

Perf. 13¾

535 A177 $3.85 multi 7.75 7.75
536 A177 $5 multi 10.00 10.00
537 A177 $13.65 multi 27.50 27.50
Nos. 525-537 (13) 56.05 56.05

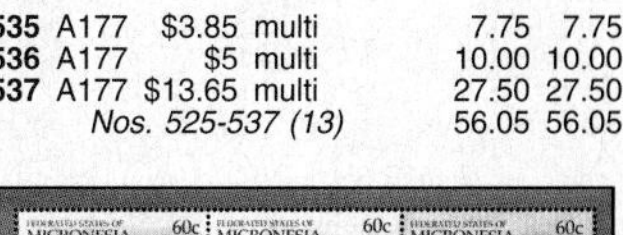

First Non-stop Solo Transatlantic Flight, 75th Anniv. (in 2002) — A178

No. 538: a, Charles Lindbergh, Donald Hall, Spirit of St. Louis. b, Spirit of St. Louis, Apr. 28, 1927. c, Towing of Spirit of St. Louis, May 20. d, Lindbergh taking off from Roosevelt Field, May 20. e, Lindbergh's arrival in Paris, May 21. f, Lindbergh in ticker tape parade, New York.

2003, Jan. 13 **Litho.** *Perf. 14*
538 A178 60c Sheet of 6, #a-f 7.25 7.25

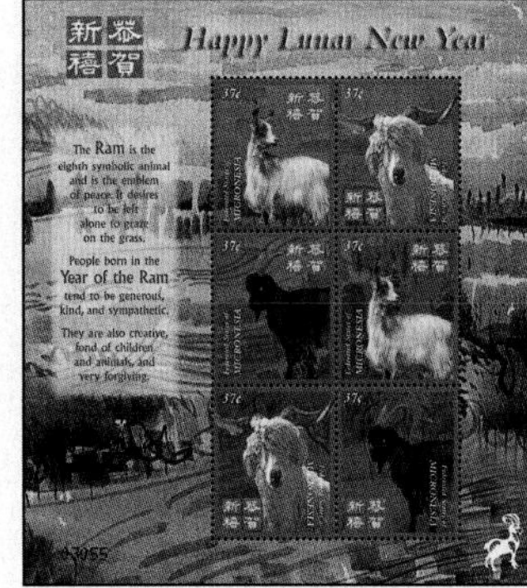

New Year 2003 (Year of the Ram) — A179

No. 539: a, Black ram facing left, country name at left. b, Black ram facing left, country name at right. c, White ram facing right, country name at left. d, White ram facing forward, country name at right.

2003, Feb. 1 **Litho.** *Perf. 14¼x14*
539 A179 37c Sheet of 6, #a-b, 2 each #c-d 4.50 4.50

Astronauts Killed in Space Shuttle Columbia Accident — A180

No. 540: a, Mission Specialist 1 David M. Brown. b, Commander Rick D. Husband. c, Mission Specialist 4 Laurel Blair Salton Clark. d, Mission Specialist 4 Kalpana Chawla. e, Payload Commander Michael P. Anderson. f,

Pilot William C. McCool. g, Payload Specialist Ilan Ramon.

2003, Apr. 7 *Perf. 13½x13¼*
540 A180 37c Sheet of 7, #a-g 5.25 5.25

Coronation of Queen Elizabeth II, 50th Anniv. — A181

No. 541: a, Wearing pearl necklace. b, Wearing sash and tiara. c, Wearing robe.
$2, Wearing crown.

2003, May 13 *Perf. 14x14¼*
541 A181 $1 Sheet of 3, #a-c 6.00 6.00

Souvenir Sheet

542 A181 $2 multi 4.00 4.00

Prince William, 21st Birthday — A182

No. 543: a, Wearing checked shirt and striped sweater. b, Facing right, wearing sweater, shirt and tie. c, Wearing suit and tie.
$2, Wearing raincoat.

2003, May 14
543 A182 $1 Sheet of 3, #a-c 6.00 6.00

Souvenir Sheet

544 A182 $2 multi 4.00 4.00

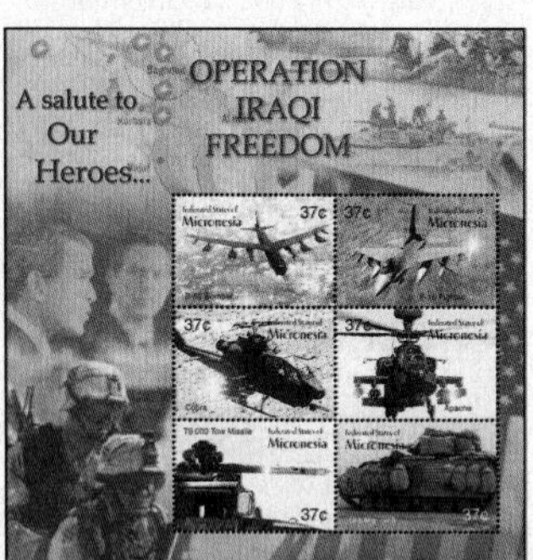

Operation Iraqi Freedom — A183

No. 545, 37c: a, B-52 Bomber. b, F-16 Fighter. c, Cobra Helicopter. d, Apache Helicopter. e, T8000 Tow Missile. f, Bradley Tank.
No. 546, 37c: a, Stealth Fighter. b, AC-130 Cargo plane. c, MH-53j Pave Low II Helicopter. d, Predator. e, Challenger Two Tank. f, Aegis Cruiser.

2003, May 14 *Perf. 14*

Sheets of 6, #a-f

545-546 A183 Set of 2 9.00 9.00

Tour de France Bicycle Race, Cent. — A184

No. 547: a, Greg LeMond, 1990. b, Miguel Indurain, 1991. c, Indurain, 1992. d, Indurain, 1993.
$2, Marco Pantani, 1998.

2003, July 1 *Perf. 13½*
547 A184 60c Sheet of 4, #a-d 5.00 5.00

Souvenir Sheet

548 A184 $2 multi 4.00 4.00

Intl. Year of Fresh Water — A185

No. 549: a, Kosrae mangroves. b, Chuuk Lagoon. c, Pohnpei's waterfalls.
$2, Pohnpei Lagoon.

2003, July 21 *Perf. 13½*
549 A185 $1 Sheet of 3, #a-c 6.00 6.00

Souvenir Sheet

550 A185 $2 multi 4.00 4.00

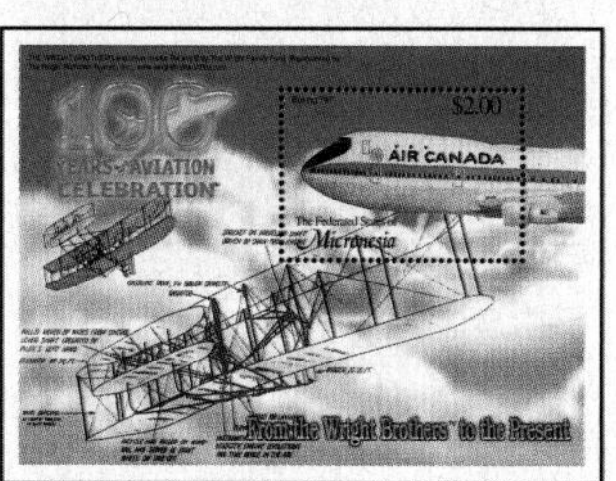

Powered Flight, Cent. — A186

No. 551: a, Concorde. b, Boeing 757. c, Junkers F13a. d, Martin M-130 China Clipper. e, Handley Page H.P.42W. f, Wright Flyer II.
$2, Boeing 747.

2003, Aug. 7 *Perf. 14*
551 A186 55c Sheet of 6, #a-f 6.75 6.75

Souvenir Sheet

552 A186 $2 multi 4.00 4.00

2003 APS Stampshow, Columbus, Ohio (No. 551).

Circus Performers — A187

No. 553, 80c: a, Glen Little. b, Joseph Grimaldi. c, Beverly Rebo Bergeron. d, Coco Michael Polakov.
No. 554, 80c: a, Jana Mandana. b, Maxim Papazov. c, Harry Keaton. d, Giraffe.

2003, Aug. 25 *Perf. 14*

Sheets of 4, #a-d

553-554 A187 Set of 2 13.00 13.00

Paintings of Boy Scouts by Norman Rockwell (1894-1978) — A188

No. 555: a, Scout with plaid neckerchief, from 1963 Boy Scout Calendar. b, A Scout is Helpful. c, The Scoutmaster. d, Scout with red neckerchief, from 1963 Boy Scout Calendar.
$2, No Swimming.

2003, Sept. 8 *Perf. 14*
555 A188 80c Sheet of 4, #a-d 6.50 6.50

Imperf

556 A188 $2 multi 4.00 4.00

No. 555 contains four 28x42mm stamps.

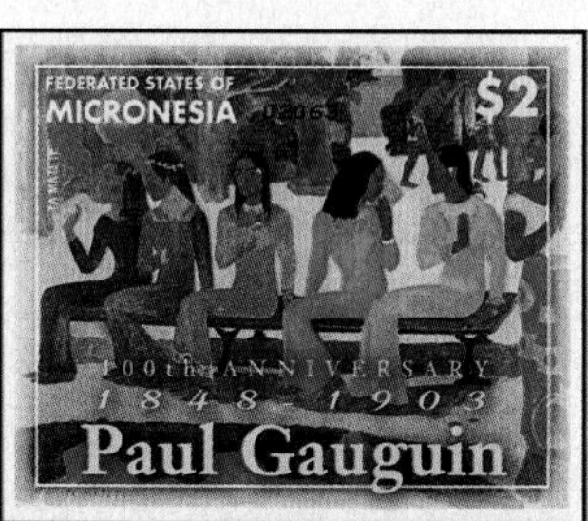

Paintings by Paul Gauguin (1848-1903) — A189

No. 557: a, Vahine No Te Tiare. b, Les Amants. c, Trois Tahitiens Conversation. d, Arearea.
$2, Ta Matete.

2003, Sept. 8 *Perf. 13¾*
557 A189 80c Sheet of 4, #a-d 6.50 6.50

Imperf

558 A189 $2 multi 4.00 4.00

No. 557 contains four 51x38mm stamps.

Paintings of James McNeill Whistler (1834-1903) — A190

Designs: 37c, Blue and Silver Blue: Wave, Biarritz. 55c, Brown and Silver: Old Battersea Bridge. 60c, Nocturne in Blue and Silver: The Lagoon, Venice. 80c, Crepuscule in Flesh Color and Green: Valparaiso.
No. 563: a, Symphony in White No. 2: The Little White Girl, vert. b, At the Piano (75x50mm). c, Symphony in White No. 1: The White Girl, vert.
$2, Portrait of Thomas Carlyle: Arrangement in Gray and Black No. 2, vert.

2003, Oct. 6 *Perf. 14¼*
559-562 A190 Set of 4 4.75 4.75
563 A190 $1 Sheet of 3, #a-c 6.00 6.00

Size: 83x104mm

Imperf

564 A190 $2 multi 4.00 4.00

Christmas A191

Designs: 37c, Madonna of the Carnation, by Leonardo da Vinci. 60c, Madonna with Yarn Winder, by da Vinci. 80c, Litta Madonna, by da Vinci. $1, Madonna of the Grand Duke, by Raphael.
$2, The Adoration of the Magi, by Giambattista Tiepolo.

2003, Nov. 5 *Perf. 14¼*
565-568 A191 Set of 4 5.75 5.75

Souvenir Sheet

569 A191 $2 multi 4.00 4.00

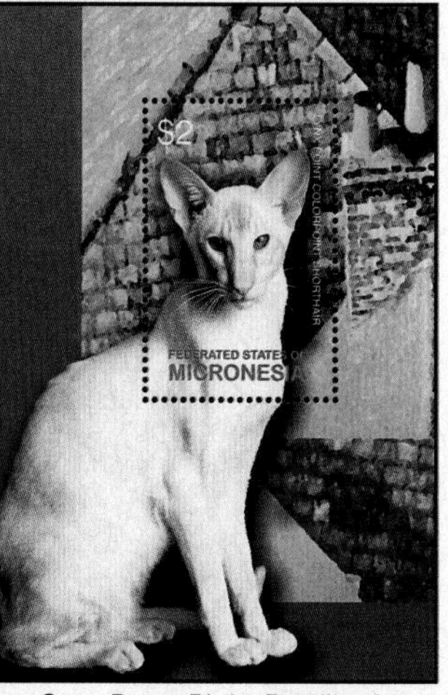

Cats, Dogs, Birds, Reptiles & Amphibians — A192

No. 570, 80c — Cats: a, Ragdoll. b, Calico Shorthaired Japanese Bobtail. c, Blue Mackerel Taffy Exotic Shorthair. d, Dilute Calico.

No. 571, 80c — Dogs: a, Australian shepherd. b, Greyhound. c, English bulldog. d, Schnauzer.
No. 572, 80c, horiz. — Birds: a, Green-winged macaw. b, American flamingo. c, Blue and gold macaw. d, Abyssinian ground hornbill.
No. 573, 80c, horiz. — Reptiles and amphibians: a, Leopard gecko. b, Red-eyed tree frog. c, Panther chameleon. d, Green and black poison frog.
No. 574, $2, Lynx Point Colorpoint Shorthair. No. 575, $2, Toy poodle. No. 576, $2, American flamingo. No. 577, $2, Madagascan chameleon, horiz.

2003, Dec. 22 ***Perf. 14***

Sheets of 4, #a-d

570-573 A192 Set of 4 26.00 26.00

Souvenir Sheets

574-577 A192 Set of 4 16.00 16.00

Pres. Bailey Olter (1932-99) — A193

2004, Feb. 16 **Litho.** ***Perf. 14***

578 A193 37c multi .75 .75

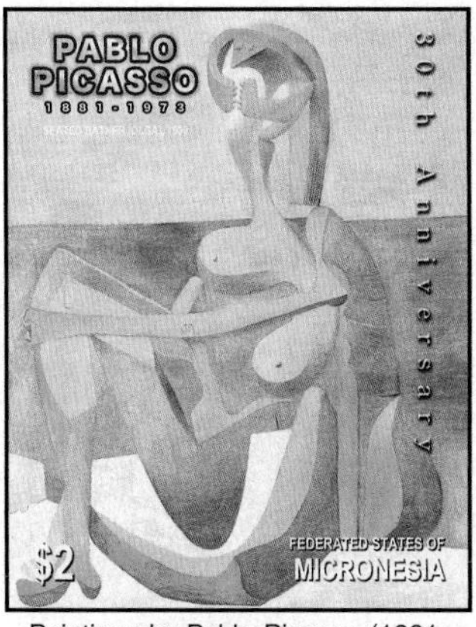

Paintings by Pablo Picasso (1881-1973) — A194

No. 579: a, Marie-Thérèse Leaning on One Elbow. b, Portrait of Jaime Sabartés. c, Portrait of Emilie Marguerite Walter (Mémé). d, Bust of a Woman Leaning on One Elbow.
$2, Seated Bather (Olga).

2004, Mar. 8 ***Perf. 14¼***

579 A194 80c Sheet of 4, #a-d 6.50 6.50

Imperf

580 A194 $2 multi 4.00 4.00

No. 579 contains four 37x50mm stamps.

Paintings in the Hermitage, St. Petersburg, Russia A195

Designs: 22c, A Young Lady in a Theatrical Costume, by Alexis Grimou. 37c, Portrait of Mrs. Harriet Greer, by George Romney. 80c, Portrait of Prince Nikolai Yusupov, by Friedrich Heinrich Füger. $1, Portrait of Richard Brinsley Sheridan, by John Hoppner.
$2, Spanish Concert (Conversation Espagnole), by Carle Vanloo.

2004, Mar. 8 ***Perf. 14¼***

581-584 A195 Set of 4 5.00 5.00

Imperf

Size: 64x81mm

585 A195 $2 multi 4.00 4.00

New Year 2004 (Year of the Monkey) — A196

Designs: 50c, Moon-struck Gibbon, by Gao Qi-feng. $1, Detail from Moon-struck Gibbon.

2004, Mar. 9 ***Perf. 13¼***

586 A196 50c multi 1.00 1.00

Souvenir Sheet

Perf. 13¼x13

587 A196 $1 multi 2.00 2.00

No. 587 contains one 30x40mm stamp. No. 586 printed in sheets of four.

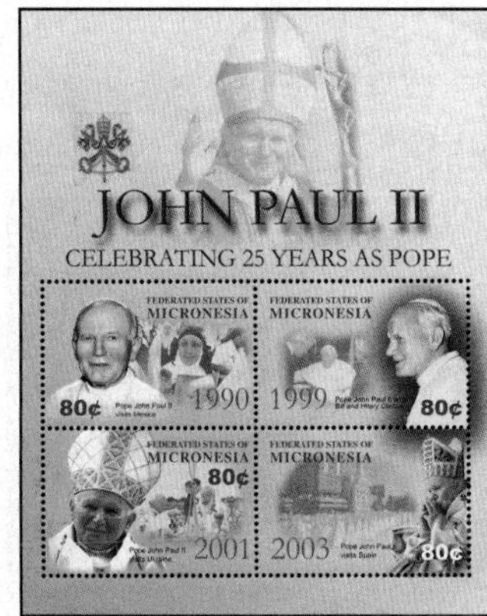

Election of Pope John Paul II, 25th Anniv. (in 2003) — A197

No. 588 — Pope John Paul II: a, Visiting Monaco, 1990. b, With Bill and Hillary Clinton, 1999. c, Visiting Ukraine, 2001. d, Visiting Spain, 2003.

2004, Sept. 1 ***Perf. 14¼x14***

588 A197 80c Sheet of 4, #a-d 6.50 6.50

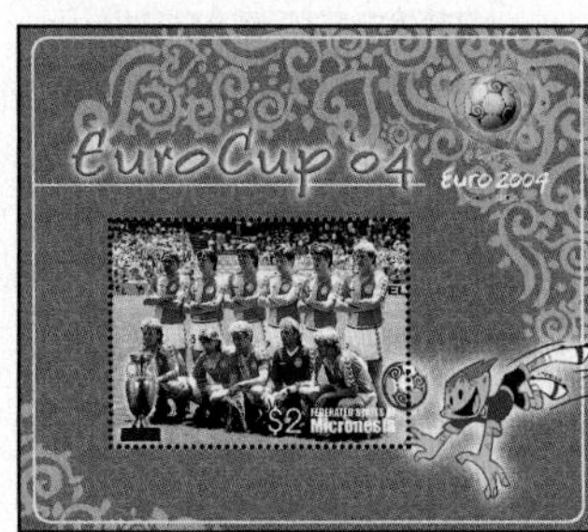

2004 European Soccer Championships, Portugal — A198

No. 589: a, Lars Olsen. b, Juergen Klinsmann. c, Peter Schmeichel. d, Nya Ullevi Stadium.
$2, 1992 Denmark team, horiz.

2004, Sept. 1 ***Perf. 14***

589 A198 80c Sheet of 4, #a-d 6.50 6.50

Souvenir Sheet

Perf. 14¼

590 A198 $2 multi 4.00 4.00

No. 589 contains four 28x42mm stamps.

D-Day, 60th Anniv. — A199

No. 591: a, Landing craft vehicle personnel. b, Destroyer Thompson. c, LST-391. d, Rhino Ferry 2, Rhino Tug 3. e, HMS Mauritius. f, Battleship Arkansas.
$2, LCI 1539.

2004, Sept. 1 ***Perf. 14***

591 A199 50c Sheet of 6, #a-f 6.00 6.00

Souvenir Sheet

592 A199 $2 multi 4.00 4.00

Souvenir Sheet

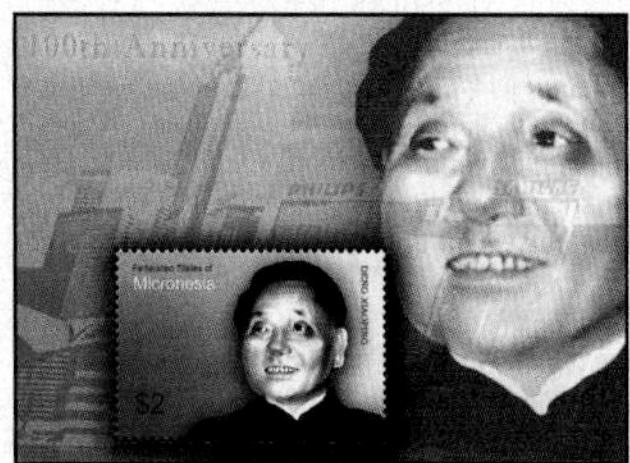

Deng Xiaoping (1904-97), Chinese Leader — A200

2004, Sept. 1 **Litho.** ***Perf. 14***

593 A200 $2 multi 4.00 4.00

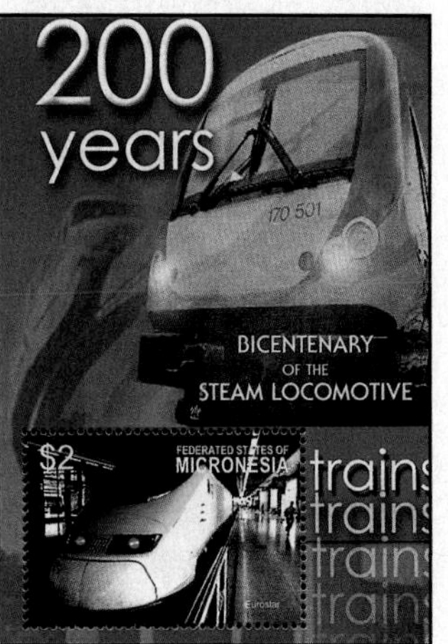

Locomotives, Bicent. — A201

No. 594, 80c: a, CFL N5520. b, Inter-region trains. c, SW-600. d, WSOR 3801.
No. 595, 80c: a, Baldwin 2-8-0. b, F-10 #1114 Diesel. c, BNSF locomotive (incorrectly inscribed "Okinawa Hitachi trains". d, Shinkansen.
No. 596, 80c: a, RS-1 #22. b, Diesel class 630. c, Okinawa Hitachi train. d, Eurostar.
No. 597, $2, Eurostar, diff. No. 598, $2, Locomotive 231-065. No. 599, $2, Michigan Central locomotive.

2004, Sept. 1 **Sheets of 4, #a-d**

594-596 A201 Set of 3 19.50 19.50

Souvenir Sheets

597-599 A201 Set of 3 12.00 12.00

Birds Type of 2002

Designs: 2c, Blue-gray gnatcatcher. 10c, Clapper rail.

2004, Nov. 1 ***Perf. 13¼***

600 A177 2c multi .25 .25
601 A177 10c multi .25 .25

Miniature Sheet

Intl. Year of Peace — A202

No. 602: a, Nelson Mandela. b, Dalai Lama. c, Pope John Paul II.

2004, Nov. 1 ***Perf. 14***

602 A202 80c Sheet of 3, #a-c 5.00 5.00

2004 Summer Olympics, Athens — A203

Designs: 37c, Ancient bronze sculpture of horse and rider. 55c, Pin from 1912 Stockholm Olympics, vert. 80c, Baron Pierre de Coubertin, Intl. Olympic Committee President, vert. $1, Poster from 1968 Mexico City Olympics, vert.

2004, Nov. 1 ***Perf. 14¼***

603-606 A203 Set of 4 5.50 5.50

Miniature Sheets

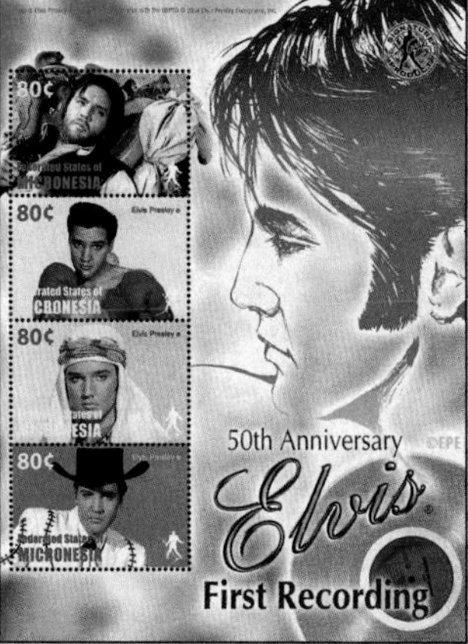

Elvis Presley's First Recording, 50th Anniv. — A204

No. 607, 80c — Presley with: a, Beard. b, Boxing gloves. c, Kaffiyeh. d, Cowboy hat.
No. 608, 80c, vert. — Presley with denomination in: a, Red. b, Purple. c, Blue. d, Orange yellow.

2004, Nov. 1 ***Perf. 14***

Sheets of 4, #a-d

607-608 A204 Set of 2 13.00 13.00

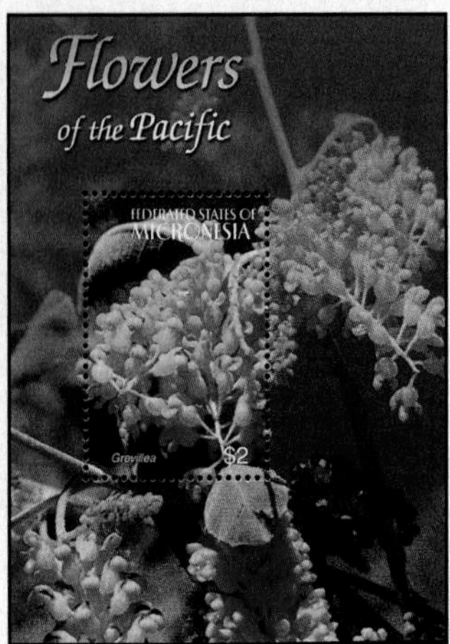

Flowers — A205

No. 609, horiz.: a, Epiphytic aeschynanthus. b, Darwinia collina. c, Rhododendron. d, Rhododendron retusum. e, Eucryphia lucida. f, Microporus xanthopus.
$2, Grevillea.

2004, Nov. 1 ***Perf. 13¼x13½***
609 A205 55c Sheet of 6, #a-f 6.75 6.75

Souvenir Sheet

Perf. 13½x13¼

610 A205 $2 multi 4.00 4.00

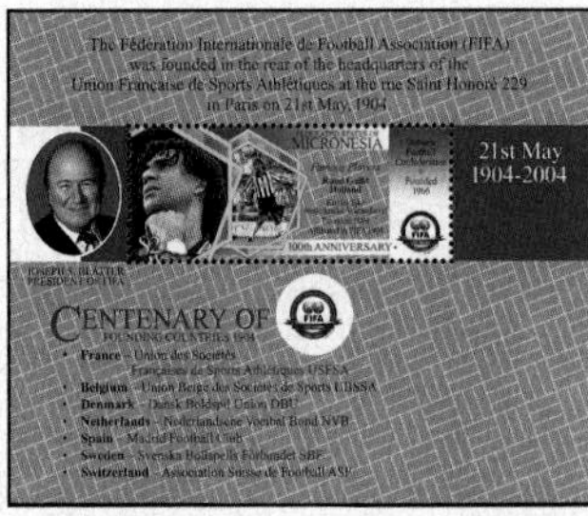

FIFA (Fédération Internationale de Football Association), Cent. — A206

No. 611: a, Herman Crespo. b, Peter Shilton. c, Klaus Augenthaler. d, Bryan Robson.
$2, Ruud Gullit.

2004, Nov. 1 ***Perf. 12¾x12½***
611 A206 80c Sheet of 4, #a-d 6.50 6.50

Souvenir Sheet

612 A206 $2 multi 4.00 4.00

National Basketball Association Players — A207

Designs: No. 613, 20c, Dirk Nowitzki, Dallas Mavericks. No. 614, 20c, Vince Carter, Toronto Raptors.

2004 ***Perf. 14***
613-614 A207 Set of 2 .80 .80

Issued: No. 613, 11/2; No. 614, 11/3. Each stamp issued in sheets of 12.

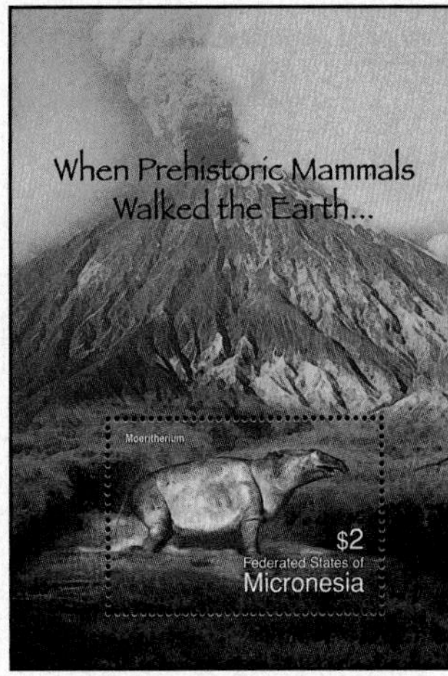

Prehistoric Animals — A208

No. 615, 80c: a, Indricotheres. b, Hyaenodons. c, Deinotherium. d, Chalicotheres.
No. 616, 80c: a, Apatosaurus. b, Pachyrhinosaurus. c, Kentrosaurus. d, Saltasaurus.
No. 617, 80c, vert.: a, Allosaurus. b, Tyrannosaurus. c, Troodon. d, Carnotaurus.
No. 618, $2, Moeritherium. No. 619, $2, Coelophysis. No. 620, $2, Deinonychus.

Perf. 14½x14, 14x14½

2004, Dec. 13 **Litho.**

Sheets of 4, #a-d

615-617 A208 Set of 3 19.50 19.50

Souvenir Sheets

618-620 A208 Set of 3 12.00 12.00

Fish and Coral — A209

No. 621: a, Clown triggerfish. b, Striped-face unicornfish. c, Firefish. d, Longnose hawkfish. e, Annella mollis. f, Dendronephthya.
$2, Great barracuda.

2004, Nov. 1 **Litho.** ***Perf. 13½***
621 A209 55c Sheet of 6, #a-f 6.75 6.75

Souvenir Sheet

622 A209 $2 multi 4.00 4.00

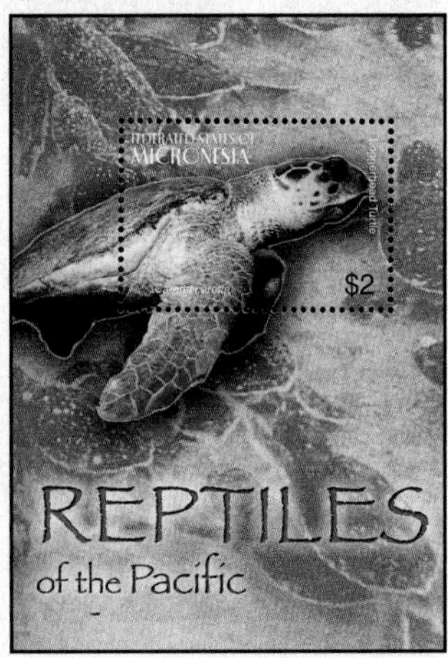

Reptiles and Amphibians — A210

No. 623: a, Blue coral snake. b, Solomon Islands horned frog. c, Levuka wrinkled ground frog. d, Flying lizard. e, Platymantis vitensis. f, Pacific ground boa.
$2, Loggerhead turtle.

2004, Nov. 1
623 A210 55c Sheet of 6, #a-f 6.75 6.75

Souvenir Sheet

624 A210 $2 multi 4.00 4.00

No. 623c has incorrect inscription as stamp depicts a lizard.

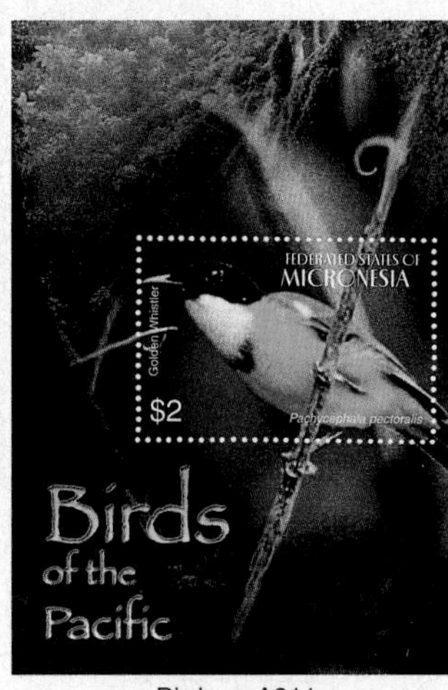

Birds — A211

No. 625, vert.: a, Black-faced woodswallows. b, Brown boobies. c, Rainbow lorikeets. d, Wandering albatross. e, Kagu. f, Great frigatebird.
$2, Golden whistler.

2004, Nov. 1
625 A211 55c Sheet of 6, #a-f 6.75 6.75

Souvenir Sheet

626 A211 $2 multi 4.00 4.00

Christmas A212

Madonna and Child paintings by: 37c, Giovanni Battista Tiepolo. 60c, Raphael. 80c, Jan Gossaert (Mabuse). $1, Fra Filippo Lippi.
$2, Unknown artist.

2004, Dec. 27 ***Perf. 14¼***
627-630 A212 Set of 4 5.75 5.75

Souvenir Sheet

631 A212 $2 multi 4.00 4.00

Diplomatic Relations Between Micronesia and People's Republic of China, 15th Anniv. — A212a

Designs: No. 631A, FSM-China Friendship Sports Center. No. 631B, Arms of People's Republic of China and Micronesia.

2004, Dec. 29 **Litho.** ***Perf. 13x13¼***
631A A212a 37c multi —
631B A212a 37c multi —
c. Horiz. pair, #631A-631B — —

New Year 2005 (Year of the Rooster) — A213

2005, Jan. 17 ***Perf. 12¾***
632 A213 50c multi 1.00 1.00

Printed in sheets of 4.

Basketball Players Type of 2004

Design: Luke Walton, Los Angeles Lakers.

2005, Feb. 24 ***Perf. 14***
633 A207 20c multi .40 .40

Pres. Ronald Reagan (1911-2004) — A214

No. 634: a, With British Prime Minister Margaret Thatcher. b, With Israeli Prime Minister Yitzhak Shamir.

2005, Mar. 21 ***Perf. 13¼x13½***
634 A214 55c Horiz. pair, #a-b 2.25 2.25

Printed in sheets containing 3 each Nos. 634a and 634b.

Elvis Presley (1935-2005) — A215

No. 635, 60c — Photos from: a, 1955. b, 1956. c, 1960 (with arm outstretched). d, 1968. e, 1970. f, 1973.
No. 636, 60c — Photos from: a, 1957. b, 1960 (in army uniform). c, 1963. d, 1965. e, 1967. f, 1969.

2005, Mar. 21 ***Perf. 13½x13¼***

Sheets of 6, #a-f

635-636 A215 Set of 2 14.50 14.50

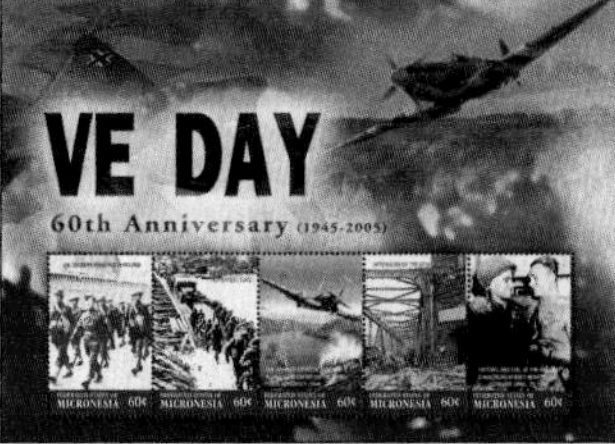

End of World War II, 60th Anniv. — A216

No. 637, 60c: a, U.S. soldiers marching in Ireland. b, British troops cross Volturno River, Italy. c, Hawker Typhoon attacks enemy on the Rhine River. d, Damaged Remagen Bridge. e, Meeting of Russian and American armies near Torgau, Germany.
No. 638, 60c: a, Poster remembering Pearl Harbor. b, Chula Beach, Tinian Island. c, Paul Tibbets and the Enola Gay. d, Hiroshima atomic bomb mushroom cloud. e, Newspaper announcing Japanese surrender.

2005, Mar. 31 ***Perf. 14***

Sheets of 5, #a-e

637-638 A216 Set of 2 12.00 12.00

Friedrich von Schiller (1759-1805), Writer — A217

No. 639: a, Wearing red cape. b, Statue. c, With head on hand.

2005, Mar. 31
639 A217 $1 Sheet of 3, #a-c 6.00 6.00

Souvenir Sheet

640 A217 $2 shown 4.00 4.00

Battle of Trafalgar, Bicent. — A218

Various depictions of ships in battle: 37c, 55c, 80c, $1.
$2, Death of Admiral Horatio Nelson.

2005, Mar. 31 ***Perf. 14¼***
641-644 A218 Set of 4 5.50 5.50

Souvenir Sheet

645 A218 $2 multi 4.00 4.00

Pope John Paul II (1920-2005) A219

2005, June 27 ***Perf. 13½x13¼***
646 A219 $1 multi 2.00 2.00

Printed in sheets of 6.

Rotary International, Cent. — A220

No. 647, vert.: a, Child. b, Emblem. c, 2004-05 Rotary International President Glenn E. Estess, Sr.
$2, 2002-03 Rotary International President Bhichai Rattakul.

2005, July 12 ***Perf. 12¾***
647 A220 $1 Sheet of 3, #a-c 6.00 6.00

Souvenir Sheet

648 A220 $2 multi 4.00 4.00

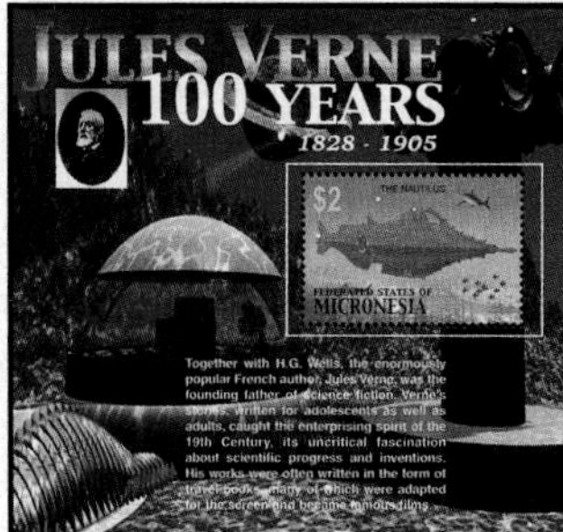

Jules Verne (1828-1905), Writer — A221

No. 649, vert.: a, Around the World in 80 Days. b, Phineas Fogg in India. c, Phineas Fogg, explorer and adventurer.
$2, Nautilus.

2005, June 7 **Litho.** ***Perf. 12¾***
649 A221 $1 Sheet of 3, #a-c 6.00 6.00

Souvenir Sheet

650 A221 $2 multi 4.00 4.00

Souvenir Sheet

Expo 2005, Aichi, Japan — A222

No. 651: a, Gray nurse shark. b, Surfer. c, Krakatoa Volcano. d, Yellow coral.

2005, June 27 ***Perf. 12x12¼***
651 A222 80c Sheet of 4, #a-d 6.50 6.50

Boats — A223

No. 652: a, 37c, Papyrus boat. b, 55c, Outrigger canoe. c, 80c, Papyrus sailboat. d, $1, Arab dhow.
$2, Lateen-rigged Nile riverboat.

2005, June 27 ***Perf. 12¾***
652 A223 Sheet of 4, #a-d 5.50 5.50

Souvenir Sheet

653 A223 $2 multi 4.00 4.00

Kosrae Government Building Complex — A224

Views of various buildings with frame colors of: 4c, Light yellow. 10c, Light blue. 22c, Pink. 37c, Light green.

2005, July 8 ***Perf. 14***
654-657 A224 Set of 4 1.50 1.50

Vatican City No. 67 — A225

2005, Aug. 9 ***Perf. 13x13¼***
658 A225 37c multi .75 .75

Pope John Paul II (1920-2005). Printed in sheets of 12.

Worldwide Fund for Nature (WWF) — A226

No. 659: a, Stephanometra echinus. b, Oxycomanthus bennetti. c, Alloeocomatella polycaldia. d, Dichrometra flagellata.

2005, Aug. 31 ***Perf. 14***
659 A226 50c Block or vert. strip of 4, #a-d 4.00 4.00
e. Souvenir sheet, 2 each #659a-659d 8.00 8.00

Souvenir Sheet

Albert Einstein (1879-1955), Physicist — A227

No. 660 — Various portraits with "Albert Einstein (1879-1955)" in: a, Orange. b, Blue. c, Red. d, Black.

2005, Sept. 20 ***Perf. 12¾***
660 A227 $1 Sheet of 4, #a-d 8.00 8.00

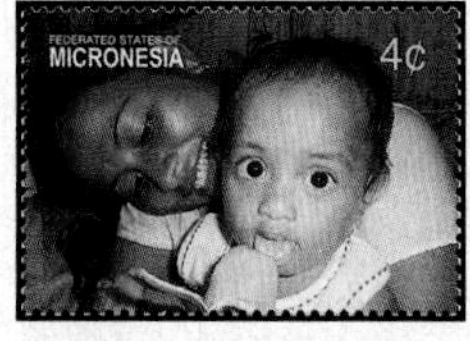

Bananas A228

Designs: 4c, Mother feeding banana to child. 10c, Four bananas. 22c, Bunch of bananas. 37c, Banana plant.

2005, Oct. 14 ***Perf. 14***
661-664 A228 Set of 4 1.50 1.50

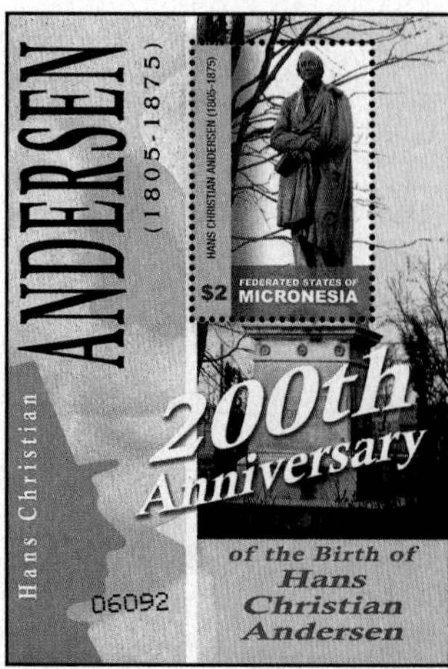

Hans Christian Andersen (1805-75), Author — A229

No. 665: a, Bust of Andersen. b, Statue of seated Andersen. c, Bust of Andersen on pedestal.
$2, Statue of standing Andersen.

2005, Nov. 15 ***Perf. 12¾***
665 A229 80c Sheet of 3, #a-c 5.00 5.00

Souvenir Sheet

666 A229 $2 multi 4.00 4.00

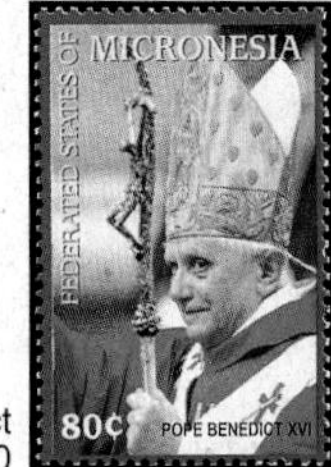

Pope Benedict XVI — A230

2005, Nov. 21 **Litho.** ***Perf. 13½***
667 A230 80c multi 1.60 1.60

Printed in sheets of 4.

Christmas — A231

Painting details: 37c, Kanigani Madonna, by Raphael. 60c, Madonna with the Fish, by Raphael. 80c, The Holy Family, by Bartolomé Esteban Murillo. $1, Madonna with the Book, by Raphael.
$2, The Holy Family, by Murillo, diff.

2005, Dec. 1 **Litho.** ***Perf. 14***
668-671 A231 Set of 4 5.75 5.75

Souvenir Sheet

672 A231 $2 multi 4.00 4.00

Flowers — A232

Designs: 4c, Tecoma stans. 10c, Ipomoea fistulosa. 22c, Hibiscus rosa-sinensis. 37c, Gerbera jamesonii. No. 677, 80c, Helianthus annuus. $1, Ixora casei.
No. 679, 80c: a, Tapeinochilos ananassae. b, Bauhnia monandra. c, Galphimia gracilis. d, Hibiscus rosa-sinensis, diff.
No. 680, $2, Helianthus annuus, diff. No. 681, $2, Phinia variegata.

2005, Nov. 15 Litho. *Perf. 12*

673-678 A232 Set of 6 5.25 5.25
679 A232 80c Sheet of 4, #a-d 6.50 6.50

Souvenir Sheets

680-681 A232 Set of 2 8.00 8.00

New Year 2006 (Year of the Dog) — A233

Paintings by Liu Jiyou: 50c, Wolf Dog. $1, Wolf Dog, horiz.

2006, Jan. 3 *Perf. 13¼*

682 A233 50c multi 1.00 1.00

Souvenir Sheet

683 A233 $1 multi 2.00 2.00

No. 683 contains one 48x35mm stamp.
No. 682 was issued in sheets of 4.

Birds — A234

Designs: No. 684, Glaucous-winged gull. No. 685, Slaty-headed parakeet. No. 686, Harlequin duck. No. 687, Purple sunbird. 75c, Plum-headed parakeet. 84c, Yellow-wattled lapwing. $4.05, Eurasian collared dove, horiz.

2006 *Perf. 12*

684	A234	24c multi	.50	.50
685	A234	24c multi	.50	.50
686	A234	39c multi	.80	.80
687	A234	39c multi	.80	.80
688	A234	75c multi	1.50	1.50
689	A234	84c multi	1.75	1.75
690	A234	$4.05 multi	8.25	8.25
		Nos. 684-690 (7)	14.10	14.10

Issued: Nos. 684, 686, 2/21; others, 4/20.

Vice-President Petrus Tun (1936-99) — A235

2006, Mar. 19 *Perf. 12¾*

691 A235 39c multi .80 .80

Printed in sheets of 4.

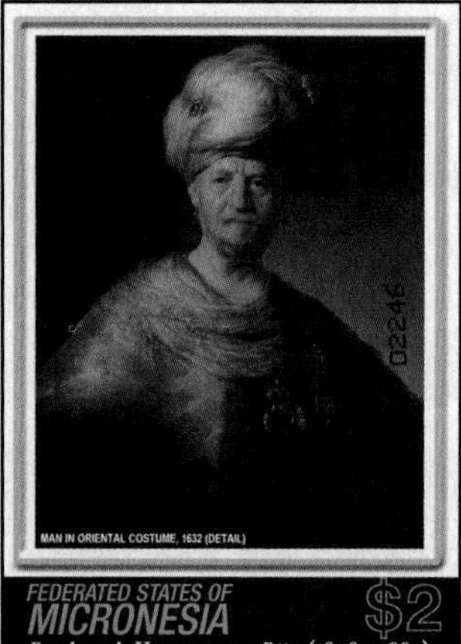

Rembrandt (1606-69), Painter — A236

No. 692: a, Saskia as Flora. b, Young Girl at a Window. c, Girl with a Broom. d, Prodigal Son in the Tavern.
$2, Man in Oriental Costume.

2006, June 22 *Perf. 13¼*

692 A236 $1 Sheet of 4, #a-d 8.00 8.00

Imperf

693 A236 $2 multi 4.00 4.00

No. 692 contains four 38x50mm stamps.

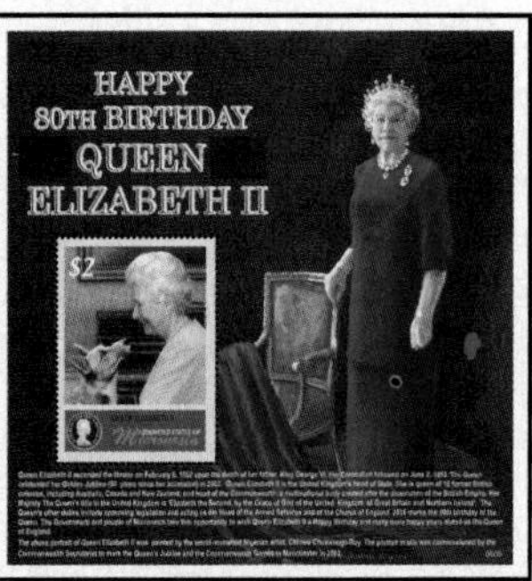

Queen Elizabeth II, 80th Birthday — A237

No. 694 — Dogs and Queen in: a, Red violet dress. b, Beige dress. c, Purple dress. d, Light blue dress.
$2, Green dress.

2006, June 22 *Perf. 14¼*

694 A237 84c Sheet of 4, #a-d 6.75 6.75

Souvenir Sheet

695 A237 $2 multi 4.00 4.00

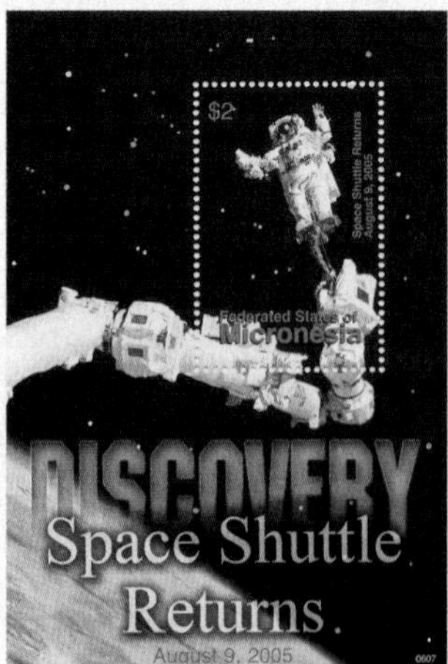

Space Achievements — A238

No. 696 — Various views of Venus Express: a, Text in black. b, Country name in black, denomination in white. c, Country name in white, denomination in black. d, Country name and denomination in white. e, Country name and denomination in red, "Venus Express" at left. f, Country name and denomination in red, "Venus Express" at right.

No. 697, $1, horiz. — Return to space of Space Shuttle Discovery: a, Denomination in white. b, Shuttle arm. c, Shuttle with cargo bay open. d, Shuttle tail.

No. 698, $1, horiz. — Spacecraft for future trips to: a, Moon, black denomination. b, Moon, blue denomination. c, Mars, red denomination. d, Mars, white denomination.

No. 699, $2, Space Shuttle Discovery astronaut space-walking. No. 700, $2, Mars Reconnaissance Orbiter. No. 701, $2, Stardust probe, horiz.

2006, July 11 *Perf. 14¼*

696 A238 75c Sheet of 6, #a-f 9.00 9.00

Sheets of 4, #a-d

697-698 A238 Set of 2 16.00 16.00

Souvenir Sheets

699-701 A238 Set of 3 12.00 12.00

Butterflies A239

Designs: 1c, Papilio euchenor. 2c, Golden birdwing. 4c, Delias henningia. 5c, Bassarona duda. 10c, Common bluebottle. 19c, Arhopala cleander. 20c, Arhopala argentea. 22c, Danaus aspasia. 75c, Arhopala aurea. 84c, Caleta mindaurus. $1, Black and white tit. $4.05, Grand imperial. $5, Jamides abdul. $10, Paralaxita lacoon.

2006, Nov. 15 *Perf. 12*

702	A239	1c multi	.25	.25
703	A239	2c multi	.25	.25
704	A239	4c multi	.25	.25
705	A239	5c multi	.25	.25
706	A239	10c multi	.25	.25
707	A239	19c multi	.40	.40
708	A239	20c multi	.40	.40
709	A239	22c multi	.45	.45
710	A239	75c multi	1.50	1.50
711	A239	84c multi	1.75	1.75
712	A239	$1 multi	2.00	2.00
713	A239	$4.05 multi	8.25	8.25
714	A239	$5 multi	10.00	10.00
715	A239	$10 multi	20.00	20.00
		Nos. 702-715 (14)	46.00	46.00

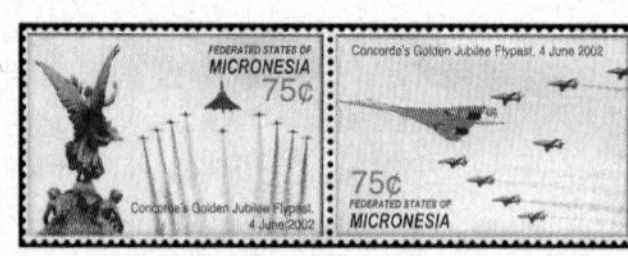

Christmas — A240

Designs: 22c, Christmas tree. 24c, Stocking. 39c, Snowman. 75c, Candle. 84c, Ornament.

2006, Dec. 4 *Perf. 13½*

716-720 A240 Set of 5 5.00 5.00

Concorde — A241

No. 721, 75c — Concorde's Jubilee Flypast: a, With statue. b, Without statue.
No. 722, 75c — Concorde 001: a, In flight. b, On ground.

Perf. 13¼x13½

2006, Dec. 20 Litho.

Pairs, #a-b

721-722 A241 Set of 2 6.00 6.00

New Year 2007 (Year of the Pig) — A242

2007, Jan. 3 *Perf. 13¼*

723 A242 75c multi 1.50 1.50

Printed in sheets of 4.

Souvenir Sheet

Wolfgang Amadeus Mozart (1756-91), Composer — A243

2007, Jan. 11

724 A243 $2 multi 4.00 4.00

Souvenir Sheet

Ludwig Durr (1878-1956), Engineer — A244

No. 725 — Durr and: a, Walrus Hula airship. b, Walrus heavy transport blimp. c, Hindenburg.

2007, Jan. 11

725 A244 $1 Sheet of 3, #a-c 6.00 6.00

Souvenir Sheet

Marilyn Monroe (1926-62), Actress — A245

No. 726: a, Looking right. b, With puckered lips. c, Wearing beret. d, With eyes closed, facing left.

2007, Jan. 11
726 A245 $1 Sheet of 4, #a-d 8.00 8.00

Scouting, Cent. — A246

2007, Jan. 11
727 A246 $1 shown 2.00 2.00

Souvenir Sheet

728 A246 $2 Scouts, flag 4.00 4.00

No. 727 was printed in sheets of 3. No. 728 contains one 37x50mm stamp.

Pope Benedict XVI, 80th Birthday — A247

2007, May 25
729 A247 50c multi 1.00 1.00

Printed in sheets of 8.

Miniature Sheet

Wedding of Queen Elizabeth II and Prince Philip, 60th Anniv. — A248

No. 730 — Queen and Prince: a, Standing, red frame. b, Seated, red frame. c, Seated, white frame. d, Standing, white frame. e, Standing, blue frame. f, Seated, blue frame.

2007, May 25
730 A248 60c Sheet of 6, #a-f 7.25 7.25

Princess Diana (1961-97) — A249

No. 731 — Various portraits with background color of: a, Pink. b, Lilac. c, Bister. d, Light green.
$2, Diana wearing tiara.

2007, May 25
731 A249 90c Sheet of 4, #a-d 7.25 7.25

Souvenir Sheet

732 A249 $2 multi 4.00 4.00

Bananas — A250

Inscriptions: 22c, Utim was. 26c, Utin lap. 41c, Mangat. 58c, Ipali. 80c, Daiwang. 90c, Akadahn Weitahta, horiz. $1.14, Peleu. $4.60, Utin Kerenis.

Perf. 14x14¾, 14¾x14

2007, June 12

733	A250	22c multi	.45	.45
734	A250	26c multi	.55	.55
735	A250	41c multi	.85	.85
736	A250	58c multi	1.25	1.25
737	A250	80c multi	1.60	1.60
738	A250	90c multi	1.90	1.90
739	A250	$1.14 multi	2.40	2.40
740	A250	$4.60 multi	9.25	9.25
		Nos. 733-740 (8)	18.25	18.25

Miniature Sheet

Elvis Presley (1935-77) — A251

No. 741 — Various portraits with denomination color of: a, Blue (country name in gray). b, Pink. c, Blue (country name in blue). d, Green. e, Buff. f, Lilac.

2007, June 20 ***Perf. 14¼***
741 A251 75c Sheet of 6, #a-f 9.00 9.00

Fish — A252

No. 742: a, Longnose hawkfish. b, Fingerprint sharpnose puffer. c, Ornate butterflyfish. d, Longnose filefish.
$2, Multi-barred goatfish.

2007, June 21 ***Perf. 13¼***
742 A252 90c Sheet of 4, #a-d 7.25 7.25

Souvenir Sheet

743 A252 $2 multi 4.00 4.00

Flowers — A253

No. 744: a, White plumeria. b, Yellow plumeria. c, White lily. d, Yellow ginger lily.
$2, Bougainvillea glabra.

2007, June 21
744 A253 90c Sheet of 4, #a-d 7.25 7.25

Souvenir Sheet

745 A253 $2 multi 4.00 4.00

Souvenir Sheet

Peace Corps in Micronesia, 40th Anniv. (in 2006) — A254

No. 746 — Inscriptions: a, Yap State. b, Kosrae State. c, Pohnpei State. d, Chuuk State.

2007, June 22
746 A254 90c Sheet of 4, #a-d 7.25 7.25

Miniature Sheet

Pres. Gerald R. Ford (1913-2006) — A255

No. 747 — Ford: a, With hand raised. b, Seated, reading documents. c, With Pres. Richard Nixon, denomination at UL. d, With Nixon, denomination at UR. e, With wife, Betty. f, Signing Nixon's pardon.

2007, Aug. 7
747 A255 $1 Sheet of 6, #a-f 12.00 12.00

Intl. Polar Year — A256

No. 748: a, African penguins. b, Emperor penguins. c, Galapagos penguin. d, Humboldt penguin. e, Magellanic penguin. f, Rockhopper penguin.
$3.50, Gentoo penguins.

2007, Aug. 7
748 A256 75c Sheet of 6, #a-f 9.00 9.00

Souvenir Sheet

749 A256 $3.50 multi 7.00 7.00

Souvenir Sheet

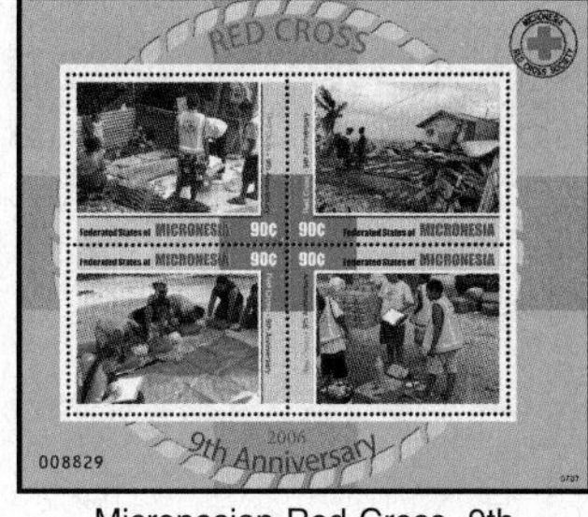
Micronesian Red Cross, 9th Anniv. — A257

No. 750 — Various pictures of relief efforts with denomination at: a, LR. b, LL. c, UR. d, UL.

2007, Aug. 20
750 A257 90c Sheet of 4, #a-d 7.25 7.25

Cats — A258

Designs: 22c, Scottish Fold. 26c, Munchkin. 41c, Abyssinian. 90c, Somali, horiz.
$2, Blue Silver Shaded Tiffanie.

Perf. 13½x13, 13x13½

2007, Sept. 24 **Litho.**
751-754 A258 Set of 4 3.75 3.75

Souvenir Sheet

Perf. 12½x12¾

755 A258 $2 multi 4.00 4.00

No. 755 contains one 29x42mm stamp.

Christmas A259

Churches: 22c, Mother Church, United Church of Christ, Pohnpei. 26c, St. Mary's Church, Yap, horiz. 41c, Sapore Bethesca Church, Fefan, Chuuk, horiz. 90c, Lelu Congregational Church, Kosrae, horiz.

Perf. 14¼x14¾, 14¾x14¼

2007, Nov. 12
756-759 A259 Set of 4 3.75 3.75

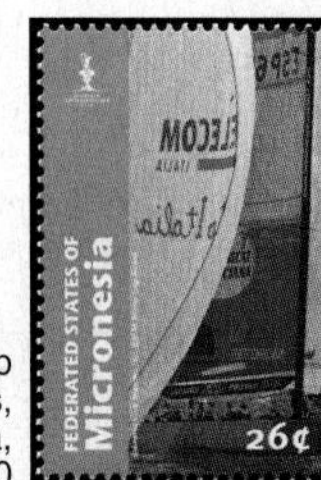
America's Cup Yachting Races, Valencia, Spain — A260

Sails of various sailboats.

2007, Dec. 12 ***Perf. 13¼***

760	Strip of 4	8.50	8.50
a.	A260 26c aquamarine & multi	.50	.50
b.	A260 80c red & multi	1.60	1.60
c.	A260 $1.14 yellow & multi	2.40	2.40
d.	A260 $2 orange & multi	4.00	4.00

First Helicopter Flight, Cent. — A261

No. 761: a, AH-1 Huey Cobra. b, 206 Jet Ranger. c, H-43 Huskie. d, AS-350 Ecureuil. $2.50, Fa 223 Drache.

2007, Dec. 12 ***Perf. 13¼***
761 A261 $1 Sheet of 4, #a-d 8.00 8.00

Souvenir Sheet

762 A261 $2.50 multi 5.00 5.00

Princess Diana (1961-97) — A262

Serpentine Die Cut 7¾
2007, Dec. 12 Litho. & Embossed
Without Gum

763 A262 $8 multi 16.00 16.00

Miniature Sheet

Pres. John F. Kennedy (1917-63) — A263

No. 764 — Kennedy: a, With curtain at left. b, Color portrait. c, With Presidential Seal. d, At microphones.

2008, Jan. 2 Litho. ***Perf. 14***
764 A263 90c Sheet of 4, #a-d 7.25 7.25

New Year 2008 (Year of the Rat) — A264

2008, Jan. 2 Litho. ***Perf. 12***
765 A264 90c multi 1.90 1.90

Printed in sheets of 4.

Miniature Sheet

2008 Olympic Games, Beijing — A265

No. 766: a, Cover of book with music from 1904 World's Fair. b, Poster for 1904 Olympic Games and World's Fair. c, Jim Lightbody. d, Martin Sheridan.

2008, Jan. 8 ***Perf. 14***
766 A265 50c Sheet of 4, #a-d 4.00 4.00

Souvenir Sheet

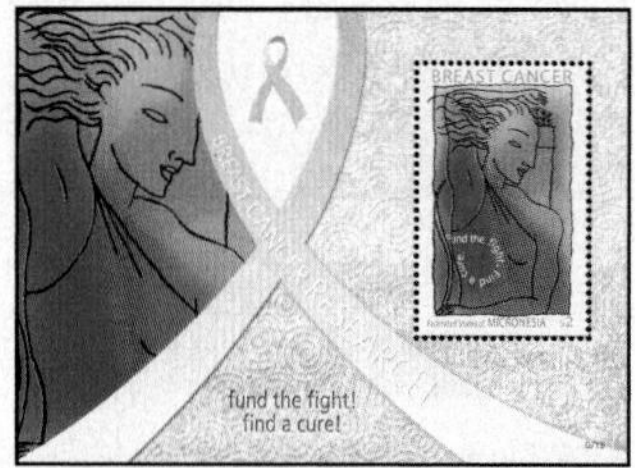

Breast Cancer Awareness — A266

2008, Mar. 12
767 A266 $2 multi 4.00 4.00

Hummer Vehicles — A267

No. 768: a, Front bumper of Hummer H3x, denomination at UR. b, Side view of Hummer H3x, denomination at LR. c, Front view of Hummer H3x, denomination at LR. d, Rear view of Hummer H3x, denomination at UR. $2, Hummer H3.

2008, May 6 ***Perf. 13¼***
768 A267 90c Sheet of 4, #a-d 7.25 7.25

Souvenir Sheet

769 A267 $2 multi 4.00 4.00

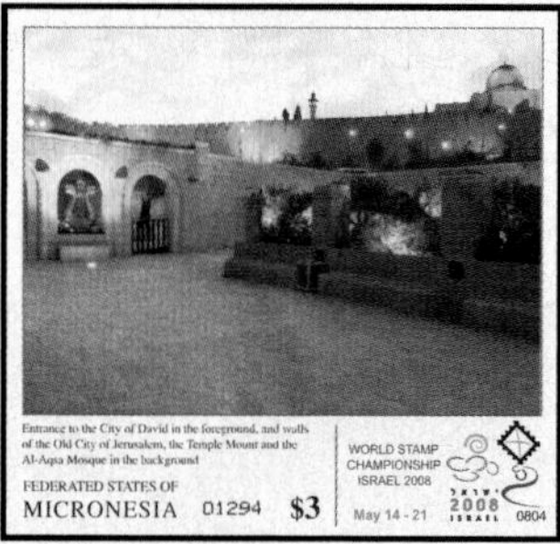

Jerusalem — A268

2008, May 14 ***Imperf.***
770 A268 $3 multi 6.00 6.00

World Stamp Championship, Israel, 2008.

Miniature Sheet

Elvis Presley (1935-77) — A269

No. 771 — Presley: a, With head on hand, buff background. b, Sitting in director's chair, gray background. c, Wearing striped jacket, brown background. d, Wearing brown shirt, red brown background. e, Wearing gray suit, yellow orange background. f, Wearing gray suit, blue gray background.

2008, June 12 ***Perf. 13¼***
771 A269 75c Sheet of 6, #a-f 9.00 9.00

Miniature Sheet

Members of Phoenix Suns Basketball Team — A270

No. 772 — Emblem of National Basketball Association and: a, Amare Stodemire. b, Boris Diaw. c, Brian Skinner. d, D. J. Strawberry. e, Shaquille O'Neal. f, Grant Hill. g, Leandro Barbosa. h, Raja Bell. i, Steve Nash.

2008, June 19
772 A270 42c Sheet of 9, #a-i 7.75 7.75

Miniature Sheet

Royal Air Force, 90th Anniv. — A271

No. 773 — Aircraft: a, Tornado. b, Harrier. c, Typhoon. d, Hawk.

2008, May 6 Litho. ***Perf. 13¼***
773 A271 90c Sheet of 4, #a-d 7.25 7.25

Miniature Sheet

Visit of Pope Benedict XVI to United States — A272

No. 774 — Pope Benedict XVI and one quarter of Papal arms at: a, LR. b, LL. c, UR. d, UL.

2008, Sept. 9 ***Perf. 13¼***
774 A272 94c Sheet of 4, #a-d 7.75 7.75

Miniature Sheets

A273

Muhammad Ali, Boxer — A274

No. 775 — Ali: a, Wearing protective headgear. b, Receiving adjustment of headgear. c, Looking right. d, In boxing ring, looking right. e, In boxing ring, looking left. f, With trainer, looking at hands.

No. 776 — Ali fighting: a, Throwing left jab. b, Ready to deliver punch. c, With hands in front of his chest. d, With opponent's punch missing.

2008, Sept. 9 ***Perf. 11½x11¼***
775 A273 75c Sheet of 6, #a-f 9.00 9.00

Perf. 13¼

776 A274 94c Sheet of 4, #a-d 7.75 7.75

Star Trek — A275

No. 777: a, U.S.S. Enterprise. b, Mr. Spock and woman. c, Captain Kirk. d, Uhura and Chekov. e, Starbase 11. f, Dr. McCoy and Mr. Spock.

No. 778: a, Scotty. b, Captain Kirk. c, Dr. McCoy and Uhura. d, Chekov.

2008, Sept. 9 ***Perf. 12x11½***
777 A275 75c Sheet of 6, #a-f 9.00 9.00

Perf. 13¼

778 A275 94c Sheet of 4, #a-d 7.75 7.75

No. 778 contains four 38x60mm stamps.

Christmas A276

Ornaments: 22c, Angel. 27c, Snowflake. 42c, Cross. 94c, Angel, diff.

2008, Sept. 9 ***Perf. 14x14¾***
779-782 A276 Set of 4 3.75 3.75

Famous Men — A277

No. 783: a, Ioanis Artui, Palikiri chief. b, Dr. Eluel K. Pretrick, Human Resources Secretary.

2008, Oct. 17 ***Perf. 13¼***
783 A277 94c Pair, #a-b 3.75 3.75

Miniature Sheet

Inauguration of US Pres. Barack Obama — A278

No. 784: a, 42c, Obama facing right. b, 42c, Obama facing left, one side of shirt collar showing. c, 42c, Obama facing left, both sides of shirt collar showing. d, 75c, As "c." e, 75c, As "b." f, 75c, As "a."

2009, Jan. 20 Litho. *Perf. 11½*

784	A278	Sheet of 6, #a-f	7.25	7.25

Miniature Sheet

Marilyn Monroe (1926-62), Actress — A279

No. 785: a, Monroe in dressing gown. b, Head of Monroe. c, Monroe in lilac sweater. d, Monroe in automobile.

2009, Jan. 22

785	A279	94c Sheet of 4, #a-d	7.75	7.75

Surfing — A280

Ocean waves and various surfers. Waves only on 20c, 22c, 59c, 83c.

2009, Jan. 26 *Perf. 14x14¾*

786	A280	1c	multi	.25	.25
787	A280	2c	multi	.25	.25
788	A280	17c	multi	.35	.35
789	A280	20c	multi	.40	.40
790	A280	22c	multi	.45	.45
791	A280	27c	multi	.55	.55
792	A280	42c	multi	.85	.85
793	A280	59c	multi	1.25	1.25
794	A280	72c	multi	1.50	1.50
795	A280	83c	multi	1.75	1.75
796	A280	94c	multi	1.90	1.90
797	A280	$1.17	multi	2.40	2.40
798	A280	$4.80	multi	9.75	9.75
799	A280	$16.50	multi	33.00	33.00
	Nos. 786-799 (14)			54.65	54.65

Miniature Sheet

New Year 2009 (Year of the Ox) — A281

No. 800: a, Denomination next to yellow arc, three leaves at top. b, Denomination even with yellow curlicues, two tan arcs going beneath denomination. c, Denomination next to yellow arc, one leaf between yellow and pink curlicues at top. d, Denomination even with yellow curlicues, tip of brown leaf touching "9" in denomination.

2009, Jan. 26 *Perf. 11½*

800	A281	94c Sheet of 4, #a-d	7.75	7.75

Peonies A282

2009, Apr. 10 *Perf. 13¼*

801	A282	42c multi	.85	.85

Printed in sheets of 6.

Miniature Sheets

A283

China 2009 World Stamp Exhibition — A284

No. 802 — Olympic sports: a, Triathlon. b, Diving. c, Equestrian. d, Table tennis.

No. 803 — Tang Dynasty art: a, Portrait of Emperor Taizong (Li Shih-min). b, Portrait of Emperor Taizong and his subjects. c, Calligraphy of Emperor Taizong. d, Mural of Emperor Taizong, Dunhuang.

2009, Apr. 10 *Perf. 12*

802	A283	59c Sheet of 4, #a-d	4.75	4.75
803	A284	59c Sheet of 4, #a-d	4.75	4.75

Souvenir Sheets

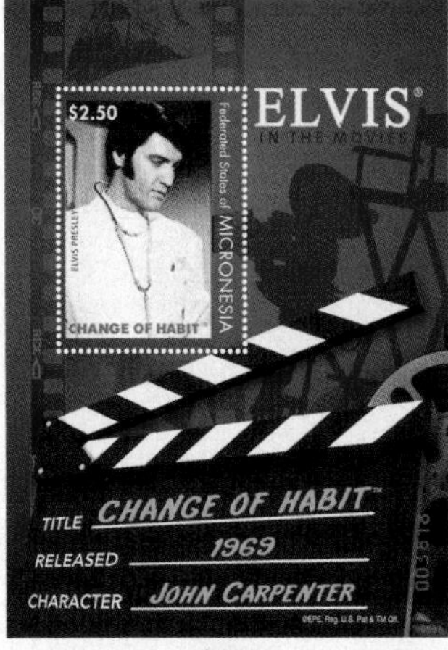

A285

A286

A287

Elvis Presley (1935-77) — A288

2009, June 10 *Perf. 13¼*

804	A285	$2.50 multi	5.00	5.00
805	A286	$2.50 multi	5.00	5.00
806	A287	$2.50 multi	5.00	5.00
807	A288	$2.50 multi	5.00	5.00
	Nos. 804-807 (4)		20.00	20.00

Miniature Sheets

A289

Michael Jackson (1958-2009) — A290

No. 808 — Shirt color: a, 28c, Yellow. b, 28c, Black. c, 75c, Yellow. d, 75c, Black.

No. 809 — Shirt color: a, 28c, Tan. b, 28c, White. c, 75c, Tan. d, 75c, White.

2009, July 7 Litho. *Perf. 13¼x13*

808	A289	Sheet of 4, #a-d	4.25	4.25
809	A290	Sheet of 4, #a-d	4.25	4.25

Miniature Sheets

A291

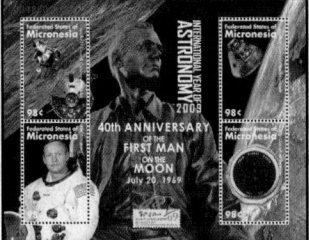

First Man on the Moon, 40th Anniv. — A292

No. 810: a, Apollo 11 lift-off. b, Neil Armstrong in space. c, Bust of Armstrong by Paula Slater. d, Apollo 11 Command Module. e, Apollo 11 Lunar Module. f, Buzz Aldrin on moon.

No. 811: a, Apollo 11 Lunar and Command Modules. b, Apollo 11 Command Module. c, Armstrong. d, Silicon disc left on Moon.

2009, July 20 *Perf. 13¼*

810 A291 75c Sheet of 6, #a-f 9.00 9.00
811 A292 98c Sheet of 4, #a-d 8.00 8.00

Butterflies A293

Designs: 28c, Great orange tip. 44c, Red pierrot. 98c, Plains cupid. $1.05, Blue admiral.

No. 816: a, Tree nymph sinharaja. b, Great Mormon. c, Blue Mormon. d, Tailed jay. e, Gladeye bushbrown. f, Ceylon rose.

2009, Sept. 4 *Perf. 12*

812-815 A293 Set of 4 5.50 5.50
816 A293 75c Sheet of 6, #a-f 9.00 9.00

Fish A294

Designs: 22c, Powder blue surgeon. 28c, Maroon clownfish. 61c, Flame angelfish. 78c, Moon wrasse. $1.24, Regal angelfish. $2.30, Firefish.

No. 823: a, Clown triggerfish. b, Wreckfish. c, Purple firefish. d, Regal tang.

2009, Sept. 4

817-822 A294 Set of 6 11.00 11.00
823 A294 94c Sheet of 4, #a-d 7.75 7.75

A295

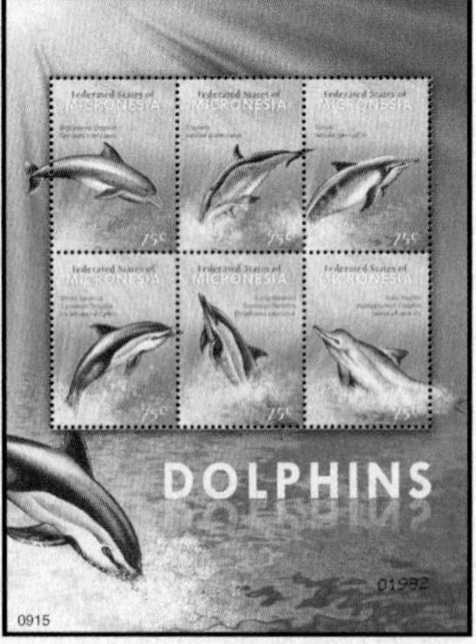

Dolphins — A296

Designs: 22c, Indo-Pacific bottlenose dolphin. 88c, Chinese white dolphin. 95c, Southern right whale dolphin. $2.80, Northern right whale dolphin.

No. 828: a, Bottlenose dolphin. b, Costero. c, Tucuxi. d, Short-beaked common dolphin. e, Long-beaked common dolphin. f, Indo-Pacific humpbacked dolphin.

2009, Sept. 4

824-827 A295 Set of 4 9.75 9.75
828 A296 75c Sheet of 6, #a-f 9.00 9.00

A297

Shells — A298

Designs: 22c, Clea nigericans. 79c, Achatina fulica. $1.39, Pomacea canaliculata. $1.56, Cyclophorus diplochilus.

No. 833: a, Thais bitubercularis. b, Conus caracteristicus. c, Amphidromus glaucolarynx. d, Anadara pilula. e, Cypraea erronea pyriformis. f, Thais aculeata.

2009, Sept. 4

829-832 A297 Set of 4 8.00 8.00
833 A298 75c Sheet of 6, #a-f 9.00 9.00

Corals A299

Designs: 27c, Flat leather coral. 55c, Strawberry coral. 83c, Discosoma sp. 3. $1.44, Porous lettuce coral.

No. 838, vert.: a, Lobophytum sp. 1. b, Nara nematifera. c, Leuconia palaoensis. d, Dendronephthya sp. 1.

No. 839, vert.: a, Sarcophyton sp. 1. b, Echinopora lamellosa.

2009, Sept. 24 *Perf. 14¾x14*

834-837 A299 Set of 4 5.75 5.75

Perf. 14x14¾

838 A299 98c Sheet of 4, #a-d 8.00 8.00

Souvenir Sheet

839 A299 98c Sheet of 2, #a-b 4.00 4.00

Miniature Sheet

Pres. Abraham Lincoln (1809-65) — A300

No. 840 — Photographs of Lincoln: a, Without beard. b, With beard, top of head not showing. c, With beard, looking right. d, With beard, profile.

2009, Oct. 16 *Perf. 13¼*

840 A300 98c Sheet of 4, #a-d 8.00 8.00

Chinese Aviation, Cent. — A301

No. 841 — Airplanes: a, CJ-5. b, CJ-6. c, JJ-5. d, JJ-6.

$2, JL-8.

2009, Nov. 12 **Litho.** *Perf. 14¼*

841 A301 75c Sheet of 4, #a-d 6.00 6.00

Souvenir Sheet

842 A301 $2 multi 4.00 4.00

No. 841 contains four 42x28mm stamps. Aeropex 2009 Philatelic Exhibition, Beijing.

Christmas A302

Designs: 22c, Santa Claus and palm tree. 44c, Christmas ornaments. 98c, Christmas stocking. $4.80, Decorated Christmas tree.

2009, Nov. 30 *Perf. 14x14¾*

843-846 A302 Set of 4 13.00 13.00

Miniature Sheet

Visit of Pope Benedict XVI to Czech Republic — A303

No. 847: a, Pope and Czech Pres. Vaclav Klaus. b, Pope in red vestments. c, Pope and Miroslav Cardinal Vlk. d, Pope in green vestments.

2009, Dec. 2 *Perf. 13x13¼*

847 A303 98c Sheet of 4, #a-d 8.00 8.00

Worldwide Fund for Nature (WWF) — A304

No. 848 — Mandarinfish: a, Male. b, Female. c, Unspecified gender. d, Unspecified gender, diff.

2009, Dec. 2 *Perf. 13½*

848 Block or strip of 4 4.25 4.25
a. A304 28c orange & multi .60 .60
b. A304 35c yellow & multi .70 .70
c. A304 44c green & multi .90 .90
d. A304 98c blue & multi 2.00 2.00
e. Sheet of 8, 2 each #848a-848d 8.50 8.50

Turtles A305

Designs: 22c, Hawksbill turtle. 88c, Australian flatback turtle. 95c, Loggerhead turtle. $2.80, Green sea turtle.

No. 853: a, Kemp's ridley turtle. b, Leatherback turtle. c, Loggerhead turtle, diff. d, Olive ridley turtle.

No. 854: a, Green sea turtle, diff. b, Hawksbill turtle, diff.

2009, Sept. 4 **Litho.** *Perf. 14¾x14*

849-852 A305 Set of 4 9.75 9.75
853 A305 98c Sheet of 4, #a-d 8.00 8.00

Souvenir Sheet

854 A305 $1.56 Sheet of 2, #a-b 6.25 6.25

Birds — A306

Designs: 28c, Brown booby. 44c, Sacred kingfisher. 98c, White-face heron. $1.05, Rainbow lorikeet.

No. 859, horiz.: a, Brandt's cormorant. b, Red-footed booby. c, Beach thick-knee. d, Common noddy.

No. 860, horiz.: a, Blue-footed booby. b, Australian pelican.

2009, Sept. 4 *Perf. 14x14¾*

855-858 A306 Set of 4 5.50 5.50

Perf. 14¾x14

859 A306 98c Sheet of 4, #a-d 8.00 8.00

Souvenir Sheet

860 A306 $1.56 Sheet of 2, #a-b 6.25 6.25

A306a

A306b

A306c

A306d

A306e

A306f

A306g

Diplomatic Relations Between Micronesia and People's Republic of China, 20th Anniv. — A306h

2009 Litho. *Perf. 12*

860C	A306a	44c multi	—	
860D	A306b	44c multi	—	
860E	A306c	44c multi	—	
860F	A306d	44c multi	—	
860G	A306e	44c multi	—	
860H	A306f	44c multi	—	
860I	A306g	44c multi	—	
860J	A306h	44c multi	—	
k.	Block of 8, #860C-860J		—	—

Litho. Affixed to 3-Dimensional Plastic

Souvenir Sheet

Without Gum

860L	Sheet of 2, #860I-860m	—	—
m.	A306c 44c multi	—	—
n.	A306b 44c multi	—	—

Miniature Sheet

Chinese Zodiac Animals — A307

No. 861: a, Rat. b, Ox. c, Tiger. d, Rabbit. e, Dragon. f, Snake. g, Horse. h, Ram. i, Monkey. j, Cock. k, Dog. l, Pig.

2010, Jan. 4 *Perf. 13¼*

861 A307 22c Sheet of 12, #a-l 5.50 5.50

Souvenir Sheet

New Year 2010 (Year of the Tiger) — A308

No. 862: a, Tiger. b, Chinese character for "tiger."

2010, Jan. 4 *Perf. 11½*

862 A308 $2 Sheet of 2, #a-b 8.00 8.00

Miniature Sheet

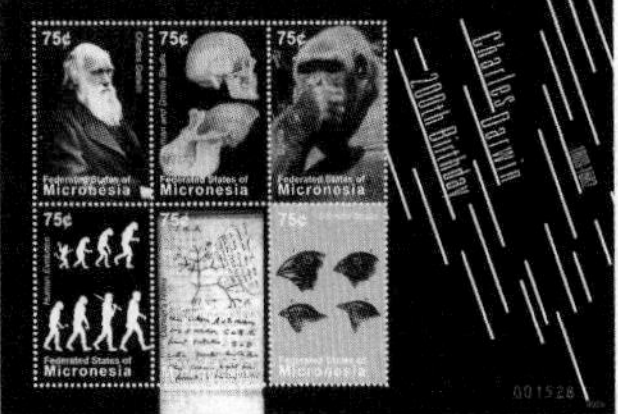

Charles Darwin (1809-82), Naturalist — A309

No. 863: a, Photograph of Darwin. b, Human and gorilla skulls. c, Gorilla. d, Human evolution. e, Darwin's notes. f, Darwin's drawings of finch beaks.

2010, Feb. 17 *Perf. 13¼*

863 A309 75c Sheet of 6, #a-f 9.00 9.00

Miniature Sheet

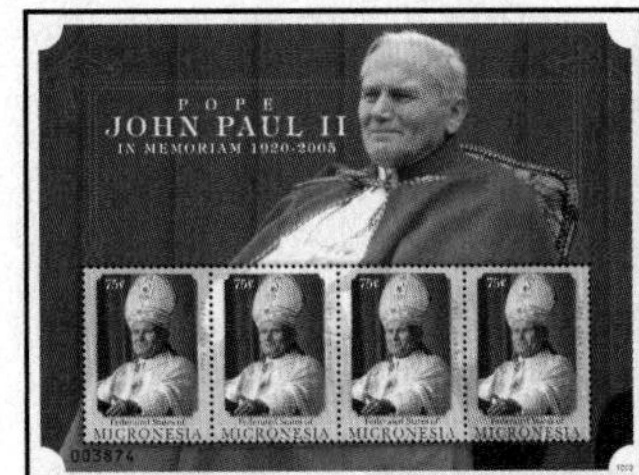

Pope John Paul II (1920-2005) — A310

No. 864 — Pope John Paul II with: a, Faint vertical line at left, white area at right. b, White area at left and top. c, White area at UL corner and at left, gray area at right. d, Gray area at left and bottom, faint vertical line at right.

2010, Apr. 23 *Perf. 11½*

864 A310 75c Sheet of 4, #a-d 6.00 6.00

A311

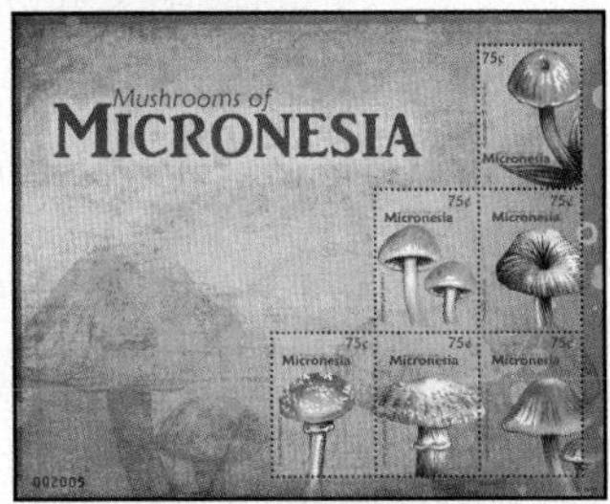

Mushrooms — A312

Designs: 28c, Galerina decipiens. 44c, Amanita pekeoides. 75c, Rhodocollybia laulaha. 98c, Amanita nothofagi.

No. 869: a, Hygrocybe aff. minutula. b, Hygrocybe pakelo. c, Amanita nehuta. d, Amanita muscaria. e, Amanita australis. f, Hygrocybe constrictospora.

2010, June 8 *Perf. 11½*

865-868 A311 Set of 4 5.00 5.00

Perf. 12x11½

869 A312 75c Sheet of 6, #a-f 9.00 9.00

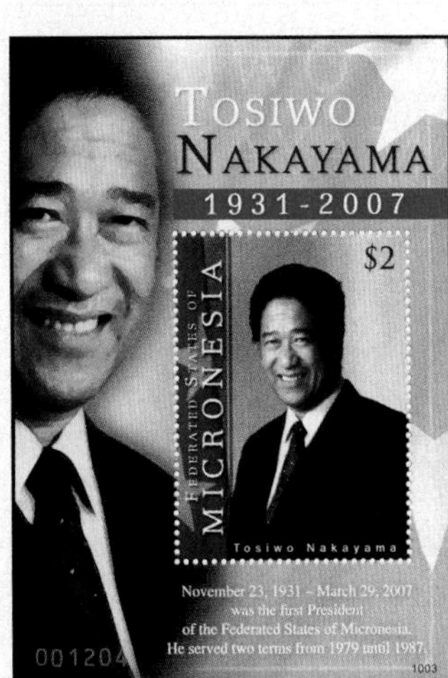

Pres. Tosiwo Nakayama (1931-2007) — A313

No. 870 — Photos of Pres. Nakayama: a, On Saipan, 1970. b, In Washington, DC, 1986. c, On Pohnpei, 1970. d, On Saipan, 1975.
$2, Color photograph.

2010, June 8 *Perf. 11½*

870 A313 80c Sheet of 4, #a-d 6.50 6.50

Souvenir Sheet

Perf. 13½

871 A313 $2 multi 4.00 4.00

No. 870 contains four 30x40mm stamps.

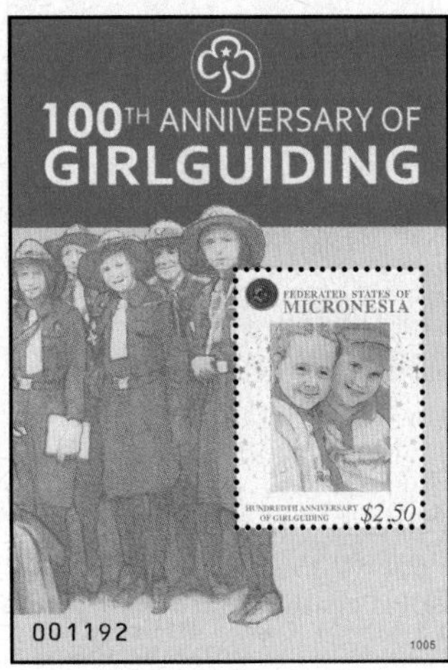

Girl Guides, Cent. — A314

No. 872, horiz.: a, Two Girl Guides holding hands. b, Two Girl Guides with yellow neckerchiefs. c, Three Girl Guides with balloons. d, Three Girl Guides writing.
$2.50, Two Rainbows.

2010, June 8 *Perf. 11½x12*

872 A314 94c Sheet of 4, #a-d 7.75 7.75

Souvenir Sheet

Perf. 11½

873 A314 $2.50 multi 5.00 5.00

Flowers and Fruit — A315

Designs: 1c, Bougainvillea. 2c, Yellow plumeria. 4c, White ginger. 5c, Guettardia speciosa. 10c, Mangat bananas. 19c, Akadahn Weitahta bananas. 20c, Peleu bananas. 22c, Three unopened coconuts. 28c, Utin Kerenis bananas. 40c, Unopened coconut. 44c, Opened coconut. 70c, Coconut out of shell. $1, Opened and unopened coconuts. $3.85, Opened coconut, diff. $4.60, Soursop. $4.80, Partially opened soursop.

2010, June 18 *Perf. 13¼*

874	A315	1c multi	.25	.25
875	A315	2c multi	.25	.25
876	A315	4c multi	.25	.25
877	A315	5c multi	.25	.25
878	A315	10c multi	.25	.25
879	A315	19c multi	.40	.40
880	A315	20c multi	.40	.40
881	A315	22c multi	.45	.45
882	A315	28c multi	.60	.60
883	A315	40c multi	.80	.80
884	A315	44c multi	.90	.90
885	A315	70c multi	1.40	1.40
886	A315	$1 multi	2.00	2.00
887	A315	$3.85 multi	7.75	7.75
888	A315	$4.60 multi	9.25	9.25
889	A315	$4.80 multi	9.75	9.75
		Nos. 874-889 (16)	34.95	34.95

Miniature Sheet

British Monarchs — A316

No. 890: a, Queen Anne. b, King George I. c, King George II. d, King George III. e, King George IV. f, King George V.

2010, Aug. 26 *Perf. 11½*

890 A316 75c Sheet of 6, #a-f 9.00 9.00

Miniature Sheet

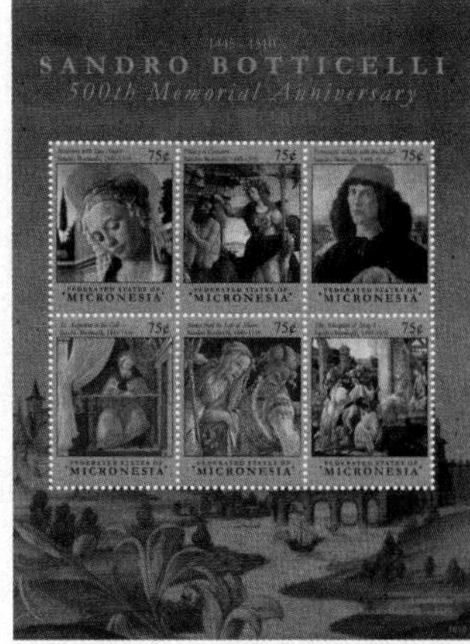

Paintings by Sandro Botticelli (1445-1510) — A317

No. 891: a, Madonna and Two Angels. b, Pallas and the Centaur. c, Portrait of a Man with the Medal. d, St. Augustine in His Cell. e, Scenes from the Life of Moses. f, Adoration of the Magi.

2010, Aug. 26 Litho.

891 A317 75c Sheet of 6, #a-f 9.00 9.00

Henri Dunant (1828-1910), Founder of the Red Cross — A318

No. 892 — Various depictions of the Battle of Solferino and Dunant's photograph in: a, Gray green. b, Brown. c, Red violet. d, Gray blue.
$2.50, Violet.

2010, Aug. 26 *Perf. 11½x12*

892 A318 94c Sheet of 4, #a-d 7.75 7.75

Souvenir Sheet

Perf. 11½

893 A318 $2.50 multi 5.00 5.00

Miniature Sheet

Princess Diana (1961-97) — A319

No. 894 — Princess Diana: a, In beige dress, embracing child. b, In plaid suit, meeting child. c, In blue green suit, meeting child. d, In pink suit.

2010, Aug. 26 Litho. *Perf. 12x11½*
894 A319 75c Sheet of 4, #a-d 6.00 6.00

Souvenir Sheet

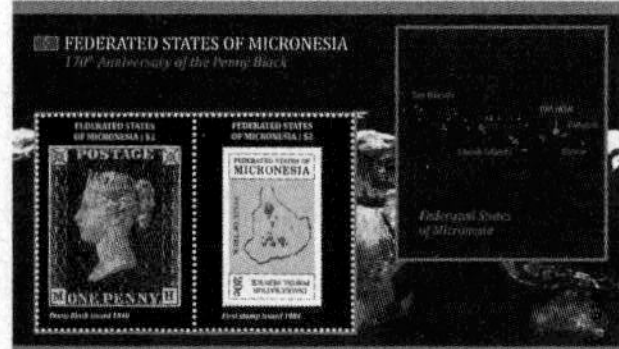

Issuance of the Penny Black, 170th Anniv. — A320

No. 895: a, Great Britain #1. b, Micronesia #2.

2010, Oct. 6 *Perf. 13x13¼*
895 A320 $2 Sheet of 2, #a-b 8.00 8.00

Christmas A321

Paintings: 22c, Adoration of the Magi, by Corrado Giaquinto. 28c, Polyptych with the Nativity, by Rogier van der Weiden. 44c, The Nativity, by Federico Barocci. 98c, The Newborn Christ, by Georges de La Tour. $4.95, The Flight into Egypt, by Giotto di Bondone.

2010, Nov. 1 *Perf. 13¼x13*
896-900 A321 Set of 5 14.00 14.00

Pope John Paul II (1920-2005) A322

2010, Dec. 16 *Perf. 12*
901 A322 75c multi 1.50 1.50

Printed in sheets of 4.

Miniature Sheet

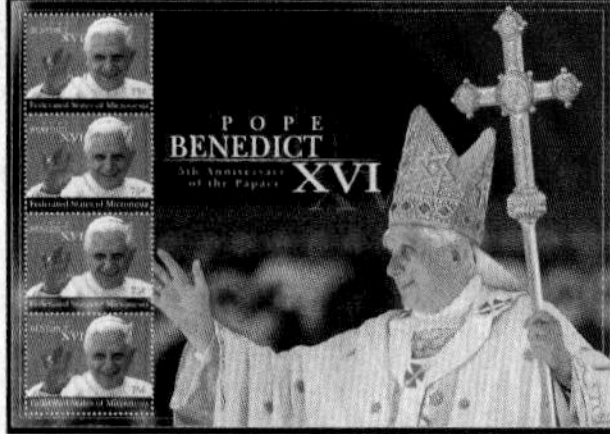

Pope Benedict XVI — A323

No. 902 — Pope Benedict XVI with lower panel: a, In solid black. b, In black and dark gray at LR. c, In brown and black with "d" over black area, finger partially visible at right. d, In brown and black with "of" over black area.

2010, Dec. 16
902 A323 75c Sheet of 4, #a-d 6.00 6.00

Miniature Sheet

Pres. Abraham Lincoln (1809-65) — A324

No. 903 — Lincoln: a, Giving Gettysburg Address. b, With wife, Mary. c, Reading draft of the Emancipation Proclamation. d, Meeting General George McClellan in tent at Antietam.

2010, Dec. 16 *Perf. 12½x12*
903 A324 75c Sheet of 4, #a-d 6.00 6.00

Miniature Sheets

2010 World Cup Soccer Championships, South Africa — A325

No. 904, 61c: a, Dani Alves. b, Dirk Kuyt. c, Lucio. d, Gregory Van Der Wiel. e, Robinho. f, Mark Van Bommel.

No. 905, 61c: a, Diego Perez. b, Isaac Vorsah. c, Egidio Arevalo. d, Kevin-Prince Boateng. e, Luis Suarez. f, Kwadwo Asamoah.

2010, Dec. 30 Litho. *Perf. 12*
Sheets of 6, #a-f
904-905 A325 Set of 2 15.00 15.00

Souvenir Sheet

New Year 2011 (Year of the Rabbit) — A326

2011, Jan. 27
906 A326 Sheet of 2 #906a 6.00 6.00
a. $1.50 Single stamp 3.00 3.00

Miniature Sheet

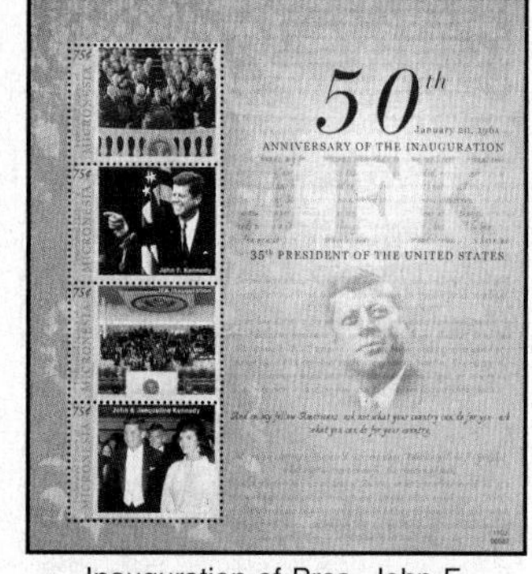

Inauguration of Pres. John F. Kennedy, 50th Anniv. — A327

No. 907: a, Kennedy taking oath. b, Kennedy pointing. c, Kennedy on reviewing stand. d, Kennedy with wife, Jacqueline.

2011, Jan. 27
907 A327 75c Sheet of 4, #a-d 6.00 6.00

Miniature Sheet

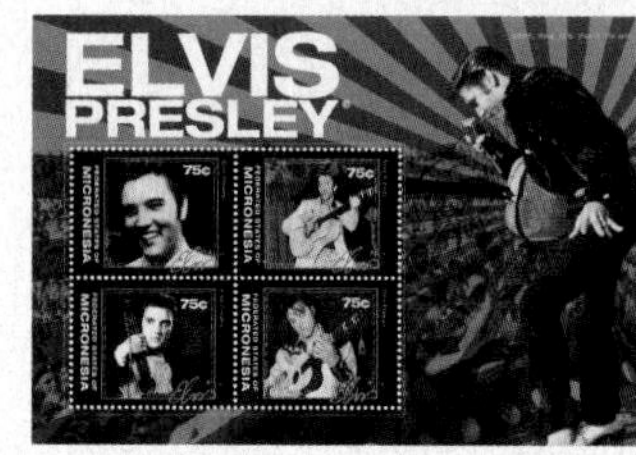

Elvis Presley (1935-77) — A328

No. 908 — Presley: a, Without guitar. b, Playing guitar, wearing jacket with plain shoulders. c, Holding guitar. d, Playing guitar, wearing shirt with decorated shoulders.

2011, Jan. 27
908 A328 75c Sheet of 4, #a-d 6.00 6.00

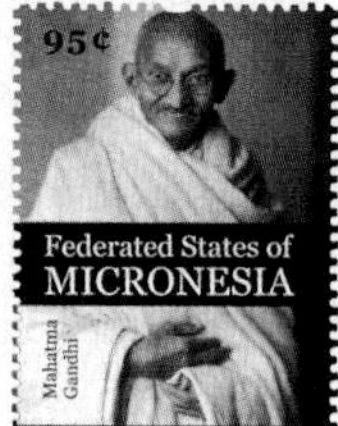

Mohandas K. Gandhi (1869-1948) A329

2011, Jan. 27 *Perf. 13 Syncopated*
909 A329 95c shown 1.90 1.90

Souvenir Sheet

910 A329 $2.50 Gandhi, horiz. 5.00 5.00

Indipex 2011, New Delhi (No. 910). No. 909 was printed in sheets of four.

A330

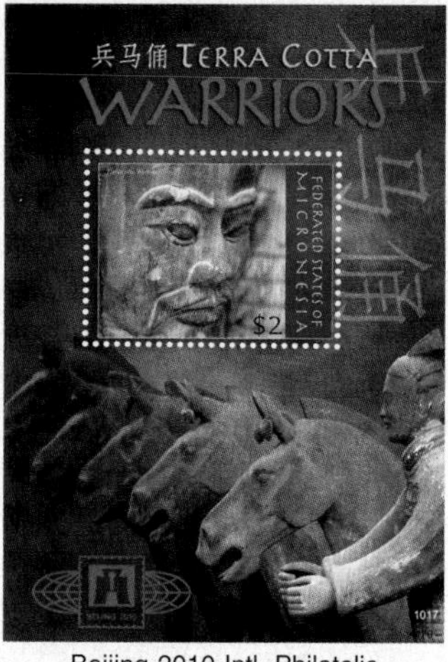

Beijing 2010 Intl. Philatelic Exhibition — A331

No. 911 — Three Gorges Dam and: a, Reservoir, denomination in red. b, Fountain, denomination in white. c, Denomination in black. d, Boats, denomination in white.
$2, Face of terra cotta warrior, Xi'an.

2011, Jan. 27 *Perf. 12*
911 A330 75c Sheet of 4, #a-d 6.00 6.00

Souvenir Sheet

912 A331 $2 multi 4.00 4.00

Engagement of Prince William and Catherine Middleton — A332

No. 913: a, Royal arms of the United Kingdom, blue background. b, Arms of Prince William of Wales, blue background. c, Couple, Middleton without hat.

No. 914: a, Royal arms of the Untied Kingdom, brown background. b, Arms of Prince William of Wales, brown background. c, Couple, Middleton with hat.

No. 915, $1.50: a, Couple. b, Royal arms of the Untied Kingdom.

No. 916, $1.50: a, Arms of Prince William of Wales. b, Prince William.

2011, Jan. 27 *Perf. 13 Syncopated*
913 A332 94c Sheet of 4, #913a-913b, 2 #913c 7.75 7.75
914 A332 94c Sheet of 4, #914a-914b, 2 #914c 7.75 7.75

Souvenir Sheets of 2, #a-b

915-916 A332 Set of 2 12.00 12.00

Miniature Sheets

A333

A334

Travels of U.S. Pres. Barack Obama — A335

No. 917 — Pres. Obama at United Nations General Assembly with: a, Viet Nam Pres. Nguyen Minh Triet, Philippines Pres. Benigno Aquino III. b, Azerbaijan Pres. Ilham Aliyev. c, Colombia Pres. Juan Manuel Santos Calderón. d, Kyrgyzstan Pres. Roza Otunbayeva.

No. 918 — Pictures from 2010 G20 Summit in Seoul: a, Pres. Obama waving. b, Pres. Obama with France Pres. Nicolas Sarkozy. c, Pres. Obama with South Korea Pres. Lee Myung-bak. d, Pres. Obama with Russia Pres. Dmitry Medvedev.

No. 919 — Pictures from 2010 G20 Summit: a, Pres. Obama facign right. b, South Korea Pres. Lee. c, Pres. Obama and others holding certificate. d, Pres. Obama at lectern, flags in background.

2011, Jan. 27 Litho. *Perf. 12*

917 A333 75c Sheet of 4, #a-d 6.00 6.00
918 A334 75c Sheet of 4, #a-d 6.00 6.00

Perf. 13 Syncopated

919 A335 75c Sheet of 4, #a-d 6.00 6.00
Nos. 917-919 (3) 18.00 18.00

Miniature Sheet

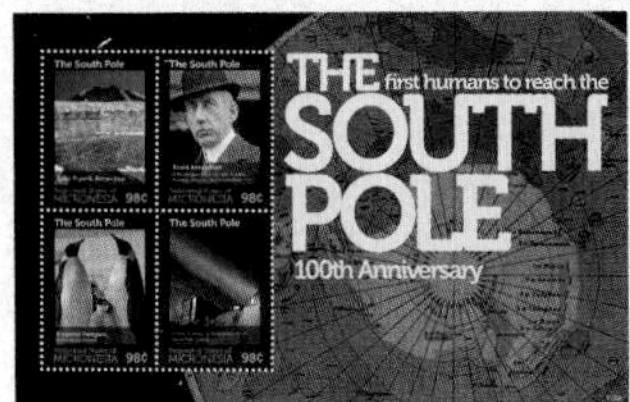

Roald Amundsen's Expedition to the South Pole, Cent. — A336

No. 920: a, Lake Fryxell, Antarctica. b, Amundsen. c, Emperor penguins. d, Aurora Australis at Amundsen-Scott South Pole Station.

2011, Apr. 6 *Perf. 12*

920 A336 98c Sheet of 4, #a-d 8.00 8.00

Miniature Sheets

U.S. Civil War, 150th Anniv. — A337

No. 921, 98c — Eagle, shield, Union and Confederate flags, Commodore George N. Hollins and Capatin John Pope from Battle of the Head of Passes, Oct. 12, 1861, and: a, The CSS Manassas attacks the USS Richmond. b, USS Richmond. c, CSS Manassas. d, USS Water Witch.

No. 922, 98c — Eagle, shield, Union and Confederate flags, Colonel Nathan G. Evans and General Charles F. Stone from Battle of Ball's Bluff, Oct. 21, 1861, and: a, General Stone's forces at Ball's Bluff. b, Union artillery fires shells across Potomac River. c, Battle map of Ball's Bluff. d, Death of Col. Edward D. Baker.

2011, Apr. 6 *Perf. 13 Syncopated*
Sheets of 4, #a-d

921-922 A337 Set of 2 16.00 16.00

U.S. Pres. Abraham Lincoln (1809-65) A338

2011, Apr. 6 *Perf. 13 Syncopated*

923 A338 75c shown 1.50 1.50

Souvenir Sheet
Perf. 12½

924 A338 $2.50 Lincoln, diff. 5.00 5.00

No. 923 was printed in sheets of 4. No. 924 contains one 38x51mm stamp.

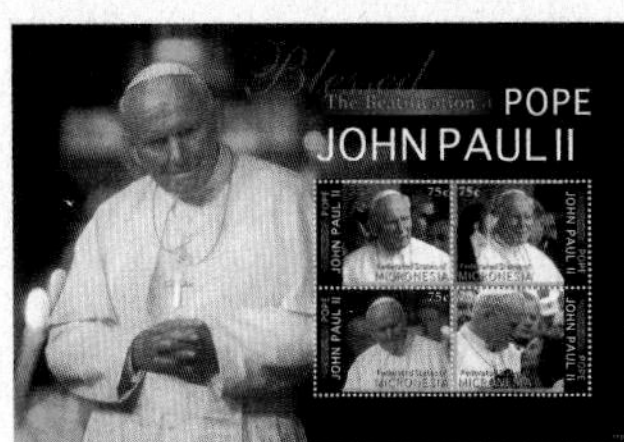

Beatification of Pope John Paul II — A339

No. 925 — Pope John Paul II: a, With archway in background at left. b, Waving. c, With man's head in background at left. d, Holding child.

$2.50, Pope John Paul II wearing miter, vert.

2011, Apr. 6 *Perf. 12*

925 A339 75c Sheet of 4, #a-d 6.00 6.00

Souvenir Sheet

926 A339 $2.50 multi 5.00 5.00

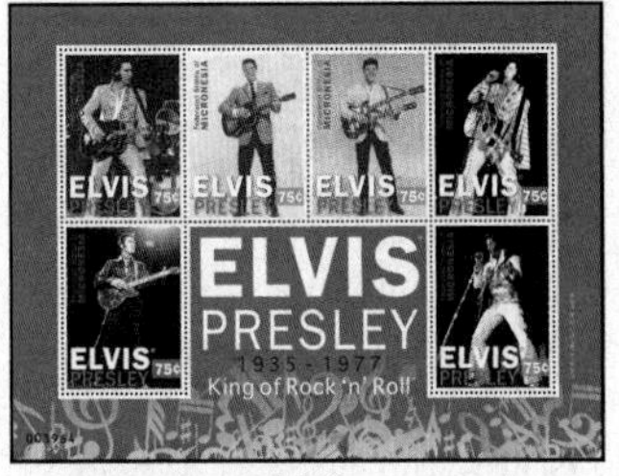

A340

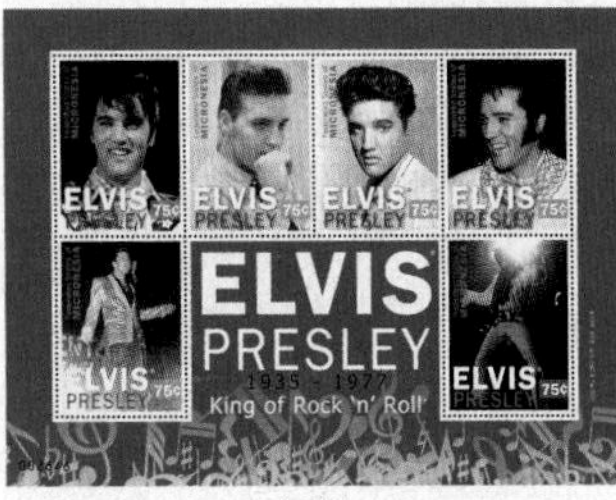

A341

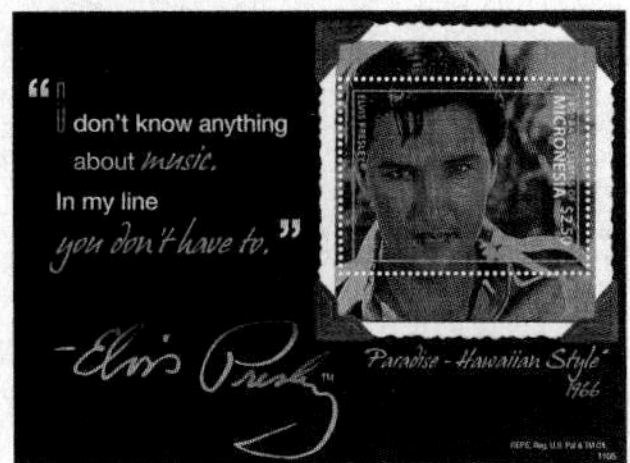

A342

A343

A344

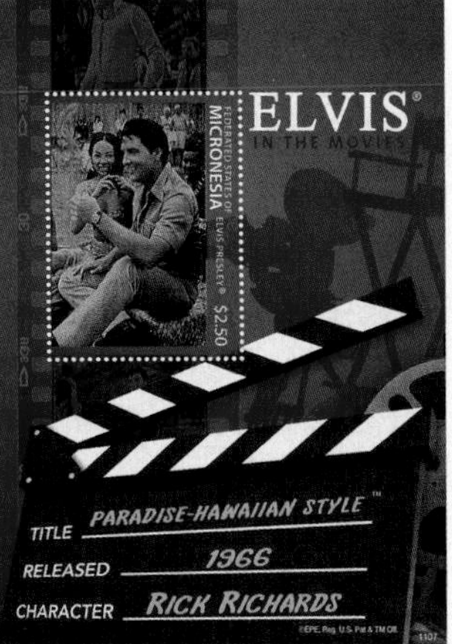

Elvis Presley (1935-77) — A345

No. 927 — Presley: a, With drums in background. b, Wearing suit with handkerchief in pocket. c, Playing double-necked guitar. d, Singing, holding microphone, wearing spotted and decorated jacket and pants. e, With red guitar. f, Singing, wearing decorated shirt and pants.

No. 928 — Presley: a, Wearing Western shirt with flower on shoulder. b, With hand in front of mouth. c, Wearing light-colored jacket. d, Wearing necklaces. e, Singing, with sign in background. f, With spotlight behind head.

2011 *Perf. 13½*

927 A340 75c Sheet of 6, #a-f 9.00 9.00
928 A341 75c Sheet of 6, #a-f 9.00 9.00

Souvenir Sheets
Perf. 12½

929 A342 $2.50 multi 5.00 5.00
930 A343 $2.50 multi 5.00 5.00
931 A344 $2.50 multi 5.00 5.00
932 A345 $2.50 multi 5.00 5.00
Nos. 929-932 (4) 20.00 20.00

Issued: Nos. 927-928, 5/16; Nos. 929-932, 4/6.

Wedding of Prince William and Catherine Middleton — A346

No. 933, 98c — Couple kissing with: a, Light gray design above denomination, white area to left of denomination. b, Dark gray design below and around denomination. c, Light gray design under and around denomination. d, White area under and around denomination.

No. 934, 98c: a, Groom, light gray design above denomination, white area to left of denomination. b, Bride, dark gray design under and around denomination. c, Groom, light gray design under and around denomination. d, Bride, white area under and around denomination.

$2.50, Couple, diff.

2011, Aug. 29 *Perf. 13 Syncopated*
Sheets of 4, #a-d

933-934 A346 Set of 2 16.00 16.00

Souvenir Sheet

935 A346 $2.50 multi 5.00 5.00

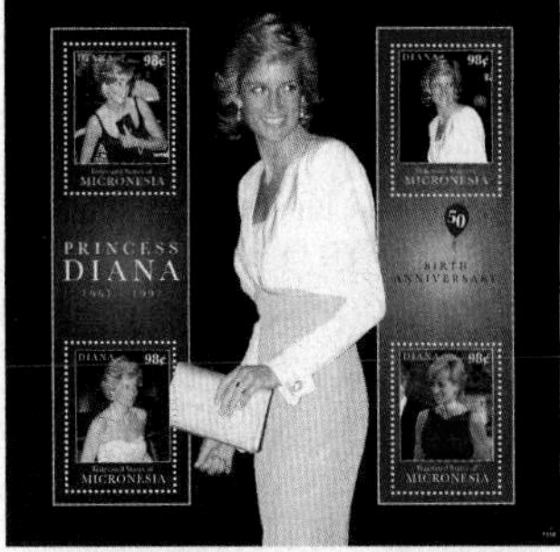

A347

Princess Diana (1961-97) — A348

No. 936 — Princess Diana wearing: a, Black dress, holding clutch purse. b, White blouse covering shoulders. c, Strapless white dress. d, Purple dress.

No. 937 — Princess Diana: a, As child, wearing red headband. b, Wearing black and white dress. c, Wearing red dress and hat. d, Wearing beige hat and beige checked jacket.

2011, July 14 *Perf. 12*

936 A347 98c Sheet of 4, #a-d 8.00 8.00
937 A348 98c Sheet of 4, #a-d 8.00 8.00

Reptiles — A349

No. 938: a, Stripe-necked turtle. b, Oceanic gecko. c, Tropical gecko. d, Four-clawed gecko. e, Mourning gecko.

No. 939: a, Marianas blue-tailed skink. b, Green sea turtle.

2011, July 14 **Litho.**

938 A349 50c Sheet of 5, #a-e 5.00 5.00

Souvenir Sheet

939 A349 $1.25 Sheet of 2, #a-b 5.00 5.00

September 11, 2011 Terrorist Attacks, 10th Anniv. — A350

No. 940 — American flag and: a, Silhouette of Pentagon Building. b, World Trade Center in black. c, World Trade Center in gray. d, Map of Stonycreek Township, Pennsylvalnia.

$2.50, World Trade Center, horiz.

2011, Sept. 9 ***Perf. 13¼x13***

940 A350 98c Sheet of 4, #a-d 8.00 8.00

Souvenir Sheet

Perf. 12

941 A350 $2.50 multi 5.00 5.00

Miniature Sheets

Japanese Team, Winners of 2011 Women's World Cup Soccer Tournament — A351

Finalists of 2011 Women's World Cup Soccer Tournament — A352

No. 942: a, Two women, woman at right wearing black headband. b, Woman wearing headband. c, Two women, woman at left wearing head bandage, woman at ridght wearing headband. d, Woman wearing yellow and black uniform. e, Woman in front of players wearing uniform numbers 10 and 7. f, Two women in front of player wearing uniform number 6. g, Woman in front of player wearing uniform number 17. h, Woman in front of woman wearing yellow and black uniform.

No. 943: a, Japan goalie Ayumi Kaihori. b, Team Japan. c, Team USA. d, USA goalie Hope Solo.

2011, Sept. 21 ***Perf. 13½x13***

942 A351 50c Sheet of 8, #a-h 8.00 8.00

Perf. 12x12½

943 A352 98c Sheet of 4, #a-d 8.00 8.00

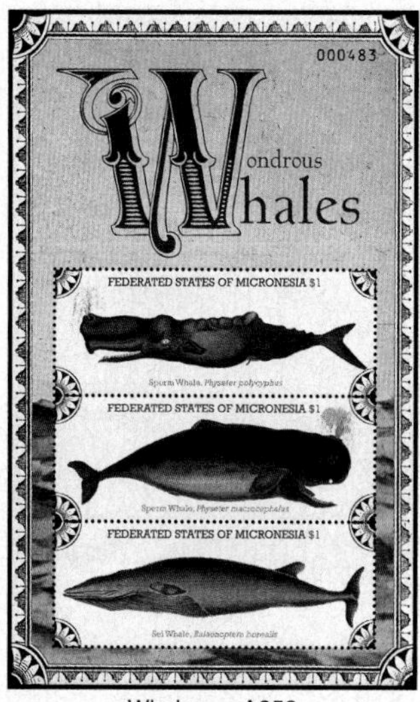

Whales — A353

No. 944: a, Physeter polycyphus. b, Physeter macrocephalus. c, Sei whale.

No. 945: a, Tail of sperm whale. b, Head of sperm whale.

2011, Sept. 21 ***Perf. 12½x12***

944 A353 $1 Sheet of 3, #a-c 6.00 6.00

Souvenir Sheet

Perf.

945 A353 $1.25 Sheet of 2, #a-b 5.00 5.00

No. 945 contains two 35mm diameter stamps.

A354

A355

Dr. Sun Yat-sen (1866-1925), President of Republic of China — A355a

No. 946: a, Blue background. b, Pink background.

No. 947: a, Denomination at UR. b, Denomination at UL.

No. 947C: a, Dr. Sun Yat-sen. b, Flag of Wuchang Uprising.

2011, Sept. 27 ***Perf. 13 Syncopated***

946 A354 63c Horiz. pair, #a-b 2.60 2.60

947 A355 63c Pair, #a-b 2.60 2.60

Souvenir Sheet

Imperf

Without Gum

947C A355a $2 Sheet of 2, #d-e 8.00 8.00

No. 946 was printed in sheets containing two pairs. No. 947 was printed in sheets containing three pairs.

Sharks — A356

No. 948: a, Sharpnose seven-gill shark. b, Basking shark. c, Porbeagle. d, Bluntnose six-gill shark.

$2.50, Sand tiger shark.

2011, Oct. 6 ***Perf. 13x13¼***

948 A356 75c Sheet of 4, #a-d 6.00 6.00

Souvenir Sheet

949 A356 $2.50 multi 5.00 5.00

Game Fish — A357

No. 950: a, Houndfish. b, Pacific agujon needlefish. c, Keeltail needlefish.

No. 951, $2.50, Swordfish. No. 952, $2.50, Rainbow runner.

2011, Oct. 6 ***Perf. 12***

950 A357 $1 Sheet of 3, #a-c 6.00 6.00

Souvenir Sheets

Perf. 13x13¼

951-952 A357 Set of 2 10.00 10.00

Christmas A358

Designs: 22c, Fish and sea anemone. 44c, Perfume flower tree branch. 98c, Palm tree. $4.95, Sea shell.

2011, Nov. 1 ***Perf. 12***

953-956 A358 Set of 4 13.50 13.50

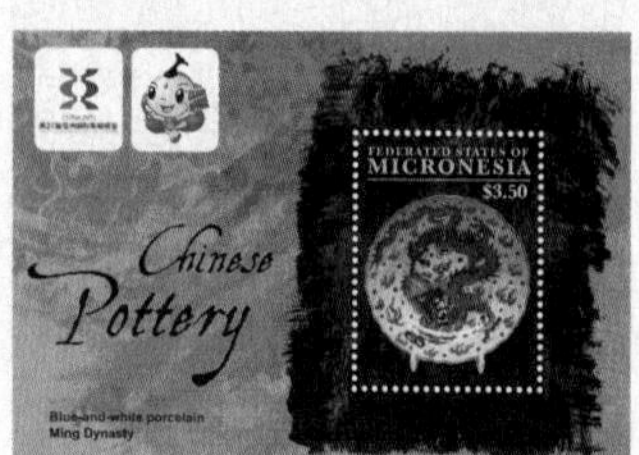

Chinese Pottery — A359

No. 957: a, Tang Dynasty ceramic offering plate with six eaves. b, Song Dynasty Celadon vase. c, Ming Dynasty porcelain plate. d, Qing Dynasty porcelain vase.

$2.50, Ming Dynasty blue and white porcelain plate.

2011, Nov. 7 ***Perf. 12***

957 A359 $1.25 Sheet of 4, #a-d 10.00 10.00

Souvenir Sheet

958 A359 $3.50 multi 7.00 7.00

Chinal 2011 Intl. Philatelic Exhibition, Wuxi.

New Year 2012 (Year of the Dragon) — A360

2011, Nov. 7 **Embroidered** ***Imperf.***

Self-Adhesive

959 A360 $8 red & yellow 16.00 16.00

Miniature Sheet

Peace Corps, 50th Anniv. — A361

No. 960 — Winning art in children's stamp design contest: a, People in canoe, by Arvin Helgenberger. b, People with sign, by Alex Alexander. c, Trees, people in canoe, and fish, by Ashly-Ann Alfons. d, Ship and flag, by Leonard Klingen.

2011, Nov. 15 **Litho.** ***Perf. 12½x12***

960 A361 44c Sheet of 4, #a-d 3.75 3.75

Erhart Aten (1932-2004), Governor of Chuuk State — A362

2011, Nov. 28 ***Perf. 11¼x11½***

961 A362 44c multi .90 .90

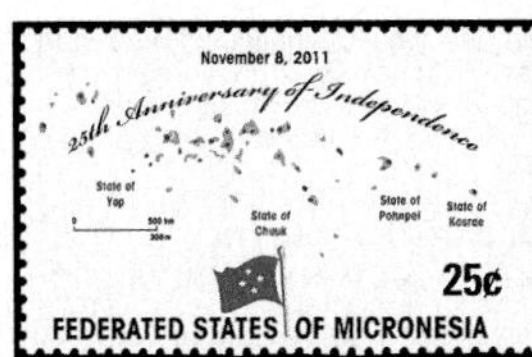

Independence, 25th Anniv. (in 2011) — A363

2012, Mar. 1 *Perf. 12*
962 A363 25c multi .50 .50

Pope Benedict XVI — A364

No. 963: a, Denomination at R. b, Denomination at L.
$3.50, Pope Benedict XVI, vert.

2012, Apr. 4 *Perf. 14*
963 A364 $1.25 Horiz. pair, #a-b 5.00 5.00

Souvenir Sheet
Perf. 12
964 A364 $3.50 multi 7.00 7.00

No. 963 was printed in sheets containing two pairs.

Pres. Ronald Reagan (1911-2004) A365

2012, Apr. 4 *Perf. 12*
965 A365 $1.25 shown 2.50 2.50

Souvenir Sheet
966 A365 $3.50 Reagan, diff. 7.00 7.00

No. 965 was printed in sheets of 4.

Reign of Queen Elizabeth II, 60th Anniv. — A366

No. 967 — Queen Elizabeth II wearing Army uniform in 1945: a, Wearing cap, looking right. b, Wearing cap, looking left. c, Without cap. d, Wearing cap, hands visible.
$3.50, Queen Elizabeth II wearing cap, vert.

2012, Apr. 4 *Perf. 13 Syncopated*
967 A366 $1.25 Sheet of 4, #a-d 10.00 10.00

Souvenir Sheet
968 A366 $3.50 multi 7.00 7.00

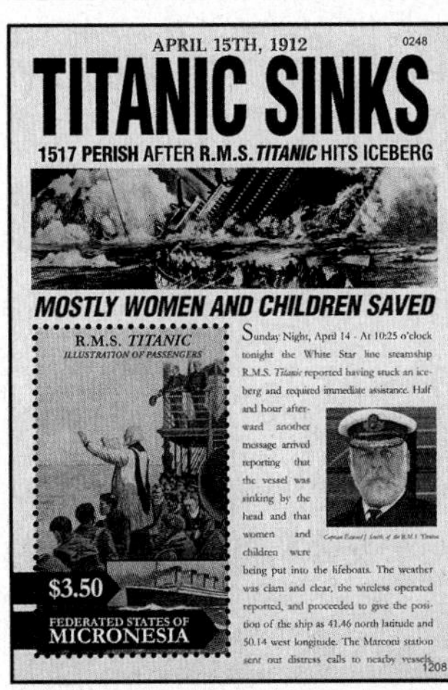

Sinking of the Titanic, Cent. — A367

No. 969, horiz.: a, Titanic sinking. b, People waiting for survivors. c, Last known photograph of the Titanic.
$3.50, Passengers on deck.

2012, Apr. 4 *Perf. 12*
969 A367 $1.25 Sheet of 3, #a-c 7.50 7.50

Souvenir Sheet
970 A367 $3.50 multi 7.00 7.00

Hindenburg Disaster, 75th Anniv. — A368

No. 971 — Hindenburg in color and: a, "D-LZ129" and Olympic rings on side of zeppelin. b, Name "Hindenburg" on side of zeppelin. c, Mooring mast.
$3.50, Hindenburg, diff.

2012, Apr. 4 *Perf. 13 Syncopated*
971 A368 $1.50 Sheet of 3, #a-c 9.00 9.00

Souvenir Sheet
972 A368 $3.50 multi 7.00 7.00

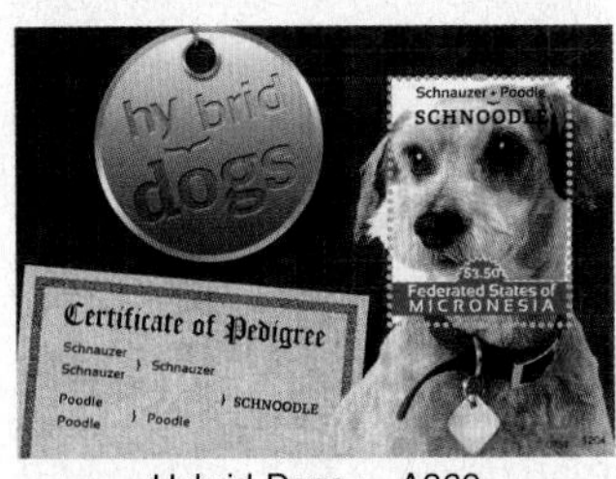

Hybrid Dogs — A369

No. 973: a, Mal-shi. b, Puggle. c, Labradoodle. d, Chiweenie.
$3.50, Schnoodle.

2012, Apr. 4 **Litho.**
973 A369 $1.25 Sheet of 4, #a-d 10.00 10.00

Souvenir Sheet
974 A369 $3.50 multi 7.00 7.00

Mother Teresa (1910-97), Humanitarian A370

Designs: $1.25, Mother Teresa. $3.50, Mother Teresa holding infant.

2012, Apr. 11 *Perf. 12*
975 A370 $1.25 multi 2.50 2.50

Souvenir Sheet
976 A370 $3.50 multi 7.00 7.00

No. 975 was printed in sheets of 4.

Premiere of Movie "The Three Stooges" — A371

No. 977, vert.: a, Sean Hayes as Larry. b, Chris Diamantopoulos as Moe. c, Will Sasso as Curly. d, Moe grabbing Curly and Larry. e, Stooges on bicycle.
$3.50, Stooges with hands against faces.

2012, Apr. 17 *Perf. 13 Syncopated*
977 A371 $1 Sheet of 5, #a-e 10.00 10.00

Souvenir Sheet
978 A371 $3.50 multi 7.00 7.00

Miniature Sheet

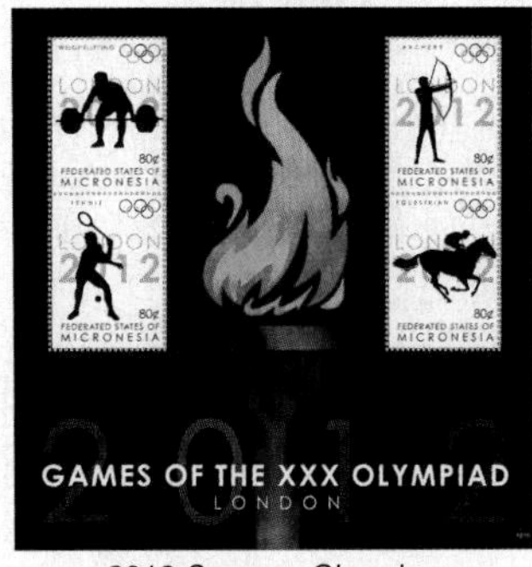

2012 Summer Olympics, London — A372

No. 979: a, Weight lifting. b, Archery. c, Tennis. d, Equestrian.

2012, May 30 *Perf. 14*
979 A372 80c Sheet of 4, #a-d 6.50 6.50

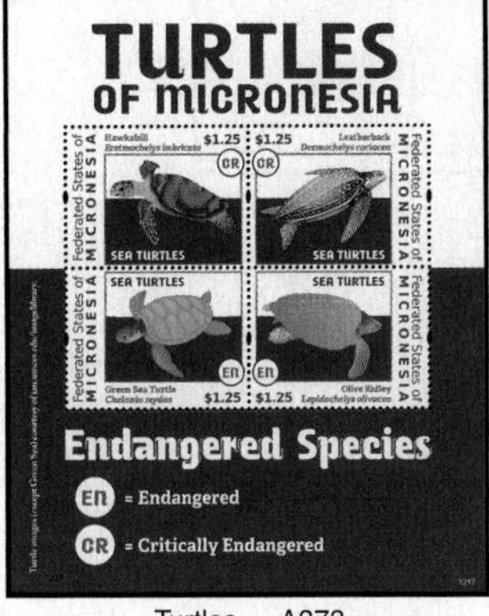

Turtles — A373

No. 980: a, Hawksbill turtle. b, Leatherback turtle. c, Green sea turtle. d, Olive ridley turtle.
No. 981: a, Loggerhead turtle. b, Flatback turtle.

2012, June 27 *Perf. 13 Syncopated*
980 A373 $1.25 Sheet of 4, #a-d 10.00 10.00

Souvenir Sheet
981 A373 $1.25 Sheet of 2, #a-b 5.00 5.00

Souvenir Sheets

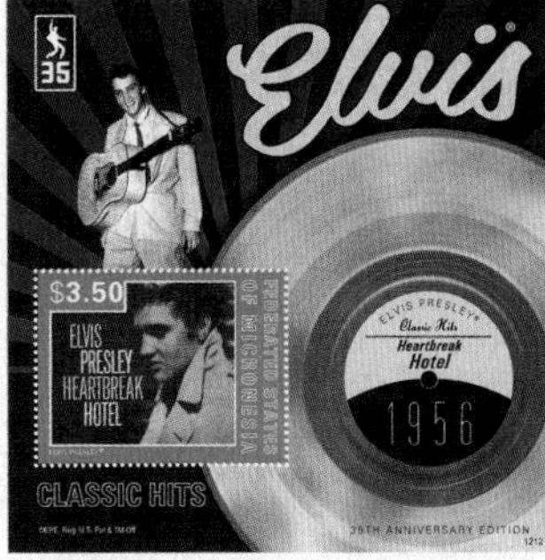

Elvis Presley (1935-77) — A374

Presley: No. 982, $3.50, On Heartbreak Hotel record cover. No. 983, $3.50, On Hound Dog record cover. No. 984, $3.50, On Teddy Bear record cover. No. 985, $3.50, Playing guitar. No. 986, $3.50, Wearing striped shirt.

2012, Aug. 7 *Perf. 12½*
982-986 A374 Set of 5 35.00 35.00

Miniature Sheets

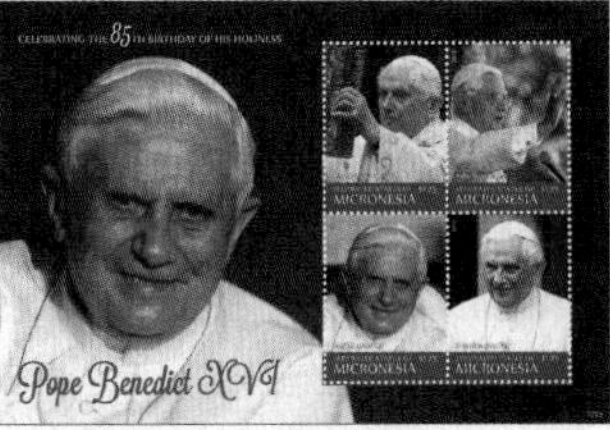

A375

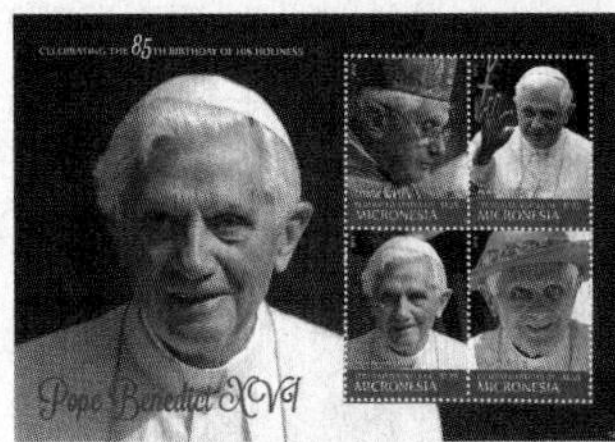

Pope Benedict XVI — A376

No. 987 — Pope Benedict XVI: a, Holding Bible. b, Waving, microphone visible. c, With white horizontal panel in background. d, With white vertical panel in background.
No. 988 — Pope Benedict XVI: a, Wearing miter. b, Waving, cross in background. c, With brown, black and gray areas in background. d, Wearing red hat.

2012, Aug. 28 *Perf. 12*
987 A375 $1.25 Sheet of 4, #a-d 10.00 10.00
988 A376 $1.25 Sheet of 4, #a-d 10.00 10.00

Space Flight Speech of Pres. John F. Kennedy, 50th Anniv. — A377

No. 989, $1.25: a, Astronaut on Moon. b, Kennedy behind microphones and Presidential seal. c, Mercury capsule. d, Gemini capsule.
No. 990, $1.25: a, Lunar Module orbiting Moon. b, Apollo service and command modules orbiting moon. c, Lunar Module and astronaut on Moon. d, Kennedy and flag.

2012, Aug. 28 *Perf. 12*
Sheets of 4, #a-d
989-990 A377 Set of 2 20.00 20.00

Ranger Moon Program, 50th Anniv. — A378

No. 991, $1.25: a, Atlas Agena rocket lifting off. b, Moon targets. c, Ranger Lander above Moon, denomination at LL. d, Ranger 3 above Moon, country name at bottom.

No. 992, $1.25: a, Ranger 3 above Moon, country name at top. b, Ranger 7. c, Ranger lander above Moon, denomination at LR. d, Ranger 4.

2012, Aug. 28 ***Perf. 13 Syncopated***

Sheets of 4, #a-d

991-992 A378 Set of 2 20.00 20.00

Carnivorous Plants — A379

No. 993: a, Pitcher plant. b, Fairy apron. c, Spoon-leaved sundew. d, Tropical sundew.

No. 994: a, Bladderwort. b, Common swamp pitcher plant.

Perf. 13 Syncopated

2012, Aug. 28 **Litho.**

993 A379 $1.25 Sheet of 4, #a-d 10.00 10.00

Souvenir Sheet

994 A379 $1.25 Sheet of 2, #a-b 5.00 5.00

Christmas — A380

Inscriptions: No. 995, 25c, Kosrae. No. 996, 25c, Yap Stone Money, vert. No. 997, 45c, Chuuk. No. 998, 45c, Pohnpei, vert.

2012, Nov. 1 **Litho.** ***Perf. 12½***

995-998 A380 Set of 4 2.80 2.80

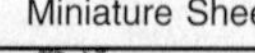

Miniature Sheet

Octopi — A381

No. 999: a, Longarm octopus. b, Common octopus. c, Giant octopus. d, Red octopus. e, Day octopus.

2012, Nov. 28 ***Perf. 13¾***

999 A381 $1 Sheet of 5, #a-e 10.00 10.00

Raphael Paintings — A382

No. 1000: a, Saint John in the Wilderness. b, The Sistine Madonna. c, Cardinal Bernardo Dovizi da Bibbiena. d, Madonna dell'Impannata.

$3.50, The Transfiguration.

2012, Nov. 28 ***Perf. 12½***

1000 A382 $1 Sheet of 4, #a-d 8.00 8.00

Souvenir Sheet

1001 A382 $3.50 multi 7.00 7.00

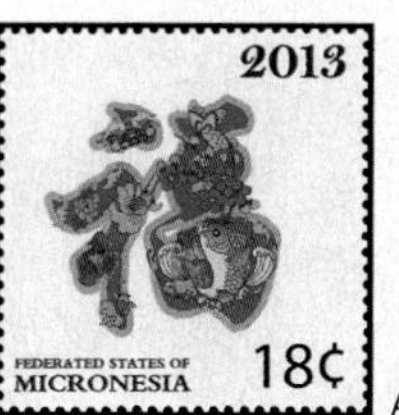

A383

A384

A385

A386

New Year 2013 (Year of the Snake) A387

2012, Oct. 10 **Litho.** ***Perf. 13¼***

1002 Sheet of 20, #1002a-1002d, 16 #1002e 8.00 8.00

a. A383 18c multi .40 .40
b. A384 18c multi .40 .40
c. A385 18c multi .40 .40
d. A386 18c multi .40 .40
e. A387 18c multi .40 .40

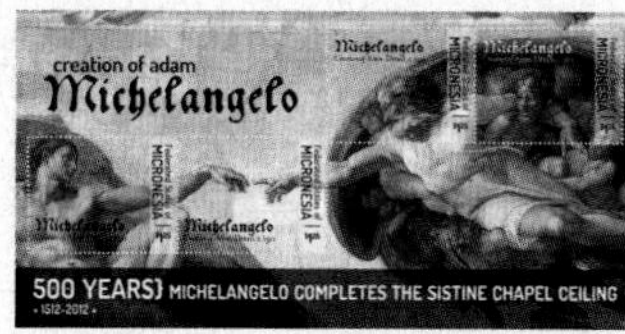

Michelangelo's Completion of the Sistine Chapel Ceiling Paintings, 500th Anniv. — A388

No. 1003 — Details from *The Creation of Adam*: a, Adam. b, Hands of Adam and God. c, Head of God. d, Feminine figure.

No. 1004: a, Separation of Land and Water. b, Creation of the Sun, Moon and Earth. c, Separation of Light and Darkness.

2012, Nov. 28 **Litho.** ***Perf. 12½***

1003 A388 $1.25 Sheet of 4, #a-d 10.00 10.00

Souvenir Sheet

1004 A388 $1.25 Sheet of 3, #a-c 7.50 7.50

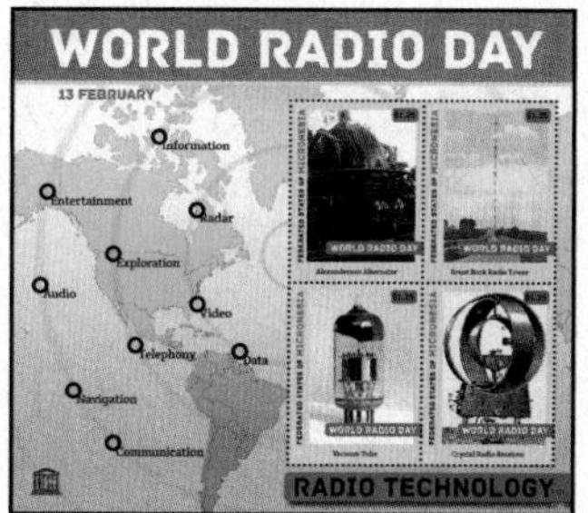

World Radio Day — A389

No. 1005: a, Alexanderson alternator. b, Brant Rock Radio Tower, Massachusetts. c, Vacuum tube. d, Crystal radio receiver.

$3.50, Telstar communications satellite.

2013, Jan. 8 **Litho.** ***Perf. 12½***

1005 A389 $1.25 Sheet of 4, #a-d 10.00 10.00

Souvenir Sheet

Perf.

1006 A389 $3.50 multi 7.00 7.00

No. 1006 contains one 38mm diameter stamp.

A390

Paintings by Vincent van Gogh (1853-90) — A391

No. 1007 — Details from: a, Self-portrait, 1889. b, Starry Night, 1889. c, Still Life: Vase with Irises, 1889. d, Willows at Sunset, 1888.

No. 1008: a, Entrance Hall of Saint-Paul Hospital, 1889. b, Café Terrace at Night, 1888. c, Still Life with Oranges, Lemons and Blue Gloves (Früchtekorb und Handschuhe), 1889. d, Vincent's Bedroom in Arles, 1888.

$3.50, The Painter on His Way to Work, 1888.

2013, Jan. 8 **Litho.** ***Perf. 13¾***

1007 A390 $1.20 Sheet of 4, #a-d 9.75 9.75

Perf. 12½

1008 A391 $1.20 Sheet of 4, #a-d 9.75 9.75

Souvenir Sheet

1009 A391 $3.50 multi 7.00 7.00

Sarah Bernhardt (1844-1923), Actress — A392

No. 1010 — Illustrations by Alfons Mucha showing Bernhardt with: a, Vase. b, Staff. c, Dagger. d, Palm frond.

$3.50, Bernhardt with lilies in hair.

2013, Feb. 20 **Litho.** ***Perf. 12***

1010 A392 $1.20 Sheet of 4, #a-d 9.75 9.75

Souvenir Sheet

Perf. 12½

1011 A392 $3.50 multi 7.00 7.00

No. 1011 contains one 38x51mm stamp.

Pres. John F. Kennedy (1917-63) — A393

No. 1012 — Pres. Kennedy: a, Facing right. b, Pointing. c, Facing slightly left, chin above top of diamond. d, Facing slightly left, chin even with top of diamond.

$3.50, Pres. Kennedy, diff.

2013, Apr. 3 **Litho.** ***Perf. 12***

1012 A393 $1.20 Sheet of 4, #a-d 9.75 9.75

Souvenir Sheet

1013 A393 $3.50 multi 7.00 7.00

LOUIS COMFORT TIFFANY

MICRONESIA $1.20

80th Memorial Anniversary

Details of Stained Glass Windows by Louis Comfort Tiffany — A394

No. 1014 — Stained-glass window with: a, Green piece of glass just below "MIC." b, Pink and red flower. c, Numerous green pieces of glass. d, Purple and yellow pieces of glass. $3.50, Stained-glass window, vert.

2013, Apr. 4 Litho. *Perf. 13¾*

1014 A394 $1.20 Sheet of 4, #a-d 9.75 9.75

Souvenir Sheet

Perf. 12½

1015 A394 $3.50 multi 7.00 7.00

No. 1015 contains one 38x51mm stamp.

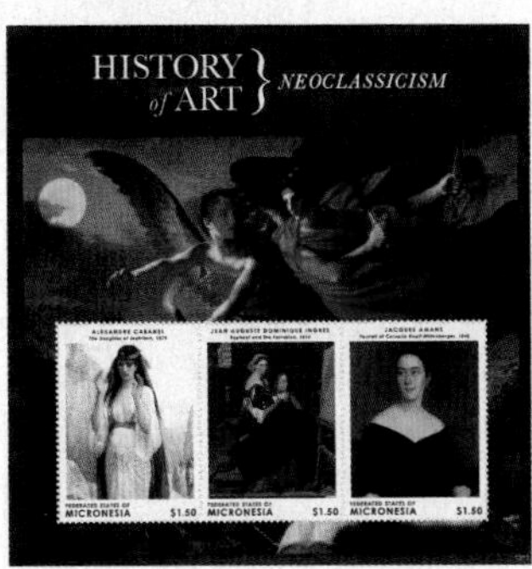

History of Art — A395

No. 1016, $1.50 — Neoclassical paintings: a, The Daughter of Jephthah, by Alexandre Cabanel. b, Raphael and the Fornarina, by Jean Auguste Dominique Ingres. c, Portrait of Cornelia Knott Miltenberger, by Jacques Amans.

No. 1017, $1.50 — Neoclassical paintings: a, Nanna, by Anselm Feuerbach. b, Portrait of Madame de Verninac, by Jacques-Louis David. c, François Marius Gronet, by Ingres.

No. 1018, $3.50, Wanderer Above the Sea of Fog, by Caspar David Friedrich. No. 1019, $3.50, Caspar David Friedrich in his Studio, by Georg Friedrich Kersting, horiz.

2013, Apr. 4 Litho. *Perf. 12½*

Sheets of 3, #a-c

1016-1017 A395 Set of 2 18.00 18.00

Souvenir Sheets

1018-1019 A395 Set of 2 14.00 14.00

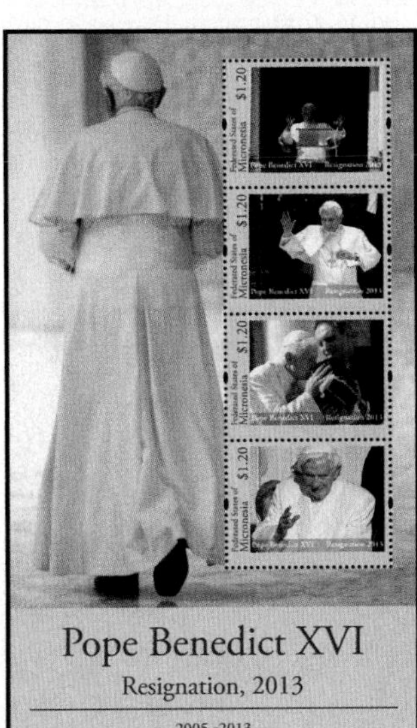

A396

Resignation of Pope Benedict XVI — A397

No. 1020 — Pope Benedict XVI: a, Behind lectern. b, Waving, wristwatch visible. c, Kissing person. d, Waving, person wearing red cap in background.

No. 1021 — Pope Benedict XVI: a, Seated in chair. b, Facing forward, white background. c, Waving, grass in background. d, Waving, hand above eyes.

No. 1022, $3.50, In arched doorway, waving. No. 1023, $3.50, Facing right, waving.

Perf. 13 Syncopated

2013, Apr. 29 Litho.

1020 A396 $1.20 Sheet of 4, #a-d 9.75 9.75

1021 A397 $1.20 Sheet of 4, #a-d 9.75 9.75

Souvenir Sheets

1022-1023 A397 Set of 2 14.00 14.00

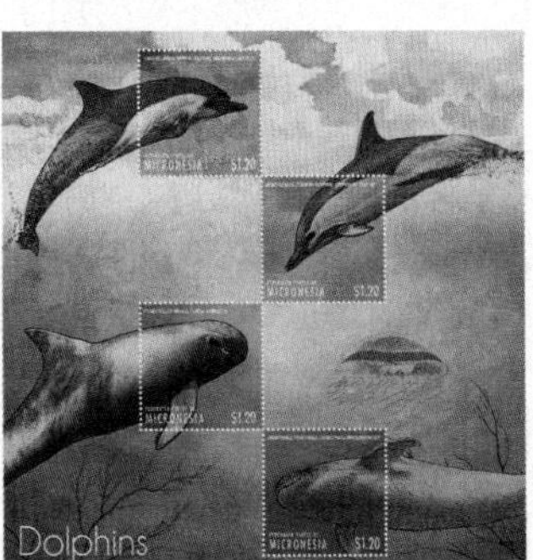

Dolphins — A398

No. 1024, $1.20: a, Long-beaked common dolphin. b, Short-beaked common dolphin. c, Pygmy killer whale. d, Short-finned pilot whale.

No. 1025, $1.20: Dusky dolphin. b, Hector's dolphin. c, Bottlenose dolphin. d, Pantropical spotted dolphin.

No. 1026, $3.50, Spinner dolphin, horiz. No. 1027, $3.50, Rough-toothed dolphin, horiz.

2012, May 7 Litho. *Perf. 13¾*

Sheets of 4, #a-d

1024-1025 A398 Set of 2 19.50 19.50

Souvenir Sheets

1026-1027 A398 Set of 2 14.00 14.00

Fish — A399

No. 1028, $1.20: a, Mandarinfish. b, Neon damselfish. c, Man-of-war fish. d, Banggai cardinalfish.

No. 1029, $1.20: a, Australasian snapper. b, Australian herring. c, Saddletail grouper. d, Tasmanian clingfish.

No. 1030, $3.50, Slender-spined porcupine fish. No. 1031, $3.50, Ocellaris clownfish.

Perf. 13 Syncopated

2013, May 7 Litho.

Sheets of 4, #a-d

1028-1029 A399 Set of 2 19.50 19.50

Souvenir Sheets

1030-1031 A399 Set of 2 14.00 14.00

Dr. Lois Englberger (1948-2011), Acting Director and Research Advisor of Island Food Community A400

Perf. 13 Syncopated

2013, May 8 Litho.

1032 A400 $1.20 multi 2.40 2.40

Souvenir Sheet

1033 A400 $3.50 multi 7.00 7.00

No. 1032 was printed in sheets of 4.

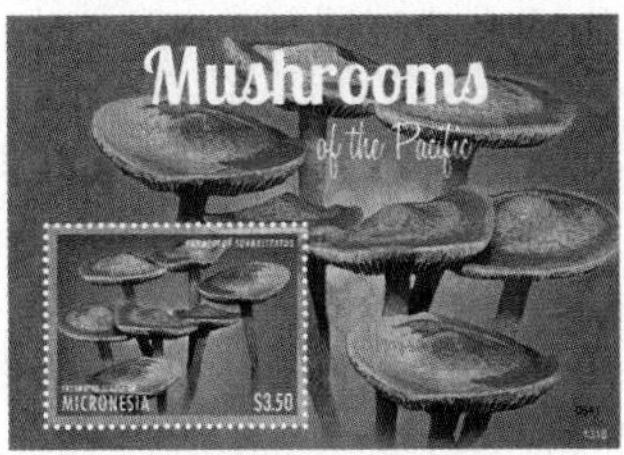

Mushrooms — A401

No. 1034, $1.25: a, Psilocybe subaerugi-nosa. b, Gymnopilus luteofolius. c, Gymnopilus junonius. d, Panaeolus cyanescens.

No. 1035, $1.25: a, Psilocybe aucklandii. b, Entoloma hochstetteri. c, Amanita citrina. d, Agaricus bernardii.

No. 1036, $3.50, Panaeolus subbalteatus. No. 1037, $3.50, Weraroa novae, vert.

2013, June 3 Litho. *Perf. 12*

Sheets of 4, #a-d

1034-1035 A401 Set of 2 20.00 20.00

Souvenir Sheets

1036-1037 A401 Set of 2 14.00 14.00

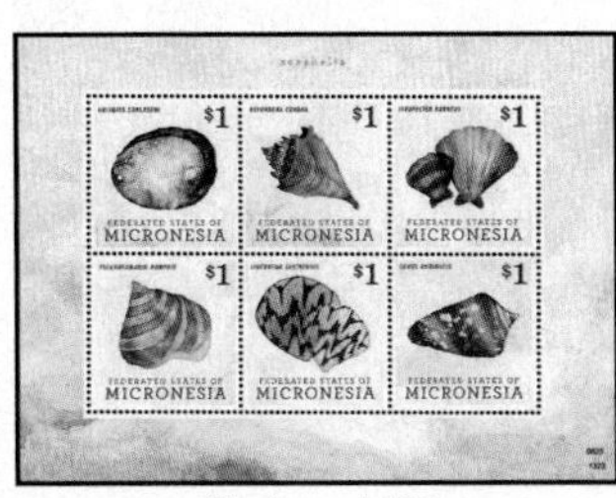

John De Avila Mangefel (1932-2007), First Governor of Yap — A402

Perf. 13¼x12½

2013, June 13 Litho.

1038 A402 46c multi .95 .95

No. 1038 was printed in sheets of 4.

Shells — A403

No. 1039: a, Haliotis sorenseni. b, Melongena corona. c, Lyropecten nodosus. d, Pleurotomaria rumphii. e, Lioconcha castrensis. f, Conus ammiralis.

$3.50, Echinus melo, vert.

2013, July 7 Litho. *Perf. 13¾*

1039 A403 $1 Sheet of 6, #a-f 12.00 12.00

Souvenir Sheet

Perf. 12½

1040 A403 $3.50 multi 7.00 7.00

No. 1040 contains one 38x51mm stamp.

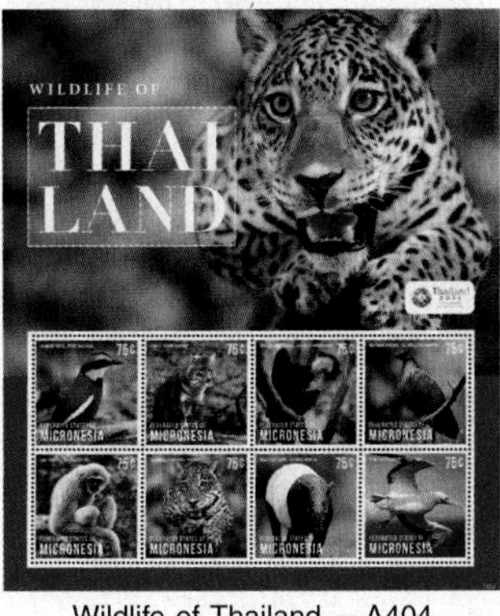

Wildlife of Thailand — A404

No. 1041: a, Banded pitta. b, Dhole. c, Wrinkled hornbill. d, Nicobar pigeon. e, Lar gibbon. f, Leopard. g, Malaysian tapir. h, Red-footed booby.

No. 1042, vert.: a, Dugong. b, Red-breasted parakeet.

2013, July 7 Litho. *Perf. 13¾*

1041 A404 75c Sheet of 8, #a-h 12.00 12.00

Souvenir Sheet

Perf. 12½

1042 A404 $1.75 Sheet of 2, #a-b 7.00 7.00

2013 Thailand World Stamp Exhibition, Bangkok. No. 1042 contains two 38x51mm stamps.

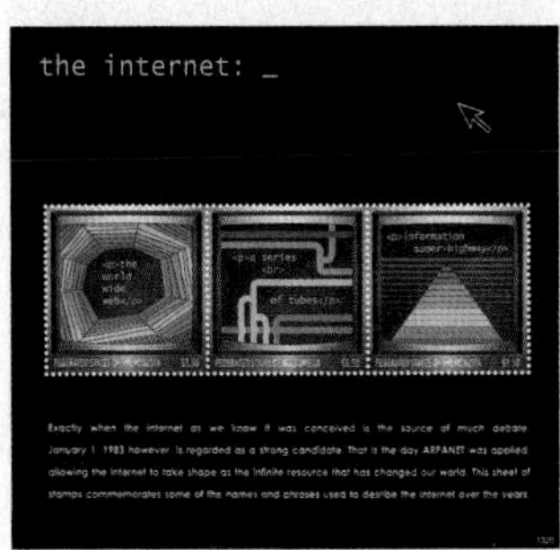

Internet, 30th Anniv. — A405

No. 1043 — Inscriptions: a, The World Wide Web. b, A series of tubes. c, Information super-highway.

3.50, Computer, vert.

2013, Aug. 12 Litho. *Perf. 13¾*

1043 A405 $1.50 Sheet of 3, #a-c 9.00 9.00

Souvenir Sheet

Perf. 12½

1044 A405 $3.50 multi 7.00 7.00

No. 1044 contains one 38x51mm stamp.

Souvenir Sheet

Elvis Presley (1935-77) — A406

Litho., Margin Embossed With Foil Application

2013, Aug. 12 *Imperf.*

Without Gum

1045 A406 $10 black 20.00 20.00

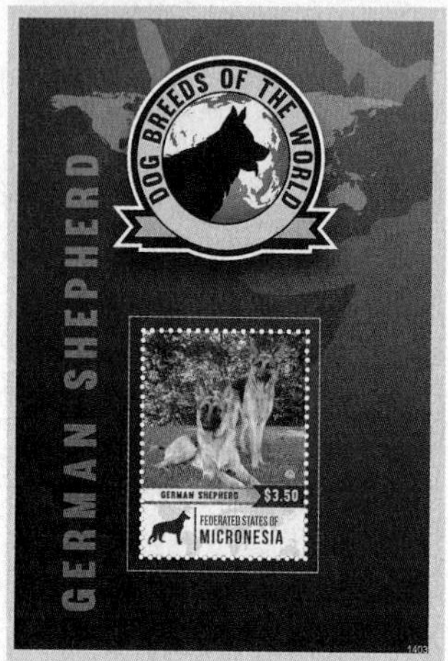
Dogs — A407

No. 1046: a, Basset hounds. b, Jack Russell terrier. c, Alaskan huskies. d, Yorkshire terrier.
$3.50, Germen shepherds.

2014, Mar. 24 **Litho.** *Perf. 14*

1046 A407 $1.20 Sheet of 4, #a-d 9.75 9.75

Souvenir Sheet

Perf. 12

1047 A407 $3.50 multi 7.00 7.00

Parrots — A408

No. 1048: a, Alisterus amboinensis. b, Geoffroyus geoffroyi geoffroyi. c, Loriculus camiguinensis. d, Loriculus calculus. e, Psittacula alexandri alexandri. f, Psittacula alexandri.
$3.50, Alisterus amboinensis, diff.

2014, Mar. 24 **Litho.** *Perf. 12½*

1048 A408 $1 Sheet of 6, #a-f 12.00 12.00

Souvenir Sheet

1049 A408 $3.50 multi 7.00 7.00

World War I, Cent. — A409

No. 1050, $1.20: a, Belgian soldier throwing Mills grenade. b, Head of Belgian soldier. c, Head of German soldier. d, German soldier charging.

No. 1051, $1.20, horiz.: a, HMS C1 submarine. b, HMS E5 submarine. c, HMS K17 submarine. d, HMS R3 submarine.

No. 1052, $2: a, King Albert I of Belgium. b, Kaiser Wilhelm II of Germany.

No. 1053, $2, horiz.: a, HMS B11 submarine. b, HMS C27 submarine.

2014, Mar. 24 **Litho.** *Perf. 14*

Sheets of 4, #a-d

1050-1051 A409 Set of 2 19.50 19.50

Souvenir Sheets of 2, #a-b

Perf. 12½

1052-1053 A409 Set of 2 16.00 16.00

No. 1052 contains two 38x51mm stamps. No. 1053 contains two 51x38mm stamps.

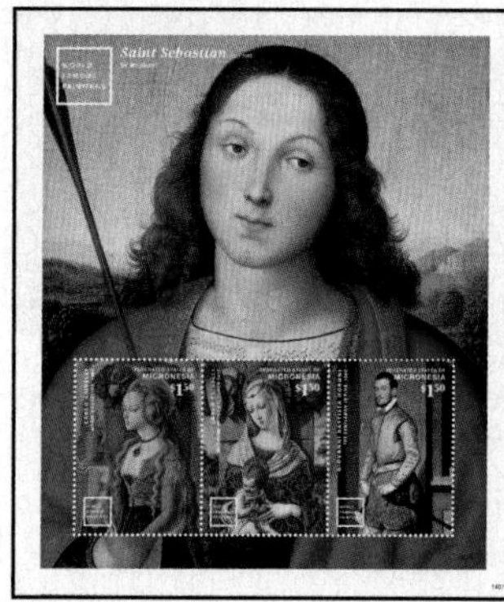
Paintings — A410

No. 1054, $1.50: a, Maria Magdalena, by Carlo Crivelli. b, Madonna of the Goldfinch, by Crivelli. c, The Gentleman in Pink, by Giovanni Battista Moroni.

No. 1055, $1.50: a, Portrait of a Woman with a Winged Bonnet, by Rogier van der Weyden. b, Annunciation, by Peter Paul Rubens. c, St. Augustine, by Caravaggio.

No. 1056, $4, Henry VII, by Hans Holbein the Younger. No. 1057, $4, The Dance Lesson, by Edgar Degas.

2014, Mar. 24 **Litho.** *Perf. 12½*

Sheets of 3, #a-c

1054-1055 A410 Set of 2 18.00 18.00

Size: 100x100

Imperf

1056-1057 A410 Set of 2 16.00 16.00

A411

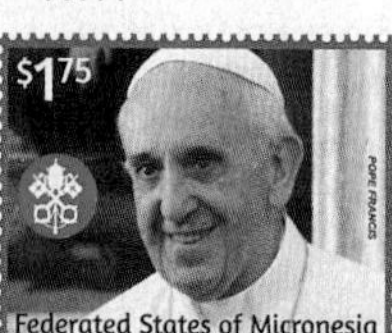
A412

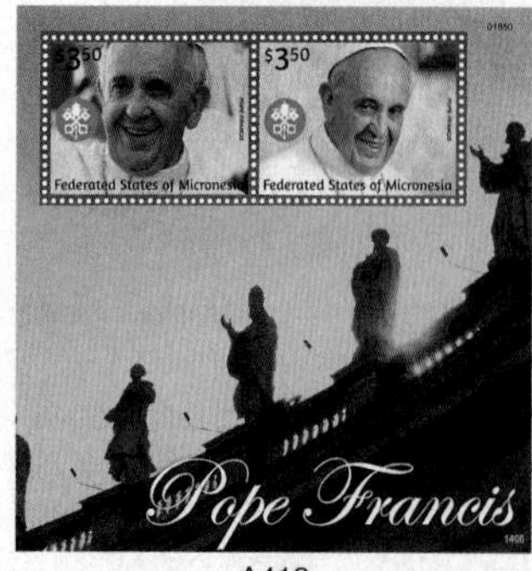
A413

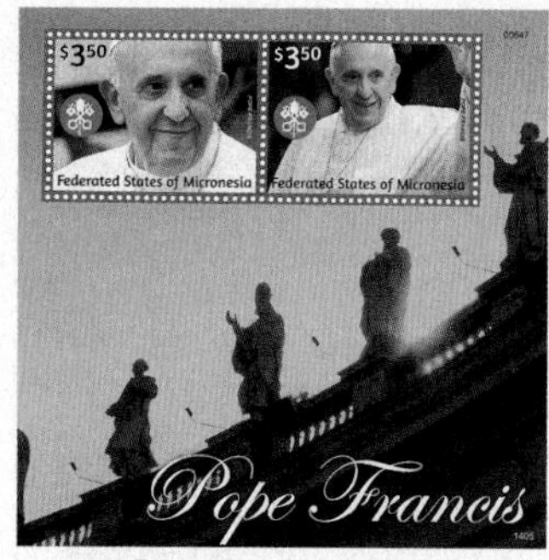
Pope Francis — A414

No. 1058: a, One ear visible. b, Both ears visible.

No. 1059, Pope wearing zucchetto.

No. 1060: a, Pink area in background. b, White area in background.

No. 1061: a, Denomination in black. b, Denomination in white.

2014, Mar. 24 **Litho.** *Perf. 14*

1058 A411 $1.75 Horiz. pair, #a-b 7.00 7.00

1059 A412 $1.75 multi 3.50 3.50

a. Horiz. pair, #1058b, 1059 7.00 7.00

Souvenir Sheets

Perf. 12

1060 A413 $3.50 Sheet of 2, #a-b 14.00 14.00

1061 A414 $3.50 Sheet of 2, #a-b 14.00 14.00

No. 1058 and 1059a each were printed in sheets containing two pairs.

A415

College of Micronesia, 20th Anniv. — A416

2014, Apr. 5 **Litho.** *Perf. 12½*

1062 A415 49c multi 1.00 1.00

1063 A416 49c multi 1.00 1.00

Birth of Prince George of Cambridge — A417

No. 1064: a, Prince George in arms of Duchess of Cambridge. b, Duchess of Cambridge and Prince George. c, Prince George, Duke and Duchess of Cambridge. d, Prince, Duke and Duchess, face of Duchess not visible.
$4, Prince, Duke and Duchess, horiz.

2014, Apr. 29 **Litho.** *Perf. 13¾*

1064 A417 $1.20 Sheet of 4, #a-d 9.75 9.75

Souvenir Sheet

Perf. 12½

1065 A417 $4 multi 8.00 8.00

No. 1065 contains one 51x38mm stamp.

Birds — A418

Designs: 1c, Black tern. 2c, Black-headed gull. 4c, Sabine's gull. 5c, Caspian tern. 10c, Common gull. 49c, White-winge black tern. 50c, Wilson's storm petrel. $1, Great skua.

2014, May 8 **Litho.** *Perf. 13¾*

1066-1073 A418 Set of 8 4.50 4.50

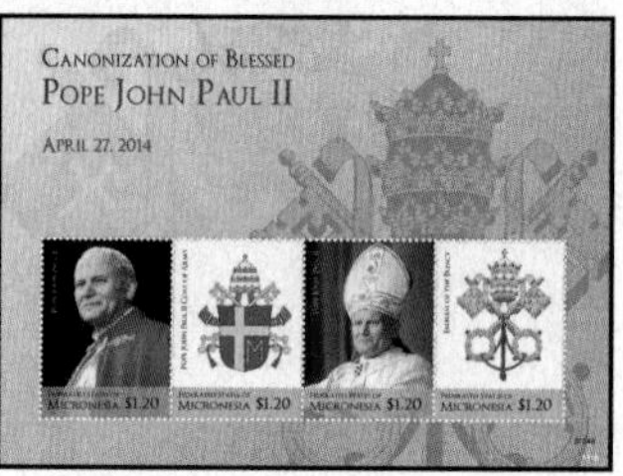
Canonization of Pope John Paul II — A419

No. 1074, $1.20: a, Pope John Paul II in red robe. b, Coat of arms of Pope John Paul II. c, Pope John Paul II wearing miter, color photograph. d, Emblem of the papacy.

No. 1075, $1.20: a, St. Peter's Basilica clock. b, Pope John Paul II wearing miter, black-and-white photograph. c, Papal arms on St. Peter's Basilica. d, Pope John Paul wearing zucchetto.

No. 1076, $2: a, Pope John Paul II in red robe, diff. b, Dome of St. Peter's Basilica.

No. 1077, $2, horiz.: a, Pope John Paul II, color photograph. b, Pope John Paul II, black-and-white photograph.

Perf. 14, 12 (#1077)

2014, May 12 **Litho.**

Sheets of 4, #a-d

1074-1075 A419 Set of 2 19.50 19.50

Souvenir Sheets of 2, #a-b

1076-1077 A419 Set of 2 16.00 16.00

A420

Nelson Mandela (1918-2013), President of South Africa — A421

No. 1078 — Mandela: a, Wearing shirt and sweater. b, Wearing black shirt with white polka dots. c, In black-and-white photograph. d, Wearing suit and tie.

No. 1079 — Mandela: a, On book cover at left, in black-and white photograph at right. b, In black-and-white photograph at left, in color photograph wearing sweater at right. c, Wearing tribal neck covering in black-and-white photograph at left, wearing jacket with Olympic emblem in color photograph at right. d, In two colro photographs.

No. 1080, $7, Mandela wearing green shirt, waving. No. 1081, $7, Mandela wearing blue and white shirt.

2014, May 12 Litho. *Perf. 13¾*

1078 A420 $1.75 Sheet of 4, #a-d 14.00 14.00
1079 A421 $1.75 Sheet of 4, #a-d 14.00 14.00

Souvenir Sheets

1080-1081 A421 Set of 2 28.00 28.00

Keitani Graham (1980-2012), Wrestler — A422

Graham: No. 1082, $1, Close-up. No. 1083, $1, With numbered sign in background. No. 1084, $1, Wrestling opponent.

2014, June 4 Litho. *Perf. 14*

1082-1084 A422 Set of 3 6.00 6.00

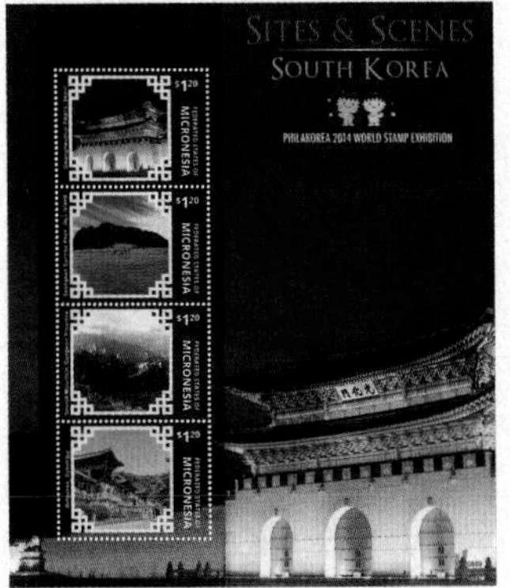

South Korean Tourist Attractions — A423

No. 1085: a, Gwanghwamun Palace, Seoul. b, Seongsan Sunrise Peak, Jeju Island. c, Seorak Mountain, Gangwon Province. d, Bulguksa, Gyeongju.

No. 1086, vert.: a, N Seoul Tower, Seoul. b, Gwangan Bridge, Busan.

2014, June 30 Litho. *Perf. 14*

1085 A423 $1.20 Sheet of 4, #a-d 9.75 9.75

Souvenir Sheet

1086 A423 $2 Sheet of 2, #a-b 8.00 8.00

Philakorea 2014 World Stamp Exhibition, Seoul.

A424

A425

A426

Caroline Kennedy, U.S. Ambassador to Japan — A427

Various photographs of Caroline Kennedy, as shown.

2014, June 30 Litho. *Perf. 12*

1087 A424 $1.20 Sheet of 4, #a-d 9.75 9.75
1088 A425 $1.20 Sheet of 4, #a-d 9.75 9.75

Souvenir Sheets

1089 A426 $2 Sheet of 2, #a-b 8.00 8.00

Perf. 14

1090 A427 $2 Sheet of 2, #a-b 8.00 8.00

Miniature Sheet

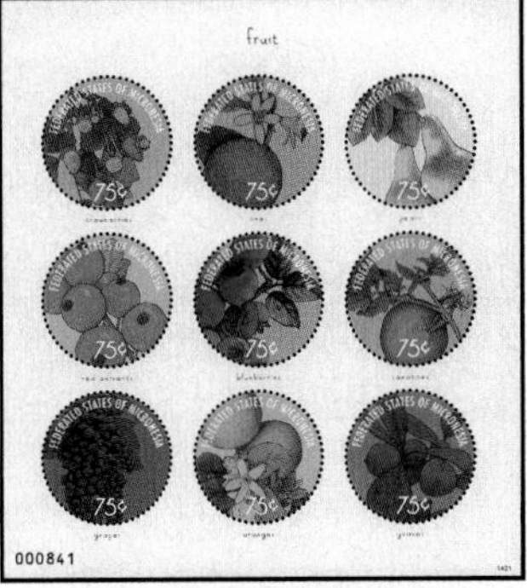

Fruit — A428

No. 1091: a, Strawberries. b, Limes. c, Pears. d, Red currants. e, Blueberries. f, Tomatoes. g, Grapes. h, Oranges. i, Guavas.

2014, July 9 Litho. *Perf.*

1091 A428 75c Sheet of 9, #a-i 13.50 13.50

Polar Bears — A429

No. 1092 — Polar bear: a, Underwater, denomination at UR. b, Underwater, head at right, denomination at UL. c, With nose above water, denomination at UR. d, Underwater, head at left, denomination at UL.

$2.50, Head of polar bear.

2014, July 31 Litho. *Perf. 14*

1092 A429 75c Sheet of 4, #a-d 6.00 6.00

Souvenir Sheet

Perf. 12½

1093 A429 $2.50 multi 5.00 5.00

No. 1093 contains one 51x38mm stamp.

A430

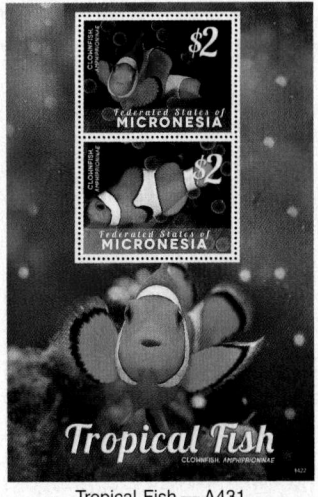

Tropical Fish — A431

No. 1094, 75c: a-d, Various depictions of clownfish in anemone, as shown.

No. 1095, 75c: a, Barcheek unicornfish. b, Discus. c, Old woman angelfish. d, Lined surgeonfish.

No. 1096, $2: a-b, Various depictions of clownfish in anemone, as shown.

No. 1097, $2, vert.: a, Clownfish, anemone at right of fish. b, Clownfish, anemone at left and right of fish

2014, Aug. 27 Litho. *Perf. 14*

Sheets of 4, #a-d

1094-1095 A430 Set of 2 12.00 12.00

Souvenir Sheets of 2, #a-b

Perf. 12½

1096-1097 A431 Set of 2 16.00 16.00

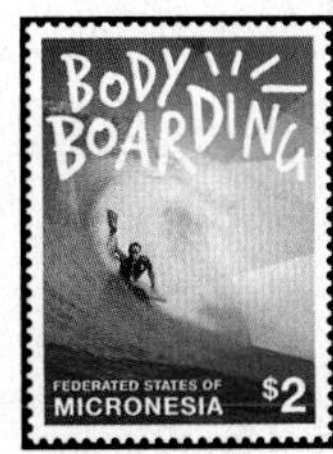

Bodyboarding A432

2014, Sept. 6 Litho. *Perf. 14*

1098 A432 $2 multi 4.00 4.00

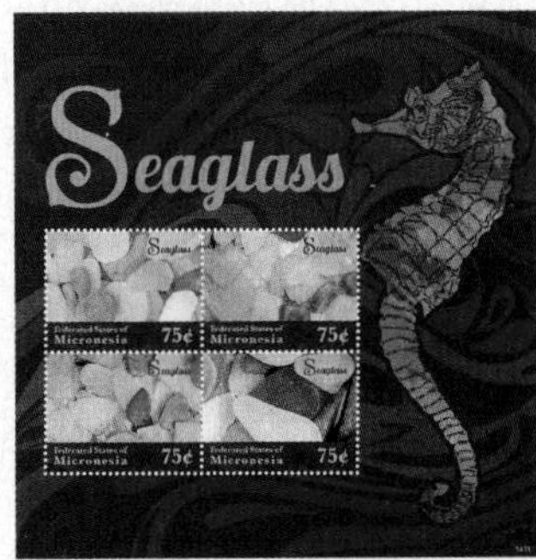

A433

Seaglass — A434

Nos. 1099, 1100, Various depictions of seaglass, as shown.

No. 1101, $4, Seaglass with black rock at left. No. 1102, $4, Seaglass with black rock at top.

Perf. 12, 14 (#1100)

2014, Sept. 15 Litho.

1099 A433 75c Sheet of 4, #a-d 6.00 6.00
1100 A434 75c Sheet of 6, #a-f 9.00 9.00

Souvenir Sheets

1101-1102 A434 Set of 2 16.00 16.00

A435

Paintings by Qi Baishi (1864-1957) — A436

No. 1103: a, Flowers on branch. b, Flowers and cricket. c, Basket of fruit. d, Mushrooms and flowers.

No. 1104: a, Flowers and beetle. b, Flowers and dragonfly. c, Flowers and dragonfly, diff. d, Flowers and grsasshopper.

No. 1105, $4, Flowers. No. 1106, $4, Rocks and boats.

2014, Sept. 15 Litho. *Perf. 14*

1103 A435 $1.20 Sheet of 4, #a-d 9.75 9.75
1104 A436 $1.20 Sheet of 4, #a-d 9.75 9.75

Souvenir Sheets

Perf. 12

1105-1106 A436 Set of 2 16.00 16.00

Nos. 1105-1106 each contain one 30x50mm stamp.

Sharks — A437

No. 1107, $1: a, Blacktip reef shark. b, Dogfish shark. c, Lemon shark. d, Tiger shark.

No. 1108, $1 — Whale shark with: a, Tail fin touching edge of design below "M" in "Micronesia." b, Tail fin not near edge of design. c, Mouth open, tail fin not visible. d, Tail fin at right.

No. 1109, $3, Great white shark. No. 1110, $3, Great hammerhead shark.

Perf. 12, 14 (#1108, 1110)

2014, Oct. 14 Litho.

Sheets of 4, #a-d

1107-1108 A437 Set of 2 16.00 16.00

Souvenir Sheets

1109-1110 A437 Set of 2 12.00 12.00

Miniature Sheets

A438

Illustrations by Alphonse Mucha (1860-1939) — A439

Various unnamed illustrations, as shown.

2014, Oct. 14 Litho. *Perf. 14*

1111 A438 $1 Sheet of 4, #a-d 8.00 8.00
1112 A439 $1 Sheet of 4, #a-d 8.00 8.00

Butterflies — A440

No. 1113, $1: a, Milbert's tortoise-shell butterfly. b, Blue morpho butterfly. c, Tiger swallowtail butterfly. d, Monarch butterfly. e, Goliath birdwing butterfly. f, Striped albatross butterfly.

No. 1114, $1: a, Emerald swallowtail butterfly. b, Gold rim swallowtail butterfly. c, Scalloped grass yellow butterfly. d, European peacock butterfly. e, Blue mountain butterfly. f, Orange-tip butterfly.

No. 1115, $3.50, Postman butterfly, horiz. No. 1116, $3.50, Richmond birdwing butterfly, horiz.

2014, Oct. 20 Litho. *Perf. 13¾*

Sheets of 6, #a-f

1113-1114 A440 Set of 2 24.00 24.00

Souvenir Sheets

Perf. 12½

1115-1116 A440 Set of 2 14.00 14.00

Nos. 1115-1116 each contain one 51x38mm stamp.

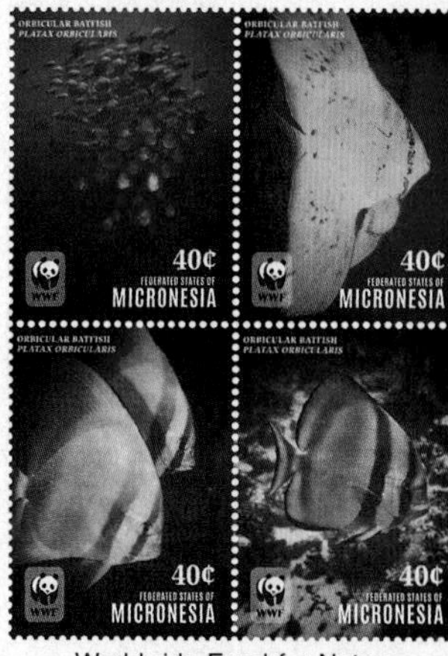

Worldwide Fund for Nature (WWF) — A441

Nos. 1117 and 1118 — Orbicular batfish: a, School. b, One yellow fish. c, Two fish. d, One gray and black fish.

2014, Nov. 11 Litho. *Perf. 14*

1117 A441 40c Block or horiz. strip of 4, #a-d 3.25 3.25
1118 A441 90c Block or horiz. strip of 4, #a-d 7.25 7.25

Souvenir Sheets

Elvis Presley (1935-77) — A442

Inscriptions: No. 1119, $4, Elvis' network television debut. No. 1120, $4, Elvis' fist live concert in NYC. No. 1121, $4, "Heartbreak Hotel" goes gold. No. 1122, $4, Elvis named honorary colonel.

2014, Nov. 11 Litho. *Perf. 14*

1119-1122 A442 Set of 4 32.00 32.00

Christmas A446

Designs: No. 1123, 49c, Boat and presents (shown). No. 1124, 49c, Boat and presents, side view of boat. $1, Presents under palm tree. $2, Boat and presents inside boat, gold garland.

2014, Nov. 24 Litho. *Perf. 14*

1123-1126 A446 Set of 4 8.00 8.00

A447

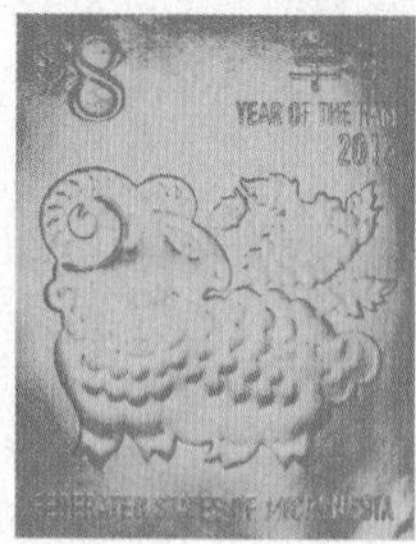

New Year 2015 (Year of the Ram) A448

No. 1127 — Various depictions of rams as shown.

2014, Nov. 24 Litho. *Perf. 14*

1127 A447 90c Sheet of 4, #a-d 7.25 7.25

Embossed

Imperf

Without Gum

1128 A448 $8 gold 16.00 16.00

Trans-Siberian Railway — A449

No. 1129 — Inscriptions: a, Construction between Yekaterinburg and Chelyabinsk. b, Convicts, as well as soldiers, worked to build the railroad. c, Construction of the Trans-Siberian Railroad by the Angara River. d, The Trans-Siberian Railway undergoing construction in 1929.

$3.50, Workers layin the last ties for the Trans-Siberian Railway.

2014, Dec. 31 Litho. *Perf. 12*

1129 A449 $1 Sheet of 4, #a-d 8.00 8.00

Souvenir Sheet

1130 A449 $3.50 multi 7.00 7.00

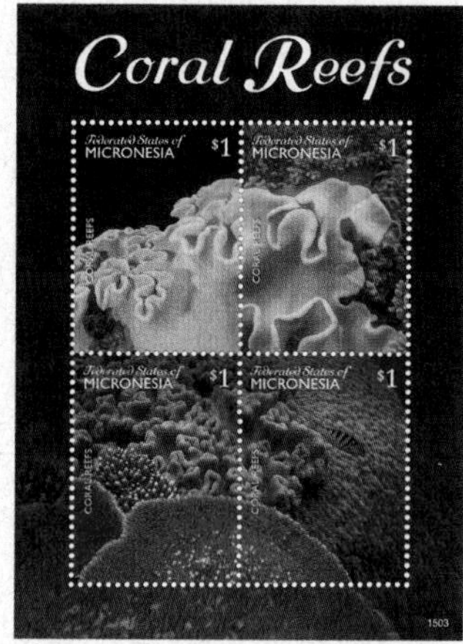

A450

A451

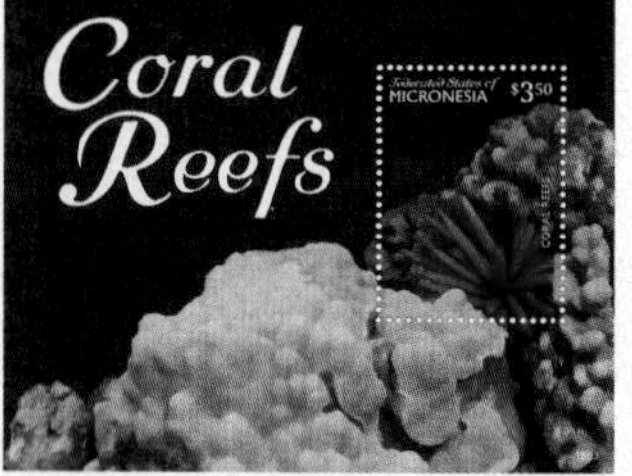

A452

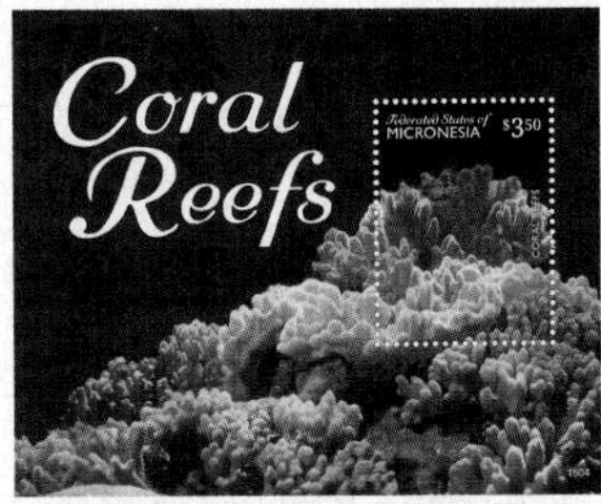

Coral Reefs — A453

Nos. 1131 and 1132 — Various corals as shown.

2014, Dec. 31 Litho. *Perf. 12*

1131	A450	$1 Sheet of 4, #a-d	8.00	8.00
1132	A451	$1 Sheet of 4, #a-d	8.00	8.00

Souvenir Sheets

1133	A452	$3.50 multi	7.00	7.00
1134	A453	$3.50 multi	7.00	7.00

Sharks
A454

Designs: 26c, Scalloped hammerhead shark. 49c, Oceanic whitetip shark. $1.15, Tiger shark. $3, Gray reef shark.

2015, Jan. 1 Litho. *Perf. 14¾x14¼*

1135-1138	A454	Set of 4	10.00	10.00

Miniature Sheet

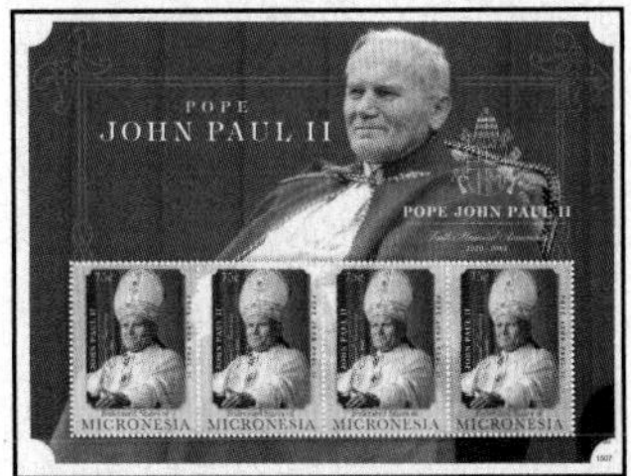

St. John Paul II (1920-2005) — A455

No. 1139 — St. John Paul II with: a, White area to right of "Pope" in red. b, White area at UR corner. c, White area at UL corner. d, Dark gray area under left part of country name.

2015, Feb. 2 Litho. *Perf. 14*

1139	A455	75c Sheet of 4, #a-d	6.00	6.00

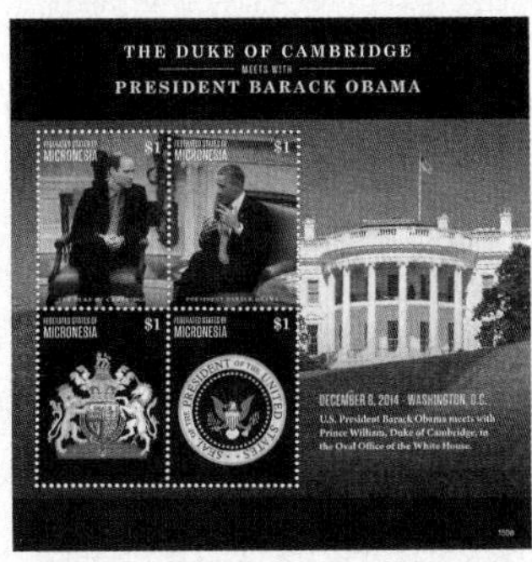

Meeting of Duke of Cambridge and U.S. Pres. Barack Obama — A456

No. 1140: a, Duke of Cambridge. b, Pres. Obama. c, Coat of arms of Duke of Cambridge. d, Presidential seal.

No. 1141: a, Duke of Cambridge, diff. b, Pres. Obama, diff.

2015, Mar. 2 Litho. *Perf. 12*

1140	A456	$1 Sheet of 4, #a-d	8.00	8.00

Souvenir Sheet

Perf. 14

1141	A456	$1.75 Sheet of 2, #a-b	7.00	7.00

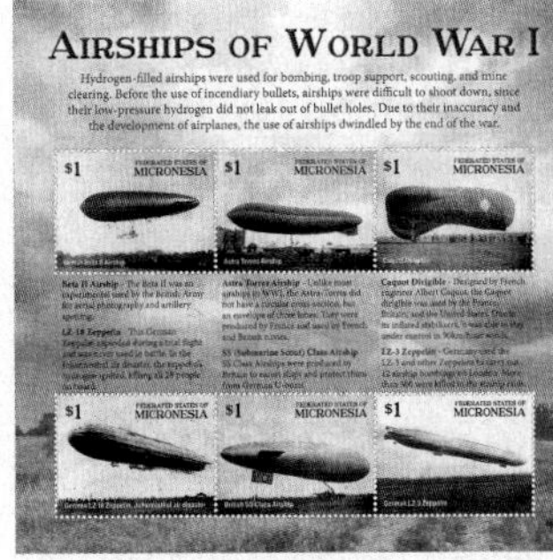

World War I Airships — A457

No. 1142: a, British Beta II airship. b, Astra Torres airship. c, Caquot dirigible. d, German LZ-18 Zeppelin. e, British SS Class airship. f, German LZ-3 Zeppelin.

$3.50, WWI Reconnaisance balloon, vert.

2015, Mar. 2 Litho. *Perf. 14*

1142	A457	$1 Sheet of 6, #a-f	12.00	12.00

Souvenir Sheet

Perf. 12

1143	A457	$3.50 multi	7.00	7.00

No. 1143 contains one 30x50mm stamp.

BMX Cycling — A458

No. 1144 — Rider: a, With black shirt and helmet. b, With white shirt and black helmet, seated on bicycle. c, With black stocking cap. d, With yellow helmet. e, Without helmet. f, With white shirt and black helmet, not on bicycle seat.

$3.50, Rider with blue shirt and helmet, horiz.

2015, Mar. 9 Litho. *Perf. 14*

1144	A458	$1 Sheet of 6, #a-f	12.00	12.00

Souvenir Sheet

Perf. 12½

1145	A458	$3.50 multi	7.00	7.00

No. 1145 contains one 51x38mm stamp.

Marine Life — A459

Designs: 1c, Achilles surgeonfish. 2c, Yellow finger sponge. 4c, Spotted eagle ray. 5c, Green sea turtle. 10c, Box jellyfish.

2015, Apr. 1 Litho. *Perf. 12½*

1146-1150	A459	Set of 5	.45	.45

A460

A461

A462

A463

A464

A465

A466

A467

A468

Hibiscus Flowers — A469

Various hibiscus flowers: No. 1151, 20c. No. 1152, 25c. No. 1153, 26c. No. 1154, 27c.

2015, Apr. 1 Litho. *Perf. 13¼x12½*

1151-1154	A460	Set of 4	2.00	2.00
1155		Vert. strip of 5	5.00	5.00
a.		A460 50c multi	1.00	1.00
b.		A461 50c multi	1.00	1.00
c.		A462 50c multi	1.00	1.00
d.		A463 50c multi	1.00	1.00
e.		A464 50c multi	1.00	1.00
f.		Souvenir sheet of 5, #1155a-1155e	5.00	5.00
1156		Vert. strip of 5	10.00	10.00
a.		A465 $1 multi	2.00	2.00
b.		A466 $1 multi	2.00	2.00
c.		A467 $1 multi	2.00	2.00
d.		A468 $1 multi	2.00	2.00
e.		A469 $1 multi	2.00	2.00
f.		Souvenir sheet of 5, #1156a-1156e	10.00	10.00

Illustrations of British Warblers by Henrik Grönvold (1858-1940) — A470

No. 1157: a, Common chiffchaff. b, Lesser whitethroat. c, Great reed warbler. d, Aquatic warbler. e, Common whitethroat. f, Melodious warbler.

$3.50, Radde's bush warblers, horiz.

2015, Apr. 16 Litho. *Perf. 13¼x12½*

1157	A470	$1 Sheet of 6, #a-f	12.00	12.00

Souvenir Sheet

Perf. 13¼

1158	A470	$3.50 multi	7.00	7.00

Europhilex 2015 Stamp Exhibition, London. No. 1158 contains one 51x38mm stamp.

Queen Elizabeth II and World Leaders — A471

No. 1159 — Queen Elizabeth II with: a, British Prime Minister Sir Winston Churchill and Baroness Spencer-Churchill. b, Irish Pres. Mary McAleese. c, Pope John Paul II. d, Pope Francis. e, South African Pres. Nelson Mandela. f, U.S. Pres. John F. Kennedy and wife, Jacqueline.

$3.50, Queen Elizabeth II and U.S. Pres. Barack Obama, vert.

2015, May 25 Litho. *Perf. 14*

1159	A471	$1 Sheet of 6, #a-f	12.00	12.00

Souvenir Sheet

Perf. 12

1160	A471	$3.50 multi	7.00	7.00

Masks — A472

No. 1161: a, K'inich Janaab' Pakal death mask. b, Japanese demon mask. c, Tapuanu mask. d, Sicán mask. e, Alutiiq mask. f, Mask of Anubis.
$3.50, Mask of Agamemnon.

2015, June 1 Litho. *Perf. 14*
1161 A472 $1 Sheet of 6, #a-f, + 6 labels 12.00 12.00

Souvenir Sheet
Perf. 12
1162 A472 $3.50 multi 7.00 7.00

Miniature Sheets

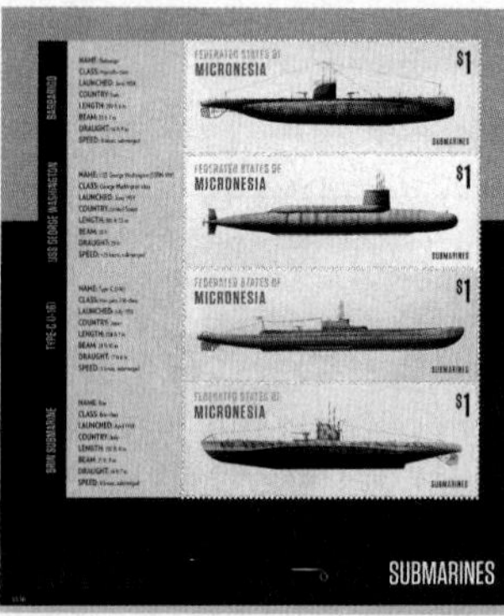

A473

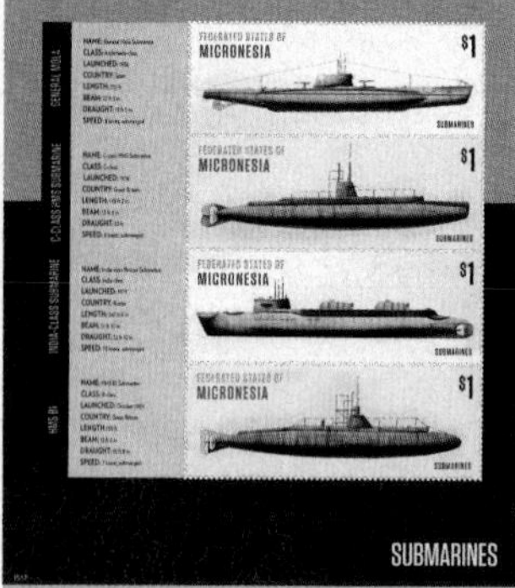

Submarines — A474

No. 1163: a, Barbarigo, Italy. b, USS George Washington, United States. c, Type C (I-16), Japan. d, Brin, Italy.
No. 1164: a, General Mola, Spain. b, C Class HMS, Great Britain. c, India Class Rescue, Russia. d, HMS B1, Great Britain.

2015, July 13 Litho. *Perf. 14*
1163 A473 $1 Sheet of 4, #a-d 8.00 8.00
1164 A474 $1 Sheet of 4, #a-d 8.00 8.00

Sir Winston Churchill (1874-1965), British Prime Minister — A475

No. 1165 — Photograph of Churchill from: a, 1895. b, 1904. c, 1914. d, 1924. e, 1940. f, 1951.
No. 1166 — Photograph of Churchill from: a, 1881. b, 1960.

2015, July 13 Litho. *Perf. 14*
1165 A475 $1 Sheet of 6, #a-f 12.00 12.00

Souvenir Sheet
Perf. 12
1166 A475 $1.75 Sheet of 2, #a-b 7.00 7.00

Birth of Princess Charlotte of Cambridge — A476

No. 1167: a, King George VI, Queen Mother and Princess Elizabeth. b, Princess Elizabeth and Prince Charles. c, Prince Charles, Princess Diana and Prince William. d, Duke and Duchess of Cambridge with Princess Charlotte.
$3.50, Duke and Duchess of Cambridge with Princess Charlotte, diff.

2015, July 13 Litho. *Perf. 12*
1167 A476 $1 Sheet of 4, #a-d 8.00 8.00

Souvenir Sheet
Perf. 14
1168 A476 $3.50 multi 7.00 7.00

Birds — A477

No. 1169: a, White tern. b, Red junglefowl. c, Little pied cormorant. d, Purple swamphen. e, Chestnut munia. f, Reunion gray white-eye.
$3.50, Blue-faced parrotfinch.

2015, July 13 Litho. *Perf. 12*
1169 A477 $1 Sheet of 6, #a-f 12.00 12.00

Souvenir Sheet
1170 A477 $3.50 multi 7.00 7.00

Miniature Sheets

Stamps of United Nations Countries — A478

No. 1171, $1: a, Great Britain #1. b, Brunei #1. c, Bulgaria #1. d, Burkina Faso #1. e, Burundi #1. f, Cape Verde #1.
No. 1172, $1: a, Cambodia #1. b, Cameroun #1. c, Canada #1. d, Central African Republic #1. e, Chad #1. f, Chile #1.
No. 1173, $1: a, People's Republic of China #1. b, Colombia #6. c, Comoro Islands #30. d, Congo Democratic Republic #323. e, Congo Republic #89. f, Costa Rica #1.
No. 1174, $1: a, Croatia #1. b, Cuba #1. c, Cyprus #1. d, Czech Republic #2877. e, Denmark #1. f, Djibout #439.
No. 1175, $1: a, Dominica #1. b, Domincan Republic #1. c, Ecuador #2. d, Egypt #1. e, El Salvador #1. f, Equatorial Guinea #1.
No. 1176, $1: a, Eritrea #1. b, Estonia #1. c, Ethiopia #1. d, Fiji #1. e, Finland #83. f, France #1.
No. 1177, $1: a, Gabon #1. b, Gambia #1. c, Georgia #7. d, Germany #1. e, Ghana #1. f, Greece #1.
No. 1178, $1: a, Grenada #1. b, Guatemala #1. c, Guinea-Bissau #345. d, Guinea #168. e, British Guiana #13. f, Haiti #1.

2015, July 13 Litho. *Perf. 12½*
Sheets of 6, #a-f
1171-1178 A478 Set of 8 96.00 96.00

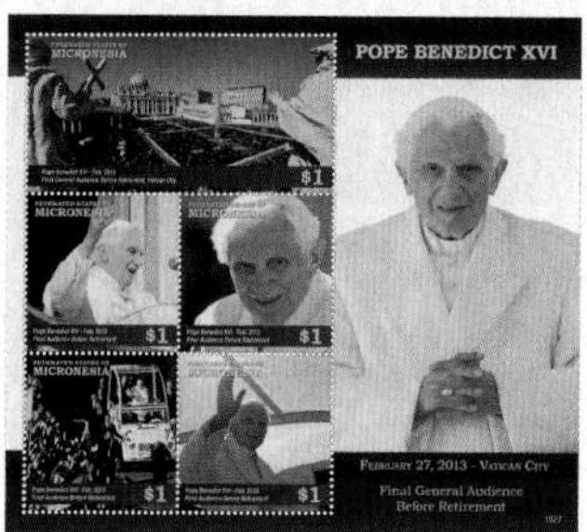

Pope Benedict XVI — A479

No. 1179: a, Crowd at St. Peter's Square (70x35mm). b, Pope Benedict XVI waving, microphone at right (35x35mm). c, Head of Pope Benedict XVI (35x35mm). d, Crowd watching Pope Benedict XVI in Popemobile (35x35mm). e, Pope Benedict XVI waving under roof of Popemobile (35x35mm).
$3.50, Pope Benedict XVI on balcony.

2015, Sept. 8 Litho. *Perf. 13¾*
1179 A479 $1 Sheet of 5, #a-e 10.00 10.00

Souvenir Sheet
1180 A479 $3.50 multi 7.00 7.00

No. 1180 contains one 35x35mm stamp.

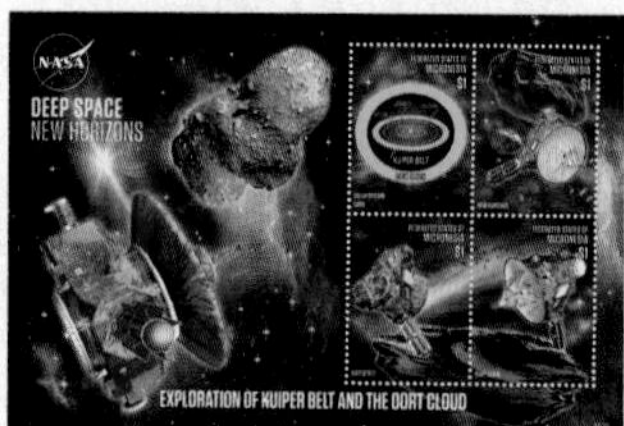

New Horizons Space Probe — A480

No. 1181 — Inscriptions: a, Solar system card. b, New Horizons. c, Kuiper Belt. d, Oort Cloud.
$3.50, Jan. 19, 2006 launch of New Horizons.

2015, Sept. 8 Litho. *Perf. 12*
1181 A480 $1 Sheet of 4, #a-d 8.00 8.00

Souvenir Sheet
1182 A480 $3.50 multi 7.00 7.00

Paintings by Vincent van Gogh (1853-90) — A481

No. 1183: a, Cypresses with Two Women, 1889. b, Vase with Red Poppies, 1886. c, Avenue of Poplars in Autumn, 1884. d, The Good Samaritan (after Delacroix), 1890. e, Plaster Statuette of a Female Torso, 1886. f, Portrait of a Man (Joseph-Michel Ginoux), 1888.
$3.50, Wheat Field with Cypresses, 1889, horiz.

2015, Sept. 8 Litho. *Perf. 12*
1183 A481 $1 Sheet of 6, #a-f 12.00 12.00

Souvenir Sheet
Perf. 12½
1184 A481 $3.50 multi 7.00 7.00

No. 1184 contains one 51x38mm stamp.

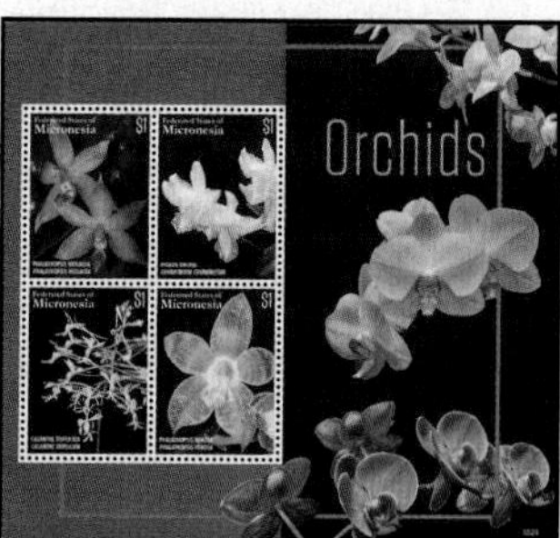

Orchids — A482

No. 1185: a, Phalaenopsis violacea. b, Pigeon orchid. c, Calanthe triplicata. d, Phalaenopsis venosa.
$3.50, Moth orchid.

2015, Sept. 8 Litho. *Perf. 12*
1185 A482 $1 Sheet of 4, #a-d 8.00 8.00

Souvenir Sheet
Perf. 13¾
1186 A482 $3.50 multi 7.00 7.00

No. 1186 contains one 35x35mm stamp.

Flowers — A483

No. 1187: a, Spider lily. b, Garden croton. c, Sea hibiscus. d, Frangipani. e, Wild ginger. f, Dauerleng.
$3.50, Frangipani, diff.

2015, Sept. 8 Litho. *Perf. 14*
1187 A483 $1 Sheet of 6, #a-f 12.00 12.00

Souvenir Sheet
Perf. 12½
1188 A483 $3.50 multi 7.00 7.00

No. 1188 contains one 51x38mm stamp.

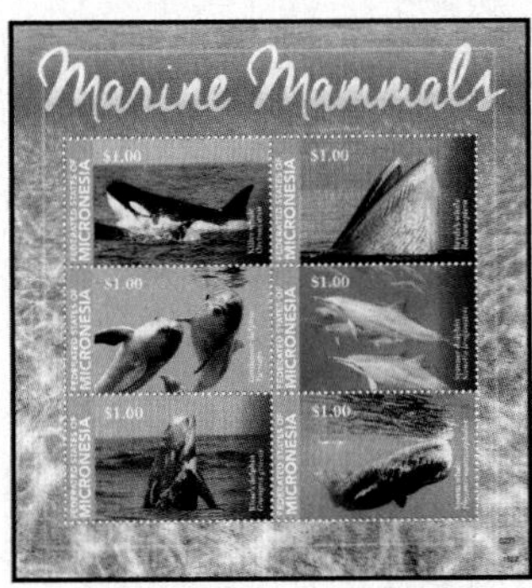

Marine Mammals — A484

No. 1189: a, Killer whale. b, Bryde's whale. c, Bottlenose dolphins. d, Spinner dolphins. e, Risso's dolphin. f, Sperm whale.
$3.50, Dugong, vert.

2015, Sept. 8 Litho. *Perf. 12*
1189 A484 $1 Sheet of 6, #a-f 12.00 12.00

Souvenir Sheet

Perf. 12½

1190 A484 $3.50 multi 7.00 7.00

No. 1190 contains one 38x51mm stamp.

Battle of Waterloo, 200th Anniv. — A485

No. 1191 — Lion's Mound Monument with outer frame color of: a, Dull scarlet. b, Blue black. c, light blue. d, Blue green. e, Carmine. f, Yellow orange.
$3.50, Purple brown.

2015, Sept. 30 Litho. *Perf. 13¾*
1191 A485 $1 Sheet of 6, #a-f 12.00 12.00

Souvenir Sheet

1192 A485 $3.50 multi 7.00 7.00

Christmas A486

Paintings by Bartolomé Esteban Murillo (1617-82): 34c, Adoration of the Shepherds, 1657. 49c, Adoration of the Shepherds, 1646-50. $1, Adoration of the Magi, 1655-60. $2, Madonna and Child, 1670.

2015, Nov. 2 Litho. *Perf. 12½*
1193-1196 A486 Set of 4 7.75 7.75

AIR POST STAMPS

Boeing 727, 1968 AP1

35c, SA-16 Albatross, 1960. 40c, PBY-5A Catalina, 1951.

1984, July 12 Litho. *Perf. 13½*
C1 AP1 28c shown .60 .60
C2 AP1 35c multi .80 .80
C3 AP1 40c multi 1.00 1.00
Nos. C1-C3 (3) 2.40 2.40

Ausipex Type of 1984

Ausipex '84 emblem and: 28c, Caroline Islands No. 4. 35c, No. 7. 40c, No. 19.

1984, Sept. 21 Litho. *Perf. 13½*
C4 A4 28c multicolored .65 .65
C5 A4 35c multicolored .85 .85
C6 A4 40c multicolored 1.10 1.10
Nos. C4-C6 (3) 2.60 2.60

Christmas Type

Children's drawings: 28c, Illustrated Christmas text. 35c, Decorated palm tree. 40c, Feast preparation.

1984, Dec. 20
C7 A5 28c multi .65 .65
C8 A5 35c multi .90 .90
C9 A5 40c multi 1.10 1.10
Nos. C7-C9 (3) 2.65 2.65

Ships Type

1985, Aug. 19
C10 A6 33c L'Astrolabe .65 .65
C11 A6 39c La Coquille .80 .80
C12 A6 44c Shenandoah 1.00 1.00
Nos. C10-C12 (3) 2.45 2.45

Christmas Type

33c, Dublon Protestant Church. 44c, Pohnpei Catholic Church.

1985, Oct. 15 Litho. *Perf. 13½*
C13 A7 33c multi .90 .90
C14 A7 44c multi 1.25 1.25

Audubon Type

1985, Oct. 31 *Perf. 14½*
C15 A8 44c Sooty tern 1.00 1.00

Ruins Type

33c, Nan Tauas inner courtyard. 39c, Outer wall. 44c, Tomb.

1985, Dec. Litho. *Perf. 13½*
C16 A16 33c multi .70 .70
C17 A16 39c multi .80 .80
C18 A16 44c multi .90 .90
Nos. C16-C18 (3) 2.40 2.40

Halley's Comet AP2

1986, May 16
C19 AP2 44c dk bl, bl & blk 1.40 1.25

Return of Nauruans from Truk, 40th Anniv. AP3

1986, May 16
C20 AP3 44c Ship in port 1.40 1.25

AMERIPEX '86 Type

Bully Hayes (1829-1877), buccanneer: 33c, Forging Hawaiian stamp. 39c, Sinking of the Leonora, Kosrae. 44c, Hayes escapes capture. 75c, Biography, by Louis Becke.
$1, Hayes ransoming chief.

1986, May 22
C21 A18 33c multi .55 .55
C22 A18 39c multi .70 .70
C23 A18 44c multi .75 .75
C24 A18 75c multi 1.50 1.50
Nos. C21-C24 (4) 3.50 3.50

Souvenir Sheet

C25 A18 $1 multi 3.25 3.25

Christmas Type

Virgin and child paintings: 33c, Austria, 19th cent. 44c, Italy, 18th cent., diff.

1986, Oct. 15 Litho. *Perf. 14½*
C26 A20 33c multicolored 1.00 1.00
C27 A20 44c multicolored 1.40 1.40

Anniversaries and Events Type

33c, US currency, bicent. 39c, 1st American in orbit, 25th anniv. 44c, US Constitution, bicent.

1987, June 13 Litho. *Perf. 14½*
C28 A21 33c multi .60 .60
C29 A21 39c multi 1.00 1.00
C30 A21 44c multi 1.10 1.10
Nos. C28-C30 (3) 2.70 2.70

Christmas Type

1987, Nov. 16 Litho. *Perf. 14½*
C31 A22 33c Holy Family .80 .80
C32 A22 39c Shepherds .90 .90
C33 A22 44c Three Wise Men 1.00 1.00
Nos. C31-C33 (3) 2.70 2.70

Bird Type

33c, Great truk white-eye. 44c, Blue-faced parrotfinch. $1, Yap monarch.

1988, Aug. 1 Litho. *Perf. 13½*
C34 A9 33c multi .55 .55
C35 A9 44c multi .70 .70
C36 A9 $1 multi 1.75 1.75
Nos. C34-C36 (3) 3.00 3.00

Colonial Era Type

No. C37, Traditional skills (boat-building). No. C38, Modern Micronesia (tourism).

1988, July 20 *Perf. 13x13½*
C37 A23 44c multi .95 .95
C38 A23 44c multi .95 .95
a. Pair, #C37-C38 1.90 1.90

Printed se-tenant in sheets of 28 plus 4 center labels picturing flags of Kosrae (UL), Truk (UR), Pohnpei (LL) and Yap ((LR).

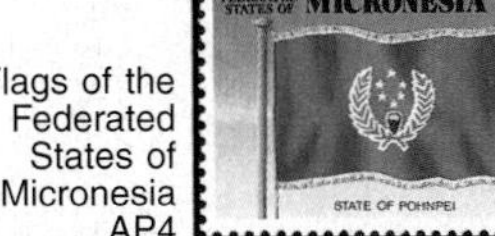

Flags of the Federated States of Micronesia AP4

1989, Jan. 19 Litho. *Perf. 13x13½*
C39 AP4 45c Pohnpei .70 .70
C40 AP4 45c Truk .70 .70
C41 AP4 45c Kosrae .70 .70
C42 AP4 45c Yap .70 .70
a. Block of 4, #C39-C42 2.80 2.80

This issue exists with 44c denominations but was not issued.

Aircraft Serving Micronesia AP5

1990, July 16 Litho. *Perf. 14*
C43 AP5 22c shown .40 .40
C44 AP5 36c multi, diff. .65 .65
C45 AP5 39c multi, diff. .75 .75
C46 AP5 45c multi, diff. .85 .85

No. C47, Propeller plane, outrigger canoe. No. C48, Passenger jet, sailboat.

1992, Mar. 27
C47 AP5 40c multicolored .70 .70
C48 AP5 50c multicolored .85 .85
Nos. C43-C48 (6) 4.20 4.20

Souvenir Sheet

First Manned Moon Landing, 25th Anniv. — AP6

1994, July 20 Litho. *Perf. 13½*
C49 AP6 $2.90 US #C76 4.25 4.25

MIDDLE CONGO

'mi-dəl 'käŋ-gō

LOCATION — Western Africa at the Equator, bordering on the Atlantic Ocean
GOVT. — Former French Colony
AREA — 166,069
POP. — 746,805 (1936)
CAPITAL — Brazzaville

In 1910 Middle Congo, formerly a part of French Congo, was declared a separate colony. It was grouped with Gabon and the Ubangi-Shari and Chad Territories and officially designated French Equatorial Africa. This group became a single administrative unit in 1934. See Gabon.

See Congo People's Republic for issues of 1959 onward.

100 Centimes = 1 Franc

See French Equatorial Africa No. 191 for additional stamp inscribed "Moyen Congo" and "Afrique Equatoriale Francaise."

Leopard — A1

Bakalois Woman — A2

Coconut Grove — A3

Perf. 14x13½

1907-22		Typo.		Unwmk.
1	A1	1c ol gray & brn	.35	.45
2	A1	2c vio & brn	.35	.45
3	A1	4c blue & brn	.70	*.85*
4	A1	5c dk grn & bl	.70	.70
5	A1	5c yel & bl ('22)	.70	.75
6	A1	10c car & bl	1.00	.70
7	A1	10c dp grn & bl grn ('22)	4.00	4.00
a.		Imperf pair	300.00	
8	A1	15c brn vio & rose ('17)	2.10	1.00
9	A1	20c brown & bl	3.50	2.75
10	A2	25c blue & grn	1.40	1.10
11	A2	25c bl grn & gray ('22)	1.00	1.00
12	A2	30c scar & grn	2.10	1.75
13	A2	30c dp rose & rose ('22)	1.75	*2.10*
14	A2	35c vio brn & bl	1.75	1.40
15	A2	40c dl grn & brn	1.75	1.75
16	A2	45c violet & red	6.00	3.50
17	A2	50c bl grn & red	2.10	2.10
18	A2	50c bl & grn ('22)	1.75	2.10
19	A2	75c brown & bl	8.50	5.50
20	A3	1fr dp grn & vio	13.00	9.00
21	A3	2fr vio & gray grn	14.00	10.00
22	A3	5fr blue & rose	42.50	37.50
		Nos. 1-22 (22)	111.00	90.45

For stamps of types A1-A3 in changed colors, see Chad and Ubangi-Shari. French Congo A4-A6 are similar but inscribed "Congo Francais."

For overprints and surcharges see Nos. 23-60, B1-B2.

Stamps and Types of 1907-22 Overprinted in Black, Blue or Red

1924-30

23 A1 1c ol gray & brn .35 .50
a. Double surcharge 150.00
24 A1 2c violet & brn .35 .50
25 A1 4c blue & brn .35 .50
b. Imperf pair 350.00
26 A1 5c yellow & bl .50 .50
27 A1 10c grn & bl grn (R) 1.10 .35
28 A1 10c car & gray ('25) .35 *.50*
29 A1 15c brn vio & rose (Bl) .70 .50
a. Double surcharge 175.00
30 A1 20c brown & blue .70 .65
31 A1 20c bl grn & yel grn ('26) .35 .35
32 A1 20c dp brn & rose lil ('27) 1.40 1.00

Nos. 10-22 Overprinted in Black, Red (R), and Blue (Bl)

33 A2 25c bl grn & gray 1.00 .40
34 A2 30c rose & pale rose (Bl) 1.40 .70
35 A2 30c gray & bl vio (R) ('25) .70 .65
36 A2 30c dk grn & grn ('27) 1.75 1.40
37 A2 35c choc & bl .70 .70
38 A2 40c ol grn & brn 1.40 1.40
a. Double overprint 300.00
39 A2 45c vio & pale red (Bl) 1.40 1.00
a. Inverted overprint 200.00
40 A2 50c blue & grn (R) 1.40 1.00
41 A2 50c org & blk ('25) .70 .65
a. Without overprint 220.00 *225.00*
42 A2 65c org brn & bl ('27) 2.75 2.10
43 A2 75c brown & blue 1.40 1.40
44 A2 90c brn red & pink ('30) 4.25 3.50
45 A3 1fr green & vio 1.40 1.40
a. Double overprint 275.00
46 A3 1.10fr vio & brn ('28) 3.50 4.25
47 A3 1.50fr ultra & bl ('30) 7.00 5.00
48 A3 2fr vio & gray grn 2.10 1.40
b. Imperf pair 300.00
49 A3 3fr red violet ('30) 7.00 5.00
50 A3 5fr blue & rose 5.00 5.00
Nos. 23-50 (28) 51.00 42.30

Nos. 48 and 50 Surcharged with New Values

1924

51 A3 25c on 2fr vio & gray grn 1.00 1.00
52 A3 25c on 5fr bl & rose (Bl) 1.25 1.25

Types of 1924-27 Surcharged with New Values in Black or Red

1925-27

53 A3 65c on 1fr red org & ol brn 1.00 1.00
a. Without surcharge 275.00
54 A3 85c on 1fr red org & ol brn 1.00 1.00
a. Double surcharge 175.00
55 A2 90c on 75c brn red & rose red ('27) 2.00 *2.40*
56 A3 1.25fr on 1fr dl bl & ultra (R) 1.40 1.40
a. Without surcharge 200.00 200.00
57 A3 1.50fr on 1fr ultra & bl ('27) 2.00 2.00
a. Without surcharge 200.00 *200.00*
58 A3 3fr on 5fr org brn & dl red ('27) 4.00 *4.00*
a. Without surcharge 275.00
59 A3 10fr on 5fr ver & bl grn ('27) 13.00 13.00
60 A3 20fr on 5fr org brn & vio ('27) 13.50 13.50
Nos. 53-60 (8) 37.90 38.30

Bars cover old values on Nos. 56-60.

Common Design Types pictured following the introduction.

Colonial Exposition Issue

Common Design Types

1931 Engr. *Perf. 12½*

Name of Country in Black

61 CD70 40c deep green 4.00 4.00
62 CD71 50c violet 5.50 5.50
63 CD72 90c red orange 5.50 5.50
64 CD73 1.50fr dull blue 5.50 5.50
Nos. 61-64 (4) 20.50 20.50

Viaduct at Mindouli A4

Pasteur Institute at Brazzaville A5

Government Building, Brazzaville — A6

1933 Photo. *Perf. 13½*

65 A4 1c lt brown .25 .25
66 A4 2c dull blue .25 .25
67 A4 4c olive grn .30 .30
68 A4 5c red violet .50 .35
69 A4 10c slate .70 .40
70 A4 15c dk violet 1.40 1.00
71 A4 20c red, *pink* 8.50 6.00
72 A4 25c orange 1.00 1.00
73 A4 30c yellow grn 2.50 1.75
74 A5 40c orange brn 2.50 1.40
75 A5 45c blk, *green* 2.50 1.75
76 A5 50c black violet .90 .70
77 A5 65c brn red, *grn* 2.50 1.75
78 A5 75c black, *pink* 13.00 9.50
79 A5 90c carmine 2.50 1.75
80 A5 1fr dark red 1.00 .70
81 A5 1.25fr Prus blue 2.10 1.40
82 A5 1.50fr dk blue 14.00 7.00
83 A6 1.75fr dk violet 2.75 1.40
84 A6 2fr grnsh blk 2.10 1.40
85 A6 3fr orange 7.00 4.00
86 A6 5fr slate blue 35.00 25.00
87 A6 10fr black 50.00 35.00
88 A6 20fr dark brown 35.00 27.50
Nos. 65-88 (24) 188.25 131.55

SEMI-POSTAL STAMPS

No. 6 Surcharged in Black

1916 Unwmk. *Perf. 14x13½*

B1 A1 10c + 5c car & blue 1.40 1.40
a. Double surcharge 140.00 140.00
b. Inverted surcharge 120.00 120.00
e. As "a," One inverted 175.00 175.00
f. In pair with unsurcharged stamp 360.00

A printing with the surcharge placed lower and more to the left was made and used in Ubangi.

No. 6 Surcharged in Red

B2 A1 10c + 5c car & blue 1.40 1.40

POSTAGE DUE STAMPS

Postage Due Stamps of France Overprinted

1928 Unwmk. *Perf. 14x13½*

J1 D2 5c light blue .50 *.70*
J2 D2 10c gray brn .60 *.70*
J3 D2 20c olive grn 1.00 *1.40*
J4 D2 25c brt rose 1.40 *1.75*
J5 D2 30c lt red 1.40 *1.75*
J6 D2 45c blue grn 1.40 *1.75*
J7 D2 50c brown vio 1.40 *1.75*
J8 D2 60c yellow brn 2.50 2.75
J9 D2 1fr red brn 2.50 *2.75*
J10 D2 2fr orange red 3.50 *4.00*
J11 D2 3fr brt violet 5.00 *7.00*
Nos. J1-J11 (11) 21.20 26.30

Village on Ubangi, Dance Mask — D3

Steamer on Ubangi River — D4

1930 Typo.

J12 D3 5c dp bl & ol .70 *1.40*
J13 D3 10c dp red & brn 1.40 *1.40*
J14 D3 20c green & brn 2.75 *2.75*
J15 D3 25c lt bl & brn 3.50 *3.50*
J16 D3 30c bis brn & Prus bl 5.00 *5.00*
J17 D3 45c Prus bl & ol 6.00 *5.50*
J18 D3 50c red vio & brn 5.50 *6.00*
J19 D3 60c gray lil & bl blk 8.50 *9.00*
J20 D4 1fr bis brn & bl blk 10.00 *14.00*
J21 D4 2fr violet & brn 14.00 *14.00*
J22 D4 3fr dk red & brn 12.00 *10.00*
Nos. J12-J22 (11) 69.35 *72.55*

Rubber Trees and Djoué River — D5

1933 Photo. *Perf. 13½*

J23 D5 5c apple green .70 .70
J24 D5 10c dk bl, *bl* .70 .70
J25 D5 20c red, *yel* 1.40 1.40
J26 D5 25c chocolate 1.40 1.40
J27 D5 30c orange red 1.75 *2.10*
J28 D5 45c dk violet 1.75 *2.10*
J29 D5 50c gray black 2.50 *2.75*
J30 D5 60c blk, *orange* 3.75 *4.00*
J31 D5 1fr brown rose 5.50 *6.25*
J32 D5 2fr orange yel 7.00 *8.50*
J33 D5 3fr Prus blue 12.00 *15.00*
Nos. J23-J33 (11) 38.45 44.90

MOHELI

mo-'ā-lē

LOCATION — One of the Comoro Islands, situated in the Mozambique Channel midway between Madagascar and Mozambique (Africa)
GOVT. — French Colony
AREA — 89 sq. mi.
POP. — 4,000
CAPITAL — Fomboni
See Comoro Islands

100 Centimes = 1 Franc

Navigation and Commerce — A1

Perf. 14x13½

1906-07 Typo. Unwmk.

Name of Colony in Blue or Carmine

1 A1 1c blk, *lil bl* 3.75 2.40
2 A1 2c brn, *buff* 2.50 1.75
3 A1 4c claret, *lav* 3.75 2.40
4 A1 5c yellow grn 4.25 2.40
5 A1 10c carmine 6.00 2.40
6 A1 20c red, *green* 13.00 7.25
7 A1 25c blue 13.00 5.50
8 A1 30c brn, *bister* 17.50 14.50
9 A1 35c blk, *yellow* 10.50 4.00
10 A1 40c red, *straw* 17.50 13.50
11 A1 45c blk, *gray grn* ('07) 75.00 60.00
a. Perf 11 300.00
12 A1 50c brn, *az* 24.00 14.50
13 A1 75c dp vio, *org* 27.50 24.00
14 A1 1fr brnz grn, *straw* 24.00 17.50
15 A1 2fr vio, *rose* 35.00 35.00
16 A1 5fr lil, *lavender* 140.00 140.00
a. Imperf pair 700.00
Nos. 1-16 (16) 417.25 347.10

Perf. 13½x14 stamps are counterfeits.

No. 12, affixed to pressboard with animals printed on the back, was used as emergency currency in the Comoro Islands in 1920.

Issue of 1906-07 Surcharged in Carmine or Black

1912

17 A1 5c on 4c cl, *lav* (C) 2.40 *3.25*
18 A1 5c on 20c red, *grn* 3.50 *3.50*
19 A1 5c on 30c brn, *bis* (C) 2.25 *3.50*
20 A1 10c on 40c red, *straw* 2.25 *3.50*
21 A1 10c on 45c blk, *gray grn* (C) 2.00 2.00
a. "Moheli" double 475.00
b. "Moheli" triple 475.00
22 A1 10c on 50c brn, *az* (C) 3.50 *4.50*
Nos. 17-22 (6) 15.90 20.25

Two spacings between the surcharged numerals are found on Nos. 17 to 22. For detailed listings, see the *Scott Classic Specialized Catalogue of Stamps and Covers.*

The stamps of Mohéli were supposed to have been superseded by those of Madagascar, January, 1908. However, Nos. 17-22 were surcharged in 1912 to use up remainders. These were available for use in Madagascar and the entire Comoro archipelago. In 1950 stamps of Comoro Islands came into use.

MOLDOVA

mäl-'dō-və

(Moldavia)

LOCATION — Southeastern Europe, bounded by Romania and the Ukraine
GOVT. — Independent republic, member of the Commonwealth of Independent States
AREA — 13,012 sq. mi.
POP. — 4,460,838 (1999 est.)
CAPITAL — Chisinau

With the breakup of the Soviet Union on Dec. 26, 1991, Moldova and ten former Soviet republics established the Commonwealth of Independent States.

100 Kopecks = 1 Ruble
100 Bani = 1 Leu (1993)

Catalogue values for all unused stamps in this country are for Never Hinged items.

Coat of Arms — A1

Flag — A2

1991, June 23 Litho. *Imperf.*
Without Gum

1 A1 7k grn & multi .25 .25
2 A1 13k blue & multi .25 .40
3 A2 30k multi .40 .40
Nos. 1-3 (3) .90 1.05

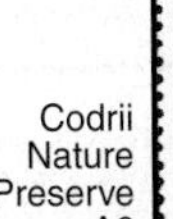

Codrii Nature Preserve A6

1992, Feb. 8 Litho. *Perf. 12*
25 A6 25k multicolored .40 .40

For surcharge see No. 547.

Natl. Arms — A7

1992, May 24 Photo. *Perf. 13½*
26 A7 35k green .25 .25
27 A7 50k red .25 .25
28 A7 65k brown .25 .25
29 A7 1r purple .25 .25
30 A7 1.50r blue .25 .25
Nos. 26-30 (5) 1.25 1.25

Birds — A8

Designs: 50k, Merops apiaster. 65k, Oriolus oriolus. 2.50r, Picus viridis. 6r, Coracias garrulus. 7.50r, Upupa epops. 15r, Cuculus canorus.

1992, Aug. 5 Litho. *Perf. 13½x14*
31 A8 50k multicolored .40 .40
32 A8 65k multicolored .40 .40
33 A8 2.50r multicolored .60 .60
34 A8 6r multicolored 1.00 1.00
35 A8 7.50r multicolored 1.30 1.30
36 A8 15r multicolored 2.75 2.75
Nos. 31-36 (6) 6.45 6.45

No. 31 incorrectly inscribed "ariaster." See Nos. 75-81.

Church of St. Panteleimon, Cent. — A9

1992, Aug. 10 Photo. *Perf. 11½*
37 A9 1.50r multicolored .40 .40

She-Wolf Suckling Romulus and Remus — A10

1992, Aug. 10 *Perf. 12x11½*
38 A10 5r multicolored 1.00 1.00

Russia Nos. 4598-4599, 5839 Surcharged "MOLDOVA" and New Value in Black or Red

1992, Aug. 31 Litho. *Perf. 12x12½*
39 A2138 2.50r on 4k #4599 .40 .40
40 A2139 6r on 3k #4598 .45 .45
41 A2138 8.50r on 4k #4599 .60 .60
42 A2765 10r on 3k #5839 (R) .70 .70
a. Black surcharge .70 .70
b. Brown red surcharge .70 .70
Nos. 39-42 (4) 2.15 2.15

Sheets of Nos. 39, 41 had row 5 inverted. On No. 40 only the 1st 5 stamps of row 5 were inverted. Counterfeit inverts were made using the original plates but with all 100 surcharges inverted. All inverts on No. 42 are fakes.

Russia Nos. 4596-4598 Surcharged in Black, Green or Red

1992, Oct. 20 Litho. *Perf. 12x12½*
43 A2138 45k on 2k #4597 (G) .40 .40
44 A2138 46k on 2k #4597 .40 .40
45 A2138 63k on 1k #4596 (R) .40 .40
46 A2138 63k on 3k #4598 .70 .70
47 A2138 70k on 1k #4596 (R) .40 .40
50 A2138 4r on 1k #4596 .70 .70
a. Red surcharge .70 .70
Nos. 43-50 (6) 3.00 3.00

Nos. 45-46 exist with overprint inverted (6th row of sheet).

1992 Summer Olympics, Barcelona — A11

1992, Oct. 24 Litho. *Perf. 13*
53 A11 35k High jump .30 .30
54 A11 65k Wrestling .35 .35
55 A11 1r Archery .35 .35
56 A11 2.50r Swimming .75 .75
57 A11 10r Equestrian 2.50 2.50
a. Souvenir sheet, #53-57 + label 4.75 4.75
Nos. 53-57 (5) 4.25 4.25

Nos. 55-56 Ovptd. with Name of Medalist, Medal and Olympic Rings in Bronze or Silver

1992, Oct. 24
58 A11 1r "NATALIA VALEEV / bronz" (BR) .55 .55
59 A11 2.50r "IURIE BAS-CATOV / argint" 1.00 1.00

Souvenir Sheet

Tudor Casapu, 1992 Weight Lifting Gold Medalist — A12

1992, Oct. 24 *Perf. 14½*
60 A12 25r multicolored 4.75 4.75

Admission of Moldova to UN — A13

Designs: 12r, UN Headquarters at left, Statue of Liberty, UN emblem, Moldovan flag.

1992, Oct. 24 *Perf. 13*
61 A13 1.30r multicolored *.85 .85*
62 A13 12r multicolored *1.75 1.75*

Moldovan Participation in Conference on European Security and Cooperation — A14

2.50r, Flag, Prague Castle. 25r, Helsinki Cathedral, flag.

1992, Oct. 24
63 A14 2.50r multi *1.25 1.25*
64 A14 25r multicolored *3.25 3.25*

Traditional Folk Art — A15

1992, Nov. 21 *Perf. 12x11½*
65 A15 7.50r Rug, pottery *1.25 1.25*

Admission of Moldova to UPU A16

1992, Dec. 26 *Perf. 12*
66 A16 5r Train, flag, emblem .30 .30
67 A16 10r Plane, flag, emblem .60 .60

Discovery of America, 500th Anniv. — A17

1992, Dec. 26 Litho. *Perf. 12*
68 A17 1r Galleon .25 .25
69 A17 6r Carrack .50 .50
70 A17 6r Caravel .50 .50
a. Pair, #69-70 3.25 3.25
Nos. 68-70 (3) 1.25 1.25

Souvenir Sheet

71 A17 25r Columbus 2.50 2.50

Elaphe Longissima A18

Denominations at: a, UL. b, UR. c, LL. d, LR.

1993, July 3 Litho. *Perf. 13½*
72 A18 3r Block of 4, #a.-d. 1.50 1.50
73 A18 15r Natrix natrix .60 .60
74 A18 25r Vipera berus .85 .85
Nos. 72-74 (3) 2.95 2.95

Bird Type of 1992

1993, July 24 Litho. *Perf. 13x13½*
75 A8 2r like #31 .30 .30
76 A8 3r like #32 .30 .30
77 A8 5r like #33 .30 .30
78 A8 10r like #34 .30 .30
79 A8 15r like #35 .35 .35
80 A8 50r like #36 .60 .60
81 A8 100r Hirundo rustica 1.25 1.25
Nos. 75-81 (7) 3.40 3.40

Nos. 75-81 exist imperf. Value, set *$100.*

Natl. Arms — A19

1993, Aug. 7 Photo. *Perf. 12x12½*
82 A19 2k blue .25 .25
83 A19 3k purple .25 .25
84 A19 6k green .25 .25
85 A19 10k olive & purple .25 .25
86 A19 15k olive & purple .25 .25
87 A19 20k gray & purple .25 .25
88 A19 30k yellow & purple .25 .25
89 A19 50k pink & purple .25 .25

Size: 21x32½mm
Perf. 12½x12

90 A19 100k multicolored .35 .35
91 A19 250k multicolored .85 .85
Nos. 82-91 (10) 3.20 3.20

For surcharges see Nos. 558-559.

Butterflies — A20

1993, Dec. 22 Litho. *Perf. 13*
94 A20 6b Pyrameis atalanta .25 .25
95 A20 10b Papilio machaon .25 .25
96 A20 50b Vanessa jo .40 .40
97 A20 250b Saturnia pavonia 1.75 1.75
Nos. 94-97 (4) 2.65 2.65

Flowers — A21

Designs: 6b, Tulipa bibersteiniana. 15b, Convallaria majalis. 25b, Galanthus nivalis. 30b, Paeonia peregrina. 50b, Galanthus plicatus. 90b, Pulsatilla grandis. 250b, Cypripedium calceolus.

1993, Dec. 25 Litho. *Perf. 13½*

98	A21	6b multicolored	.25	.25
99	A21	15b multicolored	.25	.25
100	A21	25b multicolored	.30	.30
101	A21	30b multicolored	.35	.35
102	A21	50b multicolored	.40	.40
103	A21	90b multicolored	.65	.65
		Nos. 98-103 (6)	2.20	2.20

Souvenir Sheet

104	A21	250b multicolored	1.80	1.80

No. 104 contains one 30x45mm stamp.

A22

Famous Men: 6b, Dragos Voda. 25b, Bogdan Voda I. 50b, Latcu Voda. 100b, Petru I Musat. 150b, Roman Voda Musat. 200b, Stefan I.

1993, Dec. 29 Litho. *Perf. 13*

105	A22	6b multicolored	.25	.25
106	A22	25b multicolored	.25	.25
107	A22	50b multicolored	.25	.25
108	A22	100b multicolored	.30	.30
109	A22	150b multicolored	.45	.45
110	A22	200b multicolored	.75	.75
		Nos. 105-110 (6)	2.25	2.25

A23

Europa (Contemporary art): 3b, History of Man, by M. Grecu. 150b, Springtime, by I. Vieru.

1993, Dec. 29 Litho. *Perf. 13*

111	A23	3b multicolored	.50	.50
112	A23	150b multicolored	4.00	4.00
a.		Souvenir sheet, 4 each #111-112 + label	20.00	20.00

1994 Winter Olympics, Lillehammer A24

1994, Feb. 12 Litho. *Perf. 13½*

113	A24	3b Biathlete, skiiers	.25	.25
114	A24	150b Biathlete, diff.	1.00	1.00

Russia No. 4596 Surcharged in Dark Blue

1994, Apr. 11 Litho. *Perf. 12x12½*

114A	A2138	3b on 1k olive grn	.25	.25
114B	A2138	25b on 1k olive grn	.25	.25
114C	A2138	50b on 1k olive grn	.35	.35
		Nos. 114A-114C (3)	.85	.85

First Manned Moon Landing, 25th anniv. — A25

Europa: 1b, Gemini space mission, Titan II rocket. 45b, Ed White, Gemini IV. 2.50 l, Lunar landing module.

1994, June 18 Litho. *Perf. 14*

115	A25	1b multicolored	.50	.50
116	A25	45b multicolored	2.40	2.40
117	A25	2.50 l multicolored	5.25	5.25
		Nos. 115-117 (3)	8.15	8.15

Natl. Arms — A26

1994 *Perf. 13½x14*

118	A26	1b multicolored	.25	.25
119	A26	10b multicolored	.25	.25
120	A26	30b multicolored	.25	.25
121	A26	38b multicolored	.25	.25
122	A26	45b multicolored	.55	.55
123	A26	75b multicolored	.65	.65
125	A26	1.50 l multicolored	1.20	1.20
126	A26	1.80 l multicolored	1.20	1.20
127	A26	2.50 l multi, size: 23½x29mm	1.90	1.90
128	A26	4.50 l multicolored	3.75	3.75
128A	A26	5.40 l multicolored	4.00	4.00
128B	A26	6.90 l multicolored	5.00	5.00

Size: 23½x29mm

128C	A26	7.20 l multicolored	5.00	5.00
129	A26	13 l multicolored	9.25	9.25
130	A26	24 l multicolored	17.50	17.50
		Nos. 118-130 (15)	51.00	51.00

Issued: 1b, 45b, 1.50 l, 4.50 l, 6/11/94; 10b, 30b, 5.40 l, 6.90 l, 13 l, 7/16/94; 38b, 75b, 1.80 l, 2.50 l, 7.20 l, 8/13/94.

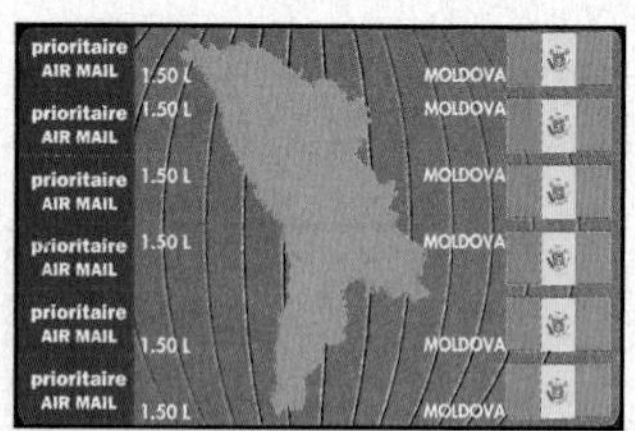

Stamp Card — A27

Designs: 1.50 l, 4.50 l, Map of Moldova.

Rouletted 26 on 2 or 3 Sides

1994, Dec. 22 Litho.

Self-Adhesive

Cards of 6 + 6 labels

131	A27	1.50 l #a.-f., lt vio & multi	6.25
132	A27	4.50 l #a.-f., dp red vio & multi	16.00

Individual stamps measure 70x9mm and have a card backing. Se-tenant labels inscribed "AIR MAIL."

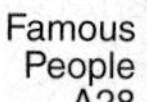

Famous People A28

Designs: 3b, Maria Cibotari (1910-49), singer. 90b, Dumitru Caraciobanu (1937-80), actor. 150b, Eugeniu Coca (1893-1954), composer. 250b, Igor Vieru (1923-83), painter.

1994, June 30 Litho. *Perf. 13½*

133	A28	3b multicolored	.25	.25
134	A28	90b multicolored	.30	.30
135	A28	150b multicolored	.40	.40
136	A28	250b multicolored	.70	.70
		Nos. 133-136 (4)	1.65	1.65

Stamp Day A29

Designs: 10b, Designing stamp. 45b, Printing stamps. 2 l, Inspecting finished sheets.

1994, July 22 Litho. *Perf. 14*

137	A29	10b multicolored	.30	.30
138	A29	45b multicolored	.75	.75
139	A29	2 l multicolored	2.25	2.25
		Nos. 137-139 (3)	3.30	3.30

Intl. Olympic Committee, Cent. — A30

60b, Pierre de Coubertin. 1.50 l, Olympic rings, symbol.

1994, Aug. 29 Litho. *Perf. 13½x14*

140	A30	60b multi	.45	.45
141	A30	1.50 l multi	1.10	1.10

Moldova's Entrance into NATO — A31

Designs: 60b, Moldova Pres. Mircea Snegur, NATO Secretary General Manfred Worner signing documents. 2.50 l, World map centered on Europe.

1994, Nov. 8 Litho. *Perf. 13½*

142	A31	60b multicolored	.85	.85
143	A31	2.50 l multicolored	3.25	3.25

Intl. Year of the Family — A32

30b, Family. 60b, Mother breast-feeding. 1.50 l, Child painting.

1994, Nov. 26 *Perf. 14*

144	A32	30b multi	.50	.50
145	A32	60b multi	1.00	1.00
146	A32	1.50 l multi	2.00	2.00
		Nos. 144-146 (3)	3.50	3.50

1996 European Soccer Championships, England — A33

Designs: 10b, Handshaking. 40b, Players legs, soccer ball. 1.20 l, Goalie.

No. 150: a, 1.10 l, Soccer federation, German flags. b, 2.20 l, Soccer ball, German, Moldovan flags. c, 2.40 l, Players.

1994, Dec. 10

147	A33	10b multicolored	.25	.25
148	A33	40b multicolored	.45	.45
149	A33	2.40 l multicolored	2.00	2.00
		Nos. 147-149 (3)	2.70	2.70

Souvenir Sheet

150	A33	Sheet of 3, #a.-c.	3.75	3.75

Christmas A34

Paintings of Birth of Christ by: 20b, unknown artist, 18th cent. 3.60 l, Gherasim, 1808.

1994, Dec. 29

151	A34	20b multicolored	.40	.40
152	A34	3.60 l multicolored	3.75	3.75

Mushrooms — A35

4b, Russula virescens. 10b, Boletus luridus. 20b, Cantherellus cibarius. 90b, Leccinum aurantiacum. 1.80 l, Leccinum duriusculum.

1995, Feb. 8

153	A35	4b multi	.45	.45
154	A35	10b multi	.70	.70
155	A35	20b multi	1.45	1.45
156	A35	90b multi	4.25	4.25
157	A35	1.80 l multi	8.00	8.00
		Nos. 153-157 (5)	14.85	14.85

European Nature Conservation Year — A36

Designs: 4b, Hieraaetus pennatus. 45b, Capreolus capreolus. 90b, Sus scrofa.

1995, Mar. 18 Litho. *Perf. 14*

158	A36	4b multicolored	.85	.85
159	A36	45b multicolored	4.00	4.00
160	A36	90b multicolored	8.25	8.25
		Nos. 158-160 (3)	13.10	13.10

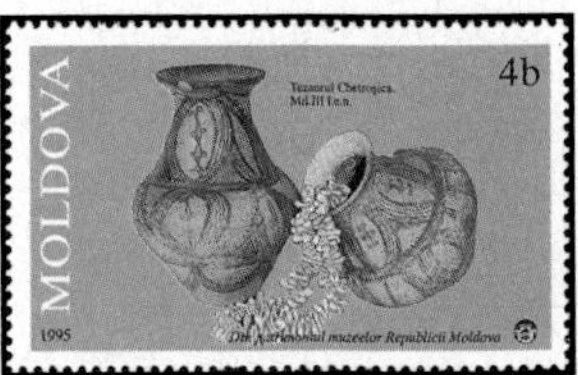

Museum of Natural Sciences — A37

Designs: 4b, Jars. 10b+2b, Dinotherium gigantissimum. 1.80 l+30b, Silver coin, 3rd-2nd cent. BC.

1995 Litho. *Perf. 14*

161	A37	4b multicolored	.45	.45
162	A37	10b +2b multi	.90	.90
163	A37	1.80 l +30b multi	6.25	6.25
		Nos. 161-163 (3)	7.60	7.60

Peace & Freedom — A38

Paintings: 10b, May 1945, by Igor Vieru. 40b, Linistea, by Sergiu Cuciuc. 2.20 l, Primavara 1944, by Cuciuc.

1995, May 9 Litho. *Perf. 14*

164	A38	10b multicolored	.40	.40
165	A38	40b multicolored	2.50	2.50
166	A38	2.20 l multicolored	4.75	4.75
		Nos. 164-166 (3)	7.65	7.65

Europa.

A39

Famous People: 9b, Constantin Stere (1865-1936), writer. 10b, Tamara Ceban (1914-90), musician. 40b, Alexandru Plamadeala (1888-1940), sculptor. 1.80 l, Lucian Blaga (1895-1961), writer.

1995, June 17 Litho. *Perf. 14*

167	A39	9b dp cl & gray	.35	.35
168	A39	10b brt mag & gray	.35	.35
169	A39	40b violet & gray	1.40	1.40
170	A39	1.80 l dk grn & gray	6.75	6.75
		Nos. 167-170 (4)	8.85	8.85

A40

Kings of Moldova, reign: No. 171, Alexandru Cel Bun, 1400-32. No. 172, Petru Aron, 1451-52, 1454-57. No. 173, Stefan Cel Mare, 1457-1504. 45b, Petru Rares, 1527-38, 1541-46. 90b, Alexandru Lapusneanu, 1552-61, 1564-68. 1.80 l, Ion Voda Cel Cumplit, 1572-74. 5 l, Stefan Cel Mare, 1457-1504.

1995, July 2 Litho. *Perf. 14*

171	A40	10 b multicolored	.40	.40
172	A40	10 b multicolored	.40	.40
173	A40	10 b multicolored	.40	.40
174	A40	45 b multicolored	1.75	1.75
175	A40	90 b multicolored	3.00	3.00
176	A40	1.80 l multicolored	7.00	7.00
		Nos. 171-176 (6)	12.95	12.95

Souvenir Sheet

177	A40	5 l multicolored	3.50	3.50

No. 177 contains one 24x29mm stamp.

Citadels of Moldova A41

1995, July 29

178	A41	10 b Soroca	.30	.30
179	A41	20 b Tighina	.60	.60
180	A41	60 b Alba	1.25	1.25
181	A41	1.30 l Hotin	3.50	3.50
		Nos. 178-181 (4)	5.65	5.65

A42

UN, 50th Anniv. — A43

Designs inside of stylized eye: No. 182, Forest stream. No. 183, Fighter plane. No. 184, Black child, barbed wire fence.

Nos. 185-186: a, 1. b, 2. c, 3. d, 4. e, 5. f, 6. g, 7. h, 8. i, 9. j, 10.

1995, Oct. 24 Litho. *Perf. 14*

182	A42	10b yellow & multi	.40	.40
183	A42	10b blue & multi	.40	.40
184	A42	1.50 l green & multi	5.25	5.25
		Nos. 182-184 (3)	6.05	6.05

Stamp Cards

Rouletted 15 on 2 or 3 Sides

Self-Adhesive

Cards of 10

185	A43	90b #a.-j.	*15.00*	*15.00*
186	A43	1.50 l #a.-j.	*25.00*	*25.00*

Background color of stamps gradually shifts from light blue (#1) to dark blue (#10). Each stamp is individually numbered.

Motion Pictures, Cent. — A44

Films: 10b, Last Moon of Autumn. 40b, Lautarii. 2.40 l, Dimitrie Cantemir.

1995, Dec. 28 Litho. *Perf. 14*

187	A44	10b red brn & blk	.65	.65
188	A44	40b olive & black	2.00	2.00
189	A44	2.40 l ultra & black	6.50	6.50
		Nos. 187-189 (3)	9.15	9.15

Mushrooms — A45

No. 190, Amanita muscaria. No. 191, Boletus satanas. 65b, Amanita phalloides. 1.30 l, Hypholoma fasciculare. 2.40 l, Amanita virosa.

1996, Mar. 23 Litho. *Perf. 14*

190	A45	10b multicolored	.95	.95
191	A45	10b multicolored	.95	.95
192	A45	65b multicolored	1.45	1.45
193	A45	1.30 l multicolored	2.25	2.25
194	A45	2.40 l multicolored	6.25	6.25
		Nos. 190-194 (5)	11.85	11.85

1996 Summer Olympic Games, Atlanta — A46

1996, Mar. 30

195	A46	10b Weight lifting	.45	.45
196	A46	20b +5b Judo	.45	.45
197	A46	45b +10b Running	.85	.85
198	A46	2.40 l +30b Canoeing	4.75	4.75
		Nos. 195-198 (4)	6.50	6.50

Souvenir Sheet

199	A46	2.20 l Archery	3.00	3.00
a.		With added inscription in sheet margin	3.75	3.75

No. 199 contains one 34x29mm stamp.

No. 199a inscribed "Nicolae JURAVSCHI Victor RENEISCHI / -canoe, argint- / Serghei MUREICO/ -lupte greco-romane,bronz-".

Monasteries A47

10b, Rudi, 18th cent. 90b, Japca, 17th cent. 1.30 l, Curchi, 18th cent. 2.80 l, Saharna, 18th cent. 4.40 l, Capriana, 16th cent.

1996, Apr. 26

200	A47	10b multi	.45	.45
201	A47	90b multi	.80	.80
202	A47	1.30 l multi	1.40	1.40
203	A47	2.80 l multi	3.00	3.00
204	A47	4.40 l multi	4.75	4.75
		Nos. 200-204 (5)	10.40	10.40

Birds — A48

Designs: 9b, Gallinula chloropus. 10b, Anser anser. No. 207, Streptopelia turtur. 4.40 l, Anas platyrhynchos.

No. 209, Phasianus colchicus.

1996, May 17

205	A48	9b multicolored	.35	.35
206	A48	10b multicolored	.35	.35
207	A48	2.20 l multicolored	2.50	2.50
208	A48	4.40 l multicolored	4.25	4.25
		Nos. 205-208 (4)	7.45	7.45

Souvenir Sheet

209	A48	2.20 l multicolored	2.50	2.50

Europa

A49

Famous Women: 10b, Elena Alistar (1873-1955), president of women's league. 3.70 l, Marie Curie (1867-1934), chemist, physicist. 2.20 l, Julia Hasdeu (1869-1888), writer.

1996, June 21 Litho. *Perf. 14*

210	A49	10b multicolored	.60	.60
211	A49	3.70 l multicolored	5.75	5.75

Souvenir Sheet

212	A49	2.20 l multicolored	4.75	4.75

A50

Famous Men: #213, Gavriil Banulescu-Bodoni (1746-1821). #214, Mihail Eminescu (1850-69), poet. 2.20 l, Ion Creanga (1837-89). 3.30 l, Vasile Alecsandri (1821-90). 5.40 l, Petru Movila (1596-1646), theologian.

1.80 l, Eminescu, diff., vert.

1996, July 30 Litho. *Perf. 14*

213	A50	10b gray vio & brn	.35	.35
214	A50	10b lt brn & dk brn	.35	.35
215	A50	2.20 l gray & brn	2.25	2.25
216	A50	3.30 l ol & brn	3.00	3.00
217	A50	5.40 l red brn & brn	5.00	5.00
		Nos. 213-217 (5)	10.95	10.95

Souvenir Sheet

218	A50	1.80 l brn	2.00	2.00

City of Chisinau, 560th Anniv. — A51

Building, year erected: 10b, City Hall, 1902. 1.30 l, Palace of Culture, 1911. 2.40 l, Mazarache Church, 1752.

1996, Oct. 6 Litho. *Perf. 14*

219	A51	10b multicolored	.75	.75
220	A51	1.30 l multicolored	2.50	2.50
221	A51	2.40 l multicolored	5.75	5.75
		Nos. 219-221 (3)	9.00	9.00

A52

Christmas: 10b, Children carrying star. 2.20 l+30b, Mother and child in center of star. 2.80 l+50b, Children decorating Christmas tree.

1996, Dec. 12 Litho. *Perf. 14*

222	A52	10b multicolored	.45	.45
223	A52	2.20 l +30b multicolored	3.25	3.25
224	A52	2.80 l +50b multicolored	4.00	4.00
		Nos. 222-224 (3)	7.70	7.70

A53

Wines of Moldova: 10b, Feteasca. 45b, Cabernet-Sauvignon. 65b, Sauvignon. 3.70 l, Rara neagra.

1997, Jan. 17 Litho. *Perf. 14*

225	A53	10b multi	.45	.45
226	A53	45b multi	.55	.55
227	A53	65b multi	.90	.90
228	A53	3.70 l multi	4.75	4.75
		Nos. 225-228 (4)	6.65	6.65

Easter — A54

Designs: 3.30b, Colored eggs, grass on plate. 5 l, Basket of eggs, food.

1997, Apr. 25 Litho. *Perf. 13½*

229	A54	10b multicolored	.35	.35
230	A54	3.30 l multicolored	2.75	2.75

Souvenir Sheet

231	A54	5 l multicolored	5.00	5.00

Composers — A55

Designs: No. 232, Franz Schubert (1797-1828). No. 233, Gavriil Musicescu (1847-1903). 45b, Sergei Rachmaninoff (1873-1943). 4.40 l, Georges Enescu (1881-1955).

1997, Feb. 22 Litho. *Perf. 14*

232	A55	10b slate & bl grn	.35	.35
233	A55	10b slate & bl grn	.35	.35
234	A55	45b slate & bl grn	.50	.50
235	A55	4.40 l slate & bl grn	4.00	4.00
		Nos. 232-235 (4)	5.20	5.20

Stories and Legends A56

Europa: 10b, Man holding up arms, goose flying, arrows from fortress. 2.80 l, Man upside down, church, sun in sky with stars and eye. 5 l, Angel touching flowers during winter.

1997, June 20 Litho. *Perf. 13½*

236	A56	10b multicolored	*1.00*	*1.00*
237	A56	2.80 l multicolored	*6.50*	*6.50*

Souvenir Sheet

238	A56	5 l multicolored	*8.50*	*8.50*

Red Book Insects — A57

Insects on plants, flowers: 25b, Mantis religiosa. 80b, Ascalphus macaronius scop. 1 l, Calosoma sycophanta. 2.20 l, Liometopum microcephalum. 5 l, Scolia maculata drury.

1997, July 26 Litho. *Perf. 14*

239	A57	25b multicolored	.35	.35
240	A57	80b multicolored	.95	.95
241	A57	1 l multicolored	1.10	1.10
242	A57	2.20 l multicolored	2.50	2.50
		Nos. 239-242 (4)	4.90	4.90

Souvenir Sheet

243	A57	5 l multicolored	5.00	5.00

World Post Day — A58

Designs: 10b, Chisinau post office building, 1997. 2.20 l, Mail coach, Chisinaupost office building. 3.30 l, Heinrich von Stephan (1831-97), vert.

1997, Oct. 18 Litho. *Perf. 14*

244	A58	10b multicolored	.40	.40
245	A58	2.20 l multicolored	2.50	2.50
246	A58	3.30 l multicolored	4.00	4.00
		Nos. 244-246 (3)	6.90	6.90

Christmas A59

Designs: 10b, Noul Neamt Monastery. 45b, "Adoration of the Shepherds," Noul Neamt Monastery. 5 l, "Nativity," Natl. Museum of Plastic Arts.

1997, Dec. 17 Litho. *Perf. 13½*

247	A59	10b multicolored	.25	.25
248	A59	45b multicolored	.30	.30
249	A59	5 l multicolored	2.75	2.75
		Nos. 247-249 (3)	3.30	3.30

A60

Cultural Heritage Sites: 7b, Nicolai Zelinski High School, Tiraspol. No. 251, Railway station, Tighina. No. 252, Cathedral, Balti. 90b, Church, Causeni. 1.30 l, Cathedral, Kagul. 3.30 l, Art Institute, Chisinau.

1997, Dec. 16 Litho. *Perf. 14*

250	A60	7b black & lilac	.40	.40
251	A60	10b black & red violet	.40	.40
252	A60	10b black & grn blue	.40	.40
253	A60	90b black & yel org	.80	.80
254	A60	1.30 l black & blue	1.25	1.25
255	A60	3.30 l black & gray	3.00	3.00
		Nos. 250-255 (6)	6.25	6.25

A61

Princes of Moldova, reign: No. 256, Petru Schiopul (1574-77, 78-79, 82-91). No. 257, Ieremia Movila (1595-1606). 45b, Stefan Tomsa (1611-15, 1621-23). 1.80 l, Radu Mihnea (1616-19, 1623-26). 2.20 l, Miron Barnovschi Movila (1626-29, 1633). 2.80 l, Bogdan Orbul (1504-17).

5 l, Mihai Viteazul, 1600.

1997, Dec. 17

256	A61	10b multicolored	.30	.30
257	A61	10b multicolored	.30	.30
258	A61	45b multicolored	.40	.40
259	A61	1.80 l multicolored	1.50	1.50
260	A61	2.20 l multicolored	2.00	2.00
261	A61	2.80 l multicolored	2.50	2.50
		Nos. 256-261 (6)	7.00	7.00

Souvenir Sheet

262	A61	5 l multicolored	5.00	5.00

No. 262 contains one 23x29mm stamp.

1998 Winter Olympic Games, Nagano A62

1998, Feb. 28

263	A62	10b Slalom skiing	.45	.45
264	A62	45b Figure skating	.90	.90
265	A62	2.20 l Biathlon	3.50	3.50
		Nos. 263-265 (3)	4.85	4.85

A63

Famous People: 10b, Alexei Mateevici (1888-1917). 40b, Pantelimon Halippa (1883-1979). 60b, Stefan Ciobanu (1883-1950). 2 l, Constantin Stamati-Ciurea (1828-98).

5 l, Nicolae Milescu-Spatarul (1636-1708).

1998, May 9 Litho. *Perf. 14*

266	A63	10b multicolored	.25	.25
267	A63	40b multicolored	.45	.45
268	A63	60b multicolored	.60	.60
269	A63	2 l multicolored	1.80	1.80
		Nos. 266-269 (4)	3.10	3.10

Souvenir Sheet

270	A63	5 l multicolored	4.50	4.50

A64

Monuments and Works of Art: 10b, Monument to Stefan cel Mare, by Alexandru Plamadeala. 60b, The Resurrected Christ, by 19th cent. artist. 1 l, Steel column, by Constantin Brancusi. 2.60 l, Trajan's Column, by Apollodorus of Damascus, Rome.

1998, May 13 *Perf. 14½x14*

271	A64	10b multicolored	.25	.25
272	A64	60b multicolored	.65	.65
273	A64	1 l multicolored	.90	.90
274	A64	2.60 l multicolored	2.50	2.50
		Nos. 271-274 (4)	4.30	4.30

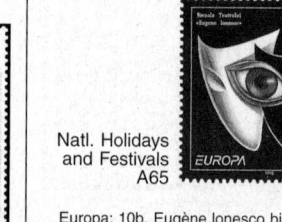

Natl. Holidays and Festivals A65

Europa: 10b, Eugène Ionesco biennial Theater Festival. 2.20 l, Lurceni ceramics, Nisporeni.

5 l, Music Festival, Martisor.

1998, July 18 Litho. *Perf. 14*

275	A65	10b multicolored	.75	.75
276	A65	2.20 l multicolored	4.75	4.75

Souvenir Sheet

277	A65	5 l multicolored	8.25	8.25

Fruit — A66

1998, Aug. 15

278	A66	7b Cerasus avium	.35	.35
279	A66	10b Prunus domestica	.35	.35
280	A66	1 l Malus domestica	.90	.90
281	A66	2 l Cydonia oblonga	1.80	1.80
		Nos. 278-281 (4)	3.40	3.40

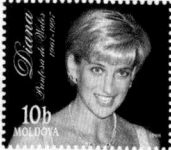

Diana, Princess of Wales (1961-97) A67

Various portraits: a, 10b. b, 90b. c, 1.80 l. d, 2.20 l. e, 1.80 l.

1998, Aug. 31 Litho. *Perf. 14*

282	A67	Sheet of 5, #a.-e. + label	6.00	6.00

First Stamps Used in Moldova, 140th Anniv. A68

Stamps on stamps: 10b, Romania #1-2, Type A2. 90b, Romania #2, #329, Type A177. 2.20 l, Romania #4, Russia #4132, #5916. 2.40 l, Moldova #122, #214, Romania #3.

Photo. & Engr.

1998, Oct. 9 *Perf. 14*

283	A68	10b multicolored	.25	.25
284	A68	90b multicolored	.45	.45
285	A68	2.20 l multicolored	1.80	1.80
286	A68	2.40 l multicolored	2.25	2.25
		Nos. 283-286 (4)	4.75	4.75

Medieval Fortresses — A69

1998, Sept. 26 Litho. *Perf. 14*

287	A69	10b Chilia	.40	.40
288	A69	60b Orhei	.70	.70
289	A69	1 l Suceava	1.10	1.10
290	A69	2 l Ismail	2.40	2.40
		Nos. 287-290 (4)	4.60	4.60

Birds A70

25b, Bubo bubo, vert. 2 l, Anthropoides virgo.

1998, Oct. 31

291	A70	25b multicolored	.55	.55
292	A70	2 l multicolored	3.50	3.50

Regional Costumes A71

1998, Nov. 28 Litho. *Perf. 14*

293	A71	25b Vara	.35	.35
294	A71	90b Vara, diff.	.80	.80
295	A71	1.80 l Iarna	1.60	1.60
296	A71	2 l Iarna, diff.	1.75	1.75
		Nos. 293-296 (4)	4.50	4.50

Annexation of Bessarabia to Romania, 80th Anniv. — A72

1998, Dec. 10

297	A72	90b multicolored	.75	.75

Universal Declaration of Human Rights, 50th Anniv. — A73

1998, Dec. 10

298	A73	2.40 l multicolored	2.75	2.75

UPU, 125th Anniv. A74

1999, Apr. 9 Litho. *Perf. 14*

299	A74	25b multicolored	.65	.65

Council of Europe, 50th Anniv. A75

1999, Apr. 9

300	A75	2.20 l multicolored	3.50	3.50

Nature Reserves — A76

Europa: 25b, Prutul de Jos. 2.40 l, Padurea Domneasca. 5 l, Codru.

1999, May 5 Litho. *Perf. 14*

301	A76	25b multicolored	.60	.60
302	A76	2.40 l multicolored	3.25	3.25

Souvenir Sheet

303	A76	5 l multicolored	7.00	7.00

Honoré de Balzac (1799-1850), Writer — A77

1999, May 20

304	A77	90b multicolored	1.00	1.00

Aleksandr Pushkin (1788-1837), Poet — A78

1999, June 6

305	A78	65b brown & black	.80	.80

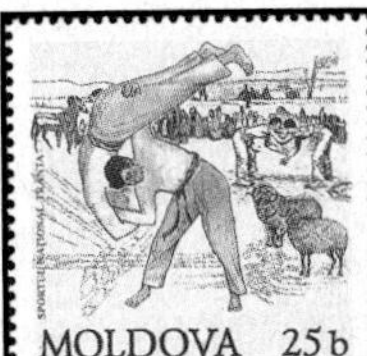

National Sports — A79

1999, June 26 Litho. *Perf. 13¾*

306	A79	25b Wrestling	.55	.55
307	A79	1.80 l Oina	2.75	2.75

First Manned Moon Landing, 30th Anniv. A80

1999, July 20 Litho. *Perf. 14*

308	A80	25b Michael Collins	.30	.30
309	A80	25b Neil Armstrong	.30	.30
310	A80	5 l Edwin Aldrin	4.75	4.75
		Nos. 308-310 (3)	5.35	5.35

Medals — A81

1999, July 31 Litho. *Perf. 14*

311	A81	25b Meritul Militar	.30	.30
312	A81	25b Pentru Vitejie	.30	.30
313	A81	25b Meritul Civic	.30	.30
314	A81	90b Mihai Eminescu	.30	.30
315	A81	1.10 l Gloria Muncii	.90	.90
316	A81	2.40 l Stefan cel Mare	2.25	2.25
		Nos. 311-316 (6)	4.35	4.35

Souvenir Sheet

317	A81	5 l Ordinul Republicii	4.50	4.50

Crafts — A82

1999, Aug. 7

318	A82	5b Wood carving	.25	.25
319	A82	25b Embroidery	.30	.30
320	A82	95b Pottery	.55	.55
321	A82	1.80 l Wicker furniture	1.60	1.60
		Nos. 318-321 (4)	2.70	2.70

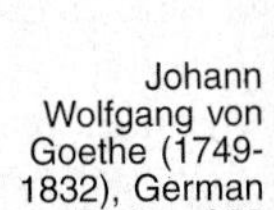

Johann Wolfgang von Goethe (1749-1832), German Poet — A83

1999, Aug. 20

322	A83	1.10 l multicolored	1.40	1.40

Return to Use of Latin Letters for Moldavian Language, 10th Anniv. — A84

1999, Aug. 31 *Perf. 13¾*

323	A84	25b multicolored	.30	.30

A85

Metropolitans: 25b, Varlaam (1590-1657). 2.40 l, Gurie Grosu (1877-1943).

1999, Sept. 12 Litho. *Perf. 14*

324	A85	25b multicolored	.25	.25
325	A85	2.40 l multicolored	2.50	2.50

A86

Moldavian Rulers, dates ruled: No. 326, Bogdan II (1449-51). No. 327, Bogdan IV (1568-72). No. 328, Constantin Cantemir (1685-93). 1.50 l, Simion Movila (1606-07). 3 l, Duke Gheorghe III (1665-66, 1668-72, 1678-84). 3.90 l, Ilias Alexandru (1666-68). 5 l, Vasile Lupu (1634-53).

1999, Oct. 16 Litho. *Perf. 14¼x14*

326	A86	25b multi	.25	.25
327	A86	25b multi	.25	.25
328	A86	25b multi	.25	.25
329	A86	1.50 l multi	.80	.80
330	A86	3 l multi	1.60	1.60
331	A86	3.90 l multi	2.60	2.60
		Nos. 326-331 (6)	5.75	5.75

Souvenir Sheet

Perf. 13¾x14

332	A86	5 l multi	3.75	3.75

No. 332 contains one 24x30mm stamp. Compare with Type A110.

Fauna A87

Designs: 25b, Lutra lutra. 1.80 l, Huso huso. 3.60 l, Rhinolophus ferrumequinum.

1999, Nov. 20 *Perf. 14x14¼*

333	A87	25b multi	.40	.40
334	A87	1.80 l multi	2.00	2.00
335	A87	3.60 l multi	3.75	3.75
		Nos. 333-335 (3)	6.15	6.15

1999 Women's Chess Championships, Chisinau — A88

1999, Nov. 27 *Perf. 13¾*

336	A88	25b Woman	.25	.25
337	A88	2.20 l Building	2.50	2.50

A89

Items From National History Museum: 25b, Helmet, candleholder. 1.80 l, Ceramic jug. 3.60 l, Bible.

Perf. 14¼x13¾

1999, Dec. 11 Litho.

338	A89	25b multi	.25	.25
339	A89	1.80 l multi	1.00	1.00
340	A89	3.60 l multi	2.75	2.75
		Nos. 338-340 (3)	4.00	4.00

A90

a, 20b, Raluca Eminovici. b, 5 l, Mihail Eminescu (1850-89), Poet. c, 25b, Gheorghe Eminovici. d, 3 l, Veronica Micle. e, 1.50 l, Iosif Vulcan.

2000, Jan. 15 Litho. *Perf. 13¾x14*

341	A90	Sheet of 5, #a.-e., + label	6.00	6.00

Fairy Tales A91

Designs: 25b, Ileana Cosinzeana. 1.50 l, Fat Frumos. 1.80 l, Harap Alb.

2000, Feb. 15 Litho. *Perf. 14*

342	A91	25b multi	*.25*	*.25*
343	A91	1.50 l multi	*1.50*	*1.50*
344	A91	1.80 l multi	*1.90*	*1.90*
		Nos. 342-344 (3)	*3.65*	*3.65*

Famous People — A92

Designs: No. 345, Henri Coanda (1886-1972), physicist. No. 346, Toma Ciorba (1864-1936), doctor. 2 l, Guglielmo Marconi (1874-1937), physicist. 3.60 l, Norbert Wiener (1894-1964), mathematician.

2000, Feb. 26 *Perf. 13¾x14*

345	A92	25b multi	*.25*	*.25*
346	A92	25b multi	*.25*	*.25*
347	A92	2 l multi	*1.50*	*1.50*
348	A92	3.60 l multi	*2.75*	*2.75*
		Nos. 345-348 (4)	*4.75*	*4.75*

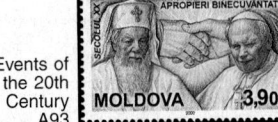

Events of the 20th Century A93

Designs: 25b, Moon landing, vert. 1.50 l, Nuclear fission, vert. 3 l, Global computerization, vert. 3.90 l, Reconciliation between Patriarch Teoctist and Pope John Paul II.

2000, Apr. 12 *Perf. 14*

349 A93 25b multi .25 .25
350 A93 1.50 l multi 1.00 1.00
351 A93 3 l multi 2.00 2.00
352 A93 3.90 l multi 2.75 2.75
Nos. 349-352 (4) 6.00 6.00

Easter — A94

Religious artwork from: 25b, 1841. 3 l, 19th cent.

2000, Apr. 30 *Perf. 14x13¾*

353 A94 25b multi .25 .25
354 A94 3 l multi 2.50 2.50

Europa, 2000

Common Design Type

2000, May 9 Litho. *Perf. 14¼x14*

355 CD17 3 l multi 3.50 3.50
Booklet, 6 #355 19.00

Exhibitions A95

Designs: 25b, Faces, Expo 2000 emblem. 3.60 l+25b, WIPA 2000 Emblem, No. 118.

2000, May 30 Litho. *Perf. 14x13¾*

356 A95 25b multi .25 .25
357 A95 3.60 l +25b multi 1.50 1.50

Churches and Monasteries — A96

Designs: 25b, Monastery, Tipova, 16th-17th Cent. 1.50 l, Church, Heciul Vechi, 1791. 1.80 l, Church, Palanca, 18th-19th Cent. 3 l, Monastery, Butuceni, 15th-16th Cent.

2000, Aug. 12 Litho. *Perf. 14*

358-361 A96 Set of 4 4.75 4.75

2000 Summer Olympics, Sydney — A97

Olympic flag and: 25b, Judo. 1.80 l, Wrestling. 5 l, Weight lifting.

2000, Sept. 15 Litho. *Perf. 14x13¾*

362-364 A97 Set of 3 5.00 5.00

Teacher's Day A98

25b, Child, teacher, class. 3.60 l, Teacher.

2000, Oct. 5 *Perf. 14x14¼*

365-366 A98 Set of 2 2.75 2.75

Christmas A99

Icons: 25b, Adoration of the Shepherds. 1.50 l, Nativity.

2000, Nov. 11 Litho. *Perf. 13¾*

367-368 A99 Set of 2 1.25 1.25

Souvenir Sheet

Perf. 13¾x14

369 A99 5 l Madonna and Child 3.50 3.50

No. 369 contains one 27x33mm stamp.

UN High Commissioner for Refugees, 50th Anniv. — A99a

2001, Jan. 19 *Perf. 14*

369A A99a 3 l multi 1.25 1.25

Worldwide Fund for Nature (WWF) — A100

Crex crex: a, On rock. b, With mouth open. c, With eggs. d, With chicks.

2001, Mar. 31 Litho. *Perf. 14x14¼*

370 A100 3 l Block of 4, #a-d 6.00 6.00

First Manned Spaceflight, 40th Anniv. — A101

2001, Apr. 12 *Perf. 14*

371 A101 1.80 l Yuri Gagarin 1.25 1.25

See No. 377. For surcharge, see No. 903.

Famous Women A102

Designs: 25b, Maria Dragan (1947-86), singer. 1 l, Marlene Dietrich (1901-92), actress. 2 l, Ruxandra Lupu (1630?-87). 3 l, Lidia Lipkovski (1884-1958).

2001, Apr. 28 *Perf. 14x14¼*

372-375 A102 Set of 4 4.75 4.75

Europa — A103

2001, May 5 *Perf. 14*

376 A103 3 l multi 2.00 2.00
Booklet, 6 #376 16.50

Space Anniversary Type of 2001

Design: Dumitru Prunariu, first Romanian cosmonaut.

2001, May 14

377 A101 1.80 l multi 1.25 1.25

Prunariu's flight, 20th anniv.

Children's Art — A104

Art by: No. 378, 25b, Cristina Mereacre. No. 379, 25b, Ion Sestacovschi. No. 380, 25b, Aliona-Valeria Samburic. 1.80 l, Andrei Sestacovschi.

2001, June 1

378-381 A104 Set of 4 3.50 3.50

Souvenir Sheet

Moldovan Stamps, 10th Anniv. — A105

Pre-independence era stamps: a, 40b, 7c Arms stamp (27x32mm). b, 2 l, 13c Arms stamp (27x32mm). c, 3 l, 30c Flag stamp (42x25mm).

2001, June 23 *Perf. 13¾x14, 14 (3 l)*

382 A105 Sheet of 3, #a-c 3.00 3.00

Animals in Chisinau Zoo — A106

Designs: 40b, Panthera tigris tigris. 1 l Equus quagga. 1.50 l, Ursus arctos. 3 l+30b, Boselaphus tragocamelus.
5 l, Panthera leo.

2001, July 14 *Perf. 13¾*

383-386 A106 Set of 4 5.75 5.75

Souvenir Sheet

387 A106 5 l multi 4.50 4.50

Declaration of Independence, 10th Anniv. — A107

2001, Aug. 27 Litho. *Perf. 14x13¾*

388 A107 1 l multi 1.25 1.25

Musical Instruments — A108

Designs: 40b, Cimpol. 1 l, Fluier. 1.80 l, Nai. 3 l, Taragot.

2001, Oct. 6 *Perf. 14x13¾*

389-392 A108 Set of 4 6.75 6.75

Year of Dialogue Among Civilizations — A109

Designs: 40b, Heads, spacecraft, horiz. 3.60b, Emblem.

2001, Oct. 9 *Perf. 14x14¼, 14¼x14*

393-394 A109 Set of 2 3.25 3.25

A110

Moldavian Rulers — A111

Ruler, dates ruled: No. 395, 40b, Mihai Racovita (1703-05, 1707-09, 1716-26). No. 396, 40b, Nicolae Mavrocordat (1709-10, 1711-15). No. 397, 40b, Constantin Mavrocordat (1733-35, 1741-43, 1748-49, 1769). No. 398, 40b, Grigore Callimachi (1761-64, 1767-69). 1 l, Grigore Alexandru Ghica (1764-67, 1774-77). 3 l, Antion Cantemir (1695-1700, 1705-07).

5 l, Dimitrie Cantemir (1710-11).

2001, Oct. 27 *Perf. 14¼x14*
395-400 A110 Set of 6 *3.75 3.75*

Souvenir Sheet

Perf. 14x14¼

401 A111 5 l multi *3.25 3.25*

Compare with type A86.

Christmas — A112

Designs: 40b, Church, 1821. 1 l, Church, 1841. 3 l, Church, 1636. 3.90 l, Cathedral, 1836.

2001, Nov. 10 *Perf. 13¾x14*
402-405 A112 Set of 4 *6.75 6.75*

Commonwealth of Independent States, 10th Anniv. — A113

2001, Dec. 14 *Perf. 14¼x14*
406 A113 1.50 l multi *1.25 1.25*

2002 Winter Olympics, Salt Lake City — A114

Designs: 40b, Cross-country skiing. 5 l, Biathlon.

2002, Feb. 8 **Litho.** *Perf. 13¾x14*
407-408 A114 Set of 2 *3.00 3.00*

Dances A115

Designs: 40b, Hora. 1.50 l, Sirba.

2002, Mar. 16 *Perf. 14x14¼*
409-410 A115 Set of 2 *4.00 4.00*

Paintings A116

Designs: No. 411, 40b, Fetele din Ceadir-lunga, by Mihai Grecu. No. 412, 40b, Meleag Natal, by Eleonora Romanescu. 1.50 l, Fata la Fereastra, by Valentina Rusu-Ciobanu. 3 l, In Doi, by Igor Vieru.

2002, Apr. 20 **Litho.** *Perf. 13¾*
411-414 A116 Set of 4 *4.00 4.00*

Europa — A117

2002, May 9 *Perf. 14*
415 A117 3 l multi *1.50 1.50*
Booklet, 6 #415 *9.00 9.00*

Souvenir Sheet

Botanical Gardens, Chisinau — A118

No. 416: a, 40b, Rose. b, 40b, Peony. c, 1.50 l, Aster. d, 3 l, Iris.

2002, June 14 *Perf. 13¾x14*
416 A118 Sheet of 4, #a-d *3.75 3.75*

Souvenir Sheet

Leonardo da Vinci (1452-1519) — A119

No. 417: a, 40b, Lady with an Ermine. b, 1.50 l, Virgin and Child with St. Anne. c, 3 l, Mona Lisa.

2002, July 25
417 A119 Sheet of 3, #a-c *3.25 3.25*

Famous Men — A120

Designs: No. 418, 40b, Grigore Ureche (1590-1647), chronicler. No. 419, 40b, Nicolae Costin (1660-1712). No. 420, 40b, Ion Neculce (1672-1745), chronicler. No. 421, 40b, Nicolae Testemiteanu (1927-86). 1.50 l, Sergiu Radautan (1926-98), scientist. 3.90 l, Alexandre Dumas (father) (1802-70), novelist.

2002, Aug. 24
418-423 A120 Set of 6 *5.00 5.00*

Horses A121

Designs: 40b, Vladimir. 1.50 l, Orlov. 3 l, Arabian.

2002, Sept. 20 *Perf. 14*
424-426 A121 Set of 3 *4.00 4.00*

The Post in Children's Art — A122

Art by: 40b, Alexandry Catranji. 1.50 l, Natalia Corcodel. 2 l, Dana Lungu.

2002, Oct. 3 **Litho.** *Perf. 14*
427-429 A122 Set of 3 *3.00 3.00*

Commonwealth of Independent States Summit — A123

CIS emblem and: 1.50 l, National leaders and flags. 3.60 l, Handshake.

2002, Oct. 6 **Litho.** *Perf. 13½*
430-431 A123 Set of 2 *3.25 3.25*

Cricova Wine Industry, 50th Anniv. A124

Designs: No. 432, 40b, Truck in warehouse. No. 433, 40b, Entrance to underground warehouse. 1.50 l, Wine glasses on table, vert. 2 l, Dusty wine bottles, wine cellar, statue. 3.60 l, Wine glasses and bottles, vert.

2002, Oct. 11 *Perf. 13¼x13, 13x13¼*
432-436 A124 Set of 5 *5.00 5.00*

Dirigibles — A125

Designs: 40b, Tissandier dirigible, France, 1883. 2 l, Ucebnii dirigible, Russia, 1908. 5 l, Graf Zeppelin, Germany, 1928.

2003, Apr. 22 **Litho.** *Perf. 13¼*
437-439 A125 Set of 3 *4.00 4.00*

Butterflies — A126

Designs: 40b, Iphiclides podalirius. 2 l, Calimorpha quadripunctaria. 3 l, Marumba quercus. 5 l, Polyommatus daphnis.

2003, Apr. 30 *Perf. 13¼x13*
440-443 A126 Set of 4 *6.50 6.50*
443a Souvenir sheet, #440-443 *6.50 6.50*
443b Booklet pane, #441-442, 2 each #440, 443 *11.00 —*
Complete booklet, #443b *11.00*

Europa — A127

Poster art: 3 l, Popular Dance Ensemble poster. 5 l, Eminescu Exhibition poster.

2003, June 12 *Perf. 13¼*
444-445 A127 Set of 2 *5.00 5.00*
445a Booklet pane, 3 each #444-445 *15.00 —*
Complete booklet, #445a *15.00*

Souvenir Sheet

Moldovan Europa Stamps, 10th Anniv. — A128

No. 446: a, 1.50 l, Rural landscape. b, 5 l, Chisinau.

2003, June 12 *Perf. 13½*
446 A128 Sheet of 2, #a-b + label *4.00 4.00*

Red Cross A129

Emblem and: 40b, Flag. 5 l, Red Cross workers at disaster site.

2003, July 4 *Perf. 13¼x13*
447-448 A129 Set of 2 *2.10 2.10*

Youth Olympics, Paris — A130

Designs: 40b, Runner. 3 l, Cyclists. 5 l, Gymnast.

2003, July 25 *Perf. 13½*
449-451 A130 Set of 3 *4.50 4.50*

Battle Against Terrorism A131

Art: 40b, Luminari, by A. Ahlupin, vert. 3.90 l, Pax Cultura, by N. Roerich.

2003, Oct. 21
452-453 A131 Set of 2 *2.75 2.75*

Dimitrie Cantemir (1673-1723), Historian A132

2003, Oct. 24 ***Perf. 13***
454 A132 3.60 l multi *2.25 2.25*

Visit of Pres. Vladimir Voronin to European Union — A133

2003, Nov. 5 ***Perf. 13½***
455 A133 3 l multi *2.25 2.25*

Famous Men — A134

Designs: 40b, Nicolae Donici (1874-1956), astronomer. 1.50 l, Nicolae Dimo (1873-1959), agronomist. 2 l, Nicolai Costenco (1913-93), writer. 3.90 l, Lewis Milestone (1895-1980), film director. 5 l, Vincent van Gogh (1853-90), painter.

2003, Nov. 14
456-460 A134 Set of 5 *7.50 7.50*

Birds From Red Book of Moldova A135

Designs: 40b, Cygnus olor. 2 l, Egretta alba. 3 l, Aquila rapax, vert. 5 l, Tetrax tetrax, vert.

2003, Dec. 18 **Litho.** ***Perf. 13¾***
461-464 A135 Set of 4 *5.00 5.00*
464a Souvenir sheet, #461-464, perf. 13 *5.00 5.00*

Famous People — A136

Designs: 40b, Natalia Gheorghiu (1914-2001), surgeon. 1.50 l, Metropolitan Dosoftei (1624-93).

2004, Apr. 30 **Litho.** ***Perf. 14x14½***
465-466 A136 Set of 2 *1.75 1.75*

Europa A137

Designs: 40b, Archaeological dig. 4.40 l, Tourists at winery.

2004, June 25 **Litho.** ***Perf. 14x14½***
467-468 A137 Set of 2 *4.50 4.50*
468a Booklet pane, 2 each #467-468 *9.00 —*
Complete booklet, #468a *9.00*

Stephen the Great (1437-1504), Prince of Moldavia — A138

Stephen the Great and: 40b, Soroca Fortress. 2 l, Capriana Monastery. 4.40 l, Map of Moldova.

2004, July 2 ***Perf. 14½x14***
469-470 A138 Set of 2 *1.75 1.75*

Souvenir Sheet

471 A138 4.40 l multi + 2 labels *3.00 3.00*

FIFA (Fédération Internationale de Football Association), Cent. — A139

No. 472: a, 2 l, Goalie catching ball. b, 4.40 l, Player dribbling ball.

2004, Aug. 14
472 A139 Horiz. pair, #a-b, + central label *3.75 3.75*

Souvenir Sheet

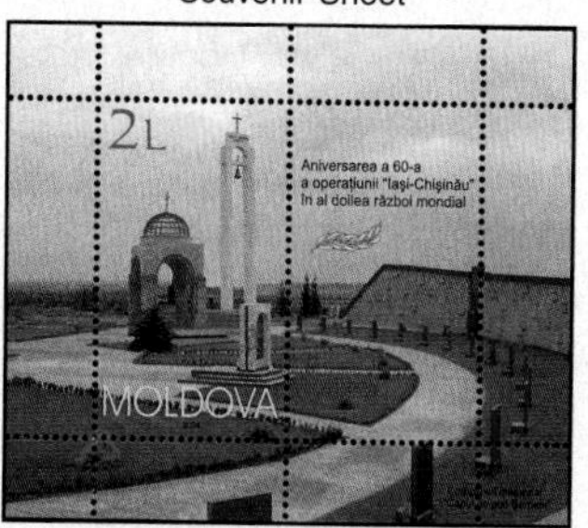

Iasi-Chisinau Operation Memorial — A140

2004, Aug. 22
473 A140 2 l multi + label *1.50 1.50*

Iasi-Chisinau Operation, 60th anniv.

2004 Summer Olympics, Athens — A141

Designs: 40b, Boxing. 4.40 l, Weight lifting.

2004, Dec. 28 ***Perf. 14x14½***
474-475 A141 Set of 2 *3.00 3.00*

Ancient Jewelry A142

Designs: 40b, Earrings, 4th cent. B.C. 1 l, Necklace, 4th-3rd cent. B.C. 1.50 l, Silver temple earring, 14th-15th cent. 2 l, Bronze bracelet, 4th cent. B.C.

2004, Dec. 28
476-479 A142 Set of 4 *3.00 3.00*

Flowering Bushes — A143

Designs: 40b, Ephedra distachya. 1.50 l, Pyrus elaeagrifolia. No. 482, 2 l, Padus avium. No. 483, 2 l, Crataegus pentagyna.

2004, Dec. 29 ***Perf. 14½x14***
480-483 A143 Set of 4 *3.50 3.50*

Locomotives — A144

Designs: 60b, ER. 1 l, ChME3. 1.50 l, D 777-3. 4.40 l, 3TE10M.

2005, Apr. 2 **Litho.** ***Perf. 14x14½***
484-487 A144 Set of 4 *4.50 4.50*

St. George's Church, Capriana Monastery — A145

2005, May 6 ***Perf. 14½x14***
488 A145 40b multi *.75 .75*

End of World War II, 60th Anniv. — A146

2005, May 9
489 A146 1.50 l multi *.90 .90*

Europa A147

Designs: 1.50 l, Cheese, corn meal mush, pitcher and cup. 4.40 l, Pies, stein and bottle of wine.

2005, May 20 ***Perf. 14x14½***
490-491 A147 Set of 2 *3.75 3.75*
491a Miniature sheet, 3 each #490-491 *14.50 —*

No. 491a was sold with, but not attached to, a booklet cover.

European Women's Chess Championships, Chisinau — A148

2005, June 10 ***Perf. 14½x14***
492 A148 4.40 l multi *3.00 3.00*

Composers — A149

Designs: 40b, Serghei Lunchevici (1934-95). 1 l, Valeriu Cupcea (1929-89). 2 l, Anton Rubinstein (1829-94).

2005, July 1 ***Perf. 14x14½***
493-495 A149 Set of 3 *3.00 3.00*

First Europa Stamps, 50th Anniv. (in 1996) — A150

Designs: No. 496, 1.50 l, Moldovan landmarks, flag and map. 15 l, Vignette of 1956 Europa stamps.
No. 498a, Moldoveanca, by Anatol Silitkii.

2005, July 20 **Litho.** ***Perf. 14½x14***
496-497 A150 Set of 2 *5.00 5.00*

Souvenir Sheet

498 Sheet, #497, 498a *5.00 5.00*
a. A150 1.50 l multi *.55 .55*

World Summit on the Information Society, Tunis — A151

2005, Sept. 14
499 A151 4.40 l multi *2.50 2.50*

Souvenir Sheet

Moldovan Passports, 10th Anniv. — A152

No. 500: a, 40b, Three passport pages with pictures. b, 1.50 l, Two closed passports. c, 4.40 l, Two passport pages with pictures.

2005, Sept. 16
500 A152 Sheet of 3, #a-c *3.75 3.75*

Endangered Reptiles and Amphibians — A153

Designs: Nos. 501, 505a, 40b, Emys orbicularis. Nos. 502, 505b, 1 l, Eremias arguta. Nos. 503, 505c, 1.50 l, Pelobates fuscus. Nos. 504, 505d, 2 l, Vipera ursini.

2005, Sept. 29 *Perf. 14x14½*
With White Frames

501-504 A153 Set of 4 *3.25 3.25*

Souvenir Sheet
Without White Frames

505 A153 Sheet of 4, #a-d, + 2 labels *3.25 3.25*

St. Nicholas Church — A154

2005, Oct. 30 *Perf. 14½x14*

506 A154 40b multi *.75 .75*

Christmas — A155

Designs: 40b, St. Ierarh Nicolae Church, Falesti. 6 l, Varzaresti Monastery.

2005, Dec. 19 Litho. *Perf. 14x14½*

507-508 A155 Set of 2 *3.25 3.25*

Makler Newspaper, 15th Anniv. — A156

2006, Jan. 20

509 A156 60b multi .30 .30

2006 Winter Olympics, Turin — A157

Designs: 60b, Luge. 6.20 l, Skiing.

2006, Feb. 10

510-511 A157 Set of 2 3.00 3.00

Buildings — A158

Designs: 22b, Post Office No. 21, Balti. 40b, Saint Gates, Chisinau. 53b, Museum of History, Cahul. 57b, Old Post and Telegraph Office, Soroca. 60b, Adormirea Maicii Domnului Church, Copceac. 3.50 l, National Museum of Fine Arts, Chisinau.

2006, Mar. 23 *Perf. 14½x14*

512 A158 22b dark blue *.75 .75*
513 A158 40b brown *.75 .75*
514 A158 53b dark blue *.75 .75*
515 A158 57b green *.75 .75*
516 A158 60b olive green *.75 .75*
517 A158 3.50 l red brown *2.50 2.50*
Nos. 512-517 (6) 6.25 6.25

Textile Arts and Native Costumes — A159

Designs: 40b, Crocheting. 60b, Moldavian woman, 19th cent., vert. 3 l, Moldavian man, 19th cent., vert. 4.50 l, Embroidery.

2006, Apr. 14 *Perf. 14x14½, 14½x14*

518-521 A159 Set of 4 3.25 3.25

Gheorghe Mustea, Conductor — A160

2006, Apr. 28 *Perf. 14x14½*

522 A160 60b multi .30 .30

Europa A161

Designs: 60b, Children and town on globe. 4.50 l, Artist and musicians, vert.

2006, May 6 *Perf. 14x14½, 14½x14*

523-524 A161 Set of 2 2.75 2.75
524a Miniature sheet, 3 each #523-524 8.25 8.25

No. 524a was sold with, but not attached to, a booklet cover.

37th Chess Olympiad, Turin — A162

2006, May 24 *Perf. 14x14½*

525 A162 4.50 l multi 1.75 1.75

2006 World Cup Soccer Championships, Germany — A163

World Cup, emblem and: 2 l, Players. 3 l, Mascot. 4.50 l, Players, diff.

2006, June 28

526-528 A163 Set of 3 4.00 4.00

Famous People — A164

Designs: 40b, Ion Halippa (1871-1941), archaeologist. 1 l, Eufrosinia Cuza (1856-1910), singer. 2 l, Petre Stefanuca (1906-42), folklorist. 4.50 l, Wolfgang Amadeus Mozart (1756-91), composer.

2006, Aug. 11 *Perf. 14½x14*

529-532 A164 Set of 4 5.00 5.00

Endangered Animals — A165

Designs: 60b, Martes martes. 1 l, Mustela erminea. 2 l, Mustela lutreola. 3 l, Mustela eversmanni.
6.20 l, Felis silvestris, vert.

2006, Aug. 16 *Perf. 14x14½*

533-536 A165 Set of 4 3.00 3.00

Souvenir Sheet
Perf. 14½x14

537 A165 6.20 l multi + label 3.00 3.00

Independence, 15th Anniv. — A166

2006, Aug. 27 *Perf. 14½x14*

538 A166 2.60 l multi 1.25 1.25

Dogs A167

Designs: 40b, German shepherd. 60b, Collie. 2 l, Standard poodle. 6.20 l, Hungarian greyhound.

2006, Sept. 8 *Perf. 14x14½*

539-542 A167 Set of 4 3.75 3.75
542a Sheet, 2 each #539-542 7.50 7.50

National Wine Day — A168

2006, Oct. 7

543 A168 60b multi .35 .35

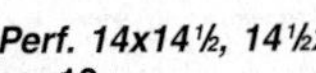

Christmas — A169

Paintings by: 40b, Valerii, Metleaev, 1988. 3 l, Mihail Statnii, 1986, vert. 6.20 l, Elena Bontea, 1973.

Perf. 14x14½, 14½x14

2006, Dec. 12 Litho.

544 A169 40b multi .30 .30
545 A169 3 l multi .80 .80
546 A169 6.20 l multi 1.90 1.90
a. Strip of 3, #544-546 3.00 3.00

Nos. 544 and 545 were each printed in sheets of 10 and in sheets of 9 containing 3 each of Nos. 544-546.

No. 25 Surcharged

Methods and Perfs As Before

2007, Jan. 11

547 A6 85b on 25k #547 1.25 1.25

Portraits in Natl. Art Museum — A170

Designs: 65b, Petrarch, by Raphael Morghen. 85b, Napoleon Bonaparte, by unknown artist. 2 l, Friedrich von Schiller, by Johann Gotthard Muller. 4.50 l, Johann Wolfgang von Goethe by James Hopwood.

2007, Feb. 28 Litho. *Perf. 14½x14*

548-551 A170 Set of 4 2.75 2.75

Mushrooms — A171

Designs: 65b, Morchella steppicola. 85b, Phylloporus rhodoxantus. 2 l, Amanita solitaria. 6.20 l, Boletus aereus.

2007, Apr. 23 Litho. *Perf. 14x14½*

552-555 A171 Set of 4 3.00 3.00

Europa A172

Designs: 2.85 l, Scouts with pencil and paint brush. 4.50 l, Scouts examining butterfly.

2007, May 8

556-557 A172 Set of 2 2.25 2.25

Scouting, cent.

No. 83 Surcharged in Blue or Black

Methods and Perfs As Before

2007, June 7

558 A19 25b on 3k #83 (Bl) .30 .30
559 A19 85b on 3k #83 (Bk) .30 .30

Cats
A173

Designs: 65b, Mixed breed. 1 l, Siamese, vert. 1.50 l, Birman, vert. 6.20 l, Persian.

Perf. 14x14½, 14½x14

2007, June 20 **Litho.**
560-563 A173 Set of 4 3.00 3.00

Birds
A174

Designs: 75b, Otis tarda. 1 l, Neophron percnopterus. 2.50 l, Lyrurus tetrix. 5 l, Gyps fulvus.
6.20 l, Tetrao urogallus.

2007, Aug. 14 **Litho.** ***Perf. 14x14½***
564-567 A174 Set of 4 3.25 3.25

Souvenir Sheet

568 A174 6.20 l multi + label 2.25 2.25

Dniester River Fish Preservation — A175

No. 569: a, Acipenser gueldenstaedtii. b, Zingel zingel.

2007, Sept. 6
569 Horiz. pair + central label 1.25 1.25
a. A175 1 l multi .30 .30
b. A175 3 l multi .95 .95

See Ukraine No. 694.

Famous People — A176

Designs: 75b, Ion Luca Caragiale (1852-1912), writer. 1 l, Anastasia Dicescu (1887-1945), opera singer. 3 l, Mircea Eliade (1907-86), historian.
6.20 l, Maria Biesu, opera singer, vert.

2007, Sept. 15 ***Perf. 14x14½***
570-572 A176 Set of 3 1.50 1.50

Souvenir Sheet

Perf. 14½x14

573 A176 6.20 l multi + label 2.00 2.00

World Chess Championships, Mexico — A177

2007, Sept. 29 ***Perf. 14x14½***
574 A177 6.20 l multi 1.90 1.90

A178

Christmas — A179

2007, Dec. 1 **Litho.** ***Perf. 14x14½***
575 A178 1 l multi .25 .25
576 A179 4.50 l multi 1.25 1.25
a. Miniature sheet, 6 #575, 3 #576 5.00 5.00

Covered Wells — A180

Well in: 10b, Peresecina. 75b, Duruitoarea. 1 l, Ciripcau, vert. 3 l, Ocnita, vert.

2008, Feb. 19 ***Perf. 14½x14, 14x14½***
577-580 A180 Set of 4 1.50 1.50

2008 Summer Olympics, Beijing — A181

Designs: 1 l, Cycling. 6.20 l, Boxing. 15 l, Weight lifting.

2008, Mar. 5 ***Perf. 14x14½***
581-583 A181 Set of 3 5.75 5.75

For overprint see No. 607.

Europa
A182

Designs: 3.50 l, Post rider, scroll, castle. 4.50 l, Letters, computer screen.

2008, Apr. 30 **Litho.** ***Perf. 14x14½***
584-585 A182 Set of 2 2.00 2.00
585a Sheet, 2 each #584-585 4.00 4.00

No. 585a was sold with, but not attached to, a booklet cover.

First Postage Stamps of Moldavia, 150th Anniv. — A183

Designs: 1 l, Romania #1-2. 3 l, Romania #3-4.

2008, May 23
586-587 A183 Set of 2 1.25 1.25
587a Booklet pane of 4, 2 each #586-587 2.50 2.50
Complete booklet, #587a 2.50

UEFA Euro 2008 Soccer Championships, Austria and Switzerland — A184

2008, June 28
588 A184 4.50 l multi 1.40 1.40

Flowers — A185

Designs: 1 l, Maianthemum bifolium. 3 l, Hepatica nobilis. 5 l, Nymphaea alba.

2008, Aug. 19 **Litho.** ***Perf. 14x14½***
589-591 A185 Set of 3 3.00 3.00
591a Souvenir sheet of 3, #589-591, + 3 labels 3.00 3.00

Famous People
A186

Designs: 1.20 l, Onisifor Ghibu (1883-1972), teacher. 1.50 l, Ciprian Porumbescu (1853-83), composer. 3 l, Leo Tolstoy (1828-1910), author. 4.50 l, Maria Tanase (1913-63), singer.

2008, Sept. 5
592-595 A186 Set of 4 4.00 4.00

Deer — A187

No. 596: a, Cervus nippon. b, Cervus elaphus sibiricus.

2008, Sept. 18
596 A187 3 l Horiz. pair, #a-b 2.25 2.25

See Kazakhstan No. 577.

Souvenir Sheet

Bender (Tighina), 600th Anniv. — A188

2008, Oct. 8
597 A188 4.20 l brn & buff + 3 labels 1.60 1.60

Princes — A189

Designs: 1.20 l, Prince Antiokh Cantemir (1708-44). 3 l, Prince Dimitrie Cantemir (1673-1723).

2008, Oct. 27 ***Perf. 14½x14***
598 A189 1.20 l brown .45 .45

Souvenir Sheet

599 A189 3 l brown + label 1.10 1.10

Princes — A190

Designs: 85b, Prince Mihail Grigore Sutu (1784-1864). 1.20 l, Prince Grigore Alexandru Ghica (1807-57). 1.50 l, Prince Mihail Sturza (1795-1884). 2 l, Prince Alexandru Ipsilanti (1726-1807). 3 l, Prince Ioan Sandu Sturza (1761-1842). 4.50 l, Prince Scarlat Callimachi (1773-1821).
6.20 l, Prince Alexandru Ioan Cuza (1820-73).

2008, Nov. 14
600-605 A190 Set of 6 4.25 4.25

Souvenir Sheet

606 A190 6.20 l multi + 5 labels 2.00 2.00

No. 582 Overprinted in Bronze

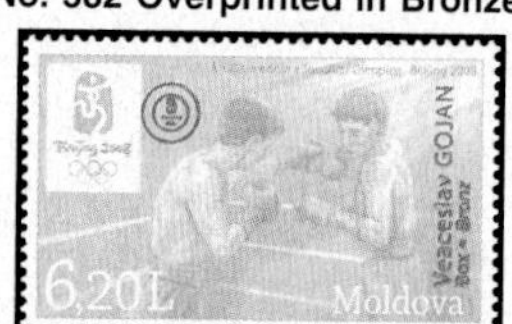

2008, Nov. 21 ***Perf. 14x14½***
607 A161 6.20 l multi 2.00 2.00

Souvenir Sheet

Moldovan Presidency of the Central European Initiative — A191

No. 608 — CEI emblems and map of: a, 1.20 l, Western Europe. b, 4.50 l, Eastern Europe.

2008, Nov. 27 ***Perf. 14½x14***
608 A191 Sheet of 2, #a-b 1.90 1.90

A192

Christmas — A193

2008, Dec. 5 Litho. *Perf. 14x14½*
609 A192 1.20 l multi .45 .45

Souvenir Sheet

610 A193 6.20 l multi 2.00 2.00

Universal Declaration of Human Rights, 60th Anniv. — A194

2008, Dec. 10
611 A194 4.50 l multi 1.50 1.50

Moldavian State, 650th Anniv. — A195

Designs: 1.20 l, Moldovan arms and flag, Presidential offices. 6.20 l, Bogdan I Voda, Prince of Moldavia.

2009, Jan. 20
612 A195 1.20 l multi .45 .45

Souvenir Sheet

613 A195 6.20 l multi + label 2.00 2.00

Ancient Weapons — A196

Weapons from: 1.20 l, 10th-14th cents. 4.50 l, 8th-13th cents.

2009, Feb. 24
614-615 A196 Set of 2 1.90 1.90

Preservation of Polar Regions and Glaciers — A197

Question mark, emblem and: 1.20 l, Penguin. 6.20 l, Polar bear.

2009, Mar. 18 Litho. *Perf. 14½x14*
616-617 A197 Set of 2 2.50 2.50

Easter A198

Decorated Easter eggs: 1.20 l, In basket. 3 l, In bowl.

2009, Apr. 2 *Perf. 14x14½*
618-619 A198 Set of 2 1.25 1.25

Council of Europe, 60th Anniv. — A199

2009, Apr. 15 *Perf. 14½x14*
620 A199 4.50 l multi 1.45 1.45

Europa A200

Designs: 4.20 l, Nicolae Donici (1874-1956), astrophysicist, observatory, planetary diagram and eclipse. 4.50 l, Galileo Galilei (1564-1642), astronomer, armillary sphere and star.

2009, May 7 *Perf. 14x14½*
621-622 A200 Set of 2 2.00 2.00
622a Sheet. 3 each #621-622 6.00 6.00

Intl. Year of Astronomy. No. 622a was sold with, but not attached to, a booklet cover.

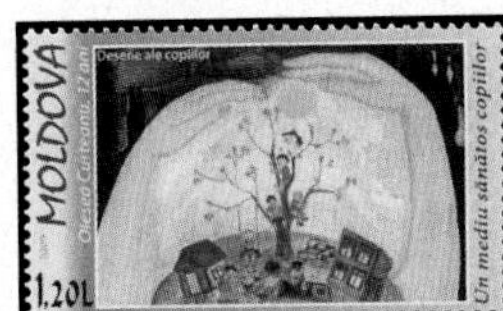

Children's Art — A201

Children's art on clean environment theme by: 1.20 l, Olesea Curteanu. 1.50 l, Iulia Struta, vert. 5 l+20b, Irina Simion, vert.

2009, June 1 *Perf. 14x14½, 14½x14*
623-625 A201 Set of 3 2.25 2.25

Flowers A202

Designs: 1.20 l, Viola suavis. 1.50 l, Adonis vernalis. 3 l, Campanula persicifolia. 4.50 l, Papaver rhoeas.

2009, June 18 *Perf. 13 Syncopated*
626-628 A202 Set of 3 1.50 1.50

Souvenir Sheet

629 A202 4.50 l multi + label 1.25 1.25
a. Sheet of 4, #626-629, + 2 labels 2.75 2.75

Insects A203

Designs: 1.20 l, Bombus paradoxus. 1.50 l, Xylocopa valga. 3 l, Carabus clathratus. 4.50 l, Coenagrion lindeni.

Perf. 13 Syncopated

2009, Sept. 24 Litho.
630-633 A203 Set of 4 2.75 2.75

A204

Personalizable Stamps — A205

Designs: No. 636, Statue of Prince Stephen the Great. No. 637, Cathedral. No. 638, Roses, wedding rings. No. 639, Basket of flowers.

2009, Aug. 5 *Perf. 13 Syncopated*

634	A204	1.20 l	lt bl & dk bl	*2.00*	*2.00*
635	A204	1.20 l	red & dk red	*2.00*	*2.00*
636	A205	1.20 l	multi + label	*2.00*	*2.00*
637	A205	1.20 l	multi + label	*2.00*	*2.00*
638	A205	1.20 l	multi + label	*2.00*	*2.00*
639	A205	1.20 l	multi + label	*2.00*	*2.00*
			Nos. 634-639 (6)	*12.00*	*12.00*

Vignettes of Nos. 634-635 and labels of Nos. 636-639 could be personalized. The vignette image shown in illustration A204 and label image shown in illustration A205 are generic.

Nuts and Fruit — A206

Designs: 50b, Walnuts. 85b, Mulberries. 1.20 l, Pears. 5 l, Apricots.

2009, Aug. 28 *Perf. 14½x14*
640-643 A206 Set of 4 2.00 2.00

Houses A207

House in: 1.20 l, Briceni. 4.50 l, Comrat. 7 l, Orhei.

2009, Oct. 1 *Perf. 14x14½*
644-646 A207 Set of 3 3.25 3.25

Moldova Grapes — A208

2009, Oct. 9 *Perf. 14½x14*
647 A208 4.50 l multi 1.25 1.25

European Day Against Human Trafficking — A209

2009, Oct. 18 *Perf. 14x14½*
648 A209 4.50 l multi 1.25 1.25

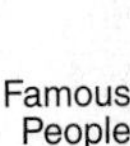

Famous People A210

Designs: No. 649, 1.20 l, Eugene Ionescu (1909-94), playwright. No. 650, 1.20 l, Eufrosinia Kersnovskaia (1907-95), writer. 4.50 l, Nicolai Gogol (1809-52), writer. 7 l, Charles Darwin (1809-92), naturalist.

2009, Nov. 26 Litho. *Perf. 14x14½*
649-652 A210 Set of 4 4.00 4.00

Christmas — A211

Designs: 1.20 l, Capra. 4.50 l, Plugusorul.

2009, Dec. 1
653-654 A211 Set of 2 1.40 1.40

Famous People A212

Designs: No. 655, 1.20 l, Grigore Vieru (1935-2009), writer. No. 656, 1.20 l, Natalia Dadiani (1865-1903), founder of school for girls. 5.40 l, Ivan Zaikin (1880-1948), wrestler and aviator. 7 l, Maria Cebotari (1910-49), singer and actress.

4.50 l, Mihai Eminescu (1850-89), writer, vert.

2010, Jan. 15 Litho. *Perf. 14x14½*
655-658 A212 Set of 4 4.00 4.00

Souvenir Sheet

Perf. 14½x14

659 A212 4.50 l multi + label 1.50 1.50

2010 Winter Olympics, Vancouver — A213

Designs: 1.20 l, Alpine skiing. 8.50 l, Biathlon, vert.

2010, Feb. 12 *Perf. 14x14½, 14½x14*
660-661 A213 Set of 2 2.50 2.50

Jewelry in National Museum of Archaeology and History — A214

Designs: 1.20 l, Shell necklace, 5th cent. B.C. 7 l, Headband and pendant, 5th cent. B.C.

2010, Feb. 23 *Perf. 13 Syncopated*
662-663 A214 Set of 2 2.25 2.25

Frédéric Chopin (1810-49), Composer — A215

2010, Mar. 1 *Perf. 14x14½*

664 A215 5.40 l multi 1.40 1.40

Mushrooms A216

Designs: 1.20 l, Lactarius piperatus. 2 l, Amanita pantherina. 5.40 l, Russula sanguinea. 7 l, Coprinus picaceus.

2010, Mar. 27 *Perf. 14½x14*

665-668 A216 Set of 4 4.50 4.50
668a Souvenir sheet, #665-668 4.50 4.50

Birds — A217

Designs: 85b, Carduelis carduelis. 1 l, Passer domesticus. 1.20 l, Strix uralensis. 4.50 l, Pica pica.
8.50 l, Columba livia.

2010, Apr. 8 *Perf. 13 Syncopated*

669-672 A217 Set of 4 2.50 2.50

Souvenir Sheet

673 A217 8.50 l multi 2.75 2.75

Europa A218

Children's books: 1.20 l, Punguta cu doi Bani, by Ion Creanga. 5.40 l, Guguta Si Prietenii Sai, by Spiridon Vangheli.

2010, Apr. 30 *Perf. 14x14½*

674-675 A218 Set of 2 1.75 1.75
675a Sheet, 3 each #674-675 5.25 5.25

No. 675a was sold with, but unattached to, a booklet cover.

End of World War II, 65th Anniv. — A219

2010, May 9 *Perf. 14½x14*

676 A219 4.50 l multi 1.40 1.40

2010 World Cup Soccer Championships, South Africa — A220

Soccer player and: 1.20 l, Mascot. 8.50 l, Emblem, vert.

Perf. 14x14½, 14½x14

2010, June 11

677-678 A220 Set of 2 2.50 2.50

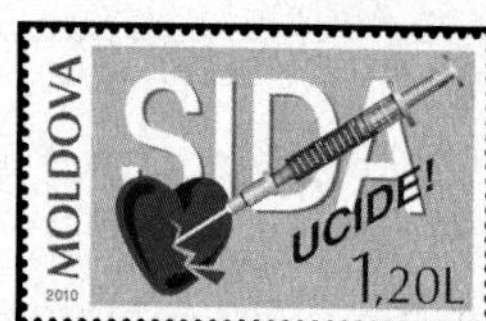

Campaign Against AIDS — A221

2010, July 1 *Perf. 14x14½*

679 A221 1.20 l multi .40 .40

Paintings Depicting Flowers A222

Designs: 1 l, Flowers, by Ion Tabirta. 1.20 l, Bouquet of Poppies, by Oleg Cojocari. 2 l, Flowers, by Mihail Statnii. 5.40 l, Chrysanthemums, by Leonid Grigorasenco.

Perf. 13 Syncopated

2010, Aug. 6 **Litho.**

680-683 A222 Set of 4 2.50 2.50

Dances — A223

Designs: 85b, Moldovanesca. 5.40 l, Calusarii, vert.

Perf. 14x14½, 14½x14

2010, Sept. 18

684-685 A223 Set of 2 1.60 1.60

Feteasca Grapes — A224

2010, Oct. 9 *Perf. 14½x14*

686 A224 4.50 l multi 1.20 1.20

National Symbols A225

Perf. 13 Syncopated at Top

2010, Nov. 3

687 A225 1.20 l Arms .25 .25
a. Perf. 13, syncopation at sides .25 .25
688 A225 4.50 l Flag 1.00 1.00
a. Perf. 13, syncopation at sides 1.00 1.00
b. Sheet of 6, 3 each #687a, 688a 3.75 3.75

Prehistoric Animals — A226

Designs: 85b, Mammuthus. 1 l, Ursus spelaeus. No. 691, 1.20 l, Panthera leo spelaea. 4.20 l, Bison.

No. 693: a, 1.20 l, Pontoceros. b, 1.50 l, Anancus. c, 5.40 l, Stephanorhinus. d, 8.50 l, Homotherium.

2010, Nov. 30 **Litho.** *Perf. 14x14½*

689-692 A226 Set of 4 1.50 1.50

Souvenir Sheet

693 A226 Sheet of 4, #a-d, + 2 labels 3.50 3.50

Christmas A227

Designs: 1.20 l, Child at window, angel holding gift. 5.40 l, Cathedral.

2010, Dec. 7 *Perf. 13 Syncopated*

694 A227 1.20 l multi .25 .25

Souvenir Sheet

695 A227 5.40 l multi 1.10 1.10

Items in National Museum of Archaeology and History A228

Designs: 85b, Amphora with lid, 5th cent. B.C. 1.20 l, Vessel with animal design, 4th cent. B.C. 8.50 l, Vessel depicting person, 4th cent. B.C.

2011, Jan. 25

696-698 A228 Set of 3 2.50 2.50
698a Sheet of 4, #696, 698, 2 #697 + 2 labels 2.75 2.75

Buildings — A229

Designs: 10b, Ralli family house, 19th cent., Dolna. 25b, Mirzoian family house, 19th cent., Hincesti. 85b, Balioz family house, 1847, Ivancea, 1 l, High school, 1916, Soroca. 1.20 l Pommer family house, 20th cent., Taul. 1.50 l, Hasnas family house, 19th cent., Sofia.

2011, Feb. 15 *Perf. 14½x14*

699	A229	10b chocolate	.25	.25
700	A229	25b deep blue	.25	.25
701	A229	85b greenish blue	.25	.25
702	A229	1 l plum	.25	.25
703	A229	1.20 l dark blue	.25	.25
704	A229	1.50 l dark green	.30	.30
		Nos. 699-704 (6)	1.55	1.55

Handicrafts A230

Designs: 1.20 l, Decorated rope, by Ludmila Berezin. 4.20 l, Straw head, by Natalia Cangea. 7 l, Rug, by Ecaterina Popescu.

2011, Mar. 1

705-707 A230 Set of 3 3.25 3.25

Self-Portraits A231

Self-portrait of: 85b, Eugenia Malesevschi (1866-1942). 1.20 l, Nicolae Grigorescu (1838-1907). 2 l, Alexandru Piamadeala (1888-1940). 5.40 l, Mihail Grecu (1916-98).

2011, Apr. 1 *Perf. 13 Syncopated*

708-711 A231 Set of 4 2.50 2.50

Miniature Sheet

First Manned Space Flight, 50th Anniv. — A232

No. 712 — Pioneer cosmonauts and astronauts: a, 1.20 l, Yuri Gagarin. b, 5.40 l, Gherman Titov. c, 7 l, Virgil I. Grissom. d, 8.50 l, Alan B. Shepard, Jr.

2011, Apr. 9 *Perf. 14½x14*

712 A232 Sheet of 4, #a-d, + 2 labels 6.00 6.00

Europa — A233

Designs: 4.20 l, Leaf depicting forest fire, healthy forest and buck. 5.40 l, Owl, forest, cut tree.

2011, May 7 *Perf. 13 Syncopated*

713-714 A233 Set of 2 2.40 2.40
714a Sheet of 6, 3 each #713-714 7.50 7.50

No. 714a was sold with, but unattached to, a booklet cover.

Flowers — A234

2011, May 20 *Perf. 14x14½*

715 A234	70b Hyacinth	.25	.25
716 A234	85b Tulips	.25	.25
717 A234	1.20 l Narcissi	.30	.30
718 A234	2 l Violas	.45	.45
	Nos. 715-718 (4)	1.25	1.25

Deportation of Moldovans to Siberia by the Soviet Union, 70th Anniv. — A235

2011, June 12 *Perf. 14½x14*
719 A235 1.20 l multi .30 .30

Souvenir Sheet

First Moldovan Stamps, 20th Anniv. — A236

No. 720: a, 85b, Moldova #1. b, 1.20 l, Moldova #2. c, 4.20 l, Moldova #3.

2011, June 23 *Perf. 13 Syncopated*
720 A236 Sheet of 3, #a-c 1.50 1.50

Mammals and Birds — A237

Designs: No. 721, 85b, Meles meles. No. 722, 1.20 l, Erinaceus europaeus. 3 l, Canis lupus. 4.20 l, Vulpes vulpes.
No. 725: a, 85b, Plegadis falcinellus. b, 1.20 l, Pelecanus onocrotalus. c, 5.40 l, Platalea leucorodia. d, 8.50 l, Aythya nyroca.

2011, July 29
721-724 A237 Set of 4 2.10 2.10
725 A237 Sheet of 4, #a-d, + 2 labels 3.75 3.75

Souvenir Sheet

Independence, 20th Anniv. — A238

2011, Aug. 27 *Perf. 14½x14*
726 A238 4.20 l multi + 2 labels 1.10 1.10

Campaign Against Smoking — A239

2011, Sept. 10
727 A239 1.20 l multi .30 .30

Diplomatic Relations Between Moldova and Romania, 20th Anniv. A240

Designs: 1.20 l, Holy Gates, Chisinau. 4.50 l, Arch of Triumph, Bucharest, Romania.

2011, Oct. 11 *Perf. 13 Syncopated*
728-729 A240 Set of 2 1.50 1.50
729a Sheet of 2, #728-729, + 4 labels 1.50 1.50

See Romania Nos. 5301-5302.

Miniature Sheet

Chisinau, 575th Anniv. — A241

No. 730: a, 85b, Palace of Culture. b, 1.20 l, National Opera and Ballet Theater. c, 2 l, Mihai Emenscu National Theater. d, 3.85 l, National Palace. e, 5.40 l, Patria Movie Theater.

2011, Oct. 13 *Perf. 14x14½*
730 A241 Sheet of 5, #a-e, + label 3.50 3.50

UN High Commisioner for Refugees, 60th Anniv. — A242

2011, Nov. 25 *Perf. 14½x14*
731 A242 1.20 l multi .25 .25

A243

Christmas — A244

2011, Dec. 3 *Perf. 14½x14*
732 A243 1.20 l multi .25 .25

Souvenir Sheet
Perf. 14x14½
733 A244 4.50 l multi 1.10 1.10

Famous People — A245

Designs: 85b, Magda Isanos (1916-44), poet. 1.20 l, Nicolae Sulac (1936-2003), musician. 3 l, Cleopatra Hrsanovschi (1861-1939), musician. 4.50 l, Franz Liszt (1811-86), composer.

2011, Dec. 17 *Perf. 14x14½*
734-737 A245 Set of 4 2.25 2.25

Paintings Depicting Children A246

Designs: 85b, Pokrovka Boy, by Igor Vieru. 1.20 l, Orphan, by Pavel Piscariov. 2.85 l, Portrait of a Child, by Lidia Arionescu-Baillayre. 4.50 l, Boy with Hat, by Constantin Kitaika.

2012, Feb. 4 *Perf. 13 Syncopated*
738-741 A246 Set of 4 2.25 2.25

Souvenir Sheet

Ion (1954-92) and Doina (1958-92) Aldea-Teodorovici, Musicians — A247

2012, Mar. 3 *Perf. 14x14½*
742 A247 7 l multi + label 1.75 1.75

Souvenir Sheet

Mihai Dolgan (1942-2008), Musician — A248

2012, Mar. 14 *Perf. 14½x14*
743 A248 4.50 l multi + label 1.10 1.10

Traditional Costumes — A249

Designs: 85b, Woman. 1.20 l, Man. 3 l, Woman, diff.
8.50 l, Man and woman.

2012, Apr. 7
744-746 A249 Set of 3 1.25 1.25

Souvenir Sheet
747 A249 8.50 l multi + label 1.90 1.90

Regional Communications Commonwealth, 20th anniv.

Europa A250

Designs: 4.20 l, Curchi Monastery. 5.40 l, Winery.

2012, Apr. 18 *Perf. 14x14½*

748 A250 4.20 l multi	.90	.90
a. Souvenir sheet of 3 + label	2.75	2.75
749 A250 5.40 l multi	1.25	1.25
a. Souvenir sheet of 3 + label	3.75	3.75

Nos. 748a and 749a were sold with, but unattached to, a booklet cover.

Medieval Military Scenes — A251

Designs: 85b, Battering ram. 1.20 l, Soldier with spear and shield, vert. 1.50 l, Military commander on horseback, vert. 5.40 l, Catapult.

Perf. 14x14½, 14½x14
2012, May 31 **Litho.**
750-753 A251 Set of 4 2.25 2.25

Pigeons — A252

Designs: 85b, Jucator de Chisinau. 1.20 l, Jucator de Balti. 3 l, Jucator basarbean. 4.20 l, Roller de Chisinau.

2012, June 21 *Perf. 14x14½*
754-757 A252 Set of 4 2.25 2.25

2012 Summer Olympics, London — A253

Designs: 4.50 l, Wrestling. 5.40 l, Cycling.

2012, July 21
758-759 A253 Set of 2 2.50 2.50

Rose Varieties A254

Designs: 85b, Mildred Scheel. 1.20 l, Friesia. 3 l, Priscilla. 4.20 l, Caribia.

2012, Aug. 10 *Perf. 13 Syncopated*
760-763 A254 Set of 4 1.90 1.90
763a Sheet of 6, #762-763, 2 each #760-761 2.40 2.40

Famous Men A255

Designs: 85b, Eugeniu Ureche (1917-2005), actor. 1.20 l, Spiridon Mocanu (1932-2007), dancer. 4.50 l, George Emil Palade (1912-2008), 1974 Nobel laureate for Physiology or Medicine. 8.50 l, Jean-Jacques Rousseau (1712-78), political philosopher.

2012, Aug. 27 *Perf. 14x14½*
764-767 A255 Set of 4 3.25 3.25

Maria Biesu (1935-2012), Opera Singer — A256

2012, Sept. 7 **Litho.**
768 A256 1.20 l multi .25 .25

Natural Monuments — A257

Designs: 1.20 l, Cheile Butesti Canyon. 4.20 l, Suta de Movile. 7 l, Emil Racovita Caves.

2012, Sept. 21 *Perf. 14x14½*
769-771 A257 Set of 3 2.50 2.50

Christmas A258

Icons from: 1.75 l, 1903. 5.40 l, 19th cent.

2012, Dec. 1 *Perf. 13 Syncopated*
772-773 A258 Set of 2 1.50 1.50

Nos. 772-773 each were printed in sheets of 8 + central label.

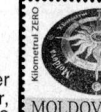

Zero Kilometer Marker, Chisinau — A259

2012, Dec. 12 *Perf. 14½x14*
774 A259 1.75 l multi .40 .40

Paintings Depicting Mihai Eminescu (1850-89), Poet — A260

Designs: 1.75 l, Mihai Eminescu, by Emil Childescu. 5.75 l, Dedication, by Vasile Nascu.

2013, Jan. 15 *Perf. 13 Syncopated*
775-776 A260 Set of 2 1.60 1.60

Nos. 775-776 each were printed in sheets of 8 + label.

Regional Communications Commonwealth Emblem, Communications Tower, Map of Moldova — A261

2013, Feb. 28 *Perf. 14½x14*
777 A261 4.50 l multi .95 .95

Berries — A262

Designs: 55b, Ribes uva-crispa. 1.50 l, Vaccinium myrtillus. No. 780, Rubus idaeus. No. 781, Viburnum opulus. 2 l, Hippophae rhamnoides. 4 l, Ribes rubrum.

2013, Mar. 30 *Perf. 14x14½*
778 A262 55b multi .25 .25
779 A262 1.50 l multi .30 .30
780 A262 1.75 l multi .35 .35
781 A262 1.75 l multi .35 .35
782 A262 2 l multi .40 .40
783 A262 4 l multi .80 .80
Nos. 778-783 (6) 2.45 2.45

Europa A263

Postal vehicles: 4.50 l, Van. 5.75 l, Horse-drawn carriage.

2013, Apr. 30
784 A263 4.50 l multi .95 .95
a. Souvenir sheet of 4 4.00 4.00
785 A263 5.75 l multi 1.25 1.25
a. Souvenir sheet of 4 5.00 5.00

Nos. 784a and 785a were sold with, but unattached to, a booklet cover.

Animals in the Chisinau Zoo — A264

Designs: 1.75 l, Panthera uncia. 2 l, Macropus rufogriseus, vert. 5.75 l, Pavo cristatus.

2013, May 18 *Perf. 14x14½, 14½x14*
786-787 A264 Set of 2 .75 .75

Souvenir Sheet

788 A264 5.75 l multi + label 1.25 1.25

Illustrations From Guguta Stories by Spiridon Vangheli — A265

Designs: No. 789, 1.75 l, Cusma. No. 790, 1.75 l, Datoria.

2013, June 1 *Perf. 14½x14*
789-790 A265 Set of 2 .70 .70

Folk Traditions — A266

Designs: No. 791, 1.75 l, Cleaning of the well. No. 792, 1.75 l, Rain dance, vert.

Perf. 14x14½, 14½x14

2013, June 20
791-792 A266 Set of 2 .70 .70

Butterflies — A267

Designs: 1 l, Thysania agrippina. No. 794, 1.75 l, Papilio blumei. No. 795, 1.75 l, Salamis temora. 5.75 l, Cymothoe excelsa.

Perf. 13 Syncopated

2013, July 5 **Litho.**
793-796 A267 Set of 4 2.10 2.10
796a Souvenir sheet of 8, 2 each #793-796, + label 4.25 4.25

Famous People A268

Designs: No. 797, 1.75 l, Adrian Paunescu (1943-2010), poet and politician. No. 798, 1.75 l, Anton Crihan (1893-1993), politician. No. 799, 1.75 l, Ion Bass (1933-2005), folk singer. No. 800, 1.75 l, Angela Paduraru (1938-95), folk singer. 4.50 l, Giuseppe Verdi (1813-1901), composer. 5.40 l, Richard Wagner (1813-83), composer.

2013 **Litho.** *Perf. 14x14½*
797-802 A268 Set of 6 3.50 3.50

Issued: Nos. 797-798, 7/20; Nos. 799-802, 8/2.

Souvenir Sheet

Alexei Mateevici (1888-1917), Poet — A269

2013, Aug. 28 **Litho.** *Perf. 14½x14*
803 A269 5.75 l multi + label 1.10 1.10

Muscat Grapes — A270

2013, Sept. 13 **Litho.** *Perf. 14½x14*
804 A270 1.75 l multi .35 .35

Urban Mass Transportation — A271

Designs: 1.75 l, Bus. 3 l, Trolleybus. 5.75 l, Tram.

2013, Oct. 12 **Litho.** *Perf. 14x14½*
805-806 A271 Set of 2 .95 .95

Souvenir Sheet

807 A271 5.75 l multi + label 1.10 1.10

First tram in Chisinau, cent. (No. 807).

Christmas — A272

2013, Nov. 22 **Litho.** *Perf. 14x14½*
808 A272 1.75 l multi .35 .35

Forget-me-nots — A273

Tree of Life Embroidery Design — A274

A275

A276

2013, Dec. 20 Litho. *Perf. 14x14½*

809	A273	1.75 l multi + label	.35	.35
810	A274	1.75 l multi + label	.35	.35

Perf. 13 Syncopated

811	A275	1.75 l multi	.35	.35
812	A276	1.75 l multi	.35	.35
		Nos. 809-812 (4)	1.40	1.40

Nos. 809-810 each were printed in sheets of 8 + 8 labels that could be personalized. The labels shown are generic.

Nos. 811-812 each were printed in sheets of 8 stamps + 4 labels that could not be personalized. The image areas of Nos. 811-812 could be personalized. Illustrations show a generic image in the image area.

The frame portion of No. 811 has eight slightly different types. Values are for any of the frame types.

Traditional Crafts — A277

Designs: 1.20 l, Pottery. 1.75 l, Basket weaving. 5.75 l, Carpet weaving.

2014, Jan. 18 Litho. *Perf. 14x14½*

813-815 A277 Set of 3 1.60 1.60

2014 Winter Olympics, Sochi, Russia — A278

Designs: 4.50 l, Skiing, bobsledding, snowboarding. 5.40 l, Ice hockey, figure skating, biathlon.

2014, Feb. 7 Litho. *Perf. 14x14½*

816-817 A278 Set of 2 1.90 1.90

Europa A279

Musical instruments: 3 l, Tambal (dulcimer). 5.75 l, Cobza (lute).

2014, Mar. 22 Litho. *Perf. 14x14½*

818-819	A279	Set of 2	1.75	1.75
818a		Sheet of 3 + label	1.90	1.90
819a		Sheet of 3 + label	3.50	3.50

Nos. 818a and 819a were sold with, but unattached, to a booklet cover.

Easter — A280

Perf. 13 Syncopated

2014, Apr. 5 Litho.

820 A280 1.75 l multi .35 .35

No. 820 was printed in sheets of 8 + central label.

Museums — A281

Designs: 1.20 l, National Museum of Ethnography and Natural History. 2 l, National History Museum. 4 l, National Art Museum.

2014, May 3 Litho. *Perf. 14x14½*

821-823 A281 Set of 3 1.40 1.40

Nos. 821-823 each were printed in sheets of 10 + 5 labels.

Arrival of German Settlers in Bessarabia, 200th Anniv. — A282

2014, May 15 Litho. *Perf. 14x14½*

824 A282 1.75 l multi .35 .35

Famous People — A283

Designs: 1.20 l, Tamara Ceban (1914-90), singer. 1.75 l, Dumitru Matcovschi (1939-2013), writer. 3 l, Toma Ciorba (1864-1936), physician. 8.50 l, Elena Cernei (1924-2000), opera singer.

Perf. 13 Syncopated

2014, June 7 Litho.

825-828 A283 Set of 4 2.60 2.60

Souvenir Sheet

Mihai Eminescu and Ion Creanga, Painting by Mihai Grecu — A284

Perf. 13 Syncopated

2014, June 14 Litho.

829 A284 5.75 l multi 1.10 1.10

Deportation of Germans from Bessarabia, 65th Anniv. — A285

2014, July 5 Litho. *Perf. 14x14½*

830 A285 1.75 l multi .35 .35

Association Agreement Between Moldova and European Union — A286

2014, Aug. 9 Litho. *Perf. 14x14½*

831 A286 1.75 l multi .35 .35

Sheep Breeds — A287

Designs: 1.20 l, Karakul sheep. 5.75 l, Tigaie sheep.

Perf. 13 Syncopated

2014, Aug. 16 Litho.

832-833 A287 Set of 2 1.25 1.25

Traditional Dishes — A288

Designs: 1 l, Fried fish with garlic sauce. 1.20 l, Bean soup with thyme. 4 l, Cheese and dill pies. 7 l, Chicken broth with parsley.

2014, Sept. 30 Litho. *Perf. 14x14½*

834-837 A288 Set of 4 2.25 2.25

Fauna — A289

Designs: 1.20 l, Helix pomatia. 1.50 l, Ciconia ciconia (46x28mm). 1.75 l, Stizostedion lucioperca (46x28mm). 2 l, Cyprinus carpio (46x28mm). 3 l, Viviparus viviparus. 8.50 l, Motacilla flava (46x28mm).

2014, Nov. 7 Litho. *Perf. 14x14½*

838-843	A289	Set of 6	3.00	3.00
843a		Souvenir sheet of 6, #838-843	3.00	3.00

Famous Men In World War I — A290

Designs: 1.75 l, Dimitrie Bogos (1889-1946), politician. 4 l, General Constantin Braescu (1873-1927). 5.75 l, Marshal Alexandru Averescu (1859-1938).

2014, Nov. 22 Litho. *Perf. 14x14½*

844-846 A290 Set of 3 1.90 1.90

New Year 2015 — A291

Designs: 1.75 l, Snowman. 5.75 l, Santa Claus in sleigh.

2014, Dec. 12 Litho. *Perf. 14½x14*

847-848 A291 Set of 2 1.25 1.25

Souvenir Sheet

Grigore Vieru (1935-2009), Poet — A292

2015, Feb. 14 Litho. *Perf. 14½x14*

849 A292 5.75 l multi + label .80 .80

International Year of Soils — A293

International Year of Light — A294

Perf. 13 Syncopated

2015, Feb. 21 Litho.

850	A293	1.75 l multi	.25	.25
851	A294	4.50 l multi	.65	.65

Composer Eugen Doga, Dancers and Musical Score for Movie *My Sweet and Tender Beast* — A295

2015, Mar. 1 Litho. *Perf. 14x14½*

852 A295 1.75 l multi .25 .25

Coats of Arms — A296

Arms of: 10b, Causeni. 25b, Hîncesti. 1 l, Ungheni. 1.20 l, Orhei. 3 l, Balti. 5 l, Chisinau.

2015, Mar. 7 Litho. *Perf. 14½x14*

853-858 A296 Set of 6 1.50 1.50

Europa A297

Old toys: 5.75 l, Wooden rocking horse and stackable rings. 11 l, Clay bird and ram figurines.

2015, Apr. 15 Litho. *Perf. 14x14½*

859-860 A297 Set of 2 2.40 2.40
860a Booklet pane of 4, 2 each #859-860 5.00 —
Complete booklet, #860a 5.00

International Telecommunication Union, 150th Anniv. — A298

2015, Apr. 29 Litho. *Perf. 14x14½*

861 A298 1.75 l multi .25 .25

End of World War II, 70th Anniv. — A299

2015, May 5 Litho. *Perf. 14½x14*

862 A299 1.75 l multi .25 .25

Intl. Children's Day — A300

Children's art by: 1.20 l, Catalina Munteanu. 1.75 l, Cristina Isacov. 5.75 l, Ana Vlas, vert.

Perf. 14x14½, 14½x14

2015, June 1 Litho.

863-865 A300 Set of 3 1.25 1.25

Traditional Embroidered Blouses A301

Blouse from: 1.75 l, 20th century. 11 l, 1925.

Perf. 13 Syncopated

2015, June 24 Litho.

866-867 A301 Set of 2 1.75 1.75

Famous People — A302

Designs: 1.20 l, Constanta Tirtau (1930-2014), actress. 1.75 l, Gica Petrescu (1915-2006), composer and singer. 4 l, Nicolae Corlateanu (1915-2005), linguist. 11 l, Pyotr Ilich Tchaikovsky (1840-93), composer. 5.75 l, Alexandru Cristea (1890-1942), composer of Moldovan national anthem.

Perf. 13 Syncopated

2015, July 17 Litho.

868-871 A302 Set of 4 2.40 2.40

Souvenir Sheet

872 A302 5.75 l multi .80 .80

Helsinki Accords, 40th Anniv. — A303

Perf. 13 Syncopated

2015, July 30 Litho.

873 A303 11 l multi 1.50 1.50

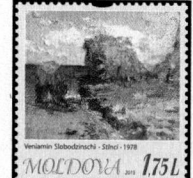

Paintings A304

Designs: 1.75 l, Rocks, by Veniamin Slobodzinschi, 1978. 3 l, Evening in the Field, by Eleonora Romanescu, 1967. 5.75 l, On the Outskirts of the Village of Dolna, by Dimitrie Peicev, 2008. 9.50 l, Landscape, by Vasile Nascu, 2004.

Perf. 13 Syncopated

2015, Aug. 15 Litho.

874-877 A304 Set of 4 2.60 2.60

Birds A305

Designs: 1.20 l, Sturnus vulgaris. 1.75 l, Pyrrhula pyrrhula. 4 l, Parus caeruleus. No. 881, 5.75 l, Bombycilla garrulus.
No. 882, 5.75 l, Alauda arvensis.

2015, Sept. 25 Litho. *Perf. 14x14½*

878-881 A305 Set of 4 1.60 1.60

Souvenir Sheet

882 A305 5.75 l multi .75 .75

Dancers — A306

No. 883: a, 1.75 l, Dancers from Moldova. b, 11 l, Dancers from Azerbaijan.

2015, Oct. 16 Litho. *Perf. 14x14½*

883 A306 Horiz. pair, #a-b 1.60 1.60

See Azerbaijan No. 1094.

Mihai Volontir (1934-2015), Actor — A307

2015, Oct. 21 Litho. *Perf. 14x14½*

884 A307 1.75 l multi .25 .25

United Nations, 70th Anniv. — A308

Perf. 13 Syncopated

2015, Oct. 24 Litho.

885 A308 15.50 l multi 2.00 2.00

A309

Personalized Stamps — A310

Perf. 13 Syncopated

2015, Nov. 17 Litho.

Panel Color

886 A309 1.75 l lt bl green .25 .25
887 A309 1.75 l dark green .25 .25
888 A309 1.75 l dark blue .25 .25
889 A309 1.75 l pinkish org .25 .25

Perf. 14x14½

890 A310 1.75 l light green .25 .25
891 A310 1.75 l pink .25 .25
892 A310 1.75 l light blue .25 .25
Nos. 886-892 (7) 1.75 1.75

Vignette portions could be personalized for an additional fee. Vignette images shown are generic.

Motor Sports — A311

No. 893: a, 1.20 l, Motocross. b, 5.75 l, Autocross.

2015, Nov. 27 Litho. *Perf. 14x14½*

893 A311 Horiz. pair, #a-b .90 .90

Christmas A312

Designs: 1.75 l, Star procession. 9.50 l, Plugusorul carolers.

Perf. 13 Syncopated

2015, Dec. 4 Litho.

894-895 A312 Set of 2 1.50 1.50

Blood Donation Campaign — A313

2016, Feb. 2 Litho. *Perf. 14½x14*

896 A313 1.75 l multi .25 .25

Souvenir Sheet

Struve Geodetic Arc UNESCO World Heritage Site, 200th Anniv. — A314

2016, Feb. 11 Litho. *Perf. 14½x14*

897 A314 5.75 l multi + label .75 .75

Martisor (Spring Celebration) A315

Martisor string on: 1.20 l, Snowdrops. 5.75 l, Cherry blossoms.

Perf. 13 Syncopated

2016, Mar. 1 Litho.

898-899 A315 Set of 2 .90 .90

Nos. 898-899 were both printed in sheets of 8 + central label.

1951 Soviet Deportation of Bessarabians, 65th Anniv — A316

2016, Mar. 31 Litho. *Perf. 14½x14*

900 A316 1.75 l multi .25 .25

A317

Europa A318

2016, Apr. 5 Litho. *Perf. 14x14½*

901 A317 5.75 l multi .75 .75
902 A318 9.50 l multi 1.25 1.25
a. Souvenir sheet of 6, 3 each #901-902 6.00 6.00

Think Green Issue.
No. 902a was sold with, but unattached to, a booklet cover.

No. 371 Surcharged in Gold

2016, Apr. 12 **Litho.**
903 A101 11 l on 1.80 l #371 1.40 1.40

First space flight by Yuri Gagarin, 55th anniv.

Flowers — A319

Designs: 10b, Xeranthemum annuum. 25b, Matricaria recutita. 1 l, Cichorium intybus. 2 l, Taraxacum officinale. 3 l, Achillea millefolium. 5 l, Salvia nemorosa.

2016, Apr. 15 **Litho.** ***Perf. 14x14½***
904-909 A319 Set of 6 1.50 1.50
909a Souvenir sheet of 6, #904-909, + 3 labels 1.50 1.50

Palm Sunday A320

2016, Apr. 24 **Litho.** ***Perf. 14x14½***
910 A320 1.75 l multi .25 .25

Worldwide Fund for Nature (WWF) — A321

No. 911 — Gladiolus imbricatus: a, Sky and flowers on seven stems. b, Sky and flowers on one stem. c, Five flowers on one stem, no sky. d, Two flowers on one stem, no sky.

Perf. 13 Syncopated

2016, May. 27 **Litho.**
911 A321 11 l Block of 4, #a-d 5.75 5.75

Pentecost — A322

2016, June 19 **Litho.** ***Perf. 14x14½***
912 A322 1.75 l multi .25 .25

Famous Men A323

Designs: No. 913, 1.20 l, Carol Schmidt (1846-1928), mayor of Chisinau. No. 914, 1.20 l, Nicolae Anestiadi (1916-68), surgeon. 1.75 l, Grigore Grigoriu (1941-2003), actor. 5.75 l, Emil Loteanu (1936-2003), film director.

2016, June 29 **Litho.** ***Perf. 14x14½***
913-916 A323 Set of 4 1.25 1.25

Souvenir Sheet

Putna Monastery, 550th Anniv. — A324

Perf. 13 Syncopated

2016, July 2 **Litho.**
917 A324 5.75 l multi .75 .75

Nativity of St. John the Baptist A325

2016, July 7 **Litho.** ***Perf. 14x14½***
918 A325 1.75 l multi .25 .25

2016 Summer Olympics, Rio de Janeiro — A326

Designs: 5.75 l, Women's discus and hammer throw. 15.50 l, Rowing.

2016, July 25 **Litho.** ***Perf. 14x14½***
919-920 A326 Set of 2 2.75 2.75

Souvenir Sheet

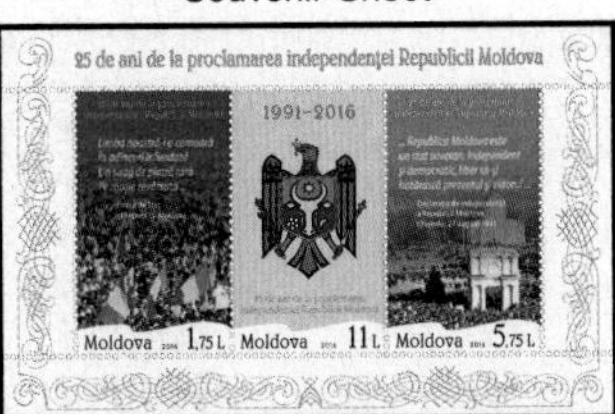

Independence, 25th Anniv. — A327

No. 921: a, 1 l, Flags and words from national anthem. b, 5.75 l, Triumphal Arch, Chisinau, and words from Moldovan Declaration of Independence. c, 11 l, Moldova coat of arms.

Litho. With Foil Application

2016, Aug. 27 ***Perf. 14½x14***
921 A327 Sheet of 3, #a-c 2.40 2.40

Woodworking — A328

No. 922 — Woodworker with mallet and: a, 1.75 l, Wooden flasks. b, 11 l, Carving of a bull.

2016, Sept. 8 **Litho.** ***Perf. 14x14½***
922 A328 Horiz. pair, #a-b 1.60 1.60

See Belarus No. 1010.

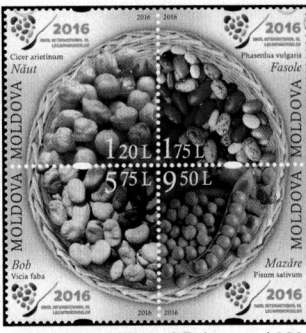

International Year of Pulses — A329

No. 923: a, 1.20 l, Cicer arietinum. b, 1.75 l, Phaseolus vulgaris. c, 5.75 l, Vicia faba. d, 9.50 l, Pisum sativum.

Perf. 13 Syncopated

2016, Sept. 27 **Litho.**
923 A329 Block of 4, #a-d 2.40 2.40

Extinct Animals of Moldova — A330

Designs: 1.20 l, Tapir. 1.75 l, Dolichopithecus ruscinensis. 4 l, Crocuta crocuta spelaea. 5.75 l, Paracamelus alexejevi.

15.50 l, Megaloceros giganteus.

2016, Oct. 29 **Litho.** ***Perf. 14x14½***
924-927 A330 Set of 4 1.60 1.60

Souvenir Sheet

928 A330 15.50 l multi 2.00 2.00

Souvenir Sheet

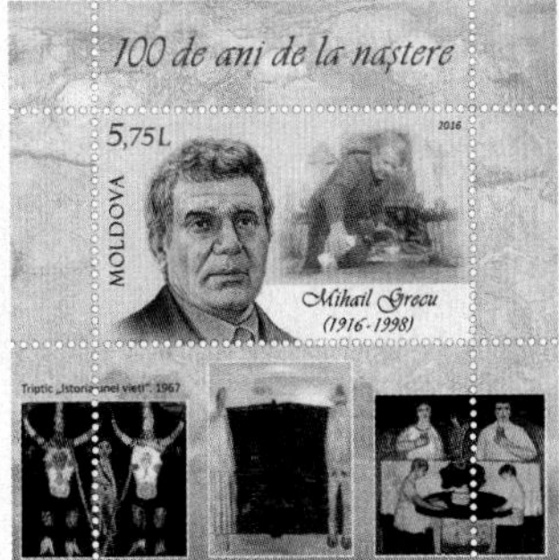

Mihail Grecu (1916-98), Painter — A331

2016, Nov. 22 **Litho.** ***Perf. 14x14½***
929 A331 5.75 l multi .75 .75

New Year 2017 A332

Ornaments: 1.75 l, Spherical with snowflakes. 5.75 l, Bells.

Perf. 13 Syncopated

2016, Dec. 2 **Litho.**
930-931 A332 Set of 2 .95 .95

Nos. 930-931 were each printed in sheets of 8 + label.

AIR POST STAMPS

TU-144 — AP1

1992-93	**Litho.**	***Perf. 12***	
C1	AP1 1.75r maroon	.40	.40
C2	AP1 2.50r red vio	.45	.45
C3	AP1 7.75r blue	1.50	1.50
C4	AP1 8.50r blue green	1.90	1.90
C5	AP1 25r red brown	.45	.45
C6	AP1 45r brown	.75	.75
C7	AP1 50r olive green	.90	.90
C8	AP1 90r blue	1.90	1.90
	Nos. C1-C8 (8)	8.25	8.25

Issued: #C1-C4, 7/20/92; #C5-C8, 7/24/93.

POSTAGE DUE STAMPS

Dove, Envelope — D1

1994, Nov. 12 **Litho.** ***Perf. 14***
J1 D1 30b lt olive & brown .55 .55
J2 D1 40b pale vio & slate .65 .65

In use, Nos. J1-J2 were torn apart, one half being affixed to the postage due item and the other half being pasted into the postman's record book. Values are for unused and canceled-to-order pairs.

MONACO

'mä-nə-,kō

LOCATION — Southern coast of France, bordering on the Mediterranean Sea
GOVT. — Principality
AREA — 481 acres
POP. — 31,842 (2001 est.)
CAPITAL — Monaco

100 Centimes = 1 Franc
100 Cents = 1 Euro (2002)

Catalogue values for unused stamps in this country are for Never Hinged items, beginning with Scott 182 in the regular postage section, Scott B51 in the semi-postal section, Scott C2 in the airpost section, Scott CB1 in the airpost semi-postal section, and Scott J28 in the postage due section.

Values for unused stamps are for examples with original gum as defined in the catalogue introduction. Very fine examples of Nos. 1-181, B1-B50, C1 and J1-J27 will have perforations clear of the design and/or frameline. Very well centered are worth more than the values quoted.

Prince Charles III — A1

1885 Unwmk. Typo. *Perf. 14x13½*

1 A1 1c olive green 25.00 17.50
2 A1 2c dull lilac 57.50 27.50
3 A1 5c blue 70.00 35.00
4 A1 10c brown, *straw* 85.00 40.00
5 A1 15c rose 350.00 18.00
6 A1 25c green 700.00 75.00
7 A1 40c slate, *rose* 85.00 45.00
8 A1 75c black, *rose* 275.00 125.00
9 A1 1fr black, *yellow* 1,750. 500.00
10 A1 5fr rose, *green* 3,000. 2,000.

Prince Albert I — A2

1891-1921

11 A2 1c olive green .70 .70
12 A2 2c dull violet .80 .80
13 A2 5c blue 50.00 6.00
14 A2 5c yel grn ('01) .50 .35
15 A2 10c brown, *straw* 100.00 16.00
16 A2 10c carmine ('01) 4.00 .70

17 A2 15c rose 175.00 8.00
a. Double impression *1,400.*
18 A2 15c vio brn, *straw* ('01) 3.00 1.00
19 A2 15c gray grn ('21) 2.00 *2.50*
20 A2 25c green 275.00 32.50
21 A2 25c dp blue ('01) 15.00 5.00
22 A2 40c slate, *rose* ('94) 4.00 2.40
23 A2 50c vio brn (shades), *org* 7.00 4.75
24 A2 75c vio brn, *buff* ('94) 27.50 18.00
25 A2 75c ol brn, *buff* ('21) 20.00 *24.00*
26 A2 1fr black, *yellow* 19.00 11.00
27 A2 5fr rose, *grn* 100.00 87.50
c. Double impression 1,500.
28 A2 5fr dull vio ('21) 200.00 *250.00*
29 A2 5fr dk grn ('21) 22.50 *27.50*
Nos. 11-29 (19) 1,026. 498.70

The handstamp "OL" in a circle of dots is a cancellation, not an overprint.

For shades, see the *Scott Classic Specialized Catalogue of Stamps and Covers.*

See No. 1782. For overprints and surcharges see Nos. 30-35, 57-59, B1.

Stamps of 1901-21Overprinted or Surcharged

1921, Mar. 5

30 A2 5c lt green .70 *.70*
31 A2 75c brown, *buff* 5.25 *6.25*
32 A2 2fr on 5fr dull vio 32.50 *52.50*
Nos. 30-32 (3) 38.45 *59.45*

Issued to commemorate the birth of Princess Antoinette, daughter of Princess Charlotte and Prince Pierre, Comte de Polignac.

Stamps and Type of 1891-1921 Surcharged

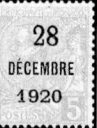

1922

33 A2 20c on 15c gray green 1.10 *1.40*
34 A2 25c on 10c rose .70 *.90*
35 A2 50c on 1fr black, *yel* 6.00 *6.50*
Nos. 33-35 (3) 7.80 *8.80*

Prince Albert I — A5

Oceanographic Museum — A6

"The Rock" of Monaco — A7

Royal Palace — A8

1922-24 Engr. *Perf. 11*

40 A5 25c deep brown 4.00 *4.75*
41 A6 30c dark green .90 .90
42 A6 30c scarlet ('23) .50 .45
43 A6 50c ultra 4.25 4.25
44 A7 60c black brown .35 .35
45 A7 1fr black, *yellow* .25 .25
46 A7 2fr scarlet ver .50 .45
47 A8 5fr red brown 32.50 *37.50*
48 A8 5fr green, *bluish* 10.50 10.50
49 A8 10fr carmine 14.00 18.00
Nos. 40-49 (10) 67.75 *77.40*

Nos. 40-49 exist imperf.

For shades, see the *Scott Classic Specialized Catalogue of Stamps and Covers.*

Prince Louis II
A9 A10

St. Dévote Viaduct ("Bridge of Suicides") A11

1923-24 Engr.

50 A9 10c deep green .35 *.55*
51 A9 15c car rose ('24) .45 *.70*
52 A9 20c red brown .35 *.55*
53 A9 25c violet .25 *.45*
a. Without engraver's name 27.50 27.50
54 A11 40c orange brn ('24) .65 .55
55 A10 50c ultra .35 *.45*
Nos. 50-55 (6) 2.40 *3.25*

The 25c comes in 2 types, one with larger "5" and "c" touching frame of numeral tablet.

Stamps of the 1922-24 issues sometimes show parts of the letters of a papermaker's watermark.

The engraved stamps of type A11 measure 31x21½mm. The typographed stamps of that design measure 36x21½mm.

See #86-88. For surcharges see #95-96.

Stamps and Type of 1891-1921 Surcharged

1924, Aug. 5 *Perf. 14x13½*

57 A2 45c on 50c brn ol, *buff* .60 *.70*
a. Double surcharge 775.00 775.00
58 A2 75c on 1fr blk, *yel* .60 *.70*
a. Double surcharge 550.00 *550.00*
59 A2 85c on 5fr dk green .60 *.70*
a. Double surcharge *650.00* *650.00*
Nos. 57-59 (3) 1.80 2.10
Set, never hinged 2.25

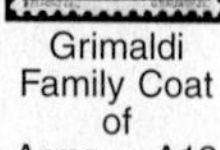

Grimaldi Family Coat of Arms — A12

Prince Louis II — A13

Louis II — A14

View of Monaco A15

1924-33 Typo.

60 A12 1c gray black .25 .25
61 A12 2c red brown .25 .25
62 A12 3c brt violet ('33) 2.75 1.90
63 A12 5c orange ('26) .35 .30
64 A12 10c blue .25 .25
65 A13 15c apple green .25 .25
66 A13 15c dull vio ('29) 2.75 1.90
67 A13 20c violet .25 .25
68 A13 20c rose .35 .25
69 A13 25c rose .25 .25
70 A13 25c red, *yel* .25 *.25*
71 A13 30c orange .25 .25
72 A13 40c black brown .25 .25
73 A13 40c lt bl, *bluish* .35 .35
74 A13 45c gray blk ('26) .90 .70
75 A14 50c myrtle grn ('25) .25 *.25*
76 A13 50c brown, *org* .25 .25
77 A14 60c yel brn ('25) .25 *.25*
78 A13 60c ol grn, *grnsh* .25 *.25*
79 A13 75c ol grn, *grnsh* ('26) .70 .35
80 A13 75c car, *straw* ('26) .35 .25
81 A13 75c slate .90 .55
82 A13 80c red, *yel* ('26) .40 .30
83 A13 90c rose, *straw* ('27) 2.00 1.60
84 A13 1.25fr bl, *bluish* ('26) .25 .25
85 A13 1.50fr bl, *bluish* ('27) 3.75 1.90

Size: 36x21½mm

86 A11 1fr blk, *orange* .25 *.25*
87 A11 1.05fr red violet ('26) .25 *.25*
88 A11 1.10fr blue grn ('27) 8.00 6.00
89 A15 2fr vio & ol brn ('25) 2.75 1.00
90 A15 3fr rose & ultra, *yel* ('27) 22.50 11.00
91 A15 5fr grn & rose ('25) 8.50 6.00
92 A15 10fr yel brn & bl ('25) 25.00 17.50
Nos. 60-92 (33) 86.30 55.85
Set, never hinged 175.00

Nos. 60 to 74 and 76 exist imperforate.

For surcharges see Nos. 93-94, 97-99, C1.

Type of 1924-33 Surcharged in Black

1926-31

93 A13 30c on 25c rose .30 .25
94 A13 50c on 60c ol grn, *grnsh* ('28) 1.50 .35
95 A11 50c on 1.05fr red vio ('28) 1.10 .70
a. Double surcharge 65.00
96 A11 50c on 1.10fr bl grn ('31) 14.00 8.75
97 A13 50c on 1.25fr bl, *bluish* (R) ('28) 1.60 .65
98 A13 1.25fr on 1fr bl, *bluish* .80 .50
99 A15 1.50fr on 2fr vio & ol brn ('28) 7.00 5.25
Nos. 93-99 (7) 26.30 16.45
Set, never hinged 40.00

Princes Charles III, Louis II and Albert I A17

1928, Feb. 18 Engr. *Perf. 11*

100 A17 50c dull carmine 2.50 *4.75*
101 A17 1.50fr dark blue 2.50 *4.75*
102 A17 3fr dark violet 2.50 *4.75*
Nos. 100-102 (3) 7.50 14.25
Set, never hinged 18.00

Nos. 100-102 were sold exclusively at the Intl. Phil. Exhib. at Monte Carlo, Feb., 1928.

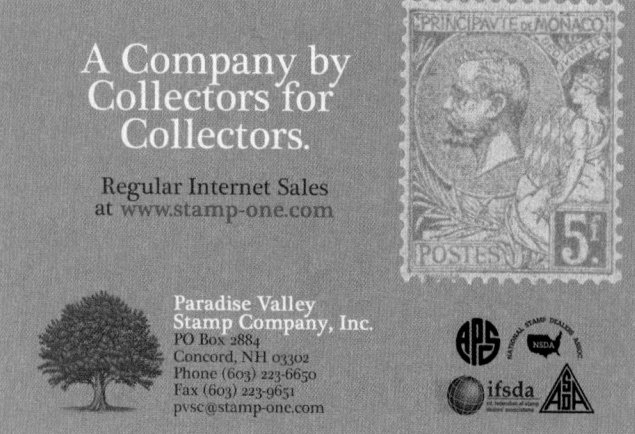

One set was sold to each purchaser of a ticket of admission to the exhibition which cost 5fr.
Exist imperf. Value, set $27.50.

Old Watchtower A20

Royal Palace A21

Church of St. Dévote — A22

Prince Louis II — A23

"The Rock" of Monaco A24

Gardens of Monaco A25

Fortifications and Harbor — A26

1932-37 *Perf. 13, 14x13½*

110	A20	15c lilac rose	.80	.25
111	A20	20c orange brn	.80	.25
112	A21	25c olive blk	1.10	.35
113	A22	30c yellow grn	1.40	.35
114	A23	40c dark brown	3.25	1.40
115	A24	45c brown red	3.50	1.10
a.		45c red	425.00	425.00
116	A23	50c purple	3.25	.85
117	A25	65c blue green	3.50	1.10
118	A26	75c deep blue	4.00	1.75
119	A23	90c red	9.50	3.25
120	A22	1fr red brn ('33)	27.50	7.75
121	A26	1.25fr rose lilac	6.75	4.50
122	A23	1.50fr ultra	40.00	10.50
123	A21	1.75fr rose lilac	35.00	9.50
124	A21	1.75fr car rose ('37)	24.00	13.00
125	A24	2fr dark blue	13.50	4.75
126	A20	3fr purple	20.00	9.00
127	A21	3.50fr orange ('35)	47.50	32.50
128	A22	5fr violet	27.50	20.00
129	A21	10fr deep blue	125.00	70.00
130	A25	20fr black	175.00	140.00
		Nos. 110-130 (21)	572.85	332.15
		Set, never hinged	1,150.	

Postage Due Stamps of 1925-32 Surcharged or Overprinted in Black

1937-38 *Perf. 14x13*

131	D3	5c on 10c violet	1.00	1.00
132	D3	10c violet	1.00	1.00
133	D3	15c on 30c bister	1.00	1.00
134	D3	20c on 30c bister	1.00	1.00
135	D3	25c on 60c red	1.50	1.50
136	D3	30c bister	2.40	2.40
137	D3	40c on 60c red	2.40	2.40
138	D3	50c on 60c red	2.40	2.40
139	D3	65c on 1fr lt bl	2.25	2.00
140	D3	85c on 1fr lt bl	5.00	4.50
141	D3	1fr light blue	7.75	7.75
142	D3	2.15fr on 2fr dl red	7.75	7.75
143	D3	2.25fr on 2fr dl red ('38)	19.00	19.00
144	D3	2.50fr on 2fr dl red ('38)	29.00	29.00
		Nos. 131-144 (14)	83.45	82.70
		Set, never hinged	175.00	

Grimaldi Arms — A27

Prince Louis II — A28

1937-43 **Engr.**

145	A27	1c dk vio brn ('38)	.25	.25
146	A27	2c emerald	.25	.25
147	A27	3c brt red violet	.25	.25
148	A27	5c red	.25	.25
149	A27	10c ultra	.25	.25
149A	A27	10c black ('43)	.25	.25
150	A27	15c violet ('39)	1.75	1.50
150A	A27	30c dull grn ('43)	.25	.25
150B	A27	40c rose car ('43)	.25	.25
150C	A27	50c brt vio ('43)	.25	.25
151	A28	55c red brn ('38)	5.75	2.25
151A	A27	60c Prus blue ('43)	.25	.25
152	A28	65c violet ('38)	30.00	13.00
153	A28	70c red brn ('39)	.35	.35
153A	A27	70c red brn ('43)	.25	.25
154	A28	90c violet ('39)	.35	.30
155	A28	1fr rose red ('38)	18.50	10.50
156	A28	1.25fr rose red ('39)	.35	.35
157	A28	1.75fr ultra ('38)	18.50	10.50
158	A28	2.25fr ultra ('39)	.35	.25
		Nos. 145-158 (20)	78.65	41.75
		Set, never hinged	150.00	

Nos. 151, 152, 155, 157 exist imperf.

Souvenir Sheet

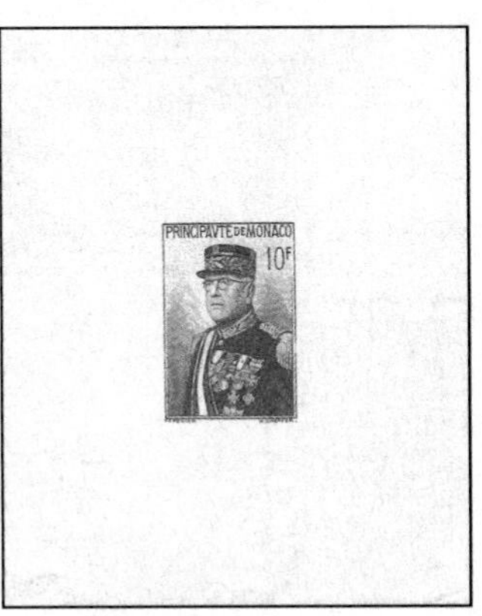
Prince Louis II — A29

1938, Jan. 17 **Unwmk.** ***Imperf.***

159	A29	10fr magenta	65.00	65.00
		Never hinged	175.00	

"Fête Nationale" 1/17/38. Size: 99x120mm.

Cathedral of Monaco — A30

St. Nicholas Square — A31

Palace Gate — A32

Palace of Monaco — A34

Panorama of Monaco A33

Harbor of Monte Carlo A35

1939-46 *Perf. 13*

160	A30	20c rose lilac	.25	.25
161	A31	25c gldn brown	.45	.30
162	A32	30c dk blue grn	.35	.30
162A	A32	30c brown red ('40)	.35	.25
163	A31	40c henna brn	.70	.50
164	A33	45c brt red vio	.50	.50
165	A34	50c dk blue grn	.35	.25
166	A32	60c rose carmine	.40	.35
166A	A32	60c dk green ('40)	.90	.70
166B	A35	70c brt red vio ('41)	.40	.25
167	A35	75c dark green	.40	.25
167A	A30	80c dull green ('43)	.25	*.25*
168	A34	1fr brown black	.40	.25
168A	A33	1fr claret ('43)	.25	.25
168B	A35	1.20fr ultra ('46)	.25	*.35*
168C	A34	1.30fr brown blk ('41)	.40	.35
168D	A31	1.50fr ultra ('46)	.40	.40
169	A31	2fr rose violet	.40	.30
169A	A35	2fr lt ultra ('43)	.25	.25
169B	A34	2fr green ('46)	.35	.25
170	A33	2.50fr red	27.50	17.50
171	A33	2.50fr dp blue ('40)	1.75	1.75
172	A35	3fr brown red	.45	.35
172A	A31	3fr black ('43)	.25	.25
172B	A30	4fr rose lilac ('46)	1.25	.55
172C	A34	4.50fr brt violet ('43)	.25	.25
173	A30	5fr Prus blue	5.25	4.00
173A	A32	5fr deep green ('43)	.25	.25
173B	A34	6fr lt violet ('46)	.70	.55
174	A33	10fr green	1.40	*1.60*
174A	A30	10fr deep blue ('43)	.25	*.25*
174B	A35	15fr rose pink ('43)	.40	*.25*
175	A32	20fr brt ultra	1.60	1.25
175A	A33	20fr sepia ('43)	.40	.25
175B	A35	25fr blue green ('46)	1.40	1.25
		Nos. 160-175B (35)	51.10	36.85
		Set, never hinged	100.00	

See Nos. 214-221, 228-232, 274-275, 319-320, 407-408, 423, 426, 428-429, B36-B50.

Louis II Stadium A36

1939, Apr. 23 **Engr.**

176	A36	10fr dark green	100.00	*110.00*
		Never hinged	175.00	

Inauguration of Louis II Stadium.

Louis II Stadium A37

1939, Aug. 15

177	A37	40c dull green	1.25	1.25
178	A37	70c brown black	1.60	1.60
179	A37	90c dark violet	2.25	2.25
180	A37	1.25fr copper red	3.00	3.00
181	A37	2.25fr dark blue	4.25	4.25
		Nos. 177-181 (5)	12.35	12.35
		Set, never hinged	22.50	

8th International University Games.

Imperforates

Many Monaco stamps from 1940 to 1999 exist imperforate. Officially 20 sheets, ranging from 25 to 100 subjects, were left imperforate.

Catalogue values for unused stamps in this section, from this point to the end of the section, are for Never Hinged items.

Prince Louis II — A38

1941-46 *Perf. 14x13*

182	A38	40c brown carmine	.65	.50
183	A38	80c deep green	.65	.50
184	A38	1fr rose violet	.25	.25
185	A38	1.20fr green ('42)	.25	.25
186	A38	1.50fr rose	.25	.25
187	A38	1.50fr violet ('42)	.25	.25
187A	A38	2fr lt green ('46)	.65	.35
188	A38	2.40fr red ('42)	.25	.25
189	A38	2.50fr deep ultra	1.10	*1.25*
190	A38	4fr blue ('42)	.25	.25
		Nos. 182-190 (10)	4.55	4.10

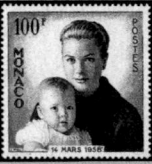

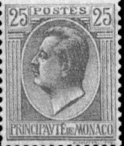

Prince Louis II — A39

1943 *Perf. 13*
191 A39 50fr purple 2.00 1.10

A40

Prince Louis II — A41

1946 Unwmk. Engr. *Perf. 14x13*
192 A40 2.50fr dk blue green .70 .25
193 A40 3fr brt red violet .70 .25
194 A40 6fr brt red .70 .35
195 A40 10fr brt ultra .70 .35

Perf. 13
196 A41 50fr dp Prus green 4.00 2.10
197 A41 100fr red 5.25 2.75
Nos. 192-197 (6) 12.05 6.05

Nos. 196-197 exist imperforate.
See Nos. 222-227, 233-236. For overprints see Nos. C8-C9.

Franklin D. Roosevelt — A42

Harbor of Monte Carlo A43

Palace of Monaco A44

Map of Monaco — A45

1946, Dec. 13 Unwmk. *Perf. 13*
198 A42 10c red violet .50 .45
199 A43 30c deep blue .50 .45
200 A44 60c blue black .50 .45
201 A45 1fr sepia 1.50 1.25
202 A45 3fr lt violet 2.25 1.75
Nos. 198-202,B93,C14-C15,CB6 (9) 10.35 8.65

Issued in tribute to the memory of Franklin D. Roosevelt.

Prince Louis II — A46

1947, May 15
203 A46 10fr dark blue green 3.50 3.50

25th anniv. of the reign of Prince Louis II.
See Nos. B94, C20a.

Hurdler A47

Runner — A48

Designs: 2fr, Discus thrower. 2.50fr, Basketball. 4fr, Swimmer.

1948, July 1 *Perf. 13*
204 A47 50c blue green .25 .25
205 A48 1fr rose brown .25 .25
206 A48 2fr grnsh blue 1.00 .75
207 A48 2.50fr vermilion 2.75 2.00
208 A48 4fr slate gray 3.25 3.00
Nos. 204-208,CB7-CB10 (9) 72.00 70.75

Issued to publicize Monaco's participation in the 1948 Olympic Games held at Wembley, England, during July and August.

Nymph Salmacis A49

Hercules — A50

Aristaeus — A51

Hyacinthus A52

François J. Bosio and Louis XIV Statue — A53

1948, July 12
209 A49 50c dark green .55 .35
210 A50 1fr red .55 .35
211 A51 2fr deep ultra 1.90 .75
212 A52 2.50fr deep violet 4.75 2.25
213 A53 4fr purple 4.75 2.50
Nos. 209-213,CB11-CB14 (9) 94.50 88.20

Issued to honor François J. Bosio (1768-1845), sculptor. No. 213 inscribed "J F Bosio."

Scenic Types of 1939

1948 **Engr.**
214 A30 50c sepia .35 .25
215 A31 60c rose pink .35 .25
216 A32 3fr violet rose 1.10 .35
217 A31 4fr emerald 1.10 .35
218 A34 8fr red brown 4.25 2.00
219 A34 10fr brown red 6.00 2.00
220 A33 20fr carmine rose 1.50 .65
221 A35 25fr gray black 35.00 17.50
Nos. 214-221 (8) 49.65 23.35

Louis II Type of 1946

1948, July *Perf. 14x13*
222 A40 30c black .30 .25
223 A40 5fr orange brown .45 .30
224 A40 6fr purple 5.00 1.75
225 A40 10fr orange .45 .30
226 A40 12fr deep carmine 6.00 2.50
227 A40 18fr dark blue 9.50 6.00
Nos. 222-227 (6) 21.70 11.10

Scenic Types of 1939

1949 *Perf. 13*
228 A33 5fr blue green .85 .35
229 A35 10fr orange 1.75 .65
230 A32 25fr blue 52.50 16.00
231 A30 40fr brown red 9.25 4.75
232 A30 50fr purple 5.75 1.00
Nos. 228-232 (5) 70.10 22.75

Louis II Type of 1946

1949, Mar. 10 *Perf. 14x13*
233 A40 50c olive .35 .25
234 A40 1fr dk violet bl .25 .25
235 A40 12fr dk slate grn 10.00 7.00
236 A40 15fr brown carmine 10.00 3.75
Nos. 233-236 (4) 20.60 11.25

Hirondelle I A54

Cactus Plants — A55

Designs: 4fr, Oceanographic Museum. 5fr, Princess Alice II at Spitzbergen. 6fr, Albert I Monument. 10fr, Hirondelle II. 12fr, Albert I whaling. 18fr, Bison.

1949, Mar. 5 *Perf. 13*
237 A54 2fr brt blue .25 .25
238 A55 3fr dark green .25 .25
239 A54 4fr blk brn & bl .25 .25
240 A54 5fr crimson 1.00 1.00
241 A55 6fr dark violet .90 .90
242 A54 10fr black brown 1.10 1.10
243 A54 12fr brt red violet 2.50 2.50
244 A54 18fr dk brn & org brn 3.50 3.50
Nos. 237-244 (8) 9.75 9.75

See Nos. C21-C26.

Palace, Globe and Pigeon A56

1949-50 Engr. Unwmk.
245 A56 5fr blue green .60 .60
245A A56 10fr orange 7.00 7.00
246 A56 15fr carmine .60 .60
Nos. 245-246,C30-C33 (7) 16.70 16.70

75th anniversary of the UPU.
Nos. 245, 245A and 246 exist imperf.
Issued: 5fr, 15fr, 12/27; 10fr, 9/12/50.

Prince Rainier III — A57

1950, Apr. 11
247 A57 10c red & blk brn .25 .25
248 A57 50c dp yel & dk brn .25 .25
249 A57 1fr purple .45 .35
250 A57 5fr dark green 3.50 1.90
251 A57 15fr carmine 5.25 5.25
252 A57 25fr ultra, ol grn & ind 5.25 5.25
Nos. 247-252,C34-C35 (8) 27.45 25.75

Enthronement of Prince Rainier III.

Prince Rainier III — A58

1950, Apr. Engr. *Perf. 14x13*
253 A58 50c purple .35 .25
254 A58 1fr orange brown .35 .30
255 A58 8fr blue green 9.00 2.40
256 A58 12fr blue 2.25 .50
257 A58 15fr crimson 4.25 .70
Nos. 253-257 (5) 16.20 4.15

1951, Apr. 31 **Typo.**
258 A58 5fr emerald 12.00 4.75
259 A58 10fr orange 20.00 7.75

See Nos. 276-279.

Statue of Prince Albert I — A59

1951, Apr. 11 Engr. *Perf. 13*
260 A59 15fr deep blue 11.00 6.50

Edmond and Jules de Goncourt A60

1951, Apr. 11
261 A60 15fr violet brown 8.00 5.00

50th anniversary of the foundation of Goncourt Academy.

St. Vincent de Paul — A61

Judgment of St. Dévote — A62

Symbolizing Monaco's Adoption of Catholicism — A63

Mosaic of the Immaculate Conception A64

Blessed Rainier of Westphalia A65

Holy Year, 1951: 50c, Pope Pius XII. 12fr, Prince Rainier III at Prayer. 15fr, St. Nicholas de Patare. 20fr, St. Roman. 25fr, St. Charles Borromée. 40fr, Cross, arms and Roman Coliseum. 50fr, Chapel of St. Dévote.

Inscribed: "Anno Santo"

1951, June 4 Unwmk. *Perf. 13*

262 A61 10c ultra & red .25 .25
263 A61 50c dk rose lake & pur .25 .25
264 A62 1fr brown & dk grn .30 .30
265 A63 2fr vio brn & ver .35 .35
266 A64 5fr blue green .45 .45
267 A63 12fr rose violet .70 .70
268 A63 15fr vermilion 4.00 4.00
269 A63 20fr red brown 6.00 6.00
270 A63 25fr ultra 8.00 8.00
271 A63 40fr dk car rose & pur 9.50 9.50
272 A63 50fr ol grn & dk vio brn 12.50 12.50
273 A65 100fr dk violet brn 25.00 25.00
Nos. 262-273 (12) 67.30 67.30

Scenic Types of 1939-46

1951, Dec. 22 *Perf. 13*

274 A31 3fr deep turq green 2.75 .90
275 A32 30fr slate black 8.50 3.50

Rainier Type of 1950

1951, Dec. 22 *Perf. 14x13*

276 A58 6fr blue green 1.75 .75
277 A58 8fr orange 1.75 .75
278 A58 15fr indigo 2.50 .45
279 A58 18fr crimson 6.25 1.50
Nos. 276-279 (4) 12.25 3.45

Radio Monte Carlo — A66

1951, Dec. 22 *Perf. 13*

280 A66 1fr blue, car & org 1.00 .35
281 A66 15fr pur, car & rose vio 4.00 1.25
282 A66 30fr indigo & red brn 17.50 6.50
Nos. 280-282 (3) 22.50 8.10

Knight in Armor — A67

1951, Dec. 22

283 A67 1fr purple 1.10 .50
284 A67 5fr gray black 3.50 2.00
285 A67 8fr deep carmine 7.00 3.50
286 A67 15fr emerald 11.50 6.50
287 A67 30fr slate black 19.00 13.50
Nos. 283-287 (5) 42.10 26.00

See Nos. 328-332, 2025-2026.

Nos. B96-B99a Surcharged with New Values and Bars in Black

1951, Dec. *Perf. 13½x13, Imperf.*

288 SP51 1fr on 10fr + 5fr 12.50 12.50
289 SP52 3fr on 15fr + 5fr 12.50 12.50
290 SP52 5fr on 25fr + 5fr 13.00 12.50
291 SP51 6fr on 40fr + 5fr 13.00 12.50
b. Block of 4, #288-291 51.00 50.00

Gallery of Hercules, Royal Palace A68

1952, Apr. 26 Engr. *Perf. 13*

292 A68 5fr red brn & brn 2.00 .55
293 A68 15fr purple & lil rose 2.50 .60
294 A68 30fr indigo & ultra 2.90 .75
Nos. 292-294 (3) 7.40 1.90

Opening of a philatelic museum at the royal palace, Apr. 26, 1952.

Basketball — A69

2fr, Soccer. 3fr, Sailing. 5fr, Cyclist. 8fr, Gymnastics. 15fr, Louis II Stadium.

1953, Feb. 23 Unwmk. *Perf. 11*

295 A69 1fr dk purple & mag .25 .25
296 A69 2fr dk grn & sl bl .25 .25
297 A69 3fr blue & lt blue .25 .25
298 A69 5fr dk brn & grnsh blk .80 .25
299 A69 8fr brown lake & red 2.00 1.00
300 A69 15fr bl, brn blk & dk grn 1.00 .90
Nos. 295-300,C36-C39 (10) 70.55 37.90

Issued to publicize Monaco's participation in the Helsinki Olympic Games.

Books, Pens and Proof Pages A70

1953, June 29 *Perf. 13*

301 A70 5fr dark green .55 .45
302 A70 15fr red brown 3.75 .70

Publication of a first edition of the unexpurgated diary of Edmond and Jules Goncourt.

Physalia and Laboratory Ship Hirondelle II — A71

1953, June 29

303 A71 2fr Prus grn, pur & choc .25 .25
304 A71 5fr dp mag, red & Prus grn .80 .30
305 A71 15fr ultra, vio brn & Prus grn 2.90 1.60
Nos. 303-305 (3) 3.95 2.15

50th anniversary of the discovery of anaphylaxis by Charles Richet and Paul Portier.

Frederic Ozanam — A72

Nun — A73

1954, Apr. 12 Engr. *Perf. 13*

306 A72 1fr bright red .25 .25
307 A73 5fr dark blue .50 .50
308 A72 15fr black 2.10 1.90
Nos. 306-308 (3) 2.85 2.65

Centenary of the death of Frederic Ozanam, founder of the Society of Saint Vincent de Paul.

Jean Baptiste de la Salle
A74 A75

1954, Apr. 12

309 A74 1fr dark carmine .25 .25
310 A75 5fr black brown .50 .50
311 A74 15fr bright ultra 2.10 1.90
Nos. 309-311 (3) 2.85 2.65

Jean Baptiste de la Salle, founder of the Christian Brothers Institute and saint.

A76

A77

Grimaldi Arms — A78

Various Forms of Grimaldi Arms in Black and Red or Black, Red and Deep Plum (5fr)

Perf. 13½x14, 14x13½

1954, Apr. 12 Typo.

312 A76 50c black & mag .25 .25
313 A77 70c black & aqua .25 .25
314 A76 80c black, red & dk grn .25 .25
315 A77 1fr violet blue .25 .25
316 A77 2fr black & dp org .25 .25
317 A77 3fr black & green .25 .25
318 A78 5fr black & lt grn .25 .25
Nos. 312-318 (7) 1.75 1.75

Scenic Types of 1939-46

1954, Apr. 12 Engr. *Perf. 13*

319 A34 25fr bright red 3.25 .50
320 A31 75fr dark green 23.00 7.50

Knight in Armor — A79

1954, Apr. 12 Unwmk. *Perf. 13*

321 A79 4fr dark red 1.50 .40
322 A79 8fr dark green 1.50 .80
323 A79 12fr dark purple 6.00 1.75
324 A79 24fr dark maroon 11.00 4.75
Nos. 321-324 (4) 20.00 7.70

Nos. 321-324 were issued precanceled only. Values for precanceled stamps in first column are for those which have not been through the post and have original gum. Values in the second column are for postally used, gumless stamps.

See Nos. 400-404, 430-433, 466-469.

Lambarene Landing, Gabon — A80

Dr. Albert Schweitzer — A81

Design: 15fr, Lambarene hospital.

1955, Jan. 14 *Perf. 11x11½*

325 A80 2fr ol grn, bl grn & ind .30 .25
326 A81 5fr dk grnsh bl & grn 1.25 .90
327 A81 15fr dk bl grn, dp cl & brn blk 3.50 2.50
Nos. 325-327 (3) 5.05 3.65

Issued to honor Dr. Albert Schweitzer, medical missionary. See No. C40.

Knight Type of 1951

1955, Jan. 14 *Perf. 13*

328 A67 5fr purple 3.25 .75
329 A67 6fr red 5.00 1.50
330 A67 8fr red brown 6.00 3.00
331 A67 15fr ultra 13.00 4.50
332 A67 30fr dark green 22.50 14.00
Nos. 328-332 (5) 49.75 23.75

Automobile and Representation of Eight European Cities — A82

1955, Jan. 14 **Unwmk.**

333 A82 100fr dk brown & red 75.00 50.00

25th Monte Carlo Automobile Rally.

Prince Rainier III — A83

1955, June 7 **Engr.** ***Perf. 13***

334 A83 6fr green & vio brn .70 .40
335 A83 8fr red & violet .70 .40
336 A83 12fr carmine & green .70 .40
337 A83 15fr purple & blue 1.40 .40
338 A83 18fr orange & blue 4.50 .40
339 A83 30fr ultra & gray 14.00 7.75
Nos. 334-339 (6) 22.00 9.75

See Nos. 405-406, 424-425, 427, 462-465, 586, 603-604A, 725-728, 730, 789, 791.

"Five Weeks in a Balloon" — A84

"A Floating City" and Jules Verne — A85

"Michael Strogoff" A86

"Around the World in 80 Days" — A87

USS Nautilus and Verne — A88

Designs (Scenes from Jules Verne's Books): 3fr, The House of Vapors. 6fr, The 500 Millions of the Begum. 8fr, The Magnificent Orinoco. 10fr, A Journey to the Center of the Earth. 25fr, Twenty Thousand Leagues under the Sea.

1955, June 7

340 A84 1fr red brn & bl gray .25 .25
341 A85 2fr blue, ind & brn .25 .25
342 A85 3fr red brn, gray & sl .25 .25
343 A86 5fr car & blk brn .25 .25
344 A84 6fr blk brn & bluish gray .45 .45
345 A86 8fr ol grn & aqua .35 .35
346 A85 10fr indigo, turq & brn 1.25 1.00
347 A87 15fr rose brn & ver 1.00 .70
348 A85 25fr bl grn, grn & gray 2.50 1.75
349 A88 30fr violet, turq & blk 6.25 5.25
Nos. 340-349,C45 (11) 37.80 35.50

50th anniv. of the death of Jules Verne.

Virgin by Francois Brea A89

Blessed Rainier — A90

Marian Year: 10fr, Pieta by Louis Brea.

1955, June 7

350 A89 5fr vio brn, gray & dk grn .25 .25
351 A89 10fr vio brn, gray & dk grn .40 .35
352 A90 15fr black brn & org brn .60 .55
Nos. 350-352 (3) 1.25 1.15

Rotary Emblem, World Map — A91

1955, June 7

353 A91 30fr blue & orange 1.00 1.00

50th anniv. of the founding of Rotary Intl.

George Washington A92

Franklin D. Roosevelt — A93

Dwight D. Eisenhower — A94

Palace of Monaco, c. 1790 — A95

Palace of Monaco, c. 1750 — A96

Designs: 3fr, Abraham Lincoln. 30fr, Columbus landing in America. 40fr, Prince Rainier III. 100fr, Early Louisiana scene.

1956, Apr. 3 **Engr.** ***Perf. 13***

354 A92 1fr dark purple .25 .25
355 A93 2fr claret & dk pur .25 .25
356 A93 3fr vio & dp ultra .25 .25
357 A94 5fr brown lake .25 .25
358 A95 15fr brn blk & vio brn .25 .25
359 A95 30fr ind, blk & ultra 3.75 2.00
360 A94 40fr dk brn & vio brn 5.00 2.50
361 A96 50fr vermilion 5.00 2.50
362 A96 100fr Prus green 5.00 3.50
a. Strip of 3, #360-362 19.00 19.00
Nos. 354-362 (9) 20.00 11.75

5th Intl. Phil. Exhib. (FIPEX), NYC, Apr. 28-May 6, 1956.

Ski Jump, Cortina d'Ampezzo — A97

Design: 30fr, Olympic Scenes.

1956, Apr. 3

363 A97 15fr brn vio, brn & dk grn 1.10 .55
364 A97 30fr red orange 2.25 1.60

Issued to publicize Monaco's participation in the 1956 Olympic Games.

"Glasgow to Monte Carlo" A98

1956, Apr. 3 **Unwmk.**

365 A98 100fr red brn & red 20.00 20.00

The 26th Monte Carlo Automobile Rally.

See Nos. 411, 437, 460, 483, 500, 539, 549, 600, 629.

Princess Grace and Prince Rainier III — A99

1956, Apr. 19 **Engr.** ***Perf. 13***

Portraits in Black

366 A99 1fr dark green .25 .25
367 A99 2fr dark carmine .25 .25
368 A99 3fr ultra .40 .25
369 A99 5fr brt yellow grn .90 .55
370 A99 15fr redsh brown 1.25 .65
Nos. 366-370,C46-C48 (8) 8.55 5.15

Wedding of Prince Rainier III to Grace Kelly, Apr. 19, 1956.

Nos. J41-J47, J50-J56 Overprinted with Bars and Surcharged in Indigo, Red or Black

Unwmk.

1956, Apr. 3 **Engr.** ***Perf. 11***

Designs: Early Transportation.

371 D6 2fr on 4fr (I) .45 .45
a. Pair, #371, 381 1.00 1.00
372 D6 3fr (R) .45 .45
a. Pair, #372, 382 1.00 1.00
373 D6 5fr on 4fr .65 .65
a. Pair, #373, 383 1.40 1.40
374 D6 10fr on 4fr (R) 1.25 1.25
a. Pair, #374, 384 2.75 2.75
375 D6 15fr on 5fr (I) 1.60 1.60
a. Pair, #375, 385 3.50 3.50
376 D6 20fr (R) 2.50 2.50
a. Pair, #376, 386 5.50 5.50
377 D6 25fr on 20fr 4.50 4.50
a. Pair, #377, 387 10.00 10.00
378 D6 30fr on 10fr (I) 8.50 8.50
a. Pair, #378, 388 19.00 19.00
379 D6 40fr on 50fr (R) 12.00 12.00
a. Pair, #379, 389 27.00 27.00
380 D6 50fr on 100fr 14.00 14.00
a. Pair, #380, 390 32.00 32.00

Designs: Modern Transportation.

381 D7 2fr on 4fr (I) .45 .45
382 D7 3fr (R) .45 .45
383 D7 5fr on 4fr .65 .65
384 D7 10fr on 4fr (R) 1.25 1.25
385 D7 15fr on 5fr (I) 1.60 1.60
386 D7 20fr (R) 2.50 2.50
387 D7 25fr on 20fr 4.50 4.50
388 D7 30fr on 10fr (I) 8.50 8.50
389 D7 40fr on 50fr (R) 12.00 12.00
390 D7 50fr on 100fr 14.00 14.00
Nos. 371-390,C49-C50 (22) 109.80 109.80

Pairs se-tenant at the base.

Princess Grace — A100

1957, May 11 Engr. *Perf. 13*

391 A100 1fr blue violet .25 .25
392 A100 2fr lt olive grn .25 .25
393 A100 3fr yellow brown .25 .25
394 A100 5fr magenta .30 .25
395 A100 15fr pink .60 .25
396 A100 25fr Prus blue .75 .65
397 A100 30fr purple 1.00 .90
398 A100 50fr scarlet 1.60 .90
399 A100 75fr orange 2.75 2.50
Nos. 391-399 (9) 7.75 6.20

Birth of Princess Caroline of Monaco.

Knight Type of 1954

1957 Unwmk. *Perf. 13*

400 A79 5fr dark blue .40 .25
401 A79 10fr yellow green .30 .25
402 A79 15fr brt orange 1.40 .90
403 A79 30fr brt blue 2.00 .90
404 A79 45fr crimson 3.25 1.75
Nos. 400-404 (5) 7.35 4.05

Nos. 400-404 were issued precanceled only. See note after No. 324.

Types of 1955 and 1939-46

1957

405 A83 20fr greenish blue 2.00 .50
406 A83 35fr red brown 4.00 1.60
407 A33 65fr brt violet 10.00 6.50
408 A30 70fr orange yellow 9.50 6.00
Nos. 405-408 (4) 25.50 14.60

Princesses Grace and Caroline
A101

1958, May 15 Engr. *Perf. 13*

409 A101 100fr bluish black 6.50 5.00

Birth of Prince Albert Alexander Louis, Mar. 14.

Order of St. Charles — A102

1958, May 15

410 A102 100fr carmine, grn & bis 1.75 1.50

Cent. of the Natl. Order of St. Charles.

Rally Type of 1956

Design: 100fr, "Munich to Monte Carlo."

1958, May 15

411 A98 100fr red, grn & sepia 7.00 6.00

27th Monte Carlo Automobile Rally.

Virgin Mary, Popes Pius IX and XII — A103

Bernadette Soubirous
A104

Tomb of Bernadette, Nevers
A105

Designs: 3fr, Shepherdess Bernadette at Bartres. 5fr, Bouriette kneeling (first miracle). 8fr, Stained glass window showing apparition. 10fr, Empty grotto at Lourdes. 12fr, Grotto with statue and altar. 20fr, Bernadette praying. 35fr, High Altar at St. Peter's during canonization of Bernadette. 50fr, Bernadette, Pope Pius XI, Mgr. Laurence and Abbe Peyramale.

1958, May 15 Unwmk.

412 A103 1fr lilac gray & vio brn .25 .25
413 A104 2fr blue & violet .25 .25
414 A104 3fr green & sepia .25 .25
415 A104 5fr gray brn & vio bl .25 .25
416 A104 8fr blk, ol bis & ind .25 .25
417 A105 10fr multicolored .25 .25
418 A105 12fr ind, ol bis & ol grn .25 .25
a. Strip of 3, #416-418 3.50 3.50
419 A104 20fr dk sl grn & rose .40 .35
420 A104 35fr ol, gray ol & dk sl grn .50 .45
421 A103 50fr lake, ol grn & ind .80 .55
422 A105 65fr indigo & grnsh bl 1.10 .75
Nos. 412-422,C51-C52 (13) 8.80 7.75

Centenary of the apparition of the Virgin Mary at Lourdes.

Sizes: Nos. 413-415, 419-420 26x36mm. No. 416 22x36mm. Nos. 417-418 48x36mm. No. 422 36x26mm.

Types of 1939-46 and 1955

1959 Engr. *Perf. 13*

423 A32 5fr copper red 1.10 .55
424 A83 25fr orange & blk 1.10 .55
425 A83 30fr dark violet 4.25 2.10
426 A34 35fr dark blue 8.50 3.25
427 A83 50fr bl grn & rose cl 5.50 2.10
428 A31 85fr dk carmine rose 12.50 6.50
429 A33 100fr brt grnsh blue 12.50 6.50
Nos. 423-429 (7) 45.45 21.55

Knight Type of 1954

1959

430 A79 8fr deep magenta .75 .35
431 A79 20fr bright green 1.40 1.25
432 A79 40fr chocolate 2.75 1.10
433 A79 55fr ultra 4.50 2.75
Nos. 430-433 (4) 9.40 5.45

Nos. 430-433 were issued precanceled only. See note after No. 324.

Princess Grace Polyclinic — A106

1959, May 16

434 A106 100fr gray, brn & grn 3.00 2.00

Opening of Princess Grace Hospital.

UNESCO Building, Paris, and Cultural Emblems — A107

50fr, UNESCO Building, children of various races.

1959, May 16

435 A107 25fr multicolored .30 .30
436 A107 50fr ol, bl grn & blk brn .40 .40

Opening of UNESCO Headquarters in Paris, Nov. 3, 1958.

Rally Type of 1956

Design: 100fr, "Athens to Monaco."

1959, May 16

437 A98 100fr vio bl, red & sl grn, *bl* 5.50 5.00

28th Monte Carlo Automobile Rally.

Carnations — A108

Bougainvillea — A109

Flowers: 10fr on 3fr, Princess Grace Carnations. 15fr on 1fr, Mimosa, vert. 25fr on 6fr, Geranium, vert. 35fr, Oleander. 50fr, Jasmine. 85fr on 65fr, Lavender. 100fr, Grace de Monaco Rose.

1959, May 16

438 A108 5fr brn, Prus grn & rose car .25 .25
439 A108 10fr on 3fr brn, grn & rose .25 .25
440 A109 15fr on 1fr dk grn & cit .30 .25
441 A109 20fr ol grn & mag .75 .55
442 A109 25fr on 6fr yel grn & red 1.25 .75
443 A109 35fr dk grn & pink 2.00 1.75
444 A109 50fr dk brn & dk grn 2.75 2.10
445 A109 85fr on 65fr ol grn & gray vio 3.00 3.00
446 A108 100fr green & pink 4.00 4.00
Nos. 438-446 (9) 14.55 12.90

Nos. 439-440, 442 and 445 were not issued without surcharge.

View of Monaco and Uprooted Oak Emblem — A110

1960, June 1 Unwmk. *Perf. 13*

447 A110 25c bl, olive grn & sepia .35 .25

World Refugee Year, 7/1/59-6/30/60.

Entrance to Oceanographic Museum — A111

Museum and Aquarium — A112

Designs: 15c, Museum conference room. 20c, Arrival of equipment, designed by Prince Albert I. 25c, Research on electrical qualities of cephalopodes. 50c, Albert I and vessels Hirondelle I and Princesse Alice.

1960, June 1 Engr. *Perf. 13*

448 A111 5c blue, sepia & cl .55 .25
449 A112 10c multicolored .70 .35
450 A112 15c sep, ultra & bis .70 .35
451 A112 20c rose lil, blk & bl 1.00 .55
452 A112 25c grnsh blue 1.50 1.00
453 A112 50c lt ultra & brown 2.50 1.75
Nos. 448-453 (6) 6.95 4.25

Inauguration of the Oceanographic Museum of Monaco, 50th anniv. See #475.

Horse Jumping — A113

Sports: 10c, Women swimmers. 15c, Broad jumper. 20c, Javelin thrower. 25c, Girl figure skater. 50c, Skier.

1960, June 1

454 A113 5c dk brn, car & emer .25 .25
455 A113 10c red brn, bl & grn .25 .25
456 A113 15c dl red brn, ol & mag .35 .35
457 A113 20c black, bl & grn 2.75 2.75
458 A113 25c dk grn & dull pur .70 .70
459 A113 50c dk bl, grnsh bl & dl pur 1.10 1.10
Nos. 454-459 (6) 5.40 5.40

Nos. 454-457 for the 17th Olympic Games, Rome, Aug. 25-Sept. 11; Nos. 458-459 for the 8th Winter Olympic Games, Squaw Valley, Feb. 18-29.

Rally Type of 1956

Design: 25c, "Lisbon to Monte Carlo."

1960, June 1
460 A98 25c bl, brn & car, *bluish* 2.00 2.00

29th Monte Carlo Automobile Rally.

Stamps of Sardinia and France, 1860, and Stamp of Monaco, 1885
A114

1960, June 1 Engr. & Embossed
461 A114 25c violet, blue & ol .75 .65

75th anniv. of postage stamps of Monaco.

Prince Rainier Type of 1955

1960 Engr. *Perf. 13*
462 A83 25c orange & blk .55 .25
463 A83 30c dark violet .55 .25
464 A83 50c bl grn & rose lil 2.25 .35
465 A83 65c yel brn & slate 14.00 4.25
Nos. 462-465 (4) 17.35 5.10

Knight Type of 1954

1960
466 A79 8c deep magenta 1.60 .55
467 A79 20c brt green 2.75 .55
468 A79 40c chocolate 4.50 1.10
469 A79 55c ultra 6.75 1.60
Nos. 466-469 (4) 15.60 3.80

Nos. 466-469 were issued precanceled only. See note after No. 324.

Sea Horse — A115

#471 Cactus (Cereanee). #472, Cactus (Nopalea dejecta). #473, Scorpion fish, horiz.

1960, June 1
470 A115 15c org brn & sl grn .80 .25
471 A115 15c ol grn, yel & brn .95 .25
472 A115 20c maroon & ol grn .95 .25
473 A115 20c brn, red brn, red & ol .80 .35
Nos. 470-473 (4) 3.50 1.10

See Nos. 581-584.

Type of 1960 and

Palace of Monaco
A116

Designs: 10c, Type A111 without inscription. 45c, Aerial view of Palace. 85c, Honor court. 1fr, Palace at night.

1960, June 1 Engr.
474 A116 5c green & sepia .25 .25
475 A111 10c dk bl & vio brn .55 .35
476 A116 45c dk bl, sep & grn 6.75 .70
477 A116 85c slate, gray & bis 8.75 2.10
478 A116 1fr dk bl, red brn & sl grn 1.10 .40
Nos. 474-478 (5) 17.40 3.80

See #585, 602, 729, 731, 731A, 790, 792.

Sphinx of Wadi-es-Sebua — A117

1961, June 3 Unwmk. *Perf. 13*
479 A117 50c choc, dk bl & ocher 1.25 .80

Issued as publicity to save historic monuments in Nubia.

Murena, Starfish, Sea Urchin, Sea Cucumber and Coral — A118

1961, June 3
480 A118 25c vio buff & dk red .25 .25

Issued to commemorate the World Congress of Aquariology, Monaco, Nov. 1960.

Medieval Town and Leper — A119

1961, June 3
481 A119 25c ol gray, ocher & car .25 .25

Issued to honor the Sovereign Order of the Knights of Malta.

Hand and Ant
A120

1961, June 3
482 A120 25c magenta & dp car .40 .40

Issued to publicize "Respect for Life."

Rally Type of 1956

Design: 1fr, "Stockholm to Monte Carlo."

1961, June 3
483 A98 1fr multicolored 1.50 1.50

30th Monte Carlo Automobile Rally.

Turcat-Mery, 1911 Winner, and 1961 Car — A121

1961, June 3
484 A121 1fr org brn, vio & rose red 1.50 1.50

50th anniv. of the founding of the Monte Carlo Automobile Rally.

Chevrolet, 1912
A122

Automobiles (pre-1912): 2c, Peugeot. 3c, Fiat. 4c, Mercedes. 5c, Rolls Royce. 10c, Panhard-Levassor. 15c, Renault. 20c, Ford. 25c, Rochet-Schneider. 30c, FN-Herstal. 45c, De Dion Bouton. 50c, Buick. 65c, Delahaye. 1fr, Cadillac.

1961, June 13 Engr.
485 A122 1c org brn, dk brn & grn .25 .25
486 A122 2c org red, dk bl & brn .25 .25
487 A122 3c multicolored .25 .25
488 A122 4c multicolored .25 .25
489 A122 5c ol bis, sl grn & car .25 .25
490 A122 10c brn, sl & red .25 .25
491 A122 15c grnsh bl & dk sl grn .25 .25
492 A122 20c pur, blk & red .25 .25
493 A122 25c dk brn lil & red .75 .75
494 A122 30c ol grn & dl pur .95 .95
495 A122 45c multicolored 1.25 1.25
496 A122 50c brn blk, red & ultra 1.75 1.75
497 A122 65c multicolored 2.00 2.00
498 A122 1fr brt pur, ind & red 2.75 2.75
Nos. 485-498 (14) 11.45 11.45

See Nos. 648-661.

Bugatti, First Winner, and Course — A123

1962, June 6 Unwmk. *Perf. 13*
499 A123 1fr lilac rose 1.50 1.50

20th Automobile Grand Prix of Monaco.

Rally Type of 1956

Design: 1fr, "Oslo to Monte Carlo."

1962, June 6
500 A98 1fr multicolored 1.50 1.50

31st Monte Carlo Automobile Rally.

Louis XII and Lucien Grimaldi
A124

50c, Document granting sovereignty. 1fr, Seals of Louis XII & Lucien Grimaldi.

1962, June 6 Engr.
501 A124 25c ver, blk & vio bl .30 .30
502 A124 50c dk bl, brn & mag .40 .40
503 A124 1fr dk brn, grn & car .60 .60
Nos. 501-503 (3) 1.30 1.30

450th anniversary of Monaco's reception of sovereignty from Louis XII.

Mosquito and Swamp
A125

1962, June 6
504 A125 1fr brn ol & lt grn .60 .60

WHO drive to eradicate malaria.

Aquatic Stadium at Night
A126

1962, June 6
505 A126 10c dk bl, ind & grn .25 .25

Sun, Flowers and Hope Chest
A127

1962, June 6
506 A127 20c multicolored .25 .25

Issued to publicize the National Multiple Sclerosis Society of New York.

Wheat Harvest
A128

1962, June 6
507 A128 25c dk bl, red brn & brn *.30 .30*
508 A128 50c ind, ol bis & dk bl grn *.50 .35*
509 A128 1fr red lil & olive bister *1.00 .65*
Nos. 507-509,C61 (4) 3.30 2.30

Europa. See No. C61.

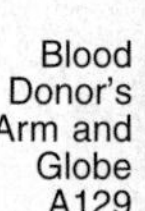

Blood Donor's Arm and Globe
A129

1962, Nov. 15 Engr. *Perf. 13*
510 A129 1fr dk red, blk & orange .90 .90

3rd International Blood Donors' Congress, Nov. 15-18 at Monaco.

Yellow Wagtails — A130

Birds: 10c, European robins. 15c, European goldfinches. 20c, Blackcaps. 25c, Great spotted woodpeckers. 30c, Nightingale. 45c, Barn owls. 50c, Common starlings. 85c, Red crossbills. 1fr, White storks.

1962, Dec. 12 **Unwmk.**

511 A130 5c green, sep & yel .25 .25
512 A130 10c bis, dk pur & red .25 .25
513 A130 15c multicolored .25 .25
514 A130 20c mag, grn & blk .35 .35
515 A130 25c multicolored .70 .70
516 A130 30c brn, sl grn & bl .90 .90
517 A130 45c vio & gldn brn 1.10 1.10
518 A130 50c bl grn, blk & yel 1.50 1.50
519 A130 85c multicolored 1.75 1.75
520 A130 1fr blk, grn & red 2.75 2.75
Nos. 511-520 (10) 9.80 9.80

Protection of useful birds.

Divers A131

10c, Galeazzi's turret, vert. 25c, William-son's photosphere, 1914 & bathyscape "Trieste," 1962. 45c, Diving suits. 50c, Diving chamber. 85c, Fulton's "Nautilus," 1800 and modern submarine. 1fr, Alexander the Great's underwater chamber and bathysphere of the N. Y. Zoological Society.

1962, Dec. 12

521 A131 5c bluish grn, vio & blk .25 .25
522 A131 10c multicolored .25 .25
523 A131 25c bis, bluish grn & sl grn .25 .25
524 A131 45c green, ind & blk .45 .45
525 A131 50c cit & dk bl .70 .70
526 A131 85c Prus grn & dk vio bl 1.25 1.25
527 A131 1fr dk bl, dk brn & dk grn 2.00 2.00
Nos. 521-527 (7) 5.15 5.15

Issued in connection with an exhibition at the Oceanographic Museum "Man Under Water," showing ancient and modern methods of under-water exploration.

Dancing Children and UN Emblem — A132

Children on Scales A133

Designs: 10c, Bird feeding nestlings, vert. 20c, Sun shining on children of different races, vert. 25c, Mother and child, vert. 50c, House and child. 95c, African mother and child, vert. 1fr, Prince Albert and Princess Caroline.

1963, May 3 **Unwmk.** ***Perf. 13***

528 A132 5c ocher, dk red & ultra .25 .25
529 A133 10c vio bl, emer & ol gray .25 .25
530 A133 15c ultra, red & grn .25 .25
531 A133 20c multicolored .25 .25
532 A133 25c blue, brn & pink .25 .25
533 A133 50c multicolored .40 .40
534 A133 95c multicolored .80 .80
535 A132 1fr multicolored 1.60 1.60
Nos. 528-535 (8) 4.05 4.05

Publicizing the UN Children's Charter.

Figurehead with Red Cross, Red Crescent and Red Lion and Sun — A134

1fr, Centenary emblem, Gustave Moynier, Henri Dunant and Gen. Henri Dufour, horiz.

1963, May 3 **Engr.**

536 A134 50c bluish grn, red & red brn .50 .50
537 A134 1fr blue, sl grn & red .50 .50

Centenary of International Red Cross.

Racing Cars on Monte Carlo Course and Map of Europe A135

1963, May 3

538 A135 50c multicolored .70 .45

European Automobile Grand Prix.

Rally Type of 1956

Design: 1fr, "Warsaw to Monte Carlo."

1963, May 3

539 A98 1fr multicolored 1.50 1.50

32nd Monte Carlo Auto Race.

Lions International Emblem — A136

1963, May 3

540 A136 50c bis, lt vio & bl .60 .60

Issued to commemorate the founding of the Lions Club of Monaco, Mar. 24, 1962.

Hôtel des Postes, Paris, and UPU Allegory — A137

1963, May 3

541 A137 50c multicolored .60 .40

1st Intl. Postal Conference, Paris, 1863.

Globe and Telstar A138

1963, May 3

542 A138 50c grn, dk pur & maroon .60 .50

1st television connection of the US and Europe through the Telstar satellite, July 11-12, 1962.

Holy Spirit over St. Peter's and World A139

1963, May 3

543 A139 1fr grn, red brn & bl .60 .60

Vatican II, the 21st Ecumenical Council of the Roman Catholic Church.

Wheat Emblem and Dove Feeding Nestlings A140

1963, May 3 **Engr.**

544 A140 1fr multicolored .70 .70

FAO "Freedom from Hunger" campaign.

Henry Ford and 1903 Model A — A141

1963, Dec. 12 **Unwmk.** ***Perf. 13***

545 A141 20c slate grn & lil rose .75 .50

Centenary of the birth of Henry Ford, American automobile manufacturer.

Bicyle Racer in Town A142

Design: 50c, Bicyclist on country road.

1963, Dec. 12

546 A142 25c bl, sl grn & red brn .30 .30
547 A142 50c bl, gray grn, & blk brn .60 .60

50th anniv. of the Bicycle Tour de France.

Pierre de Coubertin and Myron's Discobolus A143

1963, Dec. 12

548 A143 1fr dp cl, car & ocher .75 .75

Baron Pierre de Coubertin, organizer of the modern Olympic Games, birth cent.

Rally Type of 1956

Design: 1fr, "Paris to Monte Carlo."

1963, Dec. 12

549 A98 1fr multicolored 1.10 1.10

33rd Monte Carlo Automobile Rally.

Children with Stamp Album and UNESCO Emblem A144

1963, Dec. 12

550 A144 50c dp ultra, red & vio .45 .45

International Philatelic and Educational Exposition, Monaco, Nov.-Dec., 1963.

Europa Issue

Woman, Dove and Lyre — A145

1963, Dec. 12

551 A145 25c brn, grn & car *1.50* .35
552 A145 50c dk brn, bl & car *2.00* .60

Wembley Stadium and British Football Association Emblem — A146

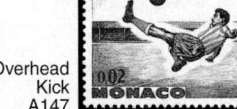

Overhead Kick A147

Soccer Game, Florence, 16th Century A148

Tackle A149

Designs: 3c, Goalkeeper. 4c, Louis II Stadium and emblem of Sports Association of Monaco, with black overprint: "Championnat /1962-1963/Coupe de France." 15c, Soule Game, Brittany, 19th century. 20c, Soccer, England, 1827. 25c, Soccer, England, 1890. 50c, Clearing goal area. 95c, Heading the ball. 1fr, Kicking the ball.

1963, Dec. 12

553 A146 1c grn, vio & dk red .25 .25
554 A147 2c black, red & grn .25 .25
555 A147 3c gray ol, org & red .25 .25
556 A146 4c bl, red, grn, pur & blk .25 .25
557 A148 10c dk bl, car & sep .25 .25
558 A148 15c sepia & car .25 .25

559 A148 20c sepia & dk bl .25 .25
560 A148 25c sepia & lilac .25 .25
a. Block of 4 1.00 1.00
561 A149 30c green, sep & red .45 .45
562 A149 50c sepia, grn & red .70 .70
563 A149 95c sepia, grn & red 1.00 1.00
564 A149 1fr sepia, grn & red 1.25 1.25
a. Block of 4 4.00 4.00
Nos. 553-564 (12) 5.40 5.40

Cent. of British Football Assoc. (organized soccer). No. 556 also for the successes of the soccer team of Monaco, 1962-63 (overprint typographed). No. 556 was not regularly issued without overprint. Value $750.

The 4 stamps of No. 560a are connected by an 1863 soccer ball in red brown; the stamps of No. 564a by a modern soccer ball.

Design from 1914 Rally Post Card — A150

Farman Biplane over Monaco — A151

Designs: 3c, Nieuport monoplane. 4c, Breguet biplane. 5c, Morane-Saulnier monoplane. 10c, Albatros biplane. 15c, Deperdussin monoplane. 20c, Vickers-Vimy biplane and map (Ross Smith's flight London-Port Darwin, 1919). 25c, Douglas Liberty biplane (first American around-the-world flight. 4 planes, 1924). 30c, Savoia S-16 hydroplane (De Pinedo's Rome-Australia-Japan-Rome flight, 1925). 45c, Trimotor Fokker F-7 monoplane (first aerial survey of North Pole, Richard E. Byrd and James Gordon Bennett, 1925). 50c, Spirit of St. Louis (first crossing of Atlantic, New York-Paris, Charles Lindbergh, 1927). 65c, Breguet 19 (Paris-New York, Coste and Bellonte, 1930). 95c, Laté 28 hydroplane (first South Atlantic airmail route, Dakar-Natal, 1930). 1fr, Dornier DO-X, (Germany-Rio de Janeiro, 1930).

1964, May 22 Engr. *Perf. 13*

565 A150 1c green, bl & ol .25 .25
566 A151 2c bl, bis & red brn .25 .25
567 A151 3c olive, grn & bl .25 .25
568 A151 4c red brn, bl & Prus grn .25 .25
569 A151 5c gray ol, vio & mag .25 .25
570 A151 10c violet, bl & ol .25 .25
571 A151 15c blue, org & brn .25 .25
572 A151 20c brt grn, blk & bl .35 .25
573 A151 25c red, bl & ol .35 .35
574 A151 30c bl, sl grn & dp cl .45 .45
575 A151 45c red brn, grnsh bl & blk .75 .55
576 A151 50c purple, ol & bis .90 .75
577 A151 65c steel bl, blk & red 1.20 1.00
578 A151 95c ocher, sl grn & red 1.60 1.25
579 A151 1fr sl grn, bl & vio brn 2.25 1.60
Nos. 565-579,C64 (16) 12.35 10.70

50th anniv. of the 1st airplane rally of Monte Carlo. Nos. 565-571 show planes which took part in the 1914 rally, Nos. 572-579 and C64 show important flights from 1919 to 1961.

Ancient Egyptian Message Transmitters and Rocket — A152

1964, May 22 Unwmk.

580 A152 1fr dk bl, indigo & org brn .70 .70

Issued to publicize "PHILATEC", International Philatelic and Postal Techniques Exhibition, Paris, June 5-21, 1964.

Types of 1955-60

1c, Crab (Macrocheira Kampferi), horiz. 2c, Flowering cactus (Selenicereus Gr.). 12c, Shell (Fasciolaria trapezium). 18c, Aloe ciliaris. 70c, Honor court of palace (like #477). 95c, Prince Rainier III.

1964, May 19 *Perf. 13*

581 A115 1c bl grn & dk red .25 .25
582 A115 2c dk grn & multi .25 .25
583 A115 12c vio & brn red .50 .25
584 A115 18c grn, yel & car .55 .25
585 A116 70c lt grn, choc & red org .70 .40
586 A83 95c ultra 1.50 .50
Nos. 581-586 (6) 3.75 1.90

Rainier III Aquatic Stadium A153

1964-67 Engr. *Perf. 13*

587 A153 10c dk car, rose, bl & blk 1.75 .25
587A A153 15c dk car, rose, brt bl & blk ('67) 1.00 .25
588 A153 25c dl grn, dk bl & blk 1.00 .25
589 A153 50c lil, bl grn & blk 1.75 1.00
Nos. 587-589 (4) 5.50 1.75

Nos. 587-589 were issued precanceled only. See note after No. 324. The "1962" date has been obliterated with 2 bars. See Nos. 732-734, 793-796, 976-979.

Common Design Types pictured following the introduction.

Europa Issue, 1964
Common Design Type

1964, Sept. 12

Size: 22x34½mm

590 CD7 25c brt red, brt grn & dk grn *1.00* .25
591 CD7 50c ultra, ol bis & dk red brn *1.50 .45*

Weight Lifter — A154

1964, Dec. 3 Unwmk. *Perf. 13*

592 A154 1c shown .25 .25
593 A154 2c Judo .25 .25
594 A154 3c Pole vault .25 .25
595 A154 4c Archery .25 .25
Nos. 592-595 (4) 1.00 1.00

18th Olympic Games, Tokyo, 10/10-25. See #C65.

Pres. John F. Kennedy and Mercury Capsule — A155

1964, Dec. 3

596 A155 50c brt bl & indigo .60 .60

Pres. John F. Kennedy (1917-63).

Television Set and View of Monte Carlo A156

1964, Dec. 3

597 A156 50c dk car rose, dk bl & brn .50 .50

Fifth International Television Festival.

Frédéric Mistral, (1830-1914), Provençal Poet — A157

1964, Dec. 3 Engr.

598 A157 1fr gray olive & brn red .55 .55

Scales of Justice and Code A158

1964, Dec. 3

599 A158 1fr gldn brn & slate grn .60 .60

Universal Declaration of Human Rights.

Rally Type of 1956

Design: 1fr, "Minsk to Monte Carlo."

1964, Dec. 3

600 A98 1fr bl grn, ocher & brn .90 .90

34th Monte Carlo Automobile Rally.

International Football Association Emblem — A159

1964, Dec. 3

601 A159 1fr red, bl & ol bister .85 .85

60th anniv. of FIFA, the Federation Internationale de Football (soccer).

Types of 1955 and 1960

Designs: 40c, Aerial view of palace. 60c, 1.30fr, 2.30fr, Prince Rainier III.

1965-66 Engr. *Perf. 13*

602 A116 40c sl grn, dl cl & brt grn .75 .25
603 A83 60c sl grn & blk 1.10 .35
604 A83 1.30fr dk red & blk 3.25 .75
604A A83 2.30fr org & rose lil ('66) 2.75 .75
Nos. 602-604A (4) 7.85 2.10

Telstar and Pleumeur-Bodou Relay Station — A160

Alexander Graham Bell and Telephone A161

Designs (ITU Emblem and): 5c, Syncom II and Earth. 10c, Echo II and Earth. 12c, Relay satellite and Earth, vert. 18c, Lunik III and Moon. 50c, Samuel Morse and telegraph. 60c, Edouard Belin, belinograph and newspaper. 70c, Roman signal towers and Chappe telegraph. 95c, Cable laying ships; "The Great Eastern" (British, 1858) and "Alsace" (French, modern). 1fr, Edouard Branly, Guglielmo Marconi and map of English Channel.

1965, May 17

605 A161 5c vio bl & slate grn .25 .25
606 A161 10c dk bl & sepia .25 .25
607 A161 12c gray, brn & dk car .25 .25
608 A161 18c ind, dk car & plum .25 .25
609 A160 25c vio, ol & rose brn .25 .25
610 A161 30c dk brn, ol & bis brn .25 .25
611 A161 50c green & indigo .25 .25
612 A161 60c dl red brn & brt bl .25 .25
613 A160 70c brn blk, org & dk bl .55 .55
614 A160 95c indigo, blk & bl .55 .55
615 A160 1fr brn, blk & ultra .75 .75
Nos. 605-615,C66 (12) 7.35 7.35

International Telecommunication Union, cent.

Europa Issue, 1965
Common Design Type

1965, Sept. 25 Engr. *Perf. 13*

Size: 36x22mm

616 CD8 30c red brn & grn *1.25 .65*
617 CD8 60c violet & dk car *2.00 1.00*

Palace of Monaco, 18th Century A162

Views of Palace: 12c, From the Bay, 17th century. 18c, Bay with sailboats, 18th century. 30c, From distance, 19th century. 60c, Close-up, 19th century. 1.30fr, Aerial view, 20th century.

1966, Feb. 1 Engr. *Perf. 13*

618 A162 10c vio, dl grn & ind .25 .25
619 A162 12c bl, bis brn & dk brn .25 .25
620 A162 18c blk, grn & bl .25 .25
621 A162 30c vio bl, sep & red brn .25 .25
622 A162 60c bl, grn & brn .65 .65
623 A162 1.30fr dk grn & red brn .80 .80
Nos. 618-623 (6) 2.45 2.45

750th anniversary of Palace of Monaco.

Dante Alighieri — A163

Designs: 60c, Dante facing Panther of Envy. 70c, Dante and Virgil boating across muddy swamp of 5th Circle. 95c, Dante watching the arrogant and Cross of Salvation. 1fr, Invocation of St. Bernard; Dante and Beatrice.

1966, Feb. 1

624 A163 30c crimson & dp grn .35 .35
625 A163 60c dl grn, Prus bl & ind .50 .50
626 A163 70c black, sep & car .70 .70
627 A163 95c red lilac & blue .75 .75
628 A163 1fr ultra & bluish grn 1.10 1.10
Nos. 624-628 (5) 3.40 3.40

700th anniv. (in 1965) of the birth of Dante (1265-1321), poet.

Rally Type of 1956

Design: 1fr, "London to Monte Carlo."

1966, Feb. 1

629 A98 1fr purple, red & indigo .95 .75

The 35th Monte Carlo Automobile Rally.

Nativity by Gerard van Honthorst A164

1966, Feb. 1

630 A164 30c brown .30 .30

Issued to honor the World Association for the Protection of Children.

Casino, Monte Carlo A165

View of La Condamine, 1860, and Francois Blanc — A166

Designs: 12c, Prince Charles III, vert. 40c, Charles III monument, Bowling Green Gardens. 60c, Seaside Promenade and Rainier III. 70c, René Blum, Sergei Diaghilev and "Petroushka." 95c, Jules Massenet and Camille Saint-Saens. 1.30fr, Gabriel Fauré and Maurice Ravel.

1966, June 1 Engr. *Perf. 13*

631 A165 12c dp blue, blk & mag .25 .25
632 A165 25c multicolored .25 .25
633 A166 30c bl, plum, grn & org .25 .25
634 A165 40c multicolored .25 .25
635 A166 60c multicolored .25 .25
636 A166 70c rose cl & ind .25 .25
637 A165 95c purple & blk .25 .25
638 A165 1.30fr brn org, ol bis & brn .65 .65
Nos. 631-638,C68 (9) 5.15 5.15

Centenary of founding of Monte Carlo.

Europa Issue, 1966
Common Design Type

1966, Sept. 26 Engr. *Perf. 13*
Size: 21½x35½mm

639 CD9 30c orange *.75* .25
640 CD9 60c light green *1.25* .40

Prince Albert I, Yachts Hirondelle I and Princess Alice — A167

1966, Dec. 12 Engr. *Perf. 13*

641 A167 1fr ultra & dk vio brn .75 .75

1st Intl. Congress of the History of Oceanography, Monaco, Dec. 12-17. Issued in sheets of 10.

Red Chalk Drawing by Domenico Zampieri — A168

1966, Dec. 12

642 A168 30c brt rose & dk brn .25 .25
643 A168 60c brt bl & yel brn .35 .35

20th anniv. of UNESCO.

Television Screen and Cross over Monaco — A169

1966, Dec. 12

644 A169 60c dk car rose, lil & red .35 .25

10th meeting of "UNDA," the International Catholic Association for Radio and Television.

Precontinent III and Divers on Ocean Floor — A170

1966, Dec. 12

645 A170 1fr Prus bl, yel & dk brn .60 .35

First anniversary of the submarine research station Precontinent III.

WHO Headquarters, Geneva — A171

1966, Dec. 12

646 A171 30c dp bl, ol brn & dp bl grn .25 .25
647 A171 60c dk grn, crim & dk brn .35 .35

Opening of WHO Headquarters, Geneva.

Automobile Type of 1961

Automobiles (Previous Winners): 1c, Bugatti, 1931. 2c, Alfa Romeo, 1932. 5c, Mercedes, 1936. 10c, Maserati, 1948. 18c, Ferrari, 1955. 20c, Alfa Romeo, 1950. 25c, Maserati, 1957. 30c, Cooper-Climax, 1958. 40c, Lotus-Climax, 1960. 50c, Lotus-Climax, 1961. 60c, Cooper-Climax, 1962. 70c, B.R.M., 1963-66. 1fr, Walter Christie, 1907. 2.30fr, Peugeot, 1910.

1967, Apr. 28 Engr. *Perf. 13x12½*

648 A122 1c ind, red & brt bl .25 .25
649 A122 2c green, red & blk .25 .25
650 A122 5c red, ind & gray .25 .25
651 A122 10c violet, red & ind .25 .25
652 A122 18c indigo & red .25 .25
653 A122 20c dk grn, red & ind .25 .25
654 A122 25c ultra, red & ind .25 .25
655 A122 30c brown, ind & grn .25 .25
656 A122 40c car rose, ind & grn .40 .40
657 A122 50c lilac, ind & grn .60 .60
658 A122 60c carmine, ind & grn .60 .60
659 A122 70c dl yel, bl grn & ind .80 .80
660 A122 1fr brn red, blk & gray 1.20 1.20
661 A122 2.30fr multicolored 2.00 2.00
Nos. 648-661,C73 (15) 10.35 10.35

25th Grand Prix of Monaco, May 7.

Dog, Egyptian Statue — A172

1967, Apr. 28 *Perf. 12½x13*

662 A172 30c dk grn, brn & blk .55 .40

Congress of the International Dog Fanciers Federation, Monaco, Apr. 5-9.

View of Monte Carlo — A173

1967, Apr. 28 *Perf. 13*

663 A173 30c slate grn, brt bl & brn .40 .40

International Tourist Year, 1967.

Chessboard and Monte Carlo Harbor — A174

1967, Apr. 28

664 A174 60c brt bl, dk pur & blk .85 .85

International Chess Championships, Monaco, Mar. 19-Apr. 1.

Melvin Jones, View of Monte Carlo and Lions Emblem — A175

1967, Apr. 28

665 A175 60c ultra, slate bl & choc .60 .40

50th anniversary of Lions International.

Rotary Emblem and View of Monte Carlo — A176

1967, Apr. 28

666 A176 1fr brt bl & lt ol grn .60 .50

Issued to publicize the Rotary International Convention, Monaco, May 21-26.

EXPO '67 Monaco Pavilion — A177

1967, Apr. 28

667 A177 1fr multicolored .55 .45

EXPO '67, International Exhibition, Montreal, Apr. 28-Oct. 27, 1967.

Map of Europe A178

1967, Apr. 28

668 A178 1fr choc, lemon & Prus bl .55 .45

Issued to publicize the International Committee for European Migration, CIME.

Europa Issue, 1967
Common Design Type

1967, Apr. 28 *Perf. 12½x13*

669 CD10 30c brt car, rose lil & brt vio *1.00* .30
670 CD10 60c grn ol & bl grn *1.75* .40

Skier and Olympic Emblem — A179

1967, Dec. 7 Engr. *Perf. 13*

671 A179 2.30fr red brn, gray & brt bl 1.25 1.25

10th Winter Olympic Games, Grenoble, France, Feb. 6-18, 1968.

Sounding Line and Map — A180

1967, Dec. 7
672 A180 1fr dk bl, grn & ol .55 .45

9th International Hydrographic Conference, Monte Carlo, April-May, 1967.

Marie Curie, Chemical Apparatus and Atom Symbol — A181

1967, Dec. 7
673 A181 1fr brn, ultra & ol .70 .50

Marie Curie (1867-1934), discoverer of radium and polonium.

Princes of Monaco Issue

Rainier I, by Eugene Charpentier — A182

#675, Lucien Grimaldi, by Ambrogio di Predis.

1967, Dec. 7 ***Perf. 12x13***
674 A182 1fr multicolored .75 .75
675 A182 1fr multicolored .75 .75

See Nos. 710-711, 735-736, 774-775, 813-814, 860-861, 892-893, 991-992, 1035-1036, 1093, 1135-1136, 1187-1188, 1246-1247, 1302-1303.

Shot Put — A183

Sport: 30c, High jump. 60c, Gymnast on rings. 70c, Water polo. 1fr, Wrestling. 2.30fr, Gymnast.

1968, Apr. 29 **Engr.** ***Perf. 13***
676 A183 20c brt bl, grn & brn .25 .25
677 A183 30c vio bl, sep & brn vio .25 .25
678 A183 60c car, brt rose lil & dp bl .25 .25
679 A183 70c ocher, brn org & Prus bl .25 .25
680 A183 1fr brn org, brn & ind .45 .45
681 A183 2.30fr dk car, vio bl & ol .95 .95
Nos. 676-681,C74 (7) 3.65 3.65

19th Olympic Games, Mexico City, 10/12-27.

St. Martin and the Beggar A184

1968, Apr. 29
682 A184 2.30fr brn red, Prus bl & blk brn 1.25 1.00

Red Cross of Monaco, 20th anniversary.

Anemones, by Raoul Dufy — A185

1968, Apr. 29 **Photo.** ***Perf. 12x13***
683 A185 1fr lt blue & multi .75 .60

International Flower Show in Monte Carlo. See Nos. 766, 776, 815-816, 829, 865.

Arms of Pope Pius IX and Prince Charles III — A186

St. Nicholas — A187

Designs: 30c, St. Benedict. 60c, Benedictine Monastery, Subiaco (Italy). 1fr, Church of St. Nicholas, Monaco, 13th century, horiz.

Perf. 12½x13, 13x12½
1968, Apr. 29 **Engr.**
684 A186 10c red & brown .25 .25
685 A187 20c sl grn, ocher & car .25 .25
686 A187 30c ultra & ol grn .25 .25
687 A187 60c lt bl, brn & dk grn .30 .30
688 A187 1fr ind, bl & ol bis .35 .35
Nos. 684-688 (5) 1.40 1.40

Centenary of the elevation of St. Nicholas Church to an Abbey *Nullius*, directly subject to the Holy See.

Europa Issue, 1968
Common Design Type

1968, Apr. 29 ***Perf. 13***
Size: 36x22mm
689 CD11 30c dp orange & car *.90* *.25*
690 CD11 60c carmine & ultra *2.25* *.30*
691 CD11 1fr green & red brn *2.25* *.40*
Nos. 689-691 (3) *5.40* .95

Locomotive 030, 1868 — A188

Locomotives and Views: 30c, Type "C"-220, 1898. 60c, Type 230-"C", 1910. 70c, Type 231-"F," 1925. 1fr, Type 241-"A," 1932. 2.30fr, Type "BB," 1968.

1968, Dec. 12 **Engr.** ***Perf. 13***
692 A188 20c vio bl, brn & blk .45 .45
693 A188 30c dk ol grn, bl & blk .45 .45
694 A188 60c bl, bis & blk 2.25 1.90
695 A188 70c vio, red brn & blk 2.25 1.90
696 A188 1fr bl, brn red & blk 3.25 2.25
697 A188 2.30fr sal pink, brt bl & blk 3.25 2.25
Nos. 692-697 (6) 11.90 9.20

Centenary of the Nice-Monaco Railroad.

Chateaubriand and Combourg Castle — A189

Scenes from Chateaubriand Novels: 20c, The Genius of Christianity. 25c, René. 30c, The Last Abencerage. 60c, The Martyrs. 2.30fr, Atala.

1968, Dec. 12
698 A189 10c dk grn, grn & pur .25 .25
699 A189 20c brt bl, vio & mag .25 .25
700 A189 25c slate, pur & brn .25 .25
701 A189 30c dp brn, brn & pur .25 .25
702 A189 60c brn red, bl grn & dk brn .35 .35
703 A189 2.30fr dk bl, ol & mag 1.10 1.10
Nos. 698-703 (6) 2.45 2.45

Vicomte François René de Chateaubriand (1768-1848), novelist and statesman.

"France" and "Fidelity" by Bosio — A190

François Joseph Bosio (1768-1845), Sculptor — A191

25c, Henri IV as a boy. 60c, Louis XIV on horseback, Place des Victoires. 2.30fr, Busts of Louis XVIII, Napoleon I and Charles X.

1968, Dec. 12
704 A190 20c brown .25 .25
705 A191 25c sal pink & dk brn .25 .25
706 A191 30c slate & vio bl .25 .25
707 A191 60c dk ol grn & gray grn .40 .40
708 A190 2.30fr black & slate .90 .90
Nos. 704-708 (5) 2.05 2.05

WHO Emblem — A192

1968, Dec. 12 **Photo.**
709 A192 60c multicolored .35 .25

World Health Organization, 20th anniv.

Princes of Monaco Type of 1967

Designs: 1fr, Charles II (1581-89). 2.30fr, Jeanne Grimaldi (1596-1620).

1968, Dec. 12 **Engr.** ***Perf. 12x13***
710 A182 1fr multicolored .70 .70
711 A182 2.30fr multicolored .70 .70

Faust and Mephistopheles — A193

Scenes from "Damnation of Faust" by Berlioz: 10c, Rakoczy March. 25c, Auerbach's Cellar. 30c, Dance of the Sylphs. 40c, Dance of the Sprites. 50c, Faust and Marguerite. 70c, Woods and Meadows. 1fr, The Ride to the Abyss. 1.15fr, Heaven.

1969, Apr. 26 **Engr.** ***Perf. 13***
712 A193 10c bl grn, pur & org brn .25 .25
713 A193 20c mag, dk ol & lt brn .25 .25
714 A193 25c ind, brn & mag .25 .25
715 A193 30c yel grn, sl & blk .25 .25
716 A193 40c org red, sl & blk .25 .25
717 A193 50c ol, plum & sl .25 .25
718 A193 70c dp grn, sl & lt brn .25 .25
719 A193 1fr mag, blk & ol bis .40 .40
720 A193 1.15fr Prus bl, blk & ultra .40 .40
Nos. 712-720,C75 (10) 3.30 3.30

Hector Berlioz (1803-69), French composer.

St. Elizabeth and Husband, Louis IV, Landgrave of Thuringia A194

1969, Apr. 26
721 A194 3fr dk red, slate & gray 1.40 1.40

Issued for the Red Cross.
See Nos. 767, 812, 830, 905, 963, 1037, 1094, 1189.

Europa Issue, 1969
Common Design Type

1969, Apr. 26
Size: 36x26mm
722 CD12 40c scarlet & purple *2.00* .30
723 CD12 70c brt blue & blk *4.25* .85
724 CD12 1fr yel bis, brn & bl *4.25* .85
Nos. 722-724 (3) *10.50* 2.00

Prince Rainier Type of 1955 and Palace Type of 1960

Designs: 80c, Aerial view of Palace. 1.15fr, 1.30fr, Honor Court.

1969-70 **Engr.** ***Perf. 13***

725 A83 40c olive & rose red .30 .25
726 A83 45c slate & ocher .50 .25
727 A83 50c ocher & mar .70 .35
728 A83 70c dk pur & brt vio bl .70 .70
729 A116 80c bl, red brn & grn 1.10 .70
730 A83 85c dk vio & brt grn 1.10 .70
731 A116 1.15fr blk, bl & mar 1.75 .75
731A A116 1.30fr ol brn, lt bl & dl grn ('70) .75 .75
Nos. 725-731A (8) 6.90 4.45

Aquatic Stadium Type of 1964-67, "1962" Omitted

1969 **Engr.** ***Perf. 13***

732 A153 22c choc, brt bl & blk .50 .25
733 A153 35c Prus bl, brt bl & blk .50 .25
734 A153 70c black & vio bl .80 .35
Nos. 732-734 (3) 1.80 .85

Nos. 732-734 were issued precanceled only. See note after No. 324.

Princes of Monaco Type of 1967

Designs: 1fr, Honoré II (1604-1662), by Philippe de Champaigne. 3fr, Louise-Hippolyte (1697-1731), by Pierre Gobert.

1969, Nov. 25 **Engr.** ***Perf. 12x13***

735 A182 1fr multicolored .60 .60
736 A182 3fr multicolored 1.25 1.25

Woman's Head, by Leonardo da Vinci — A195

Drawings by Leonardo da Vinci: 40c, Self-portrait. 70c, Head of old man. 80c, Study for head of St. Magdalene. 1.15fr, Man's head. 3fr, Professional soldier.

1969, Nov. 25 ***Perf. 13***

737 A195 30c dull brown .25 .25
738 A195 40c brn & rose red .25 .25
739 A195 70c gray green .30 .30
740 A195 80c dk brown .40 .35
741 A195 1.15fr orange brn .75 .55
742 A195 3fr olive brown 1.10 .90
Nos. 737-742 (6) 3.05 2.60

Leonardo da Vinci (1452-1519), Florentine painter, sculptor and scientist.

Alphonse Daudet and Scenes from "Letters from My Windmill" — A196

Various Scenes from "Letters from My Windmill" (Lettres de Mon Moulin).

1969, Nov. 25

743 A196 30c blue grn & multi .25 .25
744 A196 40c brn, vio bl & ol .40 .40
745 A196 70c pur, brn & ol gray .40 .40
746 A196 80c sl grn, vio bl & mar .40 .40
747 A196 1.15fr ocher, sep & blk .55 .55
Nos. 743-747 (5) 2.00 2.00

Centenary of publication of "Letters from My Windmill," by Alphonse Daudet (1840-1897).

ILO Emblem A197

1969, Nov. 25 ***Perf. 13x12½***

748 A197 40c dk blue & dk pur .35 .30

50th anniv. of the ILO.

World Map and JCI Emblem A198

1969, Nov. 25

749 A198 40c olive, dk bl & bl .35 .25

25th anniversary of the Junior Chamber of Commerce in Monaco.

Television Camera and View of Monte Carlo A199

1969, Nov. 25

750 A199 40c red brn, lil & bl .35 .25

10th International Television Festival in 1970.

King Alfonso XIII, Prince Albert I and Underwater Scene — A200

1969, Nov. 25 ***Perf. 12½x13***

751 A200 40c dk brn, blk & grnsh bl .45 .45

50th anniv. of the International Commission for the Scientific Exploration of the Mediterranean.

Congress Building, Princes Albert I and Rainier III — A201

1970, Feb. 21 **Engr.** ***Perf. 13***

752 A201 40c gray & carmine .35 .25

Meeting of the Interparliamentary Union, Monaco, Mar. 30-Apr. 5.

EXPO '70 Emblem, Japanese Scroll — A202

Designs (EXPO '70 Emblem and): 30c, Red-crowned crane. 40c, Torii. 70c, Cherry blossoms, horiz. 1.15fr, Palace and arms of Monaco, Osaka Castle and arms, horiz.

1970, Mar. 16

753 A202 20c brn, yel grn & car .25 .25
754 A202 30c brn, yel grn & buff .30 .30
755 A202 40c olive bis & pur .35 .35
756 A202 70c lt gray & red .45 .45
757 A202 1.15fr red & multi .50 .50
Nos. 753-757 (5) 1.85 1.85

Issued to publicize EXPO '70 International Exposition, Osaka, Japan, Mar. 15-Sept. 13.

Harbor Seal Pup A203

1970, Mar. 16

758 A203 40c red lil, bl & gray .75 .55

Protection of seal pups.

Doberman Pinscher A204

1970, Apr. 25

759 A204 40c ocher & black 1.40 .75

International Dog Show, Monte Carlo, Apr. 25. See No. 996.

Basque Ponies A205

Designs: 30c, Parnassius Apollo butterfly. 50c, Harbor seal in Somme Bay. 80c, Pyrenean chamois, vert. 1fr, Whitetailed sea eagles, vert. 1.15fr, European otter, vert.

1970, May 4

760 A205 30c Prus bl & multi .40 .25
761 A205 40c blue & multi .65 .35
762 A205 50c grnsh bl, bis & brn .90 .50
763 A205 80c gray grn, sl bl & brn 1.90 1.00
764 A205 1fr gray, brown & bis 2.50 2.00
765 A205 1.15fr dk brn, lt bl & yel grn 3.25 2.25
Nos. 760-765 (6) 9.60 6.35

20th anniversary of the International Federation of Animal Protection.

Flower Type of 1968

Roses and Anemones, by Vincent van Gogh.

1970, May 4 **Photo.** ***Perf. 12x13***

766 A185 3fr black & multi 2.00 1.75

International Flower Show, Monte Carlo.

Red Cross Type of 1969

3fr, St. Louis giving alms to the poor.

1970, May 4 **Engr.** ***Perf. 13***

767 A194 3fr dk gray, ol gray & slate grn 1.50 1.50

Issued for the Red Cross.

Europa Issue, 1970

Common Design Type

1970, May 4

Size: 26x36mm

768 CD13 40c deep rose lilac *.85* *.30*
769 CD13 80c bright green *2.75* *.90*
770 CD13 1fr deep blue *2.75* *.90*
Nos. 768-770 (3) *6.35* 2.10

UPU Headquarters and Monument, Bern — A206

1970, May 4

771 A206 40c brn ol, gray & bl grn .25 .25

New UPU Headquarters in Bern opening.

Plaque and Flag on the Moon, Presidents Kennedy and Nixon — A207

Design: 80c, Astronauts and landing module on moon, and Apollo 11 emblem.

1970, May 4 **Photo.**

772 A207 40c multicolored .60 .50
773 A207 80c multicolored .80 .70

Man's first landing on moon, July 20, 1969. US astronauts Neil A. Armstrong and Col. Edwin E. Aldrin, Jr., with Lt. Col. Michael Collins piloting Apollo 11.

Princes of Monaco Type of 1967

Designs: 1fr, Louis I (1662-1701), by Jean Francois de Troy. 3fr, Charlotte de Gramont (1639-1678), by Sebastian Bourdon.

1970, Dec. 15 **Engr.** ***Perf. 12x13***

774 A182 1fr multicolored .55 .55
775 A182 3fr multicolored 1.25 1.25

Painting Type of 1968

Design: 3fr, Portrait of Dédie, by Amedeo Modigliani (1884-1920).

1970, Dec. 15

776 A185 3fr multicolored 2.00 2.00

Beethoven and "Ode to Joy" A208

1970, Dec. 15

777 A208 1.30fr brown & maroon 1.50 1.10

Ludwig van Beethoven (1770-1827), composer.

Dumas and Scene from "Three Musketeers" — A209

Designs: 40c, Henri Rougier and biplane over Monaco. 80c, Alphonse de Lamartine and scenes from his works.

1970, Dec. 15

778 A209 30c blue, brown & gray .35 .25
779 A209 40c blue, sepia & gray .35 .25
780 A209 80c multicolored .35 .35
Nos. 778-780 (3) 1.05 .85

Alexandre Dumas, père (1802-70), novelist; 1st flight over the Mediterranean by Henri Rougier, 60th anniv.; publication of "Méditations Poétiques" by Alphonse de Lamartine (1790-1869), poet, 150th anniv.

Camargue Horse A210

Horses: 20c, Anglo-Arabian thoroughbred. 30c, French saddle horse. 40c, Lippizaner. 50c, Trotter. 70c, English thoroughbred. 85c, Arabian. 1.15fr, Barbary.

1970, Dec. 15 Engr. *Perf. 13*

781 A210 10c bl, ol bis & dk bl .25 .25
782 A210 20c vio bl, brn & ol .25 .25
783 A210 30c blue, brn & grn .25 .25
784 A210 40c gray, ind & ol bis .35 .25
785 A210 50c blue, dk brn & ol .85 .45
786 A210 70c dk grn, ol brn & red brn 1.00 .85
787 A210 85c dk grn, ol & sl 1.75 1.50
788 A210 1.15fr blue, emer & blk 2.10 1.75
Nos. 781-788,C77 (9) 11.05 8.55

Prince Rainier Type of 1955 and Palace Type of 1960

90c, Honor Court. 1.40fr, Aerial view of Palace.

1971 Engr. *Perf. 13*

789 A83 60c plum & blk 1.75 1.00
790 A116 90c dk car, ultra & blk 1.75 1.00
791 A83 1.10fr gray & ultra 2.50 1.75
792 A116 1.40fr pur, org & grn 2.50 1.75
Nos. 789-792 (4) 8.50 5.50

Aquatic Stadium Type of 1964-67, "1962" Omitted

1971

793 A153 26c pur, ultra & blk .45 .25
794 A153 30c cop red, bl, lil & blk .55 .25
795 A153 45c sl grn, vio bl & blk .90 .35
796 A153 90c ol, Prus bl & blk 1.40 .55
Nos. 793-796 (4) 3.30 1.40

Nos. 793-796 were issued precanceled only. See note after No. 324.

For surcharges, see Nos. 976-979.

Europa Issue, 1971

Common Design Type

1971, Sept. 6

797 CD14 50c carmine rose *2.50 .50*
798 CD14 80c brt blue *6.25 .80*
799 CD14 1.30fr slate green *6.25 1.50*
Nos. 797-799 (3) *15.00* 2.80

Old Bridge at Sospel — A211

80c, Roquebrune Castle. 1.30fr, Grimaldi Castle. 3fr, Roman Monument, La Turbie, vert. All views in Alpes-Maritimes Department, France.

1971, Sept. 6

800 A211 50c sl grn, bl & ol brn .35 .35
801 A211 80c sl grn, sl & brn .40 .40
802 A211 1.30fr brn, sl grn & red .65 .65
803 A211 3fr brt bl, sl & olive 1.10 1.10
Nos. 800-803 (4) 2.50 2.50

Protection of historic monuments.

Theodolite, Underwater Scene and Coast Line — A212

1971, Sept. 6

804 A212 80c blue grn & multi .55 .45

International Hydrographical Bureau, 50th anniv.

Sea Bird Covered with Oil — A213

1971, Sept. 6

805 A213 50c dp blue & indigo .55 .45

Against pollution of the seas.

"Arts" (Organ Pipes and Michelangelo's Creation of Adam) — A214

"Science" (Alchemist, Radar and Rocket) — A215

Design: 80c, "Culture" (medieval scholar, book, film and television).

1971, Sept. 6 Engr. *Perf. 13*

806 A214 30c brt bl, pur & brn .25 .25
807 A215 50c slate & brn org .25 .25
808 A214 80c emerald & brn .25 .25

Prince Pierre of Monaco — A216

1971, Sept. 6 Photo. *Perf. 12½x13*

809 A216 1.30fr gray green .50 .25
Nos. 806-809 (4) 1.25 1.00

25th anniv. of UNESCO.

Cocker Spaniel A217

1971, Sept. 6 *Perf. 13x12½*

810 A217 50c multicolored 2.50 1.60

Intl. Dog Show. See Nos. 826, 879, 910.

Hand Holding Blood Donor Emblem A218

1971, Sept. 6 Engr. *Perf. 13*

811 A218 80c red, violet & gray .45 .45

7th International Blood Donors Congress, Monaco, Oct. 21-24.

Red Cross Type of 1969

3fr, St. Vincent de Paul appearing to prisoners.

1971, Sept. 6

812 A194 3fr bl grn, ol grn & dp grn 1.40 1.25

Princes of Monaco Type of 1967

Designs: 1fr, Antoine I (1701-1731), by Hyacinthe Rigaud. 3fr, Marie de Lorraine (1674-1724), French School.

1972, Jan. 18 *Perf. 12x13*

813 A182 1fr multicolored .70 .70
814 A182 3fr multicolored 1.40 1.40

Painting Type of 1968

Designs: 2fr, The Cradle, by Berthe Morisot. 3fr, Clown, by Jean Antoine Watteau.

1972, Jan. 18

815 A185 2fr green & multi .50 .50
816 A185 3fr multicolored 1.40 1.40

No. 815 issued for 25th anniv. (in 1971) of UNICEF.

Christ Before Pilate, by Dürer A219

1972, Jan. 18 *Perf. 13*

817 A219 2fr lt brown & blk 1.25 1.00

500th anniv. of the birth of Albrecht Dürer (1471-1528), German painter and engraver.

La Fontaine and Animals — A220

Saint-Saens and "Samson et Dalila" — A221

1.30fr, Charles Baudelaire, nudes and cats.

1972, Jan. 18

818 A220 50c brn, grn & sl grn .65 .35
819 A221 90c dk brn & yel brn .60 .45
820 A220 1.30fr blk, red & vio brn .95 .70
Nos. 818-820 (3) 2.20 1.50

350th anniv. of the birth of Jean de La Fontaine (1621-1695), fabulist; 50th anniv. of the death of Camille Saint-Saens (1835-1921), composer; 150th anniv. of the birth of Charles Baudelaire (1821-1867), poet.

Father Christmas A222

1972, Jan. 18

821 A222 30c bis, slate bl & red .25 .25
822 A222 50c vio brn, grn & red .25 .25
823 A222 90c ocher, indigo & red .55 .35
Nos. 821-823 (3) 1.05 .85

Christmas 1971.

Battle of Lepanto — A223

1972, Jan. 18

824 A223 1fr dull bl, red & brn .65 .45

400th anniversary of the Battle of Lepanto against the Turks.

Steam and Diesel Locomotives, UIC Emblem — A224

1972, Apr. 27 Engr. *Perf. 13*

825 A224 50c dk car, lilac & choc 1.00 .75

50th anniversary of the founding of the International Railroad Union (UIC).

Dog Type of 1971

1972, Apr. 27 Photo. *Perf. 13x12½*

826 A217 60c Great Dane 2.50 1.60

International Dog Show.

Serene Landscape, Pollution, Destruction — A225

1972, Apr. 27 Engr. *Perf. 13*
827 A225 90c grn, brn & blk .60 .45

Anti-pollution fight.

Ski Jump, Sapporo '72 Emblem — A226

1972, Apr. 27
828 A226 90c bl grn, dk red & blk .60 .50

11th Winter Olympic Games, Sapporo, Japan, Feb. 3-13.

Flower Type of 1968

3fr, Flowers in Vase, by Paul Cezanne.

1972, Apr. 27 Photo. *Perf. 12x13*
829 A185 3fr multicolored 2.75 2.75

International Flower Show, Monte Carlo.

Red Cross Type of 1969

3fr, St. Francis of Assisi comforting poor man.

1972, Apr. 27 Engr. *Perf. 13*
830 A194 3fr dk purple & brn 1.75 1.40

For the Red Cross.

Europa Issue 1972
Common Design Type

1972, Apr. 27 *Perf. 12½x13*
Size: 26x36mm
831 CD15 50c vio blue & org *1.75* .60
832 CD15 90c vio blue & emer *3.25* .80

Church of Sts. John and Paul (detail), by Canaletto A227

Designs: 60c, Church of St. Peter of Castello, by Francesco Guardi. 2fr, St. Mark's Square, by Bernardo Bellotto.

1972, Apr. 27 *Perf. 13*
Sizes: 36x48mm (30c, 2fr); 26½x48mm (60c)
833 A227 30c rose red .40 .25
834 A227 60c brt purple .50 .35
835 A227 2fr Prus blue 1.90 1.25
Nos. 833-835 (3) 2.80 1.85

UNESCO campaign to save Venice.

Dressage A228

Equestrian Events: 90c, Jump over fences. 1.10fr, Jump over wall. 1.40fr, Jump over gates.

1972, Apr. 27
836 A228 60c rose car, vio bl & brn .85 .85
837 A228 90c vio bl, rose car & brn 1.10 1.10
838 A228 1.10fr brn, rose car & vio bl 1.75 1.75
839 A228 1.40fr vio bl, rose car & brn 2.75 2.75
a. Block of 4 + 2 labels 10.00 10.00

20th Olympic Games, Munich, Aug. 26-Sept. 10. Nos. 836-839 printed se-tenant in sheets of 24 stamps and 6 labels.

Auguste Escoffier and his Birthplace A229

1972, May 6 Engr. *Perf. 13*
840 A229 45c black & olive .50 .25

125th anniversary of the birth of Georges Auguste Escoffier (1846-1935), French chef.

Young Drug Addict — A230

1972, July 3
841 A230 50c carmine, sep & org .40 .25
842 A230 90c slate grn, sep & ind .60 .45

Fight against drug abuse.

Congress Emblem, Birds and Animals — A231

Designs: 50c, Congress emblem, Neptune, sea, earth and land creatures, horiz. 90c, Globe, land, sea and air creatures.

1972, Sept. 25
843 A231 30c ol, brt grn & car .25 .25
844 A231 50c ocher, brn & org brn .35 .25
845 A231 90c org brn, bl & ol .55 .45
Nos. 843-845 (3) 1.15 .95

17th Intl. Zoology Cong., Monaco, 9/24-30.

Arrangement of Lilies and Palm — A232

Designs: Floral arrangements.

1972, Nov. 13 Photo. *Perf. 13*
846 A232 30c orange red & multi .65 .40
847 A232 50c multicolored 1.00 .60
848 A232 90c black & multi 1.50 1.00
Nos. 846-848 (3) 3.15 2.00

International Flower Show, Monte Carlo, May, 1973. See Nos. 894-896.

Child and Adoration of the Kings A233

1972, Nov. 13 Engr.
849 A233 30c gray, vio bl & brt pink .25 .25
850 A233 50c dp car, lil & brn .25 .25
851 A233 90c violet bl & pur .45 .35
Nos. 849-851 (3) .95 .85

Christmas 1972.

Louis Bleriot and his Monoplane — A234

50c, Roald Amundsen & Antarctic landscape. 90c, Louis Pasteur & laboratory.

1972, Dec. 4
852 A234 30c choc & brt blue .25 .25
853 A234 50c Prus blue & ind .35 .30
854 A234 90c choc & ocher .70 .55
Nos. 852-854 (3) 1.30 1.10

Louis Bleriot (1872-1936), French aviation pioneer (30c); Roald Amundsen (1872-1928), Norwegian polar explorer (50c); Louis Pasteur (1822-1895), French chemist and bacteriologist (90c).

Gethsemane, by Giovanni Canavesio — A235

Frescoes by Canavesio, 15th century, Chapel of Our Lady of Fountains at La Brigue: 50c, Christ Stripped of His Garments. 90c, Christ Carrying the Cross. 1.40fr, Resurrection. 2fr, Crucifixion.

1972, Dec. 4
855 A235 30c bright rose .25 .25
856 A235 50c indigo .35 .25
857 A235 90c slate green .50 .50
858 A235 1.40fr bright red .65 .65
859 A235 2fr purple 1.00 .70
Nos. 855-859 (5) 2.75 2.35

Protection of historic monuments.

Princes of Monaco Type of 1967

1fr, Jacques I, by Nicolas de Largillière. 3fr, Louise Hippolyte (1697-1731), by Jean Baptiste Vanloo.

1972, Dec. 4 *Perf. 12x13*
860 A182 1fr multicolored .75 .55
861 A182 3fr multicolored 1.50 1.25

Girl, Syringe, Addicts A236

1973, Jan. 5 Engr. *Perf. 13*
862 A236 50c brt bl, claret & sl grn .35 .25
863 A236 90c orange, lil & emer .55 .45

Fight against drug abuse.

Souvenir Sheet

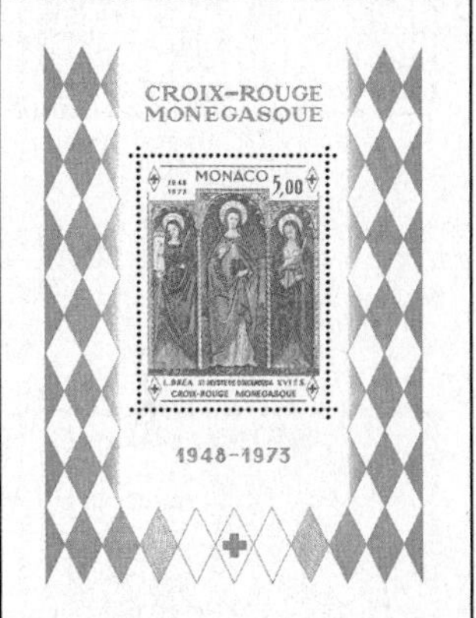

Sts. Barbara, Dévote and Agatha, by Louis Brea — A237

1973, Apr. 30
864 A237 5fr dull red 10.00 10.00

Red Cross of Monaco, 25th anniv.

Flower Type of 1968

Flowers in Vase, by Ambrosius Bosschaert.

1973, Apr. 30 Photo. *Perf. 12x13*
865 A185 3.50fr multicolored 4.75 3.25

International Flower Show, Monte Carlo.

Europa Issue 1973
Common Design Type

1973, Apr. 30 Engr. *Perf. 13*
Size: 36x26mm
866 CD16 50c orange *6.00* .90
867 CD16 90c blue green *9.00* *1.50*

Molière, Scene from "Le Malade Imaginaire" A238

1973, Apr. 30
868 A238 20c red, vio bl & brn .45 .35

Tricentenary of the death of Molière (1622-1673), French actor and writer.

Costumed Players and Mask — A239

1973, Apr. 30
869 A239 60c red, lilac & blue .50 .35

5th International Amateur Theater Festival.

Virgin Mary, St. Teresa, Lisieux Basilica — A240

1973, Apr. 30
870 A240 1.40fr indigo, ultra & brn .80 .55

Centenary of the birth of St. Teresa of Lisieux (Thérèse Martin, 1873-1897), Carmelite nun.

Charles Peguy and Cathedral of Chartres — A241

1973, Apr. 30
871 A241 50c dp claret, ol brn & sl .40 .35

Centenary of the birth of Charles Pierre Peguy (1873-1914), French writer.

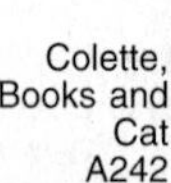

Colette, Books and Cat A242

Designs: No. 873, Eugene Ducretet and transmission from Eiffel Tower to Pantheon. 45c, Jean Henri Fabre and insects. 50c, Blaise Pascal, vert. 60c, Radar installation and telegraph wire insulators. No. 877, William Webb Ellis and rugby. No. 878, Sir George Cayley and early model plane.

1973, Apr. 30
872 A242 30c dp org, bl & dk bl .80 .50
873 A242 30c brown & multi .25 .25
874 A242 45c dp blue & multi 1.25 1.25
875 A242 50c vio bl, lil & dk pur .25 .25
876 A242 60c brn, bl blk & brt bl .35 .35
877 A242 90c brown & car rose .50 .50
878 A242 90c red & multi .50 .50
Nos. 872-878 (7) 3.90 3.60

Anniversaries: Colette (1873-1954), French writer (#872); 75th anniv. of 1st Hertzian wave transmission (#873); Fabre (1823-1915), entomologist (45c); Pascal (1623-1662), scientist and philosopher (50c); 5th Intl. Telecommunications Day (60c); Sesquicentennial of the invention of rugby (#877); Cayley (1821-95), aviation pioneer (#878).

Dog Type of 1971

45c, German shepherd.

1973, Apr. 30 Photo. *Perf. 13x12½*
879 A217 45c multicolored 9.00 5.00

International Dog Show.

The First Crèche, by Giotto — A243

Paintings of the Nativity by: 45c, School of Filippo Lippi. 50c, Giotto. 1fr, 15th century miniature, vert. 2fr, Fra Angelico, vert.

Perf. 13x12, 12x13

1973, Nov. 12 Engr.
880 A243 30c purple .40 .35
881 A243 45c rose magenta .60 .60
882 A243 50c brown orange .75 .75
883 A243 1fr slate green .90 .90
884 A243 2fr olive green 2.25 1.90
Nos. 880-884,C78 (6) 7.65 6.75

750th anniversary of the first crèche assembled by St. Francis of Assisi.

Picnic and View of Monte Carlo — A244

Designs: 20c, Dance around maypole, vert. 30c, "U Brandi" folk dance. 45c, Dance around St. John's fire. 50c, Blessing of the Christmas bread. 60c, Blessing of the sea. 1fr, Good Friday procession.

1973, Nov. 12 *Perf. 13*
885 A244 10c sl grn, dk bl & sep .25 .25
886 A244 20c blue, ol & lil .25 .25
887 A244 30c lt grn, bl & brn .25 .25
888 A244 45c dk brn, vio & red brn .25 .25
889 A244 50c black, brn & ver .25 .25
890 A244 60c blue, mag & vio bl .50 .50
891 A244 1fr ind, vio & ol bis .65 .65
Nos. 885-891 (7) 2.40 2.40

Monegasque customs.

Princes of Monaco Type of 1967

Paintings of Charlotte Grimaldi, by Pierre Gobert, 1733: No. 892, in court dress, No. 893, in nun's habit.

1973, Nov. 12 *Perf. 12x13*
892 A182 2fr multicolored 1.75 1.50
893 A182 2fr multicolored 1.75 1.50

Flower Type of 1972

Designs: Floral arrangements.

1973, Nov. 12 Photo. *Perf. 13*
894 A232 45c vio blue & multi 1.25 .80
895 A232 60c dk brown & multi 2.00 1.10
896 A232 1fr brown org & multi 3.50 2.00
Nos. 894-896 (3) 6.75 3.90

Intl. Flower Show, Monte Carlo, May 1974.

Children, Syringes, Drug Addicts A245

1973, Nov. 12 Engr.
897 A245 50c blue, grn & brn .25 .25
898 A245 90c red, brn & indigo .70 .45

Fight against drug abuse.

Souvenir Sheet

Prince Rainier III — A246

1974, May 8 Engr. *Imperf.*
899 A246 10fr black 6.50 6.50

25th anniv. of the accession of Prince Rainier III.

Art from Around the World — A247

70c, Hands holding letters. 1.10fr, Famous buildings, Statue of Liberty and Sphinx.

1974, May 8 *Perf. 13*
900 A247 50c choc & org brn .35 .25
901 A247 70c aqua & multi .35 .45
902 A247 1.10fr indigo & multi .80 .70
Nos. 900-902 (3) 1.50 1.40

Centenary of the Universal Postal Union.

King of Rome (Napoleon's Son), by Bosio — A248

Europa: 1.10fr, Madame Elisabeth (sister of Louis XVI), by Francois Josef Bosio.

1974, May 8
903 A248 45c slate grn & sep *1.50 .50*
904 A248 1.10fr brn & ol brn *3.00 .85*
a. Souv. sheet, 5 #903, 5 #904 *45.00 25.00*

Red Cross Type of 1969

Design: St. Bernard of Menthon rescuing mountain traveler.

1974, May 8
905 A194 3fr Prus bl & vio brn 1.50 1.25

For the Red Cross.

Henri Farman and Farman Planes A249

Designs: 40c, Guglielmo Marconi, circuit diagram and ships which conducted first tests. 45c, Ernest Duchesne and penicillin. 50c, Fernand Forest and 4-cylinder motor.

1974, May 8
906 A249 30c multicolored .25 .25
907 A249 40c multicolored .35 .25
908 A249 45c multicolored .35 .25
909 A249 50c multicolored .35 .25
Nos. 906-909 (4) 1.30 1.00

Farman (1874-1934), French aviation pioneer; Marconi (1874-1937), Italian inventor; Duchesne (1874-1912), French biologist; Forest (1851-1914), inventor.

Dog Type of 1971

1974, May 8 Photo. *Perf. 13x12½*
910 A217 60c Schnauzer 5.00 3.25

Intl. Dog Show, Monte Carlo, Apr. 6-7.

Ronsard and Scenes from his Sonnet à Hélène — A250

1974, May 8 Engr. *Perf. 13*
911 A250 70c choc & dk car .55 .35

450th anniversary of the birth of Pierre de Ronsard (1524-1585), French poet.

Winston Churchill — A251

1974, May 8
912 A251 1fr gray & brn .65 .45

Centenary of the birth of Sir Winston Churchill (1874-1965), statesman.

Palaces of Monaco and Vienna — A252

1974, May 8
913 A252 2fr multicolored 1.40 1.00

60th anniversary of the first International Police Congress, Monaco, Apr. 1914.

The Box, by Auguste Renoir A253

Rising Sun, by Claude Monet — A254

Impressionist Paintings: No. 915, Dancing Class, by Edgar Degas. No. 917, Entrance to Voisins Village, by Camille Pissarro. No. 918, House of the Hanged Man, by Paul Cezanne. No. 919, The Flooding of Port Marly, by Alfred Sisley.

Perf. 12x13, 13x12

1974, Nov. 12 **Engr.**

No.	Type	Value	Color	Unused	Used
914	A253	1fr	multicolored	3.00	2.50
915	A253	1fr	multicolored	3.00	2.50
916	A254	2fr	multicolored	3.00	2.50
917	A254	2fr	multicolored	3.00	2.50
918	A254	2fr	multicolored	3.00	2.50
919	A254	2fr	multicolored	3.00	2.50
			Nos. 914-919 (6)	18.00	15.00

Trainer and Tigers A255

Prancing Horses — A256

Perf. 13x12½, 12½x13

1974, Nov. 12

No.	Type	Value	Design	Unused	Used
920	A255	2c	shown	.25	.25
921	A256	3c	shown	.25	.25
922	A255	5c	Elephants	.25	.25
923	A256	45c	Equestrian act	.25	.25
924	A255	70c	Clowns	.70	.70
925	A256	1.10fr	Jugglers	1.75	1.75
926	A256	5fr	Trapeze act	3.50	3.50
			Nos. 920-926 (7)	6.95	6.95

International Circus Festival.

Honoré II Coin A257

1974, Nov. 12 ***Perf. 13***

No.	Type	Value	Color	Unused	Used
927	A257	60c	rose red & blk	.50	.35

350th anniversary of coins of Monaco.

Underwater Fauna and Flora — A258

Designs: 45c, Fish, and marine life. 1.10fr, Coral.

1974, Nov. 12 Photo. ***Perf. 13x12½***

Size: 35x25mm

No.	Type	Value	Color	Unused	Used
928	A258	45c	multicolored	1.00	.65

Size: 48x27mm

Perf. 13

No.	Type	Value	Color	Unused	Used
929	A258	70c	multicolored	1.25	1.10
930	A258	1.10fr	multicolored	1.90	1.50
			Nos. 928-930 (3)	4.15	3.25

Congress of the International Commission for the Scientific Exploration of the Mediterranean, Monaco, Dec. 6-14.

A259

Floral Arrangements A260

1974, Nov. 12 ***Perf. 13x12½***

No.	Type	Value	Color	Unused	Used
931	A259	70c	multicolored	.85	.60
932	A260	1.10fr	multicolored	1.25	.90

International Flower Show, Monte Carlo, May 1975. See Nos. 1003-1004, 1084-1085.

Prince Rainier III — A261

1974-78 **Engr.** ***Perf. 13***

No.	Type	Value	Color	Unused	Used
933	A261	60c	slate green	1.25	.35
934	A261	80c	red	1.25	.45
935	A261	80c	brt green	.45	.25
936	A261	1fr	brown	2.00	.90
937	A261	1fr	scarlet	.50	.30
938	A261	1fr	slate green	.50	.35
939	A261	1.20fr	violet bl	5.00	1.25
940	A261	1.20fr	red	.65	.40
941	A261	1.25fr	blue	.90	.75
942	A261	1.50fr	black	.80	.65
943	A261	1.70fr	dp blue	1.00	.70
944	A261	2fr	dk purple	3.50	2.25
945	A261	2.10fr	olive bister	1.25	.75
946	A261	2.50fr	indigo	2.00	1.50
947	A261	9fr	brt violet	4.50	3.50
			Nos. 933-947 (15)	25.55	14.35

Issued: 60c, #934, 936, 939, 2fr, Dec. 23; #935, 937, 1.25fr, 2.50fr, Jan. 10, 1977; #938, 940, 1.50fr, 1.70fr, 2.10fr, 9fr, Aug. 18, 1978. See Nos. 1200-1204, 1255-1256.

Monte Carlo Beach A262

Prince Albert I Statue and Museum — A264

50c, Clock tower. 1.70fr, All Saints' Tower. 3fr, Fort Antoine. 5.50fr, La Condamine (view).

1974-77

No.	Type	Value	Design	Unused	Used
948	A262	25c	shown	.90	.40
949	A264	50c	multi	1.40	.80
950	A262	1.10fr	Like #948 ('77)	2.25	1.10
951	A264	1.40fr	shown	1.75	1.00
952	A262	1.70fr	multi	2.25	2.00
953	A264	3fr	multi	5.50	3.00
954	A262	5.50fr	multi	11.00	5.00
			Nos. 948-954 (7)	25.05	13.30

Issue: 1.10fr, Jan. 10; others, Dec. 23.

See Nos. 1005-1008, 1030-1033, 1069-1072, 1095-1098, 1138-1152.

Haageocereus A265

1974, Dec. 23 Photo. ***Perf. 12½x13***

No.	Type	Value	Design	Unused	Used
955	A265	10c	shown	.40	.40
956	A265	20c	Matucana	.40	.40
957	A265	30c	Parodia	.40	.40
958	A265	85c	Mediolobivia	2.25	1.50
959	A265	1.90fr	Matucana	3.00	2.25
960	A265	4fr	Echinocereus	5.75	4.50
			Nos. 955-960 (6)	12.20	9.45

Plants from Monaco Botanical Gardens.

Europa Issue

Sailor, by Philibert Florence — A266

St. Dévote, by Ludovic Brea — A267

1975, May 13 **Engr.** ***Perf. 13***

No.	Type	Value	Color	Unused	Used
961	A266	80c	brt red lilac	*1.75*	*.50*
962	A267	1.20fr	brt blue	*2.25*	*.85*
a.			Souv. sheet, 5 ea #961-962	*40.00*	*20.00*

Red Cross Type of 1969

Design: St. Bernardino of Siena (1380-1444) burying the dead.

1975, May 13

No.	Type	Value	Color	Unused	Used
963	A194	4fr	pur & Prus bl	2.75	1.75

For the Red Cross.

Carmen, at the Tavern A268

Scenes from Carmen: 30c, Prologue, vert. 80c, The smugglers' hide-out. 1.40fr, Entrance to bull ring.

1975, May 13

No.	Type	Value	Color	Unused	Used
964	A268	30c	multicolored	.25	.25
965	A268	60c	multicolored	.35	.25
966	A268	80c	multicolored	.55	.45
967	A268	1.40fr	multicolored	1.00	.90
			Nos. 964-967 (4)	2.15	1.85

Centenary of first performance of opera Carmen by George Bizet (1838-1875).

Louis de Saint-Simon A269

Albert Schweitzer A270

1975, May 13

No.	Type	Value	Color	Unused	Used
968	A269	40c	bluish black	.35	.30
969	A270	60c	black & dull red	.65	.50

300th birth anniversary of Louis de Saint-Simon (1675-1755), statesman and writer, and birth centenary of Albert Schweitzer (1875-1965), medical missionary.

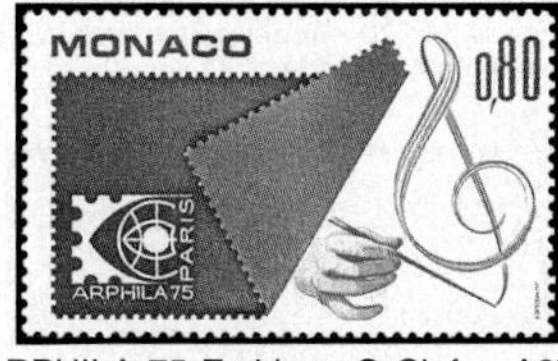

ARPHILA 75 Emblem, G Clef — A271

1975, May 13

No.	Type	Value	Color	Unused	Used
970	A271	80c	sepia & org brn	.70	.45

ARPHILA 75 International Philatelic Exhibition, Paris, June 6-16.

Seagull and Rising Sun A272

1975, May 13 **Photo.**

No.	Type	Value	Color	Unused	Used
971	A272	85c	multicolored	.85	.65

Oceanexpo 75, International Exhibition, Okinawa, July 20, 1975-Jan. 1976.

Charity Label and "1f" Destroying Cancer A273

1975, May 13 **Engr.**

No.	Type	Value	Color	Unused	Used
972	A273	1fr	multicolored	.85	.60

Fight against cancer.

Jesus with Crown of Thorns, Holy Year Emblem — A274

1975, May 13

No.	Type	Value	Color	Unused	Used
973	A274	1.15fr	lilac, bis & ind	1.00	.70

Holy Year 1975.

Villa Sauber, by Charles Garnier A275

1975, May 13

No.	Type	Value	Color	Unused	Used
974	A275	1.20fr	multicolored	1.10	.70

European Architectural Heritage Year 1975.

Woman, Globe, IWY Emblem A276

1975, May 13

975 A276 1.20fr multicolored 1.10 .70

International Women's Year.

Nos. 793-796 Surcharged

1975, Apr. 1 Engr. *Perf. 13*

976	A153	42c on 26c multi	2.50	1.10
977	A153	48c on 30c multi	3.25	1.75
978	A153	70c on 45c multi	3.75	2.25
979	A153	1.35fr on 90c multi	5.75	3.00
		Nos. 976-979 (4)	15.25	8.10

Nos. 976-979 were issued precanceled only. See note after No. 324.

Rolls Royce "Silver Ghost" 1907 — A277

10c, Hispano Suiza, 1926. 20c, Isotta Fraschini, 1928. 30c, Cord L. 29. 50c, Voisin, 1930. 60c, Duesenberg, 1933. 80c, Bugatti, 1938. 85c, Delahaye, 1940. 1.20fr, Cisitalia, 1946. 1.40fr, Mercedes Benz, 1955. 5.50fr, Lamborghini, 1974.

1975, Nov. Engr. *Perf. 13*

980	A277	5c shown	.45	.45
981	A277	10c multi	.45	.45
982	A277	20c multi	.45	.45
983	A277	30c multi	.45	.45
984	A277	50c multi	.90	.90
985	A277	60c multi	1.40	1.40
986	A277	80c multi	1.60	1.60
987	A277	85c multi	1.60	1.60
988	A277	1.20fr multi	2.75	2.75
989	A277	1.40fr multi	3.50	3.50
990	A277	5.50fr multi	9.00	9.00
		Nos. 980-990 (11)	22.55	22.55

Development of the automobile.

Princes of Monaco Type of 1967

Paintings (Unknown Artists): 2fr, Prince Honoré III (1733-1795). 4fr, Princess Catherine de Brignole (1759-1813).

1975, Nov.

991	A182	2fr multicolored	1.90	1.10
992	A182	4fr multicolored	3.75	3.00

Caged Dog A278

Designs: 80c, Cat chased up a tree, vert. 1.20fr, Horses pulling heavy load.

1975, Nov.

993	A278	60c black & brown	.90	.70
994	A278	80c blk, gray & brn	1.40	1.00
995	A278	1.20fr mag & sl grn	2.25	1.60
		Nos. 993-995 (3)	4.55	3.30

125th anniv. of the Grammont (J. P. Delmas Grammont) Law against cruelty to animals.

Dog Type of 1970

1975, Nov.

996 A204 60c Poodle 4.00 3.25

International Dog Show, Monte Carlo.

Maurice Ravel — A279

1.20fr, Johann Strauss and dancers.

1975, Nov.

997	A279	60c maroon & sepia	1.00	.60
998	A279	1.20fr maroon & indigo	2.10	1.40

Maurice Ravel (1875-1937), birth centenary, and Johann Strauss (1804-1849), sesquicentennial of birth, composers.

Clown — A280

1975, Nov. Photo. *Perf. 12½x13*

999 A280 80c multicolored 1.25 .55

2nd Intl. Circus Festival, Monte Carlo, Dec. 1975.

Honoré II Florin, 1640 — A281

1975, Nov. Engr. *Perf. 13*

1000 A281 80c slate & gray .75 .55

See Nos. 1040, 1088, 1234.

Ampère and Ampère Balance A282

1975, Nov.

1001 A282 85c ultra & indigo .75 .60

André Marie Ampère (1775-1836), physicist, birth bicentennial.

Lamentation for the Dead Christ, by Michelangelo — A283

1975, Nov.

1002 A283 1.40fr black & ol gray 1.25 .80

Michelangelo Buonarroti (1475-1564), Italian sculptor, painter and architect.

Flower Types of 1974

Designs: Floral arrangements.

1975, Nov. Photo. *Perf. 13x12½*

1003	A259	60c multicolored	1.10	.60
1004	A260	80c multicolored	1.60	.85

Intl. Flower Show, Monte Carlo, May 1976.

Clock Tower Type, 1974

1976, Jan. 26 Engr. *Perf. 13*

1005	A263	50c brown lake	.65	.35
1006	A263	60c olive green	.75	.50
1007	A263	90c purple	1.10	.75
1008	A263	1.60fr brt blue	1.60	1.40
		Nos. 1005-1008 (4)	4.10	3.00

Nos. 1005-1008 were issued precanceled only. See note after No. 324.

Prince Pierre — A284

André Maurois and Colette — A285

Writers: 25c, Jean and Jerome Tharaud. 30c, Emile Henriot, Marcel Pagnol, Georges Duhamel. 50c, Philippe Heriat, Jules Supervielle, L. Pierard. 60c, Roland Dorgeles, Marcel Achard, G. Bauer. 80c, Franz Hellens, André Billy, Msgr. Grente. 1.20fr, Jean Giono, Louis Pasteur-Vallery-Radot, Maurice Garcon.

1976, May 3 Engr. *Perf. 13*

1009	A284	10c black	.25	.25
1010	A285	20c red & slate	.30	.25
1011	A285	25c red, dk bl & blk	.30	.25
1012	A285	30c brown	.30	.30
1013	A285	50c brn, red & vio bl	.30	.25
1014	A285	60c grn, brn & lt brn	.35	.30
1015	A285	80c blk & mag	.70	.55
1016	A285	1.20fr blk, vio & cl	1.10	.85
		Nos. 1009-1016 (8)	3.60	3.00

Literary Council of Monaco, 25th anniv.

Dachshunds — A286

1976, May 3 Photo.

1017 A286 60c multicolored 5.00 4.25

International Dog Show, Monte Carlo.

Bridge Table, Coast A287

1976, May 3 Engr.

1018 A287 60c multicolored .60 .45

Fifth Bridge Olympiade, Monte Carlo.

A. G. Bell, Telephone, 1876, Satellite Dish A288

1976, May 3

1019 A288 80c multicolored .55 .35

Centenary of first telephone call by Alexander Graham Bell, Mar. 10, 1876.

Federation Emblem — A289

1976, May 3

1020 A289 1.20fr multicolored .85 .55

International Federation of Philately (F.I.P.), 50th anniversary.

US Liberty Bell Type of 1926 — A290

1976, May 3

1021 A290 1.70fr carmine & blk 1.40 .95

American Bicentennial.

Fritillaria, by Vincent van Gogh A291

1976, May 3 Photo. *Perf. 12x13*

1022 A291 3fr multicolored 8.00 5.50

Intl. Flower Show, Monte Carlo, May 1976.

Plate with Lemon Branch — A292

Europa: 1.20fr, The Peddler, 19th century figurine, and CEPT emblem.

1976, May 3 *Perf. 12½x13*

1023	A292	80c sal & multi	*1.25*	.35
1024	A292	1.20fr ultra & multi	*1.75*	.50
a.		Souv. sheet of 10, 5 each #1023-1024	*32.50*	*25.00*

21st Summer Olympic Games, Montreal, Canada — A293

60c, Diving. 80c, Athlete on parallel bars. 85c, Hammer throw. 1.20fr, Rowing, horiz. 1.70fr, Boxing, horiz.

1976, May 3 Engr. *Perf. 13*
1025 A293 60c multicolored .35 .35
1026 A293 80c multicolored .45 .35
1027 A293 85c multicolored .55 .45
1028 A293 1.20fr multicolored .80 .60
1029 A293 1.70fr multicolored 1.40 1.10
a. Souv. sheet of 5, #1025-1029, perf. 14 4.25 4.25
Nos. 1025-1029 (5) 3.55 2.85

Clock Tower Type, 1974

1976, Sept. 1 Engr. *Perf. 13*
1030 A263 52c bister .45 .25
1031 A263 62c red lilac .55 .45
1032 A263 95c scarlet 1.10 .55
1033 A263 1.70fr blue green 1.75 1.00
Nos. 1030-1033 (4) 3.85 2.25

Nos. 1030-1033 were issued precanceled only. See note after No. 324.

Princes of Monaco Type of 1967

Paintings: 2fr, Honoré IV (1815-1819), by Francois Lemoyne. 4fr, Louise d'Aumont-Mazarin (1750-1826), by Marie Verroust.

1976, Nov. 9 *Perf. 12½x13*
1035 A182 2fr violet brown 2.00 1.50
1036 A182 4fr multicolored 3.00 2.00

Red Cross Type of 1969

Design: St. Louise de Marillac and children.

1976, Nov. 9 *Perf. 13*
1037 A194 4fr grn, gray & plum 2.50 2.00

St. Vincent de Paul, View of Monaco A294

1976, Nov. 9
1038 A294 60c multicolored .45 .35

St. Vincent de Paul Conference, Monaco, July 31, 1876, centenary.

Marquise de Sevigné — A295

1976, Nov. 9
1039 A295 80c multicolored .55 .35

Marie de Rabutin-Chantal, Marquise de Sevigné (1626-1696), writer.

Coin Type of 1975

Design: 80c, Honoré II 2-gros coin.

1976, Nov. 9
1040 A281 80c grn & steel bl .75 .45

Richard E. Byrd, Roald Amundsen, North Pole — A296

1976, Nov. 9
1041 A296 85c olive, blk & bl 1.75 1.25

1st flights over the North Pole, 50th anniv.

Gulliver Holding King, Queen and Enemy Fleet — A297

1976, Nov. 9
1042 A297 1.20fr indigo, bl & brn .80 .55

250th anniversary of the publication of Gulliver's Travels, by Jonathan Swift.

Child and Christmas Decorations A298

1976, Nov. 9 *Perf. 13x12½*
1043 A298 60c multicolored .40 .25
1044 A298 1.20fr multicolored .85 .50

Christmas 1976.

"Trapped by Drugs" A299

1976, Nov. 9
1045 A299 80c grn, ultra & org .60 .35
1046 A299 1.20fr red brn, vio & car .85 .50

Fight against drug abuse.

Floral Arrangement A300

Design: 1fr, Floral arrangement. Designs by Princess Grace.

1976, Nov. 9 Photo. *Perf. 13½x13*
1047 A300 80c yellow grn & multi 1.50 .90
1048 A300 1fr lt blue & multi 2.25 1.50

International Flower Show, Monte Carlo, May 1977. See Nos. 1124-1125, 1191.

Clown and Circus Acts — A301

1976, Nov. 9
1049 A301 1fr multi 1.90 1.10

3rd Intl. Circus Festival, Dec. 26-30.

L'Hirondelle I — A302

Prince Albert I — A303

Designs (Gouaches by Louis Tinayre): 30c, Crew of L'Hirondelle. 80c, L'Hirondelle in Storm. 1fr, The Helmsman, vert. 1.25fr, L'Hirondelle in Storm. 1.40fr, Shrimp Fishermen in Boat. 1.90fr, Hauling in the Net, vert. 2.50fr, Catching Opah Fish.

1977, May 3 Engr. *Perf. 13*
1050 A302 10c multicolored .25 .25
1051 A303 20c multicolored .25 .25
1052 A302 30c multicolored .25 .25
1053 A302 80c multicolored .35 .35
1054 A302 1fr multicolored .90 .90
1055 A302 1.25fr multicolored 1.10 1.10
1056 A302 1.40fr multicolored 1.40 .75
1057 A302 1.90fr multicolored 1.75 1.75
1058 A302 2.50fr multicolored 2.75 2.75
Nos. 1050-1058 (9) 9.00 8.35

75th anniversary of publication of "The Career of a Sailor," by Prince Albert I. See Nos. 1073-1081.

Pyreneean Mountain Dogs — A304

1977, May 3 Photo.
1059 A304 80c multicolored 5.00 3.75

International Dog Show, Monte Carlo. See No. 1199.

Motherhood, by Mary Cassatt — A305

1977, May 3 Engr.
1060 A305 80c multicolored .90 .90

World Association of the Friends of Children.

Archers, Target and Monte Carlo — A306

1977, May 3
1061 A306 1.10fr multicolored .80 .55

10th Intl. Rainier III Archery Championships.

Spirit of St. Louis and Lindbergh — A307

1977, May 3
1062 A307 1.90fr multicolored 1.75 1.25

50th anniversary of first transatlantic flight by Charles Lindbergh.

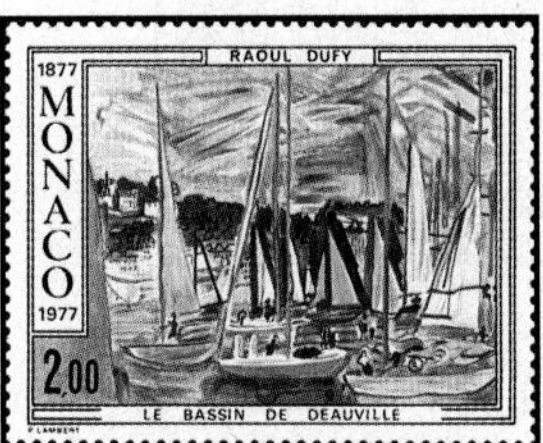
The Dock at Deauville, by Dufy — A308

1977, May 3 Photo.
1063 A308 2fr multicolored 4.50 3.00

Raoul Dufy (1877-1953), painter, birth centenary.

Young Girl, by Rubens — A309

Rubens Paintings: 1fr, Duke of Buckingham. 1.40fr, Rubens' son Nicolas, 2 years old.

1977, May 3 Engr.
1064 A309 80c multicolored .65 .55
1065 A309 1fr multicolored .95 .70
1066 A309 1.40fr multicolored 1.75 1.25
Nos. 1064-1066 (3) 3.35 2.50

Peter Paul Rubens (1577-1640).

Helmet Tower, Monaco — A310

Europa: 1.40fr, St. Michael's Church, Menton.

1977, May 3
1067 A310 1fr multicolored *1.25 .50*
1068 A310 1.40fr multicolored *3.00 .80*
a. Souv. sheet, 5 each #1067-1068 *35.00 25.00*

Clock Tower Type of 1974

1977, Apr. 1 Engr. *Perf. 13*

1069 A263 54c brt green .45 .35
1070 A263 68c orange .55 .45
1071 A263 1.05fr olive 1.10 .55
1072 A263 1.85fr brown 1.75 1.00
Nos. 1069-1072 (4) 3.85 2.35

Nos. 1069-1072 were issued precanceled only. See note after No. 324.

Career of a Sailor Types of 1977

Designs (Gouaches by Louis Tinayre): 10c, Yacht Princess Alice II, Kiel harbor. 20c, Laboratory on board ship. 30c, Yacht amidst ice floes. 80c, Crew in arctic outfits. 1fr, Yacht in polar region. 1.25fr, Yacht in snow storm. 1.40fr, Building camp on ice. 1.90fr, Yacht under steam amidst ice floes. 3fr, Yacht passing iceberg.

1977, Nov. Engr. *Perf. 13*

1073 A302 10c blk & brt bl .25 .25
1074 A302 20c Prus blue .25 .25
1075 A302 30c blk & brt bl .25 .25
1076 A303 80c multicolored .55 .45
1077 A302 1fr brt grn & blk .70 .55
1078 A302 1.25fr vio, sep & blk 1.00 .75
1079 A302 1.40fr ol, bl & pur 1.60 1.25
1080 A302 1.90fr blk & brt bl 2.75 2.25
1081 A302 3fr dk grn, ol & brt bl 4.00 3.00
Nos. 1073-1081 (9) 11.35 9.00

75th anniversary of publication of "The Career of a Sailor," by Prince Albert I.

Santa Claus A311

1977, Nov.

1082 A311 80c multicolored .60 .25
1083 A311 1.40fr multicolored .80 .40

Christmas 1977.

Flowers Types of 1974

Designs: 80c, Snapdragons and bellflowers. 1fr, Ikebana arrangement.

1977, Nov. Photo. *Perf. 13½x13*

1084 A259 80c multicolored 1.25 .70
1085 A260 1fr multicolored 1.75 1.10

Intl. Flower Show, Monte Carlo, May 1978.

Face (Van Gogh), Syringe, Hallucination Pattern — A312

1977, Nov. Engr. *Perf. 13*

1086 A312 1fr multicolored .75 .45

Fight against drug abuse.

Clown, Flags of Participants A313

1977, Nov. Photo. *Perf. 13½x13*

1087 A313 1fr multicolored 1.75 1.25

Fourth International Circus Festival. Monte Carlo, December 1977.

Coin Type of 1975

Design: 80c, Doubloon of Honoré II, 1648.

1977, Nov. Engr. *Perf. 13*

1088 A281 80c lil & brn .70 .45

Mediterranean Landscape and Industrial Pollution — A314

1977, Nov.

1089 A314 1fr multicolored .85 .50

Protection of the Mediterranean. Meeting of the UN Mediterranean Environmental Protection Group, Monte Carlo, Nov. 28-Dec. 6.

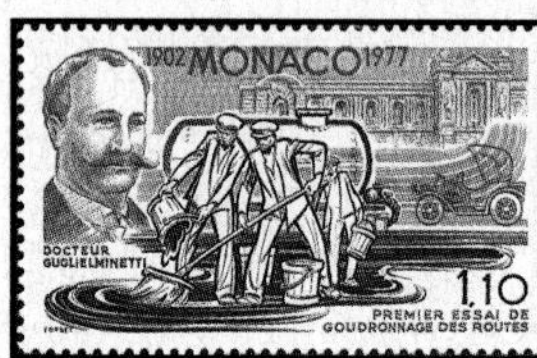

Men Spreading Tar, Dr. Guglielminetti, 1903 Car — A315

1977, Nov.

1090 A315 1.10fr multicolored .80 .45

75th anniversary of first tarred roads, invented by Swiss Dr. Guglielminetti.

View of Monaco and Tennis Emblem — A316

First Match at Wimbledon and Stadium — A317

1977, Nov.

1091 A316 1fr multicolored 1.25 .70
1092 A317 1.40fr multicolored 1.50 1.00

Lawn Tennis Federation of Monaco, 50th anniv. and cent. of 1st intl. tennis match at Wimbledon.

Prince of Monaco Type of 1967

Honoré V (1819-1841), by Marie Verroust.

1977, Nov. *Perf. 12½x13*

1093 A182 6fr multicolored 4.50 3.25

Red Cross Type of 1969

Design: 4fr, St. John Bosco and boys.

1977, Nov. *Perf. 13*

1094 A194 4fr multicolored 2.50 2.00

Nos. 1069-1072 Surcharged

1978, Jan. 17

1095 A263 58c on 54c brt grn .55 .40
1096 A263 73c on 68c orange .90 .55
1097 A263 1.15fr on 1.05fr olive 1.25 .90
1098 A263 2fr on 1.85fr brn 2.10 1.40
Nos. 1095-1098 (4) 4.80 3.25

See note after No. 324.

Illustrations, Novels by Jules Verne — A318

5c, Shipwreck. 25c, The Abandoned Ship, from "Mysterious Island". 30c, Secret of the Island. 80c, Robur, the Conqueror. 1fr, Master Zacharius. 1.40fr, The Castle in the Carpathians. 1.70fr, The Children of Capt. Grant. 5.50fr, Jules Verne and allegories.

1978, May 2 Engr. *Perf. 13*

1099 A318 5c multicolored .25 .25
1100 A318 25c multicolored .30 .25
1101 A318 30c multicolored .30 .25
1102 A318 80c multicolored .55 .50
1103 A318 1fr multicolored 1.00 .60
1104 A318 1.40fr multicolored 1.20 .85
1105 A318 1.70fr multicolored 1.75 1.40
1106 A318 5.50fr multicolored 4.25 3.25
Nos. 1099-1106 (8) 9.60 7.35

Jules Verne (1828-1905), science fiction writer, birth sesquicentennial.

Congress Center and Monte Carlo A319

1.40fr, Congress Center, view from the sea.

1978, May 2

1107 A319 1fr multicolored .60 .50
1108 A319 1.40fr multicolored .80 .50

Inauguration of Monaco Congress Center.

Soccer Players and Globe — A320

1978, May 2

1109 A320 1fr multicolored .75 .75

11th World Soccer Cup Championship, Argentina, June 1-25.

Vivaldi and St. Mark's Place, Venice — A321

1978, May 2

1110 A321 1fr dk brown & red .90 .80

Antonio Vivaldi (1675?-1741), Italian violinist and composer.

Control Ship and Grimaldi Palace — A322

1fr, Map of coastal area and city emblems.

1978, May 2 Size: 26x36mm

1111 A322 80c multi .60 .50

Size: 48x27mm

1112 A322 1fr multi, horiz. .60 .50

Protection of the environment, signing of "Ra Mo Ge" agreement for the protection of the Mediterranean Coast between Saint-Raphael, France, and Genoa, Italy (including Monaco).

Monaco Cathedral A323

Europa: 1.40fr, View of Principality from East.

1978, May 2 *Perf. 12½x13*

1113 A323 1fr multicolored *1.75* .40
1114 A323 1.40fr multicolored *3.25* .70
a. Souv. sheet, 5 each #1113-1114 *40.00 25.00*

Cinderella — A324

Mother Goose Tales: 25c, Puss in Boots. 30c, Sleeping Beauty. 80c, Fairy tale princess. 1fr, Little Red Riding Hood. 1.40fr, Bluebeard. 1.70fr, Tom Thumb. 1.90fr, Riquet with the Tuft of Hair. 2.50fr, The Fairies.

1978, Nov. 8 Engr. *Perf. 13*

1115 A324 5c multicolored .25 .25
1116 A324 25c multicolored .25 .25
1117 A324 30c multicolored .25 .25
1118 A324 80c multicolored .60 .50
1119 A324 1fr multicolored .80 .60
1120 A324 1.40fr multicolored 1.00 .85
1121 A324 1.70fr multicolored 1.25 1.10
1122 A324 1.90fr multicolored 1.75 1.25
1123 A324 2.50fr multicolored 2.40 1.75
Nos. 1115-1123 (9) 8.55 6.80

Charles Perrault (1628-1703), compiler of Mother Goose Tales.

Flower Type of 1976

Van Gogh Paintings: 1fr, Sunflowers. 1.70fr, Iris.

1978, Nov. 8 Photo. *Perf. 12½x13*

1124 A300 1fr multicolored 2.50 2.25
1125 A300 1.70fr multicolored 3.50 2.25

Intl. Flower show, Monte Carlo, May 1979, and 125th birth anniv. of Vincent van Gogh (1853-1890), Dutch painter.

Afghan Hound A325

Design: 1.20fr, Russian wolfhound.

1978, Nov. 8 *Perf. 13x12½*

1126 A325 1fr multicolored 3.00 2.40
1127 A325 1.20fr multicolored 4.50 3.00

International Dog Show, Monte Carlo.

Child Holding Gift of Shoes — A326

1978, Nov. 8 Engr. *Perf. 12½x13*
1128 A326 1fr multicolored .80 .50

Christmas 1978.

Catherine and William Booth, Salvation Army Band — A327

1978, Nov. 8 Engr. *Perf. 13*
1129 A327 1.70fr multicolored 1.20 1.00

Centenary of founding of Salvation Army.

Trained Seals A328

1fr, Lions, vert. 1.40fr, Equestrian act. 1.90fr, Monkey music band. 2.40fr, Trapeze act.

1978, Nov. 8 *Perf. 13x12½*
1130 A328 80c multicolored .70 .50
1131 A328 1fr multicolored 1.00 .80
1132 A328 1.40fr multicolored 1.60 1.00
1133 A328 1.90fr multicolored 2.00 2.00
1134 A328 2.40fr multicolored 2.75 2.40
Nos. 1130-1134 (5) 8.05 6.70

5th Intl. Circus Festival, Monte Carlo.

Princes of Monaco Type of 1967

Paintings: 2fr, Florestan I (1841-1856), by G. Dauphin. 4fr, Caroline Gilbert de Lametz (1793-1879), by Marie Verroust.

1978, Nov. 8 Engr. *Perf. 12½x13*
1135 A182 2fr multicolored 2.00 1.40
1136 A182 4fr multicolored 3.00 3.00

Souvenir Sheet

Henri Dunant and Battle Scene — A329

1978, Nov. 8 Engr. *Perf. 13*
1137 A329 5fr multicolored 4.25 4.25

Henri Dunant (1828-1910), founder of Red Cross.

View Types of 1974

25c, All Saints' Tower. 65c, Monte Carlo Beach. 70c, Exotic Garden, cacti. 1.10fr, Palais de Justice. 1.30fr, Cathedral. 1.50fr, Prince Albert Statue and Museum. 1.80fr, La Condamine. 2.30fr, Palace. 6.50fr, Monte Carlo Auditorium.

1978-80
1138 A262 25c multi .25 .25
1139 A262 65c multi .25 .25
1140 A264 70c multi ('80) .55 .35
1142 A262 1.10fr multi ('80) .60 .35
1144 A264 1.30fr multi .75 .40
1145 A264 1.50fr multi ('80) 1.10 1.10
1146 A262 1.80fr multi 1.10 .90
1148 A262 2.30fr multi ('80) 1.90 1.50
1152 A262 6.50fr multi 3.00 2.75
Nos. 1138-1152 (9) 9.50 7.85

Convention Center, Monte Carlo A330

1978-79
1154 A330 61c vermilion .30 .25
1155 A330 64c green .35 .25
1156 A330 68c brt blue .30 .25
1157 A330 78c dp rose lilac .35 .25
1158 A330 83c violet blue .30 .25
1159 A330 88c orange .35 .25
1160 A330 1.25fr brown .60 .45
1161 A330 1.30fr purple .75 .35
1162 A330 1.40fr brt yel grn .55 .35
1163 A330 2.10fr violet blue 1.00 .75
1164 A330 2.25fr brown org .75 .60
1165 A330 2.35fr lilac rose .80 .65
Nos. 1154-1165 (12) 6.40 4.65

Issued precanceled only. See note after No. 324.

Issue dates: 61c, 78c, 1.25fr, 2.10fr, July 10, 1978. Others, 1979.

Souvenir Sheet

Prince Albert — A331

1979, Apr. 30 Engr. *Perf. 12½x13*
1166 A331 10fr multicolored 6.50 6.50

21st birthday of Hereditary Prince Albert.

The Juggler of Notre Dame, by Jules Massenet A332

1.20fr, Hans, the Flute Player, by Gaston L. Ganne. 1.50fr, Don Quichotte, by Massenet. 1.70fr, L'Aiglon, by Jacques Ibert & Arthur Honegger, vert. 2.10fr, The Child & the Sorcerer, by Maurice Ravel. 3fr, Monte Carlo Opera & Charles Garnier, architect.

1979, Apr. 30 *Perf. 13*
1167 A332 1fr multicolored .80 .45
1168 A332 1.20fr multicolored .80 .55
1169 A332 1.50fr multicolored 1.20 .90
1170 A332 1.70fr multicolored 1.50 1.25
1171 A332 2.10fr multicolored 1.50 1.50
1172 A332 3fr multicolored 2.25 2.25
Nos. 1167-1172 (6) 8.05 6.90

Centenary of the Salle Garnier, Monte Carlo Opera.

Flower, Bird, Butterfly, IYC Emblem A333

Children's Drawings (IYC Emblem and): 1fr, Horse and child. 1.20fr, Children shaking hands, and heart. 1.50fr, Children of the world for peace. 1.70fr, Children against pollution.

1979, Apr. 30
1173 A333 50c multicolored .25 .25
1174 A333 1fr multicolored .45 .35
1175 A333 1.20fr multicolored .70 .50
1176 A333 1.50fr multicolored 1.00 .80
1177 A333 1.70fr multicolored 1.00 .80
Nos. 1173-1177 (5) 3.40 2.70

International Year of the Child.

Armed Messenger, 15th-16th Centuries A334

Europa (designs similar to 1960 postage dues); 1.50fr, Felucca, 18th cent. 1.70fr, Arrival of 1st train, Dec. 12, 1868.

1979, Apr. 30
1178 A334 1.20fr multicolored *1.25* *.40*
1179 A334 1.50fr multicolored 5.00 *.60*
1180 A334 1.70fr multicolored 5.00 *.85*
a. Souv. sheet of 6, 2 each #1178-1180, perf. 13x12½ *27.50* *18.00*
Nos. 1178-1180 (3) 11.25 1.85

Les Biches, by Francis Poulenc A335

Ballets: 1.20fr, Les Matelots, by George Auric. 1.50fr, Le Spectre de 1a Rose, by Carl Maria Weber, vert. 1.70fr, Gaieté Parisienne, by Jacques Offenbach. 2.10fr, Dance of Salomé, by Richard Strauss, vert. 3fr, Instrumental Music, ceiling decoration of Salle Garnier.

1979, Nov. 12
Size: 26x36mm, 36x26mm
1181 A335 1fr multicolored .70 .50
1182 A335 1.20fr multicolored .85 .65
1183 A335 1.50fr multicolored 1.25 1.00
1184 A335 1.70fr multicolored 1.60 1.40
1185 A335 2.10fr multicolored 2.75 2.25
Size: 48x27mm
1186 A335 3fr multicolored 4.00 3.25
Nos. 1181-1186 (6) 11.15 9.05

Salle Garnier, Monte Carlo Opera, cent.

Princes of Monaco Type of 1967

Paintings: 3fr, Charles III (1856-1889). 4fr, Antoinette de Merode (1828-1864).

1979, Nov. 12 *Perf. 12½x13*
1187 A182 3fr multicolored 2.25 1.75
1188 A182 4fr multicolored 3.25 2.40

Red Cross Type of 1969

5fr, St. Peter Claver preaching to slaves.

1979, Nov. 12 *Perf. 13*
1189 A194 5fr multicolored 3.25 2.40

Princess Grace Orchid — A336

1979, Nov. 12 Photo.
1190 A336 1fr multicolored 2.75 1.75

Intl. Orchid Exhibition, Monte Carlo, Apr. 1980.

Flower Type of 1976

Design: 1.20fr, Princess Grace rose.

1979, Nov. 12
1191 A300 1.20fr multicolored 2.75 1.75

Intl. Flower Show, Monte Carlo, May 1980.

Clown Balancing on Globe — A337

1979, Nov. 12
1192 A337 1.20fr multicolored 2.00 1.25

6th International Circus Festival, Monte Carlo, Dec. 6-10.

Rowland Hill, Penny Black — A338

1979, Nov. 12 Engr. *Perf. 13*
1193 A338 1.70fr multicolored 1.00 .65

Sir Rowland Hill (1795-1879), originator of penny postage.

Albert Einstein, Equations A339

1979, Nov. 12
1194 A339 1.70fr multicolored 1.40 .80

Albert Einstein (1879-1955), theoretical physicist.

St. Patrick's Cathedral, New York City, Cent. — A340

1979, Nov. 12
1195 A340 2.10fr multicolored 1.25 .75

Nativity A341

1979, Nov. 12
1196 A341 1.20fr multicolored .80 .65

Christmas 1979.

Bugatti, Monte Carlo, 1929 Winner A342

1979, Nov. 12
1197 A342 1fr multicolored 1.10 .70

50th anniv. of Grand Prix auto race, Monte Carlo.

Arms of Charles V and Monaco, View of Monaco — A343

1979, Nov. 12
1198 A343 1.50fr multicolored .90 .65

Emperor Charles V visit to Monaco, 450th anniversary.

Dog Type of 1977

Design: 1.20fr, Setter and pointer.

1979, Nov. 12 **Photo.**
1199 A304 1.20fr multicolored 5.00 3.50

International Dog Show, Monte Carlo.

Prince Rainier Type of 1974

1980, Jan. 17 **Engr.** ***Perf. 13***
1200 A261 1.10fr emerald .70 .25
1201 A261 1.30fr rose red .70 .25
1202 A261 1.60fr dk blue gray 1.25 .55
1203 A261 1.80fr grnsh blue 2.00 1.90
1204 A261 2.30fr red lilac 2.50 1.40
Nos. 1200-1204 (5) 7.15 4.35

Chestnut Branch in Spring A344

Designs of 1980, 1981 stamps show chestnut branch. 1982 stamps show peach branch. 1983 stamps show apple branch.

1980-83 **Engr.** ***Perf. 13x12½***
1205 A344 76c shown .50 .40
1206 A344 88c Spring ('81) .50 .40
1207 A344 97c Spring ('82) .50 .40
1208 A344 99c Summer .80 .60
1209 A344 1.05fr Spring ('83) .80 .60
1210 A344 1.14fr Summer ('81) .80 .60
1211 A344 1.25fr Summer ('82) .80 .60
1212 A344 1.35fr Summer ('83) .85 .60
1213 A344 1.60fr Autumn 1.25 .85
1214 A344 1.84fr Autumn ('81) 1.25 .85
1215 A344 2.03fr Autumn ('82) 1.25 .85
1216 A344 2.19fr Autumn ('83) 1.40 1.00
1217 A344 2.65fr Winter 1.75 1.20
1218 A344 3.05fr Winter ('81) 1.60 1.25
1219 A344 3.36fr Winter ('82) 1.75 1.25
1220 A344 3.63fr Winter ('83) 1.60 1.60
Nos. 1205-1220 (16) 17.40 13.05

Issued precanceled only. See note after No. 324. See Nos. 1406-1409, 1457-1460.

Gymnast — A345

1980, Apr. 28
1221 A345 1.10fr shown .40 .25
1222 A345 1.30fr Handball .50 .35
1223 A345 1.60fr Shooting .65 .45
1224 A345 1.80fr Volleyball .85 .60
1225 A345 2.30fr Ice hockey 1.00 .85
1226 A345 4fr Slalom 1.60 1.25
Nos. 1221-1226 (6) 5.00 3.75

22nd Summer Olympic Games, Moscow, July 19-Aug. 3; 13th Winter Olympic Games, Lake Placid, NY, Feb. 12-24.

Colette, Novelist — A346

Europa: 1.80fr, Marcel Pagnol (1895-1974), French playwright.

1980, Apr. 28 ***Perf. 12½x13***
1227 A346 1.30fr multicolored 1.00 *.35*
1228 A346 1.80fr multicolored 1.50 *.35*
a. Souv. sheet, 5 each #1227-1228 *15.00 10.00*

The Source, by Ingres A347

1980, Apr. 28
1229 A347 4fr multicolored 7.00 5.50

Jean Auguste Dominique Ingres (1780-1867).

Michel Eyquem de Montaigne A348

1980, Apr. 28 ***Perf. 13***
1230 A348 1.30fr multicolored .65 .45

Essays of Montaigne (1533-1592), 400th anniversary of publication.

Guillaume Apollinaire (1880-1918), French Writer — A349

1980, Apr. 28
1231 A349 1.10fr multicolored .65 .45

Paul P. Harris, Chicago Skyline, Rotary Emblem — A350

1980, Apr. 28
1232 A350 1.80fr multicolored .65 .55

Rotary International, 75th anniversary.

Convention Center, Map of Europe, Kiwanis Emblem — A351

1980, Apr. 28
1233 A351 1.30fr multicolored .65 .50

Kiwanis International, European Convention, Monte Carlo, June.

Coin Type of 1975

Design: 1.50fr, Honoré II silver ecu, 1649.

1980, Apr. 28
1234 A281 1.50fr multicolored .75 .55

Lhasa Apso and Shih-Tzu — A352

1980, Apr. 28 **Photo.**
1235 A352 1.30fr multicolored 4.00 3.25

International Dog Show, Monte Carlo.

The Princess and the Pea — A353

Hans Christian Andersen (1805-1875) Fairy Tales: 1.30fr, The Little Mermaid. 1.50fr, The Chimneysweep and the Shepherdess. 1.60fr, The Brave Little Tin Soldier. 1.80fr, The Little Match Girl. 2.30fr, The Nightingale.

1980, Nov. 6 **Engr.** ***Perf. 13***
1236 A353 70c multicolored .35 .25
1237 A353 1.30fr multicolored .65 .60
1238 A353 1.50fr multicolored .95 .85
1239 A353 1.60fr multicolored 1.10 .85
1240 A353 1.80fr multicolored 1.40 1.10
1241 A353 2.30fr multicolored 1.75 1.20
Nos. 1236-1241 (6) 6.20 4.85

Women on Balcony, by Van Dongen — A354

Paintings from 1905 Paris Fall Salon: 2fr, The Road, by de Vlaminck. 4fr, Woman Reading, by Matisse. 5fr, Three Figures Sitting on the Grass, by Andrè Derain.

1980, Nov. 6 ***Perf. 13x12***
1242 A354 2fr multicolored 2.75 1.75
1243 A354 3fr multicolored 3.25 2.50
1244 A354 4fr multicolored 4.75 4.25
1245 A354 5fr multicolored 5.00 5.00
Nos. 1242-1245 (4) 15.75 13.50

Princes of Monaco Type of 1967

Paintings: No. 1246, Prince Albert I (1848-1922), by Leon Bonnat. No. 1247, Princess Alice (1857-1925), by L. Maeterlinck.

1980, Nov. 6 ***Perf. 12½x13***
1246 A182 4fr multicolored 2.75 2.40
1247 A182 4fr multicolored 2.75 2.40

Sun and Birds, by Perrette Lambert — A355

1980, Nov. 6 ***Perf. 13***
1248 A355 6fr multicolored 3.50 3.25

Red Cross.

7th International Circus Festival — A356

1980, Nov. 6 ***Perf. 13x12½***
1249 A356 1.30fr multicolored 2.00 1.25

Christmas 1980 A357

1980, Nov. 6
1250 A357 1.10fr multicolored .50 .35
1251 A357 2.30fr multicolored 1.00 .75

Princess Stephanie of Monaco Rose — A358

1980, Nov. 6 Photo. *Perf. 12½x13*
1252 A358 1.30fr shown 1.00 .65
1253 A358 1.80fr Ikebana 1.50 1.40

International Flower Show, Monte Carlo, May 1981.

Prince Rainier Type of 1974

1980 Engr. *Perf. 13*
1255 A261 1.20fr bright green .90 .25
1256 A261 1.40fr red 1.10 .25

Issue dates: 1.20fr, Aug. 19; 1.40fr, Aug. 11.

Spirographis Spallanzanii A359

Paramuricea Clavata — A359a

10c, Anemonia sulcata. 15c, Leptosammia pruvoti. 20c, Pteroides. 40c, Alcyonium. 50c, Corallium rubrum. 60c, Caliactis parisitica. 70c, Cerianthus membranaceus. 1fr, Actinia equina. 2fr, Protula.

1980, Nov. 6 *Perf. 13x12½*
1259 A359 5c multi .25 .25
1260 A359 10c multi .25 .25
1261 A359 15c multi .25 .25
1262 A359 20c multi .25 .25
1263 A359a 30c shown .25 .25
1264 A359 40c multi .35 .25
1265 A359 50c multi .55 .45
1266 A359a 60c multi 1.00 .65
1267 A359a 70c multi 1.25 .90
1268 A359a 1fr multi 1.25 .90
1269 A359a 2fr multi 2.50 1.10
Nos. 1259-1269 (11) 8.15 5.50

See Nos. 1316-1321, 1380.

25th Wedding Anniversary of Prince Rainier and Princess Grace — A360

1981, May 4 *Perf. 13*
1270 A360 1.20fr green & blk 1.50 1.00
1271 A360 1.40fr carmine & blk 2.00 1.50
1272 A360 1.70fr olive grn & blk 2.50 1.90
1273 A360 1.80fr brown & blk 2.75 2.25
1274 A360 2fr brt blue & blk 3.75 2.75
Nos. 1270-1274 (5) 12.50 9.40

Mozart with his Father and Sister, by Carmontelle — A361

Wolfgang Amadeus Mozart (1756-1791), 225th Birth Anniversary (Paintings): 2fr, Portrait, by Lorenz Vogel (26x36mm). 3.50fr, Conducting his Requiem Two Days Before his Death, by F.C. Baude.

1981, May 4 Engr. *Perf. 13½x13*
1275 A361 2fr multicolored 1.65 1.50
1276 A361 2.50fr multicolored 2.40 2.00
1277 A361 3.50fr multicolored 3.25 2.50
a. Strip of 3, #1275-1277 8.50 8.50

Cross of Palms — A362

Europa (Palm Sunday Traditions): 2fr, Children with palms at benediction.

1981, May 4 *Perf. 12½x13*
1278 A362 1.40fr multicolored .75 *.35*
1279 A362 2fr multicolored 1.25 *.55*
a. Souv. sheet, 5 ea #1278-1279 *18.00 9.00*

European Soccer Cup, 25th Anniversary A363

1981, May 4 *Perf. 13*
1280 A363 2fr black & blue 1.25 .85

International Year of the Disabled — A364

1981, May 4
1281 A364 1.40fr brt grn & bl 1.00 .60

Monegasque National Pavilion Centenary — A365

1981, May 4
1282 A365 2fr multicolored 1.25 .85

Oceanographic Institute, Monaco and Museum, Paris — A366

1981, May 4
1283 A366 1.20fr multicolored .95 .80

75th anniversary of the Oceanographic Institute (Monaco-France).

50th Anniversary of the International Hydrographic Bureau — A367

1981, May 4
1284 A367 2.50fr multicolored 1.75 1.25

Rough Collies and Shetland Sheepdogs — A368

1981, May 4 Photo.
1285 A368 1.40fr multicolored 5.00 4.00

International Dog Show, Monte Carlo.

Marine Life Preservation A369

1981, Mar. 21 Photo.
1286 A369 1.20fr multicolored 1.00 .70

Prince Rainier III and Hereditary Prince Albert — A370

1981-84 Engr. *Perf. 13*
1287 A370 1.40fr dark green 1.00 .25
1288 A370 1.60fr carmine 1.40 .25
1289 A370 1.60fr ol grn ('82) 1.00 .25
1290 A370 1.70fr bluish grn ('84) 1.00 .25
1291 A370 1.80fr mag ('82) 1.20 .25
1292 A370 2fr red ('83) 1.50 .25
1293 A370 2.10fr red ('84) 1.50 .25
1294 A370 2.30fr blue 2.00 1.10
1295 A370 2.60fr violet bl ('82) 1.75 .80
1296 A370 2.80fr steel bl ('83) 2.00 1.25
1297 A370 3fr sky blue ('84) 3.00 1.60
1298 A370 4fr brown 1.75 .75
1299 A370 5.50fr black 2.50 1.50
Nos. 1287-1299 (13) 21.60 8.75

See Nos. 1505-1515.

Hauling Ice Floes, 17th Cent. Map Arctic A371

1981, Oct. 5
1301 A371 1.50fr multicolored 1.60 1.25

First Intl. Arctic Committee Congress, Rome, Oct. 5-9.

Princes of Monaco Type of 1967

Paintings by P.A. de Laszlo, 1929: 3fr, Prince Louis II. 5fr, Princess Charlotte.

1981, Nov. 5 Engr. *Perf. 12½x13*
1302 A182 3fr multicolored 2.50 1.25
1303 A182 5fr multicolored 3.50 2.40

Ettore Bugatti, Auto Designer and Racer, Birth Centenary A372

1981, Nov. 5 *Perf. 13*
1304 A372 1fr multicolored 1.25 .85

George Bernard Shaw (1856-1950) A373

2.50fr, Fernand Leger, painter, birth cent.

1981, Nov. 5
1305 A373 2fr multicolored 1.25 1.00
1306 A373 2.50fr multicolored 1.25 1.00

Self-portrait, by Pablo Picasso (1881-1973) — A374

#1308, Self-portrait, by Rembrandt (1606-69).

1981, Nov. 5 *Perf. 12½x13*
1307 A374 4fr multicolored 4.50 3.25
1308 A374 4fr multicolored 4.50 3.25

Ikebana, Painting by Ikenobo, 1673 — A375

Intl. Flower Show, Monte Carlo, 1982: 1.40fr, Elegantines, morning glories.

1981, Nov. 5 Photo. *Perf. 12½*
1309 A375 1.40fr multicolored 1.40 1.00
1310 A375 2fr multicolored 2.25 1.75

Catherine Deneuve Rose A376

1981, Nov. 5 *Perf. 13x12½*
1311 A376 1.80fr multicolored 4.00 2.50

First Intl. Rose Competition, Monte Carlo, June 12-14.

8th Intl. Circus Festival, Monte Carlo, Dec. 10-14 — A377

1981, Nov. 5 Engr. *Perf. 13*
1312 A377 1.40fr multicolored 2.50 1.40

Christmas 1981 A378

1981, Nov. 5
1313 A378 1.20fr multicolored .65 .60

50th Monte Carlo Auto Race — A379

1981, Nov. 5
1314 A379 1fr Lancia-Stratos 1.25 .90

Souvenir Sheet

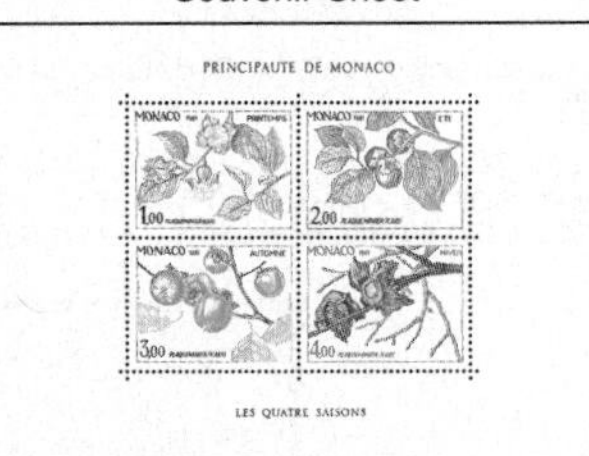

Persimmon Branch in Different Seasons — A380

1981, Nov. 5 *Perf. 13x12½*
1315 A380 Sheet of 4 8.50 8.50
a. 1fr Spring .80 .80
b. 2fr Summer 1.50 1.50
c. 3fr Autumn 2.50 2.50
d. 4fr Winter 3.00 3.00

Coral Type of 1980

Exotic Plants. 1.40fr, Hoya bella, vert. 1.60fr, Bolivicereus sam-aipatanus, vert. 1.80fr, Trichocereus grandi-florus. 2.30fr, Euphorbia milii, vert. 2.60fr, Echinocereus fitchii. 2.90fr, Rebutia heliosa. 4.10fr, Echinopsis multiplex.

Perf. 12½x13, 13x12½
1981-82 Photo.
1316 A359 1.40fr multi 3.25 1.60
1317 A359 1.60fr multi 2.75 1.10
1317A A359a 1.80fr multi 2.25 1.10
1318 A359 2.30fr multi 2.75 1.10
1319 A359a 2.60fr multi 2.75 1.10
1320 A359a 2.90fr multi 2.75 1.10
1321 A359a 4.10fr multi 3.25 2.75
Nos. 1316-1321 (7) 19.75 9.85

Issued: 1.80fr, 6/7; others 12/10.

Miniature Sheet

1982 World Cup — A381

Designs: Various soccer players.

1982, May 3 *Perf. 13*
1322 A381 Sheet of 4 8.00 8.00
a. 1fr multicolored .75 .75
b. 2fr multicolored 1.50 1.50
c. 3fr multicolored 2.25 2.25
d. 4fr multicolored 2.75 2.75

Mercantour Natl. Park Birds — A382

60c, Nutcracker. 70c, Black grouse. 80c, Rock partridge. 90c, Wall creeper, horiz. 1.40fr, Ptarmigan, horiz. 1.60fr, Golden eagle.

1982, May 3 *Perf. 12½x13, 13x12½*
1323 A382 60c multi 1.00 .85
1324 A382 70c multi 1.20 1.10
1325 A382 80c multi 1.20 1.10
1326 A382 90c multi 2.25 1.75
1327 A382 1.40fr multi 3.00 2.40
1328 A382 1.60fr multi 3.75 2.40
Nos. 1323-1328 (6) 12.40 9.60

Europa — A383

1.60fr, Guelph attacking Fortress of Monaco, 1297. 2.30fr, Treaty of Peronne, 1641.

1982, May 3 *Perf. 12½x13*
1329 A383 1.60fr multi *1.50* .40
1330 A383 2.30fr multi *1.50* .50
a. Souv. sheet, 5 ea #1329-1330 *18.00* *9.00*

Fontvielle Landfill Project A384

1982, May 3 *Perf. 13x12½*
1331 A384 1.40fr Old coastline 1.00 .50
1332 A384 1.60fr Landfill site 1.00 .60
1333 A384 2.30fr Completed site 1.50 1.00
Nos. 1331-1333 (3) 3.50 2.10

Fontvielle Stadium — A385

1982, May 3 *Perf. 13*
1334 A385 2.30fr multicolored 1.25 1.00

PHILEXFRANCE '82 Stamp Exhibition,Paris, June 11-21 — A386

1982, May 3
1335 A386 1.40fr multicolored 1.00 .80

Intl. Dog Show, Monte Carlo A387

60c, Old English sheepdog. 1fr, Briard terrier.

1982, May 3 Photo. *Perf. 13x12½*
1336 A387 60c multi 3.25 1.75
1337 A387 1fr multi 3.25 1.75

See Nos. 1366, 1431, 1479, 1539, 1676, 1704, 1756, 1806, 1855, 1900, 1940, 1990, 2035, 2069A, 2108.

Monaco Cathedral, Arms of Pope John Paul II and Monaco A388

1982, May 3 Engr.
1338 A388 1.60fr multicolored .85 .80

Creation of archbishopric of Monaco, July 25, 1981.

800th Birth Anniv. of St. Francis of Assisi — A389

1982, May 3 *Perf. 12½x13*
1339 A389 1.40fr multicolored .75 .75

TB Bacillus Cent. — A390

1982, May 3
1340 A390 1.40fr multicolored 1.10 .85

Scouting Year — A391

1982, May 3
1341 A391 1.60fr dk brown & blk 1.60 1.00

Intl. Hunting Council, 29th Meeting — A392

1982, June 11 Photo. *Perf. 12½*
1342 A392 1.60fr St. Hubert 1.20 1.00

Intl. Bibliophile Assoc. General Assembly — A393

1982, Sept. 30 Engr. *Perf. 13*
1343 A393 1.60fr multicolored .80 .60

Monte Carlo and Monaco During the Belle Epoch (1870-1925), by Hubert Clerissi — A394

1982, Nov. 8 Engr. *Perf. 13x12½*
1344 A394 3fr Casino, 1870 1.75 1.25
1345 A394 5fr Palace, 1893 3.25 2.00

See Nos. 1385-1386, 1436-1437, 1488-1489, 1546-1547, 1605-1606, 1638-1639, 1695-1696.

Nicolo Paganini (1782-1840), Composer and Violinist — A395

1.80fr, Anna Pavlova (1881-1931), ballerina. 2.60fr, Igor Stravinsky (1882-1971), composer.

1982, Nov. 8 Engr. *Perf. 12½x13*
1346 A395 1.60fr multicolored 1.25 1.00
1347 A395 1.80fr multicolored 1.75 1.20
1348 A395 2.60fr multicolored 2.00 1.40
Nos. 1346-1348 (3) 5.00 3.60

In a Boat, by Manet (1832-1883) — A396

Design: No. 1350, Les Poissons Noir, by Georges Braque (1882-1963).

1982, Nov. 8 Engr. *Perf. 13x12½*
1349 A396 4fr multicolored 3.50 3.00
1350 A396 4fr multicolored 3.50 3.00

Souvenir Sheet

10th Intl. Circus Festival, Dec. 6-10 — A439

1984, Nov. 8 Photo. *Perf. 13*
1446 A439 5fr Poster 4.00 4.00

La Femme a la Potiche, by Degas A440

1984, Nov. 8 Engr. *Perf. 12x13*
1447 A440 6fr multicolored 5.00 2.75

Christmas 1984 — A441

Figurines from Provence: 70c, Shepherd. 1fr, Blind man. 1.70fr, Happy man. 2fr, Woman spinning. 2.10fr, Angel. 2.40fr, Garlic seller. 3fr, Drummer. 3.70fr, Knife grinder. 4fr, Elderly couple.

1984, Nov. 8 *Perf. 12½x13*

1448	A441	70c multi	.45	.40
1449	A441	1fr multi	.55	.50
1450	A441	1.70fr multi	1.20	1.00
1451	A441	2fr multi	1.25	1.10
1452	A441	2.10fr multi	1.40	1.20
1453	A441	2.40fr multi	1.60	1.40
1454	A441	3fr multi	1.90	1.60
1455	A441	3.70fr multi	2.40	2.00
1456	A441	4fr multi	2.75	2.40
		Nos. 1448-1456 (9)	13.50	11.60

See Nos. 1737-1739, 1766-1768, 1838-1840, 1883-1885, 1919-1921, 1976-1978.

Cherry Tree A442

1985, Mar. 1 Engr. *Perf. 13*

1457	A442	1.22fr Spring	.50	.50
1458	A442	1.57fr Summer	.50	.50
1459	A442	2.55fr Fall	1.10	.80
1460	A442	4.23fr Winter	2.00	1.50
		Nos. 1457-1460 (4)	4.10	3.30

Issued precanceled only. See note after No. 324.

No. 1 in Green A443

1985, Mar. 25

1461	A443	1.70fr shown	.85	.50
1462	A443	2.10fr #1 in scarlet	1.00	.25
1463	A443	3fr #1 in lt peacock bl	1.20	.85
		Nos. 1461-1463 (3)	3.05	1.60

Stamp centenary, Natl. Stamp Exhibition, Dec. 5-8, Monte Carlo.

Europa 1985 — A444

Portraits: 2.10fr Prince Antoine I (1661-1731), Founder of Monaco Palace, music library. 3fr, Jean-Baptiste Lully (1632-1687), composer, violinist, superintendent of music to King Louis XIV.

1985, May 23 *Perf. 12½x13*

1464	A444	2.10fr brt blue	1.75	*.50*
1465	A444	3fr dark carmine	3.00	*.75*
a.		Souv. sheet, 5 #1464, 5 #1465	*25.00*	*15.00*

Flowers in Mercantour Park A444a

1.70fr, Berardia subacaulis. 2.10fr, Saxifraga florulenta, vert. 2.40fr, Fritillaria moggridgei, vert. 3fr, Sempervivum allionii, vert. 3.60fr, Silene cordifolia, vert. 4fr, Primula allionii.

Perf. 13x12½, 12½x13

1985, May 23 Photo.

1466	A444a	1.70fr multi	.85	.80
1467	A444a	2.10fr multi	1.00	.85
1468	A444a	2.40fr multi	1.20	1.00
1469	A444a	3fr multi	1.75	1.20
1470	A444a	3.60fr multi	2.40	1.60
1471	A444a	4fr multi	3.00	2.00
		Nos. 1466-1471 (6)	10.20	7.45

Japanese Medlar A445

1985, May 23 Engr. *Perf. 13x12½*

1472		Sheet of 4	6.50	6.50
a.	A445	1fr Spring	.55	.55
b.	A445	2fr Summer	1.25	1.25
c.	A445	3fr Autumn	1.90	1.90
d.	A445	4fr Winter	2.40	2.40

Nadia Boulanger (1887-1979), Musician, Composer, Conductor A446

Portraits, manuscripts and music: 2.10fr, Georges Auric (1899-1983), composer of film, ballet music, Music Foundation council president.

1985, May 23 *Perf. 13*

1473	A446	1.70fr brown	1.00	.60
1474	A446	2.10fr brt ultra	1.25	.90

Prince Pierre de Monaco Music Foundation composition prize, 25th anniv.

Natl. Oceanographic Museum, 75th Anniv. — A447

1985, May 23
1475 A447 2.10fr brt bl, grn & blk 1.00 .80

Graphs, Fish, Molecular Structures, Lab Apparatus — A448

1985, May 23
1476 A448 3fr dk bl grn, blk & dk rose lil 1.25 .70

Prince Rainier III Scientific Research Center, 25th anniv.

Intl. Athletic Championships, May 25-26 — A449

1985, May 23

1477	A449	1.70fr Running	.70	.55
1478	A449	2.10fr Swimming	1.00	.55

Opening of Louis II Stadium, May 25.

Monte Carlo Dog Show Type

1985, May 3 Photo. *Perf. 13x12½*
1479 A387 2.10fr Boxer 3.25 2.00

Intl. Youth Year A450

1985, May 23 Engr. *Perf. 13*
1480 A450 3fr fawn, sepia & dp grn 1.25 .75

Fish, Natl. Oceanographic Museum Aquarium A451

1.80fr, Pygoplites diacanthus. 2.20fr, Acanthurus leucosternon. 3.20fr, Chaetodon collare. 3.90fr, Balistoides conspicillum. 7fr, Aquarium.

1985, Aug. 13 Photo. *Perf. 12½x13*

1481	A451	1.80fr multi	1.40	1.10
1482	A451	2.20fr multi	1.40	1.10
1483	A451	3.20fr multi	2.25	1.60
1484	A451	3.90fr multi	2.75	2.25

Size: 40x52mm

Perf. 13

1485	A451	7fr multi	4.75	3.50
		Nos. 1481-1485 (5)	12.55	9.55

See Nos. 1560-1561, 1610-1615.

Souvenir Sheet

Transatlantic Yachting Race, Oct. 13 — A452

Yacht classes: a, Catamaran. b, Monocoque. c, Trimaran.

1985, Oct. Engr. *Perf. 13*

1486	A452	Sheet of 3	6.00	6.00
a.-c.		4fr, any single	1.75	1.75

Monaco-New York competition.

ITALIA '85, Rome, Oct. 25-Nov. 3 — A453

Design: Exhibition emblem, St. Peter's Cathedral and Temple of Castor ruins.

1985, Oct. 25 *Perf. 13½x13*
1487 A453 4fr int blk, brt grn & red rose 1.60 1.00

Belle Epoch Type of 1982

Illustrations by Hubert Clerissi: 4fr, Port of Monaco, 1912. 6fr, La Gare Vers Avenue, 1920.

1985, Nov. 7 Engr. *Perf. 13x12½*

1488	A394	4fr multi	3.00	1.75
1489	A394	6fr multi	3.50	3.00

11th Intl. Circus Festival, Dec. 5-9 — A454

1985, Nov. 7 Photo. *Perf. 13*
1490 A454 1.80fr multi 1.50 1.10

Intl. Flower Show Type of 1984

2.20fr, Roses, tulips, jonquils. 3.20fr, Ikebana of chrysanthemums, bryony.

1985, Nov. 7

1491	A435	2.20fr multi	1.40	1.00
1492	A435	3.20fr multi	2.10	1.90

Dated 1986.

Factory, Ship, Fish, Crustaceans
A455

1985, Nov. 7 Engr. *Perf. 13x13½*
1493 A455 2.20fr brt bl, dp brn & dk grnsh bl 1.00 .60

Monagasque fishing industry, Fontvieille District. See No. 1555.

Christmas 1985 — A456

1985, Nov. 7 Photo. *Perf. 12½x13*
1494 A456 2.20fr multi 1.25 .50

EUTELSAT Orbiting Earth — A457

1985, Nov. 7 Engr. *Perf. 13*
1495 A457 3fr int blk, dp rose lil & dk bl 1.40 1.00

European Telecommunications Satellite Org.

Sacha Guitry (1885-1957), Actor, Dramatist — A458

Authors, composers: 4fr, Brothers Grimm. 5fr, Frederic Chopin and Robert Schumann, composers. 6fr, Johann Sebastian Bach and George Frideric Handel, composers.

1985, Nov. 7
1496 A458 3fr brn blk & gldn brn 1.50 1.20
1497 A458 4fr dp rose lil, sep & turq bl 2.00 1.20
1498 A458 5fr stl bl, dp bl & grnsh bl 2.50 1.90
1499 A458 6fr blk, brn & stl bl 3.00 2.40
Nos. 1496-1499 (4) 9.00 6.70

Souvenir Sheet

Natl. Postage Stamp Cent. — A459

Altered designs: a, Type A1. b, Type A2. c, Type A13. d, Type A83.

1985, Dec. 5
1500 A459 Sheet of 4 8.00 8.00
a.-d. 5fr, any single 2.00 2.00

Rainier and Albert Type of 1981-84

1985-88 Engr. *Perf. 13*
1505 A370 1.80fr brt grn 1.10 .25
1506 A370 1.90fr ol grn ('86) 1.90 .55
1507 A370 2fr emer grn ('87) 1.25 .25
1508 A370 2.20fr red rose 1.25 .25
1509 A370 2.50fr dk brn 1.50 .75
1510 A370 3.20fr brt bl 2.75 2.25
1511 A370 3.40fr ind ('86) 4.25 2.25
1512 A370 3.60fr dp ultra ('87) 2.75 1.25
1513 A370 10fr claret ('86) 4.75 1.10
1514 A370 15fr dk bl grn ('86) 9.25 2.25
1515 A370 20fr brt blue ('88) 11.00 2.75
Nos. 1505-1515 (11) 41.75 13.90

Views of Old Monaco Type of 1984

Illustrations by Hubert Clerissi: 50c, Port of Monaco. 60c, St. Charles Church. 70c, Promenade. 80c, Harbor, olive trees. 90c, Quay. 1fr, Palace Square. 2fr, Ships, harbor mouth. 4fr, Monaco Tram Station. 5fr, Mail coach.

1986, Jan. 23
1516 A425 50c red .25 .25
1517 A425 60c Prus blue .25 .25
1518 A425 70c orange .55 .35
1519 A425 80c brt yel grn .35 .25
1520 A425 90c rose violet .35 .25
1521 A425 1fr brt blue .45 .25
1522 A425 2fr black .95 .45
1523 A425 4fr ultramarine 1.90 .75
1524 A425 5fr olive green 2.40 .75
Nos. 1516-1524 (9) 7.45 3.55

Hazel Nut Tree
A460

1986, Feb. 24 Engr. *Perf. 13x12½*
1525 A460 1.28fr Spring .70 .45
1526 A460 1.65fr Summer .90 .55
1527 A460 2.67fr Fall 1.40 1.00
1528 A460 4.44fr Winter 2.00 1.60
Nos. 1525-1528 (4) 5.00 3.60

Nos. 1525-1528 known only precanceled. See note after No. 324.

See Nos. 1580-1583, 1616-1619, 1685-1688, 1719-1722, 1809-1812.

Port of Monaco, 18th Cent.
A461

1986, Feb. 24
1529 A461 2.20fr ultra, gray & brown 1.10 .45

Publication of Annales Monegasques, 10th anniv.

Europa 1986 — A462

2.20fr, Ramoge Nature Protection Treaty. 3.20fr, Natl. marine reserve.

1986, May 22 Engr. *Perf. 12½x13*
1530 A462 2.20fr multi 1.75 *.40*
1531 A462 3.20fr multi 2.25 *.75*
a. Souv. sheet, 5 each #1530-1531 25.00 *14.00*

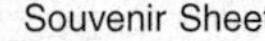

Souvenir Sheet

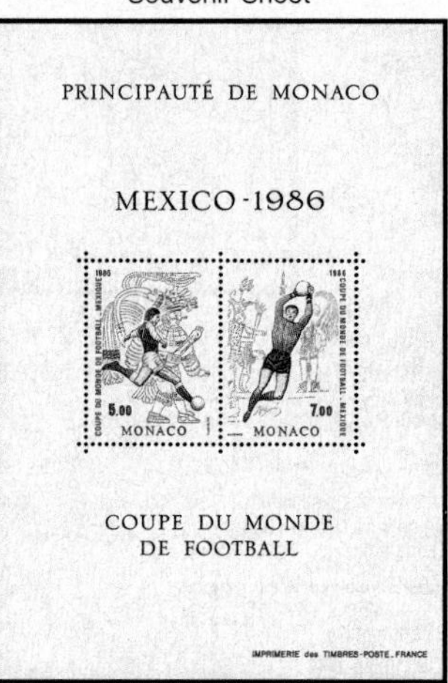

1986 World Cup Soccer Championships, Mexico — A463

1986, May 22
1532 A463 Sheet of 2 6.50 6.50
a. 5fr Player 2.50 2.50
b. 7fr Goalie 3.50 3.50

Ovis Musimon
A464

2.50fr, Capra ibex. 3.20fr, Rupicapra rupicapra. 3.90fr, Marmota marmota. 5fr, Lepus timidus varronis. 7.20fr, Mustela erminea.

1986, May 22 *Perf. 13x12½*
1533 A464 2.20fr shown 1.25 .60
1534 A464 2.50fr multi 1.25 1.00
1535 A464 3.20fr multi 1.75 1.60
1536 A464 3.90fr multi 2.50 2.00
1537 A464 5fr multi 3.00 2.75
1538 A464 7.20fr multi 3.75 3.25
Nos. 1533-1538 (6) 13.50 11.20

Nos. 1536-1538 vert.

Monte Carlo Dog Show Type

1986, May 22 Photo. *Perf. 13x12½*
1539 A387 1.80fr Terriers 5.00 3.25

Prince Albert I, Parliament — A465

1986, May 22 *Perf. 13*
1540 A465 2.50fr brn & ol grn 1.10 .75

First Constitution, 75th anniv.

Serge Diaghilev, Founder — A466

1986, May 22 *Perf. 13*
1541 A466 3.20fr brn blk, carm rose & blk 1.90 1.60

Diaghilev's first permanent ballet company, 75th anniv., and creation of Monte Carlo Ballet Company, 1986.

1st Monte Carlo Auto Rally, 75 Anniv. — A467

Winner Henri Rougier and Turcat-Mery, 1911.

1986, May 22
1542 A467 3.90fr rose mag & car 2.50 2.00

Statue of Liberty, Cent. — A468

1986, May 22
1543 A468 5fr multi 2.00 1.40

Halley's Comet — A469

10fr, Sightings, 1986, 1352.

1986, May 22
1544 A469 10fr multi 3.50 3.00

AMERIPEX '86, Chicago, May 22-June 1 — A470

1986, May 22
1545 A470 5fr US flag, skyline 2.00 1.20

Belle Epoch Type of 198?

Illustrations by Hubert Clerissi: 6fr, Pavilion, 1920, vert. 7fr, Beau Rivage Avenue, 1925, vert.

1986, Oct. 28 Engr. *Perf. 12½x13*
1546 A394 6fr multi 4.00 2.40
1547 A394 7fr multi 5.00 3.00

Premiere of El Cid, by Pierre Corneille, 350th Anniv. — A471

1986, Oct. 28 Engr. *Perf. 13*
1548 A471 4fr Scenes 1.50 1.20

Franz Liszt, Composer — A472

1986, Oct. 28
1549 A472 5fr dk red brn & brt ultra 2.00 1.40

The Olympic Diver, 1961, by Emma de Sigaldi A473

1986, Oct. 28 ***Perf. 12½x13***
1550 A473 6fr multi 2.50 1.60

Intl. Insurers Congress, Monte Carlo, Sept. 30 — A474

1986, Oct. 28 ***Perf. 13½x13***
1551 A474 3.20fr brn, dp grn & brt bl 1.50 1.00

Intl. Flower Show Type of 1984

2.20fr, Bouquet of roses, acidenthera. 3.90fr, Ikebana of lilies, beech branches.

1986, Oct. 28 Photo. ***Perf. 12½x13***
1552 A435 2.20fr multi 1.40 .80
1553 A435 3.90fr multi 2.25 1.75

Dated 1987.

12th Intl. Circus Festival, Dec. 4-8 — A475

1986, Oct. 28 ***Perf. 13***
1554 A475 2.20fr multi 1.75 1.00

Industries Type of 1985

Design: 3.90fr, Plastics industry.

1986, Oct. 28 **Engr.**
1555 A455 3.90fr dk red, dk gray & bl grn 1.75 1.20

Christmas A476

1986, Oct. 28 Photo. ***Perf. 12½x13***
1556 A476 1.80fr Holly .60 .30
1557 A476 2.50fr Poinsettia 1.25 .50

Ascent of Mt. Blanc by J. Balmat and M.G. Paccard, Bicent. — A477

1986, Oct. 28 Engr. ***Perf. 13***
1558 A477 5.80fr red, brt bl & slate bl 2.50 1.75

Miniature Sheet

Arbutus Tree — A478

1986, Oct. 28 ***Perf. 13x12½***
1559 A478 Sheet of 4 9.50 9.50
a. 3fr Spring 1.25 1.25
b. 4fr Summer 1.90 1.90
c. 5fr Fall 2.75 2.75
d. 6fr Winter 2.50 2.50

See Nos. 1645, 1680, 1736, 1775, 1804, 1852, 1934, 1943.

Aquarium Type of 1985

1986, Sept. 25 Photo. ***Perf. 12½x13***
1560 A451 1.90fr like No. 1481 2.25 1.00
1561 A451 3.40fr like No. 1483 4.00 2.50

Prince Rainier III — A479

Villa Miraflores, Seat of the Philatelic Bureau — A480

#1562b, Prince Louis II, founder of the bureau.

1987, Apr. 23 Engr. ***Perf. 12½x13***
1562 Strip of 3 8.50 8.50
a. A479 4fr bright blue 1.90 1.90
b. A479 4fr dark red 1.90 1.90
c. A480 8fr black 3.75 3.75

Philatelic Bureau, 50th anniv.
See No. 1607.

Louis II Stadium A481

1987, Apr. 23 ***Perf. 13x12½***
1563 A481 2.20fr Exterior 1.75 *.40*
1564 A481 3.40fr Interior 2.00 *.75*
a. Min. sheet, 5 each #1563-1564 25.00 *13.00*

Europa 1987.

Insects — A482

1fr, Carabe de solier. 1.90fr, Guepe dorec. 2fr, Cicindele. 2.20fr, Grande aeschne. 3fr, Chrysomele. 3.40fr, Grande sauterelle verte.

1987, Apr. 23 **Photo.**
1565 A482 1fr multi .55 .55
1566 A482 1.90fr multi 1.00 .90
1567 A482 2fr multi 1.25 1.00
1568 A482 2.20fr multi 1.50 1.00
1569 A482 3fr multi 2.40 1.75
1570 A482 3.40fr multi 3.25 2.50
Nos. 1565-1570 (6) 9.95 7.70

Nos. 1565, 1567 and 1569 horiz.

St. Devote Parish, Cent. — A483

1987, Apr. 23 Engr. ***Perf. 12½x13***
1571 A483 1.90fr black .90 .45

Monaco Diocese, Cent. — A484

1987, Apr. 23
1572 A484 2.50fr dk yellow grn 1.00 .55

50th Intl. Dog Show, Monte Carlo A485

1987, Apr. 23 ***Perf. 13x12½***
1573 A485 1.90fr Dog breeds 2.00 1.25
1574 A485 2.70fr Poodle 3.50 1.90

Stamp Day — A486

1987, Apr. 23 ***Perf. 13***
1575 A486 2.20fr multi 1.00 .45

Red Curley Tail, Mobile by Alexander Calder (1898-1976), Sculptor — A487

1987, Apr. 23 **Photo.**
1576 A487 3.70fr multi 1.60 1.00

Sculpture Exhibition, Monte Carlo.

2nd Small European Countries Games, May 14-17 — A488

1987, Apr. 23 **Engr.**
1577 A488 3fr Tennis 2.00 1.60
1578 A488 5fr Windsurfing 2.50 1.75

Miniature Sheet

Grape Vines — A489

1987, Apr. 23 ***Perf. 13x12½***
1579 A489 Sheet of 4 11.00 11.00
a. 3fr Spring 1.50 1.50
b. 4fr Summer 1.50 1.50
c. 5fr Autumn 2.00 2.00
d. 6fr Winter 2.50 2.50

Four Seasons Type of 1986

Life cycle of the chestnut tree.

1987, Mar. 17 Engr. ***Perf. 13x12½***
1580 A460 1.31fr Spring .50 .45
1581 A460 1.69fr Summer .80 .70
1582 A460 2.74fr Fall 1.25 1.10
1583 A460 4.56fr Winter 2.00 1.60
Nos. 1580-1583 (4) 4.55 3.85

Nos. 1580-1583 known only precanceled. See note after No. 324.

The Life of St. Devote, Patron Saint of Monaco A490

Text: 4fr, Born in 283, in Quercio, Devote was martyred in Mariana, Corsica. 5fr, Devote's nurse teaches the saint about Christianity.

1987, Nov. 13 Photo. ***Perf. 13x12½***
1584 A490 4fr multi 1.25 .85
1585 A490 5fr multi 1.50 1.40

Red Cross of Monaco.
See Nos. 1643-1644, 1692-1693, 1714-1715, 1776-1777, 1836-1837.

Philately A491

Butterflies and butterflies on simulated stamps.

1987, July 28 **Engr.**

1586 A491 1.90fr brt grn & dk gray .90 .40
1587 A491 2.20fr rose red & rose lake .95 .50
1588 A491 2.50fr red lil & vio 1.25 .80
1589 A491 3.40fr brt bl & bluish blk 1.90 .85
Nos. 1586-1589 (4) 5.00 2.55

13th Int'l. Circus Festival, Monte Carlo, Jan. 28-Feb. 1 — A492

1987, Nov. 13 **Photo.** ***Perf. 12½x13***

1590 A492 2.20fr multi 1.90 1.00

1988 Int'l Flower Show — A493

1987, Nov. 13

1591 A493 2.20fr Ikebanas 1.00 .60
1592 A493 3.40fr multi, horiz. 1.40 1.20

Dated 1988. See Nos. 1651, 1749.

Christmas A494

1987, Nov. 13 **Engr.** ***Perf. 13x12½***

1593 A494 2.20fr crimson 1.00 .50

5-Franc Prince Honoré V Coin A495

1987, Nov. 13 ***Perf. 13***

1594 A495 2.50fr scar & dk gray .90 .45

Recapture of the Mint, 150th anniv.

Electronics Industry — A496

1987, Nov. 13

1595 A496 2.50fr henna brn, vio bl & grn .90 .80

Int'l. Marine Radioactivity Laboratory, 25th Anniv. — A497

Design: Monaco Oceanographic Museum and Int'l. Agency of Atomic Energy, Vienna.

1987, Nov. 13

1596 A497 5fr brt bl, red brn & blk 2.00 1.40

Louis Jouvet (b.1887), French Actor A498

1987, Nov. 16 ***Perf. 13x12½***

1597 A498 3fr black 1.25 1.10

The River Crossing A499

1987, Nov. 16

1598 A499 3fr multi 1.25 1.10

Paul and Virginia, by Bernardin de Saint-Pierre, first edition bcent. (in 1988).

Marc Chagall (1887-1985), Painter — A500

1987, Nov. 16 ***Perf. 13***

1599 A500 4fr terra cotta & bl gray 1.75 1.25

Jean Jenneret (Le Corbusier, 1887-1965), French Architect — A501

4fr, Architect, Ronchamp Chapel.

1987, Nov. 16

1600 A501 4fr multi 1.60 1.20

Newton's Theory of Gravity, 300th Anniv. — A502

Invention of the Telegraph by Samuel Morse, 150th Anniv. — A503

1987, Nov. 16

1601 A502 4fr magenta & dk bl 1.75 1.10
1602 A503 4fr brt vio, turq bl & brn 1.75 1.10

Don Juan, Opera by Mozart, Bicent. — A504

Mass of the Dead, by Berlioz — A505

1987, Nov. 16

1603 A504 5fr ind, vio brn & sage grn 2.00 1.50
1604 A505 5fr sl grn, vio brn & bl 2.00 1.50

Belle Epoch Type of 1982

Illustrations by Hubert Clerissi. 6fr, Rampe Major, vert. 7fr, Old Monte Carlo Station, vert.

1987, Nov. 16 **Engr.** ***Perf. 12½x13***

1605 A394 6fr multi 3.75 2.50
1606 A394 7fr multi 4.50 3.75

Philatelic Bureau Type of 1987

1987, Nov. 13 **Engr.** ***Perf. 12½x13***

1607 Sheet of 3 7.50 7.50
a. A479 4fr blk vio, like #1562a 1.75 1.75
b. A479 4fr blk vio, like #1562b 1.75 1.75
c. A480 8fr blk vio, like #1562c 3.50 3.50

Postage Due Arms Type of 1985 Booklet Stamps

1987-88 **Photo.** ***Perf. 13 on 3 Sides***

Size: 17x23mm

1608 D10 2fr multi ('88) 1.00 .40
a. Bklt. pane of 10 11.00
1609 D10 2.20fr multi 1.00 .60
a. Bklt. pane of 10 11.00

Issued: 2fr, Jan. 15; 2.20fr, Nov. 13.

Aquarium Type of 1985

2fr, Bodianus rufus. 2.20fr, Chelmon rostratus. 2.50fr, Oxymonacanthus longirostris. 3fr, Ostracion lentiginosum. 3.70fr, Pterois volitans. 7fr, Thalassoma lunare, horiz.

Perf. 13x12½, 12½x13

1988, Jan. 15 **Photo.**

1610 A451 2fr multi 1.00 .80
1611 A451 2.20fr multi 1.50 .50
1612 A451 2.50fr multi 2.00 1.10
1613 A451 3fr multi 1.50 .80
1614 A451 3.70fr multi 2.50 2.10
1615 A451 7fr multi 3.50 2.25
Nos. 1610-1615 (6) 12.00 7.55

Four Seasons Type of 1986

Life cycle of the pear tree.

1988, Feb. 15 ***Perf. 13x12½***

1616 A460 1.36fr Spring .45 .45
1617 A460 1.75fr Summer .45 .45
1618 A460 2.83fr Fall 1.40 1.10
1619 A460 4.72fr Winter 2.25 1.60
Nos. 1616-1619 (4) 4.55 3.60

Nos. 1616-1619 known only precanceled. See note after No. 324.

Souvenir Sheet

Biathlon, 1988 Winter Olympics, Calgary — A506

1988, Feb. 15 **Engr.** ***Perf. 13***

1620 A506 Sheet of 2 12.00 12.00
a. 4fr Skiing 4.00 4.00
b. 6fr Shooting 4.00 4.00

51st Intl. Dog Show, Monte Carlo — A507

1988, Mar. 30 **Photo.** ***Perf. 12½x13***

1621 A507 3fr Dachshunds 3.00 2.00

World Assoc. of the Friends of Children (AMADE), 25th Anniv. A508

1988, Mar. 30 **Engr.** ***Perf. 13***

1622 A508 5fr dk vio bl, dk brn & brt ol grn 2.50 1.75

Europa 1988 — A509

Transport and communication: 2.20fr, Globe picturing hemispheres, man, brain, telecommunications satellite. 3.60fr, Plane propeller and high-speed locomotive.

1988, Apr. 21 ***Perf. 12½x13***

1623 A509 2.20fr multi *1.50 .50*
1624 A509 3.60fr multi *2.75 1.00*
a. Souv. sheet, 5 each #1623-1624 *27.50 12.50*

Mushrooms of Mercantour Natl. Park A510

2fr, Leccinum rotundifoliae. 2.20fr, Hygrocybe punicea. 2.50fr, Pholiota flammans. 2.70fr, Lactarius lignyotus. 3fr, Cortinarius traganus. 7fr, Russula olivacea.

Perf. 13x12½, 12½x13

1988, May 26 **Photo.**

1625 A510 2fr multicolored 1.25 .90
1626 A510 2.20fr multicolored 1.50 .85
1627 A510 2.50fr multicolored 1.75 1.50
1628 A510 2.70fr multicolored 2.10 1.75
1629 A510 3fr multicolored 2.50 2.25
1630 A510 7fr multicolored 4.25 4.25
Nos. 1625-1630 (6) 13.35 11.50

Nos. 1629-1630 vert.

Nautical Soc., Cent. — A511

1988, May 26 Engr. *Perf. 13*
1631 A511 2fr dk red, lt blue & dk grn 1.00 .70

5th Year of Restoration of Our Lady of Laghet Sanctuary A512

1988, May 26 *Perf. 12½*
1632 A512 5fr multicolored 2.00 1.40

World Health Organization, 40th Anniv. — A513

1988, May 26 *Perf. 13*
1633 A513 6fr brt blue & lake 2.50 1.75

Intl. Red Cross and Red Crescent Organizations, 125th Annivs. — A514

1988, May 26 Photo. *Perf. 13x12½*
1634 A514 6fr dull red, blk & gray 2.50 1.75

Jean Monnet (1888-1979), Nobel Peace Prize Winner in 1922 — A515

Maurice Chevalier (1888-1972), Actor — A516

1988, May 26 Engr. *Perf. 12½x13*
1635 A515 2fr brt blue, dk ol bister & blk 3.00 1.75
1636 A516 2fr blk & dark blue 3.25 1.75

1st Crossing of Greenland by Fridtjof Nansen (1861-1930), Cent. — A517

1988, May 26 *Perf. 13*
1637 A517 4fr bright violet 2.25 1.60

Belle Epoch Type of 1982

Illustrations by Hubert Clerissi: 6fr, Packet in Monte Carlo Harbor, 1910. 7fr, Monte Carlo Station, c. 1910.

1988, Sept. 8 Engr. *Perf. 13x12½*
1638 A394 6fr multi 3.25 2.50
1639 A394 7fr multi 4.00 3.25

Souvenir Sheet

1988 Summer Olympics, Seoul — A518

Woman wearing Korean regional costume, Games emblem and event: 2fr, Women's tennis. 3fr, Women's table tennis. 5fr, Women's yachting. 7fr, Women's cycling.

1988, Sept. 8 Engr.
1640 A518 Sheet of 4 9.50 9.50
a. 2fr blk, light ultra & brown 1.10 1.10
b. 3fr blk, light ultra & brown 1.40 1.40
c. 5fr blk, light ultra & brown 2.40 2.40
d. 7fr blk, light ultra & brown 3.25 3.25

Monte Carlo Congress Center, 10th Anniv. — A519

1988, Sept. 8 *Perf. 13*
1641 2fr dark blue grn 1.00 1.00
1642 3fr henna brn 1.25 1.25
a. A519 Pair, #1641-1642 2.50 2.50

Monegasque Red Cross Type of 1987

The Life of St. Devote, patron saint of Monaco: 4fr, Devote witnessing the arrival of the governor of Rome. 5fr, Devote and the governor.

1988, Oct. 20 Photo. *Perf. 13x12½*
1643 A490 4fr multicolored 2.00 1.00
1644 A490 5fr multicolored 2.50 1.50

Tree Type of 1986

Life cycle of the olive tree.

1988, Oct. 20 Engr. *Perf. 13x12½*
1645 A478 Sheet of 4 12.00 12.00
a. 3fr Spring 2.00 2.00
b. 4fr Summer 2.50 2.50
c. 5fr Fall 3.00 3.00
d. 6fr Winter 3.50 3.50

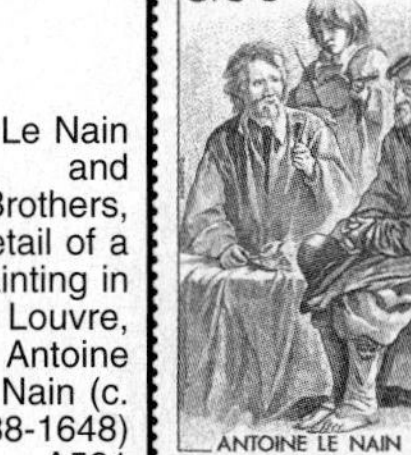
Le Nain and Brothers, Detail of a Painting in the Louvre, by Antoine Le Nain (c. 1588-1648) A521

1988, Oct. 20 *Perf. 12½x13*
1646 A521 5fr ol brn, dull brn & car rose 3.25 1.90

Les Grands Archeologues, Bronze Sculpture by Giorgio De Chirico (1888-1978), Italian Painter and Sculptor — A522

1988, Oct. 20 *Perf. 13*
1647 A522 5fr ol bis, blk brn & dark bl 3.25 1.90

Pierre Carlet de Chamblain de Marivaux (1688-1763), French Playwright, Novelist — A523

1988, Oct. 20
1648 A523 3fr dull ol & ultra 1.50 1.00

Lord Byron (1788-1824), English Poet — A524

1988, Oct. 20
1649 A524 3fr grnsh bl, brn & blk 1.75 .85

14th Intl. Circus Festival, Monte Carlo, Feb. 2-6, 1989 — A525

1988, Oct. 20 Photo. *Perf. 12½x13*
1650 A525 2fr multi 1.75 1.00

Intl. Flower Show Type of 1987

1988, Oct. 20
1651 A493 3fr Ikebana 1.75 1.25

22nd Intl. Flower Show and Flower Arranging Contest, Monte Carlo.

Textile Industry (Ready-to-Wear Clothes by Bettina and Le Squadra) A526

1988, Oct. 20 Engr. *Perf. 13*
1652 A526 3fr blk, yel org & dk ol grn 1.50 1.00

Christmas A527

1988, Oct. 20 Litho. *Perf. 12½x13*
1653 A527 2fr black & lemon 1.25 .70

Petroglyphs, Mercantour Natl. Park — A528

2fr, Magician. 2.20fr, Team of oxes. 3fr, Tools. 3.60fr, Chieftain. 4fr, Jumping jack, vert. 5fr, Christ., vert.

Perf. 13x12½, 12½x13
1989, Feb. 8 Litho.
1654 A528 2fr multi 1.00 .80
1655 A528 2.20fr multi 1.00 .80
1656 A528 3fr multi 1.40 1.20
1657 A528 3.60fr multi 2.00 1.50
1658 A528 4fr multi 2.00 1.75
1659 A528 5fr multi 2.50 2.00
Nos. 1654-1659 (6) 9.90 8.05

St. Nicolas Place — A528a

2fr, Rue des Spelugues.

Booklet Stamps

1989, Feb. 8 Litho. *Perf. 13½x13*
1660 A528a 2fr multi 1.00 .50
b. Booklet pane of 10 12.00
1660A A528a 2.20fr shown 1.25 .60
c. Booklet pane of 10 14.00

See Nos. 1702-1703, 1826-1827.

Prince Rainier III — A529

1989-91 Engr. *Perf. 13*
1661 A529 2fr pale blue grn & Prus grn .80 .35
1662 A529 2.10fr lt blue & Prus blue 1.00 .25
1663 A529 2.20fr pink & rose brn 1.00 .25

1664 A529 2.20fr pale grnsh bl & grnsh bl 1.00 .35
1665 A529 2.30fr pale pink & car lake 1.00 .25
1666 A529 2.50fr pale rose & rose lake 1.00 .25
1667 A529 3.20fr pale blue & brt blue 1.50 .90
1668 A529 3.40fr lt bl & dk bl 1.50 1.00
1669 A529 3.60fr lt blue & sapphire 1.50 1.25
1670 A529 3.80fr pale pink & dk lil rose 1.75 .55
1671 A529 4fr pale vio & rose vio 1.90 1.25
1672 A529 5fr buff & dark vio brn 2.00 .55
1673 A529 15fr pale vio & indigo 6.00 1.75
1673A A529 20fr pink & rose car 7.50 2.75
1674 A529 25fr pale gray & blk 8.00 2.00
Nos. 1661-1674 (15) 37.45 13.70

Issued: 2fr, #1663, 3.60fr, 5fr, 15fr, 3/14; 2.10fr, 2.30fr, 25fr, 1/11/90; 3.20fr, 3.80fr, 3/15/90; 20fr, 4/26/91; #1664, 2.50fr, 3.40fr, 4fr, 9/24/91.

See Nos. 1790-1799.

5th Magic Grand Prix, Monte Carlo, Mar. 17-19 A530

1989, Mar. 14 Engr. *Perf. 13x12½*
1675 A530 2.20fr multi 1.25 .80

Dog Show Type of 1982

1989, Mar. 14 Photo.
1676 A387 2.20fr Yorkshire terrier 2.00 1.10

Our Lady of Mercy Soc., 350th Anniv. A531

1989, Mar. 14 Engr. *Perf. 13*
1677 A531 3fr choc, dark red & blk 1.25 .75

Theater & Film — A532

Designs: 3fr, Jean Cocteau (1889-1963), French writer, artist. 4fr, Charlie Chaplin (1889-1977), English actor, film producer.

1989, Mar. 14
1678 A532 3fr Prus grn, olive grn & dp rose lil 1.40 1.10
1679 A532 4fr dk grn, dk vio & dk red 2.75 1.60

Tree Type of 1986

Life cycle of the pomegranate tree.

1989, Mar. 14 *Perf. 13x12½*
Miniature Sheet
1680 A478 Sheet of 4 10.00 10.00
a. 3fr Spring 1.40 1.40
b. 4fr Summer 2.00 2.00
c. 5fr Fall 2.75 2.75
d. 6fr Winter 3.00 3.00

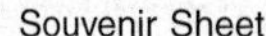
Souvenir Sheet

Reign of Prince Rainier III, 40th Anniv. — A533

1989, May 9 Engr. *Perf. 13*
1681 A533 20fr rose vio 11.00 11.00

See No. 2128.

Europa 1989 — A534

Children's games: 2.20fr, Marbles. 3.60fr, Jumping rope.

1989, May 9 *Perf. 12½x13*
1682 A534 2.20fr multi 1.50 *.40*
1683 A534 3.60fr multi 2.75 *.70*
a. Souv. sheet, 5 each #1682-1683 27.50 *14.00*

Souvenir Sheet

French Revolution, Bicent., PHILEXFRANCE '89 — A535

a, Liberty. b, Equality. c, Fraternity.

1989, July 7 Engr. *Perf. 12½x13*
1684 A535 Sheet of 3 6.50 6.50
a. 5fr sapphire 2.00 2.00
b. 5fr black 2.00 2.00
c. 5fr dark red 2.00 2.00

Four Seasons Type of 1986

Life cycle of the pear tree.

1989, July 27 Photo. *Perf. 13x12½*
1685 A460 1.39fr like No. 1616 .50 .50
1686 A460 1.79fr like No. 1617 .60 .60
1687 A460 2.90fr like No. 1618 1.25 1.25
1688 A460 4.84fr like No. 1619 2.25 1.75
Nos. 1685-1688 (4) 4.60 4.10

Nos. 1685-1688 known only precanceled. See note after No. 324.

Portrait of the Artist's Mother, by Philibert Florence A536

Regatta at Molesey, by Alfred Sisley (1839-1899) — A537

Paintings: 8fr, *Enclosed Courtyard, Auvers,* by Paul Cezanne (1839-1906), vert.

Perf. 13, 13x12½ (6fr), 12½x13 (8fr)
1989, Sept. 7 Engr.
1689 A536 4fr olive black 2.50 1.75
1690 A537 6fr multi 3.00 2.00
1691 A537 8fr multi 4.50 3.00
Nos. 1689-1691 (3) 10.00 6.75

Birth sesquicentennials of painters.

Monegasque Red Cross Type of 1987

The life of St. Devote, patron saint of Monaco: 4fr, Eutychius refuses to betray Devote to Barbarus and is poisoned. 5fr, Devote is condemned to torture by Barbarus when she refuses to make sacrifices to the Gods.

1989, Sept. 7 Photo. *Perf. 13x12½*
1692 A490 4fr multi 1.75 1.20
1693 A490 5fr multi 2.50 1.40

Interparliamentary Union, Cent. — A538

1989, Oct. 26 Engr. *Perf. 13*
1694 A538 4fr multi 1.75 1.00

Belle Epoch Type of 1982

Illustrations by Hubert Clerissi: 7fr, Ship in Monaco Port. 8fr, Gaming hall, Monte Carlo Casino.

1989, Oct. 26 *Perf. 12½x13*
1695 A394 7fr multi 3.50 2.50
1696 A394 8fr multi 4.25 3.00

Souvenir Sheet

Princess Grace Foundation, 25th Anniv. — A539

a, Princess Grace. b, Princess Caroline.

1989, Oct. 26
1697 A539 Sheet of 2 9.00 9.00
a.-b. 5fr any single 3.50 3.50

20th UPU Congress — A540

Design: Views of the Prince of Monaco's palace and the White House.

1989, Oct. 26 *Perf. 13*
1698 A540 6fr multicolored 2.50 1.75

Christmas A541

1989, Oct. 26 Litho. *Perf. 12½x13*
1699 A541 2fr Poinsettia 2.25 .80

15th Intl. Circus Festival, Monte Carlo, Feb. 1-5, 1990 — A542

1989, Dec. 7 Photo. *Perf. 12½x13*
1700 A542 2.20fr multicolored 3.50 1.00

Monaco Aid and Presence, 10th Anniv. A543

1989, Dec. 7 Engr. *Perf. 13x12½*
1701 A543 2.20fr brown & red 2.25 1.00

Avenues Type of 1989

2.10fr, The Great Stairs. 2.30fr, Mayoral Court of Honor.

1990, Feb. 8 Litho. *Perf. 13½x13*
1702 A528a 2.10fr multi .90 .50
a. Bklt. pane of 10 + 2 labels 9.50
1703 A528a 2.30fr multi 1.00 .50
a. Bklt. pane of 10 + 2 labels 11.00

Dog Show Type of 1982

1990, Mar. 15 *Perf. 13x12½*
1704 A387 2.30fr Bearded collie 2.25 1.25

Sir Rowland Hill, Great Britain No. 1 — A544

1990, Mar. 15 Engr. *Perf. 13*
1705 A544 5fr royal bl & blk 2.75 2.00

Penny Black, 150th anniv.

Flowers Named for Members of the Royal Family — A545

1990, Mar. 15 Litho. ***Perf. 12½x13***

1706 A545 2fr Princess Grace .95 .55
1707 A545 3fr Prince Rainier III 1.40 .70
1708 A545 3fr Grace Patricia 1.40 .90
1709 A545 4fr Principessa Grace 1.90 1.10
1710 A545 5fr Caroline of Monaco 2.50 1.75
Nos. 1706-1710 (5) 8.15 5.00

Intl. Telecommunications Union, 125th Anniv. — A546

1990, Mar. 15 Engr. ***Perf. 13***

1711 A546 4fr pink, dp vio & dull blue grn 1.75 1.50

Antony Noghes (1890-1978), Creator of the Monaco Grand Prix and Monte Carlo Rally — A547

1990, Mar. 15

1712 A547 3fr deep vio, blk & dark red 1.25 1.00

Automobile Club, Cent. — A548

1990, Mar. 15

1713 A548 4fr brt pur, sepia & brt blue 2.10 1.40

Monegasque Red Cross Type of 1987

The life of St. Devote, patron saint of Monaco: 4fr, Devote tortured to death (whipped). 5fr, Body layed out in a small boat.

1990, Mar. 15 Litho. ***Perf. 13x12½***

1714 A490 4fr multicolored 1.90 1.25
1715 A490 5fr multicolored 2.50 1.75

Europa — A549

1990, May 3 Engr. ***Perf. 12½x12***

1716 A549 2.30fr multicolored 1.50 *.35*
1717 A549 3.70fr multicolored 2.25 *.55*
a. Souv. sheet, 4 each, perf. 12½x13 27.50 *13.00*

Souvenir Sheet

World Cup Soccer Championships, Italy — A550

1990, May 3 ***Perf. 13x12½***

1718 A550 Sheet of 4 13.00 13.00
a. 5fr Players, trophy 3.25 3.25
b. 5fr Player dribbling ball 3.25 3.25
c. 5fr Ball 3.25 3.25
d. 5fr Players, stadium 3.25 3.25

Four Seasons Type of 1986

Life cycle of the plum tree.

1990, Sept. 17 ***Perf. 13***

1719 A460 1.46fr Spring .80 .50
1720 A460 1.89fr Summer 1.00 .80
1721 A460 3.06fr Fall 1.60 1.25
1722 A460 5.10fr Winter 2.25 1.75
Nos. 1719-1722 (4) 5.65 4.30

Nos. 1719-1722 known only precanceled. See note after No. 324.

Minerals, Mercantour Natl. Park A551

Perf. 13x12½, 12½x13

1990, Sept. 4 Litho.

1723 A551 2.10fr Anatase 1.00 .50
1724 A551 2.30fr Albite 1.00 .50
1725 A551 3.20fr Rutile 1.50 1.10
1726 A551 3.80fr Chlorite 2.00 1.25
1727 A551 4fr Brookite 2.00 1.75
1728 A551 6fr Quartz 3.50 2.75
Nos. 1723-1728 (6) 11.00 7.85

Nos. 1727-1728 vert.

Pierrot Ecrivain — A552

1990, Sept. 4 Engr. ***Perf. 12½x13***

1729 A552 3fr dark blue 1.50 .80

Helicopter, Monaco Heliport A553

5fr, Helicopters, Monte Carlo skyline.

1990, Sept. 4 ***Perf. 13***

1730 A553 3fr red, brn & blk 1.25 .60
1731 A553 5fr blk, gray bl & brn 2.00 1.40

30th World Congress of Civilian Airports, Monte Carlo.

C. Samuel Hahnemann (1755-1843), Physician — A554

1990, Sept. 4

1732 A554 3fr multicolored 1.40 .85

Homeopathic medicine, bicentennial.

Jean-Francois Champollion (1790-1832), Egyptologist — A555

1990, Sept. 4

1733 A555 5fr blue & brown 2.25 1.25

Offshore Power Boating World Championships A556

6fr, Petanque World Championships.

1990, Sept. 4

1734 A556 2.30fr brt ultra, brn & red 1.00 .70
1735 A556 6fr brn org, brn & bl 2.50 1.60

Tree Type of 1986

Miniature Sheet

Life cycle of the lemon tree.

1990, Oct. 17 Litho. ***Perf. 13x12½***

1736 A478 Sheet of 4 9.50 9.50
a. 3fr Spring 1.25 1.25
b. 4fr Summer 1.75 1.75
c. 5fr Fall 2.40 2.40
e. 6fr Winter 2.75 2.75

Type of 1984

2.30fr, Miller riding donkey. 3.20fr, Woman carrying firewood. 3.80fr, Baker.

1990, Oct. 17 Litho. ***Perf. 12½x13***

1737 A441 2.30fr multi 1.00 .45
1738 A441 3.20fr multi 1.50 .80
1739 A441 3.80fr multi 2.00 1.25
Nos. 1737-1739 (3) 4.50 2.50

The Cathedral, by Auguste Rodin (1840-1917) A558

1990, Oct. 17 Engr. ***Perf. 12½***

1740 A558 5fr bl & cream 2.25 1.25

La Pie by Claude Monet (1840-1926) — A559

1990, Oct. 17 ***Perf. 13x12***

1741 A559 7fr multicolored 4.00 4.00

Peter Ilich Tchaikovsky (1840-1893), Composer A560

1990, Oct. 17 ***Perf. 12½x13***

1742 A560 5fr dark grn & bl 2.25 1.25

16th Intl. Circus Festival, Monte Carlo — A561

1991, Jan. 2 Photo. ***Perf. 13***

1743 A561 2.30fr multicolored 1.50 .85

See No. 1801.

Intl. Symposium on Migratory Birds — A562

Migratory birds and their continents: 2fr, Ciconia abdimii, Africa. 3fr, Selasphorus platycercus, America. 4fr, Anas querquedula, Asia. 5fr, Eurystomus orientalis, Australia. 6fr, Merops apiaster, Europe.

1991, Feb. 22 Litho. ***Perf. 12½x13***

1744 A562 2fr multicolored 1.00 .60
1745 A562 3fr multicolored 1.25 1.00
1746 A562 4fr multicolored 2.00 1.25
1747 A562 5fr multicolored 2.50 2.00
1748 A562 6fr multicolored 3.25 2.50
Nos. 1744-1748 (5) 10.00 7.35

Intl. Flower Show Type of 1987

1991, Feb. 22

1749 A493 3fr Cyclamen 1.50 .85

Views of Old Monaco Type of 1984

Designs: 20c, Cliffs of Monaco, Port de Fontvieille. 40c, Place du Casino. 50c, Place de la Cremaillere. 70c, Prince's Palace. 80c, Avenue du Beau Rivage. 1fr, Place d'Armes.

1991, Feb. 22 Engr.

1750 A425 20c rose violet .25 .25
1751 A425 40c dk green .25 .25
1752 A425 50c claret .25 .25
1753 A425 70c ol green .25 .25
1754 A425 80c ultramarine .30 .25
1755 A425 1fr dk blue .40 .25
Nos. 1750-1755 (6) 1.70 1.50

Dog Show Type of 1982

1991, Feb. 22 Litho. ***Perf. 12***

1756 A387 2.50fr Schnauzer 2.00 1.40

Oceanographic Museum — A563

1991, Feb. 22

1757 A563 2.10fr Phytoplankton 1.25 .80

1992 Olympics A564

Design: No. 1758b, Cross country skiiers, diff. No. 1759a, Relay runner receiving baton. No. 1759b, Runner passing baton.

1991, Apr. 26 Engr. *Perf. 13x12½*

1758	Pair	3.50	3.50
a.	A564 3fr dark green, blue & olive	1.40	1.25
b.	A564 4fr dark green, blue & olive	1.75	1.60
1759	Pair	4.00	4.00
a.	A564 3fr brown & Prussian blue	1.40	1.25
b.	A564 5fr brown & Prussian blue	2.50	2.00

Nos. 1758 and 1759 have continuous designs.

Europa A565

1991, Apr. 26

1760	A565 2.30fr Eutelsat	1.75	*.45*
1761	A565 3.20fr Inmarsat	3.00	*.60*
a.	Min. sheet, 5 ea. #1760-1761	30.00	*13.00*

25th Intl. Contemporary Art Competition A566

1991, Apr. 26 Engr. *Perf. 12½x13*

1762 A566 4fr multicolored 2.00 1.25

Prince Pierre Foundation, 25th Anniv. — A567

1991, Apr. 26

1763 A567 5fr multicolored 2.25 1.25

Coral — A568

1991, Apr. 26 Photo. *Perf. 12*

1764	A568 2.20fr shown	1.00	.80
1765	A568 2.40fr Coral necklace	1.25	.85

Christmas Type of 1984

2.50fr, Consul. 3.50fr, Woman from Arles. 4fr, Mayor.

1991, Nov. 7 Litho. *Perf. 12*

1766	A441 2.50fr multi	1.25	.50
1767	A441 3.50fr multi	2.00	1.10
1768	A441 4fr multi	2.25	1.40
	Nos. 1766-1768 (3)	5.50	3.00

Conifers, Mercantour Natl. Park A569

2.50fr, Epicea. 3.50fr, Sapin. 4fr, Pin a crochets. 5fr, Pin sylvestre, vert. 6fr, Pin cembro. 7fr, Meleze, vert.

1991, Nov. 7

1769	A569 2.50fr multi	.95	.35
1770	A569 3.50fr multi	1.40	.70
1771	A569 4fr multi	1.50	.90
1772	A569 5fr multi	1.90	1.10
1773	A569 6fr multi	2.25	1.50
1774	A569 7fr multi	2.75	1.75
	Nos. 1769-1774 (6)	10.75	6.30

Tree Type of 1986
Miniature Sheet

Life cycle of an orange tree.

1991, Nov. 7 Engr. *Perf. 13x12½*

1775	A478 Sheet of 4	9.50	9.50
a.	3fr Spring	1.25	1.25
b.	4fr Summer	1.75	1.75
c.	5fr Fall	2.50	2.50
d.	6fr Winter	2.75	2.75

Monagasque Red Cross Type of 1987

Life of St. Devote, Monaco's Patron Saint: 4.50fr, The Storm is Rising. 5.50fr, Arrival of the Rock of Monaco.

1991, Nov. 7 Photo.

1776	A490 4.50fr multicolored	2.00	.90
1777	A490 5.50fr multicolored	2.25	1.25

Testudo Hermanni A570

No. 1778, Two crawling right. No. 1779, Peering from shell. No. 1780, Walking in grass. No. 1781, Walking amid plants.

1991, Nov. 7 Litho. *Perf. 12*

1778	A570 1.25fr multi	1.40	.80
1779	A570 1.25fr multi	1.40	.80
1780	A570 1.25fr multi	1.40	.80
1781	A570 1.25fr multi	1.40	.80
a.	Block or strip of 4, #1778-1781	7.00	7.00

Prince Albert I Type of 1891
Miniature Sheet

1991, Nov. 7 Engr. *Perf. 13*

Stamp size: 22½x28mm

1782	Sheet of 3	12.00	12.00
a.	A2 10fr dark red	3.50	3.50
b.	A2 10fr dark blue green	3.50	3.50
c.	A2 10fr deep violet	3.50	3.50

Portrait of Claude Monet by Auguste Renoir A571

1991, Nov. 7 Engr. *Perf. 12½x13*

1783 A571 5fr multicolored 2.40 1.75

Treaty of Peronne, 350th Anniv. A572

Portraits by Philippe de Champaigne (1602-1674): 6fr, Honore II (1604-1662), Monaco. 7fr, Louis XIII (1610-1643), France.

1991, Nov. 7

1784	A572 6fr multicolored	3.00	2.50
1785	A572 7fr multicolored	3.75	2.50

Princess Grace Theatre, 10th Anniv. A573

1991, Nov. 7 Litho.

1786 A573 8fr Princess Grace 4.25 3.75

Prince Rainier III Type of 1989

1991-96 Engr. *Perf. 13*

1790	A529	2.40fr pale grnsh bl & dk Prus bl	.80	.50
1791	A529	2.70fr pale bl grn, dk bl grn	1.60	.80
1791A	A529	(2.70fr) pale & Prus grn	1.00	.50
b.		With strengthened lines in military ribbon at LR	1.00	.50
1792	A529	2.80fr pale rose & rose lake	1.00	.60
1793	A529	3fr pale red, red brn	1.00	.90
1793A	A529	(3fr) pink & red	1.10	.55
1794	A529	3.70fr pale bl & dk bl	1.25	.80
1795	A529	3.80fr pale bl & dk bl	1.50	1.10
1796	A529	(3.80fr) pale & dk bl	1.50	.70
1797	A529	10fr lt bl grn & dp bl grn	3.25	1.90
1799	A529	40fr pale brn & dk brn	13.00	8.25
		Nos. 1790-1799 (11)	27.00	16.60

Nos. 1791A, 1793A, 1796 are dated "1999."

Issued: 10fr, 11/7/91; 2.40fr, 2.80fr, 3.70fr, 40fr, 7/28/93; 2.70fr, 3/18/96; 3fr, 3.80fr, 7/8/96; #1791A, 1793A, 1796, 11/28/98. No. 1791Ab, Apr. 2003.

No. 1791Ab sold for 41c on day of issue and has other strengthened lines other than those in the military ribbon.

See No. 1863b.

This is an expanding set. Numbers will change if necessary.

16th Intl. Circus Festival Type

1992, Jan. 6 Photo. *Perf. 12½x13*

1801 A561 2.50fr multicolored 1.60 1.00

1992 Winter and Summer Olympics, Albertville and Barcelona A574

Designs: 7fr, Two-man bobsled. 8fr, Soccer.

1992, Feb. 7 Engr. *Perf. 13*

1802	A574 7fr multicolored	3.25	1.50
1803	A574 8fr multicolored	3.75	2.00

Tree Type of 1986
Miniature Sheet

Life cycle of a cactus plant.

1992, Apr. 24 Photo. *Perf. 13x12½*

1804	A478 Sheet of 4	10.00	10.00
a.	3fr Spring	1.25	1.25
b.	4fr Summer	1.75	1.75
c.	5fr Fall	2.50	2.50
d.	6fr Winter	3.50	3.50

60th Monte Carlo Rally A575

1992, Mar. 13 Engr. *Perf. 13x12½*

1805 A575 4fr dk bl grn, blk & red 1.75 1.25

Intl. Dog Show Type of 1982

2.20fr, Labrador retriever.

1992, Mar. 13 Litho. *Perf. 13x12½*

1806 A387 2.20fr multi 1.75 1.00

50th Grand Prix of Monaco A576

1992, Mar. 13 Engr.

1807 A576 2.50fr vio brn, blk & brt bl 1.50 .80

25th Intl. Flower Show, Monte Carlo — A577

1992, Mar. 13 Photo. *Perf. 12½x13*

1808 A577 3.40fr multicolored 1.75 1.25

See No. 1848.

Four Seasons Type of 1986

Life cycle of a walnut tree.

1992, Mar. 13 Photo.

1809	A460 1.60fr Spring	.80	.50
1810	A460 2.08fr Summer	1.00	.80
1811	A460 2.98fr Fall	1.25	1.25
1812	A460 5.28fr Winter	2.00	1.75
	Nos. 1809-1812 (4)	5.05	4.30

Nos. 1809-1812 known only precanceled. See the note after No. 324.

Souvenir Sheet

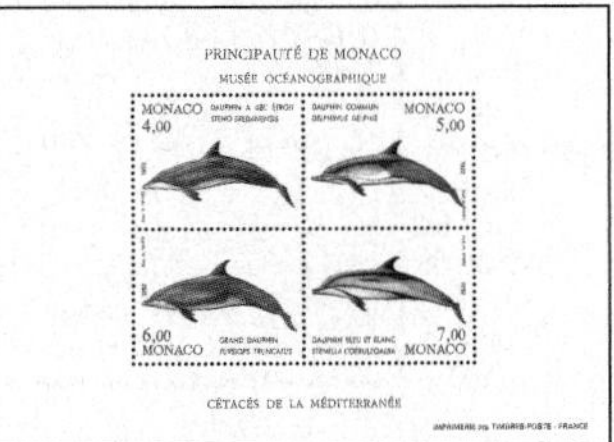

Dolphins — A578

1992, Mar. 13

1813 A578 Sheet of 4 11.50 11.50
a. 4fr Steno bredanensis 1.90 1.90
b. 5fr Delphinus delphis 2.40 2.40
c. 6fr Tursiops truncatus 3.00 3.00
d. 7fr Stenella coeruleoalba 3.50 3.50

See Nos. 1853, 1898.

Discovery of America, 500th Anniv. A579

1992, Apr. 24

1814 A579 2.50fr Pinta 1.00 *.45*
1815 A579 3.40fr Santa Maria 2.00 *.80*
1816 A579 4fr Nina 3.00 *1.25*
a. Sheet, 2 each #1814-1816 15.00 *13.50*
Nos. 1814-1816 (3) 6.00 2.50

Europa.

Ameriflora Intl. Flower Show, Columbus, Ohio A580

4fr, Fruits & vegetables. 5fr, Vase of flowers.

1992, Apr. 24 Litho. *Perf. 12½x13*

1817 A580 4fr multi 2.00 1.10
1818 A580 5fr multi 2.50 1.75

Columbus Exposition, Genoa '92 — A581

1992, Apr. 24 Engr. *Perf. 13*

1819 A581 6fr multicolored 3.00 1.75

Expo '92, Seville — A582

1992, Apr. 24

1820 A582 7fr multicolored 3.25 2.00

Views of Old Monaco Type of 1984

Illustrations by Hubert Clerissi: 60c, National Council. 90c, Port of Fontvieille. 2fr, Condamine Market. 3fr, Sailing ship. 7fr, Oceanographic Museum.

1992, May 25 Engr. *Perf. 12½x13*

1821 A425 60c dark blue .25 .25
1822 A425 90c violet brown .25 .25
1823 A425 2fr vermilion .35 .30
1824 A425 3fr black 1.10 .60
1825 A425 7fr gray blue & blk 2.50 1.40
Nos. 1821-1825 (5) 4.45 2.80

Avenues Type of 1989

2.20fr, Porte Neuve, horiz. 2.50fr, Placette Bosio, horiz.

1992, May 25 Litho. *Perf. 13x13½*
Booklet Stamps

1826 A528a 2.20fr multi 1.00 .40
a. Bklt. pane of 10 + 2 labels 10.00
1827 A528a 2.50fr multi 1.00 .45
a. Bklt. pane of 10 + 2 labels 10.00

Genoa '92 — A583

Roses: 3fr, Christopher Columbus. 4fr, Prince of Monaco.

1992, Sept. 18 Litho. *Perf. 12*

1828 A583 3fr multicolored 1.75 1.10
1829 A583 4fr multicolored 1.75 1.10

Gypaetus Barbatus, Mercantour Natl. Park A584

1992, Oct. 20 Engr. *Perf. 13x12½*

1830 A584 2.20fr grn, org & blk 1.50 1.00

Seabus A585

1992, Oct. 20

1831 A585 4fr multicolored 1.75 1.40

Phytoplankton A586

Designs: 2.20fr, Ceratium ranipes. 2.50fr, Ceratium hexacanthum.

1992, Oct. 20 Litho. *Perf. 12*

1832 A586 2.20fr multicolored 1.40 .80
1833 A586 2.50fr multicolored 1.40 .40

Baron de Coubertin's Call for Modern Olympics, Cent. — A587

1992, Oct. 20 Engr. *Perf. 13*

1834 A587 10fr blue 4.00 2.50

Chapel of St. Catherine — A588

Prince of Monaco, the Marquisat of Baux-de-Provence.

1992, Oct. 20 Litho. & Engr.

1835 A588 15fr multicolored 6.00 3.50

Monagasque Red Cross Type of 1987

The life of St. Devote, patron saint of Monaco: 6fr, Fire aboard ship. 8fr, Procession of the reliquary.

1992, Oct. 20 Engr.
Size: 48x36mm

1836 A490 6fr multicolored 2.25 1.75
1837 A490 8fr multicolored 3.25 2.50

Christmas Type of 1984

1992, Oct. 20 Litho. *Perf. 12*

1838 A441 2.50fr Basket maker 1.25 .50
1839 A441 3.40fr Fishmonger 1.75 .85
1840 A441 5fr Drummer 2.25 1.50
Nos. 1838-1840 (3) 5.25 2.85

Miniature Sheet

Postal Museum — A589

Litho. & Engr.

1992, Oct. 20 *Perf. 13*

1841 A589 Sheet of 2 9.00 9.00
a. 10fr Sardinia Type A4 4.25 4.25
b. 10fr France Type A3 4.25 4.25

17th Intl. Circus Festival, Monte Carlo — A590

1993, Jan. 5 Litho. *Perf. 13½x13*

1842 A590 2.50fr multicolored 1.40 .60

Birds, Mercantour Natl. Park — A591

Designs: 2fr, Circaetus gallicus, horiz. 3fr, Falco peregrinus, horiz. 4fr, Bubo bubo. 5fr, Pernis apivorus. 6fr, Aegolius funereus.

Perf. 13x12½, 12½x13

1993, Feb. 15 Engr.

1843 A591 2fr multicolored .95 .55
1844 A591 3fr multicolored 1.40 .70
1845 A591 4fr multicolored 1.75 1.10
1846 A591 5fr multicolored 2.10 1.50
1847 A591 6fr multicolored 2.60 1.75
Nos. 1843-1847 (5) 8.80 5.60

Intl. Flower Show Type of 1992

1993, Mar. 1 Photo. *Perf. 12½x13*

1848 A577 3.40fr multicolored 1.50 .85

10th World Amateur Theater Festival — A592

1993, Mar. 1 Litho. *Perf. 13*

1849 A592 4.20fr multicolored 2.00 .85

Intl. Civil Protection Day — A593

1993, Mar. 1 Engr. *Perf. 12½x13*

1850 A593 6fr multicolored 3.50 1.75

A594

1993, Mar. 24 Engr. *Perf. 13*

1851 A594 5fr Princess Grace 2.40 1.40

See US No. 2749.

Tree Type of 1986
Miniature Sheet

Life cycle of an almond tree: a, Spring. b, Summer. c, Autumn. d, Winter.

1993, Feb. 15 Photo. *Perf. 13x12½*

1852 A478 Sheet of 4 10.50 10.50
a.-d. 5fr any single 2.40 2.40

Marine Mammals Type of 1992
Miniature Sheet

1993, Mar. 24

1853 A578 Sheet of 4 11.50 11.50
a. 4fr Balaenoptera physalus 1.90 1.90
b. 5fr Balaenoptera acutorostrata 2.40 2.40
c. 6fr Physeter catodon 3.00 3.00
d. 7fr Ziphius cavirostris 3.25 3.25

10th Monte Carlo Open Golf Tournament A595

1993, Mar. 24 Photo. *Perf. 12*

1854 A595 2.20fr multicolored 1.00 .70

Dog Show Type of 1982

1993, Mar. 24 Litho. *Perf. 13x13½*

1855 A387 2.20fr Newfoundland 1.75 1.10

10th Biennial of Antique Dealers of Monte Carlo A596

1993, Mar. 24 *Perf. 12*

1856 A596 7fr multicolored 2.60 1.60

Flowering Cacti — A597

No. 1857, Echinopsis multiplex. No. 1858, Zygocactus truncatus. No. 1859, Echinocereas procumbens. No. 1860, Euphorbia virosa.

1993, May 4 Engr. *Perf. 13x13½*

Booklet Stamps

1857 A597 2.50fr multicolored 1.00 .70
1858 A597 2.50fr multicolored 1.00 .70
1859 A597 2.50fr multicolored 1.00 .70
1860 A597 2.50fr multicolored 1.00 .70
a. Booklet pane, 2 each #1857-1860 8.50
Nos. 1857-1860 (4) 4.00 2.80

See Nos. 1889-1892, 1914-1918, 2007-2009, 2086-2089.

Europa A598

2.50fr, Monte Carlo Ballet. 4.20fr, Sigaldi sculpture.

1993, May 4 *Perf. 12½x12*

1861 A598 2.50fr multicolored .90 *.40*
1862 A598 4.20fr multicolored 1.25 *.70*
a. Souvenir sheet, 3 each, #1861-1862, perf. 13x12½ 7.50 *7.50*

Souvenir Sheet

Admission to the UN — A599

1993, July 28 Engr. *Perf. 13*

1863 A599 Sheet of 3 12.50 12.50
a. 10fr light blue 4.00 4.00
b. 10fr brn vio (Design A529) 4.00 4.00
c. 10fr brown violet & red 4.00 4.00

Intl. Olympic Committee, 101st Session A600

Litho. & Engr.

1993, Sept. 20 *Perf. 13½x13*

Booklet Stamps

1864 A600 2.80fr Coat of arms 1.00 1.00
1865 A600 2.80fr Bobsledding 1.00 1.00
1866 A600 2.80fr Skiing 1.00 1.00
1867 A600 2.80fr Sailing 1.00 1.00
1868 A600 2.80fr Rowing 1.00 1.00
1869 A600 2.80fr Swimming 1.00 1.00
1870 A600 2.80fr Cycling 1.00 1.00
1871 A600 2.80fr shown 1.00 1.00
a. Bklt. pane of 8, #1864-1871 8.00
1872 A600 4.50fr like #1864 1.50 1.50
1873 A600 4.50fr Gymnastics 1.50 1.50
1874 A600 4.50fr Judo 1.50 1.50
1875 A600 4.50fr Fencing 1.50 1.50
1876 A600 4.50fr Hurdles 1.50 1.50
1877 A600 4.50fr Archery 1.50 1.50
1878 A600 4.50fr Weight lifting 1.50 1.50
1879 A600 4.50fr like #1871 1.50 1.50
a. Bklt. pane of 8, #1872-1879 12.00

See No. 1899.

Red Cross of Monaco — A601

Design: 6fr, Red, white crosses.

1993, Nov. 10 Litho. *Perf. 13½x13*

1880 A601 5fr red, black & yellow 2.10 1.25
1881 A601 6fr red & black 2.50 2.00

Monaco Philatelic Union, Cent. A602

1993, Nov. 10 *Perf. 13x13½*

1882 A602 2.40fr multicolored 1.00 .45

Christmas Type of 1984

1993, Nov. 10 *Perf. 13½x13*

1883 A441 2.80fr Donkey 1.00 .50
1884 A441 3.70fr Shepherd 1.50 .85
1885 A441 4.40fr Cow 1.50 1.25
Nos. 1883-1885 (3) 4.00 2.60

Edvard Grieg (1843-1907), Composer — A603

Joan Miro (1893-1943), Artist — A604

Georges de La Tour (1593-1652), Painter — A605

Litho. (#1887), Engr.

1993, Dec. 10 *Perf. 13*

1886 A603 4fr blue 2.50 1.25
1887 A604 5fr multicolored 2.50 1.60

Perf. 12x13

1888 A605 6fr multicolored 2.75 1.75

Flowering Cacti Type of 1993

1994, Jan. 7 Engr. *Perf. 13*

1889 A597 20c like #1857 .25 .25
1890 A597 30c like #1858 .25 .25
1891 A597 40c like #1860 .25 .25
1892 A597 4fr like #1859 1.25 .40
Nos. 1889-1892 (4) 2.00 1.15

18th Intl. Circus Festival, Monte Carlo — A606

1994, Jan. 7 Litho. *Perf. 13½x13*

1893 A606 2.80fr multicolored 1.40 .60

Figurines, Natl. Museum — A607

Designs: No. 1894, Poet. No. 1895, Japanese geisha. No. 1896, Shepherdess with lamb. No. 1897, Parisian woman.

1994, Jan. 7 Engr. *Perf. 12½x13*

1894 A607 2.80fr blue 1.00 .60
1895 A607 2.80fr magenta 1.00 .60
1896 A607 2.80fr purple 1.00 .60
1897 A607 2.80fr blue green 1.00 .60
Nos. 1894-1897 (4) 4.00 2.40

Marine Mammals Type of 1992

Miniature Sheet

1994, Feb. 11 Photo. *Perf. 13x12½*

1898 A578 Sheet of 4 12.00 12.00
a. 4fr Orcinus orca 2.10 2.10
b. 5fr Grampus griseus 2.50 2.50
c. 6fr Pseudorca crassidens 2.90 2.90
d. 7fr Globicephala melas 3.50 3.50

Intl. Olympic Committee Type of 1993

Souvenir Sheet

1994, Feb. 11 Engr. *Perf. 13*

1899 Sheet of 2 10.00 10.00
a. A600 10fr like #1866 4.50 4.50
b. A600 10fr like #1865 4.50 4.50

1994 Winter Olympics, Lillehammer.

Intl. Dog Show Type of 1982

2.40fr, King Charles spaniel.

1994, Mar. 14 Litho. *Perf. 13x13½*

1900 A387 2.40fr multi 1.50 .80

27th Intl. Flower Show — A608

1994, Mar. 14 *Perf. 13½x13*

1901 A608 4.40fr Iris 2.00 1.25

See Nos. 1941, 1989, 2028.

10th Grand Prix of Magic, Monte Carlo A609

1994, Mar. 14 Engr. *Perf. 13x12½*

1902 A609 5fr lake, black & blue 2.00 1.50

25th Conference of the Grand Cordon of French Cuisine A610

1994, Mar. 14 *Perf. 12½*

1903 A610 6fr multicolored 2.50 1.75

Prince Albert I, Research Ship Princess Alice II — A611

Europa: 4.50fr, Opisthoproctus Grimaldii, Eryoneicus Alberti, Oceanographic Museum, Monaco.

1994, May 5 Engr. *Perf. 13x12½*

1904 A611 2.80fr multicolored 1.25 *.75*
1905 A611 4.50fr multicolored 2.10 *1.10*
a. Min. sheet, 3 each #1904-1905 12.00 *9.00*

Intl. Olympic Committee, Cent. — A612

1994, May 17 Engr. *Perf. 12½x12*

1906 A612 3fr multicolored 1.40 .75

Institute for Preservation of the Sea — A613

1994, May 17 Litho. *Perf. 13*

1907 A613 6fr multicolored 2.25 1.75

Intl. Year of the Family — A614

1994, May 17 Engr. *Perf. 13*

1908 A614 7fr multicolored 2.75 2.00

1994 World Cup Soccer Championships, US — A615

1994, May 17 *Perf. 12½x13*
1909 A615 8fr red & black 3.25 2.25

Intl. Amateur Athletic Federation — A616

1994, June 10 *Perf. 13*
1910 A616 8fr multicolored 3.00 2.25

1903 De Dion Bouton A617

1994, Aug. 22 Engr. *Perf. 13x12½*
1911 A617 2.80fr lil, blk & brn 1.25 .85

Intl. Assoc. of Philatelic Catalogue Editors (ASCAT) — A618

1994, Aug. 22 Litho. *Perf. 13*
1912 A618 3fr blk, lil rose & grn 1.25 .75

21st UPU Congress, Seoul, Korea — A619

1994, Aug. 22
1913 A619 4.40fr bl, red & blk 2.25 1.25

Flowering Cacti Type of 1993

50c, Selenicereus grandiflorus. 60c, Opuntia basilaris. 70c, Aloe plicatilis. 80c, Opuntia hybride. 2fr, Aporocactus flagelliformis.

1994, Oct. 17 Engr. *Perf. 13*

1914	A597	50c multi	.40	.25
1915	A597	60c multi	.40	.25
1916	A597	70c multi	.40	.25
1917	A597	80c multi	.40	.25
1918	A597	2fr multi	.40	.40
		Nos. 1914-1918 (5)	2.00	1.40

Christmas Type of 1984

1994, Oct. 17 Litho. *Perf. 13*

1919	A441	2.80fr Mary	1.25	.55
1920	A441	4.50fr Christ child	2.10	.90
1921	A441	6fr Joseph	2.75	1.10
		Nos. 1919-1921 (3)	6.10	2.55

Currency Museum — A620

3fr, Prince Albert. 4fr, Arms of Grimaldi. 7fr, Prince Rainier III.

1994, Oct. 17 Engr. *Perf. 12½*

1922	A620	3fr multi	1.00	.85
1923	A620	4fr multi	1.50	1.25
1924	A620	7fr multi	3.00	2.00
		Nos. 1922-1924 (3)	5.50	4.10

Souvenir Sheet

Perf. 12½x13

1925	Sheet of 3	14.00	14.00
a.	A620 10fr like #1922	4.50	4.50
b.	A620 10fr like #1923	4.50	4.50
c.	A620 10fr like #1924	4.50	4.50

Red Cross Campaigns — A621

Designs: 6fr, Fight against cancer. 8fr, Fight against AIDS.

1994, Oct. 17 Litho. *Perf. 13*
1926 A621 6fr lake, blue & black 1.75 1.40
1927 A621 8fr lake, grn & blk 2.50 1.75

See Nos. 1983-1984.

ICAO, 50th Anniv. A622

Helicopters and: 5fr, Monaco Heliport. 7fr, Monaco skyline.

1994, Oct. 17 Engr. *Perf. 13*
1928 A622 5fr multicolored 2.00 1.50
1929 A622 7fr multicolored 3.00 2.00

Voltaire (1694-1778), Writer — A623

Sarah Bernhardt (1844-1923), Actress — A624

Publication of Robinson Crusoe, by Daniel Defoe, 275th Anniv. — A625

The Snake Charmer, by Henri Rousseau (1844-1910) — A626

1994, Oct. 17 Engr. *Perf. 13*
1930 A623 5fr olive green 2.00 1.25
1931 A624 6fr multicolored 2.25 1.50

Litho.

1932	A625	7fr multicolored	2.75	1.90
1933	A626	9fr multicolored	3.75	2.25
		Nos. 1930-1933 (4)	10.75	6.90

Tree Type of 1986

Miniature Sheet

Life cycle of an apricot tree.

1994, Oct. 17 Photo. *Perf. 13x12½*

1934	A478 Sheet of 4	12.00	12.00
a.	6fr Spring	2.50	2.50
b.	7fr Summer	2.75	2.75
c.	8fr Autumn	3.25	3.25
d.	9fr Winter	3.50	3.50

19th Intl. Circus Festival, Monte Carlo — A627

1995, Jan. 3 Litho. *Perf. 13½x13*
1935 A627 2.80fr multicolored 1.40 .60

Monte Carlo Television, 35th Festival — A628

1995, Feb. 13 Engr. *Perf. 12½x13*
1936 A628 8fr Prince Albert 3.00 1.75

European Nature Conservation Year — A629

1995, Apr. 3 Litho. *Perf. 13x13½*
1937 A629 2.40fr multicolored 1.10 .55

Intl. Special Olympics A630

1995, Apr. 3
1938 A630 3fr multicolored 1.10 .80

Rotary Intl. Convention, Nice A631

1995, Apr. 3 Engr. *Perf. 13x12½*
1939 A631 4fr blue 1.75 1.00

Intl. Dog Show Type of 1982

4fr, American cocker spaniel.

1995, Apr. 3 Litho. *Perf. 13x13½*
1940 A387 4fr multi 2.25 1.25

Intl. Flower Show Type of 1993

1995, Apr. 3 *Perf. 13½x13*
1941 A608 5fr Perroquet tulips 2.00 1.25

European Bonsai Congress A632

1995, Apr. 3 *Perf. 12*
1942 A632 6fr Acer palmatum 2.50 1.40

Tree Type of 1986

Miniature Sheet

Life cycle of a jujube tree.

1995, Apr. 3 Photo. *Perf. 12x12½*

1943	A478 Sheet of 4	10.50	10.50
a.	4fr Spring	1.90	1.90
b.	5fr Summer	2.40	2.40
c.	6fr Fall	2.75	2.75
d.	7fr Winter	3.25	3.25

Peace & Liberty A633

Europa: 2.80fr, Dove with olive branch, Alfred Nobel. 5fr, Chain broken over concentration camp, flowers.

Photo. & Engr.

1995, May 8 *Perf. 12x12½*
1944 A633 2.80fr multicolored 1.25 .80
1945 A633 5fr multicolored 2.40 1.25

50th anniversaries: End of World War II (#1944), liberation of the concentration camps (#1945).

A634

Designs: 5fr, Jean Giono (1895-1970), writer. 6fr, Marcel Pagnol (1895-1974), film producer, writer.

1995, May 8 Engr. *Perf. 12½x13*

1946 A634 5fr multicolored 1.75 1.00
1947 A634 6fr multicolored 2.00 1.40

Princess Caroline, Pres. of World Assoc. of Friends of Children — A635

1995, May 8 Photo. *Perf. 13½x13*

1948 A635 7fr blue 2.50 2.00

Intl. Council of Wildlife Conservation — A636

1995, May 8 Engr. *Perf. 13*

1949 A636 6fr St. Hubert, stag 2.00 1.25

IAAF Track & Field Championships, Louis II Stadium — A637

1995, May 8

1950 A637 7fr multicolored 2.50 1.60

Alps Monument A638

1995, May 8

1951 A638 8fr multicolored 3.00 2.00

Prince Pierre of Monaco (1895-1964) A639

1995, May 8

1952 A639 10fr lake 3.50 2.40

Souvenir Sheet

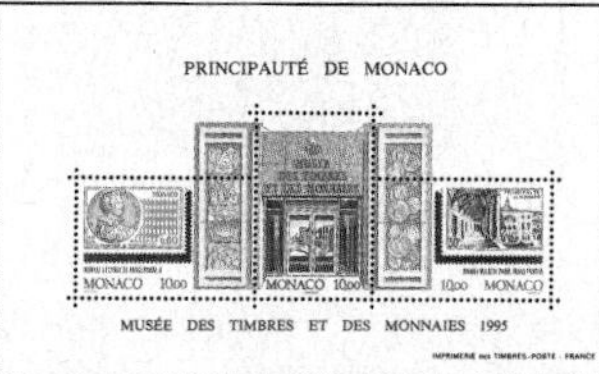

Stamp & Coin Museum — A640

a, #927. b, Museum entrance. c, #294.

1995, May 8

1953 A640 Sheet of 3, #a.-c. 13.50 13.50
a.-c. 10fr any single 4.50 4.50

St. Anthony of Padua (1195-1231) A641

1995, Sept. 25 Litho. *Perf. 13½*

1954 A641 2.80fr multicolored 1.00 .60

UN, 50th Anniv. A642

Designs: #1955, 1963a, Soldiers, UN Charter. #1956, 1963b, Grain, child. #1957, 1963c, Childrens' faces. #1958, 1963d, Musical notes, temple of Abu Simbel. #1959, 1963e, UN Security Council. #1960, 1963f, Hand holding grain, field. #1961, 1963g, Letters from various languages. #1962, 1963h, UNESCO Headquarters.

1995, Oct. 24 Engr. *Perf. 13*

1955 A642 2.50fr multicolored 1.00 .50
1956 A642 2.50fr multicolored 1.00 .50
1957 A642 2.50fr multicolored 1.00 .50
1958 A642 2.50fr multicolored 1.00 .50
1959 A642 3fr multicolored 1.25 .70
1960 A642 3fr multicolored 1.25 .70
1961 A642 3fr multicolored 1.25 .70
1962 A642 3fr multicolored 1.25 .70
Nos. 1955-1962 (8) 9.00 4.80

Miniature Sheet

1963 Sheet of 8 15.00 15.00
a.-d. A642 3fr any single 1.25 1.25
e.-h. A642 4.50fr any single 2.00 2.00

A643

Flowers: No. 1964, Rose *Grace of Monaco.* No. 1965, Fuschia *Lakeland Princess.* No. 1966, Carnation *Century of Monte Carlo.* No. 1967, Fuschia *Grace.* No. 1968, Rose *Princess of Monaco.* No. 1969, Alstroemeria *Gracia.* No. 1970, Lily *Princess Grace.* No. 1971, Carnation *Princess Caroline.* No. 1972, Rose *Stephanie of Monaco.* No. 1973, Carnation *Prince Albert.* No. 1974, Sweet pea *Grace of Monaco.* No. 1975, Gerbera *Gracia.*

1995, Oct. 24 Litho. *Perf. 13½*

Booklet Stamps

1964 A643 3fr multicolored 1.20 .80
1965 A643 3fr multicolored 1.20 .80
1966 A643 3fr multicolored 1.20 .80
1967 A643 3fr multicolored 1.20 .80
1968 A643 3fr multicolored 1.20 .80
1969 A643 3fr multicolored 1.20 .80
1970 A643 3fr multicolored 1.40 .80
1971 A643 3fr multicolored 1.20 .80
1972 A643 3fr multicolored 1.20 .80
1973 A643 3fr multicolored 1.20 .80
1974 A643 3fr multicolored 1.20 .80
1975 A643 3fr multicolored 1.20 .80
a. Bklt. pane, #1964-1975 + 2 labels 15.00
Complete booklet, #1975a 16.00

Christmas Type of 1984

1995, Oct. 24 Litho. *Perf. 13½x13*

1976 A441 3fr Balthazar 1.00 .65
1977 A441 5fr Gaspard 1.50 1.10
1978 A441 6fr Melchior 2.00 1.25
Nos. 1976-1978 (3) 4.50 3.00

Monagasque Assoc. for Protection of Nature, 20th Anniv. — A644

1995, Oct. 24 Engr. *Perf. 13*

1980 A644 4fr green, black & red 1.50 .85

Wilhelm Röntgen (1845-1923), Discovery of X-Rays, Cent. — A645

1995, Oct. 24

1981 A645 6fr multicolored 2.50 1.25

Motion Pictures, Cent. — A646

1995, Oct. 24

1982 A646 7fr dark blue 3.00 1.75

Red Cross Campaigns Type of 1994

Designs: 7fr, World fight against leprosy. 8fr, Drs. Prakash and Mandakini Amte, Indian campaign against leprosy.

1995, Oct. 24 Litho.

1983 A621 7fr multicolored 2.00 1.50
1984 A621 8fr multicolored 3.00 1.75

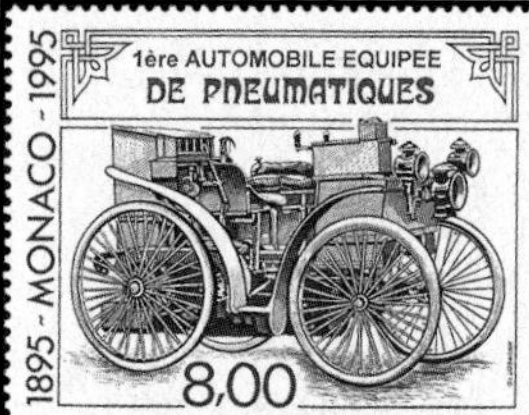

Pneumatic Automobile Tires, Cent. — A647

1995, Oct. 24 Engr.

1985 A647 8fr claret & dk purple 3.00 1.75

Springtime, by Sandro Botticelli (1445-1510) — A648

1995, Oct. 24

1986 A648 15fr blue 9.25 5.25
a. Souvenir sheet of 1 9.25 5.25

No. 1986 printed in sheets of 10 + 5 labels.

No. 1986a inscribed in sheet margin as a winner of the 4th World Cup of Stamps, portrait of Botticelli. Issued 11/6/97.

20th Intl. Circus Festival, Monte Carlo — A649

1996, Jan. 10 Litho. *Perf. 13*

1987 A649 2.40fr multicolored 1.10 .50

Compare with No. 2825b.

Magic Festival, Monte Carlo A650

1996, Jan. 10 Engr.

1988 A650 2.80fr black & gray 1.25 .55

Intl. Flower Show Type of 1994

1996, Jan. 26 Litho.

1989 A608 3fr Rhododendron 1.25 .65

Intl. Dog Show Type of 1982

1996, Jan. 26

1990 A387 4fr Fox terrier 1.75 1.00

Opening of Chapel of Notre Dame of Miséricorde, 350th Anniv. — A651

1996, Jan. 26 Engr. *Perf. 12x13*

1991 A651 6fr multicolored 2.40 2.00

Oceanographic Voyages of Prince Albert I of Monaco and King Charles I of Portugal, Cent. — A652

3fr, Fish in sea, net, Prince Albert I holding binoculars, ship. 4.50fr, Ship, King Charles I holding sextant, microscope, sea life.

1996, Feb. 1 Litho. *Perf. 12*

1992 A652 3fr multicolored 1.40 .70
1993 A652 4.50fr multicolored 2.10 1.25

See Portugal Nos. 2084-2085.

Prince Rainier III Type of 1974 Inscribed "MUSEE DES TIMBRES ET DES MONNAIES"

1996, Mar. 11 Engr. *Perf. 13*

1994 AP37 10fr purple 3.00 2.00
1995 AP37 15fr henna brown 5.00 3.50
1996 AP37 20fr ultra 7.00 4.75
Nos. 1994-1996 (3) 15.00 10.25

Stamp and Currency Museum.

Princess Grace — A653

1996, Apr. 29

1997 A653 3fr red & brown 2.00 .70

Europa.

RAMOGE Agreement Between France, Italy, Monaco, 20th Anniv. A654

Photo. & Engr.

1996, May 14 *Perf. 13*

1998 A654 3fr multicolored 1.25 .65

See France #2524, Italy #2077.

Annales Monegasques, 20th Anniv. — A655

Famous people: a, Saint Nicolas of Myra, by Louis Brea. b, Guillaume Apollinaire (1880-1918), poet. c, Jean-Baptiste Francois Bosio (1764-1827), painter. d, Francois-Joseph Bosio (1768-1845), sculptor. e, Hector Berlioz (1803-69), composer. f, Niccolo Machiavelli (1469-1527), writer. g, Sidonie-Gabrielle Colette (1873-1954), writer. h, Michael Montaigne (1533-92), essayist.

1996, May 14 Engr. *Perf. 12½x13*

1999 A655 Sheet of 8 15.00 15.00
a., e. 3fr any single 1.00 1.00
b., f. 4fr any single 1.50 1.50
c., g. 5fr any single 1.75 1.75
d., h. 6fr any single 2.00 2.00

Souvenir Sheet

CHINA '96, 9th Asian Intl. Philatelic Exhibition — A656

Designs: a, Chinese acrobats in Monaco. b, Fuling Tomb, Shenyang.

1996, May 14 Litho. *Perf. 13*

2000 A656 Sheet of 2 4.00 4.00
a.-b. 5fr any single 1.50 1.50

Introduction of Telephone Area Code 377 for Monaco — A657

1996, June 21 Engr. *Perf. 13*

2001 A657 3fr dark blue 1.00 .75
2002 A657 3.80fr vermilion 1.50 1.00

1996 Summer Olympic Games, Atlanta — A658

No. 2003, Javelin, 1896. No. 2004, Women's softball, 1996. No. 2005, Runners, 1896. No. 2006, Cycling, 1996.

1996, July 19 Litho. *Perf. 13½x13*

2003 A658 3fr multi 1.00 .90
2004 A658 3fr multi 1.00 .90
2005 A658 4.50fr multi 1.60 1.40
2006 A658 4.50fr multi 1.60 1.40
Nos. 2003-2006 (4) 5.20 4.60

Flowering Cacti Type of 1993

Designs: 10c, Bromelia brevifolia. 1fr, Stapelia flavirostris. 5fr, Cereus peruvianus.

1996, Sept. 16 Engr. *Perf. 13*

2007 A597 10c multicolored .25 .25
2008 A597 1fr multicolored .40 .25
2009 A597 5fr multicolored 1.50 .75
Nos. 2007-2009 (3) 2.15 1.25

Tree Type of 1986

Life cycle of thorn (ronce) tree.

1996, Oct. 14 Photo. *Perf. 13*

2010 A478 Sheet of 4 11.00 11.00
a. 4fr Spring 1.75 1.75
b. 5fr Summer 2.25 2.25
c. 6fr Fall 2.75 2.75
d. 7fr Winter 3.25 3.25

Red Cross Campaigns Type of 1994

Designs: 7fr, Fight against tuberculosis. 8fr, Camille Guérin, Albert-Leon C. Calmette, developers of BCG vaccine against tuberculosis.

1996, Oct. 14

2011 A621 7fr multicolored 3.00 1.50
2012 A621 8fr multicolored 3.00 2.00

UNICEF, 50th Anniv. — A658a

1996, Oct. 14 Engr. *Perf. 12½x13*

2013 A658a 3fr multicolored 1.25 .70

Discovery of the Planet, Neptune, 150th Anniv. — A659

Photo. & Engr.

1996, Oct. 14 *Perf. 13x12½*

2014 A659 4fr multicolored 2.00 .80

René Descartes (1596-1650), Philosopher, Mathematician — A660

1996, Oct. 14 Engr. *Perf. 13*

2015 A660 5fr blue & carmine 2.25 1.25

Christmas A661

1996, Oct. 14 Litho. *Perf. 13*

2016 A661 3fr Angel 1.25 .65
2017 A661 6fr Angels 2.50 1.25

Self-Portrait, by Corot (1796-1875) — A662

7fr, Self-portrait (detail), by Goya (1746-1828).

Photo. & Engr.

1996, Oct. 14 *Perf. 12x13*

2018 A662 6fr multicolored 2.50 1.50
2019 A662 7fr multicolored 3.25 1.75

Stamp and Coin Museum — A663

Designs: No. 2020, Printing and engraving stamps. No. 2021, Coins, screw press. 10fr, Front entrance to museum.

1996, Oct. 14 Engr. *Perf. 13*

2020 A663 5fr dk olive & violet 2.00 2.00
2021 A663 5fr dk ol & dk bl 2.00 2.00
2022 A663 10fr dk ol & dk bl 4.00 4.00
a. Souvenir sheet, #2020-2022 8.50 8.50
Nos. 2020-2022 (3) 8.00 8.00

No. 2022 is 48x36mm.

Grimaldi Dynasty, 700th Anniv. A664

No. 2023: a, Francois Grimaldi, 1297. b, Rainier I, d. 1314. c, Charles I, d. 1357. d, Rainier II, 1350-1407. e, Jean I, 1382-1454. f, Catalan, d. 1457. g, Lambert, d. 1494. h, Jean II, 1468-1505. i, Lucien, 1481-1523. j, Augustin, d. 1532. k, Honoré I, 1522-1581. l, Charles II, 1555-1589. m, Hercule I, 1562-1604.

No. 2024: a, Honoré II (1597-1662). b, Louis I (1642-1701). c, Antoine (1661-1731). d, Louise-Hippolyte (1697-1731). e, Jacques I (1689-1751). f, Honoré III (1720-95). g, Honoré IV (1758-1819). h, Honoré V (1778-1841). i, Florestan I (1785-1856). j, Charles III (1818-89). k, Albert I (1848-1922). l, Louis II (1870-1949). m, Rainier III.

1997 Litho. *Perf. 13*

2023 Sheet of 13 + 2 labels 30.00 30.00
a. A664 7fr multicolored 2.50 2.50
b.-d. A664 1fr multi, each .30 .30
e, g. A664 2fr multi, each .75 .75
f. A664 9fr multicolored 3.50 3.50
h.-j A664 9fr multi, each 3.50 3.50
k.-m. A664 7fr multi, each 2.50 2.50
2024 Sheet of 13 + 2 labels 30.00 30.00
a.-c. A664 1fr multi, each .35 .35
d. A664 9fr multicolored 3.50 3.50
e. A664 2fr multicolored .75 .75
f.-i. A664 9fr multi, each 3.50 3.50
j.-m. A664 7fr multi, each 2.50 2.50

Portions of the designs on Nos. 2023-2024 were applied by a thermographic process producing a shiny, raised effect.

Issued: #2023, 1/8; #2024, 7/3.

Knight in Armor Type of 1951 Inscribed "1297-1997"

1996-97 Engr. *Perf. 13*

2025 A67 2.70fr bl, brn & red 1.00 .60

Sheet of 8

2026 2 ea #a.-c., 2025 9.00 9.00
a. A67 2.70fr red 1.25 1.25
b. A67 2.70fr brown 1.25 1.25
c. A67 2.70fr blue 1.25 1.25

Issued: #2025, 12/19/96; #2026, 1/8/97.

Yacht Club of Monaco — A665

1996, Dec. 12 Litho. *Perf. 13*

2027 A665 3fr multicolored 1.25 .70

Intl. Flower Show Type of 1993

1996, Dec. 19 *Perf. 13½x13*

2028 A608 3.80fr Camellia 1.50 .75

Tennis Tournaments in Monaco, Cent. — A666

1997, Feb. 1 Litho. ***Perf. 13***
2029 A666 4.60fr multicolored 1.90 1.00

Portions of the design on No. 2029 were applied by a thermographic process producing a shiny, raised effect.
For overprint see No. 2049.

37th Festival of Television in Monte Carlo — A667

1996, Dec. 19 ***Perf. 13½x13***
2030 A667 4.90fr multicolored 2.00 1.00

Campanula "Medium" — A668

1996, Dec. 19 Litho. ***Perf. 13***
2031 A668 5fr multicolored 2.00 1.10

Auto Sports in Monaco — A669

1996, Dec. 19 Litho. ***Perf. 13***
2032 A669 3fr multicolored 1.40 .65

Philatelic Events A670

Stamp & Coin Museum and: No. 2033, Pictures, engraving tools, picture on stamps. No. 2034, Stamp, magnifying glass, envelopes.

1996, Dec. 19 Engr. ***Perf. 13***
2033 A670 3fr multicolored 2.00 .60
2034 A670 3fr multicolored 2.00 .60
a. Pair, #2033-2034 5.00 5.00

Monaco Philatelic Office, 60th anniv. (#2033). Monaco Intl. Philatelic Exhibition (#2034).

Dog Show Type of 1982

1996, Dec. 19 Litho. ***Perf. 13x13½***
2035 A387 4.40fr Afghan hound 2.40 1.00

21st Intl. Circus Festival, Monte Carlo — A671

1996, Dec. 19 Litho. ***Perf. 13½x13***
2036 A671 3fr multicolored 1.50 .60

Intl. Grand Prix of Philately — A672

1997, Apr. 5 Litho. ***Perf. 13***
2041 A672 4.60fr multicolored 1.75 1.25

Red Cross Campaign Against Drug Abuse — A673

1997, May 5 ***Perf. 13½x13***
2042 A673 7fr multicolored 3.25 1.60

Europa (Stories and Legends) A674

No. 2043, Legend of St. Devote. No. 2044, Port Hercules named for mythological Hercules.

1997, May 5 Engr. ***Perf. 12½x13***
2043 A674 3fr multicolored 1.50 .65
2044 A674 3fr multicolored 1.50 .65
a. Pair, #2043-2044 3.00 3.00

PACIFIC 97 Intl. Philatelic Exhibition A675

Design: US types A2 & A1, Monaco #1995.

1997, May 29 ***Perf. 13x12½***
2045 A675 4.90fr multicolored 2.25 1.25

Uniforms of the Carabiniers (Palace Guards) A676

Years uniforms used: 3fr, 1997. 3.50fr, 1750-1853. 5.20fr, 1865-1935.

1997, May 31 Litho. ***Perf. 13x13½***
2046 A676 3fr multicolored 1.25 .50
2047 A676 3.50fr multicolored 1.40 .60
2048 A676 5.20fr multicolored 2.25 .90
Nos. 2046-2048 (3) 4.90 2.00

No. 2029 Ovptd. "M. RIOS"

1997 ***Perf. 13***
2049 A666 4.60fr multicolored 2.10 1.40

13th Grand Prix of Magic, Monte Carlo — A677

1997 Litho. ***Perf. 13½x13***
2050 A677 4.40fr multicolored 1.75 1.25

Monaco Soccer Assoc., 1996 French Division 1 Champions — A678

1997 ***Perf. 13***
2051 A678 3fr multicolored 1.40 .80

Francois Grimaldi, by Ernando Venanzi A679

9fr, Saint Peter and Saint Paul, by Rubens.

1997, Sept. 8 Engr. ***Perf. 13½x13***
2052 A679 8fr multicolored 2.25 2.00
2053 A679 9fr multicolored 3.25 2.50

Evolution of the Geographic Territory of Monaco — A680

Designs: a, 13th century. b, 15th-19th century. c, Map of western half of Monaco, panoramic view. d, Map of eastern half of Monaco, panoramic view.

1997, Oct. 6 Litho. & Engr. ***Perf. 13***
2054 A680 5fr Sheet of 4, #a.-d. 8.00 8.00

Grimaldi Dynasty, 700th anniv.

49th Session of Intl. Whaling Commission — A681

1997, Oct. 20 Photo. ***Perf. 13x13½***
2055 A681 6.70fr multicolored 2.25 1.75

22nd Intl. Circus Festival, Monte Carlo — A682

1997, Nov. 30 Litho. ***Perf. 13½x13***
2057 A682 3fr multicolored 1.75 .70

Princess Charlotte (1898-1977) — A683

1997, Nov. 28 Engr. ***Perf. 13x12½***
2058 A683 3.80fr brown 1.50 .90

A684

Designs by Monagasque Students — A685

Perf. 13½x13, 13x13½

1997, Nov. 29 Litho.
2059 A684 4fr Under 13 group 1.40 .90
2060 A685 4.50fr Over 13 group 1.75 .90

31st Intl. Flower Show — A686

1997, Nov. 30 ***Perf. 13½x13***
2061 A686 4.40fr multicolored 1.50 1.00

1998 Winter Olympic Games, Nagano — A687

Designs: No. 2062, 4-Man bobsled, speed skating, ice hockey, figure skating. No. 2063, Downhill skiing, biathlon, luge, ski jumping, slalom skiing.

1997, Nov. 28 Photo. *Perf. 12½*
2062 4.90fr multicolored 1.90 1.25
2063 4.90fr multicolored 1.90 1.25
a. A687 Pair, #2062-2063 4.00 4.00

Moscow '97 — A688

Ballet Russes de Monte Carlo.

1997, Nov. 28 Photo. *Perf. 13½x13*
2064 A688 5fr multicolored 2.10 1.25

J.L. David (1748-1825), Painter — A689

1997, Nov. 30 Engr. *Perf. 12½x13*
2065 A689 5.20fr red brn & dk grn 2.00 1.10

Papal Bull for the Parish of Monaco, 750th Anniv. A690

7.50fr, Pope Innocent IV.

1997, Nov. 30 *Perf. 12½x13*
2066 A690 7.50fr brn, lt blue 3.00 1.90

Prince Albert I (1848-1922) — A691

1997, Nov. 29 Photo. *Perf. 13x12½*
2067 A691 8fr multicolored 3.00 2.40

38th Television Festival — A692

1998, Feb. 4 Litho. *Perf. 13½x13*
2068 A692 4.50fr multicolored 1.75 1.00

Marcel Kroenlein Arboretum, 10th Anniv. — A693

1997, Nov. 28 Photo. *Perf. 13*
2069 A693 9fr multicolored 3.50 2.50

No. 2069 was issued in sheets of 2.

Dog Show Type of 1987

2.70fr, Boxer, Doberman.

1998, Mar. 19 Litho. *Perf. 13x13½*
2069A A387 2.70fr multi 1.25 .80

Intl. Academy of Peace A694

1998, Mar. 19 Litho. *Perf. 13*
2070 A694 3fr green & blue 1.25 .70

Portions of the design of No. 2070 were applied by a thermographic process producing a shiny, raised effect.

15th Spring Arts Festival A695

1998, Mar. 19 Litho. *Perf. 13x13½*
2071 A695 4fr multicolored 1.40 .90

Pierre and Marie Curie, Discovery of Radium, Cent. A696

1998, Mar. 19 Engr. *Perf. 13x12½*
2072 A696 6fr lilac & green blue 2.25 1.40

Monegasque Red Cross, 50th Anniv. — A697

Prince Albert, Prince Louis II, Princess Grace, Prince Rainier III.

1998, Mar. 3 Litho. *Perf. 13*
2073 A697 5fr sepia, red & dk brown 2.00 1.25

Prince Albert I (1848-1922) — A698

1998, May 6 Engr.
2074 A698 7fr dark brown 3.25 1.50

Charles Garnier (1825-98), Architect, Designer of Casino of Monte Carlo — A699

1998, May 6 Litho.
2075 A699 10fr multicolored 4.00 2.25

Festival of St. Dévote — A700

1998, May 6 Litho. *Perf. 13x13½*
2076 A700 3fr multicolored 1.25 .65
a. Tete-beche pair 2.50 1.30

Europa.

Portions of the design on No. 2076 were applied by a thermographic process producing a shiny, raised effect.

Joseph Kessel (1898-1979), Writer and Journalist A701

1998, May 6 Engr. *Perf. 13½*
2077 A701 3.90fr multicolored 1.40 .90

Expo '98, Lisbon A702

1998, May 6 Litho. *Perf. 13x13½*
2078 A702 2.70fr multicolored 1.10 .60

1st Formula 3000 Grand Prix in Monaco A703

1998, May 20 Engr. *Perf. 12*
2079 A703 3fr red & black 1.40 .70

European Conference of the Youth Chamber of Economics A705

1998, May 6 Litho. *Perf. 13½x13*
2081 A705 3fr multicolored 1.25 .70

World Music Awards — A706

1998, May 6
2082 A706 10fr multicolored 4.00 2.75

Porcelain — A707

1998, June 24 *Perf. 13*
2083 A707 8fr multicolored 2.75 1.75

Publication of Monaco's Works of Art — A708

1998, June 24
2084 A708 9fr multicolored 3.25 2.00

National Festival — A709

Europa: Prince Albert, Prince Rainier III, national palace.

1998, May 31 Litho. *Perf. 13*
2085 A709 3fr multicolored 1.40 .70

Portions of the design on No. 2085 were applied by a thermographic process producing a shiny, raised, effect.

Flowering Cacti Type of 1993

2.70fr, Opuntia dejecta. 4fr, Echinocereus blanckii. 6fr, Euphorbia milii. 7fr, Stapelia variegata.

1998, Aug. 3 Engr. *Perf. 13*

2086	A597	2.70fr multicolored	1.00	.50
2087	A597	4fr multicolored	1.50	.75
2088	A597	6fr multicolored	2.00	1.10
2089	A597	7fr multicolored	2.50	1.25
		Nos. 2086-2089 (4)	7.00	3.60

1998 World Cup Soccer Championships, France — A710

1998, Aug. 3
2090 A710 15fr multicolored 6.00 3.50

No. 2090 contains hexagonal perforated label in center.

Enzo Ferrari (1898-1988), Automobile Manufacturer — A711

1998, Aug. 14 Litho.
2091 A711 7fr multicolored 2.50 1.75

George Gershwin (1898-1937), Composer — A712

1998, Aug. 14 Engr. *Perf. 13x12½*
2092 A712 7.50fr bl, bl grn & blk 3.00 1.75

Intl. College for Study of Marine Pollution, Marine Environment Laboratory — A713

1998, Sept. 4 Litho. *Perf. 13x13½*
2093 A713 4.50fr multicolored 1.75 .90

Plenary Assembly of the European Post, Monte Carlo A714

1998, Sept. 4
2094 A714 5fr multicolored 1.90 .90

Expo '98, World Philatelic Exhibition, Lisbon A715

1998, Sept. 4 Litho. & Engr.
2095 A715 6.70fr multicolored 2.50 1.50

Intl. Assoc. Against Violence in Sports, 30th Anniv. A716

Photo. & Engr.
1998, Sept. 14 *Perf. 13x13½*
2096 A716 4.20fr multicolored 1.60 1.00

Magic Stars Magic Festival, Monte Carlo — A717

1998, Sept. 26 Litho. *Perf. 13½x13*
2097 A717 3.50fr red & bister 1.40 .80

See No. 2140.

Giovanni Lorenzo Bernini (1598-1680), Architect, Sculptor — A718

1998, Sept. 26 Engr. *Perf. 13x12½*
2098 A718 11.50fr blue & brown 4.50 3.25

Italia '98, Intl. Philatelic Exhibition, Milan — A719

1998, Oct. 23 *Perf. 12½x13*
2099 A719 4.90fr Milan Cathedral 2.00 1.10

Christmas A720

3fr, Ornament. 6.70fr, Nativity scene, horiz. 15fr, Icon of Madonna and Child, 18th cent.

Perf. 13½x13, 13x13½
1998, Oct. 26 Litho.

2100	A720	3fr multicolored	1.25	.50
2101	A720	6.70fr multicolored	2.25	1.25

Souvenir Sheet
Engr.
Perf. 13
2102 A720 15fr multicolored 5.75 5.75

No. 2102 contains one 36x49mm stamp.

23rd Intl. Circus Festival, Monte Carlo — A721

1998, Nov. 20 Litho. *Perf. 13½x13*
2103 A721 2.70fr multicolored 1.25 .50

Grimaldi Seamounts A722

1998, Nov. 20 *Perf. 13*
2104 A722 10fr multicolored 3.50 2.00

Souvenir Sheet

Reign of Prince Rainier III, 50th Anniv. — A723

1998, Nov. 20 Engr.
2105 A723 25fr red & yel bister 9.00 9.00

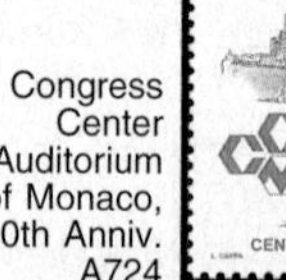

Congress Center Auditorium of Monaco, 20th Anniv. A724

1999, Feb. 12 Litho. *Perf. 13x13½*
2106 A724 2.70fr multicolored 1.25 .50

39th Intl. Television Festival, Monte Carlo — A725

1999, Jan. 18 Litho. *Perf. 13½x13*
2107 A725 3.80fr multicolored 1.75 .80

Dog Show Type of 1982

Cocker spaniel and American cocker spaniel.

1999, Jan. 18 Litho. *Perf. 13x13½*
2108 A387 4fr multicolored 2.00 1.10

Geneva Conventions, 50th Anniv. — A726

1999, Jan. 18 Engr. *Perf. 13½x13*
2109 A726 4.40fr black & red 1.90 .80

32nd Intl. Flower Show, Monte Carlo — A727

1999, Jan. 18 Litho. *Perf. 13½x13*
2110 A727 4.50fr multicolored 1.90 1.10

Monaco '99, Intl. Philatelic Exhibition — A728

Photo. & Engr.
1999, Jan. 18 *Perf. 13x12*
2111 A728 3fr multicolored 1.25 .50

Beginning with No. 2112, denominations are indicated on the stamps in both Francs and Euros. The listing value is shown in Francs.

10th Piano Masters Competition, Monte Carlo — A729

1999, Feb. 12 *Perf. 13x13½*
2112 A729 4.60fr multicolored 1.75 .80

Flowers — A730

Designs: 4.90fr, Prince of Monaco Jubilee Rose. 6fr, Paphiopedilum Prince Rainier III, Prince of Monaco and Grimaldi Roses.

1999 Litho. *Perf. 13½x13*

2113	A730	4.90fr multicolored	1.75	1.25
2114	A730	6fr multicolored	2.25	1.40

Issued: 4.90fr, 2/14; 6fr, 2/13.

Monaco Charity Assoc., 20th Anniv. A731

1999, Jan. 28 Litho. *Perf. 13*
2115 A731 6.70fr multicolored 2.50 1.50

Formula 1 Grand Prix of Monaco, 70th Anniv. — A732

1999, Apr. 16 Photo. *Perf. 12¼*
2116 A732 3fr multicolored 1.25 .80

Intl. Grand Prix of Philately, Monaco — A733

1999, Apr. 16 *Perf. 13¼*
2117 A733 4.40fr multicolored 1.75 1.10

Fifth Intl. Show Jumping Championships, Monte Carlo — A734

1999, Apr. 16 Engr. *Perf. 13x12½*
2118 A734 5.20fr blk, dk grn & red 2.00 1.50

ASM Sports Club, 75th Anniv. — A735

Cutouts of soccer players over: No. 2119, Palace. No. 2120, Aerial view of city.

1999, Apr. 16 Litho. *Perf. 13x12¾*
2119 A735 7fr multicolored 2.75 1.90
2120 A735 7fr multicolored 2.75 1.90
a. Pair, #2119-2120 6.00 6.00

Grimaldi Forum A736

1999, Apr. 25 Photo. *Perf. 13¼*
2121 A736 3fr multicolored 1.10 .50

Oceanography Museum, Cent. — A737

1999, Apr. 25 Engr. *Perf. 13¼x13*
2122 A737 5fr multicolored 2.00 1.25

Philexfrance '99, Intl Philatelic Exhibition A738

France #1, Eiffel Tower, map of France, exhibition emblem, arms of Monaco.

1999, May 5 Engr. *Perf. 13¼*
2123 A738 2.70fr multicolored 1.00 .60

See No. 2133.

Europa — A739

No. 2124, Casino, Cliffs. No. 2125, Park in Fontvieille.

1999, May 5 Photo. *Perf. 13*
2124 A739 3fr multi 1.25 .65

Size: 51x28mm

2125 A739 3fr multi 1.25 .65
a. Pair, #2124-2125 3.00 3.00

Monegasque Economic Growth — A740

Chart and: No. 2126, Fontveille and underground train station. No. 2127, Larvotto and Grimaldi Forum.

1999, May 5 Photo. *Perf. 13x13¼*
2126 5fr multi 1.75 .95
2127 5fr multi 1.75 .95
a. A740 Pair, #2126-2127 4.00 4.00

Souvenir Sheet

Reign of Prince Rainier III, 50th Anniv. — A741

1999, May 9 Engr. *Perf. 13*
2128 A741 20fr blue & gold 8.00 8.00

See No. 1681.

Honoré de Balzac (1799-1850), Writer — A742

Design: 5.20fr, Countess of Ségur (1799-1874), children's storyteller.

1999 *Perf. 12¾x13*
2129 A742 4.50fr red & blue 1.90 1.10
2130 A742 5.20fr multicolored 2.10 1.25

Reign of Prince Rainier III, 50th Anniv. — A743

Design: #256, 337, 427, 937, 1287, 1669.

1999 Engr. *Perf. 12¾x13*
2131 A743 30fr multicolored 12.00 12.00

UNESCO, 50th Anniv. A744

1999, July 2 Engr. *Perf. 13x12½*
2132 A744 4.20fr multicolored 1.60 .80

PhilexFrance Type of 1999

7fr, France #4, 92, Monaco #3.

1999, July 2 Engr. *Perf. 13¼*
2133 A738 7fr multi 2.50 1.50

Sportel, 10th Anniv. A745

1999, July 2 Litho. *Perf. 12¼*
2134 A745 10fr multicolored 3.50 2.40

Sovereign Military Order of Malta, 900th Anniv. A746

1999, July 2 Engr. *Perf. 11*
2135 A746 11.50fr multicolored 4.50 2.75

UPU, 125th Anniv. — A747

1999, July 2 Engr. *Perf. 13¼*
2136 A747 3fr multicolored 1.10 .70

Rose, Iris Named After Prince Rainier III — A748

1999, July 2 Litho. *Perf. 13¼x13*
2137 A748 4fr multicolored 1.60 .90

Stamp, Coin and Postcard Show, Fontvieille A749

3fr, Aerial photograph, coin obverse, No. 1793A. 6.50fr, Aerial photograph, 100fr coin, #257.

1999 Photo. *Perf. 13¼*
2138 A749 3fr multicolored 1.10 .50

Perf. 13¼x13½

2139 A749 6.50fr multicolored 2.50 1.75

Jubilee Bourse (#2139).
Issued: 3fr, 7/3; 6.50fr, 9/26.

Magic Stars Type of 1998

Inscribed "99"

Litho. & Typo.

1999, Sept. 6 *Perf. 13¼x13*
2140 A717 4.50fr red & gold 1.60 1.00

Development Projects — A750

Designs: a, Fontveille 1 & 2. b, La Digue (with jetty). c, Grimaldi Forum. d, La Gare.

1999, Sept. 26 Photo. *Perf. 13*

2141 Sheet of 4 + label 15.00 15.00
a. A750 4fr multicolored 1.50 1.50
b.-c. A750 9fr Any single 3.00 3.00
d. A750 19fr multicolored 6.00 6.00

No. 2141d is 80x40mm.

24th Intl. Circus Festival, Monte Carlo — A751

1999, Dec. 13 Litho. *Perf. 13¼x13*

2142 A751 2.70fr multi 1.40 .55

A752

1999, Dec. 13 Engr. *Perf. 13¼*

2143 A752 3fr Christmas 1.10 .60

Holy Year 2000 A753

1999, Dec. 13 Litho. *Perf. 13x13¼*

2144 A753 3.50fr multi 1.25 .95

33rd Intl. Flower Show — A754

1999, Dec. 13 *Perf. 13¼x13*

2145 A754 4.50fr multi 1.75 1.00

Monaco 2000 Intl. Philatelic Exposition A755

1999, Dec. 23 Engr. *Perf. 13¼x13*

2146 A755 3fr multi 1.10 .55

Bust of Napoleon, by Antonio Canova — A756

Litho. & Embossed

2000, Jan. 17 *Perf. 13¼*

2147 A756 4.20fr multi 2.00 .90

40th Intl. Television Festival, Monte Carlo — A757

2000, Jan. 17 Litho. *Perf. 13¼x13*

2148 A757 4.90fr multi 2.00 .95

The Twelve Apostles — A758

Saints: 4fr, Peter and James the Great. 5fr, John and Andrew. 6fr, Philip and Bartholomew. 7fr, Matthew and Thomas. 8fr, James the Less and Judas. 9fr, Simon and Matthias.

Engr. with Foil Application

2000, Apr. 3 *Perf. 13¼*

2149 A758 4fr multi 1.50 .80
2150 A758 5fr multi 2.00 .95
2151 A758 6fr multi 2.00 1.25
2152 A758 7fr multi 3.00 1.50
2153 A758 8fr multi 3.00 2.00
2154 A758 9fr multi 3.50 2.40
Nos. 2149-2154 (6) 15.00 8.90

Intl. Dog Show, Monte Carlo A759

6.50fr, Labrador Retriever and Golden Retriever.

2000, Apr. 3 Engr. *Perf. 13¼*

2155 A759 6.50fr multi 3.00 1.50

1993 Intl. Olympic Committee Meeting Awarding 2000 Games to Sydney A760

2000, Apr. 25 Photo.

2156 A760 7fr multi 2.50 1.50

Souvenir Sheet

Art Depicting Monaco and the Sea — A761

Artwork by: a, Adami. b, Arman. c, Cane. d, Folon. e, Fuchs. f, E. De Sigaldi. g, Sosno. h, Verkade.

2000, Apr. 25 *Perf. 13x12½*

2157 A761 Sheet of 8 + label 20.00 20.00
a.-h. 6.55fr Any single 2.50 1.50

2nd Historic Automobile Grand Prix — A762

2000, May 9 Litho. *Perf. 13½x13*

2158 A762 4.40fr multi 1.90 1.00

Monaco Pavilion, Expo 2000, Hanover A763

2000, May 9 *Perf. 13x13¼*

2159 A763 5fr multi 2.00 1.25

Saints Mark, Matthew, John and Luke — A764

2000, May 9 Engr. *Perf. 12¾x13*

2160 A764 20fr multi 8.00 8.00

Europa, 2000

Common Design Type and

Flags and Map of Europe — A765

2000, May 9 Litho. *Perf. 13¼x13*

2161 CD17 3fr multi 1.40 .70
2162 A765 3fr multi 1.40 .70
a. Pair, #2161-2162 3.00 3.00

WIPA 2000 Philatelic Exhibition, Vienna — A766

2000, May 30 Engr. *Perf. 13¼*

2163 A766 4.50fr multi 1.40 1.00

Professional-Celebrity Golf Tournament, Monte Carlo — A767

2000, June 19 Photo. *Perf. 13¼*

2164 A767 4.40fr multi 1.75 1.00

Club de Monte Carlo Exhibition of Rare Philatelic Material — A768

2000, June 23

2165 A768 3.50fr multi 1.40 .75

Red Cross — A769

2000, June 23

2166 A769 10fr multi 3.50 2.00

2000 Summer Olympics, Sydney A770

Olympic rings and: 2.70fr, Fencing, emblem of Monegasque Fencing Federation. 4.50fr, Rowers, flag of Monegasque Nautical Society.

2000, June 23 Engr. & Embossed

2167-2168 A770 Set of 2 2.50 1.75

Automobiles in Prince Rainier III Collection — A771

Woman and: 3fr, 1911 Humber Type Beeston. 6.70fr, 1947 Jaguar 4 cylinder. 10fr, 1956 Rolls-Royce Silver Cloud. 15fr, 1986 Lamborghini Countach.

2000, June 23 Engr. ***Perf. 13x13¼***
2169-2172 A771 Set of 4 13.00 10.50

See Nos. 2186-2188.

World Stamp Expo 2000, Anaheim — A772

2000, July 7 Litho. ***Perf. 13¼x13***
2173 A772 4.40fr multi 1.50 .90

Magic Stars Magic Festival, Monte Carlo — A773

2000, Sept. 4 Photo. ***Perf. 13¼***
2174 A773 4.60fr multi 1.75 1.25

Intl. Mathematics Year — A774

2000, Sept. 4 Engr.
2175 A774 6.50fr brown 2.50 1.50

Souvenir Sheet

Retable of St. Nicholas, by Ludovic Bréa, Monaco Cathedral — A775

No. 2176: a, Two figures, (31x52mm). b, Three figures, (53x52mm).

2000, Sept. 4 Photo.
2176 A775 Sheet of 2 12.00 12.00
a. 10fr multicolored 3.50 1.75
b. 20fr multicolored 6.50 4.50

New Aquarium, Oceanographic Museum — A776

2000, Oct. 2 Engr.
2177 A776 3fr multi 2.00 .70

España 2000 Intl. Philatelic Exhibition A777

2000, Oct. 2
2178 A777 3.80fr multi 1.50 .80

Observatory Grotto, 50th Anniv. and Anthropological Museum, 40th Anniv. — A778

2000, Oct. 2
2179 A778 5.20fr multi 2.00 .80

Fish A779

5fr, Fish, coral. 9fr, Fish, starfish, seaweed.

2000, Oct. 2 Photo.
2180-2181 A779 Set of 2 5.50 3.00

Fifth Congress of Aquariums (No. 2180), Monegasque Nature Protection Association, 25th anniv. (No. 2181).

Fifth Congress of Aquariums — A780

2000, Nov. 25 Photo. ***Perf. 13x12¾***
2182 A780 7fr multi 2.50 1.75

Christmas A781

2000, Dec. 1 Photo. ***Perf. 13¼***
2183 A781 3fr multi 1.40 .50

Princess Stephanie, President of AMAPEI — A782

2000, Dec. 1 Engr.
2184 A782 11.50fr red & slate 4.25 3.00

Souvenir Sheet

Monaco 2000 Intl. Philatelic Exhibition — A783

2001, Dec. 1 Photo. ***Imperf.***
2185 A783 Sheet of 2 #2185a 17.00 17.00
a. 20fr multi 8.00 8.00

Prince's Automobiles Type of 2000

Woman and: 5fr, 1989 Ferrari F1. 6fr, 1955 Fiat 600 Type Jolly. 8fr, 1929 Citroen C4F Autochenille.

2000, Dec. 1 Engr. ***Perf. 13x13¼***
2186-2188 A771 Set of 3 7.50 4.50

Exhibit of Chinese Terra-cotta Figures, Grimaldi Forum — A784

2000, Dec. 2 Photo. ***Perf. 13¼***
2189 A784 2.70fr multi 1.00 .40

Postal Museum, 50th Anniv. — A785

2000, Dec. 2
2190 A785 3fr multi 1.25 .50

Coat of Arms — A786

Serpentine Die Cut 11
2000, Dec. 4 Photo.
Booklet Stamp
Self-Adhesive
2191 A786 (3fr) red & black 1.25 .30
a. Booklet of 10 12.50

See Nos. 2389, 2410, 2673, 2775, 2863. Compare with Type A1076.

Princess Caroline of Monaco Iris — A787

2000, Dec. 2 Photo. ***Perf. 13¼***
2192 A787 3.80fr multi 1.50 .70

34th Intl. Flower Show.

Sardinian Postage Stamps, 150th Anniv. (in 2001) A788

2000, Dec. 2 Engr. ***Perf. 13x12½***
2193 A788 6.50fr Sardinia #1-3 2.50 1.75

RAMOGE Agreement, 25th Anniv. A789

2000, Dec. 2
2194 A789 6.70fr multi 2.50 1.75

Awarding of ASCAT Grand Prize to Bertrand Piccard — A790

2000, Dec. 2 Photo. ***Perf. 13¼***
2195 A790 9fr Balloon, #1433 3.50 2.00

Monaco Team, 2000 French Soccer Champions A791

2000, Dec. 3
2196 A791 4.50fr multi 1.75 .90

French, Italian and Monegasque Marine Mammal Sanctuary — A792

2000, Dec. 3
2197 A792 5.20fr multi 2.25 1.25

Neapolitan Creche, Natl. Museum — A793

2000, Dec. 3 ***Perf. 13x12½***
2198 A793 10fr multi 3.50 3.00

25th Intl. Circus Festival, Monte Carlo — A794

No. 2200: a, Clown with guitar. b, Clown. c, Tiger and tent top. d, Acrobats, tiger, lion, horses, clowns. e, Chimpanzee and high-wire acrobat.

2000, Dec. 3 ***Perf. 13¼***
2199 A794 2.70fr shown 1.25 .60
2200 A794 6fr Sheet of 5, #a-e + label 12.00 12.00

41st Intl. Television Festival, Monte Carlo — A795

2001, Feb. 5 Photo. ***Perf. 13½x13***
2201 A795 3.50fr multi 1.75 .90

Leonberger and Newfoundland — A796

2001, Apr. 14 Litho. ***Perf. 13x13¼***
2202 A796 6.50fr multi 2.50 1.25

Euroflora Flower Show — A797

2001, Apr. 21 Photo. ***Perf. 13¼***
2203 A797 6.70fr multi 2.50 1.25

Europa — A798

Designs: No. 2204, 3fr, Palace of Monaco, water droplets. No. 2205, 3fr, Wash house.

2001, May 7 Litho. ***Perf. 13½x13***
2204-2205 A798 Set of 2 2.75 1.10

Prince Rainier III Literary Prize, 50th Anniv. — A799

2001, May 14 Engr. ***Perf. 13¼***
2206 A799 2.70fr multi 1.00 .45

André Malraux (1901-76), Novelist — A800

2001, May 14 Litho. ***Perf. 13¼x13***
2207 A800 10fr black & red 3.50 1.75

Belgica 2001 Intl. Stamp Exhibition, Brussels — A801

2001, June 9 Engr. ***Perf. 13¼***
2208 A801 4fr brt blue & red 1.50 .70

2001 Philatelic and Numismatic Bourse — A802

2001, July 2 Photo. ***Perf. 13¼***
2209 A802 2.70fr multi 1.00 .45

Princess Grace Dance Academy, 25th Anniv. — A803

2001 July 2 Photo. ***Perf. 13¼***
2210 A803 4.40fr multi 1.75 .90

Naval Museum A804

2001, July 2 Photo. ***Perf. 13¼***
2211 A804 4.50fr multi 1.75 .90

37th Petanque World Championships — A805

2001, July 2 ***Perf. 13x13¼***
2212 A805 5fr multi 1.90 .80

Emile Littré, Denis Diderot, and Reference Books A806

2001, Aug. 1 Engr. ***Perf. 13¼***
2213 A806 4.20fr multi 1.50 .95

Prince Albert I Oceanography Prize, 30th Anniv. — A807

2001, Aug. 1 Engr. ***Perf. 13¼***
2214 A807 9fr bright blue 3.50 1.50

David, by Michelangelo, 500th Anniv. — A808

2001, Aug. 1 Engr. ***Perf. 13***
2215 A808 20fr multi 7.50 7.50

Palace of Monaco — A809

Designs: 3fr, Fireplace, Throne Hall. 4.50fr, Blue Hall. 6.70fr, York Chamber. 15fr, Fresco, ceiling of Throne Hall.

2001, Aug. 1 Photo. ***Perf. 13x13¼***
2216-2219 A809 Set of 4 10.00 6.50

A810

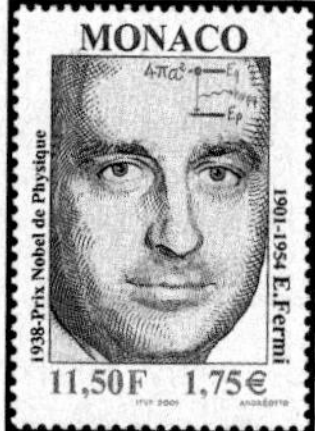

Nobel Prizes, Cent. — A811

Designs: 5fr, Alfred Nobel. 8fr, Jean-Henri Dunant, 1901 Peace laureate. 11.50fr, Enrico Fermi, 1938 Physics laureate.

2001, Sept. 3 Engr. ***Perf. 13¼***
2220 A810 5fr multi 2.00 .95
2221 A810 8fr multi 3.00 1.50
2222 A811 11.50fr multi 4.00 3.25
Nos. 2220-2222 (3) 9.00 5.70

36th Meeting of Intl. Commission for Scientific Exploration of the Mediterranean — A812

2001, Oct. 1 Photo. ***Perf. 13x13¼***
2223 A812 3fr multi 1.25 .50

Christmas — A813

2001, Oct. 1 ***Perf. 13¼***
2224 A813 3fr multi 1.25 .50

100 Cents = 1 Euro (€)

Flora & Fauna A814

Designs: 1c, Arctia caja, vert. 2c, Luria lurida. 5c, Thunbergia grandiflora, vert. 10c, Parus major. 20c, Anthias anthias. 50c, Charaxes jasius, vert. €1, Mitra zonata. €2, Datura sanguinea, vert. €5, Parus cristatus, vert. €10, Macroamphosus scolopax.

2002, Jan. 1 Engr. ***Perf. 13¼***
2225 A814 1c multi .25 .25
2226 A814 2c multi .25 .25
2227 A814 5c multi .25 .25
2228 A814 10c multi .25 .25
2229 A814 20c multi .45 .25
2230 A814 50c multi 1.10 .75
2231 A814 €1 multi 2.25 1.50
2232 A814 €2 multi 4.50 3.00
2233 A814 €5 multi 11.00 7.50
2234 A814 €10 multi 22.50 15.00
Nos. 2225-2234 (10) 42.80 29.00

See Nos. 2275, 2323-2324.

Palace of Monaco A815

Designs: 41c, Gallery of Mirrors, vert. 46c, Throne room. 58c, Painting in Gallery of Mirrors.

2002, Jan. 1 **Photo.**
2235-2237 A815 Set of 3 3.50 2.00

26th Intl. Circus Festival — A816

2002, Jan. 1
2238 A816 41c multi 1.00 .60

35th Intl. Flower Show A817

2002, Jan. 1
2239 A817 53c multi 1.25 .75

Souvenir Sheet

Automobile Club of Monaco — A818

No. 2240: a, Old and new cars, emblem of 70th Monte Carlo Rally. b, Racing cars in 3rd Historic Grand Prix and 60th Grand Prix races.

2002, Jan. 16 ***Perf. 13¼x13***
2240 A818 Sheet of 2 5.50 5.50
a. €1.07 multi 2.25 1.50
b. €1.22 multi 3.00 1.75

Prehistoric Anthropology Museum, Cent. — A819

2002, Feb. 8 ***Perf. 13¼***
2241 A819 64c multi 1.60 .95

La Carrière d'un Navigateur, by Prince Albert I, Cent. A820

2002, Feb. 8
2242 A820 67c multi 1.75 1.00

2002 Winter Olympics, Salt Lake City — A821

No. 2243: a, Denomination at UL. b, Denomination at UR.

2002, Feb. 8 ***Perf. 12¼***
2243 A821 Horiz. pair 1.00 1.00
a.-b. 23c Either single .50 .50

Jules Cardinal Mazarin (1602-61) A822

2002, Feb. 18
2244 A822 69c multi 2.00 1.00

Legion of Honor, Bicent. — A823

2002, Feb. 18 ***Perf. 13¼***
2245 A823 70c multi 1.75 1.00

Cetacean Conservation Accord — A824

2002, Feb. 18 **Engr.**
2246 A824 75c multi 2.25 1.10

Leonardo da Vinci (1452-1519) — A825

2002, Mar. 21 **Photo.**
2247 A825 76c multi 2.25 1.10

St. Bernard and Swiss Bouvier A826

2002, Mar. 21 **Engr.**
2248 A826 99c multi 2.50 1.50

Intl. Dog Show. See Nos. 2286, 2491.

Police, Cent. — A827

2002, Apr. 23 **Photo.**
2249 A827 53c multi 1.50 .70

European Academy of Philately, 25th Anniv. A828

2002, Apr. 27 **Engr.**
2250 A828 58c multi 1.25 .85

20th Intl. Swimming Meet — A829

2002, May 3 **Photo.** ***Perf. 13¼***
2251 A829 64c multi 1.60 .95

Europa — A830

Designs: No. 2252, 46c, Clown on globe, juggler, elephant, tent tops. No. 2253, 46c, "Jours de Cirque," circus acts.

2002, May 3
2252-2253 A830 Set of 2 *2.75 1.25*

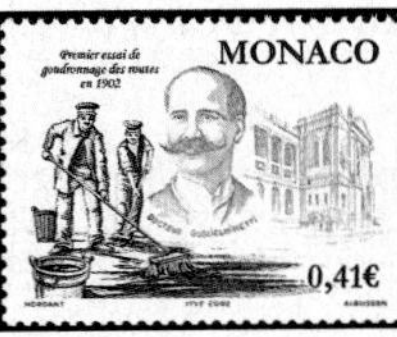

First Experiment with Tar Roads, Cent. A831

2002, May 31 **Engr.**
2254 A831 41c multi 1.00 .60

MonacoPhil 2002 Intl. Philatelic Exhibition — A832

2002, May 31
2255 A832 46c multi 1.00 .65

42nd Intl. Television Festival, Monte Carlo — A833

2002, May 31 **Photo.** ***Perf. 13¼x13***
2256 A833 70c multi 1.50 1.00

2002 World Cup Soccer Championships, Japan and Korea — A834

2002, May 31 **Engr.** ***Perf. 13¼***
2257 A834 75c multi 1.50 1.10

"Pelléas et Mélisande," Opera by Claude Debussy, Cent. of Debut — A835

2002, June 21
2258 A835 69c multi 1.40 1.00

Saint Dévote, Dove and Boat A836

2002, June 21
2259 A836 €1.02 multi 2.50 1.50

Red Cross.

Intl. Year of Mountains A837

2002, June 21 **Litho.** ***Perf. 13x13¼***
2260 A837 €1.37 multi 3.25 2.00

Euro Coinage — A838

No. 2261: a, Obverse of 1c, 2c, and 5c coins and reverse. b, Obverse of 10c, 20c, and 50c coins and reverse.

No. 2262: a, Obverse and reverse of €1 coin. b, Obverse and reverse of €2 coin.

Litho. & Embossed

2002, June 21 ***Perf. 13¼***
2261 A838 Horiz. pair 3.00 3.00
a.-b. 46c Either single 1.40 .70
2262 A838 Horiz. pair 9.25 9.25
a.-b. €1.50 Either single 4.50 4.50

Victor Hugo (1802-85), Writer — A839

No. 2263: a, Hugo and illustration from *Notre-Dame de Paris.* b, Hugo and illustration from *La Légende de Siécles.*

2002, July 1 Engr. *Perf. 13¼*
2263 A839 Horiz. pair 2.50 2.50
a. 50c multi 1.25 .75
b. 57c multi 1.25 .85

Alexandre Dumas (Father) (1802-70), Writer — A840

No. 2264: a, Dumas. b, Characters, manuscript.

2002, July 1 Photo.
2264 A840 Horiz. pair 2.50 2.50
a.-b. 61c Either single 1.25 .85

26th Publication of "Annales Monegasques" A841

2002, July 15
2265 A841 €1.75 multi 4.25 2.50

Christmas — A842

2002, Sept. 2
2266 A842 50c multi 1.25 .75

Debut of Movie "Le Voyage dans le Lune," by Georges Méliès, Cent. — A843

2002, Sept. 2 *Perf. 13¼*
2267 A843 76c multi 1.75 1.10

17th Magic Stars Magic Festival, Monte Carlo — A844

2002, Sept. 2
2268 A844 €1.52 multi 3.50 2.25

Awarding of ASCAT Grand Prize to Luis Figo — A845

2002, Nov. 29 Engr.
2269 A845 91c multi 1.90 1.25

Automobiles in Prince Rainier III Collection A846

Designs: 46c, 1949 Mercedes 220A Cabriolet. 69c, 1956 Rolls-Royce Silver Cloud I. €1.40, 1974 Citroen DS 21.

2002, Nov. 29 Photo.
2270-2272 A846 Set of 3 6.50 3.75

Souvenir Sheet

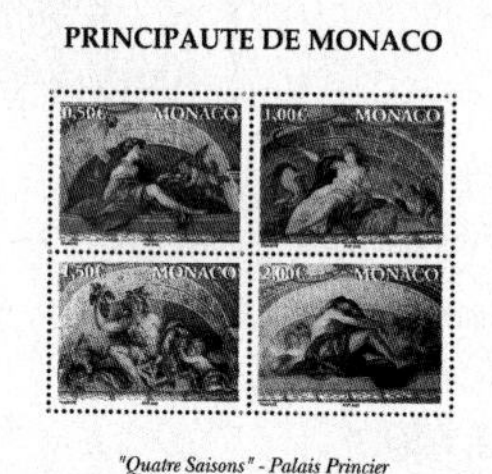

The Four Seasons, Frescos in Prince's Palace — A847

2002, Nov. 29 *Perf. 13x13¼*
2273 A847 Sheet of 4 12.00 12.00
a. 50c Spring 1.00 .75
b. €1 Summer 2.00 1.50
c. €1.50 Autumn 3.00 2.25
d. €2 Winter 4.00 3.00

Souvenir Sheet

MonacoPhil 2002 Intl. Philatelic Exhibition — A848

No. 2274: a, Monaco attractions. b, Emblem of Club de Monte Carlo.

2002, Nov. 29 *Imperf.*
2274 A848 Sheet of 2 14.00 14.00
a.-b. €3 Either single 6.00 6.00

Flora & Fauna Type of 2002

41c, Helix aspersa, vert.

2002, Nov. 30 Engr. *Perf. 13¼*
2275 A814 41c multi 1.00 .60

36th Intl. Flower Show — A849

2002, Nov. 30 Photo.
2276 A849 67c multi 1.75 1.00

World Association of Friends of Children, 40th Anniv. (in 2003) A850

2002, Nov. 30
2277 A850 €1.25 multi 3.00 1.75

Martyrdom of St. George, 1700th Anniv. — A851

2002, Dec. 1
2278 A851 53c multi 1.30 .70

Saint Cyr Military School, Bicent. — A852

2002, Dec. 1
2279 A852 61c multi 1.50 .85

27th Intl. Circus Festival — A853

2003, Jan. 2 Photo. *Perf. 13¼*
2280 A853 59c multi 1.25 .70

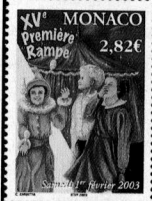

15th New Circus Artists' Festival — A854

2003, Feb. 1
2281 A854 €2.82 multi 6.50 4.00

10th World Bobsled Push Championships, Ilsenberg, Germany — A855

2003, Feb. 3
2282 A855 80c multi 1.75 .95

Monaco Yacht Club, 50th Anniv. — A856

2003, Feb. 5
2283 A856 46c multi 1.00 .60

Intl. Institute for Peace, Cent. — A857

2003, Mar. 3
2284 A857 €1.19 multi 2.75 1.75

Tennis Tournament at Monte Carlo Country Club, 75th Anniv. — A858

2003, Mar. 3
2285 A858 €1.30 multi 3.00 2.00

Dog Show Type of 2002

2003, Mar. 24 Litho. *Perf. 13x13½*
2286 A826 79c Rough collie 2.00 1.25

Junior Economic Chamber of Monaco, 40th Anniv. A859

2003, Apr. 5 Photo. *Perf. 13¼*
2287 A859 41c multi 1.00 .60

Monte Carlo Country Club, 75th Anniv. A860

2003, Apr. 12
2288 A860 46c multi 1.00 .70

General Bathymetric Charts of the Oceans, Cent. — A861

No. 2289: a, Prince Albert I, map of Arctic region, chart of Northern hemisphere. b, Oceanographic museum, map of Antarctica, chart of Southern hemisphere.

2003, Apr. 14 ***Perf. 13x12½***
2289 A861 €1.25 Vert. pair, #a-b 5.50 5.50

Poster by Alfons Mucha — A862

Poster by Jean-Gabriel Domergue — A863

2003, May 5 ***Perf. 13¼***
2290 A862 50c multi 1.50 .75
2291 A863 50c multi 1.50 .75

Europa.

Grand Bourse 2003 — A864

2003, June 2
2292 A864 45c multi 1.00 .70

43rd Intl. Television Festival, Monte Carlo — A865

2003, June 2 ***Perf. 13¼x13***
2293 A865 90c multi 2.00 1.25

15th Antiques Biennale — A866

2003, June 2 ***Perf. 13¼***
2294 A866 €1.80 multi 4.00 2.75

Navigation of Northwest Passage by Roald Amundsen, Cent. A867

2003, June 30
2295 A867 90c multi 2.00 1.40

Powered Flight, Cent. A868

2003, June 30
2296 A868 €1.80 multi 4.00 2.75

Hector Berlioz (1803-69), Composer A869

2003, July 21 **Engr.**
2297 A869 75c red & black 1.75 1.10

Aram Khatchaturian (1903-78), Composer — A870

2003, July 21
2298 A870 €1.60 multi 4.00 2.40

Portrait of a Woman, by François Boucher (1703-70) A871

Self-portrait, by Vincent van Gogh (1853-90) — A872

Self-portrait, by Francesco Mazzola, "Il Parmigianino" (1503-40) — A873

2003, Aug. 6 ***Perf. 13¼x13***
2299 A871 €1.30 multi 3.00 1.90
2300 A872 €3 black & pink 7.00 4.25
2301 A873 €3.60 black & tan 8.00 5.00
Nos. 2299-2301 (3) 18.00 11.15

Discovery of Structure of DNA Molecule, 50th Anniv. — A874

2003, Sept. 1 ***Perf. 13¼***
2302 A874 58c multi 1.25 .85

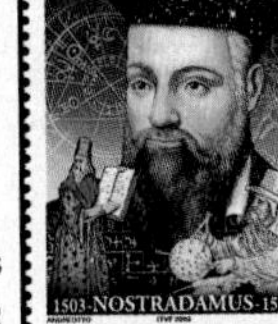

Nostradamus (1503-66), Astrologer — A875

2003, Sept. 1 **Photo.**
2303 A875 70c multi 1.60 1.00

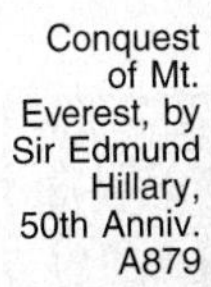

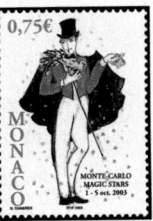

2003 Magic Stars Festival, Monte Carlo — A876

2003, Sept. 1 **Litho.** ***Perf. 13½x13***
2304 A876 75c multi 1.75 1.10

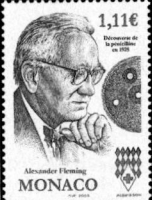

Discovery of Penicillin by Alexander Fleming, 75th Anniv. — A877

2003, Sept. 1 **Engr.** ***Perf. 13¼***
2305 A877 €1.11 multi 2.50 1.60

Awarding of Nobel Physics Prize to Pierre and Marie Curie, Cent. A878

2003, Sept. 1 **Photo.**
2306 A878 €1.20 multi 2.75 1.75

Conquest of Mt. Everest, by Sir Edmund Hillary, 50th Anniv. A879

2003, Sept. 29 **Engr.** ***Perf. 13¼***
2307 A879 €1 multi 2.25 1.50

Saint Dévote — A880

No. 2308: a, Kneeling before cross. b, Standing before soldiers. c, Boat and dove. d, Standing in front of church.

2003, Sept. 29
2308 A880 45c Block of 4, #a-d 4.00 4.00

Christmas — A881

2003, Oct. 13 **Photo.**
2309 A881 50c multi 1.25 .75

MonacoPhil 2004 Intl. Philatelic Exhibition — A882

2003, Dec. 15

2310	A882	50c multi	1.25	.75

28th Intl. Circus Festival, Monte Carlo — A883

2003, Dec. 15

2311	A883	70c multi	1.60	1.00

Beausoleil, France, Cent. A884

2004, Jan. 5 **Photo.** ***Perf. 13¼***

2312	A884	75c multi	1.75	1.10

Saint Dévote A885

Designs: 50c, Arrest of St. Dévote, vert. 75c, Proceedings against St. Dévote. 90c, Stoning of St. Dévote. €1, St. Dévote in boat, vert. €4, Protection of St. Dévote.

2004, Jan. 5 **Engr.**

2313	A885	50c red brn & red	1.10	.75
2314	A885	75c brn & orange	1.75	1.10
2315	A885	90c dk brn & brn	2.00	1.50
2316	A885	€1 dk brn & yel brn	2.50	1.50
2317	A885	€4 dk brn & red brn	9.00	6.00
		Nos. 2313-2317 (5)	16.35	10.85

6th Monegasque Biennale of Cancerology — A886

2004, Jan. 29 **Photo.** ***Perf. 13¼***

2318	A886	€1.11 multi	2.50	1.50

Princess Grace Foundation, 40th Anniv. — A887

Princess Grace Irish Library, 20th Anniv. A888

Statue of Princess Grace, by Daphné du Barry — A889

Princess Grace Rose Garden, 20th Anniv. — A890

Photo., Litho. (#2320-2321)

2004, Jan. 29

2319	A887	50c multi	1.25	.75
2320	A888	€1.11 grn & brown	2.50	1.50
2321	A889	€1.45 multi	3.25	2.00
2322	A890	€1.90 multi	4.50	2.75
		Nos. 2319-2322 (4)	11.50	7.00

Flora & Fauna Type of 2002

Designs: 75c, Hyla meridionalis, vert. €4.50, Lacerta viridis, vert.

2004, Mar. 8 **Engr.** ***Perf. 13¼***

2323	A814	75c multi	2.00	1.10
2324	A814	€4.50 multi	10.00	6.75

20th Spring of Arts A891

2004, Apr. 2

2325	A891	€1 multi	2.50	1.50

Cathedral Choir School, Cent. — A892

2004, Apr. 5 **Photo.**

2326	A892	45c multi	1.00	.70

37th Intl. Flower Show — A893

2004, Apr. 5

2327	A893	58c multi	1.40	.85

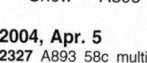

Dog Show Type of 2002

90c, Cavalier King Charles Spaniel.

2004, Apr. 9 **Litho.** ***Perf. 13x13¼***

2328	A826	90c multi	2.00	1.40

Monaco Grand Prix, 75th Anniv. A894

2004, Apr. 14 **Photo.** ***Perf. 13¼***

2329	A894	€1.20 multi	2.75	1.75

International School of Monaco, 10th Anniv. — A895

2004, Apr. 26 **Litho.** ***Perf. 13x13¼***

2330	A895	50c multi	1.25	.75

Europa — A896

Travel posters: No. 2331, 50c, Shown. No. 2332, 50c, Women in bathing suits at beach.

2004, May 3 **Photo.** ***Perf. 13¼***

2331-2332	A896	Set of 2	3.00	1.50

Order of Grimaldi, 50th Anniv. — A897

Litho. & Embossed

2004, May 3 ***Perf. 13¼x13***

2333	A897	90c multi	2.25	1.40

2004 Summer Olympics, Athens — A898

No. 2334: a, Stadium, modern runners. b, Stadium, ancient runners.

2004, May 3 ***Perf. 13x13¼***

2334	A898	45c Vert. pair, #a-b	2.25	1.40

Napoleon I and Monegasque Princes in Imperial Army — A899

Stéphanie de Beauharnais, by Baron Gérard — A900

Designs: 75c, Imperial symbols of Napoleon I, horiz. €2.40, Napoleon I, by Gérard.

Perf. 12¼x13, 13x13¼ (75c)

2004, May 28 **Photo.**

2335	A899	58c multi	1.40	.85
2336	A899	75c multi	1.75	1.10
2337	A900	€1.90 multi	4.50	2.75
2338	A900	€2.40 multi	5.50	3.50
		Nos. 2335-2338 (4)	13.15	8.20

Sergey Diaghilev (1872-1929), George Balanchine (1904-83) and Dancers of Ballet Russes de Monte Carlo — A901

2004, June 14 **Engr.** ***Perf. 13¼***

2339	A901	€1.60 multi	4.00	2.40

44th Television Festival, Monte Carlo — A902

2004, June 14 **Litho.** ***Perf. 13¼x13***

2340	A902	€1.80 multi	4.25	2.75

Frédéric Mistral (1830-1914), 1904 Nobel Laureate in Literature — A903

2004, June 26 **Engr.** ***Perf. 13¼***

2341	A903	45c multi	1.10	.70

23rd UPU Congress, Bucharest, Romania A904

2004, June 26
2342 A904 50c multi 1.25 .75

Marco Polo (1254-1324), Explorer — A905

2004, June 26
2343 A905 50c multi 1.25 .75

Salon du Timbre, Paris A906

2004, June 26
2344 A906 75c multi 1.75 1.10

Translation into French of *A Thousand and One Nights*, 300th Anniv. — A907

Litho. & Silk Screened
2004, June 26 ***Perf. 13x13¼***
2345 A907 €1 deep blue & gray 2.50 1.50

Monte Carlo Beach Hotel, 75th Anniv. A908

2004, July 5 **Photo.** ***Perf. 13¼***
2346 A908 45c multi 1.00 .70

FIFA (Fédération Internationale de Football Association), Cent. — A909

2004, Aug. 2
2347 A909 €1.60 multi 4.00 2.40

Magic Stars Magic Festival, Monte Carlo A910

2004, Sept. 6 **Litho.** ***Perf. 13x13¼***
2348 A910 45c multi 1.10 .70

Souvenir Sheet

Princess Grace (1929-82) — A911

Portraits of Princess Grace engraved by: a, 75c, Pierre Albuisson. b, €1.75, Czeslaw Slania. c, €3.50, Martin Mörck.

2004, Oct. 4 **Engr.** ***Perf. 13¼x13***
2349 A911 Sheet of 3 + label 14.00 14.00
a. 75c green & blue 1.75 1.10
b. €1.75 green & blue 4.00 2.50
c. €3.50 green & blue 7.50 5.25

See No. 2367.

Christmas A912

2004, Oct. 4 **Photo.** ***Perf. 13¼***
2350 A912 50c multi 1.25 .75

Admission to Council of Europe A913

2004, Oct. 5 **Engr.** ***Perf. 13x12½***
2351 A913 50c red & blue 1.25 .75

29th Intl. Circus Festival, Monte Carlo — A914

2004, Dec. 3 **Photo.** ***Perf. 13¼***
2352 A914 45c multi 1.10 .70

Louis II Stadium, 20th Anniv. — A915

2004, Dec. 3 **Engr.** ***Perf. 12½x13***
2353 A915 50c multi 1.25 .75

University of Paris Student Hostel, 70th Anniv. — A916

2004, Dec. 3 ***Perf. 13¼***
2354 A916 58c multi 1.40 .85

Palace of Justice, 75th Anniv. — A917

2004, Dec. 3 **Photo.**
2355 A917 75c multi 1.75 1.10

French Alliance of Monaco, 25th Anniv. — A918

2004, Dec. 3
2356 A918 75c multi 1.75 1.10

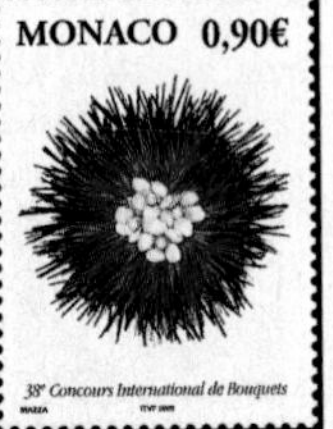
38th Intl. Flower Show — A919

2004, Dec. 3 **Photo.** ***Perf. 13¼***
2357 A919 90c multi 2.25 1.40

Luigi Valentino Brugnatelli (1761-1818), Inventor of Electroplating — A920

Litho. & Engr.
2004, Dec. 3 ***Perf. 13¼***
2358 A920 €1 blk & brn 2.50 1.50

Jean-Paul Sartre (1905-80), Author A921

2004, Dec. 3 **Photo.**
2359 A921 €1.11 multi 2.50 1.60

Invention of Safety Matches by Johan Edvard Lundstrom, 150th Anniv. A922

2004, Dec. 3
2360 A922 €1.20 multi 2.75 1.75

Publication of Don Quixote, by Miguel de Cervantes, 400th Anniv. — A923

2004, Dec. 3 **Engr.**
2361 A923 €1.20 multi 3.00 1.75

Léo Ferré (1916-93), Singer A924

2004, Dec. 3 **Photo.**
2362 A924 €1.40 multi 3.50 2.10

Invention of Hypodermic Syringe by Alexander Wood, 150th Anniv. — A925

2004, Dec. 3 **Engr.**
2363 A925 €1.60 multi 3.75 2.40

Development of Carbon 14 Dating by Willard F. Libby, 50th Anniv. — A926

2004, Dec. 3 ***Perf. 12½x13***
2364 A926 €1.80 multi 4.25 2.75

Princes and Palace of Monaco — A927

No. 2365: a, Prince Rainier III (30x31mm). b, Palace of Monaco (60x31mm). c, Hereditary Prince Albert (30x31mm).

2004, Dec. 3 ***Perf. 13¼***
2365 A927 50c Horiz. strip of 3, #a-c 3.50 3.00

First World Cup Soccer Championships, 75th Anniv. — A928

No. 2366: a, World Cup, goalie catching soccer ball. b, Flag of Uruguay, player dribbling ball.

2004, Dec. 3 Photo. *Perf. 13¼*
2366 A928 €1 Horiz. pair, #a-b 4.50 3.00

Princess Grace Type of 2004 in Changed Colors with "MonacoPhil 2004" Added in Sheet Margin
Souvenir Sheet

Designs like No. 2349.

2004, Dec. 3 Engr. *Imperf.*
2367 A911 Sheet of 3 14.00 14.00
a. 75c blue & emerald 1.75 2.25
b. €1.75 blue & emerald 4.00 5.25
c. €3.50 blue & emerald 8.50 10.50

Rotary International, Cent. — A929

Designs: 55c, Rotary emblem, founder, president, treasurer and secretary of original club. 70c, Rotary emblem, vert.

Litho. & Engr., Litho. (70c)
Perf. 13¼, 13¼x13 (70c)
2005, Feb. 23
2368-2369 A929 Set of 2 2.75 1.90

UNESCO Fine Arts Committee, 50th Anniv. — A930

2005, Mar. 1 Photo. *Perf. 13¼*
2370 A930 48c multi 1.25 .70

Publication of Albert Einstein's Theory of Relativity, Cent. — A931

2005, Mar. 1
2371 A931 53c multi 1.25 .80

First Awarding of Diplomas From School of Fine Arts — A932

2005, Mar. 1 Litho. *Perf. 13¼x13*
2372 A932 64c black & red 1.60 .95

Dog Show Type of 2002

82c, Dachshund (teckel).

2005, Mar. 1 Photo. *Perf. 13¼*
2373 A826 82c multi 2.00 1.25

Intl. Automobile Federation, Cent. — A933

2005, Apr. 1 Photo. *Perf. 13¼*
2374 A933 55c multi 1.25 1.60

21st World Exhibition of Hybrid and Electric Vehicles A934

Designs, 75c, Fetish, first electric sports car. €1.30, Stylized automobile with electric plug.

2005, Apr. 1
2375-2376 A934 Set of 2 5.00 5.00

Tenth Horse Jumping International, Monte Carlo — A935

2005, Apr. 1 Engr. *Perf. 13¼*
2377 A935 90c multi 2.25 1.40

Food — A936

No. 2378, 53c: a, Pissaladière. b, Barbaguians.
No. 2379, 55c: a, Tourte de blettes. b, Desserts.

2005, May 3 Photo.
Horiz. Pairs, #a-b
2378-2379 A936 Set of 2 *5.00 4.00*
Europa (#2378).

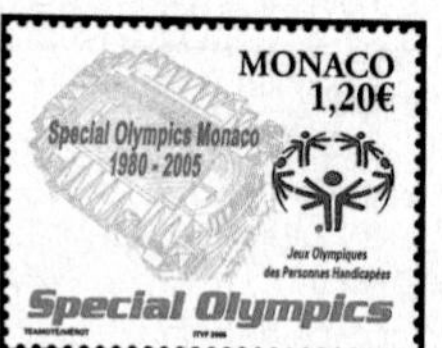

Monegasque Special Olympics, 25th Anniv. — A937

2005, June 3 Litho. *Perf. 13x13¼*
2380 A937 €1.20 multi 3.00 1.75

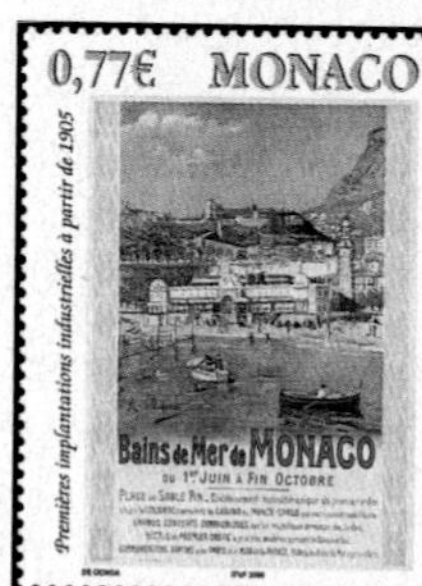

Early 20th Century Advertising Art A938

Advertisements for: 77c, Bains de Mer de Monaco. €2.50, English Sanitary Co. €3.10, Scapini Biscuits.

2005, June 3 Photo. *Perf. 12¼x13*
2381-2383 A938 Set of 3 15.00 9.50

Monaco Yacht Show — A939

2005, July 4 *Perf. 13¼*
2384 A939 82c multi 2.00 1.25

Admission to UPU, 50th Anniv. — A940

2005, July 4 Engr.
2385 A940 €3.03 multi 7.50 4.50

Astronomers A941

Designs: €1.22, Edmond Halley (1656-1742). €1.98, Gerard P. Kuiper (1905-73). €3.80, Clyde Tombaugh (1906-97).

2005, July 4 *Perf. 12½x13*
2386-2388 A941 Set of 3 17.00 10.50

Coat of Arms Type of 2000 Inscribed "20g Ecopli" at Top
Serpentine Die Cut 11
2005, July 12 Photo.
Booklet Stamp
Self-Adhesive
2389 A786 (48c) grn, blk & red 1.10 1.10
a. Booklet pane of 10 11.00

10th European Patrimony Day — A942

2005, Sept. 5 Engr. *Perf. 13¼*
2390 A942 48c multi 1.10 1.00

20th Magic Stars Festival, Monte Carlo A943

2005, Sept. 5 Litho. *Perf. 13x13¼*
2391 A943 €1.45 red, gold & blk 3.50 3.00

Christmas A944

2005, Oct. 3 Engr. *Perf. 13¼*
2392 A944 53c blk & red 1.40 1.10

Monte Carlo Bay Hotel and Resort A945

2005, Oct. 7 Photo.
2393 A945 55c multi 1.40 1.10

Nadia Boulanger (1887-1979), Conductor, and Lili Boulanger (1893-1918), Composer — A946

2005, Oct. 21 Engr.
2394 A946 90c multi 2.25 1.75

Miniature Sheet

Restoration of Garnier Hall, Monte Carlo Opera — A947

No. 2395: a, "Song." b, Garnier Hall. c, "Comedy." d, "Dance." e, Charles Garnier (1825-98), architect. f, "Music."

2005, Nov. 16
2395 A947 82c Sheet of 6, #a-f 14.50 14.50

Souvenir Sheet

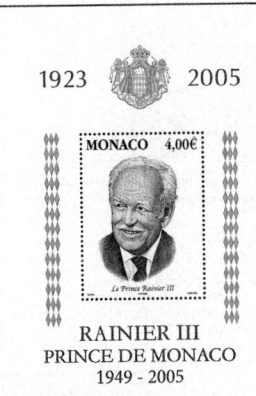

Prince Rainier III (1923-2005) — A948

2005, Nov. 19 *Perf. 13*
2396 A948 €4 black 12.00 12.00

Prince Albert II — A949

2005, Nov. 19 *Perf. 13x13¼*

2397 A949 (48c) green	1.10	1.10
2398 A949 (53c) red	1.25	1.25
2399 A949 (75c) blue	1.75	1.75
Nos. 2397-2399 (3)	4.10	4.10

National Day — A950

No. 2400: a, Fontveille (26x27mm, country name at UL). b, Palace (56x27mm). c, La Condamine and Monte Carlo (26x27mm, country name at UR).

2005, Nov. 19 **Photo.** *Perf. 13¼*
2400 A950 €1.01 Horiz. strip of 3, #a-c 7.00 7.00

MonacoPhil 2006 Philatelic Exhibition A951

2005, Dec. 12
2401 A951 55c multi 1.25 1.25

30th Intl. Circus Festival, Monte Carlo — A952

A952a

No. 2403: a, Charles Rivel, 1974 Golden Clown. b, Fredy Knie, 1977 Golden Clown. c, Alexis Gruss, Sr., 1975 Golden Clown. d, Golden Clown award. e, Georges Carl, 1979 Golden Clown.

2005, Dec. 14
2402 A952 64c shown 1.75 1.40
2403 A952a 75c Sheet of 5, #a-e, + label 11.00 11.00

The label on No. 2403 has the same vignette as No. 2402, lacking country name and denomination, but with a gray background. Compare No. 2402 with No. 2825c.

A953

2006 Winter Olympics, Turin A954

No. 2404: a, Red mascot. b, Blue mascot.

2006, Jan. 9 **Photo.** *Perf. 13¼*
2404 A953 55c Horiz. pair, #a-b 2.75 2.75
2405 A954 82c multi 2.40 1.75

Museum of Postage Stamps and Money, 10th Anniv. A955

2006, Jan. 30 **Engr.**
2406 A955 53c multi 1.25 1.25

5th Intl. Film and Literature Forum — A956

2006, Feb. 6 **Photo.** *Perf. 13¼*
2407 A956 82c multi 2.00 1.75

Léopold Sédar Senghor (1906-2001), First President of Senegal — A957

Litho. & Engr.

2006, Mar. 6 *Perf. 13x13¼*
2408 A957 €1.45 multi 3.25 3.00

100th Monte Carlo Tennis Tournament A958

2006, Mar. 8 **Photo.** *Perf. 13¼*
2409 A958 55c multi 1.25 1.25

Coat of Arms Type of 2000 Inscribed "20g Zone A" at Top

Serpentine Die Cut 11

2006, Apr. 6 **Photo.**

Self-Adhesive

Booklet Stamp

2410 A786 (55c) red & black 1.25 1.25
a. Booklet pane of 10 12.50

Monte Carlo Philharmonic Orchestra, 150th Anniv. — A959

2006, Apr. 6 *Perf. 13¼*
2411 A959 64c multi 1.75 1.40

Arctic Oceanographic Expeditions of Prince Albert I, Cent. — A960

Litho. & Engr.

2006, Apr. 10 *Perf. 13x13¼*
2412 A960 €1.60 multi 4.00 3.50

Dog Show Type of 2002

64c, Special schnauzer.

2006, Apr. 14 **Photo.** *Perf. 13¼*
2413 A826 64c multi 1.75 1.25

39th Intl. Flower Show — A961

2006, Apr. 18
2414 A961 77c multi 2.00 1.60

2006 World Cup Soccer Championships, Germany — A962

No. 2415: a, World Cup, stadium. b, Stadium and 2006 World Cup emblem.

2006, Apr. 18
2415 A962 90c Horiz. pair, #a-b 4.50 3.00

A963

Europa A964

2006, May 5 **Photo.** *Perf. 13¼*
2416 A963 53c multi 1.25 1.25
2417 A964 55c multi 1.40 1.40

RAMOGE Agreement, 30th Anniv. — A965

2006, May 9 *Perf. 12¼x13*
2418 A965 €1.75 multi 4.50 4.50

Washington 2006 World Philatelic Exhibition A966

2006, May 27 **Engr.** *Perf. 13¼*
2419 A966 90c blue & red 2.25 1.75

John Huston (1906-87), Film Director — A967

2006, May 27 *Perf. 13x12¼*
2420 A967 €1.80 blk & hen brn 4.50 3.50

Prince Albert Challenge Sabre Tournament — A968

2006, June 6 Photo. ***Perf. 13¼***
2421 A968 48c multi 1.20 1.00

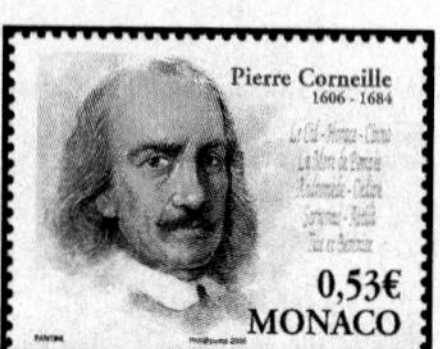

Pierre Corneille (1606-84), Dramatist A969

2006, June 17
2422 A969 53c multi 1.40 1.00

46th Intl. Television Festival, Monte Carlo — A970

2006, June 17
2423 A970 82c multi 2.00 1.75

Wolfgang Amadeus Mozart (1756-91), Composer — A971

2006, June 17 Engr. ***Perf. 13x12¼***
2424 A971 €1.22 org red & blue 3.00 2.50

Prince Pierre Foundation, 40th Anniv. — A972

2006, June 20 ***Perf. 12½x13***
2425 A972 €2.50 multi 6.25 5.50

Dino Buzzati (1906-72), Writer A973

2006, July 17 Photo. ***Perf. 13¼***
2426 A973 55c multi 1.40 1.10

Cetacean Conservation Accord, 10th Anniv. — A974

2006, July 17 ***Perf. 13x12¼***
2427 A974 90c multi 2.25 1.75

Luchino Visconti (1906-76), Film Director A975

2006, July 17 Engr. ***Perf. 12¼x13***
2428 A975 €1.75 henna brn 4.50 3.50

Rolls-Royce Automobiles, Cent. — A976

2006, Sept. 4 Engr. ***Perf. 13¼***
2429 A976 64c multi 1.75 1.40

2006 Magic Stars Festival, Monte Carlo — A977

2006, Sept. 4 Photo.
2430 A977 77c multi 2.00 1.50

Monaco Red Cross — A978

2006, Oct. 2
2431 A978 48c multi 1.20 1.00

Christmas A979

Perf. 13½x13¼

2006, Oct. 2 Litho. & Engr.
2432 A979 53c multi 1.40 1.00

Prince Albert II — A980

2006, Dec. 1 Engr. ***Perf. 13x13¼***
2433 A980 (49c) green 1.10 .75
2434 A980 (54c) red 1.50 1.10
a. Dated "2009" 1.50 1.10
2435 A980 (60c) blue 1.60 1.60
Nos. 2433-2435 (3) 4.20 3.45

Dated 2007.
No. 2434a sold for 56c when issued.

Prince Albert II and Coat of Arms A981

2006, Dec. 1 Photo. ***Perf. 13¼x13***
2436 A981 60c multi 1.50 1.20

Souvenir Sheet

Perf. 13x13¼

2437 A981 €6 multi 15.00 15.00

MonacoPhil 2006 Intl. Philatelic Exhibition. Dated 2007.

World AIDS Day A982

2006, Dec. 1 Litho. ***Perf. 13x13¼***
2438 A982 49c multi 1.20 1.00

Dated 2007.

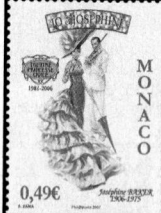

Josephine Baker (1906-75), Singer and Dancer — A983

2006, Dec. 1 ***Perf. 13¼x13***
2439 A983 49c multi 1.20 1.00

Princess Grace Theater, 25th anniv. Dated 2007.

Philatelic Anniversaries A984

2006, Dec. 1 Photo. ***Perf. 13¼***
2440 A984 54c multi 1.40 1.10

Creation of Philatelic Bureau, 70th anniv. (in 2007), Consultative Commission of the Prince's Philatelic Collection, 20th anniv. (in 2007). Dated 2007.

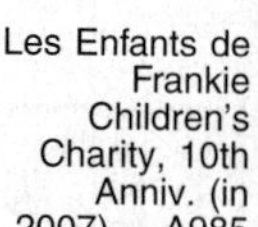

Les Enfants de Frankie Children's Charity, 10th Anniv. (in 2007) — A985

2006, Dec. 1
2441 A985 70c multi 1.75 1.50

Dated 2007.

Albert Camus (1913-60), 1957 Nobel Literature Laureate — A986

2006, Dec. 1 Engr.
2442 A986 84c multi 2.25 1.75

Dated 2007.

Auguste Escoffier (1846-1935), Chef — A987

2006, Dec. 1
2443 A987 85c multi 2.25 1.75

Dated 2007.

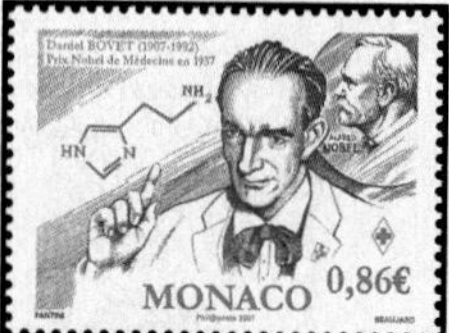

Daniel Bovet (1907-92), 1957 Nobel Medicine Laureate A988

2006, Dec. 1
2444 A988 86c dk blue & red 2.25 1.75

Dated 2007.

Cardiothoracic Center, 20th Anniv. (in 2007) — A989

2006, Dec. 1
2445 A989 €1.15 multi 3.00 2.50

Dated 2007.

Rudyard Kipling (1865-1936), 1907 Nobel Literature Laureate — A990

2006, Dec. 1
2446 A990 €1.57 multi 4.00 3.25

Dated 2007.

Opening of Institute of Sports Medicine and Surgery A991

2006, Dec. 1
2447 A991 €1.70 multi 4.25 3.50

Dated 2007.

Meeting of Prince Albert II and Pope Benedict XVI, 1st Anniv. — A992

2006, Dec. 1 Photo. ***Perf. 13x13¼***
2448 A992 €1.70 multi 4.25 4.00

Dated 2007.

Paul-Emile Victor (1907-95), Explorer — A993

2006, Dec. 1 Engr. ***Perf. 13x12¼***
2449 A993 €2.11 multi 5.25 4.50

Dated 2007.

European Philatelic Academy, 30th Anniv. (in 2007) — A994

2006, Dec. 1 Photo. ***Perf. 13x13¼***
2450 A994 €2.30 multi 5.75 5.00

Dated 2007.

Awarding of 2006 Grand Prix of Philately to Alexander D. Kroo — A995

2006, Dec. 1 Litho. ***Perf. 13¼x13***
2451 A995 €3 multi 7.50 6.50

Dated 2007.

Auto Racing — A996

No. 2452: a, 65th Monaco Grand Prix. b, 75th Monte Carlo Rally.

2006, Dec. 1
2452 A996 60c Horiz. pair, #a-b 3.00 2.75

Dated 2007.

Art in Grimaldi Forum by Nall — A997

No. 2453: a, Purple Flower. b, Yellow Flower

2006, Dec. 1 Photo. ***Perf. 13¼***
2453 A997 €1.70 Pair, #a-b 8.00 7.00

Printed in panes of 2 pairs. Dated 2007.

A998

31st Intl. Circus Festival, Monte Carlo — A999

2006, Dec. 1 Photo. ***Perf. 13¼***
2454 A998 60c multi 1.50 1.20

Litho.

Perf. 13¼x13
2455 A999 84c multi 2.25 1.75

Dated 2007.

Souvenir Sheet

40th Intl. Flower Show — A1000

No. 2456: a, Classic composition. b, Modern composition. c, Contemporary composition. d, Japanese composition.

2006, Dec. 1 Photo. ***Perf. 13¼***
2456 A1000 €1.30 Sheet of 4, #a-d 16.00 16.00

Dated 2007.

Stenella Coeruleoalba — A1001

2007, Jan. 2 Litho. ***Perf. 13x13¼***
2457 A1001 (36c) multi .95 .95

Issued precanceled only. See note after No. 324.

Giuseppe Garibaldi (1807-82), Italian Nationalist Leader A1002

2007, Mar. 16 Engr. ***Perf. 13¼***
2458 A1002 €1.40 ol brn & red 3.50 3.25

Carlo Goldoni (1707-93), Playwright A1003

Litho. & Silk-screened

2007, Mar. 16 ***Perf. 13x13¼***
2459 A1003 €4.54 multi 11.00 10.00

Monaco Olympic Committee, Cent. — A1004

2007, Apr. 2 Photo. ***Perf. 13¼***
2460 A1004 60c multi 1.40 1.20

Dalmatian A1005

2007, Apr. 2 ***Perf. 13x13¼***
2461 A1005 70c multi 1.75 1.40

Intl. Dog Show.

12th Games of Small European States A1006

2007, Apr. 2 ***Perf. 13¼***
2462 A1006 86c multi 2.00 1.75

Princess Grace Exposition, Grimaldi Forum A1007

2007, May 4 Litho. ***Perf. 13***
2463 A1007 85c multi 2.00 1.75

First Flight of Helicopter Designed by Maurice Leger, Cent. — A1008

2007, May 4 Engr. ***Perf. 12½x13***
2464 A1008 €1.15 multi 2.75 2.25

47th Television Festival, Monte Carlo — A1009

2007, May 4 Litho. ***Perf. 13¼x13***
2465 A1009 €2.90 multi 6.75 6.00

Scouting, Cent. — A1010

No. 2466: a, Scouts and campfire. b, Lord Robert Baden-Powell.

2007, May 4 Photo. ***Perf. 13¼***

2466 A1010 60c Horiz. pair, #a-b 3.75 3.75

Cartophily, Numismatics and Philately Grand Bourse — A1011

Litho. & Silk-Screened

2007, June 25 ***Perf. 13¼x13***

2467 A1011 49c multi 1.20 1.00

22nd Magic Stars Festival, Monte Carlo — A1012

2007, June 25 Litho.

2468 A1012 €1.30 red & black 3.00 2.50

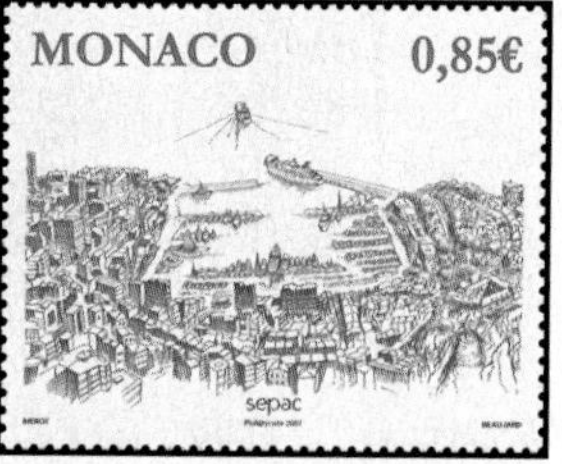

Monaco Harbor — A1013

2007, Oct. 1 Engr. ***Perf. 13x12½***

2469 A1013 85c multi 2.00 1.75

Christmas A1014

Litho. & Silk-screened

2007, Oct. 1 ***Perf. 13¼x13***

2470 A1014 54c multi 1.25 1.10

32nd Intl. Circus Festival, Monte Carlo — A1015

2007, Oct. 15 Photo. ***Perf. 13¼***

2471 A1015 60c multi 1.40 1.25

Giacomo Puccini (1858-1924), Composer A1016

2007, Dec. 7 Engr. ***Perf. 13¼***

2472 A1016 €1.40 blue & red 3.25 2.75

41st Intl. Flower Show — A1017

2008, Jan. 3 Photo.

2473 A1017 49c multi 1.10 1.00

Reformed Church of Monaco, 50th Anniv. — A1018

2008, Jan. 3 Engr. ***Perf. 13¼***

2474 A1018 49c blue & brown 1.10 1.10

Consecration of St. Charles Church, 125th Anniv. — A1019

2008, Mar. 3

2475 A1019 54c gray blue & red 1.25 1.10

Arc de Triomphe du Carrousel Quadriga, Paris, by François Joseph Bosio A1020

2008, Jan. 3

2476 A1020 54c multi 1.25 1.10

Andrea Palladio (1508-80), Architect A1021

2008, Jan. 3 Photo. ***Perf. 13¼***

2477 A1021 60c multi 1.25 1.25

10th Special Session of United Nations Environment Program, Monaco A1022

2008, Jan. 3 Photo. ***Perf. 13¼***

2478 A1022 85c multi 2.00 1.75

Johannes Brahms (1833-97), Composer A1023

2008, Jan. 3 Engr. ***Perf. 13¼***

2479 A1023 €1.15 Prus grn & red 2.75 2.25

Return of Comet Predicted by Edmond Halley, 250th Anniv. A1024

2008, Jan. 3 Photo. ***Perf. 13¼***

2480 A1024 €1.57 multi 3.50 3.00

Marcel Kroenlein Arboretum, Roure, France, 20th Anniv. — A1025

2008, Jan. 3 Engr. ***Perf. 13¼***

2481 A1025 €2.11 multi 4.75 4.00

Poster for Monte Carlo Country Club, by Raymond Gid A1026

Poster for Monte Carlo Beach Hotel, by Raymond Gid A1027

Poster for Monte Carlo Golf Club, by Raymond Gid A1028

Poster for Monte Carlo Tourism, by Louis Rué A1029

Perf. 12¼x13, 13 (#2483)

2008, Jan. 3 Photo., Litho. (#2483)

2482 A1026 70c multi 1.60 1.25
2483 A1027 85c multi 2.00 1.50
2484 A1028 €1.15 multi 2.75 2.25
2485 A1029 €2.90 multi 6.50 5.50
Nos. 2482-2485 (4) 12.85 10.50

Gen. André Massena (1758-1817) A1030

2008, Jan. 21 Engr. ***Perf. 13¼***

2486 A1030 86c grn & yel brown 2.00 1.50

Apparition at Lourdes, France, 150th Anniv. A1031

2008, Feb. 11 Engr. ***Perf. 13x12¾***

2487 A1031 €1.30 dark blue & blue 3.00 2.25

Introduction of the Ford Model T, Cent. — A1032

2008, Mar. 10 ***Perf. 13¼***

2488 A1032 €1.70 multi 3.75 3.25

National Aeronautics and Space Administration, 50th Anniv. — A1033

2008, Mar. 10
2489 A1033 €2.30 multi 5.00 4.00

Alfred Nobel (1833-1906), Inventor and Philantropist A1034

2008, Mar. 10
2490 A1034 €4 blk & claret 9.00 6.50

Dog Show Type of 2002

2008, Mar. 17 Photo. *Perf. 13¼*
2491 A826 88c Greyhound, vert. 2.00 1.50

Expo Zaragoza 2008 A1035

2008, Mar. 18 Litho. *Perf. 13x13¼*
2492 A1035 65c multi 1.50 1.00

Mother's Day — A1036

2008, Apr. 8 *Perf. 13¼x13*
2493 A1036 55c multi 1.25 .90

Stendhal (Marie-Henri Beyle) (1783-1842), Writer — A1037

2008, Apr. 8 Engr. *Perf. 13¼*
2494 A1037 €1.33 multi 3.00 2.25

Boris Pasternak (1890-1960), Writer — A1038

2008, Apr. 8
2495 A1038 €2.18 multi 5.00 3.50

2008 Summer Olympics, Beijing — A1039

No. 2496 — Olympic rings and: a, Pagoda, basketball, tennis, javelin. b, Beijing Olympics emblem, baseball, fencing, shooting.

2008, Apr. 8 *Perf. 13x12½*
2496 A1039 Horiz. pair 3.25 3.25
a. 55c red & black 1.25 1.00
b. 85c red & black 1.90 1.25

Cap d'Ail, France, Cent. A1040

2008, Apr. 21 Litho. *Perf. 13x13¼*
2497 A1040 55c multi 1.25 1.00

Exotic Garden, 75th Anniv. A1041

2008, May 2 Engr. *Perf. 13¼*
2498 A1041 50c multi 1.20 .90

2008 Magic Stars Festival, Monte Carlo — A1042

2008, May 5 Photo.
2499 A1042 72c multi 1.60 1.10

Europa A1043

Designs: 55c, Letters encircling globe. 65c, Postmen, letter, means of postal communication.

2008, May 5 Engr.
2500-2501 A1043 Set of 2 2.75 2.00

Intl. Skating Union, 52nd Congress A1044

2008, May 16 Litho. *Perf. 13¼x13*
2502 A1044 50c multi 1.25 1.00

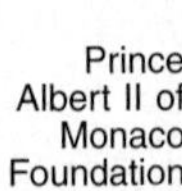

Prince Albert II of Monaco Foundation A1045

Litho. & Engr.

2008, May 16 *Perf. 13x13¼*
2503 A1045 88c multi 2.00 1.50

48th Intl. Television Festival, Monte Carlo — A1046

2008, June 2 Photo. *Perf. 13¼*
2504 A1046 €2.80 multi 6.25 4.50

Monegasque International Cooperation — A1047

Designs: 65c, Education. €1, Health. €1.25, Campaign against poverty. €1.70, Campaign against desertification.

2008, June 5 Engr.
2505-2508 A1047 Set of 4 10.00 7.50

Monaco 2008 Intl. Numismatic Exhibition A1048

Litho. & Embossed With Foil Application

2008, June 16 *Perf. 13½x13*
2509 A1048 65c multi 1.50 1.00

Schönbrunn Palace, Vienna — A1049

2008, Sept. 18 Engr. *Perf. 13¼*
2510 A1049 65c multi 1.50 1.00

WIPA 2008 Intl. Philatelic Exhibition, Vienna.

Order of Saint Charles, 150th Anniv. A1050

Photo. & Embossed With Foil Application

2008, Sept. 18 *Perf. 13x13¼*
2511 A1050 €1.50 multi 3.50 2.75

Coins of Monaco A1051

Obverse and reverse of: 50c, 1837 Franc. 55c, 1943 Franc. 72c, 1950 Franc. €1.25, 1960 Franc. €1.64, Euro coinage of 2002. €1.70, Euro coinage of 2006.

Litho. & Embossed With Foil Application

2008, Sept. 18
2512-2517 A1051 Set of 6 14.00 10.00

Christmas A1052

2008, Sept. 19 Photo. *Perf. 13¼*
2518 A1052 55c multi 1.25 1.00

33rd Intl. Circus Festival, Monte Carlo — A1053

2008, Dec. 19 Photo. *Perf. 13¼*
2519 A1053 85c multi 2.00 1.50

Prince Albert I — A1054

Flag of Monaco and Intl. Polar Year Emblem A1055

Prince Albert II — A1056

2008, Dec. 19 *Perf. 13x12¼*
2520 Horiz. strip of 3 6.00 6.00
a. A1054 85c multi 1.90 1.50
b. A1055 85c multi 1.90 1.50
c. A1056 85c multi 1.90 1.50

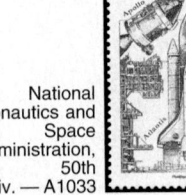

Admiral Robert E. Peary (1856-1920), Arctic Explorer, and Dog Sleds — A1057

Peary, Flag of US and Map of Arctic Area A1058

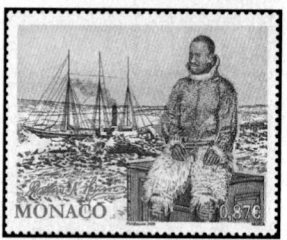

Matthew Henson (1866-1955), Arctic Explorer and Ship — A1059

Litho. & Engr.

2008, Dec. 19 ***Perf. 13¼***

2521	Horiz. strip of 3	6.00	6.00
a.	A1057 87c multi	2.00	1.50
b.	A1058 87c multi	2.00	1.50
c.	A1059 87c multi	2.00	1.50

Monaco Firefighting Corps, Cent. A1060

Designs: 50c, Railway and road emergency vehicle. 72c, Ladder truck, 1909. 87c, Fireman, ladder truck.

2009, Jan. 5 **Photo.** ***Perf. 13¼***
2522-2524 A1060 Set of 3 4.75 3.50

Princess Grace Rose Garden, 25th Anniv. — A1061

2009, Jan. 5 ***Perf. 13¼x13***
2525 A1061 €1.25 multi 2.75 2.25

Spring Arts Festival, 25th Anniv. — A1062

2009, Jan. 5
2526 A1062 €1.33 multi 3.00 2.50

First Flight Across English Channel by Louis Blériot, Cent. A1063

Litho. & Engr.

2009, Jan. 29 ***Perf. 13x12½***
2527 A1063 87c multi 2.00 1.50

Felix Mendelssohn Bartholdy (1809-47), Composer A1064

2009, Jan. 29 **Engr.** ***Perf. 13¼***
2528 A1064 €1.50 ol grn & blue 3.50 2.50

Beatification of Joan of Arc, Cent. — A1065

2009, Jan. 29
2529 A1065 €2.22 multi 5.00 4.00

MonacoPhil 2009 Philatelic Exhibition A1066

2009, Feb. 7 **Litho.** ***Perf. 13¼x13***
2530 A1066 56c multi 1.25 1.00

Chihuahua and Cavalier King Charles Spaniel A1067

2009, Feb. 7 **Photo.** ***Perf. 13¼***
2531 A1067 72c multi 1.60 1.25

Intl. Dog Show.

2009 Intl. Cat Show A1068

2009, Feb. 7 **Litho.** ***Perf. 13x13¼***
2532 A1068 88c multi 2.00 1.50

Association of Members of the Order of Academic Palms World Conference — A1069

2009, Feb. 7 **Engr.** ***Perf. 13x12½***
2533 A1069 88c multi 2.00 1.50

Barbie Doll, 50th Anniv. — A1070

2009, Feb. 7 **Photo.** ***Perf. 13¼***
2534 A1070 88c multi 2.00 1.50

42nd Intl. Flower Show — A1071

2009, Feb. 7 **Photo.** ***Perf. 13¼***
2535 A1071 89c multi 2.00 1.50

Monaco Fencing and Handgun Club, Cent. — A1072

2009, Feb. 16 **Litho. & Engr.**
2536 A1072 55c multi 1.25 1.00

Giro d'Italia Bicycle Race, Cent. — A1073

2009, Feb. 16 **Photo.**
2537 A1073 70c multi 1.60 1.25

Sir Arthur Conan Doyle (1859-1930), Writer — A1074

2009, Feb. 16 **Engr.** ***Perf. 12¼***
2538 A1074 85c multi 2.00 1.50

Edgar Allan Poe (1809-49), Writer — A1075

2009, Feb. 16
2539 A1075 €1.70 red & dk grn 3.75 2.75

Coat of Arms — A1076

Serpentine Die Cut 11

2009, Apr. 6 **Photo.**

Booklet Stamp

Self-Adhesive

2540	A1076 (70c) multi	1.60	1.25
a.	Booklet pane of 10	16.00	

Louis Notari Library, Cent. A1077

2009, Apr. 29 **Engr.** ***Perf. 13x12½***
2541 A1077 51c red & purple 1.20 .90

Monaco Grand Prix Auto Race, Cent. — A1078

2009, Apr. 29 **Photo.** ***Perf. 13x13¼***
2542 A1078 70c multi 1.60 1.20

Monaco's Admission to UNESCO, 60th Anniv. — A1079

2009, Apr. 29
2543 A1079 €1.70 multi 3.75 2.75

Louis Braille (1809-52), Educator of the Blind A1080

2009, Apr. 29 Engr. ***Perf. 12¼x13***
2544 A1080 €3.80 multi 8.50 6.50

Concerts at the Prince's Palace, 50th Anniv. A1081

2009, May 4 ***Perf. 13x13¼***
2545 A1081 51c purple & black 1.20 .90

Europa A1082

Astronomers: 56c, Francesco Maria Grimaldi (1618-63), map of Moon showing crater named after Grimaldi. 70c, Galileo Galilei (1564-1642), telescope.

Litho. & Engr.
2009, May 4 ***Perf. 13x12½***
2546-2547 A1082 Set of 2 2.75 2.25

Intl. Year of Astronomy.

Ballets de Monte-Carlo — A1083

2009, May 11 Photo. ***Perf. 13¼x13***
2548 A1083 73c multi 1.60 1.25

Ballets Russes, Cent. A1084

Designs: 89c, Fifteen performers. €1.35, Nine performers.

2009, May 11
2549-2550 A1084 Set of 2 5.00 4.00

Georges Seurat (1859-91), Painter A1085

Litho. & Engr.
2009, May 14 ***Perf. 13x13¼***
2551 A1085 73c multi 1.60 1.25

St. Francis of Assisi (c. 1181-1226) A1086

2009, May 14 Engr. ***Perf. 13¼***
2552 A1086 90c blue & black 2.00 1.50

Franciscan Order, 800th anniv.

John Calvin (1509-64), Theologian and Religious Reformer A1087

2009, May 14 ***Perf. 13x13¼***
2553 A1087 €1.67 multi 3.75 2.75

49th Intl. Television Festival, Monte Carlo — A1088

2009, May 29 Photo. ***Perf. 13¼***
2554 A1088 €1.60 multi 3.50 2.75

Italian Writers A1089

Emblem of Monaco Dante Alighieri Society and: 70c, Niccolò Machiavelli (1469-1527). 85c, Giovanni Boccaccio (1313-75). €1.30, Francesco Petrarca (Petrarch) (1304-74).

2009, June 3 Engr. ***Perf. 12¼x13***
2555-2557 A1089 Set of 3 6.25 4.50

Monaco Dante Alighieri Society, 30th anniv.

Grande Bourse 2009 — A1090

2009, June 17 Photo. ***Perf. 13¼***
2558 A1090 51c multi 1.20 .90

Youth Hostels, Cent. A1091

2009, June 17 Litho. ***Perf. 13x13¼***
2559 A1091 90c multi 2.00 1.50

Tuiga, Flagship of Monaco Yacht Club, Cent. A1092

2009, June 18 Photo. ***Perf. 13¼***
2560 A1092 70c multi 1.50 1.10

Start of Tour de France Bicycle Race in Monaco A1093

2009, July 2 Litho. ***Perf. 13¼x13***
2561 A1093 56c multi 1.25 1.00

2009 Magic Stars Festival, Monte Carlo — A1094

2009, Sept. 16 Litho. ***Perf. 13¼x13***
2562 A1094 73c multi 1.60 1.20

Place de la Mairie — A1095

2009, Sept. 16 Photo.
2563 A1095 85c multi 1.90 1.25

Big Ben, 150th Anniv. — A1096

2009, Sept. 16 Engr.
2564 A1096 €1 red & black 2.25 1.50

Christmas A1097

2009, Oct. 5 ***Perf. 13x13¼***
2565 A1097 56c multi 1.25 1.00

2010 Intl. Cat Show — A1098

2009, Dec. 4 Photo. ***Perf. 13¼***
2566 A1098 56c multi 1.25 1.00

Dated 2010.

Jean Anouilh (1910-87), Playwright — A1099

2009, Dec. 4 Engr. ***Perf. 13x12¼***
2567 A1099 73c multi 1.50 1.25

Dated 2010.

Ayrton Senna (1960-94), Race Car Driver — A1100

2009, Dec. 4 Engr. *Perf. 13x12¼*

2568	A1100	73c multi	1.50	1.25

Dated 2010.

Auguste Rodin (1840-1917), Sculptor — A1101

2009, Dec. 4 Engr. *Perf. 13x12¼*

2569	A1101	85c multi	1.90	1.50

Dated 2010.

Princess Grace (1929-82) A1102

2009, Dec. 4 Engr. *Perf. 12¼x13*

2570	A1102	89c red & black	2.00	1.50

Dated 2010.

Gustav Mahler (1860-1911), Composer — A1103

2009, Dec. 4

2571	A1103	90c brown & blue	2.00	1.50

Dated 2010.

2010 Winter Olympics, Vancouver — A1104

No. 2572 — 2010 Winter Olympics emblem and: a, Slalom skier. b, Snowboarder and figure skater.

2009, Dec. 4 Engr. *Perf. 13¼x13½*

2572	A1104	Horiz. pair	4.00	4.00
a.-b.		90c Either single	2.00	1.50

Dated 2010.

Monte Carlo Vu de Roquebrune, by Claude Monet (1840-1926) — A1105

2009, Dec. 4 Photo. *Perf. 13x13¼*

2573	A1105	€1.30 multi	3.00	2.25

Dated 2010.

US No. 85A, Trophy A1106

2009, Dec. 4 Litho.

2574	A1106	€1.35 multi	3.00	2.25

Awarding of Intl. Association of Stamp Catalogue Publishers Grand Prix for Philately to William H. Gross. Dated 2010.

The Birth of Venus, by William Bouguereau (1825-1905) — A1107

2009, Dec. 4 Photo. *Perf. 13¼x13*

2575	A1107	€1.60 multi	3.50	2.75

Dated 2010.

Anton Chekhov (1860-1904), Writer — A1108

2009, Dec. 4 Engr. *Perf. 13x12¼*

2576	A1108	€1.67 multi	3.50	2.75

Dated 2010.

Souvenir Sheet

Prince Albert II — A1109

Litho. (Margin) & Engr.

2009, Dec. 4 *Perf. 13¼x13*

2577	A1109	€4 red & black	9.00	7.00

MonacoPhil 2009 Intl. Philatelic Exhibition. Dated 2010.

Souvenir Sheet

Automobile Club of Monaco, 120th Anniv. — A1110

No. 2578: a, Race car. b, Formula 1 race car.

2009, Dec. 4 Photo. *Perf. 13x13¼*

2578	A1110	Sheet of 2	6.50	6.50
a.		€1.30 multi	3.00	2.50
b.		€1.70 multi	3.00	2.50

Dated 2010.

34th Intl. Circus Festival, Monte Carlo — A1111

2009, Dec. 10 Photo. *Perf. 13¼*

2579	A1111	70c multi	1.50	1.10

Dated 2010.

Australian Shepherd A1112

2010, Feb. 8 Photo. *Perf. 13¼*

2580	A1112	51c multi	1.10	.80

Intl. Dog Show.

Intl. Flower Arrangement Festival — A1113

2010, Feb. 8

2581	A1113	70c multi	1.50	1.10

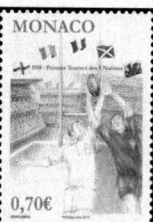

Five Nations Rugby Championships, Cent. — A1114

2010, Feb. 8 Litho. *Perf. 13¼x13*

2582	A1114	70c multi	1.50	1.10

Scenes From "The Seven Samurai," Film by Akira Kurosawa (1910-98) — A1115

2010, Feb. 24 Engr. *Perf. 13x12¼*

2583	A1115	51c ol grn & black	1.10	.80

Monte Carlo Rolex Masters Tennis Tournament A1116

2010, Mar. 4 Photo. *Perf. 13¼*

2584	A1116	85c multi	1.90	1.50

2010 World Cup Soccer Championships, South Africa — A1117

No. 2585 — Flag of South Africa, players in stadium with denomination at: a, LL. b, UR.

2010, Mar. 4

2585	A1117	Horiz. pair	4.00	4.00
a.-b.		89c Either single	2.00	1.50

Souvenir Sheet

2008 Monaco Coin — A1118

Litho. & Embossed With Foil Application

2010, Mar. 4 *Perf. 13½*

2586	A1118	€1 multi	2.25	1.75

Expo 2010, Shanghai.

Miniature Sheet

Oceanographic Museum of Monaco, Cent. — A1119

No. 2587: a, Prince Albert I. b, Stuffed Ursus maritimus. c, Pterapogon kauderni, horiz. d, Hands pointing at starfish, horiz.

Litho. & Engr.

2010, Mar. 29 *Perf. 13¼x13*

2587	A1119	Sheet of 4	6.00	6.00
a.		51c multi	1.10	.80
b.		56c multi	1.25	1.00
c.		73c multi	1.60	1.20
d.		90c multi	2.00	1.50

Miniature Sheet

Former Grimaldi Family Fiefs in France — A1120

No. 2588: a, County of Thann. b, Barony of Altkirch. c, County of Rosemont. d, County of Ferrette.

2010, Apr. 23 **Photo.** *Perf. 13x13¼*

2588 A1120 €1 Sheet of 4, #a-d 9.00 9.00

Flora and Fauna — A1121

Designs: 2c, Pinna nobilis, Submarine Reserve of Larvotto. €2, Lis martagon, Mercantour National Park, France.

2010, Apr. 29 **Engr.** *Perf. 13¼*

2589 A1121 2c multi .25 .25
2590 A1121 €2 multi 4.00 3.00

Mother Teresa (1910-97), Humanitarian A1122

2010, Apr. 29 **Photo.** *Perf. 13¼*

2591 A1122 €1.70 multi 3.75 2.75

UNAIDS Program, 15th Anniv. — A1123

2010, May 5 **Photo.** *Perf. 13¼*

2592 A1123 89c multi 2.00 1.50

Europa A1124

Map of Europe, books and: 56c, Five children. 70c, One child.

2010, May 5 **Engr.** *Perf. 13x13¼*

2593-2594 A1124 Set of 2 2.75 2.25

London 2010 Festival of Stamps — A1125

2010, May 7

2595 A1125 €1.30 multi 2.75 2.25

50th Television Festival, Monte Carlo — A1126

Litho. With Foil Application

2010, May 26 *Perf. 13¼x13*

2596 A1126 €2.80 multi 5.75 3.75

Human Paleontology Institute, Paris, Cent. — A1127

2010, June 1 **Engr.** *Perf. 13x12¾*

2597 A1127 56c multi 1.25 1.00

See France No. 3821.

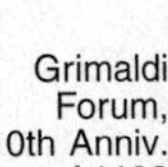

Grimaldi Forum, 10th Anniv. A1128

2010, June 22 **Litho.** *Perf. 13x13¼*

2598 A1128 75c multi 1.60 1.25

Youth Olympic Games, Singapore — A1129

2010, June 22 **Photo.**

2599 A1129 87c multi 1.90 1.50

Maritime and Airport Police Division, 50th Anniv. — A1130

2010, July 1 **Engr.** *Perf. 13¼*

2600 A1130 53c multi 1.10 .75

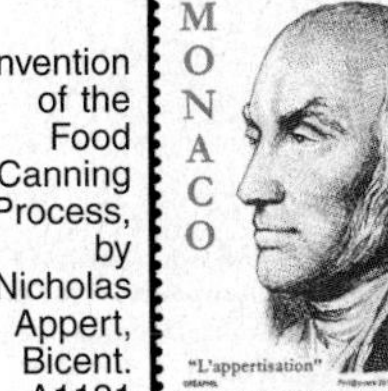

Invention of the Food Canning Process, by Nicholas Appert, Bicent. A1131

2010, July 1 *Perf. 12¼*

2601 A1131 95c red & purple 2.10 1.60

Invention of First Practical Internal Combustion Engine by Jean-Joseph-Etienne Lenoir, 150th Anniv. — A1132

2010, July 1

2602 A1132 €1.75 multi 4.00 3.00

Little Africa Gardens, Monaco — A1133

2010, July 1 *Perf. 13x13¼*

2603 A1133 €2.30 multi 5.00 4.00

First International Electric Postal Flight, Monaco to Nice — A1134

2010, Aug. 23 **Litho.** *Perf. 13*

2604 A1134 95c multi 2.00 1.50

Monaco Scientific Center, 50th Anniv. A1135

2010, Sept. 17 **Photo.** *Perf. 13¼*

2605 A1135 58c multi 1.25 1.00

25th Magic Stars Festival, Monte Carlo — A1136

2010, Sept. 17 **Litho.** *Perf. 13¼x13*

2606 A1136 €1.40 multi 3.00 2.25

Monaco Regional Express Transport A1137

2010, Sept. 19 **Engr.** *Perf. 13x13¼*

2607 A1137 €1.35 multi 3.00 2.25

Albert I High School, Cent. A1138

2010, Oct. 4 *Perf. 13x13¼*

2608 A1138 75c multi 1.60 1.20

Christmas A1139

2010, Oct. 4 **Photo.** *Perf. 13¼*

2609 A1139 58c multi 1.25 1.00

35th Intl. Circus Festival, Monte Carlo — A1140

2010, Dec. 20 ***Perf. 13¼***
2610 A1140 75c multi 1.60 1.10

Constitution of Monaco, Cent. — A1141

2011, Jan. 4
2611 A1141 53c multi 1.20 .90

Egyptian Mau Cat — A1142

2011, Jan. 4
2612 A1142 87c multi 1.90 1.25

Intl. Cat Show.

Juan Manuel Fangio (1911-95), Race Car Driver — A1143

Indianapolis 500, Cent. — A1144

Monte Carlo Rally, Cent. — A1145

2011, Jan. 12 **Engr.** ***Perf. 13x13¼***
2613 A1143 95c multi 2.00 1.50

Photo.
2614 A1144 €1.35 multi 3.00 2.25
2615 A1145 €1.40 multi 3.00 2.25
Nos. 2613-2615 (3) 8.00 6.00

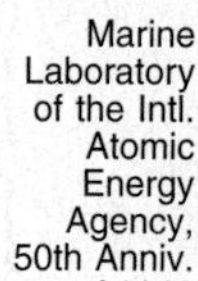

Marine Laboratory of the Intl. Atomic Energy Agency, 50th Anniv. A1146

2011, Jan. 20 **Photo.** ***Perf. 13¼***
2616 A1146 87c multi 1.90 1.25

Renewable Energy A1147

2011, Jan. 20 **Litho.** ***Perf. 13x13¼***
2617 A1147 €1.80 multi 4.00 3.00

Mission Enfance Association, 20th Anniv. — A1148

2011, Jan. 28
2618 A1148 53c multi 1.10 .75

Labrador Retriever A1149

2011, Feb. 7 **Photo.** ***Perf. 13¼***
2619 A1149 53c multi 1.10 .75

Intl. Dog Show.

A1150

Sculptors and Their Sculptures — A1151

No. 2620: a, Antoine Bourdelle (1861-1929). b, Horse's head from Monument to General Alvear.

No. 2621: a, Aristide Maillol (1861-1944). b, The Night.

2011, Feb. 21 **Engr.** ***Perf. 13¼***
2620 A1150 Horiz. pair 3.25 3.25
a.-b. 75c Either single 1.60 1.10
2621 A1151 Horiz. pair 4.25 4.25
a.-b. 95c Either single 2.00 1.50

State Visit of Prince Albert II to Ireland A1152

2011, Feb. 21 **Photo.** ***Perf. 13¼***
2622 A1152 €1.40 multi 3.00 2.25

Monte Carlo Rolex Masters Tennis Tournament A1153

2011, Mar. 2
2623 A1153 75c multi 1.60 1.10

Napoleon II (1811-32), Titular King of Rome — A1154

2011, Mar. 2 **Engr.**
2624 A1154 €1 brown & blue 2.25 1.60

44th Intl. Flower Show, Monte Carlo — A1155

Chelsea Flower Show, London — A1156

Japanese Garden of Monaco A1157

Photo., Litho. (#2626)
2011, Mar. 24 ***Perf. 13¼***
2625 A1155 95c multi 2.00 1.50
Perf. 13¼x13
2626 A1156 €1.75 multi 3.75 2.75
Perf. 13x13¼
2627 A1157 €2.35 multi 5.00 3.50
Nos. 2625-2627 (3) 10.75 7.75

Consecration of Monaco Cathedral, Cent. — A1158

2011, Mar. 31 **Engr.** ***Perf. 13x13¼***
2628 A1158 58c red & black 1.25 1.00

Lions Club of Monaco, 50th Anniv. A1159

2011, Mar. 31 **Photo.** ***Perf. 13¼***
2629 A1159 75c multi 1.60 1.10

Souvenir Sheet

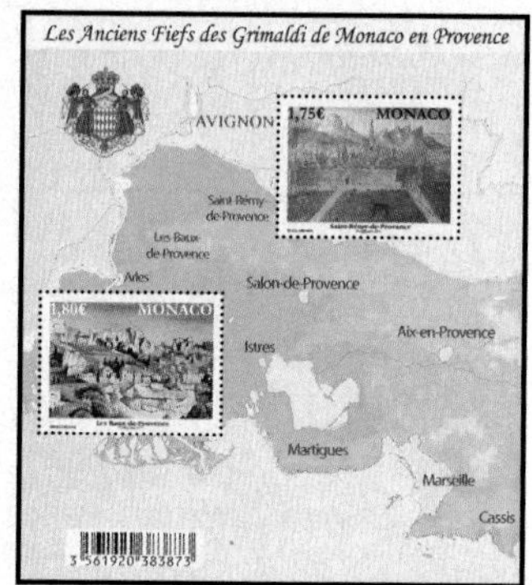

Former Grimaldi Family Fiefs in Provence — A1160

No. 2630: a, Saint-Rémy-de-Provence. b, Les Baux-de-Provence.

2011, Apr. 4 ***Perf. 13x13¼***
2630 A1160 Sheet of 2 8.00 8.00
a. €1.75 multi 3.75 2.75
b. €1.80 multi 3.75 2.75

Aquilegia Bertolonii, Mercantour National Park — A1161

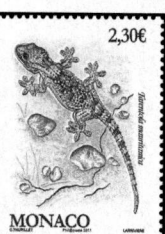

Tarentola Mauritanica A1162

2011, Apr. 20 **Photo.** ***Perf. 13¼***
2631 A1161 3c multi .25 .25

Engr.
Perf. 13¼x13
2632 A1162 €2.30 multi 5.00 3.50

Europa — A1163

Designs: 58c, Alpine forest. 75c, Mediterranean forest.

2011, May 3 Photo. *Perf. 13¼*
2633-2634 A1163 Set of 2 3.00 2.25
Intl. Year of Forests.

Winning Artwork in Environment and Ecology in Monaco Children's Stamp Design Contest — A1164

2011, May 18 Litho. *Perf. 13x13¼*
2635 A1164 53c multi 1.20 .90

A1165

Wedding of Prince Albert II and Charlene Wittstock — A1166

Engr. With Foil Application
2011, July 1 *Perf. 13x13¼*

2636	A1165	55c blk & grn	1.25	1.00
2637	A1165	60c blk & red	1.25	1.00
2638	A1165	77c blk & pur	1.75	1.25
2639	A1165	89c blk & blue	2.00	1.50
2640	A1165	€4.10 brn, gold & red	9.00	7.00
	Nos. 2636-2640 (5)		15.25	11.75

Souvenir Sheet
Photo.
2641 A1166 €5 multi 11.00 8.00

Prince's Company of Carabiniers — A1167

2011, July 18 Photo. *Perf. 13¼*
2642 A1167 77c multi 1.75 1.25

Monte Carlo Golf Club, Cent. — A1168

2011, Aug. 9 Litho. *Perf. 13¼*
2643 A1168 60c multi 1.25 .90

Monegasque Alpine Club, Cent. — A1169

2011, Aug. 9 Photo.
2644 A1169 60c multi 1.25 .90

2011 Grande Bourse, Salle du Canton — A1170

2011, Aug. 12
2645 A1170 60c multi 1.25 .90

Zeus Faber — A1171

2011, Aug. 16 Litho.
2646 A1171 (39c) multi .85 .65

No. 2646 was issued precanceled only. See note after No. 324.

MonacoPhil 2011 Intl. Philatelic Exhibition A1172

2011, Aug. 29 *Perf. 13¼*
2647 A1172 55c multi 1.25 .90

Paris Institute of Oceanography, Cent. — A1173

2011, Sept. 19 Engr. *Perf. 13x13¼*
2648 A1173 77c multi 1.75 1.25

Exotic Garden, Monaco A1174

2011, Sept. 28 Photo. *Perf. 13¼*
2649 A1174 75c multi 1.75 1.25

First Man in Space, 50th Anniv. A1175

2011, Sept. 28 Engr. *Perf. 13x13¼*
2650 A1175 €2.78 blue 6.00 4.50

Georges Méliès (1863-1938), Film Maker — A1176

2011, Sept. 28
2651 A1176 €1.45 multi 3.25 2.40

Franz Liszt (1811-86), Composer — A1177

2011, Oct. 10 *Perf. 13x12¼*
2652 A1177 €1 multi 2.25 1.75

Théophile Gautier (1811-72), Poet — A1178

2011, Oct. 10 Litho. *Perf. 13*
2653 A1178 €1.75 multi 4.00 3.00

Prince Antoine I (1661-1731) — A1179

Litho. & Embossed With Foil Application
2011, Oct. 10
2654 A1179 €1.80 multi 4.00 3.00

Henri Troyat (1911-2007), Writer — A1180

2011, Oct. 10 Engr. *Perf. 12¼x13*
2655 A1180 €2.40 multi 5.25 3.75

Christmas A1181

2011, Oct. 17 Litho. *Perf. 13¼*
2656 A1181 60c multi 1.25 .90

25th Telethon A1182

2011, Dec. 2
2657 A1182 60c multi 1.25 .90

Intl. Association of Philatelic Catalogue Editors (ASCAT) Grand Prix — A1183

2011, Dec. 2 Photo.
2658 A1183 78c multi 1.75 1.25

Souvenir Sheet

Prince Albert II and Princess Charlene — A1184

2011, Dec. 2
2659 A1184 €5 multi 11.00 11.00

MonacoPhil 2011 Intl. Philatelic Exhibition.

36th Intl. Circus Festival, Monte Carlo — A1185

2011, Dec. 19
2660 A1185 77c multi 1.75 1.25

Intl. Flower Arrangement Festival — A1186

2012, Jan. 10 **Litho.**
2661 A1186 55c multi 1.25 .90

2012 Intl. Cat Show — A1187

2012, Jan. 10 **Photo.** ***Perf. 13¼***
2662 A1187 77c multi 1.75 1.25

St. Martin's Gardens A1188

2012, Jan. 10
2663 A1188 89c multi 2.00 1.50

Miniature Sheet

Frescoes of the Monte Carlo Opera — A1189

No. 2664: a, Comedy, by Frédéric Lix. b, Music, by Gustave Boulanger. c, Dance, by Georges Clairin. d, Song and Eloquence, by François Feyen-Perrin.

2012, Jan. 25 ***Perf. 13x13¼***
2664 A1189 €1.45 Sheet of 4, #a-d 13.00 13.00

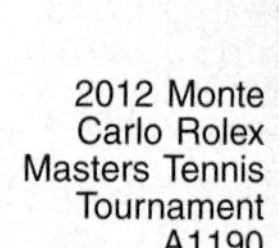

2012 Monte Carlo Rolex Masters Tennis Tournament A1190

2012, Feb. 2 ***Perf. 13¼***
2665 A1190 89c multi 2.00 1.50

Collie — A1191

2012, Feb. 2 **Engr.**
2666 A1191 89c multi 2.00 1.50

Intl. Dog Show.

Florestan Company, 25th Anniv. — A1192

2012, Feb. 20 **Litho.** ***Perf. 13¼***
2667 A1192 55c multi 1.25 .90

Recognition by France of Monaco's Independence, 500th Anniv. — A1193

2012, Feb. 20 **Engr.** ***Perf. 13x13¼***
2668 A1193 55c red & black 1.25 .90

Carabine de Monaco (Rifle Shooting Association), Cent. — A1194

2012, Feb. 20
2669 A1194 €1.35 multi 3.00 2.25

75th Bazaar for the Work of Sister Mary A1195

2012, Mar. 16 **Litho.** ***Perf. 13¼***
2670 A1195 60c multi 1.25 .90

70th Monaco Grand Prix A1196

2012, Mar. 20 **Engr.** ***Perf. 13x13¼***
2671 A1196 77c multi 1.75 1.25

First Seaplane Competition, Cent. — A1197

2012, Mar. 20
2672 A1197 €1.80 multi 4.00 3.00

Coat of Arms Type of 2000 Inscribed "20g écopli" at Top

Serpentine Die Cut 11

2012, Apr. 20 **Photo.**

Booklet Stamp Self-Adhesive

2673 A786 (55c) blue & multi 1.25 .90
a. Booklet pane of 10 12.50

Compare with No. 2863.

Arrival of PlanetSolar Boat in Monaco — A1198

2012, Apr. 20 **Engr.** ***Perf. 13x13¼***
2674 A1198 77c multi 1.75 1.25

Expo 2012, Yeosu, South Korea A1199

2012, Apr. 20 **Photo.** ***Perf. 13¼***
2675 A1199 78c multi 1.75 1.25

Europa A1200

Rooms in the Prince's Palace: 60c, Louis XV Bedroom. 77c, Mazarin Room.

2012, May 9 **Litho.**
2676-2677 A1200 Set of 2 3.00 2.25

Rotary Club of Monaco, 75th Anniv. A1201

2012, June 9
2678 A1201 77c multi 1.75 1.25

United Nations Rio + 20 Conference on Sustainable Development, Rio de Janeiro — A1202

2012, June 9
2679 A1202 78c multi 1.75 1.25

Prince of Monaco Islands, French Southern and Antarctic Territories — A1203

No. 2680: a, Giant Antarctic petrel. b, Coastline of Prince of Monaco Islands.

2012, June 9 **Litho. & Engr.**
2680 A1203 Sheet of 2 4.50 4.50
a.-b. €1 Either single 2.25 1.60

See French Southern and Antarctic Territories No. 467.

Souvenir Sheet

Cabaret on the Banks of the River, by Jan Breughel — A1204

2012, June 25 **Photo.**
2681 A1204 €3 multi 6.50 5.00

Exhibition of philatelic collection of Prince Albert II, Bruges, Belgium. See Belgium No. 2577.

Fort-la-Laffe, Matignon, France — A1205

2012, July 5 **Engr.** ***Perf. 13x13¼***
2682 A1205 €1.75 multi 3.75 2.75

Visit of Prince Albert II to Matignon.

Intl. Association of Athletics Federations, Cent. — A1206

2012, July 17 Photo. *Perf. 13¼*
2683 A1206 89c multi 2.00 1.50

2012 Summer Olympics, London A1207

2012, July 17 Litho. & Engr.
2684 A1207 €1.35 multi 3.00 2.25

Tenth World Council of Consuls, Monaco A1208

2012, Aug. 22 Photo. *Perf. 12¼*
2685 A1208 55c multi 1.25 .90

Claude Debussy (1862-1918), Composer — A1209

2012, Aug. 22 Engr. *Perf. 13x12¼*
2686 A1209 €1 red & black 2.25 1.60

Crucifixion, by Louis Brea — A1210

2012, Aug. 22 Litho. *Perf. 12¼x13*
2687 A1210 €1.35 multi 3.00 2.25

Bird Protection League, Cent. — A1211

2012, Sept. 10 Engr. *Perf. 13¼*
2688 A1211 €1 multi 2.25 1.60

Opening of New National Council Building A1212

2012, Sept. 12 *Perf. 13x13¼*
2689 A1212 78c brown & black 1.75 1.25

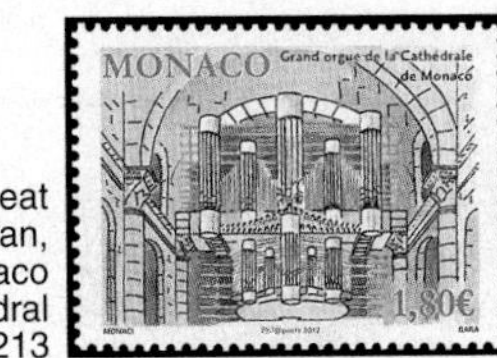

Great Organ, Monaco Cathedral A1213

Litho. & Engr.

2012, Sept. 12 *Perf. 13¼*
2690 A1213 €1.80 multi 4.00 3.00

Title of Prince of Monaco, 400th Anniv. A1214

2012, Sept. 12 Engr. *Perf. 13x13¼*
2691 A1214 €2.40 multi 5.25 3.75

Consecration of St. Charles Church, Monaco, Cent. — A1215

2012, Oct. 19 *Perf. 13¼*
2692 A1215 €1.45 multi 3.25 2.50

Auguste Lumière (1862-1954), Filmmaker — A1216

2012, Oct. 19 *Perf. 12¼*
2693 A1216 €2.35 multi 5.25 4.00

Discovery of Bust of Nefertiti, Cent. — A1217

2012, Oct. 19
2694 A1217 €3.78 multi 8.50 6.50

Timbres Passion 2012 Philatelic Exhibition, Belfort, France — A1218

No. 2695 — Coat of arms and: a, Duchess Louise d'Aumont Mazarin (1759-1826), wife of Prince Honoré IV. b, Prince Honoré IV of Monaco (1758-1819).

2012, Nov. 2 Litho. *Perf. 13¼*
2695 A1218 Horiz. pair 2.40 1.75
a.-b. 55c Either single 1.20 .90

Christmas A1219

2012, Nov. 2 Photo.
2696 A1219 60c multi 1.25 .90

Release of Third Volume of *Adventures of Tintin* — A1220

2012, Nov. 21 *Perf. 13x13¼*
2697 A1220 77c multi 1.75 1.25

Prince Albert II — A1221

Inscription: (56c), Ecopli 20g. (63c), Prioritaire 20g. No. 2700, Europa 20g. No. 2701, Ecopli 50g. (€1.05), Prioritaire 50g.

2012, Dec. 1 Engr. *Perf. 13x13¼*

2698	A1221	(56c) blue	1.25	.90
2699	A1221	(63c) red	1.40	1.10
a.		Dated "2015"	1.40	1.10
2700	A1221	(80c) red violet	1.75	1.25
2701	A1221	(80c) green	1.75	1.25
2702	A1221	(€1.05) black	2.40	1.75
		Nos. 2698-2702 (5)	8.55	6.25

Issued: No. 2699a, 1/2/15. No. 2699a sold for 76c on day of issue. See Nos. 2826-2828.

Painting by Patients of Speranza-Albert II Alzheimer's Disease Day Care Center — A1222

2012, Dec. 3 Photo. *Perf. 13¼x13*
2703 A1222 €1.35 multi 3.00 2.25

Olympia, by Edouard Manet — A1223

2012, Dec. 3 Litho. *Perf. 13x13¼*
2704 A1223 €1.80 multi 4.00 3.00

37th Intl. Circus Festival, Monte Carlo — A1224

2013, Jan. 2 Photo. *Perf. 13¼*
2705 A1224 63c multi 1.40 1.10

Pierre de Coubertin (1863-1937), Founder of Intl. Olympic Committee — A1225

2013, Jan. 2 Engr. *Perf. 13x13¼*
2706 A1225 €2.55 multi 5.75 4.50

Turkish Angora Cat — A1226

2013, Jan. 16 Photo. *Perf. 13¼*
2707 A1226 56c multi 1.25 .90

Intl. Cat Show.

Nautical Society of Monaco, 125th Anniv. — A1227

2013, Jan. 16 **Engr.**
2708 A1227 95c multi 2.00 1.50

Intl. Flower Arrangement Festival — A1228

2013, Jan. 16 **Photo.**
2709 A1228 €1.75 multi 3.75 3.00

French Bulldog — A1229

2013, Feb. 7 **Engr.**
2710 A1229 80c red & black 1.75 1.25

Intl. Dog Show.

Monte Carlo Casino Terraces A1230

2013, Feb. 7 **Photo.**
2711 A1230 80c multi 1.75 1.25

Monte Carlo Rolex Masters Tennis Tournament A1231

2013, Feb. 7
2712 A1231 €1.05 multi 2.25 1.60

World Association of Children's Friends, 50th Anniv. — A1232

2013, Feb. 18
2713 A1232 €1.55 multi 3.25 2.50

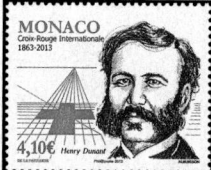

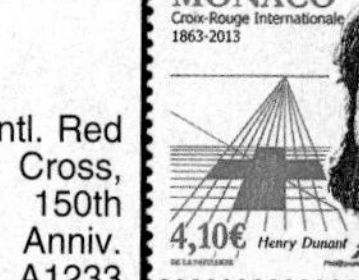
Intl. Red Cross, 150th Anniv. A1233

2013, Feb. 18 **Engr.** ***Perf. 13x13¼***
2714 A1233 €4.10 red & blk 9.00 7.00

Formula 1 Race Cars A1234

Designs: €1.05, Maserati 250F. €1.75, Tyrrell P34.

2013, Mar. 14 **Litho.** ***Perf. 13¼***
2715-2716 A1234 Set of 2 6.00 4.50

Clean Transportation — A1235

No. 2717: a, Solar-powered shuttle boat. b, Electric bicycle.

Litho. & Silk-screened

2013, Apr. 5
2717 A1235 Horiz. pair 8.00 8.00
a.-b. €1.85 Either single 4.00 3.00

Archconfraternity of Misericordia, Bicent. — A1236

2013, Apr. 27 **Photo.** ***Perf. 13¼***
2718 A1236 80c multi 1.75 1.25

Junior Chamber International Monaco, 50th Anniv. — A1237

2013, May 10 **Litho.**
2719 A1237 56c multi 1.25 .90

Europa A1238

2013, May 10
2720 A1238 63c multi 1.40 1.00

Grimaldi Family Coat of Arms and Tower of Crest, France A1239

2013, May 17 **Photo.**
2721 A1239 €1.05 multi 2.25 1.60

Visit of Prince Albert II to Duchy of Valentinois and Crest, France.

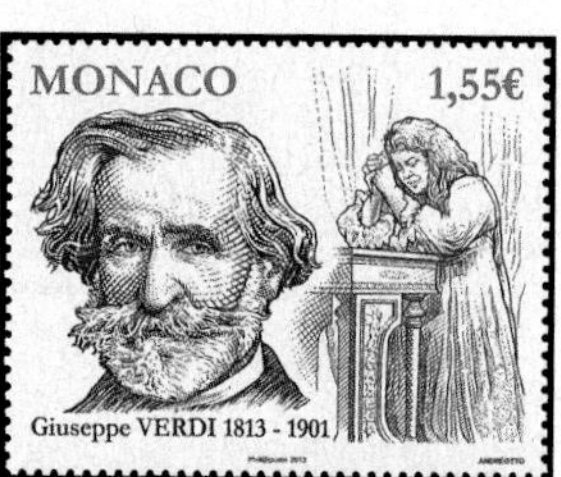
Giuseppe Verdi (1813-1901), Composer — A1240

Richard Wagner (1813-83), Composer — A1241

Premiere of *The Rite of Spring,* Ballet by Igor Stravinsky, Cent. — A1242

2013, May 22 **Engr.** ***Perf. 13x12¼***
2722 A1240 €1.55 multi 3.25 2.50
2723 A1241 €1.85 multi 4.00 3.00
2724 A1242 €2.55 multi 5.50 4.00
Nos. 2722-2724 (3) 12.75 9.50

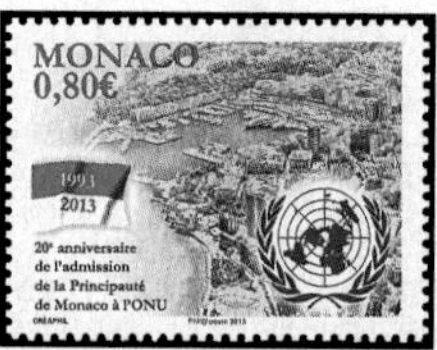
Admission to United Nations, 20th Anniv. A1243

2013, May 28 **Litho.** ***Perf. 13¼***
2725 A1243 80c multi 1.75 1.25

15th World Festival of Amateur Theater A1244

2013, June 5
2726 A1244 63c multi 1.40 1.00

Larus Michahellis A1245

2013, June 5
2727 A1245 80c multi 1.75 1.25

Discovery of Otiorhynchus Monoecirupus in Monaco — A1246

2013, June 5
2728 A1246 €1 multi 2.00 1.50

Miniature Sheet

Sharks — A1247

No. 2729: a, Blacktip shark (requin bordé). b, Tiger shark (requin-tigre). c, Whale shark (requin-baleine). d, Great white shark (grand requin blanc).

2013, June 8 **Photo.**
2729 A1247 Sheet of 4 7.50 7.50
a.-b. 63c Either single 1.40 1.00
c.-d. €1.05 Either single 2.25 1.60

Miniature Sheet

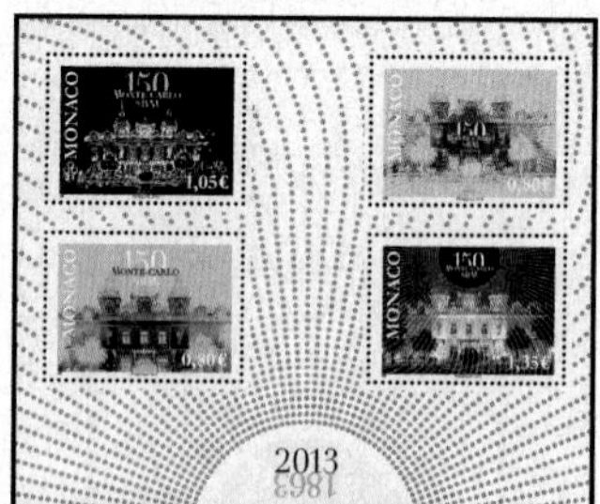
Monte Carlo Société des Bains de Mer, 150th Anniv. — A1248

No. 2730 — Monte Carlo Casino with: a, Beige background and white dots. b, Beige background. c, Black background. d, Black background and white dots.

Photo., (Sheet Margin Photo., Silk-screened and Embossed)

2013, July 5
2730 A1248 Sheet of 4 8.00 8.00
a.-b. 80c Either single 1.75 1.25
c. €1.05 multi 2.25 1.60
d. €1.35 multi 3.00 2.25

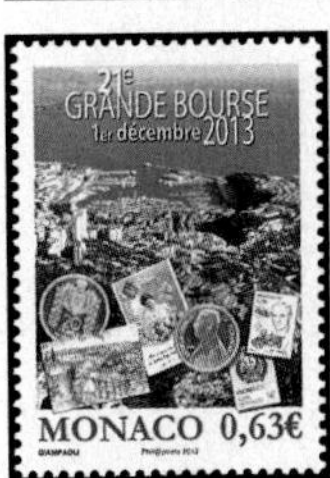

2013 Grande Bourse — A1249

2013, July 10 Photo. *Perf. 13¼*
2731 A1249 63c multi 1.40 1.00

MonacoPhil 2013 Intl. Philatelic Exhibition, Fontveille Terraces — A1250

2013, July 10 Litho.
2732 A1250 80c multi 1.75 1.25

First Trans-Mediterranean Flight by Roland Garros, Cent. — A1251

2013, Sept. 23 Litho. & Engr.
2733 A1251 €1.35 multi 3.00 2.25

Yachts — A1252

2013, Sept. 23 Engr. *Perf. 13x13¼*
2734 A1252 Horiz. pair 5.50 5.50
a. €1 Yacht without sails 2.00 1.50
b. €1.55 Yacht with sails 3.25 2.50

Jules Richard (1863-1945), Director of Monaco Oceanographic Museum A1253

2013, Oct. 9 *Perf. 13¼*
2735 A1253 €1 multi 2.00 1.50

Charles Pathé (1863-1957), Sound Recording and Film Entrepreneur A1254

2013, Oct. 9
2736 A1254 €1.85 pur & black 4.00 3.00

Crossword Puzzles, Cent. A1255

2013, Oct. 9 *Perf. 13x13¼*
2737 A1255 €2.78 black & red 6.00 4.50

Christmas A1256

2013, Oct. 30 Photo. *Perf. 13¼*
2738 A1256 63c multi 1.40 1.00

Awarding of 2013 ASCAT Grand Prix of Philately to Jacques Rogge, Pres. of Intl. Olympic Committee A1257

2013, Dec. 5 Litho. *Perf. 13¼*
2739 A1257 95c multi 2.00 1.50

Automobiles — A1258

No. 2740: a, Sunbeam Alpine. b, ZIL-111V.

2013, Dec. 5 Litho. *Perf. 13*
2740 A1258 Horiz. pair 4.00 4.00
a.-b. 95c Either single 2.00 1.50

See Russia No. 7501.

Miniature Sheet

MonacoPhil 2013 Intl. Philatelic Exhibition — A1259

No. 2741: a, Prince Albert II facing right, country name at LL. b, Prince Albert II facing forward. c, Prince Albert II facing right, country name at bottom center. d, Monogram of Prince Albert II.

Engr. With Foil Application

2013, Dec. 5 *Perf. 13*
2741 A1259 Sheet of 4 8.50 8.50
a.-d. €1 Any single 2.00 1.50

38th Intl. Circus Festival, Monte Carlo — A1260

2014, Jan. 6 Photo. *Perf. 13¼*
2742 A1260 83c multi 1.75 1.25

Posters for Movies Starring Grace Kelly A1261

Designs: €1.38, The Country Girl (Une Fille de la Province). €2.40, Dial M for Murder (Le Crime Etait Presque Parfait).

2014, Jan. 16 Litho. *Perf. 13¼*
2743-2744 A1261 Set of 2 8.00 6.00

See Nos. 2783-2784, 2845-2846, 2865-2866.

British Shorthair Cat A1262

2014, Jan. 30 Litho. *Perf. 13¼*
2745 A1262 61c multi 1.25 .90

Intl. Cat Show.

2014 Winter Olympics, Sochi, Russia A1263

2014, Jan. 30 Engr. *Perf. 13x13¼*
2746 A1263 €1.78 multi 3.75 3.00

Monte Carlo Rolex Masters Tennis Tournament A1264

2014, Feb. 5 Photo. *Perf. 13¼*
2747 A1264 €1.10 multi 2.25 1.60

Bull Terrier A1265

2014, Feb. 20 Litho. *Perf. 13¼*
2748 A1265 87c multi 1.75 1.25

Intl. Dog Show.

Intl. Flower Arrangement Festival — A1266

2014, Feb. 20 Photo. *Perf. 13¼*
2749 A1266 €2.10 multi 4.50 3.50

Gilles Villeneuve (1950-82), Formula 1 Race Car Driver — A1267

Ayrton Senna (1960-94), Formula 1 Race Car Driver — A1268

No. 2750: a, Villeneuve (31x31mm). b, Villeneuve (52x31mm).

No. 2751: a, Senna (31x31mm). b, Senna (52x31mm).

2014, Mar. 5 Photo. *Perf. 13*
2750 A1267 Horiz. pair 2.75 2.75
a.-b. 66c Either single 1.25 .90
2751 A1268 Horiz. pair 3.50 3.50
a.-b. 83c Either single 1.75 1.25

Princess Grace Foundation, 50th Anniv. — A1269

2014, Mar. 14 Litho. *Perf. 13¼*
2752 A1269 66c multi 1.25 .90

Printemps des Arts Festival (Spring Arts Festival), 30th Anniv. — A1270

2014, Mar. 14 Litho. *Perf. 13¼*
2753 A1270 €1.20 multi 2.50 1.75

Marsupilami, Comic Book Character by André Franquin — A1271

2014, Apr. 1 Photo. *Perf. 13x13¼*
2754 A1271 83c multi 1.75 1.25

Diana at the Bath, by Carlo Maratti — A1272

No. 2755: a, 18th cent. engraving of painting (denomination at LR). b, Painting, 1684 (denomination at LL).

2014, Apr. 1 Litho. *Perf. 13¼*
2755 A1272 Horiz. pair 7.00 7.00
a.-b. €1.65 Either single 3.50 2.75

Monaco Air Rally, Cent. — A1273

2014, Apr. 1 Engr. *Perf. 13¼*
2756 A1273 €2.65 multi 5.75 4.25

Old Tram and Modern Bus — A1274

Litho. & Silk-Screened
2014, Apr. 30 *Perf. 13*
2757 A1274 59c multi 1.25 .90

Europa A1275

2014, May 7 Litho. *Perf. 13¼*
2758 A1275 83c multi 1.75 1.25

Souvenir Sheet

Ancient Grimaldi Fiefdoms in France — A1276

No. 2759: a, House of the Princes of Monaco, Vic-sur-Cère, France. b, Rocher de Carlat.

2014, May 14 Photo. *Perf. 13¼*
2759 A1276 Sheet of 2 8.00 8.00
a. €1.65 multi 3.50 2.75
b. €2.10 multi 4.50 3.50

2014 World Cup Soccer Tournament, Brazil A1277

2014, May 30 Photo. *Perf. 13*
2760 A1277 98c multi 2.00 1.50

Values are for stamp with surrounding selvage.

Prince Honoré IV (1758-1819) — A1278

2014, May 30 Engr. *Perf. 13x13¼*
2761 A1278 €2.10 multi 4.50 3.50

Treaty of Paris, 200th anniv., which restored Prince Honoré IV to Monegasque throne.

Souvenir Sheet

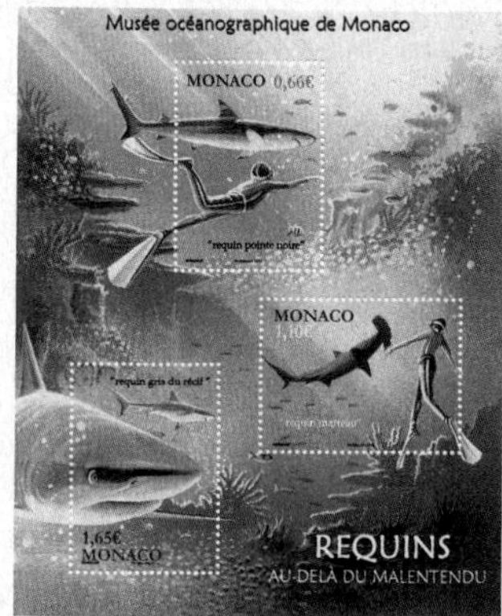

Sharks — A1279

No. 2762: a, Blacktip reef shark and diver. b, Hammerhead shark and diver, horiz. c, Gray reef sharks.

2014, June 10 Photo. *Perf. 13¼*
2762 A1279 Sheet of 3 7.50 7.50
a. 66c multi 1.25 .90
b. €1.10 multi 2.25 1.60
c. €1.65 multi 3.50 2.75

Princess Grace Rose Garden, 30th Anniv. — A1280

Litho. & Silk-Screened
2014, June 14 *Perf. 13¼*
2763 A1280 66c multi 1.25 .90

No. 2763 is impregnated with a rose scent.

Protea Flowers A1281

2014, June 14 Litho. *Perf. 13¼*
2764 A1281 83c multi 1.75 1.25

New Clubhouse of Yacht Club of Monaco A1282

Litho. & Engr.
2014, June 20 *Perf. 13¼*
2765 A1282 83c multi 1.75 1.25

Scorpionfish — A1283

2014, June 25 Litho. *Perf. 13¼*
2766 A1283 (40c) multi .85 .65

No. 2766 is known only precanceled. See note after No. 324.

Ceratonia Siliqua — A1284

2014, July 12 Photo. *Perf. 13¼*
2767 A1284 61c multi 1.25 .90

Princess Stephanie and Elephants Baby and Nepal A1285

2014, July 12 Engr. *Perf. 13x13¼*
2768 A1285 €1.10 multi 2.25 1.60

Baby & Nepal Association, 1st anniv.

World War I, Cent. A1286

Designs: €1.85, Hotel Alexandra (military hospital during war). €2.40, Prince Louis II, volunteer in French Army, and soldiers.

2014, Aug. 1 Engr. *Perf. 13x13¼*
2769-2770 A1286 Set of 2 9.00 7.50

2014 Grande Bourse — A1287

2014, Aug. 22 Litho. *Perf. 13¼x13*
2771 A1287 59c multi 1.25 .90

Opera Set Designed by Eugène Frey (1864-1930) — A1288

Litho., Silk-Screened & Embossed
2014, Aug. 22 *Perf. 13x13¼*
2772 A1288 €1.38 multi 3.00 2.25

Sportel Monaco (World Sports Content Media Convention), 25th Anniv. — A1289

2014, Sept. 1 Litho. *Perf. 13¼*
2773 A1289 59c multi 1.25 .90

Children's Day — A1290

2014, Sept. 1 Engr. *Perf. 13¼*
2774 A1290 66c multi 1.40 1.00

Intl. Convention on the Rights of the Child, 25th Anniv.

Coat of Arms Type of 2000 Inscribed "20g prioritaire" at Top
Serpentine Die Cut 11
2014, Sept. 17 Photo.
Booklet Stamp Self-Adhesive
2775 A786 (66c) red & black 1.40 1.00
a. Booklet pane of 10 14.00

83rd Interpol General Assembly, Monaco — A1291

2014, Nov. 3 Litho. *Perf. 13¼x13*
2776 A1291 66c multi 1.40 1.00

Adoration of the Magi, by Taddeo di Bartolo A1292

2014, Nov. 3 Photo. *Perf. 13¼*
2777 A1292 66c multi 1.40 1.00

Christmas.

Exhibition on Prince Albert I's Exploration of Morocco, Rabat — A1293

No. 2778: a, Hassan Tower, Rabat. b, Oceanographic Museum, Monaco.

2014, Nov. 7 Photo. *Perf. 13¼*
2778 A1293 Horiz. pair 3.50 3.50
a. 66c multi 1.40 1.00
b. 98c multi 2.00 1.50

See Morocco No.

127th International Olympic Committee Session, Monaco — A1294

Litho. & Engr.
2014, Dec. 1 *Perf. 13¼*
2779 A1294 66c multi 1.40 1.00

Fight AIDS Monaco, 10th Anniv. — A1295

Litho. & Silk-Screened With Flocking Application
2014, Dec. 1 *Perf. 13¼*
2780 A1295 €1 red & black 2.00 1.50

39th Intl. Circus Festival, Monte Carlo — A1296

2015, Jan. 7 Photo. *Perf. 13¼*
2781 A1296 95c multi 2.00 1.50

Russian Year in Monaco — A1297

No. 2782: a, Text (30x30mm). b, Buildings in Russia and Monaco (41x30mm).

2015, Jan. 7 Photo. *Perf. 13¼*
2782 A1297 Horiz. pair 5.00 5.00
a.-b. €1.20 Either single 2.50 1.75

Posters for Movies Starring Grace Kelly Type of 2014

Designs: €1.50, The Swan (Le Cygne). €2, To Catch a Thief (La Main au Collet).

2015, Jan. 14 Litho. *Perf. 13¼*
2783-2784 A1261 Set of 2 7.50 6.00

Posidonia Oceanica A1298

2015, Jan. 21 Photo. *Perf. 13¼*
2785 A1298 68c multi 1.50 1.10

Kiwanis International, Cent. — A1299

2015, Jan. 21 Litho. *Perf. 13¼*
2786 A1299 95c multi 2.00 1.50

Princess Antoinette Park A1300

2015, Jan. 21 Photo. *Perf. 13¼*
2787 A1300 €1.45 multi 3.00 2.25

German Shorthaired Pointer A1301

2015, Feb. 5 Litho. *Perf. 13¼*
2788 A1301 €1.05 multi 2.25 1.60

Intl. Dog Show.

Monte Carlo Rolex Masters Tennis Tournament A1302

2015, Feb. 5 Litho. *Perf. 13¼*
2789 A1302 €1.25 multi 2.75 1.75

Intl. Flower Arrangement Festival — A1303

2015, Feb. 5 Engr. *Perf. 13¼*
2790 A1303 €1.45 multi 3.00 2.25

Souvenir Sheet

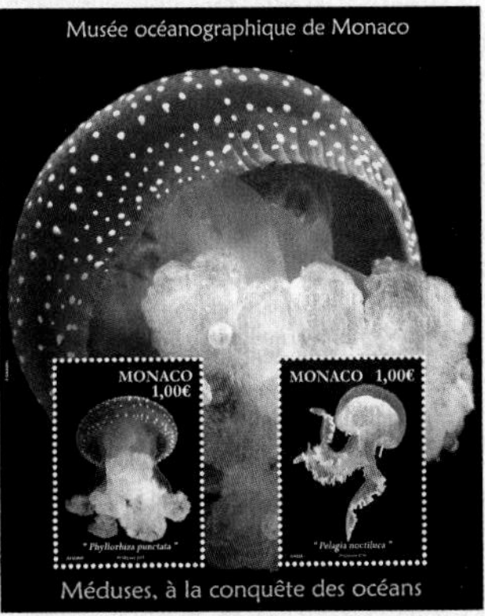

Jellyfish — A1304

No. 2791: a, Phyllorhiza punctata. b, Pelagia noctiluca.

2015, Feb. 25 Photo. *Perf. 13¼*
2791 A1304 Sheet of 2 4.50 4.50
a.-b. €1 Either single 2.25 2.25

Monaco Pavilion at Expo Milan 2015 A1305

2015, Mar. 5 Litho. *Perf. 13¼*
2792 A1305 €1 multi 2.25 2.25

Michele Alboreto (1956-2001), Formula 1 Race Car Driver — A1306

Graham Hill (1929-75), Formula 1 Race Car Driver — A1307

No. 2793: a, Alboreto wearing helmet (31x31mm). b, Alboreto in race car (52x31mm).

No. 2794: a, Hill wearing helmet (31x31mm). b, Hill in race car (52x31mm).

2015, Mar. 5 Engr. *Perf. 13*
2793 A1306 Horiz. pair 4.00 4.00
a. 76c multi 1.75 1.75
b. 95c multi 2.10 2.10
2794 A1307 Horiz. pair 5.50 5.50
a. 95c multi 2.10 2.10
b. €1.50 multi 3.25 3.25

Monacosat A1308

2015, Mar. 23 Litho. *Perf. 13¼*
2795 A1308 76c multi 1.75 1.75

Caritas Monaco, 25th Anniv. — A1309

2015, Mar. 23 Litho. *Perf. 13¼*
2796 A1309 76c multi 1.75 1.75

La Nymphe Salamacis, Sculpture by François-Joseph Bosio (1768-1845) — A1310

2015, Apr. 9 Engr. *Perf. 13x12¼*
2797 A1310 €1.25 red & black 3.00 3.00

Dante Alighieri (1265-1321), Writer — A1311

Litho. & Engr.
2015, Apr. 9 *Perf. 13x13¼*
2798 A1311 €1.90 dp car, blk & brn 4.25 4.25

Souvenir Sheet

Birth of Prince Jacques and Princess Gabriella — A1312

No. 2799 — Prince Albert II, Princess Charlène and twins: a, Color photograph. b, Sepia-toned photograph.

2015, Apr. 27 Litho. *Perf. 13¼*
2799 A1312 Sheet of 2 9.00 9.00
a.-b. €2 Either single 4.50 4.50

Formula E Race Car — A1313

2015, May 9 Litho. *Perf. 13¼*

2800 A1313 €1.05 multi 2.40 2.40

2015 Monaco ePrix race for electric cars.

Europa A1314

2015, May 11 Litho. *Perf. 13¼*

2801 A1314 95c multi 2.10 2.10

International Telecommunications Union, 150th Anniv. — A1315

2015, May 11 Litho. *Perf. 13¼*

2802 A1315 €1.25 purple 2.75 2.75

Miniature Sheet

Old Travel Posters for Granville, France — A1316

No. 2803 — Poster by: a, Jacquier. b, Pazy. c, Commarmond. d, Dorival.

2015, June 15 Photo. *Perf. 13¼x13*

2803 A1316 Sheet of 4 6.50 6.50
a.-b. 66c Either single 1.50 1.50
c.-d. 76c Either single 1.75 1.75

Visit of Prince Albert II to Grimaldi Family fiefdom of Granville.

Rainier III Academy for Music and Theater — A1317

2015, June 17 Litho. *Perf. 13¼*

2804 A1317 66c multi 1.50 1.50

Dancers, Building and Theater Curtains A1318

2015, June 17 Litho. *Perf. 13¼*

2805 A1318 €1.20 multi 2.75 2.75

Miniature Sheet

Automobile Club of Monaco, 125th Anniv. — A1319

No. 2806 — Club emblem and race car in: a, Red. b, Blue. c, Yellow brown. d, Green.

2015, June 25 Photo. *Perf. 13x13¼*

2806 A1319 Sheet of 4 11.00 11.00
a.-d. €1.25 Any single 2.75 2.75

Monaco Oceanographic Museum — A1320

2015, July 1 Photo. *Perf. 13x13¼*

2807 A1320 76c multi 1.75 1.75

50,000,000th visitor at Monaco Oceanographic Museum.

Fortress of Monaco (Prince's Residence), 800th Anniv. — A1321

2015, July 11 Litho. *Perf. 13¼*

2808 A1321 95c multi 2.10 2.10

Souvenir Sheet

Reign of Prince Albert II, 10th Anniv. — A1322

No. 2809: a, Prince Albert II, whales, map, flag on ice sheet (41x30mm). b, Fortress, flags, monogram of Prince Albert II (30x30mm). c, Monaco skyline (41x30mm).

2015, July 11 Photo. *Perf. 13¼*

2809 A1322 Sheet of 3 6.75 6.75
a.-c. €1 Any single 2.25 2.25

2015 Rugby World Cup, Great Britain A1323

2015, Aug. 17 Photo. *Perf. 13*

2810 A1323 €1.20 multi 2.75 2.75

Values are for stamps with surrounding selvage.

MonacoPhil 2015 Intl. Philatelic Exhibition — A1324

2015, Sept. 3 Litho. *Perf. 13¼*

2811 A1324 76c multi 1.75 1.75

2015 Grand Bourse — A1325

2015, Sept. 3 Litho. *Perf. 13¼*

2812 A1325 76c multi 1.75 1.75

25th Monaco Yacht Show, Port Hercule A1326

2015, Sept. 3 Litho. *Perf. 13¼*

2813 A1326 €1.20 multi 2.75 2.75

Alliance Between Grimaldi and Matignon Families, 300th Anniv. A1327

2015, Sept. 3 Engr. *Perf. 13x13¼*

2814 A1327 €1.50 multi 3.50 3.50

Pyotr Ilyich Tchaikovsky (1840-93), Composer A1328

2015, Sept. 10 Engr. *Perf. 13¼*

2815 A1328 €2 multi 4.50 4.50

Francesco Tamagno (1850-1905), Opera Singer — A1329

Adelina Patti (1843-1919), Opera Singer — A1330

2015, Sept. 10 Engr. *Perf. 13x12¼*

2816 A1329 €2.60 multi 6.00 6.00
2817 A1330 €3.05 multi 7.00 7.00

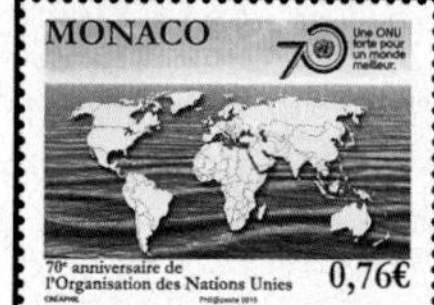

United Nations, 70th Anniv. A1331

2015, Oct. 24 Litho. *Perf. 13¼*

2818 A1331 76c multi 1.75 1.75

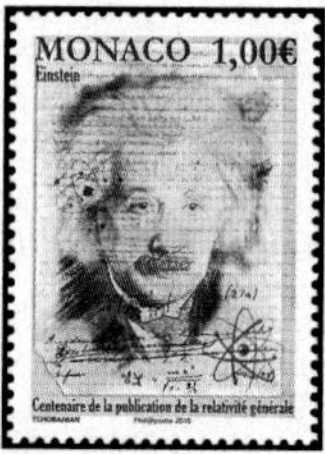

Publication of Albert Einstein's Works on General Relativity, Cent. — A1332

2015, Oct. 24 Litho. *Perf. 13¼*

2819 A1332 €1 multi 2.25 2.25

Christmas A1333

2015, Nov. 3 Litho. *Perf. 13¼*

2820 A1333 76c multi 1.60 1.60

Princess Charlene of Monaco Rose — A1334

2015, Dec. 3 Photo. *Perf. 13¼*

2821 A1334 68c multi 1.50 1.50

Princess Charlene A1335

2015, Dec. 3 Engr. *Perf. 13¼*
2822 A1335 €1.60 brn pur 3.50 3.50

Souvenir Sheet

MonacoPhil 2015 — A1336

No. 2823: a, Prince Albert I's Arctic expedition. b, Prince Albert I (1848-1922), vert.

Engr., Sheet Margin Litho. & Engr.
2015, Dec. 3 *Perf. 13x13¼, 13¼x13*
2823 A1336 Sheet of 2 11.00 11.00
a.-b. €2.50 Either single 5.50 5.50

5th New Generation Circus Festival — A1337

40th Intl. Circus Festival, Monte Carlo — A1338

No. 2825 — Posters for: a, 10th Intl. Circus Festival. b, 20th Intl. Circus Festival. c, 30th Intl. Circus Festival. d, 40th Intl. Circus Festival.

2016, Jan. 5 Litho. *Perf. 13¼*
2824 A1337 80c multi 1.75 1.75
2825 A1338 Sheet of 4 8.00 8.00
a.-b. 80c Either single 1.75 1.75
c.-d. €1 Either single 2.25 2.25

Prince Albert II Type of 2012

Inscription: (68c), Ecopli. (80c), Prioritaire. (€1), Europe.

2016, Jan. 15 Engr. *Perf. 13x13¼*
2826 A1221 (68c) blue 1.50 1.50
2827 A1221 (80c) red 1.75 1.75
2828 A1221 (€1) red violet 2.25 2.25
Nos. 2826-2828 (3) 5.50 5.50

2016 Winter Youth Olympics, Lillehammer, Norway — A1339

2016, Feb. 3 Photo. *Perf. 13¼*
2829 A1339 €1.25 multi 2.75 2.75

Monte Carlo Rolex Masters Tennis Tournament A1340

2016, Feb. 3 Litho. *Perf. 13¼*
2830 A1340 €1.60 multi 3.50 3.50

Princess Grace Rose Garden A1341

2016, Feb. 5 Litho. *Perf. 13¼*
2831 A1341 70c multi 1.50 1.50

Continental Toy Spaniel A1342

2016, Feb. 5 Litho. *Perf. 13¼*
2832 A1342 €1.25 multi 2.75 2.75

Intl. Dog Show.

Sciaena Umbra A1343

2016, Feb. 5 Engr. *Perf. 13x13¼*
2833 A1343 €1.60 multi 3.50 3.50

Race Cars A1344

Designs: 80c, March 711. €1.36, Auto Union Type C.

2016, Mar. 1 Photo. *Perf. 13¼*
2834-2835 A1344 Set of 2 4.75 4.75

Ronnie Peterson (1944-78), Formula 1 Race Car Driver — A1345

No. 2836: a, Peterson (31x31mm). b, Peterson (52x31mm).

2016, Mar. 1 Photo. *Perf. 13*
2836 A1345 Horiz. pair 4.00 4.00
a. 80c multi 1.75 1.75
b. €1 multi 2.25 2.25

Prince Pierre of Monaco (1895-1964) A1346

2016, Mar. 16 Engr. *Perf. 13¼*
2837 A1346 68c multi 1.60 1.60

Prince Pierre of Monaco Foundation, 50th anniv.

Orchestra of the Palace Guards, 50th Anniv. A1347

2016, Mar. 16 Photo. *Perf. 13¼*
2838 A1347 €1 multi 2.25 2.25

Prince Charles III (1818-89) and Sovereign Order Creating Monte Carlo — A1348

2016, Mar. 16 Engr. *Perf. 13x13¼*
2839 A1348 €1.36 multi 3.25 3.25

Foundation of Monte Carlo, 150th anniv.

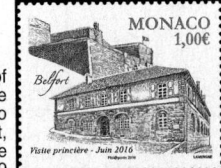

Visit of Prince Albert II to Belfort, France A1349

2016, Apr. 1 Engr. *Perf. 13x13¼*
2840 A1349 €1 multi 2.25 2.25

Miniature Sheet

Lifecycle of Caretta Caretta — A1350

No. 2841: a, Juvenile at sea, denomination at UR. b, Adult at sea, denomination at UL. c, Hatchlings leaving shell. d, Female laying eggs, vert.

Photo. & Thermography
2016, Apr. 1 *Perf. 13¼*
2841 A1350 Sheet of 4 10.00 10.00
a.-b. 80c Either single 1.90 1.90
c. €1 multi 2.25 2.25
d. €1.60 multi 3.75 3.75

Intl. Flower Arrangement Festival — A1351

2016, Apr. 29 Litho. *Perf. 13¼*
2842 A1351 80c multi 1.90 1.90

Europa A1352

2016, May 9 Litho. *Perf. 13¼*
2843 A1352 €1 multi 2.25 2.25

Think Green Issue.

Mercury Teaching Geography to Love, by Louis-Jean-François Lagrenée, the Elder (1725-1805) — A1353

2016, May 12 Litho. *Perf. 13¼*
2844 A1353 €2 multi 4.50 4.50

Posters for Movies Starring Grace Kelly Type of 2014

Designs: €1.60, Rear Window (Fenêtre sur Cour). €2, The Bridges at Toko-Ri (Les Ponts de Toko-Ri).

2016, May 19 Litho. *Perf. 13¼*
2845-2846 A1261 Set of 2 8.00 8.00

Nellie Melba (1861-1931), Opera Singer — A1354

Enrico Caruso (1873-1921), Opera Singer — A1355

2016, May 19 Engr. *Perf. 13x13¼*
2847 A1354 €1.36 multi 3.00 3.00

Perf. 13¼
2848 A1355 €2.50 multi 5.75 5.75

2016 European Soccer Championships, France — A1356

2016, June 1 Photo. *Perf. 13*
2849 A1356 €1 multi 2.25 2.25

Values are for stamps with surrounding selvage.

2016 Summer Olympics, Rio de Janeiro A1357

2016, June 1 Litho. *Perf. 13¼*
2850 A1357 €1.25 multi 2.75 2.75

Tree, La Rocher A1358

2016, June 24 Litho. *Perf. 13¼*
2851 A1358 €1 multi 2.25 2.25

Prince Albert I, Observatory Cave Archaeological Excavations — A1359

2016, June 24 Engr. *Perf. 13x13¼*
2852 A1359 €1.60 multi 3.75 3.75

Observatory Cave archaeological excavations, cent.

Emblem of Prince Albert II Foundation A1360

Conservation Efforts of Prince Albert II Foundation — A1361

No. 2854: a, Polar bear. b, Desert landscape. c, Tiger. d, Forest.

Litho. & Silk-Screened

2016, June 30 *Perf. 13¼*
2853 A1360 70c multi 1.60 1.60
2854 A1361 Sheet of 4 11.00 11.00
a.-d. €1.25 Any single 2.75 2.75

10th Anniv. of Prince Albert II of Monaco Foundation.

Princess Grace and Child — A1362

2016, July 5 Litho. *Perf. 13¼*
2855 A1362 68c multi 1.50 1.50

Association Mondial des Amis de l'Enfance, 50th anniv.

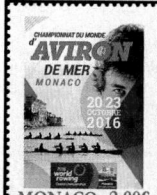

2016 World Rowing Coastal Championships, Monaco — A1363

2016, July 21 Litho. *Perf. 13¼*
2856 A1363 €2 multi 4.50 4.50

Monte Carlo Ballet Company Dancer — A1364

2016, July 21 Litho. *Perf. 13x13¼*
2857 A1364 €2.72 multi 6.25 6.25

24th Grande Bourse — A1365

2016, Aug. 24 Litho. *Perf. 13¼*
2858 A1365 80c multi 1.90 1.90

Léo Ferré (1916-93), Singer — A1366

2016, Aug. 24 Engr. *Perf. 13¼*
2859 A1366 €1.36 red & brnish blk 3.00 3.00

Miniature Sheet

Worldwide Fund for Nature (WWF) — A1367

No. 2860 — Thalassoma pavo: a, One facing right. b, One facing left. c, Two facing left and coral. d, Two fish and starfish.

Perf. 13¼x13½

2016, Sept. 15 Photo.
2860 A1367 Sheet of 4 9.00 9.00
a.-d. €1 Any single 2.25 2.25

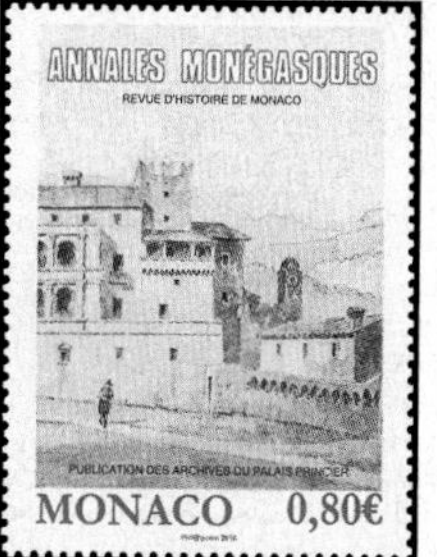

Monégasque Annals, 40th Anniv. of Publication — A1368

2016, Nov. 4 Litho. *Perf. 13¼x13*
2861 A1368 80c multi 1.75 1.75

Christmas A1369

2016, Nov. 4 Litho. *Perf. 13¼*
2862 A1369 80c multi 1.75 1.75

Coat of Arms Type of 2000 Inscribed "écopli" at Top

Serpentine Die Cut 11

2017, Jan. 3 Photo.

Booklet Stamp Self-Adhesive

2863 A786 (71c) blue & multi 1.50 1.50
a. Booklet pane of 10 15.00

Compare with No. 2673.

41st Intl. Circus Festival, Monte Carlo — A1370

Photo. & Embossed With Foil Application

2017, Jan. 3 *Perf. 13¼*
2864 A1370 €1.10 multi 2.40 2.40

Grace Kelly Movie Posters Type of 2013

Designs: €1.42, Mogambo. €2.20, High Noon (Le Train Siffera 3 Fois).

2017, Jan. 16 Litho. *Perf. 13¼*
2865-2866 A1261 Set of 2 7.75 7.75

SEMI-POSTAL STAMPS

No. 16 Surcharged in Red

1914, Oct. Unwmk. *Perf. 14x13½*
B1 A2 10c + 5c carmine 5.00 5.00

View of Monaco — SP2

1919, Sept. 20 Typo.

B2	SP2 2c + 3c lilac	32.50	*32.50*
B3	SP2 5c + 5c green	17.50	*17.50*
B4	SP2 15c + 10c rose	17.50	*17.50*
B5	SP2 25c + 15c blue	37.50	*37.50*
B6	SP2 50c + 50c brn, buff	175.00	*150.00*
B7	SP2 1fr + 1fr blk, *yel*	275.00	*150.00*
B8	SP2 5fr + 5fr dull red	925.00	*1,050.*
	Nos. B2-B8 (7)	1,480.	*1,455.*

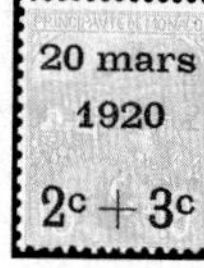

Nos. B4-B8 Surcharged

1920, Mar. 20

B9	SP2 2c + 3c on #B4	37.50	*37.50*
a.	"c" of "3c" inverted	*1,500.*	*1,500.*
b.	Pair, Nos. 9, 9a	*2,250.*	*2,250.*
B10	SP2 2c + 3c on #B5	37.50	*37.50*
a.	"c" of "3c" inverted	*1,500.*	*1,500.*
b.	Pair, Nos. 10, 10a	*2,250.*	*2,250.*
B11	SP2 2c + 3c on #B6	37.50	*37.50*
a.	"c" of "3c" inverted	*1,500.*	*1,500.*
b.	Pair, Nos. 11, 11a	*2,250.*	*2,250.*
B12	SP2 5c + 5c on #B7	37.50	*37.50*
B13	SP2 5c + 5c on #B8	37.50	*37.50*

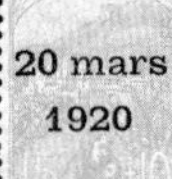

Overprinted

B14	SP2 15c + 10c rose	25.00	25.00
B15	SP2 25c + 15c blue	10.50	10.50
B16	SP2 50c + 50c brn, *buff*	50.00	50.00
B17	SP2 1fr + 1fr blk, *yel*	67.50	67.50
B18	SP2 5fr + 5fr red	5,800.	5,800.
	Nos. B9-B17 (9)	340.50	340.50

Marriage of Princess Charlotte to Prince Pierre, Comte de Polignac.

Palace Gardens SP3

"The Rock" of Monaco SP4

Bay of Monaco SP5

Prince Louis II — SP6

1937, Apr. Engr. *Perf. 13*

B19	SP3	50c + 50c green	2.10	2.10
B20	SP4	90c + 90c car	2.10	2.10
B21	SP5	1.50fr + 1.50fr blue	5.00	5.00
B22	SP6	2fr + 2fr violet	8.50	8.50
B23	SP6	5fr + 5fr brn red	60.00	60.00
		Nos. B19-B23 (5)	77.70	77.70
		Set, never hinged	225.00	

The surtax was used for welfare work.

Pierre and Marie Curie — SP7

Monaco Hospital, Date Palms SP8

1938, Nov. 15 *Perf. 13*

B24	SP7	65c + 25c dp bl grn	9.00	9.00
B25	SP8	1.75fr + 50c dp ultra	9.00	9.00
		Set, never hinged	35.00	

B24 and B25 exist imperforate.

The surtax was for the International Union for the Control of Cancer.

Lucien — SP9

Honoré II — SP10

Louis I — SP11

Charlotte de Gramont — SP12

Antoine I — SP13

Marie de Lorraine — SP14

Jacques I SP15

Louise-Hippolyte SP16

Honoré III — SP17

"The Rock," 18th Century SP18

1939, June 26

B26	SP9	5c + 5c brn blk	1.25	.75
B27	SP10	10c + 10c rose vio	1.25	.75
B28	SP11	45c + 15c brt grn	4.50	3.50
B29	SP12	70c + 30c brt red vio	6.75	6.00
B30	SP13	90c + 35c vio	6.75	6.00
B31	SP14	1fr + 1fr ultra	17.00	16.00
B32	SP15	2fr + 2fr brn org	17.00	16.00
B33	SP16	2.25fr + 1.25fr Prus bl	20.00	20.00
B34	SP17	3fr + 3fr dp rose	27.50	*27.50*
B35	SP18	5fr + 5fr red	50.00	*50.00*
		Nos. B26-B35 (10)	152.00	146.50
		Set, never hinged	400.00	

Types of Regular Issue, 1939 Surcharged in Red

1940, Feb. 10 Engr. *Perf. 13*

B36	A30	20c + 1fr violet	1.75	1.75
B37	A31	25c + 1fr dk grn	1.75	1.75
B38	A32	30c + 1fr brn red	1.75	1.75
B39	A31	40c + 1fr dk blue	1.75	1.75
B40	A33	45c + 1fr rose car	1.75	1.75
B41	A34	50c + 1fr brown	1.75	1.75
B42	A32	60c + 1fr dk grn	2.25	2.25
B43	A35	75c + 1fr brn blk	2.25	2.25
B44	A34	1fr + 1fr scarlet	3.00	3.00
B45	A31	2fr + 1fr indigo	3.00	3.00
B46	A33	2.50fr + 1fr dk grn	7.00	7.00
B47	A35	3fr + 1fr dk blue	7.00	7.00
B48	A30	5fr + 1fr brn blk	9.50	9.50
B49	A33	10fr + 5fr lt blue	18.00	18.00
B50	A32	20fr + 5fr brn vio	18.00	18.00
		Nos. B36-B50 (15)	80.50	80.50
		Set, never hinged	240.00	

The surtax was used to purchase ambulances for the French government.

Catalogue values for unused stamps in this section, from this point to the end of the section, are for Never Hinged items.

Symbol of Charity and View of Monaco SP19

Symbol of Charity and View of Monaco — SP20

1941, May 15

B51	SP19	25c + 25c brt red vio	3.25	1.60
B52	SP20	50c + 25c dk brn	3.25	1.60
B53	SP20	75c + 50c rose vio	5.75	2.00
B54	SP19	1fr + 1fr dk blue	5.75	2.00
B55	SP20	1.50fr + 1.50fr rose red	6.00	2.00
B56	SP19	2fr + 2fr Prus grn	6.25	2.75
B57	SP20	2.50fr + 2fr brt ultra	7.75	3.50
B58	SP19	3fr + 3fr dl red brn	10.00	4.00
B59	SP20	5fr + 5fr dk bl grn	14.50	5.75
B60	SP19	10fr + 8fr brn blk	21.00	11.50
		Nos. B51-B60 (10)	83.50	36.70

The surtax was for various charities.

Rainier Grimaldi — SP21

Designs: 5c, Charles II. 10c, Jeanne Grimaldi. 20c, Charles-August Goyon de Matignon. 30c, Jacques I. 40c, Louise-Hippolyte. 50c, Charlotte Grimaldi. 75c, Marie-Charles Grimaldi. 1fr, Honore III. 1.50fr, Honore IV. 2.50fr, Honore V. 3fr, Florestan I. 5fr, Charles III. 10fr, Albert I. 20fr, Marie-Victoire. Frames differ.

1942, Dec. 10

B61	SP21	2c + 3c ultra	.35	.35
B62	SP21	5c + 5c org ver	.35	.35
B63	SP21	10c + 5c blk	.35	.35
B64	SP21	20c + 10c brt grn	.35	.35
B65	SP21	30c + 30c brn vio	.35	.35
B66	SP21	40c + 40c rose red	.35	.35
B67	SP21	50c + 50c vio	.35	.35
B68	SP21	75c + 75c brt red vio	.35	.35
B69	SP21	1fr + 1fr dk grn	.35	.35
B70	SP21	1.50fr + 1fr car brn	.35	.35
B71	SP21	2.50fr + 2.50fr pur	4.25	3.50
B72	SP21	3fr + 3fr turq bl	4.50	3.50
B73	SP21	5fr + 5fr sepia	5.00	4.50
B74	SP21	10fr + 5fr rose lil	5.50	5.00
B75	SP21	20fr + 5fr ultra	6.50	5.75
		Nos. B61-B75 (15)	29.25	25.75

Saint Dévote SP36

Procession SP37

Procession SP38

Church of St. Dévote — SP39

Burning of Symbolic Boat — SP40

Blessing of the Sea SP41

Church of St. Dévote SP42

Trial of St. Barbara — SP43

Arrival of St. Dévote at Monaco — SP44

1944, Jan. 27 Unwmk. *Perf. 13*

B76	SP36	50c + 50c sepia	.25	.25
B77	SP37	70c + 80c dp ultra	.25	.25
B78	SP38	80c + 70c green	.25	.25
B79	SP39	1fr + 1fr rose vio	.25	.25
B80	SP40	1.50fr + 1.50fr red	.35	.35
B81	SP41	2fr + 2fr brn vio	.65	.65
B82	SP42	5fr + 2fr violet	.65	.65
B83	SP43	10fr + 40fr royal bl	.65	.65
B84	SP44	20fr + 60fr chlky bl	4.50	4.50
		Nos. B76-B84 (9)	7.80	7.80

Issued in honor of St. Dévote.

Type SP43 is inscribed "Jugement de Sainte Dévote," but actually shows the trial of St. Barbara in 235 A.D.

Needy Child — SP45

1946, Feb. 18 Engr.

B85	SP45	1fr + 3fr dp bl grn	.30	.30
B86	SP45	2fr + 4fr rose pink	.30	.30
B87	SP45	4fr + 6fr dk bl	.30	.30
B88	SP45	5fr + 40fr dk vio	.90	.75
B89	SP45	10fr + 60fr brn red	.90	.75
B90	SP45	15fr + 100fr indigo	1.40	1.10
		Nos. B85-B90 (6)	4.10	3.50

The surtax was for child welfare.

Nurse and Child — SP46

1946, Feb. 18

B91 SP46 2fr + 8fr brt blue .75 .70

The surtax was used for prevention of tuberculosis.

19th Century Steamer and Map SP47

1946

B92 SP47 3fr + 2fr deep blue .50 .50

Stamp Day, June 23, 1946.

Harbor of Monte Carlo SP48

1946, Dec. 13

B93 SP48 2fr + 3fr dk bluish grn 1.40 1.40

Issued in tribute to the memory of Franklin D. Roosevelt. The surtax was for a fund to erect a monument in his honor.

Prince Louis II Type

Souvenir Sheet

Unwmk.

1947, May 15 Engr. *Imperf.*

B94 A46 200fr + 300fr dk red & choc 30.00 19.00

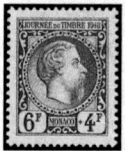

Prince Charles III — SP50

1948, Mar. 6 *Perf. 14x13*

B95 SP50 6fr + 4fr dk bl grn, *lt bl* .50 .50

Issued for Stamp Day, Mar. 6.

Princess Charlotte SP51

Prince Rainier III SP52

Perf. 13½x13, Imperf.

1949, Dec. 27 Engr.

Cross Typo. in Red

B96 SP51 10fr + 5fr red brown 10.00 10.00
B97 SP52 15fr + 5fr brt red 10.00 10.00
B98 SP52 25fr + 5fr dk vio bl 10.00 10.00
B99 SP51 40fr + 5fr dull green 10.00 10.00
a. Block of 4, #B96-B99 45.00 45.00

Printed in sheets measuring 151x173mm, perf. and imperf., containing 4 of No. B99a.
The surtax was for the Red Cross.
For surcharges see Nos. 288-291.

Hercules Strangling the Lion of Nemea — SP53

Twelve Labors of Hercules: No. B101, Killing the Hydra of Lerna. No. B102, Capturing the Erymanthean boar. No. B103, Killing Stymphalian birds. No. B104, Hercules and the Ceryneian Hind. No. B105, The Augean Stables. No. B106, Hercules and the Cretan Bull. No. B107, Wild horses of Diomedes. No. B108, Hercules and the Oxen of Geryon. No. B109, Hercules and the Belt of Hippolytus. No. B110, Winning the golden apple of Hesperides. No. B111, Battling Cerberus.

1981, Nov. 5 Engr. *Perf. 13*

B100 SP53 2.50fr + 50c multi 1.25 1.25
B101 SP53 3.50fr + 50c multi 1.25 1.25

1982, Nov. 8

B102 SP53 2.50fr + 50c multi 1.25 1.25
B103 SP53 3.50fr + 50c multi 1.25 1.25

1983, Nov. 9

B104 SP53 2.50fr + 50c multi 1.25 1.25
B105 SP53 3.50fr + 50c multi 1.25 1.25

1984, Nov. 8

B106 SP53 3fr + 50c multi 1.25 1.25
B107 SP53 4fr + 50c multi 1.25 1.25

1985, Nov. 7

B108 SP53 3fr + 70c multi 1.25 1.25
B109 SP53 4fr + 80c multi 1.25 1.25

1986, Oct. 28

B110 SP53 3fr + 70c multi 1.25 1.25
B111 SP53 4fr + 80c multi 1.25 1.25
Nos. B100-B111 (12) 15.00 15.00

Surtax on #B100-B111 for the Red Cross.

Monegasque Committee to Fight Tuberculosis and Respiratory Diseases — SP54

1994, Mar. 14 Litho. *Perf. 13½x13*

B112 SP54 2.40fr +60c multi 1.00 1.00

AIR POST STAMPS

No. 91 Srchd. in Black

Perf. 14x13½

1933, Aug. 22 Unwmk.

C1 A15 1.50fr on 5fr 16.00 16.00
a. Imperf., pair 350.00

Catalogue values for unused stamps in this section, from this point to the end of the section, are for Never Hinged items.

Plane over Monaco — AP1

Plane Propeller and Buildings — AP2

Pegasus — AP3

Sea Gull — AP4

Plane, Globe and Arms of Monaco AP5

1942, Apr. 15 Engr. *Perf. 13*

C2 AP1 5fr blue green .30 .30
C3 AP1 10fr ultra .30 .30
C4 AP2 15fr sepia .60 .60
C5 AP3 20fr henna brown .85 .85
C6 AP4 50fr red violet 4.25 3.50
C7 AP5 100fr red & vio brn 4.25 3.50
Nos. C2-C7 (6) 10.55 9.05

For surcharges see Nos. CB1-CB5.

Nos. 196-197 Overprinted in Blue

1946, May 20

C8 A41 50fr dp Prus green 4.00 4.00
C9 A41 100fr red 4.00 4.00
a. Inverted overprint 37,500.
b. Double overprint 22,500.

Douglas DC-3 and Arms AP6

1946, May 20

C10 AP6 40fr red 1.00 .50
C11 AP6 50fr red brown 2.00 .70
C12 AP6 100fr dp blue grn 2.50 1.25
C13 AP6 200fr violet 2.75 2.00
Nos. C10-C13 (4) 8.25 4.45

Exist imperforate. See Nos. C27-C29.

Harbor of Monte Carlo AP7

Map of Monaco — AP8

1946, Dec. 13

C14 AP7 5fr carmine rose .40 .40
C15 AP8 10fr violet black .55 .55

Issued in tribute to the memory of Franklin D. Roosevelt.

Franklin D. Roosevelt Examining his Stamp Collection AP9

Main Post Office, New York City AP10

Oceanographic Museum, Monaco — AP11

Harbor of Monte Carlo — AP12

Statue of Liberty and New York City Skyline — AP13

1947, May 15 Unwmk.

C16 AP9 50c violet 1.25 1.25
C17 AP10 1.50fr rose violet .55 .55
C18 AP11 3fr henna brown .55 .55
C19 AP12 10fr deep blue 3.00 3.00
C20 AP13 15fr rose carmine 6.00 6.00
a. Strip of 3, #C20, 203, C19 13.00 13.00
Nos. C16-C20 (5) 11.35 11.35

Monaco's participation in the Centenary Intl. Philatelic Exhibition, NYC, May, 1947.

Crowd Acclaiming Constitution of 1911 AP14

Anthropological Museum — AP15

Designs: 25fr, Institute of Human Paleontology, Paris. 50fr, Albert I. 100fr, Oceanographic Institute, Paris. 200fr, Albert I medal.

1949, Mar. 5 Engr. *Perf. 13*

C21 AP14 20fr brown red .85 .85
C22 AP14 25fr indigo .85 .85
C23 AP15 40fr blue green 1.40 1.40
C24 AP15 50fr blk, brn & grn 2.10 2.10
C25 AP15 100fr cerise 6.50 6.50
C26 AP14 200fr deep orange 9.00 9.00
Nos. C21-C26 (6) 20.70 20.70

Plane-Arms Type of 1946

1949, Mar. 10

C27 AP6 300fr dp ultra & ind 45.00 45.00
C28 AP6 500fr grnsh blk & bl grn 37.50 30.00
C29 AP6 1000fr black & red vio 67.50 45.00
Nos. C27-C29 (3) 150.00 120.00

UPU Type of Regular Issue

1949-50

C30 A56 25fr deep blue .50 .50
C31 A56 40fr red brown & sep 1.00 1.00
C32 A56 50fr dk green & ultra 2.00 2.00
C33 A56 100fr dk car & dk grn 5.00 5.00
Nos. C30-C33 (4) 8.50 8.50

75th anniv. of the UPU.

Nos. C30-C33 exist imperforate, also No. C30 in deep plum and violet, imperforate.

Issued: 25fr, 12/27; others, 9/12/50.

Rainier Type of Regular Issue

1950, Apr. 11 Unwmk.

C34 A57 50fr black & red brn 4.50 4.50
C35 A57 100fr red brn, sep & ind 8.00 8.00

Entronement of Prince Rainier III.

Runner — AP18

Designs: 50fr, Fencing. 100fr, Target Shooting. 200fr, Olympic Torch.

1953, Feb. 23 *Perf. 11*

C36 AP18 40fr black 11.00 8.00
C37 AP18 50fr brt purple 13.50 9.00
C38 AP18 100fr dk slate grn 17.50 9.00
C39 AP18 200fr deep carmine 24.00 9.00
Nos. C36-C39 (4) 66.00 35.00

Issued to publicize Monaco's participation in the Helsinki Olympic Games.

Dr. Albert Schweitzer and Ogowe River Scene, Gabon — AP19

1955, Jan. 14 *Perf. 13*

C40 AP19 200fr multicolored 28.00 21.00

Dr. Albert Schweitzer, medical missionary.

Mediterranean Sea Swallows — AP20

Birds: 200fr, Sea gulls. 500fr, Albatross. 1000fr, Great cormorants.

1955-57 *Perf. 11*

C41 AP20 100fr dp blue & indigo 21.00 11.00
a. Perf. 13 24.00 19.00
C42 AP20 200fr bl & blk 21.00 11.00
a. Perf. 13 300.00 150.00
C43 AP20 500fr gray & dk grn 37.50 30.00

Perf. 13

C44 AP20 1000fr dk bl grn & blk brn 90.00 60.00
a. Perf. 11 240.00 190.00
Nos. C41-C44 (4) 169.50 112.00

Issued: Perf. 11, 1/14/55; Perf. 13, 1957.

"From the Earth to the Moon" and Jules Verne — AP21

1955, June 7 Unwmk.

C45 AP21 200fr dp blue & slate 25.00 25.00

50th anniv. of the death of Jules Verne.

Wedding Type of Regular Issue

1956, Apr. 19 Engr.

Portraits in Brown

C46 A99 100fr purple 1.00 .45
C47 A99 200fr carmine 1.25 .75
C48 A99 500fr gray violet 3.25 2.00
Nos. C46-C48 (3) 5.50 3.20

Wedding of Prince Rainier III to Grace Kelly, Apr. 19, 1956.

Nos. J45 and J54 Surcharged and Overprinted "Poste Aerienne" and bars

1956, Apr. *Perf. 11*

C49 D6 100fr on 20fr 9.00 9.00
a. Double surcharge 475.00
C50 D7 100fr on 20fr 9.00 9.00
a. Double surcharge 475.00
b. Pair, #C49, C50 22.50 22.50

See footnote after No. 390.

Basilica of Lourdes — AP23

200fr, Pope Pius X, underground basilica.

1958, May 15 Unwmk. *Perf. 13*

C51 AP23 100fr dk bl, grn & gray 1.75 1.40
C52 AP23 200fr red brn & sepia 2.50 2.50

Centenary of the apparition of the Virgin Mary at Lourdes.

Prince Rainier III and Princess Grace — AP24

1959, May 16

C53 AP24 300fr dark purple 9.00 6.00
C54 AP24 500fr blue 13.00 10.50

St. Dévote — AP25

1960, June 1 Engr. *Perf. 13*

C55 AP25 2fr green, bl & vio 1.00 .65
C56 AP24 3fr dark purple 34.00 16.00
C57 AP24 5fr blue 34.00 24.00
C58 AP25 10fr green & brown 5.75 3.50
Nos. C55-C58 (4) 74.75 44.15

1961, June 3

C59 AP25 3fr ultra, grn & gray ol 2.10 1.10
C60 AP25 5fr rose carmine 4.50 2.10

Europa Issue

Mercury over Map of Europe AP26

1962, June 6 Unwmk. *Perf. 13*

C61 AP26 2fr dk grn, sl grn & brn *1.50 1.00*

Oceanographic Museum, Atom Symbol and Princes Albert I and Rainier III — AP27

1962, June 6

C62 AP27 10fr violet, bl & bis 5.50 6.00

Establishment of a scientific research center by agreement with the Intl. Atomic Energy Commission.

Roland Garros AP28

1963, Dec. 12 Engr. *Perf. 13*

C63 AP28 2fr dk blue & dk brn 1.25 1.25

50th anniversary of the first airplane crossing of the Mediterranean by Roland Garros (1888-1918).

Type of Regular Issue, 1964

Design: 5fr, Convair B-58 Hustler (New York-Paris in 3 hours, 19 minutes, 41 seconds, Maj. William R. Payne, USAF, 1961).

1964, May 22 Unwmk. *Perf. 13*

C64 A151 5fr brown, blk & bl 2.75 2.75

1st airplane rally of Monte Carlo, 50th anniv.

Bobsledding — AP29

1964, Dec. 3 Engr. *Perf. 13*

C65 AP29 5fr multicolored 2.50 2.50

9th Winter Olympic Games, Innsbruck, Austria, Jan. 29-Feb. 9, 1964.

ITU Type of Regular Issue

Design: 10fr, ITU Emblem and Monte Carlo television station on Mount Agel, vert.

1965, May 17 Engr. *Perf. 13*

C66 A161 10fr bis brn, sl grn & bl 3.50 3.50

Princess Grace with Albert Alexander Louis, Caroline and Stephanie — AP30

1966, Feb. 1 Engr. *Perf. 13*

C67 AP30 3fr pur, red brn & Prus bl 2.00 1.25

Birth of Princess Stephanie, Feb. 1, 1965.

Opera House Interior AP31

1966, June 1 Engr. *Perf. 13*

C68 AP31 5fr Prus bl, bis & dk car rose 2.75 2.75

Centenary of founding of Monte Carlo.

Prince Rainier III and Princess Grace — AP32

1966-71 Engr. *Perf. 13*

C69 AP32 2fr pink & slate 1.10 .40
C70 AP32 3fr emer & slate 2.10 .80
C71 AP32 5fr lt blue & slate 2.75 1.10
C72 AP32 10fr lemon & sl ('67) 4.00 3.50
C72A AP32 20fr org & brn ('71) 42.50 35.00
Nos. C69-C72A (5) 52.45 40.80

Issue dates: 10fr, Dec. 7, 1967; 20fr, Sept. 6, 1971. Others, Dec. 12, 1966.

Panhard-Phenix, 1895 — AP33

1967, Apr. 28 Engr. *Perf. 13*

C73 AP33 3fr Prus blue & blk 2.75 2.75

25th Grand Prix of Monaco.

Olympic Games Type of Regular Issue

1968, Apr. 29 Engr. *Perf. 13*

C74 A183 3fr Field hockey 1.25 1.25

Berlioz Monument, Monte Carlo — AP34

1969, Apr. 26 Engr. *Perf. 13*

C75 AP34 2fr green, blk & ultra .75 .75

Hector Berlioz (1803-69), French composer.

Napoleon, by Paul Delaroche AP35

1969, Apr. 26 Photo. *Perf. 12x13*

C76 AP35 3fr multicolored 1.60 1.60

Bicentenary of birth of Napoleon I.

Horses, Prehistoric Drawing from Lascaux Cave — AP36

1970, Dec. 15 Engr. *Perf. 13*

C77 AP36 3fr multicolored 4.25 3.00

Nativity Type of Regular Issue

Design: 3fr, Nativity, Flemish School, 15th century, vert.

1973, Nov. 12 Engr. *Perf. 12x13*

C78 A243 3fr Prus green 2.75 2.25

Prince Rainier III — AP37

1974, Dec. 23 Engr. *Perf. 12½x13*

C81	AP37	10fr dark purple	4.50	2.00
C82	AP37	15fr henna brown	6.00	4.00
C83	AP37	20fr ultra	10.00	5.50
		Nos. C81-C83 (3)	20.50	11.50

See Nos. 1994-1996.

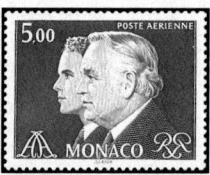

Prince Rainier and Hereditary Prince Albert AP38

1982-84 Engr. *Perf. 13x13½*

C84	AP38	5fr deep violet	1.60	.60
C85	AP38	10fr red	5.00	1.10
C86	AP38	15fr dk blue grn	6.00	1.75
C87	AP38	20fr brt blue	7.00	2.25
C88	AP38	30fr brown ('84)	11.00	4.50
		Nos. C84-C88 (5)	30.60	10.20

AIR POST SEMI-POSTAL STAMPS

Catalogue values for unused stamps in this section are for Never Hinged items.

Types of 1942 Air Post Stamps Surcharged with New Values and Bars

Unwmk.

1945, Mar. 27 Engr. *Perf. 13*

CB1	AP1	1fr + 4fr on 10fr rose red	.60	.60
CB2	AP2	1fr + 4fr on 15fr red brn	.60	.60
CB3	AP3	1fr + 4fr on 20fr sepia	.60	.60
CB4	AP4	1fr + 4fr on 50fr ultra	.60	.60
CB5	AP5	1fr + 4fr on 100fr brt red vio	.60	.60
		Nos. CB1-CB5 (5)	3.00	3.00

Surtax for the benefit of prisoners of war.

Franklin D. Roosevelt Type

1946, Dec. 13

CB6 A42 15fr + 10fr red 2.25 1.50

The surtax was for a fund to erect a monument in his honor.

1948 Olympic Type

1948, July

CB7	A48	5fr +5fr Rowing	9.00	9.00
CB8	A48	6fr +9fr Skiing	12.00	12.00
CB9	A48	10fr +15fr Tennis	17.50	17.50
CB10	A47	15fr +25fr Sailing	26.00	26.00
		Nos. CB7-CB10 (4)	64.50	64.50

Salmacis Nymph SPAP4

Designs similar to regular issue.

1948, July

CB11	A50	5fr + 5fr blk bl	11.00	11.00
CB12	A51	6fr + 9fr dk grn	11.00	11.00
CB13	A52	10fr + 15fr crim	22.50	22.50
CB14	SPAP4	15fr + 25fr red brown	37.50	37.50
		Nos. CB11-CB14 (4)	82.00	82.00

François J. Bosio (1769-1845), sculptor.

POSTAGE DUE STAMPS

D1

Perf. 14x13½

1905-43 Unwmk. Typo.

J1	D1	1c olive green	.45	.55
J2	D1	5c green	.45	.55
J3	D1	10c rose	.45	.55
J4	D1	10c brn ('09)	350.00	125.00
J5	D1	15c vio brn, *straw*	3.50	1.75
J6	D1	20c bis brn, *buff* ('26)	.35	.35
J7	D1	30c blue	.45	.55
J8	D1	40c red vio ('26)	.35	.35
J9	D1	50c brn, *org*	4.50	4.00
J10	D1	50c blue grn ('27)	.35	.35
J11	D1	60c gray blk ('26)	.35	.65
J12	D1	60c brt vio ('34)	21.00	27.50
J13	D1	1fr red brn, *straw* ('26)	.35	.25
J14	D1	2fr red org ('27)	1.00	1.50
J15	D1	3fr mag ('27)	1.00	1.50
J15A	D1	5fr ultra ('43)	.80	1.00
		Nos. J1-J15A (16)	385.35	166.40

For surcharge see No. J27.

Prince Albert I — D2

1910

J16	D2	1c olive green	.25	.45
J17	D2	10c light violet	.45	.60
J18	D2	30c bister	190.00	160.00

In January, 1917, regular postage stamps overprinted "T" in a triangle were used as postage due stamps.

Nos. J17 and J18 Surcharged

1918

J19	D2	20c on 10c lt vio	3.75	7.50
a.		Double surcharge	1,000.	
J20	D2	40c on 30c bister	4.50	8.50

D3

1925-32

J21	D3	1c gray green	.40	.50
J22	D3	10c violet	.40	.55
J23	D3	30c bister	.50	.75
J24	D3	60c red	.70	.75
J25	D3	1fr lt bl ('32)	75.00	75.00
J26	D3	2fr dull red ('32)	75.00	75.00
		Nos. J21-J26 (6)	152.00	152.55

Nos. J25 and J26 have the numerals of value double-lined.

"Recouvrements" stamps were used to recover charges due on undelivered or refused mail which was returned to the sender.

No. J9 Surcharged

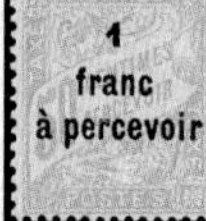

1925

J27	D1	1fr on 50c brn, *org*	.75	.50
a.		Double surcharge	*750.00*	

Catalogue values for unused stamps in this section, from this point to the end of the section, are for Never Hinged items.

D4

D5

1946-57 Engr. *Perf. 14x13, 13*

J28	D4	10c sepia	.25	.25
J29	D4	30c dark violet	.25	.25
J30	D4	50c deep blue	.25	.25
J31	D4	1fr dark green	.25	.25
J32	D4	2fr yellow brn	.25	.25
J33	D4	3fr brt red vio	.30	.30
J34	D4	4fr carmine	.45	.45
J35	D5	5fr chocolate	.35	.35
J36	D5	10fr deep ultra	.65	.65
J37	D5	20fr grnsh blue	.70	.70
J38	D5	50fr red vio & red ('50)	55.00	55.00
J38A	D5	100fr dk grn & red ('57)	12.00	12.00
		Nos. J28-J38A (12)	70.70	70.70

Sailing Vessel — D6

S. S. United States — D7

Early Postal Transport (D6): 1fr, Carrier pigeons. 3fr, Old railroad engine. 4fr, Old monoplane. 5fr, Steam automobile. 10fr, daVinci's flying machine. 20fr, Balloon. 50fr, Post rider. 100fr, Old mail coach.

Modern Postal Transport (D7): 1fr, Sikorsky S-51 helicopter. 3fr, Modern locomotive. 4fr, Comet airliner. 5fr, Sabre sports car. 10fr, Rocket. 20fr, Graf Zeppelin. 50fr, Motorcyclist. 100fr, Railroad mail car.

1953-54 *Perf. 11*

J39	D6	1fr dk grn & brt red ('54)	.25	.25
a.		Pair, Nos. J39, J48	.25	.25
J40	D6	2fr dp ultra & bl grn	.25	.25
a.		Pair, Nos. J40, J49	.40	.40
J41	D6	3fr Prus grn & brn lake	.25	.25
a.		Pair, Nos. J41, J50	.40	.40
J42	D6	4fr dk brn & Prus grn	.25	.25
a.		Pair, Nos. J42, J51	.55	.55
J43	D6	5fr ultra & pur	.60	.60
a.		Pair, Nos. J43, J52	1.40	1.40
J44	D6	10fr dp ultra & dk bl	6.00	6.00
a.		Pair, Nos. J44, J53	15.00	15.00
J45	D6	20fr indigo & pur	4.00	4.00
a.		Pair, Nos. J45, J54	9.50	9.50
J46	D6	50fr red & dk brn	8.00	8.00
a.		Pair, Nos. J46, J55	19.00	19.00
J47	D6	100fr vio brn & dp grn	13.50	13.50
a.		Pair, Nos. J47, J56	32.50	32.50
J48	D7	1fr brt red & dk grn ('54)	.25	.25
J49	D7	2fr bl grn & dp ultra	.25	.25
J50	D7	3fr brn lake & Prus grn	.25	.25
J51	D7	4fr Prus grn & dk brn	.25	.25
J52	D7	5fr purple & ultra	.60	.60

J53 D7 10fr dk bl & dp ultra 6.00 6.00
J54 D7 20fr purple & indigo 4.00 4.00
J55 D7 50fr dk brn & red 8.00 8.00
J56 D7 100fr dp grn & vio brn 13.50 13.50
Nos. J39-J56 (18) 66.20 66.20

Pairs se-tenant at the base.
For overprints see Nos. 371-390.

Felucca, 18th Century D8

2c, Paddle steamer La Palmaria, 19th cent. 5c, Arrival of 1st train. 10c, Armed messenger, 15th-16th cent. 20c, Monaco-Nice courier, 18th cent. 30c, "Charles III," 1866. 50c, Courier on horseback, 17th cent. 1fr, Diligence, 19th cent.

1960-69 Engr. *Perf. 13*

J57 D8 1c bl grn, bis brn & bl .25 .25
J58 D8 2c sl grn, sep & ultra .25 .25
J59 D8 5c grnsh bl, gray & red brn .25 .25
J60 D8 10c vio bl, blk & grn .25 .25
J61 D8 20c blue, brn & grn .90 .90
J62 D8 30c brn, brt grn & brt bl ('69) 1.40 1.40
J63 D8 50c dk bl, brn & sl grn 1.90 1.90
J64 D8 1fr sl grn, bl & brn 2.50 2.50
Nos. J57-J64 (8) 7.70 7.70

Knight in Armor D9

1980-83 Engr. *Perf. 13*

J65 D9 5c red & gray .25 .25
J66 D9 10c salmon & red .25 .25
J67 D9 15c violet & red .25 .25
J68 D9 20c lt green & red .25 .25
J69 D9 30c blue & red .25 .25
J70 D9 40c lt brown & red .25 .25
J71 D9 50c lilac & red .35 .35
J72 D9 1fr black & blue .55 .55
J73 D9 2fr dk brn & org ('82) .85 .85
J74 D9 3fr sl bl & rose car ('83) 1.20 1.20
J75 D9 4fr red & dk grn ('82) 1.75 1.75
J76 D9 5fr magenta & brn ('83) 2.00 2.00
Nos. J65-J76 (12) 8.20 8.20

Nos. J65-J76 printed in horizontal rows with princely coat of arms between stamps. Sold in strips of 3 only.

Issued: #J65-J72, 2/8; #J73, J75, 2/15; 3J74, J76, 1/3.

Natl. Coat of Arms — D10

1985-86 Photo. *Perf. 13x12½*

J77 D10 5c multicolored .25 .25
J78 D10 10c multicolored .25 .25
J79 D10 15c multicolored .25 .25
J80 D10 20c multicolored .25 .25
J81 D10 30c multicolored .25 .25
J82 D10 40c multicolored .25 .25
J83 D10 50c multicolored ('86) .25 .25
J84 D10 1fr multicolored ('86) .35 .35
J85 D10 2fr multicolored ('86) .55 .55
J86 D10 3fr multicolored .95 .95
J87 D10 4fr multicolored ('86) 1.20 1.20
J88 D10 5fr multicolored 1.75 1.75
Nos. J77-J88 (12) 6.55 6.55

See Nos. 1608-1609.

MONGOLIA

män-ˈgōl-yə

(Mongolian People's Republic)

(Outer Mongolia)

LOCATION — Central Asia, bounded on the north by Siberia, on the west by Sinkiang, on the south and east by China proper and Manchuria
GOVT. — Republic
AREA — 604,250 sq. mi.
POP. — 2,617,379 (1999 est.)
CAPITAL — Ulan Bator

Outer Mongolia, which had long been under Russian influence although nominally a dependency of China, voted at a plebescite on October 20, 1945, to sever all ties with China and become an independent nation. See Tannu Tuva.

100 Cents = 1 Dollar
100 Mung = 1 Tugrik (1926)

Catalogue values for unused stamps in this country are for Never Hinged items, beginning with Scott 149 in the regular postage section, Scott B1 in the semi-postal section, Scott C1 in the airpost section, and Scott CB1 in the airpost semi-postal section.

Watermark

Wmk. 170 — Greek Border and Rosettes

Scepter of Indra — A1

1924 Litho. Unwmk. *Perf. 10, 13½*

Surface Tinted Paper

1	A1	1c multi, *bister*	12.00	12.00
2	A1	2c multi, *brnsh*	10.50	5.50
a.		Perf. 13½	47.50	40.00
3	A1	5c multi	40.00	24.00
a.		Perf. 10	47.50	35.00
4	A1	10c multi, *gray bl*	20.00	16.00
a.		Perf. 10	20.00	16.00
5	A1	20c multi, *gray*	27.50	17.50
6	A1	50c multi, *salmon*	40.00	24.00
7	A1	$1 multi, *yellow*	55.00	40.00
b.		Perf. 10	650.00	190.00
		Nos. 1-7 (7)	205.00	139.00

These stamps vary in size from 19x25mm (1c) to 30x39mm ($1). They also differ in details of the design.

Errors of perforating and printing exist.

Some quantities of Nos. 1-2, 4-7 were defaced with horizontal perforation across the center.

The 5c exists perf 11½. Value, $325 unused, hinged, $190 used.

Revenue Stamps Handstamp

A2

Sizes: 1c to 20c: 22x36mm
50c, $1: 26x43½mm
$5: 30x45½mm

Overprinted in Violet

1926 *Perf. 11*

16	A2	1c blue	12.00	12.00
17	A2	2c orange	16.00	11.00
18	A2	5c plum	16.00	13.00
19	A2	10c green	20.00	17.00
20	A2	20c yel brn	24.00	20.00
21	A2	50c brn & ol grn	*190.00*	*175.00*
22	A2	$1 brn & salmon	*550.00*	*475.00*
23	A2	$5 red, yel & gray	*650.00*	—
		Nos. 16-23 (8)	*1,478.*	*723.00*

Black Overprint

16a	A2	1c blue	20.00	13.50
17a	A2	2c orange	32.50	20.00
18a	A2	5c plum	36.00	20.00
19a	A2	10c green	47.50	24.00
20a	A2	20c yellow brown	65.00	45.00
21a	A2	50c brown & olive grn	*1,200.*	*325.00*
22a	A2	$1 brown & salmon	*600.00*	*400.00*
23a	A2	$5 red, yellow & gray		
		Nos. 16a-22a (7)	*2,001.*	*847.50*

Red Overprint

16b	A2	1c blue
17b	A2	2c orange
18b	A2	5c plum
19b	A2	10c green
20b	A2	20c yellow brown

The preceding handstamped overprints may be found inverted, double, etc. Counterfeits abound.

For overprints and surcharges see #48-61.

A3 A4

Soyombo

TYPE I — The pearl above the crescent is solid. The devices in the middle of the stamp are not outlined.

TYPE II — The pearl is open. The devices and panels are all outlined in black.

1926-29 *Perf. 11*

Type I

Size: 22x28mm

32	A3	5m lilac & blk	12.00	12.00
33	A3	20m blue & blk	20.00	24.00

Type II

Size: 22x29mm

34	A3	1m yellow & blk	3.25	3.25
35	A3	2m brn org & blk	4.00	3.25
36	A3	5m lilac & blk	4.75	4.00
37	A3	10m lt blue & blk	4.00	2.00
a.		Imperf, pair		
39	A3	25m yel grn & blk	8.00	4.00
a.		Imperf, pair	125.00	110.00

Size: 26x34mm

40	A3	40m lemon & blk	11.00	4.75
41	A3	50m buff & blk	16.00	6.50

Size: 28x37mm

42	A4	1t brown, grn & blk	32.50	12.00
43	A4	3t red, yel & blk	72.50	47.50
44	A4	5t brn vio, rose & blk	95.00	60.00
		Nos. 32-44 (12)	283.00	183.25

In 1929 a change was made in the perforating machine. Every fourth pin was removed, which left the perforation holes in groups of three with blank spaces between the groups. Nos. 44A-44D have only this interrupted perforation. Nos. 37 and 39 are found with both perforations.

For overprints and surcharges see #45-47.

Soyombo — A5

1929, July *Interrupted Perf 11*

44A	A5	5m lilac & black	25.00	20.00
44B	A5	10m lt grnish blue & black	100.00	65.00
a.		imperf, pair	—	
44C	A5	20m blue & black	35.00	27.50
a.		imperf, pair	—	
b.		Horiz. pair, imperf btwn.		—
44D	A5	25m yel grn & black	32.50	27.50
a.		imperf, pair	—	

See note after No. 44.

Nos. 34, 35, 40 Handstamped With New Values in Black

1930

45	A3	10m on 1m	32.50	30.00
46	A3	20m on 2m	45.00	40.00
47	A3	25m on 40m	52.50	47.50
		Nos. 45-47 (3)	130.00	117.50

Soyombo — A6

Violet Overprint, Handstamped

1931

48	A6	1c blue	24.00	12.00
a.		Blue overprint	87.50	47.50
49	A6	2c orange	27.50	9.50
50	A6	5c brown vio	35.00	9.50
a.		Blue overprint	65.00	22.50
51	A6	10c green	32.50	9.50
a.		Blue overprint	65.00	37.50
52	A6	20c bister brn	47.50	12.00
53	A6	50c brown & ol yel	130.00	120.00
54	A6	$1 brown & salmon	200.00	160.00
		Nos. 48-54 (7)	496.50	332.50

Soyombo — A7

Revenue Stamps Surcharged in Black, Red or Blue

1931

59	A7	5m on 5c brn vio (Bk)	40.00	16.00
a.		Inverted surcharge		35.00
b.		Imperf., pair	225.00	225.00
60	A7	10m on 10c grn (R)	55.00	27.50
a.		Inverted surcharge	90.00	50.00
b.		Imperf., pair	225.00	225.00
61	A7	20m on 20c bis brn (Bl)	65.00	35.00
a.		Inverted surcharge		55.00
b.		Imperf., pair	225.00	225.00
		Nos. 59-61 (3)	160.00	78.50

On Nos. 59-61, "Postage" is always diagonal, and may read up or down.

Weaver at Loom — A8

Telegrapher A9

Sukhe Bator A10

Lake and Mountains — A11

Designs: 5m, Mongol at lathe. 10m, Government building, Ulan Bator. 15m, Young Mongolian revolutionary. 20m, Studying Latin alphabet. 25m, Mongolian soldier. 50m, Monument to Sukhe Bator. 3t, Sheep shearing. 5t, Camel caravan. 10t, Chasing wild horses.

Perf. 12½x12

1932 Photo. Wmk. 170

62	A8	1m brown	3.25	1.50
63	A9	2m red violet	3.25	1.50
64	A8	5m indigo	2.00	.80
65	A8	10m dull green	2.00	.80
66	A9	15m dp brown	2.00	.80
67	A9	20m rose red	2.40	.80
68	A9	25m dull violet	2.40	.80
69	A10	40m gray black	2.00	1.20
70	A10	50m dull blue	2.40	.80

Perf. 11x12

71	A11	1t dull green	2.75	1.20
72	A11	3t dull violet	5.50	2.00
73	A11	5t brown	19.50	12.00
74	A11	10t ultra	40.00	20.00
		Nos. 62-74 (13)	89.45	44.20

Used values are for canceled-to-order stamps.

Nos. 70-74 Handstamped With New Values in Black or Violet

1941 Black handstamp

74A	A11	5m on 5t	—	—
74B	A10	10m on 50m	—	—
74C	A11	10m on 10t	—	—
74D	A11	15m on 5t	—	—
74E	A11	20m on 1t	—	—
74F	A11	30m on 3t	—	—

Violet handstamp

74G	A11	5m on 5t	—	—
74H	A11	15m on 5t	—	—
74I	A11	20m on 1t	—	—
74J	A11	30m on 3t	—	—

Mongolian Man — A12

Mongolian Woman — A13

Soldier — A14

Camel Caravan A15

Modern School A16

Arms of the Republic — A17

Sukhe Bator — A18

Pasture Scene — A19

Paper with network as in italics

1943		**Typo.**	***Perf. 12½***	
75	A12	5m green, *green*	12.00	10.00
76	A13	10m dp blue, *lt bl*	20.00	11.00
77	A14	15m rose, *lt rose*	22.50	15.00
78	A15	20m org brn, *org*	32.50	27.50
79	A16	25m red brn, *buff*	32.50	32.50
80	A17	30m carmine, *red*	37.50	37.50
81	A18	45m purple, *mauve*	50.00	50.00
82	A19	60m dp green, *grn*	90.00	90.00
		Nos. 75-82 (8)	297.00	273.50

Marshal Kharloin Choibalsan — A21

1945		**Unwmk.**	***Perf. 12½***	
83	A21	1t black brown	60.00	70.00

Choibalsan A22

Victory Medal A24

Sukhe Bator and Choibalsan A23

Designs: #86, Choibalsan as young man. #87, Choibalsan University, Ulan Bator. 1t, Anniversary medal. 2t, Sukhe Bator.

1946, July		**Photo.**	***Perf. 12½***	
84	A22	30m olive bister	6.50	6.50
85	A23	50m dull purple	7.75	7.75
86	A24	60m black	8.00	8.00
87	A23	60m orange brown	14.00	14.00
88	A24	80m dk orange brn	12.50	12.50
89	A24	1t indigo	16.00	16.00
90	A24	2t deep brown	22.50	22.50
		Nos. 84-90 (7)	87.25	87.25

25th anniversary of independence.

New Housing A25

School Children — A26

Mongolian Arms and Flag — A27

Sukhe Bator — A28

Flags of Communist Countries — A29

Lenin — A30

Designs: 15m, Altai Hotel. No. 94, State Store. No. 95, Like 30m. 25m, University. 40m, National Theater. 50m, Pedagogical Institute. 60m, Sukhe Bator monument. Sizes of type A25: Nos. 91, 93-94, 98-99, 32½x22mm. 25m, 55x26mm.

1951, July				
91	A25	5m brn, *pink*	6.75	6.75
92	A26	10m dp bl, *pink*	8.25	8.25
93	A25	15m grn, *grnsh*	10.00	10.00
94	A25	20m red org	10.00	10.00
95	A27	20m dk bl & multi	10.00	10.00
96	A25	25m bl, *bluish*	10.00	10.00
97	A27	30m red & multi	10.00	10.00
98	A25	40m pur, *pink*	10.00	10.00
99	A25	50m brn, *grysh*	20.00	20.00
100	A28	60m brn blk	20.00	20.00
101	A29	1t multi	20.00	20.00
102	A28	2t dk brn & org brn	25.00	25.00
103	A30	3t multi	25.00	25.00
		Nos. 91-103 (13)	185.00	185.00

30th anniversary of independence.

Choibalsan — A31

Choibalsan and Farmer — A32

Choibalsan in uniform — A32a

Choibalsan and Sukhe Bator — A33

Designs: No. 108, 30m, Choibalsan and factory worker (47x33mm). 50m, Choibalsan and Young Pioneer. No. 112, 2t, Choibalsan in uniform.

1953, Dec.		**Photo.**	***Perf. 12½***	
104	A31	15m dull blue	5.00	5.00
105	A32	15m dull green	5.00	5.00
106	A31	20m dull green	10.00	10.00
107	A32	20m sepia	10.00	10.00
108	A32	20m violet blue	10.00	10.00
109	A32	30m dark brown	10.00	10.00
110	A33	50m orange brn	10.00	10.00
111	A33	1t carmine rose	10.00	10.00
112	A32a	1t sepia	15.00	15.00
113	A32a	2t red	15.00	15.00
114	A33	3t sepia	20.00	20.00
115	A33	5t red	40.00	40.00
		Nos. 104-115 (12)	160.00	160.00

First anniversary of death of Marshal Karloin Choibalsan (1895-1952).

Arms of Mongolia — A34

1954, Mar.		**Litho.**	***Perf. 12½***	
116	A34	10m carmine	12.00	7.00
117	A34	20m carmine	60.00	50.00
118	A34	30m carmine	12.00	8.00
119	A34	40m carmine	40.00	40.00
120	A34	60m carmine	12.00	10.00
		Nos. 116-120 (5)	136.00	115.00

Sukhe Bator and Choibalsan — A35

Lake Hubsugul A36

Guard with Dog — A37

#122, Lenin Statue, Ulan Bator. 50m, Choibalsan University. 1t, Arms and flag of Mongolia.

1955, June		**Photo.**	***Perf. 12½***	
121	A35	30m green	1.25	1.00
122	A35	30m orange ver	2.50	1.00
123	A36	30m brt blue	2.25	1.25
124	A37	40m dp red lilac	5.00	1.75
125	A36	50m ocher	5.00	2.25
126	A37	1t red & multi	9.00	7.00
		Nos. 121-126 (6)	25.00	14.25

35th anniversary of independence.

1955

Design: 2t, Lenin.

127	A35	2t bright blue	10.00	5.00

85th anniversary of birth of Lenin.

Flags of Communist Countries A38

1955

128	A38	60m blue & multi	5.00	4.00

Fight for peace.

Arms of Mongolia — A39

1956		**Photo.**	***Perf. 12½***	
129	A39	20m dark brown	3.00	2.00
130	A39	30m dark olive	4.00	3.00
131	A39	40m bright blue	5.00	4.00
132	A39	60m blue green	6.00	4.50
133	A39	1t deep carmine	10.00	8.00
		Nos. 129-133 (5)	28.00	21.50

Kremlin, Moscow, Train and Sukhe Bator Monument A40

Design: 2t, Flags of Mongolia and USSR.

1956				
134	A40	1t dk blue & multi	25.00	15.00
135	A40	2t red & multi	10.00	8.00

Establishment of railroad connection between Moscow and Ulan Bator.

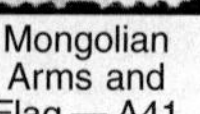
Mongolian Arms and Flag — A41

Hunter with Golden Eagle — A42

Wrestlers A43

Designs: No. 138, 3 children (33x26½mm).

1956, July **Typo.** ***Perf. 9***

136	A41	30m blue	10.00	5.00
137	A42	30m pale brown	50.00	50.00
138	A42	60m orange	20.00	20.00
139	A43	60m yellow green	20.00	20.00
		Nos. 136-139 (4)	100.00	95.00

35th anniversary of independence.

Types A41 and A43 without "XXXV"

1958

140	A41	20m red	5.00	3.00
141	A43	50m brown, *pink*	12.50	3.00

Nos. 140-143 were issued both with and without gum.

Poster — A44

1958, Mar. **Litho.** ***Perf. 9***

142	A44	30m maroon & salmon	5.00	4.00

13th Congress of Mongolian People's Party.

Globe and Dove — A45

1958, May

143	A45	60m deep blue	5.00	4.00

4th Congress of International Democratic Women's Federation, Vienna, June, 1958. Nos. 142-143 exist imperf.

Yak — A46

No. 144, Pelicans, vert. No. 145, Siberian ibex, vert. No. 147, Yak. No. 148, Camels.

1958, July **Typo.** ***Perf. 9***

144	A46	30m lt blue	15.00	3.50
145	A46	30m brt green	4.00	2.50
146	A46	60m orange	4.00	2.50
147	A46	1t blue	4.00	3.50
148	A46	1t rose	4.00	3.50
		Nos. 144-148 (5)	31.00	15.50

Shades exist.

Canceled to Order
Some quantity of all issues not printed by the State Printing Works, Ulan Bator, except Nos. 296-303, were canceled to order.
Used values are for c-t-o. Postally used stamps sell for considerably more.

Catalogue values for unused stamps in this section, from this point to the end of the section, are for Never Hinged items.

Stallion A47

Designs: 5m, 40m, Goat. 10m, 30m, Ram. 15m, 60m, Stallion. 20m, 50m, Bull. 25m, 1t, Bactrian camel.

Perf. 10½x11½

1958, Nov. 11 **Litho.**

149	A47	5m yellow & brn	.25	.25
150	A47	10m lt grn & brn	.25	.25
151	A47	15m lilac & brn	.35	.25
152	A47	20m lt bl & brn	.35	.25
153	A47	25m rose & brn	.40	.25
154	A47	30m lilac & pur	.50	.25
155	A47	40m lt & dk green	.50	.25
156	A47	50m salmon & brn	.55	.25
157	A47	60m lt blue & ind	.95	.25
158	A47	1t yellow & brn	1.75	.50
		Nos. 149-158 (10)	5.85	2.75

Holy Flame (Tulaga) — A48

1959, May 1 **Litho.** ***Perf. 9***

159	A48	1t multi	4.50	3.50

See No. C36.

Archer — A49

Mongol Sports: 5m, Taming wild horse. 10m, Wrestlers. 15m, Horseback riding. 25m, Horse race. 30m, Archers. 70m, Hunting wild horse. 80m, Proclaiming a champion.

1959, June 6 **Photo.** ***Perf. 11***

160	A49	5m multi	.25	.25
161	A49	10m multi	.25	.25
162	A49	15m multi	.25	.25
163	A49	20m multi	.25	.25
164	A49	25m multi	.40	.25
165	A49	30m multi	.55	.25
166	A49	70m multi	.75	.35
167	A49	80m multi	1.10	.55
		Nos. 160-167 (8)	3.80	2.40

Young Wrestlers A50

Youth Festival Emblem — A51

Designs: 5m, Young musician, horiz. 20m, Boy on horseback. 25m, Two opera singers. 40m, Young Pioneers with flags, horiz.

Photo.; Litho. (30m)

1959, July ***Perf. 12, 11 (30m)***

168	A50	5m vio bl & rose car	.25	.25
169	A50	10m bl grn & brn	.25	.25
170	A50	20m claret & grn	.25	.25
171	A50	25m green & vio bl	.35	.25
172	A51	30m lil & lt bl	.35	.25
173	A50	40m green & pur	1.10	.50
		Nos. 168-173 (6)	2.55	1.75

Mongolian Youth Festival.
The 30m was printed by State Printing Works, Ulan Bator.
Issue dates: 30m, July 11; others July 10.

"Mongol" in Stylized Uighur Script — A52

"Mongol" in Various Scripts: 40m, Soyombo. 50m, Kalmuck. 60m, Square (Pagspa). 1t, Cyrillic.
Printed by State Printing Works, Ulan Bator.

1959, Sept. 1 **Litho.** ***Perf. 11***

Size: 29x42½mm

174	A52	30m black & multi	6.50	6.50
175	A52	40m black & multi	6.50	6.50
a.		Horiz. pair, imperf between and at right	*150.00*	
176	A52	50m black & multi	8.50	8.50
177	A52	60m black & multi	14.00	14.00

Size: 21x31mm

Perf. 9

178	A52	1t black & multi	17.50	17.50
		Nos. 174-178 (5)	53.00	53.00

1st Intl. Mongolian Language Congress.

Battle Emblem A53

Battle Monument A54

1959, Sept. 15 **Photo.** ***Perf. 12½x12***

179	A53	40m yellow, brn & car	.60	.25
180	A54	50m multicolored	.60	.25

Ha-lo-hsin (Khalka) River Battle, 20th anniv.

Congress Emblem A55

Printed by State Printing Works, Ulan Bator.

1959, Dec. **Litho.** ***Perf. 11***

181	A55	30m green	4.50	4.50

2nd meeting of rural economy cooperatives of Mongolia.

Sable — A56

Pheasants — A57

Perf. 15, 11x13

1959, Dec. 21 **Photo.**

182	A56	5m shown	.25	.25
183	A57	10m shown	.25	.25
184	A56	15m Muskrat	.25	.25
185	A57	20m Otter	.55	.25
186	A56	30m Argali	.55	.25
187	A57	50m Saigas	1.00	.35
188	A57	1t Musk deer	2.00	.75
		Nos. 182-188 (7)	4.85	2.35

Lunik 3 — A58

50m, Lunik 3 with path around moon, horiz.

1959, Dec. 30 **Photo.** ***Perf. 12***

189	A58	30m violet & yel grn	.80	.80
190	A58	50m red, dk bl & grn	1.25	1.25

Lunik 3 Russian moon mission, Oct. 7, 1959.

Motherhood Badge — A59

Flower Emblem — A60

1960, Mar. 8 — *Perf. 11, 12½x11½*

No.	Type	Description	Unused	Used
191	A59	40m blue & bister	.75	.25
192	A60	50m blue, grn & yel	1.10	.40

International Women's Day.

Lenin — A61

1960, Apr. 22 Photo. — *Perf. 11½x12*

No.	Type	Description	Unused	Used
193	A61	40m dk rose car	.60	.25
194	A61	50m rose violet	.80	.35

90th anniversary, birth of Lenin.

Jacob's-ladder — A62

1960, May 31 — *Perf. 11½x12*

No.	Type	Description	Unused	Used
195	A62	5m Larkspur	.25	.25
196	A62	10m Tulips	.25	.25
197	A62	15m shown	.25	.25
198	A62	20m Globeflowers	.25	.25
199	A62	30m Bellflowers	.35	.25
200	A62	40m Parnassia	.65	.25
201	A62	50m Geranium	.90	.35
202	A62	1t Begonia	1.25	.80
		Nos. 195-202 (8)	4.15	2.65

For overprints see Nos. 296-303.

Equestrian — A63

Running — A64

15m, Diving. 20m, Wrestling. 30m, Hurdling. 50m, Gymnastics, women's. 70m, High jump. 1t, Discus, women's.

1960, Aug. 1 — *Perf. 15, 11*

No.	Type	Description	Unused	Used
203	A63	5m shown	.25	.25
204	A64	10m shown	.25	.25
205	A63	15m multi	.25	.25
206	A64	20m multi	.30	.25
207	A63	30m multi	.50	.25
208	A64	50m multi	.65	.30
209	A63	70m multi	.80	.35
210	A64	1t multi	1.25	.40
		Nos. 203-210 (8)	4.25	2.30

17th Olympic Games, Rome, 8/25-9/11.

Red Cross A65

1960, Aug. 29 — *Perf. 11*

No.	Type	Description	Unused	Used
211	A65	20m blue, red & yel	.80	.40

Newspaper "Unen" (Truth) — A66

1960, Dec. 19 — *Perf. 12x11½*

No.	Type	Description	Unused	Used
212	A66	20m red, yel & sl grn	.35	.25
213	A66	30m grn, yel & red	.45	.25

40th anniversary of Mongolian press.

Golden Orioles — A67

Songbirds: 5m, Rose-colored starling. 10m, Hoopoe. 20m, Black-billed capercaillie. 50m, Oriental broad-billed roller. 70m, Tibetan sandgrouse. 1t, Mandarin duck.

Triangle points down on 5m, 50m, 70m, 1t.

1961, Jan. 3 — *Perf. 11*

No.	Type	Description	Unused	Used
214	A67	5m multi	.60	.25
215	A67	10m multi	.70	.25
216	A67	15m multi	.85	.25
217	A67	20m multi	1.00	.25
218	A67	50m multi	1.50	.50
219	A67	70m multi	2.00	.70
220	A67	1t multi	2.10	.85
		Nos. 214-220 (7)	8.75	3.05

Federation Emblem — A68

Design: 30m, Worker and emblem, vert.

Perf. 11½x12, 12x11½

1961, Jan. 29 — **Photo.**

No.	Type	Description	Unused	Used
221	A68	30m dk gray & rose	.35	.25
222	A68	50m ultra & red	.45	.25

World Federation of Trade Unions, 15th anniv.

Patrice Lumumba (1925-1961), Premier of Congo — A69

1961, Apr. 8 — *Perf. 11½x12*

No.	Type	Description	Unused	Used
223	A69	30m brown	2.25	1.25
224	A69	50m violet gray	2.75	1.75

Bridge A70

Designs: 10m, Shoemaker. 15m, Department Store, Ulan Bator. 20m, Government building. 30m, State Theater, Ulan Bator. 50m, Machinist. 1t, Modern and old buildings.

Sizes: 31½x21mm, 59x20mm (20m)

1961, Apr. 30 — *Perf. 11½x12, 15*

No.	Type	Description	Unused	Used
225	A70	5m emerald	.25	.25
226	A70	10m blue	.25	.25
227	A70	15m rose red	.25	.25
228	A70	20m brown	.25	.25
229	A70	30m blue	.25	.25
230	A70	50m olive green	.35	.25
231	A70	1t violet	.60	.35
		Nos. 225-231 (7)	2.20	1.85

40th anniversary of independence; modernization of Mongolia.

Yuri Gagarin and Globe — A71

Designs: 20m, Gagarin with rocket, vert. 50m, Gagarin making parachute descent, vert. 1t, Gagarin wearing helmet, globe.

1961, May 31 — *Perf. 15*

No.	Type	Description	Unused	Used
232	A71	20m multi	.50	.25
233	A71	30m multi	.80	.40
234	A71	50m multi	1.00	.60
235	A71	1t multi	1.50	.65
		Nos. 232-235 (4)	3.80	1.90

Yuri A. Gagarin, 1st man in space, 4/12/61.

Postman on Reindeer A72

15m, #241a, Postman on camel. 10m, 20m, Postman with yaks. 25m, #241c, Postman with ship. 30m, 50m, Diesel train.

1961, June 5 — *Perf. 15*

No.	Type	Description	Unused	Used
236	A72	5m multi	.25	.25
237	A72	15m multi	.25	.25
238	A72	20m multi	.25	.25
239	A72	25m multi	.25	.25
240	A72	30m multi	4.00	2.00
		Nos. 236-240,C1-C3 (8)	7.00	3.90

Souvenir Sheet

Perf. 11

No.	Type	Description	Unused	Used
241		Sheet of 4	6.00	6.00
a.	A72	5m light blue & brown	1.50	1.00
b.	A72	10m green, brown & blue	1.50	1.00
c.	A72	15m green, violet & brown	1.50	1.00
d.	A72	50m violet, green & black	1.50	1.00

40th anniv. of independence; postal modernization. See No. C4b for 25m, perf. 11.

Souvenir Sheet

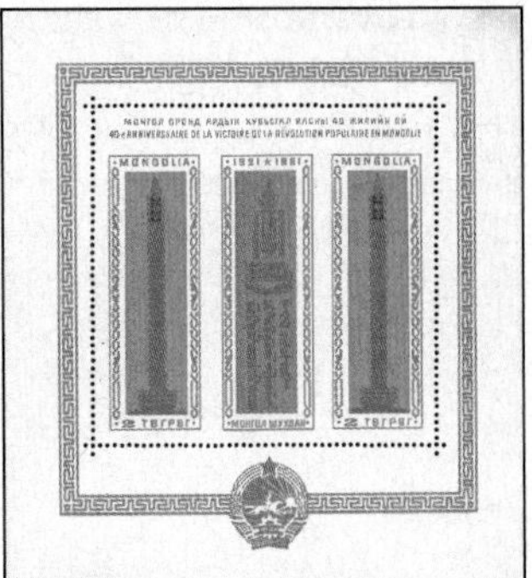
Ornamental Column — A73

1961, June 20 — *Perf. 12*

No.	Type	Description	Unused	Used
242	A73	Sheet of 2 + label	6.00	6.00
a.		2t blue, red & gold	2.75	2.00

40th anniversary of the Mongolian People's Revolution. No. 242 contains two No. 242a and label, imperf. between.

Herdsman and Oxen — A74

Designs: Herdsmen and domestic animals (except 1t and No. 252a).

1961, July 10 — *Perf. 13*

No.	Type	Description	Unused	Used
243	A74	5m Rams	.25	.25
244	A74	10m shown	.25	.25
245	A74	15m Camels	.25	.25
246	A74	20m Pigs and geese	.30	.25
247	A74	25m Angora goats	.30	.25
248	A74	30m Horses	.30	.25
249	A74	40m Sheep	.50	.25
250	A74	50m Cows	.75	.30
251	A74	1t Combine harvester	1.10	.75
		Nos. 243-251 (9)	4.00	2.80

Souvenir Sheets

Perf. 12

No.	Type	Description	Unused	Used
252		Sheet of 3	2.50	2.50
a.	A74	5m Combine harvester	.75	.50
b.	A74	15m Angora goats	.75	.50
c.	A74	40m Oxen	.75	.50
253		Sheet of 3	2.50	2.50
a.	A74	10m Pigs and geese	.75	.50
b.	A74	20m Horses	.75	.50
c.	A74	30m Cows	.75	.50
254		Sheet of 3	3.00	3.00
a.	A74	25m Camels	.90	.75
b.	A74	50m Rams	.90	.75
c.	A74	1t Sheep	.90	.75

40th anniversary of independence. Nos. 252-254 each contain 3 stamps imperf. between.

Horseback Riders — A75

5m, Young wrestlers & instructor. 15m, Camel & pony riders. 20m, Falconers. 30m, Skier. 50m, Archers. 1t, Male dancers.

1961, Aug. 10 — *Perf. 11*

No.	Type	Description	Unused	Used
255	A75	5m multi	.25	.25
256	A75	10m multi	.25	.25
257	A75	15m multi	.25	.25
258	A75	20m multi	.80	.25
259	A75	30m multi	.35	.35
260	A75	50m multi	.45	.35
261	A75	1t multi	.75	.50
		Nos. 255-261 (7)	3.10	2.20

Independence, 40th anniv.; Mongolian youth sports.

Statue of Sukhe Bator — A76

Designs: 5m, Mongol youth. 10m, Mongol chieftain. 20m, Singer. 30m, Dancer. 50m, Dombra player. 70m, Musicians. 1t, Gymnast. 5m, 10m, 70m, 1t, horiz.

Perf. 12x11½, 11½x12

1961, Sept. 16

262 A76 5m brt grn & red lil .25 .25
263 A76 10m red & dk bl .25 .25
264 A76 15m bl & lt brn .25 .25
265 A76 20m pur & brt grn .25 .25
266 A76 30m vio bl & car .30 .25
267 A76 50m ol & vio .55 .25
268 A76 70m brt lil rose & ol .65 .35
269 A76 1t dk bl & ver 1.25 .75
Nos. 262-269 (8) 3.75 2.60

40th anniv. of independence; Mongolian culture.

Arms of Mongolia — A77

1961, Nov. 17 *Perf. 11½x12*

270 A77 5m multi .25 .25
271 A77 10m multi .25 .25
272 A77 15m multi .25 .25
273 A77 20m multi .25 .25
274 A77 30m multi .25 .25
275 A77 50m multi .35 .25
276 A77 70m multi .45 .35
277 A77 1t multi .50 .45
Nos. 270-277 (8) 2.55 2.30

For surcharges see Nos. 2144A, 2302D.

Congress Emblem A78

1961, Dec. 4 **Litho.** *Perf. 11½*

278 A78 30m vio bl, yel & red .30 .25
279 A78 50m brn, yel & red .40 .30

5th World Congress of Trade Unions, Moscow, Dec. 4-16.

UN Emblem and Arms of Mongolia — A79

10m, Globe, map of Mongolia, dove. 50m, Flags of UN & Mongolia. 60m, UN Headquarters, New York. Parliament, Ulan Bator. 70m, UN assembly, UN & Mongolian flags.

1962, Mar. 15 **Photo.** *Perf. 11*

280 A79 10m gold & multi .25 .25
281 A79 30m gold & multi .30 .25
282 A79 50m gold & multi .55 .35
283 A79 60m gold & multi .65 .35
284 A79 70m gold & multi .75 .50
Nos. 280-284 (5) 2.50 1.70

Mongolia's admission to UN.

Soccer — A80

Designs: 10m, Soccer ball, globe and flags. 30m, Soccer players, globe and ball. 60m, Goalkeeper. 70m, Stadium.

1962, May 15 **Litho.** *Perf. 10½*

285 A80 10m multi .25 .25
286 A80 30m multi .30 .25
287 A80 50m multi .45 .30
288 A80 60m multi .55 .35
289 A80 70m multi .75 .35
Nos. 285-289 (5) 2.30 1.50

World Soccer Championship, Chile, 5/30-6/17.

D. Natsagdorji — A81

1962, May 15 **Photo.** *Perf. 15x14½*

290 A81 30m brown .30 .25
291 A81 50m bluish grn .40 .25

Mongolian writers' congress.
For overprints see Nos. 430-431.

Solidarity Emblem — A82

1962, May 22 **Litho.** *Perf. 11½x10½*

292 A82 20m yel grn & multi .30 .25
293 A82 30m bl & multi .40 .25

Afro-Asian Peoples' solidarity.

Flags of USSR and Mongolia — A83

Perf. 11½x10½

1962, June 25 **Litho.**

294 A83 30m brn & multi .30 .25
295 A83 50m vio bl & multi .40 .25

Mongol-Soviet friendship.

Nos. 195-202 Overprinted

1962, July 20 **Photo.** *Perf. 11½x12*

296 A62 5m multi .60 .30
297 A62 10m multi .65 .35
298 A62 15m multi .75 .35
299 A62 20m multi .75 .35
300 A62 30m multi .80 .50
301 A62 40m multi .90 .50
302 A62 50m multi 1.10 .50
303 A62 1t multi 1.75 .90
Nos. 296-303 (8) 7.30 3.75

WHO drive to eradicate malaria.

Military Field Emblem — A84

Designs: 30m, Tablets with inscriptions. 50m, Stone column. 60m, Genghis Khan.

1962, July 20 *Perf. 11½x12*

304 A84 20m blue & multi *1.50 1.50*
305 A84 30m red & multi *1.50 1.50*
306 A84 50m pink, brn & blk *3.50 3.50*
307 A84 60m blue & multi *3.50 3.50*
Nos. 304-307 (4) *10.00 10.00*

Genghis Khan (1162-1227), Mongol conqueror.

For overprints see Nos. 1846-1849. For surcharge, see No. 2378A.

River Perch — A85

10m, Burbot. 15m, Arctic grayling. 20m, Shorthorn sculpin. 30m, Marine zander. 50m, Siberian sturgeon. 70m, Waleck's chub minnow. 1.50t, Cottocomephorid.

1962, Dec. 28 *Perf. 11*

308 A85 5m shown .25 .25
309 A85 10m multi .25 .25
310 A85 15m multi .25 .25
311 A85 20m multi .25 .25
312 A85 30m multi .30 .25
313 A85 50m multi .30 .30
314 A85 70m multi .40 .35
315 A85 1.50t multi .65 .35
Nos. 308-315 (8) 2.65 2.25

Sukhe Bator (1893-1923), National Hero — A86

1963, Feb. 2 **Photo.** *Perf. 11½x12*

316 A86 30m blue .25 .25
317 A86 60m rose car .40 .25

Laika and Rocket — A87

Designs: 15m, Rocket launching, vert. 25m, Lunik 2, vert. 70m, Andrian G. Nikolayev and Pavel R. Popovich. 1t, Mars rocket.

1963, Apr. 1 **Litho.** *Perf. 12½x12*

Size: 46x32mm

318 A87 5m multicolored .25 .25

Size: 20x68mm

319 A87 15m multicolored .25 .25
320 A87 25m multicolored .40 .25

Size: 46x32mm

321 A87 70m multicolored .75 .30
322 A87 1t multicolored 1.00 .60
Nos. 318-322 (5) 2.65 1.65

Soviet space explorations.

Blood Transfusion — A88

20m, Packing Red Cross parcels. 50m, Vaccination. 60m, Ambulance service. 1.30t, Centenary emblem.

1963, Aug. 15 *Perf. 10½*

323 A88 20m multi .25 .25
324 A88 30m shown .25 .25
325 A88 50m multi .50 .30
326 A88 60m multi .60 .40
327 A88 1.30t multi .90 .50
Nos. 323-327 (5) 2.50 1.70

Red Cross centenary.

Karl Marx — A89

1963, Sept. 16 **Photo.** *Perf. 11½x12*

328 A89 30m blue .30 .25
329 A89 60m dk car rose .40 .30

145th anniversary of birth of Karl Marx.

Mongolian Woman — A90

1963, Sept. 26

330 A90 30m blue & multi .50 .25

5th Intl. Women's Cong., Moscow, 6/24-29.

Inachis
A91

Mongolian butterflies: 10m, Gonepteryxrhamni. 15m, Aglais urticae. 20m, Parnassius apollo. 30m, Papilio machaon. 60m, Agrodiaetus damon. 1t, Limenitis populi.

1963, Nov. 7 Litho. *Perf. 11½*

331	A91	5m shown	.45	.25
332	A91	10m multi	.50	.25
333	A91	15m multi	.70	.25
334	A91	20m multi	.75	.25
335	A91	30m multi	1.20	.25
336	A91	60m multi	1.75	.50
337	A91	1t multi	2.25	.75
		Nos. 331-337 (7)	7.60	2.50

UNESCO Emblem, Globe and Scales — A92

1963, Dec. 10 Photo. *Perf. 12*

338	A92	30m multicolored	.40	.25
339	A92	60m multicolored	.60	.40

Universal Declaration of Human Rights, 15th anniversary.

Mushrooms — A93

Designs: 5m, Coprinus Comatus. 10m, Lactarius torminosus. 15m, Psalliota campestris. 20m, Russula delica. 30m, Ixocomus granulatus. 50m, Lactarius scrobiculatus. 70m, Lactarius deliciosus. 1t, Ixocomus variegatus.

1964, Jan. 1 Litho. *Perf. 10½*

340	A93	5m shown	.50	.25
341	A93	10m multi	.75	.40
342	A93	15m multi	.95	.50
343	A93	20m multi	1.10	.55
344	A93	30m multi	1.25	.60
345	A93	50m multi	1.50	.75
346	A93	70m multi	1.75	.90
347	A93	1t multi	2.25	2.10
		Nos. 340-347 (8)	10.05	6.05

Souvenir Sheet

Skier — A94

1964, Feb. 12 Photo. *Perf. 12x11½*

348	A94	4t gray	4.50	4.50

9th Winter Olympic Games, Innsbruck, Jan. 29-Feb. 9.

Lenin — A95

1964 Photo. *Perf. 11½x12*

349	A95	30m salmon & multi	.60	.25
350	A95	50m blue & multi	.80	.40

60th anniversary of Communist Party. Nos. 349-350 printed with alternating label showing Lenin quotation.

Javelin — A96

5m, Gymnastics, women's. 15m, Wrestling. 20m, Running, women's. 30m, Equestrian. 50m, Diving, women's. 60m, Bicycling. 1t, Olympic Games emblem.
4t, Wrestling.

1964, Apr. 30 Litho. *Perf. 10½*

351	A96	5m multi	.25	.25
352	A96	10m shown	.25	.25
353	A96	15m multi	.25	.25
354	A96	20m multi	.25	.25
355	A96	30m multi	.40	.25
356	A96	50m multi	.60	.25
357	A96	60m multi	.80	.30
358	A96	1t multi	1.00	.60
		Nos. 351-358 (8)	3.80	2.40

Souvenir Sheet

Perf. 12x11½

359	A96	4t multi	3.50	3.50

18th Olympic Games, Toyko, Oct. 10-25. No. 359 contains one horizontal stamp, 37x27½mm. Issued Sept. 1.

Congress Emblem — A97

1964, Sept. 30 Photo. *Perf. 11*

360	A97	30m multicolored	.40	.30

4th Mongolian Women's Congress.

Lunik 1 — A98

Space Research: 10m, Vostok 1 and 2. 15m, Tiros weather satellite, vert. 20m, Cosmos circling earth, vert. 30m, Mars probe, vert. 60m, Luna 4, vert. 80m, Echo 2. 1t, Radar and rockets.

1964, Oct. 30

361	A98	5m multicolored	.25	.25
362	A98	10m multicolored	.25	.25
363	A98	15m multicolored	.25	.25
364	A98	20m multicolored	.35	.25
365	A98	30m multicolored	.50	.35
366	A98	60m multicolored	.65	.40
367	A98	80m multicolored	.95	.45
368	A98	1t multicolored	1.25	.55
		Nos. 361-368 (8)	4.45	2.75

Rider Carrying Flag — A99

1964, Nov. 26 Photo. *Perf. 11½x12*

369	A99	25m multicolored	.40	.25
370	A99	50m multicolored	.50	.40

40th anniversary of Mongolian constitution.

Weather Balloon A100

Designs: 5m, Oceanographic exploration. 60m, Northern lights and polar bears. 80m, Geomagnetism. 1t, I.Q.S.Y. emblem and Mercator map.

1965, May 15 Photo. *Perf. 13½*

371	A100	5m gray & multi	.25	.25
372	A100	10m grn & multi	.25	.30
373	A100	60m blue, blk & pink	.70	.25
374	A100	80m citron & multi	.85	.35
375	A100	1t brt green & multi	1.25	.60
		Nos. 371-375,C6-C8 (8)	7.20	2.85

International Quiet Sun Year.

Horses — A101

Designs: Mares and Foals.

1965, Aug. 25 *Perf. 11*

376	A101	5m shown	.25	.25
377	A101	10m Falconers	.25	.25
378	A101	15m Taming wild horse	.25	.25
379	A101	20m Horse race	.35	.25
380	A101	30m Hurdles	.50	.35
381	A101	60m Wolf hunt	.65	.40
382	A101	80m Milking a mare	.95	.45
383	A101	1t Mare and foal	1.25	.55
		Nos. 376-383 (8)	4.45	2.75

Girl Holding Lambs — A102

10m, Boy and girl drummers. 20m, Camp fire. 30m, Wrestlers. 50m, Emblem.

1965, Oct. 10 Photo. *Perf. 11*

384	A102	5m shown	.25	.25
385	A102	10m multi	.25	.25
386	A102	20m multi	.30	.25
387	A102	30m multi	.40	.30
388	A102	50m multi	.70	.50
		Nos. 384-388 (5)	1.90	1.55

40th anniv. of Mongolian Youth Org.

Chinese Perch — A103

1965, Nov. 25

389	A103	5m shown	.25	.25
390	A103	10m Lenok trout	.25	.25
391	A103	15m Siberian sturgeon	.25	.25
392	A103	20m Amur salmon	.40	.25
393	A103	30m Bagrid catfish	.60	.25
394	A103	60m Siluri catfish	.95	.25
395	A103	80m Northern pike	1.10	.45
396	A103	1t River perch	1.50	.65
		Nos. 389-396 (8)	5.30	2.60

Marx and Lenin — A104

1965, Dec. 15 *Perf. 11½x12*

397	A104	10m red & blk	.35	.25

6th Conference of Postal Ministers of Communist Countries, Peking, June 21-July 15.

Sable — A105

10m, Fox. 15m, Otter, vert. 20m, Cheetah, vert. 30m, Pallas's cat. 60m, Stone marten. 80m, Ermine, vert. 1t, Woman in mink coat, vert.

1966, Feb. 15 Photo. *Perf. 12½*

398 A105 5m shown .25 .25
399 A105 10m multi .25 .25
400 A105 15m multi .30 .25
401 A105 20m multi .30 .25
402 A105 30m multi .40 .25
403 A105 60m multi .60 .30
404 A105 80m multi .80 .40
405 A105 1t multi 1.25 .75
Nos. 398-405 (8) 4.15 2.70

Opening of WHO Headquarters, Geneva — A106

1966, May 3 Photo. *Perf. 12x11½*

406 A106 30m bl grn, bl & gold .30 .25
407 A106 50m red, bl & gold .50 .30

For overprints see Nos. 483-484.

Soccer — A107

Designs: 30m, 60m, 80m, Various soccer plays. 1t, British flag and World Soccer Cup emblem. 4t, Wembley Stadium, horiz.

1966, May 31 Photo. *Perf. 11*

408 A107 10m multicolored .25 .25
409 A107 30m multicolored .25 .25
410 A107 60m multicolored .35 .30
411 A107 80m multicolored .55 .40
412 A107 1t multicolored .75 .50
Nos. 408-412 (5) 2.15 1.70

Souvenir Sheet

Perf. 12½, Imperf.

413 A107 4t gray & brown 2.75 2.00

World Soccer Championship for Jules Rimet Cup, Wembley, England, July 11-30. No. 413 contains one stamp 61x83mm.

Sukhe Bator, Parliament Building, Ulan Bator — A108

1966, June 7 Litho. *Perf. 12x12½*

414 A108 30m red, bl & brn .40 .25

15th Congress of Mongolian Communist Party.

Wrestling A109

Designs: Various wrestling holds.

1966, June 15 Photo. *Perf. 11½x12*

415 A109 10m multicolored .25 .25
416 A109 30m multicolored .25 .25
417 A109 60m multicolored .40 .25
418 A109 80m multicolored .45 .25
419 A109 1t multicolored .60 .25
Nos. 415-419 (5) 1.95 1.25

World Wrestling Championship, Toledo, Spain.

Emblem and Map of Mongolia A110

Sukhe Bator, Grain and Factories A111

Perf. 11½x12, 12x11½

1966, July 11 Litho.

420 A110 30m red & multi 1.10 .80
421 A111 50m red & multi 2.75 1.00

45th anniversary of independence.
For overprints see Nos. 552-553.

Lilium Tenuifolium — A112

5m, Physochlaena physaloides. 10m, Allium polyrrchizum. 20m, Thermopsis lanceolata. 30m, Amygdalus mongolica. 60m, Caryopteris mongolica. 80m, Piptanthus mongolicus. 1t, Iris bungei.

1966, Oct. 15 Photo. *Perf. 12x11½*

422 A112 5m multi .25 .25
423 A112 10m multi .30 .25
424 A112 15m shown .40 .25
425 A112 20m multi .50 .25
426 A112 30m multi .60 .30
427 A112 60m multi .85 .40

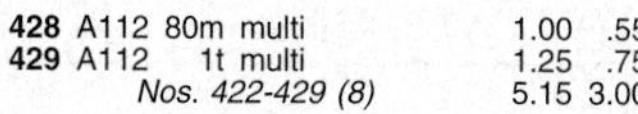
428 A112 80m multi 1.00 .55
429 A112 1t multi 1.25 .75
Nos. 422-429 (8) 5.15 3.00

Nos. 290-291 Overprinted: "1906/1966"

1966, Oct. 26 Photo. *Perf. 15x14½*

430 A81 30m brown 8.00 8.00
431 A81 50m bluish grn 10.00 10.00

60th anniv. of birth of D. Natsagdorji, writer. 50m exists double, one inverted.

Children's Day — A113

10m, Child with dove. 15m, Children with reindeer. 20m, Boys wrestling, vert. 30m, Horseback riding. 60m, Children riding camel, vert. 80m, Child with sheep. 1t, Boy archer, vert.

1966, Dec. 2 *Perf. 11½x12, 12x11½*

432 A113 10m shown .25 .25
433 A113 15m multi .35 .25
434 A113 20m multi .40 .25
435 A113 30m multi .45 .25
436 A113 60m multi .70 .40
437 A113 80m multi .95 .50
438 A113 1t multi 1.25 .75
Nos. 432-438 (7) 4.35 2.65

Proton 1 — A114

Perf. 11½x12½, 12½x11½

1966, Dec. 28 Photo.

439 A114 5m Vostok 2, vert. .25 .25
440 A114 10m shown .25 .25
441 A114 15m Telstar 1, vert. .25 .25
442 A114 20m Molniya 1, vert. .30 .25
443 A114 30m Syncom 3, vert. .40 .30
444 A114 60m Luna 9 .50 .30
445 A114 80m Luna 12, vert. .60 .40
446 A114 1t Mariner 4 .80 .50
Nos. 439-446 (8) 3.35 2.50

Space exploration.

Tarbosaurus — A115

1967, Mar. 31 *Perf. 12x11½*

447 A115 5m shown .35 .25
448 A115 10m Talarurus .40 .25
449 A115 15m Proceratops .45 .25
450 A115 20m Indricotherium .45 .25
451 A115 30m Saurolophus .70 .30
452 A115 60m Mastodon 1.60 .40
453 A115 80m Mongolotherium 1.75 .60
454 A115 1t Mammoth 2.00 .90
Nos. 447-454 (8) 7.70 3.20

Prehistoric animals.

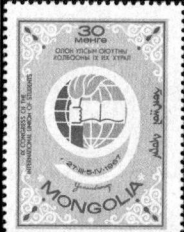

A116

Congress emblem.

1967, June 9 Litho. *Perf. 12*

455 A116 30m lt blue & multi .40 .25
456 A116 50m pink & multi .60 .40

9th Youth Festival for Peace and Friendship, Sofia.

A117

Design: 40m, Sukhe Bator and soldiers. 60m, Lenin and soldiers.

1967, Oct. 25 Litho. *Perf. 11½x12*

457 A117 40m red & multi .45 .25
458 A117 60m red & multi .75 .35

Russian October Revolution, 50th anniv.

Ice Hockey and Olympic Rings A118

5m, Figure skating. 10m, Speed skating. 20m, Ski jump. 30m, Bobsledding. 60m, Figure skating, pair. 80m, Slalom.
4t, Women's figure skating.

1967, Dec. 29 *Perf. 12x12½*

459 A118 5m multi .25 .25
460 A118 10m multi .25 .25
461 A118 15m shown .35 .25
462 A118 20m multi .45 .25
463 A118 30m multi .75 .35
464 A118 60m multi .90 .40
465 A118 80m multi 1.10 .50
Nos. 459-465 (7) 4.05 2.25

Souvenir Sheet

Perf. 12

466 A118 4t multi 3.50 3.50

10th Winter Olympic Games, Grenoble, France, Feb. 6-18.

Bactrian Camels A119

1968, Jan. 15 Photo. *Perf. 12*

467 A119 5m shown .25 .25
468 A119 10m Yak .25 .25
469 A119 15m Lamb .25 .25
470 A119 20m Foal .35 .25
471 A119 30m Calf .40 .25
472 A119 60m Bison .55 .25
473 A119 80m Roe deer .80 .35
474 A119 1t Reindeer 1.40 .45
Nos. 467-474 (8) 4.25 2.30

Young animals.

Black Currants — A120

Berries: 5m, Rosa acicularis. 15m, Gooseberries. 20m, Malus. 30m, Strawberries. 60m, Ribes altissimum. 80m, Blueberries. 1t, Hippophae rhamnoides.

Lithographed & Engraved

1968, Feb. 15

475	A120	5m blue & ultra	.25	.25
476	A120	10m buff & brn	.25	.25
477	A120	15m lt grn & grn	.25	.25
478	A120	20m yel & red	.25	.25
479	A120	30m pink & car	.40	.25
480	A120	60m sal & org brn	.45	.25
481	A120	80m pale & dl bl	.80	.30
482	A120	1t lt yel & red	.95	.45
		Nos. 475-482 (8)	3.60	2.25

Nos. 406-407 Overprinted

1968, Apr. 16 Photo. *Perf. 12x11½*

483	A106 30m bl grn, bl & gold	6.00	4.00
484	A106 50m red, blue & gold	6.00	4.00

WHO, 20th anniversary.

Human Rights Flame — A121

1968, June 20 Litho. *Perf. 12*

485 A121 30m turq & vio bl .50 .25

International Human Rights Year.

"Das Kapital," by Karl Marx A122

Design: 50m, Karl Marx.

1968, July 1 Litho. *Perf. 12*

486	A122 30m blue & multi	.30	.25
487	A122 50m red & multi	.50	.25

Karl Marx (1818-1883).

Artist, by A. Sangatzohyo — A123

Paintings: 10m, On Remote Roads, by Sangatzohyo. 15m, Camel calf, by B. Avarzad. 20m, Milk, by Avarzad. 30m, The Bowman, by B. Gombosuren. 80m, Girl Sitting on Yak, by Sangatzohyo. 1.40t, Cagan Dara Eke, by Janaivajara. 4t, Meeting, by Sangatzohyo, horiz.

1968, July 11 Litho. *Perf. 12*

488	A123 5m brown & multi	.25	.25
489	A123 10m brown & multi	.25	.25
490	A123 15m brown & multi	.25	.25
491	A123 20m brown & multi	.40	.25
492	A123 30m brown & multi	.55	.35
493	A123 80m brown & multi	1.10	.55
494	A123 1.40t brown & multi	2.10	1.00
	Nos. 488-494 (7)	4.90	2.90

Miniature Sheets

Perf. 11½, Imperf.

495 A123 4t brown & multi 5.00 5.00

Paintings from national museum, Ulan Bator. #495 contains one 54x84mm stamp.

Volleyball — A124

Olympic Rings and: 10m, Wrestling. 15m, Bicycling. 20m, Javelin, women's. 30m, Soccer. 60m, Running. 80m, Gymnastics, women's. 1t, Weight lifting. 4t, Equestrian.

1968, Sept. 1 Litho. *Perf. 12*

496	A124 5m multicolored	.25	.25
497	A124 10m multicolored	.25	.25
498	A124 15m multicolored	.25	.25
499	A124 20m multicolored	.25	.25
500	A124 30m multicolored	.35	.25
501	A124 60m multicolored	.50	.30
502	A124 80m multicolored	.70	.35
503	A124 1t multicolored	1.00	.40
	Nos. 496-503 (8)	3.55	2.30

Souvenir Sheets

Perf. 11½, Imperf.

504 A124 4t orange & multi 3.50 3.50

19th Olympic Games, Mexico City, Oct. 12-27. #504 contains one 52x44mm stamp.

A125

Hammer, spade & cogwheel.

1968, Sept. 17 Litho. *Perf. 11½*

505 A125 50m blue & vermilion .40 .25

Industrial development in town of Darhan.

A126

1968, Nov. 6 Litho. *Perf. 12*

506 A126 60m turquoise & sepia .40 .25

Maxim Gorki (1868-1936), Russian writer.

Madonna and Child, by Boltraffio A127

Paintings: 10m, St. Roch Healed by an Angel, by Brescia. 15m, Madonna and Child with St. Anne, by Macchietti. 20m, St. John on Patmos, by Cano. 30m, Lady with Viola da Gamba, by Kupetzky. 80m, Boy, by Amerling. 1.40t, Death of Adonis, by Furini. 4t, Portrait of a Lady, by Renoir.

1968, Nov. 20 Litho. *Perf. 12*

507	A127 5m gray & multi	.25	.25
508	A127 10m gray & multi	.25	.25
509	A127 15m gray & multi	.30	.25
510	A127 20m gray & multi	.35	.25
511	A127 30m gray & multi	.45	.30
512	A127 80m gray & multi	.85	.40
513	A127 1.40t gray & multi	1.25	.75
	Nos. 507-513 (7)	3.70	2.45

Miniature Sheet

514 A127 4t gray & multi 4.00 4.00

UNESCO, 22nd anniv.

Jesse Owens, US — A128

Olympic Gold Medal Winners: 5m, Paavo Nurmi, Finland. 15m, Fanny Blankers-Koen, Netherlands. 20m, Laszlo Papp, Hungary. 30m, Wilma Rudolph, US. 60m, Boris Shakhlin, USSR. 80m, Donald Schollander, US. 1t Akinori Nakayama, Japan. 4t, Jigjidin Munkhbat, Mongolia.

1969, Mar. 25 Litho. *Perf. 12*

515	A128 5m multicolored	.25	.25
516	A128 10m multicolored	.25	.25
517	A128 15m multicolored	.25	.25
518	A128 20m multicolored	.25	.25
519	A128 30m multicolored	.30	.25
520	A128 60m multicolored	.50	.30
521	A128 80m multicolored	.75	.50
522	A128 1t multicolored	1.00	.50
	Nos. 515-522 (8)	3.55	2.55

Souvenir Sheet

523 A128 4t green & multi 4.00 4.00

Bayit Woman A129

Regional Costumes: 10m, Torgut man. 15m, Dzakhachin woman. 20m, Khalkha woman. 30m, Dariganga woman. 60m, Mingat woman. 80m, Khalkha man. 1t, Bargut woman.

1969, Apr. 20 Litho. *Perf. 12*

524	A129 5m multicolored	.25	.25
525	A129 10m multicolored	.25	.25
526	A129 15m multicolored	.30	.25
527	A129 20m multicolored	.50	.25
528	A129 30m multicolored	.60	.25
529	A129 60m multicolored	.70	.25
530	A129 80m multicolored	.90	.40
531	A129 1t multicolored	1.25	.75
	Nos. 524-531 (8)	4.75	2.65

Red Cross Emblem and Helicopter — A130

50m, Emblem, Red Cross car, shepherd.

1969, May 15 Litho. *Perf. 12*

532	A130 30m multicolored	1.25	.30
533	A130 50m multicolored	1.25	.40

30th anniversary of Mongolian Red Cross.

Landscape and Edelweiss — A131

Mongolian landscapes and flowers: 10m, Pinks. 15m, Dianthus superbus. 20m, Geranium. 30m, Dianthus ramosissimus. 60m, Globeflowers. 80m, Delphinium. 1t, Haloxylon.

1969, May 20

534	A131 5m shown	.25	.25
535	A131 10m multi	.25	.25
536	A131 15m multi	.30	.25
537	A131 20m multi	.30	.25
538	A131 30m multi	.45	.25
539	A131 60m multi	.55	.25
540	A131 80m multi	.70	.40
541	A131 1t multi	.90	.45
	Nos. 534-541 (8)	3.70	2.35

See No. 1105.

Bull Fight, by Tsewegdjaw — A132

Paintings from National Museum: 10m, Fighting Colts, by O. Tsewegdjaw. 15m, Horseman and Herd, by A. Sangatzohyo. 20m, Camel Caravan, by D. Damdinsuren. 30m, On the Steppe, by N. Tsultem. 60m, Milking Mares, by Tsewegdjaw. 80m, Going to School, by B. Avarzad. 1t, After Work, by G. Odon. 4t, Horses, by Damdinsuren.

1969, July 11 **Litho.** ***Perf. 12***

542 A132 5m multicolored .25 .25
543 A132 10m multicolored .25 .25
544 A132 15m multicolored .25 .25
545 A132 20m multicolored .25 .25
546 A132 30m multicolored .30 .25
547 A132 60m multicolored .60 .25
548 A132 80m multicolored .80 .40
549 A132 1t multicolored 1.25 .60
Nos. 542-549 (8) 3.95 2.50

Souvenir Sheet

550 A132 4t multicolored 4.00 4.00

10th anniversary of cooperative movement. No. 550 contains one stamp 65x42mm.

Mongolian Flag and Emblem A133

1969, Sept. 20 **Litho.** ***Perf. 11½***

551 A133 50m multicolored .50 .30

Battle of Ha-lo-hsin (Khalka) River, 30th anniversary.
For surcharge, see No. 2384A.

Nos. 420-421 Overprinted

Perf. 11½x12, 12x11½

1969, Nov. 26 **Photo.**

552 A110 30m red & multi *8.00 8.00*
553 A111 50m red & multi *10.00 10.00*

45th anniv. of Mongolian People's Republic.

Mercury 7 — A134

Designs: 5m, Sputnik 3. 10m, Vostok 1. 20m, Voskhod 2. 30m, Apollo 8. 60m, Soyuz 5. 80m, Apollo 12.

1969, Dec. 6 **Photo.** ***Perf. 12x11½***

554 A134 5m multicolored .25 .25
555 A134 10m multicolored .25 .25
556 A134 15m multicolored .25 .25
557 A134 20m multicolored .25 .25
558 A134 30m multicolored .25 .25
559 A134 60m multicolored .45 .25
560 A134 80m multicolored .60 .25
Nos. 554-560 (7) 2.30 1.75

Souvenir Sheet

561 A134 4t multicolored 3.50 2.50

Space achievements of US and USSR.

Wolf — A135

Designs: 10m, Brown bear. 15m, Lynx. 20m, Wild boar. 30m, Moose. 60m, Bobac marmot. 80m, Argali. 1t, Old wall carpet showing hunter and dog.

1970, Mar. 25 **Photo.** ***Perf. 12***

562 A135 5m multicolored .25 .25
563 A135 10m multicolored .25 .25
564 A135 15m multicolored .35 .25
565 A135 20m multicolored .40 .25
566 A135 30m multicolored .45 .25
567 A135 60m multicolored .75 .40
568 A135 80m multicolored 1.00 .60
569 A135 1t multicolored 1.25 .80
Nos. 562-569 (8) 4.70 3.05

Lenin and Mongolian Delegation, by Sangatzohyo — A136

Designs: 20m, Lenin, embroidered panel, by Cerenhuu, vert. 1t, Lenin, by Mazhig, vert.

1970, Apr. 22 **Photo. & Litho.**

570 A136 20m multicolored .30 .25
571 A136 50m multicolored .50 .25
572 A136 1t lt bl, blk & red 1.25 .50
Nos. 570-572 (3) 2.05 1.00

Centenary of the birth of Lenin.

Souvenir Sheet

EXPO '70 Pavilion of Matsushita Electric Co. and Time Capsule — A137

1970, May 26 **Photo.** ***Perf. 12½***

573 A137 4t gold & multi 4.50 4.50

EXPO '70 International Exposition, Osaka, Japan, Mar. 15-Sept. 13.

Sumitomo Fairy Tale Pavilion — A138

1970, June 5 **Photo.** ***Perf. 12x11½***

574 A138 1.50t multi + label 1.00 1.00

EXPO '70 International Exposition, Osaka. No. 574 printed in sheets of 20 (5x4) with alternating horizontal rows of tabs showing various fairy tales and EXPO '70 emblem.

Soccer, Rimet Cup — A139

Soccer players of various teams in action.

1970, June 20 ***Perf. 12½x11½***

575 A139 10m multi .25 .25
576 A139 20m multi .25 .25
577 A139 30m multi .25 .25
578 A139 50m multi .40 .25
579 A139 60m multi .50 .25
580 A139 1t multi .90 .25
581 A139 1.30t multi 1.00 .45
Nos. 575-581 (7) 3.55 1.95

Souvenir Sheet

Perf. 12½

582 A139 4t multi 3.50 3.50

World Soccer Championship for Jules Rimet Cup, Mexico City, May 30-June 21. No. 582 contains one stamp 51x37mm.

Old World Buzzard A140

Birds of Prey: 20m, Tawny owls. 30m, Northern goshawk. 50m, White-tailed sea eagle. 60m, Peregrine falcon. 1t, Old world kestrel. 1.30t, Black kite.

1970, June 30 **Litho.** ***Perf. 12***

583 A140 10m bl & multi .75 .25
584 A140 20m pink & multi 1.00 .25
585 A140 30m yel grn & multi 1.10 .25
586 A140 50m bl & multi 1.20 .25
587 A140 60m yel & multi 1.60 .50
588 A140 1t grn & multi 2.00 .50
589 A140 1.30t bl & multi 2.50 .65
Nos. 583-589 (7) 10.15 2.65

Russian War Memorial, Berlin — A141

1970, July 11 **Litho.** ***Perf. 12***

590 A141 60m blue & multi .60 .30

25th anniversary of end of World War II.

Bogdo-Gegen Palace — A142

Designs: 10m, Archer. 30m, Horseman. 40m, "White Mother" Goddess. 50m, Girl in national costume. 60m, Lion statue. 70m, Dancer's mask. 80m, Detail from Bogdo-Gegen Palace, Ulan Bator.

1970, Sept. 20 **Litho.** ***Perf. 12***

591 A142 10m multi .35 .25
592 A142 20m multi .35 .25
593 A142 30m multi .35 .25
594 A142 40m multi .35 .30
595 A142 50m multi .75 .65
596 A142 60m multi .90 .75
597 A142 70m multi 1.00 .85
598 A142 80m multi 1.25 1.10
a. Block of 4, #595-598
Nos. 591-598 (8) 5.30 4.40

Souvenir Sheet

Recovery of Apollo 13 Capsule — A143

1970, Nov. 1 **Litho.** ***Perf. 12***

599 A143 4t blue & multi 4.50 4.50

Space missions of Apollo 13, Apr. 11-17, and Soyuz 9, June 1-10, 1970.

Mongolian Flag, UN and Education Year Emblems — A144

1970, Nov. 7

600 A144 60m multi .60 .30

International Education Year.

Mounted Herald A145

1970, Nov. 7 **Litho.** ***Perf. 12***

601 A145 30m gold & multi .50 .30

50th anniv. of newspaper Unen (Truth).

Apollo 11 Lunar Landing Module — A146

Designs: 10m, Vostok 2 & 3. 20m, Voskhod 2, space walk. 30m, Gemini 6 & 7 capsules. 50m, Soyuz 4 & 5 docking in space. 60m, Soyuz 6, 7 & 8 group flight. 1t, Apollo 13 with damaged capsule. 1.30t, Luna 16 unmanned moon landing. 4t, Radar ground tracking station.

1971, Feb. 25 **Litho.** ***Perf. 12***

602 A146 10m multi .25 .25
603 A146 20m multi .25 .25
604 A146 30m multi .25 .25
605 A146 50m multi .35 .25
606 A146 60m multi .45 .25
607 A146 80m multi .60 .25

608 A146 1t multi .75 .30
609 A146 1.30t multi .95 .40
Nos. 602-609 (8) 3.85 2.20

Souvenir Sheet

610 A146 4t vio bl & multi 3.50 3.50

US and USSR space explorations.

Rider with Mongolian Flag — A147

Designs: 30m, Party meeting. 90m, Lenin with Mongolian leader. 1.20t, Marchers, pictures of Lenin and Marx.

1971, Mar. 1 Photo. *Perf. 12½*

611 A147 30m gold & multi .30 .25
612 A147 60m gold & multi .40 .30
613 A147 90m gold & multi .50 .40
614 A147 1.20t gold & multi .60 .50
Nos. 611-614 (4) 1.80 1.45

Mongolian Revolutionary Party, 50th anniv.

Souvenir Sheet

Lunokhod 1 on Moon — A148

Design: No. 615b, Apollo 14 on moon.

1971, Apr. 15 Photo. *Perf. 14*

615 A148 Sheet of 2 3.50 3.50
a.-b. 2t any single 1.50 1.50

Luna 17 unmanned automated moon mission, Nov. 10-17, 1970, and Apollo 14 moon landing, Jan. 31-Feb. 9, 1971.

Dancer's Mask A149

Designs: Various masks for dancers.

1971, Apr. 25 Litho. *Perf. 12*

616 A149 10m gold & multi .25 .25
617 A149 20m gold & multi .30 .25
618 A149 30m gold & multi .40 .25
619 A149 50m gold & multi .40 .25
620 A149 60m gold & multi .50 .30
621 A149 1t gold & multi .90 .40
622 A149 1.30t gold & multi 1.00 .55
Nos. 616-622 (7) 3.75 2.25

Red Flag and Emblems A150

1971, May 31 Photo. *Perf. 12x11½*

623 A150 60m bl, red & gold .40 .25

16th Congress of Mongolian Revolutionary Party.

Steam Locomotive — A151

1971, July 11 Litho. *Perf. 12*

624 A151 20m shown .50 .25
625 A151 30m Diesel locomotive .60 .25
626 A151 40m Truck .65 .25
627 A151 50m Automobile .75 .25
628 A151 60m Biplane PO-2 .85 .30
629 A151 80m AN-24 plane 1.00 .40
630 A151 1t Fishing boat 1.75 1.00
Nos. 624-630 (7) 6.10 2.70

50th anniversary of modern transportation.

For overprints and surcharge, see Nos. 850A-850G, 2825.

Arms of Mongolia and Soldier — A152

Design: 1.50t, Arms, policeman and child.

1971, July 11 Litho. *Perf. 12*

631 A152 60m multi .50 .25
632 A152 1.50t multi .65 .30

50th anniversary of the people's army and police.

Mongolian Flag and Emblem — A153

1971, Aug. 25 Photo. *Perf. 12x11½*

633 A153 60m lt bl & multi .40 .25

International Year Against Racial discrimination.

Flag of Youth Organization — A154

1971, Aug. 25 Litho. *Perf. 12*

634 A154 60m org & multi .60 .30

50th anniversary of Mongolian revolutionary youth organization.

The Woodsman and the Tiger A155

Designs: Various Mongolian fairy tales.

1971, Sept. 15 Litho. *Perf. 12*

635 A155 10m gold & multi .25 .25
636 A155 20m gold & multi .25 .25
637 A155 30m gold & multi .30 .25
638 A155 50m gold & multi .35 .25
639 A155 60m gold & multi .50 .25
640 A155 80m gold & multi .65 .25
641 A155 1t gold & multi .90 .35
642 A155 1.30t gold & multi 1.10 .50
Nos. 635-642 (8) 4.30 2.35

Bactrian Camel — A156

1971, Nov. 1 Litho. *Perf. 12½*

643 A156 20m Yaks .25 .25
644 A156 30m shown .25 .25
645 A156 40m Sheep .35 .25
646 A156 50m Goats .40 .25
647 A156 60m Cattle .55 .35
648 A156 80m Horses .65 .35
649 A156 1t White horse 1.00 .50
Nos. 643-649 (7) 3.45 2.20

Mongolian livestock breeding.

Cross-country Skiing — A157

Designs (Sapporo Olympic Emblem and): 20m, Bobsledding. 30m, Women's figure skating. 50m, Slalom. 60m, Speed skating. 80m, Downhill skiing. 1t, Ice hockey. 1.30t, Figure skating, pairs. 4t, Ski jump.

Perf. 12½x11½

1972, Jan. 20 Photo.

650 A157 10m multi .25 .25
651 A157 20m ol & multi .25 .25
652 A157 30m ultra & multi .30 .25
653 A157 50m brt bl & multi .35 .25
654 A157 60m multi .45 .25
655 A157 80m grn & multi .55 .25
656 A157 1t bl & multi .70 .30
657 A157 1.30t vio & multi .90 .35
Nos. 650-657 (8) 3.75 2.15

Souvenir Sheet

Perf. 12½

658 A157 4t lt bl & multi 2.50 2.50

11th Winter Olympic Games, Sapporo, Japan, Feb. 3-13.

Taming Wild Horse A158

Paintings: 20m, Mythological animal in winter. 30m, Lancer on horseback. 50m, Athletes. 60m, Waterfall and horses. 80m, The Wise Musician, by Sarav. 1t, Young musician. 1.30t, Old sage with animals.

1972, Apr. 15 Litho. *Perf. 12*

659 A158 10m multi .25 .25
660 A158 20m multi .25 .25
661 A158 30m multi .25 .25
662 A158 50m multi .35 .25
663 A158 60m multi .40 .25
664 A158 80m multi .65 .35
665 A158 1t multi .70 .35
666 A158 1.30t multi .85 .40
Nos. 659-666 (8) 3.70 2.35

Paintings by contemporary artists in Ulan Bator Museum.

Calosoma Fischeri A159

Designs: Various insects.

1972, Apr. 30 Litho. *Perf. 12*

667 A159 10m multi .25 .25
668 A159 20m multi .30 .25
669 A159 30m multi .40 .25
670 A159 50m multi .50 .25
671 A159 60m multi .70 .25
672 A159 80m multi 1.00 .50
673 A159 1t multi 1.25 .75
674 A159 1.30t multi 1.75 .95
Nos. 667-674 (8) 6.15 3.45

UN Emblem A160

1972, Aug. 30 Photo. *Perf. 12*

675 A160 60m multi .60 .40

ECAFE (UN Economic Commission for Asia and the Far East), 25th anniv.

Slow Lizard — A161

Designs: 15m, Radd's toad. 20m, Pallas's viper. 25m, Toad-headed agamid. 30m, Siberian wood frog. 60m, Przewalski's lizard. 80m, Taphrometopon lineolatum (snake). 1t, Stoliczka's agamid.

1972, Sept. 5 Litho. *Perf. 12*

676	A161	10m multi	.25	.25
677	A161	15m multi	.25	.25
678	A161	20m multi	.25	.25
679	A161	25m multi	.40	.25
680	A161	30m multi	.45	.25
681	A161	60m multi	.60	.30
682	A161	80m multi	.95	.45
683	A161	1t multi	1.50	.55
		Nos. 676-683 (8)	4.65	2.55

Symbols of Technical Knowledge — A162

Design: 60m, University of Mongolia.

1972, Sept. 25

684	A162	50m org & multi	.40	.25
685	A162	60m lil & multi	.50	.25

30th anniversary of Mongolian State University.

Virgin and Child with St. John, by Bellini — A163

Paintings by Venetian Masters: 20m, Transfiguration, by Bellini, vert. 30m, Virgin and Child, by Bellini, vert. 50m, Presentation in the Temple, by Bellini. 60m, St. George, by Mantegna, vert. 80m, Departure of St. Ursula, by Carpaccio, vert. 1t, Departure of St. Ursula, by Carpaccio.

1972, Oct. 1

686	A163	10m multi	.25	.25
687	A163	20m multi	.25	.25
688	A163	30m multi	.30	.25
689	A163	50m multi	.50	.25
690	A163	60m multi	.70	.25
691	A163	80m multi	.80	.40
692	A163	1t multi	1.00	.70
		Nos. 686-692 (7)	3.80	2.35

Save Venice campaign. See No. B3.

Manlay Bator Damdinsuren — A164

Designs: 20m, Ard Ayus, horiz. 50m, Hatan Bator Magsarzhav. 60m, Has Bator, horiz. 1t, Sukhe Bator.

1972, Oct. 20 Litho. *Perf. 12*

693	A164	10m gold & multi	.25	.25
694	A164	20m gold & multi	.30	.25
695	A164	50m gold & multi	.40	.25
696	A164	60m gold & multi	.50	.30
697	A164	1t gold & multi	1.00	.40
		Nos. 693-697 (5)	2.45	1.45

Paintings of national heroes.

Spasski Tower, Moscow — A165

1972, Nov. 7 Photo. *Perf. 11*

698	A165	60m multi + label	.75	.25

50th anniversary of USSR.

Mark Spitz, US, Gold Medal — A166

Designs (Medal and): 10m, Ulrike Meyfarth, Germany. 20m, Sawao Kato, Japan. 30m, András Balczó, Hungary. 60m, Lasse Viren, Finland. 80m, Shane Gould, Australia. 1t, Anatoli Bondarchuk, USSR. 4t, Khorloo Baianmunk, Mongolia.

1972, Dec. 15 Photo. *Perf. 12½*

699	A166	5m grn & multi	.25	.25
700	A166	10m ver & multi	.25	.25
701	A166	20m bl & multi	.30	.25
702	A166	30m multi	.30	.25
703	A166	60m lt vio & multi	.50	.25
704	A166	80m ol & multi	.70	.30
705	A166	1t lem & multi	.90	.40
		Nos. 699-705 (7)	3.20	1.95

Souvenir Sheet

706	A166	4t red & multi	2.50	2.50

Winners in 20th Olympic Games, Munich.

Chimpanzee on Bicycle — A167

Circus Scenes: 10m, Seal playing ball. 15m, Bear riding wheel. 20m, Woman acrobat on camel. 30m, Woman equestrian. 50m, Clown playing flute. 60m, Woman gymnast. 1t, Circus building, Ulan Bator, horiz.

1973, Jan. 29 Litho. *Perf. 12*

707	A167	5m multi	.25	.25
708	A167	10m multi	.25	.25
709	A167	15m multi	.30	.25
710	A167	20m multi	.40	.25
711	A167	30m multi	.50	.25
712	A167	50m multi	.60	.25
713	A167	60m multi	.80	.40
714	A167	1t multi	1.00	.70
		Nos. 707-714 (8)	4.10	2.60

Postrider A168

Designs: 60m, Diesel locomotive. 1t, Truck.

1973, Jan. 31 Photo. *Perf. 12x11½*

715	A168	50m brown	.55	.25
716	A168	60m green	2.00	.25
717	A168	1t rose claret	1.00	.30
		Nos. 715-717,C34 (4)	5.15	1.20

For surcharges, see Nos. 2405-2407.

Sukhe Bator and Merchants A169

Paintings of Sukhe Bator: 20m, With elders. 50m, Leading partisans. 60m, With revolutionary council. 1t, Receiving deputation, horiz.

1973, Feb. 2 Photo. *Perf. 11½x12*

718	A169	10m gold & multi	.25	.25
719	A169	20m gold & multi	.25	.25
720	A169	50m gold & multi	.40	.25
721	A169	60m gold & multi	.50	.25
722	A169	1t gold & multi	.80	.30
		Nos. 718-722 (5)	2.20	1.30

Sukhe Bator (1893-1923).

Nicolaus Copernicus A170

Designs: 60m, 2t, Copernicus in laboratory, by Jan Matejko, horiz., 55x35mm. Nos. 725, 726b, Portrait. No. 726a, like 50m.

1973, Mar. Litho. *Perf. 12*

723	A170	50m gold & multi	.50	.25
724	A170	60m gold & multi	.60	.30
725	A170	1t gold & multi	1.00	.40
		Nos. 723-725 (3)	2.10	.95

Souvenir Sheet

726		Sheet of 3	*4.00*	*3.00*
a.		A170 1t multi	.60	.60
b.		A170 1t multi	.60	.60
c.		A170 2t multi	1.50	1.50

500th anniversary of the birth of Nicolaus Copernicus (1473-1543), Polish astronomer.

Marx and Lenin — A171

1973, July 15 Photo. *Perf. 11½x12*

727	A171	60m gold, car & ultra	.75	.40

9th meeting of postal administrations of socialist countries, Ulan Bator.

Aquatic Birds — A172

Designs: 5m, Common Shelducks. 10m, Arctic loons. 15m, Bar-headed geese. 30m, Great crested grebe. 50m, Mallards. 60m, Mute swans. 1t, Greater scaups.

1973, Aug. 10 Litho. *Perf. 12x11*

728	A172	5m shown	.45	.25
729	A172	10m multi	.60	.25
730	A172	15m multi	1.00	.25
731	A172	30m multi	1.20	.30
732	A172	50m multi	1.60	.40
733	A172	60m multi	1.90	.45
734	A172	1t multi	2.25	.60
		Nos. 728-734 (7)	9.00	2.50

1973, Aug. 25 Litho. *Perf. 12x11*

Designs: Fur-bearing animals: 5m, Siberian weasel. 10m, Siberian chipmunk. 15m, Flying squirrel. 20m, Eurasian badger. 30m, Eurasian red squirrel. 60m, Wolverine. 80m, Mink. 1t, White hare.

735	A172	5m multi	.25	.25
736	A172	10m multi	.25	.25
737	A172	15m multi	.25	.25
738	A172	20m multi	.35	.25
739	A172	30m multi	.50	.25
740	A172	60m multi	.85	.40
741	A172	80m multi	1.00	.60
742	A172	1t multi	1.50	.70
		Nos. 735-742 (8)	4.95	2.95

1973, Dec. 15 Litho. *Perf. 12x11*

Designs: Flowers: 5m, Alpine aster. 10m, Mongolian silene. 15m, Rosa davurica. 20m, Mongolian dandelion. 30m, Rhododendron dahuricum. 50m, Clematis tangutica. 60m, Siberian primula. 1t, Pasqueflower.

743	A172	5m multi	.25	.25
744	A172	10m multi	.25	.25
745	A172	15m multi	.25	.25
746	A172	20m multi	.30	.25
747	A172	30m multi	.45	.25
748	A172	50m multi	.75	.35
749	A172	60m multi	.90	.50
750	A172	1t multi	1.50	.65
		Nos. 743-750 (8)	4.65	2.75

Globe and Red Flag Emblem — A173

1973, Dec. 10 Photo. *Perf. 12x12½*

751	A173	60m gold, red & blue	.60	.25

15th anniversary of the review "Problems of Peace and Socialism," published in Prague.

Limenitis Populi A174

Butterflies: 10m, Arctia hebe. 15m, Rhyparia purpurata. 20m, Catocala pacta. 30m, Isoceras kaszabi. 50m, Celerio costata. 60m, Arctia caja. 1t, Diacrisia sannio.

1974, Jan. 15 Litho. *Perf. 11*

752 A174 5m lil & multi .30 .25
753 A174 10m brn & multi .35 .25
754 A174 15m bl & multi .35 .25
755 A174 20m brn org & multi .55 .25
756 A174 30m lt vio & multi .75 .25
757 A174 50m dl red & multi 1.00 .30
758 A174 60m yel grn & multi 1.20 .40
759 A174 1t ultra & multi 1.50 .50
Nos. 752-759 (8) 6.00 2.45

"Hehe Namshil" by L. Merdorsh A175

Designs (Various Scenes from): 20m, "Sive Hiagt," by D. Luvsansharav. 25m, 80m, 1t, "Edre," by D. Namdag. 30m, "The 3 Khans of Sara-Gol" (legend). 60m, "Amarsana," by B. Damdinsuren. 20m and 30m horizontal.

1974, Feb. 20 Litho. *Perf. 12*

760 A175 15m sil & multi .25 .25
761 A175 20m sil & multi .30 .25
762 A175 25m sil & multi .40 .25
763 A175 30m sil & multi .50 .25
764 A175 60m sil & multi .60 .25
765 A175 80m sil & multi .80 .30
766 A175 1t sil & multi 1.00 .80
Nos. 760-766 (7) 3.85 2.35

Mongolian operas and dramas.

Government Building and Sukhe Bator — A176

1974, Mar. 1 Photo. *Perf. 11*

767 A176 60m gold & multi .75 .40

50th anniv. of renaming capital Ulan Bator.

Juggler A177

10m, Circus horses, horiz. 30m, Trained elephant. 40m, Yak pushing ball, horiz. 60m, Acrobats with ring. 80m, Woman acrobat on unicycle.

1974, May 4 Litho. *Perf. 12*

768 A177 10m multi .25 .25
769 A177 20m multi .40 .25
770 A177 30m multi .50 .30
771 A177 40m multi .80 .40
772 A177 60m multi 1.00 .50
773 A177 80m multi 1.60 .75
Nos. 768-773,C65 (7) 5.80 3.05

Mongolian Circus. No. 773 has se-tenant label, with similar design.

Girl on Bronco — A178

Children's Activities: 20m, Boy roping calf. 30m, 40m, Boy taming horse (different designs). 60m, Girl with doves. 80m, Wrestling. 1t, Dancing.

1974, June 2 Litho. *Perf. 12*

774 A178 10m dl yel & multi .25 .25
775 A178 20m lt bl & multi .25 .25
776 A178 30m grn & multi .30 .25
777 A178 40m yel & multi .40 .25
778 A178 60m pink & multi .60 .25
779 A178 80m bl & multi .80 .35
780 A178 1t dl bl & multi 1.00 .50
Nos. 774-780 (7) 3.60 2.10

Children's Day.
For surcharges see Nos. 2577-2578.

Archer — A179

National Sports: 20m, Two horsemen fighting for goatskin. 30m, Archer on horseback. 40m, Horse race. 60m, Riding wild horse. 80m, Rider chasing riderless horse. 1t, Boys wrestling.

1974, July 11 Photo. *Perf. 11*

781 A179 10m vio bl & multi .25 .25
782 A179 20m yel & multi .25 .25
783 A179 30m lil & multi .30 .25
784 A179 40m multi .40 .25
785 A179 60m multi .60 .25
786 A179 80m multi .80 .40
787 A179 1t multi 1.00 .60
Nos. 781-787 (7) 3.60 2.25

Nadom, Mongolian national festival.

Grizzly Bear A180

20m, Common panda. 30m, Giant panda. 40m, Two brown bears. 60m, Sloth bear. 80m, Asiatic black bears. 1t, Giant brown bear.

1974, July Litho. *Perf. 12*

788 A180 10m shown .25 .25
789 A180 20m multi .30 .25
790 A180 30m multi .35 .25
791 A180 40m multi .50 .35
792 A180 60m multi .75 .35
793 A180 80m multi 1.00 .50
794 A180 1t multi 1.50 .75
Nos. 788-794 (7) 4.65 2.70

Stag in Zuun Araat Wildlife Preserve — A181

20m, Beaver. 30m, Leopard. 40m, Great black-backed gull. 60m, Deer. 80m, Mouflon. 1t, Deer and entrance to Bogd-uul Preserve.

1974, Sept. Litho. *Perf. 12*

795 A181 10m shown .25 .25
796 A181 20m multi .30 .25
797 A181 30m multi .35 .25
798 A181 40m multi .50 .35
799 A181 60m multi .75 .35
800 A181 80m multi 1.00 .50
801 A181 1t multi 1.50 .75
Nos. 795-801 (7) 4.65 2.70

Protected fauna in Mongolian wildlife preserves.

Buddhist Temple, Bogdo Gegen Palace — A182

Mongolian Architecture: 15m, Buddhist Temple, now Museum. 30m, Entrance to Charity Temple, Ulan Bator. 50m, Mongolian yurta. 80m, Gazebo in convent yard.

1974, Oct. 15 Litho. *Perf. 12*

802 A182 10m bl & multi .30 .25
803 A182 15m multi .35 .25
804 A182 30m grn & multi .45 .30
805 A182 50m multi .60 .40
806 A182 80m yel & multi 1.00 .50
Nos. 802-806 (5) 2.70 1.70

Spasski Tower, Sukhe Bator Statue A183

1974, Nov. 26 Photo. *Perf. 11½x12*

807 A183 60m multi .75 .40

Visit of General Secretary Brezhnev and a delegation from the USSR to participate in celebration of 50th anniversary of People's Republic of Mongolia.

Sukhe Bator Proclaiming Republic A184

Designs: No. 808, "First Constitution," symbolic embroidery. No. 809, Flag over landscape, plane and communications tower.

1974, Nov. 28 Litho.

808 A184 60m multi .65 .25
809 A184 60m multi .65 .25
810 A184 60m multi .65 .25
Nos. 808-810 (3) 1.95 .75

50th anniv. of People's Republic of Mongolia.

Decanter A185

Designs: 20m, Silver jar. 30m, Night lamp. 40m, Tea jug. 60m, Candelabra. 80m, Teapot. 1t, Silver bowl on 3-legged stand.

1974, Dec. 1 Photo.

811 A185 10m blue & multi .25 .25
812 A185 20m claret & multi .30 .25
813 A185 30m multi .35 .25
814 A185 40m dp bl & multi .50 .25
815 A185 60m multi .60 .25
816 A185 80m grn & multi .80 .40
817 A185 1t lilac & multi 1.00 .60
Nos. 811-817 (7) 3.80 2.25

Mongolian 19th century goldsmiths' work.

Lapwing (plover) — A186

1974, Dec. Litho. *Perf. 11*

818 A186 10m shown .35 .25
819 A186 20m Fish .45 .25
820 A186 30m Marsh marigolds .55 .25
821 A186 40m White pelican .75 .25
822 A186 60m Perch .75 .30
823 A186 80m Mink .90 .40
Nos. 818-823,C66 (7) 4.95 2.20

Water and nature protection.

American Mail Coach, UPU Emblem — A187

Designs (UPU Emblem and): 20m, French two-wheeled coach. 30m, Changing horses, Russian coach. 40m, Swedish caterpillar mail truck. 50m, First Hungarian mail truck. 60m, German Daimler-Benz mail truck. 1t, Mongolian dispatch rider.

1974, Dec. Litho. *Perf. 12*

824 A187 10m multi .25 .25
825 A187 20m multi .25 .25
826 A187 30m multi .30 .25
827 A187 40m multi .40 .30
828 A187 50m multi .60 .35
829 A187 60m multi .75 .40
830 A187 1t multi 1.00 .65
Nos. 824-830 (7) 3.55 2.45

Cent. of the UPU and Stockholmia 74.

Soviet Flag, Broken Swastika A188

1975, May 9 Photo. *Perf. 11½x12*

832 A188 60m multi .75 .40

30th anniversary of the end of World War II and victory over fascism.

Mongolian Woman A189

1975, May

833 A189 60m multi .75 .45

International Women's Year 1975.

Zygophyllum Xanthoxylon — A190

Medicinal Plants: 20m, Ingarvillea potaninii. 30m, Lancea tibetica. 40m, Jurinea mongolica. 50m, Saussurea involucrata. 60m, Allium mongolicum. 1t, Adonis mongolica.

1975, May 24 Photo. *Perf. 11x11½*

834 A190 10m dp org & multi .25 .25
835 A190 20m grn & multi .30 .25
836 A190 30m yel & multi .45 .25
837 A190 40m vio & multi .60 .25
838 A190 50m brn & multi .65 .30
839 A190 60m bl & multi .90 .30
840 A190 1t multi 1.50 .60
Nos. 834-840 (7) 4.65 2.20

12th International Botanists' Conference.

Shepherd — A191

Puppet Theater: 20m, Boy on horseback. 30m, Boy and disobedient bull calf. 40m, Little orphan camel's tale. 50m, Boy and obedient little yak. 60m, Boy riding swan. 1t, Children's choir.

1975, June 30 Litho. *Perf. 12*

841 A191 10m multi .25 .25
842 A191 20m multi .30 .25
843 A191 30m multi .40 .25
844 A191 40m multi .60 .25
845 A191 50m multi .70 .30
846 A191 60m multi .80 .30
847 A191 1t multi 1.25 .50
Nos. 841-847 (7) 4.30 2.10

For surcharges see Nos. 2575-2576.

Pioneers Tending Fruit Tree — A192

60m, Pioneers studying, and flying model plane. 1t, New emblem of Mongolian Pioneers.

1975, July 15 *Perf. 12x11½*

848 A192 50m multi .40 .25
849 A192 60m multi .50 .25
850 A192 1t multi .70 .40
Nos. 848-850 (3) 1.60 .90

Mongolian Pioneers, 50th anniversary.

Nos. 624-630 Overprinted

1975, July 15 Litho. *Perf. 12*

850A A151 20m multi 5.00 5.00
850B A151 30m multi 5.00 5.00
850C A151 40m multi 4.00 4.00
850D A151 50m multi 4.00 4.00
850E A151 60m multi 5.00 5.00
850F A151 80m multi 5.00 5.00
850G A151 1t multi 6.00 6.00
Nos. 850A-850G (7) 34.00 34.00

Fifty years of communication.

Golden Eagle Hunting Fox — A193

Hunting Scenes: 20m, Dogs treeing lynx, vert. 30m, Hunter stalking marmots. 40m, Hunter riding reindeer, vert. 50m, Boar hunt. 60m, Trapped wolf, vert. 1t, Bear hunt.

1975, Aug. 25 Litho. *Perf. 12*

851 A193 10m multi .45 .25
852 A193 20m multi .50 .25
853 A193 30m multi .60 .25
854 A193 40m multi .65 .30
855 A193 50m multi .75 .35
856 A193 60m multi .85 .40
857 A193 1t multi 1.00 .60
Nos. 851-857 (7) 4.80 2.40

Hunting in Mongolia.

Mesocottus Haitej — A194

Various Fish: 20m, Pseudaspius lepto cephalus. 30m, Oreoleuciscus potanini. 40m, Tinca tinca. 50m, Coregonus lavaretus pidschian. 60m, Erythroculter mongolicus. 1t, Carassius auratus.

1975, Sept. 15 Photo. *Perf. 11*

858 A194 10m multi .25 .25
859 A194 20m multi .30 .25
860 A194 30m multi .45 .25
861 A194 40m bl & multi .60 .30
862 A194 50m grn & multi .75 .30
863 A194 60m lil & multi .90 .40
864 A194 1t vio bl & multi 1.50 .60
Nos. 858-864 (7) 4.75 2.35

Neck and Bow of Musical Instrument (Morin Hur) — A195

National Handicraft: 20m, Saddle. 30m, Silver headgear. 40m, Boots. 50m, Tasseled Woman's cap. 60m, Pipe and tobacco pouch. 1t, Sable cap.

1975, Oct. 10 Litho. *Perf. 11½x12½*

865 A195 10m multi .25 .25
866 A195 20m multi .25 .25
867 A195 30m multi .30 .25
868 A195 40m multi .40 .25
869 A195 50m multi .50 .30
870 A195 60m multi .60 .30
871 A195 1t multi 1.00 .60
Nos. 865-871 (7) 3.30 2.20

Revolutionists with Flags — A196

1975, Nov. 15 Litho. *Perf. 11½x12*

872 A196 60m multi .75 .40

70th anniversary of Russian Revolution.

Ski Jump, Olympic Games Emblem A197

Winter Olympic Games Emblem and: 20m, Ice hockey. 30m, Skiing. 40m, Bobsled. 50m, Biathlon. 60m, Speed skating. 1t, Figure skating, women's. 4t, Skier carrying torch.

Perf. 11½x12½

1975, Dec. 20 Litho.

873 A197 10m multi .25 .25
874 A197 20m multi .25 .25
875 A197 30m brn & multi .30 .25
876 A197 40m grn & multi .40 .25
877 A197 50m multi .50 .30
878 A197 60m ol & multi .60 .30
879 A197 1t multi 1.00 .40
Nos. 873-879 (7) 3.30 2.00

Souvenir Sheet

880 A197 4t multi 3.00 3.00

12th Winter Olympic Games, Innsbruck, Austria, Feb. 4-15, 1976.

Taming Wild Horse A198

Mongolian Paintings: 20m, Camel caravan, horiz. 30m, Man playing lute. 40m, Woman adjusting headdress, horiz. 50m, Woman wearing ceremonial costume. 60m, Women fetching water. 1t, Woman musician. 4t, Warrior on horseback.

1975, Nov. 30 *Perf. 12*

881 A198 10m brown & multi .25 .25
882 A198 20m blue & multi .25 .25
883 A198 30m olive & multi .35 .25
884 A198 40m lilac & multi .45 .25
885 A198 50m blue & multi .55 .30
886 A198 60m lilac & multi .65 .30
887 A198 1t silver & multi 1.00 .50
Nos. 881-887 (7) 3.50 2.10

Souvenir Sheet

888 A198 4t bl & multi 4.00 3.50

House of Young Technicians A199

Designs: 60m, Hotel Ulan Bator. 1t, Museum of the Revolution.

1975, Dec. 30 Photo. *Perf. 12x11½*

893	A199 50m ultra		.50	.25
894	A199 60m bl grn		.60	.25
895	A199 1t brick red		1.00	.40
	Nos. 893-895 (3)		2.10	.90

Camels in Gobi Desert — A200

20m, Horse taming. 30m, Herding. 40m, Pioneers' camp. 60m, Young musician. 80m, Children's festival. 1t, Mongolian wrestling.

1976, June 1 Litho. *Perf. 12*

896	A200 10m multi	.25	.25
897	A200 20m multi	.30	.25
898	A200 30m multi	.35	.25
899	A200 40m multi	.50	.25
900	A200 60m multi	.60	.25
901	A200 80m multi	.90	.40
902	A200 1t multi	1.00	.50
	Nos. 896-902 (7)	3.90	2.15

International Children's Day.

Red Star — A201

1976, May 1 Photo. *Perf. 11x12½*

903 A201 60m red, maroon & silver .75 .40

17th Congress of the Mongolian People's Revolutionary Party, June 14.

Archery, Montreal Games' Emblem, Canadian Flag — A202

20m, Judo. 30m, Boxing. 40m, Vaulting. 60m, Weight lifting. 80m, High Jump. 1t, Target shooting.

1976, May 20 Litho. *Perf. 12½x11½*

904	A202 10m yel & multi	.25	.25
905	A202 20m yel & multi	.25	.25
906	A202 30m yel & multi	.25	.25
907	A202 40m yel & multi	.40	.25
908	A202 60m yel & multi	.55	.30
909	A202 80m yel & multi	.80	.35
910	A202 1t yel & multi	1.00	.50
	Nos. 904-910 (7)	3.50	2.15

21st Olympic Games, Montreal, Canada, July 17-Aug. 1. See No. C81.

Partisans A203

Fighter and Sojombo Independence Symbol — A204

Perf. 12x11½, 11½x12

1976, June 15 Litho.

911	A203 60m multi	.60	.30
912	A204 60m multi	.60	.30

55th anniversary of Mongolia's independence. See No. C82.

Souvenir Sheet

Sukhe Bator Medal — A205

1976, July 11 *Perf. 11½*

913 A205 4t multi 4.00 4.00

Mongolian honors medals.

Osprey — A206

Protected Birds: 20m, Griffon vulture. 30m, Bearded lammergeier. 40m, Marsh harrier. 60m, Black vulture. 80m, Golden eagle. 1t, Tawny eagle.

1976, Aug. 16 Litho. *Perf. 12*

914	A206 10m multi	.60	.25
915	A206 20m multi	.90	.25
916	A206 30m multi	1.10	.30
917	A206 40m multi	1.40	.30
918	A206 60m multi	1.75	.40
919	A206 80m multi	1.90	.50
920	A206 1t multi	2.25	.60
	Nos. 914-920 (7)	9.90	2.60

"Nadom" Military Game — A207

Paintings by O. Cevegshava: 10m, Taming Wild Horse, vert. 30m, Hubsugul Lake Harbor. 40m, The Steppe Awakening. 80m, Wrestlers. 1.60t, Yak Descending in Snow, vert.

1976, Sept. Litho. *Perf. 12*

921	A207 10m multi	.25	.25
922	A207 20m multi	.25	.25
923	A207 30m multi	.30	.25
924	A207 40m multi	.40	.25
925	A207 80m multi	.70	.30
926	A207 1.60t multi	1.25	.70
	Nos. 921-926 (6)	3.15	2.00

Interlocking Circles, Industry and Transport — A208

1976, Oct. 15 Photo. *Perf. 12x11½*

927 A208 60m brn, bl & red 1.25 .30

Soviet-Mongolian friendship.

John Naber, US Flag, Gold Medals A209

Designs: 20m, Nadia Comaneci, Romanian flag. 30m, Kornelia Ender, East German flag. 40m, Mitsuo Tsukahara, Japanese flag. 60m, Gregor Braun, German flag. 80m, Lasse Viren, Finnish flag. 1t, Nikolai Andrianov, Russian flag.

1976, Nov. 30 Litho. *Perf. 12*

928	A209 10m multi	.25	.25
929	A209 20m multi	.25	.25
930	A209 30m multi	.25	.25
931	A209 40m multi	.30	.25
932	A209 60m multi	.50	.30
933	A209 80m multi	.75	.40
934	A209 1t multi	.90	.50
	Nos. 928-934 (7)	3.20	2.20

Gold medal winners, 21st Olympic Games, Montreal. See No. C83.

Stone Tablet on Tortoise A210

Carved Tablet, 6th-8th Centuries A211

1976, Dec. 15 Litho. *Perf. 11½x12*

935	A210 50m brn & lt bl	1.00	.35
936	A211 60m gray & brt grn	1.50	.40

Intl. Archaeological Conference, Ulan Bator.

R-1 Plane — A212

Designs: Various Mongolian planes.

1976, Dec. 22 *Perf. 12*

937	A212 10m multi	.25	.25
938	A212 20m multi	.25	.25
939	A212 30m multi	.30	.25
940	A212 40m multi	.35	.25
941	A212 60m multi	.55	.30
942	A212 80m multi	.70	.30
943	A212 1t multi	.80	.50
	Nos. 937-943 (7)	3.20	2.10

Dancers — A213

Folk Dances: 20m, 13th century costumes. 30m, West Mongolian dance. 40m, "Ekachi," or horse-dance. 60m, "Bielge," West Mongolian trunk dance. 80m, "Hodak," or friendship dance. 1t, "Dojarka."

1977, Mar. 20 Litho. *Perf. 12½*

944	A213 10m multi	.25	.25
945	A213 20m multi	.30	.25
946	A213 30m multi	.45	.25
947	A213 40m multi	.55	.25
948	A213 60m multi	.75	.25
949	A213 80m multi	1.00	.40
950	A213 1t multi	1.10	.45
	Nos. 944-950 (7)	4.40	2.10

Miniature Sheet

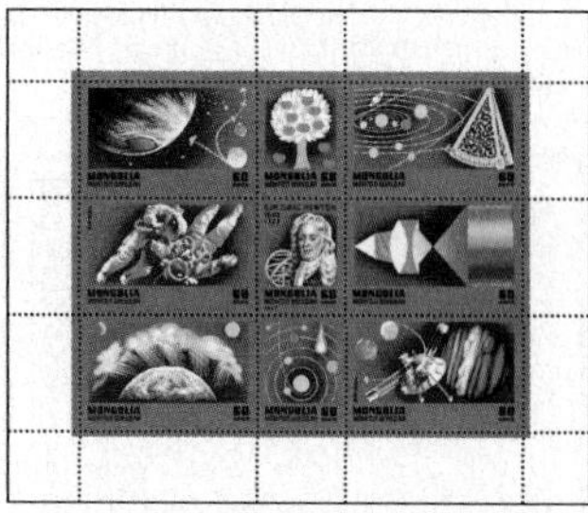

A214 & A215 Designs

a, Path of Pioneer from Earth to Jupiter, deflected by Mars. b, Apple tree. c, Sextant and planets. d, Astronauts in space. e, Isaac Newton. f, Prism and spectrum. g, Rain falling on earth. h, Motion of celestial bodies. i, Pioneer 10 over Jupiter.

1977, Mar. 31 Litho. *Perf. 11½x12*

951	Sheet of 9	4.50	2.50
a.	A214 60m multi	.40	.25
b.	A215 60m multi	.40	.25
c.	A214 60m multi	.40	.25
d.	A214 60m multi	.40	.25
e.	A215 60m multi	.40	.25
f.	A214 60m multi	.40	.25
g.	A214 60m multi	.40	.25
h.	A215 60m multi	.40	.25
i.	A214 60m multi	.40	.25

Sir Isaac Newton (1642-1727), English natural philosopher and mathematician.

Nos. 951a-951i arranged in 3 rows of 3. Nos. 951d and 951i inscribed AIR MAIL.

D. Natsagdorji, Writer, and Quotation — A216

Design: No. 953, Grazing horses, landscape, ornament and quotation.

1977 *Perf. 11½x12*

952	A216 60m multi	1.00	.50
953	A216 60m multi	1.00	.50

D. Natsagdorji, founder of modern Mongolian literature. Label and vignette separated by simulated perforations.

Primitive Tortoises — A217

Prehistoric Animals: 20m, Ungulate (titanothere). 30m, Beaked dinosaurs. 40m, Entelodon (swine). 60m, Antelope. 80m, Hipparion. 1t, Aurochs.

1977, May 7 Photo. *Perf. 12½*

954 A217 10m multi .35 .25
955 A217 20m multi .50 .25
956 A217 30m multi .55 .25
957 A217 40m multi .75 .30
958 A217 60m multi 1.25 .30
959 A217 80m multi 1.50 .60
960 A217 1t multi 1.75 .90
Nos. 954-960 (7) 6.65 2.85

Souvenir Sheet

Mongolia, Type A2 and Netherlands No. 1 — A218

1977, May 20

961 A218 4t multi 3.00 2.00

AMPHILEX '77 International Philatelic Exhibition, Amsterdam, May 27-June 5. No. 961 contains one 37x52mm stamp.

Boys on Horseback — A219

20m, Girl on horseback. 30m, Hunter on horseback. 40m, Grazing horses. 60m, Mare & foal. 80m, Grazing horse & student. 1t, White stallion.

1977, June 15 Litho. *Perf. 12*

962 A219 10m multi .25 .25
963 A219 20m multi .30 .25
964 A219 30m multi .35 .25
965 A219 40m multi .45 .25
966 A219 60m multi .60 .30
967 A219 80m multi .85 .40
968 A219 1t multi 1.00 .50
Nos. 962-968 (7) 3.80 2.20

Copper and Molybdenum Plant, Vehicles A220

1977, June 15 Litho. *Perf. 12*

969 A220 60m multi 1.50 .50

Erdenet, a new industrial town.

Bucket Brigade Fighting Fire — A221

Fire Fighting: 20m, Horse-drawn fire pump. 30m, Horse-drawn steam pump. 40m, Men in protective suits fighting forest fire. 60m, Modern foam extinguisher. 80m, Truck and ladder. 1t, Helicopter fighting fire on steppe.

1977, Aug. Litho. *Perf. 12*

970 A221 10m multi .25 .25
971 A221 20m multi .25 .25
972 A221 30m multi .40 .25
973 A221 40m multi .55 .25
974 A221 60m multi .65 .30
975 A221 80m multi .85 .35
976 A221 1t multi 1.10 .50
Nos. 970-976 (7) 4.05 2.15

Radar and Molniya Satellite on TV Screen — A222

1977, Sept. 12 Photo. *Perf. 12x11½*

977 A222 60m gray, bl & blk .50 .30

40th anniversary of Technical Institute.

Lenin Museum, Ulan Bator — A223

1977, Oct. 1 Litho. *Perf. 12*

978 A223 60m multi .60 .30

Inauguration of Lenin Museum in connection with the 60th anniversary of the Russian October Revolution.

Dove, Globe, Decree of Peace A224

Designs: 50m, Cruiser Aurora and Russian flag, vert. 1.50t, Globe and "Freedom."

Perf. 11½x12, 12x11½

1977, Oct. 1 Photo.

979 A224 50m gold & multi .80 .25
980 A224 60m gold & multi .70 .25
981 A224 1.50t gold & multi 1.25 .60
Nos. 979-981 (3) 2.75 1.10

60th anniversary of the Russian Revolution.

Aporia Crataegi — A225

Moths: 20m, Gastropacha quercifolia. 30m, Colias chrysoteme. 40m, Dasychira fascelina. 60m, Malocosoma neustria. 80m, Diacrisia sanno. 1t, Heodes virgaureae.

1977, Sept. 25 Photo. *Perf. 12½*

982 A225 10m multi .25 .25
983 A225 20m multi .45 .25
984 A225 30m multi .60 .25
985 A225 40m multi .90 .25
986 A225 60m multi 1.20 .30
987 A225 80m multi 1.50 .40
988 A225 1t multi 1.90 .55
Nos. 982-988 (7) 6.80 2.25

Giant Pandas — A226

Pandas: 10m, Eating bamboo, vert. 30m, Female and cub in washtub, vert. 40m, Male and cub playing with bamboo. 60m, Female and cub, vert. 80m, Family. 1t, Male, vert.

1977, Nov. 25 Litho. *Perf. 12*

989 A226 10m multi .25 .25
990 A226 20m multi .30 .25
991 A226 30m multi .45 .25
992 A226 40m multi .60 .30
993 A226 60m multi .90 .35
994 A226 80m multi 1.50 .55
995 A226 1t multi 1.75 .75
Nos. 989-995 (7) 5.75 2.70

Souvenir Sheet

Helen Fourment and her Children, by Rubens — A227

1977, Dec. 5 *Perf. 11½x10½*

996 A227 4t multi 4.50 4.50

Peter Paul Rubens (1577-1640).

Ferrari Racing Car — A228

Experimental Racing Cars: 30m, Ford McLaren. 40m, Madi, USSR. 50m, Mazda. 60m, Porsche. 80m, Russian model car. 1.20t, The Blue Flame, US speed car.

1978, Jan. 28 Litho. *Perf. 12*

997 A228 20m multi .25 .25
998 A228 30m multi .25 .25
999 A228 40m multi .30 .25
1000 A228 50m multi .40 .30
1001 A228 60m multi .60 .30
1002 A228 80m multi .80 .40
1003 A228 1.20t multi 1.25 .50
Nos. 997-1003 (7) 3.85 2.25

Boletus Variegatus — A229

Mushrooms: 30m, Russula cyanoxantha. 40m, Boletus aurantiacus. 50m, Boletus scaber. 60m, Russula flava. 80m, Lactarius resimus. 1.20t, Flammula spumosa.

1978, Feb. 28 Photo. *Perf. 11x11½*

1004 A229 20m yel & multi .35 .25
1005 A229 30m yel & multi .55 .25
1006 A229 40m yel & multi .80 .30
1007 A229 50m yel & multi 1.00 .35
1008 A229 60m yel & multi 1.40 .40
1009 A229 80m yel & multi 1.90 .45
1010 A229 1.20t yel & multi 2.50 .75
Nos. 1004-1010 (7) 8.50 2.75

Young Couple with Youth Flag — A230

1978, Apr. Litho. *Perf. 11½x12*

1011 A230 60m multi .80 .30

17th Congress of Mongolian Youth Organization, Ulan Bator, Apr. 1978.

Soccer, Sugar Loaf Mountain, Rio de Janeiro, Brazil 1950 Emblem — A231

Designs (Various Soccer Scenes and): 30m, Old Town Tower, Bern, Switzerland, 1954. 40m, Town Hall, Stockholm, Sweden, 1958. 50m, University of Chile, Chile, 1962. 60m, Parliament and Big Ben, London, 1966. 80m, Degolladeo Theater, Guadalajara, Mexico, 1970. 1.20t, Town Hall and TV Tower, Munich, Germany.

1978, Apr. 15 *Perf. 12*

1012 A231 20m multi .25 .25
1013 A231 30m multi .25 .25
1014 A231 40m multi .30 .25
1015 A231 50m multi .35 .30
1016 A231 60m multi .45 .30
1017 A231 80m multi .60 .30
1018 A231 1.20t multi .90 .50
Nos. 1012-1018 (7) 3.10 2.15

11th World Cup Soccer Championship, Argentina, June 1-25. See No. C109.

Capex Emblem, Eurasian Beaver and Canada #336 — A232

30m, Tibetan sand grouse & Canada #478. 40m, Red-throated loon & Canada #369. 50m, Argali & Canada #324. 60m, Eurasian brown bear & Canada #322. 80m, Moose & Canada #323. 1.20t, Great black-backed gull & Canada #343.

1978, June Litho. *Perf. 12*

1019 A232 20m multi .25 .25
1020 A232 30m multi .35 .25
1021 A232 40m multi .55 .30
1022 A232 50m multi .75 .40
1023 A232 60m multi .90 .50
1024 A232 80m multi 1.00 .60
1025 A232 1.20t multi 1.50 .80
Nos. 1019-1025 (7) 5.30 3.10

CAPEX '78 International Philatelic Exhibition, Toronto, June 9-18. See No. C110.

Marx, Engels and Lenin A233

1978, July 11 Photo. *Perf. 12x11½*
1026 A233 60m gold, blk & red .70 .30

50th anniversary of publication in Prague of "Problems of Peace and Socialism."

Souvenir Sheet

Outdoor Rest, by Amgalan — A234

Paintings by D. Amgalan: No. 1027b, Winter Night (dromedary and people in snow). No. 1027c, Saddling up.

1978, Aug. 10 Litho. *Perf. 12*
1027 A234 Sheet of 3 3.75 3.75
a.-c. 1.50t any single 1.00

Philatelic cooperation between Hungary and Mongolia, 20th anniversary. No. 1027 contains 3 stamps and 3 labels.

Papillon — A235

Dogs: 20m, Black Mongolian sheepdog. 30m, Puli. 40m, St. Bernard. 50m, German shepherd. 60m, Mongolian watchdog. 70m, Samoyed. 80m, Laika (1st dog in space) and rocket. 1.20t, Cocker spaniel and poodles.

1978, Sept. 25 Litho. *Perf. 12*
1028 A235 10m multi .30 .25
1029 A235 20m multi .30 .25
1030 A235 30m multi .50 .25
1031 A235 40m multi .60 .30
1032 A235 50m multi .80 .30
1033 A235 60m multi .90 .30
1034 A235 70m multi 1.00 .50
1035 A235 80m multi 1.25 .50
1036 A235 1.20t multi 1.50 .80
Nos. 1028-1036 (9) 7.15 3.45

Open Book and Pen — A236

1978, Oct. 20 Photo. *Perf. 12x11½*
1037 A236 60m car & ultra .60 .30

Mongolian Writers' Association, 50th anniversary.

Souvenir Sheets

Paintings — A237

Melancholy, by Dürer — A238

Paintings: No. 1038a, Clothed Maya, by Goya. No. 1038b, "Ta Matete," by Gauguin. No. 1038c, Bridge at Arles, by Van Gogh.

1978, Oct. 30 Litho. *Perf. 12*
1038 A237 Sheet of 3 + 3 labels 4.50 4.50
a.-c. 1.50t any single + label 1.25 1.25

Perf. 11½
1039 A238 4t black 4.50 4.50

Anniversaries of European painters: Francisco Goya; Paul Gauguin; Vincent van Gogh; Albrecht Dürer.

Camel and Calf — A239

Bactrian Camels: 30m, Young camel. 40m, Two camels. 50m, Woman leading pack camel. 60m, Old camel. 80m, Camel pulling cart. 1.20t, Race.

1978, Nov. 30 Litho. *Perf. 12*
1040 A239 20m multi .25 .25
1041 A239 30m multi .30 .25
1042 A239 40m multi .45 .30
1043 A239 50m multi .60 .30
1044 A239 60m multi .75 .40
1045 A239 80m multi 1.00 .60
1046 A239 1.20t multi 1.40 .75
Nos. 1040-1046 (7) 4.75 2.85

Flags of Comecon Members, Globe — A240

1979, Jan. 2 Litho. *Perf. 12*
1047 A240 60m multi + label .60 .30

30th anniversary of the Council of Mutual Assistance (Comecon).
Label and vignette separated by simulated perforations.

Silver Tabby — A241

Domestic Cats: 30m, White Persian. 50m, Red Persian. 60m, Cream Persian. 70m, Siamese. 80m, Smoky Persian. 1t, Burmese.

1979, Feb. 10
1048 A241 10m multi .25 .25
1049 A241 30m multi .35 .25
1050 A241 50m multi .50 .25
1051 A241 60m multi .75 .30
1052 A241 70m multi .90 .35
1053 A241 80m multi 1.00 .45
1054 A241 1t multi 1.10 .60
Nos. 1048-1054 (7) 4.85 2.45

Potaninia Mongolica — A242

Flowers: 30m, Sophora alopecuroides. 50m, Halimodendron halodendron. 60m, Forget-me-nots. 70m, Pincushion flower. 80m, Leucanthemum Sibiricum. 1t, Edelweiss.

1979, Mar. 10 Litho. *Perf. 12*
1055 A242 10m multi .25 .25
1056 A242 30m multi .45 .25
1057 A242 50m multi .55 .25
1058 A242 60m multi .65 .25
1059 A242 70m multi .70 .30
1060 A242 80m multi .80 .35
1061 A242 1t multi .90 .50
Nos. 1055-1061 (7) 4.30 2.15

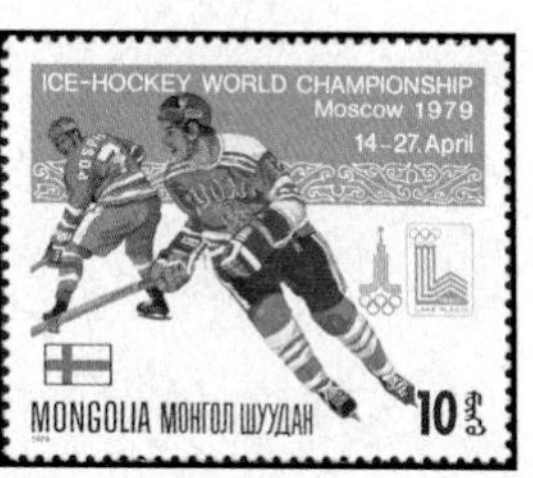

Finland-Czechoslovakia, Finnish Flag — A243

Ice Hockey Games and 1980 Olympic Emblems: 30m, German Fed. Rep.-Sweden, German flag. 50m, US-Canada, US flag. 60m, USSR-Sweden, Russian flag. 70m, Canada-USSR, Canadian flag. 80m, Swedish goalie and flag. 1t, Czechoslovakia-USSR, Czechoslovak flag.

1979, Apr. 10 Litho. *Perf. 12*
1062 A243 10m multi .25 .25
1063 A243 30m multi .25 .25
1064 A243 50m multi .35 .25
1065 A243 60m multi .45 .25
1066 A243 70m multi .55 .25
1067 A243 80m multi .65 .30
1068 A243 1t multi .90 .40
Nos. 1062-1068 (7) 3.40 1.95

Ice Hockey World Championship, Moscow, Apr. 14-27.

Lambs — A244

Paintings: 30m, Milking, camels. 50m, Plane bringing supplies in winter. 60m, Herdsmen and horses. 70m, Milkmaids, vert. 80m, Summer Evening (camels). 1t, Landscape with herd. 4t, After the Storm.

Perf. 12x11½, 11½x12
1979, May 3 Litho.
1069 A244 10m multi .25 .25
1070 A244 30m multi .25 .25
1071 A244 50m multi .35 .25
1072 A244 60m multi .45 .25
1073 A244 70m multi .50 .30
1074 A244 80m multi .75 .30
1075 A244 1t multi .95 .40
Nos. 1069-1075 (7) 3.50 2.00

Souvenir Sheet
1076 A244 4t multi 3.50 3.50

20th anniv. of 1st agricultural cooperative.

Souvenir Sheet

A245

Designs (Rowland Hill and): No. 1077a, Mongolia No. 4, Bulgaria No. 1, Philaserdica Emblem. No. 1077b, American mail coach. No. 1077c, Mail car, London-Birmingham railroad, 1838. 1077d, Packet leaving Southampton, Sept. 24, 1842, opening Indian mail service.

1979, May 15 Litho. *Perf. 12*
1077 A245 Sheet of 4, multi 4.50 4.50
a.-d. 1t any single 1.00 .90

Philaserdica '79, Sofia, May 18-27, and Rowland Hill (1795-1879), originator of penny postage.

Rocket, Manchester, 1829 — A246

Locomotives: 20m, "Adler" Nuremberg-Furth, 1835. 30m, American engine, 1860. 40m, Ulan Bator-Nalajh run, 1931. 50m, Moscow-Ulan Bator run, 1936. 60m, Moscow-Ulan Bator, 1970. 70m, Tokyo-Osaka run, 1963. 80m, Orleans Aerotrain, 1967. 1.20t, Soviet Rapidity, experimental train.

1979, June 8 Litho. *Perf. 12*
1078 A246 10m multi .25 .25
1079 A246 20m multi .30 .25
1080 A246 30m multi .45 .25
1081 A246 40m multi .50 .25
1082 A246 50m multi .60 .30
1083 A246 60m multi .65 .30
1084 A246 70m multi .90 .30

1085 A246 80m multi .95 .45
1086 A246 1.20t multi 1.00 .60
Nos. 1078-1086 (9) 5.60 2.95

Intl. Transportation Exhibition, Hamburg.
For surcharge see No. 2144B.

Mongolian and Russian Flags — A247

Battle Scene and Emblem A248

1979, Aug. 10 Photo. ***Perf. 11½x12***
1087 A247 60m multi .75 .30
1088 A248 60m multi .75 .30

Battle of Ha-lo-hsin River, 40th anniversary.

Manuls A249

Wild Cats: 30m, Lynx. 50m, Tigers. 60m, Snow leopards. 70m, Black panthers. 80m, Cheetahs. 1t, Lions.

1979, Sept. 10 Litho. ***Perf. 12***
1089 A249 10m multi .25 .25
1090 A249 30m multi .35 .25
1091 A249 50m multi .55 .25
1092 A249 60m multi .60 .25
1093 A249 70m multi .75 .30
1094 A249 80m multi .85 .40
1095 A249 1t multi 1.25 .50
Nos. 1089-1095 (7) 4.60 2.20

Souvenir Sheet

A250

a, Brazil No. 1582. b, Brazil #1144 (Pele). c, Mongolia #C1.

1979, Sept. 15 Litho. ***Perf. 11***
1096 A250 Sheet of 3 + 3 labels 6.75 6.75
a.-c. 1.50t any single + label 2.00 2.00

Brasiliana '79, 3rd World Thematic Stamp Exhibition, Rio de Janeiro, Sept. 15-23.

Cross-Country Skiing, Lake Placid '80 Emblem — A251

30m, Biathlon. 40m, Ice hockey. 50m, Ski jump. 60m, Downhill skiing. 80m, Speed skating. 1.20t, Bobsledding. 4t, Figure skating.

1980, Jan. 20 Litho. ***Perf. 11½x12½***
1097 A251 20m multi .25 .25
1098 A251 30m multi .35 .25
1099 A251 40m multi .45 .25
1100 A251 50m multi .60 .25
1101 A251 60m multi .60 .25
1102 A251 80m multi .85 .30
1103 A251 1.20t multi 1.00 .40
Nos. 1097-1103 (7) 4.10 1.95

Souvenir Sheet

1104 A251 4t multi 2.50 2.50

13th Winter Olympic Games, Lake Placid, NY, Feb. 12-24.

Flower Type of 1969

Souvenir Sheet

Design: Landscape and edelweiss.

1980, May 5 Litho. ***Perf. 11***
1105 A131 4t multi 2.50 2.50

London 1980 Intl. Stamp Exhib., May 6-14. No. 1105 contains one stamp 43x26mm.

Weightlifting, Moscow '80 Emblem — A252

1980, June 2 Litho. ***Perf. 12***
1106 A252 20m shown .25 .25
1107 A252 30m Archery .25 .25
1108 A252 40m Gymnast .30 .25
1109 A252 50m Running .40 .25
1110 A252 60m Boxing .50 .30
1111 A252 80m Judo .60 .30
1112 A252 1.20t Bicycling .70 .50
Nos. 1106-1112 (7) 3.00 2.10

Souvenir Sheet

1113 A252 4t Wrestling 2.50 2.00

22nd Summer Olympic Games, Moscow, July 19-Aug. 3.

Gold Medal, Swimmer, Moscow '80 Emblem — A253

Gold Medal, Moscow '80 Emblem and Number of Medals won by Top Countries: 30m, Fencing. 50m, Judo. 60m, Track. 80m, Boxing. 1t, Weight lifting. 1.20t, Kayak.

1980, Sept. 15 Litho. ***Perf. 12½***
1114 A253 20m multi .25 .25
1115 A253 30m multi .25 .25
1116 A253 50m multi .30 .25
1117 A253 60m multi .40 .25
1118 A253 80m multi .50 .30
1119 A253 1t multi .70 .40
1120 A253 1.20t multi .90 .50
Nos. 1114-1120 (7) 3.30 2.20

See No. C144.

A254

No. 1121, Jumdshaigiin Zedenbal. No. 1122, Zedenbal, 1941. No. 1123, Zedenbal, 1979. No. 1124, With Brezhnev, horiz. No. 1125, With children. No. 1126, Sukhe Bator. No. 1127, Choibalsan.

1980, Sept. 17 ***Perf. 11½x12***
1121 A254 60m blue green .30 .25
1122 A254 60m gray green .30 .25
1123 A254 60m blk, gray .30 .25
1124 A254 60m reddish brown .30 .25
1125 A254 60m carmine .30 .25
1126 A254 60m brown purple .30 .25
1127 A254 60m ultra .30 .25
Nos. 1121-1127 (7) 2.10 1.75

Miniature Sheet

A255

Cosmonauts from various Intercosmos flights: a, A. Gubarjev. b, Czechoslovakia #2222. c, P. Klimuk. d, Poland #2270. e, V. Bykovsky. f, DDR #1947. g, N. Rukavishnikov. h, Bulgaria #2576. i, V. Kubasov. j, Hungary #C417.

1980, Oct. 10 Litho. ***Perf. 12***
1128 A255 Sheet of 10 3.50 3.50
a.-j. 40m any single .30 .30

Intercosmos cooperative space program.
See No. 1232.

Benz, Germany, 1885 — A256

Antique Cars: 30m, President, Austria-Hungary, 1897. 40m, Armstrong Siddley, 1904. 50m, Russo-Balt, 1909. 60m, Packard, United States, 1909. 80m, Lancia, Italy, 1911. 1.60t, Marne taxi, France, 1914. 4t, Nami-1, Russia, 1927.

1980, Nov. 20 Litho. ***Perf. 12½***
1129 A256 20m multi .25 .25
1130 A256 30m multi .25 .25
1131 A256 40m multi .45 .25
1132 A256 50m multi .50 .35
1133 A256 60m multi .60 .40
1134 A256 80m multi .80 .50
1135 A256 1.60t multi 1.75 .75
Nos. 1129-1135 (7) 4.60 2.75

Souvenir Sheet

1136 A256 4t multi 3.50 3.50

Penguins A257

30m, Giant blue whale. 40m, Albatross. 50m, Weddell seals. 60m, Emperor penguins. 70m, Skua. 80m, Grampus. 1.20t, Penguins, Soviet plane.
4t, World map showing continental drift.

1980, Dec. 1 ***Perf. 12***
1137 A257 20m shown .90 .25
1138 A257 30m multi 1.25 .40
1139 A257 40m multi 1.50 .50
1140 A257 50m multi 1.75 .60
1141 A257 60m multi 2.00 .70
1142 A257 70m multi 2.25 .80
1143 A257 80m multi 2.75 1.00
1144 A257 1.20t multi 3.25 1.25
Nos. 1137-1144 (8) 15.65 5.50

Souvenir Sheet

1145 A257 4t multi 7.50 7.50

Antarctic animals and exploration. No. 1145 contains one 44mm circular stamp.

Souvenir Sheet

A258

1980, Dec. 20 Litho. ***Perf. 11***
1146 Sheet of 2 3.50 2.00
a. A258 2t shown 1.50 .85
b. A258 2t Old Marketplace 1.50 .85

The Shepherd Speaking the Truth, IYC Emblem A259

IYC Emblem and Nursery Tales: 30m, Above Them the Sky is Always Clear. 40m, Winter's Joys. 50m, Little Musicians. 60m, Happy Birthday. 80m, The First Day of School. 1.20t, May Day. 4t, The Wonder-working Squirrels.

1980, Dec. 29 ***Perf. 12***
1147 A259 20m multi .25 .25
1148 A259 30m multi .25 .25
1149 A259 40m multi .30 .25
1150 A259 50m multi .40 .25
1151 A259 60m multi .50 .30
1152 A259 80m multi .60 .40
1153 A259 1.20t multi .75 .50
Nos. 1147-1153 (7) 3.05 2.20

Souvenir Sheet

1154 A259 4t multi 3.00 2.00

Intl. Year of the Child (1979).

60th Anniversary of People's Army — A260

1981, Jan. 31 Litho. *Perf. 12*

1155	A260	60m multi	.75	.30

60th Anniversary of People's Revolutionary Party — A261

1981, Feb. 2

1156	A261	60m multi	.75	.30

Ice Racing — A262

Designs: Various racing motorcycles.

1981, Feb. 28 *Perf. 12½*

1157	A262	10m multi	.25	.25
1158	A262	20m multi	.25	.25
1159	A262	30m multi	.30	.25
1160	A262	40m multi	.40	.25
1161	A262	50m multi	.40	.25
1162	A262	60m multi	.50	.25
1163	A262	70m multi	.50	.25
1164	A262	80m multi	.60	.30
1165	A262	1.20t multi	.60	.30
		Nos. 1157-1165 (9)	3.80	2.35

Rocket Designer Koroljov — A263

Designs: 20m, Cosmonauts boarding Soyuz 39. 40m, Vostok I, Yuri Gagarin. 50m, Salyut space station. 60m, Satellite photographing earth. 80m, Light crystallization from Salyut spacecraft. 1.20t, Salyut, Kremlin, Sukhe Bator statue. 4t, Soviet and Mongolian cosmonauts.

1981, Mar. 22 Litho. *Perf. 12*

1166	A263	20m multi	.25	.25
1167	A263	30m multi	.30	.25
1168	A263	40m multi	.30	.25
1169	A263	50m multi	.40	.30
1170	A263	60m multi	.40	.30
1171	A263	80m multi	.60	.40
1172	A263	1.20t multi	.80	.60
		Nos. 1166-1172 (7)	3.05	2.35

Souvenir Sheet

Perf. 11½

1173	A263	4t multi	2.50	2.50

Intercosmos cooperative space program (Mongolia-USSR). No. 1173 contains one 29x39mm stamp.

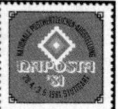

A264

1981, Apr. 28 Litho. *Perf. 12*

1174		Sheet of 4 + 4 labels	6.00	6.00
a.		A264 1t No. 240, Ulan Bator + label	1.40	1.25
b.		A264 1t Germany #8N4, 8NB10 + label	1.40	1.25
c.		A264 1t Austria #B110 + label	1.40	1.25
d.		A264 1t Japan #827 + label	1.40	1.25

1981 Stamp Exhibitions: Mongolian Natl., Ulan Bator; Naposta, Stuttgart; WIPA, Vienna; Japex, Tokyo.

Star Shining on Factories and Sheep A265

1981, May 5

1175	A265	60m multi	.75	.30

18th Congress of Revolutionary People's Party, May.

Souvenir Sheet

Statue of Sukhe Bator, Mongolian Flag — A266

1981, May 20 *Perf. 12½*

1176	A266	4t multi	2.50	1.50

Mongolian Revolutionary People's Party, 60th anniv.

Sheep Farming (Economic Development) — A267

30m, Transportation. 40m, Telecommunications. 50m, Public health service. 60m, Agriculture. 80m, Power plant. 1.20t, Public housing.

1981, June 1 *Perf. 12½x11½*

1177	A267	20m shown	.25	.25
1178	A267	30m multi	.30	.25
1179	A267	40m multi	.40	.25
1180	A267	50m multi	.50	.35
1181	A267	60m multi	.60	.30
1182	A267	80m multi	.80	.40
1183	A267	1.20t multi	1.25	.60
		Nos. 1177-1183 (7)	4.10	2.40

Souvenir Sheet

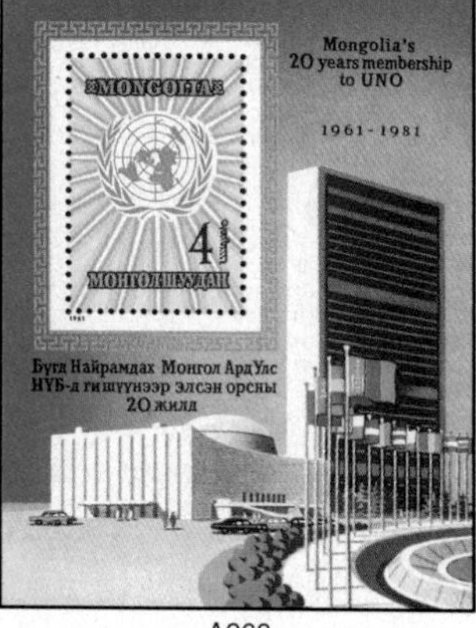

A268

1981, July 11 Litho. *Perf. 12½x11½*

1184	A268	4t multi	2.50	2.50

20th anniv. of UN membership.

A269

Designs: Sailing ships: 10m, Egyptian, 15th cent. BC, horiz. 20m, Mediterranean, 9th cent., horiz. 40m, Hansa Cog, 12th cent. 50m, Venitian, 13th cent. 60m, Santa Maria. 80m, Endeavor. 1t, Poltava, 18th cent. 1.20t, US schooner, 19th cent.

1981, Aug. 1 *Perf. 12*

1185	A269	10m multi	.25	.25
1186	A269	20m multi	.25	.25
1187	A269	40m multi	.35	.30
1188	A269	50m multi	.50	.30
1189	A269	60m multi	.60	.40
1190	A269	80m multi	.70	.40
1191	A269	1t multi	.85	.45
1192	A269	1.20t multi	1.00	.50
		Nos. 1185-1192 (8)	4.50	2.85

Mongolian-USSR Friendship Pact — A270

1981, Sept. 1 *Perf. 11½x12*

1193	A270	60m multi	.75	.30

Flora, by Rembrandt A271

30m, Hendrickje in the Bed. 40m, Young Woman with Earrings. 50m, Young Girl in the Window. 60m, Hendrickje like Flora. 80m, Saskia with Red Flower. 1.20t, Holy Family with Drape.

4t, Self-portrait with Saskia.

1981, Sept. 1 *Perf. 11½x12½*

1194	A271	20m shown	.25	.25
1195	A271	30m multi	.35	.25
1196	A271	40m multi	.40	.25
1197	A271	50m multi	.50	.30
1198	A271	60m multi	.75	.30
1199	A271	80m multi	1.00	.50
1200	A271	1.20t multi	1.25	.60
		Nos. 1194-1200 (7)	4.50	2.45

Souvenir Sheet

1201	A271	4t multi	4.50	4.50

375th birth anniv. of Rembrandt.

Goat (Pawn) — A272

Designs: Wood chess pieces.

1981, Sept. 30 Litho. *Perf. 12½*

1202	A272	20m shown	.25	.25
1203	A272	40m Cart (castle)	.50	.25
1204	A272	50m Camel (bishop)	.60	.30
1205	A272	60m Horse (knight)	.70	.40
1206	A272	80m Lion (queen)	.95	.50
1207	A272	1.20t Man and dog (king)	1.25	.75
		Nos. 1202-1207 (6)	4.25	2.45

Souvenir Sheet

1208	A272	4t Men playing	4.25	4.25

Camel and Circus Tent A273

1981, Oct. 30 Litho. *Perf. 12*

1209	A273	10m shown	.25	.25
1210	A273	20m Horsemen	.25	.25
1211	A273	40m Wrestlers	.35	.25
1212	A273	50m Archers	.45	.30
1213	A273	60m Folksinger	.55	.35
1214	A273	80m Girl playing jat-ga	.65	.35
1215	A273	1t Ballet dancers	.95	.50
1216	A273	1.20t Statue	1.10	.60
		Nos. 1209-1216 (8)	4.55	2.85

Wolfgang Amadeus Mozart and Scene from his Magic Flute — A274

Composers and Scenes from their Works: 30m, Beethoven, Fidelio. 40m, Bartok, Miraculous Mandarin. 50m, Verdi, Aida. 60m, Tchaikovsky, Sleeping Beauty. 80m, Dvorak, New World Symphony score. 1.20t, Chopin, piano.

1981, Nov. 16

1217 A274 20m shown .30 .25
1218 A274 30m multi .40 .25
1219 A274 40m multi .40 .25
1220 A274 50m multi .50 .30
1221 A274 60m multi .50 .30
1222 A274 80m multi .80 .40
1223 A274 1.20t multi 1.25 .50
Nos. 1217-1223 (7) 4.15 2.25

Ribbon Weaver A275

Designs: Mongolian women.

Perf. 11½x12½

1981, Dec. 10 **Litho.**

1224 A275 20m multi .25 .25
1225 A275 30m multi .35 .25
1226 A275 40m multi .45 .25
1227 A275 50m multi .50 .25
1228 A275 60m multi .60 .40
1229 A275 80m multi .60 .50
1230 A275 1.20t multi 1.25 .75
Nos. 1224-1230 (7) 4.00 2.65

Souvenir Sheet

1231 A275 4t multi 4.00 4.00

For surcharge, see No. 2728.

Intercosmos Type of 1980

Designs: a, V. Gorbatko. b, Y. Romanenko. c, V. Dzhanibekov. d, L. Popov. e, Vietnamese stamp. f, Cuban stamp. g, No. 1173. h, Romania No. C241.

1981, Dec. 28 ***Perf. 12***

1232 A255 Sheet of 8, multi 4.50 4.50
a.-h. 50m, any single .50 .35

Historic Bicycles A276

10m, Germany, 1816. 20m, Scotland, 1838. 40m, US, 1866. 50m, France, 1863. 60m, "Kangaroo", 1877. 80m, England, 1870. 1t, 1878. 1.20t, Modern bike.
4t, Racing.

1982, Mar. 25 **Litho.** ***Perf. 11***

1233 A276 10m multi .25 .25
1234 A276 20m multi .25 .25
1235 A276 40m multi .30 .25
1236 A276 50m multi .40 .25
1237 A276 60m multi .50 .30
1238 A276 80m multi .60 .30
1239 A276 1t multi .70 .40
1240 A276 1.20t multi .80 .40
Nos. 1233-1240 (8) 3.80 2.40

Souvenir Sheet

Perf. 12½

1241 A276 4t multi 3.50 3.50

No. 1241 contains one stamp 47x47mm.

1982 World Cup A277

10m, Brazil, 1950. 20m, Switzerland, 1954. 40m, Sweden, 1958. 50m, Chile, 1962. 60m, England, 1966. 80m, Mexico, 1970. 1t, Germany, 1974. 1.20t, Argentina, 1978.
4t, Spain, 1982.

1982, Apr. 20 ***Perf. 12***

1242 A277 10m multi .25 .25
1243 A277 20m multi .25 .25
1244 A277 40m multi .30 .25
1245 A277 50m multi .40 .25
1246 A277 60m multi .50 .30
1247 A277 80m multi .60 .30
1248 A277 1t multi .70 .40
1249 A277 1.20t multi .80 .40
Nos. 1242-1249 (8) 3.80 2.40

Souvenir Sheet

Perf. 11

1250 A277 4t multi 3.00 3.00

No. 1250 contains one stamp 48x48mm.

12th Trade Union Congress, Ulan Bator A278

1982, May 20 **Litho.** ***Perf. 11½x12½***

1251 A278 60m multi 1.40 .50

Souvenir Sheet

PHILEXFRANCE Intl. Stamp Exhibition, Paris, June 11-21 — A279

1982, June 11 ***Imperf.***

1252 A279 4t No. B13 design 3.00 3.00

George Dimitrov (1882-1949), First Prime Minister of Bulgaria — A280

1982, June 18 ***Perf. 12***

1253 A280 60m gold & blk .75 .30

Chicks — A281

1982, June 25 ***Perf. 11***

1254 A281 10m shown .25 .25
1255 A281 20m Colt .25 .25
1256 A281 30m Lamb .40 .25
1257 A281 40m Fawn .45 .25
1258 A281 50m Camel calf .55 .25
1259 A281 60m Kid .60 .25
1260 A281 70m Calf .70 .30
1261 A281 1.20t Young boar .90 .30
Nos. 1254-1261 (8) 4.10 2.10

Coal Mining Industry — A282

1982, July 5 ***Perf. 12***

1262 A282 60m Mine, truck .75 .30

18th Mongolian Youth Org. Congress A283

1982, Aug. 14 ***Perf. 11½x12***

1263 A283 60m multi .75 .30

Siberian Pine A284

30m, Abies sibirica. 40m, Populus diversifolia. 50m, Larix sibirica. 60m, Pinus silvestris. 80m, Betula platyphylla. 1.20t, Picea obovata.

1982, Aug. 16

1264 A284 20m shown .25 .25
1265 A284 30m multi .25 .25
1266 A284 40m multi .40 .25
1267 A284 50m multi .55 .25
1268 A284 60m multi .65 .25
1269 A284 80m multi .80 .30
1270 A284 1.20t multi 1.20 .40
Nos. 1264-1270 (7) 4.10 1.95

60th Anniv. of Mongolian Youth Org. — A285

1982, Aug. 30

1271 A285 60m multi .75 .30

Iseki-6500 Tractor, Japan — A286

20m, Deutz-DX-230, Germany. 40m, Bonser, Gt. Britain. 50m, Intl.-884, US. 60m, Renault TX-145-14, France. 80m, Belarus-611, USSR. 1t, K-7100, USSR. 1.20t, DT-75, USSR.

1982, Oct. 1 **Litho.** ***Perf. 12½***

1272 A286 10m shown .25 .25
1273 A286 20m multi .25 .25
1274 A286 40m multi .30 .25
1275 A286 50m multi .40 .25
1276 A286 60m multi .50 .30
1277 A286 80m multi .60 .30
1278 A286 1t multi .70 .40
1279 A286 1.20t multi .80 .40
Nos. 1272-1279 (8) 3.80 2.40

Scenes from The Foal and The Hare Folktale A287

1983, Jan. 1 **Litho.** ***Perf. 14***

1280 A287 10m multi .25 .25
1281 A287 20m multi .25 .25
1282 A287 30m multi .30 .25
1283 A287 40m multi .35 .30
1284 A287 50m multi .45 .30
1285 A287 60m multi .55 .40
1286 A287 70m multi .75 .40
1287 A287 80m multi .95 .40
1288 A287 1.20t multi 1.10 .50
Nos. 1280-1288 (9) 4.95 3.05

Souvenir Sheet

Imperf

1289 A287 7t multi 4.50 4.50

No. 1289 contains one stamp 58x58mm.

Scenes from Walt Disney's The Sorcerer's Apprentice — A288

1983, Jan. 1

1290 A288 25m multi .25 .25
1291 A288 35m multi .30 .25
1292 A288 45m multi .35 .25
1293 A288 55m multi .45 .30
1294 A288 65m multi .55 .30

1295 A288 75m multi .65 .30
1296 A288 85m multi .85 .30
1297 A288 1.40t multi 1.00 .40
1298 A288 2t multi 1.10 .45
Nos. 1290-1298 (9) 5.50 2.80

Souvenir Sheet

1299 A288 7t multi 4.50 4.50

Fish, Lake Hevsgel — A289

30m, Sheep, Zavhan Highlands. 40m, Beaver, Lake Hovd. 50m, Horses, Lake Uvs. 60m, Chamois, Bajanhongor Steppe. 80m, Mounted hunter, eagle, Bajan-Elgij Highlands. 1.20t, Camels, Gobi Desert.

1982, Nov. 30 ***Perf. 12***

1300 A289 20m shown .25 .25
1301 A289 30m multi .25 .25
1302 A289 40m multi .30 .25
1303 A289 50m multi .40 .35
1304 A289 60m multi .50 .45
1305 A289 80m multi 1.40 .45
1306 A289 1.20t multi 1.40 .50
Nos. 1300-1306 (7) 4.50 2.50

Mongolian Skin Tent (Yurt) — A290

20m, Antonov AN-24B plane. 40m, Deer. 50m, Bighorn sheep. 60m, Eagle. 80m, Museum of the Khans, Ulan Bator. 1.20t, Sukhe Bator monument, Ulan Bator.

1983, Mar. 30 **Litho.** ***Perf. 14***

1307 A290 20m multi .30 .25
1308 A290 30m shown .40 .25
1309 A290 40m multi .50 .25
1310 A290 50m multi .60 .30
1311 A290 60m multi .75 .50
1312 A290 80m multi .90 .55
1313 A290 1.20t multi 1.10 .60
Nos. 1307-1313 (7) 4.55 2.70

For surcharge, see No. 2670.

Souvenir Sheet

90th Birth Anniv. of Sukhe Bator — A291

1983 ***Perf. 13x14***

1314 A291 4t multi 4.50 4.50

No. 1314 with "1893-1993" overprinted in the sheet margin was produced in limited quantities.

Local Flowers — A292

20m, Rose. 30m, Dahlias. 40m, Tagetes faula. 50m, Narcissus. 60m, Violets. 80m, Tulips. 1.20t, Heliopsis helianthoides.

1983, Feb. 4 **Photo.** ***Perf. 13***

1315 A292 20m multi .25 .25
1316 A292 30m multi .30 .25
1317 A292 40m multi .35 .25
1318 A292 50m multi .40 .25
1319 A292 60m multi .50 .30
1320 A292 80m multi .65 .30
1321 A292 1.20t multi .75 .40
Nos. 1315-1321 (7) 3.20 2.00

50th Anniv. of Border Forces — A293

1983, Feb. 9 **Litho.** ***Perf. 14***

1322 A293 60m multi .75 .30

Souvenir Sheet

BRASILIANA, Philatelic Exhibition — A294

1983, July 10 **Litho.** ***Perf. 14***

1323 A294 4t multi 3.00 2.50

Karl Marx — A295

1983, Oct. 1 **Litho.** ***Perf. 14***

1324 A295 60m gold, dp car & bl .75 .30

18th Party Congress, Ulan Bator — A296

10m, Cattle. 20m, Coal. 30m, Garment. 40m, Agricultural. 60m, Communications. 80m, Transportation. 1t, Educational System.

1983, Nov. 1 **Litho.** ***Perf. 14***

1325 A296 10m multi .25 .25
1326 A296 20m multi .25 .25
1327 A296 30m multi .30 .25
1328 A296 40m multi .40 .30
1329 A296 60m multi .60 .30
1330 A296 80m multi 1.50 .60
1331 A296 1t multi 1.00 .60
Nos. 1325-1331 (7) 4.30 2.55

Souvenir Sheet

Sistine Madonna, by Raphael (1483-1520) — A297

1983, Dec. 15 **Litho.** ***Perf. 14x13½***

1332 A297 4t multi 4.00 4.00

A298

Children in Various Activities.

1984, Jan. 1 **Photo.** ***Perf. 13***

1333 A298 10m multi .25 .25
1334 A298 20m multi .25 .25
1335 A298 30m multi .30 .25
1336 A298 40m multi .45 .25
1337 A298 50m multi .75 .35
1338 A298 70m multi 1.10 .50
1339 A298 1.20t multi 1.50 .75
Nos. 1333-1339 (7) 4.60 2.60

Rodents — A299

Various rodents.

1984, Jan. 15 **Litho.** ***Perf. 13½x13***

1340 A299 20m multi .30 .25
1341 A299 30m multi .50 .25
1342 A299 40m multi .70 .30
1343 A299 50m multi .80 .40
1344 A299 60m multi 1.00 .50
1345 A299 80m multi 1.25 .75
1346 A299 1.20t multi 1.60 1.00
Nos. 1340-1346 (7) 6.15 3.45

1984 Winter Olympics — A300

20m, Bobsledding. 30m, Cross-country skiing. 40m, Hockey. 50m, Speed skating. 60m, Downhill skiing. 80m, Figure skating. 1.20t, Biathlon. 4t, Ski jumping.

1984, Feb. 15 **Litho.** ***Perf. 14***

1347 A300 20m multi .25 .25
1348 A300 30m multi .25 .25
1349 A300 40m multi .35 .25
1350 A300 50m multi .35 .25
1351 A300 60m multi .50 .25
1352 A300 80m multi .70 .25
1353 A300 1.20t multi .75 .40
Nos. 1347-1353 (7) 3.15 1.90

Souvenir Sheet

1354 A300 4t multi 3.25 3.25

Size of No. 1354: 134x106mm. Nos. 1347-1352 vert.

Children Feeding Lambs — A301

20m, Ice skating. 40m, Planting tree. 50m, Playing on beach. 60m, Carrying pail. 80m, Three dancers. 1.20t, Two dancers.
4t, Boy, girl.

1984, Mar. 1 **Litho.** ***Perf. 12***

1355 A301 20m multi .25 .25
1356 A301 30m shown .30 .25
1357 A301 40m multi .40 .25
1358 A301 50m multi .40 .25
1359 A301 60m multi .50 .30
1360 A301 80m multi .60 .30
1361 A301 1.20t multi 1.00 .40
Nos. 1355-1361 (7) 3.45 2.00

Souvenir Sheet

1362 A301 4t multi 3.00 3.00

No. 1362 contains one stamp 48x46mm. Compare with Type SP3. For surcharges, see Nos. 2656-2657.

Mail Car, Communications Emblems — A302

20m, Earth satellite receiving station. 40m, Airplane. 50m, Central PO. 1t, Radar station. 1.20t, Train.
4t, Dish antenna.

1984, Apr. 15 ***Perf. 13½x14***

1363 A302 10m shown .25 .25
1364 A302 20m multi .30 .25
1365 A302 40m multi .40 .25
1366 A302 50m multi .50 .35
1367 A302 1t multi .90 .40
1368 A302 1.20t multi 2.00 1.00
Nos. 1363-1368 (6) 4.35 2.50

Souvenir Sheet

Imperf

1369 A302 4t multi 4.50 3.50

1984 Summer Olympics — A303

1984, June 1 **Photo.** ***Perf. 14***

1370 A303 20m Gymnastics .25 .25
1371 A303 30m Bicycling .25 .25
1372 A303 40m Weight lifting .35 .25
1373 A303 50m Judo .35 .25
1374 A303 60m Archery .50 .25

No.	Design	Description	Unused	Used
1375	A303	80m Boxing	.50	.25
1376	A303	1.20t High jump	.75	.35
		Nos. 1370-1376 (7)	2.95	1.85

Souvenir Sheet

No.	Design	Description	Unused	Used
1377	A303	4t Wrestling	3.25	2.25

Souvenir Sheet

AUSIPEX '84 and ESPANA '84 — A304

1984, May Litho. *Perf. 14*

No.	Design	Description	Unused	Used
1378	A304	4t Jet	4.00	4.00

Cuban Revolution, 25th Anniv. — A304a

1984, June 2 Litho. *Perf. 14*

No.	Design	Description	Unused	Used
1378A	A304a	60m multi	.75	.30

State Bank, 60th Anniv. A304b

60m, Commemorative coins, 1981.

1984, Sept. 25 *Perf. 13½x13*

No.	Design	Description	Unused	Used
1378B	A304b	60m multi	.75	.30

Radio Broadcasting in Mongolia, 50th Anniv. — A304c

1984, Sept. 1 Litho. *Perf. 13x13½*

No.	Design	Description	Unused	Used
1378C	A304c	60m multicolored	.90	.30

Scenes from Walt Disney's Mickey and the Beanstalk — A305

1984, Dec. 20 Litho. *Perf. 11*

No.	Design	Description	Unused	Used
1379	A305	25m multi	.30	.25
1380	A305	35m multi	.40	.25
1381	A305	45m multi	.55	.25
1382	A305	55m multi	.65	.25
1383	A305	65m multi	.75	.30
1384	A305	75m multi	.85	.40
1385	A305	85m multi	.95	.50
1386	A305	1.40t multi	1.10	.65
1387	A305	2t multi	1.40	.80
		Nos. 1379-1387 (9)	6.95	3.65

Miniature Sheet

Perf. 14

No.	Design	Description	Unused	Used
1388	A305	7t multi	4.00	4.00

Fairy Tales — A306

1984, Dec. 20 Litho. *Perf. 13½*

No.	Design	Description	Unused	Used
1389	A306	10m multi	.25	.25
1390	A306	20m multi	.30	.25
1391	A306	30m multi	.35	.25
1392	A306	40m multi	.40	.25
1393	A306	50m multi	.45	.25
1394	A306	60m multi	.50	.25
1395	A306	70m multi	.60	.35
1396	A306	80m multi	.75	.40
1397	A306	1.20t multi	.90	.55
		Nos. 1389-1397 (9)	4.50	2.80

Miniature Sheet

No.	Design	Description	Unused	Used
1398	A306	4t multi	4.00	4.00

Souvenir Sheet

60th Anniv. of Mongolian Stamps — A308

1984, Dec. 20 Litho. *Perf. 14*

No.	Design	Description	Unused	Used
1400	A308	4t No. 1	4.50	3.50

Ulan Bator, 60th Anniv. — A309

Mongolian People's Republic, 60th Anniv. — A310

1984, Nov. 26 Litho. *Perf. 13x13½*

No.	Design	Description	Unused	Used
1401	A309	60m multicolored	.75	.40

Perf. 14

No.	Design	Description	Unused	Used
1402	A310	60m multicolored	.75	.40

Mongolian People's Party, 60th Anniv. — A311

1984, Nov. 26 Litho. *Perf. 14*

No.	Design	Description	Unused	Used
1403	A311	60m multi	.90	.30

Native Masks — A312

1984, Dec. 31 Litho. *Perf. 14*

No.	Design	Description	Unused	Used
1404	A312	20m multi	.25	.25
1405	A312	30m multi	.30	.25
1406	A312	40m multi	.45	.25
1407	A312	50m multi	.55	.25
1408	A312	60m multi	.75	.30
1409	A312	80m multi	1.00	.30
1410	A312	1.20t multi	1.25	.50
		Nos. 1404-1410 (7)	4.55	2.10

Souvenir Sheet

No.	Design	Description	Unused	Used
1411	A312	4t multi	4.50	4.50

Dogs A313

20m, Collie. 30m, German Sheepdog. 40m, Papillon. 50m, Cocker Spaniel. 60m, Puppy. 80m, Dalmatians. 1.20t, Mongolian Sheepdog.

1984, Dec. 31 Litho. *Perf. 13*

No.	Design	Description	Unused	Used
1412	A313	20m multi	.25	.25
1413	A313	30m multi	.30	.25
1414	A313	40m multi	.45	.25
1415	A313	50m multi	.55	.25
1416	A313	60m multi	.75	.30
1417	A313	80m multi	1.00	.30
1418	A313	1.20t multi	1.25	.50
		Nos. 1412-1418 (7)	4.55	2.10

Cattle — A314

20m, Shar tarlan. 30m, Bor khaliun. 40m, Sarlag. 50m, Dornod taliin bukh. 60m, Char tarlan. 80m, Nutgiin uulderiin unee. 1.20t, Tsagaan tolgoit.

1985, Jan. *Perf. 14*

No.	Design	Description	Unused	Used
1419	A314	20m multi	.25	.25
1420	A314	30m multi	.35	.25
1421	A314	40m multi	.45	.25
1422	A314	50m multi	.50	.25
1423	A314	60m multi	.60	.25
1424	A314	80m multi	.80	.35
1425	A314	1.20t multi	.95	.35
		Nos. 1419-1425 (7)	3.90	1.95

1984 Olympic Winners — A315

Gold medalists: 20m, Gaetan Boucher, Canada, 1500-meter speed skating. 30m, Eirik Kvalfoss, Norway, 10-kilometer biathlon. 40m, Marja-Lissa Haemaelainen, Finland, 5-kilometer Nordic skiing. 50m, Max Julen, Switzerland, men's giant slalom. 60m, Jens Weissflog, German Democratic Republic, 70-meter ski jump. 80m, W. Hoppe and D. Schauerhammer, German Democratic Republic, 2-man bobsled. 1.20t, Elena Valova and Oleg Vasiliev, USSR, pairs figure skating. 4t, USSR, ice hockey. Nos. 1430-1432 vert.

1985, Apr. 25

No.	Design	Description	Unused	Used
1426	A315	20m multi	.25	.25
1427	A315	30m multi	.30	.25
1428	A315	40m multi	.40	.30
1429	A315	50m multi	.40	.30
1430	A315	60m multi	.60	.40
1431	A315	80m multi	.70	.50
1432	A315	1.20t multi	.80	.60
		Nos. 1426-1432 (7)	3.45	2.60

Souvenir Sheet

No.	Design	Description	Unused	Used
1433	A315	4t multi	3.50	3.00

Souvenir Sheet

Girl, Fawn — A316

1985, Apr. 25

No.	Design	Description	Unused	Used
1434	A316	4m multi	4.00	4.00

Birds — A317

20m, Ciconia nigra. 30m, Haliaetus albicilla. 40m, Grus leucogeranus. 50m, Paradoxornis heudei. 60m, Grus monacha. 80m, Grus vipio. 1.20t, Buteo lagopus.

1985, May 1 *Perf. 12½x13*

No.	Design	Description	Unused	Used
1435	A317	20m multi	.25	.25
1436	A317	30m multi	.35	.25
1437	A317	40m multi	.50	.25
1438	A317	50m multi	.60	.25
1439	A317	60m multi	.80	.30
1440	A317	80m multi	1.00	.40
1441	A317	1.20t multi	1.25	.50
		Nos. 1435-1441 (7)	4.75	2.20

National Wildlife Preservation Association.

World Youth Festival, Moscow A318

60m, Girls in folk costumes.

1985, June *Perf. 14*
1442 A318 60m multi .80 .40

Camelus Bactrianus — A319

Panthera Unicias — A320

Cervus Elaphus — A321

Camels, leopards and deer.

1985
1443 A319 50m Adults, young 1.50 .40
1444 A319 50m Facing right 1.50 .40
1445 A319 50m Facing left 1.50 .40
1446 A319 50m Trotting 1.50 .40
1447 A320 50m Hunting .60 .40
1448 A320 50m Standing in snow .60 .40
1449 A320 50m Female, young .60 .40
1450 A320 50m Adults .60 .40
1451 A321 50m Fawn 1.25 .40
1452 A321 50m Doe in woods 1.25 .40
1453 A321 50m Adult male 1.25 .40
1454 A321 50m Adults, fawn 1.25 .40
Nos. 1443-1454 (12) 13.40 4.80

#1443-1446 show the World Wildlife Fund emblem, #1447-1454 the Natl. Wildlife Preservation emblem. Issue dates: #1443-1446, July 1; #1447-1454, Aug. 1.

UN, 40th Anniv. A322

60m, Flags, UN building.

1985, Aug. 1 *Perf. 13½x13*
1455 A322 60m multi .75 .40

Indigenous Flowering Plants — A323

20m, Rosa davurica. 30m, Matricaria chamomilla. 40m, Taraxacum officinale. 50m, Saxzifraga hirculus. 60m, Vaccinium vitis idaea. 80m, Sanguisorba officinalis. 1.20t, Plantago major.
4t, Hippophae rhamnoides.

1985, Aug. 1 *Perf. 14*
1456 A323 20m multi .25 .25
1457 A323 30m multi .35 .25
1458 A323 40m multi .50 .25
1459 A323 50m multi .60 .25
1460 A323 60m multi .70 .25
1461 A323 80m multi .90 .35
1462 A323 1.20t multi 1.25 .40
Nos. 1456-1462 (7) 4.55 2.00

Souvenir Sheet

1463 A323 4t multi 4.00 4.00

Defeat of Nazi Germany, 40th Anniv. — A324

1985, Sept. 15 *Perf. 13x13½*
1464 A324 60m Monument .75 .30

A325

Various soccer plays. No. 1472 horiz.

1985, Oct. 1 *Perf. 14*
1465 A325 20m multi .25 .25
1466 A325 30m multi .25 .25
1467 A325 40m multi .25 .25
1468 A325 50m multi .35 .25
1469 A325 60m multi .40 .25
1470 A325 80m multi .50 .25
1471 A325 1.20t multi .55 .25
Nos. 1465-1471 (7) 2.55 1.75

Souvenir Sheet

1472 A325 4t multi 3.00 2.50

1985 Junior World Soccer Championships, Moscow.

Souvenir Sheet

ITALIA '85 — A326

1985, Oct. 1
1473 A326 4t Horseman 3.25 2.50

Conquest of Space — A327

Russian spacecraft.

1985, Nov. 1
1474 A327 20m Soyuz .25 .25
1475 A327 30m Cosmos .25 .25
1476 A327 40m Venera 9 .30 .25
1477 A327 50m Salyut .35 .25
1478 A327 60m Luna 9 .45 .25
1479 A327 80m Train 1.25 .55
1480 A327 1.20t Dish receiver 1.00 .25
Nos. 1474-1480 (7) 3.85 2.05

Souvenir Sheet

1985, Dec. 15
1481 A327 4t Cosmonaut on space walk 3.25 2.50

Mushrooms — A328

20m, Tricholoma mongolica. 30m, Cantharellus cibarius. 40m, Armillariella mellea. 50m, Amanita caesarea. 70m, Xerocomus badius. 80m, Agaricus silvaticus. 1.20t, Boletus edulis.

1985, Dec. 1 *Perf. 13½*
1482 A328 20m multi .35 .25
1483 A328 30m multi .45 .25
1484 A328 40m multi .55 .25
1485 A328 50m multi .65 .25
1486 A328 70m multi .85 .30
1487 A328 80m multi 1.10 .30
1488 A328 1.20t multi 1.60 .40
Nos. 1482-1488 (7) 5.55 2.00

Souvenir Sheet

Phalacrocorax Penicillatus — A329

1986, Jan. 15 *Perf. 12½x13*
1489 A329 4t multi 3.50 3.50

No. 1489 contains one stamp plus 2 labels picturing various bird species.

Young Pioneers — A330

1985, Dec. 31 **Litho.** *Perf. 13x13½*
1490 A330 60m multi .70 .30

Victory Monument — A331

1985, Dec. 31 *Perf. 12½x13*
1491 A331 60m multi .70 .30

Victory over Japan ending WWII, 40th anniv.

Natl. Costumes A332

1986, Mar. 1 **Litho.** *Perf. 14*
Background Color
1492 A332 60m yel grn, shown .50 .25
1493 A332 60m red .50 .25
1494 A332 60m pale yel grn .50 .25
1495 A332 60m violet .50 .25
1496 A332 60m ultra .50 .25
1497 A332 60m bluish grn .50 .25
1498 A332 60m pale org brn .50 .25
Nos. 1492-1498 (7) 3.50 1.75

Ernst Thalmann (1886-1944) A333

1986, May 15 **Litho.** *Perf. 14*
1499 A333 60m gold, redsh brn & dk brn .75 .30

Natl. Revolution, 65th Anniv. — A334

60m, Statue of Sukhe Bator.

1986, May 15

1500 A334 60m multi .70 .30

19th Socialist Party Congress A335

1986, May 15

1501 A335 60m multi .70 .30

1986 World Cup Soccer Championships, Mexico — A336

FIFA emblem and various soccer plays. Nos. 1502-1503, 1505-1508 vert.

1986, May 31

1502 A336 20m multi .25 .25
1503 A336 30m multi .25 .25
1504 A336 40m multi .35 .25
1505 A336 50m multi .45 .25
1506 A336 60m multi .55 .25
1507 A336 80m multi .65 .25
1508 A336 1.20t multi .80 .30
Nos. 1502-1508 (7) 3.30 1.80

Souvenir Sheet

1509 A336 4t multi 1.90

Mink, Wildlife Conservation — A337

1986, June 15

1510 A337 60m Spring .60 .30
1511 A337 60m Summer .60 .30
1512 A337 60m Autumn .60 .30
1513 A337 60m Winter .60 .30
Nos. 1510-1513 (4) 2.40 1.20

Flowers — A338

20m, Valeriana officinalis. 30m, Hyoscymus niger. 40m, Ephedra sinica. 50m, Thymus gobica. 60m, Paeonia anomala. 80m, Achilea millefolium. 1.20t, Rhododendron adamsii.

1986, June 1 Litho. ***Perf. 14***

1514 A338 20m multi .25 .25
1515 A338 30m multi .30 .25
1516 A338 40m multi .35 .25
1517 A338 50m multi .40 .25
1518 A338 60m multi .50 .25
1519 A338 80m multi .75 .30
1520 A338 1.20t multi 1.00 .40
Nos. 1514-1520 (7) 3.55 1.95

Butterflies — A339

20m, Neptis coenobita. 30m, Colias tycha. 40m, Leptidea amurensis. 50m, Oeneis tarpenledevi. 60m, Mesoacidalia charlotta. 80m, Smerinthus ocellatus. 1.20t, Pericalia matronula.

1986, Aug. 1 ***Perf. 13½***

1521 A339 20m multi .25 .25
1522 A339 30m multi .25 .25
1523 A339 40m multi .35 .25
1524 A339 50m multi .40 .25
1525 A339 60m multi .45 .25
1526 A339 80m multi .55 .30
1527 A339 1.20t multi .85 .40
Nos. 1521-1527 (7) 3.10 1.95

Circus — A340

Animal trainers & acrobats. #1531-1534 vert.

1986, Aug. 1 ***Perf. 14***

1528 A340 20m multi .25 .25
1529 A340 30m multi .30 .25
1530 A340 40m multi .35 .25
1531 A340 50m multi .40 .25
1532 A340 60m multi .50 .25
1533 A340 80m multi .75 .25
1534 A340 1.20t multi 1.00 .30
Nos. 1528-1534 (7) 3.55 1.80

Przewalski's Horses — A341

No. 1535, Two horses, foal. No. 1536, One facing left, two facing right. No. 1537, Three facing right. No. 1538, Four in storm.

1986, Aug. 1 Litho. ***Perf. 14***

1535 A341 50m multi .75 .40
1536 A341 50m multi .75 .40
1537 A341 50m multi .75 .40
1538 A341 50m multi .75 .40
Nos. 1535-1538 (4) 3.00 1.60

Pelicans (Pelecanus) — A341a

No. 1538A, Crispus feeding. No. 1538B, Crispus wading. No. 1538C, Onocrotalus flying. No. 1538D, Onocrotalus on land.

1986, Sept. 1 Litho. ***Perf. 14***

1538A A341a 60m multi .80 .50
1538B A341a 60m multi .80 .50
1538C A341a 60m multi .80 .50
1538D A341a 60m multi .80 .50
Nos. 1538A-1538D (4) 3.20 2.00

Saiga Tatarica Mongolica — A341b

No. 1538E, Spring (doe, fawn). No. 1538F, Summer (buck, doe). No. 1538G, Fall (buck). No. 1538H, Winter (buck, doe).

1986, Sept. 15

1538E A341b 60m multi .75 .40
1538F A341b 60m multi .75 .40
1538G A341b 60m multi .75 .40
1538H A341b 60m multi .75 .40
Nos. 1538E-1538H (4) 3.00 1.60

Musical Instruments — A342

1986, Sept. 4

1539 A342 20m Morin khuur .25 .25
1540 A342 30m Bishguur .30 .25
1541 A342 40m Ever buree .35 .25
1542 A342 50m Shudarga .40 .25
1543 A342 60m Khiil .50 .25
1544 A342 80m Janchir .75 .30
1545 A342 1.20t Jatga 1.00 .30
Nos. 1539-1545 (7) 3.55 1.85

Souvenir Sheet

1546 A342 4t like 20m, vert. 3.50 3.50

STOCKHOLMIA '86. Nos. 1539-1543 vert.

Intl. Peace Year — A342a

1986, Sept. 20 Litho. ***Perf. 13x13½***

1546A A342a 10m multicolored .75 .30

North American Bird Species — A343

No. 1547, Anthus spinoletta. No. 1548, Aythya americana. No. 1549, Bonasa umbellus. No. 1550, Olor columbianus.

1986, Oct. 1

1547 A343 60m multi .80 .50
1548 A343 60m multi .80 .50
1549 A343 60m multi .80 .50
1550 A343 60m multi .80 .50
Nos. 1547-1550 (4) 3.20 2.00

Eastern Architecture — A343a

Various two-story buildings.

1986, Oct. 1 **Color of Border**

1551 A343a 60m dark grn & blk .75 .40
1552 A343a 60m beige & blk .75 .40
1553 A343a 60m apple grn & blk .75 .40
1554 A343a 60m red brn & blk .75 .40
Nos. 1551-1554 (4) 3.00 1.60

Classic Automobiles — A344

20m, 1922 Alfa Romeo RL Sport, Italy. 30m, 1912 Stutz Bearcat, US. 40m, 1902 Mercedes Simplex, Germany. 50m, 1923 Tatra 11, Czechoslovakia. 60m, 1908 Ford Model T, US. 80m, 1905 Vauxhall, England. 1.20t, 1913 Russo-Baltik, Russia.

1986, Oct. 1 Litho. ***Perf. 14***

1554A A344 20m multi .25 .25
1554B A344 30m multi .30 .25
1554C A344 40m multi .35 .25
1554D A344 50m multi .40 .25
1554E A344 60m multi .50 .25
1554F A344 80m multi .75 .30
1554G A344 1.20t multi 1.00 .40
Nos. 1554A-1554G (7) 3.55 1.95

Souvenir Sheet

1554H A344 4t like 1.20t 3.00 3.00

Woodpeckers A344a

20m, Picus canus. 30m, Jynx torquilla. 40m, Dryobates major. 50m, Dryobates leucotos. 60m, Dryobates minor. 80m, Dryocopus martius. 1.20t, Picoides tridactylus.
4t, Saphopipo noguchi.

1986, Nov. 1

1555 A344a 20m multi .25 .25
1556 A344a 30m multi .30 .25
1557 A344a 40m multi .35 .25
1558 A344a 50m multi .40 .25
1559 A344a 60m multi .50 .25
1560 A344a 80m multi .75 .30
1561 A344a 1.20t multi 1.00 .40
Nos. 1555-1561 (7) 3.55 1.95

Souvenir Sheet

1562 A344a 4t multi 4.00 4.00

Chess Champions — A345

Portraits and chessmen on boards in match-winning configurations: 20m, Steinitz, Austria. 30m, Lasker, Germany. 40m, Alekhine, France. 50m, Botvinnik, USSR. 60m, Karpov, USSR. 80m, N. Gaprin-dashvili. 1.20t, M. Chibur-danidze. No. 1562H, Chess champions Gary Kasparov, Jose R. Capablanca, Max Euwe, Vassily Smyslow, Mikhail Tal, Tigran Petrosian, Boris Spasski and Bobby Fischer; W. Menchik, L. Rudenko, E. Bykowa and O. Rubzowa.

1986, Nov. 1 ***Perf. 14***

1562A A345 20m multi .25 .25
1562B A345 30m multi .25 .25
1562C A345 40m multi .25 .25
1562D A345 50m multi .35 .25
1562E A345 60m multi .45 .25
1562F A345 80m multi .55 .25
1562G A345 1.20t multi .90 .30

Size: 110x100mm
Imperf

1562H	A345	4t multi	4.00	4.00
		Nos. 1562A-1562H (8)	7.00	5.80

Souvenir Sheet

Halley's Comet — A346

1986, Nov. 30 Litho. *Perf. 14*

1563	A346	4t multicolored	4.00	2.50

Ovis Ammon Ammon — A347

No. 1565, In the mountains. No. 1566, Close-up of head. No. 1567, Male, female, lamb.

1987, Jan. 1

1564	A347	60m shown	.75	.40
1565	A347	60m multi	.75	.40
1566	A347	60m multi	.75	.40
1567	A347	60m multi	.75	.40
		Nos. 1564-1567 (4)	3.00	1.60

For surcharges, see Nos. 2779-2782.

Children's Activities A348

20m, Backpacking, hunting butterflies. 30m, Playing with calves. 40m, Chalk-writing on cement. 50m, Playing soccer. 60m, Go-cart, model rocket, boat. 80m, Agriculture. 1.20t, Playing the morin khuur, dancing.

1987, Feb. 1

1568	A348	20m multi	.25	.25
1569	A348	30m multi	.30	.25
1570	A348	40m multi	.35	.25
1571	A348	50m multi	.40	.25
1572	A348	60m multi	.45	.25
1573	A348	80m multi	.55	.25
1574	A348	1.20t multi	.80	.30
		Nos. 1568-1574 (7)	3.10	1.80

Int'l. Peace Year (40m); Child Survival Campaign (50m).

13th Trade Unions Congress — A349

1987, Feb. 15 *Perf. 13½x13*

1575	A349	60m multi	1.50	1.00

Equestrian Sports — A350

1987, Mar. 1

1576	A350	20m Lassoer	.25	.25
1577	A350	30m Breaking horse	.25	.25
1578	A350	40m Shooting bow	.30	.25
1579	A350	50m Race	.40	.25
1580	A350	60m Retrieving flags	.45	.25
1581	A350	80m Tug-of-war	.55	.25
1582	A350	1.20t Racing wolf	.85	.30
		Nos. 1576-1582 (7)	3.05	1.80

Admission into Comecon, 25th Anniv. — A351

1987, Apr. 15 *Perf. 13x13½*

1583	A351	60m multi	.75	.40

Fruit — A352

A353

20m, Hippophae rhamnoides. 30m, Ribes nigrum. 40m, Ribes rubrus. 50m, Ribes altissimum. 60m, Rubus sachalinensis. 80m, Padus asiatica. 1.20t, Fragaria orientalis.
4t, Malus domestica.

1987, June 1 *Perf. 13½*

1584	A352	20m multi	.35	.25
1585	A352	30m multi	.50	.25
1586	A352	40m multi	.65	.25
1587	A352	50m multi	.75	.25
1588	A352	60m multi	.90	.25
1589	A352	80m multi	1.00	.25
1590	A352	1.20t multi	1.40	.25
		Nos. 1584-1590 (7)	5.55	1.75

Souvenir Sheet
Perf. 14

1591	A353	4t multicolored	3.25	3.25

Soviet-Mongolian Diplomatic Relations, 50th Anniv. — A354

1987, July 1 *Perf. 13x13½*

1592	A354	60m multi	.75	.45

Russian Revolution, 70th Anniv. — A355

1987, July 1

1593	A355	60m multi	.75	.45

Folk Dances — A356

1987, Aug. 1 *Perf. 14*

1594	A356	20m multi	.25	.25
1595	A356	30m multi, diff.	.25	.25
1596	A356	40m multi, diff.	.35	.25
1597	A356	50m multi, diff.	.45	.25
1598	A356	60m multi, diff.	.55	.25
1599	A356	80m multi, diff.	.65	.25
1600	A356	1.20t multi, diff.	.80	.30
		Nos. 1594-1600 (7)	3.30	1.80

Antiques A357

Full costume and accessories: 20m, Folk costumes. 30m, Gilded nunchaku. 40m, Brooches. 50m, Draw-string pouch, rice bowl. 60m, Headdress. 80m, Pouches, bottle, pipe. 1.20t, Sash, brooch.

1987, Aug. 10

1601	A357	20m multi	.25	.25
1602	A357	30m multi	.25	.25
1603	A357	40m multi	.35	.25
1604	A357	50m multi	.45	.25
1605	A357	60m multi	.55	.25
1606	A357	80m multi	.65	.25
1607	A357	1.20t multi	.80	.30
		Nos. 1601-1607 (7)	3.30	1.80

Souvenir Sheet

HAFNIA '87 — A358

1987, Aug. 10

1608	A358	4t multi	3.50	3.00

Swans — A359

No. 1609, Cygnus olor on land. No. 1610, Cygnus olor in water. No. 1611, Cygnus bewickii. No. 1612, Cygnus bewickii, gunus and olor.

1987, Aug. 15

1609	A359	60m multi	.75	.30
1610	A359	60m multi	.75	.30
1611	A359	60m multi	.75	.30
1612	A359	60m multi	.75	.30
		Nos. 1609-1612 (4)	3.00	1.20

Domestic and Wild Cats — A360

1987, Oct. 1 Litho. *Perf. 14*

1613	A360	20m multi, vert.	.30	.25
1614	A360	30m multi, vert.	.35	.25
1615	A360	40m multi, vert.	.40	.25
1616	A360	50m shown	.50	.25
1617	A360	60m multi	.60	.25
1618	A360	80m multi	.75	.30
1619	A360	1.20t multi	1.10	.30
		Nos. 1613-1619 (7)	4.00	1.85

Miniature Sheet

1620	A360	4t multi, vert.	4.00	3.00

Helicopter — A361

20m, B-12. 30m, Westland-WG-30. 40m, Bell-S-206L. 50m, Kawasaki-369HS. 60m, KA-32. 80m, MI-17. 1.20t, MI-10K.

1987, Oct. 3 *Perf. 12½x11½*

1621	A361	20m multi	.25	.25
1622	A361	30m multi	.25	.25
1623	A361	40m multi	.35	.25
1624	A361	50m multi	.45	.25

1625 A361 60m multi .55 .25
1626 A361 80m multi .65 .25
1627 A361 1.20t multi .80 .30
Nos. 1621-1627 (7) 3.30 1.80

Disney Cartoons — A362

The Brave Little Tailor (25m-55m, 2t, No. 1637), and The Celebrated Jumping Frog of Calaveras County (65m-1.40t, No. 1638).

1987, Nov. 23 *Perf. 14*

1628 A362 25m multi .25 .25
1629 A362 35m multi .35 .25
1630 A362 45m multi .50 .25
1631 A362 55m multi .60 .25
1632 A362 65m multi .70 .25
1633 A362 75m multi .85 .25
1634 A362 85m multi .95 .30
1635 A362 1.40t multi 1.10 .50
1636 A362 2t multi 1.40 .75
Nos. 1628-1636 (9) 6.70 3.05

Souvenir Sheets

1637 A362 7t multi 5.50 5.50
1638 A362 7t multi 5.50 5.50

A363

Tropical Fish — A364

20m, Betta splendens. 30m, Carassius auratus. 40m, Rasbora hengeli. 50m, Aequidens. 60m, Xiphophorus macalatus. 80m, Xiphophorus helleri. 1.20t, Pterophyllum scalare, vert.
4t, Crenuchus spilurus.

1987, Oct. *Perf. 13x12½, 12½x13*

1639 A363 20m multi .25 .25
1640 A363 30m multi .35 .25
1641 A363 40m multi .45 .25
1642 A363 50m multi .60 .25
1643 A363 60m multi .70 .25
1644 A363 80m multi .90 .25
1645 A363 1.20t multi 1.00 .30
Nos. 1639-1645 (7) 4.25 1.80

Miniature Sheet

Perf. 14

1646 A364 4t multi 4.25 3.75

19th Communist Party Congress A365

1987, Dec. *Perf. 14*

1647 A365 60m Family .40 .25
1648 A365 60m Construction .75 .25
1649 A365 60m Jet, harvesting, produce .40 .25
1650 A365 60m Education .40 .25
1651 A365 60m Transportation .40 .25
1652 A365 60m Heavy industry .40 .25
1653 A365 60m Science and technology .40 .25
Nos. 1647-1653 (7) 3.15 1.75

Vulpes Vulpes (Fox) — A366

1987, Dec.

1654 A366 60m Adult in snow .65 .30
1655 A366 60m Adult, young .65 .30
1656 A366 60m Adult in field .65 .30
1657 A366 60m Close-up of head .65 .30
Nos. 1654-1657 (4) 2.60 1.20

Souvenir Sheet

INTERCOSMOS — A367

1987, Dec. 15 **Litho.** *Perf. 14*

1658 A367 4t multi 3.00 2.50

Souvenir Sheet

PRAGA '88 — A368

1988, Jan. 30

1659 A368 4t 1923 Tatra 11 3.00 2.50

Sukhe Bator — A369

1988, Feb. 2 *Perf. 13x13½*

1660 A369 60m multi .80 .50

For surcharge, see footnote after No. 2764.

Roses — A370

1988, Feb. 20 *Perf. 14*

1661 A370 20m Invitation .30 .25
1662 A370 30m Meilland .55 .25
1663 A370 40m Pascali .40 .25
1664 A370 50m Tropicana .50 .25
1665 A370 60m Wendy Cussons .55 .25
1666 A370 80m Blue moon .60 .25
1667 A370 1.20t Diorama .90 .30
Nos. 1661-1667 (7) 3.80 1.80

Souvenir Sheet

1668 A370 4t multicolored 3.25 2.75

19th Communist Youth Congress — A371

1988, Apr. 15 *Perf. 12½x13*

1669 A371 60m multicolored .80 .50

Puppets — A372

Folk tales: 20m, Ukhaant Ekhner. 30m, Altan Everte Mungun Turuut. 40m, Aduuchyn Khuu. 50m, Suulenkhuu. 60m, Khonchyn Khuu. 80m, Argat Byatskhan Baatar. 1.20t, Botgochyn Khuu.

1988, Apr. 1 **Litho.** *Perf. 14*

1670 A372 20m multi .25 .25
1671 A372 30m multi .30 .25
1672 A372 40m multi .40 .25
1673 A372 50m multi .45 .25
1674 A372 60m multi .60 .25
1675 A372 80m multi .80 .25
1676 A372 1.20t multi 1.25 .30
Nos. 1670-1676 (7) 4.05 1.80

1988 Summer Olympics, Seoul — A373

20m, Judo. 30m, Women's archery. 40m, Weight lifting. 50m, Women's gymnastics. 60m, Cycling. 80m, Running. 1.20t, Wrestling.
4t, Boxing.

1988, Feb. 15

1677 A373 20m multi .25 .25
1678 A373 30m multi .25 .25
1679 A373 40m multi .40 .25
1680 A373 50m multi .45 .25
1681 A373 60m multi .50 .25
1682 A373 80m multi .60 .25
1683 A373 1.20t multi 1.00 .30
Nos. 1677-1683 (7) 3.45 1.80

Souvenir Sheet

1684 A373 4t multi 3.00 2.50

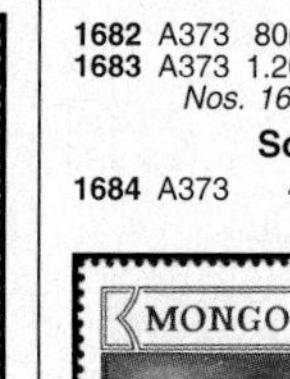

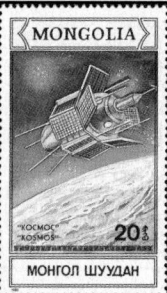

Soviet Space Achievements A374

1988, May 15

1685 A374 20m Cosmos .25 .25
1686 A374 30m Meteor .25 .25
1687 A374 40m Salyut-Soyuz .40 .25
1688 A374 50m Prognoz-6 .45 .25
1689 A374 60m Molniya-1 .50 .25
1690 A374 80m Soyuz .60 .25
1691 A374 1.20t Vostok 1.00 .25
Nos. 1685-1691 (7) 3.45 1.75

Effigies of Buddhist Deities — A375

Various statues.

1988, June 15 **Litho.** *Perf. 14*

1692 A375 20m multi .25 .25
1693 A375 30m multi, diff. .25 .25
1694 A375 40m multi, diff. .35 .25
1695 A375 50m multi, diff. .50 .25
1696 A375 60m multi, diff. .65 .25
1697 A375 70m multi, diff. .85 .25
1698 A375 80m multi, diff. 1.00 .30
1699 A375 1.20t multi, diff. 1.50 .30
Nos. 1692-1699 (8) 5.35 2.10

Wildlife Conservation — A376

Eagles — Haliaeetus albicilla: No. 1700, Eagle facing left, diff., vert. No. 1701, Landing on branch, vert. No. 1702, Facing right, vert.

1988, Aug. 1 **Litho.** *Perf. 14*

1700 A376 60m multi .80 .50
1701 A376 60m multi .80 .50
1702 A376 60m multi .80 .50
1703 A376 60m shown .80 .50
Nos. 1700-1703 (4) 3.20 2.00

Souvenir Sheet

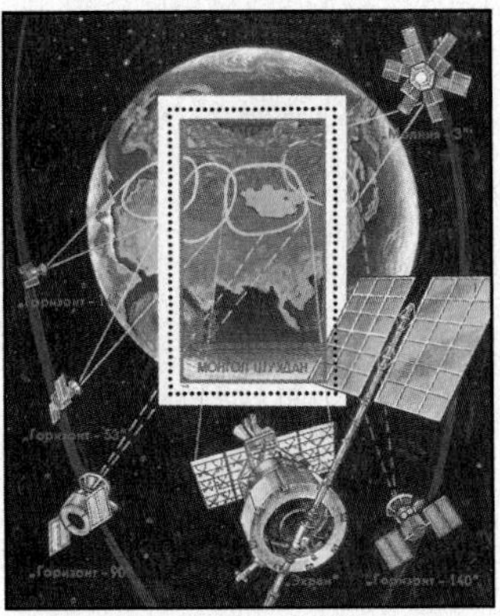

Cosmos — A377

1988, Sept. 15 Litho. ***Perf. 14***

1704 A377 4t Satellite links 4.00 4.00

Opera — A378

1988, Oct. 1 Litho. ***Perf. 13x12½***

1705 A378 60m multi + label 1.50 .75

Equus hemionus — A380

1988, May 3

1713 A380 60m Mare, foal .80 .50
1714 A380 60m Ass's head .80 .50
1715 A380 60m Ass galloping .80 .50
1716 A380 60m Ass cantering .80 .50
Nos. 1713-1716 (4) 3.20 2.00

Winners of the 1988 Winter Olympics, Calgary — A381

No. 1717, Matti Nykaenen, Finland. No. 1718, Bonnie Blair, US, vert. No. 1719, Alberto Tomba, Italy, vert. No. 1720, USSR hockey team, vert.
No. 1721, Katarina Witt, DDR.

1988, July 1

1717 A381 1.50t multicolored .70 .30
1718 A381 1.50t multicolored .70 .30
1719 A381 1.50t multicolored .70 .30
1720 A381 1.50t multicolored .70 .30
Nos. 1717-1720 (4) 2.80 1.20

Souvenir Sheet

1721 A381 4t multicolored 3.00 3.00

A382

20m, Horsemanship. 30m, Archery. 40m, Wrestling. 50m, Archery, diff. 70m, Horsemanship, diff. 1.20t, Horsemanship, wrestling, archery.

1988, Sept. 1

1722 A382 10m shown .25 .25
1723 A382 20m multi .30 .25
1724 A382 30m multi .35 .25
1725 A382 40m multi .45 .25
1726 A382 50m multi .55 .25
1727 A382 70m multi .60 .25
1728 A382 1.20t multi .75 .30
Nos. 1722-1728 (7) 3.25 1.80

Socialism and Peace — A383

1988, Dec. 1 ***Perf. 13x13½***

1729 A383 60m multicolored .85 .30

Goats — A384

Various species.

1989, Jan. 15 ***Perf. 14***

1730 A384 20m multi .30 .25
1731 A384 30m multi .35 .25
1732 A384 40m multi .45 .25
1733 A384 50m multi .50 .25
1734 A384 60m multi .60 .25
1735 A384 80m multi .75 .25
1736 A384 1.20t multi 1.00 .30
Nos. 1730-1736 (7) 3.95 1.80

Souvenir Sheet

1737 A384 4t multi, vert. 3.25 3.25

Souvenir Sheet

Child Survival — A385

4t, Drawing by H. Jargalsuren.

1989, Jan. 28 Litho. ***Perf. 14***

1738 A385 4t multicolored 3.50 2.00

Karl Marx — A386

1989, Feb. 25 Litho. ***Perf. 13x13½***

1739 A386 60m multicolored .75 .30

Miniature Sheet

A387

Mongolian Airline Jet — A388

1989, July 1 ***Perf. 14***

1740 A387 Sheet of 3 7.50 7.50
a. 20m Concorde jet .75 .50
b. 60m TGV high-speed train 2.00 1.75
c. 1.20t Statue of Sukhe Bator 4.50 4.00

Souvenir Sheet

1741 A388 4t multicolored 4.50 4.50

PHILEXFRANCE '89, BULGARIA '89.
For overprint see No. 1756.

World War II Memorial A389

1989, Sept. 2

1742 A389 60m multicolored 1.00 .50

For surcharge, see No. 2384B.

Cacti — A390

20m, O. microdasys. 30m, E. multipiex. 40m, R. tephracanthus. 50m, B. haselbergii. 60m, G. mihanovichii. 80m, C. strausii. 1.20t, Horridocactus tuberisvicatus.
4t, Astrophytum ornatum.

1989, Sept. 7

1743 A390 20m multi .25 .25
1744 A390 30m multi .25 .25
1745 A390 40m multi .45 .25
1746 A390 50m multi .60 .25
1747 A390 60m multi .70 .25
1748 A390 80m multi .85 .25
1749 A390 1.20t multi 1.10 .30
Nos. 1743-1749 (7) 4.20 1.80

Souvenir Sheet

1750 A390 4t multi 4.00 4.00

A391

Winners at the 1988 Summer Olympics, Seoul: No. 1751, Kristin Otto, East Germany. No. 1752, Florence Griffith-Joyner, US. No. 1753, Gintaoutas Umaras, USSR. No. 1754, Stefano Cerioni, Italy.
No. 1755, N. Enkhbat, Mongolia.

1989, Oct. 1

1751 A391 60m multi .75 .30
1752 A391 60m multi .75 .30
1753 A391 60m multi .75 .30
1754 A391 60m multi .75 .30
Nos. 1751-1754 (4) 3.00 1.20

Souvenir Sheet

1755 A391 4t multi 4.00 4.00

No. 1740 Overprinted for WORLD STAMP EXPO '89

1989, Nov. 17 Miniature Sheet

1756 A387 Sheet of 3 8.00 8.00
a. 20m multicolored .75 .50
b. 60m multicolored 2.00 1.50
c. 1.20t multicolored 4.50 4.00

Books, Fountain Pen — A392

1989, Dec. 1

1757 A392 60m multicolored .75 .45

Beavers (Castor fiber birulai) — A393

No. 1758, Cutting down saplings. No. 1759, Rolling wood across ground. No. 1760, Beaver on land, in water. No. 1761, Beaver and young.

1989, Dec. 10

1758	A393	60m multi	.70	.30
1759	A393	60m multi	.70	.30
1760	A393	60m multi	.70	.30
1761	A393	60m multi	.70	.30
		Nos. 1758-1761 (4)	2.80	1.20

Medals and Military Decorations — A394

1989, Dec. 31 ***Perf. 13x13½***

1762	A394	60m pink & multi	1.00	.30
1763	A394	60m lt blue grn & multi	1.00	.30
1764	A394	60m vio & multi	1.00	.30
1765	A394	60m org & multi	1.00	.30
1766	A394	60m brt blue & multi	1.00	.30
1767	A394	60m ver & multi	1.00	.30
1768	A394	60m vio blue & multi	1.00	.30
		Nos. 1762-1768 (7)	7.00	2.10

Bears and Giant Pandas — A395

20m, Ursus pruinosis. 30m, Ursus arctos syriacus. 40m, Ursus thibetanus. 50m, Ursus maritimus. 60m, Ursus arctos bruinosus. 80m, Ailuropus melanoleucus. 1.20t, Ursus arctos isabellinus.

4t, Ailuropus melanoleucus, diff.

1990, Jan. 1 ***Perf. 14***

1769	A395	20m multi	.25	.25
1770	A395	30m multi	.25	.25
1771	A395	40m multi	.30	.25
1772	A395	50m multi	.35	.30
1773	A395	60m multi	.55	.45
1774	A395	80m multi	.75	.60
1775	A395	1.20t multi	1.10	1.00
		Nos. 1769-1775 (7)	3.55	3.10

Souvenir Sheet

1776	A395	4t multi	5.00	3.00

Winter Sports — A396

20m, 4-man bobsled. 30m, Luge. 40m, Women's figure skating. 50m, 1-man bobsled. 60m, Pairs figure skating. 80m, Speed skating. 1.20t, Ice speedway.

4t, Ice hockey.

1990, Jan. 6

1777	A396	20m multi	.25	.25
1778	A396	30m multi	.25	.25
1779	A396	40m multi	.35	.25
1780	A396	50m multi	.40	.25
1781	A396	60m multi	.45	.25
1782	A396	80m multi	.65	.25
1783	A396	1.20t multi	.95	.30
		Nos. 1777-1783 (7)	3.30	1.80

Souvenir Sheet

1784	A396	4t multi	4.00	3.00

Space Exploration — A397

Rockets and spacecraft: 20m, Soyuz, USSR. 30m, Apollo-Soyuz, US-USSR. 40m, *Columbia* space shuttle, US, vert. 50m, *Hermes*, France. 60m, *Nippon*, Japan, vert. 80m, *Energy*, USSR, vert. 1.20t, *Buran*, USSR, vert. 4t, *Sanger*, West Germany.

1990, Jan. 30

1785	A397	20m shown	.25	.25
1786	A397	30m multicolored	.25	.25
1787	A397	40m multicolored	.35	.25
1788	A397	50m multicolored	.45	.25
1789	A397	60m multicolored	.55	.30
1790	A397	80m multicolored	.75	.30
1791	A397	1.20t multicolored	1.10	.40
		Nos. 1785-1791 (7)	3.70	2.00

Souvenir Sheet

1792	A397	4t multicolored	4.00	4.00

Jawaharlal Nehru, 1st Prime Minister of Independent India — A398

1990, Feb. 10

1793	A398	10m gold, blk & dark red brn	1.50	.75

Statue of Sukhe Bator — A399

1990, Feb. 27

1794	A399	10m multicolored	1.50	.75

Mongolian Ballet — A400

Dancers in scenes from various ballets. 40m, 80m, 1.20t vert.

1990, Feb. 28

1795	A400	20m shown	.25	.25
1796	A400	30m multi	.25	.25
1797	A400	40m multi	.40	.25
1798	A400	50m multi	.50	.25
1799	A400	60m multi	.60	.25
1800	A400	80m multi	.65	.25
1801	A400	1.20t multi	.90	.30
		Nos. 1795-1801 (7)	3.55	1.80

Automobiles — A401

20m, Citroen, France. 30m, Volvo 760 GLF, Sweden. 40m, Honda, Japan. 50m, Volga, USSR. 60m, Ford Granada, US. 80m, VAZ 21099, USSR. 1.20t, Mercedes Class 190, West Germany.

1990, Mar. 26

1802	A401	20m multi	.25	.25
1803	A401	30m multi	.25	.25
1804	A401	40m multi	.35	.25
1805	A401	50m multi	.45	.25
1806	A401	60m multi	.50	.25
1807	A401	80m multi	.55	.25
1808	A401	1.20t multi	.85	.30
		Nos. 1802-1808 (7)	3.20	1.80

Souvenir Sheet

1809	A401	4t like 50m	4.50	3.00

Lenin — A402

1990, Mar. 27 ***Perf. 13x13½***

1810	A402	60m gold, black & ver	1.00	.50

Unen Newspaper, 70th Anniv. — A403

1990, Apr. 1 ***Perf. 14***

1811	A403	60m multicolored	.90	.50

End of World War II, 45th Anniv. — A404

1990, Apr. 1

1812	A404	60m multicolored	1.00	.60

Buddhist Deities (18th-20th Cent. Paintings) A405

20m, Damdin Sandub. 30m, Pagwa Lama. 40m, Chu Lha. 50m, Agwanglobsan. 60m, Dorje Dags Dan. 80m, Wangchikdorje. 1.20t, Buddha.

4t, Migjed Jang-Rasek.

1990, Apr. 1

1813	A405	20m multi	.25	.25
1814	A405	30m multi	.40	.25
1815	A405	40m multi	.50	.25
1816	A405	50m multi	.60	.30
1817	A405	60m multi	.75	.30
1818	A405	80m multi	.85	.40
1819	A405	1.20t multi	1.10	.50
		Nos. 1813-1819 (7)	4.45	2.25

Souvenir Sheet

1820	A405	4t multi	6.50	6.50

A406

Aspects of a Cooperative Settlement — A407

Paintings: 20m, Animals on plain, rainbow. 30m, Workers, reindeer, dog, vert. 40m, Two men, mountains, Bactrian camels. 50m, Man, Bactrian camels. 60m, Huts, animal shelter, corral. 80m, Breaking horses, vert. 1.20t, Sheep, shepherd girl on horse. 4t, Wrestling match.

1990, Apr. 1

1821	A406	20m shown	.25	.25
1822	A406	30m multicolored	.30	.25
1823	A406	40m multicolored	.50	.25
1824	A406	50m multicolored	.60	.30
1825	A406	60m multicolored	.70	.40
1826	A406	80m multicolored	.90	.50
1827	A406	1.20t multicolored	1.40	.55
		Nos. 1821-1827 (7)	4.65	2.50

Souvenir Sheet

1828	A407	4t shown	6.00	6.00

Scenes from Various Mongolian-made Films — A408

1990, Apr. 1

1829	A408	20m shown	.30	.25
1830	A408	30m multi, diff.	.40	.25
1831	A408	40m multi, diff.	.60	.30
1832	A408	50m multi, diff.	.80	.40
1833	A408	60m multi, diff.	1.10	.50

1834 A408 80m multi, diff. 1.25 .65
1835 A408 1.20t multi, diff. 1.75 1.00
Nos. 1829-1835 (7) 6.20 3.35

Souvenir Sheet

1836 A408 4t multi, diff., vert. 7.00 7.00

Souvenir Sheet

Stamp World London '90 — A409

1990, Apr. 1

1837 A409 4t multicolored 5.00 5.00

1990 World Cup Soccer Championships, Italy — A410

Trophy and various athletes.

1990, Apr. 30

1838 A410 20m multicolored .25 .25
1839 A410 30m multicolored .25 .25
1840 A410 40m multicolored .30 .25
1841 A410 50m multicolored .40 .25
1842 A410 60m multicolored .45 .25
1843 A410 80m multicolored .65 .25
1844 A410 1.20t multicolored .95 .25
Nos. 1838-1844 (7) 3.25 1.75

Souvenir Sheet

1845 A410 4t Trophy, vert. 4.00 2.50

Nos. 304-307 Ovptd.

1990, May 1 Photo. ***Perf. 11½x12***

1846 A84 20m multicolored *3.50*
1847 A84 30m multicolored *4.00*
1848 A84 50m multicolored *5.00*
1849 A84 60m multicolored *6.00*
Nos. 1846-1849 (4) *18.50*

Coronation of Genghis Khan, 800th anniv. (in 1989).

Souvenir Sheet

Genghis Khan — A411

1990, May 8 Litho. ***Perf. 13½***

1850 A411 7t multicolored 7.50 7.50

Stamp World London '90. Exists imperf. Exists without "Stamp World London '90" and Great Britain No. 1.

Cranes *(Grus vipio pallas)* — A412

1990, May 23 ***Perf. 14***

1851 A412 60m brt blue & multi .90 .60
1852 A412 60m brt rose lil & multi .90 .60
1853 A412 60m red lil & multi .90 .60
1854 A412 60m car rose & multi .90 .60
Nos. 1851-1854 (4) 3.60 2.40

Nos. 1853-1854 are vert.

Marine Mammals — A413

20m, Balaenoptera physalus. 30m, Megaptera novaeangliae. 40m, Monodon monoceros. 50m, Grampus griseus. 60m, Tursiops truncatus. 80m, Lagenorhynchus acutius. 1.20t, Balaena mysticetus. 4t, Killer whale.

1990, June 20 Litho. ***Perf. 14***

1855 A413 20m multi .30 .25
1856 A413 30m multi .40 .25
1857 A413 40m multi .45 .25
1858 A413 50m multi .55 .30
1859 A413 60m multi .70 .40
1860 A413 80m multi .95 .50
1861 A413 1.20t multi 1.40 .55
Nos. 1855-1861 (7) 4.75 2.50

Souvenir Sheet

1861A A413 4t multi 4.00 4.00

A414

Cultural Heritage — A415

No. 1864, Fire ring. No. 1865, Genghis Khan. No. 1866, Tent. No. 1867, Horses. No. 1868, Royal family. No. 1869, Royal court.

1990, Aug. 13 ***Perf. 13x12½***

1862 A414 10m shown .25 .25
1863 A414 10m Like No. 1862, arrows at left .25 .25
1864 A415 40m multi .45 .25
1865 A415 60m multi .65 .25
1866 A414 60m multi .65 .25
1867 A414 60m multi .65 .25
1868 A414 80m green panel .95 .40
1869 A414 80m dk bl panel .95 .40
a. Souv. sheet, #1862-1869 + label 8.00 8.00
Nos. 1862-1869 (8) 4.80 2.30

20th Party Congress A416

1990, Mar. 1 Litho. ***Perf. 14***

1870 A416 60m multicolored .90 .50

Dinosaurs — A417

1990, Aug. 25

1871 A417 20m shown .40 .25
1872 A417 30m multi, diff. .50 .25
1873 A417 40m multi, diff. .65 .25
1874 A417 50m multi, diff .75 .30
1875 A417 60m multi, vert. 1.00 .40
1876 A417 80m multi, diff. 1.25 .50

Size: 60x21mm

Perf. 13

1877 A417 1.20t multi, diff. 1.75 .55
Nos. 1871-1877 (7) 6.30 2.50

Souvenir Sheet

1878 A417 4t multi, diff. 6.00 6.00

Giant Pandas — A418

10m, Adult on rock, vert. 20m, Adult, eating, vert. 30m, Adult and cub, vert. 50m, Adult and cub, resting. 60m, Adult, mountains. 80m, Adult and cub, playing. 1.20t, Adult, in winter. 4t, Family.

1990, Aug. 15 Litho. ***Perf. 14***

1879 A418 10m multi .25 .25
1880 A418 20m multi .30 .25
1881 A418 30m multi .45 .25
1882 A418 40m shown .60 .30
1883 A418 50m multi .70 .40
1884 A418 60m multi .90 .50
1885 A418 80m multi 1.25 .65
1886 A418 1.20t multi 1.75 1.00
Nos. 1879-1886 (8) 6.20 3.60

Souvenir Sheet

1887 A418 4t multi 6.00 6.00

Pyramids of Egypt — A419

Seven wonders of the ancient world: 20m, Lighthouse of Alexander, vert. 40m, Statue of Zeus, vert. 50m, Colossus of Rhodes, vert. 60m, Mausoleum of Halicarnassus, vert. 80m, Temple of Artemis. 1.20t, Hanging gardens of Babylon, vert. 4t, Pyramids of Egypt, vert.

1990, Sept. 25

1888 A419 20m multicolored .35 .25
1889 A419 30m shown .45 .25
1890 A419 40m multicolored .65 .25
1891 A419 50m multicolored .75 .25
1892 A419 60m multicolored 1.00 .25
1893 A419 80m multicolored 1.25 .40
1894 A419 1.20t multicolored 1.75 .65
Nos. 1888-1894 (7) 6.20 2.30

Souvenir Sheet

1895 A419 4t multicolored 6.00 6.00

Moschus Moschiferus — A419a

No. 1895B, In snow. No. 1895C, Facing left. No. 1895D, Two, one on ground.

1990, Sept. 26 Litho. ***Perf. 14***

1895A A419a 60m shown .80 .50
1895B A419a 60m multi .80 .50
1895C A419a 60m multi .80 .50
1895D A419a 60m multi .80 .50
Nos. 1895A-1895D (4) 3.20 2.00

Parrots — A420

1990, Oct. 25 Litho. ***Perf. 14***

1896 A420 20m shown .25 .25
1897 A420 30m multi, diff. .25 .25
1898 A420 40m multi, diff. .45 .25
1899 A420 50m multi, diff. .60 .30
1900 A420 60m multi, diff. .75 .40
1901 A420 80m multi, diff. 1.00 .50
1902 A420 1.20t multi, diff. 1.50 .55
Nos. 1896-1902 (7) 4.80 2.50

Souvenir Sheet

1903 A420 4t multi, diff. 4.75 4.00

Butterflies — A421

Designs: 20m, Purpurbar. 30m, Grosses nachtpfauenauge. 40m, Grosser C-Falter. 50m, Stachelbeerspanner. 60m, Damenbrett. 80m, Schwalbenschwanz. 1.20t, Aurorafalter. 4t, Linienschwarmer, vert.

1990, Nov. 25 Litho. ***Perf. 14***

1904 A421 20m multicolored .25 .25
1905 A421 30m multicolored .30 .25
1906 A421 40m multicolored .45 .25
1907 A421 50m multicolored .60 .30

1908	A421	60m multicolored	.70	.40
1909	A421	80m multicolored	.85	.50
1910	A421	1.20t multicolored	1.20	.55
		Nos. 1904-1910 (7)	4.35	2.50

Souvenir Sheet

1911	A421	4t multicolored	4.25	3.75

Flintstones Visit Mongolia — A422

Designs: 25m, Dino, Bamm-Bamm. 35m, Dino, Bamm-Bamm, diff., vert. 45m, Betty, Wilma, Bamm-Bamm, Pebbles. 55m, Fred, Barney, Dino. 65m, Flintstones & Rubbles. 75m, Bamm-Bamm riding Dino. 85m, Fred, Barney, Bamm-Bamm. 1.40t, Flintstones, Rubbles in car. 2t, Fred, Barney. No. 1921, Wilma, Betty & Bamm-Bamm. No. 1922, Bamm-Bamm, Pebbles riding Dino.

1991, Feb. 10 Litho. *Perf. 14*

1912	A422	25m multicolored	.30	.25
1913	A422	35m multicolored	.30	.25
1914	A422	45m multicolored	.45	.25
1915	A422	55m multicolored	.50	.25
1916	A422	65m multicolored	.70	.25
1917	A422	75m multicolored	.70	.30
1918	A422	85m multicolored	.85	.30
1919	A422	1.40t multicolored	1.20	.40
1920	A422	2t multicolored	1.75	.40
		Nos. 1912-1920 (9)	6.75	2.65

Souvenir Sheets

1921	A422	7t multicolored	4.50	4.50
1922	A422	7t multicolored	4.50	4.50

The Jetsons A423

Designs: 20m, Jetsons blasting off in spaceship. 25m, Jetsons on planet, horiz. 30m, George, Jane, Elroy & Astro. 40m, George, Judy, Elroy & Astro. 50m, Jetsons in spaceship, horiz. 60m, George, Jane, Elroy & Mr. Spacely, horiz. 70m, George, Elroy wearing jet packs. 80m, Elroy. 1.20t, Elroy, Judy & Astro. No. 1932, Elroy, red flowers. No. 1933, Elroy, blue flowers.

1991, Feb. 10

1923	A423	20m multicolored	.25	.25
1924	A423	25m multicolored	.25	.25
1925	A423	30m multicolored	.35	.25
1926	A423	40m multicolored	.45	.25
1927	A423	50m multicolored	.50	.30
1928	A423	60m multicolored	.55	.30
1929	A423	70m multicolored	.65	.30
1930	A423	80m multicolored	.70	.40
1931	A423	1.20t multicolored	1.10	.40
		Nos. 1923-1931 (9)	4.80	2.70

Souvenir Sheets

1932	A423	7t multicolored	4.50	4.50
1933	A423	7t multicolored	4.50	4.50

Mongolian People's Revolutionary Party, 70th Anniv. — A423a

1991, Mar. 1 Litho. *Perf. 14*

1933A	A423a	60m multicolored	.90	.40

A424

Stamp World London '90 — A425

Various birds.

1991, Mar. 3 Litho. *Perf. 14½*

1934	A424	25m multicolored	.25	.25
1935	A424	35m multicolored	.35	.25
1936	A424	45m multicolored	.50	.25
1937	A424	55m multicolored	.60	.25
1938	A424	65m multicolored	.75	.25
1939	A424	75m multi, horiz.	.80	.30
1940	A424	85m multicolored	1.00	.40
1941	A424	1.40t multicolored	1.50	.50
1942	A424	2t multicolored	2.25	.55
		Nos. 1934-1942 (9)	8.00	3.00

Souvenir Sheets

1943	A424	7t multicolored	7.00	7.00
1944	A425	7t multicolored	7.00	7.00

Butterflies and Flowers of Mongolia — A426

Designs: 20m, 30m-60m, various butterflies. Others, various flowers.

1991, Mar. 3 Litho. *Perf. 14½*

1945	A426	20m multicolored	.45	.25
1946	A426	25m multicolored	.50	.25
1947	A426	30m multicolored	.65	.25
1948	A426	40m multicolored	.85	.25
1949	A426	50m multicolored	1.00	.25
1950	A426	60m multicolored	1.25	.25
1951	A426	70m multicolored	1.50	.30
1952	A426	80m multicolored	1.75	.30
1953	A426	1.20t multicolored	2.25	.40
		Nos. 1945-1953 (9)	10.20	2.50

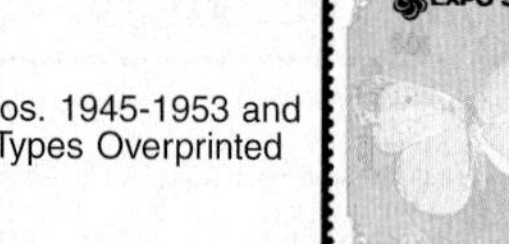

Nos. 1945-1953 and Types Overprinted

1991, Mar. 3

1954	A426	20m multicolored	.45	.25
1955	A426	25m multicolored	.50	.25
1956	A426	30m multicolored	.65	.25
1957	A426	40m multicolored	.85	.25
1958	A426	50m multicolored	1.00	.25
1959	A426	60m multicolored	1.25	.25
1960	A426	70m multicolored	1.50	.30
1961	A426	80m multicolored	1.75	.30
1962	A426	1.20t multicolored	2.25	.40
		Nos. 1954-1962 (9)	10.20	2.50

Souvenir Sheets

1963	A426	7t Butterfly	10.00	10.00
1964	A426	7t Flower	10.00	10.00

Nos. 1963-1964 were not issued without overprint which appears in sheet margin only.

Mongolian People's Army, 70th Anniv. — A426a

People's Army — A426b

1991, Mar. 18 Litho. *Perf. 14*

1964A	A426a	60m multicolored	.90	.40

Souvenir Sheet

1964B	A426b	4t multicolored	3.00	3.00

Issue date: No. 1964B 7/11/91.

Birds — A427

20m, Lururus tetrix. 30m, Tadorna tadorna. 40m, Phasianus colchicus. 50m, Clangula byemalis. 60m, Tetrastes bonasia. 80m, Mergus serrator. 1.20t, Bucephaia clangula. 4t, Anas crecca, vert.

1991, Apr. 1 *Perf. 14*

1965	A427	20m multi	.30	.25
1966	A427	30m multi	.45	.25
1967	A427	40m multi	.55	.25
1968	A427	50m multi	.75	.30
1969	A427	60m multi	.90	.40
1970	A427	80m multi	1.25	.50
1971	A427	1.20t multi	1.60	.75
		Nos. 1965-1971 (7)	5.80	2.70

Souvenir Sheet

1972	A427	4t multi	5.50	5.50

Flowers — A428

20m, Dianthus superbus. 30m, Gentiana puenmonanthe. 40m, Taraxacum officinale. 50m, Iris sibrica. 60m, Lilium martagon. 80m, Aster amellus. 1.20t, Cizsium rivulare. 4t, Campanula persicifolia.

1991, Apr. 15

1973	A428	20m multi	.25	.25
1974	A428	30m multi	.35	.25
1975	A428	40m multi	.55	.25
1976	A428	50m multi	.70	.30
1977	A428	60m multi	.70	.40
1978	A428	80m multi	1.00	.50
1979	A428	1.20t multi	1.40	.55
		Nos. 1973-1979 (7)	4.95	2.50

Souvenir Sheet

1980	A428	4t multi	4.50	4.50

Buddhist Effigies — A429

20m, Defend. 30m, Badmasanhava. 40m, Avalokitecvara. 50m, Buddha. 60m, Mintugwa. 80m, Shyamatara. 1.20t, Samvara. 4t, Lamidhatara.

1991, May 1

1981	A429	20m multi	.25	.25
1982	A429	30m multi	.30	.25
1983	A429	40m multi	.50	.25
1984	A429	50m multi	.70	.30
1985	A429	60m multi	.80	.40
1986	A429	80m multi	1.10	.50
1987	A429	1.20t multi	1.20	.55
		Nos. 1981-1987 (7)	4.85	2.50

Souvenir Sheet

1988	A429	4t multi	5.00	5.00
a.		With Phila Nippon '91 emblem overprinted in sheet margin	—	—

For surcharge, see No. 2658.

Insects — A430

20m, Neolamprima adolphinae. 30m, Chelorrhina polyphemus. 40m, Coptolabrus coelestis. 50m, Epepeotes togatus. 60m, Cicindela chinensis. 80m, Macrodontia cervicornis. 1.20t, Dynastes hercules. 4t, Cercopis sanguinolenta, vert.

1991, May 22

1989	A430	20m multi	.35	.25
1990	A430	30m multi	.40	.25
1991	A430	40m multi	.55	.25
1992	A430	50m multi	.75	.30
1993	A430	60m multi	.80	.40
1994	A430	80m multi	1.25	.50
1995	A430	1.20t multi	1.50	.55
		Nos. 1989-1995 (7)	5.60	2.50

Souvenir Sheet

1995A	A430	4t multi	4.50	4.50

African Animals — A431

1991, May 23

1996	A431	20m Zebras	.25	.25
1997	A431	30m Cheetah	.35	.25
1998	A431	40m Black rhinos	.55	.25
1999	A431	50m Giraffe, vert.	.70	.30
2000	A431	60m Gorilla	.80	.40
2001	A431	80m Elephants	1.00	.50
2002	A431	1.20t Lion, vert.	1.25	.55
		Nos. 1996-2002 (7)	4.90	2.50

Souvenir Sheet

2003	A431	4t Gazelle	5.00	5.00

No. 1997 is incorrectly spelled "Cheetan."

Exhibition of Meiso Mizuhara's Mongolian Stamp Collection — A432

1991, June Litho. *Perf. 13½*
2004 A432 1.20t multicolored 3.00 1.00

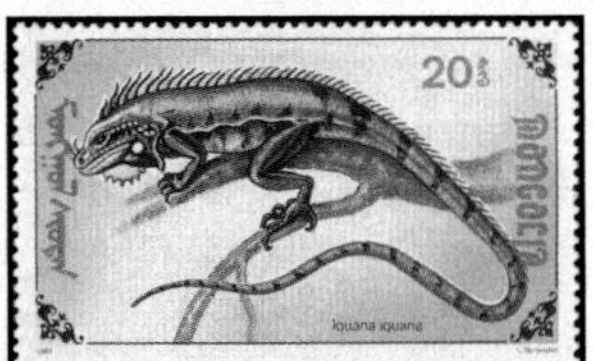

Lizards — A433

20m, Iguana iguana. 30m, Ptychozoon kihli. 40m, Chlamydosaurus kingii. 50m, Cordylus cordylus. 60m, Basiliscus basilisus. 80m, Tupinambis teguixin. 1.20t, Amblyrhynchus cristatus.
4t, Varanus bengalensis, vert.

1991, Oct. 29 *Perf. 14*
2005 A433 20m multi .25 .25
2006 A433 30m multi .30 .25
2007 A433 40m multi .45 .25
2008 A433 50m multi .60 .30
2009 A433 60m multi .75 .40
2010 A433 80m multi .90 .50
2011 A433 1.20t multi 1.60 .55
Nos. 2005-2011 (7) 4.85 2.50

Souvenir Sheet

2012 A433 4t multi 4.50 4.50

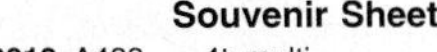

Masks and Costumes A434

Various masks and costumes.

1991, Oct. 1
2013 A434 35m multicolored .40 .25
2014 A434 45m multicolored .50 .25
2015 A434 55m multicolored .65 .25
2016 A434 65m multicolored .75 .30
2017 A434 85m multicolored 1.00 .50
2018 A434 1.40t multicolored 1.65 .80
2019 A434 2t multicolored 2.35 1.00
Nos. 2013-2019 (7) 7.30 3.35

Souvenir Sheet

2020 A434 4t multicolored 5.50 5.50

Phila Nippon '91 — A435

1991, Oct. 29
2021 A435 1t Pagoda .55 .50
2022 A435 2t Japanese beauty .80 .75
2023 A435 3t Mongolian woman 1.10 .75
2024 A435 4t Mongolian building 1.50 1.00
Nos. 2021-2024 (4) 3.95 3.00

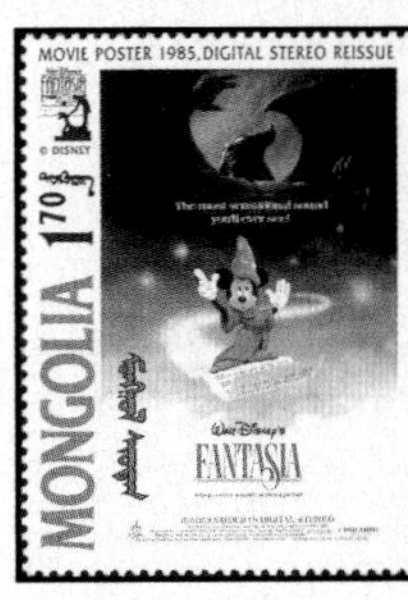

Fantasia, 50th Anniv. A436

Designs: 1.70t, Poster, 1985. 2t, Poster, 1940. 2.30t, Poster, 1982. 2.60t, Poster, 1981. 4.20t, Poster, 1969. 10t, Poster, 1941. 15t, Drawing of Mlle. Upanova, 1940. 16t, Sketch of Mickey as Sorcerer's Apprentice.
No. 2033, Mickey as Sorcerer's Apprentice. No. 2034, Dinosaurs from "The Rite of Spring," horiz. No. 2035, Thistles and orchids from "Russian Dance," horiz. No. 2036, Dancing mushrooms from "Chinese Dance," horiz.

1991, Dec. 31 *Perf. 13½x14, 14x13½*
2025 A436 1.70t multicolored .40 .25
2026 A436 2t multicolored .60 .25
2027 A436 2.30t multicolored .75 .25
2028 A436 2.60t multicolored 1.00 .25
2029 A436 4.20t multicolored 1.25 .40
2030 A436 10t multicolored 1.75 .50
2031 A436 15t multicolored 2.75 1.20
2032 A436 16t multicolored 3.00 1.20
Nos. 2025-2032 (8) 11.50 4.30

Souvenir Sheets

2033 A436 30t multicolored 7.50 7.50
2034 A436 30t multicolored 7.50 7.50
2035 A436 30t multicolored 7.50 7.50
2036 A436 30t multicolored 7.50 7.50

1992 Winter Olympics, Albertville — A437

60m, Speed skating, vert. 80m, Ski jumping, vert. 1t, Hockey, vert. 1.20t, Figure skating, vert. 1.50t, Biathlon. 2t, Downhill skiing. 2.40t, Two-man bobsled.
8t, Four-man bobsled, vert.

1992, Feb. 1 *Perf. 14*
2037 A437 60m multi .25 .25
2038 A437 80m multi .35 .25
2039 A437 1t multi .40 .25
2040 A437 1.20t multi .50 .25
2041 A437 1.50t multi .65 .25
2042 A437 2t multi .90 .25
2043 A437 2.40t multi 1.10 .25
Nos. 2037-2043 (7) 4.15 1.75

Souvenir Sheet

2044 A437 8t multi 4.00 2.50

Dogs — A438

Various breeds of dogs.

1991, Dec. 1 Litho. *Perf. 14*
2045 A438 20m multi .25 .25
2046 A438 30m multi, vert. .30 .25
2047 A438 40m multi, vert. .50 .25
2048 A438 50m multi .65 .30
2049 A438 60m multi .80 .40
2050 A438 80m multi .95 .50
2051 A438 1.20t multi 1.50 .70
Nos. 2045-2051 (7) 4.95 2.65

Souvenir Sheet

2052 A438 4t multi 5.00 5.00

Cats — A439

Various breeds of cats.

1991, Dec. 27
2053 A439 20m multi .25 .25
2054 A439 30m multi, vert. .30 .25
2055 A439 40m multi .50 .25
2056 A439 50m multi, vert. .65 .30
2057 A439 60m multi, vert. .80 .40
2058 A439 80m multi, vert. .95 .50
2059 A439 1.20t multi, vert. 1.50 .70
Nos. 2053-2059 (7) 4.95 2.65

Souvenir Sheet

2060 A439 4t multi 5.00 5.00

Alces Alces — A440

1992, May 1 Litho. *Perf. 14*
2061 A440 3t Male 1.00 .50
2062 A440 3t Two females 1.00 .50
2063 A440 3t One female, vert. 1.00 .50
2064 A440 3t Male's head, vert. 1.00 .50
Nos. 2061-2064 (4) 4.00 2.00

Souvenir Sheet

Ferdinand von Zeppelin (1838-1917), Airship Designer — A441

1992, May 1
2065 A441 16t multicolored 4.00 4.00

Souvenir Sheets

People and Events — A442

No. 2066, Pres. Punsalmaagiin Ochirbat visiting Pres. George Bush at White House. No. 2067, Mother Teresa helping poor in Calcutta. No. 2068, Pope John Paul II at mass. Nos. 2069-2070, Boy Scout blowing bugle.

1992, May 22 *Perf. 14x13½*
2066 A442 30t silver & multi 5.00 4.50

Perf. 14
2067 A442 30t silver & multi 5.00 4.50
2068 A442 30t silver & multi 5.00 4.50
2069 A442 30t silver & multi 5.00 4.50
2070 A442 30t silver & multi 5.00 4.50
Nos. 2066-2070 (5) 25.00 22.50

Nos. 2067-2070 each contain one 43x28mm stamp. Nos. 2069-2070 exist with gold inscription and border. No. 2069, 17th World Boy Scout Jamboree, Korea. No. 2070, 18th World Boy Scout Jamboree, Netherlands, 1995.

Souvenir Sheet

Discovery of America, 500th Anniv. — A443

Designs: a, Columbus. b, Sailing ship.

1992, May 22
2071 A443 30t Sheet of 2, #a.-b. 7.50 6.00

World Columbian Stamp Expo '92, Chicago, Genoa '92.

Miniature Sheets

Railways of the World — A444

Designs: No. 2072a, 3t, Tank locomotive, Darjeeling-Himalaya Railway, India. b, 3t, Royal Scot, Great Britain. c, 6t, Bridge on the River Kwai, Burma-Siam Railway. d, 6t, Baltic tank engine, Burma. e, 8t, Baldwin locomotive, Thailand. f, 8t, Western Railway locomotive, Pakistan. g, 16t, P.36 class locomotive, USSR. h, 16t, Shanghai-Beijing Express, China.
Orient Express: No. 2073a, 3t, 1931 Advertising poster. b, 3t, 1928 poster. c, 6t, Dawn departure. d, 6t, Golden Arrow departing Victoria Station. e, 8t, Waiting at station in Yugoslavia. f, 8t, Turn of the century picture of train. g, 16t, Fleche d'Or locomotive approaching Etaples, France. h, 16t, Arrival in Istanbul, Turkey.
No. 2074, New Tokaido line, Japan. No. 2075, TGV, France. No. 2076a, Emblem of Pullman Car Company. b, Emblem of Intl. Wagons-lits Company. No. 2077, Passengers waiting to board Orient Express.

1992, May 24
2072 A444 Sheet of 8, #a.-h. 12.00 9.00
2073 A444 Sheet of 8, #a.-h. 12.00 9.00

Souvenir Sheets

2074 A444 30t multicolored 6.00 5.00
2075 A444 30t multicolored 6.00 5.00
2076 A444 30t Sheet of 2, #a.-b. 12.00 11.00
2077 A444 30t black & gold 6.00 5.00

Nos. 2074-2075 contain one 58x42mm stamp.

Miniature Sheet

Birds — A445

Various birds: a, 3t. b, 3t, Owl. c, 6t, Gull, horiz. d, 6t, horiz. e, 8t. f, 8t, horiz. g, 16t. h, 16t, horiz.

1992, May 24

2078 A445 Sheet of 8, #a.-h. 15.00 10.00

Souvenir Sheet

Perf. 14x13½

2079 A445 30t Ducks, 30t in UR 4.50 4.50
2080 A445 30t Duck, 30t in LR 4.50 4.50

Nos. 2079-2080 contain one 50x38mm stamp.

Miniature Sheet

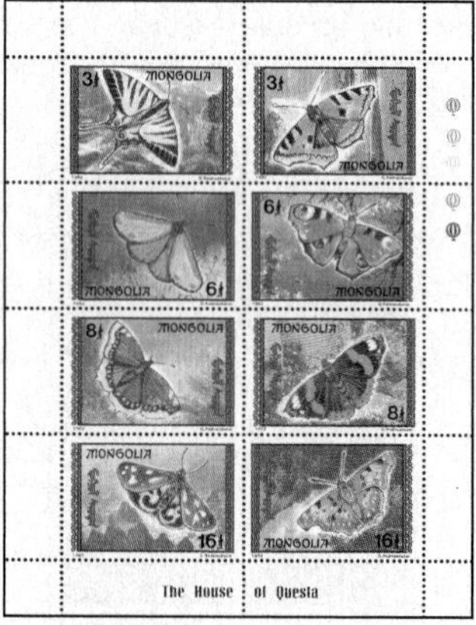

Butterflies and Moths — A446

Various butterflies or moths and: a, 3t, Mountains. b, 3t, Desert. c, 6t, Grass. d, 6t, Lake. e, 8t, Mountain, diff. f, 8t, Flowers. g, 16t, Rocks. h, 16t, Lake, diff.

1992, May 24 ***Perf. 14***

2081 A446 Sheet of 8, #a.-h. 15.00 10.00

Souvenir Sheet

Perf. 14x13½

2082 A446 30t pink & multi 6.00 5.00
2083 A446 30t blue & multi 6.00 5.00

Nos. 2082-2083 contain one 50x38mm stamp.

1992 Summer Olympics, Barcelona — A447

Designs: a, Gold medal. b, Torch.

1992, Jan. 22 **Litho.** ***Perf. 14***

2084 A447 30t Sheet of 2, #a.-b. 8.75 8.75

Souvenir Sheet

Genghis Khan — A448

1992, June 15 **Litho.** ***Perf. 14***

2085 A448 16t multicolored *20.00 20.00*

Mushrooms — A449

Designs: 20m, Marasmius oreades. 30m, Boletus luridus. 40m, Hygrophorus marzuelus. 50m, Cantharellus cibarius. 60m, Agaricus campester. 80m, Boletus aereus. 1.20t, Amanita caesarea. 2t, Tricholoma terreum. 4t, Mitrophora hybrida.

1991, June 18 **Litho.** ***Perf. 13***

2086	A449	20m	multicolored	.25	.25
2087	A449	30m	multicolored	.30	.25
2088	A449	40m	multicolored	.45	.25
2089	A449	50m	multicolored	.50	.25
2090	A449	60m	multicolored	.60	.30
2091	A449	80m	multicolored	.75	.40
2092	A449	1.20t	multicolored	1.10	.55
2093	A449	2t	multicolored	1.60	.80
			Nos. 2086-2093 (8)	5.55	3.05

Souvenir Sheet

2094 A449 4t multicolored 5.50 5.50

Dated 1990. No. 2094 contains one 32x40mm stamp.

Discovery of America, 500th Anniv. — A450

Columbus and: 3t, Two sailing ships. 7t, Natives approaching Santa Maria. 10t, Pinta. 16t, Santa Maria, vert. 30t, Santa Maria, diff. 40t, Santa Maria, dolphins. 50t, Nina.
#2102, Ship, vert. #2103, Portrait, vert.

1992, Aug. **Litho.** ***Perf. 14***

2095	A450	3t	multicolored	.25	.25
2096	A450	7t	multicolored	.50	.25
2097	A450	10t	multicolored	.75	.25
2098	A450	16t	multicolored	1.00	.30
2099	A450	30t	multicolored	1.75	.80
2100	A450	40t	multicolored	2.00	1.40
2101	A450	50t	multicolored	3.00	1.75
			Nos. 2095-2101 (7)	9.25	5.00

Souvenir Sheets

Perf. 13½x14

2102 A450 80t multicolored 5.00 5.00
2103 A450 80t multicolored 5.00 5.00

Nos. 2102-2103 each contain one 38x52mm stamp.

Miniature Sheet

Butterflies A451

#2104: a, 3t, Anthocharis cardamines. b. 8t, Inachis io. c, 10t, Fabriciana adippe. d, 16t, Limenitis reducta. e, 30t, Agrumaenia carniolica. f, 40t, Polyommatus icarus. g, 50t, Parnassius apollo. h, 60t, Saturnia pyri.
No. 2105, Limenitis populi. No. 2106, Heodes virgaureae.

1992, Dec. **Litho.** ***Perf. 14***

2104 A451 Sheet of 8, #a.-h. 12.00 11.00

Souvenir Sheets

Perf. 14x13½

2105 A451 80t multicolored 5.00 4.00
2106 A451 80t multicolored 5.00 4.00

Nos. 2105-2106 each contain one 51x38mm stamp.

1992 Summer Olympics, Barcelona — A452

1993, Jan. **Litho.** ***Perf. 13½***

2107	A452	3t	Long jump	.25	.25
2108	A452	6t	Pommel horse	.25	.25
2109	A452	8t	Boxing	.35	.25
2110	A452	16t	Wrestling	.35	.25
2111	A452	20t	Archery, vert.	.55	.25
2112	A452	30t	Cycling	.60	.25
2113	A452	40t	Equestrian	.70	.30
2114	A452	50t	High jump	.90	.30
2115	A452	60t	Weight lifting	1.10	.40
			Nos. 2107-2115 (9)	5.05	2.50

Souvenir Sheet

Perf. 15x14

2116 A452 80t Judo 4.00 3.50
2117 A452 80t Javelin 4.00 3.50

Nos. 2116-2117 contain one 40x30mm stamp.

Miniature Sheet

Birds A453

Designs: No. 2118a, 3t, Tetrae tetrix. b, 8t, Gallinula chloropus. c, 10t, Regulus satrapa. d, 16t, Alcede atthis. e, 30t, Gavia stellata. f, 40t, Ardes cinerea. g, 50t, Upupa epops. h, 60t, Niltava rubeculoides. No. 2119, Gyps fulvus. No. 2120, Podiceps cristatus.

1993, Feb. **Litho.** ***Perf. 14***

2118 A453 Sheet of 8, #a.-h. 11.00 10.00

Souvenir Sheets

Perf. 14x13½

2119 A453 80t multicolored 4.50 4.00
2120 A453 80t multicolored 4.50 4.00

Nos. 2119-2120 each contain one 51x38mm stamp.

Souvenir Sheets

Polska '93 — A454

#2121a, 2122, Copernicus. #2121b, Chopin. #2121c, 2123, Pope John Paul II.

1993, May 1 **Litho.** ***Perf. 13½x14***

2121 A454 30t Sheet of 3, #a.-c. 9.00 7.00
2122 A454 80t multicolored 8.00 7.00
2123 A454 80t multicolored 8.00 7.00
Nos. 2121-2123 (3) 25.00 21.00

Animals, Sports, & Transportation — A455

Designs in gold: No. 2124, Cats, dogs. No. 2125, Turtle, bee, wildcat, butterfly. No. 2126, Owl, butterfly, mushroom, dinosaur. Nos. 2127, Chessmen, archer, baseball player, wrestlers, horse and rider. Nos. 2128, Modern transportation.
No. 2129, Dinosaur, whales, butterflies. No. 2130, Mushroom, turtle, flowers.

1993, Jan. 5 **Embossed** ***Perf. 9***

2124-2128 A455 200t Set of 5 75.00 75.00

Nos. 2124-2128 exist in silver and in either gold or silver imperf. souvenir sheets of 1.

Embossed

1993, June 1 ***Perf. 8½x9***

Size: 79x53mm

2129 A455 200t silver 15.00 15.00

Souvenir Sheet

Imperf

Litho. & Embossed

2130 A455 200t gold 25.00 20.00

No. 2130, Topex '93, Madison, WI. No. 2129 exists in imperf. souvenir sheet of 1. No. 2130 exists in silver.

Souvenir Sheets

Taipei '93 — A456

1993, Aug. 14 **Litho.** ***Perf. 13½x14***

2137 A456 80t Genghis Khan *15.00*
2138 A456 80t Sun Yat-Sen *20.00*

Dirigible Flight Over Ulan Bator — A457

1993, Aug. 27 **Litho.** ***Perf. 14***

2139 A457 80t multicolored 3.00 3.00

No. 2139 has a holographic image. Soaking in water may affect the hologram.
Issued in sheets of 4

Buddhist Deities A458

Various statues and paintings.

1993, Oct. 3 *Perf. 13½x14*

2140	A458	50t multicolored	.35	.25
2141	A458	100t multicolored	.70	.30
2142	A458	150t multicolored	1.00	.50
2143	A458	200t multicolored	1.40	.65
a.		Miniature sheet of 4	5.25	5.25
		Nos. 2140-2143 (4)	3.45	1.70

Souvenir Sheet

2144	A458	300t multicolored	2.00	2.00

Bangkok '93.

Nos. 276 & 1084 Surcharged

1993 *Perfs., Etc. as Before*

2144A	A77	8t on 70m #276	*7.50*
2144B	A246	15t on 70m #1084	*15.00*

No. 2144A exists with double surcharge. The surcharge on No. 2144B exists with four different type fonts.

New Year 1994 (Year of the Dog) — A459

No. 2146, Stylized dog running, vert.

1994, Jan. 10 *Perf. 14x13½, 13½x14*

2145	A459	60t multicolored	3.00	.75
2146	A459	60t multicolored	3.00	.75

1994 World Cup Soccer Championships, U.S. — A460

Championship teams: #2147, Uruguay, 1930, 1950. #2148, Italy, 1954. #2149, Brazil, 1959. #2150, West Germany, 1954. #2151, Argentina, 1978, 1986. #2152, Italy, 1938. #2153, Brazil, 1962. #2154, West Germany, 1974. #2155, Brazil, 1970. #2156, Italy, 1982. #2157, West Germany, 1990.

1994, Jan. 15 *Perf. 14x13½*

2147	A460	150t multicolored	.70	.25
2148	A460	150t multicolored	.70	.25
2149	A460	150t multicolored	.70	.25
2150	A460	150t multicolored	.70	.25
2151	A460	150t multicolored	.70	.25
a.		Souv. sheet of 2, #2147, 2151	2.00	2.00
2152	A460	200t multicolored	.90	.40
2153	A460	200t multicolored	.90	.40
2154	A460	200t multicolored	.90	.40
2155	A460	250t multicolored	1.20	.55
a.		Souvenir sheet of 3, #2149, 2153, 2155	3.50	3.50
2156	A460	250t multicolored	1.20	.55
a.		Souvenir sheet of 3, #2148, 2152, 2156	3.50	3.50
2157	A460	250t multicolored	1.20	.55
a.		Souvenir sheet of 3, #2150, 2154, 2157	3.50	3.50
b.		Miniature sheet of 4, #2151, 2155-2157	5.50	6.25
		Nos. 2147-2157 (11)	9.80	4.10

Souvenir Sheet

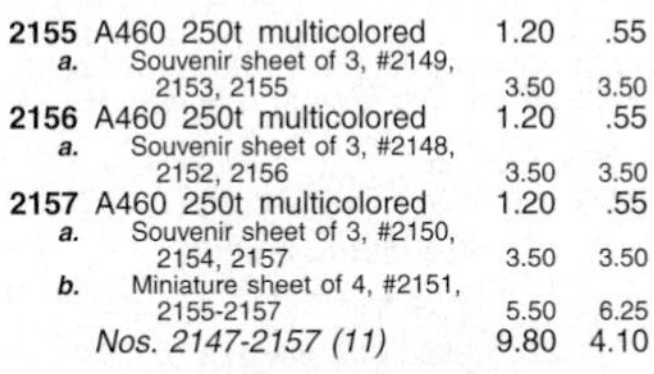

Punsalmaagiin Ochirbat, First President of Mongolia — A461

1994, Apr. 1 *Perf. 14*

2158	A461	150t multicolored	2.00	2.00

1994 Winter Olympics, Lillehammer A462

50t, Biathlon. 60t, Two-man bobsled. 80t, Slalom skiing. 100t, Ski jumping. 120t, Pairs figure skating. 200t, Speed skating.
400t, Ice hockey.

1994, Apr. 10 **Litho.** *Perf. 13½*

2159	A462	50t multi	.35	.25
2160	A462	60t multi	.45	.25
2161	A462	80t multi	.60	.40
2162	A462	100t multi	.75	.50
2163	A462	120t multi	.80	.55
2164	A462	200t multi	1.10	.90
		Nos. 2159-2164 (6)	4.05	2.85

Souvenir Sheet

2165	A462	400t multi	4.00	4.00

Souvenir Sheet

Dalai Lama, 1989 Nobel Peace Prize Winner — A463

1994, June 27 **Litho.** *Perf. 13½*

2166	A463	400t multicolored	*30.00*

Miniature Sheet of 18

Wildlife — A466

Designs: a, Brown raptor. b, Woodpecker. c, Cranes in flight. d, White raptor. e, Yellow bird on tree branch (i). f, Two birds flying left. g, Raptor perched on rock. h, Two birds flying right. i, Squirrel. j, Dragonfly (f). k, Water bird standing near pond (o). l, Duck in flight over pond. m, Brown bird. n, Ground hog. o, Ladybug on flower. p, Bird's eggs. q, Grasshopper (m). r, Butterfly.

1994, July 15

2169	A466	60t #a.-r. + 2 labels	10.00	7.00

First Manned Moon Landing, 25th Anniv. A467

No. 2170, Trans-lunar injection. No. 2171, Astronaut on moon. No. 2172, Space shuttle, earth. No. 2173, Astronaut, shuttle.

1994, July 20 **Litho.** *Perf. 13½*

2170	A467	200t multi	.90	.50
2171	A467	200t multi	.90	.50
2172	A467	200t multi	.90	.50
2173	A467	200t multi	.90	.50
a.		Miniature sheet of 4, #2170-2173	4.50	2.50
		Nos. 2170-2173 (4)	3.60	2.00

Singpex '94 — A468

1994, Aug. 31

2174	A468	300t Butterfly	1.50	1.00

Souvenir Sheet

2175	A468	400t Dog	*6.00*	*5.00*

New Year 1994 (Year of the Dog).

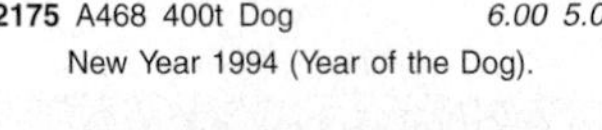

A469

PHILAKOREA '94 — A470

1994 **Litho.** *Perf. 14*

2176	A469	600t Korea #1749	2.50	.75
2177	A469	600t #433	2.50	.75
2178	A470	600t #1	2.50	.75
2179	A470	600t Korea #1	2.50	.75
		Nos. 2176-2179 (4)	10.00	3.00

Souvenir Sheets

Perf. 13½x14

2180	A470	400t #5	4.00	4.00

Perf. 14

2181	A469	600t Yong Sik Hong	4.50	4.00

First Mongolian Stamp, 70th anniv. (#2180). No. 2180 contains one 34x46mm stamp.
Issued: No. 2180, 11/23, others, 8/16.
For surcharges see #2247C-2247G.

Dinosaurs — A471

60t, Mammuthus, vert. 80t, Stegosaurus, vert. 100t, Talararus. 120t, Gorythosaurus. 200t, Tyrannosaurus.
400t, Triceratops.

1994, Nov. 30 *Perf. 14*

2182	A471	60t multi	.40	.25
2183	A471	80t multi	.50	.30
2184	A471	100t multi	.55	.40
2185	A471	120t multi	.75	.55
2186	A471	200t multi	1.10	.90
		Nos. 2182-2186 (5)	3.30	2.40

Souvenir Sheet

2187	A471	400t multi	*4.50*	*4.50*

Nos. 2182-2187 exist in imperf. sheets of 1.
No. 2182 is misspelled.

Mongolian-Japanese Friendship — A472

1994, Dec. 15 *Perf. 14x13½*

2188	A472	20t multicolored	*1.00*	.30

New Year 1995 (Year of the Boar) — A474

1995, Jan. 1 *Perf. 14x13½, 13½x14*

2190	A474	200t shown	.85	.30
2191	A474	200t Boar, diff, vert.	.85	.30

A475

Nos. 2192, 2192A, Flower. Nos. 2193, 2196-2197 Ram. Nos. 2194-2195, Airplane.

Litho. & Typo.

1994, July 25 *Perf. 15x14*

Denomination in Black

2192	A475	10t green	—	—
2192A	A475	10t grn, red denomination	—	—

2193 A475 18t magenta — —
2194 A475 22t blue — —
2195 A475 22t blue, red denomination — —
2196 A475 44t like #2193 — —
2197 A475 44t magenta, blue denomination — —

Dated 1993.
No. 2192A issued 1994(?).

Religious Masked Dancing — A476

Various masked dancers in traditional costumes.

1995, Feb. 25 Litho. *Perf. 14*

2201	A476 20t multicolored	.25	.25
2202	A476 50t multicolored	.30	.25
2203	A476 60t multicolored	.35	.25
2204	A476 100t multicolored	.60	.30
2205	A476 120t multicolored	.70	.30
2206	A476 150t multicolored	.85	.40
2207	A476 200t multicolored	1.10	.50
	Nos. 2201-2207 (7)	4.15	2.25

Souvenir Sheet

2208 A476 400t multicolored 4.00 4.00

Saiga Tatarica A477

1995, Mar. 30 Litho. *Perf. 14*

2209	A477 40t shown	.40	.25
2210	A477 55t Two adults	.50	.25
2211	A477 70t One running left	.60	.30
2212	A477 200t One up close	1.60	.80
a.	Block of 4, #2209-2212	3.50	3.50

World Wildlife Fund.

Souvenir Sheet

First Philately & Collections Fair, Hong Kong '95 — A478

Designs: a, Butterfly. b, Flowers.

1995, June 6 Litho. *Perf. 14*

2213 A478 200t Sheet of 2, #a.-b. + 2 labels 4.25 4.25

Goldfish — A479

Designs: 20t, Yellow oranda. 50t, Red and white wen-yu. 60t, Brown oranda with red head. 100t, Calico pearl-scale with phoenix tail. 120t, Red lion-head. 150t, Brown oranda. 200t, Red and white oranda with narial.
400t, White and gold unidentified fish.

1995, Sept. 1 Litho. *Perf. 14*

2214-2220 A479 Set of 7 *5.50 4.00*

Souvenir Sheet

2221 A479 400t multicolored *5.50 4.00*

No. 2221 contains one 50x38mm stamp.

Miniature Sheet

Motion Pictures, Cent. — A480

Various portraits of Marilyn Monroe (1926-62): No. 2222a, 60t. b, 80t. c, 100t. d, 120t. e, 150t. f, 200t. g, 250t. h, 300t. i, 350t.
No. 2223, In white-collared blouse. No. 2224, With lion. No. 2225, In black lace dress. No. 2226, In scene from movie, Niagara.

1995, Oct. 20

2222 A480 Sheet of 9, #a.-i. 8.50 7.00

Souvenir Sheets

2223	A480 200t multi	4.50	4.50
2224-2226	A480 300t each	4.50	4.50

Miniature Sheet

UN, 50th Anniv. — A481

Exterior views of UN complexes, Secretaries General: a, Trygve Lie. b, Dag Hammarskjold. c, U Thant. d, Kurt Waldheim. e, Jose Perez de Cuellar. f, Boutros Boutros-Ghali.

1995, Oct. 15

2227 A481 60t Sheet of 6, #a.-f. 6.50 5.00

Miniature Sheet

Elvis Presley (1935-77) — A482

Various portaits: No. 2228a, 60t. b, 80t. c, 100t. d, 120t. e, 150t. f, 200t. g, 250t. h, 300t. i, 350t.

No. 2229, Wearing yellow sweater. No. 2230, With dancing girl. No. 2231, With guitar. No. 2232, In army uniform, wife Priscilla.

1995, Oct. 20

2228 A482 Sheet of 9, #a.-i. 9.00 8.00

Souvenir Sheets

2229	A482 200t multi	5.00	5.00
2230	A482 300t multi	5.00	5.00
2231-2232	A482 400t each	6.50	5.00

Miniature Sheet

X-Men Comic Characters — A483

Designs: No. 2233a, 30t, Bishop. b, 50t, Beast. c, 60t, Rogue. d, 70t, Gambit. e, 80t, Cyclops. f, 100t, Storm. g, 200t, Professor X. h, 250t, Wolverine.
No. 2234: a, Wolverine, horiz. b, Magneto, horiz.

1995, Sept. 15

2233 A483 Sheet of 8, #a.-h. 3.50 3.00

Souvenir Sheet of 2

2234 A483 250t #a.-b. 3.50 3.00

New Year 1996 (Year of the Rat) A484

1996, Jan. 1 Litho. *Perf. 14*

2235	A484 150t Rat, diff., vert.	1.00	.60
2236	A484 200t shown	1.50	.85

CHINA '96 — A485

Designs: a, Monument of Sukhe Bator. b, Temple of Heaven, Beijing. c, Migjed Jang-Rasek. d, Great Wall.

1996, Apr. 25 Litho. *Perf. 13½x14*

2237 A485 65t Sheet of 4, #a.-d. *10.00 10.00*

1996 Summer Olympic Games, Atlanta A486

30t, Cycling. 60t, Women's shooting. 80t, Weight lifting. 100t, Boxing. 120t, Women's archery, vert. 150t, Rhythmic gymnastics, vert. 200t, Hurdles, vert. 350t, Equestrian. 400t, Wrestling.
500t, Basketball. 600t, Judo.

1996 Litho. *Perf. 14*

2238	A486 30t multicolored	.25	.25
2239	A486 60t multicolored	.25	.25
2240	A486 80t multicolored	.25	.25
2241	A486 100t multicolored	.30	.25
2242	A486 120t multicolored	.30	.25
2243	A486 150t multicolored	.40	.25
2244	A486 200t multicolored	.50	.30
2245	A486 350t multicolored	1.00	.70
2246	A486 400t multicolored	1.10	.80
	Nos. 2238-2246 (9)	4.35	3.30

Souvenir Sheets

2246A	A486 500t multicolored	3.50	2.50
2246B	A486 600t multicolored	4.00	4.00

No. 2246A contains one 37x53mm stamp, No. 2246B one 52x39mm stamp.
Olymphilex '96 (#2246A-2246B).

Mongolian postal authorities have declared as "unauthorized" two sheets of nine 350t Train stamps similar to Nos. 2442-2443, two souvenir sheets of one 2000t Train stamps similar to Nos. 2444-2445, and one sheet of six 300t Ferrari stamps similar to No. 2446.

Genghis Khan — A486a

Die Cut Perf. 7½

1996, Aug. 28 Embossed

Self-Adhesive

2246C A486a 10,000t gold *60.00 60.00*

CAPEX '96 — A487

Designs: a, 350t, #2. b, 400t, Canada #1.

1996 Litho. *Perf. 12½*

2247 A487 Sheet of 2, #a.-b. 8.00 8.00

No. 2247b is 40x30mm. No. 2247 exists with blue at upper right margin corner and different colored margin picture of CN Tower.

Nos. 2176-2179, 2181 Overprinted

1996, Sept. 8 Litho. *Perf. 14*

2247C	A469 600t On #2176	2.50	2.50
2247D	A469 600t On #2177	2.50	2.50
2247E	A470 600t On #2178	2.50	2.50
2247F	A470 600t On #2179	2.50	2.50
	Nos. 2247C-2247F (4)	10.00	10.00

Souvenir Sheet

2247G A469 600t On No. 2181 4.00 4.00

Mongolian National Democratic and Social Democratic Parties
A487a

1996, Sept. 25 Litho. *Perf. 13¾*
2247H A487a 100t multicolored .60 .50

Souvenir Sheet

Taipei '96 — A487b

1996, Oct. 21 Litho. *Perf. 12¾*
2247I A487b 750t multicolored 5.00 5.00
r. Overprinted "Taipei 2005" in margin in silver 5.00 5.00

No. 2247Ir issued 8/19/2005.

Children & Scouting Emblem — A487c

1996, Dec. 16 Litho. *Perf. 14*

Country Flags

2247J A487c 250t Mongolia 1.50 .40
2247K A487c 250t US 1.50 .40
2247L A487c 250t Germany 1.50 .40
2247M A487c 250t Russia 1.50 .40
2247N A487c 250t Japan 1.50 .40
2247O A487c 250t PRC 1.50 .40
q. Souvenir sheet, #2247J-2247O 15.00 15.00
Nos. 2247J-2247O (6) 9.00 2.40

Souvenir Sheet

Perf. 12¾x12¾

2247P A487c 700t No flag 4.25 4.25

UNICEF (#2247P).

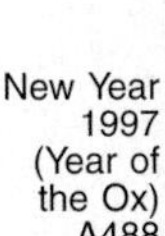

New Year 1997 (Year of the Ox)
A488

1997 Litho. *Perf. 14*
2248 A488 300t Ox, vert. 1.25 1.00
2249 A488 350t shown 1.50 1.25

Souvenir Sheet

Total Solar Eclipse Over Mongolia, Mar. 9, 1997 — A489

1997 Litho. *Perf. 12½*
2250 A489 1000t Map of Mongolia 5.00 4.75

Return of Hong Kong to China
A490

Designs: 200t, Former Chinese Pres. Deng Xioaping, Queen Elizabeth II. 250t, Chinese Pres. Jiang Zemin and Chief Executive of the Special Administrative Region of Hong Kong, Tung Chee-hwa.

1997 Litho. *Perf. 13½*
2251 A490 200t multicolored 1.00 1.00
2252 A490 250t multicolored 1.50 1.50
a. Pair, #2251-2252 2.50 2.50

Seven Joys — A491

Designs: a, Wheel. b, Gem. c, Minister. d, Queen. e, Elephant. f, Horse. g, General.

1997 Litho. *Perf. 11*
2253 A491 200t Sheet of 7, #a.-g., + 2 labels 6.00 6.00

Souvenir Sheet

Moscow '97 — A492

1997 *Perf. 12½x11½*
2254 A492 1000t No. 264 5.00 5.00
a. With Irkutsk 2007 emblem and inscirption added in sheet margin ('07) 1.75 1.75

No. 2254a issued 6/8/2007.

Monument to the Politically Repressed
A493

1997 *Perf. 13x13½*
2255 A493 150t black & gray .95 .60

Trains
A493a

Designs: 20t, VL-80 electric locomotive. 40t, Japanese high speed electric train. 120t, BL-80 Diesel locomotive. 200t, German steam locomotive. 300t, Lass "FDp" steam locomotive. 350t, 0-6-0 tank locomotive. 400t, Diesel locomotive. 500t, T6-106 Diesel locomotive. 600t, Magnetic train.

No. 2255K, "Rocket." No. 2255L, London-Paris train.

1997, Dec. 5 Litho. *Perf. 14x14¼*
2255A A493a 20t multi .45 .25
2255B A493a 40t multi .55 .25
2255C A493a 120t multi .65 .25
2255D A493a 200t multi .85 .30
2255E A493a 300t multi .90 .40
2255F A493a 350t multi 1.00 .60
2255G A493a 400t multi 1.25 .70
2255H A493a 500t multi 1.40 .75
2255I A493a 600t multi 1.75 1.00
j. Sheet of 9, #2255A-2255I 11.00 11.00
Nos. 2255A-2255I (9) 8.80 4.50

Souvenir Sheets

Perf. 11¼

2255K A493a 800t multi 3.75 2.50
2255L A493a 800t multi 3.75 2.50

Nos. 2255K, 2255L each contain one 59x43mm stamp.

Emperors of Mongolia
A494

a, Genghis Khan. b, Ogadai Khan. c, Guyuk Khan. d, Mangu Khan. e, Kublai Khan.

Perf. 11½x12½

1997, Dec. 25 Litho.
2256 A494 1000t Strip of 5, #a.-e. 20.00 20.00

Nos. 2256a-2256e exist in souvenir sheets containing 1 or 2 21x33mm stamps.

New Year 1998 (Year of the Tiger)
A495

Various stylized tigers.

1998, Feb. 1 *Perf. 12*
2257 A495 150t multicolored 1.00 1.00
2258 A495 200t multicolored 1.50 1.50
2259 A495 300t multicolored 2.00 2.00
Nos. 2257-2259 (3) 4.50 4.50

Design on No. 2259 is oriented point down.

Mongolian Yaks
A496

Various yaks: 20t, Three. 30t, One white. 50t, With carts. 100t, One male. 150t, Female with calf. 200t, Three, campsite. 300t, One with horns, flowing hair. 400t, Brown yak looking back.

800t, Carrying children and supplies.

1998, Mar. 15 Litho. *Perf. 12*
2260 A496 20t multicolored .25 .25
2261 A496 30t multicolored .25 .25
2262 A496 50t multicolored .25 .25
2263 A496 100t multicolored .35 .35
2264 A496 150t multicolored .55 .55
2265 A496 200t multicolored .75 .75

Size: 50x36mm

2266 A496 300t multicolored 1.10 1.10
2267 A496 400t multicolored 1.50 1.50
Nos. 2260-2267 (8) 5.00 5.00

Souvenir Sheet

Perf. 11

2268 A496 800t multicolored 5.50 5.50

No. 2268 contains one 60x47mm stamp.

Butterflies and Orchids — A497

Designs: 100t, Adonis blue, dendrobium cunninghamii. 150t, Brown hairstreak, oncidium ampliatum. 200t, Large skipper, maxillaria triloris. 250t, Orange tip, calypso bulbosa. 300t, Painted lady, catasetum pileatum. 350t, Purple hairstreak, epidedrum fimbratum. 400t, Red admiral, cleistes rosea. 450t, Small copper, ponthieva maculata. 500t, Small tortoiseshell, cypripeium calceolus.

Each 800t: No. 2278, Red admiral, c. macranthum. No. 2279, Adonis blue, c. guttatum.

1997, Dec. 5 Litho. *Perf. 14*
2269-2277 A497 Set of 9 5.50 3.50

Souvenir Sheets

2278-2279 A497 Set of 2 8.50 5.00

Souvenir Sheet

1998 World Cup Soccer Championships, France — A498

1998, June 1 *Perf. 13*
2280 A498 1000t multicolored 5.00 5.00

Souvenir Sheet

Pres. Natsagyn Bagabandi — A499

1998, July 15 Litho. *Perf. 12½*

2281 A499 1000t multicolored 4.00 3.50

Greenpeace, 26th Anniv. — A500

Designs: 200t, Penguin in snow. 400t, Six penguins, water, mountain. 500t, Two penguins at water's edge. 800t, Large group of penguins.

No. 2286: a, like #2282. b. like #2283. c, like #2284. d, like #2285. e, like #2287.

1000t, Greenpeace ship.

1997, Sept. 15 Litho. *Perf. 13½*

2282-2285 A500 Set of 4 6.25 6.25
2286 A500 Sheet of 5, #a.-e. 7.00 7.00

Souvenir Sheet

2287 A500 1000t multicolored 6.00 6.00

Country name, denominations, "Greenpeace" in red on No. 2286. Nos. 2282-2287 exist imperf.

Diana, Princess of Wales (1961-97) A501

Various portraits with bister background — #2288: a, 50t. b, 100t. c, 150t, d, 200t. e, 250t. f, 300t. g, 350t. h, 400t. i, 450t.

Various portraits with pale brown background — #2289a, 50t. b. 100t. c, 150t. d, 200t. e, 250t. f, 300t. g, 350t. h, 400t. i, 450t.

Each 1000t: No. 2290, Diana holding infant son. No. 2291, Diana wearing tiara. No. 2292, Diana in pink dress. No. 2293, Diana in white (Mother Teresa in margin).

1997, Dec. 15 Sheets of 9, #a-i

2288-2289 A501 Set of 2 12.00 12.00

Souvenir Sheets

2290-2293 A501 Set of 4 14.00 14.00

Nos. 2288-2289 exist imperf.

Genghis Khan's Soldiers A502

Various soldiers in traditional attire, background color: 100t, tan. 150t, pale violet. 200t, green blue. 250t, green. 300t, gray. 350t, pink. 400t, blue. 600t, pale brown.

Army on the march — #2302: a, 600t, One standing, others on horses. b, 1000t, Leaders riding decorated horses. c, 600t, Two standing, leopards, others on horses.

1997, Dec. 20 *Perf. 12*

2294-2301 A502 Set of 8 8.50 8.50

Souvenir Sheet

2302 A502 Sheet of 3, #a.-c. 8.50 8.50

No. 2302b is 65x56mm.

No. 276 Surcharged

1996, Dec. 25 Photo. *Perf. 11½x12*

2302D A77 200t on 70m multi *10.00 5.00*

National Symbols — A503

1998, Jan. 1

2303 A503 300t Natl. flag, horiz. .90 .75
2304 A503 300t shown .90 .75

Ursus Arctos Gobiensis A504

100t, Adult looking forward. 150t, Adult walking left. 200t, Two bears. 250t, Mother, cubs.

1998, July 20

2305-2308 A504 Set of 4 7.00 7.00
2307a Sheet of 2, #2305, 2307 3.00 3.00
2308a Sheet of 2, #2306, 2308 4.00 4.00

Fish A505

Designs: 20t, Lebistes reticulatus. 30t, Goldfish. 50t, Balistes conspicillum. 100t, Goldfish, diff. 150t, Synchirops splendidus. 200t, Auratus. 300t, Xiphophorus helleri. 400t, Pygoplites diacanthus. 600t, Chaetodon auriga.

Various fish, denomination (800t): No. 2318, At top. No. 2319, At bottom.

1998, July 20 *Perf. 12½*

2309-2317 A505 Set of 9 6.00 6.00

Souvenir Sheets

Perf. 11

2318-2319 A505 Set of 2 12.00 12.00

Nos. 2318-2319 each contain one 95x49mm stamp.

Domestic Cats A506

Designs: 50t, Red Persian. 100t, Manx cat. 150t, Smoke Persian. 200t, Long-haired white Persian. 250t, Silver tabby. 300t, Siamese.

1000t, Kittens, basket.

1998, Sept. 1 *Perf. 12*

2320-2325 A506 Set of 6 5.00 5.00

Souvenir Sheet

2326 A506 1000t multicolored 5.00 5.00

Jerry Garcia (1942-95) and The Grateful Dead A507

Nos. 2327-2328, Various portraits of Jerry Garcia.

No. 2328A — Black and white photos: f, 100t. g, 150t. h, 50t.

No. 2328B — Blue guitar: i, 150t. j, 200t. k, 100t.

No. 2328C — Red guitar: l, 200t. m, 250t. n, 150t.

No. 2328D — White guitar: o, 200t. p, 250t. q, 150t.

No. 2328E — Dark background: r, 300t. s, 350t. t, 250t.

No. 2329: Various portraits of Garcia: a, 50t. b, 100t. c, 150t. d, 200t. e, 250t. f, 300t. g, 350t. h, 400t. i, 450t.

No. 2330: Various pictures of bears (Grateful Dead emblem) in sports activities: a, 50t, Dirt biking. b, 100t, Soccer. c, 150t, Basketball. d, 200t, Golf. e, 250t, Baseball. f, 300t, Roller blading. g, 350t, Ice hockey. h, 400t, Football. i, 450t, Skiing.

Each 1000t: No. 2331, Garcia holding guitar. No. 2331A, Garcia with left hand on guitar, right hand in air.

1998-99 *Perf. 12½*

2327 A507 100t multicolored 1.00 .50
2328 A507 200t multicolored 1.00 .50

Strips of 3

2328A-2328E A507 Set of 5 9.00 9.00

Sheets of 9, #a-i

2329-2330M A507 Set of 2 11.50 11.50

Souvenir Sheets

2331-2331A A507 Set of 2 5.00 5.00

Nos. 2327-2328 were each issued in sheets of 9. Nos. 2331-2331A contain one 51x76mm.

Dot of "I" in Garcia is a diamond on Nos. 2327-2329, 2331-2331A. "Jerry Garcia" is in pink letters with rose shadowing on Nos. 2328A-2328E.

Issued: No. 2331A, 1/1/99; #2328A-2328E, 1999; others 10/15/98.

See Nos. 2385-2389.

Bob Marley (1947-81) A508

Portraits: 200t, Up close. 1000t, At microphone.

1998, Oct. 15

2332 A508 200t multicolored 1.25 1.25

Souvenir Sheet

2333 A508 1000t multicolored 3.00 3.00

No. 2332 was issued in sheets of 9. No. 2333 contains one 51x76mm stamp.

Carlos Santana A509

1998, Oct. 15

2334 A509 200t multicolored 1.50 1.50

No. 2334 was issued in sheets of 9.

The Three Stooges — A510

Scenes from "The Three Stooges" motion pictures — #2335: a, 50t, Guns, cigars. b, 100t, Road signs. c, 150t, Dynamite. d, 200t, Golf clubs. e, 240t, Medals on uniform. f, 300t, Dove. g, 350t, Flower bouquets. h, 400t, Bright green cap. i. 450t, Whisk broom, cigar.

No. 2336: a, 50t, Doctor's equipment. b, 100t, Musical instruments. c, 150t, Clothes press. d, 200t, Long cord. e, 250t, Vise. f, 300t, Brick wall. g, 350t, Pliers. h, 400t, Turkey. i, 450t, Door.

No. 2337: a, 50t, Union soldiers. b, 100t, French Foreign Legion. c, 150t, Confederate soldiers, women. d, 200t, Horse. e, 250t, Army uniform, grenade. f, 300t, Cannon. g, 350t, Confederate soldiers, whiskey flask. 400t, Army uniforms, officer. 450t, Scarecrow.

Each 800t: No. 2338, like #2335b. No. 2339, like #2336c, vert. No. 2340, With football.

1998, Nov. 25 Litho. *Perf. 13½*

Sheets of 9, #a-i.

2335-2337 A510 Set of 3 22.50 22.50

Souvenir Sheets

2338-2340 A510 Set of 3 9.00 9.00

Nos. 2335-2340 exist imperf. Nos. 2338-2340 each contain one 51x41mm stamp.

Eight Offerings of Buddha — A511

#2341, The White Sign of Luck. #2342, The Auspicious Wheel. #2343, The Auspicious Cup. #2344, The White Couch. #2345, The White Umbrella. #2346, The Duaz of Victory. #2347, The White Lotus. #2348, The Auspicious Fish.

1998, Dec. 10 Litho. *Perf. 12*

2341-2348 A511 200t Set of 8 5.00 5.00

Howdy Doody Television Show — A512

No. 2349: a, 50t, Chief Thunderthud. b, 100t, Princess Summerfall Winterspring. c, 150t, Howdy in Mexican outfit. d, 150t, Buffalo Bob in gray shirt, Howdy. e, 200t, Buffalo Bob in red and white shirt, Howdy. f, 250t, Howdy, Buffalo Bob rubbing noses. g, 450t, Howdy in military uniform. h, 250t, Clarabell the Clown. i, 450t, Howdy lying down.

Each 800t: No. 2350, Howdy. No. 2351, Buffalo Bob, Howdy, horiz. No. 2352, Howdy, Buffalo Bob.

Perf. 13½x14, 14x13½x14

1999, Apr. 1

2349 A512 Sheet of 9, #a.-i. 6.00 6.00

Souvenir Sheets

Perf. 14 (#2352)

2350-2352 A512 Set of 3 8.00 8.00

No. 2352 contains one 48x61mm stamp.

Prime Ministers of Mongolia — A513

a, T. Namnansuren. b, Badamdorj. c, D. Chagdarjav. d, D. Bodoo. e, S. Damdinbazar. f, B. Tserendorj. g, A. Amar. h, Ts. Jigjidjav. i, P. Genden. j, Kh. Ghoibalsan. k, Yu. Tsedenbal. l, J. Batmunkh. m, D. Sodnom. n, Sh. Gungaadorj. o, D. Byambasuren. p, P. Jasrai. q, M. Enkhsaikhan. r, Ts. Elbegdorj.

1998, Dec. 1 ***Perf. 12***

2353 A513 200t Sheet of 18, #a.-r. 15.00 15.00

Natl. Wrestling Champions A514

Designs: a, D. Damdin. b, S. Batsuury. c, J. Munkhbat. d, H. Bayanmunkh. e, B. Tubdendorj. f, D. Tserentogtokh. g, B. Baterdne.

1998, Dec. 26 ***Perf. 12½***

2354 A514 200t Sheet of 7, #a.-g. 7.00 7.00

John Glenn's Return to Space A515

Mercury Friendship 7 — #2355: a, 50t, Mercury capsule in outer space. b, 100t, NASA emblem. c, 150t, Friendship 7 mission patch. d, 150t, Launch of Friendship 7. e, 200t, Glenn, 1962. f, 250th, Recovery of capsule. g, 450t, Moon. h, 250t, Capsule re-entering atmosphere. i, 450t, Stars.

Shuttle Discovery mission — #2356: a, 50t, NASA emblem. b, 100t, Glenn in red launch suit. c, 150t, Discovery mission patch. d, 150t, Launch of Discovery. e, 200t, Glenn, 1998. f, 250t, Discovery landing. g, 450t, Sun. h, 250t, Discovery in outer space. i, 450t, NASA "40" emblem.

Sheets of 9

1998, Dec. 31 ***Perf. 14***

2355-2356 A515 #a.-i., each 11.00 11.00

Postal Delivery — A516

Post office: a, 100t, Brown. b, 200t, Blue. c, 200t, Blue green. d, 400t, Red lilac. e, 400t, Violet.

Electronic services: f, 100t, Blue. g, 200t, Blue green. h, 200t, Red lilac. i, 400t, Violet. j, 400t, Brown.

EMS delivery: k, 100t, Blue green. l, 200t, Red lilac. m, 200t, Violet. n, 400t, Brown. o, 400t, Blue.

Mail train: p, 100t, Red lilac. q, 200t, Violet. r, 200t, Brown. s, 400t, Blue. t, 400t, Blue green.

Jet plane: u, 100t, Violet. v, 200t, Brown. w, 200t, Blue. x, 400t, Blue green. y, 400t, Red lilac.

1998, Nov. 15 ***Perf. 12***

2357 A516 Sheet of 25, #a.-y. 22.50 22.50

Universal Declaration of Human Rights, 50th Anniv. — A517

1998, Dec. 25 Litho. ***Perf. 12***

2358 A517 450t multi + label 3.50 3.50

New Year 1999 (Year of the Rabbit) A518

1999, Feb. 17

2359 A518 250t Rabbit, vert. 2.00 2.00

2360 A518 300t shown 2.00 2.00

Buddha Migjed Jankraisig, Ulan Bator A519

Designs: 200t, Temple.

Each 1000t: No. 2363, Statue. No. 2364, Statue, drawing of Temple.

1999, Apr. 15

2361 A519 200t multicolored 1.00 1.00

2362 A519 400t multicolored 2.00 2.00

Souvenir Sheets

Perf. 11

2363-2364 A519 Set of 2 8.00 8.00

Nos. 2363-2364 each contain one 49x106mm stamp.

Falcons — A520

Falcon: a, 300t, Subbuteo. b, 250t, Naumanni. c, 200t, Tinnunculus. d, 170t, Peregrinus. e, 800t, Rusticolus by nest. f, 600t, Rusticolus in flight. g, 400t, Pelegrinoides over kill. h, 350t, Pelegrinoides on branch. i, 150t, Columbarius. j, 100t, Vespertinus. k, 50t, Cherrug. l, 30t, Amurensis.

1999, Mar. 20 ***Perf. 12***

2365 A520 Sheet of 12, #a.-l. 12.00 12.00

"I Love Lucy" Television Show — A521

Various scenes — #2366: a, 50t. b, 100t. c, 150t. d, 150t. e, 200t. f, 250t. g, 450t. h, 250t. i, 450t.

Each 800t: No. 2367, Lucy talking with woman. No. 2368, Ethel looking at Lucy locked in cold storage locker.

1999, July 15 Litho. ***Perf. 13½x14***

2366 A521 250t Sheet of 9, #a.-i. 6.00 6.00

Souvenir Sheets

2367-2368 A521 Set of 2 5.50 5.50

Nos. 2367-2368 each contain one 38x51mm stamp.

Betty Boop Cartoon Character A522

Various pictures of Betty Boop — #2369: a, 50t. b, 100t. c, 150t. d, 150t. e, 200t. f, 250t. g, 450t. h, 250t. i, 450t.

Each 800t: No. 2370, Betty in dog's eyes, horiz. No. 2371, Up close, horiz.

1999, July 15

2369 A522 Sheet of 9, #a.-i. 6.00 6.00

Souvenir Sheets

Perf. 14x13½

2370-2371 A522 Set of 2 4.75 4.75

Nos. 2370-2371 each contain one 51x38mm stamp.

Folk Tales A523

Designs: 50t, Man, yurt, two demons. 150t, Chess players. 200t, Lion carrying logs. 250t, Flying horse. 300t, Archer, bird, sun. 450t, Horses, cranes.

1000t, Birds, camel in flight.

1999, June 15 Litho. ***Perf. 13x13¼***

2372-2377 A523 Set of 6 7.00 7.00

Souvenir Sheet

Perf. 12½

2378 A523 1000t multicolored 7.00 7.00

No. 2378 contains one 41x32mm stamp.

No. 307 Surcharged

Methods and Perfs as Before

1999, June 15

2378A A84 810t on 60m bl & multi *16.00 16.00*

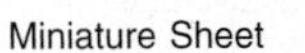

Miniature Sheet

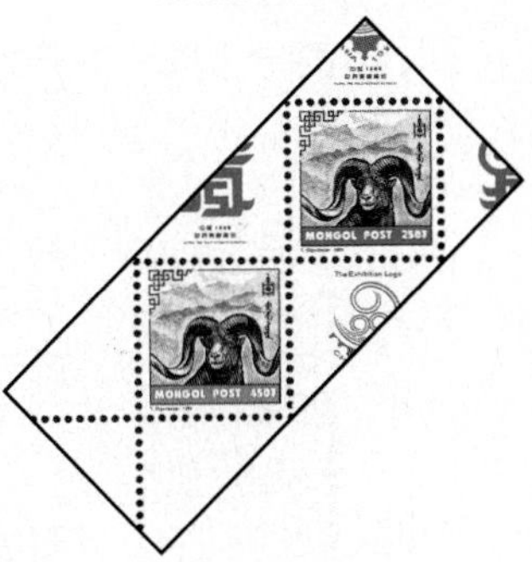

Ram — A524

Panel color: a, 250t, Blue. b, 450t, Red.

1999, Aug. 21 Litho. ***Perf. 12½***

2379 A524 Miniature sheet of 2, #a.-b. 2.00 2.00

China 1999 World Philatelic Exhibition. No. 2379 is cut from a larger sheet of alternating stamps and labels. The cutting is through the labels along the diagonal axes.

UPU, 125th Anniv. — A525

Designs: No. 2380, Rider, two horses. No. 2381, Rider, one horse. No. 2382, Train and truck. No. 2382, Airplane and computer.

800t, Ogodei Khan (1186-1241).

1999, Oct. 9

2380-2383 A525 250t Set of 4 4.00 4.00

Souvenir Sheet

2384 A525 800t multi 4.50 4.50

No. 2384 contains one 31x41mm stamp.

Nos. 551, 1742 Surcharged

Methods and Perfs. as Before

1999, Aug. 25

2384A A133 250t on 50m multi 10.00 10.00

2384B A389 250t on 60m multi 10.00 10.00

Victory in Khalkh-gol War, 60th anniv.

Genghis Khan A525a

Die Cut Perf. 11½

1999, Sept. 27 Embossed

Self-Adhesive

2384C A525a 15,000t gold & sil 60.00 —

Jerry Garcia Type of 1998

No. 2385 — Rose and blue speckled background: a, 50t. b, 100t. c, 150t.

No. 2386 — Pink-toned vignette extension backgrounds: a, 100t. b, 150t. c, 200t.

No. 2387 — Pink, blue and purple curved line backgrounds: a, 150t. b, 200t. c, 250t.

No. 2388 — Dark blue and purple straight line backgrounds: a, 150t. b, 200t, c, 250t.

No. 2389 — Blue green and green backgrounds: a, 250t. b, 300t. c, 350t.

1999 Litho. *Perf. 12½*

"Jerry Garcia" In Black-Shadowed Letters

2385-2389 A507 Set of 5 strips of 3 9.00 9.00

Stone Carvings A526

Designs: 50t, Stele with Uigur inscriptions, vert. 150t, Turtle, 13th cent. 200t, Kul Tegin burial site, 7th-8th cent., vert. 250t, Kul Tegin, 8th cent., vert. 300t, Dragon, 8th-9th cent. 450t, Man, 5th-7th cent., vert.

2000, Jan. 17 Litho. *Perf. 12*

2390-2395 A526 Set of 6 5.00 5.00

A527

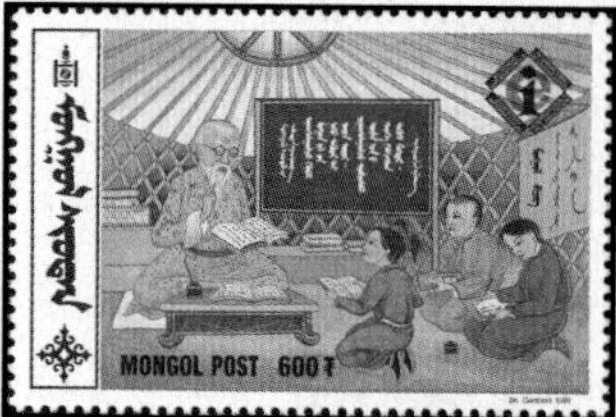

World Teachers' Day — A528

Academicians: #2396, 2398, Dr. Tsendiin Damdinsuren (1908-86). #2397, 2399, Dr. B. Rinchin (1905-77).

1999, Dec. 5

2396	A527	250t blue & blk	.50	.50
2397	A527	250t grn & blk	.50	.50
2398	A527	450t pur & blk	.85	.85
2399	A527	450t brn & blk	.85	.85
2400	A528	600t multi	1.10	1.10
		Nos. 2396-2400 (5)	3.80	3.80

Souvenir Sheet

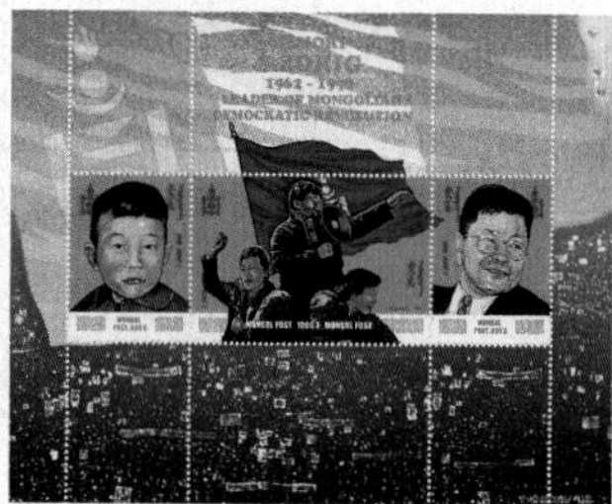

Sanjaasuregin Zorig (1962-98), Politician — A529

Designs: a, 600t, Zorig in 1968. b, 1000t, Three people, flag. c, 600t, Zorig in 1998.

1999, Oct. 1 *Perf. 13¼x13*

2401 A529 Sheet of 3, #a.-c. 5.50 5.50

Size of No. 2401b: 59x39mm.

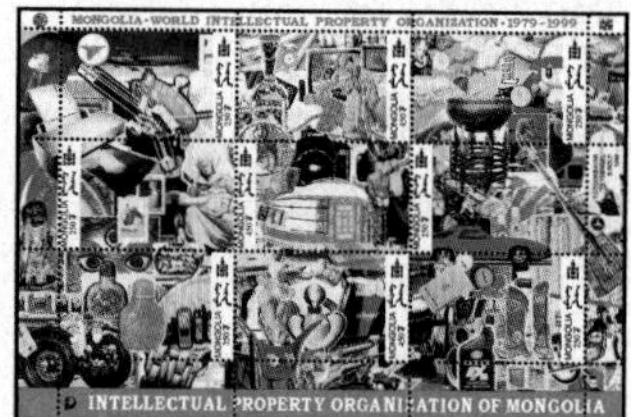

World Intellectual Property Organization, 20th Anniv. — A529a

No. 2401D: e, 250t, Satellite, airplane. f, 450t, Statue, television. g, 250t, Cauldron, toy. h, 250t, Copier, stamps. i, 450t, Camera, yurt, Mongolian couple. j, 250t, Red automobile. k, 250t, Grille of antique auto, bottles, cellular phones, wristwatch. l, 450t, Perfume bottles. m, 250t, Pack of cigarettes, soccer ball, volley ball, basketball, bottle of motor oil, boom box.

1999, Dec. 24 Litho. *Perf. 12*

2401D A529a Sheet of 9, #e-m 8.00 8.00

Souvenir Sheet

Japan-Mongolia Friendship — A530

a, Sumo wrestler. b, Symbols of countries.

1999, Dec. 28 *Perf. 13½*

2402 A530 450t Sheet of 2, #a.-b. 4.50 4.50

New Year 2000 (Year of the Dragon) — A531

Background color: 250t, Red. 450t, Blue, vert.

2000, Jan. 10 Litho. *Perf. 12*

2403-2404 A531 Set of 2 4.00 4.00

For overprint, see Nos. 2733-2734.

Nos. 715-717, C34 Surcharged

Methods and Perfs as Before

2000, Jan. 19

2405	A168	1000t on 50m brn	7.00	7.00
2406	A168	2000t on 60m grn	8.00	8.00
2407	A168	5000t on 1t rose claret	15.00	15.00
2408	AP12	10,000t on 1.50t bl	30.00	30.00
		Nos. 2405-2408 (4)	60.00	60.00

Wolves — A532

Designs: 150t, Pair, one with snout up. 250t, Eating deer. 300t, Nursing young. 450t, Snarling.

2000, Jan. 17 Litho. *Perf. 12*

2409-2412 A532 Set of 4 4.00 4.00

Souvenir Sheet

2413 A532 800t Pair baying 4.00 4.00

No. 2413 contains one 50x30mm stamp.

Sheep — A533

Breeds: 50t, Sumber. 100t, Orkhon. 150t, Baidrag. 250t, Barga. 400t, Uzemchin. 450t, Bayad.

2000, Jan. 20

2414-2419 A533 Set of 6 4.00 4.00

Souvenir Sheet

2420 A533 800t Govi-Altai 4.00 4.00

One Day of Mongolia, by Balduugiin Sharav — A534

Various parts of painting: a, 50t. b, 100t, c, 150t. d, 200t. e, 250t. f, 300t. g, 350t. h, 450t. i, 600t.

2000, Jan. 24

2421 A534 Sheet of 9, #a-i 9.00 9.00

Huts and Yurts A535

Designs: 50t, Hunters returning to hut. 100t, Mother, daughter, animals near hut. 150t, Yurt near hill. 250t, Two yurts, motorcycle, and satellite dish. 450t, Yurt construction.

No. 2427, 800t, Yurt's furnishings. No. 2428, 800t, Yurt and wagon.

2000, Jan. 25

2422-2426 A535 Set of 5 4.00 4.00

Souvenir Sheets

2427-2428 A535 Set of 2 8.00 8.00

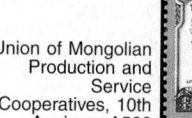

Union of Mongolian Production and Service Cooperatives, 10th Anniv. — A536

Panel colors: 300t, Blue. 450t, Green.

2000, Mar. 27 *Perf. 12*

2429-2430 A536 Set of 2 4.00 4.00

A537

A538

A539

A540

A541

A542

A543

Costumes of Mongolian Lords — A544

2000, May 11 ***Perf. 13¼***

2431	A537 550t multi	1.50	1.00
2432	A538 550t multi	1.50	1.00
2433	A539 550t multi	1.50	1.00
2434	A540 550t multi	1.50	1.00
2435	A541 550t multi	1.50	1.00
2436	A542 550t multi	1.50	1.00
2437	A543 550t multi	1.50	1.00
2438	A544 550t multi	1.50	1.00
	Nos. 2431-2438 (8)	12.00	8.00

Buddhas A545

No. 2439: a, Jigjid. b, Gombo. c, Tsamba. d, Jamsran. e, Baldanlkham. f, Ochirvani. g, Namsrai. h, Gongor. i, Damdinchoijoo. j, Shalshi.

2000, July 1 ***Perf. 13x13½***

2439	Block of 10	15.00	11.00
a.-j.	A545 550t Any single	1.50	1.10

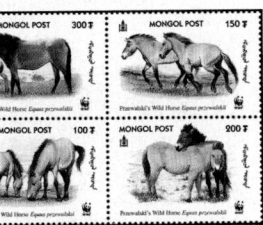

Worldwide Fund for Nature (WWF) — A546

Two Przewalski's horses: No. 2440a, 300t, No. 2441a, 100t, Standing apart. No. 2440b, 150t, No. 2441b, 250t, Galloping. No. 2440c, 100t, No. 2441d, 200t, Grazing. No. 2440d, 200t, No. 2441c, 50t, Standing together.

2000, July 5 **Litho.** ***Perf. 13½***

2440	A546 Block or strip of 4, #a-d	4.50	4.50

Litho. & Holography

Size: 50x35mm

2441	A546 Block of 4, #a-d	5.50	5.50

Illustrations on No. 2441 are mirror images of those on No. 2440.

Trains — A547

No. 2442: a, 200t, Guaari-Current electric locomotive, France. b, 400t, 2-10-0 Austerity, Great Britain. c, 300t, ALG Bo-Bo electric locomotive, Great Britain. d, 400t, Diesel-electric locomotive, Australia. e, 300t, E-10 Bo-Bo electric locomotive, Germany. f, 200t, C38 Class Pacific, US. g, 300t, 46 Class electric locomotive, US. h, 200t, Bo-Bo electric locomotive, New Zealand. i, 400t, Bo-Bo electric locomotive, Netherlands.

No. 2443: a, 300t, Italian second-clas carriage. b, 400t, Bodmin & Wadebridge Railway composite carriage. c, 200t, Stephenson 2-2-2, Russia. d, 200t, 2-2-2 Walt, US. e, 300t, The General, US. f, 400t, 4-4-0 Washington, US. g, 400t, Braithwaite 0-4-0, Great Britain. h, 200t, Ross Winans Muddigger locomotive, US. i, 300t, 4-4-0 Ramapo, US.

No. 2444, 800t, The Ringmaster, US. No. 2445, 800t, Deltic electric locomotive, Great Britain.

2000, July 7 **Litho.** ***Perf. 14***

Sheets of 9, #a-i

2442-2443	A547 Set of 2	13.00	13.00

Souvenir Sheets

2444-2445	A547 Set of 2	8.00	8.00

Ferrari Race Cars — A548

No. 2446: a, 1975 312 T. b, 1961 156 F1. c, 1979 312 T4. d, 1964 158 F1. e, 1981 126 CK. f, 1974 312 B3.

2000, July 15

2446	A548 350t Sheet of 6, #a-f	16.00	16.00

2000 Summer Olympics, Sydney A549

Designs: 100t, Boxing. 200t, Wrestling. 300t, Judo. 400t, Shooting.

2000, July 21 ***Perf. 13x13¼***

2447-2450	A549 Set of 4	4.00	4.00

Albert Einstein (1879-1955) — A550

Einstein: a, 100t, At blackboard. b, 300t, Wearing hat. c, 200t, Wearing green sweater. d, 200t, With violin. e, 550t, Close-up. f, 100t, At lectern. g, 100t, Holding pipe. h, 400t, Receiving award. i, 300t, Holding clock.

2000, Aug. 10 ***Perf. 12½***

2451	A550 Sheet of 9, #a-i	7.50	7.50

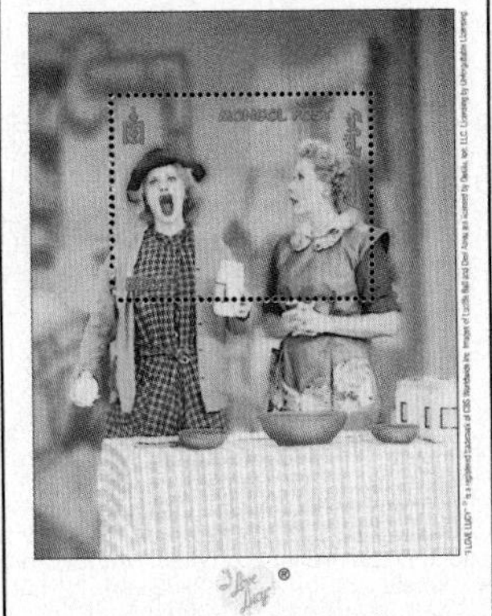
I Love Lucy — A551

No. 2452, vert.: a, 100t, Lucy, wiping hands, and Ethel. b, 400t, Lucy, reading letter, and Ethel. c, 200t, Lucy, setting table, and Fred. d, 200t, Lucy on telephone. e, 300t, Lucy with chin on fist. f, 100t, Lucy with head on hands. g, 100t, Lucy and Ethel waving. h, 550t, Lucy, holding bowl, and Ethel. i, 300t, Lucy, wearing brown sweater and holding jar, and Ethel.

No. 2453, 800t, Lucy, with mouth open, holding jar, and Ethel. No. 2454, 800t, Lucy, wearing stole, and Ethel.

2000, Aug. 15 **Litho.** ***Perf. 12½***

2452	A551 Sheet of 9, #a-i	4.00	4.00

Souvenir Sheets

2453-2454	A551 Set of 2	3.00	3.00

The Three Stooges — A552

No. 2455, horiz.: a, 100t, Moe, Larry and woman. b, 400t, Moe, Shemp and Larry attempting jail escape. c, 300t, Moe, with blow torch, Shemp and Larry. d, 200t, Moe, Larry and Joe Besser with musical instruments. e, 300t, Man knocking together heads of Shemp, Larry and Moe. f, 100t, Man with hammer, Moe, Larry and Shemp. g, 100t, Larry, Joe Besser and Moe in kitchen. h, 550t, Moe, Shemp and Larry with large wrench. i, 200t, Larry, Moe and Shemp in kitchen.

No. 2456, 800t, Moe, with fingers in ears, and Shemp. No. 2457, 800t, Shemp and Larry in army uniforms.

2000, Aug. 17

2455	A552 Sheet of 9, #a-i	8.00	8.00

Souvenir Sheets

2456-2457	A552 Set of 2	3.00	3.00

20th Century Events in Mongolia — A553

No. 2458: a, Independence, 1911. b, National revolution, 1921. c, Declaration of Mongolian People's Republic, 1924. d, Political repression, 1937. e, War years, 1939-45. f, Voting for independence, 1945. g, Agricultural reform, 1959. h, Member of UN, 1961. i, Space flight, 1981. j, Democratic revolution, 1990.

2000, Sept. 13 **Litho.** ***Perf. 13½x13***

2458	A553 300t Sheet of 10, #a-j + 2 labels	8.00	8.00

See No. 2482.

Marmota Sidisica — A554

Number of marmots: 100t, One. 200t, Three. 300t, Two. 400t, Three, diff.

2000, Sept. 15 ***Perf. 13¼x13***

2459-2462	A554 Set of 4	6.00	6.00

Souvenir Sheet

Perf. 13x13¼

2463	A554 800t One marmot, horiz.	5.50	5.50

Traditional Patterns — A555

Various designs: 50t, 200t, 250t, 300t, 400t, 550t.
50t, 250t, 550t are horiz.

Perf. 13¼x13, 13x13¼

2000, Sept. 20
2464-2469 A555 Set of 6 10.00 10.00

John F. Kennedy, Jr. (1960-99) — A556

2000, Sept. 25 ***Perf. 14***
2470 A556 300t multi 1.50 1.50

Printed in sheets of 6.

Millennium — A557

Exploration: a, 100t, Charles Darwin. b, 200t, Mollusk. c, 300t, HMS Beagle. d, 400t, Peacock. e, 400t, Dinosaur. f, 100t, Clematis. g, 200t, Orchid. h, 300t, Giant tortoise. i, 200t, Reduviid bug. j, 100t, Down House. k, 300t, Duck. l, 550t, The Origin of Species. m, 100t, Chimpanzee. n, 300t, Turkey. o, 550t, Horse. p, 600t, Ram (60x40mm). q, Vormela peregusna.

2000, Oct. 5 ***Perf. 12¾x12½***
2471 A557 Sheet of 17, #a-q + label 17.00 17.00

State Symbols — A558

No. 2472: a, Headdress on spike. b, Horn. c, Bow, arrows and quiver. d, Robe. e, Crossed swords. f, Saddle. g, Belt. h, Seated man. i, Throne.

2000, Oct. 25 Litho. ***Perf. 12***
2472 A558 300t Sheet of 9, #a-i 15.00 15.00

Queens — A559

No. 2473: a, Oulen. b, Borteujin. c, Turakana. d, Caymish. e, Chinbay.

2000, Oct. 30
2473 Horiz. strip of 5 7.50 7.50
a.-e. A559 300t Any single 1.50 1.50

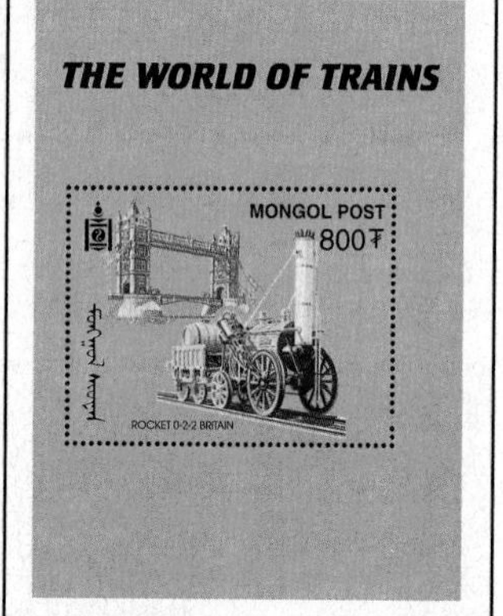

Trains — A560

No. 2474: a, 200t, TGV, France. b, 100t, X200, Sweden. c, 300t, Regio Runner, Netherlands. d, 100t, Deltic, Great Britain. e, 300t, Type M1200, Burma. f, 200t, ICE, Germany. g, 300t, G Class, Australia. h, 200t, Class E444, Italy. i, 100t, GM F7 Warbonnet, US.

No. 2475: a, 200t, Class 18 4-6-2, Germany. b, 100t, Class GS-4 4-8-4, US. c, 300t, Class 25 4-8-4, South Africa. d, 100t, Class 685 2-6-2, Italy. e, 300t, Class HP, India. f, 200t, Class SY 2-8-2, China. g, 300t, Liner A3 Pacific, Great Britain. h, 200t, Class 231C 4-6-2, France. i, 100t, Class 3700, Netherlands.

No. 2476, 800t, Rocket 0-2-2, Great Britain. No. 2477, 800t, Eurostar, France and Great Britain, vert.

2000, Nov. 25 ***Perf. 14***

Sheets of 9, #a-i

2474-2475 A560 Set of 2 13.50 13.50

Souvenir Sheets

2476-2477 A560 Set of 2 9.00 9.00

Nos. 2474-2475 each contain nine 42x28mm stamps.

Endangered Animals of Gobi Desert — A561

No. 2478: a, 100t, Scarabaeus typhon (40x30mm). b, 400t, Ursus arctos gobiensis (40x40mm). c, 300t, Camelus bactrianus ferus (40x40mm). d, 300t, Saiga tatarica mongolica (40x40mm). e, 550t, Ovis ammon (40x40mm). f, 550t, Uncia uncia (40x40mm). g, 100t, Phrynosephalus helioscopus(40x30mm). h, 200t, Coliber spinalus (40x30mm). i, 200t, Euchoreutes paso (40x30mm). j, 300t, Chlamydotis undulata (40x40mm).

2000, Dec. 25 ***Perf. 12½***
2478 A561 Sheet of 10, #a-j 15.00 15.00

Souvenir Sheet

Advent of New Millennium — A562

Litho. & Embossed with Foil Application

2001, Jan. 1 ***Perf. 13½***
2479 A562 5000t multi 15.00 15.00

New Year 2001 (Year of the Snake) — A563

Color behind snake: 300t, Pink. 400t, green, vert.

2001, Jan. 15 Litho. ***Perf. 13¼***
2480-2481 A563 Set of 2 4.00 4.00

20th Century Events Type of 2000

World events: a, First World War, 1914. b, October Revolution, 1917. c, Power seized by Fascists, 1933. d, Second World War, 1939. e, Nuclear weapons, 1945. f, Establishment of the United Nations, 1945. g, End of colonialism, 1940. h, Space travel, 1961. i, Downfall of socialism, 1989. j, Establishment of Mongolia, 1911.

2001, Mar. 15 ***Perf. 13½x13***
2482 A553 300t Sheet of 10, #a-j, + 2 labels 8.00 8.00

Armed Forces, 80th Anniv. — A564

Designs: No. 2483, 300t, Marshal G. Demid (blue green). No. 2484, 300t, Marshal J. Lhagvasuren (dark green). No. 2485, 300t, L. Dandar (olive green).

2001, Mar. 18 ***Perf. 13¾x13¼***
2483-2485 A564 Set of 3 3.00 3.00

Souvenir Sheet

Mountaineers — A565

No. 2486: a, Mountaineer waving. b, Mountaineers starting climb.

2001, Apr. 1 ***Perf. 13¼x13***
2486 A565 400t Sheet of 2, #a-b 4.00 4.00

I Love Lucy — A566

No. 2487, horiz.: a, 100t, Lucy drinking from cup, Ricky reading newspaper. b, 400t, Ricky and Fred. c, 300t, Lucy, Ethel and two candy factory workers. d, 200t, Lucy with arms outstretched, candy factory worker. e, 300t, Lucy looking at candy factory worker. f, 100t, Lucy smearing chocolate on worker's face. g, 100t, Worker smearing Lucy's face with chocolate. h, 550t, Ricky holding stocking, Fred. i, 200t, Ethel and Lucy.

No. 2488, 800t, Lucy wrapping chocolates. No. 2489, 800t, Fred and Ricky preparing dinner.

2001, Apr. 15 ***Perf. 12½***
2487 A566 Sheet of 9, #a-i 7.00 7.00

Souvenir Sheets

2488-2489 A566 Set of 2 3.00 3.00

The Three Stooges — A567

No. 2490: a, 100t, Larry. b, 400t, Larry and Shemp inserting instrument into man's mouth. c, 300t, Moe and Shemp. d, 200t, Moe, Larry and Shemp on telephones. e, 300t, Moe with chef's toque, Shemp, Larry. f, 100t, Moe looking in tube. g, 100t, Moe hitting Larry, Shemp. h, 550t, Shemp, Larry, Moe and woman. i, 200t, Moe with gavel, Curly on telephone.

No. 2491, 800t, Shemp and Larry as shown on #2490e. No. 2492, 800t, Shemp as angel, vert.

2001, Apr. 15
2490 A567 Sheet of 9, #a-i 7.00 7.00

Souvenir Sheets

2491-2492 A567 Set of 2 3.00 3.00

Philatelic Exhibitions — A568

Nomading, by T.S. Minjuur and exhibition emblem of: a, Hong Kong 2001. b, Hafnia 01. c, Phila Nippon '01. d, Belgica 2001.

2001, May 15 ***Perf. 13½***
2493 A568 400t Sheet of 4, #a-d 4.00 4.00

Souvenir Sheet

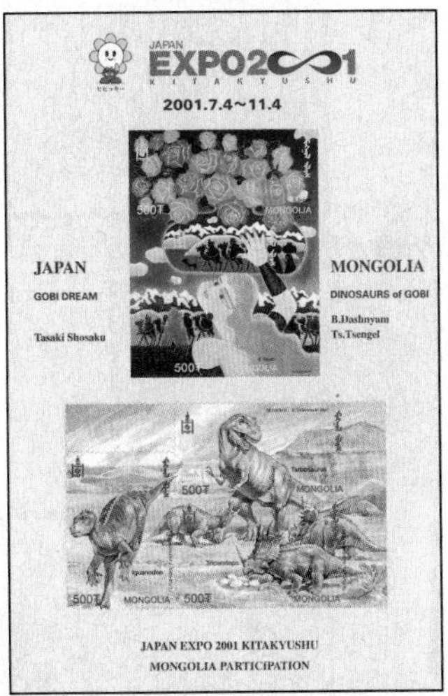

Expo 2001, Kitakyushu, Japan — A569

No. 2494: a, Roses from Gobi Dream, by Shosaku Tasaki (52x24mm). b, Dreamer from Gobi Dream, vert. (32x42mm). c, Tarbosaurus (48x25mm). d, Iguanodon, vert. (30x41mm). e, Triceratops (48x25mm).

Serpentine Die Cut 10¾, 12¼ (#2494c-2494e)

2001, July 1

Self-Adhesive

2494 A569 500t Sheet of 5, #a-e 9.00 9.00

Children and Sports — A570

No. 2495: a, Chess. b, Bicycling. c, Baseball.

No. 2496: a, 200t, Mongolian children on horses. b, 350t, Ice hockey. c, 500t, Flag, Mongolian boy on horse. d, 150t, Children playing soccer. e, 300t, Mongolian girl on horse. f, 450t, Boy playing soccer. g, 100t, Mongolian children on horses. h, 250t, Golf. i, 400t, Mongolian children on horses.

2001, Sept. 1 ***Perf. 12½***

2495 A570 500t Horiz. strip of 3, #a-c 4.00 4.00
2496 A570 Sheet of 9, #a-i 12.00 12.00

Scouting and Nature — A571

No. 2497: a, 100t, Salpingotus. b, 200t, Uncia uncia. c, 300t, Haliaeetus albicilla. d, 400t, Pandion haliatus. e, 450t, Panciawus colchicus.

No. 2498: a, 50t, Butterfly. b, 100t, Bat. c, 200t, Butterfly, diff. d, 300t, Mushrooms. e, 400t, Dinosaur. f, 450t, Puffin.

No. 2499, vert.: a, 150t, Sea shell. b, 300t, Owl. c, 450t, Sea turtle. d, 100t, Frog. e, 250t, Butterfly. f, 400t, Orchid. g, 50t, Penguins. h, 200t, Elephant. i, 350t, Whale.

2001, Sept. 1

2497 A571 Sheet of 5, #a-e, + label 5.00 5.00
2498 A571 Sheet of 6, #a-f 5.00 5.00
2499 A571 Sheet of 9, #a-i 7.50 7.50

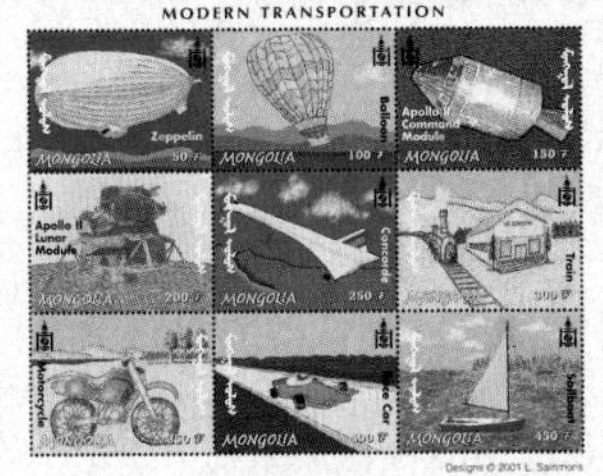

Modern Transportation — A572

No. 2500: a, 50t, Zeppelin. b, 100t, Balloon. c, 150t, Apollo 11 command module. d, 200t, Apollo Lunar Module. e, 250t, Concorde. f, 300t, Train. g, 350t, Motorcycle. h, 400t, Race car. i, 450t, Sailboat.

2001, Sept. 15

2500 A572 Sheet of 9, #a-i 7.50 7.50

Admission to United Nations, 40th Anniv. — A573

No. 2501: a, Dove, map. b, UN and Mongolian flags.

2001, Oct. 27 ***Perf. 13***

2501 A573 400t Horiz. pair, #a-b 3.00 3.00

Year of Dialogue Among Civilizations A574

2001, Dec. 20 ***Perf. 13¼x13***

2502 A574 300t multi 2.50 2.50

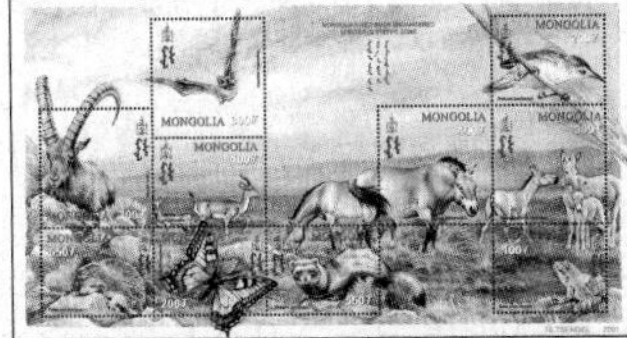

Endangered Species in Steppe Zone — A575

No. 2503: a, 300t, Vespertilio superans (40x40mm). b, 200t, Podoces hendersoni (40x30mm). c, 300t, Capra sibirica (40x40mm). d, 100t, Gazella subgutturosa (40x30mm). e, 400t, Equus przewalskii (40x40mm). f, 300t, Equus hemionus hemionus (40x40mm). g, 550t, Erinaceus dauricus (40x30mm). h, 200t, Papilio machaon (40x30mm). i, 550t, Vormela peregusna (40x30mm). j, 100t, Rana chensinensis (40x30mm).

2001, Dec. 30 ***Perf. 13½x13¼***

2503 A575 Sheet of 10, #a-j 10.00 10.00

History of Humanity — A576

Prominent features of stamps: a, Leaning Tower of Pisa, Romulus and Remus suckling she-wolf. b, Eagle, warrior with shield. c, Great Wall of China. d, Mosque, warrior on horseback. e, Celtic cross, castle, warrior with shield. f, Mona Lisa, by Leonardo da Vinci, David, by Michelangelo, other sculptures and religious paintings. g, Mask, Easter Island statues, boomerang, native, hut. h, Sir Isaac Newton, telescope, planets, Nicolaus Copernicus. i, Eiffel tower, Napoleon bonaparte on horseback, French flag, Arc de Triomphe. j, Astronaut, Earth, DNA molecule, computer. k, Greek soldier and amphora. l, Taj Mahal, Asoka pillar. m, Statue of Buddha. n, Genghis Khan. o, Yurt, Buddhist statue. p, Jesus Christ, Madonna and Child. q, Globe, ship, Christopher Columbus. r, Statue of Liberty, U.S. Capitol, Indian chief, U.S. flag, George Washington, city skyline. s, Printing press, man on horseback, letters of alphabet. t, Tower Bridge, British flag, Penny Black.

2001, Dec. 30 ***Perf. 13¼***

2504 Sheet of 20 20.00 20.00
a.-j. A576 200t Any single 1.00 1.00
k.-t. A576 300t Any single 1.00 1.00

New Year 2002 (Year of the Horse) A577

Mane color: 300t, Gray, vert. 400t, Yellow brown.

2002, Feb. 13 ***Perf. 13¼x13, 13x13¼***

2505-2506 A577 Set of 2 4.00 4.00

Birds of Prey — A578

Designs: 100t, Gyps himalayensis. 150t, Gyps fulvus. 300t, Neophron percnopterus. 400t, Aegypius monachus. 550t, Gypaetus barbatus.

2002, Apr. 1 ***Perf. 12½***

2507-2511 A578 Set of 5 5.00 5.00

Souvenir Sheets

Mongolia - Japan Diplomatic Relations, 30th Anniv. — A579

No. 2512, 550t: a, Camel. b, Przewalski's horse.

No. 2513, 550t, vert. (38x50mm): a, Rider on horseback. b, Face of cartoon character.

2002, Apr. 27 ***Perf. 12***

2512-2513 A579 Set of 2 8.00 8.00

Dogs A580

Dogs with: 100t, Sheep. 200t, Cattle. 300t, Camel and yurt. 400t, Camels. 800t, Dog.

2002, May 1 ***Perf. 13¼x13***

2514-2517 A580 Set of 4 4.00 4.00

Souvenir Sheet

2518 A580 800t multi 3.50 3.50

2002 World Cup Soccer Championships, Japan and Korea — A581

No. 2519: a, 300t, Stadium, Seoul. b, 400t, 1998 French team and flag, World Cup trophy. c, 400t, 1966 English team and flag, Jules Rimet Cup. d, 300t, Stadium, Yokohama.

2002, May 31 ***Perf. 12***

2519 A581 Sheet of 4, #a-d 4.50 4.50

Flowers — A582

Designs: 100t, Thermopsis. No. 2521, 150t, Chelidonium. No. 2522, 150t, Hypencum. 200t, Plantago. 250t, Saussurea. 300t, Rosa acicularis. 450t, Lilium.

2002, June 15 **Litho.** ***Perf. 12***

2520-2526 A582 Set of 7 7.00 7.00

Rock Paintings — A583

Various paintings with background colors of: 50t, Pink. 100t, Beige. 150t, Greenish blue. 200t, Green. 300t, Blue. 400t, Blue. 800t, Dark blue.

2002, July 1

2527-2532 A583 Set of 6 6.00 6.00

Souvenir Sheet

2533 A583 800t multi 3.50 3.50

New Year 2003 (Year of the Sheep) — A584

Sheep with background colors of: 300t, Yellow. 400t, Green, horiz.

2003, Jan. 1

2534-2535 A584 Set of 2 4.00 4.00

Mushrooms and Birds A585

Designs: 50t, Russula aeruginosa, Coccothraustes coccothraustes. 100t, Boletus edulis, Loxia curvirostra. 150t, Boletus badius, Carpodacus erythrinus. 200t, Agaricus campester, Garrulus glandarius. 250t, Marasmius onreades, Luscinia megarhynchos. 300t, Cantharellus cibarius, Locustella certhiola. 400t, Amanita phalloides, Ardea cinerea. 550t, Suillus granulatus, Accipter gentilis.

No. 2544, 800t, Lactarius tormmosus, Aeqithalos caudatus. No. 2545, 800t, Tricholoma pertentosum, Lanius collurio.

2003, Feb. 1 ***Perf. 13¼x13***
2536-2543 A585 Set of 8 12.00 12.00

Souvenir Sheets

2544-2545 A585 Set of 2 12.00 12.00

Nos. 2544-2545 each contain one 60x40mm stamp.

Visit Mongolia — A586

No. 2546: a, 100t, Statue of Sukhe Bator. b, 200t, City buildings. c, 300t, Rock formation. d, 400t, Yurts.

No. 2547: a, 100t, Camels. b, 200t, Yaks. c, 300t, Hunter with eagle. d, 400t, Snow leopard.

2003, July 11 ***Perf. 12***

Sheets of 4, #a-d

2546-2547 A586 Set of 2 8.00 8.00

Endangered Species in Khangai Zone — A587

No. 2548: a, 300t, Pandion haliaetus (40x30mm). b, 200t, Dryomys nitedula (40x30mm) c, 300t, Rangifer tarandus (40x40mm). d, 100t, Moschus moschiferus (40x40mm). e, 550t, Alces alces pfizenmayeri (40x40mm). f, 400t, Alces alces cameloides (40x40mm). g, 300t, Sus scrofa nigripes (40x40mm). h, 550t, Phasianus colchicus (40x30mm). i, 200t, Lutra lutra (40x30mm). j, 100t, Castor fiber birulai (40x30mm).

2003, Aug. 15 ***Perf. 13½***
2548 A587 Sheet of 10, #a-j 10.00 10.00

Birds, Butterflies, Orchids and Mushrooms — A588

No. 2549, 800t — Birds: a, Common bush tanager. b, Black-headed hemispingus. c, Scarlet-rumped tanager. d, Band-tailed seedeater.

No. 2550, 800t — Butterflies: a, Thecla teresina. b, Theritas cypria. c, Theritas coronata. d, Thecla phaleros.

No. 2551, 800t — Orchids: a, Vanda rothschildiana. b, Paphiopedium parishii. c, Dendrobium nobile. d, Cattleya loddigesii.

No. 2552, 800t — Mushrooms: a, Hypholoma fasciculare. b, Marasmiellus ramealis. c, Collybia fusipes. d, Kuehneromyces mutabilis.

No. 2553, 2500t, Andean hillstar. No. 2554, 2500t, Thecla pedusa. No. 2555, 2500t, Barkeria skinnerii. No. 2556, 2500t, Psathyrella multipedata, vert.

Perf. 13¼x13½, 13½x13¼
2003, Dec. 10

Sheets of 4, #a-d

2549-2552 A588 Set of 4 20.00 20.00

Souvenir Sheets

2553-2556 A588 Set of 4 16.00 16.00

Souvenir Sheet

Yang Liwei, First Chinese Astronaut — A589

2003, Dec. 25 **Litho.** ***Perf. 12***
2557 A589 800t multi 4.00 4.00

New Year 2004 (Year of the Monkey) — A590

Monkey and background in: 300t, Blue. 400t, Red.

2004, Feb. 21
2558-2559 A590 Set of 2 4.00 4.00

"Peace MANDALA" in MONGOLIA 2004

No.7188/9999

Peace Mandala — A591

No. 2560: a, 50t, Tushita Heaven. b, 100t, Elephant and Lady Maya. c, 150t, Birth of Buddha. d, 200t, Buddha as prince of Shakya clan. e, 250t, Prince shaving off hair. f, 300t, Buddha beating the devil. g, 400t, Buddha preaching for first time. h, 550t, Great Nirvana Sutra. i, 5000t, Various scenes in Buddha's life.

No. 2561, Central details of No. 2560i.

Size of Nos. 2560a-2560h, 41x38mm; No. 2560i, 132x182mm.

Serpentine Die Cut 10, 6¾ (#2560i, 2561)

2004, June 3 **Litho.**

Self-Adhesive

2560 A591 Sheet of 9, #a-i 18.00 18.00

Souvenir Sheet

Litho. With Foil Application

2561 A591 5000t gold & brn 20.00 20.00

Mammals — A592

Designs: (100t), Equus przewalskii. (300t), Camelus bactrianus ferus. (400t), Ovis ammon. (550t), Capra sibirica.

2004, July 1 **Litho.** ***Perf. 13¼x13***

2562	A592 (100t) multi	.50	.50
2563	A592 (300t) multi	.75	.75
2564	A592 (400t) multi	1.25	1.25
2565	A592 (550t) multi	1.50	1.50
	Nos. 2562-2565 (4)	4.00	4.00

Genghis Khan (c. 1162-1227) — A593

Various depictions of Genghis Khan: 200t, 300t, 350t, 550t. 300t is horiz.

2004, July 11 ***Perf. 13***
2566-2569 A593 Set of 4 4.00 4.00

Unification of Mongolia, 800th anniv. (in 2006).

2004 Summer Olympics, Athens — A594

Designs: 100t, Judo. 200t, Wrestling, horiz. 300t, Boxing. 400t, Pistol shooting, horiz.

2004, Aug. 13 ***Perf. 12***
2570-2573 A594 Set of 4 4.00 4.00

UPU, 130th Anniv. — A595

2004, Sept. 15 ***Perf. 12¾***
2574 A595 300t multi 1.50 1.50

Nos. 776, 778, 841, 842 Surcharged

Methods and Perfs as Before

2004, Oct. 5

2575	A191 550t on 10m #841	—	—
2576	A191 550t on 20m #842	—	—
2577	A178 550t on 30m #776	—	—
2578	A178 550t on 60m #778	—	—

A596

A597

A598

Soccer A599

Designs: No. 2581, Goalie making save. No. 2582, Player kicking ball. No. 2583, Three players. No. 2584, Player and goalie.

2004, Oct. 15 **Litho.** ***Perf. 12¾x13***

2579	A596 50t multi	.25	.25
2580	A597 50t multi	.25	.25
2581	A597 100t multi	.40	.40
2582	A597 100t multi	.40	.40
2583	A597 150t multi	.55	.55
2584	A597 150t multi	.55	.55
2585	A598 200t multi	.80	.80
2586	A599 200t multi	.80	.80
	Nos. 2579-2586 (8)	4.00	4.00

Souvenir Sheet

First Mongolian Stamp, 80th Anniv. — A600

2004, Dec. 4 ***Perf. 13¼x13***
2587 A600 800t multi 3.50 3.50

Miniature Sheets

Insects and Flowers — A601

No. 2588: a, 100t, Mantis religiosa. b, 100t, Aster alpina. c, 200t, Echinops humilis. d, 200t, Apis mellifera. e, 300t, Angaraeris barabensis. f, 300t, Nymphaea candida.

No. 2589: a, 100t, Lytta caraganae. b, 100t, Rosa acicularis. c, 200t, Aguilegia sibirica. d, 200t, Tabanus bovinus. e, 300t, Corizus hyoscyami. f, 300t, Lilium pumilum.

2004, Dec. 25 ***Perf. 13***

Sheets of 6, #a-f

2588-2589 A601 Set of 2 10.00 10.00

Women's Headdresses — A602

No. 2590: a, Kazakh headdress, denomination at left. b, Mongol headdress, denomination at right.

2004, Dec. 31 *Perf. 11½x11¾*

2590 A602 550t Horiz. pair, #a-b 5.00 5.00

See Kazakhstan No. 472.

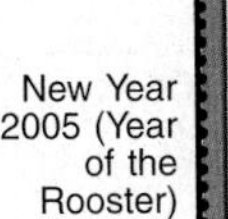

New Year 2005 (Year of the Rooster) A603

Roosters with frame color of: 300t, Red violet. 400t, Blue, vert.

2005, Jan. 1 *Perf. 12*

2591-2592 A603 Set of 2 4.00 4.00

Souvenir Sheet

Expo 2005, Aichi, Japan — A604

No. 2593: a, 100t, Butterfly on flower. b, 150t, Flower. c, 200t, Puppy. d, 550t, Kitten.

2005, Mar. 25

2593 A604 Sheet of 4, #a-d 4.50 4.50

World Vision A605

2005, Apr. 1

2594 A605 550t multi 1.50 1.00

Native Costumes — A606

No. 2595, 200t — Blue frame: a, Man with white and blue costume. b, Woman with green and white costume.

No. 2596, 200t — Green frame: a, Man with stringed instrument. b, Woman with red costume.

No. 2597, 200t — Rose pink frame: a, Man with white and blue costume. b, Woman with green costume.

2005, June 20 *Perf. 13½x13*

Horiz. pairs, #a-b

2595-2597 A606 Set of 3 5.00 5.00

Maharanza A607

No. 2595 — Color of face: a, White. b, Blue. c, Red. d, Yellow brown.

2005, July 8 *Perf. 13x12¾*

2598 Horiz. strip of 4 4.00 4.00

a.-d. A607 400t Any single 1.00 1.00

Souvenir Sheet

Asashorou, Sumo Wrestling Champion — A608

No. 2599 — Asashorou: a, 600t, Wearing baseball cap. b, 700t, On horse, vert. c, 800t, In wrestling loincloth, vert.

2005, July 18 *Perf. 13*

2599 A608 Sheet of 3, #a-c 5.00 5.00

World Vision A609

2005, Sept. 20 *Perf. 12*

2600 A609 550t multi 1.50 1.00

Headdresses A610

People wearing various headdresses: 50t, 100t, 150t, 200t, 250t, 300t.
800t, National headdress.

2005, Oct. 3 *Perf. 12¾x13*

2601-2606 A610 Set of 6 4.00 4.00

Souvenir Sheet

Perf. 12

2607 A610 800t multi 3.50 3.50

No. 2607 contains one 37x56mm stamp.

Souvenir Sheets

Shenzhou VI Space Flight — A611

No. 2608, 800t, Astronauts waving. No. 2609, 800t, Astronauts in spacecraft.

2005, Dec. 9 *Perf. 12*

2608-2609 A611 Set of 2 8.00 8.00

Souvenir Sheet

Coins of the Mongolian Empire — A612

No. 2610 — Various coins with background color of: a, Blue. b, Grayish lilac. c, Deep bister.

2006, Jan. 11 *Perf. 13x12¾*

2610 A612 550t Sheet of 3, #a-c 5.00 5.00

New Year 2006 (Year of the Dog) A613

Mongolian emblem and "Year of the Dog" at: 300t, Right. 400t, Left.

2006, Jan. 27 *Perf. 13x13¼*

2611-2612 A613 Set of 2 3.50 3.50

Miniature Sheet

Europa Stamps, 50th Anniv. — A614

No. 2613: a, Archer. b, Camels. c, Boys herding livestock. d, Goat. e, Rocks. f, Building spire. g, Dinosaur skeleton. h, Circus performers. i, Yurt. j, Two men in native costumes. k, Airplane. l, Ox.

2006, Feb. 1 *Perf. 12½x13*

2613 A614 200t Sheet of 12, #a-l 8.00 8.00

m. Souvenir sheet, #2613a-2613b, perf. 13 1.50 1.50

n. Souvenir sheet, #2613c-2613d, perf. 13 1.50 1.50

o. Souvenir sheet, #2613e-2613f, perf. 13 1.50 1.50

p. Souvenir sheet, #2613g-2613h, perf. 13 1.50 1.50

q. Souvenir sheet, #2613i-2613j, perf. 13 1.50 1.50

r. Souvenir sheet, #2613k-2613l, perf. 13 1.50 1.50

World Vision — A615

No. 2614: a, Children riding ox. b, Child riding horse.

2006, May 5 **Litho.** *Perf. 12*

2614 A615 550t Horiz. pair, #a-b 3.50 3.50

Souvenir Sheet

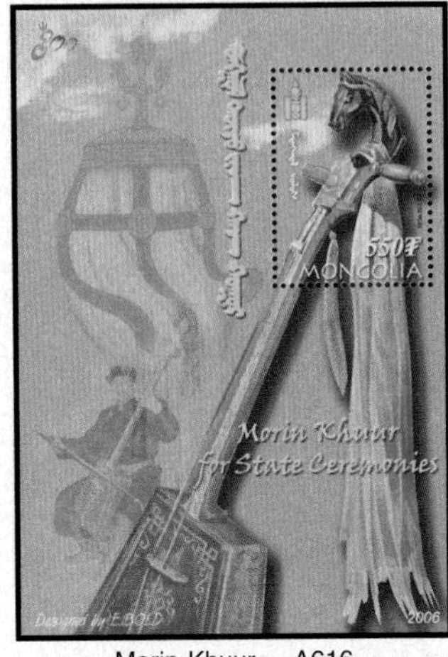

Morin Khuur — A616

2006, June 16

2615 A616 550t multi 2.00 2.00

Souvenir Sheet

Pres. Nambaryn Enkhbayar — A617

2006, June 21

2616 A617 800t multi 3.50 3.50

Souvenir Sheet

2006 World Cup Soccer Championships, Germany — A618

No. 2617 — Various stylized players: a, 200t. b, 250t. c, 300t. d, 400t.

2006, June 23

2617 A618 Sheet of 4, #a-d 5.00 5.00

Souvenir Sheet

State Visit of US Pres. George W. Bush — A619

2006, June 30 ***Perf. 13x13¼***
2618 A619 600t multi 3.00 3.00

Souvenir Sheets

A620

Famous Mongols — A621

No. 2619 — Various unnamed Mongols: a, 50t (23x33mm). b, 100t (23x33mm). c, 300t (23x33mm). d, 400t (23x33mm). e, 500t (80x56mm).

2006 ***Perf. 13, 11½ (#2619e)***
2619 A620 Sheet of 5, #a-e 6.00 6.00
f. As #2619, with sheet margin overprinted in gold with Mongolian text 1.90 1.90

Perf. 11½x11¾
2620 A621 3800t shown 12.00 12.00

Mongolian stamps, 85th anniv. (#2619). Issued: No. 2619, 7/8; No. 2619f, 7/16/09.
No. 2620, 9/19. Mongolian State, 800th anniv.

Souvenir Sheet

Horse Sculptures — A622

No. 2621: a, 300t, Horse and rider. b, 400t, Horse only.

2006, Sept. 28 ***Perf. 12***
2621 A622 Sheet of 2, #a-b 3.50 3.50

See India No. 2167.

Miniature Sheet

Friendly Exchange Philatelic Exhibition — A623

No. 2622: a, 150t, Olympic Stadium, Beijing. b, 200t, Waterfalls. c, 250t, City street at night.

2006, Oct. 25 **Litho.** ***Perf. 12***
2622 A623 Sheet of 3, #a-c 1.10 1.10

Hucho Taimen Fish — A624

No. 2623 — Various depictions of fish: a, 100t. b, 200t. c, 300t. d, 400t.

2006, Dec. 17
2623 A624 Block of 4, #a-d 1.75 1.75

New Year 2007 (Year of the Pig) — A625

Designs: 300t, Two pigs. 400t, Two pigs, diff.

2006, Dec. 17
2624-2625 A625 Set of 2 1.25 1.25

Dutch Royalty — A625a

No. 2625A: b, Prince Willem-Alexander. c, Prince Willem-Alexander and Princess Máxima. d, Princess Máxima.

2007, Jan. 7 ***Perf. 13¼x13½***
2625A Vert. strip of 3 3.75 3.75
b.-d. A625a 700t Any single 1.25 1.25

Printed in sheets containing 2 each of Nos. 2625Ab-2625Ad.

Miniature Sheet

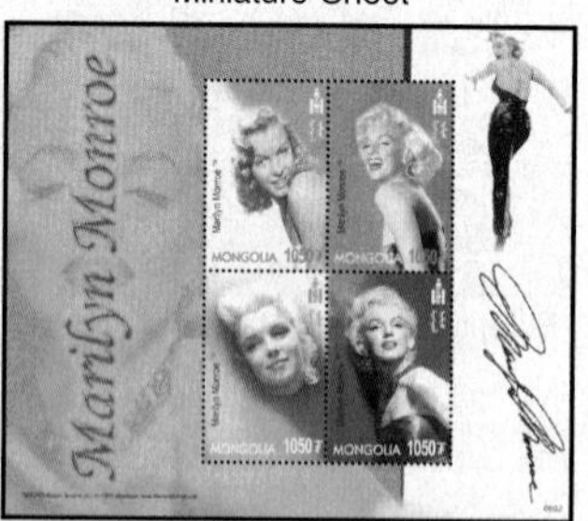

Marilyn Monroe (1926-62), Actress — A625b

No. 2625E — Monroe with: f, Background in orange in white, country name and denomination in orange. g, Background and denomination in orange, country name in white. h, Background in rose and white, country name and denomination in white. i, Background in claret, country name and denomination in white.

2007, Jan. 26
2625E A625b 1050t Sheet of 4, #f-i 7.25 7.25

Miniature Sheet

Elvis Presley (1935-77) — A625c

No. 2625J — Presley: k, Facing right, holding microphone. l, Facing forward, country name at top. m, Facing right, without microphone. n, Facing forward, country name at bottom.

2007, Jan. 26 ***Perf. 13¼***
2625J A625c 1050t Sheet of 4, #k-n 7.25 7.25

Betty Boop — A625d

No. 2625O — Betty Boop: p, Holding down dress in breeze. q, With both hands in air. r, With hands clasped. s, With one arm raised, parts of "B," "E," and "T" at top. t, Winking, with leg lifted. u, With one arm raised, parts of "B," "O," and "P" at top.
No. 2625V — Betty Boop lifting dress to expose garter: a, Without part of heart to left of "GO" in country name. b, With part of heart to left of "GO" in country name.

2007, Jan. 26 ***Perf. 13¼x13½***
2625O A625d 700t Sheet of 6, #p-u 7.25 7.25

Souvenir Sheet

2625V A625d 1500t Sheet of 2, #w-x 5.25 5.25

Souvenir Sheet

Diplomatic Relations Between Mongolia and the United States, 20th Anniv. — A626

No. 2626: a, 400t, Statue of Genghis Khan, Ulan Bator. b, 550t, Statue of Abraham Lincoln, Washington, DC.

2007, Jan. 29 ***Perf. 12***
2626 A626 Sheet of 2, #a-b 1.75 1.75

Lama Tsonghapa (1357-1419), Buddhist Teacher — A627

2007, Jan. 30 ***Perf. 12¾***
2627 A627 100t multi .25 .25

Souvenir Sheet

Diplomatic Relations Between Mongolia and Japan, 35th Anniv. — A628

No. 2628: a, 550t, Mt. Fuji, Japan. 700t, Mt. Otgontenger, Mongolia.

2007, Feb. 23 ***Perf. 12***
2628 A628 Sheet of 2, #a-b 2.25 2.25

Calligraphy A629

Designs: 50t, Light of wisdom. 100t, Butterfly. 150t, Flower. 200t, Horse. 250t, Spring. 300t, Leaves. 400t, Wow. 550t, Wild camel. 800t, Sky.

2007, Aug. 2 ***Perf. 13x12¾***
2629-2636 A629 Set of 8 3.50 3.50

Souvenir Sheet

Perf. 12¾
2637 A629 800t multi 1.40 1.40

No. 2637 contains one 43x57mm stamp.

Souvenir Sheets

Modern Art — A630

Art by: No. 2638, 400t, Ts. Tsegmid. No. 2639, 400t, S. Sarantsatsralt. No. 2640, 400t, Ts. Enkhjin. No. 2641, 400t, Do. Bold, horiz. No. 2642, 400t, Sh. Chimeddorj, horiz.

2007, Aug. 21 ***Perf. 13***
2638-2642 A630 Set of 5 3.50 3.50

Miniature Sheet

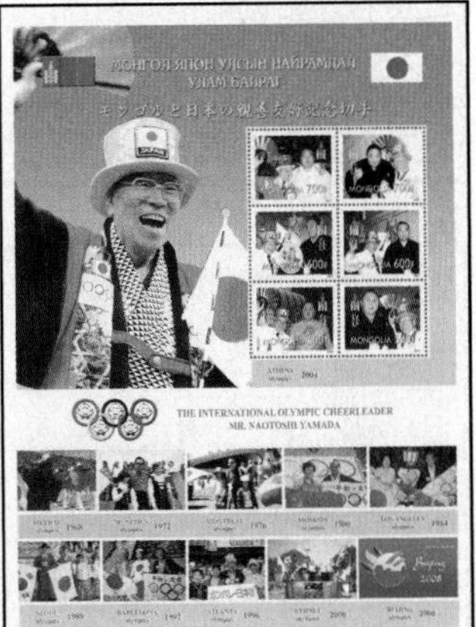

Naotoshi Yamada, Olympic Cheerleader, and Mongolian Sumo Wrestlers — A631

No. 2643 — Yamada and various wrestlers with Mongolian emblem and inscriptions at: a, 500t, Right. b, 500t, Left. c, 600t, Right. d, 600t, Left. e, 700t, Right. f, 700t, Left.

2007, Oct. 3 ***Die Cut***

Self-Adhesive

2643 A631 Sheet of 6, #a-f, + 10 labels 6.25 6.25

Genghis Khan (c. 1162-1227) — A632

Perf. 12½x12¾

2007, Nov. 29 **Litho.**

2644	Horiz. strip of 5	5.50	5.50
a.	A632 230t black	.40	.40
b.	A632 400t brown	.40	.40
c.	A632 650t blue	.40	.40
d.	A632 800t green	.40	.40
e.	A632 1000t violet	.40	.40

New Year 2008 (Year of the Rat) — A633

No. 2645 — Rat with denomination at: a, UR. b, LL.

2008, Jan. 1 ***Perf. 12¾***

2645 A633 800t Vert. pair, #a-b 2.75 2.75

Wedding of Queen Elizabeth II and Prince Philip, 50th Anniv. — A634

No. 2646: a, Queen. b, Queen and Prince.

2008, Jan. 25 ***Perf. 13¼***

2646 A634 400t Pair, #a-b 1.40 1.40

Printed in sheets of 6 containing 2 each of Nos. 2646a-2646b.

Princess Diana (1961-97) — A635

No. 2647, vert. — Princess Diana wearing: a, Necklace and black gown. b, Red hat and coat. c, Black and white dress. d, Black and white hat and jacket.

3000t, Prince Charles and Princess Diana.

2008, Jan. 25

2647 A635 1150t Sheet of 4, #a-d 8.00 8.00

Souvenir Sheet

2648 A635 3000t multi 5.25 5.25

First Helicopter Flight, Cent. — A636

No. 2649: a, Belvedere. b, AS 565 Dauphin/Panther. c, Explorer. d, Shark.

3000t, Scout.

2008, Jan. 25

2649 A636 1150t Sheet of 4, #a-d 8.00 8.00

Souvenir Sheet

2650 A636 3000t multi 5.25 5.25

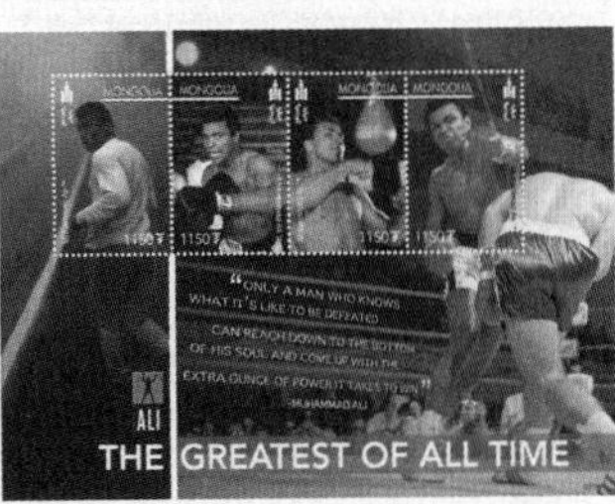

Muhammad Ali, Boxer — A637

No. 2651, 1150t — Ali: a, Wearing shirt. b, Shadow-boxing. c, Punching bag. d, Punching at opponent.

No. 2652, 1150t, horiz. — Ali with: a, Black boxing gloves punching at opponent. b, Red boxing gloves with left arm extended. c, Red boxing gloves, ring rope in background. d, Red boxing gloves, lights and ring rope in background.

No. 2653, 3000t, Ali wearing robe. No. 2654, 3000t, Close-up photograph.

Perf. 13¼, 11½ (#2652)

2008, Jan. 25

Sheets of 4, #a-d

2651-2652 A637 Set of 2 16.00 16.00

Souvenir Sheets

2653-2654 A637 Set of 2 10.50 10.50

Pope John Paul II (1920-2005) — A637a

2008, Jan. 25 Litho. ***Perf. 13½x13¼***

2654A A637a 880t multi 1.50 1.50

Miniature Sheet

Photomosaic of Pope Benedict XVI — A638

No. 2655 — Part of photomosaic with frame around it: a, At left and top in green. b, At left in green. c, At left in green and white. d, At left and bottom in white.

2008, Jan. 25 ***Perf. 13¼***

2655 A638 1150t Sheet of 4, #a-d 8.00 8.00

Nos. 1355 and 1359 Surcharged

Methods and Perfs As Before

2008, Feb. 29

2656 A301 1000t on 20m #1355 1.75 1.75

2657 A301 1000t on 60m #1359 1.75 1.75

No. 1983 Surcharged

Method and Perf. As Before

2008, Mar. 7

2658 A429 250t on 40m #1983 .45 .45

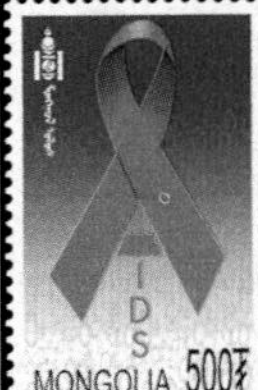

Campaign Against AIDS — A639

2008, Apr. 10 Litho. ***Perf. 12¾x13***

2659 A639 500t multi .85 .85

Handcrafted Items A640

Designs: No. 2660, 500t, Pipe and tobacco pouch (shown). No. 2661, 500t, Jar and cloth. No. 2662, 500t, Silver bowls. No. 2663, 500t, Sword and sheath. No. 2664, 500t, Saddle.

2008, June 8 ***Perf. 12¾***

2660-2664 A640 Set of 5 4.50 4.50

Miniature Sheet

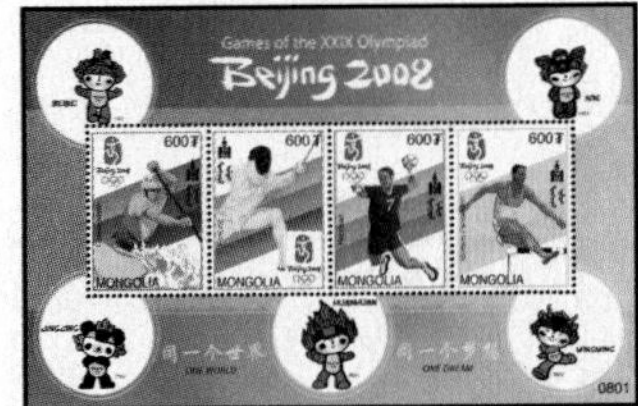

2008 Summer Olympics, Beijing — A641

No. 2665: a, Canoe-kayak. b, Fencing. c, Handball. d, Modern pentathlon.

2008, July 8 ***Perf. 12¾x12½***

2665 A641 600t Sheet of 4, #a-d 4.25 4.25

Wild Boars A642

No. 2666: a, Head of boar. b, Sow and piglets. c, Boar. d, Boar and sow.

2008, Sept. 10 ***Perf. 12½x12¾***

2666 Horiz. strip of 4 5.75 5.75
a.-d. A642 800t Any single 1.40 1.40

New Year 2009 (Year of the Ox) A643

Ox with background color of: 200t, Yellow. 300t, Blue.

2009, Jan. 19 ***Perf. 12***

2667-2668 A643 Set of 2 .75 .75

National Coat of Arms — A644

Great White Banner — A645

National Flag — A646

Soyombo A647

2009, Jan. 28 **Litho.**
2669 Horiz. strip of 4 4.00 4.00
a. A644 400t multi .60 .60
b. A645 500t multi .75 .75
c. A646 800t multi 1.10 1.10
d. A647 1000t multi 1.50 1.50

No. 1307 Surcharged

Method and Perf. As Before
2009, Apr. 6
2670 A290 1000t on 20m #1307 1.40 1.40

People in Yurt A648

2009, Apr. 6 **Litho.** ***Perf. 13x12¾***
2671 A648 1000t multi 1.40 1.40

China 2009 World Stamp Exhibition, Luoyang — A649

No. 2672: a, Giant panda. b, Ursus arctos gobiensis.

2009, Apr. 10 ***Perf. 12¾x12½***
2672 A649 300t Pair, #a-b .85 .85

Printed in sheets of 14, 7 each Nos. 2672a-2672b, + 2 labels.

Peonies A650

2009, Apr. 23 ***Perf. 13½x13¼***
2673 A650 700t multi 1.00 1.00

Printed in sheets of 6.

Earrings From Korea, 5th-6th Cent. A651

Earrings From Mongolia, 18th-19th Cent. A652

Earring From Kazakhstan, 2nd-1st Cent. B.C. — A653

2009, June 12 ***Perf. 12***
2674 Horiz. strip of 3 3.50 3.50
a. A651 800t multi 1.10 1.10
b. A652 800t multi 1.10 1.10
c. A653 800t multi 1.10 1.10

See Kazakhstan No. 595, South Korea No. 2313.

Battles of Khalkhiin Gol, 70th Anniv. — A654

2009, Aug. 20 ***Perf. 13x12½***
2675 A654 500t lil & pur .70 .70

Souvenir Sheet

Taras — A655

No. 2676: a, White Tara. b, Green Tara.

2009, Oct. 9 ***Perf. 12***
2676 A655 800t Sheet of 2, #a-b 2.25 2.25

Diplomatic Relations Between Mongolia and People's Republic of China, 60th Anniv. — A656

No. 2677 — Buildings with frame and denomination in: a, Blue. b, Red.

2009, Oct. 9 ***Perf. 12¾***
2677 Horiz. pair with central label 3.00 3.00
a.-b. A656 1000t Either single 1.50 1.50

APU Company, 85th Anniv. — A657

2009, Dec. 1 ***Perf. 12¾x13***
2678 A657 800t multi 1.10 1.10

Camel Polo A658

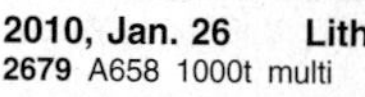

2010, Jan. 26 **Litho.** ***Perf. 11½***
2679 A658 1000t multi 1.40 1.40

A659

A660

A661

A662

A663

A664

Secrets of the Mongols — A665

Designs: No. 2686, Black banner. No. 2687, Five arrows.

2010, Feb. 5 ***Perf. 13x12¾***
2680 A659 1000t multi 1.40 1.40
2681 A660 1000t multi 1.40 1.40
2682 A661 1000t multi 1.40 1.40
2683 A662 1000t multi 1.40 1.40
2684 A663 1000t multi 1.40 1.40
2685 A664 1000t multi 1.40 1.40
Nos. 2680-2685 (6) 8.40 8.40

Souvenir Sheets
Perf. 12
2686 A665 1500t pur & multi 2.10 2.10
2687 A665 1500t grn & multi 2.10 2.10

Compare with Types A677-A683.

New Year 2010 (Year of the Tiger) — A666

No. 2688 — Tiger with background color of: a, Green. b, Blue.

2010, Feb. 14 ***Perf. 12***
2688 A666 1000t Vert. pair, #a-b 3.00 3.00

Children A667

Children with stringed instruments and: 800t, Horse. 1000t, Camel.

2010, Apr. 20 ***Perf. 13½***
2689-2690 A667 Set of 2 2.75 2.75

Mountains — A668

No. 2691: a, Sutai Khairkhan. b, Altan Khokhii. c, Khan Khokhii. d, Suvarga Khairkhan.

No. 2692: a, Burkhan Khaldun. b, Bogd Khairkhan. c, Dariganga, Dari Ovoo. d, Otgontenger.

2010 Litho. *Perf. 13¼*

2691 A668 500t Block or horiz. strip of 4, #a-d 3.00 3.00

Perf. 12

2692 A668 500t Block of 4, #a-d 3.00 3.00

Issued: No. 2691, 5/27; No. 2692, 6/15.

Flag of Mongolia A669

2010, June 15 *Perf. 13*

2693 A669 800t multi 1.25 1.25

2010 World Cup Soccer Championships, South Africa — A670

No. 2694: a, Emblem. b, Mascot.

2010, July 11 *Perf. 13¼x13*

2694 A670 800t Horiz. pair, #a-b, + central label 2.40 2.40

Souvenir Sheet

Chingunjav (1710-57), Leader of Rebellion Against Manchus — A671

2010, Aug. 27 *Perf. 12¼x12*

2695 A671 800t multi 1.25 1.25

Souvenir Sheet

Pres. Tsakhiagiin Elbegdorj — A672

2010, Oct. 22 *Perf. 12½x13*

2696 A672 500t multi .80 .80

Butterflies A673

Designs: 100t, Ornithoptera croesus. 200t, Papilio antimachus. 400t, Ornithoptera priamus urvilleanus. 500t, Papilio zalmoxis. 800t, Troides rhadamantius. 1000t, Ornithoptera victoriae epiphanes.

2010, Dec. 8 Litho. *Perf. 12*

2697-2702 A673 Set of 6 5.00 5.00

Souvenir Sheet

Taras — A674

No. 2703: a, Green tara. b, Red tara.

2010, Dec. 8 *Perf. 13x13¼*

2703 A674 800t Sheet of 2, #a-b 2.75 2.75

New Year 2011 (Year of the Rabbit) — A675

2011, Jan. 12 *Perf. 11½*

2704 A675 1000t multi 1.60 1.60

First Man in Space, 50th Anniv. A676

2011, Apr. 12 *Perf. 13¼*

2705 A676 500t multi .85 .85

Printed in sheets of 10 + 2 labels.

A677

A678

A679

A680

A681

A682

Secrets of the Mongols — A683

Designs: No. 2712, White banner. No. 2713, Khan's seal of Great Mongol.

2011, May 29 Litho. *Perf. 13x12¾*

2706 A677 1000t multi 1.60 1.60
2707 A678 1000t multi 1.60 1.60
2708 A679 1000t multi 1.60 1.60
2709 A680 1000t multi 1.60 1.60
2710 A681 1000t multi 1.60 1.60
2711 A682 1000t multi 1.60 1.60
Nos. 2706-2711 (6) 9.60 9.60

Souvenir Sheets

Perf. 12

2712 A683 1500t blue & multi 2.50 2.50
2713 A683 1500t brown & multi 2.50 2.50

Compare with Types A659-A665.

Livestock A684

Designs: No. 2714, 1000t, Yak. No. 2715, 1000t, Camel. No. 2716, 1200t, Mongolian horse. No. 2717, 1200t, Reindeer.

2011, June 13 *Perf. 13x12¾*

2714-2717 A684 Set of 4 7.25 7.25

Souvenir Sheet

Motor Sports — A685

No. 2718: a, 300t, Road rally. b, 400t, Motorcycle racing. c, 600t, Auto racing.

2011, July 8 *Perf. 13x13¼*

2718 A685 Sheet of 3, #a-c 2.10 2.10

Miniature Sheet

Mongolian People's Revolution, 90th Anniv. — A686

No. 2719: a, 600t, Kharloin Choibalsan (1895-1952), Prime Minister, 1939-52 (30x30mm). b, 600t, Dogsomyn Bodoo (1895-1922), Prime Minister, 1921-22 (30x30mm). c, 600t, Soliin Danzan (1885-1924), Central Committee chairman (30x30mm). d, 600t, Dambyn Chagdarjav (1880-1922), Prime Minister, 1921 (30x30mm). e, 600t, Dansrabilegiin Dogsom (1884-1939), President, 1936-39 (30x30mm). f, 600t, D. Losol (1898-1940), revolutionist (30x30mm). g, 1200t, Sukhe Bator (1893-1923), leader of revolution (30x40mm).

2011, July 11 *Perf. 12*

2719 A686 Sheet of 7, #a-g 7.75 7.75

Souvenir Sheets

Reign of Genghis Khan, 805th Anniv. — A687

Designs: No. 2720, 2000t, Genghis Khan (c. 1162-1227). No. 2721, 2000t, Order of Genghis Khan.

2011, July 11 Litho.

2720-2721 A687 Set of 2 6.50 6.50

Hunnu Culture, 2200th Anniv. — A688

No. 2722: a, Pottery. b, Jewelry depicting horse. c, Jewelry depicting bird. d, Wolf attacking buck. e, Arrowheads.

5000t, Modun Shanyu (c. 234 B.C.-174 B.C), emperor.

2011, July 25 *Perf. 11¾x11½*

2722 A688 1000t Sheet of 5, #a-e 8.25 8.25

Souvenir Sheet

Perf. 12¾

2723 A688 5000t multi 8.25 8.25

No. 2723 contains one 60x65mm stamp.

Wildlife A689

Wildlife of: 400t, Antarctic and Arctic regions. 600t, Mongolia. 1000t, Australia. 1200t, Africa.

2011, July 27 ***Perf. 12***
2724-2727 A689 Set of 4 5.25 5.25

No. 1231 Surcharged in Gold

Method and Perf. As Before
2011, July 28
2728 A275 800t on 4t #1231 1.40 1.40

PhilaNippon '11, Intl. Philatelic Exhibition, Yokohama.

Wedding of Prince William and Catherine Middleton A690

Designs: 1200t, Couple.
No. 2730: a, Prince William. b, Catherine Middleton.

2011, Aug. 22 **Litho.** ***Perf. 12***
2729 A690 1200t multi 2.00 2.00

Souvenir Sheet

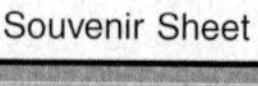

Perf. 13½x13
2730 A690 1500t Sheet of 2, #a-b 4.75 4.75

Souvenir Sheet

Education in Mongolia, 90th Anniv. — A691

No. 2731: a, Students, bugler, building. b, Girl, children at computers. c, Mongolian flag, graduates, building.

2011, Sept. 9 ***Perf. 12***
2731 A691 1200t Sheet of 3, #a-c 5.75 5.75

Souvenir Sheet

Admission to the United Nations, 50th Anniv. — A692

2011, Oct. 27 **Litho.** ***Perf. 12¾***
2732 A692 1000t multi 1.60 1.60

Nos. 2403-2404 Overprinted in Gold

Methods and Perfs As Before
2011, Nov. 11
2733 A531 250t multi on #2403 .40 .40
2734 A531 450t multi on #2404 .70 .70

China 2011 Intl. Philatelic Exhibition, Wuxi.

Souvenir Sheet

Mongolian Diplomatic Service, Cent. — A693

No. 2735: a, Mijiddorjiin Khanddorj (1869-1915), first Mongolian Foreign Minster (30x65mm). b, Flag of Mongolia, United Nations Building, dove (50x38mm). c, Golden gerege (30x65mm).

Perf. 12¾, 13¼ (#2735b)
2011, Dec. 1 **Litho.**
2735 A693 600t Sheet of 3, #a-c 2.75 2.75

Souvenir Sheet

United Nations Secretary General Ban Ki-Moon and Mongolian Prime Minister Sukhbaatar Batbold — A694

2011, Dec. 13 ***Perf. 13x13¼***
2736 A694 500t multi .75 .75

Admission to United Nations, 50th anniv.

Souvenir Sheet

Mongolian Government Palace and Flag — A695

2011, Dec. 17 ***Perf. 12¾***
2737 A695 1000t multi 1.50 1.50

Mongolian government, cent.

Souvenir Sheet

Mongolian Revolution, Cent. — A696

No. 2738: a, Bogdo Jebtsundamba VIII (Bogd Khan, 1869-1924), Emperor. b, Tögs-Ochiryn Namnansuren (1878-1919), Prime Minister.

2011, Dec. 29 ***Perf. 13¼x13***
2738 A696 1000t Sheet of 2, #a-b, + label 3.00 3.00

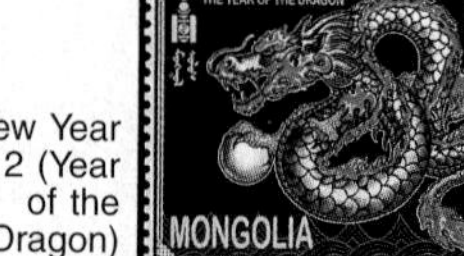
New Year 2012 (Year of the Dragon) A697

2012, Jan. 1 ***Perf. 13x13¼***
2739 A697 600t multi .90 .90

Souvenir Sheet

Fleet of Kublai Khan — A698

No. 2740: a, 1000t, Kublai Khan (1215-94), Emperor. b, 1200t, Warship.

2012, Mar. 4 ***Perf. 12***
2740 A698 Sheet of 2, #a-b 3.50 3.50

Souvenir Sheet

Diplomatic Relations Between Mongolia and Japan, 40th Anniv. — A699

No. 2741: a, Mongolian doll. b, Japanese doll.

2012, Mar. 12 ***Perf. 12¾x13***
2741 A699 600t Sheet of 2, #a-b, + label 1.90 1.90

Mythological Creatures — A700

Cats — A701

Designs: 100t, Dragon. 200t, Lion. 400t, Tiger. 600t, Khan Garuda.

2012, Apr. 22 **Litho.** ***Perf. 13¼***
2742 A700 100t multi .25 .25
2743 A701 200t multi .30 .30
2744 A701 400t multi .65 .65
2745 A700 600t multi .95 .95
Nos. 2742-2745 (4) 2.15 2.15

Souvenir Sheet

Antarctic Explorers — A702

No. 2746: a, Fabian von Bellingshausen (1778-1852). b, Mikhail P. Lazarev (1788-1851).

2012, June 17 ***Perf. 13***
2746 A702 800t Sheet of 2, #a-b 2.40 2.40

2012 Summer Olympics, London — A703

No. 2747 — Emblem of 2012 Summer Olympics, British flag and: a, London tourist attractions. b, Athletes.

2012, July 5 ***Perf. 13¼***
2747 Pair 2.40 2.40
a. A703 700t multi 1.10 1.10
b. A703 800t multi 1.25 1.25

Women in Modern National Costumes A704

Various costumes: 100t, 200t, 300t, 400t, 500t, 600t.
No. 2754: a, 700t. b, 800t.

2012, Aug. 24 *Perf. 12*
2748-2753 A704 Set of 6 3.00 3.00

Souvenir Sheet
Perf. 13x13¼

2754 A704 Sheet of 2, #a-b 2.25 2.25

No. 2754 contains two 38x50mm stamps.

Miniature Sheet

Guardians of the Days — A705

No. 2755 — Guardian and inscription: a, 100t, Moon. b, 200t, Mars. c, 300t, Mercury. d, 400t, Jupiter. e, 500t, Venus. f, 600t, Saturn. g, 700t, Sun.

Self-Adhesive

2012, Oct. 14 ***Die Cut Perf.***
2755 A705 Sheet of 7, #a-g 4.00 4.00

Souvenir Sheet

Customs Department, Cent. — A706

No. 2756: a, 800t, Three Mongolian customs officials. b, 1000t, Two modern Mongolian customs officials, flag, horiz. 1200t, Customs dog, marijuana.

2012, Oct. 20 *Perf. 13¼x13*
2756 A706 Sheet of 3, #a-c 4.50 4.50

Souvenir Sheet

Genghis Khan (1162-1227), Mongol Conqueror — A707

No. 2757: a, 350t, Horse. b, 850t, Genghis Khan.

2012, Nov. 14 *Perf. 12*
2757 A707 Sheet of 2, #a-b 1.75 1.75

Birds A708

Designs: 100t, Amazona aestiva, Ara chloroptera, Ara ararauna. 200t, Paradisaea raggiana, Paradisaea rudolphi. 300t, Cygnus atratus, Cygnus olor, Phoenicopterus roseus. 400t, Aix galericulata, Aix sponsa. 800t, Erythrura gouldiae, Pteridophora albertus, Euplectes orix. 1000t, Pavo cristatus, Chrysolophus pictus.

2012, Dec. 24 *Perf. 13¼*
2758-2763 A708 Set of 6 4.00 4.00

Flag and Emblem of Mongolia A709

2012, Dec. 29 *Perf. 13x13¼*
2764 A709 1200t multi 1.75 1.75

No. 1660 with this 500t surcharge in gold, released in Feb. 2013, was produced in limited quantities.

New Year 2013 (Year of the Snake) A710

2013, Feb. 6 **Litho.** *Perf. 12*
2765 A710 600t multi .90 .90

No. 2765 was printed in sheets of 16 + 4 labels.

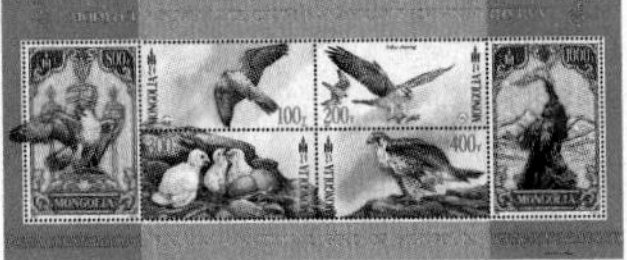

Gazelles A711

Designs: 200t, Gazella subgutturosa. 400t, Procapra gutturosa. 800t, Procapra gutturosa, diff. 1000t, Gazella subgutturosa, diff.

2013, June 4 *Perf. 13x13¼*
2766-2769 A711 Set of 4 3.50 3.50
2769a Sheet of 8, 2 each #2766-2769, + central label 7.00 7.00

Miniature Sheet

Falcons — A712

No. 2770: a, 100t, Falcon in flight (60x30mm). b, 200t, Two Falco cherrug in flight (60x30mm). c, 300t, Falcon chicks and eggs (60x30mm). d, 400t, Falcon on rock (60x30mm). e, 800t, Falcon and Mongolian regalia (40x60mm). f, 1000t, Falcon on hand of Mongolian falconer (40x60mm).

Litho., Margin Litho. With Foil Application

2013, June 19 *Perf. 12*
2770 A712 Sheet of 6, #a-f 4.00 4.00

Animals on Elephant A713

Musician A714

Mongolian Woman A715

Yurt A716

2013, July 21 **Litho.** *Perf. 12½x12¾*

2771	A713 1000t multi	1.40	1.40
2772	A714 1000t multi	1.40	1.40
2773	A715 1000t multi	1.40	1.40
2774	A716 1000t multi	1.40	1.40
	Nos. 2771-2774 (4)	5.60	5.60

No. 2363 Srchd. in Red With Thailand 2013 World Stamp Exhibition Emblem Added

Souvenir Sheet

2013, Aug. 2 *Perf. 11*
2775 A519 1500t on 1000t #2363 2.00 2.00

Thailand 2013 World Stamp Exhibition, Bangkok.

Batu Khan (c. 1207-55), Mongol Ruler — A717

2013, Oct. 16 **Litho.** *Perf. 12*
2776 A717 1000t multi 1.25 1.25

The Beatles — A718

No. 2777: a, 500t, Ringo Starr (38x50mm). b, 500t, John Lennon (38x50mm). c, 1000t, Paul McCartney and George Harrison (60x50mm).

2013, Dec. 6 **Litho.** *Perf. 13*
2777 A718 Sheet of 3, #a-c 2.40 2.40

New Year 2014 (Year of the Horse) A719

No. 2778 — Horse facing: a, Right. b, Left.

2013, Dec. 22 **Litho.** *Perf. 13xx12¾*
2778 Horiz. pair + central label 1.60 1.60
a.-b. A719 650t Either single .80 .80

Nos. 1564-1567 Surcharged

Methods and Perfs As Before

2014, Jan. 6

2779	A347 1300t on 60m #1564	1.60	1.60
2780	A347 1300t on 60m #1565	1.60	1.60
2781	A347 1300t on 60m #1566	1.60	1.60
2782	A347 1300t on 60m #1567	1.60	1.60
	Nos. 2779-2782 (4)	6.40	6.40

Mongolian postage stamps, 90th anniv.

Flowers A720

Designs: 200t, Lilium dahuricum, Cypripedium calceolus and bee. 300t, Saussurea involucrata and bird. 400t, Iris sibirica, Lilium pumilum and butterfly. 900t, Trollius asiaticus, Tulipa uniflora and dragonfly. 1000t, Cypripedium macranthum, Adonis sibirica and ladybug.

2014, Feb. 15 **Litho.** *Perf. 13x12¾*
2783-2787 A720 Set of 5 3.25 3.25
2787a Sheet of 10, 2 each #2783-2387, + 2 central labels 6.50 6.50

Scientists — A721

Designs: No. 2788, 100t, Charles Darwin (1809-82), naturalist. No. 2789, 100t, Albert Einstein (1879-1955), physicist. No. 2790, 300t, Leonardo da Vinci (1452-1519). No. 2791, 300t, Isaac Newton (1642-1727), physicist. No. 2792, 500t, Galileo Galilei (1564-

1642), astronomer. No. 2793, 500t, Niels Bohr (1885-1962), physicist.

2014, Mar. 25 Litho. *Perf. 13¼x13*
2788-2793 A721 Set of 6 2.10 2.10

No. 1400 Surcharged in Metallic Red

Method and Perf. As Before
2014, May 16
2794 A308 2000t on 4t #1400 2.25 2.25

Mongolian postage stamps, 90th anniv.

Threatened Species From Red Book of Mongolia — A722

Designs: 200t, Lynx pardinus. 300t, Podoces hendersoni. 400t, Phasianus colchicus. 500t, Vormela peregusna.

2014, May 16 Litho. *Perf. 12*
2795-2798 A722 Set of 4 1.60 1.60
2798a Souvenir sheet of 4, #2795-2798 1.60 1.60

Souvenir Sheet

Bank of Mongolia, 90th Anniv. — A723

No. 2799: a, Mongolian man. b, Bank of Mongolia emblem.

2014, May 30 Litho. *Perf. 13¼x13*
2799 A723 2000t Sheet of 2, #a-b 4.50 4.50

A724

A725

A726

A727

A728

A729

A730

Items at Bogd Khan Palace Museum A731

Design: 2000t, Bogd Khan (1869-1924), 8th Jebtsundamba, Khagan of Mongolia.

2014, June 13 Litho. *Perf. 13x13¼*
2800 A724 1000t multi 1.10 1.10
2801 A725 1000t multi 1.10 1.10
2802 A726 1000t multi 1.10 1.10
2803 A727 1000t multi 1.10 1.10
2804 A728 1000t multi 1.10 1.10
2805 A729 1000t multi 1.10 1.10
2806 A730 1000t multi 1.10 1.10
2807 A731 1000t multi 1.10 1.10
Nos. 2800-2807 (8) 8.80 8.80

Souvenir Sheet
2808 A731 2000t multi 2.25 2.25

No. 2808 contains one 40x60mm stamp.

A732

Tarbosurus Bataar — A733

Designs: No. 2809, 1000t, Tarbosaurus bataar. No. 2810, 1000t, Tarbosaurus bataar skeleton.

No. 2811: a, 200t, Tarbosaurus bataar, diff. b, 400t, Tarbosaurus bataar skull. c, 500t, Tarbosaurus bataar skeleton, diff. d, 800t, Tarbosaurus bataar, map of Mongolia highlighted on globe.

2014, July 24 Litho. *Perf. 13x13¼*
2809-2810 A732 Set of 2 2.25 2.25

Miniature Sheet
Perf. 12
2811 A733 Sheet of 4, #a-d 2.10 2.10

Souvenir Sheets

Visits to Mongolia by World Leaders — A734

No. 2812: a, Mongolia Pres. Tsakhiagiin Elbegdorj. b, Xi Jinping, President of People's Republic of China.

No. 2813a, Russian Pres. Vladimir Putin

2014 Litho. *Perf. 12¾*
2812 A734 800t Sheet of 2, #a-b 1.75 1.75
2813 A734 Sheet of 2, #2812a, 2813a 1.75 1.75
a. 800t multi .85 .85

Issued: No. 2812, 8/21, No. 2813, 9/3.

Genghis Khan (c. 1162-1227) — A735

2014, Aug. 28 Litho. *Perf. 12½*
2814 A735 100t brn & multi .25 .25
2815 A735 1300t red & multi 1.50 1.50

Battles of Khalkhiin Gol, 75th Anniv. — A736

2014, Aug. 28 Litho. *Perf. 13¼*
2816 A736 750t multi .85 .85

See Russia No. 7562.

Souvenir Sheet

Mongolian Postage Stamps, 90th Anniv. — A737

No. 2817: a, Mongolian flag, Mongolia #7. b, Great White Banner, Mongolia #1-6.

Litho., Sheet Margin Litho. With Foil Application
2014, Oct. 7 *Perf. 13¼x13*
2817 A737 1000t Sheet of 2, #a-b 2.25 2.25

Souvenir Sheet

Ulan Bator, 375th Anniv. — A738

2014, Oct. 27 Litho. *Perf. 13¼*
2818 A738 1000t multi 1.10 1.10

New Year 2015 (Year of the Ram) A739

No. 2819 — Ram with head at: a, Right. b, Left.

2014, Dec. 28 Litho. *Perf. 13x12½*
2819 Horiz. pair + central label 1.40 1.40
a.-b. A739 650t Either single .70 .70

Miniature Sheet

Snow Leopards — A740

No. 2820: a, 1000t, Two leopards, green panel. b, 1000t, Two leopards, blue panel. c, 1300t, One leopard, purple panel. d, 1300t, Three leopards, magenta panel.

2015, Jan. 21 Litho. *Perf. 12¾x13*
2820 A740 Sheet of 4, #a-d 4.75 4.75

Souvenir Sheet

3,000,000th Citizen of Mongolia — A741

No. 2821: a, Close-up of horseman on globe sculpture. b, Entire sculpture.

2015, Jan. 28 Litho. *Perf. 13¼x13*
2821 A741 1000t Sheet of 2, #a-b 2.10 2.10

Water Conservation A742

2015, Mar. 20 Litho. *Perf. 13¼x13*
2822 A742 1300t multi 1.40 1.40

Freedom Online Coalition Emblem — A743

2015, Apr. 29 Litho. *Perf. 13¼x13*
2823 A743 1300t multi 1.40 1.40

End of World War II, 70th Anniv. — A744

2015, May 9 Litho. *Perf. 11½*
2824 A744 800t multi .85 .85

No. 626 Surcharged in Black and Gold

Methods and Perfs. As Before

2015, July 19
2825 A151 900t on 40m #626 .90 .90

Transportation Department, 90th anniv.

Dogs and Yaks A745

Designs: 300t, Tibetan mastiff and yak. 500t, Two Tibetan mastiffs. 800t, Mongolian bankhar and yak. 1000t, Mongolian bankhar and taiga.

2015, Aug. 3 Litho. *Perf. 12¾*
2826-2829 A745 Set of 4 2.75 2.75

Kublai Khan (1215-94) — A746

Designs: 300t, Hand cannons, 400t, Banknote. 500t, Gerege. 800t, Golden goblet. 2000t, Portrait of Kublai Khan.

2015, Sept. 16 Litho. *Perf. 13¼x13*
2830-2833 A746 Set of 4 2.00 2.00

Souvenir Sheet

Perf. 13x13¼

2834 A746 2000t multi 2.00 2.00

No. 2834 contains one 38x50mm stamp.

Horses — A747

No. 2835: a, 800t, Gray horse, brown horse with white mane. b, 800t, Light brown horse galloping, black and white horse. c, 800t, Dappled gray horse, brown horse with saddle. d, 1000t, Dark gray horse galloping, dark brown horse. e, 1000t, Brown horse with blue ribbon. f, 1000t, Horse and foal.

2015, Dec. 4 Litho. *Perf. 12*
2835 A747 Block of 6, #a-f 5.50 5.50

Dashichoiling Monastery — A748

Designs: 100t, Traditional ger temples. 500t, Khuree Maidar procession. 800t, Khuree Tsam ritual, two people in costume. 1000t, Khuree Tsam ritual, 5 people in costume.

No. 2840, vert. a, Drawing of Maidar. b, Maidar sculpture.

2015, Dec. 14 Litho. *Perf. 12½*
2836-2839 A748 Set of 4 2.50 2.50

Souvenir Sheet

Perf. 13x13¾

2840 A748 1300t Sheet of 2, #a-b 2.60 2.60

No. 2840 contains two 40x60mm stamps.

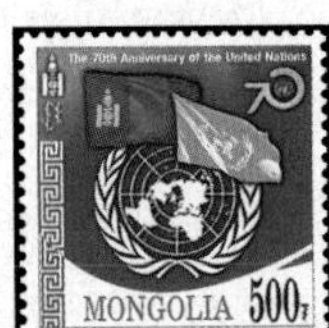

United Nations, 70th Anniv. — A749

2015, Dec. 20 Litho. *Perf. 13¼*
2841 A749 500t multi .50 .50

Paintings — A750

Paintings by unknown artists: No. 2842, 1000t, Dating. No. 2843, 1000t, Goatherd. No. 2844, 1000t, Migration. No. 2845, 1000t, Clatter. No. 2846, 1000t, Girls, vert. No. 2847, 1000t, Gorge, vert.

2015, Dec. 25 Litho. *Perf. 12¾*
2842-2847 A750 Set of 6 6.25 6.25

New Year 2016 (Year of the Monkey) A751

No. 2848 — Three monkeys with "Year of the Monkey" inscription at: a, Left. b, Right.

2015, Dec. 28 Litho. *Perf. 13x12½*
2848 Horiz. pair + central label 1.40 1.40
a.-b. A751 650t Either single .70 .70

Souvenir Sheet

Traditional Mongolian Life — A752

No. 2849: a, 1000t, Man and woman in traditional costumes, denomination at LL (30x40mm). b, 1000t, Man and woman in traditional costumes, denomination at LR (30x40mm). c, 2000t, Yurts and horses (60x40mm).

2016, Mar. 20 Litho. *Perf. 13¼x13*
2849 A752 Sheet of 3, #a-c 4.00 4.00

Mongol Information Technology, Post and Telecommunications System, 95th Anniv. — A753

2016, Mar. 30 Litho. *Perf. 13x13¼*
2850 A753 1300t multi 1.25 1.25

Souvenir Sheet

11th Asia-Europe Meeting, Ulan Bator — A754

No. 2851: a, 1300t, Emblem. b, 1500t, Statue of Genghis Khan.

2016, Apr. 15 Litho. *Perf. 12*
2851 A754 Sheet of 2, #a-b 2.75 2.75

Folklore A755

Designs: No. 2852, 900t, Woman, elephant, bulls, goats, camels and horses. No. 2853, 900t, Bearded man, birds, deer. No. 2854, 1200t, Camel, deer, swans, man holding tiger. No. 2855, 1200t, Tree, bird, rabbit, monkey, elephant.

2016, July 1 Litho. *Perf. 12¾*
2852-2855 A755 Set of 4 4.25 4.25

Anandyn Amar (1886-1941), Prime Minister — A756

2016, July 8 Litho. *Perf. 12*
2856 A756 500t multi .50 .50

People's Revolution, 95th Anniv. — A757

2016, July 10 Litho. *Perf. 13x13¼*
2857 A757 400t multi .40 .40

2016 Summer Olympics, Rio de Janeiro — A758

2016, July 28 Litho. *Perf. 13¼x13*
2858 A758 1000t multi 1.00 1.00

Souvenir Sheet

Genghis Khan (c. 1162-1227) — A759

2016, Oct. 23 Litho. *Perf. 12*
2859 A759 2000t multi 1.75 1.75

Mongol Empire, 810th Anniv.

Mammals — A760

Designs: 600t, Ram. 700t, Goat. 800t, Bull. 900t, Stallion. 1000t, Camel.

2016, Oct. 30 Litho. *Perf. 12*
2860-2864 A760 Set of 5 3.50 3.50

Souvenir Sheet

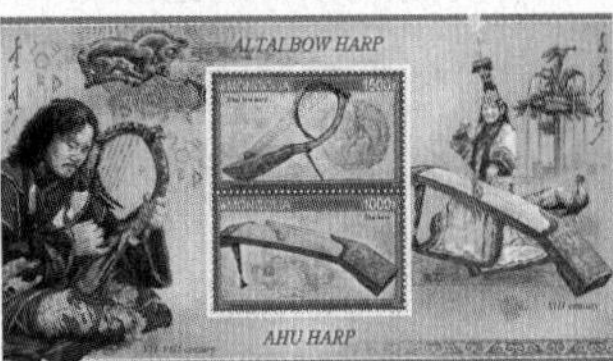

Harps — A761

No. 2865: a, 1000t, Ahu harp. b, 1500t, Altai bow harp.

2016, Nov. 11 Litho. *Perf. 12*
2865 A761 Sheet of 2, #a-b 2.10 2.10

Transportation With Animals — A762

Designs: 100t, Reindeer-drawn sled. 200t, Horse-drawn cart. 300t, Ox-drawn cart. 400t, Camel-drawn cart.

2016, Dec. 11 Litho. ***Perf. 13x13¼***

2866-2869	A762	Set of 4	.80	.80

Yumjaagiin Tsedenbal (1916-91), Prime Minister — A763

Litho., Sheet Margin Litho. With Foil Application

2016, Dec. 21 ***Perf. 13¼***

2870 A763 2000t multi		1.60	1.60

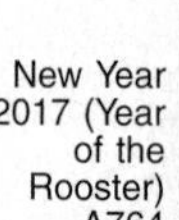

New Year 2017 (Year of the Rooster) A764

No. 2871 — Rooster and chicks with chicks at: a, Right. b, Left.

2017, Jan. 8 Litho. ***Perf. 13x12½***

2871	Horiz. pair + central label	1.10	1.10
a.-b.	A764 650t Either single	.55	.55

SEMI-POSTAL STAMPS

Catalogue values for unused stamps in this section are for Never Hinged items.

Vietnamese Mother and Child — SP1

1967, Dec. 22 Photo. ***Perf. 12x11½***

B1	SP1	30m + 20m multi	.60	.30
B2	SP1	50m + 30m multi	.60	.30

Solidarity with Vietnam.

Save Venice Type of Regular Issue

Souvenir Sheet

Departure of St. Ursula, by Carpaccio.

1972, Oct. 1 Litho. ***Perf. 12***

B3	A163	3t + 1t multi	4.00	4.00

Save Venice Campaign. No. B3 contains one horizontal stamp.

Girl Feeding Lambs SP2

UNICEF Emblem and: 20m+5m, Boy playing flute and dancing girl. 30m+5m, Girl chasing butterflies. 40m+5m, Girl with ribbon. 60m+5m, Girl with flowers. 80m+5m, Girl carrying bucket. 1t+5m, Boy going to school.

1977, June 1 Litho. ***Perf. 12***

B4	SP2	10m + 5m multi	.25	.25
B5	SP2	20m + 5m multi	.25	.25
B6	SP2	30m + 5m multi	.35	.25
B7	SP2	40m + 5m multi	.45	.30
B8	SP2	60m + 5m multi	.65	.35
B9	SP2	80m + 5m multi	.85	.55
B10	SP2	1t + 5m multi	1.10	.70
		Nos. B4-B10 (7)	3.90	2.65

Surtax was for Mongolian Children's Village. See No. CB1.

Boys on Horseback — SP3

Children and IYC Emblem: 30m+5m, Raising chickens. 50m+5m, With deer. 60m+5m, With flowers. 70m+5m, Planting tree. 80m+5m, Studying space project. 1t+5m, Dancing. 4t+50m, Girl on horseback.

1979, Jan. 10

B11	SP3	10m + 5m multi	.30	.25
B12	SP3	30m + 5m multi	.30	.25
B13	SP3	50m + 5m multi	.45	.25
B14	SP3	60m + 5m multi	.50	.25
B15	SP3	70m + 5m multi	.65	.35
B16	SP3	80m + 5m multi	.80	.40
B17	SP3	1t + 5m multi	1.10	.65
		Nos. B11-B17 (7)	4.10	2.40

Souvenir Sheet

B18	SP3	4t + 50m multi	3.25	3.25

International Year of the Child. Compare with Type A301.

1998 Winter Olympic Games, Nagano — SP4

No. B19, Speed skating. No. B20, Ski jumping. No. B21, Snowboarding. No. B22, Freestyle skiing.

1998 Litho. ***Perf. 12***

B19	SP4	150t +15t multi	.65	.50
B20	SP4	200t +20t multi	.80	.60
B21	SP4	300t +30t multi	1.30	1.00
B22	SP4	600t +60t multi	2.25	1.75
		Nos. B19-B22 (4)	5.00	3.85

Ulan Bator, 360th Anniv. — SP5

Designs, 300t +30t each: No. B23, Flags and arms. No. B24, Seated man. No. B25, Arms.

No. B26, Various views of Ulan Bator.

1999 Litho. ***Perf. 12½***

B23-B25	SP5	Set of 3	3.00	3.00

Sheet of 9

Perf. 12½x12¼

B26	SP5	200t +20t #a.-i.	8.00	8.00

No. B26 contains nine 45x27mm stamps.

Unity Against Terrorism — SP6

World Trade Center, Statue of Liberty, American flag and country name in: 300t+50t, Red. 400t+50t, Blue.

Perf. 13½x13¼

2001, Nov. 11 Litho.

B27-B28	SP6	Set of 2	3.00	3.00

AIR POST STAMPS

Catalogue values for unused stamps in this section are for Never Hinged items.

Postal Modernization Type of Regular Issue

Designs: 10m, 20m, Postman with horses. 25m, Postman with reindeer. 30m, 50m, Plane over map of Mongolia. 1t, Post horn and flag of Mongolia.

1961, June 5 Photo. ***Perf. 15***

C1	A72	10m multicolored	.30	.25
C2	A72	50m multicolored	.60	.25
C3	A72	1t multicolored	1.10	.40
		Nos. C1-C3 (3)	2.00	.80

Souvenir Sheet

Perf. 11

C4	Sheet of 4	3.50	3.50
a.	A72 20m lt blue grn & multi	.80	.80
b.	A72 25m light blue & multi	.80	.80
c.	A72 30m light green & multi	.80	.80
d.	A72 1t rose carmine & multi	.80	.80

40th anniversary of independence; postal modernization. No. C4b is not inscribed Airmail.

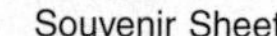

Souvenir Sheet

Austria Type SP55, Austrian and Mongolian Stamps Circling Globe — AP1

1965, May 1 Engr. ***Perf. 11½***

C5	AP1	4t brown carmine	4.50	3.50

Vienna Intl. Philatelic Exhibition, WIPA, June 4-13. #C5 contains one 61x38mm stamp.

Weather Satellite AP2

Designs: 20m, Antarctic exploration. 30m, Space exploration.

1965, May 15 Photo. ***Perf. 13½***

C6	AP2	15m lilac, gold & blk	.50	.25
C7	AP2	20m blue & multi	2.75	.60
C8	AP2	30m rose & multi	.65	.25
		Nos. C6-C8 (3)	3.90	1.05

International Quiet Sun Year, 1964-65.

ITU Emblem — AP3

Design: 4t, Communications satellite.

1965, Dec. 20 ***Perf. 11½x12***

C9	AP3	30m blue & bister	1.00	.50
C10	AP3	50m red & bister	1.00	.50

Souvenir Sheet

Perf. 11, Imperf.

C11	AP3	4t gold, bl & blk	4.00	3.00

ITU, centenary. No. C11 contains one stamp, 38x51mm. Exists imperf. Values: unused $5.50; used $4.50.

Souvenir Sheet

Luna 10, Moon and Earth — AP4

1966, July 10 Photo. *Imperf.*
C12 AP4 4t multicolored 4.50 3.50

Luna 10 Russian moon mission, Apr. 3, 1966.

Souvenir Sheet

Astronaut and Landing Module — AP5

1969, Aug. 20 Litho. *Perf. 11½*
C13 AP5 4t ultra & multi 4.00 3.00

Apollo 11 US moon mission, first man landing on moon.

Souvenir Sheet

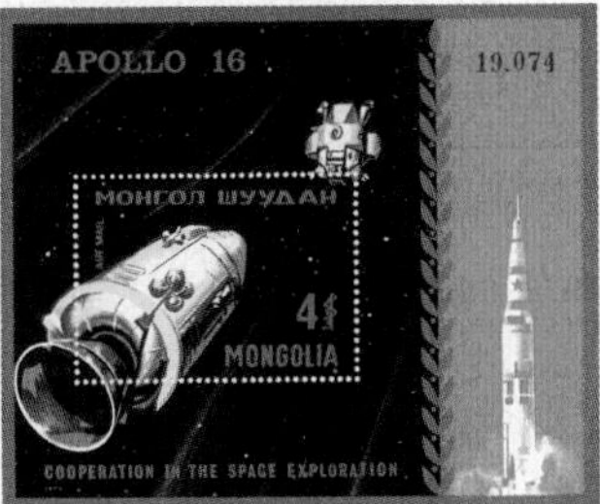

Apollo 16 — AP6

Perf. 12½x11½
1972, Apr. 16 Photo.
C14 AP6 4t multicolored 4.00 3.00

Apollo 16 moon mission, Apr. 15-27.

Souvenir Sheet

Mongolian Horse — AP7

1972, May 10 Photo. *Perf. 12½*
C15 AP7 4t multicolored 4.00 3.00

Centenary of the discovery of the Przewalski wild horse, bred in captivity in Berlin Zoo.

Telecommunication — AP8

Designs: 30m, Horse breeding. 40m, Train and plane. 50m, Corn and farm machinery. 60m, Red Cross ambulance and hospital. 80m, Actors. 1t, Factories.

1972, July 11 Litho. *Perf. 12*

C16	AP8	20m olive & multi	.40	.35
C17	AP8	30m violet & multi	.40	.35
C18	AP8	40m rose & multi	.40	.35
C19	AP8	50m red & multi	.40	.35
C20	AP8	60m multicolored	.70	.35
C21	AP8	80m lt blue & multi	.70	.35
C22	AP8	1t green & multi	1.00	.90
		Nos. C16-C22 (7)	4.00	3.00

Mongolian Achievements.

Mongolian Flag, Globe and Radar — AP9

Perf. 12½x11½
1972, July 20 Photo.
C23 AP9 60m olive & multi 1.00 .50

Intl. Telecommunications Day, May 17, 1972.

Running and Olympic Rings — AP10

Olympic Rings and: 15m, Boxing. 20m, Judo. 25m, High jump. 30m, Rifle shooting. 60m, Wrestling. 80m, Weight lifting. 1t, Mongolian flag and sport emblem. 4t, Woman archer, vert.

Perf. 12½x11½
1972, July 30 Photo.

C24	AP10	10m multicolored	.30	.30
C25	AP10	15m multicolored	.30	.30
C26	AP10	20m multicolored	.30	.30
C27	AP10	25m multicolored	.30	.30
C28	AP10	30m multicolored	.30	.30
C29	AP10	60m multicolored	.50	.30
C30	AP10	80m multicolored	.65	.50
C31	AP10	1t multicolored	.90	.70
		Nos. C24-C31 (8)	3.55	3.00

Souvenir Sheet
Perf. 11½x12½

C32 AP10 4t orange & multi 3.50 3.00

20th Olympic Games, Munich, 8/26-9/11.

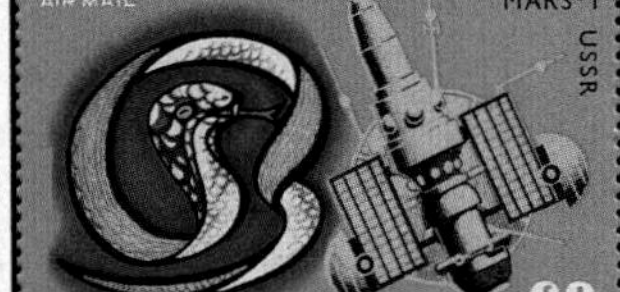

U.S./U.S.S.R. Space Achievements — AP11

Astrological Signs of the Eastern Calendar and Space Project: a, Snake, Mars 1. b, Dragon and Mariner 2. c, Hare, Soyuz 5. d, Monkey, Explorer 6. e, Cock, Venera 1. f, Rat, Apollo 15. g, Horse, Apollo 8. h, Boar, Cosmos 110. i, Tiger, Gemini 7. j, Sheep, Electron 2. k, Dog, Ariel 2. l, Ram, Venera 4.

1972, Dec. 4 Photo. *Perf. 12*
C33 Sheet of 12 7.00 5.00
a.-f. AP11 60m any single, size: 55x35mm .50 .40
g.-l. AP11 60m any single, size: 35x35mm .50 .40

Airliner — AP12

1973, Jan. Photo. *Perf. 12*
C34 AP12 1.50t blue 1.60 .40

For surcharge, see No. 2408.

Weather Satellite, Earth Station, WMO Emblem — AP13

1973, Feb. Photo. *Perf. 12x11½*
C35 AP13 60m multicolored 1.00 .50

Intl. meteorological cooperation, cent.

Holy Flame Type of 1959
Souvenir Sheet

1973, Apr. 15 Photo. *Perf. 12½*
C36 A48 4t gold & multi 4.00 3.00

IBRA München 1973 Intl. Stamp Exhibition, Munich, May 11-20. No. C36 contains one 40x63mm stamp in redrawn design of A48 with simulated perforations and wide gold margin.

Mongolia #236 — AP14

Designs: Stamps (with mail-connected designs) of participating countries: No. C37, Russia No. 3100. No. C39, Bulgaria #1047. No. C40, Hungary #B202. No. C41, Czechoslavia #C72. No. C42, German Dem. Rep. #369. No. C43, Cuba #C31. No. C44, Romania #2280. No. C45, Poland #802.

1973, July 31 Litho. *Perf. 12½*

C37	AP14	30m multi	.50	.30
C38	AP14	30m shown	.50	.30
C39	AP14	30m multi	.50	.30
C40	AP14	30m multi	.50	.30
C41	AP14	30m multi	.50	.30
C42	AP14	30m multi	.50	.30
C43	AP14	30m multi	.50	.30
C44	AP14	30m multi	.50	.30
C45	AP14	30m multi	.50	.30
		Nos. C37-C45 (9)	4.50	2.70

Conference of Permanent Committee for Posts and Telecommunications of Council for Economic Aid (COMECON), Ulan Bator, Aug. 1973.

Launching of Soyuz Spacecraft — AP15

10m, Apollo 8. 15m, Soyuz 4 & 5 docking. 20m, Apollo 11 lunar module. 30m, Apollo 14 splashdown. 50m, Soyuz 6, 7 & 8. 60m, Apollo 16 moon rover. 1t, Lunokhod 1 on moon. 4t, Soyuz and Apollo.

1973, Oct. 26 Litho. *Perf. 12½*

C46	AP15	5m shown	.30	.25
C47	AP15	10m multi	.30	.25
C48	AP15	15m multi	.30	.25
C49	AP15	20m multi	.30	.25
C50	AP15	30m multi	.50	.25
C51	AP15	50m multi	.60	.25
C52	AP15	60m multi	.70	.50
C53	AP15	1t multi	1.00	.75
		Nos. C46-C53 (8)	4.00	2.75

Souvenir Sheet

C54 AP15 4t multi 4.50 3.50

US and Russian achievements in space.

Comecon Building, Moscow — AP16

1974, Feb. 28 Photo. *Perf. 11½x12*
C55 AP16 60m blue & multi .75 .30

25th anniversary of the Council of Mutual Economic Assistance.

Souvenir Sheet

Mongolia No. 4 — AP17

1974, Mar. 15 Photo. *Perf. 12½*
C56 AP17 4t multicolored 4.00 3.00

50th anniv. of 1st stamps of Mongolia.

Postrider and UPU Emblem — AP18

UPU emblem & means of transportation: No. C58, Reindeer post. No. C59, Mail coach. No. C60, Balloon post. No. C61, Steamship and AN-2 plane. No. C62, Train, truck and city. No. C63, Rocket over North Pole.

No. C64, Globe and post horn, vert.

1974, Apr. Litho. *Perf. 12*

C57 AP18 50m shown .65 .35
C58 AP18 50m multi .65 .35
C59 AP18 50m multi .65 .35
C60 AP18 50m multi .65 .35
C61 AP18 50m multi .65 .35
C62 AP18 50m multi .65 .35
C63 AP18 50m multi .65 .35
Nos. C57-C63 (7) 4.55 2.45

Souvenir Sheet

C64 AP18 4t multi 10.00 9.00

Centenary of Universal Postal Union.

Circus Type of 1974

Design: 1t, Two women contortionists.

1974, May 4 Litho. *Perf. 12*

C65 A177 1t multicolored 1.25 .60

No. C65 has se-tenant label, with similar design.

Nature Type of Regular Issue

1t, Scientist checking water, globe. 4t, Wild rose.

1974, Dec. Litho. *Perf. 11*

C66 A186 1t multicolored 1.20 .50

Souvenir Sheet

Perf. 12½

C67 A186 4t multicolored 4.00 3.00

UPU Type of 1974

Souvenir Sheet

Design: UPU Emblem, vert.

1974, Dec. *Perf. 11½x12*

C68 A187 4t multicolored 4.50 4.50

Soyuz on Launching Pad, Project Emblem — AP19

Project Emblem and: 20m, Radar and Apollo. 30m, Apollo, Soyuz and earth. 40m, Spacecraft before docking. 50m, Spacecraft after docking. 60m, Soyuz circling earth. 1t, Spacecraft, space station and earth. 4t, Russian and American astronauts.

1975, June 14 Litho. *Perf. 12*

C69 AP19 10m blue & multi .25 .25
C70 AP19 20m multicolored .25 .25
C71 AP19 30m sepia & multi .25 .25
C72 AP19 40m silver & multi .45 .30
C73 AP19 50m multicolored .65 .40
C74 AP19 60m multicolored .80 .40
C75 AP19 1t multicolored 1.20 .80
Nos. C69-C75 (7) 3.85 2.65

Souvenir Sheet

C76 AP19 4t black & multi 2.75 2.75

Apollo Soyuz space test project (Russo-American space cooperation), launching July 15; link-up July 17.

Mongolian Mountain Sheep — AP20

1975, Aug. 4 Litho. *Perf. 12*

C77 AP20 1.50t multi + label 2.00 1.00

South Asia Tourism Year.

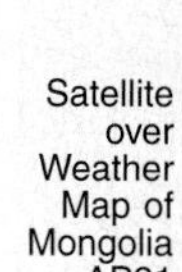
Satellite over Weather Map of Mongolia AP21

1976, Mar. 20 *Perf. 12x11½*

C78 AP21 60m blue & yellow 1.00 .30

40th anniversary of meteorological service.

Souvenir Sheet

Girl with Books and Flowers — AP22

1976, Mar. 30 *Perf. 12*

C79 AP22 4t multicolored 3.50 3.00

30th anniversary of UNESCO.

Souvenir Sheet

The Wise Musician, by Sarav — AP23

1976, May 3 Litho. *Perf. 11½x12½*

C80 AP23 4t multicolored 3.50 3.00

Interphil 76 Phil. Exhib., Philadelphia, Pa., May 29-June 6.

Olympic Games Type of 1976

Souvenir Sheet

1976, May 20 *Perf. 12½x11½*

C81 A202 4t Wrestling 3.00 2.50

Independence Type of 1976

60m, Progress in agriculture and industry.

1976, June 20 Litho. *Perf. 12x11½*

C82 A203 60m multicolored .70 .30

Olympic Medalists Type, 1976

Souvenir Sheet

Design: 4t, Oidov Zeveg, Mongolian flag.

1976, Nov. 30 Litho. *Perf. 11x11½*

C83 A209 4t multicolored 3.00 2.50

Mounting Carrier Rocket with Bell-shaped Gear — AP24

Designs: 20m, Launching of Intercosmos 3. 30m, Marine Observatory Gagarin (ship). 40m, Satellite observation of lunar eclipse. 60m, Observatory with multiple antenna system. 80m, Examination of Van Allen Zone, magnetosphere. 1t, Meteorological earth satellite. 4t, Intercosmos satellite with lines showing participating countries on globe.

1977, June 20 Litho. *Perf. 12*

C84 AP24 10m multicolored .25 .25
C85 AP24 20m multicolored .25 .25
C86 AP24 30m multicolored .35 .25
C87 AP24 40m multicolored .45 .25
C88 AP24 60m multicolored .65 .40
C89 AP24 80m multicolored .90 .50
C90 AP24 1t multicolored 1.10 .60
Nos. C84-C90 (7) 3.95 2.50

Souvenir Sheet

Perf. 12½

C91 AP24 4t multicolored 3.50 2.50

11th anniv. of Intercosmos program, cooperation of 9 socialist countries for space research. No. C91 contains one stamp 58x37mm.

Trade Union Emblem, Factory and Sheep AP25

1977, June *Perf. 12x11½*

C92 AP25 60m multicolored 1.00 .30

11th Cong. of Mongolian Trade Unions, May 12.

Montgolfier's Balloon — AP26

Dirigibles: 30m, Zeppelin over North Pole, 1931. 40m, Osoaviahim, Russian Arctic cargo. 50m, North, Russian heavy duty cargo. 60m, Aeron-340, Russian planned. 80m, Machinery transport, Russian planned. 1.20t, Flying crane, French planned. 4t, Russia No. C26 (stamp) and Sukhe Bator statue.

1977, Dec. Litho. *Perf. 12*

C93 AP26 20m multicolored .25 .25
C94 AP26 30m multicolored .25 .25
C95 AP26 40m multicolored .35 .25
C96 AP26 50m multicolored .45 .30
C97 AP26 60m multicolored .65 .30
C98 AP26 80m multicolored .90 .50
C99 AP26 1.20t multicolored 1.40 .60
Nos. C93-C99 (7) 4.25 2.45

Souvenir Sheet

Perf. 12½x11½

C100 AP26 4t multicolored 4.00 3.00

History of airships.

A. F. Mozhaiski and his Plane, 1884 — AP27

Designs: 30m, Henry Farman and his plane, 1909. 40m, Geoffrey de Havilland and D. H. 66 Hercules, 1920's. 50m, Charles A. Lindbergh, Spirit of St. Louis and route New York to Paris, 1927. 60m, Mongolian pilots Shagdarsuren and Demberel and plane over Altai Mountains, 1935. 80m, Soviet aviators Chkalov, Baidukov, Beliakov, plane and route Moscow to Vancouver, 1937. 1.20t, A. N. Tupolev, supersonic plane TU 154, route Moscow to Alma-Ata, 1968. 4t, Wilbur and Orville Wright and their plane.

1978, Mar. 25 Litho. *Perf. 12½x11*

C101 AP27 20m multi .25 .25
C102 AP27 30m multi .30 .25
C103 AP27 40m multi .35 .25
C104 AP27 50m multi .45 .30
C105 AP27 60m multi .55 .30
C106 AP27 80m multi .70 .40
C107 AP27 1.20t multi 1.10 .60
Nos. C101-C107 (7) 3.70 2.35

Souvenir Sheet

C108 AP27 4t multi 3.50 3.50

75th anniversary of first powered flight, Wright brothers, 1903.

Soccer Type of 1978

Souvenir Sheet

Design: 4t, Two soccer players.

1978, Apr. 15 *Perf. 11½*

C109 A231 4t multi 3.75 3.75

World Soccer Championships, Argentina 78, June 1-25. #C109 contains 1 45x38mm stamp.

Souvenir Sheet

Canada No. 553 and Mongolia No. 549 — AP28

1978, June Litho. *Perf. 12½*

C110 AP28 4t multi 3.50 3.50

CAPEX '78, Intl. Phil. Exhibition, Toronto, June 9-18.

Map of Cuba, Ship, Plane and Festival Emblem — AP29

1978, July 28 Litho. *Perf. 12*

C111 AP29 1t multicolored 1.50 .30

11th World Youth Festival, Havana, 7/28-8/5.

Souvenir Sheet

Aleksei Gubarev and Vladimir Remek, PRAGA '78 Emblem — AP30

1978, Sept. 5 Litho. *Perf. 12*

C112 AP30 4t multicolored 3.50 3.50

PRAGA '78 Intl. Phil. Exhib., Prague, Sept. 8-17, and Russian-Czechoslovak space cooperation, Intercosmos.

DDR Flag, TV Tower, Berlin, Satellite AP31

1979, Oct. 9 Litho. *Perf. 11½x12*

C113 AP31 60m multicolored .75 .40

German Democratic Republic, 30th anniv.

Demoiselle Crane AP32

Protected Birds: 30m, Hawk warbler. 50m, Ruddy shelduck. 60m, Blue magpie. 70m, Goldfinch. 80m, Titmouse. 1t, Golden oriole.

1979, Oct. 25

C114	AP32	10m multi	.40	.25
C115	AP32	30m multi	.60	.25
C116	AP32	50m multi	.75	.25
C117	AP32	60m multi	1.00	.25
C118	AP32	70m multi	1.10	.30
C119	AP32	80m multi	1.25	.30
C120	AP32	1t multi	1.50	.35
		Nos. C114-C120 (7)	6.60	1.95

Venera 5 and 6 — AP33

American and Russian Space Missions: 30m, Mariner 5. 50m, Mars 3. 60m, Viking 1 and 2. 70m, Luna 1, 2 and 3. 80m, Lunokhod 2. 1t, Apollo 15. 4t, Apollo 11, astronauts on moon.

Perf. 12½x11½

1979, Nov. 24 **Litho.**

C121	AP33	10m multi	.25	.25
C122	AP33	30m multi	.25	.25
C123	AP33	50m multi	.35	.25
C124	AP33	60m multi	.45	.25
C125	AP33	70m multi	.55	.30
C126	AP33	80m multi	.65	.40
C127	AP33	1t multi	.80	.40
		Nos. C121-C127 (7)	3.30	2.10

Souvenir Sheet

C128	AP33	4t multi	3.50	3.50

Apollo 11 moon landing, 10th anniversary.

Andrena Scita — AP34

Insects: 30m, Paravespula germanica. 40m, Perilampus ruficornis. 50m, Bumblebee. 60m, Honey bee. 80m, Stilbum cyanurum. 1.20t, Ruby tail.

1980, Feb. 25 **Litho.** ***Perf. 11x12***

C129	AP34	20m multi	.25	.25
C130	AP34	30m multi	.30	.25
C131	AP34	40m multi	.45	.30
C132	AP34	50m multi	.55	.30
C133	AP34	60m multi	.65	.40
C134	AP34	80m multi	.85	.50
C135	AP34	1.20t multi	1.25	.60
		Nos. C129-C135 (7)	4.30	2.60

Z-526 AFS Stunt Planes, Czechoslovakia — AP35

30m, RS-180 "Sportsman," Germany. 40m, Yanki-Anu, US. 50m, MJ-2 "Tempete," France. 60m, "Pits," Canada. 80m, "Acrostar," Switzerland. 1.20t, JAK-50, USSR.
4t, JAK-52, USSR.

1980, Aug. 4 **Litho.** ***Perf. 12***

C136	AP35	20m shown	.25	.25
C137	AP35	30m multi	.25	.25
C138	AP35	40m multi	.35	.25
C139	AP35	50m multi	.45	.25
C140	AP35	60m multi	.55	.30
C141	AP35	80m multi	.65	.40
C142	AP35	1.20t multi	1.00	.55
		Nos. C136-C142 (7)	3.50	2.25

Souvenir Sheet

C143	AP35	4t multi	3.00	2.50

10th World Aerobatic Championship, Oshkosh, Wisconsin, Aug. 17-30. No. C143 contains one 50x43mm stamp.

Olympic Type of 1980

Souvenir Sheet

1980, Sept. 15 **Litho.** ***Perf. 12½***

C144	A253	4t Wrestlers	3.50	3.50

J. Davaajav, Mongolian silver medalist, 22nd Summer Olympic Games, Moscow. Inscribed "Los Angeles '84".

Souvenir Sheet

AP36

1980, Dec. 10 **Litho.** ***Perf. 11½x11***

C145	AP36	4t multi	3.50	3.50

Johannes Kepler (1571-1630), German astronomer.

AP37

Graf Zeppelin and: 20m, Germany #C40, sea eagle. 30m, Germany #C41, polar fox. 40m, Germany #C42, walrus. 50m, Russia #C26, polar bear. 60m, Russia #C27, snowy owl. 80m, Russia #C28, puffin. 1.20t, Russia #C29, seal. 4t, Icebreaker Maligin.

1981, Oct. 5 **Litho.** ***Perf. 12x11½***

C146	AP37	20m multi	.50	.25
C147	AP37	30m multi	.60	.25
C148	AP37	40m multi	.30	.40
C149	AP37	50m multi	.90	.30
C150	AP37	60m multi	1.00	.40
C151	AP37	80m multi	1.40	.60
C152	AP37	1.20t multi	1.75	.70
		Nos. C146-C152 (7)	6.45	2.90

Souvenir Sheet

C153	AP37	4t multi	4.50	4.00

Graf Zeppelin polar flight, 50th anniv. No. C153 contains one stamp 36x51mm.

ITU Plenipotentiaries Conference, Nairobi, Sept. — AP38

1982, Sept. 27 **Litho.** ***Perf. 12***

C154	AP38	60m Map	.80	.30

2nd UN Conference on Peaceful Uses of Outer Space, Vienna, Aug. 9-21 — AP39

No. C155, Sputnik 1. No. C156, Sputnik 2. No. C157, Vostok 1. No. C158, Venera 8. No. C159, Vostok 6. No. C160, Voskhod 2. No. C161, Apollo II. No. C162, Soyuz 6.
No. C163, Soyuz 39, Salyut 6.

1982, Dec. 15 **Litho.** ***Perf. 12***

C155	AP39	60m multi	.50	.30
C156	AP39	60m multi	.50	.30
C157	AP39	60m multi	.50	.30
C158	AP39	60m multi	.50	.30
C159	AP39	60m multi	.50	.30
C160	AP39	60m multi	.50	.30
C161	AP39	60m multi	.50	.30
C162	AP39	60m multi	.50	.30
		Nos. C155-C162 (8)	4.00	2.40

Souvenir Sheet

Perf. 12½x12

C163	AP39	4t multi	3.50	3.50

Balloon Flight Bicentenary AP40

20m, Montgolfiere, 1783. 30m, Blanchard, 1785. 40m, Royal-Vauzhall, 1836. 50m, Oernen, 1897. 60m, Gordon Bennett Race, 1906. 80m, Paris, 1931. 1.20t, USSR-VR-62, 1933.
4t, Mongolia, 1977.

1982, Dec. 31 ***Perf. 11½x12½***

C164	AP40	20m multi	.25	.25
C165	AP40	30m multi	.30	.25
C166	AP40	40m multi	.40	.25
C167	AP40	50m multi	.50	.25
C168	AP40	60m multi	.65	.25
C169	AP40	80m multi	.90	.30
C170	AP40	1.20t multi	1.40	.40
		Nos. C164-C170 (7)	4.40	1.95

Souvenir Sheet

C171	AP40	4t multi	3.50	3.50

Souvenir Sheet

Revolutionary Mongolia Monument — AP41

1983 **Litho.** ***Imperf.***

C172	AP41	4t multi	3.50	3.50

Concorde — AP42

20m, DC-10, vert. 30m, Airbus A-300 B-2. 50m, Boeing 747. 60m, IL-62. 80m, TU-154. 1.20t, IL-86.
4t, Yak-42.

1984, Aug. 15 **Litho.** ***Perf. 14***

C173	AP42	20m multi	.25	.25
C174	AP42	30m multi	.30	.25
C175	AP42	40m shown	.40	.30
C176	AP42	50m multi	.50	.40
C177	AP42	60m multi	.60	.40
C178	AP42	80m multi	.80	.50
C179	AP42	1.20t multi	1.20	.60
		Nos. C173-C179 (7)	4.05	2.70

Souvenir Sheet

C180	AP42	4t multi	3.50	3.50

1988 Winter Olympics, Calgary AP43

20m, Bobsled. 30m, Ski jumping. 40m, Downhill skiing. 50m, Biathlon. 60m, Speed skating. 80m, Women's figure skating. 1.20t, Ice hockey.
4t, Cross-country skiing.

1988, Jan. 20 **Litho.** ***Perf. 14***

C181	AP43	20m multi	.25	.25
C182	AP43	30m multi	.25	.25
C183	AP43	40m multi	.35	.25
C184	AP43	50m multi	.40	.25
C185	AP43	60m multi	.55	.30
C186	AP43	80m multi	.65	.30
C187	AP43	1.20t multi	.75	.40
		Nos. C181-C187 (7)	3.20	2.00

Souvenir sheet

C188	AP43	4t multi	3.25	2.50

Souvenir Sheet

Hong Kong '94 — AP44

1994, Feb. 18 Litho. ***Perf. 14½x15***

C189	AP44	600t multicolored	4.00	4.00
a.		With Hong Kong '97 emblem in sheet margin	4.00	4.00

Issued: #C189a, 1/12/97.

No. C163 Surcharged in Red

Souvenir Sheet

2001, Mar. 22 Litho. ***Perf. 12½x12***

C190	AP39	400t on 4t multi	*25.00*	*25.00*

Joint Soviet-Mongolian space flight, 20th anniv.

AIR POST SEMI-POSTAL STAMP

Catalogue values for unused stamps in this section are for Never Hinged items.

UNICEF Type of 1977

Souvenir Sheet

Design: 4t+50m, Balloon with Mongolian flag, children and UNICEF emblem.

1977, June 1 Litho. ***Perf. 12***

CB1	SP2	4t + 50m multi	4.00	4.00

First balloon flight in Mongolia. Surtax was for Children's Village.

MONTENEGRO

ˌmän-tə-ˈnē-ˌ(ˌ)grō

LOCATION — Southern Europe, bordering on the Adriatic Sea
GOVT. — Republic in southern Europe.
AREA — 5,415 sq. mi.
POP. — 620,145 (2003)
CAPITAL — Podgorica

Montenegro maintained a precarious independence from the Ottoman Turks during the 16th-19th centuries as a theocracy, under a succession of bishop princes. In 1852 it became an independent principality. On December 1, 1918, Montenegro, along with Bosnia and Herzegovina, Croatia, Dalmatia and Slovenia, was absorbed by Serbia to form the Kingdom of the Serbs, Croats and Slovenes, which became the Kingdom of Yugoslavia in 1929.

All stamps of the Kingdom of Montenegro were printed at the State Printing Works, Vienna, Later, overprints were applied at Cetinje.

During World War II, an Italian satellite regime was established in an enlarged Montenegrin state, but after the war, Montenegro became one of the constituent republics of the Socialist Federal Republic of Yugoslavia.

In 1992, with the dissolution of the greater Yugoslav republic, only Montenegro remained associated with Serbia, first in the Federal Republic of Yugoslavia and, after 2002, in the looser federation of Serbia & Montenegro.

On May 21, 2006, Montenegrins endorsed independence and complete separation from Serbia in a national referendum, and the Republic of Montenegro declared independence on June 3.

On June 7, Serbia officially recognized Montenegro's independence.

100 Novcic = 1 Florin
100 Helera = 1 Kruna (1902)
100 Para = 1 Kruna (1907)
100 Para = 1 Perper (1910)
100 cents = 1 euro (2003)

Canceled to Order

Used values for Nos. 1-110, H1-H5, and J1-J26 are for canceled-to-order stamps. Postally used examples sell for considerably more.

Watermarks

Wmk. 91 — "BRIEF-MARKEN" (#1-14) or "ZEITUNGS-MARKEN" (#15-21) in Double-lined Capitals once across sheet

Wmk. 140 — Crown

Prince Nicholas I — A1

Early Printings

Narrow Spacing (2-2½mm)

Perf. 10½ Large Holes, pointed teeth

1874 Typo. Wmk. 91

1	A1	2n yellow	40.00	45.00
2	A1	3n green	55.00	45.00
3	A1	5n rose red	50.00	45.00
4	A1	7n lt lilac	50.00	37.50
5	A1	10n blue	140.00	92.50
6	A1	15n yel bister	160.00	140.00
7	A1	25n lilac gray	325.00	225.00
		Nos. 1-7 (7)	820.00	630.00

Middle Printings (1879)

Narrow spacing

Perf. 12, 12½, 13 and Compound

8	A1	2n yellow	11.50	7.50
a.		Perf. 12-13x10½	190.00	140.00
9	A1	3n green	9.25	6.00
10	A1	5n red	9.25	6.00
11	A1	7n rose lilac	9.25	6.00
a.		7n lilac	19.00	14.00
12	A1	10n blue	19.00	8.00
a.		Perf. 12-13x10½	65.00	52.50
13	A1	15n bister brn	19.00	11.00
14	A1	25n gray lilac	25.00	16.00
		Nos. 8-14 (7)	102.25	60.50

Late Printings (1893?)

Narrow and wide spacing (2¾-3½mm)

Perf. 10½, 11½ Small holes, broad teeth

(Perf. 11½ also with pointed teeth)

15	A1	2n yellow	4.50	3.00
a.		Perf. 11 ('94)	32.50	23.00
16	A1	3n green	4.50	3.00
17	A1	5n red	3.50	2.75
18	A1	7n rose	3.50	2.75
a.		Perf. 11 ('94)	14.50	13.50
19	A1	10n blue	4.50	3.25
20	A1	15n brown	4.50	3.50
21	A1	25n brown violet	5.75	4.50
		Nos. 15-21 (7)	30.75	22.75

Dates of issue of the late printings are still being researched.

Types of 1874-93 Overprinted in Black or Red

1893 ***Perf. 10½, 11½***

22	A1	2n yellow	32.50	8.00
a.		Perf. 11	*75.00*	*30.00*
23	A1	3n green	6.50	3.25
24	A1	5n red	4.50	2.75
25	A1	7n rose	5.75	4.50
a.		Perf. 12	110.00	72.50
b.		7n rose lilac	5.00	3.00
c.		7n lilac, perf. 12	*125.00*	
d.		Perf. 11	*40.00*	*30.00*
26	A1	10n blue	5.75	4.50
27	A1	10n blue (R)	8.50	6.25
28	A1	15n brown	4.50	3.50
a.		Perf. 12	140.00	92.50
29	A1	15n brown (R)	*2,750.*	*1,900.*
30	A1	25n brown violet	4.50	3.50
31	A1	25n brn vio (R)	8.50	5.50
a.		Perf. 12½		*275.00*
		Nos. 22-28,30-31 (9)	81.00	41.75

Introduction of printing to Montenegro, 400th anniversary.

This overprint had many settings. Several values exist with "1494" or "1495" instead of "1493", or with missing letters or numerals due to wearing of the clichés. Double and inverted overprints exist. Some printings were made after 1893 to supply a philatelic demand, but were available for postage.

The 7n with red overprint was not issued.

1894-98 Wmk. 91 ***Perf. 10½***

32	A1	1n gray blue	.65	.65
33	A1	2n emerald ('98)	.45	.45
34	A1	3n car rose ('98)	.45	.45
c.		3n analine red ('98)	.45	.75
35	A1	5n orange ('98)	2.75	.65
36	A1	7n gray lilac ('98)	.55	.55
37	A1	10n magenta ('98)	.65	.95
38	A1	15n red brn ('98)	.45	.65
39	A1	20n brown orange	.65	.65
40	A1	25n dull blue ('98)	.45	.65
41	A1	30n maroon	.65	.65
42	A1	50n ultra	.65	.45
43	A1	1fl deep green	.95	4.50
44	A1	2fl red brown	1.50	13.50
		Nos. 32-44 (13)	10.80	24.75

Perf. 11½, Small Holes

32a	A1	1n gray blue	.55	.60
33a	A1	2n emerald ('98)	.70	.65
34a	A1	3n carmine rose ('98)	.70	.65

Monastery at Cetinje (Royal Mausoleum) A3

Perf. 10½

1896, Sept. 1 Litho. Unwmk.

45	A3	1n dk blue & bis	.40	1.40
46	A3	2n magenta & yel	.40	1.40
47	A3	3n org brn & yel grn	.40	1.40
48	A3	5n bl grn & bis	.40	1.40
49	A3	10n yellow & ultra	.40	1.40
50	A3	15n dk blue & grn	.40	1.40
51	A3	20n bl grn & ultra	.40	1.50
52	A3	25n dk blue & yel	.50	1.50
53	A3	30n magenta & bis	.65	1.50
54	A3	50n red brn & gray bl	.65	1.50
55	A3	1fl rose & gray bl	1.10	1.90
56	A3	2fl brown & black	1.60	2.25
		Nos. 45-56 (12)	7.30	18.55

Perf. 11½

45a	A3	1n dark blue & bister	.95	2.25
46a	A3	2n magenta & yellow	.95	2.25
47a	A3	3n org brn & yel grn	.95	2.25
48a	A3	5n blue green & bister	.95	2.25
49a	A3	10n yellow & ultramarine	.45	1.40
50a	A3	15n dark blue & green	72.50	110.00
51a	A3	20n blue green & ultra	45.00	67.50
52a	A3	25n dk blue & yellow	1.40	2.75
53a	A3	30n magenta & bister	1.40	2.75
54a	A3	50n red brn & gray blue	1.40	2.75
55a	A3	1fl rose & gray blue	2.10	3.50
56a	A3	2fl brown & black	2.75	5.50

Bicentenary of the ruling dynasty, founded by the Vladika, Danilo Petrovich of Nyegosh.

Inverted centers and other errors exist, but experts believe these to be printer's waste.

Perf. 11½ counterfeits are common.

Prince Nicholas I — A4

Perf. 13x13½, 13x12½ (2h, 5h, 50h, 2k, 5k), 12½ (1h, 25h)

1902, July 12

57	A4	1h ultra	.45	.45
58	A4	2h rose lilac	.45	.45
59	A4	5h green	.45	.45
a.		Pair, imperf.	5.75	
60	A4	10h rose	.45	.45
61	A4	25h dull blue	.95	1.10
a.		Perf. 12½	4.50	
62	A4	50h gray green	.95	1.10
63	A4	1k chocolate	.95	.95
64	A4	2k pale brown	.95	1.10
65	A4	5k buff	1.10	2.75
		Nos. 57-65 (9)	6.70	8.80

The 2h black brown and 25h indigo were not issued. Values: 2h, $95; 25h, $65. The 25h, perf. 12½, probably was never issued. Value, $4.50.

Constitution Issue

Same Overprinted in Red or Black "Constitution" 15mm

УСТАВ
Type I

УСТАВ
Type II

УСТАВ
Type III

УСТАВ
Type IV

1905, Dec. 5

66	A4	1h ultra (R)	.45	.45
e.		Double overprint	14.00	14.00
67	A4	2h rose lilac	.45	.45
e.		Double overprint	14.00	14.00
68	A4	5h green (R)	.95	.95
e.		Double overprint	14.00	14.00
f.		Inverted overprint	37.50	
69	A4	10h rose	1.40	1.10
e.		Double overprint	14.00	
70	A4	25h dull blue (R)	.70	.65
e.		Double overprint	14.00	
71	A4	50h gray green (R)	.70	.65
e.		Double overprint	14.00	14.00
72	A4	1k chocolate (R)	.70	.65
e.		Double overprint	14.00	14.00
f.		Inverted overprint	37.50	
73	A4	2k pale brown (R)	.95	.95
e.		Double overprint	17.00	17.00
74	A4	5k buff	1.50	1.40
e.		Double overprint	17.00	
		Nos. 66-74 (9)	7.80	7.25

Overprints in other colors are proofs.

1906 "Constitution" 16½mm

Type I

67a	A4	2h rose lilac	45.00	45.00
e.		Double overprint	—	
f.		Inverted overprint	—	
69a	A4	10h rose	325.00	
70a	A4	25h dull blue (R)	29.00	27.00
e.		Double overprint	—	
f.		Inverted overprint	—	
71a	A4	50h gray green (R)	29.00	27.00
e.		Double overprint	—	
f.		Inverted overprint	—	
72a	A4	1k chocolate (R)	29.00	27.00
73a	A4	2k pale brown (R)	29.00	27.00
f.		Inverted overprint	—	
74a	A4	5k buff	1.50	1.40
f.		Inverted overprint	—	
		Nos. 67a-74a (9)	488.90	155.80

Type II

66b	A4	1h ultra (R)	.45	.45
67b	A4	2h rose lilac	.45	.45
e.		Double overprint	19.00	
f.		Inverted overprint	47.50	
68b	A4	5h green (R)	.95	.95
e.		Double overprint	19.00	
69b	A4	10h rose	1.10	1.10
f.		Inverted overprint	47.50	
70b	A4	25h dull blue (R)	.70	.65
e.		Double overprint	19.00	
f.		Inverted overprint	47.50	
71b	A4	50h gray green (R)	.70	.65
e.		Double overprint	19.00	
72b	A4	1k chocolate (R)	.70	.65
73b	A4	2k pale brown (R)	.95	.95
f.		Inverted overprint	47.50	

No.	Design	Description	Unused	Used
74b	A4	5k buff	1.50	1.40
f.		Inverted overprint	55.00	
		Nos. 66b-74b (9)	7.50	7.25

Type III

No.	Design	Description	Unused	Used
66c	A4	1h ultra (R)	2.75	2.75
67c	A4	2h rose lilac	2.75	2.75
e.		Double overprint	—	
f.		Inverted overprint	—	
68c	A4	5h green (R)	5.75	5.50
e.		Double overprint	—	
69c	A4	10h rose	7.25	6.75
f.		Double overprint	—	
70c	A4	25h dull blue (R)	3.75	3.50
e.		Double overprint	—	
f.		Inverted overprint	—	
71c	A4	50h gray green (R)	3.75	3.50
e.		Double overprint	—	
72c	A4	1k chocolate (R)	3.75	3.75
73c	A4	2k pale brown (R)	4.75	4.75
f.		Inverted overprint	—	
74c	A4	5k buff	5.75	5.50
f.		Inverted overprint	—	

Type IV

No.	Design	Description	Unused	Used
66d	A4	1h ultra (R)	.95	.95
67d	A4	2h rose lilac	.95	.95
68d	A4	5h green (R)	2.40	2.40
e.		Double overprint	—	
f.		Inverted overprint	—	
69d	A4	10h rose	2.25	6.75
f.		Inverted overprint	—	
g.		"Constitutton"	22.50	
70d	A4	25h dull blue (R)	1.90	1.90
e.		Double overprint	—	
f.		Inverted overprint	—	
71d	A4	50h gray green (R)	2.40	2.40
f.		Inverted overprint	—	
72d	A4	1k chocolate (R)	2.40	2,40
73d	A4	2k pale brown (R)	3.50	3.25
f.		Inverted overprint	—	
74d	A4	5k buff	3.75	3.50
f.		Inverted overprint	—	

Prince Nicholas I — A5

1907, June 1 Engr. *Perf. 12½*

No.	Design	Description	Unused	Used
75	A5	1pa ocher	.40	.25
76	A5	2pa black	.40	.25
77	A5	5pa yellow green	1.60	.25
78	A5	10pa rose red	2.75	.25
79	A5	15pa ultra	.45	.45
80	A5	20pa red orange	.45	.45
81	A5	25pa indigo	.45	.45
82	A5	35pa bister brown	.70	.45
83	A5	50pa dull violet	.70	.65
84	A5	1kr carmine rose	.70	.65
85	A5	2kr green	.70	.65
86	A5	5kr red brown	1.50	1.10
		Nos. 75-86 (12)	10.80	5.85

Many Montenegro stamps exist imperforate or part perforate. Experts believe these to be printer's waste.

King Nicholas I as a Youth — A6

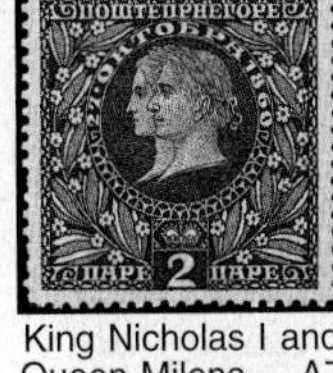

King Nicholas I and Queen Milena — A7

King Nicholas I — A11

Prince Nicholas — A12

5pa, 10pa, 25pa, 35pa, Nicholas in 1910. 15pa, Nicholas in 1878. 20pa, King and Queen, diff.

1910, Aug. 28 Engr.

No.	Design	Description	Unused	Used
87	A6	1pa black	.75	.45
88	A7	2pa purple brown	.75	.45
89	A6	5pa dark green	.75	.45
90	A6	10pa carmine	.75	.45
91	A6	15pa slate blue	.75	.45
92	A7	20pa olive green	.95	.65
93	A6	25pa deep blue	.95	.65
94	A6	35pa chestnut	1.40	.95
95	A11	50pa violet	1.40	.95
96	A11	1per lake	1.40	.95
97	A11	2per yellow green	1.75	1.10
98	A12	5per pale blue	1.90	1.40
a.		Perf. 10	25.00	
		Nos. 87-98 (12)	13.50	8.90

Proclamation of Montenegro as a kingdom, the 50th anniv. of the reign of King Nicholas and the golden wedding celebration of the King and Queen.

King Nicholas I — A13

1913, Apr. 1 Typo.

No.	Design	Description	Unused	Used
99	A13	1pa orange	.45	.65
100	A13	2pa plum	.45	.65
101	A13	5pa deep green	.50	.65
102	A13	10pa deep rose	.50	.65
103	A13	15pa blue gray	.60	.65
104	A13	20pa dark brown	.60	.65
105	A13	25pa deep blue	.95	.95
106	A13	35pa vermilion	.70	.65
107	A13	50pa pale blue	.45	.95
108	A13	1per yellow brown	.95	1.40
109	A13	2per gray violet	.95	1.40
110	A13	5per yellow green	.95	1.40
		Nos. 99-110 (12)	8.05	10.65

SERBIA & MONTENEGRO

100 Cents=1 Euro

Yugoslavia became Serbia & Montenegro Feb. 4, 2003, with each section of the country maintaining and operating their own postal service, and each having their own currency. After a referendum on independence on May 21, 2006, Montenegro seceded from Serbia and Montenegro, declaring independence on June 3. Serbia formally recognized Montenegro's independence on June 7.

The stamps below are inscribed only with euro denominations, used solely within Montenegro. Stamps inscribed with dinar denominations, issued for use in Serbia, and those denominated in both dinar and euro currencies, for use in either region, are found under the Serbia listings.

Budva A20

Durmitor A21

2003, Sept. 15 Litho. *Perf. 12½*

No.	Design	Description	Unused	Used
120	A20	25c multi	1.25	1.25
121	A21	40c multi	2.25	2.25

Christmas — A22

2003, Nov. 21 *Perf. 13¼*

No.	Design	Description	Unused	Used
122	A22	25c multi	1.75	1.75
		Complete booklet, 10 #122	17.50	

National Symbols A23

Small coat of arms, outline map of Europe and: 25c, Map of Montenegro. 40c, Parliament Building and map of Montenegro. 50c, Large coat of arms and map of Montenegro. 60c, Flag and map of Montenegro.

2005, Dec. 15 Litho. *Perf. 13*

No.	Design	Description	Unused	Used
123-126	A23	Set of 4	8.00	8.00

See Nos. 140-142.

Europa A24

Designs: 25c, Fish, shrimp, and mussels. 50c, Meat, olives, cheese and fruit.

No. 128C: d, 25c, Bee, honeycomb and honey. e, 50c, Grapes, grapevine, wine.

2005, Dec. 30 *Perf. 13½x13¾*

No.	Design	Description	Unused	Used
127	A24	25c multicolored	*4.00*	*4.00*
a.		As #127, perf. 13½x 13¾x 13½x imperf.	*18.00*	*18.00*
128	A24	50c multicolored	*8.50*	*8.50*
a.		As #128, perf. 13½x imperf. x 13½x 13¾	*25.00*	*25.00*
b.		Souvenir sheet, #127a, 128a	*45.00*	*45.00*

Souvenir Sheet

Perf. 13½x13¾

No.	Design	Description	Unused	Used
128C	A24	Sheet of 2, #d-e	*40.00*	*40.00*

A25

Europa Stamps, 50th Anniv. — A26

No. 129: a, Montenegro #100, common vignette of 1960 Europa stamps. b, Montenegro #101, common vignette of 1961-62 Europa stamps. c, Montenegro #102, bee and honeycomb. d, Montenegro #105, common vignette of 1956 Europa stamps.

No. 129E: f, Like #129a. g, Like #129b. h, Like #129c. i, Like #129d.

2006, Jan. 3 Litho. *Perf. 13½x13¾*

Stamps with Frames

No.	Design	Description	Unused	Used
129		Horiz. strip of 4	16.00	16.00
a.		A25 50c multi	1.00	1.00
b.		A25 €1 multi	2.50	2.50
c.-d.		A25 €2 Either single	4.75	4.75

Souvenir Sheet

Stamps Without Frames

No.	Design	Description	Unused	Used
129E	A25	Sheet of 4, #f-i	21.00	21.00

Litho. with Foil Application

Imperf

Size: 103x76mm

No.	Design	Description	Unused	Used
130	A26	€5.50 multi	15.00	15.00

No. 129E exists imperf. Value, *$65.*

2006 Winter Olympics, Turin A27

Designs: 60c, Figure skating. 90c, Ski jumping.

2006, Feb. 7 Litho. *Perf. 13½x13¾*

No.	Design	Description	Unused	Used
131-132	A27	Set of 2	4.00	4.0

Flowers A28

Designs: 25c, Petteria ramentacea. 50c, Viola nikolai.

2006, Mar. 15

No.	Design	Description	Unused	Used
133-134	A28	Set of 2	2.75	2.75

Introduction of Perper Currency, Cent. — A29

Central Bank of Montenegro and: 40c, 1906 1-para coin. 50c, 1906 20-para coin.

2006, Apr. 27 Litho. *Perf. 13½x13¾*

No.	Design	Description	Unused	Used
135-136	A29	Set of 2	3.50	3.50

2006 World Cup Soccer Championships, Germany — A30

Designs: No. 137, 60c, Players in match. No. 138, 90c, Players in match, diff.

No. 139: a, 60c, Players, empty stadium in background. b, 90c, Players, empty stadium in background, diff.

2006, May 30 *Perf. 13¾x13½*

No.	Design	Description	Unused	Used
137-138	A30	Set of 2	5.75	5.75

Souvenir Sheet

No.	Design	Description	Unused	Used
139	A30	Sheet of 2, #a-b	5.00	5.00

National Symbols Type of 2005 Redrawn With "Posta Crne Gore" Under Postal Emblem

Designs as before.

2006, June Litho. *Perf. 13¾*

No.	Design	Description	Unused	Used
140	A23	25c multi	1.00	1.00
a.		Perf. 13	*2.00*	*2.00*
141	A23	40c multi	1.50	1.50
a.		Perf. 13	*3.00*	*3.00*
142	A23	60c multi	2.50	2.50
		Nos. 140-142 (3)	5.00	5.00

Nos. 140a and 141a are dated "2005," while Nos. 140-142 are dated "2006."

Independent Republic

Tourism A31

Designs: 25c, Durmitor. 50c, Sveti Stefan.

2006, July 5 *Perf. 13½x13¾*

No.	Design	Description	Unused	Used
143-144	A31	Set of 2	2.75	2.75

Independence Referendum of May 21 — A32

2006, July 13
145 A32 50c multi 2.00 2.00

Europa — A33

Designs: No. 146, 60c, Women linking chain. No. 147, 90c, People and sun, horiz.
No. 148: a, 60c, Man with suitcase. b, 90c, People of different races.

2006, Aug. 30 *Perf. 13¾*
146-147 A33 Set of 2 6.00 6.00

Souvenir Sheet

148 A33 Sheet of 2, #a-b 5.75 5.75

Capt. Ivo Visin (1806-68), Circumnavigator, and Ship, Splendido — A34

2006, Sept. 5 *Perf. 13½x13¾*
149 A34 40c multi 1.60 1.60

Stamp Day — A35

2006, Oct. 2 *Perf. 13¾*
150 A35 25c multi 1.00 1.00

Mona Lisa, by Leonardo da Vinci, 500th Anniv. — A36

2006, Oct. 18 *Perf. 13¾x13½*
151 A36 50c multi 2.00 2.00

Cultural Heritage A37

Designs: No. 152, 25c, Ruins, Dukla Archaeological Site. No. 153, 25c, Glassware.

2006, Nov. 3 *Perf. 13¾x13½*
152-153 A37 Set of 2 2.00 2.00

Tara River A38

Perf. 13½x13¾

2006, Nov. 15 **Litho.**
154 A38 40c multi 1.50 1.50

Gregorian Calendar, 425th Anniv. A39

2007, Jan. 4 *Perf. 13¾x13*
155 A39 50c multi 2.00 2.00

Printed in sheets of 8 + label.

Wildlife Protection A40

2007, Feb. 7
156 A40 50c multi 2.00 2.00

Printed in sheets of 8 + label.

Europa — A41

Map of Montengro and: Nos. 157, 159a, 60c, Montengro Scouting emblem. Nos. 158, 159b, 90c, Tent and campfire.

2007, Apr. 20 **Litho.** *Perf. 13¾*
157 A41 60c multi 2.25 2.25
158 A41 90c multi 3.00 3.00
a. Souvenir sheet, #157-158 5.50 5.50

Perf. 13¾ (Imperf. Between Stamps)

159 Sheet of 2 5.50 5.50
a. A41 60c multi, 42x28mm 2.00 2.00
b. A41 90c multi, 42x28mm 2.75 2.75

Nos. 157 and 158 were each printed in sheets of 8 + label. No. 159 was sold with but not attached to a booklet cover.

Birds — A42

No. 160: a, 25c, Gull. b, 50c, Eagle.

2007, May 11 **Litho.** *Perf. 13¾*
160 A42 Pair, #a-b 3.00 3.00

Migration of Montenegrins to Istria, 350th Anniv. — A43

2007, June 21 *Perf. 13¾*
161 A43 60c multi 2.10 2.10

Printed in sheets of 8 + label.

Postal History A44

Glagolithic Text — A45

Mountains A46

Stylized Butterfly A47

2007, July 3
162 A44 25c multi .90 .90
163 A45 40c multi 1.40 1.40
164 A46 50c multi 1.75 1.75
165 A47 60c multi 2.25 2.25
Nos. 162-165 (4) 6.30 6.30

Petar Lubarda (1907-74), Painter A48

2007, July 27 *Perf. 13¾*
166 A48 40c multi 1.50 1.50

Ship — A49

2007, Aug. 1
167 A49 60c multi 2.10 2.10

Printed in sheets of 8 + label.

Joy of Europe — A50

2007, Oct. 2
168 A50 50c multi 1.90 1.90

Regional Telephone Service, Cent. — A51

Designs: 25c, Telephone dial. 50c, Telephone dial and red dots.

2007, Nov. 9 **Litho.** *Perf. 13¾*
169-170 A51 Set of 2 2.75 2.75

New Year's Day — A52

Designs: No. 171, 25c, Twisted ribbon. No. 172, 25c, Christmas ornament on tree branch. 50c, Wreath and bells. €1, Lit candle.

2007, Dec. 5 *Perf. 14x13¾*
171-174 A52 Set of 4 7.25 7.25

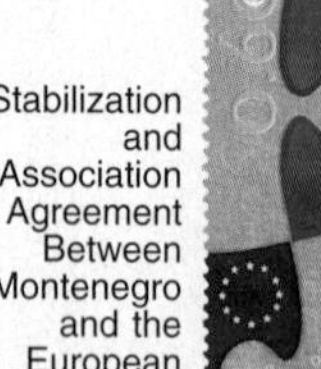

Stabilization and Association Agreement Between Montenegro and the European Union — A53

Jigsaw puzzle pieces with: 60c, Montenegro coat of arms and European Union ring of stars.

No. 176: a, 40c, Montenegro coat of arms. b, 50c, European Union ring of stars.

2008, Feb. 1 Litho. *Perf. 13¾*

175 A53 60c multi 2.10 2.10

Souvenir Sheet

176 A53 Sheet of 2, #a-b 3.25 3.25

Flowers — A54

Designs: 25c, Draba bertiscea. 40c, Edraianthus wettsteinii. 50c, Protoedriantus tarae. 60c, Dianthus nitidus.

2008, Feb. 20

177-180 A54 Set of 4 6.50 6.50

Nos. 177-180 each were printed in sheets of 5 + label.

2008 Summer Olympics, Beijing A55

Stylized athletes, Beijing Olympics emblem and: 60c, Map of Montenegro. 90c, Montenegro coat of arms.

2008, Mar. 26

181-182 A55 Set of 2 5.75 5.75

Europa — A56

Designs: No. 183, 60c, Boy, envelope with stamp. No. 184, 90c, Girl, letter.

No. 185: a, 60c, Boy, right half of envelope. b, 90c, Girl, left half of envelope.

2008, Apr. 2

183-184 A56 Set of 2 5.75 5.75

Souvenir Sheet

185 A56 Sheet of 2, #a-b 5.75 5.75

Nos. 183-184 each were printed in sheets of 8 + label.

Marko Miljanov (1833-1901), Writer — A57

2008, Apr. 24

186 A57 60c multi 2.25 2.25

Battle of Grahovac, 150th Anniv. — A58

2008, Apr. 29

187 A58 25c multi .95 .95

Tourism A59

Designs: 25c, Hillside hut. 40c, Fortress. 50c, Pier and boats. 60c, Boat on lake.

2008, May 21

188-191 A59 Set of 4 6.00 6.00

191a Sheet of 4, #188-191 6.00 6.00

Chess Olympics, Dresden, Germany A60

2008, June 18 Litho. *Perf. 13¾*

192 A60 60c multi 2.25 2.25

Ship Jadran, 75th Anniv. A61

2008, July 16

193 A61 50c multi 2.00 2.00

Victory of Montenegrin Team at European Water Polo Championships, Malaga, Spain — A62

2008, Sept. 15

194 A62 50c multi 2.00 2.00

Printed in sheets of 8 + label.

Roman Art — A63

No. 195: a, 25c, Frieze depicting faces. 50c, Mosaic depicting angel.

2008, Sept. 17

195 A63 Horiz. pair, #a-b 2.75 2.75

Stamp Day — A64

2008, Oct. 2

196 A64 60c multi 2.40 2.40

Automobile A65

Hourglass, Map of Montenegro A66

Eagle and Angel — A67

2008, Oct. 20 *Perf. 13¾x13¼*

197 A65 40c multi 1.60 1.60

198 A66 50c multi 1.75 1.75

199 A67 60c multi 2.40 2.40

Nos. 197-199 (3) 5.75 5.75

Alfred Nobel (1833-96), Inventor and Philanthropist — A68

2008, Oct. 21 *Perf. 13¾*

200 A68 50c multi 1.90 1.90

A69

A70

A71

A72

A73

First Railway in Montenegro, Cent. — A74

2008, Nov. 2

201 A69 25c multi .95 .95

202 A70 25c multi .95 .95

203 A71 25c multi .95 .95

204 A72 25c multi .95 .95

205 A73 25c multi .95 .95

206 A74 25c multi .95 .95

a. Souvenir sheet of 6, #201-206 5.75 5.75

Nos. 201-206 (6) 5.70 5.70

Nos. 201-206 each were printed in sheets of 5 + label.

Joy of Europe — A75

Designs: 25c, Shown. 40c, Towers and bridge, horiz.

2008, Nov. 20

207-208 A75 Set of 2 2.50 2.50

Nos. 207-208 each were printed in sheets of 8 + label.

Universal Declaration of Human Rights, 60th Anniv. — A76

2008, Dec. 11 *Perf. 13¾*

209 A76 50c multi 1.90 1.90

Printed in sheets of 8 + label.

Louis Braille (1809-52), Educator of the Blind A77

2009, Jan. 30

210 A77 60c multi 2.25 2.25

Kotor Churches Honoring St. Tryphon, 1200th Anniv. — A78

No. 211 — St. Tryphon and denomination in: a, Black. b, White.

2009, Feb. 3 *Perf. 14*
211 A78 50c Horiz. pair, #a-b 3.75 3.75

First Theatrical Performance in Niksic, 125th Anniv. — A79

Vita Nikolic (1934-94), Poet — A80

Zetski Dom Theater, Cetinje, 125th Anniv. A81

Crnojevic Monastery, 525th Anniv. — A82

2009 **Litho.** *Perf. 13¾*
212 A79 25c multi .90 .90
213 A80 40c multi 1.25 1.25
214 A81 50c multi 1.50 1.50
215 A82 60c multi 1.75 1.75
Nos. 212-215 (4) 4.75 4.75

Arts through the ages. Issued: 25c, 2/16; others, 4/8.

Fish A83

Designs: 25c, Alburnus scoranza. 40c, Thymallus thymallus. 50c, Salmothymus obtusirostris zetensis. 60c, Cyprinus carpio.

2009, Apr. 16
216-219 A83 Set of 4 6.00 6.00

Nos. 216-219 each were printed in sheets of 5 + label.

Europa A84

Designs: No. 220, 60c, Boy and girl looking at celestial objects. No. 221, 90c, Boy looking through telescope.

No. 222, vert.: a, 60c, Planets and constellations. b, 90c, Comet, asteroids and constellations.

2009, Apr. 16
220-221 A84 Set of 2 4.00 4.00

Souvenir Sheet

222 A84 Sheet of 2, #a-b 5.00 5.00

Intl. Year of Astronomy.

Tourism A85

Designs: 25c, Water skiing. 40c, Rock climbing in Nevidio Canyon. 50c, Paragliding. 60c, Rafting on the Tara River.

2009, Apr. 16
223-226 A85 Set of 4 6.00 6.00
226a Souvenir sheet of 4, #223-226 6.00 6.00

Nos. 223-226 each were printed in sheets of 5 + label.

25th Universiade, Belgrade — A86

2009, June 4 *Perf. 13¾*
227 A86 50c multi 1.75 1.75

Printed in sheets of 8 + label.

Prince Vasilije Petrovic-Njegos (1709-66), Bishop — A87

2009, June 4 *Perf. 13¾x13*
228 A87 40c multi 1.40 1.40

Vicko Bujovic (1660-1709), Military Leader, and Ship — A88

2009, July 10 *Perf. 13¾*
229 A88 60c multi 2.00 2.00

Printed in sheets of 8 + label.

Nature Protection A89

Bandaged plants and: 25c, Lake Plav. 50c Lake Crno.

2009, July 10 **Litho.**
230-231 A89 Set of 2 2.50 2.50

Nos. 230-231 each were printed in sheets of 8 + label.

Stamp Day — A90

2009, Oct. 2 *Perf. 13x13¾*
232 A90 25c multi 1.00 1.00

Joy of Europe — A91

Children's art with: 40c, Dialogue balloon. 50c, Thought balloon.

2009, Nov. 20 *Perf. 13¾*
233-234 A91 Set of 2 3.00 3.00

Nos. 233-234 each were printed in sheets of 8 + label.

Valtazar Bogisic (1834-1908), Jurist — A92

2009, Dec. 7 *Perf. 13x13¾*
235 A92 50c multi 1.60 1.60

700-Year-Old Historical Document in Kotor Archives — A93

2009, Dec. 20 *Perf. 13¾x13*
236 A93 25c multi .95 .95

Dado Duric (1933-2010), Painter — A94

St. Elias, Fresco in Moraca Monastery A95

2010, Jan. 28 *Perf. 13x13¾*
237 A94 50c multi 1.50 1.50
238 A95 50c multi 1.50 1.50

2010 Winter Olympics, Vancouver A96

Designs: €1, Speed skater. €1.50, Snowboarder.

2010, Feb. 12 *Perf. 13¾*
239-240 A96 Set of 2 8.00 8.00

Nos. 239-240 each were printed in sheets of 8 + label.

Danilo Kis (1935-89), Writer — A97

2010, Feb. 22 *Perf. 13¾x13*
241 A97 50c multi 1.75 1.75

Flora — A98

Designs: 25c, Salvia officialis. 50c, Satureja subspicata. 60c, Tilia tomentosa. €1, Epilobium angustifolium.

2010, Mar. 18 **Litho.**
242-245 A98 Set of 4 7.75 7.75

Nos. 242-245 each were printed in sheets of 5 + label.

Europa — A99

Stack of books and: No. 246, 60c, Girl, butterfly, castle, rainbow. No. 247, 90c, Boy, car, star, rope ladder.

No. 248: a, 60c, Books, fairy, crown, dress. b, 90c, Books, ship, ladder.

2010, Apr. 22 *Perf. 13¾*
246-247 A99 Set of 2 5.25 5.25

Souvenir Sheet

248 A99 Sheet of 2, #a-b 5.25 5.25

St. Basil of Ostrog (1610-71) A100

2010, May 12 *Perf. 13x13¾*
249 A100 50c multi 1.75 1.75

2010 World Cup Soccer Tournament, South Africa — A101

2010, June 11 ***Perf. 13¾***
250 A101 €1.50 multi 4.75 4.75

Printed in sheets of 8 + label.

Tourism A102

Designs: 25c, Canoe and trees. 50c, Mountains. 60c, Waterside straw hut. €1, Beach.

2010, June 24 **Litho.**
251-254 A102 Set of 4 8.00 8.00
254a Souvenir sheet of 4, #251-254 8.00 8.00

Nos. 251-254 each were printed in sheets of 5 + label.

Ship A103

2010, July 8
255 A103 25c multi 1.00 1.00

Printed in sheets of 8 + label.

Balsic Dynasty, 650th Anniv. — A104

2010, July 15 ***Perf. 13x13¾***
256 A104 25c multi .95 .95

First Electric Power Network in Montenegro, Cent. — A105

2010, Aug. 19
257 A105 25c multi .95 .95

Kingdom of Montenegro, Cent. — A106

2010, Aug. 28
258 A106 50c multi 1.75 1.75

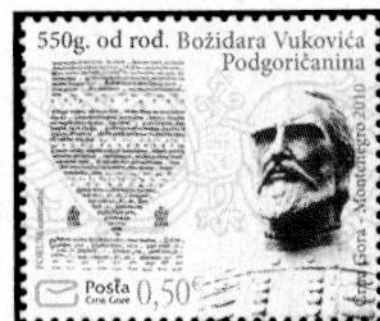

Bozidar Vukovic (c. 1466-c. 1540), Printer A107

2010, Sept. 16 **Litho.**
259 A107 50c multi 1.75 1.75

Stamp Day — A108

2010, Oct. 2 ***Perf. 13¾x13***
260 A108 30c multi 1.00 1.00

Joy of Europe A109

2010, Oct. 21 ***Perf. 13¾***
261 A109 90c multi 3.25 3.25

Printed in sheets of 8 + label.

Pasha Husein Mosque, Pljevlja — A110

Ivan Mazuranic (1814-90), Poet — A111

Reverse of Roman Reduced Sestertius Found in Duklja (Podgorica) A112

Miroslav Gospels — A113

Perf. 13¾x13, 13x13¾

2010, Nov. 12
262 A110 30c multi 1.00 1.00
263 A111 40c multi 1.25 1.25
264 A112 80c multi 2.50 2.50
265 A113 90c multi 2.75 2.75
Nos. 262-265 (4) 6.70 6.70

Art through the ages.

Nature Protection — A114

Umbrella over: 30c, Waterfall. 40c, Mountains.

2010, Dec. 16 ***Perf. 13¾x13***
266-267 A114 Set of 2 2.25 2.25

Painting by Vojo Stanic A115

Jovan Ivanisevic (1860-89), Composer A116

2011, Jan. 31 **Litho.** ***Perf. 13***
268 A115 30c multi .95 .95
269 A116 40c multi 1.25 1.25

Tripo Kokolja (1661-1713), Painter A117

2011, Feb. 22
270 A117 30c multi .95 .95

Vuk Vrcevic (1811-82), Poetry Translator A118

2011, Feb. 26
271 A118 30c multi .95 .95

Fauna A119

Map of Montenegro and: No. 272, 30c, Pina nobilis. No. 273, 30c, Triturus alpestris montenegrinus. 40c, Pelecanus crispus. 90c, Phalacrocorax pygmaeus.

2011, Mar. 17
272-275 A119 Set of 4 6.00 6.00

Europa A120

Designs: No. 276, 90c, "EU" in foliage. No. 277, 90c, Map of Europe with leaf veins, white background.

No. 278, 90c, vert.: a, "EU" in foliage. b, Map of Europe with leaf veins, green background.

2011, Apr. 21 ***Perf. 13¼x13***
276-277 A120 Set of 2 5.75 5.75

Souvenir Sheet

Perf. 13x13¼

278 A120 90c Sheet of 2, #a-b 5.75 5.75

Intl. Year of Forests.

Tourism A121

Designs: No. 279, 30c, Mountains and valley, "Turizam" at left. No. 280, 30c, Mountains and lake, "Turizam" at right. 40c, Mountains and valley, diff. 90c, Beach.

2011, May 12 ***Perf. 13***
279-282 A121 Set of 4 5.75 5.75
282a Sheet of 4, #279-282 5.75 5.75

No. 282a was sold with a booklet cover but was not attached to it.

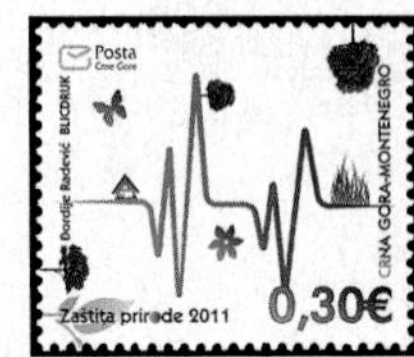

Environmental Protection — A122

Butterfly, flowers and: 30c, House, oscilloscope wave pattern. 40c, Smiling face.

2011, May 21
283-284 A122 Set of 2 2.25 2.25

Kazansky Cathedral, St. Petersburg, Russia — A123

Russian Diplomatic Mission, Cetinje — A124

2011, May 26 ***Perf. 13¼x13***
285 A123 30c multi 1.00 1.00
286 A124 30c multi 1.00 1.00
a. Horiz. pair, #285-286 2.25 2.25

Nos. 285-286 each were printed in sheets of 8 + label. See Russia No. 7272.

Games of Small European States, Liechtenstein — A125

Designs: 30c, Volleyball. 90c, Tennis ball.

2011, June 9
287-288 A125 Set of 2 3.75 3.75

Nos. 287-288 each were printed in sheets of 8 + label.

Belvedere Demonstrations, 75th Anniv. — A126

2011, June 25 *Perf. 13*
289 A126 30c multi .90 .90

Ship "Brindisi" A127

2011, July 7 *Perf. 13¼x13*
290 A127 40c multi 1.25 1.25

Printed in sheets of 8 + label.

Concordat Between Montenegro and Vatican City, 125th Anniv. A128

2011, Oct. 7 *Perf. 13*
291 A128 30c multi .95 .95

Joy of Europe A129

2011, Oct. 21 *Perf. 13¼x13*
292 A129 90c multi 2.75 2.75

Printed in sheets of 8 + label.

Fresco of King Michael A130

Crnogorac, First Montengrin Newspaper A131

Zabljak Crnojevica Fortified Town — A132

Josip Slade (1828-1911), Architect A133

2011, Nov. 11 *Perf. 13*
293 A130 30c multi .90 .90
294 A131 40c multi 1.25 1.25
295 A132 50c multi 1.50 1.50
296 A133 90c multi 2.75 2.75
Nos. 293-296 (4) 6.40 6.40

Stamp Day — A134

2011, Dec. 15 **Litho.**
297 A134 40c multi 1.25 1.25

Sculptures by Risto Stijovic (1894-1974) A135

Montenegrin Man, by Ilija Sobajic (1876-1953) A136

Painting by Nikola Vujosevic A137

Montenegrin Army Musicians A138

2012, Jan. 27 *Perf. 13*
298 A135 30c multi .90 .90
299 A136 40c multi 1.25 1.25
300 A137 80c multi 2.25 2.25
301 A138 95c multi 2.75 2.75
Nos. 298-301 (4) 7.15 7.15

Ilovik Nomocanon, 750th Anniv. — A139

2012, Feb. 23
302 A139 30c multi .90 .90

Enthronement of Durad Balsic as Lord of Zeta, 650th Anniv. — A140

2012, Feb. 27
303 A140 30c multi .90 .90

Flora A141

Designs: 30c, Nettles (kopriva). 90c, Vranac grapes (vinova loza).

2012, Mar. 16
304-305 A141 Set of 2 3.50 3.50

Nos. 304-305 each were printed in sheets of 5 + label.

Matija Zmajevic (1680-1735), Russian Admiral A142

2012, May 10
306 A142 30c multi .80 .80

Tourism A143

Designs: No. 307, 30c, Directional arrows on pole. No. 308, 30c, Ship, sun, town names. 80c, Suitcase with blue handle decorated with travel symbols. 95c, Suitcase with red handle decorated with travel symbols.

2012, May 14
307-310 A143 Set of 4 6.50 6.50
310a Souvenir sheet of 4, #307-310 7.00 7.00

No. 310a was sold with, but unattached to, a booklet cover.

Environmental Protection A144

Life preserver on: 30c, Duck. 95c, Frog.

2012, May 21 **Litho.** *Perf. 13*
311-312 A144 Set of 2 3.25 3.25

2012 Summer Olympics, London A145

Designs: 90c, Rhythmic gymnastics. 95c, Discus thrower.

2012, June 8 **Litho.** *Perf. 13¼x13*
313-314 A145 Set of 2 5.00 5.00
314a Souvenir sheet of 2, #313-314 5.00 5.00

Nos. 313-314 each were printed in sheets of 8 + central label.

Battle of Carev Laz, 300th Anniv. — A146

2012, June 25 *Perf. 13*
315 A146 30c multi .80 .80

Accession Negotiations with the European Union — A147

2012, June 29
316 A147 95c multi 2.50 2.50

Lighthouses A148

Designs: No. 317, 30c, Verige Lighthouse. No. 318, 30c, Volujica Lighthouse.

2012, July 6 *Perf. 13x13¼*
317-318 A148 Set of 2 1.60 1.60

Nos. 317-318 each were printed in sheets of 8 + central label.

2012 European Championship of ZRK Buducnost Women's Handball Team — A149

2012, July 27 **Litho.**
319 A149 30c multi .80 .80

No. 319 was printed in sheets of 8 + central label.

Fixing of Montenegrin Boundaries, 175th Anniv. — A150

2012, Oct. 10 *Perf. 13*
320 A150 30c multi .85 .85

Europa A151

Leaves and: 80c, River gorge. 95c, Sveti Stefan.

2012, Oct. 17 *Perf. 13¼x13*
321-322 A151 Set of 2 4.75 4.75
322a Souvenir sheet of 2, #321-322 4.75 4.75

Nos. 321-322 each were printed in sheets of 8 + central label.

Joy of Europe — A152

2012, Oct. 22 ***Perf. 13x13¼***
323 A152 90c multi 2.50 2.50

No. 323 was printed in sheets of 8 + central label.

Art in Piva Monastery A153

Hieromonk Makarije Printing Works A154

Legend of Pava and Ahmet — A155

Battle of Tudjemila A156

2012, Nov. 12 ***Perf. 13***
324 A153 30c multi .85 .85
325 A154 30c multi .85 .85
326 A155 40c multi 1.25 1.25
327 A156 95c multi 2.75 2.75
Nos. 324-327 (4) 5.70 5.70

Stamp Day — A157

2012, Dec. 14
328 A157 30c multi .80 .80

Success of Montenegro Women's Handball Team — A158

Women's handball team, flag of Montenegro, and: No. 329, 30c, Gold medal from 2012 European championships. No. 330, 30c, Silver medal from 2012 Olympics.

2012, Dec. 28 Litho. ***Perf. 13¼x13***
329-330 A158 Set of 2 1.60 1.60

Nos. 329-330 each were printed in sheets of 8 + central label.

Camil Sijaric (1913-89), Writer — A160

Pero Pocek (1878-1963), Painter — A161

Traditional Folk Costume — A162

Our Lady of Philerme Icon — A163

2013, Jan. 31 Litho. ***Perf. 13***
331 A160 30c multi .85 .85
332 A161 40c multi 1.10 1.10
333 A162 80c multi 2.25 2.25
334 A163 95c multi 2.60 2.60
Nos. 331-334 (4) 6.80 6.80

Prince Petar II Petrovic-Njegos (1813-51) — A164

2013, Feb. 22 Litho. ***Perf. 13x13¼***
335 A164 30c multi .80 .80

No. 335 was printed in sheets of 8 + central label.

Union of Montenegro and Kotor Bay, 200th Anniv. — A165

2013, Feb. 27 Litho. ***Perf. 13***
336 A165 30c multi .80 .80

Flora and Fauna — A166

Map of Montenegro and: 80c, Parnassius apollo. 95c, Scabiosa ochroleuca.

2013, Mar. 15 Litho. ***Perf. 13***
337-338 A166 Set of 2 4.50 4.50

Europa — A167

2013, Apr. 19 Litho. ***Perf. 13x13¼***
339 A167 95c multi 2.50 2.50

No. 339 was printed in sheets of 8 + central label.

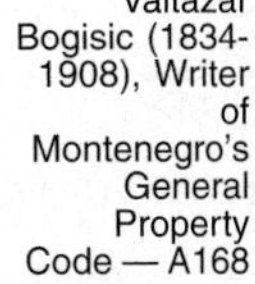

Valtazar Bogisic (1834-1908), Writer of Montenegro's General Property Code — A168

2013, May 10 Litho. ***Perf. 13***
340 A168 30c multi .80 .80

Tourism A169

Designs: 30c, Two hikers. 40c, Cyclist raising bicycle.

2013, May 14 Litho. ***Perf. 13***
341-342 A169 Set of 2 1.90 1.90
342a Souvenir sheet of 2, #341-342 1.90 1.90

Stara Maslina, Old Olive Tree, Stari Bar A170

2013, May 23 Litho. ***Perf. 13¼x13***
343 A170 30c multi .80 .80

No. 343 was printed in sheets of 8 + central label.

Sports A171

Designs: 80c, Basketball. 95c, "100", emblem of Lovcen soccer team, soccer ball.

2013, June 7 Litho. ***Perf. 13***
344-345 A171 Set of 2 4.75 4.75
345a Souvenir sheet of 2, #344-345 4.75 4.75

Participation of Montenegrin team in 2013 Euro Basket tournament, Slovenia (No. 344); Lovcen soccer team, cent. (No. 345).

Edict of Milan, 1700th Anniv. — A172

2013, June 21 Litho. ***Perf. 13***
346 A172 30c multi .80 .80

Marko Martinovic (1663-1716), Teacher of Naval Navigation — A173

2013, June 28 Litho. ***Perf. 13¼x13***
347 A173 30c multi .80 .80

No. 347 was printed in sheets of 8 + central label.

First Airplane Flight in Montenegro, Cent. — A174

2013, Sept. 5 Litho. ***Perf. 13***
348 A174 30c multi .80 .80

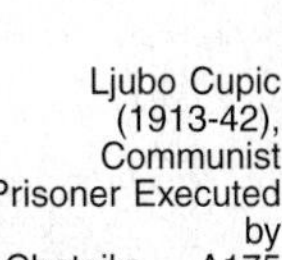

Ljubo Cupic (1913-42), Communist Prisoner Executed by Chetniks — A175

2013, Oct. 8 Litho. ***Perf. 13***
349 A175 30c multi .85 .85

Joy of Europe A176

2013, Oct. 22 Litho. ***Perf. 13¼x13***
350 A176 95c multi 2.60 2.60

No. 350 was printed in sheets of 8 + central label.

Princess Elena of Montenegro (1873-1952) A177

Map of Stari Bar — A178

2013, Nov. 12 Litho. ***Perf. 13***
351 A177 30c multi .85 .85
352 A178 40c multi 1.10 1.10

Stamp Day — A179

2013, Dec. 15 Litho. ***Perf. 13***
353 A179 30c multi .85 .85

Dobrota Lace — A180

Medieval Tombstones A181

2014, Jan. 31 Litho. *Perf. 13*
354 A180 30c multi .80 .80
355 A181 95c multi 2.60 2.60

2014 Winter Olympics, Sochi, Russia A182

2014, Feb. 17 Litho. *Perf. 13¼x13*
356 A182 95c multi 2.60 2.60

No. 356 was printed in sheets of 8 + central label.

Archbishopric of Bar, 925th Anniv. — A183

2014, Feb. 27 Litho. *Perf. 13*
357 A183 30c multi .85 .85

Edraianthus Wetstainii Ssp. Lovcenicus A184

Hypholoma Fasciculare A185

2014, Mar. 14 Litho. *Perf. 13*
358 A184 30c multi .85 .85
359 A185 95c multi 2.60 2.60

Gusle — A186

2014, Apr. 18 Litho. *Perf. 13x13¼*
360 A186 95c multi 2.60 2.60
a. Souvenir sheet of 1 2.60 2.60

Europa. No. 360 was printed in sheets of 8 + central label.

Church, Grahovac, 150th Anniv. — A187

2014, May 9 Litho. *Perf. 13*
361 A187 30c multi .85 .85

Tourism A188

Designs: 30c, Porto Montenegro, Tivat. 40c, Mount Hajla.

2014, May 14 Litho. *Perf. 13*
362-363 A188 Set of 2 1.90 1.90

Crna Poda Forest — A189

2014, May 23 Litho. *Perf. 13x13¼*
364 A189 95c multi 2.60 2.60

No. 364 was printed in sheets of 8 + central label.

2014 World Cup Soccer Championships, Brazil — A190

2014, June 9 Litho. *Perf. 13*
365 A190 95c multi 2.60 2.60
a. Souvenir sheet of 1 2.60 2.60

Podgorica Telegraph Station, Cent. — A191

2014, June 20 Litho. *Perf. 13*
366 A191 30c multi .85 .85

Reburial of King Nicholas I and Queen Milena in Montenegro, 25th Anniv. — A192

2014, June 27 Litho. *Perf. 13¼x13*
367 A192 30c multi .85 .85

No. 367 was printed in sheets of 8 + central label.

Lokanda Hotel, Cetinje, 150th Anniv. — A193

2014, Sept. 5 Litho. *Perf. 13*
368 A193 30c multi .75 .75

Mihailo Lalic (1914-92), Writer — A194

2014, Oct. 8 Litho. *Perf. 13*
369 A194 30c multi .75 .75

Joy of Europe — A195

2014, Oct. 22 Litho. *Perf. 13x13¼*
370 A195 95c multi 2.40 2.40

No. 370 was printed in sheets of 8 + central label.

Anastas Bocaric (1864-1944), Painter — A196

2014, Nov. 12 Litho. *Perf. 13*
371 A196 30c multi .75 .75

Orlov Krs Mausoleum A197

2014, Nov. 12 Litho. *Perf. 13*
372 A197 80c multi 2.00 2.00

Svac Archaeological Site — A198

2014, Nov. 12 Litho. *Perf. 13*
373 A198 95c multi 2.40 2.40

Danilovgrad Library, 125th Anniv. — A199

2014, Nov. 17 Litho. *Perf. 13*
374 A199 30c multi .75 .75

Kotor High School, 150th Anniv. — A200

2014, Nov. 28 Litho. *Perf. 13*
375 A200 30c multi .75 .75

Stamp Day — A201

2014, Dec. 15 Litho. *Perf. 13*
376 A201 30c multi .75 .75

First female postal official, cent.

National Art Museum, Cetinje A202

2015, Feb. 5 Litho. *Perf. 13¼x13¾*
377 A202 30c multi .70 .70

Jeweled Buckle — A203

2015, Feb. 5 Litho. *Perf. 13¼x13¾*
378 A203 40c multi .90 .90

Ostrog Monastery, 350th Anniv. — A204

Perf. 13¾x13¼
2015, Feb. 19 Litho.
379 A204 30c multi .70 .70

Phoenicopterus Roseus — A205

Perf. 13¼x13¾
2015, Mar. 12 Litho.
380 A205 95c multi 2.10 2.10

Europa A206

2015, Apr. 16 Litho. *Perf. 13¾*
381 A206 95c multi 2.25 2.25
a. Souvenir sheet of 1 2.25 2.25

No. 381 was printed in sheets of 8 + central label.

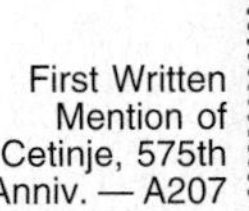

First Written Mention of Cetinje, 575th Anniv. — A207

2015, May 5 Litho. ***Perf. 13¼x13¾***
382 A207 30c multi .70 .70

Kitesurfing A208

2015, May 8 Litho. ***Perf. 13¾***
383 A208 95c multi 2.10 2.10

No. 383 was printed in sheets of 8 + central label.

Pinus Heldreichii A209

2015, May 13 Litho. ***Perf. 13¾***
384 A209 95c multi 2.10 2.10

No. 384 was printed in sheets of 8 + central label.

2015 European Basketball Championships A210

2015, May 22 Litho. ***Perf. 13¼x13¾***
385 A210 95c multi 2.10 2.10
a. Souvenir sheet of 1 2.10 2.10

Joy of Europe A211

2015, Oct. 22 Litho. ***Perf. 13x13¾***
386 A211 95c multi 2.25 2.25

Bar, Montenegro - Bari, Italy Ferry, 50th Anniv. — A212

2015, Oct. 30 Litho. ***Perf. 13¾***
387 A212 30c multi .70 .70

No. 387 was printed in sheets of 8 + label.

St. George Monastery, Berane A213

Ruins, Soko Grad — A214

Perf. 13¼x13¾
2015, Nov. 11 Litho.
388 A213 30c multi .65 .65
389 A214 95c multi 2.00 2.00

Stamp Day — A215

Perf. 13¾x13¼
2015, Dec. 15 Litho.
390 A215 95c multi 2.10 2.10

Restoration of the Montenegrin Orthodox Church, 25th Anniv. — A216

Perf. 13¾x13¼
2015, Dec. 28 Litho.
391 A216 30c multi .65 .65

ACKNOWLEDGMENT OF RECEIPT STAMPS

Prince Nicholas I — AR1

Perf. 10½, 11½
1895 Litho. Wmk. 91
H1 AR1 10n ultra & rose 1.10 1.10
a. Perf. 11½ 1.10 1.10

Prince Nicholas I — AR2

1902 Unwmk. ***Perf. 12½***
H2 AR2 25h orange & carmine 1.10 1.10
a. Double print 29.00
b. Pair, imperf. 45.00

Constitution Issue

No. H2 Overprinted in Black

1905

"Constitution" 15mm

H3 AR2 25h orange & carmine 1.10 1.10
g. Inverted overprint 85.00
h. Double overprint 24.00

"Constitution" 16½mm ('06)

H3a	Overprint Type I	32.50	35.00
H3b	Overprint Type II	1.40	1.90
H3c	Overprint Type III	5.75	6.50
H3d	Overprint Type IV	3.25	3.50

See note after 74a.

AR3

1907 Engr.
H4 AR3 25pa olive .95 1.40

Nicholas I — AR4

1913 Typo.
H5 AR4 25pa olive green .95 3.50

POSTAGE DUE STAMPS

D1

Perf. 10½
1894, Nov. Litho. Wmk. 91

J1	D1	1n red	3.75	3.50
c.		Pair, imperf.	42.50	
J2	D1	2n yellow green	1.50	1.40
J3	D1	3n orange	.95	.95
c.		Double impression	8.50	
J4	D1	5n olive green	.70	.65
J5	D1	10n violet	.70	.65
J6	D1	20n ultra	.70	.65
c.		Double impression	55.00	
J7	D1	30n emerald	.70	.65
c.		Double impression	55.00	
J8	D1	50n pale gray grn	.70	.65
		Nos. J1-J8 (8)	9.70	9.10

Perf. 11

J1a	D1	1n red	7.25	6.75
J2a	D1	2n yellow green	4.75	4.75
J3a	D1	3n orange	5.75	5.50
J5a	D1	10n violet	3.75	3.50
J6a	D1	20n ultramarine	3.75	3.50
J7a	D1	30n emerald	5.75	5.50
J8a	D1	50n pale gray green	5.75	5.50
		Nos. J1a-J8a (7)	36.75	35.00

Perf. 11½

J1b	D1	1n red	3.75	3.50
J2b	D1	2n yellow green	1.50	1.40
J3b	D1	3n orange	.95	.95
J4b	D1	5n olive green	.70	.65
J5b	D1	10n violet	.70	.65
J6b	D1	20n ultramarine	.70	.65
J7b	D1	30n emerald	.70	.65
J8b	D1	50n pale gray green	.70	.65
		Nos. J1b-J8b (8)	9.70	9.10

D2

1902 Unwmk. ***Perf. 12½***

J9	D2	5h orange	.45	.65
J10	D2	10h olive green	.45	.65
J11	D2	25h dull lilac	.45	.65
J12	D2	50h emerald	.45	.65
J13	D2	1k pale gray green	.95	1.50
		Nos. J9-J13 (5)	2.75	4.10

Constitution Issue

Postage Due Stamps of 1902 Overprinted in Black or Red "Constitution" 15mm

1905

J14	D2	5h orange	.65	1.40
a.		Inverted overprint	37.50	
b.		Double overprint	17.00	
J15	D2	10h olive green (R)	.95	2.75
a.		Double overprint	17.00	
b.		Ovpt. 16¾mm, Type II	1.90	4.00
c.		As "b," Type III	1.90	4.00
d.		As "b," Type IV	1.90	4.00
J16	D2	25h dull lilac	.65	1.40
a.		Inverted overprint	37.50	
b.		Double overprint	17.00	
J17	D2	50h emerald	.65	1.40
a.		Inverted overprint	37.50	
b.		Double overprint	14.00	
J18	D2	1k pale gray green	.95	1.90
a.		Double overprint	14.00	
		Nos. J14-J18 (5)	3.85	8.85

D3

1907 Typo. ***Perf. 13x13½***

J19	D3	5pa red brown	.45	1.40
J20	D3	10pa violet	.45	1.40
J21	D3	25pa rose	.45	1.40
J22	D3	50pa green	.45	1.40
		Nos. J19-J22 (4)	1.80	5.60

D4

1913 ***Perf. 12½***

J23	D4	5pa gray	1.40	1.90
J24	D4	10pa violet	.95	1.40
J25	D4	25pa blue gray	.95	1.40
J26	D4	50pa lilac rose	1.40	1.90
		Nos. J23-J26 (4)	4.70	6.60

ISSUED UNDER AUSTRIAN OCCUPATION

Austrian Military Stamps of 1917 Overprinted

1917 Unwmk. ***Perf. 12½***
1N1 M1 10h blue 14.50 12.00
1N2 M1 15h car rose 14.50 12.00

Austrian Military Stamps of 1917 Overprinted in Black

1918
1N3 M1 10h blue 40.00
1N4 M1 15h car rose 1.90

Nos. 1N3-1N4 were never placed in use. This overprint exists on other stamps of Austria and Bosnia and Herzegovina, and in blue or red.

ISSUED UNDER ITALIAN OCCUPATION

Yugoslavia Nos. 142, 144-154 Overprinted

1941 Unwmk. Typo. ***Perf. 12½***
2N1 A16 25p black .80 *1.40*
2N2 A16 1d yel grn .80 *1.40*
2N3 A16 1.50d red .80 *1.40*

2N4	A16	2d	dp mag	.80	*1.40*
2N5	A16	3d	dull red brn	.80	*1.40*
2N6	A16	4d	ultra	.80	*1.40*
2N7	A16	5d	dark blue	2.25	*3.25*
2N8	A16	5.50d	dk vio brn	2.25	*3.25*
2N9	A16	6d	slate blue	2.25	*3.25*
2N10	A16	8d	sepia	2.25	*3.25*
2N11	A16	12d	brt violet	2.25	*3.25*
2N12	A16	16d	dull violet	2.25	*3.25*
2N13	A16	20d	blue	160.00	*210.00*
2N14	A16	30d	brt pink	50.00	*97.50*
	Nos. 2N1-2N14 (14)			228.30	*335.40*
	Set, never hinged			425.00	

The 25p, 1d, 3d, 6d and 8d exist with inverted overprint.

Stamps of Italy, 1929, Overprinted in Red or Black

1941		**Wmk. 140**			***Perf. 14***
2N15	A90	5c	ol brn (R)	.80	*.95*
2N16	A92	10c	dark brn	.80	*.95*
2N17	A93	15c	sl grn (R)	.80	*.95*
2N18	A91	20c	rose red	.80	*.95*
2N19	A94	25c	deep grn	.80	*.95*
2N20	A95	30c	ol brn (R)	.80	*.95*
2N21	A95	50c	pur (R)	.80	*.95*
2N22	A94	75c	rose red	.80	*.95*
2N23	A94	1.25 l	dp bl (R)	1.00	*.95*
	Nos. 2N15-2N23 (9)			7.40	*8.55*
	Set, never hinged			20.00	

Yugoslavia Nos. 144-145, 147-148, 148B, 149-152 Overprinted in Black

1942	**Unwmk.**		**Typo.**		***Perf. 12½***
2N24	A16	1d	yel grn	2.00	2.75
2N25	A16	1.50d	red	95.00	65.00
2N26	A16	3d	dull red brn	2.00	2.75
2N27	A16	4d	ultra	2.00	2.75
2N28	A16	5.50d	dk vio brn	2.00	2.75
2N29	A16	6d	slate blue	2.00	2.75
2N30	A16	8d	sepia	2.00	2.75
2N31	A16	12d	brt violet	2.00	2.75
2N32	A16	16d	dull violet	2.00	2.75
	Nos. 2N24-2N32 (9)			111.00	87.00
	Set, never hinged			220.00	

Yugoslavia Nos. 142 and 146 with this overprint in red were not officially issued.

Red Overprint

2N24a	A16	1d	2.00	*2.75*
2N25a	A16	1.50d	145.00	*200.00*
2N26a	A16	3d	2.00	*2.75*
2N27a	A16	4d	2.00	*2.75*
2N28a	A16	5.50d	2.00	*2.75*
2N29a	A16	6d	2.00	*2.75*
2N30a	A16	8d	2.00	*2.75*
2N31a	A16	12d	2.00	*2.75*
2N32a	A16	16d	2.00	*2.75*
	Nos. 2N24a-2N32a (9)		161.00	*222.00*
	Set, never hinged		300.00	

Peter Nyegosh and Mt. Lovchen View OS1

Mt. Lovchen Scene OS2

Peter Petrovich Nyegosh — OS3

Designs: 15c, Mountain Church, Eve of Trinity Feast. 20c, Chiefs at Cetinje Monastery. 25c, Folk Dancing at Cetinje Monastery. 50c, Eagle dance. 1.25 l, Chiefs taking loyalty oath. 2 l, Moslem wedding procession. 5 l, Group sitting up with injured standard bearer.

Perf. 14.

1943, May 9		**Unwmk.**		**Photo.**	
2N33	OS1	5c	deep violet	2.40	*4.00*
2N34	OS2	10c	dull olive grn	2.40	*4.00*
2N35	OS1	15c	brown	2.40	*4.00*
2N36	OS1	20c	dull orange	2.40	*4.00*
2N37	OS1	25c	dull green	2.40	*4.00*
2N38	OS1	50c	rose pink	2.40	*4.00*
2N39	OS1	1.25 l	sapphire	2.40	*4.00*
2N40	OS1	2 l	blue green	3.60	*4.00*
2N41	OS2	5 l	dark red, *sal*	8.00	*14.00*
2N42	OS3	20 l	dark vio, *gray*	20.00	*27.50*
	Nos. 2N33-2N42 (10)			48.40	*73.50*
	Set, never hinged			82.50	

Quotations from national poem on backs of stamps.

For overprints and surcharges see Nos. 3N10-3N14, 3NB3-3NB8.

OCCUPATION AIR POST STAMPS

Yugoslavia Nos. C7-C14 Overprinted Like Nos. 2N1-2N14

Perf. 12½, 11½x12½, 12½x11½

1941			**Photo.**	**Unwmk.**	
2NC1	AP6	50p	brown	6.50	7.50
2NC2	AP7	1d	yel grn	4.50	7.50
2NC3	AP8	2d	blue gray	4.50	7.50
2NC4	AP9	2.50d	rose red	6.50	7.50
2NC5	AP6	5d	brn vio	35.00	55.00
2NC6	AP7	10d	brn lake	35.00	55.00
2NC7	AP8	20d	dark grn	72.50	92.50
2NC8	AP9	30d	ultra	40.00	55.00
	Nos. 2NC1-2NC8 (8)			204.50	287.50
	Set, never hinged			500.00	

Italy No. C13 Overprinted in Red Like Nos. 2N15-2N23

1941		**Wmk. 140**		***Perf. 14***	
2NC9	AP3	50c	olive brn	1.10	1.10
	Never hinged			2.75	

Yugoslavia Nos. C7-C14 Overprinted in Black

a

b

Perf. 12½, 11½x12½, 12½x11½

1942, Jan. 9				**Unwmk.**	
2NC10	AP6(a)	50p	brown	12.00	*15.00*
2NC11	AP7(a)	1d	yel grn	12.00	*15.00*
2NC12	AP8(b)	2d	blue gray	12.00	*15.00*
2NC13	AP9(b)	2.50d	rose red	12.00	*15.00*
2NC14	AP6(a)	5d	brn vio	12.00	*15.00*
2NC15	AP7(a)	10d	brn lake	12.00	*15.00*
2NC16	AP8(b)	20d	dk grn	210.00	*250.00*
2NC17	AP9(b)	30d	ultra	35.00	*60.00*
	Nos. 2NC10-2NC17 (8)			317.00	*400.00*
	Set, never hinged			700.00	

Nos. 2NC10-2NC17 exist with red overprints. Value, each $80 unused, $150 used.

c

Overprints *a*, *b* or *c* were applied in 1941-42 to the following Yugoslavia stamps under Italian occupation:

a. or *b.* Nos. B120-B123 (4 values) in black and in red.

c. Nos. B116-B119 (4 values) in black and in red.

Cetinje AP1

Mt. Durmitor — AP6

Designs: 1 l, Seacoast. 2 l, Budus. 5 l, Mt. Lovchen. 10 l, Rieka River.

1943	**Unwmk.**		**Photo.**	***Perf. 14***	
2NC18	AP1	50c	brown	6.00	*8.00*
2NC19	AP1	1 l	ultra	6.00	*8.00*
2NC20	AP1	2 l	rose pink	6.00	*8.00*
2NC21	AP1	5 l	green	8.00	*12.00*
2NC22	AP1	10 l	lake, *rose buff*	16.00	*20.00*
2NC23	AP6	20 l	indigo, *rose*	27.50	*35.00*
	Nos. 2NC18-2NC23 (6)			69.50	*91.00*
	Set, never hinged			175.00	

For overprints and surcharges see Nos. 3NC1-3NC5, 3NCB1-3NCB6.

OCCUPATION POSTAGE DUE STAMPS

Yugoslavia Nos. J28-J32 Overprinted Like Nos. 2N1-2N14

1941	**Unwmk.**		**Typo.**	***Perf. 12½***	
2NJ1	D4	50p	violet	4.00	*5.50*
2NJ2	D4	1d	dp mag	4.00	*5.50*
2NJ3	D4	2d	deep blue	4.00	*5.50*
2NJ4	D4	5d	orange	110.00	*120.00*
2NJ5	D4	10d	chocolate	12.00	*15.00*
	Nos. 2NJ1-2NJ5 (5)			134.00	*151.50*
	Set, never hinged			300.00	

1934 Postage Due Stamps of Italy Overprinted in Black Like Nos. 2N15-2N23

1942		**Wmk. 140**		***Perf. 14***	
2NJ6	D6	10c	blue	2.75	*4.50*
2NJ7	D6	20c	rose red	2.75	*4.50*
2NJ8	D6	30c	red orange	2.75	*4.50*
2NJ9	D6	50c	violet	2.75	*4.50*
2NJ10	D7	1 l	red orange	2.75	*4.50*
	Nos. 2NJ6-2NJ10 (5)			13.75	*22.50*
	Set, never hinged			28.00	

ISSUED UNDER GERMAN OCCUPATION

Yugoslavia Nos. 147-148 Surcharged

1943	**Unwmk.**		**Typo.**	***Perf. 12½***	
3N1	A16	50c	on 3d	6.00	*14.50*
3N2	A16	1 l	on 3d	6.00	*14.50*
3N3	A16	1.50 l	on 3d	6.00	*14.50*
3N4	A16	2 l	on 3d	10.00	*28.00*
3N5	A16	4 l	on 3d	10.00	*28.00*
3N6	A16	5 l	on 4d	10.00	*28.00*
3N7	A16	8 l	on 4d	24.00	*57.50*
3N8	A16	10 l	on 4d	32.50	*90.00*
3N9	A16	20 l	on 4d	65.00	*200.00*
	Nos. 3N1-3N9 (9)			169.50	*475.00*
	Set, never hinged			375.00	

Montenegro Nos. 2N37-2N41 Ovptd.

1943			**Photo.**	***Perf. 14***	
3N10	OS1	25c	dull green	18.00	*100.00*
3N11	OS1	50c	rose pink	18.00	*100.00*
3N12	OS1	1.25 l	sapphire	18.00	*100.00*
3N13	OS1	2 l	blue grn	18.00	*100.00*
3N14	OS2	5 l	dk red, *sal*	250.00	*1,250.*
	Nos. 3N10-3N14 (5)			322.00	*1,650.*
	Set, never hinged			625.00	

Counterfeits exist.

SEMI-POSTAL STAMPS

Yugoslavia Nos. 147-148 Surcharged

1944	**Unwmk.**		**Typo.**	***Perf. 12½***	
3NB1	A16	15pf + 85pf on 3d		18.00	*100.00*
3NB2	A16	15pf + 85pf on 4d		18.00	*100.00*

Montenegro Nos. 2N37-2N40 Surcharged

d

1944			**Photo.**	***Perf. 14***	
3NB3	OS1	15pf +85pf on 25c		18.00	*100.00*
3NB4	OS1	15pf +1.35m on 50c		18.00	*100.00*
3NB5	OS1	25pf +1.75m on 1.25 l		18.00	*100.00*
3NB6	OS1	25pf +1.75m on 2 l		18.00	*100.00*
	Nos. 3NB1-3NB6 (6)			108.00	*600.00*
	Set, never hinged			240.00	

Surtax on Nos. 3NB1-3NB6 aided refugees.

Montenegro Nos. 2N37-2N38 and Yugoslavia Nos. 147-148 Surcharged

e

f

1944

3NB7 OS1 15pf + 85pf on 25c (e) 15.00 *80.00*
3NB8 OS1 15pf + 1.35m on 50c (e) 15.00 *80.00*
3NB9 A16 50pf + 2.50m on 3d (f) 15.00 *80.00*
3NB10 A16 50pf + 2.50m on 4d (f) 15.00 *80.00*
Nos. 3NB7-3NB10 (4) 60.00 *320.00*
Set, never hinged 130.00

The surtax on Nos. 3NB7-3NB10 aided the Montenegro Red Cross.

AIR POST STAMPS

Montenegro Nos. 2NC18-2NC22 Overprinted Like Nos. 3N10-3N14

1943 Unwmk. Photo. *Perf. 14*

3NC1 AP1 50c brown 18.00 *100.00*
3NC2 AP1 1 l ultra 18.00 *100.00*
3NC3 AP1 2 l rose pink 18.00 *100.00*
3NC4 AP1 5 l green 18.00 *100.00*
3NC5 AP1 10 l lake, *rose buff* *3,200.* *11,000.*
Nos. 3NC1-3NC5 (5) *3,272.* *11,400.*
Set, never hinged 6,250.

Counterfeits exist.

AIR POST SEMI-POSTAL STAMPS

Montenegro Nos. 2NC18-2NC20 Surcharged Type "d"

1944 Unwmk. Photo. *Perf. 14*

3NCB1 AP1 15pf +85pf on 50c 18.00 *100.00*
3NCB2 AP1 25pf +1.25m on 1 l 18.00 *100.00*
3NCB3 AP1 50pf +1.50m on 2 l 18.00 *100.00*
Nos. 3NCB1-3NCB3 (3) 54.00 *300.00*
Set, never hinged 80.00

The surtax aided refugees.

Same Surcharged Type "e"

1944

3NCB4 AP1 25pf +1.75m on 50c 15.00 *80.00*
3NCB5 AP1 25pf +2.75m on 1 l 15.00 *80.00*
3NCB6 AP1 50pf +2m on 2 l 15.00 *80.00*
Nos. 3NCB4-3NCB6 (3) 45.00 *240.00*
Set, never hinged 100.00

The surtax aided the Montenegro Red Cross.

MONTSERRAT

ˌmänˌt̬-sə-ˈrat

LOCATION — West Indies southeast of Puerto Rico
GOVT. — British Crown Colony
AREA — 39 sq. mi.
POP. — 12,853 (1999 est.)

Montserrat was one of the four presidencies of the former Leeward Islands colony until it became a colony itself in 1956.

Montserrat stamps were discontinued in 1890 and resumed in 1903. In the interim, stamps of Leeward Islands were used. In 1903-56, stamps of Montserrat and Leeward Islands were used concurrently.

12 Pence = 1 Shilling
20 Shillings = 1 Pound
100 Cents = 1 Dollar (1951)

Catalogue values for unused stamps in this country are for Never Hinged items, beginning with Scott 104 in the regular postage section, Scott B1 in the semi-postal section, Scott O45 in the officials section.

Watermark

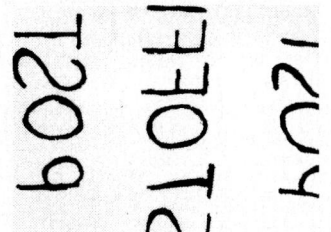

Wmk. 380 — "POST OFFICE"

Values for unused stamps are for examples with original gum as defined in the catalogue introduction. Very fine examples of Nos. 1-2, 6 and 11 will have perforations touching the design on at least one side due to the narrow spacing of the stamps on the plates. Stamps with perfs clear of the framelines on all four sides are scarce and will command higher prices.

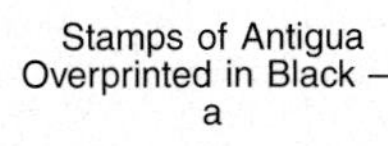
Stamps of Antigua Overprinted in Black — a

1876 Engr. Wmk. 1 *Perf. 14*

1 A1 1p red 30.00 19.00
a. Vert. or diag. half used as ½p on cover 1,650.
c. "S" inverted 1,250. 875.00
2 A1 6p green 75.00 50.00
a. Vertical half used as 3p on cover —
b. Vertical third used as 2p on cover 6,500.
c. "S" inverted 1,900. 1,350.
d. 6p blue green 1,350.
e. As "d," "S" inverted *13,000.*

Some experts consider Nos. 2d, 2e to be from a trial printing.

Queen Victoria — A2

1880 Typo.

3 A2 2½p red brown 300.00 225.00
4 A2 4p blue 160.00 47.50

See Nos. 5, 7-10.

1884 Wmk. 2

5 A2 ½p green 1.25 *11.00*

Antigua No. 18 Overprinted type "a"

1884 Engr.

6 A1 1p rose red 28.00 20.00
a. Vert. half used as ½p on cover 1,550.
b. "S" inverted 1,100. 1,100.

Type of 1880

1884-85 Typo.

7 A2 2½p red brown 275.00 77.50
8 A2 2½p ultra ('85) 29.00 22.50
9 A2 4p blue 2,100. 300.00
10 A2 4p red lilac ('85) 6.00 3.50

Antigua No. 20 Overprinted type "a"

1884 Engr. *Perf. 12*

11 A1 1p red 82.50 65.00
a. "S" inverted 2,350. 1,550.
b. Vert. half used as ½p on cover 1,900.

Symbol of the Colony — A3

King Edward VII — A4

1903 Wmk. 2 Typo. *Perf. 14*

12 A3 ½p gray green .90 19.00
13 A3 1p car & black .90 .50
14 A3 2p brown & black 6.50 *50.00*
15 A3 2½p ultra & black 1.75 2.10
16 A3 3p dk vio & brn orange 8.50 *50.00*
17 A3 6p ol grn & vio 15.00 *65.00*
18 A3 1sh vio & gray grn 12.00 *26.00*
19 A3 2sh brn org & gray green 42.50 *27.50*
20 A3 2sh6p blk & gray grn 27.50 *60.00*

Wmk. 1

21 A4 5sh car & black 160.00 *225.00*
Nos. 12-21 (10) 275.55 *525.10*

1904-08 Wmk. 3 Chalky Paper

22 A3 ½p grn & gray grn ('06) 1.00 1.25
a. Ordinary paper 13.00 4.00
23 A3 1p car & blk ('07) 17.00 *30.00*
24 A3 2p brown & black ('06) 2.50 1.40
a. Ordinary paper 3.00 *13.00*
25 A3 2½p ultra & blk ('05) 3.00 *7.75*
26 A3 3p dk vio & brn orange ('08) 13.00 2.75
a. Ordinary paper 13.00 *8.00*
27 A3 6p ol grn & vio ('08) 16.00 *6.50*
a. Ordinary paper 13.00 *42.50*
28 A3 1sh violet & gray grn ('08) 12.00 8.50
29 A3 2sh brn org & gray grn ('08) 60.00 *55.00*
30 A3 2sh6p blk & gray grn ('08) 65.00 *60.00*
31 A4 5sh car & blk ('07) 160.00 *190.00*
Nos. 22-31 (10) 349.50 *363.15*

1908-13 Ordinary Paper

31A A3 ½p deep green 12.00 1.10
32 A3 1p carmine 1.75 .35
33 A3 2p gray 2.00 *22.50*
34 A3 2½p ultramarine 2.50 4.25

Chalky Paper

35 A3 3p vio, *yellow* 1.10 *22.50*
36 A3 6p red vio & gray vio 12.00 *60.00*
37 A3 1sh blk, *green* 10.00 *55.00*
38 A3 2sh bl & vio, *bl* 50.00 *67.50*
39 A3 2sh6p car & blk, *blue* 42.50 *87.50*
40 A4 5sh grn & scar, *yel* 65.00 92.50

Surface-colored Paper

41 A3 3p vio, *yel* ('13) 4.50 *40.00*
Nos. 31A-41 (11) 203.35 *453.20*

King George V — A5

1913 Chalky Paper

42 A5 5sh green & scar, *yel* 90.00 *160.00*

King George V — A6

1916-22 Wmk. 3 *Perf. 14*

Ordinary Paper

43 A6 ½p green .45 2.75
44 A6 1p scarlet 2.50 .90
45 A6 2p gray 2.75 *5.00*
46 A6 2½p ultramarine 2.50 *26.00*

Chalky Paper

47 A6 3p violet, *yel* 1.40 *23.00*
48 A6 4p blk & red, *yel* ('22) 8.50 *42.50*
49 A6 6p dl vio & red violet 3.50 *37.50*
50 A6 1sh blk, *bl grn,* ol back 3.50 *42.50*
51 A6 2sh vio & ultra, *bl* 22.00 *60.00*
52 A6 2sh6p blk & red, *bl* 40.00 *90.00*
53 A6 5sh grn & red, *yel* 55.00 *95.00*
Nos. 43-53 (11) 142.10 *425.15*

For overprints see Nos. MR1-MR3.

1922-29 Wmk. 4 Ordinary Paper

54 A6 ¼p brown .35 6.25
55 A6 ½p green ('23) .30 .30
56 A6 1p dp violet ('23) .80 .70
57 A6 1p carmine ('29) 1.10 1.75
58 A6 1½p orange 2.50 *11.00*
59 A6 1½p rose red ('23) .60 *5.00*
60 A6 1½p fawn ('29) 3.25 .55
61 A6 2p gray .80 *2.25*
62 A6 2½p ultramarine 9.25 18.00
63 A6 2½p orange ('23) 2.75 *21.00*
64 A6 3p ultra ('23) .80 *18.00*

Chalky Paper

65 A6 3p vio, *yel* ('26) 2.00 *6.50*
66 A6 4p black & red, *yel* ('23) 1.75 *14.00*
67 A6 5p dull vio & ol grn 5.50 *11.00*
68 A6 6p dull vio & red vio ('23) 3.50 *8.50*
69 A6 1sh blk, *emer* ('23) 3.50 *8.00*
70 A6 2sh vio & ultra, *bl* 8.00 *22.50*
71 A6 2sh6p blk & red, *bl* ('23) 14.00 *65.00*
72 A6 3sh green & vio 14.00 *22.50*
73 A6 4sh black & scar 17.50 *50.00*
74 A6 5sh grn & red, *yel* ('23) 37.50 *65.00*
Nos. 54-74 (21) 129.75 *357.80*

Tercentenary Issue

New Plymouth and Harbor A7

1932, Apr. 18 Engr.

75 A7 ½p green 1.25 *16.00*
76 A7 1p red 1.25 *6.50*
77 A7 1½p orange brown 1.40 *3.00*
78 A7 2p gray 1.90 *23.00*
79 A7 2½p ultra 1.40 *21.00*
80 A7 3p orange 1.90 *21.00*
81 A7 6p violet 2.50 *37.50*
82 A7 1sh olive green 14.50 *50.00*
83 A7 2sh6p lilac rose 52.50 *87.50*
84 A7 5sh dark brown 115.00 *200.00*
Nos. 75-84 (10) 193.60 465.50
Set, never hinged 400.00

300th anniv. of the colonization of Montserrat.

Common Design Types pictured following the introduction.

Silver Jubilee Issue
Common Design Type

1935, May 6 *Perf. 11x12*

85 CD301 1p car & dk blue 1.25 4.25
86 CD301 1½p gray blk & ultra 2.00 *3.75*
87 CD301 2½p ultra & brn 2.75 *4.25*
88 CD301 1sh brn vio & ind 4.25 *18.00*
Nos. 85-88 (4) 10.25 *30.25*
Set, never hinged 19.00

Coronation Issue
Common Design Type

1937, May 12 *Perf. 13½x14*

89 CD302 1p carmine .25 1.50
90 CD302 1½p brown .40 .35
91 CD302 2½p bright ultra .35 1.50
Nos. 89-91 (3) 1.00 3.35
Set, never hinged 1.75

Carr's Bay — A8

Sea Island Cotton — A9

Botanic Station A10

1941-48 *Perf. 14*
92 A8 ½p dk grn ('42) .25 .25
93 A9 1p car ('42) .40 .35
94 A9 1½p rose vio ('42) .40 *.55*
95 A10 2p red orange 1.20 .80
96 A9 2½p brt ultra ('43) .40 .35
97 A8 3p brown ('42) 1.50 .45
98 A10 6p dull vio ('42) 2.00 .70
99 A8 1sh brn lake ('42) 1.75 .35
100 A10 2sh6p slate bl ('43) 13.50 3.00
101 A8 5sh car rose ('42) 16.00 3.50

Perf. 12
102 A10 10sh blue ('48) 10.00 *30.00*
103 A8 £1 black ('48) 10.00 *35.00*
Nos. 92-103 (12) 57.40 *75.30*
Set, never hinged 85.00

1938, Aug. 2 *Perf. 13*
92a A8 ½p 2.50 *2.00*
93a A8 1p 2.50 *.40*
94a A9 1½p 11.00 *1.00*
95a A10 2p 11.00 *1.00*
96a A9 2½p 1.25 *1.50*
97a A8 3p 3.00 *3.25*
98a A10 6p 11.50 *1.25*
99a A8 1sh 11.50 *1.25*
100a A10 2sh6p 20.00 *1.00*
101a A8 5sh 24.00 *10.00*
Nos. 92a-101a (10) 98.25 *22.65*
Set, never hinged 200.00

Catalogue values for unused stamps in this section, from this point to the end of the section, are for Never Hinged items.

Peace Issue
Common Design Type

1946, Nov. 1 Engr. *Perf. 13½x14*
104 CD303 1½p deep magenta .25 .25
105 CD303 3p brown .25 .25

Silver Wedding Issue
Common Design Types

1949, Jan. 3 Photo. *Perf. 14x14½*
106 CD304 2½p brt ultra .25 .25

Engraved; Name Typographed
Perf. 11½x11
107 CD305 5sh rose carmine 9.00 *18.00*

UPU Issue
Common Design Types

Engr.; Name Typo. on 3p and 6p
Perf. 13½, 11x11½
1949, Oct. 10 **Wmk. 4**
108 CD306 2½p ultramarine .45 *1.00*
109 CD307 3p chocolate 1.10 .75
110 CD308 6p lilac .75 .85
111 CD309 1sh rose violet 1.10 1.25
Nos. 108-111 (4) 3.40 3.85

University Issue
Common Design Types

1951, Feb. 16 Engr. *Perf. 14x14½*
112 CD310 3c rose lil & gray blk .25 *.60*
113 CD311 12c violet & black .60 *.90*

Government House A11

Designs (portrait at right on 12c, 24c and $2.40): 2c, $1.20, Cotton field. 3c, Map of Presidency. 4c, 24c, Picking tomatoes. 5c, 12c, St. Anthony's Church. 6c, $4.80, Badge of Presidency. 8c, 60c, Cotton ginning.

Perf. 11½x11
1951, Sept. 17 Engr. Wmk. 4
114 A11 1c gray .30 .30
115 A11 2c green .30 .30
116 A11 3c orange brown .30 .30
117 A11 4c rose carmine .30 .30
118 A11 5c red violet .30 .30
119 A11 6c dark brown .40 .40
120 A11 8c dark blue .60 .60
121 A11 12c red brn & blue 1.25 1.25
122 A11 24c emer & rose car 1.75 1.75
123 A11 60c rose car & gray black 3.50 3.50
124 A11 $1.20 dp bl & emer 11.00 11.00
125 A11 $2.40 dp grn & gray black 14.00 14.00
126 A11 $4.80 pur & gray blk 28.00 28.00
Nos. 114-126 (13) 62.00 62.00

Coronation Issue
Common Design Type

1953, June 2 *Perf. 13½x13*
127 CD312 2c dark green & black .65 .50

Type of 1951 with Portrait of Queen Elizabeth II

½c, 3c, "Map of Presidency." 48c, Cotton field.

1953-57 *Perf. 11½x11*
128 A11 ½c violet ('56) .30 .25
129 A11 1c gray black .30 .25
130 A11 2c green .30 .25
131 A11 3c orange brown .75 .65
132 A11 4c rose car ('55) .30 .25
133 A11 5c red vio ('55) .30 .25
134 A11 6c dk brown ('55) .80 .70
135 A11 8c dp ultra ('55) .30 .25
136 A11 12c red brn & blue ('55) .30 .25
137 A11 24c emer & rose car ('55) .90 .80
138 A11 48c rose violet & olive ('57) 1.75 1.50
139 A11 60c rose car & blk ('55) 2.25 1.75
140 A11 $1.20 bl & emer ('55) 4.50 3.50
141 A11 $2.40 dp green & blk ('55) 9.25 7.00
142 A11 $4.80 pur & gray black ('55) 40.00 30.00
Nos. 128-142 (15) 62.30 47.65

See Nos. 146-149, 156.

West Indies Federation
Common Design Type

Perf. 11½x11
1958, Apr. 22 Engr. Wmk. 314
143 CD313 3c green .45 .25
144 CD313 6c blue .65 .45
145 CD313 12c carmine rose 1.25 .65
Nos. 143-145 (3) 2.35 1.35

Type of 1953-57

As before, but inscribed: "Map of the Colony" (½c, 3c) "Badge of the Colony" (6c, $4.80).

1958 Wmk. 4 *Perf. 11½x11*
146 A11 ½c violet .65 .25
147 A11 3c orange brown .65 .75
148 A11 6c dark brown .30 .25
149 A11 $4.80 pur & gray blk 14.50 *9.00*
Nos. 146-149 (4) 16.10 *10.25*

Freedom from Hunger Issue
Common Design Type

Perf. 14x14½
1963, June 4 Photo. Wmk. 314
150 CD314 12c lilac .55 .45

Red Cross Centenary Issue
Common Design Type

1963, Sept. 2 Litho. *Perf. 13*
151 CD315 4c black & red .25 .25
152 CD315 12c ultra & red .75 .55

Shakespeare Issue
Common Design Type

1964, Apr. 23 Photo. *Perf. 14x14½*
153 CD316 12c slate blue .35 .25

Type of 1953-57
Perf. 11½x11
1964, Oct. 30 Engr. Wmk. 314
156 A11 2c green 1.20 .25

ITU Issue
Common Design Type

Perf. 11x11½
1965, May 17 Litho. Wmk. 314
157 CD317 4c ver & lilac .25 .25
158 CD317 48c emer & rose red 1.00 .90

Pineapple — A12

Wmk. 314 Upright
1965, Aug. 16 Photo. *Perf. 15x14*
159 A12 1c shown .30 .25
160 A12 2c Avacado .30 .25
161 A12 3c Soursop .30 .25
162 A12 4c Peppers .30 .25
163 A12 5c Mango .30 .25
164 A12 6c Tomatoes .30 .25
165 A12 8c Guava .30 .25
166 A12 10c Okra .30 .25
167 A12 12c Limes .30 .25
168 A12 20c Oranges .40 .25
169 A12 24c Bananas .65 .40
170 A12 42c Onion 1.30 1.25
171 A12 48c Cabbage 1.75 1.40
172 A12 60c Papayas 1.75 1.60
173 A12 $1.20 Pumpkin 2.10 2.75
174 A12 $2.40 Sweet potato 5.50 6.00
175 A12 $4.80 Eggplant 11.00 12.00
Nos. 159-175 (17) 27.15 27.90

For surcharges see Nos. 193-198.

1969 Wmk. 314 Sideways
159a A12 1c .25 .25
160a A12 2c .45 *.50*
161a A12 3c .30 .40
162a A12 4c .75 .40
163a A12 5c .90 *1.00*
166a A12 10c 1.75 *2.00*
168a A12 20c 2.10 *2.40*
Nos. 159a-168a (7) 6.50 6.95

Intl. Cooperation Year Issue
Common Design Type

1965, Oct. 25 Litho. *Perf. 14½*
176 CD318 2c lt green & claret .25 .25
177 CD318 12c lt violet & green .55 .40

Churchill Memorial Issue
Common Design Type

1966, Jan. 24 Photo. *Perf. 14*
Design in Black, Gold and Carmine Rose
178 CD319 1c bright blue .25 .25
179 CD319 2c green .25 .25
180 CD319 24c brown .35 .30
181 CD319 42c violet .75 .75
Nos. 178-181 (4) 1.60 1.55

Royal Visit Issue
Common Design Type

Perf. 11x12
1966, Feb. 4 Litho. Wmk. 314
182 CD320 14c violet blue .60 .25
183 CD320 24c dk carmine rose 1.10 .75

WHO Headquarters Issue
Common Design Type

1966, Sept. 20 Litho. *Perf. 14*
184 CD322 12c multicolored .25 .25
185 CD322 60c multicolored .75 .75

UNESCO Anniversary Issue
Common Design Type

1966, Dec. 1 Litho. *Perf. 14*
186 CD323 4c "Education" .25 .25
a. Orange omitted 60.00
187 CD323 60c "Science" .40 .40
188 CD323 $1.80 "Culture" 1.75 1.75
Nos. 186-188 (3) 2.40 2.40

On No. 186a, the squares of the lowercase letters appear in yellow.

Sailing and ITY Emblem A13

ITY Emblem and: 15c, Waterfall, Chance Mountain, vert. 16c, Beach scene. 24c, Golfers.

1967, Dec. 29 Photo. Wmk. 314
189 A13 5c multicolored .35 .35
190 A13 15c multicolored .35 .35
191 A13 16c multicolored .45 .45
192 A13 24c multicolored 1.10 1.10
Nos. 189-192 (4) 2.25 2.25

Issued for International Tourist Year.

Nos. 167, 169, 171, 173-175 and Type Surcharged

1968, May 6 *Perf. 15x14*
193 A12 15c on 12c multi .25 .25
a. Wmkd. sideways ('69) 1.50 *1.75*
194 A12 25c on 24c multi .25 .25
a. Wmkd. sideways ('69) 2.50 *3.00*
195 A12 50c on 48c multi .45 .45
a. Wmkd. sideways ('69) 5.25 *6.00*
196 A12 $1 on $1.20 multi .70 .70
197 A12 $2.50 on $2.40 multi 1.50 1.50
198 A12 $5 on $4.80 multi 3.00 3.00
Nos. 193-198 (6) 6.15 6.15

The surcharge bars are slightly thinner on the "Wmkd. sideways" varieties.

Woman Runner A14

Designs: 25c, Weight lifter. 50c, Athlete on rings. $1, Runner and Toltec sculptures, vert.

Perf. 14½x14, 14x14½
1968, July 31 Photo. Wmk. 314
199 A14 15c gold, brt grn & rose claret .25 .25
200 A14 25c gold, org & blue .25 .25
201 A14 50c gold, ver & green .25 .25
202 A14 $1 multicolored .30 .30
Nos. 199-202 (4) 1.05 1.05

19th Olympic Games, Mexico City, 10/12-27.

Albert T. Marryshow — A15

Portraits and Human Rights Flame: 5c, Alexander Hamilton. 25c, William Wilberforce. 50c, Dag Hammarskjold. $1, Rev. Martin Luther King, Jr.

1968, Dec. 2 Photo. *Perf. 14x14½*
203 A15 5c multicolored .25 .25
204 A15 15c multicolored .25 .25
205 A15 25c multicolored .25 .25
206 A15 50c multicolored .25 .25
207 A15 $1 multicolored .25 .25
Nos. 203-207 (5) 1.25 1.25

International Human Rights Year.

The Two Trinities, by Murillo — A16

Christmas: 15c, 50c, The Adoration of the Magi, by Botticelli.

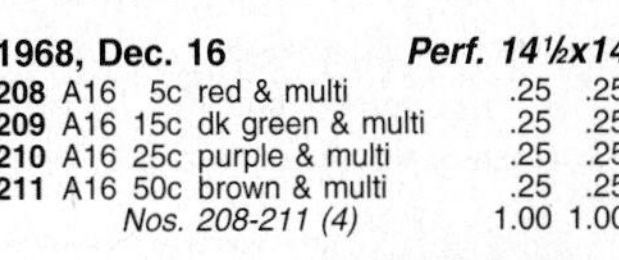

1968, Dec. 16 *Perf. 14½x14*

No.	Type	Value	Description	Unused	Used
208	A16	5c	red & multi	.25	.25
209	A16	15c	dk green & multi	.25	.25
210	A16	25c	purple & multi	.25	.25
211	A16	50c	brown & multi	.25	.25
			Nos. 208-211 (4)	1.00	1.00

Map of Caribbean — A17

Design: 35c, 50c, "Strength in Unity," horiz.

1969, May 27 **Photo.** *Perf. 14*

No.	Type	Value	Description	Unused	Used
212	A17	15c	green & multi	.25	.25
213	A17	20c	brown & multi	.25	.25
214	A17	35c	dp carmine & multi	.25	.25
215	A17	50c	multicolored	.25	.25
			Nos. 212-215 (4)	1.00	1.00

First anniversary of CARIFTA (Caribbean Free Trade Area).

Telephone and Map — A18

Development Projects (Map and): 25c, Book and "New Schools." 50c, Planes (air transport service). $1, Pylon and power lines.

Wmk. 314

1969, July 29 **Litho.** *Perf. 13½*

No.	Type	Value	Description	Unused	Used
216	A18	15c	multicolored	.25	.25
217	A18	25c	multicolored	.25	.25
218	A18	50c	multicolored	.25	.25
219	A18	$1	multicolored	.25	.25
			Nos. 216-219 (4)	1.00	1.00

Dolphin A19

Fish: 15c, Atlantic sailfish. 25c, Blackfin tuna and fishing boat. 40c, Spanish mackerel.

1969, Nov. 1 **Photo.** *Perf. 13x14*

No.	Type	Value	Description	Unused	Used
220	A19	5c	multicolored	.25	.25
221	A19	15c	multicolored	.35	.35
222	A19	25c	multicolored	.70	.70
223	A19	40c	multicolored	1.25	1.25
			Nos. 220-223 (4)	2.55	2.55

King Caspar, Virgin and Child (Stained-glass Window) — A20

Christmas: 50c, Nativity, by Leonard Limosin, horiz.

Perf. 12½x13, 13x12½

1969, Dec. 10 **Litho.** **Wmk. 314**

No.	Type	Value	Description	Unused	Used
224	A20	15c	violet & multi	.25	.25
225	A20	25c	red & multi	.25	.25
226	A20	50c	orange & multi	.25	.25
			Nos. 224-226 (3)	.75	.75

Red Cross and Distribution of Hearing Aids — A21

Red Cross and: 3c, Fund raising sale and invalid. 15c, Car bringing handicapped to work. 20c, Instruction for blind worker.

1970, Apr. 13 **Litho.** *Perf. 14½*

No.	Type	Value	Description	Unused	Used
227	A21	3c	multicolored	.25	.25
228	A21	4c	multicolored	.25	.25
229	A21	15c	multicolored	.25	.25
230	A21	20c	multicolored	.25	.25
			Nos. 227-230 (4)	1.00	1.00

Centenary of British Red Cross Society.

Red-footed Booby A22

Birds: 2c, Killy hawk, vert. 3c, Frigate bird, vert. 4c, White egret, vert. 5c, Brown pelican, vert. 10c, Bananaquit, vert. 15c, Common ani. 20c, Tropic bird. 25c, Montserrat oriole. 50c, Greenthroated carib, vert. $1, Antillean crested hummingbird. $2.50, Little blue heron, vert. $5, Purple-throated carib. $10, Forest thrush.

Wmk. 314 Upright on Horiz. Stamps, Sideways on Vert. Stamps

Perf. 14x14½, 14½x14

1970-74 **Photo.**

No.	Type	Value	Description	Unused	Used
231	A22	1c	yel org & multi	.25	.25
232	A22	2c	lt vio & multi	.25	.25
233	A22	3c	multicolored	.25	.25
234	A22	4c	lt grn & multi	.25	.25
235	A22	5c	bister & multi	.25	.25
236	A22	10c	gray & multi	.25	.25
237	A22	15c	multicolored	.50	.40
238	A22	20c	rose brn & multi	.65	.55
239	A22	25c	brown & multi	.85	.70
240	A22	50c	lt vio & multi	1.75	1.40
241	A22	$1	multicolored	3.00	2.40
242	A22	$2.50	dl bl & multi	6.75	5.50
243	A22	$5	multicolored	13.50	11.00
243A	A22	$10	blue & multi	26.00	22.50
			Nos. 231-243A (14)	54.50	45.95

Issued: $10, 10/30/74; others 7/2/70.

For surcharges and overprints see Nos. 314, 317, 337-339, O1-O4.

Wmk. Sideways on Horiz. Stamps, Upright on Vert. Stamps

1972-74

No.	Type	Value	Description	Unused	Used
231a	A22	1c	multicolored	.80	1.10
232a	A22	2c	multicolored	1.00	1.10
233a	A22	3c	multicolored	1.00	1.10
234a	A22	4c	multicolored	1.50	1.50
235a	A22	5c	multicolored	2.00	1.75
237a	A22	15c	multicolored	5.00	4.50
238a	A22	20c	multicolored	7.00	7.50
239a	A22	25c	multicolored	9.75	9.50
			Nos. 231a-239a (8)	28.05	28.05

Issued: 1c, 2c, 3c, 7/21/72; 5c, 15c, 3/8/73; 20c, 10/2/73; 4c, 2/4/74; 25c, 5/17/74.

"Madonna and Child with Animals," after Dürer — A23

Christmas: 15c, $1, Adoration of the Shepherds, by Domenichino (Domenico Zampieri).

1970, Sept. 21 **Litho.** *Perf. 14*

No.	Type	Value	Description	Unused	Used
244	A23	5c	lt blue & multi	.25	.25
245	A23	15c	red orange & multi	.25	.25
246	A23	20c	ol green & multi	.25	.25
247	A23	$1	multicolored	.50	.50
			Nos. 244-247 (4)	1.25	1.25

War Memorial, Plymouth — A24

Tourist Publicity: 15c, Fort St. George and view of Plymouth. 25c, Beach at Carrs Bay. 50c, Golf Course.

1970, Nov. 30 **Litho.** *Perf. 14*

No.	Type	Value	Description	Unused	Used
248	A24	5c	multicolored	.25	.25
249	A24	15c	multicolored	.40	.40
250	A24	25c	multicolored	.70	.70
251	A24	50c	multicolored	1.50	1.50
a.			Souvenir sheet of 4, #248-251	7.25	7.25
			Nos. 248-251 (4)	2.85	2.85

Girl Guide — A25

Girl Guides' 60th Anniv.: 15c, 25c, Brownie.

1970, Dec. 31

No.	Type	Value	Description	Unused	Used
252	A25	10c	orange & multi	.25	.25
253	A25	15c	lt blue & multi	.25	.25
254	A25	25c	lilac & multi	.25	.25
255	A25	40c	multicolored	.30	.30
			Nos. 252-255 (4)	1.05	1.05

"Noli me Tangere," by Orcagna (Andrea di Cione) — A26

Easter: 5c, 20c, Descent from the Cross, by Jan van Hemessen.

Perf. 13½x13

1971, Mar. 22 **Photo.** **Wmk. 314**

No.	Type	Value	Description	Unused	Used
256	A26	5c	orange brn & multi	.25	.25
257	A26	15c	multicolored	.25	.25
258	A26	20c	green & multi	.25	.25
259	A26	40c	blue green & multi	.25	.25
			Nos. 256-259 (4)	1.00	1.00

Distinguished Flying Cross and Medal — A27

Highest Awards for Military Personnel: 20c, Military Cross and Medal. 40c, Distinguished Service Cross and Medal. $1, Victoria Cross.

Perf. 14½x14

1971, July 8 **Litho.** **Wmk. 314**

No.	Type	Value	Description	Unused	Used
260	A27	10c	gray, vio & silver	.25	.25
261	A27	20c	green & multi	.25	.25
262	A27	40c	lt bl, dk bl & sil	.25	.25
263	A27	$1	red, dk brn & gold	.40	.40
			Nos. 260-263 (4)	1.15	1.15

50th anniversary of the British Commonwealth Ex-services League.

"Nativity with Saints" (detail), by Romanino A28

Christmas (Paintings): 15c, $1, Angels' Choir, by Simon Marmion.

1971, Sept. 16 *Perf. 14x13½*

No.	Type	Value	Description	Unused	Used
264	A28	5c	brown & multi	.25	.25
265	A28	15c	emerald & multi	.25	.25
266	A28	20c	ultra & multi	.25	.25
267	A28	$1	red & multi	.40	.40
			Nos. 264-267 (4)	1.15	1.15

Piper Apache, First Landing at Olveston Airfield — A29

Designs: 10c, Beech Twin Bonanza. 15c, De Havilland Heron. 20c, Britten Norman Islander. 40c, De Havilland Twin Otter. 75c, Hawker Siddeley 748 and stewardesses.

1971, Dec. 16 *Perf. 13½x14*

No.	Type	Value	Description	Unused	Used
268	A29	5c	multicolored	.25	.25
269	A29	10c	multicolored	.30	.30
270	A29	15c	multicolored	.45	.45
271	A29	20c	multicolored	.65	.65
272	A29	40c	multicolored	1.25	1.25
273	A29	75c	multicolored	2.00	2.00
a.			Souvenir sheet of 6, #268-273	16.00	16.00
			Nos. 268-273 (6)	4.90	4.90

14th anniversary of Leeward Islands Air Transport (LIAT).

Chapel of Christ in Gethsemane, Coventry Cathedral — A30

Easter: 10c, 75c, The Agony in the Garden, by Giovanni Bellini.

1972, Mar. 9 **Litho.** *Perf. 13½x13*

No.	Type	Value	Description	Unused	Used
274	A30	5c	red & multi	.25	.25
275	A30	10c	blue & multi	.25	.25
276	A30	20c	emerald & multi	.25	.25
277	A30	75c	lilac & multi	.75	.75
			Nos. 274-277 (4)	1.50	1.50

Iguana A31

Designs: 15c, Spotted ameiva (lizard), vert. 20c, Frog ("mountain chicken"), vert. $1, Redfoot tortoises.

1972, June 8 **Litho.** *Perf. 14½*

No.	Type	Value	Description	Unused	Used
278	A31	15c	lilac rose & multi	.60	.60
279	A31	20c	black & multi	.70	.70
280	A31	40c	blue & multi	1.50	1.50
281	A31	$1	green & multi	3.00	3.00
			Nos. 278-281 (4)	5.80	5.80

Madonna of the Chair, by Raphael A32

Christmas (Paintings): 35c, Virgin and Child with Cherubs, by Bernardino Fungai. 50c, Magnificat Madonna, by Botticelli. $1, Virgin and Child with St. John and Angel, by Botticelli.

1972, Oct. 18 ***Perf. 13½***

282	A32	10c violet & multi	.25	.25
283	A32	35c brt red & multi	.25	.25
284	A32	50c red brown & multi	.30	.30
285	A32	$1 olive & multi	.50	.50
		Nos. 282-285 (4)	1.30	1.30

Silver Wedding Issue, 1972
Common Design Type

Design: Queen Elizabeth II, Prince Philip, tomatoes, papayas, limes.

Perf. 14x14½
1972, Nov. 20 Photo. Wmk. 314

286	CD324	35c car rose & multi	.25	.25
287	CD324	$1 ultra & multi	.30	.30

Passionflower A33

Designs: 35c, Passiflora vitifolia. 75c, Passiflora amabilis. $1, Passiflora alata caerulea.

1973, Apr. 9 Litho. ***Perf. 14x13½***

288	A33	20c purple & multi	.40	.40
289	A33	35c multicolored	.75	.75
290	A33	75c brt blue & multi	1.10	1.10
291	A33	$1 multicolored	2.00	2.00
		Nos. 288-291 (4)	4.25	4.25

Easter. Black backprinting gives story of passionflower.

Montserrat Monastery, Spain — A34

35c, Columbus aboard ship sighting Montserrat. 60c, Columbus' ship off Montserrat. $1, Arms and map of Montserrat & neighboring islands.

1973, July 16 Litho. ***Perf. 13½x14***

292	A34	10c multicolored	.40	.40
293	A34	35c multicolored	.90	.90
294	A34	60c multicolored	1.40	1.40
295	A34	$1 multicolored	2.10	2.10
a.		Souvenir sheet of 4, #292-295	20.00	20.00
		Nos. 292-295 (4)	4.80	4.80

480th anniversary of the discovery of Montserrat by Columbus.

Virgin and Child, Studio of David — A35

Christmas (Paintings): 35c, Holy Family with St. John, by Jacob Jordaens. 50c, Virgin and Child, by Bellini. 90c, Virgin and Child by Carlo Dolci.

1973, Oct. 15 Litho. ***Perf. 14x13½***

296	A35	20c blue & multi	.25	.25
297	A35	35c ol bister & multi	.30	.30
298	A35	50c brt green & multi	.40	.40
299	A35	90c brt rose & multi	.55	.55
		Nos. 296-299 (4)	1.50	1.50

Princess Anne's Wedding Issue
Common Design Type

1973, Nov. 14 ***Perf. 14***

300	CD325	35c brt green & multi	.25	.25
301	CD325	$1 multicolored	.40	.40

Masqueraders A36

20c, Steel band, horiz. 60c, Girl weaving. $1, University Center, horiz.

1974, Apr. 8

302	A36	20c multi	.25	.25
303	A36	35c shown	.25	.25
304	A36	60c multi	.25	.25
305	A36	$1 multi	.40	.40
a.		Souvenir sheet of 4, #302-305	4.50	4.50
		Nos. 302-305 (4)	1.15	1.15

University of the West Indies, 25th anniv. For surcharge see No. 316.

Hands Holding Letters, UPU Emblem A37

Designs: 2c, 5c, $1, Hands and figures from UPU Monument, Bern; UPU emblem. 3c, 50c, like 1c.

1974, July 3 Litho. ***Perf. 14***

306	A37	1c violet & multi	.25	.25
307	A37	2c red & black	.25	.25
308	A37	3c olive & multi	.25	.25
309	A37	5c orange & black	.25	.25
310	A37	50c brown & multi	.25	.25
311	A37	$1 grnsh blue & black	.40	.40
		Nos. 306-311 (6)	1.65	1.65

Centenary of Universal Postal Union. For surcharges see Nos. 315-318.

Churchill, Parliament, Big Ben — A38

Churchill and Blenheim Palace — A39

Perf. 13x13½
1974, Nov. 30 Unwmk.

312	A38	35c ocher & multi	.25	.25
313	A39	70c brt green & multi	.30	.30
a.		Souvenir sheet of 2, #312-313	.75	.75

Sir Winston Churchill (1874-1965).

Nos. 241, 304, 310-311 Surcharged

Perf. 14x14½, 14
Photo., Litho.
1974, Oct. 2 Wmk. 314

314	A22	2c on $1 multi	.30	.30
315	A37	5c on 50c multi	1.40	1.40
316	A36	10c on 60c multi	3.75	3.75
317	A22	20c on $1 multi	1.25	1.25
a.		One bar in surcharge	2.75	2.75
318	A37	35c on $1 multi	2.75	2.75
		Nos. 314-318 (5)	9.45	9.45

Carib Carbet (House) A40

Carib Artifacts: 20c, Necklace (caracoli). 35c, Club. 70c, Canoe.

Wmk. 314
1975, Mar. 3 Litho. ***Perf. 14***

319	A40	5c dk red, ocher & blk	.25	.25
320	A40	20c blk, och & dk red	.25	.25
321	A40	35c blk, dk red & och	.25	.25
322	A40	70c ocher, dk red & blk	.35	.35
a.		Souvenir booklet	3.50	
		Nos. 319-322 (4)	1.10	1.10

No. 322a contains 2 self-adhesive panes printed on peelable paper backing with bicolored advertising on back. One pane of 6 contains 3 each similar to Nos. 320-321; the other pane of 4 contains one each similar to Nos. 319-322. Stamps are imperf. x roulette. Panes have commemorative marginal inscription.

One Bitt A41

Old Local Coinage (1785-1801): 10c, Eighth of a dollar. 35c, Quarter dollars. $2, One dollar.

1975, Sept. 1 Litho. ***Perf. 14***

323	A41	5c ultra, silver & blk	.25	.25
324	A41	10c brown org, sil & blk	.25	.25
325	A41	35c green, silver & blk	.35	.35
326	A41	$2 brt rose, sil & blk	1.20	1.20
a.		Souvenir sheet of 4, #323-326	2.25	2.25
		Nos. 323-326 (4)	2.05	2.05

Explanation and description of coinage printed in black on back of souvenir sheet.

Montserrat Nos. 1 and 2 — A42

10c, Post Office, Montserrat & #1a with AO8 cancel. 40c, Cover with #1a, 1b. 55c, #A4 (G.B. #27 with AO8 cancel) & #2. 70c, 2 #1, 1 #1a with AO8 cancels. $1.10, Packet "Antelope" & #2.

1976, Jan. 5 ***Perf. 13½***

327	A42	5c multicolored	.25	.25
328	A42	10c multicolored	.25	.25
329	A42	40c multicolored	.50	.50
330	A42	55c multicolored	.65	.65
331	A42	70c multicolored	.85	.85
332	A42	$1.10 multicolored	1.25	1.25
a.		Souvenir sheet of 6, #327-332	4.25	4.25
		Nos. 327-332 (6)	3.75	3.75

Centenary of Montserrat's postage stamps.

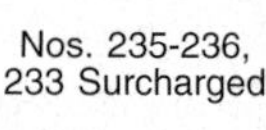
Trinity, by Orcagna — A43

Paintings by Orcagna (Andrea di Cione): 40c, Resurrection. 55c, Ascension. $1.10, Pentecost.

Perf. 14x13½
1976, Apr. 5 Litho. Wmk. 373

333	A43	15c multicolored	.25	.25
334	A43	40c multicolored	.25	.25
335	A43	55c multicolored	.25	.25
336	A43	$1.10 multicolored	.30	.30
a.		Souvenir sheet of 4	1.90	1.90
		Nos. 333-336 (4)	1.05	1.05

Easter 1976. Nos. 333-336 were prepared, but not issued in 1975. Stamps are surcharged with new values; date "1975" obliterated with heavy bar. No. 336a contains one each of Nos. 333-336; "1975" in margin obliterated with heavy bar.

Nos. 235-236, 233 Surcharged

Perf. 14½x14
1976, Apr. 12 Photo. Wmk. 314

337	A22	2c on 5c multi	.35	.35
338	A22	30c on 10c multi	.70	.70
339	A22	45c on 3c multi	1.20	1.20
		Nos. 337-339 (3)	2.25	2.25

For overprints see Nos. O3-O4.

White Frangipani — A44

Designs: Flowering trees of Montserrat.

Perf. 13½x14
1976, July 5 Litho. Wmk. 373

340	A44	1c shown	.25	.25
341	A44	2c Cannonball tree	.25	.25
342	A44	3c Lignum vitae	.25	.25
343	A44	5c Malay apple	.25	.25
344	A44	10c Jacaranda	.25	.25
345	A44	15c Orchid tree	.25	.25
346	A44	20c Manjak	.25	.25
347	A44	25c Tamarind	.25	.25
348	A44	40c Flame of the Forest	.25	.25
349	A44	55c Pink cassia	.30	.30
350	A44	70c Long John	.35	.35
351	A44	$1 Saman	.50	.50
352	A44	$2.50 Immortelle	1.25	1.25
353	A44	$5 Yellow poui	2.50	2.50
354	A44	$10 Flamboyant	5.00	5.00
		Nos. 340-354 (15)	12.15	12.15

For surcharges and overprints see Nos. 374-376, 420, 435-440, O10-O44.

Mary and Joseph on Road to Bethlehem — A45

Christmas (Map of Montserrat and): 20c, Shepherds. 55c, Virgin and Child. $1.10, Three Kings.

1976, Oct. 4 *Perf. 14½*

355 A45 15c vio blue & multi .25 .25
356 A45 20c green & multi .25 .25
357 A45 55c lilac & multi .25 .25
358 A45 $1.10 multicolored .40 .40
a. Souvenir sheet of 4, #355-358 2.00 2.00
Nos. 355-358 (4) 1.15 1.15

Hudson River Review of Opsail 76 — A46

Designs: 40c, Raleigh. 75c, HMS Druid (Raleigh attacking Druid, 1776).

1976, Dec. 13 **Litho.** *Perf. 13*

359 15c multicolored .30 .30
a. A46 Pair, #359, 362 1.90 1.90
360 40c multicolored .65 .65
361 75c multicolored 1.10 1.10
a. A46 Pair, #360-361 1.75 1.75
362 $1.25 multicolored 1.60 1.60
a. A46 Souvenir sheet of 4, #359-362, perf. 14x13½ 4.00 4.00
Nos. 359-362 (4) 3.65 3.65

American Bicentennial.

Queen Arriving for 1966 Visit, Yacht Britannia — A48

Designs: 45c, Firing of cannons at Tower of London. $1, The crowning.

1977, Feb. 7

363 A48 30c multicolored .25 .25
364 A48 45c multicolored .25 .25
365 A48 $1 multicolored .30 .30
Nos. 363-365 (3) .80 .80

25th anniv. of the reign of Elizabeth II. #363-365 were issued also in booklet panes of 4.

Epiphyllum Hookeri — A49

Flowers of the Night: 15c, Ipomoea alba, vert. 55c, Cereus hexagonus. $1.50, Cestrum nocturnum, vert.

1977, June 1 **Litho.** *Perf. 14*

366 A49 15c multicolored .25 .25
367 A49 40c multicolored .30 .30
368 A49 55c multicolored .40 .40
369 A49 $1.50 multicolored 1.25 1.25
a. Souvenir sheet of 4, #366-369 3.25 3.25
Nos. 366-369 (4) 2.20 2.20

Princess Anne at Ground-breaking Ceremony, Glendon Hospital — A50

Designs: 40c, New deep-water jetty, Plymouth. 55c, Glendon Hospital. $1.50, Freighter unloading at new jetty.

1977, Oct. 3 **Wmk. 373** *Perf. 14½*

370 A50 20c multicolored .25 .25
371 A50 40c multicolored .25 .25
372 A50 55c multicolored .30 .30
373 A50 $1.50 multicolored .80 .80
a. Souvenir sheet of 4, #370-373 2.50 2.50
Nos. 370-373 (4) 1.60 1.60

Development.

Nos. 349-350, 352 Surcharged with New Value and Bars and Overprinted: "SILVER JUBILEE 1977 / ROYAL VISIT / TO THE CARIBBEAN"

1977, Oct. **Litho.** *Perf. 13½x14*

374 A44 $1 on 55c multi .30 .30
375 A44 $1 on 70c multi .30 .30
376 A44 $1 on $2.50 multi .30 .30
Nos. 374-376 (3) .90 .90

Caribbean visit of Queen Elizabeth II. Surcharge has bars of differing thickness and length. No. 374 has two settings.

"Silent Night, Holy Night" — A51

Christmas Carols and Map of Montserrat: 40c, "We Three Kings of Orient Are." 55c, "I Saw Three Ships Come Sailing In." $2, "Hark the Herald Angels Sing."

1977, Nov. 14 **Litho.** *Perf. 14½*

377 A51 5c blue & multi .25 .25
378 A51 40c bister & multi .25 .25
379 A51 55c lt blue & multi .25 .25
380 A51 $2 rose & multi .50 .50
a. Souvenir sheet of 4, #377-380 1.25 1.25
Nos. 377-380 (4) 1.25 1.25

Four-eye Butterflyfish — A52

Fish: 40c, French angelfish. 55c, Blue tang. $1.50, Queen triggerfish.

1978, Feb. 27 **Wmk. 373** *Perf. 14*

381 A52 30c multicolored .40 .40
382 A52 40c multicolored .50 .50
383 A52 55c multicolored .70 .70
384 A52 $1.50 multicolored 2.00 2.00
a. Souvenir sheet of 4, #381-384 5.50 5.50
Nos. 381-384 (4) 3.60 3.60

Elizabeth II and St. Paul's, London — A53

Designs: 55c, Chichester Cathedral. $1, Lincoln Cathedral. $2.50, Llandaff Cathedral, Cardiff.

1978, June 2 *Perf. 13½*

385 A53 40c multicolored .25 .25
386 A53 55c multicolored .25 .25
387 A53 $1 multicolored .25 .25
388 A53 $2.50 multicolored .50 .50
a. Souvenir sheet of 4, #385-388 1.25 1.25
Nos. 385-388 (4) 1.25 1.25

25th anniversary of coronation of Elizabeth II, Defender of the Faith. Nos. 385-388 printed in sheets of 10 stamps and 2 labels. #385-388 also issued in bklt. panes of 2.

Alpinia — A54

Flowering Plants: 55c, Allamanda cathartica. $1, Blue tree petrea. $2, Amaryllis.

1978, Sept. 18 **Litho.** *Perf. 13½x13*

389 A54 40c multicolored .25 .25
390 A54 55c multicolored .35 .35
391 A54 $1 multicolored .65 .65
392 A54 $2 multicolored 1.25 1.25
Nos. 389-392 (4) 2.50 2.50

Private, 1796 — A55

Uniforms: 40c, Corporal, 1831. 55c, Sergeant, 1837. $1.50, Officer, 1784.

1978, Nov. 20 **Litho.** *Perf. 14½*

393 A55 30c multicolored .25 .25
394 A55 40c multicolored .25 .25
395 A55 55c multicolored .35 .35
396 A55 $1.50 multicolored 1.00 1.00
a. Souvenir sheet of 4, #393-396 2.10 2.10
Nos. 393-396 (4) 1.85 1.85

See Nos. 401-404.

Cub Scouts A56

Boy Scouts: 55c, Signaling. $1.25, Cooking, vert. $2, Flag folding ceremony, vert.

1979, Apr. 2 **Litho.** *Perf. 14*

397 A56 40c multicolored .25 .25
398 A56 55c multicolored .30 .30
399 A56 $1.25 multicolored .70 .70
400 A56 $2 multicolored .75 .75
a. Souvenir sheet of 4, #397-400 2.75 2.75
Nos. 397-400 (4) 2.00 2.00

50th anniversary of Scouting in Montserrat.

Uniform Type of 1978

30c, Private, 1783. 40c, Private, 1819. 55c, Officer, 1819. $2.50, Highlander officer, 1830.

1979, July 4 **Wmk. 373** *Perf. 14*

401 A55 30c multicolored .25 .25
402 A55 40c multicolored .25 .25
403 A55 55c multicolored .25 .25
404 A55 $2.50 multicolored 1.25 1.25
a. Souvenir sheet of 4, #401-404 2.50 2.50
Nos. 401-404 (4) 2.00 2.00

IYC Emblem, Learning to Walk — A56a

1979, Sept. 17 **Litho.** *Perf. 13½x14*

405 A56a $2 brown org & black .60 .60
a. Souvenir sheet 1.50 1.50

International Year of the Child.

Hill, Penny Black, Montserrat No. 1 — A57

Designs: 55c, UPU Emblem, charter. $1, UPU Emblem, cover. $2, Hill, Post Office regulations.

1979, Oct. 1 *Perf. 14*

406 A57 40c multicolored .25 .25
407 A57 55c multicolored .25 .25
408 A57 $1 multicolored .35 .35
409 A57 $2 multicolored .70 .70
a. Souvenir sheet of 4, #406-409 2.75 2.75
Nos. 406-409 (4) 1.55 1.55

Sir Rowland Hill (1795-1879), originator of penny postage; UPU membership, centenary.

Tree Lizard A58

1980, Feb. 4 **Litho.** *Perf. 14*

410 A58 40c Tree frog .30 .30
411 A58 55c shown .45 .45
412 A58 $1 Crapaud .80 .80
413 A58 $2 Wood slave 1.60 1.60
Nos. 410-413 (4) 3.15 3.15

Marquis of Salisbury, 1817; Postmarks, 1838, London 1980 Emblem — A59

Ships or Planes, Stamps of Montserrat: 55c, H.S. 748, #349. #416, La Plata, 1901, type A4. #417, Lady Hawkins, 1929, #84. #418, Avon, 1843, Gt Britain #3. #419, Aeronca, #140.

1980, Apr. 14 **Litho.** *Perf. 14½*

414 A59 40c multicolored .25 .25
415 A59 55c multicolored .30 .30
416 A59 $1.20 multicolored .55 .60
417 A59 $1.20 multicolored .55 .60
418 A59 $1.20 multicolored .55 .60
419 A59 $1.20 multicolored .55 .60
a. Souvenir sheet of 6, #414-419 3.00 3.00
Nos. 414-419 (6) 2.75 2.95

London 1980 Intl. Stamp Exhib., May 6-14. For surcharges see Nos. 736-740.

No. 352 Overprinted: 75th Anniversary of / Rotary International

1980, July 7 **Litho.** *Perf. 13½x14*

420 A44 $2.50 multicolored 1.10 1.10

Discus Thrower, Stadium, Olympic Rings — A60

Flags of Host Countries: 40c, Greece, 1896; France, 1900; U.S., 1904. 55c, Great Britain, 1908; Sweden, 1912; Belgium, 1920. 70c, France, 1924; Netherlands, 1928; US, 1932. $1, Germany, 1936; Great Britain, 1948; Finland, 1952. $1.50, Australia, 1956; Italy, 1960; Japan, 1964. $2, Mexico, 1968,; Fed. Rep. of Germany, 1972; Canada, 1976.

1980, July 7 Litho. *Perf. 14*

421	A60	40c multicolored	.25	.25
422	A60	55c multicolored	.25	.25
423	A60	70c multicolored	.30	.30
424	A60	$1 multicolored	.40	.40
425	A60	$1.50 multicolored	.50	.50
426	A60	$2 multicolored	.70	.70
427	A60	$2.50 multicolored	.90	.90
a.		Souv. sheet of 7, #421-427 + 2 labels	3.50	3.50
		Nos. 421-427 (7)	3.30	3.30

22nd Summer Olympic Games, Moscow, July 19-Aug. 3.

Lady Nelson, 1928 A61

1980 Litho. *Perf. 14*

428	A61	40c shown	.25	.25
429	A61	55c Chignecto, 1913	.40	.40
430	A61	$1 Solent, 1878	.75	.75
431	A61	$2 Dee, 1841	1.40	1.40
		Nos. 428-431 (4)	2.80	2.80

Plume Worm — A62

1980 Litho. *Perf. 14*

432	A62	40c shown	.50	.50
433	A62	55c Sea fans	.70	.70
434	A62	$2 Coral, sponges	1.75	1.75
		Nos. 432-434 (3)	2.95	2.95

Nos. 340, 342, 345, 348 Surcharged

1980, Sept. 30 Litho. *Perf. 14*

435	A44	5c on 3c (#342)	.25	.25
436	A44	35c on 1c (#340)	.25	.25
437	A44	35c on 3c (#342)	.25	.25
438	A44	35c on 15c (#345)	.25	.25
439	A44	55c on 40c (#348)	.25	.25
440	A44	$5 on 40c (#348)	1.25	1.40
		Nos. 435-440 (6)	2.50	2.65

Zebra Butterfly — A63

65c, Tropical checkered skipper. $1.50, Large orange sulphur. $2.50, Monarch.

1981, Feb. 2 Wmk. 373

441	A63	50c shown	.75	.50
442	A63	65c multi	.90	.55
443	A63	$1.50 multi	1.10	1.00
444	A63	$2.50 multi	1.60	1.40
		Nos. 441-444 (4)	4.35	3.45

Spadefish — A64

10c, Hogfish. 15c, Creole wrasse. 20c, Yellow damselfish. 25c, Sergeant major. 35c, Clown wrasse. 45c, Schoolmaster. 55c, Striped parrotfish. 65c, Bigeye. 75c, French grunt. $1, Rock beauty. $2, Blue chromis. $3, Fairy basslet, blueheads. $5, Cherubfish. $7.50, Longspine squirrelfish. $10, Longsnout butterflyfish.

Wmk. 373

1981, Mar. 20 Litho. *Perf. 13½*

445	A64	5c shown	.25	.25
446	A64	10c multi	.25	.25
447	A64	15c multi	.25	.25
448	A64	20c multi	.25	.25
449	A64	25c multi	.25	.25
450	A64	35c multi	.25	.25
451	A64	45c multi	.40	.40
452	A64	55c multi	1.25	1.25
453	A64	65c multi	.55	.55
454	A64	75c multi	.60	.60
455	A64	$1 multi	.85	.85
456	A64	$2 multi	1.75	1.75
457	A64	$3 multi	2.75	2.75
458	A64	$5 multi	4.25	4.25
459	A64	$7.50 multi	4.75	4.75
460	A64	$10 multi	7.25	7.25
		Nos. 445-460 (16)	25.90	25.90

For surcharges and overprints see Nos. 507-508, 511-512, 515, O45-O55, O95-O97.

Inscribed 1983

1983 Wmk. 380

445a	A64	5c	.30	.25
446a	A64	10c	.35	.25
449a	A64	25c	.40	.25
450a	A64	35c	.45	.30
454a	A64	75c	.65	.55
455a	A64	$1	.85	.70
458a	A64	$5	3.75	3.75
460a	A64	$10	6.75	6.75
		Nos. 445a-460a (8)	13.50	12.80

Fort St. George (National Trust) — A65

65c, Bird Sanctuary, Fox's Bay. $1.50, The Museum. $2.50, Bransby Point Battery.

1981, May 18 Wmk. 373 *Perf. 13½*

461	A65	50c shown	.30	.30
462	A65	65c multi	.30	.30
463	A65	$1.50 multi	.70	.80
464	A65	$2.50 multi	1.40	1.50
		Nos. 461-464 (4)	2.70	2.90

Prince Charles, Lady Diana, Royal Yacht Charlotte A66

Prince Charles and Lady Diana — A67

Wmk. 380

1981, July 13 Litho. *Perf. 14*

465	A66	90c shown	.35	.35
a.		Booklet pane of 4, perf. 12	1.75	
466	A67	90c shown	1.25	1.25
467	A66	$3 Portsmouth	.85	.85
468	A67	$3 like #466	2.10	2.10
a.		Booklet pane of 2, perf. 12	3.50	
469	A66	$4 Britannia	1.10	1.10
470	A67	$4 like #466	2.40	2.40
		Nos. 465-470 (6)	8.05	8.05

Royal wedding. Each denomination issued in sheets of 7 (6 type A66, 1 type A67).

For surcharges and overprints see Nos. 509-510, 513-514, 578-579, O56-O61.

Souvenir Sheet

1981, Dec. *Perf. 12*

471	A67	$5 multicolored	3.00	3.00

50th Anniv. of Airmail Service A68

50c, Seaplane, Dorsetshire. 65c, Beechcraft Twin Bonanza. $1.50, DeHaviland Dragon Rapide. $2.50, Hawker Siddeley Avro 748.

1981, Aug. 31 Wmk. 373 *Perf. 14*

472	A68	50c multicolored	.40	.40
473	A68	65c multicolored	.50	.50
474	A68	$1.50 multicolored	1.00	1.00
475	A68	$2.50 multicolored	1.60	1.60
		Nos. 472-475 (4)	3.50	3.50

Methodist Church, Bethel — A69

Christmas (Churches): 65c, St. George's Anglican, Harris. $1.50, St. Peter's Anglican, St. Peter's. $2.50, St. Patrick's Roman Catholic, Plymouth.

1981, Nov. 16 Litho. *Perf. 14*

476	A69	50c multicolored	.25	.25
477	A69	65c multicolored	.30	.30
478	A69	$1.50 multicolored	.50	.50
479	A69	$2.50 multicolored	.90	.90
a.		Souvenir sheet of 4, #476-479	2.75	2.75
		Nos. 476-479 (4)	1.95	1.95

Wild Flowers First Discovered on Montserrat — A70

50c, Rondeletia buxifolia, vert. 65c, Heliotropium ternatum. $1.50, Picramnia pentandra, vert. $2.50, Diospyros revoluta.

1982, Jan. 18 Litho. *Perf. 14½*

480	A70	50c multicolored	.25	.25
481	A70	65c multicolored	.25	.25
482	A70	$1.50 multicolored	.50	.50
483	A70	$2.50 multicolored	1.25	1.25
		Nos. 480-483 (4)	2.25	2.25

350th Anniv. of Settlement of Montserrat by Sir Thomas Warner — A70a

Jubilee Type of 1932.

Wmk. 373

1982, Apr. 17 Litho. *Perf. 14½*

483A	A70a	40c green	.25	.25
483B	A70a	55c red	.25	.25
483C	A70a	65c brown	.30	.30
483D	A70a	75c gray	.30	.30
483E	A70a	85c ultra	.35	.35
483F	A70a	95c orange	.40	.40
483G	A70a	$1 purple	.40	.40
483H	A70a	$1.50 olive	.60	.60
483I	A70a	$2 car rose	.75	.75
483J	A70a	$2.50 sepia	1.05	1.05
		Nos. 483A-483J (10)	4.65	4.65

A70b

75c, Catherine of Aragon, 1501. $1, Aragon arms. $5, Diana.

1982, June Wmk. 380 *Perf. 14*

484	A70b	75c multi	.30	.30
485	A70b	$1 multi	.30	.30
486	A70b	$5 multi	1.40	1.40
		Nos. 484-486 (3)	2.00	2.00

21st birthday of Princess Diana, July 1.

For surcharges and overprints see Nos. 574, O62-O64.

Scouting Year — A71

1982, Sept. 13 Litho. *Perf. 14*

487	A71	$1.50 Scout	.80	.80
488	A71	$2.50 Baden-Powell	1.20	1.20

Christmas A72

35c, Annunciation. 75c, Shepherds' vision. $1.50, Virgin and Child. $2.50, Flight into Egypt.

1982, Nov. 18 Wmk. 373 *Perf. 14*

489	A72	35c multi	.25	.25
490	A72	75c multi	.35	.35
491	A72	$1.50 multi	.65	.65
492	A72	$2.50 multi	1.25	1.25
		Nos. 489-492 (4)	2.50	2.50

Dragonflies — A73

50c, Lepthemis vesiculosa. 65c, Orthemis ferruginea. $1.50, Triacanthagyna trifida. $2.50, Erythrodiplax umbrata.

1983, Jan. 19 Litho. *Perf. 13½x14*

493	A73	50c multi	.55	.55
494	A73	65c multi	.70	.70
495	A73	$1.50 multi	1.50	1.50
496	A73	$2.50 multi	2.10	2.10
		Nos. 493-496 (4)	4.85	4.85

Blue-headed Hummingbird A74

75c, Green-throated carib. $2, Antillean crested hummingbird. $3, Purple-throated carib.

1983, May 24 Wmk. 373 *Perf. 14*

No.	Type	Value	Description	Unused	Used
497	A74	35c	shown	.90	.90
498	A74	75c	multi	1.25	1.25
499	A74	$2	multi	3.25	3.25
500	A74	$3	multi	4.50	4.50
			Nos. 497-500 (4)	9.90	9.90

Arms — A75

1983, July 25 Litho. *Perf. 14½*

No.	Type	Value	Description	Unused	Used
501	A75	$12	red & black	5.00	*7.50*
502	A75	$30	blue & red	15.00	*20.00*

Manned Flight Bicentenary — A76

Designs: 35c, Montgolfiere, 1783, vert. 75c, De Havilland Twin Otter 310, 1981. $1.50, Lockheed Vega's around the world flight, 1933. $2, British R34 airship transatlantic flight, 1919.

1983, Sept. 19 Litho. *Perf. 14*

No.	Type	Value	Description	Unused	Used
503	A76	35c	multicolored	.30	.30
504	A76	75c	multicolored	.40	.40
505	A76	$1.50	multicolored	.60	.60
506	A76	$2	multicolored	.90	.90
a.			Souvenir sheet of 4, #503-506	3.00	3.00
			Nos. 503-506 (4)	2.20	2.20

For surcharges see Nos. 573, 577.

Nos. 449, 446, 467-468, 453-454, 469-470, 456 Surcharged

Wmk. 373 (A64), 380

1983, Aug. 15 Litho. *Perf. 13½x14*

No.	Type	Description	Unused	Used
507	A64	40c on 25c multi	.55	.55
508	A64	70c on 10c multi	.85	.85
509	A66	70c on $3 multi	.75	.75
510	A67	70c on $3 multi	1.75	1.75
511	A64	90c on 65c multi	.95	.95
512	A64	$1.15 on 75c multi	1.20	1.20
513	A66	$1.15 on $4 multi	.95	.95
514	A67	$1.15 on $4 multi	2.25	2.25
515	A64	$1.50 on $2 multi	1.50	1.50
		Nos. 507-515 (9)	10.75	10.75

Christmas Carnival 1983 A77

1983, Nov. 18 Wmk. 380 *Perf. 14*

No.	Type	Value	Description	Unused	Used
516	A77	55c	Clowns	.25	.25
517	A77	90c	Star Bursts	.25	.25
518	A77	$1.15	Flower Girls	.30	.30
519	A77	$2	Masqueraders	.45	.45
			Nos. 516-519 (4)	1.25	1.25

See Nos. 547-550.

Nos. 503-506 were overprinted "INAUGURAL FLIGHT Montserrat — Nevis — St. Kitts." These exist on souvenir covers with first day cancel of Dec. 15, 1983. No announcement of this set was made nor were mint stamps generally available.

1984 Summer Olympics — A78

1984, Mar. 6 Litho. *Perf. 14*

No.	Type	Value	Description	Unused	Used
520	A78	90c	Discobolus	.40	.40
521	A78	$1	Torch	.50	.50
522	A78	$1.15	Stadium	.55	.55
523	A78	$2.50	Flags	.90	.90
a.			Souvenir sheet of 4, #520-523	3.00	3.00
			Nos. 520-523 (4)	2.35	2.35

Cattle Egret A79

10c, Carib grackles. 15c, Common gallinule. 20c, Brown boobys. 25c, Black-whiskered vireos. 40c, Scaly-breasted thrashers. 55c, Laughing gulls. 70c, Glossy ibis. 90c, Green heron. $1, Belted kingfisher. $1.15, Bananaquits. $3, Sparrow hawks. $5, Forest thrush. $7.50, Black-crowned night heron. $10, Bridled quail doves.

1984, May 11

No.	Type	Value	Description	Unused	Used
524	A79	5c	shown	.45	.35
525	A79	10c	multi	.45	.35
526	A79	15c	multi	.45	.35
527	A79	20c	multi	.60	.35
528	A79	25c	multi	.60	.50
529	A79	40c	multi	.90	.55
530	A79	55c	multi	1.10	.35
531	A79	70c	multi	1.40	.50
532	A79	90c	multi	1.50	.70
533	A79	$1	multi	1.90	.90
534	A79	$1.15	multi	2.40	1.60
535	A79	$3	multi	5.00	*6.00*
536	A79	$5	multi	7.00	*8.00*
537	A79	$7.50	multi	9.00	*14.50*
538	A79	$10	multi	10.50	*15.00*
			Nos. 524-538 (15)	43.25	50.00

For surcharges see Nos. 651-655, 663-666. For overprints see Nos. O65-O78.

Packet Boats A80

1984, July 9 Wmk. 380 *Perf. 14*

No.	Type	Value	Description	Unused	Used
539	A80	55c	Tagus, 1907	.30	.30
540	A80	90c	Cobequid, 1913	.45	.45
541	A80	$1.15	Lady Drake, 1942	.55	.55
542	A80	$2	Factor, 1948	.90	.90
a.			Souvenir sheet of 4, #539-542	4.25	4.25
			Nos. 539-542 (4)	2.20	2.20

Marine Life A81

90c, Top shell & hermit crab. $1.15, Rough file shell. $1.50, True tulip snail. $2.50, West Indian fighting conch.

1984, Sept. Wmk. 380 *Perf. 14*

No.	Type	Value	Description	Unused	Used
543	A81	90c	multi	1.60	1.60
544	A81	$1.15	multi	2.00	2.00
545	A81	$1.50	multi	3.00	3.00
546	A81	$2.50	multi	4.00	4.00
			Nos. 543-546 (4)	10.60	10.60

Christmas Carnival Type of 1983

55c, Bull Man. $1.15, Masquerader Captain. $1.50, Carnival Queen contestant. $2.30, Contestant, diff.

1984, Nov. 12

No.	Type	Value	Description	Unused	Used
547	A77	55c	multi	.65	.65
548	A77	$1.15	multi	1.60	1.60
549	A77	$1.50	multi	1.75	1.75
550	A77	$2.30	multi	2.75	2.75
			Nos. 547-550 (4)	6.75	6.75

National Emblems — A82

1985, Feb. 8 Litho. *Perf. 14*

No.	Type	Value	Description	Unused	Used
551	A82	$1.15	Mango	.40	*.60*
552	A82	$1.50	Lobster Claw	.50	*1.00*
553	A82	$3	Montserrat Oriole	.75	*2.25*
			Nos. 551-553 (3)	1.65	3.85

Indigenous Orchids — A83

90c, Oncidium urophyllum. $1.15, Epidendrum difforme. $1.50, Epidendrum ciliare. $2.50, Brassavola cucullata.

1985, May 9 Wmk. 380 *Perf. 14*

No.	Type	Value	Description	Unused	Used
554	A83	90c	multicolored	.60	*.70*
555	A83	$1.15	multicolored	.60	*.75*
556	A83	$1.50	multicolored	.70	*.85*
557	A83	$2.50	multicolored	.85	*1.00*
a.			Souvenir sheet of 4, #554-557	7.00	7.00
			Nos. 554-557 (4)	2.75	3.30

Queen Mother, 85th Birthday — A84

#558a, 564a, Facing right. #558b, 564b, Facing forward. #559a, Facing right. #559b, Facing left. #560a, Facing right. #560b, Glancing right. #561a, 563a, Facing right. #561b, 563b, Facing left. #562a, Facing right. #562b, Facing forward.

1985-86 Unwmk. *Perf. 12½*

No.	Type	Value	Description	Unused	Used
558	A84	55c	Pair, #a.-b.	.45	.45
559	A84	90c	Pair, #a.-b.	.75	.75
560	A84	$1.15	Pair, #a.-b.	.85	.85
561	A84	$1.50	Pair, #a.-b.	1.20	1.20
			Nos. 558-561 (4)	3.25	3.25

Souvenir Sheets of 2

No.	Type	Value	Description	Unused	Used
562	A84	$2	#a.-b.	1.75	1.75
563	A84	$3.50	#a.-b.	3.50	3.50
564	A84	$6	#a.-b.	5.50	5.50

Issued: #563-564, 1/10/86; others, 8/7/85.

For surcharges see No. 575.

Cotton Industry A85

1985, Sept. 23 Unwmk. *Perf. 15*

No.	Type	Value	Description	Unused	Used
569	A85	90c	Cotton plants	.25	*.30*
570	A85	$1	Carding	.25	*.35*
571	A85	$1.15	Automated loom	.25	*.35*
572	A85	$2.50	Hand loom	.40	*.50*
a.			Souvenir sheet of 4, #569-572	4.50	4.50
			Nos. 569-572 (4)	1.15	1.50

Nos. 504, 485, 560, 505, 469-470 Ovptd. or Surcharged "CARIBBEAN ROYAL VISIT 1985" in 2 or 3 Lines

Perf. 14, 12½ ($1.15)

Wmk. as Before

1985, Nov. 14 Litho.

No.	Type	Description	Unused	Used
573	A76	75c multi	4.75	4.75
574	A70b	$1 multi	6.75	6.75
575	A84	$1.15 Pair, #a.-b.	14.50	14.50
577	A76	$1.50 multi	9.25	9.25
578	A66	$1.60 on $4 multi	4.75	4.75
579	A67	$1.60 on $4 multi	17.00	17.00
		Nos. 573-579 (6)	57.00	57.00

No. 579 surcharged but not overprinted.

Audubon Birth Bicentenary — A86

Illustrations of North American bird species by John J. Audubon: #580a, Black-throated blue warbler. #580b, Palm warbler. #581a, Bobolink. #581b, Lark sparrow. #582a, Chipping sparrow. #582b, Northern oriole. #583a, American goldfinch. #583b, Blue grosbeak.

1985, Nov. 29 Unwmk. *Perf. 12½*

No.	Type	Value	Description	Unused	Used
580	A86	15c	Pair, #a.-b.	.25	.25
581	A86	30c	Pair, #a.-b.	.25	.25
582	A86	55c	Pair, #a.-b.	.40	.40
583	A86	$2.50	Pair, #a.-b.	1.40	1.40
			Nos. 580-583 (4)	2.30	2.30

Christmas A87

70c, Angel of the Lord. $1.15, Three wise men. $1.50, Caroling, Plymouth War Memorial. $2.30, Our Lady of Montserrat.

1985, Dec. 2 Wmk. 380 *Perf. 15*

No.	Type	Value	Description	Unused	Used
588	A87	70c	multi	.25	.25
589	A87	$1.15	multi	.35	.35
590	A87	$1.50	multi	.40	.40
591	A87	$2.30	multi	.70	.70
			Nos. 588-591 (4)	1.70	1.70

A set of 8 stamps for the 1986 World Cup was printed but not issued. Stamps became available with the liquidation of the printer.

Girl Guides, 50th Anniv. — A88

#592a, Lord Baden-Powell. #592b, Guide giving oath. #593a, Lady Baden-Powell.

#593b, Guide cutting hair. #594a, Lord and Lady Baden-Powell. #594b, Guides in public service. #595a, Troop inspection, 1936. #595b, Guides saluting.

1986, Apr. 11

592 A88 20c Pair, #a.-b. .25 .25
593 A88 75c Pair, #a.-b. .75 .75
594 A88 90c Pair, #a.-b. .85 .85
595 A88 $1.15 Pair, #a.-b. 1.10 1.10
Nos. 592-595 (4) 2.95 2.95

For overprints see Nos. 966-967.

Queen Elizabeth II, 60th Birthday — A89

Various portraits.

1986, Apr. 11 Unwmk. *Perf. 12½*

600 A89 10c multicolored .25 .25
601 A89 $1.50 multicolored .35 *.35*
602 A89 $3 multicolored .55 *.55*
603 A89 $6 multi, vert. .85 *.85*
Nos. 600-603 (4) 2.00 2.00

Souvenir Sheet

604 A89 $8 multicolored 5.00 5.00

Halley's Comet — A90

Designs: 35c, 40c (No. 613a,) Bayeux Tapestry (detail), 1066 sighting. 50c, $1.75 (No. 613b), Adoration of the Magi, by Giotto. 70c, $2 (No. 613c), Edmond Halley, trajectory diagram, 1531 sighting. $1, $3 (No. 613d), Sightings, 1066 and 1910. $1.15, 55c (No. 614a), Sighting, 1910. $1.50, 60c (No. 614b), Giotto space probe, comet, diagram. $2.30, 80c (No. 614c), U.S. Space Telescope, comet. $4, $5 (No. 614d), Computer picture of photograph, 1910.

1986 *Perf. 14*

605-612 A90 Set of 8 3.75 3.75

Souvenir Sheets

613 A90 Sheet of 4, #a.-d. 2.75 2.75
614 A90 Sheet of 4, #a.-d. 2.75 2.75

Issued: #613-614, 10/10; others, 5/9.
For overprints see Nos. 656-657.

A91

Wedding of Prince Andrew and Sarah Ferguson — A92

No. 615: a, Andrew, vert. b, Sarah, vert.
No. 616: a, Andrew wearing cowboy hat. b, Sarah wearing fur hat.

1986 Litho. *Perf. 12½x13, 13x12½*

615 A91 70c Pair, #a.-b. .70 .70
616 A91 $2 Pair, #a.-b 1.00 1.00
c. Souvenir booklet 5.00

Souvenir Sheet

617 A92 $10 multicolored 5.00 5.00

#616c contains 2 imperf panes. One pane contains 2 #615; the other 2 #616.
Issued: #617, 10/15; others, 7/23.
For overprints see Nos. 628-629.

Clipper Ships A93

90c, Antelope, 1793. $1.15, Montagu, 1840. $1.50, Little Catherine, 1813. $2.30, Hinchingbrook, 1813.

1986, Aug. 29 *Perf. 14*

618 A93 90c multi 1.90 1.25
619 A93 $1.15 multi 3.00 3.00
620 A93 $1.50 multi 3.25 3.25
621 A93 $2.30 multi 4.25 4.75
a. Souvenir sheet of 4, #618-621 12.50 12.50
Nos. 618-621 (4) 12.40 12.25

Communications — A94

Designs: 70c, Radio Montserrat, near Dagenham. $1.15, Radio Gem ZGM-FM 94, Plymouth. $1.50, Radio Antilles, O'Garro's, $2.30, Cable & Wireless telegraph office, Plymouth.

1986, Sept. 29 Wmk. 380 *Perf. 14*

622 A94 70c multicolored 1.10 .65
623 A94 $1.15 multicolored 1.60 1.25
624 A94 $1.50 multicolored 1.90 1.90
625 A94 $2.30 multicolored 2.40 *3.00*
Nos. 622-625 (4) 7.00 6.80

Nos. 615-616 Ovptd. in Silver "Congratulations to T.R.H. The Duke & Duchess of York"

Perf. 12½x13, 13x12½

1986, Nov. 14 Litho.

628 A91 70c Pair, #a.-b. 1.75 1.75
629 A91 $2 Pair, #a.-b. 4.00 4.00

Christmas — A95

70c, Christmas rose. $1.15, Candle flower. $1.50, Christmas tree kalanchoe. $2.30, Snow on the mountain.

1986, Dec. 12 Unwmk. *Perf. 14*

632 A95 70c multi .85 .85
633 A95 $1.15 multi 1.40 1.40
634 A95 $1.50 multi 2.00 2.00
635 A95 $2.30 multi 3.00 *3.50*
a. Souvenir sheet of 4, #632-635, perf. 12x12½ 11.00 11.00
Nos. 632-635 (4) 7.25 7.75

Souvenir Sheets

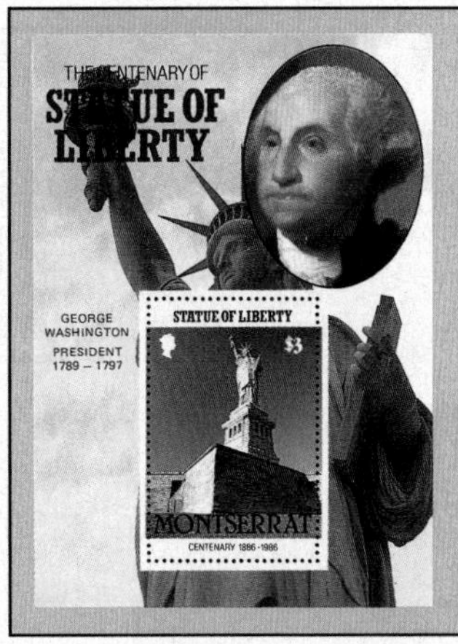

Statue of Liberty, Cent. — A96

1986, Nov. 18 Litho. *Perf. 14*

636 A96 $3 Statue, pedestal 1.75 1.75
637 A96 $4.50 Head 2.40 2.40
638 A96 $5 Statue, NYC 2.75 2.75
Nos. 636-638 (3) 6.90 6.90

Sailing A97

$1.15, Golf. $1.50, Plymouth Public Market. $2.30, Air Studios.

1986, Dec. 10 *Perf. 15*

639 A97 70c shown .55 *.60*
640 A97 $1.15 multi .80 *1.25*
641 A97 $1.50 multi .80 *1.50*
642 A97 $2.30 multi 1.60 *2.75*
Nos. 639-642 (4) 3.75 6.10

For surcharge see No. B3.

Sharks A98

1987, Feb. 2 Wmk. 380 *Perf. 14*

643 A98 40c Tiger 1.75 .50
644 A98 90c Lemon 3.00 1.25
645 A98 $1.15 White 3.50 2.00
646 A98 $3.50 Whale 7.00 *8.50*
a. Souvenir sheet of 4, #643-646, perf. 12½x12 16.00 16.00
Nos. 643-646 (4) 15.25 12.25

Butterflies A99

90c, Straight-line sulpher. $1.15, Red rim. $1.50, Hammock skipper. $2.50, Mimic.

1987, Aug. 10 Wmk. 380 *Perf. 14*

647 A99 90c multi 2.25 2.25
648 A99 $1.15 multi 3.00 3.00
649 A99 $1.50 multi 3.75 3.75
650 A99 $2.50 multi 6.00 6.00
Nos. 647-650 (4) 15.00 15.00

Nos. 531, 527, 525, 532 and 535 Surcharged

1987, Apr. 6

651 A79 5c on 70c multi .80 *1.10*
652 A79 $1 on 20c multi 2.60 1.10
653 A79 $1.15 on 10c multi 3.25 1.60
654 A79 $1.50 on 90c multi 3.75 2.25
655 A79 $2.30 on $3 multi 5.50 *6.50*
Nos. 651-655 (5) 15.90 12.55

Nos. 613-614 Ovptd. for CAPEX '87 in Red and Black

Souvenir Sheets of 4

1987, June 13 Unwmk.

656 A90 #a.-d. 3.50 3.50
657 A90 #a.-d. 3.50 3.50

Orchids — A100

90c, Oncidium variegatum, vert. $1.15, Vanilla planifolia. $1.50, Gongora quinquenervis, vert. $3.50, Brassavola nodosa. $5, Oncidium lanceanum.

1987, Nov. 13 Unwmk. *Perf. 14*

658 A100 90c multi 1.00 1.00
659 A100 $1.15 multi 1.25 1.25
660 A100 $1.50 multi 1.75 1.75
661 A100 $3.50 multi 4.25 4.25
Nos. 658-661 (4) 8.25 8.25

Souvenir Sheet

662 A100 $5 multi 17.00 17.00

Christmas.

Nos. 525, 528-529 and 532 Surcharged "40th Wedding Anniversary / HM Queen Elizabeth II / HRH Duke of Edinburgh / November 1987." and New Value

Wmk. 380

1987, Nov. 20 Litho. *Perf. 14*

663 A79 5c on 90c No. 532 .55 .55
664 A79 $1.15 on 10c No. 525 .70 .70
665 A79 $2.30 on 25c No. 528 1.60 1.60
666 A79 $5 on 40c No. 529 3.25 3.25
Nos. 663-666 (4) 6.10 6.10

Exists spelled "Edingburgh." Value, set $45.

Tropical Bats — A101

1988, Feb. 8 Wmk. 380 *Perf. 14*

667 A101 55c Free-tailed bat 1.00 1.00
668 A101 90c Fruit bat 1.75 1.75
669 A101 $1.15 Fisherman bat 2.25 2.25
670 A101 $2.30 Fruit bat, diff. 4.50 4.50
Nos. 667-670 (4) 9.50 9.50

Souvenir Sheet

671 A101 $2.50 Funnel-eared bat 10.50 10.50

Marine Birds — A102

90c, Magnificent frigatebird. $1.15, Caribbean elaenia. $1.50, Glossy ibis. $3.50, Purple-throated carib.
$5, Brown pelican.

1988, Apr. 2 **Unwmk.**

672 A102 90c multi 1.00 1.00
673 A102 $1.15 multi 1.25 1.25
674 A102 $1.50 multi 1.50 1.50
675 A102 $3.50 multi 3.25 3.25
Nos. 672-675 (4) 7.00 7.00

Souvenir Sheet

676 A102 $5 multi 5.50 5.50

Easter.

1988 Summer Olympics, Seoul — A103

Eastern architecture and events: 90c, Women's discus. $1.15, High jump. $3.50, Women's 200-meter and Seoul university building. $5, Single scull rowing, pagoda.

Unwmk.

1988, July 29 **Litho.** ***Perf. 14***

677 A103 90c multicolored .95 .95
678 A103 $1.15 multicolored 1.00 1.00
679 A103 $3.50 multicolored 3.25 3.25
Nos. 677-679 (3) 5.20 5.20

Souvenir Sheet

680 A103 $5 multicolored 5.25 5.25

Sea Shells A104

5c, Golden tulip. 10c, Little knobby scallop. 15c, Sozoni's cone. 20c, Globular coral shell. 25c, Sundial. 40c, King helmet. 55c, Channeled turban. 70c, True tulip shell. 90c, Music volute. $1, Flame auger. $1.15, Rooster-tail conch. $1.50, Queen conch. $3, Teramachi's slit shell. $5, Florida crown conch. $7.50, Beau's murex. $10, Triton's trumpet.

1988, Aug. 30

681 A104 5c multi .30 .25
682 A104 10c multi .30 .25
683 A104 15c multi .30 .25
684 A104 20c multi .30 .25
685 A104 25c multi .30 .25
686 A104 40c multi .45 .45
687 A104 55c multi .55 .60
688 A104 70c multi .70 .75
689 A104 90c multi .90 1.00
690 A104 $1 multi 1.00 1.10
691 A104 $1.15 multi 1.25 1.40
692 A104 $1.50 multi 1.50 1.75
693 A104 $3 multi 3.50 3.50
694 A104 $5 multi 5.00 5.50
695 A104 $7.50 multi 7.50 8.50
696 A104 $10 multi 10.50 11.50
Nos. 681-696 (16) 34.35 37.30

For surcharges see Nos. 698-701, 767-770.
For overprints see Nos. O79-O94.

University of the West Indies, 40th Anniv. — A105

1988, Oct. 4 **Litho.** ***Perf. 14***

697 A105 $5 multicolored 4.00 4.00

Nos. 687, 690, 693 and 694 Surcharged

Unwmk.

1988, Nov. 4 **Litho.** ***Perf. 14***

698 A104 40c on 55c No. 687 .50 .50
699 A104 90c on $1 No. 690 1.50 1.50
700 A104 $1.15 on $3 No. 693 1.75 1.75
701 A104 $1.50 on $5 No. 694 2.50 2.50
Nos. 698-701 (4) 6.25 6.25

Intl. Red Cross, 125th Anniv. A106

1988, Dec. 16

702 A106 $3.50 multicolored 2.10 2.10

Christmas — A107

Birds: 90c, Spotted sandpiper. $1.15, Ruddy turnstone. $3.50, Red-footed booby.
$5, Aububon's shearwater.

1988, Nov. 28 ***Perf. 14x13½***

703 A107 90c multi 1.00 1.00
704 A107 $1.15 multi 1.25 1.25
705 A107 $3.50 multi 3.75 3.75
Nos. 703-705 (3) 6.00 6.00

Souvenir Sheet

Perf. 13½x14

706 A107 $5 multi 6.00 6.00

Defense Force, 75th Anniv. — A108

Uniforms: 90c, Drum major. $1.15, Fatigue clothing. $1.50, Khaki uniform. $3.50, Dress uniform.
$5, Cadet (girl), woman.

1989, Feb. 24 **Litho.** ***Perf. 14***

707 A108 90c multi 1.10 1.10
708 A108 $1.15 multi 1.25 1.25
709 A108 $1.50 multi 1.60 1.60
710 A108 $3.50 multi 4.25 4.25
Nos. 707-710 (4) 8.20 8.20

Souvenir Sheet

711 A108 $5 multi 6.25 6.25

Easter Lilies A109

90c, Amazon. $1.15, Salmon blood, vert. $1.50, Amaryllis, vert. $3.50, Amaryllis, diff., vert.
$5, Resurrection, vert.

1989, Mar. 21 **Litho.** ***Perf. 14***

712 A109 90c multi .75 .75
713 A109 $1.15 multi .90 .90
714 A109 $1.50 multi 1.10 1.10
715 A109 $3.50 multi 3.00 3.00
Nos. 712-715 (4) 5.75 5.75

Souvenir Sheet

716 A109 $5 multi 7.25 7.25

Ships Built in Montserrat — A110

Designs: 90c, Schooner Morning Prince, 1942-1948. $1.15, Cargo boat Western Sun. $1.50, Cargo boat Kim G under construction. $3.50, Cargo and passenger boat MV Romaris.

1989, June 30 **Litho.** ***Perf. 13½x14***

717 A110 90c multicolored 1.50 1.50
718 A110 $1.15 multicolored 1.75 1.75
719 A110 $1.50 multicolored 2.25 2.25
720 A110 $3.50 multicolored 5.00 5.00
Nos. 717-720 (4) 10.50 10.50

For surcharges see Nos. B1-B2.

Making of the Film *The Wizard of Oz,* 50th Anniv. — A111

1989, Sept. 22 **Litho.** ***Perf. 14***

721 A111 90c Scarecrow .95 .95
722 A111 $1.15 Cowardly Lion 1.10 1.10
723 A111 $1.50 Tin Man 1.50 1.50
724 A111 $3.50 Dorothy 3.25 3.25
Nos. 721-724 (4) 6.80 6.80

Souvenir Sheet

725 A111 $5 shown 7.00 7.00

Nos. 721-724 vert.

1st Moon Landing, 20th Anniv. — A112

Designs: $1.15, Armstrong on ladder, descending from lunar module. $1.50, Eagle, astronaut on lunar surface. $3.50, Recovery of command module after splashdown. $5, Astronaut on the Moon, vert.

Perf. 13½x14, 14x13½

1989, Dec. 19 **Litho.**

726 A112 90c shown .70 .70
727 A112 $1.15 multicolored .90 .90
728 A112 $1.50 multicolored 1.20 1.20
729 A112 $3.50 multicolored 2.50 2.50
Nos. 726-729 (4) 5.30 5.30

Souvenir Sheet

730 A112 $5 multicolored 7.50 7.50

For overprints see Nos. 847-850.

World War II Battle Ships A113

70c, I.J.N. Yamato. $1.15, USS Arizona. $1.50, K.M. Bismarck on fire. $3.50, HMS Hood.
$5, K.M. Bismarck, map.

1990, Feb. 12 **Litho.** ***Perf. 14***

731 A113 70c multi 2.25 2.25
732 A113 $1.15 multi 4.25 4.25
733 A113 $1.50 multi 5.50 5.50
734 A113 $3.50 multi 12.50 12.50
Nos. 731-734 (4) 24.50 24.50

Souvenir Sheet

735 A113 $5 multi 20.00 20.00

Nos. 414-418 Surcharged in Bright Rose Lilac

1990, May 3 ***Perf. 14½***

736 A59 70c on 40c #414 1.10 1.10
737 A59 90c on 55c #415 1.40 1.40
738 A59 $1 on $1.20 #416 1.50 1.50
739 A59 $1.15 on $1.20 #417 1.75 1.75
740 A59 $1.50 on $1.20 #418 2.25 2.25
Nos. 736-740 (5) 8.00 8.00

Stamp World London '90.

Penny Black, 150th Anniv. A114

Designs: 90c, Montserrat #5, General P.O. $1.15, Montserrat #1, postal workers sorting mail, vert. $1.50, Great Britain #1, man and woman mailing letters, vert. $3.50, Great Britain #2, mailman delivering to residence. $5, Chateau Barrack cover of 1836, Great Britain #1, landscape.

1990, June 1 ***Perf. 13½x14, 14x13½***

741 A114 90c shown 1.25 1.25
742 A114 $1.15 multicolored 1.60 1.60
743 A114 $1.50 multicolored 1.90 1.90
744 A114 $3.50 multicolored 4.50 4.50
Nos. 741-744 (4) 9.25 9.25

Souvenir Sheet

745 A114 $5 multicolored 10.00 10.00

Stained-glass Windows — A115

1990, Apr. 12 **Litho.** ***Perf. 14x15***

746 A115 Strip of 3 7.00 7.00
a. $1.15 The Empty Tomb 1.25 1.25
b. $1.50 The Ascension 1.75 1.75
c. $3.50 Risen Christ with Disciples 3.75 3.75

Souvenir Sheet

747 A115 $5 The Crucifixion 7.50 7.50

World Cup Soccer Championships, Italy — A116

Designs: 90c, Montserrat vs. Antigua. $1.15, U.S. vs. Trinidad. $1.50, Montserrat team. $3.50, West Germany vs. Wales. $5, World Cup trophy.

1990, July 8 **Litho.** *Perf. 14*
748 A116 90c multicolored .90 .90
749 A116 $1.15 multicolored 1.25 1.25
750 A116 $1.50 multicolored 1.60 1.60
751 A116 $3.50 multicolored 3.75 3.75
Nos. 748-751 (4) 7.50 7.50

Souvenir Sheet

752 A116 $5 multicolored 8.75 8.75

Spinner Dolphin A117

$1.15, Common dolphin. $1.50, Striped dolphin. $3.50, Atlantic spotted dolphin. $5, Atlantic white-sided dolphin.

1990, Sept. 25 **Litho.** *Perf. 14*
753 A117 90c shown 2.10 1.10
754 A117 $1.15 multi 2.50 1.60
755 A117 $1.50 multi 3.50 3.25
756 A117 $3.50 multi 5.75 6.25
Nos. 753-756 (4) 13.85 12.20

Souvenir Sheet

757 A117 $5 multi 15.00 15.00

Fish A118

90c, Spotted goatfish. $1.15, Cushion starfish. $1.50, Rock beuaty. $3.50, French grunt. $5, Trunkfish.

1991, Feb. 7 **Litho.** *Perf. 14*
758 A118 90c multi 1.75 1.75
759 A118 $1.15 multi 2.25 2.25
760 A118 $1.50 multi 3.00 3.00
761 A118 $3.50 multi 6.50 6.50
Nos. 758-761 (4) 13.50 13.50

Souvenir Sheet

762 A118 $5 multi 14.00 14.00

For surcharges and overprints see Nos. O98-O99, O104, O107.

Birds A119

90c, Duck. $1.15, Hen, chicks. $1.50, Rooster. $3.50, Helmeted guinea fowl.

1991, Apr. 17 **Litho.** *Perf. 14*
763 A119 90c multi 1.00 1.00
764 A119 $1.15 multi 1.40 1.40
765 A119 $1.50 multi 1.60 1.60
766 A119 $3.50 multi 4.00 4.00
Nos. 763-766 (4) 8.00 8.00

For surcharges and overprints see Nos. O100, O102, O105, O108.

Nos. 684-685, 692, 695 Surcharged

1991 **Litho.** *Perf. 14*
767 A104 5c on 20c #684 .40 .40
768 A104 5c on 25c #685 .40 .40
769 A104 $1.15 on $1.50 #692 4.75 4.75
770 A104 $1.15 on $7.50 #695 4.75 4.75
Nos. 767-770 (4) 10.30 10.30

Mushrooms A120

90c, Panaeolus antillarum. $1.15, Cantharellus cinnabarinus. $1.50, Gymnopilus chrysopellus. $2, Psilocybe cubensis. $3.50, Leptonia caeruleocapitata.

1991, June 13 **Litho.** *Perf. 14*
771 A120 90c multi 1.50 1.50
772 A120 $1.15 multi 1.90 1.90
773 A120 $1.50 multi 2.50 2.50
774 A120 $2 multi 3.50 3.50
775 A120 $3.50 multi 5.75 5.75
Nos. 771-775 (5) 15.15 15.15

Lilies — A121

1991, Aug. 8
776 A121 90c Red water lily .95 .95
777 A121 $1.15 Shell ginger 1.25 1.25
778 A121 $1.50 Early day lily 1.50 1.50
779 A121 $3.50 Anthurium 3.50 3.50
Nos. 776-779 (4) 7.20 7.20

For surcharges and overprints see Nos. O101, O103, O106, O109.

Frogs and Toads — A122

$1.15, Tree frog. $2, Crapaud toad. $3.50, Mountain chicken.

1991, Oct. 9 **Litho.** *Perf. 14*
780 A122 $1.15 multi 2.75 2.75
781 A122 $2 multi 5.00 5.00
782 A122 $3.50 multi 8.00 8.00
Nos. 780-782 (3) 15.75 15.75

Souvenir Sheet

Perf. 14½x14

783 A122 $5 Sheet of 1 14.50 14.50

No. 783 contains one 81x48mm stamp that incorporates designs of Nos. 780-782.

Cats A123

90c, Black British shorthair. $1.15, Seal point siamese. $1.50, Silver tabby persian. $2.50, Birman temple cat. $3.50, Egyptian mau.

1991, Dec. 5
784 A123 90c multi 1.90 1.90
785 A123 $1.15 multi 2.50 2.50
786 A123 $1.50 multi 3.25 3.25
787 A123 $2.50 multi 5.25 5.25
788 A123 $3.50 multi 7.00 7.00
Nos. 784-788 (5) 19.90 19.90

Discovery of America, 500th Anniv. — A124

No. 789: a, $1.50, Navigating instruments. b, $1.50, Coat of arms, Columbus. c, $1.50, Columbus, Bahamian natives. d, $1.50, Queen Isabella, Columbus with petition. e, $1.50, Exotic birds. f, $1.50, Exotic plants. g, $3.00, Santa Maria, Nina & Pinta.

1992, Jan. 16 **Litho.** *Perf. 14*
789 A124 Sheet of 7, #a.-g. 17.50 17.50

No. 789g is 85x28mm. See No. 829.

Dinosaurs A125

$1, Tyrannosaurus. $1.15, Diplodocus. $1.50, Apatosaurus. $3.45, Dimetrodon. $4.60, Owen with bone, vert.

1992, Aug. 1 **Litho.** *Perf. 14*
790 A125 $1 multi 2.10 2.10
791 A125 $1.15 multi 2.40 2.40
792 A125 $1.50 multi 3.00 3.00
793 A125 $3.45 multi 7.00 7.00
Nos. 790-793 (4) 14.50 14.50

Souvenir Sheet

794 A125 $4.60 multi 12.50 12.50

Sir Richard Owen, cent. of death.

1992 Summer Olympics, Barcelona A126

$1, Torch bearer. $1.15, Flags. $2.30, Olympic flame, map. $3.60, Various events.

1992, Apr. 10
795 A126 $1 multi 1.25 1.25
796 A126 $1.15 multi 1.50 1.50
797 A126 $2.30 multi 2.75 2.75
798 A126 $3.60 multi 4.50 4.50
Nos. 795-798 (4) 10.00 10.00

Montserrat Oriole — A127

$1, Male. $1.15, Male, female. $1.50, Female feeding chicks. $3.60, Map, male.

1992, June 30 **Litho.** *Perf. 13½x14*
799 A127 $1 multi 1.50 1.50
800 A127 $1.15 multi 1.75 1.75
801 A127 $1.50 multi 2.25 2.25
802 A127 $3.60 multi 5.50 5.50
Nos. 799-802 (4) 11.00 11.00

Insects A128

5c, Grasshopper. 10c, Field cricket. 15c, Dragonfly. 20c, Red skimmer. 25c, Pond skater. 40c, Leaf weevil. 55c, Leaf cutter ants. 70c, Paper wasp. 90c, Bee fly. $1, Lacewing. $1.15, Orange-barred sulphur. $1.50, Painted lady. $3, Bella moth. $5, Plume moth. $7.50, White peacock. $10, Postman.

1992, Aug. 20 **Litho.** *Perf. 15x14*
803 A128 5c multi .30 .30
804 A128 10c multi .30 .30
805 A128 15c multi .30 .30
806 A128 20c multi .30 .30
807 A128 25c multi .30 .30
808 A128 40c multi .40 .45
809 A128 55c multi .55 .60
810 A128 70c multi .70 .75
811 A128 90c multi .95 1.10
812 A128 $1 multi 1.10 1.20
813 A128 $1.15 multi 1.20 1.30
814 A128 $1.50 multi 1.50 1.75
815 A128 $3 multi 3.00 3.50
816 A128 $5 multi 5.00 5.75
817 A128 $7.50 multi 8.00 8.75
818 A128 $10 multi 10.50 12.00
Nos. 803-818 (16) 34.40 38.65

For overprints and surcharges see Nos. 871-872, 881A, 881C, O110-O125.

Christmas — A129

Designs: $1.15, Adoration of the Magi. $4.60, Angel appearing before shepherds.

1992, Nov. 26 **Litho.** *Perf. 13½x14*
819 A129 $1.15 multicolored 1.75 1.75
820 A129 $4.60 multicolored 7.25 7.25

Coins and Bank Notes — A130

Designs: $1, One-dollar coin, twenty-dollar notes. $1.15, Ten-cent, twenty-five cent coins, ten-dollar notes. $1.50, Five-cent coin, five-dollar notes. $3.60, One-cent, two-cent coins, one-dollar notes.

1993, Feb. 10 *Perf. 14x13½*
821 A130 $1 multicolored 1.60 1.60
822 A130 $1.15 multicolored 1.75 1.75
823 A130 $1.50 multicolored 2.25 2.25
824 A130 $3.60 multicolored 5.50 5.50
Nos. 821-824 (4) 11.10 11.10

Discovery of America, 500th Anniv. (in 1992) — A131

1993, Mar. 10 **Litho.** *Perf. 14*
825 A131 $1 Coming ashore 2.25 2.25
826 A131 $2 Natives, ships 4.25 4.25

Organization of East Caribbean States.

Coronation of Queen Elizabeth II, 40th Anniv. — A132

Designs: $1.15, Queen, M.H. Bramble. $4.60, Queen riding in Gold State Coach.

1993, June 2 *Perf. 13½x14*
827 A132 $1.15 multicolored 1.50 1.50
828 A132 $4.60 multicolored 5.50 5.50

Columbus Type of 1992 with Added Text

No. 829: a, $1.15, like #789a. b, $1.15, like #789b. c, $1.15, like #789c. d, $1.50, like #789d. e, $1.50, like #789e. f, $1.50, like #789f. g, $3.45, like #789g.

1993, Sept. 7 Litho. *Perf. 14*

829 A124 Sheet of 7, #a.-g. 27.50 27.50

Nos. 829a-829g each have different added text.

Royal Air Force, 75th Anniv.

Common Design Type

Designs: 15c, Boeing Sentry, 1993. 55c, Vickers Valiant, 1962. $1.15, Handley Page Hastings, 1958. $3, 1943 Lockheed Ventura, 1943.

No. 834: a, Felixstowe F5, 1921. b, Armstrong Whitworth Atlas, 1934. c, Fairey Gordon, 1935. d, Boulton Paul Overstrand, 1936.

Wmk. 373

1993, Nov. 17 Litho. *Perf. 14*

830 CD350 15c multicolored .30 .30
831 CD350 55c multicolored .80 .80
832 CD350 $1.15 multicolored 1.75 1.75
833 CD350 $3 multicolored 4.25 4.25
Nos. 830-833 (4) 7.10 7.10

Souvenir Sheet

834 CD350 $1.50 Sheet of 4, #a.-d. 7.25 7.25

Beetles A133

Perf. 15x14

1994, Jan. 21 Litho. Unwmk.

835 A133 $1 Ground beetle 1.25 1.25
836 A133 $1.15 Click beetle 1.60 1.60
837 A133 $1.50 Harlequin beetle 1.90 1.90
838 A133 $3.45 Leaf beetle 4.50 4.50
Nos. 835-838 (4) 9.25 9.25

Souvenir Sheet

839 A133 $4.50 Scarab beetle 6.00 6.00

Hibiscus Flowers and Fruits — A134

Designs: 90c, Cotton. $1.15, Sorrel. $1.50, Okra. $3.50, Hibiscus rosa sinensis.

1994, Mar. 22 Litho. *Perf. 14x13½*

840 A134 90c multicolored 1.25 1.25
841 A134 $1.15 multicolored 1.60 1.60
842 A134 $1.50 multicolored 2.00 2.00
843 A134 $3.50 multicolored 5.00 5.00
Nos. 840-843 (4) 9.85 9.85

Aquatic Dinosaurs A135

No. 844: a, $1, Elasmosaurus. b, $1.15, Plesiosaurus. c, $1.50, Nothosaurus. d, $3.45, Mosasaurus.

1994, May 6 Litho. *Perf. 15x14*

844 A135 Strip of 4, #a.-d. 12.50 12.50

1994 World Cup Soccer Championships, U.S. — A136

No. 845: a, 90c, Montserrat youth soccer. b, $1, 1990 World Cup, US vs. England. c, $1.15, Rose Bowl Stadium, Pasadena, Calif., US. d, $3.45, German team, 1990 World Cup Winners.

No. 846: a, Jules Rimet. b, Bobby Moore, England Team Captain, 1966. c, Lew Jaschin. d, Sepp Herberger, German trainer.

1994, May 20 *Perf. 14*

845 A136 Vert. strip of 4, #a.-d. 10.00 10.00

Souvenir Sheet

Perf. 14x14½

846 A136 $2 Sheet of 4, #a.-d. 11.00 11.00

No. 845 printed in sheets of 2 strips + 4 labels.

Nos. 726-729 Ovptd. in Red or Srchd. in Red and Black

Inscribed "Space Anniversaries" and: 40c, "Yuri Gagarin / First man in space / April 12, 1961." $1.15, "First Joint US / Soviet Mission / July 15, 1975." $1.50, "25th Anniversary / First Moon Landing / Apollo XI-July 20, 1994." $2.30, "Columbia / First Space Shuttle / April 12, 1981."

1994, July 20 *Perf. 13½x14*

847 A112 40c on 90c multi .75 .75
848 A112 $1.15 multi 3.00 3.00
849 A112 $1.50 multi 3.50 3.50
850 A112 $2.30 on $3.50 multi 5.75 5.75
Nos. 847-850 (4) 13.00 13.00

Obliterator on Nos. 847, 850 is black.

Woodstock Festival, 25th Anniv. A137

1994, Oct. 20 *Perf. 12½*

851 A137 $1.15 1969 Poster 1.90 1.90
852 A137 $1.50 1994 Poster 2.10 2.10

Souvenir Sheets

853 A137 $4.50 like #851 6.00 6.00
854 A137 $4.50 like #852 6.00 6.00

Sea Vegetation A138

1995, Feb. 14 *Perf. 14x15*

855 A138 $1 Sea fan .85 .85
856 A138 $1.15 Sea lily 1.00 1.00
857 A138 $1.50 Sea pen 1.40 1.40
858 A138 $3.45 Sea fern 3.25 3.25
Nos. 855-858 (4) 6.50 6.50

Souvenir Sheet

859 A138 $4.50 Sea rose 4.50 4.50

Motion Pictures, Cent. A139

No. 860: a.-i., Various portraits of Marilyn Monroe.

$6, Marilyn Monroe & Elvis Presley.

1995, June 13 Litho. *Perf. 12½*

860 A139 $1.15 Sheet of 9, #a-i 11.50 11.50

Souvenir Sheet

861 A139 $6 multicolored 7.50 7.50

No. 861 contains one 51x57mm stamp.

1995 IAAF World Track & Field Championships, Gothenburg, Sweden — A140

No. 862: a, Jesse Owens, U.S. b, Eric Lemming, Sweden. c, Rudolf Harbig, Germany. d, Montserrat youth.

1995, Aug. 3 *Perf. 14*

862 A140 $1.50 Sheet of 4, #a-d 7.50 7.50

End of World War II, 50th Anniv. — A141

No. 863: a, Atmospheric sounding experiments using V-2 rockets. b, Space Shuttle Challenger.

No. 864: a, 1st successful nuclear reactor. b, Calder Hall Atomic Power Station, England.

No. 865: a, Ju88G-7a nightfighter equipped with SN2 radar. b, NATO Boeing E6 AWACS.

No. 866: a, Gloster Meteor III jet aircraft. b, British Airways Concorde.

1995, Aug. 15

863 A141 $1.15 Pair, #a.-b. 3.50 3.50
864 A141 $1.15 Pair, #a.-b. 3.50 3.50
865 A141 $1.50 Pair, #a.-b. 4.75 4.75
866 A141 $1.50 Pair, #a.-b. 4.75 4.75
Nos. 863-866 (4) 16.50 16.50

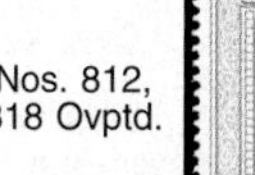

Nos. 812, 818 Ovptd.

1995 Litho. *Perf. 15x14*

871 A128 $1 multicolored 1.25 1.25
872 A128 $10 multicolored 11.00 11.00

UN, 50th Anniv. — A142

1995, Sept. 4 Litho. *Perf. 14*

873 A142 $1.15 Food 1.25 1.25
874 A142 $1.50 Education 1.50 1.50
875 A142 $2.30 Health 2.50 2.50
876 A142 $3 Peace 3.25 3.25
Nos. 873-876 (4) 8.50 8.50

Souvenir Sheet

877 A142 $6 Justice 7.00 7.00

Natl. Trust, 25th Anniv. A143

Designs: $1.15, Headquarters building. $1.50, 17th cent. cannon, Bransby Point. $2.30, Painting of original Galways sugar mill, vert. $3, Great Alps Falls, vert.

1995, Nov. 15 Litho. *Perf. 14*

878-881 A143 Set of 4 12.50 12.50

Nos. 806 and 809 Surcharged

Methods and Perfs As Before

1995

881A A128 5c on 55c #809 — —
881C A128 10c on 20c #806 — —

An additional stamp was issued in this set. The editors would like to examine any example of it.

Scavengers of the Sea — A144

1996, Feb. 14 Litho. *Perf. 15x14*

882 A144 $1 Bull shark 1.20 1.20
883 A144 $1.15 Sea mouse 1.40 1.40
884 A144 $1.50 Bristleworm 1.75 1.75
885 A144 $3.45 Prawn xiphocaris 3.75 3.75
Nos. 882-885 (4) 8.10 8.10

Souvenir Sheet

886 A144 $4.50 Man o'war 6.25 6.25

Radio, Cent. (in 1995) A145

Designs: $1.15, Guglielmo Marconi, transmitting equipment, 1901. $1.50, Wireless laboratory, Marconi's yacht, Elettra. $2.30, First transatlantic radio message, Newfoundland, 1901. $3, First air/ground radio station, Croydon, 1920.

$4.50, First radio telescope, Jodrell Bank, Cheshire, England.

1996, Mar. 19 Litho. *Perf. 14*

887-890 A145 Set of 4 8.75 8.75

Souvenir Sheet

891 A145 $4.50 multi 5.25 5.25

1996 Summer Olympic Games, Atlanta A146

1896 Medalists: $1.15, Paul Masson, cycling. $1.50, Robert Garrett, discus. $2.30, Spiridon Louis, marathon. $3, John Boland, tennis.

1996, June 24 Litho. *Perf. 14*

892-895 A146 Set of 4 7.50 7.50

Mythical Creatures — A147

1996, Aug. 15 Litho. *Perf. 14*

No.	Type	Value	Description	Unused	Used
896	A147	5c	Leprechaun	.25	.25
897	A147	10c	Pegasus	.25	.25
898	A147	15c	Griffin	.25	.25
899	A147	20c	Unicorn	.25	.25
900	A147	25c	Gnome	.25	.25
901	A147	40c	Mermaid	.40	.40
902	A147	55c	Cockatrice	.50	.50
903	A147	70c	Fairy	.65	.65
904	A147	90c	Goblin	.80	.80
905	A147	$1	Faun	.90	.90
906	A147	$1.15	Dragon	1.00	1.00
907	A147	$1.50	Giant	1.25	1.25
908	A147	$3	Elf	2.40	2.40
909	A147	$5	Centaur	4.00	4.00
910	A147	$7.50	Phoenix	6.00	6.00
911	A147	$10	Erin	7.50	7.50
			Nos. 896-911 (16)	26.65	26.65

For overprints see Nos. O126-O140.

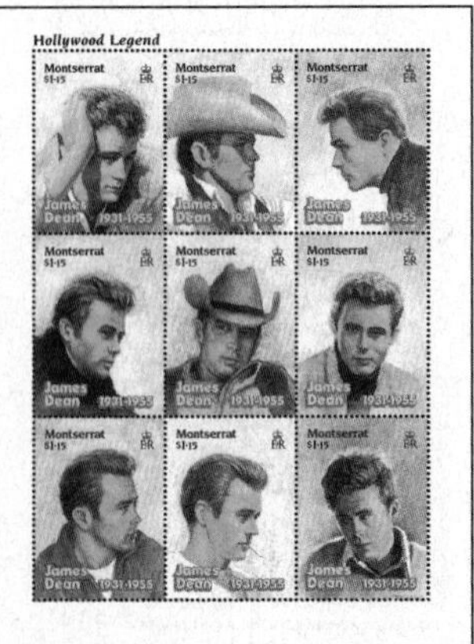

James Dean (1931-55), Actor — A148

Various portraits.

1996, June 28 Litho. *Perf. 12½*

912 A148 $1.15 Sheet of 9, #a.-i. 11.50 11.50

Souvenir Sheet

913 A148 $6 multicolored 7.50 7.50

No. 913 contains one 51x57mm stamp. For overprint see No. 921.

Dancing Bears, Emblem of "The Grateful Dead" — A149

Jerry Garcia A150

No. 914 — Color of bears: a, blue violet, green. b, yellow. c, orange, pink.

1996, Oct. 21 Litho. *Perf. 12½*

914 A149 $1.15 Strip of 3, #a.-c. 3.75 3.75
915 A150 $6 multicolored 6.75 6.75

For overprint and surcharge see #920A, 928. Compare with #955-956 and #970-83.

Scavenger Birds A151

1997, Jan. 28 Litho. *Perf. 14½x14*

No.	Type	Value	Description	Unused	Used
916	A151	$1	Turkey vulture	1.00	1.00
917	A151	$1.15	American crow	1.25	1.25
918	A151	$1.50	Great skua	1.50	1.50
919	A151	$3.45	Kittiwake	3.50	3.50
			Nos. 916-919 (4)	7.25	7.25

Souvenir Sheet

920 A151 $4.50 King vulture 5.25 5.25

No. 914 Overprinted "Hong Kong '97" Across Strip in Dark Blue

Methods and Perfs as before

1997, Mar. 26

920A A149 $1.15 Strip of 3, #b-d 4.00 4.00

No. 912 Overprinted

1997, June 2 Litho. *Perf. 12½*

921 A148 $1.15 Sheet of 9, #a.-i. 12.50 12.50

Overprints are placed over vertical perfs separating each column of stamps. Each stamp in the left and right columns has only half the overprint. The stamps in the center column contains two incomplete halves of the overprint. The overprints also appear twice in sheet margin.

Eruption of Mt. Soufriere, Endangered Species — A152

No. 922: a, Heavy ash eruption, Plymouth, 1995. b, First pyroclastic flow entering sea. c, Double venting at Castle Peak. d, Mangrove cuckoo. e, Nocturnal lava flow, Soufriere Hills, 1996. f, Antillean crested hummingbird. g, Ash cloud engulfing Plymouth. h, Lava spine extruded, Soufriere Hills, 1996. i, New land created from pyroclastic flows.

1997, June 23 *Perf. 14*

922 A152 $1.50 Sheet of 9, #a.-i. 12.50 12.50
j. Additional inscription in sheet margin 12.50 12.50

No. 922j is inscribed in sheet margin: "MUSIC FOR" and "IN AID OF THE VICTIMS OF SOUFRIERE HILLS VOLCANO," "ROYAL ALBERT HALL LONDON" and "15th SEPTEMBER 1997."

Elvis Presley (1935-77) A153

American rock stars: No. 924, Jimi Hendrix (1942-70). No. 925, Jerry Garcia (1942-95). No. 926, Janis Joplin (1943-70).

1997, Aug. 29 Litho. *Perf. 12½*

No.	Type	Value	Description	Unused	Used
923	A153	$1.15	multicolored	2.50	2.50
924	A153	$1.15	multicolored	2.50	2.50
925	A153	$1.15	multicolored	2.50	2.50
926	A153	$1.15	multicolored	2.50	2.50
			Nos. 923-926 (4)	10.00	10.00

Abstract Art — A154

1997, Aug. 29 Litho. *Perf. 12½*

927 A154 $1.50 multicolored 2.50 2.50

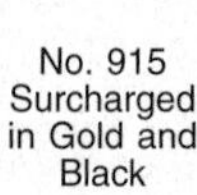

No. 915 Surcharged in Gold and Black

1997 Litho. *Perf. 12½*

928 A150 $1.50 on $6 multi 3.00 3.00

Medicinal Plants — A155

1998, Mar. 30 Litho. *Perf. 15*

No.	Type	Value	Description	Unused	Used
929	A155	$1	Prickly pear	.75	.75
930	A155	$1.15	Pomme coolie	.85	.85
931	A155	$1.50	Aloe	1.10	1.10
932	A155	$3.45	Bird pepper	2.75	2.75
			Nos. 929-932 (4)	5.45	5.45

A156

Famous People of the 20th Cent.: No. 933, Jean-Henri Dunant. No. 934, Mohandas Gandhi. No. 935, Pablo Picasso. No. 936, David Ben-Gurion. No. 937, Dwidght D. Eisenhower. No. 938, Wernher von Braun. No. 939, Eva & Juan Perón. No. 940, Konrad Adenauer. No. 941, Mao Tse-tung. No. 942, Lord Mountbatten. No. 943, Charles Lindbergh. No. 944, Anne Frank. $3, John F. Kennedy.

1998, May 18 Litho. *Perf. 12½*

No.	Type	Value	Description	Unused	Used
933	A156	$1.15	multicolored	2.00	2.00
934	A156	$1.15	multicolored	2.00	2.00
935	A156	$1.15	multicolored	2.00	2.00
936	A156	$1.15	multicolored	2.00	2.00
937	A156	$1.15	multicolored	2.00	2.00
938	A156	$1.15	multicolored	2.00	2.00
939	A156	$1.15	multicolored	2.00	2.00
940	A156	$1.50	multicolored	2.75	2.75
941	A156	$1.50	multicolored	2.75	2.75
942	A156	$1.50	multicolored	2.75	2.75
943	A156	$1.50	multicolored	2.75	2.75
944	A156	$1.50	multicolored	2.75	2.75
			Nos. 933-944 (12)	27.75	27.75

Souvenir Sheet

945 A156 $3 multicolored 5.00 5.00

No. 945 contains one 51x38mm stamp.
Issued in sheets of 4 with illustrated right margin.

1998, May 18 Litho. *Perf. 12½*

Royalty of the 20th cent.: No. 946, Grand Duchess Charlotte (1896-1985) & Felix, Luxembourg. No. 947, Leopold III (1901-83) & Astrid, Belgium. No. 948, Wilhelmina (1880-1962), Netherlands. No. 949, Gustav V (1858-1950), Sweden. No. 950, Alfonso XIII (1886-1931), Spain. No. 951, Christian X (1870-1947), Denmark. No. 952, Haakon VII (1872-1957) & Olav, Denmark. No. 953, George VI (1895-1952), Great Britain.

No.	Type	Value	Description	Unused	Used
946	A156	$1.15	multicolored	1.40	1.40
947	A156	$1.15	multicolored	1.40	1.40
948	A156	$1.50	multicolored	1.60	1.60
949	A156	$1.50	multicolored	1.60	1.60
950	A156	$1.50	multicolored	1.60	1.60
951	A156	$1.50	multicolored	1.60	1.60
952	A156	$1.50	multicolored	1.60	1.60
953	A156	$1.50	multicolored	1.60	1.60
			Nos. 946-953 (8)	12.40	12.40

Issued in sheets of 4 with illustrated right margin.

Bob Marley (1947-81) — A157

Various portraits.

1998, Aug. 6

954 A157 $1.15 Sheet of 8, #a.-h. + label 14.00 14.00

Jerry Garcia (1947-95) — A158

Various portraits.

1998, Aug. 6

955 A158 $1.15 Sheet of 9, #a.-i. 14.00 14.00

Souvenir Sheet

956 A158 $5 multicolored 8.00 8.00

No. 956 contains one 51x76mm stamp. Compare with #914-915 and #970-983.

Eclipse of the Sun, Feb. 26, 1998 — A159

Views of Mt. Soufriere volcano: No. 957, Homes near water. No. 958, Looking across mountain tops. No. 959, Ash on mountainside, home. No. 960, Ash, steam rising in air.
$6, View of eclipse, vert.

1998 Litho. *Perf. 12½*

957	A159 $1.15 multicolored	2.00	2.00
958	A159 $1.15 multicolored	2.00	2.00
959	A159 $1.15 multicolored	2.00	2.00
960	A159 $1.15 multicolored	2.00	2.00
	Nos. 957-960 (4)	8.00	8.00

Souvenir Sheet

961 A159 $6 multicolored 7.75 7.75

Diana, Princess of Wales (1961-97) A160

$1.15, As bride. $1.50, Princess of charities. $3, At Royal Ascot.
$6, Rose, Diana.

1998 Litho. *Perf. 12½*

962	A160 $1.15 multi	1.90	1.90
963	A160 $1.50 multi	2.25	2.25
964	A160 $3 multi	4.25	4.25
	Nos. 962-964 (3)	8.40	8.40

Souvenir Sheet

965 A160 $6 multi 8.00 8.00

No. 965 contains one 51x38mm stamp.

Nos. 592-593 Ovptd. in Red with emblem and "13th WORLD JAMBOREE MONDIALE CHILE 1999"

Wmk. 380

1998, Dec. 29 Litho. *Perf. 15*

966	20c Pair, #a.-b.	.75	.75
967	75c Pair, #a.-b.	2.75	2.75

Nos. 873-874 Overprinted

Unwmk.

1999, Apr. 27 Litho. *Perf. 14*

968	A142 $1.15 on #873	2.75	2.75
969	A142 $1.50 on #874	3.25	3.25

Jerry Garcia (1947-95) — A161

Garcia: No. 970, $1.15, Wearing purple shirt, microphone at right, light blue background. No. 971, $1.15, In red light, dark blue background. No. 972, $1.15, Wearing purple shirt, microphone at left. No. 973, $1.15, Like #971, blue green background. No. 974, $1.15, Wearing black shirt, playing guitar. No. 975, $1.15, Wearing red shirt. No. 976, $1.15, Wearing blue shirt, microphone at right, vert. No. 977, $1.15, Wearing blue shirt, microphone to left of face, vert. No. 978, $1.15, Wearing blue shirt, microphone partially covering face, vert. No. 979, $1.15, Wearing black shirt, orange rectangular frame, vert. No. 980, $1.15, Wearing blue shirt, orange and blue frame, vert. No. 981, $1.15, Wearing black shirt, orange and blue frame, vert.
No. 982, $6, Vignette of #980. No. 983, $6, Wearing black shirt, vert.

1999 Litho. Unwmk. *Perf. 12½*

970-981 A161 Set of 12 20.00 20.00

Souvenir Sheets

982-983 A161 Set of 2 20.00 20.00

Issued in sheets of 9 containing 3 each of Nos. 970-972, 973-975, 976-978, 979-981 respectively. Nos. 982-983 contain one 76x51mm or 51x76mm stamp, respectively. Compare with #914-915 and #955-956.

Fruit A162

1999 Litho. Wmk. 380 *Perf. 12½*

984	A162 $1.15 Mango	1.10	1.10
985	A162 $1.50 Breadfruit	1.50	1.50
986	A162 $2.30 Papaya	2.40	2.40
987	A162 $3 Lime	3.00	3.00
988	A162 $6 Akee	6.25	6.25
a.	Sheet of 5, #984-988 +label	15.00	15.00
	Nos. 984-988 (5)	14.25	14.25

Dogs A163

70c, Yorkshire terrier. $1, Welsh corgi. $1.15, King Charles spaniel. $1.50, Poodle. $3, Beagle.

1999

989	A163 70c black	1.30	1.30
990	A163 $1 black	2.25	2.25
991	A163 $1.15 black	2.25	2.25
992	A163 $1.50 black	3.25	3.25
993	A163 $3 black	6.25	6.25
a.	Sheet of 5, #989-993 + label	15.00	15.00
	Nos. 989-993 (5)	15.30	15.30

World Teachers' Day — A164

World map and: $1, Ruler, scissors, compass, pencil, paint brush. $1.15, Teacher lecturing, $1.50, Compass, flag, camera, globe, plumb bob, theodolite. $5, Pen, flask, funnel, thermometer, calipers, microscope.

1999 Litho. *Perf. 12½*

994-997 A164 Set of 4 14.00 14.00

Worldwide Fund for Nature A165

No. 998 — Great hammerhead shark: a, Pair swimming. b, Pair near ocean floor. c, Trio swimming. d, One swimming.

Perf. 13¼

1999, Nov. 29 Litho. Unwmk.

998	Horiz. strip of 4	4.00	4.00
a.-d.	A165 50c Any single	.80	.80

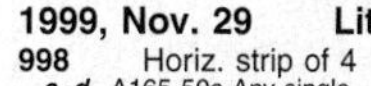

Millennium — A166

2000, Jan. 1 Unwmk.

999 A166 $1.50 multi 3.50 3.50

100th Test Cricket Match at Lord's Ground — A167

Designs: $1, Alfred Valentine. $5, George Headley.
$6, Lord's Ground, horiz.

2000, May 5 Litho. *Perf. 13½x13¼*

1000-1001 A167 Set of 2 7.50 7.50

Souvenir Sheet

Perf. 13¼x13½

1002 A167 $6 multi 10.00 10.00

The Stamp Show 2000, London A168

Battle of Britain, 60th anniv.: 70c, Scramble. $1.15, Hurricane Mk.1 overhaul. $1.50, Hurricane Mk. 1 and enemy plane. $5, Spitfire Mk. 1a of Flight Lt. Frank Howell.
$6, Plane in air.

Wmk. 373

2000, May 22 Litho. *Perf. 14*

1003	A168 70c multi	.70	.70
1004	A168 $1.15 multi	1.10	1.10
1005	A168 $1.50 multi	1.50	1.50
1006	A168 $5 multi	5.00	5.00
	Nos. 1003-1006 (4)	8.30	8.30

Souvenir Sheet

1007 A168 $6 multi 7.00 7.00

Millennium — A169

People of Montserrat and: 90c, Statue of Liberty. $1.15, Great Wall of China. $1.50, Eiffel Tower. $3.50, Millennium Dome, Great Britain.

Perf. 13½

2000, July 3 Litho. Unwmk.

1008-1011 A169 Set of 4 7.25 7.25

Queen Mother, 100th Birthday A170

Queen Mother and various buildings. Panel color under country name in: 70c, Yellow. $1.15, Purple. $3, Green. $6, Orange.

2000, Aug. 4 *Perf. 13½x13*

1012-1015	A170 Set of 4	11.50	11.50
1015a	Souvenir sheet, #1012-1015	13.50	13.50

Christmas A171

Designs: $1, The three Magi. $1.15, Cavalla Hill Methodist Church. $1.50, Shepherds. $3, $6, Mary and Joseph arriving in Bethlehem.

Perf. 14x14¾

2000, Nov. 29 **Wmk. 373**

1016-1019 A171 Set of 4 7.25 7.25

Souvenir Sheet

1020 A171 $6 multi 8.00 8.00

Birds A172

Designs: $1, Golden swallow, vert. $1.15, Crested quail dove. $1.50, Red-legged thrush. $5, Fernandina's flicker, vert.
$8, St. Vincent parrot.

2001, Mar. 26 **Litho.** *Perf. 13¼*

1021-1024 A172 Set of 4 12.00 12.00

Souvenir Sheet

1025 A172 $8 multi 10.00 10.00

Philatelic Personalities — A173

Designs: $1, Edward Stanley Gibbons, Charles J. Phillips. $1.15, John Lister. $1.50, Theodore Champion and 19th cent. French postilion. $3, Thomas de la Rue.
$8, Sir Rowland Hill, Bruce Castle.

2001, Apr. 30 *Perf. 13¼*

1026-1029 A173 Set of 4 9.00 9.00

Souvenir Sheet

1030 A173 $8 multi 10.00 10.00

Queen Elizabeth II, 75th Birthday — A174

Dress color: 90c, Black. $1.15, Yellow. $1.50, Pink. $5, Green.
$6, Lilac.

2001, June 22 *Perf. 13¼*

1031-1034 A174 Set of 4 10.00 10.00

Souvenir Sheet

1035 A174 $6 multi 9.00 9.00

Buildings — A175

Designs: 70c, Lookout community. $1, St. John's Hospital. $1.15, Tropical Mansion Suites. $1.50, Montserrat Secondary School. $3, Golden Years Home.

2001, Aug. 15 **Litho.** *Perf. 13½*

1036-1040 A175 Set of 5 10.00 10.00

Fruit A176

Designs: 5c, West Indian cherries. 10c Mammee apples. 15c, Limes. 20c, Grapefruits. 25c, Orange. 40c, Passion fruits. 55c, Bananas. 70c, Papayas. 90c, Pomegranates. $1, Guavas. $1.15, Mangos. $1.50, Sugar apple. $3, Cashews. $5, Soursops. $7.50, Watermelon. $10, Pineapple.

2001, Oct. 10 **Litho.** *Perf. 13½x13¼*

1041	A176	5c	multi	.25	.25
1042	A176	10c	multi	.25	.25
1043	A176	15c	multi	.25	.25
1044	A176	20c	multi	.25	.25
1045	A176	25c	multi	.25	.25
1046	A176	40c	multi	.40	.40
1047	A176	55c	multi	.50	.50
1048	A176	70c	multi	.65	.65
1049	A176	90c	multi	.85	.85
1050	A176	$1	multi	1.00	1.00
1051	A176	$1.15	multi	1.10	1.10
1052	A176	$1.50	multi	1.40	1.40
1053	A176	$3	multi	3.00	3.00
1054	A176	$5	multi	4.75	4.75
1055	A176	$7.50	multi	7.50	7.50
1056	A176	$10	multi	9.75	9.75
	Nos. 1041-1056 (16)			32.15	32.15

Butterflies — A177

Designs: $1, Common long-tail skipper. $1.15, Straight-line skipper. $1.50, Giant hairstreak. $3, Monarch.
$10, Painted lady.

2001, Dec. 20 **Litho.** *Perf. 13¼*

1057-1060 A177 Set of 4 8.50 8.50

Souvenir Sheet

1061 A177 $10 multi 12.50 12.50

2002 Winter Olympics, Salt Lake City — A178

No. 1062: a, $3, Downhill skiing. b, $5, Bobsled.

2002, Mar. 12 **Litho.** *Perf. 13¼*

1062 A178 Horiz. pair, #a-b 9.50 9.50

Fish A179

Designs: $1, Sergeant major. $1.15, Mutton snapper. $1.50, Lantern bass. $5, Shy hamlet.
$8, Queen angelfish.

Perf. 13¼

2002, July 29 **Litho.** **Unwmk.**

1063-1066 A179 Set of 4 11.50 11.50

Souvenir Sheet

1067 A179 $8 multi 10.50 10.50

Nos. 1012-1015 Overprinted

2002, Sept. 23 **Litho.** *Perf. 13½x13*

1068	A170	70c	on #1012	.75	.75
1069	A170	$1.15	on #1013	1.25	1.25
1070	A170	$3	on #1014	3.25	3.25
1071	A170	$6	on #1015	6.75	6.75
	Nos. 1068-1071 (4)			12.00	12.00

Wild Flowers — A180

Designs: 70c, Allamanda cathartica. $1.15, Lantana camara. $1.50, Leonotis nepetifolia. $5, Plumeria rubra.
$8, Alpinia purpurata.

Perf. 13¼

2002, Nov. 29 **Litho.** **Unwmk.**

1072-1075 A180 Set of 4 12.00 12.00

Souvenir Sheet

1076 A180 $8 multi 11.00 11.00

Coronation of Queen Elizabeth II, 50th Anniv. — A181

No. 1077: a, Queen wearing crown. b, Crown on pillow. c, Queen wearing tiara and purple sash.
$6, Queen wearing crown, diff.

2003, Apr. 30 *Perf. 14*

1077 A181 $3 Sheet of 3, #a-c 9.50 9.50

Souvenir Sheet

1078 A181 $6 multi 5.50 5.50

Powered Flight, Cent. — A182

No. 1079: a, Wright Flyer II in blue. b, Wright Flyer II in brown. c, Wright Brothers. d, Wright Flyer I.
$6, Wright Flyer II.

2003, June 30 **Litho.** *Perf. 14*

1079 A182 $2 Sheet of 4, #a-d 9.25 9.25

Souvenir Sheet

1080 A182 $6 multi 8.00 8.00

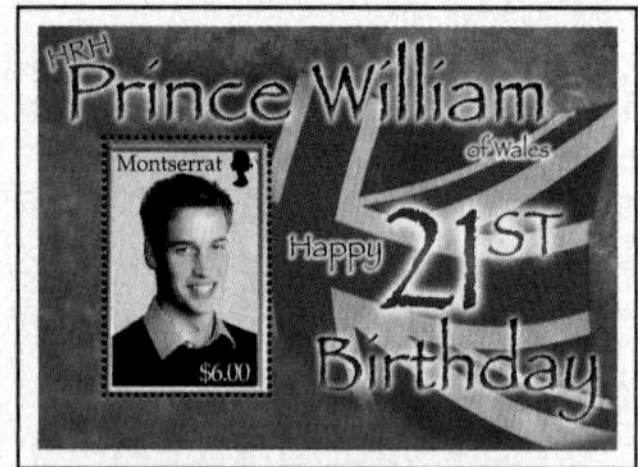

Prince William, 21st Birthday — A183

No. 1081 — Prince William in suit and tie with: a, Frame obscured at LL and LR by portrait. b, Frame obscured at LL by portrait. c, Frame not obscured.
$6, Wearing sweater and shirt with open collar.

2003, Aug. 20

1081 A183 $3 Sheet of 3, #a-c 10.00 10.00

Souvenir Sheet

1082 A183 $6 multi 8.00 8.00

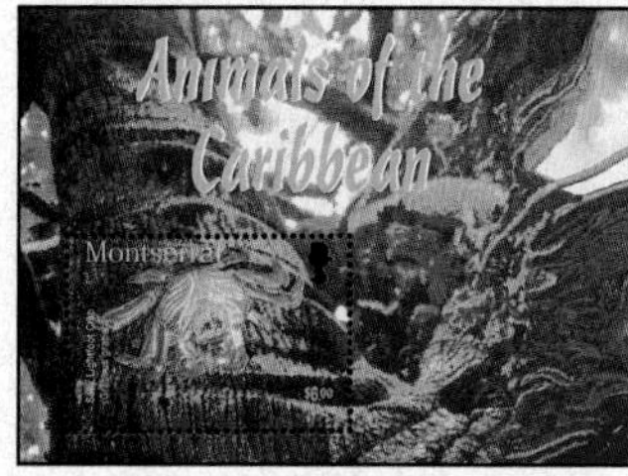

Fauna — A184

No. 1083: a, Piping frog. b, Land hermit crab. c, Spix's pinche. d, Dwarf gecko. e, Green sea turtle. f, Indian mongoose.
$6, Sally Lightfoot crab.

2003, Nov. 28

1083 A184 $1.50 Sheet of 6, #a-f 10.00 10.00

Souvenir Sheet

1084 A184 $6 multi 7.00 7.00

Mushrooms — A185

No. 1085: a, Slimy lead milk cap. b, Rosy spike cap. c, Stump puffball. d, Parasol. e, Crab russula. f, Scaly vase chanterelle.
$6, Fly agaric.

2003, Nov. 28

1085 A185 $1.50 Sheet of 6, #a-f 10.00 10.00

Souvenir Sheet

1086 A185 $6 multi 7.25 7.25

Birds A186

Designs: 90c, Belted kingfisher. $1.15, Yellow warbler. No. 1089, $1.50, Hooded warbler. $5, Cedar waxwing.
No. 1091: a, Roseate spoonbill. b, Laughing gull. c, White-tailed tropicbird. d, Bare-eyed thrush. e, Glittering-throated emerald. f, Lesser Antillean grackle.
$6, Bananaquit.

2003, Nov. 28

1087-1090 A186 Set of 4 12.00 12.00

1091 A186 $1.50 Sheet of 6, #a-f 9.50 9.50

Souvenir Sheet

1092 A186 $6 multi 7.00 7.00

2004 Summer Olympics, Greece A187

Designs: 90c, 1932 Los Angeles Olympics poster. $1.15, 1972 Munich Olympics pin.

$1.50, 1976 Montreal Olympics poster. $5, Pankration, horiz.

2004, June 30 Litho. *Perf. 13¼*
1093-1096 A187 Set of 4 9.25 9.25

Butterflies — A188

No. 1097: a, Lacewing. b, Swallowtail. c, Shoemaker. d, White peacock.
$6, Flashing astraptes.

2004, July 6 Litho. *Perf. 14*
1097 A188 $2.30 Sheet of 4, #a-d 9.25 9.25

Souvenir Sheet

1098 A188 $6 multi 5.00 5.00

Cats — A189

Designs: $1.15, Singapura. $1.50, Burmese. $2, Abyssinian. $5, Norwegian.
$6, Russian Blue.

2004, Aug. 23
1099-1102 A189 Set of 4 10.50 10.50

Souvenir Sheet

1103 A189 $6 multi 9.00 9.00

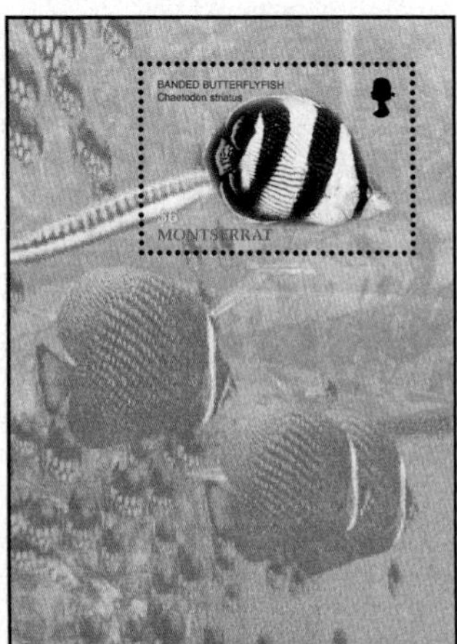

Fish — A190

No. 1104: a, Blue-girdled angelfish. b, Regal angelfish. c, Emperor angelfish. d, Blotch-eyed soldierfish.
$6, Banded butterflyfish.

2004, Sept. 30
1104 A190 $2.30 Sheet of 4, #a-d 9.50 9.50

Souvenir Sheet

1105 A190 $6 multi 8.00 8.00

Locomotives, 200th Anniv. — A191

No. 1106: a, Austerity. b, Deli Vasut. c, Class 424 No. 424.247/287. d, L-1646. e, Steam locomotive 324.1564. f, Class Ia.
No. 1107: a, Old Class TV. b, Class Va 7111. c, Class 424 No. 424.009. d, Class III.
$6, Class QR1.

2004, Oct. 29 *Perf. 14½x14*
1106 A191 $1.50 Sheet of 6, #a-f 7.75 7.75
1107 A191 $2 Sheet of 4, #a-d 6.75 6.75

Souvenir Sheet

1108 A191 $6 multi 5.00 5.00

World AIDS Day — A192

2004, Dec. 1 *Perf. 13½*
1109 A192 $3 multi 2.50 2.50

Printed in sheets of 4.

D-Day, 60th Anniv. A193

Designs: $1.15, Air assault begins. $1.50, Troops assault beaches of Normandy. $2, Field Marshal Montgomery. $5, HMS Belfast.

2004, Dec. 24 *Perf. 14*
1110-1113 A193 Set of 4 9.00 9.00

National Soccer Team — A194

2004, Dec. 24 Litho. *Perf. 12*
1114 A194 $6 multi 5.00 5.00

Nos. 1036-1040 Overprinted

2005, Feb. 21 Litho. *Perf. 13½*
1115 A175 70c multi .60 .60
1116 A175 $1 multi .80 .80
1117 A175 $1.15 multi .95 .95
1118 A175 $1.50 multi 1.25 1.25
1119 A175 $3 multi 2.50 2.50
Nos. 1115-1119 (5) 6.10 6.10

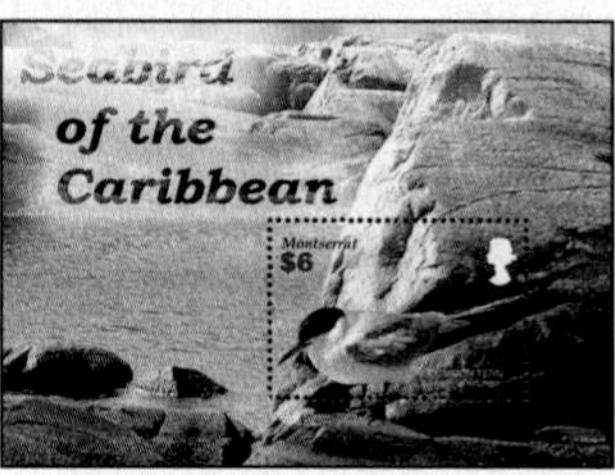

Birds — A195

No. 1120: a, Brown pelican. b, Red-billed tropicbird. c, Galapagos Island cormorant. d, Waved albatross.
$6, Common tern.

2005, Apr. 25 Litho. *Perf. 13¼x13½*
1120 A195 $2.30 Sheet of 4, #a-d 7.75 7.75

Souvenir Sheet

1121 A195 $6 multi 5.50 5.50

Orchids — A196

No. 1122: a, Cattleya lueddemanniana. b, Cattleya luteola. c, Cattleya trianaei. d, Cattleya mossiae.
$6, Cattleya mendelii.

2005, Apr. 25
1122 A196 $2.30 Sheet of 4, #a-d 7.75 7.75

Souvenir Sheet

1123 A196 $6 multi 5.00 5.00

Molluscs and Shells A197

Designs: $1.15, Liguus virgineus. $1.50, Liguus fasciatus testudineus. $2, Liguus fasciatus. $5, Cerion striatella.
$6, Liguus fasciatus, vert.

2005, June 1 *Perf. 13¼x13½*
1124-1127 A197 Set of 4 8.25 8.25

Souvenir Sheet

Perf. 13½x13¼

1128 A197 $6 multi 5.50 5.50

Miniature Sheet

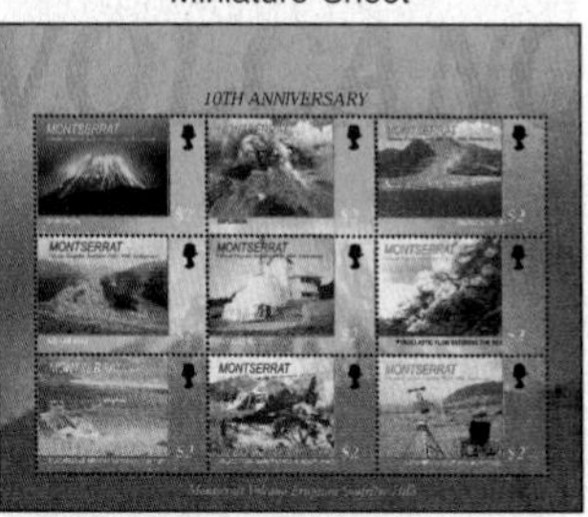

Soufriere Hills Volcanic Eruption, 10th Anniv. — A198

No. 1129: a, Dome glow. b, Explosion. c, Tar River Delta. d, Belham River. e, MVO Building. f, Pyroclastic flow entering the sea. g, Blackburne Airport, destroyed in 1997. h, Helicopter maintenance and monitoring. i, Instruments used for monitoring.

2005, July 18 Litho. *Perf. 14*
1129 A198 $2 Sheet of 9, #a-i 16.00 16.00

Rotary International, Cent. — A199

Emblem and: $1, Shamrock. $1.15, Heliconia flower. $1.50, Lady and the Harp. $5, Map of Montserrat.
$6, Medical care for children, horiz.

2005, Sept. 12 *Perf. 12¾*
1130-1133 A199 Set of 4 8.00 8.00

Souvenir Sheet

1134 A199 $6 multi 5.50 5.50

Battle of Trafalgar, Bicent. — A200

No. 1135: a, Napoleon Bonaparte. b, Admiral Horatio Nelson. c, Battle of the Nile. d, Battle of Trafalgar.
$6, Nelson, diff.

2005, Nov. 4 Litho. *Perf. 12*
1135 A200 $2 Sheet of 4, #a-d 8.00 8.00

Souvenir Sheet

1136 A200 $6 multi 6.00 6.00

Hans Christian Andersen (1805-75), Author — A201

No. 1137: a, Thumbelina. b, The Flying Trunk. c, The Buckwheat.
$6, The Little Mermaid.

2005, Dec. 23 *Perf. 12¾*
1137 A201 $3 Sheet of 3, #a-c 8.00 8.00

Souvenir Sheet

Perf. 12

1138 A201 $6 multi 6.00 6.00

No. 1137 contains three 39x25mm stamps.

Famous People A202

Designs: No. 1139, $1.15, William Henry Bramble (1901-88), first chief minister. No. 1140, $1.15, Michael Simmons Osborne (1902-67), merchant and parliamentarian. No. 1141, $1.15, Robert William Griffith (1904-96), union leader. No. 1142, $1.15, Patricia Griffin (1907-86), social worker. No. 1143, $1.15, Lilian Cadogan (1907-92), nurse. No. 1144, $1.15, Samuel Aymer (1911-79), folk musician.

2005, Dec. 5 Litho. *Perf. 12¾*
1139-1144 A202 Set of 6 6.00 6.00
1140a Inscribed "Symmons" instead of "Simmons" 1.00 1.00
1144a Souvenir sheet, #1139, 1140a, 1141-1144 6.00 6.00

Nos. 1022, 1058-1059, 1072 and 1075 Overprinted

Methods and Perfs As Before

2006, Apr. 1
1145 A180 70c on #1072 .60 .60
1146 A172 $1 on #1022 .85 .85
1147 A177 $1.15 on #1058 1.00 1.00
1148 A177 $1.50 on #1059 1.25 1.25
1149 A180 $5 on #1075 4.00 4.00
Nos. 1145-1149 (5) 7.70 7.70

Overprint is on four lines on No. 1146.

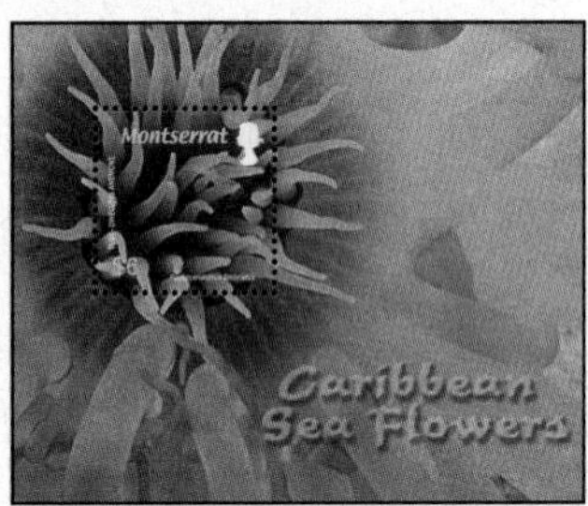

Marine Life — A203

No. 1150: a, Giant Caribbean anemone. b, Beadlet anemone. c, Golden crinoid. d, Oval cup coral.
$6, Tube-dwelling anemone.

2006, May 2 Litho. *Perf. 12*
1150 A203 $2.30 Sheet of 4, #a-d 9.00 9.00

Souvenir Sheet

1151 A203 $6 multi 5.75 5.75

Moths — A204

No. 1152: a, Cecropia moth. b, Madagascan sunset moth. c, Great peacock moth. d, Zodiac moth.
$6, White-lined sphinx moth.

2006, May 2
1152 A204 $2.30 Sheet of 4, #a-d 9.00 9.00

Souvenir Sheet

1153 A204 $6 multi 5.75 5.75

Dogs — A205

Designs: $1.15, Rottweiler. $1.50, Boxer. $2, Corgi. $5, Great Dane.
$6, St. Bernard.

2006, Aug. 16
1154-1157 A205 Set of 4 8.50 8.50

Souvenir Sheet

1158 A205 $6 multi 5.50 5.50

Worldwide Fund for Nature (WWF) — A206

No. 1159 — Various depictions of Mountain chicken frog: a, 70c. b, $1. c, $1.15. d, $1.50.

2006, Aug. 16 *Perf. 13¼*
1159 A206 Block of 4, #a-d 3.75 3.75
e. Miniature sheet, 2 #1159 7.50 7.50

Souvenir Sheet

2006 World Cup Soccer Championships, Germany — A207

No. 1160 — World Cup, emblem and: a, $1.15, FIFA World Cup Stadium, Hanover. b, $1.50, Sir Stanley Matthews, England team uniform. c, $2, Sir Ralph "Dixie" Dean, England team uniform. d, $5, Bobby Moore, England team uniform.

2006, Aug. 31 *Perf. 12*
1160 A207 Sheet of 4, #a-d 8.00 8.00

Christopher Columbus (1451-1506), Explorer — A208

Designs: $1.15, Map of North and South America, Columbus's vessels. $1.50, Columbus and map of voyage. $2, Ship, Earth, Columbus. $5, Columbus, vert.
$6, Earth, Columbus and crew with flag, vert.

2006, Oct. 27 *Perf. 12¾*
1161-1164 A208 Set of 4 8.00 8.00

Souvenir Sheet

1165 A208 $6 multi 5.00 5.00

A209

Queen Elizabeth II, 80th Birthday — A210

No. 1166: a, Queen wearing crown, country name in black. b, Queen wearing crown, country name in white, c, Queen wearing tiara. d, Queen wearing tiara and sash.

2006, Oct. 27 *Perf. 13¼*
1166 A209 $2.30 Sheet of 4, #a-d 7.00 7.00

Souvenir Sheet

1167 A210 $8 shown 6.00 6.00

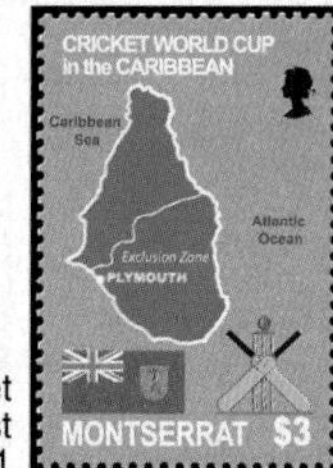

2007 Cricket World Cup, West Indies — A211

Designs: $3, 2007 Cricket World Cup emblem, map and flag of Montserrat. $5, Cricket team, horiz.
$8, 2007 Cricket World Cup emblem.

2007, Mar. 9 Litho. *Perf. 13¼*
1168-1169 A211 Set of 2 6.25 6.25

Souvenir Sheet

1170 A211 $8 multi 6.25 6.25

Scouting, Cent. — A212

No. 1171, horiz. — Scouts: a, Looking at flower. b, Working at construction site. c, In sailboat. d, Feeding goat. e, Making campfire. f, Installing birdhouse.
$6, Lord Robert Baden-Powell.

2007, Mar. 9
1171 A212 $2 Sheet of 6, #a-f 9.50 9.50

Souvenir Sheet

1172 A212 $6 multi 4.75 4.75

Flowers — A213

Designs: 10c, Poinsettia. 30c, Periwinkle. 35c, Bougainvillea. 50c, Ixora. 70c, Heliconia. 80c, Morning glory. 90c, Poinciana. $1, Cup of gold. $1.10, Chenille plant. $1.50, Oleander. $2.25, Hibiscus. $2.50, Frangipani. $2.75, Bird of paradise. $5, Madagascar jasmine. $10, Yellow poui. $20, Rose.

2007, May 14 Litho. *Perf. 12½*
1173 A213 10c multi .25 .25
1174 A213 30c multi .25 .25
1175 A213 35c multi .25 .25
1176 A213 50c multi .40 .40
1177 A213 70c multi .55 .55
1178 A213 80c multi .60 .60
1179 A213 90c multi .70 .70
1180 A213 $1 multi .75 .75
1181 A213 $1.10 multi .85 .85
1182 A213 $1.50 multi 1.10 1.10
1183 A213 $2.25 multi 1.75 1.75
1184 A213 $2.50 multi 1.90 1.90
1185 A213 $2.75 multi 2.10 2.10
1186 A213 $5 multi 3.75 3.75
1187 A213 $10 multi 7.50 7.50
1188 A213 $20 multi 15.00 15.00
Nos. 1173-1188 (16) 37.70 37.70

Princess Diana (1961-97) — A214

No. 1189 — Diana wearing tiara and: a, Blue dress. b, Black dress. c, White dress. d, White dress with high neck.
$7, Diana without tiara.

2007, Aug. 8 Litho. *Perf. 13¼*
1189 A214 $3.40 Sheet of 4, #a-d 12.00 12.00

Souvenir Sheet

1190 A214 $7 multi 6.00 6.00

Turtles — A215

No. 1191: a, Hawksbill turtle. b, Green turtle. c, Leatherback turtle. d, Loggerhead turtle.
$7, Kemp's Ridley sea turtle.

2007, Aug. 8 *Perf. 13¼x13½*
1191 A215 $3.40 Sheet of 4, #a-d 11.50 11.50

Souvenir Sheet

1192 A215 $7 multi 6.00 6.00

Parrots — A216

No. 1193: a, Green-winged macaw. b, Mitred conure. c, Sun conure. d, Blue-and-yellow macaw.
$7, Hyacinth macaw.

2007, Oct. 11 Litho. *Perf. 13½x13¼*
1193 A216 $3.40 Sheet of 4, #a-d 13.50 13.50

Souvenir Sheet

1194 A216 $7 multi 9.00 9.00

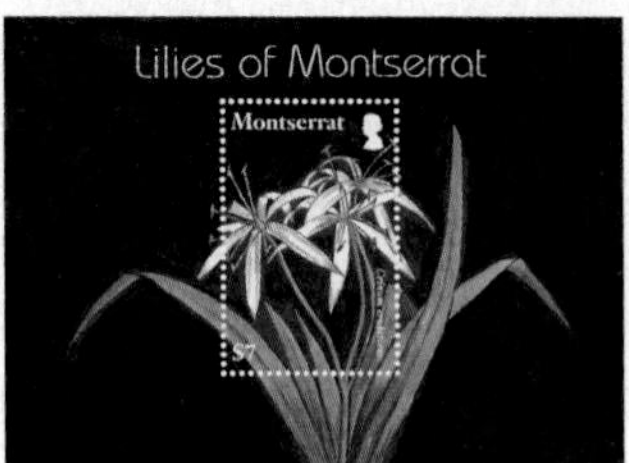

Lilies — A217

No. 1195, horiz.: a, Hippeastrum puniceum. b, Hymenocallis caribaea. c, Zephyranthes puertoricensis. d, Belamcanda chinensis.
$7, Crinum erubescens.

2007, Oct. 11 ***Perf. 13¼x13½***
1195 A217 $3.40 Sheet of 4, #a-d 11.50 11.50

Souvenir Sheet
Perf. 13½x13¼

1196 A217 $7 multi 6.00 6.00

Miniature Sheet

Charles Wesley (1707-88), Hymn Writer — A218

No. 1197: a, Portrait of Wesley by unknown artist. b, Portrait of Wesley by John Russell. c, Engraving of Wesley by Jonathan Spilsbury. d, Bethany Methodist Church.

2007, Dec. 18 Litho. ***Perf. 13¼***
1197 A218 $2.50 Sheet of 4, #a-d 8.00 8.00

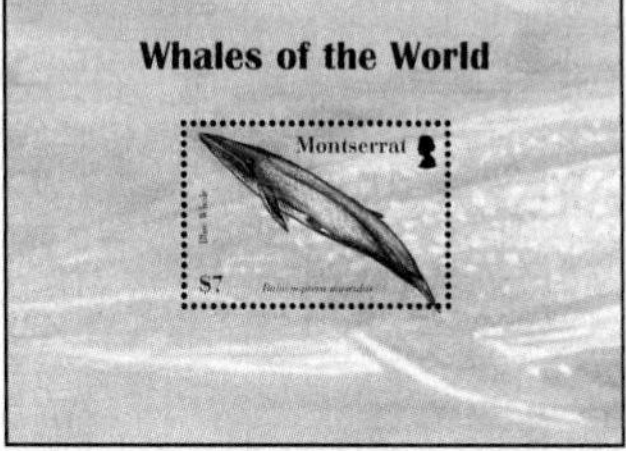

Whales — A219

No. 1198: a, Sperm whale. b, Minke whale. c, Cuvier's beaked whale. d, Humpback whale.
$7, Blue whale.

2008, May 2 ***Perf. 12¾***
1198 A219 $3.55 Sheet of 4, #a-d 13.00 13.00

Souvenir Sheet

1199 A219 $7 multi 8.00 8.00

Space Exploration, 50th Anniv. — A220

No. 1200, vert.: a, Explorer I on Juno I launch rocket. b, Dr. James Van Allen, Explorer I. c, Explorer I. d, Drs. William Pickering, James Van Allen and Wernher von Braun with Explorer I model.
$7, Explorer I, diff.

2008, May 29 ***Perf. 13¼***
1200 A220 $3.55 Sheet of 4, #a-d 12.00 12.00

Souvenir Sheet

1201 A220 $7 multi 6.00 6.00

Endangered Animals — A221

No. 1202, vert.: a, African elephant. b, Bald eagle. c, Sumatran tiger. d, Hawksbill turtle. e, Indian rhinoceros. f, Western gorilla.
$7, Rock iguana.

2008, July 3
1202 A221 $2.25 Sheet of 6, #a-f 11.00 11.00

Souvenir Sheet

1203 A221 $7 multi 6.00 6.00

Miniature Sheet

Early Postal History — A222

No. 1204: a, "Lady McLeod" stamp, early paddle packet boat. b, Early Montserrat postal card. c, Great Britain #U1-U2. d, Great Britain #1, Sir Rowland Hill. e, Montserrat #1-2. f, Montserrat cancels.

2008, July 31 Litho. ***Perf. 13½***
1204 A222 $2.75 Sheet of 6, #a-f 13.50 13.50

Miniature Sheets

Royal Air Force, 90th Anniv. — A223

No. 1205, $3.55: a, English Electric Lightning P3. b, Hurricane IIC. c, Jet Provost T3A. d, Jaguar GR3A.

No. 1206, $3.55: a, Westland Sea King HAR3 helicopter. b, Gloster Javelin FAW9. c, P-66 Pembroke C1. d, Chinook HC2 helicopter.

2008, Sept. 5 Litho. ***Perf. 13¼***
Sheets of 4, #a-d
1205-1206 A223 Set of 2 25.00 25.00

University of the West Indies, 60th Anniv. — A224

Designs: $2, Building on Montserrat campus. $5, University arms, diploma.

2008, Sept. 30
1207-1208 A224 Set of 2 6.00 6.00

Miniature Sheets

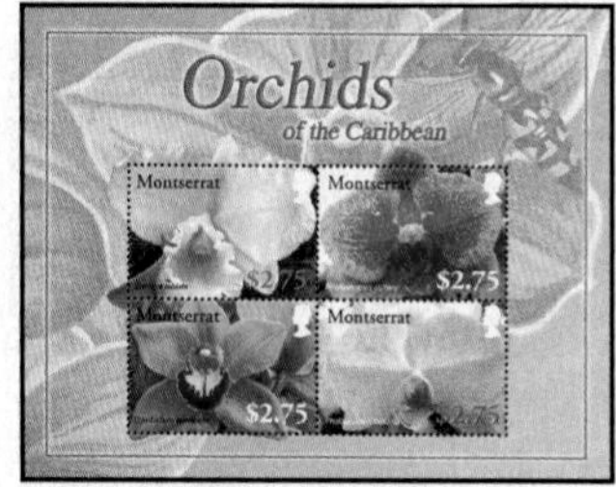

Orchids — A225

No. 1209, $2.75: a, Cattleya labiata. b, Phalaenopsis cultivar with pink spots. c, Cymbidium annabelle. d, Phalaenopsis taisuco.

No. 1210, $2.75: a, Phalaenopsis amabilis. b, Cattleya aurantiaca. c, Phalaenopsis cultivar with pink lines. d, Dendrobium nobile.

2008, Nov. 27 ***Perf. 13¼***
Sheets of 4, #a-d
1209-1210 A225 Set of 2 19.00 19.00

Dolphins — A226

No. 1211: a, Common dolphin. b, Bottlenose dolphin. c, Pantropical spotted dolphin. d, Long-snouted spinner dolphin.
$7, Risso's dolphin.

2008, Nov. 27 ***Perf. 12¾***
1211 A226 $3.55 Sheet of 4, #a-d 12.50 12.50

Souvenir Sheet

1212 A226 $7 multi 5.75 5.75

Miniature Sheet

New Year 2009 (Year of the Ox) — A227

No. 1213: a, Yellow orange ox facing right. b, Black ox facing left. c, Gray ox facing right. d, White ox facing left.

2009, Feb. 2 Litho. ***Perf. 12¾***
1213 A227 $3.55 Sheet of 4, #a-d 13.00 13.00

Miniature Sheets

Dr. Martin Luther King, Jr. (1929-68), Civil Rights Leader — A228

No. 1214, $2.50: a, King. b, King at desk. c, King wearing hat. d, King's wife, Coretta.

No. 1215, $2.50, horiz.: a, March on Washington crowd. b, King meeting Malcolm X. c, King with Pres. John F. Kennedy and other civil rights leaders. d, King waving to March on Washington crowd.

2009, Feb. 26 ***Perf. 13½***
Sheets of 4, #a-d
1214-1215 A228 Set of 2 16.00 16.00

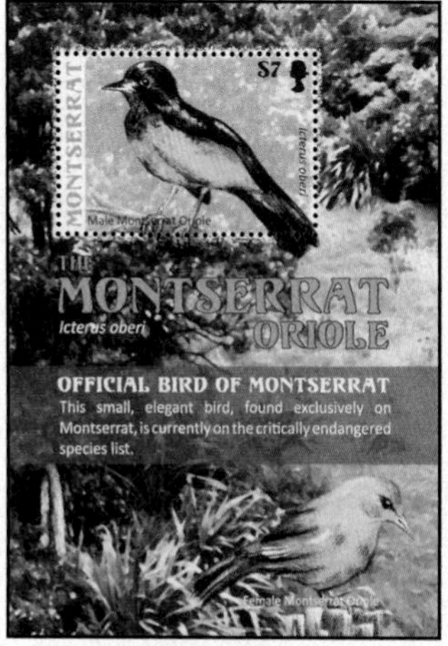

MONTSERRAT
$7
THE MONTSERRAT ORIOLE
Icterus oberi
OFFICIAL BIRD OF MONTSERRAT
This small, elegant bird, found exclusively on Montserrat, is currently on the critically endangered species list.

Birds — A229

No. 1216: a, Smooth-billed ani. b, American kestrel. c, Common moorhen. d, Cattle egret.
$7, Male Montserrat oriole.

2009, Apr. 1
1216 A229 $2.75 Sheet of 4, #a-d 9.00 9.00

Souvenir Sheet

1217 A229 $7 multi 6.50 6.50

Corals A230

Designs: $1.10, Staghorn coral. $2.25, Zoanthid coral. $2.50, Blade fire coral. $2.75, Brain coral.
$7, Orange tube coral, vert.

2009, Apr. 29
1218-1221 A230 Set of 4 7.00 7.00

Souvenir Sheet

1222 A230 $7 multi 6.00 6.00

No. 1222 contains one 37x51mm stamp.

Charles Darwin (1809-82), Naturalist — A231

No. 1223, vert.: a, Darwin. b, Coenobita clypeatus. c, Anolis lividus. d, Epidendrum montserratense.
$7, Darwin, waterfall, emblem of Montserrat Centre Hills Project.

2009, July 28
1223 A231 $2.75 Sheet of 4, #a-d 8.50 8.50

Souvenir Sheet

1224 A231 $7 multi 6.00 6.00

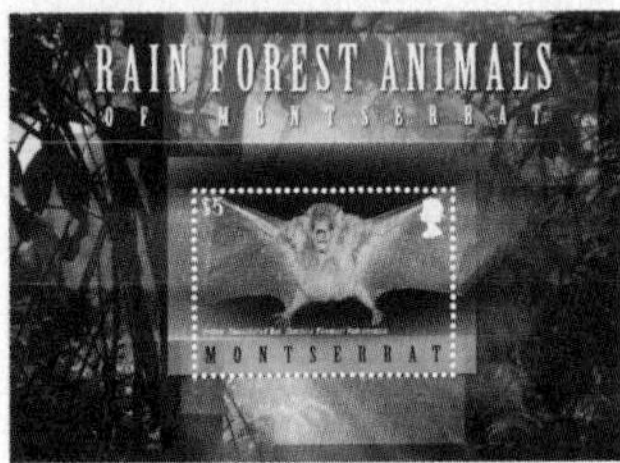

Rain Forest Animals — A232

No. 1225: a, $1.10, Green iguana. b, $2.25, Galliwasp. c, $2.50, Black snake. d, $2.75, Common agouti.
$5, Yellow-shouldered bat.

2009, Sept. 25 Litho. *Perf. 13¼*
1225 A232 Sheet of 4, #a-d 7.50 7.50

Souvenir Sheet

1226 A232 $5 multi 4.25 4.25

Trees — A233

Designs: $1.10, Tamarind. $2.25, Dwarf coconut. $2.50, Breadfruit. $2.75, Calabash. $5, Geiger.

2009, Oct. 30 *Perf. 14¼x14¾*
1227-1231 A233 Set of 5 10.50 10.50

Miniature Sheet

Naval Aviation, Cent. — A234

No. 1232 — Aircraft carriers: a, 70c, HMS Ark Royal II. b, $1.10, HMS Furious. c, $2.25, HMS Argus. d, $2.50, HMS Illustrious. e, $2.75, HMS Ark Royal IV. f, $5, HMS Invincible.

2009, Dec. 4 Litho. *Perf. 11½x11¼*
1232 A234 Sheet of 6, #a-f 11.00 11.00

A235

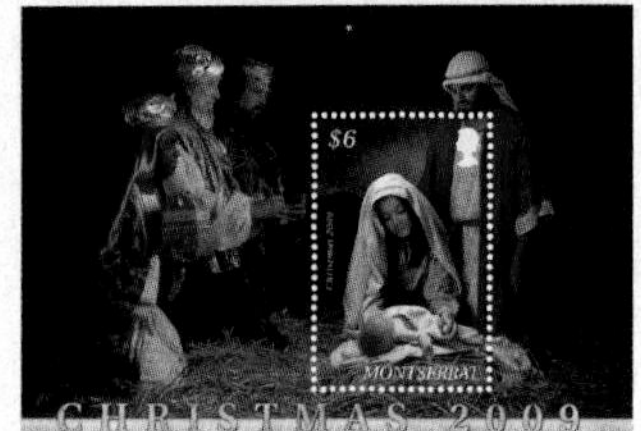

Christmas — A236

Designs: $1.10, Snowflake bush. $2.25, Carnival troupe. $2.50, Masquerade. $2.75, St. Patrick's Roman Catholic Church.
$6, Creche figurines of Holy Family.

2009, Dec. 18 *Perf. 12¾*
1233-1236 A235 Set of 4 6.75 6.75

Souvenir Sheet

1237 A236 $6 multi 5.25 5.25

Marine Life A237

Designs: $1.10, Basket star. $2.25, Spiny lobster. $2.50, Spotted drum. $2.75, Sea anemone, vert. $5, Batwing coral crab.

2010, Mar. 15 *Perf. 14¼*
1238-1242 A237 Set of 5 10.50 10.50

Miniature Sheets

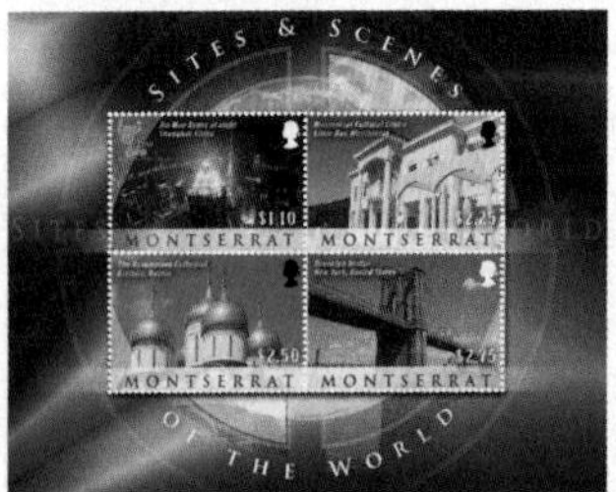

World Landmarks — A238

No. 1243: a, $1.10, Jin Mao Tower, Shanghai, China. b, $2.25, Montserrat Cultural Center, Little Bay, Montserrat. c, $2.50, Assumption Cathedral, Moscow, Russia. d, $2.75, Brooklyn Bridge.
No. 1244: a, $1.10, Fishing villages in Shanghai and Hong Kong. b, $2.25, Camelot Villa, Montserrat. c, $2.50, Buildings at Zaanse Schans Windmill Village, Zaandam, Netherlands. d, $2.75, Reichstag, Berlin, Germany.

2010, Apr. 19 *Perf. 14¼*

Sheets of 4, #a-d

1243-1244 A238 Set of 2 15.00 15.00

Miniature Sheets

A239

Michael Jackson (1958-2009), Singer — A240

No. 1245 — Jackson: a, Wearing sunglasses. b, Wearing red jacket and white shirt. c, With microphone near mouth. d, Wearing high-collared red jacket.
No. 1246 — Jackson: a, Facing right, no microphone. b, Facing left, holding microphone. c, Wearing black jacket, holding microphone. d, Facing forward, no microphone.

2010, June 25 *Perf. 13½*
1245 A239 $2.50 Sheet of 4, #a-d 8.50 8.50
1246 A240 $2.50 Sheet of 4, #a-d 8.50 8.50

A241

Flowers — A242

Designs: $1.10, Wild marigold. $2.25, Shrubby toothedthread. $2.50, Wild sweet pea. $2.75, Rosy periwinkle. $5, Measle bush.
$7, Pribby.

2010, Aug. 18
1247-1251 A241 Set of 5 12.00 12.00

Souvenir Sheet

1252 A242 $7 multi 6.50 6.50

Worldwide Fund for Nature (WWF) — A243

No. 1253 — Reddish egret: a, $1.10, Two birds in water. b, $2.25, Two birds in flight. c, $2.50, Bird preening feathers. d, $2.75, Bird running in water.

2010, Oct. 29 Litho.
1253 A243 Block or strip of 4, #a-d 7.50 7.50
e. Souvenir sheet of 8, 2 each #a-d 15.00 15.00

Giant Panda — A244

No. 1254 — Panda: a, Eating, brown in background. b, Resting on tree. c, Eating, green in background. d, Walking.
$7, Panda, diff.

2010, Nov. 22 Litho. *Perf. 12*
1254 A244 $2.50 Sheet of 4, #a-d 3.00 3.00

Souvenir Sheet

Perf. 13 Syncopated

1255 A244 $7 multi 4.50 4.50

Beijing 2010 Intl. Philatelic Exhibition.

Shells A245

Designs: $1.10, Beaded periwinkle. $2.25, Green star shell. $2.50, Smooth Scotch bonnet. $2.75, Calico scallop. $5, Hawk wing conch.
$7, Atlantic partridge tun, vert.

2011, Jan. 10 *Perf. 13 Syncopated*
1256-1260 A245 Set of 5 10.50 10.50

Souvenir Sheet

1261 A245 $7 multi 5.25 5.25

Miniature Sheet

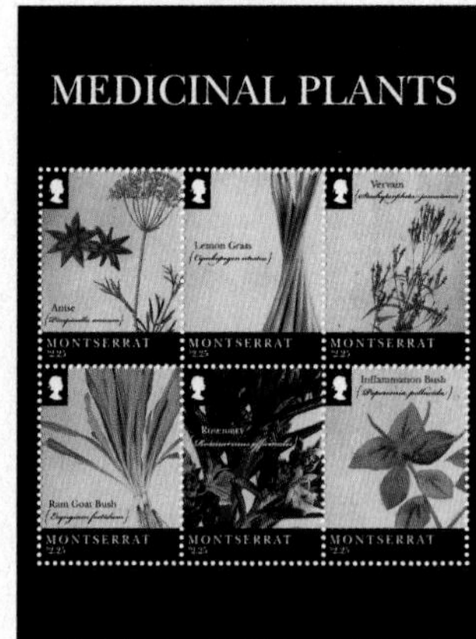

Medicinal Plants — A246

No. 1262: a, Anise. b, Lemon grass. c, Vervain. d, Ram goat bush. e, Rosemary. f, Inflammation bush.

2011, Mar. 15 *Perf. 12x11½*
1262 A246 $2.25 Sheet of 6, #a-f 10.00 10.00

Engagement of Prince William and Catherine Middleton — A247

No. 1263: a, Couple, door at left. b, Middleton. c, Prince William. d, Couple, picture frame in background.
No. 1264: a, Middleton, diff. b, Prince William, diff.

2011, Mar. 31 *Perf. 13¼*
1263 A247 $2.75 Sheet of 4, #a-d 8.25 8.25

Souvenir Sheet

1264 A247 $5 Sheet of 2, #a-b 7.50 7.50

Livestock A248

Designs: $2.25, Barbados black belly sheep. $2.50, Boer goat, horiz. $2.75, Black donkey. $5, Red cattle, horiz.
$7, Arabian horse.

2011, June 6 *Perf. 12*
1265-1268 A248 Set of 4 9.25 9.25

Souvenir Sheet

1269 A248 $7 multi 5.25 5.25

Wedding of Prince William and Catherine Middleton — A249

No. 1270: a, Groom wearing hat. b, Couple, groom without hat. c, Bride looking left. d, Groom without hat. e, Couple, groom with hat. f, Bride looking right.
$7, Couple kissing.

2011, June 29 *Perf. 13x13¼*
1270 A249 $2.25 Sheet of 6, #a-f 10.00 10.00

Souvenir Sheet

1271 A249 $7 multi 5.25 5.25

Sept. 11, 2001 Terrorist Attacks, 10th Anniv. — A250

No. 1272: a, Tribute in Washington Square, New York City, Sept. 14, 2001. b, American flag, chain-link fence, message on piece of wood. c, Messages on pillar in Union Square, New York City, Sept. 13, 2001. d, Memorial, Stonycreek Township, Pennsylvania.
$6, Keithroy Maynard (1971-2001), New York City firefighter killed in attacks.

2011, Sept. 11 *Perf. 12*
1272 A250 $2.75 Sheet of 4, #a-d 8.25 8.25

Souvenir Sheet

1273 A250 $6 multi 4.50 4.50

Alphonsus Cassell (1949-2010), Calypso and Soca Singer — A251

Designs: $2.25, Color photograph of Cassell. $2.50, Color photograph, diff.
No. 1276, horiz. — Cassell singing: a, With spotlights in background. b, Wearing headphones. c, With hand raised above head. d, Not holding microphone.

2011, Oct. 15 *Perf. 14*
1274-1275 A251 Set of 2 3.50 3.50

Perf. 12

1276 A251 $2.75 Sheet of 4, #a-d 8.25 8.25

Statue of Liberty, 125th Anniv. — A252

No. 1277 — View of: a, $1.10, Head. b, $1.10, Torch. c, $2.25, Head, diff. d, $2.25, Tablet. e, $2.50, Entire statue. f, $2.50, Head and tablet.
$6, Entire statue and base.

2011, Oct. 28 *Perf. 12*
1277 A252 Sheet of 6, #a-f 8.75 8.75

Souvenir Sheet

1278 A252 $6 multi 4.50 4.50

No. 1278 contains one 30x80mm stamp.

Miniature Sheets

Flora and Fauna of China — A253

No. 1279 — Flora: a, $1.10, Chinese plum. b, $2.25, Opium poppy. c, $2.50, Japanese camellia. d, $2.75, Pomegranate.
No. 1280 — Fauna: a, $1.10, Purple heron. b, $2.25, Indian elephant. c, $2.50, Snub-nosed monkey. d, $2.75, Royal Bengal tiger.

2011, Nov. 11 *Perf. 12*

Sheets of 4, #a-d

1279-1280 A253 Set of 2 13.00 13.00

China 2011 Intl. Philatelic Exhibition, Wuxi.

Christmas A254

Designs: $2.25, Choral group Voices. $2.50, Emerald Community Singers. $2.75, Volpanics. $5, New Ebenezer Seventh Day Adventist Church.

2011, Dec. 6 *Perf. 14*
1281-1284 A254 Set of 4 9.25 9.25

Ducks — A255

No. 1285: a, Northern pintail. b, Green-winged teal. c, Fulvous whistling duck. d, Blue-winged teal.
$6, Northern shoveler.

2012, Feb. 28 *Perf. 14*
1285 A255 $3.50 Sheet of 4, #a-d 10.50 10.50

Souvenir Sheet

Perf. 12

1286 A255 $6 multi 4.50 4.50

Cacti — A256

No. 1287: a, Queen of the night. b, Old man's whiskers. c, Devil cholla. d, Century plant.
No. 1288: Prickly pear cactus. b, Prickly pear fruit.

2012, Feb. 10
1287 A256 $2.75 Sheet of 4, #a-d 8.25 8.25

Souvenir Sheet

1288 A256 $3.50 Sheet of 2, #a-b 5.25 5.25

Reign of Queen Elizabeth II, 60th Anniv. — A257

No. 1289: a, Head of Queen Elizabeth II. b, Queen Elizabeth II waving, two men in background. c, Queen Elizabeth II on throne. d, Queen Elizabeth II and Prince Philip.
$7, Queen Elizabeth II, vert.

2012, Apr. 18 *Perf. 12*
1289 A257 $3.50 Sheet of 4, #a-d 10.50 10.50

Souvenir Sheet

Perf. 14

1290 A257 $7 multi 5.25 5.25

Bridges — A258

No. 1291, vert.: a, Sydney Harbour Bridge. b, Brooklyn Bridge. c, Golden Gate Bridge.
$6, Tower Bridge, London.

2012, June 8 *Perf. 14*
1291 A258 $4 Sheet of 3, #a-c 9.00 9.00

Souvenir Sheet

1292 A258 $6 multi 4.50 4.50

Marine Life — A259

No. 1293: a, Yellow tang. b, Spotted dolphin. c, Manatee. d, Green sea turtle.
$6, Blue-spotted grouper.

2012, June 26 **Litho.**
1293 A259 $3 Sheet of 4, #a-d 9.00 9.00

Souvenir Sheet

1294 A259 $6 multi 4.50 4.50

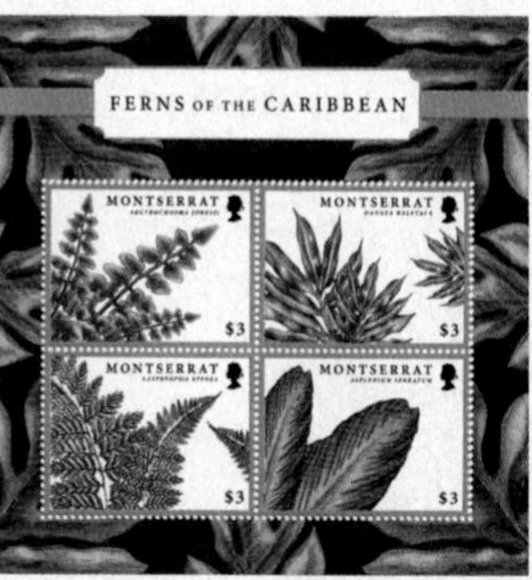

Ferns — A260

No. 1295: a, Argyrochosma jonesii. b, Danaea kalevala. c, Lastreopsis effusa. d, Asplenium serratum.

$6, Phlebodium aureum, vert.

2012, Aug. 20 *Perf. 14*

1295 A260 $3 Sheet of 4, #a-d 9.00 9.00

Souvenir Sheet

Perf. 12½

1296 A260 $6 multi 4.50 4.50

No. 1296 contains one 38x51mm stamp.

Scenes From China — A261

No. 1297 — Great Wall of China: a, Tower at right, denomination in black. b, Four towers, denomination in black. c, Wall turrets, denomination in white. d, Wall walkway, denomination in white.

No. 1298: a, Gate of Heavenly Peace. b, Forbidden City. c, Summer Palace, large rock at LL. d, Summer Palace, stairway at LL. e, Pudong skyline. f, Li River, Quangxi Province.

No. 1299, $5, Sanqingshan National Park, vert. No. 1300, $5, Dragon carving on a temple facade, vert.

2012, Nov. 15 *Perf. 13¾*

1297 A261 $2.25 Sheet of 4, #a-d 6.75 6.75

1298 A261 $2.50 Sheet of 6, #a-f 11.50 11.50

Souvenir Sheets

Perf. 12½

1299-1300 A261 Set of 2 7.50 7.50

Beijing 2012 Intl. Philatelic Exhibition. Nos. 1299-1300 each contain one 38x51mm stamp.

Minerals — A262

No. 1301: a, Amber. b, Chrysoberyl. c, Garnet. d, Microcline. e, Sunstone. f, Lapis lazuli. $6, Orpiment, vert.

2013, Jan. 31 *Perf. 13¾*

1301 A262 $2.50 Sheet of 6, #a-f 11.50 11.50

Souvenir Sheet

Perf. 12¾

1302 A262 $6 multi 4.50 4.50

No. 1302 contains one 38x51mm stamp.

Butterflies — A263

Designs: 10c, Pygmy fritillary. 30c, Cloudless sulphur. 35c, Gulf fritillary. 50c, St. Christopher's hairstreak. 70c, Nyctelius skipper. 80c, Cassius blue. 90c, Antillean crescent. $1, Polydamas swallowtail. $1.10, Flambeau. $1.50, Bronze hairstreak. $2.25, Caribbean buckeye. $2.50, Red rim. $2.75, White peacock. $5, Stub-tailed skipper. $10, Zebra. $20, Manuel's skipper.

2013, Mar. 5 *Perf. 12*

1303	A263	10c	multi	.25	.25
1304	A263	30c	multi	.25	.25
1305	A263	35c	multi	.25	.25
1306	A263	50c	multi	.40	.40
1307	A263	70c	multi	.55	.55
1308	A263	80c	multi	.60	.60
1309	A263	90c	multi	.70	.70
1310	A263	$1	multi	.75	.75
1311	A263	$1.10	multi	.85	.85
1312	A263	$1.50	multi	1.10	1.10
1313	A263	$2.25	multi	1.75	1.75
1314	A263	$2.50	multi	1.90	1.90
1315	A263	$2.75	multi	2.10	2.10
1316	A263	$5	multi	3.75	3.75
1317	A263	$10	multi	7.50	7.50
1318	A263	$20	multi	15.00	15.00
	Nos. 1303-1318 (16)			37.70	37.70

Globe Theater Fire, 400th Anniv. — A264

No. 1319 — Plays by William Shakespeare (1564-1616): a, Hamlet. b, Julius Caesar. c, Macbeth. d, Romeo and Juliet.

$7, Shakespeare, vert.

2013, May 29 *Perf. 13¾*

1319 A264 $2.75 Sheet of 4, #a-d 8.25 8.25

Souvenir Sheet

Perf. 12½

1320 A264 $7 multi 5.25 5.25

No. 1320 contains one 38x51mm stamp.

New Year 2014 (Year of the Horse) — A265

No. 1321 — Horse: a, Grazing. b, Pacing, with one front leg lifted. c, Walking, with no feet lifted. d, Galloping, with two front legs lifted.

$7, Horse, diff.

2013, July 17 *Perf. 13¾*

1321 A265 $2.75 Sheet of 4, #a-d 8.25 8.25

Souvenir Sheet

1322 A265 $7 multi 5.25 5.25

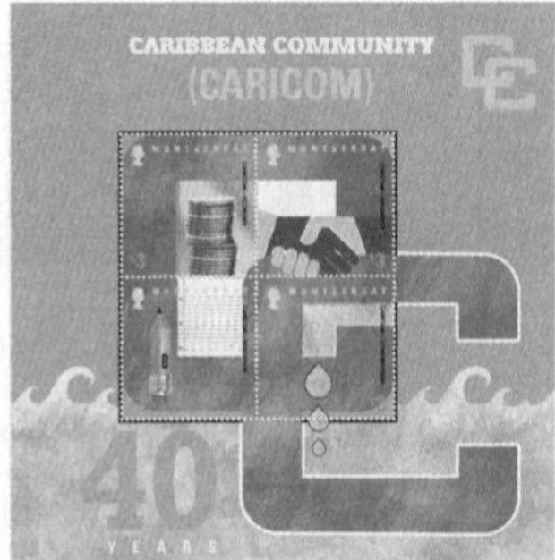

Caribbean Community, 40th Anniv. — A266

No. 1323: a, Economy. b, Diplomacy. c, Education. d, Conservation.

$7, 40th anniv. emblem.

2013, July 31

1323 A266 $3 Sheet of 4, #a-d 9.00 9.00

Souvenir Sheet

1324 A266 $7 multi 5.25 5.25

Flowers — A267

No. 1325: a, $2.75, Black pirate. b, $2.75, Cape blue water lily. c, $3, Angel's trumpet. d, $3, Emerald vine.

$7, Moon vine.

2013, Aug. 27 **Litho.** *Perf. 12½*

1325 A267 Sheet of 4, #a-d 8.50 8.50

Souvenir Sheet

1326 A267 $7 multi 5.25 5.25

Thailand 2013 World Stamp Exhibition, Bangkok — A268

No. 1326: a, $2.75, Coconut trees. b, $2.75, Sanphet Prasat Palace. c, $3, Buddha statues. d, $3, Erawan Waterfall.

$7, Elephant and riders.

2013, Sept. 2 **Litho.** *Perf. 13¾*

1327 A268 Sheet of 4, #a-d 8.50 8.50

Souvenir Sheet

1328 A268 $7 multi 5.25 5.25

Birth of Prince George of Cambridge — A269

No. 1329 — Prince George and: a, Duchess of Cambridge. b, Duke and Duchess of Cambridge.

$7, Prince George and Duke of Cambridge.

2013, Sept. 22 **Litho.** *Perf. 14*

1329 A269 $2.75 Pair, #a-b 4.25 4.25

Souvenir Sheet

1330 A269 $7 multi 5.25 5.25

No. 1329 was printed in sheets containing 2 each of Nos. 1329a and 1329b.

Kittens — A270

No. 1331: a, Bicolor tabby. b, Brown-and-white mackerel tabby. c, Calico. d, Gray-and-white mackerel tabby.

$7, Mackerel tabby, diff.

2013, Nov. 7 **Litho.** *Perf. 13¾*

1331 A270 $3 Sheet of 4, #a-d 9.00 9.00

Souvenir Sheet

1332 A270 $7 multi 5.25 5.25

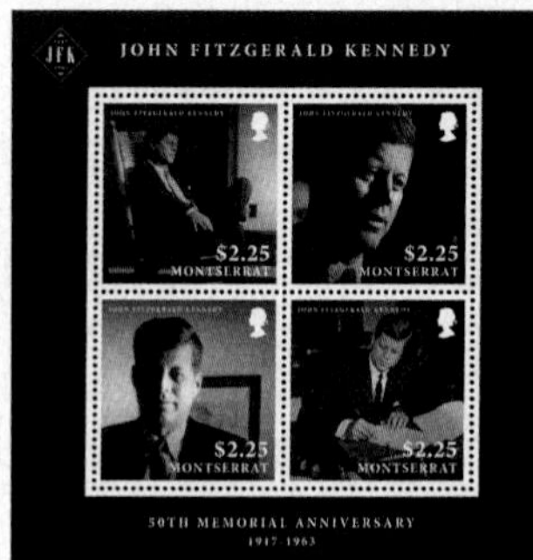

Pres. John F. Kennedy (1917-63) — A271

No. 1333 — Pres. Kennedy: a, Sitting in rocking chair. b, Facing right. c, Facing forward, picture frame in background. d, Signing paper.

$7, Pres. Kennedy at microphone.

2013, Nov. 22 **Litho.** *Perf. 13¾*

1333 A271 $2.25 Sheet of 4, #a-d 6.75 6.75

Souvenir Sheet

1334 A271 $7 multi 5.25 5.25

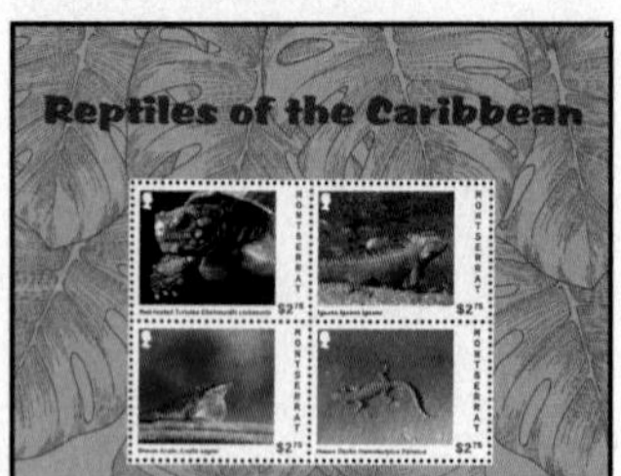

Reptiles — A272

No. 1335: a, Red-footed tortoise. b, Iguana. c, Brown anole. d, House gecko.

$7, Blue-headed anole.

2013, Dec. 23 **Litho.** *Perf. 12*

1335 A272 $2.75 Sheet of 4, #a-d 8.25 8.25

Souvenir Sheet

1336 A272 $7 multi 5.25 5.25

War Memorial, Plymouth — A273

Montserrat Coat of Arms — A274

2014, Feb. 7 Litho. *Perf. 12*

1337 A273 $50 multi 37.50 37.50
1338 A274 $100 multi 75.00 75.00

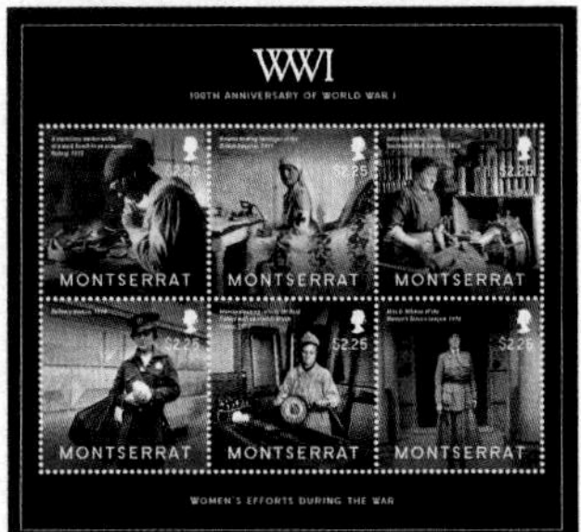

World War I, Cent. — A275

No. 1339: a, Female munitions worker welding, 1915. b, Nurse ironing bandages, 1915. c, Woman at Southwark Hall Army Recruiting Office, London, 1915. d, Delivery woman, 1914. e, Woman cleaning railway car door, 1914. f, Miss D. Milman of the Women's Sevice League, 1918.
$7, French Red Cross poster, 1915, vert.

2014, Feb. 26 Litho. *Perf. 13¾*

1339 A275 $2.25 Sheet of 6, #a-f 10.00 10.00

Souvenir Sheet

Perf. 12¾x12½

1340 A275 $7 multi 5.25 5.25

No. 1340 contains one 38x51mm stamp.

Hummingbirds — A276

No. 1341: a, Bronze-tailed plumeleteer. b, White-bellied mountaingem. c, Olivaceous thornbill. d, White-bellied emerald.
No. 1342: a, Chestnut-breasted coronet. b, Collared Inca.

2014, Apr. 22 Litho. *Perf. 13¾*

1341 A276 $3 Sheet of 4, #a-d 9.00 9.00

Souvenir Sheet

1342 A276 $3.50 Sheet of 2, #a-b 5.25 5.25

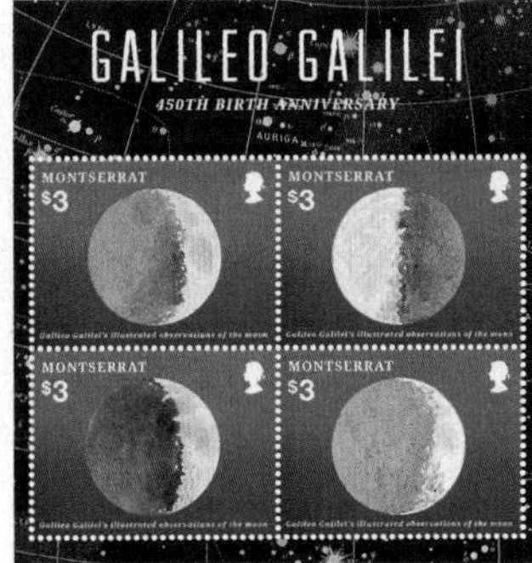

Astronomy — A277

No. 1343 — Various illustrations of Moon by Galileo Galilei, as shown.
$7, Galileo Galilei (1564-1642), astronomer.

2014, June 5 Litho. *Perf. 14*

1343 A277 $3 Sheet of 4, #a-d 9.00 9.00

Souvenir Sheet

1344 A277 $7 multi 5.25 5.25

Vegetables — A278

No. 1345: a, Lettuce. b, Corn. c, Eggplants. d, Sweet potatoes.
No. 1346: a, Cauliflower. b, Carrots.

2014, June 24 Litho. *Perf. 13¾*

1345 A278 $3 Sheet of 4, #a-d 9.00 9.00

Souvenir Sheet

1346 A278 $3.50 Sheet of 2, #a-b 5.25 5.25

Paintings — A279

No. 1347: a, Still Life Vase with Twelve Sunflowers, by Vincent van Gogh. b, Young Woman in the Garden, by Henri Lebasque. c, Dancer Arranging Her Hair, by Edgar Degas. d, The Fruit Seller, by Frederick Childe Hassam.
$7, At the Market, by Félix Vallotton.

2014, Aug. 6 Litho. *Perf. 12½*

1347 A279 $3.50 Sheet of 4, #a-d 10.50 10.50

Souvenir Sheet

1348 A279 $7 multi 5.25 5.25

Dogs — A280

No. 1349: a, Siberian husky. b, French bulldog. c, Chihuahua. d, Basset hound.
$7, Dalmatian.

2014, Aug. 27 Litho. *Perf. 12*

1349 A280 $3 Sheet of 4, #a-d 9.00 9.00

Souvenir Sheet

1350 A280 $7 multi 5.25 5.25

Sports — A281

No. 1351: a, Hurdling. b, Relay race. c, Shot put. d, Soccer.
$7, Cricket.

2014, Oct. 13 Litho. *Perf. 12½x12*

1351 A281 $3.50 Sheet of 4, #a-d 10.50 10.50

Souvenir Sheet

1352 A281 $7 multi 5.25 5.25

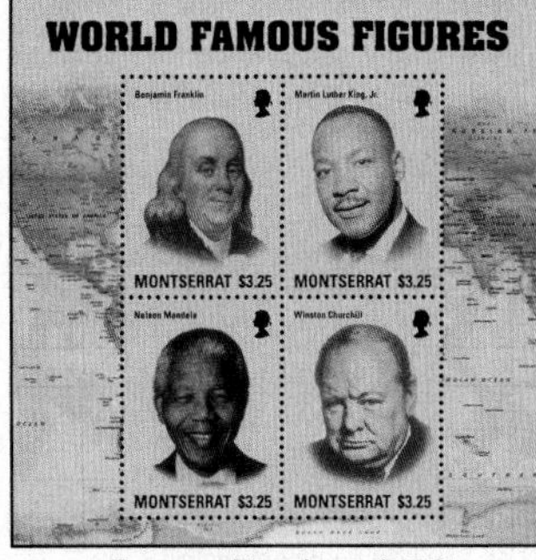

Famous People — A282

No. 1353: a, Benjamin Franklin. b, Dr. Martin Luther King, Jr. c, Nelson Mandela. d, Sir Winston Churchill.
$7, Mahatma Gandhi.

2014, Dec. 4 Litho. *Perf. 12x12½*

1353 A282 $3.25 Sheet of 4, #a-d 9.75 9.75

Souvenir Sheet

Perf. 13½

1354 A282 $7 multi 5.25 5.25

No. 1354 contains one 38x51mm stamp.

Tropical Fish — A283

No. 1355: a, Blue-girdled angelfish. b, Foxface rabbitfish. c, Powder blue tang. d, Clown triggerfish.
$7, Sixspine butterflyfish.

2014, Dec. 22 Litho. *Perf. 12½x12*

1355 A283 $3.25 Sheet of 4, #a-d 9.75 9.75

Souvenir Sheet

1356 A283 $7 multi 5.25 5.25

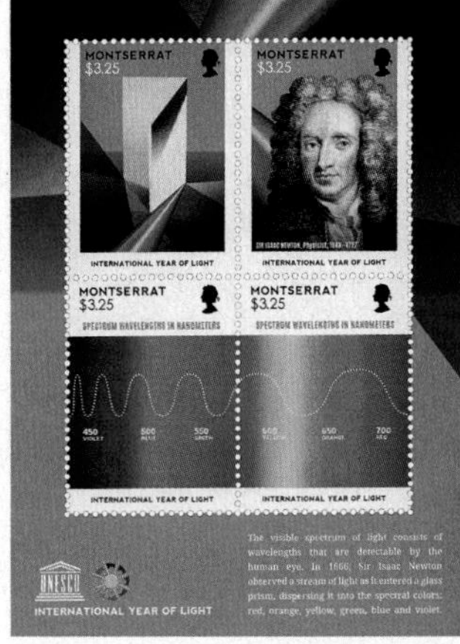

International Year of Light — A284

No. 1357: a, Prism and spectrum. b, Sir Isaac Newton (1643-1727), physicist. c, Wavelengths of violet, blue and green light. d, Wavelengths of yellow, orange and red light.
$7, Wavelengths of ultraviolet and infrared light.

2015, Jan. 29 Litho. *Perf. 12x12½*

1357 A284 $3.25 Sheet of 4, #a-d 9.75 9.75

Souvenir Sheet

Perf. 13½

1358 A284 $7 multi 5.25 5.25

No. 1358 contains one 38x51mm stamp.

Leatherback Sea Turtle — A285

No. 1359: a, Turtle in sea. b, Head of hatchling. c, Turtle heading to sea. d, Turtle returning to beach.
$7, Hatchling heading to sea.

2015, Mar. 24 Litho. *Perf. 13¾*

1359 A285 $3.25 Sheet of 4, #a-d 9.75 9.75

Souvenir Sheet

1360 A285 $7 multi 5.25 5.25

Great Britain No. O1 and Street Scene — A286

Design: $7, Great Britain No. O1.

2015, May 15 Litho. *Perf. 14*

1361 A286 $3.25 multi 2.40 2.40

Souvenir Sheet

Perf. 12

1362 A286 $7 multi 5.25 5.25

Penny Black (not shown on Nos. 1361-1362), 175th anniv. No. 1361 was printed in sheets of 4.

Seahorses — A287

No. 1363: a, Two Longsnout seahorses. b, Lined seahorse and sea grass. c, Lined seahorse. d, Two longsnout seahorses, coral in background.
$7, Dwarf seahorse.

2015, May 28 Litho. *Perf. 13¾*

1363 A287 $3.25 Sheet of 4, #a-d 9.75 9.75

Souvenir Sheet

Perf. 14x13¾

1364 A287 $7 multi 5.25 5.25

Roses — A288

No. 1365 — Color of rose: a, Yellow. b, Red. c, Pink. d, Pale pink.
$7, Two roses, horiz.

2015, July 20 Litho. *Perf. 14*

1365 A288 $3.25 Sheet of 4, #a-d 9.75 9.75

Souvenir Sheet

Perf. 12½

1366 A288 $7 multi 5.25 5.25

No. 1366 contains one 51x38mm stamp.

Photographs of Earth from Space — A289

No. 1367: a, Wildfires in central Chile. b, Kavir Desert, Iran. c, Central Saudi Arabia. d, Cancún, Mexico.
$7, Montserrat.

2015, Sept. 15 Litho. *Perf. 12*

1367 A289 $3.25 Sheet of 4, #a-d 9.75 9.75

Souvenir Sheet

1368 A289 $7 multi 5.25 5.25

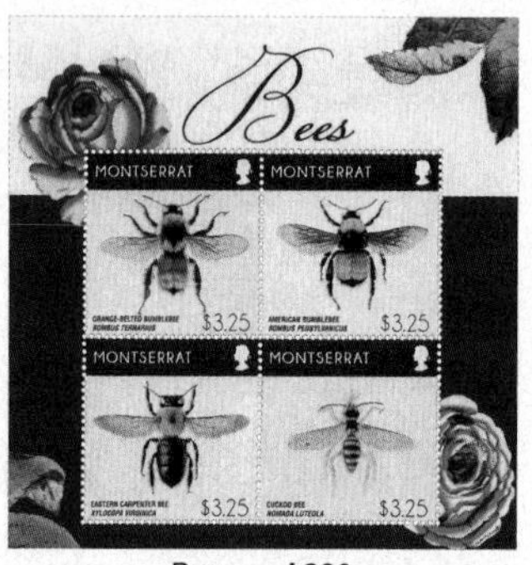

Bees — A290

No. 1369: a, Orange-belted bumblebee. b, American bumblebee. c, Eastern carpenter bee. d, Cuckoo bee.
$7, Common eastern bumblebee.

2015, Sept. 30 Litho. *Perf. 13¾*

1369 A290 $3.25 Sheet of 4, #a-d 9.75 9.75

Souvenir Sheet

1370 A290 $7 multi 5.25 5.25

Self-Portraits — A291

No. 1371: a, Jan Van Eyck, 1433. b, Peter Paul Rubens, 1623. c, William Hind, 1862-63. d, Georges Daniel de Monfreid, 1905.
$7, Paul Gauguin, 1885.

2015, Nov. 11 Litho. *Perf. 12x12½*

1371 A291 $3.25 Sheet of 4, #a-d 9.75 9.75

Souvenir Sheet

1372 A291 $7 multi 5.25 5.25

Beetles — A292

No. 1373: a, Goliathus giganteus. b, Dynastes tityus. c, Lucanus laminifer. d, Penthea pardalis.
$7, Chalcosoma atlas.

2015, Nov. 30 Litho. *Perf. 12½*

1373 A292 $3.25 Sheet of 4, #a-d 9.75 9.75

Souvenir Sheet

1374 A292 $7 multi 5.25 5.25

British Royal Family — A293

No. 1375 — Queen Elizabeth II: a, Wearing black gloves, no horse. b, Holding flowers. c, Wearing black gloves, with horse. d, Wearing purple coat, with horse.
$7, Prince George and Princess Charlotte.

2016, Jan. 22 Litho. *Perf. 14*

1375 A293 $3.25 Sheet of 4, #a-d 9.75 9.75

Souvenir Sheet

Perf. 12½

1376 A293 $7 multi 5.25 5.25

No. 1376 contains one 38x51mm stamp.

Birds — A294

No. 1377: a, Brown trembler. b, Black swift. c, Willet. d, Brown noddy.
$7, Montserrat oriole.

2016, Mar. 8 Litho. *Perf. 12½*

1377 A294 $3.25 Sheet of 4, #a-d 9.75 9.75

Souvenir Sheet

1378 A294 $7 multi 5.25 5.25

Cricket — A295

No. 1379: a, Ball. b, Glove. c, Bat and wickets. d, Helmet.
$7, Ball, vert.

2016, Mar. 17 Litho. *Perf. 13¾*

1379 A295 $3.25 Sheet of 4, #a-d 9.75 9.75

Souvenir Sheet

Perf. 12½

1380 A295 $7 multi 5.25 5.25

No. 1380 contains one 38x51mm stamp.

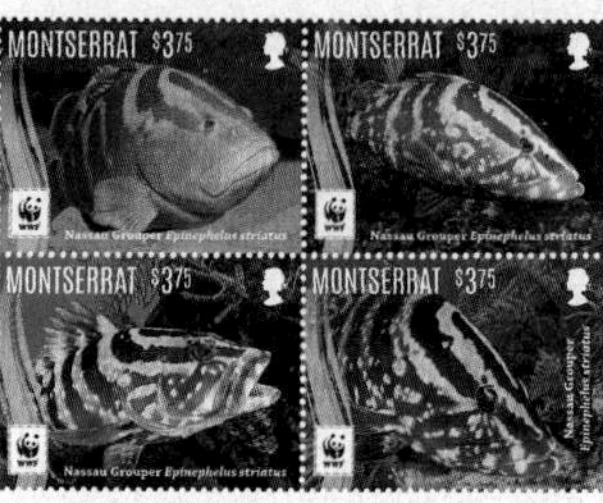

Worldwide Fund for Nature (WWF) — A296

Various depictions of Nassau grouper, as shown.

2016, May 30 Litho. *Perf. 14*

1381 A296 $3.75 Block of 4, #a-d 11.00 11.00

e. Miniature sheet of 8, 2 each #1381a-1381d 22.00 22.00

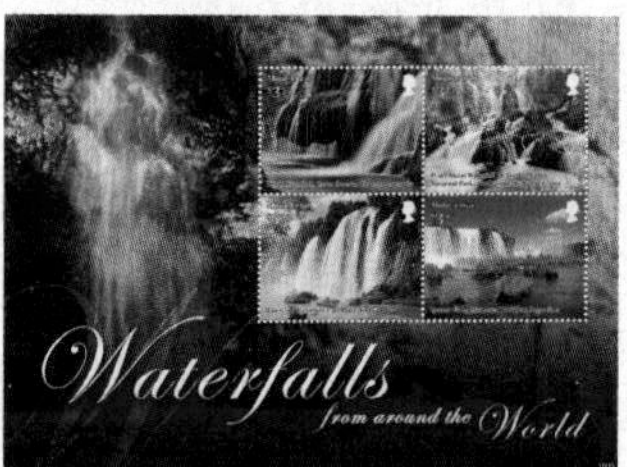

Waterfalls — A297

No. 1382: a, Bigar Waterfall, Romania. b, Pearl Shoal Waterfall, People's Republic of China. c, Ban Gioc Waterfall, Viet Nam. d, Iguazu Falls, Argentina.
$10, Great Alps Waterfall, Montserrat, vert.

2016, June 8 Litho. *Perf. 14*

1382 A297 $3.25 Sheet of 4, #a-d 9.75 9.75

Souvenir Sheet

Perf. 12½

1383 A297 $10 multi 7.50 7.50

No. 1383 contains one 38x51mm stamp.

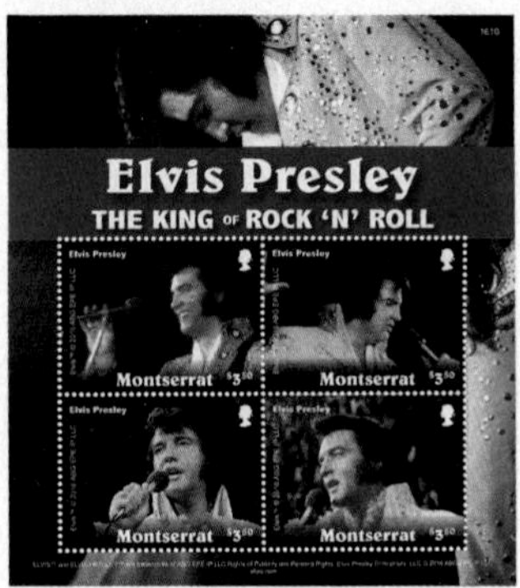

Elvis Presley (1935-77) — A298

No. 1384: Various photographs of Presley, as shown
$10, Presley on knee, spreading cape with arms.

2016, July 27 Litho. *Perf. 14*

1384 A298 $3.50 Sheet of 4, #a-d 10.50 10.50

Souvenir Sheet

Perf. 12½

1385 A298 $10 multi 7.50 7.50

No. 1385 contains one 51x38mm stamp.

Sea Turtles — A299

No. 1386: a, Green sea turtle. b, Loggerhead sea turtle. c, Olive ridley sea turtle. d, Kemp's ridley sea turtle.
$7, Hawksbill sea turtle, horiz.

2016, Sept. 23 Litho. *Perf. 13¾*

1386 A299 $3.50 Sheet of 4, #a-d 10.50 10.50

Souvenir Sheet

Perf. 12½

1387 A299 $7 multi 5.25 5.25

No. 1387 contains one 51x38mm stamp.

Transportation — A300

No. 1388: a, Ferry. b, Prison van. c, State automobile. d, Police motorcycle.
$7, Airplane.

2016, Nov. 16 Litho. *Perf. 14*

1388 A300 $3.50 Sheet of 4, #a-d 10.50 10.50

Souvenir Sheet

Perf. 12½

1389 A300 $7 multi 5.25 5.25

No. 1389 contains one 51x38mm stamp.

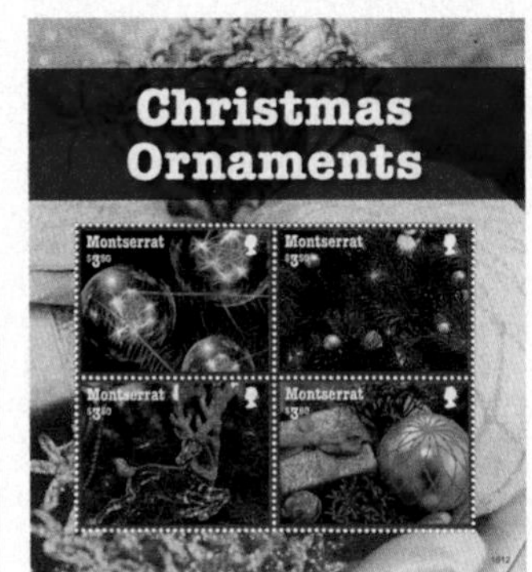

Christmas — A301

No. 1390: a, Three round silver ornaments. b, Small ornaments on Christmas tree. c, Reindeer. d, Gold ornaments.
$7, Ornament with snowflake.

2016, Nov. 29 Litho. *Perf. 14*

1390 A301 $3.50 Sheet of 4, #a-d 10.50 10.50

Souvenir Sheet

Perf. 12½

1391 A301 $7 multi 5.25 5.25

No. 1391 contains one 51x38mm stamp.

SEMI-POSTAL STAMPS

Catalogue values for unused stamps in this section are for Never Hinged items.

Nos. 719-720 Surcharged

1989, Oct. 20 Litho. *Perf. 13½x14*

B1 A110 $1.50 +$2.50 multi 3.00 3.00
B2 A110 $3.50 +$2.50 multi 4.50 4.50

Surcharge for hurricane relief.

No. 642 Surcharged

1995, Dec. 29 Litho. *Perf. 15*

B3 A97 $2.30 +$5 multi 9.00 9.00

Surcharge for volcano relief.

WAR TAX STAMPS

No. 43 Overprinted in Red or Black

1917-18 Wmk. 3 *Perf. 14*

MR1 A6 ½p green (R) .25 *1.75*
MR2 A6 ½p green ('18) .25 *2.00*

Type of Regular Issue of 1919 Overprinted

1918

MR3 A6 1½p orange & black .30 *.35*

Denomination on No. MR3 in black on white ground. Two dots under "d."

OFFICIAL STAMPS

Nos. O1-O44 used on Post Office and Philatelic Bureau mail. Not sold to public, used or unused.

Nos. 235-236, 338-339 Overprinted

Perf. 12½x14

1976, Apr. 12 Photo. Wmk. 314

O1 A22 5c multicolored 1.90
O2 A22 10c multicolored 2.50
O3 A22 30c on 10c multi 5.00
O4 A22 45c on 3c multi 6.00
Nos. O1-O4 (4) 15.40

Nos. 243-243A also received this overprint.

Nos. 343-347, 349-351, 353-354 Overprinted

Perf. 13½x14

1976, Oct. 1 Litho. Wmk. 373

O10 A44 5c multicolored .25
O11 A44 10c multicolored .25
O12 A44 15c multicolored .25
O13 A44 20c multicolored .25
O14 A44 25c multicolored .25
O15 A44 55c multicolored .40
O16 A44 70c multicolored .50
O17 A44 $1 multicolored .70
O18 A44 $5 multicolored 3.50
O19 A44 $10 multicolored 7.00
Nos. O10-O19 (10) 13.35

Nos. 343-347, 349-351, 353-354 Overprinted

1980, Sept. 30 *Perf. 14*

O20 A44 5c multicolored .25
O21 A44 10c multicolored .25
O22 A44 15c multicolored .25
O23 A44 20c multicolored .25
O24 A44 25c multicolored .25
O25 A44 55c multicolored .35
O26 A44 70c multicolored .45
O27 A44 $1 multicolored .65
O28 A44 $5 multicolored 3.00
O29 A44 $10 multicolored 6.00
Nos. O20-O29 (10) 11.70

Nos. 341-351, 353-354 Overprinted or Surcharged

1980, Sept. 30 Litho. *Perf. 14*

O30 A44 5c multicolored .25
O31 A44 5c on 3c multi .25
O32 A44 10c multicolored .25
O33 A44 15c multicolored .25
O34 A44 20c multicolored .25
O35 A44 25c multicolored .25
O36 A44 30c on 15c multi .25
O37 A44 35c on 2c multi .40
O38 A44 40c multicolored .30
O39 A44 55c multicolored .45
O40 A44 70c multicolored .60
O41 A44 $1 multicolored .80
O42 A44 $2.50 on 40c multi 2.00
O43 A44 $5 multicolored 4.00
O44 A44 $10 multicolored 8.00
Nos. O30-O44 (15) 18.30

Catalogue values for unused stamps in this section, from this point to the end of the section, are for Never Hinged items.

Fish Issue of 1981 Nos. 445-449, 451, 453, 455, 457-458, 460 Overprinted

1981, Mar. 20 Litho. *Perf. 13½*

O45 A64 5c multicolored .25 .25
O46 A64 10c multicolored .25 .25
O47 A64 15c multicolored .25 .25
O48 A64 20c multicolored .25 .25
O49 A64 25c multicolored .25 .25
O50 A64 45c multicolored .35 .35
O51 A64 65c multicolored .50 .50
O52 A64 $1 multicolored .75 .75
O53 A64 $3 multicolored 2.25 2.25
O54 A64 $5 multicolored 3.75 3.75
O55 A64 $10 multicolored 7.50 7.50
Nos. O45-O55 (11) 16.35 16.35

Nos. 465-470 Surcharged

1982, Nov. 17 Litho. *Perf. 14*

O56 A66 45c on 90c (#465) .40 .40
O57 A67 45c on 90c (#466) .40 .40
O58 A66 75c on $3 (#467) .70 .70
O59 A67 75c on $3 (#468) .70 .70
O60 A66 $1 on $4 (#469) .90 .90
O61 A67 $1 on $4 (#470) .90 .90
Nos. O56-O61 (6) 4.00 4.00

Princess Diana Issue, Nos. 484-486 Overprinted or Surcharged

1983, Oct. 19 Litho. *Perf. 14*

O62	A70b	70c on 75c (#484)	1.50	1.50
O63	A70b	$1 (#485)	1.90	1.90
O64	A70b	$1.50 on $5 (#486)	2.50	2.50
		Nos. O62-O64 (3)	5.90	5.90

Nos. 524-536, 538 Overprinted

1985, Apr. 12 Wmk. 380 *Perf. 14*

O65	A79	5c multicolored	.50	.25
O66	A79	10c multicolored	.50	.25
O67	A79	15c multicolored	.50	.25
O68	A79	20c multicolored	.50	.25
O69	A79	25c multicolored	.50	.25
O70	A79	40c multicolored	.80	.40
O71	A79	55c multicolored	.90	.45
O72	A79	70c multicolored	1.25	.65
O73	A79	90c multicolored	1.60	.80
O74	A79	$1 multicolored	1.90	.90
O75	A79	$1.15 multicolored	2.00	1.00
O76	A79	$3 multicolored	5.25	2.50
O77	A79	$5 multicolored	9.25	4.75
O78	A79	$10 multicolored	17.50	9.00
		Nos. O65-O78 (14)	42.95	21.70

Nos. 681-694 and 696 Overprinted

Unwmk.

1989, May 9 Litho. *Perf. 14*

O79	A104	5c multicolored	.25	.25
O80	A104	10c multicolored	.25	.25
O81	A104	15c multicolored	.25	.25
O82	A104	20c multicolored	.25	.25
O83	A104	25c multicolored	.25	.25
O84	A104	40c multicolored	.40	.40
O85	A104	55c multicolored	.60	.55
O86	A104	70c multicolored	.75	.70
O87	A104	90c multicolored	.95	.90
O88	A104	$1 multicolored	1.00	.95
O89	A104	$1.15 multicolored	1.25	1.25
O90	A104	$1.50 multicolored	1.60	1.40
O91	A104	$3 multicolored	3.00	2.75
O92	A104	$5 multicolored	5.25	4.75
O94	A104	$10 multicolored	10.50	9.50
		Nos. O79-O94 (15)	26.55	24.40

Nos. 446, 454a and 456 Surcharged

1989 Wmk. 373 *Perf. 13½*

O95	A64	70c on 10c multi	1.75	1.75
O96	A64	$1.15 on 75c multi	3.25	3.25
O97	A64	$1.50 on $2 multi	4.00	4.00
		Nos. O95-O97 (3)	9.00	9.00

Nos. 758-761, 763-766, 776-779 Surcharged or Overprinted "OHMS"

1992 Litho. *Perf. 14*

O98	A118	70c on 90c #758	1.50	1.50
O99	A118	70c on $3.50 #761	1.50	1.50
O100	A119	70c on 90c #763	1.50	1.50
O101	A121	70c on 90c #776	1.50	1.50
O102	A119	$1 on $3.50 #766	2.00	2.00
O103	A121	$1 on $3.50 #779	2.00	2.00
O104	A118	$1.15 on #759	2.25	2.25
O105	A119	$1.15 on #764	2.25	2.25
O106	A121	$1.15 on #777	2.25	2.25
O107	A118	$1.50 on #760	3.00	3.00
O108	A119	$1.50 on #765	3.00	3.00
O109	A121	$1.50 on #778	3.00	3.00
		Nos. O98-O109 (12)	25.75	25.75

Nos. 803-816, 818 Ovptd. "OHMS" in Red

1993, Apr. 14 Litho. *Perf. 15x14*

O110	A128	5c multicolored	.30	.30
O111	A128	10c multicolored	.30	.30
O112	A128	15c multicolored	.30	.30
O113	A128	20c multicolored	.30	.30
O114	A128	25c multicolored	.30	.30
O115	A128	40c multicolored	.50	.50
O116	A128	55c multicolored	.75	.75
O117	A128	70c multicolored	.85	.85
O118	A128	90c multicolored	1.05	1.05
O119	A128	$1 multicolored	1.20	1.20
O120	A128	$1.15 multicolored	1.40	1.40
O121	A128	$1.50 multicolored	1.75	1.75
O122	A128	$3 multicolored	3.75	3.75
O123	A128	$5 multicolored	6.00	6.00
O125	A128	$10 multicolored	12.00	12.00
		Nos. O110-O125 (15)	30.75	30.75

A number has been reserved for an additional value in this set.

Nos. 896-909, 911 Ovptd. "O.H.M.S." In Red

1997 Litho. *Perf. 14*

O126	A147	5c multicolored	.25	.25
O127	A147	10c multicolored	.25	.25
O128	A147	15c multicolored	.25	.25
O129	A147	20c multicolored	.25	.25
O130	A147	25c multicolored	.25	.25
O131	A147	40c multicolored	.40	.40
O132	A147	55c multicolored	.50	.50
O133	A147	70c multicolored	.70	.70
O134	A147	90c multicolored	.90	.90
O135	A147	$1 multicolored	.95	.95
O136	A147	$1.15 multicolored	1.10	1.10
O137	A147	$1.50 multicolored	1.40	1.40
O138	A147	$3 multicolored	3.00	3.00
O139	A147	$5 multicolored	4.75	4.75
O140	A147	$10 multicolored	9.75	9.75
		Nos. O126-O140 (15)	24.70	24.70

Nos. 1041-1054, 1056 Overprinted

Perf. 13½x13¼

2002, June 14 Litho.

O141	A176	5c multi	.30	.30
O142	A176	10c multi	.30	.30
O143	A176	15c multi	.30	.30
O144	A176	20c multi	.30	.30
O145	A176	25c multi	.30	.30
O146	A176	40c multi	.35	.35
O147	A176	55c multi	.45	.45
O148	A176	70c multi	.90	.90
O149	A176	90c multi	1.20	1.20
O150	A176	$1 multi	1.40	1.40
O151	A176	$1.15 multi	1.75	1.75
O152	A176	$1.50 multi	2.25	2.25
O153	A176	$3 multi	4.75	4.75
O154	A176	$5 multi	7.50	7.50
O155	A176	$10 multi	15.00	15.00
		Nos. O141-O155 (15)	37.05	37.05

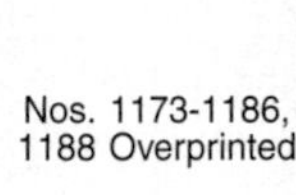

Nos. 1173-1186, 1188 Overprinted

2007, May 14 Litho. *Perf. 12½*

O156	A213	10c multi	.25	.25
O157	A213	30c multi	.25	.25
O158	A213	35c multi	.25	.25
O159	A213	50c multi	.40	.40
O160	A213	70c multi	.55	.55
O161	A213	80c multi	.60	.60
O162	A213	90c multi	.70	.70
O163	A213	$1 multi	.75	.75
O164	A213	$1.10 multi	.85	.85
O165	A213	$1.50 multi	1.10	1.10
O166	A213	$2.25 multi	1.75	1.75
O167	A213	$2.50 multi	1.90	1.90
O168	A213	$2.75 multi	2.10	2.10
O169	A213	$5 multi	3.75	3.75
O170	A213	$20 multi	15.00	15.00
		Nos. O156-O170 (15)	30.20	30.20

Size and location of overprint varies.

MOROCCO

mə-ˈrä-ˌkō

LOCATION — Northwest coast of Africa
GOVT. — Kingdom
AREA — 171,953 sq. mi.
POP. — 29,661,636 (1999 est.)
CAPITAL — Rabat

A powerful kingdom from the 8th century, during the Middle Ages, Morocco ruled large areas of northwest Africa and Spain. By the turn of the 20th century, it had contracted to roughly its present borders and was the focus of an intense rivalry between France and Germany, who actively competed for control of the country. In 1912 most of Morocco became a French protectorate, with Spain acting as protector of zones in the extreme northern and southern parts of the country. Tangier was designated an international zone, administered by France, Spain, Britain and, later, Italy.

In 1956 the three zones of Morocco, French, Spanish and Tangier, were united to form an independent nation. Nos. 1-24 and C1-C3 were intended for use only in the southern (French currency) zone. Issues of the northern zone (Spanish currency) are listed after Postage Due stamps.

For earlier issues see French Morocco and Spanish Morocco.

400 Moussonats = 1 Rial (1912)
100 Centimes = 1 Franc (1956)
100 Centimes = 1 Dirham (1962)

Catalogue values for all unused stamps in this country are for Never Hinged items, except for Nos. A1-A14.

Aissaouas Mosque, Tangier — A1a

On White Paper
Narrow Margins

1912, May 25 Litho. *Perf. 11*

A1	A1a	1m light gray	8.00	8.00
A2	A1a	2m lilac	9.00	8.00
A3	A1a	5m blue green	12.00	8.00
A4	A1a	10m vermilion	20.00	8.50
A5	A1a	25m blue	29.00	24.00
A6	A1a	50m violet	42.50	35.00
		Nos. A1-A6 (6)	120.50	91.50

On Nos. A1-A12, the 5m and 10m values always have the name of the engraver beneath the design, while the 1m, 25m and 50m always lack name, and the 2m value exists both with and without name.

Aissaouas Mosque, Tangier — A1b

On Lightly Tinted Paper

1913, Feb. Wide Margins

A7	A1b	1m gray	1.75	1.75
A8	A1b	2m brown lilac	1.75	1.75
A9	A1b	5m blue green	2.00	2.00
A10	A1b	10m vermilion	2.00	2.00
A11	A1b	25m blue	4.25	4.25
A12	A1b	50m gray violet	4.25	4.25
		Nos. A7-A12 (6)	16.00	16.00

No. A6 Surcharged

1913, Nov.

A13	A1a	.05 on 50c violet	1,750.	*2,000.*
A14	A1a	.10 on 50c violet	1,750.	*2,000.*

Sultan Mohammed V — A1

1956-57 Unwmk. Engr. *Perf. 13*

1	A1	5fr brt bl & indigo	.30	.25
2	A1	10fr bis brn & choc	.25	.25
3	A1	15fr dp grn & magenta	.35	.25
4	A1	25fr purple ('57)	1.10	.25
5	A1	30fr green ('57)	1.90	.25
6	A1	50fr rose red ('57)	2.75	.25
7	A1	70fr dk brn & brn red ('57)	4.25	.80
		Nos. 1-7 (7)	10.90	2.30

For surcharges see Nos. B1-B5, B8-B9.

Men Reading — A2

Campaign against illiteracy: 15fr, Girls reading. 20fr, Instructor and pupils. 30fr, Old man and child reading. 50fr, Girl pointing out poster.

1956, Nov. 5

8	A2	10fr pur & vio	1.75	1.20
9	A2	15fr car & rose lake	2.25	1.50
10	A2	20fr bl grn & grn	2.60	2.40
11	A2	30fr rose lake & brt red	4.25	2.75
12	A2	50fr dp bl & bl	8.25	5.25
		Nos. 8-12 (5)	19.10	13.10

Sultan Mohammed V — A3

1957, Mar. 2 Photo. *Perf. 13½x13*

13	A3	15fr blue green	1.50	1.10
14	A3	25fr gray olive	2.00	1.10
15	A3	30fr deep rose	4.00	1.90
		Nos. 13-15 (3)	7.50	4.10

Anniversary of independence.

Prince Moulay el Hassan — A4

1957, July 9 *Perf. 13*

16	A4	15fr blue	1.50	1.00
17	A4	25fr green	1.90	1.50
18	A4	30fr car rose	3.00	2.10
		Nos. 16-18 (3)	6.40	4.60

Designation of Prince Moulay el Hassan as heir to the throne.

King Mohammed V — A5

1957, Nov. *Perf. 12½*

No.	Type	Description	Unused	Used
19	A5	15fr blk & brt grn	1.40	.70
20	A5	25fr blk & rose red	1.50	.95
21	A5	30fr blk & vio	2.90	1.25
		Nos. 19-21 (3)	5.80	2.90

Enthronement of Mohammed V, 30th anniv.

Morocco Pavilion, Brussels World's Fair — A6

1958, Apr. 20 **Engr.** *Perf. 13*

No.	Type	Description	Unused	Used
22	A6	15fr brt grnsh bl	.40	.25
23	A6	25fr carmine	.40	.30
24	A6	30fr indigo	.55	.35
		Nos. 22-24 (3)	1.35	.90

World's Fair, Brussels.

UNESCO Building, Paris, and Mohammed V — A7

1958, Nov. 23

No.	Type	Description	Unused	Used
25	A7	15fr green	.40	.25
26	A7	25fr lake	.40	.25
27	A7	30fr blue	.55	.30
		Nos. 25-27 (3)	1.35	.80

UNESCO Headquarters opening, Paris, Nov. 3.

Ben Smin Sanatorium A8

1959, Jan. 18 **Unwmk.** *Perf. 13*

No.	Type	Description	Unused	Used
28	A8	50fr dk brn, car & slate grn	.90	.50

Red Cross-Red Crescent Society.

Mohammed V — A9

1959, Aug. 18 **Engr.** *Perf. 13*

No.	Type	Description	Unused	Used
29	A9	15fr dk car rose	.60	.40
30	A9	25fr brt bl	.85	.55
31	A9	45fr dk grn	1.10	.60
		Nos. 29-31 (3)	2.55	1.55

50th birthday of King Mohammed V.

Princess Lalla Amina — A10

1959, Nov. 17

No.	Type	Description	Unused	Used
32	A10	15fr blue	.40	.25
33	A10	25fr green	.50	.25
34	A10	45fr rose lil	.55	.30
		Nos. 32-34 (3)	1.45	.80

Issued for International Children's Week.

Map of Africa and Symbols of Agriculture, Industry and Commerce — A11

1960, Jan. 31 *Perf. 13*

No.	Type	Description	Unused	Used
35	A11	45fr vio, ocher & emer	1.10	.65

Issued to publicize the meeting of the Economic Commission for Africa, Tangier.

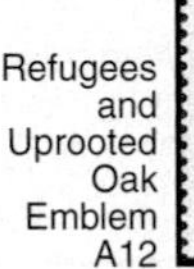

Refugees and Uprooted Oak Emblem A12

45fr, Refugee family and uprooted oak emblem.

1960, Apr. 7 **Unwmk.** *Perf. 13*

No.	Type	Description	Unused	Used
36	A12	15fr ocher, blk & grn	.30	.30
37	A12	45fr blk & grn	.50	.50

World Refugee Year, July 1, 1959-June 30, 1960.

Marrakesh A13

1960, Apr. 25 **Engr.** *Perf. 13*

No.	Type	Description	Unused	Used
38	A13	100fr grn, bl & red brn	1.40	.90

900th anniversary of Marrakesh.

Lamp — A14

Designs: 25fr, Fountain and arched door. 30fr, Minaret. 35fr, Ornamented wall. 45fr, Moorish architecture.

1960, May 12 *Perf. 13½*

No.	Type	Description	Unused	Used
39	A14	15fr rose lil	.50	.50
40	A14	25fr dk bl	.55	.55
41	A14	30fr org red	1.25	.65
42	A14	35fr black	1.40	1.10
43	A14	45fr yel grn	2.00	1.50
		Nos. 39-43 (5)	5.70	4.30

1,100th anniv. of Karaouiyne University, Fez.

Arab League Center, Cairo and Mohammed V — A15

1960, June 28 **Photo.** *Perf. 12½*

No.	Type	Description	Unused	Used
44	A15	15fr grn & blk	.60	.25

Opening of the Arab League Center and the Arab Postal Museum, Cairo.

Wrestlers — A16

Sports: 10fr, Gymnast. 15fr, Bicyclist. 20fr, Weight lifter. 30fr, Runner. 40fr, Boxers. 45fr, Sailboat. 70fr, Fencers.

1960, Sept. 26 **Engr.** *Perf. 13*

No.	Type	Description	Unused	Used
45	A16	5fr ol, vio bl & plum	.25	.25
46	A16	10fr org brn, bl & brn	.25	.25
47	A16	15fr emer, bl & org brn	.30	.25
48	A16	20fr ultra, ol & brn	.35	.25
49	A16	30fr vio bl, mar & sep	.40	.25
50	A16	40fr grnsh bl, dk pur & red brn	.65	.25
51	A16	45fr grn, plum & ultra	.80	.30
52	A16	70fr dk brn, bl & gray	1.10	.40
		Nos. 45-52 (8)	4.10	2.20

17th Olympic Games, Rome, 8/25-9/11.

Runner A17

1961, Aug. 30 **Unwmk.** *Perf. 13*

No.	Type	Description	Unused	Used
53	A17	20fr dk grn	.25	.25
54	A17	30fr dk car rose	.50	.25
55	A17	50fr brt bl	.65	.40
		Nos. 53-55 (3)	1.40	.90

3rd Pan-Arabic Games, Casablanca.

Post Office, Tangier — A18

View of Tangier and Gibraltar A19

Design: 30fr, Telephone operator.

1961, Dec. 8 **Litho.** *Perf. 12½*

No.	Type	Description	Unused	Used
56	A18	20fr red vio	.40	.25
57	A18	30fr green	.55	.25
57A	A19	90fr lt bl & vio bl	1.00	.50
		Nos. 56-57A (3)	1.95	1.00

Conference of the African Postal and Telecommunications Union, Tangier.

Mohammed V and Map of Africa — A20

1962, Jan. 4 **Unwmk.** *Perf. 11½*

No.	Type	Description	Unused	Used
58	A20	20c buff & vio brn	.30	.25
59	A20	30c lt & dk bl	.45	.25

1st anniv. of the conference of African heads of state at Casablanca.

Patrice Lumumba and Map of Congo — A21

1962, Feb. 12 *Perf. 12½*

No.	Type	Description	Unused	Used
60	A21	20c bis & blk	.30	.25
61	A21	30c dl red brn & blk	.45	.25

1st death anniv. of Patrice Lumumba, Premier of Congo Democratic Republic.

Moroccan Students — A22

1962, Mar. 5 **Engr.**

No.	Type	Description	Unused	Used
62	A22	20fr multi	.55	.30
63	A22	30fr multi	.55	.40
64	A22	90fr gray grn, indigo & brn	.90	.70
		Nos. 62-64 (3)	2.00	1.40

Issued to honor the nation's students.

Arab League Building, Cairo — A23

1962, Mar. 22 **Photo.** *Perf. 13½x13*

No.	Type	Description	Unused	Used
65	A23	20c red brn	.55	.25

Arab Propaganda Week, 3/22-28. See #146.

Malaria Eradication Emblem and Swamp A24

50c, Dagger stabbing mosquito, vert.

1962, Sept. 3 **Engr.** *Perf. 13*

No.	Type	Description	Unused	Used
66	A24	20c dk grn & grnsh blk	.35	.25
67	A24	50c dk grn & mag	.50	.30

WHO drive to eradicate malaria.

Fish and Aquarium — A25

1962, Nov. 5 **Unwmk.** *Perf. 13*

No.	Type	Description	Unused	Used
68	A25	20c shown	.60	.25
69	A25	30c Moray eel	.75	.25

Casablanca Aquarium.

Courier and Sherifian Stamp of 1912
A26

Designs: 30c, Courier on foot and round Sherifian cancellation. 50c, Sultan Hassan I and octagonal cancellation.

1962, Dec. 15 **Unwmk.**

70	A26 20c Prus grn & redsh brn	.75	.25
71	A26 30c dk car rose & blk	.75	.40
72	A26 50c bl & bister	1.10	.50
	Nos. 70-72 (3)	2.60	1.15

Stamp Day; 1st National Stamp Exhibition, Dec. 15-23; 75th anniv. of the Sherifian Post and the 50th anniv. of its reorganization.

Boy Scout — A27

1962, Aug. 8 **Litho.** ***Perf. 11½***

73	A27 20c vio brn & lt bl	.55	.25

5th Arab Boy Scout Jamboree, Rabat.

King Hassan II — A28

1962 **Engr.** ***Perf. 13½x13***

75	A28 1c gray olive	.25	.25
76	A28 2c violet	.25	.25
77	A28 5c black	.25	.25
78	A28 10c brn org	.25	.25
79	A28 15c Prus grn	.25	.25
80	A28 20c purple	.25	.25
81	A28 30c dp yel grn	.30	.25
82	A28 50c vio brn	.60	.25
83	A28 70c deep blue	.90	.25
84	A28 80c magenta	1.50	.25
	Nos. 75-84 (10)	4.80	2.50

"Mazelin" (designer-engraver) reads down on Nos. 75-84. See Nos. 110-114.

King Moulay Ismail — A29

1963, Mar. 3 ***Perf. 12½***

85	A29 20c sepia	.55	.25

Tercentenary of Meknes as Ismaili capital.

Al Idrissi, Geographer
A30

#87, 88A, Ibn Batota, explorer. #88, Ibn Khaldoun, historian and sociologist.

1963-66 **Engr.**

86	A30 20c dk sl grn	.50	.30
87	A30 20c dk car rose	.50	.30
88	A30 20c black	.50	.30
88A	A30 40c dk vio bl ('66)	.60	.30
	Nos. 86-88A (4)	2.10	1.20

Famous medieval men of Morocco (Maghreb). No. 88A also marks the inauguration of the ferryboat "Ibn Batota" connecting Tangier and Malaga.

Issued: #86-88, 5/7/63; #88A, 7/15/66.

Sugar Beet and Sugar Refinery, Sidi Slimane
A31

50c, Tuna fisherman, vert.

1963, June 10 **Unwmk.** ***Perf. 13***

89	A31 20c shown	.45	.25
90	A31 50c multicolored	.80	.35

FAO "Freedom from Hunger" campaign.

Heads of Ramses II, Abu Simbel
A32

Designs: 30c, Isis, Kalabsha Temple, vert. 50c, Temple of Philae.

1963, July 15 **Engr.** ***Perf. 11½***

91	A32 20c black	.30	.30
92	A32 30c vio, *grysh*	.55	.30
93	A32 50c maroon, *buff*	.75	.40
	Nos. 91-93 (3)	1.60	1.00

Campaign to save historic monuments in Nubia.

Agadir Before Earthquake
A33

30c, Like 20c, with "29 Février 1960" and crossed bars added. 50c, Agadir rebuilt.

Engr.; Engr. & Photo. (No. 95)

1963, Oct. 10 ***Perf. 13½x13***

94	A33 20c bl & brn red	.45	.30
95	A33 30c bl, brn red & red	.50	.40
96	A33 50c bl & brn red	1.00	.60
	Nos. 94-96 (3)	1.95	1.30

Issued to publicize the rebuilding of Agadir.

Arms of Morocco and Rabat — A35

Centenary Emblem and Plan of Agadir Hospital
A34

1963, Oct. 28 **Photo.** ***Perf. 12½x13***

97	A34 30c blk, dp car & sil	.55	.25

Centenary of the International Red Cross.

1963, Nov. 18 ***Perf. 13x12½***

98	A35 20c gold, red, blk & emer	.55	.25

Installation of Parliament.

Hands Breaking Chain
A36

1963, Dec. 10 **Engr.** ***Perf. 13***

99	A36 20c dk brn, grn & org	.55	.25

15th anniversary of the Universal Declaration of Human Rights.

Flag — A37

1963, Dec. 25 **Photo.** ***Perf. 13x12½***

100	A37 20c blk, dp car & grn	.60	.25

Evacuation of all foreign military forces from Moroccan territory.

Moulay Abd-er-Rahman, by Delacroix — A38

1964, Mar. 3 **Engr.** ***Perf. 12x13***

101	A38 1d multi	3.00	2.00

Coronation of King Hassan II, 3rd anniv.

Weather Map of Africa and UN Emblem — A39

30c, World map and barometer trace, horiz.

1964, Mar. 23 **Photo.** ***Perf. 11½***

Granite Paper

102	A39 20c multi	.50	.25
103	A39 30c multi	.55	.40

UN 4th World Meteorological Day. See No. C10.

Children on Vacation
A40

30c, Heads of boy and girl, buildings.

1964, July 6 **Litho.** ***Perf. 12½***

104	A40 20c multi	.40	.40
105	A40 30c multi	.50	.50

Issued for vacation camps for children of P.T.T. employees.

Olympic Torch — A41

1964, Sept. 22 **Engr.** ***Perf. 13***

106	A41 20c car lake, dk pur & grn	.35	.25
107	A41 30c bl, dk grn & red brn	.55	.35
108	A41 50c grn, red & brn	.70	.60
	Nos. 106-108 (3)	1.60	1.20

18th Olympic Games, Tokyo, Oct. 10-25.

Cape Spartel Lighthouse, Sultan Mohammed ben Abd-er-Rahman
A42

Perf. 12½x11½

1964, Oct. 15 **Photo.**

109	A42 25c multi	.55	.25

Centenary of the Cape Spartel lighthouse.

King Type of 1962

1964-65 **Engr.** ***Perf. 12½x13***

Size: 17x23mm

110	A28 20c purple (redrawn)	2.00	.30

Perf. 13½x13

Size: 18x22mm

111	A28 25c rose red ('65)	.35	.25
112	A28 35c slate ('65)	.55	.25
113	A28 40c ultra ('65)	.55	.25
114	A28 60c red lilac ('65)	.85	.25
	Nos. 110-114 (5)	4.30	1.30

The Arabic inscription touches the frame on No. 110. "Mazelin" (designer-engraver) reads up on No. 110, down on Nos. 111-114. No. 110 is a coil stamp with red control numbers on the back of some copies.

Iris — A43

40c, Gladiolus segetum. 60c, Capparis spinosa, horiz.

1965 **Photo.** ***Perf. 11½***

Granite Paper

115	A43 25c shown	.85	.50
116	A43 40c multi	1.10	.60
117	A43 60c multi	1.40	1.25
	Nos. 115-117 (3)	3.35	2.35

Printed in sheets of 10. Five tête-bêche pairs in every sheet; vertical stamps arranged 5x2, horizontal stamps 2x5.

See Nos. 129-131.

Mohammed V Arriving by Plane — A44

1965, Mar. 15 **Litho.** ***Perf. 12½***

118	A44 25c lt bl & dk grn	.50	.30

10th anniv. of the return of King Mohammed V from exile and the restoration of the monarchy.

ITU Emblem, Punched-Tape Writer and Telegraph Wires — A45

Design: 40c, ITU emblem, TIROS satellite, radio waves and "ITU" in Morse code.

Perf. 13x14

1965, May 17 Unwmk. Typo.

119 A45 25c multi .50 .25
120 A45 40c lt bl, dp bl & bis .60 .25

ITU, centenary.

ICY Emblem A46

1965, June 14 Engr. *Perf. 13*

121 A46 25c slate grn .30 .25
122 A46 60c dk car rose .50 .25

International Cooperation Year.

Royal Prawn A47

Designs: No. 123, Triton shell. No. 124, Varnish shell (pitaria chione). No. 125, Great voluted shell (cymbium neptuni). No. 126, Helmet crab, vert. 40c, Mantis shrimp, vert.

1965 Photo. *Perf. 11½*
Granite Paper

123 A47 25c vio & multi 1.00 .40
124 A47 25c lt bl & multi 1.00 .40
125 A47 25c org & multi 1.00 .40
126 A47 25c lt grn & multi 1.00 .40
127 A47 40c bl & multi 1.75 .60
128 A47 1d yel & multi 2.50 1.25
Nos. 123-128 (6) 8.25 3.45

Printed in sheets of 10. Nos. 126-127 (5x2); others (2x5). Five tête bêche pairs in every sheet.

Flower Type of 1965

Orchids: 25c, Ophrys speculum. 40c, Ophrys fusca. 60c, Ophrys tenthredinifera (front and side view), horiz.

1965, Dec. 13 Photo. *Perf. 11½*
Granite Paper

129 A43 25c yel & multi .90 .50
130 A43 40c dl rose & multi 1.75 .50
131 A43 60c lt bl & multi 2.25 1.50
Nos. 129-131 (3) 4.90 2.50

Note on tête bêche pairs after No. 117 also applies to Nos. 129-131.

Grain — A48

40c, Various citrus fruit. 60c, Olives, horiz.

1966 Photo. *Perf. 11½*
Granite Paper

133 A48 25c blk & bister .50 .25
136 A48 40c multi .50 .25
137 A48 60c gray & multi .55 .25
Nos. 133-137 (3) 1.55 .75

For surcharge see No. 231.

Flag, Map and Dove A49

1966, Mar. 2 Typo. *Perf. 14x13*

139 A49 25c brt grn & red .50 .25

Tenth anniversary of Independence.

King Hassan II — A50

1966, Mar. 2 Engr. *Perf. 13*

140 A50 25c red, brt grn & indigo .50 .25

Coronation of King Hassan II, 5th anniv.

Cross-country Runner — A51

1966, Mar. 20 Engr. *Perf. 13*

141 A51 25c blue green .50 .25

53rd International Cross-country Race.

WHO Headquarters from West — A52

40c, WHO Headquarters from the East.

1966, May 3 Engr. *Perf. 13*

142 A52 25c rose lil & blk .30 .25
143 A52 40c dp bl & blk .50 .25

Inauguration of the WHO Headquarters, Geneva.

Crown Prince Hassan Kissing Hand of King Mohammed V — A53

25c, King Hassan II and parachutist.

Perf. 12½x12

1966, May 14 Photo. Unwmk.

144 A53 25c gold & blk .40 .25
145 A53 40c gold & blk .55 .30
a. Strip of 2, #144-145 + label 1.10 .75

10th anniv. of the Royal Armed Forces.

Type of 1962 Inscribed: "SEMAINE DE LA PALESTINE"

1966, May 16 *Perf. 11x11½*

146 A23 25c slate blue .50 .25

Issued for Palestine Week.

Train — A54

1966, Dec. 19 Photo. *Perf. 13½*

147 A54 25c shown 1.00 .30
148 A54 40c Ship .95 .40
149 A54 1d Autobus 1.20 .55
Nos. 147-149 (3) 3.15 1.25

Twaite Shad A55

Fish: 40c, Plain bonito. 1d, Bluefish, vert.

1967, Feb. 1 Photo. *Perf. 11½*
Granite Paper

150 A55 25c yel & multi .75 .30
151 A55 40c yel & multi .85 .30
152 A55 1d lt grn & multi 1.90 .90
Nos. 150-152 (3) 3.50 1.50

Printed tête bêche in sheets of 10. Nos. 150-151 (2x5); No. 152 (5x2).

Ait Aadel Dam — A56

1967, Mar. 3 Engr. *Perf. 13*

153 A56 25c sl grn, Prus bl & gray .50 .25
154 A56 40c Prus bl & lt brn .70 .25

Inauguration of Ait Aadel Dam.

Rabat Hilton Hotel, Map of Morocco and Roman Arch — A57

1967, Mar. 3

155 A57 25c brt bl & blk .40 .25
156 A57 1d brt bl & pur .90 .25

Opening of the Rabat Hilton Hotel.

Torch, Globe, Town and Lions Emblem — A58

1967, Apr. 22 Photo. *Perf. 12½*

157 A58 40c gold & saph bl .40 .25
158 A58 1d gold & slate grn 1.10 .25

Lions International, 50th anniversary.

Three Hands Holding Pickax — A59

1967, July 9 Engr. *Perf. 13*

159 A59 25c slate green .50 .25

Community Development Campaign.

Intl. Tourism Year Emblem A60

1967, Aug. 9 Photo. *Perf. 12½*

160 A60 1d lt ultra & dk bl .90 .35

Arrow and Map of Mediterranean A61

1967, Sept. 8 *Perf. 13x12*

161 A61 25c dk bl, ultra, red & tan .50 .25
162 A61 40c blk, bl grn, red & tan .55 .25

Mediterranean Games, Tunis, Sept. 8-17.

Steeplechase — A62

1967, Oct. 14 Photo. *Perf. 12½*

163 A62 40c yel grn, blk & brt rose lilac .50 .25
164 A62 1d lt ultra, blk & brt rose lilac .80 .35

International Horseshow.

Cotton — A63

1967, Nov. 15 Photo. *Perf. 12½*

165 A63 40c lt bl, grn & yel .50 .25

Human Rights Flame — A64

1968, Jan. 10 Engr. *Perf. 13*

166 A64 25c gray .40 .25
167 A64 1d rose claret .50 .25

International Human Rights Year.

King Hassan II — A65

1968-74 Litho. *Perf. 13*

Portrait in Magenta, Brown and Black

Size: 23x30mm

169 A65 1c cream & blk .25 .25
170 A65 2c lt grnsh bl & blk .25 .25
171 A65 5c lt ol grn & blk .25 .25
172 A65 10c pale rose & blk .25 .25
173 A65 15c gray bl & blk .25 .25
174 A65 20c pink & blk .25 .25
175 A65 25c white & blk .25 .25
176 A65 30c pale rose & blk .30 .25
177 A65 35c bl & blk .50 .30
178 A65 40c gray & blk .50 .25
179 A65 50c lt bl & blk .60 .25
180 A65 60c salmon & blk .85 .25
181 A65 70c gray & blk 3.50 .90
182 A65 75c pale yel ('74) 1.00 .30
183 A65 80c ocher & blk 1.00 .30

Perf. 13½x14

Size: 26x40mm

184 A65 90c lt bl grn & blk 1.40 .45
185 A65 1d tan & blk 1.75 .30
186 A65 2d lt ultra & blk 2.50 .60
187 A65 3d bluish lil & blk 5.25 1.10
188 A65 5d apple grn & blk 8.50 3.25
Nos. 169-188 (20) 29.40 10.25

For overprints & surcharges see #224, B17-B18.

Nurse and Child — A66

1968, Apr. 8 Engr. *Perf. 13*

189 A66 25c ultra, red & olive .30 .25
190 A66 40c slate, red & olive .50 .25

WHO, 20th anniv.

Pendant — A67

1968, May 15 Photo. *Perf. 11½*

191 A67 25c shown .80 .25
192 A67 40c Bracelet 1.25 .30
a. Pair, #191-192, vertically tête-bêche 4.00 2.40

Moroccan Red Crescent Society.

See Nos. 373-374.

Map of Morocco and Rotary Emblem — A68

1968, May 23 *Perf. 13*

193 A68 40c multi .65 .25
194 A68 1d ultra & multi .95 .30

Rotary Intl. District Conference, Casablanca, May 24-25.

Ornamental Design A69

Designs: Various patterns used for sashes.

1968, July 12 Photo. *Perf. 11½*

195 A69 25c multi 2.00 .90
196 A69 40c multi 2.40 1.20
197 A69 60c multi 3.50 2.10
198 A69 1d multi 6.50 3.25
Nos. 195-198 (4) 14.40 7.45

Berber (Riff), North Morocco — A70

Regional Costumes: 10c, Man from Ait Moussa ou Ali. 15c, Woman from Ait Mouhad. No. 200, Bargeman from Rabat Salé. No. 201, Citadin man. 40c, Citadin woman. 60c, Royal Mokhazni. No. 204, Zemmours man. No. 204A, Man from Meknassa. No. 206, Msouffa woman, Sahara.

1968-74 Litho. *Perf. 13x12½*

198A A70 10c multi ('69) .75 .50
199 A70 15c yel & multi ('69) 1.25 .70
200 A70 25c bis & multi 1.25 .75
201 A70 25c tan & multi ('69) 1.40 .75
202 A70 40c lt bl & multi 1.50 1.10
203 A70 60c emer & multi 2.10 1.40
204 A70 1d lt bl & multi 2.75 1.90
204A A70 1d gray & multi ('69) 2.50 1.25

Perf. 15

205 A70 1d bis & multi 1.75 1.00
206 A70 1d grn & multi 1.75 1.00
a. Souvenir sheet of 10, #198A-206, perf. 13 20.00 20.00
b. As "a," with red overprint & surcharge 22.50 20.00
Nos. 198A-206 (10) 17.00 10.35

No. 206a issued June 30, 1970, for the opening of the National P.T.T. Museum, Rabat. Sold for 10d.

No. 206b issued Nov. 22, 1974, for the 8th Cong. of the Intl. Fed. of Blood Donors. Each stamp overprinted vertically "8eme Congres de la F.I.O.D.S." and blood container emblem. Black marginal inscription partially obliterated with lines, new Arabic inscription and price added. Sold for 20d.

Princess Lalla Meryem — A71

Children's Week: 40c, Princess Lalla Asmaa. 1d, Crown Prince Sidi Mohammed.

1968, Oct. 7 Litho. *Perf. 13½*

207 A71 25c red & multi .55 .25
208 A71 40c yel & multi .70 .40
209 A71 1d lt bl & multi .85 .70
Nos. 207-209 (3) 2.10 1.35

Wrestling, Aztec Calendar Stone and Olympic Rings — A72

1968, Oct. 25 Photo. *Perf. 12x11½*

210 A72 15c shown .35 .25
211 A72 20c Basketball .50 .25
212 A72 25c Cycling .70 .30
213 A72 40c Boxing .90 .30
214 A72 60c Running 1.40 .30
215 A72 1d Soccer 2.50 .50
Nos. 210-215 (6) 6.35 1.90

19th Olympic Games, Mexico City, 10/12-27.

10 Dirham Coin of Tetuan, 1780 — A73

Coins: 25c, Dirham, Agmat, c. 1138 A.D. 40c, Dirham, El Alya (Fes), c. 840 A.D. 60c, Dirham, Marrakesh, c. 1248 A.D.

1968, Dec. 17 Photo. *Perf. 11½*

Granite Paper

216 A73 20c dp plum, sil & blk .40 .25
217 A73 25c dk rose brn, gold & blk .50 .35
218 A73 40c dk grn, sil & blk 1.00 .45
219 A73 60c dk red, gold & blk 1.25 .65
Nos. 216-219,C16-C17 (6) 17.40 9.30

Issued with tabs.

Women from Zagora A74

Design: 25c, Women from Ait Adidou.

1969, Jan. 21 Litho. *Perf. 12*

220 A74 15c multi 1.25 .65
221 A74 25c multi 1.60 .95
Nos. 220-221,C15 (3) 5.25 2.85

Painting by Belkahya — A75

1969, Mar. 27 Litho. *Perf. 11½x12*

222 A75 1d lt grnsh bl, blk & brn .65 .40

International Day of the Theater.

King Hassan II — A76

1969, July 9 Photo. *Perf. 11½*

223 A76 1d gold & multi 1.25 .55

40th birthday of King Hassan II. A souvenir sheet contains one No. 223. Size: 75x105mm. Sold for 2.50d.

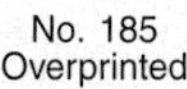

No. 185 Overprinted

1969, Sept. 22 Litho. *Perf. 13*

224 A65 1d tan & multi 5.25 3.25

First Arab Summit Conference, Rabat.

Mahatma Gandhi — A77

1969, Oct. 16 Photo. *Perf. 11½*

225 A77 40c pale vio, blk & gray 1.00 .40

Mohandas K. Gandhi (1869-1948), leader in India's struggle for independence.

ILO Emblem A78

1969, Oct. 29

226 A78 50c multi .50 .25

ILO, 50th anniv.

King Hassan II on Way to Prayer — A79

1969, Nov. 20 Photo. *Perf. 11½*

227 A79 1d multi 1.00 .55

1st Arab Summit Conference, Rabat, Sept. 1969. For overprint see No. 311.

Spahi Horsemen, by Haram al Glaoui A80

1970, Jan. 23 Engr. *Perf. 12x13*
228 A80 1d multi 1.00 .55

Main Sewer, Fez — A81

1970, Mar. 23 Litho. *Perf. 12*
229 A81 60c multi .50 .25

50th Congress of Municipal Engineers, Rabat, Mar. 1970.

Guedra Dance, by P. C. Beaubrun A82

1970, Apr. 15
230 A82 40c multi .55 .25

Folklore Festival, Marrakesh, May 1970.

No. 137 Overprinted "1970", "Census" in Arabic in Red and Surcharged in Black

1970, July 9 Photo. *Perf. 11½*
231 A48 25c on 60c multi .50 .25

Issued to publicize the 1970 census.

Radar Station at Souk El Arba des Sehoul, and Satellite — A83

1970, Aug. 20
232 A83 1d lt ultra & multi 1.10 .30

Revolution of King and People, 17th anniv.

Ruddy Shelduck — A84

1970, Sept. 25 Photo. *Perf. 11½*
233 A84 25c shown 1.20 .40
234 A84 40c Houbara bustard 1.60 .45

Campaign to save Moroccan wildlife.

Man Reading Book, Intl. Education Year Emblem — A85

1970, Oct. 20 Litho. *Perf. 12x11½*
235 A85 60c dl yel & multi .55 .25

Symbols of Peace, Justice and Progress A86

1970, Oct. 27 *Perf. 13½*
236 A86 50c multi .50 .25

United Nations, 25th anniversary.

Arab League Countries and Emblem A87

1970, Nov. 13 Photo. *Perf. 11½*
237 A87 50c multi .50 .25

Arab League, 25th anniversary.

Olive Grove, Tree and Branch A88

1970, Dec. 3 Litho. *Perf. 12*
238 A88 50c red brn & grn .80 .40

International Olive Year.

Es Sounna Mosque, Rabat A89

1971, Jan. 5 Engr. *Perf. 13*
239 A89 60c ol bis, bl & sl grn .55 .30

Restoration of Es Sounna Mosque, Rabat, built in 1785.

Heart and Horse — A90

1971, Feb. 23 Photo. *Perf. 12x12½*
240 A90 50c blk & multi .50 .25

European heart research week, Feb. 21-28.

Dam and Hassan II — A91

1971, Mar. 3 *Perf. 11½*
241 A91 25c multi .50 .25
a. Souv. sheet of 4 2.50 2.00

Accession of King Hassan II, 10th anniv. No. 241a issued Mar. 24. Sold for 2.50d.

Black and White Hands with Dove and Emblem A92

1971, June 16 Photo. *Perf. 13*
242 A92 50c brn & multi .50 .25

Intl. Year against Racial Discrimination.

Children Around the World — A93

1971, Oct. 4 Litho. *Perf. 13x14*
243 A93 40c emer & multi .50 .25

International Children's Day.

Shah Mohammed Riza Pahlavi of Iran — A94

1971, Oct. 11 Photo. *Perf. 11½*
244 A94 1d bl & multi .70 .45

2500th anniv. of the founding of the Persian empire by Cyrus the Great.

Mausoleum of Mohammed V — A95

50c, Mausoleum, close-up view, and Mohammed V. 1d, Decorated interior wall.

1971, Nov. 10 Litho. *Perf. 14*
245 A95 25c multi .35 .25
246 A95 50c multi .45 .25
247 A95 1d multi, vert. .75 .25
Nos. 245-247 (3) 1.55 .75

Soccer Ball and Games Emblem A96

1971, Nov. 30 Photo. *Perf. 13x13½*
248 A96 40c shown .55 .25
249 A96 60c Runner .80 .25

Mediterranean Games, Izmir, Turkey, Oct. 6-17.

Arab Postal Union Emblem A97

1971, Dec. 23 Litho. *Perf. 13x12½*
250 A97 25c dk & lt bl & org .50 .25

25th anniv. of the Conference of Sofar, Lebanon, establishing APU.

Sun over Cultivated Sand Dunes — A98

1971, Dec. 30 Photo. *Perf. 12½*
251 A98 70c blk, bl & yel .50 .25

Sherifian Phosphate Office (fertilizer production and export), 50th anniversary.

Torch and Book Year Emblem — A99

1972, Jan. 12 *Perf. 11½*
252 A99 1d silver & multi .55 .25

International Book Year.

National Lottery — A100

1972, Feb. 7 Photo. *Perf. 13*
253 A100 25c tan, blk & gold .50 .25

Creation of a national lottery.

Bridge of Sighs — A101

Designs: 50c, St. Mark's Basilica and waves, horiz. 1d, Lion of St. Mark.

1972, Feb. 25

254 A101 25c multi .25 .25
255 A101 50c red, blk & buff .60 .25
256 A101 1d lt bl & multi .50 .35
Nos. 254-256 (3) 1.35 .85

UNESCO campaign to save Venice.

Bridge, Road, Map of Africa — A102

1972, Apr. 21 ***Perf. 13***
257 A102 75c blue & multi .55 .25

2nd African Road Conf., Rabat, Apr. 17-22.

Morocco No. 223 — A103

1972, Apr. 27 ***Perf. 11½***
258 A103 1d lt ultra & multi .65 .25

Stamp Day.

The Engagement of Imilchil, by Tayeb Lahlou A104

1972, May 26 Litho. ***Perf. 13x13½***
259 A104 60c blk & multi .90 .50

Folklore Festival, Marrakesh, May 26-June 4.

Map of Africa, Dove and OAU Emblem — A105

1972, June 12 Photo. ***Perf. 11½***
260 A105 25c multi .50 .25

9th Summit Conference of Organization for African Unity, Rabat, June 12-15.

Landscape, Environment Emblem — A106

1972, July 20 Photo. ***Perf. 12½x12***
261 A106 50c bl & multi .50 .25

UN Conference on Human Environment, Stockholm, June 5-16

Olympic Emblems, Running A107

1972, Aug. 29 Photo. ***Perf. 13x13½***
262 A107 25c shown .25 .25
263 A107 50c Wrestling .35 .25
264 A107 75c Soccer .60 .25
265 A107 1d Cycling .75 .50
Nos. 262-265 (4) 1.95 1.25

20th Olympic Games, Munich, 8/26-9/11.

Sow Thistle — A108

40c, Amberboa crupinoides.

1972, Sept. 15 Litho. ***Perf. 14***
266 A108 25c shown .50 .25
267 A108 40c multi .65 .25

See No. 305-306.

Mountain Gazelle — A109

1972, Sept. 29 Photo. ***Perf. 11½***
268 A109 25c shown .80 .35
269 A109 40c Barbary sheep 1.10 .40

Nos. 266-269 issued for nature protection.

Rabat Rug — A110

25c, High Atlas rug. 70c, Tazenakht rug. 75c, Rabat rug, different pattern.

Perf. 13½ (25fr, 70fr), 11½

1972-73 Photo.
270 A110 25c multi .90 .25
270A A110 50c multi 1.00 .25
271 A110 70c multi 1.40 .50
271A A110 75c multi 1.50 .50
Nos. 270-271A (4) 4.80 1.50

Issued: 50c, 75c, 10/27; 25c, 70c, 12/28/73.

See Nos. 326-327.

Child and UNICEF Emblem — A111

1972, Dec. 20 Photo. ***Perf. 13½x13***
272 A111 75c brt grn & bl .50 .25

International Children's Day.

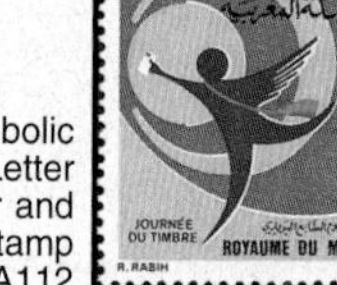

Symbolic Letter Carrier and Stamp A112

1973, Jan. 30 Photo. ***Perf. 13x13½***
273 A112 25c brn & multi .25 .25

Stamp Day.

Weather Map, Northern Hemisphere A113

1973, Feb. 23 Photo. ***Perf. 13***
274 A113 70c silver & multi .55 .30

Intl. meteorological cooperation, cent.

King Hassan II, Coat of Arms — A114

1973-76 Photo. ***Perf. 14***
275 A114 1c pale yel & multi .25 .25
276 A114 2c pale bl & multi .25 .25
277 A114 5c pale ol & multi .25 .25
278 A114 10c brn org & multi .25 .25
279 A114 15c vio gray & multi .25 .25
280 A114 20c pink & multi .25 .25
281 A114 25c pale bl & multi .25 .25
282 A114 30c rose & multi .25 .25
283 A114 35c org yel & multi .35 .25
284 A114 40c lt gray & multi 4.00 .35
285 A114 50c ultra & multi .50 .25
286 A114 60c sal & multi .60 .25
287 A114 70c yel grn & multi .50 .25
288 A114 75c lem & multi .45 .25
289 A114 80c multi .50 .30
290 A114 90c brt grn & multi .55 .25
291 A114 1d beige & multi 1.75 .25
292 A114 2d gray & multi 3.50 .50
293 A114 3d lt lil & multi 4.50 .75
294 A114 5d lt brn & multi ('75) 3.50 1.00
294A A114 5d pink & multi ('76) 3.50 1.00
Nos. 275-294A (21) 26.20 7.65

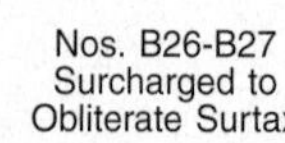

Nos. B26-B27 Surcharged to Obliterate Surtax

1973, Mar. 13 ***Perf. 11½***
295 SP1 25c multi 2.50 2.50
296 SP1 70c multi 2.75 2.75
a. Pair, #295-296, vert. tête-bêche 7.25 7.25

Tourism Conference 1973. Arabic overprint and date on one line on No. 296.
See Nos. 351-352.

Holy Ka'aba, Mecca, Mosque and Minaret, Rabat A115

1973, May 3 Photo. ***Perf. 13½x14***
297 A115 25c lt bl & multi .25 .25

Mohammed's 1,403rd birthday.

Roses and M'Gouna A116

1973, May 14 ***Perf. 13***
298 A116 25c bl & multi .25 .25

Rose Festival of M'Gouna.

Hands, Torch, OAU Emblem — A117

1973, May 25 Photo. ***Perf. 14x13***
299 A117 70c deep claret & multi .50 .25

OAU, 10th anniversary.

Dancers with Tambourines — A118

Design: 1d, Dancer with handbells, Marrakesh Minaret, Atlas Mountain.

1973, May 30 ***Perf. 12½x13***
300 A118 50c multi .50 .25
301 A118 1d multi .65 .30

Folklore Festival, Marrakesh.

Copernicus A119

70c, Heliocentric system.

1973, June 29 ***Perf. 13x13½***
302 A119 70c multi 1.25 .30

Microscope, WHO Emblem, World Map — A120

1973, July 16 Photo. *Perf. 13x12½*
303 A120 70c multi .55 .25

WHO, 25th anniversary.

INTERPOL Emblem, Fingerprint A121

1973, Sept. 12 Photo. *Perf. 13x13½*
304 A121 70c brn, sil & bl .50 .25

50th anniv. of Intl. Criminal Police Org.

Flower Type of 1972

1973, Oct. 12 Litho. *Perf. 14*
305 A108 25c Daisies, horiz. .65 .25
306 A108 1d Thistle 1.25 .50

Nature protection.

Berber Hyena A122

Design: 50c, Eleonora's falcon, vert.

1973, Nov. 23 Photo. *Perf. 14*
307 A122 25c multi 1.25 .25
308 A122 50c multi 2.50 .40

Nature protection.

Map and Colors of Morocco, Algeria and Tunisia A123

1973, Dec. 7 *Perf. 13x13½*
309 A123 25c gold & multi .50 .25

Maghreb Committee for Coordination of Posts and Telecommunications.

Fairway and Drive over Water Hazard — A124

1974, Feb. 8 Photo. *Perf. 14x13*
310 A124 70c multi 1.25 .25

International Golf Grand Prix for the Hassan II Morocco trophy.

No. 227 Overprinted in Red

1974, Feb. 25 *Perf. 11½*
311 A79 1d multi 2.75 1.50

Islamic Conference, Lahore, India, 1974.

Map of Africa, Scales, Human Rights Flame — A125

1974, Mar. 15 Photo. *Perf. 14x13½*
312 A125 70c gold & multi .50 .25

25th anniversary of the Universal Declaration of Human Rights.

Vanadinite A126

1974-75 Photo. *Perf. 13*
313 A126 25c shown 2.25 .60
313A A126 50c Aragonite 2.00 .35
314 A126 70c Erythrine 4.00 .75
314A A126 1d Agate 4.00 .60
Nos. 313-314A (4) 12.25 2.30

Issued: 25c, 70c, 4/30/74; 50c, 1d, 2/14/75.

Minaret, Marrakesh Mosque, Rotary Emblem — A127

1974, May 11 Photo. *Perf. 14*
315 A127 70c multi .55 .25

District 173 Rotary International annual meeting, Marrakesh, May 10-12.

UPU Emblem, Congress Dates — A128

1d, Scroll with UPU emblem, Lausanne coat of arms & 17th UPU Congress emblem, horiz.

1974, May 30 Photo.
316 A128 25c lt grn, org & blk .30 .25
317 A128 1d dk grn & multi .70 .25

Centenary of Universal Postal Union.

Drummer and Dancers — A129

Design: 70c, Knife juggler and women.

1974, June 7 Photo. *Perf. 14*
318 A129 25c multi .50 .25
319 A129 70c multi 1.25 .35

National folklore festival, Marrakesh.

Environment Emblem, Polution, Clean Water and Air — A130

1974, June 25 *Perf. 13*
320 A130 25c multi .40 .25

World Environment Day.

Simulated Stamps, Cancel and Magnifier A131

1974, Aug. 2 Photo. *Perf. 13*
321 A131 70c sil & multi .50 .25

Stamp Day.

No. J5 Surcharged

1974, Sept. 25 Photo. *Perf. 14*
322 D2 1d on 5c multi 2.00 1.40

Agricultural census.

World Soccer Cup — A132

1974, Oct. 11
323 A132 1d brt bl & multi .95 .65

World Cup Soccer Championship, Munich, June 13-July 7.

A stamp similar to No. 323, also issued Oct. 11, has gold inscription: "CHAMPION: R.F.A." in French and Arabic, honoring the German Federal Republic as championship winner. Value $32.50.

Double-spurred Francolin — A133

Perf. 14x13½, 13½x14

1974, Dec. 5 Photo.
324 A133 25c green & multi .60 .25
325 A133 70c Leopard, horiz. 1.25 .35

Nature protection.

Zemmour Rug — A134

Design: 1d, Beni Mguilo rug.

1974, Dec 20 *Perf. 13*
326 A134 25c multi .55 .25
327 A134 1d multi 1.20 .30

See Nos. 349-350, 398-400.

Columbine — A135

1975 Photo. *Perf. 13½*
328 A135 10c Daisies .25 .25
329 A135 25c Columbine .50 .25
330 A135 35c Orange lilies .55 .25
331 A135 50c Anemones .65 .25
332 A135 60c White starflower .80 .35
333 A135 70c Poppies .85 .35
334 A135 90c Carnations 1.20 .50
335 A135 1d Pansies 1.10 .60
Nos. 328-335 (8) 5.90 2.80

Issued: 25c, 35c, 70c, 90c, 1/10; others, 4/29.

Water Carrier, by Feu Tayeb Lahlou A136

1975, Apr. 3 *Perf. 13*
338 A136 1d multicolored 1.20 .50

Stamp Collector, Carrier Pigeon, Globe — A137

1975, May 21 Photo. *Perf. 13*

339 A137 40c gold & multi .50 .25

Stamp Day.

Musicians and Dancers — A138

1975, June 12 Photo. *Perf. 14x13½*

340 A138 1d multicolored .95 .30

16th Folklore Festival, Marrakesh, 5/30-6/15.

Guitar and Association for the Blind Emblem A139

1975, July 8 *Perf. 13x13½*

341 A139 1d purple & multi .90 .50

Week of the Blind.

Animals in Forest — A140

1975, July 25 Photo. *Perf. 13x13½*

342 A140 25c multicolored .50 .25

Children's Week.

Games' Emblem, Runner, Weight Lifter — A141

1975, Sept. 4 Photo. *Perf. 13*

343 A141 40c gold, maroon & buff .50 .25

7th Mediterranean Games, Algiers, 8/23-9/6.

Bald Ibis A142

1975, Oct. 21 Photo. *Perf. 13*

344 A142 40c shown 1.25 .40
345 A142 1d Persian lynx, vert. 1.60 .80

Nature protection.

King Mohammed V Greeting Crowd, Prince Moulay Hassan at Left — A143

King Hassan II A144

#348, King Mohammed V wearing fez.

1975, Nov. 21 Photo. *Perf. 13½*

346 A143 40c blk, sil & dk bl .55 .25
347 A144 1d blk, gold & dk bl .80 .50
348 A144 1d blk, gold & dk bl .80 .50
a. Sheet of 3, #346-348 12.50 12.50

20th anniversary of independence.

Rug Type of 1974

25c, Ouled Besseba. 1d, Ait Ouaouzguid.

1975, Dec. 11

349 A134 25c red & multi .90 .50
350 A134 1d orange & multi 1.40 .55

A number of issues have been printed se-tenant in sheets of 10 (5x2) arranged vertically tête bêche.

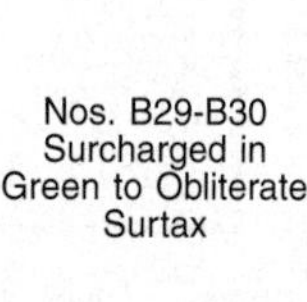
Nos. B29-B30 Surcharged in Green to Obliterate Surtax

1975 *Perf. 11½*

351 SP1 25c blue & multi 2.50 2.50
352 SP1 70c orange & multi 2.75 2.75
a. Pair, #351-352, vertically tête-bêche 7.25 7.25

March of Moroccan people into Spanish Sahara, Dec. 1975.

"Green March of the People" — A145

1975, Dec. 30 Photo. *Perf. 13½x13*

353 A145 40c multicolored .45 .25

March of Moroccan people into Spanish Sahara, Dec. 1975.

Copper Coin, Fez, 1883-84 — A146

Coins: 15c, 50c, silver coin, Rabat, 1774-75. 35c, 65c, Gold coin, Sabta, 13th-14th centuries. 1d, Square coin, Sabta, 12th-13th centuries.

1976 Photo. *Perf. 14x13½*

354 A146 5c dull rose & multi .25 .25
355 A146 15c brown & multi .25 .25
356 A146 35c gray & multi .50 .25
357 A146 40c ocher & multi .70 .25
358 A146 50c ultra & blk .80 .25
359 A146 65c yellow & multi .95 .30
360 A146 1d multicolored 1.25 .45
Nos. 354-360 (7) 4.70 2.00

Issued: #354-356, 4/26; #357-360, 1/20.

1976, Sept. 9

Designs: Various Moroccan coins.

361 A146 5c green & multi .25 .25
362 A146 15c dp rose & multi .25 .25
363 A146 20c lt bl & multi .35 .25
364 A146 30c lil rose & multi .45 .25
365 A146 35c green & multi .60 .25
366 A146 70c orange & multi .80 .25
Nos. 361-366 (6) 2.70 1.50

See Nos. 403-406A, 524B-524C.

Family — A147

1976, Feb. 12 *Perf. 14x13½*

367 A147 40c multicolored .50 .25

Family planning.

Arch, Ibn Zaidoun Mosque — A148

40c, Hall, Ibn Zaidoun Mosque, horiz.

Perf. 13½x14, 14x13½

1976, Feb. 12 Photo.

368 A148 40c multicolored .35 .25
369 A148 65c multicolored .60 .25

Ibn Zaidoun Mosque, millennium.

Medersa bou Anania, Fez A149

1976, Feb. 26 *Perf. 13x14½*

370 A149 1d multicolored .65 .25

Borobudur Temple — A150

Design: 40c, Bas-relief, Borobudur.

1976, Mar. 11 Photo. *Perf. 13*

371 A150 40c multicolored .40 .25
372 A150 1d multicolored .80 .25

UNESCO campaign to save Borobudur Temple, Java.

Islamic Conference, 6th Anniv. — A151

1976 Litho. *Perf. 13½x13*

372A A151 1d Dome of the Rock .65 .25

Jewelry Type of 1968

Designs: 40c, Pendant. 1d, Breastplate.

1976, June 29 Photo. *Perf. 14x13½*

373 A67 40c blue & multi .50 .25
374 A67 1d olive & multi .95 .30
a. Pair, #373-374, vertically tête-bêche 1.75 1.75

Moroccan Red Crescent Society.

Bicentennial Emblem, Flags and Map of US and Morocco — A152

Design: 1d, George Washington, King Hassan, Statue of Liberty and Royal Palace, Rabat, vert.

1976, July 27 Photo. *Perf. 14*

375 A152 40c multicolored .50 .25
376 A152 1d multicolored .90 .35

American Bicentennial.

Wrestling A153

1976, Aug. 11 *Perf. 13x13½*

377 A153 35c shown .25 .25
378 A153 40c Cycling .25 .25
379 A153 50c Boxing .50 .30
380 A153 1d Running .95 .45
Nos. 377-380 (4) 1.95 1.25

21st Olympic Games, Montreal, Canada, July 17-Aug. 1.

Old and New Telephones, Radar — A154

1976, Sept. 29 **Photo.** ***Perf. 14***
381 A154 1d gold & multi .65 .25

Centenary of first telephone call by Alexander Graham Bell, Mar. 10, 1876.

Blind Person's Identification A155

1976, Oct. 12 **Photo.** ***Perf. 13½x14***
382 A155 50c multicolored .50 .25

Week of the Blind.

Chanting Goshawk A156

1976, Oct. 29 ***Perf. 13x13½***
383 A156 40c shown 1.40 .40
384 A156 1d Purple gallinule 2.00 .70

Nature protection.

King Hassan, Star, Torch, Map of Morocco — A157

1976, Nov. 19 **Photo.** ***Perf. 12½x13***
385 A157 40c multicolored .55 .25

Green March into Spanish Sahara, 1st anniv.

Nos. B34-B35 Ovptd. with 2 Bars over Srch. and 4-line Arabic Inscription

1976, Nov. 29 **Photo.** ***Perf. 13½***
386 SP1 25c ultra, blk & org 2.00 2.00
387 SP1 70c red, blk & org 2.40 2.40
a. Pair, #386-387, vert. tête-bêche 5.50 5.50

5th African Tuberculosis Conference, Rabat.

Globe and Dove A158

1976, Dec. 16 ***Perf. 13***
388 A158 1d blue, blk & red .55 .25

5th Summit Meeting of Non-aligned Countries, Colombo, Aug. 9-19, and 25th anniv. of Org. of Non-aligned Countries.

African Soccer Cup — A159

1976, Dec. 29 **Photo.** ***Perf. 14***
389 A159 1d multicolored .70 .25

Letters Circling Globe, Postmark A160

1977, Jan. 24 **Photo.** ***Perf. 13½***
390 A160 40c multicolored .50 .25

Stamp Day.

Aeonium Arboreum A161

Malope Trifida — A162

1d, Hesperolaburnum platyclarpum.

Perf. 13x13½, 14 (A162)

1977, Feb. 22
391 A161 40c multicolored .55 .40
392 A162 50c multicolored 1.00 .50
393 A161 1d multicolored 1.20 .65
Nos. 391-393 (3) 2.75 1.55

Ornamental Lamps, View of Salé — A163

1977, Mar. 24 **Photo.** ***Perf. 14***
394 A163 40c multicolored .55 .25

Candle procession of Salé.

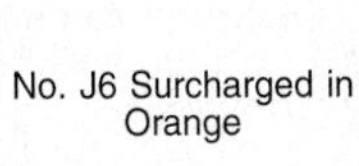

No. J6 Surcharged in Orange

1977, May 11 **Photo.** ***Perf. 14***
395 D2 40c on 10c multi .80 .40

Cherry Festival.

Map of Arab Countries, Emblem A164

1977, June 2 **Photo.** ***Perf. 14***
396 A164 50c multicolored .55 .25

5th Congress of Organization of Arab Cities.

APU Emblem, Members' Flags A165

1977, June 20
397 A165 1d multicolored .55 .25

Arab Postal Union, 25th anniversary.

Rug Type of 1974

Designs: 35c, No. 399A, Marmoucha rug, diff. No. 399, Ait Haddou rug. 1d, Salé rug.

Perf. 11½x12, 13½ (#399A)

1977-79 **Photo.**
398 A134 35c multicolored .45 .25
399 A134 40c multicolored .55 .25
399A A134 40c multicolored ('79) 1.00 .25
400 A134 1d multicolored 1.00 .40
Nos. 398-400 (4) 3.00 1.15

Issued: #399A, 3/8/79; others, 7/21/77.

Cithara — A166

1977, Aug. 18 **Photo.** ***Perf. 14***
401 A166 1d multi .90 .30

Week of the Blind.

Ali Jinnah and Map of Pakistan — A167

1977, Oct. 10 **Photo.** ***Perf. 13½x13***
402 A167 70c multi .55 .25

Mohammed Ali Jinnah (1876-1948), first Governor General of Pakistan.

Coin Type of 1976

Designs: Various Moroccan coins.

1977-81 ***Perf. 14x13½***
403 A146 10c gray & multi .35 .25
403A A146 25c ap grn & multi ('81) 1.40 .35
404 A146 60c dk red & multi ('78) 1.00 .25
405 A146 75c citron & multi .70 .25
405A A146 80c pale vio & mult ('81) 7.00 .50
406 A146 2d yel grn & multi 1.75 .35
406A A146 3d beige & multi ('81) 14.00 1.75
Nos. 403-406A (7) 26.20 3.70

Marcher with Flag, Map of Morocco and Spanish Sahara — A168

1977, Nov. 6 **Photo.** ***Perf. 14***
407 A168 1d multi .65 .25

Green March into Spanish Sahara, 2nd anniv.

Chamber of Representatives — A169

1977, Nov. 6 ***Perf. 13½***
408 A169 1d multi .65 .25
a. Souvenir sheet 3.00 3.00

Opening of Chamber of Representatives. No. 408a sold for 3d.

Enameled Silver Brooch — A170

1977, Dec. 14 **Photo.** ***Perf. 11½***
409 A170 1d multi 2.50 .25

Moroccan Red Crescent Society.

Copper Vessel — A171

1d, Standing filigree copper bowl with cover.

1978, Jan. 5 **Photo.** ***Perf. 13***
410 A171 40c gold & multi .40 .25
411 A171 1d gold & multi .90 .25
a. Pair, #410-411, vert. tête-bêche 2.00 2.00

Map of Sahara, Cogwheel Emblem — A172

1d, Map of North Africa, fish in net, camels.

1978, Feb. 27 **Photo.** ***Perf. 14***
412 A172 40c multi .40 .25
413 A172 1d multi, horiz .80 .25

Promotion of the Sahara. See Nos. 441-442 for similar stamps overprinted.

Covered Jar — A173

1978, Mar. 27 *Perf. 13½x13*
414 A173 1d shown .90 .50
415 A173 1d Vase .90 .50

Week of the Blind.

Red Crescent, Red Cross, Arab Countries A174

1978, Apr. 14 *Perf. 13x13½*
416 A174 1d multi .80 .30

10th Conference of Arab Red Crescent and Red Cross Societies, Apr. 10-15.

View of Fez, Rotary Emblem — A175

1978, Apr. 22 Photo. *Perf. 14*
417 A175 1d multi .65 .30

Rotary Intl. Meeting, Fez, District 173.

Dome of the Rock, Jerusalem — A176

1978, May 29 *Perf. 14½*
418 A176 5c multi .30 .25
419 A176 10c multi .30 .25

Palestinian fighters and their families. For overprints see Nos. 502-502A.

Folk Dancers and Flutist — A177

1978, June 15 *Perf. 13½x13*
420 A177 1d multi 2.00 .50

National Folklore Festival, Marrakesh.

Sugar Cane Field, and Conveyor Belt A178

1978, July 24 Photo. *Perf. 13*
421 A178 40c multi .45 .25

Sugar industry.

Games Emblem — A179

1978, Aug. 25
422 A179 1d multi .90 .25

World sailing championships.

Bird, Tree, Tent, Scout Emblem — A180

1978, Sept. 26 Photo. *Perf. 13*
423 A180 40c multi 1.00 .50

Pan-Arab Scout Jamboree, Rabat.

View of Fez A181

1978, Oct. 10
424 A181 40c multi .45 .25

Moulay Idriss the Great, Festival, Fez.

Flame Emblem — A182

1978, Dec. 21 Photo. *Perf. 14*
425 A182 1d multi .70 .25

30th anniversary of Universal Declaration of Human Rights.

Houses, Agadir — A183

1979, Jan. 25 Photo. *Perf. 12*
426 A183 40c shown .40 .25
427 A183 1d Old Fort, Marrakesh .80 .25

Soccer and Cup A184

1979, Mar. 2 *Perf. 13*
428 A184 40c multi .55 .25

Mohammed V Soccer Cup.

Vase — A185

1979, Mar. 29 Photo. *Perf. 14*
429 A185 1d multi .95 .25

Week of the Blind.

Procession A186

1d, Festival, by Mohamed Ben Ali Rbati, horiz.

1979, Apr. 18 *Perf. 13x13½, 13½x13*
430 A186 40c multi .45 .25
431 A186 1d multi .75 .25

Brass Containers, Red Crescent A187

1d, Heated coffee urn, vert.

Perf. 13x13½, 13½x13
1979, May 16 Photo.
432 A187 40c shown .30 .25
433 A187 1d multi .80 .30

Red Crescent Society.

Dancers — A188

1979, June 1 Photo. *Perf. 13*
434 A188 40c multi .55 .25

National Festival of Marrakech.

Silver Dagger — A189

1979, June 20 *Perf. 14*
435 A189 1d multi .80 .25

King Hassan II, 50th Birthday — A190

1979, July 9 Photo. *Perf. 14*
436 A190 1d multi .65 .25

4th Arab Youth Festival, Rabat A191

1979, July 30 Photo. *Perf. 13½x14*
437 A191 1d multi .65 .25

King Hassan II and Crowd — A192

1979, Aug. 20 *Perf. 14x13½*
438 A192 1d multi .50 .25

Revolution of the King and the People, 25th anniv.

Intl. Bureau of Education, 50th Anniv. — A193

1979, Sept. 28 Photo. *Perf. 13x13½*
439 A193 1d multi .65 .25

Pilgrimage to Mecca, Mt. Arafat, Holy Ka'aba A194

1979, Oct. 25 *Perf. 13½*
440 A194 1d multi .65 .25

No. 413 Redrawn in Smaller Size and Ovptd. in Red

1979, Nov. 7 Litho. *Perf. 14*
Size: 33x23mm

441 A172 40c multi .55 .25
442 A172 1d multi 1.10 .40

Return of Oued Eddahab province, Aug. 14.

Leucanthemum Catanance — A195

1979, Nov. 21 Photo. *Perf. 14½*

443 A195 40c Centaurium .30 .25
444 A195 1d shown .80 .25

Children, Globe, IYC Emblem — A196

1979, Dec. 3 *Perf. 14*

445 A196 40c multi .90 .30

International Year of the Child.

Otter — A197

1979, Dec. 18 *Perf. 13½x13*

446 A197 40c shown .70 .25
447 A197 1d Redstart 1.50 .25

Traffic Signs and Road — A198

1980, Jan. 3 Photo. *Perf. 14*

448 A198 40c shown .25 .25
449 A198 1d Children at curb .55 .25

Fortress A199

1980, Jan. 29 *Perf. 13x13½*

450 A199 1d multi .55 .25

Copper Bowl and Lid, Red Crescent — A200

Red Crescent Soc.: 70c, Copper kettle, brazier.

1980, Feb. 28 Photo. *Perf. 14*

451 A200 50c multi .50 .25
452 A200 70c multi .70 .25
a. Pair, #451-452, vert. tête-bêche 1.75 1.75

Week of the Blind — A201

1980, Mar. 19 Photo. *Perf. 14*

453 A201 40c multi .50 .25

Rabat Mechanical Sorting Office — A202

1980, Apr. 17

454 A202 40c multi .55 .25

Stamp Day.

Rotary Intl., 75th Anniv. — A203

1980, May 14 Photo. *Perf. 14*

455 A203 1d multi .55 .25

Cloth and Leather Goods — A204

1980, May 31 Photo. *Perf. 13½x13*

456 A204 1d multi .65 .25

4th Textile and Leather Exhibition, Casablanca, May 2-9.

Gypsum — A205

1980, June 19 Photo. *Perf. 13½x13*

457 A205 40c multi 1.25 .25

See Nos. 477-478.

Falcon — A206

1980, July 26 *Perf. 11½*

458 A206 40c multi 1.75 .30

Hunting with falcons.

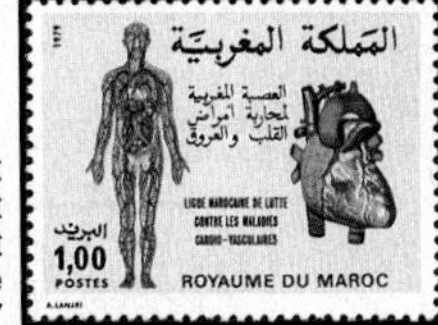

Fight against Heart Disease A207

1980, Aug. 7 Photo. *Perf. 13x13½*

459 A207 1d multi .65 .25

A208

1980, Aug. 18 *Perf. 14*

460 A208 40c shown .60 .25
461 A208 1d Emblems, diff. 1.10 .25

United Nations Decade for Women.

Ornamental Saddle and Harness A209

40c, Saddle, harness, diff.

1980, Sept. 3 *Perf. 14½*

462 A209 40c multi .35 .25
463 A209 1d shown .90 .25

World Meteorological Day — A210

1980, Sept. 18

464 A210 40c multi .55 .25

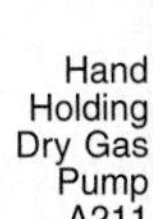

Hand Holding Dry Gas Pump A211

40c, Light bulb, gas can.

1980, Oct. 6 Photo. *Perf. 14*

465 A211 40c multi .30 .25
466 A211 1d shown .65 .25

Energy conservation.

World Tourism Conference, Manila, Sept. 27 — A212

1980, Oct. 22 *Perf. 11½x12*

467 A212 40c multi .55 .25

Symbolic Tree Rooted in Europe and Africa A213

1980, Oct. 30 *Perf. 14*

468 A213 1d multi .80 .25

Straits of Gibraltar linking Europe and Africa.

5th Anniversary of the Green March — A214

1980, Nov. 6

469 A214 1d multi .65 .25

Holy Ka'aba — A215

1980, Nov. 9

470 A215 40c shown .25 .25
471 A215 1d Mecca Mosque .70 .25
a. Souv. sheet of 2, #470-471 2.00 2.00

No. 471a sold for 3d.

Senecio Antheuphorbium A216

1980, Dec. 4 *Perf. 13*
472 A216 50c shown .70 .25
473 A216 1d Periploca laevigata 1.25 .40

Leaves, by Mahjoubi Aherdan — A217

Design: 40c. Untitled painting by Mahjoubi Aherdan (23x38mm).

1980, Dec. 18 *Perf. 12*
474 A217 40c multicolored .30 .25
475 A217 1d multicolored .75 .25

Nejjarine Fountain, Fes — A218

1981, Jan. 22 *Perf. 14x13½*
476 A218 40c multi .50 .25

Mineral Type of 1980

1981, Feb. 19 Photo. *Perf. 13½x13*
477 A205 40c Onyx 1.00 .25
478 A205 1d Malachite-azurite 2.25 .40

Inscribed 1980.

King Hassan II — A219

1981, Mar. 2 *Perf. 14*
479 A219 60c shown .30 .25
480 A219 60c Map of Morocco .30 .25
481 A219 60c King Mohammed V .30 .25
a. Strip of 3, #479-481 1.25 .75

25th anniv. of independence.

25th Anniv. of King Hassan II Coronation — A220

1981, Mar. 3
482 A220 1.30d multi .65 .25

The Source, by Jillali Gharbaoui — A221

1981, Apr. 8 *Perf. 13x12½*
483 A221 1.30d multi 1.00 .35

Anagalis Monelli — A222

70c, Bubonium intricatum.

1981, Apr. 23 *Perf. 13*
484 A222 40c shown .50 .25
485 A222 70c multicolored 1.00 .25

Army Badge — A223

Moroccan Armed Forces, 25th Anniv: No. 486, King Hassan II as army major general; No. 488, King Mohammed V.

1981, May 14 Photo. *Perf. 14x13½*
486 A223 60c multi .30 .25
487 A223 60c multi .30 .25
488 A223 60c multi .30 .25
a. Strip of 3, #486-488 1.10 .75

13th World Telecommunications Day — A224

1981, May 18 *Perf. 14x13*
489 A224 1.30d multi .65 .25

Hand-painted Plate — A225

1981, June 5 *Perf. 14*
490 A225 50c shown .35 .25
491 A225 1.30d Plate, diff. .80 .25

Week of the Blind.

22nd Marrakesh Arts Festival — A226

1981, June 18 *Perf. 13½x13*
492 A226 1.30d multi .90 .25

For overprint see No. 579.

Seboula Dagger, Oujda — A227

1981, Sept. 7 Photo. *Perf. 13½*
493 A227 1.30d multi 1.10 .25

Copper Mortar and Pestle, Red Crescent — A228

1981, Sept. 24 *Perf. 14*
494 A228 60c shown .45 .25
495 A228 1.30d Tripod 1.20 .30

Intl. Year of the Disabled — A229

1981, Oct. 15 *Perf. 13½*
496 A229 60c multi .55 .25

Iphiclides Feisthamelii A230

1.30d, Zerynthia rumina.

1981, Oct. 29 *Perf. 13½x13*
497 A230 60c shown 2.00 .50
498 A230 1.30d multi 3.50 1.00

See Nos. 528-529.

6th Anniv. of Green March — A231

1981, Nov. 6 *Perf. 13x13½*
499 A231 1.30d multi .55 .25

Intl. Palestinian Solidarity Day — A232

1981, Nov. 22 *Perf. 13½x13*
500 A232 60c multi .55 .25

Congress Emblem — A233

1981, Nov. 22 *Perf. 13½*
501 A233 1.30d multi .65 .30

World Federation of Twin Cities, 10th Congress, Casablanca, Nov. 15-18.

Nos. 418-419 Surcharged

1981, Nov. 25 Photo. *Perf. 14½*
502 A176 40c on 5c multi 8.50 6.00
502A A176 40c on 10c multi 6.50 3.75

First Anniv. of Mohammed V Airport — A234

1981, Dec. 8 Photo. *Perf. 14x13*
503 A234 1.30d multi .65 .25

Al Massirah Dam Opening A235

1981, Dec. 17 *Perf. 11½*
504 A235 60c multi .40 .25

King Hassan II — A236

1981, Dec. 28 *Perf. 13x12½*
505 A236 5c multi .25 .25
506 A236 10c multi .25 .25
507 A236 15c multi .25 .25
508 A236 20c multi .25 .25
509 A236 25c multi .25 .25
510 A236 30c multi .25 .25
511 A236 35c multi .25 .25
512 A236 40c multi .40 .25
513 A236 50c multi .25 .25
514 A236 60c multi .25 .25
515 A236 65c multi .25 .25
516 A236 70c multi .25 .25
a. Perf 12x11¾, granite paper .25 .25

517	A236	75c multi	.25	.25
518	A236	80c multi	.30	.25
519	A236	90c multi	.50	.25

No. 516a is dated 1999 and has the denomination and "Postes" closer to the shoulder than to the chin.

1983, Mar. 1 Photo. *Perf. 14½*
Size: 25x32mm

520	A236	1d multi	.30	.25
521	A236	1.40d multi	.40	.25
522	A236	2d multi	.45	.25
523	A236	3d multi	.75	.25
524	A236	5d multi	1.10	.45
524A	A236	10d multi	2.25	.80
e.		Perf 11½, granite paper	2.00	1.00
		Nos. 505-524A (21)	9.45	6.00

No. 524Ae is dated 1999 and has the denomination and "Postes" closer to the shoulder than to the chin.

See Nos. 566-575, 715-724.

Coin Type of 1976

1979-81 Photo. *Perf. 12½*
Size: 18x23mm

524B	A146	40c ocher & multi	.60	.25
d.		Bklt. pane of 10	6.00	
524C	A146	50c brt bl, blk & dk brn ('81)	.60	.25

Equestrian Sports A237

1981, Dec. 29 *Perf. 13x13½*
525 A237 1.30d multi 1.25 .40

Traditional Carpet Design — A238

50c, Glaoua pattern. 1.30d, Ouled Besseba pattern.

1982, Jan. 21

526	A238	50c multi	.25	.25
527	A238	1.30d multi	.65	.25

Butterfly Type of 1981

60c, Celerio oken lineata. 1.30d, Mesoacidalia aglaja lyauteyi.

1982, Feb. 25 *Perf. 13½x13*

528	A230	60c multi	1.60	.55
529	A230	1.30d multi	3.50	.85

World Forest Day — A240

1982, Apr. 8 *Perf. 14*
531 A240 40c multi .55 .25

Blind Week — A241

1982, May 10
532 A241 1d Jug .55 .25

Folk Dancers, Rabat — A242

1982, June 3
533 A242 1.40d multi .65 .25

Copper Candlestick, Red Crescent — A243

1982, July 1
534 A243 1.40d multi .65 .25

Women in Traditional Clothing, by M. Mezian — A244

1982, Aug. 16 Photo. *Perf. 14*
535 A244 1.40d multi .65 .30

Natl. Census A245

1982, Sept. 6 Photo. *Perf. 11½*
536 A245 60c multi .40 .25

ITU Conf., Nairobi, Sept. — A246

1982 *Perf. 13½x13*
537 A246 1.40d multi .55 .25

TB Bacillus Centenary A247

1982, Sept. 30
538 A247 1.40d multi .80 .30

World Food Day — A248

1982, Oct. 16 *Perf. 14*
539 A248 60c multi .55 .25

Unity Railroad A249

1982, Nov. 6 *Perf. 13x13½*
540 A249 1.40d multi 1.40 .50

30th Anniv. of Arab Postal Union A250

1982, Nov. 17 *Perf. 14*
541 A250 1.40d multi .55 .25

Intl. Palestinian Solidarity Day — A251

1982, Nov. 29 *Perf. 14*
542 A251 1.40d sil & multi .55 .25

Red Coral, Al-Hoceima A252

1982, Dec. 20 *Perf. 13½*
543 A252 1.40d multi 1.00 .30

Stamp Day — A253

1983, Jan. 26 *Perf. 13½x13*
544 A253 1.40d Nos. 3, 178 .55 .25

Week of the Blind — A254

1983, Apr. 20 Photo. *Perf. 14*
545 A254 1.40d multi .65 .25

Popular Arts A255

1983, June 27 Photo. *Perf. 14*
546 A255 1.40d multi .90 .25

Wrought-Iron Lectern — A256

1983, July 7 Litho. *Perf. 13½*
547 A256 1.40d multi .90 .25

Economic Commission for Africa, 25th Anniv. — A257

1983, July 18 Photo. *Perf. 14*
548 A257 1.40d multi .55 .25

Moroccan Flora — A258

1983, Aug. 1 Litho. *Perf. 14*

549	A258	60c Tecoma	.50	.25
550	A258	1.40d Strelitzia	1.00	.30

Kings Mohammed V and Hassan II — A259

1983, Aug. 20 **Litho.** ***Perf. 14***
551 A259 80c multi .55 .25
a. Souvenir sheet of 1 2.40 2.40

King and People's Revolution, 30th Anniv. No. 551a sold for 5 dinars.

Mediterranean Games — A260

80c, Stylized sportsmen. 1d, Emblem. 2d, Stylized runner, horiz.

1983, Sept. 3 **Photo.** ***Perf. 14***
552 A260 80c multi .40 .25
553 A260 1d multi .55 .30
554 A260 2d multi 1.60 .45
a. Souv. sheet of 3, #552-554, imperf. 3.00 3.00
Nos. 552-554 (3) 2.55 1.00

No. 554a sold for 5d.

Touiza A261

1983, Sept. 30 **Photo.** ***Perf. 13***
555 A261 80c Tractors .55 .25

Palestinian Solidarity — A262

1983, Nov. 10 **Photo.** ***Perf. 13½x13***
556 A262 80c multi .45 .25

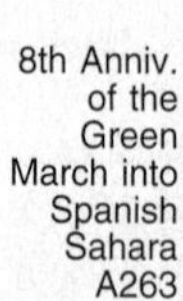

8th Anniv. of the Green March into Spanish Sahara A263

1983, Nov. 17 ***Perf. 13x13½***
557 A263 80c multi .55 .25

Ouzoud Waterfall — A264

1983, Nov. 28 ***Perf. 14***
558 A264 80c multi .45 .25

Children's Day — A265

1983, Dec. 5 **Photo.** ***Perf. 13½x13***
559 A265 2d multi .65 .25

Zemmouri Carpet — A266

Various carpets.

1983, Dec. 15 ***Perf. 13½***
560 A266 60c multi .45 .25
561 A266 1.40d multi .90 .25

World Communications Year — A267

1983, Dec. 20 ***Perf. 14***
562 A267 2d multi 1.20 .25

Twin Cities, Jerusalem and Fez A268

1984, Jan. 16 **Photo.** ***Perf. 13x13½***
563 A268 2d multi 1.00 .25

Desert Fox — A269

2d, Jumping mouse, vert.

1984, Feb. 13 ***Perf. 11½x12, 12x11½***
564 A269 80c shown 1.00 .40
565 A269 2d multi 2.25 .80

King Hassan II Type of 1981

1984-88 **Photo.** ***Perf. 14½***
Size: 25x32mm

566 A236 1.20d multi ('88) .30 .25
567 A236 1.25d multi .30 .25
568 A236 1.60d multi ('87) .45 .25
569 A236 2.50d multi ('87) .65 .35
570 A236 3.60d multi ('88) 1.25 .40
571 A236 4d multi 1.10 .65
572 A236 5.20d multi ('88) 1.75 .75
573 A236 6.50d multi ('87) 1.75 1.10
574 A236 7d multi ('87) 1.90 1.25
575 A236 8.50d multi ('87) 2.25 1.60
Nos. 566-575 (10) 11.70 6.85

Dated 1986: 1.60d, 2.50d, 6.50d, 7d, 8.50d. Issued: 1.20d, 3.60d, 5.20d, Dec. 26, 1988.

39th Anniv. of Arab League A270

1984, May 24 ***Perf. 14½x14***
578 A270 2d Emblem .65 .25

No. 492 Overprinted

1984, June 12 ***Perf. 13½x13***
579 A226 1.30d multi .90 .25

25th Anniv. of Marrakesh Arts Festival.

Local Plants — A271

1984, June 13 ***Perf. 14***
580 A271 80c Mentha viridis .30 .25
581 A271 2d Aloe .90 .40

See Nos. 602-603.

Week of the Blind A272

1984, July 10 ***Perf. 13x13½***
582 A272 80c Painted bowl .50 .25

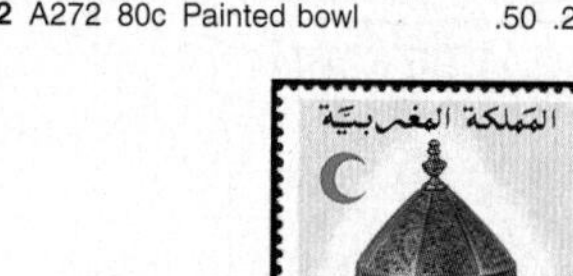

Red Crescent — A273

2d, Octagonal brass container.

1984, July 16 ***Perf. 14***
583 A273 2d multi .80 .35

1984 Summer Olympics — A274

1984, Aug. 8 ***Perf. 13½x13***
584 A274 2d Sports .90 .35

Intl. Child Victims' Day — A275

2d, Children held by dove.

1984, Aug. 22 ***Perf. 14***
585 A275 2d multi .80 .35

UPU Day — A276

1984, Oct. 9 **Photo.** ***Perf. 13½***
586 A276 2d multi .65 .25

World Food Day — A277

1984, Oct. 16 ***Perf. 14***
587 A277 80c multi .55 .25

Intl. Civil Aviation Org., 40th Anniv. — A278

1984, Oct. 20 ***Perf. 13½***
588 A278 2d multi 1.10 .50

Green March, 9th Anniv. — A279

1984, Nov. 6 ***Perf. 14***
589 A279 80c Scroll, text .55 .25

Palestinian Solidarity — A281

2d, Arab Revolt flag, 1918-19.

1984, Nov. 29 ***Perf. 13½***
591 A281 2d multi 1.00 .50

UN Human Rights Declaration, 36th Anniv. — A282

1984, Dec. 10 ***Perf. 14***
592 A282 2d multi .65 .35

Native Dogs — A283

1984, Dec. 21 **Photo.** ***Perf. 14***
593 A283 80c Aidi .70 .25
594 A283 2d Sloughi 1.40 .40

UN Child Survival Campaign A284

1985, Mar. 5 **Photo.** ***Perf. 14***
595 A284 80c Growth monitoring .55 .25

1st SOS Children's Village in Morocco A285

1985, Mar. 11 ***Perf. 13x13½***
596 A285 2d multi .65 .25

Sherifian Hand Stamp, 1892 — A287

1985, Mar. 25 **Photo.** ***Perf. 14***
597 A287 2d dl pink, blk & gray .65 .25

Souvenir Sheet

Perf. 13½

598	Sheet of 6	4.00	4.00
a.	A287 80c green, black & gray	.55	.40
b.	A287 80c yellow, black & gray	.55	.40
c.	A287 80c blue, black & gray	.55	.40
d.	A287 80c red, black & gray	.55	.40
e.	A287 80c purple, black & gray	.55	.40
f.	A287 80c brown, black & gray	.55	.40

Stamp Day. #598 sold for 5d.

See #615-616, 633-634, 668-669, 684-685, 701-702, 733-734, 756-757, 790-791, 806-807, 821-822, 835-836, 906-907.

World Environment Day — A288

1985, June 5 ***Perf. 13***
599 A288 80c Emblem, ecosystem .55 .25

Susi Dancers from Marrakesh and Kutabia, Minaret A289

1985, June 7 ***Perf. 13x13½***
600 A289 2d multi .95 .40

Folk Arts Festival.

Week of the Blind — A290

1985, June 24 ***Perf. 14***
601 A290 80c Ceramic bowl .50 .25

See type A316.

Flower Type of 1984

1985, July 1
602 A271 80c Bougainvillea 1.10 .30
603 A271 2d Red hibiscus 1.90 .50

Berber Woman — A291

1985, July 15 ***Perf. 14***
604 A291 2d multi 3.00 .35

Red Crescent Society.

6th Pan-Arab Games — A292

2d, Torch, emblem, map.

1985, Aug. 2 ***Perf. 14½x13½***
605 A292 2d multi .90 .35

UN, 40th Anniv. — A293

1985, Oct. 7 ***Perf. 13***
606 A293 2d multi 2.00 .75

Intl. Youth Year — A294

1985, Oct. 21
607 A294 2d multi 2.25 .75

Green March, 10th Anniv. — A295

2d, Commemorative medal.

1985, Nov. 6 ***Perf. 14½x13½***
608 A295 2d multi .65 .25

Palestinian Solidarity A296

1985, Nov. 29 ***Perf. 13½***
609 A296 2d multi .80 .25

Butterflies A297

80c, Euphydryas desfontainii. 2d, Colotis evagore.

1985, Dec. 16 **Photo.** ***Perf. 14***
610 A297 80c multi 1.60 .65
611 A297 2d multi 4.00 1.60

Accession of King Hassan II, 25th Anniv. — A298

Perf. 13x13½, 13½x13

1986, Mar. 3 **Litho.**
612 A298 80c Natl. arms, vert. .30 .25
613 A298 2d shown .70 .40
a. Souv. sheet of 2, #612-613, imperf. 1.25 1.25

26th Intl. Military Medicine and Pharmaceutical Congress A299

1986, Mar. 24 **Photo.** ***Perf. 14***
614 A299 2d multi .60 .45

Hand Stamp Type of 1985

Sherifian postal seals of Maghzen-Safi, 1892.

1986, Apr. 7
615 A287 80c orange & blk .30 .25
616 A287 2d green & blk .70 .30

Week of the Blind — A300

1986, Apr. 21
617 A300 1d multi 1.00 .35

1986 World Cup Soccer Championships, Mexico — A301

1d, Emblems, horiz. 2d, Soccer cup, emblems.

1986, May 31 ***Perf. 13½***
618 A301 1d multi .60 .25
619 A301 2d multi 1.10 .35

Red Crescent Soc. — A302

1986, June ***Perf. 14***
620 A302 2d multi .90 .35

Popular Arts A303

1986, June
621 A303 2d Folk band, dancers 1.00 .30

Flowers — A304

1d, Warionia saharae. 2d, Mandragora autumnalis.

1986, July 21 **Photo.** ***Perf. 14***
622 A304 1d multi 1.40 .35
623 A304 2d multi 2.75 .65

Intl. Peace Year — A305

1986, Aug. 4 ***Perf. 13***
624 A305 2d multicolored 1.10 .40

18th Skydiving Championships A306

1986, Aug. 18 ***Perf. 13½x13***
625 A306 2d multicolored 1.40 .40

Horse Week A307

1986, Oct. 10 ***Perf. 13***
626 A307 1d multicolored 1.40 .25

Green March, 11th Anniv. — A308

1986, Nov. 6 **Photo.** ***Perf. 14***
627 A308 1d multicolored 1.40 .25

World Food Day — A309

1986, Nov. 12
628 A309 2d multicolored .60 .40

Aga Khan Architecture Prize A310

1986, Nov. 24 **Litho.** ***Perf. 13***
629 A310 2d multicolored 2.50 .75

Operation Grain: One Million Hectares — A311

1986, Dec. 8
630 A311 1d multicolored .55 .25

Butterflies A312

1d, Elphinstonia charlonia. 2d, Anthocharis belia.

1986, Dec. 22 ***Perf. 14***
631 A312 1d multi 1.25 .55
632 A312 2d multi 3.25 1.50

Hand Stamp Type of 1985

Stamp Day: Sherifian postal seals of Maghzen-Tetouan, 1892.

1987, Jan. 26 **Photo.**
633 A287 1d blue & blk .75 .35
634 A287 2d red & black 1.50 .65

King Mohammed V, Flag, 1947 — A313

No. 636, King Hassan II, 1987.

1987, Apr. 9 **Photo.** ***Perf. 13½x13***
635 A313 1d shown .55 .25
636 A313 1d multi .55 .25
a. Souvenir sheet of 2, Nos. 635-636 1.20 1.20

Tangiers Conf., 40th anniv. #636a sold for 3d.

Red Crescent Society — A314

1987, May 1 **Photo.** ***Perf. 14***
637 A314 2d Brass lamp .80 .35

UN Child Survival Campaign A315

1d, Oral rehydration.

1987, May 25 ***Perf. 12½x13***
638 A315 1d multi .55 .30

See Nos. 647, 687.

Week of the Blind — A316

1987, June 8 ***Perf. 14***
639 A316 1d Porcelain cup .55 .30

Flowering Plants — A317

1d, Zygophyllum fontanesii. 2d, Otanthus maritimus.

1987, July 6 **Photo.**
640 A317 1d multi .35 .25
641 A317 2d multi .70 .35

See Nos. 661-662.

US-Morocco Diplomatic Relations, 200th Anniv. — A318

1987, July **Litho & Engr.**
642 A318 1d lt bl, blk & scar .50 .25

See United States No. 2349.

Give Blood — A319

2d, King Hassan II, map.

1987, Aug. 20 **Photo.** ***Perf. 13x13½***
643 A319 2d multi .80 .45

Desert Costumes, the Sahara — A320

1d, Woman from Melhfa. 2d, Man from Derraa.

1987, Sept. 14 ***Perf. 13***
644 A320 1d multi .50 .25
645 A320 2d multi 1.00 .50

See Nos. 711-712, 740-741.

13th Intl. Cong. on Irrigation and Drainage — A321

1987, Sept. 21
646 A321 1d multi .55 .30

UN Child Survival Type of 1987

1d, Universal immunization.

1987, Sept. 28
647 A315 1d multicolored .55 .30

Congress on Mineral Industries, Marrakesh A322

1987, Oct.
648 A322 1d Azurite .75 .25
649 A322 2d Wulfenite 1.00 .50

See No. 769.

Green March, 12th Anniv. — A323

1987, Nov. 6 Photo. *Perf. 14*
650 A323 1d multicolored .55 .25

See Nos. 667, 683, 695, 727, 750, 769, 802, 820, 834, 848, 862, 885.

Royal Armed Forces Social Services Month A324

1987, Nov. 13 *Perf. 13x12½*
651 A324 1d multicolored .55 .25

Birds — A325

1d, Passer simplex saharae. 2d, Alectoris barbara.

1987, Dec. 1 Litho. *Perf. 14*
652 A325 1d multi .75 .30
653 A325 2d multi 1.50 .45

Natl. Postage Stamp 75th Anniv. — A326

Design: Postmark and Sherifian postage stamp (French Morocco) of 1912.

1987, Dec. 31 Photo. *Perf. 14x13½*
654 A326 3d pale lil rose, blk & blue grn 1.25 .70

Cetiosaurus Mogrebiensis — A327

1988, Jan. 18 Photo. *Perf. 13½*
655 A327 2d multicolored 3.50 .95

A328

1988, Feb. 16 Litho. *Perf. 14*
656 A328 2d multicolored .65 .45

Intl. Symposium on Mohammed V, Aug. 16-Nov. 20, 1987.

A329

Perf. 14½x13½
1988, Mar. 13 Photo.
657 A329 3d multi 1.00 .75

16th Africa Cup Soccer Championships.

Horse Week A330

1988, Mar. 20 Litho. *Perf. 14*
658 A330 3d multi 1.75 .75

Intl. Red Cross and Red Crescent Orgs., 125th Annivs. — A331

1988, Apr. 30 Photo. *Perf. 12½x13*
659 A331 3d pink, blk & dark red .95 .65

Week of the Blind — A332

1988, May 25 Litho. *Perf. 14*
660 A332 3d Pottery bottle .90 .65

Flower Type of 1987

No. 661, Citrullus colocynthis. No. 662, Calotropis procera.

1988, June 27 Litho. *Perf. 14*
661 A317 3.60d multi 1.25 .75
662 A317 3.60d multi 1.25 .75

UN Child Survival Campaign A333

1988, July 18 Litho. *Perf. 12½x13*
663 A333 3d multi .90 .60

1988 Summer Olympics, Seoul — A334

Perf. 14½x13½
1988, Sept. 17 Litho.
664 A334 2d multi .80 .50

Birds — A335

1988, Oct. 26 Litho. *Perf. 14*
665 A335 3.60d Grande outarde 1.75 .75
666 A335 3.60d Flamant rose 1.75 .75

Green March Anniv. Type of 1987

1988, Nov. 6
667 A323 2d multi .65 .40

Green March, 13th anniv.

Hand Stamp Type of 1985

Sherifian postal seals of Maghzen-El Jadida, 1892: No. 668, Octagonal. No. 669, Circular.

1988, Nov. 22 Photo. *Perf. 14*
668 A287 3d olive bister & blk 1.10 .60
669 A287 3d violet & blk 1.10 .60

Stamp Day.

Housing of the Ksours and Casbahs A336

1989, Jan. 23 *Perf. 13x13½*
670 A336 2d multi .65 .40

Royal Chess Federation, 25th Anniv. — A337

1989, Apr. 17 Litho. *Perf. 14*
671 A337 2d multi .80 .40

Red Crescent Society — A338

1989, May 29 Litho. *Perf. 14x13½*
672 A338 2d multi 1.10 .40

Week of the Blind — A339

1989, June 12 *Perf. 14*
673 A339 2d multi .55 .40

A340

No. 675, King Hassan II, diff.

1989, July 9 Litho. *Perf. 13x13½*
674 A340 2d multi .75 .40
675 A340 2d multi .75 .40
a. Souvenir sheet of 2, #674-675, imperf. & embossed *15.00 15.00*

King Hassan II, 60th birthday. No. 675a sold for 5d.

Flowering Plants — A341

No. 676, Narcissus papyraceus. No. 677, Cerinthe major.

1989, Sept. 11 Litho. *Perf. 14*
676 A341 2d multi .80 .45
677 A341 2d multi .80 .45

See Nos. 709-710, 742-743.

World Telecommunications Day — A342

1989, Sept. 25 *Perf. 13x12½*
678 A342 2d multicolored .60 .45

13th World Congress on Fertility and Sterility — A343

1989, Oct. 6 *Perf. 14*
679 A343 2d multicolored .60 .45

Birds A344

1989, Oct. 16 *Perf. 14*
680 A344 2d Desert beater .70 .45
681 A344 3d Gorget lark 1.00 .70

Interparliamentary Union, Cent. — A345

1989, Oct. 27
682 A345 2d multicolored .60 .45

Green March Anniv. Type of 1987

1989, Nov. 6
683 A323 3d multicolored .90 .70

Green March, 14th anniv.

Hand Stamp Type of 1985

Sherifian postal seals of Maghzen-Casablanca, 1892: 2d, Circular. 3d, Octagonal.

1990, Jan. 15 **Photo.** *Perf. 14*
684 A287 2d orange & blk .65 .45
685 A287 3d green & blk 1.00 .70

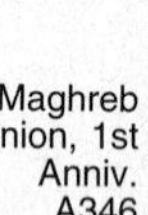

Maghreb Union, 1st Anniv. A346

1990, Feb. 17 *Perf. 13½x14*
686 A346 2d multicolored .60 .45
a. Souv. sheet of one, perf. 13½ .95 .95

No. 686a sold for 3d.

UN Child Survival Type of 1987

1990 *Perf. 12½x13*
687 A315 3d Breast feeding .95 .70

3rd World Olive Day A347

1990, May 14 **Litho.** *Perf. 14*
688 A347 2d Olive press .50 .35
689 A347 3d King Hassan II .75 .55

Week of the Blind A348

1990, May 28 **Litho.** *Perf. 14*
690 A348 2d multicolored .70 .50

Red Crescent Society A349

1990, June 11
691 A349 2d multicolored .55 .35

Intl. Literacy Year — A350

1990, Sept. 17 **Litho.** *Perf. 14*
692 A350 3d blk, yel grn & grn 1.10 .80

Birds A351

1990, Oct. 26
693 A351 2d Tourterelle, vert. .85 .50
694 A351 3d Huppe fasciee 1.25 .80

Green March Anniv. Type of 1987

1990, Nov. 5
695 A323 3d multicolored 1.10 .80

Green March, 15th anniv.

Independence, 35th Anniv. — A353

1990, Nov. 18
696 A353 3d multicolored 1.10 .80

Dam A354

1990, Nov. 26
697 A354 3d multicolored 1.10 .80

A355

1990, Dec. 28 **Litho.** *Perf. 14*
698 A355 3d multicolored 1.00 .75

Royal Academy of Morocco, 10th anniv.

A356

Opening of Postal Museum, 20th Anniv.: No. 699, Telegraph machine. No. 700, Horse-drawn mail carriage fording river.

1990, Dec. 31 **Litho.** *Perf. 13½x13*
699 A356 2d multicolored .65 .50
700 A356 3d multicolored 1.00 .75
a. Souv. sheet of 2, #699-700, imperf. 2.10 2.10

No. 700a sold for 6d, has simulated perforations.

Hand Stamp Type of 1985

Sherifian postal seals of Maghzen-Rabat, 1892: 2d, Circular. 3d, Octagonal.

1991, Jan. 25 *Perf. 14*
701 A287 2d ver & blk .65 .50
702 A287 3d blue & blk 1.00 .75

A357

1991, Feb. 18
703 A357 3d multicolored 1.00 .75

UN Development Program, 40th anniv.

A358

No. 705, Wearing business suit.

1991, Mar. 3 **Litho.** *Perf. 14½x13*
704 A358 3d shown 1.25 .35
705 A358 3d multi 1.25 .35
a. Souv. sheet of 2, #704-705, imperf. 3.00 2.35

Coronation of King Hassan II, 30th anniv. Nos. 704-705 exist tete beche. No. 705a has simulated perforations and sold for 10d.

A359

1991, Mar. 28 **Litho.** *Perf. 14*
706 A359 3d multicolored 1.00 .75

Phosphate Mining, 70th anniv.

Week of the Blind — A360

1991, May 15 **Photo.** *Perf. 14*
707 A360 3d multicolored 1.00 .75

Red Crescent Society — A361

1991, May 27 **Litho.** *Perf. 14*
708 A361 3d multicolored .95 .70

Flowering Plants Type of 1989

1991, June 27 **Litho.** *Perf. 14*
709 A341 3d Pyrus mamorensis 1.00 .70
710 A341 3d Cynara humilis 1.00 .70

Desert Costumes Type of 1987

Costumes of Ouarzazate.

1991, July 31 **Photo.**
711 A320 3d Woman 1.00 .70
712 A320 3d Man 1.00 .70

King Hassan II Type of 1981

1991-98 **Photo.** *Perf. 14½*
Size: 25x32mm

715 A236 1.35d multicolored .45 .25
717 A236 1.70d multicolored .40 .25
719 A236 2.30d multicolored .50 .25
a. Perf 11½, granite paper .50 .25
722 A236 5.50d multicolored 1.25 1.00
a. Perf 11½, granite paper 2.00 1.00
723 A236 6d multicolored 1.25 .95
724 A236 20d multicolored 5.00 3.50
Nos. 715-724 (6) 8.85 6.20

Issued: 1.35d, Sept. 2; 1.70d, 1994; 2.30d, 6d, 1998.

This is an expanding set. Numbers will change if necessary.

Nos. 719a and 722a are dated 1999, and have the denomination and "Postes" closer to the shoulder than to the chin.

A362

1991, Sept. 23 **Litho.** *Perf. 14*
725 A362 3d multicolored .95 .70

19th World Congress on Roads, Marrakesh.

A363

1991, Oct. 30 **Litho.**
726 A363 3d multicolored .95 .70

4th Session of the Council of Presidents of the Maghreb Arab Union.

Green March Anniv. Type of 1987

1991, Nov. 6 **Photo.** ***Perf. 14***
727 A323 3d multicolored .95 .70

Green March, 16th anniv.

Birds — A364

1991, Nov. 20 **Litho.** ***Perf. 14***
728 A364 3d Merops apiaster 1.75 .50
729 A364 3d Ciconia ciconia 1.75 .50

See Nos. 748-749.

Fight Against AIDS — A365

1991, Dec. 16
730 A365 3d multicolored 1.00 .80

Organization of the Islamic Conference, 20th Anniv. — A366

1991, Dec. 16
731 A366 3d multicolored 1.00 .80

African Tourism Year — A367

1991 **Litho.** ***Perf. 14***
732 A367 3d multicolored 1.00 .80

Hand Stamp Type of 1985

Sherifian postal seals of Maghzen-Essaouira, 1892: No. 733, Circular. No. 734, Octagonal.

1992, Jan. 13
733 A287 3d olive & blk 1.00 .80
734 A287 3d purple & blk 1.00 .80

Intl. Space Year — A368

1992, Feb. 17
735 A368 3d multicolored 1.00 .80

Week of the Blind — A369

1992, Mar. 19 **Photo.** ***Perf. 14***
736 A369 3d multicolored 1.00 .80

Red Crescent Society — A370

1992, Mar. 30
737 A370 3d multicolored 1.00 .80

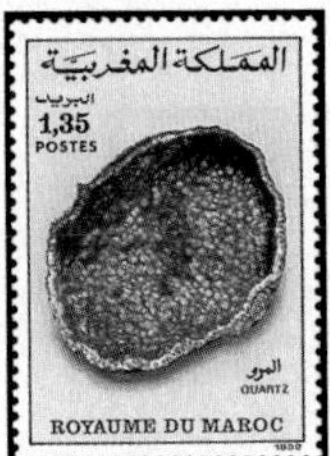

Minerals — A371

1992, May 11 **Litho.** ***Perf. 14***
738 A371 1.35d Quartz .50 .40
739 A371 3.40d Calcite 1.25 1.00

Desert Costumes Type of 1987

Costumes of Tata.

1992, May 25 **Photo.** ***Perf. 14***
740 A320 1.35d Woman .50 .40
741 A320 3.40d Man 1.25 1.00

Flowering Plants Type of 1989

1.35d, Campanula afra. 3.40d, Thymus broussonetii.

1992, July 13
742 A341 1.35d multi .50 .40
743 A341 3.40d multi 1.25 1.00

A372

1992, July 24
744 A372 3.40d multicolored 1.25 1.00

1992 Summer Olympics, Barcelona.

Modes of Transportion and Communications, Map of Africa — A373

1992, Sept. 14 **Litho.** ***Perf. 14***
745 A373 3.40d multicolored 1.40 .75

Expo '92, Seville — A374

1992, Oct. 12
746 A374 3.40d multicolored 1.40 .75

Discovery of America, 500th Anniv. A375

1992, Oct. 12
747 A375 3.40d multicolored 1.40 .75

Bird Type of 1991

1992, Oct. 26 **Litho.** ***Perf. 14***
748 A364 3d Gyps fulvus 1.50 .65
749 A364 3d Ganga cata, horiz. 1.50 .65

Green March Anniv. Type of 1987

1992, Nov. 6 **Litho.** ***Perf. 14***
750 A323 3.40d multicolored .95 .75

Green March, 17th anniv.

Sherifian Post, Cent. A377

Designs: 3.40d, Octagonal Sherifian postal seal, scroll, Sultan Moulay Hassan I. 5d, Scroll, various circular and octagonal Sherifian postal seals, Sultan.

1992, Nov. 22 **Litho.** ***Perf. 14***
751 A377 1.35d multicolored .55 .25
752 A377 3.40d multicolored .95 .75

Size: 165x115mm

Imperf

753 A377 5d multicolored 2.00 1.00
Nos. 751-753 (3) 3.50 2.00

Intl. Conference on Nutrition, Rome — A378

1992, Dec. 7 **Litho.** ***Perf. 14***
754 A378 3.40d multicolored 1.40 .75

Al Massira Airport, Agadir — A379

1992, Dec. 21 **Litho.** ***Perf. 14***
755 A379 3.40d multicolored 1.25 .80

Hand Stamp Type of 1985

Sherifian postal seals of Maghzen-Tanger, 1892: 1.70, Circular. 3.80d, Octagonal.

1993, Jan. 29 **Litho.** ***Perf. 14***
756 A287 1.70d green & black .45 .35
757 A287 3.80d orange & black 1.00 .80

Stamp Day.

Week of the Blind A380

1993, Mar. 15 **Litho.** ***Perf. 14***
758 A380 4.40d multicolored 1.25 1.00

World Meteorology Day — A381

1993, Mar. 23
759 A381 4.40d multicolored 1.25 1.00

Red Crescent Society — A382

1993, Apr. 26 **Litho.** ***Perf. 14***
760 A382 4.40d multicolored 1.25 1.00

A383

1993, June 14
761 A383 4.40d multicolored 1.25 1.00

World Telecommunications Day.

Argania Spinosa — A384

1993, July 26 Litho. *Perf. 14*

762	A384 1.70d Extracting oil	.60	.35
763	A384 4.80d Tree branch	1.75	1.00

A385

1993, Aug. 21

764 A385 4.80d multicolored 1.25 1.00

Prince Sidi Mohammed, 30th birthday.

Inauguration of the Hassan II Mosque A386

1993, Aug. 30 *Perf. 13*

765 A386 4.80d multicolored 1.25 1.00

A387

1993, Sept. 30 Litho. *Perf. 14*

766 A387 4.80d multicolored 1.25 1.00

King and People's Revolution, 40th Anniv.

World Post Day — A388

1993, Oct. 15

767 A388 4.80d multicolored 1.25 1.00

New Islamic University — A389

1993, Nov. 1 Litho. *Perf. 14*

768 A389 4.80d multicolored 1.25 1.00

Green March Anniv. Type of 1987

1993, Nov. 6

769 A323 4.80d multicolored 1.25 1.00

Green March, 18th anniv.

Water Birds A390

1993, Dec. 13 Litho. *Perf. 14*

770	A390 1.70d Sarcelle marbree	.75	.30
771	A390 4.80d Foulque a crete	1.75	.85

Manifest of Independence, 50th Anniv. — A391

1994, Mar. 31 Litho. *Perf. 14*

772 A391 4.80d multicolored 2.50 .85

A392

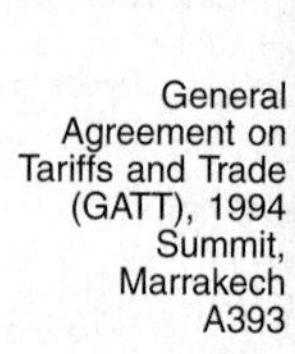

General Agreement on Tariffs and Trade (GATT), 1994 Summit, Marrakech A393

No. 774Ab, 1.70d, like #773. c, 4.80d, like #774.

1994, Apr. 29 Litho. *Perf. 14*

773	A392 1.70d multicolored	.50	.30
774	A393 4.80d multicolored	1.25	.80

Sheet of 2

Rouletted

774A A393 #b.-c. 3.50 3.00

Buildings and background are all in shades of claret on Nos. 774b-774c. No. 773 has building and background in shades of green. No. 774 has black building with claret background. No. 774A sold for 10d.

Week of the Blind — A394

1994, May 9

775 A394 4.80d multicolored 3.00 1.10

Red Crescent Society — A395

1994, May 18

776 A395 4.80d multicolored 1.40 .85

Natl. Conference on Children's Rights — A396

4.80d, Boy, girl under sun.

1994, May 25

777	A396 1.70d shown	.50	.30
778	A396 4.80d multi	1.25	.85

1994 World Cup Soccer Championships, US — A397

1994, June 17 *Perf. 13*

779 A397 4.80d multicolored 2.50 1.00

King Hassan II, 65th Birthday A398

Designs: 1.70d, Wearing business suit. 4.80d, Wearing traditional costume, vert.

1994 *Perf. 13x12½, 12½x13*

780	A398 1.70d multicolored	.90	.30
781	A398 4.80d multicolored	2.25	1.00

A399

1994, June 27 *Perf. 12½x13*

782 A399 4.80d multicolored 1.75 .60

Intl. Olympic Committee, Cent.

A400

1994

783 A400 4.80d multicolored 1.20 .60

Death of Antoine de Saint-Exupery, 50th anniv.

Flowers A401

1.70d, Chamaelon gummifer. 4.80d, Pancratium maritimum, vert.

1994 *Perf. 13x12½, 12½x13*

784	A401 1.70d multi	.60	.30
785	A401 4.80d multi	1.25	.60

Water Birds A402

1.70d, Courlis a bec grele. 4.80d, Goeland d'audouin.

1994, Oct. 24 Photo. *Perf. 13x13½*

786	A402 1.70d multi	1.50	.60
787	A402 4.80d multi	4.50	2.00

A403

Green March, 19th Anniv.: 4.80d, Marchers, map, inscription.

1994, Nov. 6 Litho. *Perf. 12½*

788	A403 1.70d multicolored	.40	.30
789	A403 4.80d multicolored	1.10	.80

Hand Stamp Type of 1985

Sherifan postal seals of Maghzen-Marrakesh: 1.70d, Circular. 4.80d, Octagonal.

1994, Nov. 22 *Perf. 12½*

790	A287 1.70d blue & black	.60	.30
791	A287 4.80d vermilion & black	1.40	.80

Stamp Day.

Week of the Blind — A404

1995, Feb. 27 Litho. *Perf. 13½*

792 A404 4.80d multicolored 2.00 .80

Arab League, 50th Anniv. — A405

1995, Mar. 22 Litho. *Perf. 13½*
793 A405 4.80d multicolored 1.40 .80

Red Crescent Society — A406

1995, Apr. 24 Litho. *Perf. 13½x13*
794 A406 4.80d multicolored 1.40 .80

Flowers — A407

1995, May 29 Litho. *Perf. 13½x13*
795 A407 2d Malva hispanica .50 .35
796 A407 4.80d Phlomis crinita 1.40 .85

Birds — A408

1.70d, Coracias garrulus. 4.80d, Carduelis carduelis.

1995, Sept. 18 Litho. *Perf. 13½x13*
797 A408 1.70d multi .45 .30
798 A408 4.80d multi 1.10 .85

See Nos. 818-819, 832-833, 846-847.

FAO, 50th Anniv. A409

1995, Oct. 16 Photo. *Perf. 13½*
799 A409 4.80d multicolored 1.40 .85

UN, 50th Anniv. A410

1.70d, "50," Moroccan, UN flags. 4.80d, Moroccan flag, UN emblem, map of Africa.

1995, Oct. 24 *Perf. 12½*
800 A410 1.70d multicolored .75 .30
801 A410 4.80d multicolored 2.25 .85

Green March Anniv. Type of 1987 and

Green March, 20th Anniv. — A411

1995, Nov. 6 Photo. *Perf. 12½*
802 A323 1.70d multicolored .40 .30
803 A411 4.80d multicolored 1.10 .85

A412

Independence, 40th anniv.: 4.80d, Crown, national flag. 10d, King Mohammed V, crown over flag, King Hassan II.

1995, Nov. 18 Litho. *Perf. 12½*
804 A412 4.80d multicolored 1.25 .85

Size: 112x83mm

Imperf

805 A412 10d multicolored 2.75 2.00

Hand Stamp Type of 1985

Sherifan postal seals of Maghzen-Meknes, 1892: 1.70d, Circular. 4.80d, Octagonal.

1995, Nov. 22 Photo. *Perf. 12½*
806 A287 1.70d olive & black .40 .30
807 A287 4.80d violet & black 1.10 .85

Stamp Day.

A413

1996, Mar. 3 Litho. *Perf. 13½*
808 A413 2d Natl. arms .45 .35
809 A413 5.50d King Hassan II 1.25 .95

Size: 134x86mm

Imperf

810 A413 10d Crown, King 2.75 1.75

Accession of King Hassan II, 35th anniv.

Traditional Crafts — A414

1996, Mar. 25 Photo. *Perf. 13½x13*
811 A414 5.50d Pottery 1.25 1.00
812 A414 5.50d Copper 1.25 1.00

Flowers — A415

2d, Cleonia lusitanica. 5.50d, Tulipa sylvestris.

1996, Apr. 25
813 A415 2d multi .50 .40
814 A415 5.50d multi 1.25 1.00

A416

King Hassan II: 2d, In uniform. 5.50d, Wearing traditional headpiece.

1996, May 14 Photo. *Perf. 13x13½*
815 A416 2d multicolored .60 .40
816 A416 5.50d multicolored 1.40 1.00

Royal Armed Forces, 40th anniv.

A417

1996, July 19 Photo. *Perf. 13½x13*
817 A417 5.50d multicolored 1.25 1.00

1996 Summer Olympics, Atlanta.

Bird Type of 1995

2d, Pandion haliaetus. 5.50d, Egretta garzetta.

1996, Oct. 21 Photo. *Perf. 13½x13*
818 A408 2d multi 1.40 .40
819 A408 5.50d multi 3.00 1.00

Green March Anniv. Type of 1987

1996, Nov. 6 Litho. *Perf. 13½*
820 A323 5.50d multicolored 1.50 1.00

Green March, 21st anniv.

Hand Stamp Type of 1985

Sherifan postal seals of Maghzen-Fes, 1892: 2d, Circular. 5.50d, Octagonal.

1996, Nov. 22 Photo. *Perf. 13½*
821 A287 2d orange & black .45 .35
822 A287 5.50d green & black 1.40 1.00

Stamp Day.

UNICEF, 50th Anniv. A418

1996, Dec. 11 *Perf. 13x13½*
823 A418 5.50d multicolored 1.25 1.00

Moroccan Pottery A419

1997, Feb. 24 Photo. *Perf. 13x13½*
824 A419 5.50d multicolored 1.25 .90

Flowers — A420

2d, Lupinus luteus. 5.50d, Silybum marianum.

1997, Mar. 24 Photo. *Perf. 13½x13*
825 A420 2d multi .90 .25
826 A420 5.50d multi 2.50 .60

A421

Speakers, 1947: No. 827, Crown Prince Hassan. No. 828, Sultan Mohammed V.

1997, Apr. 9 Litho. *Perf. 13½x13*
827 A421 2d multicolored .70 .25
828 A421 2d multicolored .70 .25

Speech in Tangier by King Hassan II, 50th anniv.

World Reading and Copyright Day — A422

1997, Apr. 23
829 A422 5.50d multicolored 1.25 .60

Intl. Meeting on Ibn Battuta (1304-77?), Traveler and Writer — A423

1997, May 9 *Perf. 13x13½*
830 A423 5.50d multicolored 1.25 .60

Moroccan Copper — A424

1997, July 21 **Photo.** ***Perf. 13½***
831 A424 5.50d multicolored 1.25 .55

Bird Type of 1995

Designs: 2d, Anthropoides virgo. 5.50d, Parus caeruleus ultramarinus.

1997, Oct. 20 **Photo.** ***Perf. 13½x13***
832 A408 2d multicolored .50 .25
833 A408 5.50d multicolored 1.40 .60

Green March Anniv. Type of 1987

1997, Nov. 6 ***Perf. 13½***
834 A323 5.50d multicolored 1.20 .60

Green March, 22nd anniversary.

Hand Stamp Type of 1985

Sherifan postal seals of Maghzen-Larache, 1892: 2d, Circular. 5.50d, Octagonal.

1997 **Photo.** ***Perf. 13½***
835 A287 2d blue & black .50 .25
836 A287 5.50d vermilion & black 1.25 .60

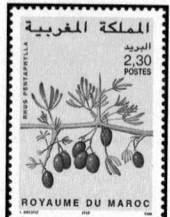

Flowers — A425

2.30d, Rhus pentaphylla. 6d, Orchis papilionacea.

1998 **Photo.** ***Perf. 13½x13***
837 A425 2.30d multi .65 .30
838 A425 6d multi 1.60 .80

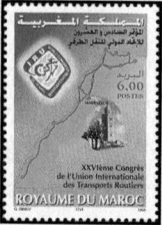

A426

1998
839 A426 6d multicolored 1.60 .80

25th Intl. Road Transportation Congress.

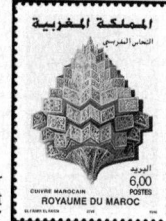

Copper Ornament A427

1998
840 A427 6d multicolored 1.60 .80

A428

1998
841 A428 6d multicolored 1.60 .80

1998 World Cup Soccer Championships, France.

Pottery A429

1998 ***Perf. 13x13½***
842 A429 6d multicolored 1.60 .80

Intl. Year of the Ocean A430

1998
843 A430 6d multicolored 1.60 .80

King & People's Revolution, 45th Anniv. A431

1998
844 A431 6d multicolored 1.60 .80

World Stamp Day — A432

1998 **Photo.** ***Perf. 13½x13***
845 A432 6d multicolored 1.60 .80

Bird Type of 1995

Designs: 2.30d, Luscinia megarhynchos. 6d, Struthio camelus.

1998 **Photo.**
846 A408 2.30d multicolored .65 .30
847 A408 6d multicolored 1.60 .80

Green March Anniv. Type

1998, Nov. 6 ***Perf. 13½***
848 A323 6d multicolored 1.60 .80

Green March, 23rd anniv.

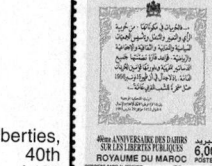

Public Liberties, 40th Anniv. — A433

1998 **Litho.** ***Perf. 13½x13***
849 A433 6d multicolored 1.60 .80

A434

1998 **Photo.**
850 A434 6d multicolored 1.60 .80

Universal Declaration of Human Rights, 50th anniv.

World Theater Day — A435

1999 **Litho.** ***Perf. 13¼***
851 A435 6d multi 1.50 .75

Flora — A436

2.30d, Eryngium triquetrum. 6d, Viscum cruciatum.

1999
852 A436 2.30d multi .60 .30
853 A436 6d multi 1.50 .75

Bab Mansour Laalej — A437

1999 ***Perf. 13x13¼***
854 A437 6d multi 1.50 .75

Jewelry A438

1999 ***Perf. 13¼***
855 A438 6d multi 1.50 .75

A439

1999
856 A439 2.30d On throne .60 .30
857 A439 6d In robes 1.50 .75
a. Souvenir sheet, #856-857, imperf, without gum 2.25 1.10

King Hassan II, 70th birthday.

World Environment Day — A440

1999
858 A440 6d multi 1.50 .75

UPU, 125th Anniv. — A441

1999, Oct. 9 **Photo.** ***Perf. 13¼***
859 A441 6d multi 1.25 .60

FAO Medal Awarded by King Hassan II — A442

1999, Oct. 16
860 A442 6d multi 1.60 .60

See No. 964.

Anti-poverty Week — A443

1999, Nov. 11 **Photo.** ***Perf. 11¾***
Granite Paper
861 A443 6d multi 1.40 1.00

Compare with type A461.

Green March Anniv. Type of 1987

1999, Nov. 6 **Photo.** ***Perf. 13¼***
862 A323 6d multi 1.60 .60

Green March, 24th anniv.

Fish
A444

Designs: 2.30d, Diplodus cervinus. 6d, Lampris guttatus.

1999, Nov. 29 **Photo.** ***Perf. 13¼***

863 A444 2.30d multi .65 .25
864 A444 6d multi 1.50 .75

Miniature Sheet

Morocco Year in France — A445

No. 865: a, Stork on nest. b, People in robes. c, Mandolin, pillars. d, Boat at dock.

1999, Dec. 13 ***Perf. 13¼x13***

865 A445 Sheet of 4 6.25 3.00
a.-d. 6d Any single 1.50 .75

African Cup Soccer Tournament — A446

2000, Jan. 25 ***Perf. 11¾x11½***
Granite Paper

866 A446 6d multi 1.50 .75

Year 2000
A447

2000, Jan. 31 **Granite Paper**

867 A447 6d multi 1.50 .75

Reconstruction of Agadir, 40th Anniv. — A448

2000, Feb. 29 **Photo.** ***Perf. 11¾***
Granite Paper

868 A448 6.50d multi 1.60 .80

Islamic Development Bank — A449

2000, Mar. 6 **Photo.** ***Perf. 11¾x11½***
Granite Paper

869 A449 6.50d multi 1.60 .80

Natl. Day of the Handicapped — A450

2000, Mar. 30 **Granite Paper**

870 A450 6.50d multi 1.60 .80

Flora
A451

Designs: 2.50d, Jasione montana. 6.50d, Pistorica breviflora.

2000, Apr. 27 **Photo.** ***Perf. 11¾***
Granite Paper

871-872 A451 Set of 2 2.50 1.10

World Meteorological Organization, 50th Anniv. — A452

2000, May 15 **Granite Paper**

873 A452 6.50d multi 1.60 .80

Marrakesh Arts Festival
A453

2000, June 5 **Photo.** ***Perf. 11¾***
Granite Paper

874 A453 6.50d multi 1.60 .80

Intl. Peace Year
A454

2000 **Photo.** ***Perf. 11¾***
Granite Paper

875 A454 6.50d multi 1.60 .80

Enthronement of King Mohammed VI, 1st Anniv. — A455

King in: 2.50d, Business suit. 6.50d, Robe.

2000, July 30 **Photo.** ***Perf. 11¾***
Granite Paper

877-878 A455 Set of 2 2.10 1.00
878a Souvenir sheet of 2, #877-878, imperf. 2.50 1.25

No. 878a sold for 10d.

Intl. Festival, Volubilis
A456

2000, Sept. 8 ***Perf. 11¾***
Granite Paper

879 A456 6.50d multi 1.90 1.60

2000 Summer Olympics, Sydney — A457

2000, Sept. 15 **Granite Paper**

880 A457 6.50d multi 1.90 1.60

SOS Children's Villages — A458

2000, Oct. 12 **Granite Paper**

881 A458 6.50d multi 1.75 .80

World Teacher's Day — A459

2000, Oct. 25 **Photo.** ***Perf. 11¾***
Granite Paper

882 A459 6.50d multi 1.75 .80

Anti-poverty Week — A461

2000, Nov. 1 **Photo.** ***Perf. 11¾***
Granite Paper

884 A461 6.50d multi 1.75 .80

Compare with type A443. Value is for stamp with surrounding selvage. See Nos. 911, 928, 953, 997, 1027, 1048, 1076, 1098, 1117, 1144, 1159.

Green March Anniv. Type of 1987 and

Map and Inscription
A462

2000, Nov. 6 **Photo.** ***Perf. 11¾***
Granite Paper

885 A323 2.50d multi .65 .25
886 A462 6.50d multi 1.75 .80

Green March, 25th anniv.

Antoine de Saint-Exupéry (1900-44), Aviator, Writer — A463

2000, Nov. 13 Photo. ***Perf. 11¾***
Granite Paper

887 A463 6.50d multi 2.00 .80

Independence, 45th Anniv. — A464

2000, Nov. 18 **Granite Paper**

888 A464 6.50d multi 1.60 .80

Fish A465

Designs: 2.50d, Apogon imberbis. 6.50d, Scorpaena loppei.

2000, Dec. 25 **Granite Paper**

889-890 A465 Set of 2 2.75 1.25

El Gharbi Gate A466

2001, Mar. 22 Photo. ***Perf. 11¾***
Granite Paper

891 A466 6.50d multi 1.75 1.00

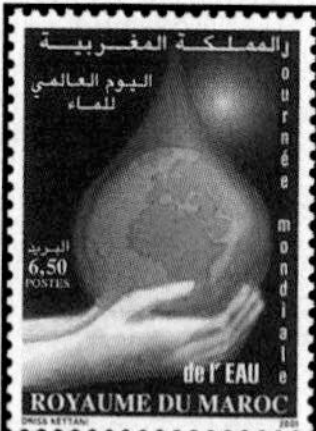

World Water Day — A467

2001, Mar. 30 **Granite Paper**

892 A467 6.50d multi 1.75 1.00

Armed Forces, 45th Anniv. — A468

Designs: 2.50d, Soldier and insignia. 6.50d, Soldier in frame.

2001, May 16 Litho. ***Perf. 14¼x13¾***

893-894 A468 Set of 2 2.40 1.25

Flora — A469

Designs: 2.50d, Euphorbia rigida. 6.50d, Glaucium flavum.

2001, June 7 Photo. ***Perf. 11¾***
Granite Paper

895-896 A469 Set of 2 2.75 1.25

Houses of Worship — A470

Designs: 2.50d, Koekelberg Basilica, Belgium. 6.50d, Hassan II Mosque, Casablanca.

2001, June 10 **Granite Paper**

897-898 A470 Set of 2 2.25 1.50

See Belgium Nos. 1855-1856.

Natl. Diplomacy Day — A471

Perf. 14¼x13¾

2001, June 29 **Litho.**

899 A471 6.50d multi 1.75 .70

A472

A473

A474

King Mohammed VI A475

Perf. 12¾x13¼, 13¼x12¾

2001, July 31 **Litho.**

Size: 24x33mm

900 A472 2.50d multi .55 .25
901 A473 6d multi 1.40 .55
902 A474 6.50d multi 1.50 .60

Size: 32x24mm
Arms 14mm Tall

903 A475 10d multi 2.40 .85
Nos. 900-903 (4) 5.85 2.25

Compare type A472 with type A687; type A473 with types A572 and A688; type A475 with type A573.

See Nos. 934A-934B, 940-943, 960-962, 1007A-1007B, 1020, 1029A.

Marine Life — A476

Designs: 2.50d, Lophius budegassa. 6.50d, Monachus monachus, horiz.

2001, Sept. 28 Litho. ***Perf. 11¾***
Granite Paper

904-905 A476 Set of 2 2.25 .95

Hand Stamp Type of 1985

Hand stamps of Ksar el Kebir, 1892: 2.50d, Round. 6.50d, Octagonal.

2001, Oct. 9 Litho. ***Perf. 14¼x13¾***

906 A287 2.50d olive & black .70 .25
907 A287 6.50d violet & black 1.75 .70

World Day to Combat Desertification A477

2001, Oct. 29 Litho. ***Perf. 13¼***

908 A477 6.50d multi 1.40 .60

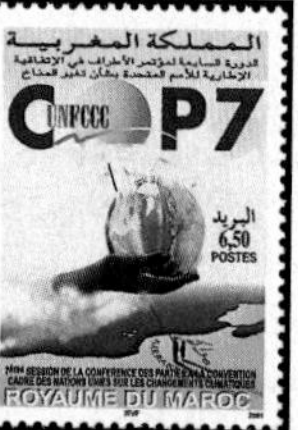

7th UN Climate Change Conference A478

2001, Oct. 29

909 A478 6.50d multi 1.40 .60

Green March, 26th Anniv. A479

2001, Nov. 7 Photo. ***Perf. 13x13¼***

910 A479 6.50d multi 1.40 .60

Anti-Poverty Week Type of 2000 and

Anti-Poverty Week A480

2001, Nov. 8 ***Perf. 12½***

911 A461 6.50d multi 1.60 .60

Perf. 13x13¼

912 A480 6.50d multi 1.60 .60

Value of No. 911 is for stamp with surrounding selvage.

Year of Dialogue Among Civilizations A481

2001, Dec. 14 ***Perf. 13¼x13***

913 A481 6.50d multi 1.40 .60

Fountains — A482

Designs: 2.50d, Wallace Fountain, Paris. 6.50d, Nejjarine Fountain, Fez.

2001, Dec. 14 ***Perf. 13¼***

914-915 A482 Set of 2 2.25 .85

See No. 963. See France Nos. 2847-2848.

Chellah Gate A483

2002, Feb. 28 ***Perf. 13x13¼***

916 A483 6.50d multi 1.60 .60

Intl. Women's Day — A484

2002, Mar. 8 ***Perf. 13¼x13***

917 A484 6.50d multi 1.60 .60

Cedar Tree — A485

2002, Mar. 29

918 A485 6.50d multi 1.60 .60

2nd World Assembly on the Elderly A486

2002, Apr. 30 ***Perf. 13x13¼***

919 A486 6.50d multi 1.60 .60

Special Session of UN General Assembly on Children — A487

2002, May 8 ***Perf. 13¼x13***
920 A487 6.50d multi 1.60 .60

Dated 2001.

Flora — A488

Designs: 2.50d, Linaria bipartita. 6.50d, Verbascum pseudocreticum.

2002, June 5 **Photo.** ***Perf. 13¼x13***
921-922 A488 Set of 2 2.75 .80

Intl. Telecommunications Union Plenipotentiary Conference, Marrakesh — A489

2002, Sept. 23 **Photo.** ***Perf. 13¼***
923 A489 6.50d multi 1.60 .60

Size: 120x90mm

Imperf

Without Gum

924 A489 10d multi 2.75 1.50

Palestinian Intifada A490

2002, Sept. 28 ***Perf. 13¼***
925 A490 6.50d multi 1.60 .70

Intl. Year of Ecotourism A491

2002, Sept. 30
926 A491 6.50d multi 1.60 .70

Green March, 27th Anniv. — A492

2002, Nov. 7
927 A492 6.50d multi 1.60 .70

Anti-Poverty Week Type of 2000 and

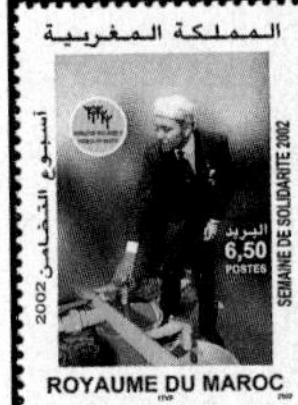

Anti-Poverty Week — A493

2002, Nov. 8 ***Perf. 12½***
928 A461 6.50d multi 1.40 .70

Perf. 13¼

929 A493 6.50d multi 1.40 .70

Value of No. 928 is for stamp with surrounding selvage.

Maghzen Post, 110th Anniv. A494

Sultan Moulay Hassan I and: 2.50d, Circular postal seal. 6.50d, Octagonal postal seal.

2002, Nov. 22 ***Perf. 12½, 13 (6.50d)***
930-931 A494 Set of 2 2.50 .95

Value of Nos. 930-931 are for stamps with surrounding selvage. No. 931 is ocatagonally shaped.

UN Year for Cultural Heritage A495

2002, Dec. 18 ***Perf. 13¼x13***
932 A495 6.50d multi 1.75 .70

Fish A496

Designs: 2.50d, Alosa alosa. 6.50d, Epinephelus marginatus.

2002, Dec. 30 ***Perf. 13¼***
933-934 A496 Set of 2 2.75 .95

King Mohammed VI Type of 2001

2002 **Litho.** ***Perf. 11½***

Granite Paper

Size: 24x30mm

934A A472 2.50d multi .75 .35
934B A473 6d multi 2.00 1.00

Bab el Okla, Tetuan A497

2003, Feb. 28 **Photo.** ***Perf. 13¼***
935 A497 6.50d multi 1.60 .70

Fir Trees A498

2003, Mar. 28
936 A498 6.50d multi 1.75 .70

Intl. Year of Fresh Water — A499

2003, Apr. 28 ***Perf. 13¼x13***
937 A499 6.50d multi 1.75 .70

Flora — A500

Designs: 2.50d, Limonium sincatum. 6.50d, Echinops spinosus.

2003, May 30 ***Perf. 13¼***
938-939 A500 Set of 2 2.75 1.25

King Mohammed VI Type of 2001

2003 **Litho.** ***Perf. 13¼x12¾***

940 A475 70c lt bl & multi .25 .25
941 A475 80c pur & multi .25 .25
942 A475 5d yel & multi 1.50 .50
943 A475 20d lil & multi 6.00 2.10
Nos. 940-943 (4) 8.00 3.10

Coat of arms on Nos. 940 and 941 is 14mm tall. See Nos. 1007A-1007B for stamps with coat of arms 11mm tall.

Salé Grand Mosque, 1000th Anniv. — A501

2003, July 11 **Photo.** ***Perf. 13x12¼***
944 A501 6.50d multi 1.60 .90

World Youth Congress A502

2003, Aug. 12 ***Perf. 13¼***
945 A502 6.50d multi 1.60 .90

Revolution of the King and People, 50th Anniv. A503

2003, Aug. 20
946 A503 6.50d multi 1.60 .90

King Mohammed VI, 40th Birthday — A504

Designs: Nos. 947, 949a, 2.50d, King in suit and tie. Nos. 948, 949b, 6.50d, King in robe.

2003, Aug. 21
947-948 A504 Set of 2 2.50 1.40

Souvenir Sheet

Stamps With Pink Frames

949 A504 Sheet of 2, #a-b 2.75 2.75

No. 949 sold for 10d.
Compare with type A545.

Fish A505

Designs: 2.50d, Sparisoma cretense. 6.50d, Anthias anthias.

2003, Sept. 30 **Photo.** ***Perf. 13¼***
950-951 A505 Set of 2 2.50 1.40

World Post Day — A506

2003, Oct. 9
952 A506 6.50d multi 1.90 .95

Anti-Poverty Week Type of 2000 and

King Mohammed VI Visiting Sick Child — A507

2003, Oct. 31 **Photo.** ***Perf. 12¾***
953 A461 6.50d multi 1.90 .95
954 A507 6.50d multi 1.90 .95

Green March, 28th Anniv. — A508

2003, Nov. 5 **Photo.** ***Perf. 13¼***
955 A508 6.50d multi 1.90 .95

Rabat, 2003 Arab Culture Capital — A509

2003, Dec. 19 Litho. *Perf. 13x13¼*
956 A509 6.50d multi 2.00 1.00

Philately at School A510

2003, Dec. 29 *Perf. 13¼*
957 A510 6.50d multi 2.00 1.00

UN Literacy Decade — A511

2003, Dec. 29 *Perf. 13x13¼*
958 A511 6.50d multi 2.00 1.00

Morocco - People's Republic of China Diplomatic Relations, 45th Anniv. — A512

2003, Dec. 31 *Perf. 12*
959 A512 6.50d multi 2.00 1.00

Types of 2001 Redrawn With Added Frame Lines

2002-03 Litho. *Perf. 11½*

Size: 24x30mm

960 A474 6.50d multi *2.50 2.50*

Size: 32x23mm

Arms 11mm Tall

961 A475 10d multi *4.00 4.00*

Booklet Stamps

Self-Adhesive

Serpentine Die Cut 11

Size: 20x23mm

962 A472 2.50d multi ('03) .70 .40
a. Booklet pane of 10 7.00
963 A482 6.50d Like #915 ('03) 1.75 1.00
a. Booklet pane of 10 17.50

Issued: 6.50d, 10d, 2002. 2.50d, 6.50d, 9/3/03.
On No. 903, arms are 9mm tall.

FAO Medal Type of 1999

2003, July Photo. *Perf. 13x13¼*

Size: 48x38mm

964 A442 6d multi *5.00 5.00*

Ibn Battutah (1304-68), Traveler and Author — A513

2004, Feb. 24 Photo. *Perf. 13x12¼*
965 A513 6.50d multi 2.00 1.00

Bab Agnaou, Marrakesh A514

2004, Mar. 18 *Perf. 13¼*
966 A514 6.50d multi 2.00 1.00

Flowers — A515

Designs: 2.50d, Linaria gharbensis. 6.50d, Nigella damascena.

2004, Mar. 29
967-968 A515 Set of 2 2.75 1.25

16th World Military Equestrian Championships, Témara — A516

2004, Apr. 18
969 A516 6.50d multi 2.00 1.00

Hassan II Tennis Grand Prix, 20th Anniv. — A517

2004, May 14
970 A517 6.50d multi 2.25 1.00

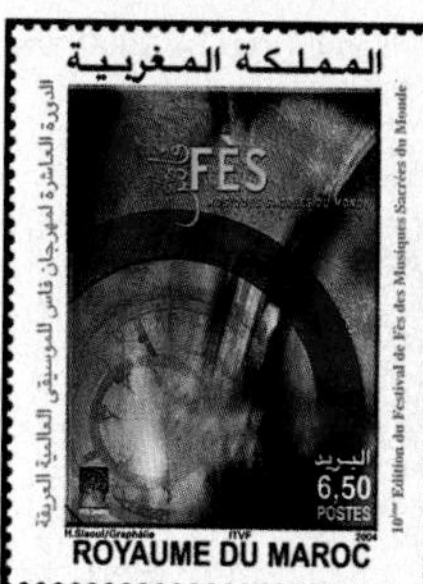
10th World Sacred Music Festival, Fez A518

2004, May 28 *Perf. 12¼x13*
971 A518 6.50d multi 2.00 1.00

Caftan — A519

2004, June 18 *Perf. 13¼*
972 A519 6.50d multi 2.00 1.00

Dinosaur Fossils Found in Tazouda A520

2004, July 12
973 A520 6.50d multi 2.00 1.00

30th Intl. Military History Congress A521

2004, July 29
974 A521 6.50d multi 2.00 1.00

Enthronement of King Mohammed VI, 5th Anniv. — A522

Designs: Nos. 975, 977a, 2.50d, King in suit. Nos. 976, 977b, 6d, King in robe.

2004, July 30
975-976 A522 Set of 2 2.75 2.75

Souvenir Sheet

Stamps With Yellow Frames

977 A522 Sheet of 2, #a-b 3.00 3.00

No. 977 sold for 10d.

Intl. Peace Day — A523

2004, Sept. 21 Photo. *Perf. 13¼*
978 A523 6d multi 1.90 .95

Anti-Poverty Week Type of 2000 and

Anti-Poverty Week — A524

2004, Oct. 22 *Perf. 12¾*
979 A461 6.50d multi 2.00 1.00

Perf. 13¼
980 A524 6.50d multi 2.00 1.00

Value for No. 979 is for stamp with surrounding selvage.

Green March, 29th Anniv. — A525

2004, Nov. 6 Photo. *Perf. 13¼*
981 A525 6d multi 2.00 1.00

Marine Life A526

Designs: 2.50d, Xiphias gladius. 6.50d, Octopus vulgaris.

2004, Nov. 16 Photo. *Perf. 13¼*
982-983 A526 Set of 2 2.75 1.25

World Children's Day — A527

2004, Nov. 24
984 A527 6.50d multi 2.00 1.00

Rotary International, Cent. — A528

2005, Feb. 23 *Perf. 13x13¼*
985 A528 6.50d multi 2.00 1.00

Arab League, 60th Anniv. — A529

2005, Mar. 22 *Perf. 13¼x13*

986 A529 6.50d multi 2.00 1.00

Bab Boujloud, Fez A530

2005, Mar. 30 *Perf. 13¼*

987 A530 6.50d multi 2.00 1.00

Amnesty International A531

2005, May 6 **Photo.** *Perf. 13¼*

988 A531 6.50d multi 2.00 1.00

Flora — A532

Designs: 2.50d, Erodium sebaceum. 6.50d, Linaria ventricosa.

2005, May 26 **Photo.** *Perf. 13¼*

989-990 A532 Set of 2 2.50 1.00

Rock Carvings, Iourarhane A533

2005, May 31

991 A533 6.50d multi 2.00 1.00

13th World Neurosurgery Congress, Marrakesh A534

2005, June 19

992 A534 6.50d multi 2.00 1.00

Phosphates Office, 80th Anniv. — A535

2005, Aug. 31 **Photo.** *Perf. 13¼*

993 A535 6.50d multi 2.00 1.00

United Nations, 60th Anniv. — A536

2005, Oct. 24

994 A536 6.50d multi 2.00 1.00

Green March, 30th Anniv. A537

Marchers and "30" in: 2.50d, Light blue. 6d, Green.

2005, Nov. 6

995-996 A537 Set of 2 2.75 2.75

Anti-Poverty Week Type of 2000 and

Anti-Poverty Week — A538

2005, Nov. 7 *Perf. 12¾*

997 A461 6.50d multi 2.00 1.00

Perf. 13¼

998 A538 6.50d multi 2.00 1.00

Values for No. 997 are for stamps with surrounding selvage.

Friendship of Morocco and the Netherlands, 400th Anniv. — A539

Designs: No. 999, 6.50d, Five tourist attractions. No. 1000, 6.50d, Arch and waterway, vert.

2005, Nov. 14 *Perf. 13¼*

999-1000 A539 Set of 2 4.00 1.90

World Summit on the Information Society, Tunis A540

2005, Nov. 16

1001 A540 6d multi 2.00 1.00

Return from Exile of King Mohammed V, 50th Anniv. — A541

Country name in: No. 1002, Red. No. 1003a, Green.

2005, Nov. 16 *Perf. 13¼x13*

1002 A541 6.50d multi 1.90 1.00

Souvenir Sheet

1003 Sheet, #1002, 1003a 4.00 2.25

a. A541 6.50d multi 1.75 .75

Souvenir Sheet

Children's Art — A542

No. 1004: a, Children and flower, by Kaoutar Azizi Alaoui. b, Children and dove, by Sara Bourquiba. c, House and trees, by Mohcine Kahyouchat. d, Sun on horizon, by Anise Anico.

2005, Nov. 21 *Perf. 13x13¼*

1004 A542 2.50d Sheet of 4, #a-d 3.00 2.00

Intl. Year of Microcredit A543

2005, Nov. 30 *Perf. 13¼*

1005 A543 6.50d multi 2.00 1.00

Marine Life A544

Designs: 2.50d, Sparus aurata. 6d, Sepia officinalis.

2005, Dec. 22

1006-1007 A544 Set of 2 2.70 1.00

King Mohammed VI Type of 2001 Redrawn With Smaller Coat of Arms

2005 **Litho.** *Perf. 11½*

Coat of Arms 11mm Tall

1007A A475 70c multi *5.00 1.00*

1007B A475 80c multi *5.00 1.00*

Nos. 1007A and 1007B are dated 2005. Coat of arms is 14mm tall on Nos. 940 and 941.

King Mohammed VI — A545

Designs: No. 1008, King in suit and tie. No. 1009, King in robe.

2005 **Litho.** *Serpentine Die Cut 11*

Booklet Stamps

Self-Adhesive

1008 A545 2.50d multi .75 .75

1009 A545 2.50d multi .75 .75

a. Booklet pane, 5 each #1008-1009 7.50

Compare type A545 with A504. See Nos. 1054A-1054B.

Bustard A546

Melierax Metabates A547

Egretta Garzetta A548

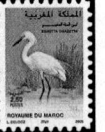

Pandion Haliaetus A549

Alectoris Barbara A550

Porphyrio Porphyrio A551

Carduelis Carduelis A552

Bird A553

Duck A554

Falcon A555

Self-Adhesive

2005 *Serpentine Die Cut 11*

1010 Booklet pane of 10 8.50

a. A546 2.50d multi .85 .40

b. A547 2.50d multi .85 .40

c. A548 2.50d multi .85 .40

d. A549 2.50d multi .85 .40

e. A550 2.50d multi .85 .40

f. A551 2.50d multi .85 .40

g. A552 2.50d multi .85 .40

h. A553 2.50d multi .85 .40

i. A554 2.50d multi .85 .40

j. A555 2.50d multi .85 .40

Two Women
A556

Ait Mouhad
A557

Saharaoui
Derraa
A558

Two Women
A559

Citadin
A560

Saharaoui
Melhfa
A561

Tata Woman
A562

Tata Man
A563

Meknassa
A564

Mokhazni
du Roi
A565

Self-Adhesive

2005 ***Serpentine Die Cut 11***

1011	Booklet pane of 10	20.00	
a.	A556 6d multi	2.00	1.10
b.	A557 6d multi	2.00	1.10
c.	A558 6d multi	2.00	1.10
d.	A559 6d multi	2.00	1.10
e.	A560 6d multi	2.00	1.10
f.	A561 6d multi	2.00	1.10
g.	A562 6d multi	2.00	1.10
h.	A563 6d multi	2.00	1.10
i.	A564 6d multi	2.00	1.10
j.	A565 6d multi	2.00	1.10

Traffic Safety
Day — A566

2006, Feb. 18 Photo. ***Perf. 13½x13***
1012 A566 6.50d multi 2.00 1.00

OPEC Intl. Development Fund, 30th
Anniv. — A567

2006, Feb. 28 ***Perf. 13¼***
1013 A567 6.50d multi 2.00 1.00

Bab
Marshan,
Tangiers
A568

2006, Mar. 30
1014 A568 6.50d multi 1.90 1.00

Foreign
Affairs
Ministry,
50th
Anniv.
A569

2006, Apr. 26
1015 A569 6d multi 1.75 1.00

Flowers — A570

Designs: 2.50d, Narcissus cantabricus. 6.50d, Paeonia mascula.

2006, Apr. 28
1016-1017 A570 Set of 2 2.50 2.50

Royal
Armed
Forces,
50th
Anniv.
A571

Kings Mohammed VI, Hassan II, and Mohammed V, anniversary emblem, airplanes and: 2.50d, Tank. 6.50d, Ships.

2006, May 14
1018-1019 A571 Set of 2 2.50 1.10
1019a Souvenir sheet, #1018-1019 2.75 2.75

No. 1019a sold for 10d.

Type of 2001 With Added Frameline and

A572

King
Mohammed
VI — A573

2006, July 1 Litho. ***Perf. 11½***
Granite Paper

1020	A472	3.25d blue & multi	.90	.50
1021	A572	7.80d lt grn & multi	2.40	1.20
1022	A573	13d lilac & multi	3.75	1.90
		Nos. 1020-1022 (3)	7.05	3.60

Designs size of No. 1020: 25x32mm.
See No. 1029A for stamp similar to No. 1020, with 22x32mm design without frameline.
See No. 1054D for stamp similar to No. 1021, with 22x32mm design, with country name in white, inscribed "Phil@poste" at bottom. Compare types A572 with types A473 and A688.
Compare type A573 with types A475 and A599a.

Barbary
Ape — A574

Atlas
Lion — A575

2006, July 31 ***Perf. 13¼x13***
1023 A574 3.25d multi .90 .50
1024 A575 7.80d multi 2.25 1.10

Green
March,
31st Anniv.
A576

Designs: No. 1025, 7.80d, King Mohammed VI waving to crowd. No. 1026, 7.80d, Mohammed VI Mosque, Boujdour.

2006, Nov. 7 Photo. ***Perf. 13¼***
1025-1026 A576 Set of 2 4.50 2.25

Anti-Poverty Week Type of 2000

2006, Nov. 10
1027 A461 7.80d multi 2.25 .95

Values are for stamps with surrounding selvage.

Stamp
Day — A577

2006, Nov. 22
1028 A577 7.80d multi 2.25 1.10

Values are for stamps with surrounding selvage.

Admission to the
United Nations,
50th
Anniv. — A578

2006, Nov. 24
1029 A578 7.80d multi 2.25 1.10

King Mohammed VI Type of 2001

2006, Nov. Litho. ***Perf. 13¼***
Size: 22x32mm
1029A A472 3.25d blue & multi 1.10 1.10

No. 1020 has a frame line around design while No. 1029A does not. No. 1029A has a printer's imprint of "Phil@poste."

World
AIDS Day
A579

2006, Dec. 1 Litho. ***Perf. 13¼***
1030 A579 7.80d multi 2.25 1.10

Diplomatic
Relations
Between
Morocco
and Japan,
50th Anniv.
A580

Designs: 3.25d, Dove, maps and flags. 7.80d, Flags, arches, pottery.

2006, Dec. 20 Photo. ***Perf. 13¼***
1031-1032 A580 Set of 2 3.25 1.50

Fish
A581

Designs: 3.25d, Thunnus thynnus. 7.80d, Sardina pilchardus.

2006, Dec. 25
1033-1034 A581 Set of 2 3.25 1.50

African Soccer Confederation, 50th
Anniv. — A582

2007, Feb. 26 Litho. ***Perf. 13¼***
1035 A582 7.80d multi 2.40 1.10

Values are for stamps with surrounding selvage.

Mohammed V
University, 50th
Anniv. — A583

2007, Mar. 15
1036 A583 3.25d multi 1.00 .50

Ibn Khaldun (1332-1406), Philosopher — A584

2007, Mar. 28
1037 A584 7.80d multi 2.40 1.10

Souvenir Sheet

Intl. Agricultural Exhibition, Meknès — A585

No. 1038: a, Palm trees. b, Argans. c, Cattle, horiz. d, Olives, horiz.

Perf. 12¾x13¼, 13¼x12¾ (horiz. stamps)

2007, Apr. 19

1038	A585	Sheet of 4	7.00	7.00
a.-b.		3.25d Either single	1.00	.50
c.-d.		7.80d Either single	2.40	1.25

No. 1038 sold for 24d.

Couscous A586

2007, June 1 ***Perf. 13¼x13***
1039 A586 7.80d multi 2.40 1.10

Andalusian Music — A587

2007, June 8 ***Perf. 13x13¼***
1040 A587 7.80d multi 2.40 1.10

Souvenir Sheet

Paintings — A588

No. 1041: a, Fulgurance, by M. Qotbi, vert. b, Horses and Riders, by, H. Glaoui. c, Symphonie d'Eté, by Qotbi. d, Horses, by Glaoui.

2007, June 21 ***Perf. 13***
1041 A588 3.25d Sheet of 4, #a-d 4.00 4.00

Scouting, Cent. — A589

2007, Aug. 7 **Litho.** ***Perf. 13¼***
1042 A589 7.80d multi 2.40 1.10

Buildings — A590

Designs: 3.25d, Silves Castle, Portugal. 7.80d, Tower, Arzila, Morocco.

2007, Sept. 26
1043-1044 A590 Set of 2 3.50 1.75

See Portugal Nos. 2955-2956.

World Post Day A591

2007, Oct. 9
1045 A591 3.25d multi 1.25 .90

Fez, 2007 Islamic Cultural Capital A592

2007, Oct. 30
1046 A592 7.80d multi 2.40 1.10

Compare with Type A618.

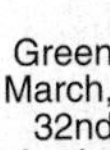

Green March, 32nd Anniv. A593

2007, Nov. 6
1047 A593 7.80d multi 2.40 1.10

Anti-Poverty Week Type of 2000

2007, Nov. 8
1048 A461 7.80d multi 2.40 1.10

Values are for stamps with surrounding selvage.

National Quality Week — A594

2007, Nov. 12
1049 A594 7.80d multi 2.40 1.10

World Children's Day — A595

2007, Nov. 20
1050 A595 7.80d multi 2.40 1.10

Supreme Court, 50th Anniv. — A596

2007, Nov. 21
1051 A596 3.25d multi 1.00 .50

Bab Lamrissa — A597

2007, Dec. 7 **Litho.** ***Perf. 13¼***
1052 A597 7.80d multi 2.40 1.10

Royal Air Morocco, 50th Anniv. A598

2007, Dec. 19
1053 A598 7.80d multi 2.40 1.10

"Morocco of Champions" — A599

2007, Dec. 28
1054 A599 7.80d multi 2.40 1.10

Values are for stamps with surrounding selvage.

King Mohammed VI Types of 2005, 2006 (Redrawn) and

King Mohammed VI — A599a

Designs: No. 1054A, King in suit and tie. No. 1054B, King in robe.

Booklet Stamps
Self-Adhesive

2007 **Litho.** ***Serpentine Die Cut 11***

1054A	A545	3.25d multi	1.00	1.00
1054B	A545	3.25d multi	1.00	1.00
c.		Booklet pane, 5 each #1054A-1054B	10.00	

Size: 22x32mm
Country Name in White
Water-Activated Gum
Perf. 13

1054D	A572	7.80d multi	2.25	1.10
f.		Dated 2009	2.25	1.00
g.		Dated 2010	2.25	.95

Compare with No. 1021, which is wider and has country name in blue.

Size: 31x23mm

1054E A599a 13d pink & multi 3.50 1.75

Compare with No. 1022, which is taller and has a lilac background.

Moroccan Travel Market A600

2008, Jan. 17
1055 A600 7.80d multi 2.40 1.10

Africa Cup of Nations Soccer Championships — A601

2008, Jan. 31
1056 A601 7.80d multi 2.40 1.10

Export Trophy — A602

2008, Apr. 4 **Litho.** ***Perf. 13¼***
1057 A602 3.25d multi 1.00 .50

Fez, 1200th Anniv. — A603

2008, Apr. 5
1058 A603 3.25d multi 1.00 .50

Flowers — A604

Designs: 3.25d, Calendula stellata. 7.80d, Convolvulus tricolor.

2008, Apr. 30 **Litho.** ***Perf. 13¼***
1059-1060 A604 Set of 2 3.25 1.60

Buildings in Morocco and Iran — A605

No. 1061: a, 3.25d, Flags of Morocco and Iran, Kasbah, Oudayas, Morocco, and Falak-Ol-Aflak Castle, Iran. b, 3,25d, Scroll and Falak-Ol-Aflak Castle. c, 7.80d, Scroll and Kasbah, Oudayas, Morocco.

2008, May 12 **Litho.** ***Perf. 13¼***
1061 A605 Horiz. strip of 3, #a-c 4.25 2.25

See Iran No. 2955.

Children's Art — A606

No. 1062: a, Earth, by Narjiss Lasfar. b, House and trees, by Chaimae Abbaich, horiz. c, Polluted sphere, by Ahmed Anas Bennis, vert. d, House and sun, by Wassim Chakou, vert.

2008, May 26
1062 Horiz. strip of 4 4.00 2.00
a.-d. A606 3.25d Any single .95 .45

World Environment Day — A607

2008, June 5
1063 A607 7.80d multi 2.40 1.10

Rug From Salé A608

Rug From Marmoucha A609

Rug From Ouled Besseba A610

Rug From Haut Atlas A611

Rug From Ait Haddou A612

Rug From Tazenakht A613

Rug From Marmoucha A614

Rug From Rabat A615

Rug From Ait Ouaouzguid A616

Rug From Rabat A617

Self-Adhesive

2008 ***Serpentine Die Cut 11***

1064	Booklet pane of 10	25.00	
a.	A608 7.80d multi	2.50	1.10
b.	A609 7.80d multi	2.50	1.10
c.	A610 7.80d multi	2.50	1.10
d.	A611 7.80d multi	2.50	1.10
e.	A612 7.80d multi	2.50	1.10
f.	A613 7.80d multi	2.50	1.10
g.	A614 7.80d multi	2.50	1.10
h.	A615 7.80d multi	2.50	1.10
i.	A616 7.80d multi	2.50	1.10
j.	A617 7.80d multi	2.50	1.10

Fez, 1200th Anniv. A618

2008, June 23 ***Perf. 13¼***
1065 A618 7.80d multi 2.40 1.10

Compare with Type A592.

Bouregreg Valley Light Rail Line — A619

No. 1066: a, 3.25d, Train, bridge. b, 7.80d, Train, fortress.

2008, July 21
1066 A619 Horiz. pair, #a-b 3.25 1.60

2008 Summer Olympics, Beijing — A620

No. 1067 — Olympic rings and: a, Four runners. b, Three hurdlers. c, Boxers. d, Runner.

2008, Aug. 8 **Photo.** ***Perf. 13¼***
1067 Horiz. strip of 4 4.00 2.00
a.-d. A620 3.25d Any single 1.00 .45

Arab Post Day — A621

No. 1068 — Emblem and: a, World map, pigeon. b, Camel caravan.

2008, Aug. 28 **Litho.** ***Perf. 12¾***
1068 Sheet of 2 4.50 2.25
a.-b. A621 7.80d Either single 2.25 1.10

Marine Life A622

Designs: 3.25d, Isurus oxyrinchus. 7.80d, Haliotis tuberculata.

2008, Sept. 18 ***Perf. 13¼***
1069-1070 A622 Set of 2 3.25 1.60

Miniature Sheet

Art and Culture — A623

No. 1071: a, Musicians. b, Ezzellij tiles. c, Haik (white garment). d, Koran school.

2008, Oct. 10 **Photo.** ***Perf. 13¼x13***
1071 A623 3.25d Sheet of 4, #a-d 4.00 2.00

Diplomatic Relations Between Morocco and People's Republic of China — A624

Designs: 3.25r, Vases and flags of Morocco and People's Republic of China. No. 1073, 7.80d, Intertwined arabesque and Chinese emblem. No. 1074, 7.80d, Arabic archway and Great Wall of China, vert.

2008, Oct. 30 **Photo.** ***Perf. 12***
1072-1074 A624 Set of 3 4.50 2.25

Green March, 33rd Anniv. A625

2008, Nov. 6 **Litho.** ***Perf. 13¼***
1075 A625 3.25d multi 1.00 .35

Anti-Poverty Week Type of 2000

2008, Nov. 12 **Photo.** ***Perf. 13¼***
1076 A461 7.80d multi 2.00 .95

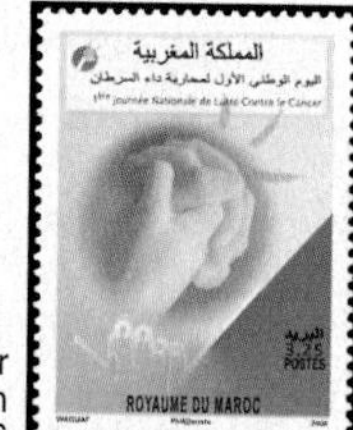
Natl. Cancer Prevention Day — A626

2008, Nov. 22 ***Perf. 13¼***
1077 A626 3.25d multi 1.00 .35

Universal Declaration of Human Rights, 60th Anniv. A627

2008, Dec. 10 **Litho.** ***Perf. 13***
1078 A627 7.80d multi 2.00 .95

Bab Al Marsa, Essaouira A628

2008, Dec. 26 **Photo.** ***Perf. 13¼***
1079 A628 7.80d multi 2.00 1.00

Louis Braille (1809-52), Educator of the Blind — A629

2009, Jan. 16
1080 A629 7.80d multi 2.00 .95

Insurance for Artisans and the Self-Employed — A630

2009, Feb. 16 ***Perf. 13x13¼***
1081 A630 3.25d multi 1.00 .35

25th Hassan II Grand Prix Tennis Tournament A631

2009, Apr. 6 ***Perf. 13¼***
1082 A631 3.25d multi 1.00 .40

Cadi Ayyad University, Marrakesh, 30th Anniv. A632

2009, Apr. 20
1083 A632 3.25d multi 1.00 .40

Sugar Industry — A633

2009, Apr. 22 **Photo.**
1084 A633 3.25d multi 1.00 .40

Leopard With Mail Bag — A633a

2009, May 6 **Litho.** ***Perf. 13x13¼***
1084A A633a 5.90d multi 2.00 .75

Natl. Theater Day A634

2009, May 14 **Photo.** ***Perf. 13¼***
1085 A634 3.25d multi 1.00 .40

Intl. Year of Astronomy A635

2009, May 15
1086 A635 7.80d multi 2.50 1.00

Protection for Children Using Computers A636

2009, May 17 **Litho.** ***Perf. 13x13¼***
1087 A636 7.80d multi 2.50 1.00

Al-Maghrib Bank, 50th Anniv. A637

2009, July 2 **Photo.** ***Perf. 13¼***
1088 A637 3.25d multi 1.00 .40

A638

Enthronement of King Mohammed VI, 10th Anniv. — A639

King Mohammed VI: 3.25d, On horse. 7.80d, Wearing suit.
15d, With images of Kings Mohammed V and Hassan II.

Photo. & Embossed With Foil Application

2009, July 30 ***Perf. 13¼***

Granite Paper (#1089-1090)

1089 A638 3.25d multi 1.00 .40
1090 A638 7.80d multi 2.50 1.00

Souvenir Sheet

Litho. with Three-Dimensional Plastic Affixed

Serpentine Die Cut 9½

Self-Adhesive

1091 A639 15d multi 6.50 6.50

Nos. 1089-1090 have gold frames with an orange cast. A souvenir sheet containing Nos. 1089-1090 having gold frames with a yellow cast sold for 36d.

Jerusalem, Capital of Arab Culture — A640

2009, Aug. 3 **Litho.** ***Perf. 13¼***
1092 A640 3.25d multi 1.00 .40

Natl. Women's Day — A641

2009, Oct. 10
1093 A641 3.25d multi 1.00 .40

Mohammedia School of Engineering, 50th Anniv. — A652

2009, Oct. 24 **Litho.** ***Perf. 13¼***
1095 A652 3.25d multi 1.00 .40

Mehdia Gate A653

2009, Oct. 30 **Photo.** ***Perf. 13¾***
1096 A653 7.80d multi 2.50 1.10

Green March, 34th Anniv. — A654

2009, Nov. 6 **Litho.** ***Perf. 13¼***
1097 A654 3.25d multi 1.10 .55

Anti-Poverty Week Type of 2001

2009, Nov. 15 **Photo.** ***Perf. 13***
1098 A461 7.80d multi 2.50 1.10

Value is for stamp with surrounding selvage.

Port of Tangiers — A655

No. 1099 — Ship in port, gear wheels in: a, 3.25d, Gray. b, 7.80d, Brown.

2009, Dec. 7 **Litho.** ***Perf. 13¼***
1099 A655 Horiz. pair, #a-b 3.50 1.50

Caisse de Dépot et de Gestion, 50th Anniv. — A656

2009, Dec. 19
1100 A656 7.80d dk blue & gold 2.50 1.00

Fish A657

Designs: No. 1101, 7.80d, Sarda sarda. No. 1102, 7.80d, Oblada melanura.

2009, Dec. 28
1101-1102 A657 Set of 2 5.00 2.00

Children's Art A658

No. 1103: a, Horses. b, Trees. c, Lake, mountain and trees. d, Building with smokestacks.

2009, Dec. 31
1103 Vert. strip of 4 4.00 1.75
a.-d. A658 3.25d Any single .85 .40

Rosa Damascena A659

Orange Blossoms A660

2010, Jan. 14 ***Perf. 13¼x13***
1104 A659 7.80d multi 2.50 1.00

Perf. 13x13¼

1105 A660 7.80d multi 2.50 1.00

Nos. 1104-1105 are each impregnated with the scent of the depicted flower.

Reconstruction of Agadir, 50th Anniv. — A661

2010, Feb. 28 ***Perf. 13¼***
1106 A661 7.80d multi 2.50 .95

Earth Day — A662

2010, Apr. 22
1107 A662 3.25d multi 1.00 .40

Alfalfa A663

2010, Apr. 22 **Litho. & Embossed**
1108 A663 10d multi 3.50 1.25

No. 1108 has a circle of adhesive tape covering a small embossed circle containing alfalfa seeds.

Miniature Sheet

Art and Culture — A664

No. 1109 — Paintings of casbahs in: a, Ibeghouzen. b, Oudaias. c, Ait ben Haddou. d, Tinzouline.

2010, May 12 ***Perf. 13x13¼***
1109 A664 3.25d Sheet of 4, #a-d 5.00 1.50

Level A Quality Certification for Morocco Post — A665

2010, May 26 ***Perf. 13¼***
1110 A665 3.25d multi 1.00 .35

National Day of Resistance A666

2010, June 18
1111 A666 3.25d multi 1.00 .35

Bab al Bahr, Abilah — A667

2010, July 10
1112 A667 7.80d multi 2.50 .95

OCP Groupe, 90th Anniv. — A668

2010, Aug. 7 ***Perf. 12¼***
1113 A668 7.80d multi 2.50 .95

Intl. Year of Biodiversity A669

2010, Oct. 11 **Litho.** ***Perf. 13¼***
1114 A669 7.80d multi 2.50 1.00

Souvenir Sheet

Green March, 35th Anniv. — A670

No. 1115: a, Marchers. b, Hand holding Moroccan flag.

2010, Nov. 6 **Litho.** ***Perf. 14***
1115 A670 7.80d Sheet of 2, #a-b 5.00 5.00

Grains of sand were applied to portions of the design by a thermographic process.

Sciaena Umbra A671

2010, Nov. 16 **Photo.** ***Perf. 13¼***
1116 A671 7.80d multi 2.50 .95

Anti-Poverty Week Type of 2001

2010, Nov. 19 **Photo.** ***Perf. 13***
1117 A461 7.80d multi 2.50 .95

Value is for stamp with surrounding selvage.

Numeric 2013 Plan — A672

2010, Nov. 30 **Litho.** ***Perf. 13¼x13***
1118 A672 7.80d multi 2.50 .95

Tenth Marrakesh Intl. Film Festival — A673

2010, Dec. 3 **Photo.** ***Perf. 13¼***
1119 A673 7.80d multi 2.50 .95

Train A674

2010, Dec. 14
1120 A674 3.25d multi 1.00 .40

Greetings A675

Inscriptions: No. 1121, 3.25d, Bonheur (happiness). No. 1122, 3.25d, Prospérité (prosperity). No. 1123, 3.25d, Santé (health).

2010, Dec. 20
1121-1123 A675 Set of 3 3.00 1.25

King Mohammed VI Type of 2007 and

A687

A688

2011, Feb. 1 **Litho.** ***Perf. 13x13¼***
1126 A687 3.50d brn org & multi 1.25 .40
1127 A688 8.40d lilac & multi 2.75 1.10

Perf. 13¼x13
1128 A599a 20d lt green & multi 6.50 2.50
Nos. 1126-1128 (3) 10.50 4.00

Compare type A687 with type A472, and type A688 with types A473 and A572.

Leopard With Mail Bag — A690

2011, Apr. 20 **Litho.** ***Perf. 13x13¼***
1130 A690 6.40d multi 2.25 .85

Miniature Sheet

Tom and Jerry Cartoons — A691

No. 1131: a, Jerry hitting tennis ball through Tom's racquet. b, Tom and Jerry in hammocks on desert island. c, Jerry shooting tennis balls at Tom with machine. d, Tom swimming with Jerry on his chest. e, Tom hitting tennis net with racquet. f, Wave approaching Tom and Jerry. g, Jerry holding tennis ball for Tom. h, Jerry listening to shell, Tom collecting shells. i, Tom slipping on tennis balls thrown by Jerry. j, Tom and Jerry building sand castles.

2011, May 4 ***Perf. 13¼***
1131 A691 3.50d Sheet of 10, #a-j 12.00 12.00

Turkeys — A692

Henna Plant — A693

2011, May 30
1132 A692 3.50d multi 1.25 .45
1133 A693 8.40d multi 2.75 1.10

A694

A695

A696

A697

A698 A699

A700 A701

Copperware

A702 A703

Serpentine Die Cut 11

2011, June 16 Self-Adhesive

1134 Booklet pane of 10 25.00
a. A694 8.40d multi 2.50 1.10
b. A695 8.40d multi 2.50 1.10
c. A696 8.40d multi 2.50 1.10
d. A697 8.40d multi 2.50 1.10
e. A698 8.40d multi 2.50 1.10
f. A699 8.40d multi 2.50 1.10
g. A700 8.40d multi 2.50 1.10
h. A701 8.40d multi 2.50 1.10
i. A702 8.40d multi 2.50 1.10
j. A703 8.40d multi 2.50 1.10

Al Barid Bank A704

2011, June 27 ***Perf. 13¼***
1135 A704 3.50d multi 1.25 .45

Famous Men A705

No. 1136: a, Moulay Abderrahmane Ben Zidane (1873-1946), historian. b, Abou Chouaib Doukkali Essadiki (1878-1938), scientist. c, Mohamed Ben Larbi Alaoui Lamdaghri (1880-1964), Justice Minister. d, Mohamed El Mokhtar Soussi (1900-63), religious scholar. e, Abdellah Ben Abdessamad Guennoune (1908-89), first governor of Tangiers.

2011, June 30 Litho.
1136 Horiz. strip of 5 6.00 6.00
a.-e. A705 3.50d Any single 1.00 .50

Campaign Against AIDS — A706

2011, July 27
1137 A706 8.40d multi 2.75 1.10

National Artisan's Week — A707

2011, Sept. 8 ***Perf. 13¼***
1138 A707 3.50d multi 1.25 .45

First Air Mail in Morocco, Cent. A708

No. 1139 — Airplane and monument in: a, Color. b, Black-and-white.

2011, Sept. 19
1139 A708 8.40d Vert. pair, #a-b 5.00 3.00

Miniature Sheet

Coins — A709

No. 1140: a, Obverse of 1893 bronze 8-fels coin (showing star). b, As "a," reverse (showing "1131" date). c, Obverse of 1609 gold dinar (26mm diameter coin with 20mm diameter inner circle, no horizontal lines). d, As "c," reverse (with long horizontal lines inside inner circle). e, Obverse of gold Almohades dinar (29mm coin with inner square, no long horizontal lines inside square). f, As "e," reverse (with long horizontal line inside square). g, Obverse of 1145 gold dinar (25mm coin with 15mm inner circle, with long horizontal lines inside inner circle). h, As "g," reverse (without long horizontal lines inside inner circle). i, Obverse of 790 silver dirham (Arabic script around edge of coin). j, As "i," reverse (five dots around edge of coin).

Litho. & Embossed

2011, Oct. 20 ***Perf. 13¼x13¾***
1140 A709 3.50d Sheet of 10, #a-j 12.00 12.00

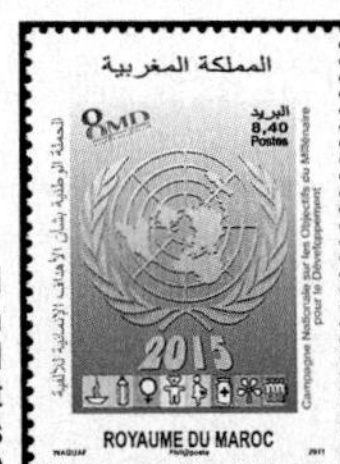

National Campaign on Millennial Development Objectives A710

2011, Oct. 24 Litho. ***Perf. 13¼***
1141 A710 8.40d multi 2.75 1.10

Children's Art — A711

No. 1142 — Various works of children's art inscribed: a, L'Ecole (school), by Ibtissam Gariate. b, L' Environmement (environment), by Ramah Damach. c, La Sante (health), by Hanane Aliouan. d, L'Enfance (childhood), by Kenza Najdaoui, horiz.

2011, Oct. 25
1142 A711 3.50d Horiz. strip of 4, #a-d 5.00 5.00

Green March, 36th Anniv. — A712

2011, Nov. 6 Photo.
1143 A712 8.40d multi 2.75 1.10

Anti-Poverty Week Type of 2001

2011, Nov. 28 Photo. ***Perf. 13***
1144 A461 8.40d multi 2.75 1.10

Values are for stamps with surrounding selvage.

Miniature Sheet

Folding Screens — A713

No. 1145 — Screen art by: a, 3.50d, Paula Cardozo. b, 3.50d, Abdellah Yacoubi. c, 8.40d, Yukako Fukuda-Ota, vert. d, 8.40d, Miki Tica, vert.

Perf. 13x13¼, 13¼x13 (vert. stamps)

2011, Dec. 1
1145 A713 Sheet of 4, #a-d 7.00 7.00

National Statistics and Applied Economics Institute, 50th Anniv. — A714

2011, Dec. 15 ***Perf. 13¼***
1146 A714 3.50d multi 1.25 .40

Animals in Rabat Zoo A715

No. 1147: a, Mouflons. b, Oryx. c, Lions, vert. d, Ibises, vert.

2012, Jan. 9 Photo. ***Perf. 13¼***
1147 Strip of 4 7.00 7.00
a.-b. A715 3.50d Either single 1.00 .40
c.-d. A715 8.40d Either single 2.25 1.00
e. Souvenir sheet of 4, #1147a-1147d 7.00 7.00

2012 African Cup of Nations Soccer Tournament, Equatorial Guinea and Gabon — A716

2012, Jan. 23 Litho. ***Perf. 13¾***
1148 A716 3.50d multi 1.25 .50

Values are for stamps with surrounding selvage.

Mohammed V Theater, Rabat, 50th Anniv. A717

2012, Mar. 27 ***Perf. 13x13¼***
1149 A717 3.50d multi 1.25 .40

Moroccan Postage Stamps, Cent. — A718

No. 1150: a, 3.50d, Anniversary emblem. b, 8.40d, Horses and riders.

2012, May 22 ***Perf. 13¼x14***
1150 A718 Vert. pair, #a-b 3.75 3.75

Arab Post Day — A719

2012, Aug. 3 ***Perf. 13x13¼***
1151 A719 8.40d multi 2.75 .95

2012 Summer Olympics, London A720

Perf. 13¼ Syncopated

2012, Aug. 17
1152 A720 8.40d multi 2.75 1.00

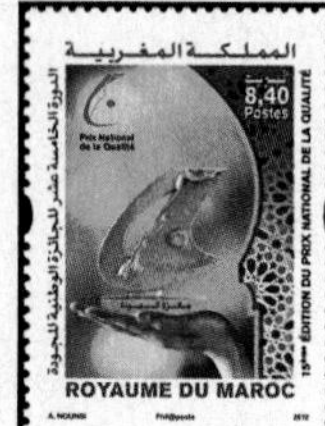

15th National Quality Prize — A721

2012, Sept. 27 **Litho.**
1153 A721 8.40d multi 2.75 1.00

Retirement Allowance Collective Plan, 35th Anniv. A722

2012, Oct. 4 ***Perf. 13¼ Syncopated***
1154 A722 3.50d multi 1.25 .40

El Jadida Horse Show A725

Perf. 13¼ Syncopated

2012, Oct. 17 **Photo.**
1157 A725 8.40d multi 2.75 1.00

Anti-Poverty Week Type of 2001

2012, Nov. 7 **Photo.** ***Perf. 13¼***
Dated "2012"

1159 A461 8.40d multi 2.75 1.00

Values are for stamps with surrounding selvage.

Maghzen Post, 120th Anniv. — A728

No. 1161 — Sherifian postal seals and their impressions: a, Purple circular. b, Purple octagonal. c, Blue green circular. d, Blue green octagonal. e, Blue circular. f, Blue octagonal. g, Red circular. h, Red octagonal. i, Black circular. j, Black octagonal. k, Orange circular. l, Orange octagonal.

Perf. 13¼x13 Syncopated

2012, Nov. 22 **Photo.**
1161 Sheet of 12 + 12 labels 15.00 15.00
a.-l. A728 3.50d Any single + label 1.00 .45

Intl. Year of Renewable Energy — A729

Perf. 13¼ Syncopated

2012, Dec. 24 **Photo.**
1163 A729 8.40d multi 2.75 1.00

SEMI-POSTAL STAMPS

Nos. 1-5 Surcharged

1960, Mar. **Unwmk.** **Engr.** ***Perf. 13***

B1 A1 5fr + 10fr brt bl & ind .45 .40
B2 A1 10fr + 10fr bis brn & choc .55 .55
B3 A1 15fr + 10fr dp grn & mag 1.25 1.10
B4 A1 25fr + 15fr purple 1.40 1.15
B5 A1 30fr + 20fr green 2.25 2.25
Nos. B1-B5 (5) 5.90 5.45

The surtax aided families whose members consumed adulterated cooking oil with crippling or fatal results.

French Morocco Nos. 321 and 322 Surcharged

1960, Sept. 12
B6 A71 15fr + 3fr on 18fr dk grn .80 .80
B7 A71 20fr + 5fr brown lake 1.25 1.25

Nos. 1 and 6 Surcharged in Red or Black

1963, Jan. 28 **Engr.** ***Perf. 13***
B8 A1 20c + 5c on 5fr brt bl & ind (R) .70 .70
B9 A1 30c + 10c on 50fr rose red .80 .45

The surtax was for flood victims.

Moroccan Brooch — SP1

Design: 40c+10c, Brooch with pendants.

1966, May 23 **Photo.** ***Perf. 11½***
Granite Paper

B10 SP1 25c + 5c ultra, sil, blk & red .90 .55
B11 SP1 40c + 10c mag, sil, blk, ultra & bl 1.40 .70
a. Pair, #B10-B11, vertically tête-bêche 3.25 3.25

Meeting in Morocco of the Middle East and North African Red Cross-Red Crescent Seminar. The surtax was for the Moroccan Red Crescent Society.

See Nos. B12-B13, B15-B16, B19-B22, B26-B27, B29-B30, B34-B35.

1967, May 15 **Granite Paper**

Designs: 60c+5c, Two brooches, by silver drapery. 1d+10c, Two bracelets.

B12 SP1 60c + 5c yel bis & multi .95 .95
a. Pair, vertically tête-bêche 3.00 3.00
B13 SP1 1d + 10c emer & multi 1.90 1.90
a. Pair, vertically tête-bêche 4.75 4.75

Surtax for the Moroccan Red Crescent Society.

Hands Reading Braille and Map of Morocco — SP2

1969, Mar. 21 **Photo.** ***Perf. 12½***
B14 SP2 25c + 10c multi .60 .25

Week of the Blind, Mar. 21-29.

Jewelry Type of 1966

Designs: 25c+5c, Silver earrings. 40c+10c, Gold ear pendant.

1969, May 9 **Photo.** ***Perf. 11½***
Granite Paper

B15 SP1 25c + 5c gray grn & multi 1.25 .65
B16 SP1 40c + 10c tan & multi 1.60 .80
a. Pair, #B15-B16, vert. tête-bêche 6.00 6.00

50th anniv. of the League of Red Cross Societies. Surtax was for Moroccan Red Crescent Society.

Nos. 173-174 Surcharged

1970, Feb. 26 **Litho.** ***Perf. 13***
B17 A65 10c + 25c multi 3.50 3.50
B18 A65 15c + 25c multi 3.50 3.50

The surtax was for flood victims.

Jewelry Type of 1966

Designs: 25c+5c, Necklace with pendants. 50c+10c, Earring with 5 pendants.

1970, May 25 **Photo.** ***Perf. 11½***
Granite Paper

B19 SP1 25c + 5c gray & multi 1.10 .90
B20 SP1 50c + 10c brt vio & multi 1.50 1.25
a. Pair, #B19-B20, vert. tête-bêche 4.00 4.00

Surtax for Moroccan Red Crescent Society.

1971, May 10 **Granite Paper**

25c+5c, Brooch. 40c+10c, Stomacher.

B21 SP1 25c + 5c gray & multi 1.10 .65
B22 SP1 40c + 10c yel & multi 1.90 1.00
a. Pair, #B21-B22, vertically tête-bêche 3.25 3.25

Globe and Map of Palestine SP3

1971, Apr. 30 ***Perf. 13***
B23 SP3 25c + 10c multi .60 .30

Palestine Week, May 3-8.

String Instrument and Bow — SP4

1971, June 28 **Photo.** ***Perf. 12***
B24 SP4 40c + 10c multi .60 .40

Week of the Blind.

Mizmar (Double Flute) — SP5

1972, Mar. 31 **Photo.** ***Perf. 13x13½***
B25 SP5 25c + 10c multi .60 .55

Week of the Blind.

Jewelry Type of 1966

Designs: 25c+5c, Jeweled bracelets. 70c+10c, Rectangular pendant with ball drop.

1972, May 8 **Photo.** ***Perf. 11½***
Granite Paper

B26 SP1 25c + 5c brn & multi .80 .80
B27 SP1 70c + 10c dp grn & multi 1.25 1.25
a. Pair, #B26-B27, vert. tête-bêche 3.25 3.25

For overprints see Nos. 295-296.

Drums SP6

1973, Mar. 30 **Photo.** ***Perf. 13x14***
B28 SP6 70c + 10c multi .65 .50

Week of the Blind.

Jewelry Type of 1966

25c+5c, Silver box pendant. 70c+10c, Bracelet.

1973, June 15 **Photo.** ***Perf. 11½***
B29 SP1 25c + 5c bl & multi 1.50 .60
B30 SP1 70c + 10c org & multi 2.25 .95
a. Pair, #B29-B30, vert. tête-bêche 4.50 4.50

Moroccan Red Crescent Society. For overprints see Nos. 351-352.

Pistol — SP7

70c+10c, Decorated antique powder box.

1974, July 8 **Photo.** ***Perf. 14x13½***
B31 SP7 25c + 5c multi .80 .80
B32 SP7 70c + 10c multi 1.25 1.25
a. Pair, #B31-B32, vert. tête-bêche 2.50 2.50

Moroccan Red Crescent Society.

Erbab (Fiddle) — SP8

1975, Jan. 10 Photo. *Perf. 13*

B33 SP8 70c + 10c multi	1.20	.50

Week of the Blind.

Jewelry Type of 1966

25c+5c, Silver pendant. 70c+10c, Earring.

1975, Mar. 13 Photo. *Perf. 13½*

B34 SP1 25c + 5c multi	.80	.80
B35 SP1 70c + 10c multi	1.25	1.25
a. Pair, #B34-B35, vert. tête-bêche	2.50	2.50

Moroccan Red Crescent Society. For overprints see #386-387.

AIR POST STAMPS

Sultan's Star over Casablanca — AP1

Unwmk.

1957, May 4 Engr. *Perf. 13*

C1 AP1 15fr car & brt grn	1.40	1.10
C2 AP1 25fr brt grnsh bl	2.10	1.40
C3 AP1 30fr red brn	3.00	1.90
Nos. C1-C3 (3)	6.50	4.40

Intl. Fair, Casablanca, May 4-19.

King Hassan II — AP2

1962

C5 AP2 90c black	.70	.25
C6 AP2 1d rose red	1.00	.25
C7 AP2 2d deep blue	1.15	.60
C8 AP2 3d dl bl grn	2.25	1.00
C9 AP2 5d purple	4.50	1.60
Nos. C5-C9 (5)	9.60	3.70

Meteorological Day Type of Regular Issue

1964, Mar. 23 Photo. *Perf. 11½*

Granite Paper

C10 A39 90c Anemometer & globe	1.10	.70

Intl. Fair, Casablanca, 20th Anniv. — AP3

1964, Apr. 30 Photo. *Perf. 12½*

C11 AP3 1d bl, bis & org	1.10	.70

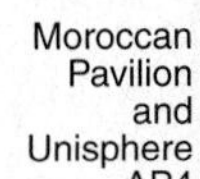

Moroccan Pavilion and Unisphere AP4

1964, May 25 Unwmk. *Perf. 12½*

C12 AP4 1d dk grn, red & bl	1.10	.80

New York World's Fair, 1964-65.

Ramses II and UNESCO Emblem — AP5

Litho. & Engr.

1966, Oct. 3 *Perf. 12x11½*

C13 AP5 1d magenta, *yel*	1.25	.80

UNESCO, 20th anniv.

Jet Plane — AP6

Perf. 12½x13½

1966, Dec. 19 Photo.

C14 AP6 3d multi	4.50	2.00

Costume Type of Regular Issue

Design: 1d, Women from Ait Ouaouzguit.

1969, Jan. 21 Litho. *Perf. 12*

C15 A74 1d multi	2.40	1.25

Coin Type of Regular Issue, 1968

Coins: 1d, King Mohammed V, 1960. 5d, King Hassan II, 1965.

1969, Mar. 3 Photo. *Perf. 11½*

Granite Paper

C16 A73 1d brt bl, sil & blk	4.75	1.60
C17 A73 5d vio blk, sil & blk	9.50	6.00

King Hassan II — AP7

1983, Mar. 1 Photo. *Perf. 12*

Granite Paper

C18 AP7 1.40d multi	.60	.25
C19 AP7 2d multi	.65	.25
C20 AP7 3d multi	.90	.30
C21 AP7 5d multi	1.40	.50
C22 AP7 10d multi	3.00	.95
Nos. C18-C22 (5)	6.55	2.25

No. C19 Overprinted

1987, Mar. 23 Photo. *Perf. 12*

Granite Paper

C23 AP7 2d multi	1.10	.65

1st World Congress of Friday Preachers, Al Joumouaa.

No. C18 Overprinted

1989, Mar. 27 Photo. *Perf. 12*

Granite Paper

C24 AP7 1.40d multi	.50	.40

Maghreb Union, agreement between Morocco, Algeria and Tunisia.

No. C18 Surcharged

2000, July 6 Photo. *Perf. 12*

Granite Paper

C25 AP7 6.50d on 1.40d multi	1.25	.60

Intl. Colloquium on King Hassan II.

POSTAGE DUE STAMPS

D1

1965 Unwmk. Typo. *Perf. 14x13½*

J1 D1 5c green	21.00	3.50
J2 D1 10c bister brown	1.00	.30
J3 D1 20c red	1.00	.30
J4 D1 30c brown black	1.50	.65
Nos. J1-J4 (4)	24.50	4.75

See French Morocco Nos. J27-J34, J46-J56.

Oranges — D2

1974-96 Photo. *Perf. 14*

J5 D2 5c shown	.30	.25
J6 D2 10c Cherries	.45	.25
J7 D2 20c Grapes	.60	.25
J8 D2 30c Peaches, horiz.	.90	.25
J9 D2 40c Grapes ('78)	.35	.25
J10 D2 60c Peaches, horiz. ('78)	1.10	.25
J11 D2 80c Oranges ('78)	1.40	.25
J12 D2 1d Apples ('86)	.50	.25
J13 D2 1.20d Cherries ('84)	.90	.25
J14 D2 1.60d Peaches ('85)	.90	.25
J15 D2 2d Strawberries ('86)	.90	.35

Litho.

J16 D2 5d like #J12 ('96)	2.10	1.00
Nos. J5-J16 (12)	10.40	3.85

For surcharges see Nos. 322, 395.

Strawberries — D3

Strawberries — D3a

Grapes D4

Apples D5

Cherries — D6

2003 Photo. *Perf. 13x13½*

J17 D3 1.50d multi	—	—
J17A D3a 1.50d multi	.90	.75
J18 D4 2d multi	—	—
J19 D5 5d multi	3.25	2.75
J20 D6 2d multi	1.20	1.10
Nos. J17-J20 (5)	5.35	4.60

Fruit Type of 1974-96

2005 ? Litho. *Perf. 14*

J21 D2 60c Peaches	—	—

No. J21 has a background of solid color. No. J10 has a background of dots. The text is thicker and heavier on No. J10 than on No. J21.

NORTHERN ZONE

100 Centimos = 1 Peseta

All Northern Zone issues except Nos. 21-22 were also sold imperforate in limited quantities.

Sultan Mohammed V — A1

Villa Sanjurjo Harbor A2

Designs: 25c, Polytechnic school. 50c, 10p, Institute of Culture, Tetuan.

Perf. 13x12½, 12½x13

1956, Aug. 23 Photo. Unwmk.

1 A1 10c deep rose	.30	.25
2 A2 15c yellow brn	.30	.25
3 A2 25c dk bl gray	.30	.25
4 A1 50c dark olive	.40	.25
5 A1 80c brt green	.80	.80
6 A2 2p brt red lil	6.50	6.50

No.	Type	Description	Unused	Used
7	A2	3p brt blue	11.00	11.00
8	A1	10p green	25.00	*40.00*
		Nos. 1-8 (8)	44.60	59.30

Value, set of Nos. 1-8 as imperf. pairs $2,500.

A3

1957, Mar. 2 ***Perf. 13½x13***

No.	Type	Description	Unused	Used
9	A3	80c blue green	.75	.75
10	A3	1.50p gray olive	1.90	1.90
11	A3	3p deep rose	4.00	4.00
		Nos. 9-11 (3)	6.65	6.65

1st anniv. of independence. See Morocco Nos. 13-15. Value, set of Nos. 9-11 as imperf. pairs $500.

Sultan Mohammed V — A4

1957 **Engr.** ***Perf. 13***

No.	Type	Description	Unused	Used
12	A4	30c brt bl & indigo	.25	.25
13	A4	70c bis, brn & choc	.35	.25
14	A4	80c brt violet	1.50	.35
15	A4	1.50p dp grn & mag	.50	.30
16	A4	3p green	.75	.65
17	A4	7p rose red	5.00	1.50
		Nos. 12-17 (6)	8.35	3.30

Value, set of Nos. 12-17 as imperf. pairs $600.

Prince Moulay el Hassan — A5

1957, July 15 **Photo.** ***Perf. 13***

No.	Type	Description	Unused	Used
18	A5	80c blue	.60	.60
19	A5	1.50p green	1.50	1.50
20	A5	3p carmine rose	4.50	4.50
		Nos. 18-20 (3)	6.60	6.60

Value, set of Nos. 18-20 as imperf. pairs $600.

Nos. 13 and 15 Surcharged in Carmine or Black

1957 **Engr.**

No.	Type	Description	Unused	Used
21	A4	15c on 70c (C)	.75	.75
22	A4	1.20p on 1.50p (Bk)	1.25	1.25

King Mohammed V — A6

1957, Nov. **Photo.** ***Perf. 12½***

No.	Type	Description	Unused	Used
23	A6	1.20p blk & brt grn	.65	.65
24	A6	1.80p blk & rose red	.65	.65
25	A6	3p black & violet	2.00	2.00
		Nos. 23-25 (3)	3.30	3.30

Enthronement of Mohammed V, 30th anniv. Value, set of Nos. 23-25 as imperf. pairs $750.

NORTHERN ZONE AIR POST STAMPS

Plane over Lau Dam AP1

1.40p, 4.80p, Plane over Nekor bridge.

Perf. 12½x13

1956, Dec. 17 **Photo.** **Unwmk.**

No.	Type	Description	Unused	Used
C1	AP1	25c rose violet	.35	.35
C2	AP1	1.40p lilac rose	.90	.90
C3	AP1	3.40p org vermilion	1.90	1.90
C4	AP1	4.80p dull violet	3.25	3.25
		Nos. C1-C4 (4)	6.40	6.40

Value, Nos. C1-C4 as set of imperf. pairs $750.

MOZAMBIQUE

mō-zəm-'bēk

LOCATION — Southeastern Africa, bordering on the Mozambique Channel
GOVT. — Republic
AREA — 308,642 sq. mi.
POP. — 16,542,800 (1997)
CAPITAL — Maputo

Formerly a Portuguese colony, Mozambique, or Portuguese East Africa, was divided into eight districts: Lourenco Marques, Inhambane, Quelimane, Tete, Mozambique, Zambezia, Nyassa and the Manica and Sofala region formerly administered by the Mozambique Company. At various times the districts issued their own stamps which were eventually replaced by those inscribed "Mocambique."

Mozambique achieved independence June 25, 1975, taking the name People's Republic of Mozambique.

1000 Reis = 1 Milreis
100 Centavos = 1 Escudo (1913)
100 Centavos = 1 Metical (1980)

Catalogue values for unused stamps in this country are for Never Hinged items, beginning with Scott 330 in the regular postage section, Scott C29 in the airpost section, Scott J51 in the postage due section, and Scott RA55 in the postal tax section.

Portuguese Crown — A1

Perf. 12½, 13½

1877-85 **Typo.** **Unwmk.**

No.	Type	Description	Unused	Used
1	A1	5r black	2.00	1.00
a.		Perf. 13½	3.00	1.60
2	A1	10r yellow	18.00	4.50
3	A1	10r green ('81)	1.50	.60
4	A1	20r bister	1.50	.75
a.		Perf. 13½	3.00	2.00
5	A1	20r rose ('85)	400.00	*125.00*
6	A1	25r rose	1.00	.35
a.		Perf. 13½	6.75	1.60
7	A1	25r violet ('85)	3.00	2.00
8	A1	40r blue	25.00	15.00
9	A1	40r yel buff ('81)	2.00	1.60
a.		Perf. 12½	3.50	3.00
10	A1	50r green	60.00	20.00
a.		Perf. 13½	125.00	60.00
11	A1	50r blue ('81)	1.00	.40
12	A1	100r lilac	1.00	.50
13	A1	200r orange	2.00	1.40
a.		Perf. 12½	5.25	4.50
14	A1	300r chocolate	2.25	2.00
		Nos. 1-4,6-14 (13)	120.25	50.10

The reprints of the 1877-85 issues are printed on a smooth white chalky paper, ungummed, with rough perforation 13½, also on thin white paper, with shiny white gum and clean-cut perforation 13½.

King Luiz — A2

Typographed and Embossed

1886 ***Perf. 12½***

No.	Type	Description	Unused	Used
15	A2	5r black	1.50	.60
16	A2	10r green	1.50	.70
17	A2	20r rose	2.00	1.50
18	A2	25r dull lilac	9.00	1.40
19	A2	40r chocolate	1.75	.85
20	A2	50r blue	2.25	.50
21	A2	100r yellow brn	2.50	.50
22	A2	200r gray violet	4.25	1.75
23	A2	300r orange	4.50	2.00
		Nos. 15-23 (9)	29.25	9.80

Perf. 13½

No.	Type	Description	Unused	Used
15a	A2	5r	4.00	2.75
16a	A2	10r	4.25	2.75
17a	A2	20r	13.00	6.00
18a	A2	25r	13.00	6.00
19a	A2	40r	15.00	9.50
20a	A2	50r	16.00	4.50
22a	A2	200r	15.00	12.50
		Nos. 15a-22a (7)	80.25	44.00

Nos. 15, 18, 19, 20, 21 and 23 have been reprinted. The reprints have shiny white gum and clean-cut perforation 13½. Many of the colors are paler than those of the originals.

For surcharges and overprints see Nos. 23A, 36-44, 46-48, 72-80, 192, P1-P5.

No. 19 Surcharged in Black

Type I

Type II

Type III

There are three varieties of No. 23A:
I — "PROVISORIO" 19mm long, numerals 4½mm high.
II — "PROVISORIO" 19½mm long, numerals 5mm high.
III — "PROVISORIO" 19½mm long, numerals of both sizes.

1893, Jan. ***Perf. 12½***

Without Gum

No.	Type	Description	Unused	Used
23A	A2	5r on 40r choc	150.00	50.00

King Carlos I — A3

1894 **Typo.** ***Perf. 11½, 12½***

No.	Type	Description	Unused	Used
24	A3	5r yellow	.50	.45
25	A3	10r red lilac	.50	.35
26	A3	15r red brown	1.25	.75
27	A3	20r gray lilac	1.25	.50
28	A3	25r blue green	1.25	.25
29	A3	50r lt blue	5.00	1.50
a.		Perf. 12½	7.50	2.00
30	A3	75r rose	1.75	1.25
31	A3	80r yellow grn	2.00	1.00
32	A3	100r brown, *buff*	1.75	1.25
33	A3	150r car, *rose*	8.00	4.00
a.		Perf. 11½		
34	A3	200r dk blue, *blue*	6.00	3.00
35	A3	300r dk blue, *salmon*	9.00	3.00
		Nos. 24-35 (12)	38.25	17.30

Nos. 28 and 31-33 have been reprinted with shiny white gum and clean-cut perf. 13½.

For surcharges and overprints see Nos. 45, 81-92, 193-198, 201-205, 226-228, 238-239.

Stamps of 1886 Overprinted in Red or Black

1895, July 1 ***Perf. 12½***

Without Gum

No.	Type	Description	Unused	Used
36	A2	5r black (R)	12.00	5.50
37	A2	10r green	14.00	6.50
38	A2	20r rose	15.00	6.00
39	A2	25r violet	16.00	6.50
a.		Double overprint	*200.00*	
40	A2	40r chocolate	20.00	7.50
41	A2	50r blue	22.00	7.50
a.		Perf. 13½	80.00	55.00
42	A2	100r yellow brown	22.00	8.25
43	A2	200r gray violet	30.00	13.00
a.		Perf. 13½	100.00	65.00
44	A2	300r orange	45.00	17.50
		Nos. 36-44 (9)	196.00	78.25

Birth of Saint Anthony of Padua, 7th cent.

No. 35 Surcharged in Black

1897, Jan. 2 ***Perf. 12½***

Without Gum

No.	Type	Description	Unused	Used
45	A3	50r on 300r dk bl, *sal*	150.00	40.00

Nos. 17, 19 Surcharged

a

b

c

1898 **Without Gum**

No.	Type	Description	Unused	Used
46	A2	(a) 2½r on 20r rose	42.50	11.00
47	A2	(b) 2½r on 20r rose	30.00	10.00
a.		Inverted surcharge	55.00	45.00
48	A2	(c) 5r on 40r choc	60.00	10.00
a.		Inverted surcharge	90.00	45.00
		Nos. 46-48 (3)	132.50	31.00

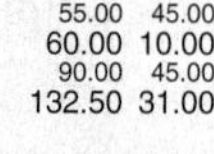

King Carlos I — A4

Name and Value in Black except 500r

1898-1903 **Typo.** ***Perf. 11½***

49 A4 2½r gray .25 .25
50 A4 5r orange .25 .25
51 A4 10r lt green .25 .25
52 A4 15r brown 2.00 1.50
53 A4 15r gray grn ('03) .70 .55
54 A4 20r gray violet .85 .40
55 A4 25r sea green .85 .40
56 A4 25r carmine ('03) .70 .30
57 A4 50r dark blue 1.50 .50
58 A4 50r brown ('03) 2.00 1.50
59 A4 65r dull blue ('03) 20.00 12.00
60 A4 75r rose 7.00 2.75
61 A4 75r red lilac ('03) 3.00 1.75
62 A4 80r violet 6.00 3.25
63 A4 100r dk blue, *bl* 2.00 1.00
64 A4 115r org brn, *pink* ('03) 10.00 5.00
65 A4 130r brown, *straw* ('03) 10.00 5.00
66 A4 150r brown, *straw* 10.00 2.75
67 A4 200r red lilac, *pnksh* 2.00 1.40
68 A4 300r dk blue, *rose* 8.00 3.25
69 A4 400r dl bl, *straw* ('03) 13.00 7.50
70 A4 500r blk & red, *bl* ('01) 20.00 8.00
71 A4 700r vio, *yelsh* ('01) 25.00 9.00
Nos. 49-71 (23) 145.35 68.55

For overprints and surcharges see Nos. 94-113, 200, 207-220.

Stamps of 1886-94 Surcharged

On Stamps of 1886
Red Surcharge

1902 ***Perf. 12½, 13½***

72 A2 115r on 5r blk 5.00 2.00

Black Surcharge

73 A2 65r on 20r rose 5.00 2.50
a. Double surcharge 50.00 50.00
74 A2 65r on 40r choc 6.00 4.00
75 A2 65r on 200r violet 5.00 1.75
76 A2 115r on 50r blue 2.00 1.00
77 A2 130r on 25r red vio 3.00 .90
78 A2 130r on 300r orange 3.00 .90
79 A2 400r on 10r green 7.50 3.25
80 A2 400r on 100r yel brn 40.00 25.00
Nos. 72-80 (9) 76.50 41.30

The reprints of Nos. 74, 75, 76, 77, 79 and 80 have shiny white gum and clean-cut perforation 13½.

On Stamps of 1894
Perf. 11½

81 A3 65r on 10r red lil 3.50 2.00
82 A3 65r on 15r red brn 3.50 2.00
a. Pair, one without surcharge
83 A3 65r on 20r gray lil 3.75 2.00
84 A3 115r on 5r yel 4.00 2.00
a. Inverted surcharge
85 A3 115r on 25r bl grn 3.50 2.00
86 A3 130r on 75r rose 4.00 2.25
87 A3 130r on 100r brn, *buff* 6.00 5.00
88 A3 130r on 150r car, *rose* 4.00 2.00
89 A3 130r on 200r bl, *bl* 5.00 3.50
90 A3 400r on 50r lt bl 1.50 1.40
91 A3 400r on 80r yel grn 1.50 1.40
92 A3 400r on 300r bl, *sal* 1.50 1.40

On Newspaper Stamp of 1893
Perf. 13½

93 N3 115r on 2½r brn 2.00 2.25
Nos. 81-93 (13) 43.75 29.20

Reprints of No. 87 have shiny white gum and clean-cut perforation 13½.

Overprinted in Black

On Stamps of 1898
Perf. 11½

94 A4 15r brown 2.00 .85
95 A4 25r sea green 2.50 .85
96 A4 50r blue 3.00 1.75
97 A4 75r rose 5.00 2.00
Nos. 94-97 (4) 12.50 5.45

No. 59 Surcharged in Black

1905

98 A4 50r on 65r dull blue 4.00 2.00

Stamps of 1898-1903 Overprinted in Carmine or Green

1911

99 A4 2½r gray .30 .25
a. Inverted overprint 15.00 15.00
100 A4 5r orange .30 .25
101 A4 10r lt green 2.00 .50
102 A4 15r gray grn .30 .25
103 A4 20r gray vio 2.00 .40
104 A4 25r carmine (G) .30 .25
a. 25r gray violet (error)
105 A4 50r brown .50 .25
106 A4 75r red lilac 1.00 .50
107 A4 100r dk blue, *bl* 1.00 .50
108 A4 115r org brn, *pink* 1.50 .85
109 A4 130r brown, *straw* 1.50 .85
a. Double overprint
110 A4 200r red lil, *pnksh* 3.00 .70
111 A4 400r dull bl, *straw* 3.50 .85
112 A4 500r blk & red, *bl* 4.00 .85
113 A4 700r vio, *straw* 4.50 .85
Nos. 99-113 (15) 25.70 8.10

King Manuel II — A5

Overprinted in Carmine or Green

1912 ***Perf. 11½x12***

114 A5 2½r violet .25 .25
115 A5 5r black .25 .25
116 A5 10r gray grn .25 .25
117 A5 20r carmine (G) .55 .40
118 A5 25r vio brn .25 .25
119 A5 50r dp blue .50 .35
120 A5 75r bis brn .50 .35
121 A5 100r brn, *lt grn* .50 .35
122 A5 200r dk grn, *salmon* 1.00 .70
123 A5 300r black, *azure* 1.00 .70

Perf. 14x15

124 A5 500r ol grn & vio brn 2.00 1.25
Nos. 114-124 (11) 7.05 5.10

Vasco da Gama Issue of Various Portuguese Colonies Common Design Types Surcharged

1913 **On Stamps of Macao**

125 CD20 ¼c on ½a bl grn 1.50 1.50
126 CD21 ½c on 1a red 1.50 1.50
127 CD22 1c on 2a red vio 1.50 1.50
128 CD23 2½c on 4a yel grn 1.50 1.50
a. Double surcharge 50.00 50.00
129 CD24 5c on 8a dk bl 2.50 2.50
130 CD25 7½c on 12a vio brn 2.00 2.00
131 CD26 10c on 16a bis brn 1.75 1.50
132 CD27 15c on 24a bis 1.50 1.50
Nos. 125-132 (8) 13.75 13.50

On Stamps of Portuguese Africa

133 CD20 ¼c on 2½r bl grn 1.25 1.25
134 CD21 ½c on 5r red 1.25 1.25
135 CD22 1c on 10r red vio 1.25 1.25
a. Inverted surcharge 45.00 45.00
136 CD23 2½c on 25r yel grn 1.25 1.25
137 CD24 5c on 50r dk bl 1.25 1.25
138 CD25 7½c on 75r vio brn 1.75 1.75
139 CD26 10c on 100r bis brn 1.50 1.50
140 CD27 15c on 150r bis 1.50 1.50
Nos. 133-140 (8) 11.00 11.00

On Stamps of Timor

141 CD20 ¼c on ½a bl grn 1.50 1.50
142 CD21 ½c on 1a red 1.50 1.50
143 CD22 1c on 2a red vio 1.50 1.50
144 CD23 2½c on 4a yel grn 1.50 1.50
145 CD24 5c on 8a dk bl 1.50 1.50
146 CD25 7½c on 12a vio brn 3.00 3.00
147 CD26 10c on 16a bis brn 1.50 1.50
148 CD27 15c on 24a bis 2.00 2.00
Nos. 141-148 (8) 14.00 14.00
Nos. 125-148 (24) 38.75 38.50

Ceres — A6

1914 **Typo.** ***Perf. 15x14***

Name and Value in Black
Chalky Paper

149 A6 ¼c olive brown .35 .25
150 A6 ½c black .35 .25
151 A6 1c blue green .35 .25
152 A6 1½c lilac brown .35 .25
153 A6 2c carmine .40 .25
154 A6 2½c lt vio .40 .25
155 A6 5c deep blue .40 .25
156 A6 7½c yel brn 1.45 .75
157 A6 8c slate 1.45 .75
158 A6 10c org brn 1.45 .75
159 A6 15c plum 3.00 1.40
160 A6 20c yellow green 1.45 .95
161 A6 30c brown, *grn* 2.00 1.10
163 A6 40c brn, *pink* 2.00 .85
164 A6 50c org, *salmon* 2.75 3.00
165 A6 1e grn, *bl,* 18.00 7.00
Nos. 149-165 (16) 36.15 18.30

1919-26 **Ordinary Paper**

166 A6 ¼c olive brown .25 .25
a. Name and value printed twice 12.00
b. Name and value printed triple —
167 A6 ½c black .25 .25
168 A6 1c blue green .25 .25
169 A6 1½c lilac brown .25 .25
170 A6 2c carmine .25 .25
171 A6 2½c lt vio .25 .25
172 A6 3c org ('21) .25 .25
a. Name and value printed twice —
173 A6 4c pale rose ('21) .25 .25
174 A6 4½c gray ('21) .25 .25
175 A6 5c deep blue .25 .25
176 A6 7c ultra ('21) .25 .25
177 A6 7½c yel brn .25 .25
178 A6 8c slate .25 .25
179 A6 10c org brn .25 .25
180 A6 30c deep green ('21) .75 .50
181 A6 1e rose 1.40 .85
Nos. 166-181 (16) 5.65 4.85

Perf. 12x11½

182 A6 ¼c olive brown .30 .25
183 A6 ½c black .25 .25
184 A6 1c blue green .50 .25
a. Name and value printed twice 16.00
185 A6 1½c lilac brown .25 .25
186 A6 2c carmine .25 .25
187 A6 2c gray ('26) .25 .25
188 A6 2½c lt vio .25 .25
189 A6 3c org ('21) .25 .25
190 A6 4c pale rose ('21) .25 .25
191 A6 4½c gray ('21) .25 .25
191A A6 6c lilac ('21) .25 .25
a. Name and value printed twice
191B A6 7c ultra ('21) .25 .25
191C A6 7½c yel brn .25 .25
191D A6 8c slate .25 .25
191E A6 10c org brn .25 .25
191F A6 12c gray brn ('21) .25 .25
191G A6 12c blue grn ('22) .25 .25
191H A6 15c plum .65 .35
191I A6 15c brn rose ('22) .25 .25
191J A6 20c yel grn .25 .25
191K A6 24c ultra ('26) 4.50 2.00
191L A6 25c choc ('26) 1.50 1.25
191M A6 30c deep green ('21) 1.00 .25
191N A6 40c turq blue ('22) 1.00 .30
191O A6 50c lt violet ('26) .50 .25
191P A6 60c dk blue ('22) 1.00 .30
191Q A6 60c rose ('26) 1.10 .25
191R A6 80c brt rose ('22) 1.60 1.25
191S A6 80c rose ('22) 1.00 .25
191T A6 1e rose ('22) 1.60 .50
Nos. 182-191T (30) 20.50 11.70

For surcharges see Nos. 232-234, 236-237, 249-250, J46-50.

1921 **Chalky Paper**

191U A6 40c brown, *pink* ('21) 1.25 .85
191V A6 60c red brn, *pink* 1.00 .60
191W A6 80c dk brn, *bl* ('21) 1.40 .60
191X A6 1e grn, *bl,* 1.40 .60
191Y A6 2e brt vio, *pink* 1.40 .60

Perf. 15x14

191Z A6 30c gray bl, *pink* ('21) 1.50 1.25
Nos. 191U-191Z (6) 7.95 4.50

Stamps of 1902 Overprinted Locally in Carmine

1915

On Provisional Stamps of 1902

192 A2 115r on 5r black 200.00 100.00
193 A3 115r on 5r yellow 1.25 .75
194 A3 115r on 25r bl grn 1.25 .75
195 A3 130r on 75r rose 1.25 .75
196 A3 130r on 100r brn, *buff* 1.25 .75
197 A3 130r on 150r car, *rose* 1.25 .75
198 A3 130r on 200r bl, *bl* 1.25 .75
199 N3 115r on 2½r brn .80 .40

On No. 97

200 A4 75r rose 1.50 1.10
Nos. 192-200 (9) 209.80 106.00

Stamps of 1902-05 Overprinted in Carmine

1915

On Provisional Stamps of 1902

201 A3 115r on 5r yellow .80 .50
202 A3 115r on 25r bl grn .80 .55
203 A3 130r on 75r rose .80 .55
204 A3 130r on 150r car, *rose* 1.00 .50
205 A3 130r on 200r bl, *bl* 1.00 .50
206 N3 115r on 2½r brn 1.00 .50

On No. 96

207 A4 50r blue 1.00 .50

On No. 98

208 A4 50r on 65r dull blue 1.00 .50
Nos. 201-208 (8) 7.40 4.10

Stamps of 1898-1903 Overprinted Locally in Carmine Like Nos. 192-200

1917

209 A4 2½r gray 20.00 17.50
210 A4 15r gray grn 15.00 12.50
211 A4 20r gray vio 15.00 12.50
212 A4 50r brown 14.00 11.00
213 A4 75r red lilac 32.50 25.00
214 A4 100r blue, *bl* 6.00 2.50
215 A4 115r org brn, *pink* 8.00 3.00
216 A4 130r brown, *straw* 7.50 3.00
217 A4 200r red lil, *pnksh* 7.50 2.50
218 A4 400r dull bl, *straw* 7.50 3.00
219 A4 500r blk & red, *bl* 7.00 2.50
220 A4 700r vio, *yelsh* 15.00 6.00
Nos. 209-220 (12) 155.00 101.00

War Tax Stamps of 1916-18 Surcharged

1918 ***Rouletted 7***

221 WT2 2½c on 5c rose 2.50 1.50

Perf. 11, 12

222 WT2 2½c on 5c red 1.10 .70
a. "PETRIA" 4.00 2.00
b. "PEPUBLICA" 4.00 2.00
c. "1910" for "1916" 9.00 4.00

War Tax Stamps of 1916-18 Surcharged

1919 ***Perf. 11***

224 WT1 1c on 1c gray grn .75 .40
a. "PEPUBLICA" 6.00 4.00

b. Rouletted 7 *300.00 100.00*

Perf. 12

225 WT2 1½c on 5c red .40 .35
a. "PETRIA" 4.00 2.00
b. "PEPUBLICA" 4.00 2.50
c. "1910" for "1916" 7.50 3.75

Stamps of 1902 Overprinted Locally in Carmine Like Nos. 192-200

1920
226 A3 400r on 50r lt blue 1.25 1.25
227 A3 400r on 80r yel grn 1.25 1.25
228 A3 400r on 300r bl, *sal* 1.25 1.25
Nos. 226-228 (3) 3.75 3.75

War Tax Stamp of 1918 Surcharged in Green

1920 ***Perf. 12***
229 WT2 6c on 5c red .60 .50
a. "1910" for "1916" 9.00 5.00
b. "PETRIA" 3.00 2.00
c. "PEPUBLICA" 3.00 2.00

Lourenco Marques Nos. 117, 119 Surcharged in Red or Bue

1921 ***Perf. 15x14***
230 A4 10c on ½c blk (R) .75 .40
231 A4 30c on 1½c brn (Bl) 1.25 .70

Same Surcharge on Mozambique Nos. 150, 152, 155 in Red, Blue or Green

232 A6 10c on ½c blk (R) 1.00 .85
233 A6 30c on 1½c brn (Bl) 1.10 .70
a. Double surcharge 30.00 30.00
234 A6 60c on 2½c vio (G) 1.50 .80
Nos. 230-234 (5) 5.60 3.45

War Tax Stamp of 1918 Surcharged in Green

1921 ***Perf. 12***
235 WT2 2e on 5c red 1.00 .50
a. "PETRIA" 2.50 2.25
b. "PEPUBLICA" 4.25 2.50
c. "1910" for "1916" 9.00 6.50

No. 190 Surcharged

1923 ***Perf. 12x11½***
236 A6 50c on 4c pale rose 1.00 .55

No. 191R Overprinted in Green

1924
237 A6 80c bright rose 1.00 .60

4th centenary of the death of Vasco da Gama.

Nos. 90 and 91 Surcharged

1925 ***Perf. 11½***
238 A3 40c on 400r on 50r .70 .70
239 A3 40c on 400r on 80r .60 .50
a. "a" omitted 42.50 42.50

Glazed Paper

1922-26 ***Perf. 12x11½***
240 A6 1e blue ('26) 1.60 .65
241 A6 2e dk violet ('22) 1.00 .35
242 A6 5e buff ('26) 9.00 2.50
243 A6 10e pink ('26) 18.00 5.00
244 A6 20e pale turq ('26) 45.00 17.50

Postage Due Stamp of 1917 Overprinted in Black and Bars in Red

1929, Jan. ***Perf. 12***
247 D1 50c gray .85 .55

No. 191Y Surcharged

1931 ***Perf. 11½***
249 A6 70c on 2e dk vio 1.50 .50
250 A6 1.40e on 2e dk vio 2.00 .50

"Portugal" Holding Volume of the "Lusiads" — A7

Wmk. Maltese Cross (232)

1933, July 13 **Typo.** ***Perf. 14***

Value in Red or Black

251 A7 1c bister brn (R) .25 .25
252 A7 5c black brn .25 .25
253 A7 10c dp violet .25 .25
254 A7 15c black (R) .25 .25
255 A7 20c light gray .25 .25
256 A7 30c blue green .25 .25
257 A7 40c orange red .25 .25
258 A7 45c brt blue .40 .25
259 A7 50c dk brown .30 .25
260 A7 60c olive grn .25 .25
261 A7 70c orange brn .25 .25
262 A7 80c emerald .25 .25
263 A7 85c deep rose 1.00 .50
264 A7 1e red brown .75 .25
265 A7 1.40e dk blue (R) 7.00 1.10
266 A7 2e dk violet 2.00 .35
267 A7 5e apple green 4.00 .50
268 A7 10e olive bister 8.00 1.00
269 A7 20e orange 22.50 2.00
Nos. 251-269 (19) 48.45 8.70

See Nos. 298-299.

Common Design Types pictured following the introduction.

Common Design Types

Perf. 13½x13

1938, Aug. **Engr.** **Unwmk.**

Name and Value in Black

270 CD34 1c gray green .25 .25
271 CD34 5c orange brn .25 .25
272 CD34 10c dk carmine .25 .25
273 CD34 15c dk vio brn .25 .25
274 CD34 20c slate .25 .25
275 CD35 30c rose vio .25 .25
276 CD35 35c brt green .30 .25
277 CD35 40c brown .40 .25
278 CD35 50c brt red vio .40 .25
279 CD36 60c gray black .50 .25
280 CD36 70c brown vio .50 .25
281 CD36 80c orange .75 .25
282 CD36 1e red .70 .25
283 CD37 1.75e blue 1.75 .30
284 CD37 2e brown car 1.50 .30
285 CD37 5e olive green 5.00 .50
286 CD38 10e blue vio 10.00 1.00
287 CD38 20e red brown 22.50 1.40
Nos. 270-287 (18) 45.80 6.75

For surcharges see Nos. 297, 301.

No. 258 Surcharged in Black

1938, Jan. 16 **Wmk. 232** ***Perf. 14***
288 A7 40c on 45c brt blue 2.50 1.40

Map of Africa — A7a

Perf. 11½x12

1939, July 17 **Litho.** **Unwmk.**

289 A7a 80c vio, *pale rose* 1.50 1.25
290 A7a 1.75e bl, *pale bl* 4.00 2.75
291 A7a 3e grn, *yel grn* 7.00 4.00
292 A7a 20e brn, *buff* *35.00 50.00*
Nos. 289-292 (4) *47.50 58.00*

Presidential visit.

New Cathedral, Lourenço Marques — A8

Railroad Station A9

Municipal Hall — A10

1944, Dec. **Litho.** ***Perf. 11½***
293 A8 50c dk brown .70 .40
294 A8 50c dk green .70 .40
295 A9 1.75e ultra 4.00 .85
296 A10 20e dk gray 8.50 .85
Nos. 293-296 (4) 13.90 2.50

4th cent. of the founding of Lourenço Marques. See No. 302. For surcharge see No. 300.

No. 283 Surcharged in Carmine

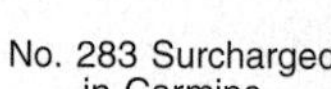

1946 **Engr.** ***Perf. 13½x13***
297 CD37 60c on 1.75e blue 1.00 .40

Lusiads Type of 1933

1947 **Wmk. 232** **Typo.** ***Perf. 14***

Value in Black

298 A7 35c yellow grn 4.00 2.00
299 A7 1.75e deep blue 4.50 2.00

No. 296 Srchd. in Pink

1946 **Unwmk.** ***Perf. 11½***
300 A10 2e on 20e dk gray 1.40 .40

No. 273 Surcharged with New Value and Wavy Lines

Perf. 13½x13

301 CD34 10c on 15c dk vio brn .70 .40
a. Inverted surcharge 30.00

Cathedral Type of 1944

Commemorative Inscription Omitted

1948 **Litho.** ***Perf. 11½***
302 A8 4.50e brt vermilion 1.75 .40

Antonio Enes — A11

1948, Oct. 4 ***Perf. 14***
303 A11 50c black & cream 1.00 .35
304 A11 5e vio brn & cream 3.00 .85

Birth centenary of Antonio Enes.

Gogogo Peak — A12

Zambezi River Bridge — A13

Zumbo River A14

Waterfall at Nhanhangare A15

Lourenço Marques A16

Plantation, Baixa Zambezia A17

Pungwe River at Beira — A18

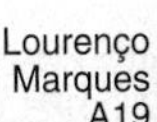

Lourenço Marques
A19

Polana Beach — A20

Malema River — A21

Perf. 13½x13, 13x13½

1948-49 Typo. Unwmk.

No.	Type	Value	Color	Unused	Used
305	A12	5c	orange brn	.25	*.50*
306	A13	10c	violet brn	.25	.25
307	A14	20c	dk brown	.25	.25
308	A12	30c	plum	.25	.25
309	A14	40c	dull green	.25	.25
310	A16	50c	slate	.25	.25
311	A15	60c	brown car	.25	.25
312	A16	80c	violet blk	.25	.25
313	A17	1e	carmine	.35	.25
314	A13	1.20e	slate gray	.35	.25
315	A18	1.50e	dk purple	.50	.25
316	A20	1.75e	dk blue ('49)	.75	.25
317	A18	2e	brown	.50	.25
318	A19	2.50e	dk slate ('49)	1.50	.25
319	A20	3e	gray ol ('49)	1.00	.25
320	A15	3.50e	olive gray	1.10	.25
321	A17	5e	blue grn	1.10	.25
322	A19	10e	choc ('49)	2.50	.35
323	A21	15e	dp carmine ('49)	8.00	1.75
324	A21	20e	orange ('49)	15.00	1.75
			Nos. 305-324 (20)	34.65	8.35

On No. 320 the "$" is reversed.

Lady of Fatima Issue

Common Design Type

1948, Oct. Litho. *Perf. 14½*

No.	Type	Value	Color	Unused	Used
325	CD40	50c	blue	1.00	.50
326	CD40	1.20e	red violet	3.00	1.00
327	CD40	4.50e	emerald	6.00	1.50
328	CD40	20e	chocolate	10.00	1.50
			Nos. 325-328 (4)	20.00	4.50

Symbols of the UPU — A21a

1949, Apr. 11 *Perf. 14*

329 A21a 4.50e ultra & pale gray 1.00 .50

75th anniversary of UPU.

Catalogue values for unused stamps in this section, from this point to the end of the section, are for Never Hinged items.

Holy Year Issue

Common Design Types

1950, May *Perf. 13x13½*

No.	Type	Value	Color	Unused	Used
330	CD41	1.50e	red orange	.75	.30
331	CD42	3e	brt blue	1.00	.55

Spotted Triggerfish
A22

Pennant Coral Fish — A22a

Fish: 10c, Golden butterflyfish. 15c, Orange butterflyfish. 20c, Lionfish. 30c, Sharpnose puffer. 40c, Porky filefish. 50c, Dark brown surgeonfish. 1.50e Rainbow wrasse. 2e, Orange-spotted gray-skin. 2.50e, Kasmir snapper. 3e, Convict fish. 3.50e, Stellar triggerfish. 4e, Cornetfish. 4.50e, Vagabond butterflyfish. 5e, Mail-cheeked fish. 6e, Pinnate batfish. 8e, Moorish idol. 9e, Triangulate boxfish. 10e, Flying gurnard. 15e, Redtooth triggerfish. 20e, Striped triggerfish. 30e, Horned cowfish. 50e, Spotted cowfish.

Photogravure and Lithographed

1951 Unwmk. *Perf. 14x14½*

Fish in Natural Colors

No.	Type	Value	Color	Unused	Used
332	A22	5c	dp yellow	.30	*.75*
333	A22	10c	lt blue	.25	*.50*
334	A22	15c	yellow	.80	*1.00*
335	A22	20c	pale olive	.40	.25
336	A22	30c	gray	.40	.25
337	A22	40c	pale green	.30	.25
338	A22	50c	pale buff	.30	.25
339	A22a	1e	aqua	.30	.25
340	A22	1.50e	olive	.25	.25
341	A22	2e	blue	.30	.25
342	A22	2.50e	brnsh lilac	.60	.25
343	A22	3e	aqua	.60	.25
344	A22	3.50e	olive grn	.60	.25
345	A22	4e	blue gray	1.40	1.00
346	A22	4.50e	green	1.25	2.00
347	A22	5e	buff	1.25	.25
348	A22a	6e	salmon pink	1.25	.25
349	A22a	8e	gray blue	2.10	.25
350	A22	9e	lilac rose	4.50	.30
351	A22	10e	gray lilac	13.50	2.00
352	A22	15e	gray	40.00	8.75
353	A22	20e	lemon	25.00	4.00
354	A22	30e	yellow grn	25.00	5.50
355	A22	50e	gray vio	42.50	12.00
			Nos. 332-355 (24)	163.15	41.05
			Set, hinged	100.00	

Holy Year Extension Issue

Common Design Type

1951, Oct. Litho. *Perf. 14*

356 CD43 5e carmine & rose + label 2.25 1.00

No. 356 without label attached sells for less.

Victor Cordon — A23

1951, Oct. *Perf. 11½*

No.	Type	Value	Color	Unused	Used
357	A23	1e	dk brown	1.75	.40
358	A23	5e	black & slate	6.50	1.10

Centenary of the birth of Victor Cordon, explorer.

Medical Congress Issue

Common Design Type

Design: Miguel Bombarda Hospital.

1952, June 19 Litho. *Perf. 13½*

359 CD44 3e dk bl & brn buff 1.10 .55

Plane and Ship — A24

1952, Sept. 15 Unwmk.

360 A24 1.50e multi .65 .45

4th African Tourism Congress.

Missionary — A25

1953

No.	Type	Value	Color	Unused	Used
361	A25	10c	red brn & pale vio	.25	.25
362	A25	1e	red brn & pale yel grn	.80	.25
363	A25	5e	blk & lt bl	1.60	.45
			Nos. 361-363 (3)	2.65	.95

Exhibition of Sacred Missionary Art, held at Lisbon in 1951.

Canceled to Order

Certain issues, including Nos. 364-383, were canceled to order under Republican administration.

Papilio Demodocus A26

Various Butterflies and Moths in Natural Colors

Photogravure and Lithographed

1953, May 28 *Perf. 13x14*

No.	Type	Value	Color	Unused	Used
364	A26	10c	lt blue	.40	.25
365	A26	15c	cream	.40	.25
366	A26	20c	yellow grn	.40	.25
367	A26	30c	lt violet	.40	.25
368	A26	40c	brown	.40	.25
369	A26	50c	bluish gray	.40	.25
370	A26	80c	brt blue	.40	.25
371	A26	1e	gray bl	.40	.25
372	A26	1.50e	ocher	.55	.25
373	A26	2e	orange brn	5.00	.50
374	A26	2.30e	blue	5.00	.35
375	A26	2.50e	citron	7.25	.35
376	A26	3e	lilac rose	2.60	.25
377	A26	4e	light blue	.50	.25
378	A26	4.50e	orange	.50	.25
379	A26	5e	green	.50	.25
380	A26	6e	pale vio	.70	.25
381	A26	7.50e	buff	5.50	.30
382	A26	10e	pink	8.75	1.25
383	A26	20e	grnsh gray	11.00	1.25
			Nos. 364-383 (20)	51.05	7.50

Value of set canceled-to-order, $1.00. For overprints see Nos. 517, 527.

Stamps of Portugal and Mozambique — A27

1953, July 23 Litho. *Perf. 14*

No.	Type	Value	Color	Unused	Used
384	A27	1e	multicolored	.95	.40
385	A27	3e	multicolored	3.25	.85

Issued in connection with the Lourenço Marques philatelic exhibition, July 1953.

Stamp of Portugal and Arms of Colonies — A27a

Stamp Centenary Issue

1953 Photo. *Perf. 13*

386 A27a 50c multicolored .70 .55

Map — A28

1954, Oct. 15 Litho.

Color of Colony

No.	Type	Value	Color	Unused	Used
387	A28	10c	pale rose lilac	.25	.25
388	A28	20c	pale yellow	.25	.25
389	A28	50c	lilac	.25	.25
390	A28	1e	orange yel	.25	.25
391	A28	2.30e	white	.65	.40
392	A28	4e	pale salmon	.65	.25
393	A28	10e	lt green	2.00	.25
394	A28	20e	brown buff	2.60	.35
			Nos. 387-394 (8)	6.90	2.25

For overprints see Nos. 516, 530.

Sao Paulo Issue

Common Design Type

1954, July 2

395 CD46 3.50e dk gray, cream & ol .40 .30

Arms of Beira — A29

Paper with network as in parenthesis

Arms in Silver, Gold, Red and Pale Green

1954, Dec. 1 *Perf. 13x13½*

No.	Type	Value	Color	Unused	Used
396	A29	1.50e	dk bl *(bl)*	.40	.30
397	A29	3.50e	brn *(buff)*	1.00	.35

Issued to publicize the first philatelic exhibition of Manica and Sofala.

Mousinho de Albuquerque — A30

2.50e, Statue of Mousinho de Albuquerque.

1955, Feb. 1 Litho. *Perf. 11½x12*

No.	Type	Value	Color	Unused	Used
398	A30	1e	gray, blk & buff	.75	.35
399	A30	2.50e	ol bis, blk & bl	1.40	.65

100th anniversary of the birth of Mousinho de Albuquerque, statesman.

A31

Eight Races Holding Arms of Portugal

1956, Aug. 4 Unwmk. *Perf. 14½*

Central Design in Multicolored

No.	Type	Value	Color	Unused	Used
400	A31	1e	pale yellow & multi	.40	.25
401	A31	2.50e	lt blue & multi	.80	.40

Issued to commemorate the visit of President Antonio Oscar de Fragoso Carmona.

A32

1957, Aug. 15 **Litho.**
402 A32 2.50e View of Beira .80 .30

50th anniversary of the city of Beira.

Brussels Fair Issue

Exhibition Emblems and View — A32a

1958, Oct. 8 **Unwmk.** ***Perf. 14½***
403 A32a 3.50e blk, grn, yel, red & bl .30 .25

Tropical Medicine Congress Issue
Common Design Type

Design: Strophanthus grandiflorus.

1958, Sept. 14 ***Perf. 13½***
404 CD47 1.50e sal brn, grn & red 4.00 .85

Caravel — A33

1960, June 25 **Litho.** ***Perf. 13½***
405 A33 5e multicolored .65 .25

500th anniversary of the death of Prince Henry the Navigator.

Technical Instruction A34

1960, Nov. 21 **Unwmk.** ***Perf. 14½***
406 A34 3e multicolored .55 .25

Commission for Technical Co-operation in Africa South of the Sahara (C.C.T.A.), 10th anniv.

Arms of Lourenço Marques — A35

Arms of various cities of Mozambique.

1961, Jan. 30 **Litho.** ***Perf. 13½***
Arms in Original Colors; Black, Ultramarine and Red Inscriptions

407	A35	5c salmon	.25	.25
408	A35	15c pale green	.25	.25
409	A35	20c lt vio gray	.25	.25
410	A35	30c buff	.25	.25
411	A35	50c bluish gray	.25	.25
412	A35	1e pale ol	.25	.25
413	A35	1.50e lt blue	.25	.25
414	A35	2e pale pink	.40	.25
415	A35	2.50e lt bl grn	1.25	.25
416	A35	3e beige	.45	.25
417	A35	4e yellow	.45	.25
418	A35	4.50e pale gray	.45	.25
419	A35	5e pale bluish grn	.45	.25
420	A35	7.50e rose	1.00	.40
a.		"CORREIOS 7$50" omitted		

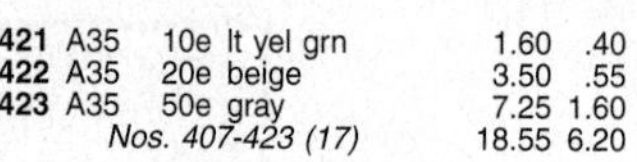

421	A35	10e lt yel grn	1.60	.40
422	A35	20e beige	3.50	.55
423	A35	50e gray	7.25	1.60
		Nos. 407-423 (17)	18.55	6.20

Sports Issue
Common Design Type

50c, Water skiing. 1e, Wrestling. 1.50e, Woman gymnast. 2.50e, Field hockey. 4.50e, Women's basketball. 15e, Speedboat racing.

1962, Feb. 10 **Unwmk.** ***Perf. 13½***
Multicolored Designs

424	CD48	50c gray green	.30	.25
425	CD48	1e dk gray	.85	.25
426	CD48	1.50e pink	.40	.25
427	CD48	2.50e buff	.90	.25
428	CD48	4.50e gray	1.25	.45
429	CD48	15e gray green	2.00	1.00
		Nos. 424-429 (6)	5.70	2.45

For overprints see Nos. 522, 526, 529.

Anti-Malaria Issue
Common Design Type

Design: Anopheles funestus.

1962, Apr. 5 ***Perf. 13½***
430 CD49 2.50e multicolored 1.40 .40

Planes over Mozambique — A36

1962, Oct. 15 **Litho.** ***Perf. 14½***
431 A36 3e multicolored .80 .25

25th anniversary of DETA airlines.

Lourenço Marques 1887 and 1962 — A37

1962, Nov. 1 ***Perf. 13***
432 A37 1e multicolored .45 .25

75th anniversary of Lourenço Marques.

Vasco da Gama Statue and Arms — A38

1963, Apr. 25 **Unwmk.** ***Perf. 14½***
433 A38 3e multicolored .40 .25

Founding of Mozambique City, 200th anniv.

Airline Anniversary Issue
Common Design Type

1963, Oct. 21 **Litho.** ***Perf. 14½***
434 CD50 2.50e brt pink & multi .40 .25
Nos. 434 (1) .40 .25

Barque, 1430 — A39

Caravel, 1436 — A40

Development of Sailing Ships: 30c, Lateen-rigged caravel, 1460. 50c, "Sao Gabriel," 1497. 1e, Dom Manuel's ship, 1498. 1.50e, Warship, 1500. 2e, "Flor de la Mar," 1511. 2.50e, Redonda caravel, 1519. 3.50e, 800-ton ship, 1520. 4e, Portuguese India galley, 1521. 4.50e, "Santa Tereza," 1639. 5e, "Nostra Senhora da Conceiçao," 1716. 6e, "Nostra Senhora do Bom Sucesso," 1764. 7.50e, Launch with mortar, 1788. 8e, Brigantine, 1793. 10e, Corvette, 1799. 12.50e, Schooner "Maria Teresa," 1820. 15e, "Vasco da Gama," 1841. 20e, Frigate "Dom Fernando II," 1843. 30e, Training Ship "Sagres," 1924.

1963, Dec. 1 **Litho.** ***Perf. 14½***

435	A39	10c multicolored	.25	.25
436	A40	20c multicolored	.25	.25
437	A40	30c multicolored	.25	.25
438	A40	50c multicolored	.25	.25
439	A40	1e multicolored	.55	.25
440	A40	1.50e multicolored	.45	.25
441	A40	2e multicolored	.45	.25
442	A39	2.50e multicolored	.50	.25
443	A40	3.50e multicolored	.45	.30
444	A39	4e multicolored	.60	.25
445	A40	4.50e multicolored	1.10	.25
446	A40	5e multicolored	10.00	.30
447	A39	6e multicolored	1.00	.30
448	A39	7.50e multicolored	1.10	.40
449	A39	8e multicolored	1.10	.40
450	A39	10e multicolored	1.25	.60
451	A39	12.50e multicolored	1.40	.75
452	A39	15e multicolored	2.00	.70
453	A40	20e multicolored	3.00	.70
454	A40	30e multicolored	6.00	1.40
		Nos. 435-454 (20)	31.95	8.35

National Overseas Bank Issue

Modern Bank Building, Luanda A40a

1964, May 16 ***Perf. 13½***
455 A40a 1.50e bl, yel gray & grn .40 .25

National Overseas Bank of Portugal, cent.

Pres. Americo Rodrigues Thomaz — A41

1964, July 23 **Litho.** ***Perf. 13½x12½***
456 A41 2.50e multicolored .40 .25

Visit of Pres. Americo Rodrigues Thomaz of Portugal to Mozambique, in July.

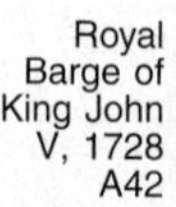

Royal Barge of King John V, 1728 A42

Designs: 35c, Barge of Dom Jose I, 1753. 1e, Customs barge, 1768. 1.50e, Sailor, 1780, vert. 2.50e, Royal barge, 1780. 5e, Barge of Dona Carlota Joaquina, 1790. 9e, Barge of Dom Miguel, 1831.

1964, Dec. 18 **Litho.** ***Perf. 14½***

457	A42	15c multicolored	.25	.25
458	A42	35c lt bl & multi	.25	.25
459	A42	1e gray & multi	.50	.25
460	A42	1.50e gray & multi	.30	.25
461	A42	2.50e multicolored	.25	.25
462	A42	5e multicolored	.40	.25
463	A42	9e multicolored	1.00	.65
		Nos. 457-463 (7)	2.95	2.15

ITU Issue
Common Design Type

1965, May 17 **Unwmk.** ***Perf. 14½***
464 CD52 1e yellow & multi .40 .25

National Revolution Issue
Common Design Type

Design: 1e, Beira Railroad Station, and Antonio Enes School.

1966, May 28 **Litho.** ***Perf. 11½***
465 CD53 1e multicolored .50 .30

Harquebusier, 1560 — A42a

30c, Harquebusier, 1640. 40c, Infantry soldier, 1777. 50c, Infantry officer, 1777. 80c, Drummer, 1777. 1e, Infantry sergeant, 1777. 2e, Infantry major, 1784. 2.50e, Colonial officer, 1788. 3e, Infantry soldier, 1789. 5e, Colonial bugler, 1801. 10e, Colonial officer, 1807. 15e, Colonial infantry soldier, 1817.

1967, Jan. 12 **Photo.** ***Perf. 14***

466	A42a	20c multicolored	.25	.25
467	A42a	30c multicolored	.25	.25
468	A42a	40c multicolored	.25	.25
469	A42a	50c multicolored	.25	.25
470	A42a	80c multicolored	.50	.25
471	A42a	1e multicolored	.40	.25
472	A42a	2e multicolored	.40	.25
473	A42a	2.50e multicolored	.60	.25
474	A42a	3e multicolored	.60	.25
475	A42a	5e multicolored	1.00	.30
476	A42a	10e multicolored	1.25	.40
477	A42a	15e multicolored	1.50	.60
		Nos. 466-477 (12)	7.25	3.55

Navy Club Issue
Common Design Type

Designs: 3e, Capt. Azevedo Coutinho and gunboat (stern-wheeler) Tete. 10e, Capt. Joao Roby and gunboat (paddle steamer) Granada.

1967, Jan. 31 **Litho.** ***Perf. 13***
478 CD54 3e multicolored .40 .25
479 CD54 10e multicolored .80 .40

Virgin's Crown, Presented by Portuguese Women — A43

1967, May 13 **Litho.** ***Perf. 12½x13***
480 A43 50c multicolored .25 .25

50th anniversary of the appearance of the Virgin Mary to 3 shepherd children at Fatima.

Cabral Issue

Raising the Cross at Porto Seguro — A44

Designs: 1.50e, First mission to Brazil. 3e, Grace Church, Santarem, vert.

1968, Apr. 22 **Litho.** ***Perf. 14***

481	A44	1e multicolored	.25	.25
482	A44	1.50e multicolored	.30	.25
483	A44	3e multicolored	.65	.25
		Nos. 481-483 (3)	1.20	.75

500th birth anniv. of Pedro Alvares Cabral, navigator who took possession of Brazil for Portugal.

Admiral Coutinho Issue
Common Design Type

Design: 70c, Adm. Coutinho and Adm. Gago Coutinho Airport.

1969, Feb. 17 **Litho.** ***Perf. 14***
484 CD55 70c multicolored .25 .25

Luiz Vaz de Camoens — A45

Sailing Ship, 1553 — A46

Designs: 1.50e, Map of Mozambique, 1554. 2.50e, Chapel of Our Lady of Baluarte, 1552. 5e, Excerpt from Lusiads about Mozambique (1st Song, 14th Stanza).

Perf. 12½x13, 13x12½

1969, June 10 **Litho.**

485	A45	15c multicolored	.25	.25
486	A46	50c multicolored	.25	.25
487	A45	1.50e multicolored	.25	.25
488	A46	2.50e multicolored	.25	.25
489	A45	5e multicolored	.50	.30
		Nos. 485-489 (5)	1.50	1.30

Visit to Mozambique of Luiz Vaz de Camoens (1524-80), poet, 400th anniv.

Vasco da Gama Issue

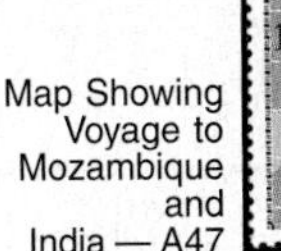

Map Showing Voyage to Mozambique and India — A47

1969, Aug. 29 **Litho.** ***Perf. 14***

490	A47	1e multicolored	.25	.25

Vasco da Gama (1469-1524), navigator.

Administration Reform Issue

Common Design Type

1969, Sept. 25 **Litho.** ***Perf. 14***

491	CD56	1.50e multicolored	.25	.25

King Manuel I Issue

Illuminated Miniature of King's Arms — A48

1969, Dec. 1 **Litho.** ***Perf. 14***

492	A48	80c multicolored	.25	.25

500th anniversary of the birth of King Manuel I.

Marshal Carmona Issue

Common Design Type

5e, Antonio Oscar Carmona in marshal's uniform.

1970, Nov. 15 **Litho.** ***Perf. 14***

493	CD57	5e multicolored	.40	.25

Fossil Fern A49

Fossils and Minerals: 50c, Fossil snail. 1e, Stibnite. 1.50e, Pink beryl. 2e, Dinosaur. 3e, Tantalocolumbite. 3.50e, Verdelite. 4e, Zircon. 10e, Petrified wood.

1971, Jan. 15 **Litho.** ***Perf. 13***

494	A49	15c gray & multi	.25	.25
495	A49	50c lt ultra & multi	.25	.25
496	A49	1e green & multi	.30	.25
497	A49	1.50e multicolored	.40	.25
498	A49	2e multicolored	1.00	.25
499	A49	3e lt bl & multi	2.00	.25
500	A49	3.50e lilac & multi	3.00	.25
501	A49	4e multicolored	4.00	.30
502	A49	10e dl red & multi	5.00	.85
		Nos. 494-502 (9)	16.20	2.90

For overprints see Nos. 525, 528.

Mozambique Island — A49a

1972, May 25 **Litho.** ***Perf. 13***

503	A49a	4e ultra & multi	.40	.25

4th centenary of publication of The Lusiads by Luiz Camoens.

Olympic Games Issue

Common Design Type

3e, Hurdles and swimming, Olympic emblem.

1972, June 20 ***Perf. 14x13½***

504	CD59	3e multi	.30	.25

For overprint see No. 523.

Lisbon-Rio de Janeiro Flight Issue

Common Design Type

1e, "Santa Cruz" over Recife harbor.

1972, Sept. 20 **Litho.** ***Perf. 13½***

505	CD60	1e multi	.25	.25

Sailboats A50

Designs: Various sailboats.

1973, Aug. 21 **Litho.** ***Perf. 12x11½***

506	A50	1e multi	.25	.25
507	A50	1.50e multi	.25	.25
508	A50	3e multi	.40	.25
		Nos. 506-508 (3)	.90	.75

World Sailing Championships, Vauriens Class, Lourenço Marques, Aug. 21-30.
For overprints see Nos. 519-520, 524.

WMO Centenary Issue

Common Design Type

1973, Dec. 15 **Litho.** ***Perf. 13***

509	CD61	2e rose red & multi	.30	.25

For overprint see No. 521.

Satellite Dishes A51

1974, June 25 **Litho.** ***Perf. 13***

510	A51	50c multi	.25	.25

Establishment of satellite communications network via Intelsat among Portugal, Angola and Mozambique.
For overprint see No. 518.

"Bird" Made of Flags of Portugal and Mozambique — A52

1975, Jan. **Litho.** ***Perf. 14½***

511	A52	1e pink & multi	.25	.25
512	A52	1.50e yel & multi	.25	.25
513	A52	2e gray & multi	.25	.25
514	A52	3.50e lem & multi	.40	.30
515	A52	6e lt bl & multi	.90	.30
a.		Souv. sheet of 5, #511-515 + label	4.50	4.50
		Nos. 511-515 (5)	2.05	1.35

Lusaka Agreement, Sept. 7, 1974, which gave Mozambique independence from Portugal, effective June 25, 1975.
No. 515a sold for 25e.
For overprints see Nos. 543-545.

Republic

Issues of 1953-74 Overprinted in Red or Black

a

b

1975, June 25

516	A28 (a)	10c (R; #387)	.40	.40
517	A26 (a)	40c (R; #368)	.25	.25
518	A51 (b)	50c (B; #510)	.30	.25
519	A50 (b)	1e (B; #506)	.50	.40
520	A50 (b)	1.50e (B; #507)	.95	.80
521	CD61 (a)	2e (B; #509)	2.75	2.75
522	CD48 (b)	2.50e (B; #427)	.55	.45
523	CD59 (a)	3e (R; #504)	.65	.55
524	A50 (b)	3e (B; #508)	.70	.65
525	A49 (b)	3.50e (B; #500)	2.75	2.75
526	CD48 (b)	4.50e (B; #428)	3.75	1.75
527	A26 (a)	7.50e (R; #381)	.90	.45
528	A49 (b)	10e (B; #502)	1.75	.60
529	CD48 (b)	15e (B; #429)	2.10	1.75
530	A28 (a)	20e (R; #394)	2.40	1.40
		Nos. 516-530,C35-C38 (19)	25.25	18.85

Workers, Farmers and Children A53

Designs: 30c, 50c, 2.50e, like 20c. 4.50e, 5e, 10e, 50e, Dancers, workers, armed family.

1975 **Litho.** ***Perf. 12x11½***

531	A53	20c pink & multi	.25	.25
532	A53	30c bis & multi	.25	.25
533	A53	50c bl & multi	.25	.25
534	A53	2.50e grn & multi	.25	.25
535	A53	4.50e brn & multi	.40	.25
536	A53	5e bis & multi	.55	.25
537	A53	10e bl & multi	1.00	.45
538	A53	50e yel & multi	4.50	2.25
a.		Souvenir sheet of 8	7.50	7.50
		Nos. 531-538 (8)	7.45	4.20

No. 538a contains 8 stamps similar to Nos. 531-538 with simulated perforation. Sold for 75e.
For overprint see No. 554.

Farm Woman — A54

1976, Apr. 7 **Litho.** ***Perf. 14½***

539	A54	1e shown	.25	.25
540	A54	1.50e Teacher	.25	.25
541	A54	2.50e Nurse	.30	.25
542	A54	10e Mother	1.10	.70
		Nos. 539-542 (4)	1.90	1.45

Day of the Mozambique Woman, Apr. 7.

Nos. 513-515 Overprinted in Red: "PRESIDENTE KENNETH KAUNDA / PRIMEIRA VISITA 20/4/1976"

1976, Apr. 20 **Litho.** ***Perf. 14½***

543	A52	2e gray & multi	.25	.25
544	A52	3.50e lem & multi	.40	.30
545	A52	6e lt bl & multi	.80	.50
		Nos. 543-545 (3)	1.45	1.05

Visit of President Kaunda of Zambia.

Pres. Machel's Arrival at Maputo — A55

Designs: 1e, Independence proclamation ceremony. 2.50e, Pres. Samora Moises Machel taking office. 7.50e, Military parade. 20e, Flame of Unity and festival.

1976, June 25

546	A55	50c multi	.25	.25
547	A55	1e multi	.25	.25
548	A55	2.50e multi	.30	.25
549	A55	7.50e multi	.80	.30
550	A55	20e multi	2.25	1.25
		Nos. 546-550 (5)	3.85	2.30

First anniversary of independence.

Mozambique No. 1 — A56

1976, July ***Perf. 11½x12***

551	A56	1.50e ocher & multi	.25	.25
552	A56	6e red & multi	.55	.30

Centenary of Mozambique postage stamps.

Flag and Weapons A57

1976, Sept. 25 **Litho.** ***Perf. 14½***

553	A57	3e multi	.40	.25

Army Day 1976.

No. 534 Overprinted in Silver: "FACIM"

1976 **Litho.** ***Perf. 12x11½***

554	A53	2.50e multi	.70	.30

FACIM, Industrial Fair.

Bush Baby — A58

Animals: 1e, Honey badger. 1.50e, Pangolin. 2e, Steinbok. 2.50e, Guenon (monkey). 3e, Cape hunting dog. 4e, Cheetah. 5e, Spotted hyena. 7.50e, Wart hog. 8e, Hippopotamus. 10e, Rhinoceros. 15e, Sable antelope. 1e, 2e, 3e, 4e, 7.50e, 8e, 10e horiz.

1977, Jan. **Litho.** ***Perf. 14½***

555	A58	50c multi	.25	.25
556	A58	1e multi	.25	.25
557	A58	1.50e multi	.25	.25
558	A58	2e multi	.25	.25
559	A58	2.50e multi	.30	.25

560	A58	3e multi	.30	.25
561	A58	4e multi	.50	.25
562	A58	5e multi	.70	.25
563	A58	7.50e multi	1.10	.30
564	A58	8e multi	1.20	.40
565	A58	10e multi	1.20	.40
566	A58	15e multi	1.75	.95
		Nos. 555-566 (12)	8.05	4.05

Congress Emblem — A59

Monument in Maputo — A60

Design: 3.50e, Monument in Macheje, site of 2nd Frelimo Congress, horiz.

1977, Feb. 7 ***Perf. 14½***

567	A59	3e multi	.40	.25

Perf. 12x11½, 11½x12

568	A60	3.50e multi	.30	.30
569	A60	20e multi	2.10	.95
		Nos. 567-569 (3)	2.80	1.50

3rd FRELIMO Party Congress, Maputo, Feb. 3-7.

Women, Child's Design — A61

1977, Apr. 7 **Litho.** ***Perf. 14½***

570	A61	5e dp org & multi	.30	.25
571	A61	15e lt grn & multi	1.40	.55

Mozambique Women's Day 1977.

Worker and Farmer — A62

1977, May 1 **Litho.** ***Perf. 14½***

572	A62	5e red, blk & yel	1.00	.30

Labor Day.

People, Flags and Rising Sun — A63

1977, June 25 **Litho.** ***Perf. 11½x12***

573	A63	50c multi	.25	.25
574	A63	1.50e multi	.25	.25
575	A63	3e multi	.30	.25
576	A63	15e multi	1.10	.45
		Nos. 573-576 (4)	1.90	1.20

2nd anniversary of independence.

Bread Palm A64

1977, Dec. 21 **Litho.** ***Perf. 12x11½***

577	A64	1e shown	.45	.25
578	A64	10e Nyala	1.10	.55

Nature protection and Stamp Day.

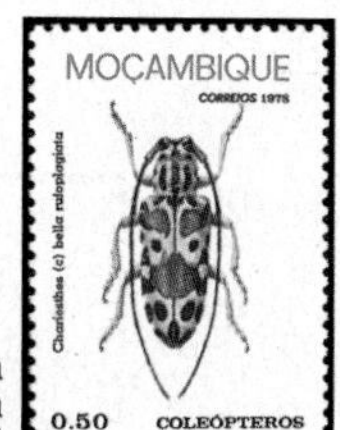
Chariesthes Bella Rufoplagiata A65

Beetles: 1e, Tragocephalus variegata. 1.50e, Monochamus leuconotus. 3e, Prospocera lactator meridionalis. 5e, Dinocephalus ornatus. 10e, Tragiscoschema nigroscriptum maculata.

1978, Jan. 20 **Litho.** ***Perf. 11½x12***

579	A65	50c multi	.45	.30
580	A65	1e multi	.45	.30
581	A65	1.50e multi	.60	.30
582	A65	3e multi	.70	.30
583	A65	5e multi	.90	.45
584	A65	10e multi	1.50	.45
		Nos. 579-584 (6)	4.60	2.10

Violet-crested Touraco — A66

Birds of Mozambique: 1e, Lilac-breasted roller. 1.50e, Weaver. 2.50e, Violet-backed starling. 3e, Peter's twinspot. 15e, European bee-eater.

1978, Mar. 20 **Litho.** ***Perf. 11½***

585	A66	50c multi	.60	.30
586	A66	1e multi	.60	.30
587	A66	1.50e multi	.80	.30
588	A66	2.50e multi	1.00	.30
589	A66	3e multi	1.50	.30
590	A66	15e multi	2.00	.55
		Nos. 585-590 (6)	6.50	2.05

Mother and Child, WHO Emblem A67

1978, Apr. 17 ***Perf. 12***

591	A67	15e multi	.80	.40

Smallpox eradication campaign.

Crinum Delagoense A68

Flowers of Mozambique: 1e, Gloriosa superba. 1.50e, Eulophia speciosa. 3e, Erithrina humeana. 5e, Astripomoea malvacea. 10e, Kigelia africana.

1978, May 16 ***Perf. 11½x12***

592	A68	50c multi	.45	.30
593	A68	1e multi	.45	.30
594	A68	1.50e multi	.45	.30
595	A68	3e multi	.45	.30
596	A68	5e multi	.90	.30
597	A68	10e multi	1.20	.60
		Nos. 592-597 (6)	3.90	2.10

No. 1, Canada No. 1 — A69

1978, June 9

598	A69	15e multi	1.00	.55

CAPEX Canadian International Philatelic Exhibition, Toronto, Ont., June 9-18.

National Flag — A70

1.50e, Coat of arms. 7.50e, Page of Constitution people. 10e, Music band & natl. anthem.

1978, June 25 ***Perf. 11½x12***

599	A70	1e multi	.30	.30
600	A70	1.50e multi	.30	.30
601	A70	7.50e multi	.45	.30
602	A70	10e multi	.70	.40
a.		Souvenir sheet of 4	2.40	2.40
		Nos. 599-602 (4)	1.75	1.30

3rd anniversary of proclamation of independence. No. 602a contains 4 stamps similar to Nos. 599-602 with simulated perforations. Sold for 30e.

Soldiers, Festival Emblem — A71

2.50e, Student. 7.50e, Farmworkers.

1978, July 28

603	A71	2.50e multi	.25	.25
604	A71	3e multi	.25	.25
605	A71	7.50e multi	.55	.40
		Nos. 603-605 (3)	1.05	.90

11th World Youth Festival, Havana, 7/28-8/5.

Czechoslovakia No. B126 and PRAGA '78 Emblem — A72

1978, Sept. 8 **Litho.** ***Perf. 12x11½***

606	A72	15e multi	.95	.55
a.		Souvenir sheet	3.50	3.50

PRAGA '78 International Philatelic Exhibition, Prague, Sept. 8-17.

No. 606a contains one stamp with simulated perforations. Sold for 30e.

Soccer A73

Stamp Day: 1.50e, Shotput. 3e, Hurdling. 7.50e, Fieldball. 12.50e, Swimming. 25e, Roller skate hockey.

1978, Dec. 21 **Litho.** ***Perf. 12x11½***

607	A73	50c multi	.25	.25
608	A73	1.50e multi	.25	.25
609	A73	3e multi	.25	.25
610	A73	7.50e multi	.55	.40
611	A73	12.50e multi	.80	.55
612	A73	25e multi	1.75	1.25
		Nos. 607-612 (6)	3.85	2.95

Carrier Pigeon, UPU Emblem A74

1979, Jan. 1 **Litho.** ***Perf. 11x11½***

613	A74	20e multi	3.00	1.00

Membership in Universal Postal Union.

Soldier Giving Gourd to Woman — A75

Edward Chivambo Mondlane A76

Designs: 3e, Frelimo soldiers. 7.50e, Mozambique children in school.

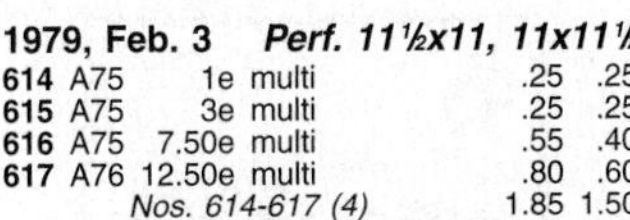

1979, Feb. 3 ***Perf. 11½x11, 11x11½***

614	A75	1e multi	.25	.25
615	A75	3e multi	.25	.25
616	A75	7.50e multi	.55	.40
617	A76	12.50e multi	.80	.60
		Nos. 614-617 (4)	1.85	1.50

Dr. Edward Chivambo Mondlane (1920-1969), educator, founder of Frelimo Party.

Shaded Silver Cat — A77

Cats: 1.50e, Manx. 2.50e, English blue. 3e, Turkish. 12.50e, Long-haired Mid-East tabby. 20e, African wild cat.

1979, Mar. 27 **Litho.** ***Perf. 11***

618	A77	50c multi	.40	.25
619	A77	1.50e multi	.45	.25
620	A77	2.50e multi	.45	.25
621	A77	3e multi	.55	.25
622	A77	12.50e multi	1.20	.60
623	A77	20e multi	1.75	1.00
		Nos. 618-623 (6)	4.80	2.60

Wrestling and Moscow '80 Emblem — A78

Sport and Moscow '80 Emblem: 2e, Running. 3e, Equestrian. 5e, Canoeing. 10e, High jump. 15e, Archery.

1979, Apr. 24 **Litho.** ***Perf. 11***

624	A78	1e gray grn & blk	.25	.25
625	A78	2e brt bl & blk	.25	.25
626	A78	3e lt brn & blk	.35	.25
627	A78	5e multi	.50	.25
628	A78	10e grn & blk	.60	.40
629	A78	15e lil rose & blk	1.25	.70
		Nos. 624-629 (6)	3.20	2.10

Souvenir Sheet

Imperf

630	A78	30e rose & dk brn	3.50	3.50

22nd Olympic Games, Moscow, July 10-Aug. 3, 1980. No. 630 contains one 47x37mm stamp.

Garden and IYC Emblem A79

Children's Drawings and IYC Emblem: 1.50e, Dancers. 3e, City. 5e, Farmers. 7.50e, Village. 12.50e, Automobiles, train and flowers.

1979, June 1 **Litho.** ***Perf. 11***

631	A79	50c multi	.30	.30
632	A79	1.50e multi	.30	.30
633	A79	3e multi	.30	.30
634	A79	5e multi	.40	.30
635	A79	7.50e multi	.55	.30
636	A79	12.50e multi	1.25	.55
		Nos. 631-636 (6)	3.10	2.05

International Year of the Child.

Flight from Colonialism — A80

Designs: 2e, Founding of FRELIMO and Pres. Eduardo Chivambo Mondlane. 3e, Advance of armed strruggle and death of Mondlane. 7.50e, Final fight for liberation. 15e, Proclamation of victory, Pres. Samora Moises Machel, flag and torch. Designs after mural in Heroes' Square, Maputo. 30e, Building up the country.

1979, June 25

637	A80	50c multi	.25	.25
638	A80	2e multi	.25	.25
639	A80	3e multi	.25	.25
640	A80	7.50e multi	.45	.30
641	A80	15e multi	.95	.70
b.		Strip of 5, #637-641	3.25	3.25

Souvenir Sheet

Imperf

641A	A80	30e multi	6.25	6.25

4th anniversary of independence. No. 641A contains one stamp with simulated perforations. No. 641b has continuous design.

Scorpion Fish A81

Tropical Fish: 1.50e, King fish. 2.50e, Gobius inhaca. 3e, Acanthurus lineatus. 10e, Gobuchthys lemayi. 12.50e, Variola louti.

1979, Aug. 7 **Litho.** ***Perf. 11***

642	A81	50c multi	.45	.30
643	A81	1.50e multi	.45	.30
644	A81	2.50e multi	.45	.30
645	A81	3e multi	.45	.30
646	A81	10e multi	1.20	.30
647	A81	12.50e multi	1.30	.45
		Nos. 642-647 (6)	4.30	1.95

For surcharge see No. 1254.

Quartz A82

Mozambique Minerals.

1979, Sept. 10

648	A82	1e shown	.50	.30
649	A82	1.50e Beryl	.75	.30
650	A82	2.50e Magnetite	1.00	.30
651	A82	5e Tourmaline	1.50	.30
652	A82	10e Euxenite	1.75	.45
653	A82	20e Fluorite	2.50	.80
		Nos. 648-653 (6)	8.00	2.45

Citizens Gathering Arms — A83

1979, Sept. 25

654	A83	5e multi	.45	.25

15th anniversary of independence.

Locomotive — A85

Designs: Historic Locomotives.

1979, Nov. 11 **Litho.** ***Perf. 11***

656	A85	50c multi	.25	.25
657	A85	1.50e multi	.25	.25
658	A85	3e multi	.40	.25
659	A85	7.50e multi	.70	.25
660	A85	12.50e multi	1.10	.40
661	A85	15e multi	1.30	.55
		Nos. 656-661 (6)	4.00	1.95

For surcharge see No. 1298.

Dalmatian — A86

50c, Basenji, vert. 3e, Boxer. 7.50e, Blue gasconha braco. 12.50e, Cocker spaniel. 15e, Pointer.

Perf. 11½x11, 11x11½

1979, Dec. 17 **Litho.**

662	A86	50c multi	.40	.30
663	A86	1.50e shown	.40	.30
664	A86	3e multi	.50	.30
665	A86	7.50e multi	.75	.30
666	A86	12.50e multi	1.10	.45
667	A86	15e multi	1.50	.65
		Nos. 662-667 (6)	4.65	2.30

For surcharge see No. 1299.

Nireus Lyaeus — A87

Butterflies: 1.50e, Amauris ochlea. 2.50e, Pinacopterix eriphia. 5e, Junonia hierta cebrene. 10e, Nephronia argia. 20e, Catacroptera cloanthe.

1979, Dec. 21

668	A87	1e multi	.40	.30
669	A87	1.50e multi	.40	.30
670	A87	2.50e multi	.55	.30
671	A87	5e multi	.75	.30
672	A87	10e multi	1.25	.35
673	A87	20e multi	2.50	.90
		Nos. 668-673 (6)	5.85	2.45

Dermacentor Rhinocerinus, Rhinoceros — A88

Ticks and Animals: 50c, Dermacentor circumguttatus cunhasilvai, elephant. 2.50e, Green tick, giraffe. 3e, Red tick, antelope. 5e, Ambloymma theilerae, cattle. 7.50e, Buffalo tick, buffalo.

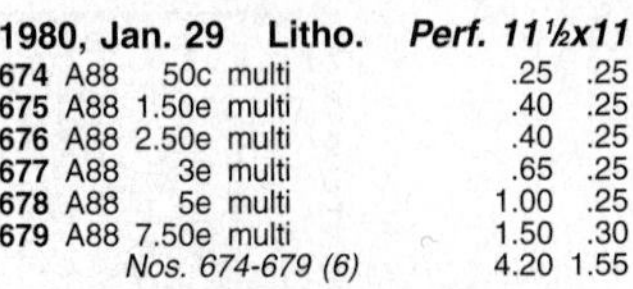

1980, Jan. 29 **Litho.** ***Perf. 11½x11***

674	A88	50c multi	.25	.25
675	A88	1.50e multi	.40	.25
676	A88	2.50e multi	.40	.25
677	A88	3e multi	.65	.25
678	A88	5e multi	1.00	.25
679	A88	7.50e multi	1.50	.30
		Nos. 674-679 (6)	4.20	1.55

Ford Hercules, 1950 — A89

Public Transportation: 1.50e, Scania Marcopolo, 1978. 3e, Bussing Nag, 1936. 5e, Articulated Ikarus, 1978. 7.50e, Ford taxi, 1929. 12.50e, Fiat 131 taxi, 1978.

1980, Feb. 29 **Litho.** ***Perf. 11***

680	A89	50c multi	.25	.25
681	A89	1.50e multi	.25	.25
682	A89	3e multi	.30	.25
683	A89	5e multi	.35	.25
684	A89	7.50e multi	.60	.25
685	A89	12.50e multi	.80	.40
		Nos. 680-685 (6)	2.55	1.65

Marx, Engels, and Lenin A90

1980, May 1 **Litho.** ***Perf. 11***

686	A90	10e multi	1.10	.30

Workers' Day.

"Heads," by Malangatana, London 1980 Emblem — A91

Paintings by Mozambique Artists: 1.50e, Crowded Market, by Moises Simbine. 3e, Heads with Helmets, by Malangatana. 5e, Women with Goods, by Machiana. 7.50e, Crowd with Masks, by Malangatana. 12.50e, Man and Woman with Spear, by Mankeu.

1980, May 6

687	A91	50c multi	.25	.25
688	A91	1.50e multi	.25	.25
689	A91	3e multi	.25	.25
690	A91	5e multi	.40	.25
691	A91	7.50e multi	.55	.25
692	A91	12.50e multi	.75	.35
		Nos. 687-692 (6)	2.45	1.60

London 1980 Intl. Stamp Exhibition, 5/6-14.

World Telecommunications Day — A92

1980, May 17 **Litho.** ***Perf. 12***

693	A92	15e multi	1.00	.45

Mueda Massacre, 20th Anniv. — A93

1980, June 16 **Litho.** ***Perf. 11***

694	A93	15e multi	1.00	.45

People with Weapons and Flag — A94

1e, Development projects, 1975. 3e, Arms, flags, 1977. 4e, Raised fists, 1978. 5e, Hand holding grain, flags, 1979. 10e, Year banners, 1980.

30e, Soldiers.

1980, June 25

695	A94	1e multi	.25	.25
696	A94	2e shown	.25	.25
697	A94	3e multi	.25	.25
698	A94	4e multi	.35	.25
699	A94	5e multi	.35	.25
700	A94	10e multi	.80	.30
		Nos. 695-700 (6)	2.25	1.55

Souvenir Sheet

Litho. ***Imperf.***

700A	A94	30e multi	3.50	3.50

5th anniv. of independence. No. 700A contains one stamp with simulated perforations.

Gymnast, Moscow '80 Emblem — A95

1980, July 19

701	A95	50c shown	.25	.25
702	A95	1.50e Soccer	.25	.25
703	A95	2.50e Running	.25	.25
704	A95	3e Volleyball	.30	.25
705	A95	10e Bicycling	.65	.25
706	A95	12.50e Boxing	.90	.40
		Nos. 701-706 (6)	2.60	1.65

22nd Summer Olympic Games, Moscow, July 19-Aug. 3.

Soldier, Map of Southern Africa Showing Zimbabwe — A96

1980, Apr. 18

707	A96	10e multi	.65	.30

Establishment of independent Zimbabwe, Apr. 18.

Narina Trogon — A97

1.50m, Crowned crane. 2.50m, Red-necked francolin. 5m, Ostrich. 7.50m, Spur-winged goose. 12.50m, Fish eagle.

1980, July 30 **Litho.** ***Perf. 11***

708	A97	1m shown	.25	.25
709	A97	1.50m multi	.50	.25
710	A97	2.50m multi	1.00	.25
711	A97	5m multi	2.00	.25
712	A97	7.50m multi	3.00	.30
713	A97	12.50m multi	4.00	.40
		Nos. 708-713 (6)	10.75	1.70

For surcharges see Nos. 1253A, 1255.

First Census, Aug. 1-15 A98

1980, Aug. 12 ***Perf. 11***

714	A98	3.5m multi	.40	.25

Brush Fire Control Campaign — A99

1980, Sept. 7

715	A99	3.5m multi	.80	.25

Harpa Major A100

1.50m, Lambis chiragra. 2.50m, Murex pecten. 5m, Architectonia perspectiva. 7.50m, Murex ramosus. 12.50m, Strombus aurisdinae.

1980, Dec. 12 **Litho.** ***Perf. 11***

716	A100	1m shown	.35	.25
717	A100	1.50m multi	.40	.25
718	A100	2.50m multi	.50	.25
719	A100	5m multi	.60	.25
720	A100	7.50m multi	.75	.25
721	A100	12.50m multi	1.25	.40
		Nos. 716-721 (6)	3.85	1.65

Pres. Machel and Symbols of Industry and Transportation — A101

Decade of Development, 1981-1990 (Pres. Machel and): 7.50m, Soldiers. 12.50m, Symbols of education.

1981, Jan. 1 **Litho.** ***Perf. 11x11½***

722	A101	3.50m red & bl	.50	.25
723	A101	7.50m grn & red brn	1.00	.25
724	A101	12.50m dk bl & lil rose	1.75	.45
		Nos. 722-724 (3)	3.25	.95

Bilbao Soccer Stadium, Soccer Player — A102

Soccer players and various stadiums.

1981, Jan. 30 **Litho.** ***Perf. 11***

725	A102	1m multi	.25	.25
726	A102	1.50m multi	.25	.25
727	A102	2.50m multi	.25	.25
728	A102	5m multi	.35	.25
729	A102	7.50m multi	.60	.25
730	A102	12.50m multi	.95	.40
c.		Souvenir sheet of 6	2.40	2.40
		Nos. 725-730 (6)	2.65	1.65

Souvenir Sheets

Imperf

730A	A102	20m multi	3.50	3.50
730B	A102	20m multi	3.50	3.50

ESPANA '82 World Cup Soccer Championship. No. 730c contains Nos. 725-730 with simulated perforations. Sizes: No. 730A, 105x85mm; 730B, 141x111mm.

For surcharge see No. 1303.

Giraffe — A103

1.50m, Tsessebe. 2.50m, Aardvark. 3m, African python. 5m, Loggerhead turtle. 10m, Marabou. 12.50m, Saddlebill stork. 15m, Kori bustard.

1981, Mar. 3 ***Perf. 11***

731	A103	50c shown	.35	.25
732	A103	1.50m multi	.40	.25
733	A103	2.50m multi	.60	.25
734	A103	3m multi	.65	.25
735	A103	5m multi	.70	.25
736	A103	10m multi	.90	.35
737	A103	12.50m multi	1.10	.50
738	A103	15m multi	1.75	.60
		Nos. 731-738 (8)	6.45	2.70

Pankwe A104

50c, Chitende, vert. 2.50m, Kanyembe, vert. 7m, Nyanga. 10m, Likuti and m'petheni.

1981, Apr. 8 **Litho.** ***Perf. 11***

739	A104	50c multi	.25	.25
740	A104	2m shown	.25	.25
741	A104	2.50m multi	.30	.25
742	A104	7m multi	.75	.30
743	A104	10m multi	1.50	.45
		Nos. 739-743 (5)	3.05	1.50

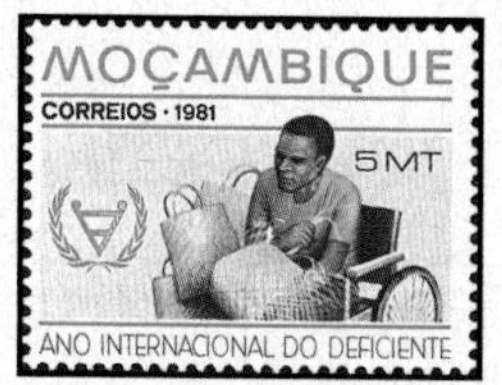

International Year of the Disabled — A105

1981, Apr. 18

744	A105	5m multi	.55	.25

African Buffalo and Helicopter, Exhibition Emblem — A106

5m, Hunters, blue kids. 6m, Hunter, impala. 7.50m, Hunters shooting. 12.50m, Elephants. 20m, Trap.

1981, June 14 ***Perf. 11***

745	A106	2m shown	.40	.25
746	A106	5m multi	.60	.25
747	A106	6m multi	.75	.25
748	A106	7.50m multi	.90	.25
749	A106	12.50m multi	1.10	.35
750	A106	20m multi	2.35	.65
a.		Souv. sheet of 6, #745-750, imperf.	6.50	6.50
		Nos. 745-750 (6)	6.10	2.00

World Hunting Exhibition, Plovdiv, Bulgaria. No. 750a sold for 60m.

For surcharge see No. 1258.

50-centavo Coin, Obverse and Reverse A107

First Anniversary of New Currency (Coins on stamps of matching denomination).

1981, June 16

751	A107	50c multi	.25	.25
752	A107	1m multi	.30	.25
753	A107	2.50m multi	.40	.25
754	A107	5m multi	.45	.25
755	A107	10m multi	.70	.30
756	A107	20m multi	1.50	.75
a.		Souv. sheet of 6, #751-756, imperf.	3.25	3.25
		Nos. 751-756 (6)	3.60	2.05

No. 756a sold for 40m.

Crops — A108

Designs: 50c, Sunflower (Helianthus annus). 1m, Cotton (Gossypium spp.). 1.50m, Sisal (Agave sisalana). 2.50m, Cashews (Anacardium occidentale). 3.50m, Tea (Camellia sinensis). 4.50m, Sugar cane (Saccharum officianum). 10m, Castor oil plant (Ricinus communis). 12.50m, Coconuts (Cocos nucifera). 15m, Tobacco (Nicotiniana tabacum). 25m, Rice (Oryza sativa). 40m, Corn (Zea mays). 60m, Peanut (Arachis hypogaea).

1981, July 24 **Litho.** ***Perf. 14½***

757	A108	50c red & org	.25	.25
758	A108	1m red & black	.25	.25
759	A108	1.50m red & Prus bl	.25	.25
760	A108	2.50m red & bis	.25	.25
761	A108	3.50m red & gray grn	.25	.25
762	A108	4.50m red & gray	.30	.25
763	A108	10m red & blue	.75	.25
764	A108	12.50m red & dk brn	1.00	.35
765	A108	15m red & ol grn	1.20	.40
766	A108	25m red & yel grn	1.50	.80
767	A108	40m red & org brn	2.50	1.10
768	A108	60m red & brn	3.75	1.75
		Nos. 757-768 (12)	12.25	6.15

For surcharges see Nos. 1034A, 1185, 1216, 1218, 1252, 1300, 1399, 1420.

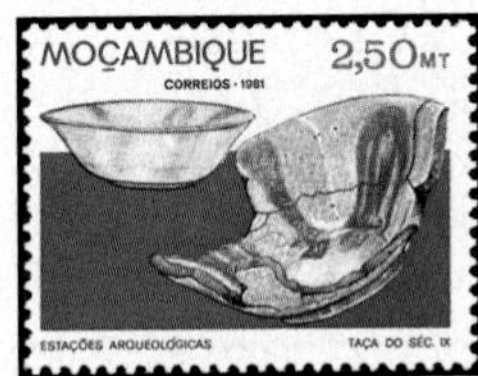

9th Cent. Persian Bowl, Chibuene Excavation Site — A109

1m, Manyikeni Museum. 1.50m, Hand ax, Massingir Dam. 7.50m, Pot, Chibuene, 9th cent. 12.50m, Gold beads, Manyikeni. 20m, Iron, Manyikeni, 15th cent.

1981, Aug. 30 *Perf. 11*

769 A109 1m multi .25 .25
770 A109 1.50m multi .25 .25
771 A109 2.50m shown .25 .25
772 A109 7.50m multi .50 .25
773 A109 12.50m multi .85 .45
774 A109 20m multi 1.40 .75
Nos. 769-774 (6) 3.50 2.20

For surcharge see No. 1213.

Sculptures A110

50c, Mapiko mask. 1m, Suffering woman. 2.50m, Mother and child. 3.50m, Man making fire. 5m, Chietane and man. 12.50m, Chietane.

1981, Sept. 25 Litho. *Perf. 11*

775 A110 50c multi .25 .25
776 A110 1m multi .25 .25
777 A110 2.50m multi .25 .25
778 A110 3.50m multi .25 .25
779 A110 5m multi .50 .30
780 A110 12.50m multi .50 .50
Nos. 775-780 (6) 2.00 1.80

World Food Day A111

1981, Oct. 16 Litho. *Perf. 11*

781 A111 10m multi .80 .40

Ocean Tanker Matchedje — A112

1.50m, Tugboat Macuti. 3m, Prawn trawler Vega 7. 5m, Freighter Linde. 7.50m, Ocean freighter Pemba. 12.50m, Dredger Rovuma.

1981, Nov. 22 Litho. *Perf. 11*

782 A112 50c shown .25 .25
783 A112 1.50m multi .25 .25
784 A112 3m multi .25 .25
785 A112 5m multi .40 .25
786 A112 7.50m multi .70 .40
787 A112 12.50m multi 1.25 .75
Nos. 782-787 (6) 3.10 2.15

Chinaman Crab — A113

50c, Portunus Pelagieus. 1.50m, Scylla serrata. 3m, Penaeus indicus. 7.50m, Palinurus delagoae. 12.50m, Lusiosquilla maculata. 15m, Panulirus ornatus.

1981, Dec. 6

788 A113 50c multi .50 .25
789 A113 1.50m multi .50 .25
790 A113 3m multi .50 .25
791 A113 7.50m multi .80 .25
792 A113 12.50m multi 1.25 .50
793 A113 15m multi 1.60 .60
Nos. 788-793 (6) 5.15 2.10

For surcharges see Nos. 1214, 1219, 1253, 1392.

Hypoxis Multiceps A114

1.50m, Pelargonium luridum. 2.50m, Caralluma melananthera. 7.50m, Ansellia gigantea. 12.50m, Stapelia leendertziae. 25m, Adenium multiflorium.

1981, Dec. 21 Litho. *Perf. 11*

794 A114 1m shown .25 .25
795 A114 1.50m multi .25 .25
796 A114 2.50m multi .25 .25
797 A114 7.50m multi .50 .35
798 A114 12.50m multi 1.00 .60
799 A114 25m multi 2.00 1.10
Nos. 794-799 (6) 4.25 2.80

For surcharges see Nos. 1215, 1217, 1251, 1301, 1390, 1303A.

First Anniv. of Posts and Telecommunications Dept. — A115

1982, Jan. 1 Litho. *Perf. 11*

800 A115 6m Phone, globe .45 .25
801 A115 15m Envelope 1.25 .80

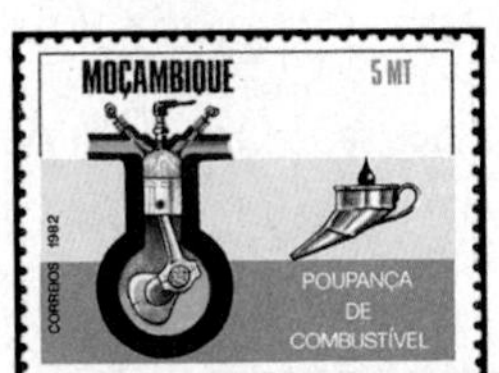

Gasoline Conservation — A116

1982, Jan. 25

802 A116 5m Piston .35 .30
803 A116 7.50m Car .55 .40
804 A116 10m Truck .75 .60
Nos. 802-804 (3) 1.65 1.30

Sea Snake A117

1.50m, Mozambique spitting cobra. 3m, Savanna vine snake. 6m, Black mamba. 15m, Boomslang. 20m, Bitis arietans.

1982, Feb. 27 Litho. *Perf. 11*

805 A117 50c shown .65 .25
806 A117 1.50m multi .65 .25
807 A117 3m multi .65 .25
808 A117 6m multi .70 .25
809 A117 15m multi 1.50 .50
810 A117 20m multi 2.10 .80
Nos. 805-810 (6) 6.25 2.30

TB Bacillus Centenary — A118

1982, Mar. 15 Litho. *Perf. 11*

811 A118 20m multi 2.00 1.10

ITU Plenipotentiary Conference, Nairobi, Sept. 28-Nov. 5 — A119

1982, Mar. 31 *Perf. 13½*

812 A119 20m multi 1.60 .80

1982 World Cup — A120

Designs: Various soccer players.

1982, Apr. 19 Litho. *Perf. 13½*

813 A120 1.5m multi .25 .25
814 A120 3.5m multi .30 .25
815 A120 7m multi .50 .25
816 A120 10m multi .85 .35
817 A120 20m multi 1.40 1.00
Nos. 813-817 (5) 3.30 2.10

Souvenir Sheet

Imperf

818 A120 50m multi 4.00 4.00

Souvenir Sheet

Two Tahitian Women, by Gauguin — A121

1982, June 11 Litho. *Imperf.*

819 A121 35m multi 6.00 5.25

PHILEXFRANCE '82 Intl. Stamp Exhibition, Paris, June 11-21.

Natl. Liberation Front, 20th Anniv. — A122

4m, Pres. Mondland addressing crowd. 8m, Guarded fields. 12m, Procession.

1982, June 25 *Perf. 13*

820 A122 4m multi .30 .25
821 A122 8m multi .60 .30
822 A122 12m multi .90 .45
Nos. 820-822 (3) 1.80 1.00

Vangueria Infausta A123

Designs: Fruits: 2m, Mimusops caffra. 4m, Sclerocarya caffra. 8m, Strychnos spinosa. 12m, Salacia kraussi. 32m, Trichilia emetica.

1982, Sept. 13 *Perf. 11*

823 A123 1m shown .25 .25
824 A123 2m multi .25 .25
825 A123 4m multi .30 .25
826 A123 8m multi .60 .30
827 A123 12m multi .90 .50
828 A123 32m multi 2.10 1.10
Nos. 823-828 (6) 4.40 2.65

25th Anniv. of Sputnik 1 Flight A124

1m, Sputnik, 1957. 2m, Yuri Gagarin's flight, 1961. 4m, A. Leonov's spacewalk, 1965. 8m, Apollo 11, 1969. 16m, Apollo-Soyuz, 1975. 20m, Salyut-6, 1978.

1982, Oct. 4 Litho. *Perf. 11*

829 A124 1m multi .25 .25
830 A124 2m multi .25 .25
831 A124 4m multi .30 .25
832 A124 8m multi .60 .30
833 A124 16m multi 1.25 .90
834 A124 20m multi 1.60 .90
a. Min. sheet of 6, #829-834 4.50 4.50
Nos. 829-834 (6) 4.25 2.85

People's Vigilance Day — A125

1982, Oct. 11 *Perf. 13½*

835 A125 4m multi .40 .25

Caique — A126

Traditional boats. 4m, 8m, 12m, 16m horiz.

1982, Nov. 29

836 A126 1m shown .25 .25
837 A126 2m Machua .25 .25
838 A126 4m Calaua .40 .25
839 A126 8m Chitatarro .75 .30
840 A126 12m Cangaia 1.00 .45
841 A126 16m Chata (flatboat) 1.75 .75
Nos. 836-841 (6) 4.40 2.25

Marine Life — A127

1m, Ophiomastix venosa. 2m, Protoreaster lincki. 4m, Tropiometra carinata. 8m, Holothuria scabra. 12m, Prionocidaris baculosa. 16m, Colobocentrotus atnatus.

1982, Dec. 21 Litho. *Perf. 11*

842 A127 1m multi .50 .25
843 A127 2m multi .50 .25
844 A127 4m multi .50 .25
845 A127 8m multi .80 .25
846 A127 12m multi 1.20 .45
847 A127 16m multi 1.60 .50
Nos. 842-847 (6) 5.10 1.95

Frelimo Party 4th Congress — A128

1983, Jan. 17

848 A128 4m Map, soldier .25 .25
849 A128 8m Voters .40 .25
850 A128 16m Farm workers 1.00 .65
Nos. 848-850 (3) 1.65 1.15

Seaweed A129

1m, Codium duthierae. 2m, Halimeda cuncata. 4m, Dictyota liturata. 8m, Encorachne bing hamiae. 12m, Laurencia flexuosa. 20m, Acrosorium sp..

1983, Feb. 28 Litho. *Perf. 11*

851 A129 1m multi .25 .25
852 A129 2m multi .25 .25
853 A129 4m multi .30 .25
854 A129 8m multi .65 .25
855 A129 12m multi 1.00 .40
856 A129 20m multi 1.25 .75
Nos. 851-856 (6) 3.70 2.15

1984 Olympic Games, Los Angeles A130

1983, Mar. 31 Litho. *Perf. 11*

857 A130 1m Diving .25 .25
858 A130 2m Boxing .25 .25
859 A130 4m Basketball .25 .25
860 A130 8m Handball .60 .25
861 A130 12m Volleyball .80 .40
862 A130 16m Running 1.10 .50
863 A130 20m Sailing 1.25 .80
Nos. 857-863 (7) 4.50 2.70

Souvenir Sheet

Imperf

864 A130 50m Discus 3.25 3.25

For surcharge see No. 1257.

Steam Locomotives — A131

1983, Apr. 29 Litho. *Perf. 11*

865 A131 1m 1912 .50 .25
866 A131 2m 1947 .50 .25
867 A131 4m 1923 .50 .25
868 A131 8m 1924 .60 .30
869 A131 16m 1924, diff. 1.40 .40
870 A131 32m 1950 2.75 1.25
Nos. 865-870 (6) 6.25 2.70

20th Anniv. of Org. of African Unity A132

1983, May 25 Litho. *Perf. 11*

871 A132 4m multi .25 .25

Mammals A133

1m, Petrodromus tetradactylus. 2m, Rhabdomys pumilio. 4m, Paraxerus vincenti. 8m, Cryptomys hottentotus. 12m, Pronolagus crassicaudatus. 16m, Eidolon helvum.

1983, May 30

872 A133 1m multi .50 .25
873 A133 2m multi .50 .25
874 A133 4m multi .50 .25
875 A133 8m multi .90 .25
876 A133 12m multi 1.25 .45
877 A133 16m multi 1.50 .60
Nos. 872-877 (6) 5.15 2.05

Souvenir Sheet

Marimba Players — A134

1983, July 29 Litho. *Perf. 11*

878 A134 30m multi 4.00 4.00

BRASILIANA '83 Intl. Stamp Show, Rio de Janeiro, July 29-Aug. 7.

World Communications Year — A135

1983, Aug. 26 Litho. *Perf. 11*

879 A135 8m multi .60 .25

Fishing Techniques — A136

1983, Oct. 29 Litho. *Perf. 11*

880 A136 50c Line fishing .25 .25
881 A136 2m Chifonho .25 .25
882 A136 4m Momba .25 .25
883 A136 8m Gamboa .50 .30
884 A136 16m Mono 1.40 .50
885 A136 20m Lema 1.60 .75
Nos. 880-885 (6) 4.25 2.30

World Communications Year, Stamp Day — A137

50c, Horn. 1m, Drum. 4m, Native mail carriers. 8m, Boat. 16m, Truck. 20m, Train.

1983, Dec. 21 Litho.

886 A137 50c multicolored .25 .25
887 A137 1m multicolored .25 .25
888 A137 4m multicolored .45 .25
889 A137 8m multicolored 1.10 .25
890 A137 16m multicolored 2.00 .55
891 A137 20m multicolored 3.00 .75
Nos. 886-891 (6) 7.05 2.30

2nd Anniv. of Mozambique Red Cross (July 10) — A138

1983, Oct. 29 Litho. *Perf. 11*

892 A138 4m Flood relief .25 .25
893 A138 8m Rescue truck .55 .25
894 A138 16m First aid 1.25 .50
895 A138 32m Field first aid 2.25 1.00
Nos. 892-895 (4) 4.30 2.00

Olympic Games 1984, Los Angeles A139

1984, Jan. 2 Litho. *Perf. 11*

896 A139 50c Swimming .25 .25
897 A139 4m Soccer .40 .25
898 A139 8m Hurdles .60 .30
899 A139 16m Basketball 1.25 .50
900 A139 32m Handball 2.60 1.50
901 A139 60m Boxing 4.25 2.10
Nos. 896-901 (6) 9.35 4.90

Indigenous Trees — A140

50c, Trichilia emetica. 2m, Brachystegia spiciformis. 4m, Androstachys johnsonii. 8m, Pterocarpus angolensis. 16m, Milletia stuhlmannii. 50m, Dalbergia melanoxylon.

1984, Mar. 30 Litho. *Perf. 11*

902 A140 50c multicolored .25 .25
903 A140 2m multicolored .25 .25
904 A140 4m multicolored .30 .25
905 A140 8m multicolored .65 .25
906 A140 16m multicolored 1.10 .55
907 A140 50m multicolored 3.25 1.75
Nos. 902-907 (6) 5.80 3.30

Nkomati Accord, Mar. 16 — A141

1984, Mar. 16

908 A141 4m Dove .40 .25

Natl. Arms A142

1984, May 1

909 A142 4m shown .30 .25
910 A142 8m Natl. flag .65 .30

Traditional Dances A143

1984, May 9

911 A143 4m Makway .25 .25
912 A143 8m Mapiko .50 .25
913 A143 16m Wadjaba 1.50 .65
Nos. 911-913 (3) 2.25 1.15

LUBRAPEX '84, May 9-17.

Museums and Artifacts — A144

Designs: 50c, Nampula Museum, African carrying water jar, wooden statue. 4m,

Museum of Natural History, preserved bird. 8m, Revolution Museum, guerrilla fighter statue. 16m, Colonial Occupation Museum, fort and cannon. 20m, Numismatic Museum, coins. 30m, Palace of St. Paul, chair, 19th cent.

1984, June 25

914	A144	50c multi	.25	.25
915	A144	4m multi	.35	.25
916	A144	8m multi	.60	.30
917	A144	16m multi	1.25	.60
918	A144	20m multi	1.40	.80
919	A144	30m multi	2.25	1.10
		Nos. 914-919 (6)	6.10	3.30

Freshwater Fish — A145

50c, Alestes imberi. 4m, Labeo congoro. 12m, Syndontis zambezensis. 16m, Notobranchius zachovii. 40m, Barbus paludinosus. 60m, Barilius zambezensis.

1984, Aug. 24

920	A145	50c multi	.25	.25
921	A145	4m multi	.40	.25
922	A145	12m multi	1.00	.45
923	A145	16m multi	1.00	.60
924	A145	40m multi	2.75	1.40
925	A145	60m multi	3.75	2.10
		Nos. 920-925 (6)	9.15	5.05

For surcharge see No. 1311.

Intl. Fair, Maputo — A145a — 925A

1984, Aug. 24 Litho. *Perf. 11*

925A A145a 16m multicolored 1.75 .60

Traditional Weapons A146

1984, Sept. 25

926	A146	50c Knife, cudgel	.30	*.25*
927	A146	4m Axes	.40	*.25*
928	A146	8m Shield, assagai	.45	*.25*
929	A146	16m Bow and arrow	2.00	.45
930	A146	32m Muzzleloader	3.00	1.10
931	A146	50m Assagai, arrow	4.00	1.75
		Nos. 926-931 (6)	10.15	4.05

Natl. Revolution, 20th anniv.
For surcharge see No. 1256.

Natl. Trade Unions, 1st Anniv. — A147

1984, Oct. 13 *Perf. 13½*

932 A147 4m Workers, emblem .40 .25

Stamp Day — A149

Cancellations on altered stamps and stationery: 4m, Barue cancel on 1885 20r postal card. 8m, Zumbo cancel on design similar to No. 52. 12m, Mozambique Co. cancel on design similar to Mozambique Company Type API. 16m, Macequece cancel on design similar to Mozambique Company No. 190.

1984, Dec. 21 *Perf. 11½x11*

936	A149	4m multi	.35	.25
937	A149	8m multi	.90	.35
938	A149	12m multi	1.50	.60
939	A149	16m multi	1.75	.75
		Nos. 936-939 (4)	4.50	1.95

African Development Bank, 20th Anniv. — A150

1984, Sept. 16 Photo. *Perf. 11½x11*

940 A150 4m multi .40 .25

Apiculture A151

4m, Beekeeper. 8m, Bee gathering pollen. 16m, Entering nest. 20m, Building honeycomb.

1985, Feb. 3

941	A151	4m multi	.30	.25
942	A151	8m multi	.70	.30
943	A151	16m multi	1.40	.60
944	A151	20m multi	2.00	.90
		Nos. 941-944 (4)	4.40	2.05

OLYMPHILEX '85, Lausanne A152

1985, Mar. 18 *Perf. 11*

945 A152 16m Shot putter 1.50 .60

World Meteorology Day — A153

1985, Mar. 23 Litho. *Perf. 11*

946 A153 4m multi .45 .25

Southern African Development Coordination Conference, 5th Anniv. — A154

4m, Map. 8m, Map, transmission tower. 16m, Industry. 32m, Flags.

1985, Apr. 1

947	A154	4m multi	.35	.25
948	A154	8m multi	1.00	.35
949	A154	16m multi	2.00	.75
950	A154	32m multi	3.25	1.25
		Nos. 947-950 (4)	6.60	2.60

Independence, 10th Anniv. — A155

Colonial resistance battles: 1m, Mujenga, 1896. 4m, Mungari, 1917. 8m, Massangano, 1868. 16m, Marracuene, 1895, and Gungunhana (c. 1840-1906), resistance leader.

1985, June 25 Litho. *Perf. 11*

951	A155	1m multi	.25	.25
952	A155	4m multi	.30	.25
953	A155	8m multi	.75	.25
954	A155	16m multi	1.60	.65
		Nos. 951-954 (4)	2.90	1.40

UN, 40th Anniv. — A156

1985, June 26

955 A156 16m multi 2.50 .70

Traditional Games — A157

1985, Aug. 28 Litho. *Perf. 11*

956	A157	50c Mathacuzana	.25	.25
957	A157	4m Mudzobo	.25	.25
958	A157	8m Muravarava	.50	.30
959	A157	16m N'Tshuwa	1.10	.60
		Nos. 956-959 (4)	2.10	1.40

Frogs and Toads A158

50c, Rana angolensis. 1m, Hyperolius pictus. 4m, Ptychadena porosissima. 8m, Afrixalus formasinii. 16m, Bufo regularis. 32m, Hyperolius marmoratus.

1985, Oct. 25 Litho. *Perf. 11*

960	A158	50c multi	.25	.25
961	A158	1m multi	.40	.25
962	A158	4m multi	.55	.25
963	A158	8m multi	1.10	.25
964	A158	16m multi	2.25	.60
965	A158	32m multi	3.75	1.10
		Nos. 960-965 (6)	8.30	2.70

Medicinal Plants — A159

50c, Aloe ferox. 1m, Boophone disticha. 3.50m, Gloriosa superba. 4m, Cotyledon orbiculata. 8m, Homeria breyniana. 50m, Haemanthus coccineus.

1985, Nov. 28 Litho. *Perf. 11*

966	A159	50c multi	.25	.25
967	A159	1m multi	.25	.25
968	A159	3.50m multi	.30	.25
969	A159	4m multi	.45	.25
970	A159	8m multi	1.10	.30
970A	A159	50m multi	6.00	1.75
		Nos. 966-970A (6)	8.35	3.05

Stamp Day A160

Stamps: 1m, Mozambique Company No. 126. 4m, Nyassa Type A6. 8m, Mozambique Company No. 110. 16m, Nyassa No. J2.

1985, Dec. 21

971	A160	1m multi	.25	.25
972	A160	4m multi	.45	.25
973	A160	8m multi	1.00	.25
974	A160	16m multi	2.00	.65
		Nos. 971-974 (4)	3.70	1.40

Halley's Comet — A161

Comet and: 4m, Space probe. 8m, Trajectory diagram. 16m, Newton's telescope, observatory, probe. 30m, Earth.

1986, Jan. 2

975	A161	4m multi	.25	.25
976	A161	8m multi	.60	.25
977	A161	16m multi	1.25	.60
978	A161	30m multi	2.50	1.25
		Nos. 975-978 (4)	4.60	2.35

1986 World Cup Soccer Championships, Mexico — A162

Players.

1986, Feb. 28 Litho. *Perf. 11½x11*

979	A162	3m Vicente	.25	.25
980	A162	4m Coluna	.25	.25
981	A162	8m Costa Pereira	.45	.30

982 A162 12m Hilario .85 .45
983 A162 16m Matateu 1.25 .60
984 A162 50m Eusebio 3.75 1.75
Nos. 979-984 (6) 6.80 3.60

Intl. Peace Year — A163

1986, Mar. 18 *Perf. 11*
985 A163 16m multi 1.25 .50

Mushrooms A164

4m, Amanita muscaria. 8m, Lactarius deliciosus. 16m, Amanita phaloides. 30m, Tricholoma nudum.

1986, Apr. 8
986 A164 4m multi .45 .25
987 A164 8m multi .30 .30
988 A164 16m multi 1.75 .75
989 A164 30m multi 3.50 1.25
Nos. 986-989 (4) 6.00 2.55

Souvenir Sheet

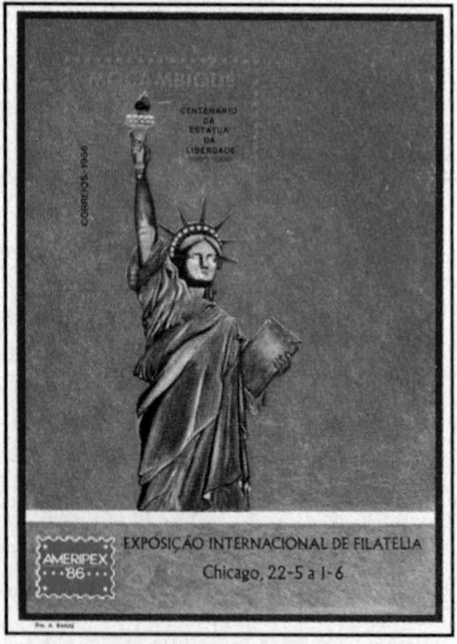

Statue of Liberty, Cent. — A165

1986, May 22 *Imperf.*
990 A165 100m multi 6.75 6.75

AMERIPEX '86. #990 has simulated perfs.

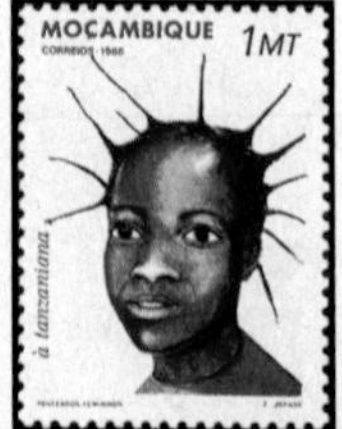

Traditional Women's Hair Styles — A166

1986, June Litho. *Perf. 11½x11*
991 A166 1m Tanzanian .25 .25
992 A166 4m Miriam .30 .25
993 A166 8m Estrelinhas .60 .25
994 A166 16m Toto 1.60 .70
Nos. 991-994 (4) 2.75 1.45

Marine Mammals — A167

1m, Dugongo dugon. 8m, Delphinus delphis. 16m, Neobalena marginata. 50m, Balaenoptera physalus.

1986, Aug. *Perf. 11*
995 A167 1m multi .25 .25
996 A167 8m multi .80 .25
997 A167 16m multi 2.75 .80
998 A167 50m multi 7.75 2.25
Nos. 995-998 (4) 11.55 3.55

Continuing Youth Education Organization, 1st Anniv. — A168

1986, Sept. 16 Litho. *Perf. 11½x11*
999 A168 4m multi .45 .25

Natl. Savings Campaign — A169

Bank notes, front and back.

1986, Oct. 22 Litho. *Perf. 11½x11*
1000 A169 4m 50m note .30 .25
1001 A169 8m 100m note .60 .25
1002 A169 16m 500m note 1.75 .60
1003 A169 30m 1000m note 3.00 1.50
Nos. 1000-1003 (4) 5.65 2.60

For surcharge see No. 1302.

Stamp Day A170

Post offices.

1986, Dec. 21 Litho. *Perf. 11*
1004 A170 3m Quelimane .30 .25
1005 A170 4m Maputo .70 .25
1006 A170 8m Beira 1.25 .35
1007 A170 16m Nampula 2.75 .75
Nos. 1004-1007 (4) 5.00 1.60

Minerals A171

1987, Jan. 2 *Perf. 11x11½*
1008 A171 4m Pyrite .80 .25
1009 A171 8m Emerald 1.50 .25
1010 A171 12m Agate 2.25 .45
1011 A171 16m Malachite 2.75 .60
1012 A171 30m Garnet 4.75 1.50
1013 A171 50m Amethyst 7.00 2.10
Nos. 1008-1013 (6) 19.05 5.15

For surcharges see #1304-1305.

Frelimo Party, 10th Anniv. — A172

1987, Feb. 3 *Perf. 11*
1014 A172 4m multi .45 .25

Pequenos Libombos Dam — A173

1987, Feb. 17 *Perf. 11½x11*
1015 A173 16m multi 1.75 .75

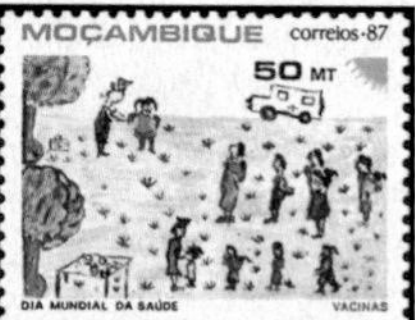

World Health Day A174

1987, Apr. 7 Litho. *Perf. 11x11½*
1016 A174 50m multi 1.20 .50

Birds — A175

3m, Granatina granatina. 4m, Halcyon senegalensis. 8m, Mellittophagus bullockoides. 12m, Perinestes minor. 16m, Coracias naevia mosambica. 30m, Cimmyris neergardi.

1987, Apr. 27 Litho. *Perf. 11½x11*
1017 A175 3m multi .25 .25
1018 A175 4m multi .30 .25
1019 A175 8m multi .60 .35
1020 A175 12m multi .95 .50
1021 A175 16m multi 1.25 .75
1022 A175 30m multi 2.50 1.25
Nos. 1017-1022 (6) 5.85 3.35

For surcharge, see No. 1299A.

Souvenir Sheet

CAPEX '87, Toronto, June 13-21 — A176

1987, June *Imperf.*
1023 A176 200m multi 4.25 4.25

No. 1023 contains one stamp having simulated perforations.

1988 Summer Olympics, Seoul — A177

12.50m, Soccer players and ball. 25m, Runner's legs. 50m, Volleyball. 75m, Chess. 100m, Basketball. 200m, Swimming.

1987, May Litho. *Perf. 11½x11*
1024 A177 12.50m multi .30 .30
1025 A177 25m multi .40 .30
1026 A177 50m multi .75 .45
1027 A177 75m multi 1.20 .70
1028 A177 100m multi 1.50 .80
1029 A177 200m multi 3.25 1.20
Nos. 1024-1029 (6) 7.40 3.75

Tapestries — A178

20m, Incomplete pattern on loom. 40m, Diamond-shaped pattern. 80m, Landscape pattern. 200m, Oriental pattern.

1987, Aug. *Perf. 11*
1030 A178 20m multi .30 .25
1031 A178 40m multi .60 .25
1032 A178 80m multi 1.20 .40
1033 A178 200m multi 2.75 1.00
Nos. 1030-1033 (4) 4.85 1.90

Maputo City A179

Early Portuguese map of Lourenco Marques.

1987, Nov. 10 Litho. *Perf. 11*
1034 A179 20m multi .55 .25

No. 762 Surcharged in Silver and Dark Red

1987 Litho. *Perf. 14½*
1034A A108 4m on 4.50m multi 2.00 2.00

1988 Summer Olympics, Seoul — A180

10m, Javelin. 20m, Baseball, horiz. 40m, Boxing, horiz. 80m, Field hockey, horiz. 100m, Gymnastic rings, horiz. 400m, Cycling, horiz.

1988, Feb. 10 Litho. *Perf. 11*
1035 A180 10m multi .25 .25
1036 A180 20m multi .25 .25
1037 A180 40m multi .40 .40
1038 A180 80m multi .80 .80
1039 A180 100m multi 1.20 1.20
1040 A180 400m multi 1.60 1.60
Nos. 1035-1040 (6) 4.50 4.50

Flowering Plants — A181

10m, Heamanthus nelsonii. 20m, Crinum polyphyllum. 40m, Boophane disticha. 80m, Cyrtanthus contractus. 100m, Nerine angustifolia. 400m, Cyrtanthus galpinnii.

1988, Mar. 18 *Perf. 11½x11*
1041 A181 10m multi .25 .25
1042 A181 20m multi .40 .30
1043 A181 40m multi .55 .40
1044 A181 80m multi 1.20 .65
1045 A181 100m multi 1.60 .80
1046 A181 400m multi 2.25 2.25
Nos. 1041-1046 (6) 6.25 4.65

World Health Organization, 40th Anniv. — A182

1988, Apr. 7
1047 A182 20m multi .45 .45

Anti-smoking campaign.

Wickerwork — A183

20m, Mat. 25m, Lidded container. 80m, Market basket. 100m, Fan. 400m, Flat basket. 500m, Funnel basket.

1988, June 16 Litho. *Perf. 11*
1048 A183 20m multi .25 .25
1049 A183 25m multi .30 .30
1050 A183 80m multi .65 .30
1051 A183 100m multi .80 .35
1052 A183 400m multi 2.00 1.60
1053 A183 500m multi 2.75 2.00
Nos. 1048-1053 (6) 6.75 4.80

Souvenir Sheet

FINLANDIA '88 — A184

1988, June 12 Litho. *Imperf.*
1054 A184 500m multi 4.00 4.00

Stamp in No. 1054 has simulated perfs.

Souvenir Sheet

State Visit of Pope John Paul II, Sept. 16-19 — A185

1988 Litho. *Perf. 13½*
1055 A185 500m multi 5.00 5.00

Horses A186

1988, Sept. 20 Litho. *Perf. 11*
1056 A186 20m Percheron .40 .30
1057 A186 40m Arab .80 .30
1058 A186 80m Thoroughbred 1.75 .40
1059 A186 100m Pony 2.50 .50
Nos. 1056-1059 (4) 5.45 1.50

Pres. Samora Machel (1933-1986) A187

1988, Oct. 19 Litho. *Perf. 11*
1060 A187 20m multi .30 .30

Stamp Day A188

1988, Dec. 21 *Perf. 11x11½, 11½x11*
1061 A188 20m P.O. trailer .30 .30
1062 A188 40m Mailbox, vert. .30 .30

Ports A189

25m, Inhambane. 50m, Quelimane, vert. 75m, Pemba. 100m, Beira. 250m, Nacala, vert. 500m, Maputo.

1988, Nov. 30 *Perf. 11*
1063 A189 25m multi .30 .30
1064 A189 50m multi .30 .30
1065 A189 75m multi .50 .30
1066 A189 100m multi .60 .30
1067 A189 250m multi 1.50 .45
1068 A189 500m multi 3.50 .90
Nos. 1063-1068 (6) 6.70 2.55

5th Frelimo Party Congress — A190

1989, Jan. 19
1069 A190 Strip of 5 3.00 3.00
a. 25m Corn .30 .30
b. 50m Axe .30 .30
c. 75m Abstract shapes .30 .30
d. 100m 2½ Gearwheels .40 .40
e. A190 250m ½ Gearwheel 1.00 1.00

Printed se-tenant in a continuous design.

French Revolution Bicent. — A191

Designs: 100m, *Storming of the Bastille,* by Thevenin. 250m, *Liberty Guiding the People,* by Delacroix. 500m, *Declaration of the Rights of Man and the Citizen,* a print by Blanchard.

1989, Feb. 16 *Perf. 11*
1070 A191 100m multi .40 .30
1071 A191 250m multi 1.20 .45

Souvenir Sheet

1072 A191 500m multi 2.40 2.40

No. 1072 is a continuous design.

Eduardo Chivambo Mondlane (1920-1969), Frelimo Party Founder, 20th Death Anniv. — A192

1989, Feb. 3 Litho. *Perf. 11*
1073 A192 25m blk, gold & dark red .30 .30

Venomous Species — A193

25m, Pandinus. 50m, Naja haje. 75m, Bombus. 100m, Paraphysa. 250m, Conus marmoreus. 500m, Pterois volitans.

1989, Mar. 23
1074 A193 25m multi .30 .30
1075 A193 50m multi .30 .30
1076 A193 75m multi .60 .30
1077 A193 100m multi 1.00 .30
1078 A193 250m multi 1.75 .45
1079 A193 500m multi 3.50 .75
Nos. 1074-1079 (6) 7.45 2.40

Coral A194

25m, Acropora pulchra. 50m, Eunicella papilosa. 100m, Dendrophyla migrantus. 250m, Favia fragum.

1989, May 2 Litho. *Perf. 11*
1080 A194 25m multi .35 .30
1081 A194 50m multi .35 .30
1082 A194 100m multi .60 .30
1083 A194 250m multi 1.40 .55
Nos. 1080-1083 (4) 2.70 1.45

1990 World Cup Soccer Championships, Italy — A195

Athletes executing various plays.

1989, June 22 Litho. *Perf. 11½x11*
1084 A195 30m multi .25 .25
1085 A195 60m multi .25 .25
1086 A195 125m multi .40 .25
1087 A195 200m multi .60 .35
1088 A195 250m multi .80 .40
1089 A195 500m multi 1.75 .90
Nos. 1084-1089 (6) 4.05 2.40

Lighthouses A196

1989, July 24 Litho. *Perf. 11*
1090 A196 30m Macuti .25 .25
1091 A196 60m Pinda .25 .25
1092 A196 125m Cape Delgado .40 .25
1093 A196 200m Isle of Goa .80 .35
1094 A196 250m Caldeira Point 1.00 .40
1095 A196 500m Vilhena 1.60 .90
Nos. 1090-1095 (6) 4.30 2.40

Filigree Workmanship in Silver — A197

1989, Aug. 30 Litho. ***Perf. 11x11½***

1096 A197 30m shown .25 .25
1097 A197 60m Flower on band .25 .25
1098 A197 125m Necklace .40 .25
1099 A197 200m Decorative box .75 .35
1100 A197 250m Utensils .90 .40
1101 A197 500m Butterfly 1.50 .90
Nos. 1096-1101 (6) 4.05 2.40

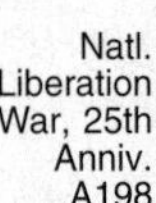

Natl. Liberation War, 25th Anniv. A198

1989, Sept. 25

1102 A198 30m multicolored .25 .25

Meteorological Instruments A199

Designs: 30m, Rain gauge. 60m, Weather system on radar. 125m, Instrument shelter. 200m, Computer monitor and keyboard.

1989, Oct. 12 ***Perf. 11½x11***

1103 A199 30m multicolored .25 .25
1104 A199 60m multicolored .30 .25
1105 A199 125m multicolored .45 .25
1106 A199 200m multicolored .90 .35
Nos. 1103-1106 (4) 1.90 1.10

Souvenir Sheet

World Stamp Expo '89, Washington, DC — A200

500m, Washington Monument.

1989, Nov. 17 ***Perf. 13½***

1107 A200 500m multi 3.00 3.00

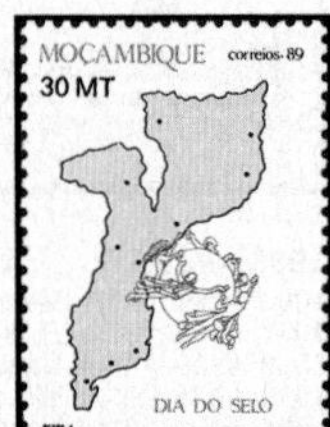

Stamp Day — A201

1989, Dec. 21 Litho. ***Perf. 11½x11***

1108 A201 30m UPU emblem .25 .25
1109 A201 60m P.O. emblem .25 .25

Southern African Development Coordination Conf. (SADCC), 10th Anniv. — A201a

1990, Jan. 31 ***Perf. 11½x11***

1109A A201a 35m multicolored .30 .25

Textile Designs A202

1990, Feb. 28 Litho. ***Perf. 11x11½***

1110 A202 42m multi, diff. .25 .25
1111 A202 90m multi, diff. .35 .25
1112 A202 150m multi, diff. .50 .30
1113 A202 200m multi, diff. .65 .35
1114 A202 400m multi, diff. 1.40 .65
1115 A202 500m multi, diff. 1.75 .90
Nos. 1110-1115 (6) 4.90 2.70

Forts A203

45m, Sena. 90m, Santo Antonio. 150m, Santo Sebastiao. 200m, Santo Caetano. 400m, Our Lady of Conceicao. 500m, Santo Luis.

1990, Mar. 20 ***Perf. 11x11½***

1116 A203 45m lt blue .25 .25
1117 A203 90m blue .35 .25
1118 A203 150m multi .50 .30
1119 A203 200m multi .65 .35
1120 A203 400m rose 1.40 .65
1121 A203 500m org red 1.75 .90
Nos. 1116-1121 (6) 4.90 2.70

Souvenir Sheet

Penny Black, Mozambique No. 1 — A204

1990, May 3 Litho. ***Perf. 11½x11***

1122 A204 1000m red, blk & bl 4.00 4.00

Penny Black, 150th anniversary. Stamp World London '90.

Bank of Mozambique, 15th Anniv. — A205

1990, May 17 Litho. ***Perf. 11x11½***

1123 A205 100m multicolored .40 .25

Natl. Independence, 15th Anniv. — A206

42.50m, Eduardo Mondlane. 150m, Samora Machel.

1990, June 25 ***Perf. 11***

1124 A206 42.50m multi .25 .25
1125 A206 150m multi .45 .25

Endangered Species — A207

42.50m, Ceratotherium simum. 100m, Dugong dugong. 150m, Loxodonta africana. 200m, Acinonix jubatus. 400m, Lutra maculicollis. 500m, Eretmochelys imbricata.

1990, Aug. 20 Litho. ***Perf. 11x11½***

1126 A207 42.50m multi .40 .25
1127 A207 100m multi .55 .25
1128 A207 150m multi .80 .30
1129 A207 200m multi 1.00 .35
1130 A207 400m multi 2.25 .65
1131 A207 500m multi 2.75 .90
Nos. 1126-1131 (6) 7.75 2.70

Trees and Plants — A208

42.50m, Dichrostachys cinerea. 100m, Queimadas. 150m, Casuariana equisetifolia. 200m, Rhizophora muronata. 400m, Estrato herbaceo. 500m, Atzelia cuanzensis.

1990, Oct. 15 Litho. ***Perf. 11½x11***

1132 A208 42.50m multi .25 .25
1133 A208 100m multi .35 .25
1134 A208 150m multi .50 .30
1135 A208 200m multi .65 .35
1136 A208 400m multi 1.40 .65
1137 A208 500m multi 1.75 .90
Nos. 1132-1137 (6) 4.90 2.70

Stamp Day — A209

No. 1138: a, Pick-up at letter box. b, Canceling letters. c, Letter carrier. d, Delivery to recipient.

1990, Dec. 21 Litho. ***Perf. 11½x11***

1138 Strip of 4 1.00 1.00
a.-d. A209 42.50m any single .25 .25

Governmental Departments A210

Designs: No. 1139, Post Office Dept., 10th anniv. No. 1140, Telecommunications Dept.

1991, Jan. 2

1139 A210 50m dk bl, red & blk .25 .25
1140 A210 50m grn, blk & brn .25 .25

Flowers — A211

50m, Strilitzia reginae. 125m, Anthurium andraeanum. 250m, Zantedeschia pentlandii. 300m, Canna indica.

1991, Feb. 25 Litho. ***Perf. 11½x11***

1141 A211 50m multi .25 .25
1142 A211 125m multi .40 .30
1143 A211 250m multi .80 .60
1144 A211 300m multi 1.00 .70
Nos. 1141-1144 (4) 2.45 1.85

Alcelaphus Lichtensteini A212

1991, Mar. 27 ***Perf. 14***

1145 Strip of 4 11.00 11.00
a. A212 50m Two adults .60 .40
b. A212 100m Adult .90 .40
c. A212 250m Adult grazing 2.25 .90
d. A212 500m Nursing calf 3.75 2.25

Fountains of Maputo — A213

Designs: 50m, Mpompine. 125m, Chinhambanine. 250m, Sao Pedro-Zaza. 300m, Xipamanine.

1991, Apr. 15 Litho. ***Perf. 11½x11***

1146 A213 50m multicolored .25 .25
1147 A213 125m multicolored .30 .25
1148 A213 250m multicolored .60 .30
1149 A213 300m multicolored .75 .40
Nos. 1146-1149 (4) 1.90 1.20

For surcharge see No. 1394.

Paintings by Mozambican Artists — A214

180m, Samale. 250m, Malangatana. 560m, Malangatana, diff.

1991, May 18 Litho. *Perf. 11½x11*

1150	A214	180m multicolored	.45	.25
1151	A214	250m multicolored	.60	.30
1152	A214	560m multicolored	1.40	.70
		Nos. 1150-1152 (3)	2.45	1.25

1992 Summer Olympics, Barcelona A215

1991, June 25 Litho. *Perf. 11½x11*

1153	A215	10m Swimming	.25	.25
1154	A215	50m Roller hockey	.25	.25
1155	A215	100m Tennis	.30	.25
1156	A215	200m Table tennis	.55	.30
1157	A215	500m Running	1.30	.60
1158	A215	1000m Badminton	2.75	1.30
		Nos. 1153-1158 (6)	5.40	2.95

For surcharges, see Nos. 1393, 1393A, 1395-1396.

British-Portuguese Agreement on Mozambique Borders, Cent. — A216

1991, Oct. 9 Litho. *Perf. 11½x11*

1159	A216	600m Map of 1890	1.00	.45
1160	A216	800m Map of 1891	1.25	.70

Souvenir Sheet

Phila Nippon '91 — A217

1991, Nov. 15 Litho. *Perf. 11½x11*

1161	A217	1500m Map of Japan	3.00	3.00

Children's Games — A218

1991, Dec. 21

1162	A218	40m Jumping rope	.25	.25
1163	A218	150m Spinning top	.25	.25
1164	A218	400m Marbles	.55	.30
1165	A218	900m Hopscotch	1.30	.70
		Nos. 1162-1165 (4)	2.35	1.50

Stained Glass Windows — A219

No. 1166 — Various designs: a, 40m. b, 150m. c, 400m. d, 900m.

1992, Jan. 22

1166	A219	Block of 4, #a.-d.	1.90	1.90

Plants — A220

300m, Rhisophora mucronata. 600m, Cymodocea ciliata. 1000m, Sophora inhambanensis.

1992, Mar. 23 Litho. *Perf. 11½x11*

1167	A220	300m multi	.60	.30
1168	A220	600m multi	1.25	.60
1169	A220	1000m multi	2.00	1.00
		Nos. 1167-1169 (3)	3.85	1.90

Traditional Tools — A221

100m, Spear, spear-thrower. 300m, Pitch forks. 500m, Hatchet. 1000m, Dagger.

1992, May 9

1170	A221	100m multi	.25	.25
1171	A221	300m multi	.60	.30
1172	A221	500m multi	1.00	.55
1173	A221	1000m multi	2.00	1.00
		Nos. 1170-1173 (4)	3.85	2.10

Lubrapex '92, Lisbon.

A222

Birds: 150m, Chalcomitra amethystina. 200m, Ceropis senegalensis. 300m, Cossypha natalensis. 400m, Lamprocolius chloropterus. 500m, Malaconotus poliocephalus. 800m, Oriolus auratus.

1992, July 24 Litho. *Perf. 11½x11*

1174	A222	150m multicolored	.40	.25
1175	A222	200m multicolored	.45	.25
1176	A222	300m multicolored	.70	.30
1177	A222	400m multicolored	.95	.45
1178	A222	500m multicolored	1.20	.45
1179	A222	800m multicolored	1.90	.90
		Nos. 1174-1179 (6)	5.60	2.60

Eduardo Mondlane University, 30th Anniv. — A223

1992, Aug. 21

1180	A223	150m grn, brn & blk	.40	.25

Traditional Musical Instruments A224

1992, Sept. 18

1181	A224	200m Phiane	.45	.25
1182	A224	300m Xirupe	.60	.25
1183	A224	500m Ngulula	1.10	.35
1184	A224	1500m Malimba	3.25	1.10
a.		Souvenir sheet of 4, #1181-1184, imperf.	6.00	6.00
		Nos. 1181-1184 (4)	5.40	1.95

Genoa '92. #1184a has simulated perfs.

No. 757 Surcharged

1992, Oct. Litho. *Perf. 14½*

1185	A108	50m on 50c #757	.70	.45

Intl. Conference on Nutrition — A225

1992, Oct. 16 *Perf. 11½x11*

1186	A225	450m multicolored	.90	.45

Parachuting A226

Various parchutists descending from sky.

1992, Nov. 10 Litho. *Perf. 11½x11*

1187	A226	50m multicolored	.25	.25
1188	A226	400m multicolored	.60	.40
1189	A226	800m multicolored	.80	.45
1190	A226	1500m multicolored	2.40	1.30
		Nos. 1187-1190 (4)	4.05	2.40

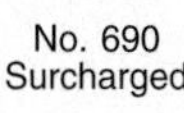

No. 690 Surcharged

Methods and Perfs As Before

1992

1190A	A91	200m on 5e #690	—

Medals — A227

400m, Order of Peace & Amity. 800m, Baga moyo. 1000m, Order of Eduardo Mondlane. 1500m, War veterans.

1993, Feb. 3 Litho. *Perf. 11½x11*

1191	A227	400m multi	.30	.25
1192	A227	800m multi	.60	.40
1193	A227	1000m multi	.85	.40
1194	A227	1500m multi	1.20	.60
		Nos. 1191-1194 (4)	2.95	1.65

Pollution A228

200m, Deforestation. 750m, Factory smoke. 1000m, Oil spill from ship. 1500m, Automobile exhaust.

1993, Apr. 8 *Perf. 11x11½*

1195	A228	200m multi	.40	.25
1196	A228	750m multi	1.10	.40
1197	A228	1000m multi	1.50	.45
1198	A228	1500m multi	2.25	.70
		Nos. 1195-1198 (4)	5.25	1.80

Natl. Parks A229

Park, animal, map: 200m, Gorongosa, lion. 800m, Banhine, giraffes. 1000m, Bazaruto, manatees. 1500m, Zinave, ostriches.

1993, May 25 Litho. *Perf. 11x11½*

1199	A229	200m multicolored	.30	.25
1200	A229	800m multicolored	.85	.40
1201	A229	1000m multicolored	1.10	.45
1202	A229	1500m multicolored	1.75	.70
		Nos. 1199-1202 (4)	4.00	1.80

Natl. Conference on Culture — A230

1993, Sept. 27 Litho. *Perf. 11½x11*

1203	A230	200m multicolored	.45	.25

Union of Portuguese Speaking Capitals A231

1993, July 30 Litho. *Perf. 11x11½*

1204	A231	1500m multicolored	2.40	.60

Brasilana '93.

Forest Plants — A232

Designs: 200m, Cycas cercinalis. 250m, Cycas revoluta. 900m, Encephalartos ferox. 2000m, Equisetum ramosissimum.

1993, Dec. 29 Litho. ***Perf. 11½x11***

1205 A232 200m multicolored .25 .25
1206 A232 250m multicolored .25 .25
1207 A232 900m multicolored .70 .40
1208 A232 2000m multicolored 1.60 .80
Nos. 1205-1208 (4) 2.80 1.70

Medicinal Plants — A233

200m, Anacardium occidentale. 250m, Sclerocarya caffra. 900m, Annona senegalensis. 2000m, Crinum delagoense.

1994 Litho. ***Perf. 11½x11***

1209 A233 200m multi .25 .25
1210 A233 250m multi .30 .25
1211 A233 900m multi 1.00 .30
1212 A233 2000m multi 2.25 .70
Nos. 1209-1212 (4) 3.80 1.50

Nos. 699, 763-764, 772, 791-792, 797-798 Surcharged

1994

Perfs. and Printing Methods as Before

1212A A94 50m on 5e #699 —
1213 A109 50m on 7.50m #772 .40 .25
1214 A113 50m on 7.50m #791 .40 .25
1215 A114 50m on 7.50m #797 .40 .25
1216 A108 100m on 10m #763 .55 .25
1217 A114 100m on 12.50m #798 .55 .25
1218 A108 200m on 12.50m #764 1.10 .25
1219 A113 250m on 12.50m #792 1.30 .25
Nos. 1213-1219 (7) 4.70 1.75

Size and location of surcharge varies. Surcharge on Nos. 1214-1215, 1219 does not contain an obliterator.

For additional surcharge, see No. 1391.

PHILAKOREA '94 — A234

Reptiles: 300m, Ichnotropis squamulosa. 500m, Lepidachelys olivacea. 2000m, Prosyma frontalis. 3500m, Rampholeon marshalli. 4000m, Snake eating a lizard.

1994, Aug. 16 Litho. ***Perf. 11½x11***

1220 A234 300m multicolored .25 .25
1221 A234 500m multicolored .40 .25
1222 A234 2000m multicolored 1.50 .45
1223 A234 3500m multicolored 2.60 .85
Nos. 1220-1223 (4) 4.75 1.80

Souvenir Sheet

1224 A234 4000m multicolored 4.25 4.25

ICAO, 50th Anniv. A235

Designs: 300d, Crop dusting. 500m, Airport terminal. 2000m, Passenger jet in flight. 3500m, Maintenance man inspecting jet engine.

1994, Oct. 12 Litho. ***Perf. 11x11½***

1225 A235 300m multicolored .25 .25
1226 A235 500m multicolored .40 .25
1227 A235 2000m multicolored 1.50 .60
1228 A235 3500m multicolored 2.75 1.10
Nos. 1225-1228 (4) 4.90 2.20

World Food Day — A236

1994, Oct. 24 ***Perf. 11½x11***

1229 A236 2000m multicolored 2.25 .60

Lubrapex '94.

National Elections — A237

1994, Oct. 26

1230 A237 900m multicolored 1.10 .40

Fight Against Illegal Drugs — A238

Designs: 500m, Couple using drugs. 1000m, Hypodermic needle, couple tied in rope, skeleton. 2000m, Man with drug dependency. 5000m, Dog apprehending man with contraband.

1994, Dec. 7

1231 A238 500m multicolored .45 .25
1232 A238 1000m multicolored .85 .30
1233 A238 2000m multicolored 1.60 .70
1234 A238 5000m multicolored 4.25 1.75
Nos. 1231-1234 (4) 7.15 3.00

Lusaka Accord, 20th Anniv. — A239

1994, Nov. 9

1235 A239 1500m multicolored 2.25 .45

Basketry — A240

300m, Two-handled basket. 1200m, Round purse. 5000m, Rectangle purse.

1995, Apr. 15 Litho. ***Perf. 11½x11***

1236 A240 250m shown .25 .25
1237 A240 300m multi .25 .25
1238 A240 1200m multi .85 .35
1239 A240 5000m multi 3.50 1.25
Nos. 1236-1239 (4) 4.85 2.10

Clothing — A241

Various styles of women's traditional clothing.

1995, May 25

1240 A241 250m blue & multi .25 .25
1241 A241 300m pink & multi .25 .25
1242 A241 1200m blue & multi .85 .35
1243 A241 5000m red & multi 3.50 1.25
Nos. 1240-1243 (4) 4.85 2.10

Inauguration of Pres. Joaquim A. Chissano, Dec. 9, 1994 — A242

No. 1244: a, 900m, Natl. arms. b, 5000m, Pres. Chissano. c, 2500m, Natl. flag.

1995, June 25 Litho. ***Perf. 11½x11***

1244 A242 Strip of 3, #a.-c. 4.00 2.00

No. 1244 has a common inscription across the bottom.

Wild Animals — A243

Designs: 500m, Crassicadautus lombergi. 2000m, Tragelaphus strepsceros, horiz. 3000m, Potamochoerus porcus nyasae, horiz. 5000m, Tragelaphus scriptus.

Perf. 11½x11, 11x11½

1995, Aug. 29 Litho.

1245 A243 500m multicolored .25 .25
1246 A243 2000m multicolored .95 .30
1247 A243 3000m multicolored 1.50 .40
1248 A243 5000m multicolored 2.50 .70
Nos. 1245-1248 (4) 5.20 1.65

FAO, 50th Anniv. — A244

1995, Oct. 16 ***Perf. 11½x11***

1249 A244 5000m multicolored 1.50 .85

UN, 50th Anniv. — A245

1995, Oct. 24

1250 A245 5000m blue & black 1.50 .85

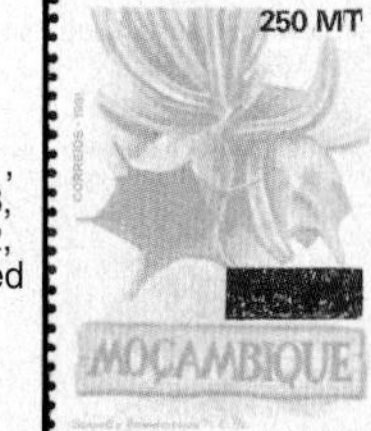

Nos. 647, 711, 713, 749, 763, 792, 798, 862, 929 Surcharged

Perfs. and Printing Methods as Before

1995, Oct. 4

1251 A114 250m on 12.50m #798 .75 .25
1252 A108 300m on 10m #763 .75 .25
1253 A113 500m on 12.50m #792 .75 .25
1253A A97 600m on 5m #711 — —
1254 A81 900m on 12.50m #647 1.00 .25
1255 A97 1000m on 12.50m #713 1.00 .25
1256 A146 1500m on 16m #929 1.00 .25
1257 A130 2000m on 16m #862 1.00 .30
1258 A106 2500m on 12.50m #749 1.20 .40
Nos. 1251-1258 (9) 7.45 2.20

UNICEF, 20th Anniv. in Mozambique A246

1995, Nov. 22 Litho. ***Perf. 11½***

1259 A246 5000m multicolored 1.50 .85

Mozambique-South Africa Soccer Match — A247

Various soccer plays.

1996, Apr. 5 Litho. *Perf. 11x11½*

No.	Type	Value	Color	Unused	Used
1260	A247	1000m	multicolored	.25	.25
1261	A247	2000m	multicolored	.45	.30
1262	A247	4000m	multicolored	.95	.55
1263	A247	6000m	multicolored	1.50	.85
		Nos. 1260-1263 (4)		3.15	1.95

Masks — A248

Various masks.

1996, July 2 Litho. *Perf. 11½x11*

No.	Type	Value	Color	Unused	Used
1264	A248	1000m	multicolored	.25	.25
1265	A248	2000m	multicolored	.45	.30
1266	A248	4000m	multicolored	.95	.55
1267	A248	6000m	multicolored	1.50	.85
		Nos. 1264-1267 (4)		3.15	1.95

Red Cross of Mozambique, 15th Anniv. — A249

1996, July 10

No.	Type	Value	Color	Unused	Used
1268	A249	5000m	multicolored	1.20	.85

Endangered Wildlife — A250

1000m, Loxodona africana. 2000m, Ceratotherum simum. 4000m, Panthera pardus. 6000m, Scotopelia peli.

1996, Sept. 3 Litho. *Perf. 11½x11*

No.	Type	Value	Color	Unused	Used
1269	A250	1000m	multi	.40	.25
1270	A250	2000m	multi	.70	.30
1271	A250	4000m	multi	1.40	.55
1272	A250	6000m	multi	2.25	.85
		Nos. 1269-1272 (4)		4.75	1.95

Removal of Land Mines — A251

Designs: 2000m, Mine, tripwire across path. 6000m, Warning sign posted. 8000m, Using mine detector. 10,000m, Removing mine.

1996, Nov. 9 Litho. *Perf. 11½x11*

No.	Type	Value	Color	Unused	Used
1273	A251	2000m	multicolored	.45	.25
1274	A251	6000m	multicolored	1.30	.80
1275	A251	8000m	multicolored	1.90	1.10
1276	A251	10,000m	multicolored	2.40	1.30
		Nos. 1273-1276 (4)		6.05	3.45

Keep The City Clean Campaign A252

1996, Dec. 16 Litho. *Perf. 11½x11*

No.	Type	Value	Color	Unused	Used
1277	A252	2000m	multicolored	.60	.30

Mozambique Postage Stamps, 120th Anniv. — A253

1996, Dec. 16 Litho. *Perf. 11½x11*

No.	Type	Value	Color	Unused	Used
1278	A253	2000m	No. 1	.60	.30

Mozambique Boats — A254

1997, Apr. 10 Litho. *Perf. 11x11½*

No.	Type	Value	Color	Unused	Used
1279	A254	2000m	Mitumbui	.45	.30
1280	A254	6000m	Muterere	1.30	.95
1281	A254	8000m	Lancha	1.90	1.30
1282	A254	10,000m	Dau	2.40	1.60
		Nos. 1279-1282 (4)		6.05	4.15

Children's Day A255

1997, June 1 Litho. *Perf. 11x11½*

No.	Type	Value	Color	Unused	Used
1283	A255	2000m	multicolored	.60	.30

Aquatic Birds A256

Designs: 2000m, Mycteria ibis. 4000m, Himantopus himantopus. 8000m, Calidris subminuta. 10,000m, Pelecanus onocrotalus.

Perf. 11½x11, 11x11½

1997, June 10

No.	Type	Value	Color	Unused	Used
1284	A256	2000m	multi, vert.	.70	.30
1285	A256	4000m	multi, vert.	1.75	.60
1286	A256	8000m	multi	3.00	1.30
1287	A256	10,000m	multi, vert.	3.50	1.75
		Nos. 1284-1287 (4)		8.95	3.95

Independence of India, 50th Anniv. — A258a

1997 Litho. *Perf. 11x11½*

No.	Type	Value	Color	Unused	Used
1287A	A258a	2000m	multi	1.20	.55

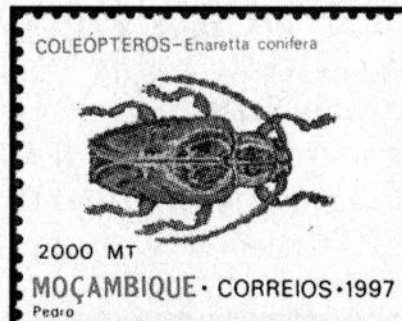

Insects A257

Designs: 2000m, Enaretta conifera. 6000m, Zographus heiroglyphicus. 8000m, Tragiscoschema bertolonii. 10,000m, Tragocephala ducalis.

1997, July 5 Litho. *Perf. 11x11½*

No.	Type	Value	Color	Unused	Used
1288	A257	2000m	multicolored	.70	.30
1289	A257	6000m	multicolored	2.00	.95
1290	A257	8000m	multicolored	2.75	1.30
1291	A257	10,000m	multicolored	3.25	1.60
a.		Souvenir sheet, #1288-1291		8.75	8.75
		Nos. 1288-1291 (4)		8.70	4.15

Labrapex '97 (#1291a).

Joao Ferreira dos Santos Group, Cent. — A258

1997, Sept. 5 Litho. *Perf. 11x11½*

No.	Type	Value	Color	Unused	Used
1292	A258	2000m	multi	*16.00*	*8.00*

Protection of the Ozone Layer — A259

1997, Sept. 16 Litho. *Perf. 11½x11*

No.	Type	Value	Color	Unused	Used
1293	A259	2000m	multicolored	.45	.30

Peace Accord, 5th Anniv. — A260

1997, Oct. 4 Litho. *Perf. 11½x11*

No.	Type	Value	Color	Unused	Used
1294	A260	2000m	multi	.55	.30

Souvenir Sheet

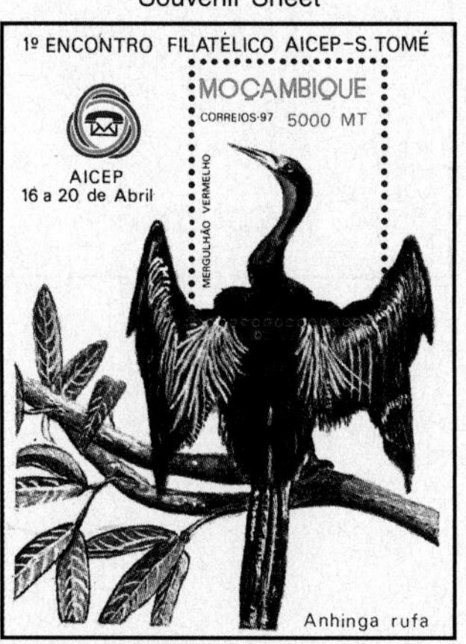

Anhinga — A261

1997 Litho. *Perf. 11½x11*

No.	Type	Value	Color	Unused	Used
1295	A261	5000m	multi	*22.50*	—

Food Products A262

1998, June 1 Litho. *Perf. 11x11½*

No.	Type	Value	Color	Unused	Used
1296	A262	2000m	multicolored	.80	.40

Expo '98, Lisbon A263

1998, May 22

No.	Type	Value	Color	Unused	Used
1297	A263	2000m	Coelacanth	.95	.40

Nos. 660, 666, 730, 764, 797, 1002, 1009, 1011, 1021 Surcharged

Printing Methods and Perfs as before

1998 (?)

No.	Type	Value	Description	Unused	Used
1298	A85	2000m	on 12.50e #660	2.75	2.75
1299	A86	2000m	on 12.50e #666	2.75	2.75
1299A	A175	2000m	on 16m #1021	—	—
1300	A108	4000m	on 12.50m #764	1.90	1.90
1301	A114	6000m	on 7.50m #797	3.25	3.25
1302	A169	7500m	on 16m #1002	3.50	3.50
1303	A102	10,000m	on 12.50m #730	2.50	2.50
1304	A171	12,500m	on 8m #1009	5.50	5.50
1305	A171	12,500m	on 16m #1011	2.75	2.75
		Nos. 1298-1305 (8)		24.90	24.90

For surcharges, see Nos. 1400-1400A.

Diana, Princess of Wales (1961-97) — A264

Nos. 1306-1308: Various portraits. No. 1309, 30,000m, Wearing Red Cross vest. No. 1310, 30,000m, Wearing purple dress.

1998 Litho. ***Perf. 13½***

1306 A264 2000m Sheet of 9, #a.-i. *5.75 5.75*

1307 A264 5000m Sheet of 9, #a.-i. *10.00 10.00*

1308 A264 8000m Sheet of 9, #a.-i. *13.00 13.00*

Souvenir Sheets

1309-1310 A264 Set of 2 12.00 12.00

Nos. 1309-1310 each contain one 42x60mm stamp.

No. 923 Surcharged in Silver

1998 Litho. ***Perf. 14***

1311 A145 500m on 16m multi — —

Promotion of Breast Feeding — A265

1998 Litho. ***Perf. 11½x11***

1312 A265 2000m multi .95 .30

Mother Teresa (1910-97) A266

1998 ***Perf. 11x11½***

1313 A266 2000m multi .95 .30

UPAP, 18th Anniv. A267

1998, Oct. 9 ***Perf. 11½x11***

1314 A267 2000m multi .80 .40

Mother's Day — A268

Designs: 2000m, Breast feeding. 4000m, Teacher. 8000m, Using computer. 10,000m, Woman in field.

1998, June 25 ***Perf. 11½x11***

1315-1318 A268 Set of 4 *8.00 8.00*

For surcharge, see No. 1417.

Plants — A269

Designs: 2000m Garcinia livingstonei. 7500m, Tabernaemontana elegans. 12,500m, Ximenia caffra. 25,000m, Syzygium guineense. 50,000m, Uapaca kirkiana.

1998, Oct. 9 ***Perf. 11¾x12***

1319-1322 A269 Set of 4 *12.00 12.00*

Souvenir Sheet

1323 A269 50,000m multi *12.00 12.00*

For surcharges, see Nos. 1418-1419, 1741-1742.

Dwellings A270

Various dwellings: 2000m, 4000m, 6000m, 8000m, 10,000m, 15,000m, 20,000m, 30,000m, 50,000m, 100,000m.

1998 Litho. ***Perf. 11x11¼***

1324-1333 A270 Set of 10 *20.00 20.00*

For surcharges and overprints, see Nos. 1399A-1399C, 1418-1419, 1420H.

Souvenir Sheets

I Love Lucy — A270a

Designs: No. 1333A, 35,000m, Lucy wearing hat. No. 1333B, 35,000m, Lucy as ballet dancer.

1999 Litho. ***Perf. 13½***

1333A-1333B A270a Set of 2 *12.00 12.00*

A271

Diana, Princess of Wales (1961-97) — A272

No. 1334: a, purple, shown. b, Dull brown, looking left. c, Orange brown, wearing pearls. d, Olive green. e, Purple, wearing feathers & hat, looking right. f, Red brown, wearing round earring.

No. 1335 — Diana with: a, Large white collar, earring (purple vignette). b, Hat, looking left (red violet vignette). c, White dress (red brown vignette). d, Dangling earrings (brown vignette). e, Patterned dress (blue violet vignette). f, Flower bouquet (olive green vignette).

1999 ***Perf. 14***

1334 A271 6500m Sheet of 6, #a.-f. *8.00 8.00*

1335 A271 6500m Sheet of 6, #a.-f. *8.00 8.00*

Litho. & Embossed

Die Cut Perf. 7

1336 A272 25,000m gold & multi *9.50 9.50*

Issued: #1336, 6/30.

The Three Stooges — A272a

No. 1336A: b, Joe Besser, Larry, Moe, frying pan. c, Shemp wearing hat. d, Moe and Larry putting pan on Joe Besser's head. e, Moe with pipe. f, Larry and Moe pouring liquids on Curly's head. g, Larry wearing hat. h, Joe Besser and Larry, pulling Moe's tooth. i, Curly. j, Shemp, Larry and Moe.

No. 1336K, 35,000m, Larry in pink shirt. No. 1336L, 35,000m, Larry holding shovel.

1999 Litho. ***Perf. 13½***

1336A A272a 5000m Sheet of 9, #b-j *7.00 7.00*

Souvenir Sheets

1336K-1336L A272a Set of 2 *12.00 12.00*

Trains — A273

2000m, DE-AC Blue Tiger, Germany. #1338, 2500m, DB 218 (red & black), Germany. #1339, 3000m, Mt. Pilatus inclined railroad car, Switzerland. 3500m, Berlin subway train, Germany.

No. 1341: a, DB V200, Germany. b, Union Pacific, US. c, Class 613, Germany. d, Canadian Pacific 4242, Canada. e, Duchess of Hamilton, Great Britain. f, Pacific Delhi, India. g, ISA, South Africa. h, DR VT 18-16-07, Germany. i, DB-DE, Australia.

No. 1342: a, DB 218 (green & yellow), Germany. b, QJ Class 2-10-2, China. c, 232 232.9, Germany. d, Flying Scotsman, Scotland. e, WR 360 CH, Germany. f, Henschel 2-8-2. g, Santa Fe 39C, US. h, Balkan Express, Greece. i, DB 218 (red & white), Germany.

No. 1343, 25,000m, Steam 2-8-2, Germany. No. 1344, 25,000m, DMU, Germany.

1999, Oct. 12 Litho. ***Perf. 14***

1337-1340 A273 Set of 4 2.10 2.10

1341 A273 2500m Sheet of 9, #a.-i. 4.00 4.00

1342 A273 3000m Sheet of 9, #a.-i. 4.75 4.75

Souvenir Sheets

1343-1344 A273 Set of 2 10.00 10.00

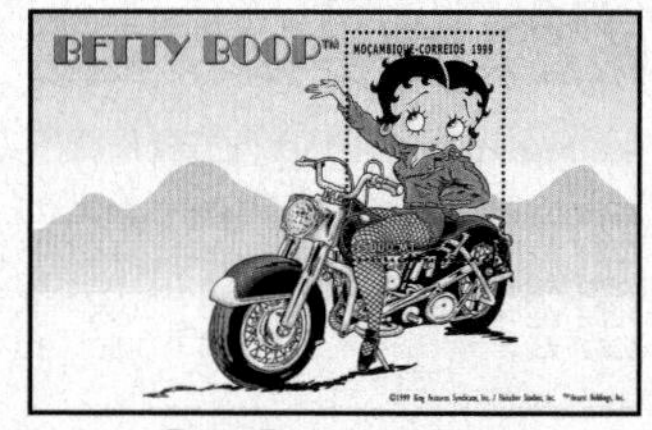

Betty Boop — A273a

No. 1344A: b, Seated on motorcycle, winking, wearing cap. c, Seated on motocycle, winking, without cap. d, Wearing cap. e, Seated on motorcycle, wearing cap, not winking. f, Hands folded across handlebars. g, Riding motorcycle. h, Hitchhiking. i, Seated on motorcycle, wearing bandana. j, Seated on motorcycle, hand raised.

No. 1344K, 35,000m, Seated on motorcycle, hand raised. No. 1344L, 35,000m, Seated next to motorcycle.

1999 Litho. ***Perf. 13½***

1344A A273a 3500m Sheet of 9, #b-j *6.50 6.00*

Souvenir Sheets

1344K-1344L A273a Set of 2 *12.00 12.00*

Cats — A274

No. 1345, 4000m: a, Chartreux. b, Australian Mist. c, Egyptian Mau. d, Scottish Fold. e, Cornish Rex. f, Abyssinian.

No. 1346, 4000m: a, Himalayan. b, Balinese. c, Persian. d, Turkish Van. e, Norwegian Forest Cat. f, Maine Coon Cat.

No. 1347, 25,000m, Ragdoll. No. 1348, 25,000m, Siamese.

2000, Mar. 29 Litho. ***Perf. 14***

Sheets of 6, #a-f

1345-1346 A274 Set of 2 9.50 9.50

Souvenir Sheets

1347-1348 A274 Set of 2 9.50 9.50

Dated 1999.

Dogs — A275

No. 1349, 4500m, vert.: a, Shetland sheepdog. b, Basenji. c, Poodle. d, St. Bernard. e, Shar Pei. f, Spinone Italiano.

No. 1350, 4500m, vert.: a, Jack Russell terrier. b, Schweizer Laufhund. c, Japanese Spitz. d, Australian Shepherd. e, Saluki. f, Siberian Husky.

No. 1351, 25,000m, Border Collie. No. 1352, 25,000m, Eurasier.

2000, Mar. 29 Litho. *Perf. 14*

Sheets of 6, #a-f

1349-1350	A275	Set of 2	10.00	10.00

Souvenir Sheets

1351-1352	A275	Set of 2	9.50	9.50

Dated 1999.

Dinosaurs — A276

No. 1353, 3000m: a, Pteranodon. b, Bothriospondylus. c, Iguanodon. d, Stegosaurus. e, Nodosaurus. f, Elaphrosaurus. g, "Petrolacisaurus." h, Procompsognathus. i, Dimetrodon.

No. 1354, 3000m: a, Plesiosaur. b, "Ceresiosaurus." c, Cryptoclidus. d, Placochelys. e, Plotosaurus. f, Ichthyosaurus. g, Platecarpus. h, Archelon. i, Mosasaur.

No. 1355, 20,000m, Tyrannosaurus Rex. No. 1356, 20,000m, "Honodus."

2000, Apr. 28 Sheets of 9, #a-i

1353-1354	A276	Set of 2	9.50	9.50

Souvenir Sheets

1355-1356	A276	Set of 2	6.50	6.50

Dated 1999.

A277

Butterflies — A278

Designs: 2000m, Palla ussheri. 2500m, Euschemon rafflesia. No. 1359, 3000m, Buttus philenor. No. 1360, 3000m, Hypolimnas bolina. 3500m, Lycorea cleobaea. 4000m, Dynastor napoleon. No. 1363, 4500m, Calimorpha dominula. 5000m, Pereute leucodrosime.

No. 1365, 4500m: a, Tisiphone abeone. b, Pseudacraea boisduvali. c, Mylothris chloris. d, Papilio glaucus. e, Mimacraea marshalli. f, Gonepteryx cleopatra.

No. 1366, 4500m: a, Palla ussheri, diff. b, Hypolimnas salmacis. c, Pereute leucodrosime, diff. d, Anteos clorinde. e, Colias eurytheme. f, Hebomoia glaucippe.

No. 1367, 4500m, horiz.: a, Thauria aliris. b, Catocala ilia. c, Colotis danae. d, Agrias claudia. e, Euploe core. f, Scoptes alphaeus.

No. 1368, 4500m, horiz.: a, Phoebis philea. b, Anteos clorinde, diff. c, Arhopala amantes. d, Mesene phareus. e, Euploea mulciber. f, Heliconius ricini.

No. 1369, 4500m, vert.: a, Euphaedra neophorn. b, Catopsilia florella. c, Charaxes bohemani. d, Junonia orithya. e, Colotis danae, diff. f, Eurytela dryope.

No. 1370, 4500m, vert.: a, Papilio demodocus. b, Kallimoides rumia. c, Danaus chrysippus. d, Palla ussheri, diff. e, Hypolimnas salmacis, diff. f, Zinina otis.

No. 1371, 20,000m, Papilio glaucus, diff. No. 1372, 20,000m, Delias mysis, horiz. No. 1373, 20,000m, Mylothris chloris, horiz. No. 1374, 20,000m, Loxura atymnus, horiz. No. 1375, 20,000m, Hemiolaus coeculus. No. 1376, 20,000m, Euxanthe wakefieldii.

2000, Apr. 28

1357-1364	A277	Set of 8	4.75	4.75

Sheets of 6, #a-f

1365-1368	A277	Set of 4	19.00	19.00
1369-1370	A278	Set of 2	9.50	9.50

Souvenir Sheets

1371-1374	A277	Set of 4	16.00	16.00
1375-1376	A278	Set of 2	6.50	6.50

Dated 1999.

Worldwide Fund for Nature — A279

No. 1377: a, Two adult gnus. b, Adult and juvenile gnus. c, Lion catching gnu. d, Adult gnu.

Illustration reduced.

2000, Apr. 28

1377	A279 6500m Block of 4, #a-d		*4.75*	*4.75*

Dated 1999.

Wild Cats — A280

No. 1378, 3000m: a, Leptailurus several. b, Panthera onca. c, Panthera tigris corbetti. d, Puma concolor. e, Panthera leo persica. f, Felis pardina. g, Lepardus pardalia. h, Acinonyx jubatus. i, Felis wrangeli.

No. 1379, 3000m: a, Felis silvestris grampia. b, Felis ourata. c, Panthera tigris tigris. d, Panthera uncia. e, Felis caracal. f, Panthera pardus. g, Panthera tigris amoyensis. h, Panthera onca (spotted). i, Neofelis nabuloso.

No. 1380, 25,000m, Panthera tigris altaica. No. 1381, 25,000m, Panthera tigris, horiz.

2000, Apr. 28 Sheets of 9, #a-i

1378-1379	A280	Set of 2	9.50	9.50

Souvenir Sheets

1380-1381	A280	Set of 2	8.00	8.00

Dated 1999.

Flowers — A281

No. 1382, 3000m: a, Laetiocattleya. b, Papaver oriental. c, Anemone blanda. d, Ipoema alba. e, Phalaenopsis luma. f, Iris ensata. g, Coenagrion puella. h, Rosa raubritter. i, Iris x daylilies hybridizers.

No. 1383, 3000m: a, Lilium auratum. b, Oncidium macianthum. c, Dendrobium. d, Cobaea scandens. e, Paphiopedilum gilda. f, Papaver nudicaule. g, Colocasia esculenta. h, Carinatum tricolor. i, Phalaenopsis.

No. 1384, vert.: a, Euanthe sanderiana. b, Torenia fourleri. c, "Amor Perfeito." d, Borboleto matizada. e, Dendrobium primulinum. f, "Lasurstern" Clematite. g, Helianthus annuus. h, Jacinto grana.

No. 1385, 20,000m, Viola x wittrockiana. No. 1386, 20,000m, Nelimbo nucifera. No. 1387, 20,000m, Gerbera jamesonii. No. 1388, 20,000m, Narcissuses and anemones.

Illustration reduced.

2000, Apr. 28 Sheets of 9, #a-i

1382-1383	A281	Set of 2	9.50	9.50
1384	A281 3500m Sheet of 8, #a-h		5.50	5.50

Souvenir Sheets

1385-1388	A281	Set of 4	12.50	12.50

Dated 1999.

Nos. 792, 797-798, 1147, 1153, 1154, 1156, 1214 Surcharged

2000 Methods & Perfs. As Before

1390	A114	10,000m on 7.50m #797	—	—
1391	A113	10,000m on 50m on 7.50m #1214	—	—
1392	A113	10,000m on 12.50m #792		—
1392A	A114	10,000m on 12.50m #798		—
1393	A215	17,000m on 10m #1153	—	—
1393A	A215	17,000m on 50m #1154	—	—
1394	A213	17,000m on 125m #1147	—	—
1395	A215	17,000m on 200m #1156	—	—
1396	A215	17,000m on 1000m #1158	—	—

No. 1393A and 1396 lack "2000" date in surcharge. No. 1391 contains "Correios — 2000) in surcharge.

The editors suspect that other surcharges may exist and would like to examine any examples.

No. 763 Surcharged in Black and Blue

No. 764 Surcharged in Black and Brown

2000 Litho. *Perf. 14½*

1398	A108	2000m on 10m #763		—
1399	A108	2000m on 12.50m #764	—	—

Nos. 1325-1327 Overprinted

No. 1399A

2000 Method and Perf. as Before

1399A	A270	4000m on #1325	—	—
1399B	A270	6000m on #1326	—	—
1399C	A270	8000m on #1327	—	—

Nos. 1300, 1301 Ovptd. in Brown or Black

2000 Litho. *Perf. 14½*

1400	A108 4000m on 12.50m #1300 (BR)		—	—
1400A	A114 6000m on 7.50m #1301		—	—

Sports and Chess — A282

No. 1401, 6500m: a, Cycling. b, Volleyball. c, Boxing. d, Weight lifting. e, Fencing. f, Judo.

No. 1402, 9000m — Chess pieces: a, Six pieces, red queen at left. b, Six pieces, gray bishop fifth from left. c, Five knights. d, Six rooks, elephant rook at left. e, Six pawns. f, Six pawns, spearholder pawn at right.

No. 1403, 9500m — Chess champions: a, Paul Morphy. b, Mikhail Botvinnik. c, Emanuel Lasker. d, Wilhelm Steinitz. e, José Raul Capablanca. f, Howard Staunton.

No. 1404, 12,500m: a, Cricket batsmen and bowler. b, Three cricket batsman, one fielder. c, Polo, rider with red shirt at left. d, Polo, player wearing #1 at right. e, Golf, flag stick at right. f, Golf, woman golfer at right.

No. 1405, 14,000m: a, Tennis, woman with headband at right. b, Table tennis, players with blue shirts. c, Table tennis, player with pink shirt in center. d, Tennis, two men at left. e, Tennis, man with cap at left. f, Table tennis, player with red shirt at left.

No. 1406, 35,000m, Table tennis. No. 1407, 35,000m, Chess player Garry Kasparov.

2000 Litho. *Perf. 13¼*

Sheets of 6, #a-f

1401-1405	A282	Set of 5	*40.00*	*40.00*

Souvenir Sheets

1406-1407	A282	Set of 2	*17.50*	*17.50*

Nos. 1401-1405 each contain six 59x29mm stamps.

A283

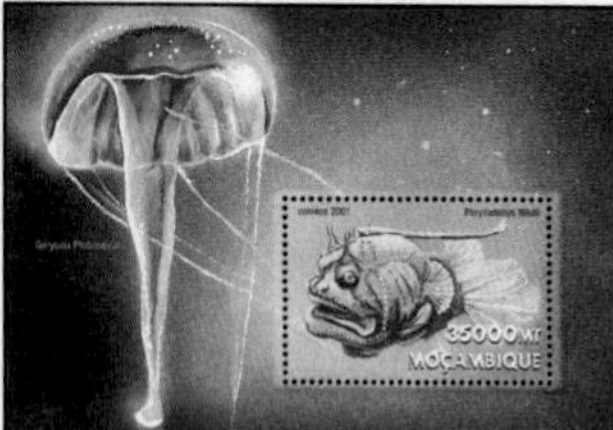

Marine Life — A284

No. 1408: a, Threadfin butterflyfish. b, Common clownfish. c, Regal tang. d, Regal angelfish. e, Copperbanded butterflyfish. f, Blue-girdled angelfish. g, Sharpnosed pufferfish. h, Humbug damselfish. i, Tailbar lionfish. j, Forcepsfish. k, Powder blue surgeon. l, Moorish idol.

No. 1409, 9500m: a, Oceanic whitetip shark. b, Gray reef shark. c, Tiger shark. d, Silky shark. e, Basking shark. f, Epaulette shark.

No. 1410, 9500m: a, Sperm whale. b, Giant squid. c, Killer whale. d, Great white shark. e, Manta ray. f, Octopus.

No. 1411, 9500m: a, Blue whale. b, Dolphinfish. c, Hammerhead shark. d, Whale shark. e, Leatherback turtle. f, Porkfish.

No. 1412, 35,000m, Wimple fish. No. 1413, 35,000m, Queen angelfish.

No. 1414, 35,000m, Phrynicthys wedli. No. 1415, 35,000m, Bull shark. No. 1416, 35,000m, Spotted trunkfish.

2001, Aug. 8 *Perf. 14*

1408	A283 4550m Sheet of 12, #a-l		*8.00*	*8.00*

Sheets of 6, #a-f

1409-1411	A284	Set of 3	*24.00*	*24.00*

Souvenir Sheets

1412-1413	A283	Set of 2	*9.50*	*9.50*
1414-1416	A284	Set of 3	*14.50*	*14.50*

Nos. 763, 1316-1317, 1328-1329 and 1330 Surcharged

Methods and Perfs As Before

2001 ?

1416A	A268 3000m on 4000m #1316		—
1417	A268 3000m on 8000m #1317	—	—
1418	A270 3000m on 15,000m #1329	—	—
1419	A270 3000m on 20,000m #1330	—	—
1420	A108 5000m on 10m #763	—	—
1420H	A270 17,000m on 10,000m #1328		—

2000 European Soccer Championships — A285

No. 1421, 10,000m: a, Luis Figo dribbling ball. b, Fernando Couto. c, Figo diving. d, Sergio Conceicao. e, Nuno Gomes. f, Rui Costa.

No. 1422, 17,000m: a, Nicolas Anelka. b, Didier Deschamps. c, Emmanuel Petit. d, Thierry Henry. e, Marcel Desailly. f, Zinedine Zidane.

No. 1422G, 75,000m, Zinedine Zidane. No. 1422H, 75,000m, Rivaldo.

2001 Litho. *Perf. 13¼x12¾*

Sheets of 6, #a-f

1421-1422	A285	Set of 2	*17.50*	*17.50*

Souvenir Sheets

1422G-1422H	A285	Set of 2	*16.00*	*16.00*

2000 Summer Olympics Medalists — A286

No. 1423, 8500m: a, Domenico Fioravanti. b, Stacy Dragila. c, Pieter van den Hoogenband. d, David O'Connor. e, Venus Williams. f, Maurice Greene. g, Joy Fawcett. h, Marion Jones. i, Patricio Ormazabal and Jeff Agoos.

No. 1424, 10,000m: a, Agnes Kovacs. b, Youila Raskina. c, Kong Linghui and Liu Guoliang. d, Nicolas Gill. e, Anky van Grunsven. f, Brian Olson. g, Wang Nan. h, Megan Quann. i, Venus Williams.

No. 1425, 17,000m: a, Vince Carter. b, Blaine Wilson. c, Steve Keir. d, Wen Xiao Wang and Chris Xu. e, Venus and Serena Williams. f, Gu Jun and Ge Fei.

No. 1426, 20,000m: a, Clara Hughes. b, Martina Hingis. c, Otilla Badescu. d, Isabel Fernandez. e, Coralie Simmons. f, Mia Hamm.

No. 1427, 28,000m: a, Patrick Rafter. b, Tadahiro Nomura. c, Seiko Iseki. d, Michael Dodge. e, Ann Dow. f, David Beckham.

No. 1428, 50,000m, Andre Agassi. No. 1429, 50,000m, Chang Jun Gao and Michelle Do. No. 1430, 50,000m, Kong Linghui. No. 1431, 100,000m, Michelle Do. No. 1432, 100,000m, Serena Williams. No. 1433, 100,000m, Christophe Legout.

2001 Sheets of 9, #a-i Litho.

1423-1424	A286	Set of 2	22.50	22.50

Sheets of 6, #a-f

1425-1427	A286	Set of 3	25.00	25.00

Souvenir Sheets

1428-1433	A286	Set of 6	47.50	47.50

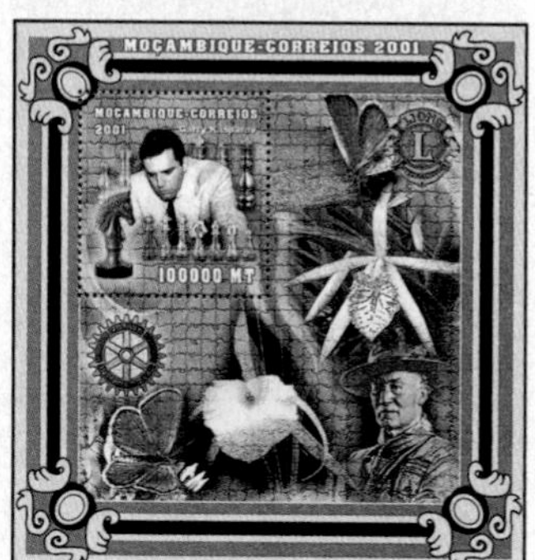

Chess Champions — A287

No. 1434, 10,000m: a, Mikhail Botvinnik. b, Garry Kasparov. c, Wilhelm Steinitz. d, Emanuel Lasker. e, Paul Morphy. f, Anatoly Karpov. g, Tigran Petrossian. h, Mikhail Tal. i, José Raul Capablanca.

No. 1435, 10,000m: a, Judith Polgar (wearing brown sweater). b, Xie Jun. c, Zsuza Polgar. d, Nana Ioseliani. e, Alisa Galliamova. f, Judith Polgar (head in hands). g, Judith Polgar (wearing blouse). h, Monica Calzetta. i, Anjelina Belakovskaia.

No. 1436, 100,000m, Kasparov. No. 1437, 100,000m, Judith Polgar.

2001 *Perf. 13¼x12¾*

Sheets of 9, #a-i

1434-1435	A287	Set of 2	*20.00*	*20.00*

Souvenir Sheets

1436-1437	A287	Set of 2	*22.00*	*22.00*

2002 Winter Olympics, Salt Lake City — A288

No. 1438, 17,000m: a, Martin Brodeur. b, Svetlana Vysokova. c, Ray Bourque and Patrik Elias. d, Rachel Belliveau. e, Scott Gomez and Janne Laukkanen. f, Sonja Nef.

No. 1439, 20,000m: a, Rusty Smith. b, Sandra Schmirler. c, Totmianina and Marinin. d, Brigitte Obermoser. e, Roman Turek. f, Jennifer Heil.

No. 1440, 28,000m: a, Kovarikova and Novotny. b, Li Song. c, Armin Zoeggeler. d, Michael von Gruenigen. e, Tami Bradley. f, Chris Drury, Turner Stevenson and Greg de Vries.

No. 1441, 50,000m, Armin Zoeggeler. No. 1442, 75,000m, Tommy Salo. No. 1443, 100,000m, Jayne Torvill and Christopher Dean.

2001 Sheets of 6, #a-f Litho.

1438-1440	A288	Set of 3	*40.00*	*40.00*

Souvenir Sheets

1441-1443	A288	Set of 3	*24.00*	*24.00*

On illustrated sheets lacking design information the lettering of minors starts with the upper left stamp, goes right and down and ends with the lower right stamp.

2002 World Cup Soccer Championships, Japan and Korea — A289

No. 1444: a, Filippo Inzaghi. b, Georghe Hagi. c, Gabriel Batistuta pointing. d, Mateja Kezman. e, Ivan Zamorano. f, Michael Owen wearing blue uniform.

No. 1445: a, Marcio Amoroso. b, Alessandro Nesta. c, Robbie Keane. d, Michel Owen kicking ball. e, Stefan Effenberg. f, Oliver Kahn.

No. 1446: a, Zinedine Zidane without ball. b, Zoran Mirkovic. c, Robbie Fowler with fist raised. d, Romario wearing red jersey. e, Francesco Totti. f, Ryan Giggs.

No. 1447: a, Javier Saviola. b, Alan Smith. c, Raul Gonzalez. d, Dwight Yorke. e, Joe Cole. f, David Beckham wearing red jersey.

No. 1448: a, Angelo Peruzzi. b, Jaap Stam. c, Jamie Redknapp. d, Rivaldo with ball at feet. e, Alan Shearer. f, Boudewijn Zenden.

No. 1449: a, Hernan Jorge Crespo. b, Gianluigi Buffon. c, Arnold Bruggink. d, Antonio Cassano. e, Mohamed Kallon. f, Jonathan Bachini.

No. 1450: a, Didier Deschamps. b, Cafu wearing green jersey. c, Dennis Bergkamp. d, Lilian Thuram. e, David Beckham wearing red jersey, diff. f, Francesco Totti, diff. g, Carsten Jancker. h, Martin Palermo. i, Andy Cole running left.

No. 1451: a, David Beckham sitting on ball. b, Edgar Davids wearing orange shirt. c, Michael Owen with hands on ball. d, Andy Cole with one leg raised. e, Ronaldo sitting. f, Emmanuel Petit with ball. g, Rivaldo with ball at chest. h, Robbie Fowler looking at ball. i, Romario wearing blue jacket.

No. 1452: a, César Manuel Rui Costa. b, Hidetoshi Nakata. c, Luis Figo. d, Michael Owen. e, Leonardo. f, Thierry Henry. g, Fabien Barthez. h, Oliver Kahn. i, Antonio Conte.

No. 1453: a, Shinji Ono. b, Rigobert Song. c, Matias Jesus Almeyda. d, Ronaldinho. e, Gabriel Batistuta wearing striped jersey. f, Rivaldo sitting on ground. g, Thierry Henry. h, Zinedine Zidane kicking ball. i, Ronaldo with ball.

No. 1454: a, Florain Maurice. b, Nicolas Anelka. c, Zinedine Zidane without ball, wearing striped jersey. d, Kazuyoshi Miura. e, Patrick Vieira. f, Gianfranco Zola. g, Emmanuel Petit without ball. h, Roberto Carlos. i, Teddy Sheringham.

No. 1455, 75,000m, Fabien Barthez. No. 1456, 75,000m, Edgar Davids wearing striped shirt. No. 1457, 75,000m, Cafu wearing red shirt.

No. 1458, 100,000m, Ronaldo wearing striped uniform. No. 1459, 100,000m, Romario wearing yellow shirt. No. 1460, 100,000m, Rivaldo dribbling ball. No. 1461, 100,000m, Nwankwo Kanu. No. 1462, 100,000m, Michael Owen wearing yellow shirt. No. 1463, 100,000m, Franz Beckenbauer. No. 1464, 100,000m, Pelé. No. 1465, 100,000m, Diego Maradona.

2001 Litho. *Perf. 13¼x12¾*

Sheets of 6, #a-f

1444	A289	5000m multi	3.25	3.25
1445	A289	10,000m multi	6.75	6.75
1446	A289	12,000m multi	8.00	8.00
1447	A289	15,000m multi	10.00	10.00
1448	A289	17,000m multi	11.50	11.50
1449	A289	20,000m multi	13.50	13.50
	Nos. 1444-1449 (6)		53.00	53.00

Sheets of 9, #a-i

1450	A289	5000m multi	5.25	5.25
1451	A289	5000m multi	5.25	5.25
1452	A289	5000m multi	5.25	5.25
1453	A289	8500m multi	8.75	8.75
1454	A289	8500m multi	8.75	8.75
	Nos. 1450-1454 (5)		33.25	33.25

Souvenir Sheets

1455-1457	A289	Set of 3	32.50	32.50
1458-1465	A289	Set of 8	115.00	115.00

On illustrated sheets lacking design information, the lettering of minors starts with the upper left stamp, continues right and down and ends with the lower right stamp.

Paintings

Madonna Paintings — A290

Alfred Sisley — A291

Hieronymus Bosch — A292

Pieter Brueghel — A293

Paul Cézanne — A294

Salvador Dali — A295

Henri Matisse — A296

Michelangelo — A297

Vincent van Gogh — A298

Johannes Vermeer — A299

Michelangelo — A300

Amadeo Modigliani — A301

Paintings of Angels — A302

Gustav Klimt — A303

Perf. 13¼x12¾

2001, Dec. 28 Litho.

Sheets of 6, #a-f

1466	A290	5000m	multi	3.25	3.25
1467	A291	10,000m	multi	6.75	6.75
1468	A292	12,000m	multi	8.00	8.00
1469	A293	12,000m	multi	8.00	8.00
1470	A294	12,000m	multi	8.00	8.00
1471	A295	12,000m	multi	8.00	8.00
1472	A296	12,000m	multi	8.00	8.00
1473	A297	12,000m	multi	8.00	8.00
1474	A298	12,000m	multi	8.00	8.00
1475	A299	12,000m	multi	8.00	8.00
1476	A300	15,000m	multi	10.00	10.00
1477	A301	15,000m	multi	10.00	10.00
1478	A302	17,000m	multi	12.00	12.00
1479	A303	28,000m	multi	19.00	19.00
	Nos. 1466-1479 (14)			125.00	125.00

Paintings

Marc Chagall — A304

Salvador Dali — A305

Edgar Degas — A306

Paul Delvaux — A307

Paul Gauguin — A308

Pablo Picasso — A309

Pierre Auguste Renoir — A310

Henri de Toulouse-Lautrec — A311

Vincent van Gogh — A312

Pablo Picasso — A313

Individual stamps depicting various works of art lack titles. On Nos. 1489-1512 artist name is in margin.

No. 1489, Pieter Breughel. No. 1490, Lucas Cranach. No. 1491, Paul Delvaux. No. 1492, El Greco. No. 1493, Wassily Kandinsky. No. 1494, Gustav Klimt. No. 1495, Johannes Vermeer. No. 1496, Paul Cézanne. No. 1497, Marc Chagall. No. 1498, Albrecht Dürer. No. 1499, Thomas Gainsborough. No. 1500, Francisco de Goya. No. 1501, Edouard Manet. No. 1502, Claude Monet. No. 1503, Henri Matisse. No. 1504, Camille Pissarro. No. 1505, Vincent van Gogh. No. 1506, Salvador Dali. No. 1507, Paul Gauguin. No. 1508, Joan Miró. No. 1509, Amadeo Modigliani. No. 1511, Picasso, diff. No. 1512, Henri de Toulouse-Lautrec. No. 1513, Religious icon.

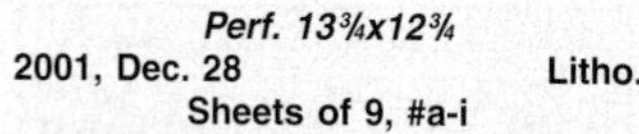

Perf. 13¾x12¾

2001, Dec. 28 **Litho.**

Sheets of 9, #a-i

1480 A304 10,000m multi 8.75 8.75
1481 A305 10,000m multi 8.75 8.75
1482 A306 10,000m multi 8.75 8.75
1483 A307 10,000m multi 8.75 8.75
1484 A308 10,000m multi 8.75 8.75
1485 A309 10,000m multi 8.75 8.75
1486 A310 10,000m multi 8.75 8.75
1487 A311 10,000m multi 8.75 8.75
1488 A312 10,000m multi 8.75 8.75
Nos. 1480-1488 (9) 78.75 78.75

Souvenir Sheets

1489 A313 50,000m multi 4.00 4.00
1490 A313 50,000m multi 4.00 4.00
1491 A313 50,000m multi 4.00 4.00
1492 A313 50,000m multi 4.00 4.00
1493 A313 50,000m multi 4.00 4.00
1494 A313 50,000m multi 4.00 4.00
1495 A313 50,000m multi 4.00 4.00
1496 A313 75,000m multi 6.25 6.25
1497 A313 75,000m multi 6.25 6.25
1498 A313 75,000m multi 6.25 6.25
1499 A313 75,000m multi 6.25 6.25
1500 A313 75,000m multi 6.25 6.25
1501 A313 75,000m multi 6.25 6.25
1502 A313 75,000m multi 6.25 6.25
1503 A313 75,000m multi 6.25 6.25
1504 A313 75,000m multi 6.25 6.25
1505 A313 75,000m multi 6.25 6.25
1506 A313 100,000m multi 8.25 8.25
1507 A313 100,000m multi 8.25 8.25
1508 A313 100,000m multi 8.25 8.25
1509 A313 100,000m multi 8.25 8.25
1510 A313 100,000m shown 8.25 8.25
1511 A313 100,000m multi 8.25 8.25
1512 A313 100,000m multi 8.25 8.25
1513 A313 100,000m multi 8.25 8.25
Nos. 1489-1513 (25) 156.50 156.50

Souvenir Sheet

Lance Armstrong, Cyclist — A314

2001 **Litho.** ***Perf. 13¼x12¾***

1514 A314 100,000m multi 11.00 11.00

2004 Olympic Games, Athens.

New Year 2002 (Year of the Horse) — A315

No. 1515 — Chinese characters in: a, Yellow. b, Purple. c, Pink. d, Brown.

22,000m, Maroon, vert.

2002, May 6 **Litho.** ***Perf. 13¼***

1515 A315 11,000m Sheet of 4, #a-d 5.25 5.25

Souvenir Sheet

Perf. 13½x13¼

1516 A315 22,000m multi 2.75 2.75

No. 1516 contains one 28x42mm stamp.

2002 Winter Olympics, Salt Lake City A316

Designs: 10,000m, Freestyle skiing. 17,000m, Freestyle skiing, vert.

Perf. 13¼x13½, 13½x13¼

2002, May 6

1517-1518 A316 Set of 2 2.75 2.75

Intl. Year of Mountains A317

Designs: No. 1519, 17,000m, Mt. Namuli. No. 1520, 17,000m, Mt. Binga.

No. 1521: a, Mt. Kenya, Kenya. b, Mt. Cook, New Zealand. c, Mt. Ararat, Turkey. d, Mt. Paine, Chile. e, Mt. Everest, Nepal. f, Mt. Kilimanjaro, Tanzania.

50,000m, Zugspitze, Germany.

2002, May 6 ***Perf. 13¼x13½***

1519-1520 A317 Set of 2 3.25 3.25
1521 A317 17,000m Sheet of 6, #a-f 9.50 9.50

Souvenir Sheet

1522 A317 50,000m multi 4.75 4.75

20th World Scout Jamboree, Thailand — A318

No. 1523, horiz.: a, 1933 Jamboree patch. b, 19th World Jamboree patch. c, Patch and mascot. d, Jamboree emblem, scout.

No. 1524, Scout.

2002, May 6 ***Perf. 13¼x13½***

1523 A318 28,000m Sheet of 4, #a-d 11.50 11.50

Souvenir Sheet

Perf. 13½x13¼

1524 A318 28,000m multi 3.00 3.00

Amerigo Vespucci (1452-1512), Explorer — A319

No. 1525, horiz.: a, Vespucci observing stars. b, Brotogeris chiriri, ship. c, Huts, ship.

50,000m, Map of voyages to South America.

2002, May 6 ***Perf. 13¼x13½***

1525 A319 30,000m Sheet of 3, #a-c 8.75 8.75

Souvenir Sheet

Perf. 13½x13¼

1526 A319 50,000m multi 4.75 4.75

Ships — A320

No. 1527, 13,500m: a-f, Various unnamed ships (shown).

No. 1528, 13,500m: a, Viking ship. b, Kayak. c, Gondola, bridge. d, Fishing boat. e, Light ship. f, Tugboat.

No. 1529, 40,000m, Aircraft carrier. No. 1530, 40,000m, Ship's figurehead, vert.

Perf. 13¼x13½, 13½x13¼

2002, May 6 **Sheets of 6, #a-f**

1527-1528 A320 Set of 2 14.50 14.50

Souvenir Sheets

1529-1530 A320 Set of 2 7.50 7.50

2002 World Cup Soccer Championships, Japan and Korea — A321

No. 1531, 28,000m: a, Zico. b, 1958 World Cup poster. c, Flag, player from Nigeria. d, Flag, player from Morocco. e, Gwangju Stadium, Korea, horiz. (56x42mm).

No. 1532, 28,000m: a, 1966 World Cup poster. b, Paolo Rossi. c, Flag, player from Denmark. d, Flag, player from Colombia. e, Inchon Munhak Stadium, Korea, horiz. (56x42mm)

No. 1533, 50,000m, Pele. No. 1534, 50,000m, Morlock, horiz.

Perf. 13½x13¼, 13¼x13½

2002, May 6 **Sheets of 5, #a-e**

1531-1532 A321 Set of 2 *27.50 27.50*

Souvenir Sheets

1533-1534 A321 Set of 2 *9.50 9.50*

A322

A323

Princess Diana (1961-97) — A324

No. 1538, 50,000m, Brown background. No. 1539, 50,000m, Purple background. No. 1540, 50,000m, Pink lilac background.

2002, May 6 *Perf. 13½x13¼*

1535 A322 28,000m Sheet of 4, #a-d *11.00 11.00*
1536 A323 28,000m Sheet of 4, #a-d *11.00 11.00*
1537 A324 28,000m Sheet of 4, #a-d *11.00 11.00*
Nos. 1535-1537 (3) 33.00 33.00

Souvenir Sheets

1538-1540 A324 Set of 3 *14.50 14.50*

Butterflies — A325

Designs: 5000m, Papilio demoleus. No, 1542, 10,000m, Euschemom rafflesia. 17,000m, Liphyra brassolis. 28,000m, Mimacraea marshalli.

No. 1545, 10,000m: a, Eurema brigitta. b, Loxura atymunus. c, Arhopala amantes. d, Junonia coenia. e, Eurides isabella. f, Hiliconius ricini. g, Zipaetis scylax. h, Cepheuptychia cephus. i, Philaethria dido.

No. 1546, 10,000m: a, Parides coon. b, Delias mysis. c, Troides brookiana. d, Syrmatia dorilas. e, Danis danis. f, Lycaena dispar. g, Mesene phareus. h, Kallima inachus. i, Morpho rhetenor.

No. 1547, 50,000m, Papilio cresphontes. No. 1548, 50,000m, Ornithoptera alexandrae caterpillar.

2002, June 17 *Perf. 14*

1541-1544 A325 Set of 4 5.25 5.25

Sheets of 9, #a-i

1545-1546 A325 Set of 2 16.00 16.00

Souvenir Sheets

1547-1548 A325 Set of 2 11.00 11.00

Fauna, Flora and Mushrooms — A326

No. 1549, 10,000m: a, Pandion haliaetus. b, Flying squirrel. c, Fox squirrel. d, Agelaius phoeniceus. e, Papilio polyxenes. f, Didelphus virginiana. g, Hyla crucifer. h, Odocoileus virginianus, standing. i, Procyon lotor.

No. 1550, 10,000m: a, Heraclides cresphontes. b, Tyto alba. c, Drocopus pileatus. d, Cypripedium parviflorum, Archilochus colobris. e, Vulpes vulpes. f, Odocoileus virginianus. g, Enallagma sp. h, Amanita muscaria. i, Tamiasciurus hudsonicus.

2002, June 17 *Perf. 14*

Sheets of 9, #a-i

1549-1550 A326 Set of 2 16.00 16.00

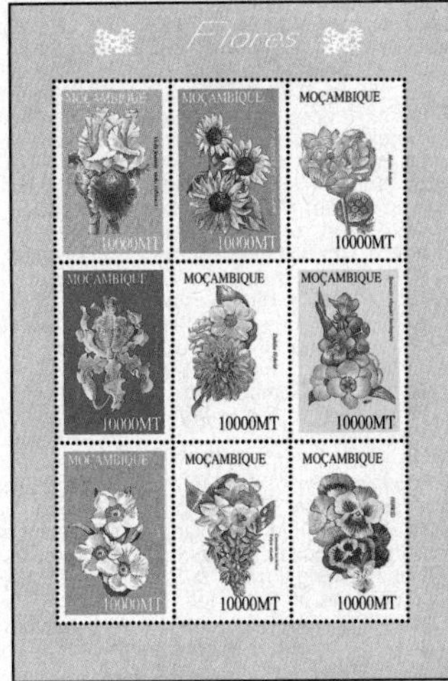

Flowers — A327

No. 1551, 10,000m: a, Viola jeannie, Viola cultivar. b, Sunflower Moonshadow. c, Momo botan. d, Schomburgkia orchid. e, Dahlia hybrid. f, Sparaxis elegans harlequin. g, Dianhus. h, Camassia leichtlinii, Tulipa saxatilis. i, Pansy hybrid.

No. 1552, 10,000m, horiz.: a, Hemerocallis. b, Narcissus (Nazcissys). c, Hybrid tea rose. d, Rainbow Promised Cayenne Capers and flying insect. e, Anemone cordnazia. f, Hymenocallis narcissiflora. g, Hymenocallis. h, Tulipa. i, Lachenalia aloides, Meconopsis poppies.

No. 1553, 10,000m, horiz.: a, Narcissus. b, L. bulbiferun var. Croceum. c, Iris purpureobractea. d, Neomarica caerulea. e, Peonia lactiflora, Primula chungensis, Viola cornuta. f, Rainbow Promised Cayenne Capers and beetle. g, Iris purpureobractea (puzpuzeobractea). h, Tuberous begonia cultivar. i, Oriental hybrid lily.

2002, June 17 *Perf. 14*

Sheets of 9, #a-i

1551-1553 A327 Set of 3 16.00 16.00

Dogs, Cats and Horses — A328

No. 1554, 17,000m — Dogs: a, Labrador retriever. b, Bulldog. c, Cocker spaniel. d, Golden retriever. e, Boxer. f, Bloodhound.

No. 1555, 17,000m — Cats: a, Maine Coon. b, Cornish Rex. c, La Perm. d, Sphynx. e, Siamese. f, Persian.

No. 1556, 17,000m — Horses: a, Hanoverian. b, Haflinger. c, Nonius. d, Belgian heavy drafts. e, Australian-bred Arab. f, Thoroughbred.

No. 1557, 40,000m, Basset hound. No. 1558, 50,000m, Chestnut Oriental Longhair cat. No. 1559, 50,000m, Don horses.

2002, June 17 *Perf. 13¼*

Sheets of 6, #a-f

1554-1556 A328 Set of 3 19.00 19.00

Souvenir Sheets

1557-1559 A328 Set of 3 15.00 15.00

Dinosaurs A329

Designs: 5000m, Protosaurus. No. 1561, 10,000m, Psittacosaurus. 17,000m, Torosaurus. 28,000m, Triceratops.

No. 1564, 10,000m: a, Diplodocus head. b, Pterosaurs. c, Diplodocuses. d, Afrovenator. e, Parasaurolophus. f, Ramphorhynchus. g, Lambeosaur. h, Euoplocephalus. i, Cynodont.

No. 1565, 10,000m: a, Brachiosaur. b, Monoclonius. c, Homalocephalus. d, Pterodactyl. e, Deinonychus. f, Archaeopteryx. g, Cretaceous landscape. h, Hypsilophodon. i, Lystrosaur.

No. 1566, 50,000m, Baryonyx. No. 1567, 50,000m, Styracosaurus, vert.

2002, June 17 *Perf. 14*

1560-1563 A329 Set of 4 5.25 5.25

Sheets of 9, #a-i, + 3 labels

1564-1565 A329 Set of 2 11.00 11.00

Souvenir Sheets

1566-1567 A329 Set of 2 11.00 11.00

A330

Birds — A331

Designs: No. 1568, 5000m, Tachymarptis melba. No. 1569, 5000m, Falco tinnunculus. No. 1570, 10,000m, Pitta angolensis. No. 1571, 10,000m, Ardea cinerea. No. 1572, 17,000m, Corythaeola cristata. No. 1573, 28,000m, Butastur rufipennis.

No. 1574, 5000m, Creagrus furcatus. No. 1575, 10,000m, Larosterna inca. No. 1576, 17,000m, Pelecanus crispus. No. 1577, 28,000m, Morus bassanus.

No. 1578, 10,000m: a, Phaeton aethereus. b, Catharacta maccormicki. c, Diomedea bulleri. d, Puffinus iherminieri. e, Oceanites oceanicus. f, Pterodroma hasitata. g, Fregata magnificens. h, Sula nebouxii. i, Uria aagle.

No. 1579, 17,000m: a, Psittacus erithacus. b, Ficedula hypleuca. c, Tchagra senegala. d, Oriolus oriolus. e, Luscinia megarhynchos. f, Halcyon malimbica.

No. 1580, 17,000m: a, Coracias garrulus. b, Estrilda astrild. c, Upupa epops. d, Merops apiaster. e, Ploceus cucullatus. f, Clamator glandarius.

No. 1581, 50,000m, Falco subbuteo. No. 1582, 50,000m, Strix varia. No. 1583, 50,000m, Butorides striatus. No. 1584, 50,000m, Actophilornis africanus, horiz.

No. 1585, 50,000m, Spheniscus demersus. No. 1586, 50,000m, Rhynchops niger, horiz.

2002, June 17

1568-1573 A330 Set of 6 6.50 6.50
1574-1577 A331 Set of 4 5.25 5.25
1578 A331 10,000m Sheet of 9, #a-i 7.75 7.75

Sheets of 6, #a-f

1579-1580 A330 Set of 2 17.50 17.50

Souvenir Sheets

1581-1584 A330 Set of 4 17.00 17.00
1585-1586 A331 Set of 2 8.50 8.50

For surcharges see Nos. 1739A, 1740, 1748.

Worldwide Fund for Nature (WWF) A332

African savannah elephant: Nos. 1587a, 1588a, Herd. Nos. 1587b, 1588b, And birds. Nos. 1587c, 1588c, With juvenile. Nos. 1587d, 1588d, With rainbow.

2002, Sept. 20 *Perf. 13¼x13½*

Size: 40x26½mm

Large Year

1587 Strip of 4 8.50 8.50
a.-d. A332 19,000m Any single 1.90 1.75

Size: 39x25mm

Small Year

1588 Miniature sheet of 4 + 4 labels 12.00 12.00
a.-d. A332 19,000m Any single 2.50 2.25

Princess Diana — A333

Pope John Paul II — A334

Elvis Presley — A335

Marilyn Monroe — A336

Marilyn Monroe — A337

Lord Robert Baden-Powell, Scout Emblem, Mushrooms and Flowers — A338

Astronauts and the Concorde — A339

Composers — A340

Louis Pasteur and Dogs — A341

Robert Stephenson and Locomotives — A342

Pope John Paul II — A343

Pope John Paul II, Madonna and Child — A344

Pope John Paul II, Madonna and Child — A345

Robert Stephenson — A346

Robert Stephenson — A347

No. 1593 — Famous men: a, Henri Dunant. b, Theodore Roosevelt. c, Albert Einstein. d, Ernest Hemingway. e, Thomas Nast. f, Albert Camus.

No. 1594 — Egyptian rulers: a, Seti I. b, Djedefre. c, Smekhkare. d, Seti II. e, Senusret III. f, Tutankhamun.

No. 1597: a, Michael Collins. b, Concorde. c, John Glenn. d, Concorde, diff. e, Neil Armstrong. f, Concorde, diff.

No. 1598 — Chess players and pieces: a, Tigran Petrosian, Lions emblem. b, Robert Fischer, Rotary emblem. c, Boris Spassky, Lions emblem. d, Raul Capablanca, Rotary emblem. e, Max Euwe, Lions emblem. f, Emanuel Lasker, Rotary emblem.

No. 1599 — Nobel Prize winners: a, Albert Einstein. b, Dalai Lama. c, Winston Churchill. d, Hideki Yukawa. e, Albert Schweitzer. f, Linus Pauling.

No. 1600 — Scout emblem and: a, Lord Robert Baden-Powell. b, Morpho aega, Baden-Powell. c, Prepona meander, Baden-Powell. d, Charaxes bernardus, Baden-Powell. e, Hypolimnas salmacis, Baden-Powell. f, Morpho rhetenor, Baden-Powell.

No. 1601 — Egyptian rulers: a, Netjenkhet Djoser. b, Tutankhamun. c, Neferefre. d, Amenhotep III. e, Pepi I. f, Amenmesses.

No. 1602 — Composers: a, Antonio Vivaldi. b, Franz Liszt. c, Ludwig van Beethoven. d, Wolfgang Mozart.

No. 1603 — Famous Men: a, Che Guevara. b, Pope John Paul II (blue gray background). c, Dr. Martin Luther King, Jr. d, Mao Zedong.

No. 1604 — Princess Diana and Pope John Paul II: a, Princess Diana in deep blue dress. b, Diana holding flowers. c, Pope John Paul II, hand showing. d, Pope John Paul II.

No. 1605 — Nelson Mandela and: a, Heulandite. b, Adamite. c, Wulfenite. d, Hemimorphite.

No. 1606 — Auto racing: a, Ayrton Senna. b, Modern race car. c, Old race car. d, Juan Manuel Fangio.

No. 1607 — Egyptian queens (tan background): a, Nefertiti facing right. b, Cleopatra VII. c, Nefertiti facing left. d, Nefertiti facing forward.

No. 1608 — Egyptian rulers (gray background): a, Nefertari. b, Tutankhamun. c, Tuthmosis. d, Nefertiti.

No. 1609 — Egyptian rulers (green background): a, Amenhotemp II. b, Merenptah. c, Amenophis IV. d, Tuthmosis.

No. 1610 — Famous people: a, Dalai Lama. b, Mother Teresa. c, Pope John Paul II. d, Mahatma Gandhi.

No. 1611 — Explorers: a, Vasco da Gama. b, Ferdinand Magellan. c, Christopher Columbus. d, Amerigo Vespucci.

No. 1612 — Aviation: a, Antoine de Saint-Exupéry. b, Charles Lindbergh standing. c, Lindbergh seated. d, Concorde.

No. 1613 — Lions and Rotary Founders: a, Paul Harris (color picture), Rotary emblem. b, Melvin Jones (sepia picture), Lions emblem. c, Harris (sepia picture), Rotary emblem. d, Jones (color picture), Lions emblem.

No. 1614 — Film personalities: a, Charlie Chaplin. b, Frank Sinatra. c, Alfred Hitchcock. d, Walt Disney.

No. 1615: a, Scipionyx. b, Beipiaosaurus. c, Haroun Tazieff and vanadinite. d, Tazieff and adamite.

No. 1616 — Famous men: a, Winston Churchill. b, John F. Kennedy. c, Konrad Adenauer. d, Charles de Gaulle.

No. 1619 — Scientists: a, Charles Darwin, Byronosaurus. b, Alexander Fleming, Tricholoma terreum. c, Fleming, Boletus edulis. d, Darwin, Irratator.

No. 1620 — Famous men: a, Albert Schweitzer. b, Claude Bernard. c, Henri Dunant. d, Raoul Follerau.

No. 1621: a, John J. Audubon. b, Audubon, Aix sponsa. c, Audubon, Toxastoma montanum, Ixoreus naevius. d, Audubon, Loxia leucoptera.

No. 1625, John Glenn. No. 1626, Lord Robert Baden-Powell. No. 1627, Victor Hugo. No. 1628, John F. Kennedy. No. 1629, Princess Diana. No. 1630, Wolfgang Mozart. No. 1631, Alexander Fleming. No. 1632, Garry Kasparov. Nos. 1633, 1634, Marilyn Monroe. No. 1635, Mother Teresa. No. 1636, Henri Dunant. No. 1637, Nelson Mandela. No. 1638, Elvis Presley. No. 1639, Vasco da Gama. No. 1640, Paul Emile Victor. No. 1641, Tutankhamun. No. 1642, Nefertiti. No. 1643, John J. Audubon, Patagioenas leucophal. No. 1644, Audubon, Quiscalus quiscula.

2002, Sept. 30 ***Perf. 13¼x12¾***

Sheets of 6, #a-f

1589	A333	15,000m	multi	8.50	8.50
1590	A334	15,000m	multi	8.50	8.50
1591	A335	15,000m	multi	8.50	8.50
1592	A336	15,000m	multi	8.50	8.50
1593	A336	15,000m	multi	8.50	8.50
1594	A336	15,000m	multi	8.50	8.50
1595	A337	17,000m	multi	9.50	9.50
1596	A338	17,000m	multi	9.50	9.50
1597	A339	17,000m	multi	9.50	9.50
1598	A339	17,000m	multi	9.50	9.50
1599	A339	17,000m	multi	9.50	9.50
1600	A339	17,000m	multi	9.50	9.50
1601	A339	17,000m	multi	9.50	9.50

Sheets of 4, #a-d

1602	A340	5000m	multi	1.90	1.90
1603	A340	20,000m	multi	7.75	7.75
1604	A340	20,000m	multi	7.75	7.75
1605	A340	20,000m	multi	7.75	7.75
1606	A340	20,000m	multi	7.75	7.75
1607	A340	20,000m	multi	7.75	7.75
1608	A340	20,000m	multi	7.75	7.75
1609	A340	20,000m	multi	7.75	7.75
1610	A340	22,000m	multi	8.50	8.50
1611	A340	22,000m	multi	8.50	8.50
1612	A340	22,000m	multi	8.50	8.50
1613	A340	25,000m	multi	9.25	9.25
1614	A340	25,000m	multi	9.25	9.25
1615	A340	25,000m	multi	9.25	9.25
1616	A340	25,000m	multi	9.25	9.25
1617	A341	25,000m	multi	9.25	9.25
1618	A342	25,000m	multi	9.25	9.25
1619	A342	33,000m	multi	12.50	12.50
1620	A342	33,000m	multi	12.50	12.50
1621	A342	33,000m	multi	12.50	12.50
	Nos. 1589-1621 (33)			292.15	292.15

Souvenir Sheets

1622	A343	88,000m	shown	8.50	8.50
1623	A344	88,000m	shown	8.50	8.50
1624	A345	88,000m	shown	8.50	8.50
1625	A345	88,000m	multi	8.50	8.50
1626	A345	88,000m	multi	8.50	8.50
1627	A345	88,000m	multi	8.50	8.50
1628	A345	88,000m	multi	8.50	8.50
1629	A345	88,000m	multi	8.50	8.50
1630	A345	88,000m	multi	8.50	8.50
1631	A345	88,000m	multi	8.50	8.50
1632	A345	88,000m	multi	8.50	8.50
1633	A345	88,000m	multi	8.50	8.50
1634	A345	110,000m	multi	10.50	10.50
1635	A345	110,000m	multi	10.50	10.50
1636	A345	110,000m	multi	10.50	10.50
1637	A345	110,000m	multi	10.50	10.50
1638	A345	110,000m	multi	10.50	10.50
1639	A345	110,000m	multi	10.50	10.50
1640	A345	110,000m	multi	10.50	10.50
1641	A345	110,000m	multi	10.50	10.50
1642	A345	110,000m	multi	10.50	10.50
1643	A345	110,000m	multi	10.50	10.50
1644	A345	110,000m	multi	10.50	10.50
1645	A346	110,000m	shown	10.50	10.50
1646	A347	110,000m	shown	10.50	10.50
	Nos. 1622-1646 (25)			238.50	238.50

World of the Sea

Ships — A348

Aircraft — A349

Sea Lions — A350

Polar Bears — A351

Killer Whales — A352

Whales — A353

Dolphins — A354

Fish — A355

Fish — A356

Fish — A357

Fish — A358

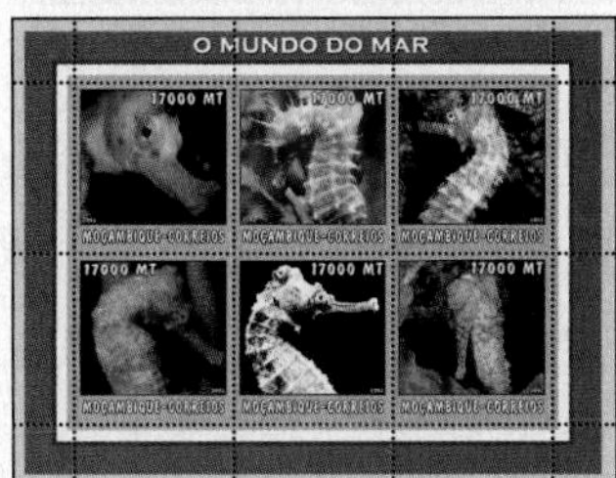

Sea Horses — A359

Penguins — A360

Penguins — A361

Sea Birds — A362

Sea Birds — A363

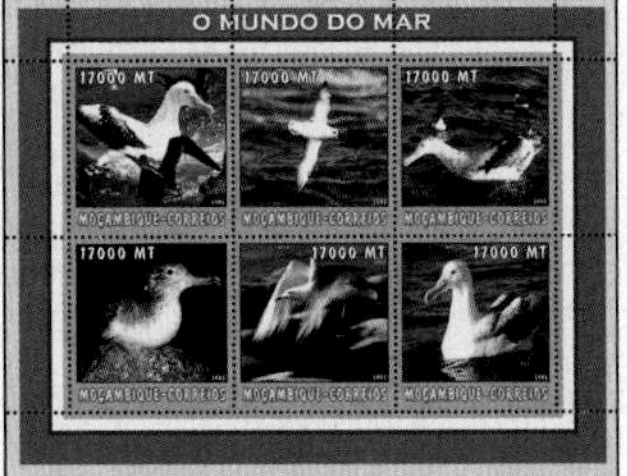

Sea Birds — A364

Crustaceans — A365

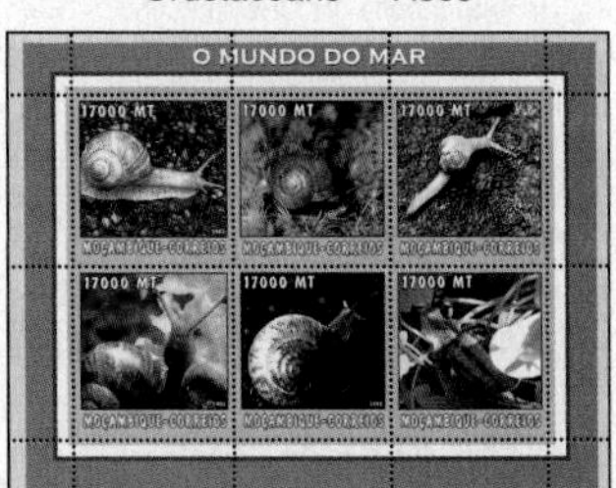

Snails — A366

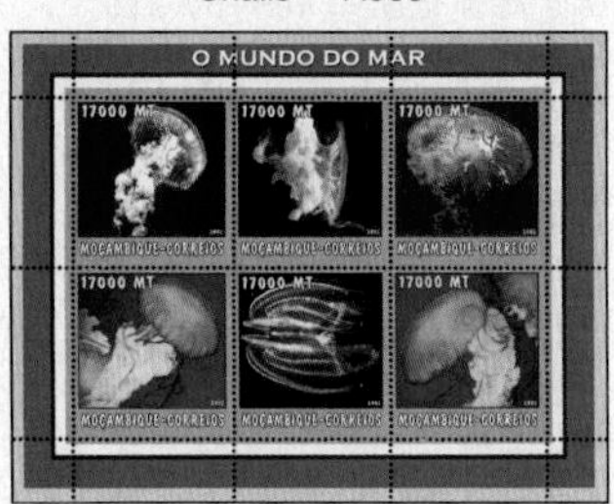

Jellyfish — A367

Coral — A368

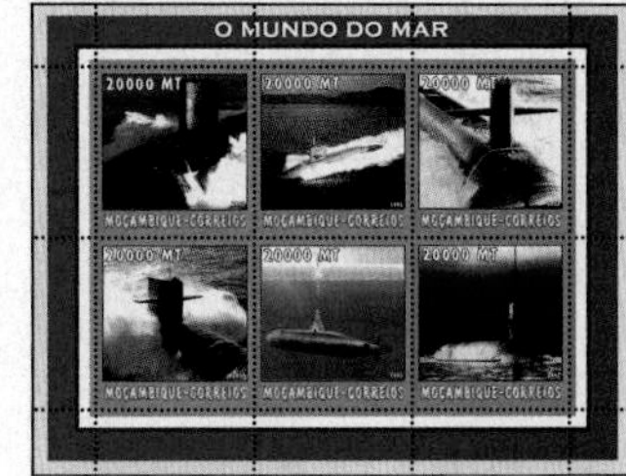

Submarines — A369

Lighthouses — A370

Ship — A371

Ship — A372

Fish — A373

Fish — A374

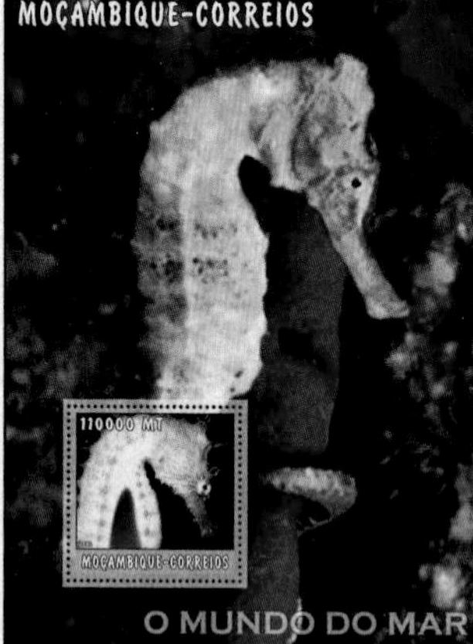

Sea Horse — A375

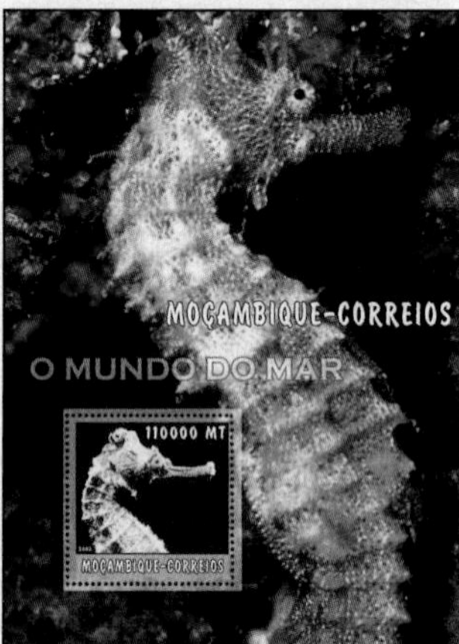

Sea Horse — A376

Penguin — A377

Penguin — A378

Sea Bird — A379

Sea Bird — A380

Sea Bird — A381

No. 1668 — Marine invertebrates: a, Phyllidia elegans. b, Phyllidia coelestis. c, Hypselodoris bullocki. d, Glossodoris hikuerensis. e, Glossodoris cruentus. f, Chromodoris leopardus.

No. 1669 — Shells: a, Murex brassica (showing shell opening). b, Cassis cornuta. c, Strombus gigas. d, Rapana rapiformis (showing shell opening). e, Chicoreus ramosus. f, Bursa bubo.

No. 1670 — Shells: a, Chicoreus virgineus. b, Tonna galea. c, Murex erythrostomus. d, Strombus gigas. e, Murex brassica (showing front of shell). f, Rapana rapiformis (showing front of shell).

No. 1671 — Tubeworms and seaweed: a, Kallymenia cribosa. b, Ulva lactuca. c, Chondrus crispus. d, Gigartina disticha. e, Palmaria palmata. f, Filogranella elatensis.

No. 1685, Seal flensing. No. 1686, Polar bear. No. 1687, Killer whale breaching surface. No. 1688, Whales underwater. No. 1689, Dolphins with open mouths. No. 1690, Lobster. No. 1691, Jellyfish. No. 1692 Coral and fish. No. 1693, Filogranella elatensis. No. 1694, Chromodoris leopardus. No. 1695, Tonna galea. No. 1696, Turbo marmoratus. No. 1697, Submarine. No. 1698, Christopher Columbus.

Perf. 12¾x13¼, 13¼x12¾

2002, Nov. 1 **Sheets of 6, #a-f**

1647	A348	5000m	multi	3.25	3.25
1648	A349	17,000m	multi	9.50	9.50
1649	A350	17,000m	multi	9.50	9.50
1650	A351	17,000m	multi	9.50	9.50
1651	A352	17,000m	multi	9.50	9.50
1652	A353	17,000m	multi	9.50	9.50
1653	A354	17,000m	multi	9.50	9.50
1654	A355	17,000m	multi	9.50	9.50
1655	A356	17,000m	multi	9.50	9.50
1656	A357	17,000m	multi	9.50	9.50
1657	A358	17,000m	multi	9.50	9.50
1658	A359	17,000m	multi	9.50	9.50
1659	A360	17,000m	multi	9.50	9.50
1660	A361	17,000m	multi	9.50	9.50
1661	A362	17,000m	multi	9.50	9.50
1662	A363	17,000m	multi	9.50	9.50
1663	A364	17,000m	multi	9.50	9.50
1664	A365	17,000m	multi	9.50	9.50
1665	A366	17,000m	multi	9.50	9.50
1666	A367	17,000m	multi	9.50	9.50
1667	A368	17,000m	multi	9.50	9.50
1668	A368	17,000m	multi	9.50	9.50
1669	A368	17,000m	multi	9.50	9.50
1670	A368	17,000m	multi	9.50	9.50
1671	A368	17,000m	multi	9.50	9.50
1672	A369	20,000m	multi	12.00	12.00
1673	A370	33,000m	multi	20.00	20.00
	Nos. 1647-1673 (27)			263.25	263.25

Souvenir Sheets

1674	A371	110,000m	shown	11.00	11.00
1675	A372	110,000m	shown	11.00	11.00
1676	A373	110,000m	shown	11.00	11.00
1677	A374	110,000m	shown	11.00	11.00
1678	A375	110,000m	shown	11.00	11.00
1679	A376	110,000m	shown	11.00	11.00
1680	A377	110,000m	shown	11.00	11.00
1681	A378	110,000m	shown	11.00	11.00
1682	A379	110,000m	shown	11.00	11.00
1683	A380	110,000m	shown	11.00	11.00
1684	A381	110,000m	shown	11.00	11.00
1685	A350	110,000m	multi	11.00	11.00
1686	A351	110,000m	multi	11.00	11.00
1687	A352	110,000m	multi	11.00	11.00
1688	A353	110,000m	multi	11.00	11.00
1689	A354	110,000m	multi	11.00	11.00
1690	A365	110,000m	multi	11.00	11.00
1691	A367	110,000m	multi	11.00	11.00
1692	A368	110,000m	multi	11.00	11.00
1693	A368	110,000m	multi	11.00	11.00
1694	A368	110,000m	multi	11.00	11.00
1695	A368	110,000m	multi	11.00	11.00
1696	A368	110,000m	multi	11.00	11.00
1697	A369	110,000m	multi	11.00	11.00
1698	A369	110,000m	multi	11.00	11.00
	Nos. 1674-1698 (25)			275.00	275.00

Zeppelins — A382

No. 1699, 28,000m, horiz.: a, Ferdinand von Zeppelin, brown and yellow background. b, LZ-2 in flight. c, LZ-10 in flight. d, LZ-1, purple background.

No. 1700, 28,000m, horiz.: a, LZ-1, blue and yellow background. b, LZ-2 tethered. c, LZ-10 above sheep. d, Ferdinand von Zeppelin with binoculars.

No. 1701, 50,000m, Ferdinand von Zeppelin, in military uniform. No. 1702, 50,000m, Ferdinand von Zeppelin, in suit.

2002, Nov. 18 *Perf. 13¼x13½*

Sheets of 4, #a-d

1699-1700	A382	Set of 2	15.00	15.00

Souvenir Sheets

Perf. 13½x13¼

1701-1702	A382	Set of 2	6.75	6.75

Locomotives — A383

No. 1703, 17,000m, horiz.: a, London, Midland and Scottish Railway, England. b, Great Northern Railway, Ireland. c, Southern Railway, England. d, Great Northern Railway, US. e, Chicago, Milwaukee, St. Paul and Pacific Railroad, US. f, London and Northeastern Railway, England.

No. 1704, 17,000m, horiz.: a, Great Southern Railway, Spain. b, Shantung Railway, China. c, Shanghai-Nanking Railway, China. d, Austrian State Railway. e, Victorian Government Railways, Australia. f, London and Northwester Railways, England.

No. 1705, 17,000m, horiz.: a, Western Railways, France. b, Netherlands State Railway (green locomotive on bridge). c, Great Indian Peninsula Railway. d, Paris-Orleans Railway, France. e, Madras and Southern Mahratta Railway, India. f, Netherlands State Railway (green locomotive).

No. 1706, 50,000m, London, Brighton and South Coast Railway, England. No. 1707, 50,000m, New York Central, US.

2002, Nov. 18 *Perf. 13¼x13½*

Sheets of 6, #a-f

1703-1705	A383	Set of 3	20.00	20.00

Souvenir Sheets

1706-1707	A383	Set of 2	6.75	6.75

A384

Automobiles — A385

No. 1708, 13,000m: a, 1912 Bentley. b, 1914 Delage Grand Prix. c, 1949, Healey Silverstone. d, 1922 Duesenberg. e, Delage 1500cc Grand Prix. f, 1961 Ferrari 375/F1.

No. 1709, 13,000m: a, 1906 Mercedes. b, 1951 Morgan. c, 1912 Sunbeam. d, 1922 Sunbeam. e, 1925 Sunbeam Tiger. f, 1908 Austin 100hp.

No. 1710, 17,000m: a, 1937, Bugatti Type 57 Alalante coupe. b, 1948 Tucker Torpedo. c, 1966 Honda S 800m. d, 1946 Cisitalia 202 GT. e, 1958 Chevrolet Impala. f, 1934 Cadillac LaSalle convertible.

No. 1711, 17,000m: a, 1908 Austin. b, 1937 Studebaker coupe. c, 1930 Bugatti Type 40GP. d, 1931 Ford Model A roadster. e, 1937 Alfa Romeo 2900B. f, 1937 Cord 812.

No. 1712, 40,000m, 1931 Alfa Romeo. No. 1713, 40,000m, 1911 Marmon Wasp.

No. 1714, 50,000m, 1957 Plymouth Fury. No. 1715, 50,000m, 1928 Mercedes-Benz SSK.

Perf. 13¼x13½, 13½x13¼

2002, Nov. 18 **Sheets of 6, #a-f**

1708-1709	A384	Set of 2	10.00	10.00
1710-1711	A385	Set of 2	12.50	12.50

Souvenir Sheets

1712-1713	A384	Set of 2	5.50	5.50
1714-1715	A385	Set of 2	6.75	6.75

Pottery — A386

Designs: 1000m, Pote. 2000m, Chaleira. 4000m, Taças. 5000m, Cantaro. 17,000m, Panela. 28,000m, Alguidar. 50,000m, Jarra. 100,000m, Bilhas.

2002, Dec. 2 *Perf. 12¾*

1716-1723	A386	Set of 8	8.00	8.00

Dated 2001.

For surcharge see No. 1739.

Justino Chemane, Composer of National Anthem — A387

2003, July 11

1724	A387	6000m multi	.55	.55

Minerals — A388

Designs: 5000m, Bauxite. 14,000m, Marble. 19,000m, shown. 33,000m, Gold.

2004, Apr. 30

1725-1728	A388	Set of 4	6.00	6.00

Dated 2003.

Paintings by Jean-Auguste Ingres — A389

Paintings by James Tissot — A390

Paintings by Pierre-Auguste Renoir — A391

Paintings by Edgar Degas — A392

Various unnamed paintings.

2004, June 17 Litho. ***Perf. 13½x13***

1729	A389	6500m Sheet of 6, #a-f	9.50	9.50
1730	A390	6500m Sheet of 6, #a-f	9.50	9.50
g.		Souvenir sheet, #1730e	1.60	1.60
1731	A391	10,000m Sheet of 6, #a-f	11.50	11.50
1732	A392	17,000m Sheet of 6, #a-f	13.00	13.00
		Nos. 1729-1732 (4)	43.50	43.50

Diplomatic Relations Between Mozambique and People's Republic of China, 30th Anniv. — A395

No. 1735: a, Flags, buildings and animals. b, Arms, Admiral Zheng He, building, vase, sculpture.

Illustration reduced.

2005, June 25 Litho. ***Perf. 13¼***

1735	A395	33,000m Pair, #a-b	5.50	5.50

Exists imperf.

Southern African Development Community, 25th Anniv. — A396

2005, Aug. 11 ***Perf. 11¼x11***

1736	A396	8000m multi	.65	.65

Traditional African Medicine Day A397

2005, Aug. 31 ***Perf. 11x11¼***

1737	A397	8000m multi	.65	.65

World Summit on the Information Society, Tunis — A398

2005, Oct. 9 ***Perf. 11¼x11***

1738	A398	8000m multi	.65	.65

Nos. 1320, 1575, 1576, 1717 Surcharged Like No. 1417 and

No. 1321 Surcharged in Black and Silver

Methods and Perfs as Before

2005 ?

1739	A386	6000m on 2000m #1717	.50	.50
1739A	A331	6000m on 10,000m #1575		—
1740	A331	8000m on 17,000m #1576	.70	.70
1741	A269	33,000m on 7500m #1320	2.75	2.75
1742	A269	33,000m on 12,500m #1321 (B&S)	2.75	2.75
		Nos. 1739-1742 (4)	6.70	6.70

Mozambique Telecommunications Company, 25th Anniv. — A399

2006, June 10 Litho. ***Perf. 11½x11***

1743	A399	8000m multi	.65	.65

No. 1743 also has denomination expressed in revalued meticals, which were put into service on July 1.

For surcharge, see No. 1747.

Presidential Initiative Against AIDS — A400

Pres. Armando Guebuza: 8m, Holding gavel. 16m, Behind microphones. 33m, With arm raised.

2006, Oct. 9 ***Perf. 11x11½***

1744-1746	A400	Set of 3	4.50	4.50

World Vision — A400a

2006 Litho. ***Perf. 11½x11***

1746A	A400a	33m multi		—

An additional stamp was issued in this set. The editors would like to examine any example.

No. 1743 Surcharged

2006 Litho. ***Perf. 11½x11***

1747	A399	33m on 8000m #1743		—

The following items inscribed "Moçambique Correios" have been declared "illegal" by Mozambique postal officials:

Sheet of nine stamps of various denominations depicting Princess Diana;

Sheet of six 5000m stamps depicting the art of Paul Delvaux;

Sheet of six 17,000m stamps depicting the art of Edgar Degas;

Stamps depicting the art of Lucas Cranach;

Six different 15,000m souvenir sheets of one depicting Pope John Paul II;

Souvenir sheet of one 30,000m stamp depicting French Pres. Nicolas Sarkozy.

A set of 12 stamps with denominations of 5,000m, 19,000m, and 33,000m depicting Europa stamps, 50th anniv.

Stamps depicting Wolfgang Amadeus Mozart; Pierre Auguste Renoir; Jean Auguste Ingres Bessieres; Marilyn Monroe; Rotary International; Lions International; Formula 1 Racing; Astronauts; 2007 Rugby World Cup.

No. 1575 Surcharged

Methods and Perfs As Before

2006 ?

1748	A331	33m on 10,000m #1575	*6.75*	*6.75*

Cahora Bassa Dam A401

Designs: 8m, Dam and reservoir. 20m, Dignitaries shaking hands. 33m, Dam and flag of Mozambique.

2007, Nov. 26 Litho. ***Perf. 11x11¼***

1749-1751	A401	Set of 3	4.75	4.75

Reign of Aga Khan, 50th Anniv. — A402

Designs: 8m, Building. No. 1753, 20m, People on beach. No. 1754, 20m, People under shelter. No. 1755, 33m, Polana Serena Hotel. No. 1756, 33m, Students in classroom, vert. (30x40mm).

Perf. 12¾, 11¼x11 (#1756)

2007, Nov.

1752-1756	A402	Set of 5	9.00	9.00

Fauna, Flora and Minerals — A403

No. 1757 — Map of Africa and wild cats: a, 8m, Acionyx jubatus. b, 8m, Panthera leo with closed mouth. c, 8m, Panthera leo with open mouth. d, 33m, Male Panthera leo. e, 33m, Female Panthera leo, diff. f, 33m, Panthera pardus.

No. 1758 — Map of Africa and elephants: a, 8m, Loxodonta cyclotis facing right. b, 8m, Loxodonta africana. c, 8m, Loxodonta cyclotis facing left. d, 33m, Loxodonta africana facing right. e, 33m, Loxodonta cyclotis, diff. f, 33m, Loxodonta africana facing left.

No. 1759 — Lighthouses and marine mammals: a, 8m, Sousa teuszii. b, 8m, Stenella frontalis. c, 8m, Stenella clymene. d, 33m, Sotalia fluviatilis. e, 33m, Stenella longirostris. f, 33m, Tursiops truncatus.

No. 1760 — Map of Africa and birds of prey: a, 8m, Haliaeetus leucocephalus. b, 8m, Terathopius ecaudatus. c, 8m, Accipiter gentilis. d, 33m, Buteo lagopus. e, 33m, Head of Aquila verreauxii. f, 33m, Aquila verreauxi on branch.

No. 1761 — Hummingbirds and orchids: a, 8m, Tachybaptus, Malaxis uniflora. b, 8m, Fregata magnificus, Coryanthes speciosa. c, 8m, Gallinula, Calochilus robertsonii. d, 33m, Veniliornis, Stanhopea. e, 33m, Basilinna leucotis, Habaneria saccata. f, 33m, Actitis macularia, Diuris filifolia.

No. 1762 — Map of Africa and bees: a, 8m, Polubia. b, 8m, Apis mellifera scutellata. c, 8m, Pompilus. d, 33m, Tiphiidae. e, 33m, Vespula vulgaris. f, 33m, Scoliidae.

No. 1763 — Map of Africa and butterflies: a, 8m, Danaus chrysippus. b, 8m, Libytheana carineta. c, 8m, Papilio morondavana. d, 33m, Danaus gilippus. e, 33m, Amblypodia tyrannus. f, 33m, Lycaena cupreus.

No. 1764 — Map of Africa and crocodiles: a, 8m, Crocodylus porosus. b, 8m, Crocodylus novaeguineae. c, 8m, Crocodylus rhombifer. d, 33m, Crocodylus niloticus. e, 33m, Osteolaemus tetraspis. f, 33m, Crocodylus siamensis.

No. 1765 — Map of Africa and frogs: a, 8m, Gastrotheca. b, 8m, Mantella. c, 8m, Rana esculenta. d, 33m, Litoria rubella. e, 33m, Dendrobatidae. f, 33m, Pyxicephalus.

No. 1766 — Dinosaurs: a, 8m, Aublysodon. b, 8m, Ornithomimus. c, 8m, Coelurus. d, 33m, Velociraptor. e, 33m, Abelisaurus. f, 33m, Saurornithoides.

No. 1767 — Map of Africa and cacti: a, 8m, Hoodia gordonii. b, 8m, Hoodia officinalis. c, 8m, Hoodia ruschii. d, 33m, Hoodia flava. e, 33m, Hoodia officinalis, diff. f, 33m, Hoodia currorii.

No. 1768 — Fruit: a, 8m, Citrus vulgaris. b, 8m, Cola acuminata. c, 8m, Cocos nucifera. d, 33m, Citrus limonum. e, 33m, Cocos nucifera, diff. f, 33m, Citrus bergamia.

No. 1769 — Map of Africa, diamonds and minerals: a, 8m, Fluorite, quartz. b, 8m, Elbaite tourmaline, quartz. c, 8m, Staurolite. d, 33m, Fluorite, pyrite. e, 33m, Benitoite, neptunite. f, 33m, Celestine.

No. 1770, 20m — Map of Africa and primates: a, Cebidae. b, Nomascus leucogenys. c, Borneo proboscis monkey. d, Symphalangus syndactylus. e, Pan troglodytes. f, Cercopithecidae.

No. 1771, 20m — Lighthouses and whales: a, Balaenoptera borealis. b, Orcinus orca. c, Eschrichtius robustus. d, Balaenoptera physalus. e, Three Orcinus orca. f, Megaptera novaeangliae.

No. 1772, 20m — Map of Africa and owls: a, Strix woodfordii. b, Tyto capensis. c, Phodilus badius on thin branch. d, Phodilus badius on thick branch. e, Tytonidae. f, Otus senegalensis.

No. 1773, 20m — Map of Africa and parrots: a, Psittacopes. b, Serudaptus. c, Pseudasturidae. d, Quercypsittidae. e, Xenopsitta. f, Palaeopsittacus.

No. 1774, 20m — Butterflies or moths and unnamed flowers: a, Inachis io. b, Saturnia pavonia. c, Papilio xuthus. d, Prepona praeneste. e, Speyeria cybele. f, Nymphalidae.

No. 1775, 20m — Map of Africa and fish: a, Scorpaenidae. b, Balistodae. c, Antennarius. d, Triglidae. e, Hydrocynus. f, Lophius.

No. 1776, 20m — Map of Africa and marine life: a, Birgus latro. b, Panulirus. c, Gecarcoidea natalis. d, Loligo opalescens. e, Genus ocypode. f, Hapalochlaena.

No. 1777, 20m — Map of Africa and reptiles: a, Vaanus niloticus. b, Chamaeleo jacksonii. c, Veranus exanthematicus. d, Scincus. e, Brookesia. f, Furcifer pardalis.

No. 1778, 20m — Map of Africa and turtles: a, Natator depressus. b, Eretmochelys imbricata. c, Lepidochelys olivacea with dark neck. d, Lepidochelys olivacea with light neck. e, Caretta caretta. f, Chelonia mydas.

No. 1779, 20m — Map of Africa and snakes: a, Bitis nasicornis. b, Bitis gabonica. c, Ophiophagus hannah. d, Thelolornis kirtlandii. e, Dendroaspis angusticeps. f, Atheris.

No. 1780, 20m — Dinosaurs: a, Therizinosaurus. b, Heterdontosaurus. c, Prosaurolophus. d, Melanorosaurus. e, Megalosaurus. f, Proceratosaurus.

No. 1781, 20m — Trees: a, Punica granatum, fruit split, and on branch. b, Elaeis guineensis. c, Cola acuminata. d, Areca catechu. e, Hevea brasiliensis. f, Punica granatum, flowers on branches and split.

No. 1782, 20m — Map of Africa and orchids: a, Purple Cattleya lueddemanniana. b, Paphiopedilum delenatii. c, Vanda coerulea. d, Pink Cattleya lueddmanniana. e, Paphiopedilum. f, Spathoglottis.

No. 1783, 20m — Map of Africa and minerals: a, Carrollite. b, Ettringite. c, Cerrusite, barite. d, Malachite. e, Carrollite, calcite. f, Dioptase.

No. 1784, 132m, Map of Africa and Nomascus nasutus. No. 1785, 132m, Map of Africa and Panthera leo. No. 1786, 132m, Loxodonta africana. No. 1787, 132m, Stenella logirostris, diff. No. 1788, 132m, Orcinus orca and lighthouse, diff. No. 1789, 132m, Lepidocolaptes, Spathoglottis plicata. No. 1790, 132m, Pulchrapollia. No. 1791, 132m, Accipiter nisus. No. 1792, 132m, Map of Africa and Polubia. No. 1793, 132m, Arctia hebe. No. 1794, 132m, Papilio homerus, Caladeria reptans. No. 1795, 132m, Map of Africa and Thassophryninae. No. 1796, 132m, Map of Africa and Chauliodus. No. 1797, 132m, Map of Africa and Dendroaspis polylepis. No. 1798, 132m, Map of Africa and Pogona vitticeps. No. 1799, 132m, Map of Africa and Crocodylus niloticus, diff. No. 1800, 132m, Map of Africa and Eretmochelys imbricata, diff. No. 1801, 132m, Map of Africa and Pychicephalus adspersus. No. 1802, 132m, Hadrosaurus. No. 1803, 132m, Adansonia tree. No. 1804, 132m, Map of Africa and Euphorbia enopla. No. 1805, 132m, Map of Africa, Diuris filifolia, Malaxis uniflora. No. 1806, 132m, Cirtus vulgaris, diff. No. 1807, 132m, Vanadinite, poldervaartite. No. 1808, 132m, Malachite, barite and malachite.

Perf. 12¾x13¼

2007, Dec. 10 **Litho.**

Sheets of 6, #a-f

1757-1769	A403	Set of 13	125.00	125.00
1770-1783	A403	Set of 14	130.00	130.00

Souvenir Sheets

Perf. 13¼ Syncopated

1784-1808	A403	Set of 25	260.00	260.00

Minerva Central Publishers, Cent. A404

Background color: 8m, Red. 20m, Olive green. 33m, Purple.

2008, Apr. 10 **Litho.** ***Perf. 11x11¼***

1809-1811	A404	Set of 3	4.75	4.75

Second Frelimo Party Congress, 40th Anniv. — A405

2008, July 25 ***Perf. 11¼x11***

1812	A405 8m multi		.65	.65

Miniature Sheets

2008 Summer Olympics, Beijing — A406

No. 1813 Surcharged

Nos. 1813 and 1814: a, Soccer. b, Basketball. c, Swimming. d, Running.

2008 ***Perf. 13¼x12¾***

1813	A406 8m Sheet of 4, #a-d		*5.00*	*5.00*
1814	A406 8m on 8m Sheet of 4, #a-d		2.50	2.50

No. 1813 shows an incorrect abbreviation for the currency, which was corrected by the surcharge.

Food — A407

Designs: 8m, Bolo de milho (corn cake). 20m, Mathapa com carangueijo (cassava with crab). 33m, Quiabo com camarao (Okra and shrimp).

2008, Oct. 9 ***Perf. 11¼x11***

1815-1817	A407	Set of 3	4.75	4.75

Maria de Lurdes Mutola, 800-Meter Gold Medalist in 2000 Summer Olympics A408

2009, Jan. 21 ***Perf. 11x11¼***

1818	A408 8m multi		.65	.65

Mozambique postal officials have declared as "illegal" stamps dated 2008 depicting chess grandmaster Bobby Fischer.

Eduardo Mondlane (1920-69), President of Mozambique Liberation Front — A409

2009, June 20 **Litho.** ***Perf. 11¼x11***

1819	A409 33m black & red		2.40	2.40

Transportation — A410

No. 1820, 33m — Transportation with animals: a, Elephants and howdah. b, Reindeer pulling sled. c, Camel and rider. d, Horse-drawn carriage. e, Donkey and rider. f, Dog sled.

No. 1821, 33m — Two-wheeled transportation: a, Rickshaw. b, Bicycle. c, Motor scooter. d, Motorcycle. e, Foot-powered scooter. f, Segway.

No. 1822, 33m — Old automobiles: a, Citroen BL 11. b, Jaguar XK-140. c, Chrysler Imperial. d, Dodge Royal Lancer. e, Mercedes-Benz 300 SL. f, Ford Custom.

No. 1823, 33m — Modern automobiles: a, Hyundai QuarmaQ. b, Lamborghini Murcielago. c, Buick Invicta. d, Ford Verve. e, Mazda RX-8. f, Cadillac CTS Sport Wagon.

No. 1824, 33m — Modern electric automobiles: a, Mitsubishi iMiEV Sport. b, Opel Meriva. c, Pickup truck (incorrectly identified as InterCity 225). d, Nissan Navara. e, Opel Insignia. f, Tesla Roadster.

No. 1825, 33m — Ancient sailing vessels: a, Phoenician bark. b, Egyptian wooden ship. c, Arab ship. d, Chinese junk. e, Greek galley. f, Roman galley.

No. 1826, 33m — Ships and maps: a, Independence, map of United States. b, Great Harry, map of Great Britain and Ireland. c, Vespucci, map of Spain. d, Norske Löwe, map of Denmark. e, Brederoe, map of Netherlands. f, Madre di Dio, map of Italy.

No. 1827, 33m — Steam-powered ships: a, SS Martha's Vineyard. b, SS America. c, SS Statendam. d, SS Brazil. e, SS Ryndam. f, SS Nieuw Amsterdam.

No. 1828, 33m — Warships: a, Warrior. b, Merrimack. c, Dreadnought. d, Lightning. e, MEKO frigate. f, Yamato.

No. 1829, 33m — Warships: a, HMS Astute. b, NS Yamal. c, USS Harry S Truman. d, Trafalgar. e, Vaygach. f, Nimitz class aircraft carrier.

No. 1830, 33m — Modern ships: a, Surcouf. b, Sea Shadow. c, Skjold class patrol boat. d, MS Radiance of the Seas. e, MS Pacific Princess. f, MS Mariner of the Seas.

No. 1831, 33m — Early locomotives: a, Trevithick. b, Blenkinsop. c, Marc Seguin. d, Puffing Billy. e, Rocket. f, Liverpool.

No. 1832, 33m — Locomotives: a, Evening Star. b, LMS Princess Royal Class. c, Russian 2TE10U. d, Atlantis. e, Cock o' the North. f, LMS Compound 4-4-0.

No. 1833, 33m — Locomotives: a, ALCO RS-1 (bister panel). b, British Rail Class 03. c, 643 Class. d, 661 Class. e, 641 Class. f, Hudswell Clarke 0-4-2ST.

No. 1834, 33m — Locomotives: a, ALCO RS-1 (gray panel). b, Re420. c, TAGAB Re2. d, EuroSprinter DB AG Class 182. e, SKODA 109. f, Re4.

No. 1835, 33m — High-speed trains: a, Thalys. b, Eurostar. c, InterCity 225. d, ICE. e, TGV. f, Pendolino.

No. 1836, 33m — High-speed trains: a, JR-Maglev. b, KTX. c, Maglev. d, 100 Series Shinkansen. e, E1 Series Shinkansen. f, N700 Series Shinkansen.

No. 1837, 33m — Pioneer aircraft: a, 1868 Albatros II glider of Jean-Marie LeBris. b, 1852 Henry Giffard balloon. c, 1849 glider of George Cayley. d, 1897 Avion III airplane of Clément Ader. e, 1874 monoplane of Félix du Temple. f, 1901 flying machine of Traian Vuia.

No. 1838, 33m — Pioneer aircraft: a, 1902 Number 21 airplane of Gustave Whitehead. b,

1904 Wright Flyer II. c, 14 Bis, 1906. c, 1908 Henry Farman biplane. d, 1909 Louis Blériot monoplane. f, 1910 Rumpler Taube.

No. 1839, 33m — Airplanes: a, Fokker D.1. b, Handley Page. c, Winstead Special. d, Boeing P26-B. e, Mitsubishi Ki-15. f, Nakajima Ki-27.

No. 1840, 33m — Military airplanes: a, Messerschmitt Bf-109. b, B-29 Superfortress. c, Yak-9. d, Avro Lancaster. e, Kawasaki Ki-61. f, Northrop P-61 Black Widow.

No. 1841, 33m — Military airplanes: a, Saab J35J. b, Sukhoi SU-30MKI. c, A-7 Corsair. d, Boeing 747 carrying Space Shuttle. e, Myasishchev M-55. f, Aero L-39 Albatros.

No. 1842, 33m — Supersonic airplanes: a, TU-144. b, F-105 Thunderbird. c, North American XB-70A. d, SR-71 Blackbird. e, Concorde 102. f, F16XL.

No. 1843, 33m — Fire vehicles: a, 1963 Magirus-Deutz Mercur 126 DL. b, 1979 Mercedes-Benz LA 1113 BR. c, 1958 Magirus-Deutz V6 Ladder. d, 1976 Dodge K1050 Somati MONIA. e, 2002 Scania 91 G310 Rosenbauer. f, 1984 Renault G300-17 Riffaul.

No. 1844, 33m — Ambulances: a, 1942 Morris Y Series. b, 1974 Citroen HB2AS 1600. c, 1942 Dodge WC54. d, 1981 Land Rover. e, 1966 Cadillac S&S48. f, 1955 Ford Kaiser V8.

No. 1845, 33m — Spacecraft: a, Sputnik I. b, Vostok I. c, Explorer I. d, Skylab. e, Mir. f, Apollo 11.

No. 1846, 33m — Spacecraft: a, Venture Star. b, Ares V. c, Space Shuttle Discovery. d, Dawn. e, SpaceShip One. f, Phoenix.

No. 1847, 175m, Camels and rider. No. 1848, 175m, Rickshaw and Segway. No. 1849, 175m, Cadillac Eldorado. No. 1850, 175m, Citroen 2CV. No. 1851, 175m, Renault Z17. No. 1852, 175m, Egyptian canoe. No. 1853, 175m, Portuguese carrack Santa Catarina do Monte Sinai and map of Portugal. No. 1854, 175m, SS Great Britain. No. 1855, 175m, Italian battleship Littorio. No. 1856, 175m, PFS Polarstern. No. 1857, 175m, F261 Magdeburg. No. 1858, 175m, North Star locomotive. No. 1859, 175m, Pannier locomotive. No. 1860, 175m, 10000 locomotive. No. 1861, 175m, CC7102 locomotive. No. 1862, 175m, Thalys, diff. No. 1863, 175m, KTX, diff. No. 1864, 175m, Triplane of John Stringfellow. No. 1865, 175m, Nieuport 28. No. 1866, 175m, Aichi D3A. No. 1867, 175m, Corsair F4U. No. 1868, 175m, EF-111. No. 1869, 175m, A2 airplane. No. 1870, 175m, 1996-2001 Mercedes Unimog 2450 L38 fire truck. No. 1871, 175m, 1956 Gurkha Red Cross Ambulance. No. 1872, 175m, Salyut 1 and Telstar. No. 1873, 175m, V-2 rocket and SS-6 Sapwood. Nos. 1847-1873 are vert.

Perf. 12¾x13¼

2009, Sept. 30 Litho.

Sheets of 6, #a-f

1820-1846 A410 Set of 27 425.00 425.00

Souvenir Sheets

Perf. 13¼ Syncopated

1847-1873 A410 Set of 27 375.00 375.00

Nos. 1847-1873 each contain one 37x38mm stamp.

Famous People and Events — A411

No. 1874, 8m — Year of the Tiger (in 2010): a, Tiger with head at bottom, Temple of Heaven. b, Tiger running, Forbidden City. c, Tiger with head at top, Temple of Heaven. d, Tiger walking, Forbidden City. e, Tiger, Yong He Gong Lama Temple. f, Tiger, Great Wall of China.

No. 1875, 8m — Shen Chou (1427-1509), painter: a, Painting of forest, sketch of tree branch with calligraphy. b, Shen Chou at R, painting at L. c, 14x19mm landscape and 13x26mm landscape. d, 17x21mm landscape and 16x20mm landscape. e, Shen Chou at L, painting at R. f, 13x15mm landscape and 16x23mm painting of man on bridge.

No. 1876, 8m — Pope John Paul II (1920-2005) and: a, Arms, sculpture. b, Dove, St. Peter's Basilica. c, Arms, dome interior. d, Arms, St. Peter's Basilica. e, Dove in flight, St. Peter's Square. f, Arms, buildings in distance.

No. 1877, 8m — Mohandas Gandhi (1869-1948) and: a, Ganesha. b, Spinning wheel. c, Taj Mahal. d, Naja naja (cobra). e, Meditating woman. f, Panthera tigris tigris (tiger).

No. 1878, 8m — Chinese film personalities: a, Sun Daolin. b, Zhao Dan. c, Ge You. d, Bai Yang. e, Ruan Lingyu. f, Zhang Yu.

No. 1879, 8m — People's Republic of China, 60th Anniv.: a, Hand holding Chinese flag, Chinese soldiers. b, Mao Zedong. c, Qian Sanqiang, Tianwan Nuclear Center. d, Deng Xiaoping, Great Wall of China. e, Hu Jintao, fireworks above Olympic Stadium. f, Jiang Zemin, Hong Kong skyline, ruins of St. Paul's Church, Macao.

No. 1880, 20m — Charlie Chaplin (1889-1977), actor, in scene from film from: a, 1915. b, 1925 (clapboard in background). c, 1918 (film reel in background). d, 1925 (film reel in background). e, 1918 (strip of film in background). f, 1925 (standing next to actress).

No. 1881, 20m — Hirohito (1901-89), emperor of Japan, in suit and tie, and in background: a, Japanese flag, Hirohito in military uniform. b, Hirohito, waving, standing next to Empress Nakano. c, Japanese flag. d, Hirohito as child, pagoda. e, Hirohito on horse, Japanese flag. f, Hirohito and Empress Nakano in gown.

No. 1882, 20m — Pres. John F. Kennedy (1917-63) and: a, Astronaut on moon. b, Kennedy at typewriter. c, Kennedy presidential campaign button. d, Family. e, Wife, Jacqueline, holding baby. f, Wedding photo.

No. 1883, 20m — Marilyn Monroe (1926-62), actress: a, Wearing costume from 1954 movie, wearing striped blouse. b, Wearing swimsuit, wearing green coat. c, Wearing top hat, wearing necklace. d, Wearing blue shorts. e, Looking through ship's porthole. f, Wearing short skirt and wearing red dress.

No. 1884, 20m — Elvis Presley (1935-77): a, Wearing white jacket and lei. b, Wearing red jacket, and jumping in air wearing cape. c, With four women. d, With arms raised, and with arms at neck. e, On telephone, wearing blue striped jacket. f, With guitar.

No. 1885, 20m — Michael Jackson (1958-2009), singer: a, Holding on to rail. b, Wearing top hat. c, Holding woman. d, As boy, with brothers. e, Speaking into microphone. f, Behind lectern, raising both arms.

No. 1886, 20m — Pope Benedict XVI: a, Facing forward, wearing miter, holding cross, arms at left. b, Wearing red hat, dove in flight. c, Facing left, wearing miter, holding cross, arms at left. d, Waving censer, arms at UR. e, With arms extended, dove on pedestal. f, Wearing red stole and zucchetto, arms at left.

No. 1887, 20m — Expo 2010, Shanghai: a, Nepal Pavilion. b, Africa Pavilion, with text beginning with "O tema." c, United Kingdom Pavilion. d, Romania Pavilion. e, African Pavilion, with text beginning with "A fachada." f, Japan Pavilion.

No. 1888, 33m — Galileo Galilei (1564-1642), astronomer, and: a, Leaning Tower of Pisa. b, Three people around telescope. c, Gear mechanism. d, Galileo's telescope. e, Telescope on wooden stand. f, Globe.

No. 1889, 33m — Johannes Kepler (1571-1630), astronomer, and: a, Moon. b, Kepler's model of the solar system and book, Mysterium Cosmographicum. c, Austrian coin depicting Kepler. d, Horoscope for General Wallenstein. e, Model of solar system. f, Model inscribed with Kepler's name.

No. 1890, 33m — George Frideric Handel (1685-1759), composer, and: a, Bust. b, Sculpture of Handel. c, Musical notes and orchestra hall in background. d, Engraving of Handel. e, Sculpture of lyre player. f, Handel's house in London.

No. 1891, 33m — William Kirby (1759-1850), entomologist: a, Kirby and Hypochrysops epicurus. b, Nicrophorus vespillo and Dytiscus marginalis. c, Kirby and unnamed butterfly. d, Kirby and Delias ninus. e, Polistes dominula and Philanthus triangulum. f, Kirby and Chilasa agestor.

No. 1892, 33m — Napoleon Bonaparte (1769-1821), emperor of France, and: a, French army. b, Battle of the Pyramids, 1798. c, Battle of Borodino, 1812. d, Imperial arms. e, Napoleon's bed. f, Battle of Arcola Bridge, 1796.

No. 1893, 33m — Joseph Haydn (1732-1809), composer, and: a, Haydn's house, Eisenstadt, Germany. b, Haydn's birthplace. c, Piano. d, Musicians. e, Esterházy Theater. f, Pianist.

No. 1894, 33m — Charles Darwin (1809-82), naturalist, and: a, Mimus trifasciatus. b, Allosaurus. c, Darwin's notes and sketches. d, Desmodus d'Orbignyi. e, Lesothosaurus. f, Microraptor gui.

No. 1895, 33m — Louis Braille (1809-52), educator of the blind: a, Braille, at left, and blind boy reading book, at right. b, Braille Institute. c, Braille, at right, and blind boy writing in Braille, at left. d, Woman and seeing-eye dogs. e, Hands and book in Braille, at left, Braille, at right. f, Braille alphabet.

No. 1896, 33m — Katsushika Hokusai (1760-1849), artist: a, Poppies, ocean waves. b, Man, red mountain. c, Sumo wrestlers. d, Man on horseback. e, Palanquin carriers. f, Man and falcon.

No. 1897, 33m — Alexander von Humboldt (1769-1859), naturalist, and: a, Simia melanocephala. b, Rhexia speciosa. c, Simia leonina. d, Hibiscus. e, Convolvulus. f, Melastoma.

No. 1898, 33m — Georges-Pierre Seurat (1859-91), painter, and paintings on tripod: a, Young woman Powdering Herself (Muher jovem a maquilhar-se). b, The Reaper (O debulhador). c, The Stonebreaker. d, Chahut (O Chabut). e, A Sunday Afternoon on the Island of La Grande Jatte (Tarde de Domingo na Ilha da Grande Jatte). f, The Bridge - View of the Seine (A vista da ponte de Seine).

No. 1899, 33m — Sir Peter Scott (1909-89), founder of Worldwide Fund for Nature: a, Scott holding dog, painting of birds in flight. b, Scott feeding ducks, painting of ducks in flight. c, Scott facing left, painting of birds in flight. d, Scott with camera, painting of birds in flight. e, Scott facing forward, painting of birds in flight. f, Scott with binoculars, painting of ducks on water.

No. 1900, 33m — First man on the Moon, 40th anniv.: a, Moon, Apollo 11 on launch pad, b, Neil Armstrong, Moon, Apollo 11 in flight. c, Apollo 11 Lunar Module above Moon. d, Apollo 11 above Moon, Edwin E. Aldrin. e, Apollo 11, astronaut and American flag on Moon. f, Apollo 11 Command Module, Michael Collins.

No. 1901, 33m — International Polar Year: a, Iceberg and Odobenus rosmarus. b, Map of Antarctica, Belgium's Princess Elisabeth Antarctic Station. c, Map of Arctic Ocean and CCGS Amundsen. d, Intl. Polar Year emblem, iceberg, Ovibos moschatus. e, Map of Antarctica, Georg von Neumayer (1826-1909) and Karl Weyprecht (1838-81), polar explorers. f, Intl. Polar Year emblem, iceberg, Ursus maritimus.

No. 1902, 175m, Tiger and Forbidden City. No. 1903, 175m, Shen Chou and painting. No. 1904, 175m, Pope John Paul II giving communion to man. No. 1905, 175m, Gandhi. No. 1906, 175m, Xie Jin (1923-2008), Chinese film director. No. 1907, 175m, Ceremony of founding of the People's Republic of China. No. 1908, 175m, Chaplin. No. 1909, 175m, Emperor Hirohito, Empress Nakano and Queen Elizabeth II. No. 1910, 175m, Pres. Kennedy, White House. No. 1911, 175m, Monroe. No. 1912, 175m, Presley. No. 1913, 175m, Jackson and Slash. No. 1914, 175m, Pope Benedict XVI. No. 1915, 175m, Chinese Pavilion at Expo 2010, Shanghai. No. 1916, 175m, Galileo Galilei and men around globe. No. 1917, 175m, Kepler, telescope, planets. No. 1918, 175m, Handel. No. 1919, 175m, Kirby and Psuedotergumia pisidice. No. 1920, 175m, Map, Napoleon on horse. No. 1921, 175m, Haydn, harpsichord. No. 1922, 175m, Darwin and Rhea darwinii. No. 1923, 175m, Braille, teacher and blind students. No. 1924, 175m, Hokusai paintings of server of sake and mountain. No. 1925, 175m, Humboldt and specimens of flora and fauna. No. 1926, 175m, Artist's palette, Bathers at Asniers, by Seurat. No. 1927, 175m, Scott with camera on tripod, painting of birds in flight. No. 1928, 175m, Astronauts on moon, American flag. No. 1929, 175m, Iceberg, Alopes lagopus.

Perf. 12¾x13¼

2009, Nov. 30 Litho.

Sheets of 6, #a-f

1874-1901 A411 Set of 28 375.00 375.00

Souvenir Sheets

Perf. 13¼ Syncopated

1902-1929 A411 Set of 28 375.00 375.00

On Nos. 1874-1901, stamps "a," "c," "d" and "f" are 37x38mm, stamps "b" and "e" are 50x38mm. Nos. 1902-1929 each contain one 50x38mm stamp.

Worldwide Fund for Nature (WWF) — A412

No. 1930 — Hippotragus equinus: a, Adult. b, Adult and juvenile. c, Adults at watering hole. d, Adults in grass.

175m, Adult grazing.

2010, Jan. 30 ***Perf. 13x13¼***

1930 A412 33m Block or strip of 4, #a-d 10.50 10.50

e. Souvenir sheet of 8, 2 each #1930a-1930d + 2 labels 21.00 21.00

Souvenir Sheet

Perf. 12¾x13¼

1931 A412 175m multi 13.50 13.50

No. 1931 contains one 37x38mm stamp.

The Natural World — A413

No. 1932, 8m — Giraffes (Giraffa camelopardalis): a, Two giraffes, giraffe at right on ground. b, Herd of giraffes. c, Two giraffes, giraffe at left on ground. d, Adult and juvenile giraffes. e, Two giraffes, giraffe at left with front legs extended. f, Two adult giraffes standing.

No. 1933, 8m — Wild pigs: a, Sus scrofa facing right. b, Brown Sus scrofa facing left. c, Gray Sus scrofa facing left. d, Phacochoerus aethiopicus. e, Potamochoerus porcus. f, Phacochoerus africanus.

No. 1934, 8m — Zebras: a, Two Equus quagga boehmi with heads pointed to left. b, Two Equus quagga burchellii standing. c, Three Equus quagga burchellii. d, Two Equus quagga crawshayi. e, Two Equus quagga burchellii, zebra on left on ground. f, Two Equus quagga boehmi, zebra at right facing right.

No. 1935, 8m — Squirrels: a, Heliosciurus gambianus. b, Atlantoxerus getulus. c, Funisciurus isabella. d, Funisciurus pyrropus. e, Funisciurus substriatus. f, Geosciurus princeps.

No. 1936, 8m — Elephants (Loxodonta africana): a, Juvenile at left with trunk raised, adult at right. b, Adult at left, juvenile at right facing right. c, Adult facing right. d, Adult facing left. e, Juvenile at left with trunk down, adult at right. f, Adult at left, juvenile at right facing forward.

No. 1937, 20m — Peonies: a, Paeonia lactiflora and Paeonia moutan. b, Paeonia albiflora and Paeonia foemina. c, Paeonia peregrina and Paeonia moutan. d, Paeonia moutan and Paeonia tenuifolia. e, Paeonia nezhnyi and Paeonia officinalis. f, Paeonia arborea and Paeonia mascula.

No. 1938, 20m — Tropical birds and plants: a, Apaloderma vittatum, Sesuvium portulacastrum. b, Corythaeola cristata, Premna leucostoma. c, Lybius bidentatus, Ehretia rigida. d, Ceyx picta, Tamarind. e, Trachyphonus erythrocephalus, Pterocarpus indicus. f, Indicator indicator, Dracaena fragrans.

No. 1939, 20m — Pigeons: a, Columba arquatrix on branch that extends to right. b, Columba guinea. c, Streptopelia senegalensis on bare branch. d, Streptopelia senegalensis on branch with foliage. e, Columba livia. f, Columba arquatrix on branch that extends to bottom.

No. 1940, 20m — Rabbits and hares: a, Oryctolagus cuniculus, three paws visible. b, Poelagus rupestris, four paws visible. c, Poelagus marjorita. d, Lepus capensis. e, Oryctolagus cuniculus, two paws visible. f, Poelagus rupestris, two paws visible.

No. 1941, 20m — Wild dogs and hyenas: a, Crocuta crocuta. b, Hyaena brunnea. c, Hyaena hyaena facing right. d, Lycaon pictus. e, Proteles cristata. f, Hyaena hyaena facing left.

No. 1942, 20m — Wild cats: a, Acinonyx jubatus. b, Panthera leo. c, Leptailurus serval. d, Profelis aurata. e, Panthera pardus. f, Felis caracal.

No. 1943, 20m — Aardvarks (Orycteropus afer): a, Facing right, tail extending to left of "2." b, Facing left, tip of ear at left under "c" of "Orycteropus." c, Facing right, tip of tail below "20." d, Facing left, snout in air, tip of ear at left under "p" of "Orycteropus." e, Facing right, tip of tail under decimal point in denomination. f, Facing left, snout on ground, tip of ear at left under "p" of "Orycteropus."

No. 1944, 20m — Bats: a, Two Rousettus aegyptiacus, bat at right with wing tip under last "0" in denomination. b, Two Rousettus aegyptiacus, bat at left hanging onto branch. c, Eidolon helvum. d, Otonycteris hemprichii. e, Two Rousettus aegyptiacus hanging onto branches. f, Barbastella barbastellus.

No. 1945, 20m — Rhinoceroses: a, Ceratotherium simum facing left. b, Diceros bicornis facing left, with all legs on ground. c, Ceratotherium simum facing right. d, Diceros bicornis with front legs raised. e, Ceratotherium simum facing forward. f, Diceros bicornis facing right.

No. 1946, 20m — Antelopes and gazelles: a, Tragelaphus buxtoni. b, Taurotragus derbianus. c, Kobus megaceros. d, Damaliscus lunatus. e, Alcelaphus buselaphus. f, Connochaetes gnou.

No. 1947, 33m — Marine birds: a, Morus capensis. b, Rynchops flavirostris. c, Thalasseus bergii. d, Sterna dougallii. e, Larus dominicanus. f, Leucophaeus pipixcan.

No. 1948, 33m — Parrots: a, Psittacus erithacus. b, Agapornis nigrigenis. c, Psittacula krameri. d, Agapornis personatus. e, Poicephalus gulielmi. f, Poicephalus senegalus.

No. 1949, 33m — Birds of prey: a, Circaetus gallicus. b, Terathopius ecaudatus. c, Melierax metabates. d, Melierax canorus. e, Pandion haliatetus, f, Elanus caeruleus.

No. 1950, 33m — Hippopotami (Hippopotamus amphibius): a, Juvenile at left, adult at right with mouth open. b, Adult at left with mouth open, juvenile at right. c, Juvenile at left, adult at right with mouth closed. d, Adult and juvenile facing right. e, Adult. f, Adult at left facing forward, juvenile at right facing right.

No. 1951, 33m — Pangolins: a, Phataginus tricuspis in ball and facing right. b, Manis gigantea facing right. c, Manis gigantea facing left. d, Uromanis tetradactyla. e, Smutsia temminckii. f, Phataginus tricuspis on branch.

No. 1952, 33m — Seals and sea lions: a, Mirounga leonina. b, Gray Monachus monachus, head at left, denomination at right. c, Monachus monachus, denomination at left. d, Brown Monachus monachus, denomination at right. e, Gray Monachus monachus, head at upper right, denomination at left. f, Hydrurga leptonyx.

No. 1953, 33m — Dolphins: a, Delphinus delphis. b, Tursiops truncatus. c, Grampus griseus. d, Stenella coeruleoalba, denomination at right. e, Stenella coeruleoalba, denomination at left. f, Delphinus capensis.

No. 1954, 33m — Whales: a, Eubalaena australis. b, Balaenoptera musculus, denomination at right. c, Caperea marginata. d, Kogia simus, Kogia breviceps. e, Balaenoptera musculus, denomination at left. f, Balaenoptera edeni.

No. 1955, 33m — Monkeys: a, Piliocolobus kirkii. b, Colobus angolensis. c, Cercopithecus solatus. d, Papio cynocephalus. e, Cercocebus torquatus. f, Cercopithecus denti.

No. 1956, 33m — Orchids: a, Neobenthamia gracilis. b, Aeranga distincta. c, Disa cardinalis. d, Mystacidium venosum. e, Phalaenopsis equestris. f, Vanda luzonica.

No. 1957, 33m — Volcanoes: a, Cattle near volcanoes. b, Lava tunnel. c, Robot exploring volcano. d, Mt. Vesuvius, Italy. e, Volcanic island. f, Sadiman Volcano, Tanzania, God-dess Pélé.

No. 1958, 33m — Global warming: a, Iceberg, Ursus maritimus. b, Haliaeetus vocifer, smokestacks. c, Panthera tigris sumatrae, forest fire. d, Sterna paradisaea, iceberg. e, Pandion haliaetus, smokestacks. f, Canis rufus, forest fire.

No. 1959, 175m, Giraffa camelopardalis, diff. No. 1960, 175m, Potamochoerus porcus, diff. No. 1961, 175m, Equus quagga boehmi, diff. No. 1962, 175m, Heliosciurus rufobrachium, Funisciurus lemniscatus. No. 1963, 175m, Three Loxodonta africana. No. 1964, 175m, Paeonia tenuifolia. No. 1965, 175m, Vidua paradisaea, Dracaena fragrans. No. 1966, 175m, Columba livia, diff. No. 1967, 175m, Pronolagus randensis. No. 1968, 175m, Lycaon pictus, diff. No. 1969, 175m, Panthera leo, diff. No. 1970, 175m, Orycteropus afer, diff. No. 1971, 175m, Eidolon helvum, diff. No. 1972, 175m, Ceratotherium simum, diff. No. 1973, 175m, Syncerus caffer. No. 1974, 175m, Pelecanus rufescens. No. 1975, 175m, Psittacus erithacus, diff. No. 1976, 175m, Haliaeetus vocifer, diff. No. 1977, 175m, Hippopotamus amphibius, diff. No. 1978, 175m, Smutsia gigantea. No. 1979, 175m, Hydrurga leptonyx, diff. No. 1980, 175m, Delphinus delphis, diff. No. 1981, 175m, Megaptera novaeangliae. No. 1982, 175m, Theropithecus gelada, Mandrillus sphinx. No. 1983, 175m, Dendrobium gonzalesii. No. 1984, 175m, Piton de la Fournaise Volcano, Reunion. No. 1985, 175m, Copenhagen Congress Center, Little Mermaid Statue, Copenhagen.

2010, Jan. 30 ***Perf. 13¼x12¾***

Sheets of 6, #a-f

1932-1958 A413 Set of 27 300.00 300.00

Souvenir Sheets

Perf. 12¾x13¼

1959-1985 A413 Set of 27 375.00 375.00

Miniature Sheet

2010 World Cup Soccer Championships, South Africa — A414

No. 1986 — Soccer players wearing: a, Dark blue shirt, orange shirt. b, Pink shirt, Light green shirt. c, Lilac shirt, light blue shirt. d, Red shirt, white shirt.

2010, Mar. 31 ***Perf. 13¼x13***

1986 A414 33m Sheet of 4, #a-d 10.50 10.50

Sports — A415

No. 1987, 8m — 2010 World Cup venues, South Africa: a, Green Point Stadium, Cape Town. b, Nelson Mandela Bay Stadium, Port Elizabeth. c, Ellis Park Stadium, Johannesburg. d, Free State Stadium, Mangaung-Bloemfontein. e, Soccer City Stadium, Johannesburg. f, Royal Bafokeng Stadium, Rustenburg.

No. 1988, 20m — 2010 Men's Winter Olympic Gold Medalists: a, Alexei Grishin, Freestyle skiing aerials. b, Felix Loch, Luge. c, Bill Demong, Large hill Nordic combined skiing. d, Jung-Su Lee, 1500-meter short-track speed skating. e, Jon Montgomery, Skeleton. f, Jasey Jay Anderson, Snowboard.

No. 1989, 20m — 2010 Women's Winter Olympic Gold Medalists: a, Lydia Lassila, Freestyle skiing aerials (incorrectly inscribed Alexei Grishin). b, Canadian team, Ice hockey. c, Amy Williams, Skeleton. d, Tatjana Huefner, Luge. e, Nicolien Sauerbreij, Snowboard. f, Martina Sablikova, 3000- and 5000-meter long track speed skating.

No. 1990, 20m — Female Table Tennis players: a, Wang Nan, denomination at left. b, Zhang Yining, denomination at right. c, Zhang Yining, denomination at left. d, Guo Yue. e, Li Xiaoxia. f, Wang Nan, denomination at right.

No. 1991, 20m — Female Cyclists: a, Linda Villumsen. b, Marianne Vos. c, Nicole Cooke. d, Victoria Pendleton. e, Simona Krupeckaite. f, Jeannie Longo.

No. 1992, 20m — Female Chess players: a, Antoaneta Stefanova. b, Xu Yuhua. c, Pia Cramling. d, Alexandra Kosteniuk. e, Viktorija Cmilyte. f, Judit Polgar.

No. 1993, 33m — Male Chess players: a, Garry Kasparov. b, Viswanathan Anand. c, Vasily Smyslov. d, Bobby Fischer. e, Anatoly Karpov. f, Veselin Topalov.

No. 1994, 33m — Male Table Tennis players: a, Wang Hao. b, Ma Lin, denomination at right. c, Ma Lin, denomination at left. d, Jorg Rosskopf. e, Wang Liqin. f, Jean-Philippe Gatien.

No. 1995, 33m — 2010 Men's Winter Olympic Gold Medalists: a, Didier Defago, Downhill skiing. b, Evgeny Ustyugov, 15-kilometer biathlon. c, Andre Lange and Kevin Kuske, two-man bobsled. d, Petter Northug, 50-kilometer cross-country skiing. e, Canadian team, Curling. f, Evan Lysacek, Figure skating.

No. 1996, 33m — 2010 Women's Winter Olympic Gold Medalists: a, Maria Riesch, Slalom and Super Combined skiing. b, Magdalena Neuner, 10-kilometer biathlon. c, Kaillie Humphries and Heather Moyse, bobsled. d, Justyna Kowalczyk, 30-kilometer cross-country skiing. e, Kim Yu-Na, Figure skating. f, Canadian team, Curling.

No. 1997, 33m — Golfers: a, Angel Cabrera. b, Padraig Harrington. c, Vijay Singh. d, Tiger Woods. e, Phil Mickelson. f, Ernie Els.

No. 1998, 33m — Tennis players: a, Dinara Safina. b, Caroline Wozniacki. c, Roger Federer wearing blue shirt. d, Rafael Nadal. e, Novak Djokovic. f, Serena Williams.

No. 1999, 33m — Baseball players: a, Ichiro Suzuki. b, Doug Mientkiewicz. c, Hideo Nomo. d, Ryan Franklin. e, Nomar Garciaparra. f, Adam Everett.

No. 2000, 33m — Ice Hockey players: a, Alexander Ovechkin. b, Sidney Crosby. c, Teemu Selanne. d, Steve Yzerman. e, Mats Sundin. f, Mario Lemieux.

No. 2001, 33m — Male Cyclists: a, Cadel Evans. b, Jan Ullrich. c, Bernard Hinault. d, Mario Cipollini. e, Marco Pantani. f, Miguel Indurain.

No. 2002, 33m — Judo: a, Alina Alexandra Dumitru. b, Ole Bischof. c, Tong Wen. d, Irakli Tsirekidze. e, Masae Ueno. f, Kosei Inoue.

No. 2003, 33m — Taekwondo: a, Cha Dong-Min. b, Guillermo Perez. c, Hadi Saei. d, Lim Su-Jeong. e, Maria Espinoza. f, Son Tae-Jin.

No. 2004, 33m — Polo players: a, Hilario Ulloa. b, Bartolomé Castagnola. c, Juan Martin Nero. d, Gonzalo Pieres. e, Nacho Figueras. f, Charles, Prince of Wales.

No. 2005, 33m — Horse racing: a, Horse #14 and rival horse. b, Horses #8 and #10. c, Horse #2. d, Horse #3. e, Horse #9 and rival horse. f, Horses #4 and #1.

No. 2006, 33m — Dog racing: a, Dog #9. b, Dog #8. c, Dog without visible number. d, Dogs #3 and #4. e, Dog #2. f, Dog #6.

No. 2007, 33m — Rugby players: a, Richie McCaw. b, Matt Giteau. c, Sergio Parisse. d, Bryan Habana. e, Victor Matfield. f, Juan Smith.

No. 2008, 33m — African soccer players: a, Player with orange shirt. b, Player with blue shirt. c, Player #17 in red shirt, player #19 in white shirt. d, Player #15 in white shirt, player in red shirt. e, Player #8 in red shirt, player #20 in blue green shirt. f, Player #5 in orange shirt, player in white shirt.

No. 2009, 33m — Soccer players: a, Samuel Eto'o. b, Kaka. c, Cesc Fabregas. d, Wayne Rooney. e, Cristiano Ronaldo. f, Lionel Messi wearing #70 on pants.

No. 2010, 33m — Lionel Messi, soccer player, dribbling soccer ball, and wearing: a, Red shirt with wide blue vertical stripe in center, at left. b, Red and blue vertically striped shirt with wide stripes, at right. c, Dark blue shirt with white trim, at left. d, Horizontally striped shirt, at right. e, Light blue shirt, at left. f, Red and blue vertically striped shirt with narrow stripes, at right.

No. 2011, 33m — Roger Federer, tennis player, with two images: a, Wearing black shirt at left, white shirt at right. b, Black shirt with blue trim at left and right. c, White shirt at left, red shirt at right. d, White shirt at left, black shirt at right. e, White shirt at left and right. f, Black shirt at left, red shirt at right.

No. 2012, 33m — Alberto Contador, cyclist, on bicycle at left, and wearing, at right: a, White shirt with blue trim. b, Yellow shirt with collar buttoned. c, Yellow shirt with open collar. d, White shirt with blue and red trim. e, Yellow shirt and blue cap. f, Yellow shirt and cap, sunglasses on cap.

No. 2013, 33m — Valentino Rossi, motorcyclist: a, Wearing blue racing uniform at left, on motorcycle at right. b, On motorcycle at left, wearing green racing uniform at right. c, On motorcycle, facing right. d, On motorcycle, facing left. e, On motorcycle at left, wearing yellow sun visor at right. f, Wearing horizontally striped shirt at left, on motorcycle at right.

No. 2014, 175m, Loftus Versfeld Stadium, Tshwane-Pretoria. No. 2015, 175m, Mark Tuitert, 1500-meter long track speed skating gold medalist. No. 2016, 175m, Torah Bright, Halfpipe gold medalist. No. 2017, 175m, Guo Yue, diff. No. 2018, 175m, Jeannie Longo, diff. No. 2019, 175m, Alexandra Kosteniuk, diff. No. 2020, 175m, Vasily Smyslov, diff. No. 2021, 175m, Wang Liqin, diff. No. 2022, 175m, Evgeny Ustygov, diff. No. 2023, 175m, Marit Bjoergen, Individual sprint and cross-country skiing gold medalist. No. 2024, 175m, Tiger Woods, diff. No. 2025, 175m, Roger Federer (one image), diff. No. 2026, 175m, Ken Griffey, Jr., baseball player. No. 2027, 175m, Wayne Gretzky, hockey player. No. 2028, 175m, Lance Armstrong, cyclist. No. 2029, 175m, Choi Min-Ho, judo. No. 2030, 175m, Wu Jingyu, taekwondo. No. 2031, 175m, Pablo MacDonough, polo player. No. 2032, 175m, Two race horses. No. 2033, 175m, Dog #8, diff. No. 2034, 175m, Shane Williams, rugby player. No. 2035, 175m, Soccer players wearing red and white shirts. No. 2036, 175m, Didier Drogba, soccer player. No. 2037, 175m, Messi, diff. No. 2038, 175m, Federer (two images), diff. No. 2039, 175m, Contador, diff. No. 2040, Rossi, diff.

2010, Mar. 30 ***Perf. 13¼x12¾***

Sheets of 6, #a-f

1987-2013 A415 Set of 27 375.00 375.00

Souvenir Sheets

Perf. 12¾x13¼

2014-2040 A415 Set of 27 375.00 375.00

Mozambique Airlines, 30th Anniv. — A416

Denominations: 8m, 20m, 33m.

2010, Apr. 14 ***Perf. 11x11¼***

2041-2043 A416 Set of 3 4.75 4.75

Rock Art — A417

No. 2044: a, Rock art, Tanum, Sweden (38x39mm). b, Altamira cave drawings, Spain (50x39mm). c, Nazca Lines, Peru (38x39mm). d, Rock art, Tadrart Acacus, Libya (38x39mm). e, Vézère Valley Caves rock art, France (50x39mm). f, Ubirr National Park rock art, Australia (38x39mm).

175m, Altamira cave drawing, Spain.

2010, June 30 **Litho.** ***Perf. 13x13¼***

2044 A417 8m Sheet of 6, #a-f 3.75 3.75

Souvenir Sheet

Perf. 13¼ Syncopated

2045 A417 175m multi 13.50 13.50

No. 2045 contains one 50x39mm stamp.

French Castles — A418

No. 2046 — Castle at: a, Chenonceau (38x39mm). b, Berzé (50x39mm). c, Montaner (38x39mm). d, Chaumont (38x39mm). e, Amboise (50x39mm). f, Brissac (38x39mm).

175m, Chambord Castle.

2010, June 30 ***Perf. 13x13¼***

2046 A418 33m Sheet of 6, #a-f 15.50 15.50

Souvenir Sheet

Perf. 13¼ Syncopated

2047 A418 175m multi 13.50 13.50

No. 2047 contains one 50x39mm stamp.

Bridges — A419

No. 2048: a, Beipanjiang Railroad Bridge, Guizhou, People's Republic of China (38x39mm). b, Sydney Harbour Bridge (50x39mm). c, Apollo Bridge, Bratislava, Slovakia (38x39mm). d, Millau Viaduct, Millau, France (38x39mm). e, Tsing Ma Bridge, Hong Kong (50x39mm). f, Coronado Bridge, San Diego, California (38x39mm).

175m, Tower Bridge, London.

2010, June 30 ***Perf. 13x13¼***

2048 A419 33m Sheet of 6, #a-f 15.50 15.50

Souvenir Sheet

Perf. 13¼ Syncopated

2049 A419 175m multi 13.50 13.50

No. 2049 contains one 50x39mm stamp.

UNESCO World Heritage Sites — A420

No. 2050, 20m — Sites in Africa: a, Rock-hewn church, Lalibela, Ethiopia (38x39mm). b, Great Zimbabwe National Monument (50x39mm). c, Old towns of Djenné, Mali (38x39mm). d, Stone Circles of Senegambia, Gambia and Senegal (38x39mm). e, Timgad, Algeria (50x39mm). f, Carthage, Tunisia (38x39mm).

No. 2051, 20m — Sites in South America: a, Tiwanaku, Bolivia (38x39mm). b, Sacsayhuamán, Cuzco, Peru (50x39mm). c, Chan Chan, Peru (38x39mm). d, Rapa Nui, Chile (38x39mm). e, Machu Picchu, Peru (50x39mm). f, Jesuit Block and Estancias of Cordoba, Argentina (38x39mm).

No. 2052, 20m — Sites in Asia: a, Kathmandu Valley, Nepal (38x39mm). b, Buddhist ruins, Takht-i-Bati, Pakistan (50x39mm). c, Horyu-ji, Japan (38x39mm). d, Nemrut Dag, Turkey (38x39mm). e, Mogao Caves, People's Republic of China (50x39mm). f, Orkhon Valley Cultural Landscape, Mongolia (38x39mm).

No. 2053, 20m — Sites in Europe: a, Olympia, Greece (38x39mm). b, Bend of the Boyne Archaeological Site, Ireland (50x39mm). c, Trulli of Alborello, Italy (38x39mm). d, Delos, Greece (38x39mm). e, Santiago de Compostela, Spain (50x39mm). f, Paphos, Cyprus (38x39mm).

No. 2054, 33m — Sites in Africa: a, Osun-Osogbo Sacred Grove, Nigeria (38x39mm). b, Carthage, Tunisia, diff. (50x39mm). c, Gorée Island, Senegal (38x39mm). d, El Jem Amphitheater, Tunisia (38x39mm). e, Dougga, Tunisia (50x39mm). f, Gebel Barkal, Sudan (38x39mm).

No. 2055, 33m — Sites in Africa: a, Cyrene, Libya (38x39mm). b, Leptis Magna, Libya (50x39mm). c, Aksum, Ethiopia (38x39mm). d, Dougga, Tunisia, diff (38x39mm). e, Sabratha, Libya (50x39mm). f, Thebes, Egypt (38x39mm).

No. 2056, 33m — Sites in North America: a, Palenque, Mexico (38x39mm). b, Uxmal, Mexico (50x39mm). c, Mesa Verde National Park, U.S. (38x39mm). d, Mayan Ruins of Copan, Honduras (38x39mm). e, Teotihuacan, Mexico (50x39mm). f, Chichen-Itza, Mexico (38x39mm).

No. 2057, 33m — Sites in South America: a, Historic Center of Santa Ana de los Ríos de Cuenca, Ecuador (38x39mm). b, Machu Picchu, Peru, diff. (50x39mm). c, Rapa Nui, Chile, diff. (38x39mm). d, Tiwanaku, Bolivia, diff. (38x39mm). e, Rapa Nui, Chile, diff. (50x39mm). f, Sacsayhuamán, Cuzco, Peru, diff. (38x39mm).

No. 2058, 33m — Sites in Asia: a, Palmyra, Syria (38x39mm). b, Persepolis, Iran (50x39mm). c, Ruins of the Buddhist Vihara, Bangladesh (38x39mm). d, Nemrut Dag, Turkey, diff. (38x39mm). e, Tyre, Lebanon (50x39mm). f, Prambanan Temples, Indonesia (38x39mm).

No. 2059, 33m — Sites in Asia: a, Koguryo Tombs, North Korea (38x39mm). b, Palmyra, Syria, diff. (50x39mm). c, Polonnaruwa, Sri Lanka (38x39mm). d, Ayutthaya, Thailand (38x39mm). e, Bosra, Syria (50x39mm). f, Borobudur, Indonesia (38x39mm).

No. 2060, 33m — Sites in Europe: a, Grand-Place, Belgium (38x39mm). b, Historic Center of Rome, Italy (50x39mm). c, Rila Monastery, Bulgaria (38x39mm). d, Gardens and Castle at Kromeríz, Czech Republic (38x39mm). e, Piazza del Duomo, Pisa, Italy (50x39mm). f, Acropolis, Athens, Greece. (38x39mm).

No. 2061, 33m — Sites in Europe: a, Paphos Castle, Cyprus, diff. (38x39mm). b, Roman Monuments, Arles, France (50x39mm). c, Las Médulas, Spain (38x39mm). d, Megalithic Temples of Malta (38x39mm). e, Pont du Gard, France (50x39mm). f, Segovia Aqueduct, Spain (38x39mm).

No. 2062, 175m, Abu Simbel Temple, Egypt. No. 2063, 175m, Volubilis, Morocco. No. 2064, 175m, Sabratha, Libya, diff. No. 2065, 175m, Monte Albán, Mexico. No. 2066, 175m, Sacsayhuamán, Cuzco, Peru, diff. No. 2067, 175m, Rapa Nui, Chile, diff. No. 2068, 175m, Sanchi Buddhist Monuments, India. No. 2069, 175m, Lakshmana Temple, Khajuraho Group of Monuments, India. No. 2070, 175m, Lesahn Giant Buddha, People's Republic of China. No. 2071, 175m, Mérida, Archaeological Complex, Spain. No. 2072, 175m, Pompeii, Italy. No. 2073, 175m, Olympia, Greece, diff.

2010, June 30 ***Perf. 13x13¼***

Sheets of 6, #a-f

2050-2061 A420 Set of 12 160.00 160.00

Souvenir Sheets

Perf. 13¼ Syncopated

2062-2073 A420 Set of 12 162.50 162.50

Nos. 2062-2073 each contain one 50x39mm stamp.

Museums and Art — A421

No. 2074, 20m — Museum of Modern Art, New York, and work of art by: a, Terry Winters (38x39mm). b, Lisa Yuskavage (50x39mm). c, Ken Price (38x39mm). d, Philip Guston (38x39mm). e, Vincent van Gogh (50x39mm). f, Robert Colescott (38x39mm).

No. 2075, 33m — Metropolitan Museum of Art, New York, and work of art by: a, Bernhard Strigel (38x39mm). b, Johannes Vermeer (50x39mm). c, Thomas Couture (38x39mm). d, Jean Baptiste Greuze (38x39mm). e, Giovanni Bellini (50x39mm). f, Adolphe-William Bouguereau (38x39mm).

No. 2076, 33m — Prado Museum, Madrid, and work of art by: a, Diego Velázquez (38x39mm). b, Francisco de Goya (50x39mm). c, Fra Angelico (38x39mm). d, Hieronymus Bosch (38x39mm). e, Bernaert van Orley (50x39mm). f, Raphael (38x39mm).

No. 2077, 33m — Uffizi Gallery (Galeria dos Ofícios), Florence, Italy, and work of art by: a, Fra Filippo Lippi (38x39mm). b, Leonardo da Vinci (50x39mm). c, Andrea del Verrocchio (38x39mm). d, Sandro Botticelli (38x39mm). e, Giovanni Bellini (50x39mm). f, Raphael (38x39mm).

No. 2078, 33m — Orsay Museum, Paris, and work of art by: a, Claude Monet (38x39mm). b, Paul Signac (50x39mm). c, Edgar Degas (38x39mm). d, Paul Gauguin (38x39mm). e, Berthe Morisot (50x39mm). f, Vincent van Gogh (38x39mm).

No. 2079, 33m — Louvre Museum, Paris, and work of art by: a, Michelangelo Merisi da Caravaggio (38x39mm). b, Hyacinthe Rigaud (50x39mm). c, Quentin Massys (38x39mm). d, Nicolas Poussin (38x39mm). e, Johannes Vermeer (50x39mm). f, Rogier van der Weyden (38x39mm).

No. 2080, 33m — National Gallery, London, and work of art by: a, Antonello da Messina (38x39mm). b, Jan van Eyck (50x39mm). c, Raphael (38x39mm). d, Thomas Gainsborough (38x39mm). e, Hans Holbein the Younger (50x39mm). f, Joseph Mallord William Turner (38x39mm).

No. 2081, 33m — National Museum, Amsterdam, and work of art by: a, Pieter Saenredam (38x39mm). b, Pieter Aertsen (50x39mm). c, Pieter de Hooch (38x39mm). d, Floris van Dijck (38x39mm). e, Jan van Scorel (50x39mm). f, Frans Hals (38x39mm).

No. 2082, 33m — Kunsthistorisches Museum, Vienna, and work of art by: a, Lucas Cranach the Elder (38x39mm). b, Jan Steen (50x39mm). c, Giuseppe Arcimboldo (Fogo, 1566) (38x39mm). d, Arcimboldo (Agua, 1566) (38x39mm). e, Pieter Bruegel the Elder (50x39mm). f, Giorgione (38x39mm).

No. 2083, 33m — Alte Pinakothek, Munich, and work of art by: a, Frans Hals (38x39mm). b, Fritz Schider (50x39mm). c, Hans Wertinger (38x39mm). d, Juan Pantoja de la Cruz (38x39mm). e, Philips Koninck (50x39mm). f, Jean Baptiste Siméon Chardin (38x39mm).

No. 2084, 33m — Gemäldegalerie, Berlin, and work of art by: a, Albrecht Dürer (38x39mm). b, Konrad Witz (50x39mm). c, Rogier van der Weyden (38x39mm). d, Raphael (38x39mm). e, Andrea Mantegna (50x39mm). f, Martin Schongauer (38x39mm).

No. 2085, 33m — Pushkin Museum of Fine Arts, Moscow, and work of art by: a, Maurice de Vlaminck (38x39mm). b, Jan Gossaert (50x39mm). c, Albert Marquet (38x39mm). d, Edgar Degas (38x39mm). e, Gustave Courbet (50x39mm). f, André Derain (38x39mm).

No. 2086, 33m — Hermitage State Museum, St. Petersburg, and work of art by: a, Thomas Gainsborough (38x39mm). b, Pieter Hendricksz de Hooch (50x39mm). c, Leonardo da Vinci (38x39mm). d, Paul Cézanne (38x39mm). e, Louis Le Nain (50x39mm). f, Unknown Egyptian sculptor (38x39mm).

No. 2087, 175m, Museum of Modern Art, work of art by Marlene Dumas. No. 2088, 175m, Metropolitan Museum of Art, work of art by Hokusai. No. 2089, 175m, Prado Museum, work of art by Bartolomé Esteban Murillo. No. 2090, 175m, Uffizi Gallery (Galeria dos Ofícios), work of art by Agnolo Bronzino. No. 2091, 175m, Orsay Museum, work of art by Maurice Denis. No. 2092, 175m, Louvre Museum, work of art by Jan van Eyck. No. 2093, 175m, National Gallery, London, work of art by William Hogarth. No. 2094, 175m, National Museum, Amsterdam, work of art by Rembrandt. No. 2095, 175m, Kunsthistorisches Museum, work of art by Pieter Bruegel the Elder. No. 2096, 175m, Alte Pinakothek, work of art by Gerard ter Borch. No. 2097, 175m, Gemäldegalerie, work of art by Hans Holbein the Younger. No. 2098, 175m, Pushkin Museum of Fine Arts, work of art by Paul Cézanne. No. 2099, 175m, Hermitage State Museum, work of art by Vincent van Gogh.

2010, June 30 ***Perf. 13x13¼***

Sheets of 6, #a-f

2074-2086 A421 Set of 13 195.00 195.00

Souvenir Sheets

Perf. 13¼ Syncopated

2087-2099 A421 Set of 13 175.00 175.00

Nos. 2087-2099 each contain one 50x39mm stamp.

Association of Portuguese-Speaking Postal and Telecommunications Organizations, 20th Anniv. — A422

2010, Nov. 10 **Litho.** ***Perf. 11x11½***

2100 A422 92m multi 7.25 7.25

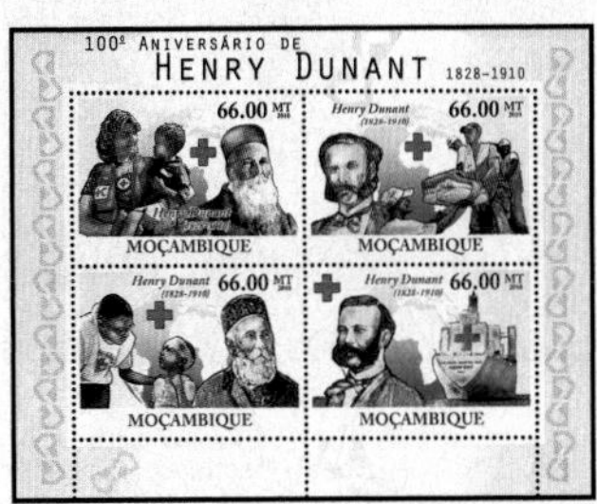

People, Anniversaries and Events — A423

No. 2101, 66m — Jean-Henri Dunant (1828-1910), founder of Red Cross, world map, Red Cross and: a, Red Cross nurse holding child. b, Red Cross workers moving supplies. c, Red Cross worker tending to injured child. d, U.S. Naval Hospital Ship Comfort.

No. 2102, 66m — Katharine Hepburn (1907-2003), actress, and scene from: a, Sea of Grass, 1947. b, Mary of Scotland, 1936. c, A Woman Rebels, 1936. d, The Philadelphia Story, 1940.

No. 2103, 66m — Jonh Lennon (1940-80), singer, and: a, Beatles, peace sign. b, Yoko Ono, protest sign. c, Yoko Ono, guitar. d, Cat.

No. 2104, 66m — Lech Kaczynski (1949-2010), President of Poland, Polish flag, and: a, Wife, Maria, and heraldic eagle. b, Pope Benedict XVI. c, Tupelov Tu-154M. d, Wife, Maria.

No. 2105, 66m — Vasily Smyslov (1921-2010), chess player, and chess board with: a, Brown red squares. b, Blue gray squares. c, Dark blue squares, cat. d, Gray squares.

No. 2106, 66m — Marshall Warren Nirenberg (1927-2010), biochemist, and: a, Macrolepiota procerea. b, Boletus luidus. c, Agaricus albus. d, Agaricus nitidus.

No. 2107, 66m — Tsutomu Yamaguchi (1916-2010), survivor of Hiroshima and Nagasaki nuclear blasts, and: a, Mushroom cloud. b, Enola Gay over Hiroshima. c, Ruins of Hiroshima. d, Mushroom cloud, statue.

No. 2108, 66m — Republic of India, 60th anniv.: a, Mother Teresa, crowd, Hindu god Ganesh. b, Statue of Ganesh, people bathing in the Ganges River. c, Cow, Taj Mahal, mangos. d, Lotus flowers, Bengal tiger.

No. 2109, 66m — Armand Razafindratandra (1925-2010), Archbishop of Antananarivo, Madagascar, and: a, St. Peter's Basilica, cross on rosary. b, Church in Madagascar. c, St. Peter's Square. d, Pope John Paul II.

No. 2110, 66m — 2010 Visit of Pope Benedict XVI to Portugal: a, Pope, cardinals. b, Pope, Papal arms. c, Pope, crowd. d, Pope waving from balcony.

No. 2111, 66m — Paintings of Johannes Vermeer (1632-1675): a, Milkmaid, 1660, and Lacemaker, 1669. b, View of Delft, 1660-61, and Girl with a Pearl Earring, 1675. c, The Art of Painting (detail), 1673, painting of a city. d, The Girl with a Wine Glass, 1659-60, The Astronomer, 1668.

No. 2112, 66m — Mask paintings of James Ensor (1860-1949) from: a, 1892, 1925-29. b, 1898, 1892. c, 1888, 1927. d, 1892, 1908.

No. 2113, 175m, Dunant, world map, Red Cross flag. No. 2114, 175m, Hepburn, scene from The Iron Petticoat, 1956. No. 2115, 175m. Lennon and Yoko Ono, diff. No. 2116, 175m, Kaczynski, cross. No. 2117, 175m, Smyslov, chessboard. No. 2118, 175m, Nirenberg, Cortinarius torvus, diagram of ribonucleic acid molecule. No. 2119, 175m, Yamaguchi, mushroom cloud. No. 2120, 175m, Mohandas K. Gandhi, Indian flag, Nelumbo nucifera. No. 2121, 175m, Razafindratandra, arms. No. 2122, 175m, Pope Benedict XVI, crowd, diff. No. 2123, 175m, The Procuress, 1656, and Girl with a Red Hat, 1666, by Vermeer. No. 2124, 175m, Mask paintings from 1890 and 1888 by Ensor.

2010, Nov. 30 ***Perf. 12¾x13½***

Sheets of 4, #a-d

2101-2112 A423 Set of 12 250.00 250.00

Souvenir Sheets

Perf. 13¼ Syncopated

2113-2124 A423 Set of 12 162.50 162.50

Nos. 2113-2124 each contain one 50x39mm stamp.

People, Anniversaries and Events — A424

No. 2125 — 70th birthday of Pelé, wearing New York Cosmos soccer jersey: a, 16m, And jacket with green collar, denomination at UR. b, 16m, Dribbling ball, denomination at UR. c, 16m, Scissor kicking, denomination at UL. d, 66m, Playing against players in green and yellow jerseys. e, 66m, Playing against player in blue, white and green uniforms. f, 66m, Playing against player in blue, orange and white uniforms.

No. 2126 — Athletes of Ninth South American Games: a, 16m, Yari Alvear. b, 16m, Facundo Argüello. c, 16m, Gustavo Tsuboi. d, 66m, Betsi Rivas. e, 66m, Mariana Pajon Londoño. f, 66m, Myke Carvalho.

No. 2127 — Princess Diana (1961-97) and: a, 16m, Tower Bridge, London. b, 16m, London Eye. sons William and Harry. c, 16m, Buckingham Palace. d, 66m, Houses of Parliament, sons William and Harry. e, 66m, Arms and British flag. f, 66m, St. Paul's Cathedral, Mother Teresa.

No. 2128 — Wedding of Prince William and Catherine Middleton: a, 16m, Windsor Castle, Prince William, Catherine Middleton. b, 16m, Princes William and Harry, Buckingham Palace. c, 16m, Palace of Westminster, Prince William, Catherine Middleton. d, 66m, Prince William, map of Great Britain. e, 66m, Prince William, Catherine Middleton, Princess Diana. f, 66m, Prince William, Catherine Middleton, Westminster Abbey.

No. 2129 — Alfred Hitchcock (1899-1988), movie director, and scene from: a, 16m, Vertigo, 1958. b, 16m, Dial M for Murder, 1954. c, 16m, Spellbound, 1945. d, 66m, Rear Window, 1954. e, 66m, Rebecca, 1940. f, 66m, The Birds, 1963.

No. 2130 — Japanese high-speed trains: a, 16m, Joetsu Shinkansen E4 Max Toki. b, 16m, Tohoku Akita Shinkansen Komachi. c, 16m, Nagano Shinkansen E2 Asama. d, 66m, Tokaido Shinkansen 700 Nozomi. e, 66m, Tokaido Shinkansen 500 Nozomi. f, 66m, Tokaido Shinkansen N700 Nozomi.

No. 2131 — European high-speed trains: a, 16m, ICE Bombardieer, Germany. b, 16m,

Thalys, Belgium. c, 16m, Eurostar, Great Britain. d, 66m, Eurostar, Italy. e, 66m, 103 Velaro E Siemens, Spain. f, 66m, TGV, France.

No. 2132 — Paintings by Amedeo Modigliani (1884-1920) from: a, 16m, 1915-16 and 1898-1920. b, 16m, 1918 and 1916. c, 16m, 1917 and 1918. d, 66m, 1917 and 1898-1920. e, 66m, 1915 and 1918. f, 66m, 1909 and 1898-1920.

No. 2133 — Vitaly Sevastyanov (1935-2010), cosmonaut: a, 16m, Wearing suit and tie, with Soyuz TMA-9. b, 16m, Wearing space suit, with Soyuz TMA-18 in space. c, 16m, Wearing suit, with Soyuz TMA-18 in space. d, 66m, Wearing space suit, with Soyuz TMA-18 in space. e, 66m, Wearing suit and tie, with Soyuz TMA-9 being prepared for launch. f, 66m, Wearing suit with military medals, with Salyut 6.

No. 2134 — IKAROS experimental spacecraft: a, 16m, In space, with text over Venus. b, 16m, With H-IIA rocket lifting off. c, 16m, In space, with Venus cut off at top. d, 66m, With rocket H-IIA lifting off, diff. e, 66m, In space, with Venus partially obscured. f, 66m, Akatsuki Vesus orbiter and Earth.

No. 2135 — World development of electrical energy: a, 16m, Earth and stylized birds. b, 16m, Greek philosopher Thales. c, 16m, Silhouettes of people, clouds. d, 66m, Hand with antique map. e, 66m, Inventor Thomas Alva Edison and lightbulb. f, 66m, Chinese Premier Sun Yat-sen and dam.

No. 2136, 175m, Pelé. No. 2137, 175m, Santiago Botero, cyclist. No. 2138, 175m, Princess Diana with youths, Red Cross. No. 2139, 175m, Prince William, Catherine Middleton, engagement ring. No. 2140, 175m, Hitchcock, scene from Psycho, 1960. No. 2141, 175m, 320 kmh Shinkansen train, 2011. No. 2142, 175m, ALSTOM AGV, France. No. 2143, 175m, Paintings by Modigliani from 1919 and 1918. No. 2144, 175m, Sevastyanov and Salyut 4. No. 2145, 175m, IKAROS and H-IIA rocket lifting off, diff. No. 2146, 175m, Luigi Galvani, and diagram of his experiments with frogs.

2010, Nov. 30 ***Perf. 12¾x13½***

Sheets of 6, #a-f

2125-2135 A424 Set of 11 210.00 210.00

Souvenir Sheets

Perf. 13¼ Syncopated

2136-2146 A424 Set of 11 150.00 150.00

People, Anniversaries and Events — A425

No. 2147, 16m — New Year 2011 (Year of the Rabbit): a, Rabbit sitting, facing right, Chinese character to right or rabbit. b, Rabbit facing left, Chinese character to left of rabbit. c, Rabbit running left, Chinese character above rabbit. d, Rabbit running right, chinese character to right of rabbit, below head, text at UL. e, Rabbit with front legs raised, Chinese character to right of rabbit. f, Rabbit leaping, Chinese character below rabbit's hind legs. g, Rabbit standing, facing left, Chinese character to left of rabbit. h, Rabbit standing, facing right, Chinese character to right of rabbit, text at LR.

No. 2148, 16m — Views of Ocean Park, Hong Kong and: a, Ailurus fulgens. b, Zalophus californianus. c, Delphinus delphis. d, Ailuropoda melanoleuca. e, Ramphastos toco. f, Chrysaora fusescens. g, Phoenicopterus roseus. h, Ara ararauna.

No. 2149, 16m — 2010 Commonwealth Games, Delhi, India: a, Achanta Sharath Kamal, table tennis player. b, Allan Davis, cyclist. c, Anastasia Rodionova, tennis player. d, Christine Girard, weight lifter. e, Paddy Barnes, boxer. f, Alicia Coutts, swimmer. g, Alison Shanks, cyclist. h, Azhar Hussain, wrestler.

No. 2150 — Details from paintings by Caravaggio (1571-1610) dated: a, 16m, 1594-95 and 1593-94. b, 16m, 1600-04 and 1593-94. c, 16m, 1607-08 and 1593-94. d, 16m, 1596 and 1601. e, 16m, 1597 and 1595-96. f, 16m, 1598 and 1596-98. g, 92m, 1598-99 and 1599. h, 92m, 1603 and 1608.

No. 2151 — Tony Curtis (1925-2010), actor, and scenes from: a, 16m, Houdini, 1953. b, 16m, Son of Ali Baba, 1952. c, 16m, The Defiant Ones, 1958. d, 16m, The Black Shield of Falworth, 1954. e, 16m, The Great Race, 1965. f, 16m, Wild and Wonderful, 1964. g, 92m, Some Like it Hot, 1959. h, 92m, Sweet Smell of Success, 1957.

No. 2152 — BP Deepwater Horizon oil spill: a, 16m, Bird standing, burning oil rig. b, 16m, Turtle in net, oil boom on water, burning rig. c, 16m, Bird in flight, ships near burning rig. d, 16m, Pelican, boat with oil boom in oil slick. e, 16m, Bird with head raised in oily water. f, 16m, Ship, bird on piling, oil burning on water's surface. g, 92m, Bird, cleanup workers on beach. h, 92m, Birds, burning rig, map of Gulf of Mexico coastline.

No. 2153 — Details of religious paintings by: a, 16m, Titian, from 1535 and 1540 . b, 16m, Alessandro Botticelli, from 1490 and 1470. c, 16m, El Greco, from 1600 and 1590-95. d, 16m, Giotto, from 1295-1300 and 1304. e, 16m, Rogier van der Weyden, from 1445 and 1435-40. f, 16m, Antonio da Correggio, from 1525 and 1520. g, 92m, Piero della Francesca, from 1450-63 and 1454-69. h, 92m, Giovanni Bellini, from 1465 and 1464-68.

No. 2154, 175m, Rabbit and Chinese character, diff. No. 2155, 175m, Stegostoma fasciatum in Ocean Park tank. No. 2156, 175m, Somdev Devvarman, tennis player. No. 2157, 175m, Painting details by Caravaggio, from 1609 and 1593-94. No. 2158, 175m, Curtis, scene from movie. No. 2159, 175m, Bird in flight near burning BP Deepwater Horizon oil rig. No. 2160, 175m, Painting details by Lorenzo Lotto from 1508 and 1530.

2010, Nov. 30 ***Perf. 12¾x13½***

Sheets of 8, #a-h

2147-2153 A425 Set of 7 120.00 120.00

Souvenir Sheets

Perf. 13¼ Syncopated

2154-2160 A425 Set of 7 95.00 95.00

Intl. Year of Forests — A426

No. 2161 — Sheet inscribed "Gibao de maos brancas": a, 16m, Hylobates lar sitting on tree branch. b, 16m, Hylobates lar hanging from tree branch. c, 16m, Hylobates lar walking. d, 16m, Hylobates lar, leaves of palm tree beneath denomination. e, 66m, Hylobates lar seated. f, 66m, Hylobates lar seated on stump.

No. 2162 — Sheet inscribed "Lémur": a, 16m, Lemur catta facing left with tail raised. b, 16m, Lemur catta, tail at bottom. c, 16m, Lemur catta facing right with tail raised. d, 16m, Lemur catta with tail over shoulder. e, 66m, Lemur catta with tail around head. f, 66m, Lemur catta with tail hanging.

No. 2163 — Sheet inscribed "Preguiça": a, 16m, Choloepus didactylus. b, 16m, Bradypus pygmaeus. c, 16m, Choloepus hoffmanni. d, 16m, Bradypus variegatus. e, 66m, Choloepus hoffmanni, diff. f, 66m, Choloepus didactylus, diff.

No. 2164 — Sheet inscribed "Rinoceronte-de-sumatra": a, 16m, Dicerorhinus sumatrensis facing right with head near ground. b, 16m, Dicerorhinus sumatrensis facing right with head raised. c, 16m, Dicerorhinus sumatrensis facing left with head near ground. d, 16m, Dicerorhinus sumatrensis facing left with head raised. e, 66m, Dicerorhinus sumatrensis facing right, diff. f, 66m, Dicerorhinus sumatrensis facing left, diff.

No. 2165 — Sheet inscribed "Morcego-Vampiro": a, 16m, Desmodus rotundus facing right, in flight . b, 16m, Desmodus rotundus on rock, blue area surrounding denomination. c, 16m, Desmodus rotundus on rock, rock under "16". d, 16m, Desmodus rotundus facing left, in flight. e, 66m, Desmodus rotundus in flight, diff. f, 66m, Desmodus rotundus on rock, diff.

No. 2166 — Sheet inscribed "Jaguar": a, 16m, Panthera onca facing left on cut off tree branch. b, 16m, Panthera onca on fallen log. c, 16m, Panthera onca on grass. d, 16m, Panthera onca walking. e, 66m, Panthera onca walking, facing left. f, 66m, Panthera onca walking, facing forward.

No. 2167 — Sheet inscribed "Peixi-boi": a, 16m, Trichechus inunguis, left fin close to frame line at bottom. b, 16m, Two Trichechus senegalensis. c, 16m, One Trichechus manatus. d, 16m, Trichechus inunguis, right fin close to frame line at bottom. e, 66m, Two Trichecus manatus. f, 66m, One Trichechus senegalensis.

No. 2168 — Sheet inscribed "Harpia": a, 16m, Harpia harpyja facing right on tree branch with leaves. b, 16m, Harpia harpyja in flight near tree. c, 16m, Harpia harpyja facing left on branch without leaves. d, 16m, Harpia harpyja facing left on tree branch with leaves. e, 66m, Harpia harpyja in flight, tree in background. f, 66m, Harpia harpyja in flight, no trees in background.

No. 2169 — Sheet inscribed "Borboleta asas de pássaro": a, 16m, Ornithoptera alexandrae on leaf, name at LL. b, 16m, Ornithoptera alexandrae in flight. c, 16m, Ornithoptera alexandrae on leaf, name at UR. d, 16m, Ornithoptera alexandrae on leaf, name at UL. e, 66m, Ornithoptera alexandrae on leaf, diff. f, 66m, Ornithoptera alexandrae in flight, diff.

No. 2170 — Sheet inscribed "Borboleta azul": a, 16m, Morpho menelaus on leaf with wings closed, name at UL. b, 16m, Morpho menelaus on tree with wings open, name at UR. c, 16m, Morpho memelaus on tree with wings partially open, name at UL. d, 16m, Morpho menelaus on rock with wings open, name at LL. e, 66m, Morpho menelaus on leaf, name at UL on two lines. f, 66m, Morpho menelaus on leaf, name in UL on one line.

No. 2171 — Sheet inscribed "Piranha": a, 16m, Pygocentrus ternetzi. b, 16m, Serrasalmus manueli. c, 16m, Pygocentrus nattereri. d, 16m, Pygocentrus cariba. e, 66m, Pygocentrus nattereri, diff. f, 66m, Pygocentrus ternetzi, diff.

No. 2172 — Sheet inscribed "Cobra-papagaio": a, 16m, Corallus caninus on branch, head at top of stamp. b, 16m, Corallus caninus on branch, head at LL. c, 16m, Corallus caninus, head at LR. d, 16m, Corallus canimus on branch, head at bottom center. e, 66m,Corallus caninus on branch, head in center, tail visible. f, 66m, Corallus caninus on branch, head at left, tail not visible.

No. 2173 — Sheet inscribed "Jacaré-açu": a, 16m, Melanosuchus niger in grass. b, 16m, Melanosuchus niger swimming. c, 16m, Melanosuchus niger standing, facing right. d, 16m, Melanosuchus niger standing, facing forward. e, 66m, Juvenile melanosuchus niger in water. f, 66m, Melanosuchus niger with mouth open.

No. 2174 — Sheet inscribed "Ra de olhos vermelhos": a, 16m, Agalychnis callidryas on vine, name at LR. b, 16m, Agalychnis callidryas facing right with rear leg extended at top, name at UR. c, 16m, Agalychnis callidryas facing left, name at UR. d, 16m, Agalychnis callidryas on vine, name at UL. e, 66m, Agalychnis callidryas on vine, name at LL. f, 66m, Agalychnus callidryas on vine, name at LR.

No. 2175 — Sheet inscribed "Tartaruga": a, 16m, Trachemys scripta elegans. b, 16m, Geochelone sulcata. c, 16m, Malaclemys terrapin. d, 16m, Chelus fimbriatus. e, 66m, Chelonoidis carbonaria. f, 66m, Terrepene carolina carolina.

No. 2176 — Sheet inscribed "Jupará": a, 16m, Potus flavus, head at UL, name at UR. b, 16m, Potos flavus, name at UL. c, 16m, Potus flavus, head at LL, name at UR. d, 92m, Potos flavus standing, name at UR, diff. e, 92m, Potos flavus, name at UL, diff. f, 92m, potos flavus in tree, name at UR.

No. 2177 — Sheet inscribed "Gorila": a, 16m, Gorilla beringei graueri, name at LR. b, 16m, Gorilla beringei. c, 16m, Gorilla gorilla diehli. d, 16m, Gorilla beringei graueri, name at UR. e, 92m, Gorilla gorilla. f, 92m, Gorilla gorilla gorilla.

No. 2178 — Sheet inscribed "Ateles": a, 16m, Ateles hybridus, name at right. b, 16m, Ateles chamek. c, 16m, Trichechus manatus. d, 16m, Ateles hybridus, name at UL. e, 92m, Ateles paniscus. f, 92m, Ateles hybridus, diff.

No. 2179 — Sheet inscribed "Társio": a, 16m, Tarsius syrichta, name at UR. b, 16m, Tarsius bancanus. c, 16m, Tarsius syrichta, name at LR. d, 16m, Tarsius tarsier. e, 92m, Tarsius dentatus. f, 92m, Tarsius syrichta, name at UL.

No. 2180 — Sheet inscribed "Tigris de Bengala": a, 16m, Panthera tigris, name at left. b, 16m, Panthera tigris tigris. c, 16m, Panthera tigris in water, name at right. d, 16m, Panthera tigris in grass, name at UR. e, 92m, Panthera tigrist tigris laying down. f, 92m, Panthera tigris tigris walking.

No. 2181 — Sheet inscribed "Calaubicórnico": a, 16m, Buceros bicornis on branch, name at UR. b, 16m, Buceros bicornis in flight, name at LR. c, 16m, Buceros bicornis on branch on tree at left, name at UR. d, 16m, Buceros bicornis on branch, name at LL. e, 92m, Buceros bicornis in flight, name at UL. f, 92m, Buceros bicornis in flight, name at LR, diff.

No. 2182 — Sheet inscribed "Casuario Austral": a, 16m, Casuarius causarius sitting, name at UL. b, 16m, Casuarius causarius standing, name at right. c, 16m, Casuarius casuarius standing, name at left. d, 16m, Casuarius casuarius with leg lifted, name at left. e, 92m, Cauarius casuarius, name at LL. f, 92m, Casuaraius casuarius, name at UL.

No. 2183 — Sheet inscribed "Coruja": a, 16m, Tyto multipunctata. b, 16m, Ninox connivens. c, 16m, Glaucidium tephronotum. d, 16m, Asio madagascariensis. e, 92m, Ninox novaeseelandiae. f, 92m, Otus rutilus.

No. 2184 — Sheet inscribed "Papagaio": a, 16m, Lorus garrulus. b, 16m, Trichoglossus chlorolepidotus. c, 16m, Trichoglottus flavoviridis. d, 16m, Trichoglossus euteles. e, 92m, Eos reticulata. f, 92m, Trichoglossus haematodus.

No. 2185 — Sheet inscribed "Quetzal-resplandecente": a, 16m, Pharomachrus mocinno on brach, name at right. b, 16m, Pharomachrus mocinno on branch, name at UR. c, 16m, Pharomachrus mocinno on branch, name at LR. d, 16m, Pharomachrus mocinno on branch, name at LL. e, 92m, Pharomachrus mocinno on branch, name at LR, diff. f, 92m, Pharomachrus mocinno on branch, name at LL, diff.

No. 2186 — Sheet inscribed "Tucano": a, 16m, Ramphastos dicolorus. b, 16m, Ramphastos toco. c, 16m, Ramphastos vitellinus. d, 16m, Ramphastos swainsonii. e, 92m, Ramphastos torquatus. f, 92m, Ramphastos sulfuratus.

No. 2187 — Sheet inscribed "Libélula": a, 16m, Anax imperator. b, 16m, Libellula depressa. c, 16m, Sympetrum fonscolombii. d, 16m, Libellula quadrimaculata. e, 92m, Ischnura heterosticta. f, 92m, Crocothemis sanguinolenta.

No. 2188 — Sheet inscribed "Borboleta-monarca": a, 16m, Danaus plexippus on flower, antennae near flower, name at right. b, 16m, Danaus plexippus on flower, antennae near denomination, name at right. c, 16m, Danaus plexippus on flower, name at UL, denomination at UR. d, 16m, Danaus plexippus on flower, name below denomination at UL. e, 92m, Danaus plexippus on branch, name at UL. f, 92m, Danaus plexippus on flower, name at LL.

No. 2189 — Sheet inscribed "Dendrobatidae": a, 16m, Epipedobates tricolor. b, 16m, Dendrobates auratus. c, 16m, Dendrobates azureus. d, 16m, Dendrobates leucomelas. e, 92m, Phyllobates terribilis. f, 92m, Oophaga pumilio.

No. 2190 — Sheet inscribed "Víbora do Gabao": a, 16m, Bitis gabonica, head at LL, name at LR. b, 16m, Bitis gabonica in grass, head in center, name at LR. c, 16m, Bitis gabonica, name at UL. d, 16m, Bitis gabonica on parched earth, head in center, name at LR. e, 92m, Bitis gabonica, name at LL. f, 92m, Bitis gabonica, name at UR.

No. 2191, 175m, Hylobates lar, diff. No. 2192, 175m, Lemur catta, diff. No. 2193, 175m, Bradypus variegatus, diff. No. 2194, 175m, Three Dicerorhinus sumatrensis. No. 2195, 175m, Desmodus rotundus, diff. No. 2196, 175m, Panthera onca, diff. No. 2197, 175m, Two Trichechus inunguis. No. 2198, 175m, Harpia harpyja in flght, diff. No. 2199, 175m, Ornithoptera alexandrae on leaf, diff. No. 2200, 175m, Two Morpho menelaus on leaves. No. 2201, 175m, Two Pygocentrus nattereri. No. 2202, 175m, Coprallus caninus on tree branch, diff. No. 2203, 175m, Melanosuchus niger, diff. No. 2204, 175m, Agalychnis callidryas, diff. No. 2205, 175m, Geochelone sulcata, diff. No. 2206, 175m, Potos flavus, diff. No. 2207, 175m, Gorilla gorilla, diff. No. 2208, 175m, Ateles hybridus, diff. No. 2209, 175m, Tarsius pumilus, diff. No. 2210, 175m, Panthera tigris, diff. No. 2211, 175m, Buceros bicornis, diff. No. 2212, 175m, Casuarius casuarius, diff. No. 2213, 175m, Asio madagascariensis, diff. No. 2214, 175m, Trichoglossus rubritorquis. No. 2215, 175m, Pharomachrus mocinno, diff. No. 2216, 175m, Ramphastos sulfuratus, diff. No. 2217, 175m, Trithemis kirbyi. No. 2218, 175m, Danaus plexippus on flower, diff. No. 2219, 175m, Dendrobates azureus, diff. No. 2220, 175m, Bitis gabonica, diff.

2011, Jan. 30 ***Perf. 12¾x13½***

Sheets of 6, #a-f

2161-2190 A426 Set of 30 525.00 525.00

Souvenir Sheets

Perf. 13½x12¾

2191-2220 A426 Set of 30 400.00 400.00

Television in Mozambique, 30th Anniv. — A427

Denominations: 66m, 92m.

2011, Feb. 28 **Litho.** ***Perf. 11x11¼***

2221-2222 A427 Set of 2 12.50 12.50

People, Events and Anniversaries — A428

No. 2223 — George Clooney, actor, and scenes from his films: a, 16m, Solaris. b, 16m, The American. c, 66m, Ocean's 12. d, 92m, The Good German.

No. 2224 — Elizabeth Taylor (1932-2011), actress: a, 16m, Wearing black dress, wearing white dress holding Oscar. b, 16m, Wearing brown dress, wearing white dress. c, 66m, Holding dog. d, 92m, With Michael Jackson.

No. 2225 — Roald Amundsen (1872-1928), Antarctic explorer and scenes from his 1911 expedition: a, 16m, Witn Norwegian flag at South Pole. b, 16m, With expedition members making scientific observations. c, 66m, Standing in hut. d, 92m, With dog team and Norwegian flag.

No. 2226 — Fridtjof Nansen (1961-1930), polar explorer, and: a, 16m, Arctocephalus gazella. b, 16m, Orcinus orca. c, 66m, Aptenodytes forsteri. d, 92m, Ship named Fridtjof Nansen.

No. 2227 — First airmail flight, cent.: a, 16m, Pilot Henri Pequet, airplane, maps. b, 16m, Pilot Earle Lewis Ovington and airplane. c, 66m, Pilot Fred J. Wiseman and airplane. d, 92m, Airplane of Fred J. Wiseman used in airmail flight from Petaluma to Santa Rosa, California.

No. 2228 — Andor Lilienthal (1911-2010), chess grandmaster, chess board and pieces, and: a, 16m, David Bronstein. b, 16m, Ruslan Ponomariov. c, 66m, Lilienthal playing chess. d, 92m, Lilienthal playing against 121 opponents.

No. 2229 — Maia Chiburdanidze, chess grandmaster, and: a, 16m, Chess board in purple. b, 16m, Chess board in gray blue. c, 66m, Knight. d, 92m, Rook and pawn.

No. 2230 — Japanese earthquake relief: a, 16m, Red Cross worker feeding infant. b, 16m, Workers carrying dead body. c, 66m, Red Cross worker watching fire. d, 92m, Fireman with hose.

No. 2231 — Chiune Sugihara (1900-86), Japanese diplomat who saved Jews in World War II, and: a, 16m, Jews, star of David. b, 16m, Sugihara in chair. c, 66m, Sugihara and his family. d, 92m, Monument to Sugihara in Vilnius, Lithuania.

No. 2232 — Rajiv Gandhi (1944-91), Indian prime minister: a, 16m, With Indians and cow. b, 16m, With family. c, 66m, With Mother Teresa. d, 92m, Standing in automobile.

No. 2233 — Paintings by Lucas Cranach, the Younger (1515-86): a, 16m, Portrait of a Woman, 1539. b, 16m, Prince Elector Moritz of Saxony, 1578. c, 66m, Elector Johann Friedrich of Saxony, 1578. d, 92m, Portrait of a Woman, diff.

No. 2234 — Paintings by Giorgio Vasari (1511-74): a, 16m, Lorenzo de Medici, 1533. b, 16m, Battle of Lepanto. c, 66m, St. Luke Painting the Virgin. d, 92m, Entombment.

No. 2235 — Franz Liszt (1811-86), composer, and: a, 16m, Liszt's house in Weimar, Germany from 1869-86. b, 16m, Budapest Opera House. c, 66m, Liszt's residence from 1863-69, Madonna del Rosario Monastery. d, 92m, Birthplace, Dobroján, Hungary.

No. 2236 — Gustav Mahler (1860-1911), composer, and: a, 16m, Symphony orchestra. b, 16m, Hofoper Building, Vienna. c, 66m, Metropolitan Oper, New York. d, 92m, Symphony orchestra, diff.

No. 2237 — Princess Diana (1961-97), and: a, 16m, Elton John. b, 16m, Baroness Chalker. c, 66m, Prince Charles, Ronald and Nancy Reagan. d, 92m, Michael Jackson.

No. 2238 — Human evolution: a, 16m, Australopithecus africanus. b, 16m, Homo habilis. c, 66m, Homo antecessor. d, 92m, Homo heidelbergensis.

No. 2239, 175m, Clooney, director's chair, projector, film reels. No. 2240, 175m, Taylor, diff. No. 2241, 175m, Amundsen and ship trapped in ice. No. 2242, 175m, Nansen, ship and Ursus maritimus. No. 2243, 175m, Pequet and airplane.No. 2244, 175m, Lilienthal playing chess, diff. No. 2245, 175m, Chiburdanidze, diff. No. 2246, 175m, Japanese firefighter holding hose at fire at industrial complex. No. 2247, 175m, Sugihara and refugees. No. 2248, 175m, Rajiv Gandhi and children. No. 2249, 175m, The Ill Matched Lovers, painting by Lucas Cranach, the Younger. No. 2250, 175m, The Walk to Emmaus, painting by Lelio Orsi. No. 2251, 175m, Liszt and Franz Liszt Music Academy, Budapest. No. 2252, 175m, Mahler and symphony orchestra, diff. No. 2253, 175m, Princess Diana, roses, Nepalese children. No. 2254, 175m, Australopithecus afarensis, map of Africa.

2011, Apr. 30 ***Perf. 13½x12¾***

Sheets of 4, #a-d

2223-2238 A428 Set of 16 240.00 240.00

Souvenir Sheets

2239-2254 A428 Set of 16 225.00 225.00

People, Events and Anniversaries — A429

No. 2255 — James Gandolfini, actor, and scenes from: a, 16m, Surviving Christmas, 2004. b, 16m, Lonely Hearts, 2006. c, 16m, The Last Castle, 2001. d, 16m, Welcome to the Rileys, 2010. e, 66m, The Sopranos, 1999-2007. f, 92m, In the Loop, 2009.

No. 2256 — Joseph Barbera (1911-2006), cartoon director, and: a, 16m, Abbott and Costello cartoon characters. b, 16m, Top Cat. c, 16m, William Hanna, production drawings of cartoon characters for Magilla Gorilla. d, 16m, Huckleberry Hound and elephant. e, 66m, Motormouse and Autocat. f, 92m, Huckleberry Hound with guitar.

No. 2257 — Ishiro Honda (1911-93), film director and scene from: a, 16m, Ghidorah, the Three-Headed Monster. b, 16m, Battle in Outer Space, 1959. c, 16m, Godzilla, 1954. d, 16m, Destroy All Monsters, 1968. e, 66m, Frankenstein Conquers the World, 1965. f, 92m, Yog: Monster from Space, 1970.

No. 2258 — American Civil War soldiers: a, 16m, Three Union soldiers and flag, 1864. b, 16m, Three Confederate soldiers with guns, 1861. c, 16m, Horse, flag and three Union soldiers, 1863. d, 16m, Three Confederate soldiers (one aiming rifle), 1861. e, 66m, Two Union cavalrymen with horses. f, 92m, Three Union soldiers, 1864, diff.

No. 2259 — Antarctic Treaty: a, 16m, Orcinus orca. b, 16m, Pygoscelis adeliae. c, 16m, Pagodroma nivea nivea. d, 16m, Channichthyidae. e, 66m, Arctocephalus gazella. f, 92m, Balaenoptera musculus.

No. 2260 — Beatification of Pope John Paul II: a, 16m, Pope grasping man around head. b, 16m, Pope pointing. c, 16m, Pope with Mother Teresa. d, 16m, Pope with St. Peter's Basilica in background. e, 66m, Pope greeting people. f, 92m, Pope wearing miter, holding crucifix.

No. 2261 — Automobiles from first Monte Carlo Rally, 1911: a, 16m, Turcat-Mery. b, 16m, Gobron 40 HP. c, 16m, Berliet 16 HP. d, 16m, Gobron-Brillié 40/60 CV. e, 66m, Delaunay-Belleville 15 HP. f, 92m, Dürkopp.

No. 2262 — Juan Manuel Fangio (1911-95), race car driver: a, 16m, Ferrari-Lancia d50. b, 16m, Flipped race car. c, 16m, Maserati 250F. d, 16m, Ferrari 166c. e, 66m, Mercedes-Benz W 196. f, 92m, Ferrari-Lancia d50, diff.

No. 2263 — Madame Tussaud Wax Museum sculptures: a, 16m, Albert Einstein. b, 16m, Princess Diana and Prince William. c, 16m, Mahatma Gandhi. d, 16m, Marilyn Monroe. e, 66m, Pope John Paul II. f, 92m, Elvis Presley.

No. 2264 — Alan B. Shepard, Jr. (1923-98), astronaut, and: a, 16m, Saturn V rocket. b, 16m, Mercury-Redstone rocket. c, 16m, Mercury 3 capsule (Freedom 7). d, 16m, Shephard in space suit. e, 66m, Pres. John F. Kennedy. f, 92m, Shepard in space capsule.

No. 2265 — Space Shuttle Challenger astronauts: a, 16m, Gregory Jarvis. b, 16m, Judith Resnik. c, 16m, Ellison Onizuka. d, 16m, Dick Scobee. e, 66m, Ronald McNair. f, 92m, Michael J. Smith.

No. 2266 — Yuri Gagarin (1934-68), first man in space: a, 16m, Gagarin and drawing of cosmonaut and space capsule. b, 16m, Vostok I. c, 16m, Gagarin and rocket launch. d, 16m, Gagarin and spacecraft in flight. e, 66m, Gagarin in Space helmet Autocat. f, 92m, Gagarin and drawing of rocket and space capsule.

No. 2267 — Mir Space Station, 25th anniv: a, 16m, Mir and rocket launch. b, 16m, Mir in space, denomination at UL. c, 16m, Mir and cosmonauts. d, 16m, Mir in space, denomination at UR. e, 66m, Mir and space shuttle. f, 92m, Mir and pieces descending to Earth.

No. 2268 — Wedding of Prince William and Catherine Middleton: a, 16m, Prince Charles and Princess Diana at UR. b, 16m, Westminster Abbey, denomination at UL. c, 16m, Prince Charles and Princess Diana at UL. d, 16m, Westminster Abbey, denomination at UR. e, 66m, Prince Charles, Princess Diana, horse. f, 92m, Westminster Abbey, denomination at UR, diff.

No. 2269, 175m, Gandolfini and scene from The Man Who Wasn't There. No. 2270, 175m, Barbera, Hanna, Autocat and Fred Flintstone. No. 2271, 175m, Honda and scene from Mothra, 1961. No. 2272, 175m, Six Confederate soldiers. No. 2273, 175m, Hydrurga leptonyx. No. 2274, 175m, Pope John Paul II, Mother Teresa. No. 2275, 175m, Turcat-Mery car in first Monte Carlo Rally. No. 2276, 175m, Fangio and Mercedes-Benz W196, diff. No. 2277, 175m, Wax sculptures of Marie Tussaud. No. 2278, 175m, Shepard, Mercury 3 rocket, Apollo 14 emblem. No. 2279, 175m, Challenger astronaut Christa McAuliffe. No. 2280, 175m, Gagarin and space capsule in flight. No. 2281, 175m, Mir in space, diff. No. 2282, 175m, Prince William, Catherine Middleton, Princess Diana and Prince Charles.

2011, Apr. 30 ***Perf. 12¾x13½***

Sheets of 6, #a-f

2255-2268 A429 Set of 14 240.00 240.00

Souvenir Sheets

Perf. 13½x12¾

2269-2282 A429 Set of 14 190.00 190.00

People, Events and Anniversaries — A430

No. 2283 — Beatification of Pope John Paul II: a, 16m, Pope John Paul II wearing miter at left. b, 16m, Pope John Paul praying at right. c, 66m, Pope John Paul II and St. Peter's Basilica. d, 92m, Pope John Paul II greeting crowd.

No. 2284 — Mohandas K. Gandhi (1869-1948), Indian independence leader, and: a, 16m, Gandhi seated, touching child. b, 16m, Gandhi standing in crowd. c, 66m, Gandhi in crowd. d, 92m, Gandhi seated in chair.

No. 2285 — Famous Indians: a, 16m, Rabindranath Tagore (1861-1941), writer and Mohandas Gandhi. b, 16m, Subhas Chandra Bose (1897-1945), nationalist leader, Bose on horseback. c, 66m, Tagore and Albert Einstein. d, 92m, Bose and Mohandas Gandhi.

No. 2286 — Intl. Year of Chemistry: a, 16m, Marie Curie (1867-1934), and model of Radium atom. b, 16m, Curie and Polonium. c, 66m, Curie and daughter, Irene. d, 92m, Curie in laboratory.

No. 2287 — Sir Alexander Fleming (1881-1955), discoverer of penicillin, and: a, 16m, Molecular model of penicillin. b, 16m, Penicillum sp. c, 66m, Vial and needle of penicillin. d, 92m, Petri dish.

No. 2288 — Princess Diana (1961-97): a, 16m, With child, Big Ben. b, 16m, Exiting automobile. c, 66m, Tower Bridge. d, 92m, And child in hospital bed.

No. 2289 — Henri Matisse (1869-1954), painter, and painting from: a, 16m, 1908. b, 16m, 1918. c, 66m, 1901. d, 92m, 1912.

No. 2290 — René Magritte (1898-1967), painter, and painting from: a, 16m, 1966. b, 16m, 1933. c, 66m, 1964. d, 92m, 1936.

No. 2291 — Ford vehicles: a, 16m, 1908 Model T. b, 16m, 1905 Delivery car. c, 66m, 1930 Model A Deluxe Sedan. d, 92m, 1927 Model T.

No. 2292 — Locomotives: a, 16m, Western Pacific 805-A, 1960, U.S. b, 16m, Alco RS-2, 1946, U.S. c, 66m, Bo-Bo Class EO, 1923, New Zealand. d, 92m, Class 103.158, 1969, Germany.

No. 2293 — World War II warships: a, 16m, HMS Hood. b, 16m, HMAS Sydney. c, 66m, DKM Bismarck. d, 92m, IJN Yamato.

No. 2294 — Jet aircraft and engines: a, 16m, F-86 Sabre, Allison J35 engine. b, 16m, Lockheed F-104 Starfighter, General Electric J79 engine. c, 66m, Grumman F9F Panther, Allison J33 engine. d, 92m, Lockheed P-80 Shooting Star, Halford H-1 engine.

No. 2295, 175m, Pope John Paul II and Mother Teresa. No. 2296, 175m, Gandhi, diff. No. 2297, 175m, Tagore and Gandhi, diff. No. 2298, 175m, Curie, diff. No. 2299, 175m, Fleming, penicillin tablets, Red Cross workers treating injured soldiers. No. 2300, 175m, Princess Diana, diff. No. 2301, 175m, Matisse and painting from 1905. No. 2302, 175m, Magritte and painting from 1941. No. 2303, 175m, Henry Ford and 1910 Model T. No. 2304, 175m, EMD GP9 locomotive, 1949, U.S and Canada. No. 2305, 175m, Admiral Graf Spee. No. 2306, 175m, Heinkel He-178, He S-3 engine.

Perf. 13¼x9¼x13¼x9¼

2011, June 30 **Litho.**

Sheets of 4, #a-d

2283-2294 A430 Set of 12 165.00 165.00

Souvenir Sheets

2295-2306 A430 Set of 12 152.50 152.50

People, Events and Anniversaries — A431

No. 2307 — Albert Einstein (1879-1955), physicist, and: a, 16m, Mass-energy equivalence equation, text starting with "Em 1919." b, 16m, Expanding universe, mass-energy equivalence equation. c, 16m, Diagram of photoelectric effect. d, 16m, Binary pulsar. e, 66m, Gravitational field. f, 92m, Circles and arrows.

No. 2308 — Musicians: a, 16m, Elvis Presley (1935-77), teddy bear, Ann-Margret. b, 16m, Frank Sinatra (1915-98), and daughter, Nancy. c, 16m, Louis Armstrong (1901-71), and Ella Fitzgerald. d, 16m, Presley and scene from movie, *Fun in Acupulco*. e, 66m, Frank Sinatra and Gene Kelly. f, 92m, Armstrong and scene from movie.

No. 2309 — Musicians: a, 16m, Michael Jackson (1958-2009). b, 16m, Freddie Mercury (1946-91). c, 16m, The Rolling Stones. d, 16m, Jackson and backup singers. e, 66m, Mercury and members of Queen. f, 92m, The Rolling Stones, diff.

No. 2310 — Film personalities: a, 16m, Alfred Hitchcock (1899-1980), director. b, 16m, James Dean (1931-55), actor. c, 16m, Greta Garbo (1905-90), actress. d, 16m, Grace Kelly (1929-82), actress. e, 66m, Clark Gable (1901-60), actor. f, 92m, Marlon Brando (1924-2004), actor.

No. 2311 — Political leaders: a, 16m, Pres. John F. Kennedy (1917-63), American astronauts. b, 16m, Sir Winston Churchill (1874-1965), British prime minister, and Pres. Franklin D. Roosevelt and Joseph Stalin. c, 16m, Charles de Gaulle (1890-1970), President of France. d, 16m, Kennedy, Lyndon B. Johnson and Sam Rayburn. e, 66m, Churchill. f, 92m, De Gaulle and Gen. George C. Marshall.

No. 2312 — Political leaders: a, 16m, Pres. Theodore Roosevelt (1858-1919), moose. b, 16m, Lech Walesa, Polish President, and Solidarity banners. c, 16m, Mikhail Gorbachev, Pres. of Soviet Union, and Pres. Barack Obama. d, 16m, Roosevelt on Wright Brothers airplane. e, 66m, Walesa, diff. f, 92m, Gorbachev and Pres. Ronald Reagan.

No. 2313 — Pioneers in communications technology: a, 16m, Guglielmo Marconi (1874-1937), radio pioneer. b, 16m, John Logie Baird (1888-1946), television pioneer. c, 16m, Thomas Edison (1847-1931), inventor of Kinetoscope. d, 16m, Alexander Graham Bell (1847-1922), inventor of telephone. e, 66m, Edward Roberts (1941-2010), computer engineer. f, 92m, Tim Berners-Lee, inventor of World Wide Web.

No. 2314 — Humanitarians: a, 16m, Mother Teresa (1910-97). b, 16m, Dr. Martin Luther King, Jr. (1929-68). c, 16m, Nelson Mandela. d, 16m, Mother Teresa and Pope John Paul II. e, 66m, King, diff. f, 92m, Mandela, diff.

No. 2315 — Writers: a, 16m, George Orwell (1903-50). b, 16m, Albert Camus (1913-60). c, 16m, Ernest Hemingway (1899-1961), with John Dos Passos, Joris Ivens and Sidney Franklin. d, 16m, Hemingway and buffalo. e, 66m, Kurt Vonnegut, Jr. (1922-2007). f, 92m, Mikhail Bulgakov (1891-1940).

No. 2316 — Sports personalities: a, 16m, Pelé, soccer player. b, 16m, Michael Jordan, basketball player. c, 16m, Ayrton Senna (1960-94), race car driver. d, 16m, Babe Ruth (1895-1948), baseball player. e, 66m, Nadia Comenici, gymnast. f, 92m, Jim Thorpe (1888-1953), Olympic track athlete.

No. 2317 — Space exploration: a, 16m, Yuri Gagarin (1934-68), Vostok 1. b, 16m, Space Shuttle. c, 16m, Valentina Tereshkova, Vostok 6. d, 16m, Mir Space Station and Space Shuttle. e, 66m, Sputnik 1. f, 92m, Neil Armstrong (1930-2012).

No. 2318 — World War II personalities: a, 16m, Charles de Gaulle (1890-1970). b, 16m, Gen. Dwight D. Eisenhower (1890-1969). c, 16m, Sir Winston Churchill (1874-1965). d, 16m, Gen. Georgy Zhukov (1896-1974). e, 66m, Harry S Truman (1884-1972). f, 92m, Gen. Bernard Montgomery (1887-1976).

No. 2319 — World War II aircraft: a, 16m, Corsair F4-U. b, 16m, Hawker Hurricane, Messerschmitt Me109, Junkers Ju-87D. c, 16m, Hawker Typhoon, Focke-Wulf Fw 190. d, 16m, Supermarine Spitfire MkXIV, Messerschmitt Me262. e, 66m, Curtiss P-40 Warhawk. f, 92m, Consolidated B-24 Liberator, Focke-Wulf 190D-9.

No. 2320 — American Impressionist painters: a, 16m, J. Ottis Adams (1851-1927), paintings from 1896 and 1901. b, 16m, Reynolds Beal (1866-1951), paintings from 1922 and 1924. c, 16m, Dennis Miller Bunker (1861-90), paintings from 1883 and 1890. d, 16m, Theodore Earl Butler (1861-1936), paintings from 1895 and 1911. e, 66m, Mary Cassatt (1844-1926), paintings from 1869 and 1880. f, 92m, Frank Weston Benson (1862-1951), paintings from 1902 and 1904.

No. 2321 — Pablo Picasso (1881-1973) and painting from: a, 16m, 1905. b, 16m, 1954. c, 16m, 1939. d, 16m, 1921-22. e, 66m, 1923. f, 92m, 1954, diff.

No. 2322 — Salvador Dalí (1904-89) and painting from: a, 16m, 1954. b, 16m, 1946. c, 16m, 1931. d, 16m, 1938. e, 66m, 1936. f, 92m, 1934.

No. 2323 — Wedding of Prince William and Catherine Middleton with: a, 16m, Horses and riders in background. b, 16m, Bride and groom walking down aisle. c, 16m, Bride and groom kissing. d, 16m, Attendant carrying train of bride's dress. e, 66m, Couple in coach. f, 92m, Couple in coach, diff.

No. 2324, 175m, Einstein, diff. No. 2325, 175m, Presley and Frank Sinatra. No. 2326, 175m, The Beatles. No. 2327, 175m, Marilyn Monroe (1926-62), actress. No. 2328, 175m, Kennedy, diff. No. 2329, 175m, Gorbachev and Pope John Paul II. No. 2330, 175m, Berners-Lee, diff. No. 2331, 175m, Dr. Albert Schweitzer (1875-1965). No. 2332, 175m, Camus, diff. No. 2333, 175m, Muhammad Ali, boxer. No. 2334, 175m, Gagarin, diff. No. 2335, 175m, Neville Chamberlain (1869-1940). No. 2336, 175m, Supermarine Spitfire battling German airplanes over Dover. No. 2337, 175m, William Merritt Chase (1849-1916), paintings from 1886 and 1894. No. 2338, 175m, Picasso and painting from 1901. No. 2339, 175m, Dalí and painting from 1947. No. 2340, Wedding of Prince William and Catherine Middleton, diff.

2011, June 30 **Sheets of 6, #a-f**

2307-2323 A431 Set of 17 275.00 275.00

Souvenir Sheets

2324-2340 A431 Set of 17 215.00 215.00

Animals of Mozambique — A432

No. 2341 — Hares: a, 16m, Two Lepus saxitilis, animal name at left. b, 16m, Two Lepus saxitilis, animal name at right. c, 16m, Three Lepus capensis. d, 16m, One Lepus capensis. e, 66m, Two Lepus capensis. f, 92m, Three Lepus capensis, diff.

No. 2342 — Rodents: a, 16m, Anomalurus derbianus. b, 16m, Hystris africaeaustralis. c, 16m, Pedetes capensis. d, 16m, Heliosciurus mutabilis. e, 66m, Paraxerus palliatus. f, 92m, Graphiurus platyops.

No. 2343 — Pangolins and aardvarks: a, 16m, Two Manis temminckii, animal name at LL. b, 16m, Two Orycteropus afer, animal name at UR. c, 16m, Two Orycteropus afer, animal name at left. d, 16m, Two Manis temminckii, animal name at UR. e, 66m, Two Manis temminckii, diff. f, 92m, Two Orycteropus afer, diff.

No. 2344 — Bovids: a, 16m, Litacranius walleri. b, 16m, Aepyceros melampus and Acinonyx jubatus. c, 16m, Oryx beisa beisa. d, 16m, Connochaetes taurinus. e, 66m, Tragelaphus spekeii. f, 92m, Taurotragus oryx.

No. 2345 — African hunting dogs: a, 16m, Three Lycaon pictus, animal name at LL. b, 16m, Two Lycaon pictus. c, 16m, Lycaon pictus chasing Connochaetes taurinus. d, 16m, Two Lycaon pictus, and animal's head with open mouth. e, 66m, Two Lycaon pictus, diff. f, 92m, Lycaon pictus, and head of animal with closed mouth.

No. 2346 — Hippopotamus amphibius: a, 16m, Animals in water and on shore with open mouths. b, 16m, Animal facing left, animal in water with open mouth, skull. c, 16m, Animals in water and on shore with closed mouths. d, 16m, Three animals. e, 66m, Adult and juvenile. f, 92m, Two animals in water.

No. 2347 — Rhinoceroses: a, 16m, Diceros bicornis, drawing of rhinoceros by Albrecht Dürer. b, 16m, Three Ceratotherium simum. c, 16m, Adult and juvenile Ceratotherium simum. d, 16m, Three Diceros bicornis, skull. e, 66m, Three Ceratotherium simum, diff. f, 92m, Three Diceros bicornis, diff.

No. 2348 — Seals: a, 16m, Two Arctocephalus pusillus, sea gull. b, 16m, Three Mirounga leonina, animal name at UL. c, 16m, Three Mirounga leonina, animal name at left. d, 16m, Three Mirounga leonina, animal name at LL. e, 66m, Three Mirounga leonina, diff. f, 92m, Pod of Arctocephalus pusillus.

No. 2349 — Primates: a, 16m, Otolemur crassicaudatus. b, 16m, Galago nyasae, Otolemur crassicaudatus. c, 16m, Chlorocebus pygerythrus. d, 16m, Cercopithecus mitis. e, 66m, Papio ursinus. f, 92m, Papio cynocephalus with Aepyceros melampus.

No. 2350 — Bats: a, 16m, Rhinolophus blasii. b, 16m, Rousettus aegyptiacus. c, 16m, Taphozous mauritianus. d, 16m, Epomophorus wahlbergi. e, 66m, Eidolon helvum. f, 92m, Nyctalus noctula.

No. 2351 — Panthera leo: a, 16m, Lion, lioness and zebra. b, 16m, Lion, two lionesses, animal carcass. c, 16m, Lion and lioness. d, 16m, Lioness with zebra carcass. e, 66m, Two lionesses. f, 92m, Lionesses, buffalo and carcass.

No. 2352 — Wild cats: a, 16m, Caracal caracal. b, 16m, Acinonyx jubatus. c, 16m, Panthera pardus. d, 16m, Leptailurus serval. e, 66m, Leptailurus serval, diff. f, 92m, Acinonyx jubatus, diff.

No. 2353 — Loxodonta africana: a, 16m, Four elephants near watering hole. b, 16m, Elephant facing left near watering hole. c, 16m, Elephant facing forward. d, 16m, Elephant facing right. e, 66m, Three elephants. f, 92m, Adult and juvenile elephants.

No. 2354 — Two Dugong dugon with animal name at: a, 16m, Center left in white. b, 16m, UL in black. c, 16m, LR in white. d, 16m, Center right in white, under denomination. e, 66m, UR in black. f, 92m, UR in black, under denomination.

No. 2355 — Dolphins: a, 16m, Sousa chinensis chinensis. b, 16m, Stenella coeruleoalba. c, 16m, Stenella longirostris. d, 16m, Steno bredanensis. e, 66m, Tursiops truncatus. f, 92m, Lagenodelphis hosei.

No. 2356 — Whales: a, 16m, Feresa attenuata. b, 16m, Orcinus orca. c, 16m, Megaptera novaeangliae. d, 16m, Physeter macrocephalus. e, 66m, Kogia sima. f, 92m, Balaenoptera borealis.

No. 2357 — Bee-eaters: a, 16m, Merops pusillus. b, 16m, Merops bullockoides. c, 16m, Merops persicus. d, 16m, Merops boehmi. e, 66m, Merops nubicoides. f, 92m, Merops apiaster.

No. 2358 — Albatrosses: a, 16m, Thalassarche melanophrys. b, 16m, Diomedea exulans. c, 16m, Phoebetria palpebrata. d, 16m, Thalassarche cauta. e, 66m, Thalassarche chlororhynchos. f, 92m, Phoebetria fusca.

No. 2359 — Storks: a, 16m, Ciconia episcopus. b, 16m, Mycteria ibis. c, 16m, Anastomus lamelligerus. d, 16m, Ciconia nigra. e, 66m, Ephippiorhynchus senegalensis. f, 92m, Ciconia abdimii.

No. 2360 — Flamingos: a, 16m, Phoenicopterus roseus, bird feeding chick in foreground, animal name at UL. b, 16m, Phoenicopterus minor, animal name at top center. c, 16m, Phoenicopterus minor, animal name at UR under denomination. d, 16m, Phoenicopterus roseus in water, animal name at UL. e, 66m, Phoenicopterus minor in flight. f, 92m, Phoenicopterus roseus, diff.

No. 2361 — Pelecanus onocrotalus: a, 16m, Pelican feeding chick with adult near water, animal name at UR. b, 16m, Three pelicans on tree branch, animal name at LL. c, 16m, Three pelicans, animal name at UL. d, 16m, Two pelicans, animal name at right. e, 66m, Two pelicans, diff. f, 92m, Four pelicans.

No. 2362 — Struthio camelus: a, 16m, Adult and juvenile ostriches. b, 16m, Two ostriches fighting. c, 16m, Head of ostrich, osctrich with wings spread. d, 16m, Two ostriches, nest with eggs. e, 66m, Ostrich running. f, 92m, Ostrich standing.

No. 2363 — Kingfishers: a, 16m, Alcedes cristata. b, 16m, Ceryle rudis. c, 16m, Halcyon senegalensis. d, 16m, Ispidina picta. e, 66m, Halcyon senegaloides. f, 92m, Halcyon leucocephala.

No. 2364 — Birds of prey: a, 16m, Haliaeetus vocifer. b, 16m, Macheiraphus alcinus. c, 16m, Circaetus cinereus. d, 16m, Aquila rapax. e, 66m, Aquila pomarina. f, 92m, Polyboroides typus.

No. 2365 — Two Pandion haliaetus with animal name at: a, 16m, UR under denomination. b, 16m, Bottom, denomination at UR. c, 16m, Bottom, denomination at UL. d, 16m, UL. e, 66m, Left. f, 92m, UL, diff.

No. 2366 — Owls: a, 16m, Tyto capensis. b, 16m, Ptilopsis granti. c, 16m, Glaucidium perlatum. d, 16m, Strix woodfordii. e, 66m, Bubo capensis. f, 92m, Bubo africanus.

No. 2367 — Butterflies: a, 16m, Papilio dardanus. b, 16m, Charaxes varanes. c, 16m, Pharmacophagus antenor. d, 16m, Papilio phorcas. e, 66m, Papilio nireus. f, 92m, Charaxes pollux.

No. 2368 — Shells: a, 16m, Mauritia arabica. b, 16m, Lambis lambis. c, 16m, Clanculus puniceus. d, 16m, Haliotis ovina. e, 66m, Morula granulata. f, 92m, Chicoreus ramosus.

No. 2369 — Sea turtles: a, 16m, Caretta caretta. b, 16m, Chelonia mydas. c, 16m, Demochelys coriacea. d, 16m, Eretmochelys imbricata. e, 66m, Lepidochelys olivacea. f, 92m, Caretta caretta, diff.

No. 2370 — Lizards: a, 16m, Two Cordylus tropidosternum, one on rock. b, 16m, Cordylus mossambicus. c, 16m, Platysaurus intermedius. d, 16m, Two Cordylus tropidosternum fighting. e, 66m, Platysaurus imperator. f, 92m, Platysaurus imperator, diff.

No. 2371, 175m, Lepus capensis, diff. No. 2372, 175m, Rhabdomys pumilio. No. 2373, 175m, Manis temminckii, diff. No. 2374, 175m, Antidoreas marsupialis. No. 2375, 175m, Lycaeon pictus, diff. No. 2376, 175m, Adult and juvenile Hippopotamus amphibius, diff. No. 2377, 175m, Ceratotherium simum, diff. No. 2378, 175m, Pod of Arctocephalus pusillus. No. 2379, 175m, Cercopithecus mitis, diff. No. 2380, 175m, Eidolon helvum, diff. No. 2381, 175m, Panthera leo, diff. No. 2382, 175m, Panthera pardus, diff. No. 2383, 175m, Loxodonta africana, diff. No. 2384, 175m, Dugong dugon, diff. No. 2385, 175m, Lissodelphis peronii. No. 2386, 175m, Feresa attenuata, diff. No. 2387, 175m, Meops hirundineus. No. 2388, 175m, Thalassarchechlororhynchus, diff. No. 2389, 175m, Mycteria ibis, diff. No. 2390, 175m, Phoenicopterus roseus, diff. No. 2391, 175m, Pelecanus onocrotalus, diff. No. 2392, 175m, Struthio camelus and egg. No. 2393, 175m, Megaceryle maxima. No. 2394, 175m, Aquila verreauxii. No. 2395, 175m, Pandion haliaetus, diff. No. 2396, 175m, Tyto alba. No. 2397, 175m, Hypolimnas salmacis. No. 2398, 175m, Stellaria solaris, Nerita plicata, Achatina vassei. No. 2399, 175m, Eretmochelys imbricata, diff. No. 2400, 175m, Papilio demodocus, Cordylus mossambicus.

2011, Aug. 30 **Sheets of 6, #a-f**

2341-2370 A432 Set of 30 500.00 500.00

Souvenir Sheets

2371-2400 A432 Set of 30 400.00 400.00

Art — A433

No. 2401, 66m — Byzantine paintings by: a, Duccio di Buoninsegna from 1285 and 1308-11. b, Giotto di Bondone. c, Andrei Rublev. d, Emmanuel Tzanes.

No. 2402, 66m — Paintings by Dutch artists: a, Pieter Claesz. b, Rembrandt van Rijn from 1655. c, Dirck Hals. d, Jacob van Ruisdael.

No. 2403, 66m — Paintings by African artists: a, George Lilanga. b, Noel Kapanda. c, Saidi Omary. d, Steven Mkumba.

No. 2404, 66m — Paintings by Chinese artists: a, Chen Hongshou. b, Gong Kai. c, Xu Wei. d, Ding Guanpeng.

No. 2405, 66m — Fauvist paintings by: a, André Derain. b, Maurice de Vlaminck. c, Henri Matisse from 1904-05 and 1905. d, Charles Camoin.

No. 2406, 66m — Cubist paintings by: a, Juan Gris. b, Georges Braque. c, Pablo Picasso from 1909 and 1937. d, Paul Cézanne from 1890-94 and 1895.

No. 2407, 66m — Pop art works by: a, Richard Hamilton. b, Andy Warhol. c, David Hockney. d, Claes Oldenburg.

No. 2408, 66m — Modern art works by: a, Roy Lichtenstein from 1961 and 1988. b, Picasso from 1927 and 1932. c, Henri Matisse from 1947. d, Joan Miró from 1917 and 1925.

No. 2409, 175m, Paintings by Duccio di Buoninsegna from 1300-05. No. 2410, 175m, Paintings by Johannes Vermeer from 1668. No. 2411, 175m, Paintings by Eduardo Saidi Tingatinga. No. 2412, 175m, Paintings by Li Gonglin. No. 2413, 175m, Paintings by Kees van Dongen. No. 2414, 175m, Painting by Picasso from 1921. No. 2515, 175m, Paintings by Lichtenstein from 1963 and 1984. No. 2416, 175m, Painting by Picasso from 1935.

2011, Oct. 30 ***Perf. 12¾x13¼***

Sheets of 4, #a-d

2401-2408 A433 Set of 8 160.00 160.00

Souvenir Sheets

2409-2416 A433 Set of 8 110.00 110.00

Art — A434

No. 2417 — Pre-historic paintings from: a, 16m, Chauvet Cave, France. b, 16m, Altamira Cave, Spain. c, 16m, Lascaux Cave, France. d, 66m, Lascaux Cave, diff. e, 66m, Niaux Cave, France. f, 66m, Chauvet Cave, diff.

No. 2418 — Paintings by Dutch artists: a, 16m, Rembrandt from 1633. b, 16m, Maarten van Heemskerck. c, 16m, Marinus van Reymerswaele. d, 66m, Vincent van Gogh from 1888. e, 66m, Lucas van Leyden. f, 66m, Johan Jongkind.

No. 2419 — Egyptian paintings from the Tomb of: a, 16m, Huy. b, 16m, Nebamun (man with tools, two women). c, 16m, Nebamun (man with staff, cattle herder and cattle). d, 66m, Nebamun, diff. e, 66m, Sebekhotep. f, 66m, Horemheb.

No. 2420 — Paintings by Flemish artists: a, 16m, Pieter Bruegel the Elder. b, 16m, Jan van Eyck. c, 16m, Frans Hals. d, 66m, Anthony van Dyck. e, 66m, Hugo van der Goes. f, 66m, Gerard David.

No. 2421 — Paintings by French artists: a, 16m, Edgar Degas from 1890. b, 16m, Paul Cézanne from 1866. c, 16m, Gustave Courbet. d, 66m, Paul Gauguin from 1892. e, 66m, Eugene Delacroix. f, 66m, Henri Matisse from 1928.

No. 2422 — Paintings by German artists: a, 16m, Hans Baldung Grien. b, 16m, Lovis Corinth. c, 16m, Ludolf Bakhuizen. d, 66m, Lucas Cranach the Elder. e, 66m, Otto Dix. f, 66m, Adam Elsheimer.

No. 2423 — Paintings by Indian artists: a, 16m, Nandalal Bose. b, 16m, Raja Ravi Varma. c, 16m, Tyeb Mehta. d, 66m, Jamini Roy. e, 66m, Abanindranath Tagore. f, 66m, S.H. Raza.

No. 2424 — Paintings by Italian artists: a, 16m, Michelangelo Buonarroti from 1508-12. b, 16m, Amadeo Modigliani from 1919. c, 16m, Titian. d, 66m, Sandro Botticelli (Minerva and Centaur, 1480). e, 66m, Tintoretto from 1540-42. f, 66m, Caravaggio.

No. 2425 — Paintings by Japanese artists: a, 16m, Toyokuni Utagawa. b, 16m, Kunimasa Utagawa. c, 16m, Toshun Kano. d, 66m, Kunisada Utagawa. e, 66m, Kiyonobu Torii. f, 66m, Shoen Uemura.

No. 2426 — Paintings by Spanish artists: a, 16m, El Greco. b, 16m, Joan Miró from 1917 and 1922-23. c, 16m, Diego Velázquez. d, 66m, Francisco Goya. e, 66m, Salvador Dalí from 1921 and 1925. f, 66m, Joaquí Sorolla.

No. 2427 — Paintings by Jewish artists: a, 16m, Modigliani from 1918. b, 16m, Moritz Daniel Oppenheim. c, 16m, Chaim Goldberg.

d, 66m, Camille Pissarro from 1901. e, 66m, Maurycy Gottlieb. f, 66m, Samuel Hirszenberg.

No. 2428 — Religious art: a, 16m, Stained-glass window depicting Jesus, 1601 painting by Caravaggio. b, 16m, Statue and fresco depicting Buddha. c, 16m, Menorah, 1638 painting of Moses, by José de Ribera. d, 66m, Ottoman calligraphy and ceiling of Ibn Battuta Mall, Dubai. e, 66m, Sculpture and fresco depicting Buddha. f, 66m, Fresco depicting Jesus, 1405 painting depicting the Annunciation by Andrei Rublev.

No. 2429 — Renaissance art by: a, 16m, Raffaello Sanzio da Urbino (Raphael). b, 16m, Botticelli (The Glorification of Mary, 1480). c, 16m, Tintoretto from 1550-53 and 1592-94. d, 66m, Leonardo da Vinci from 1480 and 1495. e, 66m, Michelangelo from 1508 and 1511. f, 66m, Giotto from 1305 and 1310.

No. 2430 — Impressionist paintings by: a, 16m, Armand Guillaumin. b, 16m, Eva Gonzalès. c, 16m, Alfred Sisley. d, 66m, Eugène Boudin. e, 66m, Stanislas Lépine. f, 66m, Edouard Manet from 1872 and 1882.

No. 2431 — Post-impressionist paintings by: a, 16m, Van Gogh from 1888 and 1889. b, 16m, Georges Seurat. c, 16m, Henri de Toulouse-Lautrec. d, 66m, Gauguin from 1888 and 1893. e, 66m, Cézanne from 1875 and 1892. f, 66m, Matisse from 1905 and 1906.

No. 2432 — Expressionist paintings by: a, 16m, Ernst Ludwig Kirchner. b, 16m, Emil Nolde. c, 16m, Franz Marc. d, 66m, Oskar Kokoscka. e, 66m, Max Beckmann. f, 66m, Wassily Kandinsky.

No. 2433 — Realist paintings by: a, 16m, Jules Breton. b, 16m, Jean-Baptiste-Camille Corot. c, 16m, Honore Daumier. d, 66m, Valentin Serov. e, 66m, Jean-François Millet. f, 66m, Ilya Repin.

No. 2434 — Surrealist paintings: a, 16m, Frida Kahlo. b, 16m, Dalí from 1963. c, 16m, Miró from 1940. d, 66m, Marc Chagall from 1911. e, 66m, Giorgio De Chirico. f, 66m, Max Ernst.

No. 2435, 175m, Pre-historic painting from Altamira Cave, diff. No. 2436, 175m, Painting by Johannes Vermeer from 1659. No. 2437, 175m, Painting from Tomb of Huy, diff. No. 2438, 175m, Painting by Peter Paul Rubens. No. 2439, 175m, Painting by Pierre-Auguste Renoir from 1890. No. 2440, 175m, Painting by Albrecht Dürer. No. 2441, 175m, Painting by Amrita Sher-Gil. No. 2442, 175m, Painting by Leonardo da Vinci from 1489-90. No. 2443, 175m, Painting by Hokusai Katsushika. No. 2444, 175m, Paintings by Picasso from 1901 and 1903. No. 2445, 175m, Painting by Chagall from 1913-14. No. 2446, 175m, 1513 painting depicting Madonna and Child by Raphael, ceiling of Farnese Palace by Annibale Carracci. No. 2447, 175m, Paintings by Leonardo da Vinci from 1489 and 1501. No. 2448, 175m, Paintings by Manet from 1878. No. 2449, 175m, Paintings by Van Gogh from 1886 and 1887. No. 2450, 175m, Paintings by Edvard Munch. No. 2451, 175m, Painting by William-Auguste Bouguereau. No. 2452, 175m, Painting by René Magritte.

2011, Oct. 30 — Sheets of 6, #a-f

2417-2434 A434 Set of 18 335.00 335.00

Souvenir Sheets

2435-2452 A434 Set of 18 240.00 240.00

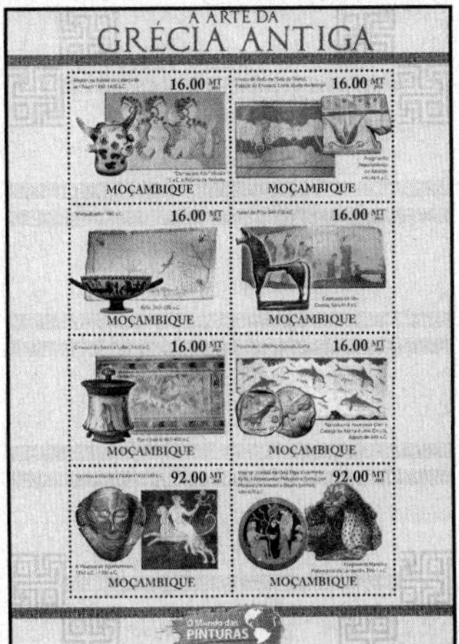

Art — A435

No. 2453 — Art of Ancient Greece: a, 16m, Bull's head rhyton, painting depicting women. b, 16m, Fresco from Knossos Palace, tile fragment. c, 16m, Painting of divers, kylix. d, 16m, Painting, sculpture of horse. e, 16m, Fresco depicting bull, pyxis. f, 16m, Fresco depicting dolphins, obverse and reverse of Athenian tetradrachm. g, 92m, Mask of Agamemnon, painting depicting Dionysius riding panther. h, 92m, Image from kylix, mosaic depicting leopard.

No. 2454 — Expensive paintings by: a, 16m, Jackson Pollock. b, 16m, Willem de Kooning. c, 16m, Gustav Klimt. d, 16m, Vincent van Gogh from 1890. e, 16m, Pierre-Auguste Renoir from 1876. f, 16m, Pablo Picasso from 1905. g, 92m, Picasso from 1932. h, 92m, Van Gogh from 1889.

No. 2455 — American Impressionist paintings by: a, 16m, Frank Weston Benson. b, 16m, Theodore Earl Butler. c, 16m, Mary Cassatt from 1879. d, 16m, Colin Campbell Cooper. e, 16m, Mary Agnes Yerkes. f, 16m, Dennis Miller Bunker. g, 92m, Childe Hassam. h, 92m, William Merritt Chase.

No. 2456 — Impressionist paintings by: a, 16m, Frederic Bazille. b, 16m, Berthe Morisot. c, 16m, Camille Pissarro from 1875. d, 16m, Claude Monet. e, 16m, Cassatt from 1873. f, 16m, Pierre-Auguste Renoir from 1882-83. g, 92m, Paul Cézanne from 1888. h, 92m, Edgar Degas from 1888.

No. 2457, 175m, Ancient Greek urn and painting. No. 2458, 175m, Painting by Picasso from 1941. No. 2459, 175m, Painting by Theodore Robinson. No. 2460, 175m, Painting by Gustave Caillebotte.

2011, Oct. 30 — Sheets of 8, #a-h

2453-2456 A435 Set of 4 85.00 85.00

Souvenir Sheets

2457-2460 A435 Set of 4 52.50 52.50

Events, People and Anniversaries — A436

No. 2461, 66m — Horse racing: a, Horses facing right, jockeys in foreground wearing black and red shirts. b, Horses in steeplechase race. c, Horses facing right, jockey in foreground wearing black shirt. d, Horses facing left, passing grandstand, jockey wearing black shirt in lead. e, Horses facing left close to rail, grandstand at left. f, Three horses near gray wall.

No. 2462, 66m — Dan Wheldon (1978-2011), race car driver: a, Wheldon in white short-sleeve shirt. b, Race car with "2012" on rear wing. c, Wheldon in red racing uniform, car #10. d, Race car, race track. e, Wheldon with arms raised, race car. f, Wheldon standing next to race car.

No. 2463, 66m — Marco Simoncelli (1987-2011), motorcycle racer: a, With Valentino Rossi. b, Touching forehead. c, Raising trophy above head. d, With motorcycle's front wheel raised. e, Kneeling next to motorcycle. f, Looking right.

No. 2464, 66m — 2012 European Soccer Championships, Poland and Ukraine: a, Denomination at UL, "2012" in yellow at LR. b, Denomination at UL, "2012" in green at UR. c, Denomination at UR, "2012" in indigo at UL, soccer players wearing red and yellow uniforms. d, Denomination at UR, "2012" in indigo at UL, soccer players wearing blue and orange univorms. e, Denomination at UR, "2012" in yellow at UL. f, Denomination at UL, "2012" in green at LR.

No. 2465, 66m — Chess champions: a, Mikhail Tal. b, Viswanathan Anand. c, Bobby Fischer. d, Vladimir Kramnik. e, Garry Kasparov. f, Boris Spassky.

No. 2466, 66m — Boy Scout: a, Hiking, trefoil at LR. b, One one knee, trefoil at left. c, Cycling, trefoil at LR. d, Inspecting small item, trefoil at LL. e, Cooking, trefoil at LR. f, In boat, trefoil at UR.

No. 2467, 66m — Steve Jobs (1955-2011), computer entrepreneur: a, With Apple II computer. b, With Steve Wozniak and computer components. c, Holding apple. d, With beard, wearing glasses. e, Seated in chair using iPad. f, With three computers.

No. 2468, 66m — Mycologists and fungi: a, Elias Magnus Fries, Crinipellis scabella. b, Heinrich Anton de Bary, Psilocybe semilanceata. c, Charles Horton Peck, Crinipellis zonata. d, Narcisse Théophile Patouillard, inocybe patouillardii. e, Miles Joseph Berkeley, Stephanospora caroticolor. f, Károly Kalchbrenner, Sarcodon fuligineoviolaceus.

No. 2469, 66m — Sir Joseph Dalton Hooker (1817-1911), botanist: a, Hooker, Banksia hookeriana, Delias eucharis. b, Charles Darwin, Pan troglodytes. c, Hooker, Liriodendron tulipifera, Junonia lemonias. d, Hooker, Magnolia campbellii. e, Walter Hood Fitch, flowers and colored pencils. f, Darwin, ship and globe.

No. 2470, 66m — 2011 Nobel laureates: a, Bruce A. Beutler, Physiology or Medicine laureate. b, Ralph M. Steinman, Physiology or Medicine laureate. c, Jules A. Hoffmann, Physiology or Medicine laureate. d, Saul Perlmutter, Physics laureate. e, Brian P. Schmidt, Physics laureate. f, Adam G. Riess, Physics laureate.

No. 2471, 66m — Russian Cosmonauts: a, Valentina Tereshkova, Vostok 6. b, Alexei Leonov, 1965 space walk. c, Pavel Popovich, Vostok 4. d, Gherman Titov, Vostok 2. e, Andriyan Nikolayev, Soyuz 9. f, Pavel Belyayev, Voskhod 2.

No. 2472, 66m — African archaeological sites: a, Altar of Osiris, Philae Island, Egypt. b, Triumphal arch, Lambaesis, Algeria. c, Temple of Minerva, Tébessa, Algeria. d, Triumphal arch, Tébessa. e, Kom Ombo Temple, Egypt. f, Gateway to the Temple of Khonsu, Luxor, Egypt.

No. 2473, 66m — Romy Schneider (1938-82), actress, and scenes from: a, Bocaccio '70, 1962. b, Monpti, 1957. c, Sissi: The Fateful Years of an Empress, 1957. d, Ludwig, 1972. e, Un Amour de Pluie, 1974. f, What's New Pussycat?, 1965.

No. 2474, 66m — Wedding of Prince William and Catherine Middleton: a, Couple and Windsor Castle, Middleton holding flowers. b, Couple, Prince William at left, at Cambridge, Prince William. c, Couple, facing forward, at Cambridge, Middleton. d, Couple facing backwards, at Cambridge, Middleton. e, Couple and Winsor Castle. f, Couple, Pippa Middleton.

No. 2475, 66m — British warships: a, HMS Vindictive. b, HMS Victoria. c, HMS Eurydice. d, HMS Powerful (Poderoso). e, HMS Queen (Rainha). f, HMS Raleigh.

No. 2476, 66m — Sinking of the Titanic, cent. (in 2012), and: a, Captain Edward John Smith, ship officers William Murdoch, Henry Wilde, and Captain Charles Bartlett of the HMHS Britannic. b, Angel. c, Lucy Noel Martha Leslie. d, Margaret (Molly) Brown. e, Captain Smith. f, Iceberg.

No. 2477, 66m — Steam locomotives: a, Cheltenham Flyer with front of locomotive in black. b, Cheltenham Flyer with yellow and red rectangle on front. c, Bombay-Poona mail train. d, Silver Jubilee. e, Royal Scot. f, Scarborough Flyer.

No. 2478, 66m — Red Cross flag and ambulance: a, Ambulance crew member removing ambulance covering. b, Ambulance crew loading person into rear of ambulance. c, Motorcycle ambulance. d, Truck ambulance with two crew members in cab. e, Ambulance with rear doors open. f, Horse entering ambulance.

No. 2479, 66m — Dirigibles: a, British Army dirigible "Baby." b, 1852 dirigible. c, Black British war dirigible. d, French dirigible "Ville de Paris." e, German dirigible "Parseval." f, German dirigible "Clouth."

No. 2480, 66m — Trees: a, Malus spp. b, Crataegus monogyna. c, Betula alleghaniensis. d, Populus alba. e, Populus nigra. f, Aesculus hippocastanum.

No. 2481, 66m — Cacti and reptiles: a, Opuntia ficus-indica, Liolaemus platei platei. b, Copiapoa megarhiza, Conolophus subcristatus. c, Copiapoa cinerea, Sistrurus catenatus edwardsii. d, Stapelia pulchellus, Arizona elegans philipi. e, Echinopsis spachiana, Heloderma suspectum. f, Astrophytum hybrid, Gopherus agassizii.

No. 2482, 66m — Phascolarctos cinereus: a, Denomination at UR, animal name at LR. b, Denomination and animal name at UL, with tree trunk and branch. c, Denomination at UL, animal name at UR. d, Denomination at UR, animal name at UL. e, Denomination and animal name at UL, with tree branch only. f, Denomination at UL, animal name at left.

No. 2483, 66m — Cat breeds: a, Bengal. b, Pixie-bob. c, Abyssinian. d, American curl. e, Ocelot. f, Sokoke.

No. 2484, 66m — Dog breeds: a, Beagle. b, Yellow Labrador retriever. c, Irish setter. d, German shepherd. e, Boston terrier. f, English galgo.

No. 2485, 66m — Sharks: a, Alopias superciliosus, Prionace glauca. b, Eugomphodus taurus, Carcharhinus limbatus. c, Stegostoma fasciatum, Carcharhinus melanopterus. d, Triaenodon obesus, Squatina squatina. e, Isurus oxyrinchus, Triakis semifasciata. f, Scyliorhynus stellaris, Carcharhinus leucas.

No. 2486, 66m — Fishing: a, Gymnura natalensis. b, Coryphaena hippurus. c, Oreochromis mossambicus. d, Wattsia mossambica. e, Xiphias gladius. f, Penaeidae.

No. 2487, 66m — DNA molecules and animals: a, Vulpes zerda. b, Arctocephalus. c, Suricata suricatta. d, Ailuropoda melanoleuca. e, Odobenus rosmarus. f, Panthera leo.

No. 2488, 66m — Endangered animals: a, Lynx rufus. b, Two Ailuropoda melanoleuca. c, Panthera tigris. d, Ovis musimon. e, Loxodonta africana. f, Ceratotherium simum.

No. 2489, 175m, Horses racing, diff. No. 2490, 175m, Wheldon, diff. No. 2491, 175m, Simoncelli, diff. No. 2492, 175m, Soccer players, diff. No. 2493, 175m, Anatoly Karpov, chess player. No. 2494, 175m, Two Scouts, trefoil at LR. No. 2495, 175m, Jobs holding iPhone. No. 2496, 175m, Lucien Quélet, mycologist, and Clavariadelphus truncatus. No. 2497, 175m, Hooker, Vanda cathcarti. No. 2498, 175m, Dan Shechtman, 2011 Nobel Chemistry laureate. No. 2499, 175m, Yuri Gagarin, Russian cosmonaut. No. 2500, 175m, Amphitheater, Timgad, Algeria. No. 2501, 175m, Schneider, scene from Triple Cross, 1966. No. 2502, 175m, Prince William, Catherine Middleton, automobile. No. 2503, 175m, HMS Juno. No. 2504, 175m, Titanic and Captain Smith, diff. No. 2505, 175m, Torbay Express. No. 2506, 175m, Fire truck. No. 2507, 175m, French dirigible "Zodiac." No. 2508, 175m, Carpinus spp. No. 2509, 175m, Copiapoa haseltoniana and snake. No. 2510, 175m, Phascolarctos cinereus, diff. No. 2511, 175m, Siamese cat. No. 2512, 175m, Rottweiler. No. 2513, 175m, Sphyrna mokarran. No. 2514, 175m, Scomberomorus plurilineatus and fishermen. No. 2515, 175m, DNA molecule and Puijila darwini. No. 2516, 175m, Delphinus delphi, Stenella coeruleoalba.

2011, Dec. 30 — *Perf. 12¾x13¼*

Sheets of 6, #a-f

2461-2488 A436 Set of 28 835.00 835.00

Souvenir Sheets

Perf. 13¼x12¾

2489-2516 A436 Set of 28 375.00 375.00

Miniature Sheets

Indonesia 2012 Intl. Philatelic Exhibition — A437

No. 2517, 66m — Like No. 2482 with exhibition emblem at: a, LR. b, LL. c, LL. d, LR. e, LL. f, LL.

No. 2518, 66m — Like No. 2488 with exhibition emblem at: a, LR. b, LL. c, LL. d, LL. e, LR. f, LL.

2011, Dec. 30 — *Perf. 12¾x13¼*

Sheets of 6, #a-f

2517-2518 A437 Set of 2 60.00 60.00

New Year 2012 (Year of the Dragon) A438

Designs: No. 2519, Dragon and clouds.

No. 2520: a, 16m, Dragon dance. b, 16m, Chinese calligraphy by Wang Xizhi. c, 16m, Drogon, guitarist Wang Lee-hom. d, 66m, Bruce Lee and Jackie Chan, actors. e, 66m, People's Republic of China banknote depicting dragon. f, Dragon boat race.

175m, Mural depicting dragons.

2011, Dec. 30 — *Perf. 13¼*

2519 A438 66m multi 5.00 5.00

Perf. 12¾x13¼

2520 A438 Sheet of 6, #a-f 18.50 18.50

Souvenir Sheet

Perf. 13¼x12¾

2521 A438 175m multi 13.50 13.50

No. 2519 was printed in sheets of 4.

People, Events and Anniversaries — A439

No. 2522 — Whitney Houston (1963-2012), singer: a, 16m, Houston and Kevin Costner, actor (38x39mm). b, 16m, Two images of Houston (50x39mm). c, 16m, Houston (38x39mm). d, 66m, Houston and Michael Jackson, singer (38x39mm). e, 66m, Houston with arms raised (50x39mm). f, 66m, Houston and Aretha Franklin, singer (38x39mm).

No. 2523 — Elvis Presley (1935-77), singer: a, 16m, Presley and automobiles (38x39mm). b, 16m, Presley as child and as adult (50x39mm). c, 16m, Presley and woman on motorcycle (38x39mm). d, 66m, Presley with guitar (38x39mm). e, 66m, Presley waving (50x39mm). f, 66m, Presley with guitar and woman (38x39mm).

No. 2524 — 70th birthday of Paul McCartney, singer: a, 16m, McCartney playing guitar (38x39mm). b, 16m, McCartney, neck of guitar (50x39mm). c, 16m, McCartney and microphone (38x39mm). d, 66m, McCartney holding guitar (38x39mm). e, 66m, McCartney playing guitar, diff. (50x39mm). f, 66m, McCartney pointing (38x39mm).

No. 2525 — Ludwig van Beethoven (1770-1827), composer: a, 16m, Beethoven and Georg Frideric Handel, composer (38x39mm). b, 16m, Beethoven conducting (50x39mm). c, 16m, Beethoven and Johann Sebastian Bach, composer (38x39mm). d, 66m, Beethoven and building (38x39mm). e, 66m, Head of Beethoven (50x39mm). f, 66m, Beethoven and Johann Wolfgang von Goethe, writer (38x39mm).

No. 2526 — Joseph Haydn (1732-1809), composer: a, 16m, Haydn, building and statue (38x39mm). b, 16m, Haydn and Wolfgang Amadeus Mozart, composer (50x39mm). c, 16m, Haydn holding quill pen, building and statue (38x39mm). d, 66m, Beethoven, Herbert von Karajan conducting (38x39mm). e, 66m, Haydn, building and statue, diff (50x39mm). f, 66m, Bach and building (38x39mm).

No. 2527 — Gene Kelly (1912-96), actor: a, 16m, Kelly (38x39mm). b, 16m, Kelly and Debbie Reynolds, actress (50x39mm). c, 16m, Kelly and Cyd Charisse, actress (38x39mm). d, 66m, Kelly and Reynolds, diff. (38x39mm). e, 66m, Kelly and Donald O'Connor, actor (50x39mm). f, 66m, Kelly, diff (38x39mm).

No. 2528 — Judy Garland (1922-69), actress: a, 16m, Garland holding Toto in *The Wizard of Oz.* (38x39mm). b, 16m, Garland and daughter, Liza Minnelli. (50x39mm). c, 16m, Garland and Margaret Hamilton as Wicked Witch of the West (38x39mm). d, 66m, Garland (38x39mm). e, 66m, Garland with Jack Haley as the Tinman and Ray Bolger as the Scarecrow (50x39mm). f, 66m, Garland holding tennis racket (38x39mm).

No. 2529 — Marilyn Monroe (1926-62), actress: a, 16m, Monroe as adult and child (38x39mm). b, 16m, Two images of Monroe (50x39mm). c, 16m, Monroe and actors Tony Curtis and Jack Lemmon in *Some Like It Hot* (38x39mm). d, 66m, Monroe in pink blouse (38x39mm). e, 66m, Two images of Monroe, diff. (50x39mm). f, 66m, Two images of Monroe, diff. (38x39mm).

No. 2530 — Elizabeth Taylor (1932-2011), actress: a, 16m, Taylor (38x39mm). b, 16m, Taylor and husband, Richard Burton, actor (50x39mm). c, 16m, Taylor in chair (38x39mm). d, 66m, Taylor and Lassie (dog) (38x39mm). e, 66m, Taylor and Burton, diff. (50x39mm). f, 66m, Taylor and James Dean, actor (38x39mm).

No. 2531 — François Truffaut (1932-84), actor and director, and: a, 16m, Scene from *The 400 Blows,* 1959 (38x39mm). b, 16m, Scene from *Close Encounters of the Third Kind,* 1977 (50x39mm). c, 16m, Scene from *The Last Metro,* 1980 (38x39mm). d, 66m, Actress Isabelle Adjani in scene from *The Story of Adele H,* 1975 (38x39mm). e, 66m, Actress Catherine Deneuve in scene from *The Last Metro* (50x39mm). f, 66m, Alfred Hitchcock, director (38x39mm).

No. 2532 — 80th birthday of Milos Forman, director: a, 16m, Tom Hulce in *Amadeus,* 1984 (38x39mm). b, 16m, Scene from *One Flew Over the Cuckoo's Nest,* 1975 (50x39mm). c, 16m, Hulce and F. Murray Abraham in *Amadeus* (38x39mm). d, 66m, Scene from *Hair,* 1979 (38x39mm). e, 66m, Forman (50x39mm). f, 66m, Jim Carrey in *Man on the Moon,* 1999 (38x39mm).

No. 2533 — Pres. John F. Kennedy (1917-63): a, 16m, Senator Robert F. Kennedy, brother, and detail from painting *Washington Crossing the Delaware* (38x39mm). b, 16m, Senator Edward M. Kennedy, brother (50x39mm). c, 16m, Pres. Bill Clinton and Indian (38x39mm). d, 66m, Pres. Barack Obama, Dr. Martin Luther King, Jr. (38x39mm). e, 66m, Kennedy and astronaut on Moon (50x39mm). f, 66m, Wife, Jacqueline, and son, John, Jr. (38x39mm).

No. 2534 — Boxers: a, 16m, Marvin Hagler (38x39mm). b, 16m, Joe Frazier (50x39mm). c, 16m, Rocky Marciano (38x39mm). d, 66m, Muhammad Ali (38x39mm). e, 66m, Joe Louis (50x39mm). f, 66m, Mike Tyson (38x39mm).

No. 2535 — St. Joan of Arc (1412-31): a, 16m, Holding lamb (38x39mm). b, 16m, In armor on one knee (50x39mm). c, 16m, Tied to stake, holding crucifix (38x39mm). d, 66m, At coronation of King Charles VII (38x39mm). e, 66m, In battle on horse (50x39mm). f, 66m, Interrogation by Cardinal Winchester (38x39mm).

No. 2536 — Leonardo da Vinci (1452-1519), artist and inventor: a, 16m, Glider, facing right (38x39mm). b, 16m, Gears (50x39mm). c, 16m, Ornithopter, view of underside (38x39mm). d, 66m, Leonardo holding model of invention (38x39mm). e, 66m, Machine gun (50x39mm). f, 66m, Paddle-wheel boat (38x39mm).

No. 2537 — Sir Isaac Newton (1642-1727), physicist and astronomer: a, 16m, Telescopes (38x39mm). b, 16m, Newton and statue (50x39mm). c, 16m, XMM-Newton orbiting observatory (38x39mm). d, 66m, Newton and house (38x39mm). e, 66m, Observatory (50x39mm). f, 66m, Newton and Zosimos of Panopolis, alchemist (38x39mm).

No. 2538 — Thomas Edison (1847-1931), inventor, and: a, 16m, Phonograph, compact disc (38x39mm). b, 16m, Edison's automobile and Infiniti Essence prototype (50x39mm). c, 16m, Motion picture camera (38x39mm). d, 66m, Phonograph, record, speakers (38x39mm). e, 66m, Lightbulb, LED light (50x39mm). f, 66m, Lightbulb, microphone (38x39mm).

No. 2539 — Nobel laureates in Chemistry: a, 16m, Ei-ichi Negishi, 2011 (38x39mm). b, 16m, Jacobus Henricus van 't Hoff, 1901 (50x39mm). c, 16m, Ernest Rutherford, 1908 (38x39mm). d, 66m, Marie Curie, 1911 (38x39mm). e, 66m, Sir William Ramsay, 1904 (50x39mm). f, 66m, Wilhelm Ostwald, 1909 (38x39mm).

No. 2540 — Jean-Jacques Rousseau (1712-78), philosopher: a, 16m, Voltaire, philosopher (38x39mm). b, 16m, Thomas Hobbes, philosopher (50x39mm). c, 16m, Voltaire and statue (38x39mm). d, 66m, Rousseau and statue (38x39mm). e, 66m, Louise d'Epinay, writer, and Denis Diderot, philosopher (50x39mm). f, 66m, Rousseau (38x39mm).

No. 2541 — Scenes from novels by Charles Dickens (1812-70): a, 16m, Group of children (38x39mm). b, 16m, Old man, crowded street (50x39mm). c, 16m, Old man and boy (38x39mm). d, 66m, Boy, people wearing hats (38x39mm). e, 66m, Boy and building (50x39mm). f, 66m, Man eating from bowl, buildings (38x39mm).

No. 2542 — Alexandre Dumas (1802-70), writer: a, 16m, Dumas, Gerard Depardieu as Edmond Dantes in *The Count of Monte Cristo* (38x39mm). b, 16m, Statue of Dumas, scene from *The Three Musketeers* (50x39mm). c, 16m, Scene from *The Vicomte de Bragelonne* (38x39mm). d, 66m, Scene from *The Lady of the Camellias,* by Alexandre Dumas (1824-95) (38x39mm). e, 66m, Auguste Maquet, writer who collaborated with Dumas, swordsman on horseback (50x39mm). f, 66m, Scene from *Queen Margot* (38x39mm).

No. 2543 — King Frederick II of Prussia (1712-86): a, 16m, Frederick II, Francesco Algarotti, philosopher (38x39mm). b, 16m, Frederick II on medal, Queen consorr Elisabeth-Christine of Brunswick-Wolfenbüttel-Bevern (50x39mm). c, 16m, Frederick II, St. Hedwig's Cathedral, Berlin (38x39mm). d, 66m, Frederick II and statue (38x39mm). e, 66m, Brandenburg Gate, Berlin (50x39mm). f, 66m, Frederick II, Pope Clement XIV (38x39mm).

No. 2544 — Napoleon III (1808-73), French emperor: a, 16m, Napoleon III, Battle of Solferino (38x39mm). b, 16m, Napoleon III at the Tuileries (50x39mm). c, 16m, Napoleon III and Emir Abdelkader, Algerian rebel leader (38x39mm). d, 66m, Napoleon III, Georges-Eugène Hausmann, Parisian civic planner (38x39mm). e, 66m, Napoleon III on horseback (50x39mm). f, 66m, Empress consort Eugénie de Montijo (38x39mm).

No. 2545 — Buildings designed by Antonio Gaudí (1852-1926): a, 16m, Bellesguard, Barcelona, Josep Fontseré, architect (38x39mm). b, 16m, Sagrada Familia Basilica, Barcelona, Joan Miró, painter (50x39mm). c, 16m, Gaudi, Güell Pavilion, Barcelona (38x39mm). d, 66m, Sagrada Familia Basilica, Henri Matisse, painter (38x39mm). e, 66m, Gaudí's Caprice, Comillas, Spain (50x39mm). f, 66m, Eugène Viollet-le-Duc, architect, Casa Vicens, Barcelona (38x39mm).

No. 2546 — Discovery of bust of Nefertiti, cent.: a, 16m, Photographer (38x39mm). b, 16m, Ludwig Borchardt, discoverer, holding bust (50x39mm). c, 16m, Archaeologists examining sculpted tile (38x39mm). d, 66m, Zahi Hawass, Egyptian Minister of Antiquities, Pyramids (38x39mm). e, 66m, Bust and Egyptian statuary (50x39mm). f, 66m, Borchardt uncovering bust (38x39mm).

No. 2547 — Paul von Hindenburg (1847-1934), German President, and Zeppelin LZ-129 Hindenburg: a, 16m, Denomination in white, Pres. Hindenburg in military uniform at LR (38x39mm). b, 16m, Denomination in black Pres. Hindenburg in military uniform at LL (50x39mm). c, 16m, Denomination in black, Pres. Hindenburg at LR (38x39mm). d, 66m, Denomination in black, Pres. Hindenburg in military uniform at LR (38x39mm). e, 66m, Denomination in black, Pres. Hindenburg at LR (50x39mm). f, 66m, Denomination in black, Pres. Hindenburg in military uniform at LL (38x39mm).

No. 2548 — Bombardment of Guernica, Spain, 75th anniv.: a, 16m, Junkers Ju-52, denomination at UL (38x39mm). b, 16m, Messerschmitt Bf-109 (50x39mm). c, 16m, Junkers Ju-52, denomination at UR (38x39mm). d, 66m, Messerschmitt Bf-109, diff. (38x39mm). e, 66m, Heinkel He-111 (50x39mm). f, 66m, Pablo Picasso, artist (38x39mm).

No. 2549 — People involved in strugtgle for black civil rights: a, 16m, John Brown, abolitionist, slaves in field (38x39mm). b, 16m, William Wilberforce, British abolitionist, slave auction (50x39mm). c, 16m, Senator Henry Clay, whipping of slave (38x39mm). d, 66m, Pres. Abraham Lincoln, U.S. Capitol, statue of chained slave (38x39mm). e, 66m, Lincoln, Pres. George Washington, Civil War battle (50x39mm). f, 66m, Frederick Douglass, Pres. John F. Kennedy (38x39mm).

No. 2550 — First solo transatlantic flight of Charles Lindbergh, 85th anniv.: a, 16m, Spirit of St. Louis, name of airplane at center bottom (38x39mm). b, 16m, Charles Lindbergh, pilot, Spirit of St. Louis (50x39mm). c, 16m, Spirit of St. Louis, name of airplane at UL (38x39mm). d, 66m, Lindbergh, Solar Impulse airplane (38x39mm). e, 66m, Lindbergh, Bernard Piccard, pilot of Solar Impulse (50x39mm). f, 66m, Lindbergh, with helmet, Spirit of St. Louis (38x39mm).

No. 2551 — Space flight of Friendship 7, 50th anniv.: a, 16m, John Glenn, NASA emblem, X-plane (38x39mm). b, 16m, Glenn in space suit and flight suit, experimental plane (50x39mm). c, 16m, Glenn and XB-70 airplane (38x39mm). d, 66m, Glenn, Friendship 7 emblem, Navy airplane (38x39mm). e, 66m, Glenn in space suit and flight suit, X-15 airplane (50x39mm). f, 66m, Glenn and airplane, diff. (38x39mm).

No. 2552, 175m, Houston, diff. No. 2553, 175m, Presley and Frank Sinatra. No. 2554, 175m, McCartney and other members of the Beatles. No. 2555, 175m, Actor Gary Oldman as Beethoven in *Immortal Beloved.* No. 2556, 175m, Haydn and Beethoven. No. 2557, 175m, Kelly and Charisse, diff. No. 2558, 175m, Garland holding Toto, Hamilton as Wicked Witch of the West, Haley as the Tinman. No. 2559, 175m, Monroe as adult and child. No. 2560, 175m, Taylor with Lassie. No. 2561, 175m, Truffaut, scene from *Jules and Jim,* 1962. No. 2562, 175m, Forman, character from *Hair,* 1979. No. 2563, 175m, Pres. Kennedy and brother, Robert, Lunar Module. No. 2564, 175m, Louis, diff. No. 2565, 175m, St. Joan of Arc, diff. No. 2566, 175m, Leonardo painting the Mona Lisa. No. 2567, 175m, Statue of Newton, XMM-Newton. No. 2568, 175m, Edison, lightbulb. No. 2569, 175m, Van 't Hoff, molecular model, building. No. 2570, 175m, Diderot, statue of Rousseau. No. 2571, 175m, Dickens, building. No. 2572, 175m, Dumas, Scene from *The Count of Monte Cristo.* No. 2573, 175m, Frederick II of Prussia, musical concert. No. 2574, 175m, Napoleon III, diff. No. 2575, 175m, Gaudí, Sagrada Familia Basilica. No. 2576, 175m, Bust of Nefertiti, Henri James Simon, German arts patron. No. 2577, 175m, Hindenburg burning. No. 2578, 175m, Junkers Ju-52 over Guernica. No. 2579, 175m, Douglass, freed slaves. No. 2580, 175m, James Stewart as Lindbergh in *The Spirit of St. Louis,* 1957, Spirit of St. Louis. No. 2581, 175m, Glenn, prehistoric man.

2012, Feb. 28 ***Perf. 12¾x13¼***

Sheets of 6, #a-f

2522-2551 A439 Set of 30 550.00 550.00

Souvenir Sheets

2552-2581 A439 Set of 30 390.00 390.00

Souvenir Sheets

Russian Flag, Agathon and Oleg Fabergé, Fabergé Eggs — A440

Litho. & Embossed With Foil Application

2012, Feb. 28 ***Perf. 13¼***

2582 A440 175m gold & multi 13.00 13.00
a. With Rossica 2013 inscription in sheet margin 13.00 13.00

2583 A440 175m silver & multi 13.00 13.00
a. With Rossica 2013 inscription in sheet margin 13.00 13.00

Extinct Animals — A441

No. 2584, 66m — Extinct European animals: a, Coelodonta antiquitatis. b, Deinotherium giganteum. c, Equus ferus ferus. d, Hippopotamus antiquus.

No. 2585, 66m, vert. — Extinct African animals: a, Hippotragus leucophorus. b, Bos primigenius. c, Elephas recki. d, Eudorcas rufina.

No. 2586, 66m, vert. — Extinct bats: a, Nyctimene sanctacrucis. b, Pteropus tokudae. c, Pteropus pilosus. d, Mystacina robusta.

No. 2587, 66m — Extinct birds: a, Chlorostilbon bracei. b, Prosobonia leucoptera. c, Hemignathus sogittirostris. d, Xenicus longipes.

No. 2588, 66m, vert. — Extinct African birds: a, Psittacula exsul. b, Alectroenas nitidissima. c, Raphus cucullatus. d, Porphyrio coerulescens.

No. 2589, 66m, vert. — Extinct parrots: a, Cyanoramphus ulietanus, Psittacula wardi. b, Ara tricolor, Psittacula exsul. c, Psephotus pulcherrimus. d, Mascarene parrot, Nestor productus.

No. 2590, 66m — Extinct reptiles: a, Desmatosuchus. b, Scaphonyx. c, Erythrosuchus. d, Dimetrodon.

No. 2591, 66m — Extinct marine life: a, Ichthyostega. b, Bothriolepsis. c, Henodus chelyops. d, Belemnitida.

No. 2592, 175m, Ursus spelaeus. No. 2593, 175m, Panthera leo leo, vert. No. 2594, 175m, Dobsonia chapmani, vert. No. 2595, 175m, Mascarenotus murivorus, Aplonis mavornata. No. 2596, 175m, Mascarinus mascarinus, vert. No. 2597, 175m, Cyanoramphus zealandicus. No. 2598, 175m, Lystrosaurus. No. 2599, 175m, Monachus tropicalis.

2012, Apr. 30 **Litho.** ***Perf. 13¼***

Sheets of 4, #a-d

2584-2591 A441 Set of 8 155.00 155.00

Souvenir Sheets

2592-2599 A441 Set of 8 105.00 105.00

Extinct and Endangered Animals — A442

No. 2600 — Extinct American animals: a, 16m, Macrauchenia patagonica. b, 16m, Bufo periglenes. c, 16m, Mammuthus columbi. d, 66m, Cuvieronius hyodon. e, 66m, Canis dirus. f, 66m, Dasypus bellus.

No. 2601 — Endangered primates: a, 16m, Pan paniscus holding plant near mouth. b, 16m, Two Pan paniscus. c, 16m, Adult and juvenile Pan paniscus. d, 66m, Pan troglodytes. e, 66m, Two Gorilla berengei. f, 66m, Two adult and one juvenile Gorilla berengei.

No. 2602 — Endangered cats: a, 16m, Panthera uncia. b, 16m, Felis planiceps. c,

16m, Panthera tigris tigris. d, 66m, Felis iriomotensis. e, 66m, Felis viverrina. f, 66m, Panthera leo persica.

No. 2603 — Endangered dolphins: a, 16m, Pontoporia blainvillei. b, 16m, Orcaella brevirostris. c, 16m, Cephalorhynchus hectori. d, 66m, Tursiops truncatus ponticus. e, 66m, Lipotes vexillifer. f, 66m, Platanista gangetica.

No. 2604 — Endangered birds: a, 16m, Buteo jamaicensis. b, 16m, Harpyhaliaetus coronatus. c, 16m, Gyps indicus. d, 66m, Pithecophaga jefferyi. e, 66m, Gyps bengalensis. f, 66m, Haliaeetus vociferoides.

No. 2605, vert. — Endangered marine birds: a, 16m, Puffinus newelli, Larus bulleri. b, 16m, Ciconia boyciana. c, 16m, Puffinus mauretanicus, Sterna lorata. d, 66m, Platalea minor. e, 66m, Hymenolaimus malacorhynchos. f, 66m, Mitu mitu.

No. 2606, vert. — Extinct birds: a, 16m, Microgoura meeki. b, 16m, Ophrysia superciliosa. c, 16m, Phalacrocorax perspicillatus, foliage in background. d, 66m, Ptilonopus mercierii. e, 66m, Ectopistes migratorius. f, 66m, Ectopistes migratorius, Columba jouyi.

No. 2607, vert. — Extinct birds: a, 16m, Fregilupus varius. b, 16m, Amazona violacea. c, 16m, Myadestes myadestinus. d, 66m, Phalacrocorax perspicillatus on rock. e, 66m, Pezophaps solitaria. f, 66m, Porphyria mantelli.

No. 2608 — Endangered insects: a, 16m, Crotchiella brachyptera. b, 16m, Cicindela marginipennis. c, 16m, Xylotoles costatus. d, 66m, Polyphylla barbata. e, 66m, Cicindela puritana. f, 66m, Polposipus herculeanus.

No. 2609 — Endangered reptiles: a, 16m, Psammobates geometricus. b, 16m, Crocodylus siamensis. c, 16m, Ceratophora tennentii. d, 66m, Varanus komodoensis. e, 66m, Callagur borneoensis. f, 66m, Cyclura pinguis.

No. 2610 — Endangered snakes: a, 16m, Aspidites ramsayi. b, 16m, Paracontias minimus. c, 16m, Montivipera albizona. d, 66m, Paracontias rothschildi. e, 66m, Thamnophis sirtalis. f, 66m, Coluber constrictor priapus.

No. 2611 — Endangered carnivores: a, 16m, Vulpes bengalensis. b, 16m, Puma concolor coryi. c, 16m, Canis lupus rufus. d, 66m, Panthera tigris sumatrae. e, 66m, Leopardus pardalis. f, 66m, Lycaon pictus.

No. 2612 — Endangered marine life: a, 16m, Neophoca cinerea. b, 16m, Phocoena sinus. c, 16m, Thunnus thynnus. d, 66m, Enhydra lutris. e, 66m, Megaptera novaeangliae. f, 66m, Oncorhynchus tshawytscha.

No. 2613 — Extinct animals: a, 16m, Dusicyon australis. b, 16m, Macrotus leucura. c, 16m, Equus quagga quagga. d, 66m, Onychogalea lunata. e, 66m, Thylacinus cynocephalus. f, 66m, Pinuinus impennis.

No. 2614, 175m, Bison antiquus. No. 2615, 175m, Three Gorilla berengei, diff. No. 2616, 175m, Lynx pardinus. No. 2617, 175m, Cephalorhynchus hectori maui, vert. No. 2618, 175m, Neophron percnopterus. No. 2619, 175m, Phalacrocorax featherstoni. No. 2620, 175m, Rhodonessa caryophyllacea. No. 2621, 175m, Ara erythrocephala, vert. No. 2622, 175m, Nicrophorus americanus. No. 2623, 175m, Crocodylus cataphractus, Pseudemys rubriventris bangsi, vert. No. 2624, 175m, Pseudechis porphyriacus. No. 2625, 175m, Carcharodon carcharias, vert. No. 2626, 175m, Monachus schauinslandi. No. 2627, 175m, Panthera leo spelaea.

2012, Apr. 30 Sheets of 6, #a-f

2600-2613	A442	Set of 14	255.00	255.00

Souvenir Sheets

2614-2627	A442	Set of 14	180.00	180.00

Extinct and Endangered Animals — A443

No. 2628 — Extinct Asian animals: a, 16m, Panthera tigris balica. b, 16m, Neofelis nebulosa brachyura. c, 16m, Gazella arabica. d, 16m, Megatapirus augustus. e, 16m, Canis lupus hodophilax. f, 16m, Cervus schomburgki. g, 92m, Dicerorhinus sumatrensis lasiotis. h, 92m, Panthera tigris virgata.

No. 2629, vert. — Extinct animals of Oceania: a, 16m, Rattus nativitatis. b, 16m, Onychogalea lunata. c, 16m, Caloprymnus campestris. d, 16m, Prototroctes oxyrhynchus. e, 16m, Peltobatrachus pustulatus. f, 16m, Hoplodactylus delcourti. g, 92m, Macrotis leucura. h, 92m, Mystacina robusta.

No. 2630 — Extinct rodents: a, 16m, Pseudomys gouldii. b, 16m, Peromyscus pembertoni. c, 16m, Orysomys nelsoni. d, 16m, Geocapromys thoracatus. e, 16m, Leporillus apicalis. f, 16m, Microtis bavaricus. g, 92m, Notomys macrotis. h, 92m, Megalomys luciae.

No. 2631 — Endangered ungulates: a, 16m, Equus hemionus. b, 16m, Gazella cuvieri. c, 16m, Hippocamelus bisculus. d, 16m, Equus africanus. e, 16m, Kobus megaceros. f, 16m, Addax nasomaculatus. g, 92m, Nilgiritragus hylocrius. h, 92m, Bubalus depressicornis.

No. 2632, vert. — Extinct birds: a, 16m, Quiscalus palustris. b, 16m, Bowdleria rufescens. c, 16m, Alectroenas nitidissima. d, 16m, Porzana palmeri. e, 16m, Nesoclopeus poecilopterus. f, 16m, Pennula sandwichensis. g, 92m, Moho nobilis. h, 92m, Gallirallus wakensis.

No. 2633, vert. — Extinct birds: a, 16m, Rhodacanthis flaviceps. b, 16m, Aplonis corvina. c, 16m, Chaunoproctus ferreorostris. d, 16m, Chaetoptila angustipluma. e, 16m, Fregilus varius. f, 16m, Chloridops kona. g, 92m, Ciridops anna. h, 92m, Zoothera terrestris.

No. 2634, vert. — Endangered butterflies: a, 16m, Speyeria zerene myrtleae. b, 16m, Manduca blackburni. c, 16m, Icaricia icarioides fenderi. d, 16m, Ornithoptera alexandrae. e, 16m, Papilio chikae. f, 16m, Ornithoptera croesus. g, 92m, Apodemia mormo langei. h, 92m, Pterourus homerus.

No. 2635 — Endangered turtles: a, 16m, Platysternon megacephalum. b, 16m, Batagur trivittata. c, 16m, Pelochelys cantorii. d, 16m, Psammobates geometricus. e, 16m, Caretta caretta. f, 16m, Mauremys sinensis. g, 92m, Dermochelys coriacea. h, 92m, Eretmochelys imbricata.

No. 2636, 175m, Panthera tigris sondaica. No. 2637, 175m, Thylacinus cynocephalus, vert. No. 2638, 175m, Notomys amplus, Rattus macleari, vert.. No. 2639, 175m, Gazella dama. No. 2640, 175m, Rhodacanthis palmeri, vert. No. 2641, 175m, Zosterops strenuus, vert. No. 2642, 175m, Ornithoptera meridionalis, vert. No. 2643, 175m, Chelonia mydas.

2012, Apr. 30 Sheets of 8, #a-h

2628-2635	A443	Set of 8	165.00	165.00

Souvenir Sheets

2636-2643	A443	Set of 8	105.00	105.00

People, Events and Anniversaries — A444

No. 2644 — Reign of Queen Elizabeth II, 60th anniv.: a, 16m, Queen waving, personal crest, with red and white areas of flag under country name. b, 16m, As "a," with red, white and blue areas of flag under country name. c, 16m, As "a," with continuation of photograph under country name. d, 66m, Queen in white dress, arms, with red, white and blue areas of flag under country name at left. e, 66m, As "d," with no part of flag under country name. f, 66m, As "d," with red, white and blue areas of flag under country name across entire panel.

No. 2645 — Airbus A380: a, 16m, Of Singapore Airlines. b, 16m, Of Transaero Airlines. c, 16m, Of Etihad Airways. d, 66m, With A380 on vertical stabilizer. e, 66m, Of British Airways. f, 66m, With white vertical stabilizer.

No. 2646 — Wilbur Wright (1867-1912), aviation pioneer, and: a, 16m, Wright Flyer, denomination in white. b, 16m, Wright and passenger seated in Wright Flyer. c, 16m, Wilbur and Orville Wright walking. d, 66m, Wright Flyer, no wheels visible. e, 66m, Wright Flyer with wheels. f, 66m, Wright Flyer, Statue of Liberty.

No. 2647 — Harriet Quimby (1875-1912), aviation pioneer, and: a, 16m, Bleriot XI. b, 16m, Nose of Bleriot XI. c, 16m, Inset photograph of Quimby, tail of airplane. d, 66m, Tail of Bleriot XI, complete Bleriot XI in flight. e, 66m, Nose of airplane, diff. f, 66m, Airplane wing tip at left, Bleriot XI at right.

No. 2648 — Hubert Latham (1883-1912), aviation pioneer: a, 16m, Dark blue Antoinette VII. b, 16m, Gray Antoinette VII. c, 16m, Lilac rose Antoinette VII. d, 66m, Latham at LL, Prussian blue Antoinette VII. e, 66m, Latham at LR, blue Antoinette VII. f, 66m, Latham at LL, gray Antoinette VII.

No. 2649 — Sinking of the Titanic, cent.: a, 16m, Lifeboats near sinking Titanic. b, 16m, Titanic, bird, ship with sails. c, 16m, Titanic and tugboat. d, 66m, Titanic at sea, other boats, lower portion of Titanic Memorial. e, 66m, Titanic hitting iceberg, ship name at LL. f, 66m, Titanic approaching iceberg, ship name at UL.

No. 2650 — Byron Nelson (1912-2006), golfer, and: a, 16m, Nelson holding golf club while walking. b, 16m, Nelson holding trophy. c, 16m, Nelson swinging golf club. d, 66m, Emblem of World Golf Hall of Fame. e, 66m, 1974 Bob Jones Award. f, 66m, Congressional medal commemorating Nelson.

No. 2651 — Marilyn Monroe (1926-62), actress: a, 16m, Holding open umbrella. b, 16m, Lying on bed, wearing white blouse with striped neckline. c, 16m, Wearing black dress. d, 66m, Wearing necklace on wrist. e, 66m, Holding closed umbrella. f, 66m, Holding beach bag.

No. 2652 — Elvis Presley (1935-77), singer: a, 16m, Pointing finger upward. b, 16m, Holding microphone stand. c, 16m, Playing guitar. d, 66m, Playing guitar, diff. e, 66m, Seated. f, 66m, On motorcycle with woman.

No. 2653 — Achille-Claude Debussy (1862-1918), composer, and painting by Claude Monet from: a, 16m, 1904. b, 16m, 1903. c, 16m, 1880. d, 66m, 1893. e, 66m, 1886. f, 66m, 1868-69.

No. 2654 — Famous Russians: a, 16m, Nikolai Rimsky-Korsakov, composer. b, 16m, Modest Mussorgsky, composer. c, 16m, César Cui, composer. d, 66m, Vladimir Stasov, critic. e, 66m, Mily Balakirev, composer. f, 66m, Alexander Borodin, composer.

No. 2655 — Igor Stravinsky (1882-1971), composer, and: a, 16m, Sculpture, score with C clef at left. b, 16m, Sculpture, musical note to left of country name. c, 16m, Sculpture, no musical note to left of country name. d, 66m, Dancers with beards. e, 66m, Dancers, score with G clef at left. f, 66m, Women dancers in red costumes.

No. 2656 — Peacemakers: a, 16m, Pope John Paul II, St. Peter's Square. b, 16m, Princess Diana, Picasso's Peace Dove. c, 16m, Pope John Paul II, Pieta, by Michelangelo. d, 66m, Mother Teresa. e, 66m, Princess Diana, British flag, Picasso's Peace Dove. f, 66m, Mother Teresa, Nobel medal.

No. 2657 — Mohandas K. Gandhi (1869-1948), Indian independence leader, and: a, 16m, Indian anti-corruption "bank note" without value. b, 16m, Lotus flower, quote written by Gandhi. c, 16m, Sun symbol. d, 66m, Gandhi and his possessions. e, 66m, Gandhi Memorial, Kanyakumari. f, 66m, Gandhi's pocket watch.

No. 2658 — Pan-African Women's Organization, 50th anniv.: a, 16m, Wangari Muta Maathai, 2004 Nobel Peace laureate, and text. b, 16m, Maathai, mother carrying infant. c, 16m, Maasai, two women. d, 66m, Assetou Koite, President of Pan-African Women's Organization, five women. e, 66m, Koite, women, tents. f, 66m, Koite, three women.

No. 2659 — Pope John Paul II (1920-2005): a, 16m, Waving. b, 16m, Two images. c, 16m, Holding infant. d, 66m, Seated, and praying. e, 66m, Holding catechism, arms of Pope John Paul II. f, 66m, Kissing icon of angel.

No. 2660 — Alexander Pushkin State Museum of Fine Arts, Moscow, cent.: a, 16m, 1888 painting by Vincent van Gogh. b, 16m, 1899 painting by Edgar Degas. c, 16m, 1901 painting by Pablo Picasso. d, 66m, Pushkin (1799-1837), writer. e, 66m, 1914 painting by Marc Chagall. f, 66m, 1626 painting by Rembrandt.

No. 2661 — Charles Darwin (1809-82), naturalist: a, 16m, Sauropelta. b, 16m, Allosaurus. c, 16m, Darwin and chimpanzee. d, 66m, Ceratosaurus. e, 66m, Darwin, pages from "On the Origin of Species," denomination in black. f, 66m, Darwin, page from "On the Origin of Species", denomination in white.

No. 2662 — Dean Arthur Amadon (1912-2003), ornithologist: a, 16m, Amadon and Haliaeetus leucocephalus. b, 16m, Amadon and Circus cyaneus. c, 16m, Amadon and Buteo magnirostris. d, 66m, Accipiter cooperii, Circus cyaneus. e, 66m, Haliaeetus albicilla. f, 66m, Accipiter gentilis.

No. 2663 — Volcanoes and vulcanologists: a, 16m, Kilauea Volcano, Hawaii, Sir William Hamilton. b, 16m, Sakurajima Volcano, Japan, Alfred Lacroix. c, 16m, Ol Doinyo Lengai Volcano, Tanzania, vulcanologist using camera. d, 66m, Mt. St. Helens, Washington, Déodat Gratet de Dolomieu. e, 66m, Gurung Merapi Volcano, Indonesia, vulcanologist in protective suit. f, 66m, Krakatoa Volcano, Indonesia, Haraldur Sigurdsson.

No. 2664 — Wernher von Braun (1912-77), rocket sceintist, and: a, 16m, Apollo 11. b, 16m, Saturn V rocket. c, 16m, Walt Disney. d, 66m, Head of Pres. John F. Kennedy, rocket launch. e, 66m, National Medal of Science, rocket launch. f, 66m, Kennedy and von Braun walking, rocket launch.

No. 2665 — Sally Ride (1951-2012), first American woman astronaut, and: a, 16m, Space Shuttle Challenger with open cargo bay doors. b, 16m, Challenger in flight. c, 16m, Challenger landing. d, 66m, Large picture of launch of Challenger, stars in background. e, 66m, Small picture of launch of Challenger. f, 66m, Challenger in orbit.

No. 2666 — Sergei Krikalev, Russian cosmonaut, and: a, 16m, LIBRAR-1. b, 16m, STS-88. c, 16m, Space Shuttle Endeavour. d, 66m, Soyuz TMA-6. e, 66m, Soyuz TMA-7. f, 66m, Space Shuttle Endeavour, diff.

No. 2667 — Liu Yang, Chinese astronaut: a, 16m, In space suit, waving, rocket. b, 16m, In space suit, saluting, Shenzhou-9, Tiangong-1. c, 16m, In space suit, Shenzhou 9 capsule. d, 66m, In uniform, Shenzhou-9. e, 66m, In uniform, saluting, Shenzhou-9. f, 66m, In uniform, waving, mission emblem.

No. 2668 — Animals of Kruger National Park, South Africa: a, 16m, Syncerus caffer. b, 16m, Hippopotamus amphibius. c, 16m, Tragelaphus strepsiceros. d, 66m, Lycaeon pictus. e, 66m, Equus quagga burchelli. f, 66m, Acinonyx jubatus.

No. 2669 — Death of Lonesome George, Pinta Island tortoise: a, 16m, With head raised. b, 16m, With head lowered, facing forward, large rock at right. c, 16m, Facing left, with head lowered. d, 66m, Facing forward, with head raised and turned left, diff. e, 66m, With head raised, facing right. f, 66m, With head lowered, facing left, diff.

No. 2670 — Paintings by Edouard Manet (1832-83) from: a, 16m, 1876. b, 16m, 1870. c, 16m, 1874. d, 66m, 1868. e, 66m, 1866. f, 66m, 1878.

No. 2671 — Jackson Pollock (1912-56), painter, and paintings from: a, 16m, 1946. b, 16m, 1950. c, 16m, 1942. d, 66m, 1940-41. e, 66m, 1943. f, 66m, 1950, diff.

No. 2672 — Art by Russian painters: a, 16m, Portrait of Konstantin Korovin, by Valentin Serov. b, 16m, Self-portrait of Mikhail Nesterov. c, 16m, Self-portrait of Ivan Kramskoi. d, 66m, Portrait of Alexander Herzen, by Nikolai Ge. e, 66m, Portrait of Ivan Goncharov, by Nikolai Yaroshenko. f, 66m, As "a," with different painting in background.

No. 2673, vert. — Paintings by Gustav Klimt (1862-1918) from: a, 16m, 1913. b, 16m, 1902. c, 16m, 1913, drawing by Egon Schiele. d, 66m, 1905. e, 66m, 1907-08. f, 66m, 1910.

No. 2674, 175m, Queen Elizabeth II, British flag. No. 2675, 175m, Airbus A380, diff. No. 2676, 175m, Wright, Wright Flyer, diff. No. 2677, 175m, Quimby, Bleriot XI, diff. No. 2678, 175m, Latham, Antoinette VII, diff. No. 2679, 175m, Titanic, Sterna paradisaea. No. 2680, 175m, Nelson, Congressional medal, diff. No.

2681, 175m, Monroe, diff. No. 2682, 175m, Presley kissing woman. No. 2683, 175m, Debussy, scene from opera *Pelléas et Mélisande*. No. 2684, 175m, Balakirev, painting by Serov. No. 2685, 175m, Stravinsky, diff. No. 2686, 175m, Kofi Annan, U.N. emblem, Nobel medal. No. 2687, 175m, Gandhi, actor Ben Kinglsey portraying Gandhi. No. 2688, 175m, Koite, Pan-African Women's Organization leaders. No. 2689, 175m, Pope John Paul II, illustration from Catechism. No. 2690, 175m, Pushkin, Alexander Pushkin State Museum of Fine Arts. No. 2691, 175m, Darwin and Euoplocephalus. No. 2692, 175m, Amadon and Accipiter striatus. No. 2693, 175m, Cross-section of volcano, Katia and Maurice Krafft, vulcanologists. No. 2694, 175m, Von Braun and his concept of circular space station. No. 2695, 175m, Ride, Space Shuttle Challenger on launch pad, STS-7 mission emblem. No. 2696, 175m, Krikalev, photograph of land and water taken from space. No. 2697, 175m, Liu Yang, Tiangong-1. No. 2698, 175m, Diceros bicornis. No. 2699, 175m, Lonesome George, diff. No. 2700, 175m, Manet painting from 1873. No. 2701, 175m, Pollock, painting from 1943, diff. No. 2702, 175m, Self-portrait of Nesterov, diff. No. 2703, 175m, Klimt and painting from 1909.

2012, Sept. 30 ***Perf. 13¼***

Sheets of 6, #a-f

2644-2673 A444 Set of 30 515.00 515.00

Souvenir Sheets

2674-2703 A444 Set of 30 375.00 375.00

Ungulani Ba Ka Khosa, Writer A445

2012, Oct. 9 ***Perf. 11x11¼***

2704 A445 92m buff & gray 6.25 6.25

Lubrapex 2012 Intl. Philatelic Exhibition, Brazil.

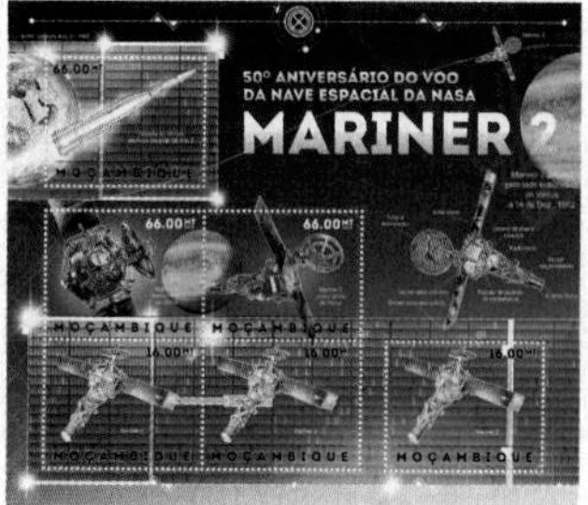

Events, Anniversaries and People — A446

No. 2705 — Mariner 2, 50th anniv., and: a, 16m, Gray vertical line, gray horizontal line at R. b, 16m, Gray horizontal line at L. c, 16m, Gray vertical line. d, 66m, Rocket, Earth. e, 66m, Venus at R. f, 66m, Venus at L.

No. 2706 — Apollo 17, 40th anniv.: a, 16m, Eugene Cernan, astronaut. b, 16m, Base of Lunar Module on Moon. c, 16m, Harrison Schmitt, astronaut. d, 66m, Ronald Evans, astronaut. e, 66m, Lunar Rover. f, 66m, Crew compartment of Lunar Module in space.

No. 2707 — Mars Rover Curiosity: a, 16m, Curiosity on Mars. b, 16m, Curiosity descending to Mars. c, 16m, Interior of Mars. d, 66m, Curiosity, diff. e, 66m, Martian rock. f, 66m, Flight Director Bobak Ferdowsi.

No. 2708 — Alouette 1 satellite, 50th anniv.: a, 16m, Engineers Colin A. Franklin, R.K. Brown and J. Barry, model of Alouette 1. b, 16m, Drs. Leroy Nelms and John Chapman, model of Alouette 1. c, 16m, Franklin and model. d, 66m, Alouette 1, maple leaf at LR. e, 66m, Five scientists studying information . f, 66m, Alouette 1, maple leaf at LL.

No. 2709 — Union Pacific Railroad, 150th anniv.: a, 16m, Big Boy No. 4014 locomotive. b, 16m, EMD DDA40X locomotive. c, 16m, Locomotive No. 844. d, 66m, GE AC6000CW locomotive. e, 66m, EMD DDA40X locomotive, diff. f, 66m, Big Boy No. 4019 locomotive.

No. 2710 — Chess match between Bobby Fischer and Boris Spassky, 40th anniv., with : a, 16m, Denomination in black, blue squares at UR. b, 16m, Red and white flag stripes at left. c, 16m, Red and white flag stripes at right. d, 66m, Red and white flag stripes at right. e, 66m, Globe, king's crown over Fischer. f, 66m, Flags of the Soviet Union and U.S.

No. 2711 — Svetozar Gligoric (1923-2012), chess player, and: a, 16m, Ludek Pachmant. b, 16m, Large magnetic chess board.. c, 16m, Vasily Smyslov. d, 66m, Mark Taimanov. e, 66m, Spassky. f, 66m, Chess board.

No. 2712 — Athletes at 2012 Paralympics, London: a, 16m, Cuiping Zhang. b, 16m, David Weir. c, 16m, Mark Rohan. d, 66m, Alan Fonteles Cardozo Oliveira. e, 66m, Esther Vergeer. f, 66m, Sarah Storey.

No. 2713 — Judo champions: a, 16m, Robert Van de Walle. b, 16m, Yasuhiro Yamashita. c, 16m, Shozo Fujii. d, 66m, Naoya Ogawa. e, 66m, David Douillet. f, 66m, Teddy Riner.

No. 2714 — Maurice Ravel (1875-1937), composer, and: a, 16m, Vaslav Nijinsky, choreographer, at piano. b, 16m, Roland Manuel, composer. c, 16m, Jacques Février, pianist. d, 66m, Ricardo Viñes, pianist. e, 66m, Eva Gauthier, opera singer, and various men. f, 66m, 1895 painting by Henri de Toulouse-Lautrec.

No. 2715 — Musicians: a, 16m, Metallica. b, 16m, Bryan Adams. c, 16m, Beyoncé. d, 66m, Shakira. e, 66m, Sir Elton John. f, 66m, Slash.

No. 2716 — Film stars and scenes from their movies: a, 16m, Johnny Depp. b, 16m, Gérard Depardieu. c, 16m, Nicole Kidman and Hugh Jackman. d, 66m, Angelina Jolie. e, 66m, Morgan Freeman and Jack Nichloson. f, 66m, Nicholson.

No. 2717 — Pope Benedict XVI: a, 16m, And painting by Raphael. b, 16m, Wearing zucchetto. c, 16m, And Vatican City arms. d, 66m, And arms of the Holy See. e, 66m, And arms of Pope Benedict XVI. f, 66m, Wearing red hat.

No. 2718 — Mother Teresa (1910-97), humanitarian, and: a, 16m, Nobel medal. b, 16m, Pope John Paul II. c, 16m, Earth. d, 66m, One child. e, 66m, Two children. f, 66m, Window of building.

No. 2719 — Princess Diana (1961-97), and London landmarks: a, 16m, Big Ben. b, 16m, St. Paul's Cathedral. c, 16m, Tower Bridge. d, 66m, Buckingham Palace. e, 66m, Big Ben, diff. f, 66m, Waterloo Bridge.

No. 2720 — Dr. Christiaan Barnard (1922-2001), first heart transplant surgeon, and: a, 16m, Operating room . b, 16m, Red cross. c, 16m, First heart transplant patient, Louis Washkansky. d, 66m, Hearts, arrow, red crosses. e, 66m, Medical helicopter. f, 66m, Cooler for transplant organs, red crosses.

No. 2721 — Red Cross campaign against AIDS: a, 16m, AIDS virus, mother holding child. b, 16m, Red Cross worker inspecting packages. c, 16m, Red Cross worker holding child. d, 66m, Child washing hands. e, 66m, Woman hugging Red Cross worker. f, 66m, People around large AIDS ribbon.

No. 2722 — Battle of Borodino, 200th anniv.: a, 16m, Napoleon Bonaparte, 1897 painting by Vasily Vereshchagin of battle. b, 16m, Four horsemen. c, 16m, Soldiers flags, one horseman. d, 66m, Horseman in blue uniform. e, 66m, Illustration of battle by unknown artist. f, 66m, Russian Field Marshal Mikhail Kutuzov, 1952 painting by Anatoly Shepelyuk.

No. 2723 — League for the Protection of Birds, cent.: a, 16m, Milvus milvus. b, 16m, Aquila fasciata. c, 16m, Falco naumanni. d, 66m, Pandion haliaetus. e, 66m, Tetrax tetrax. f, 66m, Coragyps atratus.

No. 2724 — Riga Zoo, cent.: a, 16m, Panthera leo. b, 16m, Bubo scandiaca. c, 16m, Cervus albirostris. d, 66m, Ursus arctos middendorffi. e, 66m, Tapirus terrestris. f, 66m, Amphiprion ocellaris.

No. 2725 — Sea shells: a, 16m, Spondylus princeps, Bulla striata. b, 16m, Scafander lignarius, Amusium japonicum. c, 16m, Tapes philippinarum, Murex pecten. d, 66m, Donax variabilis, Ovatella firmini, Haminoea hydalis. e, 66m, Pterynotus elongatus, Hexaplex radix. f, 66m, Hexaplex trunculus, Aplysia depilans, Isaac Lea (1792-1886), conchologist.

No. 2726 — Mary Anning (1799-1847), fossil collector: a, 16m, Dimorphodon macronyx. b, 16m, Anning, Mortoniceras inflatum fossil. c, 16m, Fossil bones. d, 66m, Ichthyosaurus fossils. e, 66m, Plesiosaurus. f, 66m, Anning, Plesiosaurus dolichodeirus fossil.

No. 2727 — Henry John Elwes (1846-1922), lepidopterist: a, 16m, Borboleta monarca. b, 16m, Grande borboleta azul, animal name at UR under denomination. c, 16m, Grande borboleta azul, animal name at UL. d, 66m, Elwes, Borboleta asa-de-pássaro. e, 66m, Borboleta "Morpho" azul. f, 66m, Elwes, Borboleta monarca.

No. 2728 — Tadas Ivanauskas (1882-1970), zoologist, and: a, 16m, Deer, Bubo bubo. b, 16m, Cygnus olor. c, 16m, Accipiter gentilis. d, 66m, Raccoon, Aquila pomarina. e, 66m, Upupa epops. f, 66m, Deer, Strix aluco, mouse.

No. 2729 — Gordon H. Cunningham (1892-1962), mycologist: a, 16m, Cunningham and Hygrophorus lucorum. b, 16m, Lycoperdon perlatum. c, 16m, Leccinum scabrum. d, 66m, Bolbitius psittacinus. e, 66m, Calocerea viscosa. f, 66m, Cunningham, Armillaria gallica.

No. 2730 — Dian Fossey (1932-85), zoologist: a, 16m, Gorilla beringei beringei. b, 16m, Fossey with forillas, head of Gorilla beringei beringei. c, 16m, Fossey with book, two Gorilla beringei beringei. d, 66m, Fossey, two Gorilla beringei beringei. e, 66m, Fossey, one Gorilla beringei beringei. f, 66m, Two Gorilla beringei beringei.

No. 2731 — Gustaf Dalén (1869-1937), 1912 Nobel Physics laureate, and: a, 16m, Celarain Lighthouse, Mexico. b, 16m, Point Stephens Lighthouse, Australia. c, 16m, Peninsula Point Lighthouse, Michigan. d, 66m, Dalén light for lighthouses. e, 66m, Barrenjoey Lighthouse, Australia. f, 66m, Skerryvore Lighthouse, Scotland.

No. 2732 — Charleston Lighthouse, South Carolina, and birds: a, 16m, Aix sponsa. b, 16m, Tringa incana. c, 16m, Larus californicus. d, 66m, Eudocimus albus. e, 66m, Lanus atricilla. f, 66m, Recurvirostra americana.

No. 2733 — UNESCO World Heritage Sites, 40th anniv.: a, 16m, Island of Mozambique. b, 16m, Osun-Osogbo Sacred Grove, Nigeria. c, 16m, Koutammakou, Land of the Battamariba, Togo. d, 66m, Royal Palaces of Abomey, Benin. e, 66m, Stone Circles of Senegambia, Gambia and Senegal. f, 66m, Kunta Kinteh Island, Gambia.

No. 2734 — Expo 2012, Yeosu, South Korea: a, 16m, Sky Tower, Thunnus thynnus. b, 16m, Ocean Pavilion, Tursiops truncatus. c, 16m, Marine Life Pavilion, Manta birostris. d, 66m, Korean Pavilion, Dugong dugon. e, 66m, Big-O, Dendrochirus zebra. f, 66m, Expo Digital Gallery, Phoca vitulina.

No. 2735, 175m, Mariner 2, Venus, diff. No. 2736, 175m, Apollo 17 Lunar Module, Lunar Rover, and astronaut on Moon. No. 2737, 175m, Mars Science Laboratory capsule containing Curiosity. No. 2738, 175m, Chapman and Alouette 1. No. 2739, 175m, Union Pacific No. 119 locomotive. No. 2740, 175m, Fischer and Spassky shaking hands. No. 2741, 175m, Gligoric and Fischer. No. 2742, 175m, Oscar Pistorius, Paralympian. No. 2743, 175m, Riner, diff. No. 2744, 175m, Ravel and Bolero dancers. No. 2745, 175m, U2. No. 2746, 175m, Brad Pitt. No. 2747, 175m, Pope Benedict XVI, crucifix. No. 2748, 175m, Mother Teresa holding child. No. 2749, 175m, Princess Diana, Buckingham Palace, diff. No. 2750, 175m, Barnard, heart, crosses. No. 2751, 175m, Africans, map, AIDS ribbon. No. 2752, 175m, Napoleon Bonaparte, 1987 Russian coin commemorating Battle of Borodino. No. 2753, 175m, Ciconia ciconia. No. 2754, 175m, Lemur catta, obverse and reverse of Latvian coin commemorating Riga Zoo. No. 2755, 175m, Lea, Venus verrucosa. No. 2756, 175m, Anning, Plesiosaurus macrocephalus fossil. No. 2757, 175m, Elwes and Borboleta "Morpho" cor-de-rosa. No. 2758, 175m, Ivanauskas, Ciconia nigra. No. 2759, 175m, Cunningham, Plectania melastoma. No. 2760, 175m, Fossey, three Gorilla beringei beringei. No. 2761, 175m, Dalén, Nobel medal. No. 2762, 175m, Charleston Lighthouse, Larus californicus, diff. No. 2763, 175m, Historic Cairo UNESCO World Heritage Site. No. 2764, 175m, Aquarium at Expo 2012.

2012, Oct. 30 ***Perf. 13¼***

Sheets of 6, #a-f

2705-2734 A446 Set of 30 500.00 500.00

Souvenir Sheets

2735-2764 A446 Set of 30 360.00 360.00

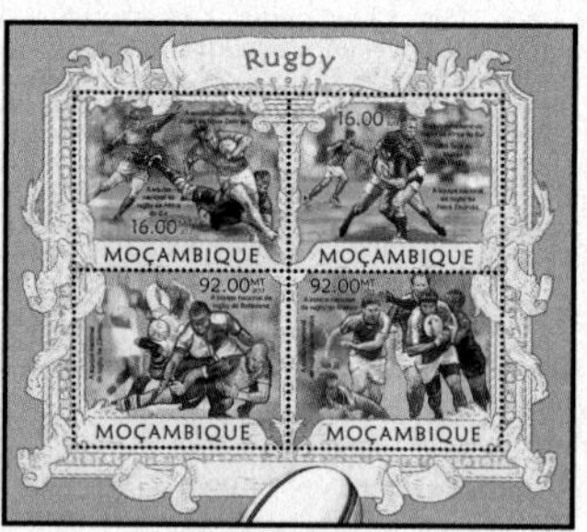

A447

No. 2765 — Rugby players from: a, 16m, New Zealand and South Africa, denomination at bottom. b, 16m, New Zealand and South Africa, denomination at top. c, 92m, Botswana and Zambia. d, 92m, Mexico and Jamaica.

No. 2766 — Rotary International emblem and cricket players: a, 16m, Adam Gilchrist. b, 16m, Donald Bradman. c, 92m, Viv Richards. d, 92m, Brian Lara.

No. 2767 — Table tennis players: a, 16m, Ding Ning. b, 16m, Wu Yang. c, 92m, Jörgen Persson, denomination at UR. d, 92m, Chinese player misidentified as Jörgen Persson, denomination at UL.

No. 2768 — Gilles Villeneuve (1950-82), race car driver, and: a, 16m, Race car, checkered flag. b, 16m, Race car. c, 92m, Race car, diff. d, 92m, Race car and track diagram.

No. 2769 — Lions International emblem and golfers: a, 16m, Ben Hogan. b, 16m, Jack Nicklaus. c, 92m, Bobby Jones. d, 92m, Arnold Palmer.

No. 2770 — Niels Bohr (1885-1962), physicist, and: a, 16m, Formula. b, 16m, Diagram of atom. c, 92m, Diagram of atom, diff. d, 92m, Albert Einstein.

No. 2771 — 2012 Nobel laureates: a, 16m, Serge Haroche, David J. Wineland, physics. b, 16m, Robert J. Lefkowitz, Brian K Kobilka, chemistry. c, 92m, Shinya Yamanaka, Sir John B. Gurdon, physiology or medicine. d, 92m, Alvin E. Roth, Lloyd S. Shapley, economics.

No. 2772 — Minerals: a, 16m, Beryl. b, 16m, Scapolite. c, 92m, Tourmaline. d, 92m, Beryl, diff.

No. 2773 — Campaign against malaria, 50th anniv. (in 2012): a, 16m, Mosquito, Brazil #C106, Ghana #128. b, 16m, Child receiving medicine, Syria #C267-C268. c, 92m, Child receiving medicine, Tunisia #404-405. d, 92m, Mosquito on globe, Democratic Republic of Congo #414-415.

No. 2774 — Orchids: a, 16m, Stanhopea insignis frost. b, 16m, Angraecum sesquipedale. c, 92m, Lycaste macrophylla. d, 92m, Miltonia vexillaria.

No. 2775 — Cat breeds: a, 16m, Singapura. b, 16m, Toyger. c, 92m, Bombay. d, 92m, Cymric.

No. 2776 — Fish: a, 16m, Signigobius biocellatus. b, 16m, Synchiropus splendidus. c, 92m, Antennarius commersoni. d, 92m, Pterois antennata.

No. 2777 — Dogs in art: a, 16m, Dogs Fighting, by Frans Snyders. b, 16m, Master Pelham, by George Romney. c, 92m, Two Hunting Dogs Tied to a Tree Stump, by Jacopo Bassano. d, 92m, Dog Pointing at a Partridge, by Jean-Baptiste Oudry.

No. 2778 — Paintings and self-portraits of Impressionist painters: a, 16m, Claude Monet. b, 16m, Edgar Degas. c, 92m, Pierre-Auguste Renoir. d, 92m, Freédéric Bazille.

No. 2779 — Paintings by Marc Chagall (1887-1985): a, 16m, The Concert, 1957, and Self-portrait, 1909-10. b, 16m, Chagall, The Madonna of the Village, 1942. c, 92m, Chagall, To My Betrothed, 1911. d, 92m, Cow with an Umbrella, 1946.

No. 2780 — Christmas art: a, 16m, Adoration of the Magi, by Gentile da Fabriano. b, 16m, The Annunciation, by Fra Filippo Lippi. c, 92m, Concert of Angels, by Matthias Grünewald. d, 92m, Adoration of the Shepherds, by Gerard von Honthorst.

No. 2781 — Sculptures by Alberto Chissano (1935-94): a, 16m, Three heads. b, 16m, One head. c, 92m, Chissano and head. d, 92m, One head, diff.

No. 2782 — Hans Werner Henze (1929-2012), composer: a, 16m, Scene from opera *The Hoopoe and the Triumph of Filial Love.*. b, 16m, Henze musical notes and clef. c, 92m, Scene from opera *Bajazzo*. d, 92m, Scene from opera *Gogo no Eiko*.

No. 2783 — Niccolò Paganini (1782-1840), composer, and: a, 16m, Paganini and La Scala Theater, Milan. b, 16m, Napoleon I, violin, score for *Napoleon Sonata*. c, 92m, Sculpture of Paganini by Sutton Betti, The Grand Canal of Venice, by J. M. W. Turner. d, 92m, Bust of Paganini, by Pierre-Jean David, violin.

No. 2784 — Genoese ship construction: a, 16m, 12th cent. Genoese ship, boat builder. b, 16m, Construction of hull. c, 92m, Construction of hull, diff. d, 92m, 11th century ship, boat builder.

No. 2785 — Venetian ship construction: a, 16m, Drawing of Venetian ship by Bernhard von Breidenbach. b, 16m, Ship and cross-section diagram. c, 92m, Drawings and Venetian galley. d, 92m, Ship under construction, boat building tools.

No. 2786 — Submarines: a, 16m, USS Gato (SS-212). b, 16m, Shchuka Class submarine, Russia. c, 92m, Japanese submarine I-506. d, 92m, German submarine U-23.

No. 2787 — Tanks: a, 16m, German Neubaufahrzeug Nr. 3-5 tank. b, 16m, Italian M 13/40 tank. c, 92m, M4 Sherman tank with 105mm howitzer, United States. d, 92m, Soviet T-34/76 tank.

No. 2788 — Japanese Shinkansen high-speed trains: a, 16m, Series N700. b, 16m, Series E6. c, 92m, Series E5. d, 92m, Series E3.

No. 2789 — European high-speed trains: a, 16m, FS Class ETR 500 Frecciarossa. b, 16m, LNER Class A4 4468 Mallard. c, 92m, AVE Class 102 Talgo 350. d, 92m, DRG Class SVT 137 Hamburg.

No. 2790 — Fire-fighting aircraft: a, 16m, Conair Turbo Firecat. b, 16m, Aerospatial AS-350B-2 Ecureuil helicopter. c, 92m, PZL-Swidnik W-3A Sokol helicopter. d, 92m, Canadair CL-215.

No. 2791 — Japanese aircraft: a, 16m, Mitsubishi F-4EJ Kai Phantom. b, 16m, Sikorsky (Mitsubishi) SH-60K (S70B-3) helicopter. c, 92m, ShinMaywa US-1A. d, 92m, Mitsubishi F-2A.

No. 2792 — Drones: a, 16m, Taurus UAV. b, 16m, MQ-1 Predator. c, 92m, Gojjet. d, 92m, MQ-4C BAMS Triton.

No. 2793 — Famous Atlantic hurricanes: a, 16m, Hurricane Katrina, 2005. b, 16m, Hurricane Felix, 2007. c, 92m, Hurricane Wilma, 2005. d, 92m, Hurricane Julia, 2010.

No. 2794 — New Year 2013 (Year of the Snake): a, 16m, Snake and yin-yang. b, 16m, Snake at right, Chinese text. c, 92m, Snake at left, Chinese text. d, 92m, Snake and "2013."

No. 2795, 175m, Percy Montgomery and South African rugby team. No. 2796, 175m, Rotary International emblem, cricket player

Sachin Tendulkar. No. 2797, 175m, Table tennis player Wu Yang. No. 2798, 175m, Villeneuve and Ferrari 312T3 race car. No. 2799, 175m, Golfer Annika Sorenstam. No. 2800, 175m, Bohr, diagram and equation. No. 2801, 175m, Mo Yan, 2012 Nobel Literature laureate. No. 2802, 175m, Scapolite and tourmaline. No. 2803, 175m, Mosquito on globe, Ryukyu Islands #95-96. No. 2804, 175m, Cypripedium orchids. No. 2805, 175m, Asian semi-longhair cat. No. 2806, 175m, Pteroidichthys amboinensis. No. 2807, 175m, The Hunting Party with Tsar Alexander III and Tsarina Maria Fedorovna, by Nikolai Semenovich Samokish. No. 2808, 175m, Garden at Sainte-Adresse, by Monet. No. 2809, 175m, Song of Songs IV, 1958, by Chagall, Portrait of Chagall, 1910, by Yury Pen. No. 2810, 175m, Adoration of the Magi, by Giotto di Bondone. No. 2811, 175m, Chissano and sculpture, diff. No. 2812, 175m, Henze and character from opera *Gisela*. No. 2813, 175m, Paganini and Il Cannone Guarnerius. No. 2814, 175m, Genoese ship under construction, 11th cent. No. 2815, 175m, Venetian galley. No. 2816, 175m, Tench Class submarine, United States. No. 2817, 175m, Soviet T-34/76 tank, diff. No. 2818, 175m, Shinkansen Series E954. No. 2819, 175m, SNCF TGV Thalys PBKA. No. 2820, 175m, Sikorsky S-70A Firehawk helicopter. No. 2821, 175m, Blue Impulse Kawasaki T4-46 5726. No. 2822, 175m, Polar Hawk and Boeing Phantom Ray drones. No. 2823, 175m, Hurricane Sandy. No. 2824, 175m, Snake, yin yand and Chinese text.

2013, Feb. 20 Litho. *Perf. 13¼*

Sheets of 4, #a-d

2765-2794 A447 Set of 30 450.00 450.00

Souvenir Sheets

2795-2824 A447 Set of 30 375.00 375.00

Worldwide Fund for Nature (WWF) A448

No. 2825 — Smutsia temmincki (Ground pangolin): a, Pangolin facing right. b, Head of pangolin, pangolin rolled in ball. c, Pangolin on rock. d, Pangolin and juvenile.

175p, Two Smutsia temmincki.

2013, Mar. 25 Litho. *Perf. 13¼*

2825	Horiz. strip of 4	15.00	15.00
a.-b.	A448 16m Either single	1.10	1.10
c.-d.	A448 92m Either single	6.25	6.25
e.	Miniature sheet of 8, 2 each #2825a-2825d, perf. 13x13¼	30.00	30.00

Souvenir Sheet

Perf. 13¼ Syncopated

2826 A448 175m multi 12.00 12.00

No. 2826 contains one 50x39mm stamp.

Transportation and Space — A449

No. 2827 — Dog teams: a, 16m, Four Canadian Eskimo dogs in harnesses. b, 16m, Two Siberian huskies in harnesses, leg of front dog behind "OC" of country name. c, 16m, Two Siberian huskies, dog sled. d, 16m, Tamaskan dogs. e, 16m, Alaskan malamute dogs. f, 16m, Two Siberian huskies in harnesses, front leg above "C" in country name.

No. 2828 — Horse transportation: a, 16m, Rider standing on two horses of four-horse team. b, 16m, Horse and sulky. c, 16m, Russian troika. d, 16m, Carriage drawn by two horses. e, 16m, Carriage drawn by six horses. f, 16m, English mail coach drawn by four horses.

No. 2829 — Famous bicycle riders in the Tour de France: a, 16m, Louison Bobet. b, 16m, Jacques Anquetil. c, 16m, Eddy Merckx. d, 16m, Bernard Hinault. e, 16m, Mark Cavendish. f, 16m, Bradley Wiggins.

No. 2830 — Ying Liwei, Chinese astronaut: a, 16m, And Shenzhou 5 re-entry capsule. b, 16m, In military uniform, with Shenzhou 5 rocket, flag of People's Republic of China. c, 16m, In spacesuit, adjusting helmet, Shenzhou 5 in space. d, 16m, In spacesuit, waving, Shenzhou 5 launch. e, 16m, In capsule wearing helmet. f, 16m, In capsule, with two fingers raised.

No. 2831 — Alan B. Shepard, Jr. (1923-98), American astronaut, and: a, 16m, Apollo 14 emblem. b, 16m, Apollo 14 plaque. c, 16m, Re-entry of Apollo 14. d, 16m, Mercury-Redstone 3 rocket. e, 16m, Mercury capsule. f, 92m, Statue of Shepard, by Robert L. Rasmussen.

No. 2832 — Apollo 8: a, 16m, Crew of Apollo 8 and launch. b, 16m, Apollo 8 orbiting Moon. c, 16m, Apollo 8 and Earth. d, 16m, Crew of Apollo 8, Apollo 8 and Earth. e, 16m, Crew in spacesuits, Apollo 8 emblem. f, 92m, Apollo 8 capsule, launch of Apollo 8.

No. 2833 — Iceboats with sail inscriptions of: a, 16m, 300. b, 16m, DM 8133. c, 16m, 44. d, 16m, DM 8931. e, 16m, 313. f, 92m, DM G-887.

No. 2834 — 2012-13 Vendée Globe Regatta: a, 16m, Crewman adjusting sails on sailboat. b, 16m, Boat with red and white sail. c, 16m, Crewman trying to keep sailboat from capsizing. d, 16m, Sailboats in line. e, 16m, Boat with black and yellow sails. f, 92m, Sailboat with blue and green hull.

No. 2835 — Rescue ships: a, 16m, 44-foot boat. b, 16m, United States Coast Guard hydrofoil. c, 16m, 45-foot boat. d, 16m, United States Coast Guard buoy tender No. 277. e, 16m, Severn Class rescue boat. f, 92m, 47-foot boat.

No. 2836 — Icebreakers: a, 16m, MV Paardeberg, Russia. b, 16m, Captain Chlebnikov, Russia. c, 16m, Oden, Sweden. d, 16m, Polarstern, Germany. e, 16m, Tempera, Finland. f, 92m, Polar Pevek, Norway.

No. 2837 — Steam locomotives: a, 16m, London & North Eastern Railway Class B17 4-6-0 Sandringham. b, 16m, London Midland & Scottish Railway 4-4-0. c, 16m, Metropolitan Railway tank locomotive. d, 16m, Johore State Railway 4-6-2. e, 16m, Dublin and South Easter Railway 4-4-2 King George. f, 92m, German State Railways 4-6-2 Pacific Express.

No. 2838 — London Metro cars: a, 16m, From 1938. b, 16m, From 1940. c, 16m, From 1973. d, 16m, From 1986. e, 16m, From 2011. f, 92m, Model of car of the future.

No. 2839 — Monorails: a, 16m, Mark VI. b, 16m, Innovia 300 on bridge. c, 16m, Mumbai monorail. d, 16m, Transrapid 09. e, 16m, Innovia 300, diff. f, 92m, Tama Toshi monorail.

No. 2840 — High-speed trains: a, 16m, ETR-500. b, 16m, TGV Réseau. c, 16m, AVE Talgo 350. d, 16m, Eurostar. e, 16m, KTX 2. f, 92m, Transrapid TR-09.

No. 2841 — Early aviators and their airplanes: a, 16m, Richard "Dick" Read Bentley and DeHavilland Moth. b, 16m, Claude Grahame-White and biplane. c, 16m, Owen Cathcart-Jones and Miles Hawk trainer. d, 16m, Alberto Santos-Dumont and Demoiselle. e, 16m, Ross Macpherson Smith and Vickers Vimy biplane. f, 92m, Alan John Cobham and Short Singapore flying boat.

No. 2842 — Small jet airplanes: a, 16m, Cessna Citation X. b, 16m, Hawker 800. c, 16m, Embraer Phenom 100. d, 16m, Gulfstream G200. e, 16m, Gulfstream G550. f, 92m, Dassault Falcon 2000.

No. 2843 — Last flight of the Concorde, 10th anniv.: a, 16m, Concorde and André Turcat, first French Concorde pilot. b, 16m, Barbara Harmer, first female Concorde pilot. c, 16m, Concorde and Sir Archibald Russell, designer of Concorde. d, 16m, Concorde and Brian Trubshaw, first British Concorde pilot. e, 16m, Concorde on fire, July 25, 2000. f, 92m, Last flight of Concorde, Nov. 26, 2003.

No. 2844 — Military helicopters: a, 16m, Mil Mi-24A. b, Boeing-Sikorsky RAH-66 Comanche. c, 16m, AgustaWestland AW-101. d, 16m, Westland Apache WAH-64D Longbow. e, 16m, Harbin Z-19. f, 92m, Mil Mi-171E.

No. 2845 — Drones: a, 16m, NASA Altair. b, 16m, General Atomics MQ-9 Reaper. c, 16m, UAV X-47B. d, 16m, Lockheed Martin RQ-170 Sentinel. e, 16m, UAV X-47A. f, 92m, General Atomics MQ-1C Gray Eagle.

No. 2846 — Dirigibles: a, 16m, Clouth, Germany. b, 16m, First British military dirigible. c, 16m, Torrres Quevedo, Spain. d, 16m, Ville de Paris, France. e, 16m, Baby, Great Britain. f, 92m, Zodiac type dirigible, France.

No. 2847 — Old race cars: a, 16m, 1954 Maserati 250F. b, 16m, 1951 Cooper Climax T51. c, 16m, 1940 Bugatti T73C. d, 16m, 1960 Lotus 18. e, 16m, 1966 Eagle-Climax T2G. f, 92m, 1952 Cooper Bristol.

No. 2848 — Popemobiles: a, 16m, FCS Star and Pope John Paul II. b, 16m, Metalpar Mercedes-Benz and motorcycle. c, 16m, Mercedes-Benz ML 430 and Pope Benedict XVI. d, 16m, Fiat Nuova Campagnola and Pope John Paul II. e, 16m, Mercedes-Benz M Class and Pope Benedict XVI. f, 92m, Pope Benedict XVI standing in Mercedes-Benz.

No. 2849 — Ferrari automobiles: a, 16m, Enzo Ferrari (1898-1988) and Auto Avio Costruzione 815. b, 16m, Ferrari 125 S. c, 16m, Ferrari 250 GTO. d, 16m, Ferrari 312 P. e, 16m, Ferrari 512 BB. f, 92m, Enzo Ferrari and Ferrari F40.

No. 2850 — Formula 1 racing champions: a, 16m, Sebastian Vettel in Renault race car. b, 16m, Vettel and Formula 1 Championship Trophy. c, 16m, Michael Schumacher and Formula 1 Championship Trophy. d, 16m, Schumacher in Mercedes race car. e, 16m, Fernando Alonso in Ferrari race car. f, 92m, Alonso and Formula 1 Championship Trophy.

No. 2851 — Motorcycles: a, 16m, 1896 Hildebrand Wolfmuller. b, 16m, 1911 Henderson. c, 16m, 1905 FN. d, 16m, 1925 DKW ZM175. e, 16m, 1920 Megola. f, 92m, 1921 Scott Flying Squirrel.

No. 2852 — Mail transport: a, 16m, English Royal Parcel Mail horse-drawn carriage. b, 16m, Workers and sacks in post office. c, 16m, Railroad mail car. d, 16m, Royal Mail truck. e, 16m, Workers and mail sacks near Royal Mail horse-drawn carriage. f, 92m, Mail sacks loaded on Royal Mail horse-drawn wagon.

No. 2853 — Police and rescue vehicles: a, 16m, Eurocopter AS-365N-3 Dauphin 2 police helicopter. b, 16m, BMW R1200RT-P police motorcycle. c, 16m, Higer KLQ6540 ambulance. d, 16m, Scania 94D fire truck. e, 16m, Lenco Bear Cat SWAT Team vehicle. f, 92m, Holden Rodeo police truck.

No. 2854 — Fire-fighting equipment: a, 16m, 1873 hose wagon. b, 16m, 1841 Paul Hodge steam-driven pumper and firefighter. c, 16m, Firemen on bicycle-chain driven vehicle, 1899 hose and ladder wagon. d, 16m, 1880 Piano pumper wagon. e, 92m, 1910 Electric fire engine, fireman in protective clothing. f, 92m, Fire truck with hoses and ladder.

No. 2855 — Military vehicles: a, 16m, Soldiers carrying kettle near Red Cross ambulance. b, 16m, Truck with open bed pulling gun. c, 16m, Red Cross workers near ambulances. d, 16m, Soldiers and Maxim motorcycle with sidecar. e, 92m, Cargo vehicle on tracks. f, 92m, Truck with ladder.

No. 2856, 175m, Siberian husky, dogs pulling sled. No. 2857, 175m, A Royal Mail Coach on a Flooded Road, by James Pollard. No. 2858, 175m, Henri Desgrange, Tour de France cyclist. No. 2859, 175m Yang Liwei, Shezhou 5, diff. No. 2860, 175m, Shepherd and Apollo 14 capsule. No. 2861, 175m, Apollo 8 orbiting Moon, diff. No. 2862, 175m, Iceboat with 221 on sail. No. 2863, 175m, Boat in Vendée Globe Regatta. No. 2864, 175m, 44-foot United States Coast Guard boat. No. 2865, 175m, Arctic Express icebreaker, Finland. No. 2866, 175m, Great Indian Peninsula Railway 4-6-0 steam locomotive. No. 2867, 175m, London Metro car from 1992. No. 2868, 175m, Mark VII monorail. No. 2869, 175m, ETR-500 train, diff. No. 2870, 175m, Amelia Earhart and Lockheed Vega. No. 2871, 175m, Learjet 65. No. 2872, 175m, Last flight of the Concorde, Nov. 26, 2003, diff.No. 2873, 175m, Boeing CH-47 Chinook helicopter. No. 2874, 175m, Firebird-9 drone. No. 2875, 175m, Capezza dirigible, France. No. 2876, 175m, 1935 Alfa Romeo Bimotore. No. 2877, 175m, Pope Benedict XVI and Mercedes-Benz ML 430 Popemobile. No. 2878, 175m, Enzo Ferrari and Ferrari F430. No. 2879, 175m, Formula 1 race car, Vettel holding Korean Grand Prix trophy. No. 2880, 175m, 1911 Indian motorcycle. No. 2881, 175m, English air mail flight, 1911. No. 2882, 175m, Ziegler Z8 airport foam spraying vehicle. No. 2883, 175m, 1863 fire wagon. No. 2884, 175m, Military truck, diff.

2013, Mar. 25 Litho. *Perf. 13¼*

Sheets of 6, #a-f

2827-2855 A449 Set of 29 325.00 325.00

Souvenir Sheets

2856-2884 A449 Set of 29 350.00 350.00

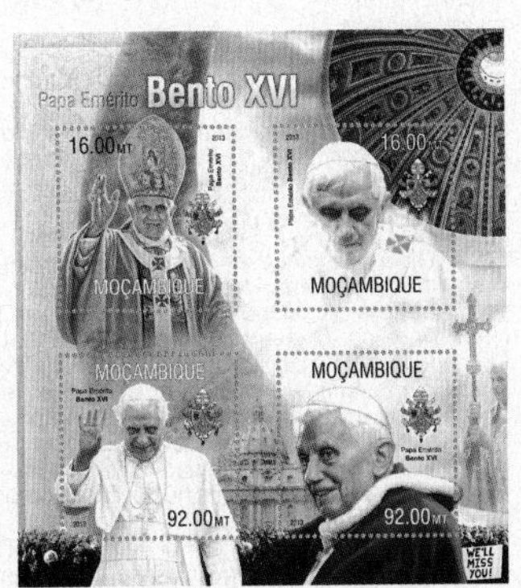

A450

No. 2885 — Coat of arms of Pope Benedict XVI and Pope Benedict XVI: a, 16m, Wearing miter. b, 16m, Wearing zucchetto, domed ceiling in background. c, 92m, Wearing zucchetto, waving. d, 92m, Wearing zucchetto and red stole.

No. 2886 — Coat of arms of Pope Francis and Pope Francis: a, 16m, Wearing miter. b, 16m, Wearing miter and holding crucifix. c, 92m, Wearing zucchetto. d, 92m, Wearing zucchetto and glasses.

No. 2887 — Marilyn Monroe (1926-62), actress: a, 16m, With husband, Joe DiMaggio. b, 16m, With bird on finger. c, 92m, Blowing bubble. d, 92m, Wearing red dress and earrings.

No. 2888 — Mohandas K. Gandhi (1869-1948), Indian independence leader: a, 16m, And Russia #3639. b, 16m, Sitting with crossed legs. c, 92m, Sitting. d, 92m, Women in background.

No. 2889 — Mao Zedong (1893-1976), Chinese communist leader: a, 16m, Reading papers. b, 16m, Wearing cap. c, 92m, With Chinese text at right. d, 92m, With flag of People's Republic of China at left.

No. 2890 — Prince William: a, 16m, Helicopter at right. b, 16m, Wearing air force uniform and flight helmet. c, 92m, Leaving helicopter, squadron emblem at right. d, 92m, Piloting helicopter.

No. 2891 — Female world chess champions: a, 16m, Zhao Xue, China. b, 16m, Humpy Koneru, India. c, 92m, Kataryna Lahno, Ukraine. d, 92m, Viktorije Cmilyte, Lithuania.

No. 2892 — Scouting trefoil and: a, 16m, Boy Scout on bicycle. b, 16m, Boy Scouts carrying canoe. c, 92m, Boy Scout with model airplane, Inachis io. d, 92m, Boy Scout at campfire, Heteronympha merope.

No. 2893 — Paintings by Raphael (1483-1520): a, 16m, Adoration of the Magi, 1502-04. b, 16m, St. George Slaying the Dragon, 1504. c, 92m, Portrait of Bindo Altoviti, 1515. d, 92m, Young Man with an Apple, 1505.

No. 2894 — Paintings by Eugene Delacroix (1798-1863): a, 16m, Christ on the Sea of Galilee, 1854. b, 16m, Orphan Girl at the Cemetery, 1823. c, 92m, Self-portrait. d, 92m, Arab Horses Fighting in a Stable, 1860.

No. 2895 — Paintings by Vincent van Gogh (1853-90): a, 16m, Memory of the Garden at Etten, 1888. b, 16m, Seascape at Saintes-Maries (Fishing Boats at Sea), 1888. c, 92m, A Pair of Shoes, 1887. d, 92m, Noon: Rest from Work, 1890.

No. 2896 — Paintings by Ivan Aivazovsky (1817-1900): a, 16m, Approximation of the Storm, 1877. b, 16m, Crimea, 1852. c, 92m, Ship Twelve Apostles, 1897. d, 92m, Morning at Sea, 1849, and Ocean, 1896.

No. 2897 — 2014 Winter Olympics, Sochi, Russia: a, 16m, Speed skating. b, 16m, Skiing. c, 92m, Curling. d, 92m, Bobsled.

No. 2898 — Intl. Red Cross, 150th anniv.: a, 16m, Rescue worker wearing gas mask carrying man. b, 16m, Jean-Henri Dunant, founder of Red Cross, and nurse carrying Red Cross flag. c, 92m, Rescue dogs at work. d, 92m, Red Cross workers caring for children.

No. 2899 — Steam locomotives: a, 16m, Empire State Express locomotive. b, 16m, 4MT, England. c, 92m, Porter 0-4-0, United States. d, 92m, Pennsylvania Railroad locomotive 4638.

No. 2900 — Volcanoes and minerals: a, 16m, Popocatépetl, Mexico, emerald and turquoise. b, 16m, Augustine Volcano, Alaska, chrysoprase and tourmaline. c, 92m, Popocatépetl, beryl and sapphire. d, 92m, Mount Bromo, Indonesia, topaz and spinel.

No. 2901 — Lighthouses and birds: a, 16m, White Shoal Lighthouse. Michigan, Rissa tridactyla. b, 16m, Portland Head Lighthouse, Maine, Columbus glacialis. c, 92m, Montauk Point Lighthouse, New York, Anas platyrhynchos. d, 92m, Lindau Harbor Lighthouse, Germany, Numenius americanus.

No. 2902 — Ailuropoda melanoleuca: a, 16m, Two pandas. b, 16m, One panda. c, 92m, Panda in tree. d, 92m, Two pandas, diff.

No. 2903 — Loxodonta africana: a, 16m, Adult and juvenile elephants. b, 16m, One elephant facing left. c, 92m, One elephant facing right. d, 92m, Two elephants, diff.

No. 2904 — Dolphins: a, 16m, Delphinus delphis, Delphinus capensis. b, 16m, Stenella attenuata. c, 92m, Lagenorhynchus obsdurus. d, 92m, Steno bredanensis, Cephalorhynchus commersonii.

No. 2905 — Parrots and plants: a, 16m, Charmosyna papou, Schefflera actinophylla. b, 16m, Polytelis swainsonii, Ara macao, Malus, Attalea maripa. c, 92m, Eclectus roratus, Cacatua moluccensis, Punica granatum. d, 92m, Ara rauna, Ara hyacinthe, Atalea funifera.

No. 2906 — Birds of prey and their prey: a, 16m, Aegypius monachus. b, 16m, Buteo buteo, lemmus lemmus. c, 92m, Buteo jamaicensis, Neotamias minimus. d, 92m, Pandion haliaetus.

No. 2907 — Owls and mushrooms: a, 16m, Surnia ulula, Coprinus comatus. b, 16m, Bubo virginianus, Peziza acetabulum. c, 92m, Tyto alba, Amanita rubescens. d, 92m, Ulula cinerea lapponica, Clitocybe inversa.

No. 2908 — Bees: a, 16m, Anthidium florentinum. b, 16m, Apis florea. c, 92m, Osmia ribifloris. d, 92m, Bombus terrestris.

No. 2909 — Insects and mushrooms: a, 16m, Choeradodis, Phrynus lunatus, Agaricus cervinus. b, 16m, Sphinx nerri, Agaricus dryophilus. c, 92m, Papilio priaunus, Sirex gigas, Cortinarius torvus. d, 92m, Heterosterne buprestoide, Russula.

No. 2910 — Butterflies and orchids: a, 16m, Papilio zelicaon, Calanthe biloba. b, 16m, Troides amphrysus. c, 92m, Alcidees metaurus, Phalaenopsis stuartiana. d, 92m, Ornithoptera victoriae, Gastrochilus spp.

No. 2911 — Marine life and seafood dishes: a, 16m, Mytilus edulis, Feijoada de mariscos. b, 16m, Penaeus monodon, Caril de camarao. c, 92m, Mercenaria mercenaria, Amêijoas em tomate. d, 92m, Callinectes sapidus, Caril de caranguejo.

No. 2912 — Frogs and snails: a, 16m, Dendrobates tinctorius, Arianta arbustorum. b, 16m, Oophaga pumilio, Planorbarius corneus. c, 92m, Phyllobates terribilis, Clea helena. d, 92m, Pelophylax shqipericus, Clithon corona.

No. 2913 — Turtles: a, 16m, Emys trinacris. b, 16m, Indotestudo elongata. c, 92m, Heosemys depressa. d, 92m, Batagur trivittata.

No. 2914 — Dinosaurs: a, 16m, Stegosaurus. b, 16m, Saurolophus. c, 92m, Rubeosaurus. d, 92m, Ankylosaurus.

No. 2915, 175m, Pope Benedict XVI and his coat of arms. No. 2916, 175m, Pope Francis and his coat of arms. No. 2917, 175m, Monroe and signature. No. 2918, 175m, Gandhi, diff. No. 2919, 175m, Mao Zedong, diff. No. 2920, 175m, Prince William in helicopter, diff. No. 2921, 175m, Anna Muzychuk, Ukrainian chess player. No. 2922, 175m, Scouting trefoil, Boy Scout with bicycle. No. 2923, 175m, St. Catherine of Alexandria, by Raphael. No. 2924, 175m, Combat of Giaour and Pasha, by Delacroix. No. 2925, 175m, The Langlois Bridge at Arles with Women Washing, by van Gogh. No. 2926, 175m, The Ninth Wave, by Aivazovsky. No. 2927, 175m, Biathlon. No. 2928, 175m, Dunant, Red Cross flag, joined hands. No. 2929, 175m, The General 4-4-0 locomotive. No. 2930, 175m, Puu Oo Volcano, Hawaii, topaz. No. 2931, 175m, Alcatraz Island Lighthouse, California, Larus argentatus. No. 2932, 175m, Ailuropoda melanoleuca, diff. No. 2933, 175m, Loxodonta africana adult and juvenile, diff. No. 2934, 175m, Sousa teuszii, Steno bredanensis. No. 2935, 175m, Deroptyus accipitrinus, Psittacula eupatria, Anacardium occidentale. No. 2936, 175m, Sarcoramphus papa. No. 2937, 175m, Tyto alba, Psalliota campestris. No. 2938, 175m, Apis mellifera. No. 2939, 175m, Calopteryx splendens, Macrothylacia rubi, Coprinopsis atramentaria. No. 2940, 175m, Papilio aegeus, Erasma pulchella, Prosthechea vitellina. No. 2941, 175m, Mytilus edulis, Arroz con mariscos. No. 2942, 175m, Hyla leucophyllata, Arianta arbustorum. No. 2943, 175m, Geoclemys hamiltonii. No. 2944, 175m, Microraptor gui.

2013, June 25 Litho. *Perf. 13¼*

Sheets of 4, #a-d

2885-2914 A450 Set of 30 450.00 450.00

Souvenir Sheets

2915-2944 A450 Set of 30 350.00 350.00

2013 China International Collection Expo (Nos. 2902, 2932).

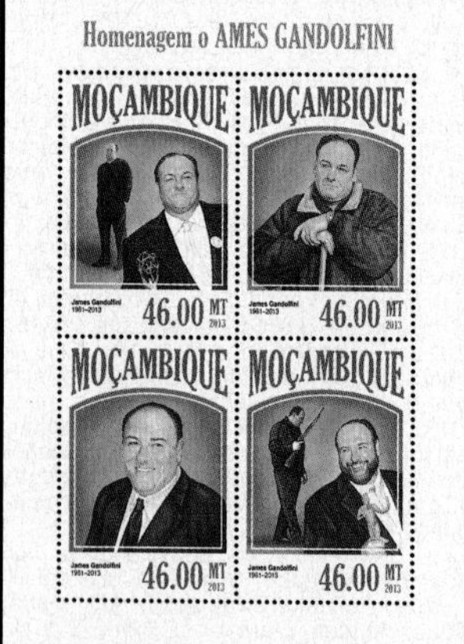

A451

No. 2945, 46m — James Gandolfini (1961-2013), actor: a, Holding Emmy award in foreground. b, Holding walking stick. c, Wearing suit and tie. d, Holding rifle in background, holding Screen Actors Guild award in foreground.

No. 2946, 46m — Giuseppe Verdi (1813-1901), composer: a, Without hat, clef at LL. b, Wearing hat, clef at LR. c, Wearing hat, clef at LL. d, Without hat, clef at LR.

No. 2947, 46m — Richard Wagner (1813-83), composer: a, Without hat, clef at LL. b, Wearing hat, clef at LR. c, Wearing hat, clef at LL. d, Without hat, clef at LR.

No. 2948, 46m — Elvis Presley (1813-1901), various images with background color of: a, Blue. b, Red. c, Orange. d, Green.

No. 2949, 46m — Russian royalty: a, Tsar Peter the Great (1672-1725). b, Heir apparent Alexei Nikolayevich (1904-18). c, Empress Catherine I (1684-1727). d, Emperor Alexander I (1777-1825).

No. 2950, 46m — Pope John Paul II: a, With hands clasped above heart, coat of arms at right. b, Holding crucifix, wearing white vestments. c, Waving, holding crucifix, wearing green vestments. d, In prayer, with hands clasped near mouth, coat of arms at right.

No. 2951, 46m — Rotary International emblem and: a, Paul Harris (1868-1947), founder, wearing hat. b, Owl, mortarboard, book, Rotary Youth Exchange emblem. c, Child receiving polio vaccine, polio eradication program emblem. d, Harris, without hat.

No. 2952, 46m — Pierre de Coubertin (1863-1937), founder of modern Olympics movement: a, Coubertin and statue. b, Table tennis. c, BMX bicycling. d, Judo.

No. 2953, 46m — Brazilian soccer players: a, Fred. b, Hulk. c, Julio Cesar. c, David Luiz.

No. 2954, 46m — Paintings depicting chess: a, The Chess Game, by Sofonisba Anguissola. b, The Veterans, by Richard Creifelds. c, Chess Game, by Marcel Duchamp. d, The Great Chess Game, by Paul Klee.

No. 2955, 46m — Post-impressionist paintings: a, Tahitian Women on the Beach, by Paul Gauguin. b, The Dining Room in the Country, by Pierre Bonnard. c, Starry Night Over the Rhone, by Vincent van Gogh. d, At the Moulin Rouge the Clowness Cha-u-kao, by Henri de Toulouse-Lautrec.

No. 2956, 46m — Paintings by Joan Miró (1893-1983): a, Miró and Vuelo de Pájaraos, 1968. b, Running Man. c, Nord-Sud, 1917. d, Waman in Front of the Sun, 1950.

No. 2957, 46m — Paintings by Pablo Picasso (1881-1973): a, Picasso and Still Life with Bottle of Anis del Mono, 1909. b, Nude Woman in Red Armchair, 1932. c, Portrait of Marie Thérèse Walter, 1937. d, Picasso and Table in a Cafe, 1912.

No. 2958, 46m — Russian art: a, Icon of Madonna and Child, by Dionisius. b, Feodor III, by Bogdan Saltanov. c, Icon of St. Sophia, Faith, Hope and Charity, by Karp Zolotaryov. d, Icon of the Trinity, by Andrej Rublev.

No. 2959, 46m — Ancient Egyptian civilization: a, Model of bark constructed in 18th Dynasty. b, King Tutankhamun and his wife. c, Tomb of King Tutankhamun. d, Bust of Nefertiti.

No. 2960, 46m — World War I: a, German submarine U-155, Winston Churchill. b, Tanks in ruined city. c, Red Cross nurse, soldiers in battle. d, T. E. Lawrence (Lawrence of Arabia), Lawrence on camel.

No. 2961, 46m — Fire trucks: a, 1939 Dennis Light 4. b, 1965 Bedford TK. c,1961 Magirus-Deutz Merkur F 25A. d, 1959 Opel Blitz LF 8.

No. 2962, 46m — Steam locomotives: a, Stourbridge Lion. b, Norris 4-2-0. c, Type 1 2-4-2. d, Problem Class 2-2-2.

No. 2963, 46m — Chinese high-speed trains: a, China Star. b, CRH2. c, CRH380B. d, CRH1.

No. 2964, 46m — Shenzhou 10: a, Shenzhou 10 in orbit. b, Zhang Xiaoguang. c, Wang Yaping. d, Nie Haisheng.

No. 2965, 46m — Minerals: a, Azurite. b, Garnet and smoky quartz. c, Yellow mineral ore. d, Amethyst and quartz.

No. 2966, 46m — Primates: a, Saguinus imperator. b, Cebus capucinus. c, Tarsius syrichta. d, Gorilla beringei graueri.

No. 2967, 46m — African animals: a, Panthera pardus. b, Loxodonta africana. c, Hippopotamus amphibius. d, Giraffa camelopardalis.

No. 2968, 46m — Whales: a, Megaptera novaeangliae. b, Balaena mysticetus. c, Eschrichtius robustus. d, Physeter macrocephalus.

No. 2969, 46m — Owls: a, Strix leptogrammica. b, Otus sagittatus. c, Strix butleri. d, Tyto soumagnei.

No. 2970, 46m — Butterflies: a, Papilio demoleus malayanus. b, Danaus chrysippus chrysippus. c, Euripus nyctelius euploeoides. d, Cethosia cyane.

No. 2971, 46m — Lighthouses and shells: a, Cape Otway Lighthouse, Australia, Cardium costatum. b, Yaquina Head Lighthouse, Oregon, Nautilides. c, Cape Hatteras Lighthouse, North Carolina, Queen conch. d, White Shoal Lighthouse, Michigan, Babylonia canaliculata.

No. 2972, 46m — Reptiles: a, Dendroaspis angusticeps. b, Agama mwanzae. c, Varanus albigularis. d, Diadophis punctatus.

No. 2973, 46m — Dinosaurs and pre-historic hominids: a, Anchiornis huxleyi. b, Homo habilis. c, Homo floresiensis. d, Velociraptor.

No. 2974, 92m — Birth of Prince George of Cambridge: a, Duke and Duchess of Cambridge, Prince George. b, Prince Charles, Duke of Cambridge holding Prince George. c, Princess Diana holding Prince William, Duke of Cambridge holding Prince George. d, Duchess of Cambridge holding Prince George.

No. 2975, 175m, Gandolfini with arms crossed. No. 2976, 175m, Verdi, diff. No. 2977, 175m, Wagner, diff. No. 2978, 175m, Presley, diff. No. 2979, 175m, Emperor Nicholas II of Russia (1868-1918). No. 2980, 175m, Pope John Paul II and his coat of arms. No. 2981, 175m, Harris, Rotary Youth Exchange emblem. No. 2982, 175m, Equestrian competitors. No. 2983, 175m, Neymar. No. 2984, 175m, The Chess Board, by Juan Gris. No. 2985, 175m, Young Women of Provence at the Well, by Paul Signac. No. 2986, 175m, Miró and Siesta, 1925. No. 2987, 175m, Picasso and House in a Garden, 1908. No. 2988, 175m, Old Jew, by Nikolai Yaroshenko. No. 2989, 175m, Bust of Egyptian Pharaoh Menes and Pyramids. No. 2990, 175m, Baron Manfed von Richthofen and Fokker Dr.I triplane in flight. No. 2991, 175m, 1914 Ford Model T fire engine. No. 2992, 175m, Jupiter locomotive. No. 2993, 175m, CHR380D high-speed train. No. 2994, 175m,Wang Yaping, diff. No. 2995, 175m, Aragonite. No. 2996, 175m, Saimiri sciureus. No. 2997, 175m, Panthera leo. No. 2998, 175m, Eubalaena australis. No. 2999, 175m, Strix nebulosa. No. 3000, 175m, Papilio polytes romulus. No. 3001, 175m, Beachy Head Lighthouse, Great Britain, Anadara corbuliodes. No. 3002, 175m, Furcier pardalis. No. 3003, 175m, Homo habilis making tool. No. 3004, 175m, Duke and Duchess of Cambridge, Prince George, diff.

2013, Sept. 25 Litho. *Perf. 13¼*

Sheets of 4, #a-d

2945-2974 A451 Set of 30 400.00 400.00

Souvenir Sheets

2975-3004 A451 Set of 30 375.00 375.00

Brasiliana 2013 Intl. Philatelic Exhibition, Rio de Janeiro (Nos. 2953, 2983); Rossica 2013 Intl. Philatelic Exhibition (Nos. 2958, 2988); 2013 China International Collection Expo (Nos. 2963, 2964, 2993, 2994).

SEMI-POSTAL STAMPS

"History" Pointing out to "the Republic" Need for Charity SP1

Nurse Leading Wounded Soldiers SP2

Veteran Relating Experiences — SP3

Perf. 11½

1920, Dec. 1 Litho. Unwmk.

B1	SP1	¼c	olive	5.00	3.50
B2	SP1	½c	olive blk	5.00	3.50
B3	SP1	1c	dp bister	5.00	3.50
B4	SP1	2c	lilac brn	5.00	3.50
B5	SP1	3c	lilac	5.00	3.50
B6	SP1	4c	green	5.00	3.50
B7	SP2	5c	grnsh blue	5.00	3.50
B8	SP2	6c	light blue	5.00	3.50
B9	SP2	7½c	red brown	5.00	3.50
B10	SP2	8c	lemon	5.00	3.50
B11	SP2	10c	gray lilac	5.00	3.50
B12	SP2	12c	pink	5.00	3.50
B13	SP3	18c	rose	5.00	3.50
B14	SP3	24c	vio brn	5.00	3.50
B15	SP3	30c	pale ol grn	5.00	3.50
B16	SP3	40c	dull red	5.00	3.50
B17	SP3	50c	yellow	5.00	3.50
B18	SP3	1e	ultra	5.00	3.50
	Nos. B1-B18 (18)			90.00	63.00

Nos. B1-B18 were used Dec. 1, 1920, in place of ordinary stamps. The proceeds were for war victims.

AIR POST STAMPS

Common Design Type

Perf. 13½x13

1938, Aug. Engr. Unwmk.

Name and Value in Black

C1	CD39	10c	scarlet	.30	.25
C2	CD39	20c	purple	.30	.25
C3	CD39	50c	orange	.30	.25
C4	CD39	1e	ultra	.40	.30
C5	CD39	2e	lilac brn	1.00	.30
C6	CD39	3e	dk green	1.75	.40
C7	CD39	5e	red brown	2.10	.70
C8	CD39	9e	rose car	4.25	.75
C9	CD39	10e	magenta	7.25	1.25
	Nos. C1-C9 (9)			17.65	4.45

No. C7 exists with overprint "Exposicao Internacional de Nova York, 1939-1940" and Trylon and Perisphere. Value $50.

No. C7 Surcharged in Black

1946, Nov. 2 *Perf. 13½x13*

C10	CD39 3e on 5e red brn		6.00	1.75
a.	Inverted surcharge			

Plane — AP1

1946, Nov. 2 Typo. *Perf. 11½*

Denomination in Black

C11	AP1	1.20e	carmine	1.10	.85
C12	AP1	1.60e	blue	1.40	.90
C13	AP1	1.70e	plum	3.50	1.40
C14	AP1	2.90e	brown	3.50	1.90
C15	AP1	3e	green	3.00	1.75
	Nos. C11-C15 (5)			12.50	6.80

Inscribed "Taxe perçue" and Denomination in Brown Carmine or Black

1947, May 20

C16	AP1	50c	blk (BrC)	.50	.25
C17	AP1	1e	pink	.50	.25
C18	AP1	3e	green	1.00	.40
C19	AP1	4.50e	yel grn	2.50	.75
C20	AP1	5e	red brown	2.50	.90
C21	AP1	10e	ultra	6.00	1.25
C22	AP1	20e	violet	11.00	4.00
C23	AP1	50e	orange	15.00	6.00
	Nos. C16-C23 (8)			39.00	13.80

Dangerous counterfeits exist.

Planes Circling Globe — AP2

1949, Mar.

C24	AP2	50c	sepia	.30	.25
C25	AP2	1.20e	violet	.50	.30
C26	AP2	4.50e	dull blue	1.25	.50
C27	AP2	5e	blue green	1.75	.50
C28	AP2	20e	chocolate	4.00	.85
	Nos. C24-C28 (5)			7.80	2.40

Catalogue values for unused stamps in this section, from this point to the end of the section, are for Never Hinged items.

Oil Refinery, Sonarep
AP3

Designs: 2e, Salazar High School, Lourenço Marques. 3.50e, Lourenço Marques harbor. 4.50e, Salazar dam. 5e, Trigo de Morais bridge. 20e, Marcelo Caetano bridge.

1963, Mar. 5 Litho. *Perf. 13*
C29 AP3 1.50e multi .60 .25
C30 AP3 2e multi .30 .25
C31 AP3 3.50e multi .60 .25
C32 AP3 4.50e multi .40 .25
C33 AP3 5e multi .50 .25
C34 AP3 20e multi 1.40 .60
Nos. C29-C34 (6) 3.80 1.85

Republic

Nos. C31-C34 Overprinted in Red

1975, June 25 Litho. *Perf. 13*
C35 AP3 3.50e multi .55 .40
C36 AP3 4.50e multi .60 .45
C37 AP3 5e multi 1.40 .80
C38 AP3 20e multi 2.00 2.00
Nos. C35-C38 (4) 3.15 1.00

DeHavilland Dragonfly, 1937 — AP4

Designs: 1.50m, Junker JU-52-3M, 1938. 3m, Lockheed Lodestar L-18-08, 1940. 7.50m, DeHavilland Dove DH-104, 1948. 10m, Douglas Dakota DC-3, 1956. 12.5m, Fokker Friendship F-27, 1962.

1981, May 14 Litho. *Perf. 11*
C39 AP4 50c multi .90 .25
C40 AP4 1.50m multi 1.10 .25
C41 AP4 3m multi 1.75 .25
C42 AP4 7.50m multi 2.50 .25
C43 AP4 10m multi 3.00 .40
C44 AP4 12.5m multi 4.50 .55
Nos. C39-C44 (6) 13.75 1.95

Piper Navajo Over Hydroelectric Dam — AP5

Designs: 40m, De Havilland Hornet trainer, 1936. 80m, Boeing 737, Maputo Airport, 1973. 120m, Beechcraft King-Air. 160m, Piper Aztec. 320m, Douglas DC-10, 1982.

1987, Oct. 28 Litho. *Perf. 11*
C45 AP5 20m multi .30 .25
C46 AP5 40m multi .60 .25
C47 AP5 80m multi 1.25 .40
C48 AP5 120m multi 1.60 .45
C49 AP5 160m multi 2.50 .60
C50 AP5 320m multi 4.00 1.10
Nos. C45-C50 (6) 10.25 3.05

POSTAGE DUE STAMPS

D1

1904 Unwmk. Typo. *Perf. 11½x12*
Name and Value in Black
J1 D1 5r yellow grn .40 .25
J2 D1 10r slate .40 .25
J3 D1 20r yellow brn .40 .25
J4 D1 30r orange .80 .70
J5 D1 50r gray brn .70 .55
J6 D1 60r red brown 3.50 1.75
J7 D1 100r red lilac 3.00 1.75
J8 D1 130r dull blue 1.50 1.20
J9 D1 200r carmine 2.00 1.20
J10 D1 500r violet 2.50 1.20
Nos. J1-J10 (10) 15.20 9.10

See J34-J43. For overprints see Nos. 247, J11-J30.

Same Overprinted in Carmine or Green

1911
J11 D1 5r yellow green .25 .25
J12 D1 10r slate .40 .25
J13 D1 20r yellow brn .30 .25
J14 D1 30r orange .30 .25
J15 D1 50r gray brown .40 .30
J16 D1 60r red brown .60 .35
J17 D1 100r red lilac .80 .55
J18 D1 130r dull blue 1.10 .80
J19 D1 200r carmine (G) 1.20 .95
J20 D1 500r violet 1.60 .95
Nos. J11-J20 (10) 6.95 4.90

Nos. J1-J10 Overprinted Locally in Carmine

1916
J21 D1 5r yellow grn 4.00 3.25
J22 D1 10r slate 5.50 3.25
J23 D1 20r yellow brn 80.00 60.00
J24 D1 30r orange 22.50 12.50
J25 D1 50r gray brown 80.00 55.00
J26 D1 60r red brown 65.00 45.00
J27 D1 100r red lilac 80.00 60.00
J28 D1 130r dull blue 2.40 2.25
J29 D1 200r carmine 2.75 3.00
J30 D1 500r violet 5.50 4.75
Nos. J21-J30 (10) 347.65 249.00

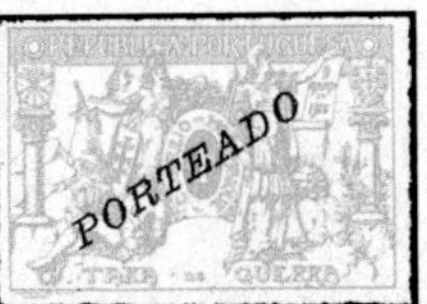

War Tax Stamps of 1916 Ovptd. Diagonally

1918 *Rouletted 7*
J31 WT1 1c gray green .95 .80
J32 WT2 5c rose .95 .80
a. Inverted overprint 8.25 7.50

Perf. 11
J33 WT1 1c gray green .95 .80
a. "PEPUBLICA" 50.00 40.00
Nos. J31-J33 (3) 2.85 2.40

Type of 1904 Issue With Value in Centavos

1917 *Perf. 12*
J34 D1 ½c yellow green .30 .30
J35 D1 1c slate .30 .30
J36 D1 2c orange brown .30 .30
J37 D1 3c orange .30 .30
J38 D1 5c gray brown .30 .30
J39 D1 6c pale brn .30 .30
J40 D1 10c red violet .30 .30
J41 D1 13c deep blue .55 .55
J42 D1 20c rose .55 .55
J43 D1 50c gray .55 .55
Nos. J34-J43 (10) 3.75 3.75

Lourenco Marques Nos. 117, 119 Surcharged in Red

1921
J44 A4 5c on ½c blk 2.00 .95
J45 A4 10c on 1½c brn 2.00 .95

Same Surcharge on Mozambique Nos. 151, 154, 190 in Red or Green

Perf. 15x14
J46 A6 6c on 1c bl grn (R) 2.00 .95
J47 A6 20c on 2½c vio (R) 1.50 .85
a. Inverted surcharge 7.50 7.50
J48 A6 50c on 4c rose (G) 1.50 .85
Nos. J44-J48 (5) 9.00 4.55

Regular Issues of 1921-22 Surcharged in Black or Red

1924 *Perf. 12x11½*
J49 A6 20c on 30c ol grn (Bk) 1.50 .45
a. Perf. 15x14 19.00 4.50
J50 A6 50c on 60c dk bl (R) 1.50 1.00

Catalogue values for unused stamps in this section, from this point to the end of the section, are for Never Hinged items.

Common Design Type
Photo. and Typo.
1952 Unwmk. *Perf. 14*
Numeral in Red Orange or Red; Frame Multicolored
J51 CD45 10c carmine (RO) .25 .25
J52 CD45 30c black brn .25 .25
J53 CD45 50c black .25 .25
J54 CD45 1e violet blue .25 .25
J55 CD45 2e olive green .25 .25
J56 CD45 5e orange brown .55 .30
Nos. J51-J56 (6) 1.80 1.55

WAR TAX STAMPS

Coats of Arms of Portugal and Mozambique on Columns, Allegorical Figures of History of Portugal and the Republic Holding Scroll with Date of Declaration of War — WT1

Prow of Galley of Discoveries. Left, "Republic" Teaching History of Portugal; Right "History" with Laurels (Victory) and Sword (Symbolical of Declaration of War) — WT2

1916 Unwmk. Litho. *Rouletted 7*
MR1 WT1 1c gray green 2.25 .55
a. Imperf., pair 15.00
MR2 WT2 5c rose 2.25 .55
a. Imperf., pair 15.00

1918 *Perf. 11, 12*
MR3 WT1 1c gray green .85 .55
a. "PEPUBLICA" 8.50 4.75
MR4 WT2 5c red 1.00 .70
a. "PETRIA" 4.00 4.00
b. "PEPUBLICA" 4.00 4.00
c. "1910" for "1916" 11.00 5.50
d. Imperf., pair
Nos. MR1-MR4 (4) 6.35 2.35

For surcharges and overprints see Nos. 221-225, 229, 235, J31-J33.

NEWSPAPER STAMPS

No. 19 Surcharged in Black, Red or Blue

a

b

1893 Unwmk. *Perf. 11½, 12½, 13½*
P1 A2 (a) 2½r on 40r 200.00 90.00
P2 A2 (a) 5r on 40r 175.00 90.00
P3 A2 (a) 5r on 40r (R) 150.00 75.00
P4 A2 (a) 5r on 40r (Bl) 180.00 75.00
P5 A2 (b) 2½r on 40r 22.50 16.00
Nos. P1-P5 (5) 727.50 346.00

Nos. P1-P5 exist with double surcharge, Nos. P2-P4 with inverted surcharge.

N3

1893 Typo. *Perf. 11½, 13½*
P6 N3 2½r brown .35 .30

For surcharge and overprint see Nos. 93, 199, 206.

No. P6 has been reprinted on chalk-surfaced paper with clean-cut perforation 13½. Value, 50 cents.

POSTAL TAX STAMPS

Pombal Commemorative Issue
Common Design Types
1925 Engr. *Perf. 12½*
RA1 CD28 15c brown & black .30 .25
RA2 CD29 15c brown & black .30 .25
RA3 CD30 15c brown & black .30 .25
Nos. RA1-RA3 (3) .90 .75

Seal of Local Red Cross Society — PT7

Surcharged in Various Colors
1925 Typo. *Perf. 11½*
RA4 PT7 50c slate & yel (Bk) 1.60 1.60

Seal of Local Red Cross Society — PT8

1926
RA5 PT8 40c slate & yel (Bk) 3.50 3.50
RA6 PT8 50c slate & yel (R) 3.50 3.50
RA7 PT8 60c slate & yel (V) 3.50 3.50
RA8 PT8 80c slate & yel (Br) 3.50 3.50
RA9 PT8 1e slate & yel (Bl) 3.50 3.50
RA10 PT8 2e slate & yel (G) 3.50 3.50
Nos. RA5-RA10 (6) 21.00 21.00

Obligatory on mail certain days of the year. The tax benefited the Cross of the Orient Society.

Type of 1926 Issue

1927 Black Surcharge

RA11 PT8 5c red & yel 3.50 3.50
RA12 PT8 10c green & yel 3.50 3.50
RA13 PT8 20c gray & yel 3.50 3.50
RA14 PT8 30c lt bl & yel 3.50 3.50
RA15 PT8 40c vio & yel 3.50 3.50
RA16 PT8 50c car & yel 3.50 3.50
RA17 PT8 60c brown & yel 3.50 3.50
RA18 PT8 80c blue & yel 3.50 3.50
RA19 PT8 1e olive & yel 3.50 3.50
RA20 PT8 2e yel brn & yel 3.50 3.50
Nos. RA11-RA20 (10) 35.00 35.00

See note after No. RA10.

PT9

1928 Litho.

RA21 PT9 5c grn, yel & blk 4.50 4.50
RA22 PT9 10c sl bl, yel & blk 4.50 4.50
RA23 PT9 20c gray blk, yel & blk 4.50 4.50
RA24 PT9 30c brn rose, yel & blk 4.50 4.50
RA25 PT9 40c cl brn, yel & blk 4.50 4.50
RA26 PT9 50c red org, yel & blk 4.50 4.50
RA27 PT9 60c brn, yel & blk 4.50 4.50
RA28 PT9 80c dk brn, yel & blk 4.50 4.50
RA29 PT9 1e gray, yel & blk 4.50 4.50
RA30 PT9 2e red, yel & blk 4.50 4.50
Nos. RA21-RA30 (10) 45.00 45.00

See note after RA10.

Mother and Children — PT10

1929 Photo. Perf. 14

RA31 PT10 40c ultra, cl & blk 3.00 3.00

The use of this stamp was compulsory on all correspondence to Portugal and Portuguese Colonies for eight days beginning July 24, 1929.

See Nos.RA39-RA47.

Mousinho de Albuquerque PT11

1930-31 Perf. 14½x14

Inscribed: "MACONTENE"

RA32 PT11 50c lake, red & gray 3.50 4.00

Inscribed: "COOLELA"

RA33 PT11 50c red vio, red brn & gray 3.50 4.00

Inscribed: "MUJENGA"

RA34 PT11 50c org red, red & gray 3.50 4.00

Inscribed: "CHAIMITE"

RA35 PT11 50c dp grn, bl grn & gray 3.50 4.00

Inscribed: "IBRAHIMO"

RA36 PT11 50c dk bl, blk & gray 3.50 4.00

Inscribed: "MUCUTO-MUNO"

RA37 PT11 50c ultra, blk & gray 3.50 4.00

Inscribed: "NAGUEMA"

RA38 PT11 50c dk vio, lt vio & gray 3.50 4.00
Nos. RA32-RA38 (7) 24.50 28.00

The portrait is that of Mousinho de Albuquerque, the celebrated Portuguese warrior, and the names of seven battles in which he took part appear at the foot of the stamps. The stamps were issued for the memorial fund bearing his name and their use was obligatory on all correspondence posted on eight specific days in the year.

Type of 1929 Issue

Denominations in Black

No. RA42 Without Denomination

1931 Perf. 14

RA39 PT10 40c rose & vio 4.00 3.25
RA40 PT10 40c ol grn & vio ('32) 5.50 4.50
RA41 PT10 40c bis brn & rose ('33) 5.50 4.50
RA42 PT10 bl grn & rose ('34) 3.75 3.50
RA43 PT10 40c org & ultra ('36) 5.50 4.50
RA44 PT10 40c choc & ultra ('37) 5.50 4.50
RA45 PT10 40c grn & brn car ('38) 7.50 5.50
RA46 PT10 40c yel & blk ('39) 7.50 5.50
RA47 PT10 40c gray brn ('40) 7.50 5.50
Nos. RA39-RA47 (9) 52.25 41.25

Allegory of Charity PT12

Denomination in Black

1942 Unwmk. Litho. Perf. 11½

RA48 PT12 50c rose carmine 8.25 2.00

White Pelican — PT13

Denomination in Black

1943-51 Perf. 11½, 14

RA49 PT13 50c rose carmine 17.00 1.25
RA50 PT13 50c emerald 10.00 1.25
RA51 PT13 50c purple 15.00 1.25
RA52 PT13 50c blue 12.00 1.25
RA53 PT13 50c red brown 50.00 1.25
RA54 PT13 50c olive bister 18.00 1.25
Nos. RA49-RA54 (6) 122.00 7.50

There are two sizes of the numeral on No. RA49.

Catalogue values for unused stamps in this section, from this point to the end of the section, are for Never Hinged items.

Inscribed: "Provincia de Mocambique"

1954-56 Perf. 14½x14

RA55 PT13 50c orange 1.40 .60
RA56 PT13 50c olive grn ('56) 1.40 .60
RA57 PT13 50c brown ('56) 1.40 .60
Nos. RA55-RA57 (3) 4.20 1.80

No. RA57 Surcharged with New Value and Wavy Lines

1956

RA58 PT13 30c on 50c brown .85 .35

Pelican Type of 1954-56

1958 Litho. Perf. 14

Denomination in Black

RA59 PT13 30c yellow .80 .60
RA60 PT13 50c salmon .80 .60

Imprint: "Imprensa Nacional de Mocambique"

1963-64

Denomination Typographed in Black

RA61 PT13 30c yellow ('64) .80 .60
RA62 PT13 50c salmon .80 .60

Women and Children — PT14

1963-65 Litho. Perf. 14

RA63 PT14 50c blk, bis & red .30 .25
RA64 PT14 50c blk, pink & red ('65) .30 .25

See Nos. RA68-RA76.

Lineman on Pole and Map of Mozambique PT15

30c, Telegraph poles and map of Mozambique.

Size: 23x30mm

1965, Apr. 1 Unwmk. Perf. 14

RA65 PT15 30c blk, salmon & lil .25 .25

Size: 19x36mm

RA66 PT15 50c blk, bl & sepia .25 .25
RA67 PT15 1e blk, yel & org .25 .25

The tax was for improvement of the telecommunications system. Obligatory on inland mail. A 2.50e in the design of the 30c was issued for use on telegrams.

Type of 1963

1967-70 Litho. Perf. 14

RA68 PT14 50c blk, lt yel grn & red .40 .25
RA69 PT14 50c blk, lt bl & red ('69) .40 .25
RA70 PT14 50c blk, buff & brt red ('70) .40 .25
Nos. RA68-RA70 (3) 1.20 .75

1972-73

RA71 PT14 30c blk, lt grn & red .25 .25
RA72 PT14 50c blk, gray & red ('73) 1.00 .25
RA73 PT14 1e blk, bis & red ('73) .25 .25
Nos. RA71-RA73 (3) 1.50 .75

1974-75

RA74 PT14 50c blue, yel & red .25 .25
RA75 PT14 1e blk, gray & ver .85 .25
RA76 PT14 1e blk, lil rose & red ('75) .40 .25
Nos. RA74-RA76 (3) 1.50 .75

Intl. Year of the Child — PT16

1979 Litho. Perf. 14¼

RA77 PT16 50e red 1.50 1.50

POSTAL TAX DUE STAMPS

Pombal Commemorative Issue

Common Design Types

1925 Unwmk. Perf. 12½

RAJ1 CD28 30c brown & black .55 .65
RAJ2 CD29 30c brown & black .55 .65
RAJ3 CD30 30c brown & black .55 .65
Nos. RAJ1-RAJ3 (3) 1.65 1.95

MOZAMBIQUE COMPANY

mō-zəm-ˈbēk ˈkəmp-nē

LOCATION — Comprises the territory of Manica and Sofala of the Mozambique Colony in southeastern Africa

GOVT. — A part of the Portuguese Colony of Mozambique

AREA — 51,881 sq. mi.

POP. — 368,447 (1939)

CAPITAL — Beira

The Mozambique Company was chartered by Portugal in 1891 for 50 years. The territory was under direct administration of the Company until July 18, 1941.

1000 Reis = 1 Milreis

100 Centavos = 1 Escudo (1916)

Mozambique Nos. 15-23 Overprinted in Carmine or Black

1892 Unwmk. Perf. 12½, 13½

1 A2 5r black (C) 4.00 .50
a. Pair, one without overprint 50.00 22.50
2 A2 10r green 4.00 .50
3 A2 20r rose 4.00 .50
a. Perf. 13½ 45.00 30.00
4 A2 25r violet 4.00 .45
a. Double overprint 27.50
5 A2 40r chocolate 4.00 .45
a. Double overprint 20.00
6 A2 50r blue 4.00 .50
7 A2 100r yellow brown 4.00 .75
8 A2 200r gray violet 4.50 .90
9 A2 300r orange 5.00 .90
Nos. 1-9 (9) 37.50 5.45

Nos. 1 to 6, 8-9 were reprinted in 1905. These reprints have white gum and clean-cut perf. 13½ and the colors are usually paler than those of the originals.

Company Coat of Arms — A2

Perf. 11½, 12½, 13½

1895-1907 Typo.

Black or Red Numerals

10 A2 2½r olive yellow .25 .25
11 A2 2½r gray ('07) 1.50 1.50
12 A2 5r orange .25 .25
a. Value omitted 15.00
b. Perf. 13½ 2.00 1.10
13 A2 10r red lilac .40 .30
14 A2 10r yel grn ('07) 2.50 .40
a. Value inverted at top of stamp 20.00 20.00
15 A2 15r red brown 1.00 .30
16 A2 15r dk green ('07) 2.50 .40
17 A2 20r gray lilac 1.50 .30
18 A2 25r green .75 .30
a. Perf. 13½ 1.90 1.25
19 A2 25r carmine ('07) 2.50 .60
a. Value omitted 15.00 10.00
20 A2 50r blue .90 .30
21 A2 50r brown ('07) 2.50 .60
a. Value omitted 15.00
22 A2 65r slate blue ('02) .75 .35
23 A2 75r rose .70 .30
24 A2 75r red lilac ('07) 5.00 1.00
25 A2 80r yellow green .50 .30
26 A2 100r brown, *buff* 1.00 .30
27 A2 100r dk bl, *bl* ('07) 4.00 1.00
28 A2 115r car, *pink* ('04) 1.25 .70
29 A2 115r org brn, *pink* ('07) 6.00 1.40
30 A2 130r grn, *pink* ('04) 1.50 .70
31 A2 130r brn, *yel* ('07) 6.00 1.40
32 A2 150r org brn, *pink* 1.00 .60
33 A2 200r dk blue, *bl* 1.00 .90
a. Perf. 13½ 2.00 1.60
34 A2 200r red lil, *pink* ('07) 7.00 1.40
35 A2 300r dk bl, *salmon* 1.10 .90
a. Perf. 13½ 2.50 1.40
36 A2 400r brn, *bl* ('04) 2.50 1.10
37 A2 400r dl bl, *yel* ('07) 9.00 3.25
38 A2 500r blk & red 1.10 .75
39 A2 500r blk & red, *bl* ('07) 9.00 1.90
a. 500r pur & red, *yel* (error)

40 A2 700r slate, *buff* ('04) 9.00 2.00
41 A2 700r pur, *yel* ('07) 5.00 2.00
42 A2 1000r violet & red 1.50 1.00
Nos. 10-42 (33) 90.45 28.75

#12b, 18a, 33a, 35a were issued without gum.
For overprints & surcharges see #43-107, B1-B7.

Nos. 25 and 6 Surcharged or Overprinted in Red

b

c

1895 *Perf. 12½, 13½*
43 A2(b) 25r on 80r yel grn 22.50 16.00
44 A2(c) 50r blue 9.00 4.00

Overprint "c" on No. 44 also exists reading from upper left to lower right.

Stamps of 1895 Overprinted in Bister, Orange, Violet, Green, Black or Brown

1898 *Perf. 12½, 13½*
Without Gum
45 A2 2½r olive yel (Bi) 6.00 1.50
a. Double overprint 40.00 25.00
b. Red overprint 60.00 50.00
46 A2 5r orange (O) 8.00 1.50
47 A2 10r red lilac (V) 8.00 1.50
48 A2 15r red brown (V) 10.00 3.00
a. Red overprint
49 A2 20r gray lilac (V) 10.00 3.00
50 A2 25r green (G) 12.00 3.00
a. Inverted overprint 65.00 40.00
51 A2 50r blue (Bk) 12.00 4.00
a. Inverted overprint 60.00 40.00
52 A2 75r rose (V) 14.00 5.00
a. Inverted overprint 75.00 40.00
b. Red overprint
53 A2 80r yellow grn (G) 19.00 5.00
a. Inverted overprint
54 A2 100r brn, *buff* (Br) 19.00 5.00
55 A2 150r org brn, *pink* (O) 19.00 5.00
a. Inverted overprint 75.00 30.00
b. Double overprint
56 A2 200r dk blue, *bl* (Bk) 17.00 7.50
57 A2 300r dk blue, *sal* (Bk) 22.50 10.00
a. Inverted overprint 60.00 50.00
b. Green overprint
Nos. 45-57 (13) 176.50 55.00

Vasco da Gama's discovery of route to India, 400th anniversary.
No. 57b was prepared but not issued.
Nos. 45 and 49 were also issued with gum.
The "Centenario" overprint on stamps perf. 11½ is forged.

Nos. 23, 12, 17 Surcharged in Black, Carmine or Violet

e

1899 *Perf. 12½*
59 A2(e) 25r on 75r rose (Bk) 4.00 2.50

f g

1900 *Perf. 12½, 12½x11½*
60 A2(f) 25r on 5r org (C) 2.10 1.40
61 A2(g) 50r on half of 20r gray lil (V) 2.00 1.00
b. Entire stamp 15.00 9.00

No. 61b is perf. 11½ vertically through center.

Stamps of 1895-1907 Overprinted Locally in Carmine or Green

1911 *Perf. 11½, 13½*
61A A2 2½r gray (C) 7.00 3.00
62 A2 5r orange (G) 6.00 3.00
63 A2 10r yellow grn (C) 1.00 .50
64 A2 15r dk green (C) 1.00 .50
a. Double overprint 40.00 20.00
65 A2 20r gray lilac (G) 2.00 .50
a. Perf. 13½ 3.00 .80
66 A2 25r carmine (G) 1.25 .60
67 A2 50r brown (G) .70 .45
68 A2 75r red lilac (G) 2.00 .45
69 A2 100r dk bl, *bl* (C) 2.00 .50
70 A2 115r org brn, *pink* (G) 2.50 1.25
71 A2 130r brn, *yel* (G) 3.00 1.25
72 A2 200r red lil, *pink* (G) 3.00 1.25
73 A2 400r dull bl, *yel* (C) 3.00 .70
74 A2 500r blk & red, *bl* (C) 4.00 1.40
75 A2 700r pur, *yel* (G) 4.00 1.40
Nos. 61A-75 (15) 42.45 16.75

Nos. 63, 67 and 71 exist with inverted overprint; Nos. 63, 72 and 75 with double overprint.

Overprinted in Lisbon in Carmine or Green

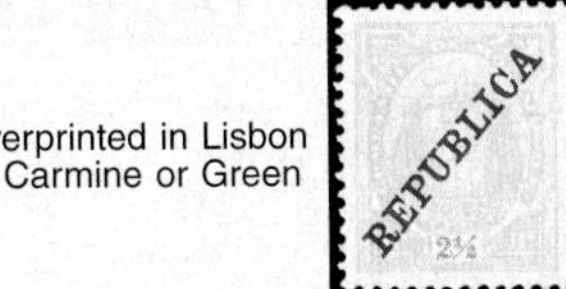

1911 *Perf. 11½, 12½*
75B A2 2½r gray .30 .25
76 A2 5r orange .30 .25
77 A2 10r yellow grn .25 .25
78 A2 15r dark green .35 .25
79 A2 20r gray lilac .40 .25
80 A2 25r carmine (G) .35 .25
a. Value inverted at top of stamp 18.00
81 A2 50r brown .70 .25
82 A2 75r red lilac .70 .25
a. Value omitted 15.00
83 A2 100r dk blue, *bl* 1.00 .25
84 A2 115r org brn, *pink* 2.50 .40
85 A2 130r brown, *yel* 3.00 .40
a. Double overprint 30.00
86 A2 200r red lil, *pink* 3.00 .40
87 A2 400r dull bl, *yel* 5.00 .40
88 A2 500r blk & red, *bl* 7.50 .40
89 A2 700r pur, *yel* 5.00 .55
Nos. 75B-89 (15) 30.35 4.80

Nos. 75B-89 Surcharged

1916 *Perf. 11½*
90 A2 ¼c on 2½r gray .25 .25
91 A2 ½c on 5r org .25 .25
a. "½c" double 20.00
92 A2 1c on 10r yel grn .40 .25
93 A2 1½c on 15r dk grn .40 .25
a. Imperf., pair 35.00
94 A2 2c on 20r gray lil .50 .25
95 A2 2½c on 25r car 1.00 .25
96 A2 5c on 50r brn .40 .25
a. Imperf., pair 40.00
97 A2 7½c on 75r red lil .65 .25
98 A2 10c on 100r dk bl, *bl* 1.25 .95
a. Inverted surcharge 40.00 40.00
99 A2 11½c on 115r org brn, *pink* 3.50 .95
a. Inverted surcharge 50.00 50.00
100 A2 13c on 130r brn, *yel* 6.50 .95
101 A2 20c on 200r red lil, *pink* 5.50 1.10
102 A2 40c on 400r dl bl, *yel* 6.50 .50
103 A2 50c on 500r blk & red, *bl* (R) 8.00 .70
104 A2 70c on 700r pur, *yel* 8.00 1.25
Nos. 90-104 (15) 43.10 8.40

Nos. 87 to 89 Surcharged

1918 *Perf. 11½*
105 A2 ½c on 700r pur, *yel* 2.50 1.30
106 A2 2½c on 500r blk & red, *bl* (Bl) 3.50 1.30
107 A2 5c on 400r dl bl, *yel* 4.50 1.30
Nos. 105-107 (3) 10.50 3.90

Native and Village — A9

Man and Ivory Tusks — A10

Corn — A11

Tapping Rubber Tree — A12

Sugar Refinery — A13

Buzi River Scene — A14

Tobacco Field — A15

View of Beira — A16

Coffee Plantation A17

Orange Tree A18

Cotton Field A19

Sisal Plantation A20

Scene on Beira R. R. — A21

Court House at Beira — A22

Coconut Palm A23

Mangroves A24

Cattle — A25

Company Arms — A26

1918-31 **Engr.** *Perf. 14, 15, 12½*
108 A9 ¼c brn & yel grn .55 .50
109 A9 ¼c ol grn & blk ('25) .30 .25
110 A10 ½c black .55 .50
111 A11 1c green & blk .55 .50
112 A12 1½c black & grn .55 .50
113 A13 2c carmine & blk .55 .50
114 A13 2c ol blk & blk ('25) .30 .25
115 A14 2½c lilac & blk .55 .50
116 A11 3c ocher & blk ('23) .30 .25
117 A15 4c grn & brn ('21) .30 .25
118 A15 4c red & blk ('25) .30 .25
119 A9 4½c gray & blk ('23) .30 .25
120 A16 5c blue & blk .55 .50
121 A17 6c claret & bl ('21) .80 .30
122 A17 6c lilac & blk ('25) .30 .25
123 A21 7c ultra & blk ('23) 1.00 .50
124 A18 7½c orange & grn .75 .70
125 A19 8c violet & blk 1.50 1.10
126 A20 10c red org & blk 1.50 1.10
128 A19 12c brn & blk ('23) 1.00 .70
129 A19 12c bl grn & blk ('25) 2.00 .35
130 A21 15c carmine & blk 1.00 .95
131 A22 20c dp green & blk 1.60 .65
132 A23 30c red brn & blk 3.50 .95
133 A23 30c gray grn & blk ('25) 2.00 .55
134 A23 30c bl grn & blk ('31) 3.50 .55
135 A24 40c yel grn & blk 1.90 1.10
136 A24 40c grnsh bl & blk ('25) .70 .85
137 A25 50c orange & blk 3.00 1.10
138 A25 50c lt vio & blk ('25) 2.25 .80
139 A25 60c rose & brn ('23) 1.50 .80
140 A20 80c ultra & brn ('23) 4.00 .80
141 A20 80c car & blk ('25) 1.10 .80
142 A26 1e dk green & blk 2.25 2.00
143 A26 1e blue & blk ('25) 2.25 .80
144 A16 2e rose & vio ('23) 6.00 1.30
145 A16 2e lilac & blk ('25) 4.00 .80
Nos. 108-145 (37) 55.05 24.80

Shades exist of several denominations.
For surcharges see Nos. 146-154, RA1.

Nos. 132, 142, 115, 120, 131, 135, 125, 137 Surcharged with New Values in Red, Blue, Violet or Black

h

i

j

1920 *Perf. 14, 15*
146 A23(h) ½c on 30c (Bk) 7.00 5.00
147 A26(h) ½c on 1e (R) 7.00 5.00
148 A14(h) 1½c on 2½c (Bl) 6.00 2.25
149 A16(h) 1½c on 5c (V) 6.00 2.25
150 A14(h) 2c on 2½c (R) 6.00 2.25
151 A22(i) 4c on 20c (V) 7.00 4.50
152 A24(i) 4c on 40c (V) 7.00 4.50
153 A19(j) 6c on 8c (R) 7.50 4.50
154 A25(j) 6c on 50c (Bk) 8.00 4.50
Nos. 146-154 (9) 61.50 34.75

The surcharge on No. 148 is placed vertically between two bars. On No. 154 the two words of the surcharge are 13mm apart.

Native — A27

View of Beira — A28

Tapping Rubber Tree — A29

Picking Tea — A30

Zambezi River — A31

1925-31 Engr. *Perf. 12*

No.	Type	Description	Unused	Used
155	A27	24c ultra & blk	1.25	1.00
156	A28	25c choc & ultra	1.25	1.00
157	A27	85c brn red & blk ('31)	.95	.80
158	A28	1.40e dl bl & blk ('31)	.90	.80
159	A29	5e yel brn & ultra	1.75	.65
160	A30	10e rose & blk	2.75	.95
161	A31	20e green & blk	3.25	1.20
		Nos. 155-161 (7)	12.10	6.40

Ivory Tusks — A32

Panning Gold — A33

1931 Litho. *Perf. 14*

No.	Type	Description	Unused	Used
162	A32	45c lt blue	3.00	1.30
163	A33	70c yellow brn	2.00	.70

Zambezi Railroad Bridge A34

1935 Engr. *Perf. 12½*

No.	Type	Description	Unused	Used
164	A34	1e dk blue & blk	8.75	1.60

Opening of a new bridge over the Zambezi River.

Airplane over Beira — A35

1935

No.	Type	Description	Unused	Used
165	A35	5c blue & blk	.55	.55
166	A35	10c red org & blk	.55	.40
a.		Square pair, imperf. between	50.00	
167	A35	15c red & blk	.55	.40
a.		Square pair, imperf. between	50.00	
168	A35	20c yel grn & blk	.55	.40
169	A35	30c green & blk	.55	.40
170	A35	40c gray bl & blk	.70	.55
171	A35	45c blue & blk	.70	.55
172	A35	50c violet & blk	.70	.70
a.		Square pair, imperf. btwn.	60.00	
173	A35	60c carmine & brn	1.10	.65
174	A35	80c carmine & blk	1.10	.65
		Nos. 165-174 (10)	7.05	5.25

Issued to commemorate the opening of the Blantyre-Beira Salisbury air service.

Giraffe — A36

Thatched Huts — A37

Rock Python — A41

Coconut Palms A50

Zambezi Railroad Bridge A52

Sena Gate — A53

Company Arms — A54

Designs: 10c, Dhow. 15c, St. Caetano Fortress, Sofala. 20c, Zebra. 40c, Black rhinoceros. 45c, Lion. 50c, Crocodile. 60c, Leopard. 70c, Mozambique woman. 80c, Hippopotami. 85c, Vasco da Gama's flagship. 1e, Man in canoe. 2e, Greater kudu.

1937, May 16 *Perf. 12½*

No.	Type	Description	Unused	Used
175	A36	1c yel grn & vio	.30	*.25*
176	A37	5c blue & yel grn	.30	*.25*
177	A36	10c ver & ultra	.30	*.25*
178	A37	15c carmine & blk	.30	*.25*
179	A36	20c green & ultra	.30	*.25*
180	A41	30c dk grn & ind	.30	*.30*
181	A41	40c gray bl & blk	.30	*.30*
182	A41	45c blue & brn	.30	*.30*
183	A41	50c dk vio & emer	.30	*.30*
184	A37	60c carmine & bl	.30	*.30*
185	A36	70c yel brn & pale grn	.30	*.30*
186	A37	80c car & pale grn	.40	.35
187	A41	85c org red & blk	.50	.40
188	A41	1e dp bl & blk	.50	.40
189	A50	1.40e dk bl & pale grn	.90	.40
190	A41	2e pale lilac & brn	1.50	.50
191	A52	5e yel brn & bl	1.25	.75
192	A53	10e carmine & blk	2.25	1.50
193	A54	20e grn & brn vio	3.00	2.75
		Nos. 175-193 (19)	13.60	10.10

Stamps of 1937 Overprinted in Red or Black

1939, Aug. 28

No.	Type	Description	Unused	Used
194	A41	30c dk grn & ind (R)	3.00	.85
195	A41	40c gray bl & blk (R)	3.00	.85
196	A41	45c blue & brn (Bk)	3.00	.85
197	A41	50c dk vio & emer (R)	4.00	1.00
198	A41	85c org red & blk (Bk)	4.00	1.00
199	A41	1e dp bl & blk (R)	4.00	1.25
200	A41	2e pale lil & brn (Bk)	4.50	1.75
		Nos. 194-200 (7)	25.50	7.55

Visit of the President of Portugal to Beira in 1939.

King Alfonso Henriques — A55

1940, Feb. 16 Typo. *Perf. 11½x12*

No.	Type	Description	Unused	Used
201	A55	1.75e blue & lt blue	1.50	.75

800th anniv. of Portuguese independence.

King John IV — A56

1940, Oct. 10 Engr. *Perf. 12½*

No.	Type	Description	Unused	Used
202	A56	40c gray grn & blk	.65	.50
203	A56	50c dk vio & brt grn	.65	.50
204	A56	60c brt car & dp bl	.65	.50
205	A56	70c brn org & dk grn	.65	.50
206	A56	80c car & dp grn	.65	.50
207	A56	1e dk bl & blk	.65	.50
		Nos. 202-207 (6)	3.90	3.00

300th anniv. of the restoration of the Portuguese Monarchy.

Mozambique Company's charter terminated July 18th, 1941 after which date its stamps were superseded by those of the territory of Mozambique.

SEMI-POSTAL STAMPS

Lisbon Issue of 1911 Overprinted in Red

1917 Unwmk. *Perf. 11½*

No.	Type	Description	Unused	Used
B1	A2	2½r gray	9.00	*10.50*
a.		Double overprint	75.00	*75.00*
B2	A2	10r yellow grn	10.00	*15.00*
B3	A2	20r gray lilac	14.00	*20.00*
B4	A2	50r brown	20.00	*25.00*
B5	A2	75r red lilac	65.00	*70.00*
B6	A2	100r dk blue, *bl*	75.00	*80.00*
B7	A2	700r purple, *yel*	175.00	*225.00*
		Nos. B1-B7 (7)	368.00	*445.50*

Nos. B1-B7 were used on July 31, 1917, in place of ordinary stamps. The proceeds were given to the Red Cross.

AIR POST STAMPS

Airplane over Beira — AP1

1935 Unwmk. Engr. *Perf. 12½*

No.	Type	Description	Unused	Used
C1	AP1	5c blue & blk	.25	.25
C2	AP1	10c org red & blk	.25	.25
C3	AP1	15c red & blk	.25	.25
C4	AP1	20c yel grn & blk	.25	.25
C5	AP1	30c green & blk	.25	.25
C6	AP1	40c gray bl & blk	.25	.25
C7	AP1	45c blue & blk	.25	.25
C8	AP1	50c dk vio & blk	.40	.25
C9	AP1	60c car & brn	.40	.25
C10	AP1	80c car & blk	.50	.25
C11	AP1	1e blue & blk	.50	.25
C12	AP1	2e mauve & blk	1.50	.40
C13	AP1	5e bis brn & bl	1.50	.50
C14	AP1	10e car & blk	2.00	.75
C15	AP1	20e bl grn & blk	3.00	1.00
		Nos. C1-C15 (15)	11.55	5.40

POSTAGE DUE STAMPS

D1

1906 Unwmk. Typo. *Perf. 11½x12*

Denominations in Black

No.	Type	Description	Unused	Used
J1	D1	5r yellow grn	.70	.40
J2	D1	10r slate	.70	.55
J3	D1	20r yellow brn	1.25	.55
J4	D1	30r orange	1.50	1.00
J5	D1	50r gray brown	1.50	1.00
J6	D1	60r red brown	22.50	9.00
J7	D1	100r red lilac	4.00	2.50
J8	D1	130r dull blue	32.50	12.00
J9	D1	200r carmine	13.00	4.00
J10	D1	500r violet	18.00	5.00
		Nos. J1-J10 (10)	95.65	36.00

Nos. J1-J10 Overprinted in Carmine or Green

1911

No.	Type	Description	Unused	Used
J11	D1	5r yellow grn	.30	.30
J12	D1	10r slate	.30	.30
J13	D1	20r yellow brn	.30	.30
J14	D1	30r orange	.30	.30
J15	D1	50r gray brown	.30	.30
J16	D1	60r red brown	.50	.50
J17	D1	100r red lilac	.50	.50
J18	D1	130r dull blue	2.00	1.40
J19	D1	200r carmine (G)	1.30	1.35
J20	D1	500r violet	2.50	1.40
		Nos. J11-J20 (10)	8.30	6.65

D2

1916 Typo.

With Value in Centavos in Black

No.	Type	Description	Unused	Used
J21	D2	½c yellow grn	.30	.30
J22	D2	1c slate	.30	.30
J23	D2	2c orange brn	.30	.30
J24	D2	3c orange	.70	.30
J25	D2	5c gray brown	.70	.30
J26	D2	6c pale brown	.70	.35
J27	D2	10c red lilac	.70	.55
J28	D2	13c gray blue	1.40	1.30
J29	D2	20c rose	1.40	1.30
J30	D2	50c gray	3.25	1.50
		Nos. J21-J30 (10)	9.75	6.50

Company Arms — D3

1919 Engr. *Perf. 12½, 13½, 14, 15*

No.	Type	Description	Unused	Used
J31	D3	½c green	.25	.25
J32	D3	1c slate	.25	.25
J33	D3	2c red brown	.25	.25
J34	D3	3c orange	.25	.25
J35	D3	5c gray brown	.25	.25
J36	D3	6c lt brown	.50	.50
J37	D3	10c lilac rose	.50	.50
J38	D3	13c dull blue	.50	.50
J39	D3	20c rose	.50	.50
J40	D3	50c gray	.50	.50
		Nos. J31-J40 (10)	3.75	3.75

NEWSPAPER STAMP

Newspaper Stamp of Mozambique Overprinted

1894 **Unwmk.** ***Perf. 11½***

P1 N3 2½r brown	.65	.55
a. Inverted overprint	30.00	30.00
b. Perf. 12½	1.50	1.10

Reprints are on stout white paper with clean-cut perf. 13½. Value $1.

POSTAL TAX STAMPS

No. 116 Surcharged in Black

1932 ***Perf. 12½***

RA1 A11 2c on 3c org & blk	1.40	*2.00*

Charity — PT2

1933 **Litho.** ***Perf. 11***

RA2 PT2 2c magenta & blk	1.40	*2.00*

PT3

1940 **Unwmk.** ***Perf. 10½***

RA3 PT3 2c black & ultra	15.00	*16.00*

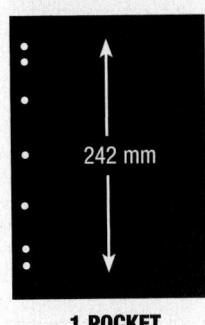

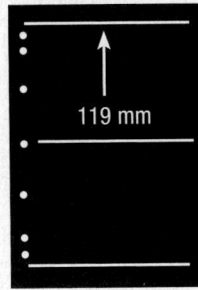

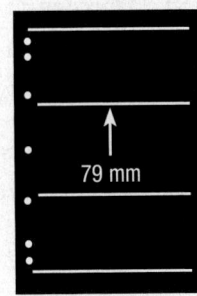

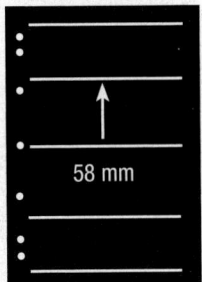

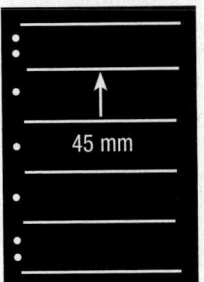

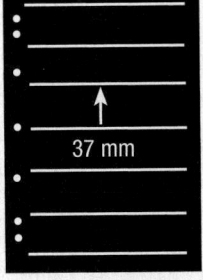

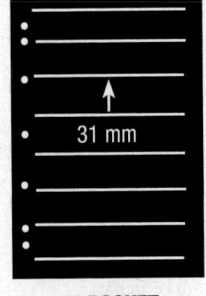

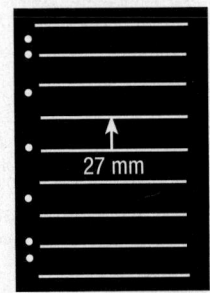

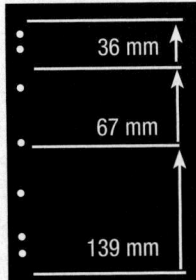

PT4

1941

RA4 PT4 2c black & brt red	15.00	*16.00*

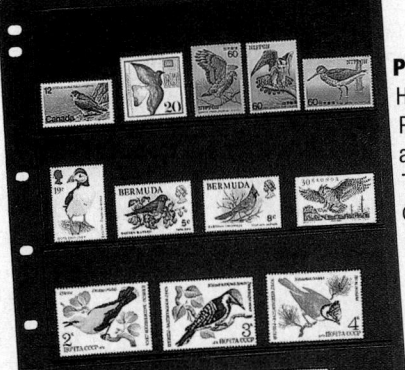

Vols. 4A-4B Number Additions, Deletions & Changes

Jamaica

Number in 2017 Catalogue	Number in 2018 Catalogue
new	79b
new	79c
new	83b
new	83c
new	84b
new	84c
new	226c

Jordan

Number in 2017 Catalogue	Number in 2018 Catalogue
2a	2
new	3a
new	4a
5a	5
6a	6
7a	7
new	7a
8a	8
new	8a
9a	9
1b	1B
1a	1Ba
2a	2B
2b	2Ba
3a	3B
4a	4B
new	4Ba
5	5B
6	6B
7	7B
8	8B
9	9B
12	13
new	12
13	14
13A	15
14	16
14a	16a
15	17
16	18
17	19
new	19a
new	19b
17A	20
18	21
19c	22
19A	23
21	24
new	24a
22	25
22A	26
23	27
new	27a
25	29
new	13C
new	13Ca
new	14C
new	15C
new	16C
new	16Ca
new	16Cb
new	17C
new	18C
new	22C
new	22Ca
new	23C
20	23D
new	23Da
20A	23E
new	29C
26	31
27	32
27A	33
28	34
29	35
new	36
30	37
31	38
35	39
33	40
34	41
39	42
new	42a
36	43
new	43a
new	43b
37	44
40	45
39	46
39A	47
42	48
41	49
47	50
new	50a
45	52
new	52a
46	53
49	54
new	54a
48	55
50B	56
new	57
new	57a
50A	58
32	36C
new	37C
new	38C
new	39C
new	40C
new	41C
new	43C
42a	48C
new	49C
43	51
44	51C
45a	52C
new	54C
48a	55C
50	57C
51A	59
51	60
52A	61
52	62
53	63
new	64
55	65
new	65a
55a	65a
new	65b
55c	65c
56	66
57a	67
new	67a
59	69
59b	69a
59a	69b
60	70
60a	70a
60b	70b
new	70c
60c	70d
61a	deleted
53	63E
53a	63Ea
54	64E
54a	64Ea
54b	64Eb
54c	64Ec
54d	64Ed
57	67E
58	68
58a	68a
58b	68b
61	71
new	71a
62	72
63	73
63a	73a
63b	73b
63c	73c
new	73d
new	73e
63d	73f
63e	73g
63f	73h
64	74A
65	74B
66	74C
67	74D
68	74E
69	74F
70	74G
71	74H
72	74I
73	74J
73B	74K

Leeward Islands

Number in 2017 Catalogue	Number in 2018 Catalogue
new	17b

Malaya — Perak

Number in 2017 Catalogue	Number in 2018 Catalogue
new	67c
new	85Ba
new	93a

Maldive Islands

Number in 2017 Catalogue	Number in 2018 Catalogue
new	7a

Mauritania

Number in 2017 Catalogue	Number in 2018 Catalogue
new	B2c

Mexico

Number in 2017 Catalogue	Number in 2018 Catalogue
new	64d

Middle Congo

Number in 2017 Catalogue	Number in 2018 Catalogue
new	7a
new	48b

Moheli

Number in 2017 Catalogue	Number in 2018 Catalogue
new	11a
new	16a

Montenegro

Number in 2017 Catalogue	Number in 2018 Catalogue
new	34c
new	32a-44a
new	34ac
new	32b-44b
new	34bc
new	45a-56a
new	59a
new	61a
new	66e
new	67e
new	68e
new	68f
new	69e
new	70e
new	71e
new	72e
new	72f
new	73e
new	74e
new	67a-74a
new	67ae
new	67af
new	70ae
new	70af
new	73af
new	74af
new	66b-74b
new	67be
new	67bf
new	68be
new	69bf
new	70be
new	70bf
new	71be
new	73bf
new	74bf
new	66c-74c
new	67ce
new	67cf
new	68ce
new	69ce
new	70ce
new	70cf
new	73cf
new	74cf
new	66d-74d
new	66dg
new	66dh
new	67dg
new	67dh
new	68de
new	68df
new	68dg
new	68dh
new	69df
new	69dg
new	69dh
new	70de
new	70df
new	70dg
new	70dh
new	71df
new	71dg
new	71dh
new	72dg
new	72dh
new	73df
new	73dg
new	73dh
new	74df
new	74dg
new	74dh
new	H1a
new	H2a
new	H2b
new	H3a-H3d
new	H3g
new	H3h
new	J1a-J8a
new	J1b-J8b
new	J14a
new	J14b
new	J15a
new	J15b-J15d
new	J16a
new	J16b
new	J17a
new	J17b
new	J18a

Illustrated Identifier

This section pictures stamps or parts of stamp designs that will help identify postage stamps that do not have English words on them.

Many of the symbols that identify stamps of countries are shown here as well as typical examples of their stamps.

See the Index and Identifier for stamps with inscriptions such as "sen," "posta," "Baja Porto," "Helvetia," "K.S.A.", etc.

Linn's Stamp Identifier is now available. The 144 pages include more than 2,000 inscriptions and more than 500 large stamp illustrations. Available from Linn's Stamp News, P.O. Box 4129, Sidney, OH 45365-4129.

1. HEADS, PICTURES AND NUMERALS

GREAT BRITAIN

Great Britain stamps never show the country name, but, except for postage dues, show a picture of the reigning monarch.

Victoria

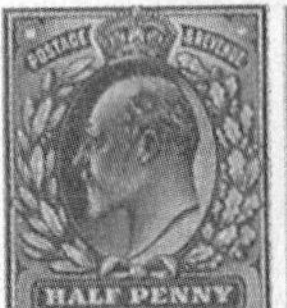

Edward VII George V Edward VIII

George VI

Elizabeth II

Some George VI and Elizabeth II stamps are surcharged in annas, new paisa or rupees. These are listed under Oman.

Silhouette (sometimes facing right, generally at the top of stamp)

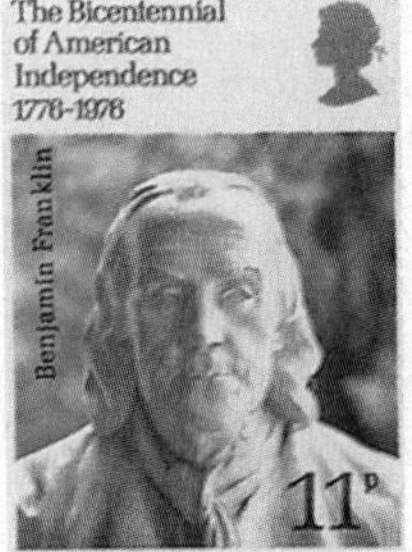

The silhouette indicates this is a British stamp. It is not a U.S. stamp.

VICTORIA

Queen Victoria

INDIA

Other stamps of India show this portrait of Queen Victoria and the words "Service" (or "Postage") and "Annas."

AUSTRIA

YUGOSLAVIA

(Also BOSNIA & HERZEGOVINA if imperf.)

BOSNIA & HERZEGOVINA

Denominations also appear in top corners instead of bottom corners.

HUNGARY

Another stamp has posthorn facing left

BRAZIL

AUSTRALIA

Kangaroo and Emu

GERMANY

Mecklenburg-Vorpommern

SWITZERLAND

PALAU

2. ORIENTAL INSCRIPTIONS

CHINA

中

Any stamp with this one character is from China (Imperial, Republic or People's Republic). This character appears in a four-character overprint on stamps of Manchukuo. These stamps are local provisionals, which are unlisted. Other overprinted Manchukuo stamps show this character, but have more than four characters in the overprints. These are listed in People's Republic of China.

Some Chinese stamps show the Sun.

Most stamps of Republic of China show this series of characters.

Stamps with the China character and this character are from People's Republic of China. 人

中国人民邮政

Calligraphic form of People's Republic of China

(一)	(二)	(三)	(四)	(五)	(六)
1	2	3	4	5	6
(七)	(八)	(九)	(十)	(十一)	(十二)
7	8	9	10	11	12

Chinese stamps without China character

REPUBLIC OF CHINA

PEOPLE'S REPUBLIC OF CHINA

Mao Tse-tung

MANCHUKUO

Temple

Emperor Pu-Yi

The first 3 characters are common to many Manchukuo stamps.

The last 3 characters are common to other Manchukuo stamps.

Orchid Crest

Manchukuo stamp without these elements

JAPAN

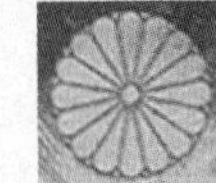

Chrysanthemum Crest

Country Name

Japanese stamps without these elements

The number of characters in the center and the design of dragons on the sides will vary.

RYUKYU ISLANDS

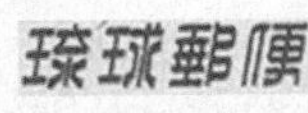

Country Name

PHILIPPINES (Japanese Occupation)

Country Name

NETHERLANDS INDIES (Japanese Occupation)

Indicates Japanese Occupation

Java **Sumatra**

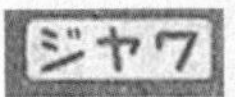

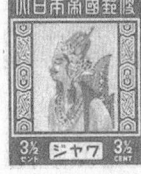

Country Name

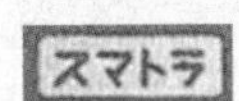

Country Name

Moluccas, Celebes and South Borneo

Country Name

NORTH BORNEO (Japanese Occupation)

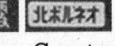

Indicates Japanese Occupation

Country Name

MALAYA (Japanese Occupation)

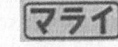

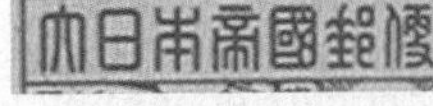

Indicates Japanese Occupation

Country Name

BURMA

Union of Myanmar

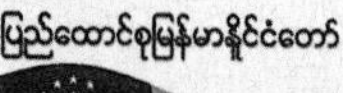

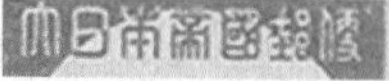

Indicates Japanese Occupation

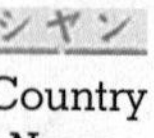

Country Name

Other Burma Japanese Occupation stamps without these elements

Burmese Script

KOREA

These two characters, in any order, are common to stamps from the Republic of Korea (South Korea) or of the People's Democratic Republic of Korea (North Korea).

This series of four characters can be found on the stamps of both Koreas. Most stamps of the Democratic People's Republic of Korea (North Korea) have just this inscription.

대한민국 우표

Indicates Republic of Korea (South Korea)

South Korean postage stamps issed after 1952 do not show currency expressed in Latin letters. Stamps wiith " HW," "HWAN," "WON," "WN," "W" or "W" with two lines through it, if not illustrated in listings of stamps before this date, are revenues. North Korean postage stamps do not have currency expressed in Latin letters.

Yin Yang appears on some stamps.

South Korean stamps show Yin Yang and starting in 1966, 'KOREA" in Latin letters

Example of South Korean stamps lacking Latin text, Yin Yang and standard Korean text of country name. North Korean stamps never show Yin Yang and starting in 1976 are inscribed "DPRK" or "DPR KOREA" in Latin letters.

THAILAND

Country Name

King Chulalongkorn

King Prajadhipok and Chao P'ya Chakri

3. CENTRAL AND EASTERN ASIAN INSCRIPTIONS

INDIA - FEUDATORY STATES

Alwar

Bhor

Bundi

Similar stamps come with different designs in corners and differently drawn daggers (at center of circle).

Dhar

Duttia

Faridkot

Hyderabad

Similar stamps exist with different central design which is inscribed "Postage" or "Post & Receipt."

Indore

Jammu & Kashmir

Text varies.

Jasdan

Jhalawar

Kotah

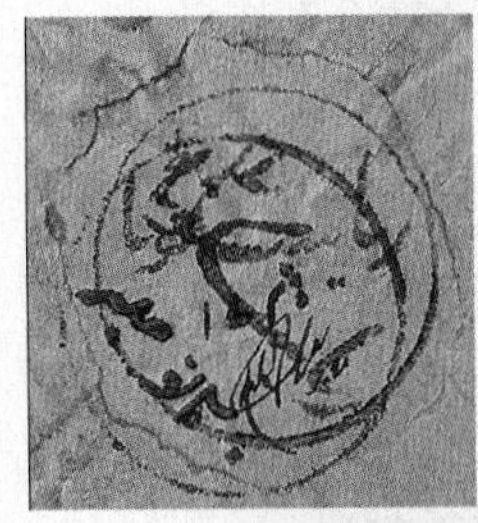

Size and text varies

Nandgaon

Nowanuggur

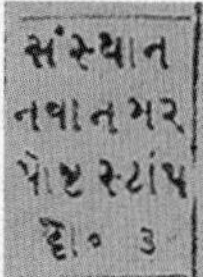

Poonch

Similar stamps exist in various sizes with different text

Rajasthan

Rajpeepla

Soruth

Tonk

BANGLADESH

বাংলাদেশ
Country Name

NEPAL

Similar stamps are smaller, have squares in upper corners and have five or nine characters in central bottom panel.

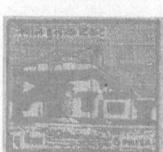

TANNU TUVA

ISRAEL

GEORGIA

This inscription is found on other pictorial stamps.

Country Name

ARMENIA

The four characters are found somewhere on pictorial stamps. On some stamps only the middle two are found.

4. AFRICAN INSCRIPTIONS

ETHIOPIA

5. ARABIC INSCRIPTIONS

١ ٢ ٣ ٤ ٥
1 2 3 4 5

٦ ٧ ٨ ٩ ٠
6 7 8 9 0

AFGHANISTAN

Many early Afghanistan stamps show Tiger's head, many of these have ornaments protruding from outer ring, others show inscriptions in black.

Arabic Script

Crest of King Amanullah

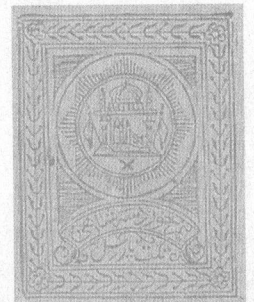

Mosque Gate & Crossed Cannons

The four characters are found somewhere on pictorial stamps. On some stamps only the middle two are found.

BAHRAIN

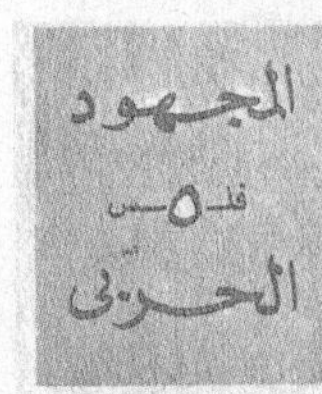

EGYPT

Postage

IRAN

Country Name

Royal Crown

Lion with Sword

Symbol

Emblem

IRAQ

JORDAN

LEBANON

Similar types have denominations at top and slightly different design.

LIBYA

Country Name in various styles

Other Libya stamps show Eagle and Shield (head facing either direction) or Red, White and Black Shield (with or without eagle in center).

Without Country Name

SAUDI ARABIA

Tughra (Central design)

Palm Tree and Swords

SYRIA

Arab Government Issues

THRACE YEMEN

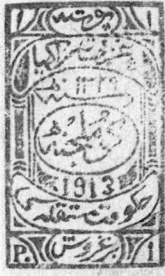

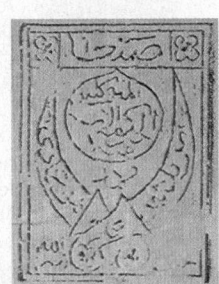

PAKISTAN

PAKISTAN - BAHAWALPUR

Country Name in top panel, star and crescent

TURKEY

Star & Crescent is a device found on many Turkish stamps, but is also found on stamps from other Arabic areas (see Pakistan-Bahawalpur)

Tughra (similar tughras can be found on stamps of Turkey in Asia, Afghanistan and Saudi Arabia)

Mohammed V

Mustafa Kemal

Plane, Star and Crescent

TURKEY IN ASIA

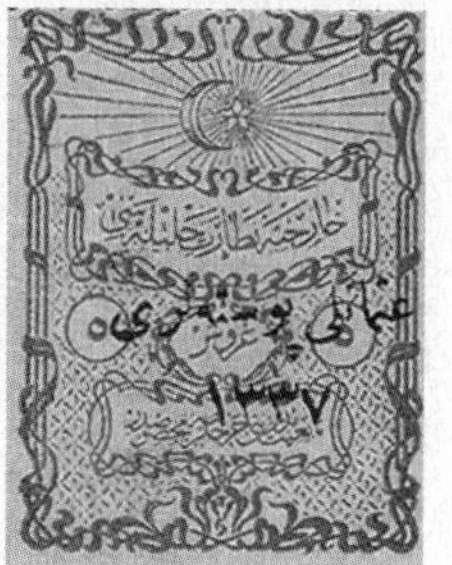

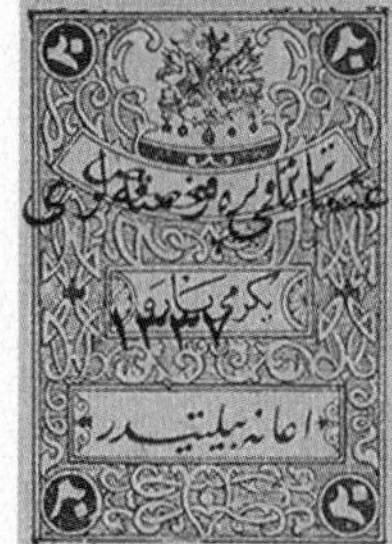

Other Turkey in Asia pictorials show star & crescent. Other stamps show tughra shown under Turkey.

6. GREEK INSCRIPTIONS

GREECE

Country Name in various styles (Some Crete stamps overprinted with the Greece country name are listed in Crete.)

Lepta

ΔΡΑΧΜΗ

ΛΕΠΤΟΝ

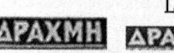

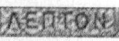

Drachma Drachmas Lepton

Abbreviated Country Name ΕΛΛ

Other forms of Country Name

No country name

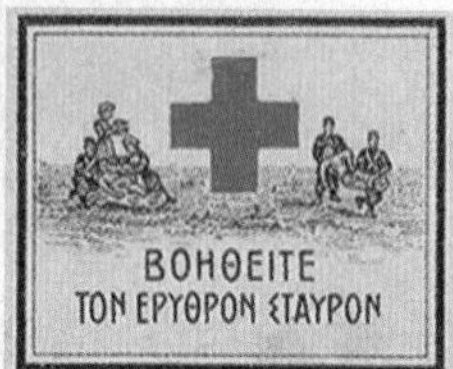

CRETE

Country Name

Crete stamps with a surcharge that have the year "1922" are listed under Greece.

EPIRUS

Similar stamps have text above the eagle.

IONIAN IS.

7. CYRILLIC INSCRIPTIONS

RUSSIA

Postage Stamp Imperial Eagle

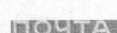

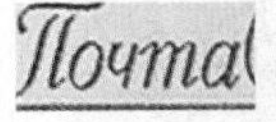

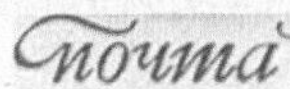

Postage in various styles

Abbreviation for Kopeck Abbreviation for Ruble Russia

Abbreviation for Russian Soviet Federated Socialist Republic RSFSR stamps were overprinted (see below)

Abbreviation for Union of Soviet Socialist Republics

This item is footnoted in Latvia

RUSSIA - Army of the North

"OKCA"

RUSSIA - Wenden

RUSSIAN OFFICES IN THE TURKISH EMPIRE

These letters appear on other stamps of the Russian offices.

The unoverprinted version of this stamp and a similar stamp were overprinted by various countries (see below).

ARMENIA

BELARUS

FAR EASTERN REPUBLIC

Country Name

FINLAND

Circles and Dots on stamps similar to Imperial Russia issues

SOUTH RUSSIA

Country Name

BATUM

Forms of Country Name

TRANSCAUCASIAN FEDERATED REPUBLICS

Abbreviation for Country Name

KAZAKHSTAN

ҚАЗАҚСТАН

Country Name

KYRGYZSTAN

КЫРГЫЗСТАН

КЫРГЫЗСТАН Country Name

ROMANIA

TAJIKISTAN

Country Name & Abbreviation

UKRAINE

Пошта України України

Україна
А. БЕЧКЕР

Country Name in various forms

УС РР

The trident appears on many stamps, usually as an overprint.

Abbreviation for Ukrainian Soviet Socialist Republic

WESTERN UKRAINE

Abbreviation for Country Name

AZERBAIJAN

AZƏRBAYCAN

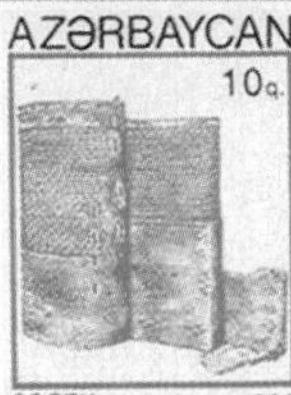

AZƏRBAYCAN

Country Name

A.C.C.P.

Abbreviation for Azerbaijan Soviet Socialist Republic

MONTENEGRO

ЦРНЕГОРЕ

ЦРНА ГОРА

Country Name in various forms

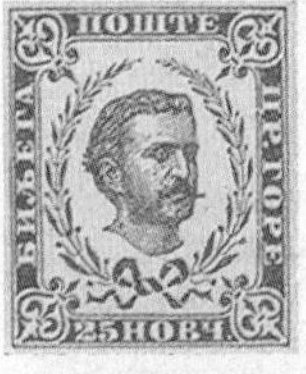

Ц.Р.ГОРЕ

Abbreviation for country name

No country name (A similar Montenegro stamp without country name has same vignette.)

SERBIA

СРПСКА СРБИЈА

Country Name in various forms

СРП. К.С.

Abbreviation for country name

No country name

MACEDONIA

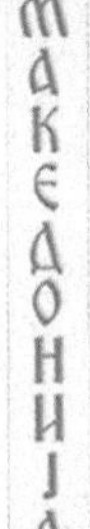

МАКЕДОНИЈА

Country Name

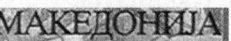

МАКЕДОНСКИ
11 Октомври 1997

Different form of Country Name

SERBIA & MONTENEGRO

YUGOSLAVIA

ЈУГОСЛАВИЈА

Showing country name

No Country Name

BOSNIA & HERZEGOVINA (Serb Administration)

РЕПУБЛИКА СРПСКА

Country Name

РЕПУБЛИКЕ СРПСКЕ

Different form of Country Name

No Country Name

BULGARIA

Country Name Postage

Stotinka

СТОТИНКИ СТОТ.

Stotinki (plural) Abbreviation for Stotinki

Country Name in various forms and styles

БЪЛГАРИЯ

НР България

No country name

Abbreviation for Lev, leva

MONGOLIA

ШУУДАН төгрөг

Country name in one word Tugrik in Cyrillic

МОНГОЛ ШУУДАН

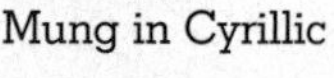

Country name in two words Mung in Cyrillic

Mung in Mongolian

Tugrik in Mongolian

Arms

No Country Name

INDEX AND IDENTIFIER

All page numbers shown are those in this Volume 4B.

Postage stamps that do not have English words on them are shown in the Illustrated Identifier.

G or GW overprinted on Cape of Good Hope .... Vol. 3A

Habilitado-1/2 (Tlacotalpan #1) 449

I.B. (West Irian) .... Vol. 3B

INDEX TO ADVERTISERS
2018 VOLUME 4B

2018
VOLUME 4B
DEALER DIRECTORY
YELLOW PAGE LISTINGS

This section of your Scott Catalogue contains advertisements to help you conveniently find what you need, when you need it...!

Accessories

BROOKLYN GALLERY COIN & STAMP, INC.
8725 4th Ave.
Brooklyn, NY 11209
PH: 718-745-5701
FAX: 718-745-2775
info@brooklyngallery.com
www.brooklyngallery.com

Appraisals

DR. ROBERT FRIEDMAN & SONS STAMP & COIN BUYING CENTER
2029 W. 75th St.
Woodridge, IL 60517
PH: 800-588-8100
FAX: 630-985-1588
drbobstamps@comcast.net
www.drbobfriedmanstamps.com

Argentina

GUILLERMO JALIL
Maipu 466,local 4
1006 Buenos Aires
Argentina
guillermo@jalilstamps.com
philatino@philatino.com
www.philatino.com
www.jalilstamps.com

Auctions

DUTCH COUNTRY AUCTIONS
The Stamp Center
4115 Concord Pike
Wilmington, DE 19803
PH: 302-478-8740
FAX: 302-478-8779
auctions@dutchcountryauctions.com
www.dutchcountryauctions.com

KELLEHER & ROGERS LTD.
4 Finance Drive, Ste. 200
Danbury, CT 06810
PH: 203-297-6056
FAX: 203-297-6059
info@kelleherauctions.com
www.kelleherauctions.com

R. MARESCH & SON LTD.
5th Floor - 6075 Yonge St.
Toronto, ON M2M 3W2
CANADA
PH: 416-363-7777
FAX: 416-363-6511
www.maresch.com

British Asia

THE STAMP ACT
PO Box 1136
Belmont, CA 94002
PH: 650-703-2342
PH: 650-592-3315
FAX: 650-508-8104
thestampact@sbcglobal.net

British Commonwealth

ARON R. HALBERSTAM PHILATELISTS, LTD.
PO Box 150168
Van Brunt Station
Brooklyn, NY 11215-0168
PH: 718-788-3978
arh@arhstamps.com
www.arhstamps.com

COLLECTORS EXCHANGE ORLANDO STAMP SHOP
1814A Edgewater Drive
Orlando, FL 32804
PH: 407-620-0908
PH: 407-947-8603
FAX: 407-730-2131
jlatter@cfl.rr.com
www.BritishStampsAmerica.com
www.OrlandoStampShop.com

ROY'S STAMPS
PO Box 28001
600 Ontario Street
St. Catharines, ON
CANADA L2N 7P8
Phone: 905-934-8377
Email: roystamp@cogeco.ca

WORLDSTAMPS/ FRANK GEIGER PHILATELISTS
PO Box 4743
Pinehurst, NC 28374
PH: 910-295-2048
info@WorldStamps.com
www.WorldStampsScott.com/British

Buying

DR. ROBERT FRIEDMAN & SONS STAMP & COIN BUYING CENTER
2029 W. 75th St.
Woodridge, IL 60517
PH: 800-588-8100
FAX: 630-985-1588
drbobstamps@comcast.net
www.drbobfriedmanstamps.com

Canada

CANADA STAMP FINDER
PO Box 92591
Brampton, ON L6W 4R1
PH: 514-238-5751
Toll Free in North America:
877-412-3106
FAX: 323-315-2635
canadastampfinder@gmail.com
www.canadastampfinder.com

ROY'S STAMPS
PO Box 28001
600 Ontario Street
St. Catharines, ON
CANADA L2N 7P8
Phone: 905-934-8377
Email: roystamp@cogeco.ca

China

THE STAMP ACT
PO Box 1136
Belmont, CA 94002
PH: 650-703-2342
PH: 650-592-3315
FAX: 650-508-8104
thestampact@sbcglobal.net

Collections

DR. ROBERT FRIEDMAN & SONS STAMP & COIN BUYING CENTER
2029 W. 75th St.
Woodridge, IL 60517
PH: 800-588-8100
FAX: 630-985-1588
drbobstamps@comcast.net
www.drbobfriedmanstamps.com

Ducks

MICHAEL JAFFE
PO Box 61484
Vancouver, WA 98666
PH: 360-695-6161
PH: 800-782-6770
FAX: 360-695-1616
mjaffe@brookmanstamps.com
www.brookmanstamps.com

German Colonies

COLONIAL STAMP COMPANY
5757 Wilshire Blvd. PH #8
Los Angeles, CA 90036
PH: 323-933-9435
FAX: 323-939-9930
Toll Free in North America
PH: 877-272-6693
FAX: 877-272-6694
info@colonialstampcompany.com
www.colonialstampcompany.com

Great Britain

COLONIAL STAMP COMPANY
5757 Wilshire Blvd. PH #8
Los Angeles, CA 90036
PH: 323-933-9435
FAX: 323-939-9930
Toll Free in North America
PH: 877-272-6693
FAX: 877-272-6694
info@colonialstampcompany.com
www.colonialstampcompany.com

British Commonwealth

British Commonwealth

Japan

THE STAMP ACT
PO Box 1136
Belmont, CA 94002
PH: 650-703-2342
PH: 650-592-3315
FAX: 650-508-8104
thestampact@sbcglobal.net

WORLDSTAMPS/ FRANK GEIGER PHILATELISTS
PO Box 4743
Pinehurst, NC 28374
PH: 910-295-2048
info@WorldStamps.com
www.WorldStampsScott.com/Japan

Katanga

WORLDSTAMPS/ FRANK GEIGER PHILATELISTS
PO Box 4743
Pinehurst, NC 28374
PH: 910-295-2048
info@WorldStamps.com
www.WorldStampsScott.com/Katanga

Kazakhstan

WORLDSTAMPS/ FRANK GEIGER PHILATELISTS
PO Box 4743
Pinehurst, NC 28374
PH: 910-295-2048
info@WorldStamps.com
www.WorldStampsScott.com/Kazakhstan

Kenya, Uganda, Tanzania

COLONIAL STAMP COMPANY
5757 Wilshire Blvd. PH #8
Los Angeles, CA 90036
PH: 323-933-9435
FAX: 323-939-9930
Toll Free in North America
PH: 877-272-6693
FAX: 877-272-6694
info@colonialstampcompany.com
www.colonialstampcompany.com

Kiauchau (German)

COLONIAL STAMP COMPANY
5757 Wilshire Blvd. PH #8
Los Angeles, CA 90036
PH: 323-933-9435
FAX: 323-939-9930
Toll Free in North America
PH: 877-272-6693
FAX: 877-272-6694
info@colonialstampcompany.com
www.colonialstampcompany.com

Kosovo

WORLDSTAMPS/ FRANK GEIGER PHILATELISTS
PO Box 4743
Pinehurst, NC 28374
PH: 910-295-2048
info@WorldStamps.com
www.WorldStampsScott.com/Kosovo

Latin America

GUY SHAW
PO Box 27138
San Diego, CA 92198
PH/FAX: 858-485-8269
guyshaw@guyshaw.com
www.guyshaw.com

Latvia

WORLDSTAMPS/ FRANK GEIGER PHILATELISTS
PO Box 4743
Pinehurst, NC 28374
PH: 910-295-2048
info@WorldStamps.com
www.WorldStampsScott.com/Latvia

Leeward Islands

COLONIAL STAMP COMPANY
5757 Wilshire Blvd. PH #8
Los Angeles, CA 90036
PH: 323-933-9435
FAX: 323-939-9930
Toll Free in North America
PH: 877-272-6693
FAX: 877-272-6694
info@colonialstampcompany.com
www.colonialstampcompany.com

Liechtenstein

HENRY GITNER PHILATELISTS, INC.
PO Box 3077-S
Middletown, NY 10940
PH: 845-343-5151
PH: 800-947-8267
FAX: 845-343-0068
hgitner@hgitner.com
www.hgitner.com

WORLDSTAMPS/ FRANK GEIGER PHILATELISTS
PO Box 4743
Pinehurst, NC 28374
PH: 910-295-2048
info@WorldStamps.com
www.WorldStampsScott.com/Liechtenstein

Luxembourg

HENRY GITNER PHILATELISTS, INC.
PO Box 3077-S
Middletown, NY 10940
PH: 845-343-5151
PH: 800-947-8267
FAX: 845-343-0068
hgitner@hgitner.com
www.hgitner.com

WORLDSTAMPS/ FRANK GEIGER PHILATELISTS
PO Box 4743
Pinehurst, NC 28374
PH: 910-295-2048
info@WorldStamps.com
www.WorldStampsScott.com/Luxembourg

Madagascar (British Issues)

COLONIAL STAMP COMPANY
5757 Wilshire Blvd. PH #8
Los Angeles, CA 90036
PH: 323-933-9435
FAX: 323-939-9930
Toll Free in North America
PH: 877-272-6693
FAX: 877-272-6694
info@colonialstampcompany.com
www.colonialstampcompany.com

Malaya

COLONIAL STAMP COMPANY
5757 Wilshire Blvd. PH #8
Los Angeles, CA 90036
PH: 323-933-9435
FAX: 323-939-9930
Toll Free in North America
PH: 877-272-6693
FAX: 877-272-6694
info@colonialstampcompany.com
www.colonialstampcompany.com

THE STAMP ACT
PO Box 1136
Belmont, CA 94002
PH: 650-703-2342
PH: 650-592-3315
FAX: 650-508-8104
thestampact@sbcglobal.net

Mariana Islands (Ger & Sp)

COLONIAL STAMP COMPANY
5757 Wilshire Blvd. PH #8
Los Angeles, CA 90036
PH: 323-933-9435
FAX: 323-939-9930
Toll Free in North America
PH: 877-272-6693
FAX: 877-272-6694
info@colonialstampcompany.com
www.colonialstampcompany.com

Marshall Islands

COLONIAL STAMP COMPANY
5757 Wilshire Blvd. PH #8
Los Angeles, CA 90036
PH: 323-933-9435
FAX: 323-939-9930
Toll Free in North America
PH: 877-272-6693
FAX: 877-272-6694
info@colonialstampcompany.com
www.colonialstampcompany.com

WORLDSTAMPS/ FRANK GEIGER PHILATELISTS
PO Box 4743
Pinehurst, NC 28374
PH: 910-295-2048
info@WorldStamps.com
www.WorldStampsScott.com/TT

Mauritius

COLONIAL STAMP COMPANY
5757 Wilshire Blvd. PH #8
Los Angeles, CA 90036
PH: 323-933-9435
FAX: 323-939-9930
Toll Free in North America
PH: 877-272-6693
FAX: 877-272-6694
info@colonialstampcompany.com
www.colonialstampcompany.com

Mesopotamia

COLONIAL STAMP COMPANY
5757 Wilshire Blvd. PH #8
Los Angeles, CA 90036
PH: 323-933-9435
FAX: 323-939-9930
Toll Free in North America
PH: 877-272-6693
FAX: 877-272-6694
info@colonialstampcompany.com
www.colonialstampcompany.com

Mexico

WORLDSTAMPS/ FRANK GEIGER PHILATELISTS
PO Box 4743
Pinehurst, NC 28374
PH: 910-295-2048
info@WorldStamps.com
www.WorldStampsScott.com/Mexico

Monaco

WORLDSTAMPS/ FRANK GEIGER PHILATELISTS
PO Box 4743
Pinehurst, NC 28374
PH: 910-295-2048
info@WorldStamps.com
www.WorldStampsScott.com/Monaco

Natal

COLONIAL STAMP COMPANY
5757 Wilshire Blvd. PH #8
Los Angeles, CA 90036
PH: 323-933-9435
FAX: 323-939-9930
Toll Free in North America
PH: 877-272-6693
FAX: 877-272-6694
info@colonialstampcompany.com
www.colonialstampcompany.com

New Britain

COLONIAL STAMP COMPANY
5757 Wilshire Blvd. PH #8
Los Angeles, CA 90036
PH: 323-933-9435
FAX: 323-939-9930
Toll Free in North America
PH: 877-272-6693
FAX: 877-272-6694
info@colonialstampcompany.com
www.colonialstampcompany.com

New Issues

DAVIDSON'S STAMP SERVICE
Personalized Service since 1970
PO Box 36355
Indianapolis, IN 46236-0355
PH: 317-826-2620
ed-davidson@earthlink.net
www.newstampissues.com

WORLDSTAMPS/ FRANK GEIGER PHILATELISTS
PO Box 4743
Pinehurst, NC 28374
PH: 910-295-2048
info@WorldStamps.com
www.WorldStampsScott.com/NI

New Zealand

COLONIAL STAMP COMPANY
5757 Wilshire Blvd. PH #8
Los Angeles, CA 90036
PH: 323-933-9435
FAX: 323-939-9930
Toll Free in North America
PH: 877-272-6693
FAX: 877-272-6694
info@colonialstampcompany.com
www.colonialstampcompany.com

Niger Coast Protectorate

COLONIAL STAMP COMPANY
5757 Wilshire Blvd. PH #8
Los Angeles, CA 90036
PH: 323-933-9435
FAX: 323-939-9930
Toll Free in North America
PH: 877-272-6693
FAX: 877-272-6694
info@colonialstampcompany.com
www.colonialstampcompany.com

Orange River Colony

COLONIAL STAMP COMPANY
5757 Wilshire Blvd. PH #8
Los Angeles, CA 90036
PH: 323-933-9435
FAX: 323-939-9930
Toll Free in North America
PH: 877-272-6693
FAX: 877-272-6694
info@colonialstampcompany.com
www.colonialstampcompany.com

Proofs & Essays

HENRY GITNER PHILATELISTS, INC.
PO Box 3077-S
Middletown, NY 10940
PH: 845-343-5151
PH: 800-947-8267
FAX: 845-343-0068
hgitner@hgitner.com
www.hgitner.com

Rhodesia

COLONIAL STAMP COMPANY
5757 Wilshire Blvd. PH #8
Los Angeles, CA 90036
PH: 323-933-9435
FAX: 323-939-9930
Toll Free in North America
PH: 877-272-6693
FAX: 877-272-6694
info@colonialstampcompany.com
www.colonialstampcompany.com

Sovereign Military Order of Malta

WORLDSTAMPS/ FRANK GEIGER PHILATELISTS
PO Box 4743
Pinehurst, NC 28374
PH: 910-295-2048
info@WorldStamps.com
www.WorldStampsScott.com/SMOM

Stamp Stores

California

BROSIUS STAMP, COIN & SUPPLIES
2105 Main St.
Santa Monica, CA 90405
PH: 310-396-7480
FAX: 310-396-7455
brosius.stamp.coin@hotmail.com

COLONIAL STAMP COMPANY
5757 Wilshire Blvd. PH #8
Los Angeles, CA 90036
PH: 323-933-9435
FAX: 323-939-9930
Toll Free in North America
PH: 877-272-6693
FAX: 877-272-6694
info@colonialstampcompany.com
www.colonialstampcompany.com

Stamp Stores

Delaware

DUTCH COUNTRY AUCTIONS
The Stamp Center
4115 Concord Pike
Wilmington, DE 19803
PH: 302-478-8740
FAX: 302-478-8779
auctions@dutchcountryauctions.com
www.dutchcountryauctions.com

Florida

DR. ROBERT FRIEDMAN & SONS STAMP & COIN BUYING CENTER
PH: 800-588-8100
FAX: 630-985-1588
drbobstamps@comcast.net
www.drbobfriedmanstamps.com

Illinois

DR. ROBERT FRIEDMAN & SONS STAMP & COIN BUYING CENTER
2029 W. 75th St.
Woodridge, IL 60517
PH: 800-588-8100
FAX: 630-985-1588
drbobstamps@comcast.net
www.drbobfriedmanstamps.com

Indiana

KNIGHT STAMP & COIN CO.
237 Main St.
Hobart, IN 46342
PH: 219-942-4341
PH: 800-634-2646
knight@knightcoin.com
www.knightcoin.com

New Jersey

BERGEN STAMPS & COLLECTIBLES
306 Queen Anne Rd.
Teaneck, NJ 07666
PH: 201-836-8987

TRENTON STAMP & COIN CO
Thomas DeLuca
Store: Forest Glen Plaza
1804 Highway 33
Hamilton Square, NJ 08690
Mail: PO Box 8574
Trenton, NJ 08650
PH: 609-584-8100
FAX: 609-587-8664
TOMD4TSC@aol.com

New York

CHAMPION STAMP CO., INC.
432 W. 54th St.
New York, NY 10019
PH: 212-489-8130
FAX: 212-581-8130
championstamp@aol.com
www.championstamp.com

CK STAMPS
42-14 Union St. # 2A
Flushing, NY 11355
PH: 917-667-6641
ckstampsllc@yahoo.com

Ohio

HILLTOP STAMP SERVICE
Richard A. Peterson
PO Box 626
Wooster, OH 44691
PH: 330-262-8907 (0)
PH: 330-262-5378 (H)
hilltop@bright.net
www.hilltopstamps.com

Supplies

BROOKLYN GALLERY COIN & STAMP, INC.
8725 4th Ave.
Brooklyn, NY 11209
PH: 718-745-5701
FAX: 718-745-2775
info@brooklyngallery.com
www.brooklyngallery.com

Topicals

E. JOSEPH McCONNELL, INC.
PO Box 683
Monroe, NY 10949
PH: 845-783-9791
FAX: 845-782-0347
ejstamps@gmail.com
www.EJMcConnell.com

WORLDSTAMPS/ FRANK GEIGER PHILATELISTS
PO Box 4743
Pinehurst, NC 28374
PH: 910-295-2048
info@WorldStamps.com
www.WorldStampsScott.com/Topic

Topicals-Columbus

MR. COLUMBUS
PO Box 1492
Fennville, MI 49408
PH: 269-543-4755
David@MrColumbus1492.com
www.MrColumbus1492.com

United Nations

BRUCE M. MOYER
Box 99
East Texas, PA 18046
PH: 610-395-8410
FAX: 610-395-8537
moyer@unstamps.com
www.unstamps.com

United States

BROOKMAN STAMP CO.
PO Box 90
Vancouver, WA 98666
PH: 360-695-1391
PH: 800-545-4871
FAX: 360-695-1616
info@brookmanstamps.com
www.brookmanstamps.com

KEITH WAGNER
ACS Stamp Company
2914 W 135th Ave
Broomfield, Colorado 80020
303-841-8666
www.ACSStamp.com

U.S.-Classics/Moderns

BARDO STAMPS
PO Box 7437
Buffalo Grove, IL 60089
PH: 847-634-2676
jfb7437@aol.com
www.bardostamps.com

U.S.-Collections Wanted

DR. ROBERT FRIEDMAN & SONS STAMP & COIN BUYING CENTER
2029 W. 75th St.
Woodridge, IL 60517
PH: 800-588-8100
FAX: 630-985-1588
drbobstamps@comcast.net
www.drbobfriedmanstamps.com

DUTCH COUNTRY AUCTIONS
The Stamp Center
4115 Concord Pike
Wilmington, DE 19803
PH: 302-478-8740
FAX: 302-478-8779
auctions@dutchcountryauctions.com
www.dutchcountryauctions.com

Want Lists-British Empire 1840-1935 German Cols./Offices

COLONIAL STAMP COMPANY
5757 Wilshire Blvd. PH #8
Los Angeles, CA 90036
PH: 323-933-9435
FAX: 323-939-9930
Toll Free in North America
PH: 877-272-6693
FAX: 877-272-6694
info@colonialstampcompany.com
www.colonialstampcompany.com

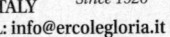

Worldwide

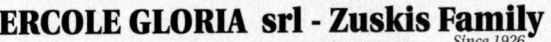

Wanted-Worldwide Collections

DUTCH COUNTRY AUCTIONS
The Stamp Center
4115 Concord Pike
Wilmington, DE 19803
PH: 302-478-8740
FAX: 302-478-8779
auctions@dutchcountryauctions.com
www.dutchcountryauctions.com

KELLEHER & ROGERS LTD.
4 Finance Drive, Ste. 200
Danbury, CT 06810
PH: 203-297-6056
FAX: 203-297-6059
info@kelleherauctions.com
www.kelleherauctions.com

Websites

KEITH WAGNER
ACS Stamp Company
2914 W 135th Ave
Broomfield, Colorado 80020
303-841-8666
www.ACSStamp.com

Worldwide-Collections

DR. ROBERT FRIEDMAN & SONS STAMP & COIN BUYING CENTER
2029 W. 75th St.
Woodridge, IL 60517
PH: 800-588-8100
FAX: 630-985-1588
drbobstamps@comcast.net
www.drbobfriedmanstamps.com